Reference Guide to

SHORT FICTION

St. James Reference Guides

American Literature

English Literature, 3 vols.

Short Fiction

World Literature, 2 vols. (in preparation)

Reference Guide to
SHORT FICTION

EDITOR
NOELLE WATSON

St J

ST. JAMES PRESS
Detroit   London   Washington D.C.

Noelle Watson, *Editor*

D. L. Kirkpatrick and James Vinson,
Series Originators, St. James Reference Guides

Gale Research Inc. Staff

Kevin S. Hile and Diane Telgen, *Project Coordinators*

Mary Beth Trimper, *Production Director*
Evi Seoud, *Assistant Production Manager*
Mary Kelley, *Production Assistant*

Cynthia Baldwin, *Art Director*
Pamela Galbreath, *Graphics Designer*
Sherrell Hobbs, *Desktop Publisher*

Library of Congress Cataloging-in-Publication Data

Reference guide to short fiction / editor, Noelle Watson.
    p. cm. -- (St. James reference guides)
    Includes bibliographical reference and index.
    ISBN 1-55862-334-5 (alk. paper) : $130.00
    1. Short story. 2. Short stories--Stories, plots, etc.
    3. Bibliography--Best books--Short stories. I. Watson, Noelle.
    II. Series.
    PN3373.R36 1994
    809.3'1--dc20   93-33650
                                                                          CIP

A CIP catalogue record of this book is available from the British Library

10 9 8 7 6 5 4 3 2 1

♾™ The paper used in this publication meets the minimum requirements of the
American National Standard for Information Sciences—Permanence Paper for
Printed Library Materials, ANSI Z39.48-1984

Printed in the United States of America
Published simultaneously in the United Kingdom

The trademark **ITP** is used under license.

CONTENTS

EDITOR'S NOTE

The *Reference Guide to Short Fiction* includes entries on the most significant writers of short fiction from the 19th and 20th centuries. The selection of writers is based on the recommendations of the advisers listed on page xi. Some living writers are included in the *Reference Guide*, but readers interested in contemporary short fiction writers should consult the St. James Press Contemporary Writers series (*Novelists* and *World Writers*).

The entry for each writer includes a biography, a complete list of the writer's published books, a selected list of bibliographies and critical studies on the writer (in English), and a signed critical essay.

In the biography, details of education, military service, and marriage(s) are given before the usual chronological summary of the writer's life; awards and honors are given last.

The Publications list includes all separately published books, though as a rule broadsheets, single sermons and lectures, minor pamphlets, exhibition catalogues, etc., are omitted. Often titles are "short." Under the heading Collections I have listed collections of the complete works and of the individual genres (stories, novels, verse, and plays); only those collections that have some editorial authority and were issued after the writer's death are cited; on-going editions are indicated by a dash after the date of publication; often a general collection from the writer's works or a selection from the individual genres mentioned above is included.

The date given is that of the first book publication, which often followed the first periodical or anthology publication by some time; I have attempted to list the actual year of publication, sometimes different from the date given on the title page. No attempt has been made to indicate which works were published anonymously or pseudonymously, or which works of fiction were published in more than one volume. I have listed plays that were produced but not published; librettos and musical plays are listed along with the other plays. Reprints of books (including facsimile editions) and revivals of plays are not listed unless a revision of text or a change of title is involved. The most recent edited version of an individual work is listed if it supersedes the collected edition cited. Introductions, memoirs, editorial matter, etc., in works cited in the Publications list are not repeated in the Critical Studies list.

For the foreign-language writers, I have listed the original edition of each book in the original language and the first English translation. Book lists for entrants in languages other than French, German, Spanish, Portuguese, and Italian contain when possible literal English translations of titles in square brackets after each title.

For certain language groups entrants have been listed by their transliterated names. Cross-references are provided as appropriate. Chinese and Japanese entrants are listed last name then first name with no separating comma, as is standard academic practice.

Some of the entries in the Writers section are supplemented in the Works section, which includes a selection of essays on the best-known short stories and novellas written in, or translated to, English, as well as on some works important chiefly for historical reasons.

The *Reference Guide* concludes with a Title Index to the Short Story section of the Publications list; the index also refers to individual short stories and novellas discussed in the writer essays and all the titles in the Works section.

I would like to thank the advisers and contributors, and, in particular, the St. James Press editors Tracy Chevalier and Lesley Henderson, for their patience and help.

ADVISERS

Christopher Barnes
Bruce Bennett
Richard P. Benton
Malcolm Bradbury
Richard P. Corballis
Peter Cowan
Eugene Current-Garcia
Leslie A. Fiedler
George Gömöri
D.C.R.A. Goonetilleke
Ian A. Gordon
Maurice Harmon
Peter Hutchison
A. Norman Jeffares
Keneth Kinnamon
Jerome Klinkowitz

Richard Kostelanetz
A.H.T. Levi
Maurice Lindsay
David Madden
Shyamala A. Narayan
W.H. New
David O'Connell
Janet Pérez
Ian Reid
Murray Sachs
Linda Wagner-Martin
Mark Williams
Jason Wilson
George Woodcock
Leon Yudkin

CONTRIBUTORS

Pamela Abee-Taulli
Wendell M. Aycock
Simon Baker
Marina Balina
Soma Banerjee
Jolene J. Barjasteh
Christopher Barnes
Peter Barta
Michael H. Begnal
Samuel I. Bellman
Gene H. Bell-Villada
Bruce Bennett
John M. Bennett
Renate Benson
Richard P. Benton
Carolyn Bliss
Anna Botta
William Broughton
Russell E. Brown
George Bruce
Eva Paulino Bueno
Nicole Buffard-O'Shea
Anthony Bushell

Lance St. John Butler
Edward Butscher
Kelly Cannon
Leonard Casper
R.V. Cassill
Ann Charters
Laurie Clancy
Barbara Clark
Stella T. Clark
Keith Clark
Joan E. Clifford
Anne Clune
David G. Coad
Robert B. Cochran
A.O.J. Cockshut
Mark L. Collins
Philip Collins
James B. Colvert
Carlo Coppola
Richard P. Corballis
George Core
Ralph J. Crane
Richard K. Cross

Donald Crowley
Eugene Current-Garcia
Renee R. Curry
Leon de Kock
Robert Dingley
John Ditsky
Livio Dobrez
Patricia Dobrez
David Dowling
Finuala Dowling
Paul A. Doyle
R.P. Draper
Charles Duncan
Grace Eckley
Wilton Eckley
Marilyn Elkins
Robert Richmond Ellis
Walter E. Evans
Welch D. Everman
James E. Falen
Peter Faulkner
Carole Ferrier
Stephen M. Finn
Felicity Firth
Joseph Flibbert
Joseph M. Flora
Kevin Foster
Sherwin S.S. Fu
Tommasina Gabriele
John Gerlach
Robert Franklin Gish
Derek Glass
Steven Goldleaf
George Gömöri
Shifen Gong
Alexander G. Gonzalez
D.C.R.A. Goonetilleke
Lois Gordon
Peter Graves
Jane Grayson
Liping Guo
Jay L. Halio
Joan Wylie Hall
James Harding
Maurice Harmon
Clive Hart
David M. Heaton
George Hendrick
Michael Herbert
David Leon Higdon
W. Kenneth Holditch
David Horrocks
William L. Howard
Peter Hutchinson
David Jackson
Regina Janes

Lawrence Jones
Chelva Kanaganayakam
Bruce Kellner
G.D. Killam
Bruce King
Kimball King
Arthur F. Kinney
David Kirby
Susanne Klingenstein
Jerome Klinkowitz
Deborah K. Kloepfer
Richard Kostelanetz
Mary Lago
Claire Larriere
Karen Lazar
Luis Leal
A.H.T. Levi
Honor Levi
Claudia M.Z. Levi
Maurice Lindsay
Joyce Lindsay
Thomas Loe
Nathan Longan
Barbara A. Looney
Dina Lowy
Sheng-mei Ma
Barbara Mabee
Craig MacKenzie
Elisabeth Mahoney
Phillip Mallett
James Mandrell
Herbert Marder
John Marney
Paul Marx
Charles E. May
Richard Mazzara
Margaret B. McDowell
David McDuff
George R. McMurray
Madonne M. Miner
Adrian Mitchell
F.C. Molloy
Robert A. Morace
Isobel Murray
Valerie Grosvenor Myer
Gwen L. Nagel
James Nagel
M.K. Naik
Susan J. Napier
Rosina Neginsky
K.M. Newton
Soňa Nováková
Harley D. Oberhelman
George O'Brien
David O'Connell
Patricia Anne Odber de
  Baubeta

Norman Page
Judith Dell Panny
Shirley Paolini
Jeffrey D. Parker
Marian Pehowski
Olga Pelensky
Genaro J. Pérez
Janet Pérez
Richard F. Peterson
Jan Pilditch
Sanford Pinsker
Glyn Pursglove
Michael Pursglove
James Raeside
Judy Rawson
Ian Reid
Karen Rhodes
Alan Riach
Ian Richards
Edward A. Riedinger
Graeme Roberts
Katharine M. Rogers
Professor Mary Rohrberger
Judith Rosenberg
Joseph Rosenblum
Francesca Ross
Trevor Royle
Patricia Rubio
Christine A. Rydel
Murray Sachs
Hana Sambrook
Stewart F. Sanderson
Linda H. Scatton
William J. Schafer
Gary Scharnhorst
Barry P. Scherr
Judith M. Schmitt
Bernice Schrank
Sydney Schultze
Irene Scobbie
Paul H. Scott

Brian Sibley
Paul Sladky
Christopher Smith
Phillip A. Snyder
Eric Solomon
John Robert Sorfleet
Hilda Spear
Carla N. Spivack
Charlotte Spivack
Rebecca Stephens
Carol Simpson Stern
Brian Stonehill
Victor Strandberg
J.R. (Tim) Struthers
Carol Summerfield
Alice Swensen
Gretchen Thies
Bruce Thompson
Laurie Thompson
Leona Toker
Richard Tuerk
Dennis Vannatta
Linda Wagner-Martin
John C. Waldmeir
Joseph J. Waldmeir
Pin P. Wan
Allan Weiss
Abby H.P. Werlock
Craig Hansen Werner
Perry D. Westbrook
John J. White
Brian Wilkie
Claire Wilkshire
Mark Williams
Jason Wilson
Sharon Wood
George Woodcock
James Woodress
Mary U. Yankalunas
Lorraine M. York
Solveig Zempel

Reference Guide to

SHORT
FICTION

ALPHABETICAL LIST OF WRITERS

Chinua Achebe
S.Y. Agnon
Ilse Aichinger
Conrad Aiken
Chingiz Aimatov
Akutagawa Ryūnosuke
Nelson Algren
Mulk Raj Anand
Hans Christian Andersen
Sherwood Anderson
Ivo Andrić
Aharon Appelfeld
Juan José Arreola
Margaret Atwood
Francisco Ayala
Marcel Aymé

Isaak Babel
James Baldwin
J.G. Ballard
Honoré de Balzac
Toni Cade Bambara
John Barth
Donald Barthelme
H.E. Bates
Barbara Baynton
Ann Beattie
Simone de Beauvoir
Samuel Beckett
Saul Bellow
Stephen Vincent Benét
Ambrose Bierce
Adolfo Bioy Casares
Clark Blaise
Heinrich Böll
María Luisa Bombal
Ruskin Bond
Jorge Luis Borges
Tadeusz Borowski
Herman Charles Bosman
Elizabeth Bowen
Kay Boyle
Ray Bradbury
George Mackay Brown
Georg Büchner
Mikhail Bulgakov

Erskine Caldwell
Hortense Calisher

Morley Callaghan
Italo Calvino
Albert Camus
Karel Čapek
Truman Capote
Peter Carey
Alejo Carpentier
Angela Carter
Raymond Carver
Rosario Castellanos
Willa Cather
John Cheever
Anton Chekhov
Charles Waddell Chesnutt
G.K. Chesterton
Kate Chopin
Austin C. Clarke
Marcus Clarke
Colette
Wilkie Collins
Joseph Conrad
Robert Coover
A.E. Coppard
Julio Cortázar
Peter Cowan
Stephen Crane

Roald Dahl
Alphonse Daudet
Dan Davin
Dazai Osamu
Walter de la Mare
Charles Dickens
Isak Dinesen
José Donoso
Fedor Dostoevskii
Arthur Conan Doyle
Annette von Droste-Hülshoff
Maurice Duggan
Daphne du Maurier

George Eliot
Ralph Ellison
Endō Shūsaku

William Faulkner
F. Scott Fitzgerald
Gustave Flaubert
E.M. Forster

Janet Frame
Mary E. Wilkin Freeman
Carlos Fuentes

Gangādhar Gādgīl
Mavis Gallant
John Galt
Gabriel García Márquez
John Gardner
Hamlin Garland
Elizabeth Gaskell
Maurice Gee
André Gide
Charlotte Perkins Gilman
Nikolai Gogol
Nadine Gordimer
Caroline Gordon
Maksim Gor'kii
Patricia Grace
R.B. Cunninghame Graham
Jacob Grimm
Wilhelm Grimm
João Guimarães Rosa

Thomas Chandler Haliburton
Dashiel Hammett
Thomas Hardy
Joel Chandler Harris
Bret Harte
L.P. Hartley
Jaroslav Hašek
Gerhart Hauptmann
Nathaniel Hawthorne
Bessie Head
Sādeq Hedāyat
Ernest Hemingway
O. Henry
E.T.A. Hoffmann
Hugh Hood
Bohumil Hrabal
Langston Hughes
Zora Neale Hurston

Yusuf Idris
Witi Ihimaera
Washington Irving

Shirley Jackson
W.W. Jacobs
Dan Jacobson
Henry James
M.R. James
Tove Jansson
Sarah Orne Jewett
Elizabeth Jolley
Glyn Jones
James Joyce

Franz Kafka
Kawabata Yasunari
Iurii Kazakov
Gottfried Keller
W.P. Kinsella
Rudyard Kipling
Danilo Kiš
Heinrich von Kleist
Milan Kundera

Pär Lagerkvist
Ring Lardner
Margaret Laurence
Mary Lavin
D.H. Lawrence
Henry Lawson
Stephen Leacock
J.-M.G. Le Clézio
Sheridan Le Fanu
József Lengyel
Siegfried Lenz
Doris Lessing
Eric Linklater
Clarice Lispector
Jack London
Lu Xun

Joaquim Machado de Assis
Alistair MacLeod
Nagīb Mahfūz
Bernard Malamud
Thomas Mann
Katherine Mansfield
Sādat Hasan Mānṭo
Mao Dun
Owen Marshall
Ana Maria Matute
W. Somerset Maugham
Guy de Maupassant
Carson McCullers
James Alan McPherson
Herman Melville
Prosper Mérimée
John Metcalf
O.E. Middleton
Mishima Yukio
Naomi Mitchison
George Moore
Frank Moorhouse
Alberto Moravia
Toshio Mori
John Morrison
Es'kia Mphahlele
Alice Munro
Robert Musil

Vladimir Nabokov
V.S. Naipaul

R.K. Narayan
Gérard de Nerval
Anais Nin

Joyce Carol Oates
Edna O'Brien
Silvina Ocampo
Flannery O'Connor
Frank O'Connor
Vladímir Odóevskii
Ōe Kenzabura
Sean O'Faolain
Liam O'Flaherty
John O'Hara
Margaret Oliphant
Tillie Olsen
Juan Carlos Onetti
István Örkény
Amos Oz
Cynthia Ozick

Grace Paley
Emilia Pardo Bazán
Dorothy Parker
Boris Pasternak
Cesare Pavese
Thomas Love Peacock
Boris Pil'niak
Luigi Pirandello
William Plomer
Edgar Allan Poe
Hal Porter
Katherine Anne Porter
J.F. Powers
Premcand
Katharine Susannah Prichard
V.S. Pritchett
Aleksandr Pushkin

Horacio Quiroga

Raja Rao
Jean Rhys
Henry Handel Richardson
Richard Rive
Charles G.D. Roberts
Mercè Rodoreda
Martin Ross
Sinclair Ross
Philip Roth
Juan Rulfo

Saki
J.D. Salinger
William Sansom
Frank Sargeson
William Saroyan

Jean-Paul Sarte
Arthur Schnitzler
Bruno Schulz
Walter Scott
Maurice Shadbolt
Varlam Shalamov
Shen Congwen
Henryk Sienkiewicz
Leslie Marmon Silko
Alan Sillitoe
Isaac Bashevis Singer
F. Sionil Jose
Pauline Smith
Iain Crichton Smith
Hjalmar Söderberg
Mario Soldati
Aleksandr Solzhenitsyn
Edith Somerville
Jean Stafford
Christina Stead
Gertrude Stein
John Steinbeck
Robert Louis Stevenson
Adalbert Stifter
Theodor Storm

Rabindranath Tagore
Tanizaki Jun'ichiro
Peter Taylor
Lygia Fagundes Telles
Abram Terts
Audrey Thomas
Dylan Thomas
James Thurber
Tatiana Tolstaia
Lev Tolstoi
Jean Toomer
Miguel Torga
William Trevor
Anthony Trollope
Tsushima Yūko
Ivan Turgenev
Mark Twain

Sabine R. Ulibarrí
Miguel de Unamuno
John Updike
Fred Urquhart

Luisa Valenzuela
Ramón del Valle-Inclán
Giovanni Verga
Bjørg Vik
Auguste Villiers de l'Isle-Adam

Alice Walker
Sylvia Townsend Warner

Robert Penn Warren
Evelyn Waugh
H.G. Wells
Eudora Welty
Albert Wendt
Edith Wharton
Patrick White
Oscar Wilde
Michael Wilding
William Carlos Williams
Angus Wilson

P.G. Wodehouse
Virginia Woolf
Richard Wright

A.B. Yehoshua
Yu Dafu

Evgenii Zamiatin
Zhang Ailing
Mikhail Zoshchenko

CHRONOLOGICAL LIST OF WRITERS

1771-1832	Walter Scott	1849-1909	Sarah Orne Jewett
1776-1822	E.T.A. Hoffmann	1850-1893	Guy de Maupassant
1777-1811	Heinrich von Kleist	1850-1894	Robert Louis Stevenson
1779-1839	John Galt	1851-1904	Kate Chopin
1783-1859	Washington Irving	1851-1921	Emilia Pardo Bazán
1785-1863	Jacob Grimm	1852-1930	Mary E. Wilkin Freeman
1785-1866	Thomas Love Peacock	1852-1936	R.B. Cunninghame Graham
1786-1859	Wilhelm Grimm	1852-1933	George Moore
1796-1865	Thomas Chandler Haliburton	1854-1900	Oscar Wilde
1797-1848	Annette von Droste-Hülshoff	1857-1929	Barbara Baynton
1799-1850	Honoré de Balzac	1857-1924	Joseph Conrad
1799-1837	Aleksandr Pushkin	1858-1932	Charles Waddell Chesnutt
1803-1870	Prosper Mérimée	1858-1949	Edith Somerville
1804-1864	Nathaniel Hawthorne	1859-1930	Arthur Conan Doyle
1804-1869	Vladímir Odóevskii	1860-1904	Anton Chekhov
1805-1875	Hans Christian Andersen	1860-1940	Hamlin Garland
1805-1868	Adalbert Stifter	1860-1935	Charlotte Perkins Gilman
1808-1855	Gérard de Nerval	1860-1943	Charles G.D. Roberts
1809-1852	Nikolai Gogol	1861-1941	Rabindranath Tagore
1809-1849	Edgar Allan Poe	1862-1910	O. Henry
1810-1865	Elizabeth Gaskell	1862-1915	Martin Ross
1812-1870	Charles Dickens	1862-1946	Gerhart Hauptmann
1813-1837	Georg Büchner	1862-1936	M.R. James
1814-1873	Sheridan Le Fanu	1862-1931	Arthur Schnitzler
1815-1882	Anthony Trollope	1862-1937	Edith Wharton
1817-1888	Theodor Storm	1863-1943	W.W. Jacobs
1818-1883	Ivan Turgenev	1864-1936	Miguel de Unamuno
1819-1880	George Eliot	1865-1936	Rudyard Kipling
1819-1890	Gottfried Keller	1866-1936	Ramón del Valle-Inclán
1819-1891	Herman Melville	1866-1946	H.G. Wells
1821-1881	Fedor Dostoevskii	1867-1922	Henry Lawson
1821-1880	Gustave Flaubert	1867-1936	Luigi Pirandello
1824-1889	Wilkie Collins	1868-1936	Maksim Gor'kii
1828-1897	Margaret Oliphant	1869-1951	André Gide
1828-1910	Lev Tolstoi	1869-1944	Stephen Leacock
1835-1910	Mark Twain	1869-1941	Hjalmar Söderberg
1836-1902	Bret Harte	1870-1946	Henry Handel Richardson
1838-1889	Auguste Villiers de l'Isle-Adam	1870-1916	Saki
1839-1908	Joaquim Machado de Assis	1871-1900	Stephen Crane
1840-1897	Alphonse Daudet	1873-1947	Willa Cather
1840-1928	Thomas Hardy	1873-1954	Colette
1840-1922	Giovanni Verga	1873-1956	Walter de la Mare
1842-1914	Ambrose Bierce	1874-1936	G.K. Chesterton
1843-1916	Henry James	1874-1965	W. Somerset Maugham
1846-1881	Marcus Clarke	1874-1946	Gertrude Stein
1846-1916	Henryk Sienkiewicz	1875-1955	Thomas Mann
1848-1908	Joel Chandler Harris	1876-1941	Sherwood Anderson

1876-1916	Jack London
1878-1957	A.E. Coppard
1878-1937	Horacio Quiroga
1879-1970	E.M. Forster
1880-1942	Robert Musil
1880-1936	Premcand
1881-1936	Lu Xun
1881-1975	P.G. Wodehouse
1882-1941	James Joyce
1882-1959	Pauline Smith
1882-1941	Virginia Woolf
1883-1923	Jaroslav Hašek
1883-1924	Franz Kafka
1883-1969	Katharine Susannah Prichard
1883-1963	William Carlos Williams
1884-1937	Evgenii Zamiatin
1885-1962	Isak Dinesen
1885-1933	Ring Lardner
1885-1930	D.H. Lawrence
1886-1965	Tanizaki Jun'ichiro
1888-1970	S.Y. Agnon
1888-1923	Katherine Mansfield
1889-1973	Conrad Aiken
1890-1938	Karel Čapek
1890-1960	Boris Pasternak
1890-1980	Katherine Anne Porter
1890-1979	Jean Rhys
1891-1940	Mikhail Bulgakov
1891-1974	Pär Lagerkvist
1892-1927	Akutagawa Ryūnosuke
1892-1975	Ivo Andrić
1892-1942	Bruno Schulz
1893-1967	Dorothy Parker
1893-1978	Sylvia Townsend Warner
1894-1941	Isaak Babel
1894-1961	Dashiel Hammett
1894-1941	Boris Pil'niak
1894-1961	James Thurber
1894-1967	Jean Toomer
1895-1981	Caroline Gordon
1895-1972	L.P. Hartley
1895-1958	Mikhail Zoshchenko
1896-1940	F. Scott Fitzgerald
1896-1975	József Lengyel
1896-1981	Mao Dun
1896-1984	Liam O'Flaherty
1896-1945	Yu Dafu
1897-1962	William Faulkner
1897-	Naomi Mitchison
1898-1943	Stephen Vincent Benét
1899-1986	Jorge Luis Borges
1899-1973	Elizabeth Bowen
1899-1961	Ernest Hemingway
1899-1972	Kawabata Yasunari

1899-1974	Eric Linklater
1899-1977	Vladimir Nabokov
1900-1991	Sean O'Faolain
1900-	V.S. Pritchett
1901(?)-1960	Zora Neale Hurston
1902-1967	Marcel Aymé
1902-1992	Kay Boyle
1902-1967	Langston Hughes
1902-1988	Shen Congwen
1902-1983	Christina Stead
1902-1968	John Steinbeck
1903-1987	Erskine Caldwell
1903-1990	Morley Callaghan
1903-1951	Sādeq Hedāyat
1903-1977	Anais Nin
1903-1966	Frank O'Connor
1903-1973	William Plomer
1903-1982	Frank Sargeson
1903-1966	Evelyn Waugh
1904-1980	Alejo Carpentier
1904-	John Morrison
1904-1991	Isaac Bashevis Singer
1905-	Mulk Raj Anand
1905-1974	H.E. Bates
1905-1951	Herman Charles Bosman
1905-	Glyn Jones
1905-1970	John O'Hara
1905-1980	Jean-Paul Sarte
1905-1989	Robert Penn Warren
1906-	Francisco Ayala
1906-1989	Samuel Beckett
1906-	R.K. Narayan
1906-	Silvina Ocampo
1906-	Mario Soldati
1907-1989	Daphne du Maurier
1907-1990	Alberto Moravia
1907-1982	Varlam Shalamov
1907-	Miguel Torga
1908-1986	Simone de Beauvoir
1908-1967	João Guimarães Rosa
1908-1950	Cesare Pavese
1908-	Raja Rao
1908-	Sinclair Ross
1908-1981	William Saroyan
1908-1960	Richard Wright
1909-1981	Nelson Algren
1909-1980	María Luisa Bombal
1909-1948	Dazai Osamu
1909-	Juan Carlos Onetti
1909-1983	Mercè Rodoreda
1909-	Eudora Welty
1910-1980	Toshio Mori
1911-	Hortense Calisher
1911-	Nagīb Mahfūz

1911-1984	Hal Porter
1912-1982	John Cheever
1912-	Mary Lavin
1912-1955	Sādat Hasan Mānṭo
1912/13	Tillie Olsen
1912-1979	István Örkény
1912-1976	William Sansom
1912-	Fred Urquhart
1912-1990	Patrick White
1913-1960	Albert Camus
1913-1990	Dan Davin
1913-	Angus Wilson
1914-	Adolfo Bioy Casares
1914-1984	Julio Cortázar
1914-	Peter Cowan
1914-	Ralph Ellison
1914-	Bohumil Hrabal
1914-	Tove Jansson
1914-1986	Bernard Malamud
1914-1953	Dylan Thomas
1915-	Saul Bellow
1915-1979	Jean Stafford
1916-1990	Roald Dahl
1916-1965	Shirley Jackson
1917-1985	Heinrich Böll
1917-1967	Carson McCullers
1917-	J.F. Powers
1917-	Peter Taylor
1918-	Juan José Arreola
1918-1986	Juan Rulfo
1918-	Aleksandr Solzhenitsyn
1919-	Doris Lessing
1919-	Es'kia Mphahlele
1919-	J.D. Salinger
1919-	Sabine R. Ulibarrí
1920-	Ray Bradbury
1920-	Zhang Ailing
1921-	Ilse Aichinger
1921-	George Mackay Brown
1922-1951	Tadeusz Borowski
1922-1974	Maurice Duggan
1922-	Mavis Gallant
1922-	Grace Paley
1923-1985	Italo Calvino
1923-	Endō Shūsaku
1923-	Gangādhar Gāḍgīl
1923-	Nadine Gordimer
1923-	Elizabeth Jolley
1924-1987	James Baldwin
1924-1984	Truman Capote
1924-	José Donoso
1924-	Janet Frame
1924-	F. Sionil Jose
1924-	Lygia Fagundes Telles

1925-1974	Rosario Castellanos
1925(?)-1977	Clarice Lispector
1925-	O.E. Middleton
1925-1970	Mishima Yukio
1925-1964	Flannery O'Connor
1925-	Abram Terts
1926-1987	Margaret Laurence
1926-	Siegfried Lenz
1926-	Ana Maria Matute
1927-1982	Iurii Kazakov
1927-1991	Yusuf Idris
1928-	Chingiz Aimatov
1928-	Carlos Fuentes
1928-	Gabriel García Márquez
1928-	Hugh Hood
1928-	Cynthia Ozick
1928-	Alan Sillitoe
1928-	Iain Crichton Smith
1928-	William Trevor
1929-	Dan Jacobson
1929-	Milan Kundera
1930-	Chinua Achebe
1930-	J.G. Ballard
1930-	John Barth
1931-1989	Donald Barthelme
1931-	Maurice Gee
1931-	Alice Munro
1931-1989	Richard Rive
1932-	Aharon Appelfeld
1932-	Robert Coover
1932-	V.S. Naipaul
1932-	Edna O'Brien
1932-	Maurice Shadbolt
1932-	John Updike
1933-1982	John Gardner
1933-	Philip Roth
1934-	Ruskin Bond
1934-	Austin C. Clarke
1935-	W.P. Kinsella
1935-1989	Danilo Kiš
1935-	Ōe Kenzabura
1935-	Audrey Thomas
1935-	Bjørg Vik
1936-	Alistair MacLeod
1936-	A.B. Yehoshua
1937-	Patricia Grace
1937-1986	Bessie Head
1938-1988	Raymond Carver
1938-	John Metcalf
1938-	Frank Moorhouse
1938-	Joyce Carol Oates
1938-	Luisa Valenzuela
1939-	Margaret Atwood
1939-	Toni Cade Bambara

ALPHABETICAL LIST OF WORKS

CHRONOLOGICAL LIST OF WORKS

The Marquise of O, Kleist, 1810
Michael Kohlhaas, Kleist, 1810
Bluebeard, Grimm, 1812
Little Red Riding Hood, Grimm, 1812
The Sand-Man, Hoffman, 1816
The Legend of Sleepy Hollow, Irving, 1820
Rip Van Winkle, Irving, 1820
Wandering Willie's Tale, Scott, 1824
The Two Drovers, Scott, 1827
The Stationmaster, Pushkin, 1830
Mateo Falcone, Mérimée, 1833
The Queen of Spades, Pushkin, 1834
Sam Slick, The Clockmaker, Haliburton, 1835
Wakefield, Hawthorne, 1835
Young Goodman Brown, Hawthorne, 1835
The Nose, Gogol, 1836
A Passion in the Desert, Balzac, 1837
The Steadfast Tin Soldier, Andersen, 1838
The Fall of the House of Usher, Poe, 1839
The Murders in the Rue Morgue, Poe, 1841
The Overcoat, Gogol, 1841
A Christmas Carol, Dickens, 1843
The Tell-Tale Heart, Poe, 1843
Rappaccini's Daughter, Hawthorne, 1844
The Cricket on the Hearth, Dickens, 1845
The Birthmark, Hawthorne, 1846
The Cask of Amontillado, Poe, 1846
The Unknown Masterpiece, Balzac, 1847
White Nights, Dostoevskii, 1848
Bezhin Meadow, Turgenev, 1852
The Old Nurse's Story, Gaskell, 1852
Bartleby, The Scrivener, Melville, 1853
Sylvie, Nerval, 1854
Benito Cereno, Melville, 1855
A Terribly Strange Bed, Collins, 1856
A Village Romeo and Juliet, Keller, 1856
The Sad Fortunes of the Rev. Amos Barton, Eliot, 1857
The Lifted Veil, Eliot, 1859
First Love, Turgenev, 1860
The Parson's Daughter of Oxney Colne, Trollope, 1861
Notes from Underground, Dostoevskii, 1864
The Signalman, Dickens, 1866
The Notorious Jumping Frog of Calaveras County, Twain, 1867
The Pope's Mule, Daudet, 1869
The Luck of Roaring Camp, Harte, 1870
The Outcasts of Poker Flat, Harte, 1870
Carmilla, Le Fanu, 1872
Green Tea, Le Fanu, 1872
A Simple Heart, Flaubert, 1877
Daisy Miller, Henry James, 1878
The Library Window, Oliphant, 1879
Ball of Fat, Maupassant, 1880
Cavalleria Rusticana, Verga, 1880
The She-Wolf, Verga, 1880

The Wonderful Tar-Baby Story, Harris, 1881
The Psychiatrist, Machado de Assis, 1882
The Suicide Club, Stevenson, 1882
Free Joe and the Rest of the World, Harris, 1884
The Piece of String, Maupassant, 1884
The Necklace, Maupassant, 1885
The Death of Ivan Ilyich, Tolstoi, 1886
A White Heron, Jewett, 1886
Markheim, Stevenson, 1887
Thrawn Janet, Stevenson, 1887
The Aspern Papers, Henry James, 1888
Lineman Thiel, Hauptmann, 1888
The Man Who Would Be King, Kipling, 1888
The Rider on the White Horse, Storm, 1888
A Tragedy of Two Ambitions, Hardy, 1888
Hautot and His Son, Maupassant, 1889
A New England Nun, Freeman, 1891
An Occurrence at Owl Creek Bridge, Bierce, 1891
The Return of a Private, Garland, 1891
Désirée's Baby, Chopin, 1892
The Speckled Band, Doyle, 1892
The Yellow Wallpaper, Gilman, 1892
The Union Buries Its Dead, Lawson, 1893
Kaa's Hunting, Kipling, 1894
On the Western Circuit, Hardy, 1894
Rothschild's Violin, Chekhov, 1894
The Revolver, Pardo Bazán, 1895
The Stolen Bacillus, Wells, 1895
A Pair of Silk Stockings, Chopin, 1897
The Bride Comes to Yellow Sky, Crane, 1898
Gooseberries, Chekhov, 1898
The Open Boat, Crane, 1898
The Turn of the Screw, Henry James, 1898
The Wife of His Youth, Chesnutt, 1898
The Goophered Grapevine, Chesnutt, 1899
The Lady with the Little Dog, Chekhov, 1899
Midnight Mass, Machado de Assis, 1899
Twenty-Six Men and a Girl, Gor'kii, 1899
The Man That Corrupted Hadleyburg, Twain, 1900
None But the Brave, Schnitzler, 1901
Water Them Geraniums, Lawson, 1901
Autumn Sonata, Valle-Inclán, 1902
Beattock for Moffat, Graham, 1902
Heart of Darkness, Conrad, 1902
The Immoralist, Gide, 1902
The Monkey's Paw, Jacobs, 1902
Typhoon, Conrad, 1902
The Beast in the Jungle, Henry James, 1903
Julia Cahill's Curse, Moore, 1903
Tonio Kröger, Mann, 1903
Mrs. Bathurst, Kipling, 1904
The Other Two, Wharton, 1904
They, Kipling, 1904
Paul's Case, Cather, 1905
The Gift of the Magi, O. Henry, 1906
Poisson d'Avril, Somerville and Martin, 1908

INTRODUCTION

INTRODUCTION
by Charles E. May

The first 120 years of the development of the short story in Europe and America divides into two almost equal periods—the movement from romanticism to realism between 1820 and 1880 and the movement from realism to impressionism between 1880 and 1940. The first period is characterized by a gradual shift from the romantic psychologizing of the old romance and folktale form in the early part of the century by Poe, Hawthorne, Gogol, and Mérimée to the emphasis on objective reality in the latter part of the century by the great realistic novelists; the second period is marked by a lyrical and metaphoric transformation of objective reality at the turn of the century by Anton Chekhov, James Joyce, Sherwood Anderson, and others. Because the story of these shifts in the form have been told so many times before, I will focus my introduction to this reference guide on the development of the short story in the last half century.

New literary movements usually begin as a reaction against whatever literary movement is predominant at the time, especially when the conventions of the existing movement become stereotyped. Realism, which dominated the writing of fiction during the latter part of the 19th century in Europe and America, was a reaction against the stereotyped sentimentalizing of the romantic movement that prevailed during the early part of the century. The basic difference between romantics and realists is a philosophic disagreement about what constitutes significant ''reality.'' For the romantics, what was meaningfully real was the ideal or the spiritual, a transcendent objectification of human desire. For the realists what mattered was the stuff of the physical world. For the romantics, pattern was more important than plausibility; thus their stories were apt to be more formal and ''literary'' than the stories of the realists. By insisting on a faithful adherence to the stuff of the external world, the realists often allowed content—which was apt to be ragged and random—to dictate form. As result, the novel, which can expand to better create an illusion of everyday reality, became the favored form of the realists, while the short story, basically a romantic form that requires more artifice and patterning, took on a secondary role. However, the nature of ''reality'' began to change around the turn of the century with the beginnings of so-called ''modernism.''

The most powerful influences on the short story in the ''modernist'' period were Russian and Irish. Ernest Hemingway, Sherwood Anderson, Katherine Anne Porter, and many others inherited from Anton Chekhov and James Joyce a technique of communicating complex emotional states by setting up artful patterns of simple concrete detail. As a result, the short story experienced a renaissance of respect not enjoyed since its beginnings half a century earlier with Hawthorne in America, Gogol in Russia, and Flaubert in France.

In the forty-year period between the publication of Sherwood Anderson's epoch-making *Winesburg, Ohio* in 1919 and Bernard Malamud's National Book Award winner *The Magic Barrel* in 1958, the ''artful approach'' initiated by Chekhov and Joyce dominated short fiction. However, in spite of this new kind of impressionistic realism introduced by Chekhov, Joyce, and Anderson early in the century, the form still retained its links to its older mythic and romance ancestors. Thus, two strains of the short story developed in the first half of the century—the stark new realistic style typical of Hemingway and his Russian compatriot Isaac Babel and the more mythic romance style of such writers as William Faulkner and Isak Dinesen.

Both styles are combined in the stories of Katherine Anne Porter, Eudora Welty, John Steinbeck, Carson McCullers, John Cheever, Richard Wright, Truman Capote, I.B. Singer, and Bernard Malamud during this period. The characteristics of the work of these writers are: a focus on the grotesque, the use of traditional folktale structures and motifs, a concern with the aesthetic experience, a fascination with the dream experience, a search for style and form, an insistence on the importance of language, the use of surrealistic imagery, and the development of a tightly unified poetic form.

This combination of both realistic and mythic styles continued up through the second half of the century, making short story writers of the period between 1960 and 1990 also roughly fall into two different groups. On the one hand, the ultimate extreme of the mythic/romance style is the fantastic anti-story of Jorge Luis Borges, John Barth, and Donald Barthelme. On the other hand, the extremes of Chekhovian realism can be seen in the so-called ''minimalism'' of Raymond Carver, Anne Beattie, and Cynthia Ozick. The very fact that the mythic/romance style of such writers as Gabriel García Márquez is sometimes called ''magical realism,'' while the minimalist style of Raymond Carver is sometimes called ''hyperrealism'' indicates that the twin streams of romance and realism are inextricably blended in the works of contemporary short story writers. The conventions of the old romance form become the very subject matter of the stories of Borges, Barth, and Barthelme; while the conventions of Chekhovian realism are practically parodied in the hyperrealism of Carver, Beattie, and Ozick.

If a major part of modernism in the early part of the century was manifested as James Joyce's frustration of conventional expectations about the cause-and-effect nature of plot and the "as-if-real" nature of character, then postmodernism pushes this tendency even further so that contemporary fiction is less and less about objective reality and more and more about its own creative processes. The primary effect of this mode of thought on contemporary fiction is that the short story loosens its illusion of reality to explore the reality of its own illusion. Rather than presenting itself "as if" it were real—a mimetic mirroring of external reality—postmodernist short fiction often makes its own artistic conventions and devices the subject of the story as well as its theme. The short story as a genre has always been more likely to lay bare its fictionality than the novel, which has traditionally tried to cover it up.

The most important precursor of the contemporary self-reflexive short story is the South American writer Jorge Luis Borges who in turn owes his own allegiance to Poe and Kafka. Because of Borges's overriding interest in aesthetic and metaphysical reality, his stories, like many of those of Poe, often resemble fables or essays. Borges's most common technique is to parody previously established genres such as the science-fiction story, the philosophical essay, or the detective story by pushing them to grotesque extremes. He realizes that reality is not the composite of the simple empirical data that we experience every day, but rather much more subjective, metaphysical, and thus mysterious than we often think that it is. Poe's detective story reminds us, says Borges, that reality is a highly patterned human construct, like fiction itself.

The most important follower of Borges is John Barth, who turned from the novel form to the short story in the late 1960's with *Lost in the Funhouse* (1968), an experimental collection in which the stories refuse to focus their attention on the external world and instead continually turn the reader's attention back to the process of fiction-making. Barth insists that the prosaic in fiction is only there to be transformed into fabulation. The artist's ostensible subject is not the main point; rather it is only an excuse or raw material for focussing on the nature of the fiction-making process. Great literature, says Barth, is almost always, regardless of what it is about, about itself.

For Donald Barthelme, the most important postmodernist writer to specialize almost solely in the short story, the problem of language is the problem of reality, for reality is the result of language processes. The problem of words, Barthelme realizes, is that so much contemporary language is used up, has become trash, dreck. Barthelme takes as his primary task the recycling of language, making metaphor out of the castoffs of technological culture. He has noted that if photography forced painters to reinvent painting, then films have forced fiction writers to reinvent fiction. Since films tell a realistic narrative so well, the fiction writer must develop a new principle. Collage, says Barthelme, is the central principle of all art in the 20th century. One of the implications of this collage process is a radical shift from the usual cause-and-effect process of fiction to the more spatial and metaphoric process of poetry. Critics have complained that Barthelme's work is without subject matter, without character, without plot, and without concern for the reader's understanding. These very characteristics, of course, have placed Barthelme with such writers as Robert Coover, William H. Gass, Ronald Sukenick, Raymond Federman, John Hawkes, and John Barth on the leading edge of postmodernist fiction.

However, alongside this extension of the Poe/Kafka fantastic story can be seen a further development of the Chekhov/Joyce realistic story, the most polished and profound practitioner of which is Raymond Carver. Since his collection of short stories, *Will You Please Be Quiet, Please?*, was nominated for the National Book Award in 1976, Carver has been the most admired short story writer in American literature and the leader of a renaissance of the form in the late 1970's and early 1980's. Part of a trend of short fiction that Barth playfully termed "hyperrealistic minimalism," or the "less-is-more" school, Carver's stories are stubbornly taciturn and reluctant to speak. Like the stories of his mentors, Chekhov and Hemingway, they communicate by indirection, suggesting much by saying little. The stories are like stark black-and-white snapshots of lives lived in a kind of quiet, even silent, desperation, told in a language that, even as it seems simple and straightforward, is highly studied and stylized. Most of Carver's stories have more of the ambience of dream than of everyday reality, yet the stories are not oneiric parables in the usual sense. His characters give us the feel of emotional reality which reaches the level of myth, even as they refuse to give us the feel of physical or simple psychological reality.

Although marital strife is perhaps the most common subject in modern American short fiction, Ann Beattie probes beyond the ordinary level of this theme by projecting the seemingly inevitable conflicts between married partners outward onto a metaphoric object or a mirror-image third party. Beattie is not interested in something so ordinary and blatant as adultery as the cause of separation; rather she focuses on the elusive emotions and subtle tensions that often underlie breakups. Because of their delicate nature, the conflicts Beattie is concerned with cannot be expressed directly and discursively, but rather must be embodied in a seemingly trivial object or an apparently irrelevant other person. One result of this realistic-minimalist technique is that although a story may begin with seemingly pedestrian details, as the details accumulate they begin to take on a lyrical tone and to assume a metaphoric importance.

A number of contemporary short story writers have combined the realism of Chekhov and Joyce with the mythic and linguistic characteristics of Hispanic, Native American, and African-American cultures. The best-known example of this combination is the South American writer Gabriel García Márquez, whose so-called "magical realism" presents events that take place within the realm of magic, even though they seem to be given a context of earthly realism. Like Franz Kafka, whom he imitated in his early works, García Márquez creates a world in which human dreams, desires, and fears are objectified as if they existed in the real world.

Leslie Marmon Silko's "Yellow Woman" is a model in some ways of this combination of styles, for, although it takes place in the modern world of jeeps and Jell-O, it also resonates with the primitive world of folktale and legend. What Silko succeeds in doing in this story is yoking a modern woman's fantasy with ancient myth. Since myth is the objectification of desire, the events of "Yellow Woman" seem mythically appropriate, for by identifying the protagonist with the mythic creature Yellow Woman, the mysterious male stranger transforms her into a goddess who represents the power of all women—huntress, moon goddess, mother of the game, and wife of war—even as she remains a character in the modern world.

Toni Cade Bambara says that her preference as a writer and a teacher is for the short story, because it "makes a modest appeal for attention, slips up on your blind side and wrassles you to the mat before you know what's grabbed you." Furthermore, she says about her own use of fiction as a method of persuading: "Writing in a rage can produce some interesting pyrotechnics, but there are other ways to keep a fire ablaze, it seems to me.... There are hipper ways to get to gut and brain than with hot pokers and pincers." One of her best-known stories, "The Lesson," communicates its lesson without leaning heavily on the lesson itself. The focus of Bambara's story, although it is based on the social issue of the disparity between the economic states of African-Americans and white Americans, is not the social issue itself, but one young girl's confrontation with it.

Cynthia Ozick, a Jewish short story writer in the tradition of Bernard Malamud, manages an almost magical blend of lyricism and realism to create a world that is both mythically distant and socially immediate at the same time. Although she is also a skilled novelist and poet, as well as the author of a number of essays on Judaism, art, and feminism, it is her short stories that most powerfully reflect her mythic imagination and her poetic use of language. Ozick's most powerful story, "The Shawl," which won first prize in 1981 in the *O. Henry Prize Stories* collection, is about a young Jewish woman in a German concentration camp whose infant is thrown into an electrical fence. It is not solely the event that creates the story's powerful impact, however, as horrible as that event is; it is also the hallucinatory style with which the fiction is created.

Ever since the beginning of the form in both Europe and America, there has always been something vaguely disturbing about short stories. Whereas novels leave us with a sense of completion, even satisfaction, short stories are apt to make us feel vexed, disconcerted, or mystified. We are not quite sure what Roderick Usher's illness is, why Bartleby "prefers not to," or why Goodman Brown must go into the forest on this one night of all nights of the year. What, we wonder, would cause ordinary people to stone someone to death in "The Lottery"? What is so important about Gogol's overcoat? Why do Hemingway's hills look like white elephants? What on earth are we to make of Kafka's human-sized cockroach?

Although we may not be sure why, we sense that the short story does not tell the same kind of story that the novel does. The novel seems to present human experience in a mostly familiar way, as if a mirror were held up to reality in which all the details of life, big and little, are reflected. Novels seem therefore relatively artless, the actions they describe motivated by cause and effect, the mere passage of time, many of them jogging along as if they could go on forever. Short stories, on the other hand, seem motivated by the inner necessity of the story, the need to recount an event that breaks up familiar experience and then moves toward an ending that is purposeful, meaningful, planned.

The short story is, on the one hand, a primitive or mythic form that seems to spring forth primarily in societies in which social structures in the broad sense have not taken over. Short stories present characters in situations in which the social does not exist to substitute social abstractions for existential confrontation. Because the short story situation is like that of dream or myth, because it is more atmosphere than events, its meaning is difficult to apprehend. As Conrad's Marlowe understands in attempting to tell the story of Kurtz and the journey into the heart of darkness, the meaning of the kind of episode on which the short story is usually built is not within like a kernel, "but outside, enveloping the tale which brought it out only as a glow brings out a haze." "Do you see the story?" Marlowe impatiently asks. "Do you see anything? It seems to me I am trying to tell you a dream—making a vain attempt. No relation of a dream can convey that notion of being captured by the incredible which is the very essence of dreams.''

However, even as these characteristics of the short story link it to its origins in the oneiric vision of myth and folktale, South African writer Nadine Gordimer suggests that the short story is a distinctively modern form, better equipped than the novel to capture ultimate reality in the modern world of truth as perspective. The strongest convention of the novel, says Gordimer, ''prolonged coherence of tone, to which even the most experimental of novels must conform unless it is to fall apart, is false to the nature of whatever can be grasped of human reality.'' Gordimer points out that even if chronology and narrative are juggled and rearranged in the novel there still is a consistency of human experience that is false to the nature of life as we experience it, in which ''contact is more like the flash of fireflies, in and out, now here, now there, in darkness.'' The short story writer sees ''by the light of the flash; theirs is the art of the only thing one can be sure of—the present moment.... A discrete moment of truth is aimed at—not the moment of truth, because the short story doesn't deal in cumulatives.''

The question of the short story form being true to reality or false to it, of being a basically primitive form or most appropriate to the modern vision, requires a reevaluation of what we mean when we define what is truly ''real.'' If we assume that reality is what one experiences every day as our well-controlled and comfortable self, then the short story often seems fantastic or hyperrealistic. If, however, we feel that immanent in the everyday is some other reality that somehow evades us, then the short story is more ''real'' than the novel can possibly be.

READING LIST

General Histories

'Abd al-Maguid, Abd al-Aziz, *The Modern Arabic Short Story: Its Emergence, Development, and Form*, 1955.

Aldrich, Earl M., *The Modern Short Story in Peru*, 1966.

Ashby, Leonard R., *History of the Short Story*, 1968.

Bates, H.E., *The Modern Short Story: A Critical Survey*, 1941; revised edition, as *The Modern Short Story from 1809 to 1953*, 1972.

Beachcroft, T.O., *The Modest Art, A Survey of the Short Story in English*, 1968.

Bennett, E.K., and H.M. Waidson, *A History of the German "Novelle"*, second edition, 1961.

Beyerl, Jan, *The Style of the Modern Arabic Short Story*, 1971.

Canby, Henry Seidel, *The Short Story in English*, 1909.

Clements, Robert J., and Joseph Gibaldi, *Anatomy of the Novella: The European Tale Collections from Boccaccio and Chaucer to Cervantes*, 1977.

Conant, Martha Pike, *The Oriental Tale in English in the Eighteenth Century*, 1907.

Crowley, J. Donald, editor, *The American Short Story 1850-1900*, 1985.

Current-García, Eugene, editor, *The American Short Story before 1850*, 1985.

Flora, Joseph M., editor, *The English Short Story 1880-1945*, 1985.

Gadpaille, Michelle, *The Canadian Short Story*, 1988.

George, A.J., *Short Fiction in France 1800-1850*, 1964.

Hanan, Patrick, *The Chinese Vernacular Short Story*, 1981.

Hanson, Clare, *Short Stories and Short Fictions 1880-1980*, 1985.

Harris, Wendell V., *British Short Fiction in the Nineteenth Century: A Literary and Bibliographic Guide*, 1979.

Hsia, C.T., *Modern Chinese Stories and Novellas: 1919-1949*, 1981.

Ikramullah, Shāista Akhtar Bānu Suhrawardy, *A Critical Survey of the Development of the Urdu Novel and Short Story*, 1945.

Kilroy, James F., editor, *The Irish Short Story: A Critical History*, 1984.

Larriere, Claire, *Victorian Short Stories* (in French and English), 1990.

Lee, Robert A., editor, *The Nineteenth-Century American Short Story*, 1985.

Lieberman, Elias, *The American Short Story: A Study of the Influence of Locality and its Development*, 1970.

Manzalaoui, Mahmud, editor, *Arabic Writing Today: The Short Story*, 1968.

Mersereau, John, Jr., *Russian Romantic Fiction*, 1983.

Moser, Charles A., editor, *The Russian Short Story: A Critical History*, 1986.

New, W.H., *Dreams of Speech and Violence: The Art of the Short Story in Canada and New Zealand*, 1987.

O'Brien, Edward J., *The Advance of the American Short Story*, revised edition, 1931.

Orel, Harold, *The Victorian Short Story: Development and Triumph of a Literary Genre*, 1986.

Pattee, Frederick L., *The Development of the American Short Story: An Historical Survey*, 1923.

Peden, Margaret Sayers, editor, *The Latin American Short Story*, 1983.

Peden, William, *The American Short Story: Front Line in the National Defense of Literature*, 1964; revised edition as *The American Short Story: Continuity and Change 1940-1975*, 1975.

Rhode, Robert D., *Setting in the American Short Story of Local Color 1865-1900*, 1975.

Ross, Danforth, *The American Short Story*, 1961.

Smith, C. Alphonso, *The American Short Story*, 1912.

Stevick, Philip, editor, *The American Short Story 1900-1945*, 1984.

Swales, Martin, *The German "Novelle"*, 1977.

Vannatta, Dennis, editor, *The English Short Story 1945-1980*, 1985.

Voss, Arthur, *The American Short Story: A Critical Survey*, 1973.

Weaver, Gordon, editor, *The American Short Story 1945-1980*, 1983.

West, Ray B., *The Short Story in America 1900-1950*, 1950.

Critical Studies

Albright, Evelyn M., *The Short-Story: Its Principles and Structure*, 1907.

Allen, Walter, *The Short Story in English*, 1981.

Aycock, Wendell M., editor, *The Teller and the Tale: Aspects of the Short Story*, 1982.

Bayley, John, *The Short Story: Henry James to Elizabeth Bowen*, 1988.

Bonheim, Helmut, *The Narrative Modes: Techniques of the Short Story*, 1982.

Bungert, Hans, editor, *Die Amerikanische Short Story: Theorie und Entwicklung* (in German and English), 1972.

Chambers, Ross, *Story and Situation: Narrative Seduction and the Power of Fiction, 1984*.

Clarey, Jo Ellyn, and Susan Lohafer, editors, *Short Story Theory at a Crossroads*, 1989.

Cross, Ethan Allen, *The Short Story: A Technical and Literary Study*, 1914.

Current-García, Eugene, and Walton R. Patrick, editors, *What Is the Short Story? Case Studies in the Development of a Literary Genre*, 1961, revised edition, 1974.

Eikhenbaum, B.M., *O. Henry and the Theory of the Short Story*, translated by I.R. Titunik, 1968.

Fagan, N. Brylion, *Short Story Writing: An Art or a Trade?*, 1923.

Foster, David William, *Studies in the Contemporary Spanish American Short Story*, 1979.

Gerlach, John, *Toward the End: Closure and Structure in the American Short Story*, 1985.

Grabo, Carl, *The Art of the Short Story*, 1913.

Hanan, Patrick, *The Chinese Short Story: Studies in Dating, Authorship, and Composition*, 1973.

Hankin, Cherry, editor, *Critical Essays on the New Zealand Short Story*, 1982.

Hanson, Clare, *Re-Reading the Short Story*, 1989.

Head, Dominic, *The Modernist Short Story: A Study in Theory and Practice*, 1992.

Huters, Theodore, editor, *Reading the Modern Chinese Short Story*, 1990.

Lanning, George, and Ellington White, editors, *The Short Story Today: A Kenyon Review Symposium*, 1970.

Liebowitz, Judith, *Narrative Purpose in the Novella*, 1974.

Lohafer, Susan, *Coming to Terms with the Short Story*, 1983.

Magill, Frank, editor, *Critical Survey of Short Fiction*, 7 vols., 1981.

Mann, Susan Garland, *The Short Story Cycle: A Genre Companion and Reference Guide*, 1988.

Matthews, Brander, *The Philosophy of the Short Story*, 1901.

May, Charles E., *Short Story Theories*, 1977.

McClare, Heather, editor, *Women Writers of the Short Story: A Collection of Critical Essays*, 1980.

Metcalf, John, and J.R. (Tim) Struthers, editors, *How Stories Mean*, 1993.

Moorhouse, Frank, editor, *The State of the Art: The Mood of Contemporary Australia in Short Stories*, 1983.

O'Brien, Edward J., *The Dance of the Machines: The American Short Story and the Industrial Age*, 1929.

O'Connor, Frank, *The Lonely Voice: A Study of the Short Story*, 1963.

O'Faolain, Sean, *The Short Story*, 1948.

O'Toole, L. Michael, *Structure, Style, and Interpretation in the Russian Short Story*, 1982.

Pain, Barry, *The Short Story*, 1916.

Reid, Ian, *Narrative Exchanges*, 1992.

Reid, Ian, *The Short Story*, 1977.

Rodax, Yvonne, *The Real and Ideal in the Novella of Italy, France, and England: Four Centuries of Change in the Boccaccian Tale*, 1968.

Rohrberger, Mary, *Hawthorne and the Modern Short Story: A Study in Genre*, 1966.

Sachs, Murray, *The French Short Story in the 19th Century*, 1969.

Shaw, Valerie, *The Short Story: A Critical Introduction*, 1983.

Stephens, Michael, *The Dramaturgy of Style: Voice in Short Fiction*, 1986.

Stummer, Peter O., editor, *The Story Must Be Told: Short Narrative Prose in the New English Literatures*, 1986.

Summers, Hollis, editor, *Discussions of the Short Story*, 1963.

Ward, Alfred C., *Aspects of the Modern Short Story: English and American*, 1924.

Welty, Eudora, *Short Stories*, 1949.

Williams, William Carlos, *A Beginning on the Short Story: Notes*, 1950.

Wright, Austin M., *The American Short Story in the Twenties*, 1961.

WRITERS

A

ACHEBE, Chinua. Nigerian. Born Albert Chinualumogu in Ogidi, 16 November 1930. Educated at Government College, Umuahia, 1944–47; University College, Ibadan, 1948–53, B.A. (London) 1953. Married Christiana Chinwe Okoli in 1961; two sons and two daughters. Talks producer, Lagos, 1954–57, controller, Enugu, 1958–61, and director, Voice of Nigeria, Lagos, 1961–66, Nigerian Broadcasting Corporation; chairman, Citadel Books Ltd., Enugu, 1967; senior research fellow, 1967–73, professor of English, 1973–81, and from 1984 professor emeritus, University of Nigeria, Nsukka; visiting professor, 1972–75, and Fulbright professor, 1987–88, University of Massachusetts, Amherst; visiting professor, University of Connecticut, Storrs, 1975–76; Regents' Lecturer, University of California, Los Angeles, 1984; visiting distinguished professor of English, City College, New York, 1989. Founding editor, Heinemann African Writers series, 1962–72, and from 1970 director, Heinemann Educational Books (Nigeria) Ltd., and Nwankwo-Ifejika Ltd. (later Nwamife), publishers, Enugu; from 1971 editor, *Okike: An African Journal of New Writing*, Nsukka; from 1983 governor, Newsconcern International Foundation, London; from 1984 founder and publisher, *Uwa Ndi Igbo: A Bilingual Journal of Igbo Life and Arts*. Member, University of Lagos Council, 1966; chairman, Society of Nigerian Authors, 1966, and Association of Nigerian Authors, 1982–86; member, Anambra State Arts Council, 1977–79; pro-chancellor and chairman of Council, Anambra State University of Technology, Enugu, 1986–88. From 1981 member of the Executive Committee, Commonwealth Arts Organisation, London; from 1983 member, International Social Prospects Academy, Geneva; from 1984 director, Okike Arts Center, Nsukka. Served on diplomatic missions for Biafra during Nigerian Civil War, 1967–69; deputy national president, People's Redemption Party, 1983. Badly injured in car accident, 1990. Recipient: Margaret Wrong Memorial prize, 1959; Nigerian National trophy, 1960; Rockefeller fellowship, 1960; Unesco fellowship, 1963; Jock Campbell award (*New Statesman*), 1965; Commonwealth Poetry prize, 1973; Neil Gunn International fellowship, 1974; Lotus award for Afro-Asian writers, 1975; Nigerian National Merit award, 1979; Commonwealth Foundation award, 1984. Litt.D.: Dartmouth College, Hanover, New Hampshire, 1972; University of Southampton, 1975; University of Ife, 1978; University of Nigeria, 1981; University of Kent, Canterbury, 1982; University of Guelph, Ontario, 1984; Mount Allison University, Sackville, New Brunswick, 1984; Franklin Pierce College, Rindge, New Hampshire, 1985; D. Univ.: University of Stirling, 1975; Open University, Milton Keynes, Buckinghamshire, 1989; LL.D.: University of Prince Edward Island, Charlottetown, 1976; D.H.L.: University of Massachusetts, 1977. Honorary fellow, Modern Language Association (U.S.), 1975; member, Order of the Federal Republic of Nigeria, 1979; honorary member, American Academy, 1982; fellow, Royal Society of Literature, 1983. Lives in Nsukka.

PUBLICATIONS

Short Stories

The Sacrificial Egg and Other Stories.   1962.
Girls at War.   1972.

Novels

Things Fall Apart.   1958.
No Longer at Ease.   1960.
Arrow of God.   1964.
A Man of the People.   1966.
Anthills of the Savannah.   1987.

Verse

Beware, Soul-Brother and Other Poems.   1971; revised edition, 1972; revised edition, as *Christmas in Biafra and Other Poems,* 1973.

Other (for children)

Chike and the River.   1966.
How the Leopard Got His Claws, with John Iroaganachi.   1972.
The Flute.   1977.
The Drum.   1977.

Other

Morning Yet on Creation Day: Essays.   1975.
In Person: Achebe, Awoonor, and Soyinka at the University of Washington.   1975.
The Trouble with Nigeria.   1983.
The World of the Ogbanje.   1986.
Hopes and Impediments: Selected Essays 1965–1987.   1988.
The University and the Leadership Factor in Nigerian Politics.   1988.
A Tribute to James Baldwin.   1989.
Beyond Hunger in Africa.   1991.

Editor, *The Insider: Stories of War and Peace from Nigeria.*   1971.
Editor, with Jomo Kenyatta and Amos Tutuola, *Winds of Change: Modern Stories from Black Africa.*   1977.
Editor, with Dubem Okafor, *Don't Let Him Die: An Anthology of Memorial Poems for Christopher Okigbo.*   1978.
Editor, with C.L. Innes, *African Short Stories.*   1985.
Editor, with others, *Beyond Hunger in Africa.*   1990.

*

Bibliography: *Achebe: A Bibliography* by B.M. Okpu, 1984.

Critical Studies: *The Novels of Achebe* by G.D. Killam, 1969, revised edition, as *The Writings of Achebe,* 1977; *Achebe* by Arthur Ravenscroft, 1969, revised edition, 1977; *Achebe* by David Carroll, 1970, revised editions, 1980, 1990; *Achebe* by Kate Turkington, 1977; *Critical Perspectives on Achebe* edited by Bernth Lindfors and C.L. Innes, 1978; *Achebe's World: The Historical and Cultural Context of the Novels of Achebe* by Robert M. Wren, 1980; *The Four Novels of Achebe: A Critical Study* by Benedict C. Njoku, 1984; *The Traditional Religion and Its Encounter with Christianity in Achebe's Novels* by E.M. Okoye, 1987; *Achebe* by C.L. Innes, 1990; *Reading Achebe* by Simon Gikandi, 1991.

*   *   *

Chinua Achebe, best-known for his five novels, has two story collections, which reveal the same interests as his longer fiction. The stories date from Achebe's undergraduate days at the University College, Ibadan, and were published as individual pieces between 1950 and 1971. The stories have been collected in *The Sacrificial Egg and Other Short Stories*, and *Girls at War*. They can be divided into three classifications: those that show the conflict between traditional and modern values, ("The Sacrificial Egg," "Dead Man's Path," and "Marriage Is a Private Affair," originally published as "The Beginning of the End"); those that display the nature of custom and belief; and those that deal with the Nigeria-Biafra civil war and its aftermath.

"The Madman," the first story in *Girls at War*, is about village life. Its hero, Nwibe, has a successful farm, wealth, several wives, and many children. He aspires to take the highest titles in his clan. Nwibe is cursed with a fierce temper and his judgement deserts him when he is under its sway. After a day's work he goes to a nearby stream to bathe, where his clothes are taken by a madman. The naked Nwibe chases the madman, now wearing Nwibe's clothing, through the market where, inadvertently, he commits an offence against a deity. This ruins his chances of taking the Afo title; even though he is purged of his madness by the local "psychiatrist" he is marked forever: "madness may indeed sometimes depart but never with all his clamorous train." The story is about pride, ambition, the nature of sanity, and the nature of tolerance. It implicitly asks what madness is, what just conduct is, and what is fit punishment.

"Uncle Ben's Choice" tells the story of a clerk of the Niger Company in the mid-1920's. "Jolly Ben," as he is known, is visited in the night by the seductive Mama Wota, the Lady of the River Niger, who promises Ben vast riches in exchange for possession of his being. Who would choose wealth over children, asks Ben? Rejected, Mama Wota bestows her favours on an eccentric, wealthy English trader. When he dies his money goes to outsiders. "Is that good wealth?" Ben asks: "God forbid."

"The Sacrificial Egg" deals with the conflict between generations and the beliefs held by each. Julius Obi, whose European education places him above a superstitious belief in the presence of the spirits, is forced through a moment of intense psychological violence and pain to re-examine his beliefs. Here, as in the "Dead Man's Path," "Marriage Is a Private Affair," and "Akueke," Achebe shows the prevalence, force, and inscrutability of traditional beliefs, which are anti-pathetic to rational scrutiny. The materials of the stories and the artist's approach to the treatment of

materials coincide: Achebe's art in these stories is one of suggestiveness rather than explicit statement.

"The Voter" shows the inability to create a democratic system of government in Nigeria. Voters collude with corrupt politicians; deceit and bribery are commonplace. Rufus Okeke, a party organiser at election time, pledges his loyalty to one candidate but accepts a huge bribe from his opposition. Fearing reprisal from both parties, "Roof" solves the problem by tearing his ballot paper in half, casting a portion for each candidate.

In "Vengeful Creditor" a three-month experiment in universal primary education ("free primadu") is undertaken in Nigeria, affecting the lives of various representative citizens. The theme provides Achebe with the opportunity for wry and ironic comment on the self-interest of supposedly disinterested public bodies—politicians who care only about political survival, hypocritical missionaries, and a public sector welfare officer who drives a Mercedes-Benz. This is a powerful attack on the simplistic, complacent, and hypocritical attitude of the Nigerian middle class whose private attitudes and actions belie their public professions and practices.

Self-interest masked by profession of public and patriotic commitment in the context of the Nigeria-Biafra civil war is the subject of "Girls at War." The story spans the civil war in Nigeria and traces its dehumanising effect; heroism and idealism are lost in the context of blood, sweat, and useless death in a fruitless cause. In "Civil Peace" Jonathan Iwegbu, a resourceful man who has survived the war, now falls victim to thugs and armed robbers who extract at gunpoint the little money with which he hopes to rebuild his life. A fatalist who believes that "nothing puzzles God," Jonathan claims he can accept his losses in peacetime as he has in war. But there is little to distinguish "civil peace" with civil war.

Achebe says in the preface to *Girls at War* that a dozen stories is a pretty lean harvest for 20 years of writing. He has added no more stories in the 20 years that have intervened. But if the harvest is small, it is not lean. The stories have a continuing and contemporary relevance. Few as they area, they have a central place in the canon of Nigerian literature.

—G.D. Killiam

See the essay on "Civil Peace."

———

AGNON, S.Y. Israeli. Pseudonym for Shmuel Yosef Halesi Czaczkes. Born in Buczacz, Galicia, Austria-Hungary (now Poland), 17 July 1888. Studied in private schools; Baron Hirsch School. Married Esther Marx in 1919; one daughter and one son. Lived in Palestine, 1907–13: first secretary of Jewish Court in Jaffa, and secretary of the National Jewish Council; lecturer and tutor in Germany, 1913–24; in Palestine again from 1924; fellow, Bar Ilan University. Recipient: Bialik prize, 1934, 1954; Hakhnasat Kala, 1937; Ussishkin prize. 1950; Israel prize, 1954, 1958; Nobel prize for literature, 1966. D.H.L.: Jewish Theological Seminary of America, 1936; Ph.D.: Hebrew University, Jerusalem, 1959. President, Mekitzei Nirdamim, 1950. Member, Hebrew Language Academy. *Died 17 February 1970.*

PUBLICATIONS

Short Stories

Kol Sirurav [Collected Fiction]. 11 vols., 1931–52; revised edition (includes additional volume *Al Kapot ha-Man'ul* [stories]), 8 vols., 1952–62.
Hachnasat Kalah (novel). 2 vols., 1931; as *The Bridal Canopy*, 1937.
Me'Az ume'Atah [From Then and from Now] (stories). 1931.
Sipurey Ahavim [Love Stories]. 1931.
Sipur Pashut (novel). 1935; as *A Simple Story*, 1985.
BeShuvah uveNachat [In Peace and Tranquillity] (stories). 1935.
Ore'ach Nata Lalun (novel). 1939; as *A Guest for the Night*, 1968.
Elu va'Elu [These and Those] (stories). 1941; section translated as *A Dwelling Place of My People*, 1983.
Temol Shilshom [The Day Before Yesterday] (novel). 1945; section published as *Kelev Chutsot*, 1950.
Samuch veNireh [Never and Apparent] (stories). 1951.
Ad Henah [Until Now] (stories). 1952.
Bilvav Yamim (novella). 1933; as *In the Heart of the Seas*, 1947.
Two Tales: The Betrothed, Edo and Enam. 1966.
Twenty-One Stories, edited by Nahum N. Glatzer. 1970; as *Selection*, 1977.

Novels

Giv'at haChol [The Hill of Sand]. 1920.
BeSod Yesharim [Among the Pious]. 1921.
MeChamat haMetsik [From the Wrath of the Oppressor]. 1921.
Al Kapot haMan'ul [Upon the Handles of the Lock]. 1922.
Polin [Poland]. 1925.
Ma'aseh rabi Gadi'el haTinok [The Tale of Little Reb Gadiel]. 1925.
Sipur haShanim haTovot. 1927.
Agadat haSofer [The Tale of the Scribe]. 1929.
Sefer, Sofer veSipur. 1938.
Shevu'at Emunim. 1943; as *The Betrothed*, in *Two Tales*, 1966.
Tehilla (in English). 1956.
Shirah [Song]. 1971; translated as *Shirah*, 1989.
Pitchey Dvarim. 1977.

Other

Me'Atsmi el Atsmi [From Me to Me]. 1976.
Esterlain yekirati: mikhatavim 684–691 (1924–1931) (letters). 1983.
Kurzweil, Baruch (letters). 1987.

Editor, with Ahron Eliasberg, *Das Buch von den polnischen Juden.* 1916.
Editor, *Yamim Nora'im.* 1938; as *Days of Awe, Being a Treasury of Traditions, Legends, and Learned Commentaries . . .* , 1948.
Editor, *Atem Re'item.* 1959.
Editor, *Sifreyhem shel Tsadikim.* 1961.

*

Critical Studies: *Nostalgia and Nightmare: A Study in the Fiction of Agnon* (includes bibliography) by Arnold J. Band, 1968; *The Fiction of Agnon* by Baruch Hochman, 1970; *Agnon* by Harold Fisch, 1975; *At the Handle of the Lock: Scenes in the Fiction of Agnon* by David Aberbach, 1984; *Agnon: Texts and Contexts in English Translation* edited by Leon I. Yudkin, 1988; *Agnon: A Revolutionary Traditionalist* by Gershon Shaked, translated by Jeffery M. Green, 1989.

* * *

When S.Y. Agnon received the Nobel prize for literature in 1966, he was the first author writing in Hebrew to be so honored. Long recognized in Palestine, later Israel, as an author who has elegantly recaptured the lost world of 19th-century, Eastern-European Jewry, he has written over 200 short stories, novels, and other miscellaneous writings.

Agnon's stories, sometime cast in the form of folk tales, usually involve a protagonist who, while engaged in a rather quotidian task, is unable to complete it due to a bizarre, sometimes magical or even mystical, happening.The protagonists are saved from their ineptitude only through their submission to God. Through language that is often drawn directly from or is a paraphrase of the Bible, and characters' and place names based on biblical and historical allusions and images, the story takes on allegorical and metaphorical significance. The reader is invited to probe into its universal, underlying meaning. The tales, set in both 19th-century Eastern Europe and modern-day Israel, possess a quality of wistfulness and longing, a desire to return to an earlier time when the world seemed a safe, ordered place, where one could pursue communion with God with impunity.

"Agunot," often translated as "Deserted Wives," is an important story for two reasons. It is Agnon's first major story published after his arrival in Palestine in 1907, at the age of 19. When he decided to take a pseudonym, the author replaced the Polish surname "Czaczkes" with *agnon*, the singular of *agunot*, which refers to a Jewish woman who, though abandoned by her husband, is still legally married to him until he is proven dead or he sends her a divorce decree. The author officially adopted Agnon as the family name in 1924, signifying a symbolic abandonment of his Eastern-European life, and the start of a new life in the promised land of Israel.

"Agunot" is the story of abandonment and desertion. Dinah, spoiled daughter of wealthy Sire Ahiezer, is emotionally abandoned by the handsome, learned groom brought for her all the way from Poland. The groom is "abandoned" by Friedele, the girl he really loves but has deserted, when she marries someone else. Ben Ari, the deft craftsman whose ark of the covenant Dinah tries to destroy because he does not return her affection, simply disappears. The major characters are all tragically attached to someone they cannot possess.

In "Fable of the Goat" (1925), which resembles the Indian *Panchatantra* tale "The Mongoose and the Cobra," an old man buys a goat for milk. Though the goat gives milk the old man describes as "sweet to my palate and the balm to my bones," it disappears every day. To find out where it goes, the son ties a string to its tail. The goat takes him to a cave that miraculously leads to the Land of Israel. He writes a note that his father should join him and puts it in the goat's ear, thinking that when the goat returns, his father will pet it and, with a flick of its ear, the note will fall out.

When the goat returns, the old man, believing the animal has led him to his death, has it slaughtered. Only when it is being skinned is the note found, but it is too late, and the old man realizes that, because of his precipitous action, he must live out his life in exile. Related succinctly in only three-and-a-half pages, the story, replete with quotes and paraphrases from the Bible, is an admonition to the rash man who, cutting himself off from the word of God, also cuts off his only link to the promised land.

The 20 stories in the tenth volume of his collected fiction, *Samuch veNireh* (also called *The Book of Deeds*), mark a major shift in Agnon's narrative style. No longer a teller of tales moving in the objective, exterior world of folklore, he is here Agnon the short story writer who draws heavily on subjective, interior, often childhood, experiences of his protagonists. The title of this collection is ironic, for in it the various unnamed first-person narrators achieve none of their deeds.

In "The Kerchief," for example, the narrator recalls how, when his father had been away a long time on business, he, the narrator, had a dream of the messiah, who sits among beggars at the gates of Rome on a rock pile binding his wounds. Shortly thereafter his father returns home with gifts, including a silk kerchief for his wife, which she wears on the Sabbath and holidays. On the day of the narrator's religious initiation ceremony (*bar mitzvah*), his mother places the kerchief around his neck. Returning home after the ceremony, he gives it to a beggar sitting on a rock pile, who uses it to bandage his running sores. The narrator turns away for a moment, and the beggar disappears. Worried about the scarf, the narrator is surprised that his mother, who has been awaiting his return, says nothing about the precious scarf; it is as if she knows what happened to it and approves.

In "To the Doctor" (1932), one of Agnon's shortest pieces, an unnamed narrator goes out at about 8:30 one evening to fetch a doctor for his ailing father. Because the doctor leaves his home at 9:00 p.m. to go drinking, the narrator is anxious to get there. On the way he is stopped by Mr. Andermann (German for "Otherman"), who says he is "just arrived from the city of Bordeaux in England," and wants to talk. Not wishing to be rude, yet anxious about his father, the narrator reluctantly stops to chat. In the meantime, it seems that the doctor leaves his home, and the father dies. One is left wondering whether the doctor would have been any help to the sick man in the first instance. Regardless of the answer, the son must live with his guilt and uncertainty.

Densely textured, lyrical, suffused with nostalgia, and highly affective, Agnon's stories bridge the two worlds of Eastern Europe and the Middle East with a seamless continuity. Translated into 16 languages—it is generally agreed that the English renderings are deficient and the German splendid—these stories are considered national treasures in Israel.

—Carlo Coppola

See the essays on "The Kerchief" and "A Whole Loaf."

————

AICHINGER, Ilse. Austrian. Born in Vienna, 1 November 1921. Educated at a gymnasium in Vienna, graduated

1939; University of Vienna, 1945/6–48. Married Günter Eich in 1953 (died 1972); two children. Publisher's reader, S. Fischer publishers, Frankfurt, East Germany, and Vienna, 1949–50; assistant to founder Inge Scholl, Hochschule für Gestaltung, Ulm. Member, Gruppe 47, from 1951. Recipient: Gruppe 47 prize, for story, 1952; Austrian State prize, 1952; City of Bremen prize, 1955; Immermann prize, 1955; Bavarian Academy of Fine Arts prize, 1961, 1991; Wildgans prize, 1969; Nelly Sachs prize, 1971; City of Vienna prize, 1974; City of Dortmund prize, 1975; Trackle prize, 1979; Petrarca prize, 1982; Belgian Europe Festival prize, 1987; Weilheim prize, 1987; Town of Solothurn prize, 1991; Roswitha medal. Lives in Vienna.

PUBLICATIONS

Short Stories

Rede unter dem Galgen.   1952; as *Der Gefesselte*, 1953; as *The Bound Man, and Other Stories*, 1955.
Selected Short Stories and Dialogue (in German), edited by James C. Alldridge.   1966.
Nachricht vom Tag: Erzählungen.   1970.
Schlechte Wörter (includes radio plays).   1976.
Meine Sprache und ich: Erzählungen.   1978.
Spiegel Geschichte: Erzählungen und Dialoge.   1979.

Novels

Die grössere Hoffnung.   1948; as *Herod's Children*, 1963.
Eliza, Eliza.   1965.

Plays

Zu keiner Stunde (dialogues).   1957; enlarged edition, 1980.
Besuch im Pfarrhaus: Ein Hörspiel, Drei Dialoge.   1961.
Auckland: 4 Hörspiele (radio plays).   1969.
Knöpfe (radio play).   In *Hörspiele*, 1978.
Weisse Chrysanthemum.   In *Kurzhörspiele*, 1979.

Radio Plays: *Knöpfe*, 1953; *Auckland*, 1969; *Gare Maritime*, 1973; *Belvedere*; *Weisse Chrysanthemum*.

Verse

Verschenkter Rat.   1978.

Other

Wo ich wohne: Erzählungen, Gedichte, Dialoge (includes stories, poems, dialogues).   1963.
Dialog, Erzählungen, Gedichte (includes dialogues, stories, poems).   1971.
Gedichte und Prosa.   1980.
Selected Poetry and Prose.   1983.
Grimmige Märchen, with Martin Walser, edited by Wolfgang Mieder.   1986.
Kleist, Moos, Fasane.   1987.
Gesemmalte Werke, edited by Richard Reichensperger.   8 vols., 1991.

Editor, *Gedichte*, by Günter Eich.   1973.

*

Critical Studies: "Aichinger as Storyteller" by Michael Kowal, in *American German Review* 33(2), 1966–67; *Aichinger* by James C. Alldridge, 1969; "A Structural Approach to Aichinger's *Spiegel Geschichte*" by Michael W. Resler, in *Unterrichtspraxis* 12(1), 1979; "Aichinger: The Sceptical Narrator" by Hans Wolfschütz, in *Modern Austrian Writing: Literature and Society after 1945*, edited by Wolfschütz and Alan Best, 1980; "Freedom vs. Meaning: Aichinger's 'Bound Man' and the Old Order Amish" by Marc A. Olshan, in *Internal and External Perspectives on Amish and Mennonite Life, II*, edited by Werner Enninger, Joachim Raith, and Karl-Heinz Wandt, 1986; "The Reception of the Works of Aichinger in the United States" by U. Henry Gerlach, in *Modern Austrian Literature* 20(3–4), 1987; "*Spiegel Geschichte*: A Linguistic Analysis" by Maurice Aldridge, in *International Review of Applied Linguistics in Language Teaching,* May 1988; "Recent Works by Aichinger" by Brian Keith-Smith, in *German Life and Letters,* July 1988.

* * *

After her debut as a writer with the novel *Die grössere Hoffnung* (*Herod's Children*), Ilse Aichinger turned to shorter works, which include short prose reflections, dialogues, radio plays, and poetry; it is, however, her short fiction that reveals best her talent and her preoccupations. Although Aichinger was a member of the "Gruppe 47," a group of young writers including Günter Grass, Heinrich Böll, Siegfried Lenz, and Ingeborg Bachmann, who set out to create a new German literature, she was never as political nor as critical of modern society as her colleagues. Her oeuvre is characterized by a search for the reality underlying those values accepted by a society that she believed to be complacent and shallow. Aichinger's mistrust of ideologies and of the use and misuse of conventional language led her to redefine narrative techniques which, at first under the influence of Franz Kafka, James Joyce, and Samuel Beckett, became progressively her own as she developed a more and more spiritualized and transcendental perception of the human condition. Her themes include the quest for one's identity, alienation from fellow human beings, and lack of understanding and communication where words have become mere signs.

"The Bound Man" explores the theme of loss of identity. The protagonist awakes one day finding himself bound by ropes which leave him just enough room to move. He accepts his bonds and becomes a circus artist acclaimed for his dexterity. He no longer knows any other identity, and when he is freed he feels himself deceived. Being unbound means not only loosing the mask which had become his alter ego but also the security which he had found in the circus. Aichinger develops this theme further in "Ghosts on the Lake," where the woman who seeks protection from the outer world by wearing sunglasses comes to realize that this is evasion; when she takes the glasses off she begins to disintegrate.

The theme of identity is picked up again, in a more positive manner, in "Moon Story," a satire on commercialized Miss Universe beauty contests, where women are subject to men's rules and desires and are valued only for their physical beauty. When one of the judges, whom the chosen Miss Universe loves, declares that she is not beautiful enough, she attempts to drown herself; in her delirium she travels to the moon and is met by Ophelia, who suggests that they exchange roles since the judges prefer the dead, still beautiful, and superficial Ophelia to a real woman. In freeing herself from her past the woman recognizes her uniqueness which cannot be attained by physical beauty or submission to set rules.

In depicting the theme of society's lack of spiritual values, Aichinger often resorts to soliloquies. "Story in a Mirror," one of her best short stories for which she received the prize of the "Gruppe 47" in 1952, has an anonymous narrator comment on the life of a young woman who has died from a botched abortion. He begins the story with her funeral service and then relates the events of a sad, unglamorous life back to the moment of her birth. Her death symbolizes a life of sterility ironically underlined by the killing of her unborn child. The narrative is interesting in that the lively flow and compassionate tone of the narrator's monologue establishes a dialogue with the dead woman unfolding her story like a movie unrolling backwards. The woman seems to arise from the dead and lives her life in reverse fashion until its beginning and end coincide.

"The Advertisement" deals with the topic of life and death in a more complex fashion. The title of the story alludes to a picture of a boy on a bill poster advertising a summer camp who becomes alive—this is typical of Aichinger's literary universe which is inhabited by speaking mice ("Die Maus"), by green donkeys ("Mein grüner Esel"), a giant milkmaid ("Das Milchmädchen von St. Louis"), and by a girl who turns out to be a newspaper ("Eliza, Eliza"). Aichinger, however, is not concerned with fairy-tale but with creating new expressions of reality as she perceives it. In "The Advertisement" a tubercular old man who puts up posters envies the young boy his eternal life. The boy, however, is terrified at the prospect of living forever because he sees his "life" as nothing more than stagnation. He is obsessed with a death wish, because for him death is the proof of life. In two grotesque sequences a little girl who invites him to dance is killed by a train, as is the boy when his poster comes unstuck and is torn to pieces by another train. The death of a young child, be it by suicide or accident, occurs in several of Aichinger's work and may suggest that only through death can the innocence and hopes of a young person be preserved and not stifled by the painful and destructive experience of life. Aichinger's own unhappy past under the Nazi regime (her mother was Jewish) may also underline her preoccupation with death and suicide.

Aichinger's work, especially her later stories, is difficult to interpret because it contains highly personal visions, so unusual and paradoxical that explanation is rarely satisfactory. Like Franz Kafka and James Joyce, she places great demands on the reader; her work is largely the domain of the literary specialist.

—Renate Benson

AIKEN, Conrad (Potter). American. Born in Savannah, Georgia, 5 August 1889. Educated at Middlesex School, Concord, Massachusetts; Harvard University, Cambridge, Massachusetts (president, *Harvard Advocate*), 1907–10, 1911–12, A.B. 1912. Married 1) Jessie McDonald in 1912 (divorced 1929), one son and two daughters, the writers Jane Aiken Hodge and Joan Aiken; 2) Clarissa M. Lorenz in 1930 (divorced 1937); 3) Mary Hoover in 1937. Contributing editor, *The Dial*, New York, 1916–19; American correspondent, *Athenaeum*, London, 1919–25, and London *Mercury*, 1921–22; lived in London, 1921–26 and 1930–39; instructor, Harvard University, 1927–28; London correspondent, *The New Yorker*, 1934–36; lived in Brewster, Massachusetts, from 1940, and Savannah after 1962. Fellow, 1947, and consultant in poetry, 1950–52, Library of Congress, Washington, D.C. Recipient: Pulitzer prize, 1930; Shelley Memorial award, 1930; Guggenheim fellowship, 1934; National Book award, 1954; Bollingen prize, 1956; Academy of American Poets fellowship, 1957; American Academy gold medal, 1958; Huntington Hartford Foundation award, 1960; Brandeis University Creative Arts award, 1967; National medal for literature, 1969. Member, American Academy, 1957. *Died 17 August 1973.*

PUBLICATIONS

Short Stories

Bring! Bring! and Other Stories.   1925.
Costumes by Eros.   1928.
Among the Lost People.   1934.
The Short Stories.   1950.
The Collected Short Stories.   1960.

Novels

Blue Voyage.   1927.
Gehenna.   1930.
Great Circle.   1933.
King Coffin.   1935.
A Heart for the Gods of Mexico.   1939.
Conversation; or, Pilgrims' Progress.   1940; as *The Conversation*, 1948.
The Collected Novels.   1964.

Verse

Earth Triumphant and Other Tales in Verse.   1914.
The Jig of Forslin: A Symphony.   1916.
Turns and Movies and Other Tales in Verse.   1916.
Nocturne of Remembered Spring and Other Poems.   1917.
The Charnel Rose, Senlin: A Biography, and Other Poems.   1918.
The House of Dust: A Symphony.   1920.
Punch: The Immortal Liar.   1921.
The Pilgrimage of Festus.   1923.
Priapus and the Pool and Other Poems.   1925.
(Poems), edited by Louis Untermeyer.   1927.
Prelude.   1929.
Selected Poems.   1929.
John Deth: A Metaphysical Legend, and Other Poems.   1930.
Preludes for Memnon.   1931.
The Coming Forth by Day of Osiris Jones.   1931.
Landscape West of Eden.   1934.
Time in the Rock: Preludes to Definition.   1936.
And in the Human Heart.   1940.
Brownstone Eclogues and Other Poems.   1942.
The Soldier.   1944.
The Kid.   1947.
The Divine Pilgrim.   1949.
Skylight One: Fifteen Poems.   1949.
Collected Poems.   1953.
A Letter from Li Po and Other Poems.   1955.
The Flute Player.   1956.
Sheepfold Hill: Fifteen Poems.   1958.

Selected Poems.   1961.
The Morning Song of Lord Zero: Poems Old and New.   1963.
A Seizure of Limericks.   1964.
Preludes.   1966.
Thee.   1967.
The Clerk's Journal, Being the Diary of a Queer Man: An Undergraduate Poem, Together with a Brief Memoir of Dean LeBaron Russell Briggs, T.S. Eliot, and Harvard, in 1911.   1971.
Collected Poems 1916–1970.   1970.
A Little Who's Zoo of Mild Animals.   1977.

Play

Mr. Arcularis (produced 1949).   1957.

Other

Scepticisms: Notes on Contemporary Poetry.   1919.
Ushant: An Essay (autobiography).   1952.
A Reviewer's ABC: Collected Criticism from 1916 to the Present, edited by Rufus A. Blanshard.   1958; as *Collected Criticism*, 1968.
Cats and Bats and Things with Wings (for children).   1965.
Tom, Sue, and the Clock (for children).   1966.
Selected Letters, edited by Joseph Killorin.   1978.

Editor, *Modern American Poets.*   1922; revised edition, 1927; revised edition, as *Twentieth Century American Poetry*, 1945; revised edition, 1963.
Editor, *Selected Poems of Emily Dickinson.*   1924.
Editor, *American Poetry 1671–1928: A Comprehensive Anthology.*   1929; revised edition, as *A Comprehensive Anthology of American Poetry*, 1944.
Editor, with William Rose Benét, *An Anthology of Famous English and American Poetry.*   1945.

*

Bibliography: *Aiken: A Bibliography (1902–1978)* by F.W. and F.C. Bonnell, 1982; *Aiken: Critical Recognition 1914–1981: A Bibliographic Guide* by Catherine Kirk Harris, 1983.

Critical Studies: *Aiken: A Life of His Art* by Jay Martin, 1962; *Aiken* by Frederick J. Hoffman, 1962; *Aiken* by Reuel Denney, 1964; *Lorelei Two: My Life with Aiken* by Clarissa M. Lorenz, 1983; *The Art of Knowing: The Poetry and Prose of Aiken* by Harry Marten, 1988; *Aiken: Poet of White Horse Vale* by Edward Butscher, 1988; *Aiken: A Priest of Consciousness* edited by Ted R. Spirey and Arthur Waterman, 1989.

*   *   *

With several poetry collections and a book of literary criticism to his credit, Conrad Aiken's turn to fiction in the early 1920's was driven by financial need, though he had published a number of stories at Harvard as an undergraduate.

His first collection of short stories, *Bring! Bring! and Other Stories*, which appeared two years before his Joycean first novel *Blue Voyage*, introduces a deft, if conventional, craftsman with a taste for domestic psychodramas in the mode of Anton Chekhov and Katherine Mansfield, prime influences. The title story, Lawrencean in its adroit probing of feminine behavior, derives significant energy from a misogynist vantage. Its weakest stories, including "The Dark City," "By My Troth, Nerissa!," and "Smith and Jones," a thin philosophical allegory as unconvincing as Poe at his most tendentious, foreshadow the difficulties Aiken would always experience when straying too far from autobiography or attempting to explore psyches too remote from his own. "Strange Moonlight" and "The Last Visit," the most effective performances in *Bring! Bring!*, are also the most personal.

"Strange Moonlight" recreates a crucial trauma from Aiken's Savannah childhood, the death of a neighborhood girl, which ushers the sensitive, prepubic hero to the brink of negation and frightening sexual knowledge in a series of musically scored events and symbols that distances the material to an almost fatal degree. Although looming ominously on a supratextual horizon, what is missing is the savage family climax that had forever warped its author's future self; the murder of his mother by his deranged father before he turned the gun on himself. The impact of "The Last Visit" is more visceral, if less ambitious, built upon a harrowing visit Aiken paid to his aged paternal grandmother during her final illness. As an early student of psychoanalytic theory as it evolved and one of the nation's pioneer Freudian critics, he was especially adept at integrating insights gained from depth psychology with traditional aesthetic machinery.

Curiously, Aiken's second collection, *Costumes by Eros*, provides no similar successes, though "Spider, Spider" achieves considerable force by exploiting a familiar fatal-siren motif. "Your Obituary, Well Written" also retains a certain fascination because it preserves Aiken's London meeting with Mansfield a few years before her untimely death in 1923, but the bulk of its companion pieces, often mere anecdotes or intellectual exercises, lack three-dimensional characters and appear willed rather than inevitable. His third collection, however, *Among the Lost People*, written while in the throes of composing the major poetry of the *Prelude* sequences and fighting off a nervous collapse, contains two recognized masterpieces, "Silent Snow, Secret Snow" and "Mr. Arcularis," and one near-classic, "Impulse."

As could be anticipated, the hypnotic surge of "Silent Snow, Secret Snow," a Poe horror story in the best sense of tapping unconscious fears, and the sad, chilling power of "Mr. Arcularis," well from the same death terror and unresolved Oedipal conflicts at the matrix of Aiken's neuroses, which abetted a profound distrust of women and dread of having inherited a father's madness. Later transformed into a play that highlights the mother's treacherous role in her son's existential despair "Mr. Arcularis" evokes the raging insecurity of a traumatized child now grown into a friendless old man. Its trick plot—recently recovered from a serious operation and sent on a sea voyage by his doctor, Mr. Arcularis is in actuality still on the operating table and sailing for oblivion—permits Aiken (and his audience) to both endure and neutralize tenacious death pressures.

In "Impulse," a smoothly narrated account of an infantile cissist's suicidal tumble into disgrace and isolation, the main character is a younger incarnation of Mr. Arcularis. With the contempt of a Nietzschean superman, he commits a minor crime to assert his superiority only to land in jail, abandoned by his supposed friends and wife, whom he has forced into a punishing-mother stance by his selfish neglect of family responsibilities. Aiken subtly illuminates this alter-ego's mental illness without any overt appeals to psychoanalytic doctrine. As a result, besides supplying a persuasive character study, "Impulse" serves as a parable vehicle for uncovering the prototypical American dilemma of immature men compelling their mature women to assume the features of a monstrous mother.

But whatever their sociological or political ramifications, the diamond virtues of Aiken's strongest short fictions reside ultimately in their lyric self-obsession and its remorse quest for psychological truths. If the protagonist of "Impulse" remains too unaware of his own culpability to achieve tragic grandeur, he and his counterparts in "Silent Snow, Secret Snow," "Mr. Arcularis," and "Strange Moonlight," touch and reflect us in ways sufficient to guarantee their literary survival.

—Edward Butscher

See the essay on "Silent Snow, Secret Snow."

AITMATOV, Chingiz (Torekulovich). Kirghizstani. Born in Sheker, Kirghizstan, 12 December 1928. Educated at Kirghiz Agricultural Institute, degree in animal husbandry 1953; Gorky Literary Institute, Moscow, 1956–58. Married 1) Keres Aitmatova, two sons; 2) Maria Urmatova in 1974, one son and one daughter. Assistant to secretary of Sheker Village Soviet, from 1943; editor, *Literaturnyi Kyrghyzstan* magazine, late 1950's; correspondent, *Pravda,* for five years; member of the Communist Party of the Soviet Union, 1959–91; deputy to Supreme Soviet, 1966–89; People's Writer of Kirghiz Soviet Socialist Republic, 1968; candidate member, 1969–71, and member, 1971–90, Central Committee, Kirghiz S.S.R.; vice chair, Committee of Solidarity with Peoples of Asian and African Countries, 1974–89; member, Congress of People's Deputies of the U.S.S.R., 1989–91; member of Mikhail Gorbachev's Presidential Council, 1990–91. Since 1990 Ambassador to Luxembourg. Member of the editorial board, *Novyi mir* and *Literaturnaia gazeta* literary journals; editor, *Druzhba narodov*; editor-in-chief, *Inostrannaia literatura,* 1988–90. First secretary, 1964–69, and chair, 1969-86, Cinema Union of Kirghiz S.S.R.; since 1986 chair, Union of Writers of Kirghizstan, and Issyk-Kul Forum. Recipient: Lenin prize, 1963; Order of the Red Banner of Labor (twice); State prize, 1968, 1977, 1983; Hero of Socialist Labour, 1978. Member of Kirghiz Academy of Science, 1974, European Academy of Arts, Science, and Humanities, 1983, and World Academy of Art and Science, 1987. Lives in Luxembourg.

PUBLICATIONS

Short Stories

Rasskazy [Stories].   1958.
Dzhamilia.   1959; as *Jamilá,* 1960.
Povesti gor i stepei.   1962; as *Tales of the Mountains and Steppes,* 1969.
Korotkie novelly [Short Novels].   1964.
Tri povesti [Three Short Stories].   1965; as *Short Novels: To Have and to Lose; Duishen; Mother-Earth,* 1965.

Povesti [Novellas].   1965.
Povesti i rasskazy [Novellas and Stories].   1970.
Izbrannoe [Collection].   1973.
Povesti [Short Stories].   1976.
Pegii pes, begushchii kraem moria.   1977; as *Piebald Dog Running Along the Shore and Other Stories,* 1989.
Izbrannoe.   1981.
Povesti [Short Stories].   1982.
Povesti [Short Stories].   1983.
Rasskazy [Stories].   1983.
Povesti, rasskazy [Novellas, Stories].   1985.
Ekho mira: povesti, rasskazy, publitsistika [Echo of the World: Novellas, Stories, Publications].   1985.
Povesti [Short Stories].   1987.
Mother Earth and Other Stories.   1989.

Novels

Melodiia [Melody].   1959.
Verbliuzhii glaz [The Camel's Eye].   1962.
Materinskoe pole.   1963; as *Mother-Earth,* in *Novels,* 1965; in *Mother Earth and Other Stories,* 1989.
Samanchy zholu.   1963.
Mlechnyi put' [Milky Way].   1963.
Pervyi uchitel' [The First Master].   1963.
Ballada o pervom uchitele [Ballad About the First Teacher].   1964.
Topolek moi v krasnoi kosynke [My Little Poplar in a Red Headscarf].   1964.
Proschai, Gul'sary!   In *Novyi mir* 3, 1966; 1967; as *Farewell, Gul'sary!,* 1970.
Syn soldata [The Son of a Soldier].   1970.
Belyi parokhod.   In *Novyi mir* 1, 1970; as *The White Ship,* 1972; as *The White Steamship,* 1972.
Posle skazki [After the Fairytale].   1971.
The Lament of a Migrating Bird.   1973; as *Rannie zhuravli,* 1976; as *The Cranes Fly Early,* 1983.
Posle skazki (Belyi parokhod); Materninskoe pole; Proshchai, Gul'sary!; Pervyi uchitel'; Litsom k litsu; Dzhamilia; Topolek moi v krasnoi kosynke; Verbliuzhii glaz; Svidanie s synom; Soldatenok.   1974.
Soldatenok [The Soldier].   1974.
Nochnoi poliv [Night Dew].   1975.
Lebedi nad Issyk-Kulem [Swans Above Issyk-Kulem].   1976.
Izbrannye proizvedeniia [Collected Works].   2 vols., 1978.
Legenda o rogatoi materi-olenizhe [The Legend of the Horned Mother Deer].   1979.
I dol'she veka dlitsia den'.   1981; as *The Day Lasts More than a Hundred Years,* 1983.
Burannyi polustanok (I dol'she veka dlitsia den') [The Snowstorm Halt].   1981.
Sobranie sochinenii v 3-kh tomakh [Collected Works in 3 Volumes].   3 vols., 1982–84.
Mat'-olenikha: legenda (iz povesti "Belyi parokhod"). [Mother Deer: Legend (from the novel *White Steamship*)].   1983.
Krasnoe iabloko [The Red Apple].   1985.
Mal'chik s pal'chik.   1985.
Plakha.   1986; as *The Place of the Skull,* 1989.
Bogoroditsa v snegakh [Madonna in the Snows].   1987.
Legenda o ptitse Donenbai: iz romana "I dol'she veka dlitsia den'" [The Legend of the Donenbay Bird: From the Novel *The Day Lasts More than a Hundred Years*].   1987.
Svidania s synom [An Appointment with the Son].   1987.
Sineglazaia volchitsa: Otr. iz romana "Plakha" [Blue-Eyed She-Wolf: From the Novel *The Block*].   1987.

Shestevo i sed'moi: Otr. iz romana "Plakha" [Sixth and Seventh: From the Novel *The Block*].   1987.
Chas slova.   1988; as *The Time to Speak Out,* 1988; as *Time to Speak,* 1989.

Play

Voskhozhdenie na Fudzhiiamu, with Kaltai Mukhamed-zhanov (produced 1973).   As *The Ascent of Mount Fuji* (produced 1975), 1975.

Other

Atadan kalgan tuiak.   1970.
V soavtorstve s zemleiu i vodoiu [In Co-Authorship with the Earth and Water] (essays and lectures).   1978.
Rasskazy, ocherki, publitsistika [Stories, Essays, Publications].   1984.
Do the Russians Want War?   1985.
My izmeniaem mir, mir izmeniaet nas [We Change the World, the World Changes Us] (essays, articles, interviews).   1985.
On Craftsmanship, with *Aitmatov* by V. Novikov.   1987.
Biz duinonu zhangyrtabyz, duino bizdi zhangyrtat.   1988.
Stat'i, vystupleniia, dialogi, interv'iu [Articles, Statements, Dialogues, Interviews].   1988.

*

Critical Studies: "Am I Not in My Own Home?" by Boris Pankin, in *Soviet Studies in Literature* 18(3), 1981; "The Child Narrator in the Novels of Aitmatov" by Nina Kolesnikoff, and "A Poetic Vision in Conflict: Aitmatov's Fiction" by Constantin V. Ponomareff, both in *Russian Literature and Criticism,* edited by Evelyn Bristol, 1982; "Aitmatov: A Feeling for the Times" by Nikolai Khokhlov, in *Soviet Literature* 4(421), 1983; "Both Are Primary: An 'Author's Translation' Is a Creative Re-Creation" by Munavvarkhon Dadazhanova, in *Soviet Studies in Literature* 20(4), 1984; "Time to Speak Out" (interview) by Vladimir Korkin, in *Soviet Literature* 5(434), 1984; "Aitmatov's First Novel: A New Departure?" by Stewart Paton, in *Slavonic and East European Review,* October 1984; "Prose Has Two Wings" by Keneshbek Asanaliyev, in *Soviet Literature* 2(443), 1985; "Aitmatov's *Proshchay, Gul'sary*" by Shellagh Duffin Graham, in *Journal of Russian Studies* 49, 1985; "India Has Become Near" by Miriam Salganik, in *Soviet Literature* 12(453), 1985; "Aitmatov's *The Execution Block*: Religion, Opium and the People," in *Scottish Slavonic Review* 8, 1987, and "The Provincial International," in *Four Contemporary Russian Writers,* 1989, both by Robert Porter; "On Aitmatov and His Characters: For the Author's 60th Birthday" by Evgenii Sidorov, in *Soviet Literature* 11(488), 1988.

* * *

Since Chingiz Aitmatov's schooling was in Kirghiz and Russian, he is completely fluent and writes in both languages, though he wrote his first story in Kirghiz. In Russia his works are regularly published and reprinted in large editions.

Aitmatov's creativity traces its origins to two diverging dynamics in the life of the Soviet republic—traditional ethnic roots and modernity. Aitmatov closely links ethnic roots with nature in the traditional life of Kirghizstan. He counterbalances this with a modernity characterized by an enthusiastic acceptance of the Soviet industrial, collectivized way of life. His main characters are unfailingly Kirghiz; his stories are set in the mountains or on the Kirghiz steppes. The spirit of his works is born either from that of Kirghiz national folklore, from the spirit and themes of 19th-century Russian literature, or from social realist themes typical of the Soviet literature of his time. He often describes the clash between the traditional Kirghiz generation of fathers and mothers, and their young sons and daughters who have been molded by Soviet ideology. In his stories the young generation is typically presented as successful, while their parents are forced to accept this success, while at the same time confronting their own "outmoded" ways of thinking. Aitmatov develops this theme in "Sypaichi" ("Dambuilders"), between the young Alembic and his father, both of whom have acquired their knowledge from their fathers. While Alembic's father trudges dutifully in his father's footsteps, showing little ingenuity, Alembic exploits his knowledge and promotes Soviet industrial progress to subdue nature, in the form of the river. Aitmatov applauds his courage in rejecting the outdated ideas of his father and the Soviet ideology that inspired Alembic to do so.

Aitmatov also affirms a modern view of women that liberates them from the patriarchal, Muslim household and arranged marriages. In "Jamila," the character of the title exemplifies this model; an attractive young woman who, like the story itself, owes a debt to Turgenev's novella, *First Love*. Jamila abandons the husband of a loveless marriage and her family to follow a man who has nothing more to recommend him than the beauty of his soul. Aitmatov also places a woman in a professional world supporting the development of a new Soviet State. Assa, a character in "On Baidamal River," exemplifies Aitmatov's view of the new Kirghiz woman, qualified and ready to take her new place along with the male comrade engineers designing the infrastructure of the modern Soviet state.

In Aitmatov's works animals often function to symbolize his conflicting attitudes toward industrial progress and the impact of Soviet civilization on the older Kirghiz culture. Aitmatov associates animals with the restoration of balance in the inner struggle of the primary characters that the authorial voice views positively. In the story "Camel's Eye" Aitmatov uses the appearance of two beautiful deer, living in harmony with themselves and nature, as an example of how humanity should live, contrasting this harmony with the troubled world of human struggle. From the point of view of deer, human "achievement," in the form of a ploughed field, represents a breach in the natural order. This breach is linked to a breach in the inner peace of the protagonist. After their appearance, the protagonist resolves his inner conflict between earthly and spiritual life, placing increasing importance on the aspirations of his dreams. In the story "The Meeting with the Son" swallows play a similar symbolic role. The main protagonist, the father, encounters swallows on the way to the village where his son, killed during the war, lived 20 years ago. The swallows appear as the father finally accepts the physical death of his son, realizing that his son's existence in his memory is more substantial than the mutability of the flesh.

Aitmatov's language is very simple. He uses accessible words and has an abrupt style alternated with lyrical sections describing nature and its relationship with humanity. With the incorporation of Kirghizia into the Russian states, Aitmatov struggles in his works to bridge two very different literary traditions through alternating elements of contrast and similarity. Through the development of specific characters he dramatizes the effects of cultural integration on the larger society and, in character development and plotting, interweaves this with universal problems of human existence such as the confrontation between generations and the search for beauty and love. Recognizing the social advances which might flow from the more modern outlook of Soviet ideology, he attempts to develop fiction that incorporates these ideals, such as equality for women and professionalism, into the fabric of traditional Kirghiz values deeply rooted in nature.

—Rosina Neginsky

See the essay on "Jamila."

———

AKUTAGAWA Ryūnosuke. Japanese. Born Niihara Ryūnosuke in Tokyo, 1 March 1892. Educated at Tokyo Imperial University, degree in English 1913–16. Married Tsukamoto Fumi in 1918; three sons. Literary staff member, *Shinshicho* (New Thought), magazine, 1914, 1916–17; English teacher, Naval Engineering College, Yokosuka, 1916–1919; literary staff member, *Osaka Mainichi,* 1919. Full-time writer, from 1919. *Died (suicide) 24 July 1927.*

PUBLICATIONS

Collections

Shū [Selected Works], edited by Nakamura Shin'ichirō. 1928; 2 vols., 1953.
Zenshū [Complete Works].   10 vols., 1934–35;   20 vols., 1954–57;   8 vols., 1964–65;   11 vols., 1967–69.
Sakuhin shū, edited by Hori Tatsuo, Kuzumaki Yoshitoshi, and Akutagawa Hiroshi.   1949.
Bungaku tokuhon, edited by Yoshida Sei ichi.   1955.
Ōchōmono zenshū.   2 vols., 1960.
Miteikō shū, edited by Kuzumaki Yoshitoshi.   1968.
Jihitsu miteikō zufo, edited by Tsunoda Chūzō.   1971.

Short Stories

Hana [The Nose].   1916.
Imogayu [Yam Gruel].   1916.
Rashōmon [name of Kyoto gateway].   1917; as *Rashomon and Other Stories,* 1952; as *Rashomon,* 1969.
Tabako to akuma [Tobacco and the Devil].   1917.
Jigokuhen.   1918; as *Hell Screen ("Jigokuhen") and Other Stories,* 1948.
Hōhyōnin no shi.   1918.
Kesa to Moritō.   1918.
Kairaishi [The Puppeteer].   1919.
Kagedōro [Street of Shadows].   1920.
Yabu no naka.   1921; as *In a Grove,* 1969.
Yarai no hana [Flowers from the Night Before].   1921.
Sara no hana [Flowers in a Dish].   1922.
Shunpuku [The Trying Winds of Spring].   1923.
Kōjakufū [May Breeze from the South].   1924.
Aru ahō no isshō.   1927; as *A Fool's Life,* illustrated by Tanaka Ryohei, 1970.
Tales Grotesque and Curious.   1930.

Japanese Short Stories, illustrated by Masakazu Kuwata.
    1961; revised edition, 1962.
Exotic Japanese Stories, illustrated by Masakazu Kuwata.
    1964.
Hell Screen, Cogwheels, and A Fool's Life.   1987.

Novel

Kappa [name of a mythical creature].   1922; translated as
    Kappa, 1947; as *Kappa: A Novel,* 1970.

Verse

Kushu [Poems].   1976.

Other

Toshishun.   1920; translated as *Tu Tze-chun* (for chil-
    dren), illustrated by Naoko Matsubara, 1965.
Shina-yuki [Notes on a Chinese Journey].   1925.
Ume, uma uguisu [The Plum, the Horse, and the Nightin-
    gale].   1926.
Bunkeitekina, amari ni bunkeitekina [Literary, All Too
    Literary].   1927.
Shuju no kotoba (essays).   1968.

*

Bibliography: in *An Introduction* by Beongcheon Yu, 1972;
in *The Search for Authenticity in Modern Japanese Literature* by Hisaaki Yamanouchi, 1978.

Critical Studies: *Akutagawa* edited and translated by Akio
Inove, 1961; "Akutagawa: The Literature of Defeatism" by
T. Arima, in *The Failure of Freedom,* 1969; "Akutagawa
and the Negative Ideal" by Howard Hibbert, in *Personality
in Japanese History,* edited by Albert Craig and Donald
Shively, 1970; *An Introduction* by Beongcheon Yu, 1972; in
Modern Japanese Writers by Makoto Ueda, 1976; "From
Tale to Short Story: Akutagawa's 'Toshishun' and its
Chinese Origins," in *Reality and Fiction in Modern Japa-
nese Literature* by Noriko Mizuta Lippit, 1980; in *Dawn to
the West: Japanese Literature of the Modern Era: Fiction* by
Donald Keene, 1984.

*   *   *

By its very brevity the short story is a difficult form.
Limited in character and situation, it aims at a single effect.
For interest, it demands a tight structure and an arresting
style that tends toward the lyrical. Its words must be
carefully chosen, and its sentences must be well constructed. The modern short story arose in Japan in the second
decade of the 20th century in deviation from the current
naturalism whose predominant form had become the
shishōsetsu or "I-novel" that centered around an author's
life. It was pioneered by the masterly work of Shiga Naoya
(1883-1971), author of the carefully-crafted short story
Kinosaki nite (1917, "At Kinosaki"). In his wake the
younger Akutagawa Ryūnosuke brought the Japanese short
story to maturity by his intelligence, imagination, and close
attention to style and form. Indeed, his accomplishment
made the short story recognized as an important part of
Japanese literature.

Akutagawa's education was two-fold. He was brought up
well grounded in Japanese history and culture and during
his writing career was often inspired by his reading of the
11th century *Konjaku monogatari* (Tales of Long Ago), its
sequel, the *Ujishui monogatari* (Tales of Uji), and the 13th
century *Heike monogatari* (The Tale of the Heike). His
favorite Japanese poet was the 17th century Basho, haiku
poet *par excellence.* At the age of ten he began to study
English and Classical (literary) Chinese (*wen yen*). And he
read some of the Chinese prose fiction written in "refined
vernacular" (*ch'ing-pa pai-hua*): Lo Kuan-chung's 14th
century *San Kuo chih yen i* (Romance of the Three
Kingdoms) and Ts'ao Hsüeh-chin's 18th century *Hung-lou
meng* (Dream of the red chamber), both novels, and P'u
Sung-ling's 18th century short stories in the *Liao Chai chih
i* (Strange Stories from a Chinese Studio). By the same
token, Akutagawa became knowledgeable in respect to
English and Continental literatures. He attended the Imperial University of Tokyo as an English major, and for
graduation he submitted the thesis *Wiriamu Morisu kenk-
yu* (A Study of William Morris). Of English language
writers, he knew Poe, Bierce, O. Henry, Swift, Browning,
Wilde, Yeats, and Shaw. Of the Continental writers he
knew Villon, Baudelaire, Verlaine, Flaubert, Mérimée,
Maupassant, Loti, France, Huymans, Goethe, Heine,
Nietzsche, Strindberg, and Kafka. Of the Russians, he
knew Gogol, Turgenev, Dostoevskii, Tolstoi, and Chekhov.
Poe and Baudelaire made lasting impressions on him. He
took Poe's "The Philosophy of Composition" to heart. Of
Baudelaire, he wrote in *Aru ahō no isshō,* (A Fool's Life):
"Life is not worth a single line of Baudelaire." The above
listings are by no means exhaustive. The important point is
that as a writer Akutagawa was able to take sustenance
from the best of the Eastern and the Western literary
traditions as he strove to create a modernist Japanese
literature.

Akutagawa's fiction can be divided into three periods
termed early (1915-1919), middle (1920-1924), and late
(1925-1927), including some posthumous publications.
The character of Akutagawa's fiction changes significantly
from one period to another as does his state of mind. He
writes stories both of ancient and modern times. His
historical stories deal with "matter" (*mono*) of three
different periods: the Late Heian (pre-feudal) period of
imperial rule, or *ochō-monō* (1068-1185); the Late Muro-
machi and Early Tokugawa eras, or *kirishitan-mono*
(ca.1549-ca.1639), when Christianity was being promoted
by Jesuit missionary activity; and the Early Meiji period
and time of the Meiji Enlightenment, or *kaika-mono*
(1868-1912), an era of reform when Western ideas began
to change the old Japan into a newly modernized nation.
For instance, such stories as *Rashōmon* (1915, "Rashomon") and *Yabu no naka* (1921, "In a Grove") take place
during the Late Heian period; *Tabako to Akuma* (1917,
"Tobacco and the Devil") and *Hōkyōnin no shi* (1918,
"The Martyr") occur during the Late Muromachi-Early
Tokugawa era; and "Hina" ("The Dolls") and "Saigo
Takamori" (1917), whose latter subject fought in the battle
of Shiroyama, take place during the Early Meiji period.
These history tales, then, contrast with Akutagawa's con-
temporary tales to form a kind of historical review from
past to present.

By the end of Akutagawa's early period in 1919, he was
regarded as the brightest star shining in the literary heaven
since those of his teacher Natsume Sōseki (1867-1916),
author of the astonishing novel narrated by a cat, *Wagahai
wa neko de aru* (1905-6, *I Am a Cat*), and short fiction
writer Shiga. Indeed, several of Akutagawa's stories of this

period are among his masterpieces: "Rashomon" suggests that people have the morality they can afford. Eerie in atmosphere and gruesome in action, the story describes the night adventure of an unemployed servant inside the south gate of Kyoto while Japan is in the throes of an economic depression. Looking for a place to sleep, he climbs the stairs to the second tier to find an old hag stripping the heads of the dead disposed there of their hair. He attacks her, demanding an explanation. She argues that she does no wrong, for from the hair she makes wigs so that she may survive. Accepting her logic, he steals her clothes and departs. Akutagawa raises certain images—the decrepit gate, the jobless poor, the abandoned corpses, the pimple on the cheek of the servant, the stripping of the old woman—to a symbolic level to render firm support to the narrative.

Jigokuhen (1918, "Hell Screen") is one of Akutagawa's greatest stories. The story of an artist who is an evil genius yet who passionately loves his daughter, it is reminiscent of Nathaniel Hawthorne's "Rappaccini's Daughter" (1844), which it exceeds in its horror. A supreme painter, Yoshihide is ordered by his patron to paint a scene of hell on a screen. After shutting himself in his studio for several months, Yoshihide emerges to inform his lord that the painting is finished except for one scene—the depiction of a young lady being burned to death in a flaming carriage. In the interest of perfection, the artist requests that his patron furnish him an actual demonstration of such an event, and his lord agrees. When the demonstration takes place, Yoshihide is at first horrified to see by the light of the fire that the young lady is his daughter; but in a few seconds he undergoes a complete transformation, his face gleaming with aesthetic joy. If "Hell Screen" and "Rashomon" project horror and mystery, other fine stories of Akutagawa's early period are quite the opposite. *Hana* (1916, "The Nose") and *Imogayu* (1916, "Yam Gruel"), although also set in the past and dependent on dramatic irony for their effects, are comic grotesques somewhat in the mode of Poe's grotesques such as "Lionizing" and "Loss of Breath" (both 1835). Like "Lionizing," "The Nose" is a satire on social status, egoism, and vanity but also with surfeit, or *what is too much*. After feeling his enormous nose impedes his social acceptance, a Buddhist monk succeeds in reducing it to normal size. Whereupon he becomes inordinately vain. Now his vanity repels everyone else. In "Yam Gruel" a Japanese petty official has an excessive fondness for a gruel made of rice porridge with yam. He wishes he could have as much as he wants. When a wealthy man gives him such an opportunity, he loses his appetite for yam gruel completely.

The stories of Akutagawa's middle period (1920–1924) show that changes were taking place in his "heart-mind" that were revising his view of the relationship between art and life. The question that was troubling him was which should take precedence. To his Yoshihide art took precedence over human life. In another such problem story, Akutagawa's charming "Shuzanzu" (1920, "An Autumn Mountain"), two old Chinese scholars discuss a painting whose aesthetics they have not understood. Eventually together they experience a mutual flash of insight, an aesthetic *satori*. They clap their hands and their faces light up with joy—they have understood! But from this point life and nature begin to win out over beauty in Akutagawa's mind. An earlier indication of his reversal can be detected in "Mikan" (1919, "The Tangerines"). This story takes place aboard a train. A teenage country girl enters the compartment of the narrator. Her plain countrified features and her ignorance in not knowing that her third-class ticket does not entitle her to ride second-class annoy him. In his mind she epitomizes the vulgarity of the lower classes. But at a railroad crossing three young boys in shabby clothes are waiting to wave to their departing sister. Leaning out of the window, she tosses several tangerines to them. The narrator is awakened and responds that "within a few minutes I felt life welling up within me." This grand feeling compensates him for the "absurdity" and "meaninglessness" of his existence. Finally, "Niwa" (1922, "The Garden") is a study of the relationships of nature, art, and human life. The beautiful formal garden of the Nakamura family has been neglected as the years go by and family members die or leave home, except for the third son who is indifferent to it. The profligate second son returns home because he is slowly dying of consumption. He decides to restore the garden, now returned to nature, to its original formal beauty. He works hard each day to the point of exhaustion—eventually being aided by his teenage nephew—until the garden is nearly the work of art it was originally; but then he dies—with a smile of satisfaction on his face. Work, creativity, and struggle are the keys to a satisfactory life, Akutagawa seems to be saying.

Until his late period (1925–1927) Akutagawa pretty well maintained his policy of self-detachment (*kokuki*) that his mentor Natsume Sōseki had taught him, advising him to "*sokuten kyoshi*" ("follow Heaven and transcend the self"). By practicing this strategy Akutagawa was able to stay out of his own stories or to be present merely as an observer or compiler. He was also able to avoid the naturalism (*shizen shugi*) he opposed as well as the *shishōsetsu* (I-novel) he disliked. Early in his middle period he had begun questioning the authenticity of participant accounts of events as well as the testimony of eye-witnesses of the same events in his complex but fascinating story "In a Grove." This tale presents seven narrative points of view of the same event, including that of a dead man who speaks through a medium. This multiplicity of viewpoints anticipates Faulkner's *As I Lay Dying* (1930) by almost a decade. Alleged crimes of rape and murder involving three participants, a young samurai, his pretty wife, and a notorious bandit named Tajomaru are under investigation by the High Commissioner of Police. But the testimony of the witnesses, including the ghost of the dead samurai speaking through a medium, varies so widely and is so contradictory that no determination of the truth can be reached, so strong is the egotism and the self-interest of each witness. Hence in this story Akutagawa is asking: How can the objective be distinguished from the subjective? How can the truth be distinguished from fiction?

Akutagawa's early period was highly successful and contained "glory and splendor." After the completion of "Hell Screen," however, self-doubt began to disturb his mind. After "Tatsu" (1919, "The Dragon"), a tale showing how easy it is to fool the public with disinformation, he felt himself artistically dead. Nevertheless, during his middle period he wrote such fine stories as "An Autumn Mountain," "In a Grove," and "The Garden." But after his four-month visit to China in 1925, he returned broken in body and spirit. His former ability to maintain self-detachment—what John Keats called "negative capability"—was gone. He now wallowed in his own ego, his work becoming increasingly confessional in character—even to the point of morbidness and self-disgust. This process is seen occurring in "Anchu mondo" (1927, "Dialogue in Darkness"), "Haguruma" (1927, "Cogwheels"), and *A Fool's Life*. In the first, three voices confront the narrator in succession. The first condemns him for not having turned out successfully, the second congratulates him for his courage, and the third claims to be his father and urges him "to write unto death." The second story portrays a neurotic man's worries, fantasies, and hallucinations. For instance, he sees the image of an empty raincoat on several occasions that apparently foretells his brother-in-law's suicide. He also repeatedly experiences half-transparent, multiplying cogwheels constantly revolving in his mind. The third piece, *A Fool's Life*, is an autobiography presented as 51 tableaus depicting significant events in the life of a literary genius resembling Akutagawa. None of these pieces is actually a successful work of art.

Perhaps the finest story of Akutagawa's late period is his accomplished satire *Kappa* (completed 11 February 1927), done in the manner of Jonathan Swift's *Gulliver's Travels* (1726) or Anatole France's *L'Ile des pîngouins* (1908, *Penguin Island*). In this story a traveller visits Kappaland. Kappas are mythical amphibious creatures. Pygmy size, they have bobbed hair, faces like tigers, bodies scaled like fish that like those of chameleons change color to suit the environment, frog-like appendages, and a saucer-like depression on top of their heads that contains water which provides them with power. The narrator of this tale is identified only as Patient No. 23, who is a resident of a mental asylum. Akutagawa explained that this work resulted from his "*dégoût*," that is, his disgust and loathing of the world. His suicide was to end his descent from Parnassus. Despite his failures, he has the right to be considered one of the foremost authors of Japan's modern era.

—Richard P. Benton

See the essays on "In a Grove" and "Rashomon."

ALGREN, Nelson. American. Born Nelson Ahlgren Abraham in Detroit, Michigan, 28 March 1909. Educated at schools in Chicago; University of Illinois, Urbana, 1928–31, B.S. in journalism 1931. Served in the U.S. Army Medical Corps, 1942–45: Private. Married 1) Amanda Kontowicz in 1936 (divorced 1939); 2) Betty Ann Jones in 1965 (divorced 1967). Worked as salesman, migratory worker, carnival shill, and part owner of a gas station, 1931–35; editor, Illinois Writers Project, WPA (Works Progress Administration), 1936–40; editor, with Jack Conroy, *New Anvil*, Chicago, 1939–41; worked for the Venereal Disease Program of the Chicago Board of Health, 1941–42; teacher of creative writing, University of Iowa, Iowa City, 1967, and University of Florida, Gainesville, 1974; columnist, Chicago *Free Press*, 1970. Recipient: American Academy grant, 1947, and Award of Merit medal, 1974; Newberry Library fellowship, 1947; National Book award, 1950; National Endowment for the Arts grant, 1976. *Died 9 May 1981.*

PUBLICATIONS

Short Stories

The Neon Wilderness.   1946.
The Last Carousel.   1973.

Novels

Somebody in Boots.   1935; as *The Jungle,* 1957.
Never Come Morning.   1942.
The Man with the Golden Arm.   1949.
A Walk on the Wild Side.   1956.
Calhoun (in German), edited by Carl Weissner.   1980; as *The Devil's Stocking,* 1983.

Other

Chicago: City on the Make.   1951.
Who Lost an American? Being a Guide to the Seamier Sides of New York City, Inner London, Paris, Dublin, Barcelona, Seville, Almería, Istanbul, Crete and Chicago, Illinois.   1963.
Conversations with Algren, with H.E.F. Donohue.   1964.
Notes from a Sea-Diary: Hemingway All the Way.   1965.
America Eats, edited by David E. Schoonover.   1992.

Editor, *Algren's Own Book of Lonesome Monsters.*   1962; as *Algren's Book of Lonesome Monsters,* 1964.

*

Bibliography: *Algren: A Checklist* by Kenneth G. McCollum, 1973; *Algren: A Descriptive Bibliography* by Matthew J. Bruccoli and Judith Baughman, 1985.

Critical Studies: *Algren* by Martha Heasley Cox and Wayne Chatterton, 1975; *Confronting the Horror: The Novels of Algren* by James R. Giles, 1989; *Algren: A Life on the Wild Side* by Bettina Drew, 1989.

* * *

Nelson Algren was best known as a novelist. His third novel, *The Man With the Golden Arm,* won the first National Book award in 1950. His fifth, *A Walk on the Wild Side* won high critical acclaim as perhaps the most influential comic novel to come out of the 1950's—as indeed, a precursor of the wild-sidedness of Ken Kesey's *One Flew Over the Cuckoo's Nest* and Joseph Heller's *Catch-22.* Both novels were successfully dramatized, *Golden Arm* as a popular Otto Preminger movie, and *Wild Side* as a staged musical drama and as a less-than-critically acclaimed movie.

But Algren has also written more than 50 short stories, many of which, only slightly altered, became episodes in the novels, just as certain novelistic episodes were published separately as short stories. They interchanged readily, since the subject matter and themes of both stories and novels are hardly distinguishable, and since Algren's sketch-like short story style is so easily adaptable to the episodic style of the novels. Algren himself once admitted that the novel itself is simply a longer, expanded short story.

The stories, sketches, and episodes appeared in such disparate publications as *The Kenyon Review* and *Noble Savage, The Atlantic, The Saturday Evening Post, Esquire, Playboy,* and *Dude.* Algren published no long fiction after *A Walk on the Wild Side.* The short pieces, lectures, reading, and, he insisted, playing the horses earned him a decent living.

For the most part, the stories are set in Algren's Chicago, not Dreiser's nor Farrell's Chicago—in the same way that *Dubliners* is set in Joyce's Dublin, not O'Casey's nor O'Faolain's. And Chicago and Dublin are more than settings in both cases; the cities circumscribe, are inseparable from, both subject matter and theme for both Algren and Joyce. Indeed, Joyce's Dublin South of the Liffey could have been compressed quite comfortably into Algren's Division Street neighborhood.

Algren's collection of short stories *The Neon Wildness* includes most of his best tales. He carefully chose the 18 stories in the collection, and he collected no others out of the dozens he wrote over the next nearly 40 years, though he included a few previously published stories, along with essays and poems, in *The Last Carousel*.

Dope addiction, alcohol abuse, prostitution, gambling, prize fighting, jail—these are the subjects of Algren's stories, both short and long. The characters are generally losers who habituate (not truly live in) bars, brothels, and flea bag tenements or hotels. It is a depressing, violent naturalistic world, but the depression is palliated by Algren's sense of the gently comic, of the realistic ironic—his feeling for his people and their plight is compassionate, like Dreiser's, rather than sentimental, like Steinbeck's.

Prostitution is one of the subjects in "Is Your Name Joe?," in "Depend on Aunt Elly," and in "Design for Departure," which also includes alcohol and drug abuse as subjects. Other examples of Algren's subjects include gambling ("Stickman's Laughter"); prize fighting ("He Swung and He Missed" and "Depend on Aunt Elly"); and crime, arrest, and incarceration ("The Captain Has Bad Dreams," "Poor Man's Pennies," "El Presidente de Méjico,"and "The Brothers' House"). And throughout the stories, among the characters, controlling them and the stories' action, slips and slides the con man, especially in stories like "Kingdom City to Cairo" and "So Help Me."

"The Face on the Barroom Floor" is the only true barroom story in *Neon Wilderness* (though barroom scenes appear in many others), and it is the most viciously violent. It also is a good example of Algren's use of episodes and characters from his short fiction as parts of the novels. Railroad Shorty, the powerful legless torso on wheels who, urged on by the drunks at the bar, avenges an insult by Fancy, the bartender, by pounding his face into "a scarlet sponge . . . a paste of cartilage and blood through which a single sinister eye peered blindly," reappears as Schmidt in *A Walk on the Wild Side*, exactly the same violent terrorist—only the name is changed.

Another episode from a short story reappears in *The Man With The Golden Arm*. It is from "The Captain Is Impaled," a story not included in *Neon Wilderness*. Unlike "The Face" it is a brief, gentle, non-dramatic moment, but it is significantly more important. In it, a defrocked priest responds to the captain-interrogator's nasty japes and gibes by stating softly that "We are all members of one another"; and with those words gives us, clearly and unmistakably, Algren's theme.

Two stories in *Neon Wilderness* (both of which incidentally include the book's title in their texts), both very naturalistic in content, illustrate this theme and the compassion at its heart especially well. In fact, "Design for Departure" seems almost to have been written as illustration. Mary, 15 years old, runs away from her drunken, abusive tenement environment, works in the stockyards, and lives in a cheap hotel. She is seduced by Christiano, a deaf non-mute (the symbolism of the names is perhaps too obvious) who gets her to work the wrathful husband-cheating wife badger game out of a night club called "The Jungle." Christy is caught and jailed for three years. Mary drifts into drugs and prostitution and contracts venereal disease. Hopeless, when Christy is sprung, Mary convinces him to spend his ten dollars release money for an overdose of drugs so that she may "depart." "The fix is in" she thinks as Christy returns with the drugs, "I'm Mary. 'N Jesus Christ himself is puttin' in the fix."

"The Captain Has Bad Dreams" is the precursor of "The Captain Is Impaled" as a lineup-interrogation story. In its sympathetic treatment of the cop as well as the criminal, it is a nearly perfect example of Algren's theme.

—Joseph J. Waldmeir

See the essay on "How the Devil Came Down Division Street."

———

ANAND, Mulk Raj. Indian. Born in Peshawar, 12 December 1905. Educated at Khalsa College, Amritsar; Punjab University, 1921–24, B.A. (honours) 1924; University College, University of London, 1926–29, Ph.D.; Cambridge University, 1929–30; League of Nations School of Intellectual Cooperation, Geneva, 1930–32. Married 1) Kathleen Van Gelder in 1939 (divorced 1948); 2) Shirin Vajifdar in 1950, one daughter. Lecturer, School of Intellectual Cooperation, Summer 1930, and Workers Educational Association, London, intermittently 1932–45; has also taught at the universities of Punjab, Benares, and Rajasthan, Jaipur, 1948–66; editor and contributor, *Marg Encyclopedia of Art,* 136 vols., 1948–81; Tagore Professor of Literature and Fine Art, University of Punjab, 1963–66; fine art chairman, Lalit Kala Akademi (National Academy of Art), New Delhi, 1965–70; visiting professor, Institute of Advanced Studies, Simla, 1967–68; editor, *Marg* magazine, Bombay, from 1946; director, Kutub Publishers, Bombay, from 1946. President of the Lokayata Trust, for creating a community and cultural centre in Hauz Khas village, New Delhi, from 1970. Recipient: Leverhulme fellowship, 1940–42; World Peace Council prize, 1952; Padma Bhushan, India, 1968; Sahitya Academy award, 1974. Member, Indian Academy of Letters. Lives in Bombay.

PUBLICATIONS

Short Stories

The Lost Child and Other Stories. 1934.
The Barber's Trade Union and Other Stories. 1944.
The Tractor and the Corn Goddess and Other Stories. 1947.
Reflections on the Golden Bed. 1947.
The Power of Darkness and Other Stories. 1958.
Lajwanti and Other Stories. 1966.
Between Tears and Laughter. 1973.
Selected Short Stories of Anand, edited by M.K. Naik. 1977.

Novels

Untouchable. 1935; revised edition, 1970.
The Coolie. 1936; as *Coolie,* 1945; revised edition, 1972.

Two Leaves and a Bud.   1937.
The Village.   1939.
Lament on the Death of a Master of Arts.   1939.
Across the Black Waters.   1940.
The Sword and the Sickle.   1942.
The Big Heart.   1945; revised edition, edited by Saros
    Cowasjee, 1980.
Seven Summers: The Story of an Indian Childhood.   1951.
Private Life of an Indian Prince.   1953; revised edition,
    1970.
The Old Woman and the Cow.   1960; as *Gauri,* 1976.
The Road.   1961.
Death of a Hero.   1963.
Morning Face.   1968.
Confession of a Lover.   1976.
The Bubble.   1984.

Play

India Speaks (produced 1943).

Other

Persian Painting.   1930.
Curries and Other Indian Dishes.   1932.
The Golden Breath: Studies in Five Poets of the New India.
    1933.
The Hindu View of Art.   1933; revised edition, 1957.
Letters on India.   1942.
Apology for Heroism: An Essay in Search of Faith.   1946.
Homage to Tagore.   1946.
Indian Fairy Tales: Retold (for children).   1946.
On Education.   1947.
The Bride's Book of Beauty, with Krishna Hutheesing.
    1947; as *The Book of Indian Beauty,* 1981.
The Story of India (for children).   1948.
*The King-Emperor's English; or, The Role of the English
    Language in the Free India.*   1948.
Lines Written to an Indian Air: Essays.   1949.
The Indian Theatre.   1950.
The Story of Mart (for children).   1952.
The Dancing Foot.   1957.
*Kama Kala: Some Notes on the Philosophical Basis of
    Hindu Erotic Sculpture.*   1958.
India in Colour.   1959.
More Indian Fairy Tales (for children).   1961.
Is There a Contemporary Indian Civilisation?   1963.
The Story of Chacha Nehru (for children).   1965.
The Third Eye: A Lecture on the Appreciation of Art.
    1966.
The Humanism of M.K. Gandhi: Three Lectures.   1967(?).
*The Volcano: Some Comments on the Development of
    Rabindranath Tagore's Aesthetic Theories.*   1968.
*Roots and Flowers: Two Lectures on the Metamorphosis of
    Technique and Content in the Indian-English Novel.*
    1972.
Mora.   1972.
Author to Critic: The Letters of Anand, edited by Saros
    Cowasjee.   1973.
Album of Indian Paintings.   1973.
Folk Tales of Punjab.   1974.
Seven Little-Known Birds of the Inner Eye.   1978.
The Humanism of Jawaharlal Nehru.   1978.
The Humanism of Rabindranath Tagore.   1979.
Maya of Mohenjo-Daro (for children).   n.d.
Conversations in Bloomsbury (reminiscences).   1981.
Madhubani Painting.   1984.

Pilpali Sahab: Story of a Childhood under the Raj (autobi-
    ography).   1985.
Poet-Painter: Paintings by Rabindranath Tagore.   1985.
Homage to Jamnalal Bajaj: A Pictorial Biography.   1988.
Amrita Sher Gill: An Essay in Interpretation.   1989.
Kama Yoga.   n.d.
Chitralakshana (on Indian painting).   n.d.

Editor, *Marx and Engels on India.*   1933.
Editor, with Iqbal Singh, *Indian Short Stories.*   1947.
Editor, *Introduction to Indian Art,* by A.K. Coomaras-
    wamy.   1956.
Editor, *Experiments: Contemporary Indian Short Stories.*
    1968.
Editor, *Annals of Childhood.*   1968.
Editor, *Grassroots.*   1968(?).
Editor, *Tales from Tolstoy.*   1978.
Editor, with Lance Dane, *Kama Sutra of Vatsyayana* (from
    translation by Sir Richard Burton and F.F. Arbuthnot).
    1982.
Editor, with S. Balu Rao, *Panorama: An Anthology of
    Modern Indian Short Stories.*   1986.
Editor, *Chacha Nehru.*   1987.
Editor, *Aesop's Fables.*   1987.
Editor, *The Historic Trial of Mahatma Gandhi.*   1987.
Editor, *The Other Side of the Medal,* by Edward Thompson.
    1989.
Editor, *Sati: A Writeup of Raja Ram Mohan Roy about
    Burning of Widows Alive.*   1989.

*

Bibliography: *Anand: A Checklist* by Gillian Packham,
1983.

Critical Studies: *Anand: A Critical Essay* by Jack Lindsay,
1948, revised edition, as *The Elephant and the Lotus,* 1954;
"Anand Issue" of *Contemporary Indian Literature,* 1965;
An Ideal of Man in Anand's Novels by D. Riemenschneider,
1969; *Anand: The Man and the Novelist* by Margaret Berry,
1971; *Anand* by K.N. Sinha, 1972; *Anand* by M.K. Naik,
1973; *Anand: A Study of His Fiction in Humanist Perspec-
tive* by G.S. Gupta, 1974; *So Many Freedoms: A Study of
the Major Fiction of Anand* by Saros Cowasjee, 1978;
Perspectives on Anand edited by K.K. Sharma, 1978; *The
Yoke of Pity: A Study in the Fictional Writings of Anand* by
Alastair Niven, 1978; *The Sword and the Sickle: A Study of
Anand's Novels* by K.V. Suryanarayana Murti, 1983; *The
Novels of Anand: A Thematic Study* by Premila Paul, 1983;
The Wisdom of the Heart: A Study of the Works of Anand
by Marlene Fisher, 1985; *Studies in Anand* by P.K. Rajan,
1986; *Anand: A Home Appraisal* edited by Atma Ram,
1988; *The Language of Anand, Raja Rao, and R.K.
Narayan* by Reza Ahmad Nasimi, 1989; *Anand: A Short
Story Writer* by Vidhya Mohan Shethi, n.d.

*   *   *

A leading Indian novelist, Mulk Raj Anand is also one of
the finest exponents of the short story. As prolific in this
genre as he is in longer fiction, Anand has so far produced
more than a hundred stories, which have appeared in seven
collections, beginning with *The Lost Child and Other
Stories.*

Anand has talked at length about the possible influences that have shaped his art as a short story writer. First among these was the Indian folk tale, which seems to him to be "the most perfect form of short story." Another influence was his mother, an "illiterate but highly skilled storyteller who could feel a situation passionately." Later models included Tolstoi and Gor'kii, especially in their evocative vignettes of real life, the prose poems of Turgenev and the fables of Theodore Powys. "While accepting the form of the [Indian] folk tale, especially in its fabulous character," Anand has said, "I took in the individual and group psychology of the European *conte* and tried to synthesise the two styles." The "neo-folk tale" is his "ideal of the short story."

Anand's short stories are remarkable for their range and variety, which are evinced not only in mood, tone and spirit, but also in locale, characters, and form. There are stories that offer an imaginative and emotional apprehension of an aspect of life, either on the human level or on that of animal creation. The themes here are elemental, such as birth and death, beauty, love, and childhood, and the treatment often reveals a symbolic dimension added to realistic presentation, the element of incident being minimal. In these stories there is an appropriate heightening of style in keeping with the mood and tone of the narrative. Representative of this mode are stories like "The Lost Child"; in which the traumatic experience of a small child lost in a fair symbolizes the eternal ordeal of the human condition. As Nanak says, "We are all children lost in the world-fair." "Birth" presents a poor peasant woman in an advanced state of pregnancy who is saved in her hour of trial by her deep-seated, simple faith in the gods. In "Five Short Fables" the scene shifts to the animal world, but not the hard, clear contours of the Aesopean fable; in Anand's fables lyrical description is steeped in symbolic overtones, as in "The Butterfly," which pinpoints the pathos of the eternal law that "beauty vanishes, beauty passes."

A group of stories elicits the pathos of the plight of men and women crushed by forces too strong for them to fight against; the treatment here is not symbolic but realistic. "Lajwanti" is the story of the plight of a newly-married girl, whose traumatic experience of life with her in-laws drives her to make an unsuccessful attempt to commit suicide; "The Parrot in the Cage" presents Rukmini, an old woman who has lost everything in the holocaust of the partition of India; and "Old Bapu" is the narrative of a landless peasant who migrates to a city in search of a livelihood, but is condemned to starve there.

These tales of pathos are also full of undertones of social criticism: thus, Lajwanti's tale is representative of the helplessness of the Indian woman in the traditional rustic joint family; but on the whole, social criticism remains subordinated to the pathos of the situation.

Social awareness is, however, central to a large number of Anand's stories, which his understanding of the complex social forces at work in modern India finds effective expression. For instance, the conflict between tradition and modernization is portrayed evocatively in "The Power of Darkness" and "The Tractor and the Corn Goddess"; feudal exploitation and social injustice in "A Kashmir Idyll" and "The Price of Bananas."

There is often an undercurrent of comedy in these stories of social awareness, because irony, satire and sarcasm are obviously the tools that social criticism often employs, but the focus is clearly on the exposure of social evils. Anand also has written many stories in which comedy holds the stage; "A Pair of Mustachios," "The Signature," and "Two Lady Rams" are fine examples of this. The comedy in the first of these stories arises out of excessive aristocratic pride, and that in the second is the result of the rigidity of feudal etiquette, while "Two Lady Rams" is a diverting take-off on bigamy.

Anand's comedy sometimes takes on farcical overtones, as in "The Liar," but another group of stories shows how he is capable of far subtler effects also. "The Tamarind Tree," "The Silver Bangles," and "The Thief" are primarily evocative studies in human psychology, though other elements include humanitarian compassion and social criticism, which are almost ubiquitous in Anand's work. The mind of an expectant mother, sexual jealousy, and deep-seated guilt respectively are the main concerns of these three stories.

Ample diversity of locale, characters, and form is one of the distinguishing features of Anand's art. The setting ranges from the Punjab to Uttar Pradesh and Kashmir, and both the village and the city are adequately represented. The men, women, and children that move through these narratives are from all social strata, from the highest to the lowest; Anand is a skilled story-teller, who can usually tell an absorbing tale. His style, both in narration and dialogue, is distinctive in its bold importation of Indianisms of various kinds into his English. These include expletives like "*acha*" and "*wah*," honorifics like "*huzoor*" and "preserver of the Poor" swear words such as "rape-mother" and "eater of your masters," and idiomatic expressions like "something black in the pulse" (something fishy) and "eating the air."

Anand's less achieved stories are marred by sentimentality and simplism inevitably accompanied by verbosity and careless writing, but his better work shows that he is a born storyteller, who has thought carefully about his craft, drawing upon several sources to shape it. His stories are a museum of human nature, and in sheer range, scope, and variety he has few peers among Indian writers of the short story in English.

—M.K. Naik

ANDERSEN, Hans Christian. Danish. Born in Odense, 2 April 1805. Educated at schools in Odense to age 14; alone in Copenhagen, and patronized by various benefactors: loosely associated with the singing and dancing schools at Royal Theater, 1819–22; attended Slagelse grammar school, 1822–26, and Elsinore grammar school, 1826–27; tutored in Copenhagen by L.C. Muller, 1827–28; completed examen artium, 1828. Freelance writer from 1828: royal grant for travel, 1833, 1834, and pension from Frederick VI, 1838; given title of professor, 1851; Privy Councillor, 1874. Knight of Red Eagle (Prussia), 1845; Order of the Danneborg, 1846; Knight of the Northern Star (Sweden), 1848; Order of the White Falcon (Weimar), 1848. *Died 4 August 1875.*

PUBLICATIONS

Collections

Samlede Skrifter [Collected Writings].   33 vols., 1853–79; 2nd edition, 15 vols., 1876–80.

Romaner og Rejseskildringer [Novels and Travel Notes], edited by H. Topsøe-Jensen.   7 vols., 1941–44.

Complete Fairy Tales and Stories, edited by Erik Haugaard. 1974.

Samlede eventyr og historier [Collected Tales and Stories], edited by Erik Dal.   5 vols., 1975.

Short Stories

Eventyr: Fortalte for Børn [Fairy Tales for Children].   6 vols., 1835–42; *Nye Eventyr* [New Fairy Tales], 4 vols., 1843–47; edited by Erik Dal and Erling Nielsen, 1963 —.

Billedbog uden Billeder [Picture Book Without Pictures]. 2 vols., 1838–40; as *Tales the Moon Can Tell,* 1955.

Eventyr og Historier [Tales and Stories].   1839; *Nye Eventyr og Historier,* 6 vols., 1858–67; edited by Hans Brix and Anker Jensen, 5 vols., 1918–20.

Later Tales.   1869.

Novels

Improvisatoren.   1835; as *The Improvisatore; or, Life in Italy,* 1845.

O.T.   1836; as *O.T.; or, Life in Denmark,* with *Only a Fiddler,* 1845.

Kun en Spillemand.   1837; as *Only a Fiddler,* with *O.T.,* 1845.

De to Baronesser.   1848; as *The Two Baronesses,* 1848.

A Poet's Day Dreams.   1853.

To Be, or Not to Be?   1857.

Lykke-Peer [Lucky Peer].   1870.

Plays

Kjaerlighed paa Nicolai Taarn [Love on St. Nicholas Tower] (produced 1829).   1829.

Skibet, from a play by Scribe.   1831.

Bruden fra Lammermoor, music by Ivar Bredal, from the novel *The Bride of Lammermoor* by Scott (produced 1832).   1832.

Ravnen [The Raven], music by J.P.E. Hartmann, from a play by Gozzi (produced 1832).   1832.

Agnete og Havmanden [Agnete and the Merman], music by Nils V. Gade, from Andersen's poem (produced 1833). 1834.

Festen paa Kenilworth [The Festival at Kenilworth], music by C.E.F. Weyse, from the novel *Kenilworth* by Scott (produced 1836).

Skilles og Mødes [Parting and Meeting] (produced 1836). In *Det Kongelige Theaters Repertoire,* n.d.

Den Usynlige paa Sprogø [The Invisible Man on Sprogø] (produced 1839).

Mulatten [The Mulatto], from a story by Fanny Reybaud (produced 1840).   1840.

Mikkels Kjaerligheds Historier i Paris [Mikkel's Parisian Love Stories] (produced 1840).

Maurerpigen [The Moorish Girl] (produced 1840).   1840.

En Comedie i det Grønne [Country Comedy], from a play by Dorvigny (produced 1840).

Fuglen i Paeretraeet [The Bird in the Pear Tree] (produced 1842).

Kongen Drømmer [Dreams of the King] (produced 1844). 1844.

Dronningen paa 16 aar [The Sixteen-Year-Old Queen], from a play by Bayard.   1844.

Lykkens Blomst [The Blossom of Happiness] (produced 1845).   1847.

Den nye Barselstue [The New Maternity Ward] (produced 1845).   1850.

Herr Rasmussen (produced 1846). Edited by E. Agerholm, 1913.

Liden Kirsten [Little Kirsten], music by J.P.E. Hartmann, from the story by Andersen (produced 1846).   1847.

Kunstens Dannevirke [The Bulwark of Art) (produced 1848).   1848.

En Nat i Roskilde [A Night in Roskilde], from a play by C. Warin and C.E. Lefevre (produced 1848).   1850.

Brylluppet ved Como-Søen [The Wedding at Lake Como], music by Franz Gläser, from a novel by Manzoni (produced 1849).   1849.

Meer end Perler og Guld [More Than Pearls and Gold], from a play by Ferdinand Raimund (produced 1849). 1849.

Ole Lukøie [Old Shuteye] (produced 1850).   1850.

Hyldemoer [Mother Elder] (produced 1851).   1851.

Nøkken [The Nix]. music by Franz Gläser (produced 1853). 1853.

Paa Langebro [On the Bridge] (produced 1864).

Han er ikke født [He Is Not Well-Born] (produced 1864). 1864.

Da Spanierne var her [When the Spaniards Were Here] (produced 1865).   1865.

Verse

Digte [Poems].   1830.

Samlede digte [Collected Poems].   1833.

Seven Poems.   1955.

Other

Ungdoms-Forsøg [Youthful Attempts].   1822.

Fodreise fra Holmens Canal til Ostpynten af Amager i 1828 og 1829 [A Walking Trip from Holmen's Canal to Amager].   1829.

Skyggebilleder af en Reise til Harzen.   1831; as *Rambles in the Romantic Regions of the Harz Mountains,* 1848.

En Digters Bazar.   1842; as *A Poet's Bazaar,* 1846.

Das Märchen meines Lebens ohne Dichtung (in collected German edition).   1847; as *The True Story of My Life,* 1847; as *Mit eget Eventyr uden Digtning,* edited by H. Topsøe-Jensen, 1942.

I Sverrig.   1851; as *Pictures of Sweden,* 1851; as *In Sweden,* 1851.

Mit Livs Eventyr.   1855; revised edition, 1859, 1877; edited by H. Topsøe-Jensen, 1951; as *The Story of My Life,* 1871; as *The Fairy Tale of My Life,* 1954.

I Spanien.   1863; as *In Spain, and A Visit to Portugal,* 1864.

Collected Writings.   10 vols., 1870–71.

Breve, edited by C.S.A. Bille and N. Bøgh.   2 vols., 1878.

Briefwechsel mit den Grossherzog Carl Alexander von Sachsen-Weimar-Eisenach, edited by Emil Jonas. 1887.

Correspondence with the Late Grand-Duke of Saxe-Weimar, Charles Dickens, etc., edited by Frederick Crawford.   1891.

Optegnelsesbog, edited by Julius Clausen.   1926.

Breve til Therese og Martin R. Henriques 1860–75 [Letters to Therese and Martha R. Henrique 1860–75], edited by H. Topsøe-Jensen.   1932.

Brevveksling med Edvard og Henriette Collin [Correspondence between Edvard and Henriette Collin], edited by H. Topsøe-Jensen.   6 vols., 1933–37.

Brevveksling med Jonas Collin den Aeldre og andre Medlemmer af det Collinske Hus [Correspondence between Jonas Collin the Elder and Other Members of the House of Collin], edited by H. Topsøe-Jensen.   3 vols., 1945–48.

Romerske Dagbøger [Roman Dairies], edited by Paul V. Rubow and H. Topsøe-Jensen.   1947.

Brevveksling [Correspondence], with Horace E. Scudder, edited by Jean Hersholt.   1948; as *The Andersen-Scudder Letters,* 1949.

Reise fra Kjøbenhavn til Rhinen [Travels from Copenhagen to the Rhine], edited by H. Topsøe-Jensen.   1955.

Brevveksling [Correspondence], with Henriette Wulff, edited by H. Topsøe-Jensen.   3 vols., 1959–60.

Breve til Mathias Weber [Letters to Mathias Weber], edited by Arne Portman.   1961.

Levnedsbog 1805–1831 [The Book of Life], edited by H. Topsøe-Jensen.   1962.

Breve til Carl B. Lorck [Letters to Carl B. Lorck], edited by H. Topsøe-Jensen.   1969.

Dagbøger 1825–75 [Diary], edited by Kåre Olsen and H. Topsøe-Jensen.   1971—.

Tegninger til Otto Zinck [Drawings for Otto Zinck], edited by Kjeld Heltoft.   2 vols., 1972.

Rom Dagbogsnotater og tegninger [Dairy and Drawings from Rome], edited by H. Topsøe-Jensen.   1980.

Album, edited by Kåre Olsen and others.   3 vols., 1980.

A Visit to Germany, Italy, and Malta.   1985.

A Poet's Bazaar: A Journey to Greece, Turkey, and Up the Danube.   1987.

Diaries, edited by Patricia L. Conroy and Sven H. Rossell.   1989.

*

Critical Studies: *Andersen and the Romantic Theatre* by Frederick J. Marker, 1971; *Andersen and His World* by Reginald Spink, 1972; *Andersen: The Story of His Life and Work* by Elias Bredsdorff, 1975; *Andersen* by Bo Gronbech, 1980.

* * *

Born in Odense, Denmark, the son of a poor journeyman shoemaker and his ill-educated wife, Hans Christian Andersen described himself in a letter to a friend as "a plant from the swamp." But, swamp plants flourish. It might be the story-line from one of his own tales in which the hero rises above his station and achieves success in a mileu other than that to which he was born. In fact, there is an element of the fairy tale about Andersen's early life. As a pauper, there should have been little chance of his meeting Prince Christian and of going to court, but meet him he did. He said of himself, "My life is a beautiful fairy tale, rich and happy." Like the hero of "The Travelling Companion" (1836) Andersen set out when very young and with little money to make his fortune, in his case as an actor. He was subsequently helped financially by King Frederik VI after his first books of poetry were published.

As a child, he had listened avidly to the tales told by the local old women, and this oral tradition no doubt provided him with the inspiration for and literary style of his future work. His first serious essay into literature was *Fodreise fra Holmens Canal til Ostpynten af Amager i 1828 og 1829* (A Walking Trip from Holmen's Canal to Amager), in which a young student meets a variety of strange characters ranging from St. Peter, the shoemaker of Jerusalem, to a talking cat. The work's imagination and literary style set the tone for his future tales, the first instalment of which contained, amongst others, "The Tinderbox" and "The Princess and the Pea," embroidered retellings of stories heard as a child. His second pamphlet included "Thumbelina," and his third, two of his most famous tales—"The Little Mermaid" and "The Emperor's New Clothes," both classics of their kind. All three instalments were published in book form in 1837.

From then on, Andersen kept writing fairy tales until shortly before his death. Their continuing fascination is explained by the author's ability to combine fantasy and realism, and his method of telling the stories as if in person to a child, in language it could comprehend. Unlike the brothers Grimm (collectors rather than creative writers, whose stories sometimes live up to their name) Andersen peoples his tales with characters who are made familiar. A king wears a dressing-gown and embroidered slippers; the Trolls have family problems and seem to be almost human, despite their being able to perform magic.

His animals (homely, familiar ones—no jungle beasts) behave as we would expect animals to behave, according to their nature and habitat. They also have problems and human characteristics. The rats, for example, are bored by Humpty Dumpty and find it "a fearfully dull story," and ask the Fir Tree if it did not know one about "pork and tallow candles." Andersen never places his creatures in an environment with which they would not normally be familiar. The mother duck in "The Ugly Duckling" has no personal knowledge of what lies beyond her own pond.

Flowers and inanimate objects, too, have their own characteristic qualities. In "The Snow Queen" (1846) the flowers tell their stories: the flamboyant Tiger Lily's is ferocious; the modest Daisy is sentimental, while the gentle Rose, Andersen's favourite flower, is content with her lot. The Market Basket in "The Flying Trunk" (1839) believes, because of its knowledge of the outside world, that it should be master of the kitchen rather than the stay-at-home pots and pans. An over-anthropomorphic approach in literature can become somewhat tedious, but this is not the case with Andersen. He does not sentimentalise his creatures. For example, the stork of "The Ugly Duckling" is "on his long red legs chattering away in Egyptian, for he had learnt the language from his mother," who wintered there.

While humans, animals, and inanimate objects are subject to failings such as vanity and pride (the needle of "The Darning Needle" (1845) was so refined that she fancied herself a superior sewing needle, and looked down on the inferior pin), Andersen does not burden his tales with moralistic strictures. In his world there is not always a happy-ever-after ending, and wickedness is not always punished. The little mermaid, for instance, does not marry the prince whose life she has saved, and the hero of "Under the Willow Tree" dies, a miserable failure. The Victorian reader must have found this over-turning of moral expectations somewhat shocking, but would have approved of the implied moral of "The Nightingale" (1843). Set in exotic China, a highly decorative mechanical nightingale is brought to court and enchants all from the emperor to the lackeys, "the most difficult to satisfy." The real bird is despised and flies away. The artificial bird breaks down and when the dying emperor longs to hear its beautiful music, it cannot oblige. But, on its return, the real nightingale wrestles with death in an effort to save the emperor's life with her song.

Of direct appeal to children is Andersen's delightful humour. "The Nightingale" begins: "You know of course that in China the Emperor is a Chinese and his subjects are Chinese too." In "The Snow Queen," the Lapp woman writes a letter on a dried cod fish, and the Finnish woman later makes supper of it. Adults can appreciate the sly humour of the flea who "had of course gentle blood in his veins and was accustomed to mix only with mankind, and that does make such a difference." Frequently the human learns from the animal; indeed, the Tom Cat says that "Grown-ups say a lot of silly things," and the storks, too, have a poor opinion of humans. Andersen never lost his ability to penetrate a child's mind.

Andersen did write other fiction and his ambition was to excel as a novelist, but it is as a writer of enchanting tales that his fame is ensured, largely because both child and adult can identify with the characters. The crows prefer security to freedom; the snails are much engaged in finding a suitable wife for their adopted son. What neurotic schoolgirl does not sympathise with the Ugly Duckling and hope that she, too, will grow into a beautiful swan?

—A.J. Lindsay

See the essay on "The Steadfast Tin Soldier."

ANDERSON, Sherwood (Berton). American. Born in Camden, Ohio, 13 September 1876. Educated at a high school in Clyde, Ohio; Wittenberg Academy, Springfield, Ohio, 1899–1900. Served in the U.S. Army in Cuba during the Spanish-American War, 1898–99. Married 1) Cornelia Pratt Lane in 1904 (divorced 1916), two sons and one daughter; 2) Tennessee Claflin Mitchell in 1916 (divorced 1924); 3) Elizabeth Prall in 1924 (separated 1929; divorced 1932); 4) Eleanor Copenhaver in 1933. Worked in a produce warehouse in Chicago, 1896–97; advertising copywriter, Long-Critchfield Company, Chicago, 1900–05; president, United Factories Company, Cleveland, 1906, and Anderson Manufacturing Company, paint manufacturers, Elyria, Ohio, 1907–12; freelance copywriter, then full-time writer, Chicago, 1913–20; visited France and England, 1921; lived in New Orleans, 1923–24; settled on a farm near Marion, Virginia, 1925: publisher, *Smyth Country News* and Marion *Democrat* from 1927; travelled extensively in the U.S. in mid-1930's reporting on Depression life. Member, American Academy, 1937. *Died 8 March 1941.*

PUBLICATIONS

Collections

Anderson Reader, edited by Paul Rosenfeld. 1947.
The Portable Anderson, edited by Horace Gregory. 1949; revised edition, 1972.
Short Stories, edited by Maxwell Geismar. 1962.

Short Stories

Winesburg, Ohio: A Group of Tales of Ohio Small Town Life. 1919; edited by John H. Ferres, 1966.

The Triumph of the Egg: A Book of Impressions from American Life in Tales and Poems. 1921.
Horses and Men. 1923.
Alice, and The Lost Novel. 1929.
Death in the Woods and Other Stories. 1933.
Certain Things Last: The Selected Short Stories, edited by Charles E. Modlin. 1992.

Novels

Windy McPherson's Son. 1916; revised edition, 1922.
Marching Men. 1917; edited by Ray Lewis White, 1972.
Poor White. 1920.
Many Marriages. 1923; edited by Douglas G. Rogers, 1978.
Dark Laughter. 1925.
Beyond Desire. 1932.
Kit Brandon: A Portrait. 1936.

Plays

Winesburg (produced 1934). In *Winesburg and Others*, 1937.
Mother (produced?). In *Winesburg and Others*, 1937.
Winesburg and Others (includes *The Triumph of the Egg*, dramatized by Raymond O'Neil; *Mother*, *They Married Later*). 1937.
Above Suspicion (broadcast 1941). In *The Free Company Presents*, edited by James Boyd, 1941.
Textiles, in *Anderson: The Writer at His Craft*, edited by Jack Salzman and others. 1979.

Radio Play: *Above Suspicion*, 1941.

Other

Mid-American Chants. 1918.
A Story Teller's Story. 1924; edited by Ray Lewis White, 1968.
The Modern Writer. 1925.
Notebook. 1926.
Tar: A Midwest Childhood. 1926; edited by Ray Lewis White, 1969.
A New Testament. 1927.
Hello Towns! 1929.
Nearer the Grass Roots. 1929.
The American County Fair. 1930.
Perhaps Women. 1931.
No Swank. 1934.
Puzzled America. 1935.
A Writer's Conception of Realism. 1939.
Home Town. 1940.
Memoirs. 1942; edited by Ray Lewis White, 1969.
Letters, edited by Howard Mumford Jones and Walter B. Rideout. 1953.
Return to Winesburg: Selections from Four Years of Writing for a Country Newspaper, edited by Ray Lewis White. 1967.
The Buck Fever Papers, edited by Welford Dunaway Taylor. 1971.
Anderson/Gertrude Stein: Correspondence and Personal Essays, edited by Ray Lewis White. 1972.
The Writer's Book, edited by Martha Mulroy Curry. 1975.
France and Anderson: Paris Notebook 1921, edited by Michael Fanning. 1976.
Anderson: The Writer at His Craft, edited by Jack Salzman and others. 1979.

Selected Letters, edited by Charles E. Modlin.   1984.
Letters to Bab: Anderson to Marietta D. Finley 1916–1933,
    edited by William A. Sutton.   1985.
The Diaries, 1936–41, edited by Hilbert H. Campbell.
    1987.
Early Writings, edited by Ray Lewis White.   1989.
Love Letters to Eleanor Copenhauer Anderson, edited by
    Charles E. Modlin.   1989.
Secret Love Letters; for Eleanor, a Letter a Day, edited by
    Ray Lewis White.   1991.

*

Bibliography: *Anderson: A Bibliography* by Eugene P.
Sheehy and Kenneth A. Lohf, 1960; *Merrill Checklist of
Anderson,* 1969, and *Anderson: A Reference Guide,* 1977,
both by Ray Lewis White; *Anderson: A Selective, Annotated
Bibliography* by Douglas G. Rogers, 1976.

Critical Studies: *Anderson: His Life and Work* by James
Schevill, 1951; *Anderson* by Irving Howe, 1951; *Anderson*
by Brom Weber, 1964; *Anderson* by Rex Burbank, 1964;
The Achievement of Anderson: Essays in Criticism edited by
Ray Lewis White, 1966; *Anderson: An Introduction and
Interpretation* by David D. Anderson, 1967, and *Anderson:
Dimensions of His Literary Art,* 1976, and *Critical Essays
on Anderson,* 1981, both edited by David D. Anderson; *The
Road to Winesburg: A Mosaic of the Imaginative Life of
Anderson* by William A. Sutton, 1972; *Anderson: A Collec-
tion of Critical Essays* edited by Walter B. Rideout, 1974;
Anderson: Centennial Studies edited by Hilbert H. Camp-
bell and Charles E. Modlin, 1976; *Anderson* by Welford
Dunaway Taylor, 1977; *Anderson: A Biography* by Kim
Townsend, 1987; *A Storyteller and a City: Anderson's
Chicago* by Kenny J. William, 1988; *New Essays on
Winesburg, Ohio* edited by John W. Crowly, 1990.

* * *

For a decade following the 1919 publication of *Winesburg, Ohio,* Sherwood Anderson was one of the most
influential American writers. As an experimenter in fiction
and member of the avant garde movement, he was much
imitated, and for a half century, his influence on writers
remained strong because of his rejection of established
literary forms, his glorification of the artists's life, and his
revitalization of the American idiom as a viable stylistic
device in fiction. Even now, when only a few Anderson
works — *Winesburg* and half a dozen short stories — are
read and when much of his fiction seems old-fashioned to
readers reared on post-modernist literature, his legacy is
evident. Richard Ford, for example, whose writing career
began almost half a century after Anderson's best work was
done, terms Anderson the major influence on his work due
to his innovative techniques and style.
   In his most productive years, Anderson published four
collections of stories — *Winesburg, Ohio, The Triumph of
the Egg, Horses and Men, Death in the Woods and Other
Stories* — and more were collected in the posthumous *The
Sherwood Anderson Reader* and, recently, in *Certain Things
Last.* Though his disciples Faulkner and Hemingway
turned against him, they continued to acknowledge their
debt, with Faulkner declaring Anderson the father of the
authors of the Lost Generation and Mark Twain the
grandfather of all of them. That cryptic tribute acknowledges Anderson's use of colloquial American English,
which he had learned from oral storytellers, the Southwest
humorists, and Mark Twain, who had broken away from
the stylized language characteristic of previous major
American authors. Anderson renewed that literary declaration of independence by taking the speech of his boyhood
and turning it into a lyrical, even incantatory prose, in
which simple words and phrases are reiterated and sense
impressions are conveyed concretely, a prose also influenced significantly by his reading of Gertrude Stein. Like
Whitman, Anderson rejected conventional literary patterns
in favor of an organic fiction in which forms and style grow
from reality rather than out of proscribed rules, and even
his narrators, whether first or third person, speak a flat
Midwestern language.
   Anderson's themes, emanating from his philosophy of
self-reliance and self-knowledge — Emerson, Thoreau, and
Whitman were strong influences — are few and simple: to
be out of touch with nature, without identity and the ability
to love, is merely to exist ("The Egg" and "The Man Who
Became a Woman," for example); people are dehumanized
by the Puritan work ethic, materialism, and practicality,
("An Ohio Pagan"). His heroes (or non-heroes) are rebels,
such as the writer and artists in "For What?" who struggle,
usually futilely, against the status quo. To know oneself
was, for Anderson, the ultimate accomplishment, but he
remained basically pessimistic about people's ability to
understand. Story after story concerns good but naive
people, such as the father in "The Egg," who vainly seek
answers to their dilemmas. Thus he breaks the pattern of
conventional stories in that his works often do not rise to a
climax in which the protagonist is blessed with an epiphany; indeed, in most of them, the protagonists are left
yearning for just such an insight, and whatever knowledge
may be granted as a result of their experiences is limited,
unenlightening, providing no solace for the lonely person.
   Anderson's stories are of several types, notably the study
of a grotesque character, a rite of passage episode, or a
picaresque tale, with some falling into more than one
category. Most are related by first person narrators, whose
revelation is understated, deceptively simple because ironic. The title of one of his most famous and often anthologized stories, "I Want to Know Why," would be appropriate for at least half his short stories. In "I'm a Fool," for
example, the narrator, who works as a swipe for an owner
of racing horses, lies to a young woman he meets at a race,
giving a false name and claiming that he is the son of a
wealthy horse owner. The story ends with the anguished
narrator denouncing himself as a fool and even, perhaps
hyperbolically, wishing he were dead. Whatever chance he
may have had with the young woman is lost, and he wants
to know why.
   In *Winesburg, Ohio,* Anderson introduced his theory of
the grotesque character, explained in the introductory
piece, "The Book of the Grotesque." The protagonist of the
piece, an elderly author, reminiscent of Mark Twain, has
determined after a long life that humanity's problem is that
at some point people became grotesques by claiming one
truth to the exclusion of others. All the *Winesburg* stories,
centered around teenaged George Willard, an aspiring
writer, deal with such people: the title character in "Mother" who spends years of frugality to save money so that her
son can move to the city, money that he never receives;
Doctor Parcival, "The Philosopher," who has determined
that "everyone in the world is Christ and they are all
crucified"; Kate Swift, "The Teacher," who, frustrated by
suppressed longings, tries in vain to impart to George
Willard a passion for life. In "Adventure," a typical

Winesburg story, Alice Hindman, a young dry goods clerk whose lover has abandoned her, spends years saving money in anticipation of his return. One evening, unable to control her suppressed sexuality and growing restlessness, Alice undresses and goes out into the rain to confront an elderly man who is merely confused by the apparation of a naked woman. She crawls back to the safety of her house, trembling with fear for what she has done, confused herself about the meaning of her adventure.

In "Certain Things Last," a story published first in 1992, Anderson expresses concisely his philosophy of writing fiction. The narrator, a writer, believes that "If I can write everything out plainly, perhaps I will myself understand better what has happened." Through an insightful experience, he recognizes that the writer's task is to deal with "certain facts" and "certain things"; if he can write "as clearly as I can the adventures of that certain moment," he will have accomplished his purpose. Anderson throughout his career was concerned with getting the reality of human experience on paper in his stories and allowing readers then to draw whatever enlightment or message they might from the certain details of the narrative.

—W. Kenneth Holditch

See the essays on "Death in the Woods," "Hands," and "I Want to Know Why."

ANDRIĆ, Ivo. Yugoslav. Born in Trávnik, Bosnia, Austria-Hungary, 9 October 1892. Educated at schools in Višegrad and Sarajevo; University of Zagreb; Vienna University; University of Krakow; Graz University, Ph.D. 1923. Married Milica Babić in 1959 (died 1968). Member of Mlada Bosna (Young Bosnia) and imprisoned for three years during World War I; in the Yugoslav diplomatic service, 1919–41: in Rome, Geneva, Madrid, Bucharest, Trieste, Graz, Belgrade, and, as Ambassador to Germany, Berlin; full-time writer, 1941–49; representative from Bosnia, Yugoslav parliament, 1949–55. Member of the Editorial Board, *Književni jug* (The Literary South). President, Federation of Writers of Yugoslavia, 1946–51. Recipient: Yugoslav Government Prize, 1956; Nobel prize for literature, 1961. Honorary Doctorate: University of Krakow, 1964. Member, Serbian Academy. *Died 13 March 1975.*

PUBLICATIONS

Collections

Sabrana djela [Collected Works], edited by Risto Trifković and others. 17 vols., 1982.

Short Stories

Pripovetke [Stories]. 3 vols., 1924–36.
Priča o vezirovom slonu. 1948; as *The Vizier's Elephant: Three Novellas,* 1962.
Nove pripovetke [New Stories]. 1949.
Novele [Short Stories]. 1951.
Pod grabićem: Pripovetke o životu bosanskog sela [Under the Elm: Stories of Life in a Bosnian Village]. 1952.
Anikina vremena [Anika's Times]. 1967.

The Pasha's Concubine and Other Tales. 1968.
The Damned Yard and Other Stories. 1992.

Novels

Gospodjica. 1945; as *The Woman from Sarajevo,* 1965.
Travnička hronika. 1945; as *Bosnian Story,* 1958; as *Bosnian Chronicle,* 1963; as *The Days of the Consuls,* 1992.
Na Drini ćuprija. 1945; as *The Bridge on the Drina,* 1959.
Priča o kmetu Simanu [The Tale of the Peasant Simon]. 1950.
Prokleta avlija. 1954; as *Devil's Yard,* 1962.
Ljubav u kasabi [Love in a Market Town]. 1963.

Verse

Ex ponto. 1918.
Nemiri [Anxieties]. 1919.

Other

Panorama: Pripovetke [Panorama: Stories] (for children). 1958.
Lica [Faces]. 1960.
Izbor [Selection]. 1961.
Kula i druge pripovetke [Children's Stories]. 1970.
Goya. 1972.
Letters. 1984.
The Development of Spiritual Life under the Turks, edited by Želimir B. Juričić and J.F. Loud. 1990.
Conversations with Goya, Signs, Bridges. 1992.

*

Bibliography: in *A Comprehensive Bibliography of Yugoslav Literature in English, 1593–1980* by Vasa D. Mihailovich and Mateja Matejič, 1984; supplement, 1988.

Critical Studies: "The French in The Chronicle of Travnik" by Ante Kadić, in *California Slavic Studies 1,* 1960; "The Work of Andrić" by E.D. Goy, in *Slavonic and East European Review 41,* 1963; "The Later Stories of Andrić" by Thomas Eekman, in *Slavonic and East European Review 48,* 1970; "Narrative and Narrative Structure in Andrić's *Devil's Yard*" by Mary P. Coote, in *Slavic and East European Journal 21,* 1977; *Andrić: Bridge Between East and West* by Celia Hawkesworth, 1985; *The Man and the Artist, Essays in Andrić* by Želimir B. Juričić, 1986; "The Short Stories of Andrić: Autobiography and the Chain of Proof" by Felicity Rosslyn, in *The Slavic and East European Review 67* (1), 1989; *Andrić: A Critical Biography* by Vanita Singh Mukerji, 1990; "Andrić, a 'Yugoslav' Writer" by Thomas Butler, in *Cross Currents,* 1991.

*   *   *

Ivo Andrić, the Nobel laureate for literature in 1961, is unquestionably the world's best-known Yugoslav writer. Andrić's ethnic heritage is as complex as that of the Bosnia in which he was born and raised, but like many intellectuals of his generation, he was a strong proponent of Yugoslav unity. He is best considered as he saw himself, a Yugoslav writer.

Although best-known in English for his epic masterpiece *Na Drini ćuprija (The Bridge on the Drina)*, Andrić's works include eight volumes of shorter works; before he became known as a novelist he was renowned in Yugoslavia as a master of the story. Before the outbreak of World War II Andrić had written some four dozen short pieces. From 1945 until his death he was to write nearly one hundred more.

Though conventional, the division of Andrić's work into pre- and post-World War II periods has little to do with any clear break in Andrić's thematics or style. Indicatively, his collected works are arranged not chronologically but by theme (with titles like "Children," "Signs," and "Thirst"). Whatever the topic, Andrić's best fiction combines universal themes with Balkan, especially Bosnian, specifics. Bosnia, with its violent history, tangled ethnic mix, and harsh landscape, was the land Andrić knew best and the setting for most of his prose fiction, but not for ethnography. Andrić used Bosnian settings and characters as a means to investigate and describe the human spiritual condition, and his writing reveals an existentialist vision influenced by the likes of Dostoevskii, Kierkegaard, and Camus.

Andrić selected for his stories material that was often violent, frequently unusual, and almost always redolent of legend. With a penchant for action, Andrić's stories, especially the earlier ones such as "Za Logorovanja," (1922, "In Camp") and "Mustafa Madžar," (1923, "Mustafa the Magyar"), describe a violence that is physical and brutal. In "Mara milošnica" (1926, "The Pasha's Concubine"), the abuse of a 15-year-old girl forced into the service of an authority she cannot fight ends in her derangement and death. In later works the explicitness of the violence is often muffled, but coercion and cruelty are almost always just below the surface. No doubt influenced by three years spent in an Austrian prison during World War I, Andrić's favored model of isolation is a prison cell itself ("The Bridge of the Žepa," "The Devil's Yard"), but the confinement can be of body or mind, in jail or in mental illness. In "Trup" (1937, "Torso"), for instance, an immobile, limbless body serves as the main character's prison.

The divers manifestations of physical duress are clear metaphors for a stifling of the spirit, an oppression of the soul, that characterizes the tone of many Andrić pieces. But Andrić's tone is not always pure gloom. The mood is usually set by the main character of a given story, and some of the best recognized figures, like the Franciscan monk Petar and the one-eyed village fool Ćorkan, who both appear in more than one work, are decidedly positive. Ćorkan, despite his limitations, has a vibrant soul, and in stories like "Ćorkan i švabica" (1921, "Ćorkan and the German Girl"), his fanciful aspirations are treated sympathetically.

Fancy, dreams, and visions are frequent ingredients in Andrić's stories. These altered perceptions offer access to a different "reality," one perhaps more authentic than the tangible world of things can provide. In stories like "Letovanje na jugu," (1959, "Summer in the South") and "Kod lekara" (1964, "At the Doctor's"), everyday reality finally bows completely to the fantastic. The victory of fantasy over empirically verifiable fact is closely related to Andrić's long standing interest in legend—the aura of which permeates the whole of his opus. Beginning with his very first story, "Put Alije Djerzeleza" (1920, "The Journey of Ali Djerzelez"), many Andrić stories derive immediately from Bosnian (Orthodox, Catholic, and Muslim) legends. Often the subject of the legend is humbled, and

human weaknesses are exposed. In other stories, like "Aska i Vuk" (1953, "Aska and the Wolf"), the genre tends toward the fable; but whether legend, myth, fable, or fantasy, nearly every Andrić story is impeccably crafted, every word in its proper place.

Andrić was a diligent collector of new words and phrases, and his generous use of folk expressions, dialecticisms, and turcisms even necessitated the appending of special glossaries to some works. His use of unusual words contributes to a style marked by subtlety and ambiguity, but his narrative usually is in a straightforward third person with intermittent use of complex framing ("Devil's Yard" and "Torso"). The prose is replete with similes, and he often employs almost aphoristic generalizations. The effect of this is reenforced by "conversations" that are seldom rendered in direct speech and a marked absence of explicit psychological portraits. This iconic atmosphere is further strengthened by repeating symbols and images. Andrić's best recognized symbol is the bridge (*Bridge on the Drina*, "Bridge on the Žepa," "Summer in the South"). A symbol for human's creativity and longing for eternity, the bridge has even come to identify Andrić's work as a whole. Other recurring symbols include the night ("the evil time" as Andrić called it), an immutable nature ("The Rzav Hills"), and the desert—a symbol of the human spirit unable or denied the right to speak ("Words").

The power and vital importance of all verbal communication, but especially of verbal art, of the tale, is central to many Andrić stories ("Words," "The Story," "Persecution," "Thirst," and "The People of Osatica"), and it is the belief in storytelling, this reverence for legends, that must be singled out as the core "meaning" of Andrić's work. In his Nobel acceptance speech Andrić made clear that only through imagination, and by extension, through art, can people, like "Scheherazade, . . . distract the executioner, . . . postpone the inevitability of the tragic fate that threatens us, and prolong the illusion of life and duration."

—Nathan Longan

See the essay on "Thirst."

———

APPELFELD, Aharon. Israeli. Born in Czernowitz, Bukovina, in 1932. Held in Transnistria concentration camp, Romania, for three years during World War II; escaped, wandered for several years, hiding in the Ukrainian countryside and then joining the Russian army; arrived in Palestine, 1947; served in Israeli army. Educated at Hebrew University, Jerusalem; visiting fellowship for Israeli Writers, St. Cross College, Oxford University, 1967–68; visiting lecturer, School of Oriental and African Studies, University of London, Oxford University, and Cambridge University, 1984; currently lecturer in Hebrew literature, Be'er Shev'a University. Recipient: Youth Aliyah prize; Prime Minister's prize for creative writing, 1969; Anne Frank literary prize (twice); Brenner prize, 1975; Milo prize; Israel prize, 1983; Jerusalem prize; H.H. Wingate literary award, 1987, 1989.

PUBLICATIONS

Short Stories

Ashan [Smoke].   1962; translated as "Ashan," in *In the Wilderness,* 1965.

Bagay haporeh [In the Fertile Valley].   1964; translated as "Bagay haporeh," in *In the Wilderness,* 1965.
In the Wilderness.   1965.
Chamishah sipurim [Five Stories].   1969–70.
Keme'ah edim: mivchar [Like a Hundred Witnesses: A Selection].   1975.
Tor hapela'ot (novella).   1978; as *The Age of Wonders,* 1981.
Badenheim, ir nofesh (novella).   1979; as *Badenheim 1939,* 1980.
To the Land of the Cattails (novella).   1986; as *To the Land of the Reeds,* 1987.
Bartfus ben ha'almavet (novella).   As *The Immortal Bartfuss,* 1988.

Novels

Kafor al ha'aretz [Frost on the Land].   1965.
Bekumat hakark'a [At Ground Level].   1968.
Ha'or vehakutonet [The Skin and the Gown].   1971.
Adoni hanahar [My Master the River].   1971.
Ke'ishon ha'ayin [Like the Pupil of an Eye].   1972.
Shanim vesha'ot [Years and Hours].   1974–75.
Michvat ha'or [A Burn on the Skin].   1980.
Tzili, the Story of a Life.   1983.
Hakutonet vehapasim [The Shirt and the Stripes].   1983.
The Retreat.   1984.
Ba'et uve'onah achat [At One and the Same Time].   1985; as *The Healer,* 1990.
Ritspat esh [Tongue of Fire].   1988.
Al kol hapesha'im.   As *For Every Sin,* 1989.
Katerinah.   1989; as *Katerina,* 1992.
Mesilat barzel [The Railway].   1991.

Other

Mas'ot beguf rish'on [Essays in First-Person].   1979.
Writing and the Holocaust.   1988.

Editor, *From the World of Rabbi Nahman of Bratslav.* 1973.

*

Critical Studies: "The Shirt and the Stripes" by Rochelle Furstenberg, in *Modern Hebrew Literature* 9(1–2), 1983; "Appelfeld, Survivor" by Ruth R. Wisse, in *Commentary* 75(8), 1983; "Appelfeld: The Search for a Language" by Sidra DeKoven Ezrahi, in *Studies in Contemporary Jewry,* 1, 1984; "Applefeld [sic] and Affirmation," in *Ariel* 61, 1985, and "Appelfeld: Not to the Left, Not to the Right" in *We Are All Close: Conversations with Israeli Writers,* 1989, both by Chaim Chertok; "Appelfeld and the Uses of Language and Silence" by Lawrence Langer, in *Remembering the Future,* 1989; "Literary Device Used for Effects of Subtlety and Restraint in an Emotion-Loaded Narrative Text: 'The Burn of Light' by Appelfeld" by Rina Dudai, in *Hebrew Linguistics,* January 1990; "Impossible Mourning: Two Attempts to Remember Annihilation" by James Hatley, in *Centennial Review* 35(3), 1990.

*   *   *

Aharon Appelfeld is an Israeli writer who has gone against the tide throughout his career. While the general ethos of modern Israeli writing calls upon authors to look forward and base their fiction in the present, Appelfeld continually returns to and recreates his past, the past of Israel and the world of pre-Holocaust European Jewry. His success in doing this has led A.B. Yehoshua to refer to him as a "world writer," that is, one who creates not just characters, but a whole universe. Appelfeld never addresses the Holocaust directly, letting it hover in the background, casting its shadows on the lives of his characters.

This backgrounding of the Holocaust allows Appelfeld to create a pervading sense of irony throughout his works. The hollow pretensions and self-delusion of his characters are tragically highlighted by the reality of looming disaster. The Jews' futile attempts to assimilate by trying to act like gentile intellectuals are revealed for the desperate, misguided gestures they are in the light of our retrospective knowledge of their future.

Badenheim 1939 was originally published in Hebrew, (*Badenheim, ir nofesh*) without a date in the title, a more appropriate rendering of the sense Appelfeld wants to convey of the characters' oblivion to the year's significance. A group of wealthy Jews at a health resort engage in social rituals and ignore the gathering storm around them. When several "Ostjuden" (Jews from the East) are transported there, as part of the displacement process, they use their energy to attack and disparage the newcomers, unable to recognize their common plight and enemy.

Similar themes appear in "The Retreat," which begins in pre-Holocaust Austria, and ends in a Mann-like sanitarium, where the characters have tried to find their "retreat," in self-hatred, and in learning to imitate the behavior of the surrounding peasants in an attempt to lose their separate identity. As the power of the Nazis begins to encroach upon their hideout, the noose tightens; they are forced to make dangerous sorties for provisions during which they are regularly attacked and beaten by the local peasants. Paradoxically, it is at this point that they begin to discover some kind of communal feeling and sense of mutual responsibility, taking turns venturing out, helping each other when they are hurt. This is one of Appelfeld's recurring ironies; his characters only regain their sense of common identity and unity at the brink, having been pushed to the utmost extremity.

Tor hapela'ot (The Age of Wonders) also shows the irony and tragedy of attempts at assimilation. The protagonist is a 12-year-old boy whose father, an anti-Semitic writer who abandons the family, is deported to Theriesenstadt, where he goes mad and dies. His mother finds a renewed sense of her Jewish identity through community acts and charity. As in most of Appelfeld's work, trains appear as sinister symbols; at the end of *Badenheim 1939* the characters catastrophically misjudge the railway cars at the end of the book, reasoning that, since they are in such bad condition, they do not have far to go.

To the Land of the Cattails is the story of a mother and her son whom she takes on a journey back to the land of her roots—and Appelfeld's—in Bukovina. The trip has an eerie quality for readers who know that the two are walking blindly straight into the inferno of the Holocaust. The final scene takes place at a railway station; though the mother is saved, the boy waits, unknowing, with a girl for the train that will carry them to their death.

Though Appelfeld's artistic mission is to recreate the world of pre-Holocaust Europe, he also deals with the many issues arising out of survival of the genocide. The protagonist of *The Immortal Bartfuss* is a survivor, but he has been unable to reconstruct a meaningful or peaceful life. He devotes his energy to forcing gifts and charity on people, in a reversal of Appelfeld's theme of the value of *Tzdkh* (charity). The protagonist is called immortal because life and death have become almost indistinguishable for him. He is living like one who is dead, estranged from his family, hiding money from his wife, unable to break the silence he imposed on himself during his smuggling days in Italy. Bartfuss's empty life reflects Appelfeld's belief that bandages will not help the Holocaust survivor—not even, as he has said, "a bandage such as the Jewish state." People expect survivors to teach them about life, but these demands for meaning are too much for them to bear and their internal feelings of guilt condemn them to a kind of living death.

What Appelfeld achieves in his writing is the re-evocation of the lost Jews of Europe and the recreation of the vanished world of his youth. He does so with lyric intensity, drawing a place and time forever poised on the edge of annihilation. His works pay homage to these human beings as they unknowingly face catastrophe.

—Carla N. Spivack

ARREOLA, Juan José. Mexican. Born in Ciudad Guzmán, Jalisco, 12 September 1918. Studied theatre in Paris, 1945. Teacher in Ciudad Guzmán, from 1941; worked on a newspaper in Guadalajara, 1943–45; editor, with Juan Rulfo, *q.v., Pan* magazine, and *Eos* magazine, 1940's; proofreader, Fondo de Cultura Económica publishing house, Mexico City, 1946; director of creative writing workshop, National Autonomous University of Mexico, Mexico City; founding member and actor, Poesía en Voz Alta group. Recipient: Institute of Fine Arts Drama Festival prize, and El Colegio de México fellowship, late 1940's; Xavier Villarrutia prize, 1963. Lives in Mexico City.

PUBLICATIONS

Short Stories

Gunther Stapenhorst: viñetas de Isidoro Ocampo.   1946.
Varia invención.   1949; enlarged edition, 1971.
Cinco cuentes.   1951.
Confabulario.   1952; revised edition, published with *Varia invención,* as *Confabulario y Varia invención: 1951–1955,* 1955; published with *Bestiario* and *Punta de plata,* as *Confabulario total, 1941–1961,* 1962; as *Confabulario and Other Inventions,* 1964; revised edition, as *Confabulario definitivo,* 1986.
Punta de plata.   1958; published with *Confabulario* and *Bestiario,* as *Confabulario total, 1941–61,* 1962.
Bestiario.   1958; published with *Confabulario* and *Punta de plata,* as *Confabulario total, 1941–1961,* 1962; revised edition, 1981.
Cuentos.   1969.
Antología de Arreola, edited by Jorge Arturo Ojeda. 1969.
Palindroma (includes play).   1971.
Mujeres, animales, y fantasías mecánicas.   1972.
Confabulario antológico.   1973.
Mi confabulario.   1979.
Confabulario personal.   1980.
Imagen y obra escogida.   1984.

Estas páginas mías.   1985.

Novel

La feria.   1963; as *The Fair,* 1977.

Play

La hora de todos: juguete cómico en un acto.   1954.

Other

La palabra educación.   1973.
Y ahora, la mujer.   1975.
Inventario.   1976.
Ramón López Velarde: una lectura parcial.   1988.
El arte de Nicolás Moreno, with Carlos Pellicer and Elisa García Barragán.   1990.

Editor, *Cuadernos del unicornio.*   5 vols., 1958–60.
Editor, *Lectura en voz alta.*   1968.
Editor, *La ciudad de Querétaro,* by Fernando Pereznieto Castro.   1975.

*

Bibliography: in *Mexican Literature: A Bibliography of Secondary Sources* by David William Foster, 1992.

Critical Studies: "The Estranged Man: Kafka's Influence on Arreola" by Thomas J. Tomanek, in *Revue des Langues Vivantes,* 37, 1971; "An Ancient Mold for Contemporary Casting: The Beast Book of Arreola," in *Hispania* 56, 1973, and *Arreola,* 1983, both by Yulan M. Washburn; "An Independent Author" by Andrée Conrad, in *Review* 14, 1975; "Continuity in Evolution: Arreola as Dramatist," in *Latin American Theatre Review* 8(2), 1975, "René Avilés Fabila in the Light of Arreola: A Study in Spiritual Affinity," in *Journal of Spanish Studies: 20th Century,* 7, 1979, and "Artistic Iconoclasm in Mexico: Countertexts of Arreola, Agustín, Avilés and Hiriart," in *Chasqui* 18(1), 1989, all by Theda Mary Herz; "Albert Camus' Concept of the Absurd and Arreola's 'The Switchman'" by George R. McMurray, in *Latin American Literary Review* 11, 1977; "The Little Girl and the Cat: 'Kafkaesque' Elements in Arreola's 'The Switchman'" by Leonard A. Cheever, in *American Hispanist* 34–35, 1979; "Absurdist Techniques in the Short Stories of Arreola" by Read G. Gilgen, in *Journal of Spanish Studies: 20th Century,* 8, 1980; "*Los de abajo* [Mariano Azuela], *La feria,* and the Notion of Space-Time Categories in the Narrative Text" by Floyd Merrel, in *Hispanófila* 79, 1983; "Arreola: Allegorist in an Age of Uncertainty" by Paula R. Heusinkveld, in *Chasqui* 13(2–3), 1984; "Arreola's 'The Switchman'—The Train and the Desert Experience" by Bettina Knapp, in *Confluencia* 3(1) 1987; "This Is No Way to Run a Railroad: Arreola's Allegorical Railroad and a Possible Source" by John R. Burt, in *Hispania* 71, 1988; "Arreola's *La feria*: The Author and the Reader in the Text" by Carol Clark D'Lugo, in *Hispanófila* 97, 1989.

* * *

Although Juan José Arreola has published a novel, two plays, and many essays, he is best known for his short fiction. He was born into a family of 14 children and at the age of eight was obliged to end his formal education and seek employment in various menial jobs. The epitome of the self-taught man, he published his first stories in Guadalajara during the early 1940's. Soon thereafter he moved to Mexico City where he established his reputation as a humorist more interested in universal themes than in the pressing social issues of his country. Because of his elegant style, frequent allusions to literature, and his addition to irony, paradox, and fantasy, he has been compared to the Argentine Jorge Luis Borges.

Some of Arreola's early stories treat regional themes in a realistic manner. "He Did Good While He Lived" portrays a man who discovers not only that his beloved's deceased husband, a highly esteemed citizen, was in reality a rascal, but also that his widow knew about his sins. In addition, the story exposes the hypocrisy of churchgoers when the president of the parish council on morality fathers the child of an unmarried woman. Arreola dismisses this tale as a naive depiction of good and evil, but critics have hailed it as a solidly structured, ironic representation of the subject. Another example of Mexican realism fraught with irony and implied social criticism is "Ballad," a brief sketch of a fatal duel between two young men courting the same girl. Blamed by the town citizens for the violence perpetrated by her would-be suitors, the innocent girl spends the rest of her life as a spinster.

The vast majority of Arreola's stories and vignettes either satirize human foibles through subtle psychological insights or treat philosophical themes in a light-hearted, fanciful manner. An example of the latter is "The Switchman," Arreola's best-known tale. Of this same mold is "Autrui," a takeoff on Sartre's *No Exit*, but instead of depicting hell as other people, hell (or the unknown enemy) turns out to be the narrator's other self. "Figment of a Dream" has Freudian as well as Sartrean overtones, the narrator being the unborn fetus of parents caught up in a love-hate relationship. The protagonist of "God's Silence," endeavoring to become the embodiment of Christian virtue, writes a letter to God asking why evil always seems to triumph over good. In his unsigned reply God explains, among other things, that humans should view the world as a grandiose experiment, that each individual should find an appropriate means of coping with life, and that it will be up to the narrator to recognize God when the latter appears before him. Arreola seems to suggest the basic existential tenets that existence precedes essence and that humans themselves must supply the missing deity.

"The Prodigious Milligram" stands out as one of Arreola's best allegories. Here a rebellious ant returns to her anthill not with the usual cargo of corn, but with a prodigious milligram she finds along the road. Her discovery is such a deviation from the norm that she is imprisoned and sentenced to death. Ultimately her life becomes legendary, inspiring other ants to reject convention and seek their own versions of the prodigious milligram. The story ends with the breakup and disintegration of the ant society. "The Prodigious Milligram" is a modern allegory replete with ambiguity; it can be read as an attack on excessive individualism, as a condemnation of capitalism, as a reworking of Ortega y Gasset's *The Revolt of the Masses*, or as a metaphor of the loss of tradition—and its disastrous results—in the contemporary world.

"The Rhinoceros" satirizes the battle of the sexes, one of Arreola's favorite subjects. In this brief sketch the ex-wife of the eponymous male gets her revenge when the aging "beast" is completely dominated by his clever second wife. Machismo receives the brunt of Arreola's satire in "Small Town Affair," in which Don Fulgencio sprouts horns and finally suffers a fate similar to that of a fighting bull. In "I'm Telling You the Truth" Arreola bases his satire of religion and science on the New Testament axiom that it would be harder for a rich person to enter heaven than for a camel to pass through the eye of a needle. Arpad Niklaus, a renowned scientist, seeks to refute this biblical metaphor by saving the souls of his rich patrons; he convinces them to fund his project of dissolving a camel, passing it through a needle's eye, and then reconstructing it in its original form.

Two of Arreola's most popular pieces, "Baby H.P." and "Announcement," parody the commercial world of advertising. In the former, which also satirizes U.S. technology ("Baby H.P." is the original title), a radio announcer touts the advantages of a gadget that can store the horse power generated by infants so that it can be used to operate home appliances. "Announcement," translated better as "advertisement," also uses commercial jargon, in this case to advertise "Plastisex," a custom-made, lifelike mannequin, with all the attributes of the ideal woman, designed as a substitute for a wife. This piece is hilarious, but it implicitly criticizes the dehumanization of women by men and, in an ironic twist, the artificial creatures women become in order to please men.

Arreola's works display a dazzling array of forms and styles ranging from the realistic and the erudite to the absurd and the fantastic. One of the most admired of Mexico's men of letters, he had undoubtedly influenced many of his younger colleagues. But because of his transnational themes and his sophisticated approach to literature, he is a writer's writer rather than a storyteller of mass appeal. He will be remembered as a keen satirist with a cosmopolitan world vision.

—George R. McMurray

See the essay on "The Switchman."

———————

ATWOOD, Margaret (Eleanor). Canadian. Born in Ottawa, Ontario, 18 November 1939. Educated at Victoria College, University of Toronto, 1957–61, B.A. 1961. Radcliffe College, Cambridge, Massachusetts, A.M. 1962. Harvard University, Cambridge, Massachusetts 1962–63, 1965–67. Divorced; one daughter. Lecturer in English, University of British Columbia, Vancouver, 1964–65; instructor in English, Sir George Williams University Montreal, 1967–68; teacher of creative writing, University of Alberta, Edmonton, 1969-70; assistant professor of English, York University, Toronto, 1971–72; editor and member of board of directors, House of Anansi Press, Toronto, 1971–73; writer-in-residence, University of Toronto, 1972–73, University of Alabama, Tuscaloosa, 1985, Macquarie University, North Ryde, New South Wales, 1987, and Trinity University, San Antonio, Texas, 1989; Berg Visiting Professor of English, New York University, 1986. President, Writers Union of Canada, 1981–82, and PEN Canadian Centre, 1984–86. Recipient: E.J. Pratt medal, 1961; President's medal, University of Western Ontario, 1965; Governor-General's award, 1966, 1986; Centennial Commission prize, 1967; Union League Civic and Arts Foundation prize, 1969, and Bess Hokin prize, 1974 (*Poetry,* Chicago); City of Toronto award, 1976, 1989;

St. Lawrence award, 1978; Radcliffe medal, 1980; Molson award, 1981; Guggenheim fellowship, 1981; Welsh Arts Council International Writers prize, 1982; Ida Nudel Humanitarian award, 1986; Toronto Arts award, 1986; Los Angeles *Times* Book award, 1986; Arthur C. Clarke Science-Fiction award, for novel, 1987; Humanist of the Year award, 1987; National Magazine award, for journalism, 1988; Harvard University Centennial medal, 1990. D.Litt.: Trent University, Peterborough, Ontario, 1973; Concordia University, Montreal, 1980; Smith College, Northampton, Massachusetts, 1982; University of Toronto, 1983; Mount Holyoke College, South Hadley, Massachusetts, 1985; University of Waterloo, Ontario, 1985; University of Guelph, Ontario, 1985; Victoria College, 1987; LL.D.: Queen's University, Kingston, Ontario, 1974. Companion, Order of Canada, 1981. Fellow, Royal Society of Canada, 1987; Honorary Member, American Academy of Arts and Sciences, 1988.

PUBLICATIONS

Short Stories

Dancing Girls and Other Stories.   1977.
Encounters with the Element Man.   1982.
Murder in the Dark: Short Fictions and Prose Poems.   1983.
Bluebeard's Egg and Other Stories.   1983.
Unearthing Suite.   1983.
Hurricane Hazel and Other Stories.   1986.
Wilderness Tips.   1991.
Good Bones.   1992.

Novels

The Edible Woman.   1969.
Surfacing.   1972.
Lady Oracle.   1976.
Life Before Man.   1979.
Bodily Harm.   1981.
The Handmaid's Tale.   1985.
Cat's Eye.   1988.

Plays

Radio Play: *The Trumpets of Summer,* 1964.

Television Plays: *The Servant Girl,* 1974; *Snowbird,* 1981; *Heaven on Earth,* with Peter Pearson, 1986.

Verse

Double Persephone.   1961.
The Circle Game (single poem).   1964.
Talismans for Children.   1965.
Kaleidoscopes: Baroque.   1965.
Speeches for Doctor Frankenstein.   1966.
The Circle Game (collection).   1966.
Expeditions.   1966.
The Animals in That County.   1968.
Who Was in the Garden.   1969.
Five Modern Canadian Poets, with others, edited by Eli Mandel.   1970.
The Journals of Susanna Moodie.   1970.
Oratorio for Sasquatch, Man and Two Androids: Poems for Voices.   1970.
Procedures for Underground.   1970.

Power Politics.   1971.
You Are Happy.   1974.
Selected Poems.   1976.
Marsh, Hawk.   1977.
Two-Headed Poems.   1978.
True Stories.   1981.
Notes Towards a Poem That Can Never Be Written.   1981.
Snake Poems.   1983.
Interlunar.   1984.
Selected Poems 2: Poems Selected and New 1976–1986.   1986.
Selected Poems 1966–1984.   1990.
Poems 1965–1975.   1991.

Other

Survival: A Thematic Guide to Canadian Literature.   1972.
Days of the Rebels 1815–1840.   1977.
Up in the Tree (for children).   1978.
Anna's Pet (for children), with Joyce Barkhouse.   1980.
Second Words: Selected Critical Prose.   1982.
Atwood: Conversations, edited by Earl G. Ingersoll.   1990.
For the Birds (for children).   1990.

Editor, *The New Oxford Book of Canadian Verse in English.*   1982.
Editor, with Robert Weaver, *The Oxford Book of Canadian Short Stories in English.*   1986.
Editor, *The Canlit Food Book: From Pen to Palate: A Collection of Tasty Literary Fare.*   1987.
Editor, with Shannon Ravenel, *The Best American Short Stories.*   1989.
Editor, *Barbed Lyres.*   1990.

*

Bibliography: "Atwood: An Annotated Bibliography" (prose and poetry) by Alan J. Horne, in *The Annotated Bibliography of Canada's Major Authors 1–2* edited by Robert Lecker and Jack David,   2 vols., 1979–80.

Critical Studies: *Atwood: A Symposium* edited by Linda Sandler, 1977; *A Violent Duality* by Sherrill E. Grace, 1979, and *Atwood: Language, Text, and System* edited by Grace and Lorraine Weir, 1983; *The Art of Atwood: Essays in Criticism* edited by Arnold E. Davidson and Cathy N. Davidson, 1981; *Atwood* by Jerome H. Rosenberg, 1984; *Atwood: A Feminist Poetics* by Frank Davey, 1984; *Forbidden Fruit: On the Relationship Between Women and Knowledge in Doris Lessing, Slema Lagerlöf, Kate Chopin, and Atwood* by Bonnie St. Andrews, 1986; *Atwood* by Barbara Hill Rigney, 1987; *Atwood: Reflection and Reality* by Beatrice Mendez-Egle, 1987; *Critical Essays on Atwood* edited by Judith McCombs, 1988; *Atwood: Vision and Forms* edited by Kathryn van Spanckeren and Jan Garden Castro, 1988.

*   *   *

Margaret Atwood is one of the best Canadian writers in her generation, and certainly the most versatile of all. As a critic in books like *Survival* and *Second Words*, she has developed a thematically based critique—particularly of Canadian fiction—that presents the victor-victim theme as a frequent though not universal motif; it has been convincing so far as her own fiction is concerned, though less so in relation to Canadian novels and stories as a whole. Atwood is also one of the three or four best poets practicing in Canada today, and her sharp ear as a poet is related to her sharp eye as a critic which in turn is related to the combination of playful wit, Jungian demonology, and penetrative psychological insight that characterizes her fiction.

Atwood's seven novels have been widely discussed, but the differences as well as the relations between her short and her major fiction are considerable; in the short stories her vision tends to sharpen rather than narrow as she turns away from the moral-historical preoccupations of her novels towards the special, intimate, often isolated behaviour of individuals. It is as if she were turning her eyes away from a telescope to a microscope, and following for a while a kind of intimate enquiry like those pursued by her entomologist father, but with the behaviour of humans rather than that of moths and beetles as subject. The kind of eye with which she looks, as well as the clear prose she uses, tends to link Atwood, in so far as an artist can be linked with a scientist, with the classic naturalist writers of the 19th and early 20th centuries. If there is anything that Atwood's short stories have in common, it is that they isolate for observation adolescents as they enter the "mature" world, or adults entering alien settings, or people limited both emotionally and mentally who have not yet made any terms with the world.

Atwood was writing stories quite early in her career, but only in 1977 did she publish her first collection, *Dancing Girls and Other Stories*, shortly after her third novel, *Lady Oracle*. It was followed in 1983 by *Bluebeard's Egg and Other Stories*, and in 1991 by *Wilderness Tips*, though these larger collections have been interspersed by small collections published by small presses, like *Encounters with the Element Man*, *Murder in the Dark: Short Fiction and Prose Poems*, *Hurricane Hazel and Other Stories*, and the recent *Good Bones*, described as "short parables, prose poems, monologues."

Atwood's short fiction ranges in its preoccupations—and its mood—from the deathly to trivial, for Atwood has the unusual ability to be chilling at one moment and jokingly playful the next, so that one is not always sure whether that skull has just been dug out of a graveyard or manufactured by a Hallowe'en mask-maker. The main common element is the enviable skill with which the writer works. Her short stories can be seen as the small (not always lesser) products of an imagination and an observation incessantly at work. (Her friends always open her new books fearing yet hoping to be somehow there.) The stories are, despite their assurance of touch, tentative in effect, even less likely to answer our questions fully than her novels. Yet there is a typical Atwood relentlessness about them, and we are meant to keep on questioning what is happening in this world between rationality and madness that we precariously inhabit when we read them.

The tourist, most often a woman alienated from her habitual past, is a character in many of these stories, and in other stories the trembling fear of being at the heart of the unfamiliar and the threatening is extended, as it is in Atwood's novels. In a 1980 essay on Atwood, published in *Essays on Canadian Writing*, Russell Brown elaborately compares one of her stories, "The Resplendent Quetzal" with her slightly later novel *Life Before Man*, and finds similar patterns of alienation. He says—and in doing so gives an important insight into Atwood's shorter fiction: "Throughout *Dancing Girls*, boarding houses, rented rooms, and hotels are almost the only accommodations mentioned, and all exude a sense of residents who 'never lived here'; nowhere is there stability; nowhere does a genuine 'home' exist."

One could of course apply this insight to all of Atwood's fiction. Nowhere does a real home exist. The terrible patriarchal collectivity of *The Handmaid's Tale* is the opposite of home, and it is surely significant that the more one can significantly link the central character of an Atwood story or a novel with its author, the more one is involved in a fluid family situation that is not based on a settled home but on a wandering existence depending on seasonal imperatives: an unsettling existence but one rich in data about human existence since awareness flourishes in instability. And so we find in Atwood's stories sharp observations on existence that resemble the occasional papers that in a scientist's career can vary her major theoretical pieces with the trivia by which her interest and her urge are sustained.

—George Woodcock

See the essays on "The Salt Garden" and "Wilderness Tips."

AYALA, Francisco. Spanish. Born in Granada, 16 March 1906. Educated at the University of Madrid, law degree 1929, doctorate 1931. Married Etelvina Silva in 1931; one daughter. Professor of law, University of Madrid, 1932–35; diplomat for Spanish Republic, 1937; exiled in Argentina, 1939–50, Puerto Rico, 1950–58, New York, 1958–66, and Chicago, 1966–73; professor, Rutgers University, New Brunswick, New Jersey, Bryn Mawr College, Pennsylvania, University of Chicago, and New York University. U.S. representative to Unesco. Recipient: National Critics' prize, 1972; National Literature prize, 1983; National Prize of Spanish Letters, 1988; Cervantes prize, 1991. Elected to the Spanish Royal Academy, 1983. Lives in Madrid.

PUBLICATIONS

Short Stories

El boxeador y un ángel.   1929.
Cazador en el alba (novella).   1930; as *Cazador en el alba y otras imaginaciones*, 1971.
El hechizado (novella).   1944; as "The Bewitched" in *Ursurpers*, 1987.
La cabeza del cordero.   1949; as *The Lamb's Head*, 1971.
Los usurpadores.   1949; as *Usurpers*, 1987.
Historia de macacos.   1955.
El as de Bastos.   1963.
De raptos, violaciones y otras inconveniencias, 1966.
Cuentos.   1966; as *El inquisidor y otras narraciones españolas*, 1970.

Novels

Tragicomedia de un hombre sin espíritu.   1925.
Historia de un amanecer.   1926.
Muertes de perro.   1958; as *Death as a Way of Life*, 1964.
El fondo del vaso.   1962.

El rapto. 1965.
Mis páginas mejores. 1965.
Obras narrativas completas, edited by Andrés Amorós. 1969.
El jardín de las delicias. 1971.
El rapto; Fragancia de jazmines; Diálogo entre el amor y un viejo, edited by Estelle Irizarry. 1974.
El jardín de las delicias; El tiempo y yo. 1978.
El jardín de las malicias. 1988.

Other

Indagación del cinema. 1929.
El derecho social en la constitución de la República española. 1932.
El pensamiento vivo de Saavedra Fajardo. 1941.
El problema del liberalismo. 1941.
Historia de la libertad. 1942.
Oppenheimer. 1942.
Razón del mundo (La preocupación de España). 1944.
Histrionismo y representación. 1944.
Los políticos. 1944.
Una doble experiencia política: España e Italia. 1944.
Jovellanos. 1945.
Ensayo sobre la libertad. 1945.
Tratado de sociología. 1947.
La invención del "Quijote." 1950.
Ensayos de sociología política. 1952.
Introducción a las ciencias sociales. 1952.
Derechos de la persona individual para una sociedad de masas. 1953.
El escritor en la sociedad de masas; Breve teoría de la traducción. 1956; as *Problemas de la traducción,* 1965.
La integración social en América. 1958.
La crisis actual de la enseñanza. 1958.
Tecnología y libertad. 1959.
Experiencia e invención. 1960.
Realidad y ensueño. 1963.
La evasión de los intelectuales, with H.A. Murena. 1963.
De este mundo y el otro. 1963.
España, a la fecha. 1965; enlarged edition, 1977.
El cine: arte y espectáculo. 1966.
España y la cultura germánica; España a la fecha. 1968.
Reflexiones sobre la estructura narrativa. 1970.
El "Lazarillo": Nuevo examen de algunos aspectos. 1971.
Confrontaciones. 1972.
Hoy ya es ayer (includes *Libertad y liberalismo; Razón del mundo; La crisis de la enseñanza*). 1972.
Los ensayos: teoría y crítica literaria. 1972.
La novela: Galdós y Unamuno. 1974.
Cervantes y Quevedo. 1974.
El escritor y su imagen: Ortega y Gasset, Azorín, Valle-Inclán, Machado. 1975.
El escritor y el cine. 1975.
Galdós en su tiempo. 1978.
España 1975-1980: conflictos y logros de la democracia. 1982.
De triunfos y penas. 1982.
Conversaciones con Francisco Ayala. 1982.
Recuerdos y olvidos. I: Del paraíso al destierro; II: El exilio (memoirs). 2 vols., 1982.
Palabras y letras. 1983.
La estructura narrativa, y otras experiencias literarias. 1984.
La retórica del periodismo y otras retóricas. 1985.
La imagen de España: continuidad y cambio en la sociedad española. 1986.
Mi cuarto a espadas. 1988.

Las plumas del fénix: estudios de literatura española. 1989.
El escritor en su siglo. 1990.

Editor, *Diccionario Atlántico.* 1977.

*

Critical Studies: *Ayala,* 1977, and "The Ubiquitous Trickster Archetype in the Narrative of Ayala," in *Hispania* 70(2), 1987, both by Estelle Irizarry; *Narrative Perspective in the Post-Civil War Novels of Ayala: "Muertes de perro" and "El fondo del vasap"* by Maryellen Bieder, 1979; "Historicity and Historiography in Ayala's *Los usurpadores*" by Nelson Orringer, in *Letras Peninsulares* 3 (1), 1990.

* * *

Francisco Ayala, Spanish author, sociologist, political scientist, and literary critic, began his literary career in his teens. Readers of Cervantes may recognize echoes of his novella, "The Glass Licentiate," and monomania in the *Quixote;* Cervantes's enduring influence pervades Ayala's works, mosaics of intertextual allusions to famous books of Spanish literature.

Innovations of Spanish vanguardist movements (1925-1935)—ultraism, Dadaism, cubism and surrealism—pervade *El boxeador y un ángel* (The Boxer and an Angel), five pieces showing influences of Freudian and Jungian psychology, cosmopolitanism, humor, and a preference for metaphor over realistic description. Vanguard word play, sensorial imagery, wit, and the cult of "pure" fiction essentially ended with the Civil War (1936-39). "The Boxer and an Angel" evinces fascination with technology and the cinema (newly introduced to Spain), on which Ayala wrote several essays. A boxer is helped by an angel when he is about to lose; the pseudo-epic treatment demythifies the idealization of modern sports heroes. "Hora muerta" (Dead Hour) and "Polar, Estrella" (Polar, Star) employ cinematic changes of scene and experiment with other possibilities offered by the cinema (e.g., slow motion, running the film backwards, and recurring visual motifs).

The novelette, *Cazador en el alba* (Hunter at Dawn), Ayala's most surrealistic experiment, employs free association of imagery, fusing dream, memory, delirium, and reality. A youthful military recruit falls madly in love with a dancehall girl, Aurora ("dawn" in Spanish). Ironic demythification equates the rustic recruit with Hercules and his love with Diana (goddess of hunters); verbal brilliance prevails over sentiment and content. "Erika ante el invierno" (Erika Facing Winter), published with *Cazador,* was written in 1930 after two years in Germany where Ayala witnessed fascism's development. His intuition of the Nazi movement's potential for violence and genocide imbues adolescent Erika's search for a childhood friend. Her discomfort upon perceiving "racial" differences between herself and ethnic Jews, plus an impressionistic interlude in which an innocent child is slaughtered in a butcher shop, augur future atrocities.

In 1932, Ayala became a professor of law at the University of Madrid, winning the chair of political law in 1934. During the Civil War, he served as secretary of the Republic's legation in Prague, and later in France and Cuba, emigrating to Argentina, then moving to Puerto

Rico, and later the United States. He wrote treatises on sociology, philosophy, and intellectual history, but no more collections of fiction until *Los usurpadores* (*Usurpers*), incorporating the masterful novelette, *El hechizado* ("The Bewitched"), and *La cabeza del cordero* (*The Lamb's Head*). These are Ayala's most significant novellas and stories. A common preoccupation with Spanish history (Medieval Renaissance in *Usurpers*, contemporary in *The Lamb's Head*) expressed in sparse, objective, realistic prose, permits Ayala to subvert official Francoist versions of Spain's past and present. In Ayala's mature works, stylistic considerations are subjected to thematic and philosophical ends as the writer masters the difficult art of simplicity and clarity, yet works are far from simple or transparent.

Usurpation of power, the theme unifying the ten tales of *Usurpers*, is less visible in the four novellas in *The Lamb's Head*, joined by motifs of the Civil War, but the Franco regime's overthrow of the legally constituted Republic was a maximum usurpation. "San Juan de Dios" pictures the dissolute Portuguese soldier's conversion to saintly founder of a charity hospital and a mendicant order, against the background of incessant violence in Granada, civil strife, and plagues. "The Invalid" portrays Enrique III of Castile (1390-1406), who trapped nobles usurping his power, but he decreed their release when suffering from fevers and delirium. "The Bell of Huesca" refers to a 12th-century legend of King Ramiro the Monk, recalled to Aragon's throne when his firstborn brother left no heir. Abhorring power, Ramiro beheads the magnates who summoned him to rule (the title describes the form in which their heads were placed). "The Impostors" recounts Portuguese King Sebastian's suicidal foray against Morocco and subsequent fraudulent claims to the crown. "The Inquisitor" portrays a former rabbi, a Catholic convert now Bishop-Inquisitor, covering his past by overzealous persecutions, including his brother-in-law, his daughter's tutor, even his daughter. His insincere Christianity surfaces upon praying to "Father Abraham" in a moment of tribulation. "The Embrace" recalls the 14th-century reign of Peter the Cruel and the fratricidal civil wars against his illegitimate half-brothers (he murders one and is treacherously killed by the other in a peace-embrace).

In *The Lamb's Head*, "The Message"—possibly meaningless scribbles on a mysterious scrap of paper left by a boardinghouse guest—provokes excitement and conflict among several small-town residents aspiring to proprietorship of the indecipherable "revelation." Other tales treat an erstwhile exile's return, and symbolically portray human shortcomings underlying events causing Spain's civil conflicts. *Historia de macacos* (Monkey Story) contains six bitterly ironic stories portraying people's petty inhumanity (abuse, ridicule, humiliation, and debasement of others). Moral and physical outrages perpetrated against one's neighbors and attendant ethical concerns unify the six sardonic stories of *El as de Bastos* (The Ace of Clubs). Although Ayala terms all his works "novels," short fiction is his forté, and in no sense a minor genre.

—Janet Pérez

See the essays on "The Bewitched" and "The Tagus."

AYMÉ, Marcel. French. Born in Joigny, 29 March 1902. Educated at school in Dôle. Married Marie-Antoinette Arnaud in 1932; one daughter. Served in the French Army, 1922–23. Worked at a variety of jobs including clerk, translator, film extra, all Paris; wrote for collaborationist newspapers during war; full-time writer, from early 1930's. Recipient: Théophraste Renaudot prize, 1933. *Died 14 October 1967.*

PUBLICATIONS

Collection

Oeuvres Romanesques complètes. 1989—.

Short Stories

Le Puits aux images. 1932.
Le Nain. 1934.
Derrière chez Martin (novellas). 1938.
Les Contes du Chat perché (for children). 1939.
Le Passe-Muraille. 1943; as *The Walker-Through-Walls and Other Stories*, 1950.
Le Vin de Paris. 1947; as *Across Paris and Other Stories*, 1950.
En arrière. 1950.
Autres Contes du Chat perché. 1950.
The Wonderful Farm (for children). 1951.
The Magic Pictures: More about the Wonderful Farm (for children). 1954.
Return to the Wonderful Farm. 1954.
Soties de la ville et des champs. 1958.
Derniers Contes du Chat perché (for children). 1958.
Oscar et Erick (story). 1961.
The Proverb and Other Stories. 1961.
Enjambées (collection). 1967.
La Fille du shérif; nouvelles, edited by Michel Lecureur. 1987.

Novels

Brûlebois. 1926.
Aller retour. 1927.
Les Jumeaux du diable. 1928.
La Table aux crevés. 1929; as *The Hollow Field*, 1933.
La Rue sans nom. 1930.
Le Vaurien. 1931.
La Jument verte. 1934; as *The Green Mare*, 1955.
Maison basse. 1935; as *The House of Men*, 1952.
Le Moulin de la Sourdine. 1936; as *The Secret Stream*, 1953.
Gustalin. 1937.
Le Boeuf clandestin. 1939.
La Vouivre. 1943; as *The Fable and the Flesh*, 1949.
Travelingue. 1941; as *The Miraculous Barber*, 1950.
La Belle Image. 1941; as *The Second Face*, 1951; as *The Grand Seduction*, 1958.
Le Chemin des écoliers. 1946; as *The Transient Hour*, 1948.
Uranus. 1948; as *The Barkeep of Blémont*, 1950; as *Fanfare in Blémont*, 1950.
Les Tiroirs de l'inconnu. 1960; as *The Conscience of Love*, 1962.

Plays

Vogue la galère (produced 1944). 1944.

Lucienne et le boucher.   1947.
Clérambard (produced 1950).   1950; translated as
    Clérambard, 1952.
La Tête des autres (produced 1952).   1952.
Les Quatre vérités (produced 1954).   1954.
Les Sorcières de Salem, from *The Crucible* by Arthur
    Miller.   1955.
Les Oiseaux de lune (produced 1955).   1956; as *Moon-
    birds*, 1959.
La Mouche bleue (produced 1957).   1957.
Vu du pont, from the play by Arthur Miller.   1958
Louisiane (produced 1961).   1961.
La Nuit de l'Iguane, from the play by Tennessee Williams.
    1962.
Les Maxibules (produced 1961).   1962.
Le Minotaure (produced 1966).   With *Consommation*
    and *La Convention Belzébir*.   1967.
La Convention Belzébir (produced 1966).   With *Le Mi-
    notaure* and *Consommation*.   1967.

Other

Silhouette du scandale (essays).   1938.
Le Trou de la serrure (essays).   1946.
Images de l'amour (essays).   1946.
Le Confort intellectuel (essays).   1949.
Paris que j'aime, with Antoine Blondin, and Jean-Paul
    Clébert.   1956; as *The Paris I Love*, 1963.

*

Critical Studies: *The Comic World of Aymé* by Dorothy
Brodin, 1964; *The Short Stories of Aymé*, 1980 and *Aymé*,
1987, both by Graham Lord.

* * *

Marcel Aymé wrote 83 short stories that were published
during his lifetime in eight major collections: *Le Puits aux
images, Le Nain, Derrière chez Martin, Les Contes du Chat
perché, Le Passe-Muraille, Autres Contes du Chat perché,
En arrière*, and *Derniers Contes du Chat perché*. Several
other stories have never been published in a collection:
"Samson" (1945), "Le Couple" (1963), "Un Crime"
(1951), "Héloïse" (1952), and "Knate" (1971).
Aymé's short stories deal with the same subjects in his
novels. Two major concerns are the country people in his
native Jura and urban prolitarians whose lives he observed
during his adult life in Montmartre. As in the novels, he
also wrote stories with a socio-political bite to them, in
which he seemed to attack both the left and the right. But
since the short stories have a wide range and vary in subject
matter and tone, there is no easy way to categorize them.
In general, however, it can be said that the use of the
fantastic and the marvelous is a hallmark of Aymé's short
fiction. A large number of these works seem like children's
stories and continue to be read as such today. These works
usually recount the interactions between two little girls,
Delphine and Marinette, and various representatives of the
animal kingdom. Aymé presents these stories as if social
intercourse with talking animals were a perfectly normal
everyday occurence. Children do indeed respond to them,
and this is why so many of these stories books remain in
print, but they can also be read as political or moral
allegories.

Aymé's stories can be divided into *féerique* and *fantas-
tique*. The former usually requires a world apart, like C.S.
Lewis's Narnia or J.R.R. Tolkien's Middle Earth. Some of
Aymé's stories belong to this genre but use of the *fantas-
tique* is more typical of his work. Here, humans are at the
center of the action, but strange things are allowed to occur,
for instance, invisibility in *Le Passe-Muraille*. The fantastic
is appealing to the modern reader because it allows
something strange and unexpected to burst upon the scene
in the midst of our humdrum existence. In his stories Aymé
helps us to look at our condition critically and to probe
beneath the surface.

The title story of *Le Passe-Muraille*, hailed as a short story
masterpiece, describes what happens in the boring existence of a civil servant, Dutilleul, when he finds out that he
has the ability to pass through walls. Because of this special
talent, he is able to overcome the mediocrity and anonymity to which our modern mass society ordinarily condemns
us. He is able to become someone.

A transforming, fantastic device dear to Aymé is to alter
the concept of time. In "Rechute" the aging leaders of
society decree that the year will contain 24 months, thus
slowing the aging process, which they see as favorable to
them. But this causes an uprising on the part of children
who do not want to have to wait so long for the unset of
puberty. In "La Carte" the state takes time away from
people who are considered less beneficial to the state and
awards more to those considered more useful. This leads to
many complicated situations which are both humorous and
troubling.

Aymé devoted so much of his creative energy to the short
story because it was an ideal way of showing the multiplicity, diversity, and contradictions of human existence. This
genre allowed him to develop an idea principally through
the projection of images without the restriction imposed by
a long narrative line, as is the case with the novel. Like
Rabelais, La Fontaine, and Voltaire, Aymé was essentially
a moralist and a philosopher who wanted to portray the
foibles of a wide spectrum of the human condition. Like his
predecessors, he found that the form of the short story
suited this aim well.

Aymé's realistic stories have received far less critical
commentary than his fantastic works. In these tales, he
usually treats Parisian lower-class people, the country folk
of his native Jura, or the school classroom, where young
minds, as yet unconditioned by society, do battle with
pedantic school teachers.

Condemned by leftists as a voice of the right in the years
after the war, because of his inability to keep silent about
brutality and hypocrisy after the Germans were chased out
of France, Aymé was blacklisted (like Céline, Brasillach,
Rebatet, and so many others), and his best work was
ignored. Aymé's short stories still rank among the best in
France in the 20th century. The ongoing publication of his
stories (and novels) in the prestigious Editions de la Pliéade
offers eloquent testimony to this distinction.

—David O'Connell

See the essay on "The Walker-Through-Walls."

B

BABEL, Isaak (Emmanuilovich). Russian. Born in Odessa, 1 July 1894. Educated in Nikolaev; Nicholas I Commercial School, Odessa, 1905–11; Institute of Financial and Business Studies, Kiev, later in Saratov, 1911-15, graduated 1915. Served in the army, 1917–18. Married Evgeniia Gronfein in 1919; one daughter; also one daughter by Antonina Pirozhkova. Lived in St. Petersburg from 1918: worked on Gor'kii's magazine *New Life*, 1918; editor, Ukranian State Publishing House, 1919–20; news service correspondent with First Cavalry on the Polish campaign, 1920, and correspondent for *Tiflis* newspaper in Caucasus; in Moscow from 1923; secretary of the village soviet at Molodenovo, 1930; out of favour in the 1930's, and arrested, 1939. *Died (allegedly) 17 March 1941.*

PUBLICATIONS

Collections

Collected Stories, edited by Walter Morison.   1955.
Izbrannoe.   1957; another edition, 1966.
Destvo i drugie rasskazy [Childhood and Other Stories], edited by Efraim Sicher.   1979.

Short Stories

Rasskazy [Stories].   1925.
Konarmiia.   1926; as *Red Cavalry*, 1929.
Odesskie rasskazy [Odessa Stories].   1931.
Benya Krik, The Gangster, and Other Stories, edited by Avrahm Yarmolinsky.   1948.
Lyubka the Cossack and Other Stories, edited by Andrew R. MacAndrew.   1963.
The Lonely Years 1925–29: Unpublished Stories and Private Correspondence, edited by Nathalie Babel.   1964.
You Must Know Everything: Stories 1915–1937, edited by Nathalie Babel.   1969.
The Forgotten Prose, edited by Nicholas Stroud.   1978; as *Zabytyy Babel*, 1979.

Novels

Bluzhdaiushchie zvezdy: Rasskaz **dlia** *kino* [Wandering Stars: A Cine-Story].   1926.
Istoriia moei golubiatni [The Story of My Dovecot].   1926.
Benia Krik: Kinopovest.   1926; as *Benia Krik: A Film-Novel*, 1935.
Korol' [The King].   1926.

Plays

Zakat (produced 1927).   1928; as *Sunset*, in *Noonday 3*, 1960.
Mariia (produced 1964).   1935; as *Marya*, in *Three Soviet Plays*, edited by Michael Glenny, 1966.

*

Critical Studies: *Babel* by Richard W. Hallett, 1972; *The Art of Babel* by Patricia Carden, 1972; *Babel, Russian Master of the Short Story* by James E. Falen, 1974; *An Investigation of Composition and Theme in Babel's Literary upd Cycle "Konarmija"* by Ragna Grøngaard, 1979; *Babel's Red Cavalry* by Carol Luplow, 1982; *Metaphor in Babel's Short Stories* by Danuta Mendelson, 1982; "Art as Metaphor, Epiphany, and Aesthetic Statement: The Short Stories of Babel," in *Modern Language Review*, 1982, "The Road to a Red Cavalry: Myth and Mythology in the Works of Babel," in *Slavonic and East European Review*, 1982, and *Style and Structure in the Prose of Babel*, 1986, all by Efraim Sicher; *The Place of Space in Narration: A Semiotic Approach to the Problem of Literary Space with an Analysis of the Role of Space in Babel's Konarmija* by J.J. von Baak, 1983; *The Field of Honour* by C.D. Luck, 1987; *Procedures of Montaine in Babel's Red Calavry* by Marc Schreurs, 1989; *Babel and His Film Work* by Jerry Heil, 1990.

*   *   *

The tradition that Isaak Babel belonged to was a comparatively young one. During the 19th century the movement of Jewish secular enlightenment called the *Haskala*, which had its origins in Germany, gave rise to a Hebrew and Yiddish literary culture in the Russian Empire, with centres in Warsaw, Vilna, and Odessa. One aim of the enlightenment was to bring about a degree of assimilation to European, non-Jewish culture. In Germany this process went much faster than in Russia, facilitated both by the similarity of German to Yiddish and by the relative prosperity of German Jews compared to their Russian counterparts. In Russia Jews had to contend with a much harsher attitude on the part of the authorities, particularly in the last decade of the century, yet even so they managed to develop Russian-language culture that ran parallel to the Yiddish and Hebrew ones, and Russian became another of the languages of the Jewish diaspora.

In 1914, with the outbreak of World War I, the territories of Russia that lay within the Jewish Pale became the battleground on which the rival armies fought out the conflict, and the result was an exodus of Jews to the south of Russia, particularly to Odessa. It was in Odessa that the flowering of Hebrew and Yiddish literature took place. Babel was personally acquainted with some of the great figures of Jewish writing who lived there; in particular, Mendele Moykher-Sforim, whose work Babel later translated into Russian. He was also familiar with the writing of Sholom Aleichem, which he also translated. Of books by the newer generation, he had read those of Klausner, Ravnitsky and Akhad Haam. His early stories show their influence: "Old Shloyme," which describes an old man's suicide after he realizes that his position within the family is untenable, and "Ilya Isaakovich and Margarita Prokof-yevna," an account of a romance between a Jewish businessman and a prostitute, both stem from this tradition.

Babel's undoubted masterpiece is the story-cycle *Konarmiia (Red Cavalry)*. This bears many similarities to other works by Soviet writers about the Civil War, like Furmanov's *Chapayev,* Fadeyev's *The Route,* and the short stories of Vsevolod Ivanov. Its experimentalism is in some ways related to that of the literary group known as the Serapion Brothers, and its pictorial vividness has a counterpart in Sholokhov's *Quiet Flows the Don.* Yet *Red Cavalry* is also the work that demonstrates Babel's dualism most forcefully and vividly, and in it his personality splits in two. Without it being immediately obvious, the stories have two narrators: one is the Jewish war correspondent, Kirill Vasilyevich Lyutov, bespectacled, bookish, and sensitive; and the other is the person whom Lyutov would like to become, and constantly strives to be—a true revolutionary and Bolshevik soldier with no fear of blood and killing. This dichotomy accounts for the extreme physical violence that is manifested in many of the stories: it is as though Babel were trying to overcome his own horror at what he has seen and witnessed, and to turn it into a kind of vivid, surreal poetry. At the opposite end of the spectrum is the character of the Jew Gedali, who believes in "the International of good men," and with whom Lyutov vainly remonstrates, more than half-convinced that the old man is right.

After *Red Cavalry,* Babel turned to writing semi-autobiographical stories that focused on memories of his childhood in Odessa. The qualifier "semi" is important, though, as much in these seemingly personal accounts is invented and fictive. In the story "Awakening" Babel describes a feature of life in the Odessa of his childhood which, almost against his will, left a deep mark on him. This was the remarkable proliferation in that city of performing musicians, in particular violinists, most of them from Russian-Jewish families. From Odessa came Mischa Elman and Jascha Heifetz, and the great violin teacher Stolyarsky, who later taught David Oistrakh. In the story, Stolyarsky becomes "Mr. Zagursky," though "Auer" is of course the real, and famous, violin virtuoso and teacher Leopold Auer. Babel's father decided that his son should become a child prodigy, and the boy was sent for lessons with Stolyarsky at an early age. Babel describes his dislike of playing the violin in no uncertain terms: "the sounds crawled out of my violin like iron filings." And he tells us, "During my violin practice I placed on my music-stand books by Turgenev or Dumas and, scraping out heaven only knows what, devoured page after page."

Thus the vicarious musical ambition of his parents became supplanted by a genuine ambition of his own—to become a writer. Yet somehow the connection between writing and music as a performing art—a connection possibly unconscious, since instilled at an early age—seems to have lingered in Babel's psyche for most of his life. One has a sense that for Babel, his own writing career was really something akin to a career as a concert artist, to be pursued regardless of social change and outer circumstances, with stoicism and dedication to an art that demanded self-effacement, hard work, discipline, and love. From one point of view, his passionate advocacy of Maupassant and Dumas may be seen as equivalent to the commitment a classical instrumentalist brings to the works of the 19th century concert repertoire: in his own writing he continued to interpret that European tradition and to sound its clear, distinctive note against the turbulence of history. Here, perhaps, we have a key to the apparent enigma of his situation. For in Babel we are presented with an extreme paradox: that of a practitioner of "art for art's sake" who tried to put himself and his writing at the service of a social and political revolution. Just what that revolution meant to him is not clear; yet at some level in his consciousness it seems to have been associated with his Jewish patrimony, and with the aspiration of generations of Jews for a better society and a better world. That the dream turned sour, threatening, and bloodily destructive was merely one more twist of history that must be faced with stoicism and courage. His adherence to the artist's moral duty to stay with his art to the end was what made Babel remain in the Soviet Union—for he had identified his art with the life and the destiny of his own people, and to uproot that art from its soil would be to desert them. And so, to the end, he continued to write of the Kriks and the Moldavanka, of the world that had died with the revolution and which the revolution was somehow, perhaps almost mystically, expected to transform and replace. Perhaps the most tragic and moving of all Babel's stories is "Froim Grach," which was written after the "great turning-point" of 1928 and describes the end of a Moldavanka gangster at the hands of the Cheka. Here, more clearly than almost anywhere else in Babel's writing, emerges a note of extreme anxiety and caution about the nature of the new world that is being built.

—David McDuff

See the essays on "Guy de Maupassant" and "My First Goose."

BALDWIN, James (Arthur). American. Born in New York City, 2 August 1924. Educated at Public School 139, Harlem, New York, and DeWitt Clinton High School, Bronx, New York, graduated 1942. Worked as handyman, dishwasher, waiter, and office boy in New York, and in defense work, Belle Meade, New Jersey, in early 1940's; full-time writer from 1943; lived in Europe, mainly in Paris, 1948–56. Member, Actors Studio, New York, National Advisory Board of CORE (Congress on Racial Equality), and National Committee for a Sane Nuclear Policy. Recipient: Saxton fellowship, 1945; Rosenwald fellowship, 1948; Guggenheim fellowship, 1954; American Academy award, 1956; Ford fellowship, 1958; National Conference of Christians and Jews Brotherhood award, 1962; George Polk award, 1963; Foreign Drama Critics award, 1964; Martin Luther King. Jr., award (City University of New York), 1978. D.Litt.: University of British Columbia, Vancouver, 1963. Member, American Academy, 1964. *Died 30 November 1987.*

PUBLICATIONS

Short Stories

Going to Meet the Man.   1965.

Novels

Go Tell It on the Mountain.   1953.
Giovanni's Room.   1956.

Another Country.   1962.
Tell Me How Long the Train's Been Gone.   1968.
If Beale Street Could Talk.   1974.
Just above My Head.   1979.

Plays

The Amen Corner (produced 1955).   1968.
Blues for Mister Charlie (produced 1964).   1964.
One Day, When I Was Lost: A Scenario Based on "The Autobiography of Malcolm X."   1972.
A Deed from the King of Spain (produced 1974).

Screenplay: *The Inheritance,* 1973.

Verse

Jimmy's Blues: Selected Poems.   1983.

Other

Notes of a Native Son.   1955.
Nobody Knows My Name: More Notes of a Native Son.   1961.
The Fire Next Time.   1963.
Nothing Personal, photographs by Richard Avedon.   1964.
A Rap on Race, with Margaret Mead.   1971.
No Name in the Street.   1972.
A Dialogue: Baldwin and Nikki Giovanni.   1973.
Little Man, Little Man (for children).   1976.
The Devil Finds Work: An Essay.   1976.
The Price of a Ticket: Collected Nonfiction 1948–1985.   1985.
The Evidence of Things Not Seen.   1985.
Conversations, edited by Fred L. Standley and Louis H. Pratt.   1989.

*

Bibliography: "Baldwin: A Checklist 1947–1962" by Kathleen A. Kindt, and "Baldwin: A Bibliography 1947–1962" by Russell G. Fischer, both in *Bulletin of Bibliography,* January-April 1965; *Baldwin: A Reference Guide* by Fred L. and Nancy Standley, 1979.

Critical Studies: *The Furious Passage of Baldwin* by Fern Eckman, 1966; *Baldwin: A Critical Study* by Stanley Macebuh, 1973; *Baldwin: A Collection of Critical Essays* edited by Keneth Kinnamon, 1974; *Baldwin: A Critical Evaluation* edited by Therman B. O'Daniel, 1977; *Baldwin* by Louis H. Pratt, 1978; *Baldwin* by Carolyn W. Sylvander, 1980; *Baldwin: Three Interviews* by Kenneth B. Clark and Malcolm King, 1985; *Black Women in the Fiction of Baldwin* by Trudier Harris, 1985; *Stealing the Fire: The Art and Protest of Baldwin* by Horace Porter, 1988; *Baldwin: Artist on Fire* by W.J. Weatherby, 1989; *Baldwin: The Legacy* edited by Quincy Troupe, 1989; *Talking at the Gates: A Life of Baldwin* by James Campbell, 1991.

*   *   *

James Baldwin has achieved his main impact as a novelist, as playwright and, above all, as essayist. However, his short stories, though inspired by similar sources of human injustice as his first novel *Go Tell It on the Mountain* and his plays in *Blues for Mister Charlie,* which deals with the Emmett Till case (the acquital of whites for the murder of a black accused of flirting with a white woman), and *The Amen Corner,* are no mere chippings from Baldwin's literary workshop. They are among the most powerful and well-constructed stories to come out of the 20th century.

The stories that make up Baldwin's early collection *Going to Meet the Man* begin with two fictionalized recollections of his fundamentalist preacher-father and his own three teen-age years spent as a Holy Roller preacher. In "The Rockpile," the child can never be forgiven its illegitimacy. "The Outing" describes a steamboat excursion on the Hudson river organized by the Mount Olives Pentacostal Assembly, which held a service on board full of glory "Hallelujas" and convictions of the benefits of having been "saved." But strange conflicts are aroused in the minds of some of the adolescent boys. It was as if "the animal, so vividly restless and undiscovered, so tense with power, ready to spring, had been already stalked and trapped and offered, a perpetual blood-sacrifice, on the altar of the Lord. Yet their bodies continued to change and grow, preparing them, mysteriously and with ferocious speed, for manhood. No matter how careful their movements, these movements suggested, with a distinctness dreadful for the redeemed to see, the pagan lusting beneath the blood-washed robes."

In "The Man Child" the murderously jealous Jamie, a failed farmer whose farm his friend Eric has bought, is unable to resist the sense of immortality successive generations bring, and he tragically kills his friend's son.

The out-of-work black actor reveals Baldwin's central concern when, in "Previous Condition," he tells his Jewish friend, "Oh, I know you're Jewish, you get kicked around, too, but you can walk into a bar and nobody *knows* you're Jewish and if you go looking for a job you'll get a better job than mine! . . . I know everybody's in trouble and nothing is easy, but how can I explain to you what it feels like to be black when I don't understand it and don't want to spend all my life trying to forget it?"

The most stylishly written story, "This Morning, This Evening, So Soon," in which a black singer movie star who made his name in a French film and who married a Swedish girl, plans to take his wife and son to America. It contains a satirical explanation of why white Americans are seemingly always so nice to each other; the humiliating image of a black girl being forced to stand in front of police car headlights, drop her pants and lift up her dress allegedly to convince the white police she really was black; and an evocative description of the sounds of New York: "the thing which most struck me was neither light nor shade, but noise. It came from a million things at once, from trucks and tyres and clutches and brakes and doors; from machines shutting and stamping and rolling and cutting and pressing; from the building of tunnels, the checking of gas works, the laying of wires, the digging of foundations . . . from the battering down and the rising up of walls; from millions of radios and television sets and juke boxes. The human voices distinguished themselves from the roar only by their note of stress and hostility."

A less stable relationship is depicted in "Come Out of the Wilderness," where a black girl in love with a white man gradually faces up to the knowledge that eventually he will leave her.

The title story builds into a horrifying description of the mutilation and murder of a black man by a gang of whites, and the dreadful coarsifying effect the spectacle has on the gloating whites who witness it; a story the force and ferocity of which no reader is ever likely to forget.

B. de Mott has described Baldwin as "one of the few genuinely indispensible American writers." And so, surely, he is. He explains the condition of being black in a predominantly white society to that society's majority with sharp analytical accuracy, a lack of rancour and a passion that never descends to self-pity. His attitude is well summed up in the introduction he wrote to the volume of his collected non-fiction, *The Price of a Ticket*:

> The will of the people of the State, is revealed by the State's institutions. There was not then (in 1943) nor is there, now, a single American institution which is not a racist institution. And most institutions—the unions, for one example, the Church, for another, and the Army—or the Military—for yet another, are meant to keep the nigger in his place. Yes: we have lived through avalanches of tokens and concessions but white power remains white. And what it appears to surrender with one hand, it obstinately clutches with the other.

Baldwin spent nearly a decade in Europe—*Giovanni's Room*, his second novel, is set in the bohemian world of the 1950's—before returning to his home country to associate himself with the Civil Rights movement and express "the alienation, the despair, the rage, the reality" of what it meant to be black in the United States. He writes with a focussed detachment which perhaps derives from his European experience—as in the novel *Another Country* and *The Fire Next Time*. At any rate, in his short stories, as in his plays, his novels, his essays, and occasional journalism, he probes relentlessly at the sources of what makes for disadvantagement, often using images and phrases that alike surprise by their rightness and startle by their equal application to the horrors whites also inflict on other whites. There is no attempt to exploit the pain of things. It is simply there, stated, as reflected in the music of "Sonny's Blues":

> All I know about music is that not many people hear it. And even then, on the rare occasions when something opens within, and the music enters, what we mainly hear, or hear corroborated, are personal, private, vanishing evocations. But the man who creates the music is hearing something else, is dealing with the roar rising from the void and the imposing order on it as it hits the air.

Hearing the roar rising from the void without imposing order on it could be an apt description of James Baldwin's powerful and permanent contribution to American literature. As Baldwin himself writes, in a later moment from the same story, he is aware that every experience is "only a moment, that the world waited outside . . . and the trouble stretched above us, larger than the sky."

—Maurice Lindsay

See the essays on "Sonny's Blues" and "This Morning, This Evening, So Soon."

———

BALLARD, J(ames) G(raham). British. Born in Shanghai, China, 15 November 1930. Educated at Leys School, Cambridge; King's College, Cambridge. Served in the Royal Air Force. Married Helen Mary Matthews in 1954 (died 1964); one son and two daughters. Recipient: *Guardian* Fiction prize, 1984; James Tait Black Memorial prize, 1985. Lives in Shepperton, Middlesex.

PUBLICATIONS

Short Stories

The Voices of Time and Other Stories.   1962.
Billenium and Other Stories.   1962.
Passport to Eternity and Other Stories.   1963.
The Four-Dimensional Nightmare.   1963.
Terminal Beach.   1964.
The Impossible Man and Other Stories.   1966.
The Disaster Area.   1967.
The Day of Forever.   1967.
The Overloaded Man.   1967.
Why I Want to Fuck Ronald Reagan.   1968.
The Atrocity Exhibition.   1970; as *Love and Napalm: Export USA,*   1972.
Chronopolis and Other Stories.   1971.
Vermilion Sands.   1971.
Low-Flying Aircraft and Other Stories.   1976.
The Best of Ballard.   1977.
The Best Short Stories of Ballard.   1978.
The Venus Hunters.   1980.
News from the Sun.   1982.
Myths of the Near Future.   1982.
Memories of the Space Age.   1988.
War Fever.   1990.

Novels

The Wind from Nowhere.   1962.
The Drowned World.   1962.
The Burning World.   1964; revised edition, as *The Drought,* 1965.
The Crystal World.   1966.
Crash.   1973.
Concrete Island.   1974.
High-Rise.   1975.
The Unlimited Dream Company.   1979.
Hello America.   1981.
Empire of the Sun.   1984.
The Day of Creation.   1987.
Running Wild.   1988.
The Kindness of Women.   1991.

*

Bibliography: *Ballard: A Primary and Secondary Bibliography* by David Pringle, 1984.

Critical Studies: *Ballard: The First Twenty Years* edited by James Goddard and David Pringle, 1976; *Re Search: Ballard* edited by Vale, 1983; *Ballard* by Peter Brigg, 1985.

* * *

J.G. Ballard is usually considered a science-fiction writer, even though there are no alien invaders in his work, no intergalactic space voyages, no projections into a distant future. And yet he consistently addresses one of the key issues of science fiction—the impact technology has on the human mind and body. His disturbing stories often suggest that what common sense sees as negative in our technological world might indeed be positive, and vice versa.

Ballard's short fiction falls into three periods—the early science-fiction stories, the experiments of the late 1960's and 1970's, and his more recent realistic works. A look at one story from each period shows how Ballard's concerns have remained constant while he has explored various ways of telling a story.

"Venus Smiles" was first published as "Mobile" in 1957. When the people of Vermillion Sands commission a work of metal sonic sculpture from local artist Lorraine Drexler, it turns out to be so ugly and noisy that they insist it be dismantled. Before this can happen, however, Mr. Hamilton of the Fine Arts Committee discovers that the work is growing rapidly like a huge metal plant, all the while emitting a distorted classical Muzak. Before it can take over the town, the sculpture is cut into small pieces and melted down.

Within a few months, however, bits of the sculpture find their way into the steel girders of the town's new courthouse and infect them, and the new building begins to make music and to grow. Hamilton realizes, "Lorraine Drexler's statue is here, in this building, in a dozen other buildings, in ships and planes and a million new automobiles. Even if it's only one screw or ball bearing, that'll be enough to trigger the rest off."

Early in the story, we learn that Drexler was an intimate of sculptor Alberto Giacometti and composer John Cage, and it seems that she has realized their dreams. The world will become a huge, metallic Giacomietti sculpture, and, true to Cage's avant garde aesthetic, every sound is to be music and music is to be in every sound. The seemingly harmless technology of art will now infect every metal structure on earth. For good or ill, the planet will become an artwork. As Hamilton says: "The whole world will be singing." This is an end-of-the-world-as-we-know-it story, but, unlike the usual science-fiction tale, this one raises the question of whether the world-as-we-know-it is really worth keeping.

Formally, "Venus Smiles" is a conventional narrative. Many stories from Ballard's second period, however, are made up of dislocated fragments that do not so much tell stories as permit readers to construct stories for themselves.

In the "The 60-Minute Zoom" (1976), an unnamed narrator has set up a camera aimed at the suite he shares with his wife in a hotel some three hundred yards away and adjusted the lens to zoom automatically from its widest field to its most narrow in the space of one hour. The fragmentary text reports what he sees through the viewfinder at four to six minute intervals ("2:15," "2:32," "2:46"). He expects to catch his wife in an infidelity and he does. In the end, we realize that he is not making a film but watching one made some time ago. In fact, at the moment of extreme close-up, he appears in the film himself and kills his wife.

Early on, it seems that the narrator is eager to film his wife with another man, that her infidelity is what he needs to become sexually aroused. "Despite everything, the degrading but exciting months of anger and suspicion, I feel the first hint of an erection." In fact, however, what arouses him is the image of his wife's body on film. He says, "I prefer her seen through a lens, emblematic of my own

needs and fantasies rather than existing in her own right." Though he has killed his wife, he has something better now—his wife filmed.

Of course, it is by way of film that most of us learn what to desire—not real human bodies but fantasies, pre-imagined by the electronic media. Is Ballard criticizing our sexual dependence on a technology that makes a cinematic sexuality seem more real than real? Or is he suggesting that electronic media, far from limiting our sexual possibilities, expand them, making possible sexual experiences that pre-media ages never could have imagined? Either reading seems possible. Ballard leaves it to us to decide.

"Running Wild" (1988) continues Ballard's ambivalent commentary on modern technology. This novella is presented as a report written by police psychiatrist Richard Greville who is investigating a strange crime. On the morning of June 25, 1988, at an exclusive, high-security residential community in west London, 32 home owners, domestics, and security guards were murdered and 13 children kidnapped, all in a matter of minutes. There are no clues about the identity of the killer or killers and no trace of the children.

Though he fails to convince his superiors, Greville proves to his own satisfaction that the adults were murdered by their own children who then escaped. He comes to believe that the adolescents were so protected by their parents and by the high-tech security arrangements at the compound that "the children existed in a state closely akin to sensory deprivation." "They killed to free themselves," he explains, "from a tyranny of love and care."

Greville knows that the children are hiding somewhere, waiting to launch another assault, but there is nothing he can do to stop it. Ballard seems to suggest that the existence of this adolescent revolutionary group is not necessarily bad, for at least it poses an alternative to our logical and technological world which is draining us of life. As Greville writes, "In a totally sane society, madness is the only freedom." Whether one agrees with him or not, J.G. Ballard values such freedom and asks his readers to consider whether, in our logical and totally sane society, all is really for the best.

—Welch D. Everman

See the essay on "Chronopolis."

———

BALZAC, Honoré de. French. Born in Tours, 20 May 1799. Educated at pension Le Guay-Pinel, Tours, 1804–07; Collège de Vendome, 1807–13; L'Institution Lepître, Paris, 1815; L'Institution Ganzer et Beuzelin, Paris, 1815–16; attended law lectures, the Sorbonne, Paris, Baccalaureat of Law 1819. Married Mme. Hanska (Eve Rzewuska) in 1850. Clerk for M. Guillonnet de Merville, 1816–18, and M. Passez, 1818–19; then writer, editor, magazine writer: obtained printer's license, 1826–28; owner, La Chronique de Paris, 1835–36; editor, La Revue Parisienne, 1840. President, Société des Gens de Lettres, 1839. Chevalier, Legion of Honor, 1985. Died 18 August 1850.

PUBLICATIONS

Collections

The Human Comedy, edited by George Saintsbury.   40
    vols., 1895–98.

Works.   1901.
Ouvres complètes, edited by Marcel Bouteron and Henri Longnon.   40 vols., 1912–40.
La Comédie humaine, edited by Marcel Bouteron.   11 vols., 1951–58; revised edition, edited by Pierre-George Castex and Pierre Citron, 1976— .
Collected Short Stories (in French), edited by A.W. Raitt. 1979.

Short Stories

Scènes de la vie privée.   1830; augmented edition, 1832.
Romans et contes philosophiques.   1831.
Contes bruns, with Philarète Chasles and Charles Rabou. 1832.
Les Salmigondis: Contes de toutes les couleurs.   1832; as *La Comtesse à deux maris*, in *Scènes de la vie privée*, 1835; as *Le Colonel Chabert*, in *Comédie humaine*, 1844.
Les Cent Contes Drolatiques.   3 (of an intended 10) vols., 1832–37; *Quatrième dixain* (fragments); 1925; translated as *Contes drolatiques* (in English), 1874.
Nouveaux contes philosophiques.   1832.
Le Provincial à Paris (includes *Gillette, Le Rentier, El Verdugo*).   1847; as *Gillette, or The Unknown Masterpiece*, 1988.
Selected Short Stories.   1977.

Novels

L'Héritage de Birague, with Le Poitevin de Saint-Alme and Etienne Arago.   1822.
Jean-Louis; ou, La Fille trouvée, with Le Poitevin de Saint-Alme.   1822.
Clotilde de Lusignan; ou, Le beau juif.   1822.
Le Centenaire; ou, Les Deux Beringheld.   1822; as *Le Sorcier*, in *Oeuvres complètes de Horace de Saint-Aubin*, 1837.
Le Vicaire des Ardennes.   1822.
La Dernière Fée; ou, La Nouvelle Lampe merveilleuse. 1823.
Annette et le criminel.   1824.
Wann-Chlore.   1825; as *Jane la pâle*, in *Oeuvres complètes*, 1836.
Le Dernier Chouan; ou, Le Bretagne au 1800.   1829; revised edition, as *Les Chouans; ou, Le Bretagne en 1799*, 1834; as *Le Chouan*, 1838; as *The Chouans*, 1893.
Mémoires pour servir à l'histoire de la révolution française, with Lheritier de l'Ain.   1829.
La Physiologie du mariage; ou, Méditations de philosophie éclectique.   1829; as *The Physiology of Marriage*, 1904.
Le Peau de chagrin.   1831; edited by S. de Sasy, 1974; as *The Magic Skin*, 1888; as *The Wild Ass's Skin*, in *Human Comedy*, 1895–98.
Le Médecin de campagne.   1833; excerpt, as *Histoire de Napoléon.*   1833; edited by Patrick Barthier, 1974.
Études de moeurs au XIXe siècle.   12 vols., 1833–37; includes reprints and the following new works:
    La Fleur des pois.   1834.
    La Recherche de l'absolu.   1834; as *Balthazar; or, Science and Love*, 1859; as *The Alchemist*, 1861; as *The Quest of the Absolute*, in *Human Comedy*, 1895–98; as *The Tragedy of a Genius*, 1912.
    Eugénie Grandet.   1833; translated as *Eugenie Grandet*, 1859.
    La Femme abandonnée.   1833.
    La Grenadière.   1833.
    L'illustre Gaudissart.   1833.
    La Vieille Fille.   1837.

Illusions perdues (part 1: *Les deux poètes*).   1837.
    Les Marana.   1834.
    Histoire des treize.   1834–35; as *History of the Thirteen*, 1974; translated in part as *The Mystery of the Rue Soly*, 1894, *The Girl with the Golden Eyes*, 1928, and *The Duchess of Langeais*, 1946.
Le Père Goriot.   1835; translated as *Pere Goriot*, 1886; as *Old Goriot*, 1991.
Le Livre mystique (includes *Louis Lambert* and *Séraphita*). 1835; translated as *Louis Lambert* and *Seraphita*,   2 vols., 1889; *Séraphita*, 1989.
Études philosophiques.   20 vols., 1835–40; includes reprints and the following new works:
    Un Drame au bord de la mer.   1835.
    Melmoth réconcilié.   1836.
    L'Interdiction.   1836.
    La Messe de l'Athée.   1837.
    Facino cane.   1837.
    Les Martyrs ignorés.   1837.
    Le Secret des Ruggieri.   1837.
    L'Enfant maudit.   1837.
    Une Passion dans le désert (novella).   1837; as *A Passion in the Desert*, 1985.
Le Lys dans la vallée.   1836; as *The Lily of the Valley*, 1891.
L'Excommuniée, with Auguste de Belloy, in *Oeuvres complètes de Horace de Saint-Aubin.*   1837.
La Femme supérieure.   1837; as *Les Employés*, 1865; as *Bureaucracy*, 1889.
Histoire de César Birotteau.   1838; as *History of the Grandeur and Downfall of Cesar Birotteau*, 1860; as *The Bankrupt*, 1959.
La Femme supérieure, La Maison Nucingen, La Torpille. 1838.
Les Rivalités en province.   1838; as *Le Cabinet des antiques* (includes *Gambara*), 1839; as *The Jealousies of a Country Town*, in *Human Comedy*, 1895-98.
Gambara; Adieu.   1839; translated as *Gambara*, in *Human Comedy*, 1895–98.
Une Fille d'Eve (includes *Massimilla Doni*).   1839; as *A Daughter of Eve* and *Massimilla Doni*, in *Human Comedy*, 1895–98.
Un Grand Homme de province à Paris (*Illusions perdues 2*). 1839; as *A Great Man of the Provinces in Paris*, 1893.
Beatrix; ou, Les Amours forcées.   1839; edited by Madeleine Fergeaud, 1979; translated as *Beatrix*, 1895.
Pierrette.   1840; translated as *Pierrette*, 1892.
Physiologie de l'employé.   1841.
Physiologie du rentier de Paris et de province, with Arnould Frémy.   1841.
Le Curé de village.   1841; as *The Country Parson*, in *Human Comedy*, 1895–98.
Oeuvres complètes: La Comédie humaine.   20 vols., 1842–53; includes reprints and the following new works:
    Albert Savarus.   1842; translated as *Albert Savarus*, 1892.
    Autre étude de femme.   1842.
    Illusions perdues (part 3).   1843; parts 1 and 3 translated as *Lost Illusions*, 1893.
    Esquisse d'homme d'affaires; Gaudissart II; Les Comédiens sans le savoir.   1846.
    Un Épisode sous la terreur; L'Envers de l'histoire contemporain; Z; Marcas.   1846; *L'Envers . . .* translated as *Love*, 1893.
Ursule Mirouët.   1842; translated as *Ursula*, 1891.
Scènes de la vie privée et publique des animaux.   1842.
Mémoires de deux jeunes mariées.   1842; as *Memoirs of Two Young Married Women*, 1894.

Une Tenebreuse Affaire.   1842; edited by René Guise, 1973; as *The Gondreville Mystery*, 1898; as *A Murky Business*, 1972.

Les Deux Frères.   1842; as *Un Ménage de garçon en province*, in *Comédie humaine*, 1843; as *La Rabouilleuse*, in *Oeuvres complètes*, 1912; edited by René Guise, 1972; as *The Two Brothers*, 1887; as *A Bachelor's Establishment*, in *Human Comedy*, 1895–98; as *The Black Sheep*, 1970.

Un Début dans la vie (includes *La fausse maîtresse).* 1844.

Catherine de Médicis expliquée; Le Martyr calviniste. 1845; translated as *Catherine de' Medici*, 1894.

Honorine (includes *Un Prince de la Bohème).*   1845.

Splendeurs et misères des courtisanes: Esther.   1845; as *A Harlot's Progress*, in *Human Comedy*, 1895–98; as *A Harlot High and Low*, 1970.

La Lune de miel.   1845.

Petites misères de la vie conjugale.   1845–46; as *The Petty Annoyances of Married Life*, 1861.

Un Drame dans les prisons.   1847.

Les Parents pauvres (includes *La Cousine Bette* and *Le Cousin Pons).*   1847–48; as *Poor Relations*, 1880; as *Cousin Pons*, 1886; as *Cousin Betty*, 1888.

La Dernière Incarnation de Vautrin.   1848.

Le Député d'Arcis, completed by Charles Rabou.   1854; as *The Deputy of Arcis*, 1896.

Les Paysans, completed by Mme. Balzac.   1855; as *Sons of the Soil*, 1890; as *The Peasantry*, in *Human Comedy*, 1895–98.

Les Petits Bourgeois, completed by Charles Rabou.   1856; as *The Lesser Bourgeoisie*, 1896; as *The Middle Classes*, 1898.

Sténie; ou, Les Erreurs philosophiques, edited by A. Prioult. 1936.

La Femme auteur et autres fragments inédits, edited by le Vicomte de Lovenjoul.   1950.

Mademoiselle du Vissard, edited by Pierre-George Castex. 1950.

Plays

Vautrin (produced 1840).   1840; translated as *Vautrin*, in *Works*, 1901.

Les Ressources de Quinola (produced 1842).   1842; as *The Resources of Quinola*, in *Works*, 1901.

Paméla Giraud (produced 1843).   1843; translated as *Pamela Giraud*, in *Works*, 1901.

La Marâtre (produced 1848).   1848; as *The Stepmother*, in *Works*, 1901.

Le Faiseur (produced 1849).   1851; translated as *Mercadet*, in *Works*, 1901.

L'École des ménages, edited by le Vicomte de Lovenjoul (produced 1910).   1907.

Other

Du droit d'ainesse.   1824.

Histoire impartiale des Jésuites.   1824.

Code des gens honnêtes; ou, L'Art de ne pas être dupe des fripons.   1825.

Mémoires de Mme. la Duchesse d'Abrantes, with the duchess.   vol. 1 only, 1831.

Maximes et pensées de Napoléon.   1838.

Traité de la vie élégante.   1853.

Lettres à l'etrangère (to Mme. Hanska).   4 vols., 1899–1950.

Cahiers balzaciens, edited by Marcel Bouteron.   8 vols., 1927–28.

Le Catéchisme social, edited by Bernard Guyon.   1933.

Traité de la prière, edited by Philippe Bertault.   1942.

Journaux à la mer, edited by Louis Jaffard.   1949.

Correspondance, edited by Roger Pierrot.   5 vols., 1960–68.

Editor, *Oeuvres complètes*, by La Fontaine.   1826.
Editor, *Oeuvres complètes*, by Moliere.   1826.

*

Bibliography: *A Balzac Bibliography and Index* by W. Hobart Royce, 1929–30; *Bibliography of Balzac Criticism, 1930–1990* by Mark W. Waggoner, 1990.

Critical Studies: *Balzac and the Novel* by Samuel G.A. Rogers, 1953; *Balzac: A Biography*, 1957, and *Balzac's Comédie Humaine*, 1959, both by Herbert J. Hunt; *Balzac the European* by Edward J. Oliver, 1959; *Prometheus: The Life of Balzac* by André Maurois, 1965; *Balzac: An Interpretation of the Comédie Humaine* by F.W.J. Hemmings, 1967; *The Hero as Failure: Balzac and the Rubempré Cycle* by Bernard N. Schilling, 1968; *Balzac* by V.S. Pritchett, 1973; *Balzac's Comedy of Words* by Martin Kanes, 1975; *Balzac's Recurring Characters* by Anthony Pugh, 1975; *Balzac Criticism in France (1850–1900)* by David Bellos, 1976; *Balzac: Fiction and Melodrama* by Christopher Prendergast, 1978; *Balzac: Illusions Perdues* by Donald Adamson, 1981; *Balzac and His Reader* by Mary Susan McCarthy, 1983; *Balzac and the Drama of Perspective: The Narrator in Selected Works of La Comédie Humaine* by Joan Dargan, 1985; *Family and Plots: Balzac's Narrative Generations* by Janet L. Beizer, 1986; *The Golden Scapegoat: Portrait of the Jew in the Novels of Balzac* by Frances Schlamovitz Grodzinsky, 1989; *Balzac and Music: Its Place and Meaning in His Life and Work* by Jean-Paul Barricelli, 1990; *A Fable of Modern Art* by Dore Ashton, 1991.

* * *

For a writer who produced such in immense amount of serious fiction in a relatively brief life, Honoré de Balzac was a slow starter. It is meaningless to impose a rigid distinction between the short stories of 1830-1835 and the longer fictional pieces into which they were often dovetailed or absorbed. They became part of the coherent description of French society known from 1840 as *La Comédie humaine* (*The Human Comedy*). In 1834, when Balzac first became aware of the inner coherence of his work, he thought it would be a general study of human behaviour, which he intended to classify in an essay on human energy.

Although he did write what were always intended to be short stories, most of Balzac's short fiction originated as drafts or episodes for works that were to be serialized, expanded, or combined into novels. It is therefore understandable that, along with the rather dubious and experimental pastiche of Rabelais's manner in *Les Cent Contes Drolatiques* (*Contes drolatiques* or the "*Droll Stories*"), most of Balzac's short fiction should have been written while he was still feeling his way from the early pseudonymous pot-boilers, through the various "physiologies," "codes," and "arts," towards the novels with recurring characters, which started with *La Père Goriot (Old Goriot)*, written in 1834-1835. Balzac's short fiction also must be seen against other contemporary vogues, for "scenes," semi-dramatic "proverbs," and for the mocking sketches of the freelance journalism to which, in articles for *Le Voleur, La Mode, La Caricature,* and *Le Charivari,* Balzac reverted round 1830. What Balzac specifically wrote as short fiction were the "contes," normally focusing on the narration of an event, and the "nouvelles," dealing with a rather more static situation or state of mind.

If Balzac had not gone on to write the novels, it is unlikely that the "Droll Stories" would be remembered. Balzac's decision to revive the bawdy medieval conte, whose point frequently lay in some mistaken, surprising, or grotesque sexual encounter, counter-balanced his increasing concern with the sentimental mystical values explored in *Séraphita* of 1834-35 and *Le Lys dans la vallée* of 1835-36. It gave expression to the sturdy, lusty side of his temperament, in some ways also both fastidious and feminine. The idea for the "Droll Stories" is contained in a satirical article printed in *La Mode,* in February 1830. In the course of that year, Balzac conceived the notion of transposing them into French renaissance language and style, both of which he sometimes got wrong, and of writing a hundred of them, as in Boccaccio's *Decameron.* The first tale, "The Archbishop," appeared in *La Caricature* in 4 November 1830, introducing Impéria, a Roman courtesan, in the early 15th century. Her adventures were going to be the subject of the first droll story, ten of which came out in April 1832, with a further ten in July 1833. Most of the third decade was destroyed in a warehouse fire in December 1835, and had to be rewritten for publication in 1837, and we have fragments of a fourth and a fifth decade.

They are almost all boisterous, and often cruel stories of lechery, sexual and pecuniary trickery involving late medieval Touraine, the homeland Balzac shared with Rabelais. Very few of the characters are anything but pruriently enthusiastic at the prospect of erotic pleasure, and the women are as salacious in their attitudes as the men. It is the rather inept pseudo-medieval pastiche, with the narrative pace and focus of the 16th-century conte, its realistic rogues and spontaneous courtiers, which keeps the robust vulgarity from being titillatingly pornographic, and which allows the coarse subject matter, with its mischievous delight in trickery, fraud, and more serious misdemeanour, to be relieved by the occasional intrusion of real delicacy of feeling and lightness of touch.

But there is a foretaste of the novels to come. Sharp perceptiveness about human motivation, wit, and self-parody betray the narrator's amusement at the naivete of his characters and even plots. There are isolated instances of heroism, and of a sense of honour or humour, and dramatic values are exploited. The narrator sometimes shows true sympathy or feeling for his characters, but on the whole the droll stories do not represent Balzac's sensibility at its most attractive. Real love overtakes Impéria, but when Véron, the most flamboyant literary and musical impresario in 19th-century Paris, was offered the story for the *Revue de Paris,* he turned it down, saying, "If possible, my dear Balzac, be chaste, even if only to show the full range of your talent."

The nouvelles, while intended for publication in the form in which they were written, differ from the contes, but still represent Balzac's real talent at an inchoate stage of its development. Of those written in the autumn of 1829, some were concerned to give impressions of domestic life and personal feelings, while others belong to the tradition of mystery, horror, and the fantastic. Six of these studies were grouped together in *Scènes de la vie privée* (Scenes of Private Life) but the titles of three were changed on subsequent rewriting.

"Domestic Peace" recounts the way in which an older woman guides a young wife to regain the lost affections of an errant husband, while "The Virtuous Woman" (later "A Double Family") notable for its anti-clericalism, examines how a wife, dominated by a puritanical devotion, drives her husband into the arms of another woman, who disillusions him. The story "La Vendetta," about a Corsican family blood-feud, was much strengthened on rewriting years later, when Balzac added the father's gloating joy at the sudden death of the son-in-law who had brought him the news of his daughter's starvation. "The Dangers of Misconduct" (now "Gobseck") had begun as the physiology of a money-lender for *Le Monde* and centres on the greed of the comtesse de Restaud. The money-lender's character is fully developed in the 1835 revision, in which he sides with the dying Restaud against the comtesse and her lover. The comtesse has sold him her diamonds, an episode which links the nouvelle to the novel *Old Goriot,* but "Gobseck" remains a violent story about adultery, culminating in family break-up, while *Old Goriot* was the conscious foundation for the later panoramic survey of French society.

The best of the nouvelles is generally thought to be "Gloire et malheur," which later became "La Maison du chat-qui-pelote," about the domestic background of Augustine, a draper's daughter who marries a painter but can never rise above her family's shopkeeper values. It is an early Balzac study of feminine feeling. By 1832, however, Balzac had almost abandoned the short story as a literary form. Six tableaux of 1831 and 1832 were put together in 1834 as "Même histoire" and in 1842 were presented in a composite novel as "La Femme de trente ans." There is plenty of outside evidence that Balzac was a brilliant raconteur, and he did contribute two further short stories to a collaborative volume, *Contes bruns,* in 1832, but gradually the storytelling skills which suited short fiction made way for the lengthier studies of human behaviour in his novels. His fictional imagination outgrew the short story.

—A.H.T. Levi

See the essays on "A Passion in the Desert" and "The Unknown Masterpiece."

———

BAMBARA, Toni Cade. American. Born Toni Cade in New York City, 25 March 1939. Educated at Queen's College, New York, 1955–59, B.A. in theater arts 1959; City College of New York, M.A. in literature 1963. One daughter. Social worker, State Department of Social Welfare, New York, 1956–59; director of recreation, psychiatry department, Metropolitan Hospital, New York City, 1961–62; program director, Colony House Community Center, New York City, 1962–65; director and adviser, Theatre of the Black Experience, New York, 1965–69; English instructor, SEEK Program, City College of New York, 1965–69; assistant professor, Livingstone College, Rutgers University, New Brunswick, New Jersey, 1969–74; visiting professor, Duke University, Durham, North Carolina, Atlanta University, and Emory University, Atlanta, 1975–79; artist-in-residence, Neighborhood Arts Center, Atlanta, 1975–79, Stephens College, Columbia, Missouri, 1976, and Spelman College, Atlanta, 1978–79; founder and director, 1976–85, Pamoja Writers Collective; instructor, filmmaker, and videomaker, Scribe Video Center, Philadelphia, since 1986. Honorary degree: SUNY-Albany, New York, 1990. Recipient: American Book award, 1981; Langston Hughes Society award, 1981, and Medallion, 1986. Lives in Philadelphia.

PUBLICATIONS

Short Stories

Gorilla, My Love.   1972.
The Seabirds Are Still Alive: Collected Stories.   1977.

Novels

The Salt Eaters.   1980.
If Blessing Comes.   1987.

Plays

Screenplays: Zora, 1971; The Johnson Girls, 1972; Victory Gardens, 1977; Transactions, 1979; The Long Night, 1981; Epitaph for Willie, 1982; Tar Baby (based on the novel by Toni Morrison), 1984; Raymond's Run (based on her own story), 1985; The Bombing of Osage, 1986; Celia B. Moore, Master Tactician of Direct Action, 1987.

Other

Raymond's Run (for children).   1990.

Editor (as Toni Cade), The Black Woman: Anthology. 1970.
Editor (for children), Tales and Stories for Black Folks. 1971.
Editor, with Leah Wise, Southern Black Utterances Today. 1975.

*

Bibliography: in American Women Writing Fiction edited by Mickey Pearlman, 1989.

Critical Studies: "Youth in Bambara's Gorilla, My Love" by Nancy D. Hargrove, in Women Writers of the Contemporary South, edited by Peggy Whitman Prenshaw, 1984; "From Baptism to Resurrection: Bambara and the Incongruity of Language" by Ruth Elizabeth Burks, in Black Women Writers (1950–1980), edited by Mari Evans, 1984; "'What It Is I Think She's Doing Anyhow:' A Reading of Bambara's The Salt Eaters" by Gloria Hull, in Conjuring: Black Women, Fiction, and Literary Tradition, edited by Marjorie Pryse and Hortense J. Spillers, 1985; "Problematizing the Individual: Bambara's Stories for the Revolution," in Specifying: Black Women Writing the American Experience, by Susan Willis, 1987; "The Dance of Characters and Community" by Martha M. Vertreace, in American Women Writing Fiction, edited by Mickey Pearlman, 1989.

*   *   *

A prolific writer of short fiction, Toni Cade Bambara began her career with stories reflecting the language, perspective, and sensibility of African-Americans and their concerns in the 1960's and 1970's. Her stories encapsulate the everyday adventures, fantasies, and aspirations of innocents on the verge of experience. Her characters, like those in many of J.D. Salinger's stories, are exuberant and eager to engage life completely, despite obstacles and inhibitions imposed by our culture. Bambara's empathy and imaginative insights give her stories distinction beyond social realism or the urban documentary.

One characteristic story, "My Man Bovanne," begins with an arresting observation: "Blind people got a hummin jones [addiction] if you notice." The story develops the outspoken, vivacious central character and narrator, Miss Hazel, who takes the "nice ole gent from the block [Bovanne]" under her tutelage at a benefit dance. Her actions outrage her politically sensitive (and priggish) children, who are embarrassed by their lively mother. Miss Hazel asks, "Is that what they call the generation gap?" She identifies her children's oppressive ageism: She decides that her attraction to Bovanne is both sexual and political. The blind man alone can see Miss Hazel's beautiful soul: "I imagine you are a very pretty woman, Miss Hazel."

Bambara also writes about the tensions and confusions of the individual and government, as in "Blues Ain't No Mockin Bird." That story depicts a rural Southern black family whose privacy is invaded by a crew "filming for the country, see. Part of the food stamp campaign. You know about the food stamps?" The self-respecting, self-sufficient Cain family watches, and Granny Cain tells her grandchildren a parable about their right to privacy, which young cousin Cathy, an incipient poet, translates as the tale of Goldilocks. Then Granddaddy Cain, the powerful patriarch of the clan, appears with a chicken hawk he has captured, which he nails to the barn door. The hawk's outraged mate is drawn to the scene and attacks the film crew, while Granddaddy Cain dismantles their camera. The children understand this as an exercise of personal power and autonomy.

A persistent emphasis on diversity of character and experience shapes Bambara's fiction. In "The Lesson," Miss Moore, the staid newcomer, takes a wild bunch of street kids on a window-shopping expedition, to teach them arithmetic and basic economics. They go to F.A.O. Schwartz, and the young black children view the amazing, outrageous toys of the rich. She encourages the children to draw their own economic and political conclusions from the price-tags around them. The strange outsider has taught the hip street urchins an important lesson in the real political meaning of their situation.

Other stories detail the lives of violent, lost characters, like Punjab the gambler and loan shark, who meets a canny opponent in Miss Ruby the white social worker, in "Playin with Punjab." Or the hopeless Sonny of "Talking About Sonny," who cuts his wife's throat and can only say, "Something came over me." Or Manny, the boy in "The Hammer Man" who threatened to kill his friends and is taken away by the police. The narrator says, "crazy or no crazy, Manny was my brother at that moment and the cop was my enemy."

Music and musical analogies shape and texture Bambara's stories. In a complex love story, "Medley," she creates a free-form jazz composition that reflects the romance between Larry, a mediocre bass player, and Sweet

Pea, a manicurist-vocalist. The story cleverly interweaves jazzy improvisation and sexuality to develop the musical-sensual characterizations. And in "Mississippi Ham Rider," she describes a legendary blues singer, who turns out to be a unique individual, not the walking cliche people expect.

Bambara's observations and concerns are politically oriented, but she is also a careful artisan, using her finely tuned ear for African-American diction and syntax to shape the rhythms of her stories and drawing characters that are both social types and individuals. Her stories are warm and funny, and she writes accurately and sympathetically about ordinary people without condescension or sentimentality. Her sharply focused snapshots of the daily lives of black people, urban and rural, in the contemporary world are important contributions to American literature.

—William J. Schafer

See the essay on "Gorilla, My Love."

BARTH, John (Simmons). American. Born in Cambridge, Maryland, 27 May 1930. Educated at the Juilliard School of Music, New York; Johns Hopkins University, Baltimore, A.B. 1951, M.A. 1952. Married 1) Anne Strickland in 1950 (divorced 1969), one daughter and two sons, 2) Shelly Rosenberg in 1970. Junior instructor in English, Johns Hopkins University, 1951–53; instructor 1953–56, assistant professor, 1957–60, and associate professor of English, 1960–65, Pennsylvania State University, University Park; professor of English, 1965–71, and Butler Professor, 1971–73, State University of New York, Buffalo; Centennial Professor of English and creative writing, Johns Hopkins University, from 1973: now emeritus. Recipient; Brandeis University Creative Arts award, 1965; Rockefeller grant, 1965; American Academy grant, 1966; National Book award, 1973. Litt.D.: University of Maryland, College Park, 1969. Member, American Academy, 1974, and American Academy of Arts and Sciences, 1974.

PUBLICATIONS

Short Stories

Lost in the Funhouse: Fiction for Print, Tape, Live Voice. 1968.
Chimera. 1972.
Todd Andrews to the Author. 1979.

Novels

The Floating Opera. 1956; revised edition, 1967.
The End of the Road. 1958; revised edition, 1967.
The Sot-Weed Factor. 1960; revised edition, 1967.
Giles Goat-Boy; or, the Revised New Syllabus. 1966.
Letters. 1979.
Sabbatical: A Romance. 1982.
The Tidewater Tales: A Novel. 1987.
The Last Voyage of Somebody the Sailor. 1991.

Other

The Literature of Exhaustion, and The Literature of Replenishment (essays). 1982.

The Friday Book: Essays and Other Nonfiction. 1984.
Don't Count on It: A Note on the Number of the 1001 Nights. 1984.

*

Bibliography: *Barth: A Descriptive Primary and Annotated Secondary Bibliography* by Josephy Weixlmann, 1976; *Barth: An Annotated Bibliography* by Richard Allan Vine, 1977; *Barth, Jerzy Kosinski, and Thomas Pynchon: A Reference Guide* by Thomas P. Walsh and Cameron Northouse, 1977.

Critical Studies: *Barth* by Gerhard Joseph, 1970; *Barth: The Comic Sublimity of Paradox* by Jac Tharpe, 1974; *The Literature of Exhaustion: Borges, Nabokov, and Barth* by John O. Stark, 1974; *Barth: An Introduction* by David Morrell, 1976; *Critical Essays on Barth* edited by Joseph J. Waldmeir, 1980; *Passionate Virtuosity: The Fiction of Barth* by Charles B. Harris, 1983; *Barth* by Heide Ziegler, 1987; *Understanding Barth* by Stan Fogel and Gordon Slethaug, 1990.

* * *

While John Barth's literary reputation rests largely upon his work as a novelist, he is most readily introduced to new readers through the short stories in *Lost in the Funhouse* and the three linked novellas of *Chimera*. Coming as the two collections did at the end of the 1960's and the start of the 1970's, Barth's experimental fictions "for print, tape, live voice" captured a spirit of mold-breaking, convention-assaulting formal innovation that both sealed off one period of literary history and opened the door to a whole series of others. As much for their exemplary as for their intrinsic merit, both the title story and "Life-Story" in *Lost in the Funhouse* are among the most frequently anthologized stories from this period in American fiction.

Barth's short stories crystallize on the interface between modernism and decadence. They occupy a moment in literary history when a certain hip awareness of the medium in which one creates threatens to turn opaque, obscuring the work's ostensible subject. His stories may usefully be compared to such post-modernist architectural pranks as the Pompidou Center in Paris, an edifice turned inside out, with all its normally hidden pipes and conduits on display.

"Without discarding what he'd already written he began his story afresh in a somewhat different manner." So begins "Life-Story," Barth's footnote-laden account of a writer grappling with the crushing weight of literary history as he endeavors to write something fresh and true. Writers, readers, and texts tend to be at the center of Barth's fiction; they remind us insistently that they have been written, confront us pointedly with the experience of our own reading, and refuse obstinately to pretend to be anything other than an artifice concocted from words. Yet Barth manages, with surprising success, to be both funny and touching even as he betrays the illusions of his fiction, largely because the writer's and reader's plight (if not that of the characters) is seen itself to be both funny and touching indeed.

Barth manages to turn even self-mockery inside out, and so mocks it: "If I'm going to be a fictional character G declared to himself I want to be in a rousing good yarn as they say, not some piece of avant-garde preciousness" ("Life-Story"). Where characters once clashed in believable settings, now genres do battle, in the ruins of rejected and worn-out traditions. The resultant exercises in wit and literary play are not for all readers' tastes, clearly, but to those of "writerly" inclination, Barth's reflexive pastiches and tours de force offer durable delights.

Formal experimentation is pushed to unprecedented extremes in some of these pieces. The first story in *Lost in the Funhouse*, "Frame-Tale," is a single line of print that runs up the right margin of one page and down the left margin on the other side of the sheet. The reader is instructed to cut it out of the book (!), and tape its ends together with a twist so as to form what topologists call a Moebius strip. If the instructions are followed correctly, the strip reads, "Once upon a time, there was a story that began, Once upon a time, there was a story . . . " etc. Barth thus celebrates the ultimate triumph of form over content: perfect symmetry, no plot, and words used to create an analog to video feedback, such as results when a camera is aimed at its own monitor. A similar fascination with the possibilities of substituting the frame for the canvas itself animates "Menelaiad," a Homer-inspired concatenation of nesting narrators whose coinciding interquotations produce such eye-boggling (but ultimately scrutable) lines as "'("') ('(("What?"))') (")'"

A fundamental preoccupation with originality runs through Barth's fictions, even as some of them dare to retell familiar classical stories, such as "Dunyazadiad" (told by Scheherazade's sister), "Perseid," and "Bellerophoniad," the three related novellas of *Chimera*. The author reminds us repeatedly of the paradox that nothing is so old as the urge to be new. He responds to the challenge by seeking out fiction's own origins—the Homeric retellings, the myths reskewed, the Arabian Nights re-imagined from the distaff side—and making the improbability of improving on them the comic dilemma of his own storytelling heroes and heroines.

Barth's short fiction marks an end to innocence in the willing suspension of the reader's disbelief, and the arrival of literary criticism as a mode of fiction itself. In a central passage of "Life-Story," the narrator observes:

> inasmuch as the old analogy between Author and God, novel and world, can no longer be employed unless deliberately and as a false analogy, certain things follow: 1) fiction must acknowledge its fictitiousness and metaphoric invalidity or 2) choose to ignore the question and deny its relevance or 3) establish some other, acceptable relation between itself, its author, its reader.

Barth's short fiction playfully and comically explores a variety of those "other, acceptable relations," and does so in full view of the reader—frequently by inserting a version of the reader into the experiment itself. The ludic (or game-playing) stories that result thus embrace esthetic virtues over mimetic ones.

—Brian Stonehill

See the essay on "Lost in the Funhouse."

BARTHELME, Donald. American. Born in Philadelphia, Pennsylvania, 7 April 1931; brother of the writer Frederick Barthelme. Educated at the University of Houston. Served in the U.S. Army, 1953–55. Married 1) Birgit Barthelme; 2) Marion Knox in 1978; two daughters. Reporter, Houston *Post*, 1951, 1955–56; worked on public relations and news service staff, and founding editor of the university literary magazine *Forum*, University of Houston, 1956–59; director, Contemporary Arts Museum, Houston, 1961–62; managing editor, *Location* magazine, New York, 1962–64; visiting professor, State University of New York, Buffalo, 1972, and Boston University, 1973; Distinguished Visiting Professor, City College, New York, from 1974; visiting professor, University of Houston, from 1981. Recipient: Guggenheim fellowship, 1966; National Book award, 1972; American Academy Morton Dauwen Zabel award, 1972. Member, American Academy. *Died 23 July 1989.*

PUBLICATIONS

Short Stories

Come Back, Dr. Caligari.   1964.
Unspeakable Practices, Unnatural Acts.   1968.
City Life.   1970.
Sadness.   1972.
Guilty Pleasures.   1974.
Amateurs.   1976.
Great Days.   1979.
The Emerald.   1980.
Presents, collages by the author.   1980.
Sixty Stories.   1981.
Overnight to Many Distant Cities.   1983.
Forty Stories.   1987.
Sam's Bar.   1987.

Novels

Snow White.   1967.
The Dead Father.   1975.
Paradise.   1986.
The King.   1990.

Play

Great Days, from his own story (produced 1983).

Other

The Slightly Irregular Fire Engine; or, The Thithering Dithering Djinn (for children).   1971.
The Teachings; The Satires, Parodies, Fables, Illustrated Stories, and Plays, edited by Kim Herzinger.   1992.

*

Bibliography: *Barthelme: A Comprehensive Bibliography and Annotated Secondary Checklist* by Jerome Klinkowitz, Asa Pieratt, and Robert Murray Davis, 1977.

Critical Studies: "Barthelme Issue" of *Critique,* vol. 16, no. 3, 1975; *Barthelme* by Lois Gordon, 1981; *Barthelme* by

Maurice Courturier and Régis Durand, 1982; *The Metafictional Muse: The Works of Robert Coover, Barthelme, and William H. Gass* by Larry McCaffery, 1982; *Barthelme's Fiction: The Ironist Saved from Drowning* by Charles Molesworth, 1982; *The Shape of Art in the Short Stories of Barthelme* by Wayne B. Stengel, 1985; *Understanding Barthelme* by Alan Trachtenberg, 1990; *Barthelme: An Exhibition* by Jerome Klinkowitz, 1991.

*   *   *

In the postmodern age of largely maximalist novels, Donald Barthelme, along with Samuel Beckett, and Jorge Luis Borges, and others, perfected the counter-movement towards minimalist attenuation and permutation. Equally, though more humorously, innovative, Barthelme was in a way just as influential as either Beckett or Borges, thanks to his long association with the mainstream *The New Yorker* magazine. Even as he made metafiction's leap from matter to manner, Barthelme managed to avoid the extreme self-reflexivity that characterized the more theory-inspired work of many like-minded writers. He understood, better than most perhaps, that contemporary fiction was under new pressure, in part because of the writer's and the reader's hyper-awareness of literary conventions as conventions and of competition with other narrative forms, film in particular. Barthelme, drawing especially on Beckett's example, explored fiction's possibilities while fully recognizing the difficulty of sustaining the interest of the easily jaded reader and no less easily jaded writer.

Like Beckett and Borges, Barthelme aims at extreme brevity. His methods are as varied as they are self-consciously employed. There is the ironically detached, comically deadpan presentation of absurdity: Beckett wrote parts for Buster Keaton; Barthelme wrote stories that embodied Keaton's comic imperturbability. At times Barthelme reduces plot development to its barest form, as in the one hundred numbered sections of "The Glass Mountain." More usually, his stories do not develop at all; instead, they accrete, like "Bone Bubbles" or his 2500-word sentence ("The Sentence"), forming a verbal bricolage. However despite the characteristic brevity and skeletal structure, his fiction often seems strangely excessive, even mockingly exhaustive, as in "Nothing: A Preliminary Account."

Both within individual stories and in all of Barthelme's works, the reader discovers an art based on small adjustments rather than special effects and literary leaps—a matter of fine tuning and formal manipulation of often slight material (or, as in the case of "Nothing," material that can be made to seem slight). Barthelme's art entails variations on a theme, a word used here in its musical rather than its literary sense, and is especially evident in his dialogue and extended monologue stories. Barthelme's relation to these and other forms is a matter less of parody than of mimicry and is generally closer to *hommage* than to satire, as in "Captain Blood," which recalls both the original Rafael Sabatini novel and the film based on it. What Barthelme as author experiences is not the anxiety of influence (Harold Bloom's term), but instead the pleasure of influence, and nowhere is this pleasure more evident than in his adapting various visual arts to his literary purposes: architecture, magazine layout, collage, pop art, action painting, and contemporary sculpture. The convergence, or rather juxtaposition, of verbal and visual modes (including the latter's "immediate impact") is most pro-

nounced in *City Life* ("At the Tolstoy Museum" in particular) and in *Guilty Pleasures*.

Although Barthelme's stories, or anti-stories, are aggressively antirealistic, they render the texture of contemporary American life—at its most urbane and up-to-date—with remarkable fidelity, however fanciful certain details may be. To read a Barthelme story is in a sense to read the larger culture which it reflects and imaginatively transcends: the sensory overload, the omnipresence not of God but of "noise," including the abundant, indeed excessive information which the reader, like the educated citizen, can access but never master. Spread out in a broadly democratic, seemingly indiscriminate way are the bits of popular and high culture, including debased myths ("The Glass Mountain," "The Emerald," *Snow White*), which the reader is too knowing to believe though not quite able to forget. Barthelme handles the absurd in a similar manner. Although recalling Kafka, the absurdity in a story like "Me and Miss Mandible" is no longer existential but instead intertextual; it is no more and no less important than Sabatini's Captain Blood: grist for the postmodern mill. This is not to imply that John Gardner (in *On Moral Fiction*) and other tradition-minded readers are correct in claiming that Barthelme's only message is, "better to be disillusioned than deluded." If the title of his first collection, *Come Back, Dr. Caligari*, suggests the densely and playfully intertextual aspect of Barthelme's fiction, then the title of his fourth collection, *Sadness*, suggests another, equally important. This is the sadness to which the postindustrial consumer society and Barthelme's stories of "never enough" seem inevitably (but in the latter case never nostalgically) to lead. While the narrator of "See the Moon" may claim that "fragments are the only forms I trust," and the dwarfs in *Snow White* may prefer "books that have a lot of dreck in them," and while Barthelme's fictions may be filled with an abundance of both, his reflection of these two features of contemporary culture do not constitute an endorsement of them. Barthelme's aim is not merely to record and reproduce; rather, it is to respond constructively, which is to say imaginatively, in order (as he says in one interview) to make "music out of noise." This is "The New Music" (title of a 1978 story), which celebrates the momentary rather than the momentous, and which makes (as Barthelme says in another interview) "the Uncertainty Principle our Song of Songs."

How to proceed in the face of uncertainty: this is the situation in which Barthelme and his readers, as well as his characters, find themselves. Defying the usual ways of making do and making sense, his stories invite the reader's participation and cooperation and are as much about the reader's efforts to disambiguate them as they about their ostensible subjects, and this is as true of those stories that, like his famous balloon, are so indefinite as to invite any and all interpretations, and those which seem so inclusive and exhaustive as to preclude any interpretive hypothesis that will account for more than a fraction of texts that seem at once too dense and too attenuated, overrich and undernourished.

—Robert A. Morace

See the essays on "The Balloon" and "The Indian Uprising."

———————

BATES, H(erbert) E(rnest). English. Born in Rushden, Northamptonshire, 16 May 1905. Educated at Kettering Grammar School, Northamptonshire, 1916–21. Served as a writer in the Air Ministry, 1941–45: squadron leader. Married Marjorie Helen Cox in 1931; two daughters and two sons. Reporter, Northampton *Chronicle*, 1922; warehouse clerk, 1922–26; lived in Little Chart, Kent, from 1931; columnist ("Country Life") from 1932, and literary editor from 1941, *Spectator*, London. Fellow, Royal Society of Literature, 1950 (resigned 1963). C.B.E. (Commander, Order of the British Empire), 1973. *Died 29 January 1974.*

PUBLICATIONS

Collections

The Best of Bates: A Selection of the Novels and Short Stories.   1980.

Short Stories

The Seekers.   1926.
The Spring Song, and In View of the Fact That ... : Two Stories.   1927.
Day's End and Other Stories.   1928.
Seven Tales and Alexander.   1929.
The Tree (story).   1930.
The Hessian Prisoner (story).   1930.
Mrs. Esmond's Life (story).   1930.
A Threshing Day.   1931.
A German Idyll (story).   1932.
The Black Boxer: Tales.   1932.
Sally Go round the Moon (story).   1932.
The House with the Apricot and Two Other Tales.   1933.
The Woman Who Had Imagination and Other Stories.   1934.
Thirty Tales.   1934.
The Duet (story).   1935.
Cut and Come Again: Fourteen Stories.   1935.
Something Short and Sweet: Stories.   1937.
I Am Not Myself (story).   1939.
The Flying Goat: Stories.   1939.
My Uncle Silas: Stories.   1939.
Country Tales: Collected Short Stories.   1940.
The Beauty of the Dead and Other Stories.   1940.
The Greatest People in the World and Other Stories. 1942; as *There's Something in the Air*, 1943.
How Sleep the Brave and Other Stories.   1943.
The Bride Comes to Evensford (story).   1943.
Thirty-One Selected Tales.   1947.
The Bride Comes to Evensford and Other Tales.   1949.
Selected Short Stories.   1951.
Twenty Tales.   1951.
Colonel Julian and Other Stories.   1951.
The Daffodil Sky.   1955.
Selected Stories.   1957.
Sugar for the Horse.   1957.
The Watercress Girl and Other Stories.   1959.
An Aspidistra in Babylon: Four Novellas.   1960; as *The Grapes of Paradise: Four Short Novels*, 1960.
Now Sleeps the Crimson Petal and Other Stories.   1961; as *The Enchantress and Other Stories*, 1961.
The Golden Oriole: Five Novellas.   1962.
Seven by Five: Stories 1926–1961.   1963; as *The Best of Bates*, 1963.
The Fabulous Mrs. V.   1964.
The Wedding Party.   1965.

The Wild Cherry Tree.   1968.
The Four Beauties.   1968.
The Song of the Wren.   1972.
The Good Corn and Other Stories, edited by Geoffrey Halson.   1974.
H.E. Bates (selected stories), edited by Alan Cattell. 1975.
The Poison Ladies and Other Stories, edited by Mike Poulton.   1976.
The Yellow Meads of Asphodel.   1976.

Novels

The Two Sisters.   1926.
Catherine Foster.   1929.
Charlotte's Row.   1931.
The Fallow Land.   1932.
The Story Without an End, and The Country Doctor. 1932.
The Poacher.   1935.
A House of Women.   1936.
Spella Ho.   1938.
Fair Stood the Wind for France.   1944.
The Cruise of The Breadwinner.   1946.
The Purple Plain.   1947.
The Jacaranda Tree.   1949.
Dear Life.   1949.
The Scarlet Sword.   1950.
Love for Lydia.   1952.
The Nature of Love: Three Short Novels.   1953.
The Feast of July.   1954.
The Sleepless Moon.   1956.
Death of a Huntsman: Four Short Novels.   1957; as *Summer in Salandar*, 1957.
Perfick, Perfick: The Story of the Larkin Family.   1985.
  The Darling Buds of May.   1958.
  A Breath of French Air.   1959.
  When the Green Woods Laugh.   1960; as *Hark, Hark, the Lark!*, 1961.
  Oh! To Be in England.   1963.
  A Little of What You Fancy.   1970.
The Day of the Tortoise.   1961.
A Crown of Wild Myrtle.   1962.
A Moment in Time.   1964.
The Distant Horns of Summer.   1967.
The Triple Echo.   1970.

Plays

The Last Bread.   1926.
The Day of Glory (produced 1946).   1945.

Screenplays: *There's a Future in It*, 1943; *The Loves of Joanna Godden*, with Angus Macphail, 1947; *Summertime* (*Summer Madness*), with David Lean, 1955.

Other

Flowers and Faces.   1935.
Through the Woods: The English Woodland—April to April.   1936.
Down the River (essays).   1937.
The Seasons and the Gardener: A Book for Children. 1940.
The Modern Short Story: A Critical Survey.   1941; revised edition, as *The Modern Short Story from 1809 to 1953*, 1972.
In the Heart of the Country.   1942.

O! More Than Happy Countryman. 1943; revised edition, as *The Country Heart* (includes *In the Heart of the Country*), 1949.
Something in the Air: Stories by Flying Officer X. 1944.
There's Freedom in the Air: The Official Story of the Allied Air Forces from the Occupied Countries. 1944.
The Tinkers of Elstow. 1946(?).
Edward Garnett: A Personal Portrait. 1950.
Flower Gardening: A Reader's Guide. 1950.
The Country of White Clover (essays). 1952.
The Face of England. 1952.
Pastoral on Paper. 1956.
Achilles the Donkey (for children). 1962.
Achilles and Diana (for children). 1963.
Achilles and the Twins (for children). 1964.
The White Admiral (for children). 1968.
The Vanished World (autobiography). 1969.
The Blossoming World (autobiography). 1971.
A Love of Flowers. 1971.
The World in Ripeness (autobiography). 1972.
A Fountain of Flowers (on gardening). 1974.

*

Bibliography: *Bates: A Bibliographical Study* by Peter Eads, 1990.

Critical Studies: *Bates* by Dennis Vannatta, 1983; *Bates: A Literary Life* by Dean R. Baldwin, 1987.

* * *

H.E. Bates summarized his own approach to the form of which he was an accomplished master in his study *The Modern Short Story* when writing of Stephen Crane: "a story is told not by the carefully engineered plot but by the implication of certain isolated incidents, by the capture and arrangement of certain episodic movements." The range and variety of Bates's "episodic movements" is indeed remarkable.

Even as a boy, the only vocation Bates wanted to follow was that of writing, though he would also have liked to become a painter, and indeed became a skilled amateur practitioner. From his father he inherited his passion for nature and the countryside.

Bates began writing in the 1920's; his first book, *The Two Sisters*, was published in 1926. During the next 15 years he gradually acquired a reputation for his stories about English country life. His own life at this time was a hard one, for he did not make much money. He had been taken up by the independently minded publisher Jonathan Cape, who later claimed that none of Bates's first 20 books earned the advances paid on them.

In 1941, Bates was recruited into the British Royal Air Force as a short story writer. He became a flight lieutenant in the Public Relations Department of the Air Ministry, a year later being promoted squadron leader. During the war years, under the pseudonym "Flying Office X," he produced a series of brilliant stories commemorating the way of life, and sometimes of death, of the men who made up "the Few," who won the Battle of Britain; these are sharply evocative prose sketches counterpointing the poems of John Pudney, using similar urgent material. The stories were collected in *The Greatest People in the World*. Under his own name Bates also wrote "The Cruise of *The*

Breadwinner," about a lugsail fishing boat used to patrol the English Channel looking for the crews of shot-down planes. The little boat turned back to pick up a German pilot from the water, and is attacked by an enemy fighter and two of three crew members are killed—the boy Snowy, a boy who loved binoculars, and the rescued British pilot. When the little book first came out, a reviewer observed that the story was really only about "the pity of it all." So, indeed, it is; but it remains a small, unsentimental wartime masterpiece of a tale.

The plight of women in the lives of the airmen is movingly celebrated in Bates's novel *Love for Lydia*. The European war was the inspiration for the novel that first brought him popular fame, *Fair Stood the Wind for France*, while his experiences in the Far Eastern theatre of war resulted in *The Purple Plain*, set in Burma, and *The Jacaranda Tree*, based on Bates's experience of India.

After the war, Bates made his home in "The Granary," a house in the Kentish Village of Little Chart—where, incidentally, he became an enthusiastic and skilful gardener—returning to his previous theme of English country life. Not that he was unaware of the other face of England: the run-down England of the small-time commercial traveller, evoked in "The Ring of Truth," in which a remembered childhood picture postcard leads George Pickford to return to Skelby to uncover unpalatable sexual truths about his late father and widowed mother.

One of Bates's skills is his ability to paint a country scene with the accurate imagery of a poet. It is a skill he also applies to urban scenes, as with the Derbyshire town of Skelby, which Pickford found to be "a place of squat terraces half in red brick, half in grimy stone, with a short main street of shops, five or six pubs, two working men's clubs and an outdoor beerhouse or two. . . .Stone walls split the surrounding countryside of hills and dales into lopsided fragments. . . .It was early August when he arrived and the wind had a grizzling winter sound."

Bates depicts the arousal of desire in all its manifestations with a sure touch, whether Pickford's desire for the sister of Mrs. Lambton, or Maisie Foster, in "The Quiet Girl," whose sensuality is disastrously aroused by a succession of shabby men stroking her hair.

Desire is also the binding element in that hauntingly captured episode "The Wedding Party." Escaping from the vulgar celebrations of the wedding of her sister to a coarse German, the girl in dark green forms an intense relationship with a stranger, which leads, not to their escape together to Venice as lovers, but to something much more tragic.

As the critic Walter Allen remarked (in *The Short Story in English*), Bates also is masterly at creating stasis, the feeling of stillness, as in "The Gleaner" and the fine "Death of a Huntsman," stories separated by a quarter of a century.

With his invention of that ripe old character Uncle Silas, Bates found a vehicle for recreating with gusty good humour the character and vanishing ways of an older rural England; the stories are none the worse for our realisation that the old man stretched the bounds of truth, even probability, in the telling. For instance, in "Sugar for the Horse," Uncle Silas and a drunken friend try to get the reluctant horse Panto up the stairs to go to bed with them.

By 1958, Bates was a hugely successful writer whose work had been translated into 16 different languages. Yet in that year he began a new, rather more earthy, type of story that was to bring him wider popularity: the first of his chronicles of Pop Larkin and his family, *The Darling Buds of May*. Perhaps vulgarised a little, it is still a successful series on television, thus bringing him before a wider, if perhaps less discerning, audience than his other books.

But it is upon the qualities of his short stories that his lasting reputation depends: a lucid prose-style, a sharpness of eye for imagery and a broad ear for dialogue, the ability to handle pathos objectively, a strong deftness for character-drawing, and the flowing invention of a natural story teller.

In his later years Bates published the three volumes of his autobiography, a racy and readable account of the life and times out of which the stories grew.

—Maurice Lindsay

See the essays on "The Daffodil Sky" and "How Sleep the Brave."

—————

BAYNTON, Barbara (Lawrence). Australian. Born in Scone, New South Wales, 4 June 1857. Educated at home. Married 1) Alexander Frater in 1880 (divorced 1890), two sons and one daughter; 2) Thomas Baynton in 1890 (died 1904); 3) Lord Headley in 1921 (separated 1922). Governess, Bible salesperson, briefly; writer from late 1890's; antique collector; lived in Melbourne and London, after second marriage, travelling between England and Australia. *Died 28 May 1929.*

PUBLICATIONS

Short Stories

Bush Studies.   1902; as *Cobbers,* 1917.

Novel

Human Toll.   1907.

Other

The Portable Baynton, edited by Alan Lawson and Sally Krimmer.   1980.

*

Bibliography: "A Bibliography of Baynton" by Sally Krimmer, in *Australian Literary Studies* 7 (4), 1976.

Critical Studies: "Baynton and the Dissidence of the Nineties" by A.A. Phillips, in *Overland* 22, December 1961; "Baynton" by Vance Palmer, in *Intimate Portraits and Other Pieces,* edited by H.P. Heseltine, 1968; "A New Light on Baynton" by Sally Krimmer, in *Australian Literary Studies* 7 (4), 1976; in *Three Australian Women* by Thea Astley, 1979; in *Who Is She? Images of Women in Australian Fiction* edited by S. Walker, 1983.

* * *

Barbara Baynton's single collection of short stories, *Bush Studies,* represents a small but unusual contribution to Australian literary history. Like Miles Franklin, who wrote *My Brilliant Career,* Baynton's work tends to defy that mood of cheery optimism asserted as central to the Australian tradition. It casts an ironical pall over Australian notions of egalitarian democracy built on ideas of mateship, by emphasizing the physical and psychological hardships of life in the Australian outback, which, in Baynton's work, dehumanizes its inhabitants. In Baynton's stories there is no nationalistic pride, no affinity between the landscape and its people, and no mateship. If the work of male writers of this period in Australian literary history is redolent with the metonymic relations of man to the land, to his fellows, and to the freedom of an egalitarian democracy, Baynton's work depicts a different Australia. It is a world of women who are the innocent victims of men, who are as brutal and pitiless as the land from which they scratch their living.

In "The Chosen Vessel" an unnamed woman is murdered by an itinerant swagman whose restless way of life directly opposes the possibility of female socialization. The woman and her baby are left in their hut on an empty landscape by her husband. Her background is clearly that of the town dweller; she is afraid of the cow, but the nearest "dismal drunken township" offers no protection, for the pursuit of the material means of survival is all engrossing to its inhabitants. The meaninglessness and malice of the landscape is reflected in its human inhabitants, the cruel and indifferent husband and the swagman, sure of his capacity to inspire fear, who demands food, money, and tobacco. It is similarly reflected in the imagery of the story, as the man and his dog, in direct correlation, worry victims and sheep respectively.

At the centre of this story lies some small affirmation. The maternal instincts of the woman survive even death, and do move the man who finds her body. There is also the hut, which often serves as an image of socialization in Australian literature. This hut also functions as an image of the woman's body within the text, which her pursuer determines to breach. Its violation by the swagman signifies a breakdown of even this small and ugly attempt at communal life. As the woman is raped and then murdered, her calls for help are ignored by a man on a horse. When her body is found, she is still clutching her living child, and is mistaken for a fallen ewe and lamb savaged by a dingo.

The analogies between animals and humans are rarely complimentary in Baynton's work, and the dissonance between love and sex is often used to exemplify the moral chaos she depicts. In the harsh Australian outback even the church is ineffectual. In "The Bush Church" the preacher who has managed, through fear of consequences, to gather together a bush congregation for the purpose of baptizing children fails against a landscape that allows only the practical. Here "little matters become distorted and the greater shrivelled" and as the congregation realizes that there is nothing to fear from this man the service degenerates into noisy altercation. The waterless outback is matched by spiritual aridity and those who dream are rendered ridiculous. Thus the man on the horse, in "The Chosen Vessel," who ignored the woman's cries for help, did so because he imagined that he had been granted a vision of the Virgin Mary, sent to persuade him to follow his mother's wishes in the matter of casting his vote. Influenced by this idealized vision of motherhood the man becomes "subdued and mildly ecstatic . . . feeling as a repentant, chastened child" until informed of his error by an enraged priest. The ironic reverberations cast upon the title of the work, "The Chosen Vessel," and the savagery of the woman's death, render all such idealizations ridiculous.

In these circumstances the category of woman has become little more than that of a hollow signifier.

Baynton's female protagonists often remain unnamed, and the promiscuity of bush life which appears in the form of lewdness and obscenity in her work is, in part, created by the absence of the feminine in all that she describes. In "Billy Skywonkie" an ugly, aging, and sick woman hopes to find employment as a housekeeper. At that time the advertising of such a post was little more than a thinly veiled request for a mistress. The woman, unaware of these possibilities, travels to the outback in the hope of employment. Imaged as victim, sheeplike and passive before the predatory instincts of men, this woman is entirely at the mercy of the land. Animals and humans alike are "drought-dulled" in this story, dialogue is sparse, and only the sun is "tireless and greedy." When the would-be housekeeper is rejected for her ugliness at the end of her long and exhausting passage into the world of men and the outback, she watches the slaughter of a sheep and notices "that the sheep lay passive, with its head back, till its neck curved in a bow, and that the glitter of the knife was reflected in its eye."

Women, in Baynton's *Bush Studies*, are the vulnerable victims of isolation and fear, and it is this unified vision that makes of her story collection a complex symbolic narrative which fluctuates between harsh social comedy and a search for realism in the empty malevolence of a hard land.

—Jan Pilditch

BEATTIE, Ann. American. Born in Washington, D.C., 8 September 1947. Educated at American University, Washington, D.C., B.A. 1969; University of Connecticut, Storrs, 1969–70, M.A. 1970. Married 1) David Gates in 1973 (divorced); 2) Lincoln Perry. Visiting lecturer, 1976–77 and 1980, University of Virginia, Charlottesville; Briggs Copeland Lecturer in English, Harvard University, Cambridge, Massachusetts, 1977–78. Recipient: Guggenheim fellowship, 1977; American University Distinguished Alumnae award, 1980; American Academy and Institute of Arts and Letters award, 1980. L.H.D.: American University, 1983; L.H.D.: Colby College, 1991. Member, American Academy and Institute of Arts and Letters, 1980. Lives in Charlottesville.

PUBLICATIONS

Short Stories

Distortions.   1976.
Secrets and Surprises.   1978.
Jacklighting.   1981.
The Burning House.   1982.
Where You'll Find Me and Other Stories.   1986.
What Was Mine and Other Stories.   1991.

Novels

Chilly Scenes of Winter.   1976.
Falling in Place.   1980.
Love Always.   1985.

Picturing Will.   1990.

Other

Spectacles (for children).   1985.
Alex Katz (monograph).   1987.

Editor, with Shannon Ravenel, *The Best American Short Stories 1987.*   1987.

*

Critical Studies: "Beattie's Magic Slate *or* The End of the Sixties" by Blanche H. Gelfant, in *New England Review* 1, 1979; "Through 'The Octascope': A View of Beattie" by John Gerlach, in *Studies in Short Fiction* 17, Fall 1980.

*   *   *

In her short stories, Ann Beattie seemingly abandons her reader, leaving a trail of unanswered questions about characters' lives. In "Skeletons" (in *Where You'll Find Me*) the main character, Nancy, never learns about Kyle's car accident, something only the reader is privy to. However, even the reader is uncertain about the outcome. Did Kyle die, or was he merely injured, and if so how seriously? The short story "In Amalfi," from Beattie's latest book *What Was Mine*, never carries out the narrator's good intentions to return the opal ring given her by the mysterious French woman. Will she return the ring, or is the "conspiracy" between herself and the waiter one of thievery?

Unanswered questions are common in the work of minimalist writers like Beattie and her contemporary Raymond Carver, whose literary craft Beattie much admired. Unanswered questions, so Beattie's work implies, haunt our lives in part because people cannot articulate their true thoughts and feelings. The frequent gaps presented to the reader are echoed in the silences between characters who stop talking because nothing meaningful can be said. In "Friends" (in *Secrets and Surprises*) all the characters are somehow inarticulate. Francie laments, "I don't know how to talk. I'm either alone and it's silent here all day, or my friends are around, and I really don't talk to them." People cannot speak their minds because they lack the situation and therefore the necessary linguistic "exercise" that would allow them to express themselves freely.

Then again, silence predominates because Beattie's characters wish things left unsaid. Often their continuing as they are depends on the coexistence of multiple but potentially conflicting relationships. Secret liaisons abound in Beattie's fiction, supporting characters with the intimacy they cannot find in their more public marriages or cohabitations. These peripheral encounters with intimacy must never become central to characters' lives for the threat they pose to a safe existence. In "Imagined Scenes" (in *Distortions*) David cheats on the narrator and by implication on the reader, who sees through the narrator's eyes only a momentary glimpse of David's unfaithfulness. With only the suggestion of an affair made by simple slips like David's reference to a friendly couple as "he" (in an awkward attempt to avoid talking about the wife with whom David is possibly having an affair), the reader is privy to the underworld of these characters' lives, but only in an atmosphere of confidentiality.

Sometimes Beattie's stories surprise the reader with brilliant flashes that in truth reveal nothing. A light is held out, guiding the reader and the characters only further into the morass of relationships. The central character in "Sunshine and Shadow" (in *The Burning House*) has a sudden brilliant recollection of a childhood tragedy. When he presses his face "nose-close to the window," he sees as an adult the spot on the driveway etched in his mind as a child where his mother had "run a hose into the car" and gassed herself with carbon monoxide. Despite the vividness of the recollection, the momentary revelation offers little aid for his present situation, and still less illumination on the past. The title "Sunshine and Shadow" suggests moments of brilliance that have all the form of revelation, but lack the significance of any religious epiphany as meaning retreats into shadow.

However, in Beattie's world, the random occurrence is often all that can be depended on for even illusory meaning. The random crossing of peoples' lives suggests meaning, and in the suggestion, characters clutch at the potential for intimacy that they cannot find in more permanent relationships. Characters turn not to their intended partners but to occasional acquaintances, and by implication, so Beattie suggests, even to the reader in the case of first-person narratives, in desperation revealing their secrets to whomever will listen and not accuse. Long-term relationships weight the dialogue between romantic partners in such a way that verbal intimacy becomes too costly. Secrets revealed to an acquaintance pose less of a risk. Ironically, a casual acquaintance turned confidant appears momentarily as a solid relationship, perhaps more meaningful than the committed relationship that now binds the speaker. In the elegantly woven story "Windy Day at the Reservoir" Beattie shows Chap confiding in a neighbor, Mrs. Brikel, a number of secrets that he could never tell his wife. Mrs. Brikel then confides in him that she has always been a person to whom casual acquaintances tell their secrets. It is something that has always mystified Mrs. Brikel, why "some people are drawn to other people. Drawn in so they want to tell them things. It comes as a great surprise to me that I seem to be one of those people that other people need to say things to." In Beattie's fiction, intimacy is both essential and deadly to relationships, so characters go on living with people that they seldom say anything meaningful to, content out of necessity to fuel the relationship, turning now and again to casual acquaintances for relief.

Acquaintance and friends often compete with the romantic other. A friend's ability to satisfy momentary cravings for intimacy may eventually suck dry the marrow of romantic attachments. Beattie cleverly symbolizes such parasitic attachments with the introduction of the drug dealer turned friend in "Fancy Flights." The main character, Michael, depends on Carlos for companionship when his relationship with his wife has gone sour. In fact, both Michael and his wife attribute the occasional success of their marriage to Carlos who brings the two back together after periods of separation. As grateful as the two are to Carlos, the story hints that Carlos is the satisfier of only Michael's desperate craving, for marijuana, the drug responsible in part for Michael's indifference to commitment and responsibility in marriage. Michael is suspended in a marijuana haze, vitiated of the will to be a good father and husband, kept in ample supply by the very man who claims to be his friend.

Michael's attitude of inaction is familiar in Beattie's fictional world. Her fiction tells the story, as Margaret Atwood describes it, of a world not of suspense but of suspension. Male characters more often than female characters epitomize the inability to act in their lives of prolonged childhood, but all are affected. Material possessions in the form of comfortable homes, or accessibility to narcotics that momentarily appease physical cravings—such substitutes for activity abound. As the narrator in "Janus" discovers, "anxiety became the operative force." One doesn't fear what will happen, but what might happen. People exist in a world of the imagination, but without the definition of physical action. Perhaps this is what many readers find most frustrating with Beattie's work. She portrays a world that offers little hope for change, in a literature that illustrates without giving solutions.

Only in her latest work *What Was Mine* do the stories offer a glimmer of hope with any frequency. This may come about because Beattie insists on contemporaneity, altering her tone as her world achieves distance from the despair of postcultural revolution. Among her more hopeful works is "Windy Day at the Reservoir," which ends with Mrs. Brikel gazing at the newly polished floorboards of her living room: "Just looking at it, she could feel the buoyance of her heart." In another story from the same collection, "The Longest Day of the Year," a Welcome Wagon lady, in the irony of her anger, amuses the narrator who treasures the memory of her visit long afterward. Of course, as one might expect from these gems of minimalism, the hope is itself minimal. In the case of "The Longest Day of the Year," the narrator and her husband separate. What would have been a shared memory of the Welcome Wagon lady now becomes "instead a story that I often remember, going over the details silently, by myself."

Ann Beattie's short stories charm less than captivate, luring an audience well-acquainted with the humdrum of yuppie life, but hungry for answers. While her stories offer few answers and raise far more questions, she reminds us of the need to treasure momentary illuminations that reflect a pulse of the life that lingers all too briefly. Such illuminations seem like answers, and for the time being, that may be all one needs.

—Kelly Cannon

See the essay on "The Cinderella Waltz."

———

BEAUVOIR, Simone (Lucie Ernestine Marie) de. French. Born in Paris, 9 January 1908. Educated at Institut Normal Catholique Adeline-Désir, Paris, 1913–25; Institut Sainte-Marie, Neuilly-sur-Seine; École Normale Supérieure, Paris, agrégation in philosophy 1929. Began lifelong relationship with the writer Jean-Paul Sartre, *q.v.,* 1929. Part-time teacher, Lycée Victor Duruy, Paris, 1929–31; philosophy teacher, Lycée Montgrand, Marseilles, 1931–32, Lycée Jeanne d'Arc, Rouen, 1932–36, Lycée Molière, Paris, 1936–39, and Lycée Camille-Sée and Lycée Henri IV, both Paris, 1939–43. Founding editor, with Sartre, *Les Temps Modernes,* Paris, from 1945. Member of the Consultative Committee, Bibliothèque Nationale, 1969; President, Choisir, 1972. President, Ligue des Droits des Femmes, from 1974. Recipient: Goncourt prize, 1954; Jerusalem prize, 1975; Austrian State Prize for European Literature, 1978. LL.D.: Cambridge University. *Died 14 April 1986.*

PUBLICATIONS

Short Stories

La Femme rompue (includes "L'Âge de discrétion" and "Monologue"). 1968; as *The Woman Destroyed* (includes "The Age of Discretion" and "The Monologue"), 1969.
Quand prime le spirituel. 1979; as *When Things of the Spirit Come First: Five Early Tales,* 1982.

Novels

L'Invitée. 1943; as *She Came to Stay,* 1949.
Le Sang des autres. 1945; edited by John F. Davis, 1973; as *The Blood of Others,* 1948.
Tous les hommes sont mortels. 1946; as *All Men Are Mortal,* 1956.
Les Mandarins. 1954; as *The Mandarins,* 1956.
Les Belles Images. 1966; translated as *Les Belles Images,* 1968.

Play

Les Bouches inutiles (produced 1945). 1945; as *Who Shall Die?,* 1983.

Other

Pyrrhus et Cinéas. 1944.
Pour une morale de l'ambiguïté. 1947; as *The Ethics of Ambiguity,* 1948.
L'Amérique au jour le jour. 1948; as *America Day by Day,* 1952.
L'Existentialisme et la sagesse des nations. 1948.
Le Deuxième Sexe: Les Faits et les mythes and L'Expérience vécue. 2 vols., 1949; as *The Second Sex,* 1953; vol. 1 as *A History of Sex,* 1961, and as *Nature of the Second Sex,* 1963.
Must We Burn de Sade? 1953; in *The Marquis de Sade,* edited by Paul Dinnage, 1953.
Privilèges (includes *Faut-il brûler Sade?*). 1955.
La Longue Marche: Essai sur la Chine. 1957; as *The Long March,* 1958.
Mémoires d'une jeune fille rangée. 1958; as *Memoirs of a Dutiful Daughter,* 1959.
Brigitte Bardot and the Lolita Syndrome. 1960.
La Force de l'âge (autobiography). 1960; as *The Prime of Life,* 1962.
Djamila Boupacha, with Gisèle Halimi. 1962; translated as *Djamila Boupacha,* 1962.
La Force des choses (autobiography). 1963; as *Force of Circumstance,* 1965.
Une Mort très douce. 1964; as *A Very Easy Death,* 1966.
La Vieillesse. 1970; as *Old Age,* 1972; as *The Coming of Age,* 1972.
Toute compte fait. 1972; as *All Said and Done,* 1974.
La Cérémonie des adieux. 1981; as *Adieux: A Farewell to Sartre,* 1984.
Letters to Sartre, edited by Quintin Hoare. 1991.

Editor, *Lettres au Castor et a quelques autres 1926–1939* and *1940–1963,* by Sartre. 2 vols., 1984; volume 1 as *Witness to My Life: The Letters of Jean-Paul Sartre to de Beauvoir 1926–1939,* 1992.

*

Bibliography: *Beauvoir: An Annotated Bibliography* by Jay Bennett and Gabriella Hochmann, 1989.

Critical Studies: *Beauvoir: Encounters with Death* by Elaine Marks, 1973; *Beauvoir* by Robert D. Cottrell, 1975; *Beauvoir on Women* by Jean Leighton, 1976; *Hearts and Minds: The Common Journey of Beauvoir and Jean-Paul Sartre* by Axel Madsen, 1977; *Beauvoir* by Konrad Bieber, 1979; *Beauvoir and the Limits of Commitment* by Anne Whitmarsh, 1981; *Beauvoir: A Study of Her Writings* by Terry Keefe, 1983; *After "The Second Sex": Conversations with Beauvoir* by Alice Schwarzer, 1984; *Beauvoir: A Feminist Mandarin* by Mary Evans, 1985; *Beauvoir* by Judith Okely, 1986; *The Novels of Beauvoir* by Elizabeth Fallaize, 1987; *Beauvoir* by Claude Francis and Fernande Gontier, 1987; *Critical Essays on Beauvoir* edited by Elaine Marks, 1987; *Beauvoir: A Critical View* by Renee Winegarten, 1987; *Beauvoir: A Life, A Love Story* by Claude Francis and Fernande Gontier, 1987; *Beauvoir: The Woman and Her Work* by Margaret Crosland, 1988; *Beauvoir* by Lisa Appignanesi, 1988; *Beauvoir and the Demystification of Motherhood* by Yolanda A. Patterson, 1989; *Beauvoir* by Jane Heath, 1989; *Feminist Theory and Beauvoir* by Tori Moi, 1989; *Beauvoir: A Biography* by Deirdre Bair, 1990.

* * *

Simone de Beauvoir's book, *Le Deuxième Sexe (The Second Sex),* has been an inspiration to women's movements since its publication in 1949. This is in spite of the fact that Beauvoir's life was marked by a refusal to become politically active. In the 1930's, she and Sartre were both against capitalism, but, Beauvoir has admitted, "we were still not actively for anything" on the grounds that humanity had to be remoulded, "created anew." When women were agitating for the vote Beauvoir would not have used hers if she had it. Unexpectedly, she did join a feminist march in France in November 1971, but her short stories were written well before this date, and are less concerned with women's politicization than with the situation of women and others in a society in which freedom is always difficult, perhaps even impossible, to attain.

Beauvoir's five early tales, collected in *Quand prime le spirituel (When Things of the Spirit Come First),* were written a little before she was 30 years old, to speak, she said, about the world she knew and "to expose some of its defects." For Beauvoir, those defects included the complacency of the bourgeoisie and the harm caused by a type of religiosity with which, she felt, her own childhood and early youth had been imbued. The collection is one of Beauvoir's many attempts to fictionalize the tragedy of her school friend, Zara (Elizabeth Mabille), who had wished to marry a young man of whom, she was convinced, her parents would never approve. Zara's sudden illness and death came to epitomise for a young Beauvoir the oppressive effects of the bourgeois family.

Each of the five stories of *When Things of the Spirit Come First* centres on a different young woman, but all of them are connected in some way. Marcelle Drouffle, whose story begins the collection, is a precociously sensitive spirit with a strong religious impulse. Her story casts an ironic eye on the way in which religious and other beliefs are subverted into different kinds of spiritual activity. Marcelle, who disliked the rough and tumble of childhood, spends much of her time reading in her aunt's lending library: her aunt "would have been astonished to learn the kind of sustenance that her niece's dreaming drew from certain harmless stories." The stories of women, suffering harsh treatment at the hands of arrogant masters, and who eventually win love by their submissiveness, delight the young Marcelle. She identified with the heroine of such tales, and she "was fond of quivering with repentance at the feet of a sinless and beautiful man."

The older Marcelle attempts to change society by educating a recalcitrant working class. This is despite of, or maybe because of, the "physical distress caused by the smell of human sweat and contact with coarse, rough bodies." She becomes engaged to Desroches who was of the opinion "that a Christian should not experience carnal joys before their sanctification by the sacrament of marriage," and even then, he thought, "the degree to which these pleasures were allowable presented a serious moral problem." Still striving for a spiritual ideal Marcelle does not marry Desroches, but falls hopelessly in love with, and eventually marries, a feckless poet, Denis, for whom she feels a strong physical attraction. Her perfect understanding and acceptance of the weaknesses, even perversities, which accompany Denis's genius does not mean, however, that he should not struggle against them. As the disastrous marriage crumbles about her, Marcelle is left to reflect that it was not happiness that had been granted her, but suffering. It was only suffering that could satisfy her heart. "Higher than happiness," she whispered. She would know how to receive it, and transform it, into beauty. Beauvoir's major concern in these short stories is to demonstrate the hold exercised by the moral and spiritual absolutes inculcated from childhood, so that by the time we see Marcelle again, in her sister's story, "Marguerite," it is as a sad and lonely woman willing her husband Denis to come back to her.

Beauvoir recognised the possibility that her own urge to write was a part of that activity which diverted the religious impulse into other sorts of activity. The emergence of Franco's Spain, however, led to some sense of guilt about her apolitical stance. Neither she nor Sartre had written against the French non-interventionist policy, because "their names were not well known, and it wouldn't have done any good." Later, as their fame grew, they both lent their name to a variety of causes. A view of the role of the writer as critic remained with Beauvoir throughout life, and her early collection of stories, *La Femme rompue (The Woman Destroyed)*, which deals with the emotional vulnerability of women, nevertheless retains a measure of critical detachment.

"The Age of Discretion" shows a woman coming to terms with aging. Her lost looks, criticism of her recent book which contained no new ideas, and an estrangement from her son, Philippe, depress her. Her son is unsuited to an intellectual life and finds acceptance from his father, but his mother is unable to reconcile the fact of her son with her own thwarted ambitions for him. She understands that her son's wife, Irene, is destroying him, and does not "want to break down in front of her." The ensuing battle for dominance is doomed to failure. Ultimately, her anger dissipated, she joins her husband for a stay with his mother, who has grown old successfully and re-establishes communication with her husband, at least.

The stories in this collection are typical of Beauvoir's preoccupation with growing old, and were condemned by feminist critics for their concentration on women who were failures of one sort or another. Beauvoir, however, has always retained the right to depict such women, and does not do so without sympathy, teasing the reader to detect the reality which lies between the lines. Finally driven to confront her problems, the protagonist of "The Age of Discretion" decides that she and her husband will "help one another to live through this last adventure. She says, "Will that make it bearable for us? I do not know. Let us hope so. We have no choice in the matter."

—Jan Pilditch

See the essay on "The Woman Destroyed."

BECKETT, Samuel (Barclay). Irish. Born at Foxrock, near Dublin, 13 April 1906. Educated at Ida Elsner's Academy, Stillorgan; Earlsfort House preparatory school; Portora Royal School, County Fermanagh; Trinity College, Dublin (foundation scholar), B.A. in French and Italian 1927, M.A. 1931. Worked at the Irish Red Cross Hospital, St. Lô, France, 1945. Married Suzanne Deschevaux-Dumesnil in 1961 (died 1989). French teacher, Campbell College, Belfast, 1928; lecturer in English, École Normale Supérieure, Paris, 1928–30; lecturer in French, Trinity College, Dublin, 1930–31; closely associated with James Joyce in Paris in the late 1920's and 1930's; settled in Paris, 1937, and wrote chiefly in French from 1945; translated his own work into English. Recipient: *Evening Standard* award, 1955; Obie award, 1958, 1960, 1962, 1964; Italia prize, 1959; International Publishers prize, 1961; Prix Filmcritice, 1965; Tours Film prize, 1966; Nobel prize for literature, 1969; National Grand prize for theatre (France), 1975; New York Drama Critics Circle citation, 1984. D.Litt.: Dublin University, 1959. Member, German Academy of Art; Companion of Literature, Royal Society of Literature, 1984; member, Aosdána, 1986. *Died 22 December 1989.*

PUBLICATIONS

Short Stories and Texts

More Pricks than Kicks.   1934.
Nouvelles et Textes pour rien.   1955; as *Stories and Texts for Nothing*, translated by Beckett and Richard Seaver, 1967.
From an Abandoned Work.   1958.
Imagination morte imaginez.   1965; as *Imagination Dead Imagine*, translated by Beckett, 1965.
Assez.   1966; as *Enough*, translated by Beckett, in *No's Knife*, 1967.
Bing.   1966; as *Ping*, translated by Beckett, in *No's Knife*, 1967.
Têtes-Mortes (includes *D'Un Ouvrage Abandonné, Assez, Bing, Imagination morte imaginez*).   1967; translated by Beckett in *No's Knife*, 1967.
No's Knife: Collected Shorter Prose 1945–1966 (includes *Stories and Texts for Nothing, From an Abandoned Work, Enough, Imagination Dead Imagine, Ping*).   1967.
L'Issue.   1968.
Sans.   1969; as *Lessness*, translated by Beckett, 1971.
Séjour.   1970.
Premier Amour (novella).   1970; as *First Love*, translated by Beckett, 1973.
Le Dépeupleur.   1971; as *The Lost Ones*, translated by Beckett, 1972.

The North. 1972.
First Love and Other Shorts. 1974.
Fizzles. 1976.
For to End Yet Again and Other Fizzles. 1976.
All Strange Away. 1976.
Four Novellas (*First Love, The Expelled, The Calmative, The End*). 1977; as *The Expelled and Other Novellas*, 1980.
Six Residua. 1978.
Company. 1980.
Mal vu mal dit. 1981; as *Ill Seen Ill Said*, translated by Beckett, 1982.
Worstward Ho. 1983.
Stirrings Still. 1988.
Nohow On (includes *Company, Ill Seen Ill Said, Worstward Ho*). 1989.

Novels

Murphy. 1938.
Molloy. 1951; as *Molloy*, translated by Beckett and Patrick Bowles, 1955.
Malone meurt. 1951; as *Malone Dies*, translated by Beckett, 1956.
L'Innommable. 1953; as *The Unnamable*, translated by Beckett, 1958.
Watt (written in English). 1953.
Molloy, Malone Dies, The Unnamable. 1960.
Comment c'est. 1961; as *How It Is*, translated by Beckett, 1964.
Mercier et Camier. 1970; as *Mercier and Camier*, translated by Beckett, 1974.
Abandonné. 1972.
Au loin un oiseau. 1973.
Dream of Fair to Middling Women, edited by Eoin O'Brien and Edith Fournier. 1993.

Plays

Le Kid, with Georges Pelorson (produced 1931).
En Attendant Godot (produced 1953). 1952; as *Waiting for Godot: Tragicomedy*, translated by Beckett (produced 1955), 1954.
Fin de partie: suivi de Acte sans paroles, music by John Beckett (produced 1957). 1957; as *Endgame: A Play in One Act; Followed by Act Without Words: A Mime for One Player*, translated by Samuel Beckett (*Endgame* produced 1958; *Act Without Words* produced 1960), 1958.
All That Fall (broadcast 1957; produced 1965). 1957.
Krapp's Last Tape (produced 1958). With *Embers*, 1959.
Embers (broadcast 1959). With *Krapp's Last Tape*, 1959.
Act Without Words II (produced 1959). In *Krapp's Last Tape and Other Dramatic Pieces*, 1960.
La Manivelle/The Old Tune (bilingual edition), from the play by Robert Pinget. 1960; Beckett's text only (broadcast 1960), in *Plays 1*, by Pinget, 1963.
Krapp's Last Tape and Other Dramatic Pieces (includes *All That Fall, Embers, Act Without Words I and II*). 1960.
Happy Days (produced 1961). 1961; bilingual edition, edited by James Knowlson, 1978.
Words and Music, music by John Beckett (broadcast 1962). In *Play and Two Short Pieces for Radio*, 1964.
Cascando, music by Marcel Mihalovici (broadcast in French, 1963). In *Dramatische Dichtungen 1*, 1963; as *Cascando: A Radio Piece for Music and Voice*, translated by Beckett (broadcast 1964; in *Beckett 3*, produced 1970), in *Play and Two Short Pieces for Radio*, 1964.

Play (as *Spiel*, produced 1963; as *Play*, 1964). In *Play and Two Short Pieces for Radio*, 1964.
Play and Two Short Pieces for Radio. 1964.
Eh Joe (televised 1966; produced 1978). In *Eh Joe and Other Writings*, 1967.
Va et vient: Dramaticule (as *Kommen und Gehen*, produced 1966; as *Va et vient*, produced 1966). 1966; as *Come and Go: Dramaticule*, translated by Beckett (produced 1968), 1967.
Eh Joe and Other Writings (includes *Act Without Words II* and *Film*). 1967.
Cascando and Other Short Dramatic Pieces (includes *Words and Music, Eh Joe, Play, Come and Go, Film*). 1968.
Film. 1969.
Breath (part of *Oh! Calcutta!*, produced 1969). In *Breath and Other Shorts*, 1971.
Breath and Other Shorts (includes *Come and Go, Act Without Words I and II*, and the prose piece *From an Abandoned Work*). 1971.
Not I (produced 1972). 1973.
Ghost Trio (as *Tryst*, televised 1976). In *Ends and Odds*, 1976.
That Time (produced 1976). 1976.
Footfalls (produced 1976). 1976.
Ends and Odds: Eight New Dramatic Pieces (includes *Not I, That Time, Footfalls, Ghost Trio, Theatre I and II, Radio I and II*). 1976; as *Ends and Odds: Plays and Sketches* (includes *Not I, That Time, Footfalls, Ghost Trio, . . . but the clouds . . . , Theatre I and II, Radio I and II*), 1977.
Rough for Radio (broadcast 1976). As *Radio II*, in *Ends and Odds*, 1976.
Theatre I and II (produced 1985). In *Ends and Odds*, 1976.
A Piece of Monologue (produced 1980). In *Rockaby and Other Short Pieces*, 1981.
Rockaby (produced 1981). In *Rockaby and Other Short Pieces*, 1981.
Rockaby and Other Short Pieces. 1981.
Ohio Impromptu (produced 1981). In *Rockaby and Other Short Pieces*, 1981.
Catastrophe et autres dramaticules: Cette fois, Solo, Berceuse, Impromptu d'Ohio. 1982.
Three Occasional Pieces (includes *A Piece of Monologue, Rockaby, Ohio Impromptu*). 1982.
Quad (as *Quadrat 1+2*, televised in German 1982; as *Quad*, televised 1982). In *Collected Shorter Plays*, 1984.
Catastrophe (produced 1982). In *Collected Shorter Plays*, 1984.
Nacht und Träume (televised 1983). In *Collected Shorter Plays*, 1984.
What Where (as *Was Wo*, produced in German, 1983; produced in English, 1983). In *Collected Shorter Plays*, 1984.
Collected Shorter Plays. 1984.
Ohio Impromptu, Catastrophe, and What Where. 1984.
The Complete Dramatic Works. 1986.

Screenplay: *Film*, 1965.

Radio Plays: *All That Fall*, 1957; *Embers*, 1959; *The Old Tune*, from a play by Robert Pinget, 1960; *Words and Music*, 1962; *Cascando*, 1963; *Rough for Radio*, 1976.

Television Plays: *Eh Joe*, 1966; *Tryst*, 1976; *Shades* (*Ghost Trio, Not I, . . . but the clouds . . .*), 1977; *Quadrat 1+2*, 1982 (Germany); *Quad*, 1982; *Nacht und Träume*, 1983.

Verse

Whoroscope. 1930.
Echo's Bones and Other Precipitates. 1935.
Gedichte (collected poems in English and French, with German translations). 1959.
Poems in English. 1961.
Poèmes. 1968.
Collected Poems in English and French. 1977; revised edition, as *Collected Poems 1930–1978,* 1984.

Other

"Dante . . . Bruno. Vico . . Joyce," in *Our Exagmination round His Factification for Incamination of Work in Progress.* 1929.
Proust. 1931; with *Three Dialogues with Georges Duthuit.* 1965.
Bram van Velde, with Georges Duthuit and Jacques Putman. 1958; as *Bram van Velde,* translated by Beckett and Olive Classe, 1960.
A Beckett Reader. 1967.
I Can't Go On: A Selection from the Work of Beckett, edited by Richard Seaver. 1976.
Disjecta: Miscellaneous Writings and a Dramatic Fragment, edited by Ruby Cohn. 1983.
Collected Shorter Prose 1945–1980. 1984.
Happy Days: The Production Notebook, edited by James Knowlson. 1985.
Production Notebooks, edited by James Knowlson. 3 vols., 1990.
As the Story Was Told: Uncollected and Late Prose. 1990.
The Theatrical Notebooks of Beckett, edited by James Knowlson. 3 vols., 1991–93.

Translator, *Anthology of Mexican Poetry,* edited by Octavio Paz. 1958.
Translator, with others, *Selected Poems,* by Alain Bosquet. 1963.
Translator, *Zone,* by Guillaume Apollinaire. 1972.
Translator, *Drunken Boat,* by Arthur Rimbaud, edited by James Knowlson and Felix Leakey. 1977.
Translator, with others, *No Matter No Fact.* 1988.

*

Bibliography: *Beckett: His Works and His Critics: An Essay in Bibliography* by Raymond Federman and John Fletcher, 1970 (through 1966); *Beckett: Checklist and Index of His Published Works 1967–1976* by Robin John Davis, 1979; *Beckett: A Reference Guide* by Cathleen Culotta Andonian, 1988.

Critical Studies: *Beckett: A Critical Study,* 1961, revised edition, 1968, and *A Reader's Guide to Beckett,* 1973 both by Hugh Kenner; *Beckett: The Comic Gamut,* 1962, *Back to Beckett,* 1974, and *Just Play: Beckett's Theater,* 1980, all by Ruby Cohn, and *Beckett: A Collection of Criticism,* 1975, and *Waiting for Godot: A Casebook,* 1987, both edited by Cohn; *Beckett: The Language of Self* by Frederick J. Hoffman, 1962; *Beckett* by William York Tindall, 1964; *Beckett* by Richard N. Coe, 1964; *The Novels of Beckett,* 1964, and *Beckett's Art,* 1967, both by John Fletcher; *Journey to Chaos: Beckett's Early Fiction* by Raymond Federman, 1965; *Beckett: A Collection of Critical Essays* edited by Martin Esslin, 1965; *Beckett at 60: A Festschrift*

edited by John Calder, 1967; *Beckett* by Ronald Hayman, 1968, revised edition, 1980; *Beckett Now: Critical Approaches to His Novels, Poetry, and Plays* edited by Melvin J. Friedman, 1970; *Beckett: A Study of His Novels* by Eugene Webb, 1970; *Beckett: A Study of His Plays* by John Fletcher and John Spurling, 1972, revised edition, 1978, as *Beckett the Playwright,* 1985; *Angels of Darkness: Dramatic Effect in Beckett* by Colin Duckworth, 1972; *The Fiction of Beckett: Form and Effect* by H. Porter Abbott, 1973; *Beckett* by A. Alvarez, 1973; *Beckett the Shape Changer* edited by Katharine J. Worth, 1975; *Art and the Artist in the Works of Beckett* by Hannah Case Copeland, 1975; *Beckett's Dramatic Language* by James Eliopulos, 1975; *Beckett and Broadcasting: A Study of the Works of Beckett for and in Radio and Television* by Clas Zilliacus, 1976; *Beckett* by John Pilling, 1976; *Beckett/Beckett* by Vivian Mercier, 1977; *A Student's Guide to the Plays of Beckett* by Beryl S. Fletcher, 1978, revised edition, with John Fletcher, 1985; *Beckett: A Biography* by Deirdre Bair, 1978; *The Shape of Paradox: An Essay on Waiting for Godot* by Bert O. Slates, 1978; *Frescoes of the Skull: The Later Prose and Drama of Beckett* edited by John Pilling and James Knowlson, 1979; *Beckett: The Critical Heritage* edited by Raymond Federman and Lawrence Graver, 1979; *The Beckett Manuscripts: A Critical Study* by Richard L. Admussen, 1979; *The Transformations of Godot* by Frederick Busi, 1980; *Waiting for Death: The Philosophical Significance of Beckett's En attendant Godot* by Ramona Cormier, 1980; *Beckett and the Voice of Species: A Study of the Prose Fiction* by Eric P. Levy, 1980; *Accommodating the Chaos: Beckett's Nonrelational Art* by J.E. Dearlove, 1982; *Abysmal Games in the Novels of Beckett* by Angela B. Moorjani, 1982; *Beckett: Humanistic Perspectives* edited by Morris Beja, S.E. Gontarski, and Pierre Astier, 1983; *Beckett* by Charles Lyons, 1983; *Beckett's Real Silence* by Hélène L. Baldwin, 1983; *Canters and Chronicles: The Use of Narrative in the Plays of Beckett and Harold Pinter* by Kristin Morrison, 1983; *The Development of Beckett's Fiction* by Rubin Rabinovitz, 1984; *Beckett's Theaters: Interpretations for Performance* by Sidney Homan, 1984; *Beckett and the Meaning of Being: A Study in Ontological Parable* by Lance St. John Butler, 1984; *Beckett on File* edited by Virginia Cooke, 1985; *The Intent of Undoing in Beckett's Dramatic Texts* by S.E. Gontarski, 1985, and *On Beckett: Essays and Criticism* edited by Gontarski, 1986; *Understanding Beckett: A Study of Monologue and Gesture in the Works of Beckett* by Peter Gidal, 1986; *Beckett at 80/Beckett in Context* edited by Enoch Brater, 1986, and *Beyond Minimalism: Beckett's Late Style in the Theater,* 1987, and *Why Beckett,* 1989, both by Brater; *Beckett* by Linda Ben-Zvi, 1986, and *Women in Beckett: Performance and Critical Perspectives* edited by Ben-Zvi, 1990; *As No Other Dare Fail: For Beckett on His 80th Birthday,* 1986; *The Broken Window: Beckett's Dramatic Perspective* by Jane Alison Hale, 1987; *Beckett's Later Fiction and Drama: Texts for Company* edited by James Acheson and Kateryna Arthur, 1987; *Beckett's New Worlds: Style in Metafiction* by Susan D. Brienza, 1987; *Beckett Translating/Translating Beckett* edited by Alan Warren Friedman, Charles Rossman, and Dina Sherzer, 1987; *Beckett in the Theatre: The Author as Practical Playwright and Director 1: From Waiting for Godot to Krapp's Last Tape* by Dougald McMillan and Martha Fehsenfeld, 1988; *Myth and Ritual in the Plays of Beckett* by Katherine H. Burkman, 1988; *Beckett's Critical Complicity: Carnival, Contestation and Tradition* by Sylvie Debevec Henning, 1988; *Beckett: Repetition, Theory, and Text* by Stephen Connor, 1988; *Beckett and Babel: An Investigation into the Status of the*

Bilingual Work by Brian T. Fitch, 1988; *Theatre of Shadows: Beckett's Drama 1956–1976* by Rosemary Pountney, 1988; *Beckett: Teleplays* (exhibition catalogue), 1988; *The Humour of Beckett* by Valerie Topsfield, 1988; *Beckett* by Andrew K. Kennedy, 1989; *Beckett: Waiting for Godot* by Lawrence Graver, 1989; *Beckett in Performance* by Jonathan Kalb, 1989; *Waiting for Godot: Form in Movement* by Thomas Cousineau, 1990; *Rethinking Beckett: A Collection of Critical Essays* edited by Lance St. John Butler and Robin J. Davies, 1990; *Beckett's Fiction: In Different Words* by Leslie Hill, 1990; *Beckett's Self-Referential Drama* by Shimon Levy, 1990; *The World of Beckett* edited by Joseph H. Smith, 1990; *Understanding Beckett* by Alan Astro, 1990; *Unwording the World: Beckett's Prose Works after the Nobel Prize* by Carla Locatelli, 1990; *Paradox and Desire in Beckett's Fiction* by David Watson, 1990.

* * *

Samuel Beckett wrote plays, novels, poems, some criticism, and a substantial body of short fiction during a career that spanned the Modernist and Postmodernist periods. His work divides fairly neatly into early, middle, and late sections corresponding roughly to prewar, postwar, and post-1960. Equally at home in English and French, Beckett translated the majority of his work (though not all of his short fiction) from one language into the other.

His first short fiction, which remained untranslated, was the English collection *More Pricks than Kicks*, a series of stories about one Belacqua Shua, a down-at-heel student and a sort of anti-gallant about Dublin. Probably quarried from the unpublished novel *A Dream of Fair to Middling Women*, the stories are written in a super-erudite, even Baroque prose, and depend for their effect on highly self-conscious tricks of language, zany characterisation, and amusing or grotesque situations. The first story in the collection, widely regarded as the best, is "Dante and the Lobster." The other stories follow Belacqua through parties, affairs, even a marriage, to his death on the operating table. The stories are linked together, thus, more strongly than those of James Joyce's *Dubliners*, on which *More Pricks than Kicks* is to some degree modelled—the Dublin setting and the themes of knowledge, religion, drink, and the flesh are what the two collections have in common, Beckett was an associate of Joyce's in Paris at the time he published his volume.

More Pricks is the only work of shorter fiction Beckett wrote in his early period; it is the work of a young man involved in the literary experiments of his time and it fits well with his novel of the period, *Murphy*. It has linguistic associations with Beckett's poetry, much of which also was written during this time.

During his middle period (the years that produced the trilogy of novels and the plays that made Beckett famous), Beckett wrote a series of short fictions that act as an excellent introduction to his major work. *Premier Amour* (*First Love*), the trio of novellas (*The Expelled*, *The Calmative*, and *The End*) and, above all, the *Novelles et Textes pour rien* (*Stories and Texts for Nothing*) show that Beckett had found his voice, a voice, as he said, in which monologue predominates. The style here is less ornate and the purpose less satirical than in the early work and the central figure of the alienated, elderly, masculine consciousness chewing the long cud of its memories more obvious. The narrators of these pieces are, for the first time, truly "Beckettian" in that they resemble the tramps in *Waiting for Godot* or Krapp in *Krapp's Last Tape*.

It is principally the voice or tone that we remember in these short fictions. It is the same tone that we hear in the trilogy—sardonic, desperate, stoical, more than a little mad. The prewar work is odd but anchored in reality while the postwar work enters into a new realm altogether. Elements of the real world are recognisable, such as hansom cabs, railway stations, fathers, home; but overall these are dream-like monologues in which the focus is on the consciousness performing its narrative task. Rejection of the world is a theme hard to miss, together with a sense of the world rejecting the protagonist. Decay of body and mind, inability to understand the world, and a sense of loss permeate these fictions.

Beckett was in an impasse by the end of the trilogy (a position signalled in the *Texts for Nothing*), and his way forward was to be through short plays and short fictional texts. It is in his late period that he becomes one of the most significant writers of short prose in the postwar world. It is hard to say what genre his later texts belong to; the plays, however bizarre (*Not I* consists of a mouth babbling alone on the stage) are clearly plays but the fictions can be read as prose-poems, or read aloud in performance versions, or regarded simply as tests. They test the limits of our literary categories. They tend to be monologues but now the consciousness is more dispersed, less definite, less identifiable, than in the earlier pieces. Most characteristic in this respect is *Company* (the only one of these later pieces written only in English) with its opening sentence ("A voice comes to one in the dark"). The title of the earlier version, *Imagination Dead Imagine*, is the same title as its first sentence. Here a consciousness, an imagination, explores a series of often-repeated words, circling round and round a few givens as if obsessively unable to abandon them.

In all Beckett's late prose familiar themes are picked up, kneaded into slightly different shapes, abandoned (a characteristic title is "From an Abandoned Work"). Beckett found these themes during his middle period and developed them: decay, age, frailty, mathematical calculations, the inability to remain silent, loneliness, and imprisonment. Typical is *The Lost Ones*, a text set in a cylinder; the inhabitants of the cylinder move through a range of quasi-ritual actions and gestures in their attempts to escape from their world; the light and heat vary in intensity; no escape is possible; some of the inhabitants give up and seem to die. We are a very long way indeed here from the stylistic fireworks of *More Pricks than Kicks*.

Beckett's last pieces were shorter fictions in this same vein. As late as December 1988, he published *Stirrings Still*, in which the same old cuds are chewed and the same haunting tone achieved. The title here is appropriate; Beckett saw himself for years as producing left-over texts and he called them "fizzles," "ends and odds," "residua," and "stirrings." Here the human condition is seen, or heard, at its last gasp, yet there is a stoical strength present that can hearten us against the odds.

—Lance St. John Butler

See the essay on "Dante and the Lobster."

———

BELLOW, Saul. American. Born in Lachine, Quebec, Canada, 10 June 1915; grew up in Montreal; moved with his family to Chicago, 1924. Educated at Tuley High School, Chicago, graduated 1933; University of Chicago, 1933-35; Northwestern University, Evanston, Illinois, 1935–37, B.S. (honors) in sociology and anthropology 1937; did graduate work in anthropology at University of Wisconsin, Madison, 1937. Served in the United States Merchant Marine, 1944–45. Married 1) Anita Goshkin in 1937 (divorced), one son; 2) Alexandra Tschacbasov in 1956 (divorced), one son; 3) Susan Glassman in 1961 (divorced), one son; 4) Alexandra Ionescu Tulcea in 1975 (divorced 1986); 5) Janis Freedman in 1989. Teacher, Pestalozzi-Froebel Teachers College, Chicago, 1938–42; member of the editorial department, "Great Books" Project, *Encyclopaedia Britannica,* Chicago, 1943–44; free-lance editor and reviewer, New York, 1945–46; instructor, 1946, and assistant professor of English, 1948–49, University of Minnesota, Minneapolis; visiting lecturer, New York University, 1950–52; creative writing fellow, Princeton University, New Jersey, 1952–53; member of the English faculty, Bard College, Annandale-on-Hudson, New York, 1953–54; associate professor of English, University of Minnesota, 1954–59; visiting professor of English, University of Puerto Rico, Rio Piedras, 1961; Romanes Lecturer, 1990; professor, and chairman, 1970–76, Committee on Social Thought, University of Chicago, from 1962; now Gruiner Distinguished Services Professor. Co-editor, *The Noble Savage,* New York, then Cleveland, 1960–62. Fellow, Academy for Policy Study, 1966; Fellow, Branford College, Yale University, New Haven, Connecticut. Recipient: Guggenheim fellowship, 1948, 1955; American Academy grant, 1952, and gold medal, 1977; National Book award, 1954, 1965, 1971; Ford grant, 1959, 1960; Friends of Literature award, 1960; James L. Dow award, 1964; International Literary prize, 1965; Jewish Heritage award, 1968; Formentor prize, 1970; Nobel prize for literature, 1976; Pulitzer prize, 1976; Neil Gunn International fellowship, 1977; Brandeis University Creative Arts award, 1978; Malaparte award (Italy), 1984; Scanno award (Italy), 1988; National Medal of Arts, 1988. D.Litt.: Northwestern University, 1962; Bard College, 1963; Litt.D.: New York University, 1970; Harvard University, Cambridge, Massachusetts, 1972; Yale University, 1972; McGill University, Montreal, 1973; Brandeis University, Waltham, Massachusetts, 1973; Hebrew Union College, Cincinnati, 1976; Trinity College, Dublin, 1976. Chevalier, 1968. and Commander, 1985. Order of Arts and Letters (France); Member, American Academy, 1970; Commander, Legion of Honor (France), 1983. Lives in Chicago.

PUBLICATIONS

Short Stories

Seize the Day, with *Three Short Stories and a One-Act Play.* 1956.
Mosby's Memoirs and Other Stories. 1968.
Him with His Foot in His Mouth and Other Stories. 1984.
A Theft (novella). 1989.
The Bellarosa Connection. 1989.
Something To Remember Me By: Three Tales. 1992.

Novels

Dangling Man. 1944.
The Victim. 1947.

The Adventures of Augie March. 1953.
Henderson the Rain King. 1959.
Herzog. 1964.
Mr. Sammler's Planet. 1970.
Humboldt's Gift. 1975.
The Dean's December. 1982.
More Die of Heartbreak. 1987.

Plays

The Wrecker (televised 1964). Included in *Seize the Day,* 1956.
Scenes from Humanitas: A Farce, in *Partisan Review.* 1962.
The Last Analysis (produced 1964). 1965.
Under the Weather (includes "Out from Under," "A Wen," and "Orange Souffle") (produced 1966; as *The Bellow Plays,* produced 1966). "A Wen" published in *Esquire,* January 1965; in *Traverse Plays,* edited by Jim Haynes, 1966; "Orange Souffle" published in *Traverse Plays,* 1966; in *Best Short Plays of the World Theatre 1968-1973,* edited by Stanley Richards. 1973.

Television Play: *The Wrecker,* 1964.

Other

Dessins, by Jesse Reichek; text by Bellow and Christian Zervos. 1960.
Recent American Fiction: A Lecture. 1963.
Like You're Nobody: The Letters of Louis Gallo to Saul Bellow, 1961-62. 1966.
Plus Oedipus-Schmoedipus, The Story That Started It All. 1966.
Technology and the Frontiers of Knowledge, with others. 1973.
The Portable Saul Bellow, edited by Gabriel Josipovici. 1974.
To Jerusalem and Back: A Personal Account. 1976.
Nobel Lecture. 1977.

Editor, *Great Jewish Short Stories.* 1963.

*

Bibliography: *Bellow: A Comprehensive Bibliography* by B.A. Sokoloff and Mark E. Posner, 1973; *Bellow, His Works and His Critics: An Annotated International Bibliography* by Marianne Nault, 1977; *Bellow: A Bibliography of Secondary Sources* by F. Lercangee, 1977; *Bellow: A Reference Guide* by Robert G. Noreen, 1978; *Bellow: An Annotated Bibliography* by Gloria L. Cronin, second edition, 1987.

Critical Studies: *Bellow* by Tony Tanner, 1965; *Bellow* by Earl Rovit, 1967, and *Bellow: A Collection of Critical Essays* edited by Rovit, 1975; *Bellow: A Critical Essay* by Robert Detweiler, 1967; *Bellow and the Critics* edited by Irving Malin, 1967, and *Bellow's Fiction* by Malin, 1969; *Bellow: In Defense of Man* by John Jacob Clayton, 1968, revised edition, 1979; *Bellow* by Robert R. Dutton, 1971, revised edition, 1982; *Bellow* by Brigitte Scheer-Schazler, 1973; *Bellow's Enigmatic Laughter* by Sarah Blacher Cohen, 1974; *Whence the Power? The Artistry and Humanity of Bellow* by M. Gilbert Porter, 1974; *Bellow: The Problem of Affirmation* by Chirantan Kulshrestha, 1978; *Critical*

Essays on Bellow edited by Stanley Trachtenberg, 1979; *Quest for the Human: An Exploration of Bellow's Fiction* by Eusebio L. Rodrigues, 1981; *Bellow* by Malcolm Bradbury, 1983; *Bellow: Vision and Revision* by Daniel Fuchs, 1984; *Bellow and History* by Judie Newman, 1984; *A Sort of Columbus: The American Voyages of Bellow's Fiction* by Jeanne Braham, 1984; *On Bellow's Planet: Readings from the Dark Side* by Jonathan Wilson, 1984; *Bellow* by Robert F. Kiernan, 1988; *Bellow in the 1980's* edited by Gloria Cronin and L.H. Goldman, 1989; *Bellow and the Decline of Humanism* by Michael K. Glenday, 1990; *Bellow: Against the Grain* by Ellen Pifer, 1990; *Bellow: A Biography of the Imagination* by Ruth Miller, 1991.

* * *

Although the novel remains Saul Bellow's most congenial form, the one most hospitable to the range of ideas and thickly layered style that are his trademarks, his two collections of short stories prove that Bellow is not only a consummate story writer but also an author well served by the constraints of the short story. Recent novels such as *The Dean's December* or *More Die of Heartbreak* suffer from Bellow's growing impatience with showing rather than telling, and his increasing habit of allowing stump speeches to wax ever longer and more tedious.

By contrast, Bellows short stories reminds us of how humanly rich his fiction can be. As a character in "Cousins" puts it, "Why were the Jews such avid anthropologists? . . . They may have believed that they were demystifiers, that science was their motive and that their ultimate aim was to increase universalism. But I don't see it that way myself. A truer explanation is the nearness of ghettos to the sphere of Revelation, an easy move for the mind from rotting street and rancid dishes, a direct ascent into transcendence."

Bellow's short fiction, moves easily from the quotidian to the higher realms. Childhood memory retains a special poignancy (one thinks of the Napolean Street sections of *Herzog*), and there is the same sense of anthropological accuracy coupled with transcendental musing in such stories as "The Old System," "Mosby's Memoirs," "A Silver Dish," and "Cousins." Each is concerned with the mysteries of family and those painful steps one takes through memory and meditation toward reconciliation.

If a novel like *The Dean's December* tries to make sense of Chicago's corruption, its noisy, public face, a story like "A Silver Dish" announces its intentions in quieter, more reflective tones: "What do you do about death—in this case, the death of an old father? [Woody Selbst, the story's protagonist asks] . . . How, against a contemporary background, do you mourn an octogenarian father, nearly blind, his heart enlarged, his lungs filling with fluid, who creeps, stumbles, gives off the odors, the moldiness or gasiness, of old men." Selbst, a tile contractor, may be an exception (the feisty Hattie Waggoner of "Leaving the Yellow House" is another) to the beleaguered intellectuals who figure in stories such as "Zeitland: By a Character Witness" (modeled on Bellow's boyhood chum, Isaac Rosenfeld), "What Kind of Day Did You Have?" (a novella revolving around a New York Jewish intellectual who is a dead ringer for the art critic, Harold Rosenberg), or "Him With His Foot in His Mouth" (a tale about an academic whose biting sarcasm is balanced by his capacity for lingering regret). Memory and the heart's deepest need for love is what gives these protagonists—and their stories—enormous power.

This is particularly true of "The Old System," a story in which Dr. Samuel Braun, an aging scientist, spends a "thoughtful day" remembering a family quarrel between his cousins Isaac and Tina. Braun discovers, much to his surprise, that he had loved them after all. But, like Bellow, he cannot keep from asking what in this low, dishonest time speaks for humans.

In "Mosby's Memoirs" Dr. Willis Mosby also broods about the past, but his is a slightly different problem. He is in Mexico, desperately trying to write his memoirs and finding himself stuck at the point where one ought "to put some humor in." At first the story of Lustgarten serves as comic relief, a way of priming the pump. After all, Lustgarten was the archetypal *schlemiel*, a schemer whose plans for success always managed to go awry. A former shoe salesman from New Jersey, Lustgarten had belonged to a seemingly infinite number of fanatical, bolshevisitic groups. Lustgarten had also given up politics, but his luck was no better as a capitalist than it had been as a Marxist. For example, he was an incompetent manipulator of the black market and had once imported a Cadillac only to find himself without a buyer or even enough money for gasoline. On another occasion he visited Yugoslavia expecting to be given V.I.P. treatment, only to end up on a labor brigade in the mountains. Like "A Father-to-Be" (in which a prospective husband imagines, in a dream that turns nightmare, what a projected son might be like), "Mosby's Memoirs" is a tale of extended secret-sharing. Readers of Bellow novels, such as *The Victim, Humbolt's Gift*, or *More Die of Heartbreak*, are familiar with this impulse toward psychic doubling.

In two stories "Looking for Mr. Green" and "The Gonzaga Manuscripts," Bellow replaces characters who brood about the past with protagonists whose quests expand into symbolic meaning. For the George Grebe of "Looking for Mr. Green," the search involves delivering a government check to an invalid named Green. At first glance it looks like an easy job: Grebe is more conscientious than the usual run of state employees, and, moreover, anxious to do well. But his search for the elusive Mr. Green turns out to be harder than he had imagined as Bellow's plot moves him through a series of irritations to a full-blown obsession. Nobody in Chicago's Negro district will give him any help and, soon, looking for Mr. Green takes on the look of a Kafkaesque problem. The story itself ends on a properly ambivalent note: Grebe hands over the check to a woman without the certainty that she is, in fact, Mrs. Green or that he has even found the right apartment.

In "The Gonzaga Manuscripts," a sense of quest takes Clarence Feiler to Madrid, in search of some lost manuscripts by the Spanish poet, Gonzaga. To Feiler, Gonzaga's poetry has been the only truly meaningful thing in his life. But (alas) Clarence soon discovers that the world at large cares very little about Gonzaga's poems, either published or in unpublished manuscript. At every turn he reminds himself of the sacredness of his mission, of how Gonzaga's poems must be recovered in the true spirit of the poet himself, but it soon becomes clear that Gonzaga's vision makes for better poetry than it does for a life.

The results are a series of serio-comic complications: Feiler is surrounded by the insensitive and the slightly clandestine. At various points he is cast as the ugly American by British guests at his hotel or as a CIA agent by his black market contacts. Worse, Gonzaga's manuscripts are lost forever (presumably buried with the woman to whom they were dedicated), but the quest itself has had its effects on Feiler. He returns to the hotel empty-handed, knowing full well the scorn he will face at dinner, and yet, curiously enough, he also knows that he will be able to face his detractors—this time, without need of the psychic crutch his quest had become.

Bellow's characteristic style is a marriage of gritty urban particulars and an itch for transcendental release, a blending of high brow ideas and tough guy postures, classical allusions and Yiddish quips. In short, he turned deliberate roughening of syntax into a personal voice, and in the process, added a distinctive note to American prose rhythms. Bellow made a serious literature about the memories and concontinuities of Jewish-American life possible in much the way that Faulkner made it possible to write about the South.

—Sanford Pinsker

See the essays on "Looking for Mr. Green" and *Seize the Day.*

BENÉT, Stephen Vincent. American. Born in Bethlehem, Pennsylvania, 22 July 1898; brother of William Rose Benét. Educated at Hitchcock Military Academy, Jacinto, California, 1910–11; Summerville Academy; Yale University, New Haven, Connecticut (chairman, *Yale Literary Magazine,* 1918), 1915–18, 1919–20, A.B. 1919, M.A. 1920; the Sorbonne, Paris, 1920–21. Married Rosemary Carr in 1921; one son and two daughters. Worked for the State Department, Washington, D.C., 1918, and for advertising agency, New York, 1919; lived in Paris, 1926–29; during 1930's and early 1940's was an active lecturer and radio propagandist for the liberal cause. Editor, Yale Younger Poets series. Recipient: Poetry Society of America prize, 1921; Guggenheim fellowship, 1926; Pulitzer prize, 1929, 1944; O. Henry award, 1932, 1937, 1940; Shelley Memorial award, 1933; American Academy gold medal, 1943. Member, 1929, and vice-president, National Institute of Arts and Letters. *Died 13 March 1943.*

PUBLICATIONS

Collections

Selected Poetry and Prose, edited by Basil Davenport. 1960.

Short Stories

The Barefoot Saint.   1929.
The Litter of Rose Leaves.   1930.
Thirteen O'Clock: Stories of Several Worlds.   1937.
The Devil and Daniel Webster.   1937.
Johnny Pye and the Fool-Killer.   1938.
Tales Before Midnight.   1939.
Short Stories: A Selection.   1942.
O'Halloran's Luck and Other Short Stories.   1944.
The Last Circle: Stories and Poems.   1946.

Novels

The Beginning of Wisdom.   1921.
Young People's Pride.   1922.
Jean Huguenot.   1923.

Spanish Bayonet.   1926.
James Shore's Daughter.   1934.

Verse

The Drug-Shop; or, Endymion in Edmonstoun.   1917.
Young Adventure.   1918.
Heavens and Earth.   1920.
The Ballad of William Sycamore 1790–1880.   1923.
King David.   1923.
Tiger Joy.   1925.
John Brown's Body.   1928.
Ballads and Poems 1915–1930.   1931.
A Book of Americans, with Rosemary Benét.   1933.
Burning City.   1936.
The Ballad of the Duke's Mercy.   1939.
Nightmare at Noon.   1940.
Listen to the People: Independence Day 1941.   1941.
Western Star.   1943.

Plays

Five Men and Pompey: A Series of Dramatic Portraits. 1915.
Nerves, with John Farrar (produced 1924).
That Awful Mrs. Eaton, with John Farrar (produced 1924).
The Headless Horseman, music by Douglas Moore (broadcast 1937).   1937.
The Devil and Daniel Webster, music by Douglas Moore, from the story by Benét (produced 1938).   1939.
Elementals (broadcast 1940–41).   In *Best Broadcasts of 1940–41,* edited by Max Wylie, 1942.
Freedom's a Hard Bought Thing (broadcast 1941).   In *The Free Company Presents,* edited by James Boyd, 1941.
Nightmare at Noon, in *The Treasury Star Parade,* edited by William A. Bacher.   1942.
A Child Is Born (broadcast 1942).   1942.
They Burned the Books (broadcast 1942).   1942.
All That Money Can Buy (screenplay), with Dan Totheroh, in *Twenty Best Film Plays,* edited by John Gassner and Dudley Nichols.   1943.
We Stand United and Other Radio Scripts (includes *A Child Is Born, The Undefended Border, Dear Adolf, Listen to the People, Thanksgiving Day—1941, They Burned the Books, A Time to Reap, Toward the Century of Modern Man, Your Army*).   1945.

Screenplays: *Abraham Lincoln,* with Gerrit Lloyd, 1930; *Cheers for Miss Bishop,* with Adelaide Heilbron and Sheridan Gibney, 1941; *All That Money Can Buy,* with Dan Totheroh, 1941.

Radio Plays: *The Headless Horseman,* 1937; *The Undefended Border,* 1940; *We Stand United,* 1940; *Elementals,* 1940–41; *Listen to the People,* 1941; *Thanksgiving Day— 1941,* 1941; *Freedom's a Hard Bought Thing,* 1941; *Nightmare at Noon; A Child Is Born,* 1942; *Dear Adolf,* 1942; *They Burned the Books,* 1942; *A Time to Reap,* 1942; *Toward the Century of Modern Man,* 1942; *Your Army,* 1944.

Other

A Summons to the Free.   1941.
Selected Works.   2 vols., 1942.
America.   1944.
Benét on Writing: A Great Writer's Letter of Advice to a Young Beginner, edited by George Abbe.   1964.

Selected Letters, edited by Charles A. Fenton.   1960.

Editor, with others, *The Yale Book of Student Verse 1910–1919.*   1919.

Editor, with Monty Woolley, *Tamburlaine the Great,* by Christopher Marlowe.   1919.

*

Bibliography: by Gladys Louise Maddocks, in *Bulletin of Bibliography* 20, September 1951 and April 1952.

Critical Studies: *Benét* by William Rose Benét, 1943; *Benét: The Life and Times of an American Man of Letters* by Charles A. Fenton, 1958; *Benét* by Parry Stroud, 1962.

*   *   *

Stephen Vincent Benét is a writer destined to be remembered for one or two works. Though he wrote 44 books, several plays, movie scripts, and opera libretti, and during his lifetime was one of the most famous American poets, his reputation rests on his attempt at a major American epic, *John Brown's Body,* and the short story "The Devil and Daniel Webster." Since his death, declining interest in fiction that is patriotic or espouses what William Faulkner termed "the old verities and truths of the heart" have led to Benét's being labeled old-fashioned, chauvinistic, and consigned to a minor position in the pantheon of American letters.

Not only the quantity of his short fiction, which covers the spectrum of American life in a quieter, simpler age, but also his range of styles, narrative methods, and subject matter make Benét worthy of attention. His fiction often echoes Emerson, Thoreau, and Whitman in its celebration of America: the dreams upon which the country is based; its potentials; its ethnic diversity. His use of irony reflects the influence of Hawthorne and, to a lesser extent, Poe. His prose, marked by lyrical style that is at once graceful and powerful, shows the influence of his own skill as a poet.

Benét's numerous short stories fall into four categories: stories of American history, stories in a Whitmanesque tradition celebrating America's ethnic and cultural diversity, contemporary narratives, and fantasies. The categories sometimes overlap, for historical and contemporary tales often partake of the fantastic, and the positive Americanism of Whitman is ubiquitous in Benét's fiction, but the four types are in many ways discrete.

Benét's historical narratives deal with a wide range of subjects and characters related to the past. In "A Tooth for Paul Revere," a satiric and fantastic retelling of the famous midnight ride, a toothache sets the American Revolution in motion. The fictional Lige Butterwick, who experiences several rebuffs reminiscent of those suffered by the protagonist of Hawthorne's "My Kinsman, Major Molineux," seeks out Paul Revere to have a tooth replaced by a silver one. Inadvertently he is involved in events preceding the battle of Lexington to such an extent that Revere asks of him, "Do you know what you've done? You've let out the American Revolution." In "The Angel Was a Yankee," a variation on "The Devil and Daniel Webster," P.T. Barnum outwits a Pennsylvania farmer who has captured an angel and wants to sell him to a circus. Barnum is himself fooled by the Yankee ingenuity of the angel, who

flies away before he can be displayed in "The Greatest Show on Earth."

Benét's stories in the Whitmanesque tradition portray in heroic stances protagonists from many ethnic groups who either immigrated or came under duress to the United States. The narrator of "Jacob and the Indians" tells of his ancestor, a German-Jewish immigrant who, to win the woman he loved, becomes a trader in the western Indian territories. After many deprivations and near-fatal experiences, he returns with a small fortune to find his beloved engaged to another man, but his sorrow is alleviated when he sees the granddaughter of the man who has financed his journey, "a dove, with dove's eyes." With no element of the fantastic, "Jacob and the Indians" celebrates the promise and opportunities the New World represented for "children of Dispersion." In "Freedom's a Hard Bought Thing," a slave named Cue endures much suffering, including separation from his girlfriend Sukey, before escaping from bondage. In Cincinnati, he contacts the Underground Railroad and is taken to Canada where he is reunited with Sukey. This first person narrative is written in stylized black dialect that is musical, even hymn-like. Again Benét celebrates the bravery, determination, and pride that, for him, are a hallmark of the American character.

The contemporary narratives, set in the 1930's or 1940's, represent Benét's reflections upon life in an America much changed from the days of the pioneers and founding fathers. In the poignant "Too Early Spring," a commentary on smalltown bigotry, young Helen and Chuck, vacationing with their parents, experience first love. Although Chuck's family disapproves of Helen's mother, it is soon accepted that when the two young people are of age, they will be married. When Helen's parents find the teenagers asleep in an innocent embrace in a darkened room, families and neighbors are scandalized, Helen is sent to a convent, and Chuck, matured by a painful rite of passage, realizes that nothing will ever be the same for him again.

Benét sometimes writes pure fantasy, as in "O'Halloran's Luck" and "By the Waters of Babylon." The first, reflecting the author's fascination with America's ethnic diversity, draws on the history of Irish immigrants. The narrator relates how his grandfather, Tim O'Halloran, comes to the United States to work on the construction of the Atlantic and Pacific Railway and, with the aid of a leprechaun, becomes a wealthy railway executive and wins the woman he loves. Though humorous, the story exemplifies Benét's devotion to the American dream, for Tim's own ingenuity, strength, and honor, combined with the leprechaun's magic, effect his rise to power and wealth. Quite a different type fantasy is "By the Waters of Babylon," a futuristic tale in which a survivor of "the Great Burning" that long ago destroyed the eastern United States, travels from the West to see the "Dead Places," Washington and New York, and tries to fathom what they were like. This apocalyptic vision differs markedly from Benét's usual optimistic tone.

The romanticism and heroism of Benét's writing is no longer fashionable, and some critics have faulted him for writing what they term "formula stories," often sentimental, patriotic, and designed to appeal to mainstream American readers. In the decades following his death, when a premium was placed on the avant garde in fiction, he came to be classified in some circles as quaint, passé. Nevertheless, it should be remembered that the formula story is not in and of itself bad art—Faulkner and Fitzgerald slanted material to meet the demands of a market—and that what Benét did, he did well. In his use of American historical and folk events and characters in an idealized, fantasized manner, he created a unique type sub-genre, "the Benét short story," that even 50 years after his death offers pleasure to many readers.

—W. Kenneth Holditch

See the essay on "The Devil and Daniel Webster."

BIERCE, Ambrose (Gwinnet). American. Born in Horse Cave Creek, Meigs County, Ohio, 24 June 1842. Educated at a high school in Warsaw, Indiana; Kentucky Military Institute, Franklin Springs, 1859–60. Served in the 9th Indiana Infantry of the Union Army during the Civil War, 1861–65: Major. Married Mollie Day in 1871 (separated 1888; divorced 1905); two sons and one daughter. Printer's devil, *Northern Indianan* (anti-slavery paper), 1857–59; U.S. Treasury aide, Selma, Alabama, 1865; served on military mapping expedition, Omaha to San Francisco, 1866–67; night watchman and clerk, Sub-Treasury, San Francisco, 1867–78; editor and columnist ("Town Crier"), *News Letter*, San Francisco, 1868–71; lived in London, 1872–75: staff member, *Fun*, 1872–75, and editor, *Lantern*, 1875; worked in the assay office, U.S. Mint, San Francisco, after 1875; associate editor, *Argonaut*, 1877–79; agent, Black Hills Placer Mining Company, Rockervill, Dakota Territory, 1880–81; editor and columnist ("Prattle"), *Wasp*, San Francisco, 1881–86; columnist, San Francisco *Examiner*, 1887–1906, and New York *Journal*, 1896–1906; lived in Washington, D.C., 1900–13: Washington correspondent, New York *American*, 1900–06; columnist, *Cosmopolitan*, Washington, 1905–09; traveled in Mexico, 1913–14; served in Villa's forces and is presumed to have been killed at the Battle of Ojinaga. *Died* (probably 11 January) *in 1914.*

PUBLICATIONS

Collections

Collected Works, edited by Walter Neale.   12 vols., 1909–12.
Complete Short Stories, edited by Ernest Jerome Hopkins. 1970.
Stories and Fables, edited by Edward Wagenknecht. 1977.
The Devil's Advocate: A Reader, edited by Brian St. Pierre. 1987.

Short Stories

Nuggets and Dust Panned Out in California.   1873.
Cobwebs from an Empty Skull.   1874.
Tales of Soldiers and Civilians.   1891; as *In the Midst of Life*, 1892; revised edition, 1898.
Can Such Things Be?   1893.
Fantastic Fables.   1899.

Novels

The Fiend's Delight.   1873.
The Dance of Death, with Thomas A. Harcourt.   1877; revised edition, 1877.
The Monk and the Hangman's Daughter, from a translation by Gustav Adolph Danziger of a story by Richard Voss. 1892.
A Son of the Gods, and A Horseman in the Sky.   1907.

Battlefields and Ghosts.   1931.

Verse

Black Beetles in Amber.   1892.
Shapes of Clay.   1903.

Other

The Cynic's Word Book.   1906; as *The Devil's Dictionary*, 1911; revised edition, by Ernest Jerome Hopkins, as *The Enlarged Devil's Dictionary*, 1967.
The Shadow on the Dial and Other Essays, edited by S.O. Howes.   1909; revised edition, as *Antepenultimata* (in *Collected Works 11*), 1912.
Write It Right: A Little Black-List of Literary Faults. 1909.
Letters, edited by Bertha Clark Pope.   1921.
Twenty-One Letters, edited by Samuel Loveman.   1922.
Selections from Prattle, edited by Carroll D. Hall.   1936.
Satanic Reader: Selections from the Invective Journalism, edited by Ernest Jerome Hopkins.   1968.
The Devil's Advocate: A Bierce Readers, edited by Brian St. Pierre.   1987.
Skepticism and Dissent: Selected Journalism, 1898–1901, edited by Lawrence I. Berkove.   1986.

*

Bibliography: *Bierce: A Bibliography* by Vincent Starrett, 1929; in *Bibliography of American Literature* by Jacob Blanck, 1955; *Bierce: Bibliographical and Biographical Data* edited by Joseph Gaer, 1968.

Critical Studies: *Bierce: A Biography* by Carey McWilliams, 1929; *Bierce, The Devil's Lexicographer*, 1951, and *Bierce and the Black Hills*, 1956, both by Paul Fatout; *Bierce* by Robert A. Wiggins, 1964; *The Short Stories of Bierce: A Study in Polarity* by Stuart C. Woodruff, 1965; *Bierce: A Biography* by Richard O'Connor, 1967; *Bierce* by M.E. Grenander, 1971; *Critical Essays on Bierce* edited by Cathy N. Davidson, 1982, and *The Experimental Fictions of Bierce: Structuring the Ineffable* by Davidson, 1984; *Bierce: The Making of a Misanthrope* by Richard Saunders, 1985.

* * *

Ambrose Bierce was a master of short forms. As a journalist, he was primarily a columnist and aphorist, and many of the titles of his collected pieces provide examples: *Nuggets and Dust, Cobwebs from an Empty Shell, Black Beetles in Amber,* and *Fantastic Fables.* Many of his most witty and sardonic judgments of the American scene appeared as *The Devil's Dictionary* after his death. Even his larger stories are quite short in comparison with the work of his contemporaries among the realists and local colorists at the end of the 19th century. And the numbers of formal short stories he wrote—exclusive of brief fables and "short-shorts"—reach 55 or so. Published within a brief period, most were printed in book form in *In the Midst of Life* (first titled *Tales of Soldiers and Civilians*) and *Can Such Things Be?*, and were written between 1888 and 1891. The sales of these books were initially very small since the publishing house seemed to collapse after printing his work.

Perhaps the tightest aspect of Ambrose Bierce's short stories is the narrowness of subject matter and technique.

The tales of soldiers are brilliant insights into the darker aspects of combat, which Bierce knew well from experience. The tales of civilians question (as do many of the military stories) matters of the uncanny, of life after death, ghosts, hauntings, and supernatural revenge. Whether writing of war in a realistic manner, drawn from personal experience, that helped inspire the imagined war stories of his younger contemporary Stephen Crane, or writing of the uneasy peace in lonely farms, deserted city mansions, abandoned mining camps, places that remind of Bierce's master Edgar Allan Poe—both believe that terror is not of a specific place but of the heart—Bierce employed for the most part a manner of overwhelming irony. These tours de force of horror depend on beliefs in the unexplainable, on deeply psychological repressions and transference. As Mark Twain, Bret Harte, Rudyard Kipling, and even Henry James joined plausible realistic settings to unknown ghostly fears, so Bierce is at once a local color artist in his backgrounds and a darkly disturbing analyst of psyche in his plots.

Thus, "Bitter Bierce," wit, cynic, savage polemicist, wrote first some of the finest fiction of the Civil War, then attempted to transfer the cosmic values natural to military combat into the settings usual for ghost stories, always seeking the same point: life and death are so weird and unnatural, the horrifying tales of immolation or out-of-body experiences can take place whatever the setting. Yet the war stories work brilliantly because horror is natural to war's barbarisms; most often the ghost stories, depending as they do on the added ironic distance between bucolic urban setting and ghostly event, are strained. Tales of soldiers seem realistic in their ironies, while tales of civilians seem pathological in their recreation of war's bloodiness in a peaceful world. The war stories make a major contribution to fiction, anticipating the tone of disillusionment that would mark the novels of post–World War I writers like Remarque, Barbusse, or Hemingway. The ghost stories at their best compare with Stevenson, Poe, or Le Fanu, but too often depend on a sardonic twist of events at the end, a technique handled more effectively by O. Henry.

Ambrose Bierce never lost the overwhelming memories of his youthful Civil War experiences. Joining the Ninth Indiana Infantry at the age of 19, he fought through the entire war with the western armies, being severely wounded at Kenesaw Mountain, serving also at Shiloh, Stone River, Murfreesboro, and Chickamauga, among other battles. In his finest war tales, recollected decades later, he displays the awful misery, the macabre ghastliness, the shocking brutality of war. The 15 stories in Tales of Soldiers strike a mean between violently contrived naturalism—replete with revolting ugliness and shocking coincidence—and the accumulation of exact, realistic, and factual observations of combat life. The vision is bleak; each story treats the death of the good and the brave. Ironies prevail: a Northern soldier kills his rebel father, a young enlisted man on guard duty discovers his brother's corpse; a gunner destroys his own house, with his wife and children inside. While the characters are flat, each story expresses a deep trauma, one that ends in madness and loss. Along with the much-anthologized "An Occurrence at Owl Creek Bridge," Bierce's "Chickamauga," "A Son of the Gods," "Parker Adderson, Philosopher," "One Officer, One Man," and "The Mocking-Bird" are superb vignettes of cosmic irony as people in all their insignificance learn the futility of so-called normal actions and aspirations in the face of the all-encompassing universe of war.

Since war has its own framework of irony, its own foreshortening of time, its own rapid transitions and swift confrontations, Tales of Soldiers show Bierce at his best in his sardonic fiction, which often approach, like Tolstoi's Sebastopol, universality.

In a story called "The Holy Terror," Bierce reflexively indicates his basic approach to his civilian tales: "When terror and absurdity make alliance, the effect is frightful." And in "The Suitable Surroundings," the author reveals his aim " . . . you must be made to feel fear—at least a strong sense of the supernatural—and that is a difficult matter." The difficulty causes the strain in the stories in Tales of Soldiers or Can Such Things Be? A skeptic is driven mad in a haunted house; ancient murders are re-enacted; a hanged man's spirit gets revenge; a murder haunts former scenes of domestic happiness. The first and longest tale in Can Such Things Be?, "The Death of Halpin Frayser," remains one of Bierce's most horrifying and perhaps most revealing. A young man is killed in a forest beside a grave—by a female figure who seems to have been his dead mother. The psychoanalytic possibilities resonate, but Bierce is not interested in depth analysis. What these stories are interested in is the refusal to accept death as the end. Whether on rural farm or in urban apartment, the living dead haunt the dying living. As in the famous "Moxon's Master," even mechanical monsters that might have been created by a Dr. Frankenstein prevail. Indeed, perhaps the special quality of these horror tales is that the bland and the normal succumb to the evil and the macabre. The titles themselves are revealing: "The Damned Thing," "Beyond the Wall," "A Diagnosis of Death." But as one reads the third volume of Bierce's Collected Works and moves from Can Such Things Be? to stories added under the rubics "The Ways of Ghosts" and "Some Haunted Houses," one comes also upon four short tales entitled "Soldier-Folk," and again the fictional story gives way to realistic irony. For Bierce, as a clear master of the American short story, war provided setting and structure in an appropriate form. He was an interesting horror and ghost story writer, certainly disturbing, but Bierce was one of the greatest military short story writers in any literature.

—Eric Solomon

See the essay on "An Occurrence at Owl Creek Bridge."

BIOY CASARES, Adolfo. Also writes as Javier Miranda; Martín Sacastru; H. Bustos Domecq; B. Lynch Davis; B. Suárez Lynch (joint pseudonym with Jorge Luis Borges, q.v.). Argentinian. Born in Buenos Aires, 15 September 1914. Educated at the University of Buenos Aires, 1933–34. Married Silvina Ocampo, q.v., in 1940; one daughter. Founder, with Jorge Luis Borges, Destiempo literary magazine, 1936, and "The Seventh Circle" detective series, Emecé Editores, Buenos Aires, 1943–56. Recipient: City of Buenos Aires municipal prize, 1941; National literature prize, 1969; Argentine Society of Writers grand prize of honour, 1975; Mondello prize, 1984; IILA prize (Italy), 1986; Cervantes prize, 1990, 1991; Echeverría prize; Konex prize. Elected to Légion d'Honneur (France), 1981. Lives in Buenos Aires.

PUBLICATIONS

Short Stories

17 disparos contra lo porvenir (as Martín Sacastru).   1933.
Caos.   1934.
La estatua casera.   1936.
Luis Greve, muerto.   1937.
La invención de Morel.   1940; with stories from *La trama celeste,* as *The Invention of Morel, and Other Stories from "La trama celeste,"* 1964.
Seis problemas para don Isidro Parodi, with Jorge Luis Borges (jointly as H. Bustos Domecq).   1942; as *Six Problems for Don Isidro,*   1981.
El perjurio de la nieve.   1945; as *The Perjury of the Snow,* 1964.
Dos fantasías memorables, with Jorge Luis Borges (jointly as H. Bustos Domecq).   1946.
La trama celeste.   1948; with *La invención de Morel,* as *The Invention of Morel, and Other Stories from "La trama celeste,"* 1964.
Las visperas de Fausto.   1949.
Historia prodigiosa.   1956; enlarged edition, 1961.
El lado de la sombra.   1962.
Guirnalda con amores: cuentos.   1959.
El gran serafín.   1967.
Crónicas de Bustos Domecq, with Jorge Luis Borges. 1967; as *Chronicles of Bustos Domecq,* 1976.
Adversos milagros: relatos.   1969.
Historias de amor.   1972.
Historias fantásticas.   1972.
Nuevos contos de Bustos Domecq, with Jorge Luis Borges. 1977.
El héroe de las mujeres.   1978.
Páginas (selections).   1985.
Historias desaforadas.   1986.
Una muñeca rusa.   1991; as *A Russian Doll and Other Stories,* 1992.

Novels

La nueva tormenta, o La vida múltiple de Juan Ruteno. 1935.
Plan de evasión.   1945; as *A Plan for Escape,* 1975.
Un modelo para la muerte, with Jorge Luis Borges (jointly as B. Suárez Lynch).   1946.
Los que aman, odian, with Silvina Ocampo.   1946.
El sueño de héroes.   1954; as *The Dream of Heroes,* 1987.
Bioy Casares (omnibus), edited by Ofelia Kovacci.   1963.
Diario de la guerra del cerdo.   1969; as *Diary of the War of the Pig,* 1972.
Dormir al sol.   1973; as *Asleep in the Sun,* 1978.
Los afanes.   1983.
La aventura de un fotógrafo en La Plata.   1985; as *The Adventures of a Photographer in La Plata,* 1989.
La invención y la trama.   1988.

Plays

Los orilleros; El paraiso de los creyentes (screenplays), with Jorge Luis Borges.   1955.
Les Autres (screenplay), with Jorge Luis Borges and Hugo Santiago.   1974.

Screenplays: *Les Autres,* with Jorge Luis Borges and Hugo Santiago, 1974; *Los orilleros,* with Jorge Luis Borges, 1975.

Other

Prólogo.   1929.
Antes del novecientos (recuerdos).   1958.
Años de mocedad (recuerdos).   1963.
La otra aventura.   1968.
Memoria sobre la pampa y los gauchos.   1970.
Breve diccionario del argentino exquisito (as Javier Miranda).   1971; enlarged edition (as Bioy Casares), 1978, 1990.
Aventuras de la imaginación (interviews), with Noemí Ulla. 1990.

Editor, with Jorge Luis Borges and Silvina Ocampo, *Antología de la literatura fantástica.*   1940; as *The Book of Fantasy,* 1988.
Editor, with Jorge Luis Borges and Silvina Ocampo, *Antología poética argentina.*   1941; as *Antología de la poesia argentina,* 1948.
Editor and translator, with Jorge Luis Borges, *Los mejores cuentos policiales.*   2 vols., 1943–51.
Editor, with Jorge Luis Borges, *Prosa y verso,* by Francisco Quevedo.   1948.
Editor and translator, with Jorge Luis Borges, *Poesía gauchesca.*   2 vols., 1955.
Editor, with Jorge Luis Borges, *Cuentos breves y extraordinarios.*   1955; as *Extraordinary Tales,* 1971.
Editor, with Jorge Luis Borges, *El libro del cielo y del infierno.*   1960.
Editor, with Jorge Luis Borges, *Hilario Ascasubi, Aniceto el gallo y Santos Vega.*   1960.

*

Critical Studies: "The Mirror and the Lie: Two Stories by Jorge Luis Borges and Bioy Casares" by Alfred J. MacAdam, in *Modern Fiction Studies* 19, 1973; "The Novels and Short Stories of Bioy Casares" by David P. Gallagher, in *Bulletin of Hispanic Studies* 52, 1975; in *Jorge Luis Borges: A Literary Biography* by Emir R. Monegal, 1978; "The Narrator as Creator and Critic in *The Invention of Morel*" by Margaret L. Snook, in *American Literary Review* 7, 1979; "Parody Island: Two Novels by Bioy Casares" by Suzanne Jill Lene, in *Hispanic Journal* 4, 1983; *From the Ashen Land of the Virgin* by Raul Galvez, 1989.

*   *   *

Adolfo Bioy Casares writes short fiction combining elements of science, philosophy, and psychology. Since the age of seven this Argentine writer has been producing original short stories and novels. He published his first work, *Prólogo,* in 1929 under the supervision of his father. The early stage of Bioy Casares's writing career did not yield any works of real merit. He published under the pseudonyms Javier Miranda and Martín Sacastres. Cultivating his skills under the tutelage of friend and mentor Jorge Luis Borges, Bioy Casares improved his writing style and in 1940 proved his literary genius with the publication of his breakthrough novella, *La in vención de Morel* (*The Invention of Morel*). Bioy Casares's friendship with Borges led to professional collaborations in which they used a variety of pseudonyms: H. Bustos Domecq, B. Suárez Lynch, and B. Lynch Davis. Borges and Bioy Casares founded the magazine *Destiempo* in 1936 and until 1956 also directed a collection of detective novels. The writer Silvina Ocampo, Bioy Casares's wife, has collaborated with Bioy Casares and Borges in other publications such as *Antología de la literatura fantástica* (which includes Bioy Casares short story, "The Squid in Its Own Ink"). Ocampo and Bioy Casares also have worked together on projects such as the novel *Los que aman, odian*. In 1990 and 1991 Bioy Casares was the recipient of the prestigious Miguel de Cervantes Literary award. His most recent collection of short stories, *Una muñeca rusa* (*A Russian Doll*), was published in 1991.

Although not as well-known by the general public as some of such contemporaries as Borges, Julio Cortázar, and Gabriel García Márquez, Bioy Casares uses many of the same techniques and themes indicative of the Latin American "boom" period. Marcelo Pichon Rivière in *La invención y la trama* (1991) identifies three characteristics that repeatedly dominate Bioy Casares's fiction: the importance of the inventor, the dominance of the narrator, and the appearance of the satirical writer. The third characteristic is seen by Rivière as an affirmation that Bioy Casares uses language on two levels, for characterization and for games of irony and satire.

Bioy Casares's use of science fiction and the fantastic facilitate his exploration of the existence of multiple realities. In *Guirnalda con amores,* a compilation of maxims and epigrams, Bioy Casares writes, "El mundo es inacabable, está hecho de infinitos mundos, a la manera de las muñecas rusas" ("The world is interminable, it is made of infinite worlds, in the manner of the Russian dolls.") The gateways to parallel worlds or alternate realities can be opened in various ways, through scientific inventions or mental powers.

An example of reality being altered by scientific invention can be seen in *The Invention of Morel,* wherein the protagonist finds himself on an island inhabited only by filmed projections. The machine that controls the filmed projections eventually consumes the protagonist's body and he becomes part of the projections. The story "The Celestial Plot" proposes the existence of multiple, almost identical, worlds, in which exist multiple identities of one man. The protagonist, Captain Morris, discovers his alternate lives by mistakenly entering one of the alternate worlds through a gateway opened by the test flight of an experimental plane. Captain Morris manages to reenter his own Buenos Aires, but from that moment on he lives with a heightened understanding of his own identity.

The mental powers that trigger the creation of recognition of infinite worlds include the ability to project images of physical objects, manipulate other people's minds with telepathy, and create reality through memory. One of the characters in "The Other Labyrinth" projects mental images and seems to recreate physical objects. His imagination allows him to leave the 20th century and live in the 17th century. "The Future Kings" and "The Idol" show how the mind can be controlled by outside forces, causing the victim to be propelled into a different reality. The seals in "The Future Kings" gain control over humans' thoughts and enslave their owners. Other unexplained powers alter characters' perceptions and dreams in "The Idol." The narrator of "In Memory of Pauline" brings his love, Pauline, back from the dead when his memory of her becomes physical reality. The illusion or the mental projection of her replaces flesh and blood. The mind is a powerful tool in Bioy Casares's creations.

The plot is the most dominant element of Bioy Casares's work. The characters are secondary, sometimes portrayed as stereotyped, one-dimensional figures who only serve to complete a plot formula. Many of Bioy Casares's plots are based on love stories in which the amorous relationships cannot possibly succeed. The love encounters, however, provide the impetus for the fantastic events which then engulf the characters. A study of the recurring narrative structures in his work highlights Bioy Casares's use of formulas. The "story within a story" framework manifests itself in two ways in his work. One use of multiple narrators is the formula in which a casual meeting between two (or more) friends prompts the telling of a story. In other stories, a narrator discovers a transcript, which is given to the reader, and then the narrator comments on it.

In "The Perjury of the Snow" the reader is given both an incomplete manuscript and commentary on it by an outside narrator. The manuscript describes the events surrounding the death of a terminally ill woman. By repeating the same schedule everyday, her family successfully suspends the passage of time. The life of the woman is spared until a curious stranger, whose identity is questionable, breaks into the house and disrupts the delicate time balance. The identity of the "murderer" is different according to the manuscript and the outside narrator.

Bioy Casares's short fiction can be categorized as science fiction, love stories, and fantasy literature. The majority of his works are a study of reality or identity. Some characters possess powers to manipulate time and physical reality and therefore control the gateways to alternate realities. The characters and the reader similarly become pawns in Bioy Casares's games of fantasy and adventures.

—Joan E. Clifford

See the essay on "A Letter about Emilia."

———

BLAISE, Clark (Lee). Canadian. Born in Fargo, North Dakota, United States, 10 April 1940; became Canadian citizen, 1973. Educated at Denison University, Granville, Ohio, 1957–61, A.B. 1961; University of Iowa, Iowa City, 1962–64, M.F.A. 1964. Married the writer Bharati Mukherjee in 1963; two sons. Acting instructor, University of Wisconsin, Milwaukee, 1964–65; teaching fellow, University of Iowa, 1965–66; lecturer, 1966–67, assistant professor, 1967–69, associate professor, 1969–72, and professor of English, 1973–78, Sir George Williams University, later Concordia University, Montreal; professor of humanities, York University, Toronto, 1978–80; professor of English, Skidmore College, Saratoga Springs, New York, 1980–81, 1982–83; visiting lecturer or writer-in-residence, University of Iowa, 1981–82, Saskatchewan School of the Arts, Saskatoon, Summer 1983, David Thompson University Centre, Nelson, British Columbia, Fall 1983, Emory University, Atlanta, 1985, Bennington College, Vermont, 1985, and Columbia University, New York, Spring 1986; currently, Director of the International Writing Program, University of Iowa. Recipient: University of Western Ontario President's medal, for short story, 1968; Great Lakes Colleges Association prize, 1973; Canada Council grant, 1973,1977, and travel grant, 1985; St. Lawrence award, 1974; Fels award, for essay, 1975; *Asia Week* award, for nonfiction, 1977; *Books in Canada* prize, 1979; National Endowment for the Arts grant, 1981; Guggenheim grant, 1983. D.Litt.: Denison University, 1979. Lives in Iowa City.

PUBLICATIONS

Short Stories

New Canadian Writing 1968, with Dave Godfrey and
David Lewis Stein.   1969.
A North American Education.   1973.
Tribal Justice.   1974.
Personal Fictions, with others, edited by Michael Ondaatje.
1977.
Resident Alien.   1986.

Novels

Lunar Attractions.   1979.
Lusts.   1983.

Play

Screenplay: *Days and Nights in Calcutta,* with Bharati
Mukherjee, 1991.

Other

Days and Nights in Calcutta, with Bharati Mukherjee.
1977.
*The Sorrow and the Terror: The Haunting Legacy of the Air
India Tragedy,* with Bharati Mukherjee.   1987.

Editor, with John Metcalf, *Here and Now.*   1977.
Editor, with John Metcalf, *78 [79, 80]: Best Canadian
Stories.*   3 vols., 1978-80.

*

Critical Studies: *On the Line: Readings in the Short Fiction
of Blaise, John Metcalf, and Hugh Hood,* 1982, and *Another
I: The Fiction of Blaise,* 1988, both by Robert Lecker.

*   *   *

Born in the United States of expatriate parents (a French-
Canadian father and English-Canadian mother), Clark
Blaise in many ways epitomizes the North American way of
life: lacking in clearly defined national roots, living in a
world of uncertainties and constant change. Because of his
father's job as a salesman Blaise's family moved often,
throughout the United States and Canada, and so as a child
Blaise never felt at home anywhere, while paradoxically
seeing the whole continent as his potential home. His very
autobiographical fiction reflects this sense of rootlessness,
and the major theme of his stories is the search for identity:
his narrators are constantly looking for who they are and
where they belong.

Few writers mine their personal experiences for their
fiction as much as Blaise does; one can almost see his
stories as forming a single exploration of his own self, and
then by extension an exploration of the sense of rootlessness we all share. His very personal fiction produces an
emphasis on narrative voice rather than plot or character;
in fact, he told Geoff Hancock in an interview, "Voice is
finally *all* that [the writer] has." In a world without
absolutes the author can only rely on imaginative vision,
expressed through voice, to give meaning to experience.

To be a North American, as Blaise makes clear throughout his first two collections of stories, *A North American
Education* and *Tribal Justice,* means to be without a
defined home. We are all immigrants, exiles, economic or
social migrants seeking a place. Blaise's strongest memories
are of his constant need to adjust to new cities and new
schools, and he has often remarked on his childhood
fascination with maps and mapmaking. His narrators
similarly lack national and social contexts, and search
frantically for them. Norman Dyer, the protagonist of the
first group of stories in *A North American Education,*
deludes himself into thinking that he has succeeded in
assimilating into the language and culture of Montreal. In
"A Class of New Canadians" he arrogantly believes that he
can now introduce others to the country. But he cannot see
that he and his immigrant students are very much alike.
His recognition appears in one of Blaise's best-known
stories, "Eyes," in which he struggles to cope with being
observer and observed in a city where he simply does not
fit. His environment is now full of possible threats, and his
initial assumptions about easy integration are burst, his
safe world violated by the foreignness of his new home.

Virtually all of Blaise's protagonists face a similar immersion in a strange culture, notably Paul Keeler in "Going to
India." Frank Thibidault's father, a furniture salesman,
flees to Canada in "The Salesman's Son Grows Older," and
Frank wonders how foreign his Canadian relatives will
prove to be. Like so many of Blaise's child narrators, Frank
must adjust to a new culture, new schools, and new
lifestyle. Philip Porter, the protagonist of the stories in
Resident Alien, also must move constantly, and relishes the
one time he is able to return to the same school in the fall
that he attended in the previous spring ("South"). "In
Leesburg, Florida, in 1946," he says, "I had a small
history."

Porter's difficulty with establishing an identity is exacerbated and symbolized by his lack of a definite name. He
learns during his family's flight to Canada that their
original name was Carrier and that he was really born in
Montreal, not the United States as he had believed. At least
Porter has a name (or two); so many of Blaise's narrators
are left nameless, to illustrate their lack of identity.
Resident Alien portrays Porter's search for identity through
his search for his parents. Like other fathers in Blaise's
fiction, Porter's father is a salesman who disappears and it
is only when Porter/Carrier is able to find his father that he
achieves some clear sense of who he is.

Blaise's dislocated characters seek something permanent
and secure—a place or society they can call home. Gerald
Gordon, of "How I Became a Jew" in *Tribal Justice,* has
been moved from the American South to Cincinnati and
learns to adjust to the tribal nature of his new school by
identifying with the Jewish students in their ongoing
competition with the African-Americans. The word "Israel" becomes a source of hope for an end to exile as much
for him as for his classmates. But this search for permanence in social structures or ideals is futile; as the narrator
of "He Raises Me Up" in the same collection comments,
"Some enormous frailty will be exposed: technology,
wealth, politics, marriage, whatever organizing idiocy that
binds us all together will come flying apart." And the sense
of rootlessness and exile will become a legacy to be passed
down to future generations, as we see at the end of "The
Salesman's Son Grows Older." To be alive is to be in a
world of flux, and so permanence can only be found in the
irretrievable world of childhood innocence, or death.

What we see throughout Blaise's fictional universe is a
dual vision: we want permanence and certainty, but know

that it does not exist except in our minds. Orderly appearances deceive us, because underlying it is a chaos we uncover, sometimes to our horror. Among the best symbols of this hidden world of the shocking and chaotic are the leeches that attack the overconfident writer in "At the Lake," and the population of cockroaches living unseen under Paul Keeler's rug in "Extractions and Contractions" —until he tries to scrub it. We may try to impose order on our chaotic world (the symbolic meaning of the title of "Grids and Doglegs"), but will inevitably fail.

As a writer, Blaise both embodies and explores these dualities. He, too, is observer and observed, voyeur and participant in what he portrays. Through imagination he can at least make some sense of his own past and the pasts of his characters, by turning memory into art.

—Allan Weiss

———

BLIXEN, Karen. See **DINESEN, Isak.**

———

BÖLL, Heinrich (Theodor). German. Born in Cologne, 21 December 1917. Educated at gymnasium, Cologne; University of Cologne. Served in the German army, 1939-45; prisoner of war, 1945. Married Annemarie Cech in 1942; three sons. Joiner in his father's shop, then apprentice in the book trade before the war; full-time writer from 1947; co-editor, *Labyrinth*, 1960-61, and *L*, from 1976; president, PEN International, 1971-74. Recipient: Bundesverband der Deutschen Industrie grant; Gruppe 47 prize, 1951; Rene Schickele prize, 1952; Tribune de Paris prize, 1953; Prix du Meilleur Roman Étranger, 1955; Heydt prize, 1958; Bavarian Academy of Fine Arts award, 1958; Nordrhein-Westfalen prize, 1959; Veillon prize, 1960; Cologne prize, 1961; Elba prize, 1965; Büchner prize, 1967; Nobel prize for literature, 1972; Scottish Arts Counsil fellowship, 1973. Honorary degrees: D.Sc.: Aston University, Birmingham, 1973; O.Tech.: Brunel University, Uxbridge, Middlesex, 1973; Litt.D.: Trinity College, Dublin, 1973. *Died 16 July 1985.*

PUBLICATIONS

Short Stories

Der Zug war pünktlich (novella).   1949; as *The Train Was on Time*, 1956, 1973.
Wanderer, kommst du nach Spa. . . .   1950; as *Traveller, If You Come to Spa*, 1956.
Unberechenbare Gäste: Heitere Erzählungen.   1956.
Doktor Murkes gesammeltes Schweigen und andere Satiren.   1958.
Die Waage der Baleks und andere Erzählungen.   1958.
Eighteen Stories.   1966.
Wo warst du, Adam? (novella).   1951; as *Adam, Where Art Thou?*, 1955; as *And Where Were You Adam?*, 1973.
Als der Krieg ausbrach, Als der Krieg zu Ende war.   1962; as *Absent Without Leave* (2 novellas).   1965.
Absent Without Leave and Other Stories.   1965.

Children Are Civilians Too.   1970.
Der Mann mit den Messern: Erzählungen (selection).   1972.
Gesammelte Erzählungen.   2 vols., 1981.
Die Verwundung und andere frühe Erzählungen.   1983; as *The Casualty*, 1986.
Der Angriff: Erzählungen 1947-1949.   1983.
Veränderungen in Staeck: Erzählungen 1962-1980.   1984.
Mein trauriges Gesicht: Erzählungen.   1984.
Das Vermächtnis (novella).   1982; as *A Soldier's Legacy*, 1985.
The Stories (selection; bilingual edition).   1986.
Der Engel schwieg (novella).   1992.

Novels

Die schwarzen Schafe.   1951.
Nicht nur zur Weihnachtszeit.   1952.
Und sagte kein einziges Wort.   1953; as *Acquainted with the Night*, 1954; as *And Never Said a Word*, 1978.
Haus ohne Hüter.   1954; as *Tomorrow and Yesterday*, 1957; as *The Unguarded House*, 1957.
Das Brot der frühen Jahre.   1955; as *The Bread of Our Early Years*, 1957; as *The Bread of Those Early Years*, 1976.
So ward Abend und Morgen.   1955.
Im Tal der donnernden Hufe.   1957.
Der Mann mit den Messern.   1958.
Der Bahnhof von Zimpren.   1959.
Billard um Halbzehn.   1959; as *Billiards at Half-Past Nine*, 1961.
Ansichten eines Clowns.   1963; as *The Clown*, 1965.
Entfernung von der Truppe.   1964.
Ende einer Dienstfahrt.   1966; as *The End of a Mission*, 1967.
Geschichten aus zwölf Jahren.   1969.
Gruppenbild mit Dame.   1971; as *Group Portrait with Lady*, 1973.
Die verlorene Ehre der Katharina Blum.   1974; as *The Lost Honor of Katharina Blum*, 1975.
Berichte zur Gesinnungslage der Nation.   1975.
Fürsorgliche Belagerung.   1979; as *The Safety Net*, 1982.
Du fährst zu oft nach Heidelberg.   1979.
Frauen vor Flusslandschaft: Roman in Dialogen und Selbstgesprächen.   1985; as *Women in a River Landscape: A Novel in Dialogues and Soliloques*, 1988.

Plays

Die Brücke von Berczaba (broadcast 1952).   In *Zauberei auf dem Sender und andere Hörspiele*, 1962.
Der Heilige und der Räuber (broadcast 1953).   In *Hörspielbuch des Nordwestdeutschen und Süddeutschen Rundfunks 4*, 1953; as *Mönch und Räuber*, in *Erzählungen, Hörspiele, Aufsätze*, 1961.
Ein Tag wie sonst (broadcast 1953).   1980.
Zum Tee bei Dr. Borsig (broadcast 1955).   In *Erzählungen, Hörspiele, Aufsätze*, 1961.
Eine Stunde Aufenthalt (broadcast 1957).   In *Erzählungen, Hörspiele, Aufsätze*, 1961.
Die Spurlosen (broadcast 1957).   1957.
Bilanz (broadcast 1957).   1961. With *Klopfzeichen*, 1961.
Klopfzeichen (broadcast 1960).   With *Bilanz*, 1961.
Ein Schluck Erde (produced 1961).   1962.
Zum Tee bei Dr. Borsig (includes *Mönch und Räuber*, *Eine Stunde Aufenthalt*, *Bilanz*, *Die Spurlosen*, *Klopfzeichen*, *Sprechanlage*, *Konzert für vier Stimmen*).   1964.

Hausfriedensbruch (broadcast 1969). 1969.
Aussatz (produced 1970). With *Hausfriedensbruch*, 1969.

Radio Plays: *Die Brücke von Berczaba*, 1952; *Ein Tag wie sonst*, 1953; *Der Heilige und der Räuber*, 1953; *Zum Tee bei Dr. Borsig*, 1955; *Anita und das Existenzminimum*, 1955, revised version, as *Ich habe nichts gegen Tiere*, 1958; *Die Spurlosen*, 1957; *Bilanz*, 1957; *Eine Stunde Aufenthalt*, 1957; *Die Stunde der Wahrheit*, 1958; *Klopfzeichen*, 1960; *Hausfriedensbruch*, 1969.

Verse

Gedichte. 1972.

Other

Irisches Tagebuch. 1957; as *Irish Journal*, 1967.
Im Ruhrgebiet, photographs by Karl Hargesheimer. 1958.
Unter Krahnenbäumen, photographs by Karl Hargesheimer. 1958.
Menschen am Rhein, photographs by Karl Hargesheimer. 1960.
Brief an einen jungen Katholiken. 1961.
Erzählungen, Hörspiele, Aufsätze. 1961.
Assisi. 1962.
Hierzulande. 1963.
Frankfurter Vorlesungen. 1966.
Aufsätze, Kritiken, Reden 1952–1967. 1967.
Leben im Zustand des Frevels. 1969.
Neue politische und literarische Schriften. 1973.
Nobel Prize for Literature (lecture). 1973.
Politische Meditationen zu Glück und Vergeblichkeit, with Dorothee Sölle. 1973.
Drei Tage in März, with Christian Linder. 1975.
Der Fall Staeck; oder, Wie politisch darf die Kunst sein?, with others. 1975.
Der Lorbeer ist immer noch bitter: Literarische Schriften. 1976.
Briefe zur Verteidigung der Republik, with Freimut Duve and Klaus Staeck. 1977.
Einmischung erwünscht: Schriften zur Zeit. 1977.
Werke, edited by Bernd Balzer. 10 vols., 1977–78.
Missing Persons and Other Essays. 1977.
Querschnitte: Aus Interviews, Aufsätzen, und Reden, edited by Viktor Böll and Renate Matthaei. 1977.
Gefahren von falschen Brüdern: Politische Schriften. 1980.
Warum haben wir aufeinander geschossen?, with Lew Kopelew. 1981.
Rendezvous mit Margaret. Liebesgeschichten. 1981.
Was soll aus dem jungen bloss werden? (memoir). 1981; as *What's to Become of the Boy?*, or, *Something to Do with Books*, 1984.
Der Autor ist immer noch versteckt. 1981.
Vermintes Gelände. 1982.
Antikommunismus in Ost und West. 1982.
Ich hau dem Mädche mix jedonn, ich han et bloss ens kräje. Texte, Bilder, Dokumente zur Verteihung des Ehrenbürgerrechts der Stadt Köln, 29 April 1983. 1983.
Ein-und Zusprüche: Schriften, Reden und Prosa 1981–83. 1984.
Weil die Stadt so fremd geworden ist. 1985.
Bild-Bonn-Boenish. 1985.
Die Fähigkeit zu trauern: Schriften und Reden 1983–1985. 1986.
Denken mit Böll. 1986.

Rom auf den ersten Blick. Landschaften, Städte, Reisen. 1987.

Editor, with Erich Kock, *Unfertig ist der Mensch.* 1967.
Editor, with Freimut Duve and Klaus Staeck, *Verantwortlich für Polen?* 1982.

Translator, with Annemarie Böll:
Kein Name bei den Leuten [No Name in the Street], by Kay Cicellis. 1953.
Ein unordentlicher Mensch, by Adriaan Morriën. 1955.
Tod einer Stadt [Death of a Town], by Kay Cicellis. 1956.
Weihnachtsabend in San Cristobal [The Saintmaker's Christmas Eve], by Paul Horgan. 1956.
Zur Ruhe kam der Baum des Menschen nie [The Tree of Man], by Patrick White. 1957.
Der Teufel in der Wüste [The Devil in the Desert], by Paul Horgan. 1958.
Die Geisel [The Hostage], by Brendan Behan. 1958.
Der Mann von Morgen früh [The Quare Fellow], by Brendan Behan. 1958.
Ein Wahrer Held [The Playboy of the Western World], by J.M. Synge. 1960.
Die Boot fahren nicht mehr aus [The Islandman], by Tomás O'Crohan. 1960.
Eine Rose zur Weihnachtszeit [One Red Rose for Christmas], by Paul Horgan. 1960.
Der Gehilfe [The Assistant], by Bernard Malamud. 1960.
Kurz vor dem Krieg gegen die Eskimos, by J.D. Salinger. 1961.
Das Zauberfass [The Magic Barrel], by Bernard Malamud. 1962.
Der Fänger im Roggen [The Catcher in the Rye], by J.D. Salinger. 1962.
Ein Gutshaus in Irland [The Big House], by Brendan Behan. Published in *Stücke*, 1962.
Franny und Zooey, by J.D. Salinger. 1963.
Die Insel der Pferde [The Island of Horses], by Eilís Dillon. 1964.
Hebt den Dachbalken hoch, Zimmerleute; Seymour wird vorgestellt [Raise High the Roof Beam, Carpenters; Seymour: An Introduction], by J.D. Salinger. 1965.
Caesar und Cleopatra, by G.B. Shaw. 1965.
Der Spanner [The Scarperer], by Brendan Behan. 1966.
Die Insel des grossen John [The Coriander], by Eilís Dillon. 1966.
Das harte Leben [The Hard Life], by Flann O'Brien. 1966.
Neun Erzählungen [Nine Stories], by J.D. Salinger. 1966.
Die schwarzen Füchse [A Family of Foxes], by Eilís Dillon. 1967.
Die Irrfahrt der Santa Maria [The Cruise of the Santa Maria], by Eilís Dillon. 1968.
Die Springflut [The Sea Wall], by Eilís Dillon. 1969.
Seehunde SOS [The Seals], by Eilís Dillon. 1970.
Erwachen in Mississippi [Coming of Age in Mississippi], by Anne Moody. 1970.
Candida, Der Kaiser von Amerika, Mensch und Übermensch [Candida, The King of America, Man and Superman], by G.B. Shaw. 1970.
Handbuch des Revolutionärs, by G.B. Shaw. 1972.

*

Bibliography: *Böll in America 1954–1970* by Ray Lewis White, 1979.

Critical Studies: *Böll, Teller of Tales: A Study of His Works and Characters* by Wilhelm Johannes Schwartz, 1969; *A Student's Guide to Böll* by Enid Macpherson, 1972; *Böll: Withdrawal and Re-Emergence*, 1973, *Böll: A German for His Time*, 1986, both by J.H. Reid; *The Major Works of Böll: A Critical Commentary* by Erhard Friedrichsmeyer, 1974; *The Writer and Society: Studies in the Fiction of Günter Grass and Böll* by Charlotte W. Ghurye, 1976; *The Imagery in Böll's Novels* by Thor Prodaniuk, 1979; *Böll* by Robert C. Conard, 1981; *Böll* by Klaus Schröter, 1982; *Böll: On His Death: Selected Obituaries and the Last Interview* translated by Patricia Crampton, 1985; *Böll and the Challange of Literature* by Michael Butler, 1988.

*　*　*

Heinrich Böll's short fiction comes predominantly from the early part of his literary career when, immediately after World War II, he was trying to scrape a living as a journalist, writing newspaper reports and columns, short fiction, and his first short novel, *Der Engel schwieg,* published in Germany only posthumously, in 1992. If coffee and cigarettes figure prominently in his early writing, he was recording a period after the German defeat during which both were expensive luxuries.

The predominantly Catholic southern "zone" of the country was administered by the U.S., and the cold war with the U.S.S.R. was beginning. In 1947 the political journal *Der Ruf,* founded by Alfred Andersch and Hans Werner Richter, was suppressed by the U.S. administration for subversive, procommunist tendencies, and the publication of another, similar journal, *Der Skorpion,* was also prevented. Andersch and Richter turned to literature, and in 1947 founded a non-political literary group interested in exploring left-wing values. Writers were invited to attend annual conferences and to read specimens of their work, with a prize awarded each year to the best contribution. Böll was first invited in 1951, by which time the group, known as the "Gruppe 47," had begun to become influential. He was awarded the prize. It was also at that time that his first volume of short fiction was published, *Wanderer kommst du nach Spa . . . (Traveller, If You Come to Spa).*

Böll uses a first-person narrator in all but three of the 25 stories, to highlight the plight of the individual against the sometimes implied background of a futile, vicious war, and a bureaucracy that reduces people to statistics. In "On the Bridge" the narrator, injured during the war, has the job of counting the pedestrians crossing a new bridge. He daily refuses to count one woman who obsesses him, to save her from relegation to the "future perfect" tense, as a statistic to be "multiplied, divided, and made a percentage of." The narrator compares his silently counting mouth to the mechanism of a clock, which dehumanizes himself as well as those who cross the bridge, just as he dehumanizes the bureaucrats by referring to them as an anonymous "they." His job seems pointless, and he has no idea of what happens to the figure he gives to his superiors, and what purpose their calculations serve, but at least for the narrator there is the daily significance of seeing the woman. She is only set apart from the dehumanized statistical mass because he endows her with human attributes, "long, brown hair, and slender feet."

There are other images of life, the horse-drawn wagons which are allowed only limited access to the bridge, and none at all during the rush hour, when they must give way to the mechanised and seemingly driverless cars that the narrator's "mate" has to count. The metaphor implies that progress leads to an ultimately impersonal goal. By being allowed to count the horse wagons the narrator can afford time to go and watch the woman work, but to be allowed to count the wagons the narrator must achieve promotion, and to achieve promotion he must provide "them" with accurate daily figures. In order to resist "their" ends, and retain a rudimentary human relationship, the narrator must therefore cooperate with their dehumanising aims. The narrator only manages himself to remain human through subversion: he falsifies the daily figure, allowing its size to depend on his mood, his generosity, his humanity.

The validity of the parable is independent of Böll's own views, although we might guess what they were. In fact we know that he was projecting his own views from the *Irish Journal* he published. He found Ireland enchanting precisely because it was so unconcerned with mechanisation. It had a railway but, as there was no route map, the number of stations yet to be reached could be discovered only by counting the number of cigarette cartons still in the guard's van, because one was thrown out at each platform. The light-heartedness of the *Journal* emphasises the contrast between the sense of community Böll encountered in Ireland, where even the bureaucrats were friendly, and Germany's preoccupation with the "economic miracle" (*Wirtschaftswunder*) and the loneliness of his earlier characters.

Böll's attitudes are made even clearer in the story "Stranger, Bear Word to the Spartans We . . . ," a vicious satire of Nazi ideology. The title comes from a translation by Schiller of the inscription to the Spartan heroes of Thermopylae which starts, "Wanderer, kommst du nach Sparta." The reference was immediately obvious in 1951. Joseph Goebbels's propaganda ministry had incessantly compared the heroic stand of Leonidas against the Persians at Thermopylae with the German efforts to hold back the Russians. Böll makes his viciously satirical comment in the story with elegant economy. Since there was no room left on the blackboard when the narrator had to write out the line as a handwriting exercise, he had simply shortened "Sparta" to "Spa," implicitly identifying the life-destroying burning German city in which the story is set with the life-restoring health resort.

The narrator knows that he will shortly join the large number of recently dead as nothing but a name on the bulk-bought war memorial, but he lacks the courage and patriotism of Leonidas, as he cannot think of a cause for which he would die. There is also a visual contract, pictures celebrating German militarism set against the Parthenon frieze. The Nazi education system had mutilated the country's classical heritage just as the Schiller translation had been mutilated, and as the narrator himself was. By the end of the story he has lost two arms and a leg.

All of Böll's short fiction works over the same underlying theme, the threat to the individual of some impersonal, all-encompassing authority, sometimes exemplified by the Nazi party and, in Böll's later work, by the Catholic Church. Böll is also concerned with hypocrisy, guilt, and the absurdity of war with such side effects as rationing and poverty. He wrote about them in a simple, engaging, everyday way, without obvious art or obtrusive literary language, so putting himself in the position from which, launched by the growing status of the "Gruppe 47," he could take up his fight for the cause of human rights. His career was also that of a polemicist, campaigning for freedom of speech and against injustice and hypocrisy. It was his stance on these issues, deriving most clearly from the early short fiction, which prompted Heinrich Vormweg to write in his obituary (in *Metall* 15, 26 July 1985):

Heinrich Böll's death affects not only his family, not only his friends and readers, but the life of every man and above all the lives of those who continue to be dependent on advocacy, protection, and help.

—Claudia Levi

See the essay on "Murke's Collected Silences."

BOMBAL, María Luisa. Chilean. Born in Viña del Mar, 8 June 1909. Educated at the Sorbonne, Paris, degrees in philosophy and literature. Married Jorge Larco in 1934; Count Raphaël de Saint-Phalle in 1944 (died 1973), one daughter. Lived in Paris, 1922–31; actress, Santiago, 1933–35; lived in Buenos Aires, 1935–41; Chilean representative, International PEN conference, 1940; screenwriter, Sonofilm, Buenos Aires, 1937–40; imprisoned for shooting Eulogio Sánchez, Santiago, 1941; screenwriter, translator, New York, 1941–73; returned to Chile, 1973. Recipient: Chilean Academy of Arts and Letters prize, 1977. *Died 6 May 1980.*

PUBLICATIONS

Short Stories

La historia de María Griselda.   1977.
The New Islands and Other Stories.   1982.

Novels

La última niebla.   1935; expanded edition, 1941; as *The House of Mist,* translated by Bombal, 1947; revised edition, 1981.
La amortajada.   1938; as *The Shrouded Woman,* translated by Bombal, 1948.

Other

Translator, *La desconocida del Sena,* by Jules Supervielle. 1962.

*

Bibliography: in *Spanish American Women Writers* edited by Diane E. Marting, 1990; in *Knives and Angels,* edited by Susan Bassnett, 1990.

Critical Studies: "The Vaporous World of Bombal" by Margaret V. Campbell, in *Hispania* 44, September 1961; "Structure, Imagery and Experience in Bombal's 'The Tree'" by Andrew P. Debicki, *Studies in Short Fiction,* winter 1971; "Bombal from a Feminist Perspective" by Linda Gould Levine, in *Revista/Review Interamericana* 4, Summer 1974; *Three Authors of Alienation: Bombal, Onetti, Carpentier* by Ian M. Adams, 1975; "Bombal: *La Amortajada*" by Lucia Fox-Lockert, in *Women Novelists in Spain and Spanish America,* 1979; "Bombal's Heroines: Poetic Neuroses and Artistic Symbolism" by Thomas O.

Bente, in *Hispanófila* 28, 1984; *The Lyrical Vision of Bombal* by Celeste Kostopulos-Cooperman, 1988; "Biography of a Story-Telling Woman" by Marjorie Agosin, in *Knives and Angels,* edited by Susan Bassnett, 1990.

*   *   *

María Luisa Bombal offers many interpretative challenges to her readers and critics, not least because she is one of the few authors who has rewritten their own novels, in another language. Unusually, neither *The House of Mist* or *The Shrouded Woman* reads like a translation: her prose, be it in Spanish or English, is flawless, elegant, and evocative.

Bombal's first published work, *La última niebla,* first appeared in Buenos Aires in 1935. An English translation, "The Final Mist," was published in *The New Islands and Other Stories* in 1982. However, Bombal herself produced a reworking of *La última niebla* in 1947, under the title of *The House of Mist.* The author extends her narrative considerably, giving it greater detail and depth, and altering various significant aspects of the story, among them the point in time at which the narrative action begins, and the way it ends, so that *The House of Mist* may be considered a different work from "The Final Mist." There are also two versions of Bombal's second novel: the Spanish original *La amortajada* was translated with some modifications by the author as *The Shrouded Woman.*

Some of Bombal's short stories have also been published in English by the translators Richard and Lucia Cunningham, in *The New Islands.* These brief narratives echo the same themes as the two main novels: even "The Unknown" takes as its point of departure a tale of pirates that recalls the references to Bluebeard in *The House of Mist,* and Bombal's customary use of fairy tales.

There is unanimous agreement among critics that her literary output, though not great in quantity, is of the highest quality, particularly in view of the coherence and treatment of her subject matter, and the unity of theme, setting, and style. Bombal is commonly credited with having introduced a new, feminist sensibility to Chilean literature. However, the extent to which she may accurately be categorized a Chilean writer is debatable: her intellectual formation was essentially European and most of her writing was done in Argentina in the company of Victoria Ocampo, Alfonsina Storni, and Jorge Luis Borges, or in the United States, with the encouragement of her French husband, the Count of St. Phalle. There are Chilean elements—the geographical reference in the prologue to *The House of Mist,* the constant mention of rain and mist, the presence of Indian servants, the allusion to *vicuña* wool ponchos, the occasional Chilean Spanish vocabulary item, such as *fundo* ("ranch"). But her depiction of characters and their conflicts transcends the local and national, becoming rather a universal comment on the situation of humanity, not a set of observations rooted in any particular society or age.

As she writes and rewrites her material, Bombal draws on an apparently finite number of characters, situations, and leitmotifs. Considered as a coherent whole, her work may be perceived as a set of variations on one specific theme. The greater part of her writing is taken up with the life, development, crises, and sufferings of women: it is almost as if each successive piece of writing offers a new facet of the same woman. The majority of her female protagonists are convent-educated, from the land-owning upper-middle class; they are not subject to any material deprivation, but are, nonetheless, circumscribed by their environment and the burden of social expectations. Moreover, almost without exception, they experience tremendous difficulties in carrying out their traditional role as dependent female, or wife, the only truly acceptable role that society seems to envisage for them. We are reminded of one of Bombal's most poignant lines, voiced by Ana María in *The Shrouded Woman:* "Why, why must a woman's nature be such that a man has always to be the pivot of her life?"

Women in Bombal's stories seem to be embarked on a permanent, and often fruitless, quest for love and companionship. Thus Brígida in "The Tree" is constantly described as clinging on to her husband Luis: "she unconsciously sought his shoulder all night long searching for his breath, groping blindly for protection as an enclosed and thirsty plant bends its tendrils towards warmth and moisture." These troubled, alienated women are driven to seek refuge in a universe of dreams or fairy tales that eventually becomes more real, more immediate, and infinitely more tolerable than their objective, physical world. Fantasy mingles with reality, until neither the protagonist nor the reader is sure which is which.

Although Bombal's work is not classifiable as fictional autobiography, in view of the number of reminiscences of her own life that we find in her writing, we will almost inevitably make a connection between the female protagonists of her narratives and the writer herself. Readers should note the advantages of reading her work in its entirety, with its recurring characters, themes, and symbols, all of which contribute to a more profound expression of the predicament of her female protagonist(s).

If Bombal writes repeatedly about one particular kind of woman, then she also reproduces other characters, with slight variations, in her narratives: the faithful Indian or peasant nurse, the cold, rejecting husband or lover (Luis in "The Tree," Juan Manuel in "New Islands"). One notable difference occurs when Bombal produces her English rewrites. Here, almost by way of a sop to a more romantically inclined readership, there is a slight attempt to justify the boorish behaviour of her male protagonists. Jealousy is, of course, a crucial, important element in the male-female relationship as depicted by Bombal. Virtually all of her characters are prone to this destructive emotion.

The two most important symbols in Bombal's writing are perhaps mist and hair. The first of these is not always a malign force, but in "The Final Mist" the encroachment of mist into the house and subsequently all areas of her life, is highly significant, reducing her world to a narrow, compressed prison, limiting her freedom, following her, sticking to her. Only when she is in the bedroom of her (dream) lover, can the mist no longer reach her. Mist is also present in "The Tree," indicative of profound unhappiness, claustrophobia, and oppression. In "New Islands" the mist is a haunting grey background for Juan Manuel's pursuit, then rejection of, Yolanda.

In Bombal's novels and stories, unbound hair is symbolic of liberation, both social and sexual. In "The Tree," before her marriage to Luis, Brígida wears her hair loose, "her chestnut braids that, unbound, cascaded to her waist." Women's hair is always unrestrained in moments of passion; in "The Final Mist" Regina's hair flows loose while the narrator-protagonist is obliged by her husband to wear hers in a tight braid that evidently represents her subjugation and lack of fulfilment, emotional and sexual. Bombal also deals with the subject of hair in "Trenzas," a whimsical essay rather than a short story; several stories are retold in this work, all linked by the motif of women's tresses, and all expressing the belief that women's power

and strength resides in their hair. Braids have magical, mystical powers that are linked to the world of nature, and are a means of attracting lovers, binding them as if in chains. By cutting her hair, a woman resigns herself to a barren, loveless existence. In "New Islands" Yolanda is said to resemble an Amazon huntress with her hair streaming around her face. As she sleeps her hair covers her face "like a latticework of luxuriant vines" and when Juan Manuel almost takes her by force, he entangles himself in "her thick, sweet-scented hair."

Women in Bombal are often likened to hunted animals. Luis married Brígida in "The Tree" because she had "the eyes of a startled fawn." And the encroaching males in "New Islands," Juan Manuel and Sylvester, have come to hunt.

Bombal's protagonists do not look forward to a contented old age, they do not enjoy a Keatsian "season of mists and mellow fruitfulness." Because they are defined by their relationships with men and these relationships tend to break down, old age looms ineluctably lonely, empty, and barren. The most dramatic realization of mortality comes in "The Tree" when Brígida suddenly notices with repugnance Luis's "wrinkled face, his hands crisscrossed with ropy discolored veins." The logical development of this motif is the link in Bombal's narratives between women and death, often violent. Thus, early in "The Final Mist," the narrator sees a dead girl in a glass-topped coffin, and her own house is described as a tomb. Her sister-in-law Regina shoots herself and the narrator tries to throw herself under the wheels of a vehicle. Juan Manuel in "New Islands" lost his wife, Elsa, through illness, Brígida in "The Tree" is left motherless at an early age, and a young widow tragically expires in "Braids." Most of the women depicted by Bombal are suffering some kind of death, if not a physical demise, then the death of their hopes and dreams.

There are also some positive symbols in Bombal's writing. The natural world in general and trees in particular are viewed as extremely positive elements. Autumn rain may induce a feeling of well-being, while trees offer shelter and protection. Hence the importance of the rubber tree in "The Tree," giving Brígida a refuge from her unhappy marriage to Luis; or the great, sheltering hazelnut tree under which the children played in "Braids." The garden is generally represented as a place of refuge, a place of freedom and safety in which the female protagonist can give expression to her thoughts and feelings, a place where there is some hope, because of the regeneration that is an integral part of the natural cycle. In some ways, it is a symbol of the heroine herself.

It should not be assumed that Bombal's women are completely passive and accepting. In her novels and short stories, there is frequently a point at which the central character becomes angry, and is somehow pushed by utter frustration or anger into affirming her own identity. This is a key moment, the act of resisting, or expressing anger, hostility, indignation. There is an underlying suggestion that women's social conditioning precludes any meaningful attempt to rebel against, challenge, or resist male authority figures. For Helga, the decisive moment comes when Daniel intrudes on one of her reveries (*The House of Mist*). For Ana María, the first outburst comes when she is abandoned by Ricardo, the second when she tires of Antonio's blatant unfaithfulness. (*The Shrouded Woman*). Brígida has reached a point when she can no longer stand being rebuffed, but does not know how to express her anger ("The Tree").

One additional aspect of her narrative should not be overlooked, the fact that in many ways it is a celebration of women's capacity for eroticism, for sensual pleasure. Nowhere is this seen more clearly than in "The Final Mist," in the incident where the narrator bathes in the pool, in her graphic description of the sexual act, and the intense satisfaction that she experiences with her dream lover.

Bombal's writing is innovative, in form as much as in content. At the same time, few women writers of her generation can have explored the question of female sexuality with the same frankness. Equally at ease with a first-person or third-person narrative focalization, her prose is intensely poetic and musical. In fact, music plays an important part throughout her writing (though nowhere as clearly as in "The Tree"). Her narrative concentrates on one essential theme that she explores with sensitivity and honesty, the limitations imposed on women—as much by women themselves, as by the men who control their lives.

—Patricia Anne Odber de Baubeta

See the essay on "The Tree."

————

BOND, Ruskin. Indian. Born in Kasauli, Himachal, 19 May 1934. Educated at Bishop Cotton School, Simla, 1943–50. Freelance writer, from 1956; managing editor, *Imprint* magazine, Bombay, 1975–79. Recipient: Rhys Memorial prize, for fiction, 1957. Lives in Mussourie.

PUBLICATIONS

Short Stories

The Neighbour's Wife and Other Stories.   1967.
My First Love and Other Stories.   1968.
The Man-Eater of Manjari.   1974.
Love Is a Sad Song.   1975.
A Girl from Copenhagen.   1977.
Ghosts of a Hill Station.   1983.
The Night Train at Deol.   1988.
Time Stops at Shamli and Other Stories.   1989.
Our Trees still Grow in Dehra.   1991.

Novels

The Room on the Roof.   1956.
An Axe for the Rani.   1972.
A Flight of Pigeons.   1980.
The Young Vagrants.   1981.

Fiction (for children)

The Hidden Pool, illustrated by Arup Das.   1966.
Grandfather's Private Zoo, illustrated by Mario Miranda. 1967.
Panther's Moon, illustrated by Tom Feelings.   1969.
The Last Tiger: New Delhi.   1971.
Angry River, illustrated by Trevor Stubley.   1972.
The Blue Umbrella, illustrated by Trevor Stubley.   1974.
Night of the Leopard, illustrated by Eileen Green.   1979.
Big Business, illustrated by Valerie Littlewood.   1979.
The Cherry Tree, illustrated by Valerie Littlewood.   1980.

The Road to the Bazaar (stories), illustrated by Valerie Littlewood.   1980.
Flames in the Forest, illustrated by Valerie Littlewood. 1981.
The Adventures of Rusty, illustrated by Imtiaz Dharker. 1981.
Tigers Forever, illustrated by Valerie Littlewood.   1983.
Earthquake, illustrated by Valerie Littlewood.   1984.
Getting Granny's Glasses, illustrated by Barbara Walker. 1985.
Cricket for the Crocodile, illustrated by Barbara Walker. 1986.
The Adventures of Rama and Sita, illustrated by Valerie Littlewood.   1987.
The Eyes of the Eagle, illustrated by Valerie Littlewood. 1987.
Ghost Trouble.   1989.
Snake Troubler.   1990.
Dust on the Mountain.   1990.

Verse

It Isn't Time That's Passing: Poems 1970–1971.   1972.
Lone Fox Dancing: Lyric Poems.   1975.
To Live in Magic (for children).   1983.

Other

The Wonderful World of Insects, Trees, and Wild Flowers (for children), illustrated by Kamal Kishore.   1968.
Strange Men, Strange Places.   1969.
Tales Told at Twilight (folktales; for children), illustrated by Madhu Powle.   1970.
World of Trees (for children), illustrated by Siddhartha Banerjee.   1974.
Who's Who at the Zoo (for children) photographs by Raghu Rai.   1974.
Once upon a Monsoon Time (autobiography; for children). 1974.
Man of Destiny: A Biography of Jawaharlal Nehru (for children).   1976.
A Garland of Memories (essays; for children).   1982.
Tales and Legends of India (for children), illustrated by Sally Scott.   1982.
Beautiful Garhwal: Heaven in Himalayas (travelogue). 1988.

*   *   *

In a writing career spanning 35 years, Ruskin Bond, a wordsmith (as he describes his calling) of rare distinction, has written more than a hundred short stories, essays, novels, and poetry. It is, however, as a master storyteller, possessing keen perception, and a deep insight into human nature, that Bond is internationally acclaimed. He has settled in Mussorie, a picturesque hill station in the Himalayas, and most of his stories are set there, and reflect his humble beginning and struggles.

Compassion and sensitivity to life's various nuances are the keynotes of Bond's stories. He is gentle in his satirical studies of people ("The Boy Who Broke the Bank") and infinitely understanding of the vagaries of human nature ("An Axe for the Rani"). His faculty of observing minute details is remarkable; he produces a starting effect such as in depicting the sinking of the crow's nest in the tremendous flood waters ("Sita and the River"). His style is fluid and so natural that we are carried along the course of the narrative.

The themes of Bond's stories can be categorised quite distinctly. They are mostly set in India, some revolving around his days of lost youth and romance, some presenting cameos of people commonly met on Indian roads. Several stories recall the halcyon days of childhood, while others are stories of adventure, set amidst the Himalayan foothills, with its exotic fauna. His style is conversational as he draws the reader in to share his experiences. Often there is an uneasy sense that Bond lives in, and writes of the past, basking in the afterglow of days that are no more ("The Last Tonga Ride," "Coming Home to Dehra," "The Story of Madhu").

The sweet-sour recollections of his childhood days are invested with a touch of fantasy characteristic of Bond. Memories of his own childhood spent in the boarding school at Shimla, of his beloved father whom he lost early in life ("Escape from Java"), and the simple joys of a youngster ("All Creatures Great and Small," "The Photograph") are recorded in his stories.

His remarkable short stories about people he met and remembered in the course of his life reveal his tolerant attitude and warm sympathy for human foibles ("The Thief Death of a Familiar"). It is Bond's uniqueness as a writer that he sees something of interest in the most common characters ("The Immortal Sardar," "The Guardian Angel"); he excels at intimately entering the course of their humdrum lives.

The people of the Himalayan foothills and the local flora and fauna find their way into his stories. Tales of animals and adventure, such as "Panther's Moon," "The Leopard," "Mountain Leopard," and "The Maneater of Manjari," rival some tales by Kipling or Jim Korbett, and they make exciting reading for both children and adults. Bond's passionate involvement with nature and his sorrow at human's willful destruction of its resources is almost palpable ("Death of the Trees"). Nature's resurrective power are evoked in stories like "My Father's Trees at Dehra" and "The Cherry Tree."

Hints of a romance—short, sweet, and unfinished—characterize many of Bond's best creations. There is a yearning nostalgia for lost youth, but little regret for "remembered passion." The passing of time is the theme that strings these stories along a similar emotional plane (*The Night Train at Deol*, "The Coral Tree," "The Story of Madhu," and "Binya Passes by"). These stories have a fey element, something wild and sweet, as though experienced in a dream. The girls seem to be symbols of an intense passion, and invariably appear with red ribbons in their black hair, always partnered with a struggling, recluse-like writer. Melancholy seeps in between the lines, there is plaintive cry for lost love for the years passing by. The same theme recurs in the enchanting novelette *Love Is a Sad Song*. A deep knowledge of Indian society and its tenderness, heartbreak, and loss is woven into the fabric of this exquisite piece of fiction. In his immitigably clear and lucid style, Bond depicts the intricacies of relationships and the nuances of people of different cultures against the backdrop of his country.

—Soma Banerjee

BORGES, Jorge Luis. Argentine. Born in Buenos Aires, 24 August 1899. Educated at Collège de Genève, Switzerland; Cambridge University. Married 1) Elsa Astete Millán in 1967 (divorced 1970); 2) María Kodama in 1986. Lived in Europe with his family, 1914–21; co-founding editor, *Proa*, 1924–26, and *Sur*, 1931; also associated with *Prisma*; columnist, *El Hogar* weekly, Buenos Aires, 1936–39; literary adviser, Emecé Editores, Buenos Aires; municipal librarian, Buenos Aires, 1939–43; poultry inspector, 1944–54; became blind, 1955; director, National Library, 1955–73; professor of English literature, University of Buenos Aires, 1955–70; Norton Professor of poetry, Harvard University, Cambridge, Massachusetts; visiting lecturer, University of Oklahoma, Norman, 1969. President, Argentine Writers Society, 1950–53. Recipient: Buenos Aires Municipal prize, 1928; Argentine Writers Society prize, 1945; National Prize for Literature, 1957; Ingram Merrill award, 1966; Bienal Foundation Inter-American prize, 1970; Jerusalem prize, 1971; Alfonso Reyes prize, 1973; Cervantes prize, 1980; Yoliztli prize, 1981. Honorary D.Litt.: University of Cuyo, Argentina, 1956; Oxford University, 1971; Columbia University, New York, 1971; University of Michigan, East Lansing, 1972; University of Chile, 1976; University of Cincinnati, 1976. Member, Argentine National Academy; Uruguayan Academy of Letters. Honorary Fellow, Modern Language Association (U.S.), 1961. Member, Legion of Honor. Order of Merit (Italy), 1968. Order of Merit (German Federal Republic), 1979. Icelandic Falcon Cross, 1979. Honorary K.B.E. (Knight Commander, Order of the British Empire). *Died 14 June 1986.*

PUBLICATIONS

Short Stories

Historia universal de la infamia.   1935; as *A Universal History of Infamy,* 1971.
El jardín de senderos que se bifurcan.   1941.
Seis problemas para don Isidro Parodi (with Adolfo Bioy Casares, as H. Bustos Domecq).   1942; as *Six Problems for Don Isidro Parodi,* 1981.
Ficciones (1935–1944).   1944; augmented edition, 1956; translated as *Ficciones,* 1962; as *Fictions,* 1965.
Dos fantasías memorables, with Adolfo Bioy Casares. 1946.
El Aleph.   1949; as *The Aleph and Other Stories 1933–1969,* 1970.
La muerte y la brújula.   1951.
La hermana de Elosía, with Luisa Mercedes Levinson. 1955.
Labyrinths: Selected Stories and Other Writings, edited by Donald A. Yates and James E. Irby.   1962; augmented edition, 1964.
Crónicas de Bustos Domecq, with Adolfo Bioy Casares. 1967; as *Chronicles of Bustos Domecq,* 1979.
El informe de Brodie.   1970; as *Dr. Brodie's Report,* 1972.
El congreso. 1971; as *The Congress,* 1974.
El libro de arena.   1975; as *The Book of Sand,* 1977; with *The Gold of the Tigers* (verse), 1979.
Nuevos cuentos de Bustos Domecq, with Adolfo Bioy Casares.   1977.

Novel

Un modelo para la muerte, with Adolfo Bioy Casares. 1946.

Play

Screenplay: *Los orilleros; El paraíso de los creyentes*, with Adolfo Bioy Casares,   1955.

Verse

Fervor de Buenos Aires.   1923.
Luna de enfrente.   1925.
Cuaderno San Martín.   1929.
Poemas 1922–1943.   1943.
Poemas 1923–1958.   1958.
El hacedor.   1960; as *Dreamtigers*, 1963.
Obra poética 1923–1964.   1964.
Para las seis cuerdas.   1965; revised edition, 1970.
Obra poética 1923–1967.   1967.
Nueva antología personal.   1968.
Obra poética.   5 vols., 1969–72.
Elogio de la sombra.   1969; as *In Praise of Darkness*, 1974.
El otro, el mismo.   1969.
El oro de los tigres.   1972; as *The Gold of the Tigers*, with *The Book of Sand*, 1979.
Selected Poems 1923–1967, edited by Norman Thomas di Giovanni.   1972.
La rosa profundo.   1975.
La moneda de hierro.   1976.
Historia de la noche.   1977.
Poemas 1919–1922.   1978.
Obra poética 1923–1976.   1978.
La cifra.   1981.
Antología poética.   1981.

Other

Inquisiciones (essays).   1925.
El tamaño de mi esperanza (essays).   1926.
El idioma de los Argentinos (essays).   1928; enlarged edition, as *El lenguaje de Buenos Aires*, with José Edmundo Clemente, 1963.
Evaristo Carriego (essays).   1930; as *Evaristo Carriego*, 1984.
Discusión.   1932.
Las Kennigar.   1933.
Historia de la eternidad (essays).   1936; enlarged edition, 1953.
Nueva refutación del tiempo.   1947.
Aspectos de la literatura gauchesca.   1950.
Antiguas literaturas germánicas, with Delia Ingenieros.   1951.
Otras inquisiciones 1937–1952.   1952; as *Other Inquisitions 1937–1952*, 1964.
El Martín Fierro, with Margarita Guerrero.   1953.
Obras completas, edited by José Edmundo Clemente.   10 vols., 1953–60;   1 vol., 1974.
Leopoldo Lugones, with Betina Edelberg.   1955.
Manual de zoología fantástica, with Margarita Guerrero.   1957; revised edition, as *El libro de los seres imaginarios*, 1967; as *The Imaginary Zoo*, 1969; revised edition, as *The Book of Imaginary Beings*, 1969.
Antología personal.   1961; as *A Personal Anthology*, edited by Anthony Kerrigan, 1968.
The Spanish Language in South America: A Literary Problem; El Gaucho Martín Fierro (lectures).   1964.
Introducción a la literatura inglesa, with María Esther Vázquez.   1965; as *An Introduction to English Literature*, 1974.

Literaturas germánicas medievales, with María Esther Vázquez.   1966.
Introducción a la literatura norteamericana, with Esther Zemborain de Torres.   1967; as *An Introduction to American Literature*, 1971.
Nueva antología personal.   1968.
Conversations with Borges, by Richard Burgin.   1968.
Borges on Writing, edited by Norman Thomas di Giovanni, Daniel Halpern, and Frank MacShane.   1973.
Obras completas: 1923–1972, edited by Carlos V. Frías.   1974.
Prólogos.   1975.
Qué es el budismo?, with Alicia Jurado.   1976.
Libros de sueños.   1976.
Adrogué (verse and prose; privately printed).   1977.
Borges oral (lectures).   1979.
Prosa completa.   2 vols., 1980.
Siete noches (essays).   1980; as *Seven Nights*, 1984.
A Reader, edited by Alastair Reid and Emir Rodríguez Monegal.   1981.
Nueve ensayos dantescos.   1982.
Atlas, with María Komada.   1985; as *Atlas*, 1985.
Los conjurados.   1985.
Conversaciones con Alicia Moreau de Justo y Borges.   1985.
Borges en dialogo, with Osvaldo Ferrari.   1985.
Conversaciones con Borges, with Roberto Alifano.   1986.
Conversaciones con Borges, with Francisco Tokos.   1986.
Textos Cautivos: Ensayos y reseñas en El Hogar (1936–1939), edited by Enrique Sacerio-Gari and Emir Rodríguez Monegal.   1987.
Paginas escogidas, edited by Roberto Fernandez Retamar.   1988.
Biblioteca personal: Prólogos.   1988.
Ultimas conversaciones con Borges, with Roberto Alifano.   1988.

Editor, with Pedro Henriques Urena, *Antología clasica de la literatura argentina.*   1937.
Editor, with Silvina Ocampo and Adolfo Bioy Casares, *Antología de la literatura fantástica.*   1940; as *The Book of Fantasy*, 1988.
Editor, with Silvina Ocampo and Adolfo Bioy Casares, *Antología poética argentina.*   1941.
Editor, with Adolfo Bioy Casares, *Los mejores cuentos policiales.*   2 vols., 1943–51.
Editor, with Silvina Bullrich Palenque, *El Campadrito: Su destino, sus barrios, su música.*   1945.
Editor, with Adolfo Bioy Casares, *Prosa y verso*, by Francisco de Quevedo.   1948.
Editor and translator, with Adolfo Bioy Casares, *Poesía gauchesca.*   2 vols., 1955.
Editor, with Adolfo Bioy Casares, *Cuentos breves y extraordinarios.*   1955; as *Extraordinary Tales*, 1971.
Editor, with Adolfo Bioy Casares, *Libro del cielo y del infierno.*   1960.
Editor, *Paulino Lucero, Aniceto y gallo, Santos Vega*, by Hilario Ascasubi.   1960.
Editor, *Macedonia Fernández (selection).*   1961.
Editor, *Páginas de historia y de autobiografía*, by Edward Gibbon.   1961.
Editor, *Prosa y poesía*, by Almafuerte.   1962.
Editor, *Versos*, by Evaristo Carriego.   1963.
Editor, with María Komada, *Breve antología anglosajona.*   1978.
Editor, *Micromegas*, by Voltaire.   1979.
Editor, *Cuentistas y pintores argentinos.*   1985.

Translator, *La metamorfosis,* by Kafka.   1938.
Translator, *Bartleby,* by Herman Melville.   1944.
Translator, *De los héroes; Hombres representativos,* by Carlyle and Emerson.   1949.

*

Bibliography: *Borges: An Annotated Primary and Secondary Bibliography* by David William Foster, 1984; *The Literary Universe of Borges: An Index to References and Illusions to Persons, Titles, and Places in His Writings* by Daniel Balderston, 1986.

Critical Studies: *Borges, The Labyrinth Maker* by Ana María Barrenchea, edited and translated by Robert Lima, 1965; *The Narrow Act: Borges' Art of Illusion* by Ronald J. Christ, 1969; *The Mythmaker: A Study of Motif and Symbol in the Short Stories of Borges* by Carter Wheelock, 1969; *Borges,* 1970, and *Borges Revisted,* 1991, both by Martin S. Stabb; *The Cardinal Points of Borges* edited Lowell Dunham and Ivor Ivask, 1971; *Borges* by J.M. Cohen, 1973; *Prose for Borges* edited by Charles Newman and Mary Kinzie, 1974; *Tongues of Fallen Angels: Conversations with Borges* by Selden Roman, 1974; *The Literature of Exhaustion: Borges, Nabokov and Barth* by John O. Stark, 1974; *Borges: Ficciones* by Donald Leslie Shaw, 1976; *Raid on the Articulate: Comic Eschatology in Jesus and Borges* by John Dominic Crossan, 1976; *Paper Tigers: The Ideal Fictions of Borges* by John Sturrock, 1977; *Borges: Sources and Illumination* by Giovanna De Garayalde, 1978; *Borges: A Literary Biography* by Emir Rodríguez Monegal, 1978; *Borges* by George R. McMurray, 1980; *Borges and His Fiction: A Guide to His Mind and Art* by Gene H. Bell-Villada, 1981; *The German Response to Latin American Literature, And the Reception of Borges and Pablo Neruda* by Yolanda Julia Broyles, 1981; *Borges at Eighty: Conversations* edited by William Barnstone, 1982; *The Prose of Borges: Existentialism and the Dynamics of Surprise,* 1984, and *The Meaning of Experience in the Prose of Borges,* 1988, both by Ion Tudro Agheana; *Borges* edited by Harold Bloom, 1986; *The Poetry and Poetics of Borges* by Paul Cheselka, 1987; *The Emperor's Kites: A Morphology of Borges's Tales* by Mary Lusky Friedman, 1987; *Critical Essays on Borges* edited by Jaime Alazraki, 1987, and *Borges and the Kaballah* by Alazraki, 1988; *In Memory of Borges* edited by Norman Thomas di Giovanni, 1988; *Borges and His Successors: The Borges Impact on Literature and the Arts* edited by Edna Aizenberg, 1990; *Borges: A Study of the Short Fiction* by Naomi Lindstrom, 1990; *A Dictionary of Borges* by Evelyn Fishburne, 1990; *Borges and Artificial Intelligence: An Analysis in the Style of Pierre Menard* by Ema Lapidot, 1991; *The Contemporary Praxis of the Fantastic: Borges and Cortázar* by Julio Rodríquez-Luis, 1991.

* * *

In the Spanish-speaking world, Jorge Luis Borges is almost as well known for his highly evocative verse and essays as he is for his fantastical short stories. Indeed, he began as a poet in the 1920's, when he set out to be the Walt Whitman of Buenos Aires. The rise of local fascists during the 1930's, however, soured him on nationalism of any stripe. He thereafter assumed a cosmopolitan stance, and turned to writing narratives instead. It is these brief fictions that eventually gained Borges his international reputation. Verbally dense and often bookish, his stories can put off a casual browser, though their erudite, other-worldly atmosphere is often commingled with touches of nostalgic warmth and a wry, subtle humor.

Borges's three-dozen best stories all date from the period 1939 to 1955, a time of personal and political torment for the author. They first appeared in the relatively slim volumes, *Ficciones* and *El Aleph.* And yet the artistic power, originality, and influence of these two books vastly exceeds their physical meagerness. Their terse, restrained prose style constitutes a distinct break from three centuries of Hispanic rhetoric and bombast. More important for writers of fiction the world over, the stories present alternatives both to traditional realism and to Modernist psychologism and "inwardness." What Borges does, in brief, is to emphasize the fantastical and imaginary, to foreground unreality itself as the essential stuff of storytelling, thereby making these traits prime movers of plot and character. The intrusion of the unreal into our everyday existence is precisely what Borges's fiction is about.

Hence, in several Borges stories, dreams and visions can occupy center stage. To the writer-protagonist of "The Secret Miracle," time seems to have stopped for exactly a year, though it may well be a vivid last-minute hallucination occurring within his head. Similarly, the jailed Mayan priest in "The God's Script" believes he has unlocked the divine secret of the universe; yet he could also be experiencing a classically religious-mystical seizure. By contrast, in "The Other Death" a one-time military coward's deathbed fantasies of battlefield courage somehow succeed in altering the historical record; and in "The Aleph" the narrator descends into a seedy basement, where he really does contemplate a wondrous one-inch square containing everything on planet Earth.

In the same way that it finds its way into daily life, the fantastical in Borges can intrude upon and affect our very sense of self, our personal identity. His protagonists are frequently depicted as finding out that they are actually somebody else ("The Theologians"). Or conversely, two seemingly separate life-stories become fused and, through Borgesian artifice, are shown to be just one, as in "Theme of the Traitor and the Hero" and "Story of the Warrior and the Captive," titles whose dual referents are then psychologically subverted in the ensuing narrative.

Another special side of Borges is his detective stories and crime fiction, a genre he raised to the level of a high art. "The Dead Man," "The Waiting," and "Emma Zunz" are hauntingly beautiful narratives of crime, in which the author brings into play his suggestive, fanciful notions concerning the role of mind and the nature of truth. On the other hand, "Death and the Compass"—one of Borges's greatest single pieces—is itself a dazzling spoof of the detective-story formula, a world in which everything is upside-down: the criminal captures the detective and preempts the latter's final role, and a bureaucratic "dumb cop" is proved right every time while a bookish, would-be Sherlock is proved sadly wrong.

Borges also can be credited with having invented an entire new genre: what we might call "essay-fiction," combining aspects of both. Many of Borges's best stories look like and have the feel of essays—yet are complete fictions. The narrator of "Tlon, Uqbar, Orbis Tertius" actually refers to its text as an "article," and its mixture of "hard" fact with unsettling fantasy serves to reinforce the essayistic impression. "Three Versions of Judas" presents itself as a learned article on theological disputes, with footnotes and all. Similarly, "The Sect of the Phoenix" seems to be an ethnographic account of an elusive tribe; it turns out to be a cosmic riddle and an elaborate sex joke.

Many of Borges's inventions have become standard items in our cultural lexicon. "Funes the Memorious" is now an obligatory reference in any psychological disquisition on the problem of absolute memory. The vast and bewildering information systems of our time are often likened to "The Library of Babel," and the notion of identical texts somehow possessing different meanings inevitably conjures up "Pierre Menard, Author of the *Quixote*." Borges's influence has also been felt in the arts worldwide. Bernardo Bertolucci and Nicholas Roeg both have feature films based on his stories, and Jean-Luc Godard in his more visionary movies quotes lines from Borges essays. Short novels like John Gardner's *Grendel* and Thomas Pynchon's *The Crying of Lot 49* take their cues directly from the Argentine master, and the works of Donald Barthelme and Robert Coover are in part the U.S. literary offspring of Borges's high artifice.

Borges in the 1960's became a world-renowned public figure, giving lectures and receiving accolades across the globe. One unfortunate result was that he lost much of his critical edge and started to repeat himself. Hence the narratives in the subsequent *El informe de Brodie* (*Doctor Brodie's Report*) and *El libro de arena* (*The Book of Sand*) are mostly pale imitations of the great writings from his middle period. So long as readers of short stories exist, however, the tales from *Ficciones*, *El Aleph*, and the English-language anthology *Labyrinths* will remain part of our literary repertoire.

—Gene H. Bell-Villada

See the essays on "The Circular Ruins," "The Garden of Forking Paths," "The Library of Babel," and "Pierre Menard, Author of the *Quixote*."

BOROWSKI, Tadeusz. Polish. Born in Żytomierz, Ukraine, 12 November 1922. Studied Polish literature at underground Warsaw University, 1940. Interned in concentration camps, Auschwitz and Dachau, 1943–45; political journalist and publicist, Munich, Germany, from 1948. *Died (suicide) 3 July 1951.*

PUBLICATIONS

Collections

Utwory zebrane [Collected Works].   5 vols., 1954.

Short Stories

Pożegnanie z Marią [Farewell to Maria].   1948.
Kamienny świat [The World of Stone].   1948.
Wybór opowiadań (selection).   1959.
This Way for the Gas, Ladies and Gentlemen, and Other Stories.   1967.
Dzień na Harmenzach.   1978.

Verse

Gdziekolwiek ziemia [Wherever the Earth].   1942.

Imiona nurtu [The Names of the Current].   1945.
Poszukiwania. Tracing, with K. Olszewski.   1945.
Selected Poems.   1990.

Other

Byliśmy w Oświęcimiu, with K. Olszewski and J. Nel Siedlecki.   1946.
Musik in Herzenburg.   1951.
Wspomnienia, wiersze, opowiadania (reminiscences, verse, and stories).   1977.

*

Critical Study: "A Discovery of Tragedy" by A. Wirth, *Polish Review* 12, 1967.

*   *   *

Tadeusz Borowski was an outstanding Polish writer in the years after World War II. Although he made his debut in German-occupied Warsaw with a clandestine collection of poems, his prose-writing talents blossomed soon after his liberation from the Dachau concentration camp in 1945. Previously Borowski was held in the mass-extermination camp of Oświęcim (Auschwitz) and, indeed, his very first piece of prose (published in a volume with works by K. Olszewski and J.N. Siedlecki) *Byliśmy w Oświęcimiu* (We were in Auschwitz), related his experiences from this camp where thousands of Poles died. Stories from Auschwitz form the nucleus of Borowski's book of short stories *Pożegnanie z Marią* (Farewell to Maria), which first established him as an important writer.

Few writers managed to capture the atmosphere of the Nazi concentration camps as faithfully as Borowski in stories like "This Way for the Gas, Ladies and Gentlemen" (the title story of a collection of his work in English) and "A Day at Harmenz." In the first of these stories a day is described in the life of the "labour Kommando" who help to unload the incoming transports of deported Jews destined for the gas chambers. It is a horrifying, almost maddening experience in human terms, but because members of the labour gang (which includes the narrator Tadek) can have some surplus food afterwards, it also enhances their chance to survive. And in Auschwitz—if one survived the first "selection"—survival takes precedence over all other human values. "A Day at Harmenz" is less intense in its depiction of "Auschwitz reality"—it relates episodes from camp life, including the theft of a goose, regular beatings of camp inmates who don't work hard enough, and a discussion of whistled tunes with a German *Kapo* (overseer) that could, but luckily will not, have dangerous consequences for the narrator. The day ends in anticipation of a new selection, when weak and ill labourers are chosen and sent to the gas chambers. In these stories Borowski stresses the banality of evil. His SS-men are not demonic, they are not even particularly sadistic; their main characteristic is cool indifference, although some of them show interest in the efficient realization of their "job." But they are all nameless: the murderer is anonymous. Auschwitz is a reified world, where the process of turning people into things reaches its apogee (even human corpses are used for the production of soap and bone products).

Borowski's second collection of stories *Kamienny świat* (The World of Stone) moved away from the technique of first-person storytelling; apparently, he was annoyed by the critics' automatic identification of narrator Tadek with the writer himself. The 20 stories of this collection are considerably shorter than the ones discussed above; they rarely run to more than three or four pages. Concentration camp themes still predominate, including episodes treated with a mixture of irony and deep understanding such as "The Death of Schillinger" (about the death of a German camp overseer and mass-murderer who is totally unable to grasp his own criminal behaviour), "The Man with the Package," and "The Supper" (which tells a case of "spontaneous" cannibalism amongst starving Russian prisoners of war). The title sketch, "The World of Stone," is about the postwar bustle of ordinary people, which fills the narrator with unease and with a sense of irreality—just as people "disappeared" during the war years for no particular reason, he can see "all this suddenly float into the air and then drop, all in a tangle, right at my feet" (translated by Barbara Vedder). In other words Borowski questions the definition of "normal" life and shows the extreme fragility of "normal" human values.

Several of Borowski's short stories deal with the end of war or postwar situations. "Śmierć powstańca" (The Death of an Insurgent), for example, shows the antagonism between the old KZ camp-inmates and some of the newly interned Polish prisoners, fighters of the 1944 Warsaw Uprising. "Bitwa pod Grunwaldem" (The Battle of Grunwald), later filmed by Andrzej Wajda as "Landscape after a Battle," is an ironic tale of frustration and disillusionment, told from the point of view of Polish soldiers and ex-camp inmates provisionally interned by the U.S. Army after the end of the war. The fireworks display at the conclusion of the story is in bitter contrast with the feeling of inner emptiness and cynicism about the results of liberation that seems to be shared by many young Poles. This story indicates also Borowski's own difficulties in adjusting to normal life, which (after his return to Poland and a period of pro-Communist journalistic fervour) eventually led to his suicide, the circumstances of which have not been fully explained to this day.

—George Gömöri

BOSMAN, Herman Charles. South African. Born at Kuil's River, Cape Town, 3 February 1905. Educated at University of Witwaterstand and Normal College, Johannesburg, 1923–25, teaching certificate 1925. Married 1) Vera Sawyer in 1926 (divorced 1932); 2) Ellaleen Manson in 1932 (divorced 1944; died 1945); 3) Helena Stegman in 1944. Teacher, Groot Marico district, Western Transvaal, 1926; incarcerated for murder of step-brother, Pretoria Central Prison, 1926: paroled, 1930; wrote under the pen name Herman Malan, in the 1930's and 1940's; founder and publisher, literary journals, *The Touleier, The New Sjambok,* and *The New L.S.D.,* Johannesburg, 1930–34; lived in London, Paris, and Brussels, 1934–39; founder, with W.W. Jacobs, Arden Godbold Press, 1934; returned to South Africa, 1939; journalist, advertising salesman, and newspaper editor, Pietersburg, 1943; literary editor, *South African Opinion,* 1944; moved to Cape Town, 1949; moved to Johannesburg, 1951. *Died 14 October 1951.*

PUBLICATIONS

Collections

Selected Stories, edited by Stephen Gray.   1980; revised edition, 1982.
Collected Works, edited by Lionel Abrahams.   2 vols., 1981.

Short Stories

Mafeking Road.   1947.
Unto Dust, edited by Lionel Abrahams.   1963.
Bosman at His Best: A Choice of Stories and Sketches, edited by Lionel Abrahams.   1965.
A Bekkersdal Marathon.   1971.
Jurie Steyn's Post Office.   1971.
Almost Forgotten Stories, edited by Valerie Rosenberg.   1979.
Makapan's Caves, edited by Stephen Gray.   1987.
Ramoutsa Road, edited by Valerie Rosenberg.   1987.

Novels

Jacaranda in the Night.   1947.
Willemsdorp.   1977.

Verse

The Blue Princess (as Herman Malan).   1931.
Mara (includes "Mara: A Play in One Act") (as Herman Malan).   1932.
Rust: A Poem (as Herman Malan).   1932.
Jesus: An Ode (as Herman Malan).   1933.
The Earth Is Waiting, edited by Lionel Abrahams.   1974.
Death Hath Eloquence, edited by Aegidius Jean Blignaut. 1981.

Other

Cold Stone Jug (autobiography).   1949.
A Cask of Jerepigo: Sketches and Essays.   1957.
Uncollected Essays, edited by Valerie Rosenberg.   1981.
Bosman's Johannesburg (stories and essays), edited by Stephen Gray.   1981.

Editor, with C. Bredell, *Veld Trails and Pavements: South African Short Stories.*   1949.

*

Critical Studies: *Sunflower to the Sun: The Life of Bosman* by Valerie Rosenberg, 1976; *My Friend Bosman* by Aegidius Jean Blignaut, 1981; *Bosman* edited by Stephen Gray, 1986.

* * *

A prolific novelist, poet, critic and short story writer, Herman Charles Bosman has some 20 published works to his name. However, it is as a short story writer that he is best known. Whether one measures his achievements in this genre in terms of sustained popular appeal or widespread critical acclaim, Bosman's stories—most of which appeared in collected form only after his premature death in 1951—are among the best South African literature has to offer.

Bosman was born of Afrikaner parents near Cape Town, but spent most of his life in the Transvaal, and it is the Transvaal milieu that permeates almost all of his writings. At the impressionable age of 21 he received a posting as a newly qualified teacher to the Groot Marico in the remote Western Transvaal. The impression that the Marico and its inhabitants made on the young teacher was clearly so strong that he was able over the last 20 years of his life to deliver a series of stories remarkable in quality and deeply redolent of the area.

Bosman's stories have appeared in a dozen collections over the years. However, *Mafeking Road,* by far his best-known collection, was the only one to appear in his own lifetime. Bosman's storyteller figure, the wily backveld raconteur Oom Schalk Lourens, features in all but three of the stories in *Mafeking Road.* Schalk Lourens was first introduced to the South African reading public in "Makapan's Caves," which memorably begins: "Kafirs? (said Oom Schalk Lourens). Yes, I know them. And they're all the same. I fear the Almighty, and I respect His works, but I could never understand why He made the kafir and the rinderpest." From the very outset, then, Bosman was to make use of his very distinctive brand of irony, a technique that has not always been properly interpreted by all readers of the Schalk Lourens stories. Between 1930 and 1951 no fewer than 72 stories appeared in this sequence, most of which have been taken up in posthumous collections of his work.

Mafeking Road is rich in memorable stories, but one in particular demonstrates the peculiar brand of humour that Bosman made his own. In "In the Withaak's Shade" Oom Schalk describes his encounter with a leopard in the veld when he is out one day looking for strayed cattle. True to character, his search takes the form of lying under the shade of the "withaak" tree. "I could go on lying there under the withaak and looking for the cattle like that all day, if necessary," he observes: "As you know, I am not the sort of farmer to loaf about the house when there is a man's work to be done." To Oom Schalk's horror, a leopard appears, inspects him closely, and then goes to sleep next to him.

Of course, Oom Schalk's attempts to convince the local farmers of the truth of this the next day render him the laughing stock of the area: "I could see that they listened to me in the same way that they listened when Krisjan Lemmer talked. And everybody knew that Krisjan Lemmer was the biggest liar in the Bushveld." In typical Bosman style, satire is subtly interwoven into Oom Schalk's narrative. Oom Schalk is partly vindicated when a leopard's spoor is discovered in the neighbourhood, and great excitement ensues. There is, we hear, "a great deal of shooting at the leopard and a great deal of running away from him." Says Oom Schalk: "The amount of Martini and Mauser fire I heard in the krantzes reminded me of nothing so much as the First Boer War. And the amount of running away reminded me of nothing so much as the Second Boer War." This deadpan rendering is typical of Oom Schalk, who always knows more than he lets on, and whose subtle digs at the Bushveld Afrikaner are heavily cloaked in layers of irony.

Bosman skillfully blends humour and pathos in his stories. "The Music-Maker," for example, concerns a Bushvelder's attempt to transcend the stifling confines of backveld life by risking his musical talent in "the great cities of the world." His venture takes him as far as Pretoria, where, in a reversal of the traditional rags to riches story, he winds up playing on the pavements outside bars. Typically, the reader receives this information in the last sentence of the story, and the concealed ending contrasts strikingly with the light-hearted hilarity that pervades the entire narrative.

Another important aspect of Bosman's stories is his artful foregrounding of narrative technique. The well known opening to the title story of *Mafeking Road* is a good example of this: "When people ask me—as they often do, how it is that I can tell the best stories of anybody in the Transvaal (Oom Schalk Lourens said, modestly), then I explain to them that I just learn through observing the way that the world has with men and women." He then punctures this spurious piece of philosophizing by conceding that it is a lie: "For it is not the story that counts. What matters is the way you tell it. The important thing is to know just at what moment you must knock out your pipe on your veldskoen, and at what stage of the story you must start talking about the School Committee at Drogevlei. Another necessary thing is to know what part of the story to leave out." This kind of direct intra-textual reference to the mechanics of fictionalizing is indicative of a self-consciousness in the way Bosman crafts his stories. With some of his later stories, this foregrounding of literary device approaches the level of metafictional experimentation.

Bosman's artistic concerns in his stories do not begin and end with a portrayal of South African backveld life. Critics have over the years argued convincingly that Bosman is insistently allegorising about wider issues that touch the entire South African population and, indeed, the world beyond.

—Craig MacKenzie

————

BOWEN, Elizabeth (Dorothea Cole). Irish. Born in Dublin, 7 June 1899. Educated at a day school in Folkestone, Kent; Harpenden Hall, Hertfordshire; Downe House School, Kent, 1914–17; London County Council School of Art, 1918–19. Worked in a hospital in Dublin, 1918, and for the Ministry of Information, London, during World War II. Married Alan Charles Cameron in 1923 (died 1952). Reviewer, the *Tatler,* London, from mid–1930's; associate editor, *London Magazine,* 1954–61. Recipient: James Tait Black Memorial prize, 1970. D.Litt.: Trinity College, Dublin, 1949; Oxford University, 1956. Member, Irish Academy of Letters, 1937; Companion of Literature, Royal Society of Literature, 1965; honorary member, American Academy. C.B.E. (Commander, Order of the British Empire), 1948. *Died 22 February 1973.*

PUBLICATIONS

Collections

Collected Stories.   1980.
The Mulberry Tree: Writings, edited by Hermione Lee. 1986.

Short Stories

Encounters: Stories.   1923.
Ann Lee's and Other Stories.   1926.

Joining Charles and Other Stories.   1929.
The Cat Jumps and Other Stories.   1934.
Look at All Those Roses: Short Stories.   1941.
The Demon Lover and Other Stories.   1945; as *Ivy Gripped
    the Steps and Other Stories,* 1946.
Selected Stories, edited by R. Moore.   1946.
Stories.   1959.
A Day in the Dark and Other Stories.   1965.
Irish Stories.   1978.

Novels

The Hotel.   1927.
The Last September.   1929.
Friends and Relations.   1931.
To the North.   1932.
The House in Paris.   1935.
The Death of the Heart.   1938.
The Heat of the Day.   1949.
A World of Love.   1955.
The Little Girls.   1964.
Eva Trout; or, Changing Scenes.   1968.

Plays

Anthony Trollope: A New Judgement (broadcast 1945).
    1946.
Castle Anna, with John Perry (produced 1948).

Radio Play: *Anthony Trollope: A New Judgement,* 1945.

Other

Bowen's Court (family history).   1942.
English Novelists.   1942.
Seven Winters.   1942; as *Seven Winters: Memories of a
    Dublin Childhood,* 1943.
*Why Do I Write? An Exchange of Views Between Bowen,
    Graham Greene, and V.S. Pritchett.*   1948.
Collected Impressions.   1950.
*The Shelbourne: A Centre in Dublin Life for More Than a
    Century.*   1951; as *The Shelbourne Hotel,* 1951.
A Time in Rome.   1960.
Afterthought: Pieces about Writing.   1962.
The Good Tiger (for children).   1965.
Pictures and Conversations.   1975.

Editor, *The Faber Book of Modern Stories.*   1937.
Editor, *Stories,* by Katherine Mansfield.   1956; as *34
    Short Stories,* 1957.

*

Bibliography: *Bowen: A Bibliography* by J'nan M. Sellery
and William O. Harris, 1981.

Critical Studies: *Bowen* by Jocelyn Brooke, 1952; *Bowen:
An Introduction to Her Novels* by William W. Heath, 1961;
Bowen by Allan E. Austin, 1971, revised edition, 1989;
Bowen by Edwin Kenney, 1975; *Patterns of Reality: Bow-
en's Novels* by Harriet Blodgett, 1975; *Bowen: Portrait of a
Writer* by Victoria Glendinning, 1977; *Bowen: An Estima-
tion* by Hermione Lee, 1981; *Bowen* by Patricia Craig,
1986; *Bowen* by Phyllis Lassner, 1990.

*   *   *

While Elizabeth Bowen's novels and short stories have
established their place in 20th-century literature, critics
may not always agree precisely what that place is. Those
who like to place writers like racehorses in some kind of
order are agreed that historically she provides a link
between Virginia Woolf and Iris Murdoch as a chronicler
of manners and a prober of sensibilities; but while her later
subject matter is often as English as that of Jane Austen,
George Elliott, or E.M. Forster, her treatment of it frequently is not. Celtic melancholy frequently creeps in.

She was an Anglo-Irish writer, an aristocratic representative of a dying species, virtually the last of her kind. She
was born into the English ascendency, inheriting the "big
house," Bowen's Court, but at a time when such houses
were becoming increasingly burdensome to maintain.
Though she eventually had to sell Bowen's Court (to a
demolishing developer), she never outgrew her Irishness.
As the American poet Howard Moss put it: "being English
in Ireland and Irish in England" enabled her to "grasp early
the colonial mentality from both sides . . . in the end it was
a mirror of the most exploitive relationship of all: that of
adult and child." Loss, and unfulfilment, the evanescent
nature of all experience, haunt her stories; her characters'
states of mind often are made more memorable by being
described with a poet's sharpness of observation and a
precise placing of evocative, sensuous imagery. Yet there is
often a kind of holding back that ensures an absence of
sentimentality.

For Bowen, houses often assume characters in their own
right, haunting the living with failed promises, imprisoning
with a false sense of permanence. Thus in "The Back
Drawing Room" an English visitor to an Ireland seared by
"the Troubles" comes upon a woman weeping in a "big
house" left unaccountably open. In "Foothold" the new
owner of a Georgian house is tormented by a "sickening
loneliness" emanating from the ghost of a previous owner.
In "No. 16" the last remaining occupied house in Medusa
Terrace (St. John's Wood, London) is sought out by Jane
Oates for a strange, disillusionery encounter. Clutching her
portfolio of poems, she comes to seek the opinion of
Maximillian, a journalist who has highly praised a prose
book by her. Maximillian, like Jane, is suffering from the
flu. When Jane reads her poems to him, he stops her. "Burn
them. You'll only lose your way," he says. "Are you lost?"
she asks. "Yes, I'm lost. You don't understand yet. We only
know when we're ill. Eternity is inside us—it's a secret that
we must never, never, try to betray." It is as if the poems
might somehow bring about betrayal.

The majority of writers, Bowen suggested in an essay,
"Sources of Influence" (included in her collection of
fugitive pieces *Afterthought,* "are haunted by the shadowy,
half-remembered landscape of early days: impressions and
feelings formed there and then underly language, dictate
choices of imagery. . . .The writer carries about in him an
inner environment which is constant; though which also, as
time goes on, tends to become more and more subjective."

Many of these feelings formed in her early years animate
her stories. Other issues include the bewilderment of young
girls growing up, and child bafflement in the face of well-
meaning adult incomprehension. An example of the latter
theme is "The Easter Egg Party," whose heroine, Hermione, is invited to stay by Eunice and Isabelle Evers,
"Amazons in homespuns . . . whose lives had been one
long vigorous walk"; it is a visit that ends in misunderstanding and unhappiness.

Bowen shows remarkable empathy, not only with the
viewpoint of children, but also for those women "ordained
to serve as their mothers," as Phyllis Lassner so aptly puts

it. Loneliness, the inescapable weight of past tradition, the anxieties resulting from claustrophobic homes, are all recurring themes. Bowen's capacity for evoking a character in a single phrase or image, her vivid and accurate use of language, and the energy of her writing (even taking account of her occasional habit of awkward inversion), together with her poet's eye, give her fiction its oddly disturbing quality. In general, her earlier stories are strongest on Irish themes and settings, and her later stories focus on mannerful character studies of upper- and middle-class Londoners. With the possible exception of her novel *The Heat of the Day*, arguably as fine a work of fiction as any capturing the atmosphere of wartime London, her collections of short stories are her finest achievement.

—Maurice Lindsay

See the essays on "The Demon Lover" and "Summer Night."

BOYLE, Kay. American. Born in St. Paul, Minnesota, 19 February 1902. Educated at the Cincinnati Conservatory of Music; Ohio Mechanics Institute, 1917–19. Married 1) Richard Brault in 1922 (divorced); 2) Laurence Vail in 1931 (divorced), five daughters and one son; 3) Baron Joseph von Franckenstein in 1943 (died 1963). Lived in Europe for 30 years. Foreign correspondent, *The New Yorker*, 1946–53; lecturer, New School for Social Research, New York, 1962; fellow, Wesleyan University, Middletown, Connecticut, 1963; professor of English, San Francisco State University, 1963–80, professor emerita, 1980–92; director, New York Writers Conference, Wagner College, New York, 1964; fellow, Radcliffe Institute for Independent Study, Cambridge, Massachusetts, 1964–65; writer-in-residence, University of Massachusetts, Amherst, 1967, Hollins College, Virginia, 1970–71, and Eastern Washington University, Cheney, 1982. Recipient: Guggenheim fellowship, 1934, 1961; O. Henry award, 1935, 1941; San Francisco Art Commission award, 1978; National Endowment for the Arts grant, 1980; Before Columbus Foundation award, 1983; Celtic Foundation award, 1984; Los Angeles *Times* Kirsch award, 1986; Lannan Foundation award, 1989. D. Litt: Columbia College, Chicago, 1971; Southern Illinois University, Carbondale, 1982; D.H.L.: Skidmore College, Saratoga Springs, New York, 1977; L.H.D.: Bowling Green State University, Ohio, 1986; Ohio State University, Columbus, 1986. Member, American Academy, 1979. *Died 27 December 1992.*

PUBLICATIONS

Short Stories

Short Stories.   1929.
Wedding Day and Other Stories.   1930.
The First Lover and Other Stories.   1933.
The White Horses of Vienna and Other Stories.   1936.
The Crazy Hunter: Three Short Novels.   1940; as *The Crazy Hunter and Other Stories*, 1940.
Thirty Stories.   1946.
The Smoking Mountain: Stories of Postwar Germany.   1951.

Three Short Novels.   1958.
Nothing Ever Breaks Except the Heart.   1966.
Fifty Stories.   1980.
Life Being the Best and Other Stories, edited by Sandra Whipple Spanier.   1988.

Novels

Plagued by the Nightingale.   1931.
Year Before Last.   1932.
Gentlemen, I Address You Privately.   1933.
My Next Bride.   1934.
Death of a Man.   1936.
Monday Night.   1938.
Primer for Combat.   1942.
Avalanche.   1944.
A Frenchman Must Die.   1946.
1939.   1948.
His Human Majesty.   1949.
The Seagull on the Step.   1955.
Generation Without Farewell.   1960.
The Underground Woman.   1975.

Verse

A Statement.   1932.
A Glad Day.   1938.
American Citizen: Naturalized in Leadville, Colorado.   1944.
Collected Poems.   1962; augmented edition, 1991.
Testament for My Students and Other Poems.   1970.
This Is Not a Letter and Other Poems.   1985.

Other

The Youngest Camel (for children).   1939; revised edition, 1959.
Breaking the Silence: Why a Mother Tells Her Son about the Nazi Era.   1962.
Pinky, The Cat Who Liked to Sleep (for children).   1966.
Pinky in Persia (for children).   1968.
Being Geniuses Together 1920–1930, with Robert McAlmon.   1968.
The Long Walk at San Francisco State and Other Essays.   1970.
Four Visions of America, with others.   1977.
Words That Must Somehow Be Said: Selected Essays 1927–1984, edited by Elizabeth S. Bell.   1985.

Editor, with Laurence Vail and Nina Conarain, *365 Days.*   1936.
Editor, *The Autobiography of Emanuel Carnevali.*   1967.
Editor, with Justine Van Gundy, *Enough of Dying! An Anthology of Peace Writings.*   1972.

Translator, *Don Juan*, by Joseph Delteil.   1931.
Translator, *Mr. Knife, Miss Fork*, by Rene Crevel.   1931.
Translator, *The Devil in the Flesh*, by Raymond Radiguet.   1932.
Translator, *Babylon*, by Rene Crevel.   1985.

Ghost-writer for the books *Relations and Complications, Being the Recollections of H.H. the Dayang Muda of Sarawak* by Gladys Palmer Brooke, 1929, and *Yellow Dusk* by Bettina Bedwell, 1937.

*

Critical Studies: *Boyle, Artist and Activist* by Sandra Whipple Spanier, 1986; *Boyle: A Study of the Short Fiction* by Elizabeth S. Bell, 1992.

* * *

With the exception of her work as a memoirist (*Being Geniuses Together*), Kay Boyle is most often recognized as a writer of short fiction. Her prolific literary career and eventful life offer a compelling profile of a 20th-century American writer: thrice married, mother of six, and an unrelenting political activist, she published almost 40 volumes of fiction, poetry, essays, translations, and children's stories. In her 70-year career, she has used various strategies and techniques that have helped her reach a wide range of audiences.

She began her apprenticeship as a short fiction writer with a brief course at Columbia University undertaken when she was also serving as Lola Ridge's editorial assistant in *Broom* in 1922. Her early fiction, much of which was collected in *Short Stories* and *Wedding Day* and is retained in *Life Being the Best* and *Fifty Stories,* was published in such avant-garde journals as *This Quarter* and *Contact* along with the work of such modernists as James Joyce, Gertrude Stein, Djuna Barnes, and Ernest Hemingway. Her later work appeared regularly in *The New Yorker, Story, The Nation, The Atlantic,* and *Harper's*.

Boyle's best work is characterized by an experimental, lyrical style which often manages to treat political themes in a nondoctrinaire way. Her first published short story, "Passeres' Paris" (*This Quarter* 1, 1925), demonstrates one of Boyle's most consistent narrative forms; it contains a series of expressionistic images and scenes that culminate in an intense moment in which the narrator and the reader share insights about a universal experience. Set in Paris, the story renders a knowing portrait of the tentative traveller or outsider who hopes to enter a new world without giving offense by her inevitable ignorance. Like many of Boyle's earlier stories, it creates a brief sequence of events and images that reverberate with meaning through her poetic language and its ordering of experience and detail. These stories provide a window on everyday life and invest it with symbolism and elucidation.

Many of her early stories also contain decidedly political undertones. In "Episode in the Life of an Ancestor," Boyle sketches the conflict between a father, who is determined to mold his daughter into the woman he and the patriarchal society expect, and a daughter, who refuses to be pigeon-holed into any predetermined role. She embodies the superior strength found with flexibility; the father's rigidity emerges as brittleness. While this story investigates the politics of gender, the stories "Ben" and "Black Boy" treat the injustice of racism.

Although her later stories also depend upon the craftsmanship of her language and her political concerns, they show the impact of Boyle's international lifestyle and its intrepid connection to 20th-century European and American political history. Set against the backdrop of Hitler's increasing power, the relationships in the mountain village of "The White Horses of Vienna" invoke a subtle dilemma of moral judgment. Written in 1935 before Hitler had come to be an international symbol of oppression, this story illustrates the prescient nature of Boyle's intelligence and her ability to handle complex political and emotional issues. The story's evocation of the friendship that results between the two doctors and its gradual mitigation of the Austrian family's assumptions about racial stereotypes displays a rare facility: Boyle evades the artificial binaries of race and creates a dialogic argument about the ways in which bigotry impinges upon personal relationships.

Having firsthand observation of the fall of Europe, Boyle also created raw and bitter fiction about the emotional cost of these events. Stories such as "Defeat," "Effigy of War," and "The Lost" deal with the practical and moral problems inherent in existing in an occupied country. Boyle provides additional resonance by showing the conflict's effect upon the sexual and familial relationships of the occupied people and by illustrating the negative aspects of overly zealous nationalism—even when it is practiced by those who resisted Nazism. The barman of "Effigy" cannot live in Italy because he did not return to serve in the Italian army, yet he cannot remain in France because he has retained his Italian citizenship. Ironically, he is denounced as a foreigner by a naturalized Greek who is more xenophobic than the French. The barman's death and the life of young Janos of "Lost" reflect the fate of many Europeans who found themselves without a country: their innocence failed to guarantee them immunity.

In other stories about the aftermath of war, Boyle writes about the American occupation of Germany. Many of the stories in *The Smoking Mountain* present subtle but indicting portraits of American officers. These men flaunt their victory and their material assets in the presence of an impoverished and defeated Germany. The Americans of "Summer Evening" and "Army of Occupation" emerge as dangerous and relentless as Hitler's Nazis. Boyle's stories suggest that unchecked patriarchal law has devastating results, regardless of the nationality of its practitioners.

The political and personal consequences of patriarchal ideology undergird much of Boyle's short fiction. She depicts the aftermath of war and its effects on survivors, even those who—as is the case of the young girl in "Winter Night"—will only encounter war through their association with its survivors. Stepping outside the definition of war stories as centering around combat, Boyle shows us that the failed human understanding that leads to war continues when war ceases. She examines the gap between myths about war and its reality, disavowing any hierarchy that privileges the oppressor, and elucidating the basic human need for understanding and for tolerating difference. In her essay "The Vanishing Short Story?," Boyle calls for the writer to sound "the inarticulate whispers of the concerned people of his time." Certainly, Boyle's short fiction articulates these whispers.

—Marilyn Elkins

See the essays on "Astronomer's Wife" and "The White Horses of Vienna."

BRADBURY, Ray (Douglas). American. Born in Waukegan, Illinois, 22 August 1920. Educated at Los Angeles High School, graduated 1938. Married Marguerite Susan McClure in 1947; four daughters. Full-time writer, from 1943. President, Science-Fantasy Writers of America, 1951–53. Member of the Board of Directors, Screen Writers Guild of America, 1957–61. Recipient: O. Henry prize, 1947, 1948; Benjamin Franklin award, 1954; American Academy award, 1954; Boys' Clubs of America Junior

Book award, 1956; Golden Eagle award, for screenplay, 1957; Ann Radcliffe award, 1965, 1971; Writers Guild award, 1974; Aviation and Space Writers award, for television documentary, 1979; Gandalf award, 1980. D.Litt.: Whittier College, California, 1979. Lives in Los Angeles.

PUBLICATIONS

Short Stories

Dark Carnival.   1947; abridged edition, 1948; abridged edition, as *The Small Assassin,* 1962.
The Martian Chronicles.   1950; as *The Silver Locusts,* 1951.
The Illustrated Man.   1951.
The Golden Apples of the Sun.   1953.
The October Country.   1955.
Sun and Shadow.   1957.
A Medicine for Melancholy.   1959; as *The Day It Rained Forever,* 1959.
The Pedestrian.   1962.
The Machineries of Joy.   1964.
The Vintage Bradbury.   1965.
The Autumn People.   1965.
Tomorrow Midnight.   1966.
Twice Twenty Two (selection).   1966.
I Sing the Body Electric!   1969.
Bloch and Bradbury, with Robert Bloch.   1969; as *Fever Dreams and Other Fantasies,* 1970.
(Selected Stories), edited by Anthony Adams.   1975.
Long after Midnight.   1976.
The Best of Bradbury.   5 vols., 1976.
To Sing Strange Songs.   1979.
The Aqueduct.   1979.
The Stories of Bradbury.   1980.
The Last Circus, and The Electrocution.   1980.
The Love Affair (includes verse).   1982.
Dinosaur Tales.   1983.
A Memory of Murder.   1984.
Fever Dream.   1987.
The Other Foot.   1987.
The Veldt.   1987.
The Fog Horn.   1987.
The April Witch.   1987.
The Dragon.   1988.
The Toynbee Convector.   1988.
There Will Come Soft Rains.   1989.
The Smile.   1991.

Novels

Fahrenheit 451.   1953.
Dandelion Wine.   1957.
Something Wicked This Way Comes.   1962.
Death Is a Lonely Business.   1985.
A Graveyard for Lunatics: Another Tale of Two Cities. 1990.
Green Shadows, White Whale.   1992.

Plays

The Meadow, in *Best One-Act Plays of 1947–48,* edited by Margaret Mayorga.   1948.
The Anthem Sprinters and Other Antics (produced 1968). 1963.
The World of Bradbury (produced 1964).

The Wonderful Ice-Cream Suit (produced 1965; musical version, music by Jose Feliciano, produced 1990). Included in *The Wonderful Ice-Cream Suit and Other Plays,* 1972.
The Day It Rained Forever, music by Bill Whitefield (produced 1988).   1966.
Christus Apollo, music by Jerry Goldsmith (produced 1969).
The Wonderful Ice-Cream Suit and Other Plays (includes *The Veldt* and *To the Chicago Abyss*).   1972.
Leviathan 99 (produced 1972).
Pillar of Fire and Other Plays for Today, Tomorrow, and Beyond Tomorrow (includes *Kaleidoscope* and *The Foghorn*).   1975.
The Foghorn (produced 1977).   Included in *Pillar of Fire and Other Plays,* 1975.
That Ghost, That Bride of Time: Excerpts from a Play-in-Progress.   1976.
Forever and the Earth (radio play).   1984.
Flying Machine.   1986.
A Device Out of Time.   1986.
The Martian Chronicles, adaptation of his own stories (produced 1977).   1986.
Fahrenheit 451, adaptation of his own novel (produced 1979).   1986.
Dandelion Wine, adaptation of his own story (produced 1977).   1988.
Falling Upward (produced 1988).   1988.
Bradbury on Stage.   1991.

Screenplays: *It Came from Outer Space,* with David Schwartz, 1952; *Moby-Dick,* with John Huston, 1956; *Icarus Montgolfier Wright,* with George C. Johnston, 1961; *Picasso Summer* (as Douglas Spaulding), with Edwin Booth, 1972; *Something Wicked this Way Comes,* 1983.

Television Plays: *Shopping for Death,* 1956, *Design for Loving,* 1958, *Special Delivery,* 1959, *The Faith of Aaron Menefee,* 1962, and *The Life Work of Juan Diaz,* 1963 (all *Alfred Hitchcock Presents* series); *The Marked Bullet* (*Jane Wyman's Fireside Theater* series), 1956; *The Gift* (*Steve Canyon* series), 1958; *Tunnel to Yesterday* (*Trouble Shooters* series), 1960; *I Sing the Body Electric!,* 1962, and *The Elevator,* 1986 (both *Twilight Zone* series); *The Jail* (*Alcoa Premier* series), 1962; *The Groom* (*Curiosity Shop* series), 1971; *Marionettes, Inc.,* 1985, *The Playground,* 1985, *The Crowd,* 1985, *Banshee,* 1986, *The Screaming Woman,* 1986, and *The Town Where No One Got Off,* 1986 (all *Bradbury Theatre* series); *Walking on Air,* 1987; *The Coffin,* 1988 (U.K.); *The Fruit at the Bottom of the Bowl,* 1988; *Skeleton,* 1988; *The Emissary,* 1988; *Gotcha!,* 1988; *The Man Upstairs,* 1988; *The Small Assassin,* 1988; *Punishment without Crime,* 1988; *On the Orient, North,* 1988; *Tyrannosaurous Rex,* 1988; *There Was an Old Woman,* 1988; *And So Died Raibouchinska,* 1988; *The Dwarf,* 1989; *A Miracle of Rare Device,* 1989; *The Lake,* 1989; *The Wind,* 1989; *The Pedestrian,* 1989; *A Sound of Thunder,* 1989; *The Wonderful Death of Dudley Stone,* 1989; *The Haunting of the New,* 1989; *To the Chicago Abyss,* 1989; *Hail and Farewell,* 1989; *The Veldt,* 1989; *Boys! Raise Giant Mushrooms in the Your Cellar!,* 1989; *Mars Is Heaven,* 1990; *The Murderer,* 1990; *Touched with Fire,* 1990; *The Black Ferris,* 1990; *Usher II,* 1990; *Exorcism,* 1990; *The Day It Rained Forever,* 1990; *A Touch of Petulance,* 1990; *—And the Moon Be Still as Bright,* 1990; *The Toynbee Convector,* 1990; *The Long Years,* 1990; *Here There Be Tygers,* 1990; *The Earth Men,* 1992; *Zero Hour,* 1992; *The Jar,* 1992; *Colonel Stonesteel and the "Desperate Empties,"* 1992; *The*

Concrete Mixer, 1992; *The Utterly Perfect Murder*, 1992; *Let's Play Poison*, 1992; *The Martian*, 1992; *The Lonely One*, 1992; *The Happiness Machine*, 1992; *The Long Rain*, 1992; *Down Wind from Gettysbury*, 1992; *Some Live like Lazarus*, 1992; *Fee Fi Fo Fum*, 1992; *Dora and the Great Wide World*, 1992.

Verse

Old Ahab's Friend, and Friend to Noah, Speaks His Piece: A Celebration. 1971.
When Elephants Last in the Dooryard Bloomed: Celebrations for Almost Any Day in the Year. 1973.
That Son of Richard III: A Birth Announcement. Privately printed, 1974.
Where Robot Mice and Robot Men Run round in Robot Towns: New Poems, Both Light and Dark. 1977.
Twin Hieroglyphs That Swim the River Dust. 1978.
The Attic Where the Meadow Greens. 1980.
The Haunted Computer and the Android Pope. 1981.
The Complete Poems of Bradbury. 1982.
October. 1983.
Long After Ecclesiastes. 1985.
Death Has Lost Its Charm for Me. 1987.
The Climate of Palettes. 1989.

Other

Switch on the Night (for children). 1955.
R Is for Rocket (for children). 1962.
S Is for Space (for children). 1966.
Teacher's Guide: Science Fiction, with Lewy Olfson. 1971.
The Halloween Tree (for children). 1972.
Zen and the Art of Writing, and The Joy of Writing. 1973.
The Mummies of Guanajuato, photographs by Archie Lieberman. 1978.
Beyond 1984: Remembrance of Things Future. 1979.
The Ghosts of Forever, illustrated by Aldo Sessa. 1981.
The Art of Playboy (text by Bradbury). 1985.
Zen in the Art of Writing (essays). 1990.
Yestermorrow: Obvious Answers to Impossible Futures (essays). 1991.

Editor, *Timeless Stories for Today and Tomorrow.* 1952.
Editor, *The Circus of Dr. Lao and Other Improbable Stories.* 1956.

*

Bibliography: in *The Bradbury Companion* by William F. Nolan, 1975; *Bradbury* edited by Joseph D. Olander and Martin H. Greenberg, 1980.

Critical Studies: introduction by Gilbert Highet to The Vintage Bradbury, 1965; "The Revival of Fantasy" by Russell Kirk, in *Triumph*, May 1968; *The Bradbury Companion* (includes bibliography) by William F. Nolan, 1975; *The Bradbury Chronicles* by George Edgar Slusser, 1977; *Bradbury* (includes bibliography) edited by Joseph D. Olander and Martin H. Greenberg, 1980; *Bradbury* by Wayne L. Johnson, 1980; *Bradbury and the Poetics of Reverie: Fantasy, Science Fiction, and the Reader* by William F. Toupence, 1984; *Bradbury* by David Mogen, 1986.

* * *

Ray Bradbury is one of the most compelling and idiosyncratic voices in contemporary American literature. In a long and prolific career, he has written novels, plays, poetry, and stories for children, but his reputation was established with his short fiction. Among that vast body of work are many of his most effective ideas and some of the finest examples of his craftsmanship.

Although Bradbury's writing shows influences—particularly in his early work—of Poe, Wells, Kipling, and Burroughs, his style is entirely his own. His prose has an arresting suddenness, a compelling urgency, and a sense of breathless wonder touched with melancholy. Bradbury uses the glittering language of romanticism, rich in simile and metaphor. For example, an old chandelier found in an attic ("A Scent of Sarsaparilla") is described as containing "rainbows and mornings and noons as bright as new rivers flowing endlessly back through Time."

Bradbury's critics have argued that his extraordinary gift for language is not matched by sufficient originality of thought; but, in his finest stories, he demonstrates an ability to see the fantastic in the ordinary and the outlandish in the mundane, and to reassert the classic belief that there is a vital, spiritual dimension to the humdrum world of daily existence.

Even when reworking traditional themes of fantasy, horror, and the macabre, he always succeeds in transforming the most commonplace device. Thus, in "Skeleton," Bradbury takes the cadaverous image associated with any number of comic and grotesque entertainments and rattles it anew, by writing about a man who, gradually and terrifyingly, becomes aware of the bones beneath his skin.

Bradbury takes the reader into the minds of his creations: a baby commits murder because it resents having been born ("The Small Assassin"); a man brings his father back from the grave to tell him that he loved him ("The Wish"); a nervous woman is literally scared to death in a Mexican village where the mummified dead are put on public display ("The Next in Line"); and a sea-monster comes from the deep to answer the siren love-call of a lighthouse ("The Fog Horn"). Repeatedly Bradbury shows the beautiful soul trapped in a twisted body and the monster lurking behind a mask of beauty.

His first stories were published in pulp fiction magazines whose taste for the sinister and sensational coincided with many of Bradbury's own youthful passions: the freaks, magicians, and exotic creatures of carnival and circus, and the fiends and monsters of the movies. Among the stories reflecting these sources of inspiration are tales of the Hollywood dream-factories ("The Meadow" and "Tyrannosaurus Rex"); and dark murmurings from the midway ("The Last Circus," "The Dwarf," and "The Illustrated Woman"). In "The Jar," a phony monstrosity from a sideshow—"one of those pale things drifting in alcohol plasma, forever dreaming and circling"—has its pseudo-gruesome contents replaced by the real horror of a dismembered body.

Some of Bradbury's fairground tales, like "The Black Ferris," about an attraction which, depending on whether you ride it backwards or forwards, makes you younger or older, were subsequently reworked for the novel *Something Wicked This Way Comes*.

A predominant Bradbury theme is a nostalgic reverie for small town life: in Ireland (including various yarns later incorporated into the novel *Green Shadows, White Whale*), Mexico, and especially middle America during the 1920's and 1930's. Set in Green Town, Illinois (a fictionalised, idealised version of Bradbury's birthplace, Waukegan), these stories range from touching, slightly sentimental, snapshots of childhood with its first loves and first sorrows ("One Timeless Spring"), to darker tales more akin to Bradbury's horror fantasies, as when a young boy encounters a possible vampire ("The Man Upstairs"), or a man with the power to devour the summer ("The Burning Man"). (Other Green Town stories were worked into a loose novel-form as *Dandelion Wine*.)

Although Bradbury has written numerous space fantasies—notably in his themed collection *The Martian Chronicles*—it is misleading to describe him as a science-fiction writer. He simply uses the far reaches of space as one of various locations for an allegorical exploration of hopes and fears. Of the first settlers on the Red Planet, he says, "They were coming to find something or leave something or get something, to dig up something or bury something. . . . They were coming with small dreams or large dreams or none at all." They confront racial prejudice ("The Other Foot"), grapple with religious mysteries ("The Man" and "The Fire Balloons"), and face loneliness and alienation ("Night Call, Collect" and "The Strawberry Window").

Bradbury is most compelling in his prophetic stories, which are foreboding glimpses of times to come, when paintings are publicly destroyed ("The Smile") and books are banned ("The Exiles"). It is a world sometimes blessed, but often cursed, by science and technology. For example, in "A Sound of Thunder" a time-travelling safari goes back to a prehistoric age to hunt a dinosaur, and, because someone treads on a butterfly, changes the future, subtly, but devastatingly.

The robot, the archetypal symbol of futurism, is, as constructed by Bradbury, occasionally benign but more probably malignant: a family buys an electronic grandmother ("I Sing the Body Electric"); a man invests in an android replica of himself to deceive his wife ("Marionettes, Inc."); a robot Abraham Lincoln is killed by an assassin's bullet ("Downwind from Gettysburg"); and, in one of several stories about robotic houses, a nursery with automated pictorial walls comes frighteningly alive ("The Veldt"). In "The Murderer" another mechanized home eventually drives its frantic occupier to kill it.

Throughout his writing, Bradbury juggles with light and dark, holding pessimism and optimism in exquisite balance. At his darkest, Bradbury can be seen working out personal phobias, such as his hatred for motor cars. This is the basis for "The Pedestrian," in which an innocent citizen of an automated city is arrested for committing the crime of "walking."

In more life-affirming stories, Bradbury expresses the conviction that humankind can be taught to save civilization, or possibly be tricked into doing so. Thus the Time-Traveller in "The Toynbee Convector," despairing of the philosophy of his age ("Melancholy was the attitude. The impossibility of change was the vogue. End of the world was the slogan"), decides to fake a time-machine to convince the world that it still has a future. Of all Bradbury's stories it is, perhaps, the most autobiographical.

—Brian Sibley

See the essay on "August 2026: There Will Come Soft Rains."

BROWN, George Mackay. British. Born in Stromness, Orkney, Scotland, 17 October 1921. Educated at Stromness Academy, 1926–40; Newbattle Abbey College, Dalkeith, Midlothian, 1951–52, 1956; Edinburgh University, 1956–60, 1962–64, B.A. (honours) in English 1960, M.A. Recipient: Society of Authors travel award, 1968; Scottish Arts Council prize, 1969; Katherine Mansfield-Menton prize, 1971; James Tait Black Memorial prize, 1988. M.A.: Open University, Milton Keynes, Buckinghamshire, 1976; LL.D.: University of Dundee, 1977; D.Litt.: University of Glasgow, 1985. Fellow, Royal Society of Literature, 1977. O.B.E. (Officer, Order of the British Empire), 1974. Lives in Orkney.

PUBLICATIONS

Short Stories

A Calendar of Love.   1967.
A Time to Keep.   1969.
Hawkfall and Other Stories.   1974.
The Sun's Net.   1976.
Witch and Other Stories.   1977.
Andrina and Other Stories.   1983.
Christmas Stories.   1985.
The Hooded Fisherman.   1985.
A Time to Keep and Other Stories.   1987.
The Golden Bird: Two Orkney Stories.   1987.
The Masked Fisherman and Other Stories.   1989.

Novels

Greenvoe.   1972.
Magnus.   1973.
Time in a Red Coat.   1984.

Plays

Witch (produced 1969).   Included in *A Calendar of Love,* 1967.
A Spell for Green Corn (broadcast 1967; produced 1970). 1970.
The Loom of Light (produced 1972).   Included in *Three Plays,* 1984.
The Storm Watchers (produced 1976).
The Martyrdom of St. Magnus (opera libretto), music by Peter Maxwell Davies, adaptation of the novel *Magnus* by Brown (produced 1977).   1977.
The Two Fiddlers (opera libretto), music by Peter Maxwell Davies, adaptation of the story by Brown (produced London, 1978).   1978.
The Well (produced 1981).   Included in *Three Plays,* 1984.
The Voyage of Saint Brandon (broadcast 1984). Included in *Three Plays,* 1984.
Three Plays.   1984.
A Celebration for Magnus (son et lumière text), music by Peter Maxwell Davies (produced 1988).   1987.
Edwin Muir and the Labyrinth (produced 1987).

Radio Plays: *A Spell for Green Corn,* 1967; *The Loom of Light,* 1967; *The Voyage of Saint Brandon,* 1984.

Television Plays: three stories from *A Time to Keep,* 1969; *Orkney,* 1971; *Miss Barraclough,* 1977; *Four Orkney Plays for Schools,* 1978; *Andrina,* 1984.

Verse

The Storm. 1954.
Loaves and Fishes. 1959.
The Year of the Whale. 1965.
The Five Voyages of Arnor. 1966.
Twelve Poems. 1968.
Fishermen with Ploughs: A Poem Cycle. 1971.
Poems New and Selected. 1971.
Lifeboat and Other Poems. 1971.
Penguin Modern Poets 21, with Iain Crichton Smith and
    Norman MacCaig. 1972.
Winterfold. 1976.
Selected Poems. 1977.
Voyages. 1983.
Christmas Poems. 1984.
Stone. 1987.
Two Poems for Kenna. 1988.
Songs for St. Magnus Day. 1988.
The Wreck of the Archangel. 1989.
Tryst on Egilsay. 1989.
Selected Poems 1954–1983. 1991.

Other

Let's See the Orkney Islands. 1948.
Stromness Official Guide. 1956.
An Orkney Tapestry. 1969.
The Two Fiddlers (for children). 1974.
Letters from Hamnavoe (essays). 1975.
Edwin Muir: A Brief Memoir. 1975.
Pictures in the Cave (for children). 1977.
Under Brinkie's Brae. 1979.
Six Lives of Fankle the Cat (for children). 1980.
Portrait of Orkney, photographs by Werner Forman.
    1981; revised edition, photographs by Gunnie Moberg,
    and drawings by Evlend Brown, 1988.
Shorelines: Three Artists from Orkney (exhibition cata-
    logue), with Tessa Jackson. 1985.
Keepers of the House (for children). 1986.
Letters to Gypsy. 1990.
Eureka! (for children). 1991.
Sea-King's Daughter. 1991.

Editor, *Selected Prose of Edwin Muir.* 1987.

*

Critical Studies: *Brown* by Alan Bold, 1978; *The Contribution to Literature of Orcadian Writer Brown: An Introduction and a Bibliography* by Osamu Yamada, Hilda D.
Spear, and David S. Robb, 1991.

* * *

Many of the themes that George Mackay Brown introduced into his poetry also find their way into his short
fiction—faith and renewal, death and resurrection, the real
and the mythical past. There are other links. In all his short
stories there is a natural fluency that extends from the
directness of his lyrical descriptions to an ornate narrative
with intricate internal rhythms, especially in his religious
work.

Indeed, many of his favourite poetic themes recur in his
short stories, most of which are firmly rooted in the

everyday communal life of his native Orkney from the time
of the Viking invasions of the 12th century to the more
recent times of the 1960's. The tales are told with a simple
lyrical intensity; they are concerned both with the matter of
everyday life and with legends from the history and
mythology of his native islands.

A Calendar of Love was his first collection and the title
story is rich with the symbolism of seed-time and harvest
and with the renewal of life through pain and suffering.
Jean Scarth, an innkeeper, is loved by two men of wildly
differing temperaments and becomes pregnant. Tormented
by the community's condemnation, she faces disgrace but
finds deliverance in the rhythms of nature after the first
snowfall of winter.

"Witch," a horrifying story set in 16th-century Orkney,
continues the theme with its account of the trial of Marian
Isbister, charged with witchcraft after refusing the advances
of Earl Patrick Stewart's factor. While the local people are
happy to participate in the barbarous execution, the only
person to show her any pity is the executioner who
strangles her before the fire is lit. The narrator is a clerk
who records all that he sees but the prose is imbued with a
lyrical quality which counterpoints the horror he is describing.

Also set in the same period is "Master Halcrow, Priest," a
fine study of an old priest's attempts to keep his faith at the
time of the Reformation. "The Three Islands," "Stone
Poems," and "The Story of Jorkel Hayforks" all take place
at the time of the Norse period in Orkney's history; the
latter involves a Viking's personal voyage from violence
and revenge to forgiveness and salvation. As with other
tales dealing with the past, there is a unity in Brown's
writing that allows him to spin several variations around a
common theme.

His second collection, *A Time to Keep,* contains two
sensitive studies of alcoholism and loneliness: "Celia" and
"The Eye of the Hurricane," in which an old sea captain
drinks himself to death and despair. In both stories the
central characters are not presented as worthless layabouts
but as ordinary beings with all humanity's failings. "The
Eye of the Hurricane" also contains a fine Ibsenesque scene
in which past and present become one as the dying skipper
imagines that he is back at sea, steering his ship through a
ferocious storm.

The narrator is a novelist based on Brown himself—a
technique he uses again in "The Tarn and the Rosary" (in
Hawkfall). During the course of his musings on the old
seaman's life Brown introduces the word "hawkfall" as a
symbol for impending death. The concept is expanded in
Brown's next collection, which not only uses "hawkfall" as
a title but takes a stage further Brown's reflections on death
and destruction, salvation and renewal.

The title story spans the centuries and follows a flat-nosed
generation from the Bronze Age to the present when it dies
out in ignominy. In "Tithonus" a laird grieves for the death
of his island and the absence of physical love in his own
life; the story is prompted by the Greek myth of Tithonus,
who is given the gift of immortality but not eternal youth.
"The Cinquefoil" contains five connected sketches about
an island community, each one building to the conclusion
that love alone can overcome tragedy and bind people
together. In three tales of the abnormal, "Sealskin," "The
Drowned Rose," and "The Interrogator," Brown goes to
the heart of the mystery of death and proves that love can
triumph over even the greatest evil.

A sense of celebration returned in the stories collected in
The Sun's Net and *Andrina.* True, the title story of the latter
collection is a ghost story with several familiar motifs—

doomed relationships, the sailor returned from the sea, the ever-changing seasons—but there is a new tenderness in the description of the old sailor's love for his ghostly granddaughter and his awareness that emotions live on from one generation to the next.

This theme had already been explored in "A Winter Tale," "Stone, Salt and Rose," "Soldier from the Wars Returning," and "Pastoral" (all in *The Sun's Net*), in which Brown presents man as the seed-provider and woman as the seed-nourisher. Both play a vital role in maintaining the sense of continuity which is vital if a community is to survive. "A Winter Tale" is as much a Christmas fable as a straight short story: for Brown, a convert to Catholicism, each birth is a matter for celebration, being a re-enactment of the advent of Christ.

Many of Brown's historical stories or fables have their origins in the *Orkneyinga Saga*, the 13th-century chronicle of the Earls of Orkney, and much of the imagery comes from the evidence of prehistoric sites on Orkney. In keeping with the themes he pursues, though, his vision remains his own, starkly original and deeply spiritual. Indeed, it could be said that by imposing history, myth, and fable onto his narrative, Brown finds in Orkney a microcosm of the general human condition.

—Trevor Royle

See the essay on "A Time to Keep."

———

BÜCHNER, Georg. German. Born in Goddelau, Duchy of Hesse Darmstadt, 17 October 1813. Educated at Carl Weitershausen's school, 1822-25; Gymnasium, Darmstadt, 1825-31; studied medicine at University of Strasbourg, 1831-33, and University of Giessen, 1833-34. Politically active as a student in Darmstadt, founded the society, Gesellschaft der Menschenrechte, 1834, and wrote the political pamphlet *Der Hessische Landbote,* 1834; fled Germany for Strasbourg to escape impending arrest for sedition, 1835; studied biology, earning membership of the Strasbourg Société d'Histoire Naturell and a doctorate from the University of Zurich, 1836. Lecturer in comparative anatomy, University of Zurich, 1836-37. *Died 19 February 1837.*

PUBLICATIONS

Collections

Nachgelassene Schriften, edited by Ludwig Büchner. 1850.
Sämtliche Werke, edited by K. Franzos.   1879.
Gesammelte Werke und Briefe, edited by Fritz Bergemann. 1922.
Complete Plays and Prose. 1963.
Sämtliche Werke und Briefe, edited by Werner R. Lehmann.   2 vols., 1967–71.
Plays. 1971.
Complete Works and Letters, edited by Walter Hinderer and Henry J. Schmidt.   1986.
Complete Plays, edited by Michael Patterson.   1987.
Werke und Briefe, edited by Kaaarl Pörnbacher.   1988.

Short Stories

Lenz.   In *Telegraph für Deutschland,* January 1839; translated as *Lenz,* in *Complete Plays and Prose,* 1963; also translated in *Three German Classics,* edited by Ronald Taylor, 1966; in *The Penguin Book of Short Stories,* 1974; in *The Complete Plays,* 1987.

Plays

Dantons Tod (produced 1902).   1835; as *Danton's Death,* 1939; also translated in *Classical German Drama,* edited by T.H. Lustig, 1963.
Leonce und Lena (produced 1895).   In *Mosaik, Novellen, und Skizzen,* edited by K. Gutzkow, 1842; as *Leonce and Lena,* in *From the Modern Repertoire 3,* 1956.
Woyzeck (produced 1913).   As *Wozzeck,* in *Sämtliche Werke,* 1879; translated as *Woyzeck,* in *The Modern Theatre 1,* edited by Eric Bentley, 1955; also translated in *Complete Plays and Prose,* 1963.

Other

Der Hessische Landbote, with Pastor Weidig (pamphlet). 1834 (privately printed); as *The Hessian Courier,* in *The Complete Plays,* 1987.

*

Bibliography: *Büchner* by Marianne Beese, 1983.

Critical Studies: *Büchner* by Arthur Knight, 1951; *Büchner* by H. Lindenberger, 1964; "A World of Suffering: Büchner" by J.P. Stern, in *Re-interpretations. Seven Studies in Nineteenth-Century German Literature,* 1964; *Satire, Caricature, and Perspectivism in the Works of Büchner* by Henry J. Schmidt, 1970; *Büchner* by Ronald Hauser, 1974; *The Drama of Revolt: A Critical Study of Büchner* by Maurice B. Benn, 1976; "Büchner's *Lenz*" by Martin Swales, in *The German Novelle,* 1977; *Büchner and the Birth of Modern Drama* by David G. Richards, 1977; "Büchner's *Lenz*—Style and Message" by Roy Pascal, in *Oxford German Studies* 9, 1978; *Büchner* by William C. Reeve, 1979; *Büchner* by Julian Hilton, 1982; *Büchner's "Dantons Tod": A Reappraisal* by Dorothy James, 1982; *Lenz and Büchner: Studies in Dramatic Form* by John Guthrie, 1984; *Love, Lust, and Rebellion: New Approaches to Büchner* by Reinhold Grimm, 1985; *Büchner in Britain: A Passport to Büchner* edited by Brian Keith-Smith and Ken Mills, 1987; *Büchner's Woyzeck* by Michael Ewans, 1989; "Modes of Consciousness Representation in Büchner's *Lenz*" by David Horton, in *German Life and Letters* 43, 1989–90; *Büchner: Tradition and Innovation* edited by Ken Mills and Brian Keith-Smith, 1990; *Büchner, Woyzeck* by Edward McInnes, 1991.

* * *

The sum of Georg Büchner's narrative prose is a single text, of some 25 pages, less fragmentary than is often alleged, but lacking final revision and polish. Yet, by its intensity, its feel of modernity and its influence on German writers from Hauptmann to the present, *Lenz* (written in 1835 and 1836, posthumously published in 1839) has a significance comparable to that of his dramas *Dantons Tod*

(*Danton's Death*) and *Woyzeck,* sharing their pioneering stylistic radicalism and their concern with human beings isolated, emotionally dislocated, subject to forces beyond their control.

Like them, it has roots in documented fact: the visit of the poet-dramatist Jakob Lenz, early in 1778, to the pastor and philanthropist Johann Friedrich Oberlin in Waldersbach, Alsace, entrusted to his care after a physical and mental collapse. Oberlin's report of Lenz's precarious stabilisation and then intensified mental breakdown became Büchner's principal source.

The strikingly abrupt beginning confronts us immediately with the tensions of a mind that has no steady, coherent relationship to the surrounding world. Lenz walks through the mountains, "indifferently" (translation by Henry J. Schmidt), then inwardly searching, "as though for lost dreams"; the earth seems to him to shrink, his sense of space and time is dislocated. Energized by a violent storm, which Büchner evokes in a magnificently turbulent sentence, he feels a surge of ecstatic, almost erotically aggressive intimacy with nature—he "lay over the earth, he burrowed into the cosmos, it was a pleasure that hurt him"—but returning sobriety dissolves such experiences into a mere "shadow-play." Later, he feels a panic sense of abandonment, "nameless" fear. He hurtles down the slopes, "as if insanity were pursuing him on horseback." He is soothed by the lights, the radiant calm, the intimate response at Oberlin's house, but then alone in a dark room his sensibility, his very sense of self, threatens to dissolve; desperate, he inflicts physical pain on himself, and plunges into icy water.

Amidst this restless agitation a play of opposites is discernible; calm and panic, vitality and apathy. Other oppositions follow: communion and isolation, eventually solipsism; lucid eloquence—above all, when Lenz expounds, at the centre-point of the text, his (and Büchner's) anti-idealist aesthetics—and cryptic, jaggedly exclamatory outbursts, or sullen silence. Comforting memories of his mother and his beloved Friederike are later beset by irrational guilt, he declares himself their "murderer." Faith yields to atheistic revolt.

Seeking a summary formula, critics invoke polarities of activity and passivity, movement and stasis. Neither such pole is simply "positive" or "negative." Stasis, for instance, can mean calm repose, but also numb ennui. Alternatively, one can find the several strands of the narrative converging in Lenz's struggle to regain or sustain vibrancy of feeling, sheer substance, against the constant threat of insubstantiality and insensateness—a *horror vacui* common to Büchner's works (and experience, as letters of March 1834 reveal) and to writings of the historical Lenz. For "the emptier, the deader he felt inwardly, the more he felt urged to ignite a blaze within himself," recalling a past when "he panted under the weight of all his sensations; and now so dead." His reawakened religious interests reflect this impulse; his would-be resurrection of a dead child embodies, symbolically, a desperate urge to self-reanimation, as well as a test of faith. Pain, though tormenting, yet affords proof that he *is*; in his "not wholly serious" suicide attempts he seeks "to bring himself to his senses through physical pain." And it is precisely to insensate indifference, a "terrible void," that Lenz finally succumbs.

Such antitheses yield a framework for the narrative structuring of what might otherwise dissolve into an inchoate flux of mood pictures. They generate the image patterns of the text, in turn underpinned by emphatic use of key-words ("alone," "empty," "cold"), most insistently words connoting peace (linked in German by the mor-

pheme-*ruh-*: *Ruhe, ruhig, ruhen*). Antithetical episodes are disposed in near-symmetry: sermon and seizure by atheism; first evening at Oberlin's and the uncannily disturbing night in a mountain hut. By such means, too, Büchner reins in the centrifugal energies of self-contained episodes abruptly juxtaposed, predominantly paratactic syntax and often elliptical constructions, which all generate their own effect of breathlessness to mirror Lenz's agitation.

Psychiatrists have praised the clinical accuracy of Büchner's portrayal of a schizophrenic psychosis. But Büchner's most memorable and influential achievement is the quite "un-clinical" intensity, the imaginative empathy with which the processes of Lenz's consciousness are represented. True, this is achieved within a firmly objective narratorial framework, given by an impersonal narrator whose most characteristic register is one of laconic reportage (after the manner of Oberlin), eschewing explanatory commentary and explicit gestures of compassion; yet laconicism too can be searing: "He felt no fatigue, but at times he was irritated that he could not walk on his head." This impersonal narrator can exercise the privilege of omniscience in orthodox, diegetic representation of Lenz's consciousness via indirect discourse, but again and again come an abrupt switch to the mimetic immediacy of free indirect discourse ("he stirred up everything inside him, but dead! Dead!"), or intermediate forms—elliptical formulations suggesting unco-ordinated sense-impressions, audacious metaphor, words so emotively charged that they seem to emanate from Lenz—in which the perspectives of narrator and protagonist fuse into what the critic Roy Pascal calls a "dual voice."

Such intimate access to Lenz's experience makes for compassionate understanding. More, his perceptions assume at times a haunting and persuasive poetry: "Do you not hear the terrible voice, usually called silence . . . ?" At times, too, Lenz voices the revolt against conventional ideological comforts—artistic or metaphysical—that is common to all Büchner's works. But the sobriety of the detached narrator's voice is equally important: to affirm the solidity of the world from which Lenz becomes every more alienated—and to which his aesthetic credo, informed by social and ethical commitments, had declared allegiance and obligation; and to register the disintegration of Lenz's mind, the loss of sensibility, the human waste.

—Derek Glass

BULGAKOV, Mikhail (Afanas'evich). Russian. Born in Kiev, 3 May 1891. Educated at First Kiev High School, 1900–09; Medical Faculty, Kiev University, 1909–16, doctor's degree 1916. Served as doctor in front-line and district hospitals, 1916–18. Married 1) Tatiana Nikolaevna Lappa in 1913; 2) Liubov' Evgenievna Belozerskaia in 1924; 3) Elena Sergeevna Shilovskaia in 1932. Doctor in Kiev, 1918–19, but abandoned medicine in 1920; organized a "sub-department of the arts," Vladikavkaz, 1920–21; in Moscow from 1921: journalist, with jobs for various groups and papers; associated with the Moscow Art Theatre from 1925: producer, 1930–36; librettist and consultant, Bolshoi Theatre, 1936–40. *Died 10 March 1940.*

PUBLICATIONS

Collections

P'esy.   1962; revised edition, as *Dramy i komedii*, 1965.
Izbrannaia proza.   1966.
Sobranie sochinenii, edited by Ellendea Proffer.   1982—.

Short Stories

Rokovye iaitsa [The Fatal Eggs].   1925.
D'iavoliada: Rasskazy.   1925; as *Diaboliad and Other Stories*, edited by Ellendea and Carl Proffer, 1972; as *Diaboliad*, 1991.
Rasskazy [Stories].   1926.
Zapiski Uinogo vracha.   1963; augmented edition, as *A Country Doctor's Notebook*, 1975.
Sobach'e serdtsa (novella).   1969; as *The Heart of a Dog*, 1968.
Notes on the Cuff and Other Stories, edited by Ellendea Proffer.   1992.

Novels

Dni Turbinykh (Belaia gvardiia).   2 vols., 1927–29; as *Day of the Turbins*, 1934; as *The White Guard*, 1971.
Teatralnyi roman, in *Izbrannaia proza.*   1966; as *Black Snow: A Theatrical Novel*, 1967.
Master i Margarita.   1967; complete version, 1969; as *The Master and Margarita*, 1967; complete version, 1967.

Plays

Dni Turbinykh, from his novel (produced 1926).   With *Poslednie dni (Pushkin)*, 1955; as *Days of the Turbins*, in *Early Plays*, edited by Ellendea Proffer, 1972; as *The White Guard*, 1979.
Zoikina kvartira (produced 1926), edited by Ellendea Proffer.   1971; as *Zoia's Apartment*, in *Early Plays*, edited by Proffer, 1972.
Bagrovyi ostrov (produced 1928).   In *P'esy*, 1971; as *The Crimson Island*, in *Early Plays*, edited by Ellendea Proffer, 1972.
Mertvye dushi [Dead Souls], from the novel by Gogol (produced 1932).   With *Ivan Vasil'evich*, 1964.
Kabala sviatosh (as *Mol'er*, produced 1936).   In *P'esy*, 1962; as *A Cabal of Hypocrites*, in *Early Plays*, edited by Ellendea Proffer, 1972; as *Molière*, 1983.
Skupoi, from *L'Avare* by Molière, in *Polnoe sobranie sochinenii 4*, by Molière.   1939.
Don Kikhot, from the novel by Cervantes (produced 1940).   In *P'esy*, 1962.
Poslednie dni (Pushkin) (produced 1943).   With *Dni Turbinykh*, 1955; as *The Last Days (Pushkin)*, in *Russian Literature Triquarterly 15*, 1976.
Rakhel, edited by Margarita Aliger, music by R.M. Glier (broadcast 1943; produced 1947).   Edited by A. Colin Wright, in *Novy zhurnal 108*, September 1972.
Beg (produced 1957).   In *P'esy*, 1962; as *Flight*, 1970; as *On the Run*, 1972.
Ivan Vasil'evich (produced 1966).   With *Mertvye dushi*, 1964.
Poloumnyi Zhurden, from *Le Bourgeois Gentilhomme* by Molière (produced 1972).   In *Dramy i komedii*, 1965.
Adam i Eva, in *P'esy.*   1971; as *Adam and Eve* (produced 1989) in *Russian Literature Triquarterly 1*, Fall 1971.
Minin i Pozharskii, edited by A. Colin Wright.   In *Russian Literature Triquarterly 15*, 1976.
Voina i mir [War and Peace], from the novel by Tolstoi, edited by A. Colin Wright.   In *Canadian-American Slavic Studies 15*, Summer-Fall 1981.
Flight, and Bliss.   1985.
The Heart of a Dog (produced 1988).
Six Plays (includes *The White Guard, Madam Zoyka, Flight, Molière, Adam and Eve, The Last Days*), edited by Lesley Milne.   1991.

Other

Zhizn' gospodina de Mol'era.   1962; as *The Life of Monsieur de Molière*, 1970.

*

Bibliography: *An International Bibliography of Works by and about Bulgakov* by Ellendea Proffer, 1976; *Bulgakov in English: A Bibliography 1891–1991* by Garth M. Terry, 1991.

Critical Studies: *Bulgakov's "The Master and Margarita": The Text as a Cipher* by Elena N. Mahlow, 1975; *The Master and Margarita: A Comedy of Victory*, 1977, and *Bulgakov: A Critical Biography*, 1990, both by Lesley Milne; *Bulgakov: Life and Interpretations* by A. Colin Wright, 1978; "Bulgakov Issue" of *Canadian-American Slavic Studies 15*, Summer-Fall 1981; *Three Russian Writers and the Irrational: Zamyatin, Pil'nyak, and Bulgakov* by T.R.N. Edwards, 1982; *Bulgakov: Life and Work* by Ellendea Proffer, 1984; *Between Two Worlds: A Critical Introduction to The Master and Margarita* by Andrew Barratt, 1987; *Bulgakov's Last Decade: The Writer as Hero*, 1987, and *Manuscripts Don't Burn. Bulgakov: A Life in Letters and Diaries*, 1991, both by J.A.E. Curtis; *The Writer's Divided Self in Bulgakov's The Master and Margarita* by Riitta H. Pittman, 1991; *The Apocalyptic Vision of Bulgakov's 'The Master and Margarita'* by Edwin Mellen, 1991.

*   *   *

Mikhail Bulgakov first acquired his reputation in Russia as a writer for the theater. His play *Dni Turbinykh (Days of the Turbins*, also *The White Guard)* became a staple production on the Soviet stage. Based on his own novel, it sympathetically portrays incidents in the life of the Turbin family during the Russian Civil War. That a play about the "losing side" enjoyed such status in Soviet Russia attests to its power and brilliance. However, Bulgakov's universally acknowledged masterpiece is his novel, *Master i Margarita (The Master and Margarita)*, a rich blend of fantasy, satire, and irony which depicts life in Russia of the 1930's. Though Bulgakov excelled in writing long forms, his shorter works—feuilletons, novellas, and stories—are not without merit.

The short stories remain valuable on many levels, most basically as a source of autobiographical details filtered through the eyes of various narrators. The stories also provide information about the literary establishment and life in general in the 1920's in Russia; Bulgakov gives to these works a satirical slant. Some of these compositions also serve as sources for his later works. Nevertheless, many are interesting on their own, especially "The Fatal Eggs" and the novella *Sobach'e serdtse (The Heart of a*

Dog). Bulgakov tells these early tales in the dual voice of a writer and a doctor.

The stories which became known collectively as "Zapiski na manzhetakh" ("Notes On The Cuff") began to appear in the periodical press in 1922 and continued through the following year; the collection remains incomplete. The stories of this cycle chronicle Bulgakov's literary apprenticeship. Here begins the theme that recurs throughout his career: the romance of being a writer, with its joys and sorrows, its pain and rewards. The fragmentary nature of the stories parallels the chaos of the times.

During the early 1920's Bulgakov published a number of feuilletons and stories in newspapers, especially the railwayworkers' gazette *Gudok* and the prestigious Berlin Russian language publication *Nakanune*. Bulgakov's stories, fragments of larger works, and journalistic pieces in the latter paper informed the émigrés about life in Russia during the period of the New Economic Policy (NEP), a source of much of his satirical work. The pieces for *Gudok* are much weaker in content and form.

Bulgakov's first substantial cycle of stories, *Zapiski Uinogo vracha (A Country Doctor's Notebook)*, began to appear in print in the mid-1920's, mainly in the journal *Meditsinskii rabotnik*. Trained as a doctor with a specialty in venereal diseases, Bulgakov himself worked among peasants in rural districts. Following the tradition of other writer/doctors, most notably Anton Chekhov, Bulgakov chronicles his first experiences as a doctor in the provinces. Except for two works, "Morfii" ("Morpheum") and "Ia ubil" ("The Murder"), the stories share a compositional unity with one narrator and recurring characters all in the same setting—the doctor/narrator's first bleak posting miles away from Moscow and the university. Fortunately the doctor has three able and sympathetic assistants with whom he quickly establishes a solid professional relationship. They help to see him through his first months on the job when he finally gets to put his passive knowledge into practice; they also help to ease his loneliness.

The various incidents of each story—an amputation in "Polotentse s petukhom" ("The Embroidered Towel"), a tracheotomy in "Stal'noe gorlo" ("The Steel Windpipe"), the battle against syphilis in "Zvezdnaia syp" ("The Speckled Rash"), an abnormal birth in "Kreshchenie povorotom" ("Baptism by Rotation"), a patient's stubborn ignorance in "T'ma egipetskaia" ("Black as Egypt's Night"), a series of his mistakes in "Propavshii glaz" ("A Vanishing Eye")—combine to recount the doctor's struggle against loneliness, frustration, and ignorance. As the narrator tells tale after tale we see him grow as a doctor and as a human being. When he first arrives he attempts to act older and more self-confident than he is; but when his self-consciousness disappears, he gains confidence and becomes a better doctor. Part of the charm of the collection lies in the narrative voice and Bulgakov's reliance on dialogue, a technique not surprising in an author who wrote primarily for the theater.

A quick-moving, dramatic, almost cinematic quality characterizes the story "D'iavoliada" ("Diaboliad"), which gave its name to the collection published in 1925. (Except for a small 1926 volume of feuilletons, this was the last time Bulgakov appeared in print until after Stalin's death.) The plot of "Diaboliad" centers on a simple mistake the main character Korotkov makes: he confuses his supervisor's name Underwarr (*Kal'soner*) with some of his warehouses inventory, underwear (*kal'sony*). This mix-up spawns mass confusion involving the hero, his boss, and their doubles, a situation not unlike those found in early works of Gogol and Dostoevskii, two writers who clearly

influenced Bulgakov. The confusion all turns out to be the work of the devil. (The device of the devil performing his magic in Moscow in the 1930's became one of the organizing principles of *The Master and Margarita*.) Korotkov gets caught up in the all-engulfing bureaucracy of the new regime, and loses his job and his documents. But in the Soviet Union without documents one does not exist; therefore, in order to realize the metaphor of non-existence, Korotkov commits suicide. A comic fantasy turns into an all too real tragedy.

Bulgakov focuses his satiric eyes on other aspects of Soviet life in the title story of *Rokovye iaitsq* ("The Fatal Eggs"), the most famous, and probably best story of the collection. Here he attacks the abuses of journalism, bureaucracy, and power. He also exposes the danger of obsession with science for the sake of science alone. Based in part on H.G. Wells's *The Food of the Gods* (1904), "The Fatal Eggs" tells the story of a scientist who has invented a special ray that enhances and accelerates growth. Reading of this invention, the director of a collective farm gets the idea of using the ray on chicken eggs to help ease the food shortage in the country. Thanks to stupidity and bungling, he unfortunately receives a shipment of snake eggs and inadvertently uses the ray to create monstrous creatures which roam the land devouring hapless citizens. To use Bulgakov's term, a "frosty *deus ex machina* saves the day."

Another work with Wellsian overtones, the novella *The Heart of a Dog* addresses some of the same problems as "The Fatal Eggs"; but here Bulgakov turns a more jaundiced eye on the system and the creature it has spawned: the New Soviet Man. Like his predecessor, Wells's Dr. Moreau, the noted Soviet surgeon, Professor Preobrazhenskii (whose name means "transfiguration") experiments with trying to make animals more human. He transplants a human pituitary gland and testicles into a dog. The experiment works and the dog Sharik gradually "evolves" into the man Shaurikov, who regrettably turns into an all too common example of New Soviet Man, a specimen more brutish than Sharik ever could be: a commissar who turns on his "creator."

Two other works in the collection, along with a number of stories which appeared in *Nakanune*, satirize life in Moscow in the 1920's under NEP. "No. 13. The Elpit-Rabkommun Building" (1922) recounts the disintegration and ultimate destruction of a once magnificent building after it becomes communal property. The horrors of communal living is also the subject of "Samogonnoe ozero" (1921, "Moonshine Lake"). "Pokhozhdeniia Chichikova" (1922, "The Adventures of Chichikov") is an amusing parody of Gogol's *Dead Souls,* whose main hero finds himself in NEP-era Russia. A swindler in the 19th century, Chichikov has no trouble at all functioning under NEP; in fact, corruption seems to flourish in the new Soviet State.

Most of Bulgakov's short works never match the artistic quality of his plays and novels. Nevertheless the early fiction provides a valuable picture of life in Russia in the 1920's; it also provides valuable insights into Bulgakov's development as a writer.

—Christine A. Rydel

BUSTOS DOMECQ, H.   See **BIOY CASARES, Adolfo,** and **BORGES, Jorge Luis.**

C

CALDWELL, Erskine (Preston). American. Born in Moreland, Georgia, 17 December 1903. Educated at Erskine College, Due West, South Carolina, 1920–21; University of Virginia, Charlottesville, 1922, 1925–26; University of Pennsylvania, Philadelphia, 1924. Married 1) Helen Lannigan in 1925 (divorced 1938), two sons and one daughter; 2) the photographer Margaret Bourke-White in 1939 (divorced 1942); 3) June Johnson in 1942 (divorced 1955), one son; 4) Virginia Moffett Fletcher in 1957. Played professional football, Wilkes-Barre, Pennsylvania, 1920's; reporter, Atlanta *Journal*, 1925–26; freelance writer from 1926; ran a bookstore in Portland, Maine, 1928; screenwriter, Hollywood, 1930–34, 1942–43; foreign correspondent in Mexico, Spain, Czechoslovakia, Russia, and China, 1938–41; editor, American Folkways series (25 vols.), 1941-55. Recipient: Order of Cultural Merit (Poland), 1981. Member, National Institute of Arts and Letters, 1942, and American Academy, 1984; Commander, Order of Arts and Letters (France), 1984. *Died 11 April 1987.*

PUBLICATIONS

Short Stories

American Earth. 1931; as *A Swell-Looking Girl*, 1951.
Mama's Little Girl (story). 1932.
A Message for Genevieve (story). 1933.
We Are the Living: Brief Stories. 1933.
Kneel to the Rising Sun and Other Stories. 1935.
The Sacrilege of Alan Kent (story). 1936.
Southways: Stories. 1938.
Jackpot: The Short Stories. 1940; abridged edition, as *Midsummer Passion*, 1948.
Georgia Boy. 1943.
A Day's Wooing and Other Stories. 1944.
Stories by Caldwell: 24 Representative Stories, edited by Henry Seidel Canby. 1944; as *The Pocket Book of Caldwell Stories*, 1947.
The Caldwell Caravan: Novels and Stories. 1946.
Where the Girls Were Different and Other Stories, edited by Donald A. Wollheim. 1948.
A Woman in the House. 1949.
The Humorous Side of Caldwell, edited by Robert Cantwell. 1951; as *Where the Girls Were Different and Other Stories*, 1962.
The Courting of Susie Brown. 1952.
The Complete Stories. 1953.
Gulf Coast Stories. 1956.
Certain Women. 1957.
When You Think of Me. 1959.
Men and Women: 22 Stories. 1961.
Stories. 1980.
Stories of Life: North and South. 1983.
The Black and White Stories of Caldwell. 1984.

Midsummer Passion and Other Tales of Maine Cussedness, edited by Charles G. Waugh and Martin H. Greenberg. 1990.

Novels

The Bastard. 1930.
Poor Fool. 1930.
Tobacco Road. 1932.
God's Little Acre. 1933.
Journeyman. 1935; revised edition, 1938.
Trouble in July. 1940.
All Night Long: A Novel of Guerrilla Warfare in Russia. 1942.
Tragic Ground. 1944.
A House in the Uplands. 1946.
The Sure Hand of God. 1947.
This Very Earth. 1948.
Place Called Estherville. 1949.
Episode in Palmetto. 1950.
A Lamp for Nightfall. 1952.
Love and Money. 1954.
Gretta. 1955.
Claudelle Inglish. 1959; as *Claudell*, 1959.
Jenny by Nature. 1961.
Close to Home. 1962.
The Last Night of Summer. 1963.
Miss Mama Aimee. 1967.
Summertime Island. 1968.
The Weather Shelter. 1969.
The Earnshaw Neighborhood. 1971.
Annette. 1973.

Plays

Screenplays: *A Nation Dances* (documentary), 1943; *Volcano*, 1953.

Other

In Defense of Myself. 1930.
Tenant Farmer. 1935.
Some American People. 1935.
You Have Seen Their Faces, photographs by Margaret Bourke-White. 1937.
North of the Danube, photographs by Margaret Bourke-White. 1939.
Say! Is This the U.S.A.?, photographs by Margaret Bourke-White. 1941.
All-Out on the Road to Smolensk. 1942; as *Moscow Under Fire: A Wartime Diary 1941*, 1942.
Russia at War, photographs by Margaret Bourke-White. 1942.
Call It Experience: The Years of Learning How to Write. 1951.
Molly Cottontail (for children). 1958.
Around About America. 1964.

In Search of Bisco.   1965.
The Deer at Our House (for children).   1966.
In the Shadow of the Steeple.   1967.
Writing in America.   1967.
Deep South: Memory and Observation (includes *In the Shadow of the Steeple*).   1968.
Afternoons in Mid-America: Observations and Impressions.   1976.
With All My Might: An Autobiography.   1987.
Conversations with Caldwell, edited by Edwin T. Arnold.   1988.

Editor, *Smokey Mountain Country,* by North Callahan.   1988.

*

Critical Studies: *The Southern Poor-White from Lubberland to Tobacco Road* by Shields McIlwaine, 1939; *Caldwell* by James Korges, 1969; *Black Like It Is/Was: Caldwell's Treatment of Racial Themes* by William A. Sutton, 1974; *Critical Essays on Caldwell* edited by Scott MacDonald, 1981; *Caldwell* by James E. Devlin, 1984; *Caldwell Reconsidered* edited by Edwin T. Arnold, 1990.

*   *   *

At the middle of the 20th century Erskine Caldwell was probably the most popular fiction writer on earth, as measured by many millions of his novels and short story collections sold in paperback editions in several countries. From the beginning of his career, around 1930, his short stories had been praised by serious critics, who found in his humor the gist and pith of traditional tall tales livened by a contemporary sensibility. His representations of Southern depravity and racial injustice earned him acclaim as a social critic. One of his earliest novels, *Tobacco Road,* was dramatized and set off on so long a run on Broadway it seemed like a permanent fixture. Another, *God's Little Acre,* reached a sale of 4.5 million copies in 13 years after publication. Both books prospered on a mixture of comic strip violence, misshapen characters, subhuman lack of compassion, and a diffuse, mystical interpretation of the human potential, which gratified the social conscience of the time.

His left-leaning journalism—including books of photojournalism done in collaboration with Margaret Bourke White—reinforced the political heft of his fiction. He was a frontrunner among young American writers. When his collection *Jackpot* was published in 1940 with 75 stories from the previous decade he was commonly compared with Hemingway and Faulkner. Rumors of a Nobel prize somewhere down the line seemed not incredible. But even in the years of inflated reputation there was controversy and dismay from many who wished him to be a forthright champion of justice and human dignity. In 1944 Jonathan Daniels wrote, "The American lower depths are very funny indeed. In *Tobacco Road* they amused more people than even *Abie's Irish Rose.*" Daniels went on to surmise there were hosts of readers who liked to guffaw at the helpless, the deformed, the spiritually castrated, and the sadistic. He spoke for many who had concluded Caldwell was not so much exposing the grim realities of the American South as misrepresenting them for the sake of profitable sensationalism.

Whatever the rising tide of critical censure, Caldwell's appeal to masses of readers did not shrivel drastically until well into the 1950's. After that, though he continued to pump out novels, travel books, and (fewer) short stories, his reputation plummeted until now he is hardly a memory in the minds of a generation well past middle age, a footnote to an era that mistook him for a giant.

This collapse of interest in his very large body of work might be explained by saying he published too much, so that his peak performances were inundated by the flood of hasty composition and exhausted conceptions. Alas, there aren't any peak performances among his novels. Obviously they once entertained millions who came to rely in book after book on his characteristic mix of comedy and violence. Tedium took over when the violence became ridiculous because it was so obviously puffed up.

His typical characters—landowners and white sharecroppers, lubricious women and virginal victims, murderous drifters and vicious lawmen—are conceived and presented as automatons, not even so much representing human types in flat silhouette as they are exemplars of swollen obsessions bedeviling the American underclass.

At the same time, these simplified figures who serve so badly in the novels function more effectively in the kind of short story he invented. The search for masterpieces gets no farther among the one hundred stories he said he published than among the novels, but in the bulk of the stories there is life and a lilt of black humor, and the stab of black melodrama in many. Teller of tall tales, he learned how to craft such material so the nimbleness of craft becomes a part of the joy. There is a fascination in watching him work, weave, and increase the tension of his material until it snaps in the denouement.

In the very brief "Midsummer Passion," a farmer driving his wagon home after his day's work comes on a car abandoned by the roadside. As he snoops in it he discovers a woman's stockings and panties. Stirred with ineffable longing, he carries these garments with him as he drives on. Presently he comes on a neighbor woman working innocently in her garden. He leaps down from his wagon, tackles her, and in a wild caricature of rape, tries to put the panties on her. She is too strong for him. He can only manage to get one of her feet into a leg of the tantalizing garment. When he is winded and bested in this unequal struggle, the woman stands up, draws on the panties over her dress, and with high civility instructs him to go on home. With equal civility he agrees to do just that. This is mastery in the use of a surprise ending, though the subject is ever so slight.

The same masterful direction of suspense and gusty humor can be found in "Where the Girls are Different," "Maud Island," "An Autumn Courtship," and "August Afternoon." Told in perfectly paced crescendo, this last story opens with a shiftless landowner waking from an afternoon's nap to be told by his black servant that there is a white stranger on the premises, leaned against a tree while he whittles and peers under the dress of the landowner's wife. When the stick is whittled down to a sliver the stranger and wife walk down a path together into the concealment of some bushes. The cogitating householder concludes he does not wish to interfere with a man who has a knife, whatever may be happening to his wife. He lapses into impotent pipe dreams and finds the better course is to go back to sleep.

Anyone wishing to savor the black melodrama of Caldwell's better stories might well begin with "Candy-Man Beechum"—more song than story, perhaps. A young black man, a hero of amorous longing, sets out one evening to go to his woman. In the town he must pass through to get to her he is, for no reason at all, shot to death by white law men. Here there is poignancy in the very lack of complication. In "Dorothy" an unemployed young man comes to believe with great sorrow that he has nudged an unemployed girl into prostitution, while in "Martha Jean" a helpless boy is witness to the rape of a girl who has come to town seeking work. In "Masses of Men" a desperate illiterate young mother prostitutes her ten-year-old daughter for money to buy food with. By and large these brief tableaux of darkness lack the sly craft of the overtly funny stories. Even so, they may have more power to shock, to poison complacency, and to convince than Caldwell's novels have.

—R.V. Cassill

See the essays on "Kneel to the Rising Sun" and "Saturday Afternoon."

———

CALISHER, Hortense. American. Born in New York City, 20 December 1911. Educated at Hunter College High School, New York; Barnard College, New York, A.B. in philosophy 1932. Married 1) H.B. Heffelfinger in 1935, one daughter and one son; 2) Curtis Harnack in 1959. Adjunct professor of English, Barnard College, 1956–57; visiting professor, University of Iowa, Iowa City, 1957, 1959–60, Stanford University, California, 1958, Sarah Lawrence College, Bronxville, New York, 1962, and Brandeis University, Waltham, Massachusetts, 1963–64; writer-in-residence, 1965, and visiting lecturer, 1968, Univeristy of Pennsylvania, Philadelphia; adjunct professor of English, Columbia University, New York, 1968–70 and 1972–73; Clark Lecturer, Scripps College, Claremont, California, 1969; visiting professor, State University of New York, Purchase, 1971–72; Regents' Professor, University of California, Irvine, Spring 1976; visiting writer, Bennington College, Vermont, 1978; Hurst Professor, Washington University, St. Louis, 1979; National Endowment for the Arts Lecturer, Cooper Union, New York, 1983; visiting professor, Brown University, Providence, Rhode Island, 1986; guest lecturer, U.S.-China Arts Exchange, Republic of China, 1986. President, PEN, 1986–87. President, American Academy of Arts and Letters, 1987–90. Recipient: Guggenheim fellowship, 1952, 1955; Department of State American Specialists grant, 1958; American Academy award, 1967; National Endowment for the Arts grant, 1967; Kafka prize, 1987; National Endowment for the Arts Lifetime Achievement award, 1989. Litt.D.: Skidmore College, Saratoga Springs, New York, 1980; Grinnell College, Iowa, 1986; Hofstra University, Hempstead, New York, 1988. Member, American Academy, 1977. Lives in New York City.

PUBLICATIONS

Short Stories

In the Absence of Angels.   1951.
Tale for the Mirror: A Novella and Other Stories.   1962.
Extreme Magic: A Novella and Other Stories.   1964.

The Railway Police, and The Last Trolley Ride (novellas). 1966.
Collected Stories.   1975.
Saratoga, Hot.   1985.

Novels

False Entry.   1961.
Textures of Life.   1963.
Journal from Ellipsia.   1965.
The New Yorkers.   1969.
Queenie.   1971.
Standard Dreaming.   1972.
Eagle Eye.   1973.
On Keeping Women.   1977.
Mysteries of Motion.   1983.
The Bobby-Soxer.   1986.
Age.   1987.
The Small Bang (as Jack Fenno).   1992.
In the Place of the Movie Queen.   1993.

Other

What Novels Are (lecture).   1969.
Herself (memoir).   1972.
Kissing Cousins: A Memory.   1988.

Editor, with Shannon Ravenel, *The Best American Short Stories 1981.*   1981.

*

Critical Studies: in *Don't Never Forget* by Brigid Brophy, 1966; article by Cynthia Ozick in *Midstream,* 1969; "Ego Art: Notes on How I Came to It" by Calisher, in *Works in Progress,* 1971; article by Kathy Brown in *Current Biography,* November 1973; interview in *Paris Review,* Winter 1987.

*   *   *

Many readers first encounter Hortense Calisher through her widely anthologized short stories, then anticipate her novels. After reading them, however, they may come away vaguely unsatisfied though seldom quite dissatisfied. She is too gifted a writer for that.

It seems impossible for Calisher to write poorly: she is a master of language. Precise, powerful verbs give scenes life and immediacy. In "The Woman Who Was Everybody" an overqualified department store employee reluctantly faces the day: "She swung sideways out of bed, clamped her feet on the floor, rose and trundled to the bathroom, the kitchenette." Calisher's imagery is bountiful, original, and appropriate. In the same story, "the mornings crept in like applicants for jobs." Equal to language, Calisher has evidently observed and experienced how truth is revealed in the course of living and can reconstruct these epiphanies readily in characters.

Then why, since hers are among the best American short stories of this century, are Calisher's novels less successful? At least two reasons are likely. One is that it is impossible to sustain in the long form the power she packs into the short form. The small cast, limited setting, single problem of the short story let her build the work to a final revelation which suggests that, for better or worse, a life will never be quite the same again. This is the classic short story.

Calisher novels often merely elongate the story format. Substituting for traditional plot and subplot, there are series of revelations related to the central situation. (A young couple disclose aspects of themselves as they cope with an ill child in *Textures of Life.* Another couple, from the novella *Saratoga, Hot* actually reveal more about their horsey social set then themselves.) Whether the reader can sustain interest in longer works whose integral logic is random and whose continuity needs occasional propulsion by fortuitous revelation is a question. Certainly that *does* work in *The New Yorkers*, often called her most successful novel, an indulgent insight into family life. What may be her least successful novel, *Mysteries of Motion*, distracts as much as discloses since six lives are revealed, and on a space journey at that. Better a bus ride in Brooklyn.

That more modest approach to setting is exactly what makes her short stories seem instantly relevant to our ordinary lives, that and the fact that each story—however brief—is also a life history of sorts. Calisher examines that life at a time of crisis and the reader comes away instructed in valuable experiences. In the classic "One of the Chosen" a successful Jewish lawyer, Davy Spanner, always popular in his college days, has believed that he never needed the support of fraternity life and had comfortably rejected the early overtures of the campus societies. At a class reunion, a gentile classmate blurts out the unsettling truth that Spanner would never have been offered a serious membership bid.

Calisher's long interest in psychology and the supernatural is evident. Her life spans Freudianism and beyond, but psychology—eclectic and non-systematic—as it appears in her work at times is close to fantasy, at other times follows accepted dogma. "Heartburn" centers on the power of suggestion; "The Scream on 57th Street" treats fear. Both "work" just as her general grasp of family relationships seems valid, however, it was acquired. On the other hand, *Standard Dreaming*, Calisher's unfortunate excursion into a dream world of searching characters, could be taken for a parody of surrealism.

Calisher's short stories and novellas may initially appear to be peopled by fully-rounded characters, but an overview of the stories reveals a high proportion of well-done types: the educated misfit, the eccentric family member, the young innocent, the at-odds mother-daughter (or husband-wife), the displaced southerner, the would-be radical. And type is all they need to be since hers are not primarily stories of character, but of complex situation, the result of long processes of cause and effect told in hints and subtleties. Where the Calisher protagonists have been, are now, and where they are probably going—or not going, depending on their revelations—*is* their story. Exactly who they are is incidental. Their external descriptions are often vivid, even witty, but their tastes and temperaments are revealed only to the degree that they serve the tale. If we flesh them out ourselves, it is a tribute to their creator's ability to write so that we *read* creatively.

The Collected Stories of Hortense Calisher, an enduring treasury of major works in her best genre, allows ready comparison of early and late works and reveals the consistency of Calisher's vision, even such traits as a vein of humor, a thread of the absurd, and a persistent interest in the power of the mind to direct fate. She is an eminently serious and concerned writer, despite the fatuous, the incompetents, the ditsy relatives, and the rattled authority figures who clamor for their share of attention in her works. Their truths are as true as anyone else's, Calisher suggests,

and their numbers among us may be greater than we want to believe.

—Marian Pehowski

See the essay on "The Railway Police."

———

CALLAGHAN, Morley (Edward). Canadian. Born in Toronto, Ontario, 22 September 1903. Educated at St. Michael's College, University of Toronto, B.A. 1925; Osgoode Hall Law School, Toronto, 1925–28, LL.B. 1928; admitted to the Ontario bar, 1928. Worked with the Royal Canadian Navy on assignment for the National Film Board during World War II. Married Lorreto Florence Dee in 1929 (died 1984); two sons. Part-time staff member, Toronto *Star,* 1923–27; lived in Paris, 1929; chairman of the radio forum *Things to Come* (later *Citizen's Forum*), 1943–47; panelist, *Beat the Champs* radio quiz show, 1947, and *Now I Ask You* radio show and *Fighting Words* television show, early 1950's. Recipient: Governor-General's award, 1952; *Maclean's* award, 1955; Lorne Pierce medal, 1960; Canada Council medal, 1966, prize, 1970; Molson prize, 1970; Royal Bank of Canada award, 1970. D.Litt.: University of Western Ontario, London, 1965; University of Windsor, Ontario, 1973; LL.D.: University of Toronto, 1966. Companion, Order of Canada, 1982. *Died 25 August 1990.*

PUBLICATIONS

Short Stories

A Native Argosy. 1929.
Now That April's Here and Other Stories. 1936.
Stories. 1959.
An Autumn Penitent (includes *In His Own Country*). 1973.
Close to the Sun Again (novella) 1977.
No Man's Meat, and The Enchanted Pimp (novellas). 1978.
The Lost and Found Stories of Callaghan. 1985.

Novels

Strange Fugitive. 1928.
It's Never Over. 1930.
No Man's Meat. 1931.
A Broken Journey. 1932.
Such Is My Beloved. 1934.
They Shall Inherit the Earth. 1935.
More Joy in Heaven. 1937.
The Varsity Story. 1948.
The Loved and the Lost. 1951.
The Many Coloured Coat. 1960.
A Passion in Rome. 1961.
A Fine and Private Place. 1975.
A Time for Judas. 1983.
Our Lady of the Snows. 1986.
The Man with the Coat. 1987.

Plays

Turn Again Home, from his novel *They Shall Inherit the Earth* (produced 1940; as *Going Home,* produced 1950).
To Tell the Truth (produced 1949).

Television Play: *And Then Mr. Jones,* 1974.

Other

Luke Baldwin's Vow (for children).   1948.
That Summer in Paris: Memories of Tangled Friendships with Hemingway, Fitzgerald, and Some Others.   1963.
Winter, photographs by John de Visser.   1974.

*

Bibliography: by Judith Kendle, in *The Annotated Bibliography of Canada's Major Authors 5* edited by Robert Lecker and Jack David, 1984.

Critical Studies: *Callaghan* by Brandon Conron, 1966, and *Callaghan* edited by Conron, 1975; *Callaghan* by Victor Hoar, 1969; *The Style of Innocence: A Study of Hemingway and Callaghan* by Fraser Sutherland, 1972; *Callaghan* by Patricia A. Morley, 1978; *The Callaghan Symposium* edited by David Staines, 1981.

* * *

It has often been said that the short story is the genre in which Canadian writers have most excelled, and from the animal stories of Charles G.D. Roberts and the social tales of Sara Jeannette Duncan in the later 19th century it has been a genre in which they have seemed much at home. Indeed, very few Canadian fiction writers have devoted themselves merely to the short story; the broader form and higher critical standing of the novel have attracted many of them, but not always with complete success.

An example is Morley Callaghan, who held his position as one of Canada's leading writers from the early 1930's to the later 1980's. Callaghan excelled from the beginning in briefer fiction—short stories and the novella. From 1937 to 1950 he went into a period of virtual literary silence. He emerged in 1951 with *The Loved and the Lost,* first of a group of ambitious quasi-romantic novels in which he battled, never quite successfully, with the larger forms. And though he returned in the 1970's to shorter and simpler kinds of novel, he never recovered the lapidary eloquence of his early stories about simple people, not all that intelligent, with their laconic speech patterns and their understated joys and sorrows.

His best later book was not in fact a work of fiction at all, but autobiographical, *That Summer in Paris,* a memoir of a few months spent in France at the end of the 1920's, largely in the company of Ernest Hemingway and F. Scott Fitzgerald. His acquaintance with Hemingway was indeed largely responsible for the course his career took; he worked as a cub reporter on the Toronto *Star* and for a time had Hemingway as a colleague. The influence of Hemingway on Callaghan's early work, and particularly on the simplification of his sentence structure, is evident, and Hemingway was the first fellow writer to acknowledge Callaghan's talents and to encourage him to continue working.

Not much was happening in Canadian short fiction at this time except for the kind of Anglicized quasi-romantic writing against which Callaghan almost naturally reacted. And because Hemingway took him up, and even arranged for the publication of his early stories in avant-garde international journals of the time like *This Quarter, Transition,* and *Exile,* Callaghan at first tended to be associated with the group of young American writers often referred to as "The Lost Generation," though the locales of his stories remained largely Canadian. People like Ezra Pound, Fitzgerald, and Sinclair Lewis would sometimes patronize him and flatter him even in 1960, at a time when Callaghan's vogue in American literary circles was long past, Edmund Wilson was rediscovering him as a "highly neglected writer" and eccentrically comparing his work with that of Chekhov and Turgenev.

By the beginning of the 1930's Callaghan's stories were appearing in more popular magazines like *Scribner's, Harpers' Bazaar, Atlantic Monthly,* and *The New Yorker.* Out of the work of this period he collected and published two books of short fiction, *A Native Argosy,* and *Now That April's Here and Other Stories.* Much later, in 1959, he collected all his work in this genre into *Morley Callaghan's Stories,* which contained no new work and marked the real end of his career as a writer of true short stories.

It was a seedy world of the unsuccessful and unattractive that Callaghan presented, not without compassion, in his short stories and the novellas of the 1930's which, we shall see, are closely related to them. His characters tend to live by their wits when they have any, and many of them are petty crooks, prostitutes, hangers-on of the sporting world with all its rackets; they often have ambiguous links with the world of financiers and politicians whose corruptions are seen as being merely of another kind. There will occasionally be a glimmer of gilt in a whore's heart, a usually fatal impulse of loyalty in a gangster's mind, and love is sometimes real, but Callaghan never tries to idealize his characters. Even if they are not rogues, they are fools. The best of them have destructive flaws and the dismalness of the lives lived by most of these people is accentuated by the deliberate simplicity of mind with which the writer approaches them, his refusal to write with either elegance or eloquence; "literary" is one of the dirtiest words in his vocabulary.

In some ways Callaghan's best writings are the sparsely written novellas he produced in the 1930's, formally intermediate works whose structures and themes were too complex for them still to be called stories but lacking in the structural and psychological complexity of a true novel. In fact, from *Such Is My Beloved* through *They Shall Inherit the Earth* to *More Joy in Heaven,* they may perhaps be claimed as parables, which their titles suggest. At this time Callaghan, a birthright Catholic, was taken up with the radical theology of Jacques Maritain, then teaching in Canada. And these works do reveal a kind of basic Christianity in which ecclesiastical institutions and potentates are rejected in favour of those humble people who grope their way towards Christian action and are martyred by the very world the churchmen support and represent. Written in the socially conscious decade of the 1930's, they are typical works of the age in so far as they imply—rather than state—the need for transforming all our values, though they do not offer a forceful means of achievement. But their leading characters are really holy fools, and overshadowing their naif efforts is a chronic pessimism on the author's part that ultimately presents the world as irredeemable because the vast mass of people are trapped in their spiritual and emotional limitations. Their efforts to change their world and even themselves, as in the case of the "reformed" bank robber in *More Joy in Heaven*, at best fail and at worst end in disaster.

—George Woodcock

See the essays on "Now that April's Here" and "Two Fishermen."

———

CALVINO, Italo. Italian. Born in Santiago de las Vegas, Cuba, 15 October 1923; grew up in San Remo, Italy. Educated at the University of Turin, graduated 1947. Conscripted into Young Facists, 1940; left and served in the Italian Resistance, 1943–45. Married Chichita Singer in 1964; one daughter. Member of the editorial staff, Einaudi, publishers, Turin, from 1947; co-editor, *Il Menabò*, Milan, 1959–66. Recipient: Viareggio prize, 1957; Bagutta prize, 1959; Veillon prize, 1963; Feltrinelli prize, 1972; Austrian State Prize for European Literature, 1976; Nice Festival prize, 1982. Honorary Member, American Academy, 1975. *Died 20 September 1985.*

PUBLICATIONS

Collections

Romanzi e Racconti, edited by Claudio Milanini. 1992—.

Short Stories

Ultimo viene il corvo. 1949; as *Adam, One Afternoon, and Other Stories*, 1957.
Fiabe italiane: Raccolte della tradizione popolare durante gli ultimi cento anni e transcritte in lingua dai vari dialetti. 1956; as *Italian Fables*, 1959; as *Italian Folk Tales*, 1975; complete translation, as *Italian Folktales*, 1980.
I racconti. 1958.
Marcovaldo; ovvero, Le stagioni in città. 1963; as *Marcovaldo; or, The Seasons in the City*, 1983.
La nuvola di smog e La formica argentina. 1965.
Le cosmicomiche. 1965; as *Cosmicomics*, 1968.
Ti con zero. 1967; as *T Zero*, 1969; as *Time and the Hunter*, 1970.
Gli amori difficili. 1970; as *Difficult Loves*, 1984.
The Watcher and Other Stories. 1971.
Le città invisibili. 1972; as *Invisible Cities*, 1974.
Il castello dei destini incrociati. 1973; as *The Castle of Crossed Destinies*, 1977.
Se una notte d'inverno un viaggiatore. 1979; as *If on a Winter's Night a Traveller*, 1981.
Palomar. 1983; as *Mr. Palomar*, 1985.
Sotto il sole giaguaro. 1986; as *Under the Jaguar Tree*, 1988.

Novels

Il sentiero dei nidi di ragno. 1947; as *The Path to the Nest of Spiders*, 1956.
I nostri antenati. 1960; as *Our Ancestors*, 1980.

Il visconte dimezzato. 1952; as *The Cloven Viscount (with The Non-Existent Knight)*, 1962.
Il barone rampante. 1957; as *The Baron in the Trees*, 1959.
Il cavaliere inesistente. 1959; as *The Non-Existent Knight (with The Cloven Viscount)*, 1962.
La giornata d'uno scrutatore. 1963.

Play

Un re in ascolto [The King Listens] (opera libretto), music by Luciano Berio. 1984.

Other

Una pietra sopra: Discorsi di letteratura e società. 1980.
Collezione di sabbia: Emblemi bizzarri e inquietanti del nostro passato e del nostro futuro gli oggetti raccontano il mondo. 1984.
The Uses of Literature. 1986.
The Literature Machine. 1987.
Six Memos for the Next Millennium (lectures). 1988.
Perchè leggere i classici (essays). 1992.

Editor, *Poesie edite e inedite*, by Cesare Pavese. 1962.
Editor, *Vittorini: Progettazione e letteratura.* 1968.

*

Critical Studies: *Calvino: A Reappraisal and an Appreciation of the Trilogy* by J.R. Woodhouse, 1968; *Calvino, Writer and Critic* by JoAnn Cannon, 1981; "Calvino" by Richard Andrews, in *Writers and Society in Contemporary Italy* edited by Michael Caesar and Peter Hainsworth, 1984; *Calvino and the Age of Neorealism: Fables of Estrangement* by Lucia Re, 1990; *Calvino: a San Remo* by Piero Ferrara, 1991.

* * *

Italo Calvino wrote of his experiences during World War II in his first novel *Il sentiero dei nidi di ragno (The Path to the Nest of Spiders)* and his war stories of the late 1940's. In the preface to the trilogy *I nostroi antenati (Our Ancestors)* Calvino describes the gatherings around camp fires, where the heroes of the day's exploits recounted their adventures. At this time there was no doubt in his narrative about the existence of a narrator and a hero. He also spoke in that preface about the hero "affirming himself as a human being." And he said that in narrative suspense (and he used the English word) was like salt, and declared his lack of interest in descriptions of interior scenes and the trappings of the psychological novel.

It is obvious even in his early works that Calvino is a storyteller. In fact, it has been pointed out that he only wrote one other novel, *La giornata d'uno scrutatore*, the story of a "teller" in the parliamentary elections. Even the historical novels of *Our Ancestors* are tales in the manner of Voltaire's *Candide*. The narrators of *Il visconte dimezzato (The Cloven Viscount)* and *Il barone rampante (The Baron in the Trees)* are both observers, members of the hero's family. But the third tale in order of composition, *Il cavaliere inesistente (The Non-Existent Knight)* turns out to have a surprisingly active narrator who balances nicely the non-entity of the hero. The question of observers, performers, and narrators took on more importance in his work.

During the 1950's Calvino worked for his publisher, Einaudi, making a collection of popular tales of the last hundred years from all over the Italian peninsula. This study, he said, taught him something about the economy of the tale. He became interested in the theory of narrative. Later when he lived in Paris he became involved in the Oulipo movement, and also followed closely the discussions of the structuralists and semioticians.

The collection *Fiabe italiane (Italian Folk Tales)* had been partly an exercise in popular culture. As a Communist until the Hungary episode, and founder with Vittorini of *Il Menabò di Letterature,* which aimed at bringing literature into closer contact with modern society, Calvino also wanted to reflect more reality in his stories. The peasant hero had fulfilled this role in the 1930's and 1940's. Calvino chose instead a city worker, gave him a fantastic Germanic-sounding name, Marcovaldo, and made him the hero of a set of stories representing the trials of the modern worker who still hankers after the countryside. Marcovaldo picks mushrooms along the pavements, poisoning half his street, and cuts down forests of advertising hoardings along the motorway in order to keep his family warm. An element of Ariostesque fantasy is still present, just as it was in the early stories and the trilogy. Marcovaldo is less successful in his undertakings than the heroes of the war stories, but both groups of tales appeared in the collected short stories (*I racconti*) of 1958 as "Difficult Idylls." There was also a series called *Gli amori difficili (Difficult Loves),* in which the hero or heroine is in some way hampered in personal relationships: a short-sighted man cannot recognise his friends without his new spectacles, but wearing them he is himself unrecognisable; a bather loses her swimming costume out at sea while bathing off a busy beach.

In the mid-1960's Calvino's fiction took a new turn. Both his parents were scientists, which perhaps accounted for his move towards a realistic science fiction in *Le cosmicomiche (Cosmicomics)* and *Ti con zero (Time and the Hunter).* In these two collections of short stories we meet for the first time a serial narrator figure named Qfwfq, like a scientific formula. Qfwfq has been present through all time, from the first "Big Bank" (a kind of primordial pasta party) to, for instance, the arrival of colours and the evolution of birds. He is a figure who is as comfortable among the dinosaurs as he is on Staten Island. His language is ordinary speech, not quite up to telling of the marvels he has witnessed, unlike the language of the scientists which prefixes each episode. The gap between the ordinary language and the strangeness creates the fantasy that brings the marvels to life. In "All at One Point" the creation and the Big Bank depend on Mrs. Ph(i)NKo's generous impulse: "Boys, the noodles I would make for you!" In the third part of *Time and the Hunter,* however, we find Qfwfq eclipsed and a more serious narrator takes over, an anonymous survivor imprisoned in time, in traffic jams, in futile night driving. The collection ends with the borrowed figure of the Count of Monte Cristo, a prisoner as ever in the appropriately named Chateau d'If, trying to find an escape route by pure reason without action, and so spiralling out through the realms of science, history, literature, and philosophical speculation.

The narrator of *Le città invisibili (Invisible Cities)* is Marco Polo, famous as a real life adventurer and the author of the first book of traveller's tales produced in Italy. He describes to Kublai Khan 55 of the cities of his great empire so that he can discern the mark of a pattern so subtle as to escape the bite of termites. Numerical patterning was becoming more and more important for Calvino. In "Cybernetics and Ghosts," an essay of 1967, he said that he considered narrative a "combinatorial process." In *Invisible Cities* the accounts are placed in nine series interspersed with discussions between storyteller and listener, ten cities at the beginning and the end, with seven collections of five each in between. The numbers "nine" and "ten" are powerful in the Dantesque tradition, and represent a way of accommodating reality to the rational mind. Marco Polo's last advice to Kublai Khan is to recognise who and what in Hell, which is around us, is not Hell, and to let that endure and give it space. The task is one of observation, recognition, and discrimination, resembling that of the Count of Monte Cristo contemplating his escape.

Il castello dei destini incrociati (The Castle of Crossed Destinies) presents another series of stories, some with very well-known heroes, like Orlando, Faust, and Parsifal. The new problem, however, is one of enunciation. The storytellers gathered in the castle are mute, and so are forced to pattern out their tales using significant objects, the 15th-century Tarot pack (in the case of the accompanying story, "Tavern of Crossed Destinies," the better-known 17th-century French pack). The language is that of the writer who observes the layout of the cards as the stories are constructed. Colloquial speech, which was Qfwfq's medium, is thus banished.

Se una notta d'inverno un viaggiatore (If on a Winter's Night a Traveller) leaves us again in the hands of the writer, not to mention the (male) Reader and the (female) Reader. At stake is not only the relationship between storyteller and Readers (and readers) but the very thread of suspense, that original salt, which is snapped ten different times by accidents occurring to texts between the manuscript stage and actual perusal. The relationship between author and Readers (each addressed in the very intimate *Tu* form) is conducted in twelve alternating chapters ending in the fulfillment of their wedding night: "And you say, 'Just a moment, I've almost finished *If on a Winter's Night a Traveller* by Italo Calvino.'"

Palomar (Mr. Palomar) is again a series. Twenty-seven pieces make nine groups of three (Dantesque numbers again), which originally appeared during the 1970's and 1980's in newspapers such as *Il Corriere della Sera* and *Le Repubblica.* Mr. Palomar is named after the giant telescope, and the name also resembles the Italian word for "diver," *palombaro.* He is essentially the reasonable observer trying to capture and set down the reality around him, from the strictly limited stretch of waves in the sea off his beach to a rock and sand garden in Kyoto. The task is to examine the limits of the powers of the writer's point of view. The experiment ends with the death of the narrator as he tries to evade time by describing it. It has been argued that Mr. Palomar and Calvino could be the same person, especially since the essays in *Collezione di sabbia* (Collection of Sand) bear the same stamp.

Sotto il solo giaguaro (Under the Jaguar Sun), published posthumously, was to have contained five stories dealing with the senses. A writer concerned with observation and description must naturally tackle perception. Only taste, hearing, and the sense of smell were finished. In another unfinished work, *Six Memos for the Next Millennium,* planned as the Charles Eliot Norton Poetry Lectures at Harvard, Calvino left six titles as aids for an understanding of his approach to fiction: Lightness, Quickness, Exactitude, Visibility, Multiplicity, and Consistency, the last unwritten. For such an experimental master of the tale, they make a fitting epitaph.

—Judy Rawson

———

CAMUS, Albert. French. Born in Mondovi, Algeria, 7 November 1913. Educated at the University of Algiers, graduated 1936. Married 1) Simone Hié in 1933 (divorced); 2) Francine Faure in 1940 (died 1979), twin son and daughter. Worked as meteorologist, ship-broker's clerk, automobile parts salesman, clerk in the automobile registry division of the prefecture, actor and amateur theatre producer, Algiers, 1935–39; member of the Communist Party, 1935–39; staff member, *Alger-Républicain*, 1938–39, and editor, *Soir-Républicain*, 1939–40, both Algiers; sub-editor for lay-out, *Paris-Soir*, 1940; teacher, Oran, Algeria, 1940–42; convalescent in central France, 1942-43; joined Resistance in Lyons region, 1943; journalist, Paris, 1943–45; reader and editor of Espoir series, Gallimard Publishers, Paris, 1943–60; co-founding editor, *Combat*, 1945–47. Recipient: Critics prize (France), 1947; Nobel prize for literature, 1957. *Died 4 January 1960.*

PUBLICATIONS

Collections

Complete Fiction.   1960.
Théâtre, récits, nouvelles; Essais, edited by Roger Quilliot. 2 vols., 1962–65.
Collected Plays.   1965.
Oeuvres complètes.   5 vols., 1983.

Short Stories

L'Exil et le royaume.   1957; as *Exile and the Kingdom*, 1958.

Novels

L'Étranger.   1942; as *The Stranger*, 1946; as *The Outsider*, 1946.
La Peste.   1947; as *The Plague*, 1948.
La Chute.   1956; as *The Fall*, 1957.
La Mort heureuse.   1971; as *A Happy Death*, 1972.

Plays

Le Malentendu (produced 1944).   With *Caligula*, 1944; as *Cross Purpose*, with *Caligula*, 1948.
Caligula (produced 1945).   With *Le Malentendu*, 1944; 1941 version (produced 1983), 1984; translated as *Caligula*, with *Cross Purpose*, 1948.
L'État de siège (produced 1948).   1948; as *State of Siege*, in *Caligula and Three Other Plays*, 1958.
Les Justes (produced 1949).   1950; as *The Just Assassins*, in *Caligula and Three Other Plays*, 1958; as *The Just*, 1965.
La Dévotion à la croix, from a play by Calderón (produced 1953).   1953.
Les Esprits, from a work by Pierre de Larivey (produced 1953).   1953.
Un Cas intéressant, from a work by Dino Buzzati (produced 1955).   1955.

Requiem pour une nonne, from a work by William Faulkner (produced 1956).   1956.
Le Chevalier d'Olmedo, from the play by Lope de Vega (produced 1957).   1957.
Caligula and Three Other Plays (includes *Cross Purpose, State of Seige, The Just Assassins*).   1958.
Les Possédés, from a novel by Dostoevskii (produced 1959).   1959; as *The Possessed*, 1960.

Other

L'Envers et L'endroit.   1937.
Noces.   1939.
Le Mythe de Sisyphe.   1942; as *The Myth of Sisyphus and Other Essays*, 1955.
Lettres à un ami allemand.   1945.
L'Existence.   1945.
Le Minotaure; ou, La Halte d'Oran.   1950.
Actuelles 1–3: Chroniques 1944–1948, Chroniques 1948–1953, Chronique algérienne 1939–1958.   3 vols., 1950–58.
L'Homme révolté.   1951; as *The Rebel: An Essay on Man in Revolt*, 1953.
L'Été.   1954.
Réflexions sur la guillotine, in *Réflexions sur la peine capitale*, with Arthur Koestler.   1957; as *Reflections on the Guillotine*, 1960.
Discours de Suède.   1958; as *Speech of Acceptance upon the Award of the Nobel Prize for Literature*, 1958.
Resistance, Rebellion, and Death (selection).   1960.
Méditation sur le théâtre et la vie.   1961.
Carnets: Mai 1935-fevrier 1942.   1962; translated as *Carnets 1935–1942*, 1963; as *Notebooks 1935–1942*, 1963.
Lettre à Bernanos.   1963.
Carnets: Janvier 1942-mars 1951.   1964; as *Notebooks 1942–1951*, edited by Justin O'Brien, 1965.
Lyrical and Critical (essays), edited by Philip Thody. 1967.
Le Combat d'Albert Camus, edited by Norman Stokle. 1970.
Selected Essays and Notebooks, edited by Philip Thody. 1970.
Le premier Camus.   1973; as *Youthful Writings*, 1977.
Journaux de voyage, edited by Roger Quilliot.   1978; as *American Journals*, 1987.
Fragments d'un combat 1938–1940: Alger-Républicain, Le Soir-Républicain, edited by Jacqueline Lévi-Valensi and André Abbou.   1978.
Correspondance 1932–1960, with Jean Grenier, edited by Marguerite Dobrenn.   1981.
Selected Political Writings, edited by Jonathan King. 1981.
Oeuvre fermée, oeuvrete, edited by Raymond Gay-Croisier and Jacqueline Lévi-Valensi.   1985.
Carnets: Mars 1951-décembre 1959.   1989.

Translator, *La dernière fleur*, by James Thurber.   1952.

*

Bibliography: *Camus: A Bibliography* by Robert F. Roeming, 1968; and subsequent edtions by R. Gay-Crosier, in *A Critical Bibliography of French Literature 6*, 1980; *Camus in English: An Annotated Bibliography of Camus's Contributions to English and American Periodicals and Newspapers* by Peter C. Hoy, 2nd edition, 1971.

Critical Studies: *Camus: A Study of His Work,* 1957, *Camus, 1913–1960: A Biographical Study,* 1962, and *Camus,* 1989, all by Philip Thody; *Camus* by Germaine Brée, 1959, and 1964, revised edition, 1972, and *Camus: A Collection of Critical Essays* edited by Brée, 1962; *Camus: The Artist in the Arena* by Emmett Parker, 1965; *Camus* by Phillip H. Rhein, 1969, revised edition, 1989; *Camus* by Conor Cruise O'Brien, 1970; *The Theatre of Camus* by Edward Freeman, 1971; *Camus: The Invincible Summer* by Albert Maquet, 1972; *The Unique Creation of Camus* by Donald Lazere, 1973; *Camus: A Biography* by Herbert R. Lottman, 1979; *Camus's Imperial Vision* by Anthony Rizzuto, 1981; *Camus: A Critical Study of His Life and Work,* 1982, and *Camus: The Stranger,* 1988, both by Patrick McCarthy; *Exiles and Strangers: A Reading of Camus's Exile and the Kingdom* by Elaine Showalter, Jr., 1984; *Exile and Kingdom: A Political Rereading of Camus* by Susan Tarrow, 1985; *The Ethical Pragmatism of Camus: Two Studies in the History of Ideas* by Dean Vasil, 1985; *Beyond Absurdity: The Philosophy of Camus* by Robert C. Trundle, 1987; *Camus: A Critical Examination* by David Sprintzen, 1988; *Camus and Indian Thought* by Sharad Chaedra, 1989; *Understanding Camus* by David R. Ellison, 1990; *Camus's L'Estranger: Fifty Years On* edited by Adele King, 1992.

*   *   *

Albert Camus was deeply attached to both his French and his Algerian origins. Generally left-wing, although he had been a member of the communist party only from 1935 to 1937, he had run a magazine, *Combat,* for the Resistance towards the end of World War II. By 1957, the year he received the Nobel prize, Camus had become virtually apolitical, and there had been a long-running public and private quarrel with Sartre, who was slowly jettisoning his existentialist philosophical reflections for hard-line Stalinist Marxism. When the Franco-Algerian war broke out in 1954, Camus felt drawn to mediate. The conflict escalated into a confrontation between terrorist insurrection and military repression, and Camus found it impossible to avoid expressing his left-wing views. The stories in *L'Exil et le royaume (Exile and the Kingdom)* were written while Camus was trying to mediate. Four of the six stories have Algerian backgrounds.

Camus's early journalism leant towards a style that was sparse and factual, almost dry. His later work, including *Exile and the Kingdom,* sometimes uses a style that is almost florid. The first story, "The Adulterous Woman" is held together by the psychology of the central character, Janine. Trivial incidents are described in ordinary third-person narrative and realistic detail, with snippets of conversation. But much of the story is related from inside Janine, and the central episode, almost grippingly narrated, is totally ambiguous. Janine is on a journey with her husband, Marcel, an ex-law student who had taken over his parents' dry-goods business, and was now trying to sell to Arab merchants.

An uncomfortable bus journey through the desert is narrated partly as Janine is experiencing it, as her thoughts pass through her mind with a touch of humour, her own and the narrator's. In a desert town they stay in a hotel with dirty windows. Janine insists on climbing up the stairs of the fort to lean over a parapet and look at the desert. Looking out, Janine thinks of the nomads in an encampment she could see, "possessing nothing but serving no one, poverty-stricken but free lords of a strange kingdom." That kingdom is almost allegorized. It is what had been promised to her but would never be hers. In the middle of the cold night she wonders what is missing: "she simply followed Marcel, pleased to know that someone needed her. The only joy he gave her was the knowledge that she was necessary. Probably he didn't love her." She feels suffocated and runs out to the parapet.

The loveless, childless marriage had left Janine unsatisfied. We know from the title that she is unfaithful. With the night? the desert? the yearned-for fulfilment? The descriptive prose approaches lushness. The reader does not know whether or not the narrator is vouching for what Janine feels, but it does not matter. The ambiguity is quite deliberately created. All that happens is that a woman does something slightly bizarre, but the narrative, quite short, moves from a point of no emotional intensity to a point at which it quivers with poignancy. The reader's interest is teased along by the title. Adultery? The parable could not be simpler. The longing for innocent fulfilment, for emotional satisfaction, and for the harmony of life turns out to be treachery, a guilty betrayal of the best that life has to offer.

"The Renegade" contains the semi-demented ravings of a tortured and broken missionary, once so ardent to convert the infidels, who is broken by pain. This is a powerful piece of writing, but its power derives largely from its ambiguity. As in "The Adulterous Woman" it makes no difference whether the ex-missionary's ravings narrate events that occurred or not. The story, the fascination, and the power lie entirely in what is going on in the speaker's mind, through which cascade a brilliant successions of images, symbols, and metaphors, giving the text resonances on every sort of political and personal level.

The collection's unity is in an attitude to life that is never more than sardonic when it ought to be violent. The satire on artistic success in "The Artist at Work" is cynically comic as Louise Poulin takes over Gilbert Jonas's life. The collection itself is undoubtedly virtuosic. Read in isolation the six stories might not seem related. Read together, they brilliantly focus quite different lights on the nostalgia for innocence and the sordid, repulsive inevitability of guilt.

—A.H.T. Levi

See the essay on "The Guest."

———

ČAPEK, Karel. Czech. Born in Malé Svatoňovice, Bohemia, 9 January 1890; brother of the writer Josef Čapek. Educated at the universities of Prague, Berlin, and Paris; Charles University, Prague, Ph.D. in philosophy 1915. Married the actress Olga Scheinpflugova in 1935. Journalist, *Lidové noviny*; stage director at Vinohrady Theatre, Prague, 1921–23. *Died 25 December 1938.*

PUBLICATIONS

Collections

Spisy bratří čapků [Collected Works of the Brothers Čapek]. 51 vols., 1928-49.

Toward the Radical Center: A Reader, edited by Peter Kussi.   1990.
Three Novels; Hordubal, Meteor, An Ordinary Life.   1990.

Short Stories

Boží muka [Stations of the Cross].   1917.
Trapné povídky.   1921; as *Money and Other Stories*, 1929.
Povídky z jedné kapsy [Tales from One Pocket], *Povídky z druhé kapsy* [Tales from the Other Pocket].   2 vols., 1929; translated in part as *Tales from Two Pockets*, 1932.
Apokryfy; Kniha apokryfů.   2 vols., 1932–45; as *Apocryphal Stories*, 1949.

Novels

Zářivé hlubiny [The Luminous Depths], with Josef Čapek. 1916.
Krakonošova zahrada [The Garden of Krakonos], with Josef Čapek.   1918.
Továrna na Absolutno.   1922; as *The Absolute at Large*, 1927.
Krakatit.   1924; translated as *Krakatit*, 1925; as *An Atomic Fantasy*, 1948.
Hordubal.   1933; translated as *Hordubal*, 1934.
Povětroň.   1934; as *Meteor*, 1935.
Obyčejný život.   1934; as *An Ordinary Life*, 1936.
Válka s mloky.   1936; as *War with the Newts*, 1937.
První parta.   1937; as *The First Rescue Party*, 1939.
Život a dílo skladatele Foltýna.   1939; as *The Cheat*, 1941.

Plays

Lásky hra osudná [The Fateful Game of Love], with Josef Čapek (produced 1930).   1916.
Loupežník [The Robber] (produced 1920).   1920.
R.U.R. (produced 1921).   1920; as *R.U.R. (Rossum's Universal Robots)*, 1923.
Ze života hmyzu, with Josef Čapek (produced 1922). 1921; as *And So ad Infinitivum (The Life of the Insects): An Entomological Review*, 1923; as *The Insect Play*, 1923; as *The World We Live In (The Insect Comedy)*, 1933.
Věc Makropulos (produced 1922).   1922; as *The Macropoulos Secret*, 1925.
Adam Stvořitel, with Josef Čapek (produced 1927).   1927; as *Adam the Creator*, 1929.
Bílá nemoc (produced 1937).   1937; as *Power and Glory*, 1939; as *The White Plague*, 1988.
Matka (produced 1938).   1938; as *The Mother*, 1939.

Other

Pragmatismus; čili, Filosofie praktického života [Pragmatism or a Philosophy of Practical Life].   1918.
Kritika slov [A Critique of Words].   1920.
Italské listy.   1923; as *Letters from Italy*, 1929.
Anglické listy: pro větší názornost provázené obrázky autorovými.   1924; as *Letters from England*, 1925.
O nejbližších věcech.   1925; as *Intimate Things*, 1935.
Jak vzniká divadelní hra a prvodce po zákulisí.   1925; as *How a Play Is Produced*, 1928.
Skandální aféra Josefa Holouška [The Scandalous Affair of Josef Holoušek].   1927.
Hovory s T.G. Masarykem.   3 vols., 1928–35; as *President Masaryk Tells His Story*, 1934, and *Masaryk on Thought and Life*, 1938.

Zahradníkův rok.   1929; as *The Gardener's Year*, 1931.
Výlet do Španěl.   1930; as *Letters from Spain*, 1931.
Minda; čili Ó Chovu psů.   1930; as *Minda; or, On Breeding Dogs*, 1940.
Devatero pohádek.   1932; as *Fairy Tales*, 1933; as *Nine Fairy Tales and One More Thrown in for Good Measure*, 1990.
Obrazky z Holandska.   1932; as *Letters from Holland*, 1933.
O věcech obecných; čili Zoon politikon [Ordinary Things, or Zoon politikon].   1932.
A Dašenka.   1933; translated as *Dashenka, or The Life of a Puppy*, 1940.
Legenda o člověku zahradníkovi [Legend of a Gardening Man].   1935.
Cesta na sever.   1936; as *Travels in the North*, 1939.
Jak se co dělá.   1938; as *How They Do It*, 1945.
Kalendář [Calendar].   1940.
O lidech [About People].   1940.
Vzrušené tance [Wild Dances].   1946.
Bajky a podpovídky [Fables and Would-Be Tales].   1946.
Sedm rozhlásků karle čapeka [Seven Notes for Wireless]. 1946.
Ratolest a vavřín [The Sprig and the Laurel].   1947.
In Praise of Newspapers and Other Essays on the Margin of Literature.   1951.
Obrázky z domova [Letters from Home].   1953.
Sloupkový ambit [The Pillared Cloister].   1957.
Poznámky o tvorbě [Comments on Creation].   1959.
Na břehu dnů [On the Boundaries of Days].   1966.
Divadelníkem proti své vůli [A Drama Expert against My Will].   1968.
V zajetí slov [In the Bondage of Words].   1969.
Čtení o T.G. Masarykovi [Readings about T.G. Masaryk]. 1969.
Místo pro Jonathana! [Make Way for Jonathan!].   1970.
Listy Olze 1920–38 [Letters to Olga].   1971.
Drobty pod stolem doby [Crumbs under the Table of the Age].   1975.
Listy Anielce [Letters to Anielce].   1978.
Nueskutečněný dialog [Selected Essays].   1978.
Dopisy ze Zasuvky [Letters Out of a Drawer] (letters to Vera Hruzová), edited by Jiří Opelik.   1980.
Cesty k přatelství [Selected Correspondence].   1987.

*

Critical Studies: *Čapek* by William E. Harkins, 1962; *Čapek: An Essay* by Alexander Matuska, 1964; *Good Men Still Live ("I Am the Other Čapek"): The Odyssey of a Professional Prisoner* by Alan Levy, 1974.

* * *

The average Western reader today will probably know Karel Čapek as the author of the robot play, *R.R.R.*, or as the co-author, with his brother Josef, of *Ze života hmyzu (The Insect Play)*. Yet his plays are only one part of Čapek's large oeuvre, which includes essays, travel books, novels—and short stories.

All of Čapek's short stories first appeared in newspapers and magazines (he was a professional journalist for much of his life), and all were reprinted in book form fairly quickly, a testimony to their popularity with the newspaper readership.

Chronologically his collections of short stories fall into two discrete groups: *Boží muka* (Stations of the Cross) and *Trapné povídky (Money and Other Stories)* belong to the period of World War I, while *Povídky z jedné kapsy* (Tales from One Pocket) and *Povídky z jedné kapsy* (Tales from the Other Pocket) both came out in 1929, followed in 1932 to 1945 by *Kniha apokryfů (Apocryphal Stories)*. The decade or so that separates the two groups brought a considerable change in the style, subject matter, and philosophical content of the stories, a change all the more striking for similarities between the tales. The difference is neatly summed up in two versions of the same incident: in the story "Šlépěj" ("Footprint") in *Boží muka* the footprint in the snow is a disturbing, meaningless miracle, a symbol of the uncertainty of human existence; in "Šlépěje" ("Footprints") in *Tales from Two Pockets* (as the combined edition is entitled in English) the mystery of the footprints comes to a sudden, homely end with the policeman's solid bootprints continuing where the footprints left off.

In *Boží muka* Čapek is preoccupied with disorientation, loss, with sudden and inexplicable appearances and disappearances—Boura's long-lost brother in "Elegie," Lída's disappearance in the story of the same name—and with human beings in despair—a woman crying out for help in "Pomoc!" ("Help!"), the sobs of a hunted murderer in "Hora" ("Mountain"). An individual's reactions and emotions are subsumed in a wider, universal despair.

In *Trapné povídky* the emphasis begins to shift towards the specific, the individual. Thus we are given a detailed, affectionate description of the eponymous Helena, or of the shy girl in "Pokušení" ("Temptation"). The small vices of little, pitiful people take the place of a vague menace—the thieving housekeeper in "Košile" ("Shirts), the humiliated civil servant who returns when his minister sends his shiny car for him in "Uražený" ("The Offended One").

In *Tales from Two Pockets* Čapek finds his true voice: the one quality lacking in the two earlier collections was humour, and there is plenty of it in the *Tales*. There is comedy in "Modrá chrysantéma" ("The Blue Chrysanthemum") and in "Ukradený kaktus" ("The Stolen Cactus"), both grounded in the collector's acquisitive mania, or in the predicament of a would-be poet thief, caught on the job while trying to think of a rhyme in "O lyrickém zloději" ("About a Lyrical Thief").

Čapek's humour is at its best in his rendering of colloquial speech. As far as the *Tales* has a framework, it is that of men sitting in a pub or a café at night, reminiscing and telling stories. The absolute genuineness of their voices, whether in dialogue or in monologue, reminds us that the author was also a playwright with a considerable reputation.

Though the framework is that of a mixed group of men, the *Tales* has a strong flavour of the law in action and of police work (comparisons have been made with G.K. Chesterton's Father Brown stories). These are well-made, amusing stories with a clever denouement, often with an ironical twist, but they are moral tales too. (It could, of course, be argued that there is a moral element in any tale of crime and detection: the guilty must be found out and punished.)

Čapek is concerned with moral judgment as distinct from the sentence passed by a judge. In "Zločin na poště" ("Crime in the Post Office") and in "Zmizení herce Bendy" ("The Disappearance of the Actor Benda") a private individual passes the sentence of unending misery and unease on those guilty of murder. In "Zločin v chalupě" ("Crime in a Cottage") the judge longs to punish the murderer who killed for a field next to his land, by ordering him to sow it with thorn and henbane. It is this moral judgment that raises Čapek's tales above anecdotal level, as much as his great skill in presenting character through colloquial speech.

His last collection, *Apocryphal Stories,* is something of an oddity. Ranging from prehistory to the Napoleonic wars Čapek presents historical events and historical or fictional characters from a new perspective, that of the accidental bystanders. By letting his biblical characters, his Greek philosophers, Roman soldiers, Venetians, and Spanish Jesuits speak in the tone and language of ordinary Czech people of his own time, he stresses their common humanity. His characters all think and talk like the people Čapek heard in the streets of Prague: the baker who deplores the miracle of loaves and fishes as a threat to his trade ("O pěti chlebích" ["On Five Loaves"], the prehistoric man who is offended by the cave drawings of animals as a waste of time better spent on sharpening flints ("O úpadku doby" ["On the Decadence of the Present Age"]).

Human stupidity and cruelty, as well as the nobility of which humans are capable, are the themes here. Nothing has changed, nothing can change because human nature remains always the same. This is Čapek's final message, and there is no grandeur in it, only the amused tolerance, the gentle compassion of the true humanitarian.

—Hana Sambrook

———————

CAPOTE, Truman. American. Born Truman Streckfus Persons in New Orleans, Louisiana, 30 September 1924; took step-father's surname. Educated at Trinity School and St. John's Academy, New York; Greenwich High School, Connecticut. Worked in the art department, and wrote for "Talk of the Town," *The New Yorker,* early 1940's; then full-time writer. Recipient: O. Henry award, 1946, 1948, 1951; American Academy grant, 1959; Mystery Writers of America Edgar Allen Poe award, 1966; Emmy award, for television adaptation, 1967. Member, American Academy. *Died 25 August 1984.*

PUBLICATIONS

Collections

A Capote Reader.   1987.

Short Stories

Other Voices, Other Rooms.   1948.
A Tree of Night and Other Stories.   1949.
Breakfast at Tiffany's: A Short Novel and Three Stories. 1958.
A Christmas Memory (story).   1966.

Novels

The Grass Harp.   1951.
Answered Prayers (unfinished novel).   1986.

Plays

The Grass Harp, from his own novel (produced 1952). 1952.

House of Flowers, music by Harold Arlen, lyrics by Capote and Arlen (produced 1954; revised version, produced 1968). 1968.
The Thanksgiving Visitor, from his own story (televised 1968). 1968.
Trilogy (screenplay, with Eleanor Perry), in *Trilogy*. 1969.

Screenplays: *Beat the Devil*, with John Huston, 1953; *Indiscretion of an American Wife*, with others, 1954; *The Innocents*, with William Archibald and John Mortimer, 1961; *Trilogy*, with Eleanor Perry, 1969.

Television Plays and Films (includes documentaries): *A Christmas Memory*, with Eleanor Perry, from the story by Capote, 1966; *Among the Paths to Eden*, with Eleanor Perry, from the story by Capote, 1967; *Laura*, from the play by Vera Caspary, 1968; *The Thanksgiving Visitor*, from his own story, 1968; *Behind Prison Walls*, 1972; *The Glass House*, with Tracy Keenan Wynn and Wyatt Cooper, 1972; *Crimewatch*, 1973.

Other

Local Color. 1950.
The Muses Are Heard: An Account of the Porgy and Bess Tour to Leningrad. 1956.
Observations, photographs by Richard Avedon. 1959.
Selected Witings, edited by Mark Schorer. 1963.
In Cold Blood: A True Account of a Multiple Murder and Its Consequences. 1966.
Trilogy: An Experiment in Multimedia, with Frank and Eleanor Perry. 1969.
The Dogs Bark: Public People and Private Places. 1973.
Then It All Came Down: Criminal Justice Today Discussed by Police, Criminals, and Correction Officers with Comments by Capote. 1976.
Music for Chameleons. 1980.
One Christmas (memoir). 1983.
Conversations with Capote, with Lawrence Grobel. 1985.
Capote: Conversations, edited by M. Thomas Inge. 1987.

*

Bibliography: *Capote: A Primary and Secondary Bibliography* by Robert J. Stanton, 1980.

Critical Studies: *The Worlds of Capote* by William L. Nance, 1970; *Capote* by Helen S. Garson, 1980; *Capote* by Kenneth Reid, 1981; *Capote* by Marie Rudisill and James C. Simmons, 1983; *Footnote to a Friendship: A Memoir of Capote and Others* by Donald Windham, 1983; *Capote: Dear Heart, Old Buddy* by John Malcolm Brinnin, 1986, as *Capote, A Memoir*, 1987; *Capote: A Biography* by Gerald Clarke, 1988.

*   *   *

In the early 1940's Truman Capote left the provincial south to seek first the sophistication of New York and then the most worldly of wisdom in the "cold blood" of Kansas. From the beginning, his stories were set in both New York and the likes of Admiral's Mill, Alabama. Indeed, most were set in the city. But this is mere physical place. The real provinces of Capote's stories are loneliness, dreams, and the unconscious. His characters' pre-eminent conflicts entail the struggle to connect with others, through love if possible. It is an aspiration generally overwhelmed by selfishness or narcissism. Frequently, however, his protagonists glimpse, in the course of their failings, the reasons for their shortcomings and ruined aspirations.

It is thus a legitimate commonplace that his stories may be divided not between geographical places but between the diurnal and nocturnal and, thence, between good and evil. Perhaps it is even better to say that his stories are either principally light or dark. These appropriately ambiguous terms dichotomize the body of his work both figuratively and literally. They capture the way those that are most amusing and social are enacted in daylight, while those that are most disturbing and psychological, whether grotesque or macabre, are enacted at night. Capote inclined to the dark variety. This and a certain effect of tour de force have provided him his share of detractors who find in his tales more that is facile than felicitous.

Capote did not write a great number of stories; nor did his talent in the genre really grow. He was skilled in the form and on a few occasions brilliant. But he was never better, either on the whole or in a single piece, than in his collection *A Tree of Night*. "Master Misery," "Miriam," and the title story are the dark tales here. The experiences recorded in these stories are essentially internal. The worlds circumscribing their protagonists exist only as mirrors of their interiority or as complements to a really psychic drama. Each story blends the macabre and the fantastic in an eerie ethos. "Master Misery" involves a lonely young woman's willingness to sell her dreams, at five dollars each, to a fabulous Mr. Revercomb. Strangely, this story has been attacked as meaningless, on the grounds that the exchange is inexplicable, a sheer gratuity. Surely we have here an allegorical romance for our times. (One needn't give it credence.) The youthful Sylvia (place of the "sylvan," the lovely natural) comes from Ohio to the big city and discovers her unalterable separation from others, save one lonely and passing drunk. Life being a flop, she sells her dreams and acquiesces in her miserable lot. They are purchased by Master Misery, the worse-than-reality principle. His name is Revercomb (comber, searcher among reveries, dreams). He is not a psychoanalyst, but a mythic figure. He rids Sylvia of any last illusion and leaves her about to be violated. The erosion of one's dreams by misery is common enough. Not happy, but a Capotean romance indeed. "Miriam" is similar. The aged and isolated Mrs. H. T. Miller speaks to a perfect-little-lady of a girl one night outside a theater. The child is surreal, but shows up at her apartment, finally inviting herself to stay. Capote grants neither that Miriam is real nor a figment of Mrs. Miller's imagination, though we don't really doubt the latter. Miriam is an alter-ego and version of the child Mrs. Miller probably was. Their bond is finally antagonistic, but indisputable and irreversible. The world outside the apartment is dark and dense with snow. Miriam is all that Mrs. Miller finally has to stave off the cold blackness of her future.

"A Tree of Night" is Capote's best story in this vein. Its eccentric characters and the palpable tackiness of the train car they inhabit convey a minimal reality that yields gradually to the story's symbolist core. The train moves through a night of metaphysical darkness, taking a young woman named Kay from an uncle's funeral toward an impossibly youthful sophomore year at college. With her in the car, which has the faded plush ambience of a coffin, rides a deathly old man who lives by doing a Lazarus trick in a carnival. He is the wizard of her childhood, the bogeyman in the human attic, with us for the long haul once we've made the acquaintance of death.

The light stories are "Children on Their Birthdays," "Jug of Silver," and "My Side of the Matter." These are rendered very colloquially in the first person. The first two are peppered with characters too cutely named, whose enterprises are the stuff of village legend. They are stereotypes of southern eccentrics, especially of youthful cut-ups and dreamers. The death of the wondrous quasi-child, Miss Bobbit, of "Children on Their Birthdays," is treated whimsically and seems a saccharin counterpoint to her transformation of the community she mesmerized for a year. These tales simply don't admit essential darkness to their milieus. "My Side of the Matter" strives for hilarity through a narrator who lies and gives offense on a big scale. He is a loafer, come to a hick town with his pregnant wife to freeload off her aunts. When he thieves from their savings, they take a stand against him. His tale is a grand and very funny rationalization of his whole person. To accuse Capote of not capturing a real voice here is to fail to measure this persona against the hyperbole the work intends. This fiction is after the manner of Welty's "Why I Live at the P.O." and, like it, is exempt from any phonographic litmus test. It is the epitome of Capote's diurnal mode.

The later stories come closer to reality. "Among the Paths to Eden" and "Mojave" explore, pessimistically, the prospects of marital wellbeing. If Eden stands for the blissful state of the human couple before the fall from grace, this Eden is a sad retort. The setting is a graveyard where a widower finds himself happier alone than he had been in his marriage. Yet he experiences loneliness and is tempted by the strange allurements of a woman for whom the cemetery is a virtual dating service. She looks to the obituaries to find a decent man and follows up by going to the cemetery when widowers make their annual visits. Her imitation of the songstress Helen Morgan tests Mr. Belli to the limit, but he goes his isolated and preferred way, while she turns hopelessly, we know, to the "new pilgrim, just entering through the gates of the cemetery."

In "Mojave" the desert serves as a metaphor for estrangement in marriage. In his youth George Whitelaw had met a blind man left on the desert by a wife who had decided on a younger one. George's wife, Sarah, would never do that to him. Instead she has affairs and arranges George's liaisons with other women. Neither person has any satisfaction, but the bond they have built is solid—and sterile. All they have together is the shred more than the nothing emanating from relationships which make them feel even lonelier than their marriage does. That Sarah had never seen George as more than a version of her father explains a little. But Sarah's judgment seems right when she says, "We all, sometimes, leave each other out there under the skies, and we never understand why." This seems a story poised at the end of a body of work always pointed toward it. Its truest antecedent is the most realistic story from the first collection, "Shut a Final Door," wherein Capote charted the dead-end course of a perfect narcissist through one exploitive relationship after another. That seems his judgment on our times.

—David M. Heaton

See the essay on "Other Voices, Other Rooms."

————

CAREY, Peter (Philip). Australian. Born in Bacchus Marsh, Victoria, 7 May 1943. Educated at Geelong Grammar School; Monash University, Clayton, Victoria, 1961. Married 1) Leigh Weetman; 2) Alison Summers in 1985, one son. Worked in advertising in Australia, 1962–68 and after 1970, and in London, 1968–70; partner, McSpedden Carey Advertising Consultants, Chippendale, New South Wales, until 1988; full-time writer, from 1988; currently professor, New York University. Recipient: New South Wales Premier's award, 1980, 1982; Miles Franklin award, 1981; National Book Council award, 1982, 1986; Australian Film Institute award, for screenplay, 1985; *The Age* Book of the Year award. 1985; Booker prize, 1988. Fellow, Royal Society of Literature. Lives in New York.

PUBLICATIONS

Short Stories

The Fat Man in History.   1974; as *Exotic Pleasures,* 1981.
War Crimes.   1979.

Novels

Bliss.   1981.
Illywhacker.   1985.
Oscar and Lucinda.   1988.
The Tax Inspector.   1991.

Plays

Bliss: The Screenplay.   1986; as *Bliss: The Film,* 1986.

Screenplays: *Bliss,* with Ray Lawrence, 1987; *Until the End of the World,* with Wim Wenders.

*

Critical Studies: "What Happened to the Short Story?" by Frank Moorhouse, in *Australian Literary Studies* 8, October 1977; "Bizarre Realities: An Interview with Carey" by John Maddocks, *Southerly* 41, March 1981.

*   *   *

In some ways, the short fiction of Peter Carey seems to have served as a warmup for his work as a novelist. The two collections upon which his reputation rests, *The Fat Man in History* and *War Crimes,* were both published in the 1970's, while in the 1980's he turned his attention more exclusively to the novels. Like his novels, the stories are speculative and fanciful, often starting from the question, "What if . . . ?" Stories ask, for example, "What if a person could buy a new and randomly selected genetic makeup?" ("The Chance"). Or, what if the psyche could be stripped of concealing layers as easily as the body can be stripped of clothing? ("Peeling"). In similar fashion, Carey's novels imagine what would happen if a man could die more than once (*Bliss*), or postulate that the whole of Australian history might be a series of lies people have conned themselves into believing (*Illywhacker*).

In Carey's fictional scenarios, metaphor is often literalized and then driven to its (il)logical extremes. In "The Fat Man in History," for instance, the obese are hated and persecuted because they are thought literally to embody the gluttonous and self-indulgent greed of capitalism, which a communistic revolution has supplanted. One group of fat men responds in kind to these assumptions, deciding to "purify" the revolution by separating its nourishing aspects from the dross. To do this, they plan to pass it through their digestive systems, "bodily consuming an official of the Revolution." Carey has likened the method he employs in stories like "Fat Man" to that of a cartoonist, exaggerating, caricaturing, and pushing things to a "ludicrous . . . extension."

Both the short fiction and the novels exhibit this cartoonist's take on reality, and they share other technical features as well. Most notable is a masterful blending of the convincingly real, the disturbingly surreal, and the unabashedly outlandish. The mix variously recalls such literary progenitors as Kafka, Faulkner, Borges, García Márquez, Donald Barthelme, and Nabokov. Kafka, we remember, turns a character into a giant insect and then with sober realism narrates what must inevitably follow. Faulkner has a corpse recount the story of her life, and García Márquez sets an ascension into heaven amidst wet sheets. Similarly, Carey supplies enough corroborative, authenticating detail in the story "'Do You Love Me?'" to make us accept the proposition that unloved regions, buildings, and people will begin to dematerialize.

A different but related effect is achieved when Carey self-consciously explores his role as artificer, as he does in "Report on the Shadow Industry." Here he sees even fiction as part of a product line of diaphanous, deceptive, unsubstantial, and unsatisfying "shadows," supplied by a consumption-based culture to meet manufactured needs.

Such techniques—sometimes grouped under the rubric "magic realism" to suggest a matter-of-fact rendering of the physically impossible and blatantly symbolic—are used to varying degrees in Carey's fiction, and he is quite capable of abandoning them altogether. When he does, it is often in favor of a probing psychological realism such as that of "A Schoolboy Prank," in which middle-aged men gather to honor, but end by tormenting, a former teacher, because he reminds them of adolescent homoerotic experiments they would rather forget. In his novels too, Carey demonstrates repeatedly that he knows as much about human nature as he does about postmodern literary pyrotechnics.

In several ways, then, the stories are kin to the novels. But they also have their own rewards for the reader. More tightly choreographed than the longer works, they shift the emphasis from character development to theme and fictional premise. In so doing, they not only delight with their inventiveness and virtuosity, but offer themselves as compact fables or parables for our times. Appropriately, the theme to which Carey recurs in the stories is power: political, financial, emotional, and psychological. As he explores its permutations, he is interested in how power is sought, acquired, wielded, defended, abused, and withheld from its victims. Many of his stories are set in a vaguely futuristic time and an ill-defined place, tactics that increase the reader's sense that these are universally applicable allegories of our age.

It may be a useful oversimplification to think of Carey's first volume of short stories, *The Fat Man in History,* as concerned with victimization and impotence, while the second collection, *War Crimes,* emphasizes the wrongly or lethally empowered. *Fat Man* is full of people caught in a variety of "Catch-22's." There is Crabs ("Crabs"), whose car is disabled by a gang of parts thieves. They leave him trapped in a drive-in theatre to which other crippled vehicles and their occupants are delivered daily. When he

finally escapes the theatre, he finds nothing outside: all life is within the drive-in, from which he is now excluded. In another story, "Life and Death in the South Side Pavilion," the first person narrator is employed by a nameless company to tend horses, who keep drowning in a pool the company won't fence. When the narrator gives up trying to save the horses and drives them into the pool, the company simply delivers another lot. The narrator's profound disorientation—his inability to grasp who, where, or what he's supposed to be—is mirrored by the protagonist of "A Windmill in the West," a soldier left alone in central Australia who shoots down a plane because he can no longer distinguish what he was ordered to guard from whom. In these stories, faceless authorities manipulate their underlings by imposing ignorance and isolation.

Those in power may also turn the disenfranchised against each other, as they do in the volume's title story. Here, the fat men's attempt to oppose the revolution by consuming it ends in their consumption of one of their own instead. Their leader is killed and eaten, and his place usurped by another member of the group. In a final irony, Carey reveals that the whole takeover was engineered by an outside agent, whose job is to inspire disruptive internal squabbling within the ranks of a potentially subversive element.

Like *Fat Man, War Crimes* is peopled with victims: the vaporizing father of "'Do You Love Me?,'" the battered young woman of "The Uses of Williamson Wood," and the retired schoolmaster whose dead dog is nailed to his door in "A Schoolboy Prank." But in this volume, Carey more thoroughly examines the dynamics by which victims may become victimizers and power may become an addictive drug. A case in point is the architect of "Krista-Du," who designs a magnificent gathering place for the feuding tribes of a third-world nation, but whose good intentions actually make him the accomplice of the brutal dictator who hired him. The architect consoles himself that when the tribes come together under the lofty dome of his "Krista-Du," they will unite to overthrow the dictator. Instead, the hot breath of so many people rises to form clouds under the dome, a phenomenon that the dictator uses to subdue his superstitious peoples with evidence of his prowess as a sorcerer.

Self-deception, Carey warns, can threaten others as much as oneself. In "The Chance" the narrator tries to convince his lover that she needn't be ugly and malformed to be a sincere ideological revolutionary. Undeterred by his arguments, she destroys her beauty and their relationship in a misconceived political act. Spectacular examples of legitimate motives run amok and power misused occur in the title story "War Crimes," whose first person narrator carries out his mandate to reverse the sales slump at a frozen foods factory by means of intimidation, torture, and treachery. Finally, he launches a full-scale war.

Critics of Carey's short fiction have frequently pointed to the surprising sense of truth and reality emanating from texts marked by fabulous plots and fantastic characters. This effect probably arises from the alchemy through which, as Carey remarked in an interview with Ray Willbanks, "lies becom[e] truths." "One can look at the fact of imagination," Carey says, "as a way of actually shaping the future." A fictional plot, in other words, can become a prediction.

He goes on in the interview to explain the "great responsibility" which accrues to the writer because of this tendency of the imagined to transmogrify into reality. The responsibility is to "tell the truth," both about those ugly lies that have already hardened into fact and about "the potential of the human spirit" to reimagine and so reinvent something better. For these reasons, as critic Robert Ross has observed, stories and storytelling really matter to Carey. He has admired the power and the potency in Borges; his own readers recognize the same qualities in Carey's work.

—Carolyn Bliss

See the essay on "American Dreams."

CARPENTIER (y Valmont), Alejo. Cuban. Born in Havana, 26 December 1904. Educated at the University of Havana. Married Andrea Esteban. Journalist, Havana, 1921–24; editor, *Carteles* magazine, Havana, 1924–28; director, Foniric Studios, Paris, 1928–39; writer and producer, CMZ radio station, Havana, 1939–41; professor of history of music, Conservatorio Nacional, Havana, 1941–43; lived in Haiti, Europe, the United States, and South America, 1943–59; director, Cuban Publishing House, Havana, 1960–67; cultural attaché, Cuban Embassy, Paris, from 1967. Columnist, *El National*, Caracas; editor, *Imam*, Paris. *Died 24 April 1980.*

PUBLICATIONS

Collections

Obras completas. 1983—.

Short Stories

Viaje a la semilla (story). 1944; as "Journey Back to the Source," in *War of Time*, 1970.
El acoso (novella). 1956; as *The Chase*, 1989.
Guerra del tiempo: Tres relatos y una novela: El Camino de Santiago, Viaje a la semilla, Semejante a la noche, y El acoso. 1958.
War of Time. 1970.
El derecho de asilo, Dibujos de Marcel Berges. 1972; *El derecho de asilo* as "Right of Sanctuary," in *War of Time,* 1970.
Cuentos. 1977.

Novels

¡Écue-yamba-Ó! 1933.
El reino de este mundo. 1949; as *The Kingdom of This World,* 1957.
Los pasos perdidos. 1953; as *The Lost Steps,* 1956.
El siglo de las luces. 1962; as *Explosion in a Cathedral,* 1963.
Los convidados de plata (unfinished novel). 1972.
Concierto barroco. 1974; translated as *Concierto barroco,* 1988.
El recurso del método. 1974; as *Reasons of State,* 1976.
La consagración de la primavera. 1979.
El arpa y la sombra. 1979; as *The Harp and the Shadow,* 1990.

Plays

Yamba-O, music by M.F. Gaillard (produced 1928).
La passion noire, music by M.F. Gaillard (produced 1932).

Verse

Dos poemas afrocubanos, music by A. Garcia Caturla. 1929.
Poèmes des Antilles, music by M.F. Gaillard. 1929.

Other

La música en Cuba. 1946.
Tientos y diferencias: Ensayos. 1964; as *Tientos, diferencias y otros ensayos,* 1987.
Literatura y consciencia política en América Latina. 1969.
La ciudad de las columnas, photographs by Paolo Gasparini. 1970.
Letra y solfa (selection), edited by Alexis Márquez Rodríguez. 1975.
Crónicas (articles). 1976.
Bajo el Signo de la Cibeles: Crónicas sobre España y los españoles 1925-1937, edited by Julio Rodríguez Puértolas. 1979.
El adjetivo y sus arrugas. 1980.
La novela latinoamericana en vísperas de un nuevo siglo y otros ensayos. 1981.
Ensayos (selected essays).
Entrevistas, edited by Virgilio López Lemus. 1985.

*

Bibliography: *Carpentier: Biographical Guide/Guía Biligráfica* by Roberto González Echevarría and Klaus Müller-Bergh, 1983.

Critical Studies: *Three Authors of Alienation: Bombal, Onetti, Carpentier* by M. Ian Adams, 1975; *Major Cuban Novelists: Innovation and Tradition* by Raymond D. Souza, 1976; *Carpentier: The Pilgrim at Home* by Roberto González Echevarría, 1977; *Carpentier and His Early Works* by Frank Janney, 1981; *Carpentier: Los pasos perdidos* (in English) by Verity Smith, 1983; *Alchemy of a Hero: A Comparative Study of the Works of Carpentier and Mario Vargas Llosa* by Bob M. Tusa, 1983; *Carpentier* by Donald L. Shaw, 1985; *Myth and History in Caribbean Fiction: Carpentier, Wilson Harris, and Edouard Glissant* by Barbara J. Webb, 1992.

* * *

Although Alejo Carpentier is best known as a novelist, he has written some very fine short stories, the most important of which are collected in English in *War of Time*. Raised in Cuba, the son of a Russian mother and a French father, Carpentier tried to synthesize in his fiction the major elements of Latin American and European cultures. He was especially interested in the blacks and Indians of the Caribbean, which made him a leading practitioner of magical realism, a poetic fusion of reality and fantasy.

Carpentier's most anthologized story, "Journey Back to the Source," attempts to negate normal temporal progression by narrating the life of its protagonist in reverse, from death to birth. Two of his best tales are "Like the Night" and "The Highroad of Saint James." In the former the five protagonists are warriors departing for war from ancient times to the 20th century. The first of these is preparing to join Agamemnon's army to lay siege to Troy and rescue Helen from her infamous captors; the second is a 16th-century Spanish youth departing for the New World to enhance the glory of God and the Spanish king; the goals of the third warrior, who is leaving for the French colonies in America, are to civilize the savages and achieve wealth and glory for himself; the 13th-century crusades motivate the departure of the fourth warrior; and the last of the five is an American determined to vanquish the "Teutonic Order" opposing the allies during World War I. In the final pages the Greek warrior reappears, but as he boards the ship for Troy, he becomes aware that his suffering will soon begin, that his true mission is not to rescue Helen, who is being used for propaganda purposes, but rather to satisfy the ambitions of politicians and businessmen seeking power and economic gain. Carpentier destroys the barriers of time by depicting archetypal situations and by suggesting that although individual identities change, human behavior (based on the desire for power, wealth, prestige, and sexual gratification) remains the same throughout history.

In some respects "The Highroad of Saint James" resembles "Like the Night," but instead of portraying different protagonists in similar situations, it depicts a single protagonist in a series of episodes that, like those of the previous tale, suggest circular instead of lineal time. Juan of Antwerp, a 16th-century Spanish soldier stationed in Flanders, falls ill with the plague and vows to do penance in Santiago de Compostela, the site of the tomb of St. James, if he recovers his health. (The story's title in Spanish, "El camino de Santiago," also means the Milky Way, which supposedly guides pilgrims to Santiago de Compostela.) In the Spanish city of Burgos, Juan of Antwerp (now Juan the Pilgrim), once again physically fit, abandons his pledge to God and surrenders to the desires of the flesh. Also in Burgos he is convinced by a charlatan recently returned from the Americas that he should proceed to Seville and from there to the Americas, where he can make his fortune. Juan sails to Cuba, but in Havana he kills a man and is forced to flee, eventually making his way back to Spain as Juan the West Indian. In Burgos again, Juan the West Indian meets a young man, also named Juan, who is on his way to Santiago de Compostela. But Juan the West Indian convinces this second Juan the Pilgrim to accompany him to Seville, from where they set out for the Americas under the "starry heavens . . . white with galaxies" (translated by Frances Partridge). In addition to the cyclical repetition of the human experience, "The Highroad of Saint James" dramatizes the struggle between earthly reality and the heavenly ideal (the latter symbolized by the story's title). Thus the two sinners' departure for the New World under star-studded skies ends the story on an optimistic note.

"Right of Sanctuary" and "The Chosen" are fine examples of satire, the former of Latin American politics and the latter of religious bigotry and war. The protagonist of "Right of Sanctuary" is the secretary to the president of a Latin American nation who manages to escape to the embassy of a small neighboring nation when the president is overthrown by General Mabillán. After several weeks of boredom in the drab embassy, the secretary becomes the lover of the ambassador's wife. Then, having gradually assumed the duties of the ambassador, he applies for citizenship of the country represented by the embassy and ultimately is named ambassador of that country to his own. Meanwhile, General Mabillán feels obliged to accept this

preposterous turn of events because he must settle a border dispute with the newly appointed ambassador's nation in order to receive aid from the United States. The absurdity of Carpentier's tale is further underscored by a series of cardboard Donald Ducks that are sold and replaced in a toy store opposite the embassy of sanctuary. This recurring image of Walt Disney's famous creation serves as a reminder of the ever-present American influence in Latin America.

"The Chosen" reflects Carpentier's research on cultures with myths similar to that of the Biblical deluge and Noah's ark. In this allegory the vessels of five "chosen ones," including Noah, meet during the flood, each captain believing that he alone has been selected by his deity to survive and repopulate a purified world. After the waters recede, the world indeed is repopulated but instead of peace, misunderstanding, violence, and war ensue.

In his short fiction Carpentier develops his principal existential preoccupations, including the archetypal patterns of human behavior, mythical as opposed to historical time, and the fusion of the real and the magical in Latin American life. Known for his baroque style and avant-garde literary techniques, he is considered a major innovator in Latin American letters and a writer of universal stature.

—George R. McMurray

See the essay on "Journey Back to the Source."

———

CARTER, Angela (Olive, née Stalker). British. Born in Eastbourne, Sussex, 7 May 1940. Educated at the University of Bristol, 1962–65, B.A. in English 1965. Married Paul Carter in 1960 (divorced 1972). Journalist, Croydon, Surrey, 1958–61; lived in Japan, 1969–70; Arts Council Fellow in creative writing, University of Sheffield, 1976–78; visiting professor of creative writing, Brown University, Providence, Rhode Island, 1980–81; writer-in-residence, University of Adelaide, Australia, 1984. Recipient: Rhys Memorial prize, 1968; Maugham award, 1969; Cheltenham Festival prize, 1979; Maschler award, for children's book, 1982; James Tait Black Memorial prize, 1985. *Died 16 February 1992.*

PUBLICATIONS

Short Stories

Fireworks: Nine Profane Pieces.   1974; revised edition, 1987.
The Bloody Chamber and Other Stories.   1979.
Black Venus's Tale.   1980.
Black Venus.   1985; as *Saints and Strangers,* 1986.
American Ghosts and Old World Wonders.   1993.

Novels

Shadow Dance.   1966; as *Honeybuzzard,* 1967.
The Magic Toyshop.   1967.
Several Perceptions.   1968.
Heroes and Villains.   1969.
Love.   1971; revised edition, 1987.

The Infernal Desire Machines of Dr. Hoffman.   1972; as
    The War of Dreams, 1974.
The Passion of New Eve.   1977.
Nights at the Circus.   1984.
Wise Children.   1991.

Plays

Vampirella (broadcast 1976; produced 1986).   Included
    in *Come unto These Yellow Sands,* 1984.
Come unto These Yellow Sands (radio plays; includes *The
    Company of Wolves, Vampirella, Puss in Boots*).   1984.

Screenplays: *The Company of Wolves,* with Neil Jordan,
1984; *The Magic Toyshop,* 1987.

Radio Writing: *Vampirella,* 1976; *Come unto These Yellow
Sands,* 1979; *The Company of Wolves,* from her own story,
1980; *Puss in Boots,* 1982; *A Self-Made Man* (on Ronald
Firbank), 1984.

Verse

Unicorn.   1966.

Other

Miss Z, The Dark Young Lady (for children).   1970.
The Donkey Prince (for children).   1970.
Comic and Curious Cats, illustrated by Martin Leman.
    1979.
The Sadeian Woman: An Exercise in Cultural History.
    1979; as *The Sadeian Woman and the Ideology of
    Pornography,*   1979.
Nothing Sacred: Selected Writings.   1982.
Moonshadow (for children).   1982.
Sleeping Beauty and Other Favourite Fairy Tales.   1982.
Expletives Deleted: Selected Writings.   1992.

Editor, *Wayward Girls and Wicked Women.*   1986.
Editor, *The Virago Book of Fairy Tales.*   1990; *The Old
    Wives' Fairy Tale Book,* 1990.

Translator, *The Fairy Tales of Charles Perrault.*   1977.

*   *   *

The early death of Angela Carter in 1992 cut short the
career of one of the most inventive and wide-ranging
English writers of recent years. A brilliant essayist and
critic (whose article on D. H. Lawrence and women's
clothing, for instance, is unforgettable in its wit and
insight), she also wrote nine novels, a book of cultural
studies, radio plays, and four volumes of short stories, as
well as being a lively collector and editor of fairy tales.
Whatever she gave her attention to came back from her
sensibility to her readers in unexpected and challenging
forms.

Her first volume of short stories, *Fireworks,* is characteristic of her strange and sometimes disconcerting range of
interests. The nine stories vary considerably in mode: "A
Souvenir of Japan" is a comparatively realistic retrospective survey of the love affair of a European woman and a
younger Japanese man, but the perception of Japanese
culture as alien and "dedicated to appearances" gives the
story a peculiarly self-reflexive quality. "The Executioner's

Beautiful Daughter" is, by contrast, a disturbing fable
about a society located somewhere "in the uplands" where
repression and sexual savagery are the norm. Realism and
the fable are the poles between which these stories move,
but Carter's imagination is drawn much more strongly to
the latter. However, what gives force and significance to the
fables is their way of suddenly seeming to allude to life as
we know it: they appear to be fantasies, but only in the
sense that fantasies are parts of real life. "Master" is
perhaps the most powerful story, that of "a man whose
vocation was to kill animals," and his relationship with a
pubescent girl from a tribe in the South American jungle
where he has gone to kill "the painted beast, the jaguar."
Nemesis finally occurs (as the reader wishes it to do), but
by the time the girl shoots him with his own rifle, she has
the "brown and amber dappled sides" of the creature the
hunter has come to destroy. A victory for nature? The
reader is challenged, but cannot find an easy reassuring
answer. This is true of the effect of the volume as a whole.

It was followed by the outstandingly successful *The
Bloody Chamber and Other Stories,* retelling some of the
fairy tales familiar within our culture; I almost added,
"from a feminist point of view." But that would be
debatable. Some feminists objected to the terms of the rewriting, finding the depiction of women politically incorrect. This is part of Carter's appeal: she is an exploratory
writer, and the reader never knows where the path will
lead. "The Bloody Chamber" itself is the most elaborate,
taking the horrific story of Bluebeard as its starting point
and telling it from the point of view of his latest bride. The
whole story is an extraordinary achievement, mingling old
fable, new psychological insight, and parodic inventiveness
with great panache. Its wit seems to deny moralistic
interpretation, but certainly we can see in the girl's courage
and the mother's decisive action a story enabling and
encouraging for the woman reader (and disturbing for the
male, unless he is prepared to accept the "blind"—castrated?—role of the piano-tuner).

All the stories—there are nine others—share the energy
and inventiveness of "The Bloody Chamber." The last
three deal with that standby of the Gothic imagination, the
wolf. "The Werewolf" is very brief: the girl-child wounds a
wolf on the way to visit her sick grandmother, and finds
that the paw she cuts off the wolf is missing from her
grandmother's hand. No doubt she is a witch, who must be
punished, killed, and replaced. "The Company of Wolves"
is a more elaborate version of the Red Riding Hood story,
with an inspiring conclusion in which the girl's courage
triumphs. When the wolf threatens to eat her, "the girl
burst out laughing; she knew she was nobody's meat."
"Wolf Alice" is a girl brought up by wolves (a Freudian
figure), taken to the household of the duke, the "damned
Duke" who "haunts the graveyard." Their consummation
is as unexpected as it is positive. Here, as so often
throughout this wonderfully imaginative and superbly
written sequence, the reader is led to see human relations in
the mirror, the "rational glass," of these traditional stories
as retold. He or she will certainly react differently according to gender, but both will find much to enjoy as well as
much to puzzle and challenge.

The same imaginative energy and intellectual curiosity is
at work in the nine stories of *Black Venus.* The opening
story concerns Baudelaire's mistress Jeanne Duval, and
combines cultural history with psychological insight: Carter
has no hesitation about mixing the modes. The choice of
subjects suggest something central to her writings, a
concern with wider horizons than those of the main
tradition of English fiction with its preference for social

realism. Other stories in this volume evoke Uzbekistan, a 17th-century North America where an English woman becomes part of an Indian tribe; the theatrical world of Edgar Allan Poe's mother, read back from its legacy to him; the characters (and actors) about to take part in a performance of *A Midsummer Night's Dream*; the horrific folk-world of "Peter and the Wolf"; the kitchen of a great house in the north of England where the cook is seduced while making a souffle but doesn't forget to slam the oven door; and the world of the murderess Lizzie Borden in Fall River, Massachusetts, in August 1892. This final story powerfully evokes the stifling world of a New England miser and his family, making the murders all too inevitable. The "angel of death roosts on the roof-tree" of the family home. Carter brilliantly integrates fiction, myth, and human reality.

This is true also of her posthumously published volume, *American Ghosts and Old World Wonders*, which contains nine pieces. Four of these are related to the United States. "Lizzie's Tiger" deals again with the world of Lizzie Borden, but this time she is a strong-willed four-year-old, taking herself to see the tiger at the traveling circus. Her confrontation with it, and its tamer, leads to a "sudden access of enlightenment" about power and its exercise in the world. Two stories provide something like scenarios for Western films, one based on the coincidence that the name John Ford is that of a 17th-century playwright as well as a 20th-century director. "The Merchant of Shadows" vividly describes the visit of a researcher to the remote home of a Garbo-like recluse, with a trick ending which is connected with Carter's delight in the artificial. "The Ghost Ships" contrasts the Puritanism of early New England with the pagan legacies of Europe. "In Pantoland" is an affectionate commentary on the imaginary world of the pantomime and its inhabitants. "Ashputtle" offers three versions of the Cinderella story, one particularly disturbing. "Alice in Prague" is a fantasy of 17th-century Prague with allusions to Jan Svankmayer's film *Alice*. And the last piece reflects on the figure of Mary Magdalene as represented by Georges de la Tour and Donatello. Its final emphasis on the skull, placed where a child would be if this Mary were the Virgin, is particularly grim in the context of Carter's early death. But the volume as a whole is worthy of a writer of great variety and inventiveness, for whom the short story form was often especially enabling.

—Peter Faulkner

———

CARVER, Raymond. American. Born in Clatskanie, Oregon, 25 May 1938. Educated at Chico State College, California (founding editor, *Selection*), 1958–59; Humboldt State University, Arcata, California, 1960–63, A.B. 1963; University of Iowa, 1963–64, M.F.A. 1966. Married 1) Maryann Burk in 1957 (divorced 1982), one daughter and one son; 2) the writer Tess Gallagher in 1988. Worked in various jobs, including janitor, saw mill worker, delivery man, and salesman, 1957–67; textbook editor, Science Research Associates, Palo Alto, California, 1967–70; visiting lecturer, University of California, Santa Cruz, 1970–71, and Santa Barbara, 1975; visiting professor of English, University of California, Berkeley 1971–72; visiting writer, University of Iowa, 1972–73, Goddard College, Vermont, 1977–78, and University of Texas, El Paso, 1978–79; professor of English, Syracuse University, New York,

1980–84. Editor, *Quarry*, Santa Cruz, 1971. Recipient: National Endowment for the Arts fellowship, for poetry, 1971, for fiction, 1979; Stanford University Stegner Fellowship, 1973; Guggenheim fellowship, 1978; O. Henry award, 1983; Strauss Living award, 1983. *Died 4 August 1988.*

PUBLICATIONS

Short Stories

Put Yourself in My Shoes.   1974.
Will You Please Be Quiet, Please?   1976.
Furious Seasons and Other Stories.   1977.
What We Talk about When We Talk about Love.   1981.
The Pheasant.   1982.
Cathedral.   1983.
The Stories.   1985.
Where I'm Calling From: New and Selected Stories.   1988.

Plays

Carnations (produced 1962).
Dostoevsky: A Screenplay, with Tess Gallagher; published with *King Dog* by Ursula K. LeGuin.   1985.

Television Play: *Feathers*, from his own story, 1987.

Verse

Near Klamath.   1968.
Winter Insomnia.   1970.
At Night the Salmon Move.   1976.
Two Poems.   1982.
If It Please You.   1984.
Where Water Comes Together with Other Water.   1985.
This Water.   1985.
Ultramarine.   1986.
In a Marine Light: Selected Poems.   1987.
A New Path to the Waterfall.   1989.

Other

Fires: Essays, Poems, Stories.   1983.
My Father's Life, illustrated by Gaylord Schanilec.   1986.
Conversations with Carver, edited by Marshall Bruce Gentry and William L. Stull.   1990.
No Heroics, Please: Uncollected Writings, edited by William L. Stull.   1991.

Editor, *We Are Not in this Together: Stories*, by William Kittredge.   1983.
Editor, with Shannon Ravenel, *Best American Short Stories 1986*.   1986.
Editor, with Tom Jenks, *American Short Story Masterpieces*.   1987.

*

Critical Studies: "Voyeurism, Dissociation, and the Art of Carver" by David Boxer, in *Iowa Review*, Summer 1979; "Carver: A Chronicler of Blue-Collar Despair" by Bruce Weber, in *New York Times Magazine*, 24 June 1984; "Beyond Hopelessville: Another Side of Carver" by William L. Stull in *Philological Quarterly*, Winter 1985; in

European Views of Contemporary American Literature edited by Marc Chénetier, 1985; *Understanding Carver* by Arthur M. Saltzman, 1988; *Carver: A Study of the Short Fiction* by Ewing Campbell, 1992.

* * *

Raymond Carver is the most important writer in the renaissance of short fiction sparked in Callaghan literature in the 1980's. A master of what has been termed "minimalist hyperrealism," he belongs to a tradition of short story writers beginning with Anton Chekhov and continuing with Ernest Hemingway—two of his acknowledged mentors.

The stories in Carver's two early collections, *Will You Please Be Quiet, Please?* and *What We Talk about When We Talk about Love*, depend very little on plot, focusing instead on seemingly trivial situations of lower-middle class characters so sparsely delineated that they seem less physical reality than shadowy presences trapped in their own inarticulateness. Because reality for Carver exists only in the hard, bare outlines of an ambiguous event, these early stories often have more the sense of dream than everyday reality.

Typical of Carver's first two collections are "Neighbors" and "Why Don't You Dance?," both of which present ordinary people in ordinary situations that Carver transforms into the mysteriously extraordinary. "Neighbors" focuses on a young couple asked to watch their neighbors' apartment and water their plants. However the husband begins to stay longer and longer in the apartment, taking trivial things and then trying on the clothes of both the vacationing man and his wife. The story comes to a climax when the husband discovers that his wife is similarly fascinated, and, against all reason, they begin to hope that maybe the neighbors won't come back. When they discover that they have locked themselves out of the apartment, they hold on to each other desperately, leaning into the door as if "against a wind."

The story offers no explanation for the fascination the apartment holds for the young couple. But the understated language makes it clear that this is not a story about sexual perversion, but rather about the fascination of visiting someone else's secret inner reality and temporarily taking on their identity. The desperation the couple feels at the conclusion suggests the impossibility of truly entering into the lives of others, except to visit and inevitably to violate.

"Why Don't You Dance?" begins with an unidentified man who has arranged all his furniture on his front lawn just as it was when it was in the house. Carver only obliquely suggests a broken marriage as the motivation for this mysterious gesture by noting that the bed has a reading lamp on "his" side of the bed and a reading lamp on "her" side of the bed—though the man's wife does not appear in the story. The minimalist drama of the story begins when a young couple stops and makes offers for some of the furnishings, all of which the man indifferently accepts. Nothing really happens; the man plays a record on the phonograph and the man and the girl dance. The story ends with a brief epilogue weeks later when the girl tells a friend about the incident: "She kept talking. She told everyone. There was more to it, and she was trying to get it talked out. After a time, she quit trying."

The story illustrates the Chekhovian tradition of embodying complex inner reality by the simple description of outer reality. By placing all his furniture on his front lawn, the man externalizes what has previously been hidden inside the house. The young couple metaphorically "replace" the older man's lost relationship by creating their own relationship on the remains of his. However, the story is not a hopeful one, for the seemingly minor conflicts between the two young people presage another doomed marriage. Indeed, as the girl senses, there is "more to it," but she cannot quite articulate the meaning of the event, can only, as storytellers must, retell it over and over again, trying to get it talked out and intuitively understood.

Carver's two later collections, *Cathedral* and *Where I'm Calling From*, represent a shift in his basic theme and style. Whereas his early stories are minimalist and bleak, his later stories are more discursive and optimistic. A particularly clear example of this shift can be seen in the revisions Carver made to an early story entitled "The Bath" and renamed "A Small, Good Thing" in the last two collections. Both versions of the story concern a couple whose son is hit by a car on his eighth birthday and who is hospitalized in a coma—an event made more nightmarish by the fact that they receive annoying calls from a baker from whom the wife had earlier ordered a custom-made birthday cake for the child. "The Bath" is very brief; told in Carver's early, neutralized style, it focuses less on the feelings of the couple than on the mysterious and perverse interruption of the persistent anonymous calls.

The revision, "A Small, Good Thing," is five times longer and sympathetically develops the emotional life of the couple, suggesting that their prayers for their son bind them together in a genuine human communion that they have never felt before. Much of the detail of the revision focuses on the parents as they anxiously wait for their son to regain consciousness. Whereas in the first version, the child's death abruptly ends the story, in the second, the couple go visit the baker after the boy's death. He shares their sorrow; they share his loneliness. The story ends in reconciliation in the warm and comfortable bakery as the couple eat bread and talk into the early morning, not wanting to leave—as if a retreat into the communal reality of the bakery marks the true nature of healing human at-oneness.

Carver's understanding of the merits of the short story form and his sensitivity to the situation of modern men and women caught in tenuous relationships and inexplicable separations has made him an articulate spokesperson for those who cannot articulate their own dilemmas. Although critics are divided over the relative merits of Carver's early bleak experimental stories and his later more conventional and morally optimistic stories, there is little disagreement that Raymond Carver is the ultimate modern master of the "much-in-little" nature of the short story form.

—Charles E. May

See the essays on "Cathedral" and "What We Talk about When We Talk about Love."

———

CASTELLANOS, Rosario. Mexican. Born in Mexico City, 25 May 1925. Educated at National University, Mexico City, M.A. in philosophy 1944–50; studied at Madrid University. Married Ricardo Guerra in 1957 (divorced); one son. Director, cultural programs, Chiapas, 1951–53; worker, Instituto Arts and Sciences, Tuxtla; theater director, Instituto Nacional Indigenista, 1956–59; writer, essayist, and columnist, various Mexico City newspapers and journals, from 1960; teacher of comparative literature, and press director, National University, 1960–66; visiting professor of Latin American literature, University of Wisconsin, University of Indiana, and University of Colorado, 1967; chair, comparative literature, National University, 1967–71; Mexican ambassador, Israel, 1971–74; professor of Mexican literature, Hebrew University, Jerusalem, 1971–74. Recipient: Mexican Critics' award, for novel, 1957; Xavier Villaurrutia prize, for stories, 1961; Woman of the Year, Mexico, 1967. *Died 7 August 1974.*

PUBLICATIONS

Collections

A Reader, edited by Maureen Ahern, with others.   1988.
Another Way To Be: Selected Works (poetry, essays, stories), edited by Myralyn F. Allgood.   1990.

Short Stories

Ciudad real: Cuentos.   1960.
Los convidados de agosto.   1964.
Álbum de familia.   1971.

Novels

Balún Canán.   1957; as *The Nine Guardians,* 1959.
Oficio de tinieblas.   1962.

Play

El eterno feminino.   1975.

Verse

Trayectoria del polvo.   1948.
Apuntes para una declaración de fe.   1948.
De la vigilia estéril.   1950.
Dos poemas.   1950.
Presentación al templo: Poemas (Madrid, 1951), with *El rescate del mundo.*   1952.
Poemas 1953–1955.   1957.
Al pie de la letra.   1959.
Salomé y Judith: Poemas dramáticos.   1959.
Lívida luz.   1960.
Poesía no eres tú: Obra poética 1948–1971.   1972.
Looking at the Mona Lisa.   1981.
Bella dama sin piedad y otros poemas.   1984.
Meditación en el umbral: Antología poética, edited by Julian Palley.   1985; as *Meditation on the Threshold* (bilingual edition), 1988.
Selected Poems, edited by Cecilia Vicuña and Magda Bogin.   1988.

Other

Sobre cultura femenina (essays).   1950.
La novela mexicana contemporánea y su valor testimonial. 1965.
Rostros de México, photographs by Bernice Kolko.   1966.
Juicios sumarios: Ensayos.   1966; revised edition as *Juicios sumarios: Ensayos sobre literatura,* 2 vols., 1984.
Materia memorable (verse and essays).   1969.

Mujer que sabe latín (criticism).   1973.
El uso de la palabra (essays).   1974.
El mar y sus pescaditos (criticism).   1975.

*

Critical Studies: "Images of Women in Castellanos' Prose" by Phyllis Rodríguez-Peralta, in *Latin American Literary Review* 6, 1977; *Homenaje* edited by Maureen Ahern and Mary Seale Vásquez, 1980; in *The Double Strand: Five Contemporary Mexican Poets* by Frank Dauster, 1987; in *Lives on the Line: The Testimony of Contemporary Latin American Authors* edited by Doris Meyer, 1988; in *Women's Voice* by Naomi Lindstrom, 1989; *Remembering Rosario: A Personal Glimpse into the Life and Works* edited and translated by Myralyn F. Allgood, 1990; "Confronting Myths of Oppression: The Short Stories of Catellanos" by Chloe Funival, in *Knives and Angels,* edited by Susan Bassnett, 1990; in *Spanish American Women Writers* edited by Diane E. Marting, 1990.

*   *   *

Rosario Castellanos's work encompasses all the traditional literary genres, yet she is mostly known as a poet, and this is reflected in the selection of her works available in English translation. The majority of her writing remains untranslated, although several excellent anthologies have appeared in English in recent years, containing some of her best-known stories.

Castellanos's writing, and her personal and professional life as well, are marked by her profound concern for social justice; always, the focus is on women and the indigenous peoples of southern Mexico, two groups marginalized by the dominant national culture. In her literary examination of human relationships in a world of glaring inequities, she probes the intricacies and paradoxes of power itself. In addition to its economic and political dimensions, she insists on the fundamental importance of language. In her essay "Language as an Instrument of Domination" Castellanos asserts that language, like race and religion, is first and foremost a privilege, used to protect some and to exclude others; real communication, she maintains, is only possible among equals. Thus her fiction is full of characters whose lives are defined by lack of communication, isolation, silence. But if language has the power to dominate and oppress, it contains as well the possibility of change; often in her stories, it is language that empowers, that begins to redefine social relations.

"The Eagle" (1960) is set in Mexico's southern-most state of Chiapas, ancestral home of the Maya. Here, the native people of a small mountain town are duped by the lazy and mean municipal secretary, a *ladino* (the regional term for a European or non-native), into paying him an enormous amount of money to replace the town stamp, the eagle of the story's title. The new rubber stamp, of course, costs only a few pesos and the official, Hector Villafuerte, indulges in numerous luxuries and then starts a business with the rest of the money. For the native people, however, the eagle is not at all a stamp, but a spirit. According to Mayan beliefs, every human being is accompanied in life by an animal that is one's protective spirit; the same is true of tribes or groups, and the people see the town symbol in this light. Both Hector and the representatives of the native society use the same words—they speak of the eagle, and it is Hector who first uses the native word *nahual*, spirit — but the words have entirely different meanings for each, based on their cultural formation. And while Hector thinks he is cleverly outwitting the natives, he is more incapable of understanding than his victims.

"The Widower Román" (1964) is one of Castellanos's best-known stories, and it has been made into a film in Mexico. Set in Chiapas, among the provincial ruling class, it is a long story which tells a horrifying tale of revenge. The occasion is the marriage of Carlos Román, one of the town's prominent men, and Romelia Orantes, the youngest of several daughters of another leading family. Here again it is language that reveals both the astonishing lack of communication between the two, and the cultural underpinnings that have shaped each of them as social beings. He is a man who believes that he deserves whatever he wants; she is a woman who believes that she is fortunate if she gets anything she wants. It is also language that protects Carlos's power — the language between father and suitor who make the decisions, the legal language of the marriage contract which protects husband but not wife. When Carlos uses words as a weapon against Romelia, they have credibility simply because he is a respectable man. She, like Cassandra, may say whatever she wishes, but no one will listen to her.

Another of Castellanos's well-known works, "Cooking Lesson" (1971), is from her last collection of stories, the last fiction she published before her death; it is also her most perfectly-constructed story. The setting is cosmopolitan Mexico City, among the comfortable, educated class. The narrator's story is one of self-discovery and it is significant that she speaks for herself, in the first person. She is a newly-married woman, unnamed, who is attempting to cook her first dinner for her husband. As she confronts a piece of meat, completely unaware of any means of preparing it, she reflects on woman's place — the kitchen where she is so obviously out of place — and on women's social roles. She ponders her identity as unmarried woman and as married woman, which seem to be the only available categories. In the process she makes connections between her personal situation and the larger cultural context, uncovering many of the most basic myths of femininity/masculinity, often with the wry humor characteristic of Castellanos's later works. The meat offers a frank reminder of the sexual dimension of marriage and of women's situation in patriarchal society; it becomes as well a metaphor for the relationship and for the narrator herself, as it undergoes a metamorphosis during the cooking process but then, ultimately, it disappears, burnt to a crisp. The story's open ending allows the reader to determine what will become of this bride and the institution of marriage, although it is clear that the weight of tradition is formidable, and that alternatives to established social roles cannot be had easily, nor without cost.

Rosario Castellanos's stories offer glimpses of very different facets of contemporary Mexico, and considerations of basic issues that transcend the national or regional. They are visions of worlds she knew, and of worlds she hoped we might create. They are also invitations to communication, for words, Castellanos concludes in the essay on language cited above, only have meaning when they are shared with others.

—Barbara A. Clark

———

CATHER, Willa (Sibert). American. Born in Wilella Back Creek Valley, near Winchester, Virginia, 7 December 1873; moved with her family to a farm near Red Cloud, Nebraska, 1883. Educated at Red Cloud High School, graduated 1890; Latin School, Lincoln, Nebraska, 1890–91; University of Nebraska, Lincoln, 1891–95, A.B. 1895. Columnist, Lincoln *State Journal*, 1893–95; lived briefly in Red Cloud, 1896; editor, *Home Monthly*, Pittsburgh, 1896–97; telegraph editor and drama critic, Pittsburgh *Daily Leader*, 1896–1900; contributor, the *Library*, Pittsburgh, 1900; Latin and English teacher, Central High School, Pittsburgh, 1901–03; English teacher, Allegheny High School, Pittsburgh, 1903–06; staff writer, later managing editor, *McClure's* magazine, New York, 1906–11; full-time writer from 1912. Recipient: Pulitzer prize, 1923; American Academy Howells medal, 1930, and gold medal, 1944; Prix Femina Americaine, 1932. Litt.D.: University of Nebraska, 1917; University of Michigan, Ann Arbor, 1922; Columbia University, New York, 1928; Yale University, New Haven, Connecticut, 1929; Princeton University, New Jersey, 1931; D.L.: Creighton University, Omaha, Nebraska, 1928; LL.D.: University of California, Berkeley, 1931; L.H.D.: Smith College, Northampton, Massachusetts, 1933. Member, American Academy. *Died 24 April 1947.*

PUBLICATIONS

Collections

Early Novels and Stories (Library of America), edited by Sharon O'Brien.   1987.
The Short Stories, edited by Hermoine Lee.   1989.
Great Short Works of Cather, edited by Robert K. Miller. 1989.
Later Novels (Library of America), edited by Sharon O'Brien.   1990.
Stories, Poems, and Other Writings (Library of America), edited by Sharon O'Brien.   1992.

Short Stories

The Troll Garden.   1905; variorum edition, edited by James Woodress, 1983.
Youth and the Bright Medusa.   1920.
The Fear That Walks by Noonday.   1931.
Obscure Destinies.   1932.
Novels and Stories.   13 vols., 1937–41.
The Old Beauty and Others.   1948.
Early Stories, edited by Mildred R. Bennett.   1957.
Collected Short Fiction 1892–1912, edited by Virginia Faulkner.   1965.
Uncle Valentine and Other Stories: Uncollected Fiction 1915–1929, edited by Bernice Slote.   1973.

Novels

Alexander's Bridge.   1912; as *Alexander's Bridges*, 1912.
O Pioneers!   1913.
The Song of the Lark.   1915.
My Ántonia.   1918.
One of Ours.   1922.
A Lost Lady.   1923.
The Professor's House.   1925.
My Mortal Enemy.   1926.
Death Comes for the Archbishop.   1927.
Shadows on the Rock.   1931.

Lucy Gayheart. 1935.
Sapphira and the Slave Girl. 1940.

Verse

April Twilights. 1903.
April Twilights and Other Poems. 1923; revised edition, 1933; edited by Bernice Slote, 1962; revised edition, 1968.

Other

The Life of Mary Baker G. Eddy, and the History of Christian Science, by Georgine Milmine (ghostwritten by Cather). 1909.
My Autobiography, by S.S. McClure (ghostwritten by Cather). 1914.
Not Under Forty. 1936.
On Writing: Critical Studies on Writing as an Art. 1949.
Writings from Cather's Campus Years, edited by James R. Shively. 1950.
Cather in Europe: Her Own Story of the First Journey, edited by George N. Kates. 1956.
The Kingdom of Art: Cather's First Principles and Critical Principles 1893-1896, edited by Bernice Slote. 1967.
The World and the Parish: Cather's Articles and Reviews 1893–1902, edited by William M. Curtin. 2 vols., 1970.

Editor, *The Best Stories of Sarah Orne Jewett.* 2 vols., 1925.

*

Bibliography: *Cather: A Bibliography* by Joan Crane, 1982.

Critical Studies: *Cather: A Critical Introduction* by David Daiches, 1951; *Cather: A Critical Biography* by E.K. Brown, completed by Leon Edel, 1953; *The Landscape and the Looking Glass: Cather's Search for Value* by John H. Randall III, 1960; *The World of Cather* by Mildred R. Bennett, 1961; *Cather's Gift of Sympathy* by Edward and Lillian Bloom, 1962; *Cather* by Dorothy Van Ghent, 1964; *Cather and Her Critics* edited by James Schroeter 1967; *Cather: Her Life and Art,* 1970, and *Cather: A Literary Life,* 1987, both by James Woodress; *Cather* by Dorothy McFarland Tuck, 1972; *Cather: A Pictorial Memoir* by Bernice Slote, 1973, and *The Art of Cather* edited by Slote and Virginia Faulkner, 1974; *Five Essays on Cather,* 1974, and *Critical Essays on Cather,* 1984, both edited by John J. Murphy; *Cather's Imagination* by David Stouck, 1975; *Cather* by Philip L. Gerber, 1975; *Chrysalis: Cather in Pittsburgh 1896–1906* by Kathleen D. Byrne and Richard C. Snyder, 1982; *Willa: The Life of Cather* by Phyllis C. Robinson, 1983; *Cather's Short Fiction,* 1984, and *Cather: A Reference Guide,* 1986, both by Marilyn Arnold; *The Voyage Perilous: Cather's Romanticism* by Susan Rosowski, 1986; *Cather: The Emerging Voice* by Sharon O'Brien, 1986; *Cather in Person: Interviews, Speeches and Letters* edited by L. Brent Bohlke, 1987; *Cather: Life as Art* by Jamie Ambrose, 1987; *Cather in France: In Search of the Last Language* by Robert J. Nelson, 1988; *Cather: A Life Saved Up* by Hermoine Lee, 1989, as *Cather: Double Lives,* 1990; *Cather* by Susie Thomas, 1989; *Cather: A Study of the Short Fiction* by Loretta Wasserman, 1991.

* * *

Although Willa Cather largely abandoned short fiction after she began writing novels, she launched her career as a writer of stories, and the last thing she completed before she died was a story. All told, she wrote 58 stories between 1892 and 1945, and in terms of total wordage, about one-third of her entire literary corpus is short fiction. She regarded her stories, however, as the lesser part of her work, and for her in fact the short story was her apprenticeship. Of the 45 stories she published through 1912 when her first novel appeared, only four of them was she willing to reprint later in her career. The rest she wanted forgotten; she would have destroyed all traces of them if she could have.

Cather was born in Back Creek, Virginia, in the Shenandoah Valley, the oldest of seven children, but when she was nine years old, her parents migrated to Nebraska, where she spent the next 13 years. First they farmed, then moved into Red Cloud, the town immortalized in both Cather's stories and novels. Her literary career began as a freshman at the University of Nebraska when she wrote a story for an English class. It so impressed her professor that he sent it off to be published in a Boston magazine. This story was "Peter," which ultimately became an important episode in *My Àntonia.*

For the next two decades Cather published only stories and poems. The early stories are amateurish and range widely in setting, subject, and style. She wrote a story of ancient Egypt, a romantic tale laid in 18th-century Virginia, a ghost story in a football setting, fairy tales, and stories of grim realism. Some of these tales are imitative of Henry James, the writer she most admired. But gradually her narrative powers grew, and she began placing her work in national magazines. By 1905 she was able to publish her first volume of fiction, *The Troll Garden,* a collection of seven stories about art and artists, a subject that preoccupied her off and on throughout her life. Among these tales are "Paul's Case" and "The Sculptor's Funeral," the latter being an attack on aesthetic sterility and smugness in a Kansas village.

The Troll Garden climaxed a decade that Cather spent in Pittsburgh editing a home magazine, writing drama and music criticism for a newspaper, and teaching high school English. In 1906 she moved on to New York to become an editor of *McClure's Magazine,* but her writing suffered because of the pressure of editorial duties. In the next six years she managed to publish only nine stories, some of which had been written before she moved to New York, but the quality is increasingly high. *McClure's, Harpers, The Century,* and *Colliers* published them, and several ("The Enchanted Bluff," "The Joy of Nelly Dean," and "The Bohemian Girl," look ahead to subjects and themes Cather would use in her celebrated Nebraska novels.

After 1912 when her first novel appeared, Cather put most of her energy into the novel, and in the next 33 years she wrote only 13 more stories. Some of these, however, are of equal quality with her long fiction. In 1920 she put together another collection of stories, *Youth and the Bright Medusa,* again stories about artists. She reprinted four tales from *The Troll Garden* and added four more recently written. Two of them, "A Gold Slipper" and "The Diamond Mine," are excellent tales reflecting Cather's great interest in opera. A third, "Coming, Aphrodite," pits an avant garde artist against an opera singer in an abortive romance.

During the 1910's and 1920's Cather wrote eight novels, but her novels often contain interest for students of the short story. The story of Pavel and Peter and the bridal couple thrown to the wolves in *My Ántonia* is a self-contained episode. "Tom Outland's Story" in *The Professor's House* is a long story that has been separately anthologized. Inserted in the middle of the novel, it is one of Cather's best fictions and evokes memorably the Southwest and the ancient cliff-dwellers of Mesa Verde. *My Mortal Enemy* is actually nouvelle length, although it was published separately as a novel. *Death Comes for the Archbishop* contains a number of inset stories that can be read separately.

After the death of her parents and a final visit to Red Cloud for a reunion with her brothers and sisters, Cather revisited the subject of her Nebraska novels and stories. The result was *Obscure Destinies,* one of her most distinguished books. It contains three stories, "Neighbour Rosicky," "Old Mrs. Harris," and "Two Friends." "Old Mrs. Harris," in the view of many Cather scholars, is the finest piece of short fiction Cather wrote. Three generations of Cather women provide prototypes for the characters. The title character is Cather's grandmother Boak, who accompanied her daughter's family to Nebraska; Victoria Templeton is Cather's mother, a Southern lady transplanted to the prairie; and Vickie is Cather herself as teenager. A fictionalized Red Cloud is the setting, and prominent characters are the Rosens, modeled on Cather's Jewish neighbors, the Wieners, whose library and European culture gave young Willa an early glimpse of the Old World. When Blanche Knopf read the story in manuscript, she wrote that it seemed to her one of the great stories of all time. "Two Friends" is a lesser tale, but it evokes memorably Red Cloud and two of its businessmen, as the narrator, Cather's adolescent self, listens to them talk on summer evenings outside the general store.

Between 1915 and 1929 Cather published six stories that she never reprinted. Two of them, "Double Birthday" and "Uncle Valentine," are well worth preserving. Both are Pittsburgh stories that draw on Cather's memory of friends from her years in Pennsylvania. "Uncle Valentine" is especially interesting, as the title character is suggested by the composer Ethelbert Nevin, whom Cather knew and admired and whose untimely death she mourned. A final trio of Cather's stories, *The Old Beauty and Others,* was published posthumously by her literary executors. The title story is one that Cather put aside when the *Woman's Home Companion* rejected it, but the other two were written at the end of her life. "The Best Years" is vintage Cather and evokes poignantly her memories of her family and Red Cloud during her youth. "Before Breakfast" is an old-age story that takes an affirmative view of life and is the only tale she wrote set on Grand Manan Island off the coast of New Brunswick where she had a summer cottage.

—James Woodress

See the essays on "Neighbour Rosicky" and "Paul's Case."

CHANG, Eileen.   See ZHANG AILING.

CHEEVER, John (William). American. Born in Quincy, Massachusetts, 27 May 1912. Educated at Thayer Academy, South Braintree, Massachusetts. Served in the U.S. Army Signal Corps, 1943–45: Sergeant. Married Mary M. Winternitz in 1941; one daughter and two sons. Full-time writer in New York City, 1930-51, Scarborough, New York, 1951–60, and Ossining, New York, after 1961; teacher at Barnard College, New York, 1956–57, Ossining Correctional Facility (Sing Sing prison), 1971–72, and University of Iowa Writers Workshop, Iowa City, 1973; visiting professor of creative writing, Boston University, 1974-75. Recipient: Guggenheim fellowship, 1951, and second fellowship; Benjamin Franklin award, 1955; O. Henry award, 1956, 1964; American Academy grant, 1956, and Howells medal, 1965; National Book award, 1958; National Book Critics Circle award, 1979; Pulitzer prize, 1979; MacDowell medal, 1979; American Book award, for paperback, 1981; National Medal for literature, 1982. Litt.D.: Harvard University, Cambridge, Massachusetts, 1978. Member, American Academy, 1958. *Died 18 June 1982.*

PUBLICATIONS

Short Stories

The Way Some People Live: A Book of Stories.   1943.
The Enormous Radio and Other Stories.   1953.
Stories, with others.   1956; as *A Book of Stories,* 1957.
The Housebreaker of Shady Hill and Other Stories.   1958.
Some People, Places, and Things That Will Not Appear in My Next Novel.   1961.
The Brigadier and the Golf Widow.   1964.
The World of Apples.   1973.
The Stories.   1978.
The Day the Pig Fell into the Well (story).   1978.
The Leaves, The Lion-Fish and the Bear (story).   1980.
The Uncollected Stories.   1988.

Novels

The Wapshot Chronicle.   1957.
The Wapshot Scandal.   1964.
Bullet Park.   1969.
Falconer.   1977.
Oh, What a Paradise It Seems.   1982.

Plays

Television Plays: scripts for *Life with Father* series; *The Shady Hill Kidnapping,* 1982.

Other

Conversations with Cheever, edited by Scott Donaldson.   1987.
The Letters, edited by Benjamin Cheever.   1988.
The Journals.   1991.

*

Bibliography: *Cheever: A Reference Guide* by Francis J. Bosha, 1981.

Critical Studies: *Cheever* by Samuel Coale, 1977; *Cheever* by Lynne Waldeland, 1979; *Critical Essays on Cheever* edited by R.G. Collins, 1982; *Cheever: The Hobgoblin Company of Love* by George W. Hunt, 1983; *Home Before Dark: A Biographical Memoir of Cheever* by Susan Cheever, 1984; *Cheever: A Study of the Short Fiction* by James Eugene O'Hara, 1989.

*   *   *

John Cheever was the author of two hundred short stories, the majority of them first published in *The New Yorker,* achieving the status of modern American master, the equal of Poe, Hawthorne, Crane, and Hemingway. Cheever's importance can be measured in terms of both the number of his stories that won awards and the number of times so many of his stories have been anthologized. The retrospective collection, *The Stories of John Cheever,* winner of a Pulitzer prize and a National Book award, revived interest in the short story on the part of publishers and readers, making it both commercially more viable and critically more respectable.

Because the simplicity of his stories is almost always deceptive, efforts to classify Cheever, particularly as a realist or a traditionalist or even a satirist, generally fail. His biographer, Scott Donaldson, rightly claims that Cheever's fiction "tells us more about people in the American middle-class during that half century [1930-1982] than any other writer has done or can do." But the writer whom one influential reviewer has called "the Chekhov of the exurbs," another has dubbed "Ovid in Ossining." Cheever's approach to the middle-class life chronicled in his fiction proves intriguingly complex, at once celebratory and satiric, realistic and fantastic, as concerned with metamorphosis as with 20th-century mores. Although no postmodernist, Cheever was far more innovative than most *New Yorker* writers, and although outside the academy (except for very brief and generally disastrous stints), he was no literary lightweight cheerfully endorsing suburban values.

His uncertain critical reputation, which lasted until the publication of *Falconer* in 1977, did little to alleviate the sense of economic, social, and psychological insecurity that Cheever began to experience at least as early as adolescence (the breakup of his parents marriage, the Depression, his fear of acknowledging his bisexuality). Despite his frequent claims that fiction is not crypto-autobiography, Cheever made his insecurity and fragile sense of self-esteem the subjects of his stories. If the shortcoming of much early criticism, at least through the publication of *Falconer,* was the failure to address the autobiographical element in the fiction, criticism since Cheever's death in 1982 runs the risk of making precisely the opposite mistake, of following the lead of the author's daughter in *Home Before Dark* and *Treetops,* seeing in the fiction nothing but autobiographical revelation.

Settings, general situations, and character types remain stable (almost obsessively so) throughout Cheever's career, as does the lyrical style he developed following a brief period of imitating Hemingway's style. Cheever's approach to his material proves more varied. "The Enormous Radio," for example, begins as a work of quiet, seemingly predictable realism. "Jim and Irene Westcott were the kind of people who seem to strike that satisfactory average of income, endeavor, and respectability that is reached by the statistical reports in college alumni bulletins." Once their radio breaks down and Jim buys a new one, realism begins to give way to Hawthornesque romance. The veneer of middle-class respectability cracks, exposing a chilling apprehensiveness lurking just below the surface of what had been the Westcotts' thoroughly average lives.

In "Goodbye, My Brother," one of several Cheever stories based on Cheever's relationship with his older brother Fred, the split between the brothers underscores the Poe-like spirit in the narrator-protagonist's own character. Understanding this division helps us to understand Cheever's habit of appending lyrical endings that seem both to affirm the existence of a spiritual (or, in the case of "Goodbye My Brother," mythic) realm, and by virtue of the strained relation between the ending and all that precedes it, to undermine this affirmation, suggesting that it may be at best wishful thinking and at worst delusion. The almost schizophrenic character of Cheever's vision also manifests itself between stories that tell essentially the same tale from two very different perspectives. "A Vision of the World" (1961), for example, reads like the comic companion piece to "The Seaside Houses," published one year later. These examples form parts of a larger pattern of opposition that includes divisions between sexuality and spirituality, absurdity and ecstasy, confinement and expansiveness, and the characters' all-too-middle-class lives and their desire "to celebrate a world spread out around us like a bewildering and stupendous dream." Like the aging poet Asa Bascomb, in "A World of Apples," who "walked like all the rest of us in some memory of prowess," Cheever's characters want to build a bridge between their present and their past, their lives and their dreams—dreams which, like his lyrical endings, Cheever often undermines by making them appear either absurd or childish. In "Artemis the Honest Well Digger" the main character goes "looking for a girl as fresh as the girl on the oleomargarine package."

Just as often the balance tips the other way as Cheever explores the disease and dread of an American dream that "hangs morally and financially from a thread." In "The Housebreaker of Shady Hill" Johnny Hake may be saved from a life of crime (burgling his affluent neighbors after being fired), but a gentle rain restores his moral sense (as well as his job); others, like Neddy Merrill in "The Swimmer" and Cash Bentley in "O Youth and Beauty," are not so fortunate. Neither is Charlie Pastern in "The Brigadier and the Golf Widow," a story in which the threat of nuclear destruction cannot begin to compare with the less apocalyptic but more personal and pervasive fear or loneliness and dispossession that afflicts so many Cheever characters, most obviously (and often humorously) the expatriate Americans in Cheever's Italian stories. The worst alienation occurs, however, not abroad but at home, where the thread by which his characters' moral and economic lives hang seems only as strong as it is tenuous.

—Robert A. Morace

See the essays on "The Country Husband" and "The Swimmer."

CHEKHOV, Anton (Pavlovich). Russian. Born in Taganrog, 17 January 1860. Educated at a school for Greek boys, Taganrog, 1867–68; Taganrog grammar school, 1868–79; Moscow University Medical School, 1879–84, graduated as doctor 1884. Married the actress Olga Knipper in 1901. Freelance writer while still in medical school, especially for humorous magazines, and later for serious ones; practicing doctor in Moscow, 1884–92, Melikhovo, 1892–99, and in Yalta after 1899. Recipient: Pushkin prize, 1888. Member, Imperial Academy of Sciences, 1900 (resigned, 1902). *Died 2 July 1904.*

PUBLICATIONS

Collections

Polnoe sobranie sochinenii i pisem [Complete Works and Letters], edited by S.D. Balukhaty and others.   20 vols., 1944–51; a new edition, 30 vols., 1974— .
The Major Plays.   1964.
The Oxford Chekhov, edited by Ronald Hingley.   9 vols., 1964–80.
Collected Works.   5 vols., 1987.
The Sneeze: Plays and Stories.   1989.

Short Stories

Pestrye rasskazy [Motley Tales].   1886; revised edition, 1891.
Nevinnye rechi [Innocent Tales].   1887.
Rasskazy [Tales].   1889.
Tales.   13 vols., 1916–22.
The Unknown Chekhov: Stories and Other Writings Hitherto Untranslated, edited by A. Yarmolinsky.   1954.
Early Stories.   1960.
The Early Stories 1883–1888, edited by Patrick Miles and Harvey Pitcher.   1984.

Novels

V sumerkakh [In the Twilight].   1887.
Khmurye liudi [Gloomy People].   1890.
Duel [The Duel].   1892.
Palata No. 6 [Ward No. 6].   1893.

Plays

Ivanov (produced 1887; revised version, produced 1889). In *P'esy,* 1897; translated as *Ivanov,* in *Plays 1,* 1912.
Lebedinaia pesnia (produced 1888).   In *P'esy,* 1897; as *Swan Song,* in *Plays 1,* 1912.
Medved' (produced 1888).   1888; as *The Bear,* 1909; as *The Boor,* 1915.
Leshii (produced 1889).   1890; as *The Wood Demon,* 1926.
Predlozhenie (produced 1889).   1889; as *A Marriage Proposal,* 1914.
Trigik ponevole (produced 1889).   1890.
Svad'ba (produced 1890).   1889; as *The Wedding,* in *Plays 2,* 1916.
Yubiley (produced 1900).   1892.
Diadia Vania (produced 1896).   In *P'esy,* 1897; as *Uncle Vania,* in *Plays 1,* 1912.
Chaika (produced 1896).   In *P'esy,* 1897; revised version (produced 1898), 1904; as *The Seagull,* in *Plays 1,* 1912.
Tri sestry (produced 1901).   1901; as *The Three Sisters,* in *Plays 2,* 1916.
Vishnevyi sad (produced 1904).   1904; as *The Cherry Orchard,* 1908.

Neizdannaia p'esa, edited by N.F. Belchikov.   1923; as *That Worthless Fellow Platonov,* 1930; as *Don Juan (in the Russian Manner),* 1952; as *Platonov,* 1964.

Other

Ostrov Sakhalin.   1895; as *The Island: A Journey to Sakhalin,* 1967.
Sobranie sochinenii.   11 vols., 1899–1906.
Pis'ma [Letters].   1909; *Sobranie pis'ma,* 1910; *Pis'ma,* 1912–16, and later editions.
Zapisnye knizhki.   1914; as *The Note-Books,* 1921.
Letters to Olga Knipper.   1925.
Literary and Theatrical Reminiscences, edited by S.S. Kotelianskii.   1927.
Personal Papers.   1948.
Selected Letters, edited by Lillian Hellman.   1955.
Letters, edited by Simon Karlinsky.   1973.

*

Bibliography: *Chekhov in English: A List of Works by and about Him* edited by Anna Heifetz and A. Yarmolinsky, 1949; *The Chekhov Centennial: Chekhov in English: A Selective List of Works by and about Him 1949–60* by Rissa Yachnin, 1960; *Chekhov Bibliography: Works in English by and about Chekhov: American, British, and Canadian Performances,* 1985, and *Chekhov Criticism: 1880 through 1986,* 1989, both by Charles W. Meister; *Chekhov: A Reference Guide to Literature* by K.A. Lantz, 1985; *Chekhov Rediscovered: A Collection of New Studies with a Complete Bibliography* edited by Savely Senderovich and Munir Sendich, 1987.

Critical Studies: *Chekhov: A Biographical and Critical Study,* 1950, and *A New Life of Chekhov,* 1976, both by Ronald Hingley; *Chekhov: A Biography* by Ernest J. Simmons, 1962; *The Breaking String: The Plays of Anton Chekhov* by Maurice Valency, 1966; *Chekhov and His Prose* by Thomas Winner, 1966; *Chekhov: A Collection of Critical Essays* edited by Robert Louis Jackson, 1967; *Chekhov* by J.B. Priestly, 1970; *Chekhov in Performance: A Commentary on the Major Plays* by J.L. Styan, 1971; *The Chekhov Play: A New Interpretation* by Harvey Pitcher, 1973; *Chekhov: The Evolution of His Art* by Donald Rayfield, 1975; *Chekhov: A Study of the Major Stories and Plays* by Beverly Hahn, 1977; *Chekhov* by Irina Kirk, 1981; *Chekhov: The Critical Heritage* edited by Victor Emeljanow, 1981; *Chekhov and the Vaudeville: A Study of Chekhov's One-Act Plays* by Vera Gottlieb, 1982; *Chekhov: A Study of the Four Major Plays* by Richard Peace, 1983; *Chekhov* (biography) by Henri Troyat, 1984, translated by Micheal Henry Heim, 1986; *Chekhov and Tagore: A Comparative Study of Their Short Stories* by Sankar Basu, 1985; *Chekhov and O'Neill: The Uses of the Short Story in Chekhov's and O'Neill's Plays* by Déter Egri, 1986; *Chekhov and Women* by Carolina de Maegd-Soëp, 1987; *Chekhov: A Spirit Set Free* by V.S. Pritchett, 1988; *Critical Essays on Chekhov* edited by Thomas A. Eekman, 1989.

*   *   *

Critics and literary historians generally agree that Anton Chekhov was the most important influence on the development of the "modern" short story at the beginning of the

20th century. Chekhov's short stories were first characterized as an offshoot of 19th-century realism—not because they reflected the social commitment or political convictions of the realistic novel, but because they seemed to focus on fragments of everyday reality and to present "slices of life." When Chekhov's stories first appeared in translation, a number of critics noted that they were so deficient in incident and plot that they lacked every element that constitutes a really good short story. However, at the same time, other critics argued that Chekhov's ability to dispense with a striking incident, his impressionism, and his freedom from the literary conventions of the highly plotted and formalized story marked the beginnings of a new kind of short fiction that somehow combined realism and romantic poetry.

This combination of the realistic and the poetic has been the most problematical aspect of Chekhov's stories. It has often reduced critics to commenting vaguely about an elusive, seamless quality that makes them resistant to analysis or interpretation. As early as 1916, critic Barry Pain noted that in the "artistic" story typical of Chekhov we find a quality rarely found in the novel in the same degree of intensity: "a very curious, haunting, and suggestive quality." Chekhov has been credited with creating the "literary" or "artistic" short story by initiating a shift from focusing on what happens to characters externally to what happens in the minds of characters. Literary historian A.C. Ward argued in 1924 that the brief prose tale since Chekhov more readily lent itself to impressionistic effects and provided a more suitable medium for excursions into the unconscious than the novel.

When Chekhov began publishing his best-known stories near the end of the 19th century, the romantic tale form with its emphasis on plot was still predominant. Although realism had laid the groundwork for Stephen Crane's experiments with impressionism and for Henry James's explorations of psychological reality, O. Henry and lesser known imitators of the patterned Poe "story of effect" dominated the short story in America at the time. In England, the short story was enjoying its first flush of success with the formalized stories of Stevenson and Kipling; Maupassant was sophisticating the patterned Poe story in France; and in Russia, Gogol was parodying and Turgenev was lyricizing the folktale.

The Chekhovian short story marks a transition from the romantic projective fiction of Poe and the patterned ironic fiction of O. Henry—in which characters are merely functions of the story—to an apparently realistic episode in which plot is subordinate to "as-if-real" character. However, because the short story is too short to allow character to be created by the multiplicity of detail and social interaction typical of the novel, Chekhov's stories focus on human experience under the influence of a particular mood; as a result, tone rather than plot becomes their unifying principle. Conrad Aiken once noted that if in retrospect, we find that Chekhov's characters have an odd way of evaporating, it is because we never saw them externally, but rather as "infinitely fine and truthful sequences of mood."

The typical Chekhov story does not realistically focus on everyday reality, but instead centers on the psychological aftermath of an event that breaks up everyday reality and leaves the involved characters helpless to understand or integrate the event and painfully inadequate to articulate their feelings about it. Some of Chekhov's best-known stories, such as "Gooseberries" and "The Lady with the Little Dog," end with characters caught in conflicting emotions that transcend their ability to understand or articulate them. Chekhov is not a realist in the usual sense of that term. In fact, after reading "The Lady with the Little Dog," Maxim Gor'kii wrote to Chekhov that he was killing realism for good, for it had outlived its time. "No one can write so simply about such simple things as you do," Gor'kii wrote: "After any of your insignificant stories everything seems crude, as though it were not written with a pen but with a log of wood."

In "Misery," one of the clearest examples of Chekhov's typical theme and structure, the everyday rhythm of the cab driver Iona's reality is broken up by the news that his son is dead, and he feels compelled to communicate the impact of this news to his fares. What the story presents is the comic and pathetic sense of the incommunicable nature of grief itself. Iona "thirsts for speech," wants to talk of the death of his son "properly, with deliberation." He is caught by the basic desire to tell a story of the break-up of his everyday reality that will express the irony he senses and that, by being deliberate and detailed, will both express his grief and control it.

What makes this story different from the typical story that came before it is that it not only does not seem like a told story of a past event, it does not emphasize an event at all but rather the lack of one. What Iona wants to tell is not a story in the usual sense of the word, but a story that expresses an inner state by being deliberate and detailed. In this sense "Misery" is not a mere lament (as the title is sometimes translated), but a controlled objectification of grief and its incommunicable nature by the presentation of deliberate details. It therefore indicates in a basic way one of the primary contributions Chekhov makes to the short story form—the expression of a complex inner state by means of the presentation of selected concrete particulars. T.S. Eliot later termed such a technique "objective correlative," and James Joyce mastered it fully in *Dubliners* (1914). With Chekhov, the short story took on a new respectability as the most appropriate narrative form to reflect the modern temperament.

—Charles E. May

See the essays on "Gooseberries," "The Lady with the Little Dog," and "Rothchild's Violin."

CHESNUTT, Charles Waddell. American. Born in Cleveland, Ohio, 20 June 1858; moved with his family to Fayetteville, North Carolina, 1866. Educated privately, and at local schools. Married Susan U. Perry in 1878; four children. Teacher, North Carolina public schools, 1873–77; assistant principal, 1877–79, and principal, 1880–83, Howard Normal School, Fayetteville; reporter, New York *Mail and Express,* 1883; clerk for railway company, Cleveland, 1883, then stenographer for the company's lawyer and studied law (admitted to Ohio bar, 1887); owned a stenographic business, mid-1880's–1899 and after 1902. Recipient: NAACP Spingarn medal, 1928. *Died 15 November 1932.*

PUBLICATIONS

Collections

The Short Fiction, edited by Sylvia Lyons Render.   1974.

Short Stories

The Conjure Woman.   1899.
The Wife of His Youth and Other Stories of the Color Line.
    1899.

Novels

The House Behind the Cedars.   1900.
The Marrow of Tradition.   1901.
The Colonel's Dream.   1905.

Other

Frederick Douglass.   1899.

*

Bibliography: "The Works of Chesnutt: A Checklist" by
William L. Andrews, in *Bulletin of Bibliography,* January
1976; *Chesnutt: A Reference Guide* by Curtis W. Ellison
and E.W. Metcalf, Jr., 1977.

Critical Studies: *Chesnutt, Pioneer of the Color Line* by
Helen M. Chesnutt, 1952; *Chesnutt: America's First Great
Black Novelist* by J. Noel Heermance, 1974; *An American
Crusade: The Life of Chesnutt* by Frances Richardson
Keller, 1978; *The Literary Career of Chesnutt* by William
L. Andrews, 1980; *Chesnutt* by Sylvia Lyons Render, 1980;
Chesnutt by Cliff Thompson, 1992.

*   *   *

A gifted novelist and short story writer, Charles Waddell
Chesnutt was the first African-American published by a
major American magazine and publishing house. He
sought to mine original literary material found in remote
locales or overlooked social strata. His treatments of
slavery and mulattos living on the "color line" were
determined attempts to revise popular stereotypes and
humanize African-American literary characters.

Chesnutt wrote during a period termed by one black
historian as the "nadir" of African-American experience in
the United States. Many of the hopes raised by emancipation and the Civil War were dispelled as white supremacy
was reasserted in the South and blacks were consigned to a
second class citizenship not demonstrably better—and
sometimes worse—than they had faced as slaves. In
literature, Southern local color writers such as Joel Chandler Harris and Thomas Nelson Page extolled the lost
plantation society and sentimentalized white and black
relationships "befo' de war." Another Southerner, Thomas
Dixon, wrote novels such as *The Clansman* that painted
freed blacks as brutes not to be trusted in politics or near
white women.

Chesnutt's work controverted these portraits. Like other
local color fiction, the stories collected in *The Conjure
Woman* attempt to capture the folkways, dialect, and social
manners of quaint peoples living in backwater America.
But Chesnutt's conjure tales are more than simply quaint.
They reveal the many disquieting aspects of slavery.

Several of the stories treat the break-up of families and
the desperate and inventive efforts of slaves to maintain
their family bonds. The creative power of conjure is often
invoked to counteract slavery's cruelty. "Po' Sandy," for

instance, is about a slave who cannot maintain his relationship with his wife because he is lent out to his master's
relatives for months at a time. His wife, a conjurer, agrees
to transform him into a pinetree so that he cannot again be
uprooted from his home. But while she is called away to
nurse Mars Marrabo's daughter-in-law on a distant plantation, Sandy is chopped down and sawed into boards for a
new kitchen. A similar theme impels "Sis' Becky's Pickan-
inny," about a mother's efforts to keep her baby. Becky's
master, Colonel Pendleton, sells her in exchange for a
racehorse. After Becky's new master refuses to buy Becky's
baby too, both mother and child sicken because of their
separation. Asked to solve the problem, the conjure woman
sends bees to make the horse lame. Pendleton, who thinks
he made a bad bargain, insists on voiding the deal. The
mother and child are reunited for life.

As William L. Andrews points out, Chesnutt's masters
transcended popular stereotypes as surely as did his slaves.
Mars Marrabo and Colonel Pendleton are neither barba-
rously cruel nor paragons of benevolence. Instead, they are
self-interested and callous toward their slaves' welfare.
Marrabo offers Sandy a dollar in compensation for selling
his first wife. And Pendleton would not have reunited
Becky and her child if he had not feared losing in a
financial transaction. Even harsh masters are redeemable if
they can be shocked out of their callousness. In "Mars
Jeem's Nightmare," a conjure woman transforms a heartless master into a slave himself; he awakens a more
humane man.

If the characteristics of the slaves and their masters are
extended beyond stereotypes, so is the character of Chesnutt's raconteur, the ex-slave Uncle Julius. Ostensibly cut
in the mold of Uncle Remus, Julius illustrates a degree of
self-interest and guile that transcends that stereotype.
Unlike the typical narrators of Southern reconciliation
fiction, he does not tell his tales because he is nostalgic for
slavery days. He is usually motivated by a desire to
manipulate his employers—transplanted Yankees—into
acting in his interests instead of their own. Julius's imaginative storytelling acts in a sense as his conjuring power
over his employers. In "The Goophered Grapevine" he
recites an elaborate tale claiming that the grapes he is
enjoying are conjured because he does not want the
Northerner owning them. In "The Gray Wolf's Ha'nt" he
claims that the woods the new owner plans to clear are
haunted by a slave changed into a wolf by a vengeful
conjure man. His real motive is to preserve for his own
enjoyment a bee tree full of honey.

Chesnutt's other famous story collection, *The Wife of His
Youth,* like *The Conjure Woman,* contradicts popular social
prejudices, but in this case they chiefly concern mulatto
characters. The stories contained in this volume are not
fabulous like *The Conjure Woman*; they provide a more
realistic treatment of the problems of people of color. Set in
the South or among the bourgeois African-American societies of Northern cities, their overriding purpose, as Chesnutt records in his journal, was to elevate America from
"the unjust spirit of caste," which was "a barrier to the
moral progress of the American people."

A common topic in *The Wife of His Youth* is the search
for identity and the ambivalences a person of mixed blood
experiences on such a search. Chesnutt portrays these
ambivalences through the extensive use of irony. For
example, "The Sheriff's Children" is an account of a young
mulatto man falsely accused of killing a white man in a
small Southern town. Ironically, the sheriff who conscientiously protects the young man from a lynch mob is the
father who, during slavery, sold the boy and his black

mother. Thus, the son's reunion with his father can only be a bitterly ironic one. Indeed, the young man's entire life has been filled with the unresolvable conflict of the tragic mulatto: "You gave me a white man's spirit, and you made me a slave, and crushed it out." Another layer of irony is added when the sheriff's daughter, the accused's half-sister, shoots her brother in order to save the sheriff. The story's title suggests that the sins of the father are visited upon his children. In historical terms, the unnatural events caused by the sheriff's original neglect of duty suggest that the postwar South continued to suffer for its prewar racial exploitation.

Chesnutt also effectively used satire to explore comic dimensions of the color line. In "A Matter of Principle" Cicero Clayton, a bourgeois gentleman of light skin, states that the solution to the race question in America is "a clearer conception of the brotherhood of man." However, it is "a matter of principle" with him that he refuses to be grouped with or associate with dark-skinned Negroes. When he fears that a congressman from South Carolina who is coming to pay suit to his daughter is dark-skinned, he feigns a case of diphtheria to get out of the situation. Ironically, it turns out that the congressman was light-skinned, eligible, and marries a rival of Cicero's daughter.

Chesnutt's preoccupation with African-Americans' attempts to maintain their dignity in the face of the dehumanizing effects of slavery and postwar color prejudice resulted in two rich collections as well as dozens of uncollected short stories. Drawing on the superstitions of folk characters, he captured the manner in which the creative imagination was employed to aid in a wholesome survival. Employing irony, he depicted the ambiguities in the lives of mulatto characters as they adjusted to a life of marginal freedom.

—William L. Howard

See the essays on "The Goophered Grapevine" and "The Wife of His Youth."

———

CHESTERTON, G(ilbert) K(eith). English. Born in Kensington, London, 29 May 1874. Educated at Colet Court School, London; St. Paul's School, London (editor, the *Debater*, 1891–93), 1887–92; a drawing school in St. John's Wood, London, 1892; Slade School of Art, London, 1893–96. Married Frances Alice Blogg in 1901. Staff member, Redway, 1896, and T. Fisher Unwin, 1896–1902, publishers, London; columnist, London *Daily News*, 1901–13, and *Illustrated London News*, 1905–36; moved to Beaconsfield, Buckinghamshire, 1909; founder, with Cecil Chesterton and Hilaire Belloc, and editor, with others, *Eye Witness*, London, 1911–12; contributor, London *Daily Herald*, 1913–14; editor, New Witness, London, 1916–23; leader of the Distributist movement from 1919, and president of the Distributist League; joined Roman Catholic church, 1922; editor, with H. Jackson and R. Brimley Johnson, Readers' Classics series, 1922; editor, *G.K.'s Weekly*, London, 1925–36; lecturer, Notre Dame University, Indiana, 1930; radio broadcaster, BBC, 1930's. Also an illustrator: illustrated some of his own works and books by Hilaire Belloc and E.C. Bentley. President, Detection Club, 1928. Honorary degrees: Edinburgh, Dublin, and Notre Dame universities. Fellow, Royal Society of Literature.

Knight Commander with Star, Order of St. Gregory the Great, 1934. *Died 14 June 1936.*

PUBLICATIONS

Collections

Selected Stories, edited by Kingsley Amis. 1972.
As I Was Saying: A Chesterton Reader, edited by Robert Knille. 1985.
The Bodley Head Chesterton, edited by P.J. Kavanagh. 1985; as *The Essential Chesterton,* 1987.
Collected Works, edited by D.J. Conlon. 1987—.

Short Stories

The Tremendous Adventures of Major Brown. 1903.
The Club of Queer Trades. 1905.
The Innocence of Father Brown. 1911; edited by Martin Gardner, 1987.
The Perishing of the Pendragons. 1914.
The Wisdom of Father Brown. 1914.
The Man Who Knew Too Much and Other Stories. 1922.
Tales of the Long Bow. 1925.
The Incredulity of Father Brown. 1926.
The Secret of Father Brown. 1927.
(Stories). 1928.
The Sword of Wood. 1928.
The Poet and the Lunatic: Episodes in the Life of Gabriel Gale. 1929.
The Moderate Murderer, and The Honest Quack. 1929.
The Ecstatic Thief. 1930.
Four Faultless Felons. 1930.
The Floating Admiral, with others. 1931.
The Scandal of Father Brown. 1935.
The Paradoxes of Mr. Pond. 1936.
The Coloured Lands (includes non-fiction). 1938.
The Vampire of the Village. 1947.
Father Brown: Selected Stories, edited by Ronald Knox. 1955.
The Penguin Complete Father Brown. 1981; as *The Father Brown Omnibus,* 1983.
Daylight and Nightmare: Uncollected Stories and Fables, edited by Marie Smith. 1986.
Thirteen Detectives: Classic Mystery Stories, edited by Marie Smith. 1987.
The Best of Father Brown, edited by H.R.F. Keating. 1987.
Seven Suspects, edited by Marie Smith. 1990.

Novels

The Napoleon of Notting Hill. 1904.
The Man Who Was Thursday: A Nightmare. 1908.
The Ball and the Cross. 1909.
Manalive. 1912.
The Flying Inn. 1914.
The Return of Don Quixote. 1927.

Plays

Magic: A Fantastic Comedy (produced 1913). 1913.
The Judgment of Dr. Johnson (produced 1932). 1927.
The Surprise (produced 1953). 1953.

Verse

Greybeards at Play: Literature and Art for Old Gentlemen: Rhymes and Sketches. 1900.
The Wild Knight and Other Poems. 1900; revised edition, 1914.
The Ballad of the White Horse. 1911.
Poems. 1915.
Wine, Water, and Song. 1915.
Old King Cole. 1920.
The Ballad of St. Barbara and Other Verses. 1922.
(Poems). 1925.
The Queen of Seven Swords. 1926.
The Collected Poems. 1927; revised edition, 1932.
Gloria in Profundis. 1927.
Ubi Ecclesia. 1929.
The Grave of Arthur. 1930.
Greybeards at Play and Other Comic Verse, edited by John Sullivan. 1974.
Collected Nonsense and Light Verse, edited by Marie Smith. 1987.

Other

The Defendant. 1901.
Twelve Types. 1902; augmented edition, as *Varied Types,* 1903; selections, as *Five Types,* 1910; and as *Simplicity and Tolstoy,* 1912.
Thomas Carlyle. 1902.
Robert Louis Stevenson, with W. Robertson Nicoll. 1903.
Leo Tolstoy, with G.H. Perris and Edward Garnett. 1903.
Charles Dickens, with F.G. Kitton. 1903.
Robert Browning. 1903.
Tennyson, with Richard Garnett. 1903.
Thackeray, with Lewis Melville. 1903.
G.F. Watts. 1904.
Heretics. 1905.
Charles Dickens. 1906.
All Things Considered. 1908.
Orthodoxy. 1908.
George Bernard Shaw. 1909; revised edition, 1935.
Tremendous Trifles. 1909.
What's Wrong with the World. 1910.
Alarms and Discursions. 1910.
William Blake. 1910.
The Ultimate Lie. 1910.
A Chesterton Calendar. 1911; as *Wit and Wisdom of Chesterton,* 1911; as *Chesterton Day by Day,* 1912.
Appreciations and Criticisms of the Works of Charles Dickens. 1911.
A Defence of Nonsense and Other Essays. 1911.
The Future of Religion: Chesterton's Reply to Mr. Bernard Shaw. 1911.
The Conversion of an Anarchist. 1912.
A Miscellany of Men. 1912.
The Victorian Age in Literature. 1913.
Thoughts from Chesterton, edited by Elsie E. Morton. 1913.
The Barbarism of Berlin. 1914.
London, photographs by Alvin Langdon Coburn. 1914.
Prussian Versus Belgian Culture. 1914.
Letters to an Old Garibaldian. 1915; with *The Barbarism of Berlin,* as *The Appetite of Tyranny.* 1915.
The So-Called Belgian Bargain. 1915.
The Crimes of England. 1915.
Divorce Versus Democracy. 1916.
Temperance and the Great Alliance. 1916.

The Chesterton Calendar, edited by H. Cecil Palmer. 1916.
A Shilling for My Thoughts, edited by E.V. Lucas. 1916.
Lord Kitchener. 1917.
A Short History of England. 1917.
Utopia of Usurers and Other Essays. 1917.
How to Help Annexation. 1918.
Irish Impressions. 1920.
The Superstition of Divorce. 1920.
Charles Dickens Fifty Years After. 1920.
The Uses of Diversity: A Book of Essays. 1920.
The New Jerusalem. 1920.
Eugenics and Other Evils. 1922.
What I Saw in America. 1922.
Fancies Versus Fads. 1923.
St. Francis of Assisi. 1923.
The End of the Roman Road: A Pageant of Wayfarers. 1924.
The Superstitions of the Sceptic. 1925.
The Everlasting Man. 1925.
William Cobbett. 1925.
The Outline of Sanity. 1926.
The Catholic Church and Conversion. 1926.
Selected Works (Minerva Edition). 9 vols., 1926.
A Gleaming Cohort, Being Selections from the Works of Chesterton, edited by E.V. Lucas. 1926.
Social Reform Versus Birth Control. 1927.
Robert Louis Stevenson. 1927.
Generally Speaking: A Book of Essays. 1928.
(Essays). 1928.
Do We Agree? A Debate, with Bernard Shaw. 1928.
A Chesterton Catholic Anthology, edited by Patrick Braybrooke. 1928.
The Thing (essays). 1929.
G.K.C. a M.C., Being a Collection of Thirty-Seven Introductions, edited by J.P. de Fonseka. 1929.
The Resurrection of Rome. 1930.
Come to Think of It: A Book of Essays. 1930.
The Turkey and the Turk. 1930.
At the Sign of the World's End. 1930.
Is There a Return to Religion? with E. Haldeman-Julius. 1931.
All Is Grist: A Book of Essays. 1931.
Chaucer. 1932.
Sidelights on New London and Newer York and Other Essays. 1932.
Christendom in Dublin. 1932.
All I Survey: A Book of Essays. 1933.
St. Thomas Aquinas. 1933.
Chesterton (selected humour), edited by E.V. Knox. 1933; as *Running after One's Hat and Other Whimsies,* 1933.
Avowals and Denials: A Book of Essays. 1934.
The Well and the Shallows. 1935.
Explaining the English. 1935.
Stories, Essays and Poems. 1935.
As I Was Saying: A Book of Essays. 1936.
Autobiography. 1936.
The Man Who Was Chesterton, edited by Raymond T. Bond. 1937.
Essays, edited by John Guest. 1939.
The End of the Armistice, edited by F.J. Sheed. 1940.
Selected Essays, edited by Dorothy Collins. 1949.
The Common Man. 1950.
Essays, edited by K.E. Whitehorn. 1953.
A Handful of Authors: Essays on Books and Writers, edited by Dorothy Collins. 1953.

The Glass Walking-Stick and Other Essays from the Illustrated London News 1905–1936, edited by Dorothy Collins.   1955.
Chesterton: An Anthology, edited by D.B. Wyndham Lewis.   1957.
Essays and Poems, edited by Wilfrid Sheed.   1958.
Lunacy and Letters (essays), edited by Dorothy Collins.   1958.
Where All Roads Lead.   1961.
The Man Who Was Orthodox: A Selection from the Uncollected Writings of Chesterton, edited by A.L. Maycock.   1963.
The Spice of Life and Other Essays, edited by Dorothy Collins.   1964.
Chesterton: A Selection from His Non-Fictional Prose, edited by W.H. Auden.   1970.
Chesterton on Shakespeare, edited by Dorothy Collins.   1971.
The Apostle and the Wild Ducks, and Other Essays, edited by Dorothy Collins.   1975.
The Spirit of Christmas: Stories, Poems, Essays, edited by Marie Smith.   1984.

Editor, *Thackeray* (selections).   1909.
Editor, with Alice Meynell, *Samuel Johnson* (selections).   1911.
Editor, *Love and Freindship* (sic) by Jane Austen.   1922.
Editor, *Essays by Divers Hands 6*.   1926.
Editor, *G.K.'s* (miscellany from *G.K.'s Weekly*).   1934.

*

Bibliography: *Chesterton: A Bibliography* by John Sullivan, 1958, supplement, 1968, and *Chesterton 3: A Bibliographical Postscript*, 1980.

Critical Studies: *On the Place of Chesterton in English Letters* by Hilaire Belloc, 1940; *Chesterton*, 1943, and *Return to Chesterton*, 1952, both by Maisie Ward; *Paradox in Chesterton* by Hugh Kenner, 1947; *Chesterton*, 1950 (revised edition, 1954, 1964), and *The Mind of Chesterton*, 1970, both by Christopher Hollis; *Chesterton: Man and Mask* by Garry Wills, 1961; *Chesterton: A Biography* by Dudley Barker, 1973; *Chesterton* by Lawrence J. Clipper, 1974; *Chesterton: A Centennial Appraisal* by John Sullivan, 1974; *The Novels of Chesterton: A Study in Art and Propaganda* by Ian Boyd, 1975; *Chesterton, Belloc, Baring* by Raymond Las Vergnas, 1975; *Chesterton: The Critical Judgments 1900–1937*, 1976, and *Chesterton: A Half Century of Views*, 1987, both edited by D.J. Conlon; *Chesterton, Radical Populist* by Margaret Canovan, 1977; *Chesterton and the Twentieth-Century English Essay* edited by Banshi Dhar, 1977; *Chesterton: Explorations in Allegory* by Lynette Hunter, 1979; *Chesterton and Hilaire Belloc: The Battle Against Modernity* by Jay P. Corrin, 1981; *The Outline of Sanity: A Biography of Chesterton* by Alzina Stone Dale, 1982; *Chesterton and the Edwardian Cultural Crisis* by John Coates, 1984; *Chesterton: A Seer of Science* by Stanley L. Jaki, 1986; *Chesterton: A Critical Study* by K. Dwarakanath, 1986; *Chesterton* by Michael Ffinch, 1986; *Chesterton: Philosopher Without Portfolio* by Quentin Laver, 1988; *The Riddle of Joy: Chesterton and C.S. Lewis* edited by Michael H. Macdonald and Andrew A. Tadie, 1989; *Gilbert: The Man Who Was Chesterton* by Michael Coren, 1989; *G.K.'s Weekly: An Appraisal* by Brocard Sewell, 1990.

*   *   *

G.K. Chesterton's stories can be divided into the secular and the religious, but both have several features in common. Both kinds have strong elements of extravagance and fantastic high spirits, tempered by sharp and sudden doses of common sense. He is always aiming to make the familiar appear in its pristine strangeness, to peel away the coarsening layers of habit, so that a weed or a London street or a suburban family may appear romantic and glorious. As we can see from his autobiography (especially the chapter entitled "How To Be a Lunatic"), he considered that he had attained sanity and religious truth by passing through something near to madness; and this is reflected in the stories as in the essays. His descriptive passages are not only sharply observed, but often imply social criticism; for instance the following contains a critique of fruitless aristocratic opulence: "outlying parts of a great house, regularly swept and garnished for a master who never comes."

Though some of the stories were written after 1918, the secular ones are usually pervaded with the atmosphere of Edwardian public life, stating or implying his dislike of the imperialism of Rhodes and Kipling (he had been among the small minority who was proud to be called a pro-Boer), the corruption of the Marconi scandal, and a society where, as he thought, power and opulence had become complacent and cynical. Often there is a leading character who expresses these views. Such is Horne Fisher in "The Man Who Knew Too Much," who says "I know too much. That's what's the matter with me," and who penetrates to the "daylight on the other side of strange scenery."

In a particularly fantastic collection *The Club of Queer Trades* there are men with professions like the "organizer of repartee" who is employed to be the feed at fashionable dinner parties for a man with a Wilde-like reputation for impromptu wit. Other characters include a man who has invented a wordless language through dancing, and a man paid to impersonate vicars and colonels, whose endless calls keep impatient but polite people at home when their presence elsewhere would be unwelcome. In "Tales of the Long Bow" the central figure is Crane, whose casual good manners contrast with the vulgarities of the new rich.

But it is on the religious stories, centred on Father Brown, that Chesterton's reputation as a story writer mainly rests. He describes the character's origin in the 16th chapter of his autobiography:

> In Father Brown, it was the chief feature to be featureless. The point of him was to appear pointless. . . .I made his appearance shabby and shapeless, his face round and expressionless, his manners clumsy. . . . At the same time I did take some of his inner intellectual qualities from my friend, Father John O'Connor of Bradford. . . . a sensitive and quick-witted Irishman, with the profound irony and some of the potential irritability of his race.

It is interesting that he thus took as a model for his character, in his own Anglo-Catholic days, a Roman Catholic priest, and one who was eventually to receive him into the Catholic Church.

The main idea of these stories was simple and fruitful, to give that popular genre of the detective story a core of Christian thought and feeling, so that criminals and victims and witnesses might be judged, not as the law courts judge, but as gifted spiritual advisers might judge. Of course, this meant that the reader had to accept the obvious improbability that Father Brown always happened to be hanging about when a murder was about to be committed, and that his parish duties never seemed onerous. The other recurrent character is Flambeau, the thief, who is outwitted by Father Brown in "The Blue Cross," and who signalizes his repentance by returning the jewels he has stolen in an atmosphere of uproarious Christmas farce in "The Flying Stars." Afterwards he is often a valued assistant in the priest's investigations.

Father Brown is a firm supporter of common sense and homely virtues, at the same time as he is, like his creator, a lover of paradox. Very characteristic is "The Scandal of Father Brown," where the priest is suspected of conniving at adultery, because the actual adulterer looks dull and elderly (like a stock idea of a husband), while the husband has the appearance of a curly-headed lover. When the American journalist shows his prejudices about "Wops and Dagos," Father Brown has his wider context:

Well, there was a Dago, or possibly a Wop, called Julius Caesar; he was afterwards killed in a stabbing match; you know these Dagos always use knives. And there was another one called Augustine, who brought Christianity to our little island.

Many of the stories are aimed against esoteric cults, pseudo-oriental magic, and cranky religions. Thus in "The Blast of the Book," the book, a glance into which is supposed to make the reader disappear, proves to consist of blank pages, and the ingenious story of its fatal effects are elaborate fabrication.

In other stories the inconsistency of the casual assumptions of the world is exposed to witty ridicule, as in "The Worst Crime in the World," where a mother's wish for a prudent marriage for her daughter would have meant mating her with a man who has murdered his father. In "The Invisible Man," the caller that no one noticed is the postman, who is also the murderer, and the story ends with Father Brown giving him spiritual counsel. Very characteristic is Father Brown's description of the postman's uniform; "He is dressed handsomely in red, blue and gold." Chesterton really did see familiar things like that.

The odd similarity in the dress of fashionable diners and those who wait on them leads, in "The Queer Feet" to an ingenious story in which a thief deceives the diners into thinking he is a waiter, and the waiters into thinking he is a diner, but the upshot, that the members of the Club agree to meet in green dinner jackets to avoid being mistaken for waiters, has a symbolic value as a critique of the meaningless extravagance of a plutocracy lacking a real social function. The conventionality of many who deem themselves bold and revolutionary thinkers is satirized in "The Crime of the Communist," where a communist don can talk of bloody revolution, but would be horrified at the thought of smoking before the port.

Few have succeeded so well as Chesterton in combining a thoughtful interpretation of life with amusing fantasies.

—A.O.J. Cockshut

CHOPIN, Kate (Katherine Chopin, née O'Flaherty). American. Born in St. Louis, Missouri, 8 February 1851. Educated at the Academy of the Sacred Heart, St. Louis,

graduated 1868. Married Oscar Chopin in 1870 (died 1883); five sons and one daughter. Lived in New Orleans, 1870–79, on her husband's plantation in Cloutierville, Louisiana, 1880–82, and in St. Louis after 1884. *Died 22 August 1904.*

PUBLICATIONS

Collections

Complete Works, edited by Per Seyersted.   2 vols., 1969.

Short Stories

Bayou Folk.   1894.
A Night in Acadie.   1897.
The Awakening and Other Stories, edited by Lewis Leary.   1970.
Portraits: Short Stories, edited by Helen Taylor.   1979.
The Awakening and Selected Stories, edited by Sandra M. Gilbert.   1984.

Novels

At Fault.   1890.
The Awakening.   1899; edited by Margaret Culley, 1976.

Other

A Chopin Miscellany, edited by Per Seyersted and Emily Toth.   1979.

*

Bibliography: in *Bibliography of American Literature* by Jacob Blanck, 1957; *Edith Wharton and Chopin: A Reference Guide* by Marlene Springer, 1976.

Critical Studies: *Chopin and Her Creole Stories* by Daniel S. Rankin, 1932; *The American 1890's: Life and Times of a Lost Generation* by Larzer Ziff, 1966; *Chopin: A Critical Biography* by Per Seyersted, 1969; *Chopin* by Peggy Skaggs, 1985; *Chopin* by Barbara C. Ewell, 1986; *Forbidden Fruit: On the Relationship Between Women and Knowledge in Doris Lessing, Slema Lagerlöf, Chopin, and Margaret Atwood* by Bonnie St. Andrews, 1986; *New Essays on The Awakening* edited by Wendy Martin, 1988; *Chopin* by Emily Toth, 1988; *Gender, Race, and Religion in the Writings of Grace King, Ruth McEnery Stuart, and Chopin* by Helen Taylor, 1989; *Verging on the Abyss: the Social Fiction of Chopin and Edith Wharton* by Mary E. Papke, 1990; *Chopin Reconsidered: Beyond the Bayou* edited by Lynda S. Boren and Sara deSaussure Davis, 1992.

* * *

Kate Chopin wrote nearly a hundred stories between her first critically undistinguished novel *At Fault* and her last major work *The Awakening*, which critics found "shocking" and "immoral." Two volumes were published in her lifetime—*Bayou Folk* and *A Night in Acadie*—and others were printed in magazines such as *Youth's Companion, Atlantic Monthly*, and *Vogue*. Recurring characters appear in many of the stories so that, according to one critic, they "maintain artistic autonomy and yet appear strangely related to one another."

Chopin's first works were ranked with those of regionalists George Washington Cable and Grace King and praised for their reflection of "the quaint and picturesque life among the Creole and Acadian folk of the Louisiana bayous" ("A Very Fine Fiddle," "Boulôt and Boulotte," "Beyond the Bayou"). The earliest stories, set primarily in Natchitoches (pronounced Nackitosh) parish, deal with both Creoles, the French-speaking, Catholic middle or upper class, and, less often, Cajuns, who tended to be a lower-class French-speaking group originally resettled from Canada ("At Chênière Caminada," "Love on the Bon-Dieu"). But while Chopin was in one sense a local colorist, later critics have also recognized her work as an early form of both social and regional realism in the tradition of Rebecca Harding Davis, Ellen Glasglow, and Willa Cather.

Chopin did not start writing seriously until she was in her late thirties. As she developed as a writer, she called on her wide reading for literary models. She admired Sarah Orne Jewett (1849–1909) and Mary E. Wilkins Freeman (1852–1930); critics agree, however, that the major influences on her work were French—Gustave Flaubert, whose *Madame Bovary* (1857) presages *The Awakening* and, particularly, Guy de Maupassant whose stories, like Chopin's, are marked by realism, detachment, economy, and irony.

The issues and themes in Chopin's work are varied. Although most of her stories emphasize character over plot, some are no more than brief character sketches ("Old Aunt Peggy," "Elizabeth Stock's One Story," "Juanita"). Some deal with family relationships, those between siblings ("Ma'ame Pélagie," "A Family Affair") and those between parent and child ("Charlie," "A Rude Awakening"). Some, such as "A Little Free-Mulatto," "Ozème's Holiday," "The Bênitous' Slave" and "Nég Créol," explore the complicated relationship between blacks and whites. "La Belle Zoraïde" is one of Chopin's most powerful stories, centered on a mistress who raises a beautiful black girl, insisting that a mulatto is the only man she should marry. When she falls in love with the black Mézor, Madame Delarivìere has him sold; when Zoraïde bears his child, her mistress tells her it died at birth. The story not only raises the issues of control and racial identity but of grief and loss in the image of the demented Zoraïde clinging to a bundle of rags which she insists is her baby. Maternity is held up throughout Chopin's work as a force which overcomes dissatisfaction, the loss of which brings pain ("Athénaïse," "Regret"). In this sense it is somewhat ironic that Chopin, who lived a rather exemplary private life, should have been condemned for her refusal to uphold, in her writing, society's moral view of marriage and motherhood.

And yet, many of her stories do involve dissatisfied women trapped in unhappy marriages with a "sense of hopelessness, an instinctive realization of the futility of rebellion against a social and sacred institution." Some women do not even recognize their unhappiness until they are unexpectedly released ("The Story of an Hour") and some, such as Mentine in "A Visit to Avoyelles," seem resigned to being dissipated by overwork and childbearing. "In Sabine" centers on 'Tite Reine, who has "changed a good deal" since her marriage—a visitor finds her thinner, uneasy, and distressed, but emboldened finally to leave her abusive husband. The most developed story constructed around this theme is "Athénaïse" in which a wife loses her "sense of duty" as Chopin explores the "Gordian knot of marriage" and Athénaïse explains, "I don't hate him . . . It's jus' being married that I detes' an' despise."

Although Chopin, whose work fell into critical neglect soon after her death in 1904, was resurrected by feminist scholars in the 1960's, her sensibilities are often channeled through male protagonists, many of whom embody or articulate not the female but the human condition. Gouvernail, for example, who appears in a number of works ("A Respectable Woman," "Athénaïse," *The Awakening*) believes the "primordial fact of existence" to be that "things seemed all wrongly arranged in this world, and no one was permitted to be happy in his own way." Many men in Chopin are patient, sensitive, considerate souls who even in the grips of human selfishness follow a gentleman's code. They fall in love easily and passionately, overly susceptible to women's charms. Numerous stories are built around a "coup de foudre" where a man suddenly "abandon[s] himself completely to his passion" against all reason, sometimes coming to his senses and sometimes finding true love ("At the 'Cadian Ball," "Love on the Bon-Dieu," "A No-Account Creole").

Both men and women in Chopin's stories are "attuned to the natural flow of their own emotions"; they are "alive and keen and responsive" in the immediacy of the moment and do not become entangled in guilt, anxiety, or anguished self-analysis. According to one biographer, Per Seyersted, "Chopin concentrated on the immutable impulses of love and sex." She was deeply influenced by Walt Whitman in this regard, and quotes him in her work. The sexuality and eroticism of some of her stories ("Lilacs," "Two Portraits," "A Vocation and a Voice") shocked editors, but Seyersted sees in stories like "The Storm" a foreshadowing of D.H. Lawrence where sexuality reflects not wantonness but "a mystic contact with the elements."

Chopin's universe, finally, is both cruel and moral in its own way, presided over by hope, faith, providence, nature, and eros. The greatest crime is perhaps indifference ("The Godmother"), as Chopin acknowledges "the supremacy of the moving power which is love; which is life."

—Deborah Kelly Kloepfer

See the essays on "Désirée's Baby" and "A Pair of Silk Stockings."

———

CLARKE, Austin C(hesterfield). Barbadian. Born in Barbados. 26 July 1934. Educated at Combermere Boys' School. Barbados; Harrison's College, Barbados; Trinity College, University of Toronto. Married Betty Joyce Reynolds in 1957; two daughters. Reporter in Timmins and Kirkland Lake, Ontario, Toronto, 1959–60; freelance producer and broadcaster, Canadian Broadcasting Corporation. Toronto, from 1963; scriptwriter, Educational Television, Toronto; Jacob Ziskind Professor of Literature, Brandeis University, Waltham, Massachusetts, 1968–69; Hoyt Fellow, 1968, and visiting lecturer, 1969, 1970, Yale University, New Haven, Connecticut; fellow, Indiana University School of Letters, Bloomington, 1969; Margaret Bundy Scott Visiting Professor of Literature, Williams College, Williamstown, Massachusetts, 1971; lecturer, Duke University, Durham, North Carolina, 1971–72; visiting professor, University of Texas, Austin, 1973–74; cultural and press attaché, Embassy of Barbados, Washington, D.C., 1974–76; writer-in-residence, Concordia University, Montreal, 1977; General manager. Caribbean Broadcasting Corporation, St. Michael, Barbados, 1975–76. Member, Board of Trustees, Rhode Island School of Design, Providence, 1970–75; Vice-Chairman, Ontario Board of Censors, 1983–85. Since 1988 member, Immigration and Refugee Board of Canada. Recipient: Belmont short story award, 1965; University of Western Ontario President's medal, 1966; Canada Council senior arts fellowship, 1967, 1970, and grant, 1977; Casa de las Americas prize, 1980; Toronto Art award, 1992. Lives in Toronto.

PUBLICATIONS

Short Stories

When He Was Free and Young and He Used to Wear Silks.
1971; expanded edition, 1973.
When Women Rule.   1985.
Nine Men Who Laughed.   1986.

Novels

The Survivors of the Crossing.   1964.
Amongst Thistles and Thorns.   1965.
The Meeting Point.   1967.
Storm of Fortune.   1973.
The Bigger Light.   1975.
The Prime Minister.   1977.
Proud Empires.   1986.

Other

The Confused Bewilderment of Martin Luther King and the Idea of Non-Violence as a Political Tactic.   1968.
Growing Up Stupid under the Union Jack: A Memoir.
1980.

*

Critical Studies: interview with Graeme Gibson, in *Eleven Canadian Novelists,* 1974; "An Assessment of Austin Clarke, West Indian-Canadian Novelist" by Keith Henry in *CLA Journal,* 29(1), 1985; *Biographical-Critical Study of Clarke* by Stella Algoo-Baken, 1992.

*   *   *

Austin C. Clarke, who was born in Barbados and emigrated to Canada in 1955, is unquestionably the most important black Canadian writer. He has written numerous novels and stories about a community that is much larger and has had a more central role in Canadian history than most Canadians realize.

Clarke's characters hold ambivalent attitudes toward both the Caribbean and Canada. Those who live in the West Indies love their home because it is their home, but despise its enervating poverty, corruption, and parochialism. They look to North America, particularly Canada, as a land of infinite possibilities, a place where fortunes and a "better life" can be made; in other words, as a source of hope. His characters who have emigrated, however, see that Canada is really a place where opportunity is limited by social position and, above all, race. Most arrive in Canada as maids (under Canada's Domestic Immigration Scheme) or unemployed, and learn that to be black in Toronto during the 1950's and 1960's is to see dreams and illusions shattered. Some look back nostalgically at their island homes, comparing them favourably to a city that is "cold" in both the literal and figurative senses. Lloyd W. Brown has called these images of the Caribbean and Canada "Paradise" and "El Dorado"—both homes are idealized when seen from a distance. Out of frustration at their failure, Clarke's characters often turn to verbal and, in many cases, physical violence.

Clarke's first collection, *When He Was Free and Young and He Used to Wear Silks,* contains a number of stories dramatizing the first encounters of West Indian immigrants with Toronto. Like Clarke himself, they were brought up in another British colony, and so arrive expecting to feel at home in a country that is as close to England itself as they can reach, and one that in addition will offer the vast opportunities they have come to expect from North American life. But they find that the Canadian version of the American Dream proves false, even when they manage to attain some material success. In "They Heard a Ringing of Bells," four friends sit on the campus of the University of Toronto reviewing how their dreams of success have led to nothing but poverty and illness. At the beginning of the story one character refers to Canada as "a damn great country," but after they revel in nostalgia over their island homes Canada becomes "chilly as hell." Enid Scantlebury, in "Waiting for the Postman to Knock," both yearns for and dreads the next such knock—what comes may be a cheque or yet another unpaid and unpayable bill. Those who do gain material success find that their new possessions—like Calvin's purchase, the title object in "The Motor Car," and Jefferson Theophillis Belle's house in "Four Stations in His Circle"—leave them fundamentally unsatisfied. The hollowness of Belle's empty Rosedale mansion symbolizes his own spiritual hollowness, and that of everyone—resident as well as immigrant—who seeks fulfillment in material wealth.

These characters experience a bewildering culture clash when their more vibrant, emotional, brashly expressive lifestyle comes up against Canadian reserve and public stoicism. "A Wedding in Toronto," for example, shows what happens when a marriage celebration in Caribbean style becomes the object of noise complaints and an eventual police raid. What immigration produces for all of Clarke's characters is a kind of cultural split personality; they are fully alienated figures, as they endeavour to abandon their earlier, West Indian identities but cannot quite become Anglo-Canadians. They exist in a cultural borderland torn between past and future, nostalgia and hope, and above all who they are, were, and would like to be.

Clarke's later collections, *When Women Rule* and *Nine Men Who Laughed,* are concerned less with the immigrant experience and more with Canadian society in general, although Clarke still focuses on immigrants, whose experiences most clearly highlight what is wrong with that society. It may be surprising to note that in Clarke's stories almost as many white as black characters are shown chasing unattainable or unworthy dreams. As a "moral idealist," in Brown's terms, Clarke sees much to criticize in North America's corrupting materialism and mass-market pressure to seek wealth and conformity. The promise of affluence and Canada's illusory cultural and social harmony—the myth of the Canadian "mosaic"—conflicts with the reality as characters find poverty and alienation rather than success and community. Pat, the Scottish-Canadian protagonist of "Give It a Shot," and the Barbadian title character of "Griff!" both strive for instant success through gambling, with predictable results. In "Doing Right" Cleveland begins his career thinking he can succeed within the system by being a Green Hornet, then turns to running a corrupt towing service when he sees how limited his opportunities for advancement are.

Perhaps the most illustrative example of the hollowness of the Canadian way of life is Joshua Miller-Corbaine of "A Man" and "How He Does It" in *Nine Men Who Laughed.* The unemployed Miller-Corbaine has crafted an elaborate false identity for himself as a successful and important lawyer, for the benefit of his mistresses and his own sense of self-worth. Like so many of Clarke's characters, Miller-Corbaine has no identity, or must adopt many identities to be accepted by white upper-class Canadian society. One striking image in "Canadian Experience," from the same collection, reflects how Canadians in general and immigrants in particular suffer from a fragmented identity in our alienated and alienating environment: on his way to a probably futile job interview, George sees a reflection in a glass office building that "tears him into strides and splatters his suit against four glass panels, and makes him disjointed."

The alienation that immigrants experience is conveyed most strikingly through their language. Clarke frequently recreates the West Indian dialect, not only in his dialogue but frequently in his narrative voice as well, to emphasize his immigrants' status as outsiders. The clash between the dialect and what is said creates much of the fiction's ironic tone and satirical thrust. But Clarke aims the satire at Canada as well as his self-deluding immigrants, and skewers academic and institutional jargon—as in "The Discipline" (*When Woman Rule*) and "What Happened" (*When He Was Free*).

But Clarke's fiction is not bleak. While he despises material ambition as a hollow pursuit, he admires the passionate energy and irrepressible hope that fuel it. While he scorns the naive search for greener pastures, he has no illusions about the physical and spiritual corruption engendered by third-world poverty. Overall, his fiction celebrates the human capacity to create ideals and then pursue them, regardless of the cost to one's health, wealth, or sense of identity.

—Allan Weiss

CLARKE, Marcus (Andrew Hislop). Australian. Born in Kensington, London, 24 April 1846. Educated at Highgate School, London, 1858–62 (school friend of Gerard Manley Hopkins). Married Marian Dunn in 1869; six children. Emigrated to Australia, 1863; staff member, Bank of Australia, Melbourne, 1863–65; worked on sheep station on the Wimmera River, 1866–67; moved to Melbourne, 1867; contributor to the *Argus* and the *Age*; columnist ("Peripatetic Philosopher"), *Australasian,* 1867–70; owner and editor, *Colonial Monthly,* 1868–69, and *Humbug,* 1869–70; editor, *Australian Journal,* 1870–71; secretary to the trustees, 1870, sub-librarian, 1873, and assistant librarian, 1876–81, Melbourne Public Library; columnist ("Atticus"), the *Leader,* from 1877; declared bankrupt, 1874 and 1881. Founding member, Yorick Club, 1868. *Died 2 August 1881.*

PUBLICATIONS

Collections

The Portable Clarke, edited by Michael Wilding.   1976.
Stories, edited by Michael Wilding.   1983.

Short Stories

Holiday Peak and Other Tales.   1873.
Sensational Tales.   1886.
Four Stories High.   1877.
Australian Tales.   1896.

Novels

Long Odds.   1869; as *Heavy Odds,* 1896.
His Natural Life.   1874; as *For the Term of His Natural Life,* 1885; edited by Stephen Murray-Smith, 1970.
'Twixt Shadow and Shine: An Australian Story of Christmas.   1875.
The Man with the Oblong Box.   1878.
The Mystery of Major Molineaux, and Human Repetends.   1881.
The Conscientious Stranger: A Bullocktown Idyll.   1881.
Chidiock Tichbourne; or, The Catholic Conspiracy.   1893.

Plays

Goody Two Shoes and Little Boy Blue.   1870.
Twinkle, Twinkle, Little Star; or, Harlequin Jack Frost, Little Tom Tucker, and the Old Woman That Lived in a Shoe.   1873.
Reverses.   1876.
Alfred the Great, with H. Keiley (produced 1878).   1879.
The Happy Land, from the play *The Wicked World* by W.S. Gilbert (produced 1880).

Other pantomimes, with R.P. Whitworth.

Other

The Peripatetic Philosopher.   1869.
Old Tales of a Young Country.   1871.
The Future Australian Race.   1877.
Civilization Without Delusion.   1880.
What Is Religion? A Controversy.   1895.
Stories of Australia in the Early Days.   1897.
A Colonial City: High and Low Life: Selected Journalism, edited by L.T. Hergenhan.   1972.

Editor, *History of the Continent of Australia and the Island of Tasmania (1787–1870).*   1877.
Editor, *We 5: A Book for the Season.*   1879.

*

Bibliography: *Clarke: An Annotated Bibliography* by Ian F. McLaren, 1982.

Critical Studies: *Clarke* by Brian Elliott, 1958; *Clarke* by Michael Wilding, 1977.

* * *

Best-known for his classic novel about the convict system in eastern colonial Australia, *For the Term of His Natural Life*, Marcus Clarke, a bohemian journalist based in Melbourne, wrote more than 40 short stories. Only two collections of his short fiction, *Holiday Peak and Other Tales* and *Four Stories High*, were published before his untimely death, at the age of 35 in 1881. His stories cover three categories: frontier sketches and stories of Australian up-country life, magazine stories that conform to Victorian melodrama, and experimental fantasy stories. They are characterized by a certain "romance of reality" that combines the wide reading of a litterateur—particularly influential are Honoré de Balzac, Charles Dickens, Bret Harte, and Edgar Allen Poe—with a vivid, eclectic response to the strange landscape and itinerant figures of colonial Australia.

"Pretty Dick" is universally recognized as his best story. The plot establishes an indigenous Australian myth: the sentimental, if not harrowing, tale of the child lost in the bush, the primitive landscape. The lost child represents the orphan or outcast identity of transplanted Europeans. Pretty Dick, a seven-year-old innocent, is a doomed victim of an archetypal environment—mysterious, grim, and indifferent. This story effectively combines frontier realism with a melodramatic plot and fantasy.

Clarke's first volume of stories, *Holiday Peak*, makes a significant contribution to the pioneering tradition of frontier realism that is developed in Henry Lawson's bush stories of the 1890's. "Bullocktown" uses a first person identification with the country inhabitants and includes the colloquial speech of workers with emphasis on the social importance of drinking at "the public-house bar." "Grumbler's Gully" presents a dark view of drinking in the dreary, even destructive, restraints of country life. It was Clark's only short story published outside Australia. "How The Circus Came to Bullocktown" depicts a carnival clash of opposites between drinkers, teetotalers, and the crazy itinerants of "Buncombe's Imperial Yanko-American Circus." The *Holiday Peak* collection is influenced by Clarke's reading of Bret Harte's *The Luck of Roaring Camp*. Clarke emphasized the importance of "poetry and pathos" in "the ordinary daily life" of a new country. "Poor Joe" imitates Harte's fictional pattern of tragic self-sacrifice in distorted or eccentric figures.

However much Clarke conveys pathos in his stories, he also maintains an ironic distance in his exploration of the macabre, the dream-like and different levels of consciousness. The title story "Holiday Peak" emphasizes a grotesque setting with Egyptian descriptions. A fanciful, most antipodean meeting includes Charles Kingsley playing cards with Newman and Swinburne at Mount Mightha-been. The exaggeration of a frontier yarn is also evident in the exuberant figure of Captain Sporboy in "Romance of Bullocktown." Two other tales, "The Dual Existence" and "The Golden Island," are reminiscent of Poe's style, but "A Haschich Trance" is a bold psychological experiment and a compelling account of writing about a drug "trip" with objective observations. Clarke refers to De Quincey's *Confessions of an English Opium Eater*, and this literary experiment by a young bohemian is an impressive, radical contribution to Australian literature.

His short fiction is most famous for a passage in "Australian Scenery." Though Clarke does not attempt to individualize the Australian landscape or explore his rather repetitive sense of its strangeness in his outback and mining stories, he cites "the dominant note of Edgar Allan Poe's poetry—Weird Melancholy" as "the dominant note of Australian Scenery." This seductive piece of rhetoric illustrates a topsy-turvy view of the new world, a fantasy version that provides a classic commentary for later Australian writers who depict an alien and hostile landscape.

This self-styled "Peripatetic Philosopher" is a very self-aware literary creator. The extremes of laconic realism and reverie explore contemporary issues and unusual experiences. Clarke's belief in scientific progress, his vivid sense of the surreal, his literary use of the archetypes and clichés of fiction reflect an accomplished writer whom Mark Twain noted aptly as "Australia's only literary genius" in his time.

—Mark L. Collins

———

COLETTE, (Sidonie-Gabrielle). French. Born in Saint-Saveur en Puisaye, 28 January 1873. Educated at local school to age 16. Married 1) the writer Henry Gauthier-Villars ("Willy") in 1893 (divorced 1910); 2) Henry de Jouvenal in 1912 (divorced 1925), one daughter; 3) Maurice Goudeket in 1935. Actress and revue performer, 1906–27; columnist, 1910–19, and literary editor, 1919–24, *Le Matin;* drama critic, *La Revue de Paris*, 1929, *Le Journal*, 1934–39, *L'Eclair*, and *Le Petit Parisien;* operated a beauty clinic, Paris, 1932–33. Recipient: City of Paris Grand Médaille, 1953. Member, Belgian Royal Academy, 1936; Member, 1945, and president, 1949, Goncourt Academy; Honorary Member, American Academy, 1953. Chevalier, 1920, Officer, 1928, Commander, 1936, and Grand Officer, 1953, Legion of Honor. *Died 3 August 1954.*

PUBLICATIONS

Collections

Works.   17 vols., 1951–64.
Oeuvres complètes.   16 vols., 1973.
Collected Stories, edited by Robert Phelps.   1983.
Oeuvres, edited by Claude Pichois.   1984—.

Short Stories

La Femme cachée.   1924; as *The Other Woman*, 1971.
Bella-Vista.   1937.
Chambre d'hôtel.   1940; in *Julie de Carneilhan and Chance Acquaintances*, 1952.
Gigi et autres nouvelles.   1944; translated as *Gigi*, 1952.
Stories.   1958; as *The Tender Shoot and Other Stories*, 1959.

Novels

Claudine à l'école, with Willy.   1900; as *Claudine at School*, 1930.
Claudine à Paris, with Willy.   1901; as *Claudine in Paris*, 1931; as *Young Lady of Paris*, 1931.
Claudine amoureuse, with Willy.   1902; as *Claudine en ménage*, 1902; as *The Indulgent Husband*, 1935; as *Claudine Married*, 1960.
Claudine s'en va, with Willy.   1903; as *The Innocent Wife*, 1934; as *Claudine and Annie*, 1962.

Minne; Les Egarements de Minne.   2 vols., 1903–05; revised version, as *L'Ingénue libertine*, 1909; as *The Gentle Libertine*, 1931; as *The Innocent Libertine*, 1968.

Le Retraite sentimentale.   1907; as *Retreat from Love*, 1974.

Les Vrilles de la vigne.   1908.

La Vagabonde.   1911; as *The Vagrant*, 1912; as *Renée la vagabonde*, 1931; as *The Vagabond*, 1954.

L'Entrave.   1913; as *Recaptured*, 1931; as *The Shackle*, 1963.

Les Enfants dans les ruines.   1917.

Dans la foule.   1918.

Mitsou; ou, Comment l'esprit vient aux filles.   1918; as *Mitsou; or, How Girls Grow Wise*, 1930.

La Chambre éclairée.   1920.

Chéri.   1920; translated as *Chéri*, 1929.

Le Blé en herbe.   1923; as *The Ripening Corn*, 1931; as *The Ripening*, 1932; as *Ripening Seed*, 1956.

Quatre saisons.   1925.

Le Fin de Chéri.   1926; as *The Last of Chéri*, 1932.

La Naissance du jour.   1928; as *A Lesson in Love*, 1932; as *Morning Glory*, 1932; as *The Break of Day*, 1961.

La Seconde.   1929; as *The Other One*, 1931; as *Fanny and Jane*, 1931.

Paradises terrestres.   1932.

La Chatte.   1933; as *The Cat*, 1936; as *Saha the Cat*, 1936.

Duo.   1934; translated as *Duo*, 1935; also translated with *The Toutounier*, 1974; as *The Married Lover*, 1935.

Le Toutounier.   1939; as *The Toutounier*, with *Duo*, 1974.

Julie de Carneilhan.   1941; translated as *Julie de Carneilhan*, in *Julie de Carneilhan and Chance Acquaintances*, 1952.

Le Képi.   1943.

Plays

En camerades (produced 1909).   In *Oeuvres complètes 15*, 1950.

Claudine, music by Rodolphe Berger, from the novel by Colette (produced 1910).   1910.

Chéri, with Léopold Marchand, from the novel by Colette (produced 1921).   1922; translated as *Cheri*, 1959.

La Vagabonde, with Léopold Marchand, from the novel by Colette (produced 1923).   1923.

L'Enfant et les sortilèges, music by Maurice Ravel (produced 1925).   1925; as *The Boy and the Magic*, 1964.

La Décapitée (ballet scenario), in *Mes Cahiers*.   1941.

Gigi, with Anita Loos, from the story by Colette (produced 1951).   1952; in French, 1954.

Jeune filles en uniform, Lac aux dames, Divine (screenplays), in *Au Cinéma*.   1975.

Screenplays: *La Vagabonde*, 1917, remake, 1931; *La Femme cachée*, 1919; *Jeunes filles en uniform* (French dialogue for German film *Mädchen in Uniform)*, 1932; *Lac aux dames*, 1934; *Divine*, 1935.

Other

Dialogues de bêtes.   1904; augmented edition, as *Sept dialogues de bêtes*, 1905; as *Douze dialogues de bêtes*, 1930; as *Barks and Purrs*, 1913; as *Creatures Great and Small*, 1951.

L'Envers du music-hall.   1913; as *Music-Hall Sidelights*, 1957.

Prrou, Poucette, et quelques autres.   1913; revised edition, as *La Paix chez les bêtes*, 1916; as *Cats, Dogs, and I*, 1924; also translated in *Creatures Great and Small*, 1951.

Les Heures longues 1914–1917.   1917.

La Maison de Claudine.   1922; as *The Mother of Claudine*, 1937; as *My Mother's House*, 1953.

Le Voyage égoïste.   1922; in part as *Journey for Myself: Selfish Memoirs*, 1971.

Rêverie du nouvel an.   1923.

Aventures quotidiennes.   1924; in *Journey for Myself: Selfish Memoirs*, 1971.

Renée Vivien.   1928.

Sido.   1929; translated as *Sido*, with *My Mother's House*, 1953.

Histoires pour Bel-Gazou.   1930.

La Treille Muscate.   1932.

Prisons et paradis.   1932; in part in *Places*, 1970.

Ces plaisirs.   1932; as *Le Pur et l'impur*, 1941; as *The Pure and the Impure*, 1933; as *These Pleasures*, 1934.

La Jumelle noire (theatre criticism).   4 vols., 1934–38.

Mes apprentissages.   1936; as *My Apprenticeships*, 1957.

Chats.   1936.

Splendeur des papillons.   1937.

Mes cahiers.   1941.

Journal à rebours.   1941; in *Looking Backwards*, 1975.

De ma fenêtre.   1942; augmented edition, as *Paris de ma fenêtre*, 1944; in *Looking Backwards*, 1975.

De la patte à l'aile.   1943.

Flore et Pomone.   1943; as *Flowers and Fruit*, edited by Robert Phelps, 1986.

Nudités.   1943.

Broderie ancienne.   1944.

Trois . . . six . . . neuf.   1944.

Belles Saisons.   1945; as *Belles Saisons: A Colette Scrapbook*, edited by Robert Phelps.   1978.

Une Amitié inattendue (correspondence with Francis Jammes), edited by Robert Mallet.   1945.

L'Étoile vesper.   1946; as *The Evening Star: Recollections*, 1973.

Pour un herbier.   1948; as *For a Flower Album*, 1959.

Oeuvres complètes.   15 vols., 1948–50.

Trait pour trait.   1949.

Journal intermittent.   1949.

Le Fanal bleu.   1949; as *The Blue Lantern*, 1963.

La Fleur de l'âge.   1949.

En pays connu.   1949.

Chats de Colette.   1949.

Paysages et portraits.   1958.

Lettres à Hélène Picard, edited by Claude Pichois.   1958.

Lettres à Marguerite Moréno, edited by Claude Pichois. 1959.

Lettres de la vagabonde, edited by Claude Pichois and Roberte Forbin.   1961.

Lettres au petit corsaire, edited by Claude Pichois and Roberte Forbin.   1963.

Earthly Paradise: An Autobiography Drawn from Her Lifetime of Writing, edited by Robert Phelps.   1966.

Places (miscellany; in English).   1970.

Contes de mille et un matins.   1970; as *The Thousand and One Mornings*, 1973.

Journey for Myself: Selfish Memoirs (selection).   1971.

Lettres à ses pairs, edited by Claude Pichois and Roberte Forbin.   1973.

Au Cinéma, edited by Alain and Odette Virmaux.   1975.

Letters from Colette, edited by Robert Phelps.   1980.

*

Critical Studies: *Madame Colette: A Provincial in Paris*, 1952, and *Colette: The Difficulty of Loving*, 1973, both by Margaret Crosland; *Colette* by Elaine Marks, 1961; *Colette* by Margaret Davies, 1961; *Colette* by R.D. Cottrell, 1974; *Colette: A Taste for Life* by Yvonne Mitchell, 1975; *Colette: Free and Fettered* by Michèle Sarde, translated by Richard Miller, 1981; *Colette: The Woman, The Writer* edited by Erica M. Eisinger and Mari McCarty, 1981; *Colette* by Joanna Richardson, 1983; *Colette: A Passion for Life* by Genevieve Dormann, translated by David Macey, 1985; *Colette* by Allan Massie, 1986; *Colette* by Nicola Ward Jouve, 1987; *Colette: A Life* by Herbert Lottman, 1991; *Colette* by Diana Holmes, 1991; *Colette and the Fantom Subject of Autobiography* by Jerry Aline Flieger, 1992.

*   *   *

Colette's reputation as a writer rests squarely on her novels, although she achieved much more besides: she acted, danced, performed in music-hall and mime; she wrote prolifically for the theatre, the cinema, newspapers, children and, autobiographically, for posterity. Her various collections of short stories and novellas form an important part of her fictional output and have been widely translated. Five major collections of stories were published in her lifetime.

Colette was married three times. After separating from her first husband she had a long and very public lesbian relationship with the Marquise de Belboeuf, known as "Missy." She divorced her second husband as well as the first, before marrying in 1935 a man nearly 17 years her junior. She had a happy childhood, had a daughter by her second husband, and retained throughout her life a strong affinity with animals. All these elements, in conjunction with her intensely varied career, influenced her work. Her short stories were often written as first-person narratives, and in many the narrator was called "Colette." Triggered though they sometimes were by incidents and memories from her life and acquaintanceship, the stories combine fact as well as fiction. Ordinary people are made to appear extraordinary beneath their everyday failings and normality. The drama underlying the apparently conventional surface is carefully and casually observed, and frequently the moral, if not the intellectual, superiority of the female protagonist is a hidden theme.

The 22 stories which make up *La Femme* cachée (*The Other Women*) are very largely narrated in the third person, unlike many of the longer stories and novellas Colette was later to publish. Restricted to about 1500 words, their brevity does not imply, however, a simple reliance on the traditional final twist for effect. About a third of the stories concern married couples, and the surprises, compromises, and intimate understanding that come with marriage. Frequently they are told from the wife's point of view. "The Hand," for instance, describes a newly-wed couple entwined in bed. The wife savours the almost scandalous excitement of being with a husband she scarcely knows, but with whom she is in love. Admiring him in the half-light, she suddenly is repelled by the crablike convulsions of his hand, but in the morning kisses his "monstrous hand" and embarks on that universal, deceitful but diplomatic course of married life.

The psychological adjustment that has to be made after the death, divorce, or departure of a partner is another theme that Colette analyses with great sensitivity. The loneliness following such a break in a relationship, whether marital or lesbian, is conveyed in such stories as "Habitude," where two women "broke up in the same way as they had become close, without knowing why." The partnership is never treated as odd or abnormal, and its ending could be that of any heterosexual couple. In "The Judge" a widow is unnerved in an attempt to mark her change of status by her manservant, who clearly but silently disapproves of a new and too youthful hairstyle. The disintegration of her confidence compels her to make another appointment with her stylist the next day.

The title story of *Belle-Vista* concerns one of those "blank pages" that Colette considered important, the times in a woman's life when she is not dominated by passion, and so can observe veiled aspects of human nature. The hotel Bella-Vista seems to be run by a pair of women, but one turns out to be a transvestite who has, moreover, made the servant pregnant. There is only one other guest when the narrator is staying there, a sinister character who disappears after throttling a cage of parakeets. The narrator feels a simultaneous attraction and repugnance; she wants to leave the hotel, but recognises the perverse fascination of danger.

"Chambre d'hôtel," the first of the two novellas which make up the volume of the same name (*translated as Chance Acquaintances*), is based on an anecdote connected with Colette's music-hall career. The melodramatic elements of the story push it beyond bare credulity on occasion, but the tension in the narrator's wish to be part of events recall a similar tug in "Bella-Vista." The second novella, "The Rainy Moon," relates a story in which coincidences, mysterious behaviour, and connections are linked with the occult. The unnamed narrator finally sees the woman who has been trying to rid herself of her estranged husband, in the distance, dressed in mourning.

"The Tender Shoot" concerns a man of 50 years who falls for a young peasant girl. She is perfectly willing to satisfy him sexually, but is determined to keep the situation from her mother. Not surprisingly, they are discovered taking refuge from a storm in the girl's house, and the mother harangues her daughter not on grounds of morality or virtue, but on account of her seducer's age and physical condition. The two women unite to pelt him with stones as he runs from the house. "The Képi," in the same volume, shows a different side of the coin in the fragile links in the male-female age gap. Here, the 45-year-old Marco, a woman who earns a sparse living ghostwriting, answers a personal advertisement, and she meets and falls in love with a young lieutenant. The affair awakens her sexuality, but one day in bed she playfully puts on his képi. This severe military cap merely emphasises her age, and the relationship comes to a swift end.

"Gigi" first appeared in the weekly magazine *Présent* in 1941, and subsequently as the title story of the last of Colette's fictional works, in 1944. It was staged, and later made into a film with Audrey Hepburn. The story's source was a real incident told to Colette 15 years earlier, but the author moves it back to the more romantic end of the 19th century, the era of the brilliant demi-mondaines. Unlike many of Colette's other short stories it is witty, charming, and ends happily and unambiguously. It is also stylishly unsentimental. The adolescent Gigi comes from a family of women who had made their way as courtesans: "I understand that we don't marry," she says to her great-aunt. She is aware of such things, but is utterly without guile. When the same future is planned for her with a rich, 33-year-old man whom the family has long held in affection, Gigi insists she will not comply with the arrangement. She changes her mind; he realises what she means to him, and asks permission to marry her. The ironic parallel to a normal girl's upbringing and expectation of marriage is made to Gigi's education: she is taught how to eat lobster, choose jewels, and move gracefully. The severity of the rules on both sides of the social divide are equal.

"The Sick Child," in the same collection, describes the hallucinatory imaginings of the boy as he escapes the restrictions of his bed. In sleep, or in the final crisis of his illness, he embroiders a world into which his wasted legs cannot carry him, flying on the lavender scented air which his mother uses to sweeten the room. He survives, and bids farewell to the make-believe dreams of his other self.

To a visitor in the last years of her life, Colette claimed, "Perhaps the most praiseworthy thing about me is that I have known how to write like a woman." Her themes of childhood, nature, and love, in their many forms, are indeed those of a female writer, and although autobiographical elements often underpin the fiction, her writing should not be interpreted only on this level. Her work can be equally appropriate to both sexes.

—Honor Levi

See the essays on "The Other Woman" and "The Rainy Moon."

COLLINS, (William) Wilkie. English. Born in London, 8 January 1824; son of the painter William Collins. Educated at Maida Hill Academy, London, 1835–36; with his parents in Italy, 1836–38; at a private school, Highbury, London, 1838–41; apprentice, Antrobus and Company, tea merchants, London, 1841–46; studied at Lincoln's Inn, London, 1846–51: called to the bar, 1851. Lived with Caroline Graves, 1859–68 and 1870–80: adopted her daughter; supported Martha Rudd ("Mrs. Dawson"), 1868–89: two daughters and one son. Friend and literary collaborator of Charles Dickens, *q.v.*, 1851–70: staff member and contributor, *Household Words* and *All the Year Round*, 1856–61; addicted to opium from mid-1860's; gave reading tour of U.S., 1873–74. Also a painter: exhibited at the Royal Academy, London, 1849. *Died 23 September 1889.*

PUBLICATIONS

Short Stories

After Dark. 1856.
Miss or Mrs.? and Other Stories in Outline. 1873; revised edition, 1875.
Readings and Writings in America: The Frozen Deep and Other Stories. 1874.
Little Novels. 1887.
The Lazy Tour of Two Idle Apprentices, No Thoroughfare, The Perils of Certain English Prisoners, with Charles Dickens. 1890.
The Best Supernatural Stories, edited by Peter Haining. 1990.

Novels

Antonina; or, The Fall of Rome. 1850.

Mr. Wray's Cash-Box; or, The Mask and the Mystery. 1852.
Basil: A Story of Modern Life. 1852; revised edition, 1862; edited by Dorothy Goldman, 1990.
Hide and Seek. 1854; revised edition, 1861.
The Dead Secret. 1857.
The Queen of Hearts. 1859.
The Woman in White. 1860; edited by Harvey Peter Sucksmith, 1975.
No Name. 1862; edited by Virginia Blain, 1986.
Armadale. 1866; edited by Catherine Peters, 1989.
The Moonstone. 1868; edited by J.I.M. Stewart, 1966.
Man and Wife. 1870.
Poor Miss Finch. 1872.
The New Magdalen. 1873.
The Law and the Lady. 1875.
The Two Destinies. 1876.
The Haunted Hotel: A Mystery of Modern Venice (with *My Lady's Money*). 1879.
A Rogue's Life, From His Birth to His Marriage. 1879.
The Fallen Leaves. 1879.
Jezebel's Daughter. 1880.
The Black Robe. 1881.
Heart and Science: A Story of the Present Time. 1883.
I Say No. 1884.
The Evil Genius: A Domestic Story. 1886.
The Guilty River. 1886.
The Legacy of Cain. 1889.
Blind Love, completed by Walter Besant. 1890.

Plays

A Court Duel, from a French play (produced 1850).
The Lighthouse, with Charles Dickens, from the story "Gabriel's Marriage" by Collins (produced 1855).
The Frozen Deep, with Charles Dickens (produced 1857). 1866; in *Under the Management of Mr. Charles Dickens: His Production of The Frozen Deep,* edited by R.L. Brannan. 1966.
The Red Vial (produced 1858).
A Message from the Sea (produced 1861).
No Name, with W.B. Bernard, from the novel by Collins. (produced 1871). 1863; revised version, by Collins alone, 1870.
Armadale, from his own novel. 1866.
No Thoroughfare, with Charles Dickens and Charles Fechter, from the story by Collins and Dickens (produced 1867). 1867.
Black and White, with Charles Fechter (produced 1869). 1869.
The Woman in White, from his own novel (produced 1870; revised version produced 1871). 1871.
Man and Wife, from his own novel (produced 1873). 1870.
The New Magdalen (produced 1873). 1873.
Miss Gwilt (produced 1875). 1875.
The Moonstone, from his own novel (produced 1877). 1877.
Rank and Riches (produced 1883).
The Evil Genius (produced 1885).

Other

Memoirs of the Life of William Collins, R.A., with Selections from His Journals and Correspondence. 2 vols., 1848.
Rambles Beyond Railways; or, Notes in Cornwall Taken A-Foot. 1851; revised edition, 1861.

My Miscellanies.   2 vols., 1863; revised edition, 1875.
Considerations on the Copyright Question Addressed to an American Friend. 1880.

*

Bibliography: *Collins: An Annotated Bibliography 1889–1976* by Kirk H. Beetz, 1978.

Critical Studies: *The Early Novels of Collins* by Walter de la Mare, 1932; *Collins: A Biography* by Kenneth Robinson, 1951; *Collins* by Robert Ashley, 1952; *The Life of Collins* by Nuel Pharr Davis, 1956; *Collins* by William H. Marshall, 1970; *Collins: The Critical Heritage* edited by Norman Page, 1974; *Collins: A Critical and Biographical Study* by Dorothy L. Sayers, edited by E.R. Gregory, 1977; *Collins: A Critical Survey of His Prose Fiction, with a Bibliography* by R.V. Andrew, 1979; *Collins and His Victorian Readers* by Sue Lunoff, 1982; *Collins: Women, Property, and Propriety* by Philip O'Neill, 1988; *The Secret Life of Collins* by William M. Clarke, 1988; *In the Secret Theatre of Home: Collins, Sensation Narrative, and Nineteenth-Century Psychology* by Jenny Bourne Taylor, 1988.

* * *

Wilkie Collins was a prolific writer of short stories, most of them appearing initially in magazines (including *Household Words*, under the editorship of his friend and mentor Charles Dickens), and most of them being collected subsequently in a series of volumes. He was very active in this genre from the early 1850's; possibly there are even earlier stories, not credited to him, which appeared anonymously in various periodicals. During the 1860's, the period during which his major novels were written, he produced few short stories, but he returned to the form in the 1870's and 1880's.

Collins's stories fall into a number of categories and bear an interesting relationship both to his full-length fiction and to established and emerging types of story. One of his most important innovations was in the field of the detective story, and his "A Stolen Letter" has been described as the first English detective story. (It appeared in 1855, in the special Christmas number of *Household Words*, written jointly by Collins and Dickens and titled "The Seven Poor Travellers"; the title "A Stolen Letter" was supplied later, Collins not infrequently changing the titles of his stories for their successive appearances.) The story, involving forgery, blackmail, plotting and counterplotting, spying, the deciphering of a cryptic message, a desperate search against the clock, last-minute success, and a practical joke at the villain's expense, contains many ingredients that were to be used again by Collins and others, including Arthur Conan Doyle in the Sherlock Holmes stories. The narrative is also characteristically given to a story teller with an idiosyncratic style, resulting in a brisk, crisp narrative pace and the sense of an audience within the story telling situation. A related but somewhat different technique is used in another detective story, "The Biter Bit" (originally titled "Who Is the Thief?" for its appearance in *The Atlantic Monthly* in 1858), where the epistolary method is employed in a narrative that uses the device of the least-likely criminal and that can even be read as a subverting of the new detective story genre.

A different kind of detective story is "The Diary of Anne Rodway" (in *Household Words*, 1856), in which the detective is a young girl anxious to discover her friend's murderer. The account of the lives of the very poor is rendered vivid by the use of Anne's diary as a vehicle for the narrative: a seamstress without parents or friends, she shows courage and resourcefulness in tracking down the man responsible for her fellow-lodger's death on the basis of a tiny, almost insignificant clue.

Collins also wrote a number of stories that owe a debt to the Gothic tradition, and these can be divided into those exploiting the supernatural or the uncanny and those simply designed to shock and thrill with their account of horrifying events which (as in his best-known story, "A Terribly Strange Bed") turn out to have a rational explanation. "The Dream Woman" (originally "The Ostler," in *Household Words*, 1855) uses one of Collins's favourite motifs, a chance meeting with a mysterious woman. Despite his mother's warning that she is "the woman of the dream"—a terrifying figure who has appeared to him during a night spent in a lonely inn seven years earlier—the protagonist marries her and narrowly escapes a murderous attack. The conclusion is open-ended: has he escaped danger once and for all, or will the woman reappear in his life? As he does so often, Collins sets the main story within a frame involving a narrator and a listener as well as the central actor in the drama, now an old man but still living in daily dread of the woman's reappearance. Collins used an expanded version of this story for his public readings given in America in 1873, though regrettably the effectively ambiguous ending was changed for one of a more decisive kind.

While some of Collins's stories are relatively short, others are virtually novellas, a good example being "Mad Monkton." The hero comes from a family suffering from "the horrible affliction of hereditary insanity" and the title turns out to be ambiguous, raising the question whether Monkton is genuinely haunted by his uncle's ghost or whether he is suffering from delusions. A family tradition holds that, if the uncle's body remains unburied, the family will become extinct; hence Monkton sets off for Italy (a favourite setting for Gothic horror stories) to find and bury it. He is accompanied by a young friend who is the story's narrator. The graphic scene of the body's discovery, involving a detailed description of a putrefying corpse, was too much for Dickens, who declined to publish "Mad Monkton" in his magazine (it appeared in *Fraser's Magazine* in 1855).

Another ghost story, "The Dead Hand," introduces another favourite motif of Collins's and of much 19th-century sensational writing, that of the double (in this case plausibly provided by a half-brother). This story, which appeared as "The Double-Bedded Room" in *Household Words* in 1857, includes several other elements that relate it to other writings by Collins and to wider traditions of storytelling: the bold introduction of the theme of illegitimacy looks forward to Collins's novel *No Name*—the phrase "no name" actually appearing in the story—while the setting of the action in an inn recalls not only Collins's own frequent use of such settings but a long tradition that extends forward at least as far as Alfred Hitchcock's *Psycho*.

As these selected examples suggest, Collins showed a marked preference for certain types of story but also showed considerable ingenuity in his variations on established themes as well as originality in his early experiments in detective fiction (anticipating, among much else, his own classic *The Moonstone*). Of particular interest to the student of fictional technique is his use of a variety of narrative voices, often set within a frame that establishes the narrative situation and hence interposes a credible intermediary between the reader and events that are in themselves often bizarre or fantastic. Many of the ideas, incidents, or character-types in the stories were used again, in modified or expanded form, in his full-length works of fiction. Moreover, the eccentric lawyer in "A Stolen Letter" has been seen as providing Dickens with suggestions for the character of Jaggers in *Great Expectations*, and Collins's story of the French Revolution, "Sister Rose," (in *Household Words*, 1855), may have been in Dickens's mind when he conceived *A Tale of Two Cities*.

Collins is, thus, not only one of the earliest substantial writers of short fiction in England but a significant innovator and a significant influence upon at least one major writer. Not only did he contribute to the expansion and popularity of the genre and to the sophistication of its technique, but he produced a number of stories (represented in several current selections) that are still highly readable today.

—Norman Page

See the essay on "A Terribly Strange Bed."

CONRAD, Joseph. British. Born Józef Teodor Konrad Korzeniowski in Berdyczów (now Berdichev), Podolia, Ukrainian Province of Poland, 3 December 1857; became British citizen, 1886. Educated at schools in Cracow, 1868–73. Married Jessie George in 1896; two sons. Moved to Marseilles, 1874; merchant seaman from 1874: sailed on a number of French merchant ships to the West Indies, 1874–76; qualified as an able seaman in England, 1878, and sailed in British ships in the Orient trade from 1879; received Master's Certificate in the British Merchant Service, 1886; received first command, 1888; first mate on the *Torrens*, 1892–93; retired from the Merchant Service and moved to England, 1894; lived in Ashford, Kent, from 1896. *Died 3 August 1924.*

PUBLICATIONS

Collections

Works (revised by Conrad).   22 vols., 1920–25.
The Portable Conrad, edited by Morton Dauwen Zabel. 1947; revised edition, edited by Frederick R. Karl, 1969.
The Complete Short Fiction, edited by Samuel Hynes.   2 vols., 1992.

Short Stories

Tales of Unrest.   1898.
Youth: A Narrative, with Two Other Stories (includes "Heart of Darkness" and "The End of the Tether"). 1902; edited by Morton Dauwen Zabel, 1959; *Heart of Darkness*, edited by Robert Kimbrough, 1971, revised, 1988.
Typhoon.   1902.
Typhoon and Other Stories.   1903.
A Set of Six.   1908.

'Twixt Land and Sea: Tales.   1912; *The Secret Sharer*, edited by Robert Kimbrough, 1963.
Within the Tides: Tales.   1915.
Tales of Hearsay.   1925.
Complete Short Stories.   1933.

Novels

Almayer's Folly: A Story of the Eastern River.   1895.
An Outcast of the Islands.   1896.
The Children of the Sea.   1897; as *The Nigger of the Narcissus: A Tale of the Sea*, 1898; edited by Robert Kimbrough, 1979.
Lord Jim.   1900; edited by John Batchelor, 1983.
The Inheritors: An Extravagant Story, with Ford Madox Ford.   1901.
Romance, with Ford Madox Ford.   1903.
Nostromo: A Tale of the Seaboard.   1904; edited by Keith Carabine, 1984.
The Secret Agent: A Simple Tale.   1907; edited by Bruce Harkness and S.W. Reid, 1990.
Under Western Eyes.   1911; edited by Jeremy Hawthorn, 1983.
Chance.   1913; edited by Martin Ray, 1988.
Victory: An Island Tale.   1915; edited by John Batchelor, 1986.
The Shadow-Line: A Confession.   1917; edited by Jeremy Hawthorn, 1985.
The Arrow of Gold: A Story Between Two Notes.   1919.
The Tale.   1919.
Prince Roman.   1920.
The Warrior's Soul.   1920.
The Rescue: A Romance of the Shallows.   1920.
The Black Mate: A Story.   1922.
The Rover.   1923.
The Nature of a Crime, with Ford Madox Ford.   1924.
Suspense: A Napoleonic Novel.   1925.
The Sisters (unfinished).   1928.

Plays

One Day More, from his own story "Tomorrow" (produced 1905; revised version produced 1918).   1917.
The Secret Agent, from his own novel (produced 1922). 1921.
Laughing Anne, from his own story "Because of the Dollars."   1923.

Other

The Mirror of the Sea: Memories and Impressions.   1906; with *A Personal Record*, edited by Zdzislaw Najder, 1988.
Some Reminiscences.   1912; as *A Personal Record*, 1912; with *The Mirror of the Sea*, edited by Zdzislaw Najder, 1988.
Notes on Life and Letters.   1921.
Notes on My Books.   1921; as *Prefaces to His Works*, edited by Edward Garnett, 1937.
Last Essays, edited by Richard Curle.   1926.
Letters to His Wife.   1927.
Letters 1895–1924, edited by Edward Garnett.   1928.
Conrad to a Friend: 150 Selected Letters to Richard Curle, edited by Curle.   1928.
Lettres Françaises, edited by Gerard Jean-Aubry.   1930.
Letters to Marguerite Poradowska 1890–1920, edited and translated by John A. Gee and Paul A. Sturm.   1940; edited by R. Rapin (in French), 1966.

Letters to William Blackwood and David S. Meldrum, edited by William Blackburn.   1958.
Conrad's Polish Background: Letters to and from Polish Friends, edited by Zdzislaw Najder.   1964.
Conrad and Warrington Dawson: The Record of a Friendship, edited by D.B.J. Randall.   1968.
Letters to R.B. Cunninghame Graham, edited by C.T. Watts.   1969.
Congo Diary and Other Uncollected Pieces, edited by Zdzislaw Najder.   1978.
Conrad: Under Familial Eyes, edited by Zdzislaw Najder.   1983.
Collected Letters, edited by Frederick R. Karl and Laurence Davies.   1983—.
Selected Literary Criticism and The Shadow-Line, edited by Allan Ingram.   1986.

Translator, *The Book of Job: A Satirical Comedy,* by Bruno Winawer.   1931.

*

Bibliography: *Conrad: An Annotated Bibliography of Writings about Him* by Bruce E. Teets and Helmut E. Gerber, 1971, and *Conrad: An Annotated Bibliography* by Teets, 1990; *An Annotated Critical Bibliography of Conrad* by Owen Knowles, 1992.

Critical Studies: *Conrad: A Personal Remembrance* by Ford Madox Ford, 1924; *Conrad: Life and Letters,* 2 vols., 1927, and *The Sea-Dreamer: A Definitive Biography of Conrad,* 1957, both by Gerard Jean-Aubry; *Conrad and His Circle* by Jessie Conrad, 1935; *Conrad: Some Aspects of the Art of the Novel* by Edward Crankshaw, 1936; *Conrad: The Making of a Novelist* by J.D. Gordan, 1940; *Conrad: Poland's English Genius* by M.C. Bradbrook, 1941; *The Great Tradition: George Eliot, Henry James, Conrad* by F.R. Leavis, 1948; *Conrad's Measure of Man* by Paul L. Wiley, 1955; *Conrad and His Characters: A Study of Six Novels* by Richard Curle, 1957; *Conrad: Achievement and Decline* by Thomas Moser, 1957; *Conrad the Novelist* by Albert Guerard, 1958; *The Thunder and the Sunshine: A Biography,* 1958, and *The Sea Years of Conrad,* 1965, both by Jerry Allen; *Conrad: A Critical Biography* by Jocelyn Baines, 1960, revised edition, 1967; *Conrad's Heart of Darkness and the Critics* edited by Bruce Harkness, 1960; *A Reader's Guide to Conrad,* 1960, and *Conrad, The Three Lives: A Biography,* 1979, both by Frederick R. Karl, and *Conrad: A Collection of Criticism* edited by Karl, 1975; *Conrad, Giant in Exile,* 1961, and *The Two Lives of Conrad,* 1965, both by Leo Gurko; *Conrad: Lord Jim* by Tony Tanner, 1963; *The Political Novels of Conrad* by E. Knapp Hay, 1963; *Conrad's Eastern World,* 1966, *Conrad's Western World,* 1971, and *Conrad and His World,* 1972 (as *Conrad,* 1988), all by Norman Sherry, and *Conrad: The Critical Heritage* edited by Sherry, 1973; *Conrad: A Psychoanalytic Biography* by Bernard Meyer, 1967; *Conrad's Politics: Community and Anarchy in the Fictions of Conrad* by Avrom Fleishman, 1967; *Conrad's Short Fiction* by Lawrence Graver, 1969; *Conrad's Models of Mind* by Bruce Johnson, 1971; *Conrad: The Modern Imagination* by C.B. Cox, 1974; *Language and Being: Conrad and the Literature of Personality* by Peter J. Glassman, 1976; *Conrad* by Martin Tucker, 1976; *Conrad: The Way of Dispossession* by H.M. Daleski, 1977; *Conrad: The Major Phase* by Jacques Berthoud, 1978; *Conrad's Early Sea Fiction: The Novelist as Navigator* by Paul Bruss, 1979; *Conrad: Language and Fictional Self-Consciousness,* 1979, and *Conrad: Narrative Technique and Ideological Commitment,* 1990, both by Jeremy Hawthorn; *Conrad in the Nineteenth Century,* 1979, and *Conrad: Nostromo,* 1988, both by Ian Watt; *Conrad's Later Novels* by Gary Geddes, 1980; *Thorns and Arabesques: Contexts for Conrad's Fiction* by William W. Bonney, 1980; *Conrad: Almayer's Folly to Under Western Eyes,* 1980, and *Conrad: The Later Fiction,* 1982, both by Daniel R. Schwarz; *Conrad: Times Remembered* by John Conrad, 1981; *Kipling and Conrad: The Colonial Fiction* by John A. McClure, 1981; *Conrad* by Gillon Adam, 1982; *A Preface to Conrad,* 1982, and *Conrad: A Literary Life,* 1989, both by Cedric Watts; *Heart of Darkness: A Critical Commentary* by Hena Maes-Jelinek, 1982; *Conrad: A Chronicle* by Zdzislaw Najder, 1983, and *Conrad under Familial Eyes* edited by Najder, 1983; *Conrad and Imperialism: Ideological Boundaries and Visionary Frontiers* by Benita Parry, 1983; *Conrad and the Paradox of Plot* by Stephen K. Land, 1984, as *Paradox and Polarity in the Fiction of Conrad,* 1984; *Conrad and Charles Darwin: The Influence of Scientific Thought on Conrad's Fiction* by Redmond O'Hanlon, 1984; *Conrad Revisited: Essays for the Eighties* edited by Ross C. Murfin, 1985; *Conrad, Ford Madox Ford, and the Making of Romance* by Raymond Brebach, 1985; *Coercion to Speak: Conrad's Poetics of Dialogue* by Aaron Fogel, 1985; *A Conrad Companion* by Norman Page, 1986; *Critical Essays on Conrad* edited by Ted Billy, 1987; *Heart of Darkness: Search for the Unconscious* by Gary Adelman, 1987; *Conrad: Consciousness and Integrity* by Steve Ressler, 1988; *Interweaving Patterns in the Works of Conrad* by Gail Fraser, 1988; *Lord Jim* by John Batchelor, 1988; *Conrad's Narrative Method* by Jakob Lothe, 1989; *A Conrad Chronology* by Owen Knowles, 1990; *Conrad: Interviews and Recollections* edited by Martin Ray, 1990; *Conrad: Third World Perspectives* edited by Robert Hamner, 1990; *Conrad's Lingard Trilogy: Empire, Race, and Women in the Malay Novels* by Heliéna Krenn, 1990; *Conrad: Beyond Culture and Background* by D.C.R.A. Goonetilleke, 1990; *Conrad and the Fictions of Skepticism* by Mark A. Wollaeger, 1991; *Conrad's Fiction as Critical Discourse* by Richard Ambrosini, 1991; *Conrad's Existentialism* by Otto Bohlmann, 1991; *Conrad: A Biography* by Jeffrey Meyers, 1991.

*   *   *

When Joseph Conrad came to England in 1878 he was a double exile; he had left Poland, the land of his birth, in 1874 to join the French Merchant Navy. Four years later, desperately in debt and perhaps disappointed in love he attempted suicide. When he was recovered he left France and joined the British Merchant Navy, though according to his biographer Jocelyn Baines, he knew at the time "no more than a few words of the language." Despite this, however, he became one of the most significant English fiction writers of the early 20th century, publishing 26 separate volumes between 1895 and 1928, the last four of these being posthumous publications.

His best-known and most significant works are "Heart of Darkness" and *Nostromo,* the former a long story, the latter a powerful novel, both published early in the century. All his fiction draws to some extent on his own experience. In particular, the exotic settings are reminiscent of his own life as son of a dissident Polish aristocrat during a time of

Russian domination, as exile from his fatherland, as merchant seaman travelling to many parts of the world.

Though he wrote short stories throughout his life, most of Conrad's best tales were written around about the turn of the century. A number of them were first published in magazines and afterwards collected into a volume. "Youth" was first published in *Blackwood's Magazine* for September 1898, and later in 1902 in a volume together with "Heart of Darkness" and "The End of the Tether"; the first and last of these are seafaring tales.

One of Conrad's favourite narrative devices is that of the "double narrator"; "Youth" is an excellent illustration of this device. In this story Conrad introduces for the first time his best-known narrator, Marlow, though both here and in "Heart of Darkness" Marlow is the central character as well. Marlow is not, however, the first narrator; another unnamed narrator sets the scene—a reunion of five seafaring friends who have gathered to drink and to reminisce. We learn nothing of Marlow but his name until he takes over the narration; what he tells is a sailor's yarn of his own youth. It is a tale of Conrad's own youth, based directly on his own experiences.

The sea, which is so often the backcloth for Conrad's fiction is here, as in *Typhoon*, a main contender; the plot revolves around a man's battle with the elements but, in battling against the sea, Marlow seeks to prove his manhood. The romance and adventure is merely the starting point; Conrad's concern is with the nature of the man himself and with the man's relationship to other men. Placed on a ship at sea, Marlow is isolated from ordinary life and has to come to terms with himself and his own identity; in the trials and disasters that he and his shipmates endure on the voyage he learns that he does not lack courage and is able to endure hardship. At the end of the voyage he is "weary beyond expression" but at the same time "exulting like a conqueror." Not only has he performed his duty, however, but every man on the ship has been shown to have done his best. Conrad is especially concerned with loyalty and "Youth" illustrates his belief that life on board ship relies on the loyalty of every man and on the acceptance of a hierarchy that creates essential order.

Particularly in the sea stories Conrad is hardly concerned with women; here, the only woman character is Mrs. Beard, the captain's wife, who appears briefly at the beginning to perform in the conventional wifely duties of darning and sewing; she then is escorted from the ship and put on a train for home.

To some extent, "Youth" may be seen as unique in Conrad's work in its exuberance and in its happy ending; Conrad rarely recaptures the unalloyed joy expressed by Marlow during the trials the Judea undergoes: "I would not have given up the experience for worlds. I had moments of exultation." Yet as Marlow looks back on the adventure from the perspective of an older man, other more typically Conradian thoughts prevail and the story ends with the regret that youth, adventure, and romance have passed from his life.

If "Youth" is an example of a directly autobiographical story, "Amy Foster" is an example of a story that, while strongly influenced by Conrad's experiences, is not autobiographical. It was first published in serial form in the *Illustrated London News* in 1901 and later in book form in the volume *Typhoon and Other Stories* in 1903. It is the only one of Conrad's stories named for a female protagonist, though its original title was "The Husband," which suggests Conrad's uncertainty as to whether Amy or her husband, Yanko Goorall, should be seen as the principal character.

The story no doubt reflects Conrad's feelings about being a foreigner in a strange land and he enlists our sympathy for the poor rejected exile who is cast away on the shore of southern England. Amy Foster's uncomprehending pity for her husband, however, never makes him easy in his exile; her later rejection of the foreignness in him, which leads to his death in sickness and despair, is one of the most moving accounts in all of Conrad's short stories.

The pessimism of this story is much more typical of Conrad than is the joy of Marlow's tale in "Youth." "Amy Foster" is the story of exile, nostalgia, regret, the failure of relationships, and, as so often in Conrad, death. It is narrated in an indirect way; the first narrator is an unknown "I" who is told the tale by Dr. Kennedy, the local doctor, and it is through the first narrator that the story comes to the reader.

Conrad's short stories, like his novels, illustrate his consuming interest in narration. The stories use various settings, draw their characters from many nationalities, and present situations that are typical of his work overall.

—Hilda D. Spear

See the essays on "Heart of Darkness," "The Secret Sharer" and *Typhoon*.

———

COOVER, Robert (Lowell). American. Born in Charles City, Iowa, 4 February 1932. Educated at Southern Illinois University, Carbondale, 1949-51; Indiana University, Bloomington, B.A. 1953; University of Chicago, 1958-61, M.A. 1965. Served in the United States Naval Reserve, 1953–57: Lieutenant. Married Maria del Sans-Mallafre in 1959; two daughters and one son. Taught at Bard College, Annandale-on-Hudson, New York, 1966–67, University of Iowa, Iowa City, 1967–69, Columbia University, New York, 1972, Princeton University, New Jersey, 1972–73, Virginia Military Institute, Lexington, 1976, and Brandeis University, Waltham, Massachusetts, 1981; writer-in-residence, Brown University, Providence, Rhode Island; since 1981. Fiction editor, *Iowa Review,* Iowa City, 1974–77. Recipient: Faulkner award, 1966; Brandeis University Creative Arts award, 1969; Rockefeller fellowship, 1969; Guggenheim fellowship, 1971, 1974; American Academy award, 1976; National Endowment for the Arts grant, 1985; Rea award, for short story, 1987.

PUBLICATIONS

Short Stories

Pricksongs and Descants.   1969.
Hair o' the Chine.   1979.
After Lazarus: A Filmscript.   1980.
Charlie in the House of Rue.   1980.
A Political Fable (novella).   1980.
The Convention.   1982.
In Bed One Night and Other Brief Encounters.   1983.
Aesop's Forest, with *The Plot of the Mice and Other Stories,*
   by Brian Swann.   1986.

A Night at the Movies; or, You Must Remember This.
1987.

Novels

The Origin of the Brunists.   1966.
*The Universal Baseball Association, Inc., J. Henry Waugh,
    Prop.*   1968.
The Public Burning.   1977.
Spanking the Maid.   1982.
Gerald's Party.   1986.
Whatever Happened to Gloomy Gus of the Chicago Bears?
    1987.
Pinocchio in Venice.   1991.

Plays

The Kid (produced 1972).   Included in *A Theological
    Position,* 1972.
A Theological Position (includes *A Theological Position,
    The Kid, Love Scene, Rip Awake*).   1972.
Love Scene (as *Scène d'amour,* produced 1973; as *Love
    Scene,* produced 1974).   Included in *A Theological
    Position,* 1972.
Rip Awake (produced 1975).   Included in *A Theological
    Position,* 1972.
A Theological Position (produced 1977). Included in *A
    Theological Position,* 1972.
Bridge Hand (produced 1981).

Other

Editor, with Kent Dixon, *The Stone Wall Book of Short
    Fiction.*   1973.
Editor, with Elliott Anderson, *Minute Stories.*   1976.

*

Critical Studies: *Fiction and the Figures of Life* by William
H. Gass, 1970; *Black Humor Fiction of the Sixties* by Max
Schulz, 1973; "Coover and the Hazards of Metafiction" by
Neil Schmitz, in *Novel 7,* 1974; "Humor and Balance in
Coover's *The Universal Baseball Association, Inc.*" by
Frank W. Shelton, in *Critique 17,* 1975; "Coover, Metafic-
tions, and Freedom" by Margaret Heckard, in *Twentieth
Century Literature 22,* 1976; "The Dice of God: Einstein,
Heisenberg, and Coover" by Arlen J. Hansen, in *Novel 10,*
1976; "Structure as Revelation: Coover's *Pricksongs and
Descants*" by Jessie Gunn, in *Linguistics in Literature,* 2(1),
1977; *The Metafictional Muse: The Works of Coover,
Donald Barthelme, and William H. Gass* by Larry McCaf-
fery, 1982; *Coover: The Universal Fictionmaking Process* by
Lois Gordon, 1983; *Coover's Fictions* by Jackson I. Cope,
1986.

*   *   *

Robert Coover, like many other writers of innovative
fiction who came to prominence in the United States
during the 1960's, was strongly influenced by the experimental fiction of such South American writers as Jorge
Louis Borges and Julio Cortázar. His earliest short stories
are crafted in tribute to their fabulative methods, in which
as much attention is given to the self-conscious mechanics
of storytelling as to the story's subject. Soon, however,

Coover was to find the same basic ingredients, including
examples of the fabulous and ridiculous passing as everyday reality, available within the most common narratives
of American popular culture, to which his later work has
been directed.

Pricksongs and Descants, Coover's first short story collection, is similar to other metafictive experiments of the
period, such as John Barth's *Lost in the Funhouse* and
Ronald Sukenick's *The Death of the Novel and Other
Stories,* all of which draw on Borges's manner of exploiting
the fictive aspects of what one has supposed is reality. In
"The Babysitter" Coover chooses an extremely simple and
familiar occasion, that of a husband and wife leaving their
children with a babysitter so they can attend a friend's
party. Without ever departing from realistic description he
allows the scene to devolve into almost absurdist chaos. His
method is to segment his narrative into discreet paragraphs, each of which contains a single incident and
perspective. As additional characters enter the story, the
narrative thus takes on additional dimensions, until the
competing nature of those dimensions (the babysitter's
wish to quiet the children, her boyfriend's desire to stop by
for sex, even the television's broadcast of a program whose
action is taken into account just as evenly as anything else
that happens) causes reality itself to be called into question.
Elsewhere in *Pricksongs and Descants* Coover achieves
similar results with almost purely formal exercises, such as
in "Seven Exemplary Fictions"; other times, especially
with "The Hat Act," he reduces character and action to a
Beckettian minimum. And in "The Gingerbread House" he
takes his first steps toward emphasizing the fabulative
elements of familiar texts, in this case the Hansel and Gretl
fairy tale. But it is in both the dynamics and subject matter
of "The Babysitter" that the future direction of his
fictionist's career is found.

That direction is clarified in one of the author's few
uncollected stories, left so to remain useable as a freshly
entertaining piece for live readings: "McDuff on the
Mound," published in *The Iowa Review* (Fall 1971), where
editorial confusion at what fabulative metafiction was led
to its categorization as "criticism." It is a critical text in
that it responds to another narrative, the famous 19th-
century doggerel poem, "Casey at the Bat." Yet by means
of altered perspective (from the batter's box to the pitcher's
mound) and a self-consciously exuberant stylistics (in
which almost every action is exaggerated to cartoonlike
proportions), Coover creates a genuinely new text, one that
uses earlier assumptions to question the nature of what had
passed for stable reality before.

Coover's penchant for fabulative embellishment has
turned three of his short stories into longer works, "The
Cat in the Hat for President" (in *New American Review,*
August 1968) becoming the 12,000 word *A Political Fable,*
a longer story called "Whatever Happened to Gloomy Gus
of the Chicago Bears" (in *New American Review,* February
1975) being expanded into a novella, and "The Public
Burning of Julius and Ethel Rosenberg" (in *Tri Quarterly,*
Winter 1973) growing from a 10-page short story into a
massive, 200,000 word novel, *The Public Burning.* The
technique is that of "McDuff on the Mound" taken to
deliberate excess, whereby a narrative voice assumed to be
stable (because known as a tradition itself) mixes with a
style of action that the voice cannot control; the fictive
chemistry that results threatens to spill off the page, much
as happens in the original Cat in the Hat doings popularized by Dr. Seuss. As with Coover's inspirations drawn
from the work of the great South American short story
masters, the approach is a self-consciously artistic one: a

challenge set by making a narration appropriate to one type of subject cope with materials that it cannot logically control.

That stories can be generated by purely intellectual problems is demonstrated in the author's small press collection, *In Bed One Night*. The pieces here collected are extremely short ones, most of them just three or four pages long and readable to an audience in about that many minutes. Coover wrote them as warmup exercises for his public readings, something that became necessary as his short stories continued growing into much longer ones. To introduce audiences to the pure essence of his method, he would now devise quick little presentations, sometimes not much longer than prose poems but eminently fictions in that their telling employs narrative sequence (such as an old man turning into one of the birds he feeds and a prototypical inventor of the human mind being run out of the universe by his unleashed creation).

Yet Coover's greatest fascination remains with how American popular culture itself accomplishes the same style of narrative happenings. Each of his stories in *A Night at the Movies* does just that, focusing on the icons and attractions of popular films in order to reveal the narratives of much greater potential that are hidden within them. Even before adulthood most Americans have seen enough movies to create an infinitude of stories; Coover demonstrates this fact in "Inside the Frame," where bits and pieces of perhaps a thousand films are collaged together to form a sequence that entertains according to the same mechanism as film, which is a succession of quickly passing frames.

Coover's genius as a short story writer, then, has been to use fabulative and metafictive devices to move his narratives as far as possible from the traditions of social realism, but then to refocus these self-consciously artistic techniques on materials most readers will have assumed to be familiar subjects from the real world, but which are now revealed to be as magically potent as the most fabulous doings of Borges, Cortázar, or others considered to be well beyond realism's pale.

—Jerome Klinkowitz

COPPARD, A(lfred) E(dgar). English. Born in Folkestone, Kent, 4 January 1878. Educated at Lewes Road Boarding School, Brighton, 1883–87; apprenticed to a tailor in Whitechapel, London, 1887–90. Married 1) Lily Annie Richardson in 1905 (died); 2) Winifred May de Kok, one son and one daughter. Paraffin vendor's assistant, auctioneer, cheesemonger, soap-agent, and carrier, in Brighton by 1898; thereafter worked for several years in the offices of an engineering firm; confidential clerk, Eagle Ironworks, 1907–19. *Died 13 January 1957.*

PUBLICATIONS

Collections

Selected Stories. 1972.

Short Stories

Adam and Eve and Pinch Me: Tales. 1921.

Clorinda Walks in Heaven: Tales. 1922.
The Black Dog and Other Stories. 1923.
Fishmonger's Fiddle: Tales. 1925.
The Field of Mustard: Tales. 1926.
Silver Circus: Tales. 1928.
Count Stefan. 1928.
The Gollan. 1929.
The Hundredth Story. 1930.
Pink Furniture. A Tale for Lovely Children with Noble Natures. 1930.
Nixeys Harlequin: Tales. 1931.
Crotty Shinkwin, The Beauty Spot. 1932.
Cheefoo. 1932.
Dunky Fitlow: Tales. 1933.
Ring the Bells of Heaven. 1933.
Emergency Exit. 1934.
Polly Oliver: Tales. 1935.
The Ninepenny Flute: Twenty-One Tales. 1937.
Tapster's Tapestry. 1938.
You Never Know, Do You? and Other Tales. 1939.
Ugly Anna and Other Tales. 1944.
Selected Tales. 1946.
Fearful Pleasures. 1946.
Dark-Eyed Lady: Fourteen Tales. 1947.
Collected Tales. 1948.
Lucy in Her Pink Jacket. 1954.

Verse

Hips and Haws. 1922.
Pelagea and Other Poems. 1926.
Yokohama Garland and Other Poems. 1926.
Collected Poems. 1928.
Easter Day. 1931.
Cherry Ripe. 1935.
Simple Day. 1978.

Other

Rummy, The Noble Game, with Robert Gibbings. 1932.
It's Me, O Lord! (autobiography). 1957.

Editor, *Songs from Robert Burns.* 1925.

*

Bibliography: *The Writings of Coppard* by Jacob Schwartz, 1931.

Critical Studies: *Coppard: His Life and His Poetry* by George Brandon Saul, 1932; *Remarks on the Style of Coppard* by A. Jehin, 1944; in *The Lonely Voice: A Study of the Short Story* by Frank O'Connor, 1963.

* * *

The deceptive simplicity of A.E. Coppard's short stories has beguiled many critics into believing that they are little more than country tales with a beginning, a middle, and an end, and an uncomplicated moral message. On one level, it is easy to understand this point of view, for Coppard was at his happiest writing about the lives of ordinary people; on another, deeper, level many of his stories are complicated allegories that display a profound compassion for the underdog, the poor, and the dispossessed.

He also knew how to write from a woman's perspective. In "The Field of Mustard" three "sere disvirgined women" find a commonality of interest and purpose while gathering kindling in a high wood outside their village. Two of them, Rose and Dinah, are drawn to each other not only through their shared experience of country life and manners, but, as they discover, through their common passion for Rufus Blackthorn, the local gamekeeper.

Far from alienating them, the knowledge that each has had a love affair with the man only serves to strengthen the bond between them. When Dinah tells Rose that she wishes she had been a man, she really means it: the emotion is not in any way prurient but merely a manifestation of their close friendship. As so often happens in a triangle, though, the third woman Amy Hardwick is excluded from their circle of intimacy and the exchanges between Rose and Dinah take place as they rest above a field of mustard with the countryside stretching out beyond it. Here, as in so many stories, Coppard proves to be a master of natural description, his prose the equal of anything written by Hardy.

Although little happens in "The Field of Mustard"—the women return to their quiet domestic ways—the experience has transformed Dinah and Rose: "Clouds were borne frantically across the heavens, as if in a rout of battle, and the lovely earth seemed to sigh in grief as some calamity all unknown to men."

A similar sense of passion shared and love denied lies at the heart of "Dusky Ruth," again set in the Cotswold country Coppard knew so well. A traveller arrives at a country inn where he is captivated by a dark-haired serving girl. Lost in passion he spends the night with her, only to surrender to some silent sadness which lies at the heart of her being. The following day he leaves, never to return, and the reader is left with the uncomfortable feeling that both the traveller and the girl have been transformed utterly by the experience.

Coppard returned to the theme of love lost in "The Higgler," in which the central character, Harvey Witlow, falls in love with the beautiful and educated daughter of a husbandless farmer. Although the girl never acknowledges his presence—in spite of his repeated visits to buy her mother's produce—Harvey dreams of winning her. However, when her mother offers the girl in marriage, together with a handsome dowry, he panics and after much prevarication, turns his back on the match and marries Sophy, his first love. Only later does he discover that the girl really wanted him and had begged her mother to arrange the match. By then it is too late and Coppard ends the story on a bitter-sweet note with the mother dead and the girl left to run the farm. As the higgler leaves, he muses on his fate: "Of course there was Sophy; but still—Sophy!" The same theme is explored in "The Man from the Caravan," in which two sisters, Marion and Rose, vie for the love of a feckless romantic novelist. Although Coppard describes the main characters as silly or vain misfits—a local colonel who is smitten by Marion is described as "an awkward oaf-like maniac"—he never loses sympathy with them and reveals himself as a profound analyst of human behaviour.

Coppard's other great strength is the technical skill with which he invokes the background. In stories like "Weep Not My Wanton," "The Wife of Ted Wickham," and "The Truant Heart," the countryside is almost a character in its own right, lovingly depicted, with a life of its own. By his own admission Coppard knew the English countryside so well because he had spent much of his young life tramping over it. As the son of poor parents he had to work hard, too. Although self-pity is entirely absent from his literary output, there are strong autobiographical echoes of his early life in the tailoring trade in his story "The Presser," which focuses on the sweatshops of London in the early days of this century.

Although it is possible to see the influence of Chekhov or Maupassant in early collections like *Adam and Eve and Pinch Me* and *The Black Dog*, Coppard's voice is very much his own. Moreover, he possesses the ability to create events that occur not so much in the lives of his characters as in his observation of them.

For example, the much-anthologised "Mordecai and Cocking" is both a pleasing vignette of rural life and a tart and subtle illustration of the injustices that face both humans and their animals in the real countryside. Not only does Eustace Cocking, the young countryman, lose his job and his living but his dog drops dead while chasing a hare, and the story ends with nemesis approaching in the shape of the menacing gamekeeper. Here, as in every other story, Coppard showed a sure ear for the rhythms and cadences of rural speech.

Above all, and this quality marks Coppard as an outstanding exponent of the short story, in all his fiction he translated the best aspects of the observed rural world into the realms of his own imagination.

—Trevor Royle

See the essays on "The Black Dog," "Fishmonger's Fiddle," and "The Poor Man."

———

CORTÁZAR, Julio. Argentine. Born in Brussels, Belgium, 26 August 1914; grew up in Argentina. Educated at teachers college, Buenos Aires, literature degree. Married 1) Aurora Bernardez in 1953; 3) Carol Dunlop. Taught in secondary schools in several small towns and in Mendoza, Argentina, 1935–45; translator for publishers, 1945–51; lived in Paris, from 1951: writer, and freelance translator for UNESCO. Recipient: Grand Aigle d'Or (Nice), 1976. *Died 12 February 1984.*

PUBLICATIONS

Short Stories

Bestiario.   1951.
Final del juego.   1956.
Las armas secretas.   1959.
Historias de cronopios y de famas.   1962; as *Cronopios and Famas,*   1969.
Cuentos.   1964.
Todos los fuegos el fuego.   1966; as *All Fires the Fire and Other Stories,*   1973.
End of the Game and Other Stories (selection).   1967; as *Blow-Up and Other Stories,*   1968.
El perseguidor y otros cuentos.   1967.
Ceremonias (selection).   1968.
Relatos (selection).   1970.
La isla a mediodia y otros relatos.   <u>1971.</u>
Octaedro.   1974.
Los relatos.   4 vols., 1976–85.
Alguien que anda por ahí y otros relatos.   1977.
Territorios.   1978.

A Change of Light and Other Stories. 1980.
Queremos tanto a Glenda. 1981; as We Love Glenda So Much and Other Tales, 1983.

Novels

Los premios. 1960; as The Winners, 1965.
Rayuela. 1963; as Hopscotch, 1966.
62: Modelo para armar. 1968; as 62: A Model Kit, 1972.
Libro de Manuel. 1973; as A Manual for Manuel, 1978.
La casilla de los Morelli, edited by Julio Ortega. 1973.
Vampiros multinacionales. 1975.
Un tal Lucas. 1979; as A Certain Lucas, 1984.
Deshoras. 1983.

Play

Los reyes. 1949.

Verse

Presencia (as Julio Denis). 1938.
Pameos y meopas. 1971.

Other

La vuelta al día en ochenta mundos. 1967; as Around the Day in Eighty Worlds, 1986.
Buenos Aires, Buenos Aires (includes English translation). 1968.
Último round. 1969.
Literatura en la revolución y revolución en la literatura, with Oscar Collazos and Mario Vargas Llosa. 1970.
Viaje alrededor de una mesa. 1970.
Prosa del observatorio, with Antonio Galvez. 1972.
Paris: The Essence of an Image. 1981.
Los autonautas de la cosmopista, o, Un viaje atemporal París-Marsella, with Carol Dunlop. 1983.
Argentina: Años de alambradas culturales. 1984.
Nicaragua, tan violentamente dulce. 1984; as Nicaraguan Sketches, 1989.
Textos políticos. 1985.
La fascinación de las palabras (interviews), with Omar Prego. 1985.
Cartas a una pelirroja, edited by Evelyn Picon Garfield. 1990.

Translator, Obras en prosa, by Edgar Allan Poe. 1956.

*

Bibiography: Cortázar: His Works and His Critics: A Bibliography by Sarah de Mundo Lo, 1985.

Critical Studies: Cortázar by Evelyn P. Garfield, 1975; Cortázar: Rayuela by Robert Brody, 1976; The Final Island: The Fiction of Cortázar (includes bibliography) edited by Ivar Ivask and Jaime Alazraki, 1978; The Novels of Cortázar by Steven Boldy, 1980; Keats, Poe, and the Shaping of Cortázar's Mythopoesis by Ana Hernández del Castillo, 1981; Cortázar by Terry J. Peauler, 1990; Cortázar's Character Mosaic: Reading the Longer Fiction by Gordana Yovanovich, 1991; The Contemporary Praxis of the Fantastic: Borges and Cortázar by Julio Rodríguez-Luis, 1991; The Politics of Style in the Fiction of Balzac, Beckett, and Cortázar by M.R. Axelrod, 1991; The Magical and the Monstrous: Two Faces of the Child-Figure in the Fiction of Cortázar and José Donoso by Sarah E. King, 1992.

* * *

In a note at the end of his second collection Final del juego (End of the Game), Julio Cortázar suggested that chronology of composition was not a way to define his stories. He appears to be a writer who came fully mature to the concision and suggestibility of the short story with his first collection, Bestiario (Bestiary) in 1951. In fact he published his first short story (under the name of Julio Denis) in 1941.

Cortázar disliked explaining his stories to critics, but did outline what he felt his 82 short stories tried to explore. He dismissed the anecdote, what the story is about, as trivial, and felt a story sought to release an "explosion of mental energy," an "archetypal babble," close to the surrealist attempt to liberate the subconscious from the repressive forces mutilating an individual. Cortázar's fiction abounds in suspicions of some deeper reality that can never be named in conventional language. However, most of his stories depend on a skilled use of realism, a believable narrator, and porteño slang (Spanish spoken in Buenos Aires) in order to invoke this alien force hidden inside people.

"House Taken Over," the opening story of Bestiario (published the year he left for Paris), is narrated by a man from a privileged background, living with his sister in a grand flat. Something is taking over their flat. The narrator resignedly accepts this invasion, and simply locks door after door, losing his books, then clothes, until he and his sister are forced out into the street, and he drops the key into a drain. Is the story a nightmare? Is there some fantastic creature taking over the house? We never know. We are left with clues about the kind of people involved; their dependence on books, their fixed routines, their lack of vitality. The story could even be a parable about Peronism and the intellectual class. However, the critic cannot clear up the mystery, and this is often the point in Cortázar's stories.

The title story, "Bestiary" is narrated by a young girl (Cortázar is masterly at catching the mentality of children approaching adolescence) who is sent off to the country to stay with relatives, and is forbidden to enter certain rooms because the grown-ups claim a tiger lurks there. This girl witnesses but does not really understand a breakdown in the relationships between the adults (some illicit affair?), and finally pretends the tiger is in another room, to take vengeance on Nene, who is killed. What is this tiger? Again a critic can only guess, for the narrator is a half-knowing child.

In Final del juego Cortázar continues his exploration of this archetypal babble, with further stories narrated by young people, like "After Lunch," (not translated) where a boy is forced to take "it" for a walk to the centre of Buenos Aires in a local bus. This "it" shifts from appearing to be a dog, or a backward brother, to something more symbolic like adolescent awkwardness. Cortázar refuses to reveal the identity of this enigmatic, threatening "it" that the boy narrator tries to abandon, but cannot. The story could be a parable about a boy's lack of freedom, about the guilt of growing up into the adult's world, but interpretation is up to the critic.

The third collection, *Las armas secretas* (Secret Weapons) takes this invisible, threatening force outside the narrator's consciousness even further. In the title story "Secret Weapons," about Pierre in Paris, trying to bed his girl friend Michèle, we find that chance associations occur in his mind from suddenly imagining a double-barrelled shotgun, to a glass ball on a staircase in a suburban house. Slowly it emerges that Michèle was once raped by a German soldier, and Pierre reminds her of this man. Then in a tricky scene, it could be that the German did not rape her, for a voice speaks about true love, and sings a recurring Schumann song; maybe the soldier was killed by the Resistance, and Michèle was ashamed of being in love with a German. The title alludes to these bizarre forces in the mind. A longer story called the "The Pursuer" about a jazz saxophonist based on Charlie Parker, narrated by a critic called Bruno, suggests more meaningful ways of looking at time, at identity, at what art really is. Despite the black jazz player's stuttering explorations into the darker side of life, Cortázar shows how the status quo asserts itself as Johnny dies with his "quest" unsolved.

A story like "The Island at Noon" from his fourth collection *Todos los fuegos el fuego (All Fires the Fire and Other Stories)*, could have been published in his first collection, as a stale air steward's dreams of a small Greek island. He finally arrives there to witness his own plane crash, as he swims out to meet himself, drowning. Cortázar plays with doubles, and split identities in a Poe-like way. The complicated story "The Other Heaven" is split between Buenos Aires of the 1940's and Paris of the 1870's, a friendly whore, a strange South American poet, a public execution, and a boring marriage, so that one narrator appears to be the fantasy projection of the other, but it is hard to know which time zone is more realistic.

"Severo's Phases" from *Octaedro*, about a local faith-healer who attracts people to his mysterious prophecies, was described by Cortázar as being the "exact narration of a nightmare I had." Cortázar's skill lies in depicting the nightmare so that it remains more vivid than any interpretation of it. Some of Cortázar's later stories do suggest some political bad-faith irrupting out of normality ("Meeting," "Apocalypse at Solentiname"), but even the more politicised Cortázar does not interpret his own storytelling. He was acutely aware of how difficult it was for his narrators and characters to change their lives, but they remain haunted by some sense of a deeper otherness threatening their orderly bourgeois lives.

—Jason Wilson

See the essays on "Apocalypse at Solentiname," "Axolotl," "Blow-Up," and "End of the Game."

English, University of Western Australia. Co-editor, *Westerly,* since 1975. Recipient: Commonwealth Literary Fund fellowship, 1963; Australian Council for the Arts fellowship, 1974, 1980. Order of Australia (AM), 1987. Lives in Mount Claremont, Australia.

PUBLICATIONS

Short Stories

Drift. 1944.
The Unploughed Land. 1958.
The Empty Street. 1965.
The Tins and Other Stories. 1973.
New Country, with others, edited by Bruce Bennett. 1976.
Mobiles. 1979.
A Window in Mrs. X's Place (selected stories). 1986.
Voices. 1988.

Novels

Summer. 1964.
Seed. 1966.
The Color of the Sky. 1986.
The Hills of Apollo Bay. 1989.

Other

A Unique Position: A Biography of Edith Dircksey Cowan 1861–1932. 1978.
Maitland Brown: A View of Nineteenth-Century Western Australia. 1988.

Editor, *Short Story Landscape: The Modern Short Story.* 1964.
Editor, with Bruce Bennett and John Hay, *Spectrum 1–2.* 2 vols., 1970; *Spectrum 3,* 1979.
Editor, *Today: Short Stories of Our Time.* 1971.
Editor, *A Faithful Picture: The Letters of Eliza and Thomas Brown at York in the Swan River Colony 1841–1852.* 1977.
Editor, *A Colonial Experience: Swan River 1839–1888 from the Diary and Reports of Walkinshaw Cowan.* Privately printed. 1979.
Editor, with Bruce Bennett and John Hay, *Perspectives One* (short stories). 1985.
Editor, *Impressions: West Coast Fiction 1829–1988.* 1989.
Editor, with Bruce Bennett, John Hay, and Susan Ashford, *Western Australian Writing: A Bibliography.* 1990.

*

Critical Studies: "The Short Stories of Cowan," 1960, and "New Tracks to Travel: The Stories of White, Porter and Cowan," 1966, both by John Barnes, in *Meanjin;* essay by Grahame Johnston in *Westerly,* 1967; "Cowan Country" by Margot Luke, in *Sandgropers* edited by Dorothy Hewett, 1973; "Behind the Actual" by Bruce Williams, in *Westerly* 3, 1973; "Regionalism in Cowan's Short Fiction" by Bruce Bennett, in *World Literature Written in English,* 1980; "Practitioner of Silence" by Wendy Jenkins, in *Fremantle Arts Review* 1, 1986; "Of Books and Covers: Cowan" by

---

COWAN, Peter (Walkinshaw). Australian. Born in Perth, Western Australia, 4 November 1914. Educated at the University of Western Australia, Nedlands, B.A. in English 1941, Dip. Ed. 1946. Served in the Royal Australian Air Force, 1943–45. Married Edith Howard in 1941; one son. Clerk, farm labourer, and casual worker, 1930–39; teacher, 1941–42; member of the faculty, University of Western Australia, 1946–50; senior English master, Scotch College, Swanbourne, Western Australia, 1950–62; senior tutor, 1964–79, and since 1979 Honorary Research Fellow in

Bruce Bennett, in *Overland 114*, 1989; *Cowan: New Critical Essays* edited by Bruce Bennett and Susan Miller, 1992.

* * *

Although Peter Cowan has written four novels and two biographies, he is best known as a short story writer. Many stories have been published in international anthologies, and his work has been translated into German, Danish, Swedish, Japanese, and Chinese. Cowan's seven volumes of short stories span a period from the 1930's to the late 1980's. He has been characterized as a regional writer of his native Western Australia, but in half a century of writing and publishing short fiction he has also demonstrated a strong interest in modernistic experiment. Cowan has written long stories verging on the novella, such as "The Unploughed Land," "The Empty Street," and "The Lake," but he has attracted most attention as a minimalist whose style is deliberately stripped bare of all ornamentation and shows lonely figures, in ones or twos, set against land- or cityscapes. Their voices sometimes seem to emerge bodiless from the land, expressing in their essential isolation something of its distances. Oddly for an Australian writer at this time, Cowan's principal influences were American, especially Hemingway. Chekhov too was an influence, showing how stories could reveal motive, mood, and irony without resort to melodrama.

Cowan's first volume *Drift* contains fifteen stories in three sections: "Yesterday," "Between," "Now." Most of the stories deal with the Depression years in Western Australia and their aftermath, but several evoke the traumas of the home front during World War II. Whereas Australian writers such as Katharine Susannah Prichard perceived the 1930's and 1940's as providing scope for group solidarity or mateship, Cowan's vision is more ironic, more sombre. His characters, usually solitary (even when they are in company) are often emotionally as well as materially deprived. Their battles are as much within themselves as with the outer environment. Yet the author's apparent detachment from them may be more apparent than real; a subdued compassion seems to inform his treatment of the men and women whose fates he evokes.

"I have always been involved in the Australian landscape," Cowan has written, "the physical landscape and everything about it, and in my short stories particularly I have tried to see an interaction of people with this landscape." In "Isolation," the opening story in *Drift,* the historical process of an increasing settlement of farming areas is deftly established, anticipating the early pages of Patrick White's novel *The Tree of Man.* Such settlement is always problematic when set against ecological concerns: "War began against the trees, the jarrah and karri valuable commercially, and against those that were given no value ... war against the trees that brought men there and kept them there" (in the southwest of Western Australia).

The desire of humans to possess this land is dramatized by Cowan; but the land answers with drought, and the depressed economic conditions force farmers from their once-prized holdings. Even in the midst of hardship, however, Cowan's farm workers seem to participate in something good. The rituals of farm work (the man and the woman picking apples together in "Isolation," for example) suggest a quality of meaningful living that city offices and suburban domesticity cannot match. In "Isolation" two farmers on neighbouring farms, a man and a woman, seem for a time to offer each other an escape from isolation, but

the man's confusion and his destructive anger lead to tragedy. The story has elements of social realism but is artfully constructed to convey changes of mood and perspective. The high-flying eagle which is shown hovering above the human figures on this extensive landscape, for example, is reminiscent of perspectives offered in some of Thomas Hardy's Wessex tales.

Two of Cowan's most anthologised stories are "The Red-Backed Spiders" and "The Tractor." In "The Tractor" (from *The Empty Street* collection) a typical Cowan antithesis between city and bush values and ways of living is exposed. The story shows a woman teacher's romantic ideas of the bush and its inhabitants, which are opposed to her fiancé's instincts as a farmer to clear the land of all trees. But Cowan's imagination is subtle and does not remain at the level of simple binary oppositions. The woman (whose conservationist values Cowan would personally endorse) becomes implicated in the destructive forces she condemns. In stories such as this one Cowan achieves lights and shades of colouring, suggesting somehow both the primacy of the Australian landscape and the ineffectual efforts of humans to achieve understanding or harmony with it. Consonant with this approach is his stripping of human character to its non-social aspects, highlighting the often-frustrated primal human needs of love and a place of belonging.

The later stories of Peter Cowan in volumes such as *Mobiles* and *Voices* illustrate his increasing drive towards compression of effect. In the volume *Voices,* earlier experiments with chiaroscuro and other techniques are renewed and sharpened. Without the trappings of normal narrative conventions, such as authorial commentary or explanation, or even quotation marks to denote direct speech, Cowan's voices speak unclothed, as if out of the darkness in which they live. They appear bare of physiological mannerisms, eccentric clothing, or the other colourful paraphernalia of conventional constructions of character. In these later short fictions, especially, Cowan's treatment indicates his belief in the fragility of human reason. In their representation of what Cowan has called "the pointlessness, frustration and bitterness of much of today's living," these stories reject the conventions of a realism deriving from historical narrative or journalism. Yet the world which Cowan's stories reveal is that which our newspapers and television regularly inform us about or moralise upon: the drug culture, prostitution, sexual abuse, commercial corruption.

In *Voices,* Cowan's settings, which are often used symbolically, range from representations of the dry interior of Western Australia to sections of its coastline, from school classrooms and their surroundings to glassed-in apartments in Perth or a hotel in one of the nearby Asian capitals. In the story "Apartment," for instance, an ex-addict and prostitute enjoys the relative luxury of an apartment where she has been asked to live with a man on weekends and evenings, apparently as a pay-off for some drug deal. Cowan's focus is not on externals, however; instead, he offers hints and clues, requiring the reader to piece together the emotional puzzles of the situation. Continually at issue are questions of freedom and responsibility; the reality of his characters' lives is their imprisonment in situations where they are forced to adopt masks or "covers" for their emotions.

Cowan's bareness of style may itself be seen as a cover for his subtle and sometimes complex explorations of Australian figures set against a variety of Western land and cityscapes. His achievement is to avoid both the cliches of a populist bush realism, and a fashionable postmodernism, in a continual wrestle with the forms of short fiction. In so doing, he shows the scope for experiment and change in this most flexible of art forms.

—Bruce Bennett

See the essay on "The Red-Backed Spiders."

———————

CRANE, Stephen. American. Born in Newark, New Jersey, 1 November 1871. Educated at schools in Port Jervis, New York, 1878–83, and Asbury Park, New Jersey, 1883–84; Pennington Seminary, 1885–87; Claverack College, and Hudson River Institute, Claverack, New York, 1888–90; Lafayette College, Easton, Pennsylvania, 1890; Syracuse University, New York, 1891. Lived with Cora Taylor from 1897. News agency reporter, New York *Tribune,* 1891–92; wrote sketches of New York life for New York *Press,* 1894; travelled in the western U.S. and Mexico, writing for the Bacheller and Johnson Syndicate, 1895; sent by Bacheller to report on the insurrection in Cuba, 1896: shipwrecked on the voyage, 1897; went to Greece to report the Greco-Turkish War for New York *Journal* and *Westminster Gazette,* London, 1897; lived in England after 1897; reported the Spanish-American War in Cuba for the New York *World,* later for the New York *Journal,* 1898. *Died 5 June 1900.*

PUBLICATIONS

Collections

The Complete Short Stories and Sketches, edited by Thomas A. Gullason.   1963.
The Portable Crane, edited by Joseph Katz.   1969.
Works, edited by Fredson Bowers.   10 vols., 1969–76.
Prose and Poetry (Library of America), edited by J.C. Levenson.   1984.

Short Stories

The Little Regiment and Other Episodes of the American Civil War.   1896.
The Open Boat and Other Tales of Adventure.   1898.
The Monster and Other Stories.   1899; augmented edition, 1901.
Whilomville Stories.   1900.
Wounds in the Rain: War Stories.   1900.
The Sullivan County Sketches, edited by Melvin Schoberlin.   1949; revised edition, edited by R.W. Stallman, as *Sullivan County Tales and Sketches,* 1968.

Novels

Maggie, A Girl of the Streets (A Story of New York).   1893; revised edition, 1896.
The Red Badge of Courage: An Episode of the American Civil War.   1895.
George's Mother.   1896.
The Third Violet.   1897.
Active Service.   1899.
Last Words.   1902.
The O'Ruddy: A Romance, with Robert Barr.   1903.

Play

The Blood of the Martyr.   1940.

Verse

The Black Riders and Other Lines.   1895.
A Souvenir and a Medley: Seven Poems and a Sketch. 1896.
War Is Kind.   1899.

Other

Great Battles of the War.   1901.
Et Cetera: A Collector's Scrap-Book.   1924.
A Battle in Greece.   1936.
Letters, edited by R.W. Stallman and Lillian Gilkes. 1960.
Uncollected Writings, edited by Olov W. Fryckstedt. 1963.
The War Despatches, edited by R.W. Stallman and E.R. Hagemann.   1964.
The New York City Sketches and Related Pieces, edited by R.W. Stallman and E.R. Hagemann.   1966.
Notebook, edited by Donald J. and Ellen B. Greiner. 1969.
Crane in the West and Mexico, edited by Joseph Katz. 1970.
The Western Writings, edited by Frank Bergon.   1979.
The Correspondence, edited by Stanley Wertheim and Paul Sorrentino.   2 vols., 1988.

*

Bibliography: *Crane: A Critical Bibliography* by R.W. Stallman, 1972; *Crane: An Annotated Bibliography* by John C. Sherwood, 1983; *Crane: An Annotated Bibliography of Secondary Scholarship* by Patrick K. Dooley, 1992.

Critical Studies: *Crane: A Study in American Letters* by Thomas Beer, 1923; *Crane,* 1950, and *Crane: The Red Badge of Courage,* 1981, both by John Berryman; "Naturalistic Fiction: 'The Open Boat'" by Richard P. Adams, in *Tulane Studies in English* 4, 1954; *The Poetry of Crane* by Daniel Hoffman, 1957; "Realistic Devices in Crane's 'The Open Boat'" by Charles R. Metzger, in *Midwest Quarterly* 4, 1962; *Crane* by Edwin H. Cady, 1962, revised edition, 1980; *Crane in England,* 1964, and *Crane: From Parody to Realism,* 1966, both by Eric Solomon; "Crane's 'The Bride Comes to Yellow Sky'" by A.M. Tibbets, in *English Journal* 54, 1965; "Interpretation Through Language: A Study of the Metaphors in Crane's 'The Open Boat'" by Leedice Kissane, in *Rendezvous* 1, 1966; *Crane: A Biography* by R.W. Stallman, 1968; *The Fiction of Crane,* 1968, and *The Red Badge of Courage: Redefining the Hero,* 1988, both by Donald B. Gibson; *A Reading of Crane* by Marston LaFrance, 1971; *Cylinder of Vision: The Fiction and Journalistic Writing of Crane* by Milne Holton, 1972; *Crane: The Critical Heritage* edited by Richard Weatherford, 1973; *Crane's Artistry* by Frank Bergon, 1975; *Crane and Literary Impressionism* by James Nagel, 1980; *The Anger of Crane: Fiction and the Epic Tradition* by Chester L. Wolford, 1983; *Crane* by James B. Colvert, 1984; "Crane's Vaudeville Marriage: 'The Bride Comes to Yellow Sky'" by Samuel I. Bellman, in *Selected Essays: International Conference on Wit and Humor,* edited by Dorothy

M. Joiner, 1986; *New Essays on The Red Badge of Courage* edited by Lee Clerk Mitchell, 1986; *Crane* by Bettina L. Knapp, 1987; *Crane* edited by Harold Bloom, 1987; *Crane: A Pioneer in Technique* by H.S.S. Bais, 1988; *The Color of the Sky: A Study of Crane* by David Haliburton, 1989; *Crane: A Study of the Short Fiction* by Chester L. Wolford, 1989; *Critical Essays on Crane* edited by Donald Pizer, 1990; *The Double Life of Crane* by Christopher E.G. Benfey, 1992.

* * *

Though Stephen Crane is best known for his innovative Civil War novel, *The Red Badge of Courage,* and a handful of superb stories, among them "The Blue Hotel," "The Bride Comes to Yellow Sky," and "The Open Boat," he was astonishingly productive. When he died in 1900 at the age of 28 from tuberculosis aggravated by his strenuous life as a freelance journalist, he had written six novels, two books of poems, six collections of stories and sketches, and several volumes of miscellaneous journalism. A relativist, ironist, and impressionist, he was the most gifted writer of his generation, and the most original, admired by generations of readers for his acute psychological insights, his bold experiments with new fictional forms, and his witty impressionistic style.

Crane's stories cover an unusually wide range of subjects and settings. He wrote of the savagery of New York slum life, of the horrors of war on imagined battlefields in Virginia and on real ones in Greece and Cuba, of the terror and despair of shipwreck, of the comedy, pathos, and cruelty of childlife in smalltown America, and of the blighting powers of social superstition and community prejudice. Yet for all this variety there is a remarkable unity in his writings, partly because of the pronounced and consistent interpenetration of theme in his work, partly because of the power of his integrating imagination. His way of seeing things was shaped by the cultural, social, and intellectual conflicts of the 1870's, 1880's, and 1890's, when the new sciences and advanced theological scholarship were sharply challenging the authority of orthodox religion and whatever faith was left in the expansive ideas of the old Romantic idealism. By the early 1890's, when Crane wrote his first stories, Emerson's notion of a godlike, self-reliant hero who enjoys an original relation to a benevolent and purposeful nature was to many no longer convincing. In Crane's perspective humans appear as diminished, standing helpless before the implacable forces of nature, raging against the hostile—or worse, indifferent—gods they hold responsible for their plight. This paradigm appears regularly in his fiction, bringing into close relationship such superficially disparate stories and sketches as "The Mesmeric Mountain" and "Four Men in a Cave" in (*The Sullivan County Tales and Sketches*), *The Red Badge of Courage,* "The Blue Hotel," "The Open Boat," "Death and the Child," "A Descent into a Coal Mine," "Mr. Bink's Holiday," and others. Many of the tropes, images, and motifs associated with the theme are ingeniously adapted from story to story, further emphasizing the connections between them and enhancing the power of imagination that informs them.

The essential traits of Crane's diminished hero appear in his earliest journalistic writings, satirical descriptions of complacent vacationers at resorts along the Jersey Coast. In an ironic phrase here, a mocking image there, he exposed their vanity by placing them in the context of a vast and indifferent nature: the narcissistic "summer girl" appears on the beach as "a bit of interesting tinsel flashing near the sombre-hued ocean"; the pompous founder of the town is certain that his beach enhances the value of the Lord's adjacent sea. The hero of several Sullivan County stories, Crane's first professional fiction, suffers similar delusions. He is "the little man" (many of Crane's characters are anonymous, or nearly so), a swaggering outdoorsman who anxiously explores the rugged Sullivan County landscape for signs of a benevolent and sympathetic nature. What his anxiety-driven fancy discovers is not reassurance but maddening ambiguity: the "black mouth" of a cave gapes at him; a hill, mysteriously sentient, glowers threateningly; yet on occasion, when the sun gleams "merrily" on a little lake, and the soughing pines sing hymns of love, the landscape is a pastoral idyll, a marvel of harmony and divine good will. Laboring under the stress of these fantasies, the "little man's" mood swings wildly between rage and despair and strutting self-assurance.

This characterization of this hero and the tropes and imagery of an ambiguous nature are the essential elements of many of Crane's stories, including his masterpieces, *The Red Badge of Courage* and "The Open Boat." Like the "little man," Henry Fleming (*The Red Badge*) desperately seeks justification for his cowardly conduct on the battlefield in the transcendent authority of nature—just as the reflective correspondent in the "The Open Boat" seeks answers to the riddle of being in the seascape. Unlike Henry, the correspondent eventually dispels his neurotic fantasies—the only character in Crane's fiction who does so—and comes to understand that nature is neither for nor against him—neither cruel, "nor beneficent, or treacherous, nor wise," but "indifferent, flatly indifferent."

In these stories the theme is central, constituting in effect the entire plot; in others it appears obliquely and incidentally. "The Blue Hotel" a good example of its ingenious adaptation in stories with very different settings and subjects. The "coxcomb" hero, the Swede, an Eastern visitor to the Nebraska frontier town of Fort Romper, takes refuge from a raging blizzard in a local hotel. His head swarming with dime-thriller fantasies of western violence, he suspects the owner and his son of plotting his murder. He beats the outraged son in a savage fistfight, and leaving the hotel makes his way into the town through the howling storm. Swelled with pride in his heroic victory over the owner's son, the Swede imagines himself as a worthy adversary of the blizzard, a sterling representative of a "conquering and elate humanity." "The conceit of man," Crane writes, neatly encapsulating his major theme, "was explained by this storm to be the very engine of life." The Swede enters a saloon, swelled with pride in his imagined victory. "I like this weather," he boasts to the barman. "It suits me. I like it. It suits me." A moment later the victor is dead, murdered by a professional gambler he tries to bully into having a drink with him.

Though the vain hero and his alienation in nature figures in his work from first to last, Crane pursued other important themes as well. The conflict between the ideals of civic order and lawlessness is the principal theme of "The Blue Hotel" and "The Bride Comes to Yellow Sky," a superb comedy that tells how the newly-wed marshal of Yellow Sky, Texas, insures the domestication of the town by subduing the local six-gun wizard, Scratchy Wilson. The power of relentless social and economic forces, the theme of Crane's first novel, *Maggie: A Girl of the Streets,* is vividly, though indirectly, evoked in descriptions of a nightmarish Bowery flophouse ("An Experiment in Misery") and of the despair of huddled men in a bread line

("The Men in the Storm"). Devastation wrought by the bigotry and cruelty of smalltown life is the theme of "The Monster" and other Whilomville stories.

Crane's ironic depiction of the tragic consequences of sentimental self-aggrandizement and his unique impressionistic style earned him the admiration of the leading literary writers of his time, among them Joseph Conrad, Ford Madox Ford, and H.G. Wells. Wells's conviction that Crane's work "was the first expression of the opening mind of a new period" proved prophetic. Some of the major writers of the brilliant 1920's, Amy Lowell, Willa Cather, Sherwood Anderson, and Ernest Hemingway, found in his high originality something of the spirit of their own revolutionary literary aims.

—James B. Colvert

See the essays on "The Bride Comes to Yellow Sky" and "The Open Boat."

———————

D

DAHL, Roald. British. Born in Llandaff, Glamorgan, Wales, 13 September 1916. Educated at Repton School, Yorkshire. Served in the Royal Air Force, 1939–45: in Nairobi and Habbanyah, 1939–40; with a fighter squadron in the Western Desert, 1940 (wounded); in Greece and Syria, 1941; assistant air attaché, Washington, D.C., 1942–43; wing commander, 1943; with British Security Co-ordination, North America, 1943–45. Married 1) the actress Patricia Neal in 1953 (divorced 1983), one son and four daughters (one deceased); 2) Felicity Ann Crosland in 1983. Member of the Public Schools Exploring Society expedition to Newfoundland, 1934; member of the Eastern staff, Shell Company, London, 1933–37, and Shell Company of East Africa, Dar-es-Salaam, 1937–39. Recipient: Mystery Writers of America Edgar Allan Poe award, 1953, 1959, 1980; Federation of Children's Book Groups award, 1983; Whitbread award, 1983; World Fantasy Convention award, 1983; Federation of Children's Book Groups award, 1989. D.Litt.: University of Keele, Staffordshire, 1988. *Died 23 November 1990.*

PUBLICATIONS

Short Stories

Over to You: 10 Stories of Flyers and Flying. 1946.
Someone Like You. 1953; revised edition, 1961.
Kiss, Kiss. 1960.
Twenty-Nine Kisses. 1969.
Selected Stories. 1970.
Penguin Modern Stories 12, with others. 1972.
Switch Bitch. 1974.
The Best of Dahl. 1978.
Tales of the Unexpected. 1979.
More Tales of the Unexpected. 1980; as *Further Tales of the Unexpected,* 1981.
A Dahl Selection: Nine Short Stories, edited by Roy Blatchford. 1980.
Two Fables. 1986.
A Second Dahl Selection: Eight Short Stories, edited by Hélène Fawcett. 1987.
Ah, Sweet Mystery of Life, illustrated by John Lawrence. 1990.

Novels

Sometime Never: A Fable for Supermen. 1948.
My Uncle Oswald. 1979.

Fiction (for children)

The Gremlins, illustrated by Walt Disney Studio. 1943.
James and the Giant Peach, illustrated by Nancy Ekholm Burkert. 1961.
Charlie and the Chocolate Factory, illustrated by Joseph Schindelman. 1964.

The Magic Finger, illustrated by William Pène du Bois. 1966.
Fantastic Mr. Fox, illustrated by Donald Chaffin. 1970.
Charlie and the Great Glass Elevator, illustrated by Joseph Schindelman. 1972.
Danny, The Champion of the World, illustrated by Jill Bennett. 1975.
The Wonderful Story of Henry Sugar and Six More. 1977; as *The Wonderful World of Henry Sugar.* 1977.
The Complete Adventures of Charlie and Mr. Willy Wonka (omnibus), illustrated by Faith Jaques. 1978.
The Enormous Crocodile, illustrated by Quentin Blake. 1978.
The Twits, illustrated by Quentin Blake. 1980.
George's Marvellous Medicine, illustrated by Quentin Blake. 1981.
The BFG, illustrated by Quentin Blake. 1982.
The Witches, illustrated by Quentin Blake. 1983.
The Giraffe and the Pelly and Me, illustrated by Quentin Blake. 1985.
Matilda, illustrated by Quentin Blake. 1988.
Esio Trot, illustrated by Quentin Blake. 1990.
The Vicar of Nibbleswicke, illustrated by Quentin Blake. 1991.

Plays

The Honeys (produced New York, 1955).

Screenplays: *You Only Live Twice,* with Harry Jack Bloom, 1967; *Chitty-Chitty-Bang-Bang,* with Ken Hughes, 1968; *The Night-Digger,* 1970; *The Lightning Bug,* 1971; *Willy Wonka and the Chocolate Factory,* 1971.

Television Play: *Lamb to the Slaughter* (Alfred Hitchcock Presents series), 1955.

Verse (for children)

Revolting Rhymes, illustrated by Quentin Blake. 1982.
Dirty Beasts, illustrated by Rosemary Fawcett. 1983.
Rhyme Stew, illustrated by Quentin Blake. 1989.

Other

Boy: Tales of Childhood (autobiography; for children). 1984.
Going Solo (autobiography; for children). 1986.

Editor, *Dahl's Book of Ghost Stories.* 1983.

*

Critical Studies: *Dahl* by Chris Powling, 1983; *Dahl* by Alan Warren, 1988.

* * *

After being severely wounded in World War II, and then resuming his career as a fighter pilot, Roald Dahl was sent to Washington as an assistant air attaché in 1942. It was in Washington that he began writing the short stories for American magazines about his wartime experience that were later collected as *Over to You*. Although Dahl later wrote more for children, his adult short fiction includes in a whole series of collections—*Someone Like You, Kiss Kiss, Twenty-Nine Kisses from Roald Dahl, Switch Bitch,* and *Ah, Sweet Mystery of Life*. Some of these stories were dramatized for television and published in the two anthologies *Tales of the Unexpected* and *More Tales of the Unexpected*. Dahl's current reputation is, however, still largely dependent on his writing for children, and in 1983 he was awarded the Whitbread prize for *The Witches*. Although the more urbane short fiction was plainly written for adults, its foreshortened psychological and emotional perspectives, as well as other techniques, often bear the hallmark of a writer whose imagination is attuned to that of children.

The short story suits Dahl's imaginative purposes for a variety of reasons. It allows forceful moral points to be made without lengthy psychological analysis or emotional profundity. It permits a reliance on conversational exchange that promotes vividness and allows swift and effective caricature to be substituted for depth of characterization. Above all, it allows Dahl's point to be made in a single episode, anecdote, or escapade, often with his characteristic type of ending. He has been described as "the absolute master of the twist in the tale." Sometimes vicious twists at the end of the stories teasingly challenge the reader's generic expectations, generated by the register and language of the foregoing narration. The need for psychological complexity is replaced by a punchy story line, incidentally making the texts ideal for dramatization.

The literary techniques nevertheless are effective for being relatively unsophisticated. First person narration is purposefully used to achieve real immediacy. In "Bitch" Dahl even introduces a mirror-system of first-person narrators in Uncle Oswald's diaries and the nephew who introduces them. The absurdity of the plot keeps the reader at a distance, while the mode of narration engages the reader's sympathies. Much the same might be said of "Pig," where the pretended literary form adds a further mine of irony. Dahl purports to be writing a fairy-tale:

Once upon a time, in the City of New York, a beautiful baby boy was born into this world, and the joyful parents named him Lexington.

The alliterative "b" sounds, banal adjectives, the child's name, the upper case for "City," and the opening four words all converge to announce a register of amused irony. Lexington is referred to throughout the story as "our hero," portrayed as being sweetly innocent, with blond hair and blue eyes, writing a vegetarian cookbook, and living in the country where he looks after his elderly Aunt Glosspan. When she dies, he buries her in the garden and goes to New York, where he is conned by a lawyer and eventually killed in an abattoir. The humour is macabre. The vegetarian not only eats meat, but becomes meat, falling into the boiling water with the other pigs. Writing about how to cook, he becomes cooked. The narrative is straight-faced, with "our hero" used in the last sentence. The fairy story pretence and faintly adolescent humour are deployed in a piece of short fiction dependent on subtle and adult ironies.

The boyishness of Dahl's humour remains conspicuous, locked into the grim period when his imagination was formed, between his famous account of being caned at his prep school (by a future archbishop of Canterbury), and his life as a beer-swilling young officer. He is fascinated by scrapes and how to get out of them, uses obsolete upper middle-class schoolboy slang, with words like "tough" and nicknames like "Stinker," and often uses pastiche of the boys' adventure story as a literary form.

The humour is bizarre, mischievous, sometimes ghoulish. In "Lamb to the Slaughter," a woman kills her husband with a joint of lamb from the freezer. With a dead husband and a frozen leg of lamb as his stage properties, Dahl sends her shopping and unfreezes the meat. The police are called as the murder weapon is roasting, and prevailed on to eat it. Mary Moloney feels genuine grief, but cannot help sharing the reader's wry giggle, as the police, thinking that the murder weapon "is probably right under our very noses," set about consuming it. That sort of humour, based on escapades and japes, runs right through Dahl's work, especially what he wrote for children.

In "The Twits," Mrs. Twit cooks "spaghetti" for her husband. In fact it is a plate of worms. Dahl is playing on what, until the quite recent past, was the average British child's unfamiliarity with pasta, and the xenophobic distaste for it. Mr. Twit invents a disease in revenge. He goes to great pains to convince Mrs. Twit that she has contracted "the dreaded shrinks," and that she is on the point of shrinking into oblivion. Once again children are always being warned against illnesses of which their age-group has no direct experience. The childish impishness of the children's stories is actually often distilled from the adult humour of more ambitious short fiction, like the resonant, alliterated names (Mr. Botibol, Mr. Buggage, Tibbs the butler, and Mrs. Tottle the secretary), or the schoolboy larks of trapping pheasants with raisins (in "The Champion of the World" from *Kiss Kiss*, which was in fact later reworked into a children's story, *Danny, The Champion of the World*).

"Vengeance Is Mine" hinges on a similar schoolboy sense of fantasy and justice. Two broke young men set up a business of wreaking revenge on gossip columnists on behalf of the rich people they have insulted in their columns. In less than a week they earn enough to retire. Only adults can know that adult values are so warped that rich people mostly like appearing in gossip columns, and that is Dahl's comment.

Not all the short fiction uses the same stereotype. "Katina" deals with the experiences of a soldier, implicitly Dahl himself, and the horrors that he witnessed in Greece. Simply and unsentimentally the narrator remembers, but the small orphaned girl of the title is used to imply a sharp accusation against the soldiers who remain unable to consider the actual consequences of their killings. At the end, when Katina is killed, the narrator stands unthinking for several hours. The implication is that at this moment he turned against war. Dahl touches on emotional profundity, but without psychological complexity.

Dahl wrote unpretentiously, and laid no claim to the moral high ground. He wanted to entertain, and wrote with great skill and wonderful directness. But it is the sharp moral focus behind the vision that elevates the entertainment into literature.

—Claudia Levi

See the essay on "Georgy Porgy."

———————

DAUDET, Alphonse. French. Born in Nîmes, 13 May 1840. Educated in Lyons. Married Julia Allard in 1867; two sons and one daughter. Pupil-teacher, 1855–56; school usher, Collège d'Alais, 1857; secretary for Duc de Morny, 1860–65; joined National Guard, 1870; full-time writer and playwright, from 1865, Paris. *Died 16 December 1897.*

PUBLICATIONS

Collections

Works. 24 vols., 1898–1900.
The Novels, Romances and Writings of Daudet. 20 vols., 1898–1903.
Oeuvres complètes. 18 vols., 1899–1901; 20 vols., 1929–31.
Oeuvres complètes illustrées. 20 vols., 1929–31.
Œuvres, edited by Jean-Louis Curtis. 12 vols., 1965–66.
Œuvres, edited by Roger Ripoll. 1986—.

Short Stories

Le Roman du Chaperon rouge: scènes et fantaisies. 1862.
Lettres de mon moulin. Impressions et souvenirs. 1869; edited by Jacques-Henry Bornecque; 2 vols., 1948; as *Stories of Provence* (selection), 1886; as *Letters from My Mill,* 1880; as *Letters from a Windmill in Provence,* 1922; as *French Stories from Daudet,* 1945; as *Letters from My Mill and Letters to an Absent One,* 1971; as *Letters from My Windmill,* 1978.
Lettres à un absent. 1871; as *Letters to an Absent One,* 1900; as *Letters to an Absent One and Letters from My Mill,* 1971.
Robert Helmont. Études et paysages. 1873; as *Robert Helmont: Diary of a Recluse, 1870–1871,* 1892.
Contes du lundi. 1873; revised edition, 1878; as *Contes militaires* (special edition), edited by J.T.W. Brown, 1892; as *Monday Tales* (bilingual edition), 1950.
Contes et récits (collection). 1873.
Les Femmes d'artistes. 1874; as *Wives of Men of Genius,* 1889; as *Artists' Wives,* 1890.
Contes choisis. La fantaisie et l'histoire (collection). 1877.
Les Cigognes, légende rhénane. 1883.
La Belle-Nivernaise. Histoire d'un vieux bateau et de son équipage, illustrated by Émile Montégut. 1886; as *La Belle-Nivernaise; The Story of an Old Boat and Her Crew (and Other Stories),* 1887; as *La Belle-Nivernaise, the Story of a River-Barge and its Crew,* edited by James Boïelle, 1888; *La Belle-Nivernaise and Other Stories,* 1895.
La Fedór. L'Enterrement d'une étoile. 1896.
La Fedór. Pages de la vie, illustrated by Faïes. 1897; in part as *Trois souvenirs,* 1896.
Le Trésor d'Arlatan, illustrated by H. Laurent Desrousseaux. 1897.

Novels

Le Petit Chose. Histoire d'un enfant. 1868; as *My Brother Jack, or the Story of What-d'ye-Call'em,* 1877; as *The Little Good-for-Nothing,* 1878.
Aventures prodigieuses de Tartarin de Tarascon. 1872; as *The New Don Quixote, or the Wonderful Adventures of Tartarin de Tarascon,* 1875.

Fromont jeune et Risler aîné. Moeurs parisiennes. 1874; as *Sidonie,* 1877.
Jack. Moeurs contemporaines. 2 vols., 1876; translated as *Jack,* 1877.
Le Nabab. Moeurs parisiennes. 1877; as *The Nabob,* 1877.
Les Rois en exil. 1879; *Kings in Exile,* 1879.
Numa Roumestan. 1881.
L'Evangéliste. Roman parisien. 1883; *Port Salvation; or, The Evangelist,* 2 vols., 1883.
Sapho. Moeurs parisiennes. 1884; as *Sappho,* 1884; as *Sappho: A Picture of Life in Paris,* 1954.
Tartarin sur les Alpes. Nouveaux exploits du héros tarasconnais. 1885; as *Tartarin on the Alps,* 1887.
L'Immortel. 1888.
Port-Tarascon. Dernières aventures de l'illustre Tartarin. 1890; as *Port-Tarascon, the Last Adventures of the Illustrious Tartarin,* 1891.
Rose et Ninette. Moeurs du jour. 1892; as *Rose and Ninette,* 1892.
La Petit Paroisse. Moeurs conjugales. 1895.
Soutien de famille. Moeurs contemporaines. 1898; as *The Head of the Family,* 1898.

Plays

La Dernière Idole, with others (produced 1862). 1862.
Les Absents (produced 1864). 1863.
L'Œillet blanc, with others (produced 1865). 1865.
Le Frère aîné, with others (produced 1867). 1868.
Le Sacrifice (produced 1869). 1869.
L'Arlésienne (produced 1872). 1872; as *L'Arlésienne (The Girl of Arles),* 1894.
Lise Tavernier (produced 1872). 1872.
Le Char, with others (produced 1878). 1878.
Théâtre. 3 vols., 1880–99.
Le Nabab, with others (produced 1880). 1881.
Jack, with others (produced 1881). 1882.
Fromont jeune et Risler aîné, with others (produced 1886). 1886.
Numa Roumestan (produced 1887). 1890.
La Lutte pour la vie (produced 1889). 1890.
L'Obstacle (produced 1889, with music by Reynaldo Hahn). 1891.
Sapho, with others (produced 1885). 1893.
La Menteuse, with others (produced 1892). 1893.

Verse

Les Amoureuses. 1858; enlarged edition, 1863; enlarged edition, as *Les Amoureuses. Poèmes et fantaisies, 1857–61,* 1873.
La Double Conversion, conte en vers. 1861.

Other

Œuvres. 16 vols., 1879–91.
Oeuvres complètes. 8 vols., 1881–87; 24 vols., 1897–99.
Souvenirs d'un homme de lettres. Pages retrouvés (memoirs). 1888; as *Recollections of a Man,* 1889.
Trente ans de Paris. A travers ma vie et mes livres (memoirs). 1888; as *Thirty Years of Paris and of My Literary Life,* 1888.
Entre les Frises et la rampe. Petites études de la vie théâtrale. 1894.

Notes sur la vie (memoirs).   1899.
Premier Voyage, Premier Mensonge. Souvenirs de mon enfance (memoirs), illustrated by Bigot-Valentin. 1900; as *My First Voyage, My First Lie,* 1901.
Pages inédites de critique dramatique, 1874–1880, edited by Lucien Daudet.   1923.
La Doulou.   1929; as *La Doulou: La vie: Extraits des carnets inédit de l'auteurs,* 1931; as *Suffering 1887–95,* 1934.
Histoire d'une amitié: Correspondance inédite entre Daudet et Frédéric Mistral 1860–1897, edited by Jacques-Henry Bornecque.   1979.

Translator, *Vie d'enfant* by Batisto Bonnet.   1894.
Translator, with others, *Valet de ferme.*   1894.

*

Bibliography: *Daudet, A Critical Bibliography* by Geoffrey E. Hare, 2 vols., 1978–79.

Critical Studies: *Daudet* (biography) by Robert H. Sherard, 1894; "Three Notes to Daudet's Stories" by T.A. Jenkins, *Modern Language Notes,* May 1907; in *The Historical Novel and Other Essays* by Brander Matthews, 1901; *Daudet,* by G.V. Dobie, 1949; in *The Short Story* by Sean O'Faolain, 1951; *The Career of Daudet: A Critical Study* by Murray Sachs, 1965; *Daudet* by Alphonse V. Roche, 1976.

* * *

For 40 years, Alphonse Daudet was an active, and highly successful, man of letters, busily publishing poems, plays, novels, short stories, and memoirs—twenty volumes' worth, in the most complete edition of his works—for which he earned a major worldwide reputation. A century later that major reputation is in sharp decline, even in France, where most of his works are no longer read, or in print; his place in French literary history, though far from negligible, is yet among those of the second rank. In addition to two or three still popular novels, only a select handful of his nearly one hundred short stories are "alive" today, having been kept steadily in print since they first appeared. But those stories are so well known, and so widely read, in France and elsewhere, that they have attained the status of classics in the genre, and are regularly studied in the schools. As a short story writer, Daudet is still a major figure.

It is an irony that would not have been lost on Daudet himself that it is only in a "minor" genre that posterity now recognizes him as a major figure. It must be added, however, that Daudet himself never considered the short story a "minor" genre. It was his genre of choice, in which he had learned his craft, and which he had gladly practiced, in some form, throughout his career, from first to last. There is, indeed, symbolic significance in the fact that his last publication was a short story. More telling still is the evidence that a "short story mindset" pervades all his work: his poems often tell a story, his plays can be seen as dramatized anecdotes, and critics have regularly noted that his novels are either episodic in structure, or have so many detachable subplots that they resemble ingeniously disguised short story collections. Storytelling was indeed second nature to Daudet, and he understood full well that it was the indispensable foundation of his literary calling.

Daudet himself believed that he owed his talent as a teller of tales to his meridional temperament: vivacity, emotional warmth, and facility with language. There is much contemporary testimony that, on social occasions, Daudet often proved himself a gifted and spellbinding raconteur. That special ability transfers itself vividly into a story writing style that is effusive yet intimate, and that gives the reader the pleasing sensation of "listening" to the author spontaneously telling the story aloud to an audience of one. The secret of this "oral" style, so carefully cultivated by Daudet in his short stories, lies in the successful creation of the right narratorial "voice" for each occasion, and for that kind of creation Daudet possessed an instinctive ease.

Daudet's first published story collection, *Lettres de mon moulin,* (*Letters from My Windmill*), was ideally suited to the fullest exploitation of this "oral" style. Each story purported to be a letter from the author to various correspondents, thus justifying an informal, warmly personal and quasi-conversational style, and enabling the author to vary mood, tone, and narratorial "voice" according to the subject of each tale. For a somber account of a tragically unrequited love, as in "The Arlesian Girl," Daudet adopted a spare and self-effacing narrative manner, using simple peasant words and short sentences, to emphasize the stark horror of the drama. Tales of minor ecclesiastical misdeeds, by contrast, such as "The Elixir of Reverend Father Gaucher," or "The Pope's Mule," are more effectively rendered in a tone of mounting, infectious gaiety, regularly undercut by sly, ironic observations that create a comfortable distance, for the reader, from the mildly scandalous events being narrated. Stories that broached the moral dilemmas of the author's own calling— "M. Seguin's Goat," and "The Legend of the Man with the Golden Brain" are the chief examples—required the sententiousness and mock solemnity of the fable, the legend, or the exemplary tale, so that the reader might be properly entertained without missing the seriousness of the story's moral insight.

There is striking variety of style, technique, and subject matter in *Letters from My Windmill,* but the common denominator of all the stories is the skill and refined craftsmanship with which each story is presented. This was the first publication in which Alphonse Daudet exhibited something more than a lively imagination and an engaging narrative manner: he proved himself a meticulous and demanding stylist, with a sense of form and structure, a keen ear for appropriate sentence rhythm, and a willingness to revise his work repeatedly, to meet his own aesthetic standards. He had become a disciplined artist.

During the 1870's, Daudet expanded his range and his productivity in the short story, finding new subject matter in the Franco-Prussian War, and in the daily life of Parisians, for example, and discovering new ways to tell a contemporary tale without losing any of the freshness and charm of his "oral" technique. In the early 1870's he published four volumes of stories and sketches, including the very successful *Contes du lundi* (*Monday Tales*), and at the end of the decade, he published revised and augmented editions of *Letters from My Windmill* and *Monday Tales* that, together, contained all of his short stories he wished to keep in print. Those two definitive volumes, and two longer novellas he published at the end of his life, *La Fédor* and *Le Trésor d'Arlatan,* (Arlatan's Treasure), represent his total surviving contribution to the art of the short story. It is a distinguished achievement by any measure. First and foremost, he reminded his fellow writers (and his readers) of the distant oral origins of storytelling, for he devised a writing style that recaptured the flavor, excitement, and intimacy of the human voice, which was the ancient world's vehicle for the transmission of tales. He also demonstrated commitment to the short story genre, when it was still a literary novelty, by treating it with high seriousness, and bringing to bear upon it all of his discipline and artistry. He had the singular capacity to probe the deepest of human emotions in his stories, with sympathy and understanding, yet with enough skeptical irony to avoid the pitfall of sentimentality. He wrote most often about unhappy love, and about the vulnerability of the innocent in a corrupt world, because those themes corresponded most closely to his own experience of the world. Hence the personal and intimate tone which characterized so many of his short stories, and which generations of readers have found to be so moving. Whatever the future may hold for the rest of his work, one must believe that Daudet's short stories will continue to live, for the world will always take time to "listen" to a storyteller who can tell a tale as entrancingly as he does.

—Murray Sachs

See the essay on "The Pope's Mule."

———

DAVIN, Dan(iel Marcus). British. Born in Invercargill, New Zealand, 1 September 1913. Educated at Marist Brothers' School, Invercargill; Sacred Heart College, Auckland; University of Otago, Dunedin, M.A. in English, Dip. M.A. in Latin 1935; Balliol College, Oxford (Rhodes scholar), 1936–39, B.A. in classics 1939, M.A. 1945. Served in the Royal Warwickshire Regiment, 1939–40, and in the New Zealand Division, 1940–45: major; M.B.E. (Member, Order of the British Empire), 1945. Married Winifred Gonley in 1939; three daughters. Junior assistant secretary, 1946–48, and assistant secretary, 1948–69, Clarendon Press, Oxford; deputy secretary to the delegates, 1970–78, and director of the Academic Division, 1974–78, Oxford University Press: retired 1978. Fellow of Balliol College, 1965, emeritus since 1978. D.Litt.: University of Otago, 1984. Fellow, Royal Society of Arts. C.B.E. (Commander, Order of the British Empire), 1987. *Died 28 September 1990.*

PUBLICATIONS

Short Stories

The Gorse Blooms Pale.   1947.
Breathing Spaces.   1975.
Selected Stories.   1981.
The Salamander and the Fire: Collected War Stories. 1986.

Novels

Cliffs of Fall.   1945.
For the Rest of Our Lives.   1947; revised edition, 1965.
Roads from Home.   1949; edited by Lawrence Jones, 1976.
The Sullen Bell.   1956.
No Remittance.   1959.
Not Here, Not Now.   1970.

Brides of Price.   1972.

Other

An Introduction to English Literature, with John Mulgan. 1947.
Crete.   1953.
Writing in New Zealand: The New Zealand Novel, with W.K. Davin.   2 vols., 1956.
Katherine Mansfield in Her Letters.   1959.
Closing Times (memoirs).   1975.
Snow upon Fire: A Dance to the Music of Time: Anthony Powell (lecture).   1976.

Editor, *New Zealand Short Stories.*   1953; as *The Making of a New Zealander,* 1989.
Editor, *Selected Stories,* by Katherine Mansfield.   1953.
Editor, *English Short Stories of Today,* second series. 1958; as *The Killing Bottle: Classic English Short Stories,* 1988.
Editor, *Short Stories from the Second World War.*   1982.

*

Critical Studies: "Davin's Roads from Home" by H. Winston Rhodes, in *Critical Essays on the New Zealand Novel* edited by Cherry Hankin, 1976; *Davin* by James Bertram, 1983; *Barbed Wire and Mirrors: Essays on New Zealand Prose* by Lawrence Jones, 1987.

*   *   *

Although in his lifetime Dan Davin was known primarily as a novelist, it may well be that he will ultimately be remembered more for his short stories. Written in the intervals of a busy life over more than 40 years, Davin's stories are more accomplished as narratives than are his novels, whether they are Joycean epiphany stories such as "The Apostate," more plot-centered yarns such as "Cassino Casualty," or more complex, longer narratives such as "The Wall of Doors." And, while the social canvas of any single story is necessarily more restricted than that of the novels, taken together the stories provide a fuller, more balanced picture of his expatriate New Zealand generation than do the novels.

The stories divide into three main historical or biographical groups. The first consists of stories of growing up, many of them dealing with the development of Mick Connolly within the Irish Catholic subculture of Invercargill in the far south of New Zealand. These stories trace Mick from his first religious experience ("The Apostate") through a series of childhood learning experiences "Death of a Dog" and "Presents" through his (or a similar character's) adolescence ("Saturday Night" and "The Quiet One") and finally to university life and his sexual initiation ("That Golden Time"). A few other stories, such as "The Hydra" or "Boarding-house Episode," take similar young New Zealand protagonists through disillusioning learning experiences in Oxford or London.

The largest group of stories is that dealing with the New Zealand Division in World War II. *The Salamander and the Fire* collects the war stories from the earlier volumes, and also includes five war stories written in the 1980's, and arranges them as an historical sequence. Thus they present moments in the lives of men in the campaigns in Greece and Crete, in North Africa, and finally in Italy. Some of these stories, such as "Below the Heavens," focus on the initiation of the young man into the horrors of war. Others, such as "The Persian's Grave," focus on the testing of more grizzled veterans in difficult situations. Such stories as "North of the Sangro" are more historically oriented survivor's yarns, usually told from the point of view of an intelligence officer (which was Davin's role through much of the war).

Davin entitled his war novel *For the Rest of Our Lives*, and in the story "Not Substantial Things," the narrator similarly muses that "We'd never give anything again what we'd given the Div....We'd used up what we had and we'd spend the rest of our lives looking over our shoulders." Certainly Davin kept looking back over his shoulder at this war experience, returning to it in his last stories. As a result of this self-confessed obsession with the war, the third group of his stories, those set after the war, are neither as numerous nor as powerful as the war stories. A few, such as "First Flight," deal with the expatriate's return visit to New Zealand. Others, such as "Growing," deal with the family man in England, and a few, such as "The Saloon Bar," deal with English public life.

The three groups of stories come together to make a kind of personal social history, but they are more than that. In his introduction to *Selected Stories*, Davin lists his three requirements for a successful story: "a passion for the exact, the authentic, detail; some intellectual power which can organise the form and weight it with a central, though not necessarily explicit, thought; and a power of feeling, a spirit, which means that the story, while avoiding a moral, is fundamentally moral." The authentic detail is there in all of the stories, with a Joycean sharpness if not a Joycean economy, whether it is the image of baby rabbits drowning in the thaw of a late snow in Invercargill, the silence of olive trees with the dead in a gully beneath them after a battle in Crete, or the sound of a motorbike disturbing the evening in an Oxford street. The intellectual power is provided by Davin, the skeptical philosopher, with his rejection of Catholicism for a bleak naturalistic vision of humans as conscious creatures in an unconscious universe, victims of the indifferent forces of sex, time, and death. That skeptical naturalism blends with the skeptical liberalism of his literary generation, a generation that learned through the betrayals of the 1930's and the horrors of World War II that no cause is to be trusted entirely, that while God does not exist original sin does, that to live in the world and act is to dirty (not to say bloody) one's hands, that nothing in the self, others, or society is ever really simple. That intellectual force is combined in the stories with an underlying moral vision, a vision involving an armed truce with reality, an ironic and unillusioned awareness and acceptance of the complexities and imperfections of world, society, and self.

In the best stories, such as "The Quiet One," authentic detail, intellectual power, and moral vision combine to produce a powerful effect. In that story, Ned, the young protagonist, learns something about sexuality and human relations through his encounter with his cousin Marty, seeing Marty's pain and remorse over the death of his girl from an abortion. Ned, himself on the brink of adolescent sexuality, playing Friday night games primarily for social approval and companionship, has a premature glimpse into what it all means; the difficulties of sexuality and the terrible tangle of human relationships and human nature. The story, a classic example of the epiphany story, with the central discovery turning on moral complexity, rich in

detail, with an implicit intellectual power, is a strong argument for the staying power of Davin's stories.

—Lawrence Jones

DAZAI Osamu. Pseudonym for Tsushima Shuji. Japanese. Born in Kanagi, 19 June 1909. Educated in Kanagi grade school; middle school in Aomori City; Higher school in Hirosaki, 1927–30; University of Tokyo, 1930. Married 1) Oyama Hatsuyo in 1931; 2) Ishihara Michiko in 1939, one son and two daughters, including the writer Tsushima Yūko, *q.v.* Journalist and writer: illness, drinking, and drugs led to several suicide attempts. *Died (suicide) 13 June 1948.*

<small>PUBLICATIONS</small>

Collections

Zenshu [Works].   12 vols., 1955–56; revised edition, 1967–68, 1979.

Short Stories

Hashire Merosu.   1940; as *Run, Melos, and Other Stories,* 1988.
Shinshaku Shokoku Banashi [A Retelling of the Tales from the Province].   1945.
Otogi Zoshi [A Collection of Fairy Tales].   1945.
Biyon No Tsuma [Villon's Wife].   1947.
Selected Stories, edited by James O'Brien.   1983.
Crackling Mountain and Other Stories.   1989.
Self-Portraits: Tales from the Life of Japan's Greatest Decadent Romantic.   1991.

Novels

Bannen [The Declining Years].   1936.
Doke No Hana [The Flower of Buffoonery].   1937.
Dasu Gemaine [Das Gemeine].   1940.
Shin Hamuretto [The New Hamlet].   1941.
Kojiki Gakusei [Beggar-Student].   1941.
Kakekomi Uttae [The Indictment].   1941.
Seigi to Bisho [Justice and Smile].   1942.
Udaijin Sanetomo [Lord Sanetomo].   1943.
Tsugaru.   1944; as *Return to Tsugaru: Travels of a Purple Tramp,* 1985.
Pandora no Hako [Pandora's Box].   1946.
Shayo.   1947; as *The Declining Sun,* 1950; as *The Setting Sun,* 1956.
Ningen Shikkaku.   1948; as *No Longer Human,* 1953.

Other

Fugaku Hyakkei [One Hundred Views of Mt. Fuji]. 1940.
Tokyo Hakkei [Eight Views of Tokyo].   1941.
Human Lost (in Japanese).   1941.

*

Critical Studies: *Landscapes and Portraits* by Donald Keene, 1971; *Accomplices of Silence: The Modern Japanese Novel* by Masao Miyoshi, 1974; *Dazai* by James A. O'Brien, 1975; *Modern Japanese Writers and the Nature of Literature* by Makoto Ueda, 1976; *The Saga of Dazai* (includes stories) by Phyllis I. Lyons, 1985; *Suicidal Narrative in Modern Japan: The Case of Dazai* by Alan Wolfe, 1990.

*   *   *

Even those who read Dazai's work with no previous knowledge of his life will rapidly start to form an image of the generic Dazai protagonist. A man relatively youthful but already feeling the weariness of age, brought up in a well-to-do family in northeastern Japan but now living in disgrace and penury, the Dazai character is usually scratching a desperate living by means of writing or drawing, or some menial bureaucratic job. He is a drunk and a womanizer, caught in an endless cycle of self-loathing, drink, misdemeanour, remorse, and further self-loathing. He usually has already attempted suicide and is thinking of trying it again.

Dazai's life and character did in fact conform very closely to this description. After dropping out of university, he lived from hand to mouth on his writings, twice married, a womanizer and drinker addicted to drugs as a result of his treatment for tuberculosis, he attempted suicide four times — twice with women — before he finally drowned himself with a mistress in 1948. It has been remarked that his life was almost the parody of the decadent artist.

The question then is what kind of writing emerged from this troubled existence. One obvious feature is that the act of writing, or of failing to write, is a central preoccupation of many of his pieces. Like many other 20th-century writers he seems to have taken his first literary steps by looking back, recording his memories of the past and trying to find how he came to want to write. Much of his writing is frankly autobiographical, presenting a linked series of vignettes from different periods of his life ("Memories," "An Almanac of Pain," "One Hundred Views of Mount Fuji," "Eight Views of Tokyo"). "Memories" (also translated as "Recollections") in particular contains many scenes from Dazai's childhood and early youth that he afterwards reexplored in more tightly organized stories.

Distinguishing between a short story and an autobiographical fragment is always difficult in Japanese literature. Certain of Dazai's pieces are narrated straightforwardly in the first-person singular and seem to conform to circumstances of his life at the time they were written, so there is no external or internal evidence for regarding them as fictional. He merely shapes the narration of the whole and lays subtle stress on certain aspects and images which may give a kind of symbolic significance to the whole. Such pieces include "Thinking of Zenzo," "My Older Brothers," "Landscapes with Figures in Gold," and "On the Question of Apparel." As his career progressed, he tended to include passages referring the readers to scenes and information given in other writings. In every one of them there is the same distinctive authorial voice, with its mixture of self-pity and self-mockery, bonhomie and hurt incomprehension.

"Thinking of Zenzo" provides a good example of his use of minor incident for symbolic effect in these largely autobiographical first-person narratives. Superficially the story is that of an occasion when the narrator was invited to attend a dinner for artists and critics from the region of northeastern Japan where he was born. Extremely self-conscious, aware that many of the distinguished guests knew him only by his bad reputation, he goes in terror of disgracing himself. When it is his turn to introduce himself he speaks in an inaudible mumble, and then, on being asked to repeat, he tells them very rudely to shut up. It is apparent from the ensuing stony silence that his words, though muttered in an undertone, have been heard.

This central tale of a humiliation foretold is enclosed by another incident. At the beginning of the story the narrator agrees to buy some roses from a woman posing as a local farmer's wife. He does this even though he is certain she is a fake and that the roses won't bloom as she has promised. And yet, after he has returned from the banquet a friend who knows about roses tells him he thinks the flowers will bloom and are worth more than he paid for them. This allows the story to end with a kind of optimism: "I felt not a little contented. God exists. . . .They say to experience sorrow at any price. That the blue sky is most beautiful when seen through a prison cell window. And so on. I gave thanks" (translated by Ralph F. McCarthy). This curious mixture of prayer and mockery is typical of Dazai. What underlies almost all of his writing is a painfully simple question — is there any point to this or not? If he can derive some sense of coherence, of warmth, from an incident like this, even one aside from the main story, then the narrator sees some point in going on. If not, then the end of the story simply opens out over a pit of despair — as it does in "Cherries," "Father," "Merry Christmas," and many others. This kind of self-absorption can be both frustrating and depressing for the reader, so it is not surprising that Dazai's best works are those in which he makes use of some device to lever the story away from the narrating ego. The simplest way to do this is to tell somebody else's story. To this end he published reworked versions of Japanese folk tales ("Crackling Mountain," "Taking the Wen Away") and stories by Japanese writers from an earlier period ("A Poor Man's Got His Pride," "The Monkey's Mound"). *Hashire Merosu* ("Melos, Run!"), inspired by a poem by Schiller, has become something of a school anthology piece in Japan, probably because it is one of the few of Dazai's works that could be described as virtuous and uplifting.

Some of Dazai's strongest and most tightly organized stories are those in which the protagonist is not the usual self-tormenting male narrator but a woman. *Biyon No Tsuma* ("Villon's Wife") is about a woman married to a ne'er-do-well writer — the title is supposedly that of a story written by her husband. Tired of staying in their squalid apartment and looking after their child while her husband spends all the money on drink and other women, she eventually ends up working at one of the bars where he is a regular customer. In this and other works such as "Magic Lantern," "Hifu to Kokoro" (Skin and the Heart), and "Osan," we can admire the astonishing psychological exactness of the twists and turns of the woman's thoughts, and the skilful construction of dialogue. Because the main focus of the women's attention is not on themselves but on another — usually the pathetic and self-deceiving male figure — it is easier to sympathize both with them and with the object of their sympathy.

—James Raeside

de la MARE, Walter. English. Born in Charlton, Kent, 25 April 1873. Educated at St. Paul's Cathedral Choristers' School, London (founder, *Choristers Journal*, 1889). Married Constance Elfrida Ingpen in 1899 (died 1943); two sons and two daughters. Clerk, Anglo-American Oil Company, London, 1890–1908; reviewer for the *Times*, *Westminster Gazette*, *Bookman*, and other journals, London. Recipient: Royal Society of Literature Polignac prize, 1911; James Tait Black Memorial prize, 1922; Library Association Carnegie medal, for children's book, 1948; Foyle Poetry prize, 1954. D.Litt.: Oxford, Cambridge, Bristol, and London universities; LL.D.: University of St. Andrews. Honorary fellow, Keble College, Oxford. Granted Civil List pension, 1908; Companion of Honour, 1948; Order of Merit, 1953. *Died 22 June 1956.*

PUBLICATIONS

Collections

de la Mare: A Selection from His Writings, edited by Kenneth Hopkins. 1956.
The Complete Poems, edited by Leonard Clark and others. 1969.
The Collected Poems. 1979.

Short Stories

The Riddle and Other Stories. 1923; as *The Riddle and Other Tales*, 1923.
Two Tales: The Green-Room, The Connoisseur. 1925.
The Connoisseur and Other Stories. 1926.
On the Edge: Short Stories. 1930.
Seven Short Stories. 1931.
The Nap and Other Stories. 1936.
The Wind Blows Over. 1936.
The Picnic and Other Stories. 1941.
Best Stories. 1942.
The Collected Tales, edited by Edward Wagenknecht. 1950.
A Beginning and Other Stories. 1955.
Ghost Stories. 1956.
Some Stories. 1962.
Eight Tales. 1971.

Novels

Henry Brocken: His Travels and Adventures in the Rich, Strange, Scarce-Imaginable Regions of Romance. 1904.
The Return. 1910; revised edition, 1922.
Memoirs of a Midget. 1921.
Lispet, Lispett, and Vaine. 1923.
Ding Dong Bell. 1924.
At First Sight. 1928.
A Forward Child. 1934.

Fiction (for children)

The Three Mulla-Mulgars. 1910; as *The Three Royal Monkeys, or, The Three Mulla-Mulgars*, 1935.
Story and Rhyme: A Selection from the Writings of de la Mare, Chosen by the Author. 1921.
Broomsticks and Other Tales. 1925.
Miss Jemima. 1925.
Old Joe. 1927.

Told Again: Traditional Tales. 1927; as *Told Again: Old Tales Told Again*, 1927; as *Tales Told Again*, 1959.
Stories from the Bible. 1929.
The Dutch Cheese and the Lovely Myfanwy. 1931.
The Lord Fish and Other Tales. 1933.
Animal Stories, Chosen, Arranged, and in Some Part Re-Written. 1939.
The Old Lion and Other Stories. 1942.
Mr. Bumps and His Monkey. 1942.
The Magic Jacket and Other Stories. 1943.
The Scarecrow and Other Stories. 1945.
The Dutch Cheese and Other Stories. 1946.
Collected Stories for Children. 1947.
A Penny a Day. 1960.

Play (for children)

Crossings: A Fairy Play, music by C. Armstrong Gibbs (produced 1919). 1921.

Verse

Poems. 1906.
The Listeners and Other Poems. 1912.
The Old Men. 1913.
The Sunken Garden and Other Poems. 1917.
Motley and Other Poems. 1918.
Flora. 1919.
Poems 1901 to 1918. 2 vols., 1920; as *Collected Poems 1901 to 1918*, 2 vols., 1920.
The Veil and Other Poems. 1921.
Thus Her Tale: A Poem. 1923.
A Ballad of Christmas. 1924.
The Hostage. 1925.
St. Andrews, with Rudyard Kipling. 1926.
(Poems). 1926.
Alone. 1927.
Selected Poems. 1927.
The Captive and Other Poems. 1928.
Self to Self. 1928.
A Snowdrop. 1929.
News. 1930.
To Lucy. 1931.
The Sunken Garden and Other Verses. 1931.
Two Poems. 1931.
The Fleeting and Other Poems. 1933.
Poems 1919 to 1934. 1935.
Poems. 1937.
Memory and Other Poems. 1938.
Two Poems, with Arthur Rogers. 1938.
Haunted: A Poem. 1939.
Collected Poems. 1941.
Time Passes and Other Poems, edited by Anne Ridler. 1942.
The Burning-Glass and Other Poems, Including The Traveller. 1945.
The Burning-Glass and Other Poems. 1945.
The Traveller. 1946.
Two Poems: Pride, The Truth of Things. 1946.
Inward Companion. 1950.
Winged Chariot. 1951.
Winged Chariot and Other Poems. 1951.
O Lovely England and Other Poems. 1953.
The Winnowing Dream. 1954.
Selected Poems, edited by R.N. Green-Armytage. 1954.
The Morrow. 1955.
(Poems), edited by John Hadfield. 1962.

A Choice of de la Mare's Verse, edited by W.H. Auden. 1963.
Envoi.   1965.

Verse (for children)

Songs of Childhood.   1902, revised edition, 1916, 1923.
A Child's Day: A Book of Rhymes.   1912.
Peacock Pie: A Book of Rhymes.   1913.
Down-Adown-Derry: A Book of Fairy Poems.   1922.
Stuff and Nonsense and So On.   1927; revised edition, 1946.
Poems for Children.   1930.
This Year, Next Year.   1937.
Bells and Grass: A Book of Rhymes.   1941.
Collected Rhymes and Verses.   1944.
Rhymes and Verses: Collected Poems for Children.   1947.
Poems, edited by Eleanor Graham.   1962.
The Voice: A Sequence of Poems, edited by Catherine Brighton.   1986.

Other

M.E. Coleridge: An Appreciation.   1907.
Rupert Brooke and the Intellectual Imagination (lecture).   1919.
Some Thoughts on Reading (lecture).   1923.
Some Women Novelists of the 'Seventies.   1929.
The Printing of Poetry (lecture).   1931.
The Early Novels of Wilkie Collins.   1932.
Lewis Carroll.   1932.
Early One Morning in the Spring: Chapters on Children and on Childhood as It Is Revealed in Particular in Early Memories and in Early Writings.   1935.
Letters from de la Mare to Form Three.   1936.
Poetry in Prose (lecture).   1936.
Arthur Thompson: A Memoir.   1938.
An Introduction to Everyman.   1938.
Stories, Essays, and Poems, edited by M.M. Bozman. 1938.
Pleasures and Speculations.   1940.
Selected Stories and Verses (for children), edited by Eleanor Graham.   1952.
Private View (essays).   1953.
Molly Whuppie (for children).   1983.

Editor, *Come Hither: A Collection of Rhymes and Poems for the Young of All Ages.*   1923; revised edition, 1928.
Editor, with Thomas Quayle, *Readings: Traditional Tales Told by the Author.*   6 vols., 1925–28.
Editor, *Desert Islands and Robinson Crusoe.*   1930; revised edition, 1932.
Editor, *Poems,* by Christina Rossetti.   1930.
Editor, *The Eighteen-Eighties: Essays by Fellows of the Royal Society of Literature.*   1930.
Editor, *Tom Tiddler's Ground: A Book of Poetry for the Junior and Middle Schools.*   3 vols., 1932.
Editor, *Old Rhymes and New, Chosen for Use in Schools.* 2 vols., 1932.
Editor, *Behold, This Dreamer! Of Reverie, Night, Sleep, Dream, Love-Dreams, Nightmare, Death, The Unconscious, The Imagination, Divination, The Artist, and Kindred Subjects.*   1939.
Editor, *Love.*   1943.

*

Critical Studies: *de la Mare: A Critical Study* by Forrest Reid, 1929; *de la Mare: An Exploration* by John Atkins, 1947; *de la Mare: A Study of His Poetry* by H.C. Duffin, 1949; *de la Mare* by David Cecil, 1951; *de la Mare* by Kenneth Hopkins, 1953; *Tea with de la Mare* by Leonard Clark, 1960; *de la Mare* by Doris Ross McCrosson, 1966.

*   *   *

Walter de la Mare, the sixth child of civil servant Edward de la Mare and Lucy Browning, was born in Charlton, Kent. His father's family was of Huguenot descent. His mother was the daughter of a naval surgeon whose family was of Scottish origin and who was distantly related to the poet, Robert Browning. Educated at the choir school of St. Paul's Cathedral, where he was a chorister, de la Mare showed early signs of literary ability in his editing of the *Choristers Journal*, to which he made a major contribution. On leaving St. Paul's, he became a clerk for 18 years in the city office of the Anglo-American Oil Company. When he received a small government pension, he devoted himself subsequently to a career of full-time writing. Much of his early work was published in magazines such as the *Cornhill*, *Pall Mall Gazette*, and the *Sketch*, under the pseudonym of Walter Ramal, an anagram of his name.

Known primarily as a poet, he wrote many collections of poetry for both children and adults. His topics range in subject matter, including animals, nature, people, the supernatural, and dreamland—subjects that figure largely in his fiction as well. Strongly rhythmic, the imaginative quality of his verse appeals to the young in heart of all ages, as does the mysterious fascination of the macabre.

In 1910, de la Mare's long story *The Three Mulla-Mulgars* was published. The book concerns three royal monkeys (Thumb, Thimble, and Nod) and their dangerous journey to the paradisiacal valleys of Tishnar. He wrote the story for and read it to his own children. It embraces that imaginative quality and fine prose style that were to stamp his adult fiction.

In addition to the *The Three Mulla-Mulgars*, de la Mare wrote 20 original stories for children and retold 60 others, which appear in such collections as *Told Again*, *Stories from the Bible*, *Animal Stories*, and *Selected Stories and Verses*.

In his essay entitled *Rupert Brooke and the Intellectual Imagination*, de la Mare wrote that children "live in a world peculiarly their own, so much so that it is doubtful if the adult can do more than very fleetingly reoccupy that far-away consciousness. There is no solitude more secluded than a child's, no absorption more complete, no insight more exquisite and, one might add, more comprehensive." It is this insight into a child's mentality that infuses all his writing for and about children. The child, frequently a lonely small boy, also inhabits de la Mare's adult fiction. He is too young to appreciate his senior's dilemma, but is sensitively aware that all is not well in the grown-up world. "The Almond Tree" (*The Riddle*) is an account of his childhood, told by a count who, as a youngster, does not realise that his mother is pregnant; nor does he appreciate why she so bitterly resents his father's regular visits to Miss Grey, a neighbour with whose brother the father plays cards. The boy is impartial in giving his affection to each of the protagonists. On finding the body of his father lying in the snow, young Nicholas remarks somewhat baldly, "I found him in the snow; he's dead." The child's grief, however, is momentary and he is glad to be his own master, to do as he pleases.

In "Miss Duveen" (in *The Riddle*), a moving and finely wrought depiction of a woman's increasing mental instability as a result of a youthful, unfortunate love affair, the child, Arthur, has an ambivalent attitude to Miss Duveen. He enjoys his meetings with her more, one feels, out of curiosity than understanding or sympathy. Indeed, when her cousin, a harsh woman, has Miss Duveen placed in a mental institution, the boy's reaction borders on relief, for no longer would he be "saddled with her company by the stream."

In "An Ideal Craftsman" (in *On the Edge*) the boy, much in awe of the intimidating butler, Jacobs, encounters in the kitchen the repulsive fat woman who, from unrequited love, has murdered a man after he said she was "not the first." The child, whose imagination has been fired by a "dingy volume of the *Newgate Calendar*," realises that by skilfully faking a hanging for the dead man he can save the woman's skin, but does not appreciate why she strangled him in the first place. The deed is accomplished, and he succumbs to panic as he awaits the return of his father and stepmother. The children behave as one would expect: they take pies and tarts; they outdare each other, as in "The Trumpet" (in *The Wind Blows Over*), but finally they give way to childish trepidation.

De la Mare sometimes adopts the device of having two people, unknown to each other, conversing in an impersonal setting such as a railway station or tearoom. One character is under a strong compulsion to tell his or her tale to the not altogether sympathetic listener. In the cases of "Missing" (in *The Connoisseur*), and "Crewe" (in *On the Edge*), the thought of murder is implicit, although the actual word is not mentioned. In "Crewe" there is the added dimension of the supernatural; the scarecrow, bearing an uncanny resemblance to the dead man, appears to move ever closer to the vicarage, which many years before had been exorcised and is thought to be haunted. Frequently, sinister events take place by moonlight or in old creaking houses.

In his novel *Memoirs of a Midget* de la Mare shows his compassion for the griefs and fears of the lonely, a repeated theme in his fiction. The woman, because of her tiny size, is alien to society. That same compassion is exhibited in the short story "The Picnic" (in *On the Edge*). The efficient, but lonely, Miss Curtis falls in love with a man sitting immobile and "almost excruciatingly alone" in the window, beneath which she eats her solitary picnic. Her disillusionment is complete when she discovers the man whom she has adored from afar is totally blind and will never reciprocate her feelings.

De la Mare is probably at his best when dealing with the intense world of the child and the isolation of the lonely relieved by recollection of happier days. His prose has a solid and purposeful, almost Biblical resonance. Indeed, Graham Greene described it as "unequalled in its richness since the death of James, or, dare one at this date say, Robert Louis Stevenson." For his imaginative insight, his descriptions of nature and his ability to enter sympathetically into the situations of his subjects, de la Mare surely deserves a wider readership than fashion at present affords him.

—A.J. Lindsay

See the essays on "A Recluse" and "Seaton's Aunt."

DICKENS, Charles (John Huffam). English. Born in Portsmouth, Hampshire, 7 February 1812; lived with his family in London, 1814–16, Chatham, Kent, 1817–21, and London, 1822. Attended a school in Chatham; worked in a blacking factory, Hungerford Market, London, while his family was in Marshalsea debtor's prison, 1824; attended Wellington House Academy, London, 1824–27, and Mr. Dawson's school, Brunswick Square, London, 1827. Married Catherine Hogarth in 1836 (separated 1858), seven sons and three daughters; possibly had a son by Ellen Ternan. Clerk in a law office, London, 1827–28; shorthand reporter, Doctors' Commons, 1828–30, and in Parliament for *True Son*, 1830–32, *Mirror of Parliament*, 1832–34, and *Morning Chronicle*, 1834–36; contributor, *Monthly Magazine*, 1833–34 (as Boz, 1834), and *Evening Chronicle*, 1835–36; editor, *Bentley's Miscellany*, 1837–39; visited the U.S., 1842; lived in Italy, 1844–45; appeared in amateur theatricals from 1845, and managed an amateur theatrical tour of England, 1847; editor, London *Daily News*, 1846; lived in Switzerland and Paris, 1846; founding editor, *Household Words*, London, 1850–59, and its successor, *All the Year Round*, 1859–70; gave reading tours of Britain, 1858–59, 1861–63, 1866–67, and 1868–70, and the U.S., 1867-68; lived in Gad's Hill Place, near Rochester, Kent, from 1860. *Died 9 June 1870.*

PUBLICATIONS

Collections

Nonesuch Dickens, edited by Arthur Waugh and others. 23 vols., 1937–38.
The Short Stories, edited by Walter Allen. 1971.
Selected Short Fiction, edited by Deborah A. Thomas. 1976.
The Supernatural Short Stories, edited by Michael Hayes. 1978.
The Portable Dickens, edited by Angus Wilson. 1983.

Short Stories

Sketches by Boz Illustrative of Every-Day Life and Every-Day People. 1836; second series, 1836.
A Christmas Carol, in Prose, Being a Ghost Story of Christmas. 1843.
The Cricket on the Hearth: A Fairy Tale of Home. 1845.
Christmas Stories from Household Words and All the Year Round, in *Works* (Charles Dickens Edition). 1874.
The Christmas Books, edited by Ruth Glancy. 1971.

Novels

The Posthumous Papers of the Pickwick Club. 1837; *The Pickwick Papers*, edited by James Kinsley, 1986.
Oliver Twist; or, The Parish Boy's Progress. 1838; edited by Kathleen Tillotson, 1966.
The Life and Adventures of Nicholas Nickleby. 1839; edited by Paul Schlicke, 1990.
Master Humphrey's Clock: The Old Curiosity Shop, Barnaby Rudge. 3 vols., 1840–41; *The Old Curiosity Shop and Barnaby Rudge* each published separately, 1841; *Barnaby Rudge* edited by Gordon W. Spence, 1973.

The Life and Adventures of Martin Chuzzlewit.   1844;
    edited by Margaret Cardwell, 1982.
The Chimes: A Goblin Story.   1844.
The Battle of Life: A Love Story.   1846.
*The Haunted Man and the Ghost's Bargain: A Fancy for
    Christmas Time.*   1848.
*Dealings with the Firm of Dombey and Son, Wholesale,
    Retail, and for Exportation.*   1848; edited by Alan
    Horsman, 1974.
The Personal History of David Copperfield.   1850; edited
    by Nina Burgis, 1981, and by Jerome H. Buckley, 1990.
Bleak House.   1853; edited by George Ford and Sylvère
    Monod, 1977.
Hard Times, for These Times.   1854; edited by George
    Ford and Sylvère Monod, 1972.
Little Dorrit.   1857; edited by Harvey Peter Sucksmith,
    1979.
A Tale of Two Cities.   1859; edited by Andrew Sanders,
    1988.
Great Expectations.   1861; edited by Louise Stevens,
    1966.
Our Mutual Friend.   1865; edited by Stephen Gill, 1971.
The Mystery of Edwin Drood.   1870; edited by Arthur J.
    Cox, 1974.
*The Lazy Tour of Two Idle Apprentices, No Thoroughfare,
    The Perils of Certain English Prisoners,* with Wilkie
    Collins.   1890.

Plays

O'Thello (produced 1833).   In *Nonesuch Dickens*,
    1937–38.
The Village Coquettes, music by John Hullah (produced
    1836).   1836.
The Strange Gentleman (produced 1836).   1837.
Is She His Wife? or, Something Singular (produced 1837).
    N.d.
Mr. Nightingale's Diary, with Mark Lemon (produced
    1851).   1851.
The Lighthouse, with Wilkie Collins, from the story
    "Gabriel's Marriage" by Collins (produced 1855).
The Frozen Deep, with Wilkie Collins (produced 1857).
    1866; in *Under the Management of Mr. Dickens: His
    Production of the Frozen Deep,* edited by R.L. Brannan,
    1966.
No Thoroughfare, with Wilkie Collins and Charles Fechter,
    from the story by Dickens and Collins (produced 1867).
    1867.
The Lamplighter.   1879.

Other

American Notes for General Circulation.   2 vols., 1842;
    edited by John S. Whitely and Arnold Goldman, 1972.
Pictures from Italy.   1846.
Works (Cheap Edition).   17 vols., 1847–67.
A Child's History of England.   3 vols., 1852–54.
The Uncommercial Traveller.   1861.
Speeches Literary and Social, edited by R.H. Shepherd.
    1870; revised edition, as *The Speeches 1841–1870,*
    1884.
Speeches, Letters, and Sayings.   1870.
The Mudfog Papers.   1880.
Letters, edited by Georgina Hogarth and Mamie Dickens.
    3 vols., 1880–82; revised edition (Pilgrim Edition),
    edited by Madeline House, Graham Storey, and Kath-
    leen Tillotson, 1965—.
Plays and Poems, edited by R.H. Shepherd.   2 vols., 1885.

*To Be Read at Dusk and Other Stories, Sketches, and
    Essays,* edited by F. G. Kitton.   1898.
Miscellaneous Papers, edited by B.W. Matz.   2 vols.,
    1908.
The Life of Our Lord (for children).   1934.
Speeches, edited by K.J. Fielding.   1960.
Uncollected Writings from Household Words 1850–1859,
    edited by Harry Stone.   2 vols., 1968.
Household Words: A Weekly Journal 1850–1859, edited by
    Anne Lohrli.   1974.
The Public Readings, edited by Philip Collins.   1975.
Dickens on America and the Americans, edited by Michael
    Slater.   1979.
Dickens on England and the English, edited by Malcolm
    Andrews.   1979.
Book of Memoranda, edited by Fred Kaplan.   1981.
Selected Letters, edited by David Paroissien.   1985.
A December Vision: Social Journalism, edited by Neil
    Philip and Victor Neuburg.   1986.
Dickens' Working Notes for His Novels, edited by Harry
    Stone.   1987.

Editor, *The Pic Nic Papers.*   3 vols., 1841.

*

Bibliography: *The First Editions of the Writings of Dickens*
by John C. Eckel, 1913, revised edition, 1932; *A Bibliography of the Periodical Works of Dickens* by Thomas Hatton
and Arthur H. Cleaver, 1933; *A Dickens Bibliography* by
Phillip Collins, 1970; *A Bibliography of Dickensian Criticism 1836–1975* by R.C. Churchill, 1975; *The Cumulated
Dickens Checklist 1970–1979* by Alan M. Cohn and K.K.
Collins, 1982; *The Critical Reception of Dickens
1833–1841* by Kathryn Chittick, 1989.

Critical Studies: *The Life of Dickens* by John Forster, 3
vols., 1872–74, edited by A.J. Hoppé, 2 vols., 1966;
Dickens by G.K. Chesterton, 1906; *The Dickens World* by
Humphry House, 1941; *Dickens: His Character, Comedy,
and Career* by Hesketh Pearson, 1949; *Dickens: His Tragedy and Triumph* by Edgar Johnson, 2 vols., 1952, revised
and abridged edition, 1 vol., 1977; *Dickens,* 1953, revised
1963, and *Dickens: A Critical Introduction,* 1958, revised
1965, both by K.J. Fielding; *Dickens and His Readers* by
George H. Ford, 1955; *Dickens at Work* by Kathleen
Tillotson and John Butt, 1957; *Dickens: The World of His
Novels* by J. Hillis Miller, 1958; *The Imagination of
Dickens* by A.O.J. Cockshut, 1961; *The Dickens Critics*
edited by George H. Ford and Lauriat Lane, Jr., 1961;
Dickens and the Twentieth Century edited by John Gross
and Gabriel Pearson, 1962; *Dickens and Crime,* 1962,
revised 1963, and *Dickens and Education,* 1963, revised
1964, both by Philip Collins, and *Dickens: The Critical
Heritage,* 1971, and *Dickens: Interviews and Recollections,*
2 vols., 1981, both edited by Collins; *The Flint and the
Flame: The Artistry of Dickens* by Earle R. Davis, 1963;
Dickens from Pickwick to Dombey by Steven Marcus, 1964;
Dickens: The Dreamer's Stance by Taylor Stoehr, 1965; *The
Dickens Theatre: A Reassessment of the Novels* by Robert
Garis, 1965; *The Making of Dickens* by Christopher
Hibbert, 1967; *Dickens the Novelist,* 1968, and *Martin
Chuzzlewit,* 1985, both by Sylvère Monod; *Dickens the
Novelist* by F.R. Leavis and Q.D. Leavis, 1970; *The Moral
Art of Dickens* by Barbara Hardy, 1970; *The World of
Dickens* by Angus Wilson, 1970; *Dickens the Craftsman*

edited by Robert Parlow, 1970; *The Melancholy Man: A Study of Dickens's Novels* by John Lucas, 1970, revised edition, 1980; *Dickens and the Art of Analogy* by H.M. Daleski, 1971; *The City of Dickens*, 1971, and *From Copyright to Copperfield: The Identity of Dickens*, 1987, both by Alexander Welsh; *Dickens Centennial Essays* edited by Ada Nisbet and Blake Nevius, 1971; *Dickens and the Rhetoric of Laughter* by James R. Kincaid, 1972; *A Reader's Guide to Dickens* by Philip Hobsbaum, 1973; *The Violent Effigy: A Study of Dickens's Imagination* by John Carey, 1973; *Dickens' Sketches by Boz: End in the Beginning* by Virgil Grillo, 1974; *Dickens at Doughty Street* by John Greaves, 1975; *Dickens's Apprentice Years: The Making of a Novelist* by Duane De Vries, 1976; *The Dickens Myth: Its Genesis and Structure* by Geoffrey Thurley, 1976; *Allegory in Dickens* by Jane Vogel, 1977; *The Confessional Fictions of Dickens* by Barry Westburg, 1977; *Dickens as a Familiar Essayist* by Gordon Spence, 1977; *Dickens and His Publishers* by Robert Patten, 1978; *Dickensian Melodrama: A Reading of the Novels* by George J. Worth, 1978; *Dickens and Reality* by John Romano, 1979; *Dickens on the City* by F.S. Schwarzbach, 1979; *Dickens: A Life* by Norman Mackenzie and Jeanne Mackenzie, 1979; *Reality and Comic Confidence in Dickens* by P.J.M. Scott, 1979; *Interpreting, Interpreting: Interpreting Dickens's Dombey* by Susan R. Horton, 1979; *Dickens and the Invisible World: Fairy Tales, Fantasy, and Novel-Making* by Harry Stone, 1979; *The Decoding of Edwin Drood* by Charles Forsyte, 1980; *Dickens and the Suspended Quotation* by Mark Lambert, 1981; *Dickens* by Harland S. Nelson, 1981; *Dickens at Play* by S.J. Newman, 1981; *A Reformer's Art: Dickens' Picturesque and Grotesque Imagery* by Nancy K. Hill, 1981; *The Reader in the Dickens World: Style and Response* by Susan R. Horton, 1981; *Excess and Restraint in the Novels of Dickens* by John Kucich, 1981; *Dickens and Religion* by Dennis Walder, 1981; *Dickens and the Short Story* by Deborah A. Thomas, 1982; *Dickens: New Perspectives* edited by Wendell Stacy Johnson, 1982; *Dickens: Novelist in the Market-Place* by James M. Brown, 1982; *Dickens and Women* by Michael Slater, 1983; *The Changing World of Dickens* by Robert Giddings, 1983; *Dickens and Phiz* by Michael Steig, 1983; *A Dickens Companion*, 1984, *A Dickens Chronology*, 1988, and *Bleak House: A Novel of Connections*, 1990, all by Norman Page; *Dickens and the Romantic Self* by Lawrence Frank, 1984; *A Preface to Dickens* by Allan Grant, 1984; *Dickens and the Broken Scripture* by Janet L. Larson, 1985; *Dickens* by Steven Connor, 1985; *Dickens and the Form of the Novel* by Graham Daldry, 1986; *Dickens* by Kate Flint, 1986; *A Companion to The Mystery of Edwin Drood* by Wendy S. Jacobson, 1986; *The Companion to Our Mutual Friend* by Michael Cotsell, 1986, and *Critical Essays on Great Expectations* edited by Cotsell, 1990; *Dickens the Designer* by Juliet McMaster, 1987; *Dickens in Search of Himself: Recurrent Themes and Characters in the Work of Dickens* by Gwen Watkins, 1987; *Bleak House* by Graham Storey, 1987; *Great Expectations: A Novel of Friendship* by Bert G. Hornback, 1987; *The Companion to A Tale of Two Cities* by Andrew Sanders, 1988; *Dickens and Popular Entertainment* by Paul Schlicke, 1988; *Circulation: Defoe, Dickens, and the Economies of the Novel* by David Trotter, 1988; *Dickens' Childhood* by Michael Allen, 1988; *The Dickens Index* edited by Nicolas Bentley, Michael Slater, and Nina Burgis, 1988; *The Companion to Bleak House* by Susan Shatto, 1988; *Dickens: A Biography* by Fred Kaplan, 1988; *Dramatic Dickens* edited by Carol Hanbery MacKay, 1989; *The Dickens Pantomime* by Edwin M. Eigner, 1989; *The Textual Life of Dickens's Characters* by James A. Davies, 1990; *A Dickens Glossary* by Fred Levit, 1990; *Dickens* by Peter Ackroyd, 1990; *Edwin Drood: Antichrist in the Cathedral* by John Thacker, 1990; *Dickens and the 1830's* by Kathryn Chittick, 1990; *Dickens's Class Consciousness: A Marginal View* by Pam Morris, 1990; *The Dickens Hero: Selfhood and Alienation in the Dickens World* by Beth F. Herst, 1990; *The Invisible Woman: The Story of Nelly Ternan and Dickens* by Claire Tomalin, 1990.

* * *

Charles Dickens's first fictional work was "A Dinner at Poplar Walk" (*Monthly Magazine*, December 1833, later retitled "Mr. Minns and His Cousin"). Further stories soon appeared in sundry journals, and were collected, sometimes in revised form, together with descriptive essays, in *Sketches by Boz* (two series, February and December 1836). The attention they caught led to his being invited to write *Pickwick Papers* (serialized 1836-37), which—following the precedent of 18th-century novels—included nine interpolated tales: controversy continues whether these were space-fillers pulled out of his drawer, or whether their themes relate contrapuntally or otherwise to the main narrative. An early instalment of *Nicholas Nickleby* (1838-39) contains two tales, and *Master Humphrey's Clock* (1840-41) has three, before full-length novels took over, to satisfy reader demand. Similarly, when editing *Bentley's Miscellany* (1837-39), Dickens wrote a few short tales before concentrating on *Oliver Twist*. In 1843 Dickens accidentally invented the Christmas Book genre with *A Christmas Carol*, followed by four others of similar format and length (about 40,000 words), later collected as *Christmas Books*. From 1850, when he established a weekly magazine, his Christmas endeavours went into their Special Christmas Numbers. Here he usually created a framework like that of *The Canterbury Tales* or *The Decameron*: a number of people are assembled—round the family hearth, or marooned in a snowed-up inn, or wherever— and they all tell tales (Dickens engaged collaborators to write most of these). This series, which included variants on this pattern, continued until 1867, when Dickens decided that the idea was exhausted. His contributions were collected as *Christmas Stories*.

A few other short narratives appeared in collections— "The Lamplighter," adapted from an unacted farce (in *Pic Nic Papers*, 1841), "To Be Read at Dusk," two supernatural tales (in *The Keepsake*, 1852)—or were written for the lucrative American magazine market, though published simultaneously in his own weekly: "Hunted Down," about the exposure of a "gentleman"-murderer (*New York Ledger*, August-September 1859), "A Holiday Romance," four tales "told" by children, embodying such childish fantasies as a reversal of roles between adults and children, and including a charming fairy story about a magic fishbone (*Our Young Folks*, January-May 1868), and *George Silverman's Explanation* (*Atlantic Monthly*, January-March 1868), an impressive story about psychological oppression. There are about 80 stories in all, and extended anecdotes occur in many essays and in character sketches (e.g., in the anonymous *Sketches of Young Gentlemen*, 1838).

A Christmas Carol is a mythological masterpiece, worthy to stand alongside Dickens's novels. This cannot be said of his other short pieces, which at best engage his talents rather than his genius. Many are humdrum: some are weak apprentice efforts, some are rather tedious hackwork pieces, over-reliant on facile comic situations and phraseology or on conventional horrifics. Dickens needed the elbow room of novel-length for his genius to flourish, involving a large cast in a multiplicity of plots and settings. Almost all the shorter fictions, however, are manifestly Dickensian—though few would now be read were Dickens's name not attached to them. *Sketches by Boz,* his first book, displays many lifelong stances and preoccupations, and its subtitle *Illustrative of Every-Day Life and Every-Day People* announces a favourite milieu, while the metropolitan setting of almost all its items recurs in the novels, where London is the predominant location. Most of the tales are comic, involving such predictable subjects as hen-pecked husbands, family tiffs, legacy-hunting, class-pretensions, inappropriate courtships, military impostors, a duel between cowards, the mistakes of a night, and the absurdities of amateur theatricals. There are two exceptions, "The Black Veil" (a mother goes mad when a physician fails to resuscitate her hanged son) and "The Drunkard's Death" (a watery grave, after a life ruinous to himself and his family). Sensation and violence are prominent in the *Pickwick* interpolated tales, emotionally at odds with the novel's high comic spirit: two more tales about drunkard's destructive lives and terrible deaths, others about a madman's murderous plans and a prisoners' implacable revenge for his and his family's sufferings. These tales release the darker propensities of Dickens's imagination: mental disturbance, crime, violence, prisons are important in later novels.

According to Harry Stone, in *Dickens and the Invisible World,* the Christmas Books centre on "a protagonist who is mistaken or displays false values is forced, through a series of extraordinary events, to see his errors." Supernatural means are used in all except *The Battle of Life:* fairystory and nursery tale influences are evident (and, as Dickens said, seasonally appropriate). After the *Carol* and *The Chimes,* however, the seasonal reference recedes, though there remains a stress on hearth and home and family affection, often temporarily rejected or disturbed. The domestic theme of *The Cricket on the Hearth* particularly appealed to its original readers. *The Chimes* has more of the topical social and political satire and protest familiar in the novels, though also in Tilly Slowboy, the dense but devoted maid-of-all-work, it has one of the broadly comic characters that were a popular ingredient in these books. Problems of personality and memory that were engaging Dickens in the late 1840's are explored in *The Haunted Man,* and in the story's terrible waif—"A baby savage, a young monster, a child who had never been a child"—Dickens, as in other books, pays seasonal attention to childhood and repeats his social message.

Most of the *Christmas Stories* (1852-67) are first person narrative, often told by a highly flavoured character. Several entered Dickens's public readings repertoire (1858-70) as successful character-monologues, some being evidently written with a view to this purpose. The stories of the garrulous boarding house-keeper Mrs. Lirriper (1863, revived 1864) and the market cheapjack Doctor Marigold (1865) are good instances: brilliantly conceived voices, but with disappointingly inconsequential or mawkish tales to tell. "Tales" better describes these short fictions than "short stories": Dickens was unaffected by the short story art then being created by Poe and others. These stories have scant reference to Christmas, though Dickens liked to "strike the chord of the season." Social and political references are only incidental now; but the Indian Mutiny inspired *The Perils of Certain English Prisoners.* "The Signalman" is one of Dickens's best supernatural stories.

Other characteristic interests appear in "Boots at the Holly-Tree Inn" (child-centered sentiment blended with humour) and *No Thoroughfare* (in collaboration with Wilkie Collins: crime, detection, melodrama). There are many incidental felicities: Dickens always becomes animated, for instance, over railways (*Mugby Junction,* and elsewhere) and over showbiz (Mr. Chops the Dwarf, in *Going into Society;* Pickleson the fairground giant, in *Doctor Marigold*). But these stories are obviously minor works, in a double sense, if read alongside the novels written at the same phase of Dickens's maturity.

—Philip Collins

See the essays on *A Christmas Carol, The Cricket on the Hearth,* and "The Signalman."

DINESEN, Isak. Pseudonym for Karen Christentze Blixen, née Dinesen. Danish. Born in Rungsted, 17 April 1885. Educated privately; studied art at Academy of Art, Copenhagen, 1902–06, in Paris, 1910, and in Rome. Married Baron Bror Blixen-Finecke in 1914 (divorced 1921). Managed a coffee plantation near Nairobi, Kenya, with her husband, 1913–21, and alone, 1921–31; lived in Rungsted after 1931. Recipient: Holberg medal, 1949; Ingenio e Arti medal, 1950; Nathansen Memorial Fund award, 1951; Golden Laurels, 1952; Hans Christian Andersen prize, 1955; Danish Critics prize, 1957. Founding Member, Danish Academy, 1960; Honorary Member, American Academy 1957; Corresponding Member, Bavarian Accademy of Fine Arts. Wrote in English and translated her own works into Danish. *Died 7 September 1962.*

PUBLICATIONS

Collections

Mindeudgave [Memorial Edition].   7 vols., 1964.

Short Stories

Seven Gothic Tales.   1934; as *Syv fantastiske Fortaellinger,* 1935.
Winter's Tales.   1942; as *Vinter Eventyr,* 1942.
Kardinalens Tredie Historie [The Cardinal's Third Tale]. 1952.
Babettes Gaestebud.   1955; as "Babette's Feast," in *Anecdotes of Destiny,* 1958.
Last Tales.   1957; as *Sidste Fortaellinger,* 1957.
Skaebne-Anekdoter.   1958; as *Anecdotes of Destiny,* 1958; as *Babette's Feast and Other Anecdotes of Destiny,* 1988.
Ehrengard.   1963; translated as *Ehrengard,* 1963.
Efterladte Fortaellinger, edited by Frans Lasson.   1975; as *Carnival: Entertainments and Posthumous Tales,* 1977.

Novel

Gengaeldelsens Veje (as Pierre Andrézel).   1944; as *The Angelic Avengers,* 1946.

Play

Sandhedens Haevn: En Marionetkomedie (produced 1936).
1960; as *The Revenge of Truth: A Marionette Comedy,* in
"Isak Dinesen" and Karen Blixen, by Donald Hannah,
1971.

Other

Out of Africa.   1937; as *Den afrikanske Farm,* 1937.
Om retskrivning: Politiken 23–24 marts 1938 [About
Spelling: Politiken 23–24 March 1938].   1949.
Farah [name].   1950.
Daguerrotypier (radio talks).   1951.
Omkring den nye Lov on Dyreforsøg [The New Law on
Vivisection].   1952.
En Baaetale med 14 Aars Forsinkelse [A Bonfire Speech 14
Years Later].   1953.
Spøgelseshestene [The Ghost Horses].   1955.
Skygger paa Graesset.   1960; as *Shadows on the Grass,*
1960.
On Mottoes of My Life.   1960.
Osceola, edited by Clara Svendsen.   1962.
Essays.   1965.
Breve fra Afrika 1914–31, edited by Frans Lasson.   2
vols., 1978; as *Letters from Africa,* 1981.
Daguerrotypes and Other Essays.   1979.
On Modern Marriage and Other Observations.   1986.

*

Bibliography: *Dinesen: A Bibliography* by Liselotte Henrik-
sen, 1977; supplement in *Blixeniana 1979,* 1979; *Karen
Blixen/Isak Dinesen: A Select Bibliography* by Nage
Jørgensen, 1985.

Critical Studies: *The World of Dinesen* by Eric O. Jo-
hannesson, 1961; *Dinesen: A Memorial* edited by Clara
Svendsen, 1964; *The Gayety of Vision: A Study of Dinesen's
Art* by Robert Langbaum, 1965; *Titania: The Biography of
Dinesen* by Parmenia Migel, 1967; *The Life and Destiny of
Blixen* by Clara Svendsen and Frans Lasson, 1970; *"Isak
Dinesen" and Karen Blixen: The Mask and the Reality* by
Donald Hannah, 1971; *Dinesen's Aesthetics* by Thomas R.
Whissen, 1973; *My Sister, Isak Dinesen* by Thomas Dine-
sen, 1975; *Dinesen: The Life of a Storyteller* by Judith
Thurman, 1982, as *Dinesen: The Life of Karen Blixen,*
1982; *The Pact: My Friendship with Dinesen* by Thorkild
Bjørning, 1984; *Karen Blixen: Isak Dinesen: A Chronology*
by Frans Lasson, 1985; *The Witch and the Goddess in the
Stories of Dinesen* by Sarah Stambaugh, 1988; *Dinesen and
the Engendering of Narrative* by Susan Hardy Aiken, 1990;
Dinesen: The Life and Imagination of a Seducer by Olga
Anastasia Pelensky, 1991.

*   *   *

Among short story writers of renown, Isak Dinesen is
unique, *sui generis,* a category in and of herself. Although
writing in a European tradition at variance with most
American literature, she achieved wide popularity in this
country, which revived with the movie of *Out of Africa.*
Dinesen bears similarities to some American authors,
notably Nathaniel Hawthorne and Edgar Allan Poe, though
her models are usually not specific writers but legends,
myths, and fairy tales, a debt she subtly acknowledges when
Hans Christian Anderson appears as a character in "The
Pearls."

A Romantic, Dinesen believed in fiction as pure and
absolute art, obligated to no standards other than those
dictated by the logic the story creates. She deemed herself a
teller of tales, charming her audience like Scherezade, and
believed that the artist, in serving humanity, parallels the
priest or aristocrat. By creating and controlling their own
cosmos, writers mimic God's creation of the universe, a
concept similar to Coleridge's theory of the imagination.
This parallel is pointed up in "The Young Man with the
Carnation" when a writer says to God that just "as the
heavens are higher than the earth, so are thy short stories
higher than our short stories." He then imagines a dialogue
in which God informs him that it is God who wants stories
written, not humans.

For Dinesen, fiction is superior to actuality, the far away
in time and place, with strange characters involved in
fantastic events, more desirable than the present. Like
Henry Adams, she dramatizes the antagonism between the
modern world of what Adams called "multiplicity" in
which humans are overly sophisticated, and the simpler,
more elemental and unified past from which we are
separated. That antagonism manifests itself as well in her
portrayals of country and city life, the so-called civilized
and the primitive. Only through art can a requisite unity be
established and opposites (life and art, dreams and reality;
good and evil; tragedy and comedy; humility and pride) be
reconciled. The artist can make us aware of the necessity of
fate and patterns, the inevitability of both the sweet and
bitter elements of life, and effect a synthesis.

Dinesen's Romanticism also embraces the Gothic and
exhibits the same fascination with the mysterious and the
supernatural as Poe's *Tales of the Grotesque and Arabesque*
(1840). In quaintly perverse, deeply symbolic narratives,
elemental and unforgettable as the myths and legends of
childhood, she creates archaic and exotic settings (castles,
mills, ships, woodlands); motifs such as dreams ("The
Dreaming Child"), obsessive love ("The Cloak"), incest
("The Caryatids"), doubling and mirror images ("The
Young Man with the Carnation"); bizarre characters such
as the gypsy seer ("The Caryatids"), the bird changed into
an old woman ("The Sailor-Boy's Tale"), Pellegrina Leoni,
"the diva who had lost her voice" ("Echoes"), and the
giantess Lady Flora ("The Cardinal's Third Tale"). Her
cast of larger-than-life figures, often ghostly, melancholy,
remote, contradictory, obsessive, are drawn in psychological depth despite their other-worldly qualities. The result is,
in totality, rather like a medieval tapestry, attractive,
colorful, yet depicting a scene strangely different from our
own world, or as if a familiar scene were viewed, reversed,
in an old and cloudy mirror.

Dinesen created her own microcosm, not governed by
rules of reality or of other literature, possessed of its own
order, sense of morality, and definitions of the abstractions
by which humans live, a world as distinctive as Faulkner's
Yoknapatawpha County, though less realistic. The hierarchy of her cosmos, with aristocrats divinely ordained, has
led to Dinesen's being criticized as an elitist, a patrician,
even a snob. A medieval acceptance of the position fate has
assigned one is dramatized in several intricately constructed stories, including "A Country Tale" and "Alkmene."
Many tales reveal a god who created aristocrats who, as
caretakers of the peasants and servants of the king, fulfill a
major role in a universal pattern. Dinesen seems to find the
medieval stratified society more functional, even more
realistic, than modern democracies. Her belief in fate is

related to her theory of tragedy, in which the human being fights destiny, and comedy, in which characters accept appointed roles. Some stories illustrate her paradoxical notion that tragedy can be a source of human happiness.

For all her belief that it is the job of the teller of tales to delight readers, divert them from sorrows, make them live in the present, Dinesen repeatedly dramatizes moral and philosophical concepts, which often run counter to those traditionally accepted in western culture. For example, although it is an essential part of her view of an ordered world, her concept of justice admits of the aristocrat's total authority over the peasant, as in "Sorrow-Acre," and the belief that morality imposes order on human society is questioned repeatedly, as in "Of Secret Thoughts and of Heaven" and "The Poet."

In style and pattern, Dinesen's stories—categorized by her as either "Gothic," tales of art with dreamlike plots, characters, and settings ("The Dreamers"), or "Winter's" tales, tales of nature, usually set in Denmark ("The Fish")—are uniquely her own. The language is deliberately quaint and archaic, possessed of remarkable clarity despite the stylized syntax quite unlike that of *Out of Africa* with its fine command of English. Structurally, they often involve a tale within a tale, a carefully framed interior narrative that serves as a parable or fable to shed light on the main story.

Her characters often seem by some simple, unconscious act to move through a veil separating reality from a world without any recognizable coordinates of time or place. A dreamlike, decidedly non-realistic quality of plots, settings, and characters in Dinesen's haunted and haunting stories results from her belief that dreams and art are similar, a concept that shapes her narrative method. As in dreams her tales create their own logic; time is foreshortened or lengthened; the subconscious emerges; and actions are sometimes surreal, even absurd. However, there emerges a sense of the inevitability and credibility of characters and actions.

Dinesen's most incisive statement about the art of writing appears in the story "The Blank Page," in which an ancient teller of tales relates how the morning after the wedding of a princess of Portugal, the bridal bed sheet was displayed before the palace as testament to her virginity, then returned to the convent where it had been woven. There the center of the sheet was framed and displayed in a gallery with those from other princesses. Only one sheet differed, because it was unstained, and the old story teller compares this to the blank page, upon which the deepest, sweetest, merriest, and most cruel tale is to be found, if the author has been loyal to the story. Within the mystery of the silence signified by the blank page, the strange uniqueness of Dinesen's talent is to be found.

—W. Kenneth Holditch

See the essays on "The Blue Jar," "The Monkey," and "Sorrow-Acre"

———

DONOSO (Yañez), José. Chilean. Born in Santiago, 5 October 1924. Educated at the Grange School, Santiago; University of Chile Instituto Pedagógio, 1947; Princeton University, New Jersey (Doherty scholar), A.B. 1951. Married María Serrano in 1961; one daughter. Worked as a shepherd in Patagonia; taught English, Catholic University of Chile, 1954, and journalism at University of Chile; staff member, *Revista Ercilla,* Santiago, 1959–64; and at Colorado State University, Fort Collins, 1969; literary critic, *Siempre* magazine, 1964–66; participant in Writers' Workshop, University of Iowa, Iowa City, 1965–67. Recipient: City of Santiago prize, 1955; Chile-Italy prize, for journalism, 1960; William Faulkner Foundation prize, 1962; Guggenheim fellowship, 1968, 1973; Critics' prize (Spain), 1979; Encomienda con Placa de la Orden de Alfonso X el Sabio, 1987; National Literature prize (Chile), 1990; Woodrow Wilson Foundation fellow, 1992. Chevalier de l'Ordre des Arts et des Lettres (France), 1986. Lives in Santiago.

PUBLICATIONS

Short Stories

Veraneo y otros cuentos.   1955.
Coronación (novella).   1957; as *Coronation,* 1965.
El charleston.   1960; as *Charleston and Other Stories,* 1977.
El lugar sin límites (novella).   1966; as *Hell Hath No Limits,* in *Triple Cross,* 1972.
Este domingo (novella).   1966; as *This Sunday,* 1967.
Los mejores cuentos.   1966.
Cuentos.   1971.
Tres novelitas burguesas.   1973; as *Sacred Families,* 1977.
Cuatro para Delfina.   1982.
Cuentos.   1985.

Novels

El obsceno pájaro de la noche.   1970; as *The Obscene Bird of Night,* 1973.
Casa de campo.   1978; as *A House in the Country,* 1984.
La misteriosa desaparición de la marquesita de Loria.   1980.
El jardín de al lado.   1981; as *The Garden Next Door,* 1992.
La desesperanza.   1986; as *Curfew,* 1988.
Taratuta; Naturaleza muerta con cachimba.   1990; as *Taratuta; Still Life with Pipe,* 1993.

Plays

Sueños de mala muerte (produced 1982).   1985.
Este domingo, with Carlos Cerda from his own novel (produced 1990).   1990.

Screenplay: *The Moon in the Mirror.*

Verse

Poemas de un novelista.   1981.

Other

Historia personal del "boom."   1972; as *The Boom in Spanish American Literature: A Personal History,* 1977.

Editor, with others, *The Tri-Quarterly Anthology of Contemporary Latin American Literature.*   1969.

Has translated works by John Dickson Carr, Isak Dinesen, Nathaniel Hawthorne, and Françoise Mallet-Joris.

*

Critical Studies: "The Novel as Happening: An Interview with Donoso" by Rodríguez Monegal, in *Review* 73, 1973; *Donoso* by George R. McMurray, 1979; "*El obsceno pájaro de la noche*: A Willed Process of Evasion" by Pamela Bacarisse, in *Contemporary Latin American Fiction,* edited by Salvador Bacarisse, 1980; "Structure and Meaning in *La misteriosa desaparición de la Marquesita de Loria*," in *BHS,* 3, 1986, and "Donoso and the Post-Boom: Simplicity and Subversion," in *Contemporary Literature* 4, 1987, both by Philip Swanson; "Countries of the Mind: Literary Space in Joseph Conrad and Donoso" by Alfred J. MacAdam, in his *Textual Confrontations,* 1987; *Studies on the Works of Donoso: An Anthology of Critical Essays* by Miriam Adelstein, 1990; "Aesthetics, Ethics, and Politics in Donoso's *El jardín de al lado*" by Ricardo Gutiérrez Mouat, in *PMLA* 106, 1991; *Understanding Donoso* by Sharon Magnarelli, 1992.

* * *

José Donoso is a Chilean novelist and short story writer. His first three novels qualify as novellas or novelettes. *Coronación* (*Coronation*), like many of this writer's works, is narrated with a studied incoherence suggesting mental or emotional disturbance and plurality of perspectives that demand much of the reader. Decadence of the Chilean aristocracy, one of Donoso's enduring concerns, is the primary theme of three interrelated story lines: the grotesque birthday celebration of the completely mad, pathologically repressed nonagenarian Miss Elisa and her death following a private party in which her drunken servants crown her; the story of her fiftyish bachelor grandson and his ill-fated, violent love for the young nursemaid, Estela; and that of Estela's love for Mario, a delinquent who uses her to rob the house. The hermetic monotony and existential inauthenticity of upper-class life, isolated from the "real" workaday world, are portrayed in almost naturalistic sequences, while social determinism appears in depiction of society's dregs from the neighboring shantytown.

Este domingo (*This Sunday*) focuses upon the deterioration of Chile's bourgeoisie and its values as seen by one of the narrators, an anonymous grandchild of the major characters, Alvaro, his wife Chepa, and Violeta (a servant of Alvaro's family, seduced in his youth, and a perennial refuge for his lifelong childishness). Physical, moral, and environmental decadence—the aging of people and property—contrast with idealized recollections of a splendid past. Adroit use of innovative techniques and more subtle thematic development, a contrapuntal effect achieved with stream-of-consciousness narration, make this work more complex than *Coronation*. Philosophical and literary theories of Henri Bergson and Marcel Proust blend with latent Freudian and existential concepts, resulting in greater aesthetic and intellectual density.

In the novella *El lugar sin límites* (*Hell Hath No Limits*), use of a deranged narrative perspective anticipates the still more nightmarish world of Donoso's longest and most critically acclaimed novel, *El obsceno pájaro de la noche* (*The Obscene Bird of Night*). The breakdown of an established order, symbolically the traditional social order, appears through the disintegrating psyches of the narrators. *Casa de campo* (*A House in the Country*), seen as an allegory of Chilean politics, won Spain's 1979 Critics' prize. Few meaningful thematic or technical distinctions

exist between Donoso's novels and short fiction; length notwithstanding, all superbly blend sociological observation and psychological analysis, and realism never eliminates fantasy, for madness, the supernatural, and the unknown lurk just beyond the uncertain limits of reason.

Veraneo y otros cuentos (Summer Vacation and Other Stories) and *El charleston* (The Charleston) are represented by tales included in *Charleston and Other Stories.* A favorite motif, the labyrinthine, decrepit mansion, haunting all of Donoso's fiction (a Jungian symbol of the psyche) and allegedly based on the home of his father's elderly great-aunts where Donoso was born, appears in several of the early stories. Upper-class, traditional Chilean families, the problem of the generation gap, a rigidly stratified society where a rich, decadent minority is cared for by an impoverished lower class, pervade the stories as well as the writer's longer works. Donoso's recurrent ulcers, prolonged psychoanalysis, and a nightmarish illness (in 1969) marked by hallucinations, schizophrenia, and paranoia due to intolerance of painkillers, all are reflected in his fiction. Following Freudian theory, Donoso stresses the importance of early childhood experiences, the power of the unconscious, and the central role of sexuality in other areas of life; much of the characters' conduct is irrational, neurotic, or motivated by repressed erotic urges, as in his long novels.

Tres novelitas burguesas (*Sacred Families*) reflecting Donoso's experience in Spain, paints the politicosocial and cultural environment of Catalonia, evincing Donoso's reactions to the intellectual and sociological ambience of the peninsula. "Chattanooga Choo-Choo," a critique of materialism, drugs, and easy eroticism among upper-class Catalans, includes an exiled Latin American novelist who fights with his publisher because his novel isn't selling (exiles of necessity "lose" their natural audiences). Sterility of the painter in "Green Atom Number Five" allegorically represents the exiled artist's frustration at separation from his homeland. "Gaspard de la Nuit" introduces other motifs common to Donoso's exile works, including homosexuality, sterility, absence, the double, estrangement, and role reversal, paradigms of exilic experience. Many of these appear in *El jardín de al lado* (*The Garden Next Door*), a longer novel painting the exile of a Chilean couple in Madrid. In *La misteriosa desaparición de la marquesita de Loria* (The Strange Disappearance of the Young Marquise of Loria), Donoso contributes an amusing bit of erotica to Spain's outpouring in this genre following the death of Franco and demise of the censorship.

Cuatro para Delfina (Four [Novelettes] for Delphine), one of Donoso's more varied collections, returns to the Santiago setting of his early stories, offering four seemingly realistic visions of the concrete socio-historical ambient of the Chilean capital. While differing in tone and shadings from festive to lugubrious and grotesque, all involve precise observations of daily existence at the same time they constitute disturbing, even visionary, allegories of national life. From farce to tragedy to parable, the varied registers of Donoso's art coincide in their masterful narrative architecture and his mastery in portraying what for most eyes is invisible.

—Janet Pérez

See the essay on *Hell Hath No Limits.*

DOSTOEVSKII, Fedor (Mikhailovich). Russian. Born in Moscow, 30 October 1821. Educated at home to age 12; Chermak's School Moscow; Army Chief Engineering Academy, St. Petersburg, 1838–43: commissioned as ensign, 1839, as 2nd Lieutenant, 1842, graduated 1843 as War Ministry draftsman; resigned 1844. Married 1) Mariia Dmitrievna Isaeva in 1857 (died 1864), one step-son; 2) Anna Grigorevna Snitkina in 1867, two daughters and two sons. Writer; political involvement caused his arrest, 1849, and imprisonment in Omsk, 1850–54; exiled as soldier at Semipalatinsk, 1854: corporal, 1855, ensign, 1856, resigned as 2nd Lieutenant for health reasons, and exile ended, 1859; editor, *Vremia* (Time), 1861–63; took over *Epokh* on his brother's death, 1864–65; in Western Europe, 1867–71; editor, *Grazhdanin [Citizen]*, 1873–74. *Died 28 January 1881.*

PUBLICATIONS

Collections

Novels.   12 vols., 1912–20.
Sobranie Sochinenii, edited by Leonid Grossman.   10 vols., 1956–58.
Polnoe sobranie sochinenii.   1972—.

Short Stories

Bednye Liudi.   1846; as *Poor Folk*, 1887.
Zapiski iz podpol'ia.   1864; as *Letters from the Underworld*, 1915; as *Notes from Underground*, in *Novels*, 1918.

Novels

Dvoinik.   1846; as *The Double*, in *Novels*, 1917; as *The Double: A Poem to St. Petersburg*, 1958.
Igrok.   1866; as *The Gambler*, 1887.
Prestuplenie i nakazanie.   1867; as *Crime and Punishment*, 1886.
Idiot.   1869; as *The Idiot*, 1887.
Vechnyi muzh.   1870; as *The Permanent Husband*, 1888; as *The Eternal Husband*, 1917.
Besy.   1872; as *The Possessed*, 1913; as *The Devils*, 1953.
Podrostok.   1875; as *A Raw Youth*, 1916.
Brat'ia Karamazovy.   1880; as *The Brothers Karamazov*, 1912.

Other

Zapiski iz mertvogo doma.   1861–62; as *Buried Alive; or, Ten Years of Penal Servitude in Siberia*, 1881; as *The House of the Dead*, 1911.
Dnevnik pisatelia.   1876–81; as *The Diary of a Writer*, 1949.
Pis'ma k zhene, edited by V.F. Pereverzev.   1926; as *Letters to His Wife*, 1930.
Occasional Writings.   1961.
The Notebooks for "The Idiot" ["Crime and Punishment," "The Possessed," "A Raw Youth," "The Brothers Karamazov"], edited by Edward Wasiolek.   5 vols., 1967–71.
The Unpublished Dostoevsky: Diaries and Notebooks 1860–1881, edited by Carl R. Proffer.   3 vols., 1973–76.
Selected Letters, edited by Joseph Frank and David Goldstein.   1987.

Complete Letters, edited by David Lowe and Ronald Meyer.   5 vols., 1988–91.

*

Bibliography: "Dostoevsky Studies in Great Britain: A Bibliographical Survey" by Garth M. Terry in *New Essays on Dostoevsky* edited by Malcolm V. Jones and Garth M. Terry, 1983.

Critical Studies: *Dostoevsky: His Life and Art* by A. Yarmolinsky, 1957; *Dostoevsky in Russian Literary Criticism 1846–1954* by Vladimir Seduro, 1957; *Dostoevsky* by David Magarshak, 1961; *Dostoevsky: A Collection of Critical Essays* edited by Rene Wellek, 1962; *The Undiscovered Dostoevsky*, 1962, and *Dostoevsky: His Life and Work*, 1978, both by Ronald Hingley; *Problems of Dostoevsky's Poetics* by Mikhail M. Bakhtin, 1963; *Dostoevsky: The Major Fiction* by Edward Wasiolek, 1964; *Dostoevsky's Quest for Form* by Robert Louis Jackson, 1966; *Dostoevsky: His Life and Work* by Konstantin Mochulsky, 1967; *Dostoevsky: An Examination of the Major Novels* by Richard Peace, 1971; *Dostoevsky: The Seeds of Revolt 1821–1848* and *The Years of Ordeal 1850–1859* by Joseph Frank,   2 vols., 1976–83; *Dostoevsky*, 1976, and *Dostoevsky After Bakhtin: Readings in Dostoevsky's Fantastic Realism*, 1990, both by Malcolm V. Jones, and *New Essays on Dostoevsky* edited by Jones and Garth M. Terry, 1983; *A Dostoevsky Dictionary* by Richard Chapple, 1983; *Dostoevsky: Myths of Quality* by Roger B. Anderson, 1986; *Dostoevsky: A Writer's Life* by Geir Kjetsaa, 1988; *Dostoevsky* by Peter Conrad, 1988; *The Political and Social Thoughts of Dostoevsky* by Stephen Carter, 1991.

* * *

In Fedor Dostoevskii, Russian literature found the authentic confirmation of its destiny and a direction that pointed beyond the purely historical towards a genuinely universal vision of humankind. Initially drawing his inspiration from Gogol, the young Dostoevskii sought to continue where his master had left off. His first work of short fiction, *Bednye Liudi (Poor Folk)* depicted a thoroughly Gogolian romance between a lowly civil servant and a young girl. The story, in epistolary form, does, however, break new ground by developing the personalities of the two principal characters in a way unknown to Gogol. The civil servant, Makar Devushkin, in particular, is seen in all his wretchedness as a human being, not as a demonic or caricature figure. The success of *Poor Folk* and its acceptance and approval by Nekrasov and Belinskii led Dostoevskii to believe that he was firmly launched on the way to becoming Gogol's heir. But the story's popularity and success were based on a misunderstanding of Dostoevskii's creative intentions. While Nekrasov and Belinskii saw the book as a work of social criticism, Dostoevskii's concerns were in fact moral and metaphysical. In his so-called St. Petersburg poem, "The Double" (1846), set in the Gogolian world of civil servants and government offices and departments, the writer explored levels of consciousness and reality not touched previously in Russian fiction. In the story of the civil servant Golyadkin and his double, it is possible to see a link with Gogol's "The Nose," but the nightmarish horror and underground claustrophobia of Dostoevskii's narrative are unprecedented in the writing of his time, and the public and critical reaction were predictably negative. The same negative judgment met his extraordinary depiction of a civil servant's fantasy world in the story "Mr. Prokharchin" (1847).

In 1847 Dostoevskii began to frequent the revolutionary circle of Petrashevskii, and this may have been brought about in part by his desire to identify more closely with the atheistic teaching of Belinskii, perhaps in the hope that this would enable him to write works that would be more acceptable to the Russian critical establishment. The works he wrote during this period were if anything, however, even more remote from the critical and artistic climate that prevailed. The story "The Landlady" (1849) is a study in inward reality that contains some very early allusions to themes that were later to be developed in *Brat'ia Karamazovy* (The Brothers Karamazov), and is entirely permeated by a Hoffmannesque romantic delirium. "*Netochka Nezvanova*" (1849), an unfinished novel, is also a Hoffmannesque narrative, concerning an artist whose talent is spent. In fact, however, the result of the writer's involvement with revolutionary politics was to propel him in a direction hitherto unknown, and produced the works of the mature Dostoevskii. The experience of being condemned to death, facing execution, and having the sentence commuted at the last moment to four years' exile and hard labour and reduction to the ranks, stayed with the writer all the rest of his life and profoundly influenced the way he perceived existence and thought and wrote about it.

The immediate fruit of the period of exile was the prison narrative *The House of the Dead*. More than any other work of Dostoevskii's, this documentary-style narrative, closely based on the writer's own experience of penal servitude, represents a cataclysmic fall from a world of dreams and fantasy to the cold facts—and the human and animal warmth—of reality. The portrayal of the convicts, many of whom were dangerous murderers who had killed several times, leaves an unforgettable impression on the reader, as do the chapters that describe the prison bathhouse, the stage show, and the prison animals.

Perhaps the most striking and characteristic shorter narratives of Dostoevskii's later years are to be found contained within much longer works. "The Meek Girl" (1876), which is based on a newspaper report on the suicide of a seamstress who plunged from a garret window, holding a religious icon in her hands, is in fact an extract from *A Writer's Diary*, the one-man literary and polemical review which Dostoevskii issued between 1876 and 1877. It was initially connected with an episode from his projected novel "The Dreamer," and only gradually did it begin to emerge as an independent narrative work. Above all, the author was concerned to present to his readers a "fantastic story" that would tell the truth about reality as seen from within, from a psychological, spiritual perspective. Dostoevskii refers to this in his author's introduction; he writes of the story's form being "fantastic," claiming that "this is neither nor a set of diary notes, but a record of a man's inward thought-processes, one which involves the "hypothesis of a stenographer who has written everything down." The story is thus very modern in conception, and relates to techniques, such as stream-of-consciousness, that were developed in European fiction much later.

The other major work of short fiction from the latter part of Dostoevskii's career is "The Legend of the Grand Inquisitor," a chapter from book five of *The Brothers Karamazov*. The "Legend" is derived from a passage in the "The Landlady," published some 40 years earlier, where the old man Murin says:

You know, master, a weak man cannot control himself on his own.

Give him everything, and he'll come of his own accord and give it back to you; give him half the world, just try it, and what do you think he'll do? He'll hide himself in your shoe immediately, that small will he make himself. Give a weak man freedom and he'll fetter it himself and give it back to you. A foolish heart has no use for freedom!

In the story of the Saviour's return to earth in Seville, at the time of the worst excesses of the Inquisition, Dostoevskii presents a sustained meditation of the meaning of freedom and power. The secret of the Grand Inquisitor is that he does not believe in God—and this is why he ultimately lets Christ go, telling him never to return to earth and interfere as he has done with the designs of those who would exercise power upon earth. The tale is given an ironic twist by the fact that it is the demented but intellectually brilliant Ivan, suffering from *delirium tremens* with hallucinations of the devil, who invents the story—even this great discussion of the ultimate themes of human history and destiny is somehow shadowy and suspect, a fever-dream. This is typical of Dostoevskii's art, and especially typical of the attitude towards reality that is developed in his short fiction.

—David McDuff

See the essays on *Notes from Underground* and "White Nights."

DOYLE, (Sir) Arthur Conan. Scottish. Born in Edinburgh, 22 May 1859. Educated at the Hodder School, Lancashire, 1868–70; Stonyhurst College, Lancashire, 1870–75; Jesuit School, Feldkirch, Austria (editor, *Feldkirchian Gazette*), 1875–76; studied medicine at the University of Edinburgh, 1877–81, M.B. 1881, M.D. 1885. Served as senior physician at a field hospital in South Africa during the Boer War, 1899–1902: knighted, 1902. Married 1) Louise Hawkins in 1885 (died 1906), one daughter and one son; 2) Jean Leckie in 1907, two sons and one daughter. Physician in Southsea, Hampshire, 1882–90; full-time writer from 1891; Unionist candidate for Parliament for Central Edinburgh, 1900, and tariff reform candidate for the Hawick Burghs, 1906. Member, Society for Psychical Research, 1893–1930 (resigned). LL.D.: University of Edinburgh, 1905. Knight of Grace of the Order of St. John of Jerusalem. *Died 7 July 1930.*

PUBLICATIONS

Short Stories

Mysteries and Adventures.   1889; as *The Gully of Bluemansdyke and Other Stories,* 1892.
The Captain of the Polestar and Other Tales.   1890.
The Adventures of Sherlock Holmes.   1892.
My Friend the Murderer and Other Mysteries and Adventures.   1893.
The Memoirs of Sherlock Holmes.   1893.

The Great Keinplatz Experiment and Other Stories.   1894.
The Exploits of Brigadier Gerard.   1896.
The Man from Archangel and Other Stories.   1898.
The Green Flag with Other Stories of War and Sport. 1900.
Adventures of Gerard.   1903.
The Return of Sherlock Holmes.   1905.
Round the Fire Stories.   1908.
The Last Galley: Impressions and Tales.   1911.
His Last Bow: Some Reminiscences of Sherlock Holmes. 1917.
Danger! and Other Stories.   1918.
Tales of the Ring and Camp.   1922; as The Croxley Master and Other Tales of the Ring and Camp, 1925.
Tales of Terror and Mystery.   1922; as The Black Doctor and Other Tales of Terror and Mystery, 1925.
Tales of Twilight and the Unseen.   1922; as The Great Keinplatz Experiment and Other Tales of Twilight and the Unseen, 1925.
Tales of Adventure and Medical Life.   1922; as The Man from Archangel and Other Tales of Adventure, 1925.
Tales of Pirates and Blue Water.   1922; as The Dealings of Captain Sharkey and Other Tales of Pirates, 1925.
Tales of Long Ago.   1922; as The Last of the Legions and Other Tales of Long Ago, 1925.
The Case-Book of Sherlock Holmes.   1927.
The Maracot Deep and Other Stories.   1929.
Historical Romances.   2 vols., 1931–32.
The Professor Challenger Stories.   1952.
Great Stories, edited by John Dickson Carr.   1959.
The Annotated Sherlock Holmes, edited by William S. Baring-Gould.   2 vols., 1967.
The Adventures of Sherlock Holmes (facsimile of magazine stories).   1976; as The Sherlock Holmes Illustrated Omnibus, 1978.
The Best Supernatural Tales of Doyle, edited by E.F. Bleiler.   1979.
Sherlock Holmes: The Published Apocrypha, with others, edited by Jack Tracy.   1980.
The Final Adventures of Sherlock Holmes, edited by Peter Haining.   1981.
The Edinburgh Stories.   1981.
The Best Science Fiction of Doyle, edited by Charles G. Waugh and Martin H. Greenberg.   1981.
Uncollected Stories, edited by John Michael Gibson and Richard Lancelyn Green.   1982.
The Best Horror Stories of Doyle, edited by Martin H. Greenberg and Charles G. Waugh.   1988.
The Supernatural Tales of Doyle, edited by Peter Haining. 1988.

Novels

A Study in Scarlet.   1888.
The Mystery of Cloomber.   1888.
Micah Clarke.   1889.
The Sign of Four.   1890.
The Firm of Girdlestone.   1890.
The White Company.   1891.
The Doings of Raffles Haw.   1892.
The Great Shadow.   1892.
The Great Shadow, and Beyond the City.   1893.
The Refugees.   1893.
Round the Red Lamp, Being Facts and Fancies of Medical Life.   1894.
The Parasite.   1894.
The Stark Munro Letters.   1895.
Rodney Stone.   1896.

Uncle Bernac: A Memory of the Empire.   1897.
The Tragedy of Korosko.   1898; as A Desert Drama, 1898.
A Duet, with an Occasional Chorus.   1899; revised edition, 1910.
Hilda Wade (completion of story by Grant Allen).   1900.
The Hound of the Baskervilles.   1902.
Sir Nigel.   1906.
The Case of Oscar Slater.   1912.
The Lost World.   1912.
The Poison Belt.   1913.
The Valley of Fear.   1915.
The Land of Mist.   1925.
The Field Bazaar.   Privately printed, 1934.

Plays

Jane Annie; or, The Good Conduct Prize, with J.M. Barrie, music by Ernest Ford (produced 1893).   1893.
Foreign Policy, from his story "A Question of Diplomacy" (produced 1893).
Waterloo, from his story "A Straggler of 15" (as A Story of Waterloo, produced 1894; as Waterloo, produced 1899). 1907.
Halves, from the story by James Payn (produced 1899).
Sherlock Holmes, with William Gillette, from works by Doyle (produced 1899).
A Duet (A Duologue) (produced 1902).   1903.
Brigadier Gerard, from his own stories (produced 1906).
The Fires of Fate: A Modern Morality, from his novel The Tragedy of Korosko (produced 1909).
The House of Temperley, from his novel Rodney Stone (produced London, 1910).
The Pot of Caviare, from his own story (produced 1910).
The Speckled Band: An Adventure of Sherlock Holmes (produced 1910).   1912.
The Crown Diamond (produced 1921).   1958.
It's Time Something Happened.   1925.

Verse

Songs of Action.   1898.
Songs of the Road.   1911.
The Guards Came Through and Other Poems.   1919.
The Poems: Collected Edition (includes play The Journey). 1922.

Other

The Great Boer War.   1900.
The War in South Africa: Its Cause and Conduct.   1902.
Works (Author's Edition).   12 vols., 1903.
The Fiscal Question.   1905.
An Incursion into Diplomacy.   1906.
The Story of Mr. George Edalji.   1907.
Through the Magic Door (essays).   1907.
The Crime of the Congo.   1909.
Divorce Law Reform: An Essay.   1909.
Doyle: Why He Is Now in Favour of Home Rule.   1911.
The Case of Oscar Slater.   1912.
Divorce and the Church, with Lord Hugh Cecil.   1913.
Great Britain and the Next War.   1914.
In Quest of Truth, Being a Correspondence Between Doyle and Captain H. Stansbury.   1914.
To Arms!   1914.
The German War.   1914.
Western Wanderings (travel in Canada).   1915.
The Outlook on the War.   1915.
An Appreciation of Sir John French.   1916.

A Petition to the Prime Minister on Behalf of Sir Roger Casement.   1916.

A Visit to Three Fronts: Glimpses of British, Italian, and French Lines.   1916.

The British Campaign in France and Flanders.   6 vols., 1916–20; revised edition, as *The British Campaigns in Europe 1914–1918,* 1 vol., 1928.

The New Revelation.   1918.

The Vital Message (on spiritualism).   1919.

Our Reply to the Cleric.   1920.

A Public Debate on the Truth of Spiritualism, with Joseph McCabe.   1920; as *Debate on Spiritualism,* 1922.

Spiritualism and Rationalism.   1920.

The Wanderings of a Spiritualist.   1921.

Spiritualism: Some Straight Questions and Direct Answers. 1922.

The Case for Spirit Photography, with others.   1922.

The Coming of the Fairies.   1922.

Three of Them: A Reminiscence.   1923.

Our American Adventure.   1923.

Our Second American Adventure.   1924.

Memories and Adventures.   1924.

Psychic Experiences.   1925.

The Early Christian Church and Modern Spiritualism. 1925.

The History of Spiritualism.   2 vols., 1926.

Pheneas Speaks: Direct Spirit Communications.   1927.

What Does Spiritualism Actually Teach and Stand For? 1928.

A Word of Warning.   1928.

An Open Letter to Those of My Generation.   1929.

Our African Winter.   1929.

The Roman Catholic Church: A Rejoinder.   1929.

The Edge of the Unknown.   1930.

Works (Crowborough Edition).   24 vols., 1930.

Strange Studies from Life, edited by Peter Ruber.   1963.

Doyle on Sherlock Holmes.   1981.

Essays on Photography, edited by John Michael Gibson and Richard Lancelyn Green.   1982.

Letters to the Press: The Unknown Doyle, edited by John Michael Gibson and Richard Lancelyn Green.   1986.

The Sherlock Holmes Letters, edited by Richard Lancelyn Green.   1986.

Editor, *D.D. Home: His Life and Mission,* by Mrs. Dunglas Home.   1921.

Editor, *The Spiritualists' Reader.*   1924.

Translator, *The Mystery of Joan of Arc,* by Léon Denis. 1924.

*

Bibliography: *The World Bibliography of Sherlock Holmes and Dr. Watson* by Ronald Burt De Waal, 1975; *A Bibliography of Doyle* by Richard Lancelyn Green and John Michael Gibson, 1983.

Critical Studies: *The Private Life of Sherlock Holmes* by Vincent Starrett, 1933, revised edition, 1960; *Doyle: His Life and Art* by Hesketh Pearson, 1943, revised edition, 1977; *The Life of Doyle* by John Dickson Carr, 1949; *In the Footsteps of Sherlock Holmes,* 1958, revised edition, 1971, *The World of Sherlock Holmes,* 1973, and *A Study in Surmise: The Making of Sherlock Holmes,* 1984, all by Michael Harrison; *The Man Who Was Sherlock Holmes* by

Michael Hardwick and Mollie Hardwick, 1964; *Doyle: A Biography* by Pierre Nordon, 1966; *Doyle: A Biography of the Creator of Sherlock Holmes* by Ivor Brown, 1972; *A Sherlock Holmes Commentary* by D. Martin Dakin, 1972; *Sherlock Holmes in Portrait and Profile* by Walter Klinefelter, 1975; *The Sherlock Holmes File* by Michael Pointer, 1976; *Doyle's Sherlock Holmes: The Short Stories: A Critical Commentary* by Mary P. De Camara and Stephen Hayes, 1976; *The Adventures of Doyle: The Life of the Creator of Sherlock Holmes* by Charles Higham, 1976; *The Encyclopedia Sherlockiana* by Jack Tracy, 1977; *Doyle: A Biographical Solution* by Ronald Pearsall, 1977; *Sherlock Holmes and His Creator* by Trevor H. Hall, 1978; *Doyle: Portrait of an Artist* by Julian Symons, 1979; *Sherlock Holmes: The Man and His World* by H.R.F. Keating, 1979; *Who's Who in Sherlock Holmes* by Scott R. Bullard and Michael Collins, 1980; *The International Sherlock Holmes* by Ronald Burt De Waal, 1980; *A Sherlock Holmes Compendium* edited by Peter Haining, 1980; *Sherlock Holmes in America* by Bill Blackbeard, 1981; *Sherlock Holmes: A Study in Sources* by Donald A. Redmond, 1982; *The Quest for Sherlock Holmes: A Biographical Study of the Early Life of Doyle* by Owen Dudley Edwards, 1983; *The Sign of Three: Dupin, Holmes, Peirce* edited by Umberto Eco and Thomas A. Sebeok, 1983; *The Baker Street Reader: Cornerstone Writings about Sherlock Holmes* edited by Philip A. Shreffler, 1984; *The Biographical Sherlock Holmes: An Anthology/Handbook* by Arthur Liebman, 1984; *Medical Casebook of Doyle: From Practitioner to Sherlock Holmes and Beyond* by Alvin E. Rodin and Jack D. Key, 1984; *Doyle* by Don Richard Cox, 1985; *The Complete Guide to Sherlock Holmes* by Michael Hardwick, 1986; *Sherlock Holmes: A Centenary Celebration* by Allen Eyles, 1986; *Elementary My Dear Watson: Sherlock Holmes Centenary: His Life and Times* by Graham Nown, 1986; *The Unrevealed Life of Doyle: A Study in Southsea* by Geoffrey Stavert, 1987; *Doyle* by Jacqueline A. Jaffe, 1987; *The Quest for Doyle: Thirteen Biographers in Search of a Life* by Jon L. Lellenberg, 1987; *Doyle and the Spirits: The Spiritualist Career of Doyle* by Kelvin I. Jones, 1989.

*   *   *

Although Arthur Conan Doyle refused to make any great claims for his short fiction and insisted that his work was inferior to Poe or Maupassant, he remains one of the great masters of the modern short story. In scope alone he was certainly one of the most prolific authors of his generation and his stories embraced a wide range of subjects, from adventure and crime to medicine and sport. And, of course, one short story in particular, "A Study in Scarlet" (1887), gave birth to Sherlock Holmes and his companion Dr. Watson.

As a struggling young medical practitioner Doyle had turned to writing short fiction as a means of supplementing his income, but what started as a prop became an all-consuming passion. His interest in the short story as a literary form had been fired by the publication of "The Mystery of the Sasassa Valley" in September 1879 while he was working as an assistant in Birmingham. Other stories of note include "The Captain of the Pole-Star" for *Temple Bar* (February 1883) and "J. Habakuk Jephson's Statement" for the *Cornhill* (January 1884), but it was in the pages of *Strand Magazine* that Doyle was to reach his most enthusiastic public through the creation of Sherlock Holmes.

Starting with the publication in July 1891 of "A Scandal in Bohemia," Doyle followed Holmes's adventures until "The Final Problem" in December 1893, when he killed him off along with his arch enemy Professor Moriarty. Such was the public demand for Holmes's genius for scientific detection, though, that Doyle had to resurrect him and he reappeared in the novel *The Hound of the Baskervilles* and again in the short story collection *The Return of Sherlock Holmes.* By then Holmes and Watson had become public property and their success helped to make Doyle one of the most popular authors of his day.

At Doyle's own admission, one of the models for Holmes was Dr. Joseph Bell (1837-1911), one of his Edinburgh teachers and a pioneer of forensic medicine, whose deductive abilities had much impressed his students. The name owed its origins to the American poet Oliver Wendell Holmes (1809-94) who was much admired by Doyle. Sherlock Holmes became, and remains, a cult figure and the concept of his powers of rapid deduction, allied to Watson's slow-thinking empiricism, was an irresistible literary invention. Moreover, Doyle developed a simple narrative formula that suited the spirit of the late Victorian age and he had the happy ability of suggesting to his readers that they too were part of the story.

In Holmes, Doyle created a believable and admirable character. Although Holmes is intellectually arrogant and occasionally pompous, he balanced those failings with attributes that made the detective attractive to the average reader. Holmes is financially independent, a thorough patriot, and strong-minded, and he possessed a flair for showmanship. Despite being a commoner, he is a confidant of royalty and the aristocracy whom he wins over by the sheer force of his personality. At the same time he has a number of failings which give him a human touch—a liking for black shag tobacco and occasional shots of cocaine. Small wonder that Doyle had difficulties breaking away from him as the subject of his best short fiction.

However, Doyle also made good use of his time away from Holmes's domination. From the 1890's until his death 40 years later, he wrote and published a wide range of stories, all with different backgrounds and styles. Although not a soldier, he wrote a number of stories of army life, enlivened by his powers of observation, not only of the physical background but also of the military type. "A Regimental Scandal" and "The Colonel's Choice" both deal with the sensitive topic of military honour. History, too, was an all-abiding concern, particularly the Regency period. His earliest stories set at that time, "The Great Shadow" and "An Impression of the Regency," prefigure the exploits and adventures of Brigadier Gerard, the cavalry officer whom Napoleon says has "the stoutest heart in my army." In stories like "The Medal of Brigadier Gerard" the soldier leaps out of history's pages to become Doyle's happiest and most amusing fictional creation.

Once he had become financially secure through the Holmes's stories, much of Doyle's short fiction was written for pleasure. The stories collected in *The Last Galley* betray his interest in archaeology and collecting fossils, concerns that were to lead to his novel *The Lost World.* Ancient history was another interest and he used it to good effect in stories like "The Centurion" (1922). His last story, "The Last Resource" (1930), is set in the underworld of America during the prohibition era and is remarkable for the way in which Doyle managed to capture the local speech rhythms.

Inevitably, given the scale of his output, some of Doyle's stories were either incorporated into later fiction or look forward to it. "The Cabman's Story" (1884) is set in London and can be read as a precursor to the Holmes's

stories; the same is true of "The Winning Shot" (1883), which contains echoes of the nighttime countryside of *The Hound of the Baskervilles.*

There are other connections. In all his fiction Doyle demonstrated great powers of observation—a consequence of his own medical training—and he showed himself to be at home in a wide variety of backgrounds. Allied to the sheer exuberance of his literary style and the range of his interests, these virtues mark Doyle as the first writer to put the short story on a professional footing.

—Trevor Royle

See the essay on "The Speckled Band."

———

DROSTE-HÜLSHOFF, Annette von. German. Born Anna Elisabeth Franziska Adolfine Wilhelmina Luisa Maria in Schloss Hülshoff near Münster, Westphalia, 10 January 1797. Educated by private tutors. Moved with her mother and sister to Rüschhaus following the death of her father in 1826; from 1840 collaborated with the writer Levin Schücking who encouraged her poetic activity; lived in Meersburg from 1846. Suffered from ill health throughout her life. *Died 24 May 1848.*

PUBLICATIONS

Collections

Gesammelte Schriften, edited by Levin Schücking.   3 vols., 1878–79.
Sämtliche Werke: historisch-kritische Ausgabe, edited by Karl Schulte Kemminghausen.   4 vols., 1925–30.
Poems, edited by Margaret Atkinson.   1968.
Historische-kritische Ausgabe: Werke, Briefweschel, edited by Winfried Woesler.   14 vols., 1978–85.
Werke, edited by Clemens Heselhaus.   1984.

Short Stories

Die Judenbuche.   1842; as *The Jew's Beech,* 1958; as *The Jew's Beech Tree,* in *Three Eerie Tales from 19th Century German,* 1975.
Ledwina (fragment).   1923.

Play

Perdu; oder, Dichter, Verlenger und Blaustrümpfe.   1840.

Verse

Walther.   1818.
Gedichte.   1838.
Das Malerische und Romantische Westfalen.   1839.
Gedichte.   1844.
Das geistliche Jahr. Nebst eine Anhang Religiöser Gedichte, edited by C.B. Schülter and Wilhelm Junkmann.   1851.
Letzte Gaben, edited by Levin Schücking.   1860.
Lebensgang, edited by Marie Silling.   1917.
Balladen.   1922.

Other

Bilder aus Westfalen.   1845.

Briefe, edited by C. Schlueter.   1877.

Die Briefe Droste-Hülshoff und Levin Schücking, edited by Theo Schücking.   1893.

Die Briefe der Dichterin Droste-Hülshoff, edited by Hermann Cardauns.   1909.

Drei-und-zwanzig neue Droste-Briefe, edited by Manfred Schneider.   1923.

Briefe, edited by Karl Schulte Kemminghausen.   2 vols., 1944.

Lieder und Gesänge, edited by Karl Gustav Fellerer. 1954.

*

Critical Studies: *Droste-Hülshoff* by Margaret Mare, 1965; *Droste-Hülshoff: A Woman of Letters in a Period of Transition,* 1981, and *Droste-Hülshoff: A Biography,* 1984, both by Mary Morgan; *Droste-Hülshoff: A German Poet Between Romanticism and Realism* by John Guthrie, 1989.

* * *

Annette von Droste-Hülshoff owes her reputation as one of Germany's greatest woman writers primarily to her mature poetry and her novella *Die Judenbuche* (*The Jew's Beech Tree*), published in 1842. Other prose fictions remained incomplete. The most interesting, an early novel-fragment, *Ledwina,* portrays a languid, consumptive heroine, prone to Romantic daydreams and "Gothick" nightmares, constricted by the conventions of aristocratic life in rural Westphalia, the author's own milieu, that is later portrayed in *Bei uns zu Lande auf dem Lande* (Our Rural Homeland) via the gently ironic perspective of a visiting relation in a mode influenced by Washington Irving's *Bracebridge Hall.* A crime story, "Joseph," barely progresses beyond the construction of an elaborate narrative frame. While these works are leisurely in narrative mode, *The Jew's Beech Tree* is all terseness, closer in style, structure, thematic concerns, and atmosphere of sinister mystery to Droste-Hülshoff's remarkable ballads and longer narrative poems.

In 1818 her uncle, August von Haxthausen, had published his "Story of an Algerian Slave," a stylized account, emphasizing patterns of fate, of an actual case with which members of the family had been involved as magistrates. Inspired by this model, *The Jew's Beech Tree* traces, episodically, the life of one Friedrich Mergel from childhood to his murder of a Jewish tradesman, Aaron, who has publicly humiliated him. He flees, and the case lapses. Twenty-eight years later a man returns to the village, infirm after years of enslavement by Turkish pirates, and accepts identification as Johannes "Nobody," Friedrich's double. Months later he is found hanged from the beech-tree under which Aaron's body was found, and on which had been carved a Hebrew curse. In a conclusion altogether harsher than Haxthausen's, the body, now identified as Friedrich's, is interred in a carrion-pit—a suicide's fate.

Thus a tale of guilt and atonement? Of retribution exacted, when earthly justice has failed, by an austere deity? Or is this suicide the distraught act of a broken man? Or do we invoke more irrational agencies of fate which find symbolic focus in the uncanny magnetism of the Jew's

Beech itself, and its inscription? The narrator refuses interpretation. Sustaining the mystery of the figure's identity precludes psychological analysis, allows only fragmentary clues from his words and gestures, none pointing directly to suicidal intent or unequivocally to remorse.

But nor is there unequivocal clarity as to Friedrich's guilt, identity, or the nature of his death. Indeed, for many critics the essential point of the tale lies rather in its very quality of obscurity, one that transcends the conventional concealments and false trails of the crime story, and expresses an epistemological scepticism. But beside strategies of mystification there are countervailing patterns of concealment and elucidation, to which the translation of the Hebrew inscription in the final sentence, with maximum emphasis, is the clearest pointer. Unobtrusive juxtapositions, parallelisms (identification of Friedrich as Johannes inverts a misidentification of Johannes on his first appearance), and interlocking motifs (in the circumstances in which Aaron's and Friedrich's bodies are discovered) insinuate meaningful connections. And—unless this be a shaggy-dog story—so does a structural logic.

The focus of two-thirds of the story is Friedrich's development from childhood and the social and moral milieu that shapes it. The "Sittengemälde" of the story's subtitle ("A Picture of Manners from Mountainous Westphalia"), the "depiction of the life and manners" of the region, is no mere local colour. A verse prologue reinforces the point, bidding the reader, raised "secure / Amid the light," not condemn a "poor wretched life": who can assess the effect of "secret, soul-destroying prejudice" implanted "in some young breast"? In this isolated region a rough and ready law of custom prevails; Friedrich's village is communally involved in the theft of timber from the surrounding forests. His mother (movingly portrayed in her demoralization by a miserable marriage: "Ten years, ten crosses") transmits to him the community's antisemitic prejudice; superstition brands his drunkard father, after death in mysterious circumstances, a ghostly bogey-man of the forests. Taunted by his peers, a dreamy solitary, he then finds in his uncle, Simon, an ersatz father-figure and, in his employ (partly as a look-out for the "Blue Smock" timber-thieves), a sense of worth, however dubious; through noisy ostentation, to compensate for early privations, he gains some dominance in the village, but such status is precarious, and aggression is his response to any humiliation, be it by Aaron or earlier by the forester, Brandis.

Yet for all that, it is its chiaroscuro quality that makes the tale compelling, and its intimation of dimensions at odds with the social and psychological realism predicated by the milieu depiction. At one level, sheer narrative concision generates mystery, and, in dialogic passages especially, an extra intensity: Friedrich's confrontation with Brandis, for one, seethes with unexplained resentments and cryptic mutual accusation. As in Droste-Hülshoff's poetry, acutely observed, vividly rendered detail abounds, but its precise significance is often elusive: a late sighting of Friedrich reports his carving a spoon from a stick until "he cut it right in two"—signalling distractedness or a moment of decision? And only rarely, and with some inconsistency, does the narrator assume a vantage point of omniscience, almost as often conceding puzzlement. Much is presented from the perspective of individual participants, with no single viewpoint privileged, or of more amorphous witnesses.

At another level, Johannes "Nobody," despite his realistic presence as the disowned illegitimate son of Simon, is essentially the Doppelgänger of German Romantic tradition—an alter ego, embodiment of the wretched outsider, the "nobody" that Friedrich had first been and will once more be. Tales of Mergel's ghost may be rationalized as superstition, but their atmospheric suggestiveness reinforces the sense of the Breder Forest, scene of all violent actions, as a heart of darkness. Quivering leaves suggest, anthropomorphically, the death agonies of a freshly-felled beech, investing the spoliation of the forests with a dimension of evil beyond mundane poaching. Above all, Simon, beyond his flesh-and-blood presence as shady entrepreneur, is portrayed with details (those coat-tails like flames!) redolent of the diabolic; his "adoption" of Friedrich is a seduction to evil and depravity, in which Friedrich's "boundless arrogance" (the primal sin of *superbia*) is the first step on an ultimately self-destructive path. Motifs suggestive of Cain or Judas lend further weight to interpretations of the text as an admonitory moral-religious exemplum, albeit one whose edificatory intent is obscured by the best instincts of a compelling storyteller.

—Derek Glass

DUGGAN, Maurice (Noel). New Zealander. Born in Auckland, 25 November 1922. Educated at the University of Auckland. Married Barbara Platts in 1945; one child. Worked in advertising from 1961: with J. English Wright (Advertising) Ltd. Auckland, 1965–72. Recipient: Hubert Church Prose award, 1957; New Zealand Library Association Esther Glen award, for children's book, 1959; Katherine Mansfield Memorial award, for short story, 1959; University of Otago Robert Burns fellowship, 1960; New Zealand Literary Fund scholarship, 1966; Buckland award, 1969. *Died 11 December 1974.*

PUBLICATIONS

Collections

Collected Stories, edited by C.K. Stead.   1981.

Short Stories

Immanuel's Land.   1956.
Summer in the Gravel Pit.   1965.
O'Leary's Orchard and Other Stories.   1970.

Other (for children)

Falter Tom and the Water Boy.   1957.
The Fabulous McFanes and Other Children's Stories.
  1974.

*

Critical Studies: "The Short Stories of Duggan" by Terry Sturm, in *Landfall* 97, March 1971; "Duggan's Summer in the Gravel Pit" by Dan Davin, in *Critical Essays in the New Zealand Short Story,* edited by Cherry Hankin, 1982; "Coming of Age in New Zealand: Buster O'Leary Among STC, Rhett Butler, Hell's Angels, and Others" by Neil Besner, in *Ariel,* January 1987.

*   *   *

Although Maurice Duggan spent much of his life trying to write a novel, none was ever completed to his satisfaction and it is almost exclusively for his short fiction, only 30 published stories, that this most self-exacting of New Zealand writers is known. Duggan was born in Auckland in 1922 and it was the loss of his leg in 1940 through osteomyelitis that seems to have generated his desire to write. The amputation ended his all-absorbing interest in sports and prevented him from following his friends into the army during World War II. By 1944 he had made contact with Frank Sargeson, New Zealand's most famous writer of the time, and the older man quickly became his mentor. Duggan evokes this period movingly in "Beginnings," which appeared in the magazine *Landfall* in 1966 as part of a series on how New Zealanders started writing.

Duggan was encouraged by Sargeson, but he never really adopted the other writer's colloquial style. From the beginning his early stories, such as "Sunbrown" and "Notes on an Abstract Arachnid," displayed a wordiness and a disinterest in conventional forms. His first attempts were weakened by what Duggan himself described as "a habit of rhetoric," but as he developed, his stories showed a stylishness and sophistication previously unknown in New Zealand fiction. "Six Place Names and a Girl," to which Sargeson contributed the title, proved a breakthrough with its almost minimal plot and its brief, evocative descriptions of areas on the Hauraki Plains. At the time of publication its one-word sentences and composite words seemed technically very daring.

In 1950 Duggan travelled to England. During his two years in Europe he attempted to write a full-length book and became more interested in concatenated prose. Parts of the uncompleted work were eventually refashioned into short stories built around the lives of the Lenihans, an Irish immigrant family living in Auckland. "Guardian" and "In Youth Is Pleasure" depict and condemn the harsh treatment meted out to boys in a Catholic boarding school. "Race Day" describes some children watching a horse race in the distance from the porch of their house, and their parents' unconcern at a fatal accident. "The Deposition" chronicles the madness and death of the same children's mother and the sudden remarriage of Mr. Lenihan to the much younger Grace Malloy. "A Small Story" goes on to make explicit the children's rejection of their new stepmother. Its rigorous, spare prose style, and the motif of the gate the children swing on reflecting the futility of all action, are typical of the stories of this period.

With some allowance for artistic licence, many of the events in these stories mirror Duggan's own early life. Despite the obvious influence of Joyce's *Dubliners,* the Lenihan stories are some of the finest series written by a New Zealander. They have been compared favourably to Katherine Mansfield's Karori works on the Burnell family, which were written under similar circumstances. The Lenihan stories were mostly published in Duggan's first book, *Immanuel's Land,* and have remained among the most popular of his works. However, he noted thereafter that "I ceased to be subject."

At the same time that Duggan was writing the Lenihan stories he was also working on a travel diary entitled "Voyage," which in three parts describes his journey by ship to England, a holiday through Italy, and adventure in Spain. It was widely admired when published in New Zealand for its lyric power and the virtuosity of its mandarin style. For the next few years Duggan seems, at least in retrospect, to be trying to bring this richness into the New Zealand realist tradition. "The Wits of Willie Graves" is the story of a debt collector's journey into the outer reaches of the New Zealand countryside, his meeting with a hillbilly family and his slow sense of collusion with the father's incestuous attitude to his eldest daughter. The descriptions of the isolated landscape and of the harsh lifestyle of the family blend effectively with the tale of corruption. "Blues for Miss Laverty" is a story of loneliness told in a prose evocative of urban desolation. Mary May Laverty, a spinsterish classical music teacher, is bedevilled by a nameless man who plays a record of the St. Louis Blues over and over again in her boarding house. Eventually, after a failed attempt at an affair with the father of one of her pupils, she confronts the nameless man briefly and they recognise the impossibility in life of "a little human warmth."

"Blues for Miss Laverty" was written during Duggan's year as Burns Fellow at Otago University, and it is during this fertile period that he produced two long monologues that effectively pushed the New Zealand short story out of its social realist rut. "Riley's Handbook" consists of the ravings of an artist named Fowler who has escaped his wife and family to become a bar-man and caretaker in a sprawling rural hotel. His attempt to revise his identity requires a new name, Riley, but "disguise and sudden departure have not been enough." Riley forms a sexual relationship with Myra, another worker in the hotel, and rails bitterly against the absurdity of both his former and adopted lives. The story's atmosphere of utter despair would be hard to take were it not for the comic exuberance of its language, its sense of revelling in melancholy and the skill with which its characters are drawn. "Along Rideout Road that Summer," a story told by a young man who has run away from home, plays with many of the themes of conventional New Zealand fiction.

In the remaining 14 years of his life Duggan completed only three further stories. Each attracted great attention when it appeared. "O'Leary's Orchard" is the often touching story of the relationship between an older man and a younger woman, and "An Appetite for Flowers" describes the tug-of-love between a divorced couple for the affections of their child. "The Magsman Miscellany," which was published in 1975 one year after Duggan's death, managed to cause a sensation with its skillful use of meta-fictional form, the story of Ben McGoldrick's relationship to his wife and of them both to fiction. This is testament, no doubt, to Duggan's ability to stay ahead of his contemporaries, to develop continually the possibilities of style, and never to be happy with less than the perfect phrase. Despite the paucity of his output he ranks with Mansfield and Sargeson as one of New Zealand's greatest exponents of short fiction.

—Ian Richards

See the essay on "Along Rideout Road that Summer."

————

du MAURIER, (Dame) Daphne. English. Born in London, 13 May 1907; daughter of the actor manager Sir Gerald du Maurier; granddaughter of George du Maurier. Educated privately and in Paris. Married lieutenant-general Sir Frederick Browning in 1932 (died 1965); two daughters and one son. Recipient: Mystery Writers of America Grand Master award, 1977. Fellow, Royal Society of Literature, 1952. D.B.E. (Dame Commander, Order of the British Empire), 1969. *Died 19 April 1989.*

PUBLICATIONS

Short Stories

Happy Christmas (story).   1940.
Come Wind, Come Weather.   1940.
Nothing Hurts for Long, and Escort.   1943.
Consider the Lilies (story).   1943.
Spring Picture (story).   1944.
Leading Lady (story).   1945.
London and Paris.   1945.
The Apple Tree: A Short Novel and Some Stories.   1952; as *Kiss Me Again, Stranger: A Collection of Eight Stories, Long and Short,* 1953; as *The Birds and Other Stories,* 1968.
Early Stories.   1954.
The Breaking Point: Eight Stories.   1959; as *The Blue Lenses and Other Stories,* 1970.
The Treasury of du Maurier Stories.   1960.
The Lover and Other Stories.   1961.
Not after Midnight and Other Stories.   1971; as *Don't Look Now,* 1971.
Echoes from the Macabre: Selected Stories.   1976.
The Rendezvous and Other Stories.   1980.
Classics of the Macabre.   1987.

Novels

The Loving Spirit.   1931.
I'll Never Be Young Again.   1932.
The Progress of Julius.   1933.
Jamaica Inn.   1936.
Rebecca.   1938.
Frenchman's Creek.   1941.
Hungry Hill.   1943.
The King's General.   1946.
The Parasites.   1949.
My Cousin Rachel.   1951.
Mary Anne.   1954.
The Scapegoat.   1957.
Castle Dor (completion of novel by Arthur Quiller-Couch).   1962.
The Glass-Blowers.   1963.
The Flight of the Falcon.   1965.
The House on the Strand.   1969.
Rule Britannia.   1972.

Plays

Rebecca, from her own novel (produced 1940).   1940.
The Years Between (produced 1944).   1945.
September Tide (produced 1948).   1949.

Screenplay: *Hungry Hill,* with Terence Young and Francis Crowdry, 1947.

Television Play: *The Breakthrough,* 1976.

Other

Gerald: A Portrait (on Gerald du Maurier).   1934.
The du Mauriers.   1937.

The Infernal World of Branwell Brontë. 1960.
Vanishing Cornwall, photographs of Christian Browning. 1967.
Golden Lads: Sir Francis Bacon, Anthony Bacon and Their Friends. 1975.
The Winding Stair: Francis Bacon, His Rise and Fall. 1976.
Growing Pains: The Shaping of a Writer (autobiography). 1977; as *Myself When Young,* 1977.
The Rebecca Notebook and Other Memories (includes stories). 1980.
Enchanted Cornwall: Her Pictorial Memoir, edited by Piers Dudgeon. 1989.

Editor, *The Young George du Maurier: A Selection of His Letters 1860–1867.* 1951.
Editor, *Best Stories,* by Phyllis Bottome. 1963.

*

Critical Studies: *du Maurier* by Richard Kelly, 1987; *The Private World of du Maurier* by Martyn Shallcross, 1991.

* * *

Daphne du Maurier wrote most of her short fiction between 1943 and 1969, originally publishing stories in women's magazines such as *Good Housekeeping* and *Ladies Home Journal.* Her tales were later collected in *The Apple Tree* (*Kiss Me Again, Stranger* in the United States), *The Breaking Point,* and *Not after Midnight* (*Don't Look Now* in the United States). These three volumes represent her best work. In 1980 she published *The Rendezvous and Other Stories* consisting of pieces written decades earlier, which one critic has claimed could only be appreciated by "her most die-hard fans, with minds clouded by her past success."

Du Maurier occupies a strange space in literature, almost entirely ignored by scholars and biographers and yet popularized by Alfred Hitchcock's film versions of *Jamaica Inn, Rebecca,* and "The Birds," and by Nicolas Roeg's 1973 adaptation of "Don't Look Now" (starring Julie Christie and Donald Sutherland). Despite an unfavorable review of her later work by Paul Ableman noting a lack of "any evidence whatsoever of true literary ability," du Maurier in her best efforts is an entertaining and gifted storyteller whose work revolves around psychological and supernatural complications and is often liminally situated at what she calls "the breaking point" where "a link between emotion and reason is stretched to the limit of endurance, and sometimes snaps."

Du Maurier had an intense, complicated, and psychologically incestuous relationship with her father, an actor and theatrical manager in whom she noted a "definite feminine strain." She herself often yearned to be a boy and as an adolescent adopted a male persona called Eric Avon. This sexual ambiguity is evident throughout her work not only in the occasional first-person male narrator ("Kiss Me Again, Stranger," "Monte Verità") but in allusions to homosexuals, transvestites, and pedophiles. One of the most striking examples is "Ganymede," in which a classics scholar on holiday in Venice succumbs to the charms of a young boy and accidentally causes his death. The detective story "A Border-Line Case" is a study in inadvertent incest as a young actress, Shelagh Money, has an affair with a mysterious recluse whom she later discovers to be her biological father.

Children are often featured in du Maurier's stories, usually dead, exploited, or abused ("The Alibi," "Ganymede," "The Lordly Ones," "No Motive," "Don't Look Now"). Sometimes they possess an uncanny ability to see truth or "the other side" of a secret world inaccessible to adults. "The Pool," for example, is a story of a young girl on her annual summer visit to her grandparents. Deborah has a passionate relationship to nature, particularly to a pool which she considers "holy ground." She creeps out of bed at night, leaving behind her those who have shut out "all the meaning and all the point" and have "forgotten the secrets." In an altered state of consciousness she almost drowns, and the significance of her desperate attempts to hold on to the "magic" becomes clear in the last scene where she lies in bed with her first menstrual period, aware that "the hidden world . . . was out of her reach forever."

Du Maurier's work is full of hidden worlds. One of the most striking examples is the extraordinary "Don't Look Now," which involves a couple vacationing in Venice after the death of one of their children. In a gothic setting of cathedrals, mistaken identities, murder, psychics, ghosts, and dwarves, du Maurier sets up an accidental encounter in a restaurant between John and Laura and two elderly twins, one of whom is blind and yet tells Laura she has "seen" her dead daughter, Christine, sitting at the table. At first Laura is exalted and relieved, believing instantly and completely in the vision, but then comes a second encounter in which the blind twin reports a warning: Christine sees danger for her father if her parents do not leave Venice immediately. Although John believes that the twins are merely exploiting his grief-stricken wife, he feels an inexplicable "sense of doom, of tragedy" as du Maurier explores the small coincidences and misunderstandings upon which humans' fate hangs.

John's sense that "this is the end, there is no escape, no future" is echoed throughout du Maurier's work in various forms. "The Birds," for example, which is significantly different in setting and focus from the movie, is a story about rhythm, ritual, and natural law ruptured by some incomprehensible force over which authority and logic have no power. In this sense it is similar to the not entirely successful "The Apple Tree," an allegorical tale about a tree which mysteriously takes on the personality of a man's dead wife.

Du Maurier has been criticized for sacrificing her characters to plot, and in a certain sense this is true; according to one critic, du Maurier is not so much interested in "depth of feeling" as she is in "a sequence of events that inextricably lead [her undefined characters] to a predestined, usually surprising, fate." A good example is "Kiss Me Again, Stranger," in which the narrator is drawn one night by an intense, irrational attraction to a mysterious young woman who is revealed in the next day's paper to be a serial killer. While some of du Maurier's stories, such as "The Apple Tree" and "The Blue Lenses," are constructed around rather strained conceits, many of them are psychologically binding, loosening her dependence on the supernatural and reflecting her keen and disturbing observations about human nature ("The Way of the Cross") and psychopathology ("The Alibi," "The Split Second," "No Motive").

It is no accident, perhaps, that many of du Maurier's characters are actors, ghosts, patients, or tourists—all people looking for truth, power, freedom, or comfort, and navigating a strange, dislocated space somewhere between their ordinary lives and the extraordinary.

—Deborah Kelly Kloepfer

E

ELIOT, George. Pseudonym for Mary Ann (later Marian) Evans. English. Born in Arbury, Warwickshire, 22 November 1819. Educated at Miss Lathom's school, Attleborough; Miss Wallington's school, Nuneaton, 1828–32; Misses Franklins' school, Coventry, 1832–35. Lived with George Henry Lewes from 1854 (died 1878); married John Walter Cross in 1880. Took charge of family household after death of her mother, 1836; lived with her father in Foleshill, near Coventry, 1841–49; lived in Geneva, 1849–50; moved to London, 1851; contributor, 1851 and 1855–57, and assistant editor, 1852–54, *Westminster Review*; lived in Germany, 1854–55, Richmond, Surrey, 1855–60, and London from 1861. *Died 22 December 1880.*

PUBLICATIONS

Collections

Works. 21 vols., 1895.
Selected Essays, Poems, and Other Writings, edited by A.S. Byatt and Nicholas Warren. 1990.
Collected Poems, edited by Lucien Jenkins. 1990.

Short Stories

Scenes of Clerical Life. 1858; edited by Thomas A. Noble, 1985.

Novels

Adam Bede. 1859; edited by John Paterson, 1968.
The Mill on the Floss. 1860; edited by Gordon S. Haight, 1980.
Silas Marner, The Weaver of Raveloe. 1861; edited by Q.D. Leavis, 1967. Romola. 1863.
Felix Holt, The Radical. 1866; edited by Fred C. Thomson, 1988.
Middlemarch: A Study of Provincial Life. 1872; edited by David Carroll, 1986.
Daniel Deronda. 1876; edited by Graham Handley, 1984.

Verse

The Spanish Gypsy. 1868.
How Lisa Loved the King. 1869.
The Legend of Jubal and Other Poems. 1874.
Complete Poems. 1889.

Other

Works (Cabinet Edition). 24 vols., 1878–85.
Impressions of Theophrastus Such. 1879.
Essays and Leaves from a Note-Book, edited by C.L. Lewes. 1884.
Early Essays. 1919.

Letters, edited by Gordon S. Haight. 9 vols., 1954–78; selections, 1985.
Essays, edited by Thomas Pinney. 1963.
Some Eliot Notebooks (for Daniel Deronda), edited by William Baker. 1976.
Middlemarch Notebooks, edited by John Clark Pratt and Victor A. Neufeldt. 1979.
A Writer's Notebook 1854–1879 and Uncollected Writings, edited by Joseph Wiesenfarth. 1981.
A George Eliot Miscellany: A Supplement to Her Novels, edited by F.B. Pinion. 1982.

Translator, with Rufa Brabant (later Mrs. Charles Hennell), *The Life of Jesus Critically Examined,* by D.F. Strauss. 3 vols., 1846; edited by Peter C. Hodgson, 1973.
Translator, *The Essence of Christianity,* by Ludwig Feuerbach. 1854.
Translator, *Ethics,* by Spinoza, edited by Thomas Deegan. 1981.

*

Bibliography: *Eliot: A Reference Guide* by Constance M. Fulmer, 1977; *An Annotated Critical Bibliography of Eliot* by George Levine, 1988; *Eliot: A Reference Guide* by Karen L. Pangallo, 1990.

Critical Studies: *Eliot's Life as Related in Her Letters and Journals* by John Walter Cross, 3 vols., 1885; *Eliot: Her Mind and Art* by Joan Bennett, 1948; *The Great Tradition: Eliot, Henry James, Joseph Conrad* by F.R. Leavis, 1948; *Eliot* by Robert Speaight, 1954; *The Novels of Eliot: A Study in Form,* 1959, and *Particularities: Readings in Eliot,* 1982, both by Barbara Hardy, and *Critical Essays on Eliot* edited by Hardy, 1970; *The Art of Eliot* by W.J. Harvey, 1961; *Eliot* by Walter Allen, 1964; *A Century of Eliot Criticism* edited by Gordon S. Haight, 1965, and *Eliot: A Biography* by Haight, 1968; *Experiments in Life: Eliot's Quest for Values* by Bernard J. Paris, 1965; *Eliot's Early Novels: The Limits of Realism* by U.C. Knoepflmacher, 1968; *Eliot: The Critical Heritage* edited by D.R. Carroll, 1971; *Eliot* by A.E.S. Viner, 1971; *Eliot: The Emergent Self* by Ruby V. Redinger, 1975; *Eliot: Her Beliefs and Her Art* by Neil Roberts, 1975; *This Particular Web: Essays on Middlemarch* edited by Ian Adam, 1975; *Will and Destiny: Morality and Tragedy in Eliot's Novels,* 1975, and *The Triptych and the Cross: The Central Myths of Eliot's Poetic Imagination,* 1979, both by Felicia Bonaparte; *Eliot's Creative Conflict: The Other Side of Silence* by Laura Comer Emery, 1976; *Who's Who in Eliot* by Phyllis Hartnoll, 1977; *The Novels of Eliot* by Robert Liddell, 1977; *Eliot's Mythmaking* by Joseph Wiesenfarth, 1977; *Eliot and the Novel of Vocation* by Alan Mintz, 1978; *Eliot and the Visual Arts* by Hugh Witemeyer, 1979; *Eliot: Centenary Essays and an Unpublished Fragment* edited by Anne Smith, 1980; *The Sympathetic Response: Eliot's*

Fictional Rhetoric by Mary Ellen Doyle, 1981; *A George Eliot Companion* by F.B. Pinion, 1981; *Eliot, Romantic Humanist: A Study of the Philosophical Structure of Her Novels* by K.M. Newton, 1981; *Making Up Society: The Novels of Eliot* by Philip Fisher, 1981; *Eliot: A Centenary Tribute* edited by Gordon S. Haight and Rosemary T. Van Arsdel, 1982; *Eliot* by Herbert Foltinek, 1982; *Eliot, 1983,* and *The Mill on the Floss: A Natural History,* 1990, both by Rosemary Ashton; *The Language That Makes Eliot's Fiction* by Karen B. Mann, 1983; *Middlemarch* by Kerry McSweeney, 1984; *Eliot and Community: A Study in Social Theory and Fictional Form* by Suzanne Graver, 1984; *Eliot and Nineteenth-Century Science* by Sally Shuttleworth, 1984; *Eliot and Blackmail* by Alexander Welsh, 1985; *A Preface to Eliot* by John Purkis, 1985; *Eliot* by Elizabeth Deeds Ermarth, 1986; *Eliot* by Simon Dentith, 1986; *Eliot and the Landscape of Time: Narrative Form and Protestant Apocalyptic History* by Mary Wilson Carpenter, 1986; *Eliot* by Gillian Beer, 1986; *Eliot* by Jennifer Uglow, 1987; *Social Figures: Eliot, Social History, and Literary Representation* by Daniel Cottom, 1987; *Middlemarch: A Novel of Reform* by Bert G. Hornback, 1988; *Reading Middlemarch: Reclaiming the Middle Distance* by Jeanie Thomas, 1988; *A George Eliot Chronology* by Timothy Hands, 1989; *Eliot: Woman of Contradictions* by Ian Taylor, 1989; *Vocation and Desire: Eliot's Heroines* by Dorothea Barrett, 1989; *Eliot: An Intellectual Life* by Valerie A. Dodd, 1990.

* * *

George Eliot came late to fiction writing; she was 37 years old when her first story appeared, though she had written widely before (intellectual journalism, reviews, translations). George Lewes, with whom she lived, himself a novelist and literary critic, assured her that she had "wit, description and philosophy—those go a good way towards the production of a novel." Unsure as ever about her creative powers, she decided first to try her hand with a short story. Its opening chapters convinced them of her ability in dialogue, but, as she wrote in "How I Came To Write Fiction," "there still remained the question whether I could command any pathos." Pathos was then a prerequisite, as Anthony Trollope's definition, in his *Autobiography,* 1883, shows: "A novel should give a picture of common life enlivened by humour and sweetened by pathos."

Eliot soon demonstrated her ability in this, with Milly's death in "The Sad Fortunes of the Rev. Amos Barton," which appeared in the prestigious *Blackwood's Magazine.* It was followed by "Mr. Gilfil's Love-Story" and "Janet's Repentance" (January to November 1857); the three stories were collected as *Scenes of Clerical Life. Adam Bede* was to have provided a fourth "scene" but became a full-length novel. All four stories drew heavily on places, personalities, and episodes from her early life and from local tradition in the Midlands, as was promptly recognized there. Thus, the Shepperton of the first two stories is based on the village of her birth, Chilvers Coton, and Cheverel Manor in "Mr. Gilfil" is based on Arbury Hall, the nearby seat of the Newdigate family (her father's employer). Clergymen in Chilvers Coton and Nuneaton, and their generally "sad fortunes," suggested central situations in all three "scenes." As in the subsequent novels—*Middlemarch* is subtitled *A Study of Provincial Life*—Eliot is at pains to present in detail the local community, but in these early stories she uses memory and observation more and

her imagination less. Fitfully, she here tries to live up to her male pseudonym by having the narrator refer to "remembering" from "his" youth some of the personalities.

"Mr. Gilfil's Love-Story" is the least impressive and least clerical of the stories: Maynard Gilfil's being a young clergyman is inessential to his function as a frustrated and then very briefly happy lover. It is a conventional tale of a love-triangle—worthy boy (Gilfil) loves girl (Caterina) who loves another (the higher-born but unworthy Captain Wybrow)—which become a quadrangle when Wybrow courts the wealthy Miss Assher and the sparks begin to fly, predictably. Miss Assher rightly suspects that "something more than friendship" exists between her suitor and Caterina, who, incensed by Wybrow's disloyalty, and being of Italian origin and thus of more passionate and impulsive nature than an English-rose heroine, decides to do something about it. Intent on murdering Wybrow, she is providentially saved from crime by his having just dropped dead. After anguish, illness, and repentance, she accepts Gilfil's love but dies soon after, leaving him to a life of sad ingrowing singleness. (Much of this situation is retreated in *Adam Bede* more fully and with greater depth.) This narrative, set in the late 18th century, is given perspective and fuller meaning by the opening and closing frame chapters, set "thirty years ago," when Gilfil is seen as a crusty if decent old clergyman with "more of the knots and ruggedness of poor human nature than there lay any hint of in the open-eyed loving Maynard."

That characteristic Eliot adjective "poor" works hard in this story, notably for the fragile and bewildered "little Tina." Other characteristic skills appear in the expansive, affectionate if ironical, presentation of old Gilfil's rural parishioners, and of the local grandees Sir Christopher and Lady Cheverel, and the sharper presentation of Miss Assher and her loquacious mother (who "went dribbling on like a leaky shower-bath") and of the tensions underlying country-house life. The introduction of "Janet's Repentance" is even more leisurely: the eponymous Janet is first heard of in chapter 3 and first seen at the end of chapter 4, the opening chapters having been concerned with the local men at their booze and local ladies over their teacups and a lively and sociologically intelligent account of the social, economic, and religious state of Milby (based on Nuneaton, though, defending herself for not offering a more cheerful story, Eliot remarked that the actual town was more vicious and the characters taken from it were more disgusting and had sadder fates in real life).

The first we hear of Janet is that she is a secret drinker (not common in Victorian heroines), though her more kindly neighbours hold that "she's druv to it" by her husband lawyer Dempster's open drunkenness and brutality. We never see Janet drinking or drunken, though her eyes had "a strangely fixed, sightless gaze" on her first appearance. The topic is handled delicately; but also we see how, though generally admirable, Janet may have contributed to the failure of the marriage and "druv" Dempster further into viciousness. Similarly original is the treatment of Evangelicalism, a religious movement antipathetic to most Victorian novelists (as killjoy, sanctimonious, hypocritical). Eliot knew it from the inside, from her youth, and presents it sympathetically though not uncritically ("Yes, the movement was good, though it had that mixture of folly and evil which often makes what is good an offense to feeble and fastidious minds"—Eliot is free with authorial comments). Her emphasis as ever is on loving direct fellow-feeling, as against "that facile psychology which prejudges individuals by means of formulae."

She wrote only two other short fictions—her strange paranormal "The Lifted Veil" (1859) and "Brother Jacob," a "trifle," as she called it, written in 1860 and published anonymously in the *Cornhill Magazine* (1864). Though its provincial settings are characteristic and its money-lust theme was a growing preoccupation of Eliot's then, "Brother Jacob" exhibits few of her strengths. Heavy polysyllabic persiflage and harsh irony predominate, with little of her gentler humour, let alone sympathy for poor errant humanity. The protagonist David Faux—his surname, like his later alias Freely, and many other proper names in the story, indicates its mode—is a wholly mean, mendacious, unscrupulous, ambitiously self-seeking young man, a confectioner by trade, who steals his mother's nest-egg to finance his emigration to the United States. Later he returns to England and begins to flourish in trade and in mercenary courtship in Grimworth town, but his past catches up with him and his world collapses—"an admirable instance of the unexpected forms in which the great Nemesis hides herself." Nemesis takes the form of David's embarrassingly clinging and vocal idiot brother Jacob, who had nearly frustrated his earlier plans. Elements of this material had been retreated in *Silas Marner*.

—Philip Collins

See the essays on "The Lifted Veil" and "The Sad Fortunes of the Rev. Amos Barton."

ELLISON, Ralph (Waldo). American. Born in Oklahoma City, Oklahoma, 1 March 1914. Educated at a high school in Oklahoma City, and at Tuskegee Institute, Alabama, 1933–36. Served in the United States Merchant Marine, 1943–45. Married Fanny McConnell in 1946. Writer from 1936; lecturer, Salzburg Seminar in American Studies, 1954; instructor in Russian and American Literature, Bard College, Annandale-on-Hudson, New York, 1958–61; Alexander White Visiting Professor, University of Chicago, 1961; visiting professor of writing, Rutgers University, New Brunswick, New Jersey, 1962–64; Whittall Lecturer, Library of Congress, Washington, D.C., 1964; Ewing Lecturer, University of California, Los Angeles, 1964; visiting fellow in American studies, Yale University, New Haven, Connecticut, 1966; Albert Schweitzer Professor in the Humanities, New York University, 1970–79; now emeritus. Chairman, Literary Grants Committee, American Academy, 1964–67; member, National Council on the Arts, 1965–67; member, Carnegie Commission on Educational Television, 1966–67; member of the editorial board, *American Scholar*, Washington, D.C., 1966–69; honorary consultant in American Letters, Library of Congress, Washington, D.C., 1966–72. Trustee, John F. Kennedy Center of the Performing Arts, Washington, D.C., New School for Social Research, New York, Bennington College, Vermont, Educational Broadcasting Corporation, and Colonial Williamsburg Foundation. Recipient: Rosenwald fellowship, 1945; National Book award, 1953; National Newspaper Publishers Association Russwarm award, 1953; American Academy Rome prize, 1955, 1956; United States Medal of Freedom, 1969; National Medal of Arts, 1985; Coordinating Council of Literary Magazines-General Electric Foundation award, 1988. Ph.D. in Humane Letters: Tuskegee Institute, 1963; Litt.D.: Rutgers University,

1966; University of Michigan, Ann Arbor, 1967; Williams College, Williamstown, Massachusetts, 1970; Long Island University, New York, 1971; College of William and Mary, Williamsburg, Virginia, 1972; Wake Forest College, Winston-Salem, North Carolina, 1974; Harvard University, Cambridge, Massachusetts, 1974; L.H.D.: Grinnell College, Iowa, 1967; Adelphi University, Garden City, New York, 1971; University of Maryland, College Park, 1974. Commandant, Order of Arts and Letters (France), 1970. Member, American Academy, 1975. Lives in New York City.

PUBLICATIONS

Novel

Invisible Man.   1952.

Excerpts form novel-in-progress: "The Roof, the Steeple and the People," in *Quarterly Review of Literature,* 1960; "And Hickman Arrives," in *Noble Savage,* March 1960; "It Always Breaks Out," in *Partisan Review,* Spring 1963; "Juneteenth," in *Quarterly Review of Literature 13,* 1965; "Night-Talk," in *Quarterly Review of Literature 16,* 1969; "Song of Innocence," in *Iowa Review,* Spring 1970; "Cadillac Flambe," in *American Review 16* edited by Theodore Solotaroff, 1973.

Other

The Writer's Experience, with Karl Shapiro.   1964.
Shadow and Act (essays).   1964.
The City in Crisis, with Whitney M. Young and Herbert Gnas.   1968.
Going to the Territory (essays).   1986.

*

Bibliography: "A Bibliography of Ellison's Published Writings" by Bernard Benoit and Michel Fabre, in *Studies in Black Literature,* Autumn 1971; *The Blinking Eye: Ellison and His American, French, German and Italian Critics 1952–1971* by Jacqueline Covo, 1974.

Critical Studies: *The Negro Novel in America,* revised edition, by Robert A. Bone, 1958; "The Blues as a Literary Theme" by Gene Bluestein, in *Massachusetts Review,* Autumn 1967; *Five Black Writers: Essays* by Donald B. Gibson, 1970; *Twentieth-Century Interpretations of Invisible Man* edited by John M. Reilly, 1970; "Ellison Issue" of *CLA Journal,* March 1970; interview in *Atlantic,* December 1970; *The Merrill Studies in Invisible Man* edited by Ronald Gottesman, 1971; *Ellison: A Collection of Critical Essays* edited by John Hersey, 1973; article by Leonard J. Deutsch, in *American Novelists since World War II* edited by Jeffrey Heltermann and Richard Layman, 1978; *Folklore and Myth in Ellison's Early Works* by Dorothea Fischer-Hornung, 1979; *The Craft of Ellison,* 1980, and "The Rules of Magic: Hemingway as Ellison's 'Ancestor,'" in *Southern Review,* Summer 1985, both by Robert G. O'Meally, and *New Essays on Invisible Man* edited by O'Meally, 1988; *Ellison: The Genesis of an Artist* by Rudolf F. Dietze, 1982; introduction by the author to 30th anniversary edition of *Invisible Man,* 1982; "Ellison and Dostoevsky" by Joseph Frank, in *New Criterion,* September 1983; *Speaking for You: The Vision of Ellison* edited by

Kimberly W. Benston, 1987; *Invisible Criticism: Ellison and the American Canon* by Alan Nadel, 1988; *Creative Revolt: A Study of Wright, Ellison, and Dostoevsky* by Michael F. Lynch, 1990.

* * *

Ellison's single novel *Invisible Man* has in the past 40 years become a classic and landmark of American literature, a fiction that summarizes, analyzes, and encompasses a large portion of the African-American experience. He has also written distinguished social and literary essays and has published a variety of short fiction. In addition to short stories, he has published a number of self-contained episodes from a long-projected second novel, while several segments from *Invisible Man* have been printed as discrete stories—notably the opening section ("Battle Royal") and an alternative draft of the surreal hospital interlude ("Out of the Hospital and Under the Bar").

Even in *Invisible Man,* a densely complex and unified vision, Ellison tended to work in episodes and short narrative segments. His short fiction reiterates and develops many themes of the novel: the perils of growing up black in a society radically self-divided, the contrasts between Northern and Southern, urban and rural cultures, the power of dreams, wishes and fantasies in the lives of dispossessed and powerless people.

Ellison has often remarked on the diversity of experience he had as a young man—as a college student, an itinerant laborer, a traveling musician, an educator and a writer. His stories reflect the breadth of experiences available to African-Americans but also comment incisively on the limitations imposed by disfranchisement and marginality on people who struggle to define and control their own destinies.

An early story, "King of the Bingo Game" (in *Tomorrow,* November 1944), describes a character much like the nameless narrator of *Invisible Man.* He has moved from the familiar, familial South—Rocky Mount, North Carolina—to the cold, alienating urban North and feels isolated and helpless, sitting in a movie theatre bingo night. He is driven by anxiety, needing money, and so he pins all his hopes on the bingo game and the turn of the wheel that awards prizes. But the uncertainty of the turning wheel of fortune and his single chance for redemption overwhelm him. He awaits the jackpot of $36.90 (lucky numbers from the Numbers Game, also echoed in the 1,369 light bulbs illuminating the Invisible Man's underground hideout). The strain crushes him, he becomes irrational, and two policemen, who look "like a tap-dance team" on the stage, beat him and drag him away, as he sees the spinning wheel stop at double zero, the winning position.

Another story about luck, superstition, and futile dreams is "Did You Ever Dream Lucky?" (in *New World Writing* 5, 1954). It is a long lie told by Mary Rambo to Portwood, a neighbor, at Thanksgiving dinner. Mary's rambling anecdote describes an auto accident in which she discovers a bag full of clinking metal she assumes to be money. She smuggles it home and hides it in her toilet tank, and then is consumed by guilt, curiosity, and anxiety. Finally, she opens the bag to find tire chains. The ironic treasure is like a dream deferred—useless tire chains for a generation without cars, slim hope for the next generation to "go to heaven in a Cadillac."

Another story reflecting the theme of growing into experience, initiation from innocence into the tragedies,

mysteries, and ambiguities of adulthood is "A Coupla Scalped Indians," (in *New World Writing* 9, 1956). It chronicles a night when two 11-year old boys are initiated into a series of mysteries. They have been circumcised by the family doctor, and the symbolism of the rite is rich: "The doctor had said it would make us men and Buster had said, hell, he was a man already—what he wanted was to be an Indian. We hadn't thought about it making us scalped ones." They go to a carnival, argue about the propriety of playing the dozens and dream of being free spirits—noble savages, either boy scouts or Indians. Thrashing through the woods with their Boy Scout hatchets, they find the shack of Aunt Mackie, the town's ancient "conjure woman," and the narrator sees her through the window—naked, with the ripe body of a young woman. Like Circe, she captures him, saying, "You peeped . . . now you got to do the rest. I said kiss me, or I'll fix you. . . .'" But Aunt Mackie, after inspecting his circumcision, finds he is only a child and rejects him. But he has learned about "being a man" and about the profound mysteries of female sexuality.

Ellison's stories revolve around the themes of fate and luck, dreams and powerlessness, the contrast between comforting family life in small, close communities and the harsh loneliness of big, dense cities. They extend and enlarge the basic thematic material of *Invisible Man* and give varied examples of the scale and breadth of African-American life in our time.

—William J. Schafer

See the essay on "King of the Bingo Game."

———

ENDŌ Shūsaku. Japanese. Born in Tokyo, 27 March 1923. Educated at Keio University, Tokyo, B.A. in French literature 1949; University of Lyon, 1950–53. Married Junko Okado in 1955; one son. Contracted tuberculosis in 1959. Former editor, *Mita bungaku* literary journal; chair, Bungeika Kyokai (Literary Artists' Association); manager, Kiza amateur theatrical troupe; President, Japan PEN. Recipient: Akutagawa prize, 1955; Tanizaki prize, 1967; Gru de Oficial da Ordem do Infante dom Henrique (Portugal), 1968; Sanct Silvestri (award by Pope Paul VI), 1970; Noma prize, 1980. Member, Japanese Arts Academy, 1981. Honorary doctorate: Georgetown University, Washington, D.C.; University of California, Santa Clara. Lives in Tokyo.

PUBLICATIONS

Short Stories

Shiroi hito [White Man].   1955.
Kiiroi hito [Yellow Man].   1955.
Obakasan.   In *Asahi shinbun,* April-August 1959; as *Wonderful Fool,* 1974.
Watashi ga suteta onna [The Girl I Left Behind].   1963; as "Mine," in *Japan Christian Quarterly* 40(4), 1974.
Aika [Elegies].   1965.
Ryūgaku.   In *Gunzō,* March 1965; as *Foreign Studies,* 1989.
Taihen daa [Good Grief!].   1969.

Endō Shūsaku bungaku zenshū [Collected Works].   11 vols., 1975.
Jūichi no iro garasu [11 Stained Glass Elegies].   1979.
Stained Glass Elegies.   1984.
Hangyaku.   2 vols., 1989.
The Final Martyrs.   1994.

Novels

Umi to dokuyaku.   1958; as *The Sea and Poison,* 1972.
Kazan.   1959; as *Volcano,* 1978.
Chimmoku.   1966; as *Silence,* 1969.
Shikai no hotori [By the Dead Sea].   1973.
Iesu no shūgai.   1973; as *A Life of Jesus,* 1978.
Yumoa shūsetsu shū.   1973.
Waga seishun ni kui ari.   1974.
Kuchibue o fuku toki.   1974; as *When I Whistle,* 1979.
Sekai kikō.   1975.
Hechimakun.   1975.
Kitsunegata tanukigata.   1976.
Gūtara mandanshū.   1978.
Marie Antoinette.   1979.
Samurai.   1980; as *The Samurai,* 1982.
Onna no isshō.   1982.
Akuryō no gogo.   1983.
Sukyandaru.   1986; as *Scandal,* 1988.

Plays

Ōgon no kuni (produced 1966).   1969; as *The Golden Country,* 1970.
Bara no yakata [A House Surrounded by Roses].   1969.

Other

Furansu no daigakusei [Students in France, 1951–52].   1953.
Seisho no naka no joseitachi.   1968.
Korian vs. Mambō, with Kita Morio.   1974.
Ukiaru kotoba.   1976.
Ai no akebono, with Miura Shumon.   1976.
Nihonjin wa kirisuto kyō o shinjirareru ka.   1977.
Kirisuto no tanjō.   1978.
Ningen no naka no X.   1978.
Rakuten taishō.   1978.
Kare no ikikata.   1978.
Jū to jūjika (biography of Pedro Cassini).   1979.
Shinran, with Masutani Fumio.   1979.
Sakka no nikki.   1980.
Chichioya.   1980.
Kekkonron.   1980.
Endō Shūsaku ni yoru Endō Shūsaku.   1980.
Meiga Iesu junrei.   1981.
Ai to jinsei o meguru dansō.   1981.
Okuku e no michi.   1981.
Fuyu no yasashisa.   1982.
Watakushi ni totte kami to wa.   1983.
Kokoro.   1984.
Ikuru gakkō.   1984.
Watakushi no aishita shōsetsu.   1985.
Rakudai bōzu no rirekisho.   1989.
Kawaru mono to kawaranu mono: hanadokei.   1990.

*

Critical Studies: "Shusaku Endo: The Second Period" by Francis Mathy, in *Japan Christian Quarterly* 40, 1974; "Tradition and Contemporary Consciousness: Ibuse, Endo, Kaiko, Abe" by J. Thomas Rimer, in *Modern Japanese Fiction and Its Traditions,* 1978; "Mr. Shusaku Endo Talks About His Life and Works as a Catholic Writer" (interview), in *Chesterton Review* 12 (4), 1986; "The Roots of Guilt and Responsibility in Shusaku Endo's *The Sea and Poison*" by Hans-Peter Breuer, in *Literature and Medicine* 7, 1988; "Rediscovering Japan's Christian Tradition: Text-Immanent Hermeneutics in Two Short Stories by Shusaku Endo" by Rolf J. Goebel, in *Studies in Language and Culture* 14 (63), 1988; "Graham Greene: *The Power and the Glory*: A Comparative Essay with *Silence* by Shusaku Endo" by Kazuie Hamada, in *Collected Essays by the Members of the Faculty (Kyoritsu Women's Junior College),* 31, February 1988; "Christianity in the Intellectual Climate of Modern Japan" by Shunichi Takayanagi, in *Chesterton Review* 14 (3), 1988; "Salvation of the Weak: Endo Shusaku," in *The Sting of Life: Four Contemporary Japanese Novelists,* 1989, and "The Voice of the Doppelgänger," in *Japan Quarterly* 38 (2), 1991, both by Van C. Gessel.

*   *   *

Ever since publication of his award-winning novel, *Chimmoku (Silence),* in 1966, Endō's international reputation as a writer of full-length fiction has remained secure. Less well documented outside Japan and yet equally important are his achievements in the short story, although publication of two collections of his short stores in English (*Stained Glass Elegies* and *The Final Martyrs*) has gone some way to decreasing this gap. Not only do these short stories add to our understanding of Endō's literary art, they also succeed in focussing on specific themes that all too often are subsumed into the more ambitious overall framework of the author's full-length novels.

This would certainly seem to be the case with the two lengthy, early stories, *Shiroi hito* ("White Man") and *Kiiroi hito* ("Yellow Man"). As the titles suggest, the stories represent an attempt to explore in literary form a division Endō perceived during the course of a prolonged period of study in France between the Christian West and the pantheistic East. At this stage in his career, this division is portrayed as unfathomable — as emphasised, for example, in Chiba, protagonist of "Yellow Man," who senses the existence of a great chasm between himself and Father Durand, the disgraced French priest. In describing the eyes of the "yellow man" as "insensitive to God, and sin — and death," Endō establishes the dichotomy between East and West that he would seek to bridge only much later in his career. Father Durand is driven to ask rhetorically, "Do you really think the Christian God can take root in this damp country, amongst this yellow race?" The implication is strong that East-West rapprochement will only be possible through rejection of the trappings of the Western religion.

To the Japanese Christian Endō, the conclusion was clearly disturbing and led to a literary questioning of the significance and validity of his own baptism (largely at the behest of his pious mother) — in a series of stories in which the protagonist is troubled by the "ill-fitting clothes" that had been forced upon him ("Forty-Year-Old Man"). Almost without exception, the protagonists of these stories are plagued by spiritual doubts as they struggle to locate "the existence of God, along these dirty, commonplace Japanese streets" ("My Belongings"). At the same time, they remain convinced, like Egi in "Despicable Bastard," that they "will probably go on betraying [their] own soul, betraying love, betraying others." It is this that leads them to empathise with the "Kakure" (Hidden) Christians. Like the Kakure, these contemporary protagonists despair—not only of ever acquiring the strength required to emulate those who were martyred for their faith, but equally of ever being able to communicate their message that "the apostate endures a pain none of you can comprehend" ("Unzen").

Such despair is not, however, unmitigated and Endō finds within "weak" characters an inner energy and consequent capacity for acts of strength. Initial examples of this trait tend to be left at the level of suggestion (the "faint-hearted" and "effeminate" Mouse in "Tsuda no Fuji," who is rumoured to have laid down his own life at Dachau in order to spare one of his comrades). But as his career has progressed, Endō has come to portray such unexpected acts of strength not so much in terms of inexplicable paradoxes, but as literary symbols of his view of human nature, itself a composite of seemingly irreconcilable forces. The result is a series of stories, epitomised by "The Shadow Man," that addresses the human duality in terms of characters confronted by their shadow being, their alter ego. Increasing emphasis is placed on the need to penetrate behind the image that his protagonists present to the world, to those elements of their being that have previously remained suppressed, in order to determine their "true" natures. In "The Shadow Man," this conclusion is seen in a priest who, for all his outward rejection of the Christian faith, finally has an inner faith as strong as, if not stronger than, that before his fall from grace. In later treatments of this theme, the focus on this inner being as essential to an understanding of the composite individual is rendered more explicit. For example, in "The Evening of the Prize Giving Ceremony" the protagonist's concern with his "shadow" being leads to a growing awareness that the realm of the unconscious is the key to his "true self."

The focus in Endō's short stories increasingly has come to rest on the true nature of a single male protagonist—with the emphasis frequently on the "indelible marks" this character leaves on the lives of those with whom he comes into contact. The shift is significant, for in coming to highlight the extent to which the lives of all human beings are linked at this deeper, unconscious level, Endō has succeeded in distancing himself from the explicitly Christian concerns that dominate his earlier stories, whilst retaining the focus on moral issues that represents the hallmark of his entire literary output.

—Mark Williams

See the essay on "Mothers."

————

F

FAULKNER, William. American. Born William Cuthbert Falkner in New Albany, Mississippi, 25 September 1897; moved with his family to Oxford, Mississippi, 1902. Educated at local schools in Oxford, and at the University of Mississippi, Oxford, 1919–20. Served in the Royal Canadian Air Force, 1918. Married Estelle Oldham Franklin in 1929; two daughters. Bookkeeper in bank, 1916–18; worked in Doubleday Bookshop, New York, 1921; postmaster, University of Mississippi Post Office, 1921–24; lived in New Orleans and contributed to New Orleans *Times-Picayune*, 1925; traveled in Europe, 1925–26; returned to Oxford, 1927; thereafter a full-time writer; screenwriter for Metro-Goldwyn-Mayer, 1932–33, 20th Century-Fox, 1935–37, and Warner Brothers, 1942–45; writer-in-residence, University of Virginia, Charlottesville, 1957, and part of each year, 1958–62. Recipient: O. Henry award, 1939, 1949; Nobel prize for literature, 1950; American Academy Howells medal, 1950; National Book award, 1951, 1955; Pulitzer prize, 1955, 1963; American Academy of Arts and Letters gold medal, 1962. Member, Nation Letters, 1939, and American Academy, 1948. *Died 6 July 1962.*

PUBLICATIONS

Collections

The Portable Faulkner, edited by Malcolm Cowley. 1946; revised edition, 1967.
The Faulkner Reader, edited by Saxe Commins. 1954.
Novels 1930–1935 (Library of America), edited by Joseph Blotner and Noel Polk. 1985.
Novels 1936–1940 (Library of America), edited by Joseph Blotner. 1990.

Short Stories

These 13: Stories. 1931.
Doctor Martino and Other Stories. 1934.
Go Down, Moses, and Other Stories. 1942.
Knight's Gambit. 1949.
Collected Stories. 1950.
Big Woods. 1955.
Jealousy and Episode: Two Stories. 1955.
Uncle Willy and Other Stories. 1958.
Selected Short Stories. 1961.
Barn Burning and Other Stories. 1977.
Uncollected Stories, edited by Joseph Blotner. 1979.

Novels

Soldiers' Pay. 1926.
Mosquitoes. 1927.
Sartoris. 1929; original version, as *Flags in the Dust,* edited by Douglas Day, 1973.
The Sound and the Fury. 1929.
As I Lay Dying. 1930.
Sanctuary. 1931.
Idyll in the Desert. 1931.
Light in August. 1932.
Miss Zilphia Gant. 1932.
Pylon. 1935.
Absalom, Absalom! 1936.
The Unvanquished. 1938.
The Wild Palms (includes *Old Man*). 1939.
The Hamlet. 1940; excerpt, as *The Long Hot Summer,* 1958.
Intruder in the Dust. 1948.
Notes on a Horsethief. 1950.
Requiem for a Nun. 1951.
A Fable. 1954.
Faulkner County. 1955.
The Town. 1957.
The Mansion. 1959.
The Reivers: A Reminiscence. 1962.
Father Abraham, edited by James B. Meriwether. 1984.

Plays

The Marionettes (produced 1920). 1975; edited by Noel Polk, 1977.
Requiem for a Nun (produced 1957). 1951.
The Big Sleep, with Leigh Brackett and Jules Furthman, in *Film Scripts One,* edited by George P. Garrett, O.B. Harrison, Jr., and Jane Gelfmann. 1971.
To Have and Have Not (screenplay), with Jules Furthman. 1980.
The Road to Glory (screenplay), with Joel Sayre. 1981.
Faulkner's MGM Screenplays, edited by Bruce F. Kawin. 1983.
The DeGaulle Story (unproduced screenplay), edited by Louis Daniel Brodsky and Robert W. Hamblin. 1984.
Battle Cry (unproduced screenplay), edited by Louis Daniel Brodsky and Robert W. Hamblin. 1985.
Stallion Road: A Screenplay, edited by Louis Daniel Brodsky and Robert W. Hamblin. 1989.

Screenplays: *Today We Live,* with Edith Fitzgerald and Dwight Taylor, 1933; *The Road to Glory,* with Joel Sayre, 1936; *Slave Ship,* with others, 1937; *Air Force* (uncredited), with Dudley Nichols, 1943; *To Have and Have Not,* with Jules Furthman, 1945; *The Big Sleep,* with Leigh Brackett and Jules Furthman, 1946; *Land of the Pharaohs,* with Harry Kurnitz and Harold Jack Bloom, 1955.

Television Play: *The Graduation Dress,* with Joan Williams, 1960.

Verse

The Marble Faun. 1924.
Salmagundi (includes prose), edited by Paul Romaine. 1932.

This Earth.   1932.
A Green Bough.   1933.
Mississippi Poems.   1979.
Helen: A Courtship, and *Mississippi Poems.*   1981.
Vision in Spring.   1984.

Other

Mirrors of Chartres Street.   1953.
New Orleans Sketches, edited by Ichiro Nishizaki,   1955; revised edition, edited by Carvel Collins, 1958.
On Truth and Freedom.   1955(?).
Faulkner at Nagano (interview), edited by Robert A. Jelliffe.   1956.
Faulkner in the University (interviews), edited by Frederick L. Gwynn and Joseph Blotner.   1959.
University Pieces, edited by Carvel Collins.   1962.
Early Prose and Poetry, edited by Carvel Collins.   1962.
Faulkner at West Point (interviews), edited by Joseph L. Fant and Robert Ashley.   1964.
The Faulkner-Cowley File: Letters and Memories 1944–1962, with Malcolm Cowley.   1966.
Essays, Speeches, and Public Letters, edited by James B. Meriwether.   1966.
The Wishing Tree (for children).   1967.
Lion in the Garden: Interviews with Faulkner 1926–1962, edited by James B. Meriwether and Michael Millgate.   1968.
Selected Letters, edited by Joseph Blotner.   1977.
Mayday.   1978.
Letters, edited by Louis Daniel Brodsky and Robert W. Hamblin.   1984.
Sherwood Anderson and Other Famous Creoles.   1986.
Thinking of Home (letters), edited by James G. Watson.   1992.

*

Bibliography: *The Literary Career of Faulkner: A Bibliographical Study* by James B. Meriwether, 1961; *Faulkner: A Reference Guide* by Thomas L. McHaney, 1976; *Faulkner: A Bibliography of Secondary Works* by Beatrice Ricks, 1981; *Faulkner: The Bio-Bibliography* by Louis Daniel Brodsky and Robert W. Hamblin, 1982; *Faulkner: An Annotated Checklist of Recent Criticism* by John Earl Bassett, 1983; *Faulkner's Poetry: A Bibliographical Guide to Texts and Criticisms* by Judith L. Sensibar and Nancy L. Stegall, 1988.

Critical Studies: *Faulkner: A Critical Study* by Irving Howe, 1952, revised edition, 1962, 1975; *Faulkner* by Hyatt H. Waggoner, 1959; *The Novels of Faulkner* by Olga W. Vickery, 1959, revised edition, 1964; *Faulkner* by Frederick J. Hoffman, 1961, revised edition, 1966; *Bear, Man, and God* edited by Francis L. Utley, Lynn Z. Bloom, and Arthur F. Kinney, 1963, revised edition, 1971; *Faulkner: The Yoknapatawpha Country,* 1963, *Faulkner: Toward Yoknapatawpha and Beyond,* 1978, and *Faulkner: First Encounters,* 1983, all by Cleanth Brooks; *Faulkner's People* by Robert W. Kirk and Marvin Klotz, 1963; *A Reader's Guide to Faulkner* by Edmond L. Volpe, 1964; *Faulkner: A Collection of Critical Essays* edited by Robert Penn Warren, 1966; *The Achievement of Faulkner* by Michael Millgate, 1966; *Faulkner: Myth and Motion* by Richard P. Adams, 1968; *Faulkner of Yoknapatawpha County* by Lewis Leary, 1973; *Faulkner's Narrative* by Joseph W.

Reed, Jr., 1973; *Faulkner: Four Decades of Criticism* edited by Linda W. Wagner, 1973, and *Hemingway and Faulkner: Inventors/Masters* by Wagner, 1975; *Faulkner: A Collection of Criticism* edited by Dean M. Schmitter, 1973; *Faulkner: The Abstract and the Actual* by Panthea Reid Broughton, 1974; *Faulkner: A Biography* by Joseph Blotner,   2 vols., 1974, revised and condensed edition,   1 vol., 1984; *A Faulkner Miscellany* edited by James B. Meriwether, 1974; *Doubling and the Incest/Repetition and Revenge: A Speculative Reading of Faulkner* by John T. Irwin, 1975; *Faulkner: The Critical Heritage* edited by John Earl Bassett, 1975; *A Glossary of Faulkner's South* by Calvin S. Brown, 1976; *The Most Splendid Failure: Faulkner's The Sound and the Fury* by André Bleikasten, 1976, and *Faulkner's The Sound and the Fury: A Critical Casebook* edited by Bleikasten, 1982; *Faulkner's Heroic Design: The Yoknapatawpha Novels* by Lynn Levins, 1976; *Faulkner's Craft of Revision* by Joanne V. Creighton, 1977; *Faulkner's Women: The Myth and the Muse* by David L. Williams, 1977; *Faulkner's Narrative Poetics* by Arthur F. Kinney, 1978, and *Critical Essays on Faulkner: The Compson Family,* 1982, and *The Sartoris Family,* 1985, both edited by Kinney; *The Fragile Thread: The Meaning of Form in Faulkner's Novels* by Donald M. Kartiganer, 1979; *Faulkner's Career: An Internal Literary History* by Gary Lee Stonum, 1979; *Faulkner: The Transfiguration of Biography* by Judith Wittenberg, 1979; *Faulkner's Yoknapatawpha Comedy* by Lyall H. Powers, 1980; *Faulkner: His Life and Work* by David Minter, 1980; *The Heart of Yoknapatawpha* by John Pilkington, 1981; *Faulkner's Characters: An Index to the Published and Unpublished Fiction* by Thomas E. Dasher, 1981; *Faulkner: The Short Story Career: An Outline of Faulkner's Short Story Writing from 1919 to 1962,* 1981, and *Faulkner: The Novelist as Short Story Writer,* 1985, both by Hans H. Skei; *A Faulkner Overview: Six Perspectives* by Victor Strandberg, 1981; *Faulkner: Biographical and Reference Guide and Critical Collection* edited by Leland H. Cox,   2 vols., 1982; *The Play of Faulkner's Language* by John T. Matthews, 1982; *The Art of Faulkner* by John Pikoulis, 1982; *Faulkner's "Negro": Art and the Southern Context* by Thadious M. Davis, 1983; *Faulkner: The House Divided* by Eric J. Sundquist, 1983; *Faulkner's Yoknapatawpha* by Elizabeth M. Kerr, 1983; *Faulkner: New Perspectives* edited by Richard Brodhead, 1983; *The Origins of Faulkner's Art* by Judith Sensibar, 1984; *Uses of the Past in the Novels of Faulkner* by Carl E. Rollyson, Jr., 1984; *Faulkner's Absalom, Absalom! A Critical Casebook* edited by Elizabeth Muhlenfeld, 1984; *A Faulkner Chronology* by Michel Gresset, 1985; *Faulkner's Short Stories* by James B. Carothers, 1985; *Faulkner* by Alan Warren Friedman, 1985; *Genius of Place: Faulkner's Triumphant Beginnings* by Max Putzel, 1985; *Faulkner's Humor,* 1986, *Faulkner and Women,* 1986, *Faulkner and Race,* 1988, *Faulkner and the Craft of Fiction,* 1989, *Faulkner and Popular Culture,* 1990, and *Faulkner and Religion,* 1991, all edited by Doreen Fowler and Ann J. Abadie; *Figures of Division: Faulkner's Major Novels* by James A. Snead, 1986; *Heart in Conflict: Faulkner's Struggles with Vocation* by Michael Grimwood, 1986; *Faulkner: The Man and the Artist,* Stephen B. Oates, 1987; *Faulkner: The Art of Stylization* by Lothar Hönnighausen, 1987; *Faulkner* by David Dowling, 1988; *Fiction, Film, and Faulkner: The Art of Adaptation* by Gene D. Phillips, 1988; *Faulkner, American Writer* by Frederick Karl, 1989; *Faulkner's Country Matters: Folklore and Fable in Yoknapatawpha* by Daniel Hoffman, 1989; *Faulkner's Marginal Couple* by John N. Duvall, 1990; *Faulkner: The Yoknapatawpha Fiction* edited by A. Robert Lee, 1990; *Faulkner's Fables of Creativity:*

The Non-Yoknapatawpha Novels by Gary Harrington, 1990; *Faulkner: Life Glimpses* by Louis Daniel Brodsky, 1990; *Faulkner's Short Fiction* by James Ferguson, 1991.

* * *

The *Collected Stories of William Faulkner,* published in 1950, comprises 900 pages and 42 stories, many of which feature the same characters that we encounter in his Yoknapatawpha County novels. In his stories, as in his novels, Faulkner's distinctive achievement was to combine a penetrating grasp of individual consciousness—getting what he called "the story behind every brow"—with a remarkable breadth of social vision, so as to encompass with equal authority aristocrats and poor whites; black people and Indians; old maids and matriarchs; Christlike scapegoats and pathological murderers; intellectuals and idiots.

In his Nobel prize address of 1950, Faulkner summarized his life's work in terms of an internal struggle—"the problems of the human heart in conflict with itself which alone can make good writing because only that is worth writing about." On one side of that conflict is the ideal self, striving to realize its potential for "love and honor and pride and compassion and sacrifice" and the other "old verities of the heart." On the other side is the weakness that prevents these ideals from being realized, among which the paramount vice is cowardice: "the basest of all things is to be afraid." Within this universal paradigm of identity-psychology—that is, the elementary human struggle to achieve a satisfactory sense of one's own worth—Faulkner portrays his individual protagonists as relating their effort to some uniquely private symbol of identity. It is crucially important that in true existentialist fashion, characters define that symbol for themselves without reference to conventional mores. Thus, in "A Rose for Emily" the symbol of Emily's worth is the bridal chamber in the attic in which her mummified lover awaits her nightly embrace; in "A Justice" it is the steamboat that Ikkemotubbe forces his people to haul overland so he can install his bride in a dwelling appropriate to a chieftain; and in "Wash" the symbol of enhanced worth is the great-grandchild whose imminent birth will fuse Wash's white trash bloodlines with those of the infant's aristocrat father, Thomas Sutpen. The fact that each of these characters (Emily, Wash Jones, Ikkemotubbe) is a murderer is secondary to the grand assertion of will—the quintessence of the heroic—which each of them invests in the chosen symbol of personal worth.

In addition to suspending conventional morality so as to enter the story behind every brow, Faulkner flouts conventional realism by according heroic status preponderantly to losers, failures, and misfits. Before rising up with scythe in hand to defend his family honor, Wash Jones is so degraded that even black slaves, who freely enter Sutpen's kitchen while blocking Wash at the door, laugh in his face over his dwelling ("dat shack down yon dat Cunnel wouldn't *let* none of us live in") and his cowardice ("Why ain't you at de war, white man?"). In "Ad Astra," Faulkner again follows the Biblical premise that the last shall be first by casting the two lowliest, most outcast characters as spiritually superior. While the so-called Allied soldiers lapse into a violent ethnic free-for-all, French versus English versus Irish versus American, the subadar (a man of color from India) and the German prisoner transcend the barriers of race, language, religion, and wartime enmity so as to establish a bond based on "music, art, the victory born of defeat" and social justice (each renounces his aristocratic heritage for the belief that "all men are brothers").

Faulkner's craft is exemplified in two extraordinarily original stories about Indian culture, "A Justice" and "Red Leaves." In "A Justice" two interracial love affairs—Pappy's with a slave woman and Ikkemotubbe's with a Creole—become entangled because of Ikkemotubbe's urgent identity-need. Having passed himself off in New Orleans as the tribal chief, a ploy that helped him win the love of the Creole woman, he has hurried home ahead of his pregnant sweetheart so as to install himself as chief before she gets there. After eliminating three relatives who stand in his way—the present chief, along with the chief's son and brother—Ikkemotubbe must get the endorsement of Pappy and Pappy's best friend, Herman Basket, who apparently have the power to name the next chief, called "The Man." In a wonderfully subtle deployment of threats and bribes, Ikkemotubbe obtains this anointing but then withholds from Herman Basket the horse he had promised and from Pappy the black woman he had used for enticement. So Pappy, aflame with desire, has to contrive his own path to satisfaction. This he does, to the outrage of the black woman's husband who appeals to Chief Ikkemotubbe for justice when a "yellow" baby is born. With Solomon-like wisdom, the chief first tries to soothe the cuckold's feelings by bestowing on the infant the name "Had-Two-Fathers." When that fails to mollify the black man, a second stage of justice does effect the purpose: Pappy and Herman Basket spend months of hard labor constructing a fence around the black man's hut, which not only keeps Pappy physically at bay but during construction makes him too tired to be a lover at night. This comic tale renders the origin of the Indian hero of *The Bear,* Sam Fathers—whose name by rights should have been "Had-Three-Fathers" inasmuch as it was the crafty Ikkemotubbe himself and not Pappy who actually was the baby's father.

Although "Red Leaves" has comic elements—it is here, not in "A Justice," that we learn of Ikkemotubbe's romantic caper in New Orleans—its extraordinary power derives from its tragic portrait of a scapegoat. As so often in Faulkner's fiction, we begin the tale sharing the perspective of an uncomprehending outsider: two Indians are in pursuit of a slave who seems shamefully reluctant to accompany his master, the tribal chief, to the next world. "They do not like to die," one complains to the other; "A people without honor and without decorum," to which the friend replies, "But then, they are savages; they cannot be expected to regard usage."

Not until part IV, at midpoint in the story, do we meet the central character, the aforesaid transgressor against usage, honor, and decorum. Only now does Faulkner's true theme come into play, a theme stated most directly in the foreword to his 1954 volume *The Faulkner Reader:* "we all write for this one purpose. . . . [to] say No to death." Hopeless beyond reprieve, the slave initially says yes to death, listening to "the two voices, himself and himself," saying "You are dead" and "Yao, I am dead." To remove any doubt, the slaves who conduct his funeral service in the swamp tell him outright, "Eat and go. The dead may not consort with the living; thou knowest that." Again, he concedes defeat: "Yao. I know that." Only when he is slashed by a snake does his will to live rise up to battle the certitude of his coming death: "'It's that I do not wish to die'—in a quiet tone of slow and low amaze, as though. . . [he] had not known the depth and extent of his desire."

Without question he is virtually a dead man, and his heroic struggle cannot be measured by his success in escape or resisting capture. It is measured instead by his stalling tactics which enable him to say no to death for perhaps 60 breaths by pretending to eat, though his throat is too constricted by fear to swallow. He then extends his lifespan perhaps another 60 breaths by pretending to drink water, again with throat constricted, until this last gambit is forcibly terminated: "'Come,' Basket said, taking the gourd from the Negro and hanging it back in the well." With the gourd gone, the slave's stalling gambit is finished, removing any further chance to forestall death.

Had he not written his great novels, stories like these would have assured Faulkner an honored place in American letters on their own account. Given his range and depth of imagination, along with extraordinary powers of expression in both traditional and experimental forms, Faulkner's total achievement is a literary canvas of truly Shakespearean scope and intensity in both the comic and tragic modes. No one in American literature has a better claim to be its greatest author; no one using the English language has a better claim to a seat beside Shakespeare.

—Victor Strandberg

See the essays on "Barn Burning," "The Bear," "Spotted Horses," and "A Rose for Emily."

———

FITZGERALD, F(rancis) Scott (Key). American. Born in St. Paul, Minnesota, 24 September 1896. Educated at St. Paul Academy, 1908–11; Newman School, Hackensack, New Jersey, 1911–13; Princeton University, New Jersey, 1913–17. Served in the U.S. Army, 1917–19: 2nd Lieutenant. Married Zelda Sayre in 1920; one daughter. Advertising copywriter, Barron Collier Agency, New York, 1919–20; full-time writer from 1920; lived in Europe, 1924–26, 1929–31; screenwriter for Metro-Goldwyn-Mayer, Hollywood, 1937–38. *Died 21 December 1940.*

PUBLICATIONS

Collections

The Bodley Head Fitzgerald, edited by Malcolm Cowley and J.B. Priestley.   6 vols., 1958–63.
The Fitzgerald Reader, edited by Arthur Mizener.   1963.
The Short Stories, edited by Matthew J. Bruccoli.   1989.

Short Stories

Flappers and Philosophers.   1920.
Tales of the Jazz Age.   1922.
All the Sad Young Men.   1926.
Taps at Reveille.   1935.
The Stories, edited by Malcolm Cowley.   1951.
The Mystery of the Raymond Mortgage (story).   1960.
The Pat Hobby Stories, edited by Arnold Gingrich.   1962.
The Apprentice Fiction of Fitzgerald 1909–1917, edited by John Kuehl.   1965.
Bits of Paradise: 21 Uncollected Stories, with Zelda Fitzgerald, edited by Matthew J. Bruccoli and Scottie Fitzgerald Smith.   1973.

The Basil and Josephine Stories, edited by Jackson R. Bryer and John Kuehl.   1973.
The Price Was High: The Last Uncollected Stories of Fitzgerald, edited by Matthew J. Bruccoli.   1979.

Novels

This Side of Paradise.   1920.
The Beautiful and Damned.   1922.
John Jackson's Arcady, edited by Lilian Holmes Stack.   1924.
The Great Gatsby.   1925; *A Facsimile of the Manuscript* edited by Matthew J. Bruccoli, 1973; *Apparatus* edited by Bruccoli, 1974.
Tender Is the Night: A Romance.   1934; revised edition, edited by Malcolm Cowley, 1951.
The Last Tycoon: An Unfinished Novel, Together with The Great Gatsby and Selected Writings, edited by Edmund Wilson.   1941.
Dearly Beloved.   1969.

Plays

Fie! Fie! Fi-Fi! (plot and lyrics only), book by Walker M. Ellis, music by D.D. Griffin, A.L. Booth, and P.B. Dickey (produced 1914).   1914.
The Evil Eye (lyrics only), book by Edmund Wilson, music by P.B. Dickey and F. Warburton Guilbert (produced 1915).   1915.
Safety First (lyrics only), book by J.F. Bohmfalk and J. Biggs, Jr., music by P.B. Dickey, F. Warburton Guilbert, and E. Harris (produced 1916).   1916.
The Vegetable; or, From President to Postman (produced 1923).   1923.
Screenplay for Three Comrades, edited by Matthew J. Bruccoli.   1978.

Screenplays: *A Yank at Oxford* (uncredited), with others, 1937; *Three Comrades,* with Edward E. Paramore, 1938.

Radio Play: *Let's Go Out and Play,* 1935.

Verse

Poems 1911–1940, edited by Matthew J. Bruccoli.   1981.

Other

The Crack-Up, with Other Uncollected Pieces, Note-Books, and Unpublished Letters, edited by Edmund Wilson.   1945.
Afternoon of an Author: A Selection of Uncollected Stories and Essays, edited by Arthur Mizener.   1957.
The Letters of Fitzgerald, edited by Arthur Turnbull.   1963.
Thoughtbook, edited by John Kuehl.   1965.
Fitzgerald in His Own Time: A Miscellany, edited by Matthew J. Bruccoli and Jackson R. Bryer.   1971.
Dear Scott/Dear Max: The Fitzgerald-Perkins Correspondence, edited by John Kuehl and Jackson R. Bryer.   1971.
As Ever, Scott Fitz—: Letters Between Fitzgerald and His Literary Agent Harold Ober 1919–1940, edited by Matthew J. Bruccoli and Jennifer Atkinson.   1972.
Ledger, edited by Matthew J. Bruccoli.   1973.
The Cruise of the Rolling Junk (travel).   1976.
The Notebooks, edited by Matthew J. Bruccoli.   1978.

Correspondence, edited by Matthew J. Bruccoli and Margaret M. Duggan.   1980.
Fitzgerald on Writing, edited by Larry W. Phillips.   1985.

*

Bibliography: *The Critical Reception of Fitzgerald: A Bibliographical Study* by Jackson R. Bryer, 1967, supplement 1984; *Fitzgerald: A Descriptive Bibliography* by Matthew J. Bruccoli, 1972, supplement 1980, revised edition, 1987; *The Foreign Critical Reception of Fitzgerald: An Analysis and Annotated Bibliography* by Linda C. Stanley, 1980.

Critical Studies: *The Far Side of Paradise: A Biography of Fitzgerald* by Arthur Mizener, 1951, revised edition, 1965, and *Fitzgerald: A Collection of Critical Essays* edited by Mizener, 1963; *The Fictional Technique of Fitzgerald* by James E. Miller, Jr., 1957, revised edition, as *Fitzgerald: His Art and His Technique,* 1964; *Beloved Infidel: The Education of a Woman* (with Gerold Frank), 1958, and *The Real Fitzgerald: Thirty-Five Years Later,* 1976, both by Sheilah Graham; *Fitzgerald* by Andrew Turnbull, 1962; *The Composition of Tender Is the Night,* 1963, *Scott and Ernest: The Authority of Failure and the Authority of Success,* 1978, and *Some Sort of Epic Grandeur: The Life of Fitzgerald,* 1981, all by Matthew J. Bruccoli, and *New Essays on The Great Gatsby* edited by Bruccoli, 1985; *Fitzgerald* by Kenneth Eble, 1963, revised edition, 1977, and *Fitzgerald: A Collection of Criticism* edited by Eble, 1973; *Fitzgerald and His Contemporaries* by William F. Goldhurst, 1963; *Fitzgerald: A Critical Portrait* by Henry Dan Piper, 1965; *The Art of Fitzgerald* by Sergio Perosa, 1965; *Fitzgerald and the Craft of Fiction* by Richard D. Lehan, 1966; *Fitzgerald: The Last Laocoön* by Robert Sklar, 1967; *Fitzgerald: An Introduction and Interpretation* by Milton Hindus, 1968; *Zelda: A Biography* by Nancy Milford, 1970, as *Zelda Fitzgerald,* 1970; *The Illusions of a Nation: Myth and History in the Novels of Fitzgerald* by John F. Callahan, 1972; *Fitzgerald: The Critical Reception,* 1978, and *The Short Stories of Fitzgerald: New Approaches in Criticism,* 1982, both edited by Jackson R. Bryer; *Candles and Carnival Lights: The Catholic Sensibility of Fitzgerald* by Joan M. Allen, 1978; *Fitzgerald* by Rose Adrienne Gallo, 1978; *Fitzgerald: Crisis in an American Identity* by Thomas J. Stavola, 1979; *The Achieving of The Great Gatsby: Fitzgerald 1920–1925* by Robert Emmet Long, 1979; *Fitzgerald and the Art of Social Fiction* by Brian Way, 1980; *Fitzgerald: A Biography* by André Le Vot, 1983; *Fool for Love: Fitzgerald* by Scott Donaldson, 1983, and *Critical Essays on Fitzgerald's The Great Gatsby* edited by Donaldson, 1984; *Invented Lives: The Marriage of F. Scott and Zelda Fitzgerald* by James R. Mellow, 1984; *The Novels of Fitzgerald* by John B. Chambers, 1989; *Fitzgerald's Craft of Short Fiction: The Collected Stories 1920–1935* by Alice Hall Petry, 1989.

* * *

F. Scott Fitzgerald often cursed his gift for producing short stories, disdaining them as mere "trash" demanded by the readers of slick-magazines. Describing his "personal public" as "the countless flappers and college kids who think I am sort of oracle," he dismissed their callow tastes by devoting his second story collection, *Tales of the Jazz Age,* to "those who read as they run and run as they read."

Entertaining such distracted readers was a living, Fitzgerald clearly implied, not a calling.

Fitzgerald felt his true calling was the novel. The fabulous sums his stories brought—up to $4000 each—bought him time to write his far less lucrative novels. The slick-magazine market called for stories about young lovers leaping hand-in-hand over life's obstacles—the precise sort of story Fitzgerald could produce with all the trimmings: snappy dialogue, sudden plot reversals, languorous descriptions replete with inventive metaphors, and a generally sophisticated, even cynical, tone.

Adhering to that slick formula usually assured him of a sale, while departing too radically from it could mean rejection, no matter how original or clever his departure was. He described his 1925 short story "Rags Martin-Jones and the Pr-nce of W-les" as "Fantastic Jazz, so good that [*Saturday Evening Post* editor George Horace] Lorimer . . . refused it." He claimed his story collection *All The Sad Young Men* was made up of stories "so good that I had difficulty selling them."

While Fitzgerald could write a bad story, as Dorothy Parker remarked, he could not write badly. His bad stories, Fitzgerald noted, came when he wrote "plots without emotion, emotions without plots."

Fitzgerald's power derives from his rhythm and imagery; and his weakness was in developing plots and characters. Emphasizing language and de-emphasizing structure is more typical of poetry than prose and Fitzgerald's stories often resemble poems. Like poems, Fitzgerald's stories are structured to maximize moments of intensity. Nearly all of Fitzgerald's short stories are divided into Roman-numeraled sections, each containing one discrete scene. These scenes are then juxtaposed, the total effect intended to exceed the separate parts. Each new beginning and ending allows Fitzgerald another opportunity to swell his prose with a richness of rhetorical and emotional peaks.

These intense moments sometimes over-reach, but Fitzgerald's most memorable prose achieves, as he put it, "some sort of epic grandeur." The early story "Head and Shoulders" (1920) shows Fitzgerald's love of language and his disdain for structure. "Although the plot actually doesn't start until the couple marry, nearly two-thirds of the story is taken up with their courtship," John A. Higgens points out. "In this story, as in many others, Fitzgerald seems to write the scene and not the story." His lush scene-painting often disguises some structural defect.

Fitzgerald's most memorable passages—the beginning and ending of *The Great Gatsby,* for example—are the emphatic points in which he concentrates his best metaphors and images. "Let me tell you about the very rich. They are different from you and me," he writes near the beginning of "The Rich Boy," a story that ends with the vivid metaphor, "I don't think he was ever really happy unless someone was in love with him, responding to him like filings to a magnet."

A metaphor that typifies Fitzgerald's sensuous poetic flourishes appears at the end of "'The Sensible Thing'," which Arthur Mizener called "vague and . . . ineffective" and which Matthew J. Bruccoli termed "a highly effective . . . story [that] closes with [the] acceptance that love is unrepeatable." Fitzgerald's lush endings strike some readers as uniformly overwritten and other readers as paragons of beauty: Bruccoli maintains that it was a "favorite Fitzgerald strategy . . . to end a story with a burst of eloquence or wit." Higgens argues that Fitzgerald's tendency is "to force emotion by rhetoric rather than imply it," which causes "his chronic inability to end a story effectively." The ending of "'The Sensible Thing'"obviously takes in a great range of critical opinion:

> though he search through eternity he could never recapture those lost April hours. He might press her close now till the muscles knotted on his arms—she was something desirable and rare that he had fought for and made his own—but never again an intangible whisper in the dusk, or on the breeze of night. . . . Well, let it pass, he thought; April is over, April is over. There are all kinds of love in the world, but never the same love twice.

"'The Sensible Thing'," like many Fitzgerald stories, has long been read for clues to his novels. *The Great Gatsby* cluster, for example, includes "Absolution," which Fitzgerald had considered publishing as a prologue to *The Great Gatsby;* "The Diamond as Big as the Ritz," a fantasy version of the theme of young love amidst monstrous wealth; "Winter Dreams," which, like *Gatsby,* tells the story of a poor ambitious boy's adoration of a rich and callous girl; and "Last of the Belles." Current criticism elevates Fitzgerald's stories from crude drafts of his novels to worthy achievements in their own right. Indeed, Fitzgerald's novels, with the arguable exception of *The Great Gatsby,* all have severe structural flaws, and he may be remembered primarily as a short story writer, which is how he was best known in his lifetime.

Fitzgerald's themes were limited, as he acknowledged. "But my God! it was my material and all I had to deal with," he bristled in 1934:

> Mostly, we authors repeat ourselves—that's the truth. We have two or three great and moving experiences in our lives—experiences so great and so moving that it doesn't seem at the time that anyone else has been so caught up and pounded and dazzled and astonished and beaten and broken and rescued and illuminated and rewarded and humbled in just that way ever before. Then we learn our trade, well or less well, and we tell our two or three stories—each time in a new disguise—maybe ten times, maybe a hundred, as long as people will listen.

Fitzgerald's disguises were more various than his self-criticism implies. His stories often used sharp contrasts to offset the ethereality of his rich prose: North/South in "The Ice Palace," brains/body in "Head and Shoulders," love/money in "The Rich Boy," and success/failure in "May Day," as well as the contrasts of East/Midwest, America/Europe, and idealism/disillusionment.

In retrospect, his stories might be grouped into series. The longest series was the first, the formulaic boy-meets-girl, boy-loses-girl, boy-wins-girl-back-again stories that he wrote for *The Saturday Evening Post* in the early 1920's. For better or for worse, this series gave Fitzgerald his reputation, though he developed in the late 1920's a new series concerned with marital crises ("The Rough Crossing," "Magnetism," "Two Wrongs") that might be called the *Tender is the Night* cluster, and a pair of series about teenagers, the "Basil" series, the adventures of a barely-disguised adolescent F. Scott Fitzgerald, and the "Josephine" series, modeled after Fitzgerald's first great love.

When the bottom fell out of the *Saturday Evening Post* short story market in the 1930's, Fitzgerald invented a most uncharacteristic series of stories set in Medieval France about a Frankish Knight named Phillipe, whose heroic nature was patterned after Ernest Hemingway. The characters in the Phillipe stories spoke a *patois* that came straight out of gangster-movies of the 1930's. Though a more interesting experiment than many critics have deemed it, the Phillipe series was rejected by magazine editors for years and remained partly unpublished until decades after Fitzgerald died.

Frustrated by his reputation as a relic of the 1920's, he asked an editor in the 1940's to try printing his work under a pseudonym: "it would fascinate me," he explained, "to have one of my stories stand on its own merits completely." That editor, Arnold Gingrich of *Esquire,* shaped the short fiction of Fitzgerald's last decade, just as Lorimer of the *Post* shaped Fitzgerald's first published stories. Gingrich advanced money to Fitzgerald, reducing Fitzgerald's indebtedness with every published story. *Esquire*'s editorial policy encouraged him to write stories quickly and at under half the length of his *Post* work. The *Esquire* stories were not only far more concise, they were sparer, clearer, and tightly plotted. "Financing Finnegan," "Three Hours Between Planes," "The Lost Decade," "The Long Way Out," and the 14-story Pat Hobby series, all published in *Esquire,* exemplify Fitzgerald's last short fiction: quality entertainment containing unadorned poetic insights into "the riotous excursions into the human heart."

—Steven Goldleaf

See the essays on "Babylon Revisited," "The Diamond as Big as the Ritz," and "Winter Dreams."

FLAUBERT, Gustave. French. Born in Rouen, 12 December 1821. Educated at Collège Royal de Rouen, 1831–39 (expelled); baccalauréat, 1840; studied law at École de Droit, Paris, 1841–45. Suffered a seizure in 1844 that left him in poor health; lived with his family at Croisset, near Rouen, after 1845 until his death; spent winters in Paris after 1856; visited Egypt and the Near East, 1849–51; publication of *Madame Bovary,* 1857, led to unsuccessful prosecution for indecency; returned to North Africa, 1858. State pension, 1879. Chevalier, Legion of Honor, 1866. *Died 8 May 1880.*

PUBLICATIONS

Collections

Oeuvres complètes (includes correspondence).   35 vols., 1926–54.
Complete Works.   10 vols., 1926.
Oeuvres, edited by A. Thibaudet and R. Dumesnil.   2 vols., 1946–48.
Oeuvres complètes, edited by Bernard Masson.   1964.
Oeuvres complètes, edited by M. Bardèche.   16 vols., 1971–76.

Short Stories

Trois contes (includes "Un coeur simple," "La Légend de Saint Julien l'hospitalier," "Hérodias").   1877; edited by S. de Sasy, 1973; as *Three Tales* (includes "A Simple Heart," "The Legend of Saint Julian the Hospitaller," and "Herodias"), 1903.

Novels

Madame Bovary.   1857; translated as *Madame Bovary,* 1881; numerous subsequent translations.
Salammbô.   1862; edited by P. Moreau, 1970; translated as *Salammbô,* 1886; numerous subsequent translations.
L'Education sentimentale.   1869; edited by C. Gothot-Mersch, 1985; as *Sentimental Education,* 1896; numerous subsequent translations.
La Tentation de Saint Antoine.   1874; edited by C. Gothot-Mersch, 1983; as *The Temptation of Saint Anthony,* 1895; numerous subsequent translations.
Bouvard et Pécuchet.   1881; edited by Alberto Cento, 1964; and by C. Gothot-Mersch, 1979; as *Bouvard and Pecuchet,* 1896; reprinted in part as *Dictionnaire des idées reçues,* edited by Lea Caminiti, 1966; as *A Dictionary of Platitudes,* edited by E.J. Fluck, 1954; as *The Dictionary of Accepted Ideas,* 1954.
Le première Education sentimentale.   1963; as *The First Sentimental Education,* 1972.

Plays

Le Candidat (produced 1874).   1874.
Le Château des coeurs, with Louis Bouilhet and Charles d'Osmoy (produced 1874).   In *Oeuvres complètes,* 1910.

Other

Par les champs et par les grèves.   1886.
Mémoires d'un fou.   1901.
Souvenirs, notes, et pensées intimes, edited by L. Chevally-Sabatier.   1965; and by J.P. Germain, 1987; as *Intimate Notebook 1840–1841,* edited by Francis Steegmuller, 1967.
November, edited by Francis Steegmuller.   1966.
Flaubert in Egypt: A Sensibility on Tour, edited by Francis Steegmuller.   1972; as *Voyage en Egypte: octobre 1849–juillet 1850,* edited by Catherine Meyer, 1986.
Correspondance, edited by Jean Bruneau.   3 vols., 1973–91.
Letters, edited by Francis Steegmuller.   2 vols., 1980–82.
Correspondance, with George Sand, edited by Alphonse Jacobs.   1981; as *Flaubert-Sand: The Correspondence,* 1993.
Flaubert and Turgenev: A Friendship in Letters: The Complete Correspondence, edited by Barbara Beaumont. 1985.
Carnets de travail, edited by Pierre-Marc de Biasi.   1988.
Flaubert-Ivan Turgenev: Correspondance, edited by Alexandre Zviguilsky, 1989.
Cahier intime de jeunesse: souvenirs, notes et pensees intimes, edited by J.P. Germain.   1987.
Early Writings, edited by Robert Berry Griffin.   1992.

Editor, *Dernières chansons,* by Louis Bouilhet.   1872.

*

Critical Studies: *Flaubert and Madame Bovary* by Francis Steegmuller, 1947; *Flaubert and the Art of Realism* by Anthony Thorlby, 1956; *On Reading Flaubert* by Margaret G. Tillett, 1961; *Flaubert: A Collection of Critical Essays* edited by Raymond D. Giraud, 1964; *The Novels of Flaubert* by Victor Brombert, 1966; *Madame Bovary and the Critics* edited by Benjamin F. Bart, 1966, *Flaubert,* 1967, and *The Legendary Sources of Flaubert's Saint Julian,* 1977, both by Bart; *Flaubert* by Stratton Buck, 1966; *Flaubert* by Enid Starkie,   2 vols., 1967–71; *The Greatness of Flaubert* by Maurice Nadeau, 1972; *The Dossier of Flaubert's Un coeur simple* by George A. Willenbrink, 1976; *Flaubert and Henry James: A Study in Contrasts* by David Gervais, 1978; *A Concordance to Flaubert's Bouvard et Pécuchet* by Charles Carlut, 1980; *Sartre and Flaubert* by Hazel E. Barnes, 1981; *The Family Idiot: Flaubert 1821–1857* by Jean-Paul Sartre, translated by Carol Cosman, 1981—; *Flaubert and the Historical Novel* by Anne Green, 1982; *Saint/Oedipus: Psychocritical Approaches to Flaubert's Art* by William J. Berg, 1982; *Towards the Real Flaubert: A Study of Madame Bovary* by Margaret Lowe, 1984; *Flaubert and the Gift of Speech: Dialogue and Drama in Four Modern Novels,* 1986, and *The Madame Bovary Blues: The Pursuit of Illusion in Nineteenth Century French Fiction,* 1987, both by Stirling Haig; *The Hidden Life at Its Source: A Study of Flaubert's L'Education sentimentale* by D.A. Williams, 1988; *Flaubert: A Biography* by Herbert Lottman, 1989; *Flaubert* by David Roe, 1989; *Madame Bovary* by Rosemary Lloyd, 1989; *Flaubert, Trois contes* by A.W. Raitt, 1991; *Flaubert's Straight and Suspect Saints: The Unity of Trios Contes* by Aimée Israel-Pelletier, 1991; *Madame Bovary* by Stephen Heath, 1992; *Flaubert* by Henri Troyat, translated by Joan Pinkham, 1992; *The Script of Decadence: Essays on the Fictions of Flaubert and the Poetics of Romanticism* by Eugenio Donato, 1993.

* * *

Gustave Flaubert is often, and with good reason, called "the founder of the modern novel," in recognition of his development of a whole new aesthetic of prose fiction, widely accepted by his successors, to the elaboration of which he seems to have single-mindedly devoted his entire career. One does not, therefore, easily or often think of Flaubert as a significant contributor to the evolution of the modern short story. After all, he published only one thin volume of three short stories, seemingly a temporary respite in a career so insistently devoted to the novel. To the literary historian, Flaubert is primarily, and quite properly, a novelist and a theorist of the novel.

Interestingly enough, in all Flaubert's writing about the theory of fiction—most of which is in his voluminous correspondence—he never once says anything to differentiate the novel from the short story. Even while he was composing the three tales that made up the thin volume he published in 1877, under the title *Trois Contes (Three Tales),* he freely discusses, with his various correspondents, the difficulties he was experiencing with these compositions, but nowhere does he attribute these difficulties to the particular form he was using. One might legitimately conclude, indeed, that Flaubert was not conscious of any difference between the novel and the short story, or did not believe in any such difference. His own words suggest that, in his mind, the theory of fiction is applicable to all narrative prose, regardless of length.

Nevertheless, it is hard to sustain the argument that Flaubert did not distinguish, in practice at least, between a novel and a short story. He made a conscious choice of the form, after all, when he started to write "The Legend of Saint Julian, Hospitaller," the first of his *Three Tales,* in the autumn of 1875, and even the most superficial of analyses will reveal that, in the writing, he made frequent—and surely conscious—concessions to the need for brevity and compression. An indicative detail is the frequency with which he uses the dramatic device of the pungent, isolated, one-sentence paragraph, throughout these three stories, compared to their relative rarity in the novels, where they are reserved for the pithy summation of only the most significant developments. An additional observation one might make is that there are very few, if any, really long paragraphs (running more than one full page, for example) in the short stories, whereas they are plentiful in the novels. There are ample signs, in short, that a principle of economy is operative in the short stories, but not in the novels. Flaubert may not have theorized about such matters, but, perhaps as a matter of artistic instinct, he certainly did not write a short story in *exactly* the same way as he did a novel.

It is certainly true that Flaubert invented no new techniques for the short story, and developed no new concept of what a short story should be, but he fully respected what his predecessors in the short story had achieved (he was not only aware of the work of Mérimée and Balzac, but also of that of the greatest Russians, thanks to this close friend, Turgenev), and that enabled him to give to his *Three Tales* a kind of classic perfection which made them an influential landmark in the history of the short story, even though they were in no obvious way innovative. All three stories, for example, strictly observe the short story principles first illustrated by Mérimée a half-century earlier, that an artistic tale must have a strong unity of focus, and a firmly disciplined, digression-free, narrative style. Other signs of Flaubert's tight artistic control are: the sharply limited cast of characters in each story, the intense focus on a single individual at the story's center, and a powerfully concentrated and concise ending which encapsulates the full meaning the story is meant to convey. More specifically Flaubertian traits, rather than requirements of short story tradition, are the deliberate absence of overt narratorial interventions, the pronounced rhythm and euphoniousness of the sentences, and the detailed accuracy and vividness of all physical descriptions, making the prose exceptionally visual and even pictorial for the reader.

Many critics have been pleased to find a coherent unity in *Three Tales,* such as one rarely sees in a collection of separate stories, and especially in a collection each of whose tales is set in a different time and in a different cultural environment, as is the case with Flaubert's little volume. The dominant unity the critics find in *Three Tales* is the theme of sainthood: a Biblical saint in the form of the menacingly prophetic John the Baptist, a medieval saint in the form of the deeply troubled Hospitaller, St. Julian, and a modern saint in the improbable form of the simple, but utterly selfless, servant Félicité. This portrait gallery of saints makes the whole volume, *Three Tales,* as much a work of art as is each tale taken separately, and constitutes one more reason for the wide influence this slender volume has had, as a model of excellence, on the evolution of the modern short story.

It remains a puzzle to this day why Flaubert, the dedicated novelist, should suddenly have interrupted a novel in progress late in his life, and written three short stories for publication, between 1875 and 1877. The full motivation can only be guessed at, but we do know that *Three Tales* were not his first composition in that form, but that the subject matter of all three stories was not new to him either, by any means, but had been worked on by Flaubert at least 30 years earlier, in each case.

Flaubert began writing when he was ten years old, and the great majority of the approximately 40 pieces he composed in his youth were what must be called short stories, though they were highly varied in form and content. Flaubert saved all his youthful work, but refused to publish them. They were published after his death, and some of them are impressively skillful, though obviously immature. They are worth reading, if only to understand better how Flaubert eventually became a great literary artist. It is evident that he learned his craft of fiction by writing short stories for a dozen years. As for *Three Tales,* the least we can say is that, when he wrote them, he was not making a new departure in his career, but rather, a pious return to his literary roots. In one sense, at least, it is plausible to argue, Flaubert was a short story writer all his life, and his very last publication, *Three Tales,* is the magnificent proof of that.

—Murray Sachs

See the essay on "A Simple Heart."

———

FORSTER, E(dward) M(organ). English. Born in London, 1 January 1879. Educated at Kent House, Eastbourne, Sussex, 1890–93; Tonbridge School, Kent, 1893–97; King's College, Cambridge (exhibitioner), 1897–1901, B.A. 1901, M.A. 1910. Travelled in Italy, 1901–02, and in Greece and Italy, 1903; lecturer, Working Men's College, London, 1902–07; contributor, and a founder, *Independent Review,* London, 1903; tutor to the children of Countess von Amim (the writer Elizabeth), Nassenheide, Germany, 1905; lived in India, 1912–13; cataloguer, National Gallery, London, 1914–15; Red Cross volunteer worker, Alexandria, Egypt, 1915–18; literary editor, London *Daily Herald,* 1920; private secretary to the Maharajah of Dewas, India, 1921. Fellow of King's College, Cambridge, and Clark lecturer, Trinity College, Cambridge, 1927; honorary fellow of King's College, 1946–70. President, National Council for Civil Liberties, 1934–35, 1944; vice-president, London Library; member, BBC General Advisory Council; president, Cambridge Humanists. Recipient: James Tait Black Memorial prize, 1925; Femina Vie Heureuse prize, 1925; Benson medal, 1937, and Companion of Literature, 1961, Royal Society of Literature. LL.D.: University of Aberdeen, 1931; Litt.D.: University of Liverpool, 1947; Hamilton College, Clinton, New York, 1949; Cambridge University, 1950; University of Nottingham, 1951; University of Manchester, 1954; Leyden University, Holland, 1954; University of Leicester, 1958. Honorary member, American Academy and Bavarian Academy of Fine Arts. Companion of Honour, 1953; Order of Merit, 1969. *Died 7 June 1970.*

PUBLICATIONS

Collections

Works (Abinger Edition), edited by Oliver Stallybrass and Elizabeth Heine. 1972— .
The New Collected Short Stories, edited by P.N. Furbank. 1985.

Short Stories

The Celestial Omnibus and Other Stories.   1911.
The Eternal Moment and Other Stories.   1928.
The Collected Tales.   1947; as *The Collected Short Stories*,
1948.
The Life to Come and Other Stories.   1972.
Arctic Summer and Other Fiction.   1980.

Novels

Where Angels Fear to Tread.   1905.
The Longest Journey.   1907.
A Room with a View.   1908.
Howards End.   1910; manuscripts edited by Oliver Stally-
brass, 1973.
The Story of the Siren.   1920.
A Passage to India.   1924; manuscripts edited by Oliver
Stallybrass, 1978.
Maurice.   1971.

Plays

Pageant of Abinger, music by Ralph Vaughan Williams
(produced 1934).   1934.
England's Pleasant Land: A Pageant Play (produced 1938).
1940.
Billy Budd, with Eric Crozier, music by Benjamin Britten,
from the story by Herman Melville (produced 1952).
1951; revised version (produced 1964), 1961.

Screenplay: *A Diary for Timothy* (documentary), 1945.

Other

Egypt.   1920.
Alexandria: A History and a Guide.   1922; revised edition,
1938.
Pharos and Pharillon.   1923.
Anonymity: An Enquiry.   1925.
Aspects of the Novel.   1927.
A Letter to Madan Blanchard.   1932.
Sinclair Lewis Interprets America.   1932.
Goldsworthy Lowes Dickinson (biography).   1934.
Abinger Harvest.   1936.
What I Believe.   1939.
Nordic Twilight.   1940.
The New Disorder.   1949.
The Hill of Devi, Being Letters from Dewas State Senior.
1953.
Two Cheers for Democracy.   1951.
Desmond MacCarthy.   1952.
I Assert That There Is an Alternative to Humanism.   1955.
Battersea Rise.   1955.
Marianne Thornton 1797–1887: A Domestic Biography.
1956.
Albergo Empedocle and Other Writings, edited by George
H. Thomson.   1971.
A View Without a Room.   1973.
Aspects of the Novel and Related Writings, edited by Oliver
Stallybrass.   1974.
Letters to Donald Windham.   1976.
Commonplace Book (manuscript facsimile).   1978; edited
Philip Gardner, 1985.
Only Connect: Letters to Indian Friends, edited by Syed
Hamid Husain.   1979.
Selected Letters, edited by P.N. Furbank and Mary Lago.
2 vols., 1983–85.

Editor, *Original Letters from India 1779–1815,* by Eliza
Fay.   1925.

*

Bibliography: *A Bibliography of Forster* by B.J. Kirkpatrick,
1965, revised edition, 1985; *Forster: An Annotated Bibliography of Secondary Materials* by Albert Borrello, 1973;
Forster: An Annotated Bibliography of Writing about Him
edited by Frederick P.W. McDowell, 1976.

Critical Studies: *Forster* by Lionel Trilling, 1943, revised
edition, 1965; *The Novels of Forster* by James McConkey,
1957; *The Art of Forster* by H.J. Oliver, 1960; *The
Achievement of Forster* by John Beer, 1962, and *A Passage
to India: Essays in Interpretation* edited by Beer, 1985;
Forster: The Perils of Humanism by Frederick Crews, 1962;
Art and Order: A Study of Forster by Alan Wilde, 1964;
Forster: A Collection of Critical Essays edited by Malcolm
Bradbury, 1966; *The Cave and the Mountain: A Study of
Forster* by Wilfred Stone, 1966; *Forster: A Passage to India,*
1967, and *Forster: The Personal Voice,* 1975, both by John
Colmer; *Forster* by Frederick P.W. McDowell, 1969, re-
vised edition, 1982; *Forster: The Critical Heritage* edited
by Philip Gardner, 1973, and *Forster* by Gardner, 1977;
Forster: A Study in Double Vision by Vasant A. Shahane,
1975, and *Approaches to Forster* edited by Shahane, 1981;
Forster's Women: Eternal Differences by Bonnie Finkel-
stein, 1975; *Forster: The Endless Journey* by J.S. Martin,
1976; *Forster's Howards End: Fiction as History* by Peter
Widdowson, 1977; *Forster's Posthumous Fiction,* 1977, and
Forster, 1987, both by Norman Page; *Alexandria Still:
Forster, Durrell, and Cavafy* by Jane Lagoudis Pinchin,
1977; *Forster: A Life* by P.N. Furbank,   2 vols., 1977–78;
Forster's India by G.K. Das, 1977; *Forster and His World*
by Francis King, 1978, as *Forster,* 1988; *Forster: A Human
Exploration: Centenary Essays* edited by G.K. Das and
John Beer, 1979; *A Reading of Forster* by Glen Cavaliero,
1979; *Forster's Passages to India* by Robin Jared Lewis,
1979; *Forster's A Passage to India: The Religious Dimension* by Chaman L. Sahni, 1981; *Forster's Narrative Vision*
by Barbara Rosecrance, 1982; *Forster: Centenary Revalua-
tions* edited by Judith Scherer Herz and Robert K. Martin,
1982; *Forster* by Claude J. Summers, 1983; *A Preface to
Forster* by Christopher Gillie, 1983; *Forster as Critic* by
Rukun Advani, 1984; *Forster: Our Permanent Contemporary* by P.J.M. Scott, 1984; *Critical Essays on Forster* edited
by Alan Wilde, 1985; *The Short Narratives of Forster* by
Judith Scherer Herz, 1988; *Challenge and Conventionality
in the Fiction of Forster* by Stephen K. Land, 1990.

* * *

E.M. Forster wrote short stories over a period of more
than half a century, the earliest belonging to the opening
years of the 20th century, the latest to the closing years of
his very long life. Their publication, too, extends over a
very long period: a number of stories appeared in Edwardian magazines and were collected in the 1911 and 1928
volumes, while others appeared only after his death.
Together the stories constitute a significant body of work,
though there is evidence that Forster also destroyed a
number of stories, circulated among his friends but never
published, on at least two occasions (the first in about
1922, when he noted in his diary that he had "burnt my

indecent writings," the second in the last decade of his life, when he was presumably tidying up his papers in anticipation of his death).

The contents of the first two volumes, brought together in the *Collected Short Stories,* share certain features with Forster's full-length novels of the Edwardian period, especially the two Italian novels and *The Longest Journey.* In particular they dramatize the disruptive power of the emotions on a highly organized and rigidly conventional society. They differ from the novels, however, in making more overt use of the supernatural and the whimsical. The title story of *The Celestial Omnibus,* for instance, is a fantasy or parable which has its starting-point in a realistic setting but soon moves into sentimentalized Wellsian science fiction. Elsewhere Forster's classical education leads him to use the Greek mythological figure of Pan to symbolize nature, and especially the anarchic effects of sexuality, as opposed to civilization, as represented by English bourgeois life. Pan's influence is explicit in the title of "The Story of a Panic," which Forster referred to as the first story he ever wrote.

These early stories are characterized by the economy, wit, and irony that are familiar to readers of his novels, as well as by his moral commitment in offering a critique of contemporary English attitudes, particularly with regard to sexuality and social class. There is no doubt, however, that their impact is somewhat diminished by an archness or sentimentality that are now recognizable as a period flavour and are no doubt the result of the original appearance of nearly all these stories in magazines intended for a popular readership. Editorial constraints must have compelled Forster to modify the sharpness of his criticism and to encode issues that he would have preferred to deal with more frankly.

This is all the more evident when one compares these early stories with some of those published posthumously. *The Life to Come* contains stories written over a period of more than 50 years, for instance, from "Albergo Empedocle," published in *Temple Bar* in December 1903 but omitted from the 1911 volume at his publisher's request, to "The Other Boat," written in 1957 and 1958. Not surprisingly, the contents of this volume are very diverse and not all reviewers regarded it as a justifiable addition to Forster's published writings. To any student of Forster, however, many of the stories are of great interest. "Ansell," one of his earliest stories and one which had to wait some 70 years for publication, questions the value of the scholarly and intellectual life as against the life of nature and impulse, and finds its climax in a symbolic incident that recalls the use of symbolism in the full-length fiction. Several of the other stories in the volume belong to the Edwardian period.

Most of the other stories belong to the interwar period, and this group includes several examples of the type of homosexual short story that Forster wrote for his own pleasure and for the entertainment of his friends; as already indicated, most of Forster's work in this genre was destroyed by him, hence the surviving examples are of particular interest. "The Obelisk" (1939) is an extended indecent joke, its seaside setting giving it something of the quality of the traditional English comic postcard analysed by George Orwell in "The Art of Donald McGill." "Arthur Snatchfold" (1928), on the other hand, is a more serious, even tragic, handling of the same theme of a casual homosexual encounter that in this case goes wrong. "The Classical Annex" (1930-31) is another story based on a phallic joke. It introduces a vein of fantasy that recalls the Edwardian stories while contrasting, in its comic explicitness, with their careful concern not to give offence.

As these comments suggest, Forster's stories cover a wide range in subject matter and treatment. They also differ markedly in the audiences for which they were intended: while some were tailored for a middle-class magazine readership, others were restricted to private circulation and hence set the author free from official or unofficial censorship—an issue to which he devoted much thought and energy. Forster's statement in the introduction to the *Collected Short Stories* that the volume includes "all that I have accomplished in a particular line" is misleading, as Forster must have been well aware; on the other hand, the social climate changed dramatically in England between 1947 and 1972, and he would probably be gratified that the stories written for private circulation eventually found a wider audience.

Forster thought highly of his stories, declaring on one occasion in a letter to Edward Garnett that "I think them better than my long books." But he was also aware that in some of the stories he had been unable to speak out as boldly as he might have wished. In another letter, to T.E. Lawrence, he remarked that "one of the stories [in *The Eternal Moment*] is a feeble timid premonition of the one which is with you"—the reference being, presumably, to one of the homosexual stories subsequently destroyed. Critics have noted the relationship of the stories to the major fiction: in her early study, *The Writings of E.M. Forster,* for instance, Rose Macaulay describes them as "abstracts and brief chronicles of the earlier novels" (she was not, of course, including the contents of *The Life to Come* in this comment). Forster did not produce as substantial a body of material in the short story form as James or Hardy, for example, nor did he write as many first-rate examples of the genre as Conrad or Kipling; but his best stories—"The Road from Colonus" and "The Other Boat"—are of very high quality and have an unusual interest in covering such a wide chronological span. Though few of Forster's critics have given the stories extended attention, they ought not to be overlooked by any serious student of his fiction.

—Norman Page

See the essays on "The Other Boat" and "The Road from Colonus."

FRAME, Janet (Paterson). New Zealander. Born in Dunedin, 28 August 1924. Educated at Oamaru North School; Waitaki Girls' High School; University of Otago Teachers Training College, Dunedin. Recipient: Hubert Church Prose award, 1952, 1964, 1974; New Zealand Literary Fund award, 1960; New Zealand scholarship in letters, 1964, and award for achievement, 1969; University of Otago Robert Burns fellowship, 1965; Buckland literary award, 1967; James Wattie award, 1983, 1985; Commonwealth Writers prize, 1989. D.Litt.: University of Otago, 1978. C.B.E. (Commander, Order of the British Empire), 1983. Lives near Levin, New Zealand.

PUBLICATIONS

Short Stories

The Lagoon: Stories.   1951; revised edition, as *The Lagoon and Other Stories,* 1961.

The Reservoir: Stories and Sketches.   1963.
Snowman, Snowman: Fables and Fantasies.   1963.
The Reservoir and Other Stories.   1966.
You Are Now Entering the Human Heart.   1983.

Novels

Owls Do Cry.   1957.
Faces in the Water.   1961.
The Edge of the Alphabet.   1962.
Scented Gardens for the Blind.   1963.
The Adaptable Man.   1965.
A State of Siege.   1966.
The Rainbirds.   1968; as *Yellow Flowers in the Antipodean
   Room,* 1969.
Intensive Care.   1970.
Daughter Buffalo.   1972.
Living in the Maniototo.   1979.
The Carpathians.   1988.

Verse

The Pocket Mirror.   1967.

Other

Mona Minim and the Smell of the Sun (for children).
   1969.
An Autobiography.   1990.
   To the Is-Land.   1982.
   An Angel at My Table.   1984.
   The Envoy from Mirror City.   1985.

*

Bibliography: by John Beston, in *World Literature Written
in English,* November 1978.

Critical Studies: *An Inward Sun: The Novels of Frame,*
1971, and *Frame,* 1977, both by Patrick Evans; *Bird,
Hawk, Bogie: Essays on Frame* edited by Jeanne Delbaere,
1978; *Frame* by Margaret Dalziel, 1981.

*   *   *

Like many New Zealand novelists, Janet Frame began her
writing career by publishing a collection of short stories.
The Lagoon won immediate recognition with the Hubert
Church award for New Zealand's finest prose fiction in
1951. A double edition of stories which followed in 1963
was entitled *Snowman, Snowman: Fables and Fantasies*
and *The Reservoir: Stories and Sketches.* The fables and
fantasies tend to illustrate ideas while paying little heed to
realism. The stories and sketches, on the other hand, pay
greater attention to the representation of the familiar
world, while conveying ideas through more realistic situations and sequences. The stories from *The Lagoon* can also
be divided into these two categories; they are illustrative or
representational in emphasis.

A later volume, *You Are Now Entering the Human Heart,*
is Janet Frame's own selection of seven stories from each of
the earlier volumes, to which she adds four further stories
previously published in periodicals.

Many of Frame's stories recreate a child's world with a
sensitivity that is always astonishing. Others offer insight

into the adult mind, depicting resourcefulness and loneliness, deception and devotion, reluctance to be generous,
and the ultimate futility of acquisitiveness.

The more representational stories show children sharing
and overcoming terrors, discovering their world and their
own wisdom. The settings are generally New Zealand
towns, beaches, or picnic places. In the stories that provide
an adult perspective, the settings include the English city as
well. Frequently, the adult character is a solitary person, or
one who has a sense of being isolated while observing
others with a critical detachment. Frame's characters enjoy
few material privileges. They are dwellers in boarding
houses, or families and individuals living in modest homes
and circumstances.

Setting is relatively unimportant in Frame's illustrative
stories: a room, a street, a town. Certainly, as in the story
"Two Sheep," New Zealand is evoked through the reference to freezing works, sheep trucks, sale yards, and "a
valley road where the surrounding hills leaned in a sun-
scorched wilderness of rock, tussock and old rabbit war-
rens." Nevertheless, in such stories, the timeless, placeless
elements are the important ones: road, valley, hill, wilderness.

Frame's originality and mythic imagination were first
apparent in a tale which she composed at the age of three to
tell to her sisters and brother.

> Once upon a time there was a bird. One day a hawk
> came out of the sky and ate the bird. The next day a
> big bogie came out from behind the hill and ate up
> the hawk for eating up the bird.

It seems that each element is more powerful than the last.
The hawk is an instinctive killer. The bogie, an apparition
from the nether world, has unknown powers.

In Frame's work, the image of the bird is often equated
with the writer. That the hawk should choose the bird as
prey may have to do with the fact that the bird sings while
the hawk can only shriek or cry. By this contrast, the song
of the bird passes judgement on those who are incapable of
song. If bird and hawk suggest the creative and destructive
members of a community, all must perish when the bogie
takes revenge. While the fragile bird sings or while the poet
speaks, the magic of words restrains the hawk and the force
lurking behind the hill. In the primitive and simple
expression of an archetypal sequence, the "Bird, Hawk,
Bogie" story is an original myth. It embodies a philosophy
that is reiterated in Frame's work, finding its fullest
expression in the novels *Scented Gardens for the Blind* and
Intensive Care.

In her thirties, Janet Frame spent seven years in England,
Spain, and France. During her return to New Zealand by
sea, she was asked by a fellow passenger to name the titles
of her published works. A "diffidence in naming titles"
which she describes in this situation had already found
expression in a fable from *The Lagoon* called "The Birds
Began to Sing." To the repeated question, "What are you
singing . . . ?" no answer is given. Like the blackbirds in
her fable, Frame resists detaching name or classification
details. Only by listening to a song or reading a story in its
entirety can the artistry and significance be appreciated.
Like the blackbirds, true artists express themselves with
spontaneity and originality, without awareness of audience,
classifiers, and critics.

Frame's longest and most complex story is in the illustrative mode. It is the novella-length "Snowman, Snowman,"
which is both a fantasy and a skilfully composed allegory.
The main characters are a snowman and a snowflake.

Snowman personifies man. His fixity of perception and his limitation of mind and vision are recognisable human failings. But from a different perspective, Snowman also personifies Christ who was "made man." Snowman says, "I have been made Man. . . . Is it not a privilege to have been made man?" Descriptions of Christ from Revelations befit Snowman: "as white as snow," Christ "cometh with clouds," Christ's "eyes were as a flame of fire." Snowman has "coal-black pine-forest eyes." The story is an ironical enactment of Christ's crucifixion, with Snowman's adversaries being the warm sun and wind. Tension derives from the irony of Snowman's belief that he will live "for ever and ever," and the reader's knowledge that he will soon melt.

Both Snowman and his mentor and Perpetual Snowflake are equivocal. This contemporary allegory reverses the familiar order, turning everything upside down. The paradoxes persuade us to consider questions of divinity and mortality.

Frame's more realistic or representational stories have received far greater attention from the critics than the cryptic illustrative fables and fantasies. Among the representational are several acclaimed masterpieces: "The Reservoir," "The Day of the Sheep," "The Bullcalf," "The Bath," and "Swans."

—Judith Dell Panny

See the essays on "The Reservoir" and "Swans."

FREEMAN, Mary E(leanor) Wilkin. American. Born in Randolph, Massachusetts, 31 October 1852; brought up in Randolph, then in Brattleboro, Vermont; returned to Randolph, 1883. Educated at Brattleboro High School, Holyoke Female Seminary, South Hadley, Massachusetts, 1870–71; Glenwood Seminary, West Brattleboro, 1871. Married Charles M. Freeman in 1902 (died 1923). Lived in Metuchen, New Jersey, after 1902. Recipient: American Academy Howells medal, 1925. Member, American Academy, 1926. *Died 13 March 1930.*

PUBLICATIONS

Collections

Selected Short Stories, edited by Marjorie Pryse.   1983.

Short Stories

A Humble Romance and Other Stories.   1887; as *A Far-Away Melody and Other Stories,* 1890.
A New England Nun and Other Stories.   1891.
Silence and Other Stories.   1898.
The Love of Parson Lord and Other Stories.   1900.
Understudies.   1901.
Six Trees.   1903.
The Wind in the Rose-Bush and Other Stories of the Supernatural.   1903.
The Givers.   1904.
The Fair Lavinia and Others.   1907.
The Winning Lady and Others.   1909.
The Copy-Cat and Other Stories.   1914.

Edgewater People.   1918.
The Best Stories, edited by Henry Wysham Lanier.   1927.

Novels

Jane Field.   1892.
Pembroke.   1894; edited by Perry D. Westbrook, 1971.
Madelon.   1896.
Jerome, A Poor Man.   1897.
The People of Our Neighborhood.   1898; as *Some of Our Neighbours,* 1898.
The Jamesons.   1899.
In Colonial Times.   1899.
The Heart's Highway: A Romance of Virginia in the Seventeenth Century.   1900.
The Portion of Labor.   1901.
The Debtor.   1905.
"Doc" Gordon.   1906.
By the Light of the Soul.   1907.
The Shoulders of Atlas.   1908.
The Butterfly House.   1912.
The Yates Pride.   1912.
An Alabaster Box, with Florence Morse Kingsley.   1917.

Play

Giles Corey, Yeoman.   1893.

Other (for children)

Goody Two-Shoes and Other Famous Nursery Tales, with Clara Doty Bates.   1883.
Decorative Plaques (verse), designs by George F. Barnes.   1883.
The Cow with Golden Horns and Other Stories.   1884(?).
The Adventures of Ann: Stories of Colonial Times.   1886.
The Pot of Gold and Other Stories.   1892.
Young Lucretia and Other Stories.   1892.
Comfort Pease and Her Gold Ring.   1895.
Once Upon a Time and Other Child-Verses.   1897.
The Green Door.   1910.
The Infant Sphinx: Collected Letters, edited by Brent L. Kendrick.   1985.

*

Bibliography: in *Bibliography of American Literature* by Jacob Blanck, 1959; "A Checklist of Uncollected Short Fiction" by P.B. Eppard and M. Reichardt, in *American Literary Realism* 23, Fall 1990.

Critical Studies: *Freeman* by Edward Foster, 1956; *Freeman* by Perry D. Westbrook, 1967, revised edition, 1988.

*   *   *

Mary Eleanor Wilkins Freeman was a popular and prolific author whose career spanned 50 years, during which she published 16 novels and 13 collections of short fiction. With the exception of her novel *Pembroke,* her best writing was confined to the short story form. For material for most of her works she drew from the environment in which she had been born and brought up—the small towns and farms and villages of New England. Her chief interest was in people and character, though she was skilled in creating atmosphere and realistic settings. She may be classed as a local colorist, but her profound insights into human nature and social relationships make that classification much too narrow. Early in her career she was recognized as a realist (e.g., by William Dean Howells and Hamlin Garland) and an accurate reporter of life and conditions in the New England of her day—a time of ruinous economic decline and social change.

In the preface to a British edition of her first collection of stories, *A Humble Romance and Other Stories,* Freeman wrote: "These little stories were written about village people of New England. They are studies of the descendants of the Massachusetts Bay Colonists, in whom can still be seen traces of those features of will and conscience, so strong as to be almost exaggerations and deformities, which characterized their ancestors."

Will and conscience, then, are ubiquitous preoccupations in Freeman's writings; for either separately or, more often, in combination, they provide the motivation of her characters, and their effects are quite varied. They may be an almost psychopathic, disabling force, or they may appear as a somewhat humorous eccentricity, or they can be directed toward the fulfillment of useful, constructive goals.

In the story "Gentian" the will in a morbid and destructive form ungrounded in conscience controls and makes miserable the lives of a married couple. The husband refuses to take the gentian prescribed for a serious illness because on principle he hates doctors and medicines. When his wife, prompted by conscience, confesses that she has been dosing him with gentian disguised in his food, he insists on cooking his own meals; and when she offers to leave and live with her sister, he answers, "Mebbe 'twould be jest as well." The husband's will is broken finally by the worsening of his illness. The wife returns and cares for him. Among other stories in which excessive willpower is exerted toward unreasonable and destructive ends are "On the Walpole Road" and "A Conflict Ended."

By contrast, in some of Freeman's fictional characters a strong will and sensitive conscience are presented as desirable assets. Such is the case in the story "Louisa." Louisa is a young woman who has lost her job as a schoolteacher. Her widowed mother wants her to marry a rich suitor, but she refuses because she does not love him. Instead she supports herself, her mother, and her senile grandfather by farming the family plot of land and by working as a field laborer for other farmers. Another better known example of a New England woman's determined will exerted for a useful end is in "The Revolt of Mother," in which a wife prevails over the greed and stubbornness of her husband in acquiring a decent home for her family. In stories like these two, in which women overcome severe handicaps by their own efforts, sometimes over the opposition of their menfolk, Freeman has attracted the attention and approval of recent feminist critics. Though she did not consider herself a feminist, she had a deep and sympathetic understanding of the difficulties and frustrations faced, and frequently surmounted, by rural village women in an economically depressed region in which they had been to some extent stranded by the exodus of large numbers of the more intelligent and ambitious men to the industrial cities and to the farmlands of the West. The world of Freeman's fiction was largely a woman's world, and she admired the way so many women coped in it.

All of Freeman's women, however, do not cope, for example, the impoverished seamstress Martha Patch in "An Honest Soul." Driven by a tyrannical conscience and an unyielding will, Martha, in sewing a patchwork quilt for each of two customers, finds that she has included in one quilt a rag belonging to the other customer. She tears apart and resews the quilts only to find that she has made the same mistake again. She once more resews the quilts; but, finishing them, she faints from hunger and lies helpless on the floor until a neighbor comes to her aid. Freeman ponders whether this were not "a case of morbid conscientiousness."

Martha Patch was only one of the victims of the poverty that blighted the New England countryside as Freeman knew it. More extreme cases, the real paupers, were gathered in town poorhouses in which the mentally deranged were also often housed. With an unsparing realism comparable to that of the naturalistic writers of her time, Freeman depicts in the story "Sister Liddy" life and conditions in one of these grim establishments. The inmates, all women or children, sit in meaningless or incoherent conversation while children play in the corridors, and in the back ground are heard the moans of the sick and the screams of the insane. The stark hopelessness of the interior scene is accentuated by the cold autumnal rain sweeping across the surrounding fields.

In "Sister Liddy" Freeman has isolated and presented to the reader the very essence of misery—misery as it might be found at any time in any place. This achievement typifies the basic strength of her writing. Her people are New England villagers or farmfolk, and their outer lives, their manners, and their speech are shaped by their environment. But their inner lives, the forces and emotions that determine their destinies are recognizable as universally human, whether fulfilling or self-defeating, joyous or despairing.

—Perry D. Westbrook

See the essay on "A New England Nun."

FUENTES, Carlos. Mexican. Born in Panama City, 11 November 1928. As a child lived in the United States, Chile, and Argentina; returned to Mexico at age 16. Educated at Colegio Frances Morelos; National Autonomous University of Mexico, Mexico City, LL.B. 1948; Institut des Hautes Études Internationales, Geneva. Married 1) Rita Macedo in 1959 (divorced 1966), one daughter; 2) Sylvia Lemus in 1973, one son and one daughter. Member, then secretary, Mexican delegation, International Labor Organization, Geneva, 1950–52; assistant chief of press section, Ministry of Foreign Affairs, Mexico City, 1954; press secretary, United Nations Information Center, Mexico City, 1954; editor, *Revista Mexicana de Literatura,* 1954–58, *El Espectador,* 1959–61, *Siempre,* from 1960, and *Política,* from 1960; secretary, then assistant director of Cultural Department, National Autonomous University of Mexico, 1955–56; head of Department of Cultural Relations, Ministry of Foreign Affairs, 1957–59; Mexican Ambassador to France, 1974–77; fellow, Woodrow Wilson International Center for Scholars, 1974; Virginia Gildersleeve Visiting Professor, Barnard College, New York, 1977; Norman Maccoll Lecturer, 1977, and Simón Bolívar Professor of Latin American Studies, 1986–87, Cambridge University; Henry L. Tinker Lecturer, Columbia University, New York, 1978; professor of English, University of Pennsylvania, Philadelphia, 1978–83; humanities fellow, Princeton University, New Jersey; professor of compara-

tive literature, 1984–86, and Robert F. Kennedy Professor
of Latin American studies, since 1987, Harvard University,
Cambridge, Massachusetts. President, Modern Humanities
Research Association, since 1989. Recipient: Mexican
Writers Center fellowship, 1956; Biblioteca Breve prize,
1967; Xavier Villaurrutia prize, 1975; Rómulos Gallegos
prize (Venezuela), 1977; Alfonso Reyes prize, 1979; Mexican National award for literature, 1984; Cervantes prize,
1987; Rubén Darío prize, 1988; Italo-Latino Americano
Instituto prize, 1988; New York City National Arts Club
Medal of Honor, 1988; Order of Cultural Independence
(Nicaragua), 1988; IUA prize, 1989. D.Litt.: Wesleyan
University, Middletown, Connecticut, 1982; Cambridge
University, 1987; D.Univ.: University of Essex, Wivenhoe,
1987; LL.D.: Harvard University; other honorary doctor-
ates: Columbia College; Chicago State University; Washington University, St. Louis. Member, El Colegio Nacional,
since 1974; American Academy and Institute of Arts and
Letters, 1986. Lives in Cambridge.

PUBLICATIONS

Short Stories

Los días emmascarados.   1954.
Aura (novella).   1962; translated as Aura, 1965.
Cantar de ciegos.   1964.
Chac Mool y otros cuentos.   1973.
Agua quemada.   1981; as Burnt Water, 1981.
Constancia y otras novelas para vírgenes.   1989; as
    Constancia and Other Stories for Virgins, 1990.

Novels

La región más transparente.   1958; as Where the Air Is
    Clear, 1960.
Las buenas conciencias.   1959; as Good Conscience, 1961.
La muerte de Artemio Cruz.   1962; as The Death of
    Artemio Cruz, 1964.
Zona sagrada.   1967; as Holy Places, in Triple Cross,
    1972.
Cambio de piel.   1967; as A Change of Skin, 1968.
Cumpleaños.   1969.
Terra nostra.   1975; translated as Terra Nostra, 1976.
La cabeza de la hidra.   1978; as The Hydra Head, 1978.
Una familia lejana.   1980; as Distant Relations, 1982.
El gringo viejo.   1985; as The Old Gringo, 1985.
Cristóbal nonato.   1987; as Christopher Unborn, 1989.
La campaña.   1990; as The Campaign, 1991.

Plays

Todos los gatos son pardos.   1970.
El tuerto es rey.   1970.
Las reinos originarios (includes Todos los gatos son pardos
    and El tuerto es rey).   1971.
Orquídeas a la luz de la luna.   1982; as Orchids in the
    Moonlight (produced 1982).

Screenplays: Pedro Paramo, 1966; Tiempo de morir, 1966;
Los caifanes, 1967.

Television Series: The Buried Mirror (on Christopher
Columbus), 1991.

Verse

Poemas de amor: Cuentos del alma.   1971.

Other

The Argument of Latin America: Words for North Ameri-
    cans.   1963.
Paris: La revolución de Mayo.   1968.
La nueva novela hispanoamericana.   1969.
El mundo de Jose Luis Cuevas.   1969.
Casa con dos puertas.   1970.
Tiempo mexicano.   1971.
Cervantes; o, La crítica de la lectura.   1976; as Don
    Quixote; or, The Critique of Reading, 1976.
Cuerpos y ofrendas.   1972.
High Noon in Latin America.   1983.
Juan Soriano y su obra, with Teresa del Conde.   1984.
On Human Rights: A Speech.   1984.
Latin America: At War with the Past.   1985.
Palacio Nacional, with Guillermo Tovar y de Teresa.
    1986.
Gabriel García Marquez and the Invention of America
    (lecture).   1987.
Myself with Others: Selected Essays.   1988.
The Buried Mirror: Reflections on Spain and the New
    World.   1992.

Editor, Los signos en rotación y otra ensayos, by Octavio
Paz.   1971.

*

Bibliography: "Fuentes: A Bibliography" by Sandra L.
Dunn, in Review of Contemporary Fiction 8, 1988; in
Mexican Literature: A Bibliography of Secondary Sources
by David William Foster, 1992.

Critical Studies: Fuentes by Daniel de Guzman, 1972; The
Archetypes of Fuentes: From Witch to Androgyne by Gloria
Durán, 1980; Fuentes: A Critical View edited by Robert
Brody and Charles Rossman, 1982; Fuentes by Wendy D.
Faris, 1983; Fuentes: Life, Work, and Criticism by Alfonso
González, 1987.

*   *   *

Carlos Fuentes's reputation transcends linguistic boundaries both for his long and short fiction. His diplomatic
family lived in Santiago, Chile, Buenos Aires, Washington,
D.C., and Geneva, affording a universal perspective few
writers have. Nevertheless, preoccupations with Mexico
and its "national unconscious" constitute motifs throughout his oeuvre.
Los días emmascarados (The Masked Days), his first
collection of short stories, enunciates prehistoric, indigenous Mexican themes and other enduring characteristics
such as the amalgamation of past and present, the supernatural, relativism, his past as a Mexican, and the human
condition. While Fuentes cultivates technical virtuosity
and experimental fiction, his urge toward conventional
resolution entices the reader along fictional paths requiring
a suspension of reality and a leap into the supernatural.
The six stories in this collection develop fantastic themes

ranging from the gruesome to the ludicrous and employ a first-person point of view.

"Chac Mool," the title story of a 1973 collection, underscores Fuentes's fascination with his Aztec roots by introducing the ancient rain god. Filiberto's diary, discovered by a friend, recounts baffling events. The protagonist's drowning is partially explained by the discovery that his home has been usurped by Chac Mool. The preColumbian rain god's corruption by contemporary decadence in Mexico appears in his using lipstick, make-up, and cheap lotion.

"In Defense of the Trigolibia," parodies the political essay, slyly subverting the values fostered and supported by two superpowers: Nusitanios (United States) and Tundriusa (the former Soviet Union). Fuentes satirizes both countries at a time when intellectuals usually accepted Marxist doctrine. "In a Flemish Garden," a precursor to *Aura,* employs a diary format. Moving into an old, sumptuous mansion from days of the French Intervention, the diarist describes the architecture and garden. But the supernatural appears: the odor of the flowers in the garden is "mournful," crypt-like, and the garden's flora and appearance suggest an alien climate. An old woman appears, leaving the message "TLACTOCATZINE," then a letter. Later he sees her on the garden bench, but upon approaching discovers only the cold wind. Reentry proves impossible: the sealed doors trap him in the garden as the woman calls him Max and speaks in Aztec. Clues link the woman with the ill-fated French "empress" Carlota, perhaps driven mad by Aztec gods. Tlactocatzine was the name given to Carlota's husband, Maximilian, by the Mexicans and this, plus the old woman's ravings in Aztec, implies that the diarist has somehow vaulted into the past and has been transformed into Maximilian.

Cantar de ciegos (Songs of the Blind) contains stories that have appeared in English in several collections. *Burnt Water* incorporates stories from *Los días emmascarados* and *Cantar de ciegos.* "Las dos Elenas," narrated in the first person, introduces young Elena, who after watching the French film, *Jules et Jim,* consults her husband Victor about a *ménage à trois,* arguing that "if morality is everything that gives life, and immorality everything that refutes it," making three people happy could not be immoral. Elena's mother, the elder Elena, criticizes her daughter's amorality and "modern" thinking, as reported by Victor, the narrator, without subjective intervention. The ending reveals that Victor is having an affair with his wife's mother. Again Fuentes employs the dichotomy of reality *vis-à-vis* illusion. Initially the modern, liberated wife seems more likely to have an affair than the old fashioned, conservative, Hispanic matron. Traditional values and morality are questioned by juxtaposing the two Elenas: are age-old deception and betrayal more acceptable then honestly examining the reasons for marital boredom and proposing unorthodox alternatives?

Constancia and Other Stories for Virgins first appeared as *Constancia y otras novelas para vírgenes* in 1989. The five stories range in length from 44 pages to almost one hundred, explaining the use of *novelas* in the Spanish title. The title story, "Constancia," reiterates the supernatural, exploited previously in *Aura,* "In a Flemish Garden," and "Chac Mool," and other tales. The narrator-diarist of "Constancia," a surgeon in his late sixties, practices in Atlanta three days a week, living in Savannah the remainder of the time. In Seville in 1946, he married reclusive Constancia Bautista, beginning a lonely existence. His only acquaintance, a Russian emigré, lived across the street. One day the Russian, Plotnikov, informs him that since he is about to die he has come to say goodbye. The doctor later investigates Plotnikov's house, to find a photograph of Plotnikov, Constancia, and a child. One bedroom contains a baroque coffin with the Russian emigré holding the skeletal remains of a two-year-old child. Returning home to obtain an explanation, he learns his wife has disappeared. Checking records later in Seville, he discovers that his wife, the Russian, and a 16-month-old child were murdered by Nationalist troops in 1939 after having emigrated in 1929 to Spain from Russia to escape the revolution. Enigma begets enigmas when he returns home after a month absence to discover that a man, a woman and a child have taken refuge in his house, claiming they escaped from El Salvador and entered the United States illegally. Henceforth, he devotes his life to them, instructing them what to do if arrested, ignoring the beckoning lights illuminating the emigré's house nightly. Fuentes stresses the will to live, which in this story overcomes the natural, allowing the uncanny to prevail.

Fuentes characteristically stresses the human condition and its need to prevail, to overcome death and aging, to surmount the norm instituted by a society, revealing (to paraphrase Fuentes) that art is the most precious symbol of life.

—Genaro J. Pérez

See the essays on *Aura* and "The Doll Queen."

G

GĀDGĪL, Gaṅgādhar (Gopāl). Indian (Marāṭhī language). Born in Bombay, 25 August 1923. Educated at Bombay University, M.A. in economics and history. Married Vasantī Gāḍgīl in 1948, two daughters and one son. Professor of Economics, Keekabhai Premchand College, 1946–48, Sydenham College, 1948–59, L.D. Ruparel College, 1959–64, Narsi Monji College, 1964-71, all in Bombay; studied at Harvard University, Cambridge, Massachussetts, and Stanford University, California, 1957–58; economic adviser, Apte Group, 1971–76, and Walchand Group, since 1976, both in Bombay. Recipient: Abhiruchi award, 1949; *Hindustan Times* National Contest award, for a story, 1954; New York *Herald Tribune* prize, for story, 1954; Maharastra State award, for story, 1956, 1957, 1960; Rockfeller Foundation Scholarship, 1957-58; N.C. Kelkar award, 1980; R.S. Jog award, 1982. Honorary professor of Marāṭhī, University of Bombay, 1977–80; president, All-India Marāṭhī Literary Conference, 1981–82; president, Mūmbai Marāṭhī Sāhitya Saṅgh, since 1983; vice-president, Sahitya Academy, 1988–93; vice-president, Mūmbai Marāṭhī Grantha Saṅgrahālay (Bombay public library), since 1986. Lives in Bombay.

PUBLICATIONS

Short Stories

Mānas-citre [Human Pictures]. 1946.
Kaḍū aṇī goḍ [Bitter and Sweet]. 1948.
Navyā vāṭā. [New Paths]. 1950.
Birbhire. 1950.
Saṃsār [Worldly Life]. 1951
Uddhvasta viśva [A World Destroyed]. 1951.
Kabutare [Pigeons]. 1952.
Talāvātle cāndaṇe [The Moon in the Lake]. 1954.
Khara sā̃gāyacë mhaṇje [To Tell the Truth]. 1954.
Varṣā [Rain]. 1956.
Ole unh [Wet Sunlight]. 1957.
Baṇḍū [Baṇḍū]. 1957.
Vegle jag [A Different World]. 1958.
Gāḍgīlā̃cyā kathā [Stories], edited by S.P. Bhagvat. 1958.
Svapnabhūmi [Dreamland]. 1959.
Kājvā [The Firefly]. 1960.
Pālṇā [Cradle]. 1961.
Guṇākār [Multiplication] (includes *Navyā vāṭā* and *Ole unh*). 1965.
Irāvaṇ [name of a month]. 1977.
Viḷakhā [The Tight Embrace]. 1978.
Aṭhvan [Remembrances]. 1978.
Khālī utarlele ākāś [The Sky Descended]. 1979.
Asaṃmām tasaṃ [This Way and That]. 1983.
Khuāvaṇāryā cāndaṇya [Glittering Stars] (includes *Varṣā* and *Ole unh*). 1984.
Amrut [Nectar]. 1986
Soneri kavaḍse [Golden Sunbeam]. 1986.

Baṇḍūce gupcup [Baṇḍs Secrets]. 1986.
Naviadak [Selected Stories], edited by Sudha Joshi. 1986.
Baṇḍūce mokal sutalo [Baṇḍs Runs Wild]. 1987.
The Woman and Other Stories, translated by Gāḍgīl and Ian Raeside. 1990.
Biravā. 1991.
Vacak Baṇḍū [Selected Stories about Baṇḍū] edited by G.M. Pawar. 1991.
Āśā catur bayak [Women so Wiley and Clever]. 1991.
Sāhityil rāsik ho. 1991.
Baṇḍū bilandar tharto. 1992.
Bugrī māzī saṇḍalī ga [My Flower-Basket Has Spilled]. 1992.
Selected Short Stories, edited by M.K. Naik. 1994.

Novels

Lilīce phūl [Lily Flowers]. 1950.
Durdamya [Indomitable]. 2 vols., 1971.

Fiction for children

Ḍhāḍśī candū (based on *The Adventures of Tom Sawyer* by Mark Twain). 1951.
Lakhūcī rojniśī [The Day to Day Diary of Little Lakhu's Exploits]. 1954.
Ratne [Jewels]. 1985.
Pakyacī gang [Pakya's Gang]. 1985.

Plays

Vedyañcā caukon [Fool's Quandrangle]. 1952.
Pāc nāṭikā [Five One-Act Plays]. 1953.
Āmhī āple thor puruṣ hoṇār [I Shall Be a Brave Man] (for children). 1957
Sāhānī mūle [Good Children] (for children). 1961.
Baṇḍū nāṭak karto [Baṇḍū Makes a Play]. 1961.
Baṇḍū, Nānū āṇi gulābī hatti [Baṇḍū, Nānū and the Pink Elephant]. 1962.
Jyotsnā āṇi Jyoti [Jyotsnā and Jyoti]. 1964.
Bābāñcā kaliṅgar aṇī mūlicā sweater [Father's Watermelon and Daughter's Sweater] (for children). 1979.
Cimṭit cimaṭlelā Baṇḍū [Baṇḍū Caught in Tongs]. 1980.
Mūle cor pakartat [Children Catch a Thief]. 1985.

Other

Gopurāñcyā Pradeśat [The Land of the Gopurams] (travelogue). 1952.
Sātā samudrāpalīkare [Beyond the Seven Seas]. 1959.
Khaḍak āṇi pāṇī [Rock and Water] (literary essays). 1960.
Sāhityāce māndaṇḍa [Standards of Literature] (essays). 1962.
Mūmbai āṇi Mūmbai kar [Bombay and Its People]. 1970.

Khaḍilkaranci tīn nāṭake [Three Plays by Khaḍilkar] (literary criticism).   1973.

Rural Employment Guarantee Scheme — Two Views. 1975.

Phirkyā (humour).   1976.

Pāṇyavarci akṣare [Words on Water] (literary criticism). 1979.

Is Nationalisation of Industries in Public Interest?   1979.

Limits of Public Sector in India.   1979.

The Consumer and the Indian Economic Environment. 1980.

Ārthik navalkathā [Wonderous Tales of Economic Folly] (essays).   1982.

Ājkālce sāhityik [Literary People of Today] (essays). 1980.

Āmhī āple Ḍhaṇḍopanta [My Name is Ḍhaṇḍopanta] (humour).   1982.

Pratibhecyā sahāvāsat (literary criticism).   1985.

Āṅkhī ārthik navalkathā [More Wonderous Tales of Economic Folly].   1985.

Sāhityapremī rāsik ho! [Ye Discriminating Lovers of Literature!].   1986.

The Consumer, Business and the Government.   1987.

The Writer and the Contemporary Environment.   1987.

A Consumer Oriented Economic Policy.   1989.

Crazy Bombay (humor), translated by Gādgīl.   1991.

Muṅgīce Mahābhārat [An Ant's Mahābhārat] (autobiography).   1993.

Editor, *Youth and Self-Employment.*   1976.

Editor, with Arvind A. Deshpande, *Maharashtra: Problems, Potential and Prospects.*   1988.

Translator, *Saṅgars,* by Henry James.   1965.

*

Critical Study: "Facets of Human Nature" by M.K. Naik, in *Indian Book Chronicle* 16, June 1991.

* * *

Gaṅgādhar Gādgīl is one of the chief writers of the modern short story in Marathi—the language of the Bombay region of Western India, which has a literature now more than eight hundred years old. Though the Marathi short story made its first appearance during the 1890's, under the influence of British literature, it came to maturity only during the 1930's, and received a distinctly modernist orientation after World War II.

The Marathi short story before Gādgīl and his contemporaries tended to be either purely anecdotal, or slick and well-made or sentimental or didactic. The new post-World War II story developed into an art-form liberated from conventional structural restrictions, and with far wider range of subject, and greater complexity and subtlety in its presentation of human life and character. In keeping with its varied subject matter, it employed a variety of appropriate formal strategies and styles in narration, dialogue, and description.

Gādgīl is an apt representative of the modern Marathi short story in that his work illustrates almost all these salient features. Gādgīl's is mostly a middle-class world, though in a story like "A Dying World," he captures the feudal ambience of the vanishing landed aristocracy with equal conviction. A story like "The Coin," which presents a homeless urchin in Bombay, offers a revealing glimpse of low-class urban life. But Gādgīl is perhaps at his most characteristic in exposing the limitations of middle-class values and probing the middle-class mind mercilessly as in "The Hollow Men," which is easily one of his most memorable efforts. "Refugee City" is another fine story; it describes a typical day in the life of Bombay with all its hurry and bustle, one-up-manship and ruthless impersonality.

Memorable as these presentations of segments of society are, Gādgīl is perhaps at his best in exposing "freckled human nature." His range is so wide that he has written stories dealing with practically the entire range of human life, from the new-born infant to the old man and woman at the end of the lives. In "A Tale of Toys" the world is seen through the consciousness of an infant; "The Sorrows of Shashi" and "The Class-Teacher Resigns" are studies of schoolboy and schoolgirl psychology respectively; in "The Musical Doorbell" and "By Stealthy Steps" we get glimpses of the world view of a teen-age boy and a girl respectively; a young man with an outsize inferiority complex (of which the outsize briefcase he sports is an apt objective correlative) is the subject of "The Runt" and a sentimental young woman that of "The Dreamworld"; "In Full Sail" and "House of Cards" present the psychology of middle age, and old age "blues" colour "Valley of Darkness" and "Leftovers."

Sex at various levels of experience is another recurrent theme: it figures as sheer animal passion in "The Camel and the Pendulum." "The Education of Rose Mathai" shows how sexual awakening transforms a nondescript girl into a self-confident young woman; the evanescent "imitations of maternity" are deftly encapsulated in the story. "How Sweet the Moonlight Sleeps upon the Waters" and "The Sky Stoops to Conquer" are engaging studies in conjugal love. Curiously enough, only romantic, premarital love somehow does not seem to interest Gādgīl at all.

Noted for his ruthless realism and subtle psychological probing, Gādgīl has also written surrealistic fantasies ("The Yakshi and Revolution"), stories of semi-mystical musings ("At the Still Point"), and of evanescent moods ("A Rainy Day"), and sheer horse-play and farce (the stories about Bandu, the office-clerk).

Gādgīl's technique is equally resourceful. He generally adopts an open form, allowing his theme to evolve its own narrative structure. The opening and the ending of his stories therefore exhibit a great deal of variety; the opening is usually brisk, but when a narrative demands an opening description to set the tone, as in "The Hollow Men," he does not shrink from providing it. A clinching comment, an ironic flourish, or a neat summing up are some of the end-strategies adopted.

Gādgīl's style, both in narration and dialogue, is eminently direct, functional, and unadorned; hence, when he employs an occasional image, the result is startling: "The clerks sitting at rows of tables in the big office looked like glass-beads woven in the string of office-work."

Gādgīl's major achievement is that he played a significant role in freeing the Marathi short story from the shackles of conventional plotting, surface realism, and facile romanticism, and he brought to the form a variety and flexibility, a depth of psychological perception, and an openness of structure, which made it truly modern in spirit and form.

—M.K. Naik

See the essay on "The Hollow Men."

———

GALLANT, Mavis. Canadian. Born Mavis Young in Montreal, Quebec, 11 August 1922. Educated at schools in Montreal and New York. Worked at National Film Board of Canada, Montreal, early 1940's; reporter, Montreal *Standard*, 1944–50; has lived in Europe since 1950, and in Paris from early 1960's; contributor, *The New Yorker*, since 1951; writer-in-residence, University of Toronto, 1983–84. Recipient: Canadian Fiction prize, 1978; Governor-General's award, 1982; Canada–Australia literary prize, 1984. Honorary degree: Université Sainte-Anne, Pointe-de-Église, Nova Scotia, 1984. Foreign honorary member, American Academy, 1988; fellow, Royal Society of Literature, 1988. Officer, Order of Canada, 1982. Lives in Paris.

PUBLICATIONS

Short Stories

The Other Paris.   1956.
My Heart Is Broken: Eight Stories and a Short Novel. 1964; as *An Unmarried Man's Summer*, 1965.
The Pegnitz Junction: A Novella and Five Short Stories. 1973.
The End of the World and Other Stories.   1974.
From the Fifteenth District: A Novella and Eight Short Stories.   1979.
Home Truths: Selected Canadian Stories.   1981.
Overhead in a Balloon: Stories of Paris.   1987.
In Transit: Twenty Stories.   1988.

Novels

Green Water, Green Sky.   1959.
A Fairly Good Time.   1970.

Play

What Is to Be Done? (produced 1982).   1984.

Other

The Affair of Gabrielle Russier, with others.   1971.
Paris Notebooks: Essays and Reviews.   1988.

*

Bibliography: by Judith Skelton Grant and Douglas Malcolm, in *The Annotated Bibliography of Canada's Major Authors 5* edited by Robert Lecker and Jack David, 1984.

Critical Studies: "Gallant Issue" of *Canadian Fiction 28*, 1978; *Gallant: Narrative Patterns and Devices* by Grazia Merler, 1978; *The Light of Imagination: Gallant's Fiction* by Neil K. Besner, 1988; *Reading Gallant* by Janice Kulyk Keefer, 1989.

*   *   *

Mavis Gallant's fiction is concerned with how we confront the past, whether our own youth or what we refer to as history—the collective sum of our memories. She portrays refugees, exiles, and expatriates, many of them North Americans living in Europe like herself. Often her characters are unsure of their identities and alienated from their families and their own past selves. Indeed, one critic, David O'Rourke, considers Gallant's characters to be exiles in time as much as in space; they feel "locked into a present situation, condition, stage of personal history, from which escape is difficult, and sometimes impossible." Many characters in her earlier stories live on the Riviera during the off-season, which becomes, as Michelle Gadpaille says, "a museum of mores, a fitting place to study the habits and the habitats of dying breeds."

The past gives us identity, and many characters in Gallant's fiction cling to their pasts to preserve their identities and lend meaning to the present or at least make it tolerable. Those who succumb to the ease of living in comfortably familiar ways end up paralyzed and lacking in vitality, like Walter of "An Unmarried Man's Summer," Miss Horeham of "The Moabitess," and the characters in "In the Tunnel." The tunnel of the latter story, according to George Woodcock, symbolizes the "self-repetition in which each of the characters lives and the narrowness of insight and view that limits their sense of life." Such characters do not grow or change; they view life in habitual ways that sap their spirits and leave them, in essence, dead—readers have been struck by the frequent symbolic use of physical illness and winter settings in Gallant's work.

Apart from being trapped by personal histories, characters find themselves caught up in historical movements which they cannot control or seldom understand. But history's movements cannot be resisted; when one interviewer suggested that Piotr, the Polish protagonist of "Potter," chooses to fall back into familiar patterns, Gallant said, "He is not hanging on to the past, the political system is hanging on to him."

How do characters respond to history or current events? Some, like Señor Pinedo of the story by the same name, maintain their early illusions despite everything falling apart around them. Pinedo continues to assert the glories of the Falange movement in the face of poverty and oppression. Many of Gallant's Riviera stories portray refugees from the crumbling British Empire during and after World War II, like the Unwins in "The Four Seasons," and the Webbs in "The Remission," who try to recreate old patrician Britain overseas. The Unwins have worked so hard to remove themselves from the flow of time that they remain wilfully blind to the meaning of Mussolini's rise—and so do many Italians. The Webbs similarly hold onto a way of life now no longer relevant, and it is significant that Barbara has an affair with an actor who plays typical prewar British gentlemen in films, while her husband—a real representative of the old gentry—lies dying. Other characters find they cannot escape the pain of the past, like Helena, the concentration camp survivor in "The Old Friends," who "stings" the German commissioner with whom she has lunch with her references to Germany's past (she is symbolized by the wasp she frees at the end of their most recent conversation). The commissioner represents a third way Gallant's characters deal with history, by trying to forget it or its implications. The commissioner cannot believe the holocaust was anything more than an administrative error; "A serious mistake was made," he thinks. In "The Latehomecomer," Thomas Bestermann returns home long after other soldiers and finds that his fellow Germans, notably Willy Wehler, want nothing more than to forget the war entirely. But that, of course, means denying him, too, since he has known almost nothing but his role as a German soldier. Ernst, who appears in "Ernst in Civilian Clothes" and "Willi," has no other identity but that provided by his uniform, and he has worn many different uniforms during his life. What is left for him when the war is relegated to a safe distance in the world's collective memory? What happens to our identities when they are largely determined by events everyone wants to forget?

Many of Gallant's stories focus on World War II and its aftermath because to her it was history's ultimate dislocation. As a journalist in Montreal she was once asked to supply captions to the first photographs to come out of the concentration camps, and she was too stunned by what she saw to do so. After the war she went to Europe, and was again struck by the war's destructive legacy. Because of the photographs, she became interested in finding out why fascism occurs, not in broad historical terms but in its personal manifestations—what she called in an interview with Geoff Hancock fascism's "small possibilities in people." She sees fascism as the ultimate form of rigid thinking, one that views the world in absolute terms, above all in abstracts that leave no room for humanity. Thus, while a small child lies crushed beneath him Señor Pinedo can only see an opportunity to reassert the glories of his old cause; as Grazia Merler says, he is "a character totally subjugated by the system," whose humanity crumbles under "his blind fidelity to rules and regulations."

Of course, what we call history is only our memory of it, and our memory distorts the truth to make it more acceptable. Many of Gallant's characters live in worlds of their own creation. Carol Frazier, of "The Other Paris," is a classic example: she refuses to see Paris as it is because the reality conflicts with the illusions she has brought with her to the city. Characters like Carol attempt to deny history by replacing it with creations of their imaginations, a hopeless task. In contrast, Linnet Muir has no choice to make her own past out of what she learns from her visits to Montreal in the series of stories about her ("In Youth Is Pleasure," "Between Zero and One," and so on).

Gallant's fiction portrays a constant struggle with the past. Those who cling to their pasts become prisoners of it; those who deny their pasts lose their identities. However her characters respond, they cannot escape the profound effects that history—personal or national—continues to have on the present.

—Allan Weiss

See the essays on "My Heart Is Broken" and "The Ice Wagon Going Down the Street."

GALT, John. Scottish. Born in Irvine, Ayrshire, 2 May 1779. Educated at Irvine Grammar School; schools in Greenock; Lincoln's Inn, London, 1809–11. Married Elizabeth Tilloch in 1813; three sons. Clerk, Greenock Customs House, 1796, and for James Miller and Company, Greenock, 1796–1804; engaged in business ventures in London, 1805–08 (bankrupt, 1808); travelled in Mediterranean and Near East, 1809–11: met Byron; agent for a merchant in Gibraltar, 1812–13; editor, *Political Review,* London, 1812, and *New British Theatre* monthly, London, 1814–15; secretary, Royal Caledonian Society, 1815; regular contrib-

utor, *Monthly Magazine,* 1817–23, and *Blackwood's Magazine,* from 1819; lobbyist for the Edinburgh and Glasgow Union Canal Company, 1819–20, and later for the United Empire Loyalists and other clients; secretary, 1823–25, and superintendent, resident in Canada, 1825–29, to the Canada Company, formed for the purchase of crown land: founded the town of Guelph, Ontario, 1827; imprisoned for debt after his return to England, 1829; editor, the *Courier* newspaper, London, 1830; contributor *Fraser's Magazine,* from 1830; lived in Greenock, 1834–39. *Died 11 April 1839.*

PUBLICATIONS

Collections

Works, edited by D.S. Meldrum and William Roughead. 10 vols., 1936.
Poems: A Selection, edited by G.H. Needler.   1954.
Collected Poems, edited by Hamilton Baird Timothy. 1969.
Selected Short Stories, edited by Ian A. Gordon.   1978.

Short Stories

The Majolo: A Tale.   1816.
The Earthquake: A Tale.   1820.
Annals of the Parish; or, The Chronicle of Dalmailing During the Ministry of the Reverend Micah Balwhidder. 1821; edited by Ian A. Gordon, 1986.
The Provost.   1822; edited by Ian A. Gordon, 1973.
The Steam-Boat.   1822.
Rothelan: A Romance of the English Histories.   1824.
Stories of the Study.   1833.
The Howdie and Other Tales, edited by William Roughead. 1923.
A Rich Man and Other Stories, edited by William Roughead.   1925.

Novels

Glenfell; or, Macdonalds and Campbells.   1820.
The Ayrshire Legatees; or, The Pringle Family.   1821.
Sir Andrew Wylie of That Ilk.   1822.
The Entail; or, The Lairds of Grippy, edited by David M. Moir.   1822; edited by Ian A. Gordon, 1970.
The Gathering of the West; or, We've Come to See the King, with *The Ayrshire Legatees.*   1823; edited by Bradford A. Booth, 1939.
Ringan Gilhaize; or, The Covenanters.   1823; edited by Patricia J. Wilson, 1984.
The Spaewife: A Tale of the Scottish Chronicles.   1823.
The Omen.   1826.
The Last of the Lairds; or, The Life and Opinions of Malachi Mailings, Esq., of Auldbiggins, completed by David M. Moir.   1826; edited by Ian A. Gordon, 1976.
Lawrie Todd; or, The Settlers in the Woods.   1830; revised edition, 1849.
Southennan.   1830.
Bogle Corbet; or, The Emigrants.   1831; Canadian section edited by Elizabeth Waterston, 1977.
The Member.   1832; edited by Ian A. Gordon, 1976.
The Radical.   1832.
Stanley Buxton; or, The Schoolfellows.   1832.
Eben Erskine; or, The Traveller.   1833.
The Stolen Child: A Tale of the Town.   1833.
The Ouranoulogos; or, The Celestial Volume.   1833.

Plays

*The Tragedies of Maddelen, Agamemnon, Lady Macbeth,
    Antonia, and Clytemnestra.*   1812.
*The Apostate; Hector; Love, Honour, and Interest; The
    Masquerade; The Mermaid; Orpheus; The Prophetess;
    The Watchhouse; The Witness, in The New British
    Theatre.*   1814–15.
The Appeal (produced 1818).   1818.

Verse

*The Battle of Largs: A Gothic Poem, with Several Miscella-
    neous Pieces.*   1804.
The Crusade.   1816.
Poems.   1833.
Efforts by an Invalid.   1835.
A Contribution to the Greenock Calamity Fund.   1835.
The Demon of Destiny and Other Poems.   1839.

Other

Cursory Reflections on Political and Commercial Topics.
    1812.
Voyages and Travels in the Years 1809, 1810, and 1811.
    1812.
The Life and Administration of Cardinal Wolsey.   1812.
Letters from the Levant.   1813.
The Life and Studies of Benjamin West.   2 vols., 1816–20;
    as *The Progress of Genius,* 1832; edited by Nathalia
    Wright, 1960.
*The Wandering Jew; or, The Travels and Observations of
    Hareach the Prolonged* (for children).   1820.
All the Voyages round the World.   1820.
A Tour of Europe and Asia.   2 vols., 1820.
George the Third, His Court and Family.   2 vols., 1820.
*Pictures Historical and Biographical, Drawn from English,
    Scottish, and Irish History* (for children).   2 vols., 1821.
The National Reader and Spelling Book.   2 vols., 1821.
A New General School Atlas.   1822.
The English Mother's First Catechism for Her Children.
    1822.
Modern Geography and History.   1823.
*The Bachelor's Wife: A Selection of Curious and Interesting
    Extracts* (essays).   1824.
The Life of Lord Byron.   1830.
The Lives of the Players.   2 vols., 1831.
*The Canadas as They at Present Commend Themselves to
    the Enterprise of Emigrants, Colonists, and Capitalists,*
    edited by Andrew Picken.   1832.
The Autobiography.   2 vols., 1833.
The Literary Life and Miscellanies.   3 vols., 1834.

Editor, *The Original and Rejected Theatre, and The New
    British Theatre.*   4 vols., 1814–15.
Editor, *Diary Illustrative of the Times of George the Fourth,*
    vols. 3–4, by Lady Charlotte Bury.   1838.
Editor, *Records of Real Life in the Palace and Cottage,* by
    Harriet Pigott.   1839.

*

Critical Studies: *Galt* by Jennie W. Aberdein, 1936; *Galt
and Eighteenth-Century Scottish Philosophy,* 1954, and
Galt's Scottish Stories, 1959, both by Erik Frykman; *Susan
Ferrier and Galt* by William M. Parker, 1965; *Galt: The*

Life of a Writer by Ian A. Gordon, 1972; *The Galts: A
Canadian Odyssey* by H.B. Timothy, 1977; *Galt* by Ruth I.
Aldrich, 1978; *Galt, romancier ecossais* by H. Gibault,
1979; *Galt* edited by Christopher A. Whatley, 1979; *Galt* by
P.H. Scott, 1985; *Galt: Reappraisals* edited by Elizabeth
Waterston, 1985.

*   *   *

John Galt, who was born in the west of Scotland, was a
man of many aspirations and achievements. He was a
contemporary of other remarkable Scottish writers, like
Walter Scott, James Hogg, and Lord Byron. Like them, his
writing was voluminous and diverse. This was by no means
his only activity. He engaged, without much success, in
commercial ventures. He travelled in the Mediterranean,
where he met Byron, of whom he wrote one of the first
biographies. In Canada he played a considerable part in the
settlement of Ontario.

Galt's work included poetry, plays, biography, history,
and economics, but his reputation rests on his fiction, more
than a dozen novels and many short stories. They were
varied in length, style, and subject and were often highly
innovative. *The Entail* is a tragedy of greed and obsession,
but with much verbal exuberance and comedy. *Ringan
Gilhaize* is a historical novel of great range, a study of the
nature and consequences of political or religious intolerance and violence. *Sir Andrew Wylie* is a mixed bag of
comedy, social observation, political satire, and (then still
an unusual theme) crime and detection. *Lawrie Todd* and
Bogle Corbet also broke new ground in exploring the early
days of Canada and the United States. From his own
experience, Galt admired the enterprise, energy, and egalitarian spirit of North America.

In spite of the interest of these longer novels, published in
three volumes as was then customary, much of Galt's finest
work is in his shorter novels and short stories. His special
strength is in imaginary autobiographies, full of apparently
unconscious irony, in which the supposed narrator gives
away more then he realises. The first and most famous was
Annals of the Parish. In this, the Rev. Mr. Balwhidder,
minister of the parish of Dalmailing, gives an account of
his ministry from 1760 to 1810, a period of rapid economic
and social change in Scotland. It is a book which can be
read in at least three ways: as an evocation of a period that
is so accurate it can be taken as a social history, as an
illustration of Scottish Enlightenment theories about the
nature of social change, or simply as a highly entertaining
comedy. In *The Provost* Galt applied the same techniques
to small town politics with sharper political satire. He dealt
with the British Parliament before the Reform Act in *The
Member,* the first specifically political novel in English.

Throughout his life Galt wrote short stories, which
appeared first in magazines and then later in a book where
they were connected by some device or other. An example
is *The Steam-Boat,* in which the stories are said to have
been told by fellow passengers in a steamer on the River
Clyde or on a journey from Scotland to London. Many of
these stories are quite slight, little more than the sort of
jokes that passengers might tell one another. Some have a
note of pathos and some experiment with different forms
of English as well as Galt's own Scots. There are several
such collections, which Galt evidently wrote with ease and
fluency.

He took up the short story more seriously in the last years
of his life, between 1832 and 1836, when he had returned

to Scotland to live in Greenock where he had spent much of his youth. (Most of them are included in *John Galt: Selected Short Stories.*) In his fiction set in Scotland, which is the best part of it, Galt had always made effective use of the Scots tongue. In the introduction to one of these stories, "The Seamstress," he explained why: "No doubt something may be due to the fortunate circumstance of the Scotch possessing the whole range of the English language, as well as their own, by which they enjoy an uncommonly rich vocabulary."

In his *Autobiography* Galt said that he spent much time in his childhood listening to the conversation of the old ladies of the neighbourhood. It was from them that he acquired his fluency in Scots and it no doubt from this source also that he was able to cast women as the narrator convincingly and sympathetically, in several of these stories, including "The Seamstress," "The Gudewife," "The Howdie," and "The Mem, or Schoolmistress." Others ("Our Borough" and "The Dean of Guild") are miniature variations of *The Provost.* Some are opening chapters of novels which he did not finish, but all read like completed works. They convey a character, an episode, or an atmosphere in a very few pages. These were early days for the modern short story, but in this, as in much else, Galt was an innovator.

—Paul H. Scott

GARCÍA MÁRQUEZ, Gabriel. Colombian. Born in Aracataca, 6 March 1928. Educated at Colegio San José, Barranquilla, 1940–42; Colegio Nacional, Zipaquirá, to 1946; studied law and journalism at the National University of Colombia, Bogotá, 1947–48; University of Cartagena, 1948–49. Married Mercedes Barcha in 1958; two sons. Journalist, 1947–50, 1954, and foreign correspondent in Paris, 1955, *El Espectador*; journalist, *El Heraldo*, Barranquilla, 1950–54; founder, Prensa Latina (Cuban press) agency, Bogotá: worked in Prensa Latina office, Havana, 1959, and New York, 1961. Lived in Venezuela, Cuba, the United States, Spain, and Mexico; returned to Colombia in 1982. Founder, 1979, and since 1979 president, Fundación Habeas. Recipient: Colombian Association of Writers and Artists award, 1954; Concurso Nacional de Cuento short story prize, 1955; Esso literary prize, 1961; Chianciano prize (Italy), 1968; Foreign Book prize (France), 1970; Gallegos prize (Venezuela), 1972; Neustadt international prize, 1972; Nobel prize for literature, 1982; Los Angeles *Times* prize, 1988. LL.D.: Columbia University, New York, 1971. Member, American Academy. Lives in Mexico.

PUBLICATIONS

Short Stories

La hojarasca (novella).   1955; as "Leafstorm," in *Leafstorm and Other Stories*, 1972.
El coronel no tiene quien le escriba (novella).   1957; as "No One Writes to the Colonel," in *No One Writes to the Colonel and Other Stories*, 1968; with *Big Mama's Funeral*, 1971.
Los funerales de la mamá grande.   1962; as *Big Mama's Funeral*, with *No One Writes to the Colonel*, 1971.
No One Writes to the Colonel and Other Stories, 1968.
No One Writes to the Colonel; Big Mama's Funeral, 1971.
La increíble y triste historia de la cándida Eréndira y de su abuela desalmada: Siete cuentos.   1972; as *Innocent Eréndira and Other Stories*, 1978.
Ojos de perro azul: Nueve cuentos desconocidos.   1972.
Leafstorm and Other Stories.   1972.
Cuatro cuentos.   1974.
Todo los cuentos 1947–1972.   1975.
Collected Stories.   1984; revised edition, 1991.
Collected Novellas.   1990.
Doce cuentos Peregrinos.   1992.

Novels

La mala hora.   1962; as *In Evil Hour*, 1979.
Isabel viendo llover en Macondo.   1967.
Cien años de soledad.   1967; as *One Hundred Years of Solitude*, 1970.
El negro qui hizo esperar a los ángeles.   1972.
El otoño del patriarca.   1975; as *The Autumn of the Patriarch*, 1976.
El ultimo viaje del buque fantasma.   1976.
Crónica de una muerte anunciada.   1981; as *Chronicle of a Death Foretold*, 1982.
El rastro de tu sangre en la nieve: el verano feliz de la señora Forbes.   1982.
El amor en los tiempos del cólera.   1985; as *Love in the Time of Cholera*, 1988.
La aventura de Migual Littín, clandestino en Chile.   1986; as *Clandestine in Chile. The Adventures of Miguel Littín,* 1987.
El general en su labertino.   1989; as *The General in His Labyrinth*, 1990.

Plays

Viva Sandino.   1982; as *El asalto: el operativo con que el FSLN se lanzo al mundo*, 1983.
El secuestro (screenplay).   1982.
María de mi corazón (screenplay) (*Mary My Dearest*), with J.H. Hermosillo.   1983.
Eréndira (screenplay, from his own novella).   1983.
Diatribe of Love Against a Seated Man (produced 1988).

Screenplays: *El secuestro,* 1982; *María de mi corazón* (*Mary My Dearest*), with J.H. Hermosillo, 1983; *Eréndira,* from his own novella, 1983.

Other

La novela en América Latina: dialogo, with Mario Vargas Llosa.   1968.
Relato de un náufrago.   1970; as *The Story of a Shipwrecked Sailor*, 1986.
Cuando era feliz e indocumentado (essays).   1973.
Chile, el golpe y los gringos.   1974.
Cuba en Angola.   1977.
Operacíon Carlota.   1977.
De viaje por los países socialistes: 90 días en la "Cortina de Hierro."   1978.
Crónicas y reportajes (essays).   1978.
Periodismo militante.   1978.
La batalla de Nicaragua, with Gregoria Selser and Daniel Waksman Schinca.   1979.
García Márquez habla de García Márquez (interviews), edited by Alfonso Rentería Mantilla.   1979.
Los Sandinistas, with others.   1979.

Así es Caracas.   1980.
Obra periodistica, edited by Jacques Gilard. (includes vol. 1: *Textos constenos*; vols. 2–3: *Entre cachacos*; vol.4: *De Europa y America (1955-1960).*   4 vols., 1981–83.
El olor de la quayaba, with Plinio Apuleyo Mendoza (interview).   1982; as *The Fragrance of Guava,* 1983.
La soledad de América Latina; Brindis por la poesía.   1983.
Viva Sandino.   1982; as *El asalto,* 1983; as *El secuestro,* 1983.
Persecución y muerte de minorías: Dos perspectivas polemicas, with Guillermo Nolando-Juárez.   1984.
El cataclismo de Damocles = The Doom of Damocles.   1986.
Textos costeños.   1987.
Dialogo sobre la novela latinoamericana, with Mario Vargas Llosa.   1988.

*

Bibliography: *García Márquez: An Annotated Bibliography 1947–1979* by Margaret Eustella Fau, 1980, and *A Bibliographic Guide to García Márquez 1979–1985* by Margaret Eustella Fau and Nelly Sfeir de Gonzáles, 1986.

Critical Studies: "The Short Stories of García Márquez" by Roger M. Peel, in *Studies in Short Fiction* 8 (1), Winter 1971; *García Márquez* by George R. McMurray, 1977; *The Presence of Faulkner in the Writings of García Márquez* by Harley D. Oberhelman, 1980; *García Márquez: Revolutions in Wonderland* by Regina Janes, 1981; *The Evolution of Myth in García Márquez from La hojarasca to Cien años de soledad* by Robert Lewis Sims, 1981; *García Márquez* by Raymond L. Williams, 1984; Special García Márquez Issue, *Latin American Literary Review* 13, January-June 1985; *Critical Perspectives in García Márquez* edited by Bradley A. Shaw and Nora Vera-Goodwin, 1986; *Critical Essays on García Márquez,* 1987; *García Márquez and Latin America* edited by Alok Bhalla, 1987; *García Márquez and the Invention of America* by Carlos Fuentes, 1987; *García Márquez: New Readings* edited by Bernard McGuirk and Richard Cardwell, 1987; *García Márquez, Writer of Colombia* by Stephen Minta, 1987; *García Márquez and the Powers of Fiction* edited by Julio Ortega, 1988; *Understanding García Márquez* by Kathleen McNerney, 1989; *García Márquez: One Hundred Years of Solitude* by Michael Wood, 1990; *García Márquez: The Man and His Work* by Gene H. Bell-Villada, 1990; *García Márquez: A Study of the Short Fiction* by Harley D. Oberhelm, 1991.

* * *

Gabriel García Márquez received the 1982 Nobel prize for literature in recognition of his creativity in the short story, the novel, and journalism. In all of his fiction he is a social critic, espousing a leftist ideological position, but he is never doctrinaire in his writing. Universal characteristics are evident in all of his fiction, and he has always contended that the revolutionary role of the writer in the 20th century is to write well.

If García Márquez had never written a single novel, he would still merit an important niche in literary history for his short fiction, often judged to be exemplary. A close reading of his early prose provides an overview of his emerging style and shows the broad vision of the mythical world behind all his fiction. These early writings contain the themes and methods that recur throughout his fiction. He starts from the reality of everyday events in Latin American life, events so surreal that he does not have to invent hyperbole. He writes about simple people in the remote reaches of the Caribbean littoral, imbuing them with a literary soul in much the same way William Faulkner dealt with the inhabitants of his Yoknapatawpha County.

The principal theme of many of García Márquez's early short stories is death, and his reading of Kafka, Hemingway, and Woolf is clearly visible. His first short story, "The Third Resignation," appeared in 1947 in the Bogotá newspaper *El Espectador.* It pulsates with an agonizing fear of death and clearly demonstrates his devotion to Kafka. By the mid-1950's García Márquez had established his reputation as a writer of short stories in the Bogotá press, as well as in his native coastal region, first in Cartagena and later in Barranquilla. Written as they were during a period of great national chaos subsequent to the 1948 assassination of the liberal political leader, Jorge Eliécer Gaitán, this early fiction shows how the common people of Colombia reacted to the violence and censorship of the time. Above all else they affirm the writer's dedication to aesthetic principles and to the precept of writing well.

Many of García Márquez's best short stories are in the 1962 collection published under the title, *Los funerales de la mamá grande* (*Big Mama's Funeral*). His first three novels together with the short stories of this volume are the antecedents of his 1967 masterpiece, *Cien años de soledad* (*One Hundred Years of Solitude*). Most of the short stories in this collection concentrate on the vicissitudes of life in the closed environment of a small Colombian town, often called Macondo or sometimes simply *el pueblo* (the town). They form a transitional work between the early fiction and the more mature writings, yet the use of reappearing characters, family clans, and recurring episodes shows the continuing influence of Faulkner. He deals with the problems of human dignity and the plight of the poor, as well as with the political violence during the decade after Gaitán's assassination. "One of These Days" is a case in point. It focuses on the unwilling visit of a small town mayor to a dentist who is his bitter political enemy. Kathleen McNerney suggests that in this story war and civil repression are both understated or unstated, a technical stratagem García Márquez learned from his early reading of Hemingway. Other themes seen in this collection are the problem of class differences ("Montiel's Widow") and the role of the artist in society ("Balthazar's Marvelous Afternoon"). Throughout this volume the struggle of the humble to maintain their personal dignity as they face the power structure above them is constantly in evidence.

"Big Mama's Funeral," the title story of this collection, is a classic example of hyperbolic humor, a technique García Márquez used extensively in later works. Many critics believe it is his most accomplished piece of short fiction, and it has been more widely examined than any of his other short stories. This raucous tale of the death of Big Mama, Macondo's absolute sovereign, and the subsequent consternation it caused in the nation as well as in the ecclesiastical realm, opens the door to a world of florid exaggeration and satiric comedy within the framework of the folktale. Likewise it creates a myth of enormous proportions as it lambastes political and social institutions and the Colombian semifeudal system of land tenure. At the same time the author takes giant steps in what David William Foster calls the conceptualization of the fictionalized reader. The story uses the technique called "magical realism" in that it requires readers to suspend their disbelief and accept the possibility of a new, extraordinary reality. This technique, so prominent in this short story, informs much of García Márquez's subsequent fiction.

In 1972 a collection of seven short stories came out with the unusually long title *La increíble y triste historia de la cándida Eréndira y de su abuela desalmada* (*The Incredible and Sad Tale of Innocent Eréndira and Her Heartless Grandmother*). As was the case with the collection *Big Mama's Funeral*, the title story contains many reappearing characters from earlier stories in the volume. This collection represents a transition from the earlier fiction of Macondo to central themes later seen in his most recent fiction: exploitation on both a personal and a national scale ("A Very Old Man with Enormous Wings," "Blacamán the Good, Vendor of Miracles"), the extraordinary power of the human imagination ("A Very Old Man with Enormous Wings," "Last Voyage of the Ghost Ship"), and the use of the sea as an enduring metaphor ("The Sea of Lost Time"). In most of these stories a kind of carnivalization takes place, a concept first delineated by Mikhail Bakhtin. Bakhtin theorizes that the carnivalization technique constitutes or reinforces a radical disequilibrium in life patterns, thereby offering the potential for transformation, after which life may either continue as it was before or be indelibly altered. The potential for change, however, is a welcome hiatus in everyday life, even if the change lasts only for the duration of the festivity.

The title story at the end of the collection has as its central theme the exploitation of Eréndira by her heartless grandmother, but there are suggestions of similar exploitation by the church, by foreign powers, and by the military establishment. There are frequent references to characters and situations in the first six stories in the collection. The tale is told by an omniscient narrator up to the sixth section where the narrative shifts to the first person and is directed to a fictionalized reader. The story of Eréndira begins when she forgets to extinguish the candelabra and the wind causes it to fall, thereby destroying her grandmother's house and all her belongings. Eréndira is obliged to repay the entire debt by working as a prostitute under her grandmother's tutelage. This paradigm of exploitation produces a myth with both classical Greek prototypes and modern archetypes.

Like most of the tales in this collection, "Innocent Eréndira" has a series of carnivalesque sequences and an open ending. The conclusions of all the short stories in this collection confirm the fictitiousness of every ending save death itself, but at the same time they offer the hope of the continuing, transforming power of ideas. They exorcise the earlier fiction of Macondo and give García Márquez the opportunity to explore new themes and stylistic techniques.

There is a clear relationship between García Márquez's short fiction and his novels. His concern with solitude and death gradually evolves as well as his interest in the irrational forces that control the lives of his protagonists. He views the deleterious effects of science and technology as he seeks a utopian world where it is possible to celebrate the power of human imagination.

—Harley D. Oberhelman

See the essays on "No One Writes to the Colonel," "Tuesday Siesta," and "A Very Old Man with Enormous Wings."

———

GARDNER, John (Champlin, Jr.). American. Born in Batavia, New York, 21 July 1933. Educated at DePauw University, Greencastle, Indiana, 1951–53; Washington University, St. Louis, A.B. 1955; University of Iowa (Woodrow Wilson Fellow, 1955–56), M.A. 1956, Ph.D. 1958. Married 1) Joan Louise Patterson in 1953, one son and one daughter; 2) Liz Rosenberg in 1980. Teacher at Oberlin College, Ohio, 1958–59, California State University, Chico, 1959-62, and San Francisco, 1962–65, Southern Illinois University, Carbondale, 1965–74, Bennington College, Vermont, 1974–76, Williams College, Williamstown, Massachusetts, and Skidmore College, Saratoga Springs, New York, 1976–77, George Mason University, Fairfax, Virginia, 1977–78; visiting professor, University of Detroit, 1970–71, and Northwestern University, Evanston, Illinois, 1973; member of the English department, State University of New York, Binghamton, 1978–82. Editor, *MSS* and Southern Illinois University Press Literary Structures series. Recipient: Danforth fellowship, 1970; National Endowment for the Arts grant, 1972; American Academy award, 1975; National Book Critics Circle award, 1976. *Died 14 September 1982.*

PUBLICATIONS

Short Stories

The King's Indian: Stories and Tales.   1974.
The Art of Living and Other Stories.   1981.

Novels

The Resurrection.   1966.
The Wreckage of Agathon.   1970.
Grendel.   1971.
The Sunlight Dialogues.   1972.
Jason and Medeia (novel in verse).   1973.
Nickel Mountain: A Pastoral Novel.   1973.
October Light.   1976.
In the Suicide Mountains.   1977.
Vlemk, The Box-Painter.   1979.
Freddy's Book.   1980.
Mickelsson's Ghosts.   1982.
Stillness, and Shadows, edited by Nicholas Delbanco. 1986.

Plays

William Wilson (libretto).   1978.
Three Libretti (includes *William Wilson, Frankenstein, Rumpelstiltskin*).   1979.

Verse

Poems.   1978.

Other

The Gawain-Poet.   1967.
Le Mort Darthur.   1967.
The Construction of the Wakefield Cycle.   1974.
Dragon, Dragon and Other Timeless Tales (for children). 1975.
The Construction of Christian Poetry in Old English. 1975.
Gudgekin the Thistle Girl and Other Tales (for children). 1976.

A Child's Bestiary (for children).   1977.
The Poetry of Chaucer.   1977.
The Life and Times of Chaucer.   1977.
The King of the Hummingbirds and Other Tales (for children).   1977.
On Moral Fiction.   1978.
On Becoming a Novelist.   1983.
The Art of Fiction: Notes on Craft for Young Writers.   1984.

Editor, with Lennis Dunlap, *The Forms of Fiction.*   1962.
Editor, *The Complete Works of the Gawain-Poet in a Modern English Version with a Critical Introduction.*   1965.
Editor, with Nicholas Joost, *Papers on the Art and Age of Geoffrey Chaucer.*   1967.
Editor, *The Alliterative Morte Arthure, The Owl and the Nightingale,* and *Five Other Middle English Poems, in a Modernized Version, with Comments on the Poems, and Notes.*   1971.
Editor, with Shannon Ravenel, *The Best American Short Stories 1982.*   1982.

Translator, with Nobuko Tsukui, *Tengu Child,* by Kikuo Itaya.   1983.
Translator, with John Maier, *Gilgamesh.*   1984.

*

Bibliography: *Gardner: A Bibliographical Profile* by John M. Howell, 1980; *Gardner: An Annotated Secondary Bibliography* by Robert A. Morace, 1984.

Critical Studies: *Gardner: Critical Perspectives* edited by Robert A. Morace and Kathryn VanSpanckeren, 1982; *Arches and Light: The Fiction of Gardner* by David Cowart, 1983; *A World of Order and Light: The Fiction of Gardner* by Gregory L. Morris, 1984; *Thor's Hammer: Essays on Gardner* edited by Jeff Henderson and Robert E. Lowrey, 1985; *The Novels of Gardner* by Leonard C. Butts, 1988; *Gardner: A Study of the Short Fiction* by Jeff Henderson, 1990.

* * *

Best-known for his novels and controversial, almost evangelical advocacy of "moral fiction," the prolific John Gardner published just two collections of short fiction. (Five additional stories remain uncollected.) Yet unlike the varied forms in which he tried his hand—librettos, translations, academic books and articles, poetry, children's stories, and a radio play—Gardner's two collections are not mere literary curiosities but essential texts and are remarkably representative of his larger concerns. Together they embody the conflicting aesthetic tendencies that characterize not only Gardner's own writing but more generally American fiction from the 1960's to the early 1980's. Like his novels, the stories mix postmodern techniques, especially parody and pastiche, and personal experiences, like the rural settings of his western New York youth, and the cultural and intellectual ambience of the colleges and universities where he taught. He was a medievalist at Southern Illinois University and, just before his death in a motorcycle accident, a director of the writing program at State University of New York at Binghamton.

His first book was the textbook-anthology *The Forms of Fiction.* One of his writing students at Chico State was Raymond Carver, whose own later fiction, so different from Gardner's, would become a major influence on American writing in the 1980's.

The stories in *The King's Indian* underscore the significant differences between Carver's reticent, gritty working class realism and Gardner's overblown tales and crafty fabulations. Clearly related to the preoccupation with parody and pastiche that characterized the work of so many other postmodernist writers, including John Barth, Donald Barthelme, Angela Carter, and Robert Coover, *The King's Indian* seems at once more accessible, more wide ranging, and more protean. Gardner was, in the words of one reviewer, "the Lon Chaney of contemporary fiction." Yet despite their wildly varied settings and the range of parodic styles, the collection's nine stories and tales achieve a subtle and surprising unity of effect. "Pastoral Care," the first of the five stories in "The Midnight Reader" section, is written in a quasi-realistic style lightly reminiscent of John Updike, but does not entirely lack the cartoonishness present in so much of Gardner's writing. The story is set in contemporary Carbondale, Illinois, where Gardner was then teaching, and introduces one of Gardner's most important themes, that of personal responsibility and commitment in the face of uncertainty. "The Ravages of Spring" is also set in southern Illinois but in the nineteenth century, and includes Kafka and cloning as well as Gothicism and Edgar Allan Poe. The collection includes stories set in several different time periods, from the Middle Ages ("The Temptation of St. Ivo,") to the contemporary ("John Napper Sailing through the Universe"). In "John Napper" the characters are all real—John Gardner and his family and John Napper, illustrator of Gardner's 1972 novel, *The Sunlight Dialogues,* —and the theme, overtly presented here but implicit throughout the collection, is the power of art to transform, indeed to redeem the world.

In the three "Tales of Queen Louisa" Gardner combines the metafictionist's self-conscious and anachronistic retelling of familiar stories and recycling of familiar forms to serve new, which is to say postmodern, purposes with this same interest in the ability of the artist (here the mad queen) to redeem the world. (This also characterizes Gardner's stories for children.) Following the interlude, of these three tales, the story "The King's Indian" explodes into a Joycean omnigatherum of stories and styles. Drawing on material borrowed from Poe, Melville, Hawthorne, and a host of other writers (and presaging the novel *Middle Passage* by the former student Charles Johnson), and employing a narrative approach reminiscent of Coleridge ("The Rime of the Ancient Mariner") and Conrad (*Heart of Darkness*), "The King's Indian" raises the issue of art as artifice, and as hoax, to new, dizzying heights.

The collection comes full circle with the story "Illinois the Changeable," back to the setting of "Pastoral Care," having traversed the entire narrative spectrum, from realism to fabulism. Gardner offers two equally plausible possibilities of the story and the collection overall (and indeed all of his fiction), as a reflection of "the magnificence of God and of all his Creation" or as "mere pyrotechnic pointlessness."

It is this "pyrotechnic pointlessness" that Gardner condemns in *On Moral Fiction,* his "table-pounding" call for an art of affirmation to counter what he saw as fiction's having strayed into the false ways of cheap nihilism and "linguistic sculpture." Gardner's best fiction—short and long—derives its power from the conflict between the desire to affirm and the possibility of "pyrotechnic pointlessness." The problem with the majority of the ten stories collected in *The Art of Living* is that they are too pointed and as a result not pyrotechnic and parodic enough. At worst they degenerate into the long-winded didacticism of "Vlemk the Box-Painter" and the sophomoric play of "The Library Horror," or else seem the product of an enfeebled fabulism ("The Art of Living"). "The Joy of the Just," originally published the same year as *The King's Indian* but written much earlier as part of *Nickel Mountain* (when it was still a collection of related stories and not yet "A Pastoral Romance"), is decidedly weak. The stories that return to the rural realism that served Gardner so well throughout his career (*The Sunlight Dialogues*, *Nickel Mountain*, *October Light*, and *Mickelsson's Ghosts*) are by far the collection's strongest. Much of their interest and power derives from their autobiographical wellsprings (which is also the case in the less successful title story). "Come on Back" draws on the Welsh community in western New York in which the Gardner family had long taken an active part. "Stillness" is drawn from a novel Gardner wrote shortly before the failure of his first marriage. And "Redemption," written at the suggestion of a psychiatrist as a form of bibliotherapy, concerns the guilt its young narrator—and Gardner—felt as the result of the accidental death of a younger brother. What these three stories share is a quiet assurance that did not so much replace as complement the stylistically different yet thematically related art of *The King's Indian*. Gardner ultimately was neither a metafictionist nor (as the term has come to be understood) a moral fictionist, neither a conventional realist nor a postmodern fabulist. He was, or tried to be, all of the above, and that may be the reason why, even a decade after his death, his literary reputation remains uncertain.

—Robert A. Morace

See the essay on "Redemption."

————

GARLAND, (Hannibal) Hamlin. American. Born near West Salem, Wisconsin, 14 September 1860. Educated at Cedar Valley Seminary, Osage, Iowa, 1876–81. Married Zulime Taft in 1899; two daughters. Taught at a country school, Grundy County, Ohio, 1882–83; homesteader in McPherson County, Dakota Territory, 1883–84; student, then teacher, Boston School of Oratory, 1884–91; full-time writer from 1891: lived in Chicago, 1893–1916, New York, 1916–30, and Los Angeles, 1930–40. Founding president, Cliff Dwellers, Chicago, 1907. Recipient: Pulitzer prize, for biography, 1922; Roosevelt Memorial Association gold medal, 1931. D.Litt: University of Wisconsin, Madison, 1926; Northwestern University, Evanston, Illinois, 1933; University of Southern California, Los Angeles, 1937. Member, 1918, and director, 1920, American Academy. *Died 5 March 1940.*

PUBLICATIONS

Short Stories

Main-Travelled Roads: Six Mississippi Valley Stories. 1891; revised edition, 1899, 1922, 1930; edited by Thomas A. Bledsoe, 1954.

Prairie Folks. 1893; revised edition, 1899.
Wayside Courtships. 1897.
Other Main-Travelled Roads (includes *Prairie Folks and Wayside Courtships*). 1910.
They of the High Trails. 1916.

Novels

A Member of the Third House. 1892.
Jason Edwards: An Average Man. 1892.
A Little Norsk; or, Ol' Pap's Flaxen. 1892.
A Spoil of Office. 1892.
Rose of Dutcher's Coolly. 1895; revised edition, 1899; edited by Donald Pizer, 1969.
The Spirit of Sweetwater. 1898; revised edition, as *Witch's Gold*, 1906.
The Eagle's Heart. 1900.
Her Mountain Lover. 1901.
The Captain of the Gray-Horse Troop. 1902.
Hesper. 1903.
The Light of the Star. 1904.
The Tyranny of the Dark. 1905.
Money Magic. 1907; as *Mart Haney's Mate*, 1922.
The Moccasin Ranch. 1909.
Cavanagh, Forest Ranger. 1910.
Victor Ollnee's Discipline. 1911.
The Forester's Daughter. 1914.

Play

Under the Wheel. 1890.

Verse

Prairie Songs. 1893.
Iowa, O Iowa! 1935.

Other

Crumbling Idols: Twelve Essays on Art. 1894; edited by Jane Johnson, 1960.
Ulysses S. Grant: His Life and Character. 1898.
The Trail of the Goldseekers: A Record of Travel in Prose and Verse. 1899.
Boy Life on the Prairie. 1899; revised edition, 1908.
The Long Trail (for children). 1907.
The Shadow World. 1908.
A Son of the Middle Border. 1917; edited by Henry M. Christman, 1962.
A Daughter of the Middle Border. 1921.
A Pioneer Mother. 1922.
Commemorative Tribute to James Whitcomb Riley. 1922.
The Book of the American Indian. 1923.
Trail-Makers of the Middle Border. 1926.
The Westward March of American Settlement. 1927.
Back-Trailers from the Middle Border. 1928.
Prairie Song and Western Story (miscellany). 1928.
Roadside Meetings. 1930.
Companions on the Trail: A Literary Chronicle. 1931.
My Friendly Contemporaries: A Literary Log. 1932.
Afternoon Neighbors: Further Excerpts from a Literary Log. 1934.
Joys of the Trail. 1935.
Forty Years of Psychic Research: A Plain Narrative of Fact. 1936.
The Mystery of the Buried Crosses: A Narrative of Psychic Exploration. 1939.

Diaries, edited by Donald Pizer.   1968.
Observations on the American Indian 1895–1905, edited by Lonnie E. Underhill and Daniel F. Littlefield, Jr. 1976.

*

Bibliography: *Garland and the Critics: An Annotated Bibliography* by Jackson R. Bryer and Eugene Harding, 1973; *Henry Blake Fuller and Garland: A Reference Guide* by Charles L.P. Silet, 1977.

Critical Studies: *Garland: A Biography* by Jean Holloway, 1960; *Garland's Early Work and Career* by Donald Pizer, 1960; *Garland: L'homme et l'oeuvre* by Robert Mane, 1968; *Garland: The Far West* by Robert Gish, 1976; *Garland* by Joseph B. McCullough, 1978; *Critical Essays on Garland* edited by James Nagel, 1982; *The Critical Reception of Garland 1891–1978* edited by Charles L.P. Silet and Robert E. Welch, 1985.

* * *

Hamlin Garland's position in the American literary canon is secure, mostly as a proponent and practitioner of American literary realism. His work on the aesthetics of the movement, *Crumbling Idols,* advanced the theory of "veritism" that represented the truths, austere as they may be, of ordinary people in the daily routines of their besieged lives.

His own experiences as a "son of the middle border," reflective both of hard times and ambitions for a better life, provided the basis for his best writings—whether as pure autobiography or autobiographical fiction. For example, Garland's hopes and fears for his mother, who led a hard existence in Dakota territory, during the farm depression of the 1880's, gave rise to his most celebrated collection of short stories, *Main Travelled Roads.* Other important works include his early novel, *Rose of Dutcher's Coolly,* and two of his autobiographies, *A Son of the Middle Border* and the Pulitzer-prize winning *A Daughter of the Middle Border.*

Garland both imagined and lived his own life myth of the ever-ambitious, always-striving youth, turning first to the promises of the literary establishment of the East and then to the hope and horizon of the West. In the process, he not only wrote some of the most representative stories of rural Midwestern existence at the turn of the century, he more or less discovered, and certainly advanced, the Western novel. His enthusiasm for the American dream (including his Klondike and Dakota gold rush adventures) took a highly romantic form in his western writings.

Main Travelled Roads offers ample evidence of Garland's realistic/romantic ambivalence and equivocations, seen in his ability to universalize the local and the regional and to expand the conventions and expectations of the 19th-century into the real and imagined transitions of the 20th-century.

Garland's often-reprinted story, "Under the Lion's Paw," serves as a complementary metaphor to his title, *Main Travelled Roads.* His characters are life-weary and are victimized, almost rodent-like in the face of the lion-like powers. In "Under the Lion's Paw" Tim Haskins and his wife, Nettie, migrate to Iowa from Kansas, driven out by crop-devouring grasshoppers and looking for a better life. The Haskins are befriended by Steven Council and his wife, Sarah, who served as examples of successful land

ownership. Haskins and his family do find a farm but suffer the exploitations of land speculator Jim Butler. When Butler increases the price of the farm—due to Haskins' own improvements—Haskins consents to pay, but with an anger that emotionally places Butler under the "paw" of Haskins.

Similar ambivalences and mitigations exist in "Among the Corn Rows," "A Branch Road," "Up the Coulee," "Mrs. Ripley's Trip," "A 'Good Fellow's' Wife," and others of Garland's stories. In "Branch Road" Garland's typical rescue plot mirrors the way he sought to save his own mother from the toil of farm life, a theme he uses at length in *The Moccasin Ranch.*

"Up the Coulee" is another manifestation of Garland's need to write about his mother's hard life. In the story Howard McLane returns from the city to find his "dear old mother" and his younger brother in relative poor straits, compared to his own good fortune. "Among the Corn Rows" presents a variation on the Cinderella motif as a bachelor, Rob Rodemaker, seeks out Julia Peterson, affording her the "rescue" of marriage.

For contemporary readers the rural interludes in Garland's stories no doubt seem overly sentimental in places. What shines through, however, is a sincere, if opportune, discovery of voice and theme which reveals Garland as a Midwestern writer determined to reconcile his life with his efforts as an artist.

—Robert Franklin Gish

See the essay on "The Return of a Private."

———

GASKELL, Elizabeth (Cleghorn, née Stevenson). English. Born in Chelsea, London, 29 September 1810; brought up in Knutsford, Cheshire, by her aunt. Educated at Byerley sisters' school, Barford, later Stratford on Avon, 1822–27. Married the Unitarian minister William Gaskell in 1832; four daughters and one son. Lived in Manchester from 1832; contributor, Dickens's *Household Words,* 1850–58; met and became a friend of Charlotte Brontë, 1850: visited her at Haworth, 1853; organized sewing-rooms during the cotton famine, 1862–63; contributor, *Cornhill Magazine,* 1860–65. *Died 12 November 1865.*

PUBLICATIONS

Collections

Works (Knutsford Edition), edited by A.W. Ward.   8 vols., 1906–11.
Novels and Tales, edited by C.K. Shorter.   11 vols., 1906–19.
Tales of Mystery and Horror, edited by Michael Ashley. 1978.

Short Stories

Lizzie Leigh and Other Tales.   1855.
Round the Sofa.   1859; as *My Lady Ludlow and Other Tales,* 1861; edited by Edgar Wright, 1989.
Right at Last and Other Tales.   1860.
Lois the Witch and Other Tales.   1861.

Cousin Phillis (novella).   1864.
Cousin Phillis and Other Tales.   1865; edited by Angus Easson, 1981.
The Grey Woman and Other Tales.   1865.

Novels

Mary Barton: A Tale of Manchester Life.   1848; edited by Edgar Wright, 1987.
The Moorland Cottage.   1850.
Ruth.   1853; edited by Alan Shelston, 1985.
Cranford.   1853; edited by Elizabeth Porges Watson, 1972.
North and South.   1855; edited by Angus Easson, 1973.
A Dark Night's Work.   1863.
Sylvia's Lovers.   1863; edited by Arthur Pollard, 1964.
Wives and Daughters.   1866; edited by Angus Easson, 1987.

Other

The Life of Charlotte Brontë.   2 vols., 1857; revised edition, 1857; edited by Alan Shelston, 1975.
My Diary: The Early Years of My Daughter Marianne. 1923.
Letters, edited by J.A.V. Chapple and Arthur Pollard. 1966.

Editor, *Mabel Vaughan,* by Maria S. Cummins.   1857.

*

Bibliography: by Clark S. Northrup in *Gaskell* by Gerald DeWitt Sanders, 1929; *Gaskell: An Annotated Bibliography 1929–1975* by Jeffrey Welch, 1977; *Gaskell: A Reference Guide* by R.L. Selig, 1977.

Critical Studies: *Gaskell: Her Life and Work* by Annette B. Hopkins, 1952; *Gaskell, Novelist and Biographer* by Arthur Pollard, 1965; *Gaskell: The Basis for Reassessment* by Edgar Wright, 1965; *Gaskell, The Artist in Conflict* by Margaret L. Ganz, 1969; *Gaskell's Observation and Invention* by John G. Sharps, 1970; *Gaskell* by John McVeagh, 1970; *Gaskell and the English Provincial Novel* by Wendy A. Craik, 1975; *Gaskell: The Novel of Social Crisis,* 1975, and *Gaskell,* 1984, both by Coral Lansbury; *Gaskell: A Biography* by Winifred Gérin, 1976; *Gaskell* by Angus Easson, 1979; *Gaskell: A Portrait in Letters* by J.A.V. Chapple and John G. Sharps, 1980; *The Themes of Gaskell* by Enid L. Duthie, 1980; *Gaskell's Mary Barton and Ruth: A Challenge to Christian England* by Monica Fryckstedt, 1982; *Gaskell* by Tessa Brodetsky, 1986; *Gaskell* by Patsy Stoneman, 1987.

*   *   *

Elizabeth Gaskell is the Victorian novelist par excellence, establishing her characters against a background drawn with care and attention to detail, and relating the events in her novels with the same detailed care. Yet there is much to reward the reader in her short fiction. It should be said that she betrays some unease, an absence of a sure touch in setting the framework of her tales, especially in the longer ones ("Mr. Harrison's Confessions," "My Lady Ludlow," and *Cousin Phillis*). "Mr. Harrison's Confessions" can be

seen as simply a dry run for *Cranford* (the first instalment of which appeared later in the same year, 1851). While it lacks the subtlety of loving characterisation of the Cranford ladies with their elegant economics, it has the advantage of a clearly defined chronological structure, from the arrival of the young physician at Duncombe to his marriage and full acceptance into the local society.

"My Lady Ludlow" is an affectionate portrait of an autocratic, self-willed yet essentially noble (in both senses) old lady, written in a straightforward chronological form. It is marred, however, by the clumsy insertion of the tragic story of the Marquise de Créquy and her son, guillotined during the French Revolution. The purpose is plain enough: to explain Lady Ludlow's fierce aversion to education for the lower classes by showing the disastrous effects of educating the mind but not the heart. Yet the argument is so palpably spurious, and the de Créquy story so intrusive that "My Lady Ludlow" fails as a construction of plot around characters. It is redeemed by Gaskell's skilful portrayal of Lady Ludlow and especially of the excellent Miss Galindo (the very excellence of whose portrayal threatens the balance of the tale further). Even in this idyllic tale we may observe the author's sympathy with, and knowledge of, the appalling conditions of the rural poor. Later Gaskell attempted to incorporate "My Lady Ludlow" along with several other pieces in a volume entitled *Round the Sofa,* but the attempt, clumsily done, was unsuccessful, and later editions abandon the unsatisfactory linking narrative.

Cousin Phillis is the most successful of these three novellas. The story flows naturally: the idyll of the Holmans' farm destroyed by the dashing Mr. Holdsworth who breaks Phillis's heart. Yet the abruptness of the ending, all the more grating in contrast to the leisurely, exquisite descriptions of the farm and its inhabitants, is clumsy, as if the author, suddenly aware of the restrictions on the length of a short story, despaired of rounding it off satisfactorily. It comes as no surprise to the reader to learn of a letter from Gaskell to her publisher in which she puts forward a much longer alternative ending to the tale.

In contrast to these three longer stories Gaskell's other short stories, relying less on characterisation and more on conventional plot development, are more satisfactory samples of the writer's craft even if they lack some of the qualities of her longer pieces—the subtlety of characterisation, the detailed observation.

In her most successful stories she returns to the North Country background of her novels *Mary Barton* and *North and South:* Rochdale and Manchester in "Lizzie Leigh," Westmoreland in "Half a Life-time Ago," and "The Old Nurse's Tale," Yorkshire in "The Crooked Branch," Cumberland in "The Half-Brothers." The life of the small North Country farmer was hard, and she describes it compassionately. Even in these shorter stories her eye for vivid detail is remarkable: for example, the identification of Lizzie Leigh's illegitimate baby which her mother is able to make because the baby's little frocks were "made out of its mother's gowns, for they were large patterns to buy for a baby."

A significant aspect of Gaskell's short fiction is the quality of her heroines, who are capable of truly heroic actions of self-denial and self-sacrifice. They are strong, loving, and patient, women of unflinching moral courage and rectitude: Mrs. Leigh searches for her lost daughter once her dying husband has sanctioned her search, Susan Dixon in "Half a Life-time Ago" sacrifices her happiness to look after her weak-minded brother, Bessy in "The Crooked Branch" serves and shields her old uncle and aunt.

There is a moral undercurrent even in Gaskell's ghost stories and Gothic fiction. Bridget Fitzgerald's curse in "The Poor Clare" can only be lifted when there is a true change in her heart. In "The Doom of the Griffiths," described by Gaskell herself as "rubbishy," the old curse is fulfilled through the pride and bitterness of the Griffiths. In "Lois the Witch" the harsh faith of the New England Puritans is roundly condemned while the gentle forgiving spirit of true Christianity is upheld.

Though the reader may find these genre stories interesting, the stories they will remember, and to which they will surely return with pleasure, are those that reveal the talents, sympathies, and powers of observation found in her novels.

—Hana Sambrook

See the essay on "The Old Nurse's Story."

————

GEE, Maurice (Gough). New Zealander. Born in Whakatane, 22 August 1931. Educated at Avondale College, Auckland, 1945–49; University of Auckland, 1950–53, M.A. in English 1953; Auckland Teachers College, 1954. Married Margaretha Garden in 1970, two daughters; one son from previous relationship. Schoolteacher, 1955–57; held various jobs, 1958–66; assistant librarian, Alexander Turnbull Library, Wellington, 1967–69; city librarian, Napier Public Library, 1970–72; deputy librarian, Teachers Colleges Library, Auckland, 1974–76; full-time writer, from 1976; writing fellow, Victoria University of Wellington, 1989. Recipient: New Zealand Literary Fund scholarship, 1962, 1976, 1986, 1987, and award for achievement, 1967, 1973; University of Otago Robert Burns fellowship, 1964; Hubert Church Prose award, 1973; New Zealand Book award, 1976, 1979, 1982, 1991; James Tait Black Memorial prize, 1979; Sir James Wattie award, 1979; New Zealand Children's Book of the Year award, 1984; New Zealand Library Association Esther Glen medal, 1986. Honorary D.Litt.: Victoria University of Wellington, 1987. Katherine Mansfield fellow, 1992. Lives in Wellington.

PUBLICATIONS

Short Stories

A Glorious Morning, Comrade.   1975.
Collected Short Stories.   1986.

Novels

The Big Season.   1962.
A Special Flower.   1965.
In My Father's Den.   1972.
Games of Choice.   1976.
Plumb.   1978.
Meg.   1981.
Sole Survivor.   1983.
Prowlers.   1987.
The Burning Boy.   1990.
Going West.   1993.

Fiction (for children)

Under the Mountain.   1979.

The World Around the Corner.   1980.
The Halfmen of O.   1982.
The Priests of Ferris.   1984.
Motherstone.   1985.
The Fire-Raiser (stories).   1986.
The Champion.   1989.

Plays

Television Series: *Mortimer's Patch,* 1980; *The Fire-Raiser,* from his own story, 1986; *The Champion,* from his own story, 1989.

Other

Nelson Central School: A History.   1978.

*

Bibliography: "Gee: A Bibliography" by Cathe Giffuni, in *Australian and New Zealand Studies in Canada* 3, Spring 1990.

Critical Studies: "Beginnings" by Gee, in *Islands,* March 1977; by Biran Boyd, in *Islands* 30–32, 1980–81; *Introducing Gee* by David Hill, 1981; "Definitions of New Zealanders: The Stories of Shadbolt and Gee" by Lauris Edmond, in *Critical Essays on the New Zealand Short Story,* edited by Cherry Hankin, 1982; Trevor James, in *World Literature Written in English* 23, 1984; Lawrence Jones, in *Landfall,* September 1984; *Gee* by Bill Manhire, 1986; *Leaving the Highway: Six Contemporary New Zealand Novelists* by Mark Williams, 1990.

* * *

Although Maurice Gee's short stories are primarily by-products of his career as a novelist, they rank among the finest stories in New Zealand literature and make a substantial contribution to the tradition of the critical realist story. Many of his stories were apprentice pieces— 11 of his 19 published stories appeared between 1955 and 1961, the years leading up to his first published novel in 1962. The others, including some of his best work, have appeared at irregular intervals between 1966 and 1986, when the last one to date, "Joker and Wife," was published in his *Collected Short Stories.*

Some of the earlier stories, such as "A Sleeping Face" (1957), the much-anthologized "The Losers" (1959), and "Eleventh Holiday" (1961), are obviously those of the budding novelist. The large cast of characters, the complex plot working towards a definite climax, and the interplay of different points of view all look towards the novels to come. In their presentation of the same or overlapping events from different perspectives, they anticipate the method of the Plumb trilogy. However, from the first, in such stories as "The Widow" (1955) and the uncollected "Evening at Home" (1956), Gee has shown that he has also mastered methods more exclusively those of the short story. All of the stories since 1966 are told from the point of view of one character, most of them lead up to a moment of recognition (or the refusal of one) by that character, and most of them depend on image and suggestion as much as on plot.

Gee's art and his vision have both developed out of the tradition of critical realism of Frank Sargeson and the other writers of that generation. As in Sargeson's stories, there is often a clear-cut division between the more individualistic and imaginative outsider and the repressive puritan majority, such as the division between the persecuted young Frank Milich and the middle-aged, middle-class "regulars" at Mayall's Cottage Resort in "Eleventh Holiday." However, as is shown by the more humorously handled revolts of the younger Trevor Jones in "Schooldays" and the older Charles Pitt-Rimmer in "A Glorious Morning, Comrade," Gee's tonal range with "Man Alone" characters is greater than that of the early Sargeson and his followers.

Gee's anti-puritanism is subordinated to a larger moral vision in most of his stories. By the time of "A Retired Life" in 1969, self-righteous puritans are seen as anachronistic, and they are placed as only one type among many who hide behind a safe conformity to evade the dangers and complexities of life and the difficulties of self-knowledge. Lew Betham, the superficial and self-deceiving race-horse owner of "The Losers," is an early non-puritan example of such a moral type. Lew diminishes himself and disappoints his wife by his blindness, whereas Stan Philpott mutilates his horse in order to get the insurance money he needs to save himself from having to face reality. In "The Champion" Eric Wilbraham seems about to cause a head-on collision in asserting the anger that he uses to evade self-knowledge. In Gee's view, then, morally blind individuals can be dangerous both to themselves and to others.

Not that self-knowledge and a recognition of the complexity of reality are easy in Gee's world, for they often lead his characters to pain and suffering, and, finally growth. Thus, Connie Reynolds in "The Losers" must face the reality of the mistakes she has made in her life if she is to redeem herself, and Vincent Brown in "Right-Hand Man" must face the fact that he has based his life on illusions before he can turn from a public life that has really been like "a game played on a board" to a more genuine concern for "what went on inside his skin." Less traumatically but more sadly, Janet in "Buried Treasure, Old Bones" looks with no illusions on a life in which the "buried treasure" of a few memories is all that she has, those at least offering "a pain that was welcome because its shape was known." More painfully, but with a similar clear-eyed honesty, Lloyd Neeley in "The Hole in the Window" and Cliff Poulson in "A Retired Life" face the loneliness and emptiness that their lives offer them, symbolized by the hole in Neeley's shop window, "an opening into nothing," and by Poulson's mental image of his own emotional state, "a stone face, broken, with blind eyes."

Maurice Shadbolt has praised Gee's work for the way in which it captures the "sight and sensation" of life in contemporary New Zealand, and the stories do provide a kind of social record. They deal with a variety of institutions and activities (schools, local politics, sports, small businesses, farming); most of all, they present a comprehensive picture of marriage and personal relationships. However, in Gee's stories, unlike Shadbolt's, the characters are more important as individuals responding to larger moral issues than they are as social types. The social history is there, but it is in the creation of character in its moral dimensions that Gee excels and earns his place as a significant contemporary continuator of the tradition of New Zealand critical realism.

—Lawrence Jones

See the essay on "A Glorious Morning, Comrade."

GIDE, André (Paul-Guillaume). French. Born in Paris, 22 November 1869. Educated at École Alsacienne, Paris, 1878–80; Lycée in Montpellier, 1881; boarder at M. Henri Bauer, 1883–85, and at M. Jacob Keller, 1886–87; École Alsacienne, 1887; École Henri IV: baccalauréat, 1890. Married Madeleine Rondeaux in 1895 (died 1938); had one daughter by Elisabeth van Bysselberghe. Mayor of a Normandy commune, 1896; juror in Rouen, 1912; special envoy of Colonial Ministry on trip to Africa, 1925–26. Helped found *Nouvelle Revue Française,* 1909. Recipient: Nobel prize for literature, 1947. Ph.D.: Oxford University. Honorary Member, American Academy, 1950. *Died 19 February 1951.*

PUBLICATIONS

Collections

Romans, récits, et soties; Oeuvres lyriques, edited by Yvonne Davet and Jean-Jacques Thierry. 1958.

Short Stories

L'Immoraliste (novella). 1902; as *The Immoralist,* 1930.
Le Retour de l'enfant prodigue (novella). 1907; as *The Return of the Prodigal,* 1953.
La Porte étroite (novella). 1909; as *Strait Is the Gate,* 1924.
Isabelle (story). 1911; as *Isabelle,* in *Two Symphonies,* 1931.
La Symphonie pastorale (story). 1919; as *The Pastoral Symphony,* in *Two Symphonies,* 1931.
Two Symphonies (includes *Isabelle* and *The Pastoral Symphony*). 1931.
Deux récits. 1938.

Novels

Les Cahiers d'André Walter. 1891; in part as *The White Notebook,* 1965; complete translation as *The Notebook of André Walter,* 1968.
La Tentative Amoureuse. 1893; as "The Lovers' Attempt," in *The Return of the Prodigal,* 1953.
Le Voyage d'Urien. 1893; as *Urien's Voyage,* 1964.
Paludes. 1895; as *Marshlands,* with *Prometheus Misbound,* 1953.
Les Nourritures terrestres. 1897; as *Fruits of the Earth,* 1949.
Le Prométhée mal enchaîné. 1899; as *Prometheus Illbound,* 1919; as *Prometheus Misbound,* with *Marshlands,* 1953.
Les Caves du Vatican. 1914; as *The Vatican Swindle,* 1925; as *Lafcadio's Adventures,* 1927; as *The Vatican Cellars,* 1952.

Les Faux-monnayeurs.   1926; as *The Counterfeiters,* 1927; as *The Coiners,* 1950.
L'École des femmes.   1929; as *The School for Wives,* 1929.
Thésée.   1946; translated as *Theseus,* 1948.

Plays

Philoctète (produced 1919).   1899; as *Philoctetes,* in *My Theatre,* 1952; also in *The Return of the Prodigal,* 1953.
Le Roi Candaule (produced 1901).   1901; as *King Candaules,* in *My Theatre,* 1952.
Saül (produced 1922).   1903; as *Saul,* in *My Theatre,* 1952; also in *The Return of the Prodigal,* 1953.
Le Retour de l'enfant prodigue (produced 1928).   1909.
Bethsabé.   1912; as *Bathsheba,* in *My Theatre,* 1952; also in *The Return of the Prodigal,* 1953.
Antoine et Cléopatre, from the play by Shakespeare (produced 1920).   In *Théâtre complet,* 1947.
Amal; ou, La Lettre du roi, from the play by Tagore (produced 1928).   1922.
Robert: Supplément a l'école des femmes (produced 1946).   1930; as *Robert; ou, L'Intérêt général,* 1949.
Oedipe (produced 1931).   1931; as *Oedipus,* in *Two Legends,* 1950.
Les Caves du Vatican, from his own novel (produced 1933).   In *Théâtre complet,* 1948.
Perséphone (libretto), music by Igor Stravinsky (produced 1934).   1934; edited by Patrick Pollard, 1977; translated as *Persephone,* in *My Theater,* 1952.
Geneviève.   1936.
Le treizième arbre (produced 1939).   In *Théâtre,* 1942; as *The Thirteenth Tree,* adapted by Diane Moore, 1987.
Théâtre.   1942; as *My Theater,* 1952.
Hamlet, from the play by Shakespeare (produced 1946).   In *Théâtre complet,* 1949.
Le Procès, with Jean-Louis Barrault, from the novel by Kafka (produced 1947).   1947; translated as *The Trial,* 1950.
Théâtre complet.   8 vols., 1947–49.

Verse

Les Poésies d'André Walter.   1892.

Other

Le Traité du Narcisse.   1891; as *Narcissus,* in *The Return of the Prodigal,* 1953.
Réflexions sur quelques points de littérature et de morale. 1897.
Feuilles de route 1895–1896.   1899.
Philoctète, suivi de Le Traité du Narcisse, La Tentative amoureuse, El Hadj.   1899; in *The Return of the Prodigal,* 1953.
De l'influence en littérature.   1900.
Lettres à Angèle (1898–1899).   1900.
Les Limites de l'art.   1901.
De l'importance du public.   1903.
Prétextes.   1903; enlarged edition, 1913; in *Pretexts: Reflections on Literature and Morality,* edited by Justin O'Brien, 1959.
Amyntas.   1906; translated as *Amyntas,* 1958.
Dostoïevsky d'après sa correspondance.   1908.
Oscar Wilde.   1910; translated as *Oscar Wilde,* 1951.
Charles-Louis Philippe.   1911.
C.R.D.N.   1911; enlarged edition as *Corydon* (privately printed), 1920; 2nd edition, 1925; translated as *Corydon,* 1950.

Nouveaux prétextes.   1911; in *Pretexts: Reflections on Literature and Morality,* edited by Justin O'Brien, 1959.
Souvenirs de la cour d'assises.   1914; as *Recollections of the Assize Court,* 1941.
Si le grain ne meurt.   2 vols., 1920–21; as *If It Die . . . ,* 1935.
Numquid et tu . . . ?   1922; translated in *Journal,* 1952.
Dostoïevsky.   1923; translated as *Dostoevsky,* 1925.
Incidences.   1924.
Caractères.   1925.
Le Journal des faux-monnayeurs.   1926; as *Journal of the Counterfeiters,* 1951; as *Logbook of the Coiners,* 1952.
Dindiki.   1927.
Émile Verhaeren.   1927.
Joseph Conrad.   1927.
Voyage au Congo.   1927; in *Travels in the Congo,* 1929.
Le Retour du Tchad, suivi du Voyage au Congo, Carnets de route.   1928; as *Travels in the Congo,* 1929.
Travels in the Congo.   1929.
Essai sur Montaigne.   1929; translated as *Montaigne: An Essay in Two Parts,* 1929.
Un Esprit non prévenu.   1929.
Lettres.   1930.
L'Affaire Redureau, suivie de Faits divers.   1930.
Le Sequestrée de Poitiers.   1930.
Jacques Rivière.   1931.
Divers.   1931.
Oeuvres complètes, edited by Louis Martin-Chauffier.   15 vols., 1932–39; *Index,* 1954.
Les nouvelles nourritures.   1935; in *Fruits of the Earth,* 1949.
Retour de l'U.R.S.S.   1936; *Retouches,* 1937; as *Return from the U.S.S.R.,* 1937; as *Back from the U.S.S.R.,* 1937.
Journal 1889–1939.   1939; *1939–1942,* 1946; *1942–1949,* 1950; translated as *Journals 1889–1949,* edited by Justin O'Brien,   4 vols., 1947–51.
Découvrons Henri Michaux.   1941.
Attendu que.   1943.
Interviews imaginaires.   1943; as *Imaginary Interviews,* 1944.
Jeunesse.   1945.
Lettres à Christian Beck.   1946.
Souvenirs littératures et problèmes actuels.   1946.
Et nunc manet in te.   1947; as *The Secret Drama of My Life,* 1951; as *Madeleine,* 1952.
Paul Valéry.   1947.
Poétique.   1947.
Correspondance 1893–1938, with Francis Jammes, edited by Robert Mallet.   1948.
Notes sur Chopin.   1948; as *Notes on Chopin,* 1949.
Préfaces.   1948.
Rencontres.   1948.
Correspondance 1899–1926, with Paul Claudel, edited by Robert Mallet.   1949; as *The Correspondence 1899–1926,* 1952.
Feuillets d'automne.   1949; as *Autumn Leaves,* 1950.
Lettres, with Charles du Bos.   1950.
Littérature engagée, edited by Yvonne Davet.   1950.
Égypte 1939.   1951.
Ainsi soit-il; ou, Les Jeux sont faits.   1952; as *So Be It; or, The Chips Are Down,* 1960.
Correspondance 1909–1926, with Rainer Maria Rilke, edited by Renée Lang.   1952.
Lettres à un sculpteur (Simone Marye).   1952.
The Return of the Prodigal (includes *Narcissus,* "The Lovers' Attempt," *El Hadj, Philoctetes, Bathsheba,* and *Saul*).   1953.

Correspondance 1890–1942, with Paul Valéry, edited by Robert Mallet.   1955.

Lettres au Docteur Willy Schuermans (1920–1928).   1955.

Correspondance 1890–1942, with Paul Valéry, edited by Robert Mallet.   1955; as *Self-Portraits: The Gide-Valéry Letters 1890–1942* (abridged edition), edited by Robert Mallet, 1966.

Lettres au Docteur Willy Schuermans (1920–1928).   1955.

Correspondance inédite, with Rilke and Verhaeren, edited by C. Bronne.   1955.

Correspondance, with Marcel Jouhandeau.   1958.

Correspondance 1905–1912, with Charles Péguy, edited by Alfred Saffrey.   1958.

Correspondence 1904–1928, with Edmund Gosse, edited by Linette F. Brugmans.   1960.

Correspondance 1908–1920, with André Suarès, edited by Sidney D. Braun.   1963.

Correspondance 1911–1931, with Arnold Bennett, edited by Linette F. Brugmans.   1964.

Correspondance 1909–1951, with André Rouveyre, edited by Claude Martin.   1967.

Correspondance 1913–1951, with Roger Martin du Gard, edited by Jean Delay.   2 vols., 1968.

Lettres, with Jean Cocteau, edited by Jean-Jacques Kihm.   1970.

Correspondance 1912–1950, with François Mauriac, edited by Jacqueline Morton.   1971.

Le Récit de Michel, edited by Claude Martin.   1972.

Correspondance, with Charles Brunard.   1974.

Correspondance 1891–1938, with Albert Mockel, edited by Gustave Vanwelkenhuyzen.   1975.

Correspondance, with Jules Romains, edited by Claude Martin.   1976; supplement, 1979.

Correspondance 1897–1944, with Henri Ghéon, edited by Jean Tipy.   2 vols., 1976.

Correspondance 1892–1939, with Jacques-Émile Blanche, edited by Georges-Paul Collet.   1979.

Correspondance, with Justin O'Brien, edited by Jacqueline Morton.   1979.

Correspondance, with Dorothy Bussy, edited by Jean Lambert.   2 vols., 1979-81; as *Selected Letters*, edited by Richard Tedeschi, 1983.

Correspondance 1907–1950, with François-Paul Alibert, edited by Claude Martin.   1982.

Correspondance 1929–1940, with Jean Giono, edited by Roland Bourneuf and Jacques Cotnam.   1983.

Correspondance 1934–1950, with Jef Last, edited by C.J. Greshoff.   1985.

La Correspondance générale de Gide, edited by Claude Martin.   1985.

Correspondance, with Harry Kessler, edited by Claude Foucart.   1985.

Correspondance 1927–1950, with Thea Sternheim, edited by Claude Foucart.   1986.

Correspondance 1891–1931, with Francis Viélé-Griffin, edited by Henri de Paysac.   1986.

Correspondance 1902–1928, with Anna de Noailles, edited by Claude Mignot-Ogliastri.   1986.

Correspondance, with Jacques Copeau, edited by Jean Claude,   2 vols., 1987-88.

Correspondance avec sa mère 1880–1895, edited by Claude Martin.   1988.

Correspondance 1903–1938, with Valery Larbaud, edited by Françoise Lioure.   1989.

Correspondance, with André Ruyters, edited by Claude Martin and Victor Martin-Schmets.   2 vols., 1990.

Editor, *The Living Thoughts of Montaigne*.   1939.

Editor, *Anthologie de la poésie française*.   1949.

Translator, *Typhon*, by Joseph Conrad.   1918.

Translator, with J. Schiffrin, *Nouvelles; Recits*, by Aleksandr Pushkin.   2 vols., 1929–35.

Translator, *Arden of Faversham*, in *Le Théâtre élizabethain*.   1933.

Translator, *Prométhée*, by Goethe.   1951.

*

Bibliography: *An Annotated Bibliography of Criticism on Gide 1973–1988* by Catharine Savage Brosman, 1990.

Critical Studies: *Gide*, 1951, and *Gide: A Critical Biography*, 1968, both by George D. Painter; *Gide* by Enid Starkie, 1953; *The Theatre of Gide* by J.C. McLaren, 1953; *Gide and the Hound of Heaven* by H. March, 1953; *Portrait of Gide* by Justin O'Brien, 1953; *Gide* by Albert Guerard, 1963, revised edition, 1969; *Gide: His Life and Work* by Wallace Fowlie, 1965; *Gide: The Evolution of an Aesthetic* by Vinio Rossi, 1967; *Gide and the Greek Myth* by Helen Watson-Williams, 1967; *Gide* by Thomas Cordle, 1969; *Gide: A Study of His Creative Writings* by G.W. Ireland, 1970; *Gide: A Collection of Critical Essays* edited by David Littlejohn, 1970; *Gide and the Art of Autobiography* by C.D.E. Tolton, 1975; *Gide and the Codes of Homotextuality* by Emily S. Apter, 1987; *Gide* by David H. Walker, 1990; *Gide: Homosexual Moralist* by Patrick Pollard, 1991.

*   *   *

André Gide was too complex a figure to be neatly pigeon-holed. Novelist, playwright, autobiographer, and philosopher, he also kept a valuable journal and translated Shakespeare, William Blake, and Joseph Conrad into French. He was born into a prosperous middle-class family and enjoyed a private income which freed him from the necessity of earning a living. This gave him the liberty to write whenever and whatever he pleased, and the result was a prolific body of work that made him one of the leading French authors and prose stylists of the 20th century. His books vary in length from *Les Faux-monnayeurs (The Counterfeiters)*, a large-scale work that anticipated Faulkner and Dos Passos in its use of the technique of simultaneity, to brief essays of reminiscence like *Oscar Wilde* and writings about travel and music. (He was a gifted amateur pianist specialising in Chopin.)

His was a divided spirit. Although a homosexual who found adventure with Arab boys on his travels in North Africa, in his late twenties he married his cousin Madeleine. The conflict between homosexuality and the state of marriage is depicted in *L'Immoraliste (The Immoralist)*, which, like most of his writing, is autobiographical. The marriage remained unconsummated, although, having been brought up in a strict, almost Calvinistic Protestantism, Gide claimed to have a deep spiritual affection for his wife.

From all the stress and turmoil of his private life, Gide distilled a series of intensely personal writings. Like Montaigne, with whom he has sometimes been compared, he could say that his main subject was himself. When he pictures the conflict between homosexuality and marriage in *The Immoralist*, he is exploring his own personal dilemma. When he charts the mysticism of love in *La Porte étroite (Strait Is the Gate)*, he is describing his own religious problems. We cannot, therefore, expect of so inward-looking an author the sort of features we look for in more conventional writers: character drawing, neat plotting, well-balanced narrative. All Gide's very diverse writings neat plotting, well-balanced narrative. All Gide's very diverse writings are merely instalments of an emotional and philosophical development which is continually unfolding. It follows, inevitably, that he does not write short stories in the sense that Maupassant or Maugham or Chekov understood the term, whereby characters are involved in situations that are resolved within the space of a few pages.

What he did write were short pieces, often called "treatises," which discuss a particular idea or put forward a commentary on life. *Le Retour de l'enfant prodigue (The Return of the Prodigal)*, for example, is typical of him in that he takes a well-known story, in this case from the Bible, and turns it into a personal statement about his own spiritual pilgrimage. With *Thésée (Theseus)*, he calls on Greek myth, and, while following the main lines of the old legend, contrives to shape it into an allegory with several layers of meaning. The narrative becomes a debate between Oedipus and Theseus, in which they discuss the nature of heroism and wisdom. Theseus draws on his experience to argue that man must always strive to overcome the obstacles that fate places in his way. By contrast, when Oedipus blinded himself, Theseus suggests, he was admitting defeat and accepting the idea of guilt. Oedipus retorts that by so doing he was affirming his superiority to destiny. Theseus remains unconvinced.

Another classical legend that Gide used for his own purpose was that of Prometheus. The scene of *Le Prométhée mal enchaîné (Prometheus Misbound)* is a Parisian café. Here a random gathering of customers is assembled by a waiter who, not being seated at a table and taking no part in the conversation, claims that he is disinterested and can describe his act as "gratuitous." This is the nub of the discussion that follows, led by Prometheus who designs to call in at the café. The idea of "gratuitous action" (*l'acte gratuit*) was one that fascinated Gide, and it appears in a number of other works, notably *Les Caves du Vatican (The Vatican Cellars)*. Is there such a thing, he keeps asking himself, as a purely disinterested action? Once an action has been performed it tends to swallow up the personality of the one who performed it, just as the eagle in the Greek legend devoured the flesh of Prometheus. In the end Gide was forced to admit that a wholly disinterested action was impossible and that "gratuitous" action was nothing more than inconsequence.

Again taking his cue from classical literature, this time from Corydon, the name of Virgil's Arcadian shepherd who has become a symbol of homosexual love, Gide wrote an apologia for his own homosexuality. *C.R.D.N. (Corydon)* appeared in 1911 and caused something of a scandal. It takes the shape of a Platonic dialogue in which Gide attempts to dispute the generally held opinion that pederasty was unnatural and a danger to society. He draws on biological evidence, some of it rather dubious, to show that since homosexuality is prevalent among many animals, this must be proof that the conditions cannot be harmful to nature. As for any danger to society, Gide claims that, while the female is confined to the biological function, the male is free to devote himself to a wide variety of other interests, such as the arts, sport and, presumably, pederasty. The argument, put thus baldly, may seem thin, but Gide clothes it in very readable and persuasive language.

"I am the only person who interests me," said Montaigne. So could Gide have remarked. His shorter writings, too formless to be called short stories, are, rather, fascinating

explorations of an intricate personality which was self-contradictory, elusive, sometimes baffling and exasperating, but always very human.

—James Harding

See the essays on *The Immoralist* and *Strait Is the Gate*.

GILMAN, Charlotte (Anna) Perkins (Stetson). American. Born in Hartford, Connecticut, 3 July 1860. Studied art, Rhode Island School of Design, Providence, 1878–79. Married 1) (Charles) Walter Stetson in 1884 (divorced 1894), one daughter (died 1979); 2) George Houghton Gilman in 1900 (died 1943). Treated for hysteria by Dr. S. Weir Mitchell, 1886; moved to Pasadena, California, 1888; playwright with Grace Channing, 1888–91; ran a boarding house, 1890's; co-editor, *The Impress* journal, San Francisco, 1894; full-time writer, activist in women's suffrage movement, public speaker, and lecturer, from mid–1890's; moved to New York City, 1900; lectured in Europe, 1905; editor and writer, *The Forerunner* magazine, 1909–1916; moved to Pasadena, 1934. *Died (suicide) 17 August 1935.*

PUBLICATIONS

Short Stories

The Yellow Wallpaper (novella).   1899; edited by Elaine Hedge, 1973.

Novels

The Crux.   1911.
Moving the Mountain.   1911.
What Diantha Did.   1912.
Herland: A Lost Feminist Utopia, edited by Ann J. Lane. 1979.

Verse

In This Our World.   1893.
Suffrage Songs and Verses.   1911.

Other

A Clarion Call to Redeem the Race!   1890.
Women and Economics.   1898.
Concerning Children.   1900.
The Home, Its Work and Influence.   1903.
Human Work.   1904.
The Punishment that Educates.   1907.
The Man-Made World; or, Our Androcentric Culture. 1911.
His Religion and Hers: A Study of the Faith of Our Fathers and the Work of Our Mothers.   1923.
The Living of Gilman (autobiography).   1935.
The Gilman Reader: "The Yellow Wallpaper" and Other Fiction, edited by Ann J. Lane.   1980.
Gilman: A Non-Fiction Reader, edited by Larry Ceplair. 1991.

*

Bibliography: *Gilman: A Bibliography* by Gary Scharnhorst, 1985.

Critical Studies: "Gilman on the Theory and Practice of Feminism" by Carl N. Degler, in *American Quarterly* 8, Spring 1956; *Gilman: The Making of a Radical Feminist* by Mary A. Hill, 1980; *Building Domestic Liberty: Gilman's Architectural Feminism* by Polly Wynn Allen, 1988; *Gilman: The Woman and Her Work* edited by Sheryl L. Meyering, 1989; *To Herland and Beyond: The Life and Work of Gilman* by Ann J. Lane, 1990; *The Captive Imagination: A Casebook on The Yellow Wallpaper* edited by Catherine Golden, 1992; *Critical Essays on Gilman* edited by Joanne B. Karpinski, 1992.

*   *   *

Charlotte Perkins Gilman, a prominent intellectual in the woman's movement in the United States early in the 20th century, began her public career as a poet and writer of short fiction during the 1890's. A skilled and versatile writer, Gilman was also an unapologetic polemicist whose writings were fundamentally didactic.

In a pair of stories published in 1891 and 1892 in *The New England Magazine,* Gilman experimented in the female gothic mode. "The Giant Wistaria" is, in its most elementary sense, a formulaic ghost story about an unwed mother, a victim of Puritan patriarchy in the person of her tyrannical father, whose spirit haunts a decaying New England mansion. Several visitors detect the presence of her ghost in and around the house. The tale is more than a superficial indictment of sexual oppression, however. By piecing together a number of disparate clues, the reader learns that the woman whose ghost stalks the house killed her child and starved to death rather than submit to her father's demand that she abandon the child and marry for appearance's sake. Under the circumstances, the murder and suicide seem acts of heroic defiance that save her and her child from lives of shame. Terrorized by men in life, the woman becomes a source of terror to men in afterlife.

The story is thus a companion piece to "The Yellow Wallpaper," Gilman's most celebrated story, which she wrote only five months later. The narrator of this tale, who suffers from severe post-partum depression, moves with her husband and child into a rented seaside estate where she might enjoy complete rest. Her physician-husband in fact prescribes the "rest cure" popularized by the nerve specialist S. Weir Mitchell, the implied villain of the story, who had treated Gilman under similar circumstances in 1886. Over the course of several weeks, the narrator becomes progressively insane. Forbidden to read or write, she begins to discern the crouching figure of a woman trapped in the patterned wallpaper of her garret-room; that is, the narrator begins to read in the paper dim inferences of her own predicament. Every few days, she records her discoveries in a concealed diary, an act of rebellion against the patriarchal strictures of her physician-husband. The tale ends as she peels yards of paper from the walls to free the trapped woman, with whom she entirely identifies in her madness.

Until recently, "The Giant Wistaria" was unknown to modern readers and "The Yellow Wallpaper" seemed little more than a tale of grotesque horror. Read as subtle critiques or subversions of gender hierarchies, however, these two stories rank as minor masterpieces. The heroine of the first no less than the narrator of the second is confined in a prisonhouse of language. Neither woman is permitted to describe her predicament as a victim of the patriarchal order; indeed, the first disappears from the story, at least in a corporeal sense, after speaking a total of three sentences while the second writes a clandestine epistolary tale, an absolutely forbidden discourse. Each of them, rather than submit to the demands of male authority, devises a set of signs that defy patriarchal control.

After these tales appeared in the early 1890's, Gilman published little fiction until she began to issue *The Forerunner* in 1909. She included a short story and an installment of a serialized novel in each monthly issue of this magazine over a period of over seven years. With rare exceptions, her short tales were either feminist fantasies or parables about the economic independence of women. The stories of the former type tend to be whimsical and satirical, those of the latter type more contrived and repetitive. The feminist fantasies include "If I Were a Man," in which "pretty little Mollie Mathewson" awakens one morning to discover that she has been transformed into her husband Gerald. S/he enjoys such novel experiences as the sensation of money in the pocket, and at the office s/he defends women from men's slanderous gossip. Similarly, in "When I Was a Witch," the narrator suddenly acquires the power to make her fondest wishes a reality. She metes out punishment to those who abuse animals, sell contaminated milk or meat, or shortchange their customers. At her bidding, newspapers print their lies in a different shade of ink. When she wishes that women "might realize their Womanhood at last," however, nothing happens because "this magic which had fallen on me was black magic—and I had wished white." Such a conclusion betrays Gilman's fear of the resiliency of traditional gender roles.

Gilman's parables of economic independence were more conventional, certainly more formulaic and predictable, than her satirical fantasies. In each of these success stories, the heroine is freed from dependence upon men, often as the result of death or temporary separation from her husband, often with the aid of another woman who acts as her patron. In "The Widow's Might," for example, a middle-aged widow declares her intention to live on the wealth she helped her late husband accumulate rather than save it for their grown children. In "Mrs. Beazley's Deeds," the heroine is counseled by "the best woman lawyer in New York" to retain control of inherited property rather than give title to her ne'er-do-well husband. She opens a boardinghouse and becomes self-reliant while he eventually flees the state to escape his creditors. And in "Mrs. Elder's Idea," the middle-aged heroine refuses to follow her husband into retirement; instead, she begins a new career as a professional buyer. Though initially disconcerted, her husband is reconciled to the change when he realizes that she is happier than she would have been unemployed. That is, Gilman illustrated her belief that the economic independence of women, rather than a threat to the family, would improve and refine the marital institution.

Gilman allowed in her autobiography that her fiction was "more difficult" to write than her essays. Still, she published some 170 "pastels" and short stories during her career, most of them in *The Forerunner.* They were not "literature," or so Gilman protested, but "propaganda" with overt purpose. They were "written to drive nails with." Her protests notwithstanding, of course, Gilman attained a level of complexity and artistry in "The Giant Wistaria" and "The Yellow Wallpaper" that none of her later stories exhibit.

—Gary Scharnhorst

See the essay on "The Yellow Wallpaper."

GOGOL (Ianovskii), Nikolai (Vasil'evich). Russian. Born in Sorochintsii, 19 March 1809. Educated at Nezhin high school, 1821–28. Civil servant, 1828–31; history teacher, Patriotic Institute, St. Petersburg, and private tutor, 1831–34; assistant lecturer in history, University of St. Petersburg, 1834–36; in Western Europe, 1836–39, 1842–48. *Died 21 February 1852.*

PUBLICATIONS

Collections

Works.   6 vols., 1922–27.
Polnoe sobranie sochinenii [Complete Works].   14 vols., 1937–52.
The Collected Plays and Tales, edited by Leonard J. Kent. 1969.
The Theatre of Gogol: Plays and Selected Writings, edited by Milton Ehre.   1980.
Selection.   1980.
The Complete Tales, edited by Leonard J. Kent.   2 vols., 1985.

Short Stories

Vechera na khutore bliz Dikanki [Evenings on a Farm near Dikanka].   1831–32.
Mirgorod.   1835; as *Mirgorod, Being a Continuation of Evenings in a Village near Dikanka,* 1928.
Arabeski.   1835; as *Arabesques,* 1982.
Cossack Tales.   1860.
St. John's Eve and Other Stories from "Evenings at the Farm" and "St. Petersburg Stories."   1886.
Taras Bulba, also St. John's Eve and Other Stories.   1887.
Tales.   1945.

Novel

Mertvye dushi.   1842; as *Home Life in Russia,* 1854; as *Tchitchikoff's Journeys,* 1886; as *Dead Souls,* 1887.

Plays

Revizor (produced 1836).   1836; as *The Inspector-General,* 1892; as *The Government Inspector,* in *Works,* 1927.
Zhenitba (produced 1842).   1841; as *The Marriage,* in *Works,* 1927.
Igroki.   1842; as *The Gamblers,* in *Works,* 1927.

Other

Sochineniia.   2 vols., 1842.
Vybrannye mesta iz perepiski s druz'iami [Selected Passages from Correspondence with Friends].   1847.
Meditations on the Divine Liturgy.   1913; as *The Divine Liturgy of the Russian Orthodox Church,* 1960.
Letters, edited by Carl R. Proffer.   1967.

*

Bibliography: *Gogol: A Bibliography* by Philip E. Frantz, 1989.

Critical Studies: *Gogol* by Vladimir Nabokov, 1944; *Gogol as a Short Story Writer* by F.C. Driessen, 1965; *Gogol: His Life and Works* by Vsevolod Setchkarev, 1965; *Gogol: The Biography of a Divided Soul* by Henri Troyat, 1974; *Gogol from the Twentieth Century* edited by Robert A. Maguire, 1974, revised edition, 1976; *The Sexual Labyrinth of Gogol* by Simon Karlinsky, 1976; *Through Gogol's Looking Glass: Reverse Vision, False Focus, and Precarious Logic* by William Woodin Rowe, 1976; *Gogol's Dead Souls,* 1978, and *The Symbolic Art of Gogol: Essays on His Short Fiction,* 1982, both by James B. Woodward; *The Creation of Gogol* by Donald Fanger, 1979; *Out from under Gogol's "Overcoat": A Psychoanalytical Study* by Daniel Rancour-Laferriere, 1982; *The Enigma of Gogol* by Richard Peace, 1981; *Such Things Happen in the World!: Something Deixis in Three Short Stories by Gogol* by P.M. Vaszink, 1988; *Gogol: Text and Context* edited by Jane Grayson and Faith Wigzell, 1989.

*   *   *

Nikolai Gogol occupies a unique place in Russian literature as a 19th-century writer whose vision of the world, while in essence a moral one, nonetheless defies any conventional categorization, and is preoccupied mainly with realms of fantasy that at times seem extraordinarily modern and surrealistic. In general it may be said that Gogol's universe, though decidedly grounded in the physical and material, is in a constant state of change and transformation that carry it towards concerns that are spiritual and metaphysical. As a short story writer, Gogol developed and extended the tradition that was established by Pushkin in his *Tales of Belkin* (1830), preserving the concision and irony of Pushkin's prose style, while allowing a freer play of imaginative resources.

Gogol's earliest mature work of fiction, the story cycle *Vechera na Khutore bliz Dikanki* (Evenings on a Farm near Dikanka), though still largely rooted in an essentially realistic narrative mode, is characterized by a sunny humour that derives from 18th-century literary models, in particular the novels of Sterne. The stories, which portray life and legend in the rural depths of the Ukraine, are full of an almost Rabelaisian earthiness and vitality. Yet several of the tales—"Christmas Eve" and "May Night" among them—have the night as their background, and dramatic and tragic narratives alternate with cheerful, lyrical ones. In most of them there is a sense of fate guiding the lives and fortunes of men and women, and there is frequent intervention by demons and devils, even in the farce-like "Sorochinsky Fair." The story "A Terrible Vengeance" shows the influence not only of Ukrainian heroic poetry, but also of German romantic writing, in particular that of Tieck and Hoffman, and also of the French "frenetic school," with its central elements of incest, daughter-murder, and descriptions of blood and horror. The tales of *Mirgorod,* written as a sequel to *Vechera na khutore bliz Dikanki,* show a retreat from the themes of love and sexuality that play a prominent role in the early stories. Hugh Maclean has suggested that Gogol established a connection between sexuality and death which brought about this change in his attitude. Perhaps the most immediately striking and memorable story in the second group of tales is "The Story of How Ivan Ivanovich Quarreled with Ivan Nikiforovich," which points the way towards a more general critique of human existence. The tale, which describes a futile and banal dispute between two equally bone-headed protagonists, develops the theme of *poshlost*, an almost untranslatable concept that contains the notions of vulgarity and complacent blindness to higher values. "It's tedious in this world, ladies and gentlemen," the narrator concludes.

In his fantastic stories, which were originally published as part of *Arabeski (Arabesques)*, a collection of historical and philosophical essays interspersed with short narratives, Gogol changed the scene of action from the countryside of the Ukraine to St. Petersburg. The model here was once again a foreign one: the French urban chronicle, in which a correspondent provides his readers with reports from the streets and side-lanes of the great city. The genre, as it developed in Russia, had a vaguely philanthropic and socially critical tendency, and the writers who practised it were sometimes referred to as the "natural school" (*natural'naya shkola*). Gogol, however, used the genre in his own way, as a vehicle for sharply delineated reflections on the purpose and significance of human life in general. The central themes of the stories are loneliness and loss, and the narrator gives an impression of being thoroughly alienated and repelled by the urban reality he describes, refusing to see in St. Petersburg's majestic prospects and facades anything but human misery—a place that is half a hell and half a madhouse, to quote one critic. Perhaps the most typical story of the collection is "The Nevsky Prospect," which gives an account of the pursuit by two friends of two women. Lieutenant Piskarev romantically woos a woman who turns out to be a prostitute and eventually brings about his death, while the painter Pirogov—the name suggests boundless materialism and is derived from the Russian word for "pie"—finds happiness with a female German artisan. At the end of the story the narrator warns his readers against the Nevsky Prospect, calling it a place of shifting illusions where the devil himself lights the lamps in order to make everything appear in a false illumination.

—David McDuff

See the essays on "The Nose" and "The Overcoat."

GORDIMER, Nadine. South African. Born in Springs, Transvaal, 20 November 1923. Educated at a convent school, and the University of the Witwatersrand, Johannesburg. Married 1) G. Gavron in 1949; 2) Reinhold Cassirer in 1954; one son and one daughter. Visiting lecturer, Institute of Contemporary Arts, Washington, D.C., 1961, Harvard University, Cambridge, Massachusetts, 1969, Princeton University, New Jersey, 1969, Northwestern University, Evanston, Illinois, 1969, and University of Michigan, Ann Arbor, 1970; adjunct professor of writing, Columbia University, New York, 1971; presenter, *Frontiers* television series, 1990. Recipient: W.H. Smith literary award, 1961; Thomas Pringle award, 1969; James Tait Black memorial prize, 1972; Booker prize, 1974; Grand Aigle d'Or prize (France), 1975; CNA award, 1975; Scottish Arts Council Neil Gunn fellowship, 1981; Common Wealth award, 1981; Modern Language Association award (U.S.), 1981; Malaparte prize (Italy), 1985; Nelly Sachs prize (Germany), 1985; Bennett award (U.S.), 1986; Royal Society of Literature Benson medal, 1990; Nobel prize for literature, 1991. D.Lit.: University of Leuven, Belgium, 1980; D.Litt.: Smith College, Northampton, Massachusetts, 1985; City College, New York, 1985; Mount Holyoke College, South Hadley, Massachusetts, 1985. Honorary member, American Academy of Arts and Sciences, 1980; honorary fellow, Modern Language Association (U.S.), 1985. Lives in Johannesburg.

PUBLICATIONS

Short Stories

Face to Face: Short Stories.   1949.
The Soft Voice of the Serpent and Other Stories.   1952.
Six Feet of the Country.   1956.
Friday's Footprint and Other Stories.   1960.
Not for Publication and Other Stories.   1965.
Livingstone's Companions.   1971.
Selected Stories.   1975; as *No Place Like*, 1978.
Some Monday for Sure.   1976.
A Soldier's Embrace.   1980.
Town and Country Lovers (story).   1980.
Something Out There.   1984.
Crimes of Conscience.   1991.
Jump and Other Stories.   1991.

Novels

The Lying Days.   1953.
A World of Strangers.   1958.
Occasion for Loving.   1963.
The Late Bourgeois World.   1966.
A Guest of Honour.   1970.
The Conservationist.   1974.
Burger's Daughter.   1979.
July's People.   1981.
A Sport of Nature.   1987.
My Son's Story.   1990.

Plays

Television Plays and Documentaries: *A Terrible Chemistry* (*Writers and Places* series), 1981; *Choosing for Justice: Allan Boesak*, with Hugo Cassirer, 1985; *Country Lovers, A Chip of Glass Ruby, Praise, and Oral History* (all in *The Gordimer Stories* series), 1985 (U.S.); *Frontier* series, 1990 (U.K.).

Other

African Lit. (lectures).   1972.
On the Mines, photographs by David Goldblatt.   1973.
The Black Interpreters: Notes on African Writing.   1973.
What Happened to Burger's Daughter; or, How South African Censorship Works, with others.   1980.
Lifetimes: Under Apartheid, photographs by David Goldblatt.   1986.
The Essential Gesture: Writing, Politics, and Places, edited by Stephen Clingman.   1988.
Conversations with Gordimer, edited by Nancy Topping Bazin and Marilyn Dallman Seymour.   1990.

Editor, with Lionel Abrahams, *South African Writing Today*.   1967.

*

Bibliography: *Gordimer, Novelist and Short Story Writer: A Bibliography of Her Works* by Racilia Jilian Nell, 1964.

Critical Studies: *Gordimer* by Robert F. Haugh, 1974; *Gordimer* by Michael Wade, 1978; *Gordimer* by Christopher Heywood, 1983; *The Novels of Gordimer: Private Lives/Public Landscapes* by John Cooke, 1985; *Gordimer* by Judie Newman, 1988; *Critical Essays on Gordimer* edited by Rowland Smith, 1990; "Feminism as 'Piffling'? Ambiguities in Some of Gordimer's Short Stories," in *Current Writing* 2, 1990, and "Something Out There/Something in There: Gender and Politics in Gordimer's Novella," in *English in Africa* 19, May 1992, both by Karen Lazar.

*   *   *

Nadine Gordimer, winner of the Nobel prize for literature in 1991, is well known as a novelist. However, her first published books were short story collections and she has continued to produce internationally-acclaimed short fiction. Gordimer's short stories constitute a detailed guide to her development as a writer. Many of the broad themes of her novels receive their first airing in short story form, as in the case of the relationship between "Six Feet of the Country" and *The Conservationist*. And, in particular, the evolution of Gordimer's social and political awareness is scrupulously charted by her successive volumes of short fiction. Moreover, although Gordimer has remained a somewhat conventional novelist, relying to a considerable extent on the assumptions of 19th-century realism, that is not quite the case in her short stories. Later collections like *A Soldier's Embrace* reveal a greater imaginative and formal range than the author's longer works.

Central as the short story is to Gordimer's reputation and significance, it is clear that the form could not always accomodate her subject. The vicious ironies of life among and between the races in South Africa are not confronted with consistent incisiveness. Early stories, such as "Is There Nowhere Else Where We Can Meet?" and "Ah, Woe Is Me," represent the tension between the races, and reveal a young writer's impressive skill in depicting both the internal and external landscapes in which her characters discover their reality. What is missing from these early stories is a sense of the characters' social dimension, an omission that is particularly eloquent in "The Soft Voice of the Serpent," with its stifling sense of unnamed trouble in white South Africa's paradise.

It is precisely this social component that Gordimer's later short stories articulate. In order to do so, the author had to acknowledge the intensely bureaucratized nature of South African social life, an instance of which forms one level of "Six Feet of the Country," as well as the human, or dehumanizing, costs of such moral policing. The difficulty of dismantling barriers is not only an obviously political one. In a more fundamental sense, it is, for the characters of this story, a moral difficulty. It is even possible to suggest that this is essentially an imaginative problem. The white couple in the story ultimately fail to imagine what the family of the dead African have to go through to in order to reclaim the body. The tacit intersection of the moral and the imaginative in the author's mind serves as a reproach to her fellow-countrymen for denying themselves the degree of humanity that such a coalition of psychological and cultural forces might potentiate.

In order to write such a story, or the more actively multi-racial story "The Smell of Death and Flowers," which cautions against a facile identification with the black struggle in South Africa on the part of naive whites, Gordimer has to represent a set of social conditions in which officialdom's barriers have already been significantly relaxed. To assume this state of affairs as an imaginative given, Gordimer enters into the minds of blacks and other non-white characters, thereby conferring on them an equality that in the mind of the South African authorities and their supporters, they should be historically, culturally, and socially denied. While Gordimer also dissects the mentality of white South Africa in such stories as "The Night the Winner Came Home" and "The Bridegroom," it is with her non-white fellow-countrymen that her work becomes increasingly concerned.

This concern has the effect of introducing a conspicuous political element into Gordimer's stories, evident in the stories in *Not for Publication*. The title story deals with the cultural formation of a black African politician. "Some Monday for Sure," represents the aspirations of militant blacks within South Africa. This radical political emphasis also is seen in the title story of *Livingstone's Companions,* in which both the regime of an emergent black African state are the superficial, though economically tenacious, white presence and ineffectual heirs of the colonial enterprise. The title novella of *Something Out There* provides a comparable though more elaborate account of that enterprise's fate in a strictly South African context. These two works provide a kind of summation of Gordimer's anatomy of her imaginative world's geo-political reality and its human consequences. Many of the stories in her later collections are noteworthy for their concentrated, parable-like brevity.

Gordimer's path-breaking short fiction is distinguished by sharp characterization, attentive and patient description of the natural phenomena surrounding her characters, and a highly developed moral sense of the elaborate social strata which constitute her country's society, in particular the city of Johannesburg, where Gordimer has spent her working life. In addition to its obvious courage, her work is notable for its intelligence. This latter quality is not merely evident in the interest Gordimer's work takes in the nature of ideas and its impact on the lives of her characters. At a more primary level, she brings a sense of impassioned cerebration to her contemplation of the anomalies, vicissitudes, challenge, and heartbreak for which her time and place have become synonymous.

—George O'Brien

See the essays on "Something Out There," "The Train from Rhodesia," and "The Ultimate Safari."

* * *

GORDON, Caroline. American. Born in Todd County, Kentucky, 6 October 1895. Educated at Bethany College, West Virginia, A.B. in Greek 1916. Married Allen Tate in 1924 (divorced and remarried 1946; separated 1955; divorced 1959); one daughter. High school teacher, 1917–19; reporter, Chattanooga *News,* Tennessee, 1920–24; secretary to the writer Ford Madox Ford, New York, 1926-28; lived in Europe, 1928–29 and 1932–33; writer-in-residence, University of North Carolina Woman's

College, Greensboro, 1938–39; lecturer in creative writing, School of General Studies, Columbia University, New York, from 1946; visiting professor of English, University of Washington, Seattle, 1953; writer-in-residence, University of Kansas, Lawrence, 1956, University of California, 1962–63, and Purdue University. Lafayette, Indiana, 1963; teacher of creative writing, University of Dallas, after 1973. Joined Catholic Church, 1947. Recipient: Guggenheim fellowship, 1932; O. Henry award, 1934; American Academy grant, 1950; National Endowment for the Arts grant, 1966. D.Litt.: Bethany College, 1946; St. Mary's College, Notre Dame, Indiana, 1964. *Died 11 April 1981.*

PUBLICATIONS

Collections

Collected Stories.   1981.

Short Stories

The Forest of the South.   1945.
Old Red and Other Stories.   1963.

Novels

Penhally.   1931.
Aleck Maury, Sportsman.   1934; as *The Pastimes of Aleck Maury: The Life of a True Sportsman,* 1935.
None Shall Look Back.   1937.
The Garden of Adonis.   1937.
Green Centuries.   1941.
The Women on the Porch.   1944.
The Strange Children.   1951.
The Malefactors.   1956.
The Glory of Hera.   1972.

Other

How to Read a Novel.   1957.
A Good Soldier: A Key to the Novels of Ford Madox Ford. 1963.
The Southern Mandarins: Letters of Gordon to Sally Wood, 1924–1937, edited by Sally Wood.   1984.

Editor, with Allen Tate, *The House of Fiction: An Anthology of the Short Story.*   1950; revised edition, 1960.

*

Bibliography: *Flannery O'Connor and Gordon: A Reference Guide* by Robert E. Golden and Mary C. Sullivan, 1977.

Critical Studies: *Gordon* by Frederick P.W. McDowell, 1966; *Gordon* by W.J. Stuckey, 1972; *The Short Fiction of Gordon: A Critical Symposium* edited by Thomas H. Landess, 1972; *Gordon as Novelist and Woman of Letters* by Rose Ann C. Fraistat, 1984; *Close Connections: Gordon and the S'ern Renaissance* by Ann Waldron, 1987; *Gordon: A Biography* by Veronica A. Makowsky, 1989.

*   *   *

Equally skilled as a novelist and a short story writer, Caroline Gordon made the complex social, psychological, and political transition from the Old South of the 19th century to the New South of the 20th century her special topic. Her studies of middle class Southerners and the passing of the old cultured agrarian squirearchy link her with writers like Eudora Welty, Peter Taylor, or Robert Penn Warren, although she has a distinctive voice and vision.

Gordon's short stories tracing the life of Aleck Maury are among the finest studies of an American sportsman, as insightful and meticulous as the hunting and fishing tales of Ernest Hemingway and William Faulkner. The episodic novel *Aleck Maury, Sportsman* contains most of this material, excepting such brilliant independent stories as "Old Red," "The Presence," "One More Day," "To Thy Chamber Window, Sweet," and "The Last Day in the Field," which complete the saga of Maury, an insouciant classics teacher, gentleman farmer, and devoted sportsman. The stories draw on Gordon's family experiences and include fictionalized glimpses of her and husband Allen Tate at the thresholds of their literary careers.

The region defined by most of Gordon's stories is southeastern Kentucky and northeastern Tennessee, a borderland of small farms—tobacco and horses—and the fields and streams of the Cumberland River valley. Many stories focus on family and social relations in the first half of the century, following the extended family and neighbors of Professor Maury. However, the past—historical and literary—obtrudes into the present culture, with many allusions to mythology and literature, ancient and modern, and to the Civil War as the great determining pivot of Southern society.

A few stories rove to the past: "The Captivity" retells Jenny Wiley's tale, perhaps the most famous Indian-captivity story, and "Hear the Nightingale Sing," "The Forest of the South," and "The Ice House." All are Civil War tales, detailing the impact of the invading Union Army on civilians in the rural South. "A Walk with the Accuser" treats Huguenots in 16th-century France, and "The Olive Garden" and "Emmanuele, Emmanuele!" treat modern French culture.

Gordon's characters are typically highly educated in the literary classics, dwelling in what she called "the forest of the South," like Shakespeare's courtly exiles in the Forest of Arden finding a pleasant, seductive pastoralism in the isolated backwoods. In "The Burning Eyes" we learn of Aleck Maury's late-19th-century childhood and initiation into hunting (by a black tenant farmer and "headlong hunter" of possums). The rural microcosm of Maury's youth is described:

> There was a broad pasture immediately in front of the house, its edges already encroached upon by old-field pines. To the right was a curving stretch of dark woodland. To the left wound away the old red road that led, I knew, to Brackets, and beyond that to Hawkwood and Grassdale. I had visited at these and various other family places in the neighborhood, knew even the savor of the houses, but I could not take these features into my landscape. For me the world as seen from my dooryard was always those woods and the pasture and the old red, winding road.

The woods and roads become means of retreat and escape from family and civilization.

In Gordon's stories, characters seek asylum from society in nature, dealing with the simple certainties of the seasons and animals. She details the intense knowledge and technique necessary for the dedicated hunter or fly fisherman. These skills and knowledge, born of observation and deep emotional experience, contrast with literary learning—the scraps of poetry, myth, the classics—that define the manners of the genteel, feminized household. Aleck Maury spends his life evading the responsibilities of home and hearth by fleeing to the fields and streams, devoting himself to the specialized learning of shotgun and flyrod, so his title of "professor" is especially ironic.

The forces defining Gordon's characters include social duties, family ties, and the weaknesses of the flesh. Marriage is one prison, in a society highly conscious of genealogy and social status. Aging is another, as chronicled in "The Last Day in the Field," when Aleck Maury realizes he has lost the eye-hand skills for wing-shooting. He can still turn to fishing, the less physical but more contemplative art. A parallel story, "All Lovers Love the Spring," describes an aging, unmarried woman raised among boys in the country. She tends an aged mother and takes up the risky hobby of mushroom-hunting and discovers the tension between her family duty and her freedom in nature:

On a mound of earth, in that black, swampy water, a tame pear tree was in bloom.... Most of the blossoms hadn't unfolded yet; the petals looked like seashells. I stood under the tree and watched all those festoons of little shells floating up, up, up into the bluest sky I've ever seen, and wished that I didn't have to go home. Mama's room always smells of camphor. You notice it after you've been out in the fresh air.

Gordon's men and women are shaped by forces of their culture but make profound connections with the earth. The basic tension in her short stories rises from the conflicting desires and needs of people and from the constraints of modern, urban civilization. "The Brilliant Leaves" tells of a failed elopement, in which a young man looks down from a mountain at the settlement below: "They looked alike, those houses. He wondered how his mother and his aunt could sit there every afternoon talking about the people who lived in them." His girl friend plummets from the mountain by Bridal Veil Falls, and Jimmy must run through the autumn woods for help:

... he did not see the leaves he ran over. He saw only the white houses that no matter how fast he ran kept always just ahead of him. If he did not hurry they would slide off the hill, slide off and leave him running forever through these woods, over these dead leaves.

Caroline Gordon's stories chronicle the choices between individual liberty and social responsibility that defined the Southern culture that was her background and her richest subject.

—William J. Schafer

See the essay on "Old Red."

GOR'KII, Maksim. Pseudonym for Alexei Maksimovich Peshkov. Russian. Born in Nizhnii Novgorod, now Gorky, 16 March 1868. Educated in parish school, Nizhnii Novgorod; Kumavino elementary school, 1877–78. Married Ekaterina Pavlovna Volzhina in 1896 (separated); one son and one daughter. Apprenticed to a shoemaker at age 12; then draughtsman's clerk and cook's boy on a Volga steamer; from 1888, associated with revolutionary politics: first arrest, 1889; travelled on foot through much of Russia; member of publishing cooperative Knowledge, and literary editor, *Lifi,* St. Petersburg, from 1899; in the U.S., 1906, and Capri, 1906–13; set up revolutionary propaganda school, 1909; returned to Russia after general amnesty, 1913: editor, *Chronicles* magazine, 1915–17, and newspaper *New Life,* 1917–18; established publishing house World Literature; involved in Petrograd Workers and Soldiers Soviet, and in writers and scholars conditions generally; left Russia in 1921: editor, *Dialogue,* Berlin, 1923–25, and in Sorrento during most of 1924–31; returned to Russia in 1931: editor, *Literary Apprenticeship* magazine, 1933. Recipient: Order of Lenin, 1932. Gorky Literary Institute established in his honor. *Died 18 June 1936.*

PUBLICATIONS

Collections

Polnoe sobranie sochinenii: Khudozhestvennaia literatura. 25 vols., 1968–76.
Collected Works. 10 vols., 1978–82.
Collected Short Stories, edited by Avrahm Yarmolinsky and Moura Budberg. 1988.

Short Stories

Ocherki i rasskazy. 3 vols., 1898–99; as *Tales,* 1902.
Orloff and His Wife: Tales of the Barefoot Brigade. 1901.
The Outcasts and Other Stories. 1902.
Twenty-Six Men and a Girl and Other Stories. 1902.
Tales of Two Countries. 1914.
Through Russia (collection). 1921.
Unrequited Love and Other Stories. 1949.

Novels

Foma Gordeev. 1899; translated as *Foma Gordeyev,* 1902; as *The Man Who Was Afraid,* 1905; as *Foma,* 1945.
Troe. 1900; as *Three of Them,* 1902; as *Three Men,* 1902; as *The Three,* 1958.
Mat'. 1906; as *Mother,* 1907; as *Comrades,* 1907.
Zhizn nenuzhnovo cheloveka. 1907–08; as *The Spy: The Story of a Superfluous Man,* 1908; as *The Life of a Useless Man,* 1971.
Ispoved'. 1908; as *A Confession,* 1909.
Gorodok Okurov [Okurov City]. 1909.
Leto [Summer]. 1909.
Zhizn' Matveia Kozhemiakina. 1910–11; as *The Life of Matvei Kozhemyakin,* 1959.
Zhizn' Klima Samgina. 1925–36; as *The Bystander, The Magnet, Other Fires,* and *The Spectre,* 4 vols., 1938.
Delo Artamonovykh. 1925; as *Decadence,* 1927; as *The Artamonov Business,* 1948; as *The Artamanovs,* 1952.

Plays

Na dne (produced 1902). 1903; as *A Night's Lodging,* 1905; as *The Lower Depths,* 1912; as *Submerged,* 1914; as *At the Bottom,* 1930.

Meshchane (produced 1902).   1902; as *The Smug Citizens*, 1906; as *The Courageous One*, 1958; as *The Petty Bourgeois*, in *Collected Works 4*, 1979.
Dachniki (produced 1904).   1904; as *Summerfolk*, 1975.
Deti solntsa (produced 1905).   1905; as *Children of the Sun*, 1912.
Varvary (produced 1906).   1905; as *Barbarians*, in *Seven Plays*, 1945.
Vragi (produced 1907).   1906; as *Enemies*, in *Seven Plays*, 1945.
Vassa Zheleznova (produced 1911).   1910; revised version, 1935; translated as *Vassa Zheleznova*, in *Seven Plays*, 1945; as *Vassa Zheleznova: A Mother*, 1988.
Vstrecha [The Meeting] (produced 1910).   1910.
Chudaki (produced 1910).   1910; as *Queer People*, in *Seven Plays*, 1945.
Zykovy (produced 1918).   1913; as *The Zykovs*, in *Seven Plays*, 1945.
Starik (produced 1919).   1915; as *The Judge*, 1924; as *The Old Man*, 1956.
Somov i drugie [Somov and the Others].   1931.
Egor Bulychov i drugie (produced 1932).   1932; as *Yegor Bulichoff and Others*, in *The Last Plays*, 1937.
Dostigaev i drugie (produced 1934).   1933; as *Dostigaeff and the Others*, in *The Last Plays*.   1937.
Seven Plays.   1945.
Five Plays, edited by Edward Braun.   1988.

Verse

Pesnia o Burevestnike [Song about Burevestnik].   1901.
Chelovek [Man].   1902.
Devushka i smert' [A Girl and Death].   1917.

Other

A.P. Chekhov.   1905; as *Anton Tchekhov: Fragments of Recollections*.   1921.
Detstvo, V liudakh, Moi universitety.   1913–22; as *My Childhood, In the World [My Apprenticeship], My University Days [My Universities]*, 1915–23; as *Autobiography*, 1949.
Vospominaniia o Tolstom.   1919; as *Reminiscences of Tolstoy*, 1920.
Revoliutsiia i kul'tura [Revolution and Culture].   1920.
O russkom krest'ianstve [On the Russian Peasantry].   1922.
Vospominaniia [Reminiscences].   1923.
Zametki iz dnevnika.   1924; as *Fragments from My Diary*, 1924.
V.I. Lenin.   1924; translated as *V.I. Lenin*, 1931; as *Days with Lenin*, 1933.
Reminiscences of Leonid Andreyev.   1928.
O literature.   1933; revised edition, 1935, 1955; as *On Literature: Selected Articles*, 1958.
Literature and Life: A Selection from the Writings.   1946.
History of the Civil War in the USSR, volume 2: The Great Proletarian Revolution, October-November 1917.   1947.
F.I. Chaliapin.   2 vols., 1957–58; as *Chaliapin: An Autobiography*, edited by Nina Froud and James Hanley, 1967.
The City of the Yellow Devil: Pamplets, Articles, and Letters about America.   1972.
Rasskazy i povesti 1892–1917 (selection).   1976.
Nesvoevremennye mysli.   1971; as *Untimely Thoughts*, edited by Herman Ermolaev, 1968.

Perepiska Gor'kogo (selected correspondence).   2 vols., 1986.

*

Bibliography: *Gorky in English: A Bibliography 1868–1986* by Garth M. Terry, 1986; *Gorky: A Reference Guide* by Edith W. Clowes, 1987.

Critical Studies: *Gorky and His Russia* by Alexander Kaun, 1931; *Gorky: Romantic Realist and Conservative Revolutionary* by Richard Hare, 1962; *Stormy Petrel: The Life and Work of Gorky* by Dan Levin, 1965; *Gorky: His Literary Development and Influence on Soviet Intellectual Life* by I. Weil, 1966; *The Bridge and the Abyss: The Troubled Friendship of Gorky and V.I. Lenin* by Bertram D. Wolfe, 1967; *Gorky, The Writer: An Interpretation* by F.M. Borras, 1967; *Three Russians Consider America: America in the Works of Gor'kii, Aleksandr Bick, and Vladimir Majakovskii* by Charles Rougle, 1976; *Gorky* (biography) by Henri Troyat, 1986, translated by Lowell Blair, 1989; *Gorky* by Barry P. Scherr, 1988; *Gorky and His Contemporaries: Memoirs and Letters* edited by Galina Belaya, 1989.

* * *

While Maksim Gor'kii is best known today for such works as his play *Na dne* (*The Lower Depths*) and his autobiographical trilogy, he first gained fame as a writer of short stories, and to this day his reputation in Russia is based in no small part on his achievements in that genre, which he continued to practice throughout his career. His early stories in particular played an important role in the history of Russian literature, for they introduced characters from a part of society that had previously been virtually ignored by writers: the rootless wanderers, or vagabonds (the Russian word, "bosiaki" means literally "the barefoot ones"), whom he had come to know during his own wanderings and then romanticized in his fiction.

From 1892, when Gor'kii published his first story, "Makar Chudra," until the 1899 appearance of his novel *Foma Gordeev*, Gor'kii was exclusively a writer of short fiction, and the bulk of his best-known stories date from this period. Many of his early works employ folklore or at least folklore-like elements for their effect ("Makar Chudra," "Old Izergil," "Song of the Falcon," "Song of the Stormy Petrel"). Thus "Old Izergil," which was to remain one of Gor'kii's favorite stories, comments upon the mundane life of Izergil, a woman who has failed to instill her own life with any lasting meaning, by surrounding it with two legends—one of which, the story of Danko, who rips his own burning heart from his body and leads his people to freedom by its light, is among Gor'kii's most famous creations.

Gor'kii's first detailed portrayal of the vagabond is found in "Chelkash," where the title character already exhibits all the chief traits of such figures. A professional thief in a large port city, Chelkash takes on as his accomplice a young peasant, who has just arrived from the country. The story ultimately focuses less on the actual robbery than on the two men's quarrel over the money afterward; the point is that the peasant—whose actions are both greedy and cowardly—comes off much worse than the free-spirited Chelkash. Typically, the vagabonds prefer to live on their own and to be beholden to no one. They reject both what they see as the docile poverty of the peasantry and the social conventions of the better educated classes. They are not necessarily people to emulate: here, as well as in "A Rolling Stone" and "Konovalov," the vagabonds may be admirable for their ability to break away from the norm, but even the strongest among them are still misfits and seem doomed to a life apart from other human beings.

In these latter two works a first-person narrator imparts a strong autobiographical element, and indeed "Konovalov," like such tales from the period as "Twenty-Six Men and a Girl" or the later "The Boss," uses Gor'kii's own experiences during his Kazan years to provide an authentic background. Typical in this regard is "Creatures That Once Were Men" (whose Russian title actually means "ex-people"), which depicts a group of people who inhabit a cheap lodging house. In the course of the story the inhabitants lose both their unofficial leader and support, the manager of the lodging house, who is arrested after a fight, and their spiritual inspiration, a person known only as the "teacher," who dies from the effects of his alcoholism. With its setting, its motley cast of down-and-outers, and its emphasis on the futility of relying on others to better one's situation in life, the story offers a preview of Gor'kii's greatest play, *The Lower Depths*.

While the semi-autobiographical works are sometimes marred by the narrator's tendency to philosophize and to state the story's moral too directly, Gor'kii also composed a generous handful of unadorned tales that bring out the harshness of the life he knew simply through the events: "Cain and Artyom," "Malva," "On a Raft," "In the Steppe." The latter two were cited by Chekhov as among his favorites; in both, the efficient action and spare dialogue take the place of extensive description, offering brutal examples of the cruelty that people can show toward one another. "Malva" provides a strikingly unsentimental portrayal of a female vagabond, who lets men fight over her, only to assert her freedom and to show an independence far greater than that of the male figures in the story.

Many of Gor'kii's stories from the 1910's and 1920's invoke the autobiographical framework that he occasionally used earlier. Indeed, his major collection in English of stories from the 1910's, *Through Russia*, is united by the consistent presence of a narrator who bears some resemblance to Gor'kii, even if the individual pieces clearly contain numerous fictional elements. Vagabonds again appear, but, like the title figures in "Kalinin" and "A Woman," they seem less attractive, often desperate, and at times simply defeated by all that life has done to them. Meanwhile, the narrator, who previously was often just an observer, or, at an even greater remove, the person to whom a story was being told, now takes more of a role in the action; this is particularly true of "Birth of a Man" and "The Deceased," the stories that open and conclude the original group of works in the collection. As the very titles of the two works indicate, Gor'kii begins with a birth and ends with a death: now he is far more concerned than before with grouping his stories into cycles. Human nature has hardly improved from the earlier tales, but little by little the narrator, depicted as a transient and an outsider at first, comes to establish ties to those around him, until in the last story he breaks his journey to read the prayers over a dead man and comes to feel a link with people whom he barely knows.

Among Gor'kii's last stories are several that mark a new direction, including "The Story of a Novel," "The Hermit," "A Sky-Blue Life," and "Karamora." Here the narrator plays a reduced role (if he appears at all), and Gor'kii allows his figures to speak directly. The social themes recede somewhat; attention is drawn instead to the psychological complexities of his chief figures, who may descend into madness (Mironov in "A Sky-Blue Life") or exhibit such a profound inner void that they are indifferent to the distinction between good and evil (Karamora). Fittingly, then, Gor'kii's final short stories, with their claustrophobic narratives and often purposeful confusion between the real and the imagined, turn out to be among his most accomplished.

—Barry P. Scherr

See the essay on "Twenty-Six Men and a Girl."

———

GRACE, Patricia (Frances). New Zealander. Born in Wellington in 1937. Educated at Green Street Convent, Newtown, Wellington; St. Mary's College; Wellington Teachers' College. Married; seven children. Has taught in primary and secondary schools in King Country, Northland, and Porirua. Writing fellow, Victoria University, Wellington 1985. Recipient: Maori Purposes Fund Board grant, 1974; New Zealand Literature Fund grant, 1975, 1983; Hubert Church Prose award, 1976; Children's Picture Book of the Year award, 1982; Victoria University Writing fellowship, 1985; Wattie award, 1986; New Zealand Fiction award, 1987; Scholarship in Letters, 1988, 1990. Literary Fund grant, 1990. H.L.D.: Victoria University, 1989. Q.S.O. (Queen's Birthday Honours), 1988. Lives in Wellington.

PUBLICATIONS

Short Stories

Waiariki. 1975.
The Dream Sleepers and Other Stories. 1980.
Electric City and Other Stories. 1987.
Selected Stories. 1991.

Novels

Mutuwhenua: The Moon Sleeps. 1978.
Potiki. 1986.
Cousins. 1992.

Other (for children)

The Kuia and the Spider. 1981.
Watercress Tuna and the Children of Champion Street. 1984.
He aha te mea nui?, Ma wai?, Ko au tenei, Ahakoa he iti (Maori readers). 4 vols., 1985.

Other

Wahine Toa: Women of Maori Myth, paintings by Robyn Kahukiwa. 1984.

*   *   *

Patricia Grace is the supreme stylist among Maori authors writing in English. From the first she has striven to recreate in prose the peculiar flavour of English as spoken by the Maori. To accentuate the impression of oral discourse, she fills her stories with dialogue, and, in the early ones, at least, she uses first person narration. Thus in *Waiariki* (her first book, and the first volume of fiction published by a Maori woman) there are 13 stories, of which all but one ("The Dream") are in the first person. In a few of these stories there is an attempt to evoke the characteristics of the Maori language itself rather than Maori *English.* Thus in "Toki," "At the River," and "Huria's Rock" she imitates traditional Maori folk tales, using the technique sometimes known as "foreignization," where the English text is made to read like a literal translation of another language (in this case Maori). The opening paragraph of "Toki," for example, illustrates the use of Maori syntax, periphrasis, and word-order:

From the north he came, Toki, in his young day. Ah yes. A boaster this one, Toki the fisherman.

In a second group of the *Waiariki* stories ("The Dream," and to a lesser extent "Holiday" and "Waiariki"), the text is peppered with Maori phrases, and one critic has—rather fancifully—likened the result to macaronics. But for the majority of the stories English is the primary medium, and Maori words and phrases appear no more than is necessary to accentuate the distinctively Maori flavour of the narration. It is these stories that provide the basis for Grace's subsequent development.

"A Way of Talking" (the opening story in *Waiariki*) highlights Grace's central preoccupation by focussing on different ways of talking English—a Maori way, evident in the private exchanges of two sisters, and what Sara/Hera (the less educated sister, who is also the narrator) calls a "Pakehafied" way, used by the other sister (Rose/Rohe) to impress people in authority. Thus, in private, Hera can refer to Rohe as "a stink thing," whereas, in public, Rose talks to a Pakeha woman about "the people from down the road whom your husband is employing to cut scrub."

In this early story the Maori voice is not sustained throughout Hera's narration or even throughout the private conversations of the sisters. Towards the end, for example, Rohe adopts an improbably formal idiom in response to Hera's point that Maori, as well as Pakeha, tend to use racial stereotypes in their everyday discourse:

It's not so much what is said, but when and where and in whose presence. Besides, you and I don't speak in this way now, not since we were little. It's the older ones: Mum, Dad, Nanny who have this habit.

The same inconsistency is evident in the other stories of *Waiariki*. In the title story, for example, a handful of Maori terms cannot disguise the conventional literary idiom used to state the moral at the end:

My regret came partly in the knowledge that we could not have the old days back again. We cannot have the simple things. . . .And there was regret in me too for the passing of innocence, for that which made me unable to say to my children, 'Put your kits in the sand little ones. Mimi on your kits and then wash them in the sea. Then we will find plenty. There will be plenty of good kai moana in the sea and your kits will always be full.'

The distinctive Maori voice that is realised imperfectly in *Waiariki* is refined and sustained in her two subsequent collections, *The Dream Sleepers* and *Electric City*. In *The Dream Sleepers* especially it is often tinged with a lyricism that seems closer to the world of Maori song or oratory than to everyday conversation. The opening paragraph of "Mirrors," for example, is an interesting blend of the poetic and the demotic:

So out under a hanging sky with my neck in danger from the holes in my slippers. Hey slippers. Watch out now, we've both seen younger days remember. Hurry me down to the end of the drive for the milk. Milk. Then turn me and we'll scuff back inside together to where the heater's plugged, pressing a patch of warmth into the corner where I'll sit with my back to the window, drinking tea. By gee.

Another interesting new development in her last two collections is the use of third person narration to supplement her customary first person technique. These third person stories still contain a high proportion of dialogue, and several (the splendid "Journey" in *The Dream Sleepers,* and "Fishing" in *Electric City*) are written in a species of free indirect discourse that suggests oral Maori usage. So the change in point of view does not compromise Grace's distinctively Maori voice.

Grace writes in a variety of genres. The early tales ("Toki") are akin to myth, and mythical elements provide a backdrop for some of the later stories like "Between Earth and Sky," where the Maori legend of creation (involving the separation of earth and sky) underlies an account of modern-day childbirth. Most of her stories, however, are miniature "slices" of contemporary life. Many of these (the delightful "Beans" and the loosely linked series involving Uncle Kepa and his extended family which constitutes part two of *The Dream Sleepers*) celebrate the imaginative, carefree world of rural Maori children. Grace is a prolific children's writer, so this focus is not surprising. On the other hand, she also depicts the seedier circumstances of urban Maori adults and adolescents (especially women), sometimes with grim realism (in "The Geranium," a study of a battered wife), sometimes with wry humour (in "Mirrors," which depicts the tribulations of a middle-aged woman on a winter's morning.)

Grace has also written a few plotty stories, the best of which ("Journey" and "Going for the Bread") trace the hardening of a protagonist's heart against the injustices suffered by contemporary Maori. These stories—along with her second novel, *Potiki,* and the grimmer slice-of-life studies, such as "The Geranium," "The Dream Sleepers," and "Electric City"—give the lie to Grace's claim (in a recent interview) that she has "never thought about the political element" of her work. The bulk of her writing may be delicate, lyrical, trivial even, but she is not totally immune from the angry, committed tone that characterises most contemporary Maori writing.

—Richard P. Corballis

———

GRAHAM, R(obert) B(ontine) Cunninghame. Scottish. Born in London, 24 May 1852; son of the laird of Ardoch, Dunbarton. Educated at Harrow School, Middlesex,

1865–67; at a private school in Brussels, 1868–69. Married the poet Gabriela Balmondière in 1878 (died 1906). Travelled in Argentina, 1870–71; surveyor and worked in tea trade, Paraguay, 1873–74; horse dealer in Uruguay, Brazil, and Argentina, 1876–77; lived in New Orleans, Texas, and Mexico, 1879–81; inherited his family's Scottish estates, 1883; Liberal member of Parliament for North-West Lanarkshire, 1886–92, but became a socialist and follower of William Morris; founder, with Keir Hardie, and first president, Scottish Labour Party, 1888; Labour parliamentary candidate for Camlachie division of Glasgow, 1892; prospected for gold in Spain, 1894; travelled in Morocco, 1897; sent by War Office to South America to buy horses for British troops, 1914; cattle surveyor in Colombia for British government, 1916–17; Liberal parliamentary candidate for Western Stirling and Clackmannan, 1918; founding member, Scottish National Party, 1918. Justice of the peace and deputy lieutenant for Dunbarton; justice of the peace for Perth and Stirling. *Died 20 March 1936.*

PUBLICATIONS

Collections

The Essential Graham, edited by Paul Bloomfield.   1952.
Selected Writings, edited by Cedric Watts.   1981.

Short Stories and Sketches

The Ipané.   1899.
Thirteen Stories.   1900.
Success.   1902.
Progress and Other Sketches.   1905.
His People.   1906.
Faith.   1909.
Hope.   1910.
Charity.   1912.
A Hatchment.   1913.
El Rio de la Plata (in Spanish).   1914.
Scottish Stories.   1914.
Brought Forward.   1916.
The Dream of the Magi.   1923.
Redeemed and Other Sketches.   1927.
Thirty Tales and Sketches, edited by Edward Garnett.   1929.
Writ in Sand.   1932.
Mirages.   1936.
Rodeo: A Collection of Tales and Sketches, edited by A.F. Tschiffely.   1936.
The South American Sketches, edited by John Walker.   1978.
Beattock for Moffat, and the Best of Graham.   1979.
The Scottish Sketches, edited by John Walker.   1982.
The North American Sketches, edited by John Walker.   1986.

Other

Notes on the District of Menteith for Tourists and Others.   1895.
Father Archangel of Scotland and Other Essays, (includes fiction) with Gabriela Graham.   1896.
Aurora la Cujiñi: A Realistic Sketch in Seville.   1898.
Mogreb-el-Acksa: A Journey in Morocco.   1898.
A Vanished Arcadia, Being Some Account of the Jesuits in Paraguay 1607 to 1767.   1901.

Hernando de Soto.   1903.
Bernal Diaz del Castillo.   1915.
A Brazilian Mystic, Being the Life and Miracles of Antonio Conselheiro.   1920.
Cartagena and the Banks of the Sinú.   1920.
The Conquest of New Granada, Being the Life of Gonzalo Jimenez de Quesada.   1922.
The Conquest of the River Plate.   1924.
Inveni Portam: Joseph Conrad.   1924.
Doughty Deeds: An Account of the Life of Robert Graham of Gartmore, Poet and Politician 1735–97.   1925.
Pedro de Valdivia, Conqueror of Chile.   1926.
José Antonio Páez.   1929.
Bibi.   1929.
The Horses of the Conquest.   1930; edited by R.M. Denhardt, 1949.
Portrait of a Dictator: Francisco Solano Lopez (Paraguay 1865–70).   1933.
With the North West Wind.   1937.
Three Fugitive Pieces, edited by H.F. West.   1960.

Translator, *Mapirunga,* by Gustavo Barroso.   1924.

*

Bibliography: *A Bibliography of the First Editions of Graham* by Leslie Chaundy, 1924; *The Herbert Faulkner West Collection of Graham,* 1938; *Graham and Scotland: An Annotated Bibliography* by John Walker, 1980.

Critical Studies: *Don Roberto* by H.F. West, 1936; *Don Roberto, Being an Account of the Life and Works of Graham* by A.F. Tschiffely, 1937, as *Tornado Cavalier,* 1955; *Graham: A Centenary Study* by Hugh MacDiarmid, 1952; *Prince-Errant and Evocator of Horizons: A Reading of Graham* by R.E. Haymaker, 1967; *Graham: A Critical Biography,* 1979, and *Graham,* 1983, both by Cedric Watts; *Robert and Gabriela Cunninghame Graham* by Alexander Maitland, 1983.

* * *

R.B. Cunninghame Graham (Don Roberto, as he was affectionately known in South America) was born into a noble Scottish family the paternal line of which went back to Robert II and the Earls of Menteith. He was also a descendant of Robert Graham (whose biography he wrote), the poet of "If Doughty Deeds my Lady Please." Between 1886 and 1892, as a Liberal Member of Parliament for the mining constituency of North-West Lanark, he rode on his horse to the House of Commons. Always a flamboyant figure, this gesture was typical of the man; as was his unremitting fight for better working conditions for the colliers, chainmakers, and others of the underprivileged whom he considered to be the victims of cruel exploitation and an appallingly unfair class system. That he himself came from an aristocratic background in no way deterred him in his struggle. Always politically active, his social conscience led to a sentence of six weeks in prison for his part in the 1888 Trafalgar Square Riots.

Although born a Scottish landowner, Graham and his Chilean-born wife, Gabriela (a writer of not inconsiderable talent) spent much of their time abroad. Fluent in Spanish and a prolific writer, in English, of sketches, essays, polemical articles, travel books, histories and stories,

Graham wrote of the pampas and grouchos, amongst whom he lived and worked, and his beloved horses in *The Horses of the Conquest,* one of his last books, and in *The Ipané,* and *Rodeo.* In these collections he describes in vivid detail the people and animals of South America. At heart an adventurer, Graham was in his element riding under the South American sun and exulting in the freedom the wide pampas offered, which he described as "all grass and sky, and sky and grass, and still more sky and grass."

In his well-known collection *Success* Graham contrasts material worldly success with gallant failure to the former's disadvantage. Perhaps his most consistently interesting volume is *Scottish Stories,* a compilation of all his stories about Scottish personalities. There is a typical and entertaining irony in "Christie Christison" (1912), which recounts the experience of a sailor home on leave and full of lust. He finds in the brothel not only his daughter but also his wife, whom he excuses on the grounds that he had given her a "daud" (hit her) before he left.

Graham included many authors among his circle of friends—Oscar Wilde, Joseph Conrad, and Bernard Shaw among others. Indeed, Shaw used Graham as a basis for Sergius in *Arms and the Man,* and he admitted that without Graham's incomparable *Mogreb-el-Acksa,* an account of his attempt to reach the forbidden city of Tarudant, *Captain Brassbound's Conversion* would not have been written.

Although Graham wrote over 30 books, he never wrote a novel, confining himself in fiction to the short story. While he enjoyed personal notoriety during his lifetime and his literary significance was recognised, his work later was sadly neglected until recently. The vitality of the man is reflected in the vigour of his prose, his meticulous eye for detail in his flashing descriptions of people and animals, and his lyric sensitivity in the manner in which he encapsulates the essence of time and place.

—A.J. Lindsay

See the essay on "Beattock for Moffat."

———

GRIMM, Brothers. GRIMM, Jacob (Ludwig Karl). German. Born in Hanau, 4 January 1785. Educated at Cassel lyceum, 1798–1802; University of Marburg, studied law, 1802–1805. Researcher for Friedrich Karl von Savigny in Paris, 1805; civil servant, secretariat of the War Office, Cassel, 1806; librarian for King Jérôme Bonaparte's private library, Wilhelmshöhe, 1808–14, 1815; co-editor with Wilhelm Grimm, *Altdeutsche Wälder,* 1813–16; legation secretary for the Hessian delegation at the Congress of Vienna, 1814–15; librarian, Cassel, 1816; chair, Archaeology and librarianship, University of Göttingen, Hanover, 1830–37, dismissed from the university for political reasons by Ernst August in 1837; lived in Cassel, 1837–41; member, Academy of Science, Berlin, 1841; president, Conferences of Germanists, Frankfurt am Main, 1846, Lubeck, 1847; elected to the Frankfurt parliament, 1848. Recipient: Order of merit, 1842. Honorary doctorate, University of Marburg, 1819; Berlin University, 1828; Berslau University, 1829. *Died 20 September 1863.*
GRIMM, Wilhelm (Karl). German. Born in Hanau, 24 February 1786. Educated at the Cassel lyceum, 1798–1803; University of Marburg, 1803–06; graduated in law 1806. Married Henriette Dorothea Wild in 1825; one daughter and three sons. Co-editor with Jacob Grimm, *Altdeutsche Wälder,* 1813–16; assistant librarian, electoral library, Cassel, 1814–29; professor, University of Göttingen, 1830, dismissed from the university for political reasons by Ernst August in 1837; lived in Cassel, 1837–41. Member: Prussian Akademie der Wissenschaften, Berlin, 1841. Honorary doctorate, Marburg University, 1819. *Died 16 December 1859.*

PUBLICATIONS

Collections

Complete Works.   62 vols., 1974—.
Die älteste Märchensammlung der Brüder Grimm, edited by Heinz Rölleke.   1975.
Grimm's Tales for Young and Old: The Complete Stories. 1977.

Short Stories

Kinder- und Hausmärchen.   1812–15; revised editions, 1819 and 1837 (includes *Anmerkungen zu den einzelnen Märchen*), 1840, 1843, 1850, 1857; as *German Popular Stories,* 1823–26; revised edition as *Gammer Grethel; or, German Fairy Tales and Popular Stories,* 1839; as *Home Stories,* 1855; *Grimm's Popular Stories,* 1868; *Grimm's Fairy Tales,* 1872; *Grimm's Goblins,* 1876; as *The Complete Grimm's Fairy Tales,* 1944; as *Complete Fairy Tales of the Brothers Grimm,* edited by Jack Zipes, 2 vols., 1987.
Altdeutsche Wälder.   1813–16.
Deutsche Sagen.   1816–18; as *The German Legends of the Brothers Grimm,* edited by Donald Ward, 1981.

Other

Deutsches Wörterbuch, with others.   32 vols., 1854–1961.
Freundesbriefe von Wilhelm und Jacob Grimm: Mit Anmerkungen, edited by Alexander Reifferscheid.   1878.
Briefwechsel des Freihern K.H.G. von Meusebach mit Jacob und Wilhelm Grimm.   1880.
Briefwechsel zwischen Jacob und Wilhelm Grimm aus der Jegenszeit, edited by Herman Grimm and Gustav Hinrichs.   1881; revised edition, 1963.
Briefwechsel der Gebrüder Grimm mit nordischen Gelehrten, edited by Ernst Schmidt.   1885.
Briefwechsel zwischen Jacob und Wilhelm Grimm, Dahlmann und Gervinus, edited by Eduard Ippel.   2 vols., 1885–86.
Briefe der Brüder Jacob und Wilhelm Grimm an Georg Friedrich Benecke aus den Jahren 1808–1829, edited by Wilhelm Müller.   1889.
Briefwechsel F. Lückes mit den Brüdern Jacob und Wilhelm Grimm.   1891.
Briefe der Brüder Grimm an Paul Wigand, edited by Edmund Stengel.   1910.
Briefwechsel Johann Kaspar Bluntschlis mit Jacob Grimm. 1915.
Briefe der Brüder Grimm, edited by Albert Leitzmann and Hans Gürtler.   1923.
Briefwechsel der Brüder Jacob und Wilhelm Grimm mit Karl Lachmann, edited by Albert Leitzmann.   2 vols., 1927.
Briefwechsel zwischen Jacob Grimm und Karl Goedeke, edited by Johannes Bolte.   1927.

Briefe der Brüder Grimm au Savigny, edited by Wilhelm Schoof. 1953.
Unbekannte Briefe der Brüder Grimm, edited by Wilhelm Schoof. 1960.
John Mitchell Kemble and Jacob Grimm: A Correspondence 1832–1852. 1971.
Briefwechsel der Bruder Grimm mit Hans Georg von Hammerstein, edited by Carola Gottzmann. 1985.

Editors, *Die beiden ältesten deutschen Gedichte aus dem achten Jahrundert: Das Lied von Hildebrand und Hadubrand und das Weissenbrunner Gebet*. 1812.
Editors, *Lieder der alten Edda*. 1815.
Editors, *Der arme Heinrich*, by Hartmann von Aue. 1815.
Editors and translators, *Irische Elfenmärchen*, by C. Croker. 1826.

PUBLICATIONS by Jacob Grimm

Collections

Auswahl aus den kleineren Schriften. 1871.
Über die deutsche Sprache. 1914.
Reden und Aufsätze, edited by Wilhelm Schoof. 1966.

Fiction

Irmenstrasse und Irmensäule: Eine mythologische Abhandlung. 1815.
Deutsche Mythologie. 1835; as *Teutonic Mythology*, 4 vols., 1883-88.
Frau Aventiure klopft an Beneckes Thür. 1842.
Der Fundevogel: Ein Märlein. 1845.

Other

Über den altdeutschen Meistergesang. 1811.
Deutsche Grammatik. 4 vols., 1819–37.
Zur Recension der deutschen Grammatik. 1826.
Deutsche Rechtsalterthümer. 1828.
Hymnorum veteris ecclesiae XXVI interpretatio Theodisca nunc primum edita. 1830.
Bericht . . . an die Hannoversche Regierung. 1833.
Reinhart Fuchs. 1834.
Über seine Entlassung (pamphlet). 1838.
Sendschrieben an Karl Lachmann über Reinhart Fuchs. 1840.
Über zwei entdeckte Gedichte aus der Zeit des deutschen Heidenthums. 1842.
Grammatik der Hochdeutschen Sprache unserer Zeit. 1843.
Deutsche Grenzalterthümer. 1844.
Über Diphthonge nach weggefallnen Consonanten. 1845.
Über Iornandes und die Geten: Eine in der Akademie der Wissenschaften am 5. März 1846 von Jacob Grimm gehaltene Vorlesung (lecture). 1846.
Geschichte der deutschen Sprache. 2 vols., 1848.
Über Marcellus Burdingalensis. 1849.
Das Wort des Besitzes: Eine linguistische Abhandlung. 1850.
Über den Liebesgott: Gelesen in der Akademie am 6. Januar 1851 (lecture). 1851.
Über den Ursprung der Sprache. 1851.
Über Frauennamen aus Blumen. 1852.
Über die Namen des Donners. 1855.
Über die Marcellischen Formeln, with Adolf Pictet. 1855.

Über den Personenwechsel in der Rede. 1856.
Über einige Fälle der Attraction. 1858.
Von Vertretug männlicher durch weibliche Namensformen. 1858.
Über Schule, Universität, Academie. 1859.
Über das Verbrennen der Leichen: Eine in der Academie der Wissenschaften am 29 November 1849 . . . (lecture). 1859.
Rede auf Schiller, gehalten in der feierlichen Sitzung der König. 1859.
Rede auf Wilhelm Grimm gehalten in der König und . . . Rede über das Alter, edited by Herman Grimm. 1863.
Kleinere Schriften (autobiography), edited by Karl Victor Müllenhoff and Eduard Ippel. 8 vols., 1864–90.
Briefwechsel zwischen Jacob Grimm und Friedrich David Graeter aus dem Jahren 1810–1813, edited by Hermann Fischer. 1877.
Briefe an Hendrik Willem Tydeman: Mit einem Anhange und Anmerkungen, edited by Alexander Reifferscheid. 1883.
Briefwechsel von Jacob Grimm und Hoffmann von Fallersleben mit Henrik van Wyn: Nebst anderen Briefen zur deutschen Literatur, edited by Karl Theodor Gaedertz. 1888.
Kopitars Briefwechsel mit Jakob Grimm, edited by Max Vasmer. 1938.

Editor, *Silva de romances viejos*. 1815.
Editor, *Zur Recension der deutschen Grammatik*. 1826.
Editor, *Taciti Germania edidit et qua as res Germanorum pertinere videntur e reliquo Tacitino oere excerpsit*. 1835.
Editor, with Andreas Schmeller, *Lateinische Gedichte des X. und XI. Jahrhunderts*. 1838.
Editor, *Andreas und Elene*. 1840.
Editor, *Gedichte des Mittelalters aus König Greidrich I., den Staufer, und aus seiner, sowie der nächstfolgenden Zeit*. 1844.

Translator, *Kleine serbische Grammatik*, by Vuk Stefanovic Karadzic. 1824.

PUBLICATIONS by Wilhelm Grimm

Other

Über deutsche Runen. 1821.
Grâve Ruodolf: Ein Altdeutsches Gedicht. 1828.
Zur Literatur der Runen. 1828.
Bruchstücke aus einem Gedichte von Assundin, 1829.
Die deutsche Heldensage. 1829.
Die Hildebrando antiquissimi carminis teutonici fragmentum. 1830.
Die sage vom ursprung der Christusbilder. 1843.
Exhoratatio ad plebem christianam Glossae Cassellanae: Über die Bedeutung der deutschen Fingernamen. 1848.
Über Freidank: Zwei Nachträge. 1850.
Altdeutsche Gespräche: Nachtrag. 1851.
Zur Geschichte des Reims. 1852.
Nachtrag zu den Casseler glossen. 1855.
Thierfabeln bei den Meistersängern. 1855.
Die Sage von Polyphem. 1857.
Kleinere Schriften (autobiography), edited by Gustav Hinrichs. 4 vols., 1881-87.
Unsere Sprachlaute als Stimmbildner. 1897.

Editor, *Vridankes Bescheidenheit*. 1834.

Editor, *Der Rosengarten.*   1836.

Editor, *Ruolandes liet.*   1838.

Editor, with Bettina von Arnim and Karl August Varnhagen von Ense, *Sämmtliche Werke,* by Ludwig Achim von Arnim.   22 vols., 1853–56; revised edition, 21 vols., 1857; reprinted, 1982.

Editor, *Wernher vom Niederrhein.*   1839.

Editor, *Goldene Schmiede,* by Konrad von Würzburg. 1840.

Editor, *Silvester,* by Konrad von Würzburg.   1841.

Editor, *Athis und Prophilias: Mit Nachtrag.*   2 vols., 1846–52.

Editor, *Altdeutsche Gespräche: Mit Nachtrag.*   2 vols., 1851.

Editor, *Bruchstücke aus einem unbekann ten Gedicht vom Rosengarten.*   1860.

Editor and translator, *Drei altschottische Lieder.*   1813.

Translator, *Altdänische Heldenlieder, Balladen und Märchen.*   1811.

Translator, *Trische Land—und Seemärchen: Gesammelt,* by Thomas Crofton Croker, edited by **Werner Moritz** and Charlotte Oberfeld.   1986.

*

Critical Studies: *The Brothers Grimm* by Ruth Michaelis-Jena, 1970; *Paths Through the Forest: A Biography of the Brothers Grimm* by Murray B. Peppard, 1971; *Jacob Grimm's Conception of German Studies* by Peter F. Ganz, 1973; *The Uses of Enchantment: The Meaning and Importance of Fairy Tales* by Bruno Bettelheim, 1977; *The German Legends of the Brothers Grimm,* edited and translated by Donald Ward, 1981; *One Fairy Story Too Many: The Brothers Grimm and Their Tales* by John M. Ellis, 1983; *Grimms' Bad Girls and Bold Boys: The Moral and Social Vision of the Tales* by Ruth B. Bottigheimer, 1987; *The Hard Facts of the Grimms' Fairy Tales* by Maria M. Tatar, 1987; *The Brothers Grimm and the Folktale* edited by James M. McGlathery, 1988, and *Fairy Tale Romance. The Grimms, Basile, and Perrault* by McGlathery, 1991; *The Brothers Grimm: From Enchanted Forests to the Modern World* by Jack Zipes, 1988; *The Grimm Brothers and the Germanic Past: International Bicentenary Symposium on the Brothers Grimm,* 1990; *The Brothers Grimm and Their Critics: Folktales and the Quest for Meaning* by Christa Kamenetsky, 1992.

* * *

The intellectual collaboration of Jacob and Wilhelm Grimm is one of the most celebrated in history and led to their honorary title "Fathers of German Studies." They gained world-wide fame through their *Kinder- und Hausmärchen* (Children's and Household Tales), which they continually expanded and revised in seven major editions between 1812 and 1857. They consist not only of magic fairy tales but also include legends, anecdotes, jokes, and religious tales. The bulk of the 210 tales and 32 omitted tales came from the oral tradition, but their collective project also included more than 20 literary sources from various ages and cultures. In the 20th century, the collection has been second only to the Bible as a best-seller in Germany. On an international scale, it is considered the second most widely-read book by a German-speaking author, following closely Karl Marx's *Das Kapital.* With their collection of tales and many significant scholarly publications, the Grimms contributed to the areas of folklore, myth, history, ethnology, religion, jurisprudence, lexicography, German and world literature, as well as literary criticism. As joint authors, they produced eight books and as individuals 35 between the two of them, eleven volumes of essays and notes and thousands of letters. Their German Dictionary, begun in 1838 extended only to the letter F in their lifetimes, was completed in 1960 and 1961 after generations of Germanists contributed to the project.

The Grimms' *Kinder- und Hausmärchen* collection must be seen against the background of the Romantic movement at the end of the 18th century with its national reaction of the people toward French hegemony in the Napoleonic era and Germans' emphasis on the discovery of folk art. The Grimm brothers' major intent was to uncover distinctive features expressed in German culture, customs, heritage, and history, and thus aid the cause of uniting the German people. Both brothers believed that they could reconstitute oral folk tales from the past by using stories that were being told in the present and in this manner recreate major elements of Germany's collective memory of its past. Critics have been eager to show how the Grimms assumed editorial authority and twisted parts of their tales to fit their nationalistic political program and appeal to the taste and moral teachings of the bourgeois class. Since Germany was divided in many different principalities when the Grimms wrote and edited their tales, one form of identity was provided by the family. Child abuse and neglect, sexual abuse, and domestic violence were common social problems of the time. These problems are frequently not treated in a straightforward manner in the Grimms' collection because the Grimms had a tendency to suppress sexual depictions. Puberty and pregnancy, secret sexual desires are rarely alluded to, indicating the Grimms' difficulties with representations of human sexuality and their strong commitment to moral teachings. After 1919, when most of the additions to the tales came from literary sources, Wilhelm Grimm assumed primary responsibilities for the stylistic, formal, and thematic changes. A major concern of Wilhelm Grimm's was to make the tales more acceptable for children since they had mostly aimed for a reading public of adult and serious people. Furthermore, they needed to make the collections more proper and sellable for the growing middle-class readership.

Contrary to popular myths, the Grimms did not collect the oral tales as itinerant folklorists wandering the landscapes of their native Hesse and talking to peasants, but by inviting storytellers from the area to their home in Kassel. As most storytellers in the early 19th century, the predominantly female storytellers acquainted with the Grimms came from educated members of the middle and aristocratic classes. The majority of the Grimm informants around Kassel were women from the Wild and Hassenpflug families (the latter was of Huguenot ancestry and spoke French at home). These women met with the Grimms regularly to tell stories they had heard from their governesses, nursemaids, and servants. However, one of the most important contributors (35 tales) was Dorothea Viehmann, an impoverished widow of a tailor and daughter of an immigrant Huguenot from Zwehrn, who came to nearby Kassel to sell fruit and died in poverty in 1815. Outside of the principality of Hesse (Hessia), the Bökendorfer Circle in Westphalia, a circle of young men and women founded by the aristocrat Wilhelm von Haxthausen (among them the famous 19th century poet Annette von Droste-Hülshoff and her sister Jenny), contributed 66 tales. Gradually, the social class of the Grimms' informants changed and included oral sources from the lower classes. As was common and acceptable in the 19th century, the Grimms appropriated anonymous women's work in their collections. Feminist critics have drawn attention to the fact that materials on the Grimms' actual informants became part of scholarly records long after the brothers' death.

The Grimms' personal struggle to overcome social prejudice and poverty after their parents' early deaths, and the example of staunch Protestant ethic, set for them by their father and grandfather, influenced their methods of editing and adapting, and reconstructing. Readers encounter the representation of the Grimms' 19th-century patriarchal society as well as the Grimms' personal ideals, desires, and beliefs in the emphasis on industriousness, order, family, and tradition. With each of their revisions, the Grimms included more sources directly from journals and books. Of great interest to them were 16th-century tale collections, particularly the folktales and books ("Volksbücher") by Hans Sachs and Johannes Pauli. Wilhelm Grimm began to enter them in adapted form into their 1815 edition and continued to include them until their last edition in 1857. The 16th-century tale collections depicted an urban world and needed many adaptations by the Grimms to fit the 19th-century context in the area of social, economic, gender, and confessional roles. The brothers changed all references to open female sexuality, increased male violence and abuse to reflect the social problems of their time, and ignored whatever conflicted with 19th-century values.

Since the early 1970's, feminist critics have particularly focused on the passive, silent, and pretty heroines in the Grimms' tales. Partnership between the sexes is rarely present. Instead, women are portrayed as the weaker sex and have to act patient, obedient, industrious, clean, and quiet if they want to fulfill their one goal in life: to meet a worthy man and to get married. Even Cinderella is only a heroine after shedding her dirty rags and dressing properly and cleaning herself up. Males function as rescuers and are portrayed as cunning, resourceful, and courageous, and can win their chosen bride as a "prize" only after much hard work. The archetype of female evil is the witch or sorceress, as in "Rapunzel," where the sorceress demands to be handed over a child. Rapunzel's patience and naiveté as a prisoner in a tower in the forest (where the sorceress locked her at the age of twelve, the onset of puberty one can assume) and the prince's endurance are rewarded in the end. The societal ideal of a happy family is achieved and justice has been restored. The fairy tale paradigm of weak, submissive femininity and strong masculinity is also upheld in the popular tale of "Hansel and Gretel." Each time the children hear their parents talking about abandoning them in the forest because of their poverty, Hansel finds comforting words: "Hush, Gretel, don't cry. God will help us." In the end they prevail together and illustrate the Protestant work ethic with Hansel's resourcefulness and Gretel's hard work in the house of the witch.

Many different types of critical approaches have been applied to the Grimms' fairy tale collections. Significant contributions to the scholarship on the tales have been made by folklorists, literary historians, educators, Jungian and Freudian scholars and psychologists, Marxists, structuralists, and literary critics with various other orientations. For some critics, the magic of the fairy tales may have faded altogether, but for children and adults in many different cultures, dreams of conquering oppressors, win-

ning out over evil, being rewarded for hard work, finding a prince or princes, and living happily ever after continue to hold fascination and a utopian dimension. Unquestionably, the Grimms' tales will offer rich sources for enjoyment, social-historical analysis, and imaginative identification for generations to come.

—Barbara Mabee

See the essays on "Bluebeard" and "Little Red Riding Hood."

GUIMARÃES ROSA, João. Brazilian. Born in Cordisburgo, Minas Gerais, 27 June 1908. Educated at Medical School of Minas Gerais, Belo Horizonte, M.D. 1925–30. Married 1) Lygia Cabral Pena in 1930; 2) Aracy Moebius de Carvalho in 1938. Public servant, Statistical Service, Minas Gerais, 1929–31; physician, private practice, 1931–32; medical officer, military service, 1932–34; joined Ministry of Foreign Affairs, 1934; vice-consul, Germany, 1938–42; interned in Baden-Baden, 1942; secretary, Brazilian Embassy in Colombia, 1942–44; head, Ministry of Foreign Affairs Documentation Service, 1944–46; secretary, Brazilian Delegation to Paris Peace Conference, 1946; secretary general, Brazilian Delegation to Ninth Pan-American Conference, Bogotá, 1948; counselor, Brazilian Embassy, Paris, 1949–51; cabinet chief, 1951-53, and budget chief, 1953–58, Ministry of Foreign Affairs; ambassador, 1958–62; chief of borders division, 1962–67. Vice-president, First Latin American Writers Conference, Mexico City, 1965. Member, Brazilian Academy of Letters, 1967. Recipient: Brazilian Academy of Letters Poetry award, 1937; Felipe d'Oliveira prize, 1946; Machado de Assis prize, 1956; Carmen Dolores Barbosa prize, 1957; Paula Brito prize, 1957; Brazilian Pen Club award, 1963. *Died 19 November 1967.*

PUBLICATIONS

Collections

Selecta, edited by Paulo Rónai.   1973.
Contos, edited by Heitor Megale and Marilena Matsuola.   1978.

Short Stories

Sagarana.   1946; revised editions, 1951, 1956, 1958; translated as *Sagarana,* by Harriet de Onís, 1966.
Corpo de baile: Sete novelas.   1956; third edition as *Manuelzão e Miguilim, No urubùquaquá, no pinhém,* and *Noites do sertão,* 3 vols., 1964–65.
Primeiras Estórias.   1962; as *The Third Bank of the River and Other Stories,* 1968.
Tutaméia: Terceiras estórias.   1967.
Estas estórias.   1969.

Novel

Grande Sertão: Veredas.   1956; as *The Devil to Pay in the Backlands,* 1963.

Other

Ave, palavra (prose and verse).   1970.
Sagarana emotiva: cartas de Guimarães Rosa [a] Paulo Dantas.   1975.

*

Critical Studies: by Mary Daniel, in *Studies in Short Fiction* 8, Winter, 1971; *Structural Perspectivism in Guimarães Rosa* by W. Martins, 1973; *Guimarães Rosa* by Jon S. Vincent, 1978; *The Synthesis Novel in Latin America: A Study of Grande Sertão* by Eduardo de Faria Coutinho, 1991.

*   *   *

João Guimarães Rosa stands as one of the dominant and most innovative of modern Brazilian prose writers, his collected works comprised primarily of short fiction. With his first book, *Sagarana,* a collection of nine short stories, he attracted critical acclaim, winning the Felipe d'Oliveira prize of the Brazilian Academy of Letters. There followed in 1956 *Corpo de baile* (Dance Corps), seven novellas later published in three volumes. In 1956 also there appeared his principal work, and only novel, *Grande Sertão (The Devil to Pay in the Backlands). Primeiras Estórias (The Third Bank of the River and Other Stories)* appeared in 1962, comprising 21 brief short stories, varying in length from a half dozen to a dozen pages. A volume of even briefer stories, *Tutaméia,* double in number, followed in 1967. Posthumously, *Estas estórias* (These Stories) was released in 1969, containing, like his first book, nine stories. In 1970 appeared his final work, *Ave, palavra* (Hail, Word), a miscellany of reminiscences, chronicles, and notes. Other short fiction of Guimarães Rosa includes stories he published in magazines during his early writing career, beginning in the late 1920's, and chapters he contributed toward the end of his career for two novels collectively written by a group of authors.

The book which first brought critical acclaim to Guimarães Rosa, *Sagarana,* contains the alluring blend of contrapuntal opposites that came to characterize his work: compelling narratives in settings of regional primitivism, quickened by a resonating treatment of sophisticated modernism. The setting and characters of the stories are of the primitive backlands. The protagonists are as easily animals as human beings, lending the narratives an air of folklore or fable. But the narrative treatment does not occur in so elementary or transparent a fashion. Well reflecting this complexity is the story "Conversation Among Oxen." This narrative about (and by) a team of oxen pulling a cart shifts in point of view from man to animal then melds between them, reinforcing tensions between truth and fiction, right and wrong, justice and revenge. Another tale, "Bulletproof," focuses on a sorcerer and the atmosphere of magical belief in the backlands. But essentially the tale is a consideration of the manipulation of diction, the irony and humor of such play upon reality, and the subtle, unsteady, gradually emerging perception of the difference between magic and reality.

The novellas or longer short stories of *Corpo de baile* elaborate upon the baroque character of Guimarães Rosa's work. Its tales, which can be reduced to spare plot lines of men and women grappling with desire, reality, or identity, are embellished with extensive subplots and marginal characters and observations. Described by the author as poems, the embellished narratives possess a prose enhanced by poetic devices of rhyme, alliteration, and invented words, yet also bear a complexity and ambiguity that can be obscure. Among the stories most commented upon in this volume is "Campo Geral," with its insightful perspective on a child viewing adults and being incorporated into adulthood.

The publication of *Corpo de baile* together with *The Devil to Pay in the Backlands* obtained for Guimarães Rosa the coveted Machado de Assis prize of the Brazilian Academy of Letters, recognizing the collective achievement of his work, his books henceforth began to be translated in Europe and the United States. The literary uniqueness and influence of his work lay in the phenomenon of tales of Aesopian frugality being told in Joycean layers of narrative dimension, with a charm that could be as homely as it was multi-faceted and challenging.

As if anticipating the brevity of life that remained to him, the last two books published by Guimarães Rosa in his lifetime present progressively leaner, briefer narratives, recounting moments of transforming discovery or epiphanies. The impact of the rapid, concise tales in *The Third Bank of the River* suggests mystical assurance and peace — or resignation. In "The Horse that Drank Beer" a man discovers the beautiful in the ugly; in "Hocus Psychocus," children acting in a school play begin to perceive the truth in illusion; and in "Sorôco, His Mother, His Daughter" a village breaks out in sympathetic song, understanding the permanence of separation as a man's mentally unstable mother and daughter depart for a distant assylum. In *Tutaméia* the brevity of its stories makes them hardly more than anecdotes bearing aphoristic insights in an atmosphere of alienation and separation. Interspersed with these tales are prefaces, reflections on writing and the sources of literary inspiration. The cumulative effect of the rapidity of insights in these works gives the reader a sense of accompanying, then becoming, a magical seer.

The posthumous *Estas estórias* is unique for having tales that take the reader outside the traditional backlands setting and atmosphere of Guimarães Rosa to the Andes and to Mato Grosso. Yet in other aspects, such as the length of the stories and appearance of animal protagonists, it harkens back to *Sagarana.* It also has a sense of the author who was so representative of and sympathetic to the Brazilian backlands, recognizing himself as having been part of the larger modern Latin American literary phenomenon of magical realism. *Ave, palavra* blends small pieces of reflection and recollection, and is only short fiction to the extent the author embellished on those memories and thoughts.

As a major figure in Brazilian literature and short fiction, Guimarães Rose is preceded only by Joaquim Maria Machado de Assis. Among the Brazilian contemporaries of his time, one of the most brilliant generations of the national culture, his modernist perspective and regionalist focus were comparable to the writings of Mário de Andrade. However, Guimarães Rosa possessed a more thorough integration with and encompassing perception of his environment together with a greater subtlety of insight and complexity of technique. Among world writers, he has been compared to James Joyce for the breadth and detail of his universe and the originality of his literary technique.

Fortunately in this comparison, however, Gumarães Rosa is not so often as opaque.

—Edward A. Riedinger

See the essay on "The Third Bank of the River."

————

H

HALIBURTON, Thomas Chandler. Canadian. Born in Windsor, Nova Scotia, 17 December 1796. Educated at the King's College School, Windsor, Ontario, and King's College, Windsor, B.A. 1815; studied law: admitted to the Nova Scotia bar, 1820. Married 1) Louisa Neville in 1816 (died 1840), 11 children; 2) Sarah Harriet Williams in 1856. Lawyer in Annapolis Royal, Nova Scotia, from 1820; member for Annapolis Royal, Nova Scotia House of Assembly, 1826–29; contributor to the *Novascotian*, 1828–31, 1835–36; judge, Inferior Court of Common Pleas, Nova Scotia, 1829–41; toured England, 1838–39, 1843; justice, Nova Scotia Supreme Court, 1841–56; moved to England, 1856; lived in Isleworth, Middlesex, from 1859; member of Parliament (U.K.) for Launceton, 1859–65. Chairman, Canadian Land and Emigration Company; member of the Board, British North American Association of London. D.C.L.: Oxford University, 1858. *Died 27 August 1865.*

Publications

Collections

Sam Slick in Pictures: The Best of the Humour of Haliburton, edited by Lorne Pierce. 1956.
The Sam Slick Anthology, edited by R.E. Watters. 1969.

Short Stories

The Clockmaker; or, The Sayings and Doings of Samuel Slick of Slickville. 3 vols., 1836–40.
The Attaché; or, Sam Slick in England. 4 vols., 1843–44.
Yankee Yarns and Yankee Letters. 1852.
Sam Slick's Wise Saws and Modern Instances; or, What He Said, Did, or Invented. 1853; as *Sam Slick in Search of a Wife,* 1855.

Novels

The Letter-Bag of the Great Western; or, Life in a Steamer. 1840.
The Old Judge; or, Life in a Colony. 1849; edited by M.G. Parks, 1978.
Nature and Human Nature. 1855.
The Season-Ticket. 1860.
The Courtship and Adventures of Jonathan Hombred; or, The Scrapes and Escapes of a Live Yankee. 1860.

Other

A General Description of Nova Scotia. 1823.
An Historical and Statistical Account of Nova Scotia. 2 vols., 1829.
The Bubbles of Canada. 1839.
A Reply to the Report of the Earl of Durham. 1839.

The English in America. 2 vols., 1851; as *Rule and Misrule of the English in America,* 1851.
An Address on the Present Condition, Resources, and Prospects of British North America. 1857.
The Letters, edited by Richard A. Davies. 1988.

Editor, *Traits of American Humor by Native Authors.* 3 vols., 1852.
Editor, *The Americans at Home; or, Byeways, Backwoods, and Prairies.* 3 vols., 1854.

*

Critical Studies: *Haliburton: A Study in Provincial Toryism* by V.L.O. Chittick, 1924 (includes bibliography); *Language and Vocabulary in Sam Slick* by Elna Bengtsson, 1956; *Canadian History and Haliburton* by Stan Bodvar Liljegren, 1969; *On Haliburton: Selected Criticism* edited by Richard A. Davies, 19; *Haliburton* by N.H. Percy, 1980; *The Haliburton Symposium* edited by Frank M. Tierney, 1984.

* * *

The accepted canon of Canadian literature begins with writers who had no idea of themselves as being Canadian. The first "Canadian" novel (*The History of Emily Montague,* 1769) was actually written by the transient Englishwoman, Frances Brooke, wife of the English military chaplain at Québec. And the first Canadian short fiction consisted of the sketches—hardly yet short stories—written by two men who would have seen themselves as British North Americans, and perhaps, with a wry smile, as "Bluenoses," but would have shuddered at the thought of being identified with either Lower or Upper Canadians. They were two Nova Scotians writing in the early 19th century, Thomas McCulloch (1776–1843) and Thomas Chandler Haliburton.

It is impossible to discuss Haliburton without first mentioning McCulloch, for between them they developed the semi-realistic sketch, heavy in characterization, adventurous in speech, and moral in humour, that has recurrently appeared as a favourite form among Canadian writers.

Both men were in a sense pillars of the Nova Scotian establishment, McCulloch principal of a Presbyterian academy, and Haliburton a judge, and both used the newspapers, which appeared earlier in Nova Scotia than elsewhere in British North America, to embark on the satirical sketches by which each of them meant to reform the Bluenose by mockery. McCulloch's "Letters of Mephibosheth Stepsure" first appeared between December 1821 and May 1822 in the pages of *The Acadian Recorder,* but afterwards were virtually ignored until a volume of them, dated 1860, was distributed in 1862. McCulloch did not in fact gain his deserved repute until the middle of the 20th century when his work (as *The Stepsure Letters*) was published in the New Canadian Library with an introduction by Northrop Frye. Frye rightly praised him as "the founder of genuine Canadian humour; that is of humour that is based on a vision of society and is not merely a series of wisecracks on a single theme."

Long before this, Haliburton, so largely inspired by McCulloch, had gained an international reputation as a humorist which extended well beyond the bounds of the Maritimes, to the United States and Britain. Haliburton, like McCulloch, began with sketches in newspapers, though he abandoned the letter form McCulloch had borrowed from 18th-century writers, but retained the single commenting voice, in his case that of the Yankee itinerant clockmaker Sam Slick, whom the narrator encounters on his journeys about Nova Scotia. Originally called "Sketches of Nova Scotia," these pieces were almost immediately reprinted as a discontinuous work of fiction, united by Sam's contemptuous criticisms, under the title of *The Clockmaker; or, The Sayings and Doings of Samuel Slick of Slickville.*

Such popularity did the volume gain that Haliburton wrote second and third series, published with the same title in 1838 and 1840 respectively. Later Sam was taken to England, and out of his visit there appeared two two-volume books, *The Attaché, or Sam Slick in England*, and dated respectively 1843 and 1844. Before he finally discarded him, Haliburton took Sam back over the Atlantic as an agent of the president of the United States, sent to examine the Nova Scotian fisheries; he offered the last of him in two more, rather sententious volumes, *Sam Slick's Wise Saws and Modern Instances; or, What He Said and Did, or Invented.*

Some critics, it must be said, see Haliburton's best writing in *The Old Judge*, two volumes that in 1849 broke the Sam Slick sequence with some witty semi-fictional, semi-autobiographical sketches of a frankly High Tory judge on his circuit and the characters he meets.

But while *The Old Judge* is less strident, more mellow and stylized, it is still the Sam Slick sketches that voluminously embody Haliburton's true contribution to British North American fiction, his acute concern for popular vernaculars (slang as it was then called) which made him the first writer really to find a North American language to deal with North American situations. Sam's rich colloquial vocabulary is built up in catalogue-like and cumulative harangues as he observes the Nova Scotian countryside while talking its complacent inhabitants into buying his over-priced timepieces and discussing them contemptuously at the same time:

> Them old geese and vet'ran owls, that are so poor the foxes won' steal 'em for fear o' hurtin' their teeth: that little yallar, lantern-jaw'd long-legg's, rabit-eared runt of a pig, that's so weak it can't curl its tail up; that old frame of a cow, a standin' there with her eyes shot to, a-comtemplatin' of her latter end; and that varmint-looking horse, with his hocks swelled bigger than his belly, that looks as if he had come to her funeral.

Haliburton shows few of the concerns that were evident in later short story writers. His human situations are simple ones, the relations he portrays mostly unpassionate ones between vain and foolish people upon whom Sam preys with his flattery and "soft sawder." But in the process he builds up the picture of a somnolent society, serving his own purpose of stirring his fellow Nova Scotians to improve their farming methods and social attitudes, and it is for Sam Slick's speech and the portrait of a society he wishes to reform that we read the Sam Slick sketches today. Much in later Canadian writing—and not merely the work of that obvious disciple Stephen Leacock—is indebted to him.

—George Woodcock

See the essay on "The Clockmaker."

HAMMETT, (Samuel) Dashiell. American. Born in St. Mary's County, Maryland, 27 May 1894. Educated at Baltimore Polytechnic Institute to age 13. Served in the Motor Ambulance Corps of the U.S. Army, 1918–19: Sergeant; also served in the U.S. Army Signal Corps in the Aleutian Islands, 1942–45. Married Josephine Annas Dolan in 1920 (divorced 1937); two daughters. Worked as a clerk, stevedore, and advertising manager; private detective, Pinkerton Agency, 1908–22; full-time writer from 1922: book reviewer, *Saturday Review of Literature,* New York, 1927–29, and New York *Evening Post,* 1930; lived in Hollywood, 1930–42; began long relationship with Lillian Hellman in 1930; teacher of creative writing, Jefferson School of Social Science, New York, 1946–56. Convicted of contempt of Congress and sentenced to six months in prison, 1951. President, League of American Writers, 1942, and Civil Rights Congress of New York, 1946–47; member of the Advisory Board, *Soviet Russia Today. Died 10 January 1961.*

PUBLICATIONS

Collections

The Big Knockover: Selected Stories and Short Novels, edited by Lillian Hellman. 1966; as *The Hammett Story Omnibus,* 1966; as *The Big Knockover and The Continental Op,* 2 vols., 1967.

Short Stories

The Adventures of Sam Spade and Other Stories, edited by Ellery Queen. 1944; as *They Can Only Hang You Once,* 1949; selection, as *A Man Called Spade,* 1945.
A Man Named Thin and Other Stories, edited by Ellery Queen. 1962.

Novels

Red Harvest. 1929.
The Dain Curse. 1929.
The Maltese Falcon. 1930.
The Glass Key. 1931.
The Thin Man. 1934.
$106,000 Blood Money. 1943; as *Blood Money,* 1943; as *The Big Knockover,* 1948.
The Continental Op, edited by Ellery Queen. 1945.
The Return of the Continental Op, edited by Ellery Queen. 1945.
Hammett Homicides, edited by Ellery Queen. 1946.
Dead Yellow Women, edited by Ellery Queen. 1947.

Nightmare Town, edited by Ellery Queen.   1948.
The Creeping Siamese, edited by Ellery Queen.   1950.
Woman in the Dark, edited by Ellery Queen.   1951.
The Continental Op, edited by Steven Marcus.   1974.

Plays

Watch on the Rhine (screenplay), with Lillian Hellman, in
   Best Film Plays of 1943-44, edited by John Gassner and
   Dudley Nichols.   1945.

Screenplays: *City Streets,* with Oliver H.P. Garrett and
Max Marcin, 1931; *Woman in the Dark,* with others, 1934;
After the Thin Man, with Frances Goodrich and Albert
Hackett, 1936; *Another Thin Man,* with Frances Goodrich
and Albert Hackett, 1939; *Watch on the Rhine,* with Lillian
Hellman, 1943.

Other

Secret Agent X-9 (cartoon strip), with Alex Raymond.   2
   vols., 1934.
The Battle of the Aleutians, with Robert Colodny.   1944.

Editor, *Creeps by Night.*   1931; as *Modern Tales of
   Horror,* 1932; as *The Red Brain,* 1961; as *Breakdown,*
   1968.

*

Bibliography: *Hammett: A Descriptive Bibliography* by
Richard Layman, 1979.

Critical Studies: *"The Black Mask School"* by Philip
Durham and *"The Poetics of the Private-Eye: The Novels of
Hammett"* by Robert I. Edenbaum, both in *Tough Guy
Writers of the Thirties* edited by David Madden, 1968;
Hammett: A Casebook, 1969, and *Hammett: A Life at the
Edge,* 1983, both by William F. Nolan; *An Unfinished
Woman,* 1969, *Pentimento,* 1973, and *Scoundrel Time,*
1976, all by Lillian Hellman; *Beams Falling: The Art of
Hammett* by Peter Wolfe, 1980; *Shadow Man: The Life of
Hammett* by Richard Layman, 1981; *Hammett* by Dennis
Dooley, 1983; *Hammett: A Life* by Diane Johnson, 1983, as
The Life of Hammett, 1984; *Hammett* by William Marling,
1983; *Private Investigations: The Novels of Hammett* by
Sinda Gregory, 1984; *Hammett* by Julian Symons, 1985.

*   *   *

Dashiell Hammett rose to fame as the leading exponent of
the so-called "hard-boiled" school of crime, writing during
a relatively brief period from 1922 to 1934. In just four
years Hammett stamped his individual style on the American crime story, mostly in the *Black Mask* popular magazine, creating the figure of the private eye who moved
through an urban landscape of corruption and violence,
dispensing his own idiosyncratic brand of justice as he saw
fit largely unimpeded by law enforcement agencies.
   Hammett's career as a short story writer probably reached
it apotheosis in 1925 when he published no fewer than five
of his best stories—"The Whosis Kid," "The Scorched
Face," "Corkscrew," "Dead Yellow Women," and "The
Gutting of Couffignal"—but he went on to write over 75
stories in all, as well as five novels built around the stories,

often first appearing in the *Black Mask* magazine as
novelettes and later joined together, or, in the case of his
most famous work *The Maltese Falcon,* a five-part serial.
After 1934 Hammett worked as a scriptwriter in Hollywood for a time, he created the comic strip character
"Secret Agent X-9," and he helped popularise his work in
radio serials. He wrote little more, except for a late,
unfinished autobiographical novel "Tulip." In the space of
little more than a decade, however, Hammett had virtually
transformed the genre of the detective and crime story and
was the acknowledged leader of a group of writers that later
included Raymond Chandler, Horace McCoy, and Erle
Stanley Gardner.
   His most talented successor, Chandler, said of Hammett's
characters that "he put these people down on paper as they
are, and he made them talk and think in the language they
customarily used for these purposes." He was frequently
compared to Hemingway—by André Gide, among others—and in *Death in the Afternoon* (1932) Hemingway
pays a tribute to him by having his wife read his novel *The
Dain Curse* to him when he was suffering from eye trouble
in Spain.
   Hammett worked as an operative during two periods in
Pinkerton's National Detective Agency, and it is unquestionably this experience that helped give his stories an
authenticity that the genre had never before had. The
stories are filled with detailed accounts of how to shadow
someone, of the use of fingerprints and varieties of poisons,
of long, boring waits outside houses and bars. They are
intricately but for the most part plausibly plotted. Everything superfluous to them has been pared away, even to the
descriptions of the San Francisco landscape, which is
reduced to street signs and the names of joints.
   His protagonist in the stories is unnamed; Hammett
wrote later that "I didn't deliberately keep him nameless,
but he got through 'Arson Plus' and 'Slippery Fingers'
without needing a name, so I suppose I may as well let him
run along that way." He is merely the Continental Op, a
short, fat man of between 35 and 40 who nevertheless is
extremely proficient with both his fists and a gun and who
is not averse to taking justice into his own hands. At the
end of "The Golden Horseshoe" (1924) the Continental Op
chats with the murderer Ed Bohannon whom he has been
unable to nail and tells him:

   "I can't put you up for the murders you engineered in
   San Francisco; but I can sock you with the one you
   didn't do in Seattle—so justice won't be cheated.
   You're going to Seattle, Ed, to hang for Ashcraft's
   suicide." And he did.

Such brutal pragmatism is characteristic of the Op, whose
allegiance is only to his agency and its representative, the
equally cynical and amoral "Old Man": we are told in one
of many similar references, "The mildness and courtesy he
habitually wore over his cold-bloodedness were in his face
and eyes and voice" ("$106,000 Blood Money").
   Women (or "girls" as they are invariably referred to) in
the world of the Op are, like almost everyone and everything else, predatory and corrupt. Though the Op can be
sensually attracted, he mostly lives a life of monastic
simplicity. Sam Spade's famous abandonment of the
woman he loves because she has murdered his despised
partner and broken the Code in *The Maltese Falcon* is
foreshadowed in many of the stories:

   I also have an idea. Mine is that when the last gong
   rings I'm going to be leading this baby and some of

her playmates to the city prison. That is an excellent reason—among a dozen others I could think of—why I shouldn't get mushy with her.

("The Whosis Kid")

Hammett changes forever the face of the American crime story and his lean, laconic, wise-cracking prose has had a host of imitators.

—Laurie Clancy

————

HARDY, Thomas. English. Born in Higher Bockhampton, Dorset, 2 June 1840. Educated at local schools, 1848–56; articled to the ecclesiastical architect John Hicks in Dorchester, 1856–62. Married 1) Emma Lavinia Gifford in 1874 (died 1912); 2) Florence Emily Dugdale in 1914. Moved to London to continue his architectural training, and worked as assistant to Arthur Blomfield, 1862–67; returned to Dorset and began writing fiction, 1867, but continued to work as architect in Dorset and London, 1867–72; full-time writer from 1872; lived at Max Gate, Dorchester, from 1885. Justice of the peace for Dorset; member, Council of Justice to Animals. Recipient: Royal Institute of British Architects medal, for essay, 1863; Architecture Association prize, for design, 1863; Royal Society of Literature gold medal, 1912. LL.D.: University of Aberdeen, 1905; University of St. Andrews, Fife, 1922; University of Bristol, 1925; Litt.D.: Cambridge University, 1913; D.Litt.: Oxford University, 1920. Honorary fellow, Magdalene College, Cambridge, 1913, and Queen's College, Oxford, 1922; honorary fellow, Royal Institute of British Architects. Order of Merit, 1910. *Died 11 January 1928.*

PUBLICATIONS

Collections

New Wessex Edition of the Works.   1974—.
Complete Poems, edited by James Gibson.   1976; *Variorum Edition,* 1979.
The Portable Hardy, edited by Julian Moynahan.   1977.
Complete Poetical Works, edited by Samuel Hynes.   3 vols., 1982–85.
(Selections), edited by Samuel Hynes.   1984.
Collected Short Stories, edited by F.B. Pinion.   1988.

Short Stories

Wessex Tales, Strange, Lively and Commonplace.   1888; revised edition, 1896, 1912.
A Group of Noble Dames.   1891; revised edition, 1896.
Life's Little Ironies: A Set of Tales.   1894; revised edition, 1896, 1912.
A Changed Man, The Waiting Supper, and Other Tales.   1913.

Novels

Desperate Remedies.   1871; revised edition, 1896, 1912.

Under the Greenwood Tree: A Rural Painting of the Dutch School.   1872; revised edition, 1896, 1912; edited by Simon Gatrell, 1985.
A Pair of Blue Eyes.   1873; revised edition, 1895, 1912, 1920; edited by Alan Manford, 1985.
Far from the Madding Crowd.   1874; revised edition, 1875, 1902; edited by James Gibson, 1975.
The Hand of Ethelberta: A Comedy in Chapters.   1876; revised edition, 1895, 1912.
The Return of the Native.   1878; revised edition, 1895, 1912; edited by Colin Temblett-Wood, 1975.
Fellow Townsmen.   1880.
The Trumpet-Major: A Tale.   1880; revised edition, 1895; edited by Ray Evans, 1975.
A Laodicean; or, the Castle of the De Stancys.   1881; revised edition, 1881, 1896, 1912.
Two on a Tower.   1882; revised edition, 1883, 1895, 1912.
The Romantic Adventures of a Milkmaid.   1883; revised edition, 1913.
The Mayor of Casterbridge: The Life and Death of a Man of Character.   1886; revised edition, 1895, 1912; edited by Dale Kramer, 1987.
The Woodlanders.   1887; revised edition, 1895, 1912; edited by Dale Kramer, 1981.
Tess of the d'Urbervilles: A Pure Woman Faithfully Presented.   1891; revised edition, 1892, 1895, 1912; edited by Scott Elledge, 1965, revised 1977.
Wessex Novels.   16 vols., 1895–96.
Jude the Obscure.   1895; revised edition, 1912; edited by Patricia Ingham, 1985.
The Well-Beloved: A Sketch of Temperament.   1897; revised edition, 1912; edited by Tom Hetherington, 1986.
An Indiscretion in the Life of an Heiress.   1934; edited by Terry Coleman, 1976.
Our Exploits at West Poley, edited by Richard Little Purdy.   1952.

Plays

Far from the Madding Crowd, with J. Comyns Carr, from the novel by Hardy (produced 1882).
The Three Wayfarers, from his own story "The Three Strangers" (produced 1893).   1893; revised edition, 1935.
Tess of the d'Urbervilles, from his own novel (produced 1897; revised version, produced 1924). In *Tess in the Theatre,* edited by Marguerite Roberts, 1950.
The Dynasts: A Drama of the Napoleonic Wars.   3 vols., 1904–08; vol. 1 revised, 1904; edited by Harold Orel, 1978.
The Play of Saint George.   1921.
The Famous Tragedy of the Queen of Cornwall (produced 1923).   1923; revised edition, 1924.

Verse

Wessex Poems and Other Verses.   1898.
Poems of the Past and the Present.   1901; revised edition, 1902.
Time's Laughingstocks and Other Verses.   1909.
Satires of Circumstance: Lyrics and Reveries, with Miscellaneous Pieces.   1914.
Selected Poems.   1916; revised edition, as *Chosen Poems,* 1929.
Moments of Vision and Miscellaneous Verses.   1917.

Collected Poems.   1919; revised edition, 1923, 1928, 1930.
Late Lyrics and Earlier, with Many Other Verses.   1922.
Human Shows, Far Phantasies, Songs, and Trifles.   1925.
Winter Words in Various Moods and Metres.   1928.

Other

The Dorset Farm Labourer, Past and Present.   1884.
Works (Wessex Edition).   24 vols., 1912–31.
Works (Mellstock Edition).   37 vols., 1919–20.
Life and Art: Essays, Notes, and Letters, edited by Ernest Brennecke, Jr.   1925.
The Early Life of Hardy 1840–1891, by Florence Hardy. 1928; *The Later Years of Hardy 1892–1928,* 1930;   1 vol. edition, as *The Life of Hardy,* 1962; revised edition, as *The Life and Works of Hardy,* edited by Michael Millgate, 1984.
The Architectural Notebook, edited by C.J.P. Beatty. 1966.
Personal Writings: Prefaces, Literary Opinions, Reminiscences, edited by Harold Orel.   1966.
The Personal Notebooks, edited by Richard H. Taylor. 1978.
Collected Letters, edited by Richard Little Purdy and Michael Millgate.   7 vols., 1978–88; *Selected Letters,* edited by Millgate, 1990.
The Literary Notebooks, edited by Lennart A. Björk.   2 vols., 1985.
Alternative Hardy, edited by Lance St. John Butler.   1989.

Editor, *Select Poems of William Barnes.*   1908.

*

Bibliography: *Hardy: A Bibliographical Study* by Richard Little Purdy, 1954, revised edition, 1968; *Hardy: An Annotated Bibliography of Writings about Him* by Helmut E. Gerber and W. Eugene Davis,   2 vols., 1973–83; *An Annotated Critical Bibliography of Hardy* by R.P. Draper and Martin Ray, 1989.

Critical Studies: *Hardy: A Study of His Writings and Their Background* by W.R. Rutland, 1938; *Hardy of Wessex* by Carl J. Weber, 1940, revised edition, 1965; *Hardy* by Edmund Blunden, 1941; *Hardy the Novelist: An Essay in Criticism* by David Cecil, 1943; *Hardy: The Novels and Stories* by Albert Guerard, 1949, revised edition, 1964, and *Hardy: A Collection of Critical Essays* edited by Guerard, 1963; *The Lyrical Poetry of Hardy* by C. Day Lewis, 1953; *Hardy: A Critical Biography* by Evelyn Hardy, 1954; *The Pattern of Hardy's Poetry* by Samuel Hynes, 1961; *Hardy* by Richard Carpenter, 1964; *Hardy* by Irving Howe, 1967; *Hardy the Novelist: A Reconsideration* by Arnold Kettle, 1967; *Hardy: Materials for a Study of His Life* edited by J. Stevens Cox,   2 vols., 1968–71; *A Hardy Companion,* 1968, revised edition, 1976, *A Commentary on the Poems of Hardy,* 1976, *Hardy: Art and Thought,* 1977, *A Hardy Dictionary,* 1989, and *Hardy the Writer: Surveys and Assessments,* 1990, all by F.B. Pinion; *Hardy: The Critical Heritage* edited by R.G. Cox, 1970; *Hardy: Distance and Desire* by J. Hillis Miller, 1970; *Hardy: The Poetic Structure* by Jean Brooks, 1971; *Hardy: His Career as a Novelist,* 1971, and *Hardy: A Biography,* 1982, both by Michael Millgate; *Hardy: A Critical Biography* by J.I.M. Stewart, 1971; *Hardy and British Poetry* by Donald Davie, 1972;

Hardy and History by R.J. White, 1974; *The Great Web: The Form of Hardy's Major Fiction* by Ian Gregor, 1974; *Moments of Vision: The Poetry of Hardy* by Paul Zietlow, 1974; *Young Hardy,* 1975, and *The Older Hardy,* 1978 (as *Hardy's Later Years,* 1978), both by Robert Gittings, and *The Second Mrs. Hardy* by Gittings and Jo Manton, 1979, revised edition, 1981; *Hardy's The Mayor of Casterbridge: Tragedy or Social History?* by Laurence Lerner, 1975; *The Shaping of Tess of the d'Urbervilles* by J.T. Laird, 1975; *Hardy: The Tragic Novels: A Casebook* edited by R.P. Draper, 1975; *Hardy: The Poetry of Perception* by Tom Paulin, 1975, revised edition, 1986; *Hardy: The Forms of Tragedy* by Dale Kramer, 1975, and *Critical Approaches to the Fiction of Hardy,* 1979, and *Critical Essays on Hardy: The Novels,* 1990, both edited by Kramer; *The Final Years of Hardy 1912–1928* by Harold Orel, 1976; *The Pessimism of Hardy* by G.W. Sherman, 1976; *A Preface to Hardy* by Merryn Williams, 1976; *The Genius of Hardy* edited by Margaret Drabble, 1976; *Hardy, Novelist and Poet,* 1976, and *Hardy's Wessex,* 1983, both by Desmond Hawkins; *Hardy's Poetic Vision in The Dynasts* by Susan Dean, 1977; *Hardy* by Norman Page, 1977, and *Hardy: The Writer and His Background* edited by Page, 1980; *An Essay on Hardy* by John Bayley, 1978; *Hardy* by Lance St. John Butler, 1978; *Hardy and the Sister Arts* by Joan Grundy, 1979; *The Novels of Hardy* edited by Anne Smith, 1979; *The Poetry of Hardy* edited by Patricia Clements and Juliet Grindle, 1980; *Hardy's Poetry,* 1981, and *Hardy's Metres and Victorian Prosody,* 1988, both by Dennis Taylor; *Hardy: Psychological Novelist* by Rosemary Sumner, 1981; *Hardy and Women: Sexual Ideology and Narrative Form* by Penny Boumelha, 1982; *The Short Stories of Hardy: Tales of Past and Present* by Kristin Brady, 1982; *Unity in Hardy's Novels,* 1982, and *Hardy's Influence on the Modern Novel,* 1987, both by Peter J. Casagrande; *The Neglected Hardy: Hardy's Lesser Novels* by Richard H. Taylor, 1982; *The Poetry of Hardy: A Study in Art and Ideas* by William E. Buckler, 1983; *Hardy's Use of Allusion* by Marlene Springer, 1983; *Hardy: Poet of Tragic Vision* by M.M. Das, 1983; *I'd Have My Life Unbe: Hardy's Self-Destructive Characters* by Frank R. Giordano, Jr., 1984; *Hardy's English* by Ralph W.V. Elliott, 1984; *The Expressive Eye: Fiction and Perception in the Work of Hardy* by J.B. Bullen, 1986; *Tess of the d'Urbervilles* edited by Terence Wright and Michael Scott, 1987; *Hardy: The Offensive Truth* by John Goode, 1988; *Hardy the Creator: A Textual Biography* by Simon Gatrell, 1988; *Women and Sexuality in the Novels by Hardy* by Rosemarie Morgan, 1988; *A Journey into Hardy's Poetry* by Joanna Cullen Brown, 1989; *Hardy* by Patricia Ingraham, 1989; *The Language of Hardy* by Raymond Chapman, 1990; *Hardy's Topographical Lexicon and Canon of Intent: A Reading of the Poetry* by Margaret Faurot, 1990; *A Critical Introduction to the Poems of Hardy* by Trevor Johnson, 1990; *Hardy and His God: A Liturgy of Unbelief* by Deborah L. Collins, 1990; *Critical Essays on Hardy: The Novels* edited by Dale Kramer and Nancy Marck, 1990.

*   *   *

Thomas Hardy wrote about 50 short stories, the period of composition extending throughout the last quarter of the 19th century and thus corresponding approximately to the period of his career as a novelist. Nearly all were published soon after composition ("Old Mrs. Chundle," published posthumously, is a notable exception), and appeared in magazines in England or America. The quick returns provided by magazine stories no doubt constituted a significant element in Hardy's income as a professional author, and some critics have been led to dismiss the stories as pot-boilers. Recent critics such as Kristin Brady have, however, taken them more seriously, and Hardy himself regarded them highly enough to collect 37 of them in a series of four volumes, from *Wessex Tales* to *A Changed Man,* and to include these volumes in the collected editions of his works.

The stories fall naturally into four groups, each of which shares certain features with Hardy's full-length novels. In the first group are those that, like *Under the Greenwood Tree* and other novels, evince an intimate, detailed, loving but also at times ironic observation and understanding of rustic and small-town life. A good example is "A Few Crusted Characters," a set of linked anecdotes (described by Hardy himself as "Colloquial Sketches") narrated in turn by various local characters. Another example is "The Distracted Preacher," a love story that also makes use of the theme of smuggling, as well as employing local dialect and topography. This type of story is predominantly humorous or at least light-hearted, in contrast to the serious and even tragic and bizarre mood of many of Hardy's other stories.

A second group can be identified in terms of period setting rather than the use of locale and regional folklife and culture. Hardy had a lifelong interest in the Napoleonic period, manifested not only in his long epic drama *The Dynasts* but in his novel *The Trumpet-Major,* and stories such as "The Melancholy Hussar of the German Legion" are by-products of this enthusiasm. A subgroup of historical tales turns to earlier periods of English history, the most impressive achievement in this area being the volume *A Group of Noble Dames.* This set of ten linked stories, told by various local characters ("the Old Surgeon," "the Rural Dean") with some attention to congruence between teller and tale, may owe something in its structure to *The Canterbury Tales,* but its world is more exclusively localized: as the title suggests, the concern is with the history of various aristocratic or genteel families of the district— further evidence of Hardy's keen response to the idea of the history and vicissitudes of a family. Many of the stories are tragic in tone, the finest of them, "Barbara of the House of Grebe," being a remarkable exercise in Gothic horror. The story is also an interesting instance of Hardy's ability, in a story intended for a middle-class Victorian readership, to handle the themes of eroticism and sadism. (It is true, however, that one contemporary critic described it as "unnatural" and "disgusting," and later T.S. Eliot referred disapprovingly to the "morbid emotion" it seemed to be intended to indulge.) At the same time it represents a striking, and typically Hardyan, blending of modes: as Kristin Brady points out, it is a "fairy tale . . . told in a realistic mode rather than a mode of romance."

This last example suggests that the second category of story that is being proposed here merges into the third: the romantic tales, often embodying some element of the supernatural and claiming kinship with the folk tale and the traditional ballad. One of the finest of these is "The Fiddler of the Reels," another story in which Hardy contrived to effect a compromise between the tolerance level of Victorian readers and editors and his own desire to explore issues of sexuality. Mop's seductive musical powers clearly represent an irresistible sexual magnetism, and the story curiously blends the ancient motif of the demon lover and a modern setting that invokes that arch-Victorian phenomenon, the Great Exhibition of 1851. In somewhat lighter vein is "The Three Strangers," the repetitive

structure of which is strongly reminiscent of the traditional tale or ballad.

In contrast to all of these categories is the final group of stories, those which present contemporary life in highly realistic and often ironic or tragic terms and have much in common with Hardy's later tragic novels such as *Jude the Obscure.* A particularly effective example is "On the Western Circuit," first published in 1891 and hence preceding that novel by only a short period; like *Jude,* too, it suffered bowdlerization on its original magazine appearance. Like so much of Hardy's later work, the story concerns an unsatisfactory marriage and the craving of a woman for the kind of fulfillment that cannot be found in the union to which custom has permanently condemned her. The central idea of the story—that a pregnant woman's strong convictions may leave their mark on her child—has an outcome that may at first sight seem fanciful but is related to Hardy's deep interest in questions of heredity. The story's ending, involving the rejection of the child by his true father, is finely ironic. Though less intense than "An Imaginative Woman," "The Son's Veto" is another notable story in this category.

As the examples cited suggest, Hardy's range as a writer of short stories is wide. In the preface to *Wessex Tales,* defending the historical accuracy of some of his stories, he remarks disarmingly that they "are but dreams, and not records." The truth seems to be that they are both dreams and records, the two elements sometimes being found within a single example. The time is certainly past when Hardy's short fiction can be ignored or dismissed as mere journeyman work, for it has both a significant and suggestive relationship to his more ambitious projects and, at its best, offers work of a quality comparable with that of contemporary writers, like Kipling and Conrad, whose short stories have been treated as a more familiar and integral part of their achievement.

—Norman Page

See the essays on "On the Western Circuit" and "A Tragedy of Two Ambitions."

HARRIS, Joel Chandler. American. Born near Eatonton, Georgia, 9 December 1848. Educated at Eatonton Academy for Boys. Married Esther LaRose in 1873; nine children. Printer's devil and typesetter, *Countryman* weekly, published at the Turnwold Plantation, 1862–66; staff member, Macon *Telegraph,* Georgia, 1866, *Crescent Monthly,* New Orleans, 1866–67, *Monroe Advertiser,* Forsyth, Georgia, 1867–70, Savannah *Morning News,* Georgia, 1870–76, and Atlanta *Constitution,* 1876–1900; founder, with his son Julian, *Uncle Remus's* magazine, Atlanta, 1907–08. L.H.D.: Emory College, Oxford, Georgia, 1902. Member, American Academy, 1905. *Died 2 July 1908.*

PUBLICATIONS

Collections

The Complete Tales of Uncle Remus, edited by Richard Chase.   1955.

Short Stories

Uncle Remus: His Songs and His Sayings: The Folklore of the Old Plantation.   1880; as *Uncle Remus and His Legends of the Old Plantation*, 1881; as *Uncle Remus; or, Mr. Fox, Mr. Rabbit, and Mr. Terrapin*, 1881; revised edition, 1895.
Nights with Uncle Remus: Myths and Legends of the Old Plantation.   1883.
Mingo and Other Sketches in Black and White.   1884.
Free Joe and Other Georgian Sketches.   1887.
Daddy Jake the Runaway and Short Stories Told after Dark.   1889.
Balaam and His Master and Other Sketches and Stories.   1891.
A Plantation Printer: The Adventures of a Georgia Boy During the War.   1892; as *On the Plantation*, 1892.
Uncle Remus and His Friends: Old Plantation Stories, Songs, and Ballads, with *Sketches of Negro Character*.   1892.
Little Mr. Thimblefinger and His Queer Country: What the Children Saw and Heard There.   1894.
Mr. Rabbit at Home.   1895.
Stories of Georgia.   1896; revised edition, 1896.
Aaron in the Wildwoods.   1897.
Tales of the Home Folks in Peace and War.   1898.
Plantation Pageants.   1899.
The Chronicles of Aunt Minervy Ann.   1899.
On the Wing of Occasions.   1900.
The Making of a Statesman and Other Stories.   1902.
Wally Wanderoon and His Story-Telling Machine.   1903.
A Little Union Scout: A Tale of Tennessee During the Civil War.   1904.
Told by Uncle Remus: New Stories of the Old Plantation.   1905.
Uncle Remus and Brer Rabbit.   1907.
The Bishop and the Boogerman.   1909; as *The Bishop and the Bogie-Man*, 1909.
Uncle Remus and the Little Boy.   1910.
Uncle Remus Returns.   1918.
The Witch Wolf: An Uncle Remus Story.   1921.

Novels

The Story of Aaron (So Named), The Son of Ben Ali, Told by His Friends and Acquaintances.   1896.
Sister Jane, Her Friends and Acquaintances.   1896.
Gabriel Tolliver: A Story of Reconstruction.   1902.
The Shadow Between His Shoulder-Blades.   1909.
Qua: A Romance of the Revolution, edited by Thomas H. English.   1946.

Verse

The Tar-Baby and Other Rhymes of Uncle Remus.   1904.

Other

Harris, Editor and Essayist: Miscellaneous Literary, Political, and Social Writings, edited by Julia C. Harris.   1931.

Editor, *Life of Henry W. Grady, Including His Writings and Speeches: A Memorial Volume.*   1890.
Editor, *The Book of Fun and Frolic.*   1901; as *Merrymaker*, 1902.
Editor, *World's Wit and Humor.*   1904.

Translator, *Evening Tales*, by Frédéric Ortoli.   1893.

*

Bibliography: in *Bibliography of American Literature* by Jacob Blanck, 1959; *Harris: A Reference Guide* by R. Bruce Bickley, Jr., and others, 1978.

Critical Studies: *The Life and Letters of Harris* by Julia Collier Harris, 1918; *Harris, Folklorist* by Stella Brewer Brookes, 1950; *Harris: A Biography* by Paul M. Cousins, 1968; *Harris* by R. Bruce Bickley, Jr., 1978, and *Critical Essays on Harris* edited by Bickley, 1981; *Sources and Analogues of the Uncle Remus Tales* by Florence E. Baer, 1980.

*   *   *

In his novels, journalism, and stories, Joel Chandler Harris tried to preserve the best of the Old South to promote America's reconciliation after the Civil War. Besides his tales of reunion, he is famous for his Uncle Remus stories, a series of African-American folktales told by a former slave.

The reunion tales are unfailingly formulaic. They typically feature a middle Georgia rural setting, a narrator who is returning from the city to a community he knew as a youth in the idyllic days before the war, a faithful ex-slave who has returned to serve former masters after his newfound freedom proves disappointing, a Yankee soldier wounded in the vicinity who remains afterward, and southern whites who are perhaps a bit too proud but are nevertheless worthy of the reader's sympathy.

Harris takes particular care in depicting those characters toward whom the white South may have had a lingering wariness or antagonism. The Yankee soldier, for example, usually faces initial antagonism, but through his wholesome good nature is eventually accepted into, and makes essential contributions to, the southern community. This acceptance may be dramatized in his being wedded to a southern woman and entrusted with the management of her family's plantation ("Aunt Fountain's Prisoner," "The Old Bascom Place," and "A Story of the War"), or in his developing a lasting friendship with a southern man ("Little Compton"). In either case, the denouement advocates a healthy union of the best of the old (southern) way of life with the best of the new (northern). Thus the reader's faith in the South's, and by extension America's, future is restored.

Harris also invests considerable time developing benevolent black characters. Often these faithful servants narrate substantial portions of the stories, a common device used in reconciliation fiction of the period. As in Thomas Nelson Page's "Marse Chan," Harris stories such as "Mingo," "Balaam and His Master," and "A Story of the War," feature a former slave who chronicles the happiness, trials, and tribulations of his or her owners with pleasure, respect, and love. These ex-slave narrators seem to have no lives or aspirations of their own; they live a vicarious existence through their former masters. Having the supposed victims of southern slavery speak adoringly of kindly masters reassured the white South that the blacks bore no grudge against them. It also reassured the North that the South could be trusted once again to rule itself and its former slaves.

One noteworthy variation on the reunion story is "Mingo." Here reconciliation is not between the North and the South but between southern social classes. Feratia Bivins is a proud poor white whose son marries the daughter of the aristocratic Wornums, who consequently disown her. After the son and daughter die during the Civil War, their child is left in the care of Feratia and the ex-slave Mingo, who returns from an aimless search for freedom to help support his former mistress's child. Eventually Mrs. Wornum, chastened by the news of her daughter's death, humbles herself before Feratia so that she can become acquainted with her granddaughter. Feratia not only swallows her resentment of the rich woman but also overcomes her poor-white prejudice against blacks, acknowledging that without Mingo, she and her granddaughter could never have survived. The story's ending portrays a union of aristocrat, poor white, and child (the product of the marriage of the two classes), presided over by the constancy, benevolence, and practical good sense of an ex-slave who has committed himself even in freedom to serving whites.

Harris is most famous for his popular Uncle Remus tales, which also have a conciliatory purpose. They are usually framed by dialogue between Uncle Remus, a kindly ex-slave who remains on his mistress and her Yankee husband's plantation after the war doing various chores, and the little son of the plantation owners. But, as several literary critics have pointed out, the tales have another dimension that transcends Harris's political purposes; inside the frame stories there are animal legends that were orally transmitted by the slaves for several generations before Harris preserved them in written form.

Spread over ten volumes, these 220 tales are a wealth of information about the folk imagination and, more specifically, about African-American efforts to preserve their humanity during slavery. Some of the tales are concerned with etiology, or how the earth and its creatures became what they are. For example, "How Mr. Rabbit Lost His Fine Bushy Tail" and "Why Mr. Possum Has No Hair on His Tail" describe the origins of the physical characteristics of animals. "The Story of the Deluge, and How It Came About" is a universal myth of a great flood. In addition, though, this story allegorizes the position of the oppressed slave in American society. Unable to get a hearing at a raucous assembly of animals and literally stepped on by the larger animals, the crawfishes gain revenge by drilling holes into the ground and unleashing a deluge. The moral of the story seems to be that the weak cannot be ignored: they are capable of undermining the strong and powerful.

The triumph of the powerless is a common theme in the tales. The slave's preference for the weaker animals is perhaps best conveyed by Brer Rabbit, a trickster—that is, a legendary hero who survives against superior force through his superior wit and ability to deceive his enemies. The rabbit's tricks are often violent and inhumane. Several critics have suggested that they are a reflection of the slave system and give vent to the slave's suppressed desire for vengeance for the abuses of slavery.

On the allegorical level, the competition between Brer Rabbit and his foes suggests real or potential disputes over power and ownership in plantation society. In "Mr. Rabbit Grossly Deceives Mr. Fox," for example, sexual competition is treated from the slave's point of view. Brer Fox would like dearly to humiliate Brer Rabbit in front of "Miss Meadows and the gals" to prove his superiority, but the rabbit pretends to be ill and tricks the fox into carrying him before the ladies on his saddled back. The rabbit wins the admiration of the women while the fox appears to be merely a beast of burden. The story ends with Brer Rabbit sauntering into the ladies' house triumphantly smoking a cigar.

Although the allegory is not consistent because the stories were not conceived by a single author nor created systematically, the animal tales give remarkable insight into the experience of the slaves and the world they lived in. These and Harris's other short fiction influenced a nation's perception of the South and the African-American.

—William L. Howard

See the essays on "Free Joe and the Rest of the World" and "The Wonderful Tar-Baby Story."

————

HARTE, (Francis) Bret(t). American. Born in Albany, New York, 25 August 1836; lived with his family in various cities in the northeast, then in New York City after 1845. Educated in local schools to age 13. Married Anna Griswold in 1862; four children. Worked in a lawyer's office, then a merchant's counting room, New York; moved to Oakland, California, 1854; teacher, LaGrange, apothecary's clerk, Oakland, and express-man in various California towns, 1854–55; private tutor, 1856; guard on Wells Fargo stagecoach, 1857; printer and reporter, Arcata *Northern Californian,* 1858–60; moved to San Francisco: typesetter, *Golden Era,* 1860–61; clerk, Surveyor General's office, 1861–63; secretary, U.S. branch mint, 1863–69; contributor and occasional acting editor, *Californian,* 1864–66; first editor, *Overland Monthly,* 1868–71; lived in New Jersey and New York, 1871–78; went on lecture tours, 1872–74; tried unsuccessfully to establish *Capitol* magazine, 1878; U.S. commercial agent, Krefeld, Germany, 1878–80; U.S. Consul, Glasgow, 1880–85; lived in London, 1885–1902. *Died 5 May 1902.*

PUBLICATIONS

Collections

Writings.   20 vols., 1896–1914.
Representative Selections, edited by Joseph B. Harrison. 1941.
The Best Short Stories, edited by Robert N. Linscott. 1967.

Short Stories

The Lost Galleon and Other Tales.   1867.
The Luck of Roaring Camp and Other Sketches.   1870; revised edition, 1871.
Stories of the Sierras and Other Sketches.   1872.
Mrs. Skaggs's Husbands and Other Sketches.   1873.
An Episode of Fiddletown and Other Sketches.   1873.
Tales of the Argonauts and Other Sketches.   1875.
Wan Lee, The Pagan and Other Sketches.   1876.
My Friend, The Tramp.   1877.
The Man on the Beach.   1878.
Jinny.   1878.
Drift from Two Shores.   1878; as *The Hoodlum Bard and Other Stories,* 1878.
An Heiress of Red Dog and Other Sketches.   1879.
The Twins of Table Mountain.   1879.

Jeff Briggs's Love Story and Other Sketches.   1880.
Flip and Other Stories.   1882.
On the Frontier.   1884.
California Stories.   1884.
The Heritage of Dedlow Marsh and Other Tales.   1889.
A Sappho of Green Springs and Other Tales.   1891.
Sally Dows, Etc.   1893.
A Protegee of Jack Hamlin's and Other Stories.   1894.
The Bell-Ringer of Angel's and Other Stories.   1894.
Barker's Luck and Other Stories.   1896.
The Ancestors of Peter Atherly and Other Tales.   1897.
Tales of Trail and Town.   1898.
Stories in Light and Shadow.   1898.
Mr. Jack Hamlin's Mediation and Other Stories.   1899.
Trent's Trust and Other Stories.   1903.

Novels

Condensed Novels and Other Papers.   1867; revised edition, 1871.
The Little Drummer; or, The Christmas Gift That Came to Rupert: A Story for Children.   1872.
Idyls of the Foothills.   1874.
Gabriel Conroy.   1876.
Thankful Blossom: A Romance of the Jerseys 1779.   1877.
Thankful Blossom and Other Tales.   1877.
The Story of a Mine.   1877.
In the Carquinez Woods.   1883.
By Shore and Sedge.   1885.
Maruja.   1885.
Snow-Bound at Eagle's.   1886.
The Queen of the Pirate Isle.   1886.
A Millionaire of Rough-and-Ready, and Devil's Ford.   1887.
The Crusade of the Excelsior.   1887.
A Phyllis of the Sierras, and A Drift from Redwood Camp.   1888.
The Argonauts of North Liberty.   1888.
Cressy.   1889.
Captain Jim's Friend, and The Argonauts of North Liberty.   1889.
A Waif of the Plains.   1890.
A Ward of the Golden Gate.   1890.
A First Family of Tasajara.   1891.
Colonel Starbottle's Client and Some Other People.   1892.
Susy: A Story of the Plains.   1893.
Clarence.   1895.
In a Hollow of the Hills.   1895.
Three Partners; or, The Big Strike on Heavy Tree Hill.   1897.
From Sand Hill to Pine.   1900.
Under the Redwoods.   1901.
Openings in the Old Trail.   1902; as *On the Old Trail,* 1902.
Condensed Novels: Second Series: New Burlesques.   1902.

Plays

Two Men of Sandy Bar, from his story "Mr. Thompson's Prodigal."   1876.
Ah Sin, with Mark Twain (produced 1877).   Edited by Frederick Anderson, 1961.
Sue, with T. Edgar Pemberton, from the story "The Judgment of Bolinas Plain" by Harte (produced 1896). 1902; as *Held Up* (produced 1903).

Verse

The Heathen Chinee.   1870.
Poems.   1871.
That Heathen Chinee and Other Poems, Mostly Humorous.   1871.
East and West Poems.   1871.
Poetical Works.   1872; revised edition, 1896, 1902.
Echoes of the Foot-Hills.   1874.
Some Later Verses.   1898.
Unpublished Limericks and Cartoons.   1933.

Other

Complete Works.   1872.
Prose and Poetry.   2 vols., 1872.
Lectures, edited by Charles Meeker Kozlay.   1909.
Stories and Poems and Other Uncollected Writings, edited by Charles Meeker Kozlay.   1914.
Sketches of the Sixties by Harte and Mark Twain from The Californian 1864–67.   1926; revised edition, 1927.
Letters, edited by Geoffrey Bret Harte.   1926.
San Francisco in 1866, Being Letters to the Springfield Republican, edited by George R. Stewart and Edwin S. Fussell.   1951.

Editor, *Outcroppings, Being Selections of California Verse.*   1865.
Editor, *Poems,* by Charles Warren Stoddard.   1867.

*

Bibliography: in *Bibliography of American Literature* by Jacob Blanck, 1959; *Harte: A Reference Guide* by Linda D. Barnett, 1980.

Critical Studies: *Harte, Argonaut and Exile* by George R. Stewart, 1931; *Mark Twain and Harte* by Margaret Duckett, 1964; *Harte: A Biography* by Richard O'Connor, 1966; *Harte,* 1972, and *Harte, Literary Critic,* 1979, both by Patrick Morrow.

*   *   *

Although Bret Harte has often been scorned as the author of unrealistic and sentimental short stories such as "The Luck of Roaring Camp," "The Outcasts of Poker Flat," and "Tennessee's Partner," some literary historians have suggested that his influence on the short story has been significant. Arthur Hobson Quinn has argued that Harte taught nearly all American writers of short stories some of the essentials of their art, and Fred Lewis Pattee has placed Harte second only to Washington Irving in his influence on the form.

Harte's short fiction represents a transition point between the romanticism of Nathaniel Hawthorne and Edgar Allan Poe and the realism of Hamlin Garland and William Dean Howells, resting uneasily in that era of American literature known as the local color movement. Harte once said he aimed to be the Washington Irving of the Pacific coast. And indeed his stories are closely related to the folklore of a region, much as Irving's "Rip Van Winkle" and "The Legend of Sleepy Hollow" are. However, Harte differs from Irving in that his characters derive not from folklore itself, but rather from actuality; indeed, this grounding of the stuff of fable in the world of fact explains how local color formed the roots of the realistic movement. Harte is a realist in that he tries to create the illusion that the events in his stories could actually happen and that the characters are as-if-real, rather than that the events were derived from folklore as they are in the stories of Irving, or that the characters are the figures of parable, as they are in the stories of Hawthorne.

This grounding of characters and events in a specific regional area creates the illusion of realism often attributed to Harte. For example, in his first story, "The Work on Red Mountain," later named "M'liss," Harte creates a character who seems to come alive with reality primarily because in her rebellion and individuality she stands out so extremely from those around her. However, the creation of a character who is an individualist does not necessarily mean the creation of an individual character. In his invention of philosophical gamblers, virginal schoolmarms, and prostitutes with hearts of gold, Harte did not draw on preexisting stereotypes so much as he created them to become stereotypes of the pulp and b-movie western ever since.

Granted, Harte makes use of a crude sort of psychology, but by presenting burly and coarse-talking miners as gentle father-figures, hard and brittle gamblers as philosophical Hamlets, and gaudily-painted prostitutes as self-sacrificing martyrs, Harte tried to show that beneath the surface of one's external persona lay unexamined depths when a crisis or a novel situation arose to stimulate them. The sentimentality that results from this simplistic psychology often constitutes the crucial turning point of Harte's stories; thus, it is the sentimentality of the gestures of Kentuck, Tennessee's Partner, and the gambler Oakhurst that remains with the reader.

However, it is the humor that usually goes along with the pathos that critics have failed to note in Harte—a humor that creates ironic effects that make his stories more complex than they first appear and that has made them so influential on the development of the short story. Harte would have been happy to accept this as his major contribution, for he once singled out humor, originating in stories and anecdotes and orally transmitted in barrooms and country stories, as the factor that finally diminished the influence of English models on the form and created the first true American short story.

The topsy turvy world of Bret Harte is primarily created by the comic intent of the point of view or voice of his stories. In her classic study of American humor, Constance Rourke notes that Harte used the traditional forms of burlesque, sketch, yarn, and episode, and particularly the monologue: "Its tone was often apparent even when the personal approach was submerged." This monologue humor is most obvious in what has been called Harte's best story, "Tennessee's Partner," for here the bipolarity of humor and pathos seems most obviously laid bare. However, the story has not always been understood this way. Mark Twain's annotations on the story focus on the central problem: "Does the artist show a clear knowledge of human nature when he makes his hero *welcome back* a man who has committed against him that sin which neither the great nor the little ever forgive? & not only welcome him back but love him with the fondling love of a girl to the last, & *then* pine for the loss of him?"

The problem with Twain's reading of the story, and that of numerous readers since, is that he has not paid careful attention to the tone of the teller. After relating how Tennessee's partner went to San Francisco for a wife and was stopped in Stockton by a young waitress who broke at least two plates of toast over his head, the narrator says that he is well aware that "something more might be made of this episode, but I prefer to tell it as it was current at Sandy Bar—in the gulches and barrooms—where all sentiment was modified by a strong sense of humor." It is from this point of view—sentiment modified by humor—that the narrator tells the entire story. Tennessee's running off with his partner's wife and his trial and execution are related in the same flippant phrases and in the same tone as used to describe Tennessee's partner's somewhat hazardous wooing. Once the reader is willing to accept this barroom point of view, the story takes on a new and not so pathetic dimension. The narrator fully intends for this story to be, not the occasion for tears, but for sardonic laughter.

Still, it is Harte's sentimentality that has most appealed to popular readers and has most alienated the serious critical establishment. Wallace Stegner has summed up Harte's critical situation admirably: "The consensus on Harte is approximately what it was at the time of his death: that he was a skillful but not profound writer who make a lucky strike in subject matter and for a few heady months enjoyed a fabulous popularity."

—Charles E. May

See the essays on "The Luck of Roaring Camp" and "The Outcasts of Poker Flat."

HARTLEY, L(eslie) P(oles). English. Born in Whittlesea, Cambridgeshire, 30 December 1895. Educated at Harrow School, Middlesex (Leaf scholar), 1910–15; Balliol College, Oxford (Williams exhibitioner; editor, *Oxford Outlook*), 1915–16, 1919–22, B.A. in history 1921. Served in the British Army, Norfolk Regiment, 1916–18: 2nd lieutenant. Fiction reviewer, *Spectator, Saturday Review, Weekly Sketch, Time and Tide,* the *Observer,* and the *Sunday Times,* all London, 1923–72; lived part of each year in Venice, 1933–39; lived in Bath and London, 1946–72; Clark lecturer, Trinity College, Cambridge, 1964. Member of the Committee of Management, Society of Authors; president, PEN English section. Recipient: James Tait Black memorial prize, 1948; Heinemann award, 1954. C.B.E. (Commander, Order of the British Empire), 1956; Companion of Literature, Royal Society of Literature, 1972. *Died 13 December 1972.*

PUBLICATIONS

Collections

The Complete Short Stories.   1973.

Short Stories

Night Fears and Other Stories.   1924.
The Killing Bottle.   1932.
The Travelling Grave and Other Stories.   1948.
The White Wand and Other Stories.   1954.
Two for the River and Other Stories.   1961.
The Collected Short Stories.   1968.
Mrs. Carteret Receives and Other Stories.   1971.

Novels

Simonetta Perkins.   1925.
Eustace and Hilda.   1958.
   The Shrimp and the Anemone.   1944; as *The West Window,* 1945.
   The Sixth Heaven.   1946.
   Eustace and Hilda.   1947.
The Boat.   1949.
My Fellow Devils.   1951.
The Go-Between.   1953.
A Perfect Woman.   1955.
The Hireling.   1957.
Facial Justice.   1960.
The Brickfield.   1964.
The Betrayal.   1966.
Poor Clare.   1968.
The Love-Adept: A Variation on a Theme.   1969.
My Sisters' Keeper.   1970.
The Harness Room.   1971.
The Collections.   1972.
The Will and the Way.   1973.

Other

The Novelist's Responsibility: Lectures and Essays.   1967.
The Cat (essay).   1986.

*

Critical Studies: *Hartley* by Paul Bloomfield, 1962, revised edition, 1970; *Hartley* by Peter Bien, 1963; *Wild Thyme, Winter Lightning: The Symbolic Novels of Hartley* by Anne Mulkeen, 1974; *Hartley* by Edward T. Jones, 1978; *Best Friends* by Julian Fane, 1990.

* * *

Often described as a stylist in the mould of Henry James (a portrayal given some edge by his Jamesian first novel *Simonetta Perkins* in which a young Bostonian falls for a handsome gondolier) L.P. Hartley is more than a simple imitator with a limited literary range. In *Night Fears,* his first collection of short stories, he provided evidence that he was an assured author with an acute yet delicate eye for the manners, morals, and harmless foibles of middle-class society.

The majority of the stories in the first collection can be described as experimental investigations into the different mental or psychological states of the main characters. The title story of *Night Fears,* for instance, explores the fears of a night watchman during the course of a single night. As the man confronts his own terrors Hartley contrasts the solidity of the environment around him with the darkness and solitude outside: for the man, one is reality and the other is the invisible world of the mind.

Fears of another kind lie at the hearts of "A Visit to the Dentist," in which an outsider convinces himself that life can only have meaning by facing up to a physical pain. In "A Tonic" a similar theme is explored; a seriously ill man attempts to persuade a distinguished physician, Sir Sigismund Keen, that he does not suffer from a serious heart condition. The story is both a perceptive study of one man's particular neurosis and a comment on every human being's fear of death. Another type of neurosis is examined

in "Talent": a man goes through life convincing himself that he is without any literary talent when all the evidence suggests otherwise.

Other stories in the volume, like "St. George and the Dragon," "The Telephone Call," "A Condition of Release," and "The Last Time," betray another Hartleian preoccupation—the realisation that life can never be tamed even though people spend most of their time attempting to bring order to their existence. In "A Condition of Release" a foppish young man attempts to be decisive by taking a swim but is discomforted by the theft of his trousers. Hartley provides an ironic vignette of the clash between other and chaos in a comic scene in which the pompous swimmer is forced to change roles with the vagabond to have his clothes returned.

"The Island," the longest story in this first collection, is also the most satisfying. Hartley makes it clear from the beginning that the life lived by Mrs. Santander, the central character, is vainglorious and self-destructive. Although she lives apart from the rest of the world, cocooned in a luxurious house, outside the environment is harsh and unforgiving. The island itself looks like "some crustacean, swallowed by an ill-turned starfish, but unassimilated," while inside her house order reigns. Of course, this is an illusion; Mrs. Santander is a flawed character who is unfaithful to her husband. When she is murdered at the story's end, Hartley makes the wind and the rain crash into the idealised world Mrs. Santander has created for herself, thereby underlining the idea that people cannot isolate themselves from real life.

Hartley's understanding of the meeting points between reality and fantasy and his absorption with the symbolism of the "otherness" of life are developed further in the later horror and ghost stories of *The Killing Bottle* and *The Travelling Grave.* Here the characters exist in a world as tangible as the one of their own creation like the country house settings of "Feet Foremost," "A Change of Ownership," or "The Travelling Grave." Italy, too, is a favourite setting and is often recreated in a fantastic way so that the islands near Venice, in "Three, Four for Dinner," are as much as exotic paradise as a real place.

Like John Buchan, Hartley is well aware of the narrow line that divides the civilised world from barbarism and in his best Gothic tales ("A Visitor from Down Under," "Podollo," "The Cotillon") evil is seen as a mysterious force impinging on the lives of ordinary people. Vengeance and revenge after death are also favourite themes of stories: in "Feet Foremost" the ghostly and possessive love of Lady Elinor for Antony is a curse and he can only be saved by the love of another woman. These macabre and fantastical elements are central to Hartley's vision.

In the later stories of *The White Wand* and *Two for the River* Hartley continues his exploration of familiar themes in a deeper and more refined way. "W.S." is typical of the author's literary bravura and tackles the idea of the doppelganger. Walter Streeter, an author, is surprised to receive a series of threatening postcards from "W.S.," one of his least pleasant characters, and he comes to the sorry understanding that his character's worst points are merely an extension of his own failings. Although the conclusion is farcical, the story is an acute examination of the conundrum that good and evil can exist side by side in the human personality.

Other stories with the writer or artist as hero/villain are "Up the Garden Path," "The Two Vaynes," "A Rewarding Experience," and "The White Wand" (all from *The White Wand*). As in "W.S.," Hartley seems to be saying that creative people have the facility to see behind appearances and to understand the moral dilemma thrown up by conflicting mental states.

Hartley's early interest in the supernatural and paranormal also informs much of his longer fiction and points the way to the moral concerns of novels like *The Go-Between* and the *Eustace and Hilda* trilogy.

—Trevor Royle

See the essay on "The Travelling Grave."

———

HAŠEK, Jaroslav. Czech. Born in Prague, Bohemia, 30 April 1883. Educated at St. Stephen's School, 1891–93; Imperial and Royal Junior Gymnasium, 1893–97, expelled; Czechoslavonic Commercial Academy, 1899–1902. Married 1) Jarmila Mayerová in 1910 (separated 1912), one son; 2) bigamous marriage with Shura Lvova in 1920. Worked for a chemist in late 1890's; wrote stories and sketches for several humorous and political magazines from 1901; also wrote and performed cabaret sketches; clerk, Insurance Bank of Slavie, 1902–03; jailed for anarchist rioting, 1907; editor, *Svět zvířat* (Animal World), 1909–10; assistant editor, *Czech Word*, 1911; conscripted, 1915; captured by the Russians: allowed to work for Czech forces in Russia, and staff member, *Čechoslovan*, Kiev, 1916–18; after a propaganda battle, 1917–18, left Czech group and entered political department of the Siberian Army: editor, *Our Path* (later *Red Arrow*), 1919, *Red Europe*, 1919, and other propaganda journals in Russia and Siberia; sent to Czechoslovakia to do propaganda work, 1920; lived in Lipnice from 1921. *Died 3 January 1923.*

PUBLICATIONS

Collections

Spisy [Works].   16 vols., 1955–68.

Short Stories

Dobrý voják švejk a jiné podivné historky [The Good Soldier švejk and Other Strange Stories].   1912.
Trampoty pana Tenkráta [The Tribulations of Mr. That-Time].   1912.
Průvodčí cizincu a jiné satiry.   1913; as *The Tourist Guide: Twenty-Six Stories*, 1961.
Můj obchod se psy [My Trade with Dogs].   1916.
Dobrý voják švejk v zajetí [The Good Soldier švejk in Captivity] (novella).   1917.
Pepíček Nový a jiné historky [Pepíček Nový and Other Stories].   1921.
Tři muži se žralokem a jiné poučné historky [Three Men and a Shark and Other Instructive Stories].   1921.
Mírová Konference [The Peace Conference].   1922.
Idylky z pekla.   1974.
The Red Commissar, Including Further Adventures of the Good Soldier Svejk and Other Stories.   1981.
Povídky (selection).   2 vols., 1988.
The Bachura Scandal and Other Stories and Sketches.   1991.

Novel

Osudy dobrého vojáka švejk za světové války [The Good Soldier švejk and His Fortunes in the World War].   4 vols., 1921–23; as *The Good Soldier Schweik,* 1930; complete version, 1973.

Other

Maloměstský pitaval.   1978.
Lidsky profil Haška [Selected Letters].   1979.
Žroutská historie.   1979.
Nejnovější český galanthomue čili krasochovník.   1985.
Tajemstuí mého pobytu v Rusku [Essays Selected].   1985.

*

Critical Studies: *The Bad Bohemian: The Life of Hašek,* 1978, and *Hašek: A Study of švejk and the Short Stories,* 1982, both by Cecil Parrott.

* * *

Jaroslav Hašek is best known as the author of the most famous Czech book, the anti war satire *Osudy dobrého vojáka Švejk za světové války (The Good Soldier Schweik).* Hašek wrote his only novel in 1921 and 1922, and its four volumes were still only a fragment at the time of his death in 1923. The book, which has since then been translated into numerous foreign languages and which for many foreigners is the only book in Czech they have ever heard of, was at first dismissed by the literary establishment of the young Czech republic as unliterary and detrimental to the national spirit. It was banned in the armies of Czechoslovakia, Poland, and Hungary.

During his life and for long after his death, Hašek's writing was on the periphery of Czech literature and he himself was not taken seriously as an artist. He was a heavy drinker who frequented many Prague pubs, known as a joker entertaining the public, an anarchist fighting against authority. Many of his pranks shocked the Prague petit-bourgeois and engaged the attention of the police, the most famous being Hašek's parliamentary candidacy for his own mock Party of Moderate Progress Within the Limits of the Law.

Hašek's principal work, *The Good Soldier Schweik,* did not come out of nowhere. His 1,300 short stories and feuilletons written before and during World War I are a preparation, in style and theme, for the masterpiece. Most of these have high merits of their own. Hand in hand with Hašek's bohemian existence goes a certain unliterariness of his style. Hašek wrote in the tradition of popular culture, the "culture of the street." His fiction is full of fascinating types placed in ludicrous situations. Having a gift for brief characterization, Hašek does not dwell on his characters' appearance but rather on their actions and manner of speech. He uses the humor and often the means of expression of the uncultured classes. The scope and variety of characters and their milieu is amazing, and so is Hašek's thorough knowledge of their idiom and his ingenuity in inventing comic plots. Hašek's creativity stems from an immediate idea and verbal improvization. The short stories read more like anecdotes, often structurally crude and obviously hurriedly written. They are mostly very short—usually less than 1,000 words—as they had to fit the space allotted a daily feuilleton in the newspaper. Brevity affects their style—a condensed narrative telling a single episode, bare of descriptions and using simple sentences with no literary adornments. The very first sentences catch the reader's attention and introduce a comic accent. For example, one of Hašek's anti-clerical stories, "The Struggle for the Soul" (1913), starts ironically: "Vicar Michalejc was a saintly man with an income of 3,000 crowns a year, apart from other benefits derived from eight additional parishes attached to his own parishes" (translated by Cecil Parrott).

Hašek's humor is not kind. His tone is sarcastic, bitter, often cynical to the point of crassness. This is part of Hašek's antibourgeois stance. His bohemian negation attacks the powerful authorities and institutions of the Austro-Hungarian Empire, of which Bohemia was then part, and the sacred symbols and myths of Czech national life. His satire targets the church, the aristocracy, the army, schools, parents, children, Germans, Czechs, politics and politicians, and the bureacracy. Typical of most 20th-century Czech and world satire, it is also a demasking of the emptiness of language, an uncompromising attack at the meaninglessness of official bureaucratic phrases and stylistic clichés of the administration, which become identified with the absurdity of the political system. Ever-present irony discloses all remnants of obsolete ideas and shatters hypetrophic applications of moral norms.

Hašek's anti-establishment ideology is aimed against convention and the absurd alienation of humanity. In this Hašek has often been compared to his Prague contemporary, Franz Kafka. Both inhabit a phantasmagoric, dehumanized world of bureaucracy. What distinguishes them is Hašek's liberating effect of humor and laughter.

The absurdities of administrative practice and its red tape are parodied in some of Hašek's best stories, especially "The Official Zeal of Mr. Štěpán Brych, Toll Collector on a Bridge in Prague" (1911), in which the thoughtless execution of orders without consideration leads to fatal consequences.

Robert Pynsent has identified as one of the most common of Hašek's types the *schlemazel*, an awkward, clumsy fellow, ridden with bad luck, who serves as a vehicle for satire directed at an institution. Such is Lindiger whose business ventures go wrong in "The Coffin-Dealer" (1914), the burglar in "Šejba the Burglar Goes on a Job" (1913), and "The Purple Thunderbolt" (1913).

Most of Hašek's stories are based on true incidents in his life. Hašek really did run a pet shop that, just as in the story "The Cynological Institute" (1915), was essentially a dog-stealing business. "The Psychiatric Puzzle" (1911) is based on another real experience when Hašek was imprisoned for a purported suicide attempt.

Although best known for an antimilitarist novel, Hašek did not concentrate on the army until World War I. Antimilitarist satire is relatively mild in Hašek's pre war stories; for example, "Infantryman Trunec's Cap" (1909) is more of a satire on army bureaucracy. "At the Barber's" (1911), a superbly written stream-of-consciousness tale, though dealing with the grotesqueness of war, is more of a satire on Czech petit-bourgeois national and racial prejudices. An anti war stance is more apparent in the first five Švejk stories (1911) and the 1917 short novel *Dobrý voják Švejk v zajetí* (The Good Soldier Švejk in Captivity), forerunners of Hašek's final masterpiece.

Hašek wrote most of his stories before the war for Prague newspapers. During the war he wrote patriotic political pamphlets for the Czech Legion's newspaper in Kiev, but those have nearly no literary value. The cycle of tales centered around the Siberian town of Bugulma, where Hašek was stationed as a Communist commissar after he had joined the Red Army, is considered by critics like Cecil Parrott to be his best. Autobiographical in character, these stories show commissar Gashek (the Russian alphabet has no *h*) trying to create order in the chaos of new revolutionary authorities.

Hašek has often been accused of misanthropy; his humor may have been sometimes vulgar and crass, his satire biting and bitter, but his outlook remains essentially optimistic. His contemporary, another famous Czech writer, Karel Čapek wrote: "In school we were taught that humor is a spice. Today it seems to me rather that humor is not an ingredient, but a basic formula which one must apply when observing the world. Hašek had humour. Hašek was a person who *saw the world.* Many others just write about it" (quoted from the introduction to *Průvodčí cizincú a jiné satiry [The Tourist Guide]*). Hašek and his humor influenced many writers, including Brecht, Heller, Hrabal, and Škvorecký.

—Soňa Nováková

HAUPTMANN, Gerhart (Johann Robert). German. Born in Ober-Salzbrunn, 15 November 1862. Educated at a school in Breslau; studied sculpture at Royal College of Art, Breslau, 1880–82; also studied at University of Jena, 1882–83. Married 1) Marie Thienemann in 1884 (divorced), three sons; 2) Margarete Marschalk in 1905, one son. Sculptor in Rome, 1883–84; also worked as actor in Berlin, before becoming a full-time writer; co-founder of the literary group *Durch.* Recipient: Grillparzer prize, 1896, 1899, 1905; Goethebünde Schiller prize, 1905; Nobel prize for literature, 1912; Goethe prize (Frankfurt), 1932. Honorary degrees: Oxford University, 1905; University of Leipzig, 1909; University of Prague, 1921; Columbia University, New York, 1932. Ordre pour le Mérite, 1922. *Died 8 June 1946.*

PUBLICATIONS

Collections

Dramatic Works, edited by Ludwig Lewisohn.   9 vols., 1912–29.
Sämtliche Werke, edited by Hans-Egon Hass.   11 vols., 1962–74.

Short Stories

Fasching.   1887.
Bahnwärter Thiel.   1888; as "Lineman Thiel" in *Lineman Thiel and Other Tales,* 1989.
Der Apostel (novella).   1890.
Der Ketzer von Soana.   1918; as *The Heretic of Soana,* 1923.
Die Hochzeit auf Buchenhorst.   1931.
Das Meerwunder.   1934.
Der Schuss im Park.   1939.
Das Märchen.   1941.
Mignon (novella).   1944.
Lineman Thiel and Other Tales.   1989.

Novels

Der Narr in Christo, Emanuel Quint. 1910; as *The Fool in Christ, Emanuel Quint,* 1911.
Atlantis. 1912; translated as *Atlantis,* 1912.
Lohengrin. 1913.
Parsival. 1914.
Phantom. 1922; translated as *Phantom,* 1923.
Die Insel der grossen Mutter. 1924; as *The Island of the Great Mother,* 1925.
Wanda. 1928.
Buch der Leidenschaft. 1930.
Im Wirbel der Berinfung. 1936.

Plays

Vor Sonnenaufgang (produced 1889). 1889; as *Before Dawn,* 1909; in *Three German Plays,* 1963; as *Before Daybreak,* 1978; as *Before Sunrise,* edited by Jill Perkins, 1978.
Das Friedenfest (produced 1890). 1890; as *The Coming of Peace,* 1900; as *The Reconciliation,* in *Dramatic Works,* 1914.
Einsame Menschen (produced 1891). 1891; as *Lonely Lives,* 1898.
Die Weber (produced 1893). 1892; as *The Weavers,* 1899; in *Five Plays,* 1961.
Kollege Crampton (produced 1892). 1892; as *Colleague Crampton,* in *Dramatic Works,* 1914.
Der Biberpelz (produced 1893). 1893; as *The Beaver Coat,* 1912; in *Five Plays,* 1961.
Hanneles Himmelfahrt (produced 1893). 1893; translated as *Hannele,* 1894; in *Five Plays,* 1961.
Florian Geyer (produced 1896). 1896; translated as *Florian Geyer,* in *Dramatic Works,* 1929.
Die versunkene Glocke (produced 1896). 1896; as *The Sunken Bell,* 1898.
Fuhrmann Henschel (produced 1898). 1898; as *Drayman Henschel,* in *Dramatic Works,* 1913; in *Five Plays,* 1961.
Schluck und Jau (produced 1900). 1900; as *Schluck and Jau,* in *Dramatic Works,* 1919.
Michael Kramer (produced 1900). 1900; translated as *Michael Kramer,* in *Dramatic Works,* 1914.
Der rote Hahn (produced 1901). 1901; as *The Conflagration,* in *Dramatic Works,* 1913.
Die arme Heinrich (produced 1902). 1902; as *Henry of Auë,* in *Dramatic Works,* 1914.
Rose Bernd (produced 1903). 1903; translated as *Rose Bernd,* in *Dramatic Works,* 1913; in *Five Plays,* 1961.
Elga (produced 1905). 1905; translated as *Elga,* in *Dramatic Works,* 1919.
Und Pippa tanzt! (produced 1906). 1906; as *And Pippa Dances,* 1907.
Die Jungfrau vom Bischofsberg (produced 1907). 1907; as *Maidens of the Mount,* in *Dramatic Works,* 1919.
Kaiser Karls Geisel (produced 1908). 1908; as *Charlemagne's Hostage,* in *Dramatic Works,* 1919.
Griselda (produced 1909). 1909; translated as *Griselda,* in *Dramatic Works,* 1919.
Die Ratten (produced 1911). 1911; as *The Rats,* in *Dramatic Works,* 1913.
Gabriel Schillings Flucht (produced 1912). 1912; as *Gabriel Schilling's Flight,* in *Dramatic Works,* 1919.
Festspiel in deutschen Reimen (produced 1913). 1913; as *Commemoration Masque,* in *Dramatic Works,* 1919.
Der Bogen des Odysseus (produced 1914). 1914; as *The Bow of Ulysses,* in *Dramatic Works,* 1919.

Winterballade (produced 1917). 1917; as *A Winter Ballad,* in *Dramatic Works,* 1925.
Der weisse Heiland (produced 1920). 1920; as *The White Savior,* in *Dramatic Works,* 1925.
Indipohdi (produced 1920). 1920; translated as *Indipohdi,* in *Dramatic Works,* 1925.
Peter Bauer (produced 1921). 1921.
Veland. 1925; translated as *Veland,* in *Dramatic Works,* 1929.
Dorothea Angermann (produced 1926). 1926.
Spuk: Die schwarze Maske (produced 1929); *Hexenritt* (produced 1928). 1929.
Vor Sonnenuntergang (produced 1932). 1932.
Die goldene Harfe (produced 1933). 1933.
Hamlet in Wittenberg (produced 1935). 1935.
Ulrich von Lichtenstein (produced 1939). 1939.
Die Tochter der Kathedrale (produced 1939). 1939.
Atridentetralogie: Iphigenie in Aulis, Agamemnons Tod, Elektra, Iphigenie in Delphi (produced 1940–44), 4 vols., 1941–48.
Magnus Garbe (produced 1942). 1942.
Die Finsternisse. 1947.
Herbert Engelmann, completed by Carl Zuckmayer (produced 1952). 1952.
Five Plays. 1961.

Verse

Promethidenlos. 1885.
Das bunte Buch. 1888.
Anna. 1921.
Die blaue Blume. 1924.
Till Eulenspiegel. 1928.
Ährenlese. 1939.
Der grosse Traum. 1942.
Neue Gedichte. 1946.

Other

Griechischer Frühling. 1908.
Ausblicke. 1922.
Gesammelte Werke. 12 vols., 1922.
Um Volk und Geist. 1932.
Gespräche, edited by Josef Chapiro. 1932.
Das Abenteuer meiner Jugend. 1937.
Diarium 1917 bis 1933, edited by Martin Machatzke. 1980.
Notiz-Kalender 1889 bis 1891, edited by Martin Machatzke. 1982.
Hauptmann—Ludwig von Hofmann: Briefwechsel 1894–1944, edited by Herta Hesse-Frielinghaus. 1983.
Otto Brahm, Hauptmann: Briefwechsel 1889–1912, edited by Peter Sprengel. 1985.
Tagebuch 1892 bis 1894, edited by Martin Machatzke. 1985.
Tagebücher 1897 bis 1905, edited by Martin Machatzke. 1987.
Ein Leben für Hauptmann: Aufsätze aus den Jahren 1929–1990, edited by Walter A. Reichart. 1991.

*

Critical Studies: *The Death Problem in the Life and Works of Hauptmann* by Frederick A. Klemm, 1939; *Hauptmann* by Hugh F. Garten, 1954; *Hauptmann: His Life and Work* by C.F.W. Behl, 1956; *Hauptmann: The Prose Plays* by Margaret Sinden, 1957; *Witness of Deceit: Hauptmann as a Critic of Society* by L.R. Shaw, 1958; *Hauptmann: Centenary Lectures* edited by K.G. Knight and F. Norman, 1964; *Hauptmann in Russia, 1889–1917: Reception and Impact* by Albert A. Kipa, 1974; *From Lessing to Hauptmann: Studies in German Drama* by Ladislaus Löb, 1974; *Hauptmann and Utopia*, 1976, and *Hauptmann: Religious Syncretism and Eastern Religions*, 1984, both by Philip Mellen; *The Image of the Primitive Giant in the Works of Hauptmann* by Carolyn Thomas Sussère, 1979; *The German Naturalists and Hauptmann: Reception and Influence* by Alan Marshall, 1982.

* * *

Primarily known as a dramatist, Gerhart Hauptmann frequently wrote in other genres like the verse epic, the novel, and the story during a prolific career spanning 65 years. In all he completed ten works of short fiction, but only *Bahnwärter Thiel* ("Lineman Thiel") and *Der Ketzer von Soana* (*The Heretic of Soana*) have received widespread public and critical acclaim. His later stories in particular have suffered neglect, partly because, having first gained a reputation as the author of social dramas ("Before Sunrise" and "The Weavers"), he remains stubbornly associated with naturalism.

In fact, apart from "Lineman Thiel" (1888), only Hauptmann's first story "Carnival," written earlier the same year, is to any extent an exemplary naturalist text. Significantly subtitled "A Study," it represents a slice of working-class life, set in a clearly identifiable rural milieu southeast of Berlin. Here a sailmaker called Kielblock, returning home in darkness across a frozen lake, loses his way and drowns, together with his wife and young child. Determined to make the most of the Shrovetide carnival—a last chance to indulge himself before spring when his workload increases—Kielblock has spent the previous 24 hours in an orgy of dancing, gaming, and drinking, and his excessive alcohol consumption contributes greatly to the catastrophe. Hauptmann's use of local dialect gives the tale verisimilitude, and his playwright's skills are evident both in the ironic devices employed to anticipate the drowning and the build-up of suspense prior to it.

Another early story, *Der Apostel* ("The Apostle"), is subtitled "A Novella-like Study," but here the dramatic action traditionally associated with the German novella is mostly in the mind of the unnamed central character, a semi-deranged itinerant preacher proclaiming a gospel of pacifism and reverence for nature. In evoking this figure's acute spiritual anguish, the narcissism and delusions of grandeur that culminate in his imitation of Christ, Hauptmann is clearly influenced by Georg Büchner's story *Lenz*, which he greatly admired. Extensive use of free indirect discourse, combined with emotionally loaded descriptions of nature, allow the reader to share the character's vision from within, and, thus, to an extent, to sympathise with him. No authorial judgement is passed on his views, but evidence from other works suggests that his Tolstoian ideals and his cultural pessimism, expressed in negative comments on war, city life, and modern technology, have Hauptmann's approval.

An even more radical rejection of modern civilisation is depicted in the longer novella *The Heretic of Soana*, which enjoyed great popularity after World War I. The main character here is not an apostle, but an apostate: a young, ascetic Catholic priest whose senses are suddenly aroused by an erotic encounter with a peasant girl living on the fringes of his parish. He abandons for her his flock and becomes a pastor in the literal sense; a goatherd enjoying a timeless, Arcadian existence high on the Monte Generoso above Lake Lugano. Hauptmann adopts the device of a neutral editor to frame the heretic's first-person narrative, but he clearly shares his character's anti-Christian, Dionysian views, which are strongly reminiscent of Nietzsche. Nature and Eros are celebrated with occasionally compelling lyricism, but the work is stylistically uneven, at points bordering on kitsch.

The six stories Hauptmann wrote in the last 20 years of his life, none of which has appeared in English translation, are technically less sophisticated than "Lineman Thiel" or "The Apostle." They owe more to traditional oral narrative, the death of which is actually bemoaned in one of them, *Der Schuss im Park* (The Shot in the Park) of 1939, by an old retired forester. This character proceeds to tell his nephew, over a bottle of wine and several pipes of tobacco, a tale from his past, involving an aristocratic German explorer guilty of bigamy. A similar yarn is encountered in *Das Meerwunder* (The Miracle of the Sea), where the raconteur is an ancient mariner, relating his adventures—this time over several bottles of wine—to an assembled group of eccentrics. In other tales the first-person narrator is undisguisedly Hauptmann himself, whether drawing heavily on memories of his student days in Jena—*Die Hochzeit auf Buchenhorst* (The Wedding at Buchenhorst)—or giving a humorously surreal account of a night spent at the very inn where he was born and which now is threatened with imminent demolition—"Die Spitzhacke" (The Pick-axe) of 1930.

The subject matter of these later stories is varied, but some thematic links are discernible. Erotic fascination and dependency, so prominent in "Thiel" and *The Heretic of Soana*, recur, for instance, in *Der Schuss im Park*, *Das Meerwunder*, and Hauptmann's last novella *Mignon*, where the aging narrator is totally captivated by the eponymous heroine, the homeless, orphaned daughter of a nobleman, who lives the life of a wandering minstrel. The cultural pessimism of earlier stories also resurfaces, sometimes in even bleaker form, as in *Das Meerwunder*, the positively misanthropic message of which may indirectly reflect Hauptmann's despair at the triumph of Nazism. Occasionally this pessimism turns to nostalgia for Germany's "good old days," whether in a eulogy about timber-framed houses in Meissen (*Die Hochzeit auf Buchenhorst*) or in the "wake" for the Hotel Krone ("Die Spitzhacke"), which is celebrated by a bizarre gathering of animals and birds, each representing a traditional German inn-sign.

The fusion of reality and fantasy in the latter story is typical of Hauptmann's tendency to introduce more and more dream-like or supernatural elements into his later work. Such effects are most extreme in *Das Meerwunder*, which at times is worthy of Edgar Allan Poe. Less horrific, but certainly uncanny, is the three-fold appearance of Goethe's ghost in *Mignon*, a story rich in allusions to "Wilhelm Meister." Another example is *Das Märchen* (The Fairy-Tale), a rather heavy-handed reworking of Goethe's symbolic fantasy of the same title. Here the contrast with the faithful representation of social realities in "Carnival" and "Lineman Thiel" could not be more marked.

—David Horrocks

See the essay on "Lineman Theil."

HAWTHORNE, Nathaniel. American. Born Nathaniel Hathorne in Salem, Massachusetts, 4 July 1804. Educated at Samuel Archer's School, Salem, 1819; Bowdoin College, Brunswick, Maine, 1821–25. Married Sophia Peabody in 1842; two daughters and one son. Lived with his mother in Salem, writing and contributing to periodicals, 1825–36; editor, *American Magazine of Useful and Entertaining Knowledge,* Boston, 1836; weigher and gager, Boston Customs House, 1839–41; invested in the Brook Farm Commune, West Roxbury, Massachusetts, and lived there, 1841–42; lived in Concord, Massachusetts, 1842–45, 1852, and 1860–64; surveyor, Salem Customs House, 1846–49; lived in Lenox, 1850–51, and West Newton, 1851, both Massachusetts; U.S. Consul, Liverpool, England, 1853-57; lived in Italy, 1858–59, and London, 1859–60. *Died 19 May 1864.*

PUBLICATIONS

Collections

Complete Writings.   22 vols., 1900.
Complete Novels and Selected Tales, edited by Norman Holmes Pearson.   1937.
The Portable Hawthorne, edited by Malcolm Cowley. 1948; revised edition, 1969; as *Hawthorne: Selected Works,* 1971.
Works (Centenary Edition), edited by William Charvat and others.   1963—.
Poems, edited by Richard E. Peck.   1967.
Tales and Sketches (Library of America), edited by Roy Harvey Pearce.   1982.
Novels (Library of America), edited by Millicent Bell. 1983.

Short Stories

Fanshawe: A Tale.   1828.
Twice-Told Tales.   1837; revised edition, 1842.
Mosses from an Old Manse.   1846.
The Snow-Image and Other Twice-Told Tales.   1851.
The Dolliver Romance and Other Pieces, edited by Sophia Hawthorne.   1876.
Fanshawe and Other Pieces.   1876.

Novels

The Celestial Rail-Road.   1843.
The Scarlet Letter: A Romance.   1850.
The House of the Seven Gables: A Romance.   1851.
The Blithedale Romance.   1852.
Transformation; or, The Romance of Monte Beni.   1860; as *The Marble Faun,* 1860.
Pansie: A Fragment.   1864.
Septimius: A Romance, edited by Una Hawthorne and Robert Browning.   1872; as *Septimius Felton; or The Elixir of Life,* 1872.
Dr. Grimshaw's Secret: A Romance, edited by Julian Hawthorne.   1883; edited by Edward H. Davidson, 1954.
The Ghost of Dr. Harris.   1900.

Other

Grandfather's Chair: A History for Youth.   1841; *Famous Old People, Being the Second Epoch of Grandfather's Chair,* 1841; *Liberty Tree,* with the *Last Words of Grandfather's Chair,* 1841, revised edition, 1842.
Biographical Stories for Children.   1842.
True Stories from History and Biography.   1851.
A Wonder-Book for Girls and Boys.   1851.
Life of Franklin Pierce (campaign biography).   1852.
Tanglewood Tales for Girls and Boys, Being a Second Wonder-Book.   1853.
Our Old Home: A Series of English Sketches.   1863; in *Works,*   1970.
Passages from the American Note-Books, edited by Sophia Hawthorne.   2 vols., 1868.
Passages from the English Note-Books, edited by Sophia Hawthorne.   2 vols., 1870.
Passages from the French and Italian Note-Books, edited by Una Hawthorne.   2 vols., 1871.
Twenty Days with Julian and Little Bunny: A Diary. 1904.
Love Letters.   2 vols., 1907.
Letters to William D. Ticknor.   2 vols., 1910.
The Heart of Hawthorne's Journal, edited by Newton Arvin.   1929.
The American Notebooks, edited by Randall Stewart. 1932; in Works, 1972.
The English Notebooks, edited by Randall Stewart.   1941.
Hawthorne as Editor: Selections from His Writings in the American Magazine of Useful and Entertaining Knowledge, edited by Arlin Turner.   1941.
Hawthorne's Lost Notebook 1835–1841, edited by Barbara S. Mouffe.   1978.
American Travel Sketches, edited by Alfred Weber and others.   1989.

Editor, with Elizabeth Hawthorne, *Peter Parley's Universal History.*   2 vols., 1837; as *Peter Parley's Common School History,* 1838.
Editor, *Journal of an African Cruiser,* by Horatio Bridge. 1845.
Editor, *The Yarn of a Yankee Privateer,* by Benjamin Frederick Browne(?).   1926.

*

Bibliography: *Hawthorne: A Descriptive Bibliography* by C.E. Frazer Clark, Jr., 1978; *Hawthorne and the Critics: A Checklist of Criticism 1900–1978* by Jeanetta Boswell, 1982; *Hawthorne: An Annotated Bibliography of Comment and Criticism Before 1900* by Gary Scharnhorst, 1988.

Critical Studies: *Hawthorne* by Henry James, 1879; *Hawthorne: A Biography* by Randall Stewart, 1948; *Hawthorne* by Mark Van Doren, 1949; *Hawthorne's Fiction: The Light and the Dark,* 1952, revised edition, 1964, and *Hawthorne's Imagery,* 1969, both by Richard Harter Fogle; *Hawthorne: A Critical Study,* 1955, revised edition, 1963, and *The Presence of Hawthorne,* 1979, both by Hyatt H. Waggoner; *Hawthorne's Tragic Vision* by Roy R. Male, 1957; *Hawthorne, Man and Writer* by Edward Wagenknecht, 1961; *Hawthorne: An Introduction and Interpretation,* 1961, and *Hawthorne: A Biography,* 1980, both by Arlin Turner; *Hawthorne Centenary Essays* edited by Roy Harvey Pearce, 1964; *Hawthorne* by Terence Martin, 1965, revised edition,

1983; *The Sins of the Fathers: Hawthorne's Psychological Themes* by Frederick Crews, 1966; *Hawthorne: A Collection of Critical Essays* edited by A.N. Kaul, 1966; *Twentieth-Century Interpretations of The Scarlet Letter* edited by John C. Gerber, 1968; *Plots and Characters in the Fiction and Sketches of Hawthorne*, 1968, and *A Hawthorne Encyclopedia*, 1991, both by Robert L. Gale; *Hawthorne, Transcendental Symbolist* by Marjorie Elder, 1969; *The Recognition of Hawthorne: Selected Criticism since 1828* edited by B. Bernard Cohen, 1969; *Hawthorne as Myth-Maker: A Study in Imagination* by Hugo McPherson, 1969; *Hawthorne: The Critical Heritage*, 1970, and *Hawthorne: A Collection of Criticism*, 1975, both edited by J. Donald Crowley; *The Pursuit of Form: A Study of Hawthorne and the Romance* by John Caldwell Stubbs, 1970; *Hawthorne's Early Tales: A Critical Study* by Neal F. Doubleday, 1972; *Hawthorne's Career* by Nina Baym, 1976; *Hawthorne: The Poetics of Enchantment* by Edgar A. Dryden, 1977; *Rediscovering Hawthorne* by Kenneth Dauber, 1977; *Hawthorne and the Truth of Dreams* by Rita K. Gollin, 1979; *A Reader's Guide to the Short Stories of Hawthorne* by Lea B.V. Newman, 1979; *Hawthorne: The English Experience 1853–1864* by Raymona E. Hull, 1980; *Hawthorne in His Times* by James R. Mellow, 1980; *The Productive Tension of Hawthorne's Art* by Claudia D. Johnson, 1981; *Hawthorne: New Critical Essays* edited by A. Robert Lee, 1982; *Family Themes in Hawthorne's Fiction* by Gloria C. Erlich, 1984; *The Province of Piety: Moral History in Hawthorne's Early Tales* by Michael J. Colacurcio, 1984, and *New Essays on The Scarlet Letter* edited by Colacurcio, 1985; *Hawthorne's Secret: An Un-told Tale* by Philip Young, 1984; *Hawthorne's Tales* edited by James McIntosh, 1987; *Secrets and Sympathy: Forms of Disclosure in Hawthorne's Novels* by Gordon Hutner, 1989; *Hawthorne and the Romance of the Orient* by Luther S. Luedtke, 1989; *Hawthorne's Early Narrative Art* by Melinda M. Ponder, 1990; *Hawthorne: Tradition and Revolution* by Charles Swann, 1991; *The Hawthorne and Melville Friendship* edited by James C. Wilson, 1991; *The Production of Personal Life: Class, Gender, and the Psychological in Hawthorne's Fiction* by Joel Pfister, 1992; *The Critical Responses to Hawthorne's The Scarlet Letter* edited by Gary Scharnhorst, 1992.

* * *

Nathaniel Hawthorne's career as a writer of short fiction began inauspiciously with his failure to publish any of three unified collections of tales and sketches ("Seven Tales of My Native Land," "Provincial Tales," and "The Story Teller"). As a result he was forced to publish most of these pieces separately—and anonymously or pseudonymously—in newspapers and the few magazines and gift-book annuals available in the American literary scene. It was not until almost a decade later, in 1837, when he had written almost 50 tales and sketches, some of them among his finest, that he published 18 under his own name as *Twice-Told Tales*. In 1842 a two-volume edition of his work added 19 others. *Mosses from an Old Manse* reprinted 22 more with an author's preface, "The Old Manse." His third major collection, *The Snow-Image*, did not appear until 1851 after Hawthorne had turned to writing full-length romances, and a number of the 15 selections—most notably, "My Kinsman, Major Molineux"—predated the 1837 volume. By this time Hawthorne had begun to enjoy widespread acclaim as author of *The Scarlet Letter*, a romance that Henry James would later describe as America's first indisputably classic work of fiction.

The story of Hester Prynne and Arthur Dimmesdale marks at once the culmination and the transformation of Hawthorne's development as a writer of tales; likewise, "The Custom-House" introduction perfects his use of the sketch form as a way, fully integrated with the fiction, of commenting on the American artist's situation and on the nature both of his materials and his creative processes. Together they define the two most essential threads of his practice in short fiction. Indeed, his original choice of title for his masterpiece, curious but instructive, is probably the best description of the work he did between 1828 and 1851: "Old Time Legends: Together with Sketches, Experimental and Ideal."

The conventions and exigencies of publication, Hawthorne's right sense of his audience's predisposition to sentimental and pietistic didacticism, and his own penchant for historical consciousness and what James called "the deeper psychology" required that Hawthorne not only create fictions but instruct his audience about the nature of those fictions. Thus was he given to frequent sub-titles such as "A Parable," "A Fantasy," "An Imaginary Retrospect," "A Moralized Legend," and "Allegories of the Heart," all of them designed to mediate between his readers and his materials; thus, too, did he write half a dozen juvenile collections, as if to prepare a serious audience for the future. Often (as in the four "Legends of the Province-House") he used framed narratives which allowed the collaborative voice and character of the narrator/persona to guarantee the reliability of the tale. One of his finest sketches, "The Haunted Mind," traces, like many of his prefaces, the processes of the creative imagination. And among the memorable tales that dramatize the plight of the artist caught between the hard-headed practicality of his audience and the subtleties of his materials are "Drowne's Wooden Image," "The Artist and the Beautiful," and "The Snow-Image." Nowhere is that collaborative, and meditative, voice more obvious than in "Wakefield," the slight sketch of a middle-aged man who, all unaware, leaves his wife of ten years and spends the next 20 years viewing her behavior in his absence: "If the reader choose," says the narrator, "let him do his own meditation; or if he prefer to ramble with me through the twenty years of Wakefield's vagary, I bid him welcome."

Hawthorne's imagination found his own contemporary scene recalcitrant: what he called "The Present, the Immediate, the Actual" offered him no fit materials. He needed, he said, "a neutral territory, somewhere between the real world and fairy-land, where the Actual and the Imaginary may meet, and each imbue itself with the nature of the other." Typical opening sentences that establish that "neutral territory" through vague distancing, include: "In the latter part of the last century," "At nightfall, once, in the olden time," "In those strange old times, when fantastic dreams and madmen's reveries were realized among the actual circumstances of life." The strategy is by no means escapist but is instead Hawthorne's indirect way of exercising his acute sense of the past to comment incisively on humankind's moral condition in the present.

It was early New England history, provincial and colonial, and the drama of Puritan consciousness that provided the richest abundance of materials, themes, and techniques. "The May-Pole of Merry Mount" dramatizes the struggle between the Puritan Endicott and the Merry Mounters allegorically: "Jollity and gloom were contending for an empire." Mr. Hooper's crepe veil in "The Minister's Black Veil" is the sort of single central symbol that anticipates

Hester's scarlet letter; like the letter, the veil is also a symbolic action expressive at once of self-concealment and self-revelation; like it, too, the veil at once alienates Hooper from his community and encloses him within it. The Puritan mistreatment of the Quaker boy Ilbrahim in "The Gentle Boy" constitutes an early version of Hawthorne's later definition of the unpardonable sin: "the violation of the sanctity of the human heart." In "My Kinsman, Major Molineux" young Robin, thinking it "high time to begin the world" with the aid of his powerful relative, leaves home only to discover himself participating symbolically in the ritual killing of his would-be benefactor. Robin discovers not only that he can't go home again but the same grim fact that so many other protagonists do. In Ralph Waldo Emerson's terms, the truth goes this way: "It is very unhappy, but too late to be helped, the discovery we have made that we exist. That discovery is called the Fall of Man."

Hawthorne's genius in developing this and other themes has made him a profound influence on other major writers as various as Herman Melville and Henry James, Robert Frost and William Faulkner, Flannery O'Connor and Jorge Luis Borges.

—J. Donald Crowley

See the essays on "The Birthmark," "Rappaccini's Daughter," "Wakefield," and "Young Goodman Brown."

HEAD, Bessie (née Emery). Citizen of Botswana. Born in Pietermaritzburg, South Africa, 6 July 1937. Educated at Umbilo Road High School. Married Harold Head in 1961; one son. Moved to Bechuanaland (now Botswana), 1964; teacher and farm worker at Swaneng Hill project, Serowe; teacher in primary schools in South Africa and Botswana, for four years; journalist, Drum Publications, Johannesburg, for two years. *Died 17 April 1986.*

PUBLICATIONS

Short Stories

The Collector of Treasures and Other Botswana Village Tales.   1977.
Tales of Tenderness and Power.   1989.

Novels

When Rain Clouds Gather.   1969.
Maru.   1971.
A Question of Power.   1973.
A Bewitched Crossroad: An African Saga.   1984.

Other

Serowe, Village of the Rain Wind.   1981.
Head: A Woman Alone: Autobiographical Writings, edited by Craig MacKenzie.   1990.

*

Bibliography: *Head: A Bibliography* by Craig MacKenzie and Catherine Woeber, 1992.

Critical Studies: "The Novels of Head" by Arthur Ravenscroft, in *Aspects of South African Literature* edited by Christopher Heywood, 1976; "Short Fiction in the Making: The Case of Head" in *English in Africa* 16 (1), 1989, "Head's *The Collector of Treasures*: Modern Storytelling in a Traditional Botswanan Village," in *World Literature Written in English* 29 (2), 1989, *Head: An Introduction,* 1989, and "Alienation, Breakdown and Renewal in the Novels of Head," in *International Literature in English: The Major Writers,* edited by Robert L. Ross, 1991, all by Craig MacKenzie, and *Between the Lines: Interviews with Head, Sheila Roberts, Ellen Kuzwayo, Miriam Tlali* edited by MacKenzie and Cherry Clayton, 1989.

*   *   *

The single collection of short stories published in Bessie Head's lifetime, *The Collector of Treasures and Other Botswana Village Tales,* has its origins in the oral history of her adopted country. The material is derived from interviews conducted by the author with the villagers of Serowe. The individual testimonies Bessie Head collected in this way serve a double purpose as the basis of her social history, *Serowe, Village of the Rainwind,* as well as of her postcolonial folktales.

The apparent simplicity of the stories belies their sophisticated construction; Head's treatment of temporal sequence, her wry or enigmatic denouements, and her unique use of the exposition to introduce not the protagonists but the social context, give her work a richly textured quality. Set against the backdrop of Botswana's troubled history of white expansionism, missionary intervention, migrant labour, and political independence, the tales also contain an account of timeless customs and beliefs which go against this grain of progress. They retain a verbal quality, partly because Head uses narrative devices that draw attention to the fact that the story is being told (for example, a fireside story), and partly because her intention is to preserve her people's memory of custom, of wedding and funeral rituals, the traditions of ploughing and harvesting, proverbial wisdom, and pre-Christian religion.

The moral of Head's tales in never unequivocal. The clash between Setswana tradition and colonial progress imbues the stories with complexity. Although she tends to support custom over innovation, her feminist brief exists in direct contradiction to the subjugated position of women in this patriarchal, conservative community.

Appropriately, the volume opens with an archetypal tale of origin and fall. "The Deep River: A Story of Ancient Tribal Migration" relates the genesis of the Talaote tribe in central Africa, and its exodus (because of a man's love of a woman) from his harmonious paradise. In a postscript, Head acknowledges that her story is an imaginative reconstruction of history based on the failing and unreliable memories of the elders of the Botaloate tribe. But it is not just the tale of how the people came to be settled in Bamangwato. The story is a portrait of a people easily divided because their very nature is a contradictory one. In addition to the jealousy of his brothers, Sebembele's action of taking one of his father's widows as his wife inspires a heated debate among the people. They are divided between those who deplore the fact that their chief could jeopardize his future over a woman, and those who respond sympathetically to this demonstration of tenderness. Sebembele is forced to leave the tribe and travel southwards to Bamangwato. The story introduces themes that recur throughout the collection, namely, the relationship of individual and community, the position of women in society, and the encroachment of civilization upon custom.

In their critique of Christianity, the following three stories also explore the themes of allegiance and betrayal. "Heaven Is Not Closed" tells the story of a devout Christian woman who is ex-communicated when she marries a man who will not be married according to the rites of the church because he represents "an ancient stream of holiness that people had lives with before any white man had set foot in the land." As the title suggests, the story becomes an occasion for a profound questioning of the motives of those who propound the Gospel in Botswana, who deprecate Setswana religious belief and presume to hold the keys of heaven. Hypocrisy is also associated with Christianity in "The Village Saint," in which an apparently devout woman torments her daughter-in-law.

A more complex treatment of Christianity is to be found in "Jacob: The Story of a Faith-Healing Priest." The story has many Old Testament parallels: the lives of the two prophets of Makaleng contains echoes of the stories of Joseph, Job, and Samuel. In relating the phases of Jacob's fortune (as a child cheated of his inheritance, a rich man robbed of his possessions, and a poor man rewarded with a virtuous wife), the narrator questions the beneficence of Jacob's God. An equivocal stance is maintained throughout the story: while Jacob is admired for the sincerity of his belief, doubt is cast upon his calm acceptance of the divine suffering meted out to him. Jacob is finally vindicated when his rival, the wealthy prophet Lebojang, is tried and sentenced to death for ritual murder. The two prophets represent the best and worst of Christianity in Head's assessment: a meek submission before the often arbitrary will of God, and a self-serving hypocrisy masking deadly evil.

Ritual murder is not completely indicted, however. In "Looking for a Rain God," a father and grandfather are driven by drought and desperation to resort to this practice. The ritual murder does not cause the rain to fall; instead, ironically, the death of the two little girls "hung like a dark cloud of sorrow over the village." The two men are tried and sentenced to death, but this act of white-ordained justice does not resolve the issue. "The subtle story of strain and starvation," which is not admitted as evidence in court, is admitted by the narrator, who looks into the hearts of all the people living off the land and concludes, "They could have killed something to make the rain fall."

In *The Collector of Treasures,* the western system of justice is seen to be a crude response to the intricate dynamics of traditional life in Botswana. While "Kgotla" recounts the respectful deliberations of the village elders as they weigh up the merits of a case, in "Life" and "The Collector of Treasures" the protagonists are imprisoned by a judiciary that is part of the problem rather than its solution. Life's husband murders her because she is so de-tribalized that she is incapable of giving up her city ways and settling down to the slow, monotonous pace of the village. The proverb that accounts for Lesego's rash action ("rivers never cross here") is given a modern slant when the beer-brewing women sing the Jim Reeves song "That's What Happens When Two Worlds Collide." Proverb and song carry two meanings: Lesego and Life are incompatible as personalities, but they are also representatives of two conflicting cultures.

In the title story, a wife kills her husband by castrating him. The story is Head's most overtly feminist statement. In it, she demonstrates how the roots of male brutality are firmly embedded in ideology. The narrator shows how ancient tradition, the colonial period, and independence all serve male interests. The story represents a corrosive attack on patriarchy as well as a triumphant celebration of the healing powers of community and neighbourliness and the resilience of women. The heroine, Dikeledi Mokopi, is a collector of treasures in that she "always found gold amidst the ash, deep loves that had joined her heart to the hearts of others." Like Dikeledi, Thato (in the final story "Hunting") has an ability "to sift and sort out all the calamities of everyday life with the unerring heart of a good story-teller." The same could be said of Head.

After her death in 1986, Head's previously unpublished writing was collected in a volume entitled *Tales of Tenderness and Power.* The collection shows her development from the early, anecdotal pieces of an apprentice writer unsure of what her subject matter ought to be, to the mature author who shaped her fine observations of Botswana village life into *The Collector of Treasures.* The awkward hesitation evident in "Let Me Tell a Story now. . . ." (1962) has disappeared in the much-anthologized story "The Prisoner Who Wore Glasses" (1973), based on an authentic case in which a white gaoler was humanized by the political prisoners in his charge. As in all her best work, Head here creatively transforms a real incident into a tale by the injection of tenderness. The posthumously published collection is well named.

—Finuala Dowling

HEDĀYAT, Sādeq. Iranian. Born in Teheran, 17 February 1903. Educated at missionary school, graduated 1925; studied dentistry and engineering in France, 1926. Scholar of ancient Iranian texts, and Zoroastrian, Hindu, and Buddhist philosophy; studied and travelled in Belgium and France, 1926–30; civil service worker, 1930–36: Bank Melli, Office of Trade, Ministry of Foreign Affairs, and State Construction Company; travelled in India, 1936-37; founder and co-editor, *Majalle-ye musīqī,* government magazine; journalist, 1941–47; moved to Paris, 1950. Member, First Iranian Writers Congress. *Died (suicide) 8 or 9 April 1951.*

PUBLICATIONS

Collections

Anthology, edited by Ehsan Yarshater.   1979.

Short Stories

Zende be-gūr [Buried Alive].   1930; expanded edition, 1952.
Seh qatreh khūn [Three Drops of Blood].   1932.
Sāyeh rowshan [Twilight].   1933.
Sag velgard [The Stray Dog].   1942.
Velengārī [Tittle-tattle].   1944; expanded edition, 1954.
Omnibus.   1972(?).

An Introduction (stories), edited by Deborah Miller Mostaghel.   1976.
The Blind Owl and Other Hedayat Stories, edited by Carol L. Sayers and Russel P. Christenson.   1984.

Novels

'Alaviyeh Khānom [Madame 'Al-viye].   1933.
Būf-e kūr.   1937; as *The Blind Owl,* 1957; as *The Blind Owl and Other Hedayat Stories,* edited by Carol L. Sayers and Russel P. Christenson, 1984.
Hāji Āqā.   1945; as *Hāji Ā ghā, the Portrait of an Iranian Confidence Man.*   1979.
Tūp-e morvāri [The Pearl Cannon].   1979.

Plays

Parvīn dokhtar-e sāsān [Parvin, Daughter of Sassan].   1930.
Māziyār, with Mojteba Minovi.   1933.
Afsāneh-ye āferīnesh [Legend of the Creation].   1946.

Other

Favā'ed-e gīyāhuhwārī [The Merits of Vegetarianism] (essays).   1930.
Esfahān Nesf-e Jahān [Isfahan, Half-of-the-World] (travelogue).   1932.
Owsāneh [The Legend].   1933.
Nayrangestān [Persian Folklore].   1933.
Vagh Vagh Sahāb [Mr. Bow Wow], with Mas'ud Farzād.   1933.
Majmu'eh-ye neveshteh-hā-ye parākandeh [Collection of Scattered Writings] (includes stories).   1955; revised edition, edited by Hasan Qa'emyan, 1963–64.

Also translator of stories by Franz Kafka, Anton Chekhov, Arthur Schnitzler, Jean-Paul Sartre, and others.

*

Bibliography: in *Modern Persian Prose Literature* by Hassan Kamshad, 1966.

Critical Studies: *Hedāyat's Ivory Tower* by Iraj Bashiri, 1974; *Hedāyat's "The Blind Owl" Forty Years After* (includes translations of the stories "Buried Alive" and "Three Drops of Blood") edited by M.C. Hillman, 1978; in *Persian Literature* edited by Ehsan Yarshater, 1988; *Hedāyat's "Blind Owl" as a Western Novel* by Michael Beard, 1990; *Hedāyat* by Homa Kutouzian, 1991.

*   *   *

Arguably the most influential writer in 20th-century Iranian letters, Sādeq Hedāyat introduced modernity into Persian fiction. He drew upon three major sources for his creative inspiration: Iran's lush literary tradition, especially folk literature; French and German fiction, notably the works of Jean-Paul Sartre and Franz Kafka, a number of whose short stories he translated into Persian; and Hindu and Buddhist thinking, which he absorbed during a stay in India.

The eight stories from his first collection *Zende be-gūr* (Buried Alive) were written while Hedāyat was studying first dentistry, then engineering, in France and Belgium. In the title story, "Buried Alive," a middle-class eccentric nonchalantly speaks of his various efforts to kill himself with cyanide and opium, among other things, none of which is effective. For him, living is death; death for him would mean freedom. This story is the first of a number of works in which the characters, overwhelmed by acute existential angst, contemplate or actually commit suicide.

"The Mongol's Shadow" appeared in the collection *Non-Iran* (1931) featuring works by Hedāyat and two other writers, and shows another his other major literary concerns: Iran's past glories. The warrior Shahrukh, seriously wounded from fighting Mongol enemies, rests in the hollow of a tree. He bitterly recalls how his fiancée was raped and cut to pieces by a Mongol. He also thinks back to happier times when the two of them walked in the rice fields holding hands, and when his dying father gave him a special sword with which to fight the Mongols. Gradually, life ebbs out of his body, and he dies with a horrific smile on his face, one similar to that of the Mongol who killed his fiancée. Years later two peasants spot the warrior's smiling skeleton in the tree trunk and run off in terror, ironically calling it "the shadow of the Mongol." An especially violent story filled with racial slurs, it shows how badly backward invaders (both Mongol and Arab) treated Iranians, but also suggests that for Iranians to respond in kind was not only futile but degrading.

In "Three Drops of Blood" (1932), the title story from Hedāyat's second collection, *Seh qatreh Khūn,* the central image is three drops of blood, a metaphor for the love triangle involving the mental-patient narrator, Khan, his best friend, and Khan's fiancée. An unreliable narrator, Khan disjointedly and inconsistently tells their story, the truth value of which is highly suspect. The reader is left to reconstruct what has really happened and to speculate as to why Khan is now in an asylum. It is likely that he went insane because his friend and his fiancée became lovers. Their sexuality, transmuted into the mating frenzy of cats, is described by the friend in an elaborate narrative presented through the filter of Khan's soliloquy. Khan's illness is projected upon the friend, supposedly the result of being jilted by the fiancée's cousin. Complex and intricate, the story is notable both for its pathos and accurate portrayal of aspects of mental illness.

"The Man Who Killed His Passion," from the same collection, is another psychological study of betrayal. The main character is the studious young teacher, Ali, who strives to lead the ascetic life of a Sufi mystic. Under the tutelage of an older colleague, an Arabic teacher, Ali eats little, sleeps on a straw bed, avoids women, and studies mystical texts. When he learns that his mentor is, in fact, a fraud, Ali is despondent, for he senses that his pursuit of mystical enlightenment is senseless. As a result, life holds no meaning for him. He wanders to a cafe where a prostitute plies him with wine, which is strictly forbidden in Islam, and then she seduces him. Two days later a newspaper notice tersely states that he has committed suicide. Critic H. Kamshad has noted that traditionally Sufism has been a way among Iranians to sidestep perversions of Islam by zealots who ignore that religion's democratic and egalitarian teachings. In this story, then, "not even this solace exists in modern Iran: he [Hedāyat] is describing the debasement, not only of formal religion, but of what might have been a satisfactory substitute for it." Or, as Sartre might have put it: there's no way out.

In "The Stray Dog," the title story from Hedāyat's final collection, published in 1942, a Scottish setter forages for food in the village square. He experiences the culturally sanctioned animosity Middle Easterners hold towards dogs: that they are lowly and unclean; therefore, worthy of mistreatment. Resting in a ditch, he remembers, as if in a dream, earlier, happier times when, as Pat, he received love from both his mother and his master. One day Pat had run away briefly from his master to copulate with a bitch in heat. When he returned, the master had gone, and Pat was left to fend for himself in this hostile environment. What he misses most was being loved. After Pat awakens from his reverie, a kind stranger feeds him, then speeds off in a car, after which Pat desperately chases. Exhausted, he limps to the side of the road, where slowly he is overtaken by death. Pat is presented in his awareness and needs as very human: he reacts to kindness and affection with joy, and suffers abandonment and ill treatment with the same despair as any human might. That he would run himself to death chasing after love is no surprise. Interpreted politically, this story is thought to be an accurate description of the common Iranian's life during the tyrannical reign of Reza Shah (1925-1941). The story could only be told metaphorically because of stern censorship and political repression.

Read in conjunction with Hedāyat's harrowing short novel, *Būf-e kūr (The Blind Owl)*, these works present a grim, alienated world where people, obsessed with isolation, seek some kind of meaning to their existence and invariably find none. Instead, they encounter only dead ends, barriers, walls, prisons, asylums, and thoughts of self-destruction. This last, given Hedāyat's own suicide, is both prophetic and poignant.

—Carlo Coppola

HEMINGWAY, Ernest (Miller). American. Born in Oak Park, Illinois, 21 July 1899. Educated at Oak Park High School, graduated 1917. Served as a Red Cross ambulance driver in Italy, 1918; also served on the western front with the Italian Arditi: wounded in action: Medaglia d'Argento al Valore Militare; Croce de Guerra; involved in anti-submarine patrol duty off the coast of Cuba, 1942–44. Married 1) Hadley Richardson in 1921 (divorced 1927), one son; 2) Pauline Pfeiffer in 1927 (divorced 1940), two sons; 3) the writer Martha Gellhorn in 1940 (divorced 1946); 4) Mary Welsh in 1946. Reporter, Kansas City *Star*, 1917; reporter, then foreign correspondent, Toronto *Star* and *Star Weekly*, 1920–23: covered the Greco-Turkish War, 1922; moved to Paris, 1921, and became associated with the expatriate community, including Gertrude Stein, *q.v.*, and Ezra Pound; correspondent in Paris for Hearst newspapers, 1924–27; settled in Key West, Florida, 1928; moved to Cuba, 1940, and to Idaho, 1958; war correspondent for North American Newspaper Alliance, in Spain, 1937–38, and for *Collier's* in Europe, 1944–45: Bronze Star. Recipient: Bancarella prize (Italy), 1953; Pulitzer prize, 1953; Nobel prize for literature, 1954; American Academy award of merit medal, 1954. *Died (suicide) 2 July 1961.*

PUBLICATIONS

Collections

A Hemingway Selection, edited by Dennis Pepper.   1972.

The Enduring Hemingway, edited by Charles Scribner, Jr. 1974.
88 Poems, edited by Nicholas Gerogiannis.   1979; as *Complete Poems*, 1983.
The Complete Short Stories, edited by Finta Vigia.   1987.

Short Stories

Three Stories and Ten Poems.   1923.
In Our Time (sketches).   1924.
In Our Time: Stories.   1925; revised edition, 1930.
Men Without Women.   1927.
God Rest You Merry Gentlemen.   1933.
Winner Take Nothing.   1933.
The Fifth Column and the First Forty-Nine Stories (includes play).   1938.
The Portable Hemingway, edited by Malcolm Cowley. 1944.
The Essential Hemingway.   1947.
The Old Man and the Sea.   1952.
Hemingway in Michigan, edited by Constance Cappel Montgomery.   1966.
The Fifth Column and Four Stories of the Spanish Civil War.   1969.
The Nick Adams Stories, edited by Philip Young.   1972.

Novels

The Torrents of Spring: A Romantic Novel in Honor of the Passing of a Great Race.   1926.
The Sun Also Rises.   1926; as *Fiesta*, 1927.
A Farewell to Arms.   1929.
To Have and Have Not.   1937.
For Whom the Bell Tolls.   1940.
Across the River and into the Trees.   1950.
Islands in the Stream.   1970.
A Divine Gesture: A Fable.   1974.
The Garden of Eden.   1986.

Plays

Today Is Friday.   1926.
The Spanish Earth (screenplay).   1938.
The Fifth Column (produced 1940).   In *The Fifth Column . . .*, 1938.

Screenplays (documentaries): *Spain in Flames*, with others, 1937; *The Spanish Earth*, 1937.

Verse

Collected Poems.   1960.

Other

Death in the Afternoon.   1932.
Green Hills of Africa.   1935.
The Hemingway Reader, edited by Charles Poore.   1953.
Hemingway: The Wild Years (newspaper articles), edited by Gene Z. Hanrahan.   1962.
A Moveable Feast (autobiography).   1964.
By-Line: Hemingway, Selected Articles and Dispatches of Four Decades, edited by William White.   1967.
Hemingway: Cub Reporter: "Kansas City Star" Stories, edited by Matthew J. Bruccoli.   1970.
The Faithful Bull (for children).   1980.
Selected Letters 1917–1961, edited by Carlos Baker. 1981.

Hemingway on Writing, edited by Larry W. Phillips. 1984.

The Dangerous Summer.   1985.

Dateline: Toronto: The Complete Toronto Star Dispatches 1920 to 1924, edited by William White.   1985.

Conversations with Hemingway (interviews), edited by Bruccoli, 1986.

Editor, *Men at War: The Best War Stories of All Time.* 1942.

*

Bibliography: *Hemingway: A Comprehensive Bibliography* by Audre Hanneman, 1967, supplement, 1975; *Hemingway: A Reference Guide* by Linda W. Wagner, 1977.

Critical Studies: *Hemingway: The Writer as Artist,* 1952, revised edition, 1972, and *Hemingway: A Life Story,* 1969, both by Carlos Baker, and *Hemingway and His Critics: An International Anthology* edited by Baker, 1961; *Hemingway* by Philip Young, 1952, revised edition, as *Hemingway: A Reconsideration,* 1966; *Hemingway* by Stewart F. Sanderson, 1961; *Hemingway: A Collection of Critical Essays* edited by Robert P. Weeks, 1962; *Hemingway* by Earl Rovit, 1963; *The Hero in Hemingway's Short Stories* by Joseph DeFalco, 1963; *Hemingway: An Introduction and Interpretation* by Sheridan Baker, 1967; *Hemingway and the Pursuit of Heroism* by Leo Gurko, 1968; *Hemingway's Nonfiction: The Public Voice* by Robert O. Stephens, 1968, and *Hemingway: The Critical Reception* edited by Stephens, 1977; "Hemingway's 'Hills Like White Elephants'" by Gary D. Elliott, in *Explicator* 35, 1977; *Hemingway: The Inward Terrain* by Richard B. Hovey, 1968; *Hemingway's Heroes* by Delbert E. Wylder, 1969; *Hemingway: The Writer's Art of Self-Defense* by Jackson R. Benson, 1969, and *The Short Stories of Hemingway: Critical Essays* edited by Benson, 1975; *A Reader's Guide to Hemingway* by Arthur Waldhorn, 1972; *Hemingway's Craft* by Sheldon Norman Grebstein, 1973; *Hemingway and Faulkner: Inventors/Masters* by Linda W. Wagner, 1975, *Hemingway: Six Decades of Criticism,* 1987, and *New Essays on The Sun Also Rises,* 1987, both edited by Linda Wagner-Martin; *By Force of Will: The Life and Art of Hemingway,* 1977, and *New Essays on A Farewell to Arms,* 1990, both by Scott Donaldson; *Scott and Ernest: The Authority of Failure and the Authority of Success* by Matthew J. Bruccoli, 1978; *Hemingway and His World* by Anthony Burgess, 1978; *The Tragic Art of Hemingway* by Wirt Williams, 1981; *Hemingway: The Critical Heritage* edited by Jeffrey Meyers, 1982, and *Hemingway: A Biography* by Meyers, 1985; *Hemingway's Nick Adams,* 1982, and *Hemingway: A Study of the Short Fiction,* 1989, both by Joseph M. Flora; *Hemingway* by Samuel Shaw, 1982; *Hemingway: New Critical Essays* edited by A. Robert Lee, 1983; *The Hemingway Women* by Bernice Kert, 1983; *Hemingway and The Sun Also Rises: The Crafting of a Style* by Frederic J. Svoboda, 1983; *Hemingway: The Writer in Context* edited by James Nagel, 1984; *Concealments in Hemingway's Work* by Gerry Brenner, 1984; *Hemingway: Life and Works* (chronology) by Gerald B. Nelson and Glory Jones, 1984; *Cassandra's Daughters: Women in Hemingway* by Roger Whitlow, 1984; *Along with Youth: Hemingway, the Early Years,* 1985, and *Less Than a Treason: Hemingway in Paris,* 1990, both by Peter Griffin; *The Young Hemingway,* 1986, *Hemingway: The Paris Years,* 1989, and *Hemingway: The American Homecoming,* 1993, by Michael Reynolds; *Hemingway* (biography) by Kenneth S. Lynn, 1987; *Hemingway and Nineteenth-Century Aestheticism* by John Gaggin, 1988; *Hemingway Rediscovered* by Norberto Fuentes, 1988; *Hemingway in Love and War: The Lost Diary of Agnes von Kurowsky, Her Letters and Correspondence of Hemingway* edited by Henry Serrano Villard and James Nagel, 1989; *Hemingway's Neglected Short Fiction: New Perspectives* edited by Susan F. Beegel, 1989; *Hemingway's Art of Non Fiction* by R. Weber, 1990; *Hemingway and His World* by A. E. Hotchner, 1990; *Hemingway: Essays of Reassessment* edited by Frank Scafella, 1991.

*   *   *

When Ernest Hemingway was awarded the Nobel prize for literature in 1954, the jury testified to his stature as one of the most important 20th-century authors. In the words of the president of the Swedish Academy, Hemingway "honestly and undauntedly reproduces the genuine features of the hard countenance of the age," displaying in the process "a natural admiration of every individual who fights the good fight in a world of reality overshadowed by violence and death." This judgment on the author's moral stance was coupled with a tribute to his "powerful style-forming mastery of the art of modern narration."

The more obvious features of Hemingway's narrative technique—the crisp reporting of action observed in sharp focus, dialogue that is colloquial in register and laconic in tone—have been imitated by writers throughout the world. In this sense his influence as a stylist has been massive. But in Hemingway, unlike many imitators of the superficialities of his style, these features grow out of and are supported by deeper narrative structures. His early shorter fiction best illustrates how he taught himself to build them.

In *Death in the Afternoon,* essential reading for its scattered comments on his aims and techniques, he recalled his apprenticeship to his craft.

> I was trying to write then and I found the greatest difficulty, apart from knowing truly what you really felt . . . , was to put down what really happened in action; what the actual things were which produced the emotion that you experienced.

His aim was to describe action in such a concentrated form that the experience would be communicated powerfully and precisely to the reader. Sequences of action were to be stated in simple declarative prose; extraneous matter must be discarded as likely to dilute the concentration. In this way the essential message to be communicated, "the real thing . . . would be as valid in a year or ten years or, with luck and if you stated it purely enough, always. . . ."

His first substantial collection of short stories, *In Our Time,* incorporates twelve experimental vignettes of this kind, dealing with a variety of violent events. The following is typical of the genre:

> We were in a garden at Mons. Young Buckley came in with his patrol across the river. The first German I saw climbed up over the garden wall. We waited till he got one leg over and then potted him. He had so much equipment on and looked awfully surprised

and fell down into the garden. Then three more came over further down the wall. We shot them. They all came just like that.

Here Hemingway has chosen to present the action through the register of a British subaltern's speech style. The strength of the sketch, however, lies in the accelerating pace of the sequence of actions: waiting while the first German climbs halfway over the wall; potting him; noting the heavy equipment, the surprised expression, the fall; then rapid action in which the narrator has no time to observe such details: "Then three more came over further down the wall. We shot them. They all came just like that."

These vignettes are interleaved between longer stories in which the narrative technique has been developed and amplified by dialogue. This also has been reduced to bare essentials. The emotional responses between speakers are implied, not described, as speech follows speech. The new stories also extend the range of subjects, exploring areas of violence and pain in which physical brutality is compounded with spiritual torment. Seven of the stories deal with events in the life of a certain Nick Adams and form a kind of loose episodic novel. Of these, "Indian Camp" and "The End of Something" are compelling studies of the loss of adolescent innocence and of painful initiation into the adult world. Equally powerful is "The Battler," in which Nick falls in with a violent punch drunk boxer and his softly spoken black protector. The story is pervaded by a suppressed hint of something sinister in the relationship between the boxer and his protector.

But "Out of Season" illustrates most clearly the direction Hemingway's narrative technique was taking. The story is presented obliquely, its effect created as much by what is omitted as by what is overtly stated. It tells how a young man and his wife set out to fish an Alpine stream. Their tippling peasant guide leads them to a stretch of water where fishing is prohibited, though he assures them that no one will object. The man is keen to fish; the woman is not and turns back to their hotel. The man finds he has no lead sinker for his line. The guide asks for money to buy supplies so that all three may go fishing next day. The man hands money over but says he may decide not to go fishing after all. The story, however, is not really about the fishing trip. It is about the relationship of the man and the woman as revealed through the action and dialogue. There is something deeply wrong between them; chasms of resentment open up between the man's expressions of solicitude and the woman's refusal to respond. We are not told what the trouble is, but we feel that it is very bad. Superficially, this is the story of an aborted fishing trip; quintessentially it is the story of a collapsing relationship whose outcome is unresolved.

Hemingway wrote of his narrative strategy that "if a writer of prose knows enough about what he is writing about he may omit things that he knows and the reader, if the writer is writing truly enough, will have a feeling of those things as strongly as if the writer had stated them. The dignity of movement of an iceberg is due to only one-eighth of it being above water."

With this and his dictum that "Prose is architecture, not interior decoration" in mind, the reader more easily perceives the submerged structures that support the visible parts of his later fiction, including "Hills Like White Elephants," "The Snows of Kilimanjaro," and the long story (for it is hardly a novel) *The Old Man and the Sea.* The submerged structures in *The Old Man and the Sea* incorporate Christian symbols and a framework of allegory to support the account of a fisherman's fight for victory and survival. This is a masterpiece from, in the Nobel jury's citation, "one of the great writers of our time."

—Stewart F. Sanderson

See the essays on "A Clean, Well-Lighted Place," "Hills Like White Elephants," "The Short Happy Life of Francis Macomber," and "The Snows of Kilimanjaro."

HENRY, O. Pseudonym for William Sydney, or Sidney, Porter. American. Born in Greensboro, North Carolina, 11 September 1862. Educated at his aunt's private school in Greensboro to age 7; apprentice pharmacist in Greensboro, 1878–81; licensed by the North Carolina Pharmaceutical Association, 1881. Married 1) Athol Estes Roach in 1887 (died 1897), one son and one daughter; 2) Sara Lindsay Coleman in 1907. Moved to Texas, 1882, and worked on a ranch in LaSalle County, 1882–84; bookkeeper in Austin, 1884–86; contributed to Detroit *Free Press,* 1887; draftsman, Texas Land office, Austin, 1887–91; teller, First National Bank, Austin, 1891–94; founding editor, *Iconoclast,* later *Rolling Stone* magazine, Houston, 1894–95; columnist ("Tales of the Town," later "Some Postscripts"), Houston *Post,* 1895–96; accused of embezzling funds from his previous employers, First National Bank, Austin, 1895; fled to Honduras to avoid trial, 1896–97; returned to Austin because of wife's illness, 1897; jailed for embezzling in the Federal Penitentiary, Columbus, Ohio, 1898–1901 (5-year sentence reduced to 3): while in prison began publishing stories as O. Henry; moved to Pittsburgh, 1901, and New York, 1902; thereafter a full-time writer; regular contributor, New York *Sunday World,* 1903–05. O. Henry Memorial award established by the Society of Arts and Sciences, 1918. *Died 5 June 1910.*

PUBLICATIONS

Collections

Complete Works.   1926.
Stories, edited by Harry Hansen.   1965.

Short Stories

Cabbages and Kings.   1904.
The Four Million.   1906.
The Trimmed Lamp and Other Stories of the Four Million. 1907.
Heart of the West.   1907.
The Voice of the City: Further Stories of the Four Million. 1908.
The Gentle Grafter.   1908.
Roads of Destiny.   1909.
Options.   1909.
Strictly Business: More Stories of the Four Million.   1910.
Whirligigs.   1910.
Let Me Feel Your Pulse.   1910.
The Two Women.   1910.
Sixes and Sevens.   1911.
Rolling Stones.   1912.
Waifs and Strays.   1917.
O. Henryana: Seven Odds and Ends: Poetry and Short Stories.   1920.

Selected Stories, edited by C. Alphonse Smith.   1922.
The Best of O. Henry.   1929.
More O. Henry.   1933.
The Best Short Stories of O. Henry, edited by Bennett Cerf
    and Van H. Cartmell.   1945.
The Pocket Book of O. Henry, edited by Harry Hansen.
    1948.
Cops and Robbers, edited by Ellery Queen.   1948.
O. Henry Westerns, edited by Patrick Thornhill.   1961.

Play

Lo, with Franklin P. Adams, music by A. Baldwin Sloane
    (produced 1909).

Other

Complete Writings,   14 vols., 1918.
Letters to Lithopolis from O. Henry to Mabel Wagnalls.
    1922.
Postschipts (from Houston *Post*), edited by Florence Strat-
    ton.   1923.
O. Henry Encore: Stories and Illustrations (from Houston
    Post), edited by Mary Sunlocks Harrell.   1939.

*

Bibliography: *A Bibliography of Porter (O. Henry)* by Paul
S. Clarkson, 1938; *Porter (O. Henry): A Reference Guide* by
Richard C. Harris, 1980; in *Bibliography of American
Literature* by Jacob Blanck, edited by Virginia L. Smyers
and Michael Winship, 1983.

Critical Studies: *O. Henry Biography* by C. Alphonse
Smith, 1916; *The Caliph of Bagdad* by Robert H. Davis and
Arthur B. Maurice, 1931; *O. Henry: The Man and His
Work,* 1949, and *O. Henry, American Regionalist,* 1969,
both by Eugene Hudson Long; *The Heart of O. Henry* by
Dale Kramer, 1954; *Alias O. Henry: A Biography* by Gerald
Langford, 1957; *O. Henry from Polecat Creek* by Ethel
Stephens Arnett, 1962; *O. Henry* by Eugene Current-Gar-
cia, 1965; *O. Henry and the Theory of the Short Story* by
B.M. Ejxenbaum, translated from the Russian by I.R.
Titunik, 1968; *O. Henry: The Legendary Life of Porter* by
Richard O'Connor, 1970; *From Alamo Plaza to Jack
Harris's Saloon: O. Henry and the Southwest He Knew* by
Joseph Gallegly, 1970; *Cheap Rooms and Restless Hearts: A
Study of Formula in the Urban Tales of Porter* by Karen
Charmaine Blansfield, 1988.

*   *   *

Like a rocket-launched spaceship, Porter's career as the
legendary O. Henry flourished during the brief span of
eight years between his arrival in New York in 1902 and his
death there in 1910. His background had supplied him with
a multitude of colorful types and adventures which, along
with many new ones, he swiftly transformed into the still
more beguiling exploits of another multitude of fictive
characters in O. Henry's glittering stories. The range of
Porter's experience, from the provincial constraints of
boyhood in an embittered Reconstruction South to ultimate creative achievement in New York, seemed limitless
as his O. Henry stories appeared in print—113 of them in
the weekly *New York Sunday World* alone between 1903
and 1905, and at least 25 longer ones published during the
same period in monthly magazines such as *Everybody's,
McClure's,* and *Munsey's.*

Porter's fame—as O. Henry—is primarily associated
with his tales of New York's "four million," the approximate population of the metropolis, aptly chosen for the title
of his second collection of stories in 1906. During his
residence in New York he produced more than 140
stories—virtually half his total output—based on the
appearance and the conduct of the throngs he observed
daily in shops and offices, hostelries and theatres, on street
corners, park benches, tenement fire-escapes, and open-air
buses. Selecting two or three such individuals who had
caught his fancy, he could quickly summon up imaginary
situations or predicaments for them to confront, and then
work out ingeniously unexpected solutions for their problems, usually with a touch of whimsy that rarely failed to
delight his grateful readers. New York challenged Porter to
record its true voice, to penetrate its mysteries, and to show
others that real worth and beauty lurked unmarked in
many unlikely places, even beneath Coney Island's span-
gled temples, which also "offered saving and apposite balm
and satisfaction to the restless human heart." Porter
eagerly accepted the challenge and strove to capture the
essence of the great city in story after story, 50 more of
them in the next two collections, *The Trimmed Lamp* and
The Voice of the City. Also published during this same time
were *Heart of the West* and *The Gentle Grafter,* containing
the stories based on his experiences in Texas and in prison;
in 1909 two more volumes of stories with varigated settings
appeared, *Roads of Destiny* and *Options.* Another collection, *Strictly Business,* containing 22 more New York
stories plus "A Municipal Report," was published in 1910,
shortly before Porter died. Still to come posthumously were
at least a half dozen more collections of stories and storied
lore, memorabilia by some of the writing folk who had
known him well.

The "O. Henry Story," as it came in time to be known,
admired, and/or condemned, owed much of its popular
appeal to Porter's sophisticated updating of two types of
short fiction that had flourished in magazines and newspapers during the decades just prior to and after the Civil
War. These were the boisterous tall tale of the Old
Southwest frontier, and the more sentimental romantic
adventure story of the postwar local color movement.
During his long apprenticeship in Texas, Porter taught
himself how to combine the most attractive features of
both types of writing parodies or burlesques of other
prominent writers' works and by transforming his own
personal encounters into far-fetched legends. While experimenting with new techniques and developing his own
individual style, he was working over in these sketches such
familiar old gambits as the disguise or impostor motif, and
he combined these motifs with variations on the theme of
disparity between rich and poor, success and misfortune,
and the idea that destiny or fate imposes inescapable roles
on the individual. This sense of determinism, treated both
seriously and comically in many of his early efforts,
remained a strong moving force throughout most of his
later writings as well.

His apprenticeship as a professional writer actually got
under way shortly after his marriage in 1887. During the
next eight years while employed in Austin, first as
draughtsman in the Texas Land Office and later as teller in
the First National Bank, Porter's random publications
elsewhere led in time to the steady flow of humorous
matter that he wrote and published in his own ambitious
weekly, *The Rolling Stone.* Here could be found during its
brief life (March to December 1894) the origins of his later
themes, plots, methods, and style; for he managed, while
holding down a full-time job at the bank, to fill its eight

pages each week with funny cartoons, squibs, and satirical barbs on people and events of local interest. In Houston the following year he continued honing these talents while writing in a daily feature column, "Some Postscripts," the kind of anecdotal humor he had done in *The Rolling Stone,* as well as longer sketches, many of them embryonic foreshadowings of his more famous later stories. In more than 50 of these, his facility for ringing changes on the familiar O. Henry themes of mistaken identity, false pretense, misplaced devotion, nobility in disguise, and the bitter irony of fate are plainly visible, along with such sentimental character types as the sensitive tramp, the ill-starred lovers, the starving artist, and the gentle grafter. Both the basic structure and tone of his more famous stories, as well as the attitudes responsible for them, were being shaped in the Houston *Post* sketches before the combined disasters occurred—his wife Athol's death, his trial and conviction that sent him to prison in 1898 an embittered man.

During the three years Porter spent in prison and the next two while becoming re-oriented in Pittsburgh and New York, he wrote more than half of some 80 new western stories that preceded his much larger production of New York tales. Most of them are set in Texas and Latin America (where he had lived nearly a year as a solitary fugitive), but virtually all of these stories reflect the conventional images associated with the Wild West. Despite realistic dialogue and specific descriptive details, their colorful dramatis personae are romanticized types; their actions are governed by a few basic passions—love, hatred, fear, greed—befitting a simplistic dichotomy of "good guys" versus "bad guys." The standard situation in most of them is a variant of the boy-meets-girl problem, involving either rivalry between two men for the possession of a woman, or discomfiture between a man and a woman which, until eliminated by some unforseen turn of events near the end, precludes any satisfactory resolution of the problem. Other situations concern the reformation or rehabilitation of jailbirds, or the opposing forces of malfeasance and the law. Porter became increasingly skilled in devising tightly knitted plots with breathless tensions relieved in last-minute, quick reversals.

Regardless of their settings, however, he skillfully shifted about and rearranged the design of his "cops-and-robbers" pattern, sometimes quite humorously, as in "A Call Loan" and "Friends in San Rosario"—both of which satirize the same lax banking laws that had also victimized him—by showing how they could be circumvented through the collusion of friendly bankers. But sometimes the pattern could be sombre, as in "The Roads We Take," a story of betrayal juxtaposing dream and reality; and brutal, too, as in "The Caballero's Way," which combines the infidelity and revenge motifs in a gruesome plot involving the deadly Cisco Kid, Porter's most attractive villain, who "killed for the love of it . . . any reason that came to his mind would suffice." So he must avenge the treachery of his mistress, Tonia, who has conspired to turn him in to her new lover, Sandridge, the Texas Ranger pursuing him. But the Kid's method of requiting her unfaithfulness is the "caballero's way—tricking Sandridge himself into performing the dirty work instead. Coldly narrated, and almost totally free of sticky sentimentality, "The Caballero's Way," not surprisingly, was long ago designated the finest of Porter's Western stories.

Despite shattered health toward the end of his life, Porter produced from 1909 to 1910 several other exceptionally fine stories, remarkable contrasts to his Texas outlaw tales. His interest having turned once again toward the broad problems of his native post-war area, he had planned an elaborate series of works to dramatize the conflicting aims and ideals of the Old South versus the New South. These never materialized, but reflections of their promise can be seen in three favorite stories that span the gamut from the deadly serious to the ridiculous—and are still anthologized favorites today. Besides "A Municipal Report," hailed as America's finest short story in 1914, there is the uproarious "Ransom of Red Chief," a farcical kidnapping venture that goes awry, and "The Rose of Dixie," a double-barreled satire of regional journalistic policies. Here, "Old South" stuffiness resides in the character of Colonel Aquila Telfair, scion of a grand old family, who plans to edit a high-minded Southern literary journal in Toombs City, Georgia. He acquires a staff of impeccably *Confederate* assistants— "a whole crate of Georgia peaches"—and adamantly refuses to sully his journal with any writings produced by Northerners; everything in it must conform to the watchword: "Of, For, and By the South." He wavers slightly when a fast-talking New York sales promotion agent, T. T. Thacker, persuades him to junk a portion of the Southern deadwood scheduled for the coming issue and to substitute in its place some popular literary piece from elsewhere so that circulation can be boosted. But in the end the Colonel fills the space tentatively agreed upon with an article entitled "Second Message to Congress/Written for/THE ROSE OF DIXIE/BY/ A Member of the Well-known/BULLOCH FAMILY OF GEORGIA/T. Roosevelt." Although "The Rose of Dixie" lacks Porter's usual romantic appeal of virtue rewarded, love requited, or innocence preserved, it still bears his trademark, the surprise ending. But better than that is the delightful spoofing that ripples through the interview between Telfair and Thacker, the one with his stiff, self-righteous Southern intransigence; the other with his brash Yankee practicality. The story is not only a splendid take-off of antebellum Southern magazines, all the funnier for being both truthful and yet kindly; but since the build-up of Thacker is equally barbed, its satire cuts both ways, exposing over-principled Southern states rightsism, poor but proud, as against unprincipled Northern commercialism, indifferent toward any ideal save that of making a "fast buck."

Of all the stories Porter ever wrote, however, he probably succeeded most effectively in the art of fusing comedy and pathos in the last one he finished before the end, "Let Me Feel Your Pulse." Based on his own search for relief during those wretched last months, the story tells of the narrator's ordeals as physicians thumped, probed, and prescribed medications for him to no avail, until at length in the Blue Ridge Mountains of North Carolina he learned about a magic flowering plant, amarylis, as a possible cure for all human ills. Almost imperceptibly the focus of the tale has shifted into the realm of allegory and fantasy and ends with a question that echoes faintly out of Milton's *Lycidas* and implies the essence of all that he had learned about himself and the world, and about his relationship to the world as an artist: "What rest more remedial than to sit with Amarylis in the shade and with a sixth sense, read the wordless Theocritan idyll?" The question subtly reminds the attentive reader that in the next few lines following that familiar allusion the poem speaks of hard-won fame and invokes a grim image of "blind Fury [who comes] and slits the thin-spun life." Death was much on Porter's mind at this point; yet with impeccable artistry his fusion of comedy and pathos shows how well the understood—and endorsed— Milton's caveat to the artist, not to expect his meed of fame in the world of his contemporaries, but in heaven as "all-judging Jove" decrees. His swan song uttered a clear, pure note.

—Eugene Current-Garcia

See the essays on "The Gift of the Magi" and "A Municiple Report."

————

HIDAYAT, Sadik. See **HEDĀYAT, Sādeq.**

————

HOFFMANN, E(rnst) T(heodore) A(madeus). German. Born Ernst Theodore Wilhelm Hoffmann in Königsberg, 24 January 1776. Educated at Burgschule, Königsberg, 1782–92; studied law at University of Königsberg, 1792–95. Married Maria Thekla Michalina Rorer-Trzynska in 1802; one daughter. In legal civil service: posts in Glogau, 1796–98, Berlin, 1798–1800, Posen, 1800–02, Plozk, 1802–04, Warsaw, 1804–08, and, after Napoleon's defeat, Berlin, 1814–22. Also a composer: Kappellmeister, 1808–09, house composer and designer, 1810–12, Bamberg Theatre, and conductor for Sekonda Company, Leipzig and Dresden, 1813–14; composer of operas, and editor of musical works by Beethoven, Mozart, Gluck, and others, 1809–21. *Died 25 June 1822.*

PUBLICATIONS

Collections

Werke, edited by Georg Ellinger. 15 vols., 1927.
Sämtliche Werke, edited by Walter Müller-Seidel and others. 5 vols., 1960–65.
Gesammelte Werke, edited by Rudolf Mingau and Hans-Joachim Kruse. 1976—.
Sämtliche Werke, edited by Wulf Segebrecht, Hartmut Steinecke, and others. 1985—.

Short Stories

Fantasiestücke in Callots Manier. 4 vols., 1814–15.
Nachtstücke. 2 vols., 1816–17.
Seltsame Leiden eines Theater-Direktors. 1819.
Klein Zaches genannt Zinnober. 1819.
Die Serapions-Brüder: Gesammelte Erzählungen und Märchen. 4 vols., 1819–21; as *The Serapion Brethren,* 1886–92.
Meister Floh. 1822; as *Master Flea,* in *Specimens of German Romance,* vol. 2, 1826.
Die letzten Erzählungen. 2 vols., 1825.
Tales, edited by Christopher Lazare. 1959.
The Tales of Hoffmann. 1963.
Tales. 1966.
The Best Tales, edited by E.F. Bleiler. 1967.
Tales, edited by R.J. Hollingdale. 1982.
Tales, edited by Victor Lange. 1982.
The Golden Pot and Other Stories, edited by Ritchie Robertson. 1992.

Novels

Die Elixiere des Teufels. 1815–16; as *The Devil's Elixir,* 1824; as *The Devil's Elixirs,* 1963.
Lebens-ansichten des Katers Murr. 1820–22.
Prinzessen Brambilla. 1821.

Play

Die Maske, edited by Friedrich Schnapp. 1923.

Verse

Poetische Werke, edited by Gerhard Seidel. 6 vols., 1958.

Other

Die Vision auf dem Schlachtfelde bei Dresden. 1814.
Briefwechsel, edited by Hans von Müller and Friedrich Schnapp. 3 vols, 1967–69.
Selected Writings, edited by Leonard J. Kent and Elizabeth C. Knight. 2 vols., 1969.
Tagebücher, edited by Friedrich Schnapp. 1971.
Juristische Arbeiten, edited by Friedrich Schnapp. 1973.
Selected Letters of Hoffmann, edited by Johanna C. Sahlin. 1977.

*

Critical Studies: *Hoffmann, Author of the Tales* by H. Hewett-Taylor, 1948; *Hoffmann* by Ronald Taylor, 1963; *Hoffmann's Other World: The Romantic Author and His "New Mythology"* by Kenneth Negus, 1965; *Music: The Medium of the Metaphysical in Hoffmann* by Pauline Watts, 1972; *The Shattered Self: Hoffmann's Tragic Vision* by Horst S. Daemmrich, 1973; *Hoffmann and the Rhetoric of Terror* by Elizabeth Wright, 1978; *Spellbound: Studies on Mesmerism and Literature* by Maria M. Tatar, 1978; *Mysticism and Sexuality: Hoffmann* by James M. McGlathery, 2 vols., 1981–85; *Hoffmann's Musical Writings: Kreisleriana, The Poet and Composer, Musical Criticism* by David Charlton, 1989.

* * *

Within five years of his death in 1822 several of E.T.A. Hoffmann's short stories had been published in English, and translations of his work (albeit variable in quality) have been continuously available since. Yet today, to English speakers at least, his writings are probably more familiar in their musical adaptations than their original form: Tchaikovskii's *Nutcracker* ballet, Delibes's *Coppélia*, and of course Offenbach's opera *The Tales of Hoffmann* are all taken from Hoffmann stories, whilst 20th-century composers from Busoni to Hindemith have also based operas upon his work. His comparative neglect as a writer, however, is regrettable not just because of the influence he exerted on others (Edgar Allan Poe and Dostoevskii were among writers who acknowledged their debt to him), but above all because, with their depth of psychological insight and their exotic mix of the realistic and the bizarre, his stories have lost none of their power to enthral. Not that these qualities have always met with uncritical approval. Sir Walter Scott, for instance, writing in 1827, talked of Hoffmann's "singularly wild and inflated fancy," and

Thomas Carlyle, who translated the story "The Golden Flower Pot" into English that same year, could still refer to Hoffmann's work as a "bright extravagance" which "less resembles the creation of a poet, than the dreams of an opium-eater." Hoffmann's writings are indeed often fanciful and flamboyant. His stories enter strange and mysterious realms peopled by ghosts and weird apparitions, and the supernatural lurks around every corner. In addition, his heroes are not solid citizens with their lives under control (such are usually presented as bourgeois philistines) but the odd and the eccentric, the mentally disturbed whose personalities are fragmenting, sometimes even the downright mad. But none of this is gratuitous or merely whimsical. Like all the Romantics, and the German Romantics more than most, Hoffmann was aware of a duality underlying human experience: the opposition of finite and infinite, the conflict between ideal and real, the gulf separating aspiration and achievement, this last dilemma embodying itself for the artist in particular in the painful deficiency of his aesthetic expression when compared with the vision that had inspired it. In addition, at a time when Franz Mesmer's experiments in hypnotism (or "mesmerism") had caught the imagination of Europe and demonstrated the precariousness of personal identity, Hoffmann was gripped by the possibility that our destinies are governed, and our desires so often thwarted, by unseen powers from another realm, whether located in the depths of the unconscious or within the elemental forces of nature.

"The Golden Flower Pot" contains many elements typical of Hoffmann's stories. Subtitled "A Fairy-tale from Modern Times," it is set in contemporary (1815) Dresden and paints a witty satirical portrait of bourgeois life and ambitions. Among the narrow worldlings, however, though quite unseen by them, there exists a very different realm, one involving magical creatures and supernatural encounters. Straddling these two worlds is a student, Anselmus, who is suffering the recurrent Hoffmannesque condition of being torn apart by conflicting impulses. In this case it is his love for the self-seeking Veronika, the embodiment of earthly values, and his simultaneous attraction to Serpentina, a little green snake, daughter of a fire spirit banished to earth. She entrances him with her blue eyes and bell-like voice and has about her the aura of poetry, yet she may be no more than a product of his fancy. He must therefore decide whether the realm of creative imagination is sufficiently real to merit his devotion or whether the prosaic and the everyday will prevail instead. On one level the conflict is played out within the mind of Anselmus, but on another it reflects the wider hostility of the material and the spiritual, a clash that in this story culminates in a spectacular battle between benign and demonic spirit-forces. The former are victorious, and Anselmus too opts for life with Serpentina in the poetic kingdom of Atlantis. Yet the story finishes, not with this picture of idyll, but with the wistful musings of the narrator in his lonely Dresden garret. An alcohol-induced trance has enabled him to glimpse, and to describe, Anselmus's bliss, but participation in it for himself is impossible. Artistic fulfillment in this life, it seems, must remain at best a dream.

Plagued by this tantalizing vision of an unreachable ideal, many of Hoffmann's heroes hide behind a facade of idiosyncrasy. Councillor Krespel, in the story of that name, is one such, the talk of the town for his scurrilous behaviour. This has been brought on by the state of his daughter, who possesses a supremely beautiful voice but who is constitutionally so weak that to indulge her music might kill her. Caught in the tension between the expression of art and the maintenance of life Krespel opts to preserve his daughter at all costs, becoming obsessive and tyrannical in the process. But the matter is taken out of his hands when, in a vision one night, he hears her singing and rushes in to find her lying quiet and peaceful, but dead. A dream has this time become spine-chilling reality.

Hoffmann is a past-master at creating an air of mystery, and few of his stories lend themselves to clear-cut interpretation. Whether, for instance, one attributes the conflicts of his heroes to their personal inadequacy or to the machinations of occult forces, both readings can usually be sustained and are equally feasible. The ambiguity is further heightened by the frequent irony of the narrative voice, a playful undertone that prefers hints to explanation and rejoices in the arcane and elusive. At the same time there is sufficient realism to prevent mere allegorizing and a sardonic note to lend bite to the text. Acute observation rubs shoulders with soaring fancy, humour exists alongside menace: it is a compelling mix.

—Peter J. Graves

See the essay on "The Sand-Man."

————

HOOD, Hugh (John Blagdon). Canadian. Born in Toronto, Ontario, 30 April 1928. Educated at De La Salle College, Toronto; St. Michael's College, University of Toronto, 1947–55, B.A. 1950, M.A. 1952, Ph.D. 1955. Married Ruth Noreen Mallory in 1957; two sons and two daughters. Teaching fellow, University of Toronto, 1951–55; associate professor, St. Joseph College, West Hartford, Connecticut, 1955–61; professor titulaire, since 1961, Department of English Studies, University of Montreal. Recipient: University of Western Ontario President's medal, for story, 1963, for article, 1968; Beta Sigma Phi prize, 1965; Canada Council grant, 1968, award, 1971, 1974, and Senior Arts grant, 1977; Province of Ontario award, 1974; City of Toronto award, 1976; Queen's Jubliee medal, 1977. Officer, Order of Canada, 1988. Lives in Montreal.

PUBLICATIONS

Short Stories

Flying a Red Kite.   1962; as volume one of *The Collected Stories,* 1987.
Around the Mountain: Scenes from Montreal Life.   1967.
The Fruit Man, The Meat Man, and The Manager.   1971.
Dark Glasses.   1976.
Selected Stories.   1978.
None Genuine Without This Signature.   1980.
August Nights.   1985.
The Collected Stories:
    A Short Walk in the Rain.   1989.
    The Isolation Booth.   1991.
You'll Catch Your Death.   1992.

Novels

White Figure, White Ground.   1964.
The Camera Always Lies.   1967.
A Game of Touch.   1970.
You Can't Get There from Here.   1972.

The New Age:
   The Swing in the Garden.   1975.
   A New Athens.   1977.
   Reservoir Ravine.   1979.
   Black and White Keys.   1982.
   The Scenic Art.   1984.
   The Motor Boys in Ottawa.   1986.
   Tony's Book.   1988.
   Property and Value.   1990.
   Be Sure To Close Your Eyes.   1993.
Five New Facts about Giorgione.   1987.

Play

Friends and Relations, in *The Play's the Thing: Four Original Television Dramas,* edited by Tony Gifford. 1976.

Other

Strength Down Centre: The Jean Beliveau Story.   1970.
The Governor's Bridge Is Closed: Twelve Essays on the Canadian Scene.   1973.
Scoring: The Art of Hockey, illustrated by Seymour Segal. 1979.
Trusting the Tale (essays).   1983.
Unsupported Assertions (essays).   1991.

Editor, with Peter O'Brien, *Fatal Recurrences: New Fiction in English from Montreal.*   1984.

*

Bibliography: by J.R. (Tim) Struthers, in *The Annotated Bibliography of Canada's Major Authors 5* edited by Robert Lecker and Jack David, 1984.

Critical Studies: "Line and Form" by Dave Godfrey, in *Tamarack Review,* Spring 1965; "Grace: The Novels of Hood" by Dennis Duffy, in *Canadian Literature,* Winter 1971; *The Comedians: Hood and Rudy Wiebe* by Patricia A. Morley, 1977; *Before the Flood: Hood's Work in Progress* by J.R. (Tim) Struthers, 1979; *On the Line: Readings in the Short Fiction of Clark Blaise, John Metcalf, and Hood* by Robert Lecker, 1982; *Hood,* 1983, and *Hood,* 1984, both by Keith Garebian; *Pilgrim's Progress: A Study of the Short Stories of Hood* by Susan Copoloff-Mechanic, 1988.

*   *   *

Perhaps Hugh Hood has not been writing short stories or novels *per se* at all. If this is so, what can we call the well over 100 richly expressive pieces of short fiction and the numerous longer works of fiction that he has created? Folk tales, imaginative histories, fictional autobiographies, meditations; odes, elegies, conversation poems, lyrical ballads; fantasies, prophecies, parables, allegories? In Canadian terms, readers of short fiction might describe his writing as a cross between the typically wry sketches of Stephen Leacock and the typically sad stories of Morley Callaghan. In American terms, readers of short fiction might describe his writing as a cross between the witty and frequently eerie fantasy-stories or memoir-stories of James Thurber and the disturbingly dark but divinely illumined revelations of Flannery O'Connor. Each of us, Hood states (in the

Contemporary Authors Autobiography Series), has four mythic sources on which to draw in constructing an identity, the lines of descent represented by four grandparental surnames. Contemplating Hood's ancestral lineage, we might justifiably imagine a quaternary consisting of Leacock, Callaghan, Thurber, and O'Connor. Other readers, wishing to trace Hood's literary descent, might just as appropriately suggest very different configurations: Dante, Wordsworth, Coleridge, and Joyce, for example, or Turgenev, Hardy, Proust, and Wodehouse.

Some of these allegiances emerged, or became more definite, at later points in Hood's career; but many were clearly marked by stories in his first collection, *Flying a Red Kite.* "Silver Bugles, Cymbals, Golden Silks," a story of the growth of a boy, a marching band, and Canadian life, all telescoped into one, strongly reflects the ironic comedy and the nostalgic lyricism of Leacock. "Where the Myth Touches Us," a story of the tragic misunderstandings between an older writer and a younger writer, though highly fictionalized, represents at some level an effort by Hood to come to terms with the direct personal influence of Callaghan. "Flying a Red Kite," like James Joyce's story "Grace," proceeds in the manner of Dante from an infernal to a purgatorial to a paradisal setting; however, unlike Joyce's story, "Flying a Red Kite" does not parody this structure but affirms it in order to move beyond irony or disbelief to a renewal of faith.

Around the Mountain: Scenes from Montreal Life, the collection of short fiction that followed *Flying a Red Kite,* presents twelve fictional sketches depicting the various rituals of Montreal life over the calendar year. Hood's next collection, *The Fruit Man, The Meat Man, and The Manager,* opens with his magnificent immortality ode "Getting to Williamstown," which was selected for *The Best American Short Stories 1966,* and its two companion pieces "The Tolstoy Pitch" and "A Solitary Ewe"; together, these stories form a triptych on the subject of eternal life, art, and love. This volume was followed by the collection *Dark Glasses,* whose title recalls the biblical passage, "Now we see through a glass darkly; but then, face to face."

In a seminal essay on Canadian poetry, "Preface to an Uncollected Anthology" (in *The Bush Garden: Essays on the Canadian Imagination*), Northrop Frye observes that the title poems of individual collections of poetry frequently provide keys to what is most important in an artist's work. Frey's argument, I believe, applies equally to the title stories of individual short story collections. Examining the title stories of several of Hood's latest collections, *None Genuine Without This Signature, August Nights,* and *You'll Catch Your Death,* allows us to perceive both the variety and the consistency of his achievement. Because these stories have been selected almost randomly for discussion, they suggest the range of focus, tone, subject, form, and method to be found in Hood's work. In addition, because the titles of these stories were chosen by the author as the titles of entire collections, it is possible to regard them as indicators directing us to fundamental aspects of Hood's oeuvre, of his work as a whole.

"None Genuine Without This Signature or Peaches in the Bathtub" is a partly romantic, partly ironic fantasy centering on four characters who develop a new line of lotion, shampoo, and handsoap, a line bearing the slogan *None Genuine Without This Signature* beneath the fake, or we might say artful, signature of the eldest partner. The story verges on parody, mockingly suggesting how modern society has created a new art form—indeed, a new religion—out of merchandising. "August Nights" is a baseball story, a dream-like, cartoon-like, innocently erotic comedy which nonetheless ends with disappointment. The story playfully but ironically depicts the intensity and the ephemerality of a different kind of worship, the infatuation of a vivacious pair of young women baseball fans for their all too human and all too temporary sports heroes. "You'll Catch Your Death" is a story of an odd but precious woman, whom society allows to die when she no longer has anything to care for or anyone to care for her. It portrays a society largely oblivious to the many forms of natural beauty and largely oblivious to its diverse responsibilities, a society capable of building massive boutique complexes but incapable of saving the life of a single soul.

As book titles, *None Genuine Without This Signature, August Nights,* and *You'll Catch Your Death* are rhythmical, euphonious, idiomatic, even lightly parodic, and for these reasons agreeable and comforting. *None Genuine Without This Signature* wittily replies to the younger writers whom Hood has discovered attempting to approximate his own method in their work. At the same time, the title provides a serious reminder of the ultimate authority and meaningfulness of the divine presence, of the holy word. And it conveys a tone of reproach, a reminder of our own corruptibility. Similarly, *August Nights,* though lyrical, offers a prophetic hint of the onset of fall. *You'll Catch Your Death* is more overtly apocalytic: the momentarily consoling familiarity of its title quickly recedes into starker apprehensions of how sadly mortal, how perversely disfigured, human life actually is. Yet in spite of all the warnings contained in his work, Hood clearly believes that we possess the capacity for salvation—through grace. From *Flying a Red Kite* onward through 30 books, Hood has dedicated his remarkable resources to nothing less than a concerted attempt to move us towards that end.

—J.R. (Tim) Struthers

HRABAL, Bohumil. Czech. Born near Brno, 28 March 1914. Educated at grammar school, and at Charles University, Prague, law degree 1946. Has worked as lawyer's clerk, railwayman, salesman, steel worker in Kladno foundries, laborer, stage hand and extra. Writer, from early 1960's. Recipient: Gottwald state prize, 1968; Artist of Merit, 1989. Lives in Liben, Czech Republic.

PUBLICATIONS

Short Stories

Hovory lidí [People's Conversations].   1956.
Taneční hodiny pro starší a pokroč ilé [Dancing Lesson for the Advanced and the Elderly].   1964.
Ostře sledované vlaky (novella).   1965; as *A Close Watch on the Trains,* 1968; as *Closely Watched Trains,* 1968.
Automat svět.   1966; as *The Death of Mr. Baltisberger,* 1975.
Morytáty a legendy [Fair Ditties and Legends].   1968.
Obsluhoval jsem anglického krále (novella).   1971; as *Jak jsem obsluhoval anglického krále,* 1980; as *I Served the King of England,* 1989.
Příliš hlučná samota (novella).   1976; as *Too Loud a Solitude,* 1990.

Hovory lidí (selection).   1984.
Vita nuova: kartinky [Vita nuova: Episodes].   1987.

Novels

Perlička na dně [A Pearl at the Bottom].   1963.
Pábitelé [Palaverers].   1964.
Inzerát na dum, ve kterém už nechci bydlet [Advertising a House I Don't Want to Live In Anymore].   1965.
Postřižiny [The Haircut].   1970; as *Cutting It Short,* 1992.
Sklenice grenadýny [A Glass of Grenadine].   197-?.
Něžný barbar [Tender Barbarian].   1973.
Krasosmutnění [Lovely Wistfulness].   1977.
Mestecko ve kterém se zastavil čas [The Town Where Time Stood Still].   1978.
Tři teskné grotesky, 1944–1953 [Three Melancholy Grosteques].   1979.
Každý den zázrak [A Miracle Every Day].   1979.
Kluby poezie [The Poetry Club].   1981.
Harlekýnovy milióny [The Harlequin's Millions].   1981.
Poupata [Burgeoning].   1982(?).
Svatby v Domě [Weddings in the House].   1984.
Proluky [Vacant Sites].   1986.
Můj svět [My World].   1988.
Kouzelná flétna [Magic Flute].   1990.

Plays

Closely Watched Trains (translation of screenplay), with Jiří Menzel.   1971; as *Closely Observed Trains,* 1971.

Screenplays: *Fádní odpoledne (A Boring Afternoon),* with Ivan Passer, 1965; *Ostře sledované vlaky (Closely Watched Trains; Closely Observed Trains),* with Jiří Menzel, 1967; *Postřižiny* [The Haircut], 1980; *Něžný barbar* (*Tender Barbarian*), from his own novel, with Václav Nyvlt, 1989.

Verse

Bambino di Praga.   1978; with *Barvotisky* and *Krásná Poldi,* 1991.
Chcete vidět zlatou Prahu? výbor z povídek.   1989.
Ztracena ulička.   1991.

Other

Toto město je ve společné péč i obyvatel [This Town Is in the Joint Care of All Its Inhabitants].   1967.
Slavnosti sněženek [Celebration of Snowdrops].   1978.
Domaci ukoly z pilnosti [Voluntary Homework] (miscellany).   1982.
Život bez smokingu [Life Without a Dinner Jacket].   1986.
Pražská ironie [Prague Irony].   1986.
Životopis trochu jinak [A Biography Done Differently].   1986.
Ponorné řičky [The Subterranean Dreams].   1990.
Kličky na kapesniku: román-interview [Knots in a Handkerchief].   1990.
Schizofrenické evangelium, 1949–1952 [Schizophrenic Gospel].   1990.
Slavná Vantochova legenda.   1991.

Editor, *Výbor z české prózy* [Selected Czech Prose].   1967.

*

Critical Study: "*The Haircutting* and *I Waited on the King of England*: Two Recent Works by Hrabal" by George Gibian, in *Czech Literature Since 1956: A Symposium,* edited by William E. Harkins and Paul I. Trensky, 1980.

* * *

Bohumil Hrabal is probably the most popular contemporary Czech novelist and short story writer. His earliest work, written in the 1940's and 1950's and for political reasons not published until the early 1960's, is heavily influenced by Dadaism and surrealism. Hrabal typically used the artistic collage, montage, or assemblage—cutting out details from everyday reality, changing their established order, and assembling them in new connections. The effect of the collage results from the confrontation of contrasting meanings. In Hrabal's stories, it is the simple, unmediated record of events and objects that affects us immediately and influences our imagination. Just as in the real world, there are contrasts: beauty with ugliness, brutality with gentleness, life with death. Their common poetic aspects become clear if we place banality into an unusual place—this is the basis of the device of the collage, which stresses the principles of play and chance, and which is essentially poetic.

Hrabal's early stories, some of which can be found in *The Death of Mr. Baltisberger*, the English translation of *Automat svět*, express the life philosophy of *pábení* (commonly but not entirely adequately translated as "palavering"). This is a word coined by Hrabal himself to describe the narrations of his simple and common characters. Their actions are sometimes eccentric, grotesque, hilarious. Their speech is that of the pub, crude, sometimes vulgar, full of slang. The stories they tell are exaggerated tall-stories. But Hrabal's humor is not crude, it is very sensitive and poetic. The grotesque atmosphere has its gentleness and emotionality. *Pábení* is a philosophy of life oscillating between plebeian roughness and surrealistic sensitivity. The main theme is the miracle of everyday reality.

Hrabal has a great admiration for the beauty of the world and its common people. He talks of "the common people that sift reality through the diamond eye of fantasy." ("The Diamond Eye" is also the title of one of Hrabal's stories.) Although Hrabal pretends to be only "the recorder and cutter of conversations" overheard in a pub or on the street, he is, in reality, the poet of urban periphery. Urban folklore is filtered through the author's own experience. Many of his stories are autobiographical or based on real-life characters ("Angel Eyes," "Prague Nativity," "Romance").

At the beginning of a long series of "palaverers" is "Little Eman," who entertains the Prague suburb of Libeň in pubs, cafeterias, and on the street—a very autobiographical type. The peak of Hrabal's achievement is Uncle Pepin, based on the author's real-life Moravian uncle of the same name, who, with the help of his stories, overcomes the handicap of his existence and position. In the story "The Death of Mr. Baltisberger" we hear his palavering bragging in juxtaposition to the image of the dying race driver Baltisberger, by means of which Hrabal creates a stronger impression on the reader's imagination.

Abroad, Hrabal is probably best known for his short novel *Ostře sledované vlaky (A Close Watch on the Trains)*. This is obviously because of the great success of the Academy Award-winning movie *Closely Watched Trains*, directed by the Czech director J. Menzel. (From the 1960's, Hrabal's stories and novels have tempted Czech directors, who with more or less success have adapted some of his work for television or the film screen.) Contextualized by a whole wave of World War II novels in 1960's Czech literature, this short novel offsets the traditional theme of the fight against the Nazis by the very intimate problems of the adolescent Miloš Hrma. His personal tragedy ironically emphasizes the tragedy of the more general historical events, and vice versa. Another part of the narrative is the mock-heroic and parodic description of the idyllic life on a railroad station in a small town at the end of the war. The narrative technique is again based on the intertwining of all plot lines.

Hrabal, wrote another short novel, *Obsluhoval jsem anglického Krále (I Served the King of England)*, in the summer of 1971, but it was not published until 1982. This text moves into levels of symbolism, allegory, and myths. The theme is the most natural of all human emotions, the desire for love and happiness. The narrator is a waiter of small stature, suffering from an inferiority complex. His aim in life is to get revenge on those that have hurt him. In his eyes, power is equated with money, and so this becomes his obsession. The emptiness of this view of life is disclosed from the outside, by paradoxical historical events. He marries a Nazi woman and this makes him a collaborator. However, by chance he participates in the underground resistance movement. Finally, he sees through the falseness of his life goals. He gains money, but he gives it all up and ends in an international camp with other "former" millionaires. In the end, he shuts himself off from the world in the mountains.

Hrabal changed his narrative technique in *I Served the King of England* from the collage to a continuous narrative. The compositional device is that of the monologue, the free flow of speech held together by lyrical association.

Hrabal's next work *Příliš hlučná samota (Too Loud a Solitude)* is another short novel that again introduces a new narrative situation to Hrabal's work. The protagonist Haňta works at a scrap paper salvage center; amidst the dirt and dust he comments on the decline of culture and education. Hrabal uses the monological form of confession and philosophical meditation. The impressions of the narrator are then commented upon by the author. The aim is not to discover the miracle of everyday reality with the help of eccentric imagination and surprising confrontations (as is the case in his short stories), or to render the sheer delight of storytelling (apparent in *I Served the King of England*), but to disclose the mysteries of life and its deepest paradoxes. In its melancholic mood this fiction differs from the previous ones.

The political climate in postwar Czechoslovakia was not friendly toward Hrabal's artistic efforts. His first works were suspect, published 20 years after they were written. In the 1960's, when political restrictions were loosened, Hrabal published his previous and new work in quick succession and was promoted to the status of a "living classic." Because of Hrabal's political stance in the Prague Spring of 1968, he fell into political disfavor again and was allowed to publish only after 1975—with great restrictions from the censorship. Hrabal frequently rewrote his stories and some were adapted by the editors. After the Velvet Revolution of 1989 the official attitude to Hrabal's work has changed again—the literary authorities have embarked on the project of publishing his collected works; they aim to reprint all his work including the original manuscript versions. Throughout all the political changes Hrabal has remained greatly popular with the reading public, which cherishes him as a national writer.

—Soňa Nováková

HUGHES, (James) Langston. American. Born in Joplin, Missouri, 1 February 1902. Educated at Central High School, Cleveland, 1916–20; Columbia University, New York, 1921–22; Lincoln University, Pennsylvania (Witter Bynner award, 1926), 1926–29, B.A. 1929. During World War II, member of the Music and Writers war boards. English teacher in Mexico, 1920–21; seaman, 1923–24; busboy, Wardman Park Hotel, Washington, D.C., 1925; Madrid correspondent, Baltimore *Afro-American*, 1937; columnist ("Simple"), Chicago *Defender*, 1943-67, and New York *Post*, 1962–67; lived in Harlem, New York, after 1947. Founder, Harlem Suitcase Theatre, New York, 1938, New Negro Theatre, Los Angeles, 1939, and Skyloft Players, Chicago, 1941. Visiting professor of creative writing, Atlanta University, 1947; poet-in-residence, University of Chicago Laboratory School, 1949. Recipient: Harmon gold medal, 1931; Rosenwald fellowship, 1931, 1940; Guggenheim fellowship, 1935; American Academy grant, 1946; Anisfield-Wolf award, 1953; NAACP Spingarn medal, 1960. D.Litt: Lincoln University, 1943; Howard University, Washington, D.C., 1963; Western Reserve University, Cleveland, 1964. Member, American Academy, 1961, and American Academy of Arts and Sciences. *Died 22 May 1967.*

PUBLICATIONS

Short Stories

The Ways of White Folks.   1934.
Simple Speaks His Mind.   1950.
Laughing to Keep from Crying.   1952.
Simple Takes a Wife.   1953.
Simple Stakes a Claim.   1957.
The Best of Simple, illustrated by Bernard Nast.   1961.
Something in Common and Other Stories.   1963.
Simple's Uncle Sam.   1965.

Novels

Not Without Laughter.   1930.
Tambourines to Glory.   1958.

Verse

The Weary Blues.   1926.
Fine Clothes to the Jew.   1927.
Dear Lovely Death.   1931.
The Negro Mother and Other Dramatic Recitations. 1931.
The Dream-Keeper and Other Poems.   1932.
Scottsboro Limited: Four Poems and a Play in Verse. 1932.
A New Song.   1938.
Shakespeare in Harlem.   1942.
Jim Crow's Last Stand.   1943.
Lament for Dark Peoples and Other Poems, edited by H. Driessen.   1944.
Fields of Wonder.   1947.

One-Way Ticket.   1949.
Montage of a Dream Deferred.   1951.
Selected Poems.   1959.
Ask Your Mama: 12 Moods for Jazz.   1961.
The Panther and the Lash: Poems of Our Times.   1967.
Don't You Turn Back (for children), edited by Lee Bennett Hopkins.   1969.

Plays

The Gold Piece, in *Brownies' Book,* July 1921.
Mulatto (produced 1935; original version produced 1939). In *Five Plays,* 1963.
Little Ham (produced 1935). In *Five Plays,* 1963.
Troubled Island (produced 1935; revised version, music by William Grant Still, produced 1949).   1949.
When the Jack Hollers, with Arna Bontemps (produced 1936).
Joy to My Soul (produced 1937).
Soul Gone Home (produced 1937?).   In *Five Plays,* 1963.
Don't You Want to Be Free?, music by Carroll Tate (produced 1937).   In *One Act Play Magazine,* October 1938.
Front Porch (produced 1938).
The Organizer, music by James P. Johnson (produced 1939).
The Sun Do Move (produced 1942).
Freedom's Plow (broadcast 1943).   1943.
Pvt. Jim Crow (radio script), in *Negro Story,* May-June 1945.
Booker T. Washington at Atlanta (broadcast 1945).   In *Radio Drama in Action,* edited by Eric Barnouw, 1945.
Street Scene (lyrics only), book by Elmer Rice, music by Kurt Weill (produced 1947).   1948.
The Barrier, music by Jan Meyerowitz (produced 1950).
Just Around the Corner (lyrics only), book by Abby Mann and Bernard Drew, music by Joe Sherman (produced 1951).
Simply Heavenly, music by David Martin (produced 1957). 1959.
Esther, music by Jan Meyerowitz (produced 1957).
Shakespeare in Harlem, with James Weldon Johnson (produced 1959).
Port Town, music by Jan Meyerowitz (produced 1960).
The Ballad of the Brown King, music by Margaret Bonds (produced 1960).
Black Nativity (produced 1961).
Gospel Glow (produced 1962).
Let Us Remember Him, music by David Amram (produced 1963).
Tambourines to Glory, music by Jobe Huntley, from the novel by Hughes (produced 1963). In *Five Plays,* 1963.
Five Plays (includes *Mulatto, Soul Gone Home, Little Ham, Simply Heavenly, Tambourines to Glory*), edited by Webster Smalley.   1963.
Jerico-Jim Crow (produced 1963).
The Prodigal Son (produced 1965).

Screenplay: *Way Down South,* with Clarence Muse, 1939.

Radio Scripts: *Jubilee,* with Arna Bontemps, 1941; *Brothers,* 1942; *Freedom's Plow,* 1943; *John Henry Hammers It Out,* with Peter Lyons, 1943; *In the Service of My Country,* 1944; *The Man Who Went to War,* 1944 (UK); *Booker T. Washington at Atlanta,* 1945; *Swing Time at the Savoy,* with Noble Sissle, 1949.

Television Scripts: *The Big Sea,* 1965; *It's a Mighty World,* 1965; *Strollin' Twenties,* 1966.

Other (for children)

Popo and Fifina: Children of Haiti, with Arna Bontemps.
1932.
The First Book of Negroes.   1952.
The First Book of Rhythms.   1954.
Famous American Negroes.   1954.
Famous Negro Music-Makers.   1955.
The First Book of Jazz.   1955; revised edition, 1962.
The First Book of the West Indies.   1956; as *The First Book of the Caribbean,* 1965.
Famous Negro Heroes of America.   1958.
The First Book of Africa.   1960; revised edition, 1964.

Other

The Big Sea: An Autobiography.   1940.
The Sweet Flypaper of Life (on Harlem), with Roy De Carava.   1955.
A Pictorial History of the Negro in America, with Milton Meltzer.   1956; revised edition, 1963, 1968.
I Wonder as I Wander: An Autobiographical Journey. 1956.
The Hughes Reader.   1958.
Fight for Freedom: The Story of the NAACP.   1962.
Black Magic: A Pictorial History of the Negro in American Entertainment, with Milton Meltzer.   1967.
Black Misery.   1969.
Good Morning, Revolution: Uncollected Social Protest Writings, edited by Faith Berry.   1973.
Hughes in the Hispanic World and Haiti, edited by Edward J. Mullen.   1977.
Arna Bontemps-Hughes: Letters 1925–1967, edited by Charles H. Nichols.   1980.

Editor, *Four Lincoln University Poets.*   1930.
Editor, with Arna Bontemps, *The Poetry of the Negro 1746–1949: An Anthology.*   1949; revised edition, as *The Poetry of the Negro 1746–1970,* 1970.
Editor, with Waring Guney and Bruce M. Wright, *Lincoln University Poets.*   1954.
Editor, with Arna Bontemps, *The Book of Negro Folklore.* 1958.
Editor, *An Africa Treasury: Articles, Essays, Stories, Poems by Black Africans.*   1960.
Editor, *Poems from Black Africa.*   1963.
Editor, *New Negro Poets: USA.*   1964.
Editor, *The Book of Negro Humor.*   1966.
Editor, *La Poésie Negro-Américaine* (bilingual edition). 1966.
Editor, *Anthologie Africaine et Malgache.*   1966.
Editor, *The Best Short Stories by Negro Writers: An Anthology from 1899 to the Present.*   1967.

Translator, with Mercer Cook, *Masters of the Dew,* by Jacques Roumain.   1947.
Translator, with Ben Frederic Carruthers, *Cuba Libre,* by Nicolás Guillén.   1948.
Translator, *Gypsy Ballads,* by Federico García Lorca. 1951.
Translator, *Selected Poems of Gabriela Mistral.*   1957.

*

Bibliography: *A Bio-Bibliography of Hughes 1902–1967* by Donald C. Dickinson, 1967, revised edition, 1972; *Hughes and Gwendolyn Brooks: A Reference Guide* by R. Baxter Miller, 1978; *Hughes: A Bio-bibliography* by Thomas A. Mikolyzk, 1990.

Critical Studies: *Hughes* by James A. Emanuel, 1967; *Hughes: A Biography* by Milton Meltzer, 1968; *Hughes, Black Genius: A Critical Evaluation* edited by Therman B. O'Daniel, 1971 (includes bibliography); *Hughes, American Poet* by Alice Walker, 1974; *Hughes: An Introduction to the Poetry* by Onwuchekwa Jemie, 1976; *Hughes: The Poet and His Critics* by Richard K. Barksdale, 1977; *Hughes: Before and Beyond Harlem* by Faith Berry, 1983; *The Life of Hughes: I, Too, Hear America Singing (1902–41),* vol. 1, 1986, and *The Life of Hughes: I Dream a World (1941–1967),* vol. 2, 1988, by Arnold Rampersad; *Hughes and the Blues* by Steven C. Hughes, 1988; *Hughes* by Jack Rummel, 1988; *The Art and Imagination of Hughes* by R. Baxter Miller, 1989.

* * *

Langston Hughes was the Harlem Renaissance man. Poet, playwright, novelist, journalist, essayist, humorist, musicologist, critic, editor, translator, and autobiographer, Hughes may be distinguished more for the breadth and variety of his literary career than for its depth. He was a celebrity, a major figure in modern American—not just African-American—literature. Harold Bloom has observed that "Hughes's principal work was his life, which is to say his literary career." Sadly, however, that life was tinged by an austere private loneliness that belied his public acceptance and acclaim. As Hughes's biographer Arnold Rampersad concludes, "If by the end [of his career] he was also famous and even beloved, Hughes knew that he had been cheated early of a richer emotional life." Nevertheless, Hughes rarely cheated his audience of the emotional richness his own life seemed to lack; rather, he displaced his personal emptiness with a fullness of literary activity marked always by the honesty of his characterizations, the energy of his dialogue, the humor of his perceptions, the dignity of his blues, and the courage of his cultural critique.

Hughes's short stories may not be quite as well-known now as his other writing, but they occupy a substantial place in his canon, comprising some eight collections, only two of which are compilations of the other six. His first collection, *The Ways of White Folks,* features revisions of stories published in *Esquire, Scribner's,* and elsewhere, and represents Hughes's intention to make his living as a writer. It signals Hughes's first consistent effort with the short story genre and initiates a critique of American culture he develops throughout his short fiction, a critique sometimes characterized by an incredulous, ironic tone as his narrators or characters expose the narrow, shortsighted ideology of his representative white characters and the shallowness of their practice; thus, he overturns the traditional white/black power structure, all without overly sentimentalizing or ennobling his African-American characters and their own cultural foibles, usually tempering his indictment of racism with a trace of humor as he, according to the blues, "laughs to keep from crying," In "A Good Job Gone," Hughes's self-centered narrator/protagonist bemoans the fate of his rich, promiscuous employer, Mr. Lloyd, who collapses into insanity over the loss of his African-American mistress, Pauline, amazed that Lloyd could misinterpret her mercenary acquiescence for love, but still placing the blame on her. "He was a swell guy when he had his right mind," the narrator concludes simplistically. "But a yellow woman sure did drive him crazy." In "Slave on the Block" and "Poor Little Black Fellow" Hughes exposes the racism inherent in supposedly liberal, progressive whites who "went in for Negroes," implying that white sponsorship merely enacts the same master/slave figure of traditional white/black relationships. Further, Hughes questions the absolute, yet ambiguous, definition of black and white which allows, in "Passing" for instance, one light-complexioned sibling to "pass for white" while it condemns his darker brother to racial servitude and the other to familial estrangement. In "Father and Son" Colonel Norwood's obituary notes that "the dead man left no heirs" despite his five children by his African-American housekeeper, Cora, two of whom were lynched by a white mob for his murder. Hughes sometimes walks on the edge of sensationalism in his stories—as in the conclusion of "Home," in which Roy Williams, a gifted violinist, is beaten and lynched on his return home from Europe, his "brown body, stark naked, strung from a tree at the edge of town . . . like a violin for the wind to play." However, Hughes generally succeeds in evoking his vision both substantively and stylistically.

Laughing to Keep from Crying features stories of similar theme: ambiguous racial identity ("Who's Passing for Who?" and "African Morning"); tenuous alliances, sexual, racial, and otherwise ("Something in Common," "Heaven to Hell," "Sailor Ashore," "Slice Him Down," and "Name in the Papers"); individual repression by bigotry ("Tain't So," "One Friday Morning," and "Professor"). *Something in Common and Other Stories* is a compilation of stories from Hughes's other collections.

The remainder of Hughes's short story collections belong to his "Simple" series, based on his column from the *Chicago Defender* (1943-66): *Simple Speaks His Mind; Simple Takes a Wife; Simple Stakes a Claim; The Best of Simple,* a compilation from the previous three; and *Simple's Uncle Sam.* These stories center on the observations and experiences of Jesse B. Semple ("Simple"), a kind of African-American Everyman and composite Harlem folk hero with more than his share of wit and wisdom, who plays a lively and loquacious Johnson to his friend Boyd's Boswell whenever they meet, typically in one of their favorite bars. With opinions on everything from lingerie and landladies to Jim Crow and the constitution of the Supreme Court, Simple creates a rich narrative world for Harlem, both imaginative and real like Garrison Keillor's Lake Wobegon or James Herriot's Yorkshire, and populates it with memorable characters such as his persistent ex-wife Isabel, his second wife Joyce, his hustling cousin Minnie, and his "nightime lady" Zarita. Susan L. Blake calls these stories "urban folktales" in the "political storytelling tradition of John-and-Old Marster cycle" that empower Simple as a commentator on the "otherwise" of African-American existence. But Hughes refrains from heavy-handed propaganda here. As he concludes in the foreword to *Simple Stakes a Claim,* "I would like to see some writers of both races write about our problems with black tongue in white cheek, or vice versa. Sometimes I try. Simple helps me."

—Phillip A. Snyder

See the essay on "The Blues I'm Playing."

————

HURSTON, Zora Neale. American. Born in Eatonville, Florida, 7 January 1901(?). Educated at Robert Hungerford School, Eatonville, and a school in Jacksonville, Florida; Morgan Academy, Baltimore, 1917–18; Howard Preparatory School, 1918–19, and Howard University, part-time 1920–24, Washington, D.C.; Barnard College, New York, 1925–28, B.A. 1928. Married 1) Herbert Sheen in 1927 (divorced 1931); 2) Albert Price III in 1939 (divorced 1943). Maid with traveling repertory company, 1915–16; waitress while at Howard Preparatory School and University, 1918–24; folklore researcher in Alabama, Florida, and Louisiana, 1927–32, and in Haiti and the British West Indies, 1936–38; drama instructor, Bethune Cookman College, Daytona, Florida, 1933–34; editor, Federal Writers Project, Florida, 1938–39; member of the drama department, North Carolina College for Negroes, Durham, 1939–40; story consultant, Paramount, Hollywood, 1941–42; part-time teacher, Florida Normal College, St. Augustine, 1942; maid in Florida, 1949–50; reporter, Pittsburgh Courier, 1952; librarian, Patrick Air Force Base, Florida, 1956–57; reporter, Fort Pierce *Chronicle,* Florida, 1957–59; substitute teacher, Lincoln Park Academy, Fort Pierce, 1958–59. Recipient: Rosenwald fellowship, 1934; Guggenheim fellowship, 1936, 1937; Anisfield Wolf award, 1942; Howard University award, 1943. Litt.D.: Morgan State College, Baltimore, 1939. *Died 28 January 1960.*

PUBLICATIONS

Collections

I Love Myself When I Am Laughing . . . and Then Again When I Am Looking Mean and Impressive: A Hurston Reader, edited by Alice Walker.   1979.
Spunk: The Selected Stories.   1985.

Novels

Jonah's Gourd Vine.   1934.
Their Eyes Were Watching God.   1937.
Moses, Man of the Mountain.   1939.
Seraph on the Suwanee.   1948.

Plays

Color Struck, in Fire!!, November 1926.
The First One, in *Ebony and Topaz,* edited by Charles S. Johnson.   1927.
The Great Day (produced 1932).
Singing Steel (produced 1934).

Other

Mules and Men.   1935.
Tell My Horse.   1938; as *Voodoo Gods: An Inquiry into Native Myths and Magic in Jamaica and Haiti,* 1939.
Dust Tracks on a Road: An Autobiography.   1942.

Editor, *Caribbean Melodies.*   1947.

*

Bibliography: *Hurston: A Reference Guide* by Adele S. Newson, 1987.

Critical Studies: *In A Minor Chord* (on Hurston, Cullen, and Toomer) by Darwin T. Turner, 1971; *Hurston: A Literary Biography* by Robert E. Hemenway, 1977; *Hurston* by Lillie P. Howard, 1980; *Hurston* edited by Harold Bloom, 1986; *New Essays on Their Eyes Were Watching God* edited by Michael Awkward, 1990; *Zora! Hurston: The Woman and Her Community* by N.Y. Nathiri, 1991.

*   *   *

Zora Neale Hurston's short fiction first appeared in some of this century's earliest African-American magazines and journals such as *Stylus* ("John Redding Goes to Sea"), *Opportunity* ("Drenched in Light," "Spunk," "Muttsy"), *Messenger* ("The Eatonville Anthology"), and *Fire!!* ("Sweat"). Hurston, Langston Hughes, and Wallace Thurman founded *Fire!!* as an avant garde journal designed to house the art of African-Americans as opposed to the politics of the race. Although the magazine was short-lived, Hurston's reputation as an African-American somewhat scornful of or indifferent to her race's political concerns remains prevalent among some modern critics.

In examining Zora Neale Hurston's short fiction as art form rather than political arena, four distinctive attributes characterize the work: an autobiographical impulse aimed at problematizing the boundaries of texts, a culminating twist designed to undo the sentimental, an individual compelled by community and relationship dynamics, and the African-American dialects displayed with fictional, rather than anthropological, accuracy.

In "Drenched in Light" profound similarities tie the short story's main character, 11-year-old Isis Watts, to the young Zora Neale Hurston as depicted in the autobiography *Dust Tracks on a Road.* In the short story, Isis daydreams about the horizon: "She rode white horses with flaring pink nostrils to the horizon, for she still believed that to be the land's end." In the autobiography, Hurston's horizon establishes a wider scope than does that of Isis: "The most interesting thing that I saw was the horizon. Every way I turned, it was there, and the same distance away. Our house, then, was in the center of the world." Hurston grew up in the same Eatonville, Florida, about which she writes, and the names of characters who appear in the short stories (Elijah Moseley and Joe Clarke of "The Eatonville Anthology") prove similar to or exactly the same as those of the folks who lived in Eatonville during her youth. This autobiographical impulse affords Hurston a way to idealize her own life as well as a way to experiment with the boundaries of genre.

To experiment with content structures, Hurston often employs a concluding twist to temper any urge to sentimentalize the people of Eatonville. "Spunk" provides a story about Spunk Banks's indiscreet affair with Lena Kanty. Joe Kanty, the husband, succumbs to coercion by his male friends to confront Spunk; Spunk kills him, and the author then proceeds to undo the killer. But Hurston does not sweet-sell a moral tale of peer pressure and guilt, nor does she tell a mere sentimental tale of the ramifications of dating married women. She displays forces worse then guilt, remorse, and gossip. In fine magical realist form, she haunts Spunk with a big black bobcat that Spunk believes is in the "h'ant" of Joe. In Hurston's hands, what begins as a tale about marital infidelity becomes a tale twisted by intervention from the beyond.

"Muttsy" seems a straightforward redemption tale in which the wealthy, gambling, drinking, and whoring Muttsy becomes so smitten by the old-fashioned youthful, and pure Pinkie, that he agrees to amend his ways in order to marry her. But Hurston demonstrates little faith in such redemptive possibilities; the story ends with the newly married Muttsy and a friend secretively rolling dice. Hurston defies sentimentality with these endings, and she opts for a seedier reality.

The individual relationships among people in Eatonville prove extremely complicated. Hurston's large scale depiction of complex relational dynamics occurs in "The Eatonville Anthology," which the *Messenger* published in three installments. The anthology includes 13 sketches with a follow-up beast fable narrative. The entire anthology has the essence of a pilgrimage; it begins as does Chaucer's *Canterbury Tales* with a description of all the independent characters involved in the community; but in contrast to Chaucer's pilgrims, these characters go nowhere. Hurston tells their tales simply to chronicle their existence in this town and thereby to take Eatonville and its inhabitants on a pilgrimage into literature. Some of the pieces are comic, some darkly humorous, and some tragic. The concluding beast fable is the tale of a dog who gets his tongue split up the middle by a rabbit, and thus "The Eatonville Anthology" ends in an ironic dispensation about split tongues. One may easily make the connection between the split tongues of the fable and Hurston's split tale-telling. Her celebration of Eatonville exudes a half-caring and half-critical attitude as she practices the art of anthologizing a beloved town and its people.

Hurston also demonstrates a proclivity for capturing African-American dialects in her writings. The anthropological accuracy of her dialects comes under question in some instances, but most critics seem comfortable with Hurston having opted for literary convention over scientific accuracy in order to procure the longevity of a piece and a wider audience for her work. A well-versed folklorist, Hurston knew the possibilities for representing dialect on the page, but she also thought that most readers did not have her background and that they needed to read the more mythologized version of a dialect. On some occasions she even allowed editorial supplements to explicate a reading such as in the opening of "Drenched in Light": "If she ain't down by de time Ah gets dere, Ah'll break huh down in de lines [loins]." The addition of the parenthetical supplement draws attention to the text as manufactured narrative and interrupts the flow of the tale, but Hurston nonetheless permits the intervention. If nothing else, it dramatizes the arduous task of employing dialect in fiction.

Hurston reportedly could not remember when she began to imagine the stories that made it to publication: "When I began to make up stories I cannot say. Just from one fancy to another, adding more and more detail until they seemed real." As an initiator of and participant in the Harlem Renaissance, Hurston sought a naked, realist accuracy in her short stories.

—Renee R. Curry

See the essay on "Sweat."

————

I

IDRIS, Yusuf. Egyptian. Born in Bairum, Sharqiva Province, 19 May 1927. Educated at Cairo University, M.D. (specialized in psychiatry) 1945–52. Physician, Kasr el Eini Hospital, 1952; practiced medicine, 1952–66; literary editor, *Ruz al-Yusuf,* 1953–53; health inspector, Ministry of Health, Darb al-Ahmar, 1956–1960; editor, *Al-Gumhuriya* newpaper, Cairo, 1960–68; joined Algerian freedom fighters, 1962; columnist and literary editor, *Al-Ahrām,* Cairo, 1973; imprisoned several times for political reasons. Member, Communist Party, 1954–56. Recipient: Egyptian Order of the Republic, 1966; Hiwar Literary prize, 1965 (refused); Medal of Republic, 1966. *Died August 1991.*

PUBLICATIONS

Short Stories

Arkhas layālī. 1954; as *The Cheapest Nights and Other Stories,* 1978; revised edition, 1978.
Al-Batal [The Hero]. 1957.
A-laysa kadhālik? [Is that not so?]. 1957.
Hādithat sharaf [A Matter of Honor]. 1958.
Qa'al-Madina [Dregs of the City]. 1959.
Al-Harqām [Guilt] (novella). 1959.
Akher al Dunya [End of the World]. 1961.
Al-'Askarī al-aswad [The Black Soldier]. 1962.
Al-'Ayb [Sin] (novella). 1962.
Lughat al-āy āy [The Ay-ay Tongue]. 1965.
Qissat hubb. 1967.
Al-Mukhattatīn. 1969.
Al-Naddāha [The Siren]. 1969.
Mashuq al-Hams [Ground Whispers]. 1970.
Al-Baydā'. 1970.
Al-Mu'allafāt al-kā milah. 1971.
Bayt min lahm [House of Flesh]. 1971.
Modern Egyptian Short Stories, with Nagīb Mahfūz and Sa'd al-Khādim. 1977.
In the Eye of the Beholder: Tales from Egyptian Life from the Writings of Idrīs, edited by Roger Allen. 1978.
Rings of Burnished Brass. 1984.
A Leader of Men; and, Abū al-rijāl (novella; bilingual edition). 1988.

Novel

Al-Harām. 1959; as *The Sinners,* 1984.

Plays

Jumbūriyyat Farahāt [The Republic of Farhāt]. 1956.
Al-Lahza al-harija [The Critical Moment]. 1957.
Al-Farāfīr (produced 1964). 1964.
Al-Mahzala al-ardiyya [The Terrestrial Comedy]. 1966.
Al-Jins al-thālith. 1971.

Other

Bi-sarāhah ghayr nutlaqah (essays). 1968.
Iktishāf qārrah (travelogue). 1972.

*

Critical Studies: in *The Style of the Modern Arabic Short Story* by Jan Beyerl, 1971; "Language and Theme in the Short Stories of Idrīs" by S. Smoekh, in *Journal of Arabic Literature* 6, 1975; introduction in *In the Eye of the Beholder* edited by Roger Allen, 1978, and *Critical Perspectives on Idris* by Allen, 1991; *The Short Stories of Idris* by P.M. Kurpershoek, 1981; *Studies in the Short Fiction of Mahfouz and Idris* by Mona N. Mikhail, 1992.

* * *

A medical student who initially wrote short stories as an avocation, Yusuf Idris burst unto the Egyptian literary scene as its enfant terrible in 1954, at the age of 27, with his first collection, *Arkhas layālī (The Cheapest Nights and Other Stories).* The volume, which caused a literary uproar, boasted a laudatory introduction by the doyen of Egyptian letters, Taha Hussein, who pronounced its author a new major talent. Though he worked as a physician and psychiatrist for over a decade, Idris gave up his medical career in the middle 1960's to devote himself fully to writing. The author of novels, dramas, and various journalistic and political tracts, Idris is best known in modern Arabic literature as its premier short story writer.

Most of Idris's most memorable characters, especially in the early works written in the 1950's, are drawn from the working class and lower socioeconomic echelons of Egyptian society, *fellahin* from small towns and the rural countryside, where Idris spent most of his youth. In "All on a Summer's Night," from the collection *Qa' al-Madina* (Dregs of the City), Idris conjures up the musky smell of cut hay, male sweat, and adolescent sexuality, when one night a group of *fellah* youth share a sexual fantasy and then disappointment as they comprehend the despair in their lives. Caught up in what seems to be an inexorable cycle of poverty and ignorance, these youth, like the characters in other stories, fight hard not only to survive, but struggle to carve out for themselves a small sense of self-respect.

Idris often describes the numbing poverty and plight of Egypt's underclass in uncomfortable detail, probably based on his medical experience and work as a health inspector for the Egyptian Ministry of Health. In "Hard Up," from *The Cheapest Nights,* Abdou starts out as a cook, but eventually works his way down the occupational scale to doorman, porter, vegetable hawker, waiter, and finally he ends up selling his blood. Eventually, however, he develops anemia, for which he is dismissed from his "job." The extraction of Abdou's blood for a price is a powerful metaphor for society's exploitation of the poor. When his blood is no longer acceptable, he is turned out and made to fend for himself.

A doctor who signs death certificates narrates "Death from Old Age," from the 1960 collection *The Shame*, a poignant, satiric story about the work of funeral assistants, elderly, underfed retirees who, to stay alive, toil at low wages to prepare corpses for burial. Funeral directors for whom they work call them "boys." In their day-to-day struggle for subsistence, these men treat death casually and have little time for courtesies and kind words which are usually offered in such circumstances.

In "The Errand,"also from *The Cheapest Nights*, the long-suffering policeman El Shabrawi, who, longing to get to the Cairo of his youth, takes a mad woman to an asylum there. Not realizing what he was in for, he finds the "errand" a dark, taxing ordeal, especially his dealings with bureaucracies at both the police station and the hospital. He cannot wait to return to his home village.

Often, not much happens in Idris's stories; little changes between the start and the end, except perhaps for insight on a character's part, if he or she is fortunate. In "The Cheapest Nights," one of Idris's most famous works, Abdel Kerim, who on a cold winter night is kept awake by a strong cup of black tea, has nothing to do and nowhere to go except home. There, as usual, he will engage in sex with his large, fecund wife, his cheapest entertainment.

Later stories written in the 1960's take on a highly symbolic, even surrealistic, quality. Often set in cities, these stories have as protagonists alienated bureaucrats and other such hallow persons, instead of farmers and workers, as in "The Omitted Letter" from the 1961 collection *Akher al Dunyg* (End of the World). "House of Flesh," the title story from the 1971 collection *Bayt min lahm*, frankly treats the centrality of sex both within and out of marriage. The three grown daughters of a widow convinces their mother to marry the blind Korean reciter who comes to their one-room home to pray. They reason that with a man in the house, suitors will come. After the marriage, no suitors come, and each of the daughters, envious of her mother, wishes to share her husband, to which she tacitly agrees. It is not certain that the blind man knows what is going on, and the morality of and responsibility for these actions is left ambiguous. Unlike in earlier works, these characters are nameless, as if to suggest anyone could be caught up in the same, or analogous, situation.

Early critics of Idris's work objected not only to Idris's depiction of the underbelly of Egyptian society, but also to his literary style, which mixed classical Arabic in the narrative with highly colloquial, often offensive, language in the dialogue. This duality of styles, called *diglossia*, is a familiar feature of many languages (Greek, Swiss German, Tamil). In such cases, an older, "pure" form of the language is used for formal situations, such as literary pursuits, recitation, broadcasting, and a contemporary, highly colloquial form of the language (which includes curses and obscenity) is used in everyday discourse and conversation. Many critics felt Idris's use of colloquial language was unliterary, but eventually came to realize that the juxtaposition of the two styles added strength, texture, and realism to his works. This later became an acceptable feature of modern Egyptian fiction.

Idris's characters seem to possess a spirit that refuses to accept their condition as permanent and unchangeable. Though often born into dire circumstances, they fight against destiny, their kismet, demonstrating, on the one hand, a seemingly infinite capacity for suffering, but on the other, an indomitable sense of hope. Commenting on

Idris's contrition to modern Arabic literature, the prominent author and critic Tawfik el-Hakim stated in the introduction to *The Cheapest Nights*, "Yusuf Idris, in my opinion, is the renovator and genius of the [Arabic] short story."

—Carlo Coppola

See the essay on "The Cheapest Nights."

IHIMAERA, Witi (Tame). New Zealander. Born in Gisborne, 7 February 1944. Educated at Te Karaka District High School, 1957–59; Church College of New Zealand, 1960–61; Gisborne Boys High School, 1962; University of Auckland, 1963–66; Victoria University, Wellington, 1968–72, B.A. 1972. Married Jane Cleghorn in 1970. Cadet reporter, Gisborne *Herald*, 1967; journalist, Post Office Headquarters, Wellington, 1968–72; information officer, 1973–74, Third Secretary, Wellington, 1975–78, Second Secretary, Canberra, 1978, and First Secretary, Wellington, 1979–85, Ministry of Foreign Affairs; New Zealand Consul, New York, 1986–88; Counsellor on Public Affairs, New Zealand Embassy, Washington, D.C., 1989; lecturer in New Zealand studies, University of Auckland, 1990–92. Recipient: Freda Buckland Literary award, 1973; James Wattie award, 1974, 1986; University of Otago Robert Burns fellowship, 1974. Lives in Auckland.

PUBLICATIONS

Short Stories

Pounamu, Pounamu.   1972.
The New Net Goes Fishing.   1977.
Dear Miss Mansfield: A Tribute to Kathleen Mansfield Beauchamp.   1989.

Novels

Tangi.   1973.
Whanau.   1974.
The Matriarch.   1986.
The Whale Rider.   1987.

Other

Maori.   1975.
New Zealand Through the Arts: Past and Present, with Sir Tosswill Woollaston and Allen Curnow.   1982.

Editor, with D.S. Long, *Into the World of Light: An Anthology of Maori Writing.*   1982.
Editor, *Te Ao Marama: Contemporary Maori Writing Since 1980.*   1992.

*

Critical Studies: "Participating" by Ray Grover, in *Islands,* Winter 1973; "Tangi" by H. Winston Rhodes, in *Landfall,* December 1973; "Maori Writers," in *Fretful Sleepers and Other Essays* by Bill Pearson, 1974; *The Maoris of New*

Zealand by Joan Metge, 1977; *Introducing Ihimaera* by Richard Corballis and Simon Garrett, 1984.

* * *

Ihimaera's early fiction followed a very rigid plan. His first book, *Pounamu, Pounamu,* was a collection of stories about the rural Maori. This was followed by two novels on the same subject: *Tangi* (an expansion of one of the stories in the earlier volume) and *Whanau.* Having, as he said, "completed writing about the rural Maori to my satisfaction," he turned his attention to "the Maori in urban areas." Again he started with a volume of short stories, *The New Net Goes Fishing,* and planned two follow-up novels, which, however, were never completed.

Pounamu, Pounamu and *The New Net Goes Fishing* thus complement each other in subject-matter, and in other respects. The central symbol of the earlier volume is greenstone (*pounamu*), the species of New Zealand jade which gives the book its title. In *The New Net Goes Fishing,* the central symbol is another green stone—the harder, gaudier emerald, which better evokes a sophisticated city milieu. The two volumes also employ complementary modes of narration. Almost all the stories in *Pounamu, Pounamu* are first-person narratives told by children or adolescents. In *The New Net Goes Fishing,* most of the stories are in the third person, and the main characters are generally a little older.

The difference between the two volumes, then, is more than just a difference between town and country. There is also a distinction between softness and harshness, between subjectivity and objectivity, between childhood and adulthood, between innocence and experience.

Pounamu, Pounamu is not, however, entirely dewy-eyed in its celebration of the traditional, communal Maori lifestyle; Ihimaera constantly reminds us that this way of life is under threat. The first three stories—all about games, and the way Maori bend the orthodox rules, whether in cards ("A Game of Cards"), hockey ("Beginning of the Tournament"), or romance ("The Makutu on Mrs. Jones")—are the happiest in the volume, but all have a sombre undertone. The climax of "A Game of Cards" is the death of Nanny Miro, who epitomises the traditional way of life. In "Beginning of the Tournament" hockey brings the community spectacularly together, but, in a telling aside, the narrator observes that "hockey's been dying in our area for some time." And while "The Makutu on Mrs. Jones" ends in a marriage, there must be some doubts about the future well-being of the feisty Irish postmistress who eventually succumbs to the tyrannical old tohunga, Mr. Hohepa.

Of the subsequent stories in the volume, the most memorable focus on destruction ("Fire and Greenstone") and death ("The Child," "The Whale" and "Tangi"). The obvious implication is that the traditional way of life on the land is doomed, and a drift to town is inevitable. Or, as an old Maori proverb puts it, "The old net is cast aside, the new net goes fishing."

The New Net Goes Fishing is framed by two stories ("Yellow Brick Road" and "Return from Oz") which draw on L. Frank Baum's story *The Wizard of Oz.* The Emerald City where Baum's Wizard lives proves much less fabulous than it seems at first; when Dorothy and her companions doff their tinted spectacles they find it to be an ordinary place presided over by an ordinary man. The superficial attractions of Ihimaera's Wellington are likewise delusive,

and life is shown to be very hard for the Maori who try to make a living there.

The 16 stories which lie inside this frame examine a wide range of interactions either between Maori and Pakeha or between rural and urban Maori. Some of the stories ("Clenched Fist," "Tent on the Home Ground," "A Sense of Belonging," "Gathering of the Whakapapa," "The Greenstone Patu," and "Catching Up") are stark demonstrations of some clear-cut point about one or other of these interactions.

A second group of stories make their points more subtly, through a delicate use of symbolism. These include "The Escalator," "Masques and Roses," and "The Seahorse and the Reef." Subtlety is achieved in a different way in a third group, which includes the most interesting stories in the volume, "The House with Sugarbag Windows," "I, Ozymandias," and "Big Brother, Little Sister." Here a narrative set in the present is interspersed with episodes from the past. The latter strand provides motivation, explanations, and human depth for the former. This technique of interweaving strands of plot constitutes Ihimaera's most distinctive contribution to the short story genre.

Ihimaera is probably New Zealand's best-known Maori writer of short fiction. (Patricia Grace would be the other contender for this honour.) The best-known Pakeha is undoubtedly Katherine Mansfield, and in *Dear Miss Mansfield* Ihimaera paid tribute to this illustrious precursor. All the stories in the volume reflect on Mansfield's work, but they do so in very different ways. The volume begins with a novella ("Maata") on the subject of the Maori princess (Maata Mahupuku) with whom Mansfield was intimate in her younger days and about whom she evidently planned a novel.

The short stories which follow "Maata" are all variations of one sort or another on stories by Mansfield. Four of the 13— "Summons to Alexandra," "His First Ball," "The Cicada," and "The Halcyon Summer" (which is presumably meant to be seen as a free imitation of Mansfield's "At the Bay")—are reworkings of early stories, published separately in 1970 ("Queen Bee" and "My First Ball"), 1973 ("Cicada") and 1971 ("Halcyon") respectively. The rest were written in 1987 and 1988 specifically for this volume. Six of the 13 rework the Mansfield originals from an explicitly Maori point of view; the rest provide evidence—most of it convincing—that Ihimaera's talent is not confined to Maori subject-matter.

—Richard Corballis

IRVING, Washington. American. Born in New York City, 3 April 1783. Educated in local schools; studied law in the offices of Henry Masterton, 1799, Brockholst Livingstone, 1801, and Josiah Ogden Hoffman, 1802; admitted to New York bar, 1806, but practised only intermittently. Served as military aide to New York Governor Tompkins in the U.S. Army during the War of 1812. Travelled in Europe, 1804–06; became partner, with his brothers, in family hardware business, New York and Liverpool, 1810; representative of the business in England, 1815 until the firm collapsed, 1818; editor, *Analectic* magazine, Philadelphia and New York, 1812–14; lived in Dresden, 1822–23, London, 1824, Paris, 1825, and Madrid, as member of the U.S. Legation, 1826-29; Secretary, U.S. Legation, London,

1829–32; returned to New York, then toured the southern and western U.S., 1832; lived at the manor house "Sunnyside," Tarrytown-on-Hudson, New York, 1836–42; U.S. Ambassador to Spain, in Barcelona and Madrid, 1842–45; then returned to Tarrytown; president, Astor Library (later New York Public Library), 1848–59. Recipient: Royal Society of Literature medal, 1830. LL.D.: Oxford University, 1831; honorary degree: Columbia University, New York; Harvard University, Cambridge, Massachusetts. Corresponding member, Royal Academy of History (Spain), 1829. *Died 28 November 1859.*

PUBLICATIONS

Collections

Works (Author's Revised Edition).   15 vols., 1848–51.
Representative Selections, edited by Henry A. Pochmann. 1934.
Complete Works, edited by Richard Dilworth Rust and others.   1969—.
Complete Tales, edited by Charles Neider.   1975.
History, Tales and Sketches (Library of America), edited by James W. Tuttleton.   1983.

Short Stories and Sketches

Salmagundi; or, The Whim-Whams and Opinions of Launcelot Langstaff, Esq., and Others, with James Kirke Paulding and William Irving.   2 vols., 1807-08; revised (by Washington Irving only), 1824.
The Sketch Book of Geoffrey Crayon, Gent.   7 vols., 1819–20; revised edition, 2 vols., 1820.
Bracebridge Hall; or, The Humourists: A Medley.   1822; edited by J.D. Colclough, 1898.
Letters of Jonathan Oldstyle, Gent.   1824.
Tales of a Traveller.   1824.
The Alhambra: A Series of Tales and Sketches of the Moors and Spaniards.   1832.
Essays and Sketches.   1837.
Chronicles of Wolfert's Roost and Other Papers.   1855.

Plays

Charles the Second; or, The Merry Monarch, with John Howard Payne, from a play by Alexandre Duval (produced 1824).   1824; edited by Arthur Hobson *Quinn*, in *Representative American Plays*, 1917.
Richelieu: A Domestic Tragedy, with John Howard Payne, from a play by Alexandre Duval (produced 1826; as *The French Libertine*, produced 1826).   1826.
Abu Hassan.   1924.
The Wild Huntsman, from a play by Friedrich Kind. 1924.
An Unwritten Play of Lord Byron.   1925.

Verse

The Poems, edited by William R. Langfeld.   1931.

Other

A History of New-York from the Beginning of the World to the End of the Dutch Dynasty.   2 vols., 1809; revised edition, 1812, 1848.

A History of the Life and Voyages of Christopher Columbus. 4 vols., 1828; edited by Winifred Hulbert, as *The Voyages of Columbus*, 1931.
A Chronicle of the Conquest of Granada.   2 vols., 1829.
Voyages and Discoveries of the Companions of Columbus. 1831.
Miscellanies (A Tour on the Prairies, Abbotsford and Newstead Abbey, Legends of the Conquest of Spain).   3 vols., 1835; *A Tour on the Prairies*, edited by John Francis McDermott, 1956.
Astoria; or, Anecdotes of an Enterprise Beyond the Rocky Mountains.   2 vols., 1836; edited by Edgeley W. Todd, 1964.
Adventures of Captain Bonneville; or, Scenes Beyond the Rocky Mountains of the Far West, based on journals of B.L.E. Bonneville.   3 vols., 1837; as *The Rocky Mountains*, 1837.
The Life of Oliver Goldsmith, with Selections from His Writings.   2 vols., 1840; revised edition, as *Oliver Goldsmith: A Biography*, in *Works II*, 1849; edited by G.S. Blakely, 1916.
Biography and Poetical Remains of the Late Margaret Miller Davidson.   1841.
A Book of the Hudson.   1849.
Mahomet and His Successors, in *Works*.   2 vols., 1850.
Life of George Washington.   5 vols., 1855–59; abridged and edited by Charles Neider, 1976.
Spanish Papers and Other Miscellanies, edited by Pierre M. Irving.   2 vols., 1866.
Letters to Mrs. William Renwick and to Her Son James Renwick.   1915.
Letters to Henry Brevoort, edited by George S. Hellman. 2 vols., 1915.
The Journals (Hitherto Unpublished), edited by William P. Trent and George S. Hellman.   3 vols., 1919.
Notes and Journal of Travel in Europe 1804–1805.   3 vols., 1921.
Diary: Spain 1828–1829, edited by Clara Louisa Penney. 1926.
Notes While Preparing Sketch Book 1817, edited by Stanley T. Williams.   1927.
Tour in Scotland 1817, and Other Manuscript Notes, edited by Stanley T. Williams.   1927.
Letters from Sunnyside and Spain, edited by Stanley T. Williams.   1928.
Journal (1823–1824), edited by Stanley T. Williams. 1931.
Irving and the Storrows: Letters from England and the Continent 1821–1828, edited by Stanley T. Williams. 1933.
Journal 1803, edited by Stanley T. Williams.   1934.
Journal 1828, and Miscellaneous Notes on Moorish Legend and History, edited by Stanley T. Williams.   1937.
The Western Journals, edited by John Francis McDermott. 1944.
Contributions to the Corrector, edited by Martin Roth. 1968.
Irving and the House of Murray (letters), edited by Ben Harris McClary.   1969.

Editor, *The Miscellaneous Works of Goldsmith.*   4 vols., 1825.
Editor, *Poems* (London edition), by William Cullen Bryant. 1832.
Editor, *Harvey's Scenes of the Primitive Forest of America.* 1841.

Translator, with Peter Irving and Georges Caines, *A Voyage to the Eastern Part of Terra Firma; or, The Spanish Main,* by F. Depons.   3 vols., 1806.

*

Bibliography: *A Bibliography of the Writings of Irving* by Stanley T. Williams and Mary Allen Edge, 1936; in *Bibliography of American Literature* by Jacob Blanck, 1969; *Irving: A Reference Guide* by Haskell Springer, 1976; *Irving Bibliography* by Edwin T. Bowden, 1989.

Critical Studies: *Life and Letters of Irving* by Pierre M. Irving, 4 vols., 1862–64; *The Life of Irving* by Stanley T. Williams,   2 vols., 1935; *The World of Irving* by Van Wyck Brooks, 1944; *Irving and Germany* by Walter A. Reichart, 1957; *Irving: Moderation Displayed* by Edward Wagenknecht, 1962; *Irving* by Lewis Leary, 1963; *Irving: An American Study 1802–1835* by William L. Hedges, 1965; *Irving Reconsidered: A Symposium* edited by Ralph Aderman, 1969; *The Worlds of Irving,* 1974, and *A Century of Commentary on the Works of Irving,* 1976, both edited by Andrew B. Myers; *Comedy and America: The Lost World of Irving* by Martin Roth, 1976; *Pierre M. Irving and Washington Irving: A Collaboration in Life and Letters* by Wayne R. Kime, 1977; *Irving* by Mary Weatherspoon Bowden, 1981; *Adrift in the Old World: The Psychological Pilgrimage of Irving* by Jeffrey Rubin Dorsky, 1988; *Tales of Adventurous Enterprise: Irving and the Poetics of Western Expansion* by Peter Antelyes, 1990.

*   *   *

Washington Irving holds a secure place in American literary history as a pioneer in the short story form and as our first important and internationally acclaimed author. During his life time, from the end of the American Revolution almost to the Civil War, his books were both popular and critically esteemed. Only James Fenimore Cooper gave him any competition. Today his reputation has faded considerably, and most of his work is no longer read; but he remains a great stylist and a master storyteller, and a few of his best tales have enduring value. Unfortunately for Irving, his work seems shallow compared with the best of the generation that followed him, such as Emerson, Thoreau, Hawthorne, Melville, and Whitman.

Irving was born in New York City, where he spent his first 32 years, received his education, and found his first literary materials. He prepared himself for writing short stories by contributing satiric pieces to his brother's newspaper at the age of 18 and later to an irregular miscellany called *Salmagundi.* His first great literary success came in 1809 when he published his *History of New-York,* supposedly written by an old Dutchman named Diedrich Knickerbocker, the same fictitious author of "Rip Van Winkle," and "The Legend of Sleepy Hollow." The history is a burlesque account of New York in the days of the Dutch colonists and mercilessly lampoons the early governors. Its separate chapters read like short pieces of historical fiction. Irving is a myth-maker in this work, and today what most people know of New York's Dutch era comes from Irving, not real history.

In 1815 Irving was sent to Europe to represent the family business, but soon after he got there the company went bankrupt. Irving then had to become a professional writer,

and the result of the family misfortune was *The Sketch Book,* the work for which he is best known. It is a collection of autobiographical pieces, essays, and stories, including his most famous tales, "Rip Van Winkle" and "The Legend of Sleepy Hollow." As in these two stories, Irving is at his best when he uses imagined or real supernatural machinery to activate his plots. "The Specter Bridegroom" is a good example of his method. It tells the story of a bride awaiting her bridegroom who dies en route to the meeting. A friend entrusted to break the sad news arrives and impersonates the bridegroom. After he leaves, the family discovers that the bridegroom has died and think they have been visited by a specter. It all ends happily when the "specter" returns and elopes with the bride.

The other type of story in *The Sketch Book* plays heavily on sentiment or pathos and is too mawkish for contemporary taste. These include "The Wife," a tale of a faithful wife who cheerfully accepts poverty when her husband loses his fortune, and "The Widow and Her Son," the story of a stalwart young man who dies young after being trapped by a press-gang and carried off to sea.

Among the autobiographical chapters in *The Sketch Book* are three essays recounting Irving's Christmas visit to a country house in Yorkshire. These gave him the idea for his next book *Bracebridge Hall,* which follows the format of the previous book. The character sketches of the squire, his servants, his neighbors read like short fiction, but the outstanding chapter in the collection is a story called "The Stout Gentleman." This is an unusual story for Irving, for it uses neither sentiment nor supernatural machinery. The narrator builds up suspense by speculating about a mysterious guest at the inn where he is staying. He is dying to see the stout gentleman but manages at the end only to see his ample posterior disappearing into a stage coach. Here Irving is again the humorist, as he was in his *History of New York.*

Irving's next book was *Tales of a Traveller,* another loose collection of pieces similar to the previous books. It resulted from a sojourn in Germany and contains some very good tales, but it was savagely reviewed and was one of Irving's least successful works. One of the successful stories, however, is a framed ghost story told to the narrator about his host's grandfather, "The Bold Dragoon." It blends nicely both humor and real or imagined supernatural business. The best tale is "The Adventure of the German Student," a bizarre yarn set in Paris during the Reign of Terror. The student meets a woman weeping beside the guillotine late one night. He takes her home with him, falls in love with her but the next morning finds a corpse in his bed. She had been one of the victims of the guillotine the day before.

In 1824 Irving began studying Spanish and went to Spain, planning to translate a work then appearing on Christopher Columbus. Instead he wrote a biography of Columbus and from that time on turned mostly to non-fiction, concentrating on history and biography. His stay in Spain, however, also resulted in *The Alhambra,* a book often called the Spanish sketchbook. It contains the familiar amalgam of autobiographical, historical, and descriptive essays, but it also recounts many stories. Irving actually lived in the Palace of the Alhambra for a time and was fascinated by the legends he was able to collect and retell. "The Legend of the Rose of the Alhambra" is a love story with a happy ending, and "The Legend of the Moor's Legacy" is an Arabian Nights kind of story with incantations and fabulous treasure. In both, Irving works the supernatural machinery hard.

After publishing *The Alhambra* Irving ended his 17-year stay in Europe and returned to the United States a celebrity. He lived another 27 years, but his days as a story writer were over. His accomplishment in this genre, however, was considerable and his influence on later writers significant. Although his reputation has dimmed, he remains a great stylist, a writer of clear, engaging prose that charms even his detractors. His aim was to produce sharp, visual images that remain in the mind after the book is closed. As a young man he once thought of being a painter, but instead he created word pictures and wrote his *Sketch Book, Bracebridge Hall,* and *Tales of a Traveller* all under the pseudonym of Geoffrey Crayon.

—James Woodress

See the essays on "The Legend of Sleepy Hollow" and "Rip Van Winkle."

————

J

JACKSON, Shirley (Hardie). American. Born in San Francisco, California, 14 December 1916. Educated at Burlingame High School, California; Brighton High School, Rochester, New York; University of Rochester, 1934–36; Syracuse University, New York, 1937–40, B.A. 1940. Married the writer Stanley Edgar Hyman in 1940; two sons and two daughters. Lived in North Bennington, Vermont, after 1945. Recipient: Mystery Writers of America Edgar Allan Poe award, 1961. *Died 8 August 1965.*

PUBLICATIONS

Collections

The Magic of Jackson, edited by Stanley Edgar Hyman. 1966.

Short Stories

The Lottery; or, The Adventures of James Harris. 1949.

Novels

The Road Through the Wall. 1948; as *The Other Side of the Street,* 1956.
Hangsaman. 1951.
The Bird's Nest. 1954; as *Lizzie,* 1957.
The Sundial. 1958.
The Haunting of Hill House. 1959.
We Have Always Lived in the Castle. 1962.

Plays

The Lottery, from her own story, in *Best Television Plays 1950–1951,* edited by William I. Kauffman. 1952.
The Bad Children: A Play in One Act for Bad Children. 1959.

Other

Life among the Savages. 1953.
The Witchcraft of Salem Village (for children). 1956.
Raising Demons. 1957.
Special Delivery: A Useful Book for Brand-New Mothers. 1960; as *And Baby Makes Three,* 1960.
9 Magic Wishes (for children). 1963.
Famous Sally (for children). 1966.
Come Along with Me: Part of a Novel, Sixteen Stories, and Three Lectures, edited by Stanley Edgar Hyman. 1968.

*

Critical Studies: *Jackson* by Lenemaja Friedman, 1975; *Private Demons: The Life of Jackson* by Judy Oppenheiner, 1988; *Jackson: A Study of the Short Fiction* by Joan Wylie Hall, 1994.

* * *

Disdainful of love stories and "junk about gay young married couples," Shirley Jackson produced a variety of short fiction, in modes ranging from the fantastic to the realistic, for magazines as diverse as *The New Yorker, Playboy,* the *Ladies' Home Journal,* and the *Yale Review.* Yet, Jackson is so exclusively identified with "The Lottery," her shocking account of a housewife's ritualistic stoning, that few readers can name another of her 100 stories or any of her six novels. Jackson claimed that, except for "The Lottery" itself, her collection *The Lottery or, The Adventures of James Harris* was "a harmless little book of short stories." The overt violence against Tessie Hutchinson is rare; still, Jackson's stories are seldom "harmless." The implicit critique of society in "The Lottery" becomes an obvious concern of such 1940's works as "After You, My Dear Alphonse" and "Flower Garden," which expose racism, and the uncollected story "Behold the Child Among His Newborn Blisses," where a doting mother is cruel to another woman's retarded son.

Typically, Jackson portrays a significant threat to at least one character's well-being. As in "The Lottery," Jackson's threatened character is usually a woman. Female protagonists of "The Tooth," "The Beautiful Stranger," "I Know Who I Love," and "A Visit" are tempted by mysterious men to abandon their colorless routine and yield to a dangerous love. Although some critics speculate that these disruptive males are hallucinations of a sexually repressed character, the ballad "James Harris, The Daemon Lover," which forms the epilogue to the 25 stories collected in *The Lottery,* suggests otherwise. Jackson implies that several of her stories are modern versions of the folktale of a young wife's abduction by the devil; references to James, Jimmy, Jamie, and a Mr. Harris recur throughout the *Lottery* volume, creating a loose unity among pieces that had first appeared in separate publications.

In "The Daemon Lover," James Harris is a handsome author who deserts his dowdy fiancée Elizabeth. The plot may be indebted to "The Demon Lover" by Elizabeth Bowen, whom Jackson ranked with Katherine Anne Porter as the best contemporary short story writers. When Jamie Harris leaves the 34-year-old Elizabeth on their wedding day, her "golden house-in-the-country future" is destroyed, and she becomes one of the several Jackson women who despair of trading their lonely city apartments for a loving home.

A happy home life does not protect women from victimization by strangers, neighbors, and even the family dog, in

266

"The Witch," "Men with Their Big Shoes," "The Renegade," and other stories. Janet Allison and her husband Robert, an older couple in "The Summer People," have a cottage in the country as well as an apartment in New York; their decision to remain at the lake after Labor Day produces an autumnal variant on the plot of "The Lottery." For no apparent reason, the New England village closes ranks, cutting off the Allisons' supplies of food and kerosene, as well as their telephone line, and the ending is ominous as the two "ordinary people" huddle against a storm in their fragile home, "and waited."

Conversely, in "Pillar of Salt," a wife's holiday in New York with her husband culminates in urban disaster and a yearning for her New Hampshire home. Entitled "Vertigo" in draft form, the story traces Margaret's growing horror of the city's dizzying speed and progressive decay. Unable to calm her final hysteria, she stands immobilized on a street corner as she tries to return to the couple's borrowed apartment. Margaret realizes, in a typical Jackson conclusion, that "she was lost," as surely as Lot's pillar-of-salt wife in the Bible.

In contrast to Janet Allison and Margaret, some of Jackson's characters are intent on permanently leaving the security of home. Elsa Dayton of "A Day in the Jungle," from the posthumous *Come Along with Me* collection, angrily walks out on a neglectful husband. Like Louisa Tether, a college-aged daughter who runs away from her family in "Louisa, Please Come Home," she feels independent in new surroundings. Yet both women regret their desperate moves. After a single day of freedom, Elsa experiences a "sudden panic" and, in relief, joins her husband for dinner. Louisa is overcome by nostalgia when a former neighbor sees her in another city and insists on taking her home. Ironically, her parents refuse to recognize her, and she reluctantly goes back to her boarding-house room and her assumed identity.

As James Egan has remarked, Jackson's fiction depicts how domestic ideals are "created, nurtured, attacked from various quarters, escaped from, weakened, parodied, and destroyed." The uncollected but often anthologized "One Ordinary Day, with Peanuts" is among Jackson's most unusual treatments of the domestic theme. After describing the kindly John Philip Johnson's long day of doing good (to a nervous single mother and her son, among others), the third-person narrator relates the man's return home to a smiling wife who has spent her day deliberately making people miserable. Mr. Johnson genially offers to "change over tomorrow." Operating from their own secure base, the two alternately improve and sabotage the personal lives of strangers.

Jackson's most positive portrayals of home occur in the humorous stories based on her own family life. During the 1950's, she worked most of these into continuous narratives in the fictionalized memoirs *Life among the Savages* and *Raising Demons*. Feminist critics have suggested that "The Third Baby's the Easiest," "On Being a Faculty Wife," and other comic sketches have a serious side in their treatment of women's fears and frustrations. The narrator of "Charles," for example, grows increasingly anxious when her son Laurie daily relates the disruptive classroom behavior of a boy named Charles. At a PTA meeting, however, the teacher responds to the narrator's concern by announcing that there is no Charles in the kindergarten and that Laurie has finally adjusted to school. In concluding with the mother's shock of recognition, "Charles" mirrors the final scenes of "The Lottery," "The Daemon Lover," "Pillar of Salt," and several other stories in which a besieged woman suffers a final, wrenching—and sometimes fatal—blow.

—Joan Wylie Hall

See the essay on "The Lottery."

————

JACOBS, W(illiam) W(ymark). English. Born in Wapping, London, 8 September 1863. Educated privately. Married Agnes Eleanor Williams in 1900; two sons and two daughters. Clerk in the Savings Bank Department of the Civil Service, London, 1883–99; thereafter a full-time writer. *Died 1 September 1943.*

PUBLICATIONS

Collections

Selected Short Stories, edited by Hugh Greene.   1975.

Short Stories

Many Cargoes.   1896.
Sea Urchins.   1898; as *More Cargoes,* 1898.
Light Freights.   1901.
The Lady of the Barge and Other Stories.   1902.
Odd Craft.   1903.
Captains All.   1905.
Short Cruises.   1907.
Sailors' Knots.   1909.
Ship's Company.   1911.
Night Watches.   1914.
Deep Waters.   19 19.
Fifteen Stories.   1926.
Sea Whisper.   1926.
Snug Harbour: Collected Stories.   1931.
Cruises and Cargoes (omnibus).   1934.

Novels

The Skipper's Wooing, and The Brown Man's Servant.   1897.
A Master of Craft.   1900.
At Sunwich Port.   1902.
Dialstone Lane.   1904.
Salthaven.   1908.
The Castaways.   1916.
The Night-Watchman and Other Longshoremen.   1932.

Plays

The Grey Parrot, with Charles Rock (produced 1899).   1908.
Beauty and the Barge, with L.N. Parker, from the story by Jacobs (produced 1904).   1910.
The Temptation of Samuel Burge, with Frederick Fenn (produced 1905).
The Boatswain's Mate, with Herbert C. Sargent (produced 1907).   1907; revised version, music by Ethel Smyth (produced 1916).
The Changeling, with Herbert C. Sargent, from the story by Jacobs (produced 1908).   1908.
The Ghost of Jerry Bundler, with Charles Rock.   1908.
Admiral Peters, with Horace Mills (produced 1908).   1909.

A Love Passage, with P.E. Hubbard (produced 1913). 1913.
In the Library, with Herbert C. Sargent, from the story by Jacobs (produced 1913).   1913.
Keeping Up Appearances (produced 1915).   1919.
The Castaway, with Herbert C. Sargent, from the story by Jacobs.   1924.
Establishing Relations.   1925.
The Warming Pan.   1929.
A Distant Relative.   1930.
Master Mariners.   1930.
Matrimonial Openings.   1931.
Dixon's Return.   1932.
Double Dealing.   1935.

*

Bibliography: *Jacobs: A Bibliography* by Chris Lamerton, 1988.

Critical Study: in *Books in General* by V.S. Pritchett, 1953.

*   *   *

W.W. Jacobs flourished at a time when it was possible for a writer to make a comfortable living from short stories alone. In England the Education Act of 1870 had created a large reading public which enjoyed a wide range of publications. The most successful among many was *The Strand Magazine,* in whose pages Conan Doyle had introduced Sherlock Holmes and boosted its circulation enormously. Jacobs, one of the highest paid short story writers of the time, also wrote for *The Strand* and *The Idler,* a periodical edited by his friend Jerome K. Jerome, himself author of that humorous classic *Three Men in a Boat.* It would take Jacobs about a month to write one of his short stories. "I first of all assemble a few sheets of paper, a bottle of ink, some pens and a blotting pad," he once said. After which he would stare into infinity and cudgel his brains. Sometimes a story dawned and seemed to write itself. "I then rewrite it," he added. These stories, which read so easily and spontaneously, were the result of long and painstaking labour, of rewriting, cutting, and endless polishing. He was reputed sometimes to take a whole morning over a sentence. Once he has completed a dozen or so stories he would collect them together for publication in book form. These volumes proved as lucrative as his magazine writing, and most of them went into many reprintings. *Many Cargoes,* for example, had been reprinted 31 times by as early as 1909, and much of his work was translated into Dutch, French, German, and Spanish.

Jacobs was born and bred in Wapping, a Thames-side district of London, where his father was a wharf manager. In those days much of its population consisted of sailors who plied barges and lighters up and down the river and out along the coast to other ports. They could be found yarning and drinking in the pubs and cheap lodging houses of Wapping. Jacobs observed them closely for his raw material, and they were to provide the lifelong subjects of his unobtrusive art. Recurrent anti-heroes in his stories were a trio of disreputable firemen, or stokers, the lowest form of seagoing life, known as whiskery old Sam Small, red-headed Ginger Dick, and Peter Russet. Once ashore they become involved in all sorts of ludicrous misadventures due to their quest for get-rich-quick schemes or free beer or rich widows with a bit of property. As someone remarks, "a sailorman is like a fish, he is safest when 'e is at

sea. When a fish comes ashore it is in for trouble, and so is a sailorman" ("Shareholders," *Deep Waters*). Sam and Dick and Peter are cunning but not quite cunning enough. "Treat me fair," says one of the dubious characters, "and I'll treat other people fair. I never broke my word without good reason for it, and that's more than everybody can say" ("Skilled Assistance," *Ship's Company*). Their exploits are related by the nightwatchman. He is idle, lazy, and henpecked. In real life he would be a bore. As presented by Jacobs he is a superbly humorous creation, sententious and drily comic. Another of Jacob's raconteurs is the oldest inhabitant of a fictional village called Claybury. A tedious old fellow, forever cadging beer and tobacco, he becomes a virtuoso of rustic malice in the hand of his creator, with his tales of artful yokels and their even more artful womenfolk. A frequent protagonist of Jacob's stories is the villainous Bob Pretty, poacher, con-man, and general trickster, who always comes out on top. He is seen at his most resourceful in "A Will and a Way" (*Light Freights*), "The Persecution of Bob Pretty" and "Odd Charges" (*Odd Craft*), "In The Family" (*Short Cruises*), and "A Tiger's Skin" (*The Lady of the Barge*).

Jacobs's characters were all drawn from what were then known as the lower classes: dockland layabouts, longshoremen, policemen, private soldiers, lower-deck sailors, shop assistants, bare-fist boxers. The men are shifty, work-shy, and not very intelligent. They spend a lot of their time trying to do each other down with plans that always backfire surprisingly and bring the story to an unexpected end. The women are invariably depicted in an unflattering light. If they are young and pretty they are also cold and calculating in their search for a husband they can nag. If they are married they are fiercely jealous termagants, more than a match for their craven husbands. As a boy, Jacobs suffered from a harsh stepmother, and as a man he was unfortunate enough to have married an unsympathetic shrew with whom he could agree on nothing. His view of women was accordingly very negative. As the nightwatchman puts it, sailormen "see so little of wimmin that they naturally 'ave a high opinion of 'em. Wait till they become nightwatchmen, and, having to be at 'ome all day, see the other side of 'em. If people on'y started life as nightwatchmen there wouldn't be 'arf the falling love that there is now" ("The Third String," *Odd Craft*).

Because he concentrated on a very small area of humanity and because he wrote primarily to entertain, Jacobs is often ignored unjustly by literary critics. He is an accomplished artist and a master of the short story. He gets his effects through a brilliant economy of means and a faultlessly controlled style. In "The Captain's Exploit" (*Many Cargoes*), the drunken skipper is rowed back to his ship by a waterman to whom, fuddled with beer, he gives four times the usual fare. "'Steady, old boy,' said the waterman affectionately." The choice and placing of the adverb "affectionately" speak volumes. Again and again Jacobs's gift for the pithy phrase arouses pleasure: the nightwatchman has "disgust written on a countenance only too well designed to express it" ("Skilled Assistance," *Ship's Company*); a group of haughty women "seemed as if they had just come off ice" ("Dual Control," *Ship's Company*); and a bottle of wine is described as "port of the look and redcurrant to the taste" ("Twin Spirits," *Light Freights*).

Jacobs also had Simenon's gift for evoking an atmosphere in very few words: "It was a wet, dreary night in the cheerless part of the great metropolis known as Wapping. The rain, which had been falling steadily for hours, fell steadily on to the sloppy pavements and roads, and joining forces in the gutter, rushed impetuously to the nearest sewer. The two or three streets which had wedged themselves in between the docks and the river, and which, as a matter of fact, really comprise the beginning and end of Wapping, were deserted except for a belated van crashing over the granite roads, or the chance form of a dock-labourer plodding doggedly along, with head bent in distaste for the rain, and hands sunk in trouser-pockets" ("The Captain's Exploit," *Many Cargoes*). He can also write lyrically: "It was a beautiful morning. The miniature river waves broke against the blunt bows of the barge, and passed by her sides rippling musically. Over the flat Essex marshes a white mist was slowly dispersing before the rays of the sun, and the trees on the Kentish hills were black and drenched with moisture" ("Mrs. Bunker's Chaperon," *Many Cargoes*).

Within the limits Jacobs set himself, he is unique. He was that rare type of artist who is successful because he chose to work entirely inside the narrow restraints he imposed. The target he aimed at, as did comic writers from Aristophanes to Dickens and onward, was human frailty. He never missed it.

—James Harding

See the essay on "The Monkey's Paw."

———

JACOBSON, Dan. British. Born in Johannesburg, South Africa, 7 March 1929. Educated at the University of the Witwatersrand, Johannesburg, 1946–49, B.A. 1949. Married Margaret Pye in 1954; two sons and one daughter. Public relations assistant, South African Jewish Board of Deputies, Johannesburg, 1951–52; correspondence secretary, Mills and Feeds Ltd., Kimberley, South Africa, 1952–54; fellow in creative writing, Stanford University, California, 1956–57; visiting professor, Syracuse University, New York, 1965–66; visiting fellow, State University of New York, Buffalo, 1971, and Australian National University, Canberra, 1980; lecturer, 1976–80, reader, 1980–88, and since 1988 professor of English, University College, London. Vice-chairman of the Literature Panel, Arts Council of Great Britain, 1974–76. Recipient: Rhys Memorial prize, 1959; Maugham award, 1964; H.H. Wingate award (*Jewish Chronicle*, London), 1978; Society of Authors travelling scholarship, 1986; J.R. Ackerley award, for autobiography, 1986; Mary Elinore Smith Poetry prize, 1992. Fellow, Royal Society of Literature, 1974. Lives in London.

PUBLICATIONS

Short Stories

A Long Way from London. 1958.
The Zulu and the Zeide. 1959.
Beggar My Neighbour. 1964.
Through the Wilderness. 1968.
A Way of Life and Other Stories, edited by Alix Pirani. 1971.
Inklings: Selected Stories (includes stories from *Beggar My Neighbour* and *Through the Wilderness*). 1973; as *Through the Wilderness,* 1977.

Novels

The Trap. 1955.
A Dance in the Sun. 1956.
The Price of Diamonds. 1957.
The Evidence of Love. 1960.
The Beginners. 1966.
The Rape of Tamar. 1970.
The Wonder-Worker. 1973.
The Confessions of Josef Baisz. 1977.
Her Story. 1987.
Hidden in the Heart. 1991.
The God-Fearer. 1992.

Play

Radio Play: *The Caves of Adullan,* 1972.

Other

No Further West: California Visited. 1959.
Time of Arrival and Other Essays. 1963.
The Story of the Stories: The Chosen People and Its God. 1982.
Time and Time Again: Autobiographies. 1985.
Adult Pleasures: Essays on Writers and Readers. 1988.

*

Bibliography: *Jacobson: A Bibliography* by Myra Yudelman, 1967.

Critical Studies: "The Novels of Jacobson" by Renee Winegarten, in *Midstream,* May 1966; "Novelist of South Africa," in *The Liberated Woman and Other Americans* by Midge Decter, 1971; "The Gift of Metamorphosis" by Pearl K. Bell, in *New Leader,* April 1974; "Apollo, Dionysus, and Other Performers in Jacobson's Circus," in *World Literature Written in English,* April 1974, and "Jacobson's Realism Revisited," in *Southern African Review of Books,* October 1988, both by Michael Wade; "A Somewhere Place" by C.J. Driver, in *New Review,* October 1977; *Jacobson* by Sheila Roberts, 1984; "Stories" by John Bayley, in *London Review of Books,* October 1987.

* * *

There are three essential ingredients in the makeup of Dan Jacobson that have affected his writing profoundly; he is South African-born (and raised up); he is Jewish, of East European extraction; and he has written virtually all his work in England. These facts about his background have become three primary factors underlying his work, and no account of it can ignore them without severe distortion. The first is undoubtedly the most significant, tending often to subsume either or both of the others. Jacobson has declared that he finds it hard to imagine he would have been a writer at all if he had stayed in South Africa. But it is impossible to imagine his writing without the stimulus given by the experience of South Africa, no matter how alienating—or even because of that very alienation.

It is obvious that Jacobson's sensibility has been influenced by England, not only by his domicile there for so much of his life, but also by his earlier reading in the literature of England in the very different surroundings of a place like Kimberley. The striking contrast between two realities, the reality of what the young Jacobson saw around him in South Africa and the reality created by his British-based reading, created in him what he has described as an almost metaphysical preoccupation, even as a child, with questions of reality. This has left him with a doubleness or split between his South African and his English selves that is very evident in his writing and is not necessarily a disadvantage. Though it can lead to a disabling self-consciousness, an over-awareness of self and worries about where this self does or does not fit in, it can also provide a creative tension, a fruitful interaction of two countries and cultures. A story dramatizing this division in the writer is "Fresh Fields," in which a dried-up older South African writer living in England tells a younger one, the narrator, to go home or he too will lose the ability to write. The older man then steals ideas for his poems from unpublished stories by the narrator, who finally hands over all his manuscripts and feels the burden of his past has been discarded, that he can stay in England and write there. This is what Jacobson himself has in fact done, but the burden of South Africa has never been entirely discarded. Indeed, it makes itself felt in his fiction, novels as well as stories, of all periods, including the most recent. It is very rare for it not to be found in these fictions in some aspect of characterization, setting, theme, and reference.

Even when there is no necessity for a South African element to appear, one seems to force its way in. "Trial and Error" (also known under the title "Live and Learn") is such a story, with Jacobson's typical themes of family relationships, guilt and betrayal, possession and freedom. There seems to be no need for the characters to be South Africans living in England, the married life of the Bothwells, threatened by Jennifer's affair with a friend's husband and temporary abandonment of Arnold and their child, is the stuff of international soap opera and could as well be about Australians or Americans as Anglo-Africans. But that would not be true of Jacobson's imaginative vision, and, once this is recognized, the reader will see that it is unfair to imagine the realm of the story as other than they are, wrong to see them as not integral. The fact of their being South Africans in England is part of the loneliness as well as the pleasure and sense of discovery of the Bothwells. It partly accounts for the conclusion, when the strongest emotion Arnold feels after Jennifer's return is not love or hatred but "fear of being left alone."

But the most striking combination of ingredients in Jacobson's stories is not the South African and the English but the South African and the Jewish. Jacobson is an acute observer of the position of Jews in South Africa. Two of his works that trace the ambivalent relationships of Jews to other South Africans of all races include, "The Example of Lipi Lippmann," about a hawker whose poverty first shames the other Jews of Lyndhurst (Jacobson's archetypal South African small inland town), and then shames and destroys himself, and "Droit de Seigneur," about a hotelier who kicks out two anti-Semitic Polish noblemen after one of them is caught in a compromising situation with a Gentile guest. In "An Apprenticeship," about a young boy who falls in love with his schoolfriend's mother, the narrator compares his own family in detail with the Gentile Pallings, to whom he feels both superior (especially intellectually) and inferior (especially socially). One striking difference applies more generally: the Pallings do not share "the burden of guilt and sympathy towards the blacks which we bore as part of our Jewishness." It is this other burden, with its honourable tradition in the history of liberal Jews in South Africa, that lies behind a story like "A Day in the Country," detailing a confrontation between a Jewish and an Afrikaner family over the teasing of a black child. It also lies behind the two most powerful and best known of Jacobson's stories: "The Zulu and the Zeide," with its touching relationship between the old grandfather (Yiddish zeide) and the young tribesman shining a revealing light on the dutiful relationships both have with old Grossman's son; and "Beggar My Neighbour" (also known as "A Gift Too Late"), poignantly showing the corruption of a possible friendship between a white boy and two black children by the gross inequalities of their situations.

The white boy in "Beggar My Neighbour" is not described as Jewish, and at this point it may be as well to turn the argument around: these stories, for all Jacobson's specific local and personal slants, are ultimately universal, their South African extremes and vividness, their Jewish nuances and humour, their English restraint and moderation combining in a wide humanity.

—Michael Herbert

———

JAMES, Henry. British. Born in New York City, 15 April 1843; brother of the philosopher William James; became British citizen, 1915. Educated at the Richard Pulling Jenks School, New York; traveled with his family in Europe from an early age: studied with tutors in Geneva, London, Paris and Boulogne, 1855–58, Geneva, 1859, and Bonn, 1860; lived with his family in Newport, Rhode Island, 1860–62; attended Harvard Law School, Cambridge, Massachusetts, 1862-63. Lived with his family in Cambridge and wrote for *Nation* and *Atlantic Monthly,* 1866–69; toured Europe, 1869–70; returned to Cambridge, 1870–72; art critic, *Atlantic Monthly,* 1871–72; lived in Europe, 1872–74, Cambridge, 1875, and Paris, 1875–76; writer for New York *Tribune,* Paris, 1875–76; moved to London, 1876, and lived in England for the rest of his life; settled in Rye, Sussex, 1896; traveled throughout the U.S., 1904–05. L.H.D.: Harvard University, 1911; Oxford University, 1912. Order of Merit, 1916. *Died 28 February 1916.*

PUBLICATIONS

Collections

Novels and Stories, edited by Percy Lubbock.   35 vols., 1921–24.
Complete Plays, edited by Leon Edel.   1949.
Complete Tales, edited by Leon Edel.   12 vols., 1962–64.
Representative Selections, revised edition, edited by Lyon N. Richardson.   1966.
Tales, edited by Maqbool Aziz.   1973—.
Novels 1871–1880 and 1881–1886 (Library of America), edited by William T. Stafford.   2 vols., 1983–85.
Literary Criticism (Library of America), edited by Leon Edel.   2 vols., 1984.
Tales, edited by Christof Wegelin.   1984.
Novels 1886–1890 (Library of America), edited by Daniel M. Fogel.   1987.

Short Stories

A Passionate Pilgrim and Other Tales.   1875.

Daisy Miller: A Study.   1878.
The Madonna of the Future and Other Tales.   1879.
A Bundle of Letters.   1880.
The Diary of a Man of Fifty, and A Bundle of Letters.
   1880.
Novels and Tales.   14 vols., 1883.
*The Siege of London, The Pension Beaurepas, and The
   Point of View.*   1883; revised edition, 1884.
Tales of Three Cities.   1884.
*The Author of Beltraffio, Pandora, Georgina's Reasons, The
   Path of Duty, Four Meetings.*   1885.
Stories Revived.   1885.
The Aspern Papers, Louisa Pallant, The Modern Warning.
   1888.
A London Life, The Patagonia, The Liar, Mrs. Temperly.
   1889.
*The Lesson of the Master, The Marriages, The Pupil,
   Brooksmith, The Solution, Sir Edmund Orme.*   1892.
The Real Thing and Other Tales.   1893.
*The Private Life, The Wheel of Time, Lord Beaupré, The
   Visits, Collaboration, Owen Wingrave.*   1893.
*Terminations: The Death of the Lion, The Coxon Fund, The
   Middle Years, The Altar of the Dead.*   1895.
*Embarrassments: The Figure in the Carpet, Glasses, The
   Next Time, The Way It Came.*   1896.
The Two Magics: The Turn of the Screw, Covering End.
   1898; *The Turn of the Screw*, edited by Robert Kim-
   brough, 1966.
The Soft Side.   1900.
The Better Sort.   1903.
Novels and Tales (New York Edition), revised by James.
   26 vols., 1907-17.
Travelling Companions, edited by Albert Mordell.   1919.
A Landscape Painter, edited by Albert Mordell.   1919.
Master Eustace.   1920.
Eight Uncollected Tales, edited by Edna Kenton.   1950.

Novels

Roderick Hudson.   1875; revised edition, 1879.
The American.   1877.
Watch and Ward.   1878.
The Europeans: A Sketch.   1878.
An International Episode.   1879.
Confidence.   1879.
Washington Square.   1881.
The Portrait of a Lady.   1881.
The Bostonians.   1886.
The Princess Casamassima.   1886.
The Reverberator.   1888.
The Tragic Muse.   1890.
The Other House.   1896.
The Spoils of Poynton.   1897; edited by Bernard Richards,
   1982.
What Maisie Knew.   1897; edited by Douglas Jefferson,
   1966.
In the Cage.   1898; edited by Morton Dauwen Zabel,
   1958.
The Awkward Age.   1899; edited by Vivien Jones, 1984.
The Sacred Fount.   1901; edited by Leon Edel, 1953.
The Wings of the Dove.   1902; edited by Peter Brooks,
   1984.
The Ambassadors.   1903; edited by Christopher Butler,
   1985.
The Golden Bowl.   1904; edited by Virginia Llewellyn
   Smith, 1983.
Julia Bride.   1909.
The Finer Grain.   1910.

The Outcry.   1911.
The Ivory Tower, edited by Percy Lubbock.   1917.
The Sense of the Past, edited by Percy Lubbock.   1917.
Gabrielle de Bergerac, edited by Albert Mordell.   1918.

Plays

Daisy Miller, from his own story.   1883.
The American, from his own novel (produced 1891).
   1891.
Guy Domville (produced 1895).   1894.
Theatricals (includes *Tenants, Disengaged*) (produced
   1909).   1894.
Theatricals: Second Series (includes *The Album, The Repro-
   bate*) (produced 1919).   1894.
The High Bid (produced 1908).   In *Complete Plays*, 1949.
The Saloon (produced 1911).   In *Complete Plays*, 1949.
The Outcry (produced 1917).   In *Complete Plays*, 1949.

Other

Transatlantic Sketches.   1875; revised edition, as *Foreign
   Parts*, 1883.
French Poets and Novelists.   1878; revised edition, 1883;
   edited by Leon Edel, 1964.
Hawthorne.   1879; edited by William M. Sale, Jr., 1956.
Portraits of Places.   1883.
Notes on a Collection of Drawings by George du Maurier.
   1884.
A Little Tour in France.   1884; revised edition, 1900.
The Art of Fiction, with Walter Besant.   1885 (?); edited
   by Leon Edel, in *The House of Fiction*, 1957.
Partial Portraits.   1888.
Picture and Text.   1893.
Essays in London and Elsewhere.   1893.
William Wetmore Story and His Friends.   2 vols., 1903.
*The Question of Our Speech, The Lesson of Balzac: Two
   Lectures.*   1905.
English Hours.   1905; edited by Alma Louise Lowe, 1960.
The American Scene.   1907; edited by Leon Edel, 1968.
View and Reviews.   1908.
Italian Hours.   1909.
The Henry James Year Book, edited by Evelyn Garnaut
   Smalley.   1911.
Autobiography, edited by F.W. Dupee.   1956.
   A Small Boy and Others.   1913.
   Notes of a Son and Brother.   1914.
   The Middle Years, edited by Percy Lubbock.   1917.
Notes on Novelists and Some Other Notes.   1914.
Letters to an Editor.   1916.
Within the Rim and Other Essays 1914–1915.   1919.
Letters, edited by Percy Lubbock.   2 vols., 1920.
Notes and Reviews.   1921.
A Most Unholy Trade, Being Letters on the Drama.   1923.
Three Letters to Joseph Conrad, edited by Gerard Jean-
   Aubry.   1926.
Letters to Walter Berry.   1928.
Letters to A. C. Benson and Auguste Monod, edited by E.F.
   Benson.   1930.
Theatre and Friendship: Some James Letters, edited by
   Elizabeth Robins.   1932.
The Art of the Novel: Critical Prefaces, edited by R.P.
   Blackmur.   1934.
Notebooks, edited by F.O. Matthiessen and Kenneth B.
   Murdock.   1947.
The Art of Fiction and Other Essays, edited by Morris
   Roberts.   1948.

James and Robert Louis Stevenson: A Record of Friendship and Criticism, edited by Janet Adam Smith.   1948.

The Scenic Art: Notes on Acting and the Drama 1872–1901, edited by Allan Wade.   1948.

Daumier, Caricaturist.   1954.

The American Essays, edited by Leon Edel.   1956.

The Future of the Novel: Essays on the Art of the Novel, edited by Leon Edel.   1956; as *The House of Fiction*, 1957.

The Painter's Eye: Notes and Essays on the Pictorial Arts, edited by John L. Sweeney.   1956.

Parisian Sketches: Letters to the New York Tribune 1875–1876, edited by Leon Edel and Ilse Dusoir Lind. 1957.

Literary Reviews and Essays on American, English, and French Literature, edited by Albert Mordell.   1957.

James and H.G. Wells: A Record of Their Friendship, Their Debate on the Art of Fiction, and Their Quarrel, edited by Leon Edel and Gordon N. Ray.   1958.

The Art of Travel: Scenes and Journeys in America, England, France, and Italy, edited by Morton Dauwen Zabel.   1958.

French Writers and American Women: Essays, edited by Peter Buitenhuis.   1960.

Selected Literary Criticism, edited by Morris Shapira. 1963.

James and John Hay: The Record of a Friendship, edited by George Monteiro.   1965.

Switzerland in the Life and Work of James: The Clare Benedict Collection of Letters from James, edited by Jörg Hasler.   1966.

Letters, edited by Leon Edel.   4 vols., 1974–84; *Selected Letters*, 1987.

The Art of Criticism: James on the Theory and Practice of Fiction, edited by William Veeder and Susan M. Griffin. 1986.

The Complete Notebooks, edited by Leon Edel and Lyall H. Powers.   1986.

The Critical Muse: Selected Literary Criticism, edited by Roger Gard.   1987.

Selected Letters to Edmund Gosse 1882–1915: A Literary Friendship, edited by Rayburn S. Moore.   1988.

Letters 1900–1915, with Edith Wharton, edited by Lyall H. Powers.   1990.

Translator, *Port Tarascon*, by Alphonse Daudet.   1891.

*

Bibliography: *A Bibliography of James* by Leon Edel and Dan H. Laurence, 1957, revised edition, 1961, 1982; *James: A Bibliography of Secondary Works* by Beatrice Ricks, 1975; *James 1917–1959: A Reference Guide* by Kristin Pruitt McColgan, 1979; *James 1960–1974: A Reference Guide* by Dorothy M. Scura, 1979; *James 1866–1916: A Reference Guide* by Linda J. Taylor, 1982; *James: A Bibliography of Criticism 1975–1981* by John Budd, 1983; *An Annotated Critical Bibliography of James* by Nicola Bradbury, 1987; *James 1975–1987: A Reference Guide* by Judith E. Funston, 1991.

Critical Studies: *James* by Rebecca West, 1916; *James: The Major Phase*, 1944, and *The James Family*, 1947, both by F.O. Matthiessen; *The Great Tradition: George Eliot, James, Joseph Conrad* by F.R. Leavis, 1948; *James* (biography) by Leon Edel,   5 vols., 1953–72, revised edition,   2

vols., 1978; *The American James* by Quentin Anderson, 1957; *The Comic Sense of James: A Study of the Early Novels* by Richard Poirier, 1960; *The Novels of James* by Oscar Cargill, 1961; *The Imagination of Disaster: Evil in the Fiction of James*, 1961, and *Search for Form: Studies in the Structure of James's Fiction*, 1967, both by J.A. Ward; *The Ordeal of Consciousness in James* by Dorothea Krook, 1962; *James and the Jacobites* by Maxwell Geismar, 1963, as *James and His Cult*, 1964; *The Expense of Vision: Essays on the Craft of James* by Laurence B. Holland, 1964; *The Caught Image: Figurative Language in the Fiction of James*, 1964, *Plots and Characters in the Fiction of James*, 1965, and *A James Encyclopedia*, 1989, all by Robert L. Gale; *Technique in the Tales of James* by K.B. Vaid, 1964; *The Imagination of Loving: James's Legacy to the Novel* by Naomi Lebowitz, 1965; *The Ironic Dimension in the Fiction of James* by John A. Clair, 1965; *An Anatomy of The Turn of the Screw* by Thomas Mabry Cranfill and Robert Lanier Clark, Jr., 1965; *James* by Bruce McElderry, 1965; *James: A Reader's Guide*, 1966, as *A Reader's Guide to James*, 1966, and *A Preface to James*, 1986, both by S. Gorley Putt; *James and the Children: A Consideration of James's The Turn of the Screw* by Eli Siegel, edited by Martha Baird, 1968; *James: The Critical Heritage* edited by Roger Gard, 1968; *James*, 1968, and *James: The Writer and His Work*, 1985, both by Tony Tanner; *The Negative Imagination: Form and Perspective in the Novels of James* by Sallie Sears, 1969; *The Early Tales of James* by James Kraft, 1969; *The Fictional Characters of James* by Muriel G. Shine, 1969; *James and the Visual Arts* by Viola Hopkins Winner, 1970; *The Grasping Imagination: The American Writings of James* by Peter Buitenhuis, 1970; *James and the Naturalist Movement* by Lyall H. Powers, 1971; *The Ambiguity of James* by Charles Thomas Samuels, 1971; *James and the Occult* by Martha Banta, 1972, and *New Essays on The American* edited by Banta, 1987; *James and the French Novel* by Philip Grover, 1973; *Reading James* by Louis Auchincloss, 1975; *James: The Drama of Fulfilment: An Approach to the Novels* by Kenneth Graham, 1975; *James and the Comic Form* by Ronald Wallace, 1975; *James, The Lessons of the Master: Popular Fiction and Personal Style in the Nineteenth Century* by William Veeder, 1975; *Communities of Honor and Love in James* by Manfred Mackenzie, 1976; *Language and Knowledge in the Late Novels of James* by Ruth Bernard Yeazell, 1976; *Who's Who in James* by Glenda Leeming, 1976; *Person, Place and Thing in James's Novels* by Charles R. Anderson, 1977; *The Crystal Cage: Adventures of the Imagination in the Fiction of James* by Daniel J. Schneider, 1978; *A Rhetoric of Literary Character: Some Women of James* by Mary Doyle Springer, 1978; *Eve and James: Portraits of Women and Girls in His Fiction*, 1978, *The Novels of James*, 1983, and *The Tales of James*, 1984, all by Edward Wagenknecht; *James and the Experimental Novel* by Sergio Perosa, 1978; *The Novels of James: A Study of Culture and Consciousness* by Brian Lee, 1978; *James: The Later Novels* by Nicola Bradbury, 1979; *Love and the Quest for Identity in the Fiction of James* by Philip Sicker, 1980; *Writing and Reading in James* by Susanne Kappeler, 1980; *Culture and Conduct in the Novels of James* by Alwyn Berland, 1981; *The Literary Criticism of James* by Sarah B. Daugherty, 1981; *James and the Structure of the Romantic Imagination* by Daniel M. Fogel, 1981; *James and Impressionism* by James J. Kirschke, 1981; *The Insecure World of James's Fiction: Intensity and Ambiguity* by Ralf Norrman, 1982; *The Drama of Discrimination in James* by Susan Reibel Moore, 1982; *The Expense of Vision: Essays on the Craft of James* edited by Laurence B. Holland, 1982;

James: The Early Novels by Robert Emmet Long, 1983; *James and the Mass Market* by Marcia Ann Jacobson, 1983; *Studies in James* by R.P. Blackmur, edited by Veronica A. Makowsky, 1983; *The Phenomenology of James* by Paul Armstrong, 1983; *James: Interviews and Recollections* edited by Norman Page, 1984; *Imagination and Desire in the Novels of James* by Carren Kaston, 1984; *James the Critic* by Vivien Jones, 1984; *James and the Art of Power* by Mark Seltzer, 1984; *A Woman's Place in the Novels of James* by Elizabeth Allen, 1984; *The Ambassadors*, 1984, and *James*, 1988, both by Alan W. Bellringer; *James: Fiction as History*, 1984, and *James and the Past*, 1990, both edited by Ian F.A. Bell; *Women of Grace: James's Plays and the Comedy of Manners* by Susan Carlson, 1985; *The Theoretical Dimensions of James* by John Carlos Rowe, 1985; *James and the Darkest Abyss of Romance* by William R. Goetz, 1986; *The Museum World of James*, 1986, and *The Book World of James*, 1987, both by Adeline R. Tintner; *Friction with the Market: James and the Profession of Authorship* by Michael Anesko, 1986; *Desire and Repression: The Dialectic of Self and Other in the Late Works of James* by Donna Przybylowicz, 1986; *Critical Essays on James* edited by James W. Gargano, 2 vols., 1987; *James and the Evolution of Consciousness: A Study of The Ambassadors* by Courtney Johnson, Jr., 1987; *Order and Design: James's Titled Story Sequences* by Richard P. Gage, 1988; *A Ring of Conspirators: James and His Literary Circle 1895–1915* by Miranda Seymour, 1988; *Desire and Love in James: A Study of the Late Novels* by David McWhirter, 1989; *Thinking in James* by Sharon Cameron, 1989; *James and the "Woman Business"* by Alfred Habegger, 1989; *James's Portrait of the Writer as Hero* by Sara S. Chapman, 1990; *New Essays on The Portrait of a Lady* edited by Joel Porte, 1990; *Professions of Taste: James, British Aestheticism, and Commodity Culture* by Jonathan Freedman, 1990; *The French Side of James* by Edwin Fussell, 1990; *James: A Study of the Short Fiction* by Richard A. Hocks, 1991; *James: The Imagination of Genius* (biography) by Fred Kaplan, 1992.

*   *   *

Henry James used his notebooks to converse with himself; in them, James the diarist upbraids, cajoles, praises, and encourages James the author. In a 19 May 1889 entry, he expresses "the desire that the literary heritage, such as it is, poor thing, that I may leave, shall consist of a large number of perfect *short* things, *nouvelles* and tales, illustrative of ever so many things in life—in the life I see and know and feel. . . ." The reader hears in these words the weariness of a writer who, in his mid-forties, had already published 23 books of one kind or another and whose most recent novels (*The Bostonians* and *The Princess Casamassima*) had not been well-received. Though James would in fact see another 32 books of his published during his lifetime, one readily sympathizes with this emphatic desire (which, incidentally, he expressed repeatedly throughout his career), to restrict himself to fictions that are "*short*" and "perfect."

In a later entry, James advised himself to "try to make use, for the brief treatment, of nothing, absolutely *nothing,* that isn't ONE, as it were—that doesn't begin and end in its little self" (8 September 1895). A master theorist as well as a consummate artist, James wrote voluminously if unsystematically about all aspects of writing, often using different terms to describe the same idea; suffice it to say that in the course of a lifetime he produced 112 shorter works, variously labeled by him as "anecdote," "tale," and "short story" (all of which are comparatively brief in length) as well as "nouvelle" (a longer work such as *Daisy Miller*). With a few exceptions, each of these has the virtue of being "perfect": as opposed to his ambiguous, open-ended, often deeply troubling novels, James's stories tend to be linear representations of complex if foreshortened actions that terminate decisively.

For his themes, James had only to look into his own celibate, cosmopolitan, highly-mannered existence ("the life I see and know and feel") and see there the nexus of all that was splendid and deadly. Art, love, money, freedom: each of these enhances and destroys in James's world. One always pays a price for whatever is worth having, and answered prayers often result in unhappiness for James's hapless protagonists. Though he often complained of his solitary state, James saw himself as a kind of high priest of art, one who rejected the conventions of career, spouse, lover, and children in order to be able to pursue a craft which required absolute solitude. Thus much of his work examines the connection between personal relations (or their lack) and the artistic or at least the aesthetic life, with the implication that the choices one makes will always be difficult and, if worthwhile in one way, costly in another.

A notable instance of this conflict between art and love is seen in "The Lesson of the Master," in which the young novelist Paul Overt is advised by his older colleague Henry St. George not to marry, as St. George himself has done. Overt takes this advice, even though he has fallen in love with Marian Fancourt, whom he renounces. Later Overt learns that Mrs. St. George has died and that the older novelist will marry Marian. The angry younger man accuses the older of betraying him, but St. George (who has, in fact, given up writing) tells Overt that he has done him a favor.

Not all of James's tormented protagonists are artists like Paul Overt, though all but a few are artistic types: sensitive, well-read men and women whose lives are governed as much by aesthetic choices as by economic, social, or moral ones. Pemberton, for example, the hero of "The Pupil" is an impoverished Oxford student who is compelled to work as tutor for the penurious Moreens, to whose eleven-year-old son, the sickly Morgan, he finds himself increasingly devoted. So great is Pemberton's affection, as a matter of fact, that he continues to tutor his charge even when the parents can no longer pay. The story ends with an instance of that sophisticated horror of which James alone is capable: the worldly, amoral parents actually try to give Pemberton their son, and Morgan Moreen dies of the shock. Even though tutor and pupil both know that Pemberton would be a better parent than either of the Moreens, the trauma of parental rejection proves fatal.

James makes difficult choices central to his art because, as his letters and notebooks make clear, they were central to his life. Too, James the consummate artist frequently wrote about the art that was the chief concern of his solitary existence. One story in particular, "The Figure in the Carpet," has attracted ample attention from critics who use its central metaphor as the basis for their own explorations of James's work. Here novelist Hugh Vereker says there is a clear pattern to his work, a discernible "figure in the carpet" he alone knows. The story's critic-narrator confesses that he cannot see the pattern, even though his fellow critic George Corvick can. Corvick marries Gwendolyn Erme but dies on their honeymoon, and she then marries the second-rate critic Drayton Deane. After her death, the narrator asks Deane if his wife had confided in him the "figure" that Corvick must have described to her, but the thickheaded Deane knows nothing of it.

Stories like "The Figure in the Carpet" suggest that the objective truth may be discernible but is likely to be beyond one's grasp, a clearly-written message buried so deeply that it can never be retrieved. This does not exonerate the Jamesian protagonist, though, who is always earnest, often to a fault. For all the refinement of James's fictional world, there is a bona fide work ethic in his major characters that makes each a strenuous seeker for something that he or she may never find. In life as in art: a handful of authors have matched James's production of "perfect *short* things" in quantity, but few have so devotedly infused craft with feeling that, though aesthetic and intellectual rather than personal and physical, is no less profound.

—David Kirby

See the essays on "The Aspern Papers," "The Beast in the Jungle," *Daisy Miller,* and *The Turn of the Screw.*

JAMES, M(ontague) R(hodes). English. Born in Goodnestone, Kent, 1 August 1862. Educated at Eton College, Berkshire (king's scholar), 1876–82 (editor, *Eton College Chronicle,* 1881–82; Wilder divinity prize, and Newcastle scholarship, 1882); King's College, Cambridge (Eton scholar; Carus divinity prize, 1882; Bell scholarship, 1883; Craven scholarship, and Septuagint prize, 1884), 1882–85, first class degrees in classical tripos, 1884–85. At Cambridge University: assistant to the director of the Fitzwilliam Museum, 1886–87; fellow of King's College, from 1887; lecturer in divinity, 1888; dean, King's College, 1889–1900; director, Fitzwilliam Museum, 1893–1908; tutor at King's College, 1900–02; Sandars reader in bibliography, 1903, 1923; provost, King's College, 1905–18; vice-chancellor of the University, 1913–15; provost, Eton College, 1918–36; Donnellan lecturer, Trinity College, Dublin, 1927; Schweich lecturer, British Academy, London, 1927; David Murray lecturer, University of Glasgow, 1931. President, Buckinghamshire Archaeological Society; trustee, British Museum; member of the royal commissions on Public Records, on the Universities of Oxford and Cambridge, and on Historical Monuments. Recipient: Bibliographical Society gold medal, 1929. D.Litt.: Trinity College, Dublin; LL.D.: University of St. Andrews, Fife; D.C.L.: Oxford University. Commander of the Order of Leopold, Belgium; fellow, British Academy, 1903; honorary member, Royal Irish Academy. Order of Merit, 1930. *Died 12 June 1936.*

PUBLICATIONS

Collections

Ghost Stories, edited by Nigel Kneale.   1973.
Ghost Stories, edited by Michael Cox.   1986.
A Warning to the Curious: The Ghost Stories of James, edited by Ruth Rendell.   1987.

Short Stories

Ghost Stories of an Antiquary.   1904.

More Ghost Stories of an Antiquary.   1911.
A Thin Ghost and Others.   1919.
A Warning to the Curious and Other Ghost-Stories.   1925.
Collected Ghost Stories.   1931.

Novels

The Five Jars.   1922.
Wailing Well.   1928.

Play

The Founder's Pageant and Play of St. Nicholas, with A.B. Ramsay.   1919.

Other

The Sculptures in the Lady Chapel at Ely.   1895.
Guide to the Windows of King's College Chapel, Cambridge. 1899.
Description of an Illuminated Manuscript of the 13th Century.   1904.
Notes on the Glass in Ashridge Chapel.   1906.
The Sculptured Bosses in the Roof of the Bauchun Chapel, Norwich Cathedral.   1908; *Cloisters,* 1911.
Old Testament Legends, Being Stories Out of Some of the Less-Known Apocryphal Books.   1913.
The Wanderings and Homes of Manuscripts.   1919.
Eton College Chapel: The Wall Paintings.   1923.
Bibliotheca Pepysiana, part 3.   1923.
Eton and King's: Recollections, Mostly Trivial 1875–1925. 1926.
Suffolk and Norfolk: A Perambulation of the Two Counties. 1930.
The Apocalypse in Art.   1931.
St. George's Chapel, Windsor: The Woodwork of the Choir. 1933.
Letters to a Friend, edited by Gwendolen McBryde. 1956.

Editor, with J.W. Clark, *The Will of King Henry VI.* 1896.
Editor, with A. Jessopp, *Life and Miracles of St. William of Norwich,* by Thomas of Monmouth.   1896.
Editor, *The Ancient Libraries of Canterbury and Dover.* 1903.
Editor, *The Second Epistle General of Peter, and The General Epistle of Jude.*   1912.
Editor, *The Chaundler Manuscripts.*   1916.
Editor, *Madam Crowl's Ghost and Other Tales of Mystery,* by Sheridan Le Fanu.   1923.
Editor, *Latin Infancy Gospels: A New Text.*   1927.
Editor, *The Bestiary.*   1928.
Editor, with A.B. Ramsay, *Letters of H.E. Luxmoore.* 1929.
Editor, *The Dublin Apocalypse.*   1932.
Editor, *The New Testament.*   4 vols., 1934–35.

Translator, with H.E. Ryle, *Psalms of the Pharisees.* 1891.
Translator, *The Biblical Antiquities of Philo.*   1917.
Translator, *Henry the Sixth,* by Joannes Blacman.   1919.
Translator, *The Lost Apocrypha of the Old Testament.* 1920.
Translator, *De Nugis Curialium,* by Walter Map.   1923.
Translator, *The Apocryphal New Testament.*   1924.
Translator, with others, *Excluded Books of the New Testament.*   1927.

Translator, *Forty Stories,* by Hans Christian Andersen. 1930; augmented edition, as *Forty-Two Stories,* 1953.

Descriptive catalogues of manuscripts in Eton College, Fitzwilliam Museum, the collection of H.V. Thompson, Rylands Library, University College, Aberdeen, and Oxford and Cambridge universities,   35 vols., 1895–1932.

*

Bibliography: "James: An Annotated Bibliography of Writings about Him" by J.R. Cox, in *English Literature in Transition* 12, 1969.

Critical Studies: *A Memoir of James* by S.G. Lubbock, 1939 (includes bibliography by A.F. Scholfield); *James* by R.W. Pfaff, 1980; *James: An Informal Portrait* by Michael Cox, 1983.

* * *

M.R. James was not primarily a writer of fiction, and the only stories he wrote were ghost stories. He was by vocation and profession first and foremost a scholar and antiquarian, an immensely learned man who specialized in classical, medieval, and Biblical studies and who achieved great distinction in many fields, including bibliography, palaeography, and architectural history. But he had been fascinated by ghosts from childhood: in a newspaper article written near the end of his life (*Evening News,* 17 April 1931) he recalled seeing a toy Punch and Judy show with cardboard figures that included the ghost, and "for years it permeated my dreams." As a schoolboy he entertained his friends by telling ghost stories, and as an adult he wrote stories to read aloud to groups of friends and subsequently published them, often first in magazines and then in volume form.

Thus his first published story, "Canon Alberic's Scrapbook" (originally titled "A Curious Book"), was written in 1892 or 1893, read aloud to friends in the latter year, published in the *National Review* in March 1895, and collected in *Ghost Stories of an Antiquary.* In many respects it sets the pattern for the stories that followed. Beginning placidly in travel-book style with a description of a French cathedral town, it describes a visit by an Englishman ("a Cambridge man") with archaeological tastes. So far, so ordinary, but the discovery of an ancient picture soon involves him in chilling experiences, and the story ends with the Englishman destroying the object that has given him a terrifying glimpse into a spirit world. The protagonist, like those in many other James stories, has much in common with the author: a man of erudition and arcane tastes, he is led by curiosity to venture beyond the limits of the rational world in pursuit of knowledge that takes him into the world of evil. There is nothing kindly about James's ghosts: they are not (as are the children in Kipling's ghost story "They") the welcome spirits of loves ones who have been lost, but evil and malevolent, coming from remote ages and impinging upon the human world of the present day, only in order to disturb, frighten, or harm. (In the article already cited, James comments that in a ghost story "you must have horror and also malevolence,")

In some stories the insight into another world proves instructive and salutary. One of the best of all James's stories is "Oh, Whistle, and I'll Come to You, My Lad," which he may have read to a group of friends at Christmas 1903. The story presents the experiences of a young and sceptical professor of ontography, whose discovery of an ancient object on a beach leads him into an unknown world. By the end of the story he is a sadder and wiser man whose "views on certain points are less clear cut then they used to be," and who has suffered a deeply disturbing, even traumatizing, experience. Again, James's method is to move from the familiar to the inexplicable, from an atmosphere of intellectual and somewhat pedantic pursuits to one of mystery and horror.

Most of James's stories are concerned with the academic or scholarly life — the life he knew best — and introduce the traditional paraphernalia of scholarship such as quotations in foreign languages (one story actually begins with a long passage in medieval Latin), footnotes, and learned bibliographical references. The deciphering of ancient inscriptions and of codes or puzzles is also a common element. As Michael Cox has suggested, while part of the purpose of this may be to suspend disbelief by initially establishing a credible world governed by its own rules, it may also be that there are elements of parody and self-parody. Cox also reminds us that, since the original listeners to these stories were mainly professional scholars and colleagues, there may have been an element of mockery directed at the teller, and possibly also at his audience.

In his preface to *More Ghost Stories of an Antiquary,* James makes clear his conviction that the most effective kind of ghost story is one set in the present day, and therefore one with whose situations the reader can readily identify. He urges that "the setting should be fairly familiar and the majority of the characters and their talk such as you may meet or hear any day," in other words, the beginning of a story should observe the conventions of literary realism, whatever may happen later. He adds that "a ghost story of which the scene is laid in the twelfth or thirteenth century may succeed in being romantic or poetical; it will never put the reader into the position of saying to himself, 'If I'm not very careful, something of this kind may happen to me!'"

A good example of these principles in practice is "Casting the Runes," one of James's most frequently anthologized stories. It opens with an exchange of formal letters and a dialogue between husband and wife written in a commonplace conversational style, but soon turns into a story of implacable and obsessive enmity and calculated revenge that entails invoking the supernatural. But the world into which the supernatural has penetrated, through the agency of an ancient book, is the world, thoroughly familiar to scholars and learned amateurs, of professional organizations and journal publication.

James was a great admirer of the stories of the Irish writer J.S. Le Fanu, whom he described as "in the first rank as a writer of ghost stories." The modern reader is likely to think that that title should properly be given to James himself, whose stories are superior in consistent quality to those of the earlier writer. In the preface to *Ghost Stories of an Antiquary* he states that his aim will have been achieved if the reader is made to "feel pleasantly uncomfortable when walking along a solitary road at nightfall, or sitting over a dying fire in the small hours," but this seems a misleading and reductive account of the effect of his stories, which often goes beyond a "pleasantly uncomfortable" sensation and conveys hints of the reality of a supernatural world of evil. It is of deep psychological interest that James, a highly successful man who followed a conventional career for his class and period, should have found such obvious satisfaction in exploring and sharing with others the darker possibilities of human experience.

—Norman Page

_____

JANSSON, Tove (Marika). Finnish (Swedish language). Born in Helsinki, 9 August 1914. Studied at art schools in Stockholm, Helsinki, and Paris. Writer and artist: creator of the Moomins in cartoon and book form; cartoon strip *Moomin* appeared in *Evening News*, London, 1953–60; several individual shows. Recipient: Lagerlöf medal, 1942, 1972; Finnish Academy award, 1959; Andersen medal, 1966; Finnish state prize, 1971; Swedish Academy prize, 1972. Lives in Helsinki.

PUBLICATIONS

Short Stories

Det Osynliga Barnet och andra berättelser.   1962; as *Tales from Moominvalley*, 1963.
Lyssnerskan [The Listener].   1971.
Dockskåpet och andra berättelser [The Doll's House and Other Stories].   1978.
Den ärliga bedragaren [The Honest Deceiver] (novella).   1982.
Brev från Klara [Letters from Klara].   1991.

Novels

Sent i November.   1970; as *Moominvalley in November*, 1971.
Sommarboken.   1972; as *The Summer Book*, 1975.
Solstaden.   1974; as *Sun City*, 1976.
Stenåkern [The Stony Field].   1984.
Resa med lätt bagage [Travelling Light].   1987.
Rent spel [Fair Play].   1989.

Other

Småtrollen och den stora översämningen [The Small Troll and the Large Flood] (stories for children).   1945.
Mumintrollet och Kometen (for children).   1946; as *Comet in Moominland*, 1951.
Trollkarlens Hatt (for children).   1949; as *Finn Family Moomintroll*, 1950; as *The Happy Moomins*, 1951.
Muminpappans Bravader (for children).   1950; as *The Exploits of Moominpappa*, 1952.
Hur Gick det Sen?   1952; as *Moomin Mymble and Little My*, 1953.
Farlig Midsommar.   1954; as *Moominsummer Madness*, 1955.
Trollvinter.   1957; as *Moominland Midwinter*, 1958.
Vem Ska trösta knyttet?   1960; as *Who Will Comfort Toffle?*, 1960.
Pappan och Havet.   1965; as *Moomin Pappa at Sea*, 1966.
Muminpappans memoarer.   1968.
Bildhuggarens Dotter (autobiography).   1968; as *Sculptor's Daughter*, 1969.
Den farliga resan.   1977; as *The Dangerous Journey*, 1978.
Vå berättelser från havet [Our Tales from the Sea] (for children).   1984.

*

Critical Studies: *Jansson: Pappan och Havet* (in English), 1979, "Jansson: Themes and Motifs," in *Proceedings of the Conference of Scandinavian Studies in Great Britain and Northern Ireland*, 1983, and *Jansson*, 1984, all by W. Glyn Jones; "Jansson: The Art of Travelling Light" by Marianne Bargum, in *Books from Finland* 21(3), 1987; "Equal to Life: Jansson's Moomintrolls" by Nancy Lyman Huse, in *Webs and Wardrobes: Humanist and Religious World Views in Children's Literature*, edited by Joseph O'Beirne Milner and Lucy Floyd Morcock Milner, 1987.

*   *   *

Tove Jansson has sometimes been characterized as a children's writer, and likened to the Swedish Astrid Lindgren (see, for example, W. Glyn Jones in *Tove Jansson*). While it cannot be denied that among the readers of Jansson's books there are many children, it is less clear that the author originally set out with the intention of writing especially or solely for them. In an interview published in 1971 she is quoted as replying to the question "who do you write for?" in these terms: "*If* my stories are addressed to any particular kind of reader it is probably to an inferior sort of one. I mean the people who find it hard to fit in anywhere, those who are outside and on the margin, rather as when one says 'small and dirty and frightened of the train.' The fish out of water. The inferior person one has oneself succeeded in shaking off or concealing."

Jansson's earliest books were fairy tales, but while appealing to children, they also had a distinctly adult flavour. *Småtrollen och den stora översämningen* (The Small Troll and the Large Flood) was the first of her Moomin books, begun during the winter of 1939, when her work as a visual artist seemed superfluous. "I excused myself by avoiding princes, princesses and small children, and chose instead my ill-natured signature figure from my humorous drawings and called him Moomintroll," the author wrote in a reminiscence. In the course of the narrative Moomintroll and his mother pass through all kinds of dangers and adventures in their quest for Pappa Moomintroll, who is eventually discovered, a victim of the Great Flood—surely a symbol of the war, and of Finland's national calamity—high up on the branch of a tree to which he has attached an S.O.S. flag. The story of how the missing father is restored to his family is founded, one feels, in a collective and individual psychology that is Jungian in content and significance (the illustrations, with their moons, trees, rivers, and phallic towers, certainly encourage such a view), while the poignancy of the concluding scenes in which Moominpappa reclaims the family home is given additional depth by the the sense of an intertwining of personal and national need and destiny.

The Moomin books that followed developed further this blend of an adult consciousness of evil and inadequacy with the child's experience of fear and joy. In the early volumes we observe the same picaresque type of narrative that characterize the story of the Great Flood. *Mumintrollet och Kometen (Comet in Moominland)* develops the character of the "little animal," Sniff, and also introduces us to the artistic, self-sufficient and sensitive Snufkin, whose tent seems to symbolise the calm with which he views the world and its perils. *Trollkarlens Hatt (Finn Family Moomintroll)* describes a journey made by the Moomintroll family to a desert island and the adventures they experience when a magician plunges them into a muddle concerning his hat. While the outline of the story resembles a children's tale, there are many features of the book, including the portrayal of the "dissolute" hattifatteners and the recurrent irony, which suggest that the author is also addressing the concerns of adults. Much of the tension centres on a dichotomy between a longing for safety and security on the one hand and a need to experience the world and its dangers on the other. This theme is particularly evident in *Muminpappans Bravader (The Exploits of Moominpappa)*, in which the hattifatteners, symbolizing the primitive human instincts, and the Groke, a kind of monster threat, play a particularly important role, and where a violent storm and a visit to an island are part of the plot in a way that was to become characteristic of the Moomin books.

Det Osynliga Barnet och andra berättelser (Tales from Moomin Valley) is a collection of short stories that signalled a change in Jansson's development as a writer. In these short pieces she concentrates more intensely on aspects of personality, and her writing is, as Glyn Jones has pointed out, "less tied to a linear action."

In general, it seems possible to say that the Moomin books are parables concerning the continuing role of childhood in adult experience, a facet of that experience that is often repressed and which, in Jansson's stories and drawings, receives expression in a way that is equally accessible to both children and adults alike. For children, after all, have some idea of the preoccupations of adults, and for them these books may serve as a kind of a hint or clue to what lies ahead in life. It is noteworthy, however, that the final volume in the Moomin series, *Sent i November (Moominvalley in November)*, is intended almost exclusively for adults, and focuses on the problems of old age, loneliness, obsession, and change. These were to become the predominant themes of Jansson's subsequent fiction, nearly all of which is intended to be read by adults and falls quite outside the category of "children's literature."

The principal works of the post-Moomin period are probably *Bildhuggarens Dotter (Sculptor's Daughter)* and *Sommarboken (The Summer Book)*. The first of these is closely related to the Moomin books, and concerns a child and her relation to fear, while the second is an extended study of old age, and describes a child's life with her grandmother. Among Jansson's more recent works (not yet translated into English in their entirety) and the short novel *Den ärliga bedragaren (The Honest Deceiver)*, about the relationship between two aged women, one of whom is despairing and helpless in her loneliness, and the other, her helper, tough, realistic and practical, and the collection of short stories *Brev från Klara (Letters from Klara)*. The title story of this collection has been translated into English (in the journal *Books from Finland*, 1992), and concerns an old woman's preparations for death and her settling of accounts with those around her.

Jansson can perhaps best be characterized as a romantic realist, for whom the creations of her imagination are always moulded and checked by a sense of practical morality. This morality is not in any sense religious or prescriptive, but derives from an ethical awareness of the uniqueness and aloneness of each human being and from a desire to penetrate to the essence of humanity through its individual manifestations.

—David McDuff

———

JEWETT, (Theodora) Sarah Orne. American. Born in South Berwick, Maine, 3 September 1849. Educated as Miss Raynes's School, 1855, and Berwick Academy, 1861–66, graduated 1866. Full-time writer in Berwick from 1866: contributed to *Atlantic Monthly* from 1869. Litt.D.: Bowdoin College, Brunswick, Maine, 1901. *Died 24 June 1909.*

PUBLICATIONS

Collections

Stories and Tales. 7 vols., 1910.
The Best Stories, edited by Willa Cather. 2 vols., 1925.
Letters, edited by Richard Cary. 1956; revised edition, 1967.
The Country of the Pointed Firs and Other Stories, edited by Mary Ellen Chase. 1968.
Best Stories, edited by Josephine Donovan, Martin Greenberg, and Charles Waugh. 1988.

Short Stories

Deephaven. 1877; edited by Richard Cary, with other stories, 1966.
Old Friends and New. 1879.
Country By-Ways. 1881.
The Mate of the Daylight, and Friends Ashore. 1883.
A White Heron and Other Stories. 1886.
The King of Folly Island and Other People. 1888.
Tales of New England. 1890.
A Native of Winby and Other Tales. 1893.
The Life of Nancy. 1895.
The Country of the Pointed Firs. 1896.
The Queen's Twin and Other Stories. 1899.
Uncollected Short Stories, edited by Richard Cary. 1971.

Novels

A Country Doctor. 1884.
A Marsh Island. 1885.
Strangers and Wayfarers. 1890.
The Tory Lover. 1901.
An Empty Purse: A Christmas Story. 1905.

Verse

Verses, edited by M.A. De Wolfe Howe. 1916.

Other

Play Days: A Book of Stories for Children. 1878.
The Story of the Normans (for children). 1887.
Betty Leicester: A Story for Girls. 1890.
Betty Leicester's English Xmas (for children). 1894; as *Betty Leicester's Christmas,* 1899.
Letters, edited by Annie Fields. 1911.
Letters Now in Colby College Library, edited by Carl J. Weber. 1947.

Editor, *Stories and Poems for Children,* by Celia Thaxter. 1895.
Editor, *The Poems of Celia Thaxter.* 1896.
Editor, *Letters of Sarah Wyman Whitman.* 1907.

*

Bibliography: *A Bibliography of the Published Writings of Jewett* by Clara Carter Weber and Carl J. Weber, 1949; in *Bibliography of American Literature* by Jacob Blanck, 1969; *Jewett: A Reference Guide* by Gwen L. Nagel and James Nagel, 1978.

Critical Studies: *Jewett* by F.O. Mattheissen, 1929; *Acres of Flint: Writers of New England 1870-1900* by Perry D. Westbrook, 1951, revised edition, as *Acres of Flint: Jewett and Her Contemporaries,* 1981; *Jewett* by John Eldridge Frost, 1960; *Jewett* by Richard Cary, 1962, and *Appreciation of Jewett: 29 Interpretive Essays* edited by Cary, 1973; *Jewett* by Margaret Farrand Thorp, 1966; "The Child in Jewett" by Eugene Hillhouse Pool, in *Colby Library Quarterly* 7, 1967; "Women and Nature in Modern Fiction" by Annis Pratt, in *Contemporary Literature* 13, 1972; "The Double Consciousness of the Narrator in Jewett's Fiction" by Catherine Barnes Stevenson, in *Colby Library Quarterly* 11, 1975; "The World of Dreams: Sexual Symbolism in 'A White Heron'" by James Ellis, in *Nassau Review* 3, 1977; "'Once Upon a Time': Jewett's 'A White Heron' as Fairy Tale" by Theodore Hovet, in *Studies in Short Fiction* 15, 1978; "Free Heron or Dead Sparrow: Sylvia's Choice in Jewett's 'A White Heron'" by Richard Brenzo, in *Colby Library Quarterly* 14, 1978; *Jewett* by Josephine Donovan, 1980; "The Necessary Extravagance of Jewett: Voices of Authority in 'A White Heron'" by Michael Atkinson, in *Studies in Short Fiction* 19, 1982; "The Language of Transcendence in Jewett's 'A White Heron'" by Gwen Nagel, in *Colby Library Quarterly* 19, 1983; *"A White Heron" and the Question of Minor Literature* by Louis A. Renza, 1984; *Critical Essays on Jewett* edited by Gwen L. Nagel, 1984; "The Shape of Violence in Jewett's 'A White Heron'" by Elizabeth Ammons, in *Colby Library Quarterly* 22, 1986; *Jewett, An American Persephone* by Sarah Way Sherman, 1989; *Jewett: Reconstructing Gender* by Margaret Roman, 1992; *Jewett: A Writer's Life* by Elizabeth Silverthorne, 1993.

*　*　*

Unlike other 19th century American women writers of short fiction such as Kate Chopin, Mary E. Wilkins Freeman, and Charlotte Perkins Gilman, whose writing was rediscovered in recent decades by feminist critics, the work of Sarah Orne Jewett has occupied a secure place in literary history since the publication of her masterpiece, *The Country of the Pointed Firs,* in 1896. For almost a century she has been considered the earliest in the series of women writers who created fiction of the highest quality in American literature. Her importance was noted 20 years after her death by Willa Cather, whose preface to a two-volume collection of Jewett's stories published by Houghton Mifflin in 1925 began with the observation that Jewett "was very conscious of the fact that when a writer makes anything that belongs to Literature," her writing goes through a process very different from that by which she "makes merely a good story."

Impressed as a teenager by the sympathetic depiction of local color (the people and life of a particular geographical setting) in Harriet Beecher Stowe's *The Pearl of Orr's Island* (1863), Jewett began to write what she considered "sketches" about people and places near her native village of South Berwick, Maine. She placed her first story in the *Atlantic Monthly* in 1869 when she was 18 years old. In 1877 she published her first collection of short fiction,

Deephaven. Reviewing this book in the *Atlantic Monthly,* William Dean Howells commended Jewett's "fresh and delicate quality" as a writer and praised her for possessing "a hand that holds itself far from every trick of exaggeration, and that subtly delights in the very tint and form of reality."

Many stories were written about New England in Jewett's time, but hers have a unique quality stemming from her deep sympathy for the native characters and her ear for local speech. Henry James recognized that Jewett was "surpassed only by Hawthorne as producer of the most finished and penetrating of the numerous short stories that have the domestic life of New England for their general and doubtless somewhat lean subject." By 1890, four years after the success of her collection *A White Heron and Other Stories,* readers like Thomas Bailey Aldrich, editor of the *Atlantic Monthly,* believed that "Hawthorne's pallid allegories will have faded away long before" Jewett's realistic sketches ceased to be read, because her work captured the flavor of the landscape and the native speech of people in her Maine community with uncommon fidelity and grace.

More recent readers of Jewett's stories, like Louis A. Renza, have investigated the category of minor literature into which Jewett was slotted after Howells, James, and later critics labeled her a "local color" or "regionalist" writer. Renza interpreted Jewett's preference for marginal characters in an isolated landscape as a subject for her fiction—the aged, widowed, or eccentric people she singled out to describe in her sketches—as a strategy she chose deliberately to foster her independence as a creative artist, enabling her to "live 'outside' stereotypical patriarchal definitions of a woman's 'proper place.'"

In 1881, after Jewett began her close friendship with Annie Fields (the widow of the eminent Boston publisher James T. Fields), her writing matured into a fuller expressiveness, culminating in the linked stories in her collection *The Country of the Pointed Firs.* Whereas earlier stories like "An Autumn Holiday" (in *Harper's Magazine,* October 1880) were relatively formless, often beginning with lengthly introductions and ending abruptly in the manner of a fluidly extended anecdote, Jewett's later work such as the stories in *The Country of the Pointed Firs* was, as Cather recognized, more "tightly built and significant in design."

Avoiding the melodramatic or didactic plots that were staple features in magazine fiction, Jewett preferred indirect portrayal of dramatic confrontation in her sketches. As a storyteller, she often positioned herself within the narrative as a character who became the conduit of another person's story. For example, in "An Autumn Holiday," Jewett goes for a long walk in the country and visits an old woman spinning in her cottage with her sister. The two older women talk about a local man they knew 50 years ago who had been a captain in the militia before he suffered a stroke and imagined he was his dead sister. He insisted on dressing in her clothes and attending the village's social functions, like church services and the Female Missionary Society. At the end of the story he thinks that the deacon, a widower, is courting him. The strangeness of the cross-dressing episodes is softened by the humorous tolerance of the two old women telling the anecdotes about the eccentric, long-dead captain to Jewett. This narrative "doubling" of a story-within-a-story lends an air of mystery to Jewett's short fiction, as if she were sketching pastels in twilight so that the darker undercurrents of deprivation, both sexual and psychological, would be less evident beneath the serenely assured surface of her material.

Stories like "The Queen's Twin" or "William's Wedding" in *The Country of the Pointed Firs* simultaneously offer and withhold an intensely shared experience, as if the narrator were reluctant to violate the privacy of her subjects' emotional lives by trespassing too closely upon them. Jewett's delicacy in suggesting more than she actually says may have resulted from the necessity in her 19th century provincial society to veil what might have been her lesbian sympathies. As Cather observed, Jewett was "content to be slight, if she could be true." Certainly her artistry in her short fiction is superb, and her sketches are among the best surviving records of everyday life in the rural New England society of her time.

—Ann Charters

See the essay on "A White Heron."

———

JOLLEY, (Monica) Elizabeth (née Knight). Australian. Born in Birmingham, England, 4 June 1923; moved to Australia, 1959; became citizen, 1978. Educated at Friends' School, Sibford, Oxfordshire, 1934–40; St. Thomas' Hospital, London (orthopaedic nursing training), 1940–43; Queen Elizabeth Hospital, Birmingham (general training), 1943–46. Married Leonard Jolley; two daughters and one son. Salesperson, nurse, and domestic, 1960's; part-time tutor in creative writing, Fremantle Arts Centre, Western Australia, from 1974; part-time tutor in English from 1978, writer-in-residence, 1982, and since 1984 half-time tutor in English, Western Australian Institute of Technology, Bentley; half-time lecturer and writer-in-residence from 1986, and honorary writer-in-residence, from 1989, Curtin University of Technology, Perth, Western Australia; writer-in-residence, Scarborough Senior High School, Winter 1980, and Western Australian College of Advanced Education, Nedlands, 1983. President, Australian Society of Authors, 1985–86. Recipient: State of Victoria prize, for short story, 1966, 1981, 1982; Sound Stage prize, for radio play, 1975; Wieckhard prize. 1975; Australian Writers Guild prize, for radio play, 1982; *Western Australia Week* prize, 1983; *The Age* Book of the Year award, 1983, 1989; Australia Council Literature Board senior fellowship, 1984; New South Wales Premier's award, 1985; Australian Bicentennial National Literary award, 1986; Miles Franklin award, 1987; Fellowship of Australian Writers Ramsden plaque, 1988. D.Tech.: Western Australian Institute of Technology, 1986; Canada Australia prize, 1990; ASAL gold medal, for novel, 1991. Officer, Order of Australia, 1988. Lives in Claremont, Western Australia.

PUBLICATIONS

Short Stories

Five Acre Virgin and Other Stories.   1976.
The Travelling Entertainer and Other Stories.   1979.
The Newspaper of Claremont Street (novella).   1981.
Woman in a Lampshade.   1983.
Miss Peabody's Inheritance (novella).   1983.
Stories.   1988.

Novels

Palomino.   1980.

Mr. Scobie's Riddle.   1983.
Milk and Honey.   1984.
Foxybaby.   1985.
The Well.   1986.
The Sugar Mother.   1988.
My Father's Moon.   1989.
Cabin Fever.   1990.

Plays

Woman in a Lampshade (broadcast 1979). Published in *Radio Quartet,* 1980.

Radio Plays: *Night Report,* 1975; *The Performance,* 1976; *The Shepherd on the Roof,* 1977; *The Well-Bred Thief,* 1977; *Woman in a Lampshade,* 1979; *Two Men Running,* 1981; *Paper Children,* 1988; *Little Lewis Has Had a Lovely Sleep,* 1990; *The Well,* 1991.

Other

Travelling Notebook: Literature Notes.   1978.
Central Mischief (essays), edited by Caroline Lurie.   1992.

*

Critical Studies: articles by Jolley and by Laurie Clancy, in *Australian Book Review,* November 1983; Helen Garner, in *Meanjin* 2, 1983; "Between Two Worlds" by A.P. Riemer, in *Southerly,* 1983; "The Goddess, the Artist, and the Spinster" by Dorothy Jones, in *Westerly* 4, 1984; Joan Kirkby, in *Meanjin* 4, 1984; Martin Harrison, in *The Age Monthly Review,* May 1985; *Jolley: New Critical Essays* edited by Delys Bird and Brenda Walker, 1991.

*   *   *

An English emigrant to Australia, Elizabeth Jolley has emerged as one of the best-known Australian fiction writers since 1980. Jolley has written nine short novels and three collections of short stories. Born in the English Midlands in 1923, Jolley was trained as a nurse. In 1959, she and her husband, Leonard, a librarian, moved to Australia with their three children. She currently lives in Perth, where she tutors at the Western Australian Institute of Technology and the Fremantle Arts Centre.

The author's fiction centers often on female characters in lesbian relationships, who live their lives without male companions. One recurrent theme in Jolley's body of work is the older/younger woman liaison; another theme plays with the author/audience relationship and the process of constructing and deconstructing the text. Jolley's work defies easy categorization, as she straddles the boundries of the tragi-comic. Her fiction notes the absurd, the hilarious, and the lonely aspects of human life. Her characters feed upon each other in meeting their needs. In an interview by Ray Wilbanks in *Antipodes* (Spring 1989), Elizabeth Jolley says, "People take what they need from each other and if they don't have a relationship in one direction they will have it in another direction." While Jolley creates idyllic female worlds where her characters are free to seek their own partners, her women characters may be trapped into dependency relationships (although her older women generally have economic strength without family attachments).

The Newspaper of Claremont Street, a novella, focuses on Newspaper or Weekly, a cleaning lady who dreams of owning land. Through her diligence she eventually buys her plot of land, but she is tormented by Nastasya, an unwelcome companion. The novella turns to violence when Weekly arranges Nastasya's death to save her privacy.

In *Miss Peabody's Inheritance*, Miss Peabody takes care of her sick mother and stays at home. Through a lively correspondence with the novelist, Diana Hopewell, Miss Peabody's life and the author's become blurred as they tell each other their two stories. When the author dies, Miss Peabody replaces her by "inheriting" her novel. Thus the author and reader roles become reversed. Again, contemplating fiction writers' problems, Jolley's work, *Foxybaby*, tells of Miss Alma Porch, who uses her current manuscript in a course at Trinity College. Here Jolley reiterates the subject of author and audience, exploring the limits of this relationship. The boundry between dream and reality disappears, causing Miss Porch to wonder if her life is a fiction.

The ironies of life appear in Jolley's short stories like "Five Acre Virgin," where the protagonist, a cleaning lady, invites her friends along to see the homes of the wealthy and then ends up in jail, or in "'Suspense! Surprise!' From Matron," where a centenarian celebrating her birthday always desired to find a honey-filled tree and never did. The solitude of a lonely woman is revealed in "The Shepherd of the Roof" when she refers to her unhappy marriage.

In her short stories and novellas Jolley creates funny but sad characters. The tragi-comic fuses in her writings, often with a dark side. With an eye for the absurd and the peculiar, her techniques of storytelling include wit, irony, suspense, and ambiguity. Where the author unnerves her reader is her refusal to present only male-dominated worlds. She examines the possibilities of female relationships, sexual and asexual, and female utopias. The claustraphobia, destructiveness, and selfishness of some of these relationships lead to the conclusion that they fail to enhance human potential. However, Jolley offers no overarching philosophy or worldview to answer the dilemmas of human existence; instead, she extends her narratives through her open-ended techniques, and her fiction poses no easy resolution for her reader.

—Shirley J. Paolini

See the essay on "Adam's Wife."

———

JONES, (Morgan) Glyn. British. Born in Merthyr Tydfil, Glamorgan, 28 February 1905. Educated at Castle Grammar School, Merthyr Tydfil; St. Paul's College, Cheltenham, Gloucestershire. Married Phyllis Doreen Jones in 1935. Formerly a schoolmaster in Glamorgan; now retired. First chair, Yr Academi Gymreig (English Section). Recipient: Welsh Arts Council prize, for nonfiction, 1969, and Premier award, 1972. D.Litt.: University of Wales, Cardiff, 1974. Lives in Cardiff.

PUBLICATIONS

Short Stories

The Blue Bed.   1937.

The Water Music.   1944.
Selected Short Stories.   1971.
Welsh Heirs.   1977.

Novels

The Valley, The City, The Village.   1956.
The Learning Lark.   1960.
The Island of Apples.   1965.

Play

The Beach of Falesa (verse libretto), music by Alun Hoddinott (produced 1974).   1974.

Verse

Poems.   1939.
The Dream of Jake Hopkins.   1954.
Selected Poems.   1975.
The Meaning of Fuchsias.   1987.
Selected Poems, Fragments, and Fictions.   1988.

Other

The Dragon Has Two Tongues: Essays on Anglo-Welsh Writers and Writing.   1968.
Profiles: A Visitor's Guide to Writing in Twentieth Century Wales, with John Rowlands.   1980.
Setting Out: A Memoir of Literary Life in Wales.   1982.
Random Entrances to Gwyn Thomas.   1982.

Editor, *Poems '76.*   1976.

Translator, with T.J. Morgan, *The Saga of Llywarch the Old.*   1955.
Translator, *What Is Worship?*, by E. Stanley John.   1978.
Translator, *When the Rose-bush Brings Forth Apples* (Welsh folk poetry).   1980.
Translator, *Honeydew on the Wormwood* (Welsh folk poetry).   1984.

*

Bibliography: by John and Sylvia Harris, in *Poetry Wales* 19(3–4), 1984.

Critical Studies: *Jones* by Leslie Norris, 1973; by Harri Pritchard-Jones, in *Welsh Books and Writers*, Autumn 1981.

*   *   *

One of a small group of pioneering Welsh writers who chose to concentrate on writing in English during the 1930's—others included Vernon Watkins and Dylan Thomas—Glyn Jones is justly considered to be one of the finest short story writers of his generation. His best work is dignified by a lyrical and evocative language and by his ability to create startling images. It also is touched by his belief in the essential goodness of humanity and by a good-natured willingness to see the best in his characters. Geographical location is also an important factor in his stories, many of which are set amongst the mining communities in or near his native Merthyr Tydfil in south Wales.

Jones first came to public notice as a short story writer with the publication of *The Blue Bed*—before that he had published mainly poetry. Indeed, the best stories betray Jones's earlier literary interests; are remarkable for their lyrical intensity and delight in language. In "Knowledge" a young man watches his wife praying in tears during a prayer meeting and is moved by a mixture of "anger and protective tenderness." Not only does he want to watch over her but he feels strangely excluded by the intensity of her passion.

Other stories are gently humorous and are marked by keen personal observation. In "Wil Thomas" the eponymous central character falls into a convoluted conversation with the wraith of a long-dead preacher as he waits for his wife to return home with his beer. Both men are described in minute and unflattering detail—Wil is egg-shaped, the preacher has broken false teeth—and the comedy centres on the preacher's uncanny possession of the eye which Wil lost in his younger days.

There is a supernatural element, too, in "Eben Isaac" and "Cadi Hughes," but Jones never allows his writing to become too serious and so in the latter story there is a touch of humour with God appearing as a one-legged man in a dirty green suit. More ambitious in intention, though less successful in execution is the story "I Was Born in Ystrad Valley," an overtly political piece about a failed revolution.

A second collection, *The Water Music*, appeared in 1944. The stories are still dominated by the passionate ornateness of Jones's language which reaches a brilliant climax in the title story, but there is, too, a harder edge to the characterisation. Whether he is dealing with drunken horse trainers ("Wat Pantathro") or strange country parsons ("Price-Parry"), the stories reveal his characters' wide-eyed reactions to the strange world around them.

Another innovation is Jones's willingness to see the world through a child's eyes. In "Bowen, Morgan and Williams" a small Welsh town and its characters are viewed with a mixture of innocent amusement and warm-hearted tolerance by a boy-narrator, now grown to man's estate. ("But all that was years ago," he comments at one stage.) However, sentimentality is kept at bay by the narrator's capacity for seeing things and people as they were and not as he would have liked them to be—his uncle has "different coloured false teeth showing like a street skyline" and Mam Evans has "baggy hands like coal-gloves."

Equally satisfying are allegories like "The Saviour" and "The Four-Loaded Man," the latter having a tender yet potent Christian significance. A small girl is visited by a stranger on a cold winter's night. She shows him kindness and is rewarded for her charity. Jones does not overplay the religious message: the visitor is not a saint but a tired old man with bloodshot eyes and a shrunken body. This close observation of humanity is typical of Jones's writing and, as in earlier stories, few of his characters are allowed to escape a gaze that makes light of physical peculiarities. For example, the preacher in "Price-Parry" has large and knuckly fingers with "the big nails flat and yellow like sheets of thin horn."

Later stories continue in the same vein. "The Boy in the Bucket" is a happy union of the most prominent elements in his writing. First, it is told from the point of view of a boy, Ceri, who is on the threshold of growing up. Second, it mixes fantasy with reality. During Sunday service in chapel Ceri daydreams about ascending the mountainside in a coal-bucket, the journey taking on the aspect of a fairy-tale adventure. The idea recalls the transformation of the swimming boys to soaring gulls in "The Water Music," but

the imagery is softer and the humour more evident. (Ceri's idyll is ended when the pew door swings open and he crashes into the aisle.)

Whether his imagination is working in the realms of fantasy or in the reality of the industrial valleys, Jones never fights shy of the emotional and cultural ties that bind him to Wales. This does not imply a narrow parochialism in his writing; rather, it explains the passionate concentration of his literary style and his capacity for creating a vividly realised world of the imagination. Jones expressed his attitude in *The Dragon Has Two Tongues*, an autobiographical account of his lifelong commitment to Welsh literature and language: "while using cheerfully enough the English language, I have never written in it a word about any country other than Wales or any people other than the Welsh people."

—Trevor Royle

JOYCE, James (Augustine Aloysius). Irish. Born in Rathgar, Dublin, 2 February 1882. Educated at Clongowes Wood College, County Kildare, 1888–91; Belvedere College, Dublin, 1893–98; University College, Dublin, 1898–1902, B.A. in modern languages 1902; briefly studied medicine in Paris, 1902–03. Married Nora Barnacle in 1931 (lived with her from 1904); one son and one daughter. Teacher in Dublin, 1903; English teacher at Berlitz schools in Pola, then in Trieste, 1904–15, Zurich, 1915–18, and again in Trieste, 1918–20; full-time writer from 1920; lived in Paris, 1920–39, and Zurich, 1940–41; suffered from glaucoma: nearly blind in later life. Recipient: Royal Literary fund grant, 1915; Civil List pension. *Died 13 January 1941.*

PUBLICATIONS

Collections

The Portable Joyce, edited by Harry Levin.   1947; revised edition, 1966; as *The Essential Joyce*, 1948.
Letters, edited by Stuart Gilbert and Richard Ellmann.   3 vols., 1957–66; *Selected Letters*, edited by Ellmann, 1975.
Poems and Shorter Writings, edited by Richard Ellmann and A. Walton Litz.   1990.

Short Stories

Dubliners.   1914; edited by Robert Scholes and A. Walton Litz, 1969.

Novels

A Portrait of the Artist as a Young Man.   1916; edited by C.G. Anderson, 1968.
Ulysses.   1922; edited by Richard Ellmann, 1969; *Ulysses: A Facsimile of the Manuscript*, edited by Clive Driver, 3 vols., 1975; Critical and Synoptic Edition edited by Hans Walter Gabler, with Wolfhard Steppe and Claus Melchior,   3 vols., 1984; corrected text, edited by Gabler, with Steppe and Melchior, 1986.

Anna Livia Plurabelle; Tales Told of Shem and Shaun; Haveth Childers Everywhere; Two Tales of Shem and Shaun; The Mime of Mick, Nick, and the Maggies (fragments from Work in Progress).   5 vols., 1928–34.

Finnegans Wake.   1939; revised edition, 1950, 1964.

Stephen Hero (first draft of *A Portrait of the Artist*), edited by Theodore Spencer.   1944; edited by John J. Slocum and Herbert Cahoon, 1955, 1963.

Anna Livia Plurabelle: The Making of a Chapter, edited by Fred H. Higginson.   1960.

Scribbledehobble: The Ur-Workbook for Finnegans Wake, edited by Thomas E. Connolly.   1961.

A First-Draft Version of Finnegans Wake, edited by David Hayman.   1963.

The Cat and the Devil (for children), edited by Richard Ellmann.   1964.

Play

Exiles (produced in German 1919; in English 1925).   1918.

Verse

Chamber Music.   1907; edited by William York Tindall, 1954.

Pomes Penyeach.   1927.

Collected Poems.   1936.

Other

Two Essays, with F.J.C. Skeffington.   1901.

James Clarence Mangan.   1930.

The Early Joyce: The Book Reviews 1902–1930, edited by Stanislaus Joyce and Ellsworth Mason.   1955.

Critical Writings, edited by Ellsworth Mason and Richard Ellmann.   1959.

Giacomo Joyce, edited by Richard Ellmann.   1968.

Joyce in Padua, edited and translated by Louis Berrone.   1977.

Joyce's Notes and Early Drafts for Ulysses, edited by Phillip F. Herring.   1977.

Letters to Sylvia Beach 1921–1940, edited by Melissa Banta and Oscar A. Silverman.   1987.

The Lost Notebook: New Evidence on the Genesis of Ulysses, edited by Danis Rose and John O'Hanlon.   1989.

Translator, *Before Sunrise,* by Gerhart Hauptmann, edited by Jill Perkins.   1978.

*

Bibliography: *A Bibliography of Joyce* by John J. Slocum and Herbert Cahoon, 1953; *A Bibliography of Joyce Studies* by Robert H. Deming, 1964, revised edition, vols., 1977; *An Annotated Critical Bibliography of Joyce* by Thomas F. Staley, 1989.

Critical Studies: *Our Exagmination round His Factification for Incamination of Work in Progress* by Samuel Beckett and others, 1929, as *An Examination of Joyce,* 1939; *Joyce's Ulysses* by Stuart Gilbert, 1930, revised edition, 1952; *Joyce and the Making of Ulysses* by Frank Budgen, 1934, revised edition, 1960; *Joyce: A Critical Introduction* by Harry Levin, 1941, revised edition, 1960; *Joyce the Artificer: Two Studies of Joyce's Methods* by Aldous Huxley

and Stuart Gilbert, 1952; *Dublin's Joyce,* 1955, *Joyce's Voices,* 1978, and *Joyce's Ulysses,* 1980, revised edition, 1987, all by Hugh Kenner; *My Brother's Keeper: Joyce's Early Years* by Stanislaus Joyce, edited by Richard Ellmann, 1958; *A Reader's Guide to Joyce,* 1959, and *A Reader's Guide to Finnegans Wake,* 1969, both by William York Tindall; *Joyce* (biography), 1959, revised edition, 1982, *Ulysses on the Liffey,* 1972, revised edition, 1984, and *The Consciousness of Joyce,* 1977, all by Richard Ellmann; *The Art of Joyce: Method and Design in Ulysses and Finnegans Wake,* 1961, and *Joyce,* 1966, revised edition, 1972, both by A. Walton Litz; *The Classical Temper: A Study of Joyce's Ulysses* by S.L. Goldberg, 1961; *Surface and Symbol: The Consistency of Joyce's Ulysses,* 1962, *Joyce: Common Sense and Beyond,* 1966, and *Afterjoyce: Studies in Fiction after Ulysses,* 1977, all by Robert Martin Adams; *Structure and Motif in Finnegans Wake,* 1962, and *Joyce's Ulysses,* 1968, both by Clive Hart, and *Joyce's Dubliners: Critical Essays* edited by Hart, 1969; *Here Comes Everybody: An Introduction to Joyce for the Ordinary Reader,* 1965 (as *Re Joyce,* 1965), revised edition, 1982, and *Joysprick: An Introduction to the Language of Joyce,* 1973, both by Anthony Burgess; *The Workshop of Daedalus: Joyce and the Raw Materials for A Portrait of the Artist as a Young Man* edited by Robert Scholes and Richard M. Kain, 1965; *The Bloomsday Book: A Guide Through Joyce's Ulysses,* 1966, revised edition as *The New Bloomsday Book,* 1988, and *Studying Joyce,* 1987, both by Harry Blamires; *The Conscience of Joyce* by Brendan O Hehir, 1967; *Joyce Remembered* by Constantine Curran, 1968; *Joyce and His World* by C.G. Anderson, 1968; *Joyce: The Critical Heritage 1902–1941* edited by Robert H. Deming, 2 vols., 1970; *Ulysses: The Mechanics of Meaning,* 1970, revised edition, 1982, and *The Wake in Transit,* 1990, both by David Hayman; *A Scrupulous Meanness: A Study of Joyce's Early Works* by Edward Brandabur, 1971; *The Ordeal of Stephen Dedalus* by Edmund L. Epstein, 1971; *The Early Joyce* by Nathan Halper, 1973; *Joyce's Ulysses* edited by Clive Hart and David Hayman, 1974; *Notes for Joyce: An Annotation of Joyce's Ulysses,* 1974, and *Joyce Annotated: Notes for Dubliners and A Portrait of the Artist as a Young Man,* 1982, both by Don Gifford; *A Conceptual Guide to Finnegans Wake* by Michael H. Begnal and Fritz Senn, 1974; *Narrator and Character in Finnegans Wake* by Michael H. Begnal and Grace Eckley, 1975; *Joyce: A Portrait of the Artist* by Stan Gébler Davies, 1975; *The Exile of Joyce* by Hélène Cixous, 1976; *Approaches to Joyce's Portrait: Ten Essays* edited by Thomas F. Staley and Bernard Benstock, 1976; *The Book as World: Joyce's Ulysses* by Marilyn French, 1976; *Epic Geography: Joyce's Ulysses* by Michael Seidel, 1976; *The Decentered Universe of Finnegans Wake* by Margot C. Norris, 1976; *The Joyce Archive* (manuscript facsimiles), edited by Michael Groden and others,   63 vols., 1977-78; *Ulysses in Progress* by Michael Groden, 1977; *The Chronicle of Leopold and Molly Bloom: Ulysses as Narrative* by J.H. Raleigh, 1977; *Third Census of Finnegans Wake: An Index of the Characters and Their Roles* by Adaline Glasheen, 1977; *Joyce: The Citizen and the Artist* by Charles H. Peake, 1977; *Joyce: The Undiscovered Country,* 1977, *Joyce,* 1985, and *Narrative Con/texts in Ulysses,* 1990, all by Bernard Benstock, and *The Seventh of Joyce,* 1982, *Critical Essays on Joyce,* 1985, *Joyce: The Augmented Ninth,* 1988, and *Critical Essays on Joyce's Ulysses,* 1989, all edited by Benstock; *Joyce's Pauline Vision* by Robert R. Boyle, 1978; *A Finnegans Wake Gazetteer* by Louis O. Mink, 1978; *Joyce and the Revolution of the Word* by Colin MacCabe, 1979, and *Joyce: New Perspectives* edited by

MacCabe, 1982; *Joyce's Exiles: A Textual Companion* by John MacNicholas, 1979; *Portraits of the Artist in Exile: Recollections of Joyce by Europeans* edited by Willard Potts, 1979; *Who's He When He's at Home: A Joyce Directory* by Bernard Benstock and Shari Benstock, 1980; *The Art of Joyce's Syntax in Ulysses* by Roy K. Gottfried, 1980; *Annotations to Finnegans Wake*, 1980, and *The Finnegans Wake Experience*, 1981, both by Roland McHugh; *The Riddles of Finnegans Wake* by Patrick A. McCarthy, 1980; *Joyce's Politics* by Dominic Manganiello, 1980; *The Odyssey of Style in Ulysses* by Karen Lawrence, 1981; *Joyce's Cities: Archaeologies of the Soul* by Jackson I. Cope, 1981; *Joyce's Metamorphoses*, 1981, and *Finnegans Wake: A Plot Summary*, 1986, both by John Gordon; *Joyce: An International Perspective* edited by S.B. Bushrui and others, 1982; *Understanding Finnegans Wake* by Danis Rose and John O'Hanlon, 1982; *A Starchamber Quiry: A Joyce Centennial Volume* edited by E.L. Epstein, 1982; *Joyce and Modern Literature* edited by W.J. McCormack and Alistair Stead, 1982; *Women in Joyce* edited by Suzette Henke and Elaine Unkeless, 1982; *Teller and Tale in Joyce's Fiction: Oscillating Perspectives* by J.P. Riquelme, 1983; *Work in Progress: Joyce Centenary Essays* edited by Richard F. Peterson and others, 1983; *The Aesthetics of Dedalus and Bloom* by Marguerite Harkness, 1984; *Light Rays: Joyce and Modernism* edited by Heyward Ehrlich, 1984; *Joyce* by Patrick Parrinder, 1984; *Joyce and Feminism*, 1984, and *Joyce*, 1987, both by Bonnie Kime Scott, and *New Alliances in Joyce Studies* edited by Scott, 1988; *A Companion to Joyce Studies* edited by Zack Bowen and James F. Carens, 1984; *Post-Structuralist Joyce: Essays from the French* edited by Derek Attridge and Daniel Ferrer, 1984; *Joyce the Creator* by Sheldon Brivic, 1985; *Joyce and Sexuality* by Richard Brown, 1985; *Children's Lore in Finnegans Wake* by Grace Eckley, 1985; *Backgrounds for Joyce's Dubliners* by Donald T. Torchiana, 1986; *Joyce's Anatomy of Culture* by Cheryl Herr, 1986; *Assessing the 1984 Ulysses* edited by C. George Sandulescu and Clive Hart, 1986; *Joyce: The Centennial Symposium* edited by Morris Beja and others, 1986; *International Perspectives on Joyce* edited by Gottlieb Gaiser, 1986; *Reading Joyce's Ulysses* by Daniel R. Schwarz, 1986; *Joyce's Book of the Dark: Finnegans Wake* by John Bishop, 1986; *Joyce's Uncertainty Principle* by Phillip F. Herring, 1987; *Joyce's Ulysses: The Larger Perspective* edited by Robert D. Newman and Weldon Thornton, 1987; *Joyce's Ulysses: An Anatomy of the Soul* by T.C. Theoharis, 1988; *Nora: A Biography of Nora Joyce* by Brenda Maddox, 1988; *Dreamscheme: Narrative and Voice in Finnegans Wake* by Michael H. Begnal, 1988; *Reauthorizing Joyce* by Vicki Mahaffey, 1988; *Dubliners: A Pluralist World* by Craig Hansen Werner, 1988; *Joyce and the Jews* by I.B. Nadel, 1988; *Ulysses: A Review of the Three Texts: Proposals for Alterations to the Texts of 1922, 1961, and 1984* by Philip Gaskell and Clive Hart, 1989; *Ulysses as a Comic Novel* by Zack Bowen, 1989; *Writing Joyce: A Semiotics of the Joyce System* by Lorraine Weir, 1989; *Joyce: Interviews and Recollections* edited by E.H. Mikhail, 1990; *Joyce and the Politics of Desire* by Suzette Henke, 1990; *The Cambridge Companion to Joyce* edited by Derek Attridge, 1990; *Joyce upon the Void* by Jean-Michel Rabeté, 1990; *Re-viewing Classics of Joyce Criticism* by Janet Egleson Dunleavy, 1991.

*   *   *

For a major novelist James Joyce published very few works of fiction and among them there is only one collection of short fiction—*Dubliners*. His novels, notably *Ulysses* and *Finnegans Wake,* are immensely long. Even *Dubliners* might in some ways be seen as doubtful for inclusion in the short fiction category as the 15 stories in the collection are closely linked to the point that they could be seen as a sort of disjointed novel. Yet Joyce is considered one of the most influential short story writers of the 20th century for *Dubliners* is an extraordinarily efficient machine for the control of the response of its readers and it is a model of the economic presentation of meaning. Katherine Mansfield and Samuel Beckett are only two of the great writers of the century to owe a considerable debt to Joyce's technique.

The stories in *Dubliners* are collectively a portrait of the Irish capital (as Joyce saw it) at the turn of the century. They are linked thematically rather than by the repetition of named characters; for example, the death of the old priest in the first story ("The Sisters") is connected to the last story in the volume ("The Dead") and numerous references to death through the stories. In particular the idea of paralysis in the first story, where the word is dwelt on by the young boy through whom "The Sisters" is focalised, hovers over the other stories. There is an element of self-portraiture in this boy—the first-person narrator of the first three stories—which must be interesting in the light of Joyce's *Portrait of the Artist as a Young Man,* and, although the other characters we encounter in the remaining (third-person) narratives are unconnected at the narrative level, there is a sense of overall structure conveyed by the fact that the collection starts in childhood and progresses through various possibilities of love, marriage, profession, political allegiance, and religion to the final tableau of stasis and mortality.

The stories, then, although they stand in their own right as miniatures of the Dublin scene, portraits of individual Dublin types in all their inadequacies, also reinforce each other in that they circle round the same topics. "The Sisters" is a boy's view of the failure and death of a priest. "An Encounter" is the same boy's view of what seems to be a sexual approach from a pervert who frightens him on a truant expedition with a school friend and then masturbates. "Araby" chronicles the boy's disillusionment when he finally manages to get to a bazaar where he expects magical delights but finds only vanity and frustration. "Eveline" shows a young woman unable to leave the dreary life that Dublin has made for her in spite of a promising offer from a young man. "After the Race" chronicles a night of "living" by a rich young Dubliner who is duped and outclassed by a quartet of foreigners (here the theme of the provinciality of the Dubliners is prominent). "Two Gallants" tells of a sordid encounter which earns one of the "gallants" half a sovereign for an evening's sexual encounter. "The Boarding House" pursues the theme of "love" by narrating the entrapment of a young man into marrying the daughter of his landlady against his own real wishes. In "A Little Cloud" an insignificant clerk with poetic pretensions meets a friend returned from success on the London press and the meeting stirs ambition in him that is at once quenched by his wailing baby and his hard-hearted wife. "Counterparts" is the counterpart of "A Little Cloud": bullied beyond endurance in his dull office job, the hero takes revenge by getting drunk and beating his little son. "Clay" is a story of a grotesque and pathetic little woman who, although she has aspirations, meets only indifference and disappointment in her circumscribed life (and for whom death is foretold as the principal thing she has to look forward to). "A Painful Case" tells of failed love—the hero is incapable of committing himself to love offered just as he is unable to engage properly with the arts of politics—he will remain "an outcast from life's feast." "Ivy Day in the Committee Room" presents (to the accompaniment of bottles being opened, as they are in many of these stories) the abject failures of Irish politics. "A Mother" shows how an artistic vocation can be nullified by a grasping materialism. "Grace" is a devastatingly ironic treatment of the Catholicism of Ireland with its tendency for details and emotion to replace clear thinking and truly religious behaviour. "The Dead" rounds off the whole sorry tale.

Joyce's Dublin, in this volume, is possessed by its past and by inertia; every word is carefully weighed so that the point is unmistakable. The first paragraph of "A Painful Case," for instance, seems to be a fairly neutral, even boring description of a Dublin bachelor, but our responses are controlled in detail; James Duffy lives in a "sombre house" looking over a "disused distillery" and a "shallow river," his furniture is largely black, iron, cold, unwelcoming, his books are ordered according to size, everything is excessively neat and, ultimately, without life or warmth. Vocabulary guides us unerringly towards character-interpretation and this in turn creates story; in Joyce the line from linguistic detail to narrative meaning is direct. We are quite unsurprised when James Duffy fails utterly in the chance of life that he is offered in the shape of Mrs. Sinico, a passionate widow. In Joyce form is content; the language and even the grammar of *Dubliners* is their meaning.

—Lance St. John Butler

See the essays on "The Dead" and "Eveline."

K

KAFKA, Franz. Austrian. Born in Prague, Austro-Hungarian Empire, 3 July 1883. Educated at Staatsgymnasium, Prague, 1893–1902; studied jurisprudence at Karl Ferdinand University, Prague, 1901-06; qualified in law, 1907: unpaid work in law courts, 1906-07. Engaged to Felice Bauer twice but never married. Worked for Assicurazioni Generali insurance company, 1907-08; Workers Accident Insurance Institute, 1908-22: developed tuberculosis, 1917, confined to a santorium, 1920–21, retired because of ill health. *Died 3 June 1924.*

PUBLICATIONS

Collections

Gesammelte Werke, edited by Max Brod and others. 11 vols., 1950—.
Parables and Paradoxes: Parabeln und Paradoxe (bilingual edition). 1961.
Shorter Works, edited by Malcolm Pasley. 1973.
Stories 1904–1924. 1981.
Schriften, Tagebücher, Briefe, edited by Nahum N. Glatzer and others. 1983—.
The Transformation and Other Stories, edited by Malcolm Pasley. 1992.

Short Stories

Betrachtung. 1913.
Der Heizer: Ein Fragment. 1913.
Die Verwandlung. 1915; edited by Peter Hutchinson and Michael Minden, 1985; as *The Metamorphosis,* 1937; edited by Stanley Corngold, 1972.
Das Urteil. 1916.
In der Strafkolonie. 1919; as *In the Penal Settlement: Tales and Short Prose Works.* 1949.
Ein Landarzt. 1919.
Ein Hungerkünstler. 1924.
Beim Bau der chinesischen Mauer. 1931; as *The Great Wall of China, and Other Pieces,* 1933.
Parables in German and English. 1947.
The Penal Colony, Stories and Short Pieces. 1948.
Wedding Preparations in the Country and Other Stories. 1953.
Dearest Father: Stories and Other Writings. 1954.
Metamorphosis and Other Stories. 1961.
Sämtliche Erzählungen, edited by Paul Raabe. 1970.
Complete Stories, edited by Nahum N. Glatzer. 1971.

Novels

Der Prozess. 1925; as *The Trial,* 1937, revised edition, 1956; edited by Malcolm Pasley, 1990.
Das Schloss. 1926; as *The Castle,* 1930, revised edition, 1953.

Amerika. 1927; original version, as *Der Verschollene,* edited by Jost Schillemeit, 1983; as *America,* 1938.
The Complete Novels. 1983.

Other

Tagebücher 1910–23. 1951; edited by Hans Gerd Koch, Michael Müller, and Malcolm Pasley, 1990; as *Diaries, 1919-1923,* edited by Max Brod, 1948; *Diaries, 1914-1923,* 1949.
Briefe an Milena, edited by Willy Haas. 1951; revised edition by Jürgen Born and Michael Müller, 1983; as *Letters to Milena,* 1953.
Briefe 1902-24, edited by Max Brod. 1958; as *Letter to Friends, Family and Editors,* 1977.
Briefe an Felice, edited by Erich Heller and Jürgen Born. 1967; as *Letters to Felice,* 1973.
Briefe an Ottila und die Familie, edited by Klaus Wagenbach and Hartmut Binder. 1975; as *Letters to Ottla and the Family,* 1982.

*

Bibliography: *A Kafka Bibliography 1908-76* by Angel Flores, 1976.

Critical Studies: *The Kafka Problem,* 1946, and *The Kafka Debate,* 1976, both edited by Angel Flores; *Kafka: A Biography* by Max Brod, 1947; *Kafka's Castle,* 1956, and *Kafka,* 1973, both by Ronald Gray, and *Kafka: A Collection of Critical Essays* edited by Gray, 1962; *Kafka: Parable and Paradox* by Heinz Politzer, 1962; *The Reluctant Pessimist: A Study of Kafka* by A.P. Foulkes, 1967; *Kafka* by Anthony Thorlby, 1972; *Moment of Torment: An Interpretation of Kafka's Short Stories* by Ruth Tiefenbrun, 1973; *The Commentator's Despair: The Interpretation of Kafka's "Metamorphosis,"* 1973, and *Kafka: The Necessity of Form,* 1988, both Stanley Corngold; *Kafka's Other Trial* by Elias Canetti, 1974; *Kafka: A Collection of Criticism* edited by Leo Hamalian, 1974; *Kafka: Literature as Corrective Punishment* by Franz Kuna, 1974, and *On Kafka* edited by Kuna, 1976; *Kafka in Context* by John Hibberd, 1975; *Kafka's "Trial": The Case Against Josef K.* by Eric Marson, 1975; *Kafka* by Meno Spann, 1976; *The World of Kafka* by J.P. Stern, 1980, and *Kafka Symposium: Paths and Labyrinths* edited by Stern and J.J. White, 1985; *The Secret Raven: Conflict and Transformation in the Life of Kafka* by Daryl Sharp, 1980; *K: A Biography of Kafka* by Ronald Hayman, 1981; *Kafka: Geometrician of Metaphor* by Henry Sussman, 1981; *Kafka's Narrators: A Study of His Stories and Sketches* by Roy Pascal, 1982; *Kafka of Prague* by Jiri Grusa, 1983; *The Nightmare of Reason: A Life of Kafka* by Ernst Pawel, 1984; *Kafka: Judaism, Politics, and Literature* by Ritchie Robertson, 1985; *Kafka's 'Landarzt' Collection: Rhetoric and Interpretation* by Gregory B. Triffitt, 1985; *Kafka,* 1986, *Kafka's The Trial,* 1987, *Kafka's The Castle,*

1988, and *Kafka's The Metamorphosis,* 1988, all edited by Harold Bloom; *Sympathy for the Abyss: A Study in the Novel of German Modernism: Kafka, Broch, Musil and Thomas Mann* by Stephen D. Dowden, 1986; *The Loves of Kafka* by Nahum N. Glatzer, 1986; *Kafka's Use of Law in Fiction: A New Interpretation of In der Strafkolonie, Der Prozess and Das Schloss* by Lida Kirchberger, 1986; *Outside Humanity: A Study of Kafka's Fiction* by Ramón G. Mendoza, 1986; *As Lonely as Kafka* by Marthe Robert, translated by Ralph Manheim, 1986; *Kafka (1883–1983): His Craft and Thought* edited by Roman Struc and J.C. Yardley, 1986; *Kafka's Contextuality* edited by Alan Udoff, 1986; *The Dove and the Mole: Kafka's Journey into Darkness and Creativity* edited by Ronald Gottesman and Moshe Lazar, 1987; *Kafka's Prussian Advocate: A Study of the Influence of Heinrich von Kleist on Kafka* by John M. Grandin, 1987; *Constructive Destruction: Kafka's Aphorisms* by Richard T. Gray, 1987; *The Jewish Mystic in Kafka* by Jean Jofen, 1987; *Kafka and the Contemporary Critical Performance: Centenary Readings* edited by Alan Udoff, 1987; *On the Threshold of the New Kabbalah: Kafka's Later Tales* by Walter A. Strauss, 1988; *Reading Kafka: Prague, Politics and the fin de siècle* edited by Mark Anderson, 1989; *A Hesitation Before Birth: The Life of Kafka* by Peter Mailloux, 1989; *Kafka's Rhetoric: The Passion of Reading* by Clayton Koelb, 1989; *After Kafka: The Influence of Kafka's Fiction* by Shimon Sandbank, 1989; *Kafka* by Pietro Citati, 1990; *Critical Essays on Kafka* by Ruth V. Gross, 1990; *Kafka and Language: In the Stream of Thoughts and Life* by Gabriele von Natamer Cooper, 1991; *Someone Like K: Kafka's Novels* by Herbert Kraft, translated by R.J. Kavanagh, 1991; *Kafka's Relatives: Their Lives and His Writing* by Anthony Northey, 1991; *A Life Study of Kafka* by Ronald Gestwicki, 1992; *Kafka's Clothes: Ornament and Aestheticism in the Habsburg fin de siècle* by Mark M. Anderson, 1992; *Kafka: Representative Man* by Frederick Karl, 1993.

* * *

W.H. Auden observed that Franz Kafka bears the same relationship to our age that Dante, Shakespeare, and Goethe bore to theirs: that is, he defines and exemplifies the modern spirit. Indeed, the modern age is too often "Kafkaesque": a nightmarish world of ethical, religious, and philosophic uncertainty. No writer has more memorably dramatized the alienation of the individual in a fathomless world than Kafka in his short fiction.

Kafka's short stories writhe with strain and struggle, with seeking, searching, questing, asking. They almost never resolve themselves by answering, finding, arriving. Inevitably the struggle ends in death ("The Metamorphosis," "Before the Law"), in the realization that the struggle is endless ("The Hunter Gracchus"), or in the even more bitter conclusion that the concept of "goal" or "end" is itself a deception ("The Departure"). In the hands of another writer the very intensity of the struggle might imply a certain existential affirmation, but not so in Kafka, where the greater the struggle, the more cruel the "punch line" at the end.

Indeed, many of Kafka's stories, especially those later collected under the title *Parables and Paradoxes,* have a sort of cosmic joke structure. Perhaps the most famous example is "Before the Law," which was also incorporated as a section of Kafka's great novel *Der Prozess (The Trial).* The law of the title can be interpreted as meaning literally the law of the land, or more generally the bureaucracy that forms so much of the unwieldy apparatus of modern life, or the fundamental governing principles of life (the answers to all the hard questions, in other words), or, perhaps, God. At the beginning of the brief parable a man appears before the open door of the law but is denied entry by the gatekeeper. It is possible he will be permitted entry later, says the gatekeeper, but perhaps not. The man is tempted to push on past (shouldn't everyone be granted free access to the law, he wonders), but decides against it. Instead, he sits on a stool provided by the gatekeeper for days, months, years. His life passes in growing exasperation and bitterness. Near death, he finally asks the question that's been troubling him for years: if everyone wants to be admitted to the law, why has no one else appeared at this particular door? Then comes the cosmic punch line: because, "roars" the gatekeeper, the door was made for that man alone. The parable ends with the gatekeeper preparing to close the door.

"Before the Law" dramatizes a typical Kafkan conflict. A man comes near to something he greatly desires but is forestalled for no very clear reasons. Indeed, the lack of any justification or explanation for the bitter thing that his life has become is at least as painful as the fact that he fails to achieve his goal. It may also occur to the reader that the man must assume a good deal of the blame for his life due to his indecisiveness (why not charge through the door?) and his obsessiveness (why not simply leave?). Hence, the end is both cruelly ironic and appropriate. The man has appeared before the law, sentence has been passed, and judgment has been carried out—only the man did not realize it was happening to him all along.

One level of despair beyond the forestalled seeker is another archetypal figure in Kafka's short fiction: the man who is beyond goals, beyond hope. One of the purest examples is a brief fiction called "The Departure." In a very few sentences Kafka dramatizes the plight of a man alienated in a world of non-understanding. His servant does not understand his simple order to saddle his horse. Only the narrator hears the sound of a distant trumpet. After the man saddles his own horse, the servant asks where he is going. He replies:

> "I don't know . . . just out of here, just out of here. Out of here, nothing else, it's the only way I can reach my goal."
> "So you know your goal?" he asked.
> "Yes," I replied, "I just told you. Out of here—that's my goal."

> (translated by Jania and James Stern)

Kafka's famous death wish is obvious in "The Departure." Indeed, although specific facts from his life rarely intrude on his fiction, Kafka was the most autobiographical of writers. "The Burrow" is a good example of a work in which we sense the writer beset by his private demons. The protagonist of the tale is a mole-like animal who constructs his labyrinthine burrow as a haven against the horrors lying in wait, supposedly, outside. Inevitably, the burrow becomes less a haven than a trap. The mole is afraid of life "outside" yet is wretchedly miserable and alone in the world of his own making. Beyond the obvious religious and philosophical parallels, it is tempting to see the mole as Kafka and the burrow as his art, which was both his relief from the pressures of living and an obsession that prevented him from living the "normal" life that he so desired. Indeed, the agony that writing too often was for Kafka (as witnessed in his diaries) is dramatized in the mole's method of "composition":

So I had to run with my forehead, thousands and thousands of times, for whole days and nights, against the ground, and I was glad when the blood came, for that was proof that the walls were beginning to harden; and in that way, as everybody must admit, I richly paid for my Castle Keep.

(translated by Willa and Edwin Muir)

Kafka richly paid for everything. It is an appropriate irony, for this crown prince of alienation, that his agonizing investment would pay little dividend until after his death. It is difficult, today, to overestimate Kafka's influence on the way we see the world and the way writers see the potential of fiction, especially short fiction. By World War II a sort of quotidian realism had come to dominate the world of short fiction to the exclusion of virtually all other modes. It was Kafka and those influenced by him, such as Jorge Luis Borges and Donald Bartheleme, who broke the stale molds and demonstrated what vivid, profound, fanciful, and provocative realms were available to writers and readers of short fiction.

—Dennis Vannatta

See the essays on "A Hunger Artist," "In the Penal Colony," "The Judgment," and "The Metamorphosis."

KAWABATA Yasunari. Japanese. Born in Osaka, 11 June 1899. Educated at Ibaragi Middle School, 1915–17, and First Higher School 1917–20, Ibaragi; Tokyo Imperial University, 1920–24, degree in Japanese literature 1924. Married Hideko; one daughter. Writer and journalist: helped found *Bungei Jidai* magazine, 1924, and Kamakura Bunko, publishers, Kamakura, later in Tokyo, 1945; author-in-residence, University of Hawaii, Honolulu, 1969. Chairman, 1948, and vice-president, 1959–69, Japan P.E.N. Recipient: Bungei Konwa Kai prize, 1937; Kikuchi Kan prize, 1944; Geijutsuin-sho prize, 1952; Japan Academy of Arts prize, 1952; Noma literary prize, 1954; Goethe medal (Frankfurt), 1959; Prix du Meilleur Livre Etranger, 1961; Nobel prize for literature, 1968. Member, Japan Academy of Arts, 1954. First Class Order of the Rising Sun, 1972. *Died 16 April 1972.*

PUBLICATIONS

Collections

Zenshu.   19 vols., 1969–74.

Short Stories

Tenohira no shōsetsu [Stories on the Palm].   1926.
Izu no odoriko.   1926; as "The Izu Dancer," in *The Izu Dancer and Others,* 1964.
Kinju.   1935; as "Of Birds and Beasts," in *House of the Sleeping Beauties and Other Stories,* 1969.
Aishu [Sorrow] (stories and essays).   1949.

Suigetsu.   1953; as "The Moon on the Water," in *The Izu Dancer and Others,* 1964.
Nemureru bijo.   1961; as "House of the Sleeping Beauties," in *House of the Sleeping Beauties and Other Stories,* 1969.
The Izu Dancer and Others.   1964.
Kata-ude.   1965; as "One Arm," in *House of the Sleeping Beauties and Other Stories,* 1969.
House of the Sleeping Beauties and Other Stories.   1969.
Palm-of-the-Hand Stories.   1988.

Novels

Kanjo shushoku [Sentimental Decoration].   1926.
Asakusa kurenaidan [The Red Gang of Asakusa].   1930.
Jojoka [Lyrical Feelings].   1934.
Hana no warutsu [The Flower Waltz].   1936.
Yukiguni.   1937; revised edition, 1948; as *Snow Country,* 1957.
Aisuru hitotachi [Lovers].   1941.
Utsukushii tabi [Beautiful Travel].   1947.
Otome no minato [Sea-Port with a Girl].   1948.
Shiroi mangetsu [White Full-Moon].   1948.
Maihime [The Dancer].   1951.
Sembazuru.   1952; as *Thousand Cranes,* 1959.
Hi mo tsuki mo [Days and Months].   1953.
Yama no oto.   1954; as *The Sound of the Mountain,* 1970.
Go sei-gen kidan.   1954; as *The Master of Go,* 1972.
Mizuumi.   1955; as *The Lake,* 1974.
Onna de aru koto [To Be a Woman].   1956–58.
Utsukushisa to kanashimi to.   1965; as *Beauty and Sadness,* 1975.
Sakuhin sen [Selected Works].   1968.
Tampopo [Dandelion].   1972.

Other

Bunsho [Prose Style].   1942.
Zenshu [collected Works].   16 vols., 1948–54; revised edition,   12 vols., 1959–61.
Asakusa monogatari [Asakusa Story].   1950.
Shōsetsu no kenkyū [Studies of the Novel].   1953.
Tōkyo no hito [The People of Tokyo].   4 vols., 1955.
Who's Who among Japanese Writers, with Aono Suekichi.   1957.
Koto [Kyoto].   1962; as *The Old Capital,* 1987.
Senshu [Selected Works], edited by Yoshiyuki Junnosuke.   1968.
Utsukushii nihon no watakushi; Japan, The Beautiful, and Myself (Nobel prize lecture).   1969.
Shōsetsu nyumon [Introduction to the Novel].   1970.

*

Critical Studies: *Accomplices of Silence: The Modern Japanese Novel* by Masao Miyoshi, 1974; *The Search for Authenticity in Modern Japanese Literature* by Hisaaki Yamanouchi, 1978; *The Moon in the Water: Understanding Tanizaki, Kawabata, and Mishima* by Gwenn Boardman Petersen, 1979.

* * *

Many of Kawabata's short stories are in the form of what he called *tanagokoro no shōsetsu,* "palm of the hand stories," a selection of which have appeared in English under the same title. He said he wrote them in the same way that others wrote poetry. However, the implications of a "palm" story, sometimes only a few paragraphs long, reach beyond the obvious reference to the scale. In Japan, as in the West, there are many people who profess to read fortunes from the pattern of lines on the hand, and with all such magical systems there are elements of synecdoche and metaphor—the hand representing the circumstances of the entire body and one small line standing for a whole complex of events.

Many of Kawabata's short short stories work in precisely this way, an apparently casual remark or trivial circumstance alluding to a crucial event in a person's past, or else predicting one in the future. In "The Sparrow's Matchmaking" a man trying to decide if he wants to marry a woman whose photograph he has been shown suddenly sees the image of a sparrow reflected in the garden pond. Somehow sure that this sparrow will be his wife in the next life, he feels that it will be right to accept the woman in the photograph as his bride in this life. The Christian reference is almost certainly intended since Kawabata read the Bible carefully and often alluded to it in his stories.

In "The Grasshopper and the Bell Cricket" this notion of an unknown fate working through casual signs is made very explicit. The narrator sees a group of children hunting insects at night using lanterns they have made themselves, and into which they have cut their names. A boy finds a grasshopper and offers it to one of the girls, who then exclaims that it is actually a rare insect— a bell cricket. As the pair stand together the narrator sees that the boy's name, cast through the cut-out in his lantern, is now lit up on the girl's breast, while hers can be seen on the boy's waist. From this symbolic instant the narrator looks forward in his imagination to the relationships the two children will have, and the moments they will be given a grasshopper and find it a bell cricket, or be given a bell cricket and find it only a grasshopper.

Almost all of Kawabata's stories concern the unknowable quality of the relationship between men and women, and even the happiest are suffused with a kind of melancholy sensuality. More precisely, it should be said that the unknowable element in relationships comes from the woman. Kawabata lost both his parents when he was too young to remember them, and critics have seen in his work the constant search for the unknown mother. "The Moon in the Water," about a young woman nursing a terminally ill husband, can be read as an attempt to comprehend one aspect of female suffering (his mother had nursed her tubercular husband before dying of the same disease a year later).

In "The Mole" the female narrator has a large mole on her back. Her habit of playing with it irritates her husband to the extent that he ends up beating and kicking her. Then, as their marriage deteriorates, he becomes indifferent even when she suddenly gives up the habit. It is the look of lonely self-absorbtion in her eyes when she does it that the husband seems to hate; but later the woman wonders if touching it reminds her of the time when her mother and sisters used to tease her about the mole and the atmosphere of family affection in which she used to live. Although talk of "fingering" is not without its sexual suggestiveness, the mole is essentially a symbol of her lovelessness and her desire to receive love from her husband.

The great importance placed on symbols leads naturally into descriptions of surreal, dream-like circumstances, to the supernatural or to some world that seems to be on the borders of all these. A late short story by Kawabata, "One Arm," begins with a young girl giving her arm to the narrator for him to spend the night with. We are to understand that she is able to detach it painlessly and it will continue to function exactly as if it were still joined to her body. This is the surreal premise of the story. All the other circumstances are described quite naturalistically, but the night in which the story takes place is, so to speak, a naturalistically strange one, one of heavy fog and dampness. The radio announcer warns that zoo animals will roar all night and clocks will go wrong. Alone in his room the narrator talks to the arm and it replies almost as if it were the girl herself; yet it is clear that although it knows the girl's thoughts, it is a separate entity—it can betray her secret feelings without embarrassment to the narrator. Finally he removes his own arm and puts the girl's in its place, so that their blood begins to mingle. Given the sensual tone of the story, this can be seen as the expression of an unattainably perfect sexual union; but with Kawabata's abiding, urgent desire to find out what is like to be a woman, the gesture transcends the physical. At the end the man wakes, horrified at the sight of his own arm lying by itself and brutally tears off the girl's arm. He replaces his own and then remorsefully cradles the delicate female arm as he lies in bed. It has become a beautiful object again, once more sad and inaccessible.

Specific dreams come to assume a more prominent role in Kawabata's writing. "The Snakes," "Eggs," "Autumn Rain," and "The White Horse" all have a dream as their centerpiece. "The White Horse" is about a man who goes to stay in a hotel every new year specifically to have the same dream about his father. One of Kawabata's most representative works, "The House of the Sleeping Beauties," concerns a house where old men pay to sleep with beautiful young girls who have been drugged into unconsciousness. "Sleep," here is not a euphemism; all they wish to do is to admire their youthful beauty and dream of their own pasts beside the innocently slumbering forms.

This last story, really a short novella, is different in length and structure from the "palm of the hand stories"— the whole nature of Kawabata's writings was always very fluid. The same short story would be reworked and appear in different versions, short stories would reappear as incidents in longer novels, and the novels themselves break off at apparently arbitrary moments. Kawabata was not much interested in relating a series of events, and not at all interested in bringing things to a clear resolution. He wanted, rather, to turn a moment or a scene around in his hand until one element of it suddenly gave off a special lustre. Something, a flower, a sound, momentarily takes on a cosmological significance, but never quite long enough for that significance to be wholly grasped.

—James Raeside

See the essay on "The Rooster and the Dancing Girl."

———

KAZAKOV, Iurii (Pavlovich). Russian. Born in Moscow, 8 August 1927. Studied cello at Gnesin Music School, Moscow, 1946-51; Gorky Institute of Literature, Moscow, 1953–58. Instructor, Moscow Conservatory; musician, 1952–54; writer, from 1952. Member, Soviet Writer's Union. *Died 1982.*

PUBLICATIONS

Short Stories

Pervoe svidanie [First Meeting].   1955.
Manka.   1958.
Adam i Eva [Adam and Eve].   1958.
Arktur—gonchii pes.   1958; as *Arcturus, The Hunting Dog,* 1968.
Zapakh khleba.   1958; as *The Smell of Bread and Other Stories,* 1965.
Trali-Vali [Silly-Billy].   1959.
Na Polustanke.   1959; as *The Small Station.* 1959.
Po Doroge [On the Road].   1961.
Tarusskie stranitsy.   1961.
Tropiki na pechke [Tropics in the Stove].   1962.
Rasskazy [Stories].   1962.
Legkaia Zhizn [Easy Life].   1963.
Krasnaia ptitsa [Beautiful Bird].   1963.
Goluboe i zelenoe [Blue and Green], with *Rasskazy i ocherk.*   1963.
Selected Short Stories (in Russian), edited by George Gibian.   1963.
Going to Town, and Other Stories.   1964.
Dvoe v dekabre [Two in December].   1966.
Kak ia stroil dom [How I Built a House].   1967.
Osen' v dubovykh lesakh.   1969; as *Autumn in the Oakwoods,* 1970.
Vo sne ty gor'ko plakal [You Bitterly Cried in Your Sleep].   1977.
Olen'i roga: rasskazy [The Deer and the Horns].   1980.
Rasskazy.   1983.
Poedemte v Lopshen'gu.   1983.
Dve Nochi [Two Nights].   1986.

Other

Severnyi dnevnik (travelogue).   1961; as *A Northern Diary,* 1973.

*

Critical Studies: in *Soviet Literature in the Sixties* by M. Hayward and E.L. Crowley, 1964; "Kazakov: The Pleasures of Isolation" by Karl Kramer, in *Slavic and East European Journal* 10, Spring 1966; "Kazakov" by George Gibian, in *Major Soviet Writers,* edited by Edward J. Brown, 1973; "The Short Stories of Kazakov" by Samuel Orth, in *Russian Language Journal* 32, Spring 1978; in *A History of Post-War Soviet Writings* by G. Svirski, 1981.

*   *   *

Iurii Kazakov published no more than 35 short stories in all, and yet this small corpus of work epitomizes the literature of the post-Stalin "Thaw" period, ushered in by Khrushchev's secret speech to the 20th Party Congress in February 1956. The mere act of writing a short story represented a major change; Stalinist prose writing had been dominated by long novels with "positive" heroes and enough space for the author to tie up all ideological loose ends. Kazakov's stories are the very reverse of this—allusive, ambiguous, and open-ended. His heroes and heroines are indecisive, unsure, vulnerable, and isolated, both physically and emotionally. They include a buoy-keeper on a Northern river (Yegor in "Fiddle Faddle," a

post girl on the White Sea (*Manka*), a blind dog (*Arkur—gonchii pes [Arcturus, The Hunting Dog]*), a plain provincial school teacher ("The Plain Girl"), and the ailing Chekhov, compelled to live apart from his wife in Yalta ("That Accursed North"). Like Chekhov, whom he acknowledged as a major influence on his work, Kazakov offers no easy solutions. Sonia, in "The Plain Girl," is painfully aware of her lack of physical attractiveness; no one asks her to dance at the party with which this story, like a number of Kazakov's stories, opens. Her subsequent encounter with a drunken—and equally lonely young man—ends in tears. Although the experience gives her a new realization of her worth as a human being, she will still be lonely and plain.

This story, like many of Kazakov's stories, is set in provincial Russia. Kazakov, whose parents were from the provinces, had a particular love of the *pomor'e* area along the White Sea coast and reproduces the local dialect in a number of stories. The contrast between the provinces and Moscow, a recurrent theme in Russian literature, is seen to best effect in "The Smell of Bread," the three chapters of which are set in Moscow and the provinces. The sophisticated Muscovite Dusia returns, somewhat reluctantly, to the village where her mother had just died. Only then does she realise the extent of her loss and the degree of her estrangement from her roots. This story, itself much influenced by Konstantin Paustovskii's *The Telegram,* prefigures much of the work of the Village Prose writers of the 1970's, particularly in its emphasis on the word *rodnoi,* meaning "native" or, in this context, "Russian." It demonstrates, too, that Kazakov is essentially a transitional writer. He looks back to 19th and early 20th century classics: Lermontov, who is the protagonist of his only historical short story "Zvon bregeta" (The Watch Chime); Turgenev, whose *A Sportsman's Sketches* (1852) clearly influenced the nature descriptions in such stories as "Old Hunting Grounds"; Anton Chekhov; Ivan Bunin, whose delicate treatment of love is echoed in *Adam i Eva* ("Adam and Eve") and *Dvoe v dekabre* ("Two in December") and Mikhail Prishvin, to whom *Arcturus the Hound,* probably Kazakov's most famous story, is dedicated.

It might be alleged that Kazakov's cope is limited, that he ploughs a very narrow furrow. What is indisputable, however, is that his handling of language is masterly. He exploits all the resources of the Russian language, particularly its prefixes, suffixes, and diminutives, in a way that it is difficult to convey in translation. For instance, every Kazakov story is saturated in sounds, which are described either by standard literary words, or by neologisms of his own invention based on standard roots, or by onomatopoeic renditions. The latter, though striking, are perhaps the least successful of Kazakov's ways of conveying sound, tending too often to resemble the attempts made in ornithological handbooks to transcribe phonetically the song of birds.

Smells also dominate Kazakov's stories, the smells of nature, people, places, and products. Kazakov regarded smell as the most evocative of the senses and even made a blind dog totally dependent on its sense of smell in order to survive, the hero of *Arcturus, The Hunting Dog.* Here again the changes rung by Kazakov on the Russian root "-pakh-" (smell) mark him as a major stylist.

In Kazakov's stories the unspoken is frequently more important than the spoken. The unspoken is conveyed by body language and facial gesture—the raising or lowering of eyes, and the offering, refusing, lighting, or smoking of cigarettes. This is particularly marked in the exchanges between Sonia and Nikolai in "The Plain Girl" and between the unnamed couple in *Na Polustanke (The Small Station)*.

Dismissed as unacceptably "pessimistic" by the Brezhnevite literary bureaucracy, Kazakov has, in the years since his death in 1982, attracted increasing attention, both in Russia and in the West.

—Michael Pursglove

See the essay on *Arcturus, The Hunting Dog*.

KELLER, Gottfried. Swiss. Born in Zurich, 19 July 1819. Educated at Armenschule zum Brunnenturm; Landknabeninstitut, to age 13; Industrieschule, 1832–33; studied painting with Peter Steiger, 1834, and Rudolf Meyer, 1837; Munich Academy, 1840–42. Gave up art for writing in Zurich, 1842: government grant to study at University of Heidelberg, 1848-50, and University of Berlin, 1850–55; Cantonal Secretary (Staatschreiber), 1861–76. Honorary doctorate: University of Zurich, 1869. Honorary Citizen, Zurich, 1878. Member, Order of Maximilian (Bavaria). 1876. *Died 15 July 1890.*

PUBLICATIONS

Collections

Sämtliche Werke, edited by Jonas Frankel and Carl Helbling.   24 vols., 1926–54.
Werke, edited by Clemens Heselhaus.   2 vols., 1982.

Short Stories and Novellas

Die Leute von Seldwyla.   1856–74; as *The People of Seldwyla*, 1911; also translated with *Seven Legends*, 1929.
Sieben Legenden.   1872; edited by K. Reichert, 1965; as *Seven Legends*, with *The People of Seldwyla*, 1929.
Züricher Novellen.   1877.
Das Sinngedicht.   1881.
Clothes Maketh Man and Other Swiss Stories.   1894.
Stories, edited by Frank G. Ryder.   1982.

Novels

Der grüne Heinrich.   1853–55; revised edition, 1880; as *Green Henry*, 1960.
Martin Salander.   1886; translated as *Martin Salander*, 1963.

Verse

Gedichte.   1846.
Neue Gedichte.   1852.
Gesammelte Gedichte.   1883.
Gedichte, edited by Albert Köster.   1922.

Other

Briefwechsel, with Theodor Storm, edited by Albert Köster. 1904.

Briefwechsel, with Paul Heyse, edited by Max Kalbeck. 1919.
Keller in seinen Briefen, edited by Heinz Amelung.   1921.
Briefwechsel, with J.V. Widmann, edited by Max Widmann.   1922.
Briefe an Vieweg, edited by Jonas Fränkel.   1938.
Gesammelte Briefe, edited by Carl Helbling.   4 vols., 1950–54.
Kellers Briefe, edited by Peter Goldammer.   1960.
Briefwechsel, with Hermann Hettner, edited by Jürgen Jahn.   1964.
Aus Kellers glücklicher Zeit: Der Dichter im Briefwechsel mit Marie und Adolf Exner, edited by Irmgard Smidt. 1981.
Mein lieber Herr und bester Freund: Keller im Briefwechsel mit Wilhelm Petersen, edited by Irmgard Smidt.   1984.
Briefwechsel, with Emil Kuh, edited by Irmgard Smidt and Erwin Streitfeld.   1988.

*

Critical Studies: *The Cyclical Method of Composition in Keller's "Sinngedicht"* by Priscilla M. Kramer, 1939; *Keller: Life and Works* by J.M. Lindsay, 1968; *Light and Darkness in Keller's "Der grüne Heinrich"* by Lucie Karcic, 1976; *Keller: Poet, Pedagogue and Humanist* by Richard R. Ruppel, 1988; *Readers and Their Fictions in the Novels and Novellas of Keller* by Gail K. Hart, 1989.

* * *

Gottfried Keller's major contribution to Swiss literature lies in the short form, and although he came to such fiction relatively late in his literary career, his particular approach reveals traces of earlier ambitions. His initial desire was to be a painter, and his detailed descriptions, obvious love of the natural world, and his eye for colour, reflects his (unsuccessful) youthful enthusiasm for art. His first success came in verse, which remained simple and direct, and these qualities are equally evident in his prose. It was actually a modest reputation in poetry which led to the award of a scholarship from his canton to study abroad, but his attempts to become a dramatist in the country he selected (Germany) proved a failure. Yet some of the best German novellas have been written by playwrights, and Keller's sense of conflict and confrontation, as well as straightforward language, which tends to avoid subordination and encapsulation, may spring from his conscientious study of drama. Only after his long autobiographical novel was published did Keller devote himself seriously to the short form, and within a year he had published the first volume of the collection on which his reputation largely rests. With some success to his credit, Keller returned to Switzerland as an independent writer. His later surprise appointment as a senior civil servant reduced his output, but he continued to compose stories, articles, and poetry.

Keller was something of an unsophisticated writer, who rarely disguised his attitudes towards his characters and who had little interest in literary theory, despite his study of literature and philosophy in Heidelberg. His presence is regularly felt in his paternalistic and moralistic tone, and he takes delight in criticising folly by means of irony. Although his plots may be grounded in reality, touches of the fairy tale are common, and his characters are often caricatured. His stories usually have a leisurely pace, not helped by the occasionally irrelevant and heavily descriptive digressions, which are detrimental to the balance of his pieces, but he is an entertaining and imaginative writer who can often draw the reader fully into the dilemma faced by his central figures.

Der grüne Heinrich (*Green Henry*) is a monument in the tradition of the German bildungsroman (novel of development); but it can be seen as a collection of episodes within a biographical frame, and the best sections are almost novellas in themselves. During its composition Keller was active in planning numerous other novellas, and the speed with which these highly successful pieces were completed suggests his inclination and talents were far better suited to the short form.

Die Leute von Seldwyla (*The People of Seldwyla*), a collection published in two separate parts, contains ten such stories, which are all satirical. Although not all of these pieces are set in this imaginary town, the name has become symbolic of middle-class narrow-mindedness and profit-seeking, with the stories exposing stupidity, greed, hypocrisy, vanity, affectation, and especially the idée fixe. The methods range from light irony to farce, mild caricature to grotesque. Incongruity is common. Three stories stand out for their forceful handling of traditional themes: "A Village Romeo and Juliet," "The Three Righteous Comb-makers," and "Clothes Maketh Man." The first approaches the Shakespearean theme in a sociological manner, tracing the forces within the lower middle class that result in the tragedy. The second is a 19th-century version of the "rat race," showing the depths to which humans can sink in their pursuit of material goals. And the third ridicules the middle-class tendency to be deceived by fine clothes and hints of grandeur. Although Keller makes much of the fact that his tales are set in Switzerland, their themes are European and, to a large extent, timeless. Men are seen as masters of their own destiny, and ridiculed for inaction or reluctance to take responsibility for their own lot. Weakness and failure are common, although catastrophe is rare. Females are on the whole superior: more sensitive, wiser and responsible in their foresight, often an indispensable crutch to their menfolk, who would go astray or even collapse without them. (Their maternal rather than sexual role may spring from Keller's own dependence on his mother, who supported him financially until his forty-second year.) Shortly before the second part of this cycle was published, Keller produced a sequence of parodies of miraculous events, *Sieben Legenden* (*Seven Legends*). The tone is at times frivolous. Good is always rewarded; folly and evil punished. Life, in line with Keller's atheistic beliefs, is to be enjoyed sensibly here and now.

Although Keller was a staunch liberal and played an active part in political conflicts in the 1840's, only his poems bear clear evidence of political ideology; his stories tend rather to be conservative in outlook and the highest goal a character can achieve is to become an active and useful member of society. This becomes more marked in his later years, when he was disturbed by what he saw as a decline of moral standards and troubled by economic expansion. His collection, the *Züricher Novellen*, (Zurich Novellas) praises traditional Swiss values, especially in "The Banner of the Upright Seven," but there is also criticism of an impractical older generation which is too obsessed with successes in its own past. The stories in this collection are framed within a narrative, and one of them, "The Governor of Greifensee," itself contains a series of separate stories. Keller's final major work, *Das Sinngedicht* (The Epigram), is a series of 13 independent tales within a frame that which is a novella itself. The majority of these are concerned with problems of marriage and compatibility. Love relationships, both failed and successful, are frequently featured in Keller's writing, and the theme was undoubtedly influenced by his own frequent and unsuccessful attempts to win a wife. Partnership is seen as a key ideal.

Keller can be at times sentimental, but the tone of his short fiction is never constant; there is often a sense of ambiguity, a hint of melancholy, even mental despair, and his irony is all-pervasive.

—Peter Hutchinson

***

KINSELLA, W(illiam) P(atrick). Canadian. Born in Edmonton, Alberta, 25 May 1935. Educated at Eastwood High School, Edmonton, graduated 1953; University of Victoria, British Columbia, B.A. in creative writing 1974; University of Iowa, Iowa City, 1976–78, M.F.A. 1978. Married 1) Myrna Salls in 1957, two children; 2) Mildred Clay in 1965 (divorced 1978); 3) Ann Knight in 1978. Clerk, Government of Alberta, 1954–56, and manager, Retail Credit Co., 1956–61, both Edmonton; account executive, City of Edmonton, 1961–67; owner, Caesar's Italian Village restaurant, 1967–72, editor, *Martlet*, 1973–74, and cab driver, 1974–76, all Victoria, British Columbia; assistant professor of English, University of Calgary, Alberta, 1978–83; full-time writer, from 1983. Recipient: *Edmonton Journal* prize, 1966; *Canadian Fiction* award, 1976; Alberta Achievement award, 1982; Houghton Mifflin Literary fellowship, 1982; *Books in Canada* prize, 1982; Canadian Authors Association prize, 1983; Leacock medal, for humor, 1987. Lives in British Columbia.

PUBLICATIONS

Short Stories

Dance Me Outside.   1977.
Scars.   1978.
Shoeless Joe Jackson Comes to Iowa.   1980.
Born Indian.   1981.
The Ballad of the Public Trustee.   1982.
The Moccasin Telegraph and Other Indian Tales.   1983.
The Thrill of the Grass.   1984.
The Alligator Report.   1985.
The Fencepost Chronicles.   1986.
Red Wolf, Red Wolf.   1987.
Five Stories.   1987.
The Further Adventures of Slugger McBatt.   1988.
The Miss Hobbema Pageant.   1989.

Novels

Shoeless Joe.   1982.
The Iowa Baseball Confederacy.   1986.
Box Socials.   1991.

Verse

Rainbow Warehouse, with Ann Knight.   1989.

Other

Two Spirits Soaring: The Art of Allen Sapp, The Inspiration of Allan Ganor.   1990.

*

Bibliography: *Kinsella: A Partially-Annotated Bibliographic Checklist (1953-1983)* by Ann Knight, 1983.

Critical Studies: "Down and Out in Montreal, Windsor, and Wetaskiwin" by Anthony Brennan, in *Fiddlehead,* Fall 1977; "Don't Freeze Off Your Leg" Spring 1979, and "Say It Ain't So, Joe" Spring-Summer 1981, both by Frances W. Kaye, in *Prairie Schooner;* article by Brian E. Burtch, in *Canadian Journal of Sociology,* Winter 1980; essay by Anne Blott, in *Fiddlehead,* July 1982; Marjorie Retzleff, in *NeWest Review,* October 1984; "Search for the Unflawed Diamond" by Don Murray, in *NeWest Review,* January 1985; *The Fiction of Kinsella: Tall Tales in Various Voices* by Don Murray, 1987; "Baseball as Sacred Doorway in the Writing of Kinsella" by Brian Aitken, in *Aethon* 8, Fall 1990.

*   *   *

W.P. Kinsella's large body of work in the short story form (more than 200 stories by his own estimate, and he's also written novels and poetry) divides nicely into three groups according to subject matter. There are first the stories about Indians, second the stories about baseball, and third the stories about neither Indians nor baseball. Only rarely do the categories overlap— "Indian Struck" is the story of an Indian baseball team's encounter with two white girls at a regional tournament, but Kinsella's Indians don't play much baseball and his baseball players are mostly not Indians.

A writer so prolific can populate and chronicle two Yoknapatawphas, and Kinsella has done so. One is in Canada, more specifically Alberta, home to the Indian stories. The other is in Iowa, more specifically Iowa City, home to the baseball stories. "My cumulative Implied Author," Kinsella has written, "would be an Indian baseball fanatic who practices magic, has kidnapped J.D. Salinger and made love to Janis Joplin."

The Indian stories are set on and around the Ermineskin Reserve, near Calgary, and told by young Silas Ermineskin, himself a writer and apprentice medicine man encouraged by his English teacher Mr. Nichols and Mad Etta the medicine lady. Other regulars include Silas's pals Frank Fence-post and Eathen Firstrider, his sister Illiana (who marries a white fool named Robert McVey and moves to Calgary where she gives Eathen's child Robert's name), his girlfriend Sadie One-wound, Frank's girlfriend Connie Bigcharles, the feminist Bedelia Coyote and her brother Robert, and Blind Louis Coyote, owner and willing lender of what often seems the only running truck on the reserve.

Kinsella has been praised as a comic writer, and it is true that some stories are very funny. "I Remember Horses," "The Four-Sky-Thunder Bundle," "Fugitives," and "The McGuffin" all center upon visits to the McVeys in Calgary. In "The McGuffin" McVey's putative son, still a baby, spends a day with Silas and Frank in the company of hookers and gamblers, while McVey's attempts to rescue the child result in his own arrest when he is mistaken for a gambler named Montana Shorty. "The Four-Sky-Thunder Bundle" describes a hilarious visit to the McVey apartment by a large group of Indians in town for the Calgary Stampede. A party develops and the police arrive in answer to a report of "Indians . . . ah . . . fornicating on your balcony." McVey himself ends up ceremonially tatooed (that's what the bundle in the title is), and his family is evicted from the apartment. "I Remember Horses" describes in detail the trashing of the new McVey home (successor to the apartment) by very nearly the same group of visitors. "I have to admit we have caused Brother Bob a certain amount of trouble in the past," allows Silas in "The Fugitives," "but we always had good intentions."

These are not the only funny stories— "The Queen's Hat," "Canadian Culture," and "Where the Wild Things Are" feature other white dummies in the Robert McVey slot, and tell hilarious stories of a buffalo hunt staged for Prince Philip, adventures with would-be movie makers in search of Indians out of James Fenimore Cooper, and an attempt by Frank and Silas to pass themselves off as "genuine Onadatchie" hunting guides to two Alabama dudes.

But most of the Indian stories, and all the best ones, are darker, deeper, less dependent on caricature whites as heavies, not at bottom funny. "Dance Me Outside" is a chilling story of murder and revenge; "Horse Collars" is darker; perhaps Kinsella's darkest is the story of "Wilbur Yellowknees and his Girls." Wilbur is a pimp whose "girls" are his daughters. "Caraway" is the tale of Joe Buffalo's revenge upon Russell Bevans for the rape of his daughter. "Gooch," "Yellow Scarf," "Goose Moon," "The Rattlesnake Express"—these too are powerful, winter-blooded stories with motives deeper than humor at their center.

The baseball stories are strikingly different, most obviously in their insistent use of fantasy. In "Shoeless Joe Jackson Comes to Iowa" a disembodied voice speaks to a man sitting on his eastern Iowa porch, assuring him a dead baseball player will visit if he will just construct a ballpark. In "The Night Manny Mota Tied the Record" a Mr. Revere suggests that baseball star Thurman Munson's recent death in a plane crash can "unhappen" if only a willing substitute can be found. In "The Last Pennant Before Armageddon" the manager of the Chicago Cubs is visited in his dreams by God, who delivers a heavy message: when the Cubs win the pennant, the world as we know it comes to end. Only one of the Indian stories, "Weasels and Ermines," with Mad Etta working heavy medicine, has anything like such magic.

The usual magic in these stories has to do with men and women, especially wild women and the men who follow them like moths to flames. "Evangeline's Mother" ends with lovers on the lam, 36-year-old Henry running off with his daughter's best friend. "Waiting for the Call" ends with its young white narrator leaving everything, planned job and planned girl, to follow his Indian girlfriend Ramona, who left for parts unknown with her family. He's on a bus, with $8.14 in his pocket, bound "to the first of many places where Ramona may be." The story ends with a young heart's defiant credo: "There are several thousand dollars worth of adrenalin coursing through my body."

"Driving Toward the Moon," "Elvis Bound," and "The Baseball Spur" are baseball stories, but they feature that same heart, bound beyond measure to its own wild girls. In "The Baseball Spur" her name is Sunny, his is Jack, and she's by her own estimate trouble. "I've done things that would curl your hair," she says. It doesn't matter. "There's nothing you can tell me that will change how I feel about you," he says. "Driving Toward the Moon" closes upon a pitcher and a woman driving away, he from his contract and ballclub, she from her husband. There's no destination closer than the moon, but here as in many a Kinsella story the moon hangs strangely near, shedding an altering, benevolent light, blessing the living who move in the dark.

—Robert B. Cochran

See the essay on "How I Got My Nickname."

———

KIPLING, (Joseph) Rudyard. English. Born in Bombay, India, 30 December 1865, of English parents; moved to England, 1872. Educated at the United Services College, Westward Ho!, Devon, 1878–82. Married Caroline Starr Balestier in 1892; two daughters and one son. Assistant editor, *Civil and Military Gazette,* Lahore, 1882–87; assistant editor and overseas correspondent, *Pioneer,* Allahabad, 1887–89; full-time writer from 1889; lived in London, 1889–92, and Brattleboro, Vermont, 1892–96, then returned to England; settled in Burwash, Sussex, 1902. Rector, University of St. Andrews, Fife, 1922–25. Recipient: Nobel prize for literature, 1907; Royal Society of Literature gold medal, 1926. LL.D.: McGill University, Montreal, 1907; D.Litt.: University of Durham, 1907; Oxford University, 1907; Cambridge University, 1907; University of Edinburgh, 1920; the Sorbonne, Paris, 1921; University of Strasbourg, 1921; D.Phil.: University of Athens, 1924. Honorary fellow, Magdalene College, Cambridge, 1932; associate member, Académie des Sciences Morales et Politiques, 1933. *Died 18 January 1936.*

PUBLICATIONS

Collections

Complete Works (Sussex Edition).   35 vols., 1937–39; as *Collected Works* (Burwash Edition), 28 vols., 1941.
Verse: Definitive Edition.   1940.
The Best Short Stories, edited by Randall Jarrell.   1961; as *In the Vernacular: The English in India and The English in England,* 2 vols., 1963.
Stories and Poems, edited by Roger Lancelyn Green.   1970.
Short Stories, edited by Andrew Rutherford.   1971.
Selected Verse, edited by James Cochrane.   1977.
The Portable Kipling, edited by Irving Howe.   1982.
Selected Stories, edited by Sandra Kemp.   1987.
A Choice of Kipling's Prose, edited by Craig Raine.   1987.

Short Stories

Plain Tales from the Hills.   1888.
Soldiers Three: A Collection of Stories.   1888.
The Phantom 'Rickshaw and Other Tales.   1888; revised edition, 1890.
Wee Willie Winkie and Other Child Stories.   1888; revised edition, 1890.
The Courting of Dinah Shadd and Other Stories.   1890.
Indian Tales.   1890.
Life's Handicap, Being Stories from Mine Own People.   1891.
Soldier Tales.   1896; as *Soldier Stories,* 1896.

The Kipling Reader.   1900; revised edition, 1901; as *Selected Stories,* 1925.
Traffics and Discoveries.   1904.
Actions and Reactions.   1909.
A Diversity of Creatures.   1917.
Selected Stories, edited by William Lyon Phelps.   1921.
Land and Sea Tales.   1923.
Debits and Credits.   1926.
Selected Stories.   1929.
Thy Servant a Dog, Told by Boots.   1930; revised edition, as *Thy Servant a Dog and Other Dog Stories,* 1938.
Humorous Tales.   1931.
Limits and Renewals.   1932; edited by Phillip Mallett, 1989.
Animal Stories.   1932.
All the Mowgli Stories.   1933.
Collected Dog Stories.   1934.
More Selected Stories.   1940.
Twenty-One Tales.   1946.
Ten Stories.   1947.
A Choice of Kipling's Prose, edited by W. Somerset Maugham.   1952; as *Maugham's Choice of Kipling's Best: Sixteen Stories,* 1953.
A Treasury of Short Stories.   1957.
(Short Stories), edited by Edward Parone.   1960.
Kipling Stories: Twenty-Eight Exciting Tales.   1960.
Famous Tales of India, edited by B.W. Shir-Cliff.   1962.
Phantoms and Fantasies: 20 Tales.   1965.
Twenty-One Tales, edited by Tim Wilkinson.   1972.
Tales of East and West, edited by Bernard Bergonzi.   1973.
Kipling's Kingdom: Twenty-Five of Rudyard Kipling's Best Indian Stories, Known and Unknown, edited by Charles Allen.   1987.

Novels

The Story of the Gadsbys: A Tale Without a Plot.   1888.
In Black and White.   1888.
Under the Deodars.   1888; revised edition, 1890.
The Light That Failed.   1890.
Mine Own People.   1891.
The Naulahka: A Story of West and East, with Wolcott Balestier.   1892.
Many Inventions.   1893.
The Day's Work.   1898.
Abaft the Funnel.   1909.

Fiction (for children)

The Jungle Book.   1894.
The Second Jungle Book.   1895; revised edition, 1895.
Captains Courageous: A Story of the Grand Banks.   1897.
Stalky & Co.   1899; revised edition, as *The Complete Stalky & Co.,* 1929.
Kim.   1901.
Just So Stories for Little Children, illustrated by Kipling.   1902.
Puck of Pook's Hill.   1906.
Kipling Stories and Poems Every Child Should Know, edited by Mary E. Burt and W. T. Chapin.   1909.
Rewards and Fairies.   1910.
Land and Sea Tales for Scouts and Guides.   1923.
Ham and the Porcupine.   1935.

Play

The Harbour Watch (produced 1913; revised version, as *Gow's Watch,* produced 1924).

Verse

Schoolboy Lyrics.   1881.
Echoes (published anonymously), with Alice Kipling. 1884.
Departmental Ditties and Other Verses.   1886; revised edition, 1890.
Departmental Ditties, Barrack-Room Ballads, and Other Verse.   1890.
Barrack-Room Ballads and Other Verses.   1892; as *Ballads and Barrack-Room Ballads,*   1892.
The Seven Seas.   1896.
Recessional.   1897.
An Almanac of Twelve Sports.   1898.
Poems, edited by Wallace Rice.   1899.
Recessional and Other Poems.   1899.
The Absent-Minded Beggar.   1899.
With Number Three, Surgical and Medical, and New Poems.   1900.
Occasional Poems.   1900.
The Five Nations.   1903.
The Muse among the Motors.   1904.
Collected Verse.   1907.
A History of England (verse only), with C.R.L. Fletcher. 1911; revised edition, 1930.
Songs from Books.   1912.
Twenty Poems.   1918.
The Years Between.   1919.
Verse: Inclusive Edition 1885–1918.   3 vols., 1919; revised edition, 1921, 1927, 1933.
A Kipling Anthology: Verse.   1922.
Songs for Youth, from Collected Verse.   1924.
A Choice of Songs.   1925.
Sea and Sussex.   1926.
St. Andrew's, with Walter de la Mare.   1926.
Songs of the Sea.   1927.
Poems 1886–1929.   3 vols., 1929.
Selected Poems.   1931.
East of Suez, Being a Selection of Eastern Verses.   1931.
Sixty Poems.   1939.
So Shall Ye Reap: Poems for These Days.   1941.
A Choice of Kipling's Verse, edited by T.S. Eliot.   1941.
Sixty Poems.   1957.
A Kipling Anthology, edited by W.G. Bebbington.   1964.
The Complete Barrack-Room Ballads, edited by Charles Carrington.   1973.
Kipling's English History: Poems, edited by Marghanita Laski.   1974.
Early Verse 1879–1889: Unpublished, Uncollected, and Rarely Collected Poems, edited by Andrew Rutherford. 1986.

Other

Quartette, with others.   1885.
The City of Dreadful Night and Other Sketches.   1890.
The City of Dreadful Night and Other Places.   1891.
The Smith Administration.   1891.
Letters of Marque.   1891; selections published 1891.
American Notes, with *The Bottle Imp,* by Robert Louis Stevenson.   1891.
Out of India: Things I Saw, and Failed to See, in Certain Days and Nights at Jeypore and Elsewhere.   1895.
The Kipling Birthday Book, edited by Joseph Finn.   1896.
A Fleet in Being: Notes of Two Trips with the Channel Squadron.   1898.
From to Sea to Sea: Letters of Travel.   2 vols., 1899; as *From Sea to Sea and Other Sketches,*   2 vols., 1900.
Works (Swastika Edition).   15 vols., 1899.

Letters to the Family (Notes on a Recent Trip to Canada). 1908.
The Kipling Reader (not same as 1900 collection of stories). 1912.
The New Army (6 pamphlets).   1914; as *The New Army in Training,*   1 vol., 1915.
France at War.   1915.
The Fringes of the Fleet.   1915.
Tales of The Trade.   1916.
Sea Warfare.   1916.
The War in the Mountains.   1917.
To Fighting Americans (speeches).   1918.
The Eyes of Asia.   1918.
The Graves of the Fallen.   1919.
Letters of Travel (1892–1913).   1920.
A Kipling Anthology: Prose.   1922.
Works (Mandalay Edition).   26 vols., 1925–26.
A Book of Words: Selections from Speeches and Addresses Delivered Between 1906 and 1927.   1928.
The One Volume Kipling.   1928.
Souvenirs of France.   1933.
A Kipling Pageant.   1935.
Something of Myself for My Friends Known and Unknown. 1937.
A Kipling Treasury: Stories and Poems.   1940.
Kipling: A Selection of His Stories and Poems, edited by John Beecroft.   2 vols., 1956.
The Kipling Sampler, edited by Alexander Greendale. 1962.
Letters from Japan, edited by Donald Richie and Yoshimori Harashima.   1962.
Pearls from Kipling, edited by C. Donald Plomer.   1963.
Kipling to Rider Haggard: The Record of a Friendship, edited by Morton Cohen.   1965.
The Best of Kipling.   1968.
Kipling's Horace, edited by Charles Carrington.   1978.
American Notes: Kipling's West, edited by Arrell M. Gibson.   1981.
O Beloved Kids: Kipling's Letters to His Children, edited by Elliot L. Gilbert.   1983.
Kipling's India: Uncollected Sketches 1884–1888, edited by Thomas Pinney.   1986.
The Illustrated Kipling, edited by Neil Philip.   1987.
Kipling's Japan, edited by Hugh Cortazzi and George Webb.   1988.
Something of Myself and Other Autobiographical Writings, edited by Thomas Pinney.   1990.
Letters, edited by Thomas Pinney.   1990— .

Editor, *The Irish Guards in the Great War.*   2 vols., 1923.

*

Bibliography: *Kipling: A Bibliographical Catalogue* by James McG. Stewart, edited by A.W. Keats, 1959; "Kipling: An Annotated Bibliography of Writings about Him" by H.E. Gerber and E. Lauterbach, in *English Fiction in Transition* 3, 1960, and 8, 1965.

Critical Studies: *Kipling: His Life and Work* by Charles Carrington, 1955, revised edition, 1978, as *The Life of Rudyard Kipling,* 1955; *Kipling* by Rosemary Sutcliff, 1960; *The Readers' Guide to Kipling's Work,* 1961, and *Kipling: The Critical Heritage,* 1971, both edited by Roger Lancelyn Green, and *Kipling and the Children* by Green, 1965; *Kipling's Mind and Art* edited by Andrew Rutherford, 1964; *Kipling and the Critics* edited by E.L. Gilbert,

1965; *Kipling* by J.I.M. Stewart, 1966; *Kipling: Realist and Fabulist* by Bonamy Dobrée, 1967; *Kipling and His World* by Kingsley Amis, 1975; *Kipling: The Glass, The Shadow, and the Fire* by Philip Mason, 1975; *The Strange Ride of Kipling: His Life and Works* by Angus Wilson, 1977; *Kipling* by Lord Birkenhead, 1978; *Kipling and Conrad: The Colonial Fiction* by John A. McClure, 1981; *Kipling* by James Harrison, 1982; *Kipling and the Fiction of Adolescence* by Robert F. Moss, 1982; *The Imperial Imagination: Magic and Myth in Kipling's India* by Lewis D. Wurgaft, 1983; *Kipling: Interviews and Recollections* edited by Harold Orel,   2 vols., 1983, and *A Kipling Chronology* by Orel, 1990; *A Kipling Companion* by Norman Page, 1984; *Kipling and Orientalism* by B.J. Moore-Gilbert, 1986; *From Palm to Pine: Kipling Abroad and at Home* by Marghanita Laski, 1987; *Kipling's Hidden Narratives* by Sandra Kemp, 1988; *Kipling* by Martin Seymour-Smith, 1989; *Kipling's Myths of Love and Death* by Nora Crook, 1989; *Kipling Considered* by Phillip Mallett, 1989; *Kipling's Indian Fiction* by Mark Paffard, 1989.

* * *

In October 1889, after seven years as a journalist in India, Rudyard Kipling returned to England determined to take the literary world by storm, and did just that. Six months later, in March 1890, he was the subject of a leading article in *The Times*: "the infant monster of a Kipling," Henry James called him. To his contemporaries, astonished at his precocity and his copiousness, the earlier stories seemed to derive from the journalism: smart, knowing, apparently realistic accounts of Anglo-Indian intrigues and flirtations, the many hardships and few pleasures of life in the barracks, the exotic but threatening world of native Indians. What strikes the modern reader, however, is rather the instability of these stories, figured in the way so many of them turn on disguise, or on lost or mistaken identities. "The Story of Morrowbie Jukes," in which an English civil engineer describes his entrapment in a sand-dune village of the living dead, is only the extreme instance of a recurrent sense of anxiety, the shifting narrative modes of the story—part nightmare Gothic, part documentary—miming the fear of dissolution which is also its subject. The epigraph to "Beyond the Pale" begins, "Love heeds not caste nor sleep a broken bed." The first sentence of the story proper reads: "A man should, whatever happens, keep to his own caste, race, and breed." This disjunction prepares for the way the story itself points to the gulf between what is so confidently known, and the impossibility of complete knowledge. The tension here between the apparent security of the narrative voice, and the sense of an India said and felt to be unknowable in Anglo-Indian terms, is one of the young Kipling's most powerful and unsettling effects. Where it is absent, other voices drowned out by the narrator's confidence, the stories shrink into yarns or anecdotes, their function merely to confirm author and reader as part of the same social and political enclave.

But Kipling's contemporaries were right to value the more overtly realist elements in these earlier stories, especially in those dealing with life in the barracks. Eighteen of these involve Kipling's "Soldiers Three," Mulvaney, Ortheris, and Learoyd: respectively Irish (sometimes stage-Irish), Cockney, and Yorkshireman. However right-wing his politics, Kipling as an artist was not afraid of the working class. He wrote of working-class life as directly as Gissing (in "Love-o'-Women" the eponymous hero dies of syphilis), but without Gissing's evident aversion. His use of the demotic, like Hardy's of the Wessex dialect, marks his sympathy with his characters, but Kipling felt less need than Hardy to remind his readers of the literary tradition (Shakespeare, Wordsworth) which sanctioned its use. "On Greenhow Hill" plays Learoyd's story of the thwarted love that drove him into the army against Ortheris's determination to shoot a native deserter. The violence, the poignancy, and the sense of waste, are all implicit in the end: Learoyd tossing aside the "scentless white violets" he had rooted up while recalling times past, Ortheris staring across the valley at his victim, shot dead from seven hundred yards, "with the smile of the artist who looks on the completed work." That last sentence wonderfully keeps the story free from condescension and sentimentality. If the brash imperialist voice which so outraged Max Beerbohm is sometimes evident in these stories, so too is a pre-Raphaelite—or Joycean—meticulousness of detail and economy of means.

The Indian stories, diverse as they are, have a number of recurring themes: the importance of work to one's sense of identity, the need to understand the codes that regulate one's society, the necessity for the young to undergo some kind of rites de passage. These are also the themes of Kipling's school stories, *Stalky & Co.*, and of *The Jungle Book* and *The Second Jungle Book*. The former sets out to subvert those works descending from *Tom Brown's Schooldays* and its successors, written to celebrate the public school ethos of cricket and the honour of the house. Kipling's "stalky" trio mock every aspect of this ethos, break all its rules, but do so, we realise, in order to find the bedrock of an authority to which they can pay more than lip service. At the heart of the book lies a clever if ultimately unpalatable redefinition of the ideas of service and Empire. The *Jungle Books* explore the paradox of the human need to obey some law (but Kipling writes of "the Law," the upper case willing it into existence), and the pain such obedience inevitably exacts. These are partly fables of adolescence, partly allegories of the "white man's burden," but both fable and allegory are subordinate, even to the adult reader, to the extraordinary richness with which Kipling imagines the Seonee jungle. *Puck of Pook's Hill* and *Rewards and Fairies,* also written for children, similarly review the themes of the Imperialist fiction—particularly the relation between heroism and sacrifice, leadership and martyrdom—but also celebrate an idea of England as the land, the healing power of a "clutch" of English earth, as Kipling began to root himself in Sussex. The best of these stories, such as "Cold Iron" and "Dymchurch Flit," shift disturbingly between the children's never-never land of old rural England, full of the smell of freshly-baked bread, and the agonised obedience to the demands of personal integrity in the tales recounted to them by the various figures called up from the past.

The Sussex setting, even in the stories addressed to adults, occasionally tempts Kipling to nostalgia. The all too charming "An Habitation Enforced" shows Kipling intent on becoming, as he put it, "one of the gentry," an insider in Sussex. The South African stories of the same period are generally harsher in tone and in subject. In "A Sahibs' War," for example, the story of a Sikh who defers reluctantly to the Sahibs' code prohibiting acts of personal vengeance, Kipling's sympathies are clearly with the outsider. Notoriously, when he came to treat this theme again, in the World War I story "Mary Postgate," he allowed Mary, unlike Umr Singh, to take her revenge, and indeed to delight in it ("She closed her eyes and drank it in"). Yet both characters are moved to hatred by a vision of love—

Umr Singh's for his Sahib, Mary's for her employer's nephew—and the power of the stories comes from the tension between the two kinds of impulse. One sees why T.S. Eliot wrote in the *Athenaeum* in 1919 that "the mind is not sufficiently curious, sufficiently brave to examine Mr. Kipling."

World War I (in which Kipling's son was killed, in 1915) seems to have released a new creative energy in Kipling. He had often written of the supernatural—sorcery ("The Mark of the Beast"), metempsychosis ("The Finest Story in the World"), and spiritual possession ("The House Surgeon")—and in the later stories this is often associated with healing, both physical and emotional. The Gardener, in the story of that name, who appears to Helen Turrell as she searches for the grave of her son is perhaps Christ; the farcical episode that restores Martin Ballart from shell shock is ascribed to Saint Jubanus; the doctors who save Mrs. Berners from death in the moving story "Unprofessional" have to rely on forces, or "tides," beyond the reach of scientific understanding. Edmund Wilson's view of the later Kipling as a man losing his hatred is overstated—the late revenge—farce "Beauty Spots" is an entirely unpleasant tale—but it is true that in the postwar stories Kipling's imaginative generosity appears in more startling forms. In "The Wish House," recounting the fiercely possessive yet utterly self-sacrificing love of Grace Ashcroft, her hope ("It *do* count, don't it—de pain?") demands our assent, as it does that of the author. In "Dayspring Mishandled" the apparent simplicities of revenge yield to a sense of the baffling complexity of human motivation, a compassionate awareness of character and destiny as "one long innuendo," endlessly defeating our attempts to explain and understand.

Kipling's more than three hundred stories exhibit a remarkable diversity of themes and interests. They also show an extraordinary technical versatility. Constrained at the beginning of his writing career by a limit of 2,000 words, he quickly developed the resources to extend his stories beyond their immediate meanings. In particular, he learned to use a prefatory epigraph (often, later, a poem of his own composition), or the frame surrounding the main body of the story, to hint at other possible perspectives, imaginative routes not taken. In the later stories, these devices serve to suggest that narrative can only partly order and control its material. The frame in "Mrs. Bathurst," by setting the narrators of a fragmented tale in a world of missed meetings and broken machinery, calls into question the reader's expectation of a single determinate explanation of events; similarly, the epigraph from Nodier used for "Dayspring Mishandled" hints at the destructive power of an obsessive love, but leaves it to the reader to decide with which of the characters in the story Nodier's verse is to be associated.

Kipling has always made the literary establishment uneasy. "The most complete man of genius . . . I have known," wrote Henry James to his brother, adding, "as distinct from fine intelligence." The nature of the genius, the quality of the intelligence, are, perhaps, questions with which criticism has not yet come to terms. It will have to do so: Kipling is our greatest storyteller.

—Phillip Mallett

See the essays on "Kaa's Hunting," "The Man Who Would Be King," "Mrs. Bathurst," and "They."

————

KIŠ, Danilo. Yugoslav. Born in Subotica, 22 February 1935. Educated at Belgrade University, degree in comparative literature 1958. Editor, *Vidici;* spent several years in France as lecturer in Serbo-Croat at various universities. Recipient: NIN prize, 1973; Goran prize, 1977. *Died October 1989.*

PUBLICATIONS

Short Stories

Rani jadi [Early Miseries].   1970.
Grobnica za Borisa Davidoviča.   1976; as *A Tomb for Boris Davidovich,* 1978.
Enciklopedija mrtvih.   1983; as *The Encyclopedia of the Dead,* 1989.

Novels

Mansarda; Psalam 44 [The Garret, Psalm 44].   1962.
Bašta, pepeo.   1965; as *Garden, Ashes,* 1976.
Peščanik.   1972; as *Hourglass,* 1990.

Plays

Elektra (produced 1969).
Noć i magla [Night and Mist] (includes *Papagaj* [The Parrot], *Drveni sanduk Tomasa Vulfa* [The Wooden Coffin of Thomas Wolfe], *Mehanički lavovi* [The Mechanical Lions]).   1983.

Other

Po-etika [Poetics] (essays).   2 vols., 1972–74.
Čas anatomije [The Anatomy Lesson] (essays).   1978.
Homo poeticus.   1983.
Sabrana dela [Collected Works].   10 vols., 1983.

Editor, with Mirjana Miočinović, *Sabrana dela* [Collected Works], by Lautréamont.   1964.

*

Bibliography: in *The Encyclopedia of the Dead,* 1989.

Critical Studies: "Imaginary-Real Lives: On Kiš" by Norbert Czarny, in *Cross Currents,* 1984; "Kiš: From 'Enchantment' to 'Documentation'" by Branko Gorjup, in *Canadian Slavic Papers,* December 1987; "Kiš: *Encyclopedia of the Dead*" by Predrag Matvejevic, in *Cross Currents,* 1988; "The Awakening of the Sleepers in Kiš's *Encyclopedia of the Dead* " by Jelena S. Bankovic-Rosul, in *Serbian Studies,* Spring 1990; "Kiš, 1935–1989" by Gyorgy Spiro, in *The New Hungarian Quarterly,* Autumn 1990.

* * *

Danilo Kiš was the son of a Hungarian Jew railroad official and a Greek-Orthodox mother from Montenegro. He spent his childhood in Novi Sad, until the family fled persecution to Western Hungary in 1942. His father was deported to Auschwitz in 1944. After the war Kiš studied at Belgrade, where he received the first degree granted in Comparative Literature in 1958. He published translations from French (Baudelaire, Lautrémont, Queneau) and Russian (Mandel'shtam, Zwetajewa). His literary debut was the novel *Mansarda* in 1962. Kiš taught Serbo-Croatian language and literature at Strassburg, Bordeaux, and Lille, then lived in Paris until his death from cancer in 1989 at age 54.

In France his work is compared with that of Nabokov and Borges, as well as to the nouveau roman, especially the novel *Peščanik (Hourglass)*; in the central European context one thinks of Bruno Schulz and Isaak Babel as kindred artists. The critic Predrag Matvejevic writes, "In the areas of policy and history he would, I believe, be a supporter of Orwell or Koestler's views."

Rane jadi (Early Miseries) was Kiš's first cycle of stories, which he wrote for "children and sensitive people." Not translated into English, it was the prototype for Kiš's thematic book of stories.

The collection of short fiction *Grobnica za Borisa Davidoviča* was published in Yugoslavia in 1976 and in the United States under the title *A Tomb for Boris Davidovich* two years later. It consists of seven stories, depicting the lives and the terrible deaths of seven men ranging from the Inquisition in France to Stalin's Russia, where most of the stories take place. All of the men who die are Jewish, all are radicals, revolutionaries, or postrevolutionary Communist officials. None of the characters is Yugoslavian; they are Russians, Poles, Rumanians, even beyond Eastern Europe, from Ireland and medieval France. The book was published in Yugoslavia only against great opposition, since it could be understood as an anti-Communist manifesto, and also because of still prevalent if latent anti-Semitic attitudes. The true grounds were masked by charges of plagiarism, as recounted by Joseph Brodsky and Ernst Pawel. Irving Howe called this book "absolutely first-rate . . . one of the best things I've ever seen on the whole experience of communism in Eastern Europe."

The collection is identified as a novel, despite the fact that all characters appear in but a single story and despite the wide range of the stories through space and time. Its subtitle "sedam poglavlja jedne zajednicke povesti" (Seven Chapters of a Single Story) is omitted in the English translation. Kiš thematic groupings of stories, which he called novels, were justified by him with reference to Babel's *Red Cavalry*, Sartre's *The Wall*, and Camus's *Exile and Kingdom*.

Despite the gruesome subject matter, the tone is ironic, full of understatement; Kiš is often pedantic in his reference to authentic or imaginary source materials, with what critic Zimmermann called a "fusion of explicit editorial commentary with poetic narration." In "The Mechanical Lions," an imaginary account of a visit by the French socialist leader Édouard Herriot to post-Revolutionary Russia, Kiš admits his sources are often fabrications, allowing the author "the deceptive idea that he is creating the world and thereby, as they say, changing it." In "The Mechanical Lions" only the Frenchman is an authentic historical personage; the story is devoted to an elaborate private staging of a religious service in the Cathedral of Saint Sofia to pander to the religious sensibilities of the Frenchman, perceived as a contradiction to his professed socialism. The later execution of the Russian planner of this deception is almost an afterthought, although it links the story with the others of horrible torture and death in the gulags of the Stalinist period: "After nine months of solitary confinement and dreadful torture, during which almost all his teeth were knocked out and his collarbone broken, Miksha finally asked to see the interrogator" (from "The Knife with the Rosewood Handle").

In the title story, the tortured Novsky, in an epic struggle with his interrogator, refuses to confess to imaginary crimes until his will is broken by having to witness a series of innocent young men being executed in his presence because of his resistance. Novsky dies much later in flight from a Siberian prison camp, at a foundry when he dives into a vat of molten steel to avoid being taken alive.

In "The Short Biography of A.A. Darmalatov" a Russian Jewish author dies a natural death, after selling out his personal integrity, publishing obsequious party-line works in order to survive. Naturally this exception to the pattern of torture and executions has a particular relevance to Kiš himself and his options as a writer in a Socialist country that sought adherence to doctrines and dogmas.

In "The Sow That Eats Her Farrow," Gould Verschoyle, an Irish leftist fighting in the Abraham Lincoln Brigade in the Spanish Civil War, is abducted to Russia and a prison camp where he dies trying to escape in 1945. His crime had been to assert that the Russians were trying to control the Republican side in the conflict (that is, he had been telling the truth).

The story "Psi i knjige" ("Dogs and Books") describes the slaughter of Jews who refused to convert to Christianity in Toulouse in 1330. The chief character Baruch David Neumann is related to the Russian character Boris Davidovich Novsky in Stalin's time by name and dates of arrest. In a note, the story is presented not as an original fictional work of Kiš, but as a found document, a chapter of a contemporary book on the Inquisition by the future pope Benedict XII. "Dogs and Books" is clearly meant to extend the topic of persecution (of Jews) on a religious or ideological basis back into history, as a general principle of Western behavior. But Kiš also remarked, "Jewishness here, as in my earlier books, is only an effect of defamiliarization. Whoever fails to understand this understands nothing of the mechanism of literary transposition."

The only other collection of short fiction by Kiš to be translated into English is *Enciklopedija mrtvih*, published in Zagreb in 1983. It appeared as *The Encyclopedia of the Dead* in New York in 1989. Here the title indicates the genre, but the random alphabetical order of an encyclopedia is belied by the single theme of death: "All the stories in this book to a greater or lesser degree reflect a theme to which I would refer as metaphysical; from the Gilgamesh epic, the question of death has been one of the obsessive themes of literature" (from "Postscript").

The Encyclopedia of the Dead comprises nine stories, and the "Post Scriptum" provides a tenth fictional text. *A Tomb for Boris Davidovich* also addressed the topic of death, but from the specific limited aspect of death as punishment meted out by the state in controlling the people; the novel *Hourglass* portrayed the persecution and death in the Holocaust of Kiš's own father, called Eduard Sam in Kiš's novel trilogy. Here Kiš undertakes an encyclopedic approach to death in its widest historical, mystical, and metaphysical dimensions. The time of the stories ranges from shortly after the death of Christ in Palestine through ancient settings in Syria, Anatolia, and Epheseus to modern Europe.

In the title story the female narrator gains access to the Royal Library in Sweden after hours, where she discovers a library dedicated to recording the death and the total previous lives of all those human beings left uncommemorated by history. The encyclopedia records begin shortly after 1789.

She rushes to the room with the records of her father, who recently died, and she experiences the events of his life in a vivid panorama of their family history, which literally springs from the page. The most minute details and facts not only from the life of the deceased but of those close to him are recorded in books chained to iron rings on the shelves. Leafing through one of the thousands of books under the letter M, the family name, she realizes that all famous persons are absent, although those famous persons she checks for are laughably obscure. Magically, the complete lives of countless millions of obscure humans have been preserved, have not been lost forever in the forward march of time. About some executions at the end of World War II, she writes, "For The Encyclopedia of the Dead, history is the sum of human destinies, the totality of ephemeral happenings. That it is why it records every action, every thought, every creative breath, every spot height in the survey, every shovelful of mud, every motion that cleared a brick from the ruins." Characteristically, Kiš has his female character seek the records of her deceased father, a project to which he himself devoted much of his creative energy, including a whole trilogy of novels.

In the concluding postscript, along with many pseudoreferences and bibliographical notes, Kiš claims that he later discovered that such an immense library actually exists, a project by the Mormon Church in Utah to record the names—they have reached 18 billion—of all human beings living and dead, on microfilm.

"The Legend of Sleepers" is an account, based on Christian, Talmudic, and Moslem sources, of a group of young men who flee from persecution, sleep in a cave for three hundred years, awake for a time, only to die again. Resurrection of the dead in Kiš's version is made possible by love: in one of the sleepers there has remained the memory of a princess. After a dreamy visit to the living, the men are buried again in their cave.

Another fantastic story is "Simon Magnus," a religious mystic and magician competing against the early Christians in Palestine. Challenged by Peter, Simon is able to ascend into the heavens physically, enabled by a great vision of the horror of the human condition, the suffering of all living things, only to fall dead to the earth. Seeking a further miracle, the people dig him up again after three days, only to find a putrefying corpse. According to his follower the prostitute Sophia, this is a final proof of the correctness of his teachings: "man's life is decay and perdition, and the world is in the hands of tyrants."

Other stories treat premonitions of death of loved ones: "The Mirror of the Unknown" and "The Story of the Master and the Disciple," a fictitious account of the genealogy of the infamous Protocols of the Elders of Zion ("The Book of Kings and Fools"). There is even a parody of scholarly research, petty and pedantic, in "Red Stamps with Lenin's Picture," in which the brief love of a deceased famous man, Mendel Osipovich, a Stalinist victim, claims her place in the footnotes of literary history. Thus the Encyclopedia collection ends in a comic vein.

—Russell E. Brown

KLEIST, (Bernd) Heinrich (Wilhelm) von. German. Born in Frankfurt an der Oder, Brandenburg (now Germany), 18 October 1777. Entered the Prussian army in 1792; took part in the seige of Mainz, 1793, promoted to second lieutenant, 1799, resigned his commission, 1799. Studied under Professor Wünsch, University of Frankfurt, 1799. Travelled throughout Germany, and to Paris and Switzerland, 1800–04; attempted to join the French army, 1803; civil servant, Königsberg, 1805–06; co-founder, with Adam Müller, and editor, *Phöbus,* Dresden, 1808–09; attempted unsuccessfully to publish the newspaper *Germania,* in Prague, 1809; editor, and *Berliner Abendblätter,* 1808–11. Suffered many nervous breakdowns. *Died (suicide) 21 November 1811.*

PUBLICATIONS

Collections

Hinterlassene Schriften, edited by Ludwig Tieck.   1821.
Gesammelte Schriften, edited by Ludwig Tieck.   3 vols., 1826.
Werke, edited by Erich Schmidt and others.   5 vols., 1904–05; revised edition,   7 vols., 1936–38.
Sämtliche Werke und Briefe, edited by Helmut Sembdner.   2 vols., 1961.

Short Stories

Erzählungen.   2 vols., 1810–11.
Michael Kohlhaas (in English).   1844.
The Marquise of O. and Other Stories.   1960.

Plays

Die Familie Schroffenstein (produced 1804).   1803; as *The Feud of the Schroffensteins,* 1916.
Amphitryon (produced 1899).   1807; translated as *Amphitryon,* 1974; in *Five Plays,* 1988.
Der zerbrochene Krug (produced 1808).   1811; as *The Broken Pitcher,* 1961; as *The Broken Jug,* in *Four Continental Plays,* edited by John P. Allen, 1964; in *Five Plays,* 1988.
Penthesilea (produced 1876).   1808; translated as *Penthesilea,* in *The Classic Theater,* edited by Eric Bentley, 1959; in *Five Plays,* 1988.
Das Käthchen von Heilbronn (produced 1810).   1810; as *Kate of Heilbronn,* in *Illustrations of German Poetry,* 1841; as *Käthchen of Heilbronn; or, the Test of Fire,* in *Fiction and Fantasy of German Literature,* 1927.
Prinz Friedrich von Homburg (produced 1821).   In *Hinterlassene Schriften,* 1821; as *The Prince of Homburg,* 1956; in *The Classic Theater,* edited by Eric Bentley, 1959; as *Prince Frederick of Homburg,* 1988.
Die Hermannsschlacht (produced 1839).   In *Hinterlassene Schriften,* 1821.
Robert Guiskard (unfinished; produced 1901).   In *Gesammelte Schriften,* 1826; as *A Fragment of the Tragedy of Robert Guiscard,* in *Five Plays,* 1988.
Five Plays (includes *Amphitryon; The Broken Jug; Penthesilea; Prince Frederick of Homburg; A Fragment of the Tragedy of Robert Guiscard*).   1988.

Other

Briefe an seine Schwester Ulrike, edited by August Koberstein.   1860.
Briefe an seine Braut, edited by Karl Biedermann and others.   1884.

Lebensspuren: Dokumente und Berichte der Zeitgenossen,
edited by Helmut Sembdner.   1964.

Über das Marionettentheater: Aufsätze und Anekdoten,
edited by Helmut Sembdner.   1935; revised edition,
1980; as *On a Theatre of Marionettes,* 1989; as *On
Puppetshows,* 1991.

An Abyss Deep Enough: Letters of Kleist, with essays, edited
by Philip B. Miller.   1982.

*

Critical Studies: *Reason and Energy* by Michael Hamburger, 1957; *Kleist's Dramas* by E.L. Stahl, 1961; *Kleist: Studies in His Work and Literary Character* by Walter Silz, 1961; *Kleist's "Prinz Friedrich von Homburg": An Interpretation Through Word Patterns* by Mary Garland, 1968; *Kleist: A Study in Tragedy and Anxiety* by John Gearey, 1968; *Kleist's Prinz Friedrich von Homburg,* 1970, and *Kleist,* 1979, both by J.M. Ellis; *From Lessing to Hauptmann: Studies in German Drama* by Ladislaus Löb, 1974; *The Major Works of Kleist* by R.E. Helbling, 1975; *Kleist and the Tragic Ideal* by H.M. Brown, 1977; *The Stories of Kleist* by Denys Dyer, 1977; *Kleist: Word into Flesh: A Poet's Quest for the Symbol* by Ilse Graham, 1977; *Kleist: A Biography* by Joachim Maass, translated by Ralph Manheim, 1983; *Desire's Sway: The Plays and Stories of Kleist* by James M. McGlathery, 1983; *Spirited Women Heroes: Major Female Characters in the Dramas of Goethe, Schiller and Kleist* by Julie D. Prandi, 1983; *Prison and Idylls: Studies in Kleist's Fictional World* by Linda Dietrick, 1985; *Kleist: A Critical Study* by Raymond Cooke, 1987; *The Manipulation of Reality in Works by Kleist* by Robert E. Glenny, 1987; *Kafka's Prusian Advocate: The Influence of Kleist on Franz Kafka* by John M. Grandin, 1987; *In Pursuit of Power: Kleist's Machiavellian Protagonists,* 1987, *Kleist's Aristocratic Heritage and Das Käthchen von Heilbronn,* 1991, and *Kleist on Stage, 1804–1987,* 1993, all by William C. Reeve; *Laughter, Comedy and Aesthetics: Kleist's Der zerbrochene Krug* by Mark G. Ward, 1989.

*   *   *

Heinrich von Kleist's standing in this century may only be a little short of adulation—Franz Kafka thought his work close to perfection and Thomas Mann considered him Germany's writer of genius—yet at the time of Kleist's suicide in 1811 contemporaries held the view of him propagated by Goethe, namely that Kleist's work was the product of a diseased mind. The contents of Kleist's handful of short prose pieces constituting his claim to being the finest short prose writer in the German language are indeed marked by the most explosive and violent spectrum of emotions and actions: brutal murders, sex crimes, hideous acts of revenge, the destruction of entire populations, race warfare, the slaughtering of innocent babes, and the rewarding of deeds of love by deeds of hate are the staple fare of his stories. A sensitive reading, however, quickly dispels the belief that Kleist is simply pandering to a mindless fascination with anarchy and evil. Behind all these prose works resides the response of a man who may best be regarded as the greatest casualty of the collapse of Enlightenment optimism. Raised in a belief in the perfectibility of humanity, Kleist encountered Kant's writing at the beginning of the 19th century and found all his convictions shattered in a Kantian philosophy that demonstrated the

limitations of human knowledge. At the heart of Kleist's prose writing is the discovery he confessed to his fiancée after reading Kant: "We cannot decide if that which we call truth is indeed truth or if it simply seems to be." In all Kleist's stories there is a dichotomy between appearance and truth. The natural disaster at the beginning of "The Earthquake in Chile" allows Jerónimo to flee prison; it appears as a divine act of intervention on his behalf, but it in fact marks the beginning of a far greater chain of disasters to come. In "The Foundling" the virtuous Elvire appears to have a lover in her room, whist in "The Duel" the noble-minded Friedrich appears to have lost the combat to the evil Count Jakob, yet it is ultimately the latter who succumbs to an apparently minor wound. And in "St. Cecilia or the Power of Music" the reader is invited to believe that the divine music that protected a convent from desecration was not conducted by Sister Antonia but by the saint who has taken on the appearance of that sister.

Acting on the strength of what they perceive to be true leads people to make hideous mistakes, thus in "The Betrothal in Santo Domingo" Gustav murders his lover Toni because he thinks he has seen her betraying him, but her actions were in fact a courageous rouse to save Gustav and his companions. Once made aware of the true situation, Gustav's reaction is pure Kleistian: he blows his own brains out.

Throughout Kleist's stories can be encountered the expression "by chance." It adds to the world of appearance a crushing dimension of apparent arbitrariness governing human existence. An identical act can lead to a belief in a world of absolute good or of absolute evil, thus in "The Earthquake in Chile" the adoption of a child at the end of a story of unmitigated horror leaves an impression that human kindness may have triumphed, but a similar act of adoption at the beginning of "The Foundling" unleashes a sequence of events that leaves the most benign of men an avenging, God-defying monster. Chance permits Kleist to introduce at every stage of his narrative sudden, dramatic changes; powerful—and often overpowering—changes or reversals of fortunes, often based on erroneous perceptions, plunge characters into greater depths of despair or momentarily elate them before their illusory hopes are crushed. Yet it would be a misreading to see his stories as essentially dramatic concepts rendered down into the short prose form, for Kleist's use of language demonstrates that these stories are neither the work of an epic writer nor a dramatist, even though Kleist the dramatist stands alongside both Goethe and Schiller as having the most profound influence upon the German theatre. As a storyteller Kleist made unrivalled use of the hypotactic possibilities of the German language. He is unmatched in the exploitation of the language's natural tendency to grammatical subordination; his sentences almost collapse under their own weight, as by use of hypotaxis he offers further information, detail, and qualifying comments. It is the prose form itself that his stories celebrate, and the psychological and metaphysical insights he offers are won as much by means of syntax and linguistic juxtaposition as by the plots of the stories themselves. To the unwary reader, however, the deliberate chronicler tone adopted in his stories can be misleading. The archaic, and seemingly unpolished, even clumsy, narrative voice belies Kleist's achievement of raising the short prose form in German to an unparalleled tool for probing the darkest recesses of humans' mind in an age that had lost its naive confidence in a loving God. Understandably, a genre that is so deeply located within its own structure and language, as Kleist's stories undoubtedly are, does not lend itself easily to adaptation to other forms, such as film, or to translation into other languages, and perhaps for this reason Kleist's influence on the development of the short prose form in European literature has not been as marked as his standing within German literature might suggest.

—Anthony Bushell

See the essays on "The Marquise of O" and "Michael Kohlhass."

KUNDERA, Milan. Czech and French. Born in Brno, Czechoslovakia, 1 April 1929; emigrated to France, 1975; became French citizen, 1981. Educated at Charles University, Prague; Academy of Music and Dramatic Arts Film Faculty, Prague, 1956. Married Věra Hrabánková in 1967. Assistant professor of film, Academy of Music and Dramatic Arts, 1958–69; professor of comparative literature, University of Rennes, France, 1975–80; since 1980, professor, École des Hautes Études, Paris. Member of the editorial board, *Literární Noviny,* 1963–68, and *Literární Listy,* 1968–69. Recipient: Writers' Publishing House prize, 1961, 1969; Klement Lukeš prize, 1963; Union of Czechoslovak Writers' prize, 1968; Médicis prize (France), 1973; Mondello prize (Italy), 1978; Commonwealth award (U.S.), 1981; Europa prize, 1982; Los Angeles *Times* award, 1984; Jerusalem prize, 1984; Académie Française Critics prize, 1987; Nelly Sachs prize, 1987; Osterichischeve State prize, 1987; *Independent* award for foreign fiction (U.K.), 1991. Honorary doctorate: University of Michigan, Ann Arbor, 1983. Member, American Academy. Lives in Paris.

PUBLICATIONS

Short Stories

Směšné lásky [Laughable Loves]; *Druhý sešit směšných lásek* [A Second Book of Laughable Loves]; *Třetí sešit směšných lásek* [A Third Book of Laughable Loves]. 3 vols., 1963–69; revised and collected as *Směšné lásky,* 1970; as *Laughable Loves,* 1974.

Novels

Zert. 1967; as *The Joke,* 1969; revised translation, by the author, 1992.
La Vie est ailleurs. 1973; as *Life Is Elsewhere,* 1974; as *Život de jinde,* 1979.
La Valse aux adieux. 1976; as *The Farewell Party,* 1976; as *Valčík na rozloučenou,* 1979.
Le Livre du rire et de l'oubli. 1979; as *The Book of Laughter and Forgetting,* 1980; as *Kniha smíchu a zapomnění,* 1981.
L'Insoutenable Légéreté de l'être. 1984; as *The Unbearable Lightness of Being,* 1984; as *Nesnesitelná lehkost bytí,* 1985.
L'Immortalité. 1990; as *Immortality,* 1991.

Plays

Majitelé klíču [The Owners of the Keys] (produced 1962). 1962.

Dvě uši dvě svatby [Two Ears and Two Weddings]. 1968; as *Ptákovina* [Cock-a-Doodle-Do] (produced 1969).
Jakub a pán (produced 1980); as *Jacques et son maître: Hommage à Denis Diderot* (produced 1981), 1981; as *Jacques and His Master,* (produced 1985), 1985.

Screenplays: *Nikdo se nebude smát* [No Laughing Matter], 1965; *Zert* [The Joke], from his own novel, with Jaromil Jires, 1968; *Já Truchlivý Bůh* [I the Sad God], 1969.

Verse

Clověk zahrada širá [Man: A Broad Garden]. 1953.
Poslední máj [The Last May]. 1955; revised edition, 1961, 1963.
Monology [Monologues]. 1957; revised edition, 1964, 1965, 1967, 1969.

Other

L'Art du roman (essays). 1986; as *The Art of the Novel,* 1988.

*

Bibliography: *Kundera: An Annotated Bibliography* by Glen Brand, 1988.

Critical Studies: *Kundera: A Voice from Central Europe* by Robert Porter, 1981; "Kundera: Dialogues with Fiction" by Peter Kussi, in *World Literature Today,* Spring 1983; "Czech Angels," in *Hugging the Store: Essays and Criticism* by John Updike, 1983; "Between East and West: A Letter to Kundera" by Robert Boyers, in *Atrocity and Amnesia, The Political Novel Since 1945,* 1985; "The Open Letter to Kundera" by Norman Podhoretz, in *The Bloody Crossroads,* 1986; "Kundera Issue" of *Salmagundi* 73, 1987; *Terminal Paradox: The Novels of Kundera* by Maria Němcová Banerjee, 1989; "Kundera Issue" of *Review of Contemporary Fiction* 9(2), Summer 1989; *Kundera and the Art of the Fiction* edited by Aron Aji, 1992.

*   *   *

Milan Kundera, renowned writer, playwright, and innovator of the novel, is of Czech origin. Born in the Moravian city of Brno in 1929, he published his first literary works in Czechoslovakia in the 1950's and 1960's. His opinions and convictions made him a spokesman for more artistic and political freedom during the Prague Spring of 1968. After the Soviet invasion, when the "normalization" process began, Kundera was banned from publication. His works were blacklisted and removed from libraries and bookstores. Kundera was forbidden to travel to the West. In 1975 he was invited to France and offered the position of assistant professor at the University of Rennes. He was granted permission to leave Czechoslovakia. However, in 1979 he was stripped of his state citizenship. Thus exiled, Kundera settled permanently in Paris, where he has been writing his fiction in Czech and essays in French. His subsequent novels have been first published by the French publishing house Gallimard in French translation and then in Czech original by the dissident Sixty-Eight Publishers of Toronto. After the political changes of 1989, Kundera has visited Czechoslovakia, but his decision to remain in

France is definite. He says that there he has found a permanent home.

Like other Czech writers forced into emigration by the political and historical circumstances after 1968, Kundera has found that many critics focus on the political context of his work. Kundera always disliked being labelled a dissident writer; when, during a 1980 television discussion *Zert (The Joke)* was referred to as "a major indictment of Stalinism," he said, "Spare me your Stalinism, please. *The Joke* is a love story." More than a description of life under Communism, Kundera's works are a statement about the modern world. As a whole, they can be seen as variations on what Peter Kussi called the themes of "awareness and self-deception, the power of human lucidity and its limits, the games of history and love," and what David Lodge called "the problematic interrelationship of sex, love, death and the ultimate mystery of being itself."

Kundera's literary reputation rests on his achievement as a novelist. Though at the beginning of his career Kundera did write some poetry, he later renounced this genre completely. Poetry, drama, or the novel are not merely artistic genres for Kundera; he said, "they are existential categories." Inherent in the lyrical mode are the dangers of narcissistic self-contemplation and emotion elevated to the only criterion of truth. Lyricism is a kind of permanent adolescence, a "state of passionate lyrical enthusiasm which, getting drunk on its frenzy, is unable to see the real world through its own grandiose haze." Thus it excludes the features of "mature mentality" like skepticism, irony, wit, or humor. The totalitarian world is like adolescence. It takes itself too seriously because it cannot tolerate humor. Humor is relativist, humor questions and mistrusts.

Kundera's first book of fiction is a collection of three short stories entitled *Směšné lásky* (Laughable Loves), published in 1963. It was followed by *Druhý sešit směšných lásek* (The Second Book of Laughable Loves) and *Třetí sešit směšných lásek* (The Third Book of Laughable Loves). By eliminating several of the original stories and changing their order, Kundera produced in 1970 the version that was subsequently published in France and was taken as the basis for the American translation of *Laughable Loves* in 1974. (The editors have changed the order of the stories again, and, in Kundera's opinion, their adaptation is not very fortunate.) *Laughable Loves* is Kundera's only collection of short stories. *Le Livve du rire et de l'oubli (The Book of Laughter and Forgetting)* may also be read as a collection of short stories, since its seven parts have different plots and characters. However, Kundera himself insists that this work is a novel and says that "the unity of a book need not stem from the plot, but can be provided by the theme." In this case the theme is the process of forgetting, of personal and collective historical amnesia, and its effects on individuals and whole nations.

In *Laughable Loves*, we have Kundera's writing at its best—with his fine instinct for detail, wry humor, comic situations, witty and ironic dialogue, biting satire, and subtle philosophizing. But amidst the humor there is an underlying melancholy and pessimism.

Most of the stories are built around the theme of seduction or erotic adventure. Erotic passion is a theme that permeates nearly all of Kundera's writing; it is seen as a crisis situation that discloses in human behavior all that is irrational and paradoxical about life.

In a world that calls for rigid morality, sex can be seen as a liberating act of rebellion against authority. Eroticism is put in opposition with sterility, just as humor is contrasted with seriousness, memory with forgetting. Trapped by circumstances and forces beyond their control, the characters try to free themselves by irresponsibility. "Womanizing" is for the male characters an expression of their "unseriousness" and a form of escape from their narrow existence. But the comedy is not joyful or, indeed, liberating. The men do not achieve their goals. Laughter and sex cannot bear the weight of being the tools for achieving personal freedom. The sexual adventure turns into a painful experience and the practical joke turns into a trap that confines the joker instead of liberating him.

In "Nobody Will Laugh," a university professor who decides to play a trick on a pathetic would-be scholar ends by being abandoned by everybody—including his beautiful mistress. She is unable to distinguish between private decency and public deception, and she leaves him "because a man who lies can't be respected by any woman." In the characters Dr. Havel ("Symposium" and "Dr. Havel After Ten Years") and Martin ("The Golden Apple of Eternal Desire"), Kundera has created the continuation of the Don Juan myth by supplanting the image of "The Great Conqueror" with that of "The Great Collector." They are both compulsive womanizers for whom the consummation itself has lost all attraction. It is the erotic chase alone that matters; even the means have become mechanical. Martin uses the depersonalized terms "registrace" (registration) and "kontaktáž" (contact) to describe the two stages of his method. The heroes realize their situation: "What does it matter that it's a futile game? What does it matter that I *know* it? Will I stop playing the game just because it is futile?," muses the unnamed hero of "The Golden Apple of Eternal Desire." The game, bringing memories of past freedom, must go on.

—Soňa Nováková

See the essay on "The Hitchhiking Game."

L

LAGERKVIST, Pär (Fabian). Swedish. Born in Växjo, 23 May 1891. Educated at the University of Uppsala, 1911–12. Married 1) Karen Dagmar Johanne Sørensen in 1918 (divorced 1925); 2) Elaine Luella Hallberg in 1925. Theatre critic, *Svenska Dagbladet*, Stockholm, 1919. Recipient: Samfundet De Nio prize. 1928; Bellman prize, 1945; Saint-Beuve prize, 946; Foreign Book prize (France), 1951; Nobel prize for literature, 1951. Honorary degree: University of Gothenburg, 1941. Member, Swedish Academy of Literature, 1940. *Died 11 July 1974.*

PUBLICATIONS

Short Stories

Två sagor om livet [Two Tales about Life]. 1913.
Järn och människor [Iron and People]. 1915.
Onda sagor [Evil Tales]. 1924.
Kämpande ande [Struggling Soul]. 1930; translated in part as *Masquerade of Souls*, 1954.
I den tiden [At That Time]. 1935.
The Eternal Smile and Other Stories. 1954.
The Marriage Feast and Other Stories. 1955.
Five Early Works (selection; bilingual edition). 1989.

Novels

Människor [People]. 1912.
Det eviga leendet. 1920; as *The Eternal Smile*, 1934.
Bödeln. 1933; as *The Hangman*, in *Guest of Reality*, 1936.
Dvärgen. 1944; as *The Dwarf*, 1945.
Barabbas. 1950; translated as *Barabbas*, 1951.
Sibyllan. 1956; as *The Sibyl*, 1958.
Pilgrimen. 1966.
  Ahasverus' död. 1960; as *The Death of Ahasuerus*, 1962.
  Pilgrim på havet. 1962; as *Pilgrim at Sea*, 1964.
  Det heliga landet. 1964; as *The Holy Land*, 1966.
Mariamne. 1967; as *Herod and Mariamne*, 1968.

Plays

Sista Mänskan [The Last Man]. 1917.
Teater: Den svåra stunden; Modern teater: Synpunkter och angrepp [The Difficult Hour; Points of View and Attack] (produced 1918). 1918; essay and play translated in *Modern Theatre*, 1966.
Himlens hemlighet (produced 1921). In *Kaos*, 1919; as *The Secret of Heaven*, in *Modern Theatre*, 1966.
Den osynlige [The Invisible One] (produced 1924). 1923.
Gäst hos verkligheten. 1925; as *Guest of Reality*, 1936.
Han som fick leva om sitt liv (produced 1928). 1928; as *The Man Who Lived His Life Over*, in *Five Scandinavian Plays*, 1971.

Konungen (produced 1950). 1932; as *The King*, in *Modern Theatre*, 1966.
Bödeln, from his own novel (produced 1934). In *Dramatik*, 1946; as *The Hangman*, in *Modern Theatre*, 1966.
Mannen utan själ (produced 1938). 1936; as *The Man Without a Soul*, in *Scandinavian Plays of the Twentieth Century 1*, 1944.
Seger i mörker [Victory in Darkness] (produced 1940). 1939.
Midsommardröm i fattighuset (produced 1941). 1941; as *Midsummer Dream in the Workhouse*, 1953.
Dramatik. 1946.
Den vises sten (produced 1948). 1947; as *The Philosopher's Stone*, in *Modern Theatre*, 1966.
Låt människan leva (produced 1949). 1949; as *Let Man Live*, in *Scandinavian Plays of the Twentieth Century 3*, 1951.
Barabbas, from his own novel (produced 1953). 1953.
Modern Theatre: Seven Plays and an Essay. 1966.

Verse

Motiv [Motifs]. 1914.
Ångest [Anguish]. 1916.
Den lyckliges väg [Happy Road]. 1921.
Hjärtats sånger [Songs of the Heart]. 1926.
Vid lägereld [By the Campfire]. 1932.
Genius. 1937.
Sång och strid [Song and Battle]. 1940.
Dikter [Verse]. 1941; revised edition, 1958, 1974.
Hemmet och stjärnan [The Home and the Stars]. 1942.
Aftonland. 1953; as *Evening Land*, 1975.
Valda dikter [Selected Poems]. 1967.

Other

Ordkonst och bildkonst [Word Art and Picture Art]. 1913.
Kaos [Chaos]. 1919.
Det besegrade livet [The Conquered Life]. 1927.
Skrifter [Writings]. 3 vols., 1932.
Den knutna näven [The Clenched Fist]. 1934.
Den befriade människan [Liberated Man]. 1939.
Prosa. 5 vols., 1945; revised edition, 1949.
Antecknat [Noted] (diary), edited by Elin Lagerkvist. 1977.

*

Bibliography: *Lagerkvist in Translation* by A. Ryberg, 1964.

Critical Studies: *Lagerkvist: An Introduction* by Irene Scobbie, 1963, and "Lagerkvist," in *Essays on Swedish Literature from 1880 to the Present Day* edited by Scobbie, 1978; *Lagerkvist: A Critical Essay* by Winston Weathers,

1968; Lagerkvist Supplement, in *Scandinavica*, 1971; *Lagerkvist* by Robert Spector, 1973; *Lagerkvist* by Leif Sjöberg, 1976; *Lagerkvist in America* by Ray Lewis White, 1979.

* * *

Pär Lagerkvist was successful as a lyric poet, playwright, and prose writer, and between 1912 and 1935 he produced several prose sketches and short stories in a variety of styles.

His first prose work, *Människor* (People), was written when Lagerkvist was in a rebellious mood. His early protests were not just left-wing political outcries but also the more personal reactions of a young man who had lost his faith and was desperately seeking a substitute. His story is a *sturm und drang* account of two brothers, the demonic, decadent Gustav at odds with his family and life generally, and Erik, a gentle dutiful home-loving son. An immature and ultimately unsuccessful work, it nevertheless contains the true Lagerkvistian elements: an intense portrayal of angst, defiance and despair, and a study in contrasts both in character and style.

In 1913 Lagerkvist visited Paris and came into contact with modern artists. He greatly admired cubist painters, particularly Picasso and Braque, and sought to adapt their principles to literature. That year he produced the tract *Ordkonst och bildkonst* (Word Art and Picture Art), in which he maintains that, like modern painters, writers should strive for simplicity of both style and content, "simple thoughts, uncomplicated emotions in the face of the eternal powers of life: sorrow and gladness, awe, reverence, love and hate, an expression of the universal which rises above the individual."

His first substantial attempt to exemplify these tenets was five short stories entitled *Järn och människor* (Iron and People). The subject in each case is the effects of war on human emotions, and the aesthetic aim is to show the contrast between iron, or weapons, and human flesh. In all five stories the characters are brought to a point where because of war their two basic emotions, love and hate, are brought into conflict, leading to a crisis in which either hatred conquers and leads to destruction, or love triumphs and brings about reconciliation.

Everything in the stories is subject to the discipline of the overall aesthetic pattern, but in some places one senses Lagerkvist's difficulty in restraining strong emotions. By 1916 those emotions were given freer rein as he struggled to come to terms with a seemingly purposeless world of mindless destruction. In this expressionistic phase Lagerkvist published a work entitled *Kaos* (Chaos) comprising a one-act play, a cycle of poems and a prose passage called "Den fordringsfulle gästen." Told in the first person, the latter is a parable on modern life. A traveller is on a short visit; he has a great deal to make sense of but "everything here is in such damned disorder." The hotel symbolises the chaotic world as Lagerkvist experienced it, while the other characters are all absorbed in their own affairs, presenting a confusing world without a focal point. The narrator in his anguish is assertive, demanding in strident language his rights, but he is humiliated and finally sees that he has no rights at all. The feeling of alienation is complete when he realises his insignificance in a vast universe. He leaves the chaotic scene and goes off into the darkness, arousing not the slightest interest among the other characters.

With the end of the war and a resolution of his marital problems in the early 1920's Lagerkvist moved from a denial to an acceptance of life. That goodness and human spirit can rise above adversity is partly reflected in *Onda sagor* (Evil Tales) where, admittedly, the dominant strain is misanthropic and shows little evidence of human dignity. "En hjältes död" ("Death of a Hero") ironically features a man pandering to the public's desire for sensationalism and record-breaking; Frälsar-Johan (John the Saviour) in the story of that name is an idiot who believes he is the Saviour and dies trying to rescue people from a burning old people's home—which is empty anyway. The autobiographical "Far och jag" ("Father and I") captures the moment when the young boy realises he is alone in a frightening and chaotic universe; "Hissen som gick ner i helvete" ("The Lift that Went down to Hell") deals with a philanderer so urbane that even being taken down to hell, described with nightmarish clarity, evokes a shallow reaction. "Källarvåningen" ("The Basement"), however, shows a positive attitude to life. The crippled Lindgren lives on charity in a poor basement, but is content with his lot for he lives literally and metaphorically on the goodness of others.

Lagerkvist had great sympathy with simple, unassuming people, a point borne out in "Bröllopsfesten" ("The Wedding Feast"), the first of four long-short stories with the general title *Kämpande ande* (Struggling Soul). Frida, a rather elderly, plain spinster who owns a little shop, is to marry Jonas, a slightly retarded porter. They no doubt make a ludicrous couple and Lagerkvist includes amusing details, such as Frida insisting on a fine bridal crown. Making love after the wedding Frida accidently bites Jonas with her false teeth: "She was rather surprised herself immediately afterwards. But it was love talking." Lagerkvist records the affair with warmth and affection, however, and shows that two lonely love-hungry souls finding each other is an occasion for happiness, not ridicule. In "Guds lille handelsresande" ("God's Little Travelling Salesman") the erring Emanual Olsson succumbs to alcohol and is saved by the Salvation Army. The search for a spiritual life is also the subject of "Själarnas maskerad," where the relationship between a businessman and a beautiful but lame woman constitutes love in its most idealistic form. However, it all takes place in the "land of souls," a land of "perpetual feasting." This is how life and love could be if our souls could escape life's paralysing trivialities. The philosophical questioning continues in "Uppbrottet" ("The Departure"), an inner monologue by a doctor who knows he is terminally ill. He discerns an afterlife but feels that the human conception of God gets in the way.

Always aware of political trends, Lagerkvist quickly reacted to the rise of totalitarianism in the 1930's. *I den tiden* (At that time) highlight its dangers in short stories showing Lagerkvist's sustained irony at its best. In "Det lilla fälttåget" ("The Tiny Tots' Campaign") the horrors of war and the pompous love of victory parades are heightened by the Swiftian device of allowing the "men" to be children going bravely into battle "armed to their milk teeth." A clever dual effect is achieved by following this with "Det märkvärdiga landet" ("The Strange Country"), the only democracy left in the world. Tourists visit it and marvel at people who are not regimented and whose thoughts and actions are embarrassingly vague in discussions about culture. The tourists enjoy the novel experience—"but it was lovely to be home again all the same."

Lagerkvist published no more short stories after 1935, but by then he had shown his mastery of the genre and had fashioned it to convey the essential dualism that runs through all his work, his constant quest for the purpose of life and a desire to fathom the fundamental good and evil aspects of humanity.

—Irene Scobbie

See the essay on "Father and I."

————

LARDNER, Ring(gold Wilmer). American. Born in Niles, Michigan, 6 March 1885. Educated at Niles High School, graduated 1901; Armour Institute of Technology (now Illinois Institute of Technology), Chicago, 1901–02. Married Ellis Abbott in 1911; four sons. Freight clerk, bookkeeper, and employee of Niles Gas Company, 1902–05; reporter, South Bend *Times,* Indiana, 1905–07; sportswriter, *Inter Ocean,* Chicago, 1907, Chicago *Examiner,* 1908, and Chicago *Tribune,* 1908–10; managing editor, *Sporting News,* St. Louis, 1910–11; sports editor, Boston *American,* 1911, Chicago *American,* 1911–12, and Chicago *Examiner,* 1912–13; columnist ("In the Wake of the News"), Chicago *Tribune,* 1913–19; moved to Long Island, New York, 1919; columnist ("Weekly Letter"), 1919–27, and wrote *You Know Me Al* comic strip, 1922–25, both for the Bell Syndicate; radio reviewer, *The New Yorker,* 1932–33. *Died 25 September 1933.*

PUBLICATIONS

Collections

The Lardner Reader, edited by Maxwell Geismar.   1963.
The Best of Lardner, edited by David Lodge.   1984.
Ring Around the Bases: The Complete Baseball Stories, edited by Matthew J. Bruccoli.   1992.

Short Stories

Gullible's Travels.   1917.
How to Write Short Stories (with Samples).   1924.
The Love Nest and Other Stories.   1926.
Round Up: The Stories.   1929; as *Collected Short Stories,* 1941.
Some Champions: Sketches and Fiction, edited by Matthew J. Bruccoli and Richard Layman.   1976.

Novels

You Know Me Al: A Busher's Letters.   1916.
Own Your Own Home.   1919.
The Real Dope.   1919.
The Big Town.   1921.

Plays

Zanzibar, music and lyrics by Harry Schmidt (produced 1903).   1903.
Elmer the Great (produced 1928).
June Moon, with George S. Kaufman, from the story "Some Like Them Cold" by Lardner (produced 1929). 1930.

Screenplay: *The New Klondike,* with Tom Geraghty, 1926.

Verse

Bib Ballads.   1915.

Other

My Four Weeks in France.   1918.
Treat 'em Rough: Letters from Jack the Kaiser Killer. 1918.
Regular Fellows I Have Met.   1919.
The Young Immigrunts.   1920.
Symptoms of Being 35.   1921.
Say It with Oil: A Few Remarks about Wives, with *Say It with Bricks: A Few Remarks about Husbands,* by Nina Wilcox Putnam.   1923.
What of It?   1925.
The Story of a Wonder Man.   1927.
Lose with a Smile.   1933.
First and Last.   1934.
Shut Up, He Explained, edited by Babette Rosmond and Henry Morgan.   1962.
Ring Around Max: The Correspondence of Lardner and Max Perkins, edited by Clifford M. Caruthers.   1973.
Letters from Ring, edited by Clifford M. Caruthers.   1979.
Lardner's You Know Me Al: The Comic Strip Adventures of Jack Keefe.   1979.

Editor, with Edward G. Heeman, March 6th, 1914: *The Home Coming of Charles A. Comisky, John J. McGraw, James J. Callahan.*   1914.

*

Bibliography: *Lardner: A Descriptive Bibliography* by Matthew J. Bruccoli and Richard Layman, 1976.

Critical Studies: *Lardner: A Biography* by Donald Elder, 1956; *Lardner* by Walton R. Patrick, 1963; *Lardner* by Otto A. Friedrich, 1965; *Lardner and the Portrait of Folly* by Maxwell Geismar, 1972; *The Lardners: My Family Remembered* by Ring Lardner, Jr., 1976; *Ring: A Biography of Lardner* by Jonathan Yardley, 1977; *Lardner* by Elizabeth Evans, 1979; *Small Town Chicago: The Comic Perspective of Finley Peter Dunne, George Ade, and Lardner* by James DeMuth, 1980.

* * *

A pioneer in investigating U.S. popular culture as an important literary topic, especially the world of sports, Ring Lardner was a meticulous miniaturist with an acute ear for the vernacular and a penetrating ironic vision of the trivia of life. His intuitive grasp of the midwestern sensibility make his short stories, parodies and excursions into home-made surrealism uniquely reflective of America from 1910 to 1930. Lardner's trademark deadpan irony and his compressed plain style, honed through years of journeyman sports journalism, influenced important younger writers (Ernest Hemingway, F. Scott Fitzgerald, Robert Benchley, and Dorothy Parker). He also was recognized as a very popular magazine humorist.

Known primarily as an acerbic clown, Lardner was a careful observer of Americana. A typical Lardner story records the speech and thoughts of semi-articulate, semi-literate people, often in the form of first-person narration by a self-serving persona (a Swiftian device) who only indirectly reveals his or her own follies, biases, and delusions in the course of storytelling. His talent for mimickry, for capturing the exact tone of earnest clumsiness in characters who attempt to inflate their ideas and their importance, is the basis of Lardner's incisive comedy, which transcends parody to become genuine social and psychological analysis.

In the epistolary novel *You Know Me Al*, Lardner invents an archetypal naif, a boastful, loudmouthed, semi-competent big-league baseball player whose awkward letters to a friend detail the trivial drama of his career. Other writers of the 1920's—Gertrude Stein, Sinclair Lewis, Sherwood Anderson, and Anita Loos—worked with mock-naive fiction to reveal the shallowness and confusion of this era of triumphant cultural expansionism, but Lardner was both the most incisive and the funniest.

Lardner used the world of professional sport, which he knew in intimate detail, as a microcosm for U.S. culture in its restless diversity. One of his best-known stories, "Champion," bluntly obliterates the icon of the sports hero by describing boxer Midge Kelly as a ruthless, brutal, and wholly egocentric character who betrays his family, his wife, and his manager to gain his title. We meet the loathesome Kelly in the story's first paragraph: "Midge Kelly scored his first knockout when he was seventeen. The knockee was his brother Connie, three years his junior and a cripple." The story details the petty nastiness of Kelly's life and ends with an ironic comment on sports journalism, the hero-minting machinery itself, as the source of all lies: "The people don't want to see him knocked. He's champion."

Other sports stories, like "Alibi Ike," "Horseshoes," and "Hurry Kane," deal with the superstition, ignorance, and close-mindedness of athletes with more humor and folksy charm. Lardner retained an ambivalent affection for the foibles and eccentricities of athletes, the self-delusion that keeps them operating under pressure, and the brilliantly inventive language of games and competition. His style parodies the zestful illiteracy of grown men playing boys' games.

Behind the mask of a casual clown, Lardner lived as a close student of U.S. culture, ideas and emotions. He loved the glitz of the musical theatre, radio, the inanely memorable cliches of Tin Pan Alley pop music, and the constant evolution of American demotic speech. His stories mimic diaries, letters, bush-league journalism, and barroom monologues. "Some Like Them Cold" depicts an epistolary romance between a self-described "handsome young man" and a "mighty pretty girlie" he woos. They progress from stiff copybook formalities to addressing one another as "Girlie" and "Mr. Man" before this correspondence between a gold-digger and a self-important shiek collapses under the weight of its hypocrisies.

In "The Golden Honeymoon" Lardner describes the falsity of sentimental ideals like marital fidelity and the joys of longevity through a couple whose life has become a cycle of bickering, petty tyrannies, and malicious manipulation. The narrator calls his wife "Mother" and reiterates a refrain—"You can't get ahead of Mother"—that anticipates Philip Wylie's studies in "Momism" and Wright Morris's quiet comic novel *Man and Boy*. In "A Caddy's Diary," a brilliant study in voice, a feckless teenage boy keeps a record of the lies, cheating, and small-town pecadilloes at a country club. The story reveals the boy's growing disillusionment with the adults who control his world and who are held up as models of ethics and behavior. One by one, they reveal themselves on the links

as small-minded, vain and selfish—cheaters at golf and at life.

A slighter, more overtly humorous study, "Contract," uses the miniature society of the bridge table as a mirror for the culture. The hapless narrator, forced to learn contract bridge as a social grace, finds that card players lose all manners and civility at the table. A target of ceaseless criticism and hectoring for his inept play, the narrator exacts revenge by criticizing the language and manners of the players. Behind the airy wit of the story, Lardner makes a strong ironic attack on social pretensions, unbridled competitiveness, the American ethos of winners and losers, the 1920's obsessions with Boosterism, Pep, and the apparatus of Babbitry.

Lardner's sympathies are always with the victims of hypocritical social structures, with those too naive or too honest to play the game of social climbing, self-aggrandizement, acquisitiveness, and egoism. In some stories, like "There Are Smiles," an O.Henry-like streak of sentimentality for "little people" or underdogs cancels the stringent irony, but in his finest stories, Lardner gives a clear-eyed, almost Olympian, overview of the human comedy and the corrupting drives of self-interest and self-deception that motivate middle-class culture.

—William J. Schafer

See the essay on "Haircut."

LAURENCE, (Jean) Margaret (née Wemyss). Canadian. Born in Neepawa, Manitoba, 18 July 1926. Educated at United College, Winnipeg, 1944–47, B.A. in English 1947. Married John F. Laurence in 1947 (separated 1962; divorced 1969); one son and one daughter. Reporter, *Winnipeg Citizen,* 1947–48; lived in England, 1949, Somaliland (now Somalia), 1950–51, Gold Coast (now Ghana), 1952–57, Vancouver, 1957–62, London and Penn, Buckinghamshire, 1962–72, and Lakefield, Ontario, from 1974; writer-in-residence, University of Toronto, 1969–70, University of Western Ontario, London, 1973, and Trent University, Peterborough, Ontario, 1974; chancellor, Trent University, 1981–83. Recipient: Beta Sigma Phi award, 1961; University of Western Ontario President's medal, 1961, 1962, 1964; Governor-General's award, 1967, 1975; Canada Council senior fellowship, 1967, 1971; Molson prize, 1975; B'nai B'rith award, 1976; Periodical Distributors award, 1977; City of Toronto award, 1978; Canadian Booksellers Association Writer of the Year award, 1981; Banff Centre award, 1983. Honorary fellow, United College, University of Winnipeg, 1967. D.Litt.: McMaster University, Hamilton, Ontario, 1970; University of Toronto, 1972; Carleton University, Ottawa, 1974; Brandon University, Manitoba, 1975; Mount Allison University, Sackville, New Brunswick, 1975; University of Western Ontario, 1975; Simon Fraser University, Burnaby, British Columbia, 1977; LL.D.: Dalhousie University, Halifax, Nova Scotia, 1972; Trent University, 1972; Queen's University, Kingston, Ontario, 1975. Companion, Order of Canada, 1971; fellow, Royal Society of Canada, 1977. *Died 6 January 1987.*

PUBLICATIONS

Short Stories

The Tomorrow-Tamer. 1963.

A Bird in the House.   1970.

Novels

This Side Jordan.   1960.
The Stone Angel.   1964.
A Jest of God.   1966; as *Rachel, Rachel,* 1968; as *Now I Lay Me Down,* 1968.
The Fire-Dwellers.   1969.
The Diviners.   1974.

Other

The Prophet's Camel Bell (travel).   1963; as *New Wind in a Dry Land,* 1964.
Long Drums and Cannons: Nigerian Dramatists and Novelists 1952–1966.   1968.
Jason's Quest (for children).   1970.
Heart of a Stranger (essays).   1976.
Six Darn Cows (for children).   1979.
The Olden-Days Coat (for children).   1979.
The Christmas Birthday Story (for children).   1980.

Editor and Translator, *A Tree for Poverty: Somali Poetry and Prose.*   1954.

*

Bibliography: by Susan J. Warwick, in *The Annotated Bibliography of Canada's Major Authors 1* edited by Robert Lecker and Jack David, 1979.

Critical Studies: *Laurence,* 1969, and *The Manawaka World of Laurence,* 1975, both by Clara Thomas; *Three Voices: The Lives of Laurence, Gabrielle Roy, and Frederick Philip Grove* by Joan Hind-Smith, 1975; *Laurence: The Writer and Her Critics* edited by W.H. New, 1977; "Laurence Issue" of *Journal of Canadian Studies,* 13 (3), 1978, and *Journal of Canadian Fiction* 27, Summer 1980; *The Work of Laurence* by John Robert Sorfleet, 1980; *Laurence* by Patricia Morley, 1981; *A Place to Stand On: Essays by and about Laurence* edited by George Woodcock, 1983; *Mother and Daughter Relationships in the Manawaka Works of Laurence* by Helen M. Buss, 1985; *Laurence: An Appreciation* edited by Christl Verduyn, 1988; *Crossing the River: Essays in Honour of Laurence* edited by Kristjana Gunnars, 1988; *Critical Approaches to the Fiction of Laurence* edited by Colin Nicholson, 1990; "Semi-autobiographical Fiction and Revisionary Realism in *A Bird in the House*" by Peter Easingwood, in *Narrative Strategies in Canadian Literature,* edited by Coral A. Howells and Lynette Hunter, 1991; "'Half War / Half Peace': Laurence and the Publishing of *A Bird in the House*" by Richard A. Davies, in *English Studies in Canada* 17, September 1991.

* * *

Margaret Laurence's literary career, even though virtually all her work was completed in Canada or England, can be divided in terms of theme and setting into two parts, African and Canadian. Apart from her novels and other larger works, each period was marked by a volume of stories: *The Tomorrow-Tamer* emanating from African memories, and *A Bird in the House,* tales of a Canadian prairie childhood which form the only work of fiction Laurence granted was partly autobiographical.

Laurence's African experience began in 1950, when she went to Somaliland with her engineer husband, who was engaged building small dams in the desert, and famine was already a subject that filled her mind when she wrote her fine travel book, *The Prophet's Camel Bell.* In 1952 she moved on to Gold Coast (now Ghana), and it was there that she began to write fiction about Africa, often seeking to perceive it through the eyes and minds of Africans, though it was in Vancouver, to which she returned in 1957, that she completed her African works, including a novel (*This Side Jordan*) and the *Tomorrow-Tamer* stories. It was with these early stories, often published in the new magazines that were appearing in Canada's literary renaissance of the 1950's and 1960's, that Laurence began to make her reputation.

Marginality is one of the most persistently repeated themes in Laurence's African stories, largely perhaps because her own attempts to know and understand Africans left her with a strong sense of her own situation as an unwilling outsider. Some of the best pieces are in fact about non-Africans "stuck" in a changing Africa, like the Levantine hairdresser in "The Perfumed Sea" who is forced to call on his wits and change his ways when the white ladies depart and his clients are all native women, and the young English missionary's son in "The Drummer of All the World," who is educated at his father's village school where all his friends were African, and who returns after independence to find these very friends are alienated from him and he is alone in a strange land with no home elsewhere. And, in what are perhaps the best stories of all, there are the Africans who have absorbed enough of the values of the west to be disturbed by those of the traditional world they reenter or have dealings with. "The Rain Child," told with wry tenderness by an old English teacher who has learnt to walk beside native ways, concerns a black girl educated in England through her early years, who is utterly lost and uncomprehending among the native girls brought up by custom. "Godman's Master" dramatically tells of the coming together of Africa's past and its possible future when a young man, acculturated by four years at a British university, comes back and rescues one of the strangest inhabitants of the old traditional society. This is the midget called Godman who has been kept in a box by his exploiter and forced to make prophetic utterances that bewilder the villagers. When the relationship between rescuer and rescued becomes impossible, it is Godman who departs into the world of freak exploitation, and who perhaps sets the keynote to this whole volume of stories when he says to Moses, his unhappy former benefactor, "I fear and fear, and yet I live." Moses answers gently, "No . . . man can do otherwise." For in spite of all the noise and colour of an Africa setting itself free, it is foreboding, uncertainty, the fears and problems of that very freedom which dominate these stories of Africa.

If in the African stories Laurence sought to enter the minds of cultures and traditions different from her own, in those that constitute *A Bird in the House* she is in the most direct way leading back to her origins. These tales, with a single leading character and her dominating family, are really a single discontinuous work. Like a novel they show the various aspects of temperament, the changing perceptions created by time and growth, yet they do not have a novel's development towards a conclusion. Each story has a tentative feel, and we learn its real significance from the stories that follow after, which gives the impression of a series of portrait photographs taken at various stages of awakening awareness rather than the narrative film a novel would provide. Still, the teller maintains her own privacy as Laurence tended to do in real life. There is a distancing to these incidents, though of a different kind from the distancing of the creative process when she finally wrote her fiction about Africa in Vancouver and her novels about Canada. And so they are perhaps more inventive than Laurence's "confession" of autobiographical intent suggests. Some critics, including the present one, find the book most convincing as a presentation of a prairie society recognizing its mortality, or of individuals and whole social groups reaching that realization. Death is so often present that one wonders what is the real bird in the house, that house which remains the constant place of so many departures, from place and from life.

—George Woodcock

See the essays on "The Loons" and "The Tomorrow-Tamer."

LAVIN, Mary. Irish. Born in East Walpole, Massachusetts, 11 June 1912; moved with her family to Athenry, Ireland, 1923. Educated at East Walpole schools; Loreto Convent, Dublin; University College, Dublin, B.A. (honours) in English 1934; National University of Ireland, Dublin, M.A. (honours) 1938. Married 1) William Walsh in 1942 (died 1954), three daughters; 2) Michael MacDonald Scott in 1969 (died 1991). French teacher, Loreto Convent, early 1940's. President, Irish PEN, 1964–65. Recipient: James Tait Black Memorial prize, 1944; Guggenheim fellowship, 1959, 1962, 1972; Katherine Mansfield-Menton prize, 1962; Ella Lynam Cabot fellowship, 1971; Eire Society gold medal (U.S.), 1974; Gregory medal, 1974; American Irish Foundation award, 1979; Allied Irish Banks award, 1981. D.Litt.: National University of Ireland, 1968. President, Irish Academy of Letters, 1971–73. Lives in Dublin.

PUBLICATIONS

Short Stories

Tales from Bective Bridge.   1942.
The Long Ago and Other Stories.   1944.
The Becker Wives and Other Stories.   1946; as *At Sallygap and Other Stories,* 1947.
A Single Lady and Other Stories.   1951.
The Patriot Son and Other Stories.   1956.
Selected Stories.   1959.
The Great Wave and Other Stories.   1961.
The Stories.   3 vols., 1964–85.
In the Middle of the Fields and Other Stories.   1967.
Happiness and Other Stories.   1969.
Collected Stories.   1971.
A Memory and Other Stories.   1972.
The Shrine and Other Stories.   1977.
Selected Stories.   1981.
A Family Likeness and Other Stories.   1985.

Novels

The House in Clewe Street.   1945.

Mary O'Grady.   1950.

Other (for children)

A Likely Story.   1957.
The Second-Best Children in the World.   1972.

*

Bibliography: by Paul A. Doyle, in *Papers of the Bibliography Society of America 63,* 1969; *Lavin: A Check List* by Ruth Krawschak, 1979.

Critical Studies: *Lavin* by Zack Bowen, 1975; *Lavin* by Richard F. Peterson, 1978; "Lavin Issue" of *Irish University Review,* Autumn 1979; *Lavin, Quiet Rebel: A Study of Her Short Stories* by A.A. Kelly, 1980.

*   *   *

For over four decades, Mary Lavin has been one of Ireland's most prolific and accomplished short story writers. Author of eleven collections of short stories, she has become a master of the short story form, though she has seldom received the critical recognition or attention accorded Frank O'Connor, Liam O'Flaherty, and Sean O'Faolain. Though often compared to Ireland's revolutionary writers, Lavin was not a part of their literary generation, and her stories are rarely about Ireland's political troubles. Born in the United States in 1912, about a decade after the births of O'Connor, O'Flaherty, and O'Faolain, Lavin did not live in Ireland until 1921, when she settled with her mother in the small town of Athenry. When she decided to become a short story writer, she turned to her mother's family and Irish middle-class life for her subject matter and, during her university days, found her literary models in the stories of Turgenev, Chekhov, Woolf, Mansfield, and Jewett.

For Lavin, the only possible condition or standard for a short story writer is the quest for the truth. She admired Katherine Mansfield's statement that the truth is the only thing worth having and the only thing that cannot fail the writer. In her own short stories, Lavin often exposes the truth of her characters' lives through an intimate study of opposed sensibilities. Usually told from the perspective of her introverted characters, her narratives focus on the failure of human beings to understand each other's emotional needs. Emerging out of these stories is a portrait of Irish small-town life populated by lonely unhappy characters who, like their city counterparts in Joyce's *Dubliners,* are paralyzed by the emotional and spiritual emptiness of their lives and are capable of little more than discovering that they have been denied life's feast by their own nature.

One of Lavin's most finely crafted stories, "A Cup of Tea" is also one of her most representative in its portrayal of the conflicting emotional needs and frustrations separating her characters from each other. The plot of "A Cup of Tea" appears to be relatively simple and insignificant—a daughter, returned after three months at the university, argues with her mother over whether or not boiled milk spoils the taste of tea. This key narrative event, however, merely serves as the flash point for the emotional problems buried within the family. While the mother, frustrated by her unhappy marriage, desperately tries to control her emotions, it takes only a small incident of disagreement for her jealousy of her daughter's life to boil to the surface. Her daughter, however, refuses to be drawn into her mother's circle of emotional failure and, after the argument, still clings to the innocent and youthful hope, rarely actualized in Lavin's stories, that people can get along if they become alike and feel the same emotions.

A major reason for the emotional intimacy of Lavin's stories is her frequent use of autobiographical material. In the middle period of her career, for example, she wrote several stories, including "Frail Vessel," that follow the lives of a merchant family based upon her mother's relatives in Athenry. The Grimes family stories, dominated by the ambitious and interfering Bedelia Grimes, represent Lavin's most extensive treatment of the Irish middle class. By the time she had finished the Grimes cycle of stories with "Loving Memory," she had exposed and developed the emotional failure of an entire family. Lavin also had retained the intimacy of her narrative by tracing the emptiness of the lives of the Grimes family not just to the conventions of small-town life but to a mother who refused to share her emotional life with her children.

As remarkable as the Grimes family stories are in capturing the emotional circumstances of Lavin's life, her later stories, especially those written after the death of her first husband, William Walsh, in 1954, represent her most personal and, in several cases, her most compelling fiction. Her widow stories, featuring Vera Traske, her most autobiographical character, form a pattern of emotional events in which women struggle to find a new life and identity after the deaths of their husbands. This pattern begins with "In a Cafe," in which a widow, bearing Lavin's own first name, reclaims her self-identity, but only after she faces her most intimate fears and needs. "In the Middle of the Fields" and "The Cuckoo-spit" actually appear to form a chronological and emotional sequence with "In a Cafe," in which Lavin's widow moves through phases of grief, loneliness, and emptiness until, through an emotional reawakening, she realizes the value and strength of the memories of her lost life in helping her form a new life. This discovery anticipates "Happiness," in which the autobiographical Vera dies, but only after passing along to her daughter a vision of life hinting that Vera's happiness has as its source the very struggles in which she has experienced so much of the pain and suffering of her life.

While "Happiness" could easily serve as a summary of her adult life and her career, Lavin has continued to write about the most painful and intimate of human experiences. In *A Family Likeness*, for example, several of her stories explore the emotional problems of growing old, especially the feeling experienced by her autobiographical character that she has no real place or value in her daughter's life. These stories also display the same narrative control and intimacy characteristic of Lavin's earlier fiction. It remains this careful balance of narrative integrity and emotional insight into the loneliness of the sensitive heart that most defines the Lavin short story and best illustrates why she deserves a place with the most accomplished short story writers produced by Ireland in the 20th century.

—Richard F. Peterson

See the essays on "Frail Vessel" and "Happiness."

———

LAWRENCE, D(avid) H(erbert). English. Born in Eastwood, Nottinghamshire, 11 September 1885. Educated at Nottingham High School, 1898–1901; University College, Nottingham (now University of Nottingham), 1906–08, teacher's certificate, 1908. Eloped with Frieda von Richthofen Weekley in 1912, married in 1914. Clerk for a firm of surgical appliance makers, Nottingham, 1901; pupil-teacher in Eastwood and Ilkeston, Nottinghamshire, 1902–06; teacher, Davidson Road School, Croydon, Surrey, 1908–12; full-time writer from 1912; lived in Germany, Italy, and Switzerland, 1912–14, and in England, 1914–19; prosecuted for obscenity (*The Rainbow*), 1915; founder, with Katherine Mansfield, *q.v.*, and John Middleton Murry, *Signature* magazine, 1916; lived in Florence, Capri, and Sicily, 1919-22; travelled to Ceylon and Australia, 1922; lived in the U.S. and Mexico, 1922–23, England, France, and Germany, 1924, New Mexico and Mexico, 1924–25, Italy, 1925–28, and France, 1928–30; also a painter: one-man show, London, 1929 (closed by the police). Recipient: James Tait Black Memorial prize, 1921. *Died 2 March 1930.*

PUBLICATIONS

Collections

Complete Poems, edited by Vivian de Sola Pinto and Warren Roberts.   2 vols., 1964.
Complete Plays.   1965.
A Selection, edited by R.H. Poole and P.J. Shepherd.   1970.
Selected Poems, edited by Keith Sagar.   1972; revised edition, as *Poems*, 1986.
Works (Cambridge Edition), edited by James T. Boulton and Warren Roberts.   1980——.
Complete Short Novels, edited by Keith Sagar and Melissa Partridge.   1982.
Selected Short Stories, edited by Brian Finney.   1982.

Short Stories

The Prussian Officer and Other Stories.   1914.
England My England and Other Stories.   1922.
The Ladybird, The Fox, The Captain's Doll.   1923; as *The Captain's Doll: Three Novelettes*, 1923.
St. Mawr, Together with The Princess.   1925.
Sun (story).   1926; unexpurgated edition, 1928.
Glad Ghosts (story).   1926.
Rawdon's Roof (story).   1928.
The Woman Who Rode Away and Other Stories.   1928.
The Escaped Cock (novella).   1929; as *The Man Who Died*, 1931.
The Virgin and the Gipsy (novella).   1930.
The Lovely Lady.   1933.
A Modern Lover.   1934.
A Prelude (story).   1949.
Love among the Haystacks and Other Pieces.   1930.
The Princess and Other Stories, and *The Mortal Coil and Other Stories*, edited by Keith Sagar.   2 vols., 1971.

Novels

The White Peacock.   1911; edited by Harry T. Moore, 1966.
The Trespasser.   1912.

Sons and Lovers. 1913; edited by Julian Moynahan, 1968; *A Facsimile of the Manuscript,* edited by Mark Schorer, 1977.
The Rainbow. 1915.
Women in Love. 1920.
The Lost Girl. 1920.
Aaron's Rod. 1922.
Kangaroo. 1923.
The Boy in the Bush, with M.L. Skinner. 1924.
The Plumed Serpent (Quetzalcoatl). 1926.
Lady Chatterley's Lover. 1928; *The First Lady Chatterley* (first version), 1944; *La Tre Lady Chatterley* (three versions), in Italian, 1954; unexpurgated edition, 1959; *John Thomas and Lady Jane* (second version). 1972.
Mr. Noon, edited by Lindeth Vasey. 1984.

Plays

The Widowing of Mrs. Holroyd (produced 1920). 1914.
Touch and Go (produced 1979). 1920.
David (produced 1927). 1926.
Keeping Barbara, in *Argosy* 14, December 1933.
A Collier's Friday Night (produced 1965). 1934.
The Daughter-in-Law (produced 1967). In *Complete Plays,* 1965.
The Fight for Barbara (produced 1967). In *Complete Plays,* 1965.
The Merry-Go-Round (produced 1973). In *Complete Plays,* 1965.
The Married Man, Altitude, and *Noah's Flood,* in *Complete Plays.* 1965.

Verse

Love Poems and Others. 1913.
Amores. 1916.
Look! We Have Come Through! 1917.
New Poems. 1918.
Bay. 1919.
Tortoises. 1921.
Birds, Beasts, and Flowers. 1923.
Collected Poems. 2 vols., 1928.
Pansies. 1929.
Nettles. 1930.
The Triumph of the Machine. 1931.
Last Poems, edited by Richard Aldington and Giuseppe Orioli. 1932.
Fire and Other Poems. 1940.

Other

Twilight in Italy. 1916.
Movements in European History. 1921; revised edition, 1926.
Psychoanalysis and the Unconscious. 1921.
Sea and Sardinia. 1921.
Fantasia of the Unconscious. 1922.
Studies in Classic American Literature. 1923; edited by Armin Arnold, as *The Symbolic Meaning: The Uncollected Versions,* 1962.
Reflections on the Death of a Porcupine and Other Essays. 1925.
Mornings in Mexico. 1927.
The Paintings of Lawrence. 1929.
My Skirmish with Jolly Roger (introduction to *Lady Chatterley's Lover*). 1929; as *A propos of Lady Chatterley's Lover,* 1930.
Pornography and Obscenity. 1929.

Assorted Articles. 1930.
Apocalypse. 1931.
Letters, edited by Aldous Huxley. 1932.
Etruscan Places. 1932.
We Need One Another. 1933.
Phoenix: The Posthumous Papers, edited by Edward D. McDonald. 1936.
Collected Letters, edited by Harry T. Moore. 2 vols., 1962.
The Paintings, edited by Mervyn Levy. 1964.
Phoenix II: Uncollected, Unpublished, and Other Prose Works, edited by Warren Roberts and Harry T. Moore. 1968.
Lawrence in Love: Letters to Louie Burrows, edited by James T. Boulton. 1968.
Centaur Letters, edited by Edward D. McDonald. 1970.
Letters to Martin Secker 1911–1930, edited by Martin Secker. 1970.
The Quest for Ranamin: Letters to S.S. Koteliansky 1914–1930, edited by G.J. Zytaruk. 1970.
Letters to Thomas and Adele Seltzer: Letters to His American Publishers, edited by Gerald M. Lacy. 1976.
Letters, edited by James T. Boulton. 1979—.
Study of Thomas Hardy and Other Essays, edited by Bruce Steele. 1985.
Memoir of Maurice Magnus. 1987.

Translator, with S.S. Koteliansky, *All Things Are Possible,* by Leo Shestov. 1920.
Translator, *Mastro-Don Gesualdo,* by Giovanni Verga. 1923.
Translator, *Little Novels of Sicily,* by Giovanni Verga. 1925.
Translator, *Cavalleria Rusticana and Other Stories,* by Giovanni Verga. 1928.
Translator, *The Story of Doctor Manente,* by A.F. Grazzini. 1929.
Translator, with S.S. Koteliansky, *The Grand Inquisitor,* by Dostoevskii. 1930.

*

Bibliography: *A Bibliography of Lawrence* by Warren Roberts, 1963, revised 1982; *Lawrence: A Bibliography* by John E. Stoll, 1977; *Lawrence: An Annotated Bibliography of Writings about Him* by James C. Cowan, 2 vols., 1982–85; *Lawrence: A Review of the Biographies and Literary Criticism* by Jill M. Phillips, 1986.

Critical Studies: *Lawrence,* 1930, *Lawrence, Novelist,* 1955, and *Thought, Words, and Creativity: Art and Thought in Lawrence,* 1976, all by F.R. Leavis; *Son of Woman: The Story of Lawrence,* 1931, and *Reminiscences of Lawrence,* 1933, both by John Middleton Murry; *The Savage Pilgrimage: A Narrative of Lawrence* by Catherine Carswell, 1932, revised edition, 1932; *Lorenzo in Taos* by Mabel Dodge Luhan, 1932; *Lawrence: An Unprofessional Study* by Anaïs Nin, 1932; *Not, but the Wind—,* 1934, and *The Memoirs and Correspondence* edited by Ernest W. Tedlock, 1961, both by Frieda Lawrence; *Lawrence: A Personal Record* by Jessie Chambers, 1935, revised edition, edited by J.D. Chambers, 1965; *Portrait of a Genius, but . . . : The Life of Lawrence* by Richard Aldington, 1950, as *Lawrence: Portrait of a Genius, but . . . ,* 1950; *The Life and Works of Lawrence,* 1951, revised edition, as *Lawrence: His Life and Works,* 1964, and *The Intelligent Heart: The Story of*

Lawrence, 1954, revised edition, as *The Priest of Love: A Life of Lawrence,* 1974, both by Harry T. Moore, and *A Lawrence Miscellany* edited by Moore, 1959; *The Love Ethic of Lawrence* by Mark Spilka, 1955, and *Lawrence: A Collection of Critical Essays* edited by Spilka, 1963; *The Dark Sun: A Study of Lawrence* by Graham Hough, 1956; *Lawrence: A Composite Biography* edited by Edward Nehls, 3 vols., 1957–59; *Lawrence* by Anthony Beal, 1961; *The Art of Perversity: Lawrence's Shorter Fictions* by Kingsley Widmer, 1962; *Lawrence: Artist and Rebel* by Ernest W. Tedlock, 1963; *The Deed of Life: The Novels and Tales of Lawrence* by Julian Moynahan, 1963; *Lawrence* by R.P. Draper, 1964, and *Lawrence: The Critical Heritage* edited by Draper, 1970; *Double Measure: A Study of the Novels and Stories of Lawrence* by George H. Ford, 1965; *The Forked Flame: A Study of Lawrence* by H.M. Daleski, 1965; *Lawrence as a Literary Critic* by David J. Gordon, 1966; *The Art of Lawrence,* 1966, *The Life of Lawrence,* 1980, and *Lawrence: Life into Art,* 1985, all by Keith Sagar, and *A Lawrence Handbook* edited by Sagar, 1982; *Sexual Politics* by Kate Millett, 1970; *Acts of Attention: The Poems of Lawrence* by Sandra M. Gilbert, 1972, revised edition, 1990; *Lawrence, The Man and His Work: The Formative Years 1885–1919* by Emile Delavenay, 1972; *Lawrence* by Frank Kermode, 1973; *The Hostile Sun: The Poetry of Lawrence* by Joyce Carol Oates, 1973; *Lawrence: Novelist, Poet, Prophet* edited by Stephen Spender, 1973; *The Plays of Lawrence* by Sylvia Sklar, 1975; *Son and Lover: The Young Lawrence* by Philip Callow, 1975; *Who's Who in Lawrence,* 1976, *Lawrence: History, Ideology and Fiction,* 1982, and *Women in Love,* 1986, all by Graham Holderness; *The Art of the Self in Lawrence* by Marguerite B. Howe, 1977; *Lawrence: The Novels* by Alastair Niven, 1978; *A Lawrence Companion: Life, Thought, and Works* by F.B. Pinion, 1978; *Lawrence and Women* edited by Anne Smith, 1978; *Lawrence: A Critical Study of the Major Novels and Other Writings* edited by A.H. Gomme, 1978; *The Composition of The Rainbow and Women in Love: A History* by Charles L. Ross, 1979; *Lawrence and the Idea of the Novel,* 1979, and *Lawrence: A Literary Life,* 1989, both by John Worthen; *The World of Lawrence: A Passionate Appreciation* by Henry Miller, edited by Evelyn J. Hinz and John J. Teunissen, 1980; *Lawrence* by George J. Becker, 1980; *The Minoan Distance: The Symbolism of Travel in Lawrence* by L.D. Clark, 1980; *Lawrence and Women* by Carol Dix, 1980; *The Moon's Dominion: Narrative Dichotomy and Female Dominance in Lawrence's Earlier Novels* by Gavriel Ben-Ephraim, 1981; *The Curve of Return: Lawrence's Travel Books* by Del Ivan Janik, 1981; *Lawrence: Interviews and Recollections* edited by Norman Page, 2 vols., 1981; *Lawrence in Australia* by Robert Darroch, 1981; *A Reader's Guide to Lawrence* by Philip Hobsbaum, 1981; *A Preface to Lawrence* by Gāmini Salgādo, 1982; *Perception in the Poetry of Lawrence* by Jillian De Vries-Mason, 1982; *Lawrence and Feminism* by Hilary Simpson, 1982; *A Reassessment of Lawrence's Aaron's Rod* by Paul G. Baker, 1983; *The Creation of Lady Chatterley's Lover* by Michael Squires, 1983; *The Poetry of Lawrence: Texts and Contexts* by Ross G. Murfin, 1983; *Lawrence: The Artist as Psychologist* by Daniel J. Schneider, 1984; *The Phoenix Paradox: A Study of Renewal Through Change in the Collected Poems and Last Poems of Lawrence* by Gail Mandell, 1984; *The Short Fiction of Lawrence* by Janice Hubbard Harris, 1984; *Lawrence and the Devouring Mother: The Search for a Patriarchal Ideal of Leadership* by Judith Ruderman, 1984; *Lawrence: A Celebration* edited by Andrew Cooper, 1985; *Lawrence: A Centenary Consideration* edited by Peter Balbert and Phillip L. Marcus, 1985;

Lawrence and Tradition, 1985, and *The Legacy of Lawrence: New Essays,* 1987, both edited by Jeffrey Meyers, and *Lawrence: A Biography* by Meyers, 1990; *Flame into Being: The Life and Work of Lawrence* by Anthony Burgess, 1985; *Lawrence's Lady: A New Look at Lady Chatterley's Lover* edited by Michael Squires and Dennis Jackson, 1985; *Lawrence: The Earlier Fiction: A Commentary* by Michael Black, 1986; *The Consciousness of Lawrence: An Intellectual Biography* by Daniel J. Schneider, 1986; *Lawrence's Leadership Politics and the Turn Against Women* by Cornelia Nixon, 1986; *Lawrence: Centenary Essays* edited by Mara Kalnins, 1986; *Lawrence: New Studies* edited by Christopher Heywood, 1987; *Sons and Lovers* by Geoffrey Harvey, 1987; *A Study of the Poems of Lawrence* by M.J. Lockwood, 1987; *Lawrence's Non-fiction: Art, Thought, and Genre* edited by David Ellis and Howard Mills, 1988; *Lady Chatterley: The Making of a Novel* by Derek Britton, 1988; *The Spirit of Lawrence: Centenary Studies* edited by Gāmini Salgādo and G.K. Das, 1988; *Critical Essays on Lawrence* edited by Dennis Jackson and Fleda Brown Jackson, 1988; *Lawrence and the Phallic Imagination: Essays on Sexual Identity and Feminist Misreadings* by Peter Balbert, 1989; *The Language of Lawrence* by Allan Ingram, 1990; *The Lady Chatterley's Lover Trial* edited by H. Montgomery Hyde, 1990; *Lawrence* by Tony Pinkney, 1990; *Lawrence's Poetry: Demon Liberated: A Collection of Primary and Secondary Material* edited by A. Banerjee, 1990; *Rethinking Lawrence* edited by Keith Brown, 1990; *The Challenge of Lawrence* edited by Michael Squires and Keith Cushman, 1990; *The Rainbow: A Search for New Life* by Duane Edwards, 1990; *Lawrence: Sexual Crisis* by Nigel Kelsey, 1991; *Lawrence: Language and Being* by Micheal Bell, 1992.

*   *   *

D.H. Lawrence was a prolific writer, who wrote important work in many different genres, including the novel, poetry, travel writing, drama, and the short story. Some critics would argue that his most important fictional work is in the novel, particularly *Sons and Lovers, The Rainbow,* and *Women in Love,* and that his short stories are distinguished by the succinctness and artistic control of insights explored more deeply and extensively in the novels. But this underestimates his innovative use of the short story form and the sheer originality of certain of his long stories, or novellas. These are no minor part of Lawrence's achievement.

The stories do, however, share with the novels Lawrence's earnest concern with the relations between the sexes, and, in particular, the influence of powerful unconscious forces (what he calls "blood consciousness," as opposed to "mental consciousness") which often determine his characters' lives at moments of emotional crisis. Their themes and settings also reflect, as those of the novels do, his personal odyssey, which took him from the Nottinghamshire and Derbyshire coalfield where he was born and brought up, to Germany and Italy, which he first visited when he eloped with Frieda Weekley, and to the American SouthWest, where, he wrote, "a new part of the soul woke up suddenly, and the old world gave way to the new." The stories also are concerned with what Lawrence felt was the inhumanly mechanical nature of the Western industrial world and its sterile subordination to a hypocritical ideal of benevolence. This, too, is a preoccupation of the novels;

but the stories seem better able to combine it with humour and satire.

The Nottinghamshire and Derbyshire stories are mostly from the early period of Lawrence's writing career—though the implication that they are therefore conditioned by attitudes he afterwards rejected, or considerably modified, can be misleading, since a number of them were revised for later publication and in the process acquired the resonances of his more mature work. (A good example is "Odour of Chrysanthemums.") These stories are steeped in working-class life; they have the virtues of an unsentimental realism and dramatic immediacy which come from Lawrence's first-hand experience of colliers and their families, and they are particularly effective in their use of the local dialect. But they are more than merely realist sketches. Even a comparatively slight piece like "Strike Pay" (1912), which recounts the escapades of a group of miners on a jaunt to a football match in Nottingham, comes to focus on the domestic tensions between husband, wife, and mother-in-law in a way that raises more serious emotional issues. In one of his early masterpieces, "Daughters of the Vicar" (1911-14), the marriage choices made by two daughters of a Midlands clergyman become the fictional means by which Lawrence probes critically, but not unsympathetically, into the twisted values of a Christian family which rates money and respectability above warm, mutually responsive feeling. There are elements in the story that suggest the distorting effect of a didactically conceived morality play: Mary's choice of an almost parodically presented caricature of a middle-class, clerical husband is perhaps too blatantly contrasted with Louisa's choice of the miner, Alfred Durant; but in the main the story's theme is worked out through discriminations that are sensitively true to the recognisable texture of ordinary life.

What is still more distinctive, however, in Lawrence's handling of the short story is the poetic power with which he imbues it. This is apparent, for example, in "The Fox" (1918-21) when March dreams of the animal to which the title alludes: "She dreamed she heard a singing outside which she could not understand, a singing that roamed round the house, in the fields, and in the darkness . . . suddenly she knew it was the fox singing. He was very yellow and bright, like corn." The level of plausible surface reality is also maintained in this story, but the experience towards which it reaches is beyond and beneath that level, requiring another linguistic dimension to communicate it. In one sense such stories seem unrealistic, for their characters are jolted out of their everyday awareness of things and compelled to behave in ways which by ordinary standards are unwise and improbable. They hear a singing outside the range of normal reality, which puts a compulsion upon them; but the imaginative heightening of Lawrence's language contrives to suggest that this is an authentically vital, rather than an hallucinatory, compulsion. Nevertheless, the conflict between the two levels continues, and creates, in fact, the substance of the tales in which it is narrated—variously exemplified by the struggle for male dominance in "The Fox" and "The Captain's Doll" (1921), the sightless versus the sighted levels of reality in "The Blind Man" (1918), and the instinct to defend natural energy against the debilitating effect of modern civilisation in "St. Mawr" (1924).

Often the outcome of this struggle remains tentatively open-ended. When it is not, as in "The Woman Who Rode Away" (1924), the reader senses a forcing of the issue. Here Lawrence makes his story the vehicle for a loaded myth. The protagonist, a representative of Western independent womanhood, seeks a different way of life from that which has made her own a dead-end one, and hopes to find it among a remote tribe of Indians. Her readiness to give them her "heart" is interpreted as a willingness to submit to a human sacrifice that will transfer power from the white race to the Indians. The story remains poised at its end at the moment when her heart will be cut out and offered to the sun. "The Woman Who Rode Away" is an impressive stylistic accomplishment, modulating from the harsh, staccato language of its sterile opening to the sinuous, incantatory rhythms and seductive repetitions that express the visionary awareness experienced by the woman under the influence of the Indians. But this is a transition rather than a balance. The poetic dimension is no longer held in tension with the more ordinary level of reality, and consequently a sense of wholeness is lost.

In "The Woman Who Rode Away," as in other of Lawrence's Mexican works, there is a marked streak of cruelty, which is fortunately subdued, if not entirely absent, from the late novellas, "The Man Who Loved Islands" (1926), *The Virgin and the Gipsy,* and *The Escaped Cock.* "The Man Who Loved Islands" is a satirical fable of idealism undermined and corrupted by its own denial of the untameable forces of nature, told in a style that, though still capable of poetry, works mainly from a base of mockingly colloquial speech. The other two novellas are intensely poetic, and again function as myths—*The Virgin and the Gipsy* as a latter-day version of the biblical flood, and *The Escaped Cock* as a bold refashioning of the Christian Resurrection combined with the pagan story of Isis and Osiris. They return, however, to the central Lawrentian theme of love (virtually ignored in "The Woman Who Rode Away"), which is a phallic, as much as a spiritual, experience. The Christ-figure in *The Escaped Cock* rises from death (the tale was published later as *The Man Who Died*) to a new-found delight in the body, preluded by a remarkable description of a black and orange cockerel, with a red comb, "leaping out of greenness . . . , his tail-feathers streaming lustrous." The brilliantly coloured, surging prose is a verbal equivalent of the paintings of Van Gogh; it signifies an affirmation of the values of the phenomenal world, leading into the quieter eloquence and subdued biblical rhythms that celebrate the man's discovery of wholeness in physical communion with the priestess of Isis.

It is arguable that *The Escaped Cock* is the most important of Lawrence's prose works after *Women in Love.* If there is a decline in his career as a novelist during the 1920's, it is not due to failure of imaginative vigour. What is missing in his novels is at least compensated by what is to be found in these stories and novellas (and also in the significantly related poems of *Birds, Beasts, and Flowers,* and *Last Poems*). There his creative vitality is unabated, and what he contributes to English short fiction is unique.

—R.P. Draper

See the essays on "The Horse Dealer's Daughter," "Odour of Chrysanthemums," "The Prussian Officer," and "The Rocking-Horse Winner."

———

LAWSON, Henry (Hertzberg). Australian. Born in Grenfell, New South Wales, 17 June 1867. Educated at the Eurunderee Public School, 1876; became deaf at age 9.

Married Bertha Bredt in 1896 (separated 1902); one son and one daughter. Held various jobs from age 13: builder, apprentice to a railway contractor, house painter, and clerk; contributed to his mother's magazines, *Republican* and *Dawn*, Sydney, 1880's, and to the *Bulletin*, Sydney, 1890's; staff member, Albany *Observer*, Western Australia, 1890, and Brisbane *Boomerang*, 1891; house painter in Bourke, 1892–93; telegraph lineman in New Zealand, 1893–94; staff member, Sydney *Worker*, 1894; gold prospector in Western Australia, 1896; teacher, Mangamaunu Maori School, 1897–98; lived in Sydney, 1898–99, London, 1900–03, and Sydney from 1904. Recipient: Commonwealth Literary Fund pension, 1920. *Died 2 September 1922.*

PUBLICATIONS

Collections

Prose Works.   2 vols., 1935.
Stories, edited by Cecil Mann.   3 vols., 1964.
Collected Verse, edited by Colin Roderick.   3 vols., 1967–69.
Short Stories and Sketches 1888–1922, edited by Colin Roderick.   1972.
Autobiographical and Other Writings 1887–1922, edited by Colin Roderick.   1972.
The World of Lawson, edited by Walter Stone.   1974.
The Essential Lawson, edited by Brian Kiernan.   1982.
The Penguin Lawson, edited by John Barnes.   1986.

Short Stories

Short Stories in Prose and Verse.   1894.
While the Billy Boils.   1896.
On the Track.   1900.
Over the Sliprails.   1900.
The Country I Come From.   1901.
Joe Wilson and His Mates.   1901.
Children of the Bush (includes poems).   1902; as *Send Round the Hat* and *The Romance of the Swag,* 2 vols., 1907.
The Rising of the Court and Other Sketches in Prose and Verse.   1910.
Mateship: A Discursive Yarn.   1911.
The Strangers' Friend.   1911.
Triangles of Life and Other Stories.   1913.

Verse

In the Days When the World Was Wide and Other Verses.   1896.
Verses, Popular and Humorous.   1900.
When I Was King and Other Verses.   1905.
The Elder Son.   1905.
The Skyline Riders and Other Verses.   1910.
A Coronation Ode and Retrospect.   1911.
For Australia and Other Poems.   1913.
My Army, O, My Army! and Other Songs.   1915; as *Song of the Dardanelles and Other Verses,* 1916.
Selected Poems.   1918.
The Auld Shop and the New.   1923.
Joseph's Dream.   1923.
Winnowed Verse.   1924.
Popular Verses.   1924.
Humorous Verses.   1924.
Poetical Works.   3 vols., 1925.

The Men Who Made Australia.   1950.

Other

A Selection from the Prose Works, edited by George Mackaness.   1928.
Letters 1890–1922, edited by Colin Roderick.   1970.

*

Bibliography: *An Annotated Bibliography of Lawson* by George Mackaness, 1951.

Critical Studies: *Lawson* by Stephen Murray-Smith, 1962, revised edition, 1975; *Lawson: The Grey Dreamer* by Denton Prout, 1963; *Lawson,* 1966, and *The Real Lawson,* 1982, both by Colin Roderick, and *Lawson: Criticism 1894–1971* edited by Roderick, 1972; *Lawson* by Judith Wright, 1967; *Lawson among Maoris* by Bill Pearson, 1968; *The Receding Wave: Lawson's Prose* by Brian E. Matthews, 1972; *In Search of Lawson* by Manning Clark, 1978, as *Lawson: The Man and the Legend,* 1985; *Out of Eden: Lawson's Life and Works: A Psychoanalytic View* by Xavier Pons, 1984; *Lawson* by Geoffrey Dutton, 1988.

*   *   *

Like several of his contemporaries, Henry Lawson's life was a relatively brief one—from 1867 to 1922. He was born at Grenfell, in central western New South Wales, around the area of the goldfields, the son of Louisa Albury and Niels Larsen (later Peter Lawson, a Norwegian seaman who jumped ship at Melbourne). Larsen became estranged from his wife in 1883 and died in 1888. Louisa lived on until 1920, by which time she had become a noted feminist.

Lawson himself became slightly deaf at the age of nine and by the time he was 14 years old was almost wholly so. He had no formal education. Lawson was socialist and egalitarian, as his mother was feminist and republican. His feelings about his father are suggested in his later story "A Child in the Dark and a Foreign Father." He began writing in 1887 and found an outlet for both his poetry (which is generally of inferior quality) and short stories in *The Bulletin.* He married Bertha Bredt in 1896 and they had two children. In 1900 he went to London but his wife left him after a nervous breakdown. Between 1905 and 1909 Lawson spent 160 days in jail on drink-related charges and arrears of maintenance, and the last 20 years of his life are a tragic story of the decline and penury of perhaps Australia's most loved writer.

Lawson's major collection of fiction, *While the Billy Boils,* contains some 87 stories, originally published in three volumes, the title volume, *On the Track,* and *Over the Sliprails* (these were also combined in the one volume, with composite title in the year in which they appeared). His art began as artlessness and anecdote. The early story "An Old Mate of Your Father's" falls in between fiction and biographical reminiscence: "You remember when we hurried home from the old bush school." The young author sets it in the past and there is mention of 1959 (the gold rush) and the Eureka Stockade. Although the prevailing tone is subdued, there are already the characteristic touches of ironic humour: "And again—mostly in the fresh of the morning—they would hang about the fences on the selection and review the live stock: five dusty skeletons of cows, a hollow-sided calf or two, and one shocking piece of equine scenery." With a few exceptions, such as the very funny story, "The Loaded Dog," in which a playful dog picks up a live piece of dynamite in its mouth and terrifies the local miners, or "Bill the Ventriloquial Rooster," in which the comedy is similarly broad, his humour is mostly downbeat, and deflationary, bringing pretensions back to earth.

Increasingly also it led towards the incongruous or even grotesque. One of his finest stories, "The Bush Undertaker," concerns an old man who discovers the corpse of his friend, Brummy; he addresses it in unself-consciously friendly tones while pulling on the bottle he has found by Brummy's side. As is common in Lawson's best stories, the strength arises from the laconic understatement of the prose as the protagonist struggles to bury his friend: "On reaching the hut the old man dumped the corpse against the wall, wrong end up." In "Rats," similarly, a demented old tramp is seen fighting furiously with his "swag," while "The Union Buries Its Dead" treats the celebrated concept of "mateship" with irony and satire.

The solitude of the bush, the monotony of landscape, and unpleasant climatic conditions are all facts of life that are treated dispassionately in Lawson's work for the most part. There is merely a vast, vacated space "where God ought to be," and in many of the stories the inscrutable Australian landscape seems to personify this absence of meaning. Despite his deafness, Lawson had an extraordinary ability to capture the rhythms and intonations of idiomatic Australian speech and many of the stories—those involving his frequent protagonist Mitchell, for instance, and many of the Steelman ones—are basically dependent upon some form of oral tradition. They are written by a man who is constantly on the move, who has no time, no inclination, no capacity to put down roots, to enter into lasting relations with other human beings or with a place. They deal often with chance, vagrant encounters, random collisions that have no possibility of developing into anything more enduring, though they are often suffused with the warmth and gentleness of the man himself.

Although Lawson never wrote a novel his most ambitious prose sequence is the so-called Joe Wilson stories, in which a melancholy and rueful Joe looks back on his younger self and the failure of his marriage with Mary. Confessedly based on the failure of his own marriage, they represent Lawson's most intense effort to explore the subtleties of male and female sexual relations, a subject he usually evaded. The theme of madness springing from isolation is never far away. *Joe Wilson and His Mates* contains most of his best work after *While the Billy Boils*.

In "Water Them Geraniums" he makes a comment about the protagonist, Mrs. Spicer: "She had many bush yarns, some of them very funny, some of them rather ghastly, but all interesting, and with a grim sort of humour about them." This could well stand as a fine description of Lawson's own art at its best.

—Laurie Clancy

See the essays on "The Drover's Wife," "The Union Buries Its Dead," and "Water Them Geraniums."

LEACOCK, Stephen (Butler). Canadian. Born in Swanmore, Isle of Wight, Hampshire, England, 30 December 1869; moved to Canada with his family, 1876. Educated at Upper Canada College, Toronto, until 1887; University of Toronto, 1887, and part-time 1888–91, B.A. in modern languages 1891; University of Chicago, 1899–1903, Ph.D. in political economy 1903. Married Beatrix Hamilton in 1900 (died 1925), one son. Teacher, Uxbridge High School, 1889, Upper Canada College, 1889–99, and University of Chicago, 1899–1903; lecturer in political science, 1903–06, associate professor of political science and history, 1906–08, William Dow Professor of political economy, and head of the department of political science and economics, 1908–36, and professor emeritus, 1936–44, McGill University, Montreal. Rhodes Trust lecturer, on tour of British empire, 1907–08; gave lecture tour of England, 1921. Recipient: Lorne Pierce medal, 1937; Governor-General's award, for non-fiction, 1937. Litt.D.: Brown University, Providence, Rhode Island, 1917; D.Litt.: University of Toronto, 1919; D.H.L.: Dartmouth College, Hanover, New Hampshire, 1920. Fellow, Royal Society of Canada, 1910. *Died 28 March 1944.*

PUBLICATIONS

Collections

The Best of Leacock, edited by J. B. Priestley.   1957; as *The Bodley Head Leacock,* 1957.
The Feast of Stephen: An Anthology of Some of the Less Familiar Writings of Leacock, edited by Robertson Davies.   1970; as *The Penguin Leacock,* 1981.

Short Stories and Sketches

Literary Lapses: A Book of Sketches.   1910.
Nonsense Novels.   1911.
Sunshine Sketches of a Little Town.   1912.
Behind the Beyond, and Other Contributions to Human Knowledge.   1913.
Arcadian Adventures with the Idle Rich.   1914.
Further Foolishness: Sketches and Satires on the Follies of the Day.   1916.
Frenzied Fiction.   1918.
The Hohenzollerns in America, with the Bolsheviks in Berlin and Other Impossibilities.   1919.
Winsome Winnie and Other New Nonsense Novels.   1920.
The Garden of Folly.   1924.
The Iron Man and the Tin Woman, with Other Such Futurities.   1929.
Laugh with Leacock: An Anthology.   1930.
The Leacock Book, edited by Ben Travers.   1930.
The Dry Pickwick and Other Incongruities.   1932.
Funny Pieces.   1936.
Here Are My Lectures and Stories.   1937.
Model Memoirs and Other Sketches from Simple to Serious.   1938.
My Remarkable Uncle and Other Sketches.   1942.
Happy Stories, Just to Laugh At.   1943.

Novels

The Methods of Mr. Sellyer: A Book Store Study.   1914.
Moonbeams from the Larger Lunacy.   1915.
Over the Footlights.   1923.
College Days.   1923.
Winnowed Wisdom.   1926.
Short Circuits.   1928.
Wet Wit and Dry Humour.   1931.

Afternoons in Utopia.   1932.
The Perfect Salesman, edited by E.V. Knox.   1934.
Too Much College; or, Education Eating Up Life.   1939.
Laugh Parade.   1940.
Last Leaves.   1945.

Play

Q, with Basil Macdonald Hastings (produced 1915). 1915.

Verse

Marionettes' Calendar 1916.   1915.
Hellements of Hickonomics in Hiccoughs of Verse Done in Our Social Planning Mill.   1936.

Other

Elements of Political Science.   1906; revised edition, 1921.
Baldwin, Lafontaine, Hincks: Responsible Government. 1907; revised edition, as *Mackenzie, Baldwin, LaFontaine, Hincks,* 1926.
Adventures of the Far North.   1914.
The Dawn of Canadian History.   1914.
The Mariner of St. Malo: A Chronicle of the Voyages of Jacques Cartier.   1914.
Essays and Literary Studies.   1916.
The Unsolved Riddle of Social Justice.   1920.
My Discovery of England.   1922.
Economic Prosperity in the British Empire.   1930.
Mark Twain.   1932.
Back to Prosperity: The Great Opportunity of the Empire Conference.   1932.
Charles Dickens: His Life and Work.   1933.
Lincoln Frees the Slaves.   1934.
Humor, Its Theory and Technique.   1935.
Humor and Humanity.   1937.
My Discovery of the West: A Discussion of East and West in Canada.   1937.
All Right, Mr. Roosevelt.   1939.
Our British Empire: Its Structure, Its History, Its Strength. 1940.
Canada: The Foundations of Its Future.   1941.
Montreal: Seaport and City.   1942.
How to Write.   1943.
My Old College, 1843–1943.   1943.
Canada and the Sea.   1944.
While There Is Time: The Case Against Social Catastrophe. 1945.
The Boy I Left Behind Me (autobiography).   1946.

Editor, *Lahontan's Voyages.*   1932.
Editor, *The Greatest Pages of Dickens.*   1934.
Editor, *The Greatest Pages of American Humor.*   1936.

*

Bibliography: *Leacock: A Check-List and Index of His Writings* by Gerhard R. Lomer, 1954.

Critical Studies: *Leacock, Humorist and Humanist* by Ralph L. Curry, 1959; *Faces of Leacock: An Appreciation* by D.A. Cameron, 1967; *Leacock: A Biography* by David M. Legate, 1970; *Leacock* by Robertson Davies, 1970; *Leacock: A Reappraisal* edited by David Staines, 1986; *Leacock: Humour and Humanity* by Gerald Lynch, 1988.

*   *   *

Stephen Leacock is best known for two short story cycles, *Sunshine Sketches of a Little Town* and *Arcadian Adventures with the Idle Rich.* While he wrote numerous volumes—mostly collections of humor, and essays and books on history, economics, and political science—it is these two works of fiction that secured his reputation and continue to be widely read.

One question often asked of Leacock's work, especially *Sunshine Sketches,* is whether it can best be classified as humorous, ironic, or satiric. Leacock certainly attacks characters and their flaws in his fiction, but does so in such a gentle way that he cannot be considered a descendent of writers of Juvenalian satire like Jonathan Swift and Rabelais. As a consequence some have labeled him a "genial humorist" or "ironist." What we have to determine is the stance of the narrator: to what extent does the narrator of these two works ridicule and disdain the characters, and to what extent does he nevertheless identify with them?

According to Gerald Lynch, Leacock was a Tory humanist; he believed in the maintenance of social order but also the need for social reform. He thus rejected both socialist radicalism with its optimistic assumptions about human nature, and the rigid conservatism that denied there were social problems or any need to address them. Above all, he rejected American-style materialism, with its amoral philosophy of rampant individualism and absence of any sense of responsibility for others. Instead, he believed that human beings needed to be reformed, and one way to do that was through humor. Life for Leacock was full of incongruities and the only possible response to its contradictions and inequities was humor that seeks to change the way people think and feel. Leacock saw himself as being in no way above his fellow human beings; their flaws were his as well. Thus, he does not take the stance of a superior belittling others, but of a sympathetic witness to humankind's follies. To be human is to fail to live up to ideals, so how can he apply standards to his characters even he himself cannot meet?

Yet Leacock does hold his characters up to a gentle form of ridicule; he does not simply indulge their all-too-human failings. He is therefore best considered a writer of Horatian satire—the sort that tempers condemnation of faults without denying the essential humanity of the targets. Leacock's narrator is never consistently superior to his satiric victims; at times he enters his characters' minds and even occasionally agrees with them. For example, many commentators have noted that in *Sunshine Sketches* Leacock pokes fun at the romantic illusions Mariposa's young women hold about love and marriage, yet proceeds to make it clear that the "enchanted" homes they seek do in fact exist. What makes them enchanted is the love that renders even the most humble house a true home. By refusing to make the women and their "princes" nothing more than objects of ridicule, by presenting their illusions as positive alternatives to the more cynical form of matrimony portrayed in *Arcadian Adventures* (compare "The Foreordained Attachment of Zena Pepperleigh and Peter Pupkin" in *Sunshine Sketches* to "The Love Story of Peter Spillikins" in *Arcadian Adventures*), he lessens the harshness of the satire.

That Leacock is a satirist is undeniable when we see the attacks on selfish materialism as embodied in Josh Smith in *Sunshine Sketches* and virtually all the characters (with the possible exception of Tomlinson) in *Arcadian Adventures*. Leacock makes fun of Mariposa's pretensions, particularly its assumptions that it ranks with the great cities of the world; the main street is so wide it shows "none of the shortsightedness which is seen in the cramped dimensions of Wall Street and Piccadilly," and it is lined with "a number of buildings of extraordinary importance." The great bank robbery never happens, and the great election is an extraordinarily provincial and cynical affair. His constant use of mock-heroic language makes his satiric purpose unmistakable. *Arcadian Adventures* is undeniably satiric, with its attacks on everything from fad religions ("The Yahi-Bahi Oriental Society of Mrs. Rasselyer-Brown") to political corruption ("The Great Fight for Clean Government"). The insidious effects of materialistic modern culture are portrayed, and wonderfully skewered, in "The Rival Churches of St. Asaph and St. Osoph" and "The Ministrations of the Rev. Uttermost Dumfarthing"; since the two churches cannot operate profitably as long as they are in competition, their boards of directors agree to a merger. All questions of doctrine and spirituality are secondary to the matter of economic viability—if they are considered at all.

Nevertheless, Leacock tempers his attacks with sentimental and romantic elements. His stories usually end happily, whereas generally satiric works derive much of their power from the portrayal of triumphant evil. Also, no real harm is ever done; the effects of most characters' flaws or outright sins are seldom persistent or serious. His characters are foolish but not evil, and cause inconvenience more than danger to others. On the other hand, *Arcadian Adventures* ends with the political victory of the plutocrats, suggesting that they have now taken control of the government as well as the religion of their city. The last line of the book ("the people of the city—the best of them—drove home to their well-earned sleep, and the others—in the lower parts of the city—rose to their daily toil") suggests the poor will continue to suffer at their hands, lending a more Juvenalian touch to the satire.

Leacock does make fun of his characters, and the more materialistic they are the more they are subjected to unmerciful ridicule. But he cannot forget that they are human beings, and that as a human being himself Leacock cannot presume to look down on them. He shares their imperfection, and cannot help sympathizing with the comforting illusions that let them cope with a reality that seldom lives up to their ideals.

—Allan Weiss

See the essay on "The Marine Excursion of the Knights of Pythias."

———

LE CLÉZIO, J(ean)-M(arie) G(ustave). French. Born in Nice, 13 April 1940. Educated at schools in Africa, 1947–50, and Nice, 1950–57; Bristol University, England, 1958–59; University of London, 1960–61; Institut d'Études Littéraires, Nice, 1959–63, licence-ès-lettres 1963; University of Aix-en-Provence, M.A. 1964; University of Perpignan, docteur-ès-lettres 1983. Married Rosalie Pi-quemal in 1961 (divorced), one daughter; remarried, one daughter. Teacher, Buddhist University, Bangkok, 1966–67, University of Mexico, Mexico City, 1967, and at Boston University, University of Texas, Austin, and University of New Mexico, Albuquerque; lived with Embera Indians, Panama, 1969–73; has lived in Nice, since 1973. Recipient: Renaudot prize, 1963; Larbaud prize, 1972; Académie Française Morand prize, 1980. Chevalier de l'Ordre des Arts et des Lettres.

PUBLICATIONS

Short Stories

La Fièvre.   1965; as *Fever*, 1966.
Le Déluge.   1966; as *The Flood*, 1967.
Mondo et autres histoires.   1978; as *Mondo*, 1990.
La Ronde et autres faits divers.   1982.
Printemps et autres saisons: nouvelles.   1989.

Novels

Le Procès-Verbal.   1963; as *The Interrogation*, 1964.
Le Jour où Beaumont fit connaissance avec sa douleur.   1964.
Terra amata.   1968; as *Terra Amata*, 1969.
Le Livre des fuites.   1969; as *The Book of Flights*, 1971.
La Guerre.   1970; as *War*, 1973.
Les Géants.   1973; as *The Giants*, 1975.
Voyages de l'autre côté.   1975.
Voyage aux pays des arbres.   1978.
Désert.   1980.
Le Chercheur d'or.   1985.
Villa aurore; Orlamondo.   1985.
Balaabilou.   1985.
Onitsha.   1991.

Other

L'Extase matérielle.   1966.
Haï.   1971.
Mydriase.   1973.
L'Inconnu sur la terre.   1978.
Vers les Icebergs.   1978.
Trois Villes saintes.   1980.
Lullaby (for children).   1980.
Celui qui n'avait jamais vu la mer; La Montagne du dieu vivant (for children).   1984.
Voyage à Rodrigues.   1986.
Les Années Cannes: 40 ans de festival.   1987.
Le Rêve mexicain, ou, La Pensée interrompue.   1988.
Sirandanes; Un Petit Lexique de la lanque créole et des oiseaux.   1990.

Translator, *Les Prophéties du chilam Balam.*   1976.
Translator, *Relation de Michocan.*   1984.

*

Critical Study: *Le Clézio* by Jennifer Waelti-Walters, 1977.

* * *

With the works of J.-M.G. Le Clézio it is not easy to know where short fiction grades off into prose poetry and meditative essay, and into what he himself describes as a "roman" (novel), that is a unified book-length text in which characters occur and events at least seem to happen. In whatever he writes that is fiction, short or long, plot is not a structure but an ingredient, alongside parable and extended metaphor. Like all really powerful original minds, Le Clézio needs new literary forms to explore the meaning of the new forms of experience endured by himself and his contemporaries, and the possible ways out of their dilemmas.

Although the new forms of experience that interest Le Clézio are not uncommon, they are none the less often personal. Le Clézio shares with many important authors, including Michaux, Kafka, and Beckett, a strong preference to keep private the actual personal experiences whose nature and consequences are imaginatively examined in the published work, which, therefore, he almost maliciously forces to stand on its own, on occasion even deliberately subverting with irony the serious purpose of his imagination.

Born in 1940, Le Clézio spent three boyhood years in Africa, taught and studied for a period in England, and finished a post-graduate diploma at Nice in 1964 with a thesis on the French poet Henri Michaux (1899-1984). In 1963 Le Clézio published a very powerful fiction, *Le Procès-Verbal,* translated (wrongly) as *The Interrogation,* which won the most important of the French literary prizes, the Prix Renaudot. The collections *La Fièvre (Fever)* and *Le Déluge (The Flood)* followed. All the volumes are concerned with the major theme of Le Clézio's writing, the abatement of hostility to society and the flight from objects and sensations towards an inner self of peaceful simplicity, from which a new relationship with humanity and nature can proceed. The most appropriate literary form in which to cast light on the causes of spiritual pressures and to examine possible ways forward from the present struggles of life within advanced industrial societies, turns out, for Le Clézio, to be the parable, in which to an unusual extent he combines a penetrating academic intelligence with great imaginative vigour.

When called up for military service Le Clézio chose the option that allowed him to teach abroad; he went to Thailand to teach at the Buddhist University at Bangkok, moving from there to the University of Mexico in 1967. He then spent four further years in Mexico, living with the Embera Indians. Much of his subsequent work has had a clearly Thai Buddhist or Mayan derivation, and more recently has been addressed to children. After 1986 he published very little for some years, until *Onitsha,* which immediately went to the top of the best-seller lists.

With one exception, all the stories in *Fever* deal with the restoration of inner serenity, as in the second story, "The Day," in which Beaumont's toothache turns into an animal attacking his brain. Serenity is achieved through alcohol, and by the end of the story Beaumont is uncomfortably sitting inside his own toth, the threat from the outside world represented by the toothache successfully repelled. In the exceptional story, "Martin" the movement towards serenity is reversed. The hydrocephalic genius allows himself to be regarded as a prophet, and the people retaliate.

For ten years Le Clézio published only novels and essays, returning to the short fiction form only in 1978 with *Mondo et autres histoires (Mondo)*. Three of the eight pieces have subsequently been issued in illustrated separate editions for children, as has one of the eleven pieces in *La Ronde et autres faits divers,* short fictional narrations based on brief news items: a group of workers illegally crossing a frontier to find work, two girls running away, a rape, a child stealing the contents of a till, a road accident, a woman giving birth in a caravan attended only by a dog, a young man revisiting the site of an accident in which the girl he loved was killed. The point in a sense is cumulative. There are no brief news items; there are only human stories, and they generally have morals.

Among the stylistic devices used by Le Clézio are typographical tricks, sketches, unusual ways of laying out print, and the general exploitation of the printed page as an artefact. Stylistically the disorientation is pursued in the switching from "I" to "you" to "he" in the course of the same narration, which has the effect of underlining the irrelevance of who is telling the story or composing the fable, as also does the apparently arbitrary order of the episodes in some of the longer fiction. As Le Clézio's oeuvre has grown, the element of violence in his work has abated, although the clash of primitive opposites—like light and dark, sun and sea, male and female, town and forest—has not. The sense of sometimes mischievous humour has dwindled in importance, and is not always as obvious as in the note prefixed to "Orlamonde" from *La Ronde*. "Any resemblance to any events which have happened is impossible." There is a sense in which Le Clézio's short fiction is unambitious, refraining from delving too deeply into the paths of flight, aggression, and withdrawal possibly open to the individual, and to the link between problems of human relationship and problems of communicating in language which is almost always discernible in the longer fiction.

Typical of the shorter pieces is "Ariane." Apparently it is just the compassionate fleshing out of a news item, the rape of a young girl by a gang of motorcyclists, just over 4,500 words, about 14 pages. In fact it is a parable. The concrete city of high-rise apartment blocks has its desolate isolation violated, as the girl is violated, as modern life violates the integrity of the individual. The first paragraph describes the agglomeration of high-rise blocks, "cliffs of grey concrete," apparently deserted, next to a dry river, far from the sea or the town. Perhaps there is nobody here, perhaps the windows are walled up and painted on?

The non-omniscient narrator tells us for three pages what it seems like: no birds, no flies, occasional flitting shadows, children in the daytime, at night motorcycles. This is high-style writing, with words the average educated French speaker goes through life without using, "alvéole" (honeycomb cell), and "the voices of telivisors" rather than TV announcers. The reader is alerted to the fact that there is more to the story than the news item, even fleshed out. Reader interest must be sustained before it becomes possible to realise that this is not just a narrated event. Le Clézio substitutes for suspense recognizable over-writing to arouse the reader's expectations. Suspense would allow the reader to suppose that the text was no more than a short story.

It is by no means certain that Le Clézio consciously selects from his repertoire means of sustaining interest until the final gang rape, which until the end seems quite likely not to be going to happen. The real meaning of the fiction cannot be clear until it has. In fact reader expectation is kept alert by the tone of the linguistic communication, the repetition of syntactical patterns, exploitation of sentence lengths, the use of question marks by the narrator, the employment of tenses, and a score of other sorts of devices which a reader would not ordinarily remark on, nor a writer necessarily be conscious of using. Not all the short fiction is parable, but none is merely a written-up news item, either. The irony of pretending that it was is one of several ways in which Le Clézio delights to tease his reader, and with which even his most straight-faced fiction is frequently spiked.

—A.H.T. Levi

LE FANU, (Joseph Thomas) Sheridan. Irish. Born in Dublin, 28 August 1814. Educated at the Royal Hibernian Military School, Dublin; at home, 1827–32; Trinity College, Dublin, 1832–37, B.A. (honours) in classics 1837; Dublin Inns of Court, called to the Irish bar, 1839, but never practised. Married Susanna Bennett in 1843 (died 1858); four children. Staff member from 1837, and editor and owner, 1869–72, *Dublin University Magazine*; owner, the *Warder*, 1839–70, the *Statesman*, 1840–46, and the *Evening Packet*, all Dublin; part-owner and co-editor, Dublin *Evening Mail*, from 1861. *Died 7 February 1873.*

PUBLICATIONS

Collections

The Poems, edited by Alfred Perceval Graves.   1896.
Madam Crowl's Ghost and Other Tales of Mystery, edited by M.R. James.   1923.
Ghost Stories and Mysteries, edited by E.F. Bleiler.   1975.
The Illustrated Le Fanu: Ghost Stories and Mysteries, edited by Michael Cox.   1988.

Short Stories

Ghost Stories and Tales of Mystery.   1851.
Chronicles of Golden Friars.   1871.
In a Glass Darkly.   1872.
The Purcell Papers.   1880.
The Watcher and Other Weird Stories.   1894.

Novels

The Cock and Anchor, Being a Chronicle of Old Dublin City.   1845; as *Morley Court*, 1873; edited by B.S. Le Fanu, 1895.
The Fortunes of Colonel Torlogh O'Brien.   1847.
The House by the Church-Yard.   1863.
Wylder's Hand.   1864.
Uncle Silas: A Tale of Bartram-Haugh.   1864; edited by W.J. McCormack, 1981.
Guy Deverell.   1865.
All in the Dark.   1866.
The Tenants of Malory.   1867.
A Lost Name.   1868.
Haunted Lives.   1868.
The Wyvern Mystery.   1869.
Checkmate.   1871.
The Rose and the Key.   1871.
Willing to Die.   1873.
The Evil Guest.   1895.

*

Critical Studies: *Le Fanu* by Nelson Browne, 1951; *Le Fanu* by Michael H. Begnal, 1971; *Le Fanu and Victorian Ireland* by W.J. McCormack, 1980; *Le Fanu* by Ivan Melada, 1987.

* * *

Sheridan Le Fanu spent most of his career as a busy journalist and editor, and much of his fiction appeared initially in newspapers and periodicals, especially the *Dublin University Magazine,* with which he had a long connection. Most of his work in volume form, and all his best-known novels and stories, were published during the last ten years of his life or posthumously, during the heyday of the sensation fiction popularized by Wilkie Collins and others. However, he had been writing stories since his undergraduate days and some of his significant early work belongs to the 1830's (for example, "A Strange Event in the Life of Schalken the Painter"). Although he began by writing historical novels and stories of Irish life, he discovered his real strength to be in the area of the tale of mystery and terror. Historically he can be seen as one of the pioneers of this genre and an influence on those who practiced it in the second half of the 19th century and afterwards. M.R. James, the leading English writer of the ghost story in the 20th century, was a great admirer of Le Fanu and edited a selection of his stories, published in 1923. It has been argued that Le Fanu's work represents a landmark in Irish writing in its strong sense of form: rejecting the looser narrative forms based on the oral tradition and favoured by earlier writers of fiction, he shows a concern with structure, point of view, and narrative framing.

His best stories are to be found in the collection *In a Glass Darkly,* which was originally issued in three volumes in 1872 and has been frequently reprinted. Introducing a 1947 reprint, V.S. Pritchett comments that Le Fanu "had the gift of brevity, the talent for the poetic sharpness and discipline of the short tale." The stories of the collection include "Green Tea," "Carmilla," "The Familiar," "Mr. Justice Harbottle," and "The Room in the Dragon Volant." All five are linked by the device of a first-person narrator who has edited the papers of Dr. Martin Hesselius—"a wanderer like myself, like me a physician, and like me an enthusiast in his profession." The references to wanderings and enthusiasm create a romantic aura that is deliberately tempered by the spirit of scientific enquiry in which the various "case-histories" are presented, and the effect of the framing is to provide an apparently clinical and objective standpoint for the recounting of stories of mystery and horror, as well as distancing the fictional events by furnishing a plausible contemporary intermediary between the action and the reader.

The cases presented have been selected, we are told, from "about two hundred and thirty" to be found among the late physician's notes. This detail is given at the opening of "The Familiar," the prologue to which mentions that Hesselius has had the story from an "unexceptionable narrator," a "venerable Irish Clergyman"—yet another credible intermediary between tale and audience—and offers the physician's generalized reflections, in the language of medical or psychological discourse, on the story that follows. The story itself begins in the late 18th century (another form of distancing) and concerns a man persecuted by a mysterious presence that dogs his footsteps and eventually drives him to his death. The chilling climax comes when one of those who find him dead exclaims that "there was something else on the bed with him" and points to "a deep indenture, as if caused by a heavy pressure, near the foot of the bed." As befits a story of supernatural malevolence, the cause of the persecution is never fully explained, though there is a hint that punishment has been exacted for a moral offence in the victim's earlier life.

"Mr. Justice Harbottle" similarly leads the reader to the heart of the narrative through an elaborate series of informants and eye-witnesses and is another striking example of Le Fanu's interest in fictional structures as a means of compelling a suspension of disbelief. The subject is an elderly judge, "dangerous and unscrupulous" in the execution of his office, who had "the reputation of being about the wickedest man in England." There are strong implications that his death, attributed officially to suicide, has been caused by a ghostly visitant who has been one of the victims of his judicial severity. Again, the ending has a noncommittal quality, not forcing a supernatural interpretation upon the reader but presenting a final ambiguity.

"The Room in the Dragon Volant" is the longest story in the collection, in effect a novella. Set in Paris and opening in 1815, it is cast in the form of an autobiographical narrative and has elements in common with Wilkie Collins's well-known story "A Terribly Strange Bed."

Le Fanu's combination in his stories of mystery and a sense of evil has led to his being compared to Hawthorne. His great popularity in the late 19th century is attested by Henry James's comment in a story of 1888, with reference to an English country house, that "there was the customary novel of Mr. Le Fanu for the bedside, the ideal reading in a country house for the hours after midnight." A modern critic, Harold Orel, has said of *In a Glass Darkly* that it "still retains the power to change a reader's attitude toward the possibility of vengeful ghosts and the lurking dangers of darkness in both city streets and one's own home." As the last phrase suggests, Le Fanu, like Wilkie Collins, domesticated the Gothic tale of terror, transposing mysterious happenings from remote castles in Europe to more familiar scenes (though "Carmilla" is a notable exception to this rule) and from the Middle Ages to the 19th century. And, again like Wilkie Collins, his concern with authenticity led him to engage in experiments in fictional structure and point of view that were well in advance of normal practice in his time.

—Norman Page

See the essays on "Carmilla" and "Green Tea."

LENGYEL, József. Hungarian. Born in Marcali, Somogy County, 4 August 1896. Studied philosophy at University of Budapest and University of Vienna. Took part in Communist Revolution of 1919; arrested and consequently fled to Vienna, 1919; moved to Berlin, 1927: worked as journalist, dramaturge, Prometheus Film Studio, and editor, *Film und Volk*; emigrated to Moscow, 1930; editorial staff member, *Sarló és Kalapács*; imprisoned in work camps, Siberia, 1938; released, rearrested, and released again, worked as night watchman, 1953; rehabilitated and allowed to return to Hungary, 1955. Founding member, Hungarian Communist Party, 1918. Co-editor, *Vörös újság* and *Ifjú Gárda*. Recipient: Attila József prize, 1957;

Central Council of Hungarian Trade Union prize, 1958; Kossuth prize, 1963. *Died 14 July 1975.*

PUBLICATIONS

Short Stories

Igéző; elbeszélés (novella).   1961; as *Igéző,* 1962; as *The Spell,* with *From Beginning to End,* 1966.
Elejétől végig (novella).   1963; as *From Beginning to End,* with *The Spell,* 1966.
Elévült tartozás (includes *Igéző* and *Elejétől végig*).   1964; as *Acta Sanctorum and Other Tales,* 1970.
Ézsau mondja [Esau Sayeth].   1969.

Novels

Visegrádi utca [Visegrád Street].   1932; revised, 1957.
Prenn Ferenc hányatott élete avagy minden tovább mutat.   1930; revised edition, 1958; as *Prenn Drifting,* 1966.
Három hídépítő; elbeszélés egy alkota´s eléletéről [Three Bridge Builders].   1960.
Újra a kezdet.   1964; as *The Judge's Chair,* 1968.
Mit bír az ember (Újra a kezdet, Trend Richárd vallomásai) [How Much Can a Man Bear?].   1965.
Szembesítés.   1972; as *Confrontation,* 1973.

Other

Keresem Kína közepét; útinapló [I Am Looking for the Centre of China: Travel Diary].   1963.
Mérni a mérhetetlent [To Measure the Immeasurable] (collection).   2 vols., 1966.
Bécsi portyák [Visits to Vienna] (travelogue).   1970.
Neve, Bernhard Reisig; föld és külföld [His Name, Bernhard Reisig; Home and Abroad].   1979.

*

Bibliography: in *Hungarian Authors: A Bibliographical Handbook,* by A. Tezla, 1970.

Critical Studies: "The Return of Lengyel" by P. Ignotus, in *Encounter,* 1965; "Lengyel: Chronicler of Cruel Years" by George Gömöri, in *Books Abroad* 49(3), Summer 1975.

*   *   *

The fiction of the 20th century would be much poorer without authors who wrote mainly about the world of Soviet concentration camps and detention centres known, since Solzhenitsyn, as the "Gulag." This theme lies in the centre of József Lengyel's work, too. Lengyel was one of the founders of the Hungarian Communist Party in 1918. After the failure of the Hungarian Soviet Republic he emigrated to Vienna and from there, via Germany, to Moscow. He was arrested in 1938 and spent the following 18 years in jail and in Soviet labour camps; he could return to Hungary only in 1955 and began to publish his stories connected with camp experiences only some years later.

All these biographical details have to be recalled, for Lengyel is, indeed, a "biographical" writer, someone who based most of his writing on experiences of his own. His most favoured genre was the short novel or the long story, differences between the two often being blurred. It was with the long story *Igézö (The Spell)* that he first made an impact. This is the story of a nameless political exile, a foreigner who lives in the Siberian forest and works there as a charcoal-burner. Through patience and kindness he wins the affection of a neighbour's dog and also earns the confidence (and the animosity) of some of the local inhabitants. *The Spell* is a melancholy tale, scenes of which are built up by what the critic L. Czigány called "the accumulation of visual detail." The short novel *Elénjetol végig (From Beginning to End)* deals with the vicissitudes of Lengyel's favourite alter-ego György Nekeresdi (Do-Not-Look-For-Him George), a foreign Communist, innocently arrested and jailed in one of Stalin's great purges. The narrator tells his story in the first person, recounting his horrifying experiences in overcrowded, putrid Russian prisons, Arctic labour camps where people freeze to death or die of sheer exhaustion or of pellagra. Bread is the leitmotif in the ballad-like tale of the hero's life; it links seemingly unrelated episodes. In the Siberian camp, bread is "life, itself"—respected with an almost religious awe—and for stealing bread the punishment is death. Lengyel's message at the end of this story is simple: "May there be bread for everybody!"

Lengyel's best stories are certainly those that deal with his personal tribulations: they all belong to his "Russian cycle" collected in the volume *Elévült tartozás* (Barred Debt). The hero of "Kicsi, mérges öregúr" ("Acta Sanctorum") is an old professor of physics who is arrested on trumped charges and subjected to beatings and humiliation by the interrogators. The little professor, who himself hates smoking, steals cigarette butts for his fellow-prisoners in the interrogation room—an act of saintly compassion in the eyes of Lengyel. The story "Sárga pipacsok" ("Yellow Poppies"), which takes place in an Arctic camp, is narrated in the first person; the narrator works as nurse in the camp hospital. A patient tells him about the mass executions that happened in Norilsk only a year or two earlier. Now yellow poppies grow on the unmarked graves of the victims. Lengyel ends the story on a cautious note: he is not sure whether the patient told the truth, but what if "even if a small fraction of what he had told were true . . . I myself also saw those yellow poppies."

Yet another labour camp story "Hohem és freier" (1964, "'Hohem' and 'Freier'") is, according to the author, a description that "has more in common with natural history than with literature" (translated by Edna Lenart). It highlights two distinct species of camp-dwellers, the professional thief and criminal ("Hohem") and the average simpleton without camp experience ("Freier"). The story describes the way in which the latter is robbed without noticing it at all. In this small piece of labour camp sociology Lengyel exhibits a sense of humour that colours only very few of his otherwise sombre and melancholic stories.

In the small collection *Ézsau mondja* (Esau Sayeth) published in 1969 Lengyel included more Siberian and other sketches that he characterized as "being half-way between fiction and truthful chronicles of reality." These stories bear the collective title "Obsitosok szökésröl beszélnek" (Veterans Talk About Escapes) and include the dramatic account of a Communist's escape from counter-revolutionary Hungary in 1919. For all the crimes of Stalin and the monolithic horror of Soviet Communism, Lengyel remained a (somewhat embittered and intensely critical) Communist to the end of his life. This fact, unfortunately, impaired his ability to write stories about postwar reality in Hungary with the same intensity as he had handled the

Gulag themes. The only striking story in *Ézsau mondja* that is not connected with prison life or Siberian escapes is entitled "Neszesszer" (Vanity Bag). It tells, in an anecdotic form, what particular impulse made a young man, the son of a colonel in the army of the Austro-Hungarian Monarchy, turn into a Communist. Social injustice was the initial theme of the young Lengyel, but protest against inhumanity and political injustice became the main thrust of his work after his release from captivity and return to his native country, where he could at last tell his own painful and terrifying story.

—George Gömöri

LENZ, Siegfried. German. Born in Lyck, East Prussia (now Elk, Poland), 17 March 1926. Educated at the University of Hamburg, 1945–48. Served in the navy during World War II. Married Lieselotte Lenz in 1949. Reporter, 1948–50, and editor, 1950–51, *Die Welt* newspaper, Hamburg; freelance writer, from 1951; campaign speaker for Social Democratic party, from 1965; visting lecturer, University of Houston, Texas, 1969. Member, Gruppe 47. Recipient: Schickele prize, 1952; Lessing prize, 1953; Hauptmann prize, 1961; Mackensen prize, 1962; Schickele prize, 1962; City of Bremen prize, 1962; State of North Rhine-Westphalia arts prize, 1966; Gryphius prize, 1979; German Free Masons prize, 1979; Thomas Mann prize, 1984; Raabe prize, 1987; Federal Booksellers peace prize, 1988; Galinsky Foundation prize, 1989. Honorary doctorate: University of Hamburg, 1976. Lives in Hamburg.

PUBLICATIONS

Short Stories

So zärtlich war Suleyken.   1955.
Das Feuerschiff.   1960; title story as *The Lightship,* 1962.
Der Hafen ist voller Geheimnisse: Ein Feature in Erzählungen und zwei masurische Geschichten.   1963.
Lehmanns Erzählungen; oder, So schön war mein Markt: Aus den Bekenntnissen eines Schwarzhändlers.   1964.
Das Wrack, and Other Stories, edited by C.A.H. Russ.   1967.
Die Festung und andere Novellen.   1968.
Lukas, sanftmütiger Knecht.   1970.
Gesammelte Erzählungen.   1970.
Erzählungen.   1972.
Meistererzählungen.   1972.
Der Geist der Mirabelle: Geschichten aus Bollerup.   1975.
Die Erzählungen: 1949–1984.   3 vols., 1986.
Selected Stories.   1989.

Novels

Es waren Habichte in der Luft.   1951.
Duell mit dem Schatten.   1953.
Der Mann im Strom.   1957.
Dasselbe.   1957.
Jäger des Spotts.   1958; as *Jäger des Spotts, und andere Erzählungen,* edited by Robert H. Spaethling, 1965.
Brot und Spiele.   1959.
Das Wunder von Striegeldorf: Geschichten.   1961.

Stimmungen der See.   1962.
Stadtgespräch, adapted from his play *Zeit der Schuldlosen.*
   1963; as *The Survivor,* 1965.
Der Spielverderber.   1965.
Begegnung mit Tieren, with Hans Bender and Werner
   Bergengruen.   1966.
Deutschstunde.   1968; as *The German Lesson,* 1971.
Hamilkar Schass aus Suleyken.   1970.
So war es mit dem Zirkus: Fünf Geschichten aus Suleyken.
   1971.
Ein Haus aus lauter Liebe.   1973.
Das Vorbild.   1973; as *An Exemplary Life,* 1976.
Einstein überquert die Elbe bei Hamburg.   1975.
Die Kunstradfahrer und andere Geschichten.   1976.
Heimatmuseum.   1978; as *The Heritage,* 1981.
Der Verlust.   1981.
Der Anfang von etwas.   1981.
Ein Kriegsende.   1984.
Exerzierplatz.   1985; as *Training Ground,* 1991.
Der Verzicht.   1985.
Das serbische Mädchen.   1987.
Geschichten ut Bollerup.   1987.
Motivsuche.   1988.
Die Klangprobe.   1990.

Plays

Das schönste Fest der Welt (radio play).   1956.
Zeit der Schuldlosen; Zeit der Schuldigen (radio play).
   1961; stage adaptation (in German), 1966.
Das Gesicht: Komödie (produced 1964).   1964.
Haussuchung (radio play).   1967.
*Die Augenbinde; Schauspiel; Nicht alle Förster sind froh:
   Ein Dialog.*   1970.
Drei Stücke.   1980.
Zeit der Schuldlosen und andere Stücke.   1988.

Radio Plays: *Zeit der Schuldlosen/Zeit der Schuldigen,*
1961; *Das schönste Fest der Welt.*

Other

So leicht fängt man keine Katze.   1954. *Der einsame
   Jäger.*   1955.
Das Kabinett der Konterbande.   1956.
Flug über Land und Meer: Nordsee—Holstein—Nordsee,
   with Dieter Seelmann.   1967; as *Wo die Möwen
   schreien: Flug über Norddeutschlands Küsten und
   Länder,* 1976.
Leute von Hamburg: Satirische Porträts.   1968.
Versäum nicht den Termin der Freude.   1970.
Lotte soll nicht sterben (for children).   1970; as *Lotte
   macht alles mit,* 1978.
Beziehungen: Ansichten und Bekenntnisse zur Literatur.
   1970.
Die Herrschaftssprache der CDU.   1971.
*Verlorenes Lang—gewonnene Nachbarschaft: zur Ostpoli-
   tik der Bundesregierung.*   1972.
Der Amüsierdoktor.   1972.
Der Leseteufel.   1972(?).
*Elfenbeinturm und Barrikade: Schriftsteller zwischen Liter-
   atur und Politik.*   1976.
Die Wracks von Hamburg: Hörfunk-Features.   1978.
*Himmel, Wolken, weites Land: Flug über Meer, Marsch,
   Geest und Heide,* with Dieter Seelmann.   1979.
Waldboden: Sechsunddreissig Farbstiftzeichnungen, illus-
   trated by Liselotte Lenz.   1979.

Gespräche mit Manès Sperber und Leszek Kołakowski,
   edited by Alfred Mensak.   1980.
*Über Phantasie: Lenz, Gespräche mit Heinrich Böll, Günter
   Grass, Walter Kempowski, Pavel Kohout,* edited by
   Alfred Mensak.   1982.
Fast ein Triumph: Aus einem Album.   1982.
*Elfenbeinturm und Barrikade: Erfahrungen am Schreib-
   tisch.*   1983.
Manès Sperber, sein letztes Jahr, with Manès and Jenka
   Sperber.   1985.
Etwas über Namen (address).   1985.
Kleines Strandgut, illustrated by Liselotte Lenz.   1986.
Am Rande des Friedens.   1989.

Editor, with Egon Schramm, *Wippchens charmante Schar-
   mützel,* by Julius Stettenheim.   1960.

*

Critical Studies: "From the Gulf Stream in the Main
Stream: Lenz and Hemingway" by Sumner Kirshner, in
Research Studies, June 1967; "Narrowing the Distance:
Lenz's *Deutschstunde*" by Robert H. Paslick, in *German
Quarterly,* March 1973; "The Macabre Festival: A Consid-
eration of Six Stories by Lenz" by Colin Russ, in *Deutung
und Bedeutung: Studies in German and Comparative Liter-
ature,* edited by Brigitte Schludermann and others, 1973;
"How It Seems and How It Is: Marriage in Three Stories by
Lenz" by Esther N. Elstun, in *Orbis litterarum* 29(2), 1974;
"Ironic Reversal in the Short Stories of Lenz," in *Neophilo-
logus* 58(4), 1974, and *Lenz,* 1978, both by Brian O.
Murdoch; "Lenz's *Deutschstunde*: A North German Nov-
el," in *German Life and Letters,* July 1975, and "The
'Lesson' in Lenz's *Deutschstunde,*" in *Seminar,* February
1977, both by Peter Russell; "Zygmunt's Follies? On Lenz's
Heimatmuseum" by Geoffrey P. Butler, in *German Life
and Letters,* January 1980; "Captive Creator in Lenz's
Deutschstunde: Writer, Reader, and Response" by Todd
Kontje, in *German Quarterly* 53, 1980; "The Interlocutor
and the Narrative Transmission of the Past: On Lenz's
Heimatmuseum" by Marilyn Sibley Fries, in *Monatshefte,*
Winter 1987; "The Eye of the Witness: Photography in
Lenz's Short Stories" by Hanna Geldrich-Leffmann, in
Modern Language Review, April 1989.

*   *   *

Siegfried Lenz is one of Germany's best known and most
widely-read authors of the postwar period. His vast oeuvre
includes many literary genres. It is, however, his fiction
that brought him world fame; his novel *Deutschstunde* (*The
German Lesson*) has been translated into some 20 languages.
   Lenz's formative years, as well as those of other writers of
his generation, notably Günter Grass, Martin Walser, Ilse
Aichinger, and Hans Magnus Enzensberger, were overshadowed by the Nazi regime. At the age of 17 Lenz was
drafted into the German Navy where he witnessed the
collapse of the Third Reich. In his early works he tried to
come to terms not only with the horrors of Nazism but
especially with the moral guilt of those who gave tacit
approval to the regime. His subsequent work deals with
past and present socio-political conflicts. Lenz's literary
technique is guided by his desire to establish close contact
with the reader. He does not openly accuse and condemn,

since he wishes to establish "an effective pact with the reader in order to reduce existing evils." To this end his protagonists are never heroes but rather ordinary people who have become victims of conflict. The basic reason for this conflict, Lenz maintains, is that individuals are never able to determine their own identity; it is shaped by others and by the outside world. This results in lack of understanding and communication, in wrong and often tragic decisions.

In the story "Luke, Gentle Servant" Lenz depicts this dilemma in a single episode that hints at a universal situation. The action takes place in Kenya, Africa, in 1952, at the time of the Mau Mau rebellion against the white settlers. The story is told in the first person which is meant to draw the reader closely into the events, a device used in a number of Lenz's stories ("The Great Wildenberg," "A Friend of the Government," and "Sixth Birthday"); in all of them the narrator either witnesses the tragedy of a victim's fall, or becomes a victim himself. The latter is the case in "Luke, Gentle Servant." The title of the story is ironic in that "gentle" Luke, as his white master (and the narrator of the story) characterized him, is the leader of the Kikuju tribe who exacts vengeance for years of colonial exploitation. The narrator's long and painful journey back to his farm and the fact that Luke betrays him symbolizes the white man's guilt for which he is now punished. "Luke, Gentle Servant" is one of the best examples of Lenz's gift as a short fiction writer: he defines his characters with great psychological insight and the metaphorical and the realistic are tightly interwoven to create tension and suspense.

That Lenz is also a born storyteller becomes evident in his delightfully humourous collections *So zärtlich war Suleyken*, in which he depicts episodes from his Prussian homeland, and *Der Geist der Mirabelle*, in which the village Bollerup stands symbolically for a peaceful and uncorrupted country life. However, Lenz's humour is seldom so unrestricted; in the rest of his work it is often supplanted by moralistic and humanitarian concerns.

"The Lightship," another major story, deals with the conflict between power and order, a common theme in Lenz's work. Three shipwrecked men who have been taken aboard the ship turn out to be dangerous criminals. The conflict that develops is twofold: the criminals' brutality is opposed by the captain, Freytag, representative of established order. That order is also threatened when members of the lightship's crew turn against Freytag out of fear of the criminals. Lenz conveys several messages in "The Lightship"—heroic actions are senseless against a murderous power once it has established itself. The order the captain seems to maintain on his ship (symbol of a trusted societal system) is an illusion, since power can so easily fall into wrong hands. The story warns against society's uncritical trust in political institutions and demands political awareness and vigilance from every citizen, in order not to fall prey to abusive powers.

In "The Lightship" Lenz touches also on a theme that is at the centre of a number of his stories—the father-son relationship. The father is either perceived as overpowering ("The Laughingstock"), or as weak ("Das Wrack" [The Shipwreck], "The Lightship"), or he is overly doting ("Die Nacht im Hotel" [The Night in the Hotel], "The Dictator's Son"). In every case, though, the son goes through a transformation process which will turn him into a responsible adult. "The Laughingstock," for example, depicts Atoq's attempt to free himself from the mighty image of his father, once a great hunter, who has crippled him psychologically and turned him into the worst hunter of the village and the laughing stock of his fellow Eskimos. The develop-

ment of the story is also typical of Lenz's narrative where an unexpected twist of fate creates suspense and heightens the tragedy of the victim. The meat of the musk-ox, which Atoq finally kills and which will prove his prowess to the villagers, is eaten by bears. However, the killing has broken the father's power and Atoq, transformed, will set out again on the hunt.

Lenz's work is characterized throughout by a sustained social criticism; he depicts "the moment of truth," as critic Colin Russ points out, in which his characters are exposed to a situation where everything which was taken for granted is suddenly doubtful, endangered, or is destroyed. Put to the test, many of these characters break. However, Lenz's compassion and sympathy for his characters and their misfortune is also characteristic of his work because, as he notes, "In our world the artist also has become an accessory—to unlawfulness, hunger, persecution and perilous dreams." It is his solidarity with those fellow human beings who have fallen victims to a harsh reality that has contributed to Lenz's success as a humane observer of his time.

—Renate Benson

LESSING, Doris (May, née Tayler). British. Born in Kermansha, Persia, 22 October 1919; moved with her family to England, then to Banket, Southern Rhodesia, 1924. Educated at Dominican Convent School, Salisbury, Southern Rhodesia, 1926–34. Married 1) Frank Charles Wisdom in 1939 (divorced 1943), one son and one daughter; 2) Gottfried Lessing in 1945 (divorced 1949), one son. Au pair, Salisbury, 1934–35; telephone operator and clerk, Salisbury, 1937–39; typist, 1946–48; journalist, Cape Town Guardian, 1949; moved to London, 1950; secretary, 1950; member of the Editorial Board, *New Reasoner* (later *New Left Review*), 1956. Recipient: Maugham award, for fiction, 1954; Médicis prize (France), 1976; Austrian State prize, 1981; Shakespeare prize (Hamburg), 1982; W.H. Smith literary award, 1986. Honorary degree, Princeton, 1989. Associate member, American Academy, 1974; honorary fellow, Modern Language Association (U.S.), 1974; distinguished fellow in literature, University of East Anglia, 1991.

PUBLICATIONS

Short Stories

This Was the Old Chief's Country: Stories.   1952.
Five: Short Novels.   1953.
No Witchcraft for Sale: Stories and Short Novels.   1956.
The Habit of Loving.   1957.
A Man and Two Women: Stories.   1963.
African Stories.   1964.
Winter in July.   1966.
The Black Madonna.   1966.
Nine African Stories, edited by Michael Marland.   1968.
The Story of a Non-Marrying Man and Other Stories.   1972; as *The Temptation of Jack Orkney and Other Stories,*   1972.
Collected African Stories.   1981.
   This Was the Old Chief's Country.   1973.

The Sun Between Their Feet.   1973.
(Stories), edited by Alan Cattell.   1976.
Collected Stories: To Room Nineteen and The Temptation of Jack Orkney.   2 vols., 1978; as *Stories,* 1 vol., 1978.
The Real Thing: Stories and Sketches.   1992.
London Observed: Stories and Sketches.   1992.

Novels

The Grass Is Singing.   1950.
Children of Violence:
  Martha Quest.   1952.
  A Proper Marriage.   1954.
  A Ripple from the Storm.   1958.
  Landlocked.   1965.
  The Four-Gated City.   1969.
Retreat to Innocence.   1956.
The Golden Notebook.   1962.
Briefing for a Descent into Hell.   1971.
The Summer Before the Dark.   1973.
The Memoirs of a Survivor.   1974.
Canopus in Argos: Archives:
  Shikasta.   1979.
  The Marriages Between Zones Three, Four, and Five.   1980.
  The Sirian Experiments.   1981.
  The Making of the Representative for Planet 8.   1982.
  The Sentimental Agents.   1983.
The Diaries of Jane Somers.   1984.
  The Diary of a Good Neighbour.   1983.
  If the Old Could—.   1984.
The Good Terrorist.   1985.
The Fifth Child.   1988.

Plays

Before the Deluge (produced 1953).
Mr. Dollinger (produced 1958).
Each His Own Wilderness (produced 1958).   In *New English Dramatists,* 1959.
The Truth about Billy Newton (produced 1960).
Play with a Tiger (produced 1962).   1962.
The Storm, from a play by Alexander Ostrovsky (produced 1966).
The Singing Door (for children), in *Second Playbill 2,* edited by Alan Durband.   1973.
The Making of the Representative for Planet 8 (opera libretto), music by Philip Glass, from the novel by Lessing (produced 1988).

Television Plays: *The Grass Is Singing,* from her own novel, 1962; *Care and Protection* and *Do Not Disturb* (both in *Blackmail* series), 1966; *Between Men,* 1967.

Verse

Fourteen Poems.   1959.

Other

Going Home.   1957; revised edition, 1968.
In Pursuit of the English: A Documentary.   1960.
Particularly Cats.   1967; as *Particularly Cats—and Rufus,* 1991.
A Small Personal Voice: Essays, Reviews, Interviews, edited by Paul Schlueter.   1974.
Prisons We Choose to Live Inside.   1986.

The Wind Blows Away Our Words (on Afghanistan).   1987.
The Lessing Reader.   1989.
African Laughter: Four Visits to Zimbabwe (memoir).   1992.

*

Bibliography: *Lessing: A Bibliography* by Catharina Ipp, 1967; *Lessing: A Checklist of Primary and Secondary Sources* by Selma R. Burkom and Margaret Williams, 1973; *Lessing: An Annotated Bibliography of Criticism* by Dee Seligman, 1981; *Lessing: A Descriptive Bibliography of Her First Editions* by Eric T. Brueck, 1984.

Critical Studies: *Lessing* by Dorothy Brewster, 1965; *Lessing,* 1973, and *Lessing's Africa,* 1978, both by Michael Thorpe; *Lessing: Critical Studies* edited by Annis Pratt and L.S. Dembo, 1974; *The City and the Veld: The Fiction of Lessing* by Mary Ann Singleton, 1976; *Boulder-Pushers: Women in the Fiction of Margaret Drabble, Lessing, and Iris Murdoch* by Carol Seiler-Franklin, 1979; *Notebooks / Memoirs / Archives: Reading and Re-reading Lessing* edited by Jenny Taylor, 1982; *Lessing* by Lorna Sage, 1983; *Lessing* by Mona Knapp, 1984; *Lessing and Women's Appropriation of Science Fiction* by Mariette Clare, 1984; *The Unexpected Universe of Lessing: A Study in Narrative Technique* by Katherine Fishburn, 1985; *Lessing* edited by Eve Bertelsen, 1985; *Critical Essays on Lessing* edited by Claire Sprague and Virginia Tiger, 1986; *Forbidden Fruit: On the Relationship Between Women and Knowledge in Lessing, Slema Lagerlöf, Kate Chopin, and Margaret Atwood* by Bonnie St. Andrews, 1986; *Rereading Lessing: Narrative Patterns of Doubling and Repetition* by Claire Sprague, 1987, and *In Pursuit of Lessing: Nine Nations Reading* edited by Sprague, 1990; *Lessing: Life, Work, and Criticism* by Katherine Fishburn, 1987; *The Theme of Enclosure in Selected Works of Lessing* by Shirley Budhos, 1987; *Lessing: The Alchemy of Survival* edited by Carey Kaplan and Ellen Cronan Rose, 1988; *Lessing* by Ruth Whittaker, 1988; *Lessing* by Jeannette King, 1989; *Understanding Lessing* by Jean Pickering, 1990.

*   *   *

Doris Lessing is a vigorous and prolific writer, with a high sense of the writer's social and political responsibility, which comes out in both her themes and her narrative modes. In addition to her numerous novels, she had published enough short stories by 1978 to fill four volumes. These were divided, as is her overall oeuvre, between the earlier stories dealing with Africa, where she was born, and later stories mainly set in London, where she came to live.

The African stories show Lessing to be a writer in the realist tradition keen to draw her readers' attention to what is going on in a particular community well-known to the writer. The stories reflect the colonial history of Africa and deal with its natural features. One such story is "The Old Chief Mshlanga," narrated in the third-person, but from a position close to that of the girl who is the protagonist. The daughter of English parents, she is brought up to think of England as home, and Africa as strange and foreign. But of course that strange and foreign landscape must be explored, and its exploration will involve contact with its people, otherwise known only in the form of household servants.

The girl ventures out on her own, and meets a chief, who addresses her with a respectful courtesy she is too immature to reciprocate. On a later trip, she finds herself in the village of the old chief again. This time their conversation leaves her with a sense of self-criticism. The landscape seems to be accusing her: "it seemed to say to me: you walk here as a destroyer." There is one more sight of the chief, when he comes to her father's farm to protest against the farmer's demand for 20 of his goats in restitution for damage done to crops. When the farmer proves intractable, the old chief leaves. His last words are translated: "All this land, this land you call yours, is his land, and belongs to our people." Soon afterwards, the chief and his people are moved two hundred miles away, "to a proper native reserve." The story ends with the girl visiting the deserted village a year or so later, to find it "a festival of pumpkins," and she speculates that "the settler lucky enough to be allotted the lush warm valley" would find there an "unsuspected vein of richness."

The political point is made with no unnecessary rhetoric; and since we are kept close to the girl's point of view, the implications can be left open for the reader to spell out. This is of course true of most interesting stories, but Lessing is particularly good at controlling her endings. "The Black Madonna" is, as she herself remarked, much fuller of bile. It tells of the relationship between a released Italian prisoner with some artistic abilities and a British captain, who is in charge of erecting a mock village for bombarding as part of a military tatoo. The captain becomes unintentionally drawn to the sentimental yet capable Italian, who paints a black peasant Madonna in his mock church. ("'Good God', said the captain, 'you can't do that . . . You can't have a black Madonna'.") At the end the captain is in hospital, and although he is drawn to the Italian's warmth and honesty, he cannot accept his offer of friendship. But the "stiff upper lip" is triumphant: "Not a sound escaped him, for the fear the nurses might hear." If the reader feels here something of D.H. Lawrence's criticism of British rigidity, that is evidence of Lessing's power.

The African stories overlap in their themes and concerns with those set elsewhere. A story with something of the bile of "The Black Madonna" is "Mrs. Fortescue." This concerns a 16-year-old schoolboy, Fred Danderlea, whose parents keep an off-license in London. An unhappy adolescent, he finds himself distant from his parents and no longer at ease with his older sister. The other occupant of the house is the long-time lodger, Mrs. Fortescue, who frequently goes out in the evenings and is regularly visited by an elderly gentleman. Fred comes to realize that she is a prostitute, and this arouses an uncontrollable response in him. One evening he makes conversation with Mrs. Fortescue, and then forces himself physically on her. The narrative vividly conveys his adolescent need and his crudity, and gives Mrs. Fortescue's plaintive words ("That wasn't very nice, was it?") a curious pathos. The story's focus is on the instabilities, pains, and cruelties of adolescence, and certainly does not suggest that the life of suburban London offers more vivid human possibilities than its colonial counterpart in Africa. Nevertheless in Lessing's stories we are usually aware of human potentialities trying to break through psychological and social restraints to achieve some kind of harmony.

Lessing's short stories do not always employ the realist mode. "Side Benefits of an Honourable Profession," for example, is narrated by a sophisticated unidentified voice of someone in the world of the theatre, and tells in gossipy style a number of stories to do with the vagaries of human relationships. "Report on the Threatened City" is in the mixed mode of the later science fiction about Canopus, and takes us into a world on the verge of self-destruction. In a variety of ways, and in many varied settings, Lessing's fiction consistently attempts to make us face the disturbing facts about ourselves and the world we create. Since she is so prolific, not all the stories are of equal value. Nevertheless, her overall achievement in the genre is worthy of attention and respect. The quality and interest of her longer works of fiction should not deter readers from the many pleasures to be found in her short fiction.

—Peter Faulkner

See the essays on "The Black Madonna," "To Room 19," and "A Woman on a Roof."

———————

LINKLATER, Eric (Robert Russell). British. Born in Penarth, Glamorganshire, Wales, 8 March 1899; grew up in Cardiff and Aberdeen. Educated at Aberdeen Grammar School, 1913–16; University of Aberdeen (Seafield, Minto, and Senatus prizes), 1918–25, M.A. in English 1925. Served in the Black Watch, 1917–19: private; served in the Royal Engineers, commanding Orkney Fortress, 1939–41: major; staff member, War Office Directorate of Public Relations, 1941–45; temporary lieutenant in Korea, 1951: territorial decoration. Married Marjorie MacIntyre in 1933; two daughters and two sons. Assistant editor, *Times of India,* Bombay, 1925–27; assistant to the professor of English literature, University of Aberdeen, 1927–28; Commonwealth fellow, Cornell University, Ithaca, New York, and the University of California, Berkeley, 1928–30; full-time writer from 1930; lived in Italy, then in Dounby, Orkney, until 1947, Easter Ross, 1947–72, and Aberdeenshire, 1972–74. Scottish Nationalist parliamentary candidate for East Fife, 1933; rector, University of Aberdeen, 1945–48; deputy lieutenant of Ross and Cromarty, Scotland, 1968–73. Recipient: Library Association Carnegie medal, for children's book, 1945. L.L.D.: University of Aberdeen, 1946. Fellow, Royal Society of Edinburgh, 1971. C.B.E. (Commander, Order of the British Empire), 1954. *Died 7 November 1974.*

PUBLICATIONS

Short Stories

The Crusader's Key.   1933.
The Revolution.   1934.
God Likes Them Plain: Short Stories.   1935.
Sealskin Trousers and Other Stories.   1947.
A Sociable Plover and Other Stories and Conceits.   1957.
The Stories.   1968.

Novels

White-Maa's Saga.   1929.
Poet's Pub.   1929.
Juan in America.   1931.
The Men of Ness: The Saga of Thorlief Coalbiter's Sons.   1932.
Magnus Merriman.   1934.
Ripeness Is All.   1935.

Juan in China.   1937.
The Sailor's Holiday.   1937.
The Impregnable Women.   1938.
Judas.   1939.
Private Angelo.   1946.
A Spell for Old Bones.   1949.
Mr. Byculla.   1950.
Laxdale Hall.   1951.
The House of Gair.   1953.
The Faithful Ally.   1954; as *The Sultan and the Lady,* 1955.
The Dark of Summer.   1956.
Position at Noon.   1958; as *My Fathers and I,* 1959.
The Merry Muse.   1959.
Roll of Honour.   1961.
Husband of Delilah.   1962.
A Man over Forty.   1963.
A Terrible Freedom.   1966.

Fiction (for children)

The Wind on the Moon.   1944.
The Pirates in the Deep Green Sea.   1949.

Plays

The Devil's in the News (produced 1930's).   1934.
The Crisis in Heaven: An Elysian Comedy (produced 1944). 1944.
To Meet the MacGregors (produced 1946?).   In *Two Comedies,* 1950.
Love in Albania (produced 1948).   1950.
Two Comedies: Love in Albania and To Meet the MacGregors.   1950.
The Mortimer Touch, from *The Alchemist* by Jonson (as *The Atom Doctor,* produced 1950; as *The Mortimer Touch,* produced 1952).   1952.
Breakspear in Gascony.   1958.

Screenplay: *The Man Between,* with Harry Kurnitz, 1953.

Verse

Poobie.   1925.
A Dragon Laughed and Other Poems.   1930.

Other

Ben Jonson and King James: Biography and Portrait. 1931.
Mary, Queen of Scots.   1933.
Robert the Bruce.   1934.
The Lion and the Unicorn; or, What England Has Meant to Scotland.   1935.
The Cornerstones: A Conversation in Elysium.   1941.
The Defence of Calais.   1941.
The Man on My Back: An Autobiography.   1941.
The Northern Garrisons: The Defence of Iceland and the Faroe, Orkney and Shetland Islands.   1941.
The Raft, and Socrates Asks Why: Two Conversations. 1942.
The Highland Division.   1942.
The Great Ship, and Rabelais Replies: Two Conversations. 1944.
The Art of Adventure (essays).   1947.
The Campaign in Italy.   1951.
Our Men in Korea.   1952.
A Year of Space: A Chapter in Autobiography.   1953.

The Ultimate Viking (essays).   1955.
Karina with Love (for children), photographs by Karl Werner Gullers.   1958.
Edinburgh.   1960.
Gullers' Sweden, photographs by Karl Werner Gullers. 1964.
Orkney and Shetland: An Historical, Geographical, Social, and Scenic Survey.   1965.
The Prince in the Heather.   1965.
The Conquest of England.   1966.
The Survival of Scotland: A Review of Scottish History from Roman Times to the Present Day.   1968.
Scotland.   1968.
The Secret Larder; or, How a Salmon Lives and Why He Dies.   1969.
The Royal House of Scotland.   1970; as *The Royal House,* 1970.
Fanfare for a Tin Hat: A Third Essay in Autobiography. 1970.
The Music of the North.   1970.
The Corpse on Clapham Common: A Tale of Sixty Years Ago.   1971.
The Voyage of the Challenger.   1972.
The Black Watch: The History of the Royal Highland Regiment, with Andro Linklater.   1977.

Editor, *The Thistle and the Pen: An Anthology of Modern Scottish Writers.*   1950.
Editor, *John Moore's England: A Selection from His Writings.*   1970.

*

Critical Study: *Linklater: A Critical Biography* by Michael Parnell, 1984.

*   *   *

Eric Linklater was a prolific writer who wrote 23 novels and several volumes of short stories, as well as poetry, plays, biographies, histories, and essays. He also had an active and eventful life: he served in World Wars I and II, he was a journalist in India and an academic in Aberdeen, and he took part in Scottish politics in the cause of self-government. He was born in Wales as the son of a shipmaster with roots in the Orkney islands to the north of Scotland, but for most of his life Linklater fostered the notion that he was a native-born Orcadian. He had a strong emotional attachment towards Orkney and its ancient association with the Vikings.

All these various strands in Linklater's life are reflected in his novels and short stories: his medical knowledge, his wide literary erudition, his military experience, his affection for Scotland and Orkney in particular, and his travels in many parts of the world. Orkney and Aberdeen, for instance, appear in *White-Maa's Saga,* the United States in *Juan in America,* Scottish politics in *Magnus Merriman,* and wartime Italy in *Private Angelo.*

If his addiction to old legends suggest the romantic, he was a sophisticated romantic, given to mixing the legendary with a witty and ironic look at contemporary reality. Because of this blend of realism and fantasy he has often been compared to the 18th-century Scottish novelist, Tobias Smollet. He also has been called Rabelaisean because his evident delight in copiousness of language and the pleasures of the flesh, although there is always a fastidious reticence in his descriptions. He was a conscious stylist. As he remarked in one of his stories, "God Likes Them Plain," "whatever its subject a story is a good story or a bad story only by virtue of the style in which it is told." He varied his style to suit the theme. It could be rich and ornate, but also direct and muscular. This applies equally to his novels and his short stories, but it was in his short stories that he was most successful.

Linklater published two major collections of short stories: *God Likes Them Plain* and *Sealskin Trousers and Other Stories*. A selection from these and other sources later was published as *The Stories of Eric Linklater*.

A reviewer of one of these collections remarked that Linklater's stories have modern settings but that they have "roots which strike down into myth and ballad and poetry." This is not his invariable technique, but it is one which he often uses. "Kind Kitty," for example, goes back to a 15th-century Scottish ballad. "The Dancers" involves some very solid 20th-century characters with the Orcadian legend of Peerie Men, dwarfs who live happy but subterranean lives. In "Sealskin Trousers" a sensible modern girl is easily persuaded to live under the sea with a selkie, a mythical creature, half seal and half man. Both of these stories carry overtones of discontent with the contemporary world. The most remarkable story of the supernatural is "The Goose Girl." This combines a tale of a soldier returning from the war and his difficulty in adjusting to peaceful life, with strong hints that the girl he marries has, Leda-like, been seduced by Zeus in the shape of a goose.

"The Crusader's Key" is set in the distant past, but has nothing of the supernatural. It is a delicate and ironic tale of a knight's lady locked in a chastity belt, who is wooed by a persistent troubador. Like many of Linklater's stories, it has an unexpected turn at the end. The lady eventually wants to escape from the belt, not because of a desire of love, but to eat. "The Duke," based on an actual event, is a powerful denunciation of the Highland landowners who cleared the people from the land to make way for sheep.

Other stories are set firmly in the present. "The Wrong Story" is a sharply observed account of a relationship, which ends in disaster, between a tourist and a guide in New Orleans. "Joy as It Flies" is a charming love story set in Edinburgh and Dublin. All of the stories, even the slightest, are told with wit and style, and they have the feel of a warm and tolerant personality.

—Paul H. Scott

See the essay on "Kind Kitty."

LISPECTOR, Clarice. Brazilian. Born in Tchetchelnik, Ukraine, 10 December 1925(?). Educated at National Faculty of Law, Rio de Janeiro, degree in law 1941–44. Married Mauri Gurgel Valente in 1944 (separated 1959); two sons. Editor, *Agência Nacional* and *A noite* newspapers, 1941–44; lived in Europe, 1944–49, in the United States, 1952–59; writer, journalist, and translator. Recipient: Graça Aranha prize, 1944; Cármen Dolores Barbosa prize, 1961; Golfinho de Ouro prize, 1969; Tenth National Literary Library Competition prize, 1976. *Died 9 December 1977.*

PUBLICATIONS

Short Stories

Alguns contos.   1952.
Laços de família.   1960; as *Family Ties*, 1972.
A legião estrangiera (includes essays).   1964; as *The Foreign Legion*, 1986.
Felicidade clandestina.   1971.
A imitação da rosa.   1973.
Onde estivestes de noite.   1974.
A via crucis do corpo.   1974.
A bela e a fera.   1979.
Soulstorm (includes stories from *A via crucis do corpo* and *Onde estivestes de noite*).   1989.

Novels

Perto do coração selvagem.   1944; as *Near to the Wild Heart*, 1990.
O lustre.   1946.
A cidade sitiada: romance.   1948; revised edition, 1964.
A maçã no escuro.   1961; as *The Apple in the Dark*, 1967.
A paixão segundo G.H.   1964; as *The Passion According to G.H.*, 1988.
Uma aprendizagem; ou, o livro dos prazeres.   1969; as *An Apprenticeship, or The Book of Delights*, 1986.
Água viva.   1973; as *The Stream of Life*, 1989.
A hora da estrela.   1977; as *The Hour of the Star*, 1986.
Um sopro de vida: pulsações.   1978.

Fiction for children

O mistério do coelho pensante.   1967.
A mulher que matou os peixes (story).   1968; as *The Woman who Killed the Fish*, in *Latin American Literary Review* 32, July-December 1988.
A vida íntima de Laura (story), illustrated by Sérgio Matta. 1974.
Quase de verdade, illustrated by Cecília Jucá.   1978.

Other

Visao do esplendor: impressôes leves.   1975.
Para não esqueser (essays).   1978.

Translator, *O retrato de Dorian Gray*, by Oscar Wilde. 1974.

*

Critical Studies: introduction by Gregory Rabassa to *The Apple in the Dark*, 1967; "Lispector: Fiction and Comic Vision" by Massuad Moisés, translated by Sara M. McCabe, in *Studies in Short Fiction* 8, Winter 1971; *Lispector*, edited by Samira Y. Campedello and Benjamin Abdalla, 1981; *Lispector* by Earl E. Fitz, 1985; in *Women's Voice* by Naomi Lindstrom, 1989; *Reading with Lispector* by Helene Cixous, edited and translated by Verena A. Conley, 1990; "Lispector: An Intuitive Approach to Fiction" by Giavanni Pontiero, in *Knives and Angels*, edited by Susan Bassnett, 1990.

* * *

Except for the names of people and places—Otavio, Lucia, Ipanema, and Rio, for instance—there is little that would place Clarice Lispector's writings in a specifically Brazilian context. In fact, Lispector is often credited as one of the first to move Brazilian fiction from its historically regional focus toward the dramatization of universal human questions and themes.

Writing and publishing from 1942 until her death in 1977, Lispector spans the late modern and early postmodern literary periods. Her novels, stories, chronicles, and nonfictional essays reflect a movement from the "well-made stories" in the *Laços de família (Family Ties)* collection to the lyrical, narratively chaotic contemplations of *A via crucis do corpo* and *Onde estivestes de noite.*

The early stories deal almost exclusively with the tensions of familial and other close relationships. Through epiphanic insights, usually triggered by an insignificant object or occurrence, Lispector's characters find themselves momentarily severed from the traditional roles and relationships which until that moment have defined their lives. The sight of a blind man chewing gum, for instance, launches the protagonist of "Love" into a frenzied reassessment of her orderly domestic life. The eggs in Anna's shopping bag fall and break, she misses her train stop, and she finds herself wandering, dazed, in the Botanical Garden, facing with horror the knowledge that "she belonged to the strong part of the world." In a similar vein, the 89-year-old protagonist of "Happy Birthday" explodes with fury at the "spineless" progeny gathered to celebrate her passage towards death. Choked by the thought that she has produced these "weak creatures," she spits on the floor and shatters the fragile and superficial unity of the party.

It has been observed that Lispector's characters generally return to their traditional roles, often showing no sign of change or heightened awareness. The circular pattern of the stories, together with numerous unsettling shifts in point of view, can leave the reader wondering exactly what has actually occurred, and by whom it has been perceived. Has the young protagonist of "Preciousness" been physically touched or even assaulted by the young men on the street, or is this "touching" a metaphor for the sound of voices that she dreads? Does Catherine in the story "Family Ties" leave her husband permanently or only for the short walk she says she will take? Neither character projects sufficient thought to clarify these ambiguities. Instead, the perception and narration move to other minds. Catherine's departure from the house, an action that follows a personally liberating interior monologue, comes to the reader through the eyes of her husband. As a result, the tone of the story melts Catherine's exuberance into her husband's anxiety and regret. Earl E. Fitz suggests that shifts of this kind push the stories beyond a circular return by adding depth to the protagonists and by implicating others into their dilemmas.

This involvement of pairs and groups of characters also reveals the failure of communication, which for Lispector typifies contemporary urban life. Flowing interior monologues contrast with sparse, hesitant dialogues, suggesting the privacy of the protagonists' new insights. And traditional gender roles, even if they are left unresolved, or, as some feminists scholars suggest, portrayed with a negative sense that change is impossible, are clearly tested by the isolating experiences that structure the stories.

Lispector's repeated examinations of gender roles and familial relationships also push gently at the boundaries of narrative realism. Although she is not a magical realist in the manner of Gabriel García Márquez or Jose Luis Borges, she does experiment with the horizons of being through the use of literal and figurative animals. An unnamed family and a hen in "The Chicken" act out the same patterns of entrapment and desire that shape the lives of Lispector's human characters. The protagonist in "The Crime of the Mathematics Professor" finds his Other in a dead dog—a surrogate, in fact, for a dog he once loved and abandoned. A.M. Wheeler suggests that the use of animals allows Lispector to magnify tensions which would require more subtlety in the development of fully rounded human characters. In this sense, the animal stories are not parables, but rather the literary equivalent of animation in film.

Operating at the boundaries of animal/human perceptions and impulses, "The Smallest Woman in the World" serves as a thematic bridge between these worlds. This story alternates an African explorer's discovery of a 24-inch pregnant tree-dwelling woman with reactions to a photo of this woman in an urban newspaper. The newspaper readers devour the image, while the woman herself struggles daily not to be devoured by neighboring cannibals. The readers find the woman "black as a monkey," suitable for a family pet. For the most part, children seem drawn to the photo—in fascination, sympathy, or horror—while their parents avert their eyes and seek distance. The explorer, meanwhile, learns to feel the joy the woman finds in having "a tree to live in all by herself." In this story motifs of the body, of literal and figurative devouring, and of the animal-like purity that separates innocence from experience reveal the tense desires that underlie familial intimacy.

Interspersed as they are with the traditional narratives in *Family Ties* and *A legião estrangiera (The Foreign Legion),* the animal stories also mark a transition to other generic experiments. *The Foreign Legion* includes not only fictional stories, but also a number of chronicles, sketches, dialogues, and personal narratives, some written for publication in Brazilian newspapers and magazines. The blending of genres continues in the *Soulstorm* stories, which tend to contemplate concepts and objects—silence, horses, a train, dignity, gentleness, and a full afternoon—rather than develop or even name individual characters.

Helene Cixous has embraced Lispector's intense, rhythmic narrative as truly feminine writing, or ecriture feminine. Some readers and theorists would consider this the highest accolade possible for a contemporary writer. Yet even Cixous grants the writings a thematic richness. This wealth opens Lispector's work to a broad spectrum of readings, from existentialist, religious, mystical, and gender-based to the political, fantastical and sensual.

—Rebecca Stephens

See the essays on "The Imitation of the Rose" and "Where You Were at Night."

——————

LONDON, Jack (John Griffith London). American. Born in San Francisco, California, 12 January 1876. Educated at a grammar school in Oakland, California; Oakland High School, 1895–96; University of California, Berkeley, 1896–97. Married 1) Bessie Maddern in 1900 (separated 1903; divorced 1905), two daughters; 2) Charmian Kittredge in 1905, one daughter. Worked in a cannery in Oakland, 1889–90; oyster "pirate," then member of the California Fisheries Patrol, 1891–92; sailor on the *Sophia Sutherland,* sailing to Japan and Siberia, 1893; returned to Oakland, wrote for the local paper, and held various odd jobs, 1893–94; tramped the U.S. and Canada, 1894–96; arrested for vagrancy in Niagara Falls, New York; joined the gold rush to the Klondike, 1897–98, then returned to Oakland and became a full-time writer; visited London, 1902; war correspondent in the Russo-Japanese War for the San Francisco *Examiner*, 1904; moved to a ranch in Sonoma County, California, 1906; attempted to sail round the world on a 45-foot yacht, 1907–09; war correspondent in Mexico, 1914. *Died 22 November 1916.*

PUBLICATIONS

Collections

Short Stories, edited by Maxwell Geismar.   1960.
(*Works*; Fitzroy Edition), edited by I.O. Evans.   18 vols., 1962–68.
The Bodley Head London, edited by Arthur Calder-Marshall.   4 vols., 1963–66; as *The Pan London*,   2 vols., 1966–68.
Novels and Stories (Library of America), edited by Donald Pizer.   1982.
Novels and Social Writings (Library of America), edited by Donald Pizer.   1984.

Short Stories

The Son of the Wolf: Tales of the Far North.   1900; as *An Odyssey of the North*, 1915.
The God of His Fathers and Other Stories.   1901; as *The God of His Fathers: Tales of the Klondike*, 1902.
Children of the Frost.   1902.
The Faith of Men and Other Stories.   1904.
Tales of the Fish Patrol.   1905.
Moon-Face and Other Stories.   1906.
The Apostate (story).   1906.
Love of Life and Other Stories.   1907.
The Road.   1907.
Lost Face.   1910.
When God Laughs and Other Stories.   1911.
South Sea Tales.   1911.
The Strength of the Strong (story).   1911.
The House of Pride and Other Tales of Hawaii.   1912.
A Son of the Sun.   1912; as *The Adventures of Captain Grief*, 1954.
Smoke Bellew.   1912; as *Smoke and Shorty*, 1920.
The Dream of Debs (story).   1912(?).
The Night-Born. . . .   1913.
The Strength of the Strong (collection).   1914.
The Turtles of Tasman.   1916.
The Human Drift.   1917.
The Red One.   1918.
On the Makaloa Mat.   1919; as *Island Tales*, 1920.
Dutch Courage and Other Stories.   1922.
Tales of Adventure, edited by Irving Shepard.   1956.
Stories of Hawaii, edited by A. Grove Day.   1965.
Great Short Works, edited by Earle Labor.   1965.
Goliah: A Utopian Essay.   1973.
Curious Fragments: London's Tales of Fantasy Fiction, edited by Dale L. Walker.   1975.
The Science Fiction of London, edited by Richard Gid Powers.   1975.
The Unabridged London, edited by Lawrence Teacher and Richard E. Nicholls.   1981.
London's Yukon Women.   1982.
Young Wolf: The Early Adventure Stories, edited by Howard Lachtman.   1984.

In a Far Country: London's Western Tales, edited by Dale L. Walker.   1986.

Novels

The Cruise of the Dazzler.   1902.
A Daughter of the Snows.   1902.
The Kempton-Wace Letters, with Anna Strunsky.   1903.
The Call of the Wild.   1903.
The Sea-Wolf.   1904.
The Game.   1905.
White Fang.   1906.
Before Adam.   1907.
The Iron Heel.   1908.
Martin Eden.   1909.
Burning Daylight.   1910.
Adventure.   1911.
The Abysmal Brute.   1913.
John Barleycorn.   1913; as *John Barleycorn; or, Alcoholic Memoirs*, 1914.
The Valley of the Moon.   1913.
The Mutiny of the Elsinore.   1914.
The Scarlet Plague.   1915.
The Jacket (The Star Rover).   1915, as *The Star Rover*, 1915.
The Little Lady of the Big House.   1916.
Jerry of the Islands.   1917.
Michael, Brother of Jerry.   1917.
Hearts of Three.   1918.
The Assassination Bureau Ltd., completed by Robert L. Fish.   1963.

Plays

The Great Interrogation, with Lee Bascom (produced 1905).
Scorn of Women.   1906.
Theft.   1910.
The Acorn-Planters: A California Forest Play. . . .   1916.
Daughters of the Rich, edited by James E. Sisson.   1971.
Gold, with Herbert Heron, edited by James E. Sisson.   1972.

Other

The People of the Abyss.   1903.
The Tramp.   1904.
The Scab.   1904.
London: A Sketch of His Life and Work.   1905.
War of the Classes.   1905.
What Life Means to Me.   1906.
The Road.   1907.
London: Who He Is and What He Has Done.   1908(?).
Revolution.   1909.
Revolution and Other Essays.   1910.
The Cruise of the Snark.   1911.
London by Himself.   1913.
London's Essays of Revolt, edited by Leonard D. Abbott.   1926.
London, American Rebel: A Collection of His Social Writings. . . ., edited by *Philip S. Foner*.   1947.
Letters from London, Containing an Unpublished Correspondence Between London and Sinclair Lewis, edited by King Hendricks and Irving Shepard.   1965.
London Reports: War Correspondence, Sports Articles, and Miscellaneous Writings, edited by King Hendricks and Irving Shepard.   1970.

*London's Articles and Short Stories in the (Oakland) High
    School Aegis,* edited by James E. Sisson.   1971.
*No Mentor But Myself: A Collection of Articles, Essays,
    Reviews, and Letters on Writing and Writers,* edited by
    Dale L. Walker.   1979.
Revolution: Stories and Essays, edited by Robert Barltrop.
    1979.
*London on the Road: The Tramp Diary and Other Hobo
    Writings,* edited by Richard W. Etulain.   1979.
*Sporting Blood: Selections from London's Greatest Sports
    Writing,* edited by Howard Lachtman.   1981.
*London's California: The Golden Poppy and Other Writ-
    ings,* edited by Sal Noto.   1986.

*

Bibliography: *London: A Bibliography* by Hensley C.
Woodbridge, John London, and George H. Tweney, 1966,
supplement by Woodbridge, 1973; in *Bibliography of
American Literature* by Jacob Blanck, 1969; *The Fiction of
London: A Chronological Bibliography* by Dale L. Walker
and James E. Sisson, 1972; *London: A Reference Guide* by
Joan R. Sherman, 1977.

Critical Studies: *London: A Biography* by Richard
O'Connor, 1964; *London and the Klondike: The Genesis of
an American Writer* by Franklin Walker, 1966; *The Alien
Worlds of London* by Dale L. Walker, 1973; *London* by
Earle Labor, 1974; *White Logic: London's Short Stories* by
James I. McClintock, 1975; *London: The Man, The Writer,
The Rebel* by Robert Barltrop, 1976; *Jack: A Biography of
London* by Andrew Sinclair, 1977; *London: Essays in
Criticism* edited by Ray Wilson Ownbey, 1978; *London: An
American Myth* by John Perry, 1981; *Solitary Comrade:
London and His Work* by Joan D. Hedrick, 1982; *The
Novels of London: A Reappraisal* by Charles N. Watson, Jr.,
1983; *Critical Essays on London* edited by Jacqueline
Tavernier-Courbin, 1983; *London* by Gorman Beauchamp,
1984; *London: An American Radical?* by Carolyn Johnston,
1984; *London, Adventures, Ideas, and Fiction* by James
Lundquist, 1987; *American Dreamers: Charmian and Lon-
don* by Clarice Stasz, 1988.

*   *   *

In 1898 Jack London sold "To the Man on the Trail," his
first story, to the *Overland Monthly* for five dollars. It
appeared in January 1899, and in August of that year he
sold "An Odyssey of the North," to *Atlantic Monthly* for
$120.00. Largely because of the influence of the *Atlantic*,
his writing career was launched. *The Son of the Wolf*, a
collection of London's Klondike tales, and his first book,
appeared in 1900. Another collection of Klondike stories,
The God of His Fathers, followed in 1901.

London's first novel, *A Daughter of the Snows*, was
published in 1902. Based on this sequence of works, it is
possible to argue that London—whether viewed as novelist, essayist, journalist, or apologist/propagandist—is also
due considerable attention as a writer of short stories. His
entire professional writing career spanned less than two
decades (17 years from the date of his first published story);
he died of uremia in 1916. He was one of those writers,
almost eponymic and certainly mythic in reputation, whose
life crossed over into fiction and in the crossing became
larger and more legendary.

Assuredly London's position in the American literary
canon is due to the fact that he honed and perfected his
talents as a novelist with the aid of the short story form. He
worked, throughout his career, masterfully in both short
and long forms of fiction and his themes and techniques in
both forms are reciprocal. Not all novelists are as comfortable in shorter forms as London was and some might even
hold that his short stories will, certainly for students of
introductory literature classes, outlive his name as a
novelist.

In any event, his short stories achieve some of the highest
potential of the form, notwithstanding what to some is an
excessive reliance on manliness and what might be regarded as a celebration of the primitive and the animalistic side
of humanity.

Within the short story form London displays considerable
variety, both in length and in setting. Recognized most
often as a writer of the Far North and the Klondike or as a
writer of the Far West of California, London also capitalized on the even more remote and exotic settings of his
travels to the Far East, the South Seas, and Australia. The
stories growing out of his farthest travels, however, remain
generally less satisfying than do his Klondike and California stories.

The variety of settings found in London's stories is not
evenly matched when it comes to plot, characterization,
and themes. These aspects of his stories are predictable and
almost formulaic due to London's belief in a naturalistic
universe. In keeping with Zola's tenets about what literary
naturalism achieves, London's characters (programmed by
him) realize all too soon that they are doomed, subject to
biological and cosmic forces much beyond their influence.

One of London's shortest stories, "War," typifies this
universal, albeit one-sided struggle. The young soldier in
the story, out on a scouting expedition, benevolently
refrains from killing an enemy scout he happens to hold,
quite close up, in his carbine's sights. London does not
moralize about the act, comment on its rightness or
wrongness. It seems a humane thing for the soldier to do. In
a reversed situation a few days later, the soldier who was
spared takes aim, at an almost impossible distance, and
kills his benevolent nemesis. Such is what the fates have in
store: death at its least deserving and most ironic.

Other ironies consistently beset and shape London's
characters. In "All Gold Canyon," an idyllic canyon—
much at peace in its seclusion—is discovered by a gold
prospector. As he revels in the abundant gold he discovers,
another interloper shoots him. But the prospector, reviving
at the most unlikely time, is able to kill the interloper. He
then packs up his gold and leaves the canyon to its solitude.
But with a corpse and some utensils left in exchange for
sacks of gold. Any moral judgments about the incident are
left entirely to the reader, for both the narrator and the
universe appear indifferent among the ironies.

London's mastery of cosmic, ironic, and relative points of
view that underscore the existence of a godhead either
vengeful or asleep at the wheel can be witnessed in stories
with urban settings as well. The Darwinian struggle occurs
with considerable severity in cities. In "South of the Slot"
the warfare orients itself around class differences: the poor
in combat with the rich. Here the protagonist, Professor
Freddie Drummond, literally is transformed (again, ironically) into becoming one of the lower class, living on the
south side of town, one of the classes which are the basis of
his sociological investigation. He becomes his alias, his
fabricated double, Bill Totts, and heroically leads the
workers as new "brothers" in arms.

In one of London's longer stories, "The Mexican," the reader is privileged to know secrets that some of the story's characters can only surmise. Here also combat, in the form of prize fighting and the Mexican Revolution, provides the basis of the story. Felipe Rivera is able to contribute money to the revolution—much to the puzzlement of the coordinating Junta—through his winnings as a boxer in Los Angeles. Rivera's dedication to the cause is matched by his hatred of gringos. These two motives enable him to defeat Danny Ward in a "winner take all" contest, which nets enough money to supply the revolution with a major shipment of guns.

Predictable and formulaic as London's stories may be, they are near flawless in their effect when judged on their own terms. Seldom does message, heavy as it is, truly outweigh technique, causing it to collapse. Rather, technique works as an integral part of the substance of the story, providing much of the pleasure in what is recognizably and uniquely "Londonesque." Never an in-door-boy, hardly a Henry James or a Howells, and ever eschewing drawing room conflicts, London infuses his stories with the vitality of life in the raw. Admittedly, he is vulnerable to criticism for what he does not do—especially in a time when more refined sensibilities rule. But for what he does, he stands shoulder to shoulder with the best of the authors in United States literary history.

—Robert Franklin Gish

See the essays on "A Piece of Steak" and "To Build a Fire."

LU HSUN. See **LU XUN.**

LU XUN. Pseudonym for Zhou Shuren. Chinese. Born in Shao-xing, Zhejiang province, China, in 1881. Educated at Kiangnan Naval Academy, Nanjing, 1898–99; School of Railways and Mines, Nanjing, 1899–1902; studied Japanese language in Japan, 1902–04, and medicine at Sendai Provincial Medical School, Japan, 1904–06; continued private studies in Japan, 1906–09. Teacher in Shao-xing, 1910–11; served in the Ministry of Education, Beijing, 1912–26, and taught Chinese literature at National Beijing University, 1920-26; taught at Amoy University, 1926, and University of Canton, 1927; then lived in international settlement of Shanghai: editor, *Ben-lin* (The Torrent), 1928, and *Yiwen* (Translation), 1934; also a translator of Japanese and western works, and a draftsman/designer. *Died 19 October 1936.*

PUBLICATIONS

Collections

Hsienshang chuanchi [Complete Works].   20 vols., 1938; supplements edited by Tang Tao,   2 vols., 1942–52.
Selected Works.   4 vols., 1956–60.
Chuan ji [Complete Works].   10 vols., 1957–58.
The Complete Stories.   1981.

Short Stories

Na han.   1923; as *Call to Arms,* 1981.
Pang huang.   1925; as *Wandering,* 1981.
Gushi xin bian.   1935; as *Old Tales Retold,* 1961.
Ah Q and Others: Selected Stories.   1941.
Selected Stories.   1954.
Wild Grass (prose poems).   1974.
Diary of a Madman and Other Stories.   1990.

Other

Zhong gno xiaoshuo shi lueh.   1924; as *A Brief History of Chinese Fiction,* 1959.
Silent China: Selected Writings, edited by Gladys Yang. 1973.
Dawn Blossoms Plucked at Dusk.   1976.

*

Bibliography: in *A History of Modern Chinese Fiction 1917–1957* by C.T. Hsia, 1961.

Critical Studies: *Lu Hsün and the New Culture Movement of Modern China* by Huang Sung-k'ang, 1957; *Gate of Darkness* by T.A. Hsia, 1974; "The Technique of Lu Hsun's Fiction" by Patrick D. Hanan, *Harvard Journal of Asiatic Studies* 34, 1974; *The Social Thought of Lu Hsün 1881–1936* by Pearl Hsia Chen, 1976; in *Modern Chinese Literature in the May Fourth Era,* edited by Merle Goldman, 1977; *Lu Hsün's Vision of Reality* by William A. Lyell, 1976; *The Style of Lu Hsun* by Raymond S.W. Hsu, 1979; *Lu Xun and His Legacy* edited by Leo Ou-fan Lee, 1985, and *Voices from the Iron House: A Study of Lu Xun* by Lee, 1987.

* * *

China's earliest practitioner of Western-style fiction, Lu Xun is also generally regarded as his country's greatest modern writer. Lu Xun was drawn to Western literature and philosophy while studying medicine in Japan, and he finally chose writing as his profession. His creative energies focused on the short story and the essay. The essays, a direct reflection of the contemporary Chinese hunger for national revival, helped guide the course of modern China's cultural development. It is his short stories, however, that have lasting influence and abiding value as art.

His short stories fill three collections: *Na Han (Call to Arms), Pang huang, (Wandering),* and *Gushi xin bian (Old Tales Retold).* Lu Xun, who considered his works a vehicle for social reform, draws his materials from the victims of a sickly culture; he aims to reveal contemporary China's diseases and pains, and to call attention to possible cures.

The first story in *Call to Arms,* "The Diary of a Madman" (which borrows its title from the Russian writer Gogol), conveys most succinctly Lu Xun's attitude toward Chinese tradition. Couched in the words of a madman, the fierce indignation with which he stigmatizes the man-eating society of his time energizes the story, which is the first notable example of social protest in China's modern literature. Suffering from a persecution mania, the madman believes that all those around him, including his immediate family, intend to kill and eat him. Targeting feudal society, Lu Xun has the madman delve into a book of Chinese history only to discover that the whole book is filled with two words: "Eat people!" With the madman as mouthpiece, Lu Xun shows that, despite his culture's profession of benevolence and righteousness, traditional Chinese life consists of cannibalism.

Most of Lu Xun's stories reveal dynamic characters—generally simple folk enduring the gray and tragic life of the Chinese masses. The protagonists tend to be helpless victims of their fate, unaware even of their true position and miserable plight. Meekly swallowing insults and silently suffering injuries, they labor day and night for a bare existence and finally fade away like fallen leaves disappearing into the mud without ever evoking any sympathy or expressing any surprise. In the rural village Lu-chuen ("My Native Place"), nothing astonishing or startling occurs; the life that goes on in the village is familiar to people who have lived on the land.

Other stories highlight Lu Xun's unique artistic exaggeration: as a consequence of stealing books, Kong Yi Ji, a victim of feudalism's traditional Examination system, is beaten till his legs are broken ("Kong Yi Ji"); the widow of Xiang Lin loses her son, the only hope of her life ("Benediction"); Seven-pound regrets that Tai Ping Jun has cut off his queue ("Storm"); Ah Q is executed for joining the movement against feudal society, a movement he neither understands nor participates in ("The True Story of Ah Q").

The stories express Lu Xun's conflicted love and hatred for the ignorant peasants. He honors their innate goodness and simplicity; still, he hates their callous indifference towards reform and their submissiveness to oppressive feudal rule. "Medicine," a complex story, offers a realistic exposé of traditional Chinese life, a symbolic parable on revolution, and a touching tale of parents' grief over their children. A young man named Xia has just been decapitated for his part in the revolutionary conspiracy against the Qing Government. Meanwhile, a youth named Hua is dying of consumption. Hua's aged father buys from the executioner a roll of bread soaked with the dead Xia's blood in the vain belief that this blood will give his son a new lease on life. Hua gobbles down the bread, but dies nevertheless. "Medicine" suggests that revolutionaries sacrifice their lives struggling for the ignorant masses. The story is a suffocating tragedy enveloped in a heavy mist of mass ignorance.

Faithful to his material and to himself, Lu Xun describes what he sees without false pretense or concealment. His memory is precious to the majority of the Chinese people because his stories so faithfully reflect the life and customs of old China. Though traditional China has passed away, people of today and tomorrow may always discover it anew in Lu Xun's stories.

—Liping Guo

See the essays on "The Diary of a Madman," "Regret for the Past," and "The True Story of Ah Q."

M

MACHADO de Assis, Joaquim Maria. Brazilian. Born in Rio de Janeiro, 21 June 1839. Married Carolina de Novaes in 1869 (died 1904). Journalist from age 15: proofreader, typesetter, writer and editor; editor and columnist, *Diário do Rio de Janeiro*, and *A Semana Ilustrada*, 1860–75; clerk, then director of accounting division, Ministry of Agriculture, Commerce, and Public Works, 1874–1908. Member, and censor, 1862–64, Conservatório Dramático Brasileiro; founding president, Academia Brasileira de Letras, 1897–1908. Order of the Rose, 1888. *Died 29 September 1908.*

PUBLICATIONS

Collections

Obras completas. 31 vols., 1937–42.
Obra completa, edited by Afrânio Coutinho. 3 vols., 1959–62; edited by Henrique de Campos, with others, 31 vols., 1955.

Short Stories

Contos fluminenses. 1872.
Histórias da Meia-Noite. 1873.
Papéis avulsos. 1882.
Histórias sem data. 1884.
Várias histórias. 1896.
Páginas recolhidas. 1899.
Relíquias de Casa Velha. 1906.
Brazilian Tales. 1921.
The Psychiatrist and Other Stories, edited by Jack Schmitt and Lorie Chieko Ishimatsu. 1963.
The Devil's Church and Other Stories. 1977.

Novels

Resurreição. 1872.
A mão e a luva. 1874; as *The Hand and the Glove,* 1970.
Helena. 1876; translated as *Helena,* 1984.
Yayá Garcia. 1878; translated as *Yayá Garcia,* 1976.
Memórias póstumas de Bráz Cubas. 1881; as *The Posthumous Memoirs of Braz Cubas,* 1951; as *Epitaph of a Small Winner,* 1952.
Quincas Borba. 1891; as *Philosopher or Dog?,* 1954; as *The Heritage of Quincas Borba,* 1954.
Dom Casmurro. 1899; translated as *Dom Casmurro,* 1953.
Esaú e Jacó. 1904; as *Esau and Jacob,* 1965.
Memorial de Ayres. 1908; as *Counselor Ayres' Memorial,* 1982; as *The Wager: Aires' Journal,* 1990.
Casa Velha. 1968.

Plays

Pipelet, from the novel *Les Mystères de Paris* by Eugène Sue (produced 1859).

As bodas de Joaninha, with Luíz Olona, music by Martin Allu (produced 1861).
Desencantos: Phantasia dramatica. 1861.
O caminho da porta (produced 1862). In *Teatro,* 1863.
O protocolo (produced 1862). In *Teatro,* 1863.
Gabriella (produced 1862).
Quase ministro (produced 1863). 1864(?).
Montjoye, from a play by Octave Feuillet (produced 1864).
Suplício de uma mulher, from a play by Émile de Girardin and Dumas fils (produced 1865). In *Teatro,* 1937.
Os deuses de casaca (produced 1865). 1866.
O barbeiro de Sevilha, from the play by Beaumarchais (produced 1866).
O anjo de Meia-Noite, from a play by Théodore Barrière and Edouard Plouvier (produced 1866).
A família Benoiton, from a play by Victorien Sardou (produced 1867).
Como elas são tôdas, from a play by Musset (produced 1873).
Tu só, tu, puro amor (produced 1880). 1881.
Não consultes médico (produced 1896). In *Teatro,* 1910.

Verse

Chrysálidas. 1864.
Phalenas. 1870.
Americanas. 1875.
Poesias completas. 1901.

Other

Correspondência, edited by Fernando Nery. 1932.
Adelaide ristori. 1955.

Translator, *Os trabalhadores do mar,* by Victor Hugo. 1866.

*

Critical Studies: *The Brazilian Othello of Machado de Assis: A Study of Dom Casmurro,* 1960, and *Machado de Assis: The Brazilian Master and His Novels,* 1970, both by Helen Caldwell; *The Craft of an Absolute Winner: Characterization and Narratology in the Novels of Machado de Assis* by Maris Luisa Nunes, 1983; *The Deceptive Realism of Machado de Assis* by John Gledson, 1984; *The Poetry of Machado de Assis* by Lorie Chieko Ishimatsu, 1984; *Machado de Assis* by Earl E. Fitz, 1989.

* * *

Joaquin Maria Machado de Assis is Brazil's most famous author but until fairly recently was hardly known in the western world except for his classic novel *Memórias póstumas de Bráz Cubas (Epitaph of a Small Winner).* A prolific novelist, poet, and essayist, he is also the author of over two hundred short stories, of which, however, only a handful are available in English translation: the only recent collections in English are *The Psychiatrist and Other Stories* and *The Devil's Church and Other Stories.* Machado's work in fiction, particularly that done after 1880, has frequently led critics to cite him as a forerunner of such modernists as James Joyce and Franz Kafka. He is even postmodernist in his preoccupation with language and its ambiguous relationship to experience, and many of his stories represent a fierce attack on scientific rationalism and its excesses.

One of his longest and most famous stories, "The Psychiatrist" (1881), concerns a brilliant scientist, Simao Bacamarte, who is determined to investigate and establish objectively the actual nature of insanity. Steadily widening the grounds for the illness, Bacamarte eventually discovers that he has now confined four-fifths of the population of his town to the Green House, as his asylum has become known. Thereupon, with Kafkaesque logic, he turns around and decides that "a theory that classified as sick all people who were mentally unbalanced" was wrong and that "normality lay in a lack of equilibrium and that the abnormal, the really sick, were the well balanced, the thoroughly rational." Following the argument to its extreme, he finally decides that he himself is the only perfect man and confines himself to the asylum.

Machado's fierce attack on reductive forms of logic and rationalism has been inevitably compared to Swift—in fact, one critic claims that the story was directly influenced by Swift's "A Serious and Useful Scheme to Make a Hospital for Incurables." The same preoccupation emerges in other stories, such as "Alexandrian Tale" (1884) and "The Secret Heart" (1885), with their depiction of sadism practised on animals in the name of science, but which, in fact, is the product of pathological needs. However, "The Psychiatrist" also displays a fascination with language in itself and in the way it can be used to mislead. The author tells us that "one of the Councilmen who had supported the President was so impressed by the figure of speech, 'Bastille of the human reason,' that he changed his mind." Later, however, when the president speaks of "what was so far merely a whirlwind of uncoordinated atoms," we are told that "this figure of speech counterbalanced to some extent the one about the Bastille."

The satiric comedy in "The Psychiatrist" is common to many of Machado's stories but he is capable of a great range of effects. A recurring theme is that of repressed love or sexual desire, sometimes between an adolescent boy and an older woman. "A Woman's Arms" concerns the 15-year-old Ignacio who falls in love with Dona Severina, the 27-year-old wife of the lawyer who employs him. When she becomes aware of his infatuation she resists it but is drawn to his room one night and kisses him on the lips, and the boy responds in his dreams. Ignacio is forced to depart from the lawyer's service and the story ends: "And down the years, in other love adventures, more real and lasting, he never again found the thrill of that Sunday on the Rua da Lapa, when he was only fifteen. To this day he often exclaims, without knowing he is mistaken, 'And it was a dream! Just a dream!'"

The same strange mixture of irony and tenderness in dealing with a similar theme emerges in one of Machado's finest stories, "Midnight Mass" (1894). This begins in the apparently artless, anecdotal style of many of the later stories: "I have never quite understood a conversation that I had with a lady many years ago, when I was seventeen and she was thirty." The narrator recalls a night when he had stayed up to attend midnight Mass and was visited in his room by the young wife of the man in whose house he was living. As in "A Woman's Arms," Machado uses subtle detail—the narrator is reading *The Three Musketeers,* Conceição's modest white negligee is described in detail—to create an atmosphere of stifled and ambiguous, dreamlike sensuality.

Machado can write stories that are broadly satirical, like "Education of a Stuffed Shirt" (1881), or that hinge directly and painfully around a moral judgment, such as "Father Versus Mother" (1905) and "The Rod of Justice" (1891), in which he exposes ironically the different moral standards that exist when oneself or others are involved. In the first story, a slave catcher returns a pregnant woman to slavery so that he can keep his own child, while in the second, a young seminarian refuses to intercede for a slave who is to be beaten by his aunt, as the aunt had earlier interceded for him. But the implications of even the most personal stories extend out to comment on Machado's own society. There is little doubt that had he written in a language such as English, rather than Portugese, he would be acclaimed as one of the masters of the short story, along with his great contemporaries such as Maupassant and Kafka.

—Laurie Clancy

See the essays on "Midnight Mass" and "The Psychiatrist."

———

MACLEOD, Alistair. Canadian. Born in North Battleford, Saskathchewan, 20 July 1936. Nova Scotia Teacher's College, Truro, Teaching certificate 1956; St. Francis Xavier University, Antigonish, B.A., B.ED. 1960; University of New Brunswick, M.A. 1961; University of Notre Dame, Ph.D. 1968. Married Anita MacLellan; six sons. Professor of English, Nova Scotia Teacher's College, 1961–63; teacher, University of Indiana, Fort Wayne, 1966–69; teacher of English and writing, University of Windsor, and editor, *The University of Windsor Review,* since 1969. Canada's Exchange Writer to Scotland, 1984–84. Lives in Windsor, Ontario.

PUBLICATIONS

Short Stories

The Lost Salt Gift of Blood. 1976; revised addition, 1988.
As Birds Bring Forth the Sun and Other Stories. 1986.

Plays

The Lost Salt Gift of Blood (produced 1982).
The Boat (produced 1983).

*

Critical Study: "Signatures of Time: MacLeod and His Short Stories" by Colin Nicholson, in *Canadian Literature* 107, Winter 1985.

* * *

In his three collections, Alistair MacLeod tells the stories of miners, farmers, and fishermen, those who inhabit the harsh, unforgiving Canadian Maritime provinces and their descendents, some of whom have escaped the unrelenting natural elements to modern cities, yet who are still haunted by their heritage and traditions. Along with brilliantly describing these regions and their inhabitants, MacLeod, a native of Canada, shows how his characters live in the harsh, unrelenting environment as well as how they face death and realize the importance of close family ties while learning to deal with loss and regret. Many of MacLeod's stories are told by the younger generations, and through the process of memory, readers discover what haunts them. Other stories come to readers through the eyes of the older generations, who reveal a dignity and strength of character in honoring their heritage despite their isolation.

Tradition plays a large role in "The Boat," which is the older narrator's memoir of his family and how they all were affected by the father's work as a fisherman. The narrator, haunted by his memories, emphasizes how the fishing boat encompassed their lives; it both supported them and isolated them in what the narrator describes as a "chain of tradition." The story ends ambiguously with the sick father falling over board, ironically on the last day of the fishing season. Was it suicide to release his son from his promise to follow the family tradition, or was the father's drowning simply an accident? MacLeod doesn't reveal the father's intentions, and the boy is left to make a decision: to pursue his natural interest in literature or to keep his promise. He chooses the former and is forever haunted by his past.

"Second Spring" is concerned with the practical workings of a farm and the young narrator's desire to join the calf club. In his attempts to produce the perfect calf for the club, he manipulates nature and fails, as in "The Boat," because chance and luck are the governing laws of nature. As with other MacLeod characters, the narrator takes his dashed hopes stoically. Nature is what controls lives in this harsh, gruelling environment.

"In the Fall" presents a common theme for MacLeod's stories, the ambiguity of life. The selling of the father's beloved and loyal horse illustrates to the young narrator the realities of the family's harsh, improvised existence. The young boy accepts the denial of loyalty on the part of the father to ensure his family's well-being. MacLeod points out the harshness of life and how emotional attachments have no place in the scheme of things when basic survival is at stake. The same occurs in the story "Winter Dog," where childhood memories force the narrator to realize the frailty of human life.

Another tale of the loss of innocence and the destruction of the belief that youth has all the advantages is "To Everything There Is a Season," about a young boy disillusioned about Santa Claus because of his father's illness. The father says, "Every man moves on, but there is no need to grieve. He leaves good things behind." The narrator, at the time, believes that his father speaks of Santa Claus, but the older narrator looking back in memory knows that his father spoke of himself.

"As Birds Bring Forth the Sun" also tells of the eminent death of a family member. MacLeod employs myth and mysticism in this story, which involves the grandfather's big gray dog that the family believes is the foreteller of death. The narrator recalls the stories of the strangely intertwined deaths of his grandfather and two uncles as he and his brothers spend a vigil at the bedside of their dying father.

"Vision" is a tale about not understanding reality. Vision is lost literally and metaphorically, revealing that we all are children of uncertainty. The story ends with an analogy to life and love that goes beyond the mere telling of a fishing story as the narrator muses: "[It was] difficult to be ever certain in our judgments or to fully see or understand. . . . And forever difficult to see and understand the tangled twisted strands of love."

In the title story of MacLeod's first collection, "The Lost Salt Gift of Blood," the narrator debates the choices and opportunities that he can offer his son, trying to decide if he will take the child back to the city with him or allow him to remain with his grandparents. After reviewing his life in the city now and life in the tiny fishing village, he decides that the grandparents' way of life (simple and honest, though poor) has more to offer his son than the "land of the Tastee Freeze," with its alarm systems and guard dogs. "Return to Rankin's Point" also condemns modern life in a clearly stated preference for the rural isolation where the past has such a strong hold on the narrator.

The short, thought-provoking story "Island" is one of the few MacLeod stories in which the main character is a woman. As the story opens, we see that long ago Agnes MacPhedran had inherited the duties of lighthouse keeper from her father. Before that time, she had had a child out of wedlock who she gave to her sister to raise, and Agnes stayed on the island to care for her ailing parents. The father of the child had promised to return but was tragically killed in an accident. By the end of the story, her grandson comes for her and fulfills his grandfather's promise, unknowingly removing her from her isolation. He uses the same words that her lover had used years before: "Would you like to live somewhere else?" The story ends: "I told you I'd come back."

In "The Tuning of Perfection" MacLeod displays the strength and dignity of the main character, the 78-year-old Archibald. The story revolves around a common MacLeod theme, the preservation of tradition, in this case represented by the Gaelic songs that symbolize the dignity and importance of Archibald's heritage.

Isolation, both literal and figurative, plays a role in "The Closing Down of Summer." A miner faces his return to the depths of the mines, which have isolated him from his wife and children, and could at any time take his life or his livelihood through an accident. Ancestry becomes more important as the men lose their hearing in the mines. They communicate using Gaelic, which the miner had heard as a child and dismissed. As in "The Tuning of Perfection," the mining men sing Gaelic songs for a crowd who cannot understand the lyrics. The miner regains the heritage that others have lost.

In these and other stories, MacLeod creates striking portraits of individual strength and endurance in a harsh environment while emphasizing the importance of family, tradition, and heritage. MacLeod, in an interview with Colin Nicholson, reflected that "Although my wife has adequate Gaelic, we are really the first generation where the breakdown of that culture is beginning to occur." Perhaps MacLeod's artfully written short stories are his attempt to preserve the Gaelic culture that seems to be diminishing in his homeland.

—Judith M. Schmitt

MAHFŪZ, Nagīb (Abdel Azīz al-Sabilgi). Name anglicised: Naguib Mahfouz. Egyptian. Born in Gamaliya, Cairo, 11 December 1911. Educated at the University of

Cairo, 1930–34, degree in philosophy 1934, post-graduate study 1935–36. Married Atjyya 'Alla' in 1954; two daughters. Secretary, University of Cairo, 1936–38; journalist: staff member, *Ar-Risāla,* and contributor to *Al-Hilāl* and *Al-Ahrām;* civil servant, Ministry of Islamic Affairs, 1939–54; director of censorship, Department of Art; director of Foundation for Support of the Cinema for the State Cinema Organization, 1959–69; consultant for cinema affairs to the Ministry of Culture, 1969–71; retired from civil service, 1971. Member of board, Dār Al-Maāref publishing house. Recipient: Egyptian state prize, 1956; National prize for letters, 1970; Collar of the Republic (Egypt), 1972; Nobel prize for literature, 1988. Named to Egyptian Order of Independence and Order of the Republic. Lives in Cairo.

PUBLICATIONS

Short Stories

Hams al-junūn [The Whispers of Madness].   1939.
Dunya Allah [The World of God].   1963.
Bayt sayyi' al-sum'a [A House of Ill-Repute].   1965.
Khammarat al-qiṭṭ al-aswad [The Black Cat Tavern].   1968.
Taht al-midhalla [Under the Awning].   1969.
Hikāya bi-la bidāya wa-la nihāya [A Story Without Beginning or End].   1971.
Shahr al-asal [Honeymoon].   1971.
God's World: An Anthology of Short Stories, edited by Akef Abadir and Roger Allen.   1973.
Al-jarīma [The Crime].   1973.
Hikāyāt hāratina [Stories of Our District].   1975.
Modern Egyptian Short Stories, with Yusuf Idris and Sa'd al-Khādim.   1977.
Al-hubb fawqa Hadabat al-Haram [Love on Pyramid Mount].   1979.
Al-shayṭān ya'iḍ [Satan Preaches].   1979.
Ra'aytu fīma yara al-nā'im [I Have Seen What a Sleeper Sees].   1982.
Al-tanḍīm al-sirri [The Secret Organization].   1984.
Ṣabāh al-ward [Good Morning].   1987.

Novels

'Abāth al aqdār [The Mockery of Fate].   1939.
Radubis.   1943.
Kifāh Ṭība [Thebes's Struggle].   1944.
Al-Qāhira al-jadīda [New Cairo].   1945.
Khān al-Khalīli.   1946.
Zuqāq al-Midaqq.   1947; as *Midaq Alley,* 1966; revised edition, 1975.
Al-Sarāb [Mirage].   1948.
Bidāya wa-nihāya.   1949; as *The Beginning and the End,* 1985.
Al-thulāthiya [The Cairo Trilogy]:
   Bayn al-Qasrayn.   1956; as *Palace Walk,* 1990.
   Qasr al-shawq.   1957; as *Palace of Desire,* 1991.
   Al-sukkariya.   1957; translated as *Sugar Street,* 1992.
Al-liṣ wa-l-kilāb.   1961; revised edition, as *The Thief and the Dogs,* 1984.
Al-sammān wa-l-kharīf.   1962; as *Autumn Quail,* 1985.
Al-Ṭarīq [The Way].   1964; as *The Search,* 1987.
Al-shahhaz.   1965; as *The Beggar,* 1986.
Tharthara fawq al-Nīl [Chit-Chat on the Nile].   1966.
Awlād hāratina.   1967; as *Children of Gebelawi,* 1981.

Miramār.   1967; translated as *Miramar,* 1978.
Al-marāya.   1972; as *Mirrors,* 1977.
Al-hubb tahta al-maṭar [Love in the Rain].   1973.
Al-karnak [Karnak].   1974; translated as *Al-karnak,* in *Three Contemporary Egyptian Novels,* edited by Saad El-Gabalawy, 1979.
Hikāyāt hāratina.   1975; as *Fountain and Tomb,* 1988.
Qalb al-layl [In the Heart of the Night].   1975.
Hadrat al-muhtaram.   1975; as *Respected Sir,* 1986.
Malhamat al harāfīsh.   1977.
'Asr al-hubb [Age of Love].   1980.
Layāli alf laylah [A Thousand and One Nights].   1981.
Afrāh al-qubbah.   1981; as *Wedding Song,* revised and edited by Mursi Saad El Dīn and John Rodenbeck, 1984.
Bāqi min al-zaman sā'ah [One Hour Left].   1982.
Amāma al'arsh [In Front of the Throne].   1982.
Rihlat Ibn Faṭṭūmah.   1983; as *The Journey of Ibn Fattouma,* 1992.
Al-ā'ish fī al-haqī qah [Living with the Truth].   1985.
Yawm qutila al-za'īm.   1985; as *The Day the Leader Was Killed,* 1989.
Hadīth al ṣabāh wa-al-masā' [Morning and Evening Talk].   1987.
Qushtumor.   1989.

Play

One-Act Plays.   1989

Other

Mahfuz-yataẓakkar [Mahfouz Remembers], edited by Gamal al-Gaytani.   1980.

*

Critical Studies: *The Changing Rhythm: A Study of Mahfuz's Novels* by Sasson Somekh, 1973; "Mahfuz's Short Stories" by Hamdī Sakkout, in *Studies in Modern Arabic Literature,* edited by R.C. Ostle, 1975; "Reality, Allegory and Myth in the Work of Mahfuz" by Mehahern Milson, in *African and Asian Studies,* 11, 1976; "Mahfuz's *Al-karnak:* The Quiet Conscience of Nassir's Egypt Revealed" by T. Le Gassick, in *Middle Eastern Journal,* 31(3), 1977; *Religion, My Own: The Literary Works of Mahfuz* by Matityahu Peled, 1983; *Critical Perspectives on Mahfūz* edited by Trevor Le Gassick, 1989; *Mahfouz, Nobel 1988: Egyptian Perspectives: A Collection of Critical Essays,* edited by Maher Shafiq Farid, 1989; *Studies in the Short Fiction of Mahfouz and Idris* by Mona N. Mikhail, 1992.

* * *

Though generally recognized as a writer of novels, Nagīb Mahfūz made his literary debut in 1934 with the publication of a short story, and has returned to this genre sporadically throughout his lengthy career. Most of his short stories, however, cluster into two distinct periods of political crisis: when he started to write in the 1930's, and from 1967 to 1971, in the wake of Egypt's defeat by Israel.

The stories of his first collection, *Hams al-junūn* (The Whispers of Madness) show raw, unsophisticated attempts at presenting Egyptian social reality. Here, against a background in which rapacious middle-class Egyptians were seeking to accommodate British imperialism and betraying their Revolution of 1919, Mahfūz treats a variety of themes, notably poverty, marital infidelity, and outmoded social conventions, and their deleterious effects on tormented people. These initial stories demonstrated a propensity to sermonizing and moralistic platitudes, and a lack of conciseness and art.

In subsequent collections, however, Mahfūz achieves a sophistication of theme and a mastery of the genre, especially in terms of economy of expression. Many of these works explore the daily lives of Egyptian civil servants, which Mahfūz, himself a civil servant, knew intimately. Through these characters and many others from various strata of society, he comments on the basically tragic nature of the human condition, due most often to poverty but sometimes to wealth, and the ultimate insignificance of humans as they struggle against forces greater than they. Many of these stories reveal symbolic, metaphorical, and metaphysical meanings, often mixing dreams and visions with reality, the distinction between the two frequently left undefined.

In "Zaabalawi" the first-person narrator is ill with an undisclosed disease and searches out a local mystic, Zaabalawi, from whom he expects a cure. In his lengthy search for the peripatetic mystic, the narrator meets a sheikh, a musician, and a drunkard. Because the latter has had the most recent experience with the mystic but will not disclose anything unless the narrator gets drunk with him, the narrator reluctantly does so. Coming out of his stupor, during which he has an ineffable experience of sorts, he learns that Zaabalawi had visited the cafe while he was passed out. The narrator hastily returns to his search. This story has overtones of an on-going quest for the divine, here the elusive mystic Zaabalawi. Wine, forbidden in Islam, functions in this story as it does traditionally in Islamic mysticism: an immediate means to transcendence, even though drinking it breaks the formal rules of the religion.

Much-anthologized in the West, "The Conjurer Made Off with the Dish," one of Mahfūz's many works with a child as the protagonist, features an unnamed boy who is sent off with a dish and money to buy cooked beans. He must return home twice to learn which kind to purchase. A conjurer, demanding payment for the performance the lad stops to watch, steals the dish. The boy then spends the bean money on a children's peep show about chivalry, love, and daring deeds, during which he stands next to a girl towards whom he has "new, strange and obscure" feelings. After the performance they go for a walk, then kiss. He returns home a third time, takes money from his savings and another dish, and goes to buy beans, only to learn that they are sold out. Angered, he throws the dish at the bean seller and runs off to the place where he kissed the girl. There he watches a tramp and a gypsy woman make love, after which they argue about money, and the tramp chokes the woman to death. Horrified, the youth runs off but finds that he is lost. He prays for a miracle to save him from the "mysterious darkness" that is about to descend. A story about growing up and taking responsibilities for one's actions in the unpredictable, adult world motivated by greed and brutality, it is also a tale of the awakening to love in both its ecstatic and destructive forms.

One of Mahfūz's notable political stories is "The Time and the Place," about a law student living in an old home who has a vision in which he and another unknown person bury a box under the palm tree in the courtyard. The law student is told to wait a year before digging the box up, which he does. It contains a note instructing him to go to a

religious master in another part of the city for a secret password. There he encounters security agents, who treat him as a criminal. Unable to make sense out of their charges, he refuses to believe that his earlier vision was false and laughs nervously while everyone else remains silent. In this story Mahfūz succeeds in combining the fairy tale ambience of the *1001 Nights* with modern-day, Kafkaesque overtones of disillusionment, political repression, and psychological intimidation.

One of the most notable features of Mahfūz's novels is his virtuosic treatment of time, which is sometimes found in his short stories as well. In "Half a Day" a diffident boy is taken to his first day of school by his father, who promises to meet him afterwards to take him home. Initially afraid, the child gradually enjoys school, where he is fascinated by his many new experiences. His father does not show up at the end of the school day, so the youngster decides to make his own way home. He is astounded how the neighborhood has changed in just a few hours. As he is about to cross a busy street, a young boy comes up to him and says, "Grandpa, let me take you across." An emotional and technical tour de force, the four-page story telescopes nearly an entire lifetime into a single half day.

Many of the themes Mahfūz explores in depth his novels are treated in miniature in his short stories. On this smaller canvas, these themes are reduced to their essence, which, in turn, produces an immediacy of impact that is unattainable in the novel.

—Carlo Coppola

MALAMUD, Bernard. American. Born in Brooklyn, New York, 26 April 1914. Educated at Erasmus Hall High School, New York; City College of New York, 1932–36, B.A. 1936; Columbia University, New York, 1937–38, M.A. 1942. Married Ann de Chiara in 1945; one son and one daughter. Teacher, New York high schools, evenings 1940–49; instructor to associate professor of English, Oregon State University, Corvallis, 1949–61; member of the division of languages and literature, Bennington College, Vermont, 1961–86; visiting lecturer, Harvard University, Cambridge, Massachusetts, 1966–68. President, PEN American Center, 1979–81. Recipient: Rosenthal award, 1958; Daroff Memorial award, 1958; Ford fellowship, 1959, 1960; National Book award, 1959, 1967; Pulitzer prize, 1967; O. Henry award, 1969, 1973; Jewish Heritage award, 1977; Vermont Council on the Arts award, 1979; Brandeis University Creative Arts award, 1981; American Academy gold medal, 1983; Bobst award, 1983; Mondello prize (Italy), 1985. Member, American Academy, 1964, and American Academy of Arts and Sciences, 1967. *Died 18 March 1986.*

PUBLICATIONS

Short Stories

The Magic Barrel.   1958.
Idiots First.   1963.
Rembrandt's Hat.   1973.
Two Fables.   1978.
The Stories.   1983.

The People, and Uncollected Short Stories, edited by Robert Giroux.   1990.

Novels

The Natural.   1952.
The Assistant.   1957.
A New Life.   1961.
The Fixer.   1966.
Pictures of Fidelman: An Exhibition.   1969.
The Tenants.   1971.
Dubin's Lives.   1979.
God's Grace.   1982.

Other

A Malamud Reader.   1967.
Conversations with Malamud, edited by Lawrence Lasher. 1991.

*

Bibliography: *Malamud: An Annotated Checklist,* 1969, and *Malamud: A Descriptive Bibliography,* 1991, both by Rita N. Kosofsky; *Malamud: A Reference Guide* by Joel Salzburg, 1985.

Critical Studies: *Malamud* by Sidney Richman, 1967; *Malamud and Philip Roth: A Critical Essay* by Glenn Meeter, 1968; *Malamud and the Critics,* 1970, and *Malamud: A Collection of Critical Essays,* 1975, both edited by Leslie A. and Joyce W. Field; *Art and Idea in the Novels of Malamud* by Robert Ducharme, 1974; *Malamud and the Trial by Love* by Sandy Cohen, 1974; *The Fiction of Malamud* edited by Richard Astro and Jackson J. Benson, 1977 (includes bibliography); *Rebels and Victims: The Fiction of Richard Wright and Malamud* by Evelyn Gross Avery, 1979; *Malamud* by Sheldon J. Hershinow, 1980; *The Good Man's Dilemma: Social Criticism in the Fiction of Malamud* by Iska Alter, 1981; *Understanding Malamud* by Jeffrey Helterman, 1985; *Theme of Compassion in the Novels of Malamud* by M. Rajagopalachari, 1988; *Malamud: A Study of the Short Fiction* by Robert Solotaroff, 1989.

*   *   *

Most of Bernard Malamud's short stories are love stories, though love stories of an unusual kind. They are not the typical Romeo and Juliet tales in which boy meets girl. They deal with different kinds of love—between older men and women, or between men and men. Most often they are about agape rather than eros, or the charity humans should show one another. They are typically very moving and often very sad.

Good examples of Malamud's kind of love story are "The Loan" (from his first collection of stories, *The Magic Barrel*), and "The Death of Me" (from his second collection, *Idiots First*). In "The Loan" Kobotsky visits his erstwhile friend, Lieb the baker, after a lapse of 15 years, to borrow two hundred dollars for a gravestone for his dead wife. The hiatus in their friendship, occasioned by an earlier loan of a hundred dollars, is immediately brushed aside as the two oldtimers become reunited. But Lieb has since remarried, and Bessie, his second wife, who handles

their money, refuses the loan, however moved she is by Kobotsky's plight. Like many of Malamud's characters, all three have suffered terribly, and charity must be severely rationed.

In "The Death of Me" Marcus, a clothier, tries to mediate between two excellent workers in his shop, Emilio Vizo, the tailor, and Josip Bruzak, the presser, who (for reasons Marcus cannot plumb) develop a fierce hatred for each other. Though the tailor and the presser have both respect and affection for old Marcus and listen attentively to his admonitions and pleas, as soon as he steps aside their feud breaks out anew. The charity Marcus feels for each of them cannot be extended from one to the other, however, leaving Marcus eventually broken and finally dead.

More like a traditional love story, though still quite different, is "The First Seven Years" (from *The Magic Barrel*). Feld the shoemaker has an only child, 19-year-old Miriam who he hopes will find a better life than the poor one he ekes out in his shop, where he is assisted by Sobel, a refugee. Feld tries to interest Miriam in Max, a college boy studying accounting. He is unaware that Sobel and Miriam already have a relationship based mostly on shared reading of the great literature of the world. When Sobel discovers Feld's plans to match Miriam with Max, he leaves in a huff, and only with difficulty does Feld persuade him to return. In the process he learns of Sobel's devotion to Miriam, extracting a promise that the assistant will wait another two years before asking Miriam to marry him.

Though simply told in sparse language—dialogue is often limited to a few, heavily weighted words—Malamud's stories frequently suggest wider dimensions. Not only the title, but the substance of "The First Seven Years" recalls Jacob's love for Rachel and his willingness to serve her father for her sake. "Take Pity" similarly suggests other realms, those of Dante's *Inferno*. Rosen, an ex-coffee salesman, tells his story to Davidov the census-taker in a cell-like room with the window shade firmly drawn. Having fallen in love with Eva, Rosen valiantly tried to help her and her family, both before and after Alex Kalish, her husband, a Polish refugee, died. But Eva stubbornly refused his help, even as the little shop her husband started and she takes over steadily failed to earn them a living. In desperation, Rosen, a single man, put his head in the oven, leaving all his possessions and his life insurance to Eva and her two little girls. At this point, Davidov, "before Rosen could cry no, idly raised the window shade." There stood Eva, staring at Rosen with "haunted, beseeching eyes." But Rosen, damned for his sins, curses her now, and rams down the shade, imprisoned by his bitterness as earlier he was imprisoned by his obsession.

Occasionally, Malamud is less subtle but still effective in the use of fantasy in his otherwise realistic fiction. For example, in "The Jewbird" (from *The Magic Barrel*) a poor, skinny crow flies into the Cohens' apartment window in the Bronx, begging for a piece of herring and a crust of bread. That the bird talks, in Yiddish, evokes only a mild surprise from Cohen, who takes an immediate dislike to the bird, though his wife and son are more charitable. Cohen is convinced that the bird is nothing but a *schnorrer,* despite the fact that over the next few months Schwartz, as the Jewbird calls himself, helps little Maurie with his homework so that the boy gets the knack of studying and does much better in school. Exasperated by the Jewbird's *chutzpah,* as he sees it, Cohen harasses and finally murders the bird—an example, perhaps, of Jewish anti-Semitism and certainly a dismal failure of human charity.

"Angel Levine" (from *The Magic Barrel*), the title story in *Idiots First,* and "Talking Horse" (from *Rembrandt's Hat*) also mingle fantasy and fiction. In these stories and others Malamud shows his kinship with the tradition of Jewish folklore and folktales as seen in the fiction of Sholem Aleichem, I.L. Peretz, and Isaac Bashevis Singer, though his style is peculiarly his own. The austerity, even bleakness, of his characters is such that one would never mistake a Malamud story for anyone else's. Malamud did not limit himself to Jewish characters and events, as "The Bill" (from *The Magic Barrel*) and "Life Is Better Than Death" (from *Idiots First*) illustrate. But whether he deals with Jewish immigrants or Italians in Rome, Malamud has an unfailing ear for the rhythms and accents of their speech as well as a sympathetic understanding of the difficulties and hardships they endure. If his most characteristic theme is that of human suffering brought on by failed communication and failed charity, his typical response to such situations is an unsentimental insistence that the realities of human existence must be faced.

—Jay L. Halio

See the essays on "The Jewbird" and "The Magic Barrel."

———

MANN, (Paul) Thomas. German. Born in Lübeck, 6 June 1875; brother of the writer Heinrich Mann. Educated at Dr. Bussenius's school, 1882–89; Gymnasium, Lübeck, 1889–94. Military service, 1898–99. Married Katja Pringsheim in 1905; six children, including the writers Erika and Klaus. Worked in insurance company, Munich, 1894–95, then writer; lived in Switzerland, 1933–36 (deprived of German citizenship, 1936), Princeton, New Jersey, 1938–41, Santa Monica, California, 1941–52, and Switzerland, 1952-55. Recipient: Bauernfeld prize, 1904; Nobel prize for literature, 1929; Goethe prize (Frankfurt), 1949; Feltrinelli prize, 1952. Honorary degree: University of Bonn (rescinded, 1936). Honorary Citizen, Lübeck, 1955. *Died 12 August 1955.*

PUBLICATIONS

Collections

Gesammelte Werke.   14 vols., 1974.
Gesammelte Werke, edited by Peter de Mendelssohn. 1980—.

Short Stories and Novellas

Der kleine Herr Friedemann: Novellen.   1898; enlarged edition, 1909.
Tristan: Sechs Novellen.   1903.
Der Tod in Venedig.   1912; as *Death in Venice,* 1925.
Das Wunderkind: Novellen.   1914.
Novellen.   2 vols., 1922.
Death in Venice and Other Stories.   1925.
Mario und der Zauberer: Ein tragisches Reiseerlebnis. 1930; as *Mario and the Magician,* 1930.
Stories of Three Decades.   1936; enlarged edition, as *Stories of a Lifetime,* 1961.
Das Gesetz: Erzählung.   1944; as *The Tables of the Law,* 1945.
Ausgewählte Erzählungen.   1945.

Die Betrogene.   1953; as *The Black Swan,* 1954.

Novels

Buddenbrooks: Verfall einer Familie.   1900; as *Buddenbrooks: The Decline of a Family,* 1924.
Königliche Hoheit.   1909; as *Royal Highness: A Novel of German Court-Life,* 1916; revised translation, 1979.
Herr und Hund: Ein Idyll.   1919; enlarged edition, 1919; as *Basham and I,* 1923; as *A Man and His Dog,* 1930.
Wälsungenblut.   1921.
Bekenntnisse des Hochstaplers Felix Krull; Buch der Kindheit.   1922; additional chapter published as *Die Begegnung,* 1953; complete version, 1953; as *Confessions of Felix Krull, Confidence Man: The Early Years,* 1955.
Der Zauberberg.   1924; as *The Magic Mountain,* 1927.
Children and Fools.   1928.
Joseph und seine Brüder: Die Geschichten Jaakobs, Der junge Joseph, Joseph in Ägypten, Joseph der Ernährer. 4 vols., 1933–43; as *Joseph and His (Joseph and His Brethren): The Tale of Jacob (Joseph and His Brothers), Young Joseph, Joseph in Egypt, Joseph the Provider,* 4 vols., 1934–44.
Nocturnes.   1934.
Lotte in Weimar.   1939; translated as *Lotte in Weimar,* 1940; as *The Beloved Returns,* 1940.
Die vertauschten Köpfe: Eine indische Legende.   1940; as *The Transposed Heads: A Legend of India,* 1941.
Doktor Faustus: Das Leben des deutschen Tonsetzers Adrian Leverkühn, erzählt von einem Freunde.   1947; as *Doctor Faustus: The Life of the German Composer, Adrian Leverkühn, as Told by a Friend,* 1948.
Der Erwählte.   1951; as *The Holy Sinner,* 1951.

Play

Fiorenza.   1906.

Other

Bilse und Ich.   1908.
Friedrich und die grosse Koalition.   1915.
Betrachtungen eines Unpolitischen.   1918; as *Reflections of a Nonpolitical Man,* 1983.
Rede und Antwort: Gesammelte Abhandlungen und kleine Aufsätze.   1922.
Vor deutscher Republik.   1923.
Okkulte Erlebnisse.   1924.
Bemühungen.   1925.
Pariser Rechenschaft.   1926.
Three Essays.   1929.
Die Forderung des Tages: Reden und Aufsätze aus den Jahren 1925-1929.   1930.
Lebensabriss. 1930; as *A Sketch of My Life.*   1930.
Goethe und Tolstoi: Zum Problem der Humanität.   1932.
Past Masters and Other Papers.   1933.
Leiden und Grösse der Meister: Neue Aufsätze.   1935.
Freund und die Zukunft: Vortrag.   1936.
Achtung, Europa! Aufsätze zur Zeit.   1938.
Dieser Friede.   1938; as *This Peace,* 1938.
Schopenhauer.   1938.
Dieser Krieg: Aufsatz. 1940; as *This War.*   1940.
Order of the Day: Political Essays and Speeches of Two Decades.   1942.
Deutsche Hörer! 25 Radiosendungen nach Deutschland. 1942; as *Listen, Germany! Twenty-Five Radio Messages*

to the German People over B.B.C., 1943; enlarged edition (55 messages), 1945.

Adel des Geistes: Sechsehn Versuche zum Problem der Humanität. 1945; enlarged edition, 1956.

Leiden an Deutschland: Tagebuchblätter aus den Jahren 1933 und 1934. 1946.

Essays of Three Decades. 1947.

Neue Studien. 1948.

Die Entstehung des Doktor Faustus: Roman eines Romans. 1949; as The Story of a Novel: The Genesis of Doctor Faustus, 1961.

Goethe und die Demokratie (lecture). 1949.

Michelangelo in seinen Dichtungen. 1950.

The Mann Reader, edited by Joseph Warner Angel. 1950.

Altes und Neues: Kleine Prosa aus fünf Jahrzehnten. 1953; revised edition, 1956.

Ansprache im Schillerjahr 1955. 1955.

Versuch über Schiller. 1955.

Zeit und Werk: Tagebücher und Schriften zum Zeitgeschehen. 1956.

Nachlese: Prosa 1951-55. 1956.

Last Essays. 1959.

Briefe an Paul Amann 1915-1952, edited by Herbert Wegener. 1959; as Letters, 1961.

Gespräch in Briefen, with Karl Kerenyi, edited by Kerenyi. 1960; as Mythology and Humanism: Correspondence, 1975.

Briefe an Ernst Bertram 1910-1955, edited by Inge Jens. 1960.

Briefe 1899-1955, edited by Erika Mann. 3 vols., 1961-65; as Letters, edited by Richard and Clara Winston, 2 vols., 1970.

Briefwechsel, with Robert Faesi, edited by Faesi. 1962.

Wagner und unsere Zeit, edited by Erika Mann. 1963; as Pro and Contra Wagner, 1985.

Briefwechsel 1900-1949, with Heinrich Mann, edited by Hans Wysling, revised edition, edited by Ulrich Dietzel. 1968; revised edition, 1975.

Briefwechsel, with Hermann Hesse, edited by Anni Carlsson. 1968; revised edition, 1975; as Letters, 1975; also edited by Hans Wysling, 1984; as The Hesse/Mann Letters: The Correspondence of Hermann Hesse and Mann, 1910-1955, 1975.

Das essayistische Werk, edited by Hans Bürgin. 8 vols., 1968.

Briefwechsel im Exil, with Erich Kahler, edited by Hans Wysling. 1970; as An Exceptional Friendship: Correspondence, 1975.

The Letters to Caroline Newton, edited by Robert F. Cohen. 1971.

Briefwechsel 1932-1955, with Gottfried Bermann Fischer, edited by Peter de Mendelssohn. 1973.

Briefe an Otto Grautoff 1894-1901, und Ida Boy-Ed, 1903-1928, edited by Peter de Mendelssohn. 1975.

Briefwechsel, with Alfred Neumann, edited by Peter de Mendelssohn. 1977.

Tagebücher, edited by Peter de Mendelssohn. 1977—; as Diaries, 1918-1939, edited by Hermann Keston, 1982—.

Briefwechsel mit Autoren: Rudolf Georg Binding, edited by Hans Wysling. 1988.

Dichter oder Schriftsteller? der Briefwechsel zwischen Mann und Josef Ponten, 1919-1930, edited by Hans Wysling. 1988.

Jahre des Unmuts: Mann's Briefwechsel mit René Schickele, 1930-1940, edited by Hans Wysling and Cornelia Bernini. 1992.

Editor, The Living Thoughts of Schopenhauer. 1939.
Editor, The Permanent Goethe. 1948.

*

Bibliography: Fifty Years of Mann Studies by Klaus Werner Jonas, 1955, and Mann Studies by Klaus Werner and Ilsedore B. Jonas, 1967.

Critical Studies: Mann: An Introduction to His Fiction, 1952, revised edition, 1962, and From "The Magic Mountain": Mann's Later Masterpieces, 1979, both by Henry Hatfield; Mann: The World as Will and Representation by Fritz Kaufmann, 1957; The Ironic German: A Study of Mann by Erich Heller, 1958, revised edition, 1981; The Last Year of Mann by Erika Mann, translated by Richard Graves, 1958; The Two Faces of Hermes, 1962, and Understanding Mann, 1966, both by Ronald D. Miller; Essays on Mann by Georg Lukács, translated by Stanley Mitchell, 1964; Mann by J.P. Stern, 1967; Mann: A Chronicle of His Life by Hans Bürgin and Hans-Otto Mayer, translated by Eugene Dobson, 1969; Mann: Profile and Perspectives by André von Gronicka, 1970; Mann: A Critical Study by Reginald J. Hollingdale, 1971; Mann: The Uses of Tradition by Terence J. Reed, 1974; Unwritten Memories by Katia Mann, edited by Elisabeth Plessen and Michael Mann, translated by Hunter and Hildegarde Hannum, 1975; Montage and Motif in Mann's "Tristan" by Frank W. Young, 1975; The Devil in Mann's "Doktor Faustus" and Paul Valéry's "Mon Faust" by Lucie Pfaff, 1976; Mann: The Devil's Advocate by T.E. Apter, 1978; The Preparation of the Future: Techniques of Anticipation in the Novels of Theodor Fontane and Mann by Gertrude Michielsen, 1978; The Brothers Mann: The Lives of Heinrich and Mann, 1871-1950 and 1875-1955 by Nigel Hamilton, 1978; The Ascetic Artist: Prefiguratios in Mann's "Der Tod in Venedig" by E.L. Marson, 1979; Mann: A Study by Martin Swales, 1980; Mann: The Making of an Artist 1875-1911 by Richard Winston, 1981; Brother Artist: A Psychological Study of Mann's Fiction by James R. McWilliams, 1983; Myth and Politics in Mann's Joseph und seine Brüder by Raymond Cunningham, 1985; Mann's Recantation of Faust: "Doctor Faustus" in the Context of Mann's Relationship to Goethe by David J.T. Ball, 1986; Mann edited by Harold Bloom, 1986; Sympathy for the Abyss: A Study in the Novel of German Modernism: Kafka, Broch, Musil and Mann by Stephen D. Dowden, 1986; Mann the Magician; or, the Good Verus the Interesting by Alan F. Bance, 1987; Vision and Revision: The Concept of Inspiration in Mann's Fiction by Karen Draybeck Vogt, 1987; Critical Essays on Mann edited by Inta M. Ezergailis, 1988; Mann's Short Fiction: An Intellectual Biography by Esther H. Léser, edited by Mitzi Brunsdale, 1989; Mann and His Family by Marcel Reich-Ranicki, translated by Ralph Manheim, 1989; Music, Love, Death, and Mann's Doctor Faustus by John F. Fetzer, 1990; Mann's Doctor Faustus: A Novel at the Margin of Modernism edited by Herbert Lehnert and Peter C. Pfeiffer, 1991; Approaches to Teaching Mann's "Death in Venice" and Other Short Fiction edited by Jeffrey B. Berlin, 1993.

* * *

Thomas Mann, renowned as the author of Buddenbrooks, Der Zauberberg (The Magic Mountain), and Doktor Faus-

tus, is arguably better known for these novels than his short fiction. Although his reputation as a story-writer rests on a handful of early masterpieces ("Tristan," "Tonio Kröger," "Death in Venice"), Mann's output of over 30 works spans six decades—from the prose-sketch "Vision" (1893) to his final novella *Die Betrogene* (*The Black Swan*) in 1953.

Until the appearance of *Buddenbrooks,* Mann devoted his energies exclusively to short fiction, producing a series of cynical cameo-portraits of eccentrics and artistic dilettantes whose background very often prefigured that of Hanno Buddenbrook, the sensitive final member of a declining merchant family. A master of psychological character-dissection, Mann created a whole gallery of fragile, introspective misfits and failures, unable to compete with their successful counterparts in the Hanseatic trading world, invariably struggling to survive in a society whose Protestant work ethic and unquestioningly healthy normality tended to marginalize such outsiders, leaving them assailed not only by corrosive self-doubt, but often by a profound sense of metaphysical inadequacy. Even when their tales do not end in death or suicide, Mann's early protagonists usually attain little more than a precarious protection against a world they continue to shun and fear.

Whether they are *artistes manqués* (Spinell in "Tristan," the unnamed hero of "Der Bajazzo" ("The Dilettante"), unsuccessful in love ("Little Herr Friedemann," Hofmann in "The Will to Happiness"), unable to get on even with a dog ("Tobias Mindernickel"), or maladjusted to their North German environments ("Tonio Kröger"), such figures are given to viewing their predicaments as symptomatic of life's destructiveness and, on the whole, seem to derive little consolation from any compensatory cultivation of the spiritual realm.

Physically and psychologically crippled, the hero of "Little Herr Friedemann" (1897) is typical of Mann's early characters. Having at an early age renounced all hope of love and rejecting the bourgeois concerns of those around him, Friedemann establishes a self-insulating lifestyle, only to have his world shattered when he falls in love with Gerda, a virago-like newcomer to his small town. He rapidly goes to pieces, no longer able to bear the burdens of a reality here represented, as so often in Mann's fiction, by the challenge of love, and commits suicide. Against the backdrop of such a bleak world (in some part influenced by Schopenhauer's pessimistic philosophy), Mann offers an unsympathetic treatment—if not satirical demolition—of fashionable *fin-de-siècle* decadence.

Gradually emerging in the early fiction, especially from "Tristan" onwards, is a fundamental contrast between the normal citizen ("der Bürger"), biologically robust, successful in the practical world, and able to relate socially, and the sickly introspective central figures with their artistic inclinations. It is a polarity representing the realms of life and spirit, often underscored by leitmotifs, the most salient being the symbolism of blond hair and blue eyes depicting the carefree "Bürger," and dark hair, brown eyes, and pronounced veins to suggest the artist-figures. (A characteristic of much of Mann's writing is the assumption that bourgeois normality goes hand in hand with health, and consequently characters representing the realm of the spirit and creative potential axiomatically manifest symptoms of either physical or psychological sickness or an amalgam of both.) Yet despite such a predilection for the schematic and the typical, even Mann's early writings rejoice in an amazingly fertile set of illustrative variations on a limited number of themes—the "Bürger" versus the artist, the conjunction of sickness and spirituality, and the decline of the "Bürgertum" due to increased introspection and aes-

thetic proclivities—subject matter that remains the author's stock-in-trade for virtually his entire creative life.

With his first story of substance, "Tristan," Mann continues to explore the dualism of spirit and life, but now by applying an even-handed form of irony that treats the representatives of both camps with an admixture of sympathy and criticism. Spinell, the artist-protagonist, is thus presented as more sensitive than those around him, even if he may cosmeticize reality and be of dubious artistic integrity, but we are nevertheless made aware that there are moments in this love-story (a burlesque version of Wagner's *Tristan und Isolde*) where he looks impossibly narcissistic and unworldly when set alongside the pragmatic "Bürger"-husband of Frau Klöterjahn, the delicate patient with whom he falls in love. Such calculatingly ironic presentation is the predominant feature of Mann's stories from this point onwards—a narrative stance whose sophistication increases beyond the early parochial treatment of artist-figures in a North German context to the more political material that emerges with the depiction of Gustav von Aschenbach's downfall and its cultural-political implications, in "Death in Venice" (1912).

With the hypnotist Cipolla in *Mario und der Zauberer* ("Mario and the Magician"), Mann goes on to create a powerful image of the totalitarianism threatening Europe at the time and of the complicity of those acquiescing to such a change in climate. Partly a continuation of the artist-theme from the early fiction, Mann's political parable gives a sense of the seductive hold of early fascism and the xenophobia gripping the Italian seaside resort where the German narrator and his family are staying. Through a bravura account of Cipolla's performance Mann satirizes the irrational politics of the day. If Cipolla is Mann's response to Europe's cult of the mesmerizing leader-figure, the German family witnessing these events clearly represent, in their vacillations, those caught up in the mood of the moment, despite their better instincts. Gone now are the intricate layers of intertextuality and elaborate symbol-laden patterns, the hall-marks of "Tonio Kröger" and "Death in Venice"; the writing has become less convoluted, and the parable-dimension more pronounced.

After "Mario," Mann's energies in exile were divided between the fight against national socialism and the need to complete his two remaining major novels: the Joseph-tetralogy and *Doktor Faustus.* His few subsequent sallies into short fiction ("The Law," a humorous account of Moses bringing down the tablets from the mountain, and *The Black Swan,* an account of an ageing woman's Roman spring, shattered by the discovery that she has a fatal illness, lack the conviction and representativeness of the early stories or the novels. As his sweep became more epic, Mann evidently regarded the short story as a lesser genre, more appropriate to the anecdotal and the whimsical than it had been for him up to the start of the 1930's.

—John J. White

See the essays on "Death in Venice," "Mario and the Magician," and "Tonio Kröger."

———

MANSFIELD, Katherine. Pseudonym for Kathleen Mansfield Beauchamp. New Zealander. Born in Wellington, 14 October 1888. Educated at a school in Karori; Girls' High

School, Wellington, 1898–99; Miss Swainson's School, Wellington, 1900–03; Queen's College, London, 1903–06; Wellington Technical College, 1908. Married 1) George Bowden in 1909 (separated 1909; divorced 1918); 2) the writer and editor John Middleton Murry in 1918 (lived with him from 1912). Settled in London, 1908; contributed to the *New Age*, 1910–11, and to Murry's *Rhythm* and its successor, the *Blue Review*, and later became his partner, 1911–13; reviewer, *Westminster Gazette*, 1911–15; founder, with Murry and D.H. Lawrence, *q.v.*, *Signature* magazine, 1916; tubercular: lived for part of each year in the south of France, then Switzerland, from 1916; contributed to the *Athenaeum*, edited by Murry, 1919–20. *Died 9 January 1923.*

PUBLICATIONS

Collections

Collected Stories. 1945.
Selected Stories, edited by Dan Davin. 1953.
The Stories, edited by Anthony Alpers. 1984.
Works (Centenary Edition), edited by Cherry Hankin. 1988—.

Short Stories

In a German Pension. 1911.
Je ne parle pas français. 1918.
Bliss and Other Stories. 1920.
The Garden Party and Other Stories. 1922.
The Dove's Nest and Other Stories. 1923.
Something Childish and Other Stories. 1924; as *The Little Girl and Other Stories*, 1924.
The Aloe. 1930; edited by Vincent O'Sullivan, 1982.
Undiscovered Country: The New Zealand Stories, edited by Ian A. Gordon. 1974.

Verse

Poems. 1923; edited by Vincent O'Sullivan, 1990.

Other

Journal, edited by J. Middleton Murry. 1927; revised edition, 1954.
Letters, edited by J. Middleton Murry. 2 vols., 1928.
Novels and Novelists (reviews), edited by J. Middleton Murry. 1930.
Scrapbook, edited by J. Middleton Murry. 1939.
Letters to John Middleton Murry 1913–1922, edited by J. Middleton Murry. 1951.
Passionate Pilgrimage: A Love Affair in Letters: Mansfield's Letters to John Middleton Murry from the South of France 1915–1920, edited by Helen McNeish. 1976.
Letters and Journals: A Selection, edited by C.K. Stead. 1977.
The Urewera Notebook, edited by Ian A. Gordon. 1978.
Collected Letters, edited by Vincent O'Sullivan and Margaret Scott. 1984—.
The Critical Writings, edited by Clare Hanson. 1987.
Letters Between Mansfield and John Middleton Murry, edited by Cherry Hankin. 1988.
Selected Letters, edited by Vincent O'Sullivan. 1989.

Translator, with S.S. Koteliansky, *Reminiscences of Leonid Andreyev*, by Maksim Gor'kii. 1928.

*

Bibliography: *Mansfield: Publications in Australia 1907–1909* by Jean E. Stone, 1977; "A Bibliography of Mansfield References 1970–1984" by N. Wattie, in *Journal of New Zealand Literature*, 1985; *A Bibliography of Mansfield* by B.J. Kirkpatrick, 1989.

Critical Studies: *Mansfield: A Critical Study* by Sylvia Berkman, 1951; *Mansfield: A Biography*, 1953, and *The Life of Mansfield*, 1980, both by Antony Alpers; *Mansfield* by Ian A. Gordon, 1954, revised edition, 1971; *Mansfield in Her Letters* by Dan Davin, 1959; *Mansfield* by Saralyn R. Daly, 1965; *Mansfield: An Appraisal* by Nariman Hormasji, 1967; *The Edwardianism of Mansfield* by Frederick J. Foot, 1969; *The Fiction of Mansfield* by Marvin Magalaner, 1971; *The Art of Mansfield* by Mary Rohrberger, 1977; *Mansfield: A Biography* by Jeffrey Meyers, 1978; *Gurdjieff and Mansfield* by James Moore, 1980; *Mansfield* by Clare Hanson and Andrew Gurr, 1981; *Mansfield and Her Confessional Stories* by Cherry Hankin, 1983; *A Portrait of Mansfield* by Nora Crone, 1985; *Mansfield* by Kate Fullbrook, 1986; *Mansfield: A Secret Life* by Claire Tomalin, 1987; *Mansfield* by Rhoda B. Nathan, 1988; *Mansfield: The Woman and the Writer* by Gillian Boddy, 1988; *Mansfield and Literary Impressionism* by Julia Van Gunsteren, 1990; *Mansfield: A Study of the Short Fiction* by J.F. Kobler, 1990.

*   *   *

Born in New Zealand in 1888 as Kathleen Mansfield Beauchamp, Mansfield managed in her brief life to establish a reputation as one of the finest practitioners of short fiction in English. Five collections of her work were published during her life time and her *Collected Stories* appeared in 1945. (She died of tuberculosis in 1923). Mansfield mingled stories of delicate poetic evocation, often based on her childhood and adolescence, with others of hard-edged, satiric comedy, such as "The Daughters of the Later Colonel." Her deceptive simplicity and subtlety of style showed the thoroughness with which she had learnt the lessons of Chekhov, and to a lesser extent the Joyce of *Dubliners*, (though she is not above writing wickedly funny parodies of Chekhov in stories like "Green Goggles").

The title story of her second collection, "Bliss," is a fair sample of her work. Thirty-year-old Bertha Young is ecstatically in love with life: "Really—really—she had everything." Mansfield skilfully captures the brittle charm and good humour of the guests at Bertha's dinner party, "just a trifle too much at their ease, a trifle too unaware," and has Bertha imagining that her friend Pearl Fulton shares her own feelings of joy in life. Only at the end does she discover that Miss Fulton, whom her husband Harry affects to despise, is having an affair with him. Less important then the action, however, is the motif of the pear tree that she and Miss Fulton admire. The story ends ambiguously:

"Oh, what is going to happen now?" she cried. But the pear tree was as lovely as ever and as full of flower and as still.

There is little or no action in most of Mansfield's stories. They work instead by suggestion and evocation. Her adult characters especially are often trapped in unhappy situations they cannot escape, although more hope lies with the children, who often recognise the imperfections of their elders.

Josephine and Constantia in "The Daughters of the Late Colonel" are so traumatised by the memory of their tyrannical father that even after his death they are unable to shake off his influence, and this becomes the source of the story's often acerbic comedy:

> Josephine had had a moment of absolute terror at the cemetery, while the coffin was lowered, to think that she and Constantia had done this thing without asking his permission. What would father say when he found out? . . . "Buried. You two girls had me buried!"

As in many of Mansfield's stories the ending is ambiguous, with at least a slim hope held out that the two women will be able to free themselves from the colonel's posthumous influence.

Many of Mansfield's finest stories go back to her childhood in a New Zealand, which she portrays as having a surprisingly deep class consciousness. In "The Garden-Party," the title story of perhaps her finest collection, the adolescent Laura learns to reject the condescending response of her mother to the news that a young working man has died. "The Doll's House" examines the way in which adults impose their class values upon their children and the latter resist them:

> For the fact was, the school the Burnell children went to was not at all the kind of place their parents would have chosen if there had been any choice. But there was none. It was the only school for miles. And the consequence was all the children of the neighbourhood, the Judge's little girls, the doctor's daughters, the storekeeper's children, the milkman's, were forced to mix together.

When the Burnell children receive a wonderful doll's house and disobediently allow the ragged Kelveys to come and see it for a few minutes, a moment of Joycean epiphany occurs to end the story.

Meanings and significances seem to stretch beyond the boundaries of Mansfield's stories. If her comedy is sometimes cruel and her vision bleak, there are often redemptive moments of discovery and hope that counteract the pessimistic tone.

—Laurie Clancy

See the essays on "At the Bay," "The Daughters of the Late Colonel," "The Garden Party," and "Prelude."

MANTO, Sādat Hasan. Indian-Pakistani (Urdū language). Born in Sambrāla, Punjab, India, 11 May 1912. Studied in Muslim High School, Amritsar, India, 1931; Hindu Sabha College, 1931–33 (failed); Aligarh Muslim University, 1934. Married Safiyah in 1939; one son and one daughter. Writer and translator, from 1931; worked for newspapers and local government, Amritsar, 1931–36; editor, *Musawwar* (Painter) film magazine, and *Samāj* (Society), Bombay, 1936–40; radio writer and staff writer, Saroj Movietone, 1937–41, and Imperial Film Company, 1938–40, Bombay; radio writer, All India Radio, New Delhi, 1941; editor, *Musawwar,* and freelance screenplay dialogue writer, 1942, Bombay; screenwriter, Filmistan, 1943–47, and Bombay Talkies Studios, 1947, Bombay; worked in film and radio, Lahore, Pakistan, 1948–55. Member, All India Progressive Writers' Association. *Died 18 January 1955.*

PUBLICATIONS

Collections

Mānto ke bahtarīn kahāniyā.   1963.

Short Stories

Ātish pāre [Sparks].   1936.
Mānto ke afsāne [Mānto's Stories].   1940.
Dhūā.   1941(?); as *Kāla shalwār* [Black Trousers], 1941.
Afsāne aur drāme [Stories and Plays].   1943; as *Ek mard* [One Man], 1956.
Cughd.   1948.
Lazzat-e sang [The Pleasure of Company].   1948(?).
Siyāh hāshiye [Black Margins].   1948.
Bādshāhshat ke khātimah.   1950(?); as *Kingdom's End and Other Stories,* 1987.
Khālī botl, khālī dibbe [Empty Bottles, Empty Boxes].   1950.
Nimrūd kī khudāī [Nimrūd's Divinity]. n.d.; second edition, 1950.
Tandā gosht.   1950.
Yazīd.   1951.
Parde ke pīche [Behind the Veil-Curtain].   1953.
Sarak ke kināre [At the Roadside].   1953.
Baghair 'unwān ke [Without Title].   1954.
Baghair ijāzat [Without Permission].   1955.
Burqe [Burqas].   1955.
Phundne.   1955.
Sarkandõ ke pīche [Behind the Reeds].   1955(?).
Shaitān [Devil].   1955.
Shikārī 'aurat [Female Hunters].   1955.
Black Milk.   1955.
Rattī, māshah, tolāh [Three Measures for Gold].   1956.
Tāhirah se tāhir.   1971.
Mere asfāne [My Stories]. n.d.
Another Lonely Voice: The Urdu Short Stories of Manto, by Leslie A. Flemming, 1979.

Plays

Radio Plays: *Āo* [Come], 1940; *Mānto ke drāme* [Mānto's Plays], 1940; *Janāze* [Funerals], 1942; *Tīn 'aurat* [Three Women], 1942; *Karvat* [Side], 1946; *Katārī,* 1975.

Screenplay: *Āth din* [Eight Days], 1947.

Other

Mānto ke mazāmīn [Mānto's Essays].   1942; as *Mānto ke adabīmazāmīn,* 1962.
Ismat Chugtāī.   1948.
Nūr Jahān, Surūr Jān.   1952.
Ganje farishte [Bald Angels].   1953.
Talkh, tursh aur shīrīn [Bitter, Sour, and Sweet].   1954.
Ūpar, nīce aur darmiyā [Up, Down, and In-Between].   1954.
Lāūdspīkar [Loudspeaker].   1955.

Mānṭo ke khuṭūt [Mānṭo's Letters], edited by Ahmad Nadīm Qāsmī.   1962.

Translator, *Saruzasht-e asīr,* by Victor Hugo.   1933.
Translator, *Do drāme,* by Anton Chekhov. n.d.
Translator, with Hasan 'Abbās, *Verā,* by Oscar Wilde. 1934.
Translator, *Rūsī afsānr* [Russian Stories].   1934.

*

Critical Study: in *Another Lonely Voice: The Urdu Short Stories of Manto* by Leslie A. Flemming, 1979.

*   *   *

Sādat Hasan Mānṭo is one of the most innovative writers in modern Urdu fiction. The author of over two hundred works in this genre published in about 24 collections, together with six volumes of plays and several books of essays, translations, and criticism, he was considered during his lifetime a renegade writer by both the powerful, Marxist-oriented progressive literary movement and the Urdu bourgeois literary establishment, which often criticized him for what they considered a preoccupation with sex and violence in his fiction. Judging many of his stories shocking, even pornographic, they seemed to be uncomfortable with his characters, mostly people on the fringes of bourgeois society (Mānṭo himself came from a family of lawyers) who have been marginalized by poverty or cataclysmic political events: prostitutes, pimps, laborers, unwed mothers, rape victims, runaway lovers, drunkards, to name but a few.

The partition of British-dominated India into the independent countries of India and Pakistan in 1947 was a seminal event in the lives and writings of Mānṭo and many of the authors of his generation. Thus, his stories fall into roughly two groups, the early ones written prior to partition, between 1935 and 1947, which include many of his best-known works, and those written after he immigrated to Pakistan from Bombay in 1948 till his death from alcoholism in 1955.

The early short story "The New Constitution" (1937), set in Lahore, is considered one of his finest, combining politics with both humor and pathos. Its main character, the poor, illiterate tonga-driver Mangu, believes that the much-touted, new Government of India Act of 1935 will bring new freedom to India, including the right for him to defend himself against a bellicose, drunken British soldier who insults him. As the police arrive to restrain Mangu, he invokes the new constitution. They respond, "What rubbish you are talking. What new constitution? It's the same old constitution, you fool." And they drag him off to jail. The story derives its humor from the fact that Mangu garbles his facts about history and the new constitution. However, the reader empathizes with him fully as Britain's great colonialist lie to India, the 1935 Government of India Act, is played out in microcosm in this work.

"Toba Tek Singh," written in the early 1950's, is considered one of the best short stories to deal with the theme of partition, important in many of North India's many languages, especially Urdu, Bengali, Hindi, and Punjabi. In it, the Indian and Pakistani governments want to exchange Muslim lunatics in India for Hindu and Sikh lunatics in Pakistan. Initially, the lunatics' seemingly bizarre comprehension of the partition and the prisoner exchange is humorous. But as one thinks about what they say and do, it seems that their understanding and actions are no worse than those of the politicians who effected the partition— an insane act—in the first place. The asylum in which they are kept is a metaphor for a world mad from the partition experience, and the ambiguous ending suggests the tentativeness of any answers to any questions asked about the partition.

Several of Mānṭo's most successful stories deal with some of society's most marginalized people—prostitutes. The heroin of "The Insult" is Saugandhi, one of Mānṭo's most sympathetically drawn characters. Tired from a long evening with an important client and not feeling well, she agrees with her pimp's request to take one last wealthy customer, who, when he sees her, rejects her. Angry over this insult, Saugandhi returns to her room, where her lover, Madho, just in from Poona, awaits her and asks, as he always does, for money. Finally understanding that her pimp and lover also insult her by exploiting her, she severs her relationship with Madho, whom she turns out, curls up with her mange-infested dog instead, and goes to sleep. The language of the story, replete with obscenities, and the disturbing, even sickening, details of the dirt and filth on Saugandhi's body and in her room, were shocking to middle-class sensibilities. In spite of these, Saughandi carries herself with dignity, and Mānṭo does not judge her. One is left to speculate what the real obscenity here is: Saugandhi's prostitution or the society that allows the exploitation and degradation implicit in prostitution?

In some stories Mānṭo mixes politics, violence, and sex. "Cold Like Ice" (1949), a terse, powerful partition story for which he was tried on obscenity charges, is the story of Ishwar Singh, a hot-blooded Sikh just returned from a six-day spree of looting and murder. He is stabbed by his woman, Kalwant Kaur, who believes that he is unable to become sexually aroused because he has been with another woman. Dying, he recounts how he murdered six men in a Muslim household, then carried off the beautiful daughter, who he thought had fainted. As he raped her, he discovered that she was dead. Traumatized into impotence, he dies taking Kalwant Kaur's hand into his. The story ends: "It was colder than ice." Whose hand is "colder than ice," his or hers, is purposely ambiguous.

While early stories show the influence of Chekhov ("Amusement"), whose works Mānṭo translated into Urdu, other later stories reflect the influence of Maupassant, especially the shocking denouement ("Colder Than Ice," "Open Up"). These works derive their power from the sharp focus on a single character or incident that the author draws. Objective in their description of events and characters, they show none of the didacticism that was considered an important component of contemporary Marxist fiction of the period. Some stories even juxtapose considerable humor alongside stark horror ("Black Borders").

Toward the end of his life, Mānṭo also experimented with a number of modernist techniques, notably the interior monologue and stream-of-consciousness ("Tassels," "The Angel"). Though some of these are noteworthy, others are marred by technical carelessness and inconsistencies, and are often rambling. Such works were often rapidly written in order to get money for alcohol. At his best, however, Mānṭo is a powerful practitioner of stories in the realist mode. Such works have moved Salman Rushdie to call

Mānṭo "the undisputed master of the modern Indian short story."

—Carlo Coppola

See the essay on "Mozail."

MAO DUN (Pseudonym of Shen Yanbing). Chinese. Born in Qingzhen, Cong xiang, Zhejiang Province, Central China, 4 July 1896. Educated at Peking University, 1914-1916. Married Kong Dezhi in 1918. Proofreader, editor, translator, Commercial Press, Shanghai, 1916-20; editor, *Xiaoshuo Yuebao* (Short Story Monthly), 1921-23; member, Communist Party, from 1921, party press officer and propagandist, National Party, Guomindang, 1923-27; English teacher, Common People's School, 1922; instructor, Shanghai University, 1923; lived in Tokyo, 1928-30; returned to Shanghai, 1930; literary editor, *Libao* newspaper, Hong Kong; dean, Xinjiang University; lecturer, Lu Xun Institute of the Arts, Yanan; government worker, Chongqing, 1942; visited Soviet Union, 1946; vice-chairman, All-China Congress of Writers and Artists, Peking, 1949; Minister of Culture, Central People's Government, 1949-65. Founder, Literary Association, 1920. Founder and member, League of Left-Wing Writers, 1930-36. Co-founder, Society for the Study of Literature. Founder or co-founder, *Yiwen* (Translated Literature) magazine, 1934, 1953; *Xiaoshuo Yuekan,* literary magazine, Hong Kong, 1948; with Lu Xun, q.v., *Chinese Literature,* 1951; *Renmin Wenxue* (People's Literature), 1951. Chair, Chinese Writers Union, 1949. Vice chair, Executive Board of the Sino-Soviet Friendship Association, from 1956. *Died 27 March 1981.*

PUBLICATIONS

Collections

Wenji [Collected Works].   10 vols., 1958-61.
Pinglunji [Collected Critical Essays].   2 vols., 1978.
Quanji.   14 vols., 1985.

Short Stories

Ye qiangwei [The Wild Roses].   1929.
Shi [Eclipse].   1930.
  Huanmie [Disillusionment].   1930.
  Dongyao [Vacillation].   1930.
  Zhuiqiu [Pursuit].   1930.
Chun can.   1933; as "Spring Silkworms," in *Spring Silkworms and Other Stories,* 1956.
Su-mang.   1935.
Duanpian xiaoshuoji [Collections].   2 vols., 1934.
Xuanji [Selected Works].   1935.
Chuangzuo xuan [Selection of Creative Writings].   1936.
Paomo [Foams and Other Stories].   1936.
Xiaocheng chunshi [Story from a Small Town].   1937.
Shaonu de xin [Heart of the Maiden].   1937.
Kuling zhi qiu [Autumn in Kuling].   1937; expanded edition, 1975.
Can dong [Winter Days].   1937.
Daibiaozuo [Representative Works].   1937.
Yanyunji [Misty Clouds and Other Stories].   1937.
Shendi miewang [The Death of God].   1944.

Weiju [Grievance and Other Stories].   1945.
Tianshuhua [Flower from the Barren Tree].   1945.
Yesu zhi si [The Death of Jesus].   1945.
Wenji [Collected Works].   1947.
Xuanji [Selected Works].   1952.
Duanpian xiaoshuo xuan [Selection of Short Stories].   1955.
Spring Silkworms and Other Stories.   1956.
Zixuanshi [Selected Works].   1962.
Duanpian xiaoshuoji [Collections of Short Stories].   2 vols., 1980.

Novels

Hong.   1930; as *Rainbow,* 1992.
San ren xing [In Company of Three].   1931.
Lu [The Road].   1932.
Ziye.   1933; as *Midnight,* 1957.
Duojiao guanxi [Polygonal Relations].   1937.
Di yi jie duan de gushi [Story of the First Stage of the War].   1939(?).
Fushi [Putrefaction].   1941.
Shuang ye hong shi er yue hua [Frosty Leaves Red as February Flowers].   1943.
Duan lian [Discipline].   1980.

Other

Chu ci xuanzhu [Annotated Selections from the Songs of Chu].   1928.
Zhongguo shenhua yanjiu ABC [Introduction to the Study of Chinese Mythology].   1929.
Qishi wenxue ABC [Introduction to Chivalric Literature].   1929.
Shenhua zalun [Miscellaneous Notes on Mythology].   1929.
Xiyang wenxue tonglun [Outline of Western Literature] (as Fang bi).   1930.
Sanwenji [Collected Essays].   1933.
Zhongguo wenxue bianqianshi [History of the Development of Chinese Literature].   1934.
Huaxiazi [Chatterbox] (essays).   1934.
Suxie yu suibi [Sketches and Notes].   1935.
Zhongguo di yi ri [One Day in China and Other Essays].   1936.
Yixiang, ganxiang, huiyi [Impressions, Reflections, Reminiscences].   1936.
Paohuo de xili [Baptism by Gunfire] (essays).   1939.
Jiehou shii yi [Pieces Picked-up after the Calamity] (essays).   1942.
Jianwen zaji [Miscellaneous Notes on What I See and Hear].   1945.
Wen xuan [Selected Essays].   1946.
Baiyang lizan [Odes to the Poplar Trees] (essays).   1946.
Fangsheng weisi zhijian [Between Coming to Life and Death] (essays).   1947.
Sulian jianwen lu [Travels in the Soviet Union].   1949.
Zi xuan sanwenji [Selected Essays].   1954.
Ye du ouji [Notes while Reading at Night].   1958.
One Day in China: May 21, 1936, edited by Sherman Cochran, Janis Cochran, and Andrew C.K. Hsieh.   1973.
Shijie mingzhu zalun [Essays on Great Works of World Literature].   1980.
Lun chuangzuo [Essays on Creative Writing], edited by Yeh Tsu-ming.   1980.
Lun Zhongguo xiandai zuojia zuopin [On the Works of Contemporary Chinese Writers], edited by Yue Daiyun.   1980.

Yiwen xuanji [Selection of Translated Works].   1981.
Wenyi pinglunji [Essays on Literature and Arts].   2 vols., 1981.
Wo zuoguo de daolu [Roads I Have Traveled on] (autobiography).   2 vols., 1981-84.
Guanyu lishi he liju [On History and Historical Plays]. n.d.
Chuangzuo de zhunbei [Preparation for Creative Writing]. n.d.

*

Bibliography: in *A History of Modern Chinese Fiction 1917-1957* by C.T. Hsia, 1961; in *Realism and Allegory in the Early Fiction of Mao Dun* by Yushi Zhen, 1986.

Critical Studies: *Mao Tun and Modern Chinese Literary Criticism* by Marian Gálik, 1969; in *Modern Chinese Literature in the May Fourth Era*, edited by Merle Goldman, 1977; in *Modern Chinese Fiction* by W. Yang and N.K. Mao, 1981; *Realism and Allegory in the Early Fiction of Mao Dun* by Yushi Zhen, 1986; *Fictional Realism in 20th-Century China: Mao Dun, Lao She, Shen Congwen* by David Der-wei Wang, 1992.

* * *

Mao Dun was one of the few truly exceptional Chinese writers of the post-May Fourth (1919) Movement. His massive literary corpus includes all forms of fiction, short stories, novelettes, and novels like *Ziye (Midnight)*, of Tolstoian scope. He published extensively in the magazine *Xiaoshuo Yuebao*, of which, in his early career, he had served as an editor.

Mao Dun's short fiction is inspired by his attraction to China's leftist causes of the 1920's, and his disappointment and pessimism over the human failure to realize those ideals. His heroes, more often heroines, are for the most part educated youngsters eager to take responsible part in the "New Order," but they typically end up disillusioned, even corrupted, by the realities of their revolution. Whether set in a small town or big city, the stories chronicle a cross-section of contemporary China. This is the hallmark of Mao Dun's writing.

A common focus of critical analysis is Mao Dun's heroine. Typically, the woman enters the story as a naive innocent, whose inner self is tested against the pressures of the traditional family and the turmoil of rapid social change. Unlike other, iconoclastic writers of the day, Mao Dun does not dwell upon the trials of the feudal wife. Instead, his heroine chooses sturdy, Ibsen-like independence in the modern world of new political ideals but collapsing moral values. However, her experiences corrupt her innocence and harden her into sophisticated cynicsm. She loses her confidence and from a nadir of despair (one heroine contracts syphilis), she emerges either, in Mao Dun's more nihilistic moods, into negative bitterness, or into what has been described as a caricature of positive socialist idealism.

The collection *Shi (Eclipse)*, which includes "Disillusion," "Vacillation," and "Pursuit," pits the idealistic, innocent ingenue against the older, sophisticated but disillusioned woman. *Ye qiangwei (The Wild Roses)* is a similar collection of short stories exploring the contrasting reactions of five young women to their experience in 1920's China. One story has the heroine abandon her husband, who has fallen behind her own progressive socialist views. By contrast, another heroine, the well-to-do Miss Huan, given an unfettered choice, cannot reconcile her traditional morality with her new "revolutionary" lifestyle. Shamed by her unwed pregnancy, she hangs herself (so the title "Suicide"). A third type of reaction is portrayed in "A Girl." This heroine, a proud, self-confident local beauty, becomes embittered against all men when her family falls on hard times and her former suitors reject her.

Mao Dun's menfolk, by and large, serve as antithetical weakness. When the woman relies on the strength of their support, they collapse; when the woman seeks their understanding of her modern views they exemplify feudal tyranny; when she needs stability in her shifting social environment, they exploit her, vacillate, or plunge her further into profligate decadence. In "Disillusion," for example, the young heroine is repeatedly disappointed by her eventually worthless men friends; in "A Girl" the girl's suitors all desert her when she most needs their approval.

Strong men in Mao Dun's fiction are merely authoritarian. Male family members exhibit obstinate resistance to new freedoms; civil and military officers of the anticommunist Nationalist society, like those in *Rainbow*, beneath their apparent magnanimity, to exploit the woman's naivety and misfortune. The alternative, demanded by communist doctrine, is Mao Dun's occasional Byronic superman: the young Communist Party activist. Impervious to temptation and corruption, wholly perfect, he is hence incredible and unrealistic. But in his aloof perfection, apart from offering the impossible shining example that plunges the woman equally unrealistically into selfless devotion to the cause, he too is of no personal help to the woman in her despair.

However, Mao Dun was capable of portraying a male protagonist sympathetically. The author recognised that "fiction is people," and he wrote at least one, more subtle, character, in the novel *Hong (Rainbow)*, that emerges memorably from the writing of the time. Admittedly, the character plays the "weak husband" role, but his pathetic attempts to regain the affection of his "progressive" wife, particularly the irony of his purchasing for her every publication he could find with the work "new" in the title, portray a human sincerity quite rare in the politicized fiction of Mao Dun's milieu.

The intense, internecine political rivalries among the revolutionary, leftist youth, the established Nationalist authority, reactionary local civil and military power-holders, and Japanese invaders that often provide the motivation for Mao Dun's characters are also seen conversely to diminish those characters by the vastness of their scope against which the individual is impotent. In story after story, the denouement results, if not deus ex machina, then at least from forces far beyond the protagonist's own determination. In "A Girl," for example, the rejection of the heroine and her eventual misanthropy develops not from her own conceit, but from the decline of her family, that too resulting from circumstances entirely outside the family's ability to remedy. The same is true of the peasant family's bankruptcy in "Spring Silkworms," caused not by shortcomings of character, but by irresistible national upheaval. However Mao Dun had portrayed the girl or the silk-raising peasant, their characters would not have affected the outcome. The litterateur Mao Dun intuitively portrays personal psychology with its search for expression and fulfilment, and paints riotous varieties of the human condition; Mao Dun the socialist-realist, disillusioned by the failures of the Left to realize its aims, pessimistically crushes individual volition beneath the drive, as he sees it, of inevitable social development. Marx's message he makes manifest in fiction if not in fact.

Mao Dun's highly literary style of composition on precisely contemporary events, engaging a recognizably European naturalism (notably Émil Zola), was addressed essentially to China's educated middle-class youth, uncertain of their prospects and values in their rapidly changing world. Women faced the greatest challenge, and Mao Dun's stories were most successful, as in *Ye qiangwei,* in specifically exploring their circumstances and psychology. Typically, Mao Dun was criticized by both sides of the political conflict: on the one side, for espousing the revolutionary cause; and conversely, for not providing clear-cut model political hero rules, or an optimistic vision of a bright socialist future. His accomplishment lies in realistically recording the vast canvas of his times and portraying a credible, complex psychology for his often memorable protagonists.

—John Marney

See the essay on "Spring Silkworms."

———————

MARSHALL, Owen (Owen Marshall Jones). New Zealander. Born in Te Kuiti, 17 August 1941. Educated at Timaru Boy's High School; University of Canterbury, Christchurch, 1960–63, M.A. (honours) in history 1963; Christchurch Teachers College, teaching diploma, 1964. Married Jacqueline Hill in 1965; two daughters. Deputy rector, Waitaki Boys High School, Oamaru, 1983-85; since 1986 deputy principal, Craighead Diocesan School, Timaru. Literary fellow, University of Canterbury, 1981. Recipient: Lillian Ida Smith award, 1986, 1988; *Evening Standard* award, for short story, 1987; American Express award, for short story, 1987; New Zealand Literary Fund scholarship, 1988, and achievement award, 1989; Robert Burns fellowship, University of Otago, 1992. Lives in Timaru, New Zealand.

PUBLICATIONS

Short Stories

Supper Waltz Wilson and Other New Zealand Stories. 1979.
The Master of Big Jingles and Other Stories.   1982.
The Day Hemingway Died.   1984.
The Lynx Hunter and Other Stories.   1987.
The Divided World: Selected Stories.   1989.
Tomorrow We Save the Orphans.   1991.

Play

Radio Play: *An Indirect Geography.*   1989.

*

Critical Studies: in *Barbed Wire and Mirrors: Essays on New Zealand Prose* by Lawrence Jones, 1987; "The Naming of Parts: Marshall" by Vincent O'Sullivan, in *Sport 3,* 1989.

*   *   *

In less than 15 years, Owen Marshall has established himself as one of the most important writers of the short story in contemporary New Zealand. From the time of his first collection in 1979 he has been recognised as a significant talent, and awards and critical accolades have ensured a high profile for all his subsequent books. A total of five collections to date, one wider-ranging selection, *The Divided World*, as well as the anthologising of a number of his best stories, have sustained this reputation.

Part of his stories' appeal is the evident recognizability of the fictional worlds that they so frequently delineate. Marshall writes of middle New Zealand. His characters are members of a society that clings, in spite of radical changes around and within it, to values that have been entrenched since the early 20th century. The values are those of a property-owning lower middle class, Anglo Saxon in its cultural origins and male-dominated in its point of view. The society so depicted is a conservative one, and within it Marshall is able to observe the experiences and the necessary recognitions of his characters with considerable compassion.

The appeal of many of these stories may be that they evoke a world that is passing from us; Marshall frequently records the world of childhood or adolescence, the world of time recently past, and the adult world in which the knowledge of loss and compromise habitually is borne with resignation rather than with anger or despair. Such a world may be identified by the reader on a personal level, though it is a broader social recognizability that gives the stories a wide reader appeal. It was perhaps this that led Frank Sargeson, reviewing Marshall's first book in what was to be the older writer's last piece of published criticism, to remark that the stories could make the reader "experience an environment which has mysteriously become a character in its own right." If the mystery is explicable in the light of close scrutiny of Marshall's texts, the assertion is nevertheless still useful, and appropriate to Marshall's work throughout his career.

His work is seldom experimental or in any obvious sense self-consciously post-modern; he seems little concerned with the inventiveness that would emphasize textuality before narrative. Nor has he altered his techniques of story telling greatly during his career, though there is the expected evidence of an enhancement of stylistic confidence that comes with experience. Experiment for Marshall seems to be confined thus far to a jeux d'esprit such as in "Off by Heart," a sequence of episodes linked by the recital of lists of names drawn from the narrator's memory, or "The Divided World," a virtuoso incantation of epigrams that declare all human experience to be divided in a way that both shares what is divided up and isolates those who would share. "The Divided World" is an important work, not so much because of its confident control of its whimsical and often ironic examples, but because it suggests a view of human endeavour in a manichaean universe which is finally at heart melancholic. Its use as the title story of Marshall's volume of selected stories seems to confirm its centrality to his work thus far.

Most commonly in a Marshall story, though, the reader may expect to find the tale of a male narrator or protagonist whose experiences identify the realities of a world that is indifferent to human ambition and distress. In some of his most successful stories, such as "The Master of Big Jingles" and "Kenneth's Friend," his characters recall childhood and adolescence, the rites of passage and the awareness of an impinging adult world of which the young must take account. There are similar epiphanic moments in "The Day Hemingway Died." Stories that consider the relationship of parents and children ("Supper Waltz Wilson," "A Poet Dream of Amazons," and "The Seed Merchant," which is among Marshall's finest single achievements) seem to recognize the inevitable sadness of love that fails to bridge the gap between the generations.

There can be humour in Marshall's world, as both the events and the narrative style in "Cabernet Sauvignon with my Brother" attest; indeed, a wry irony pervades many of the stories as the characters scrutinize human absurdity with a gently satirical gaze. The literary establishment of Marshall's own country does not escape, as shown in the short satire "Glasnost." Occasionally, in a story such as "Mumsy and Zip," there can be the recognition of a moral darkness that is fraught with horror when human ambitions and hopes are too cruelly or too long thwarted. But for the most part, the stories eschew either of the extremes of delight and despair, and evoke an emotion close to quiet poignancy.

Marshall's stories seem rooted in the tradition of the naturalistic short story whose lineage in New Zealand is traced back to Frank Sargeson. That naturalism has frequently been used in fiction that adopts the techniques of social realism, with a style of narration that involves the pretence of observational neutrality and the actuality of a humanist sympathy. Authorial sympathy in New Zealand fiction has tended to favour the suffering individual rather than the dominating social forces that may be the cause of the suffering, acknowledging a liberalism that was for a long time at the heart of both the country's literature and its social opinions. If Marshall is to be located within that tradition, it is because the sympathetic examination of individual experience and emotion seems so central to his stories. The protagonist is of interest because of what he or she will discover and feel, rather than because of what a closely plotted narrative will show happening. This is not to say that Marshall's plots are inadequate but only that the stories establish character and setting before all else. Plot is valued less for its own sake than for its use in revealing character in action. As a result, the reader often seems invited to concentrate upon characteristic behaviour, the nuances and quirky eccentricities that make for simultaneous familiarity and individuality. It is here that Marshall's greatest imaginative strengths lie, and it is here that the explanation of his popularity can most readily be sought.

—William Broughton

MATUTE (Ausejo), Ana María. Spanish. Born in Barcelona, 26 July 1926. Educated at Damas Negras French Nuns College and schools in Barcelona and Madrid. Married Ramón Eugenio de Goicoechea in 1952 (separated 1963); one son. Member of the Turia literary group, with Juan Goytisolo and others, Barcelona, 1951. Visiting professor, Indiana University, Bloomington, 1965–66, and University of Oklahoma, Norman, 1969; writer-in-residence, University of Virginia, Charlottesville, 1978–79. Recipient: Café Gijón prize, 1952; Planeta prize, 1954; National Critics' prize, for novel, 1959; March Foundation grant, 1959; Cervantes prize, 1959; Nadal prize, 1960; Lazarillo prize, for children's writing, 1965; Fastenrath prize, 1969. Honorary Fellow, American Association of Teachers of Spanish and Portuguese; corresponding member, Hispanic Society of America, 1960. Lives in Barcelona.

PUBLICATIONS

Short Stories

Fiesta al noroeste (novella).   1953.
La pequeña vida (novella).   1953.
Los cuentos, Vagabundos.   1956.
Los niños tontos.   1956.
El tiempo.   1957.
Tres y un sueño.   1961.
Historias de la Artámila.   1961.
El arrepentido.   1961.
Algunos muchachos y otros cuentos.   1968; as *The Heliotrope Wall and Other Stories,* 1989.
La vírgen de Antioquía y otros relatos.   1990.

Novels

Los Abel.   1948.
Pequeño teatro.   1954.
En esta tierra.   1955.
Los hijos muertos.   1958; as *The Lost Children,* 1965.
Los mercaderes: Primera memoria.   1959; as *Awakening,* 1963; as *School of the Sun,* 1963.
Los soldados lloran de noche.   1964.
La trampa.   1969.
A la mitad del camino.   1961.
El río.   1963.
La torre vigía.   1971.
Olvidado rey Gudú.   1980.
Diablo vuelve a casa.   1980.

Other

El país de la pizarra (for children).   1957.
Paulina, el mundo, y las estrellas (for children).   1960.
El saltamontes verde: El aprendiz (stories; for children).   1960.
Libro de juegos para los niños de los otros, photographs by Jaime Buesa.   1961.
Caballito loco; Carnivalito (stories; for children).   1962.
El polizón del "Ulises" (for children).   1965.
Obra completa.   5 vols., 1971–77.
Sólo un pie descalzo (for children).   1983.
Sino España.   1991.

Translator, *Frederick; Nadarín* (for children), by Leo Lionni.   2 vols., 1986.

*

Critical Studies: "Antipathetic Fallacy: The Hostile World of Matute's Novels," in *Romance Quarterly* 13 (Supplement), 1967, and *The Literary World of Matute,* 1970, both by Margaret E.W. Jones; *The World of Matute* by M. Weitzner, 1970; *Matute* by Rosa Roma, 1971; *Matute* by Janet W. Díaz, 1971; "Forms of Alienation in Matute's *La trampa*" by Elizabeth Ordóñez, in *Journal of Spanish Studies: 20th Century,* 4, 1976; "Adolescent Friendship in Two Contemporary Spanish Novels" by Phyllis Zatlin-

Boring, in *Hispanófila* 60, 1977; "Retrospection as a Technique in Matute's *Los hijos muertos* and *En esta tierra*" by J. Townsend Shelby, in *Revista de Estudios Hispánicos* 14(2), 1980; "Trace-Reading the Story of María/Matute in *Los mercaderes*" by Michael Scott Doyle, in *Revista de Estudios Hispánicos* 19(2), 1985; "Privation in Matute's Fiction for Children," in *Symposium* 39(2), 1985, "Codes of Exclusion, Modes of Equivocation: Matute's *Primera memoria*," in *Ideologies and Literature* 1(1–2), 1985, and "Stranger than Fiction: Fantasy in Short Stories by Matute, Rodoreda, Riera," in *Monographic Review/Revista Monográfica* 4, 1988, all by Geraldine Cleary Nichols; "*Los hijos muertos*: The Spanish Civil War as a Perpetuator of Death" by Eunice D. Myers, in *Letras Femeninas* 12(1–2), 1986; "From Freedom to Enclosure: 'Growing Down' in Matute's *Primera memoria*" by Lucy Lee-Bonanno, in *Kentucky Philological Review* 13, 1986; "Notes of Hans Christian Andersen Tales in Matute's *Primera memoria*" by Suzanne Gross Reed, in *Continental, Latin-American and Francophone Women Writers*, edited by Eunice D. Myers and Ginette Adamson, 1987; "Two Mourners for the Human Spirit: Matute and Flannery O'Connor" by Mary S. Vásquez, in *Monographic Review/Revista Monográfica* 4, 1988; "The Fictional World of Matute" by Janet Pérez, in *Women Writers of Contemporary Spain*, edited by Joan L. Brown, 1991.

* * *

One of five children of a prosperous Catalan industrialist, Ana María Matute was deeply scarred by the Spanish Civil War (1936-39), an obsessive motif in her fiction. Her social consciousness results from childhood experience of bombardments, hunger, factional violence, political and social terrorism, and religious persecution, combined with the discovery of rural poverty and social injustice (during summers spent at her maternal grandparents' farm in the backward, mountainous countryside of Old Castile, a frequent setting for her stories).

Los Abel (The Abel Family) contains constants of much Matute fiction: the Cain-Abel archetype (violence between brothers, symbolizing the Spanish Civil War), rural Castile's backwardness and misery, childhood and adolescence, rites of passage, divided families, solitary and alienated youth and inept, frustrated, bitter adults. Her early novella, *Fiesta al noroeste* (Celebration in the Northwest), surprisingly mature and complex, investigates *caciquismo* (rural political bossism) and traditional Spanish social structure via the landlord's rambling confession of rape, near-incest, avarice, and betrayal. Conflict between idealism and materialism, another Matute constant, appears most clearly in her children's tales (often recalling Hans Christian Andersen): *El saltamontes verde* (The Green Grasshopper) and *Caballito loco* (Little Crazy Horse).

Los niños tontos (The Stupid Children), Matute's most lyric collection, contains sketches painting children and their imaginary, emotional worlds. Termed prose poems by critics, these 21 brief tales portray misunderstood, rejected, rebellious, or unloved children, at odds with the world, victims of their own imaginations. Many are sick, abnormal, or deformed, often treated with great cruelty or indifference. The author's tender handling ranges from lyric indirectness to understated matter-of-factness, without separating fantasy from reality. Twelve (possibly 14) sketches involve the deaths of children, due usually to

psychological rather than physical causes, symbolizing the loss of innocence or passage to adulthood. By contrast, *Libro de juegos para los niños de los otros* (Book of Games for Others' Children) looks realistically at how street children live.

El tiempo (Time) contains a novella earlier published separately, *La pequeña vida* (The Small Life), presenting two orphaned adolescents' difficult existence in a fishing village. When their only human warmth—their friendship—is threatened, they attempt to flee together but are run down by a train in the fog. Other tales often anthologized include "The Good Children" whose eight-year-old narrator is considered shocking and reprehensible until she learns the art of deception, and "Fausto" in which an orphan girl, forced by her grandfather to get rid of her sick cat, spontaneously establishes a parallel between the "useless" dead pet and old man, auguring his demise. Time (existential being-toward-death) is obsessive, and social elements loom large in this collection, with hunger, child labor, loneliness and misery appearing repeatedly. Drunkenness, lonely old age, the importance of illusions, adolescent infatuation, first love, and lies that unexpectedly prove true are other repetitive themes.

The 22 stories of *Historias de la Artámila* (Tales of Artámila) possess a common setting (the mountain village of Matute's childhood summers), and most portray social or economic problems of the peasant sharecroppers. Others describe an illusion or its loss, an awakening, injustice, disappointment; the general tone is melancholic. Protagonists are usually children or adolescents, invalids or orphans, isolated, lonely, alienated or rejected; the few adults are in unhappy relationships, unable to communicate, and burdened by guilt. The relativity of wealth, connections between love and hate, and the total separation between the worlds of childhood and adulthood are major themes. Matute's stories evoke the atmosphere and structure of the folktale, or combine realism with the marvelous and supernatural.

El arrepentido (The Repentant One) lacks linking motifs or common setting; repentance is not important although most stories concern something regrettable: socio-economic injustice, the Civil War, terminal illness, suicide, deceit, poverty, children victimized by juvenile gangs, peer pressure, egotism, stereotyping, and false charity. The circus, traveling players, mountebanks, and the fascination of itinerant entertainers are frequent Matute motifs found here. Deliberate juxtapositions of opposites (life-death, joy-grief, lyricism-the grotesque) create ironic and artistic effect.

Tres y un sueño (Three [Tales] and One Dream), three independent novellas, examine the "dream" of childhood from the perspective of the child who grows up, one who dies, and one who refuses to grow up psychologically although maturing physically. The unreal atmosphere evokes the world of fairy tales and fantasy, suggesting reason is incompatible with the magical childhood world.

Algunos muchachos y otros cuentos (The Heliotrope Wall and Other Stories), features new elements making this collection a milestone in Matute's evolution. Each tale highlights an epigraph, an enigmatic commentary on what follows. Most narrate a crime (usually murder or arson), motivated by hate, envy, or mixed emotions, recreated lyrically, vaguely, and allusively, barely hinting at violence. Emotional background and climate, motivation, and characters' situation are nebulous, slightly out-of-focus, requiring a sophisticated reader. Fantastic and supernatural touches combine with realistic settings and down-to-earth personalities or characters of mythic dimensions. Fragmentary technique and hallucinatory narrative suggest nightmares or drug-induced hallucination, constituting puzzles readers must reconstruct. Fantasy and social preoccupations, two extremes of Matute's writing, combine with familiar themes and heightened technical mastery in her most significant collection to date.

—Janet Pérez

MAUGHAM, W(illiam) Somerset. English. Born in Paris, of English parents, 25 January 1874. Educated at King's School, Canterbury, Kent, 1885-89; University of Heidelberg, 1891–92; studied medicine at St. Thomas's Hospital, London, 1892–97: intern in Lambeth, London; qualified as surgeon, L.R.C.P., M.R.C.S., 1897. Served in a Red Cross ambulance unit in Flanders, 1914–15, and in the British Intelligence Corps, 1916–17. Married the interior designer Syrie Barnardo Wellcome in 1917 (divorced 1927); one daughter. Accountant, briefly, 1892; writer from 1896; lived mainly in Paris, 1897–1907; travelled widely from 1916: visited the South Seas, China, Malaya, and Mexico; lived at Villa Mauresque, Cap Ferrat, France, from 1928; lived in the U.S. during World War II; instituted annual prize for promising young British writer, 1947. D.Litt.: Oxford University, 1952; University of Toulouse. Fellow, and Companion of Literature, 1961, Royal Society of Literature. Commander, Legion of Honour; honorary senator, University of Heidelberg; honorary fellow, Library of Congress, Washington, D.C.; honorary member, American Academy of Arts and Letters. Companion of Honour, 1954. *Died 16 December 1965.*

PUBLICATIONS

Short Stories

Orientations.   1899.
The Trembling of the Leaf: Little Stories of the South Sea Islands.   1921; as *Sadie Thompson and Other Stories of the South Seas,* 1928; as *Rain and Other Stories,* 1933.
The Casuarina Tree: Six Stories.   1926; as *The Letter: Stories of Crime,* 1930.
Ashenden; or, The British Agent.   1928.
Six Stories Written in the First Person Singular.   1931.
Ah King: Six Stories.   1933.
The Judgement Seat (story).   1934.
East and West: Collected Short Stories.   1934; as *Altogether,* 1934.
Cosmopolitans.   1936.
Favorite Short Stories.   1937.
The Mixture as Before: Short Stories.   1940; as *Great Stories of Love and Intrigue,* 1947.
The Unconquered (story).   1944.
Creatures of Circumstance: Short Stories.   1947.
East of Suez: Great Stories of the Tropics.   1948.
Here and There.   1948.
Complete Short Stories.   3 vols., 1951.
The World Over: Stories of Manifold Places and People.   1952.
Best Short Stories, edited by John Beecroft.   1957.
A Maugham Twelve: Stories, edited by Angus Wilson.   1966; with *Cakes and Ale,* 1967.

Malaysian Stories, edited by Anthony Burgess.   1969.
Seventeen Lost Stories, edited by Craig V. Showalter.   1969.

Novels

Liza of Lambeth.   1897; revised edition, 1904.
The Making of a Saint.   1898.
The Hero.   1901.
Mrs. Craddock.   1902.
The Merry-Go-Round.   1904.
The Bishop's Apron: A Study in the Origins of a Great Family.   1906.
The Explorer.   1907.
The Magician.   1908; with *A Fragment of Autobiography,* 1956.
Of Human Bondage.   1915.
The Moon and Sixpence.   1919.
The Painted Veil.   1925.
Cakes and Ale; or, The Skeleton in the Cupboard.   1930.
The Book-Bag.   1932.
The Narrow Corner.   1932.
Theatre.   1937.
Christmas Holiday.   1939.
Up at the Villa.   1941.
The Hour Before the Dawn.   1942.
The Razor's Edge.   1944.
Then and Now.   1946.
Catalina: A Romance.   1948.
Selected Novels.   3 vols., 1953.

Plays

Marriages Are Made in Heaven (as *Schiffbrüchig,* produced 1902).   In *The Venture Annual,* edited by Maugham and Laurence Housman, 1903.
A Man of Honour (produced 1903).   1903.
Mademoiselle Zampa (produced 1904).
Lady Frederick (produced 1907).   1911.
Jack Straw (produced 1908).   1911.
Mrs. Dot (produced 1908).   1912.
The Explorer: A Melodrama (produced 1908; revised version produced 1909).   1912.
Penelope (produced 1909).   1912.
The Noble Spaniard, from a work by Ernest Grenet-Dancourt (produced 1909).   1953.
Smith (produced 1909).   1913.
The Tenth Man: A Tragic Comedy (produced 1910).   1913.
Landed Gentry (as *Grace,* produced 1910).   1913.
Loaves and Fishes (produced 1911).   1924.
A Trip to Brighton, from a play by Abel Tarride (produced 1911).
The Perfect Gentleman, from a play by Molière (produced 1913).   In *Theatre Arts,* November 1955.
The Land of Promise (produced 1913).   1913.
The Unattainable (as *Caroline,* produced 1916).   1923.
Our Betters (produced 1917).   1923.
Love in a Cottage (produced 1918).
Caesar's Wife (produced 1919).   1922.
Home and Beauty (produced 1919; as *Too Many Husbands,* produced 1919).   1923.
The Unknown (produced 1920).   1920.
The Circle (produced 1921).   1921.
East of Suez (produced 1922).   1922.
The Camel's Back (produced 1923).
The Constant Wife (produced 1926).   1927.
The Letter, from his own story (produced 1927).   1927.

The Sacred Flame (produced 1928).   1928.
The Bread-Winner (produced 1930).   1930.
Dramatic Works.   6 vols., 1931–34; as *Collected Plays*, 3 vols., 1952.
For Services Rendered (produced 1932).   1932.
The Mask and the Face, from a play by Luigi Chiarelli (produced 1933).
Sheppey (produced 1933).   1933.
Six Comedies.   1937.
Trio: Stories and Screen Adaptations, with R.C. Sherriff and Noel Langley.   1950.

Screenplay: *The Verger* (in *Trio*), 1950.

Other

The Land of the Blessed Virgin: Sketches and Impressions of Andalusia.   1905.
On a Chinese Screen.   1922.
The Gentleman in the Parlour: A Record of a Journey from Rangoon to Haiphong.   1930.
The Non-Dramatic Works.   28 vols., 1934–69.
Don Fernando; or, Variations on Some Spanish Themes.   1935.
My South Sea Island.   1936.
The Summing Up.   1938.
Books and You.   1940.
France at War.   1940.
Strictly Personal.   1941.
The Maugham Sampler, edited by Jerome Weidman.   1943; as *The Maugham Pocket Book*, 1944.
Of Human Bondage, with a Digression on the Art of Fiction (address).   1946.
Great Novelists and Their Novels: Essays on the Ten Greatest Novels of the World and the Men and Women Who Wrote Them.   1948; revised edition, as *Ten Novels and Their Authors*, 1954; as *The Art of Fiction*, 1955.
A Writer's Notebook.   1949.
A Maugham Reader, edited by Glenway Wescott.   1950.
The Writer's Point of View (lecture).   1951.
The Vagrant Mood: Six Essays.   1952.
Mr. Maugham Himself, edited by John Beecroft.   1954.
The Partial View (includes *The Summing Up* and *A Writer's Notebook*).   1954.
Points of View.   1958; as *Points of View: Five Essays*, 1959.
Purely for My Pleasure.   1962.
Selected Prefaces and Introductions.   1963.
Wit and Wisdom, edited by Cecil Hewetson.   1966.
Essays on Literature.   1967.
Letters to Lady Juliet Duff, edited by Loren D. Rothschild.   1982.
A Traveller in Romance: Uncollected Writings 1901–1964, edited by John Whitehead.   1984.

Editor, with Laurence Housman, *The Venture Annual of Art and Literature.*   2 vols., 1903–04.
Editor, *The Truth at Last*, by Charles Hawtrey.   1924.
Editor, *The Travellers' Library.*   1933; as *Fifty Modern English Writers*, 1933.
Editor, *Tellers of Tales: 100 Short Stories from the United States, England, France, Russia, and Germany.*   1939; as *The Greatest Stories of All Times*, 1943.
Editor, *A Choice of Kipling's Prose.*   1952; as *Maugham's Choice of Kipling's Best: Sixteen Stories*, 1953.

*

Bibliography: *Theatrical Companion to Maugham: A Pictorial Record of the First Performance of the Plays of Maugham* by Raymond Mander and Joe Mitchenson, 1955; *A Bibliography of the Works of Maugham* by Raymond Toole Scott, 1956, revised edition, 1973; *Maugham: An Annotated Bibliography of Writings about Him* by Charles Saunders, 1970.

Critical Studies: *Maugham* by J. Brophy, 1952, revised edition, 1958; *The Maugham Enigma*, 1954, and *The World of Maugham*, 1959, both edited by K.W. Jonas; *Maugham: A Candid Portrait* by K.G. Pfeiffer, 1959; *Maugham: A Biographical and Critical Study* by Richard A. Cordell, 1961, revised edition, 1969; *Maugham: A Guide* by Laurence Brander, 1963; *The Two Worlds of Maugham* by Wilmon Menard, 1965; *Remembering Mr. Maugham* by Garson Kanin, 1966; *Somerset and All the Maughams*, 1966, and *Conversations with Willie: Recollections of Maugham*, 1978, both by Robin Maugham; *Maugham* by M.K. Naik, 1966; *A Case of Human Bondage* by Beverley Nichols, 1966; *The Dramatic Comedy of Maugham* by Robert E. Barnes, 1968; *Maugham* by Ivor Brown, 1970; *Maugham and the Quest for Freedom*, 1972, and *Willie: The Life of Maugham*, 1989, both by Robert L. Calder; *The Pattern of Maugham*, 1974, and *Maugham*, 1977, both by Anthony Curtis; *Maugham and His World* by Frederic Raphael, 1976, revised edition, 1989; *Maugham* by Ted Morgan, 1980; *Maugham: The Critical Heritage* edited by Anthony Curtis and John Whitehead, 1987; *Maugham* by Archie K. Loss, 1987.

*   *   *

Somerset Maugham was born in France and lived there until the age of ten. He spoke, read, and wrote French with fluency, and his early intimacy with the language and the literature was to be an important factor in shaping his art. The French taste for logic and clarity appealed to him, and he liked a short story to have what he called "a beginning, a middle, and an end." One of his models was Guy de Maupassant, who specialised in the technique of the surprise ending. A vivid example of how Maugham uses this device is to be found in "Honolulu" (*The Trembling of the Leaf*), ostensibly a tale of passion and black magic, which concludes with a brief exchange of dialogue where the import of the story is abruptly reversed and one is left admiring his nonchalant skill. Maugham elaborated this device by using the medium of the short story to show how the force of circumstance can reveal totally unexpected traits in a character. In "The Lion's Skin" (*The Mixture as Before*), a jumped-up snob who marries for money displays nobility and courage by dying in the attempt to rescue his wife's beloved dog from a fire. "Mr. Know-All" (*Cosmopolitans*) tells how the vain, flashy protagonist gallantly saves the reputation of a lady at the cost of his own limitless self-esteem. "Mr. Harrington's Washing" (*Ashenden*) has for its hero a dull, pompous, conventional businessman who not only commits a heroic deed but also, to his genuine astonishment, inspires the love of a passionate Russian woman.

Long before the days of speedy air travel Maugham had ranged the world, often at some discomfort and danger, exploring remote countries in the Far East, Asia, China, the South Seas, and Russia. Here he found ample material. The bulk of his tales with exotic settings are in *The Trembling of the Leaf, Ashenden, Ah King*, and *The Casuarina Tree*. One should not look to them for penetrating analyses of the Malay or the Chinese character. Maugham is only interested in white people, the colonial civil servants and the planters, who are confronted with situations involving sex, passion, and class distinction that would never have faced them in the genteel surroundings of Esher or Chislehurst. Maugham is concerned to study their reactions, which are often quite different from what you might expect. In "The Vessel of Wrath" (*Ah King*), set on a tropical island, a missionary, a middle-aged, puritanical spinster, falls in love with the local drunk, a layabout of appalling habits, who, duly reformed, returns her affection. A situation like this, which delighted Maugham's cynical sense of humour (another example is "Winter Cruise" in *Creatures of Circumstance*), is less common than the drama, the tragedy even, which haunts most of his stories about far-off places. In "The Force of Circumstance" (*The Casuarina Tree*) a newly married young Englishwoman sails out to join her husband, a long-established colonial administrator. Gradually she comes to realise that in years past he has lived with a native girl who has given birth to two children by him. Her world collapses. In bitter disgust she leaves him and the native girl moves back in to share his bed. Another favourite theme of Maugham's Malayan stories is the behaviour of people under the stress of crisis. "The Door of Opportunity" (*Ah King*) draws a portrait of a brilliantly gifted man with a first-class brain, handsome, ambitious, able to solve any problem in a flash. But he does not suffer fools gladly and is unpopular with his less clever colleagues. A native uprising takes place and he refuses to intervene immediately because cold logic tells him that the risk is not justified. Unfortunately common sense would have taken a different view, and that is the opinion of the governor, who dismisses him for cowardice. His wife, full of contempt, walks out on him: she would prefer to have as husband a second-rate planter with common human virtues rather than an intellectual iceberg.

When a literary critic dismissed a volume of Maugham's short stories with the phrase "the mixture as before," the author amusedly chose it for the title of his next collection. It is true that a formula can be discerned in his stories, largely due to his love of paradox. When he introduces two brothers, one a conscientious hard worker and the other a charming ne'er-do-well, the reader knows that it is the latter who will prosper and end up, quite undeservedly, rich and successful ("The Ant and the Grasshopper," *Cosmopolitans*). If Maugham's protagonist has a young son, handsome and clever, whom he solemnly advises to avoid gambling, lending money, and women, on his first trip to Monte Carlo, readers somehow guess that the boy will indulge without harm in all these activities and will confound his worldly-wise father. ("The Facts of Life," *The Mixture as Before*). The pleasure lies in the telling of the story and the incidental detail so skilfully placed. Pomposity discomfited is another preferred topic, as in "The Colonel's Lady" (*Creatures of Circumstance*), where the faded, middle-aged wife suddenly publishes a sensational book of poems about a youthful love affair she once had. Her embarrassed country-gentleman husband, long accustomed to finding sex elsewhere than in the marriage bed, can only gasp unbelievingly: "What in the name of heaven did the fellow ever see in her?" Maugham had a sharp eye for the negative aspects of women: their bitchiness, their shamelessness, their lack of humour and their vanity ("The Three Fat Women of Antibes," *The Mixture as Before*). Yet there were times when even he, as in "Jane" (*First Person Singular*), had to express wry admiration for their strength of character and their ability to use men.

"Since the beginning of history," Maugham observed in the preface to *Creatures of Circumstance*, "men have gathered round the camp fire or in a group in the market place to listen to the telling of stories. The desire to listen to them appears to be as deeply rooted in the human animal as the sense of property. I have never pretended to be anything but a story teller." Some of the stories he told were written over 70 years ago. Apart from occasional stilted phrases and outdated slang they remain as compulsively readable as they were when they first appeared. He always makes you want to turn over the page and find out how the story ends. And that, in the last resort, is the only worthwhile test of a writer's skill that matters.

—James Harding

See the essays on "The Letter" and "The Outstation."

MAUPASSANT, (Henri René Albert) Guy de. French. Born in the Château de Miromesnil, near Rouen, 5 August 1850. Educated at Lycée Impérial Napoléon, Paris, 1859–60; Institution Ecclésiastique, Yvetot, 1863–68; Lycée Pierre Corneille, Rouen, 1868–69; studied law, University of Paris, 1869–70. Messenger, then orderly, in the army, 1870–71. Clerk in Ministry of the Navy: in library, 1872–73, and in Department for the Colonies, 1873–77; transferred to Ministry of Education, 1878–80; writer, especially for Gaulois and Gil-Blas newspapers; confined to insane asylum, Passy, 1892. *Died 6 July 1893.*

PUBLICATIONS

Collections

Complete Works.   9 vols., 1910.
Works.   10 vols., 1923–29.
Oeuvres complètes.   29 vols., 1925–47.
Contes et nouvelles, edited by Albert-Marie Schmidt.   2 vols., 1956–57.

Short Stories

La Maison Tellier.   1881.
Mademoiselle Fifi.   1882.
Contes de la Bécasse.   1883.
Miss Harriet.   1883.
Clair de lune.   1884.
Les Soeurs Rondoli.   1884.
Contes et nouvelles.   1885.
Contes du jour et de la nuit.   1885.
Yvette.   1885.
Monsieur Parent.   1885.
Toine.   1886.
La Petite Roque.   1886.
Le Horla.   1887.
Le Rosier de Madame Husson.   1888.
La Main gauche.   1889.
L'Inutile Beauté.   1890.
88 Short Stories.   1928.
Complete Short Stories.   3 vols., 1970.
Tales of Supernatural Terror, edited by Arnold Kellett. 1972.
The Diary of a Madman and Other Tales of Horror.   1976; as *The Dark Side of Maupassant,* 1989.
A Day in the Country and Other Stories.   1990.

Novels

Une Vie.   1883; as *A Woman's Life,* 1965.
Bel-Ami.   1885; translated as *Bel-Ami,* 1891.
Mont-Oriol.   1887; translated as *Mont-Oriol,* 1891.
Pierre et Jean.   1888; as *Pierre and Jean,* 1890.
Fort comme la mort.   1889; as *Strong as Death,* 1899; as
    The Master Passion, 1958.
Notre coeur.   1890; as *Notre Coeur (The Human Heart),*
    1890.

Plays

Une Répétition.   1879.
Histoire du vieux temps (produced 1879).   In *Des vers,*
    1880.
Musotte, with Jacques Normand, from a story by Maupas-
    sant (produced 1891).   In *Oeuvres complètes illustrées,*
    1904.
La Paix du ménage, from his own story (produced 1893).

Verse

Des vers.   1880.

Other

Au soleil.   1884.
Sur l'eau.   1888.
La Vie errante.   1890.
Correspondance, edited by J. Suffel.   3 vols., 1973.

*

Bibliography: *Maupassant Criticism in France 1880–1940*
by Artine Artinian, 1941; *Maupassant Criticism: A Centennial Bibliography 1880–1979* by Robert Willard Artinian,
1982.

Critical Studies: *Maupassant: A Biographical Study* by
Ernest Boyd, 1928; *Maupassant: A Lion in the Path* by
Francis Steegmuller, 1949; *Maupassant the Novelist,* 1954,
and *Maupassant: The Short Stories,* 1962, both by Edward
D. Sullivan; *The Private Life of Guy de Maupassant* by R.
de L. Kirkbridge, 1961; *The Paradox of Maupassant* by
Paul Ignotus, 1967; *Illusion and Reality: A Study of the
Descriptive Techniques in the Works of Maupassant* by John
R. Dugan, 1973; *Maupassant* by Albert H. Wallace, 1973;
Style and Vision in Maupassant's Nouvelles by Matthew
MacNamara, 1986; *A Woman's Revenge: The Chronology
of Dispossession in Maupassant's Fiction* by Mary Donald-
son-Evans, 1986; *Love and Nature, Unity and Doubling in
the Novels of Maupassant* by Bertrand Logan Bell, 1988;
Maupassant by Michael G. Lerner, 1975; *Bel-Ami and
Maupassant* by Christopher Lloyd, 1988; *Maupassant,
Boule de suif* by P.E. Chaplin, 1988; *Maupassant in the
Hall of Mirrors* by T.A. Le V. Harris, 1990.

*   *   *

With more than three hundred short stories to his credit,
Guy de Maupassant was incomparably the most prolific
short story writer of 19th-century France. It only increases
one's incredulity to learn that all of his stories were
produced within the span of just ten years. The quality of
his stories was certainly uneven, but enough of them—
perhaps as many as one-quarter—were of such high
quality, and a number of them so innovative in concept
and technique, that Maupassant is today generally accorded the distinction of having made the greatest contribution
in its history to the development of the French short story.
Outside of France, too, Maupassant is widely regarded as a
major figure in the short story, and as an inescapable
influence. Few are the 20th-century writers, in Europe or
America, who do not acknowledge having studied Maupassant's work, and learned something of the craft of storytelling from him.

In the 19th century, when the history of the modern
artistic short story began, few writers could have conceived
the ambition of specializing in the short story at the outset
of their careers, since it was not a viable option at the time.
Maupassant certainly did not set out to be the short story
specialist he eventually became. He did not even start out
as a writer of any kind. In his twenties he earned his living
as a civil servant, and dabbled in literature in his spare
time, trying his hand at poems, plays, and stories, and
writing occasional reviews for various journals, hoping to
attract attention and make a start. Meanwhile, he eagerly
availed himself of the offer of a family friend and fellow-
Norman, Gustave Flaubert, who proposed to help him with
his writing, and encourage him in his ambition to become a
novelist, like Flaubert himself. Afterwards, Maupassant
always acknowledged Flaubert as his master and his model,
and was wont to say that Flaubert taught him everything he
knew about writing fiction. Although his mentor did not
live to see his pupil's success, Maupassant did indeed go on
to write six successful novels, three of which are still widely
read and admired. Nevertheless, at the age of 30, Maupassant discovered his own talent for the shorter forms of
fiction, when a novella he had written about the Franco-
Prussian War won wide and enthusiastic acclaim. This was
the story called "Ball-of-Fat," which first appeared in 1880
as one in a volume of six anti-war stories, and made
Maupassant a literary celebrity overnight.

His career thus launched, and his storytelling talent
uncovered, Maupassant became a regular contributor to
several journals, turning out stories at an amazing rate,
most of them relatively short—about 3,000 words—to
meet the stringent space needs of journals. By 1882, he had
enough stories that met his personal artistic standards
(learned from his mentor, Flaubert) to publish a first
collection. It would be followed by at least a dozen more
such volumes before illness put an end to his career.

The most conspicuous hallmarks of Maupassant's storytelling skill were rapidity of movement and precise observation. He learned to "set up" a story situation with just a
few brief sentences, carefully selecting and describing the
details of character and place most essential for grasping
the significance of the story, then moved the reader swiftly,
and with stunning economy, through the action of the plot,
stopping the moment the meaning of the narrative had
become fully revealed to the alert reader. This procedure
demanded tremendous discipline of the author, to prune
his prose of superfluous verbiage without loss of clarity, but
produced in return a narrative that accumulated dramatic
force by its speed and concentration, and gave the reader
the pleasure of sudden enlightenment at the dénouement.
The procedure also had the advantage of transforming the
handicap of space limitation imposed by journals into a
rich source of narrative power. Maupassant developed to a
high degree of perfection the art of making enforced brevity

work to his own advantage. The celebrated tale, "The Necklace," can be profitably studied as a consummate example of what Maupassant's techniques of precise observation and rapid narration can accomplish. The ending of that story is particularly noteworthy, because it not only brings sudden enlightenment to the reader but to the story's characters as well.

Maupassant was, of course, not content to let his basic storytelling techniques decline into a formula to be applied mechanically to any number of different plots. He became ingeniously inventive at finding ways to shift attention away from the ending, for example, by placing a dramatic climax in the center of a story, and allowing the ending to be quietly reflective, as happens in the farcical novella about a house of prostitution called "La Maison Tellier." And he could be slow and deliberate in his narrative pace, when it suited his purposes, as in a story about fear of the unknown, called "On the Water," which depended on the slow build-up of a kind of atmosphere for its effect, but needed no rapid narration and no dramatic revelation at the end.

The variety of means, in Maupassant's stories, is more than matched by the variety of the subjects he managed to treat, and the variety of narrative manners, from frivolous to solemn, from satirical to compassionate, from ribald to sentimental, that he was capable of employing. One could, for example, make up a sizable anthology of Maupassant's stories about the Franco-Prussian War, and they would reveal the many moods, both gay and bitter, with which Maupassant, who served in the war, regarded his experiences. Another anthology could be constructed of Maupassant's stories about the fantastic and the terrifying, including the most famous example, "Le Horla," all of which have often been read as foreshadowings of the insanity Maupassant suffered at the end of his life, thus investing those tales with a prophetic spookiness the author never intended. An objective reading of those tales would reveal, instead, a very objective and clear-headed attempt to analyze the irrational fear of the unknown in human nature.

The two largest thematically-related story groups, in all of Maupassant's vast output of stories, are those that concern the peasants of Normandy ("The Piece of String" is the best-known example of that group), and those that concern the Parisian *petite bourgeoisie:* clerks, shopkeepers, civil servants, and such ("The Necklace" is the best-known story set in that milieu). Those two different worlds, both of which he knew intimately, from personal experience, seemed to bring out the very best in Maupassant, and that very best is certainly an uncanny ability to penetrate into the deepest and darkest secrets of the human soul, and, by deft and sensitive narrative techniques, to bring those secrets to the surface, where others can see and understand what otherwise goes unnoticed in the human comedy. It is that talent that made Maupassant the greatest storyteller of his age, and that will preserve his reputation as a great storyteller for as long as people are interested in understanding the innermost secrets of human nature through the enchantment of art, and the medium of the short story.

—Murray Sachs

See the essays on "Ball of Fat," "Hautot and His Son," "The Necklace," and "The Piece of String."

McCULLERS, (Lula) Carson (née Smith). American. Born in Columbus, Georgia, 19 February 1917. Educated at Columbus High School, graduated 1933; attended classes at Columbia University, New York, and New York University, 1934–36. Married James Reeves McCullers, Jr., in 1937 (divorced 1941); remarried in 1945 (died 1953). Lived in Charlotte, 1937–38, and Fayetteville, 1938–39, both North Carolina, and in New York City, 1940–44, and Nyack, New York, after 1944. Recipient: Bread Loaf Writers Conference fellowship, 1940; Guggenheim fellowship, 1942, 1946; American Academy grant, 1943; New York Drama Critics Circle award, 1950; Donaldson award, for drama, 1950; Theatre Club gold medal, 1950; University of Mississippi grant, 1966; Bellamann award, 1967. Member, American Academy, 1952. *Died 29 September 1967.*

PUBLICATIONS

Short Stories

The Member of the Wedding (novella). 1946.
The Ballad of the Sad Café: The Novels and Stories of McCullers. 1951; as *Collected Short Stories,* 1961; as *The Shorter Novels and Stories of McCullers,* 1972.
Seven. 1954.

Novels

The Heart Is a Lonely Hunter. 1940.
Reflections in a Golden Eye. 1941.
Clock Without Hands. 1961.

Plays

The Member of the Wedding, from her own novel (produced 1949). 1951.
The Square Root of Wonderful (produced 1957). 1958.

Television Plays: *The Invisible Wall,* from her story "The Sojourner," 1953; *The Sojourner,* from her own story, 1964.

Verse

The Twisted Trinity, music by David Diamond. 1946.
Sweet as a Pickle and Clean as a Pig (for children). 1964.

Other

The Mortgaged Heart (uncollected writings), edited by Margarita G. Smith. 1971.

*

Bibliography: *Katherine Anne Porter and McCullers: A Reference Guide* by Robert F. Kiernan, 1976; *McCullers: A Descriptive Listing and Annotated Bibliography of Criticism* by Adrian M. Shapiro, Jackson R. Bryer, and Kathleen Field, 1980.

Critical Studies: *McCullers: Her Life and Work* by Oliver Evans, 1965, as *The Ballad of McCullers,* 1966; *McCullers* by Lawrence Graver, 1969; *McCullers* by Dale Edmonds, 1969; *The Lonely Hunter: A Biography of McCullers* by Virginia Spencer Carr, 1975; *McCullers* by Richard M. Cook, 1975; *McCullers' The Member of the Wedding: Aspects of Structure and Style* by Eleanor Wikborg, 1975; *McCullers* by Margaret B. McDowell, 1980.

* * *

Carson McCullers identified herself as a Southern realist influenced by the mature work of Ellen Glasgow and by the 19th-century Russian realists. In her short fiction—her stories, her first novel, *The Heart Is a Lonely Hunter,* and the second of her two novellas, *Member of the Wedding*—she does pursue a sharp and detailed realism. However, in her first novella, *The Ballad of the Sad Café,* and all of her novels after *The Heart Is a Lonely Hunter,* she exhibited a penchant for the fantastic, the romantic, the grotesque, and the bizarre. The topics and themes in her novels and her short fiction are similar—guilt, death, rejection, complicated love, and the psychic conflict between freedom and security ("belonging" or becoming a "joined person" allows you to be "caught," while being an "unjoined" or free person makes you vulnerable to loneliness). Miss Amelia in *The Ballad of the Sad Café,* and Frankie and Berenice in *Member of the Wedding* are all dominated by this psychic struggle, and none finds a balance between freedom and captivity. Frankie struggles to belong by fantasizing about "the we of me," by becoming a blood donor so her blood will flow in the veins of people all over the world, by aspiring to join many clubs, and by changing her name to F. Jasmine so that her *J* initial will link her with Jarvis and Janice as she joins them at the wedding and flies away to adventure but also remains safe with them. Berenice struggles to recreate her blissful marriage with Ludie, who died, by entering three disastrous marriages. She longs to "bust free" but settles for security with a good man, though he can't make her shiver. Reality cannot be escaped at any point in this novella, as the presence of war and death hover over the hot kitchen in which Berenice, Frankie, and little John Henry cling together during the "scared summer" in 1942.

McCullers's best story is "Madame Zilensky and the King of Finland." In it she develops a complex pattern of contrasts and similarities between two college music teachers, the conventional Mr. Brook, "a somewhat pastel" figure, who lectures on Mozart minuets and explains demonished seventies and triads, and Madame Zilensky, a flamboyant woman newly-arrived from Europe with three small sons. Imaginative and inspired, she teaches with dramatic force and fitful energy, losing no time in setting four dazed students at four pianos to play Bach fugues simultaneously. She shocks Brook with stories about the three men who fathered her boys, and shocks him further when he realizes nothing she says is factual. Gradually, McCullers reveals the divided selves within each of the two individuals. Zilensky denies her secret life—working to the point of exhaustion in her room each night on what Brook discovers are 12 "immense and beautiful symphonies"—though she brags each morning about her lively social life. Though he thinks he will catch her in a big lie and victoriously confront her, he never does. His determination to expose her dishonesty fades into an amusing game for him, and we recognize him as basically kind and tolerant.

Madame Zilensky alters his quiet routine into a more zestful and creative world, and McCullers reveals that Brook also has secret evenings, indulging himself in the romantic by reading Blake poems as he rests by the fireside. He becomes far less pastel as we learn that when the music faculty departed for summer study in Salzburg, he inexplicably vanished—to go alone to Peru. McCullers's intricate techniques, convoluted comic effects, and exploration of the divided inner self of each of the two characters is superb, as is her shifting of contrasts and similarities and her intertwining use of music symbols—metronomes, loud pianos, delicate minuets, and contrapuntal patterns. The vital presence of music draws every thread of the story into place, making it one of the most thoughtful and complex comedies in American short fiction.

"The Jockey," another satire, incongruously juxtaposes tragedy and comedy. In the elegant Saratoga Hotel dining room, Bitsy Barlow, a tiny long-time jockey, in a startling climax confronts three heavy-set men who have grown rich through exploitation of the jockeys. As they drink and eat rich foods, they complain that Bitsy may have gained three pounds. Bitsy watches them haughtily from the other side of the room as he drinks his liquor in two neat swallows, closes his cigarette case with a definite snap, and holds his body rigid as he marches to their table, pointedly digging sharp heels into the rug. His "precisely tailored" suit cloaks his grief and anger over the severe and permanent crippling of a younger jockey. His unwavering propriety gives the men no warning as he tells them of his friend's shrunken leg and then calls them libertines, and with aplomb takes two of their French fries, chews them, and deliberately spits them on the beautiful rug. He again assumes his formal impeccable manner as he bows and with an air of hauteur marches past the curious diners, leaving the embarrassed men in silence. The precision of Bitsy's every move and the precision of McCullers's style remarkably produce shock, pity, and laughter.

The finest of McCullers's stories about adolescents are "Wunderkind," written when she was in high school, and "Correspondence," written not long after her graduation. Frances, the Wunderkind, is McCullers herself, slightly masked, and through Frances, McCullers expressed her frustration at her inability to interpret feeling in music, in spite of long hours of practice. Frances's anxiety, revealed in her unspoken memories, her nervous behavior, and her cold hands, builds to a climax of despair, and the story suddenly stops. "Correspondence," McCullers's only epistolary fiction, presents a less-engaging adolescent, Henky Evans. The story's distinction lies in its humorous satire and subtle revelation of Henky's failure to even suspect that she is narcissistic, really writing to herself rather than to the pen pal who never answers her letters.

Of McCullers's stories associated with alcohol abuse, "Domestic Dilemma" is artistically effective because of the depth of her characterization of Martin. The ambivalence of Martin's love-hate feelings for his alcoholic young wife, Emily, who neglects their children, and his sense of being caught in an unsolvable problem are movingly communicated. He himself seems surprised that his love still exists and that there is still some urgency in his cherishing of her, since the bond between them has become so fragile. Love in this story is a dominant and incomprehensible force, too complex to be separated from hatred, pity, memory, hope, or despair. "The Sojourner," written about the same time, also effectively characterizes a man's ambivalence about marriage and family, but Faris's selfishness makes the story more superficial and far less gripping.

It could be argued that McCullers's best works of short fiction—*Member of the Wedding, The Ballad of the Sad Café*, "Wunderkind," and "Madame Zilensky and the King of Finland"—gain much of their strength through her subtle intertwining of realistic characters and action with meaningful imagery. The imagery is often related to snow, ice, or heat but even more significantly to music. Her musical imagery is usually kinetic and transitory, rather than static, and holds complexities and richness that deepen the simple text. It often relates to blues themes, to sudden stops that parallel the end of a dream or hope, or suggest the incompleteness of human personality and human life. Usually in the background, the music produces anxiety and restlessness, rather than satisfaction in the listener, as when a scale is not completed or when a blues tune stops "just at the time the tune should be laid." If blues tunes are characteristic in the short fiction, as in the sound of a chain gang's work song, so also is the merry tune of an organ grinder—a tune that amuses children and awakens childlikeness in adults, but which also directs the behavior of a trapped monkey, ominously diverts the listener's attention from danger, and, like a Pied-Piper, lures the innocents, the dreamers, and the trusting toward the perils of human life.

—Margaret McDowell

See the essays on *The Ballad of the Sad Café* and "A Tree, A Rock, A Cloud."

McPHERSON, James A(lan). American. Born in Savannah, Georgia, 16 September 1943. Educated at Morris Brown College, Atlanta, 1961–63, 1965, B.A. 1965; Morgan State College, Baltimore, 1963–64; Harvard University, Cambridge, Massachusetts, LL.B. 1968; University of Iowa, Iowa City, M.F.A. 1971. Married in 1973 (divorced); one daughter. Instructor, University of Iowa Law School, 1968–69; lecturer in English, University of California, Santa Cruz, 1969–70; assistant professor of English, Morgan State University, 1975–76; associate professor of English, University of Virginia, Charlottesville, 1976–81; professor of English, University of Iowa, from 1981. Guest editor of fiction issues of *Iowa Review,* Iowa City, 1984, and *Ploughshares,* Cambridge, Massachusetts, 1985, 1990. Since 1969 contributing editor, *Atlantic Monthly,* Boston. Recipient: *Atlantic* Firsts award, 1968; American Academy award, 1970; Guggenheim fellowship, 1972; Pulitzer prize, 1978; MacArthur Foundation award, 1981. Lives in Iowa City.

PUBLICATIONS

Short Stories

Hue and Cry.   1969.
Elbow Room.   1977.

Other

Railroad: Trains and Train People in American Culture, with Miller Williams.   1976.

* * *

The short stories of James Alan McPherson first appeared in such periodicals as *Playboy, The Atlantic Monthly, The Harvard Advocate, The Iowa Review, The Massachusetts Review,* and *Ploughshares*. His stories have been reprinted with additional stories published for the first time in two collections. McPherson's first collection, *Hue and Cry,* contains ten stories, and a remarkable commentary appearing on the dust-jacket written by Ralph Ellison. Ellison writes: "Indeed as he makes his 'hue and cry' over the dead ends, the confusions of value and failures of sympathy and insight of those who inhabit his fictional world, McPherson's stories are in themselves a hue and cry against the dead, publicity-sustained writing which has come increasingly to stand for what is called 'black writing.'"

Ellison's assessment of McPherson's talents as a writer of short fiction is supported by the wide range of issues his stories explore and the many awards his stories have received. For those published in *Hue and Cry* McPherson won the O. Henry prize, the *Playboy* fiction award, and a grant from the American Institute of Art and Letters. It is not just craftsmanship that make McPherson's stories so successful at breaking the boundaries of "the dead, publicity-sustained writing" that Ellison deplores. McPherson's stories are about people whose lives and actions can rarely if ever be encapsulated or contained within easy and convenient generalizations or explained away on the basis of race or gender. McPherson writes about all kinds of people, including blacks, whites, men, women, janitors, lawyers, criminals, prostitutes, gays, and homophobics. His insights are those of an intelligent and informed observer who seeks to render life as he sees it rather than offer judgement or condemnation. This perspective, however, is not without its problems since the reader sometimes feels bewildered by McPherson's distancing from his characters, while at the same time making astute, highly particularized observations. The result occasionally produces rather flat, two-dimensional characters whose actions seem to warrant further exploration. The short story "Hue and Cry" from which McPherson's first collection draws its title, serves as a case in point.

In "Hue and Cry" Eric Carney who is a white has been jilted for another black man by Margot Payne, who is also black. It would be easy to approach this story as one focusing on the problems of maintaining a relationship between a black and white couple, but as the story progresses it becomes clear that the ethnic identity of any of the characters, and the presence of an inter-racial relationship has more to do with the cultural malaise of the 1960's that McPherson explores in his other stories than a "hue and cry" against a racism that might make this relationship untenable.

In the story, Margot refuses to marry Eric and instead begins to develop a relationship with a rather shy black named Charles, who showers her with attention because she is one of the few women who have ever been attracted to him. After Charles's success with Margot, he finds that other women also become attracted to him. At the beginning of their relationship Charles wants to marry Margot, who responds by being aloof and she tries to put him off by saying she is not ready. In the meantime Charles learns to play the field by capitalizing on his new popularity. Because of Charles's interest in other women, Margot changes her mind and decides to accept Charles's marriage proposal. Charles puts her off because of his desire to play the field, and his affairs with other women finally catch up to him. In the end, Margot abandons Charles and ends up by sleeping with a rather repulsive character named Jerry who was not only Eric's roommate but a man she earlier despised.

With all of the changing partners, all the jealousy, and what at times appears to be complete lack of feelings by the characters, the reader searches in vain for a character or a moral perspective to endorse. The last page of the story offers a commentary between the narrator and his audience on the events of the story. This is not particularly helpful unless one is a Zen Master whose expectations do not include a resolution of conflict in any recognizable fashion. The key to approaching events in the narrative is to be found in the quotation from Friedrich Nietzsche appearing on the story's title page: "A joke is an epigram on the death of feeling." The characters appear flat, superficial, and two-dimensional, because they are unravelling rather than becoming—the story is about losses of feeling, personality, motivation, and character.

McPherson's second collection of short stories, *Elbow Room*, contains 12 stories dealing with the same wide range of black and white characters in rural and urban settings, inter-racial relationships, and a similar line of experimentation developed in the story "Hue and Cry." In this collection, as well as in the first, the short story from which the anthology takes its name is included last. "Elbow Room" concerns a marriage between a black woman named Virginia Valentine and Paul Frost.

Despite the potential for symbolic value suggested by the character's names, which is never developed, of interest here is McPherson's inclusion of commentary, presumably by an editor who notes the lack of clarity and focus on the part of the author, which is found at the beginning, end, and at various other points in the story.

The story's conflict revolves around the fact that Paul's and Virginia's parents are not willing to accept the marriage of a white man to a black woman, who is soon to give birth. Paul assumes that he can hold out against his parents objections or just ignore them until they come around to his way of thinking. Virginia is caught between trying to support her husband and maintaining her sense of pride and personal dignity. The story ends with Paul and Virginia and their child in Kansas, with Paul's family apparently willing to accept the situation. The events in the story are not particularly interesting or imaginative; but the conflict takes place on a different level—between the author and his subject matter, or more specifically, between the narrator and his interactions with the two central characters.

The narrator journeys to the West coast to "renew my supply of stories," and his personal interactions with the characters reflect a detached skepticism mingled with an impersonal curiosity. He offers advice in rather vague and unclear ways and eventually becomes alienated from Paul, whom he seems to care for. What becomes evident from the narrator's comments and actions is that he values these people and their experiences only because of their potential for being assimilated into a work of fiction. After a conversation with Virginia, the narrator finally reaches a conclusion: "I did not care about them and their problems anymore. I did not think they had a story worth telling." The story continues with Paul's rejection of the narrator, and a period of time elapses before a picture of Paul, his wife, and child arrives through the mail. In the final paragraph of the story the editor asks the narrator to comment on the inscription "He will be a classic kind of nigger," which was written on the back of the photograph.

The narrator responds "I would find it difficult to do. It was from the beginning not my story."

One might well wonder if "Hue and Cry" is McPherson's swan song, suggesting the impossibility of assimilating the experiences of others into a work of fiction. If so, the many excellent stories collected in both anthologies should be highly valued and re-read, where the richness and variety of experiences portrayed there produces a feeling that, even "if it was not from the beginning my story," it is nonetheless true to human experience.

—Jeffrey D. Parker

MELVILLE, Herman. American. Born in New York City, 1 August 1819. Educated at New York Male School; Albany Academy to age 12. Married Elizabeth Knapp Shaw in 1847; two sons and two daughters. Worked from age 12 as clerk, farmhand, and schoolteacher; ship's boy on the *St. Lawrence*, bound for Liverpool, 1839–40; travelled in midwest, 1840; ordinary seaman on the whaler *Achushnet*, 1841 until he jumped ship in the Marquesas, 1842; left the islands on the Sydney whaling barque *Lucy Ann*, and jumped ship in Tahiti, 1842; harpooner on whaler *Charles and Henry*, from Nantucket, in southern Pacific, 1842–43; clerk and bookkeeper in general store, Honolulu, 1843; shipped back to Boston on U.S. Navy frigate *United States*, 1843–44; writer from 1844; lived in New York, 1847–50, and Pittsfield, Massachusetts, 1850–63; travelled in Near East and Europe, 1856–57; on lecture circuits in the U.S., 1857–60; lived in Washington, D.C., 1861–62, and in New York after 1863; district inspector of customs, New York, 1866–85. *Died 28 September 1891.*

PUBLICATIONS

Collections

Works. 16 vols., 1922–24.
Collected Poems, edited by Howard P. Vincent. 1947.
The Portable Melville, edited by Jay Leyda. 1952.
Selected Poems, edited by Hennig Cohen. 1964.
Great Short Works, edited by Warner Berthoff. 1966.
Writings, edited by Harrison Hayford, Hershel Parker, and G. Thomas Tanselle. 1968—.
Selected Poems, edited by Robert Penn Warren. 1970.
Typee, Omoo, Mardi (Library of America), edited by G. Thomas Tanselle. 1982.
Redburn, White-Jacket, Moby-Dick (Library of America), edited by G. Thomas Tanselle. 1983.
Pierre, Israel Potter, The Confidence-Man, Tales and Billy Budd (Library of America), edited by Harrison Hayford. 1985.
The Essential Melville, edited by Robert Penn Warren. 1987.

Short Stories

The Piazza Tales. 1856.
The Apple-Tree Table and Other Sketches. 1922.
Billy Budd and Other Prose Pieces, edited by Raymond M. Weaver, in *Works.* 1924.

Novels

Narrative of Four Months' Residence among the Natives of a Valley in the Marquesas Islands; or, A Peep at Polynesian Life. 1846; as *Typee,* 1846; revised edition, 1846.
Omoo: A Narrative of Adventures in the South Seas. 1847.
Mardi, and a Voyage Thither. 1849.
Redburn, His First Voyage. 1849.
White Jacket; or, The World in a Man-of-War. 1850; as *White-Jacket,* 1850.
The Whale. 1851; as *Moby-Dick; or, The Whale,* 1851.
Pierre; or, The Ambiguities. 1852.
Israel Potter, His Fifty Years of Exile. 1855.
The Confidence-Man, His Masquerade. 1857.

Verse

Battle-Pieces and Aspects of the War. 1866; edited by Hennig Cohen, 1963.
Clarel: A Poem, and Pilgrimage in the Holy Land. 1876; edited by Walter E. Bezanson, 1960.
John Marr and Other Sailors, with Some Sea-Pieces. 1888.
Timoleon Etc. 1891.

Other

Journal up the Straits October 11, 1856-May 5, 1857, edited by Raymond M. Weaver. 1935; as *Journal of a Visit to Europe and the Levant,* edited by Howard C. Horsford, 1955.
Journal of a Visit to London and the Continent 1849–1850, edited by Eleanor Melville Metcalf. 1948.
Letters, edited by Merrell R. Davis and William H. Gilman. 1960.

*

Bibliography: *The Merrill Checklist of Melville* by Howard P. Vincent, 1969; in *Bibliography of American Literature* by Jacob Blanck, 1973; *Melville: An Annotated Bibliography 1: 1846–1930,* 1979, and *Melville: A Reference Guide, 1931–1960,* 1987, both by Brian Higgins; *Melville and the Critics: A Checklist of Criticism 1900–1978* by Jeanetta Boswell, 1981; *Melville's Foreign Reputation: A Research Guide* by Leland R. Phelps, 1983.

Critical Studies: *Melville: The Tragedy of Mind* by William E. Sedgwick, 1944; *Call Me Ishmael: A Study of Melville* by Charles Olson, 1947; *The Trying-Out of Moby-Dick* by Howard Vincent, 1949; *Melville* by Richard Chase, 1949; *Melville* by Newton Arvin, 1950; *The Melville Log: A Documentary Life of Melville 1819-1891* by Jay Leyda, 2 vols., 1951, revised edition, 1969; *Melville: A Biography* by Leon Howard, 1951; *Melville's Quarrel with God* by Lawrance Thompson, 1952; *The Fine-Hammered Steel of Melville* by Milton R. Stern, 1957; *Melville's Billy Budd and the Critics* edited by William T. Stafford, 1961, revised edition, 1968; *The Example of Melville* by Warner Berthoff, 1962; *A Reader's Guide to Melville* by James E. Miller, Jr., 1962; *Melville* by Tyrus Hillway, 1963, revised edition, 1979; *Ishmael's White World: A Phenomenological Reading of Moby-Dick* by Paul Brodtkorb, Jr., 1965; *Melville's Thematics of Form: The Great Art of Telling the Truth* by Edgar A. Dryden, 1968; *Plots and Characters in the Fiction and Narrative Poetry of Melville* by Robert L. Gale, 1969;

Melville: The Ironic Diagram by John D. Seelye, 1970; *Moby-Dick as Doubloon: Essays and Extracts 1851–1970* edited by Hershel Parker and Harrison Hayford, 1970; *An Artist in the Rigging: The Early Works of Melville,* 1972, *Melville's Short Fiction,* 1977, and *Melville's Later Novels,* 1986, all by William B. Dillingham; *Melville: The Critical Heritage* edited by W.G. Branch, 1974; *The Early Lives of Melville* by Merton M. Sealts, Jr., 1974, and *Pursuing Melville 1940–1980* edited by Sealts, 1982; *Melville* (biography) by Edwin Haviland Miller, 1975; *The Method of Melville's Short Fiction* by R. Bruce Bickley, Jr., 1975; *Twentieth-Century Interpretations of Moby-Dick* edited by Michael T. Gilmore, 1977; *New Perspectives on Melville* edited by Faith Pullin, 1978; *The Body Impolitic: A Reading of Four Novels by Melville* by R.M. Blau, 1979; *Melville* by Edward H. Rosenberry, 1979; *Exiled Waters: Moby-Dick and the Crisis of Allegory* by Bainard Cowan, 1982; *Subversive Genealogy: The Politics and Art of Melville* by Michael Paul Rogin, 1983; *Melville: Reassessments* edited by A. Robert Lee, 1984; *Melville* edited by Harold Bloom, 1986; *A Companion to Melville Studies* edited by John Bryant, 1986; *New Essays on Moby-Dick* edited by Richard H. Brodhead, 1987; *Melville's Reading* by Merton M. Sealts, Jr., 1987; *Mourning, Gender, and Creativity in the Art of Melville* by Neal L. Tolchin, 1988; *Melville's Sources* by Mary K. Bercaw, 1988; *Melville's Marginalia,* by Walker Cowen, 2 vols., 1988; *On Melville: The Best from "American Literature"* edited by Edwin H. Cody and Louis Budd, 1989; *Empire for Liberty: Melville and the Poetics of Individualism* by Wai-chee Dimock, 1989; *Some Other World To Find: Quest and Negation in the Works of Melville* by Bruce L. Grenberg, 1989; *Reading Billy Budd* by Hershel Parker, 1990; *The Hawthorne and Melville Friendship* edited by James C. Wilson, 1991.

* * *

Best-known for the colossal epic *Moby-Dick*, Herman Melville actually began his writing career with two very short works that appeared in a small-town newspaper in New York. On May 4, 1839, and then again on May 18, the *Democratic Press and Lansingburgh Advertiser* printed "Fragments from a Writing-Desk," evidently the first of what might have been a regular column had its author not had to turn his hand to more profitable pursuits. Today the "Fragments" are read only by Melville scholars; in a way, though, these early short works predict what was to come in Melville's lengthy, uneven career.

The first of the "Fragments" is a preening letter to a fictional friend in which the author describes three attractive young women in overblown terms. A jocular yet learned piece, liberally sprinkled with quotes from and allusions to classical authors, this "Fragment" is very much in the tradition of letters written throughout history by young men eager to let their friends know that they are connoisseurs of feminine pulchritude, but even more of their own rhetoric.

The second "Fragment" is more substantive. A genuine mystery, it is the story of a man who gets a summons to a clandestine rendezvous; entering a grove, he approaches a villa and is drawn up into it via a basket. Inside, he enters an exquisitely-appointed apartment, where he encounters a silent and melancholy beauty before whom he prostrates himself. While the first fragment is largely an expression of a speaker's self-love, the second treats themes that will figure largely in Melville's writing, namely the pursuit of an ideal and the failure to achieve it.

These two fragments illustrate the extremes of Melville's writing: the first is a largely empty piece driven more by self-enchantment than anything else, whereas the second is a tensely-written and masterful (if incomplete) approach to some important themes. Throughout the rest of his career, Melville vacillated between these two positions: high-blown and self-regarding rhetoric, and careful craft and significant themes.

Following the publication of the "Fragments," Melville took to the sea and later wrote his celebrated full-length maritime adventures. However, he stumbled with *Pierre*, his only book-length fiction set on land; neither reviewers nor readers were kind. Fortunately, there was an escape available to the beleaguered author, and this was the opportunity of magazine publication, which was plentiful in the 19th century. The magazine fiction he produced falls into two categories: the less substantial sketches, similar to the first of the "Fragments," and the more or less completely realized stories, which favor the second.

Five of Melville's magazine fictions are collected in *The Piazza Tales*. The first two, "Bartleby, the Scrivener" and "Benito Cereno" are among the three best-known stories by Melville (the third is the posthumously-published *Billy Budd*). "The Lightning-Rod Man," the third of the five *Piazza Tales*, is a curious centerpiece, since it offers a lighthearted contrast to the portentousness that haunts the better-known stories. Based on a visit from a real lightning-rod salesman as well as encounters with religious preachings that threatened God's wrath, this brief sketch concludes with a prospect telling the lightning-rod man to peddle his wares—and his fears—elsewhere.

The remaining works in *The Piazza Tales*, if not as celebrated as "Bartleby, the Scrivener" and "Benito Cereno," nonetheless partake of the doom-laden atmosphere and sense of woe which characterize those stories. "The Encantadas" consists of ten sketches based on Melville's visit to the Galápagos archipelago lying some six hundred miles off the Ecuadorian coast when he was abroad the *Acushnet* (later he passed near the islands again while aboard the *Charles and Henry* and the *United States*); as usual, he added material from other accounts to his own recollections. Volcanically formed, these "enchanted isles" are picturesque though desolate; the few renegades and runaways who live there are not organized into the rigid social systems of "Bartleby" and "Benito Cereno." In Melville's cosmos, it seems that one is either a doomed partaker of a blighted social system or else a solitary seeker destined to vacillate eternally.

The last of *The Piazza Tales*, "The Bell-Tower," is an explicit tribute to Nathaniel Hawthorne. The story's protagonist, Bannadonna, is, like many of Melville's central characters, an "unblest foundling." But he also recalls the protagonists of "Dr. Heidegger's Experiment," "Rappaccini's Daughter," and the other stories in *Twice-Told Tales* and *Mosses from an Old Manse* in which scientists make the Faustian bargains for which they must eventually pay some enormous price. (Melville had enthusiastically reviewed Hawthorne's *Mosses from an Old Manse* in 1850, five years before he wrote "The Bell-Tower.")

Bannadonna is the victim of an overly complex system of his own creation. He kills one of his workers while constructing a bell tower and is himself killed by a bell-ringing automaton he has devised; the belfry itself collapses at the end of the story. In contrast to the other *Piazza Tales*, "The Bell-Tower" recalls *The Confidence-Man*, Melville's final novel and the one in which, after a complex series of novels that examine the individual's failure to find a place in the existing world, Melville invents his own world, a dark and treacherous place. Bartleby and Benito Cereno are defeated by the social systems in which they live; Bannadonna tries to transcend his surroundings by attempting not to fathom nature but "to rival her, outstrip her, and rule her." He makes his own world; it destroys him and itself.

In addition to the works discussed already, two more sketches deserve mention: "I and My Chimney," which describes husband-wife conflict in terms too personal to be entirely invented, and "The Paradise of Bachelors and the Tartarus of Maids," where the optimism of affluent bachelors is contrasted with the numbing factory labor practiced by the zombie-like maids.

Significantly, at the very end of his life and after three decades of relatively scant production following the discouraging reception of *Pierre* and *The Confidence-Man*, Melville returned to the themes of his major fiction—and, in the process, wrote one of his greatest stories—in *Billy Budd*.

—David Kirby

See the essays on "Bartleby, The Scrivener," "Benito Cereno," and *Billy Budd*.

MÉRIMÉE, Prosper. French. Born on 28 September 1803. Received law degree in 1823. Served in the National Guard, 1831 and 1848. Writer for numerous French journals, from 1820's; secretary to the minister of the navy, 1831; Maître des Requêtes, 1832–34; inspector-general of historic monuments, from 1834; held various positions in the court of Louis-Napoléon, from 1855. Member, Académie des Inscriptions, French Academy, Legion of Honor (France). *Died 23 September 1870.*

PUBLICATIONS

Collections

Writings. 1905.
Oeuvres complètes. 1927—.
Correspondance générale. 17 vols., 1941–64.
Romans et nouvelles. 2 vols., 1967.
Théâtre, romans, nouvelles. 1978.

Short Stories

Mosaïque. 1833; as *Mosaic*, 1903.
La Double Méprise. 1833; as *A Slight Misunderstanding*, 1959.
Carmen. 1847; translated as *Carmen*, 1878.
Nouvelles. 1852.
Dernières nouvelles. 1873.

Novels

Chronique de règne de Charles IX. 1829; revised edition, with "1572" prefixed, 1832; as *A Chronicle of the Reign of Charles IX*, 1853.
Colomba. 1841; translated as *Colomba*, 1853.

Verse

La Guzla.   1827.

Plays

Théâtre de Clara Gazul.   1825; revised editions, 1830, 1842.
La Jacquerie, scènes féodales.   1828.
Le Carosse du Saint Sacrement.   1850.
Les Deux héritages.   1867.

Other

Translator, *The Inspector General* by Gogol.   1853.

*

Critical Studies: *Mérimée: Heroism, Pessimism, Irony* by F.P. Bowman, 1962; *The Poetics of Mérimée* by R.C. Dale, 1966; *Mérimée* by A.W. Riatt, 1970; *Mérimée* by Maxwell A. Smith, 1972.

* * *

A Parisian born and bred, Prosper Mérimée grew up in an artistic and literary milieu, and after taking a law degree (never used), he dabbled in the literary world with some journalistic criticism, plays, and poetry, before discovering his vocation as a storyteller. At the age of 25, Mérimée composed a short historical romance, in the manner of Scott, about the St. Bartholomew's massacre that took place in 1572, during the wars of religion in France. The novel was published in 1829 under the title *Chronique de règne de Charles IX (Chronicle of the Reign of Charles IX).*

The novel won some modest praise, but its greatest significance is that it enabled Mérimée to discover, in himself, the impulses that attracted him to the writing of fiction. Composing a narrative about the Renaissance expressed his fascination with times and places remote from his own, an exoticism that came to dominate his creative work. The choice of the St. Bartholomew's massacre as subject corresponded to his instinctive conviction as an artist that situations of extreme violence, whether physical, emotional, or moral, were the most likely to reveal the deepest truths of human nature. Finally, there was the bantering tone in which the novel was written, suggesting the author's refusal to take his tale very seriously, and culminating in the impudent conclusion in which he invited each reader to invent his own ending, since he did not wish to impose one. This ironic mockery of his own creation, now identified as romantic irony, developed into his personal narrative manner, and became his instantly recognizable signature as a storyteller.

Equipped with the literary impulses that were basic to his temperament: exoticism, a focus on violence, and ironic mockery, Mérimée seems to have decided, in 1829, that the genre that was most suited to his temperament was not the historical novel—he never wrote another one—but the *conte,* and the *nouvelle,* the two short narrative forms then existing in France, both of which we now include in the short story. Beginning in May 1829, with a story about the exotic island of Corsica, called "Mateo Falcone," Mérimée published a series of short narratives in journals of the era, one every two or three months, until well into 1830.

Pleased with his results, he proceeded to revise the best narratives, arranging them in some kind of sequence, and bringing them out as a book, in 1833, entitled *Mosaïque (Mosaic),* perhaps to indicate that the seven stories it contained were each unique in shape, color, and subject matter, yet they formed a harmonious whole when assembled.

The title, at the very least, suggested Mérimée's pride in the artistic quality of his work, and the volume was indeed acclaimed for its disciplined craftsmanship throughout. The volume also displayed fully Mérimée's signature hallmarks: exotic settings (except for "The Etruscan Vase," which is set in Paris—a rarity in Mérimée's work), thematic violence, and a wittily playful narrative voice, present even in the starkly shocking tragedy of "Mateo Falcone." The publication of *Mosaic* can therefore be said to have established Mérimée's public reputation as France's first unmistakably artistic and gifted practitioner of the short story form, for Mérimée had preceded his equally gifted friend, Balzac, into the short story limelight by only a few months. One can add, moreover, that, in contrast to Balzac's earliest short stories, *Mosaic* really determined Mérimée's future as a writer. Balzac, of course, wrote some brilliant short stories in his early years, but he made his real mark as a very great novelist, whereas Mérimée embraced the short story as his true vocation, after *Mosaic,* and, with one notable exception—the short novel *Colomba* published in 1841—his creative writing was restricted to the short story form for the rest of his life.

What Mérimée brought to the short story that was distinctive was a glimpse of the potential poetics that the form seemed capable of developing, to make it into a separate, definable literary genre, governed by rules and standards, like the poem, the play, and the novel. Mérimée's principal discovery was that a story had to have a single focus, on which all of the author's creative energy had to be concentrated, in a disciplined way, free of digressions and diversions of any kind, in order to achieve the full power inherent in the story material. This formal unity, and firmly disciplined control, can be strongly sensed by every reader in the stories of *Mosaic,* and that became one of the standards by which French short stories were judged after Mérimée.

Following the acclaimed publication of *Mosaic,* Mérimée enjoyed a richly productive decade or more as a storyteller, but tending more to the relatively longer version of the short story, which the French often called a *nouvelle,* to distinguish it from the more succinct *conte,* and which it has become customary, in English, to call a novella. As early as 1833, he offered the public a mildly scandalous tale that ran nearly to a hundred pages, and appeared in a separate, thin volume under the title *La Double Méprise (A Slight Misunderstanding).* It was at least four times as long as the longest tale in *Mosaic,* but it had the same unity and careful style, and was, in every essential respect, a typical Mérimée short story. It enjoyed only a modest success. Nearly a dozen stories of similar dimensions followed, mostly in the 1830's and 1840's, a scattered few coming later, and appearing in book form only after the author's death in 1870. Of all the stories published after 1833, the best-known is certainly *Carmen,* first published in 1845, and definitely revised in 1847. *Carmen* is a powerful novella, of considerable length, focused on an unforgettably tempestuous female protagonist of peculiarly complex character: passionate, fiercely independent, yet fatalistic, who dies by the hand of a lover she has spurned. Bizet's opera of 1875 made Mérimée's tale even better known, yet is no substitute for Mérimée's hauntingly tragic original, which creates one of the most memorable character types in all literature.

Mérimée wrote only 19 short stories in his career, but they were enough to constitute one of the most distinguished and influential bodies of work in the short story form in existence. He is a delightfully satisfying storyteller, who can hold his own in any company, and he has the additional distinction, historically, of being the discoverer of the first rules of the short story genre: the rule of the unity of focus, and the rule of the tightly disciplined style.

—Murray Sachs

See the essay on "Mateo Falcone."

METCALF, John (Wesley). Canadian. Born in Carlisle, Cumberland, England, 12 November 1938. Educated at Bristol University, 1957–61, B.A. (honours) in English 1960, Cert. Ed. 1961. Married 1) Gale Courey in 1965 (marriage dissolved 1972), one daughter; 2) Myrna Teitelbaum in 1975, one stepson and two adopted children. Taught at a secondary school and a boys' borstal, Bristol, 1961, Rosemount High School, Montreal, 1962–63, Royal Canadian Air Force Base, Cold Lake, Alberta, 1964–65, at a Catholic comprehensive school in England, 1965, and at schools and universities in Montreal, part-time, 1966–71; writer-in-residence, University of New Brunswick, Fredericton, 1972–73, Loyola College, Montreal, 1976, University of Ottawa, 1977, Concordia University, Montreal, 1980–81, and University of Bologna, Italy, 1985. Recipient: Canada Council award, 1968, 1969, 1971, 1974, 1976, 1978, 1980, 1983, 1985; University of Western Ontario President's medal, for short story, 1969; Ottawa-Carleton Literary award, 1987. Lives in Ottawa, Ontario.

PUBLICATIONS

Short Stories

New Canadian Writing 1969, with C.J. Newman and D.O. Spettigue.   1969.
The Lady Who Sold Furniture.   1970.
The Teeth of My Father.   1975.
Dreams Surround Us: Fiction and Poetry, with John Newlove.   1977.
Girl in Gingham (novellas).   1978; as *Private Parts: A Memoir*, 1980; as *Shooting the Stars*, 1993.
Selected Stories.   1982.
Adult Entertainment.   1986.

Novels

Going Down Slow.   1972.
General Ludd.   1980.

Other

Kicking Against the Pricks (essays).   1982.
Freedom from Culture.   1987.
What Is A Canadian Literature?   1988.
Volleys (critical essays), with Sam Solecki and W.J. Keith.   1990.

Acts of Kindness and of Love, with Tony Calzetta.   1993.
A Passion and Delight: Selected Essays.   1993.

Editor, with others, *Wordcraft 1–5* (textbooks).   5 vols., 1967–77.
Editor, *Razor's Edge*, by Somerset Maugham.   1967.
Editor, *The Flight of the Phoenix*, by Elleston Trevor.   1968.
Editor, *Daughter of Time*, by Josephine Tey.   1968.
Editor, with Gordon Callaghan, *Rhyme and Reason.*   1969.
Editor, with Gordon Callaghan, *Salutation.*   1970.
Editor, *Sixteen by Twelve: Short Stories by Canadian Writers.*   1970.
Editor, *The Narrative Voice: Short Stories and Reflections by Canadian Authors.*   1972.
Editor, *Kaleidoscope: Canadian Stories.*   1972.
Editor, *The Speaking Earth: Canadian Poetry.*   1973.
Editor, with Joan Harcourt, *76 [77]: Best Canadian Stories.*   2 vols., 1976–77.
Editor, with Clark Blaise, *Here and Now.*   1977.
Editor, with Clark Blaise, *78 [79, 80]: Best Canadian Stories.*   3 vols., 1978–80.
Editor, *Stories Plus: Canadian Stories with Authors' Commentaries.*   1979.
Editor, *New Worlds: A Canadian Collection of Stories.*   1980.
Editor, *First [Second, Third] Impressions.*   3 vols., 1980–82.
Editor, with Leon Rooke, *81 [82]: Best Canadian Stories.*   2 vols., 1981–82.
Editor, *Making It New: Contemporary Canadian Stories.*   1982.
Editor, with Leon Rooke, *The New Press Anthology 1–2: Best Canadian Short Fiction.*   2 vols., 1984–85.
Editor, *The Bumper Book.*   1986.
Editor, with Leon Rooke, *The Macmillan Anthology 1–2.*   2 vols., 1988–89.
Editor, *Carry On Bumping.*   1988.
Editor, *Writers in Aspic.*   1988.
Editor, with Kent Thompson, *The Macmillan Anthology 3.*   1990.
Editor, *The New Story Writers.*   1992.
Editor, with J.R. Struthers, *How Stories Mean.*   1993.
Editor, with J.R. Struthers, *Canadian Classics.*   1993.

*

Critical Studies: "Metcalf Issue" of *Fiddlehead Magazine*, Summer 1977; *On the Line: Readings in the Short Fiction of Clark Blaise, Metcalf, and Hugh Hood* by Robert Lecker, 1982, and article by Douglas Rollins, in *Canadian Writers and Their Works 7* edited by Lecker, Jack David, and Ellen Quigley, 1985; "Metcalf Issue" of *Malahat Review 70*, March 1985; in *The Montreal Story Tellers* edited by J.R. Struthers, 1985; *Metcalf* by Barry Cameron, 1986; by Louis K. MacKendrick, in *Profiles in Canadian Literature 8* edited by Jeffrey Heath, 1991; *Coming of Age: Metcalf and the Canadian Short Story* edited by J.R. Struthers, 1993.

*   *   *

John Metcalf emigrated from England to Canada in 1962. Since that time he has edited anthologies and textbooks of Canadian literature, promoted the work of Canadian authors, written provocative critiques of the Canadian literary and academic establishments, and, most importantly, made his own distinctive contribution to Canadian fiction.

A satirist with a keen eye for the absurd, Metcalf sets many of his novellas and short stories in post-war Britain and/or contemporary central Canada; the old world is targeted for its hypocritical sense of propriety, the new world for its philistine commercialism. Metcalf's earlier fictions often culminate in epiphanies having to do with the loss of childhood innocence and the sudden awareness of mortality. Later works tend to address the frustrations of the writer: the epiphanies become muted and the stories are marked, increasingly, by a meticulous attention to and experimentation with the specifics of diction and typography. "I have a deep and probably neurotic interest in what you might call the *calligraphic* look of words on a page," Metcalf said in a 1981 interview with Geoff Hancock. Thematically, much of Metcalf's fiction is preoccupied with a few key issues: the distinction between art and life, between truth and fiction, and fiction and autobiography; the isolation of the writer; and the nature and function of language as an artistic medium and a means of communication.

Characteristic of Metcalf's stories about youth is "Single Gents Only," in which a young man escapes the constriction of his family when he leaves to attend university. The protagonist, David, is embarrassed by the appearance and behaviour of his parents at the train station, where his mother wears "a hat that looked like a pink felt Christmas pudding." (While they are not arranged to form an obvious sequence, Metcalf's stories often feature a child or adolescent called David: see "The Estuary," "The Teeth of My Father," "Beryl," "The Children Green and Golden," "Keys and Watercress." In these stories, David at various ages shows an interest in the precise names of things, an appreciation for the rare and beautiful, and an artistic sensibility.) Excitement at the prospect of a new life is quickly replaced by depression when David discovers the house in which he is to rent a room; the bedsheets are wet, his fellow-residents bizarre, and the geyser in the bathroom explodes. David is saved from all this by the arrival of his more experienced roommate, the sophisticated Jeremy, who pronounces the lodgings a "*lazar-house*" and proposes they find something else the next day. The story closes with a renewed sense of anticipation: David, who has found a friend and the assurance of more amenable surroundings, reads to Jeremy from *The Wind in the Willows*: "Oh what a flowery track lies spread before me, henceforth!"

"The Teeth of My Father" illustrates a number of images and concerns that recur in Metcalf's fiction. A lyrical expression of the relationship between the first-person narrator and his father, the story is also an investigation into the process of writing. The protagonist recalls his childhood and the eccentricities of his father, a minister who has all his teeth extracted to save on dental bills. He experiments with do-it-yourself denture kits, none of which produces satisfactory results: "Soon the teeth were melted down and recast every Saturday in readiness for the Sunday sermons. It was not until years later that I understood that had he produced an undeniably perfect pair it would have broken his heart." Perfection is never reached, but a dedication to its pursuit is the inheritance the narrator receives, along with a sense of rhetoric provided by the weekly sermons. While the father's eccentricities and religious sentiment are benign, the mother is an oppressive zealot who stands in the way of her son's destiny. (Methodism and youth also form an unhappy combination in *Private Parts* and "The Children Green and Golden"; mothers are further associated with prudishness, poor taste in clothes, books, or home furnishings, and the dispensing of maxims in "Private Parts" and "Single Gents Only.")

"The Teeth of My Father" is a fragmented narrative; framed by the story's present, it is interrupted by authorial interventions, flashback, excerpts from other stories, and a short section in italics dominated by the voice of someone who is apparently a critic commenting on one of the story excerpts. The critic assumes that the story is "autobiographical either in fact or impulse." Metcalf's interest in the relation between autobiography and fiction manifests itself in a number of his works; in "The Estuary" the narrator, David, describes a librarian's analysis of genre: "Fiction means a story book that isn't true and Non-Fiction means for example a book about history or science; and, no madam, biography is Non-Fiction although yet it *is* a story—the story of somebody's life—but the difference is that it's a true story and not an untrue story. Which *is* a funny way of dividing things up . . . " The problematic distinction between autobiography and fiction resurfaces in "The Eastmill Reception Centre," in which Cresswell, a university graduate, takes a teaching job at a boys' reformatory whose employees are mad, paranoid, or alcoholic. The boys' relative good humour in an institution that combines the discipline of a military school with the absurdity of a Beckett play renders them more engaging than the staff. Cresswell identifies increasingly with a 15-year-old arsonist named Dennis and sympathizes with his captives to the extent of allowing an entire cricket team to escape one afternoon. Here the conventional narrative ends and the "author" intervenes with a meditation on endings in general, this one in particular, desire, freedom, and the difficulty of expressing what he wants to say. "There *was* a Dennis," he claims, although that was not his real name, and he may or may not have burned houses. The voice of the author-narrator makes repeated assertions concerning the veracity of details in the first part of the story, but since these allegations occur within the context of a work of fiction, the reader has no more reason to believe the "truth" of the story's second section than that of the first. Here, as in "The Teeth of My Father," Metcalf pushes the distinctions between truth and falsehood, fact and fiction, to their limits in an exploration of meaning and genre.

Metcalf's fiction combines a profoundly serious interest in art, life, language and truth with a gleeful delight in the accidents and absurdities of existence.

—Claire Wilkshire

MIDDLETON, O(sman) E(dward Gordon). New Zealander. Born in Christchurch, 25 March 1925. Educated at New Plymouth Boys High School, 1939-41; Auckland University, 1946, 1948; the Sorbonne, Paris (New Zealand Government bursary), 1955–56. Served in the Royal New Zealand Air Force, 1944; New Zealand Army, 1945. Married Maida Edith Jones (marriage dissolved 1970); two children. Resident, Karolyi Memorial Foundation, Vence, France, Summer 1983; lectured at several European universities, 1983. Recipient: New Zealand award of achievement, 1960, and scholarship in letters, 1965; Hubert Church Prose award, 1964; University of Otago Robert Burns fellowship, 1970–71; New Zealand Prose Fiction award, 1976; University of Auckland John Cowie Reid award, 1989. Lives in Dunedin.

PUBLICATIONS

Short Stories

Short Stories. 1954.
The Stone and Other Stories. 1959.
A Walk on the Beach. 1964.
The Loners. 1972.
Selected Stories. 1975.
Confessions of an Ocelot, Not for a Seagull (novellas). 1978.

Verse

Six Poems. 1951.

Other

From the River to the Tide (for children). 1964.

*

Critical Studies: *New Zealand Fiction since 1945* by H. Winston Rhodes, 1968; "Middleton: Not Just a Realist" by Jim Williamson, in *Islands,* Winter 1973; *Middleton: The Sympathetic Imagination and the Right Judgements,* 1980, "Out from Under My Uncle's Hat: Gaskell, Middleton and the Sargeson Tradition," in *Critical Essays on the New Zealand Short Story* edited by Cherry Hankin, 1982, and *Barbed Wire and Mirrors: Essays on New Zealand Prose,* 1987, all by Lawrence Jones.

*   *   *

From his first published story in 1949 to his most recent collection in 1979, O.E. Middleton has published over 50 short stories and novellas. While some of these remain uncollected in little magazines, the majority appear in one or more of his six overlapping collections.

From the first, Middleton's stories could be seen to belong to the tradition of critical proletarian social realism initiated by Frank Sargeson, but they are not derivative, for Middleton succeeded for the most part in his stated aim of writing in "a voice [he] strove to make . . . [his] own." His method resembles Sargeson's—a first-person or third-person limited point of view, a vernacular style in keeping with that perspective, a relatively lightly-plotted slice-of-life structure from which the themes often emerge indirectly, although a structure rather richer in sensuous detail, less spare than Sargeson's. The range of character also resembles Sargeson's, with the emphasis on male characters from outside the middle class. Some are children, as in "Down by the River" or "First Adventure." Many are working men, as with the coopers in "Coopers' Christmas" and "A Married Man," or the seaman of "The Doss-House and the Duchess." Some are inmates of prisons, as in "My Thanksgiving" and "The Collector," or of mental hospitals, as in "Cutting Day." Some are Maori, as in "Drift" or *Not for a Seagull,* or Islanders, as in "The Loners." This range is

extended in the later stories, with the depiction of a German immigrant in "The Man Who Flew Models," or the female German student in France in "For Once in Your Life," or the Spanish artist and the female American tourist in "The Crows."

Middleton's stories are likewise in the Sargeson tradition in their underlying attitude, an attitude that might be broadly identified (in Sargeson's terms) as "a sort of humanism, although a rather special colonial variety," with a strong egalitarian strain. As in Sargeson's work, there is a clear dualism involved, a valuing of those who uphold the humanist code and a criticism of those who betray or violate it. The primary quality that furthers the code is sympathetic imagination. Sometimes this is manifested as a sympathetic understanding of one's mates, as in the secular communion among the unemployed seamen in "The Doss-House and the Duchess." Sometimes it is manifested as an imaginative understanding of another culture, as in the boy's reaching out towards Maori culture in "First Adventure," culminating in his intuitively right reburying of the Maori skeleton discovered in the sandhills. In some stories the imagination is revealed in an aesthetic awakening, as in "A Means of Soaring." All of these expressions of the sympathetic imagination are valued in the stories, while those who fail to exercise it are criticized. Sometimes the failure is in relation to the natural world, as with the objectionable middle-class father in "Killers," who intentionally runs down the harrier hawk in the road. This failure of imagination can appear as racial prejudice, as when the police in "Not for a Seagull" persecute Sonny, the Maori protagonist. In some stories, this failure is represented as sexual exploitation, as with the homosexual rapist Karel in *Confessions of an Ocelot.* More frequently it has to do with economic exploitation and class privilege, like in "The Doss-House and the Duchess."

The persistent critical problem that these stories present is that of authorial distance. Sometimes Middleton identifies too much with his positive characters and/or stereotypes his negative ones, so that the didactic design becomes too obvious and simplistic, as in "One for the Road," or, in its loaded ending, "The Crows." However, in his best stories Middleton is able to maintain a double perspective by which the reader can sympathize with the main character and share that point of view, while at the same time retaining some outside perspective, not in order to view the main character ironically but rather simply to see and understand more. Thus in "A Married Man," the reader shares the points of view of Tony and Colleen as they anticipate the birth of a first child and then mourn its loss when it is born prematurely and dies. At the end of the story the reader can both share and sympathize with Tony's experience of burying his own child while at the same time seeing more clearly than Tony can that his sympathetic workmate's attempt to cheer him up with drink and a bar-room pick-up is inappropriate to Tony's own deeper feelings. In "The Loners" the reader can share the point of view of Luke, the unemployed Islander, and comprehend more clearly than Luke can how inadequate New Zealand society is to his social needs. In the novella *Confessions of an Ocelot,* the reader can share the sensuous and emotional immediacy of Peter's long hot summer in Auckland while sensing well before Peter is aware of it that he is going to be faced with the discovery both of his own homosexuality and of the extent of human evil and suffering in the world around him. In stories such as these, Middleton's method triumphantly succeeds in presenting his vision with neither partisanship nor irony, and he demonstrates that he has found his own particular way of working within the Sargeson tradition.

—Lawrence Jones

MISHIMA Yukio. Pseudonym for Hiraoka Kimitake. Japanese. Born in Tokyo, 14 January 1925. Educated at Peers School and College, graduated 1944; Tokyo University, degree in jurisprudence 1947. Married Sugiyama Yoko in 1958; one daughter and one son. Civil servant, Finance Ministry, 1948; then freelance writer; also film director, designer, and stage producer and actor. Recipient: Shincho prize, 1954; Kishida Drama prize, 1955; Yomiuri prize, 1957, 1961; Mainichi prize, 1965. *Died (suicide) 25 November 1970.*

PUBLICATIONS

Collections

Zenshu [Collected Works], edited by Shoichi Saeki and Donald Keene,   36 vols., 1973–76.

Short Stories

Misaki nite no monogatari [Tales at a Promontory].   1947.
Kinjiki; Higyo.   2 vols., 1951–53; as *Forbidden Colours,* 1968.
Manatsu no shi.   1953; as "Death in Midsummer," in *Death in Midsummer and Other Stories,* 1966.
Death in Midsummer and Other Stories.   1966.
Acts of Worship: Seven Stories.   1989.

Novels

Hanazakari no mori [The Forest in Full Bloom].   1944.
Yoru no Shitaku [Preparations for the Night].   1948.
Tozoku [Thieves].   1948.
Shishi [Lion].   1948.
Kamen no Kokuhaku.   1949; as *Confessions of a Mask,* 1958.
Hōseki Baibai [Precious-Stone Broker].   1949.
Magun no tsuka [Passing of a Host of Devils].   1949.
Ai no kawaki.   1950; as *Thirst for Love,* 1969.
Kaibutsu [Monster].   1950.
Janpaku no Yoru [Snow-White Nights].   1950.
Ao no jidai [The Blue Period].   1950.
Natsuko no bōken [Natsuko's Adventures].   1951.
Nipponsei [Made in Japan].   1953.
Shiosai.   1954; as *The Sound of Waves,* 1956.
Shizumeru taki [The Sunken Waterfall].   1955.
Kinkakuji.   1956; as *The Temple of the Golden Pavilion,* 1959.
Kofuku go shuppan.   1956.
Bitoku no yorimeki [The Tottering Virtue].   1957.
Hashizukushi [A List of Bridges].   1958.
Kyōko no Ie [Kyoko's House].   1959.
Utage no ato.   1960; as *After the Banquet,* 1963.
Suta [Movie Star].   1961.
Nagasugita haru [Too Long a Spring].   1961.
Utsukushii hoshi [Beautiful Star].   1962.
Gogo no eikō.   1963; as *The Sailor Who Fell from Grace with the Sea,* 1965.

Ken [The Sword].   1963.
Nikutai no gakkō [The School of Flesh].   1964.
Kinu to meisatsu [Silk and Insight].   1964.
Han-teijo Daigaku [College of Unchasteness].   1966.
Eirei no Koe [Voices of the Spirits of the War Dead].   1966.
Fukuzatsuma Kare [A Complicated Man].   1966.
Yakaifuku [Evening Dress].   1967.
Taiyo to tetsu.   1968; as *Sun and Steel,* 1970.
Hojo no umi; as *The Sea of Fertility:*
   Haru no yuki.   1969; as *Spring Snow,* 1972.
   Homba.   1969; as *Runaway Horses,* 1973.
   Akatsuki no tera.   1970; as *The Temple of Dawn,* 1973.
   Tenninjosui.   1971; as *The Decay of the Angel,* 1974.
Kemono no tawamure [The Play of Beasts].   1971.

Plays

Kataku [Burning Houses] (produced 1949).   In *Ningen* (magazine), 1948.
Tōdai [Lighthouse] (produced 1950).   1950.
Kantan (produced 1950).   In *Kindai Nogakushu,* 1956; translated as *Kantan,* in *Five Modern Nō Plays,* 1957.
Setjo [Saintess].   1951.
Aya no tsuzumi (produced 1952).   1953; as *The Damask Drum,* in *Five Modern No Plays,* 1957.
Sotoba komachi (produced 1952).   In *Kindai Nogakushu,* 1956; translated as *Sotoba komachi,* in *Five Modern No Plays,* 1957.
Yoru no himawari (produced 1953).   1953; as *Twilight Sunflower,* 1958.
Wakodo yo yomigaere [Young Man Back to Life] (produced 1955).   1954.
Aoi no ue (produced 1955).   In *Kindai Nōgakushu,* 1956; as *The Lady Aoi,* in *Five Modern No Plays,* 1957.
Shiroari no su [Nest of White Ants] (produced 1955).   1956.
Fuyo no Tsuyu Ouchi Jikki [True History of the House of Ouchi] (produced 1955).
Kindai Nogakushu.   1956; as *Five Modern No Plays,* 1957.
Yuya (produced 1957).   In *Kindai Nogakushu,* 1956.
Rokumeikan [Rokumei Mansion] (produced 1956).   1957.
Hanjo (produced 1957); translated as *Hanjo,* in *Five Modern No Plays,* 1957.
Bara to kaizoku [Rose and Pirates] (produced 1958).   1958.
Nettaiju (produced 1961); in *Koe* (magazine), 1960; as *Tropical Tree,* in *Japanese Quarterly 11,* 1964.
Toka no kiku [Late Flowering Chrysanthemum] (produced 1961).
Kurotokage [Black Lizard], from a story by Edogawa Rampo (produced 1962).
Gikyoku zenshu [Collected Plays].   1962.
Yorokobi no Koto [Koto of Rejoicing] (produced 1964).
Sado kōshaku fujin (produced 1965).   1965; as *Madame de Sade,* 1967.
Suzaku-ke no Metsubo [Downfall of the Suzaku Family] (produced 1967).   1967.
Waga tomo Hitler [My Friend Hitler] (produced 1968).   1968.
Raio no Terasu [Terrace of the Leper King] (produced 1969).   1969.
Chinsetsu yumiharizuki [The Strange Story of Tametomo] (produced 1969).   1969.

Screenplay: *Yukoku* [Patriotism], 1965.

Other

Karl to emono [The Hunter and His Prey].   1951.
Aporo no sakazuki [Cup of Apollo].   1952.
Sakuhin-shu [Works].   6 vols., 1953–54.
Koi no miyako [City of Love].   1954.
Megami [Goddess].   1955.
Seishun o dō ikiru ka [How To Live as a Young Man]. 1955.
Senshu [Selected Works].   19 vols., 1957–59.
Gendai shōsetsu wa koten tari-uru ka [Can a Modern Novel Be a "Classic"?].   1957.
Fudōtoku kyōiku kōza [Lectures on Immoralities].   1959.
Hayashi Fusao Ron [Study of Hayashi Fusao].   1963.
Watashi no Henreki Jidai [My Wandering Years].   1964.
Tampen zenshu [Short Pieces].   1964.
Mikuma no Mōde [Pilgrimage to the Three Kumano Shrine].   1965.
Hyōron zenshū [Collected Essays].   1966.
Hagakure nyumon.   1967; as *The Way of the Samurai: Mishima on Hagakure in Modern Life,* 1977.
Taido. 1967; as *Young Samurai,* 1967.
Taidan, ningen to bungaku, with Mitsuo Nakamura. 1968.
Wakaki samurai no tame ni [Spiritual Lectures for the Young Samurai].   1968.
Bunka boeiron [Defense of Culture].   1969.
Yūkoku no genri [The Theory of Patriotism].   1970.
Sakkaron [Essays on Writers].   1970.
Gensen no kanjō [The Deepest Feelings].   1970.
Kodogaku nyūmon [An Introduction to Action Philosophy].   1970.
Shōbu no kokoro [Heart of Militarism].   1970.
Waga shishunki [My Adolescence].   1973.

Editor, *Rokusei nakamura utaemon.*   1959.
Editor, with Geoffrey Bownas, *New Writing in Japan.* 1972.

*

Critical Studies: *Mishima: A Biography* by John Nathan, 1974; *The Life and Death of Mishima* by Henry Scott-Stokes, 1974; *Accomplices of Silence: The Modern Japanese Novel* by Masao Miyoshi, 1974; *The Moon in the Water: Understanding Tanizaki, Kawabata, and Mishima* by Gwenn Boardman Petersen, 1979; *A Vision of the Void: Mishima* by Marguerite Yourcenar, translated by Alberto Manguel, 1985; *Mishima* by Peter Wolfe, 1989; *Escape from the Wasteland: Romanticism and Realism in Mishima and Ōe Kenzaburo* by Susan J. Napier, 1991.

*   *   *

A useful place to start in considering Mishima as a short story writer, or, indeed, to understand his oeuvre as a whole, is with the story "Patriotism." This story (later made into a film that Mishima both directed and starred in) is based on a real incident in which a young army lieutenant and his wife committed ritual suicide, or seppuku, after the failure of the "patriotic" rebellion in 1936. Following the introduction, in which the perfect beauty of the young couple is emphasised, the rest of the story is devoted entirely to a description of the preparations for suicide and, in shockingly exact detail, the act of suicide

itself. It is a paean to unswerving devotion to an accepted code and to the beauty of a young and noble death.

There is no undercurrent of irony here, no balancing of the passion of life with the necessity of death: the essential point is that the passion of life is only achieved through such a violent death. Death in the prime of youth is the fit culmination, the justification and the true glory of life, and the narrator takes enormous pains to make us assent to this point of view and emotionally participate in it.

Dying the beautiful death, the beautiful body of death, the instant of death that gives meaning to everything else— these were ideas to which Mishima constantly returned. This does not mean, of course, that all his short stories contained such meticulous and anatomically exact descriptions of suicide, but the beloved immensity of death works its influence on all his writings in one way or another.

There are other stories that deal directly with the subject of death itself, or in which the principle character dies: "Death in Midsummer," "Sword," "Kujaku" (The Peacocks). Death's numinous presence, usually more a promise than a threat, underlies and gives coherence to a story. Its absoluteness makes the everyday concerns of those struggling to avoid death seem absurd and foolish by contrast. "Death in Midsummer," one of Mishima's best-known stories, contains all these elements. The tragedy comes at the beginning. Two of Tomoko and Masaru's three children are drowned when the aunt watching them has a heart attack just as she sees them being swept out to sea; she dies before she can give warning. The rest of the story shows how the agony of grief is dulled gradually by the humdrum circumstances of life and the adjustments of the ego. Mishima convincingly shows the mother's anger and disbelief fading into a state where she has to remind herself to feel sad. Then she becomes pregnant again: "While true forgetfulness had not come, something covered Tomoko's sorrow as thin ice covers a lake" (translated by Edward G. Seidensticker). The roles have been reversed: "It attacked the organism like an invisible germ." "The organism" here means her grief and despair, and it attacks forgetfulness, what would normally be regarded as the healing processes of life. The end of the story comes after the new baby is born and Tomoko suddenly feels an urge to return to the beach where the deaths occurred. As she stands gazing out to sea and the horizon of massed clouds, her husband observes her expression, as if she were waiting for something: "'What are you waiting for?' he wanted to ask lightly. But the words did not come. He thought he knew without asking. He clutched tighter at Katsuo's hand." Katsuo is the one child who was not swept out to sea at the time, and it seems clear that what Tomoko is waiting for here is the death meted out to her other children, waiting to be borne out toward the infinity of sea and cloud and golden light— elements of landscape that occur frequently in Mishima's tales.

Another example, and one that illustrates the breadth of Mishima's reading and his eclectic use of sources, is the short tale "Sea and Sunset." Set in medieval Japan, it is about an old man who climbs to the top of a hill every evening to view the sunset over the sea. He is not Japanese, but a Frenchman, once a shepherd boy from the Cevennes who had a vision urging him to lead a crusade. He was captured and brought as a slave to India, eventually ending in the service of a wandering Japanese monk. In his vision the sea would part for him and allow him to walk to the holy land. But it does not happen, and this is all he remembers, the fact that the sea would not part and that all experiences and memories now have disappeared into the glowing sea.

It is hard to deny that many of Mishima's ideas boil down to a kind of romantic nihilism. But however intellectually confused, and often simply adolescent his philosophy may seem, an anarchic and nihilistic view of society allowed him to produce sharp and witty satires. This is the reverse side of the romanticism of death—the burlesquing of life. Some stories are simply comedies of manners, such as "The Pearl," which describes the vindictiveness, injured pride, and social manoeuvering of four wealthy, middle-aged women at a tea party. Mishima captures the icy hypocrisy of the exchanges between these women with an exactness that, even in translation, rivals Saki or Waugh at their best. Other of his stories, such as "Act of Worship," "Dojoji," and "The Seven Bridges," contain many examples of the same witty social observation, although their overall tone is soberer: Mishima was even capable of a kind of Rabelasian grotesque, as in the tale of five monstrous students in "Tamago."

But in the majority of Mishima's mature stories the main point is the ironic contrast between the characters' hopes and their real circumstances. Often they are engrossed in their trivial everyday concerns, until something brings them up against the emptiness at the centre. This is especially true of the characters identified with what Mishima saw as the decadent materialism of post-occupation Japan. In "Kyuteisha" (Emergency Stop) a young man who wanted to be an artist, instead makes his living creating lamps for the rich and tasteless. In "Thermos Bottles" a former Geisha with a talent for traditional dance is turned into just another westernized Japanese mistress, as though "the great vermilion-lacquered, black-riveted gate of some noble lady's mansion were suddenly to change into a slick revolving door." Although Mishima is better known for his novels he, like Lawrence, is a writer whose best qualities and principle ideas can be easily understood from his short fiction. For someone who tended to lapse into long passages of speculative philosophy, and equally long, and rather overcontrived and schematic descriptions, the constraints of the short story often did him a service, forcing him to make his effects cleaner and his ideas clearer, as well as bringing to the fore his talent for dialogue, which tends to go ignored in his longer works.

—James Raeside

See the essays on "Patriotism" and "Three Million Yen."

MITCHISON, Naomi (Margaret, née Haldane). British. Born in Edinburgh, 1 November 1897; daughter of the scientist John Scott Haldane; sister of the writer J.B.S. Haldane. Educated at Lynam's School, Oxford; St. Anne's College, Oxford. Served as a volunteer nurse, 1915. Married G.R. Mitchison (who became Lord Mitchison, 1964) in 1916 (died 1970); three sons and two daughters. Labour candidate for Parliament, Scottish Universities constituency, 1935; member, Argyll County Council, 1945–66; member, Highland Panel, 1947–64, and Highlands and Islands Development Council, 1966–76. Tribal adviser, and Mmarona (Mother), to the Bakgatla of Botswana, 1963–89. D. Univ.: University of Stirling, Scotland, 1976; University of Dundee, Scotland, 1985; D.Litt.: University of Strathclyde, Glasgow, 1983. Honorary Fellow, St. Anne's College, 1980, and Wolfson College, 1983, both Oxford. Officer, French Academy, 1924. C.B.E. (Commander, Order of the British Empire), 1985. Lives in Campbeltown, Scotland.

PUBLICATIONS

Short Stories

When the Bough Breaks and Other Stories.   1924.
Black Sparta: Greek Stories.   1928.
Barbarian Stories.   1929.
The Delicate Fire: Short Stories and Poems.   1933.
The Fourth Pig: Stories and Verses.   1936.
Travel Light (novella).   1952.
Five Men and a Swan: Short Stories and Poems.   1958.
Images of Africa.   1980.
What Do You Think Yourself? Scottish Short Stories.   1982.
Beyond This Limit: Selected Shorter Fiction of Mitchison, edited by Isobel Murray.   1986.
Early in Orcadia.   1987.
A Girl Must Live, edited by Isabel Murray.   1990.
Sea-Green Ribbons (novella).   1991.

Novels

The Conquered.   1923.
Cloud Cuckoo Land.   1925.
The Corn King and the Spring Queen.   1931; as *The Barbarian,* 1961.
The Powers of Light.   1932.
Beyond This Limit.   1935.
We Have Been Warned.   1935.
The Blood of the Martyrs.   1939.
The Bull Calves.   1947.
Lobsters on the Agenda.   1952.
To the Chapel Perilous.   1955.
Behold Your King.   1957.
Memoirs of a Spacewoman.   1962.
When We Become Men.   1965.
Cleopatra's People.   1972.
Solution Three.   1975.
Not by Bread Alone.   1983.
The Oath Takers.   1991.

Plays

Nix-Nought-Nothing: Four Plays for Children (includes *My Ain Sel', Hobyah! Hobyah!, Elfen Hill*).   1928.
Kate Crackernuts: A Fairy Play.   1931.
The Price of Freedom, with L.E. Gielgud (produced 1949).   1931.
Full Fathom Five, with L.E. Gielgud (produced 1932).
An End and a Beginning and Other Plays (includes *The City and the Citizens, For This Man Is a Roman, In the Time of Constantine, Wild Men Invade the Roman Empire, Charlemagne and His Court, The Thing That Is Plain, Cortez in Mexico, Akbar, But Still It Moves, The New Calendar, American Britons*).   1937; as *Historical Plays for Schools,*   2 vols., 1939.
As It Was in the Beginning, with L.E. Gielgud.   1939.
The Corn King, music by Brian Easdale, adaptation of the novel by Mitchison (produced 1951).   1951.
Spindrift, with Denis Macintosh (produced 1951).   1951.

Verse

The Laburnum Branch.   1926.

The Alban Goes Out.   1939.
The Cleansing of the Knife and Other Poems.   1978.

Other (for children)

The Hostages and Other Stories for Boys and Girls.   1930.
Boys and Girls and Gods.   1931.
The Big House.   1950.
Graeme and the Dragon.   1954.
The Swan's Road.   1954.
The Land the Ravens Found.   1955.
Little Boxes.   1956.
The Far Harbour.   1957.
Judy and Lakshmi.   1959.
The Rib of the Green Umbrella.   1960.
The Young Alexander the Great.   1960.
Karensgaard: The Story of a Danish Farm.   1961.
The Young Alfred the Great.   1962.
The Fairy Who Couldn't Tell a Lie.   1963.
Alexander the Great.   1964.
Henny and Crispies.   1964.
Ketse and the Chief.   1965.
A Mochudi Family.   1965.
Friends and Enemies.   1966.
The Big Surprise.   1967.
Highland Holiday.   1967.
African Heroes.   1968.
Don't Look Back.   1969.
The Family at Ditlabeng.   1969.
Sun and Moon.   1970.
Sunrise Tomorrow.   1973.
The Danish Teapot.   1973.
Snake!   1976.
The Little Sister, with works by Ian Kirby and Keetla Masogo.   1976.
The Wild Dogs, with works by Megan Biesele.   1977.
The Brave Nurse and Other Stories.   1977.
The Two Magicians, with Dick Mitchison.   1978.
The Vegetable War.   1980.

Other

Anna Comnena.   1928.
Comments on Birth Control.   1930.
The Home and a Changing Civilisation.   1934.
Vienna Diary.   1934.
Socrates, with Richard Crossman.   1937.
The Moral Basis of Politics.   1938.
The Kingdom of Heaven.   1939.
Men and Herring: A Documentary, with Denis Macintosh.   1949.
Other People's Worlds (travel).   1958.
A Fishing Village on the Clyde, with G.W.L. Paterson.   1960.
Presenting Other People's Children.   1961.
Return to the Fairy Hill (autobiography and sociology).   1966.
The Africans: A History.   1970.
Small Talk: Memories of an Edwardian Childhood.   1973.
A Life for Africa: The Story of Bram Fischer.   1973.
Oil for the Highlands?   1974.
All Change Here: Girlhood and Marriage (autobiography).   1975.
Sittlichkeit (lecture).   1975.
You May Well Ask: A Memoir 1920–1940.   1979.
Mucking Around: Five Continents over Fifty Years.   1981.
Margaret Cole 1893–1980.   1982.

Among You, Taking Notes: The Wartime Diary of Naomi Mitchison 1939–1945, edited by Dorothy Sheridan.   1985.
Naomi Mitchison (autobiographical sketch).   1986.
As It Was.   1988.

Editor, *An Outline for Boys and Girls and Their Parents.*   1932.
Editor, with Robert Britton and George Kilgour, *Re-Educating Scotland.*   1944.
Editor, *What the Human Race Is Up To.*   1962.

*

Critical Study: *Mitchison: A Century of Experiment in Life and Letters* by Jill Benton, 1990.

*   *   *

Naomi Mitchison has been writing short fiction for 70 years, along with a flood of other genres, novels mainly historical, plays, poems, biography, documentary, and a wide range of books for children, from the openly didactic to the richly entertaining. Just as her adult novels can approach epic sweep at times, her short stories tend to be longer than some, and she has written fine novellas, from *Travel Light* to *Sea-Green Ribbons.*

The short stories often mirror the concerns and settings of the novels. So early collections are mainly concerned with history, especially the ancient world. Mitchison characteristically uses earlier time periods for investigation of the contemporary and topical human issues close to her heart—conflicts of loyalties, the justice of political systems, and the way people obtain and use power over each other in relationships, openly, obliquely, or unconsciously. The ultimate image here is slavery: this is the ultimate test of civilisations, even her admired Athens at its best.

A good example is "The Wife of Aglaos," one of a series of stories set on "Lovely Mantinea" in *The Delicate Fire* (reprinted in *Beyond This Limit: Selected Shorter Fiction*). All five of these stories concern Greek citizens brought up with every refinement of luxury, culture, and learning, pitched suddenly into slavery and violent oppression when the city is conquered by the Macedonians. Kleta is sold, raped, ill-treated; she bears a child by her owner before escaping with her firstborn and a fellow slave to the mountains, where a band of male fugitives are hiding. She learns to adapt to the needs of the situation. On the run she gives her superfluous breast-milk to her fellow slave, and in the mountains she cooks for and sleeps with all the men, and has two more children by them. She begins to understand the political implications of her former life. This story is characteristic of Mitchison's work. It is told in a very direct conversational tone by Kleta to her niece, while the reader eavesdrops and gradually begins to understand the issues.

Most of the best short fiction is historical, or science fiction. But in 1935 Mitchison produced a contemporary fantasy, "Beyond This Limit," in a unique collaboration with artist Wyndham Lewis. Set in Paris, Oxford, and London, it deals with Phoebe Bathurst's experience of loss and betrayal when her lover is to marry someone else. Lewis produced the illustrations. Mitchison tells how the fantasy grew: "What we did was that one or other of us would get ahead. He would do a picture and I would say, what's that of?—perhaps what was going to happen, and then *I* rushed ahead . . . and so on." The major characters are so clearly in some sense Lewis and Mitchison themselves that she did not bother to say that: "He was acting as the guide of souls and with this great black hat that he always wore, and I was wearing this headscarf that I always wore. . . . It was a bouncy book, and I think the way we both enjoyed doing it is reflected." The fantasy is satiric, light-hearted, and allusive; it could be described as Mitchison's flirtation with modernism.

Mitchison comes from a very distinguished Scottish family, accustomed to great houses and public affairs, and her values include Scottish nationalism and a particular sense of responsibility, as well as feminism and socialism. Her work is always widely approachable, but she writes often with special messages for "the intelligentsia, the people who should be giving a lead." In the 1930's she began to give Scotland a greater place in her writing concerns, and the stories of *Five Men and a Swan* (written in 1940 but published in 1958) adopt a kind of Scottish English, the intonations she learned after making her home in Carradale, Kintyre, in 1937. "Five Men and a Swan," one of her best stories, is a modern fairy tale of a traditional type, about a swan who could be mastered if a man found her shed feathers at full moon. It is a story of good intentions hopelessly failing as one after another of a fishing boat crew goes to meet the swan and responds to her beauty with brutality and violence. Both local fishermen and novelist Neil Gunn praised it highly, but it was rejected by *New Writing* in London in 1941. Mitchison had to learn that her increasing Scottishness would not endear her to London publishers and media.

Mitchison has strong ties to Africa, and is mother to a tribe in Botswana. Stories like "The Coming of the New God" can shift the reader's perspective dramatically; the story is about how the multiple wives of a chief enjoy happiness in community, and how the women are totally dismayed by the acceptance, from political necessity, of a missionary regime that deprives the wives of status, home, role, and function.

Mitchison also uses elements of science fiction to disorientate the reader and disrupt expectations. "Mary and Joe" is a tense story of the future, in which Joe learns that their daughter Jaycie is in fact biologically a clone of Mary only.

In "Conversation with an Improbable Future" children outgrow their mother; they live in natural time, while her growing-processes are suspended during space journeys.

Other important qualities of Mitchison's work include an impish sense of fun and her frequent use of irony. Brought up in a scientific family, she was writing urgent environmental messages before ecology was a word in common usage. The stories often celebrate science and logic as well as the irrational, the religious, or the magic. Frequent consideration is given to ancestral gifts and powers, and to future generations, mutant or naturally evolved. The importance of communication and understanding is central. The stories often have first person narrators, most but not all female, most but not all human. Their voices are urgent or gentle, insistent or comic. Voices that seem to be heard, not read.

—Isobel Murray

MOORE, George (Augustus). Irish. Born at Moore Hall, Ballyglass, County Mayo, 24 February 1852; moved with his family to London, 1869. Educated at Oscott College, Birmingham, 1861–67; attended evening classes in art, South Kensington Museum, and studied with an army tutor, 1870; studied painting in London, 1870–73, and at Academie Julian and Ecole des Beaux Arts, Paris, 1873-74. Lived in Paris, 1873–79, and in London and Ireland from 1879; wrote for the *Spectator* and the *Examiner*; art critic, the *Speaker,* 1891–95; co-founder, with Lady Gregory, Edward Martyn, and William Butler Yeats, Irish Literary Theatre, 1899, which became the Irish National Theatre Society at the Abbey Theatre, Dublin, 1904; lived in Dublin, 1901–11, and in London from 1911; High Sheriff of Mayo, 1905. *Died 21 January 1933.*

PUBLICATIONS

Collections

Works (Carra Edition).   21 vols., 1922–24.
Works (Uniform Edition).   20 vols., 1924–33.
Works (Ebury Edition).   20 vols., 1937.

Short Stories

Celibates.   1895.
The Untilled Field.   1903; revised edition, 1903, 1914, 1926, 1931.
A Story-Teller's Holiday.   1918; revised edition,   2 vols., 1928.
In Single Strictness.   1922; revised edition, 1923; as *Celibate Lives,* 1927.
Peronnik the Fool (story).   1926; revised edition, 1928.
A Flood (story).   1930.
In Minor Keys: The Uncollected Short Stories, edited David B. Eakin and Helmut E. Gerber.   1985.

Novels

A Modern Lover.   1883; revised edition, 1885; as *Lewis Seymour and Some Women,* 1917.
A Mummer's Wife.   1884; revised edition, 1886, 1917; as *An Actor's Wife,* 1889.
A Drama in Muslin: A Realistic Novel.   1886; revised edition, as *Muslin,* 1915.
A Mere Accident.   1887.
Spring Days: A Realistic Novel—A Prelude to Don Juan. 1888; revised edition, 1912; as *Shifting Love,* 1891.
Mike Fletcher.   1889.
Vain Fortune.   1891; revised edition, 1892, 1895.
Esther Waters.   1894; revised edition, 1899, 1920; edited by David Skilton, 1983.
Evelyn Innes.   1898; revised edition, 1898, 1901, 1908.
Sister Theresa.   1901; revised edition, 1909.
The Lake.   1905; revised edition, 1906, 1921.
The Brook Kerith: A Syrian Story.   1916; revised edition, 1927.
Héloïse and Abélard.   1921; Fragments, 1921.
Ulick and Soracha.   1926.
Aphrodite in Aulis.   1930; revised edition, 1931.

Plays

Martin Luther, with Bernard Lopez.   1879.

Les Cloches de Corneville (lyrics only, with Augustus Moore), from a play by Robert Planquette and Louis Claireville (produced 1883).   1883.
The Fashionable Beauty, with J.M. Glover (produced 1885).
Le Sycamore (in French), with Paul Alexis, from the play *Sweethearts* by W.S. Gilbert (produced 1886?).
The Honeymoon in Eclipse, from a work by Mrs. G.W. Godfrey (produced 1888).
Thérèse Raquin, from a play by A. Texeira de Mattos based on the novel by Zola (produced 1891).
The Strike at Arlingford (produced 1893).   1893.
Journeys End in Lovers Meeting, with John Oliver Hobbes (produced 1894).   In *Tales without Temperaments* by Hobbes, 1902.
The Fool's Hour: The First Act of a Comedy, with John Oliver Hobbes, in *Yellow Book 1,* 1894.
The Bending of the Bough (produced 1900).   1900.
Diarmuid and Grania, with W.B. Yeats (produced 1901). 1951; edited by Anthony Farrow, 1974.
Esther Waters, from his own novel (produced 1911). 1913; edited by W. Eugene Davis, in *The Celebrated Case of Esther Waters,* 1984.
The Apostle.   1911; revised version, 1923; revised version, as *The Passing of the Essenes* (produced 1930), 1930.
Elizabeth Cooper (produced 1913).   1913; revised version, as *The Coming of Gabrielle* (produced 1923), 1920.
The Making of an Immortal (produced 1928).   1927.

Verse

Flowers of Passion.   1877.
Pagan Poems.   1881.

Other

Literature at Nurse; or, Circulating Morals.   1885.
Parnell and His Island.   1887.
Confessions of a Young Man.   1888; revised edition, 1889, 1904, 1917, 1926; edited by Susan Dick, 1972.
Impressions and Opinions.   1891; revised edition, 1913.
Modern Painting.   1893; revised edition, 1896.
The Royal Academy.   1895.
Memoirs of My Dead Life.   1906; revised edition, 1921.
Reminiscences of the Impressionist Painters.   1906.
Hail and Farewell: A Trilogy (Ave, Salve, Vale) (autobiography).   3 vols., 1911–14; revised edition, 1925; edited by Richard Allen Cave, 1 vol., 1976.
Avowals (autobiography).   1919.
Moore Versus Harris: An Intimate Correspondence Between Moore and Frank Harris.   1921.
Conversations in Ebury Street (autobiography).   1924: revised edition, 1930.
Letters to Edouard Dujardin 1866–1922 (in French), translated by John *Eglinton.*   1929.
The Talking Pine.   1931.
A Communication to My Friends.   1933.
Letters (to John Eglinton).   1942.
Letters to Lady Cunard 1895–1933, edited by Rupert Hart-Davis.   1957.
Moore in Transition: Letters to T. Fisher Unwin and Lena Milman 1894–1910, edited by Helmut E. Gerber. 1968.
Moore's Correspondence with the Mysterious Countess, edited by David B. Eakin and Robert Langenfeld. 1984.
Moore on Parnassus: Letters (1900–1933) to Secretaries, Publishers, Printers, Agents, Literati, Friends, and Ac- quaintances, edited by Helmut E. Gerber and O.M. Brack, Jr.   1988.

Editor, *Pure Poetry: An Anthology.*   1924.

Translator, *The Pastoral Loves of Daphnis and Chloe,* by Longus.   1924.

*

Bibliography: *A Bibliography of Moore* by Edwin Gilcher, 1970, supplement, 1988; *Moore: An Annotated Secondary Bibliography of Writings about Him* by Robert Langenfeld, 1987.

Critical Studies: *The Life of Moore* by Joseph M. Hone, 1936; *Moore: A Reconsideration* by Malcolm J. Brown, 1955; *GM: Memories of Moore* by Nancy Cunard, 1956; *Moore* by A. Norman Jeffares, 1965; *Moore: L'Homme et l'oeuvre* by J.C. Nöel, 1966; *Moore's Mind and Art* edited by Graham Owens, 1968; *The Man of Wax: Critical Essays on Moore* edited by Douglas Hughes, 1971; *Moore: The Artist's Vision, The Storyteller's Art* by Janet Dunleavy, 1973, and *Moore in Perspective* edited by Dunleavy, 1983; *A Study of the Novels of Moore* by Richard Allen Cave, 1978; *Moore* by Anthony Farrow, 1978; *The Way Back: Moore's The Untilled Field and The Lake* edited by Robert Welch, 1982; *Moore and German Romanticism* by Patrick Bridgewater, 1988.

*   *   *

George Moore is almost universally acknowledged as the originator of the modern short story in Ireland. Moore's first efforts in establishing the genre appeared in *Parnell and His Island,* a vicious and immature series of sketches that pillories both urban and rural Ireland. Taking the 19th-century naturalist writer's approach, Moore, being a great admirer of Emile Zola, mercilessly limned the worst, most degrading scenes he could, which gained him lasting enmity among his countrymen, both in his own upper class and in the peasant classes. "Dublin" is a criticism of the dilapidated lifestyle led by the old ascendancy in the nation's capital, while sketches such as "An Eviction" criticize not only the heartlessness of landlords evicting destitute peasants from their holdings, so that the land could be used more profitably for grazing sheep and cattle, but also the peasants themselves, who are depicted as stupid, filthy, and without any of the innate nobility credited to them by writers such as Yeats and Lady Gregory. But the collection also established the beginnings of a dominating cultural symbol: the image of physical paralysis or sluggishness as a representation of spiritual inertia.

This theme became a virtually lifelong preoccupation with Moore, who was also the first Irish writer to link paralysis with exile: those who could escape the disease before becoming trapped by their own weakness and lack of resolve did so. Until relatively recently, James Joyce received all the credit for originating and developing this thematic dialectic, but Moore is finally receiving his due as the first to base a literary work upon it, both in novel form—*A Drama in Muslin* and *The Lake*—and in the short story genre with *Celibates* and *The Untilled Field.* The latter, modelled on Turgenev's *Sportman's Sketches,* is considered the first modern collection of Irish short stories ever published, and this is certainly true if we think in terms of collections of discrete stories that make some attempt at thematic unity. *Celibates*, though published eight years earlier, is not accorded this distinction because its stories are too few and too long, even though they are thematically unified as the collection's title clearly indicates.

The title of *The Untilled Field* similarly suggests its content and acts as a symbol to reinforce its dominant theme. Barrenness—agricultural, sexual, and spiritual—inactivity, paralysis, and potential going to waste are all primary interpretations of this symbol. Although some stories, such as "The Clerk's Quest," have urban settings, most are purely rural and devoted to analyzing the factors that continued to deplete Ireland's population despite the end of extreme famine conditions. Most centrally, in stories such as "Some Parishioners" and "Julia Cahill's Curse," the Irish clergy are assailed for helping to increase the flow of exiles—by stifling and controlling the people, especially any of independent spirit and enterprising nature. Through such tactics as denunciation, arranged marriages, and stiff fees charged for performance of the sacraments, the priests are depicted as more concerned with the preservation of clerical power than with national or even communal well being.

This would all seem to suggest a writer as out of control here as he had been 15 years earlier in *Parnell and His Island*, but such is not the case. Balancing the various unsavory priests are a number who are restrained, benevolent, and quite likeable. Father Stafford, in "Some Parishioners," for example, neutralizes much of the antipathy we feel for Father Maguire, who cares more about theological technicalities than about the day-to-day happiness of his people. In "A Letter to Rome" and "A Playhouse in the Waste," Father MacTurnan is shown making sincere, selfless, and sometimes naive efforts on behalf of his poor parishioners, though he is in many ways a broken man by the end of the second story. Still, a sense of balance does generally prevail in the collection and not all of Ireland's woes are laid on the clerical doorstep, as in "The Exile," where the able brother emigrates—more out of a broken heart than anything else—while the inept brother remains and is eventually to inherit the family farm. These stories, and virtually all others in the collection, are also markedly modern for the minimal importance of plot and the emphasis instead on theme and character.

Moore's final Irish short story collection, *A Story-Teller's Holiday*, is a long series of stories in two volumes that are woven together as told by an old peasant Irish storyteller to his engrossed upper-class listener. Emulating the form of the oral tradition, Moore created the collection as one long, continuous piece of work that gives evidence of Moore's capacity for creating both pathos, as in "The Nuns of Crith Gaille," and salacious humor, as in "Father Moling and the Immaculate Conception." These are all medieval tales, at times reminiscent of Boccaccio's *The Decameron* (1351), that show the sexual temptations of nuns and priests among those of more conventional romantic lovers. Continuing in this collection is evidence of Moore's frequent tendency—in various literary forms, to delve into the past for creative materials, and of his persistent, indeed lifelong, anticlerical posture.

Some readers approaching Moore for the first time will perhaps be surprised at his versatility in short story writing, exceeding that of even Joyce; generally Joyce may give us higher quality, but Moore attempts more forms—usually succeeding in those attempts—and employs a far broader scope of subject matter, including both urban and rural perspectives on his themes.

—Alexander G. Gonzalez

See the essay on "Julia Cahill's Curse."

MOORHOUSE, Frank. Australian. Born in Nowra, New South Wales, 21 December 1938. Educated at the University of Queensland, 1959–61. Served in the Australian Army and Reserves, 1957–59. Divorced. Journalist, Sydney *Daily Telegraph,* 1956–59; editor, *Lockhart Review,* New South Wales, 1960, and *Australian Worker,* Sydney, 1963; assistant secretary, Workers' Educational Association, Sydney, 1963–65; union organiser, Australian Journalists' Association, 1966; editor, *City Voices,* Sydney, 1966; contributor and columnist, 1970–79, and night club writer, 1980, *Bulletin,* Sydney; co-founding editor, *Tabloid Story,* Sydney, 1972–74; writer-in-residence, University of Melbourne and other Australian universities; travelled in Europe and Middle East, late 1980's; moved to France, 1991. Vice-president, 1978–80, and president, 1979–82, Australian Society of Authors; chairman, Copyright Council of Australia, 1985. Recipient: Lawson Short Story prize, 1970; National Book Council Banjo award, for fiction, 1975; Senior Literary fellowship, 1976; *Age* Book of the Year, 1988; Australian Literature Society gold medal, 1989. Member, Order of Australia, 1985.

PUBLICATIONS

Short Stories

Futility and Other Animals.   1969.
The Americans, Baby.   1972.
The Electrical Experience.   1974.
Conference-ville.   1976.
Tales of Mystery and Romance.   1977.
The Everlasting Secret Family and Other Secrets.   1980.
Selected Stories.   1982; as *The Coca Cola Kid: Selected Stories,*   1985.
Room Service: Comic Writings.   1985.
Forty-Seventeen.   1988.
Lateshows.   1990.

Plays

Screenplays: *Between Wars,* 1974; *The Disappearance of Azaria Chamberlain,* 1984; *Conference-ville,* 1984; *The Coca Cola Kid,* 1985; *The Everlasting Secret Family,* 1988.

Television Plays: *Conference-ville,* 1984; *The Disappearance of Azaria Chamberlain,* 1984; *Time's Raging,* 1985.

Other

Editor, *Coast to Coast.*   1973.
Editor, *Days of Wine and Rage.*   1980.
Editor, *The State of the Art: The Mood of Contemporary Australia in Short Stories.*   1983.
Editor, *A Steele Rudd Selection: The Best Dad and Dave Stories, with Other Rudd Classics.*   1986.

Critical Studies: "The Short Stories of Wilding and Moorhouse" by Carl Harrison-Ford, in *Southerly* 33, 1974; "Frank Moorhouse's Discontinuities" by D. Anderson, in *Southerly* 35, 1975; "Some Developments in Short Fiction 1969–80" by Bruce Clunies Ross, in *Australian Literary Studies* 10 (3), 1981; "Moorhouse: A Retrospective" by Brian Kiernan, in *Modern Fiction Studies* 27 (1), 1981; interview in *Sideways from the Page* edited by J. Davidson, 1983; "The Thinker from the Bush" by Humphrey McQueen, in *Gallipoli to Petroiv,* 1984; "Form and Meaning in the Short Stories of Moorhouse" by C. Kanaganayakam, in *World Literature Written in English* 25 (1), 1985; Interview by Candida Baker, in *Yacker 3: Australian Writers Talk About Their Work,* 1989; "The Short Story Cycles of Moorhouse" by Gay Raines, in *Australian Literary Studies* 14, 1990.

* * *

Frank Moorhouse is arguably the most influential post-World War II writer of short fiction in Australia. His experiments with the genre have given vitality and relevance to the short story and he is one of its strongest advocates.

Moorhouse has a special interest in the hints and clues that short fiction can provide on the changing myths of region or nation. His main focus is not on the Australian bush legend but on the evolving social styles and outlooks of an urban generation that he, as a country boy, had joined in the mid-1960's when he moved from the New South Wales south coast to Australia's largest city, Sydney. Moorhouse's various fictional or semi-fictional representations of the inner-city suburb of Balmain have given it a place in the national literary consciousness, reinforced by the work there (especially in short fiction) of Michael Wilding, Peter Carey, and Murray Bail.

Moorhouse's work as a journalist and editor, both in country towns and the city, contributed to his literary style and his view of short fiction as a way of exposing truths about a society and its subcultures. Literary influences on Moorhouse are difficult to discern, but some of his early work especially parallels the concerns of Tom Wolfe and the New Journalists of the 1960's and 1970's. Hemingway may be an earlier influence. Moorhouse is not a spinner of timeless fables or a Borgesian puzzle-maker. Rather, he is an artful renovator of realism, constructing his tales from the bric à brac of contemporary life—images, slogans, headlines, and remembered conversations, highlighting the emotions and moral dilemmas of his generation.

In his first volume *Futility and Other Animals*, Moorhouse presents himself as an ironic chronicler of the "urban tribes" of young Australians experimenting with new lifestyles in the late 1960's. This first book, like Moorhouse's next two, is sub-titled "a discontinuous narrative," indicating his attempt to link stories loosely by various means, including location, theme and character. Later, the practice of linking (or even repeating) stories across different volumes contributes to a view of his work as a combination of autobiography and reportage, circling (or cycling) around certain key obsessions and desires. Gay Raines has placed Moorhouse's books in a wider literary history by calling them short short story cycles and linking them with the work of Sherwood Anderson, James Joyce, William Faulkner, and J.D. Salinger.

One of Moorhouse's recurrent topics is the influence of American styles and attitudes on contemporary Australians. In his second volume, *The Americans, Baby*, his urban independents are more swayed in their sex, drug-taking, protest marches, and communes than they know. The ironic, observant narrator in "The American Poet's Visit" is more independent than his confreres when he contemplates, in a semi-drunken state, the fate of his nation: "Actually we're Anglo-American. A composite mimic culture. Miserable shits." Yet why should not Australians constitute "a remarkably rich synthesis," he reflects resiliently. In other stories, American corporate institutions such as Coca-Cola, Rotary and the *Reader's Digest* are shown to enter the common discourse of Australians, achieving a distinctive inflection and reverberations in the "new" country.

Moorhouse's short fiction may be seen as a species of dialogue. As the author has himself remarked, his work comprises "dialogues with gender, with the notion of 'commitment', with nationality, with self—and with form." His work has been criticized for lacking moral passion, but Moorhouse's approach is subtle, various, and clever in a mode of truth-telling that strips the illusions from cherished assumptions and beliefs. Humour is a major weapon in this campaign, which resists authoritarianism in all its forms. Consistent with this outlook, Moorhouse resists the role of authoritarian author, preferring those kinds of short fiction that are "an arrangement of fragments within a personal field, which have a carefully judged incompletion." Moorhouse's apparently autobiographical persona nevertheless achieves a persuasive presence in many of his stories.

Screenwriting has been an important complementary activity to Moorhouse's short fiction and an interaction of techniques is evident. His use of "time-frame traps," cross-cutting of images, and compressed dialogue are elements of this. In *The Electrical Experience* a principal focus is the changing technologies of small-town Australia in the inter-war years, but the wireless and refrigerator are only precursors to the post-war invasion of film and video technology. *Conference-ville* holds up for ironic inspection the principal roadshow of our times—the conference or congress. Here, as elsewhere in society, the video-camera and the interview are integral, even determining elements of behaviour.

Moorhouse's short stories continually scrutinise the fissures between private and public cultures. In a typically humorous, dialogic story of the 1970's, "The Commune Does Not Want You," Moorhouse's first person narrator is driven to ask: "Is there a commune for people who do not fit very well into communes?" This question reverberates through the volume *The Everlasting Secret Family*, which interrogates the private and public cultures of homosexuality: the strength of community here, it is suggested, is in its secrecy.

Moorhouse's most powerful scrutiny of personal behaviour is relation to public expectations occurs in his ninth volume, *Forty-Seventeen*. The stories in this volume revolve around a love-affair that commences between a 40-year-old man and a 17-year-old schoolgirl in Australia and proceeds discontinuously across a number of nations for some years. Fascinated by ageing and the desires and expectations of different generations, Moorhouse continually interrogates the romance genre as he questions the possibilities of erotic and emotional satisfaction. In Moorhouse, the private life is always linked to a wider public life. Thus the opening piece in *Forty-Seventeen*, "Buenaventura Durruti's Funeral" reveals the narrator's personal canons of anarchism and libertarianism as being linked to his reading about the Spanish anarchist's life and death and films by Bunuel and Antonioni. When the secret romance, culminating in a rendezvous of the lovers in Madrid, seems suddenly possible, it is aborted by a postcard from the girl, who says she has fallen in love and will marry someone else. Nevertheless, the remembered romance flares recurrently through the book, providing a counterpoint to the narrator's more frequent state of "numbed control."

Frank Moorhouse has travelled widely in the 1980's and 1990's. The literary, social, and political styles which he now entertains are from Europe, Asia, and North America, as well as Australia. He has found a receptive audience in France. His hard-edged tales of mystery and romance continue to probe the taboos of personal and social experience.

—Bruce Bennett

MORAVIA, Alberto. Pseudonym for Alberto Pincherle. Italian. Born in Rome, 28 November 1907. Educated at home; received high school equivalency diploma 1967. Contracted tuberculosis in 1916 and spent much time in sanatoriums. Married 1) Elsa Morante in 1941 (divorced 1962; died 1985); 2) Dacia Maraini in 1963; 3) Carmen Llera in 1986. Foreign correspondent, *La Stampa*, Milan, and *Gazzetta del Popolo*, Turin, in the 1930's; film critic, *La Nuova Europa*, 1944–46; editor, with Alberto Carocci, *Nuovi Argomenti*, Milan, from 1953; film critic, *L'Espresso*, Milan, from 1955; State Department lecturer in the United States, 1955. President, International P.E.N., 1959. Recipient: Corriere Lombardo prize, 1945; Strega prize, 1952; Marzotto prize, 1954; Viareggio prize, 1961. Honorary Member, American Academy; Chevalier, 1952, and Commander, 1984, Legion of Honor (France). *Died 26 September 1990.*

PUBLICATIONS

Short Stories

L'epidemia: Racconti surrealistici e satirici.   1944.
L'amore coniugale e altri racconti.   1949; selection as *Conjugal Love*, 1951; in *Five Novels*, 1955.
Two Adolescents: The Stories of Agostino and Luca (includes *Agostino* and *Disobedience*).   1950.
I racconti.   1952; selections as *Bitter Honeymoon and Other Stories*, 1954; and *The Wayward Wife and Other Stories*, 1960.
Racconti romani.   1954; translated in part as *Roman Tales*, 1956.
Nuovi racconti romani.   1959; selection as *More Roman Tales*, 1963.
L'automa.   1963; as *The Fetish and Other Stories*, 1964.
Una cosa è una cosa.   1967; selection as *Command and I Will Obey You*, 1969.
Il paradiso.   1970; as *Paradise and Other Stories*, 1971; as *Bought and Sold*, 1973.
Io e lui.   1971; as *Two: A Phallic Novel*, 1972; as *The Two of Us*, 1972.
Un'altra vita.   1973; as *Lady Godiva and Other Stories*, 1975.

Boh!   1976; as *The Voice of the Sea and Other Stories*, 1978.
La cosa e altri racconti.   1983; as *Erotic Tales*, 1986.
La villa del venerdì; e altri racconti.   1990; as *The Friday Villa*, 1990.

Novels

Gli indifferenti.   1929; as *The Indifferent Ones*, 1932; as *The Time of Indifference*, 1953.
Le ambizioni sbagliate.   1935; as *The Wheel of Fortune*, 1937; as *Mistaken Ambitions*, 1955.
La bella vita.   1935.
L'imbroglio.   1937.
I sogni del pigro.   1940.
La mascherata.   1941; as *The Fancy Dress Party*, 1947.
L'amante infelice.   1943.
Agostino.   1944; translated as *Agostino*, 1947.
Due cortigiane; Serata di Don Giovanni.   1945.
La romana.   1947; as *The Woman of Rome*, 1949.
La disubbidienza.   1948; as *Disobedience*, 1950.
Il conformista.   1951; as *The Conformist*, 1951.
Il disprezzo.   1954; as *A Ghost at Noon*, 1955.
Five Novels.   1955.
La ciociara.   1957; as *Two Women*, 1958.
La noia.   1960; as *The Empty Canvas*, 1961.
Cortigiana stanca.   1965.
L'attenzione.   1965; as *The Lie*, 1966.
La vita interiore.   1978; as *Time of Desecration*, 1980.
1934.   1982; translated as *1934*, 1983.
Storie della preistoria Favole.   1983.
L'uomo che guarda.   1985; as *The Voyuer*, 1986.

Plays

Gli indifferenti, with Luigi Squarzini, from the novel by Moravia (produced 1948).   In *Sipario*, 1948.
Il provino (produced 1955).
Non approfondire (produced 1957).
Teatro (includes *Beatrice Cenci* and *La mascherata*, from his own novel).   1958; *Beatrice Cenci* (in English), 1965.
Il mondo è quello che è (produced 1966).   1966.
Il dio Kurt (produced 1969).   1968.
La vita è gioco (produced 1970).   1969.

Screenplays: *Un colpo di pistola*, 1941; *Zazà*, 1942; *Ultimo incontro*, 1951; *Sensualità*, 1951; *Tempi nostri*, 1952; *La provinciale (The Wayward Wife)*, 1952; *Villa Borghese*, 1953; *La donna del Fiume*, 1954; *La romana (The Woman of Rome)*, 1955; *Racconti romani (Roman Tales)*, 1956; *Racconti d'estate (Love on the Riviera)*, 1958; *I delfini (The Dauphins)*, 1960; *La giornata balorda (From a Roman Balcony)*, 1960; *Una domenica d'estate*, 1961; *Agostino*, 1962; *Ieri oggi domani (Yesterday, Today, and Tomorrow)*, 1963; *Le ore nude*, 1964; *L'occhio selvaggio (The Wild Eye)*, 1967.

Other

La speranza: Ossia cristianesimo e comunismo.   1944.
Opere complete.   17 vols., 1952–67.
Un mese in U.R.S.S.   1958.
I moralisti moderni, with Elemire Zolla.   1960.
Women of Rome, photographs by Sam Waagenaar.   1960.
Un'idea dell'India.   1962.
Claudia Cardinale.   1963.

L'uomo come fine e altri saggi.   1964; as *Man as an End: A Defence of Humanism,* 1965.
La rivoluzione culturale in Cina ovvero il convitato di pietra. 1967; as *The Red Book and the Great Wall: An Impression of Mao's China,* 1968.
A quale tribù appartieni?   1972; as *Which Tribe Do You Belong To?,* 1974.
Al cinema: Centoquarantotto film d'autore.   1975.
La mutazione femminile: Conversazione con Moravia sulla donna, by Carla Ravaiola.   1975.
Intervista sullo scrittore scomodo, edited by Nello Ajello. 1978.
Quando Ba Lena era tanto piccola.   1978.
Cosma e i briganti.   1980.
Impegno controvoglia: Saggi, articoli, interviste, edited by Renzo Paris.   1980.
Lettere del Sahara.   1981.
La tempesta.   1984.
L'angelo dell'informazione e altri testi teatrali.   1986.
L'inverno nucleare, edited by Renzo Paris.   1986.
Opere, 1927–1947, edited by Geno Pampaloni.   1986.
Passeggiate africane (autobiography).   1987.
Il viaggio a Roma.   1988.
Opere, 1948–1968, edited by Enzo Siciliano.   1989.
La donna leopardo.   1991.

Editor, with Elemire Zolla, *Saggi italiani.*   1960.

*

Bibliography: *An Annotated Bibliography of Moravia Criticism in Italy and in the English-Speaking World (1929–1975)* by Ferdinando Alfonsi, 1976.

Critical Studies: *Moravia* by Giuliano Dego, 1966; *Three Italian Novelists* by Donald W. Heiney, 1968; *The Existentialism of Moravia* by Joan Ross and D. Freed, 1972; *Moravia* by Jane E. Cottrell, 1974; *Women as Object: Language and Gender in the Work of Moravia* by Sharon Wood, 1990.

*   *   *

The life and career of Alberto Moravia spanned some of the most turbulent years and events of recent Italian history. Novelist, short story writer, essayist, journalist and cultural observer, Moravia constantly engaged with the social, cultural, and political life of his country. While the experimentation in literature of recent decades makes Moravia's more gritty realism look a little dated, his best works offer an acute analytical insight into a society, and a class, in moral decay.

Moravia burst upon the literary scene in 1929, when he was barely 20 years old, with *Gli indifferenti,* a novel immediately perceived, if not consciously intended, as a violent social polemic against a decadent Italian bourgeoisie which provided fascism with its most fertile soil. The novel's attack on the bankrupt morality of the bourgeoisie, for whom sex and money had displaced any higher value, had inevitable political implications that went to the heart of the fledgling fascist state.

Moravia's writing continued to be dominated by the social and moral impact of fascism on the class he knew best, the bourgeoisie. After a brief period of experimentation with surrealism and political satire (*I sogni del pigro,* and *La mascherata*), he began writing in a realist, moralist mode in short stories such as "Inverno di malato" (1935), which drew on his own youth spent in a tuberculosis sanatorium, "L'amante infelice" (1943); and *Agostino,* a masterly short novel describing vividly an adolescent's emergence from innocence, the discovery of his mother's femininity, his initiation into sexuality by a group of urchins he meets at the seaside resort where he is on vacation. *La romana (The Woman of Rome)* is about the life of Adriana told from her own perspective, that of a working-class girl drawn into prostitution; her character is in stark contrast to the torbid morality of her middle-class clients. This perspective on the impotent middle classes is maintained in *La ciociara.* Based on Moravia's own experience when he was forced to flee Rome in 1943, when the city was taken over by the Nazis after the fall of Mussolini, the novel deals powerfully with the experience of war, the loss of innocence symbolised by a brutal rape. Compassion, the wisdom of experience, is the only way out of the moral quagmire of war and the selfishness and greed it generates. In *Il conformista (The Conformist)* Moravia addressed himself less to the drastic effects than to the psychosexual underpinning of allegiance to a specific ideology: Marcello, the protagonist, identifies himself with fascism in a desperate attempt to appear normal, only gradually realising that so-called normality consists precisely of perversion and aberration.

While writing these last novels, Moravia was also writing a large number of short stories, the *Racconti romani,* considered by some to be his best work, first published in 1954. They have been compared to the work of the Milanese Belli with their sense of historical and psychological authenticity, and their mixture of standard language and dialect. Here Moravia is not writing to demonstrate a thesis or a philosophical point, as he increasingly appeared to do in his later work, and the stories retain both freshness and spontaneity in their evocation of a lower middle-class Rome in the postwar years. Three later volumes of short stories, *Il paradiso (Paradise and Other Stories), Un'altra vita (Lady Godiva and Other Stories),* and *Boh! (The Voice of the Sea and Other Stories),* were collected from stories published in the *Corriere della Sera* in the 1950's and 1960's. These stories are all linked by their use of a first-person female narrator; if his dramatic characters are women, he has declared, it is because women live most dramatically the tensions and contradictions of the modern world. Many of the stories portray family life and marriage, which is seen as collective violence by society on the woman, or as a systematic means of exploitation. The role of mother is seen to be inconsistent with an autonomous female identity, and the other side of bourgeois marriage is prostitution. Women are constantly denied subjectivity and autonomy by the world of men and work. In search of their identity, they lose it.

Moravia's achievement was to probe and reveal the relationship between the economic, the erotic, and the political. While his narratives owed much intellectually to Freud and Marx, it is the dramatic events of 20th-century Italy, and the artist's response to the spiritual and material conflicts of the modern world, that form the heart of his work.

—Sharon Wood

MORI, Toshio. American. Born in Oakland, California, 20 March 1910. Graduated from Oakland High School. Interned with family, Topaz Relocation Center, Millard, Utah, during World War II: editor and contributor, *Trek, Topaz Camp* magazine. Worked in family nursery business. *Died in 1980.*

PUBLICATIONS

Short Stories

Yokohama, California.   1949.
The Chauvinist and Other Stories, edited by Hisaye Yamamoto.   1979.

Novel

Woman from Hiroshima.   1979.

*

Bibliography: in *Asian American Literature: An Annotated Bibliography* by King-Kok Cheung and Stan Yogi, 1988.

Critical Studies: "Mori's California Koans" by Margaret Bedrosian, in *Journal of the Society for the Study of the Multi-Ethnic Literature of the United States,* Summer 1988; "Short Stories Mori" by David R. Mayer, in *Fu Jen Studies: Literature and Linguistics* 21, 1988.

*   *   *

Originally published in 1949, Toshio Mori's *Yokohama, California* was hailed by Lawson Fusao Inada as "the first real Japanese American book." Mori indeed excels in the portrayal of the Japanese-American community in California in the early decades of this century. Most of his characters are immigrants and their children involved in agriculture and small business—farmers, nursery workers, and green grocers. In recounting the quiet lives and dreams of these decent and humane Japanese-Americans, the narrative voice remains patient, understated, and compassionate. Unlike John Okada's *No-No Boy* (1957), which is permeated with blind rage and self-hatred sparked by the internment of Japanese-Americans, Mori seldom dwells on his experience at the Topaz Relocation Center, devoting his stories instead to the ordinary people—their joy and aspiration, their pain and disillusionment.

However, Mori is neither a prolific nor a major writer. Many stories in *Yokohama, California* are no more than character sketches and throughout his career Mori continued to recycle his materials. The opening episodes of his novel *Woman From Hiroshima,* for instance, are derived almost verbatim from "Grandpa and the Promised Land," published on 25 December 1948 in *Pacific Citizen,* and from "Tomorrow Is Coming," the first story in *Yokohama, California.* What Mori does exceptionally well is the depiction of humaneness and warmth in seemingly unimpressive characters. In this sense, Mori greatly resembles Hisaye Yamamoto, a Japanese-American female writer, whose *Seventeen Syllables and Other Stories* (1988) is a collection of 15 short stories, some published as early as the late-1940's.

In Mori's collection, the narrator's gentle voice becomes the center, rippling outward to individuals, to families, and finally to the closely-knit community. Many vignettes of characters are indelibly etched in the reader's mind, all with a tinge of sadness. The savvy and hard-working newspaper boy in "Business at Eleven" is forced to move away from the network of clients he has established because of his mother's second marriage; the aging nursery worker in "The Chessman" collapses in his effort to prove his usefulness to keep up the murderous pace of a young colleague. But the most significant group of such unforgettable characters are dreamers. Mori seems to have reserved a tender spot in his heart for these failed idealists, all of whom are described with utmost sympathy and absolutely no cynicism. The protagonist in "Akira Yano" boldly travels to New York and finances the publication of his own collection of essays, only to sink into oblivion, like countless other young writers. In "The Seventh Street Philosopher" the philosopher expounds "The Apology of Living" to a nearly empty stadium, despite his invitation to a sizable Japanese-American community. The lover of flowers and truth in "Say It with Flowers" prefers losing his job to lying to customers about the freshness of flowers—a common practice in that profession. The self-anointed economic wizard in "The Finance over at Doi's" dreams about making it big on Wall Street, but he is left with little of his savings after the venture. All these dreamers appear slightly clownish and insane, yet all the more endearing because of their flaws.

The representation of the harmonious Japanese-American family is underpinned by two types of characters in Mori's stories. The idealized motherhood emerges in "My Mother Stood on Her Head" and "The Woman Who Makes Swell Doughnuts." The former recounts how a housewife continues to patronize a vegetable vender who possibly is taking advantage of her kindness. The latter ennobles womanhood even further by turning the woman's doughnuts into a symbol for the nurturing, self-sacrificing femininity. Mori also deals with the role of fathers as the perfect patriarchs. The happy family of "Nodas in America" sustains itself through the care and love of the father. The uncle in "The Six Rows of Pompons" wisely channels the energy of his unruly nephew into the tending of pompons, believing that the waste of six rows of his garden is worthwhile "till he [the nephew] comes to his senses." Even sibling rivalry in "The Brothers" is looked upon by the father of the story as part of the elation of life.

The Japanese-American community is delineated with both sorrow and optimism. "The End of the Line" introduces an ever-shrinking ethnic group where many *Issei,* first-generation Japanese-Americans, have returned to Japan. But in "Lil' Yokohama," the national pastime of baseball is embraced wholeheartedly. With each district of this community rooting for its team, Mori demonstrates well the level of assimilation and Americanization of Japanese-Americans, yet subtly points out the discrimination still in existence—these teams compete with each other, never with teams of Caucasian players. In fact, there are very few references to racism or Japanese-American's identity problem, perhaps with the mild exception of "Slanted-Eyed Americans," on the attack of Pearl Harbor. This ought to be viewed less as an inadequacy than as Mori's style marked by gentleness and sensitivity in a world of fury.

The Chauvinist and Other Stories, published just months before he died, is Mori's only other volume. It collects 20 of his several hundred stories.

—Sheng-mei Ma

———

MORRISON, John (Gordon). Australian. Born in Sunderland, England, 29 January 1904. Educated at Valley Road School, Sunderland. Married 1) Frances Morrison in 1928 (died), one son, one daughter 2) Rachel Gordon in 1969. Moved to Australia in 1923; worked as bush worker, 1923–28, gardener, wharfie, 1928-38; full-time writer. Recipient: Commonwealth Literary Fund fellowship, 1947, 1949; Australian Literature Society gold medal, 1962; Patrick White award, 1986. Lives in St. Kilda, Victoria.

PUBLICATIONS

Short Stories

Sailors Belong Ships.   1947.
Black Cargo.   1955.
Twenty-Three.   1962.
Selected Stories.   1972.
Australian by Choice.   1973.
North Wind.   1982.
Stories of the Waterfront.   1984.
This Freedom.   1985.
Best Stories.   1986.

Novels

The Creeping City.   1949.
Port of Call.   1950.

*

Critical Studies: "Three Realists in Search of Reality" by David Martin, in *Meanjin* 18, 1959; "The Short Stories of Morrison" by A.A. Phillips, in *Overland* 58, 1974.

*   *   *

Born in England in 1904, John Morrison travelled to Australia in 1923, returned home briefly but then came out again to Australia in 1928, and has lived there since, like the title of one of his books, *Australian by Choice*. He began writing when he was only 15 years old but did not begin to publish until he was in his early 30's.

Although he wrote two novels, Morrison is known as the author of many fine stories, written largely in a social realist mode. His collections are: *Sailors Belong Ships, Black Cargo, 23, Selected Stories*, and *Australian by Choice*. During the 1980's Penguin Australia reprinted most of his stories under the titles *North Wind, Stories of the Waterfront, This Freedom*, and the very misleadingly titled *The Best Short Stories of John Morrison*, which is virtually a reprint of *North Wind*. In 1986 Morrison won the Patrick White award for writers of distinction.

Morrison's stories are best considered not according to when they were written but to the period of his life with which they deal; the two are often not the same. There are

his experiences in the outback when he first arrived in Australia and later when he returned, as reflected in "The Prophet of Pandaloo," set in 1924. In this story, one of Morrison's rare departures from strict realism, a tramp-prophet, a kind of bush seer, becomes the catalyst for an almost miraculously sudden series of changes on an outback station.

Then there is his struggle as a young married man during the Depression years and after, for instance, in perhaps his most famous story, "Christ, the Devil and the Lunatic." There is the fierce pride he took, as a dedicated Communist for many years, in unionism, reflected in stories such as "Lena" and "The Ticket." Related to this is his work during the 1940's as a "wharfie" (longshoreman), ranging from the warm optimism of "The Welcome" to the cold rage of "The Compound" which details the exploitation of the workers by their bosses in graphic terms. There are stories based on Morrison's later work as a gardener, such as the delightfully ironic "To Margaret," in which a bitter father breaks up a love affair between his daughter Margaret and a gardener named Hans. The narrator-gardener who replaces Hans refuses to obey his employer's instructions to uproot the linaria seedlings, lovingly arranged to spell "To Margaret." After he has been fired, he has his revenge: he leaves the same message in the viburnums.

There are the so-called "commuter" stories, pieces Morrison worked up from careful observation of and conversation with his fellow passengers on trains to and from Melbourne. An example is "The Blind Man's Story," in which a man explains to the narrator how he is happy he has become blind because his wife, who had a martyr complex, has changed completely towards him, now that she has a real cross to bear. The story ends with the narrator's uncharacteristically cold observation about "how little of life some men are driven to settle for." Finally, there are a number of stories based on the theme of the consequences to friendship when two men win a lottery on a shared ticket.

Schematic as they can sometimes be, the lottery stories are significant because they reveal most starkly the strongly ethical nature of Morrison's vision. His stories are preoccupied with that moment in an individual's life when the decision he makes (it is usually a "he" and, in the title of one of his stories, he writes mostly about "a man's world"), will reveal what kind of man he is, to what he degree he will stand by his principles or compromise them.

Although the choice is a crucial one in many stories, and is usually presented through the balanced and sympathetic view of a first person narrator who remains outside the centre of the action, it comes out most clearly in a powerful story called "The Children." Here a man delays rescuing a group of school children in order to fetch his own from out of a bush fire; he genuinely believes he has time to go back for the others. However, they perish and, in the ultimate irony, it turns out that his own would have been safe anyway. The question the agonised and ostracised man asks the sympathetic reporter who is interviewing him is one that comes up in some form or other in most of Morrison's stories: "Supposing it had been you . . . what would you have done?"

The question of moral choice is closely related to that of freedom. In "The Busting of Rory O'Mahony," for instance, Rory finally achieves the freedom he wants by leaving his wife and setting out on the road, thus destroying her happiness. Rory feels compromised by his family: "I got everything a man wants—except a bit of freedom," he says, but although the narrator even-handedly stresses the wife's complacency, the reader is left with the sense that O'Mahony's action was less than admirable. "This Freedom" is virtually a variation on the same theme, with Joe Abbs discovering after the death of his wife that he is able to pursue the kind of shiftless, irresponsible life that Rory desires. The concept of freedom in both cases is a masculine one, a flight from domesticity.

Morrison's own personality and vision are probably exemplified in the closing statement of "The Welcome": "Human decency will always come to the top if it gets even the ghost of a chance. There's mountains of evidence to prove it." Though the stories are in some ways limited, their strength lies in the nicely laconic, under-stated style, the scrupulously accurate rendering of dialogue, and the subtle use of detail to illuminate character, as here: "Two seamen who have been uptown for a lunch-hour drink push through to get off at the gasworks' berth. They're covered with coal-dust just as they left the stokehold, and you can't help noticing how carefully they avoid brushing against a man who is wearing a good grey suit." There is a lovely unaffected naturalness about the best of the stories that conceals the art.

—Laurie Clancy

MPHAHLELE, Es'kia (Ezekiel Mphahlele). South African. Born in Pretoria, 17 December 1919. Educated at St. Peter's Secondary School, Johannesburg; Adam's College, Natal, 1939–40; University of South Africa, Pretoria, 1946–49, 1953–54, 1956, B.A. (honours) 1949, M.A. in English 1956; University of Denver, 1966–68, Ph.D. in English 1968. Married Rebecca Mochadibane in 1945; five children. Clerk in institution for the blind, 1941–45; English and Afrikaans teacher, Orlando High School, Johannesburg, 1945–52; lecturer in English literature, University of Ibadan, Nigeria, 1957–61; director of African Programmes, International Association for Cultural Freedom, Paris, 1961–63; director, Chemchemi Creative Centre, Nairobi, Kenya, 1963–65; lecturer, University College, Nairobi, 1965–66; senior lecturer in English, University of Zambia, Lusaka, 1968–70; associate professor of English, University of Denver, 1970–74; professor of English, University of Pennsylvania, Philadelphia, 1974–77; inspector of Education, Lebowa, Transvaal, 1978–79; professor of African literature, University of the Witwatersrand, Johannesburg, 1979–87; director of a community education project in Soweto for the Council for Black Education and Research, from 1987. Fiction editor, *Drum,* Johannesburg, 1955–57; editor, *Black Orpheus,* Ibadan, 1960–66, and *Journal of New African Literature and the Arts.* D.Litt.: University of Natal, Durban; Rhodes University, Grahamstown; L.H.D.: University of Pennsylvania. Lives in Johannesburg.

PUBLICATIONS

Short Stories

Man Must Live and Other Stories. 1947.
The Living and Dead and Other Stories. 1961.
In Corner B and Other Stories. 1967.
The Unbroken Song: Selected Writings of Es'kia Mphahlele (includes verse). 1981.

Renewal Time (includes essays). 1988.

Novels

The Wanderers. 1971.
Chirundu. 1979.

Other

Down Second Avenue (autobiography). 1959.
The African Image (essays). 1962; revised edition, 1974.
The Role of Education and Culture in Developing African Countries. 1965.
A Guide to Creative Writing. 1966.
Voices in the Whirlwind and Other Essays. 1972.
Let's Write a Novel. 1981.
Bury Me at the Marketplace: Selected Letters of Es'kia Mphahlele 1943–1980. edited by N. Chabani Manganyi. 1984.
Father Come Home (for children). 1984.
Afrika My Music: An Autobiography 1957–1983. 1984.
Let's Talk Writing: Prose [Poetry]. 2 vols., 1986.
Poetry and Humanism: Oral Beginnings (lecture). 1986.

Editor, with Ellis Komey, *Modern African Stories.* 1964.
Editor, *African Writing Today.* 1967.

*

Critical Studies: *Seven African Writers,* 1962, and *The Chosen Tongue,* 1969, both by Gerald Moore; "The South African Short Story," by Mphahlele in *Kenyon Review,* 1969; *Mphahlele* by Ursula A. Barnett, 1976; "South African History, Politics and Literature: Mphahlele's *Down Second Avenue* and Rive's *Emergency*" by O O. Obuke, in *African Literature Today* 10, 1979; *Exiles and Homecomings: A Biography of Mphahlele* by N. Chabani Manganyi, 1983.

* * *

The short stories published by Ezekial (Es'kia) Mphahlele between 1946 and 1967 raise issues inherent in the production of literature by black South Africans in the early years of grand apartheid. The short story was a medium of necessity rather than choice to a writer whose night studies and political involvement precluded any longer genre. For this reason, his stories do not fit organically into the traditional mould. Some, like "Mrs. Plum" or "Grieg on a Stolen Piano," verge on the novella. In others, notably "Man Must Live," "Out, Brief Candle," and "Unwritten Episodes," the temporal span and range of settings sit uneasily in a condensed framework.

Mphahlele's themes and plots came increasingly to reflect South African realities—dispossession, the effects of apartheid on ordinary existence, racial conflict, the shaping of destinies by oppressive laws—and sharper and more focussed writing was the result of this shift. However, Mphahlele has stated that in his early stories, he was interested "in people, in their own ghetto life and their own little dramas and tragedies, which would not necessarily have to do with the racial issue."

His first volume of stories, *Man Must Live,* concentrates almost exclusively on life in black townships or rural settlements. These youthful stories are crudely structured and episodic. Mphahlele himself described the publication as a clumsy piece of writing.

Nevertheless, the title story introduces the theme and pattern of much of Mphahlele's work: the imperative of survival seen in the context of an individual odyssey. Khalima Zungu's rise (through labour as opposed to study) to a position in the railway police, and his fall from grace after marrying a wealthy, educated woman, exemplify Mphahlele's preoccupation with life's ironies. Zungu's aptitude for manual labour (which set him on the road to success) becomes his sole means of survival when he is abandoned by his wife and adopted family.

A more heavy-handed irony is evident in "Unwritten Episodes," a tale of a young couple who fall in love only to discover they are siblings, the final twist emerging when this revelation is shown to be false. "Out, Brief Candle" reveals how a childhood taunt, repeated in adulthood, leads to a murder. Though not directly autobiographical, as indeed much of Mphahlele's most representative and acclaimed work was to be, there is in these early attempts a restlessness and rootlessness characteristic of the author's life, and of the lives of dispossessed people in general.

The next phase of Mphahlele's story writing career was the result of his position as a journalist on the famous black periodical, *Drum*. Mphahlele claims that in the *Drum* stories (some of which appeared in his later collections), he "put the ghetto people aside, by themselves, acting out their dramas but at the same time implying the political pressure over them. Thus a note of protest entered his fiction at this point.

The anomalies of black urban existence emerge in "Lesane," where a wedding provides an opportunity for examining the pressures exerted by racist bureaucracy on individual guests. In a brilliant exposé of the absurdity of the system, we encounter Ma-Ntoi, "who came from a mining town in the Free state from which she had been expelled because she couldn't own a house as she was a widow." Other guests similarly are afflicted by apartheid legislation.

Both "Blind Alley" and "Across the Down Stream" (later reprinted as "The Coffee-Cart Girl") set a love-triangle against the backdrop of political demonstration, and the underlying warning of these stories is that there can be no normal relationships in an abnormal society. Simple romantic tales are not possible since the ties between people are jeopardized by a repressive regime. In "Blind Alley," Ditsi sees the irony of agitating for more housing when his political activities have sent his wife into another man's arms and led to his own arrest, and realizes the sheer hopelessness of "wanting a descent house with no home to house."

The Living and Dead introduces white characters for the first time, and dwells at some length upon racial conflict. The author's disillusionment and bitterness are detectable in the title story, where the character of the white boss, Stoffel Visser (working on a report "on kaffir servants in the suburbs") is held up to ridicule and finally dismissed with revulsion. Visser's black servant, Jackson, who "served him with the devotion of a trained animal," is injured, and, simultaneously, a letter from his impoverished father falls into his employer's hands. Visser is momentarily tempted to treat his servant with kindness, but concludes: "Better continue treating him as a name, not as a human being." "The Master of Doornvlei" examines a similar relationship between a farmer and his foreman. Once again the concluding reflection of the master is indicative of the economic basis of entrenched racism: "And then he was glad. He had got rid of yet another threat to his authority." Mphahlele's deep-seated resentment against the nation that enslaved his people must be seen against the background of the master-servant relationship that was not just material for stories but a living reality. Admitting his tendency to caricature the white man, Mphahlele said: "I will still enjoy engineering my own poetic justice against him."

In Corner B contains stories from earlier collections and publications, as well as two of Mphahlele's most successful stories, "A Point of Identity," and "Mrs. Plum." The first of these traces the destructive effects of the infamous Population Registration Act, according to which people had to be racially classified, often by arbitrary means: "a comb was put into their hair; if it fell out, they must have straight or curly hair and so one condition was fulfilled." Karl Almeida, the product of mixed parentage, lives contentedly in a Pretoria township with his African wife until he succumbs to the convenience of being classified "coloured" as opposed to "black." The subsequent association of sickness and death with the iniquitous policy of racial segregation enriches the story and imbues it with a painful but salutary logic.

Ezekial Mphahlele described "Mrs. Plum" as "the best thing" he "ever pulled off." The story's point of view (a black servant recounts the history of her relationship with her employer, Mrs. Plum) is its strongest and most convincing feature. The liberal Mrs. Plum, who is even briefly incarcerated for her refusal to permit the police to investigate past offences on her property, is subtly exposed as an ignorant, self-deluding, self-aggrandizing, hypocritical individual. This is achieved through Karabo's detached observation of her employer's relationship with her two pet dogs, who are accorded a higher status than the servants she patronizes. At the climax of the story, Karabo's feelings of revulsion are dramatically conveyed to the reader when she peeps through a keyhole and witnesses her mistress performing a sexual act with the pampered "gentlemen," the dogs Monty and Malan.

Mrs. Plum's well-meaning efforts to educate Karabo backfire; as her refrain ("I learned. I grew up") indicates, Karabo's education heightens her awareness of her mistress's foibles. She leaves Mrs. Plum's employment after this self-appointed liberal defender of the oppressed African refuses to grant her compassionate leave. Mrs. Plum is eventually forced to negotiate with Karabo, who returns on her own terms.

"Mrs. Plum" is a success not only in its exposé of the hypocrisy of white liberals, but in its sophisticated interweaving of social injustice (migratory labour, pass laws) with the real behind-the-scenes drama of black existence in white suburbs. The confidence that this achievement gave Mphahlele enabled him to embark on the longer autobiographical writings that mark the pinnacle of his literary career.

—Finuala Dowling

MUNRO, Alice (Anne, née Laidlaw). Canadian. Born in Wingham, Ontario, 10 July 1931. Educated at Wingham public schools; University of Western Ontario, London, 1949–51. Married 1) James Armstrong Munro in 1951 (separated 1972; divorced 1976), three daughters; 2) Gerald Fremlin in 1976. Lived in Vancouver, 1951–63, Victoria, British Columbia, 1963–71, London, Ontario, 1972–75, and Clinton, Ontario, from 1976; artist-in-residence, University of Western Ontario, 1974–75, and University of British Columbia, Vancouver, 1980. Recipient: Governor-General's award, 1969, 1978, 1987; Great Lakes Colleges Association award, 1974; Province of Ontario award, 1974; Canada-Australia literary prize, 1978. D.Litt.: University of Western Ontario, 1976.

PUBLICATIONS

Short Stories

Dance of the Happy Shades.   1968.
Something I've Been Meaning to Tell You: Thirteen Stories.
    1974.
Who Do You Think You Are?   1978; as *The Beggar Maid:
    Stories of Flo and Rose,* 1979.
The Moons of Jupiter.   1982.
The Progress of Love.   1986.
Friend of My Youth   1990.

Novel

Lives of Girls and Women.   1971.

Plays

How I Met My Husband (televised 1974).   In *The Play's
    the Thing,* edited by Tony Gifford, 1976.

Television Plays: *A Trip to the Coast,* 1973; *How I Met My
Husband,* 1974; *1847: The Irish* (*The Newcomers* series),
1978.

*

Bibliography: by Robert Thacker, in *The Annotated Bibliography of Canada's Major Authors 5* edited by Robert Lecker and Jack David, 1984.

Critical Studies: *The Art of Munro: Saying the Unsayable* edited by Judith Miller, 1984; *Probable Fictions: Munro's Narrative Acts* edited by Louis K. MacKendrick, 1984; *Munro and Her Works* by Hallvard Dahlie, 1985; *Munro: Paradox and Parallel* by W.R. Martin, 1987; *Controlling the Uncontrollable: The Fiction of Munro* by Ildiko de Papp, 1989.

*   *   *

Given the vast size of Canada, the overbearing extremities of its climate, and the great variety of its habitats, from the lushly rain-forested mountains of British Columbia to the broad semi-desert plains of its prairie provinces, it would be surprising if *place* did not play a great role in its fiction and poetry alike. And indeed it does, to such an extent that *geo-historical* has been accepted as a definition of much recent Canadian writing, from the Maritimes to the Pacific Coast.

It is a definition that is peculiarly fitting since the various patterns of settlement in Canada have combined with the habitat to produce a series of relatively autonomous cultures that affect both literature and art. There is indeed a Québec society, reinforced in this case by the dominance of the French language, but there are also recognizably distinct West Coast and Prairie, Maritime, and Newfoundland societies. And, though Ontario is often thought of as the quintessence of a faceless, generalized Canada, one of the most distinct of the country's local traditions is in fact that of the old Loyalist areas of the central province. Poets like James Reaney and Al Purdy have celebrated the rise and fall of its agrarian society since the early days of the 19th century. And a wide range of writers of fiction and of prose memoirs has also flourished in the rich loam of Ontario's agrarian past and its industrial present. Among them, a fine short story writer and a good novelist, is Alice Munro, who has been one of the region's—and of the country's—most important writers for a long generation since the 1960's.

There is nothing accidental in this juxtaposition of fiction and prose memoirs in Munro's case, for her writing has an extraordinary dual quality. It is fiction in the classic sense of imaginatively exploring character and the conflicts and contradictions to which it gives rise, and thus creating an imagined society, a world of the mind whose inhabitants attract or repel us, and in whose relationships we become as emotionally involved as we might in those of our neighbours. Yet, at the same time, Munro in her stories and novels is offering the portrait of a rural Protestant society the like of which existed and drew to an end during her lifetime. Critics have speculated on how much in fiction, and particularly of the romantic realist kind that Munro offers us, where the lyrical evocation of the background can be as important as the shrewdly plotted psychology, we are dealing with a kind of authenticity that depends on memory and experience. In fact, as Munro's work shows, the genres of autobiography and fiction run more closely together than the protagonists of inventiveness as a criterion appear to realize.

Alice Munro's first book, a collection of short stories, appeared in 1968, but she was already well known in literary circles by this time because her stories had been produced on Canadian Broadcasting Corporation programmes like *Anthology* and in magazines like *Tamarack Review,* both of which were directed by Robert Weaver. Weaver indeed can be regarded as a kind of unofficial impresario for Munro, as he was for the short story as a whole in Canada, providing places to be read and heard and even offering a little money for writers at a time when neither publishers nor editors were generally favourable to short fiction.

Munro's earliest volume, *Dance of the Happy Shades,* won her a Governor-General's award and critical praise in 1968, and has been followed by a succession of other collections of stories, from *Something I've Been Meaning To Tell You,* through *The Moons of Jupiter* (perhaps her finest group of stories), to *Friend of My Youth.*

Twice she has ventured into larger and longer forms. *Lives of Girls and Women* is presented as a novel and such, dealing as it does with the development of a woman striving to escape from a small-town upbringing, it is. Yet here Munro's ability as a short story writer has really held her back, for she takes a whole novel to develop a character no more complex or interesting than those of her short pieces, and the effort to keep up an interest and maintain a structure tends to diffuse the novel's impact and urgency. She returned halfway to the novel form in *Who Do You Think You Are?,* a group of stories centering on a single character—Rose—and on various aspects of her attempt to change from a country girl to an urban woman.

The matter of "Who?" raised in the title and indeed in the substance of this work, brings up the question of ultimate identity which faces so many of the girls and young women who are the principal characters of Munro's stories. They are often introduced living in their original environment, which is that of a traditional, closely knit rural society barely a generation away from the pioneer age and founded on a mutual recognition of everyone's place in the community, including even the recognized eccentrics. The price of their rebellion is adaptation to a different social model in which the conflicts of a more natural past are muted, but in which seeking one's self may lead to a surrender to anonymity, the fate of so many of the characters of whom Munro writes with such clear emotional insight and in such limpid prose.

—George Woodcock

See the essays on "How I Met My Husband" and "Royal Beatings."

_____

MUNRO, Hector Hugh.   See SAKI.

_____

MUSIL, Robert. Austrian. Born in Klagenfurt, 6 November 1880. Educated at a school in Steyr; military school in Eisenstadt, 1892–94, and in Mährisch-Weisskirchen, 1895–98; studied engineering at Technische Nochschule, Brno, 1898–1901; studied philosophy, University of Berlin, 1903–05, Ph.D. 1908. Military service: 1901–02; served in Austrian army, 1914–16; hospitalized, 1916, then editor of army newspaper, 1916–18; bronze cross. Married Martha Marcovaldi in 1911. Engineer in Stuttgart, 1902–03; in Berlin until 1911; archivist, 1911–13; editor, *Die neue Rundschau,* Berlin, 1914; in press section of Office of Foreign Affairs, Vienna, 1919–20, and consultant to Defense Ministry, 1920–23; then freelance writer: in Berlin, 1931–33, Vienna, 1933–38, and Switzerland, 1938–42. Recipient: Kleist prize, 1923; City of Vienna prize, 1924. *Died 15 April 1942.*

PUBLICATIONS

Collections

Gesammelte Werke, edited by Adolf Frisé.   3 vols., 1952–57; revised edition,   2 vols., 1978.

Short Stories

Die Verwirrungen des Zöglings Törless (novella).   1906; as *Young Törless,* 1955.
Vereinigungen.   1911; as *Unions,* 1965.
Drei Frauen (includes "Grigia"; "Die Portugiesin," and "Tonka").   1924; as *Three Women,* 1965; as *Tonka and Other Stories* (also includes translation of *Vereinigungen*), 1965.

Novel

Der Mann ohne Eigenschaften, completed by Martha Musil.   3 vols., 1930–43; edited by Adolf Frisé, 1952, revised edition, 1965; as *The Man without Qualities,*   3 vols., 1953–60.

Plays

Die Schwärmer.   1921; as *The Enthusiasts,* 1982.
Vinzenz und die Freundin bedeutender Männer.   1923.

Other

Das hilflose Europa.   1922.
Nachlass zu Lebzeiten.   1936; as *Posthumous Papers of a Living Author,* 1987.
Theater: Kritisches und Theoretisches, edited by Marie-Louise Roth.   1965.
Der Deutsche Mensch als Symptom, edited by Karl Corino and Elisabeth Albertsen.   1967.
Briefe nach Prag, edited by Barbara Köpplova and Kurt Krolop.   1971.
Tagebücher, edited by Adolf Frisé.   2 vols., 1976.
Texte aus dem Nachlass.   1980.
Beitrag zur Beurteilung der Lehren Machs (dissertation), edited by Adolf Frisé.   1980; as *On Mach's Theories,* 1983.
Briefe 1901–1942, edited by Adolf Frisé.   1981.
Selected Writings, edited by Burton Pike.   1986.
Precision and Soul: Essays and Addresses, edited by Burton Pike and David S. Luft.   1990.

*

Critical Studies: *Musil: An Introduction to His Work* by Burton Pike, 1961; *Femininity and the Creative Imagination: A Study of Henry James, Musil, and Marcel Proust* by Lisa Appignanesi, 1973; *Musil, Master of the Hovering Life* by Frederick G. Peters, 1978; *Musil: "Die Mann ohne Eigenschaften": An Examination of the Relationship Between Author, Narrator, and Protagonist* by Alan Holmes, 1978; *Musil and the Crisis of European Culture 1880–1942* by David S. Luft, 1980; *Musil and the Ineffable: Hieroglyph, Myth, Fairy Tale, and Sign* by Ronald M. Paulson, 1982; *Musil in Focus: Papers from a Centenary Symposium,* 1982, and *Musil and the Literary Landscape of His Time: Papers of an International Symposium,* 1991, both edited by Lothar Huber and John J. White; *Musil and the Culture of Vienna* by Hannah Hickman, 1984; *Proust and Musil: The Novel as Research Instrument* by Gene M. Moore, 1985; *Sympathy for the Abyss: A Study in the Novel of German Modernism: Kafka, Broch, Musil and Thomas Mann* by Stephen D. Dowden, 1986; *Musil's Works, 1906–1924: A Critical Introduction,* 1987, and *Musil's "The Man Without Qualities": A Critical Study,* 1988, both by Philip Payne; *Musil* by Lowell A. Bangerter, 1988; "Images of Woman in Musil's *Tonka*: Mystical Encounters and Borderlines Between Self and Other" by Barbara Mabee, in *Michigan Academician,* 1992.

* * *

As a writer, Robert Musil was too academic and analytic to excel in the conventional literary genres. All his work turns on the effort to resolve by action the tension between intellection and feeling. It is that tension that is Törless's weakness in Musil's first, successful short novel, *Die Verwirrungen des Zöglings Törless* (*Young Törless*). In the final, unfinished three-volume panorama of life in Austro-Hungarian Vienna just before World War I, *Der Mann ohne Eigenschaften* (*The Man without Qualities*), finished by his wife, this same tension causes Ulrich's withdrawal from any situation requiring decisive action.

Musil left mounds of personal papers that tell us about his life and reflections, and we have his notebooks, drafts, and sketches, but very little published work: the early *Young Törless* of 1906, which had been rejected by several publishing houses and succeeded thanks only to Alfred Kerr's review in *Der Tag*; two short stories published in 1911 as *Vereinigungen* (*Unions*); two plays, one a disastrous failure, the other only a moderate success; three other short stories in *Drei Frauen* (*Three Women*); a final short story "The Blackbird," first published in 1927; and the vast masterpiece, *The Man without Qualities.*

The rest of Musil's published work consisted of essays, prose poems, fables, sketches, speeches, and journalism. Although he was formed in a Vienna where Wedekind was examining psycho-sexual problems on the stage at the same time that Freud was writing his first papers, and his interest in experimental psychology can be traced to that city, Musil regarded himself primarily as a German-speaking European. It is in an anonymous review in *The Times Literary Supplement* of London (October 1949), that his subsequent fame is rooted. In postwar Europe, Musil's fame spread back to German-speaking Europe from England.

The short fiction, written between the decision to make a career of writing and the gestation of the great novel, must be seen as part of Musil's quest to define his own personal style in such a way as to integrate as far as possible the affective and intellectual sides of his personality. There are only five stories, six with the enigmatic "The Blackbird." The first started as "The Enchanted House," and was published in *Hyperion* in 1908. The editor asked for a second piece. Called "The Perfecting of a Love," its 40 pages cost Musil most of his energy for over two years. It was published together with the reworked version of the first story, retitled "The Temptation of Quiet Veronica" as *Unions* in 1911, and the volume was not well received. In "The Perfecting of a Love" the central figure, Claudine, incorporates into a life of complete devotion to her husband a brief adulterous relationship with a stranger.

The story starts at home, the day before Claudine goes off to the boarding school to visit her 13-year-old child, Lilli, the result of a casual affair during her first marriage. On her journey she begins to feel revulsion against the rational perfection of her tranquil, happy marriage. She needs to give in to the world of passion within her, from which she has become alienated, and does so with a shadowy senior official she meets on the train, and with whom she is cut off by the snow in the remote village near the school. He is proud of what he regards as his conquest. She forgets Lilli, whom she does not try to see; the man she is with is unimportant to her; and she feels at peace with her absent husband and with the world. The interest of the story resides in the way in which the narrator recounts Claudine's thoughts and feelings in minute detail, drawing on his knowledge of human psychological mechanisms. By the use of images, metaphors, and other stylistic devices, he achieves a powerful fictionalization of the precise experience he is describing. It is a complex, obviously brilliant account of emotionally sterilized events.

"The Temptation of Quiet Veronica" is closer to being case notes. Veronica lives with her elderly aunt. The precise status of two male characters, the aggressive Demeter and the meditative Johannes, is left undefined. What makes the story is again not the clinical state, but its emotional context, as communicated through the imagery. What little happens is filtered by the narrator through Veronica's consciousness, so that the reader is left with the chiaroscuro of her vision. Her life, clearly monotonous and emotionally empty, is evoked in her unbidden recollections of fragments of earlier conversation with Johannes. Indeed, just as Musil derived from the Vienna of Freud and Wedekind, so also he shares, during the same time period, Proust's fascination of the workings of indeliberate memory.

Veronica begins to discover the stirrings of a repressed sensuality. She had once nearly yielded to Demeter when he taunted her with inevitable sexlessly senile dessication in the old house, but she had remembered Johannes. Johannes had suggested leaving with him, but in the end she refuses, and he goes off, threatening to commit suicide. Through stylistic effects of remarkable brilliance, very clear in a series of paragraph openings, we learn how Veronica, for one night, feels herself ecstatically and sensually united with the external world. Wind, blood, animals, "streams of life," light-headedness come into her feelings, somehow connected with her speculations about the time and manner of Johannes's suicide. She undresses, just for the fun of it. Then the letter came, "as it had to come." Johannes had rediscovered himself. Veronica's semi-autism returns. From the arrival of the letter to the end takes scarcely two pages out of nearly thirty.

Three Women, comprising "Grigia," "The Lady from Portugal," and "Tonka," sees the women through the eyes of the men involved. In "Grigia" the man, called simply "Homo," a geologist. He has a liaison with Grigia while remaining mentally faithful to his wife. Grigia refuses to meet him in the habitual barn, but consents to make love for the last time in a disused mine-shaft. Her husband appears; a boulder falls, blocking the way out; Grigia escapes, but Homo dies. The writing is less experimental than in *Unions,* but the point of the brief story is the build-up to death, the event that consummates the skillfully delineated disintegration of Homo's relationship with the world. The male character's relationship to the world is also the focus of "The Lady from Portugal," in which the medieval warrior lord, nearly dead after a mere mosquito sting, fights his way back to physical fitness, a frequently recurring Musil theme, often associated with animals. In the final story of *Three Women,* "Tonka," there is specific allusion to Novalis, but also to Nietzsche. The unnamed male scientist in revolt is deeply disturbed by the apparent infidelity of the girl with whom he has run away, and realises the rights of instinct only after her death.

—A.H.T. Levi

N

NABOKOV, Vladimir. Pseudonym (for works in Russian): V. Sirin. American. Born in St. Petersburg, Russia, 23 April 1899; emigrated in 1919; became U.S. citizen, 1945. Educated at the Prince Tenishev School, St. Petersburg, 1910–17; Trinity College, Cambridge, 1919–22, B.A. (honours) 1922. Married Véra Slonim in 1925; one son. Lived in Berlin, 1922–37, and Paris, 1937–40; moved to the U.S., 1940; instructor in Russian literature and creative writing, Stanford University, California, Summer 1941; lecturer in comparative literature, Wellesley College, Massachusetts, 1941–48; part-time research fellow, Museum of Comparative Zoology, Harvard University, Cambridge, Massachusetts, 1942–48; professor of comparative literature, Cornell University, Ithaca, New York, 1948–59; visiting lecturer, Harvard University, Spring 1952; lived in Montreux, Switzerland, 1961–77. Recipient: Guggenheim fellowship, 1943, 1953; American Academy grant, 1951, and Award of Merit medal, 1969; Brandeis University Creative Arts award, 1953; National Medal for Literature, 1973. Translated or collaborated in translating his own works into English. *Died 2 July 1977.*

PUBLICATIONS

Collections

Sobranie sochinenii [Works]. 1987— .

Short Stories

Vozvrashchenie Chorba: Rasskazy i Stikhi [The Return of Chorb: Stories and Poems]. 1930.
Sogliadatai [The Spy] (novella). 1938; as *The Eye,* translated by the author and Dmitri Nabokov, 1965.
Nine Stories. 1947.
Vesna v Fial'te i drugie rasskazi [Spring in Fialta and Other Stories]. 1956.
Nabokov's Dozen: A Collection of 13 Stories. 1958.
Nabokov's Quartet. 1966.
A Russian Beauty and Other Stories, translated by the author, Dmitri Nabokov, and Simon Karlinsky. 1973.
Tyrants Destroyed and Other Stories, translated by the author and Dmitri Nabokov. 1975.
Details of a Sunset and Other Stories. 1976.
The Enchanter (novella), translated by Dmitri Nabokov. 1986.

Novels

Mashen'ka. 1926; as *Mary,* translated by the author and Michael Glenny, 1970.
Korol' Dama Valet. 1928; as *King Queen Knave,* translated by the author and Dmitri Nabokov, 1968.
Zashchita Luzhina [The Luzhin Defense]. 1930; as *The Defense,* translated by the author and Michael Scammell, 1964.

Kamera Obskura. 1932; as *Camera Obscura,* translated by W. Roy, 1936; as *Laughter in the Dark,* revised and translated by the author, 1938.
Podvig' [The Exploit]. 1933; as *Glory,* translated by the author and Dmitri Nabokov, 1971.
Otchaianie. 1936; as *Despair,* translated by the author, 1937; revised edition, 1966.
Priglashenie na Kazn'. 1938; as *Invitation to a Beheading,* translated by the author and Dmitri Nabokov, 1959; revised edition in Russian, 1975.
The Real Life of Sebastian Knight. 1941.
Bend Sinister. 1947.
Dar. 1952; as *The Gift,* translated by the author and Michael Scammell, 1963.
Lolita. 1955; translated into Russian by the author, 1967; as *The Annotated Lolita,* edited by Alfred Appel, Jr., 1970.
Pnin. 1957.
Pale Fire. 1962.
Ada; or Ardor: A Family Chronicle. 1969.
Transparent Things. 1972.
Look at the Harlequins! 1974.

Plays

Smert' [Death], 1923, *Dedushka* [Grandad], 1923, *Agaspher* [Agasfer], 1923, *Tragediia Gospodina Morna* [The Tragedy of Mr. Morn], 1924, and *Polius* [The South Pole], 1924, all in *Rul'* [The Rudder] magazine.
Skital'tsy [The Wanderers], in *Grani II* [Facets II] magazine, 1923.
Chelovek iz SSSR [The Man from the USSR] (produced 1926). In *Rul'* [The Rudder] magazine, 1927.
Sobytie [The Event] (produced 1938). In *Russkie Zapiski,* 1938.
Izobretenie Val'sa (produced 1968). In *Russkie Zapiski,* 1938; translated as *The Waltz Invention* (produced 1969), 1966.
Lolita: A Screenplay. 1974.
The Man from the USSR and Other Plays, translated by Dmitri Nabokov. 1984.

Screenplay: *Lolita,* 1962.

Verse

Stikhi [Poems]. 1916.
Dva Puti: Al'manakh [Two Paths: An Almanac]. 1918.
Gornii Put' [The Empyrean Path]. 1923.
Grozd' [The Cluster]. 1923.
Stikhotvoreniia 1929–1951 [Poems]. 1952.
Poems. 1959.
Poems and Problems. 1971.
Stikhi [Poems]. 1979.

Other

Nikolai Gogol. 1944.

Conclusive Evidence: A Memoir.   1951; as *Speak, Memory: A Memoir,* 1952; revised edition, as *Speak, Memory: An Autobiography Revisited,* 1966.
Nabokov's Congeries: An Anthology, edited by Page Stegner.   1968; as *The Portable Nabokov,* 1977.
Strong Opinions (interviews and essays).   1973.
The Nabokov-Wilson Letters: Correspondence Between Nabokov and Edmund Wilson 1940-1971, edited by Simon Karlinsky.   1979.
Lectures on Literature, edited by Fredson Bowers.   1980.
Lectures on "Ulysses": A Facsimile of the Manuscript. 1980.
Lectures on Russian Literature, edited by Fredson Bowers. 1981.
Nabokov's Fifth Arc: Nabokov and Others on His Life's Work, edited by J.E. Rivers and Charles Nicol.   1982.
Lectures on Don Quixote, edited by Fredson Bowers. 1983.
Perepiska s sestroi [Correspondence with His Sister]. 1985.
Selected Letters   1940-1977, edited by Dmitri Nabokov and Matthew J. Bruccoli.   1989.

Editor and Translator, *Eugene Onegin,* by Alexander Pushkin.   4 vols.,   1964; revised edition,   4 vols., 1976.

Translator, *Nikolka Persik* [Colas Breugnon], by Romain Rolland.   1922.
Translator, *Ania v Strane Chudes* [Alice in Wonderland], by Lewis Carroll.   1923.
Translator, *Three Russian Poets: Verse Translations from Pushkin, Lermontov and Tyutchev.*   1945; as *Poems by Pushkin, Lermontov and Tyutchev,*   1948.
Translator, with Dmitri Nabokov, *A Hero of Our Time,* by Mikhail Lermontov.   1958.
Translator, *The Song of Igor's Campaign: An Epic of the Twelfth Century.*   1960.

*

Bibliography: *Nabokov: Bibliographie des Gesamtwerks* by Dieter E. Zimmer, 1963, revised edition, 1964; *Nabokov: A Reference Guide* by Samuel Schuman, 1979; *Nabokov: A Descriptive Bibliography* by Michael Juliar, 1986.

Critical Studies: *Escape into Aesthetics: The Art of Nabokov* by Page Stegner, 1966; *Nabokov: His life in Art: A Critical Narrative,* 1967, *Nabokov: His Life in Part,* 1977, and *VN: The Life and Art of Nabokov,* 1986, all by Andrew Field; *Nabokov: The Man and His Work* edited by L.S. Dembo, 1967; *Keys to Lolita* by Carl R. Proffer, 1968, and *A Book of Things about Nabokov* edited by Proffer, 1974; *Nabokov: Criticism, Reminiscences, Translations, and Tributes* edited by Alfred Appel, Jr., and Charles Newman, 1970, and *Nabokov's Dark Cinema* by Appel, 1974; *Nabokov* by Julian Moynahan, 1971; *Nabokov's Deceptive World* by W. Woodlin Rowe, 1971; *Crystal Land: Artifice in Nabokov's English Novels* by Julia Bader, 1972; *Nabokov's Garden: A Guide to Ada* by Bobbie Ann Mason, 1974; *Nabokov* by Donald E. Morton, 1974; *Reading Nabokov* by Douglas Fowler, 1974; *Nabokov* by L.L. Lee, 1976; *The Real Life of Nabokov* by Alex de Jonge, 1976; *Nabokov Translated: A Comparison of Nabokov's Russian and English Prose* by Jane Grayson, 1977; *Nabokov: America's Russian Novelist* by George Malcolm Hyde, 1977; *Fictitious Biographies:* *Nabokov's English Novels* by Herbert Grabes, 1977; *Nabokov: The Dimensions of Parody* by Dabney Stuart, 1978; *Blue Evenings in Berlin: Nabokov's Short Stories of the 1920's* by Marina Naumann, 1978; *Nabokov: His Life, His Work, His World: A Tribute* edited by Peter Quennell, 1979; *Nabokov and the Novel* by Ellen Pifer, 1980; *Nabokov: The Critical Heritage* edited by Norman Page, 1982; *Nabokov's Novels in English* by Lucy Maddox, 1983; *The Novels of Nabokov* by Laurie Clancy, 1984; *Nabokov: A Critical Study of the Novels* by David Rampton, 1984; *Critical Essays on Nabokov* edited by Phyllis A. Roth, 1984; *Problems of Nabokov's Poetics: A Narratological Analysis* by Pekka Tammi, 1985; *Nabokov: Life, Work, and Criticism* by Charles Stanley Ross, 1985; *Worlds in Regression: Some Novels of Nabokov* by D. Barton Johnson, 1985; *A Nabokov Who's Who* by Christine Rydel, 1986; *Nabokov* by Michael Wood, 1987; *Understanding Nabokov* by Stephen Jan Parker, 1987; *Nabokov: The Mystery of Literary Structures* by Leona Toker, 1989; *Nabokov: The Russian Years 1899-1940,* 1990, and *Nabokov: The American Years,* 1991, both by Brian Boyd; *A Small Alpine Form: Studies in Nabokov's Short Fiction* edited by Charles Nicol and Gennady Barabtarlo, 1993.

*   *   *

The privileged first son of an aristocratic family, Vladimir Nabokov grew up fluent in Russian, English, and French. His early introduction to the glories of language developed into a lifelong fascination with words and word play. The rich texture of his style and the highly allusive and parodic quality of his prose produce a body of work so recondite that it requires multiple rereading, good dictionaries, and shelves full of reference books in order to appreciate fully its meaning and structure. Though Nabokov's stories are weaker on the whole than his novels, they still serve as excellent examples of his art. The short stories generally appear less interesting than the novels, mainly because they are more straightforward; however, several of them do reach the high creative level of the longer works.

Nabokov wrote the majority of his stories in his native tongue during his Berlin exile (1922-37), during which time he also wrote his nine Russian novels. The stories first appeared in the émigré periodical press and a number of them came out in two collections, *Vozvrashchenie Chorba* ("The Return of Chorb") and *Sogliadatai (The Eye).* Most of this early fiction deals with the complicated, poignant, sad, and often lonely aspects of émigré life. After having arrived in the United States, Nabokov wrote in English the novels that secured his fame and led his adopted country to claim him as her own: *Lolita, Pale Fire,* and *Ada.* Nevertheless, émigré life remains a theme in some of his English short stories ("The Assistant producer," "That in Aleppo Once," "Conversation Piece, 1945"). Émigré life serves as a metaphor for the more general themes of displacement and dislocation of time and space.

Nabokov's own concerns over such issues as the suffering of the weak at the hands of the cruel, the human reluctance to accept responsibility for one's actions, the nature of individuality and freedom, and the role fate plays in individual lives place him in the great tradition of 19th-century Russian literature. These subjects also belie both the critical commonplace that he is merely a literary gameplayer and his own contention that there are no "messages" in his work. Never blatantly didactic, Nabokov's fiction nevertheless rests on a firm moral basis.

Perhaps the most prevalent themes in Nabokov's fiction deal with the nature of art, consciousness, and reality. He also writes about love, sexuality, and madness. But most of all Nabokov teaches his audience how to read literature, especially his own, by concentrating on the details which reveal the patterns of his work. And though Nabokov vehemently denies the presence of symbols in his work, motifs such as his favorite butterflies and moths recur in his fictive universe. These patterns in turn provide his ideal readers with the clues necessary to perceive the created reality of each of his stories and novels.

The characters who inhabit Nabokov's special world generally do not fit into their social milieu. Because they usually do not concern themselves with current affairs or the "eternal questions," some critics accuse them of being solipsistic. Other critics contend that all of Nabokov's heroes are artists and writers. But his heroes come from all walks of life and all levels of intelligence and sensitivity— from the most sensitive poet to the least perceptive Philistine, or *poshliak*. His secondary characters also make up a wide range of types and function on many levels. Especially in the novels and stories of exile, these characters form the background for the action of the heroes. In addition, they fit into the society alien to the heroes and thereby accentuate their dislocation and displacement.

One of Nabokov's best stories, "A Guide to Berlin" ("Putevoditel' po Berlinu," 1925) does not dwell on the standard sights to which a Baedeker might direct a tourist: railway stations, hotels, restaurants, churches. This guide does not even mention the well-known street *Unter den Linden* or the landmark situated on Berlin's western end, the Brandenburg Gate. Instead the nameless narrator points out to his nameless companion the harmony of black water pipes covered in snow which unites them to the outer edge of the sidewalk on which they are lying; he then boards a tram and concentrates on the conductor's hands and the images they awake in his consciousness. From the tram he observes people at work and takes us with him into his synesthetic view of the city. His next stop is the zoo, which he describes as an artificial Eden, but an Eden that stimulates his imagination. At the end we see the narrator and his drinking companion in a pub, the details of which he sees in a mirror. This sight causes him to speculate on how he might be a future memory in the mind of a child he is observing in the present. "Guide to Berlin" not only presents us with a way of looking at the city Nabokov called home for many years, it also shows us how to perceive the reality of Nabokov's world by teaching us how to read his fiction. One apprehends the entire picture by concentrating on separate details.

The German city in "The Return of Chorb" becomes a modern day Hades for the protagonist who returns to tell his parents-in-law that his wife has died in a freak accident. Chorb checks into the seedy hotel where he spent his wedding night and later takes a prostitute there, but only sleeps with her quite innocently. When he awakens from a troubled dream, he turns and imagines his late wife is at his side. He screams, she takes fright and runs out of the room just as Chorb's in-laws are arriving. The details of the story evoke an aura of death: the parents walk along "lifeless streets"; Chorb sees everything in shadows and shades. Everywhere he notices leaves, withering trees, the black masses of the city park, black pavement. He sees a "young lady, as light as a dead leaf." It even "seemed to him that happiness itself had . . . the smell of dead leaves." Mice scurry and spider webs hang about. But one particular detail takes what could be seen as a typical late autumn scene and transforms the surroundings into Chorb's per-

sonal hell. From the hotel window "one could make out . . . a corner of the opera house, the black shoulder of a stone Orpheus," the man who went to Hades to bring is wife back from the dead—Chorb's very quest.

A view from another hotel window offers the main character of "Cloud, Castle, Lake" ("Oblako, ozero, bashnia," 1937) a glimpse of paradise. The narrator's "representative," Vasili Ivanovich, wins a "pleasuretrip" at an émigré raffle. He tries to give the ticket back, but to no avail. He must travel around Germany with a group of louts who torture him because he scorns their collective activities and simply wishes to be alone to read the Russian poet Tiutchev. While hiking he leaves the group and finds an inn from whose window he could see cloud, castle, and lake (cloud, lake, and *tower* in the Russian version) "in a motionless and perfect correlation of happiness." He tells the group he wants to stay behind, but they force him to return and badly beat him. Not only does this story express Nabokov's hatred of cruelty, it also serves as a prologue to and source of the title of his novel *Priglashenie na Kazn' (Invitation to a Beheading)*. In addition many allusions and parodies provide numerous subtexts to one of Nabokov's favorite and finest stories.

Other stories that deserve critical attention include "Spring in Fialta," "Signs and Symbols," "The Potato Elf," and "The Vane Sisters." The remaining stories are not without merit; they simply suffer in comparison with the brilliance of his best short fiction and novels.

—Christine A. Rydel

See the essay on "Signs and Symbols."

NAIPAUL, (Sir) V(idiadhar) S(urajprasad). Trinidadian. Born in Trinidad, 17 August 1932; brother of the writer Shiva Naipaul. Educated at Tranquillity Boys School, 1939–42; Queen's Royal College, Port of Spain, Trinidad, 1943–49; University College, Oxford, 1950–54, B.A. (honours) in English 1953. Married Patricia Ann Hale in 1955. Editor, "Caribbean Voices," BBC, London, 1954–56; fiction reviewer, *New Statesman,* London, 1957–61. Recipient: Rhys Memorial prize, 1958; Maugham award, 1961; Phoenix Trust award, 1962; Hawthornden prize, 1964; W.H. Smith literary award, 1968; Arts Council grant, 1969; Booker prize, 1971; Bennett award (*Hudson Review*), 1980; Jerusalem prize, 1983; T.S. Eliot award, 1986; Trinity Cross (Trinidad), 1989. D.Litt.: University of the West Indies, Trinidad, 1975; St. Andrews University, Fife, Scotland, 1979; Columbia University, New York, 1981; University of London, 1988; Litt.D.: Cambridge University, 1983. Honorary Fellow, University College, Oxford, 1983. Knighted, 1990.

PUBLICATIONS

Short Stories

Miguel Street. 1959.
A Flag on the Island. 1967.
In a Free State. 1971.

Novels

The Mystic Masseur.   1957.
The Suffrage of Elvira.   1958; in Three Novels, 1982.
A House for Mr. Biswas.   1961.
Mr. Stone and the Knights Companion.   1963.
The Mimic Men.   1967.
Guerrillas.   1975.
A Bend in the River.   1979.
The Enigma of Arrival.   1987.

Other

The Middle Passage: Impressions of Five Societies—British, French and Dutch—in the West Indies and South America.   1962.
An Area of Darkness: An Experience of India.   1964.
The Loss of El Dorado: A History.   1969; revised edition, 1973.
The Overcrowded Barracoon and Other Articles.   1972.
India: A Wounded Civilization.   1977.
The Return of Eva Perón, with The Killings in Trinidad (essays).   1980.
A Congo Diary.   1980.
Among the Believers: An Islamic Journey.   1981.
Finding the Centre: Two Narratives.   1984.
A Turn in the South.   1989.
India: A Million Mutinies Now.   1990.

*

Bibliography: Naipaul: A Selective Bibliography with Annotations by Kelvin Jarvis, 1989.

Critical Studies: by David Pryce-Jones, in London Magazine, May 1967; Karl Miller, in Kenyon Review, November 1967; The West Indian Novel by Kenneth Ramchand, 1970; Naipaul: An Introduction to His Work by Paul Theroux, 1972; Naipaul by Robert D. Hamner, 1973, and Critical Perspectives on Naipaul edited by Hamner, 1977; Naipaul by William Walsh, 1973; Naipaul: A Critical Introduction by Landeg White, 1975; Paradoxes of Order: Some Perspectives on the Fiction of Naipaul by Robert K. Morris, 1975; Naipaul by Michael Thorpe, 1976; Four Contemporary Novelists by Kerry McSweeney, 1982; Naipaul: A Study in Expatriate Sensibility by Sudha Rai, 1982; Contrary Awareness: A Critical Study of the Novels of Naipaul by K.I. Madhusudana Rao, 1982; Naipaul: In Quest of the Enemy by Anthony Boxill, 1983; "Naipaul Issue" of Modern Fiction Studies (West Lafayette, Indiana), Autumn 1984; The Fiction of Naipaul by Nonditor Mason, 1986; Journey Through Darkness: The Writing of Naipaul by Peggy Nightingale, 1987; The Web of Tradition: Uses of Allusion in Naipaul's Fiction by John Thieme, 1987; Naipaul by Peter Hughes, 1988; Naipaul: A Materialist Reading by Selwyn R. Cudjoe, 1988; Naipaul by Richard Kelly, 1989; The Novels of Naipaul: A Study of Theme and Form by Shashi Kamra, 1990.

*   *   *

V.S. Naipaul has spoken of the difficulty of writing novels about the "unformed" societies of the former colonies and he does not write longer works of fiction with ease. His concern with form, language, exact detail, and narrative rhythm results in understated, economical, carefully structured, densely textured narrative, similar to the modern short story. His longer works are built from self-contained episodes that, like "Jack's Garden" in The Enigma of Arrival, could be published on their own. Even his travel and autobiographical books, such as An Area of Darkness, are made of linked stories in which a incident starts with elaborate preparations and expectations only to end in disillusionment and hasty retreat. Although he has only published three books of short stories—Miguel Street, A Flag on the Island, and In a Free State—other books, such as The Loss of El Dorado, an historical work, consist mostly of discrete stories linked by theme and an episodic chronology.

He was for some years a reader for the BBC Caribbean Voices program, where he contributed to the development of the West Indian short story by advising others on the use of dialect and local subject matter. Among his early models were James Joyce and the short stories of Naipaul's father. Seepersad Naipaul's Gurudeva and Other Indian Tales (1943) was effectively the beginning of writing by East Indian Trinidadians about their community. Objective, unsentimental, with a touch of satire, Seepersad Naipaul showed an impoverished local community whose rituals and customs were in decay, confused and inappropriate to the new world of the West Indies. Some of V. S. Naipaul's earliest stories, such as "My Aunt Gold Teeth" (1954) satirically record incidents in his own extended family where Hindu orthodoxy is used cruelly against those who confusedly mimic the ways of other religions and cultures.

Miguel Street, the third book he published but actually the first he wrote, is based on life in Port of Spain. It offers amusing stories about eccentric local characters who attempt to impress others by bragging, posing, or pretending, but who are usually jobless idlers, failures, or fakes. The stories are linked, covering a decade, by the memories of the narrator, who, as he matures, sees that Trinidad is a colonial backwater offering no opportunities for achievement; people he formerly thought amusing he now sees as hopeless and trapped. There is nothing to do in Trinidad but get drunk and go with whores; he decides he must leave the island. The stories are carefully structured, usually with a first half in which the character is introduced, appears amusing but does nothing; then in the second half the character finds some objective to pursue which turns out to be a fantasy and ends in humiliation, flight, or jail. Sexual attraction is at times the start of a change in life that leads to disaster. The volume as a whole is organized by chronology and by a progression from simpler stories of idleness and self-deception to a second half of more complex stories concluding with or bordering on tragedy.

The stories of an impoverished colony in Miguel Street were followed by criticism of the neo-colonialism that accompanied independence as British rule was replaced by Americanization. A Flag on the Island consists of miscellaneous short stories that Naipaul wrote over the years, some satirical sketches about the lower middle-class life he observed as an immigrant in England, and a novella, the title story, originally written for a film that was never made. "A Flag on the Island" concerns the contrast between the ways of a British West Indian colony during World War II and its Americanization after national independence, when its local bars are turned into hotels and nightclubs for rich American tourists. Its local writers, instead of imitating British novels about lords and ladies, now write "I hate you white man" protest novels funded by American foundations which will not support writing that accurately portrays the complexities and truth of life on the island, especially the complex racial situation. The story is obviously related to themes in *An Area of Darkness* and *The Mimic Men*, in which Naipaul is concerned with the ways colonialism and independence resulted in unstable societies without authentic cultures and wills of their own, where the assertion of national identity is an irrational mixture of pseudo-traditionalism and an unearned veneer of modernization taken from others.

The analysis of the problems of freedom is developed further in the linked stories and two "diary" entries that comprise *In a Free State*. In the prologue Naipaul is on a ship between Greece and Egypt where an impoverished older English traveler is being cruelly harassed by others, mostly from the Middle East. A symbol for the reduced state of the formerly carefree, secure English international traveler, the vagabond is now prey for the "free" in a world without political order. In the epilogue Naipaul tries to rescue some Egyptian children from humiliation, but finds himself regarded by the locals as an eccentric foreigner. Although Egypt is politically free it lacks the resources or will to spare its population from the humiliation of living off the leavings of tourists. The three fictional stories in the collection concern the Indian diaspora. In "One out of Many" an Indian servant from Bombay is taken to Washington, D.C., where he becomes free by working in a restaurant, but he loses his sense of security and community. His existentialist freedom has left him with a sense of life having no purpose beyond the trouble and pain of surviving. In "Tell Me Who to Kill" there is no enemy beyond the central character's own delusions about others and the consequences of his actions. A poor, uneducated West Indian, jealous of more successful members of his family, ruins his life to send his younger brother to study in England; he follows in the hope of continuing to help, but his brother exploits him instead. "In a Free State" is set in postcolonial East Africa where freedom leads to intertribal warfare and secessionist movements. Foreign experts and advisors replace the settlers, build nothing, and move on to other new nations. Indians drive the trucks and run the shops that keep the country operating, but are hated by the Africans and looked down upon by the Europeans. The diaspora Indians, badly governed Africans, and rootless Europeans, often unable to return to secure lives at home, are all casualties of freedom.

—Bruce King

NARAYAN, R(asipuram) K(rishnaswamy). Indian. Born in Madras, 10 October 1906. Educated at Collegiate High School, Mysore; Maharaja's College, Mysore, graduated 1930. Married Rajam c. 1934 (died 1939); one daughter. Teacher, then journalist, early 1930's; owner, Indian Thought Publications, Mysore. Recipient: Sahitya Academy award, 1961; Padma Bhushan, India, 1964; National Association of Independent Schools award (U.S.), 1965; English-Speaking Union award, 1975; Royal Society of Literature Benson medal, 1980. Litt.D.: University of Leeds, Yorkshire, 1967; D.Litt.: University of Delhi; Sri Venkateswara University, Tirupati; University of Mysore. Fellow, Royal Society of Literature, 1980; honorary member, American Academy, 1982. Lives in Mysore.

PUBLICATIONS

Short Stories

Malgudi Days.   1943.
Dodu and Other Stories.   1943.
Cyclone and Other Stories.   1944.
An Astrologer's Day and Other Stories.   1947.
Lawley Road.   1956.
Gods, Demons, and Others.   1964.
A Horse and Two Goats.   1970.
Old and New.   1981.
Malgudi Days (not same as 1943 book).   1982.
Under the Banyan Tree and Other Stories.   1985.

Novels

Swami and Friends: A Novel of Malgudi.   1935.
The Bachelor of Arts.   1937.
The Dark Room.   1938.
The English Teacher.   1945; as *Grateful to Life and Death*, 1953.
Mr. Sampath.   1949; as *The Printer of Malgudi*, 1957.
The Financial Expert.   1952.
Waiting for the Mahatma.   1955.
The Guide.   1958.
The Man-Eater of Malgudi.   1961.
The Vendor of Sweets.   1967; as *The Sweet-Vendor*, 1967.
The Painter of Signs.   1976.
A Tiger for Malgudi.   1983.
Talkative Man.   1986.
The World of Nagaraj.   1990.

Other

Mysore.   1939.
Next Sunday: Sketches and Essays.   1956.
My Dateless Diary: A Journal of a Trip to the United States in October 1956.   1960.
The Ramayana: A Shortened Modern Prose Version of the Indian Epic.   1972.
Reluctant Guru (essays).   1974.
My Days: A Memoir.   1974.
The Emerald Route (includes play *The Watchman of the Lake*).   1977.
The Mahabharata: A Shortened Modern Prose Version of the Indian Epic.   1978.
A Writer's Nightmare: Selected Essays 1958–1988.   1988.

*

Bibliography: *Narayan* by Hilda Pontes, 1983.

Critical Studies: *Narayan: A Critical Study of His Works* by Harish Raizada, 1969; *Narayan*, 1971, and *Narayan: A Critical Appreciation*, 1982, both by William Walsh; *The Novels of Narayan* by Lakshmi Holmstrom, 1973; *Narayan*, 1973, and *Narayan as a Novelist*, 1988, both by P.S. Sundaram; *Perspectives on Narayan* edited by Atma Ram, 1981; *Narayan: A Critical Spectrum* edited by Bhagwat S. Goyal, 1983; *The Ironic Vision: A Study of the Fiction of Narayan* by M.K. Naik, 1983; *Narayan: His World and His Art* by Shiv K. Gilra, 1984; *The Novels of Narayan* by Cynthia Vanden Driesen, 1986; *A Critical Study of the Novels of Narayan* by J.K. Biswal, 1987.

* * *

R.K. Narayan is known primarily as the writer of novels set in Malgudi, a mythical town corresponding to his own native city of Mysore in southern India. But he has also written more than two hundred short stories, favoring the form as a "welcome diversion" after the labor of the stricter and more taxing form of the novel; he claims short stories allow him to present "concentrated miniatures of human experience in all its opulence." In these stories characters usually live on the brink of economic disaster, and fate often deals very cruelly with even the most reasonable and unselfish of them, but Narayan's treatment of harsh circumstance is often comic or elegiac.

Initially Narayan wrote stories in the form of brief anecdotes, incidents, or parables twice a week for *The Hindu*, a Madras newspaper. More recently some of his stories have appeared in *The New Yorker*. Sometimes brevity precludes impact—in "The House Opposite" a religious hermit is obsessed with a whore across the street, but no sooner is the conflict introduced than it is resolved by the woman's request for devotional assistance, which unlocks the hermit's pity. Sometimes characters are too bound within the parables they illustrate to come alive, as with the main character from "Another Community," whose fastidious desire to avoid conflict incites it.

Narayan can, however, achieve a remarkable resonance within a brief form. "Watchman" is a brief tale of a watchman's effort to keep a young woman from drowning herself in a tank he watches. He urges her to marry and give up her hopes of becoming a doctor, and he leaves her to drown. But he's consumed afterward with fears that she did die. Years later, when he sees her again at the tank with children and obvious signs of wealth, her refusal to recognize him implies her unhappiness. Here the economical form is a fitting vehicle for insight into the way circumstance leads to human frustration; the world cannot accommodate our wishes. Another story, "Mute Companions," about a deaf-mute who acquires a monkey to help him beg and then loses the monkey, verges on pathos, but when Narayan attends strictly to detail and plausibility with a compassionate and comprehensive objectivity, he depicts a very appealing mix of sorrow and acceptance.

The more recent longer stories, saturated with diversity, are the most successful. In "A Horse and Two Goats," aging Muni, who once had 40 goats, comes into a windfall when an American Indian buys an ancient village statue of a horse in a state of decline parallel to Muni's. Thinking the statue belongs to Muni, the American carts it away in his station wagon. The bartering between two men who don't speak any language in common is a masterpiece of the paradox of communicative incomprehension. Another tale, "Annamalai," about a gardener-factotum whose connection to the earth is mostly a matter of guesswork and superstition, is equally rich and well developed.

"Uncle" is perhaps the best of these longer stories. From the outset the mystery to be solved is the identity of the boy's uncle. Tales at school suggest Uncle may have been an impersonator, and a curious meeting with a Muslim tailor reveals that some have regarded him as a doctor, as a benefactor. But the uncle we see directly is proud of his boy, eager to have a photograph of him from school, trying to get him dressed appropriately, then eager to have the photograph properly framed. The framer, Jayraj, is a mysterious, dominating fellow, contending that "mounting and framing is my duty, even if you bring the photo of a donkey's rear," but he sets strict terms under which he will work to produce the best possible frame. The boy stays all night after his father leaves, hoping for an adventure, but finds Jayraj suddenly unfriendly. The boy overhears a tale about his uncle as houseboy who fled with a doctor, his wife, and a child from the Japanese invasion of Burma. The houseboy may have caused the deaths of the parents, impersonated a doctor, and kept the child and the family fortune.

The boy flees Jayraj, then asks the aunt about the truth of what he's heard. She tells him not to inquire, and as we discover in a coda that completes the story, he does not. Uncle has put him through college; Uncle and Aunt have shown him nothing but love all his life, and for the boy, now a man, this is enough. The tale is a satisfying revision of the myth of the traditional Western theme of the search for the father. The boy does not seek the endlessly receding purity of truth, but lives instead within the strange nurturing of an ambiguous reality. He will not question the terms under which he has been loved, but accept them and offer his gratitude. He thrives among strangely magical assistants, and even opponents like the malevolent Jayraj are ultimately benefactors, part of a grander design.

In all of these tales, Narayan's subjects and method of telling hardly seem to belong to the 20th century. As R.K. Jeurkar has pointed out, Narayan does not respond to social, political, and economic changes of the 20th century, nor has he experimented with contemporary narrative devices. His language seems largely transparent, and Narayan writes in English sometimes quaint enough, as several critics have noted, to read as a translation. William Walsh cautions that this transparency is deceptive, that we may not grasp as much of the Indian view of life as we believe, but even so, the best of Narayan's tales, brimming with pathos and acceptance, are thoroughly engaging for a Western audience.

—John Gerlach

See the essays on "An Astrologer's Day" and "A Horse and Two Goats."

NERVAL, Gérard de. Pseudonym for Gérard Labrunie. French. Born in Paris, 22 May 1808. Educated at Lycée Charlemagne, Paris, 1820–28; possibly apprenticed to a printer and studied law; studied medicine to 1834. Led a life of wandering; after inheriting money from his grandfather in 1834 founded *Le Monde Dramatique*, 1835; drama critic, *La Presse*, and contributor to other journals from 1838; hospitalized in mental clinics, 1841, 1849, 1851, 1853, 1854. *Died (suicide) 26 January 1855.*

PUBLICATIONS

Collections

Oeuvres complètes.   6 vols., 1867–77.
Oeuvres complètes, edited by Aristide Marie, Jules Marsan, and Édouard Champion.   6 vols., 1926–32.
Oeuvres.   2 vols., 1952–56.
Oeuvres.   2 vols., 1958.

Short Stories

Contes et facéties.   1852; as *Dreams and Life,* 1933.
Les Filles du feu.   1854; as *Daughters of Fire: Sylvie,
   Emilie, Octavie,* 1922.

Novels

Les Fauc Saulniers.   1850.
Aurélia.   1855; translated as *Aurelia,* 1933; in *Dreams and
   Life,* 1933.
Le Prince des sots, edited by Louis Ulbach.   1866.

Plays

L'Académie: ou, Les Membres introuvables.   1826.
Piquillo, with Alexandre Dumas, père, music by Hippolyte
   Monpou (produced 1837).   1837.
Léo Burckart, with Alexandre Dumas, père (produced
   1839).   1839.
L'Alchimiste, with Alexandre Dumas, père (produced
   1839).   1839.
Les Monténégrins, with E. Alboize, music by Armand
   Limnander (produced 1849).   1849.
Le Chariot d'enfant, with Joseph Méry (produced 1850).
L'Imagier de Harlem, with Joseph Méry and Bernard
   Lopez, music by Adolphe de Groot (produced 1851).
   1852.
Nicolas Flamel (in English).   1924.

Verse

Napoléon et la France guerrière: élégies nationales.   1826.
La Mort de Talma: élégies nationales.   1826.
Les Hauts Faits des Jésuites: dialogue en vers.   1826.
Monsieur Deutscourt: ou, Le Cuisinier d'un grand homme.
   1926.
Les Chimères, in *Les Filles du feu.*   1854; edited by
   Norma Rinsler, 1973; as *The Chimeras,* 1966.
Fortune's Fool: Thirty-Five Poems.   1959.

Other

Scènes de la vie orientale: Les Femmes du Caire.   1824;
   Les Femmes du Liban, 1850.
Etudes sur les poètes allemands (as Gérard).   1830.
Nos adieux à la Chambre des Députés de l'an 1830 (as le
   Père Gérard).   1831.
Voyage en Orient.   1851; translated in part as *The Women
   of Cairo,* 1929; as *Journey to the Orient,* edited by
   Norman Glass, 1972.
Les Illuminés; ou, Les Précurseurs du socialisme.   1852.
Lorély: souvenirs d'Allemagne.   1852.
Petits châteaux de Bohème: Prose et poésie.   1853.
La Correspondance de Nerval (1830–1855).   1911.
Selected Writings, edited by G. Wagner.   1958.
Le Carnet de Dolbreuse, edited by Jean Richer.   1967.

Editor, *Choix des poésies de Ronsard, du Bellay, Baïf,
   Belleau, du Bartas, Chassignet, Desportes, Régnier* (as
   Gérard).   1830.
Editor, *Le Diable amoureux.*   1830.

Translator, *Faust* (as Gérard), by Goethe.   1828; aug-
   mented edition, *Faust, et Le Second Faust,* 1840.
Translator, *Poésies allemandes* (as Gérard).   1830.
Translator, *La Damnation de Faust.*   1846.

*

Bibliography: *Nerval: A Critical Bibliography 1900–1967*
by James Villas, 1968.

Critical Studies: *Nerval and the German Heritage* by Alfred
Dubreck, 1965; *The Disinherited: The Life of Nerval* by
Benn Sowerby, 1973; *Nerval* by Norma Rinsler, 1973; *The
Style of Nerval's Aurelia* by William Beauchamp, 1976;
Aspects of the Double in the Works of Nerval by Jolene J.
Barjasteh, forthcoming.

*   *   *

Writing during the height of the romantic period in
French literature, Gérard de Nerval distinguished himself
as primarily an author of short fiction and verse. Critics
generally agree that personal grief and guilt, associated with
the death of Nerval's mother and the loss of his beloved
Jenny Colon, find expression in every aspect of his fiction.
His most compelling works draw upon the bouts of mental
illness from which he suffered much of his adult life.
Certainly, the search for self-identity linked to the quest for
the ideal woman figure among the most prominent themes
in his works.

Voyage en Orient (Journey to the Orient) represents more
than a volume of travel literature based on Nerval's year-
long trip to Egypt in 1843. Rather, the exotic sights,
customs, and Middle Eastern oral tradition provide rich
and powerful material for the author's imagination. "The
Story of Caliph Hakem," for example, focuses on the
protagonist's identity crisis linked to the appearance of a
physical double, a rival for his sister's hand in marriage.
Although Nerval uses the doppelgänger motif elsewhere in
his works, he associates it explicitly with incestuous desire
in this text. Death, suggests Nerval, is the only possible
resolution to the internal conflict created by delusions of
grandeur and unacceptable desires.

In retelling another legend ("Queen of the Morning")
Nerval emphasizes the Promethean hero's belief in his own
great destiny. Adoniram is fated to descend into the
underworld where fiery spirits ("les génies du feu") dwell in
order to unite in marriage with his spiritual sister and
feminine ideal, Balkis. As descendants of a divine race,
Adoniram and the Queen of Sheba substantiate their claim
to divinity through an incestuous union, sanctioned by the
spirits. Nerval presents Adoniram's eventual death as a
victory over the antithetical self (Solomon, his unworthy
rival), an assurance of immortality, and a fulfillment of
divine destiny.

In his volume *Les Filles du feu (Daughters of Fire)* Nerval
attempts to fuse aspects of myth and memory, dream and
reality, in the creation of a range of feminine archetypes. In
stories like "Angélique," "Sylvie," "Isis," and "Octavie,"
the author develops the myth of the ideal woman in a
progressive fashion. While "Sylvie" has received considerable attention from critics, "Octavie" is equally rich in
symbolic value. In this story, the narrator recollects a series
of events that took place during his trips to Italy. Rejected
by Aurélie, a Parisian actress, the protagonist flees the
reality of duplicitous affection and seeks comfort in the
illusion of perfection symbolized by the siren-like Octavie
("this daughter of the waters"). However, realizing that this
English girl is merely a poor substitute for his idealized
beloved, the hero is filled with an inordinate sense of guilt
and reproaches himself for imaginary transgressions. Is it

not possible through death, he asks, to attain a purer and more sacred love, one which leads to a transcendent happiness and eternal peace? The narrator's disillusionment with love leads him to consider suicide as a possible solution. Yet, he is saved by the memory of Octavie, whose purity and goodness remind him of the goddess Isis and suggest the hope for salvation. In the end, the narrator rejects the potential happiness offered by Octavie and seeks to preserve an image of perfection. The words of the narrator in "Sylvie" apply equally well to this text: "It is an image that I pursue, nothing more."

Nerval weaves various thematic elements of his earlier fiction into *Aurélia,* his literary masterpiece, a text concerned primarily with absence or loss. The autobiographical nature of this work is impossible to ignore. After all, Nerval considered it a transcription of the dreams and hallucinations he experienced during periods of mental crisis. His account of the descent into madness ("la descente aux enfers") is a surprisingly lucid one. "Dream is a second life," Nerval states simply in the opening paragraph of the text. In exploring the existence of a realm beyond real life, the author hopes to convince the reader of the reality of his visions. The narrating hero embarks on a bizarre psychic journey to recover his lost love, Aurélia. Early on, the narrator encounters a rival, like the *ferouer* of Middle Eastern myth, who usurps his rightful place with Aurélia. Filled with a sense of culpability for the loss of his beloved, the narrator sinks into despair and fears eternal damnation for imagined sins committed against his ideal.

Part two of *Aurélia* is crucial to an understanding of Nerval's own perception of his illness. Although the text begins with the narrator's despondency and the temptation of suicide, it soon evolves into a journey back from madness. The narrator's efforts to help another troubled patient, a double of himself, lead to a divine vision of salvation. Aurélia, as female archetype, serves as intercessor on the narrator's behalf to ensure God's pardon for transgressions committed in the past. Nerval ends the text on a triumphant note; he has been delivered from Hell, purified and redeemed by the ideal woman Aurélia symbolizes for him. Has redemption lead to a reintegration of the narrator's disparate selves, the good and the bad? The reader remains dissatisfied with the conclusion. (Ironically, *La Revue de Paris* published *Aurélia*'s final pages three weeks after Nerval killed himself.)

When treating an author such as Nerval, it is a difficult task indeed to separate fictional elements in his writing from autobiographical ones. Nerval's obsession with the past, his feelings of culpability (made manifest by the recurring theme of the double), and his desire to recover the lost ideal not only permeate his work but serve as the source of creative power within him.

—Jolene J. Barjasteh

See the essay on "Sylvie."

NIN, Anaïs. American. Born in Paris, France, 21 February 1903; moved to the U.S. in 1914; later became U.S. citizen. Educated at John Jasper Elementary School, New York, 1914–18. Married Hugh Guiler (also called Ian Hugo) in 1924(?). Fashion and artist's model, 1918–20; lived in Paris, 1930–40; established Siana Editions, Paris, 1935;

moved to New York, 1940, and established Gemor Press. Member, American Academy. *Died 14 January 1977.*

PUBLICATIONS

Short Stories

The Winter of Artifice (novellas).   1939.
Under a Glass Bell.   1944; augmented edition, as *Under a Glass Bell and Other Stories,* 1948.
This Hunger (novellas).   1945.
Waste of Timelessness and Other Early Stories.   1977.
The White Blackbird and Other Writings, with *The Tale of an Old Geisha and Other Stories* by Kanoko Okamoto. 1985.

Novels

The House of Incest (prose poem).   1936.
Ladders to Fire.   1946.
Children of the Albatross.   1947.
The Four-Chambered Heart.   1950.
A Spy in the House of Love.   1954.
Solar Barque.   1958; expanded edition as *Seduction of the Minotaur,* 1961.
Cities of the Interior (collection).   1959; expanded edition, 1974.
Collages.   1964.
Delta of Venus: Erotica.   1977.
Little Birds: Erotica.   1979.

Other

D.H. Lawrence: An Unprofessional Study.   1932.
Realism and Reality.   1946.
On Writing.   1947.
The Diary, edited by Gunther Stuhlmann.   6 vols., 1966–76; as *The Journals,*   6 vols., 1966–77; *A Photographic Supplement,* 1974.
The Novel of the Future.   1968.
Unpublished Selections from the Diary.   1968.
Nuances.   1970.
An Interview with Nin, by Duane Schneider.   1970.
Paris Revisited.   1972.
Nin Reader, edited by Philip K. Jason.   1973.
A Woman Speaks: The Lectures, Seminars, and Interviews of Nin, edited by Evelyn J. Hinz.   1975.
In Favor of the Sensitive Man and Other Essays.   1976.
Aphrodisiac, with John Boyce.   1978.
Linotte: The Early Diary 1914–1920.   1978; *The Early Diary 1920–1931,*   3 vols., 1982–85.
Henry and June: From the Unexpurgated Diary.   1986.
A Literate Passion: Letters of Nin and Henry Miller 1932–1953, edited by Gunther Stuhlmann.   1987.
Incest: From A Journal of Love: The Unexpurgated Diary of Nin 1932–24.   1992.

*

Bibliography: *Nin: A Bibliography* by Benjamin Franklin V, 1973; *Nin: A Reference Guide* by Rose Marie Cutting, 1978.

Critical Studies: *Nin* by Oliver Evans, 1968; *The Mirror and the Garden: Realism and Reality in the Writings of Nin* by Evelyn J. Hinz, 1971; *A Casebook on Nin* edited by

Robert Zaller, 1974; *Collage of Dreams: The Writings of Nin* by Sharon Spencer, 1977; *Nin: An Introduction* by Benjamin Franklin V and Duane Schneider, 1979; *Nin* by Bettina L. Knapp, 1979; *Nin* by Nancy Scholar, 1984.

*   *   *

Although the publication of Anaïs Nin's *Diary* elevated her to the status of a cult figure in the late 1960's, she had long been admired by a coterie of American and European avant-garde artists who recognized her talents as a writer of lyrical, experimental fiction and short stories. Lawrence Durrell, Henry Miller, Edmund Wilson, Maxwell Geismer, and William Carlos Williams all celebrated Nin for her "authentic female approach." Williams delighted in what he called her ability to express "infinity in the single cell . . . she harbors, warms, and implants that it may proliferate." Writers like Rebecca West and Djuna Barnes were startled by Nin's capacity to set herself up to serve the genius of some other man while her own talents were so often much stronger and more sure than the talents of those she worshipped. Elizabeth Hardwick and Diane Trilling were more severe. Hardwick called *Under a Glass Bell* "vague, dreamy, mercilessly pretentious; the sickly child of distinguished parents—the avant garde of the twenties—and unfortunately a great bore."

Study of the many versions of her life that she has offered in different forms—the short story, the novelette, the reweaving and republication of the novelettes into her continuous novel, *Cities of the Interior,* and, of course, her amazing diaries—shows how obsessively narcissistic she was, and yet also affords fascinating material for the scholar of the creative process. Close comparisons of the multiple versions of the same kernel event or the multiple attempts to describe the significant people in her life offer evidence of her craft. Many of Nin's early male critics mythologized her, explicating her work in terms of Freudian and Jungian concepts. Her detractors, often female, found her narcissism annoying, if not unbearable. A reexamination of her writings almost 50 years after many of the stories were first written serves her well. She is frank, fascinated with the theatrical construction of multiple selves, and concerned with craft and the intermingling of the arts. Her struggle with issues of gender, control, and sexuality make her writing of particular interest to women. The magical quality of her imaginings and her arduous journeys through psychological interiorities are well worth attention.

Her stories, at their best, are marked by keen powers of observation and an ability to write two kinds of prose, one a lyrical, transcendent sort of verbal alchemy, rich in its sensuous detail and musical in its sounds and rhythms; the other, a realistic, almost naturalistic prose describing ragpickers, or orphans, or the Parisian prostitutes, much more in the manner of a realist than a surrealist. Influenced by Martha Graham's style and *mise-en-scéne,* Nin frequently sets her characters dancing, sometimes narcissistically and, as in *The House of Incest,* without arms, at other times flamboyantly, doing the cancan. One of her most remarkable musical passages occurs in her novélette, "Winter of Artifice," from the collection of stories by the same name. A comparison of the account of her relationship with her father as rendered in this particular story against the version offered in the unexpurgated diary, *Incest,* shows that Nin has created this highly lyrical, fantastical, prose style full of synesthesia to replace the explicit language she uses in the diary to describe her sexual intercourse with her father. Nin often complained that women writers had not had a chance to invent the language of sex and the senses. She admits that her pornographic writings were largely written to fulfill a male formula; however, she does experiment with a language of the erotic in her short stories. Her brilliant description of the orchestra in which a woman draws a bow across her public hairs is one of her most successful attempts to find a symbol and language to register the complicated sexual feelings that her relationship with her father had aroused.

The recent publication of both *Henry and June* (which led to a movie of that title) and *Incest* testify to an enduring appetite for her diaries. Narcissistic and often embarrassingly badly written, these latest diaries nonetheless offer intriguing insights into Nin's theatricality and processes of self-construction. Henry Miller rightly praised Nin for the frankness of her talk about sexuality. More important, these unexpurgated diaries remove some of the mystery that enshrouded her personal and sexual life, her affair with both Henry Miller and his wife June and with both her analysts, Dr. Allendy and Otto Rank, as well as with many artists. Her story "Je Suis La Plus Malade des Surrealistes" in *Under a Glass Bell* is based on her affair with artist Antonin Artaud. The diaries also clarify the nature of her unwanted pregnancy with Miller's child (although there is a possibility that her husband, Hugh Guiler, is the father) and her dangerous surgical abortion coming in the sixth month of her pregnancy. Again, a story, "Birth," grew out of this experience. Printed as the closing story in *Under a Glass Bell,* it is little different from the version she recorded in her diary. These recently published diaries also disclose much more fully and explicitly the circumstances of her sexual relationship with her father, which began in 1933 and concluded, or so she wants us to believe, with her punishing dismissal and neglect of the Don Juan father whose combination of cruelty and love had wrought such damage on her hypersensitive, highly imaginative nature.

These unexpurgated diaries show Nin as a Scheherazade, enthralling her lovers with her tales of her sexuality to stave off the moment when she fears they will abandon her. Ever manipulative and emotionally needy and yet intellectually cunning, Nin claims to have seduced her father by telling him of Allendy's whipping of her—"flagellation" as she wants to call it—as a means to possess her sexually in ways no other of her lovers or husband will permit. She charts the feelings of anger as well as bitter amusement that this whipping has caused her, permanently altering her feelings about Allendy, making him in some ways too ridiculous to sustain the fictions about him that she has created in order to make him the suitable lover and protector that she always seeks. She moves away from Allendy and seeks out Otto Rank in order to explore the incest with her father. Later she reports with candor that Allendy blames her for luring him into this perverse fantasy and goading him on to literally enact it upon her. Her own self-construction in the *Diary* leads this reader to suspect he is partially correct, but it is difficult to justify either Rank's or Allendy's affair with a patient. Nin, however, always seems to know that she has sought out these analytic figures in order to make conquests of them and give herself material for her books. As she says in *Incest:* "I am interested not in the physical possession but in the game, as Don Juan was, *the game of seduction, of maddening, of possessing men not only physically but their souls, too*—I demand more than the whores." She needs them but she also uses them, giving herself a live auditor for her words and creations to supplement the audience afforded by her diary.

Scholars often talk of the continental influences upon Nin's writings—Proust, Artaud, and Jung—but Nin insisted on being compared with women artists and image-makers, with Jane Austen, George Eliot, Amy Lowell, Ruth Draper, Djuna Barnes, and Virginia Woolf, as well as with feminine men such as D.H. Lawrence. For Nin, these women writers, along with Madame de Stael and George Sand, were "absolute self-created individualities." Nin's stories and the stories-recast-as-novels testify to her powers of self-creation. Her women, either herself, thinly disguised as an unnamed narrator, or her characters, Djuna, Stella, Lillian, Sabina and the others, afford her the opportunity to explore women's dreams and fantasies. Her vocabulary of dreams—the mirror in the garden, labyrinths, the house-boat, ladders, and the four elements of water, air, earth and fire—all give her access to realms of the unconscious and allow her to probe relationships. Her stories at their finest, such as "Houseboat," or "Ragpicker," "Winter of Artifice," or "Birth," are marked by the originality of her imagination and her economy of style.

—Carol Simpson Stern

O

OATES, Joyce Carol. American. Born in Millersport, New York, 16 June 1938. Educated at Syracuse University, New York, 1956–60, B.A. in English 1960 (Phi Beta Kappa); University of Wisconsin, Madison, M.A. in English 1961; Rice University, Houston, 1961. Married Raymond J. Smith in 1961. Instructor, 1961–65, and assistant professor of English, 1965–67, University of Detroit; member of the Department of English, University of Windsor, Ontario, 1967–78. Since 1978 writer-in-residence, and currently Roger S. Berlind Distinguished Professor, Princeton University, New Jersey. Since 1974 publisher, with Raymond J. Smith, *Ontario Review,* Windsor, later Princeton. Recipient: National Endowment for the Arts grant, 1966, 1968; Guggenheim fellowship, 1967; O. Henry award, 1967, 1973, and Special Award for Continuing Achievement, 1970, 1986; Rosenthal award, 1968; National Book award, 1970; Rea award, for short story, 1990. Member, American Academy, 1978. Lives in Princeton.

PUBLICATIONS

Short Stories

By the North Gate. 1963.
Upon the Sweeping Flood and Other Stories. 1966.
The Wheel of Love and Other Stories. 1970.
Cupid and Psyche. 1970.
Marriages and Infidelities. 1972.
A Posthumous Sketch. 1973.
The Girl. 1974.
Plagiarized Material (as Fernandes/Oates). 1974.
The Goddess and Other Women. 1974.
Where Are You Going, Where Have You Been? Stories of Young America. 1974.
The Hungry Ghosts: Seven Allusive Comedies. 1975.
The Poisoned Kiss and Other Stories from the Portuguese (as Fernandes/Oates). 1975.
The Triumph of the Spider Monkey. 1976.
The Blessing. 1976.
Crossing the Border. 1976.
Daisy. 1977.
Night-Side. 1977.
A Sentimental Education. 1978.
The Step-Father. 1978.
All the Good People I've Left Behind. 1979.
The Lamb of Abyssalia. 1979.
A Middle-Class Education. 1980.
A Sentimental Education (collection). 1980.
Funland. 1983.
Last Days. 1984.
Wild Saturday and Other Stories. 1984.
Wild Nights. 1985.
Raven's Wing. 1986.
The Assignation. 1988.
Heat: And Other Stories. 1991.
Where Is Here? 1992.

Where Are You Going, Where Have You Been?: Selected Early Stories. 1993.

Novels

With Shuddering Fall. 1964.
A Garden of Earthly Delights. 1967.
Expensive People. 1968.
Them. 1969.
Wonderland. 1971.
Do with Me What You Will. 1973.
The Assassins: A Book of Hours. 1975.
Childwold. 1976.
Son of the Morning. 1978.
Cybele. 1979.
Unholy Loves. 1979.
Bellefleur. 1980.
Angel of Light. 1981.
A Bloodsmoor Romance. 1982.
Mysteries of Winterthurn. 1984.
Solstice. 1985.
Marya: A Life. 1986.
You Must Remember This. 1987.
Lives of the Twins (as Rosamond Smith). 1987.
Soul-Mate (as Rosamond Smith). 1989.
American Appetites. 1989.
Because It Is Bitter, and Because It Is My Heart. 1990.
I Lock My Door upon Myself. 1990.
The Rise of Life on Earth. 1991.
Black Water. 1992.

Plays

The Sweet Enemy (produced 1965).
Sunday Dinner (produced 1970).
Ontological Proof of My Existence, music by George Prideaux (produced 1972). Included in *Three Plays,* 1980.
Miracle Play (produced 1973). 1974.
Daisy (produced 1980).
Three Plays (includes *Ontological Proof of My Existence, Miracle Play, The Triumph of the Spider Monkey*). 1980.
The Triumph of the Spider Monkey, from her own story (produced 1985). Included in *Three Plays,* 1980.
Presque Isle, music by Paul Shapiro (produced 1982).
Lechery, in *Faustus in Hell* (produced 1985).
In Darkest America (*Tone Clusters* and *The Eclipse*) (produced 1990; *The Eclipse* produced 1990). 1991.
Twelve Plays (includes *Tone Clusters, The Eclipse, How Do You Like Your Meat?, The Ballad of Love Canal, Under/ground, Greensleeves, The Key, Friday Night, Black, I Stand Before You Naked, The Secret Mirror, American Holiday*). 1991.

Verse

Women in Love and Other Poems. 1968.

Anonymous Sins and Other Poems.   1969.
Love and Its Derangements.   1970.
Woman Is the Death of the Soul.   1970.
In Case of Accidental Death.   1972.
Wooded Forms.   1972.
Angel Fire.   1973.
Dreaming America and Other Poems.   1973.
The Fabulous Beasts.   1975.
Public Outcry.   1976.
Season of Peril.   1977.
Abandoned Airfield 1977.   1977.
Snowfall.   1978.
*Women Whose Lives Are Food, Men Whose Lives Are
    Money.*   1978.
The Stone Orchard.   1980.
Celestial Timepiece.   1980.
Nightless Nights: Nine Poems.   1981.
Invisible Woman: New and Selected Poems 1970–1982.
    1982.
Luxury of Sin.   1984.
The Time Traveller: Poems 1983–1989.   1989.

Other

The Edge of Impossibility: Tragic Forms in Literature.
    1972.
The Hostile Sun: The Poetry of D.H. Lawrence.   1973.
*New Heaven, New Earth: The Visionary Experience in
    Literature.*   1974.
The Stone Orchard.   1980.
Contraries: Essays.   1981.
The Profane Art: Essays and Reviews.   1983.
Funland.   1983.
On Boxing, photographs by John Ranard.   1987.
(Woman) Writer: Occasions and Opportunities.   1988.
Conversations with Joyce Carol Oates, edited by Lee
    Milazzo.   1989.

Editor, *Scenes from American Life: Contemporary Short
    Fiction.*   1973.
Editor, with Shannon Ravenel, *The Best American Short
    Stories 1979.*   1979.
Editor, *Night Walks: A Bedside Companion.*   1982.
Editor, *First Person Singular: Writers on Their Craft.*
    1983.
Editor, with Boyd Litzinger, *Story: Fictions Past and
    Present.*   1985.
Editor, with Daniel Halpern, *Reading the Fights* (on
    boxing).   1988.
Editor, with Daniel Halpern, *The Sophisticated Cat: A
    Gathering of Stories, Poems, and Miscellaneous Writings
    about Cats.*   1992.
Editor, *The Oxford Book of American Short Stories.*
    1992.

*

Bibliography: *Oates: An Annotated Bibliography* by Francine Lercangee, 1986.

Critical Studies: *The Tragic Vision of Oates* by Mary
Kathryn Grant, 1978; *Oates* by Joanne V. Creighton, 1979;
Critical Essays on Oates edited by Linda W. Wagner, 1979;
*Dreaming America: Obsession and Transcendence in the
Fiction of Oates* by G.F. Waller, 1979; *Oates* by Ellen G.
Friedman, 1980; *Oates's Short Stories: Between Tradition
and Innovation* by Katherine Bastian, 1983; *Isolation and
Contact: A Study of Character Relationships in Oates's
Short Stories 1963–1980* by Torborg Norman, 1984; *The
Image of the Intellectual in the Short Stories of Oates* by
Hermann Severin, 1986; *Oates: Artist in Residence* by
Eileen Teper Bender, 1987; *Understanding Oates* by Greg
Johnson, 1987.

*   *   *

By the early 1990's, though still only in her early fifties
and going as strong as ever, Joyce Carol Oates had
produced 16 volumes of stories, along with more than 20
novels and an assortment of books in other genres. Readers
exploring her short fiction for the first time might start with
The Wheel of Love and *Marriages and Infidelities,* sometimes regarded as among the best short story collections
ever published in the United States. Both these books
illustrate impressively the extraordinary range of Oates's
work (and most of the points made in the present essay).
The Wheel of Love includes wonderful stories: "In the
Region of Ice," about a college-teacher nun and her
troublesome and troubling Jewish student; "Where Are
You Going, Where Have You Been?" about an eerie
Sunday-afternoon encounter between a teenage girl and a
sinister visitor who finds her alone at home; "Convalescing," about the relationship between a man mentally and
physically maimed by an auto accident and his wife, who
has fallen in love with another man; "Shame," about a visit
paid by a priest to the "common" but appealing young
widow of his boyhood chum; "Wild Saturday," about a
child taken by his divorced father to a sleazy hippie
gathering; and "How I Contemplated the World from the
Detroit House of Correction and Began My Life Over
Again," about a female juvenile delinquent from a well-to-
do family. Outstanding stories in *Marriages and Infidelities*
include "Did You Ever Slip on Red Blood?" about a draft-
evasion conspiracy trial and an airplane hijacking; "The
Sacred Marriage," a sexy and haunting tale of an affair
between a literary researcher and his subject's devoted
young widow; "By the River," in which a young woman
who had run away from her husband is murdered by her
brooding and unbalanced father; "Stalking," about an
imaginative young shoplifter; "The Children," about a
"normal" suburban household riven by generational terrors and violence; "Happy Onion," which concludes with a
young woman observing the autopsy performed on the
body of her fiancé, a rock music star; and "The Dead"
(one of a sequence of stories taking off from literary
masterpieces), an amusing but disturbing account of an
overnight-successful woman writer who downs pills like
candy. Very nearly in the same class of excellence are the
volumes *The Goddess and Other Women,* especially notable
for the terrible yet lyrical story "Assault," about a rape
victim's return to the scene of her trauma; *All the Good
People I've Left Behind,* an under-appreciated part of the
Oates canon; and *Last Days,* some of which is set in the
unfamiliar (for Oates) region of eastern Europe under the
Communists.

It is hard to generalize about Oates's short fiction, since it
is so various, in subject and method; it is as though Oates
had set out to write all the stories, and kinds of stories, that
it is possible to write. Certain settings recur, particularly
the slums and affluent suburbs of big cities (often Detroit),
the rural backwaters and small cities of the Erie Canal
region in upper New York State, and the professional

milieus of the American northeast; but probably no more than a plurality of Oates's stories are set in these places. The same goes for her characters: she is drawn especially to attractively trampy, sinister, or delinquent adolescents, from underclass or well-to-do backgrounds, rural rednecks and their floozy female counterparts, urban professionals and intellectuals living on the edge of mental or moral collapse, and obsessively driven lovers of every age and kind; but, again, such a catalogue leaves out a good many of Oates's protagonists. In narrative technique, Oates is among the more traditionally realistic of the major recent writers, but it is not uncommon for her to fracture narrative continuity or to write in the stream-of-consciousness mode. While her prose style has a characteristic haste, urgency, and breathlessness, she can equally well, as narrator or through a persona, speak in a suave, urbane, or casual voice. To find an *oeuvre* of such breadth and variety one must take an extravagantly long view, far beyond the current fiction lists, toward such writers as Chaucer, Balzac, Dostoevskii, even Shakespeare.

Despite this variety, almost all of Oates's stories could be recognized as hers even if they appeared anonymously. There is, for one thing, her terrible intensity. To enter the world of her stories is to invite a torrent of life to overwhelm us, usually in a frightening way. The mode of detached irony so prevalent in 20th-century fiction is essentially foreign to Oates, who has been known to express dissatisfaction with the myth and sensibility of the isolated, alienated artist. (When we do get irony, it is typically of a sinister kind, and even then not the narrator's but a persona's, for example the level-headed voice of the cruise ship captain in "Ladies and Gentlemen," in *Heat*, as he tells his senior-citizen passengers that they are all to be put ashore to die, at their money-hungry children's behest, on a Pacific island.) Oates accepts the utter truth, reality, and existential importance of her material and her characters, however "grotesque" they may seem (the word is a favorite among scholars and critics of her work), as though life were made up mainly of the kind of sensational or appalling incidents reported or imagined in the supermarket tabloids (I HAD MY BOSS'S BABY—TO SAVE HIS MAR-RIAGE!!!) or in the grimmer annals of social work, pathological psychology, and crime. Oates finds sex, violence, psychosis, and extreme or obsessive behavior everywhere—in the city slums, weed-surrounded rural shacks, the dingy enclaves of the counterculture, honky-tonk roadhouses, suburban shopping malls, the urban citadels of Yuppiedom, high-school corridors, the genteel common-rooms of universities and think-tanks, the light-and-air-filled chateaux of Michigan auto tycoons.

For all their sensationalism, Oates's stories never suggest merely cheap effects; on the contrary, our impression—which is cumulative, ever increasing as we read more and more of her work and learn to trust her—is of a great mental power. In part, this mental power is of the same kind possessed by all good fiction writers: that of imagination and of artistic craftsmanship. The remarkable fecundity and energy of Oates's imagination are the most salient facts about her, since, clearly, her personal life (largely as an academic) cannot have exposed her directly to more than a small part of what she writes about. Her artistic craftsmanship, easily lost in the sheer explosiveness of her work, is nonetheless formidable; one notes, for example, that the lurid story of an airplane hijacking in "Did You Ever Slip on Red Blood?" is also a sustained imagistic treatment of tactile, visual, and technological modes of knowing and experiencing. Her store of sheer factual information seems endless—from the two-part inventions

of Bach to all the cheap lipsticks, from the rarefactions of the great philosophers to the minutiae of jukebox music past and present. One has the sense of a truly penetrating and original thinker behind her stories, one who could draw from her own stories innumerable insights of authentic intellectual value (of the kind she draws frequently in her published literary criticism of other authors).

A nonjudgmental openness to every kind of feeling and experience is probably the most distinctive and arresting thing about Oates, and it helps explain why, for all the power and originality of her work, she gets less attention in the highbrow literary journals than many a writer of slighter genius; pundits seem not to know what to make of her. It has been said of Oates that, if we did not know who wrote her stories, we would not be able to tell whether our anonymous author was liberal or conservative, young or old, male or female (her male characters are as fully realized as her female ones). Her creative work in itself cannot easily, if at all, be enlisted in the service of a cause or movement, despite the many stands she takes, outside that work, on all manner of current questions about life, society (boxing, for example, on which she is an authentic expert), and literature. As a result, many readers are left at a loss by Oates's refusal to judge her characters, even those who are most politically controversial or who commit the most appalling deeds, like the murderous twelve-year-old girl in "In the Warehouse" (*The Goddess*) who, having calculatedly pushed her girlhood chum to a horrible death, never feels any sorrow over the incident. One realizes, after reading Oates, just how much moral and ideological selectivity operates even in the boldest of other writers, how much of the torrent of life flows unchecked through Oates's work that, in other authors, is more safely channeled by the dams and causeways of an implicit, enlightened morality.

—Brian Wilkie

See the essays on "Did You Ever Slip on Red Blood?," "How I Contemplated the World from the Detroit House of Correction and Began My Life Over Again," and "Where Are You Going, Where Have You Been?"

O'BRIEN, Edna. Irish. Born in Tuamgraney, County Clare, 15 December 1932. Educated at National School, Scariff; Convent of Mercy, Loughrea; Pharmaceutical College of Dublin: Licentiate, Pharmaceutical Society of Ireland; practiced pharmacy briefly. Married Ernest Gebler in 1952 (marriage dissolved 1967); two sons. Recipient: Kingsley Amis award, 1962; *Yorkshire Post* award, 1971. Lives in London.

PUBLICATIONS

Short Stories

The Love Object.   1968.
A Scandalous Woman and Other Stories.   1974.
Mrs. Reinhardt and Other Stories.   1978; as *A Rose in the Heart*, 1979.
Returning.   1982.
A Fanatic Heart: Selected Stories.   1984.

Lantern Slides.   1990.

Novels

The Country Girls.   1960.
The Lonely Girl.   1962; as *Girl with Green Eyes,* 1964.
Girls in Their Married Bliss.   1964.
August Is a Wicked Month.   1965.
Casualties of Peace.   1966.
A Pagan Place.   1970.
Night.   1972.
Johnny I Hardly Knew You.   1977; as *I Hardly Knew You,* 1978.
The Country Girls Trilogy and Epilogue.   1986.
The High Road.   1988.
Time and Tide.   1992.

Plays

A Cheap Bunch of Nice Flowers (produced 1962). In *Plays of the Year 1962-1963,* 1963.
The Wedding Dress (televised 1963).   In *Mademoiselle* (New York), November 1963.
Zee & Co. (screenplay).   1971.
A Pagan Place, adaptation of her own novel (produced 1972).   1973.
The Gathering (produced 1974).
The Ladies (produced 1975).
Virginia (produced 1980).   1981.
Flesh and Blood (produced 1985).
Madame Bovary, adaptation of the novel by Flaubert (produced 1987).

Screenplays: *Girl with Green Eyes,* 1964; *I Was Happy Here* (*Time Lost* and *Time Remembered*), with Desmond Davis, 1965; *Three into Two Won't Go,* 1969; *Zee & Co.* (*X, Y, & Zee*), 1972; *The Tempter,* with others, 1975; *The Country Girls,* 1984.

Television Plays: *The Wedding Dress,* 1963; *The Keys of the Cafe,* 1965; *Give My Love to the Pilchards,* 1965; *Which of These Two Ladies Is He Married To?,* 1967; *Nothing's Ever Over,* 1968; *Then and Now,* 1973; *Mrs. Reinhardt,* from her own story, 1981.

Verse

On the Bone.   1989.

Other

Mother Ireland.   1976.
Arabian Days, photographs by Gerard Klijn.   1977.
The Collected O'Brien (miscellany).   1978.
The Dazzle (for children).   1981.
James and Nora: A Portrait of Joyce's Marriage.   1981.
A Christmas Treat (for children).   1982.
The Rescue (for children).   1983.
Vanishing Ireland, photographs by Richard Fitzgerald. 1986.
Tales for the Telling: Irish Folk and Fairy Tales.   1986.

Editor, *Some Irish Loving: A Selection.*   1979.

*

Critical Study: *O'Brien* by Grace Eckley,   1974.

* * *

While Edna O'Brien's first three novels assured her fame, they also established the major topics and themes that have been continued in her short stories: the childhood in County Clare, Ireland, tense relationships with the parents, and failed love. The scene changes when the heroine resides in London and travels elsewhere ("Paradise"), but the memories persist. In "The Bachelor" the young girl caught in an unwanted embrace struggles to escape, having "no idea that no matter how distant the flight or how high I soared those people were entangled in me." In "Ghosts," which is reminiscent of three County Clare women, they continue to live "in that faroff region called childhood, where nothing ever dies, not even oneself."

More so than with many other writers, assessment of her art has been intricately interwoven with assessment of her person. Known as a "smashing Irish beauty," much photographed and much interviewed, she has worn down early parochial Irish opposition to the "sinfulness" of sex in her fiction and has seen all her books reprinted many times in paperback. Her short stories have been published in *Cosmopolitan,* *The Atlantic Monthly,* and *The New Yorker.*

Largely because of her very intimate narration, much of it in first-person, early reviewers and many of her reading public believed that she experienced everything she wrote; more recent critics have adopted the term "quasi-autobiographical," which still implies more autobiography than can be defended, with, for example, the death of a mother or a son still living at the time of writing and parallel stories celebrating the same persons living.

In general, O'Brien uses the ingenuousness of history to enhance the conviction, but "A Rose in the Heart" is more than this. It reaffirms the attraction of the nun in "Sister Imelda" and the mother's visit to London in "Cords." The story offers a suspenseful tale of the child's inauspicious birth, increasing affection for the mother and then gradual estrangement, and the sudden death of the mother with the tensions unresolved; even the mother's carefully-hoarded bequest creates a "new wall" between them. Knowledge acquired after the mother's death increases the pain of separation in "Love Child." The stories reiterate that the appetite for tenderness is insatiable; and those who should make the gestures are too much attached to their own weaknesses, sorrows, and restraints to see the need and make the gesture.

"Savages" provides an ironic twist on the local opposition to unwed pregnancy: the romance of Mabel's return from Australia, her increasing weight tokening guilt and demanding ostracism, and banishment after false labor reveals no pregnancy. Had the provincials not been so opposed to assisting a sinful woman, she would have seen a doctor sooner and they would have been spared their malice and their double shame.

Childhood in County Clare means an unreasoning dominance of the Catholic faith in matters of love and conduct; drunken rages in which fathers turn violent toward mother and daughter ("A Scandalous Woman," "A Rose in the Heart"); precarious financial existence with money lost to land, to horses, to drink ("Sisters"); many rural touches like slugs in the cabbage; and a mixture of attitudes about the validity of escape and the pain of return (the collection *Returning*). Innocence and naiveté in the choices the characters make, while most frequently faults of the females, turns comical among the males of "Irish Revel" and "Tough Men."

In the early fiction, men are often active enemies of women, and women—while combating pregnancy, loss, loneliness, and economics—try to overcome vengeance against men; psychological abuse with lovers and husbands replaces the physical abuse of the father in childhood. On her honeymoon, Elizabeth of "Honeyman" learns the mistake of her love and expects chastisement. But the psychological bruises, and especially the necessity to write the divorced husband and his treachery out of the heroine's life, are vastly diminished in the later stories. "The Connor Girls" features the mother's attempt to placate socially-superior neighbors with an invitation that is repulsed; some years later the malicious husband, by rejecting the Connor girl's offer, unknowingly repays the earlier breach.

The loss of love of a prospective mate is a theme in "Over" and "A Journey," in which the heroine's own foibles and sensitivities damage her prospects and defeat her. In "Paradise" the heroine's inability to swim leads to a series of small failures that destroy the romance. In "The Creature" a mother's love for her son smothers him and turns him against her, leaving her a very pathetic and lonely creature. The child of "My Mother's Mother" enjoys the summer visit with the grandmother until taunted with an alarming falsity—that her mother is not her real mother; homesick, she runs home, expecting a welcome from her mother, only to confront the mother's anger at her unexpected presence.

One character's goals and aspirations, whatever they are, seem always inextricably linked to another's affections and leaves the characters extremely pathetic and vulnerable. In "An Outing" the mother plans a day at her home with a former lover in her husband's absence, with all the anticipated enjoyment contingent upon purchase of new living room furniture; when after much sacrifice and contrivance the furniture arrives, it appears unbearably ugly, and they must walk the streets to be together. "The Rug" promotes a mystery of a parcel delivered by mistake, but in the meantime the mother has imagined that it was sent to her as a reward for kindness.

These defeats, both small and large, naturally precipitate a question whether anyone achieves happiness. The woman of "The Favorite" is "in all sorts of ways lucky" and seems to have the perfect existence, with personal achievement, love of husband, and healthy children; but after the age of 40 she fights against boredom.

Whether anyone is likely to live happily ever after a successful mating seems extremely unlikely. Michael in "Courtship" is the ideal male partner—handsome, athletic, suave, hard-working, devoted to his mother. A notable flirt among the local belles and beyond the teenager's reach, he introduces her to the joys of love, inhabiting her universe with "some new and invigorating pulse of life." The man of "The Love Object," solidly married to another woman, remains the ideal while the relationship wobbles in temporary and infrequent meetings; he is "the man that dwells somewhere within me" and will keep the hope alive.

—Grace Eckley

See the essays on "The Doll" and "A Scandalous Woman."

OCAMPO, Silvina. Argentinian. Born in Buenos Aires, in 1906; sister of the writer Victoria Ocampo. Studied painting in Paris with Giorgio de Chirico and Fernand Léger. Married Adolfo Bioy Casares, q.v., in 1940; one daughter. Writer and painter. Recipient: Municipal prize for poetry, 1945; National Poetry prize, 1962; Club de los XIII prize, 1988; PEN Club Gold Pen. Lives in Buenos Aires.

PUBLICATIONS

Short Stories

Autobiografía de Irene.   1948.
La furia y otros cuentos.   1959.
Las invitadas.   1961.
Los días de la noche.   1970.
Leopoldina's Dream (selection).   1988.

Novels

Viaje olvidado.   1937.
Los que aman, odian, with Adolfo Bioy Casares.   1946.
El pecado mortal.   1966.
Informe del cielo y del infierno.   1970.
Canto escolar.   1979.
Y así sucesivamente.   1987.
Cornelia frente al espejo.   1988.

Verse

Enumeración de la patria, y otros poemas.   1942.
Espacios métricos.   1945.
Los sonetos del jardín.   1946.
Poemas de amor desesperado.   1949.
Los nombres.   1953.
Pequeña antología.   1954.
Lo amargo por dulce.   1962.
Amarillo celeste.   1972.
Arboles de Buenos Aires, with Aldo Sessa.   1979.

Plays

Los traidores, with Juan Rudolfo Wilcock (drama in verse).   1956.
No solo el perro es mágico (for children; produced 1958).

Other

El caballo alado (for children).   1972.
El cofre volante (for children).   1974.
El tobogán (for children).   1975.
La naranja maravillosa: cuentos para chicos grandes y para grandes chicos (for children).   1977.
La continuación y otras páginas.   1981.
Breve santoral.   1984.
Páginas (selections).   1984.

Editor, with Jorge Luis Borges and Adolfo Bioy Casares, *Antología de la literatura fantástica.*   1940; as *The Book of Fantasy,* 1988.
Editor, with Jorge Luis Borges and Adolfo Bioy Casares, *Antología poética argentina.*   1941.

*

Critical Studies: "The Initiation Archetype in Arguedas, Roa Bastos and Ocampo" by Barbara A. Aponte, in *Latin American Literary Review* 11(21), 1982; "A Portrait of the Writer as Artist: Ocampo," in *Perspectives on Contemporary Literature* 13, 1987, "The Twisted Mirror: The Fantastic Stories of Ocampo," in *Letras Femeninas* 13(1–2), 1987, and "The Mad Double in the Stories of Ocampo," in *Latin American Literary Review* 16(32), 1988, all by Patricia N. Klingenberg; *From the Ashen Land of the Virgin: Conversations with Bioy Casares, Borges, Denevi, Etchecopar, Ocampo, Orozco, Sabato* by Raul Galvez, 1989.

*   *   *

Jorge Luis Borges, Silvina Ocampo's friend and countryman, finds in her short fictions a "strange taste for a certain kind of innocent and oblique cruelty." There seems to be a paradox here. What might an innocent cruelty involve? Is a cruelty that is innocent, unintentional, oblique really cruelty? Is innocence that is cruel truly innocent?

Much of Ocampo's fiction draws its energy and its power to disturb from this paradox and from her refusal to resolve it. She offers no solutions to the problem of human cruelty, and perhaps, as a fiction writer, that is not her job. She suggests, however, that what we call crime is often less a function of human design than it is of inattention, a momentary lack of control, or, worse, destiny which may or may not be open to change.

As Borges noted, there is something both innocent and cruel about Ocampo's style, about the way she uses words and sentences, and about the ways in which those words and sentences work on the reader. She often writes in a voice that is purposely discontinuous, associative, and innocent of literary devices, as if the narrator were not accustomed to expressing himself or herself in words.

As a result of gaps between the sentences, the reader always senses that something is missing, that something is not being told, perhaps the very something that would bring order to the events being related, an order that would explain why the characters do what they do. But that order is never forthcoming. What happens at any given point in an Ocampo story is not necessarily the result of what has come before, nor does it necessarily determine what will follow. Often, what happens is simply what happens, beyond accounting, beyond explanation.

When cruelty appears in Ocampo's world, it is often inadvertent. In "The Clock House," a group of drunken partiers take the hunchback Estanislao to the laundry and, for no good reason, try to iron out his hump. We never find out what happens once the operation begins—the narrator simply says that he never saw the hunchback again—but it is certainly possible to imagine. Indeed, Ocampo encourages us to do so, and, in the process, she (innocently? cruelly?) places the responsibility for what has happened to Estanislao on us.

In another story, Mercedes is waiting for her beloved dog Mimoso to die so she can have it stuffed. She sits with it through the night:

> The next morning Mercedes put the dog in a sack. It was perhaps not yet dead. She made a package with burlap and newspaper so as not to attract attention in the bus and took him to the taxidermist's.

Has Mercedes inadvertently killed her dog in her eagerness to have it stuffed? Again, we cannot be sure. The dog is dead when the taxidermist opens the bundle, and the story merely goes on from there.

In Ocampo's work, the cruelest characters are often children, though, again, it is never clear whether or not they are really aware of what they are doing. In "The Prayer," Laura, a wife who does not love her husband, sees two young boys fighting over a kite. One pushes the other's face into the water in a ditch and holds him there until he drowns. "I discovered I had watched a crime, a crime in the midst of games that looked so innocent," and she takes the criminal child into her home to protect him. The boy quickly comes to hate her husband who insists upon disciplining him. Then she leaves the boy and her husband alone in the house and goes to church, where she prays and thinks to herself, "I don't know why I am afraid that something has happened in my house; I have premonitions."

Is Laura really unaware of what the boy is going to do to her husband? Would she or the child be guilty of any impending crime? Has anything happened in her house at all? Again, we never find out, and, again, we are the ones responsible for what might happen to the husband, because we are in the position of making it happen, of imagining it.

Sometimes Ocampo suggests that cruelty is a kind of metaphysical principle for which no one is responsible, that human time itself is cruel. Many of her characters seem not to be at home in the present, either because they are trapped in the past (in memory) or in the future (in prophecy). The title character in "The Autobiography of Irene" sees the future so perfectly that her life is virtually meaningless: she says, "I'll never arrive anywhere for the first time. I recognize everything." The narrator of "Magush" meets a young prophet who tells his fortune: he says, "Later when I met up with these [predicted] events, the reality seemed a little faded to me . . . my interest in living what was destined for me diminished."

The fact that many of Ocampo's characters are prophets suggests that the future is already established and waiting for us, that we are victims of a destiny that is cruel precisely because it is knowable. But even this is not assured. As one of Ocampo's prophets admits, "I suspect at times that I don't merely see the future, but that I provoke it."

Morally, Ocampo's fictions are ambiguous and paradoxical, disquieting and yet somehow magical. As in the magic realism of Gabriel García Márquez, Carlos Fuentes, Julio Cortázar, and other Latin American writers, Ocampo brings the possible and the impossible together in ways that test the limits of what we think we know about the world and our place in it. She writes, "Will we always be students of ourselves?" Despite the ambiguity in her fictions, the answer to this question at least is clear.

—Welch D. Everman

See the essay on "Leopoldina's Dream."

———

O'CONNOR, (Mary) Flannery. American. Born in Savannah, Georgia, 25 March 1925. Educated at Peabody High School, Milledgeville, Georgia, graduated 1942; Georgia State College for Women (now Georgia College at Milledgeville), 1942–45, A.B. 1945; University of Iowa, Iowa

City, 1945–47, M.F.A. 1947. Suffered from disseminated lupus after 1950. Recipient: American Academy grant, 1957; O. Henry award, 1957, 1963, 1964; Ford Foundation grant, 1959; National Catholic Book award, 1966; National Book award, 1972. D.Litt.: St. Mary's College, Notre Dame, Indiana, 1962; Smith College, Northampton, Massachusetts, 1963. *Died 3 August 1964.*

PUBLICATIONS

Collections

Complete Stories, edited by Robert Giroux.   1971.
Collected Works (Library of America), edited by Sally Fitzgerald.   1988.

Short Stories

A Good Man Is Hard to Find and Other Stories.   1955; as *The Artificial Nigger and Other Tales,* 1957.
Everything That Rises Must Converge.   1965.

Novels

Wise Blood.   1952.
The Violent Bear It Away.   1960.

Other

Mystery and Manners: Occasional Prose, edited by Sally and Robert Fitzgerald.   1969.
The Habit of Being: Letters, edited by Sally Fitzgerald. 1979.
The Presence of Grace and Other Book Reviews, edited by Carter W. Martin and Leo J. Zuber.   1983.
The Correspondence of O'Connor and the Brainard Cheneys, edited by C. Ralph Stephens.   1986.
Conversations with O'Connor, edited by Rosemary M. Magee.   1987.

Editor, *A Memoir of Mary Ann.*   1961; as *Death of a Child,* 1961.

*

Bibliography: *O'Connor and Caroline Gordon: A Reference Guide* by Robert E. Golden and Mary C. Sullivan, 1977; *O'Connor: A Descriptive Bibliography* by David Farmer, 1981.

Critical Studies: *O'Connor: A Critical Essay* by Robert Drake, 1966; *O'Connor* by Stanley Edgar Hyman, 1966; *The Added Dimension: The Art and Mind of O'Connor* edited by Melvin J. Friedman and Lewis A. Lawson, 1966, and *Critical Essays on O'Connor* edited by Friedman and Beverly L. Clark, 1985; *The True Country: Themes in the Fiction of O'Connor* by Carter W. Martin, 1969; *The World of O'Connor* by Josephine Hendin, 1970; *The Eternal Crossroads: The Art of O'Connor* by Leon Driskell and Joan T. Brittain, 1971; *The Christian Humanism of O'Connor* by David Eggenschwiler, 1972; *Nightmares and Visions: O'Connor and the Catholic Grotesque* by Gilbert Muller, 1972; *O'Connor: Voice of the Peacock* by Kathleen Feeley, 1972, revised edition, 1982; *Invisible Parade: The Fiction of O'Connor* by Miles Orvell, 1972, as *O'Connor: An Introduc-*

tion, 1991; *O'Connor* by Dorothy Walters, 1973; *The Question of O'Connor* by Martha Stephens, 1973; *O'Connor* by Preston M. Browning, Jr., 1974; *O'Connor* by Dorothy Tuck McFarland, 1976; *The Pruning Word: The Parables of O'Connor* by John R. May, 1976; *O'Connor's Dark Comedies: The Limits of Inference* by Carol Shloss, 1980; *O'Connor: Her Life, Library, and Book Reviews,* 1980, and *Nature and Grace in O'Connor's Fiction,* 1982, both by Lorine M. Getz; *O'Connor's South* by Robert Coles, 1980; *O'Connor's Georgia* by Barbara McKenzie, 1980; *The O'Connor Conpanion* by James A. Grimshaw, Jr., 1981; *O'Connor: The Imagination of Extremity* by Frederick Asals, 1982; *O'Connor: Images of Grace* by Harold Fickett and Douglas Gilbert, 1986; *O'Connor's Religion of the Grotesque* by Marshall Bruce Gentry, 1986; *O'Connor: A Study of the Short Fiction* by Suzanne Morrow Paulson, 1988; *O'Connor and the Mystery of Love* by Richard Giannone, 1989.

*   *   *

Even in her tragically brief lifetime, Flannery O'Connor came to be recognized as one of the most distinguished and distinctive writers of modern American fiction. Stricken in 1950 with disseminated lupus, an incurable tubercular disorder, she nonetheless saw published two novels, *Wise Blood* and *The Violent Bear It Away,* and a collection of ten stories, *A Good Man Is Hard to Find.* A second collection of ten stories originally printed separately in magazines and journals, *Everything That Rises Must Converge,* appeared in 1965; other posthumous publications include *Mystery and Manners,* a selection of lectures and occasional prose edited by Sally and Robert Fitzgerald; *The Complete Stories,* 31 in all, including the six that had made up her master's thesis as well as an incomplete novel; and *The Habit of Being,* a collection of her letters edited by Sally Fitzgerald.

Rarely has a writer with so relatively small a corpus attracted such intense and sustained critical engagement and controversy as she has. Although some of her early stories are generally seen as apprentice work and numerous readers find her unorthodox novels to resemble collections of intertwined stories, it is long since generally agreed that she wrote a number of the finest short stories in American literature. The lively range and variety of analytical commentary about her work (some of it, to be sure, erroneous or wrong-headed) is a tribute to the rich, dense complexity of her voice, methods, and vision. A native of Georgia (she grew up, and died there, having spent just a few years in Iowa City earning an M.F.A. degree, in Saratoga Springs, New York at the writers' workshop Yaddo, and then at the Connecticut home of her friends the Fitzgeralds), she was a regionalist of a new stripe in her South, the fundamentalist, Bible-belt, "Christ-haunted" areas of northern Georgia and eastern Tennessee. She was at the same time, to use one of her titles, her own "Displaced Person" there, a relentlessly committed Catholic with a steadfast view of history and existence as incarnational, sacramental, and redemptive. These two determinants, coupled with her first-hand experience with pain, suffering, and the knowledge of imminent death.

Her aesthetic states baldly that "Fiction can transcend its limitations only by staying within them." In the "local," then, however commonplace, tawdry, ugly, cliché-ridden, debased, and violent, would she find the essential conditions of the "transcendental," the inspiriting occasions of sanctifying grace that is for her always present and that her characters are free to accept or reject. Throughout her practice there is an insistence on mystery: "The fiction writer," she says, "presents mystery through manners, grace through nature, but when he finishes, there has to be left over that sense of Mystery which cannot be accounted for by any human formula." She has here in her sights the character of the postmodern world as steeped in the values of gnosticism and secular humanism: "part of it [is] trying to eliminate mystery . . . while another part tries to rediscover it in disciplines less personally demanding than religion." Given the deeply problematic relationship her aesthetic and her practice prompt with the unbelieving reader, O'Connor's stature is astonishing.

Her fictional worlds are an original extension of the modes of Southern Gothic and the Grotesque; and the terms used to describe her vision—black humor, black comedy, sadistic wit, the banal, the absurd, Freud's "Uncanny"—are legion. Violence, whether physical or psychological or both, and of the most shocking kinds, abounds. In "A Good Man Is Hard to Find" The Misfit sees to the mass murder of a family of five; Mr. Shiftlet in "The Life You Save May Be Your Own," having abandoned his new child-bride in a road-side diner called "The Hot Spot," feels that "the rottenness of the world was about to engulf him"; in "The Displaced Person" three bystanders neglect to help and instead hear "the little noise the Pole [Mr. Guizac] made as the tractor wheel broke his back"; the nihilistic con-artist Manley Pointer of "Good Country People" steals Joy/Hulga Hopewell's artificial leg, which is for both of them the signature of her being, and leaves her stranded in a barn loft; "Greenleaf" has Mrs. May gored to death by her tenant farmer's bull, which "had buried his head in her lap, like a wild tormented lover"; in "The Comforts of Home" the 35-year-old-son, Thomas, ostensibly trying to rid his home of Sarah Ham, shoots his mother "accidentally" when she rushes to defend the young woman; another son, Julian, in "Everything That Rises Must Converge" watches hysterically as his overweight mother succumbs to a heart attack after he has ceaselessly bullyragged her; and so on, from rapes through self-mutilations to drownings by baptism.

O'Connor's density of interconnected images, her subtle allusions to, say, texts both sacred and profane, and her carefully controlled omniscient authorial voice empower each of these horrific incidents to be epiphanic, even theophanic, depending on the dramatized perception and free choice of her characters. Citing Teilhard de Chardin's radically Christological theory of evolution, she contends that everything that rises must converge. But convergence comes only after an elevated redeeming insight and a movement of will. No rise, no convergence—but, instead, only a continuing desperately obsessive conflict.

The violence and the sacramental merge in O'Connor's vision. They are not presented dualistically as banal profane and numinous sacred but are absorbed alike under the grotesque. They function in tandem in O'Connor's anagogic and typological imagination, the visible traces of the violence having a correspondence in the invisible movements of grace. One of her most persistent techniques in dramatizing this extraordinary paradox is her masterful configuration of "doubles" that frequently define her recognition scenes. Thomas and Sarah Ham, embattled antagonists throughout "The Comforts of Home," can stand as an example. Sheriff Farebrother rushes into the house to see Thomas's mother lying "on the floor between the girl and Thomas," sees too that "the fellow had intended all along to kill his mother and pin it on the girl,"

and sees, finally, that "Over her body, the killer and the slut were about to collapse into each other's arms." That Freudian and/or Jungian criticism and other "human formulas" can and should yield understanding here goes without saying. When they do, however, O'Connor's uncannily inverted Pietà imbues the scene, the gesture with that left-over sense of mystery still unaccounted for.

—J. Donald Crowley

See the essays on "Everything That Rises Must Converge," "Good Country People," "A Good Man Is Hard to Find," and "Revelation."

———

O'CONNOR, Frank. Pseudonym for Michael Francis O'Donovan. Irish. Born in Cork, 17 September 1903. Educated at the Christian Brothers College, Cork. Served with the Republicans in the Irish civil war: imprisoned in Gormanstown. Married 1) Evelyn Bowen in 1939 (divorced), two sons and one daughter; 2) Harriet Randolph Rich in 1953, one daughter. Teacher of Irish, founder of a theatre group in Cork, and librarian in Sligo, Wicklow, and Cork prior to 1928, then librarian in Dublin; frequent contributor, *Irish Statesman,* 1930's; member of the Board of Directors, Abbey Theatre, Dublin, resigned 1939; lived in Wicklow, 1940's; poetry editor, the *Bell,* Dublin, early 1940's; teacher in the U.S., 1951–60; returned to Ireland, 1961. Litt.D.: University of Dublin, 1962. *Died 10 March 1966.*

PUBLICATIONS

Collections

Day Dreams and Other Stories and The Holy Door and Other Stories, edited by Harriet Sheehy.   2 vols., 1973.
Collected Stories.   1981.

Short Stories

Guests of the Nation.   1931.
Bones of Contention and Other Stories.   1936.
Three Tales.   1941.
Crab Apple Jelly: Stories and Tales.   1944.
Selected Stories.   1946.
The Common Chord: Stories and Tales.   1947.
Traveller's Samples: Stories and Tales.   1951.
The Stories.   1952.
More Stories.   1954.
Stories.   1956.
Domestic Relations: Short Stories.   1957.
My Oedipus Complex and Other Stories.   1963.
Collection Two.   1964.
Collection Three.   1969; as *A Set of Variations,* 1969.
The Cornet-Player Who Betrayed Ireland and Other Stories.   1981.

Novels

The Saint and Mary Kate.   1932.
Dutch Interior.   1940.

Plays

The Invincibles, with Hugh Hunt (produced 1938).
    Edited by Ruth Sherry, 1980.
Moses' Rock, with Hugh Hunt (produced 1938).
In the Train, with Hugh Hunt (produced 1954).   In *The
    Genius of the Irish Theatre,* edited by S. Barnet and
    others, 1960.
The Statue's Daughter (produced 1971).   In *Journal of
    Irish Literature 4,* January 1975.

Verse

Three Old Brothers and Other Poems.   1936.

Other

The Big Fellow: A Life of Michael Collins.   1937; as *Death
    in Dublin: Michael Collins and the Irish Revolution,*
    1937; revised edition, 1965.
A Picture Book (on Ireland).   1943.
Towards an Appreciation of Literature.   1945.
The Art of the Theatre.   1947.
Irish Miles.   1947.
The Road to Stratford.   1948; revised edition, as *Shake-
    speare's Progress,* 1960.
Leinster, Munster and Connaught.   1950.
The Mirror in the Roadway: A Study of the Modern Novel.
    1956.
An Only Child (autobiography).   1961.
The Lonely Voice: A Study of the Short Story.   1963.
The Backward Look: A Survey of Irish Literature.   1967;
    as *A Short History of Irish Literature,* 1967.
My Father's Son (autobiography).   1968.
W. B. Yeats: A Reminiscence.   1982.

Editor, *Modern Irish Short Stories.*   1957.
Editor, *A Book of Ireland.*   1959.
Editor and Translator, *Kings, Lords, and Commons: An
    Anthology from the Irish.*   1959.
Editor and Translator, with David Greene, *A Gold Trea-
    sury of Irish Poetry A.D. 600 to 1200.*   1967.

Translator, *The Wild Bird's Nest.*   1932.
Translator, *Lords and Commons.*   1938.
Translator, *The Fountain of Magic.*   1939.
Translator, *A Lament for Art O'Leary,* by Eileen O'Connell.
    1940.
Translator, *The Midnight Court: A Rhythmical Bacchana-
    lia,* by Bryan Merriman.   1945.
Translator, *The Little Monasteries: Poems.*   1963.

*

Critical Studies: *Michael/Frank: Studies on O'Connor*
edited by Maurice Sheehy, 1969 (includes bibliography);
O'Connor, 1976, and *Voices: A Life of O'Connor,* 1983,
both by James H. Matthews; *O'Connor: An Introduction* by
Maurice Wohlgelernter, 1977; *Five Irish Writers* by John
Hildebidle, 1989; *O'Connor at Work* by Michael Steinman,
1990.

*   *   *

Frank O'Connor was prolific in many literary genres,
producing some notable translations, uneven novels, passionate reviews, and influential criticism over four decades.
However, it is his short fiction that will remain his finest
achievement, over two hundred stories in seven major
collections and various selected editions. The critical
appraisal of his stories proves the truth of Valery's observation that "there is no theory that is not a fragment,
carefully prepared, of some autobiography," for commentators invariably measure O'Connor's tales against the
yardstick of his own theories on the subject, set out in *The
Lonely Voice.*

His opinion that the intense and oblique focus of short
fiction falls most naturally on "the submerged population"
of lonely, marginal figures, victims of society or their own
sensibility, has become one of the commonplaces of the
genre, and a reasonably useful tool for analysing his own
efforts. Of more interest is what O'Connor goes on to say
about narrative technique and the ambivalence between
the objective and subjective voice. He believed that a story
must have "a point," "the basic anecdote," even if it was
"smothered at birth." Yet later this is counterbalanced by
his assertion that a great story was "like a sponge; it sucks
up hundreds of impressions that have nothing whatever to
do with the anecdote." This debate, between the oral
storytelling tradition "with the tone of a man's voice,
speaking," and the more objective, precise detachment of
the Chekhovian narrative, is reflected throughout his
career, the tension producing some of his finest stories.

The most pervasive theme of O'Connor's fiction is
human lives that are governed by desires, aspirations, and
illusions, but which always seem to be overwhelmed by the
actuality of social, religious, and political pressures. As one
of his characters says, "Choice was an illusion," and the
romantic impulses of the protagonists in his first collection,
Guests of the Nation, invariably end in sadness and despair.
Eleven out of the fifteen stories have a first-person point of
view, ranging from the famous title story in which an adult
tells of his tragic, youthful, Republican experiences, to
"The Patraiarch," in which those roles are reversed. The
great strength of the collection is the subtlety with which
O'Connor manages to convey the different attitudes implicit in the narrative voice and the experiences that voice
recounts, a talent likely to remind the contemporary reader
of Milan Kundera, and his acute observation that "the
struggle of man against power is the struggle of memory
against forgetting."

The next collection of stories, *Bones of Contention,* also
has an Irish background, as indeed have virtually all of
O'Connor's stories, even to the extent of rewriting tales
collected elsewhere to add an Irish setting. D.H. Lawrence
once said that a writer's "passion" is always searching for
some form that will express or hold it better, and the
various narrative strategies deployed by O'Connor in this
collection illustrate his continuing search for a natural
fictive voice. As the title indicates, the struggles depicted
are no longer dramatic and revolutionary but domestic and
seemingly insignificant. In "Peasants" the difference between a community's internal wrangles and its solid
opposition to external power stands as a metaphor for all
the individual struggles taking place, usually against the
legal system. Dan Bride's casual dismissal of officialdom in
"The Majesty of the Law" suggests that the time-honoured
rituals of tribal custom remain untouched by an abstract
judicial system.

The most mature volume of stories produced by
O'Connor, and coincidently the moment when the lonely,
frustrated individual becomes his dominant interest, is

Crab Apple Jelly, the suggestive title once again hinting at the bittersweet, entertainingly serious nature of the stories. The finest two stories portray different aspects of the same theme. "The Long Road to Ummera" centres on an old woman's determined triumph over her own isolated loneliness, whilst "Uprooted" sullenly reflects on the inability of two brothers, a teacher and a priest, to lift themselves out of a bitter sense of failure. *The Common Chord* extends the thematic range to the sexual repression of the Irish middle class. The state censorship that followed drew the pithy remark from O'Connor that "an Irish writer without contention is a freak of nature. All the literature that matters to me was written by people who had to dodge the censor." The lonely young girls in stories like "The Holy Door" are comically dramatised in their priest-induced sexual confusion and frustration, although the engaging narratorial voice reassures the reader of its basically sympathetic attitude to the characters.

This sympathy with adolescent and adult disillusionments continued into the next decade with *Traveller's Samples* and *Domestic Relations*. The quixotic Larry Delaney, a character initially introduced in "The Procession of Live" (from O'Connor's first collection), narrates almost half of the stories, which tend to focus on outcasts of every kind. Displaced, deluded, and socially inadept, the protagonists suffer the consequences of loveless marriages and unhappy families, as denoted by the titles: "The Pariah," "Orphans," "The Man of the House," "The Drunkard," and "A Bachelor's Story." The later stories collected in *My Oedipus Complex* and *A Set of Variations* (published posthumously) are even more strongly anchored in the first-person narrative. O'Connor once said that he knew to the last syllable how any Irishman would say anything—not what he would say, but how he would say it. The character of Kate, the old woman who adopts two illegitimate boys in the title story of the last volume, might be taken as his final affirmation of the imagination in the face of the destructive forces both within and outside of the individual; what he called his "lyric cry in the face of destiny." His quest to capture the isolated subject in an objective narration never completely blended with his fascination for the oral tale, but the tension generated some of the most memorable stories ever produced by an Irish writer—no mean achievement given the company. O'Connor wrote that whereas Yeats and Synge had their "presences," he had "only my voices." It was enough.

—Simon Baker

See the essays on "First Confession," "Guests of the Nation," and "My Oedipus Complex."

ODÓEVSKII, Vladímir (Fёdorovich) (Prince). Russian. Born in Moscow, 30 July 1804. Educated in Moscow, 1816–1822. Married Ol'ga Stepanovna Lanskaia in 1826. Amateur composer and musicologist; publisher and co-editor, *Mnemozina,* 1924–25; moved to St. Petersburg, 1926; editor, writer, and critic, from 1926; librarian, St. Petersburg Public Library, from 1946; director, Rumiantsev Museum, from 1846; appointed to Moscow Senate, 1862. Co-founder, Society of Wisdom Lovers, president, 1923–25. Member, Free Society of Amateurs of Russian Letters. *Died 27 February 1869.*

PUBLICATIONS

Collections

Povesti [Novellas].   3 vols., 1890.
Povesti i rasskazy [Novellas and Stories], edited by E. Iu. Khin.   1959.
Povesti [Novellas], edited by V.I. Sakharov.   1977.
Sochineniia v dvukh tomakh [Works].   2 vols., 1981.

Short Stories

Pestrye skazki s krasnym slovtsom sobrannye Irineem Modestovichem Gomozeikoiu, magistrom filosofi i chlenom raznykh uchonykh obshchestv, izdannye V. Bezglasnym [Motley Fairy Tales].   1833.
Kniazhna Mimi; domashnie razgovory [Princess Mimi; Home Conversation].   1834(?).
Russkie nochi.   1844; as *Russian Nights,* edited by Ralph Matlaw, 1965.
Romanticheskie povesti [Romantic Novels], edited by Orest Tsekhnovitser.   1929.
Deviat' povestei [Nine Novellas].   1954.

Novel

4338 god: Fantasticheskii roman [The Year 4338. Letters from Petersburg (1835 and 1840)], edited by Orest Tsekhnovitser.   1926.

Fiction for children

Detskaia knizhka dlia voskresnykh dnei [A Child's Book for Sundays].   1833.
Gorodok v tabakerke. Detskaia skazka dedushki Irineia [The Little Town in the Snuffbox. Children's Fairy Tale of Grandfather Irinei].   1834.
Detskie Skazki dedushki Irineia [Children's Tales of Grandfather Irinei].   1840.
Skazki i povesti dlia detei Dedushki Irineia [Fairy Tales and Stories of Grandfather Irinei for Children].   1841.
Sbornik detskikh pesen Dedushki Irineia [A Book of Grandfather Irinei's Songs for Children] (verse).   1847.
Dedushki Irineia skazki i sochineniia dlia detei [Grandfather Irinei's Fairy Tales and Selections for Children].   1871.
Skazki i rasskazy dedushki Irineia [Fairy Tales and Stories of Grandfather Irinei].   1889.

Other

Chetyre apologa [Four Apologies].   1824.
Sochineniia kniazia [Works].   3 vols., 1844.
Lettre et plaidoyer en faveur de l'abonné russe.   1857.
Nedovol'no [Not Good Enough].   1867.
Publichnye lektsii professora Liubimova [Public Lectures of the Professor of Love].   1868.
Izbrannye muzykal'no-kriticheskie stat'i [Collection of Musical Critical Articles].   1951.
Stat'i o M.I. Glinke [Articles on M.I. Glinke].   1953.
Izbrannye pedagogicheskie sochineniia, edited by V. Ia. Struminskii.   1955.
Muzykal'no-literaturnoe nasledie [Musical Literary Heritage], edited by G. Bernandt.   1956.

Editor, with A.P. Zablotskii, *Sel'skoe chtenie.*   4 vols., 1863.

*

Critical Studies: Introduction to *Russian Nights* by Ralph Matlaw, 1965; "A Hollow Shape: The Philosophical Tales of Prince Odoevsky" by Simon Karlinsky, *Studies in Romanticism* 5, 1966; "Odoevsky's Russian Nights," in *Essays in Poetics* 8, 1983, and *The Life, Times, and Milieu of Odoevsky 1804–1869,* 1986, both by Neil Cornwell.

* * *

Named the "Russian Faust" after one of his own characters, Vladímir Odóevskii demonstrated an unusually deep knowledge of a wide range of subjects: music, bibliography, education, literature, science, economics, and philosophy, especially of the German idealists. He fell under the spell of German romantic philosophy while being educated in Moscow, his native city. There Odóevskii founded the *Obshchestvo liubomudriia* (Society of Wisdom Lovers), which debated philosophical problems put forth by Kant, Fichte, Spinoza, and Schilling. With his friend Wilhelm Kiukhelbeker, he published and edited the literary almanac *Mnemozina* (1824-25) dedicated to the ideals of the *liubomudrii* group.

In 1826 Odóevskii moved to St. Petersburg where he entered the civil service in the Ministry of Justice; he continued his career in service as the director of the Rumiantsev Museum and of its most important library. A man of seemingly endless activity, Odóevskii became a writer, scholar, and music critic; he also engaged in the field of publishing. He was a beloved literary figure and his salon became a forum for the best artists and minds of his day. But his fame rests mainly on the popularity of his short stories.

Odóevskii's fiction explored a number of themes, mainly gleaned from German romanticism. In his stories he tried to imbue reality with a sense of the ideal and the transcendental. He also expressed in them his dissatisfaction with the compartmentalization of knowledge and people's total reliance either on the materialistic side of existence or on the poetic ideal. Because his own proclivities tended toward aesthetic needs, much of his work deals with the role of art in society, the qualities that make up the artist, and the ramifications of creative ecstasy with its close proximity to madness and insanity. He also pondered the utopian ideal. In addition his interests included speculation on religion, government, and the fundamental meaning of human existence.

The types of stories Odóevskii wrote are as numerous as his themes: satires, fantasies, philosophical sketches, society tales, *Künstlernovellen,* anti-utopias, and even children's stories. Grandpa Irinei is the delightful narrator of the tales for youngsters, which were informative as well as entertaining. In his desire to inform the masses, Odóevskii wrote a series of anthologies for the uneducated. These were basic texts on a variety of subjects. His utopian fantasy is a fragment of another major project he set out to write: a trilogy depicting Russia's past, present, and future. *4338 god: Fantasticheskii roman* ("The Year 4338. Letters from Petersburg [1835 and 1840]") describes the world one year before Biela's Comet will collide with the earth and destroy human civilization. On the eve of destruction the world is divided into two camps: the Russian and the Chinese, with the latter sphere acting as disciple of the former. A Chinese student visits Russia's main city, a massive fusion of Moscow and St. Petersburg. In letters to a friend the student describes a world not unlike those envisioned by H.G. Wells and Aldous Huxley. An effective political system, with various ministries of philosophy, fine arts, the air forces, and conciliation, governs a Russia where people with extraordinary talents get special training to help them serve. For relaxation the workers still drink alcohol, but the upper classes inhale special gasses and take "magnetic baths," electronic stimulators that act on a group to free minds from inhibitions, induce heightened sensations, and foster love and friendship. On the whole this literary experiment shows Odóevskii's keen philosophical interest in the future of the world.

His fondness for narrative experimentation led him to create a voluble storyteller, Irinei Modestovich Gomozeiko, Odóevskii's alter-ego, another "Renaissance man," who serves as the unifying element of the *Pestrye skazki* (Motley Fairy Tales). A compendium of German romanticism, the tales tend to be whimsical, satirical, grotesque, and "supernatural." Probably one of the most well-known pieces of the collection, "A Tale of Why It Is Dangerous for Young Girls to Go Walking in a Group Along Nevsky Prospect," is a fantasy/satire against the pernicious influence of society "mamas" and foreign culture on young Russian girls. In this story Odóevskii takes a homogenized Russian beauty and turns her into a doll under a glass jar. She nods her head along with all of the other dolls in the window of a shop in which objects, foreign and fantastic, are sold. Clearly, Odóevskii makes the point that the women of Petersburg have no individuality.

A fantastic story of a much higher intellectual level, "Sil'fida" ("The Sylph"), describes the consequences of being transported to higher realms while still earth bound. Mikhail Platonovich goes to the estate of his late uncle to convalesce after some illness. Bored by lack of reading material, he orders the servants to open boxes of books packed away by his aunt because of their evil influence. He discovers a cache of alchemical and occult books and soon becomes absorbed in their mysteries. He forgets everything, even the fiancée he courts in the country; he loses himself in experiments, one of which yields a perfectly formed miniature woman who initiates him into the mysteries of higher beauty and truth. His friend brings a doctor who successfully cures him of his malaise. But instead of being grateful, Mikhail Platonovich lashes out at his friend for depriving him of the world of perfection the tiny woman revealed to him. In this story we see Odóevskii's frustration at humankind's inability to reconcile real and the ideal.

In contrast to his philosophical stories, Odóevskii wrote a series of society tales, of which the best are "Princess Zizi" and "Princes Mimi" (1834). In the latter he experiments further with narrational technique. Gone is the conventional framing device; "Princess Mimi" begins right in the middle of a ball, one of his favorite targets of satire. Odóevskii displays more narrative self-confidence when he stops the action at the most exciting part and interjects the preface to the story along with a Sternean discourse on the trials of writing novels—a good example of romantic irony, a reminder that we indeed are reading fiction. His use of this device calls to our attention the main theme of the story, appearance versus reality. Princess Mimi, an old maid "guardian of morality" in St. Petersburg *beau monde,* preserves outward decorum while slandering an innocent victim of her spite. In this story the author lashes out against Petersburg society with its superficial, hypocritical standards of human worth.

A summary of Odóevskii's views on many issues provides the thematic thread that runs through his collection *Russkie nochi (Russian Nights).* Though the stories appeared at various times, he brought them together with interspersed commentary of four men who debate the merits of scientific empiricism versus mystical idealism. He uses Plato's dialogues as his model for the stories he arranges in an order designed to develop the argument. Faust, Odóevskii's spokesman, argues on the side of idealism with the support of Rostislav who stresses the importance of love and faith. Victor and Vyacheslav become spokesmen for rationalism and utilitarianism. In three nights they tell stories that demonstrate the destructive powers of a materialistic view of the world: "Opere del Cavaliere Giambattista Piranesi," "The Brigadier," "The Ball," "The Avenger," "The Mockery of a Corpse," "The Last Suicide," "Cecelia," and "A City Without Name," an indictment of the theories of Malthus and Bentham. The economist who presents these tales becomes disillusioned as he realizes his arguments are inadequate.

The next three nights Faust tells stories dealing with the higher realm of art, which also ultimately proves to be inadequate. The three stories are about artists: Beethoven, who feels frustration with musical instruments that limit the infinite possibilities of music ("Beethoven's Last Quartet"); a poet/improvisor, who sees the component parts of everything so clearly he cannot visualize the entire picture ("The Improvvisatore"); Sebastian Bach, who sacrificed family and happiness to become perfection in art ("Sebastian Bach"). Unfortunately his art lacks human passion.

Odóevskii's stories about the artist and his role in society rank among his best. They most clearly testify to his status as the foremost disseminator of ideas of the romantic movement in Russia. Of all his contemporaries he best represents his age.

—Christine A. Rydel

OE Kenzaburō. Japanese. Born in Ōse village, Shikoku island, 31 January 1935. Educated at Tokyo University, 1954–59, B.A. in French literature 1959. Married Itami Yukari in 1960; three children. Travelled to China as member of Japan-China Literary Delegation, 1960; travelled to Eastern and Western Europe, 1961, United States, 1965, Australia and U.S., 1968, and Southeast Asia, 1970; visiting professor, Collegio de México, Mexico City, 1976; freelance writer. Recipient: May Festival prize, 1954; Akutagawa prize, 1958; Shinchōsha prize, 1964; Tanizaki prize, 1967; Noma prize, 1973; Osaragi Jirō award. Lives in Tokyo.

PUBLICATIONS

Short Stories

Shisha no Ogori [The Arrogance of the Dead].   1958.
Miru mae ni Tobe [Leap Before You Look].   1958.
Okurete kita seinen [The Youth Who Arrived Late].   1962.
Sakebigoe [Outcries].   1963.
Warera no kyōki o ikinobiru michi o oshieyo (novella).   1969; augmented edition, 1975; as "Teach Us to Outgrow Our Madness," in *Teach Us to Outgrow Our Madness: Four Short Novels,* 1977.

Waganamida o nuguitamaū hi (novella).   1972; as "The Day He Himself Shall Wipe My Tears Away," in *Teach Us to Outgrow Our Madness,* 1977.
Sora no kaibutsu Aguii.   1972; as "Aghwee the Sky Monster," in *Teach Us to Outgrow Our Madness,* 1977.
Teach Us to Outgrow Our Madness: Four Short Novels (includes "Teach Us to Outgrow Our Madness," "The Day He Himself Shall Wipe My Tears Away," "Prize Stock," "Aghwee the Sky Monster").   1977.
Gendai denkishū [Modern Tales of Wonder].   1980.

Novels

Memushiri kouchi [Pluck the Flowers, Gun the Kids].   1958.
Warera no jidai [Our Age].   1959.
Seinen no omei [The Young Man's Stigma].   1959.
Kodoku na seinen no kyūka.   1960.
Seiteki ningen [The Sexual Man].   1963.
Nichijō seikatsu no bōken [Adventures of Everyday Life].   1963.
Kojinteki na taiken.   1964; as *A Personal Matter,* 1968.
Man'nen gannen no futtobōru.   1967; as *The Silent Cry,* 1974.
Kōzui wa waga tamashii ni oyobi [The Flood Has Reached My Soul].   2 vols., 1973.
Pinchiranna chōsho.   1976; as *The Pinch-Runner Memorandum,* 1993.
Dōjidai gemu [The Game of Contemporaneity].   1979.
"Ame no ki" o kiku onnatachi [Women Listening to "Rain Tree"].   1982.
Atarashi hito yo mezameyo [Rouse Up O Young Men of the New Age!].   1983.
Natsukashii toshi e no tegami [Letters to the Lost Years].   1986.
Chiryō no tō [Tower of Healing].   1991.

Other

Sekai no wakamonotachi.   1962.
Hiroshima nōto [Hiroshima Notes].   1965.
Genshuku na tsunawatari [The Solemn Tightrope Walking].   1965.
Zensakuhin [Collected Works].   6 vols., 1966–67; 2nd series, 1977—.
Jizokusuru kokorozashi [Enduring Volition].   1968.
Kowaremono to shite no ningen [Fragile Human].   1970.
Okinawa nōto [Okinawa Notes].   1970.
Kakujidai no sōzōryoku [The Imagination of the Nuclear Age].   1970.
Genbakugo no ningen [Homo sapien After the A-Bomb].   1971.
Kujira no shimetsusuru hi [The Day the Whales Shall Be Annihilated].   1972.
Dōjidai to shite no sengo [Post-War as the Contemporaneity].   1973.
Jōkyō e [Toward Situations].   1974.
Bungaku nōto [Literary Notes].   1974.
Kotoba ni yotte: Jōkō/Bungaku [Via Words: Situations/Literature].   1976.
Shōsetsu no hōhō [The Method of a Novel].   1978.
Ōe Kenzaburō dōjidaironshū [An Essay on the Contemporary Age].   10 vols., 1981.
Shomotsu—sekai no in'yu, with Yujiro Nakamura and Masao Yamaguchi.   1981.
Chūshin to shūen, with Yujiro Nakamura and Masao Yamaguchi.   1981.

Bunka no kasseika, with Yujiro Nakamura and Masao Yamaguchi.   1982.

Hiroshima kara Oiroshima e: '82 Yōroppa no hankaku heiwa undo o miru.   1982.

Kaku no taika to "ningen" no koe [The Nuclear Conflagration and the Voice of "Man"].   1982.

Ika ni ki o korosu ka [How to Kill a Tree].   1984.

Nihon gendai no yumanisuto Watanabe Kazuo o yomu. 1984.

Ikikata no teigi: futatabi jokyo e.   1985.

Shōsetsu no takurami chi no tanoshimi.   1985.

Kaba ni kamareru.   1985.

M/T to mori no fushigi no monogatari.   1986.

Atarashii bungaku no tame no.   1988.

Kirupu no gundan.   1988.

Saigo no shōsetsu.   1988.

Editor, *Itami Mansaku essei shu,* by Mansaku Itami. 1971.

Editor, *Atomic Aftermath: Short Stories About Hiroshima-Nagasaki.*   1984; as *The Crazy Iris and Other Stories of the Atomic Aftermath,* 1985; as *Fire from the Ashes: Short Stories About Hiroshima and Nagasaki,* 1985.

*

Critical Studies: "Circles of Shame: 'Sheep' by Ōe Kenzaburō" by Frederick Richter, in *Studies in Short Fiction* 11, 1974; in *The Search for Authenticity in Modern Japanese Literature,* 1978, and *Oe Kenzaburo and Contemporary Japanese Literature,* 1986, both by Hisaaki Yamanouchi; "The 'Mad' World of Ōe Kenzaburō" by Iwamoto Yoshio, in *Journal of the Association of Teachers of Japanese* 14 (1), 1979; "Toward a Phenomenology of Ōe Kenzaburō: Self, World, and the Intermediating Microcosm" by Earl Jackson, Jr., in *Transactions of the International Conference of Orientalists in Japan* 25, 1980; "Ōe's Obsessive Metaphor, Mori the Idiot Son: Toward the Imagination of Satire, Regeneration, and Grotesque Realism" by Michiko N. Wilson, in *Journal of Japanese Studies* 7 (1), 1981; "Kenzaburo Oe: A New World of Imagination" by Yoshida Sanroku, in *Comparative Literature Studies* 22 (1), 1985; *The Marginal World of Oe Kenzaburo: A Study in Themes and Techniques* by Michiko N. Wilson, 1986; in *Off Center* by Miyoshi Masao, 1991; *Escape from the Wasteland: Romanticism and Realism in the Fiction of Mishima Yukio and Oe Kenzaburo* by Susan J. Napier, 1991.

*   *   *

Ōe Kenzaburo, arguably Japan's most important contemporary writer, is known for his short stories and novels celebrating the marginal and the oppressed, in often violent opposition to a central establishment. It is perhaps not surprising, therefore, that Ōe was born in a mountain village of Shikoku, the smallest and still most rural of Japan's four major islands. Although Ōe now lives in Tokyo, the village in the valley and the forest surrounding it have continued to empower Ōe's fictional imagination. Works highlighting a rural background range from his early so-called "pastoral fiction," such as his 1958 Akutagawa prize-winning story, "Shiiku" ("Prize Stock and the Catch") to his nostalgic 1986 novel, *Natsukashii toshi e no tegami,* (Letters to the Lost Years). While his pastoral works were largely realistic in their treatment of the village

and the valley, Ōe's later fiction increasingly began to attach a mythological significance to these places. In *Man'nen gannen no futtobōru,* (The Silent Cry), two urban brothers return to their village in the mountains to forge new lives: the older brother searches for a "thatched hut," a retreat away from the world, while the younger brother mixes village history and legends to anoint himself leader over the increasingly apathetic villagers.

The possibilities inherent in rural folk legends became increasingly important in Ōe's fiction in the 1970's and 1980's, leading to his controversial novel, *Dōjidai gemu,* (The Game of Contemporaneity), which describes a hidden mountain village's relentless opposition toward what they call the Greater Japanese Empire. *Dōjidai gemu* offers the inspiration of the folklore and legends of the village as a substitute to what Ōe considers to be the pernicious influence of the elitist myths of the Japanese emperor system.

In fact, Ōe's strong opposition to the emperor system has been another important element in his writing, often combined with the events of the summer of 1945 when Japan acknowledged defeat and the Allied Occupation began. Ōe's Japanese critics have pointed to 1945 as a watershed year in the young Ōe's life, creating a bifurcation in his personal ideology, between the "patriotic boy" who had loved the emperor and the "democratic boy" who believed in the liberal principles fostered by the Occupation. Many of his early works show this bifurcation.

Perhaps Ōe's most fascinating fictional comment on the emperor system is his brilliant novella *Waganamida o nuguitamaū hi* ("The Day He Himself Shall Wipe My Tears Away"). Inspired by the emperor-oriented suicide of Ōe's fellow novelist and personal *bête noire* Mishima Yukio, the novella is a savage attack on both the emperor system and the insane romanticism that lay behind Mishima's death. At the same time, however, the novella betrays a certain empathy towards that very romanticism, suggesting that traces of the "patriotic boy" still remain in Ōe's personality, although Ōe is a committed leftwing humanist.

Ōe's portraits of romantic protagonists, lost in dreams of violence or escape, are among his most effective. Perhaps his most successful characterization of this sort is contained in his bildungsroman, *Kojinteki na taiken (A Personal Matter).* A darkly humourous, yet extraordinarily affecting account of a young man's struggle to come to terms with having fathered a brain-damaged child, *A Personal Matter* contains strongly autobiographical elements. But Bird, as the young father is called, is ultimately far more than Ōe's alter ego. A dreamer who initially wants only to escape his marriage and travel to Africa, Bird grows up in the course of the book through a series of grotesque and memorable encounters that range from the erotic to the comic. *A Personal Matter* is one of Ōe's funniest and most moving novels, and its hero, irritating and self-pitying though he may be, is one of the most brilliantly realized characters in modern Japanese fiction.

The theme of father and brain-damaged son has remained an important element in Ōe's fiction, from the surreal fantasy *Sora no kaibutsu Aguii,* ("Aghwee the Sky Monster,") in which a father is unable to overcome his guilt for having murdered his brain-damaged baby, to the carnivalesque epic *Pinchiranna chōsho (The Pinch-Runner Memorandum),* in which a father and idiot son lead an army of marginals and grotesques against the Japanese establishment.

In recent years Ōe's work has continued to mine these themes, although the tone has become increasingly elegiac rather than angry. Ōe's recent work, especially the 1991 science fiction novel *Chiryō no tō*, (Tower of Healing), set in a dystopian future where a hidden valley exists as a final escape, suggests that his favorite themes may increasingly be combined with new departures. Whatever Ōe's next direction will be, it seems certain that he will remain committed to producing fiction that is simultaneously politically controversial and highly imaginative.

—Susan J. Napier

See the essay on "Aghwee the Sky Monster."

————————

O'FAOLAIN, Sean. Irish. Born John Francis Whelan in Cork, 22 February 1900. Educated at University College, Dublin, B.A. in English 1921, M.A. in Irish 1924, M.A. in English 1926; Harvard University, Cambridge, Massachusetts (Commonwealth fellow, 1926–28; John Harvard fellow, 1928–29), 1926–29, M.A. 1929. Served in the Irish Republican Army, 1918–21: director of publicity, 1923. Married Eileen Gould in 1928 (died 1988); one daughter, the writer Julia O'Faolain, and one son. Teacher at Christian Brothers School, Ennis, 1924; lecturer in English, Boston College and Princeton University, New Jersey, 1929, and St. Mary's College, Strawberry Hill, Twickenham, Middlesex, 1929–33; full-time writer from 1933; editor, the *Bell*, Dublin, 1940–46. Director, Arts Council of Ireland, 1957–59. D. Litt.: Trinity College, Dublin, 1957. *Died 21 April 1991.*

PUBLICATIONS

Short Stories

Midsummer Night Madness and Other Stories.   1932; as *Stories of O'Faolain*, 1970.
There's a Birdie in the Cage (story).   1935.
A Born Genius (story).   1936.
A Purse of Coppers: Short Stories.   1937.
Teresa and Other Stories.   1947; as *The Man Who Invented Sin and Other Stories*, 1948.
The Finest Stories.   1957; as *The Stories*, 1958.
I Remember! I Remember!   1961.
The Heat of the Sun: Stories and Tales.   1966.
The Talking Trees.   1970.
Foreign Affairs and Other Stories.   1976.
Selected Stories.   1978.
The Collected Stories 1–3.   3 vols., 1980–82.

Novels

A Nest of Simple Folk.   1933.
Bird Alone.   1936.
Come Back to Erin.   1940.
And Again?   1979.

Plays

She Had to Do Something (produced 1937).   1938.
The Train to Banbury (broadcast 1947).   In *Imaginary Conversations*, edited by Rayner Heppenstall, 1948.

Radio Play: *The Train to Banbury*,   1947.

Other

The Life Story of Eamon De Valera.   1933.
Constance Markievicz; or, The Average Revolutionary: A Biography.   1934; revised edition, 1968.
King of the Beggars: A Life of Daniel O'Connell.   1938.
De Valera: A Biography.   1939.
An Irish Journey.   1940.
The Great O'Neill: A Biography of Hugh O'Neill, Earl of Tyrone 1550–1616.   1942.
The Story of Ireland.   1943.
The Irish: A Character Study.   1947; revised edition, 1969.
The Short Story.   1948.
A Summer in Italy.   1949.
Newman's Way: The Odyssey of John Henry Newman.   1952.
South to Sicily.   1953; as *An Autumn in Italy*, 1953.
The Vanishing Hero: Studies in Novelists of the Twenties.   1956.
Vive Moi! (autobiography).   1964.

Editor, *Lyrics and Satires from Toni Moore.*   1929.
Editor, *The Autobiography of Theobald Wolfe Tone.*   1937.
Editor, *The Silver Branch: A Collection of the Best Old Irish Lyrics.*   1938.
Editor, *Handy Andy* (abridgement) by Samuel Lover.   1945.
Editor, *Short Stories: A Study in Pleasure.*   1961.

*

Critical Studies: *O'Faolain: A Critical Introduction* by Maurice Harmon, 1966, revised edition, 1985; *O'Faolain* by Paul A. Doyle, 1968; *The Short Stories of O'Faolain: A Study in Descriptive Techniques* by Joseph Storey Rippier, 1976; "O'Faolain Issue" of *Irish University Review*, Spring 1976; "Sean at Eighty" by Julia O'Faolain, in *Fathers: Reflections by Daughters* edited by Ursula Owen, 1983; *O'Faolain: A Critical Introduction* by Maurice Harmon, 1985; *O'Faolain's Irish Vision* by Richard Bonaccorso, 1987.

*   *   *

Sean O'Faolain's first collection of stories seems to romanticize events that take place during the Anglo-Irish War and the Civil War—escapes, a kidnapping, an assassination, bombmaking, military engagements. But they are not so much evocations of youthful rebellion as condemnations of rebel irresponsibility and violence. O'Faolain, once an idealistic rebel, recaptures that idealism in the earliest story "Fugue," but the final story, "The Patriot," clearly states his preference for love and a stable existence.

In that first collection he distances himself from rebellion. For years, through stories, novels, historical biographies, and articles, he tried to understand the forces that drove him to devote himself passionately to revolutionary violence. His second collection of stories, *A Purse of Coppers*, is a dispassionate examination of the Ireland that emerged from the revolution. In this collection he relies more on suggestion, indirection, and compression, and he is at ease with the conventions of story writing. The stories are linked by the theme of loneliness, a metaphor for the ways in which Irish society restricts individual development. Every man, Hanafin says in "Admiring the Scenery," lives out his own imagination of himself and every imagination needs its background—not just any background but a context in which he can reach his capacity as a whole man. It is a characteristic of these stories that men are shown to exist in a cul-de-sac.

O'Faolain's alienation from Irish society prevented him from seeing people in a more complex manner. But through his biography of Daniel O'Connell, *King of the Beggars*, he came to recognise the convoluted nature of the Irish mind. He accepted in O'Connell the blend of the admirable and the disgusting and saw that as a true measure of the man. He began to explore human nature for its own sake, to delight in it, to satirise it. After the war, when his horizons expanded, he enlarged his canvas. He liked to examine so-called ethnic traits and to reveal that the stereotype was not always accurate: the licentious Italian in "The Sweet Colleen" is more chaste than the Irish maiden; the amorous Frenchman in "The Faithless Wife" is much slower at getting the Irish woman to bed than she expects.

O'Faolain moved away from peasant life in his story "Lovers of the Lake," an account of a pilgrimage made by a successful Dublin surgeon and his well-to-do mistress. Along the way he reveals the complexities of human nature and differences between the sexes. A similar recognition of subliminal and ancestral forces permeates "The Silence of the Valley," a story about the wonder of remote western regions in Ireland where remnants of the older life linger on.

One of the most remarkable aspects of O'Faolain's work is that he improved with age. The six collections published between 1962 and 1982, including the six previously unpublished stories in *Collected Stories*, reveal a writer at the top of his form. He bursts through the conventions of the short story as he had discussed them in *The Short Story*, writes complex, expansive stories and episodic, more leisurely tales. He packs both with incident and detail, and turns their themes over and over, ever fascinated by human eccentricity and excess, by emotional shifts and feints. He can be mocking, exaggerating appearance, gesture, language, and response, as in "Falling Rocks, Narrowing Road, Cul-de-Sac, Stop"; or exactly tender, as in "The Talking Trees," in which a little boy races down a street after he has seen the beauty of a girl's naked body, his head alive with images: "Like birds. Like stars. Like music."

The beginnings of this late flowering are seen in *I Remember! I Remember!*, in the troubling persistence of memories for reasons impossible to understand. In "Love's Young Dream" the narrator recreates his youthful attachment to two girls with the aches and hopes, the longings and the despairs of adolescence. In "A Touch of Autumn in the Air" O'Faolain makes the point that life has to be imagined. One girl hoards facts; her sister, like O'Faolain, uses facts to create an imagined world in which to live her life. One is free, the other trapped.

His characters often pursue the unattainable. In "An Outside Inside Complex" Bertie Bolger desires to be part of a world seen through a window, but when he succeeds in possessing that world and its desirable occupant, it is the world outside, seen through her window, that fills him with longing. One of O'Faolain's favorite characters is a sophisticated, cosmopolitan male, educated, travelled, analytical, a lover of female beauty. But in his pursuit of beauty he is often deceived and disappointed as much by his own lack of guile and timidity as by the woman's reluctance to be won. Through this attractive, amusing figure O'Faolain can

demonstrate his fundamental belief that humans are endlessly varied and fascinating.

—Maurice Harmon

See the essays on "The Faithless Wife," "Lovers and the Lake," and "The Man Who Invented Sin."

O'FLAHERTY, Liam (William O'Flaherty). Irish. Born in Gort na gCapall, Inishmore, Aran Islands, 28 August 1896. Educated at Rockwell College, Cashel, County Tipperary, 1908–12; Blackrock College, County Dublin, 1912–13; Dublin Diocesan Seminary and University College, Dublin, 1913–14. Served in the Irish Guards in France, 1917–18: wounded and invalided out of service, 1918; served with the Republicans in the Irish civil war, 1921. Married Margaret Barrington in 1926 (separated 1932); one child. Travelled around the world, working as deckhand, porter, filing clerk, and farm labourer, in Asia, South America, the U.S., and Canada, 1918–21; returned to Ireland and lived in Dublin and Cork, then London; full-time writer from 1922; co-editor, *To-morrow* magazine, Dublin, 1924; lived in the Caribbean, South America, and later Connecticut during World War II; from 1946 lived mainly in Dublin, with periods in France. Recipient: James Tait Black Memorial prize, 1926; Allied Irish Banks-Irish Academy of Letters award, 1979. Founding member, Irish Academy of Letters, 1932. *Died 7 September 1984.*

PUBLICATIONS

Short Stories

Spring Sowing. 1924.
Civil War (story). 1925.
The Terrorist (story). 1926.
The Child of God (story). 1926.
The Tent and Other Stories. 1926.
The Fairy-Goose and Two Other Stories. 1927.
Red Barbara and Other Stories. 1928.
The Mountain Tavern and Other Stories. 1929.
The Ecstasy of Angus (story). 1931.
The Wild Swan and Other Stories. 1932.
The Short Stories. 1937.
Two Lovely Beasts and Other Stories. 1948.
Dúil [Desire] (story in Gaelic). 1953.
The Stories. 1956.
Selected Stories, edited by Devin A. Garrity. 1958.
Irish Portraits: 14 Short Stories. 1970.
More Short Stories. 1971.
The Wounded Cormorant and Other Stories. 1973.
The Pedlar's Revenge and Other Stories, edited by A.A. Kelly. 1976.
The Wave and Other Stories, edited by A.A. Kelly. 1980.
The Short Stories. 1986.

Novels

Thy Neighbour's Wife. 1923.
The Black Soul. 1924.
The Informer. 1925.
Mr. Gilhooley. 1926.

The Assassin.   1928.
The House of Gold.   1929.
Return of the Brute.   1929.
The Puritan.   1931.
Skerrett.   1932.
The Martyr.   1933.
Hollywood Cemetery.   1935.
Famine.   1937.
Land.   1946.
Insurrection.   1950.
The Wilderness, edited by A.A. Kelly.   1978.

Plays

Darkness.   1926.

Screenplays: *The Devil's Playground,* with others, 1937; *Last Desire,* 1939, *Jacqueline,* with others, 1956.

Other

The Life of Tim Healy.   1927.
A Tourist's Guide to Ireland.   1929.
Two Years.   1930.
Joseph Conrad: An Appreciation.   1930.
I Went to Russia.   1931.
A Cure for Unemployment.   1931.
Shame the Devil (autobiography).   1934.
All Things Come of Age: A Rabbit Story (for children).   1977.
The Test of Courage (for children).   1977.

*

Bibliography: *O'Flaherty: An Annotated Bibliography* by Paul A. Doyle, 1972; *A Bibliography of the Writings of O'Flaherty* by George Jefferson, 1988.

Critical Studies: *The Literary Vision of O'Flaherty* by John Zneimer, 1970; *O'Flaherty* by Paul A. Doyle, 1971; *O'Flaherty* by James H. O'Brien, 1973; *The Novels of O'Flaherty: A Study in Romantic Realism* by Patrick F. Sheeran, 1976; *O'Flaherty the Storyteller* by A.A. Kelly, 1976.

*   *   *

Liam O'Flaherty is best known for his popular novel *The Informer,* which also won several Academy awards when it was turned into a film by John Ford in 1935. Recent critics, however, tend to maintain that O'Flaherty's permanent literary standing will be based on the stature of his short stories.

His short stories may conveniently be divided into two types—realistic descriptions of rural Irish life and documentary-style sketches of animals. Both of these topics originate from his background of growing up on the primitive Aran Islands off the western coast of Ireland. John Millington Synge described the unique wildness and desolation of these islands "warring" on the inhabitants, and O'Flaherty speaks of the poverty of the farmers and the ever present ocean storms.

One of O'Flaherty's earliest successful short stories is "Spring Sowing," which describes the planting of seeds by the newly married Martin and Mary Delany. The young farm couple participate in this ritual for the first time with their love for each other in full flower. Despite the hard work involved, the seed planting is now a joyful activity, but the author reflects on the future when this work will be burdensome, unrelieved by initial love. The grandfather in the narrative who is badly bent from years of such toil symbolizes the future. Nevertheless, the laborious task is a spiritual joining with the land, a holy link with the soil. At this moment humans are in harmony with nature, but nature will eventually exact its toil.

"Red Barbara" also links the primitive forces of nature with human's own mysterious instincts. The widow Barbara had been married to a barbaric and alcoholic fisherman and conceived several children by him. When she remarries a civil, respectable, hard working weaver, she finds that he is unable to arouse her passions because he lacks a savagery that she needs. Eventually the situation drives him to his death. Her third husband is like the first. Their passionate sensual natures mingle, and Barbara is once more in harmony with her primitive instincts. She is happily satisfied although she must often lead her inebriated husband to bed. O'Flaherty frequently emphasizes primitive delights and instincts that unhappily, from his point of view, become hampered and restricted by the artificialities of civilization. Humans must remain close to nature and nature's often harsh and vicious realities.

In "The Tramp" the harmony with nature theme is continued. For 22 years the tramp has successfully wandered about the Irish countryside, a happy man in tune with the forces of life. Stopping briefly in a workhouse hostel, he attempts to convince two of the paupers, who are educated and regard themselves as superior to the other residents, to join him on the open road. They cannot, however, surrender their notions of false and pompous respectability even when it means continuing to live in the confinement and limitations of a state-funded poorhouse.

In "The Tent" a traveller takes refuge during a rainstorm with a tinker and his two wives. When, after sharing a bottle of whiskey, the visitor makes a pass at one of the women, the tinker beats him badly, fighting and kicking barbarically. After the traveller is thrown from the tent, he hears the tinker battering the same woman. The occupants of the tent have found their proper niche with nature.

O'Flaherty often appears to be a Irish version of D.H. Lawrence in that "the language of the blood" is paramount in his fiction. The primitive, he argues, should take precedence over civilized overintellualization. Apart from the influence that the wild and desolate Aran Islands had on his temperament, O'Flaherty was much influenced by the criticism and suggestions of Edward Garnett, who was O'Flaherty's first editor and who had served as an editor for Lawrence. Garnett favored an instinctive, almost animalistic, and very passionate approach to writing.

While admiring nature's sometimes mystical approach to humankind, O'Flaherty, nevertheless, recognized that nature is ambivalent. In "The Landing," for example, a fisherman's curragh is trapped in a turbulent storm. As the wind and engulfing waves threaten the boat, the fishermen work with equal elemental force to reach shore, and for a time wind, sea, and men blend in struggle. In O'Flaherty's stories nature cannot only dominate and unify but also torment and destroy.

Besides focusing on human's and nature's ambivalent combat, O'Flaherty also writes stories with a calm and reasoned but no less emotional approach. In "Going into Exile," for example, two of the children must leave the farm and emigrate to America to seek employment. A party celebrating the event is bittersweet. The two immigrants are distressed because they have to leave their native land, but there is a sense of adventure which they anticipate with an understated excitement. The parents, on the other hand, can ponder only the melancholy of loss. O'Flaherty effectively encapsulates the sorrow of immigration in a very thoughtful and perceptive manner.

"The Mountain Tavern," in the story so entitled, had always been a place of warmth and convivial joy. It now has been destroyed during the war between the Republicans and the Free Staters. In O'Flaherty's portrayal the ruined building and the snow that covers it symbolize the emptiness and desolation that has prevailed in Ireland through centuries of various military skirmishes.

The second type of short story O'Flaherty writes involves animal sketches. Following editor Garnett's advice to write about what he knew at first hand, O'Flaherty turned to the occupations of the Aran Islands—farming and fishing, as well as to the considerable number of wild birds that inhabit the land and the sea cliffs. He set about to describe these materials in a naturalistic documentary style.

"The Cow's Death" is a fairly typical example. When the cow's calf is stillborn, the dead calf is dragged through several fields and then thrown over a cliff. When the mother eventually recovers from her apathetic confusion of birth, she begins to seek the calf, not realizing that it is dead. She smells the trail of blood and arrives at the cliff where she sees the body of the calf resting on some rocks far below. Her calls to the calf are unheeded, and she seeks a way to descend the steep and rocky cliff. When she sees a larger wave approaching the calf, she attempts to warn the calf, and then in a fit of maternal protection, she jumps from the cliff as the calf is pulled by a wave into the ocean.

On the surface, such a story would appear to be almost a simplistic child's tale, but O'Flaherty's gift for closely observed details and his seriousness of purpose about nature's treachery raise the story to the level of a primitive but highly effective artistic woodcut.

Similar animal sagas comprise much of his work. In "The Wounded Cormorant" the bird's leg is severely injured by a rock accidentally knocked off a cliff by a wild goat. Although it is part of a group, the other cormorants attack and kill it. In "The Water Hen" two roosters fight while the hen settles herself complacently to await and welcome the victor. "The Hawk" portrays the hawk as a conqueror as it kills a lark, but when he attempts to protect his mate's eggs from being stolen by a farmer, he is severely injured by a stinging blow from the man's arm and falls to his death over a cliff. On some occasions the animal is fortunate. In "The Conger Eel" a huge eel is captured unintentionally in a fisherman's net. He struggles and rips the net but is pulled aboard the boat. The men attempt to kill the intruder but he manages to elude them and slip back into the sea.

O'Flaherty seeks to present his cameos without authorial intrusion, but it is evident that he inserts himself imaginatively into his animals, conveying their reactions and feelings, usually in a decidedly convincing manner. The portraits are slice-of-life descriptions of nature at work. Nature is the ultimate author; the writer is only the medium, the depictor of nature in action. It appears that the scenes depicted have actually been observed. The author is a documentary cameraman capturing in detail every minute occurrence.

It must be admitted that many of the animal stories are not successful because, as Frank O'Connor has noticed, the pattern of two or three thousand word sketches describing a single episode can "in quantity" become monotonous. It would have helped too if O'Flaherty's style had been more varied and more lyrical. At times the matter-of-face

vocabulary is realistically appropriate; at other times even closely observed detail cannot compensate for a flat, plain recounting of facts.

As with his stories of rural life, his animal sketches reveal the considerable unevenness in the corpus of O'Flaherty's writings. Admittedly he wrote too much in a *furor scribendi*, and one seeks in vain for a consistent polished style. The portraits of rural Irish life and the animal vignettes are often naturalistic in tone with intimations of the work of Emile Zola, for whom O'Flaherty professed admiration. At the same time the narratives often contain romantic qualities. As Sean O'Faolain was to observe, O'Flaherty has "the inflated ego of the Romantic, as well as the self-pity and the unbalance." O'Flaherty is unable to give total allegiance to either style, and it is this confluence of the naturalistic with the romantic that gives his writings their unique, distinctive tone.

—Paul A. Doyle

See the essays on "The Post Office" and "Two Lovely Beasts."

O'HARA, John (Henry). Born in Pottsville, Pennsylvania, 31 January 1905. Educated at Fordham Preparatory School; Keystone State Normal School; Niagara Preparatory School, Niagara Falls, New York, 1923–24. Married 1) Helen Petit in 1931 (divorced 1933); 2) Belle Mulford Wylie in 1937 (died 1954), one daughter; 3) Katharine Barns Bryan in 1955. Reporter, Pottsville *Journal,* 1924–26, and Tamaqua *Courier,* Pennsylvania, 1927; reporter, New York *Herald-Tribune,* and *Time* magazine, New York, 1928; rewrite man, New York *Daily Mirror,* radio columnist (as Franey Delaney), New York *Morning Telegraph,* and managing editor, *Bulletin Index* magazine, Pittsburgh, 1928–33; full-time writer from 1933; film writer, for Paramount and other studios, from 1934; columnist ("Entertainment Week"), *Newsweek,* New York, 1940–42; Pacific war correspondent, *Liberty* magazine, New York, 1944; columnist ("Sweet and Sour"), Trenton *Sunday Times-Adviser,* New Jersey, 1953–54; lived in Princeton, New Jersey, from 1954; columnist ("Appointment with O'Hara"), *Collier's,* New York, 1954–56, ("My Turn"), *Newsday,* Long Island, New York, 1964–65, and ("The Whistle Stop"), *Holiday,* New York, 1966–67. Recipient: New York Drama Critics Circle award, 1952; Donaldson award, for play, 1952; National Book award, 1956; American Academy award of merit medal, 1964. Member, American Academy, 1957. *Died 11 April 1970.*

PUBLICATIONS

Collections

Collected Stories, edited by Frank MacShane.   1985.
O'Hara: Gibbsville, Pa.: The Classic Stories, edited by Matthew J. Bruccoli.   1992.

Short Stories

The Doctor's Son and Other Stories.   1935.
Files on Parade.   1939.

Pal Joey.   1940.
Pipe Night.   1945.
Here's O'Hara (omnibus).   1946.
Hellbox.   1947.
All the Girls He Wanted.   1949.
The Great Short Stories of O'Hara.   1956.
Selected Short Stories.   1956.
A Family Party (novella).   1956.
Sermons and Soda Water (includes *The Girl on the Baggage Truck, Imagine Kissing Pete, We're Friends Again*).   3 vols., 1960.
Assembly.   1961.
The Cape Cod Lighter.   1962.
49 Stories.   1963.
The Hat on the Bed.   1963.
The Horse Knows the Way.   1964.
Waiting for Winter.   1966.
And Other Stories.   1968.
The O'Hara Generation.   1969.
The Time Element and Other Stories, edited by Albert Erskine.   1972.
Good Samaritan and Other Stories, edited by Albert Erskine.   1974.

Novels

Appointment in Samarra.   1934.
BUtterfield 8.   1935.
Hope of Heaven.   1938.
A Rage to Live.   1949.
The Farmers Hotel.   1951.
Ten North Frederick.   1955.
From the Terrace.   1958.
Ourselves to Know.   1960.
The Big Laugh.   1962.
Elizabeth Appleton.   1963.
The Lockwood Concern.   1965.
The Instrument.   1967.
Lovey Childs: A Philadelphian's Story.   1969.
The Ewings.   1972.
The Second Ewings.   1977.

Plays

Pal Joey (libretto), music by Richard Rodgers, lyrics by Lorenz Hart, from the stories by O'Hara (produced 1940).   1952.
Five Plays (includes *The Farmers Hotel, The Searching Sun, The Champagne Pool, Veronique, The Way It Was*).   1961.
Two by O'Hara (includes *The Man Who Could Not Lose* and *Far from Heaven*).   1979.

Screenplays: *I Was an Adventuress,* with Karl Tunberg and Don Ettlinger, 1940; *He Married His Wife,* with others, 1940; *Moontide,* 1942; *On Our Merry Way* (episode), 1948; *The Best Things in Life Are Free,* with William Bowers and Phoebe Ephron, 1956.

Other

Sweet and Sour (essays).   1954.
My Turn (newspaper columns).   1966.
A Cub Tells His Story.   1974.
An Artist Is His Own Fault: O'Hara On Writers and Writings, edited by Matthew J. Bruccoli.   1977.
Selected Letters, edited by Matthew J. Bruccoli.   1978.

*

Bibliography: *O'Hara: A Checklist,* 1972, and *O'Hara: A Descriptive Bibliography,* 1978, both by Matthew J. Bruccoli.

Critical Studies: *The Fiction of O'Hara* by Russell E. Carson, 1961; *O'Hara* by Sheldon Norman Grebstein, 1966; *O'Hara* by Charles C. Walcutt, 1969; *O'Hara: A Biography* by Finis Farr, 1973; *The O'Hara Concern: A Biography* by Matthew J. Bruccoli, 1975; *The Life of O'Hara* by Frank MacShane, 1980; *O'Hara* by Robert Emmet Long, 1983.

*   *   *

Trained as a journalist, and proud of his craft, John O'Hara wrote unadorned short stories that could have passed as reportage. His first collection, *The Doctor's Son and Other Stories,* contained at least one piece of non-fiction, "Of Thee I Sing, Baby," originally published as a 1932 *New Yorker* profile. O'Hara's very earliest published stories took the form of seemingly improvised speeches to a paint-manufacturing company and a ladies' social club. His deadly accurate ear for the American vernacular got him labeled a mere stenographer, but O'Hara's naturalistic dialogue strove for more than accuracy. It revealed traits his speakers felt they were cleverly concealing. O'Hara did use reportorial techniques, but he used them to create art.

Naturalistic speech—a technique popularized in the 1920's by O'Hara's satiric models Ring Lardner, Dorothy Parker, and Sinclair Lewis—gradually faded from his repertoire. Although the device recurred in "Walter T. Carriman," "Mrs. Whitmen," and in the "Pal Joey" series (all stories published by 1945) and even in the novella *A Family Party,* O'Hara's next story collections, *Files on Parade, Pipe Night,* and *Hellbox,* sympathized with their subjects rather than satirizing them. The lonely schoolboy in "Do You Like It Here?" wrongly accused of theft, the workingman in "Bread Alone" whose quiet son secretly gives him a present, the doctor who wastes his life waiting to make "The Decision," are presented critically but compassionately.

Many of O'Hara's best short stories take place in Gibbsville, Pennsylvania, a thinly disguised version of O'Hara's hometown of Pottsville, and throughout his career, O'Hara told many of these Gibbsville stories through a thinly disguised version of himself named James Malloy. In these stories, O'Hara helped invent his own sub-genre, the prototypical *New Yorker* magazine story—full of contemporary dialogue, focussed on everyday events, indeterminate in its resolution, and sometimes maddeningly elliptical. "I write little pieces for the *New Yorker*," O'Hara jokingly wrote in 1936, "some of them so vague that when I send them away I almost include a plea to the editors that if they can understand them, please to let me in on the secret." Actually, O'Hara's short fiction was lucid enough by current standards, but 1930's readers of popular fiction were accustomed to stories with explicit endings. O'Hara often ended his stories on a flat or jarring non sequitur. "Trouble in 1949," about a man who spends a nervewracking afternoon with his now-married girlfriend of a decade ago, ends with him wondering about their relationship in another ten years.

Although "1949" in that title meant only some distant future time, the year 1949 did turn out to be full of trouble for O'Hara. *The New Yorker*, which had published some 200 O'Hara pieces by then, was the market he geared his stories for, making them, as he put it, "simply not saleable anywhere else." So when *The New Yorker* reviewed his 1949 novel *A Rage to Live* harshly, he felt he could no longer contribute to it, which effectively ended his short story writing for the next eleven years.

But after a decade spent mostly writing long novels, O'Hara published a long Jim Malloy story in *The New Yorker*, later collected with two other linked Malloy stories in *Sermons and Sodawater*, and entered his golden decade of short story writing. In the 1960's he published six collections of short stories, several thousand printed pages, almost every one of which was at a remarkable level of quality.

His focus shifted slightly in that final productive decade. His Malloy stories no longer concerned events in Malloy's life, as they had in "Transaction," "Miss W.," and other early Malloy stories. Starting with *Sermons and Sodawater*, the stories took the form of memoirs about Malloy's old friends taking ill or dying. A particularly mournful collection is *The Cape Cod Lighter*, many of whose stories are set 30 or 40 years earlier, but are framed in the present. A man is persuaded by his wife and daughter to attend an old friend's funeral in "Appearances"; his vague antipathy towards the old friend, O'Hara slowly reveals, is founded more solidly than he knows. "The Lesson" is taught by a divorced father who travels to his hometown, also for a funeral, as he justifies his life to his estranged adult daughter. "Your Fah Neefah Neeface" is an especially sad tale about a woman outliving her high-spirited brother—a middle-aged Malloy narrates it, piecing together the brother's life, the woman's, and the lives of several witnesses to their youthful gaiety. "Exterior: With Figure" in the next year's collection, *The Hat on the Bed*, is another story about a family that has died out since Malloy knew them 50 years earlier. Whether narrated by Malloy or not, these stories keep the past alive by remembering it vividly in the present. "Pat Collins," "The Professors," "The Nothing Machine," and others have at their centers a long-ago event that continues troubling the protagonists in their old age.

O'Hara arranged these short story collections alphabetically, as if in contempt of the notion that any ordering might improve the stories themselves—or detract from them. He knew how good they were, and his prefaces conveyed his satisfaction with his reputation as a master of short fiction. Ever the consummate professional, O'Hara had kept his pre-1960's short stories tightly focussed and consistent in length. Now his prestige allowed him the liberties of widening the narrative scope and expanding the length of some stories: 50 printed pages was not at all unusual, and one Malloy-told monster, "A Few Trips and Some Poetry," ran 122 pages. He was writing more than he could place in magazines, and no longer needed to write for a market.

Some of these lengthy stories were as artful as any he ever wrote. *Waiting For Winter*, his 1966 collection, included several long stories never published in magazines. "Natica Jackson" and "James Francis and the Star" are two long looks at Hollywood scandals. Natica Jackson, a movie star, has a love affair resulting in the violent deaths of two children, and James Francis Hatter is a successful scriptwriter whose life is changed when he must shoot and kill a burglar. O'Hara's Hollywood stories show not only insight into the behaviour of stars, but also characterize various hangers-on and people outside the movie industry who happen to get involved with movie people. O'Hara, who had worked for years as a Hollywood script doctor, intuited

the sociology of show business. In "The Friends of Miss Julia" a studio executive's lonely mother-in-law strikes up a friendship with a woman she meets at her hairdresser. Very little happens in that story—the mother-in-law decides to leave Hollywood—but plot rarely dominates an O'Hara short story. The plot of another show business story, "John Barton Rosedale, Actor's Actor," is also slight—the title character insults a theatrical manager and costs himself a part—but that story, like "Miss Julia," is about the hierarchies and the pettiness of the entertainment world. O'Hara is concerned with relationships, not events, because events are capable of being simplified. People, no matter how simple, are always intricate.

Another show business story, "The Portly Gentleman," introduces a self-absorbed actor whose proposal of marriage gets turned down; the kicker comes when the woman's personal reasons summon up his genuine concern. Several late stories—("Andrea," "A Few Trips and Some Poetry," "The Gunboat and Madge," "The Flatted Saxophone"), concern mature people's tender feelings towards each other, entire generations after their initial passions for (and against) each other have passed. Other late stories end with characters improbably finding a kinship with strangers. "Mrs. Stratton of Oak Knoll" ends when the dignified matron of the title places on her breast the hand of a man who has befriended her and asks him, "Why does this endure?" The wise friend's answer: "Something must." O'Hara's short stories certainly will.

—Steven Goldleaf

See the essay on "Fatimas and Kisses."

OLIPHANT, Margaret (Oliphant, née Wilson). Scottish. Born in Wallyford, Midlothian, 4 April 1828. Married her cousin Francis Wilson Oliphant in 1852 (died 1859); two sons and one daughter. Full-time writer from 1849; regular contributor, *Blackwood's Magazine*, Edinburgh, from 1853. Granted Civil List pension, 1868. *Died 25 June 1897.*

PUBLICATIONS

Short Stories

Passages in the Life of Mrs. Margaret Maitland.   1849.
The Rector and the Doctor's Family (Chronicles of Carlingford series).   1863.
The Two Mrs. Scudamores.   1879.
A Beleaguered City.   1879.
Two Stories of the Seen and the Unseen (Old Lady Mary, The Open Door).   1885; expanded edition, *Stories of the Seen and the Unseen*,   1902.
The Land of Darkness, along with Some Further Chapters in the Experience of the Little Pilgrims.   1888.
Neighbours on the Green: A Collection of Stories.   1889.
The Two Marys.   1896.
The Lady's Walk.   1897.
The Ways of Life: Two Stories.   1897.
A Widow's Tale and Other Stories.   1898.
That Little Cutty and Two Other Stories.   1898.

Selected Stories of the Supernatural, edited by Margaret K. Gray.   1985.
The Doctor's Family and Other Stories, edited by Merryn Williams.   1986.
A Beleaguered City and Other Stories, edited by Merryn Williams.   1988.

Novels

Caleb Field: A Tale of the Puritans.   1851.
Merkland.   1851.
Memoirs and Resolutions of Adam Graeme of Mossgray.   1852.
Katie Stewart.   1853.
Harry Muir: A Story of Scottish Life.   1853.
Quiet Heart.   1854.
Magdalen Hepburn.   1854.
Lilliesleaf.   1855.
Zaidee.   1856.
The Athelings; or, The Three Gifts.   1857.
The Days of My Life.   1857.
Sundays.   1858.
The Laird of Norlaw.   1858.
Orphans.   1858.
Agnes Hopetoun's Schools and Holidays.   1859.
Lucy Crofton.   1860.
The House on the Moor.   1861.
The Last of the Mortimers.   1862.
Chronicles of Carlingford:
    Salem Chapel.   1863.
    The Perpetual Curate.   1864.
    Miss Marjoribanks.   1866.
    Phoebe, Junior.   1876.
Heart and Cross.   1863.
A Son of the Soil.   1865.
Agnes.   1866.
Madonna Mary.   1866.
The Brownlows.   1868.
The Minister's Wife.   1869.
John: A Love Story.   1870.
The Three Brothers.   1870.
Squire Arden.   1871.
At His Gates.   1872.
Ombra.   1872.
May.   1873.
Innocent.   1873.
A Rose in June.   1874.
For Love and Life.   1874.
The Story of Valentine and His Brother.   1875.
Whiteladies.   1875.
The Curate in Charge.   1876.
Carità.   1877.
Mrs. Arthur.   1877.
Young Musgrave.   1877.
The Primrose Path: A Chapter in the Annals of the Kingdom of Fife.   1878.
The Fugitives.   1879.
Within the Precincts.   1879.
The Greatest Heiress in England.   1879.
He That Will Not When He May.   1880.
Harry Joscelyn.   1881.
In Trust: The Story of a Lady and Her Lover.   1882.
A Little Pilgrim in the Unseen.   1882.
Hester.   1883.
It Was a Lover and His Lass.   1883.
The Ladies Lindores.   1883.
Sir Tom.   1883.
The Wizard's Son.   1883.

Madam.   1885.
Oliver's Bride.   1885.
The Prodigals and Their Inheritance.   1885.
A Country Gentleman and His Family.   1886.
Effie Ogilvie: The Story of a Young Life.   1886.
A House Divided Against Itself.   1886.
A Poor Gentleman.   1886.
The Son of His Father.   1886.
Joyce.   1888.
The Second Son, with Thomas Bailey Aldrich.   1888.
Cousin Mary.   1888.
Lady Car.   1889.
Kirsteen: The Story of a Scottish Family Seventy Years Ago.   1890.
The Duke's Daughter, and The Fugitives.   1890.
Sons and Daughters.   1890.
The Mystery of Mrs. Blencarrow.   1890.
Janet.   1891.
The Railway Man and His Children.   1891.
The Heir Presumptive and the Heir Apparent.   1891.
Diana Trelawney.   1892; as *Diana,* 1892.
The Cuckoo in the Nest.   1892.
The Marriage of Elinor.   1892.
Lady William.   1893.
The Sorceress.   1893.
A House in Bloomsbury.   1894.
Who Was Lost and Is Found.   1894.
Sir Robert's Fortune.   1894.
Two Strangers.   1894.
Old Mr. Tredgold.   1895.
The Unjust Steward; or, The Minister's Debt.   1896.

Other

The Life of Edward Irving, Minister of the National Scotch Church, London.   2 vols., 1862.
Francis of Assisi.   1868.
Historical Sketches of the Reign of George II.   2 vols., 1869.
Memoirs of the Count de Montalembert: A Chapter of Recent French History.   1872.
The Makers of Florence: Dante, Giotto, Savonarola, and Their City.   1876.
Dress.   1876.
Dante.   1877.
Molière, with F. Tarver.   1879.
Cervantes.   1880.
Literary History of England in the End of the Eighteenth and the Beginning of the Nineteenth Century.   3 vols., 1882.
Sheridan.   1883.
The Makers of Venice: Doges, Conquerors, Painters, and Men of Letters.   1887.
Memoir of the Life of John Tulloch.   1888.
Royal Edinburgh: Her Saints, Kings, Prophets, and Poets.   1890.
Jerusalem, The Holy City: Its History and Hope.   1891; reprinted in part as *The House of David,* 1891.
Memoirs of the Life of Laurence Oliphant and Alice Oliphant, His Wife.   1891.
The Victorian Age of English Literature, with F.R. Oliphant.   2 vols., 1892.
Thomas Chalmers, Preacher, Philosopher, and Statesman.   1893.
Historical Sketches of the Reign of Queen Anne.   1894; as *Historical Characters,* 1894.
A Child's History of Scotland.   1895; as *A History of Scotland for the Young,* 1895.

The Makers of Modern Rome.   1895.
Jeanne d'Arc: Her Life and Death.   1896.
Annals of a Publishing House: William Blackwood and His Sons, Their Magazine and Friends.   2 vols., 1897.
The Autobiography and Letters, edited by Mrs. Harry Coghill.   1899; revised edition, 1899; *The Autobiography* edited by Elizabeth Jay, 1990.
Queen Victoria: A Personal Sketch.   1901.

Editor, *Memoirs of the Life of Anna Jameson,* by Geraldine Macpherson.   1878.

*

Bibliography: *Oliphant: A Bibliography* by John Stock Clarke, 1986.

Critical Studies: *The Equivocal Virtue: Oliphant and the Victorian Literary Market Place* by Vineta Colby and Robert A. Colby, 1966; *Everywhere Spoken Against: Dissent in the Victorian Novel* by Valentine Cunningham, 1975; *Oliphant: A Critical Biography* by Merryn Williams, 1986.

*   *   *

Although her reputation declined after her death, and remained at a low ebb throughout much of the 20th century, Margaret Oliphant was unquestionably one of the great Victorian storytellers, as the gradual republication of her best work shows. She wrote almost a hundred novels and about 36 short stories — the dividing line is sometimes difficult to establish, because while most of the novels were of the "three-decker" Victorian variety, some of the best were really novellas or extended short stories, in which there was no need for padding. In addition, she wrote literally hundreds of articles and reviews, many of them from 1849 onwards for *Blackwood's Edinburgh Magazine* (the "Maga," as it was familiarly known), all of which are listed in an appendix to Q.D. Lewis's 1974 edition of *The Autobiography and Letters of Mrs. Margaret Oliphant.*

Widowed after a decade of marriage to Francis Oliphant — she was, so to say, twice an Oliphant, that also having been her mother's name — a weak stained-glass artist (some of whose work survives in Ely Cathedral, England) she bore six children, three of whom did not survive and another of whom died in childhood. Her two surviving sons were both failures and predeceased her. She also took on the support of a succession of impecunious relatives: brothers, cousins, a nephew, and a niece. Whilst there is some evidence that from an early age she was something of a compulsive writer, and plenty that she enjoyed a good life style (her sons went to Eton and Oxford), she had to keep writing to meet all her pecuniary needs. As a result, she overwrote, like John Galt (though for other reasons), turning out some works that were far below her best. As one of her contemporaries, the novelist Howard Sturges, put it, "Her work at its best was injured by her immense productiveness. Her best work was of a very high order of merit. The harm that she did to her literary reputation seems rather the surrounding of her best with so much which she knew to be of inferior quality."

While she enjoyed considerable success in the 1860's with the series of stories and novels that make up the *Chronicles of Carlingford,* she never again reached quite this level of acceptance by a public eager for fiction with a happy ending.

Two things militated against the recognition of her qualities as a novelist. In her own day she was in some ways an "outsider" from the cosiness of Victorian assumptions. She was a Scotswoman, born in Midlothian and brought up there and in Glasgow. Though most of her adult life was spent in England, she never lost the blunt edge of her Scots tongue, nor her questioning sharpness of mind. Indeed Sir J.M. Barrie, in his introduction to a memorial edition of her short stories, recorded that "she was of an intellect so sharp that one wondered whether she ever fell asleep." Her stories were unsentimental and unromantic.

She had been brought up in the Free Church of Scotland, whose beliefs she soon discarded because of their narrowness. As the wife of an artist in Rome and in London, she experienced the ways of Bohemianism, though they did nothing to sap her tough-minded common sense. She was thus able to view with amusement and a sense of sound proportion the rival graduations between High and Low then racking the Anglican Church; as a former extreme Presbyterian she understood the cause of dissent.

She also understood, and despised, the English class system (much less rigid in the Scotland of her day), and consequently was able to treat it with a sociological insight not always shown by writers like Trollope. Towards the end of her life (which she thought had dealt her a more rigorous hand than that given to Charlotte Brontë), she manifested some interest in the burgeoning suffragette movement. Certainly, many of her heroines work, even if only within the confines of the home, not for them the suffocating boredom of idle parlour and of gossiping drawingroom.

She was fascinated by the spectacle of weak men finding themselves confronted with responsibilities for others stronger than themselves; in "The Rector" the Reverend Morton Proctor finds that his heart and tongue fail him in the presence of a dying woman seeking comfort, and he retires to the safety of his Oxford Fellowship, aware, however, that he has brought back something of his failure with him. No doubt as a result of her own experience, many of her men are weak self-doubters while her women are lively-minded and strong.

The second factor causing further delay in the acknowledgement of Oliphant's qualities and the current restitution of her reputation, was the appearance in 1966 of what Q.D. Lewis rightly called "a denigrating account of Mrs. Oliphant and her words," *The Equivocal Virtue; Mrs. Oliphant and the Victorian Literary Market* by V. and R.A. Colby. The superficiality of their approach is balanced by *Margaret Oliphant* (1986) by Merryn Williams, who has also played a leading editorial role in the Oliphant revival.

Oliphant's break-through from conventional competence to individual greatness came with *The Doctor's Family and Other Stories,* part of the *Chronicles of Carlingford,* which also includes one of her first novels, *Miss Marjoribanks* (pronounced "Marchbanks"). Thereafter, her great works, whether novels or stories, appear at intervals, standing out from the sea of mere money-spinners and the steady flow of her journalism. They include *Miss Marjoribanks, Salam Chapel, Hester, Kirsteen, A Beleaguered City,* and a selection of her tales of the supernatural, *Selected Stories of the Supernatural,* all of which have been recently republished. *Phoebe Junior, A Last Chronicle of Carlingford, The Ladies Lindores,* and *A Country Gentleman and His Family* also should certainly be reissued. Significantly, many of these new editions are in various series of acknowledged "classics."

As the Victorian age wore on and Darwinism introduced an irradicable strain of doubt to all levels of Anglican belief, the Victorians developed a taste for ghost stories (though the genre itself goes to Defoe); to quote J.A. Cuddon's introduction to *The Penguin Book of Ghost Stories* (1982) in which Oliphant is represented, it is almost "as if the possibility of ghosts was a reassurance of an after-life." Oliphant wrote a dozen stories of the supernatural, mostly in later life, though she neither claimed to have seen a ghost herself nor sought to terrify her readers with improbably spine-chilling horrors. She probably believed, and certainly hoped, there was some sort of after-life, even if not reached by any of the routes preached by orthodox religion. Her supernatural stories explore issues raised in her other fiction: bereavement (of which she had had plentiful experience) in "The Beleaguered City" selfishness in "Old Lady May" and "The Land of Darkness," and the longing for unachievable perfection in "The Library Window," her most popular story.

At her best, Oliphant could produce dialogue as sharply pointed as Jane Austen, a social comment often more acutely informed than Anthony Trollope, and a sense of the broad surge and sweep of human change as evoked by George Eliot. Oliphant was admired by all the leading writers among her contemporaries, including James and Barrie. She is proving a stimulating and exciting rediscovery for us today, almost a century after her death.

—Maurice Lindsay

See the essay on "The Library Window."

———

OLSEN, Tillie (née Lerner). American. Born in Omaha, Nebraska, 14 January 1912 or 1913. High school education. Married Jack Olsen in 1943 (died); four daughters. Has worked in the service, warehouse, and food processing industries, and as an office typist. Visiting professor, Amherst College, Massachusetts, 1969–70; visiting instructor, Stanford University, California, Spring 1971; writer-in-residence, Massachusetts Institute of Technology, Cambridge, 1973; visiting professor, University of Massachusetts, Boston, 1974; visiting lecturer, University of California, San Diego, 1978; International Visiting Scholar, Norway, 1980; Hill Professor, University of Minnesota, Minneapolis, 1986; writer-in-residence, Kenyon College, Gambier, Ohio, 1987; Regents' Professor, University of California, Los Angeles, 1988; creative writing fellow, Stanford University, 1956–57; fellow, Radcliffe Institute for Independent Study, Cambridge, Massachusetts, 1962–64. Recipient: Ford grant, 1959; O. Henry award, 1961; National Endowment for the Arts grant, 1966, and senior fellowship, 1984; American Academy award, 1975; Guggenheim fellowship, 1975; Unitarian Women's Federation award, 1980; Bunting Institute fellowship, 1986. Doctor of Arts and Letters: University of Nebraska, Lincoln, 1979; Litt.D.: Knox College, Galesburg, Illinois, 1982; Albright College, Reading, Pennsylvania, 1986; L.H.D.: Hobart and William Smith Colleges, Geneva, New York, 1984; Clark University, Worcester, Massachusetts, 1985; Wooster College, Ohio, 1991. Lives in San Francisco.

PUBLICATIONS

Short Stories

Tell Me a Riddle: A Collection.   1961; enlarged edition, 1964.

Novel

Yonnondio: From the Thirties.   1974.

Other

Silences (essays).   1978.
Mothers and Daughters: That Special Quality: An Exploration in Photographs, with Julie Olsen-Edwards and Estelle Jussim.   1987.

Editor, *Mother to Daughter, Daughter to Mother: Mothers on Mothering.*   1984.

*

Critical Studies: *Olsen* by Abigail Martin, 1984; *Olsen and a Feminist Spiritual Vision* by Elaine Neil Orr, 1987; *Olsen* by Abby Werlock and Mickey Pearlman, 1991.

*   *   *

Tillie Olsen is author of one novel, numerous essays, a few poems, and the highly influential nonfiction work, *Silences.* On balance, however, she is best known in the literary world as a writer of short fiction. Writers ranging from Margaret Atwood to Tim O'Brien admire the superb quality of her small but highly distinguished literary achievement.

The daughter of Russian revolutionaries who immigrated to Nebraska, Olsen combines in her writing her socialist upbringing, her concern for the poor, and her love of language. Her stories repeatedly embrace and affirm the humanity of underprivileged individuals who suffer the exigencies of subsistence-level work, grueling hours, and lack of free time to devote either to the development of creative talents or to the sensitive rearing of children. Olsen particularly focuses on the lot of working-class women and their frequently heroic ability to persevere.

Her work may be divided into three periods. First, in the 1930's, Olsen published several politically polemical essays and poems, and wrote her unfinished novel *Yonnondio: From the Thirties,* which remained unpublished until 1974. The second and greatest period of her fiction writing occurred in the 1950's and early 1960's when Olsen wrote and published the four short stories that comprise *Tell Me a Riddle*: "I Stand Here Ironing," "Hey Sailor, What Ship?," "O Yes," and "Tell Me a Riddle." In the third period, from the 1970's into the 1990's, Olsen has published little fiction: only "Requa I" and the rediscovered and unfinished *Yonnondio.* She has instead channeled her talents into nonfiction writing, edited collections, and numerous speaking engagements.

The four stories in *Tell Me a Riddle* are linked by the aching hardship of poverty, the difficulties of motherhood, and the themes of exile or exclusion. Relentlessly Olsen presents us with the inexorable riddle of human existence: it paradoxically includes not merely the endurance of poverty, bigotry, illness, and pain, but the ultimate ability to surmount these debilitating circumstances. Her style is dense, rich, and experimental, as Olsen employs imagistic language, meaningful refrains, innovative structure and a variety of monologues, dialogues and narrative interruptions to convey the components of her themes, her characters, her "riddles."

In "I Stand Here Ironing," a story anthologized over one hundred times, Olsen moves our attention back and forth in an echo of the ironing rhythm as the ironing mother ponders the way she raised her eldest daughter Emily. Silently accusing herself of neglecting Emily, she searches deliberately through her memories for explanations. Her flashbacks, which recall scenes during the Depression and World War II, reveal past events that rendered her powerless: her desertion by Emily's father, her insecure series of jobs, her constant need of caretakers for Emily, her remarriage and the births of four additional children.

She returns to the postwar present and Emily's off-hand reference to the atom bomb. The mother concludes by voicing a prayer-like hope for her daughter: "Only help her to know . . . that she is more than this dress on the ironing board, helpless before the iron." Mother and daughter emerge as survivors as well as victims. Olsen's implication is that Emily has developed talents and independent strategies that, like those of her mother, will help her survive.

The next story, "Hey Sailor, What Ship?," is experimental and complex by comparison with the first, for here, Olsen employs modernist literary allusions and motifs reminiscent of Virginia Woolf's *The Waves* and T.S. Eliot's *The Waste Land*. That Olsen has never returned to these techniques isolates "Hey Sailor, What Ship?" from the rest of her work, and may suggest why Olsen critics have virtually neglected the tale.

Olsen repeatedly uses the title question to illustrate the dilemma of Michael (Whitey) Jackson, the main character. Whitey, an aging merchant seaman, agonizes between two ways of life: the itinerant life of the alcoholic sailor he has become, and the middle-class existence he used to enjoy with his old friends Lennie and Helen, and their three children Jeannie, Carol, and Allie. This family appears in three of the stories in the collection. The aging Whitey, like Emily of "I Stand Here Ironing," at the end asserts his independence, preferring his "otherness" to allowing his old friends to dictate his behavior.

Lennie, Helen, Carol, and Jeannie reappear in the third story, "O Yes," which takes place two years after the episode with Whitey, and focuses on the now twelve-year-old Carol and her metaphorical baptism into the riddle of life. Counterbalancing the white family with a black family, Olsen relates the story of the friendship between the black mother Alva and the white mother Helen, and their two daughters Parry and Carol. As Carol hovers on the threshold of womanhood, she wavers between her natural feelings of love for Parry, and the social reality of white racism and middle-class elitism.

Beginning in a black church service, Olsen imagistically evokes Carol and Parry's affectionate childhood friendship, then succinctly and poignantly portrays their painful final meeting as Carol and Parry helplessly draw apart to enter their separate worlds. At the end, Helen invokes her adult friendship with Alva as a model for her daughter and a testament to some future time when class and racial prejudice will disappear.

"Tell Me a Riddle" is frequently cited as one of the most sensitive and artistically rendered of American short stories. Olsen herself testifies to its impact: "People read it for the 20th time and they weep." The chief characters are David and Eva, Russian immigrant parents of Lennie and grandparents of Jeannie, Carol, and Allie. As Eva and her family cope with her imminent death from cancer, she grudgingly embarks with David on a westward journey which culminates in her death. Along the way, her final visits with each of her adult children elicit past memories of herself as young girl, ardent Russian revolutionary, young wife and mother whose intellectual talents and interests remain unrealized.

Eva embodies Olsen's understanding of life as the commingling of hope with pain. Grandmother and mother, Eva is linked with all Olsen's fictional women. The connections among generations of women become clear as Jeannie, through her love and understanding of her grandmother, both honors the dying woman and suggests a brighter future for the descendants of hardworking immigrants.

In "Requa I," Olsen continues to write of the working poor, but this time she creates a "family" of two marginalized men—the 14-year old Stevie and his bachelor uncle Wes with whom he goes to live after his mother's death. Departing from the relatively stable families of the other stories, in "Requa" Olsen pairs these two emotionally needy and motherless men in this ironically-named town of Requa, a Native American word for "broken in body and spirit." Just as the young girls Emily, Jeannie, and Carol learn to surmount obstacles aided by caring parents, nearly always either mothers or grandmothers, Stevie and Wes learn not only to survive, but to care for one another.

Although Olsen herself might be disconcerted about the comparisons, her fiction shares surprising affinities with such different American writers as Edith Wharton, in her close attention to the pain of wife- and motherhood, and William Faulkner, in her esteem for those who endure and prevail. At the age of 80—even if she never writes again—Olsen has persuaded us that the stories of the underprivileged as well as the elite constitute a fitting subject for literary depiction and celebration.

—Abby H.P. Werlock

See the essay on "Tell Me a Riddle."

ONETTI, Juan Carlos. Uruguayan. Born in Montevideo, 1 July 1909. Married Dolly Muhr in 1955; one son and one daughter. Lived in Buenos Aires, 1930–34; editor, *Marcha,* Montevideo, 1939–42, and *Vea y Lea,* Buenos Aires, 1946–55; editor for Reuters, Montevideo, 1941–43, and Buenos Aires, 1943–46; manager of an advertising firm, Montevideo, 1955–57; director of municipal libraries, Montevideo, 1957; lived in Spain, from 1975. Recipient: National Literature prize, 1962; William Faulkner Foundation Ibero-American award, 1963; Casa de las Américas prize, 1965; Italian-Latin American Institute prize, 1972. Lives in Buenos Aires.

PUBLICATIONS

Short Stories

Un sueño realizado y otros cuentos.   1951.

Los adioses (novella).   1954; as *Goodbyes,* in *Goodbyes and Other Stories,* 1990; as *Farewells* with *A Grave with No Name,* 1992.
Una tumba sin nombre (novella).   1959; as *A Grave with No Name,* with *Farewells,* 1992.
La cara de la desgracia.   1960.
Tan triste como ella (novella).   1963.
Jacob y el otro: un sueño realizado y otros cuentos.   1965.
Tres novelas (includes *La cara de la desgracia; Tan triste como ella; Jacobo y el otro*).   1967.
Cuentos completos (selections).   1967; revised edition, 1974; as *Goodbyes and Other Stories,* 1990.
Novelas [and Cuentos] cortas completas.   2 vols., 1968.
La novia robada y otros cuentos.   1968.
Tiempo de abrazar y los cuentos de 1933 a 1950.   1974.
Tan triste como ella y otros cuentos.   1976.
Cuentos secretos: Periquito el Aguador y otras máscaras. 1986.
Presencia y otros cuentos.   1986.

Novels

El pozo.   1939; as *The Pit,* with *Tonight,* 1991.
Tierra de nadie.   1941.
Para esta noche.   1943; as *Tonight,* with *The Pit,* 1991.
La vida breve.   1950; as *A Brief Life,* 1976.
El astillero.   1961; as *The Shipyard,* 1968.
El infierno tan temido.   1962.
Juntacadáveres.   1964; as *The Body Snatcher,* 1991.
Los rostros del amor.   1968.
La muerte y la niña.   1973.
Dejemos hablar al viento.   1979.
Cuando entonces.   1987.

Other

Obras completas, edited by Emir Rodríguez-Monegal. 1970.
Requiem por Faulkner y otros escritos (essays).   1976.

*

Critical Studies: "The Shorter Works of Onetti" by John Deredita, in *Studies in Short Fiction* 8 (1), 1971; *The Formal Expression of Meaning in Onetti's Narrative Art* by Yvonne P. Jones, 1971; Onetti issues of *Crisis,* 6, 1974, and *Review* 16, 1975; *Three Authors of Alienation: Bombal, Onetti, Carpentier* by M. Ian Adams, 1975; *Onetti* by Djelal Kadir, 1977; *Reading Onetti: Language, Narrative and the Subject* by Mark Millington, 1985; "Onetti and the Auto-Referential Text" by Bart L. Lewis, in *Hispanófila* 96, 1989.

*   *   *

Juan Carlos Onetti once stated that all he wanted to express in his fiction was humankind's adventure. His fictional characters, typically "outsiders," struggle with and are alienated from their milieu, in which they find themselves isolated, disenchanted, and lonely. His most prominent themes identified by critics, included disillusionment, desire, and deceit. His fiction exudes an ambience of decadence and decay, moral, physical and psychological. Onetti's characters typically attempt to recuperate their past, a time of lost youth or opportunities and unfulfilled promises, in the hope of recuperating a squandered life and overcoming their fear of death. His characters often strive to escape the monotonous routine of their daily lives. These characters, seldom identified by name, must be recognized by their psychological characteristics or some particular aspect of their appearance.

Onetti's short fiction usually follows a single pattern, so structured that the first half of the story (the exposition) suggests alternatives and possible motivation for the character's behavior, while the second half presents the course of action taken and elaborates potential reasons for such an election. Characteristically little happens in Onetti's fiction; plots usually revolve around an event, a decision taken or an action fulfilled, after which the testimonial that follows serves to elucidate the anecdote. In his long fiction, as well as shorter narratives, Onetti uses as a backdrop or setting the mythical town of Santa María, where most of his characters encounter, cross, and crisscross each other. Most of Onetti's fiction is open-ended: he offers no definite solutions and some mysteries remain.

"Welcome, Bob," first published in 1944 in the Argentinean newspaper *La Nación,* portrays the idealism of youth turning into conformity and disenchantment as a result of aging. The narrator is insulted by the young, idealistic brother of the woman he loves. Bob prevents the marriage between the narrator and Inez because he feels the former is too old for his sister. With passing years, as the narrator sees how Bob ages, with his naive idealism eroding and illusions of conquering the world disappearing, his anger fades with the growing conviction that Bob has been punished by nature.

"A Dream Come True," also published in *La Nación* in 1941, presents a middle-aged woman who hires a disreputable small town director to stage a extremely pleasurable dream she has had. The unreliable narrator fails to understand the woman's desires and, consequently, misinforms the reader. Not until the end, when the woman dies during the private performance of her dream, does the reader discover and comprehend her motivation, her search for happiness.

"Hell Most Feared" first appeared in the literary journal *Ficción* in 1957. The title comes from a poem of colonial Mexico probably written in the 17th century. On its most obvious level of interpretation, the story deals with spiteful revenge. Some critics have suggested a misogynous streak in Onetti's fiction and this story falls within that category. Risso, the protagonist, a newspaperman in the town of Santa María, divorces his second wife because she committed adultery. Her intention, however, was to employ contrasts to augment her love for him. The woman disappears but soon initiates limited correspondence with him, friends, and relatives, including photographs of herself engaged in different types of intercourse. The photographs document her degradation and decadence as time and the missives progress. Ironically, Risso interprets the chronicle of depravity as a testimony of her love for him, almost inviting her to return. With the last photograph, he concludes he was mistaken: she sends it to the boarding school Risso's young daughter from his first marriage attends. The narrator's violent adjectives describing the woman contradict Risso's perspective and his masochistic belief she loves him.

"Sad as She," the title story of a collection published in 1963, a long novella of some 92 pages, also has some misogynous touches. An older well-to-do man who sells spare machinery parts in Santa María is married to a younger woman, but no longer cares for her sexually. The reader discovers that the house and its large garden were inherited by the woman from her parents. Furthermore, she was pregnant by another man when they married and the husband was aware of it. He spends evenings in town with other women, arriving home late at night. Her only enjoyment comes from taking care of her son and working in her garden. He decides to build some aquariums and in the process destroys the garden she has cultivated for many years. She seduces the younger construction worker—a rustic, rough and witless man, unable to perform sexually. One day, exasperated, she asks her husband why he married her, and he replies that it was not her money, not pity, but love and she commits suicide shortly afterward.

—Genaro J. Pérez

See the essay on "Jacob and the Other."

———————

ÖRKÉNY, István. Hungarian. Born in Budapest, 5 April 1912. Educated at Technical University of Budapest, certificate in pharmacy, degree in chemistry. Served in labor battalion, World War II: spent nearly three years as a prisoner of war in Soviet camp. Married Zsuzsa Radnóti in 1965; one son, one daughter. Writer and dramatic adviser, various theatres, Budapest, 1947–56; factory chemist, 1958–61. Recipient: József Attila prize, 1955, 1967; Grand Prize for Black Humor (France), 1970; Kossuth prize, 1973. *Died June 1979.*

PUBLICATIONS

Short Stories

Tengertánc [Sea-Dance].   1941.
Budai böjt [The Fast of Buda].   1948.
Idegen föld [Alien Land].   1949.
Ezüstpisztráng [Silver Trout].   1956.
Macskajáték [Cat's Play] (novella; from his play).   1966.
Jeruzsálem hercegnője [Princess of Jerusalem].   1966.
Nászutasok a légypapiron [Newlyweds Stuck in Flypaper].   1967.
Egyperces novellák [One Minute Stories], illustrated by Réber László.   1968.
Időrendben: arcképek, korképek [In Order of Time: Portraits and Sketches].   1971.
Meddig él eoy fa? [How Long Does a Tree Live?] (selection).   1976.
Rózsakiállítás (novella).   1977; as *The Flower Show [and] The Toth Family,* 1982.
Novellák [Short Stories].   2 vols., 1980.
Búcsú: kiadatlan novellák [Parting: Unpublished Short Stories].   1989.

Novels

Házastársak [The Married Couple].   1951.
Egy négykezes regény tanulságos története [The Instructive Story of a Four-handed Novel].   1979.

Plays

Voronyezs [Voronezh].   1948.
Sötét galamb [Dark Pigeon].   1958.

Macskajáték (from his novella; produced 1979).   1966; as *Catsplay: A Tragi-comedy in Two Acts,* 1976.
Tóték [The Toth Family] (from his story; produced 1968).   1967.
Pisti a vérzivatarban.   1969; as "Stevie in the Bloodbath," in *A Mirror to the Cage,* 1993.
Vérrokonok [Blood Relations].   1974.
Kulcskeresok [Searching for Keys].   1976.
Élőszóval.   1978.
Forgatókònyyv [Scenario].   1979.
Drámák [Plays].   3 vols., 1982.

Other

Amíg idejutottunk . . . Magyarok emlékeznek hadifogságban [The Road to Captivity . . . Hungarian Prisoners of War Remember].   1946.
Lágerek népe [People of the Camps].   1947.
Az utolsó vonat [The Last Train].   1977.
Önéletrajzom töredékekben: befejezetlen regények [Fragmented Autobiography: Unfinished Novels].   1983.

*

Critical Studies: "New Developments in the Hungarian Drama" by George Gömöri, in *Mosaic* 6(4), Summer 1973; in *Ocean at the Window* edited by Albert Tezla, 1980.

* * *

István Örkény was a Hungarian prose writer and playwright of the generation that grew up during a period of increasing political strife and division in Europe and that experienced World War II as a major, formative event. Örkény's first book of short stories, *Tengertánc* (Sea-Dance), was published as early as 1941. His experiences at the Russian front (where he served as a member of the notorious labour batallions organized by the government for Jews and Communists) and the following years spent in a Russian prisoner-of-war camp provided much material for his later writing. After a feeble attempt to write in a "Socialist Realist" vein, which more or less ended with József Révai's attack on his short story "Lila tinta" (Purple Ink) for its allegedly "bourgeois" outlook, Örkény began to search for not only a distinctive new style, but for a new type of short fiction that could best encapsulate the paradoxes and absurdities of the 20th century. This he found by the mid-1960's in the genre *egyperces novella* (one-minute story), a grotesque and often absurd sketch that usually "told" a story. These "one-minute" pieces, the first of which were included in the collection *Jeruzsálem hercegnöje* (Princess of Jerusalem) became the hallmark of Örkény's shorter fiction.

In one of his sketches Örkény gave instructions as to "How to Use One-Minute Stories": "The enclosed stories may be short, but they offer full value. . . . A one-minute story may be read either standing or sitting, in the wind or in the rain, or even when riding a crowded bus. Most of them can be enjoyed while walking from one place to another" (translated by Carl R. Erickson). Thematically, these are either wartime anecdotes ("In Memoriam Professor G.H.K.," "Two Cupolas in a Snow-Covered Landscape," "Let Us Learn Foreign Tongues!"), tales of the unexpected with an ironical twist ("A Brief Course in Foreign Affairs," "Satan at Lake Balaton"), or straightforward parodies and absurd mini-dramas ("Public Opinion Research" and "The Last Cherry Stone" respectively). Most of these one-minute stories are informed by a kind of black humor, which critics detect in the work of other Central European authors from Havel to Mrożdek. What makes Örkény's work idiosyncratic is his feel for everyday situations and everyday characters. Because of this, the reader accepts the internal logic of his stories, however absurd they may seem when taken out of their "realistic" context.

Some of Örkény's longer stories are also memorable. "The Hundred and Thirty-Seventh Psalm" is the story of a bungled appendix operation, at the Russian front, carried out without aenesthetics by a former medical student. "Fohász" (Prayer) is the moving story of a Hungarian couple who have to identify the body of their son, one of the young men killed in the street fights of the 1956 uprising. While these stories are, by and large, kept within the framework of the realistic tradition, Örkény also produced some that are close to the spirit of the one-minute pieces: "Az ember melegsegre vágyik" (One Would Like to Have Some Warmth) tells the bizarre story of a doctor getting obsessed with a superior stove, whereas "Café Niagara," Örkény's most Kafkaesque piece, is a symbolic representation of the situation that totalitarianism imposes upon all its subjects. "Café Niagara" is a place where people are regularly beaten and humiliated for crimes they have not committed—yet the fact that they have already been punished liberates them from their previous fears and anxieties.

Örkény was also an accomplished playwright. One of his early plays Tóték (The Toth Family) was first written as a novella. It is based on a wartime anecdote of a half-crazed major of the Hungarian Army who, when on leave, visits the family of one of his soldiers. The family, in their effort to help their son (who at the time is already dead), submits to all the whims and wishes of the major, including the manic folding of great quantities of cardboard boxes every night. In the end the Toths revolt against the major and kill him; the absurd story has a grotesque and macabre conclusion.

Another long story by Örkény, Rózsakiállítás (The Flower Show), tackles the problem of dying and its representation by the media. A young filmmaker decides to shoot a documentary film on dying and selects three real characters to appear in his film: a professor of linguistics, a woman whose job is flower-packing, and a popular TV news commentator. The novella not only traces the process of their dying but also raises the issue of art influencing life, even the manner in which people actually die. While informed by irony The Flower Show remains within the realist tradition; for all his penchant for the grotesque Örkény was a writer interested in the everyday life of average people whose problems he depicted against the unreal backdrop of Central European history.

—George Gömöri

See the essay on "Café Niagara."

OZ, Amos. Israeli. Born in Jerusalem, 4 May 1939. Educated at Hebrew University, Jerusalem, B.A. in Hebrew literature and philosophy 1963. Served in the Israeli Army, 1957–60; fought as reserve soldier in tank corps in Sinai, 1967, and in the Golan Heights, 1973. Married Nily Zuckerman in 1960; two daughters and one son. Teacher of literature and philosophy, Hulda High School, Kibuts Hulda, and Regional High School, Givat Brenner, 1963–86; also tractor driver, youth instructor, Kibuts Hulda; visiting fellow, St. Cross College, Oxford, 1969–70; writer-in-residence or visiting professor, Hebrew University, Jerusalem, 1975, University of California, Berkeley, 1980, Colorado College, Colorado Springs, 1984–85, Boston University, 1987, and Hebrew University, Jerusalem, 1990; professor of Hebrew literature, Ben Gurion University, Beersheva, since 1987. Recipient: Holon prize, 1965; Israel-American Cultural Foundation award, 1968; B'nai B'rith award, 1973; Brenner prize, 1976; Ze'ev award for childrens' books, 1978; Bernstein prize, 1983; Bialik prize, 1986; H.H. Wingate award, 1988; Prix Femina Étranger (France), 1988; German Publishers' Union international peace prize, 1992. Honorary doctorate: Hebrew Union College, Cincinnati, 1988; Western New England College, Springfield, Massachusetts, 1988; Tel Aviv University, 1992. Chevalier de l'Ordre des Arts et des Lettres (France), 1984. Member, Catalan Academy of the Mediterranean, Barcelona, 1989, and Academy of Hebrew Language, 1991. Lives in Arad.

PUBLICATIONS

Short Stories

Artsot hatan.   1965; as Where the Jackals Howl, and Other Stories, 1981.
Ahavah me'ucheret (novellas).   1971; as Unto Death, 1975.
Anashim acherim [Different People].   1974.
Har ha'etsah hara'ah (novellas).   1976; as The Hill of Evil Counsel, 1978.

Novels

Makom acher.   1966; as Elsewhere, Perhaps, 1973.
Micha'el sheli.   1968; as My Michael, 1972.
Laga'at bamayim, laga'at baruach.   1973; as Touch the Water, Touch the Wind, 1974.
Menuchah nechonah.   1982; as A Perfect Peace, 1985.
Kufsah shechorah.   1987; as Black Box, 1988.
Lada'at ishah.   1989; as To Know a Woman, 1991.
Hamatsav hashelishiy [The Third Condition].   1991.

Other

Soumchi (story; for children).   1978; translated as Soumchi, 1980.
Be'or hakelet he'azah [Under This Blazing Light] (essays). 1979.
Po vesham b'eretz Yisra'el (essays).   1983; as In the Land of Israel, 1983.
Mimordot haLevanon (essays).   1987; as The Slopes of Lebanon,   1989.

Editor, with Richard Flantz, Until Daybreak: Stories from the Kibbutz.   1984.

*

Critical Studies: "On Oz: Under the Blazing Light" by Dov Vardi, in *Modern Hebrew Literature* 5(4), 1979; "The Jackal and the Other Place: The Stories of Oz" by Leon I. Yudkin, in his *1948 and After: Aspects of Israeli Fiction,* 1984; "An Interview with Oz" by Anita Susan Grossman, in *Partisan Review* 53(3), 1986; "The Mythic Pattern in the Fiction of Oz" by Avraham Balaban, and "*My Michael —* from Jerusalem to Hollywood via the Red Desert" by Nurith Gertz, both in *Modern Hebrew Literature in English Translation,* edited by Leon I. Yudkin, 1987; "Oz in Arad: A Profile" by Shuli Barzilai, in *Southern Humanities Review* 21(1), 1987; "Oz: The Lack of Conscience" by Esther Fuchs, in *Israeli Mythogynies: Women in Contemporary Hebrew Fiction,* 1987; "Oz: Off the Reservation" by Chaim Chertok, in his *We Are All Close: Conversations with Israeli Writers,* 1989; in *The Arab in Israeli Literature* by Gila Ramras-Rauch, 1989; in *Voices of Israel* by Joseph Cohen, 1990; "Oz" (interview) by Eleanor Wachtel, in *Queens Quarterly* 98(2), 1991.

*   *   *

Amos Oz published his first short story in 1962, and three years later, *Artsot hatan (Where the Jackals Howl, and Other Stories),* eight tales about life on a kibbutz. Of these, "Upon This Evil Earth" is a reworking of the biblical story of Jephthah, who, promising God that he will sacrifice the first thing he meets upon his return from his victory over the Ammonites, is first greeted by his only daughter. The forlorn father must contend with this bitter irony. In "Nomad and Viper" Geula, a middle-aged, unmarried woman living on a kibbutz, comes upon a Bedouin. Warned against his kind, she is both repulsed and fascinated. He is courteous, even courtly, and they smoke together. When he starts to pray, she plies him with inappropriate questions, not realizing that it is sinful to interrupt a Muslim at prayer. Because he rushes off, she reconstructs the reality of their encounter to assuage her thwarted desires: she imagines that he wised to have sex with her, for which she, initially, calls for revenge not only against him, but all of "them." Later, she regrets such feelings and even wonders about going to him. The jackals of the collection's title represent forces both outside and inside the kibbutz that seek to destroy it. Recurring in Oz's later works, this animal symbolizes threats to Israel's existence. This volume provoked considerable critical comment, some of it negative, because it empathically presented the "other," who, prior to that time, had not been so treated to any extent in Israeli literature. Since then, Oz's well-known stance of seeking political accommodation with Palestinians makes both him and his writings a target for right-wing political and religious ideologues.

A later work, "The Trappist Monastery," draws from Oz's experience as a soldier in the tank corps in both the 1967 and 1973 Arab-Israeli wars. Loud and bear-like, the prankster-soldier Itshe loves the beautiful Bruria. Kirsch, a weak, ineffective sick-bay orderly who longs to go on a military mission with Itshe, is Bruria's rival for Itshe. Kirsch lies to Itshe, saying that she has gone off to Jerusalem with someone else. The frenzied trip in a jeep to find her is a foray into the heart of darkness, during which the truck breaks down close to the enemy border. In the blackness, the men see the outline of a Trappist monastery, whose inhabitants observe permanent silence, thereby avoiding language, which, they believe, creates lies and deception. The glib Kirsch initially is delighted with Itshe's growing discomfort with the silence. Eventually, however,

he is nauseated by his hero's terror, a reversal of the David and Goliath archetypes conjured up earlier in the story.

The two novellas in *Ahavah me'ucheret (Unto Death)* and the three in *Har ha'etsah hara'ah (The Hill of Evil Counsel)* are Oz's best works of short fiction. The former treats the theme of self-deception. In both works, the chief characters are unable to achieve the laudable goals they seek because their quest is based on delusions and lies, which end up destroying them. In "Crusade," set in 1096 C.E., the French nobleman Guillaume of Touron sets off with the high-minded intention of freeing Jerusalem from "the infidel," when, in fact, he leaves for pressing personal and financial reasons. On the way, he and his men murder many Jews. He eventually goes mad and dies, possibly a suicide; most of the others kill one another, until, finally, only nine continue on their journey to an undetermined other-worldly realm. The disparity between the knights' pious, religious language and their horrific deeds underscores the moral emptiness of their undertaking.

"Late Love," set in modern Israel, is an extended interior monologue by the slovenly, unappealing Shraga Unger, an old Russian emigre who lectures on Russian Jewry at various kibbutzim. Thinking himself "redundant," he feels he is being edged out of his position by people who have no further use for him. Living in the past and unable to cope with the present, he sits alone in his filthy room overtaken by terror and panic, longing to be loved, waiting to die.

The three stories in *The Hill of Evil Counsel* "Mr. Levi," "Longing," and "The Hill of Evil Counsel," are set in Jerusalem shortly after World War II and just prior to the 1948 Arab-Israeli war. These works are interrelated through the character of the young boy Uri, who in "Mr. Levi," loses his childhood idealism and trust of those adults who encourage him in his vehemently anti-British attitudes. When the mysterious Mr. Levi arrives, Uri is told a lie: that Mr. Levi is his uncle. Moreover, Uri must say nothing about him to anyone. Levi spends a single night at Uri's home. The next day when Uri asks where Mr. Levi has gone, his parents meticulously avoid all talk of the man, as if to deny that anyone had been there at all. Horrified, Uri realizes their lie and betrayal.

"Longing" is a series of eight letters written by Dr. Emanuel Nussbaum, a prim, weak-willed doctor who is dying of cancer, to Dr. Hermine Oswald, an aggressive, self-assured psychologist who has left Palestine for the United States. Nussbaum recalls their meeting, their affair, her departure, and the longing he feels at having lost her. He describes the daily events in the neighborhood, which reflect Zionist longings for independence; his own physical deterioration, which provoke his longing for good health; and his growing affection for Uri, whom he comes to look upon as his and Hermine's secret son in whom Nussbaum invests all his hopes for Israel's future. The doctor is also pleased with Uri's return of affection for him. This is one of Oz's most poignant and affective works.

Some features of Oz's short fiction — the destructiveness of anti-Semitism on both the hated and the hater, reality versus unreality, personal needs versus national agendas — are worked out in further detail and with greater intricacy and depth in his various novels. His works, whether short or long, show Oz to be one of Israel's world-class writers of fiction.

—Carlo Coppola

See the essay on "The Hill of Evil Counsel."

OZICK, Cynthia. American. Born in New York City, 17 April 1928. Educated at New York University, B.A. (cum laude) in English 1949 (Phi Beta Kappa); Ohio State University, Columbus, M.A. 1951. Married Bernard Hallote in 1952; one daughter. Instructor in English, New York University, 1964–65; Stolnitz Lecturer, Indiana University, Bloomington, 1972; distinguished artist-in-residence, City University, New York, 1982; Phi Beta Kappa Orator, Harvard University, Cambridge, Massachusetts, 1985. Recipient: National Endowment for the Arts fellowship, 1968; Wallant award, 1972; B'nai B'rith award, 1972; Jewish Book Council Epstein award, 1972, 1977; American Academy award, 1973; Hadassah Myrtle Wreath award, 1974; Lamport prize, 1980; Guggenheim fellowship, 1982; Strauss Living award, 1983; Rea award, for short story, 1986. L.H.D.: Yeshiva University, New York, 1984; Hebrew Union College, Cincinnati, 1984; Williams College, Williamstown, Massachusetts, 1986; Hunter College, New York, 1987; Jewish Theological Seminary, New York, 1988; Adelphi University, Garden City, New York, 1988; State University of New York, 1989; Brandeis University, Waltham, Massachusetts, 1990; Bard College, Annandale-on-Hudson, New York, 1991. Lives in New Rochelle, New York.

PUBLICATIONS

Short Stories

The Pagan Rabbi and Other Stories.   1971.
Bloodshed and Three Novellas.   1976.
Levitation: Five Fictions.   1982.
The Shawl: A Story and a Novella.   1989.

Novels

Trust.   1966.
The Cannibal Galaxy.   1983.
The Messiah of Stockholm.   1987.

Other

Art and Ardor (essays).   1983.
Metaphor and Memory (essays).   1989.

*

Bibliography: "A Bibliography of Writings by Ozick" by Susan Currier and Daniel J. Cahill, in *Texas Studies in Literature and Language*, Summer 1983.

Critical Studies: "The Art of Ozick" by Victor Strandberg, in *Texas Studies in Literature and Language*, Summer 1983; *Ozick* edited by Harold Bloom, 1986; *The Uncompromising Fictions of Ozick* by Sanford Pinsker, 1987; *Ozick* by Joseph Lowin, 1988.

*   *   *

When Cynthia Ozick finished her first novel, *Trust*, in 1963, after six and a half years of intensive work, she vowed never to engage herself in something so long. "After such an extended immolation," she said in an interview in 1983, "I needed frequent spurts of immediacy—that is,

short stories which could get published right away." Since the mid-1960's, Ozick published some 25 stories in leading American magazines like *Commentary*, *Esquire*, and *The New Yorker*. Most of her stories are not short, however, but have novella length, and two tales have actually grown into novels (*The Cannibal Galaxy* and *The Messiah of Stockholm*).

Ozick's first collection of short fiction, *The Pagan Rabbi*, contains some of her best-known stories. They have become classics of Jewish-American literature. "The Pagan Rabbi" (first published in 1966) opens with a rabbi's suicide in a public park. When a former classmate at the rabbinic seminariy visits Rabbi Kornfeld's widow, he learns from her that his pious friend had fallen in love with nature, more specifically, with a dryad of eggplant-like skin. From the rabbi's diary his friend gathers that the talmudic scholar believed nature to be suffused with divinity ("Great Pan lives") and that he craved to liberate his soul from the burden of history and Jewish learning, a desire that eventually led to his suicide. In this story, Ozick establishes the antithesis of Pan and Moses, of pantheism and monotheism, of nature and history, of poetry and law, of self-indulgence and social responsibility. These pairs form the basic dichotomies in much of her early work: for instance, in *Trust*, "The Dock Witch" (1971), "Levitation" (1979), "Puttermesser and Xanthippe" (1982). These dichotomies reflect a split in Ozick's self-perception: as a Jew she is committed to history, moral seriousness, and rationality; but as a writer, she explained in an interview in 1985, "I absolutely wallow in mystery religion." As a committed Jew, story writing with its free flight of fancy remains for her an "illicit practice for which I have never actually truly given myself permission."

It is not surprising then that many of Ozick's stories are either about writers or about the process of writing and the power of the imagination. One of her most famous stories, the exquisitely funny "Envy; or, Yiddish in America" (1969, collected in *The Pagan Rabbi*), shows the plight of two Yiddish poets, Edelshtein and Baumzweig, who have no audience because nobody reads Yiddish anymore. They envy their prose-writing colleague Ostrover, whom Edelshtein calls "a pantheist, a pagan, a goy," because as an acculturated Jew—"a Freudian, a Jungian, a sensibility. No little love stories"—Ostrover is translated into English and becomes a tremendous success. In "Virility" (1971, reprinted in *The Pagan Rabbi*), another story about an immigrant poet, writing and assimilation are correlated in a similar way, and the theme of the literary fraud is introduced. Ozick refines this theme in later stories and uses it to great effect in *The Messiah of Stockholm*.

The title story of Ozick's second collection, *Bloodshed*, and the long novella "Usurpation (Other People's Stories)" (1974, reprinted in *Bloodshed*), are probably Ozick's most difficult poetological stories. "Bloodshed" revolves around the dynamics of "instead of," that is, around the function of metaphor, and demonstrates how mistaking the image for the thing, or confusing fiction and reality, can lead to crimes as horrendous as the Holocaust, engineered by men who mistook human beings for vermin and exterminated them. Similarly, "Usurpation" is a story that argues against story writing. "The point being," wrote Ozick in her preface to *Bloodshed*, "that the storymaking faculty itself can be a corridor to the corruptions and abominations of idol-worship, of the adoration of magical event." And storytelling, Ozick claims, "is a kind of magical act."

This last statement is a clue to Ozick's novella "Puttermesser and Xanthippe" (1982; reprinted in Ozick's third collection, *Levitation*). In an act of frenzied worry about the corrupt state of New York City the rationalist and lawyer Ruth Puttermesser creates a female golem, an anthropoid made from clay. This creature, self-named Xanthippe, helps Puttermesser to become the mayor of New York and to clean up and reform the city. But soon enough the golem's libidinal drive runs amok and wrecks the paradise Xanthippe had helped build. Like Rabbi Loew, the creator of a golem in 17th-century Prague, Puttermesser is forced to destroy her own creation in order to control it. During a talk in New York's Jewish Museum in 1988, Ozick called Xanthippe "a metaphor for art." Art, her story claims, unfolds its destructive potential as soon as it leaves the realm of the imagination and enters the real world.

Ozick most recent Puttermesser-story (there are now three of them), "Puttermesser Paired" (1990), presents another instance of such perilous boundary crossing. The still unmarried Puttermesser is now "fifty plus" and madly in love with the life and work of George Eliot. Thus she becomes the half-willing victim of a copyist, Rupert Rabeeno, who is obsessed with the idea of "reenacting the masters" and who seduces Puttermesser into copying the love life of George Eliot. After an imaginary honeymoon in the tracks of Eliot, Ruth is abruptly deserted by her new husband Rupert. She discovers that Rupert had not been playing Eliot's loving companion George Lewes, but the young Johnny Cross, whom Eliot married at the age of 61, and who on their honeymoon in Venice was seized with a sudden mental derangement and jumped from his balcony into the Grand Canal. Rupert, however, is sane enough not to jump out of Ruth's apartment window—he leaves through the door.

Throughout her short fiction, Ozick has offered one impediment to check the flight of fancy, and that is the fact of death, or more particularly, of deliberate murder, with which the imagination may not toy. In many of her stories the Holocaust serves as the event that tests her characters' moral seriousness (*Trust*, "The Pagan Rabbi," "The Suitcase," "A Mercenary," "Levitation," and "The Laughter of Akiva," which became *The Cannibal Galaxy*). With one exception, namely the title story of *The Shawl*, Ozick has not written directly about the Holocaust. She considers fiction the realm of human folly, of magic, and of levity, for which the destruction of the European Jews is an inappropriate subject.

—Susanne Klingenstein

See the essay on "The Shawl."

————

P

PALEY, Grace (née Goodside). American. Born in New York City, 11 December 1922. Educated at Evander Childs High School, New York; Hunter College, New York, 1938–39. Married 1) Jess Paley in 1942, one daughter and one son; 2) the playwright Robert Nichols in 1972. Has taught at Columbia University, New York, and Syracuse University, New York. Since 1966 has taught at Sarah Lawrence College, Bronxville, New York, and since 1983 at City College, New York. New York State Author, 1986–88. Recipient: Guggenheim grant, 1961; National Endowment for the Arts grant, 1966; American Academy award, 1970; Edith Wharton award, 1988, 1989; Rea award, 1993. Member, American Academy, 1980. Lives in New York City.

PUBLICATIONS

Short Stories

The Little Disturbances of Man: Stories of Men and Women
    in Love.   1959.
Enormous Changes at the Last Minute.   1974.
Later the Same Day.   1985.

Verse

Leaning Forward.   1985.
New and Collected Poems.   1992.

Other

365 Reasons Not to Have Another War.   1989.
Long Walks and Intimate Talks (stories and poems).
    1991.

*

Critical Studies: *Paley: Illuminating the Dark Lives* by Jacqueline Taylor, 1990; *Paley: A Study of the Short Fiction* by Neil Isaacs, 1990.

* * *

Grace Paley's collected short fiction thus far amounts to 45 stories in three volumes. Many had been published before, in *The New Yorker*, *Esquire*, *The Atlantic*, and a host of other periodicals. *The Little Disturbances of Man*, with eleven stories, appeared in 1959, followed by *Enormous Changes at the Last Minute* (17 stories) in 1974, and *Later the Same Day* (17 stories) in 1985.

From first to last, from the Aunt Rose of "Goodbye and Good Luck," the first volume's first story, to the Faith Darwin of "Listening," the last volume's close, it is talk that wells up from Paley's pages, distinctive voices raised in a spiffy demotic spanning life's wide octaves, the whole scale from *pianissimo comfort* to *forte vituperation*. Most usually the voices are varieties of female, from young Shirley Abramowitz ("The Loudest Voice"), star of a wonderful Christmas pageant staged mostly by Jewish schoolchildren, to old, black Mrs. Grimble ("Lavinia: An Old Story"), crying out her disappointment over a bright favorite daughter too "busy and broad" with babies to ever "be a lady preacher, a nurse, something great and have a name."

Shirley's loud voice is full of hope. "I was happy," she says in closing. "I had prayed for everybody: my talking family, cousins far away, passersby, and all the lonesome Christians. I expected to be heard." Mrs. Grimble's is a darker voice, chastened and dismayed, ending on a low note: "Then I let out a curse, Lord never heard me do in this long life. I cry out loud as my throat was made to do, Damn you Lavinia—for my heart is busted in a minute— damn you Lavinia, ain't nothing gonna come of you neither."

But talking, even hard talking, is living on, is holding free from despair—this would seem to be a fundamental Paley credo. "Tell!" says Zagrowsky ("Zagrowsky Tells"). "That opens up the congestion a little—the lungs are for breathing, not secrets." Only the very darkest story, a story featuring chosen death, centers upon a title character who at the end has nothing to say, employs the voice of a narrator who at one point has heard too much: "I said, All right, Hector. Shut up. Don't speak" ("The Little Girl").

There are occasional male voices, too—Zagrowsky ("Zagrowsky Tells") is the most voluble, but there's also Charlie ("The Little Girl"), and Vicente ("A Man Told Me the Story of His Life"). But not so many. In Paley's world mostly women are talking, the men are mostly walking, and much of the talking is about the walking. "A man can't talk," says sour Mrs. Grimble, nailing male conversation and sexual performance in one deft shot—"That little minute in his mind most the time." Virginia, the proto-Faith Darwin protagonist of "An Interest in Life," goes on more gently in the same vein: "A woman counts her children and acts snotty, like she invented life, but men *must* do well in the world."

Faith Darwin, Paley's greatest character, makes her debut, however pseudonymously, in this story. After one more run as Virginia ("Distance"), she resurfaces in "Faith in the Afternoon" with the gone husband christened Ricardo, Virginia's four children reduced to two boys, Richard and Anthony (Tonto), and parents in the Children of Judea retirement home. In Faith and her friends, in the details of their personal and political concerns (all are left-sprawling activists, especially in the *Later the Same Day* stories), Paley finds her fictional center.

Time passes. Richard goes from visiting grandparents to calling collect from Paris. Faith and her friends—Selena Retelof, Ruth Larsen, Ann Reyer, Edie Seiden—go from tending young babies in the park to being grandparents themselves. Parents die (Faith's mother, in "Friends"),

418

friends die (Ellen in "Living" and Selena in "Friends"), and sometimes children die (Samuel in "Samuel," Juniper in "The Little Girl," Selena's daughter Abby in "Friends").

Lovers and husbands come and go, Ricardo for example being succeeded by at least John, Clifford, Philip, Jack, and Nick (also Pallid the husband and Livid the ex-husband in "The Used Boy Raisers"). "You still have him-itis," Faith tells Susan, "the dread disease of females." "Yeah?" Susan replies. "And you don't?" In "Listening," the final story of *Later the Same Day*, Faith, even as she's upbraided by her lesbian friend Cassie for leaving her out of her stories (character Faith and author Paley merging here), has just been moved by the sight of a man "in the absolute prime of life" to wonder "why have you slipped out of my sentimental and carnal grasp?" The man, appropriately enough, is walking.

At last, in a dazzling move that unites the stories with the deep motives of their telling, Paley celebrates the brassy talk of Faith and her friends and offers her own preservation of that talk as an act of moral witness, a right thing. Ruth's bravery toward mounted police at a draft-board protest demonstration, as reported by Ann in "Ruthy and Edie," is verbal at its heart: "You should have been trampled to death. And you grabbed the captain by his gold buttons and you hollered, You bastard! Get your goddamn cavalry out of here." Talk saves the day, here loudly and with drama, elsewhere quietly, as when a grandchild is loved for "her new shoes and her newest sentence, which was Remember dat?" For Paley as a writer this child's interrogative shifts to imperative; by memories preserved in talk and writing, "the lifelong past is invented, which, as we know, thickens the present and gives all kinds of advice to the future." The direct affirmative statement at the end of "Friends" is quiet enough, but certainly firm, and surely clear, an endorsement of all the little human disturbances as worthy of loving attention: "But I was right to invent for my friends and our children a report on these private deaths and the condition of our lifelong attachments."

—Robert B. Cochran

See the essays on "A Conversation with My Father" and "Faith in a Tree."

PARDO BAZÁN, Emilia (Countess). Spanish. Born in La Coruña, Galicia, 16 September 1851. Self-educated. Married José Fernando Quiroga in 1868 (separated 1885; died 1921); two daughters and one son. Writer, contributor, and editor, various magazines and journals, including *La ciencia cristiana*, 1876–81, *Revista de España* and *España Moderna*, 1879–1902; lecturer, 1887–1906, and first female president, 1906, Literary Section of the Antheneum, Madrid; founding editor, *El nuevo teatro crítico*, Madrid, 1891–93; held various government positions; adviser, Ministry of Education, from 1910; professor of romance literatures, Central University of Madrid, from 1916. Created Countess, 1907. *Died 12 May 1921.*

PUBLICATIONS

Collections

Obras completas (novelas y cuentos), edited by Federico Carlos Sáinz de Robles.   2 vols., 1947; 3 vols., 1973.

Short Stories

La dama joven, illustrated by M. Obiols Delgado.   1885.
Insolación, with *Morriña*, illustrated by J. Cuchy.   1889; *Morriña* as *Homesickness*, 1891; *Insolación* as *Midsummer Madness*, 1907; expanded edition, 1923.
Cuentos escogidos.   1891.
Cuentos de Marineda.   1892.
Cuentos nuevos.   1894.
Arco iris.   1895.
Novelas ejemplares.   1895.
Cuentos de amor.   1898.
Cuentos sacro-profanos.   1899.
Un destripador de antaño y otros cuentos.   1900.
En tranvía: Cuentos dramáticos.   1901.
Cuentos de Navidad y Reyes.   1902.
Cuentos de la patria.   1902.
Cuentos antiguas.   1902.
Cuentos del terruño.   1907.
El fondo de alma.   1907.
Sud exprés.   1909.
Belcebú: Novelas breves.   1912.
Cuentos trágicos.   1913.
Cuentos de la tierra.   1923.
Cuadros religiosas.   1925.
Short Stories.   1935.
Pardo Bazán (selected stories), edited by Carmen Castro.   1945.
Las setas y otros cuentos (selection), edited by Carmen Bravo-Villasante.   1988.
Cuentos (selection), edited by Juan Paredes Nunez.   1984.
Cuentos completos, edited by Juan Paredes Nunez.   4 vols., 1990.

Novels

Pascual López, Autobiografía de un estudiante de medicina.   1879.
Un viaje de novios.   1881; as *A Wedding Trip*, 1891.
La tribuna.   1883.
El cisne de Vilamorta.   1885; as *The Swan of Vilamorta*, 1891; as *Shattered Hope, or The Swan of Vilamorta*, 1900.
Los pazos de Ulloa.   1886; as *The Son of the Bondwoman*, 1908; as *The House of Ulloa*, 1990.
La madre naturaleza.   1887.
Una cristiana.   1890; as *A Christian Woman*, 1891; as *Secret of the Yew Tree; or, A Christian Woman*, 1900.
La prueba.   1890.
La piedra angular.   1891; as *The Angular Stone*, 1892.
Adán y Eva: Doña Milagros.   1894.
Adán y Eva: Memorias de un solterón.   1896.
El tesoro de Gastón.   1897.
El saludo de las brujas.   1897.
El niño de Guzmán.   1899.
Misterio.   1903; as *The Mystery of the Lost Dauphin (Louis XVII)*, 1906.
La Quimera.   1905.
La sirena negra.   1908.
Dulce dueño.   1911.

Plays

La suerte.   1904.
Cuesta abajo.   1906.
Verdad.   1906.

Verse

Jáime.   1876.

Other

Estudio crítico de las obras del Padre Feijoo (criticism).
   1876.
San Francisco de Asís.   1882.
La cuestión palpitante (criticism).   1883.
Folklore gallego, with others.   1884.
La leyenda de la Pastoriza.   1887.
La revolución y la novela en Rusia.   3 vols., 1887; as
   Russia, its People, and its Literature, 1890.
Mi romería (articles).   1888.
De mi tierra (criticism).   1888.
Los pedagogos del renacimiento.   1889.
Al pie de la torre Eiffel (articles).   1889.
Por Francia y por Alemania.   1890.
Obras completas.   43 vols., 1891–1926.
El P. Luis Coloma (biography).   1891.
Españoles ilustres.   1891.
Los franciscanos y Colón.   1892.
Alarcón (biography).   1892.
Polémicas y estudios literarios.   1892.
Campoamor (biography).   1893.
Los poetas épicos cristianos (criticism).   1895.
Por la España pintoresca.   1895.
Hombres y mujeres de antaño.   1896.
Vida contemporánea.   1896.
La España de ayer y la de hoy.   1899.
Cuarenta días en la exposición.   1900.
De siglo á siglo.   1902.
Los franciscanos y el descubrimiento de América.   1902.
Por la Europa católica.   1902.
Goya y la espontaneidad española.   1905.
Lecciones de literatura.   1906.
Retratos y apuntes literarios.   1908.
Teatro.   1909.
La literatura franscesca moderna.   2 vols., 1910–11; vol.3,
   1914.
Arrastrado.   1912.
La cocina española antigua.   1913.
Hernán Cortés y sus hazañas (for children).   1914.
La cocina española moderna.   1916.
El porvenir de la literatura después de la guerra (lectures).
   1917.
El lirismo en al poesía francesa.   1923.
Cartas a Benito Pérez Galdos (1889–1890), edited by
   Carmen Bravo-Villasante.   1975.
La mujer española y otros articulos femistas (essays), edited
   by de Leda Schiavo.   1976.
Cartas inéditas a Pardo Bazán (letters), edited by Ana
   Maria Freire Lopez.   1991.

*

Critical Studies: *Two Modern Spanish Novelists: Pardo
Bazán and Armando Palacio Valdés* by C.C. Glasnock,
1926; "Pardo Bazán and the Literary Polemics about
Feminism" by Ronald Hilton, in *Romantic Review,* 44,
1953; *The Catholic Naturalism of Pardo Bazán* by Donald
Fowler Brown, 1957; "Observations on the Narrative
Method, the Psychology, and the Style of *Los Pazos de
Ulloa*" by Robert E. Lott, in *Hispania* 52, 1969; *Pardo
Bazán* by Walter Pattison, 1971; "Pardo Bazán's Pessimis-
tic View of Love as Revealed in *Cuentos de Amor*" by
Thomas Feeny, in *Hispanófila* 23, September 1978; "Femi-
nism and the Feminine in Pardo Bazán's Novels" by Mary
E. Giles, in *Hispania* 63, 1980; *Pardo Bazán: The Making
of a Novelist* by Maurice Hemingway, 1983; *In the Femi-
nine Mode* edited by Nöel Valis and Carol Maier, 1990.

* * *

Emilia Pardo Bazán was a spanish novelist, short story
writer, essayist, and critic. The only child of a well-to-do
family, her education (like most Spanish women of the day)
was limited to boarding school, but she thereafter continued self-instruction through systematic readings in literature, contemporary affairs, and science, learning English,
French, and Italian. Although women were denied access to
Spanish universities, she became the first woman ever to
hold a professorship of Romance literatures at the University of Madrid and the first woman director of the Madrid
Atheneum. She wrote on subjects as varied as St. Francis
and Christian mysticism, feminism, popular science, contemporary French and Russian literature, and the Russian
revolution. She also was a first-rate historian.

Credited with introducing Naturalism to Spain (without
breaking with Catholic orthodoxy), Pardo Bazán was an
ardent polemicist whose position occasionally involved
contradictions. She defended women's rights and the poor
but also social stratification, popularized Naturalism but
rejected its ideological core, especially determinism. Although usually classed as a Naturalist, Pardo Bazán was an
electic who wrote under many influences, ranging from an
early post-Romanticism and Realism through an end-of-
the-century spiritual-mystic mode, Symbolism, and early
Modernism. Although married and the mother of three
children, she broke with her husband in 1885 following his
ultimatum that she must quit writing. A prolific essayist,
she founded a literary magazine for which she wrote all the
material for several years. Early editions of her complete
works included 41 to 44 volumes: 19 or 20 long novels
(there is disagreement whether one is a novelette), several
volumes of literary criticism and history, 17 novellas (by
the writer's count), and some 600 short stories. Her most
significant model was Maupassant, whom she considered
her master.

The two best-known aspects of Pardo Bazán's work are
her Naturalism and Galician regionalism which characterize her most popular novels and together account for some
80 percent of her criticism. Few of Pardo Bazán's short
stories (or collections thereof) have been studied, but they
usually have been approached as Naturalist or regional;
Pardo Bazán suggests the Galician focus herself with short
story collections such as *Cuentos de la patria* (Tales of the
Fatherland), *Cuentos del terruño* (Tales of the Homeland),
and *Cuentos de la tierra* (Tales of the Soil). Galician stories
typically emphasize superstition, apparitions, or "miracles," fantasy, mystery, and the misty landscape, but some
present the brutality, poverty, and backwardness of rural
areas, or portray crimes of avarice, abuse, and revenge.
Numerous other thematic nucleii exist among Pardo
Bazán's stories, including those grouped around major
dates (New Year's, Epiphany, Carnival, Holy Week, Christmas) in ancient and modern times; tales of religious
inspiration or allusion, featuring biblical motifs; fantastic
tales; humorous stories; historical incidents or personages
(and, following Spain's defeat in 1898, several with patriotic themes); stories about children or animals; peasant life
and social themes; morally edifying events or implications;

male-female relations and/or love stories; psychological and moral tales.

Comparably few Pardo Bazán stories offer happy endings, although a minority do so; most of her tales of courtship treat deception or disappointment in love, abandonment or broken engagements, abusive or jealous suitors, and defects in the beloved leading to drastic escapes through emigration or entering a convent. The marriage of convenience appears often, sometimes motivated by trivial considerations indeed: a disputed dog, a lottery ticket, a specific bit of land. Misalliances, unhappy or abusive marriages abound, and frequent forms of marital conflict include internal power struggles, jealousy, suspicion, infidelities from the trivial to adultery, abandonment, and the ultimate abuse, spousal murder. Pardo Bazán clearly does not idealize the married state, and despite the paucity of alternatives for women in Spain, numerous stories suggest that matrimony is no bargain. Neglect or abuse of children is another focus, making certain stories especially timely.

Novelettes include "La gota de sangre" (The Drop of Blood), modeled after English detective stories, whose narrator is accosted by a man with blood on his shirt; the narrator later discovers a body and becomes a suspect, so that he is compelled to solve the mystery to clear himself. *Crimen libre* (Unpunished Crime), which deals with penology, anticipates the novel *La piedra angular* (*The Angular Stone*) in the author's opposition to capital punishment and her interest in criminology. As with Naturalism, Pardo Bazán's incursion into crime fiction occurred when women were not supposed to write of such things. "Finafrol" depicts Galician beggars and their sub-culture, while *Belcebú* (Beelzebub) offers an historical portrait of witchcraft, poisons, and alchemy. "Bucólica" (Bucolic), an interesting antecedent of *Los pazos de Ulloa* (*The House of Ulloa*), Pardo Bazán's masterpiece, is similarly set in a ruinous Galician country manor and portrays the decadent rural aristocracy. About half the works Pardo Bazán called novelettes are generally considered long short stories.

Insolación (Midsummer Madness) shares a common background with *En el santo* (On the Saint's Day), that of Madrid's colorful Fair of St. Isidro. *Insolación* literally means "sunstroke," and the time is not midsummer but a late spring celebration devoted to St. Isidore the Plowman, abounding in picturesque and folkloric touches. Given the prominent role of the blinding sun and the heroine's fainting spell brought on by heat and over-indulgence in alcohol, the novelette is usually termed Naturalistic. But Asís, the heroine, a wealthy young widow, and Pacheco, the Andalusian playboy who seduces her, are hardly typical Naturalistic characters. None of the sordidness, misery, and violence associated with Naturalism appear, and the only "social" problem concerns the convention obliging the widow to observe prolonged, solitary mourning and the potential ostracism if it is known she became drunk at the fair and allowed herself to be seduced.

Morriña (Homesickness), commonly classified as Naturalistic, is usually published together with *Midsummer Madness*, as in the first edition. Strictly speaking, *Homesickness* is less than Naturalistic, scarcely hinting at determinism: Esclavitud, the illegitimate daughter of a servant-girl and the priest for whom she worked, is seduced by her employer, perhaps suggesting biological predisposition (for 19th-century readers). Homesick in Madrid for her native Galicia, Esclavitud is sent to work for a Galician widow whose pampered, weakling son exploits the girl's loneliness to establish his masculinity. Left behind when the family undertakes an extended vacation (planned by her employer to abort the incipient romance), Esclavitud commits suicide. Pardo Bazán wrote these two works around the same time and may have been responsible for their appearing in a single volume; if so, she could have intended for readers to compare the very different results of the two seductions, leading to early remarriage for the wealthy widow and to the grave for the hapless maid.

As Spain's outstanding short story writer in the 19th century, Pardo Bazán is unrivalled in quality and abundance. She strove for naturalness, true-to-life vocabulary and expression, simplicity, exact and succinct descriptions, adroit organization of plot, and maximum narrative economy. Her stories develop rapidly and maintain their interest despite passing time.

—Janet Pérez

See the essay on "The Revolver."

PARKER, Dorothy (née Rothschild). American. Born in West End, New Jersey, 22 August 1893. Educated at Blessed Sacrament Convent, New York; Miss Dana's School, Morristown, New Jersey, 1907–11, graduated 1911. Married 1) Edwin Pond Parker II in 1917 (divorced 1928); 2) Alan Campbell in 1933 (divorced 1947; remarried 1950; died 1963). Played piano at a dancing school, New York, 1912–15; editorial staff member, *Vogue*, New York, 1916–17; staff writer and drama critic, *Vanity Fair*, New York, 1917–20; theatre columnist, *Ainslee's*, 1920–33; book reviewer ("Constant Reader" column), *New Yorker*, 1925–27; columnist, *McCall's*, New York, late 1920's; book reviewer, *Esquire*, New York, 1957–62. Founder, with Robert Benchley, Robert E. Sherwood, and others, Algonquin Hotel Round Table, 1920. Recipient: O. Henry award, 1929; Marjorie Peabody Waite award, 1958. *Died 7 June 1967.*

PUBLICATIONS

Short Stories

Laments for the Living. 1930.
Here Lies: The Collected Stories. 1939.
Collected Stories. 1942.

Novel

After Such Pleasures. 1933.

Plays

Chauve-Souris (revue), with others (produced 1922).
Round the Town (lyrics only; revue) (produced 1924).
Close Harmony; or, The Lady Next Door, with Elmer Rice (produced 1924). 1929.
Business Is Business, with George S. Kaufman (produced 1925).
Sketches, in *Shoot the Works* (revue) (produced 1931).
The Coast of Illyria, with Ross Evans (produced 1949). 1990.
The Ladies of the Corridor, with Arnaud d'Usseau (produced 1953). 1954.

Candide (lyrics only, with Richard Wilbur and John LaTouche), book by Lillian Hellman, music by Leonard Bernstein, from the novel by Voltaire (produced 1956). 1957.

Screenplays: *Here Is My Heart* (uncredited), with others, 1934; *One Hour Late,* with others, 1935; *The Big Broadcast of 1936,* with others, 1935; *Mary Burns, Fugitive,* with others, 1935; *Hands Across the Table,* with others, 1935; *Paris in Spring,* with others, 1935; *The Moon's Our Home,* with others, 1936; *Lady Be Careful,* with others, 1936; *Three Married Men,* with Alan Campbell and Owen Davis, Sr., 1936; *Suzy,* with others, 1936; *A Star Is Born,* with others, 1937; *Sweethearts,* with Alan Campbell, 1938; *Trade Winds,* with others, 1938; *The Little Foxes,* with others, 1941; *Weekend for Three,* with Alan Campbell and Budd Schulberg, 1941; *Saboteur,* with Peter Viertel and Joan Harrison, 1942; *Smash-Up—The Story of a Woman,* with others, 1947; *The Fan,* with Walter Reisch and Ross Evans, 1949.

Television Plays: *The Lovely Leave, A Telephone Call,* and *Dusk Before Fireworks,* from her own stories, 1962.

Verse

Enough Rope.   1926.
Sun set Gun.   1928.
Death and Taxes.   1931.
Collected Poems: Not So Deep as a Well.   1936; as *Collected Poetry,* 1944.

Other

High Society, with George S. Chappell and Frank Crowninshield.   1920.
Men I'm Not Married To, with *Women I'm Not Married To,* by Franklin P. Adams.   1922.
The Portable Parker.   1944; as *The Indispensable Parker,* 1944; as *Selected Short Stories,* 1944; revised edition, as *The Portable Parker,* 1973; as *The Collected Parker,* 1973.
Constant Reader.   1970; as *A Month of Saturdays,* 1971.

Editor, *The Portable F. Scott Fitzgerald.*   1945.
Editor, with Frederick B. Shroyer, *Short Story: A Thematic Anthology.*   1965.

*

Critical Studies: *An Unfinished Woman: A Memoir* by Lillian Hellman, 1969; *You Might as Well Live: The Life and Times of Parker* by John Keats, 1970; *Parker* by Arthur F. Kinney, 1978; *The Late Mrs. Parker* by Leslie Frewin, 1986; *Parker: What Fresh Hell Is This?* by Marion Meade, 1988.

*   *   *

At her best as a witty, suave satirist of urban life in the 1920's, Dorothy Parker depicted in several volumes of light verse and many short stories the conditions of life for alienated city-dwellers. As a skilful reviewer and critic, Parker developed a scathingly epigrammatic style, best displayed in demolishing inept or pretentious literary or dramatic productions. Her criticism of life, like her criticism of literature, was based on ideals of grace and quality that she rarely discovered in practice. Like most effective satirists, Parker was something of a frustrated or disappointed idealist, always amazed that the world is so invaryingly fraudulent.

Associated with the urbane wits of the Algonquin Round Table and the fledgling *New Yorker* magazine, Parker was an acute observer of the manners and mores of New York culture and a precursor of such realist-satirist commentators as John O'Hara, John Cheever, and John Updike. Her verse is acrid and in the tradition of neoclassical epigrammatic social satire, and this spare, telegraphic quality is also characteristic of her understated, elegant stories.

Parker's fiction often consists of interior monologues, like "A Telephone Call," in which an anxious woman prays desperately to hear from her beloved: "Please, God, let him telephone me now. Dear God, let him call me now. I won't ask anything else of You, truly I won't." Or the witty and allusive "The Little Hours," in which an insomniac invokes La Rouchefoucauld (also one of Swift's masters) and a horde of half-remembered literary citations, in lieu of counting sheep. Or the mordant "Just a Little One," a drunken soliloquy from a speakeasy in 1928.

Other stories are skeletal dialogues, as directly dramatic as one-act plays, like "The Sexes," which outlines a jealous debate, or "Here We Are," which develops the same idea through a young man and woman who have been married only three hours and who argue vituperatively on their honeymoon train ride, ending with an ominous *entente*:

> "We're not going to have any bad starts. Look at us—we're on our honeymoon. Pretty soon we'll be regular old married people. I mean. I mean, in a few minutes we'll be getting into New York, and then everything will be all right. I mean—well, look at us! Here we are married! Here we are!"

> "Yes, here we are," she said. "Aren't we?"

Another dialogue, "New York to Detroit," based on the newfangled idea of long-distance telephone calls, underscores the basic Parker theme of alienation in the midst of communication.

In 1927, Parker listed three of the greatest American short stories as Ernest Hemingway's "The Killers," Sherwood Anderson's "I'm a Fool," and Ring Lardner's "Some Like Them Cold." These choices show her critical acumen and the style and substance she admired and emulated in her own stories. In a story like "The Lovely Leave," written early in World War II, she achieves some of the effects of these three sardonic, tough-minded observers of the American scene. It depicts Mimi, a young wife, and her self-absorbed husband, Lt. Steve McVicker, home for a brief leave. He revels in the comforts of home, while his mind and heart are with the fliers he trains. She realizes she cannot compete with the intense male world of the war, and he seems impossible to reach. Finally, as he departs he explains:

> "I can't talk about it. I can't even think about it—because if I did I couldn't do my job. But just because I don't talk about it doesn't mean I want to be doing what I'm doing. I want to be with you, Mimi. That's where I belong."

The brief moment of revelation breaks down the impermeable barrier between the sexes and reassures her in her loneliness and isolation.

The loneliness of individuals cut off from each other is a quintessential Parker theme, often coupled with examples of the human capacity for self-delusion and hypocrisy. For example, "The Waltz," is a monologue story that contrasts the bright social chit-chat of a woman dancing and her darker inner thoughts:

> I hate this creature I'm chained to. I hated him the moment I saw his leering, bestial face. And here I've been locked in his noxious embrace for the thirty-five years this waltz has lasted. Is that orchestra never going to stop playing? Or must this obscene travesty of a dance go on until hell burns out?
>
> *Oh, they're going to play another encore. Oh, goody. Oh, that's lucky. Tired? I should say I'm not tired. I'd like to go on like this forever.*

As in most of Parker's stories, the light comedy of the scene is underlined by despair, a feeling of the futility of decorum and manners in a world driven by baseness, selfishness, and deceit.

Her fiction has remained popular, often more widely read than the work of her peers of the 1920's; *The Portable Dorothy Parker* has been continuously in print since 1944. Her fiction is accessible and in many ways timeless, unlike much social satire or domestic realism. The very basic emotions and situations at the heart of her writing—sexual jealousy and inconstancy, the pressures of aging and change, the bedrock human needs for affection and security—make her stories seem classic, detached from the frivolity and fecklessness of the "roaring twenties." And her liberal sociopolitical concerns are still alive, like those expressed in "Arrangement in Black and White," which exposes the shallow, unconscious racism of middle America. Such incisive observation and portraiture is enduring.

—William J. Schafer

See the essay on "Big Blonde."

PASTERNAK, Boris (Leonidovich). Russian. Born in Moscow, 29 January 1890. Educated at Moscow Fifth Gymnasium, 1901–08; University of Moscow, 1909–13; also studied at University of Marburg, 1912. Married 1) Evgeniia Vladimirovna Lourie in 1922, one son; 2) Zinaida Nikolaevna Neuhaus in 1934, one son. Tutor; worked in management in chemical factories in the Urals, 1915–17; librarian, Soviet Ministry of Education, 1918; official duties for Union of Writers from 1932, but expelled, 1958. Recipient: Medal for Valiant Labor, 1946; Nobel prize for literature (refused), 1958. *Died 30 May 1960.*

PUBLICATIONS

Collections

Sochineniia, edited by Gleb Struve and Boris Filippov. 3 vols., 1961.
Stikhotvoreniia i poemy, edited by L.A. Ozerov. 1965.

Stikhi, edited by Z. and E. Pasternak. 1966.
Collected Short Prose, edited by Christopher Barnes. 1977.
The Voice of Prose, edited by Christopher Barnes. 1986; 2nd vol., as *People and Propositions*, edited by Barnes, 1990.

Short Stories

Detstvo Liuvers. 1922; as *Childhood*, 1941; as *The Childhood of Luvers*, in *Collected Prose Works*, 1945.
Rasskazy [Stories]. 1925; as *Vozdushnye puti* [Aerial Ways], 1933.
Povest' [A Tale]. 1934; as *The Last Summer*, 1959.
Zhenia's Childhood and Other Stories. 1982.

Novel

Doktor Zhivago. 1957; as *Doctor Zhivago*, 1958.

Play

Slepaia krasavitsa. 1969; as *The Blind Beauty*, 1969.

Verse

Bliznets v tuchakh [Twin in the Clouds]. 1914.
Poverkh bar'erov [Above the Barriers]. 1917.
Sestra moia zhizn': Leto 1917 goda. 1922; as *Sister My Life: Summer, 1917*, 1967; complete version, as *My Sister—Life*, 1983.
Temy i variatsii [Themes and Variations]. 1923.
Deviat'sot piati god [Nineteen Five]. 1927.
Spektorskii. 1931.
Vtoroe rozhdenie [Second Birth]. 1932.
Stikhotvoreniia [Verse]. 1933; revised edition, 1935–1936.
Poemy [Poems]. 1933.
Na rannikh poezdakh [On Early Trains]. 1943.
Zemnoi prostor [Earth's Vastness]. 1945.
Selected Poems. 1946.
Poems. 1959.
The Poetry. 1959.
In the Interlude: Poems 1945–1960. 1962.
Fifty Poems. 1963.
The Poems of Doctor Zhivago. 1965.
Selected Poems. 1983.

Other

Karusel [The Carrousel] (for children). 1925.
Zverinets [The Menagerie] (for children). 1929.
Okhrannaia gramota. 1931; as *The Safe Conduct*, in *Collected Prose Works*, 1945.
Knizhka dlia detei [Little Book for Children]. 1933.
Izbrannie perevody [Selected Translations]. 1940.
Collected Prose Works, edited by Stefan Schimanski. 1945.
Selected Writings. 1949.
Safe Conduct: An Early Autobiography, and Other Works. 1959.
Prose and Poems, edited by Stefan Schimanski. 1959.
An Essay in Autobiography. 1959; as *I Remember*, 1959; partial Russian text, as *Liudi i polozheniia*, in *Novy Mir*, January 1967.
Letters to Georgian Friends, edited by David Magarshack. 1968.

Marina Cvetaeva, Pasternak, Rainer Maria Rilke: Lettere 1926. 1980.

Perepiska s Olga Freidenberg, edited by Elliott Mossman. 1981; as *Correspondence with Olga Freydenberg,* 1982.

Translator, *Gamlet prints datskii,* by Shakespeare.   1941.
Translator, *Romeo i Dzhulietta,* by Shakespeare.   1943.
Translator, *Antonii i Kleopatra,* by Shakespeare.   1944.
Translator, *Otello, venetsy ansky maur,* by Shakespeare. 1945.
Translator, *Genrikh chetverty* [Henry IV, parts I and II], by Shakespeare.   1948.
Translator, *Korol' Lir* [King Lear], by Shakespeare.   1949.
Translator, *Faust* (part 1), by Goethe.   1950; complete version, 1953.
Translator, *Vitiaz ianoshch,* by Sándor Petofi.   1950.
Translator, *Makbet,* in *Tragedii,* by Shakespeare.   1951.
Translator, *Mariia Stiuart,* by Schiller.   1958.

Editor and translator, with Nikolai Tikhonov, *Gruzinskie liriki.*   1935.

*

Critical Studies: *Pasternak's Lyric: A Study of Sound and Imagery* by Dale L. Plank, 1966; *Pasternak's Doctor Zhivago* by Mary F. and Paul Rowland, 1967; *Pasternak: Modern Judgements* edited by Donald Davie and Angela Livingstone, 1969; *Pasternak* by J.W. Dyck, 1972; *The Poetic World of Pasternak* by Olga R. Hughes, 1974; *Themes and Variations in Pasternak's Poetics* by Krystyna Pomarska, 1975; *Pasternak: A Critical Study* by Henry Gifford, 1977; *Pasternak: A Collection of Critical Essays* edited by Victor Erlich, 1978; *Pasternak: His Life and Art* by Guy de Mallac, 1982; *Pasternak: A Biography* by Ronald Hingley, 1983; *Pasternak: A Literary Biography* by Christopher Barnes, 1989.

* * *

To Russian readers, Boris Pasternak is best known as a lyric poet and verse translator (Shakespeare, Goethe's *Faust,* and lyrics by various European poets). To a world readership he is known mainly for the novel *Doktor Zhivago (Doctor Zhivago).* However, he also produced a dozen or so masterly and idiosyncratic works of short prose that occupy a unique place in his output and in the history of the genre in Russia. In addition to the examples written and published between the mid-1910's and 1930's, a score or more (sometimes lengthy) early prose fragments still await publication and translation.

Surprisingly, all but one of the published short fiction works are "fragmentary." Though usually complete in themselves, they are usually part of a larger novelistic conception. Pasternak's composition and publication of short prose diminished in the late 1930's, after which he worked with more successful persistence on the novel *Doctor Zhivago.* In the words of Nikolai Vilmont, Pasternak's short prose thus has the status, perhaps, of Leonardo's cartoons. Characters, events, and situations also often migrate between this prose fiction and Pasternak's lyric verse and autobiographies, as well as the completed novel.

Almost throughout his career, Pasternak worked simultaneously on poetry and prose, regarding them as "two polarities, indivisible one from the other." But his first

successes were as a poet, and his earlier prose style—up to about 1930—has characteristic "poetic" qualities: convoluted style, high incidence of metaphor and impressionistic imagery, mercurial changes of voice and narratorial point of view, and a penchant for description and "atmosphere" rather than character-drawing and storytelling. The central characters are also usually authorial self-projections—as poets or musicians; settings are also often identifiable with Pasternak's own familiar Muscovite intelligentsia milieu.

Although "The Mark of Apelles" and "Aerial Ways" reach pointed conclusions, the plot line of most of Pasternak's stories is open-ended. Structural coherence is usually derived by use of situational rhyme, such as a situation or motif followed by its own repetition in varied form.

Pasternak's three earliest stories reflect the author's attempt to escape the allurement of romantic fantasizing or spectacular self-dramatization that typified much contemporary art. In "The Mark of Apelles" (1915), the posturing poet Relinquimini is rendered stupid by a rival, who answers his challenge to a literary contest by transferring it to the realm of real life and by seducing Relinquimini's mistress and muse. In "Suboctave Story" (1917) the organist Knauer is ruled by romantic inspiration as he improvises, and he unwittingly causes the death of his son, trapped in the organ's internal mechanism; the crime of serving only art causes Knauer's final ignominious dismissal by outraged German provincial Burgers. "Letters from Tula" (1918) introduces a young poet who battles unsuccessfully with the vulgarity of his own verbal excesses, while a more seasoned elderly actor achieves a complete "silence within the soul," not by self-projection but by self-sacrifice to the demands of a theatrical role.

"Aerial Ways" (1924) is Pasternak's most consciously modernistic prose, and until the appearance of *Doctor Zhivago* it was his only work dealing with post-revolutionary Russia. Stylistically, and in theme, it has some common ground with Zamiatin's contemporary "A Story about the Most Important Thing," particularly in its macabre imagery, leitmotif usage, rapid switches of voice between Tolstoiian omniscience, mystification and explicit tantalizing of the reader, and in its unequivocal picture of dehumanization by the forces of a Marxist-inspired revolution.

Apart from the novel fragments of the 1930's, Pasternak's last important short story, or novella, appeared in 1929. Its material is closely bound up with some earlier published "Chapters from a Tale" (1922) and the narrative poem *Spektorskii.* Its Russian title, *Povest',* meaning "the tale" or "the story" (usually known in English in George Reavey's none too accurate rendering as "The Last Summer"), not only describes the genre of the work but also refers to the central character's major undertaking: the writing of a story. The hero, Sergei, is another self-embodiment of the author, and the story takes place in the pre-World War I Muscovite setting familiar to Pasternak. He is a budding author, and plans to write a work of prose, part of which is actually presented—a story within a story (see the later verses of Doctor Zhivago contained in the novel). He intends to use the fictional author's artistic earnings in a charitable bid to rescue all the suffering and exploited women of Moscow.

The new element of self-sacrifice and moral commitment by the artist, first registered in "The Story," became a constant feature of all Pasternak's subsequent writings, and it laid the first obvious basis for the strong religious strain in his later work. Another feature of "The Story" was the clearer texture of its prose. Less vigorously metaphoric and not so consciously virtuosic, Pasternak's style was approaching what he himself later designated as a form of "realism" whose best fulfillment came, however, in the novel *Doctor Zhivago*.

—Christopher Barnes

See the essay on "Zhenia Luvers' Childhood."

PAVESE, Cesare. Italian. Born in Santo Stefano Belbro, 9 September 1908. Educated at a Jesuit school, Turin; Ginnasio Moderno, Turin; Liceo Massimo d'Azeglio, 1924–27; University of Turin, 1927–30, degree in letters 1930. Translator and teacher in the early 1930's; editor, *La Cultura review*, Turin, 1934–35; confined for association with communists to Brancaleone Calabro for 8 months, 1935–36; staff member, Einaudi, publishers, Turin, from 1942. Recipient: Strega prize, 1950. *Died (suicide) 27 August 1950.*

PUBLICATIONS

Collections

Opere.   16 vols., 1960–68.

Short Stories

Feria d'agosto.   1946; translated in part as *Summer Storm and Other Stories*, 1966.
Prima che il gallo canti (includes "Il carcere" and "La casa in collina").   1949; "Il carcere" as "The Political Prisoner," in *The Political Prisoner*, 1959; "La casa in collina" as *The House on the Hill*, 1961.
La bella estate (includes "La bella estate," "Il diavolo sulle colline," "Tra donne sole").   1949; "La bella estate" as "The Beautiful Summer," in *The Political Prisoner*, 1959; "Il diavolo sulle colline" as *The Devil in the Hills*, 1959; "Tra donne sole" as *Among Women Only*, 1953, and *For Women Only*, 1959.
Notte di festa.   1953; as *Festival Night and Other Stories*, 1964.
The Political Prisoner.   1959.
Fuoco grande, with Bianca Garufi.   1959; as *A Great Fire*, in *The Beach*, 1963.
Racconti.   1960; as *Told in Confidence and Other Stories*, 1971.
The Leather Jacket: Stories, edited by Margaret Crosland. 1980.

Novels

Paesi tuoi.   1941; as *The Harvesters*, 1961.
La spiaggia.   1942; as *The Beach*, 1963.
Dialoghi con Leucò.   1947; as *Dialogues with Leucò*, 1965.
Il compagno.   1947; as *The Comrade*, 1959.
La luna e i falò.   1950; as *The Moon and the Bonfires*, 1952; as *The Moon and the Bonfire*, 1952.
Ciau Masino.   1969.

Verse

Lavorare stanca.   1936; revised edition, 1943; as *Hard Labor*, 1979.

Verrà la morte e avrà i tuoi occhi (includes *La terra e la morte*).   1951.
Poesie edite e inedite, edited by Italo Calvino.   1962.
A Mania for Solitude: Selected Poems 1930–1950, edited by Margaret Crosland.   1969; as *Selected Poems*, 1971.

Other

La letteratura americana e altri saggi.   1951; as *American Literature: Essays and Opinions*, 1970.
Il mestiere di vivere: Diario 1935–1950.   1952; as *The Burning Brand: Diaries 1935–1950*, 1961; as *This Business of Living*, 1961.
8 poesie inedite e quattro lettere a un'amica.   1964.
Lettere 1924–50, edited by Lorenzo Mondo.   2 vols., 1966; as *Selected Letters 1924–1950*, edited by A.E. Murch, 1969.
Selected Works, edited by R.W. Flint.   1968.
Vita attraverso le lettere, edited by Lorenzo Mondo. 1973.
La collana viola: lettere 1945–1950.   1991.

Translator, *Il nostro signor Wrenn*, by Sinclair Lewis. 1931.
Translator, *Moby Dick*, by Melville.   1932.
Translator, *Riso nero*, by Sherwood Anderson.   1932.
Translator, *Dedalus*, by Joyce.   1934.
Translator, *Il 42° parallelo*, by John Dos Passos.   1935.
Translator, *Un mucchio de quattrini*, by John Dos Passos. 1937.
Translator, *Autobiografia di Alice Toklas*, by Gertrude Stein.   1938.
Translator, *Moll Flanders*, by Defoe.   1938.
Translator, *David Copperfield*, by Dickens.   1939.
Translator, *Tre esistenze*, by Gertrude Stein.   1940.
Translator, *Benito Cereno*, by Melville.   1940.
Translator, *La rivoluzione inglese del 1688–89*, by G.M. Trevelyan.   1941.
Translator, *Il cavallo di Troia*, by Christopher Morley. 1941.
Translator, *Il borgo*, by Faulkner.   1942.
Translator, *Capitano Smith*, by R. Henriques.   1947.

*

Critical Studies: *Three Italian Novelists: Moravia, Pavese, Vittorini* by Donald W. Heiney, 1968; *The Smile of the Gods: A Thematic Study of Pavese's Works* by Gian-Paolo Biasin, 1968; *The Narrative of Realism and Myth: Verga, Lawrence, Faulkner, Pavese* by Gregory L. Lucente, 1981; *Pavese: A Study of the Major Novels and Poems* by Doug Thompson, 1982; *An Absurd Vice: A Biography of Pavese* by Davide Lajolo, 1983; *Pavese* by Áine O'Healy, 1988.

* * *

The novels and short fiction of Cesare Pavese feature the recurring, tormented figure that is by now legendary. The motifs in his short fiction, often elaborated in his novels, radiate around a knot of irresolvable conflicts and spiritual angst, that is both autobiographical and reflective of the social and literary tenor of Italy in the 1930's and 1940's. Pavese's work is informed by his anti-Fascist experience— which takes a number of forms, including the development of the myth of America, common to other writers, such as

Vittorini; his internment ("Land of Exile"); and his many disappointments in love. He depicts the cruelty of human nature, of man toward woman ("Wedding Trip," "Suicides") and woman toward man ("The Idol"), as well as the natural cycles that govern our world. The poignancy and power of Pavese's writing stems from the lyricism of a remote past that is revisited, and from the often tragic mire of irreconcilable elements. These include a host of mutually-exclusive impulses within the male protagonist. The desire to return to his homeland and his childhood is offset by the sense of non-belonging that follows him everywhere. His inability to put down roots undermines his need for roots. His desire for happiness shrivels under his hopelessness. The fulcrum on which these conflicts balance is the theme of solitude: Pavese's male protagonists fashion for themselves a self-containment that breeds that very solitude from which they suffer.

Perhaps the short story "The Family" is the best exemplification of just such an emotional trap. At the age of almost thirty, Corradino begins to revisit the river where he and his friends had often gone boating in their youth. The motif of a return (elsewhere in the form of an immigrant returning from America) is characteristic of Pavese's narrative. Corradino's friends know that Corradino hates to be alone, and that in the evening he abandons his furnished room for his friends' homes. Nonetheless, he decides to spend July, when his friends are away on vacation, in Turin and goes alone each day to the river to smoke and swim and meditate.

His simultaneous love and horror of solitude become more evident as Corradino struggles with the reality, rooted in a vision of Freudian predeterminism, of his own—and presumably a universal—inability to change. He tells his friend's wife that he would have to be deeply-tanned if he were ever to get married: "Because it changes me. I feel a different man" (translated by A. E. Murch). Yet he has a longing "for something to happen to change his life without robbing him of a single of his old habits."

Corradino affirms that a child of six already has all the characteristics of the man. Yet soon Corradino meets Cate, an old girlfriend he dropped years ago, who has changed; she is now a sophisticated, self-confident, and financially self-sufficient woman of 28 years.

Confronted by his past in Cate, Corradino feels at a loss, discomfited by the conviction that it is now she who no longer seems to desire or need him. Cate's new independence grows more alarming when she suddenly announces that she has a son, Dino, and shortly thereafter, that the child is his. Cate further confounds him by making absolutely no demands on him, and Corradino is torn by disbelief, resentment that the three women in her family raised Dino without him, and fear that he will be imposed upon, that he is now trapped. In an ironic parallel storyline, his lover Ernesta calls and he treats her with the same coolness and indifference with which he must once have treated Cate.

Corradino acknowledges to himself that he has never been involved with anyone, that he has had plenty of women but has dropped them all, that he has "shirked all . . . [his] responsibilities." The ultimate irony is that when he finally decides to ask the elusive Cate to marry him, she rejects him, for she is in love with another man. She explains to him that in fact she has changed while he has not. His decision to drop her in the past has had irreversible consequences. Revisiting the past has shown him that he lived only a fraction of what there was to be lived, and Corradino is left on the fringes of "the family."

Many of Pavese's male protagonists share this feeling of exile—emotional, social, and familial. This exile is internal and to some extent self-inflicted, as well as external. In "Land of Exile" the protagonist's restlessness follows him into the internment and home again to Piedmont (Pavese's birthplace). Often, this sense of restlessness revolves around the female figure, for woman in Pavese is fundamentally different from man, alternately cause and victim of the protagonists' unhappiness. It would perhaps not be going too far to say that in Pavese's narrative the woman functions as the man's natural enemy. She is both threat to his solitude and relief from it. In "Wedding Trip" Cilia's husband, the narrator, laments his solitude even more than her untimely death. Yet his killing indifference through their marriage was caused by his thwarted desire for freedom from all commitments, as embodied in the freeroaming, adventurous figure of Malagigi.

In "Suicides" another story of the cruel war between the sexes, the spurned Carlotta kills herself. Her lover, torn between guilt and bitterness, reveals the impossibility of harmony in Pavese's narrative when he confesses, "So, having been treated unjustly, I revenged myself, not on the guilty one but on another woman, as happens in this world."

—Tommasina Gabriele

PEACOCK, Thomas Love. English. Born in Weymouth, Dorset, 18 October 1785; moved with his mother to Chertsey, Surrey, 1788. Educated at Mr. Wicks's school in Englefield Green, Surrey. Married Jane Gryffydh in 1820 (died 1852); four children. Moved to London, 1802, continued his studies on his own, and worked for merchants to support himself while writing; Secretary to Sir Home Riggs Popham, in Flushing, 1808–09; lived in North Wales, 1810–11; met Shelley, 1812, accompanied him on a visit to Edinburgh, 1813, and settled near him in Great Marlow, 1816; received a pension from Shelley and subsequently acted as the executor of Shelley's estate; staff member, 1819–35, and chief examiner, 1836–56, East India Company, London; contributed to *Fraser's Magazine* until 1860; lived in Halliford, near Shepperton, Middlesex. *Died 23 January 1866.*

PUBLICATIONS

Collections

Works (Halliford Edition), edited by H.F.B. Brett-Smith and C.E. Jones.   10 vols., 1924–34.
The Novels, edited by David Garnett.   1948; as *The Complete Peacock,* 1989.
A Selection, edited by H.L.B. Moody.   1966.

Short Stories and Short Novels

Headlong Hall.   1816; revised editions, 1816, 1823, 1837; with *Gryll Grange,* edited by Michael Baron and Michael Slater, 1987.
Nightmare Abbey.   1818; revised edition, 1837; edited Raymond Wright, with *Crotchet Castle,* 1969.
Maid Marian.   1822; revised edition, 1837.

The Misfortunes of Elphin. 1829.

Novels

Melincourt. 1817.
Crotchet Castle. 1831; edited by Raymond Wright, with *Nightmare Abbey,* 1969.
Gryll Grange. 1861; with *Headlong Hall,* edited by Michael Baron and Michael Slater, 1987.

Plays

Plays (includes *The Dilettanti, The Three Doctors, The Circle of Leda*), edited by A. B. Young. 1910.

Verse

The Monks of St. Marks. 1804.
Palmyra and Other Poems. 1806.
The Genius of the Thames: A Lyrical Poem in Two Parts. 1810.
The Genius of the Thames, Palmyra, and Other Poems. 1812.
The Philosophy of Melancholy: A Poem in Four Parts, with a Mythological Ode. 1812.
Sir Hornbook; or, Childe Launcelot's Expedition: A Grammatico-Allegorical Ballad. 1813.
Sir Proteus: A Satirical Ballad. 1814.
The Round Table; or, King Arthur's Feast. 1817.
Rhododaphne; or, The Thessalian Spell. 1818.
The Stable Boy. 1820.
Paper Money Lyrics and Other Poems. 1837.
Songs from the Novels. 1902.
A Bill for the Better Promotion of Oppression on the Sabbath Day. 1926.

Other

The Four Ages of Poetry. 1863; edited by J.E. Jordan, 1965.
A Whitebait Dinner at Lovegrove's at Blackwall (Greek and Latin text by Peacock, English version by John Cam Hobhouse). 1851.
Calidore and Miscellanea, edited by Richard Garnett. 1891.
Memoirs of Shelley, with Shelley's Letters to Peacock, edited by H. F. B. Brett-Smith. 1909; edited by Humbert Wolfe, in *The Life of Shelley* by Peacock, Hogg, and Trelawny, 1933.
Letters to Edward Hookham and Shelley, with Fragments of Unpublished Manuscripts, edited by Richard Garnett. 1910.
Memoirs of Shelley and Other Essays and Reviews, edited by Howard Mills. 1970.

Translator, *Gl'Ingannati, The Deceived: A Comedy Performed at Siena in 1531, and Aelia Laelia Crispis.* 1862; edited by H.H. Furness, in *New Variorum Edition of Shakespeare,* vol. 13, 1910.

*

Critical Studies: *The Life of Peacock* by Carl Van Doren, 1911; *Peacock* by J.B. Priestley, 1927; *The Critical Reputation of Peacock* by Bill Read, 1959 (includes bibliography); *Peacock* by J.I.M. Stewart, 1963; *Peacock* by Lionel Mad-den, 1967; *Peacock: His Circle and His Age* by Howard Mills, 1968; *His Fine Wit: A Study of Peacock* by Carl Dawson, 1970; *Peacock* (biography) by Felix Felton, 1973; *Peacock: The Satirical Novels: A Casebook* edited by Lorna Sage, 1976; *Peacock Displayed: A Satirist in His Context* by Marilyn Butler, 1979; *The Novels of Peacock* by Bryan Burns, 1985; *Peacock* by James Mulvihill, 1987.

*   *   *

Thomas Love Peacock enjoys a secure, if not secondary place in the English literary canon as a writer of poetry and prose satires. He is perhaps best remembered today for his association with Percy Byshe Shelley and for his essay "The Four Ages of Poetry," which inspired Shelley's well-known "Defense of Poetry." Although Peacock has been the subject for a substantial amount of scholarly attention, it is certainly eclipsed by the number of loyal and enthusiastic readers who return again and again to his satiric fiction for entertaining and humorous portrayals of various intellectual figures and their particular brand of social, political, and literary philosophy.

One of Peacock's greatest strengths as a writer lies in his extraordinary awareness of the ideas and actions of his contemporaries that shaped his lifetime as one of the most revolutionary periods in English history. His short novels *Headlong Hall, Melincourt, Nightmare Abbey,* and *Maid Marian,* all emerge from the years immediately following the Napoleonic wars with their revolutionary threats and subsequent suppression of civil liberties. *The Misfortunes of Elphin, Crotchet Castle,* and several articles were composed in the years immediately preceding the passage of the Reform Bill of 1832. But Peacock's contemporaries, as well as his audience during the 19th and 20th centuries, branded Peacock as an author lacking in serious intellectual commitment. His fiction, they argued, resists any commitment to a particular philosophy or aesthetic ideology. He has also been described as a novelist of character, but this too is misleading since Peacock fails to provide the reader with anything but superficial analysis of motive or action, tending instead to focus largely on description. Peacock himself stated that he cared little for the serious analysis of personality and at least one of Peacock's contemporaries referred to him as "a laughing bystander," as a way of characterizing the author's relationship to the subject matter of his fiction.

Peacock's reputation also suffers as a result of shifting relationships between writer and reader during the early 19th century. At the time Peacock was developing the form he is most famous for, the prose satire, it was a common ploy of the literary marketplace to mount campaigns exposing the personal life of the artist to increase the public interest and consumption of the literary work. This is certainly one factor that lead to the vastly increased interest in literary biography during Peacock's lifetime. In short, if one's life could be made interesting, this interest might be profitably redirected to the author's works. Peacock, who was never concerned with the demands of the literary marketplace, maintained a high degree of privacy to the point of being accused of personal coldness and indifference, and lived the last years of his life as a virtual recluse.

Serious discussion of Peacock's fiction remains limited by the practice continued well into the mid-20th century of identifying his fictional characters with their originals, a practice which began as early as 1840 with the identification of Shelley as the model for Scythrop Glowry in

Nightmare Abbey. In *Headlong Hall* Miss Philomela Poppyseed is often identified with the novelist Amelia Opie, and Mr. Panscope as Coleridge. In *Melincourt* Robert Southy appears as Mr. Feathernest, Wordsworth as Mr. Paperstamp, and Shelley as Mr. Forester. Until recently, critics were content to rest on these discoveries and continued to clutter editions with footnotes identifying models for Peacock's characters. The result was a collection of wearisome, antiquated clutter that obscured any real critical insights into Peacock's work.

There is no denying that Peacock's characters are modeled after originals drawn from real life, but Peacock is not interested in the individual personality, despite the fact that they are humorously and even ridiculously portrayed. Instead, Peacock portrays ideas and conversations of individuals in juxtaposition, which generally results in a widening gap between what they say and what they actually do. His characters are abstractions or personifications of ideas rather than individuals. With the exception of *Melincourt* and *Gyrll Grange* he rarely relies on sub-plot, we learn little of the outward appearance of characters, and the action of his stories are largely conversations. Peacock's earliest attempt at the prose satire, *Headlong Hall*, is an excellent case in point.

Headlong Hall came out of Peacock's discarded farces, *The Dilettanti* and *The Three Doctors*. Instead of characters, the story contains philosophers, good food, and conversation. The story begins with four individuals travelling in the Holyhead Mail. Mr. Escot is "a deteriorationist," Mr. Foster a "perfectibilian," Mr. Jenkison a "status-quo-ite," and Dr. Gastor is a "worldly clergyman." In the opening scene the characters are identified by their philosophies as they are exposed in conversation. These four are not individuals, but philosophers as Jonathan Swift defined them, "men of infinite systems" on their way to Headlong Hall, a Welsh castle now in the possession of Harry Headlong, a man named after a waterfall. In *Headlong Hall* the reader becomes no more acquainted with the narrator than he does with any of the characters who engage in conversation at all times and at any cost. Any action taking place in the story is there to create opportunities for conversation and for allowing the narrator to cut the speakers off.

Peacock's most famous work in fiction, *Nightmare Abbey*, falls between the two forms of satiric romance, and the conversation novella, or novellas of talk. In *Nightmare Abbey* Coleridge returns as Mr. Flosky, who immerses himself in "transcendental darkness," and claims that "tea has shattered our nerves." Shelley appears as Scythrop Glowry, who after being disappointed in love secludes himself in Nightmare Abbey, reading German tragedies and transcendental philosophy, and is infected with a desire to reform the world. He is also the author of a book that has sold seven copies and he becomes obsessed with the mystic significance of that number.

Nightmare Abbey satirizes much of what will later be identified with Romanticism in Britain, particularly the value of literature and its place in the world. The interest here, and in all of Peacock's fiction, is not the lampooning of individuals, but a critique of ideas and their effect on contemporary culture. Peacock is especially concerned with the tendency of his contemporaries to respond only to ideas and literature rather than to life itself. Peacock exposes, through the conversations of his characters, the debilitating effect of an excess of ideas at the expense of personal feeling and the individual's experience in the world. The high achievement of *Nightmare Abbey* was not matched by Peacock again until *Gyrll Grange*, published serially in *Fraser's Magazine* between April and December 1860. *Gyrll Grange* also appeared in book form in 1861.

—Jeffrey D. Parker

PIL'NIAK, Boris (Boris Andreevich Vogau). Russian. Born in Mozhaisk, Moscow Province, 11 October 1894. Educated at Nizhnii Novgorod Academy of Modern Languages, 1913; University of Kolomna; Moscow Commercial Institute, degree in economics 1920. Married three times; three children. Writer, from 1920 (used pen name from 1915); chairman, Krug Publications, 1923–23; travelled in Europe, the Arctic, U.S., Middle East, and Far East, 1922–32. President, All-Russian Writers Union (expelled 1929). Arrested and disappeared 6 October 1937. *Died (official date) 9 September 1941.*

PUBLICATIONS

Collections

Izbrannye proizvedeniia [Selected Works].   1976.

Short Stories

S poslednim parokhodom i drugie rasskazy [With the Last Steamer and Other Stories].   1918.
Ivan-da-Mar'ia [Ivan and Mary].   1922.
Byl'e [Existed in the Past].   1922.
Nikola-na-Posadiakh.   1923.
Povesti o chernom khlebe [Stories about Black Bread].   1923.
Mat' syra zemlia.   1924; as *Mother Earth and Other Stories*, 1968.
Angliiskie rasskazy [English Tales].   1924.
Tales of the Wilderness.   1924.
Sperantso.   1927.
Rasskazy [Short Stories].   1927; revised edition, 1929; revised edition, 1933.
Kitaiskaia povest'.   1927; as *Chinese Story and Other Tales*, 1988.
Povest' nepogachenoi luny.   1927; as *The Tale of the Unextinguished Moon*, 1967.
Ivan-Moskva.   1927; as *Ivan Moscow*, 1935.
Raplesnutoe vremia [Spilled Time].   1927.
Krasnoe derevo (novella).   1929; as "Mahogany," in *Mother Earth and Other Stories*, 1968.
Shtoss v zhizn' [A Chance on Life].   1929.
Rozhdenie cheloveka [The Birth of Man] (novella).   1935.
Izbrannye rasskazy [Selected Stories].   1935.

Novels

Golyi god.   1922; as *The Naked Year*, 1928.
Mashiny i volki [Machines and Wolves].   1923–24.
Dertseylungen.   1928.
Volga vpadaet v Kaspiiskoe more.   1930; as *The Volga Falls to the Caspian Sea*, 1931; as *The Volga Flows to the Caspian Sea*, 1932.

Other

Sobranie sochinenii [Collected Works].   3 vols., 1923.
Korni iaponskogo solntsa [Roots of the Japanese Sun].
    1926.
Kamni i korni [Stones and Roots].   1927.
Sobranie sochinenii [Collected Works].   8 vols., 1929–30.
O'kei: amerikanskii roman [O.K. An American Novel].
    1932.

*

Critical Studies: "The Pioneers: Pil'nyak and Ivanov" by Robert Maquire, in *Red Virgin Soil: Soviet Literature in the 1920s,* 1968; "The Enigma of Pil'nyak's *The Volga Falls to the Caspian Sea*" by Kenneth N. Brostrom, in *Slavic and East European Journal* 18, 1974, and "Pil'nyak's *Naked Year:* The Problem of Faith" by Brostrom, in *Russian Language Triquarterly* 16, 1979; *Pil'nyak: A Soviet Writer in Conflict with the State* by Vera T. Reck, 1975; "Pilnyak's *A Chinese Tale*: Exile as Allegory" by Kenneth N. Brostrom, in *Mosaic* 9 (3), 1976; *Nature as Code: The Achievement of Pilnyak* by Peter Alberg Jansen, 1979; *Pilniak: Scythian at a Typewriter* by Gary Browning, 1985.

* * *

Although Boris Pil'niak wrote five large novels, he is better known as a writer of short fiction. He began to write at the age of nine and his first two short stories were published when he was eleven. From 1915, when he was 21 years old, until the end of his life, in 1937, his short stories appeared regularly in a variety of Russian-Soviet journals such as *Krasnaia Niva, Zvezda, Novyi Mir, Russkii Sovremennik, Mirskoe Delo, Literaturnyi Sovremennik,* and *Zori,* in single volume collections and two editions of his collected works.

Though his writing style has elements of ornamental prose, a touch of Leskov's storytelling, Chekhovien short fiction, and Belyi's musicality, Pil'niak developed his own original narrative style, congenial to his personal values and to his world view. That style is characterized by musical dissonance, primitive expression of complex ideas, and a Chekhovien atmosphere. He often alternates narrational voices within a story to create a narrative mosaic and enriches this with diary and epistolary styles to further the effect. He also mixes tenses and often his writing seems not to be rhetorically consistent: he switches from narrational past tense to the present, making the style more journalistic. While his themes take different shapes and undergo variations in form, they remain remarkably similar throughout the writing of his short fiction.

Always present in Pil'niak's stories is the interaction of humans and nature—how humanity affects nature and how nature molds the conditions in which humanity exists. Pil'niak is preoccupied with the importance of elemental, instinctive laws of nature, as they affect the fortunes of animals and humans. The short stories "Above the Ravine" and "One Year of Their Life" are representative of these themes. Both are reminiscent of primitive pagan painting, when nature was the ruling force and humanity was of only modest significance. In these stories, Pil'niak emphasizes the power of instinct: nature holds a primacy with its eternal circle of birth, death, and rebirth. In the story "Above the Ravine" the central figures are birds

whose function is to illustrate this circle. Pil'niak describes the life of a mother-bird, the bearer of life, as a function of her procreational instinct. There is no attachment, there are no emotions, there are no years of shared life; there is only the instinct driving the mother-bird to attract and then to follow the most able, the strongest, and the most powerful male bird, the one who will best promote the fulfillment of her instinctive goals of life, of procreation. In the story, "One Year of Their Life," Pil'niak shows that human life is also centered around the instinct of procreation. His protagonists in this story, though human, are described in a most simplistic way. There is no character development. The characters are like the birds, two animals put together by nature to continue its eternal circle, to procreate. In these stories, Pil'niak's lack of differentiation in presenting lives of birds and people is a clue to the significance of procreation to his universal demands of nature.

In the stories "Snow" and "Lesnaia dacha" ("Forest Country House") Pil'niak maintains his views of the important function of nature, but expresses them differently. These stories have Chekhovien atmosphere and even a Chekhovien method of expressing the ideas. If "Above the Ravine" and "One Year of Their Life" have a pantheistic orientation, with the main characters merging into nature, the stories "Snow" and "Forest Country House" are centered around people, focusing on aspects of their individuality and character. Although they are surrounded by nature—by snow in "Snow"; by the forest in "Forest Country House"—they are exclusive of their environment, and this exclusion is the reason for their unhappiness. Just as Chekhov's protagonists are often victims of life because they lack will, Pil'niak's protagonists are victims of life as well, not because they lack will, but because they have betrayed nature by ignoring its universal laws and their own place within it. Pil'niak's nature, with its laws and demands, often takes revenge on those who reject it. For him, only those who reconcile themselves with nature find harmony and happiness in life; only for them, life becomes useful and meaningful. "Snow" illustrates these views with a story of two people. Kseniia Ippolitovna, an attractive, cultured woman, the product of the most civilized part of Russian society, is a failure because she has wasted her life for her selfish "civilized" pleasures and did not fulfill her "natural" function: she did not procreate. In the twilight of her life this failure to accommodate nature's laws comes back on her; nature seeks its retribution through a meaningless and empty life. Kseniia is a foil to the man, Plunin, who is also a cultured intellectual and originally was in love with Kseniia. In contrast he "saves" himself and finds balance in his life by living with a simple woman and by having a child by her. His wife is a symbol of life and nature, *das ewig weibliche,* saving Plunin's lost soul from the "corruption" of culture.

The theme of natural instinct and the responsibility to recognize the primacy of nature in all living things, including humanity, reappears in Pil'niak's later stories, especially in "The Cheshire Cheese" (1923) and "The Birth of a Man" (1935). In both stories Pil'niak shows the power of instinct and the positive response of nature for those who, in spite of their inclination toward trading intellectual and cultural development for instinctive behavior, recognize their responsibility to nature, follow their instinct, and fulfill their duty. Nature is kind to those who surrender themselves to the fabric of its universal purpose. In both stories, women are forced by circumstances to have children and are at first resistant to the idea; at the approach of birth they accept their situations and, in doing so, realize profound happiness, a feeling of fulfillment of their destiny.

Pil'niak has a deep distrust of civilization and reflects this in some of his stories by undercutting its apparent progressive function. He develops action and characters that show civilization as destructive, not only of nature, but also of Pil'niak's perception of the true nature of humankind. In the story "Big Heart" (1926) Pil'niak characterizes white civilized people as narrowminded, powerless, and cowardly, in contrast to wild mongols, who he shows as courageous and beautiful and devoted to the protection of their land and their relationships with it. Pil'niak's mongols are an elemental part of nature. They live in harmony with natural forces and feel a stewardship toward nature, particularly when it is threatened by a civilization, bent on exploitation of nature for "civilized" greed. In Pil'niak's battle between nature and artifice, "Big Heart" describes the confrontation of nature with civilization, which comes in a poor second when confronted with the unlimited power of nature.

Pil'niak had a complex and evolving reaction to the Russian revolution. His views of the revolution and of its function parallel his changing perception of social development and the kind of individual needed to effect this development. It is the children of Pil'niak's protagonists who will become the basis for a new and better humanity and who will realize a better society. In his early works, such as "Snow" (1917), Pil'niak develops this scheme of second generation renewal. The progeny of an intellectual cultured father, the bearer of Russian intellectual tradition, and of a simple mother, a child of nature, is the hope for an invigorated Russia. By the time he completed "Death Beckons" (1918), Pil'niak had become more skeptical. The new world could not be built by the product of this union; the father's blood carries with it far too much weight of human civilization. The figure who will renovate human existence must be freed from the past and must look only to the future. This evolving view first appears in Pil'niak's story, "Death Beckons," and continues the development of his perception of the origin of this new figure in his stories, "Cheshire Cheese" (1923), and "Birth of a Man" (1935). "Death Beckons" is the continuation of "Snow," but in this story, death of Plunin's child can be interpreted as a necessity for developing Pil'niak's evolving concept of society and those who will be responsible for the construction of that new society. In "Cheshire Cheese" this figure is begotten of a mother, Marie, who, though she belongs to the cultured intelligentsia of pre-Revolutionary Russia, has lost her part. She confronts the future with her child, conceived with an unknown man, a bandit from the Kirghiz steppes who raped her, killed those whom she loved, and burned her home, wiping out her past. Though the child does not know his father, he is genetically linked to that father, who symbolizes the powerful force of nature. In "Birth of a Man" Pil'niak's views become more radical. His new "savior" no longer has an intellectual or cultured past; he is the child of the mother, another Marie, who is a Soviet lawyer, a communist, herself a child of revolution and without a cultural past; but she has a present and a future. She is strong, independent, knowledgeable, and the *raison d'etre* of her life is service to the new Communist state. Though only a minor character, the child's father is also a Communist and serves the new Socialist state. Marie writes in her diary: "I did not have a family which might in its roots give me the means to live. And apparently my race is not continuing but beginning—be-gin-ning. It is enclosed by a very narrow and restricted circle, by my son, who does not even have a father: but this race has an advantage, it does not look back but forward!" The Christian symbolism and its allusion to salvation is clear. Both mothers are named Marie. In the first story, the father is a figure closely linked to nature; in the second, though the natural father is not named, Pil'niak introduces a character who has the function of the biblical Joseph, a man who is not the father of the child, but who cares for Marie before she gives birth, marries her later, and adopts the child.

Although Pil'niak's views on life and his set of values change throughout his literary career, his views toward individuality remain constant. Initially humanity is only a consistent element in the larger fabric of the universe. Later the revolution, embodied by the construction of the new Soviet industrial state, becomes a paradigm for this general view. In the majority of his stories he emphasizes the insignificance of human destiny in contrast to the grandeur of the universe and grandiose projects of revolution. Pil'niak illustrates this schema in "The City of Wind," which is set against the background of a city beset by winds and fire, elements eventually tamed by people who are building the new Soviet state. Pil'niak describes the fruitless though stubborn search of a young Russian man, Pavel, who was brought up in Germany and returns to Russia to trace his roots. Though Pavel makes an enormous but unsuccessful effort to find his father, Pil'niak shows this failure as unimportant; what is important is that Pavel has discovered the city of wind and fire that for generations has subjugated the city's inhabitants, claiming many lives; now these elements are partly tamed by the industrialization made possible by the Soviet revolution.

It is Pil'niak's achievement to illustrate, using his own original style, the immensity of the universe, the fatality of its laws, and the grandiosity of the power of the revolution in comparison to the smallness of the human being. Pil'niak reminds humanity of its strong connection to nature and its secondary, rather than central, function in the universe. Throughout his creativity the human being remains merely the vehicle, and never becomes the purpose for the realization of the superior goal of universal existence.

—Rosina Neginsky

See the essay on "Mahogany."

PIRANDELLO, Luigi. Italian. Born in Agrigento, Sicily, 28 June 1867. Educated at schools in Agrigento to 1882, and Palermo to 1886; University of Palermo, 1886–87; University of Rome, 1887–89; University of Bonn, 1889–91, received doctorate. Married Antonietta Portulano in 1894 (she was committed to a mental clinic from 1919); two sons and one daughter. Writer in Rome from 1891; teacher, Regio Istituto Superiore di Magistero Femminile, 1897–1922; co-editor, *Ariel,* 1898; financial disaster in 1903 forced him to increase his income by tutoring and working as traveling examination commissioner; became involved in the theatre during World War I; director, with Nino Martoglio, Teatro Mediterraneo troupe, Rome, 1919; co-founder, Teatro d'Arte di Roma, 1924–28; joined Fascist party, 1924, but his relations with it were strained; lived outside Italy, mainly in Berlin and Paris, 1928–33. Recipient: Nobel prize for literature, 1934. Member,

Italian Academy; Legion of Honor (France). *Died 10 December 1936.*

PUBLICATIONS

Collections

Opere. 6 vols., 1956–60.
Collected Plays. 1985—.

Short Stories

Amori senza amore. 1894.
Beffe della morte e della vita. 2 vols., 1902–03.
Quand'ero matto. . . . 1902.
Bianche e nere. 1904.
Erma bifronte. 1906.
La vita nuda. 1910; as *The Naked Truth,* 1934.
Terzetti. 1912.
La trappola. 1913.
Le due maschere. 1914; as *Tu Ridi,* 1920.
Erba del nostro orto. 1915.
E domani lunedi. 1917.
Un cavallo nella luna. 1918; as *The Horse in the Moon,* 1932.
Berecche e la guerra. 1919.
Il carnevale dei morti. 1919.
Novelle per un anno. 15 vols., 1922–38; 2 vols., 1944.
Better Think Twice about It. 1933.
Four Tales. 1939; as *Limes from Sicily and Other Stories,* 1942.
Short Stories, edited by Frederick May. 1965.
Tales of Madness, edited by Giovanni R. Bussino. 1984.
Tales of Suicide, edited by Giovanni R. Bussino. 1988.

Novels

L'esclusa. 1901; as *The Outcast,* 1925.
Il turno. 1902.
Il fu Mattia Pascal. 1904; revised edition, 1921; as *The Late Mattia Pascal,* 1923.
Suo marito. 1911; as *Giustino Roncella nato Boggiolo,* 1953.
I vecchi e i giovani. 2 vols., 1913; as *The Old and the Young,* 2 vols., 1928.
Si gira. . . . 1916; as *Quaderni di Serafino Gubbio, operatore,* 1925; as *Shoot!,* 1926; as *The Notebook of Serafino Gubbio, or Shoot!,* 1990.
Uno, nessuno, e centomila. 1926; as *One, None and a Hundred Thousand,* 1933; as *One, No One and One Hundred Thousand,* 1990.
A Character in Distress. 1938.

Plays

L'epilogo. 1898; as *La morsa* (produced 1910), 1926; as *The Vise,* in *One-Act Plays,* 1928.
Samandro (produced 1928). 1909.
Lumie di Sicilia (produced 1910). 1911; as *Sicilian Limes,* in *One-Act Plays,* 1928.
Il dovere di medico. 1912; as *The Doctor's Duty,* in *One-Act Plays,* 1928.
Se non cosi (produced 1915). 1915; revised version, as *Le ragione degli altri,* 1921.
L'aria del continente, with Nino Martoglio (produced 1916).
Pensaci Giacomino! (produced 1916). 1917.

La giara (produced 1916). 1925; as *The Jar,* in *One-Act Plays,* 1928.
Il berretto a sonagli (produced 1916). 1918.
Liolà (produced 1916). 1917; translated as *Liola,* in *Naked Masks,* 1952; revised version, music by Giuseppe Mule (produced 1935).
'A vilanza, with Nino Martoglio (produced 1917).
Cosi e (si vi pare) (produced 1917). 1918; as *Right You Are (If You Think So),* in *Three Plays,* 1922; as *It Is So (If You Think So),* in *Naked Masks,* 1952.
Il piacere dell'onesta (produced 1918). 1918; as *The Pleasure of Honesty,* in *Each in His Own Way and Two Other Plays,* 1923.
Il giuoco delle parti (produced 1918). 1919; as *The Rules of the Game,* in *Three Plays,* 1959.
Ma non e una cosa seria (produced 1918). 1919.
La patente (produced 1919). 1918; as *By Judgment of the Court,* in *One-Act Plays,* 1928.
L'uomo, la bestia, e la virtu (produced 1919). 1922.
'U ciclopu, from *Cyclops* by Euripides (produced 1919). 1967.
L'innesto (produced 1919). 1921.
Come prima, meglio di prima (produced 1920). 1921.
Tutto per bene, from his novella (produced 1920). 1920; as *All for the Best,* 1960.
La signora Morli, una e due (produced 1920). 1922.
Cece (produced 1920). 1926; as *Chee-Chee,* in *One-Act Plays,* 1928.
Sei personaggi in cerca d'autore, from his novella (produced 1921). 1921; as *Six Characters in Search of an Author,* in *Three Plays,* 1922.
Vestire gl'ignudi (produced 1922). 1923; as *Naked,* in *Each In His Own Way and Two Other Plays,* 1923; as *To Clothe the Naked,* 1962.
Enrico IV (produced 1922). 1922; as *Henry IV,* in *Three Plays,* 1922.
L'imbecile (produced 1922). 1926; as *The Imbecile,* in *One-Act Plays,* 1928.
All'uscita (produced 1922). 1926; as *At the Gate,* in *One-Act Plays,* 1928.
La vita che ti diedi (produced 1923). 1924; as *The Life I Gave You,* in *Three Plays,* 1959.
L'altro figlio (produced 1923). 1925; as *The House with the Column,* in *One-Act Plays,* 1928.
L'uomo dal fiore in bocca, from his novella (produced 1919). 1926; as *The Man with the Flower in His Mouth,* in *One-Act Plays,* 1928.
Ciascuno a suo modo (produced 1924). 1924; as *Each in His Own Way,* 1923.
La sagra del signore della nave (produced 1925). 1925; as *Our Lord of the Ship,* in *One-Act Plays,* 1928.
Diana e la Tuda (produced 1926). 1927; as *Diana and Tuda,* 1950.
L'amica delle mogli (produced 1927). 1927; as *The Wives' Friend,* 1960.
La nuova colonia (produced 1928). 1928; as *The New Colony,* in *The Mountain Giants and Other Plays,* 1958.
Lazzaro (produced 1928). 1929; as *Lazarus,* 1952.
La salamandra, music by Massimo Bontempelli (produced 1928).
Bellavita (produced 1928?). 1937.
O di uno o di nessuno (produced 1929?). 1929.
Questa sera si recita a soggetto (produced 1930). 1930; as *Tonight We Improvise,* 1932.
Come tu mi vuoi. 1930; as *As You Desire Me,* 1931.
Sogno (ma forse no) (produced 1931). 1936.
Trovarsi. 1932; as *To Find Oneself,* 1960.

Quando si e qualcuno (produced 1933).   1933; as *When Someone Is Somebody*, in *The Mountain Giants and Other Plays*, 1958.
La favola del figlio cambiato, music by Malpiero (produced 1933).   1938.
Non si sa come (produced 1934).   1935; as *No One Knows How*, 1963.
I giganti della montagna (unfinished).   1938; as *The Mountain Giants*, 1958.
Naked Masks: Five Plays, edited by Eric Bentley.   1952.

Screenplays: *Pantera nera*, with Arnaldo Frateili, 1920; *Acciaio*, with Stefano Landi, 1933; *Pensaci Giacomino!*, with others, 1935.

Verse

Mal giocondo.   1889.
Pasqua di Gea.   1891.
Pier Gudrò.   1894.
Elegie renane.   1895.
Zampogna.   1901.
Fuori di chiave.   1912.

Other

Laute und Lautentwicklung der Mundart von Girgenti. 1891; as *The Sounds of the Girgenti Dialect, and Their Development*, edited by Giovanni R. Bussino, 1992.
Arte e Scienza.   1908.
L'umorismo.   1908; as *On Humor*, edited by Antonio Illiano and Daniel P. Testa, 1974.
Pirandello in the Theatre: A Documentary Record, edited by Jennifer Lorch and Susan Basnett.   1988.
Pirandello e il cinema; con una raccolta completa degli scritti teorici e creativi, edited by Francesco Callari. 1991.

Translator, *La filologia romanza*, by Fed. Neumann. 1893.
Translator, *Elegie romane*, by Goethe.   1896.

*

Critical Studies: *The Drama of Pirandello* by D. Vittorini, 1935; *The Age of Pirandello* by Lander McClintock, 1951; *Pirandello and the French Theatre* by Thomas Bishop, 1960; *Pirandello* by Oscar Büdel, 1966; *Pirandello: A Collection of Critical Essays* edited by Glauco Cambon, 1967; *Pirandello 1867–1936* by Walter Starkie, 4th edition, 1967; *Pirandello's Theatre: The Recovery of the Modern Stage for Dramatic Art* by Anne Paolucci, 1974; *Pirandello: A Biography* by Gaspare Giudici, 1975; *The Mirror of Our Anguish: A Study of Pirandello's Narrative Writings* by Douglas Radcliff-Umstead, 1978; *Pirandello: An Approach to His Theatre* by Olga Ragusa, 1980; *Pirandello, Director: The Playwright in the Theatre* by A. Richard Sogliuzzo, 1982; *Pirandello* by Susan Basnett-McGuire, 1983.

* * *

Luigi Pirandello entitled his collected short stories *Novelle per un anno* (Stories for a Year), as it was his original intention to write 365 of them. He had written 233 when he died in 1936, having contributed steadily to the genre throughout his lifetime. While he is better known for his plays, which were nearly all written in his last 20 years, the short story remained for him an irreplaceable vehicle because of the quality of concentration necessitated by its brevity and discipline. His relativism—the passionate commitment to uncertainty which rendered authorial omniscience an impossibility—led him increasingly to cast his stories in the form of monologues, in which either the protagonist tells the tale in first person direct to the reader, or within some dramatic framing device to a fictive listener; alternatively it may be told in the third person by means of free indirect speech, or, still from a single standpoint, by an observer who is in some way connected with the protagonist. All writing, for Pirandello, was a subjective exercise, and his short stories in particular derive their note of urgency and intensity from the personal involvement of the fictional narrator.

The inexhaustible diversity of narrative voices does not hide the common factor: the dark nihilistic vision that permeates Pirandello's short fiction, which is darker perhaps than the best-known and most often-translated stories might lead the general reader to suspect. At the bottom of the pit are stories like "The Trap," "Nothing," "Destruction of the Man," "The Little Red Notebook," "The Fly," and "In Silence," in which life is held cheap, humanity is brutish, and death sets in at birth, coming quickly for those who are lucky. Every form of suffering is portrayed, from the physical and factual (disease, deformity, idiocy, bereavement, poverty, bankruptcy, and starvation), to the metaphysical (despair, awareness of mortality, and the all-pervasive sense of the meaninglessness of life). There are countless stories of suicide. For two reasons misery is universal: the world is the plaything of chance, and human consciousness is in itself a source of pain.

Paradox and the unexpected play a large part in these stories. Not the least paradoxical feature is their humour, or that blend of irony and compassion that Pirandello called *umorismo*. He has a rare eye for life's contradictions, for its incongruous characters (the visionary lawyer, the pagan priest, the euphoric prisoner, the murderous child, the peace-loving soldier, and the often-recurring lucid madman), and for its incongruous ceremonies (marriages are frequently despairing while funerals can be hilarious). Animals are often introduced to demonstrate the perverse irrationality of life. In "The Black Kid," a farcical threnody on the passingness of human attachments, the English girl abroad is enchanted by the graceful young creature of the title, and on her return to England sends for it. The literal-minded vice-consul in Agrigento carries out her wishes and despatches the adult, stinking, and dung-encrusted billy-goat as requested. In "Cinci" a child murders another, provoked to indignation on behalf of a threatened lizard. A good many stories are set in Sicily, and in these particularly animals are the agents of chance; dogs, cats, flies, horses, and crows are all unwitting destroyers.

A corollary of this is that in a world without purpose or pattern, in which all experience is subjective, random objects can suddenly assume a disproportionate significance: a blade of grass ("Chants the Epistle") or a torn sleeve ("The Tight Frock-Coat") can change the course of a life, while sanity can be lost or calm restored by the observation of a pair of shoes ("Somebody's Died in the Hotel") or a sheet of wrapping-paper ("The Man with the Flower in His Mouth"). Recurring inanimate symbols stress life's littleness and limitations (traps, cages, ill-fitting garments, dim claustrophobic interiors, the fly struggling in the glass of water), and its transience; from layettes and trousseaus preserved but never worn, to all the paraphernalia of ageing. Often a chance encounter between strangers in a café or a railway train prompts the confessional urge, and the story's setting appears in itself as an image of impermanence. In contrast, a large number of Pirandello's characters in their insignificance and ugliness are moved to raise their sights and draw some consolation, with or without a telescope, from the contemplation of the stars.

The compelling quality in Pirandello's stories that keeps his reader turning the pages is a sense of vision, the suggestion that in spite of all disclaimers to omniscience, the author, in whatever person he is writing, has access to some secret knowledge, some key to an understanding of the universe. And from time to time a character experiences something very close to a mystical revelation. In "The Wheelbarrow" the sober lawyer-protagonist is travelling by train, staring with unseeing eyes at the passing countryside. He becomes aware that his spirit is somehow floating free in some distant dimension, where it is able to apprehend a new and alien mode of being which promises spiritual wholeness and fulfilment. The moment of vision permanently alters the lawyer's perspective. He sees his physical existence and family circumstances as irrelevant and constricting and, thereafter he feels the need to devote five minutes of every day to an act of complete irrationality. To reassure himself of his existential freedom, he locks his study door and plays at wheelbarrows with his dog.

The caricatural element is strong. Grotesque faces and contorted bodies abound to reinforce the sense of the irrelevance of physical appearance and the discrepancy that exists for Pirandello in every sphere between the inner world and the outer. The fat bore at the watering-spa maintains that his mountainous flesh conceals "a cherubic infant soul" ("Bitter Waters"), and the brutalised one-eyed sulphur miner shed tears of consolation at his first sight of the moon ("Ciaula Discovers the Moon"). Inwardly triumphant, a short-sighted theologian vindicates the scholarship of a lifetime in "Professor Lamis' Vengeance," unaware that he is addressing only a bunch of steaming macintoshes, while a love-lorn bridegroom on his wedding night expires in the moonlight beside the carcass of a dead horse.

In his 15 volumes of short stories Pirandello demonstrates through a multitude of disparate narratives voices that there is no limit to the number of ways in which the world may be perceived.

—Felicity Firth

See the essay on "War."

———————

PLOMER, William (Charles Franklyn). South African. Born in Pietersburg, Transvaal, 10 December 1903. Educated at Spondon House School; Beechmont, Sevenoaks, Kent; Rugby School, Warwickshire; St. John's College, Johannesburg. Served in the Royal Navy Intelligence Division, 1940–45. Farmer in South Africa, early 1920's; founding editor, with Roy Campbell, *Voorslag* (Whiplash), Durban, 1926; teacher in Japan, 1926–29; moved to England, 1929; fiction reviewer, *Spectator*, London, 1933–38; literary adviser, Jonathan Cape, publishers, London, 1937–73; lecturer, University of the Witwatersrand, Johannesburg, 1956. President, Poetry Society, 1968–71; president, Kilvert Society, 1968–73. Recipient: Queen's gold medal for poetry, 1963; Whitbread award, 1973.

D.Litt.: University Of Durham, 1958. Fellow, Royal Society of Literature, 1951. C.B.E. (Commander, Order of the British Empire), 1968. *Died 21 September 1973.*

PUBLICATIONS

Collections

Electric Delights (selections), edited by Rupert Hart-Davis. 1978.
Selected Stories, edited by Stephen Gray. 1984.

Short Stories

I Speak for Africa. 1927.
Paper Houses. 1929.
The Child of Queen Victoria and Other Stories. 1933.
Curious Relations, with Anthony Butts. 1945.
Four Countries. 1949.

Novels

Turbott Wolfe. 1926.
Sado. 1931; as *They Never Came Back,* 1932.
The Case Is Altered. 1932.
The Invaders. 1934.
Museum Pieces. 1952.

Plays (opera librettos, music by Benjamin Britten)

Gloriana (produced 1953). 1953.
Curlew River: A Parable, from a play by Juro Motomasa (produced 1964). 1964.
The Burning Fiery Furnace (produced 1966). 1966.
The Prodigal Son (produced 1968). 1968.

Verse

Notes for Poems. 1927.
The Family Tree. 1929.
The Fivefold Screen. 1932.
Visiting the Caves. 1936.
Selected Poems. 1940.
The Dorking Thigh and Other Satires. 1945.
A Shot in the Park. 1955; as *Borderline Ballads,* 1955.
Collected Poems. 1960; revised edition, 1973.
A Choice of Ballads. 1960.
Taste and Remember. 1966.
Celebrations. 1972.

Other

Cecil Rhodes. 1933.
Ali the Lion: Ali of Tebeleni, Pasha of Jannina 1741–1822. 1936; as *The Diamond of Jannina: Ali Pasha 1741–1822,* 1970.
Double Lives: An Autobiography. 1943.
At Home: Memoirs. 1958.
Conversation with My Younger Self. 1963.
The Butterfly Ball and the Grasshopper's Feast (for children). 1973.
The Autobiography (revised versions of *Double Lives* and *At Home*). 1975.

Editor, *Japanese Lady in Europe,* by Haruko Ichikawa. 1937.

Editor, *Kilvert's Diary 1870–1879.*   3 vols., 1938–40; abridged edition, 1944; revised edition, 3 vols., 1960.

Editor, *Selected Poems of Herman Melville.*   1943.

Editor, with Anthony Thwaite and Hilary Corke, *New Poems 1961: A P.E.N. Anthology.*   1961.

Editor, *A Message in Code: The Diary of Richard Rumbold 1932–1960.*   1964.

Editor, *Burn These Letters: Alice Lemon to Winifred Nicol 1959–1962.*   1973.

Translator, with Jack Cope, *Selected Poems of Ingrid Jonker.*   1968.

*

Critical Studies: *Plomer* by John R. Doyle, 1969; *Plomer: A Biography* by Peter Alexander, 1989.

* * *

The stories of William Plomer are set in four countries, South Africa, Japan, Greece, and England, providing both a framework and an indication of the chief characteristic of his writings, that they are the product of a man frequently transplanted from one country to another. As a result, his stories tend to focus on the restless and rootless, misfits and outcasts, and to explore cultural conflicts. His most important stories are those of his birthplace, for in his South African fictions Plomer founded the two dominant "schools" of subsequent South African writing: that of relationships across the colour bar, as shown in his pioneering novel *Turbott Wolfe* and the story "The Child of Queen Victoria" (1933); and that of the black migrant who comes to the white man's city in search of work, as in "Ula Masondo" (1927). Apart from the two major—and lengthy—stories, Plomer also wrote a number of lesser fictional responses to the South African racial situation; he was the first writer to tackle the subject in a radical and uncompromising way. This made him a controversial figure even as a very young man, and his first book of short stories, *I Speak for Africa*, enraged many whites for the critical treatment they received and his sympathetic treatment of blacks, presented as fully human in the stories and in *Turbott Wolfe* for the first time (astonishingly) in South African literature.

"Black Peril," even in its title confronting a deep-seated white fear, is one of the most disturbing and hence memorable of these stories, adopting a flashback technique by which Vera Corneliussen reviews her life during the delirium before her death, her memories flooding back in an approximation of her "stream of consciousness." It emerges that the newspaper version of her death "of shock" is false: this is no case of vicious black man raping virtuous white woman, for the sexual consummation of her relationship with Charlie, her black servant, is revealed as something Vera has herself desired and made inevitable. Similarly shocking and savage but less mature are stories like "Portraits in the Nude," culminating in the brutal beating of a black farm worker, with sharp and even vitriolic depictions of his white countrymen (and women, apart from Lily du Toit, who stops the torturing of Shilling and has him laid on her bed) and the stifling constrictions with which they surround themselves, but also with the evocative natural descriptions of South Africa at which Plomer excelled. In some later stories some white South Africans escape Plomer's castigation: for example, in "When the Sardines Came," which celebrates an event that breaks down the usual barriers of race, Reymond has a good name among the black people for treating them "with fairness and even kindness"; and in "Down on the Farm" Tom Stevens finds that his "coloured" servant, Willem Plaatjes, means "everything" to him (more typical is Stevens's racist neighbour, the odious Kimball).

In the fictions of Japan, black versus white gives way to East versus West, and it is perhaps inevitable that most of the stories in *Paper Houses* share an interest in suicide, that source of fascination to the occidental mind, particularly in its ritual oriental forms. The most thoughtful treatment is in "Nakamura," with its ironic twist at the end—a fatal accident takes over from an abandoned plan of suicide and murder. More typical is the satirical treatment, in connection with emperor-worship, in "The Portrait of an Emperor," in which a lost photograph leads to the consumption of rat-poison. But in Japan, as in South Africa, Plomer's main significance is as a pioneer, writing about his Japanese characters without exoticism or condescension. The displaced person is again a focus of interest, notably the uprooted rural Japanese in the city, as in "A Piece of Good Luck," perhaps the most sensitive of these stories. Cumulatively the stories reveal insights into many facets of Japanese life, including the subjection of women, the rise of militarism, and what he saw as the Japanese split personality, summed up in the title "A Brutal Sentimentalist."

Greece for Plomer was the land of love, which also provides material for his last analyses of the clash of cultures, and particularly of the impingement on the natural primitivism of the Greeks of what he described as "individuals from ostensibly more sophisticated levels of civilization," who appear ludicrous by comparison, like the caricature American, Fletcher B. Raper, contrasted with gentle blind beggars, Nikos and Timos, in "The Crisis," or like the coxcombical and insincere Napoleon Emmanuelides contrasted with the attractive young boatman, Spiros, whose lost sister gives the title to "Nausicaa." The Homeric name is apt for a story set in Corfu, description of which distorts the narrative structure; it is better subsumed into "The Island," a reverie of male friendship, with a suppressed homosexual element that is another of Plomer's characteristics.

After such studies of fundamental conflicts in three continents, with what critics have described as "uncanny" insights into the "foreigners" among whom Plomer found himself living, there is a descent into the English stories and their concerns with more superficial matters, and especially what Plomer called "the comedy of class distinctions." There is some harmless fun and pleasant, if often puerile, humour in these trivial stories, as well as some less attractive snide chortles at the seamier side of sex, but none seem to rise above superficiality and ephemerality. Sean O'Faolain thought the English stories in *Four Countries* "all flops" compared with the successes from the earlier countries, and it is to those successes that attention is most fruitfully paid. In them Plomer gave lasting expression to new perceptions of human experience, thereby fulfilling his own definition of the artist's function: "to add new forms to life, to show life in a new light, to perceive and illuminate some small part of the universal design."

—Michael Herbert

See the essays on "The Child of Queen Victoria" and "Ula Masondo."

POE, Edgar Allan. American. Born in Boston, Massachusetts, 19 January 1809; orphaned, and given a home by John Allan, 1812. Educated at the Dubourg sisters' boarding school, Chelsea, London, 1816–17; Manor House School, Stoke Newington, London, 1817–1820; Joseph H. Clarke's School, Richmond, 1820–23; William Burke's School, Richmond, 1823–25; University of Virginia, Charlottesville, 1826; U.S. Military Academy, West Point, New York, 1830–31 (court-martialled and dismissed). Served in the U.S. Army, 1827–29: Sergeant-Major. Married his 13-year-old cousin Virginia Clemm in 1836 (died 1847). Lived in Baltimore, 1831–35; assistant editor, 1835, and editor, 1836-37, *Southern Literary Messenger,* Richmond; lived in New York, 1837 and after 1843, and Philadelphia, 1838–43; assistant editor, *Gentleman's Magazine,* 1839-40, and editor, *Graham's Magazine,* 1841–42, both Philadelphia; sub-editor, New York *Evening Mirror,* 1844; editor and briefly proprietor, *Broadway Journal,* New York, 1845–46. Lecturer after 1844. *Died 7 October 1849.*

PUBLICATIONS

Collections

Complete Works (Virginia Edition), edited by James A. Harrison. 17 vols., 1902.
Poems, edited by Floyd Stovall. 1965.
Collected Works, edited by Thomas Ollive Mabbott. 3 vols., 1969–78.
Short Fiction, edited by Stuart and Susan Levine. 1976.
Collected Writings, edited by Burton R. Pollin. 1981 —.
Poetry and Tales (Library of America), edited by Patrick F. Quinn. 1984.
Essays and Reviews (Library of America), edited by G.R. Thompson. 1984.

Short Stories

Tales of the Grotesque and Arabesque. 1840.
The Prose Romances 1: The Murders in the Rue Morgue, and The Man That Was Used Up. 1843.
Tales. 1845.

Novels

The Narrative of Arthur Gordon Pym of Nantucket. 1838.
The Literati: Some Honest Opinions about Autorial Merits and Demerits. 1850.

Verse

Tamerlane and Other Poems. 1827.
Al Aaraaf, Tamerlane, and Minor Poems. 1829.
Poems. 1831.
The Raven and Other Poems. 1845.

Play

Politian: An Unfinished Tragedy, edited by Thomas Ollive Mabbott. 1923.

Other

The Conchologist's First Book; or, *A System of Testaceous Malacology* (textbook; revised by Poe). 1839; revised edition, 1840.

Eureka: A Prose Poem. 1848; edited by Richard P. Benton, 1973(?).
Letters, edited by John Ward Ostrom. 2 vols., 1948; revised edition, 2 vols., 1966.
Literary Criticism, edited by Robert L. Hough. 1965.
The Unknown Poe: An Anthology of Fugitive Writings, edited by Raymond Foye. 1980.
The Annotated Poe, edited by Stephen Peithman. 1981.
The Other Poe: Comedies and Satires, edited by David Galloway. 1983.

*

Bibliography: *Bibliography of the Writings of Poe* by John W. Robertson, 1934; *A Bibliography of First Printings of the Writings of Poe* by Charles F. Heartman and James R. Canny, 1940, revised edition, 1943; *Poe: A Bibliography of Criticism 1827–1967* by J. Lesley Dameron and Irby B. Cauthen, Jr., 1974; *Poe: An Annotated Bibliography of Books and Articles in English 1827–1973* by Esther F. Hyneman, 1974; in *Bibliography of American Literature* by Jacob Blanck, edited by Virginia L. Smyers and Michael Winship, 1983.

Critical Studies: *Poe: A Critical Biography* by Arthur Hobson Quinn, 1941; *Poe as a Literary Critic* by John Esten Cooke, edited by N. Bryllion Fagin, 1946; *Life of Poe* by Thomas Holley Chivers, edited by Richard Beale Davis, 1952; *Poe: A Critical Study* by Edward H. Davidson, 1957; *The French Face of Poe* by Patrick F. Quinn, 1957; *Poe* by Vincent Buranelli, 1961, revised edition, 1977; *Poe: A Biography* by William Bittner, 1962; *Poe: The Man Behind the Legend* by Edward Wagenknecht, 1963; *Poe's Literary Battles: The Critic in the Context of His Literary Milieu* by Sidney P. Moss, 1963; *Poe as Literary Critic* by Edd Winfield Parks, 1964; *Poe* by Geoffrey Rans, 1965; *The Recognition of Poe: Selected Criticism since 1829* edited by Eric W. Carlson, 1966; *Poe: A Collection of Critical Essays* edited by Robert Regan, 1967; *Poe, Journalist and Critic* by Robert D. Jacobs, 1969; *Poe the Poet: Essays New and Old on the Man and His Work* by Floyd Stovall, 1969; *Plots and Characters in the Fiction and Poetry of Poe* by Robert L. Gale, 1970; *Twentieth-Century Interpretations of Poe's Tales* edited by William L. Howarth, 1971; *Poe Poe Poe Poe Poe Poe Poe* by Daniel Hoffman, 1972; *Poe: A Phenomenological View* by David Halliburton, 1973; *Poe's Fiction: Romantic Irony in the Gothic Tales* by G.R. Thompson, 1973; *Poe* by David Sinclair, 1977; *Building Poe Biography* by John Carl Miller, 1977; *The Tell-Tale Heart: The Life and Works of Poe* by Julian Symons, 1978; *The Extraordinary Mr. Poe* by Wolf Mankowitz, 1978; *The Rationale of Deception in Poe* by David Ketterer, 1979; *A Psychology of Fear: The Nightmare Formula of Poe* by David R. Saliba, 1980; *A Poe Companion: A Guide to the Short Stories, Romances, and Essays* by J.R. Hammond, 1981; *Poe* by Bettina L. Knapp, 1984; *The Genius of Poe* by Georges Zayed, 1985; *Poe : The Critical Heritage* edited by I.M. Walker, 1986; *Poe, Death and the Life of Writing* by J. Gerald Kennedy, 1987; *Fables of Mind: An Inquiry into Poe's Fiction* by Joan Dayan, 1987; *The Poe Log: A Documentary Life of Poe 1809–1849* by Dwight Thomas and David Jackson, 1987; *Poe: The Design of Order* by A. Robert Lee, 1987; *A World of Words: Language and Displacement in the Fiction of Poe* by Michael J.S. Williams, 1988; *Poe: His Life and Legacy* by Jeffrey Meyers, 1992; *Poe: Mournful and Never-Ending Remembrance* by Kenneth Silverman, 1992.

* * *

In the history of the short story, Edgar Allan Poe's position is secure. Not only did he author a remarkable number of excellent stories, he also wrote what is considered to be the first theoretical statement on the short story itself. Moreover, many literary historians assigned to Poe the honor of having been the so-called "father" of the genre. There were, it is true, several other short story writers, more or less contemporary with Poe, like Nikolai Gogol in Russia and Nathaniel Hawthorne in the United States, who are also considered to have produced the "first" short story. Perhaps more important than who was first is the setting down of definition that served to distinguish what came to be called the short story from the "tale," a kind of short fiction that includes such forms as fairy tales, parables, loosely constructed narratives, and sketches. The reader should not be confused by Poe's use of "tale" as nomenclature. It was some 40 years after Poe's definition was published that "the short story" was actually named by another American writer named Brander Matthews.

Poe's definition appears in his review of Hawthorne's *Twice Told Tales*. The most relevant paragraph in the review is important enough to be quoted here:

> A skillful literary artist has constructed a tale. If wise, he has not fashioned his thoughts to accommodate his incidents; but having conceived, with deliberate care, a certain unique or single effect to be wrought out, he than invents such incidents—he then combines such events as may best aid him in establishing this preconceived effect. If his very initial sentence tend not to the outbringing of this effect, then he has failed in his first step. In the whole composition there should be no word written, of which the tendency, direct or indirect, is not to the one pre-established design. And by such means, with such care and skill, a picture is at length painted which leaves in the mind of him who contemplates it with a kindred art, a sense of the fullest satisfaction.

In insisting upon absolute unity and coherence Poe emphasizes the tightness of the form, the texture of the fabric, as it were. Just as important as the fabric, however, is Poe's insistence on the active participation of the reader who becomes a kind of co-creator to interpret symbolic substructures that provide for the story complex meanings, thus allowing depth as well as breadth.

Poe was one of the few American writers able to make a living from his writing and a dismal living it was. It did, however, encourage him to write in a tremendous variety of forms—both fiction and nonfiction. In the latter category few readers know of his editing capabilities, the range of his essays, the extent of his reviews, or the depth of his metaphysical probings. Of his fiction, it is said that he is probably the most popular American author; most every school child has read one or another of his stories. Unfortunately in the past some literary historians and critics mistakenly confusing "popular" with simple, denigrated Poe's achievements. Few such scholars exist today.

Poe's stories are of several kinds: the tales of terror, sometimes classified as "arabesque"; mysteries, sometimes classified as "tales of ratiocination"; satires; and tales of the future, sometimes referred to as flights and fancies. Poe's stories most often read are the ones most often anthologized and those most often anthologized are selections from his tales of the arabesque, tales of ratiocination, and very occasionally, satires.

"Mask of the Red Death" is plainly arabesque. Most who read it are mesmerized by it to the extent that they often fail to notice the absence of the point of view most often used by Poe, a first person narrator who is the central character in the story. A moment of consideration will explain the need for a different kind of point of view. At the end of the story no one is alive of Prince Prospero's group to recount the tale. Often Poe's stories contain little dialogue; but this one contains less than others—one sentence—a question: "Who dares?"

Many critics have attempted to attach allegoric significance to the various colors of each of the rooms or to the precise movements of the chase through the rooms. What is generally agreed upon is the tale's mesmerizing effect and the surreal setting with its dreamlike and lyrical elements that suffuse the story.

This is not to say the story is without allegoric meaning. Prince Prospero takes a group of knights and ladies of his court to the deep seclusion of one of his abbeys. The abbey is well protected by lofty walls and gates of iron. Once inside, Prospero's courtiers weld the bolts so that they cannot get out and, they think, nothing can get in. Their fear is the "Red Death," a plague that has devastated the country. The masque that Prospero devises to celebrate his safety becomes instead a dance macabre whose choreography climaxes when the Red Death chases Prospero from room to room and catches him in the ebony room. The clock ticks for the last time; the unnamed detached narrator says, "Darkness and Decay and the Red Death held illimitable dominion over all."

Poe's most famous contribution to "double" literature is "William Wilson." In "double" stories one person seems to be a reflected image of another. Often images are counterparts, often in counterpoint. In "William Wilson" the double is an exact image of the narrator's corrupt, unscrupulous, and perverted self. The story line exists on two levels. On the one hand, the double is a real person interacting with others and being seen by them. On the other hand, the double seems to be but a surreal projection arising from the mazes of the corridors and rooms, and the house itself, incomprehensible in its windings and subdivisions, that seem a reflection of the human mind in a labyrinth-like dream state.

"The Man of the Crowd" is often said to be in the style and thrust of a Hawthorne story rather than one typically Poe's. Hawthorne's "Wakefield," for example, is about a man who leaves his wife for some unaccountable reason and then just as unaccountably returns many years later expecting to be welcomed as usual by a faithful wife. There are, however, important differences. One is point of view. In Poe's story the narrator is a character who is recovering from a recent illness and who is mesmerized by the behavior of the man of the crowd. The narrator follows the old man like a shadow through the whole of night and a day until he is "wearied onto death"; but the narrator still is unable to fathom the old man's behavior and he concludes with a quotation in German: "*er lässt sich nicht lesen*" ("it does not permit itself to be read"). But the story can be read if the narrator is realized to be an image of the old man, a double. The narrator follows the man of the crowd who is unable to make commitments to a few but desires to be one among many and detached from all. This is the deep crime, a metaphor for ultimate isolation. The narrator sees his shadow self in the old man but cannot face the truth, so he turns to an excuse that what is there cannot be understood.

"Hop Frog" is sometimes characterized as one of the arabesque tales, but the story seems to fit best under the category satire or even, perhaps, under the category flights and fancies. Not so often read as Poe's most popular stories, "Hop Frog" is nevertheless a perfect gem of a story making use of a basic comic situation where the jokester is made the butt of the joke. In this story the king's prize fool makes a fool of the king. Hop Frog is a dwarf, in himself a comic contrast. Crippled, he walks between a "leap and a wriggle," but he has prodigious strength in his arms. His intellect and cunning are juxtaposed against his position as fool in the court. Like the dwarf, the king and his ministers are described in comic terms. The very idea that a ruling monarch and his ministers should have practical jokes as their main interest is incongruous with their positions. Hop Frog is willing to accept his ill treatment but when the king insults the female dwarf, Trippetta, Hop Frog uses his intellect and great strength to concoct a situation where a masquerade becomes the occasion for a frenzied scene. The king and his ministers, costumed as apes, face one another chained together while the ape-like dwarf taunts them and finally sets them on fire, and the reader watches, horrified, and yet somehow understanding the dwarf's satisfaction as he makes his last jest for the doomed king.

Poe's influence on psychoanalytic approaches to thematic materials is clear; so is his influence on the modern detective story of the Sherlock Holmes variety. Poe's brilliant detective is C. Auguste Dupin. Dupin's Watson is the narrator of the Dupin mysteries, the one who makes it possible for the detective to explain his inductive leaps. Another essential ingredient is a representative of the police, in "The Purloined Letter," for example, the prefect who heads up a competent group whose major fault is they are simply competent. In fact, the police can make use of reason; but they have no imagination and consequently can make no inductive leaps. When "The Purloined Letter" begins, the crime has been committed; the guilty one is already known. The problem involves the question of where a purloined letter is hidden after it is stolen. The greater part of the story functions to show the great detective at work and in his glory as he reveals the solution to the mystery and the superiority of his own mind.

—Mary Rohrberger

See the essays on "The Cask of Amontillado," "The Fall of the House of Usher," "The Murders in the Rue Morgue," and "The Tell-Tale Heart."

————

PORTER, Hal. Australian. Born in Albert Park, Melbourne, Victoria, 16 February 1911. Educated at Kensington State School, 1917; Bairnsdale State School, Victoria, 1918–21, Bairnsdale High School, 1922–26. Married Olivia Parnham in 1939 (divorced 1943). Cadet reporter, Bairnsdale *Advertiser,* 1927; schoolmaster, Victorian Education Department, 1927–37 and 1940, Queen's College, Adelaide, 1941–42, Prince Alfred College, Kent Town, South Australia, 1943–46, Hutchins School, Hobart, Tasmania, 1946–47, Knox Grammar School, Sydney, 1947, Ballarat College, Victoria, 1948–49, and Nijimura School, Kure, Japan (Australian Army Education), 1949–50; manager, George Hotel, St. Kilda, Victoria, 1949; director, National Theatre, Hobart, 1951–53; municipal librarian, 1953–57, and regional librarian, 1958–61, Bairnsdale and Shepparton, Victoria; from 1961 full-time writer; Australian writers representative, Edinburgh Festival, 1962; Australian Department of External Affairs lecturer, Japan, 1967. Recipient: Sydney Sesquicentenary prize, 1938; Commonwealth Literary Fund fellowship, 1956, 1960, 1964, 1968, 1972, 1974, 1977, 1980, and subsidy, 1957, 1962, 1967; Sydney *Morning Herald* prize, 1958; Sydney Journalists' Club prize, for fiction, 1959, for drama, 1961; Adelaide *Advertiser* prize, for fiction, 1964, 1970, for nonfiction, 196 Britannica-Australia award, 1967; Captain Cook Bi-centenary prize, 1970; Australia and New Zealand Bank award, for local history, 1977. Member, Order of Australia, 1982. *Died 29 September 1984.*

PUBLICATIONS

Short Stories

Short Stories.   1942.
A Bachelor's Children.   1962.
The Cats of Venice.   1965.
Mr. Butterfly and Other Tales of New Japan.   1970.
Selected Stories, edited by Leonie Kramer.   1971.
Fredo Fuss Love Life.   1974.
An Australian Selection, edited by John Barnes.   1974.
The Clairvoyant Goat and Other Stories.   1981.

Novels

A Handful of Pennies.   1958; revised edition in *Porter* (selection), 1980.
The Tilted Cross.   1961.
The Right Thing.   1971.

Plays

The Tower (produced 1964).   In *Three Australian Plays,* 1963.
The Professor (as *Toda-San,* produced 1965; as *The Professor,* produced 1965).   1966.
Eden House (produced 1969; as *Home on a Pig's Back,* produced 1972).   1969.
Parker (produced 1972).   1979.

Screenplay: *The Child* (episode in *Libido*), 1973.

Television Play: *The Forger,* 1967.

Verse

The Hexagon.   1956.
Elijah's Ravens.   1968.
In an Australian Country Graveyard and Other Poems. 1975.

Other

The Watcher on the Cast-Iron Balcony (autobiography). 1963.

Stars of Australian Stage and Screen.   1965.
The Paper Chase (autobiography).   1966.
The Actors: An Image of the New Japan.   1968.
The Extra (autobiography).   1975.
Bairnsdale: Portrait of an Australian Country Town.
    1977.
Seven Cities of Australia.   1978.
Porter (selection), edited by Mary Lord.   1980.

Editor, *Australian Poetry 1957.*   1957.
Editor, *Coast to Coast 1961–1962.*   1963.
Editor, *It Could Be You.*   1972.

*

Bibliography: *A Bibliography of Porter* by Janette Finch,
1966; "A Contribution to the Bibliography of Porter" by
Mary Lord, in *Australian Literary Studies,* October 1970;
Papers of Hal Porter 1924–1975, n.d.

Critical Studies: *Porter* by Mary Lord, 1974; *Speaking of
Writing* edited by R. D. Walshe and Leonie Kramer, 1975;
Australian Writers by Graeme Kinross Smith, 1980.

*   *   *

Although Hal Porter worked in a variety of modes, it is
his autobiographical trilogy and his short stories that
established his reputation. The stories work through the
actual experiences of his life, but the material is less
important than the extraordinarily exotic and individual
style, with all its bravura, its foregrounding of language
over subject, its list-making and its delight in arcane,
anachronistic, self-invented, and hyphenated words. The
delight is in the journey, not the arrival, the process, not the
product.

Porter was born in Melbourne in 1911 but moved to
Gippsland in the southeast of Victoria at the age of six.
After working for a time as a cadet reporter he shifted to
Melbourne and became a school teacher, moving around
Australia and eventually suffering a bad injury in an
accident that kept him from taking an active part in World
War II. After the war, Porter taught in Japan, a country
with which he fell in love, before returning to Gippsland
and the full-time occupation of a writer. He died, after
again being struck by a car, in 1984.

Most of these experiences make their way into his fiction,
as they do his autobiography, especially the first volume,
The Watcher on the Cast-Iron Balcony: critics have noted as
many 16 of his short stories that are based on experiences
similar to those described in his autobiographical trilogy.
The most traumatic event of his life, the death of his
mother, is the point around which his autobiography is
structured and makes its way, in different versions, into at
least four of his stories. In "Act One, Scene One" the
account is almost identical to that of the autobiography. In
"A Double Because It's Snowing" the narrator gives a
drunken account in a bar in Hobart of how he escaped his
mother for a year by going to Japan as a lecturer and falling
in love with a Japanese girl. But a cable arrives "Mother
gravely ill, return at once" and he falls for the ruse. In
"Francis Silver" the mother dies in much the same
circumstances as in the autobiography but asks her son to
take a memento of herself to a lover remembered in her
youth. When he does so he discovers that the lover has

completely forgotten the woman who cherished his memory for over 20 years. And, in "Gretel" a cable finds the 45-
year-old narrator in Athens and he hurries home to be
confronted, not with the drama of his mother but with a
completely different memory of a beautiful young girl who
is also, he now realises, retarded and in a lunatic asylum.

The factual basis is unimportant. Many of the stories are
largely actionless and are built around what would seem in
the hands of another writer, a trivial event or action. For
instance, one of the most moving stories, "The Cuckoo,"
concerns a man of around 40 years remembering himself
30 years before at an idyllically happy period in his life. In
a lyrical yet melancholy opening, Porter invokes what is the
central theme of all his fiction—the triumph of time over
everything except imagination, especially as it is evoked in
memory. The boy-narrator of the past steals a cuckoo egg
from a nest in the idyllic garden of his friend Miss Reede
and is discovered by her in the act. She banishes him from
paradise, and in a postscript we learn that shortly afterwards she fell and smashed her hip; because there was no
one to discover her, she lay in pain for two days, leading
her to become crippled. But the real action is in the
repeated threnodies on time that recur throughout the
story: "What else could I do, O Time, what else?," "Time,
that day, thirty years ago, *then*, did I hear Miss Reed?" Like
Vladimir Nabokov, a writer he much admired, Porter
could well have titled his autobiography *Speak, Memory.*

The theme, with variations, resounds in the fiction. In
"The Cuckoo" time is irredeemable, though in other stories
there is sometimes a relief, even if it is only in the
narrator's act of self-forgiveness. But they are similarly
actionless, except for such action as has already taken place
and is recalled. They deal with moments of retrospection,
recollection, reconstruction, and the frankly autobiographical nature of the stories is emphasised by the use of a thinly
concealed persona in many of them: the names Gregory
and Marcus frequently recur, or there is the transparent
Hal-Pal ("Party Forty-Two and Miss Brewer") and Perrot.
Many of the stories deal with either particular human
beings ("Miss Rodda," "Otto Ruff"), or places ("Country
Town"), or both ("At Aunt Sophia's"). The characteristic
perspective is that of a middle-aged man looking back on
his younger self and recreating the past through various
stylistic devices. Porter makes frequent use of the present
tense, establishing the immediacy and even-presentness of
the past. There is the constant change of person, from first
to third to second ("I see—and how I should like to warn
him!—the adolescent") and of question-answer ("Now I
am in love with a little girl. Name? Nameless?"), establishing a certain intimacy with the reader. Finally, there is the
use of certain controlling metaphors, especially those to do
with the protagonist as observer, "watcher," and almost
incessant theatrical metaphors that postulate the lives of
the protagonists as a kind of performance. In an age of
often drab and anonymous prose, his writing stands out in
its originality and adventurousness. A shrewd self-critic, he
said, "Posterity will probably see me . . . as a passable
novelist, a fair playwright, man, but a pretty *good* short
story writer."

—Laurie Clancy

See the essays on "The House on the Hill" and "Francis
Silver."

PORTER, Katherine Anne. American. Born Callie Russell Porter in Indian Creek, Texas, 15 May 1890. Educated at Thomas School, San Antonio, Texas. Married 1) John Henry Koontz in 1906 (separated 1914; divorced 1915); 2) Ernest Stock in 1925; 3) Eugene Dove Pressly in 1933 (divorced 1938); 4) Albert Russell Erskine, Jr., in 1938 (divorced 1942). Journalist and film extra in Chicago, 1911–14; tuberculosis patient, Dallas and San Angelo, Texas, and New Mexico, 1915–17; worked with tubercular children in Dallas, 1917; staff member, Fort Worth *Critic,* Texas, 1917–18; reporter, 1918, and drama critic, 1919, *Rocky Mountain News,* Denver; lived in New York, 1919, and mainly in Mexico, 1920–31, and Europe in 1930's; copy editor, Macauley and Company, publishers, New York, 1928–29; taught at Olivet College, Michigan, 1940; contract writer for MGM, Hollywood, 1945–46; lecturer in writing, Stanford University, California, 1948–49; guest lecturer in literature, University of Chicago, Spring 1951; visiting lecturer in contemporary poetry, University of Michigan, Ann Arbor, 1953–54; Fulbright lecturer, University of Liège, Belgium, 1954–55; writer-in-residence, University of Virginia, Charlottesville, Autumn 1958; Glasgow Professor, Washington and Lee University, Lexington, Virginia, Spring 1959; lecturer in American literature for U.S. Department of State, in Mexico, 1960, 1964; Ewing Lecturer, University of California, Los Angeles, 1960; Regents' Lecturer, University of California, Riverside, 1961. Library of Congress Fellow in Regional American Literature, 1944; U.S. delegate, International Festival of the Arts, Paris, 1952; member, Commission on Presidential Scholars, 1964; consultant in poetry, Library of Congress, 1965–70. Recipient: Guggenheim fellowship, 1931, 1938; New York University Libraries gold medal, 1940; Ford Foundation grant, 1959, 1960; O. Henry award, 1962; Emerson-Thoreau medal, 1962; Pulitzer prize, 1966; National Book award, 1966; American Academy gold medal, 1967; Mystery Writers of America Edgar Allan Poe award, 1972. D.Litt.: University of North Carolina Woman's College, Greensboro, 1949; Smith College, Northampton, Massachusetts, 1958; Maryville College, St. Louis, 1968; D.H.L.: University of Michigan, Ann Arbor, 1954; University of Maryland, College Park, 1966; Maryland Institute, 1974; D.F.A.: La Salle College, Philadelphia, 1962. Vice-president, National Institute of Arts and Letters, 1950–52; member, American Academy, 1967. *Died 18 September 1980.*

PUBLICATIONS

Short Stories

Flowering Judas. 1930; augmented edition, as *Flowering Judas and Other Stories,* 1935.
Hacienda: A Story of Mexico. 1934.
Noon Wine (novella). 1937.
Pale Horse, Pale Rider: Three Short Novels (includes *Noon Wine* and "Old Mortality"). 1939.
The Leaning Tower and Other Stories. 1944.
Selected Short Stories. 1945.
The Old Order: Stories of the South. 1955.
A Christmas Story. 1958.
Collected Stories. 1964; augmented edition, 1967.

Novel

Ship of Fools. 1962.

Other

My Chinese Marriage. 1921.
Outline of Mexican Popular Arts and Crafts. 1922.
What Price Marriage. 1927.
The Days Before: Collected Essays and Occasional Writings. 1952; augmented edition, as *The Collected Essays and Occasional Writings,* 1970.
A Defense of Circe. 1955.
The Never-Ending Wrong (on the Sacco-Vanzetti case). 1977.
Conversations with Porter, Refugee from Indian Creek, with Enrique Hank Lopez. 1981.
Porter: Conversations, edited by Joan Givner. 1987.
Letters, edited by Isabel Bayley. 1990.
The Strange Old World and Other Book Reviews by Porter, edited by Darlene Unrue. 1991.

Translator, *French Song-Book.* 1933.
Translator, *The Itching Parrot,* by Fernandez de Lizárdi. 1942.

*

Bibliography: *A Bibliography of the Works of Porter* and *A Bibliography of the Criticism of the Works of Porter* by Louise Waldrip and Shirley Ann Bauer, 1969; *Porter and Carson McCullers: A Reference Guide* by Robert F. Kiernan, 1976; *Porter: An Annotated Bibliography* by Kathryn Hilt and Ruth M. Alvarez, 1990.

Critical Studies: *The Fiction and Criticism of Porter* by Harry John Mooney, Jr., 1957, revised edition, 1962; *Porter* by Ray B. West, Jr., 1963; *Porter and the Art of Rejection* by William L. Nance, 1964; *Porter* by George Hendrick, 1965, revised edition, with Willene Hendrick, 1988; *Porter: The Regional Sources* by Winifred S. Emmons, 1967; *Porter: A Critical Symposium* edited by Lodwick Hartley and George Core, 1969; *Porter's Fiction* by M.M. Liberman, 1971; *Porter* by John Edward Hardy, 1973; *Porter: A Collection of Critical Essays* edited by Robert Penn Warren, 1979; *Porter: A Life* by Joan Givner, 1982, revised edition, 1991; *Porter's Women: The Eye of Her Fiction* by Jane Krause DeMouy, 1983; *Truth and Vision in Porter's Fiction,* 1985, and *Understanding Porter,* 1988, both by Darlene H. Unrue; *The Texas Legacy of Porter* by James T. Tanner, 1990.

* * *

Katherine Anne Porter's short novels *Noon Wine,* "Old Mortality," and "Pale Horse, Pale Rider" brought her great artistic praise and her long novel *Ship of Fools* was a commercial success, but much of her best work was in short fiction. She began writing about Mexico, her "familiar country," in her first story "María Concepción" (1922). In that story she showed a complete mastery of form, plunging the reader into the amoral-moral world of the Indian and by extension plumbing the depth of all human existence. As is often the case in her fiction, a strong woman triumphs over a weak man. The two stories that followed—"The Martyr" (1923) and "Virgin Violeta" (1924)—are slight, as is "That Tree" (1934).

"Flowering Judas" (1930), also set in Mexico, has been recognized as one of her best stories. She then finished a lost-generation story—"Hacienda" (1932, published as *Hacienda: A Story of Mexico*, 1934), a thinly disguised account of Sergei Eisenstein's filming of *Que Viva Mexico!* This story of spiritual, physical, moral, and psychological isolation is one of her most underrated works.

Alienated from Mexican culture, Porter turned to recreating and mythologizing her Southern heritage and her own past in Texas. "The Source" (1941) is the first story in a series called "The Old Order" and is a remarkable sketch of the grandmother's power and control over the family, revealing the grandmother as the source of the strengths and weaknesses of the whole family. The fictional grandmother, based largely on Porter's own grandmother Porter who took over the rearing of the Porter children after the death of Katherine Anne Porter's mother, was portrayed as a strong woman married to a weak man. Family history, including the relationships with slaves who in the fictional version remained with the family after they had been freed, was explored in "The Witness" (1944), "The Journey" (1936), and "The Last Leaf" (1944). "The Jilting of Granny Weatherall" (1929) is a presentation of the grandmother figure, but it is not a Miranda story.

Porter wrote several autobiographic stories in which she appears as the character Miranda: "The Fig Tree" (1960), "The Circus" (1935), "The Grave" (1935), "Old Mortality" (1938), and "Pale Horse, Pale Rider" (1938). In these often anthologized stories Porter traced the growth of Miranda from early childhood to maturity, from innocence to her initiation into the mysteries of the world. These stories about the family and Miranda, taken together, are equal to the artistic achievement of her two best Mexican stories, "María Concepción" and "Flowering Judas."

Porter, born in poverty into a family that had seen better days before the Civil War, also wrote a series of stories about the rural South she knew as a child—"He" (1927), *Noon Wine*, and "Holiday" (1960). The first two are tragic stories of Anglo families, and "Holiday," set on the farm of a German family, reflects her loathing of Germans, an attitude shown even more definitively in "The Leaning Tower" (1941) and *Ship of Fools*.

Another story, "Magic" (1928), uses the form of the dramatic monologue, and as Joan Givner, Porter's biographer, has noted, the theme is "the passive promotion of evil by innocent people, which would run through [Porter's] works in a steady, unbroken line until it reached its fullest expression in *Ship of Fools*."

Porter's stories "Rope" (1928), about a failed marriage, "The Downward Path to Wisdom" (1939), based on a childhood memory of Glenway Wescott's, "The Cracked Looking-Glass" (1932), a Joycean-like story, and "A Day's Work" (1940), set among the Irish poor in New York, though interesting, lack the vitality of Porter's best work.

"Theft" (1929) has been one her most explicated stories. The search for love, both profane and sacred, is an important theme in this complex story. The central character is a wasteland figure, an alienated woman left finally without any kind of love.

Porter's best stories are marked by a mastery of technique, by honesty, and by an exploration of the human heart and mind and society itself without lapsing into popular clichés. She had developed her fictional techniques by the time she published "María Concepción" and technically she showed little change in the decades that followed. She was a conscious writer, in the tradition of Joyce, James, and Cather. She rightly considered herself an artist: "I'm one of the few living people not afraid to pronounce that word," she said in 1958. Her literary production was not great in volume, but several of her stories are considered by most critics as belonging in that small group called America's best.

—George Hendrick

See the essays on "Flowering Judas," *Noon Wine*, and "Old Mortality."

———

PORTER, William Syndey.   See **HENRY, O.**

———

POWERS, J(ames) F(arl). American. Born in Jacksonville, Illinois, 8 July 1917. Educated at Quincy College Academy, Illinois; Northwestern University, Chicago campus, 1938–40. Married the writer Betty Wahl in 1946; three daughters and two sons. Worked in Chicago, 1935–41; editor, Illinois Historical Records Survey, 1938; hospital orderly during World War II; teacher at St. John's University, Collegeville, Minnesota, 1947 and after 1975, Marquette University, Milwaukee, 1949–51, and University of Michigan, Ann Arbor, 1956–57; writer-in-residence, Smith College, Northampton, Massachusetts, 1965–66. Recipient: American Academy grant, 1948; Guggenheim fellowship, 1948; Rockefeller fellowship, 1954, 1957, 1967; National Book award, 1963. Member, American Academy.

PUBLICATIONS

Short Stories

Prince of Darkness and Other Stories.   1947.
The Presence of Grace.   1956.
Look How the Fish Live.   1975.

Novels

Morte d'Urban.   1962.
Wheat That Springeth Green.   1988.

*

Critical Studies: *Powers* by John F. Hagopian, 1968; *Powers* edited by Fallon Evans, 1968.

* * *

J.F. Powers is noteworthy for having brought his penetrating gaze and straightforward style to recording life in the northern midwest, beginning in the 1940's. His stories should be compared to the best modern southern fiction, which so depends upon locale for its tenor and profundity. The name of one of his fictional towns, Sherwood, brings to mind Sherwood Anderson, whose *Winesburg, Ohio* seems an early forerunner of Powers's enterprise. Powers's tone is as wryly humorous and serious, but the life of his towns is different. It is modern and, thus, depicted as under the pressure of suburbanization.

Apart from a handful of stories in *Prince of Darkness* and *The Presence of Grace*, his main characters are priests or people significantly related to the Roman Catholic Church. For example, Myles in "The Devil Was the Joker," is a would-be priest, and Didymus in "Lions, Harts, Leaping Does," is an aged monk tortured by doubts of his worthiness. Most characters are parish pastors and their curates. It is their quotidien lives, dense with Church politics, rivalry, and the banalities of the rectory, that fascinate Powers. The narrator of "The Presence of Grace" remarks that "there was little solidarity among priests—a nest of tables scratching each other."

These stories of the "spiritual" life trace situations in which connivance and venality abound, making any hint of grace under pressure an ironic or astounding occurrence. Broadly speaking, they show that at every level of social interaction, no matter how low the stakes, the struggle for power surfaces, tainting everyone, including those with a yearning or capacity to transcend vicious or petty motives. But Powers is never ponderously serious. His approach is humorous, his arguments carried in a satire often tempered by mercy. Even when he is able to report some honorable conduct or motive, however, he does not sully his objectivity, moral judgment, or wit with an easy sentiment. His amusing seriousness is kin to Joyce's in "Grace" and "Ivy Day." We never doubt his characters' vices, but we are bound to smile at the distance between their estimations of themselves and the truth, a gap minutely and trenchantly observed through his exceptional narrative voices.

The dramatization of hypocrisy and of the failed imitation of Christ takes up a good deal of Powers's interest. Properly supplicated by the demonic Mac, various pastors give him entre to parishes where he peddles a low-brow religious magazine ("The Devil Was the Joker"). But Mac gets in because he also deals in a line of ill-gotten commodities for the domestic empires of those clerics. The goods range from appliances to vulgar bric-a-brac, and the deal is often cut during a poker game. The priests are properly loath to discuss either the marketplace origins of these items or the "friends" who provide them to Mac. In a pair of tour de force tales told by a cat (Fritz), Father Burner, a curate under the pastorate of Father Malt, spends his time coveting his senior's office and reading *Church Property Administration* through all the "seasons" of the Church calendar: "baseball, football, Christmas, basketball, and Lent" ("Death of a Favorite" and "Defection of a Favorite"). His is the temporal Church. And while his basic goodness asserts itself by the end of the second story, the cat's eye view has by then probed every nook and cranny of the rectory, and of the worldly ecclesiastical psyches that haunt it.

Yet all of these failings are, as Didymus muses, "indelible in the order of things: the bingo game going on under the Cross for the seamless garment of the Son of Man." Consequently, Powers searches for the presence of grace amidst the "grossest distractions" and the "watered down suburban precautions and the routine pious exercises." And he often does locate it, frequently to the amazement of a protagonist hardened by cynical habit. That is the essence of Father Fabre's realization that his rector's well practiced casuistry is deeply moral when it needs to be ("The Presence of Grace").

While these matters dominate, Powers's few excursions into nonclerical settings are excellently accomplished and deserve more note than they have received. In particular, "Trouble" and "He Don't Plant Cotton," stories about racial conflict written early in his career, are enormously compelling. The first gets inside the sensibility of a black boy, the storyteller, as he watches his mother die from a beating administered by a white mob during a riot in New Orleans. The story thoroughly realizes and champions the boy's perspective, which is characterized by a righteous anger temporized by his grandmother's astute morality. The Church is important, albeit secondarily, because the family is Catholic and knows that among Louisiana's white priests there are a few antipathetic to bigotry. Their presence, however, in no way undercuts the story's focus on the racial basis of the boy's experience, a focus finely maintained by the first person narration. This work has no truck with the hollow peace many whites—and blacks— were still making with racism at mid-century.

"He Don't Plant Cotton" deals with the confrontation, in a Chicago bar, between three black musicians and a group of white drunks from Mississippi. Two focuses are kept in balance. The musicians inhabit their music in a pure devotion to its authenticity, even as economic necessity compels them to perform the degenerate version of it constantly "requested" by the racists and fashion plates out on the town and slumming. On the other hand, the feigning is emotionally too expensive and the social control on their hostility erodes as the evening wears on. Powers conveys their artistic conviction as a moral dictate and esteems their choice to be fired rather than be manipulated and degraded by bigots and a boss who would have them pander, for his own benefit. It is certainly interesting that the female among the three, and the one under the most overt pressure, is the prime mover of their rebellion. In her youth she complements the grandmother of "Trouble" in the moral sphere. These are not the works of an author outdistanced by time.

—David M. Heaton

See the essay on "The Valiant Woman."

PREMCAND. Pseudonym for Dhanpat Ray Śrīvāstava. Indian (Hindī and Urdū languages). Born in Lahmī, near Beanres, 31 July 1880. Educated at Teachers' Training College, Allahabad, 1902–04; Allahabad University, B.A. 1919. Married second wife Ś ivrānī Dev in 1906; one daughter and two sons. Schoolteacher, Chunār, 1899, and Pratāpgarh, 1900–02; writer and contributor to Urdu journals, including *Zamānā,* from 1903; teacher, Kanpur, 1904–09; assistant deputy school inspector, Hamīrpur district, 1909–14; used pen name, from 1910; headmaster, Marwari High School, Kanpur, 1921–22; held series of jobs in publishing, from 1922; editor, *Mādhurī,* Lucknow, 1927–31; editor, *Jāgaran,* 1932–34; screenplay writer, Ajanta Cinetone, Bombay, 1934–35. Founder, Sarasvatī Press, 1923; *Hans* (Royal Swan) magazine, 1930–35. Founding member, Hindustānī Academy, 1928. President, First All-India Progressive Writers' Association, 1936. *Died 8 October 1936.*

PUBLICATIONS

Collections

Mānsarovar (collected stories).   8 vols.,   1936–50.
Kafan aur śeṣ kahāniyā̃ [Kafan and Other Stories].   1937.

Grāmya jīvan kī kahāniyā̃ [Stories of Village Life].   1938.
Nāri jīvan kī kahāniyā̃ [Stories of Women's Life].   1938.
Lailā aur dūsrī kahāniyā̃ [Laila and Other Stories].   1945.
Nimantraṇ aur dūsrī kahāniyā̃ [The Invitation and Other Stories].   1945.
Maṅglācaraṇ [The Invocation] (collected novels), edited by Amṛt Rāy.   1962.
Premcand kī pacās kahāniyā̃ [Fifty Stories by Premcand].   1963.
An Anthology, edited by Nagendra.   1981.

Short Stories

Soz-e-vatan [Passion for the Homeland] (as Nawāb Rāi).   1908.
Prem-pacīsī [Premcand's Twenty-Five Stories].   1914.
Sapta-saroj [Seven Lotuses].   1917.
Nav-nidhi [New Treasure].   1917.
Prem-pūrnimā [Premcand's Full Moon].   1918.
Prem-pacīsī II.   1919.
Prem-battīsī [Thirty-Two Stories by Premcand].   2 vols., 1920.
Prem-prasūn [Premcand's Flowers].   1924.
Prem-dvadśō [Twenty Stories by Premcand].   1926.
Prem-pramod [Premcand's Delight].   1926.
Prem-pratimā [Premcand's Image/Image of Love].   1926.
Prem-caturthī [Four Stories by Premcand].   1928.
Pā̃c phūl [Five Flowers].   1929.
Prem-pratigyā [Premcand's Vow/Love's Vow].   1929.
Agni-samādhi [Purification by Fire].   1929.
Prem kuñj [The Pool of Love/Premcand's Pool].   1930.
Prem pañcmī [Five Stories by Premcand].   1930.
Sapta-suman [Seven Flowers].   1930.
Prerṇā tathā anya kahāniyā̃ [Inspiration and Other Stories].   1932.
Samar-yātrā aur kahāniyā̃ [War-Journey and Other Stories].   1932.
Sohāg kā śav aur anya kahāniyā̃ [Death on the Marriage Day and Other Stories].   1932.
Vidrohī tathā anya kahāniyā̃ [The Rebel and Other Stories].   1932.
Premcand kī sarvaśrestha kahāniyā̃ [Premcand's Best Stories].   1934.
Pā̃c prasūn [Five Flowers].   1934.
Nav-jīvan [New Life].   1935.
Prem pīyūṣ [The Nectar of Love].   1935.
Grām-sāhitya-mālā [Series on Village Literature].   n.d.
Short Stories.   1946.
A Handful of Wheat and Other Stories.   1955.
The Secret of Culture, and Other Stories.   1960.
Guptadhan [Hidden Treasure] (unpublished stories in Hindī and Urdū), edited by Amṛt Rāy.   2 vols., 1962.
The Chessplayers and Other Stories.   1967.
The World of Premchand.   1969; revised edition as *Deliverance and Other Stories,*   1988.
The Shroud, and Twenty Other Stories.   1972.
Twenty-Four Stories.   1980.

Novels

Hamkhurmā o hamsawab.   1906.
Premā [The Vow].   1907.
Kiśnā.   1907.
Jalvā-e-Īsar [Benediction].   1912.
Premāśram [The Abode of Love].   1921.
Raṅgabhumi [The Stage].   1925.
Kāyākalpa [Metamorphosis].   1926.

Nirmālā.   1927; translated as *Nirmala.*
Pratigyā [The Vow].   1929.
Gaban [Embezzlement].   1931.
Karmabhūmi [The Arena].   1932.
Godān.   1936; translated as *Godan,*   1957; as *The Giving of the Cow,*   1968; as *The Gift of a Cow,*   1968.
Maṅgal-sūtra va anya racna [The Auspicious Bond and Other Works].   1948.

Plays

Saṅgrām [Battle].   1923.
Karbalā.   1924.
Prem kī vedi [Altar of Love].   1933.

Other

Mahātmā Shaikhsādī (biography).   1917.
Rām carcā [About Rām].   1928.
Bākamālō ke darśan.   1929; as *Kalam, talvār aur tyāg* [The Pen, the Sword, and Sacrifice], 1940.
Durgā Dās. 2nd edition,   1938.
Ciṭṭhī-patrī [Letters], edited by Madan Gopāl and Amṛt Rāy.   3 vols.,   1962.
Vividh prasaṅg [Miscellaneous Articles], edited by Amṛt Rāy.   3 vols.,   1962.
Sāhitya kā uddeśya [The Aim of Literature] (essays).   1967.
Kuch vicār [Some Thoughts] (essays).   1967.
Premcand kā aprāpya sāhitya [Premcand's Unavailable Literature], edited by Kamal Kiśor Goyinkā.   2 vols., 1988.

Translator, *Sukhdās* [Silas Marner], by George Eliot. 1920.
Translator, *Ahaṅkār,* by Anatole France.   1923.
Translator, *Āzād kathā,* by Sarśār.   2 vols., 1925–26.
Translator, *Cā̃dī ki ḍibiyā* [The Silver-Box], by John Galsworthy.   1930.
Translator, *Nyāy* [Justice], by John Galsworthy.   1930.
Translator, *Hartāl* [Strike], by John Galsworthy.   1930.

Also translated into Hindī short stories by Lev Tolstoi, Charles Dickens, Oscar Wilde, and others.

*

Critical Studies: *A Premchand Reader* by N.H. Zide and others, 1965; *Premchand* by P. Gupta, 1968; *Munshi Premchand of Lamhi Village* by Robert O. Swan, 1969; "Premchand's Urdu-Hindi Short Stories" by Mohammed Azam, in *Indian Literature* 21, 1975, and "Premchand's Mood and His Urdu Short Stories," in *Indian Literature* 18, 1978; *Prem Chand* by Govind Narain, 1978; *Munshi Premchand* by G. Sharma, 1978; *His Life and Work* by V.S. Naravane, 1980; *A Western Appraisal* by Siegfried A. Schulz, 1981; *Between Two Worlds* by Geetanjali Pandey, 1989.

*   *   *

Premcand, pseudonym of Dhanpat Ray Śrīvāstava, wrote novels and short fiction in both Urdu and Hindi. Though the author of over a dozen novels, Premcand is best known for his major and lasting contributions to both Urdu and

Hindi literature in the form of more than three hundred short stories. Most of these were published in his prestigious, if financially unsuccessful, literary journal, *Hans* (Royal Swan), and later collected into ten volumes. In these stories he managed to bring this genre from fantastic and romantic tales and fables to well-constructed, realistic stories about human beings living out their lives engaged in the search and struggle for survival and love.

An overriding concern of the short stories is to reform the social ills of India such as caste, superstition, and poverty, as well as to terminate Britain's political domination. Because this strain of didacticism, sometimes deep, sometimes superficial, permeates his work, his literary career is essentially the evolution of Premcand the propagandist to Premcand the artist, a development that is lucidly played out in his literary corpus.

Premcand's short fiction divides roughly into three phases. The years 1907 to 1920 are a learning period. Here stories are long on didacticism, especially related to the topic of patriotism, but short on art. Generally lacking in subtlety, they tend to be set in romantic, foreign environments, and characters are stereotypical rather than individuated persons. For example, his first volume of *Soz-e-vatan* (Passion for the Homeland) was so unabashedly anti-British that the colonial authorities proscribed the book and ordered the unsold copies burned. In the first story in this collection, "The Most Precious Object in the World," set in a country that is probably Persia, a beautiful princess refuses to love a handsome courtier until he brings her the most precious object in the world. He goes out on a long journey and returns with what Premcand feels is the most precious thing in the world: the last drop of blood shed by an Indian warrior fighting for his country.

"The Power of a Curse" (1911) combines social criticism with the supernatural. Ramsevak, a village lawyer, drives an old Brahman woman, Munga, to madness by duping her out of her life savings. In her madness she regularly visits his house, repeatedly cursing him ("I'll drink your blood"). She dies insane and destitute at his doorstep, and her ghost seems to haunt him and his wife, who dies of fright from seeing the bloodthirsty Munga in a dream. Ostracized by the villagers for having caused a Brahman's death and unable to make a living, Ramsevak goes on pilgrimage. Several months later a holy man looking very much like Ramsevak returns to the village, burns down Ramsevak's house, then disappears.

Ramsevak's unconvincing change of heart is an example of the unabashed idealism that permeates both stories and novels of this period. Such unexplained changes of heart, prevalent in the stories of the early and middle periods, are thought to be Premcand's chief artistic flaw. Such reversals do not emerge from the character's thinking, but rather from the author's ideology.

The stories of the middle period (1920-1932) mark a growth in Premcand's art. While still didactic in nature, they no longer take place in circumscribed, romantic settings, but rather in the stark area of the Indian village, the milieu Premcand knew best. With a marked increase in satire, especially through the use of irony, and a decrease in editorializing, he continues to treat themes of nationalism, social reform, and respect for what it good in India's traditions. Plots are influenced by Tolstoi and Maupassant, and the political philosophy of non-violence as espoused by M.K. Gandhi. He portrays village life and characters with realism, insight, and compassion. "The Road to Salvation" (1924), for example, depicts with both empathy and biting humor the senseless feud between the rich farmer Jhingur

and the boastful shepherd Buddhu, which ends only when both are reduced to poverty. In "A Little Trick" (1922) Premcand pokes fun at both Indians who do not join the Gandhian movement to oust the British from India, and gullible Gandhians who feel that the very popular boycott of British cloth would alone get rid of the British.

"A Desparate Case" (1924), with its Maupassant *coup de canon* ending, is one of many stories that depict the psychological and physical abuse of Indian women by autocratic husbands who threaten to abandon them if they do not produce male heirs. Hoping to bear a male child after the birth of four daughters, Nirupma seeks assistance from a holy man, rituals, and prayer. Assured that her fifth child will be a boy, her husband's otherwise hostile family elaborately prepares for his birth. When she learns the child is a girl, Nirupma dies, either from the effects of childbirth or out of fear of her husband and in-laws.

The late period (1932-1936) was a time of financial stress and failing health for Premcand. Works from this mature phase are didactic by implication rather than outright statement. Terse, understated, and focused, these stories feature a wide variety of well-delineated characters from village, town, and city, whose motivation and actions spring from their individual personalities rather than from a preconceived mindset of the author.

"My Big Brother" (1934) is a humorous, even touching, portrayal of the warm, caring relationship of a not-very-bright older brother who, by bullying his younger brother into playing little and studying hard, takes credit for the younger's academic success. Without patronizing his older sibling, the younger allows him his illusions and shows him the respect due him by virtue of birth order.

"The Shroud" (1936), Premcand's last story, is a powerful portrayal of the soul-numbing effects of poverty and religion on the lower classes. This story reflects Premcand's fascination with Marxism late in life as a possible means of solving India's myriad ills.

Although Premcand's short stories are sometimes uneven in quality, they are, at their best, well-wrought, powerful commentaries on the sufferings and follies of human beings. For this reason Premcand is considered the major short story writer of both Urdu and Hindi during the first half of the 20th century.

—Carlo Coppola

See the essay on "The Shroud."

———

PRICHARD, Katharine Susannah. Australian. Born in Levuka, Fiji, 4 December 1883; moved with her family to Australia, 1886. Educated at home, and at South Melbourne College. Married Hugo Throssell in 1919 (died 1933); one son. Governess in South Gippsland and at Turella sheep station, New South Wales; teacher, Christ Church Grammar School, Melbourne; journalist, Melbourne *Herald* and *New Idea,* Sydney; freelance journalist in London and Europe, 1908; editor, "Women's Work" column, Melbourne *Herald,* 1910–12; returned to London, and worked as a freelance journalist, 1912–16: correspondent in France, 1916; full-time writer from 1916; settled in Greenmount, Western Australia, 1919; founding member, Communist Party of Australia, 1920. Recipient: *Bulletin* prize, 1928. *Died 20 October 1969.*

PUBLICATIONS

Short Stories

Kiss on the Lips and Other Stories.   1932.
Potch and Colour.   1944.
N'Goola and Other Stories.   1959.
Happiness: Selected Short Stories.   1967.

Novels

The Pioneers.   1915; revised edition, 1963.
Windlestraws.   1916.
The Black Opal.   1921.
Working Bullocks.   1926.
The Wild Oats of Han (for children).   1928; revised edition, 1968.
Coonardoo, The Well in the Shadow.   1929.
Haxby's Circus, The Lightest, Brightest Little Show on Earth.   1930; as *Fay's Circus*, 1931.
Intimate Strangers.   1937.
Moon of Desire.   1941.
The Roaring Nineties: A Story of the Goldfields of Western Australia.   1946.
Golden Miles.   1948.
Winged Seeds.   1950.
Subtle Flame.   1967.
Moggie and Her Circus Pony (for children).   1967.

Plays

The Burglar (produced 1909).
Her Place (produced 1913).
For Instance (produced 1914).
The Great Man (produced 1923).
The Pioneers (produced 1923).   In *Best Australian One-Act Plays*, 1937.
Forward One (produced 1935).
Women of Spain (produced 1937).
Penalty Clause (produced 1940).
Brumby Innes (produced 1972).   1940.
Good Morning (produced 1955).
Bid Me to Love (produced 1973).   Edited by Katharine Brisbane, with *Brumby Innes*, 1974.

Verse

Clovelly Verses.   1913.
The Earth Lover and Other Verses.   1932.

Other

The New Order.   1919.
Marx: The Man and His Work.   1921(?).
The Materialist Conception of History.   1921(?).
The Real Russia.   1934.
Why I Am a Communist.   1957(?).
Child of the Hurricane: An Autobiography.   1963.
On Strenuous Wings: A Half-Century of Selected Writings, edited by Joan Williams.   1965.
Straight Left: Articles and Addresses on Politics, Literature, and Women's Affairs 1910–1918, edited by Ric Throssell.   1982.

Editor, with others, *Australian New Writing 1–3.*   3 vols., 1943–45.

*

Critical Studies: *The Rage for Life: The Work of Prichard* by Jack Beasley, 1964, *Prichard* by Henrietta Drake Brockman, 1967; *Wild Weeds and Windflowers: The Life and Letters of Prichard* by Ric Throssell, 1975; *Prichard: Centenary Essays* edited by John Hay and Brenda Walker, 1984; *As Good as a Yarn With You: Letters Between Miles Franklin, Prichard, Jean Devanny, Marjorie Barnard, Flora Eldershaw and Eleanor Dark* edited by Carole Ferrier, 1992.

*   *   *

Most of the short fiction of Katharine Susannah Prichard deals with rural working class life in Western Australia. It often focuses on the struggle for survival and demonstrates the brutalisation that may occur in the course of this; simultaneously implicit is the desire for a better life unmarked by the racism, sexism and prejudice that distort and deform human relationships. Prichard wrote to H. M. Green in 1938, a comment that in many ways sums up the essence and tone of her work:

I am impelled to interpret life and the ways of the people of my own time in their essential aspects: the struggle for existence and organisation for a social system which will enable them to grow in beauty and strength of mind and body, and knowledge and reason, with all the spiritual blossoming that involves.

Nonetheless, Prichard's short fiction is rarely didactic. The fact that she was part of the group that formed the Australian Communist Party in 1920 and remained an active member until her death has coloured many of the critical accounts of her work; a book about her by her friend and fellow writer (of a very different political persuasion) Henrietta Drake-Brockman described her as "still the most controversial figure in Australian literature." A counterposing of the perceived commitment of her work to the critical hegemony of what Frank Hardy has called the Patrick White Australia Policy has led to her being read as a key exponent of the realist mode of Australian writing.

Prichard did see her own work as relating organically to the lives of the Australian working class: "I know every phase of life in Australia I write of . . . I absorb the life of our people and country with love and an intense and intimate sympathy; I strive to express myself from these sources" (from Green's book *A History of Australian Literature*, 1962). Certainly, this suggests a dominant orientation towards realism, but her stories mingle romantic and realist modes. There are affinities with the writing of D. H. Lawrence, though Prichard denied any explicit influence. (Her story "The Grey Horse," for example, has been seen as resembling *The Boy in the Bush*, but she points out in a letter to the critic Hartley Grattan that it had been submitted for a literary competition long before the Lawrence-Skinner collaboration was available for her to read.) In another comment on her own work, (from G. A. Wilkes's article in *Southerly*), Prichard states she was attempting a complex type of realism, if not something more hybrid: "I dream of a literature to grow up in this country which will have all the reactions to truth of a many-faceted mirror." Implied here is that there are many angles from which reality can be represented. Though the insistence remains that it is crucially important that the representations seek to be "reactions to truth," this is a rather more complicated notion than that of reflections of truth.

The majority of the stories deal with everyday incidents of rural life. In her foreword to *Potch and Colour*, Prichard describes the book as "yarns that have been told to me [that] belong to a time that is passing . . . folk-lore really." Many of her stories have this quality of recording rural popular culture or mythology; a notable example is "The Frogs of Quirra-Quirra," in which a return joke is played on the local practical joker of Quirra, a town infested with frogs. He is fooled by a fake request for frogs from a French restaurant in Kalgoorlie, and dispatches hundreds of them in boxes. A laconic humour pervades the more light-hearted stories such as this one, but even in the more sombre stories (many of which are in *N'Goola*) that deal with madness and death, such as "The White Turkey," "A Devout Lover," or "The Long Shadow," about the campaign against the execution of the Rosenbergs, a kind of gaiety transfigures the dread.

Prichard's stories include some of the most effective and powerful representations of the Aboriginal population and the consequences of the forcible appropriation of their land and the breaking up of their families. One particularly moving piece, the title story of *N'Goola*, tells how a young girl, N'Goola, taken away from her father at the age of six and put into a mission school, is searched for by him for 25 years, and found shortly before his death. In this story, as in others, such as "The Cooboo" or "Happiness" from her first collection *Kiss on the Lips*, or "Flight" (also in *N'Goola*), the devastation wrought on Aboriginal people by colonisation is communicated without any of the sentiment or paternalism that marks much other writing by white Australians about Aborigines. Vance Palmer's comment in his foreword to *N'Goola* that "if a change has come over our attitudes to the Aborigines it is largely due to the way Katharine Prichard has brought them near us," is probably overstated; nonetheless, these stories, along with *Coonardoo*, stand out in their time as particularly sensitive and complex renderings of race relations and the situation of the Aboriginal people.

Prichard faced many difficulties in her own life. Her husband committed suicide in the early 1930's and she was plagued by financial worries for a long period. There were conflicting demands upon her time; as a dedicated activist she needed to relate politically to the lives and struggles of working class people—and this nourished her writing—but she also needed space to work at the art of fiction. Her correspondence with other women writers (some of which is collected in *As Good as a Yarn With You*) give an indication of how she responded to some of these pressures, exacerbated often by the fact of her being a woman writer. While Prichard cannot be read specifically as a feminist, several strong women acting independently of the sexual politics of their times are depicted in her short fiction. A notable example is Susan in "The Siren of Sandy Gap" (*Potch and Colour*).

The power of Prichard's stories could be seen as not unconnected to their motivating impulse, which she summed up in this way:

People should only write when they can't help writing: have something definite to say, some rage, or vision of beauty they are bursting with.

—Carole Ferrier

PRITCHETT, (Sir) V(ictor) S(awdon). English. Born in Ipswich, Suffolk, 16 December 1900. Educated at Alleyn's School, Dulwich, London. Married Dorothy Rudge Roberts in 1936; one son and one daughter. Worked in the leather trade in London, 1916–20, and in the shellac, glue, and photographic trade in Paris, 1920–32; correspondent in Ireland and Spain for the *Christian Science Monitor*, Boston, 1923–26; critic from 1926, permanent critic from 1937, and director, 1946–78, *New Statesman*, London; Christian Gauss Lecturer, Princeton University, New Jersey, 1953; Beckman Professor, University of California, Berkeley, 1962; writer-in-residence, Smith College, Northampton, Massachusetts, 1966, 1970–72; visiting professor, Brandeis University, Waltham, Massachusetts, 1968; Clark Lecturer, Cambridge University, 1969; visiting professor, Columbia University, New York, 1972; writer-in-residence, Vanderbilt University, Nashville, 1981. President, PEN English Centre, 1970, and president of International PEN, 1974–76; president, Society of Authors, from 1977. Recipient: Heinemann award, for non-fiction, 1969; PEN award, for non-fiction, 1974; W.H. Smith award, 1990; Silver Pen award, 1990; Elmer Holmes Bobst special award (U.S.), 1991. D.Litt.: University of Leeds, 1972; Columbia University, 1978; University of Sussex, Brighton, 1980; Harvard University, Cambridge, Massachusetts, 1985. Fellow, 1969, and Companion of Literature, 1987, Royal Society of Literature; honorary member, American Academy, 1971, and American Academy of Arts and Sciences, 1971. C.B.E. (Commander, Order of the British Empire), 1968. Knighted, 1975. Lives in London.

PUBLICATIONS

Short Stories

The Spanish Virgin and Other Stories. 1930.
You Make Your Own Life. 1938.
It May Never Happen and Other Stories. 1945.
Collected Stories. 1956.
The Sailor, Sense of Humour, and Other Stories. 1956.
When My Girl Comes Home. 1961.
The Key to My Heart. 1963.
The Saint and Other Stories. 1966.
Blind Love and Other Stories. 1969.
The Camberwell Beauty and Other Stories. 1974.
Selected Stories. 1978.
On the Edge of the Cliff. 1979.
Collected Stories. 1982.
More Collected Stories. 1983.
A Careless Widow and Other Stories. 1989.
Complete Short Stories. 1990; as *Complete Collected Stories,* 1991.

Novels

Clare Drummer. 1929.
Shirley Sanz. 1932; as *Elopement into Exile,* 1932.
Nothing like Leather. 1935.
Dead Man Leading. 1937.
Mr. Beluncle. 1951.

Plays

The Gambler (broadcast 1947). *In Imaginary Conversations,* edited by Rayner Heppenstall, 1948.

La Bohème, adaptation of the libretto by Giuseppe Giacosa and Luigi Illica, music by Puccini.   1983.

Screenplays: *Essential Jobs* (documentary), 1942; *The Two Fathers,* with Anthony Asquith, 1944.

Radio Play: *The Gambler,* 1947.

Other

Marching Spain.   1928.
In My Good Books.   1942.
Build the Ships: The Official Story of the Shipyards in War-Time.   1946.
The Living Novel.   1946; revised edition, 1964.
Why Do I Write: An Exchange of Views Between Elizabeth Bowen, Graham Greene, and Pritchett.   1948.
Books in General.   1953.
The Spanish Temper.   1954.
London Perceived.   1962.
Foreign Faces.   1964; as *The Offensive Traveller,* 1964.
New York Proclaimed.   1965.
The Working Novelist.   1965.
Dublin: A Portrait.   1967.
A Cab at the Door: Childhood and Youth 1900–1920.   1968.
George Meredith and English Comedy.   1970.
Midnight Oil (autobiography).   1971.
Balzac: A Biography.   1973.
The Gentle Barbarian: The Life and Work of Turgenev.   1977.
Autobiography (address).   1977.
The Myth Makers: Essays on European, Russian, and South American Novelists.   1979.
The Tale Bearers: Essays on English, American, and Other Writers.   1980.
The Turn of the Years, with Reynolds Stone.   1982.
The Other Side of a Frontier: A Pritchett Reader.   1984.
A Man of Letters: Selected Essays.   1985.
Chekhov: A Spirit Set Free.   1988; as *Chekhov: A Biography,* 1990.
At Home and Abroad (essays).   1989.
Lasting Impressions: Selected Essays.   1990.
Complete Collected Essays.   1992.

Editor, *This England.*   1938.
Editor, *Novels and Stories,* by Robert Louis Stevenson.   1945.
Editor, *Turnstile One: A Literary Miscellany from the New Statesman.*   1948.
Editor, *The Oxford Book of Short Stories.*   1981.

*

Critical Study: *Pritchett* by Dean R. Baldwin, 1987.

*   *   *

Considered one of the finest writers of short stories in English in the 20th century, V.S. Pritchett is very much a writer's writer who places great importance on technique, linguistic vitality, and the necessity of close observation to record life in all its many moods. His methods are summed up in a general statement about the modern short story in his introduction to *The Oxford Book of Short Stories*: "Because the short story has to be succinct and has to suggest things that have been 'left out,' are, in fact, there all the time, the art calls for a mingling of the skills of the rapid reporter or traveller with an eye for incident and ear for real speech, the instincts of the poet or the ballard-maker, and the sonnet writer's concealed discipline of form."

It is instructive to compare Pritchett's own advice with the story he has selected for inclusion in the anthology. "Many Are Disappointed" was first published in his collection *The Sailor, Sense of Humour, and Other Stories,* and it is a typical example of the combination of realism and imagination he brings to his best writing. Four men, all office workers, dream of the beer to come at the end of the day's hard cycling but are only offered tea when they reach the tavern—hence the story's title. Other than that, nothing else happens of any note, but the story remains in the mind because the characters are vividly realised, their speech is natural and idiomatic, and the background details have been vivaciously sketched. Although the language of the story is not poetic in the strict sense, it is rich with the instincts of poetry and it has a lingering sub-text which leaves the reader feeling that there is more to the characters—and what has happened to them—than has been revealed in the story.

Pritchett's shrewd observation and his compassion for his characters have led critics to compare him to Charles Dickens and there is much to the conceit. The resemblance is particularly acute when the background is London, especially the city itself, and when the characters are lower middle-class office-workers or commercial travellers. Above all, he is sympathetic to his creations, not merely breathing life into them—as Dickens did to his best characters–but also remaining sensitive even when they are outsiders or behave in a bizarre manner. Saxon in "Our Oldest Friend" exemplifies this type; as does McDowell during the painful yet comic set-piece interview in "The Vice-Consul."

In this respect, the ability to remain involved with characters who are basically flawed or foolish, H.G. Wells also comes to mind—although the influence is felt more strongly in his novel *Mr. Beluncle* than in the short stories.

Many of Pritchett's best short stories are psychological studies of unworthy enthusiasms and they build up to comic scenes which dispel any possibility of impending gloom. The insufferable businessman father in "The Fly in the Ointment" is a good example. As he tumbles through a maelstrom of emotions during the uneasy confrontation with his son, his sudden attempts to kill a fly lighten the mood by revealing a mass of petty obsessions. The tone is sympathetic; the analysis of the two characters incisive but understanding. The same is true of the vulgar and garrulous married couple, the Seugars, in "The Landlord": although they are snobbish and vain and deserve to be duped by their odd landlord, they retain the reader's compassion mainly because they are utterly believable.

Pritchett's ability to catch the rhythms and patterns of speech is also central to his art. Whenever Mr. Seugar opens his mouth he becomes the effusive suburban shop-keeper whom his wife despises yet needs for her own financial security. His overeagerness and her lack of refinement help the reader to overcome the disbelief that they could simply walk into a coveted house and buy it from a stranger. (The contrast between their crudeness and the landlord's prim silence underlines the odd nature of the subsequent relationship.)

Indeed, most of Pritchett's characters reveal themselves initially through the way they speak. This can range from the virtuoso performance of Mr. Pollfax, the dentist, who uses his patient's enforced silence to mask his true personality ("The Oedipus Complex"), to the suburban pretensions of the faintly absurd characters in "The Accompanist."

During the dinner party, which is the centre-piece of the latter story, the conversation around the table is given an added edge by the knowledge that two of them, William and Joyce (a married woman) are having a clandestine affair. This use of a subtext is also typical of Pritchett's unobtrusive approach to the short story, for it becomes increasingly clear that although Joyce is willing to have a sexual relationship with a man who is basically an outsider, she is finally more committed to upholding the values of her own social class.

Above all, Pritchett is able to keep a sufficient distance from her subject: he observes and accepts his characters without casting blame or becoming overly involved in their actions. This does not imply cold-hearted cynicism; rather, Pritchett remains a detached yet humorous observer who casts his eye on whatever life has to throw at him with irony, sympathy, and not a little humour.

—Trevor Royle

See the essays on "The Saint" and "The Wedding."

PUSHKIN, Aleksandr (Sergeevich). Russian. Born in Moscow, 26 May 1799. Educated at home, and at lycée in Tsarskoe Selo, 1811–17. Married Natalia Goncharova in 1831. Civil servant, St. Petersburg, 1817–20; exiled in southern Russia and Pskov province, 1820–26; editor, *Sovremennik* (Contemporary), 1836–37. *Died (in duel) 29 January 1837.*

PUBLICATIONS

Collections

Polnoe sobranie sochinenii, edited by B.V. Tomachevskim. 10 vols., 1977–79.
Complete Prose Fiction, edited by Paul Debreczeny. 1983.
The Captain's Daughter and Other Stories. 1992.

Short Stories

Povesti pokoinogo I.P. Belkina. 1830; as *Tales of P. Bielkin,* 1947; as *The Tales of Belkin, and The History of Goryukhino,* 1983.
Pikovaia dama (novella). 1834; as *The Queen of Spades,* with *The Captain's Daughter,* 1858.
Complete Prose Tales. 1966.

Novels

Kapitanskaia dochka. 1836; as *The Captain's Daughter,* 1846; as *Marie: A Story of Russian Love,* 1877.

Dubrovskii (fragment). 1841.
Russian Romances. 1875.

Plays

Boris Godunov. 1831; translated as *Boris Godunov,* in *Translations from Pushkin,* 1899.
Motsart i Sal'eri. 1831; as *Mozart and Salieri,* in *Translations from Pushkin,* 1899.
Pir vo vremia chumy. 1832; as *The Feast During the Plague,* in *The Little Tragedies,* 1946.
Skupoi rytsar'. 1836; as *The Covetous Knight,* in *The Works,* 1939.
Kamennyi gost'. 1839; as *The Statue Guest,* in *Translations from Pushkin,* 1899; as *The Stone Guest,* in *The Works,* 1939.

Verse

Stikhotvoreniia. 1826; revised edition, 4 vols., 1829–35, and later editions.
Evgenii Onegin. 1833; translated as *Eugene Onegin,* 1881.
Selections from the Poems, edited by Ivan Panin. 1888; as *Poems,* 1888.
Pushkin Threefold: Narrative, Lyric, Polemic, and Ribald Verse. 1972.
The Bronze Horseman: Selected Poems. 1982.
Narrative Poems by Pushkin and Lermontov. 1983.
Collected Narrative and Lyrical Poetry. 1984.
Epigrams and Satirical Verse, edited by Cynthia H. Whittaker. 1984.

Other

Puteshestvie v Arzrum [The Journey to Arzrum]. 1836.
The Works: Lyrics, Narrative Poems, Folk Tales, Prose, edited by A. Yarmolinsky. 1939.
Letters. 1964.
Pushkin in Literature, edited by Tatiana Wolff. 1971.
The History of Pugachev. 1983.
Secret Journal 1836–1837. 1986.

*

Critical Studies: *Pushkin and Russian Literature* by Janko Lavrin, 1947; *Pushkin's Bronze Horseman: The Story of a Masterpiece* by W. Lednecki, 1955; *Pushkin* by E.J. Simmons, 1964; *Pushkin: A Biography* by David Magarshack, 1967; *Pushkin* by Walter Vickery, 1970; *Pushkin: A Comparative Commentary* by John Bayley, 1971; *Pushkin* by Henri Troyat, 1974; *Pushkin and His Sculptural Myth* by Roman Jakobson, 1975; *Russian Views of Pushkin* edited by D.J. Richards and C.R.S. Cockrell, 1976; *Pushkin: A Critical Study,* 1982, and *Eugene Onegin,* 1992, both by A.D.P. Briggs; *The Other Pushkin: A Study of Pushkin's Prose Fiction* by Paul Debreczeny, 1983; *Distant Pleasures: Pushkin and the Writing of Exile* by Stephanie Sandler, 1989; *The Contexts of Pushkin* edited by Peter I. Barta and Ulrich Goegel, 1990.

* * *

Though known mainly as Russia's national poet, Aleksandr Pushkin set the standard for her prose. When he began in earnest to write prose in the late 1820's, Russian fiction, still dependent on Western models, had reached only its adolescent stage. Prose first gained importance in Russia during the late 18th century with the advent of sentimentalism; it continued to develop during the age of romanticism when various prose genres gained popularity. This period saw the rise of adventure stories, society tales, supernatural episodes, travel accounts, *künstlernovellen,* and love stories. Pushkin tried his hand at all of them; some he parodied, others he surpassed with masterpieces of genius such as *The Queen of Spades* and "The Stationmaster."

Pushkin's first serious foray into fiction, "The Blackamoor of Peter the Great" (of which only a lengthy fragment survives), exhibits a great deal of narrative sophistication for its day. Flouting the popular convention of a narrator/fictional personality who must reveal the sources of his stories, the omniscient, highly objective narrator begins without excuses and generally stays in the background. The writing is spare, without any special adornment, a consequence of Pushkin's attitude that prose, as opposed to poetry, should remain a humble medium. He continued to experiment with straightforward narration in a couple of fragments, whose focus on complex psychology and serious ideas simply did not correspond to the mode of storytelling he chose. In addition Pushkin had not yet mastered the techniques of objective narration.

Yet another fragment, "A Novel in Letters," which consists of only ten short missives, reverts to the more facile epistolary form. Unlike works that rely on letters between the protagonists of the tale, usually lovers, Pushkin's attempt at an epistolary narrative relies on letters among friends to advance the story. Here a young girl, Liza, writes to her acquaintance to explain her reasons for leaving Petersburg. At first she conceals the truth, but later she reveals she was fleeting a romantic entanglement. However, her young man follows her to the provinces and writes to his friend to report on his activities in the country. The letters are engaging and pique the reader's interest. Pushkin's female letter writer/heroine Liza is highly articulate and discerning in her literary tastes, which are clearly Pushkin's own. Her wry comments about *Clarissa* also reveal a sense of humor.

On the other hand, the narrator of Pushkin's only collection of stories, the late Ivan Petrovich Belkin, lacks sophistication, literary or otherwise. With him Pushkin ostensibly goes backward to rely on literary conventions of the day. A publisher, known only by the initials A.P., provides an introduction to the tales as well as to the narrator. He employs a convoluted, pompous style to tell the readers he has no substantial information about Belkin. He does, however, manage to write to a friend of Belkin's whose letter he appends without comment. The muddle-headed friend informs A.P. that on the twenty-third of the month he was pleased to receive the publisher's letter of the fifteenth. This would not be remarkable, except for the fact that the friend's letter is dated the sixteenth, a clue that our second narrator may be less than reliable.

Nevertheless we do find out from him in spite of his overly digressive style, that Belkin received an elementary education from the sexton, served in the military, came back to manage the estate after the death of his parents, enjoyed reading, tried his hand at writing, was sober in habits and very rarely tipsy; he also admitted a certain fondness for the ladies, though he was as "shy as a maiden." This "dear friend of our author" also provides us with clues to the identities of the original storytellers who had entertained Belkin with their tales. In the stories themselves we can see the voices and attitudes of the original narrators, but occasionally we can discern Belkin's voice.

All of the stories, in one way or another, parody prevailing modes and trends in romantic fiction. "The Shot" debunks the mysterious Byronic hero in its portrayal of Silvio, whose own actions ultimately trivialize the revenge he metes out to a young nobleman who had offended him years before. In "The Undertaker," while attending a neighbor's party, Adrian Prokhorov takes offense when a guest suggests that he propose a toast to the health of his clients. The drunken undertaker goes home and invites the corpses he has buried to a housewarming party. He takes fright when they arrive, but then awakes from his dream just as he pushes away an advancing skeleton. Pushkin treats a potentially grisly tale with grotesque humor and thereby undercuts its fantastic and macabre features. The two comic tales, "The Blizzard" and "The Squire's Daughter" (or "Mistress into Maid"), both stories of mistaken identity that ultimately result in recognition scenes and happy endings, parody female narrators. Belkin's flat style diffuses the enthusiastic raptures of the original narrator, Miss K.I.T., over these sentimental romantic tales. Also a parody of sentimental stories of romantic love, "The Stationmaster" transcends the model and stands out among *Povesti pokoinogo I.P. Belkina (The Tales of Belkin)* as the best and most original of the lot.

Pushkin resurrected Belkin to narrate the unfinished "History of the Village of Goriukhino," a parody of works by two contemporary historians, Karamzin and Polevoi. In the introduction to his history, Belkin provides us with a more detailed picture of his life than we had previously received. Unfortunately the anecdotes he relates, while making him more endearing, render him a more ridiculous and ludicrous character than we had already imagined. In spite of the fact that he might be a most inappropriate candidate for historian, Belkin's account reveals genuine social abuses of the times.

For a while Pushkin devoted his time to serious study of history and found Peter the Great and the rebel Pugachev subjects worthy of investigation. Indeed, Pugachev also appears as a pivotal character in his novel *Kapitanskaia dochka (The Captain's Daughter)*. In his last years Pushkin combined historical facts with fiction, legend, and ethnographical digressions in the short story, "Kirdzhali." However complex its structure may seem, it ends up basically as an anecdote glorifying a brigand. An anecdote about Cleopatra in a fragment of one tale becomes the basis for one of Pushkin's last and most intriguing prose works, the unfinished "Egyptian Nights." A meeting between a poet and Italian improvisator investigates a theme long prevalent in Pushkin's work — the role of the poet in society. The "collaboration" between the two artists at a literary soirée, which the poet helps organize in aid of the impoverished improvisator, results in a stunning improvisation on Cleopatra, another theme Pushkin earlier investigated at some length.

Even a brief survey of Pushkin's fiction brings to light the rich variety of his relatively small body of prose. While not always as devoid of ornament as some critics have said, nothing superfluous appears in his works. His precise use of details provides clues to further understanding of characters and themes. Pushkin's seemingly simple tale always demand close reading and rereading.

Though more than half of Pushkin's prose output consists of fragments, he exerted a profound influence on the development of Russian fiction. Writers as diverse as Gogol, Turgenev, Dostoevskii, and Tolstoii have all acknowledged their debt to him. In his first experimental fragments as well as in *Pikovaia dama (The Queen of Spades)* and his novel in verse *Evgenii Onegin (Eugene Onegin)*, Pushkin laid the groundwork for what was to become the great Russian psychological novel of the 19th century.

—Christine A. Rydel

See the essays on *The Queen of Spades* and "The Station-master."

————

Q

QUIROGA, Horacio (Sylvestre). Uruguayan. Born in Salto, 31 December 1878. Educated at University of Montevideo. Married 1) Ana María Cires in 1909 (died 1915), one daughter, one son; 2) María Elena Bravo in 1927 (separated 1936), one daughter. Founding editor, *Revista del Salto,* 1899; teacher of Spanish, Colegio Nacional, Buenos Aires, 1903; government worker, Misiones, Argentine, 1903; cotton farmer, Chaco, Argentina; professor of Spanish language and literature, Escuela Normal, Buenos Aires, 1906–11; farmer, civil servant, and justice of the peace, San Ignacio, Misiones province; worked at Uruguayan consulates, Argentina, from 1917. *Died (suicide) 19 February 1937.*

PUBLICATIONS

Collections

Selección de cuentos, edited by Emir Rodriguez Monegal. 2 vols., 1966.
Obras inéditas y desconocidas, edited by Angel Rama. 3 vols., 1967.
Novelas completas. 1979.
Cuentos completas. 1979.

Short Stories

Los arrecifes de coral (includes verse). 1901.
El crimen del otro. 1904.
Los perseguidos. 1905.
Cuentos de amor, de locura y de muerte. 1917; edited by Peter R. Beardsell, 1988.
Cuentos de la selva (para niños). 1918; as *South American Jungle Tales,* 1922.
El savaje y otros cuentos. 1920; as *El savaje y otros historias,* 1937.
Anaconda. 1921; as *Anaconda y otros cuentos,* 1953.
El desierto. 1924.
La gallina degollada y otros cuentos. 1925; as *The Decapitated Chicken and Other Stories,* illustrated by Ed Lindlof, 1976.
Los desterrados, cuentos. 1926; as *Los desterrados: Tipos de ambiente,* 1927; as *The Exiles and Other Stories,* edited by J. David Danielson and Elsa K. Gambarini, 1987; as *Los desterrados y otros textos,* edited by Jorge Lafforgue, 1990.
Más allá, cuentos. 1935; as *El más allá,* 1952.
Cuentos, edited by C. García. 13 vols., 1937–45.
Quiroga: Sus mejores cuentos, edited by John A. Crow. 1943.
Cuentos escogidos, edited by Guillermo de Torre. 1950; edited by Jean Franco, 1968.
El regreso de Anaconda y otros cuentos. 1960.
Anaconda, El salvaje, Pasado amor. 1960.
La patria y otros cuentos. 1961.
Cuentos de horror. 1968.

A la deriva, y otros cuentos. 1968; edited by Olga Zamboni, 1989.
Cuentos 1905–1910 [and] 1910–35, edited by Jorge Ruffinelli. 2 vols., 1968.
Los cuentos de mis hijos. 1970.
El desafio de las Misiones. 1970.
Quiroga (stories), edited by Maria E. Rodes de Clerico and Ramon Bordoli Dolci. 1977.
Más cuentos, edited by Arturo Souto Alabarce, 1980.
El síncope blanco y otros cuentos. 1987.
Cuentos, edited by Leonor Fleming. 1991.

Novels

Historia de un amor turbio. 1908.
Pasado amor. 1929.

Play

Los sacrifadas, cuentos escénico en cuatro actos. 1920.

Other

Suelo natal (essays). 1931.
Diario de viaje a París de Quiroga, edited by Emir Rodríguez Monegal. 1949.
Cartas inéditas de Quiroga, edited by Arturo Sergio Visca and Roberto Ibáñez. 2 vol., 1959.
La vida en Misiones, prologue by Jorge Ruffinelli. 1969.
Sobre literatura. 1970.
Cartas inéditas y evocación de Quiroga, edited by Arturo Sergio Visca. 1970.
El mundo ideal de Quiroga y cartas inéditas de Quiroga a Isidoro Escalera, edited by Antonio Hernán Rodríguez. 1971.
Cartas desde la selva. 1971.
Epoca modernista, edited by Jorge Ruffinelli. 1973.
Our First Smoke. 1972.
La abeja haragana (for children), illustrated by Rogelio Naranjo. 1985.
Cartas de un cazador. 1986.

* * *

After a disappointing visit in 1900 to Paris, and publishing in 1901 a decadent collection *Los arrecifes de coral* (Coral Reefs), Horacio Quiroga turned his back on literary fashions to write a body of gripping short stories (some 200 in all) that recreated his two passions, pioneer life and fantastic literature. In 1927 he published a "Decalogue of the perfect short story writer," based on Edgar Allan Poe's self-conscious manipulation of the reader's responses. Quiroga sought a literature of experience, where a short story was written in "blood," without false padding. He wanted to shock the reader from armchair torpor and catch "real life."

Quiroga's trip as photographer with the poet Lugones to the abandoned Jesuit missions in the Argentine province of Misiones in 1903 revealed how little known the hinterland of Argentina was. Most of his fellow writers preferred to travel to Europe than know their own continent. In 1906 Quiroga settled on 185 hectares of land near San Ignacio, and began placing many stories in this pioneer area.

In 1917 he published *Cuentos de amor, de locura y de muerte* (Stories of Love, Madness, and Death), stories written mainly in Misiones between 1906 and 1914 that deal with sudden moments of danger, even death, that test his characters, often tragically. An early ironic story can be read as a parable of what happens when a city person tries to adventure into the wilds. In "Wild Honey" (written 1911, but not translated) an accountant, who loves tea and cakes, visits a god-father in Misiones hoping to test himself. In preparation for the jungle he arrives with smart boots and a Winchester rifle, to hunt wild animals but soon discovers that the jungle is impenetrable without a *machete*. However, he discovers and gorges on wild honey guarded by stingless bees. His greed is vividly evoked until he discovers that the honey is narcotic just when carnivorous ants arrive, and clean him to the bone. As an amateur field naturalist Quiroga had also written an article on these army ants. In this story these ants are known as "la corrección," and relentlessly "correct" the accountant Benincasa's view of nature, and life. His name in Spanish means "Bien en casa" (at ease at home). He epitomises the middle-class urban values and people, living in far-off Buenos Aires, that Quiroga wanted to punish.

In 1912 he wrote his laconic "Drifting," which narrates how a squatter in Misiones on the banks of the river Paraná is bitten by a snake. Quiroga vividly describes the effect of the poison on the man, his swelling leg like "blood pudding," his incredible thirst where he mistakes brandy for water, until he paddles down stream to get help, and in the middle of an utterly banal thought, dies. The story suggests humans' inability to adapt to the extremes of nature, and is an elegy to the indifferent magnificence of Misiones. One small mistake, not noticing a deadly snake, can lead to death. Quiroga had also written a newspaper article listing the local poisonous snakes.

Following Kipling, Quiroga evoked his view of life by making animals talk. In "Sunstroke" (written 1908), set in the blistering heat of the Chaco, terrier dogs survive better than their master, killed by sunstroke. A collection named after the giant snake of the region, *Anaconda*, came out in 1921. Following Kipling's *Just So Stories*, Quiroga wrote *Cuentos de la selva* (South American Jungle Tales), where animals show how perfectly adapted they are to their environment. This despised animal side to humans fasci-

nated Quiroga. In "The Contract Labourers" we follow two Guarani-speaking Indians, Cayetano and Podeley, working at a logging camp, who spend their wages in an orgy in Posadas, get into debt, and work their debt off in the jungle. Quiroga does not only denounce the fate of these Indians in a vicious system of debt repayment, but also explores their absurd courage in escaping through the flooded jungle to get caught up again in the same system. The story shows how close to animals they are, and thus paradoxically makes them admirable. In *Los desterrados* (The Exiles and Other Stories), about local characters around Misiones, the story "The Incense Tree Roof" deals with a leaking roof, and heroically trying to bring the birth and death records up to date for a government inspection, in such a hostile, tropical environment.

Violence haunted Quiroga's actual life: in 1879 his father was accidentally shot dead; in 1896 his step-father committed suicide; in 1902 Quiroga shot dead a friend by mistake; in 1915 his first wife committed suicide. The violence implicit in these dates frames many stories which, like his masters Poe and Maupassant, are not realistically situated in pioneer lands. Quiroga was fascinated by horror, from his Poesque *El crimen del otro* (The Other's Crime) in 1904 to his last collection *Más allá* (Beyond) in 1935. Typical is "The Large Feather Pillow," written in 1907, and published in *Cuentos de amor, de locura y de muerte*, where, after getting married, a couple live in a large, silent house. The wife Alicia catches some strange illness which her husband Jordan cannot cure. She gets thinner and thinner, hallucinates about apes jumping on her, and dies. Only when the maid remakes the bed do we discover that her feather pillow weighed a ton, with a huge parasite bloated with her blood inside it. Quiroga ends the story addressing the readers, hinting that they too could find such a parasite in their pillows.

Quiroga's art of story telling sought to shock his readers out of comfortable values; the short story's economy could produce the required shock, and all Quiroga's skills were subservient to making his readers believe in what they read, down to his use of Spanish that refused to be "polished" and literary, reproducing local speech, packed with specific plant and animal names, in an attempt to capture what Quiroga called "real life."

—Jason Wilson

See the essays on "The Dead Man" and "The Decapitated Chicken."

R

RAO, Raja. Indian. Born in Hassan, Mysore, 5 November 1908. Educated at Madarasa-e-Aliya School, Hyderabad, 1915–25; Aligarh Muslim University, 1926–27; Nizam College, Hyderabad (University of Madras), B.A. in English 1929; University of Montpellier, France, 1929–30; the Sorbonne, Paris, 1930–33. Married 1) Camille Mouly in 1931; 2) Katherine Jones in 1965, one son. Editor, *Tomorrow*, Bombay, 1943–44; lived in France for many years; now lives half the year in India and half in Europe and the United States; professor of philosophy, University of Texas, Austin, from 1965, now professor emeritus. Recipient: Sahitya Academy award, 1964; Padma Bhushan, India, 1969; Neustadt International prize, 1988.

PUBLICATIONS

Short Stories

The Cow of the Barricades and Other Stories.   1947.
The Policeman and the Rose.   1978.
On the Ganga Ghat.   1989.

Novels

Kanthapura.   1938.
The Serpent and the Rope.   1960.
The Cat and Shakespeare: A Tale of India.   1965.
Comrade Kirillov.   1976.
The Chessmaster and His Moves.   1988.

Other

The Chess Master and His Moves.   1978.
Alien Poems and Stories.   1983.

Editor, with Iqbal Singh, *Changing India.*   1939.
Editor, with Iqbal Singh, *Whither India?*   1948.
Editor, *Soviet Russia: Some Random Sketches and Impressions,* by Jawaharlal Nehru.   1949.

*

Critical Studies: *Rao* by M.K. Naik, 1972; *Rao: A Critical Study of His Work* (includes bibliography) by C.D. Narasimhaiah, 1973; *The Fiction of Rao* by K.R. Rao, 1980; *Perspectives on Rao* edited by K.K. Sharma, 1980; *Indo-Anglian Literature and the Works of Rao* by P.C. Bhattacharya, 1983; *Rao* by Shiva Niranjan, 1985; *Rao and Cultural Tradition* by Paul Sharrad, 1987; *Rao: The Man and His Works* by Shyamala A. Narayan, 1988; *The Language of Mulk Raj Anand, Rao, and R.K. Narayan* by Reza Ahmad Nasimi, 1989.

*   *   *

Youngest of the "Big Three" of Indian English fiction (the other two being Mulk Raj Anand and R. K. Narayan), Raja Rao is better known as a novelist than a short story writer; but his contribution to the short story is perhaps as distinctive and substantial as that to longer fiction, though his actual output in both the forms remains equally restricted.

Of Rao's two short story collections, the first, *The Cow of the Barricades and Other Stories*, appeared in 1947, and the second, *The Policeman and the Rose*, published some 30 years later, actually contains as many as seven of the nine stories in the earlier collection, with only three new additions, but these additions constitute a new departure in the direction of philosophical statement in symbolic fictional terms.

Most of the stories in *The Cow of the Barricades* were written during the 1930's, and some of them belong to that transitional period when the author was changing over from Kannada (his mother tongue) to English as his medium of expression. As the publisher's note declares, "One of the stories—'A Client'—is translated from the Kannada, and the rest, although first written in English, are translations too: through the medium of the English language the author seeks to communicate Indian modes of feeling and expression."

These early stories are sharply etched vignettes of Indian rural life in pre-Independence days. "Javani" and "Akkayya" are touching character sketches of widows. Javani is a low-class widow, while Akkayya belongs to the Brahmin caste, but both lead equally miserable and meaningless lives. Javani's husband has died of snake-bite; hence she is universally considered to be an ill-fated woman, and is forbidden to touch her sister-in-law's child. Akkayya, who has spent her long life in bringing up other people's children, is, in death as in life only an irritating nuisance to her relatives.

The political unrest of the 1930's is mirrored in three stories: the title story, "The Cow of the Barricades," "Narsiga," and "In Khandesh." The holy cow named after the goddess Gauri, in the first story, is an expressive symbol of the Indian synthesis of tradition and modernity. The sacred cow dedicated to a god is a part of ancient Indian tradition; but Gauri, who dies of a British officer's bullet during the freedom riots, becomes a martyr in the cause of the modern Indian nationalism. "Narsiga" shows how the national consciousness roused by the Gandhian movement percolates in the simple mind of an illiterate urchin, though in the process, the ancient legend of Rama the Ideal Inidian King-god gets inextricably mixed with Gandhi's life and character, as Narsiga imagines the modern Indian leader "going in the air . . . in a flower-chariot drawn by sixteen steeds." "In Khandesh" recaptures evocatively the commotion caused in a sleepy little village by which the British Viceroy's special train is to pass.

"The True Story of Kanakapala, Protector of God" and "Companions" are legends from serpent-lore, a traditional subject in a land where a "serpent-festival" is still celebrated today. "The Little Gram Shop," on the other hand, is a starkly realistic study of Indian village life; and "A Client," the only story in the collection with an urban setting, provides an amusing glimpse into the Indian system of arranged marriages.

The narrative technique in this collection shows Rao experimenting in the direction that was to lead to the finished triumph of his mature novels. His attempt to adapt the ancient Indian folktale to fictional expression in English perhaps succeeds only partially, when he recounts old-world legends, as in "Companions"; but when he applies the architectonics of this form to a narrative of modern life, as in "The Cow of the Barricades," he achieves something much more meaningful. An equally fruitful experiment is the deliberate attempt to capture, both in dialogue and narration, the actual feel of rustic Indian speech, by the literal translation into English of Indian idiom, oaths, nicknames, and imagery, imbuing the entire book with strong flavour of authentic local colour.

Two of the three new stories in *The Policeman and the Rose* show how in his later work Rao's interest shifted from the social and political planes to a metaphysical apprehension of life. Only one story in this collection is a character sketch in the manner of earlier efforts like "Javani" and "Akkayya." "Nimka" is a portrait of a White Russian refugee, whom the Indian narrator meets in Paris. A princess by blood, she now ekes out a living by serving as a waitress in a restaurant. Drawn to India through Tolstoy and the narrator, she declares that India for her is "the land where all that is wrong everywhere goes right."

It is in "India: A Fable" and the title story, "The Policeman and the Rose" that Rao has successfully made shorter fiction the vehicle of profound metaphysical statement. The central theme in both the stories is humankind's quest for self-realization, though "A Fable" presents the theme with far greater economy of narrative content. The narrative in "The Policeman" makes strange reading, until one understands the key symbols in it. The narrator, who declares that every man is arrested at the moment of his birth by a "policeman," recounts the story of his several births in his past lives, since the day he was a contemporary of ancient Rama. In his latest birth in modern India, he goes to Paris, opens a "shop of Hindu eyes," and earns a reputation as a man of God. Upon his return to India, he falls ill, and comes back to Paris a much chastened man, only to find that he has been declared deceased and a statue erected to him there. His return in flesh being now inconvenient, he is compelled to go back to India, where at last he offers his "red rose" at the "lotus feet" of his Guru at Travancore, "the Retired Police Commissioner," and becomes free, finally getting rid of his "policeman." The major symbols here are: the "policeman," who arrests every one at birth, is the ego-sense (the Guru, who has overcome his ego, is a retired police commissioner); the "red rose" is *rajas* or passion; the "Lotus" stands for truth; the "Eye" is the eye of religious faith. The entire narrative is thus a fictional statement indicating that salvation lies in surrendering one's ego at the feet of the Guru.

Rao's short stories, though small in number, encompass Indian life and culture on individual, social, political, and metaphysical planes, and offer authentic glimpses of Indian character and thought, also imbuing English with a strong Indian flavour.

—M.K. Naik

See the essay on "India: A Fable."

———

RHYS, Jean. English. Born Ella Gwendolyn Rees Williams in Roseau, Dominica, West Indies, 24 August 1890. Educated at The Convent, Roseau; Perse School, Cambridge, England, 1907–08; Academy (now Royal Academy) of Dramatic Art, London, 1909. Married 1) Jean Lenglet in 1919 (divorced 1932), one son and one daughter; 2) Leslie Tilden Smith in 1934 (died 1945); 3) Max Hamer in 1947 (died 1966). Toured England in chorus of *Our Miss Gibbs*, 1909-10; volunteer worker in soldiers' canteen, 1914–17, and worked in a pension office, 1918, both London; lived in Paris, 1919 and 1923–27, and Vienna and Budapest, 1920–22; lived mainly in England after 1927: in Maidstone, Kent, 1950–52, London, 1952–56, Bude and Perranporth, Cornwall, 1956–60, and Cheriton Fitzpaine, Devon, from 1960. Recipient: Arts Council bursary, 1967; W.H. Smith award, 1967; Royal Society of Literature Heinemann award, 1967; Séguier prize, 1979. C.B.E. (Commander, Order of the British Empire), 1978. *Died 14 May 1979.*

PUBLICATIONS

Collections

Collected Short Stories. 1987.

Short Stories

The Left Bank and Other Stories. 1927.
Tigers Are Better-Looking, with a Selection from The Left Bank. 1968.
Sleep It Off Lady. 1976.
Tales of the Wide Caribbean, edited by Kenneth Ramchand. 1985.

Novels

Postures. 1928; as *Quartet,* 1929.
After Leaving Mr. Mackenzie. 1931.
Voyage in the Dark. 1934.
Good Morning, Midnight. 1939.
Wide Sargasso Sea. 1966.

Other

My Day (essays). 1975.
Smile Please: An Unfinished Autobiography. 1979.
Letters 1931–1966, edited by Francis Wyndham and Diana Melly. 1984.

Translator, *Perversity,* by Francis Carco. 1928 (translation attributed to Ford Madox Ford).
Translator, *Barred,* by Edward de Nève. 1932.

*

Bibliography: *Rhys: A Descriptive and Annotated Bibliography of Works and Criticism* by Elgin W. Mellown, 1984.

Critical Studies: *Rhys* by Louis James, 1978; *Rhys: A Critical Study* by Thomas F. Staley, 1979; *Rhys* by Peter Wolfe, 1980; *Rhys, Woman in Passage: A Critical Study of the Novels* by Helen E. Nebeker, 1981; *Difficult Women: A Memoir of Three* by David Plante, 1983; *Rhys* by Arnold E. Davidson, 1985; *Rhys*, 1985, and *Rhys* (biography), 1990, both by Carole Angier; *Rhys: The West Indian Novels* by Teresa F. O'Connor, 1986; *Rhys and the Novel as Women's Text* by Nancy R. Harrison, 1988; *Rhys, Stead, Lessing, and the Politics of Empathy* by Judith Kegan Gardiner, 1989; *The Unspeakable Mother: Forbidden Discourse in Rhys and H.D.* by Deborah Kelly Kloepfer, 1989; *The Rhys Woman* by Paula Le Gallez, 1990; *Critical Perspectives on Rhys* edited by Pierrette Frickey, 1990; *Rhys at World's End: Novels of Colonial and Sexual Exile* by Mary Lou Emery, 1990.

* * *

Jean Rhys, the author of five novels and 46 stories, had "no faith" in her short fiction. "Too bitter," she wrote in 1945, adding, "who wants short stories?" Rhys was often self-effacing and apologetic about her writing; it was not, in fact, until she moved to Europe, more than a decade after she had left her native Dominica for England in 1907, that she even began to think of herself as a writer. Rhys's career began somewhat accidentally when she approached Pearl Adam, wife of the *Times* Paris correspondent, for help in placing three articles written by her husband, Jean Lenglet, which she had translated from the French. Adam was more interested in whether Rhys had work of her own; Rhys revealed some sketches written between 1910 and 1919, which her new mentor tried to revise into a narrative she then sent to Ford Madox Ford. Ford, who did not publish the ultimately abandoned *Triple Sec*, nonetheless became the most significant literary influence of Rhys's early career, encouraging her writing and printing, finally, her story "Vienne," in the *Transatlantic Review* (December 1924).

"Vienne," as Judith K. Gardiner has noted, introduces "the most important Rhys character, a first-person autobiographical hero who is the victim of men, fate, circumstance, and her own good nature." Reprinted in a much longer version in *The Left Bank*, Rhys's first collection of stories, "Vienne" establishes the Rhysian principle "that 'eat or be eaten' is the inexorable law of life." It also opens the recurring issues of poverty, addiction, exclusion, "middle-class judgement," aging, suicide, and misogyny, particularly the "fiction of the 'good' woman and the 'bad' one." Although some of the stories in *The Left Bank* are set in Dominica ("Trio," "Mixing Cocktails," "Again the Antilles"), most, as the subtitle suggests, unfold in "Bohemian Paris," and replay episodes form Rhys's early life as an exile: transgression ("From a French Prison"), the struggle for economic survival ("Mannequin," "Hunger"), the "poisonous charm of the life beyond the pale" ("Tea with an Artist"), rejection and sexual exploitation ("A Night," "The Blue Bird," "A Spiritualist," "La Grosse Fifi"). As Ford Madox Ford wrote in his preface, the stories have a terrifying insight and a terrific—an almost lurid!—passion for stating the case of the underdog." Nine of the original 22 stories were reprinted in her second volume of short stories, *Tigers Are Better-Looking*.

Although Rhys's work has been compared to Maupassant, Anatole France, Katherine Mansfield, Colette, and even, as

Gardiner says, "the sensational, debased style of the crime tabloid," trying to set Rhys in a literary context is difficult. Critics have noted that her fiction is oddly disengaged socially and politically. Thomas Staley observes that although one finds a greater "aesthetic control and authorial distance" in later pieces, "her work was never very closely attuned to the technical innovations of modernism; her art developed out of an intensely private world—a world whose sources of inspiration were neither literary nor intellectual."

In the eight new stories comprising *Tigers Are Better-Looking*, both the author and the characters have aged: loss of innocence ("The Day They Burned the Books"), premonition ("The Sound of the River"), and futility are recurring themes. The title story explodes into misanthropy as a cynical journalist looking for "words that will mean something" negotiates in a world where people are "tigers waiting to spring the moment anybody is in trouble or hasn't any money." "The Lotus," likewise, centers on a writer who is humiliated, drunk, and aging. Gardiner calls it "bitter self-parody." Illness and emotional disturbance, which along with alcoholism haunted Rhys throughout her life, emerge more explicitly in these later stories; in "A Solid House" Teresa is recuperating in London during the blitz, flirting with madness and suicide as she searches for something "solid." "Outside the Machine" is set in a women's ward in a hospital and explores not only illness as metaphor but women's relationships with each other and Rhys's preoccupation with the outsider.

This collection contains two of Rhys's finest stories, "Till September Petronella" and "Let Them Call It Jazz." The latter is distinguished by the narrative voice of Selina whose Creole dialect encodes the split so characteristic in Rhys: "I see myself and I'm like somebody else." This cultural and psychological split echoes throughout her work, as in "The Insect World," where Audrey confesses, "It's as if I'm twins." "Let Them Call It Jazz" hinges on a stolen song, which Selina hears sung by a woman inmate in Holloway Prison and comes to feel is the only thing that really belongs to her. When she whistles it to a stranger, he "jazzes" it up, later informing Selina that he has sold it. "Now I've let them play it wrong," she thinks, "and it will go from me . . . like everything. Nothing left for me at all."

Thomas Staley sees the 16 stories of *Sleep It Off, Lady* (1976) as a "Thematic coda" to Rhys's previous work. Most of the stories set in Dominica are no more than sketches ("The Bishop's Feast," "On Not Shooting Sitting Birds," "I Used to Live Here Once," "Heat") but several of them initiate variations on the theme of violation, such as miscegenation ("Pioneers, Oh, Pioneers") and child abuse ("Good-bye Marcus, Good-bye Rose," "Fishy Waters"). One can trace in these stories the movement from childhood to old age, often in strikingly autobiographical pieces where Rhys has not even bothered to disguise identities. "Ouverture and Beginners Please," for example, is set at the Perse School, which Rhys attended when she arrived in England before joining the chorus of a touring musical comedy. "Before the Deluge" also is a sketch of her life in the theatre, related in tone to the "same old miseries" of the demimonde described in "Night Out 1925" and throughout Rhys's short fiction.

In Rhys's last stories, old age becomes not just the fear harbored by the younger protagonists but the fate that none of them can avoid. The title story of her last collection perhaps best exemplifies the danger and humiliation of growing old, especially for a woman, whose looks, in Rhys's world, are her only real currency. The loneliness, helplessness, and terror witnessed and feared throughout her canon come home in "Sleep It Off Lady" where Miss Verney, suffering from a heart condition, collapses in her yard and is left to die by a neighbor child who dismisses her as an old drunk deserving of no pity.

Rhys, who claimed she hated everything she wrote when it was finished, died in 1979 before she could complete a collection of autobiographical vignettes to "set the record straight," which was published posthumously as *Smile Please*. Except for brief moments, Rhys never experienced personal happiness, nor did she ever find sustained literary success; "it was always the most ordinary things that suddenly turned round and showed you another face," she wrote in "The Insect World," "a terrifying face. That was the hidden horror, the horror everybody pretended did not exist, the horror that was responsible for all the other horrors."

—Deborah Kelly Kloepfer

See the essay on "Till September Petronella."

RICHARDSON, Henry Handel. Pseudonym for Ethel Florence Lindesay Richardson. Australian. Born in Melbourne, Victoria, 3 January 1870. Educated at Presbyterian Ladies' College, Melbourne, 1883–86; studied music at the Leipzig Conservatorium, 1889–92. Married John George Robertson in 1895 (died 1933). Lived in Strasbourg, 1896–1903, London, 1903–32, and Sussex from 1933; visited Australia, 1912. Recipient: Australian Literature Society gold medal, 1929. *Died 20 March 1946.*

PUBLICATIONS

Short Stories

Two Studies. 1931.
The End of a Childhood and Other Stories. 1934.
The Adventures of Cuffy Mahony and Other Stories. 1979.

Novels

Maurice Guest. 1908.
The Getting of Wisdom. 1910.
The Fortunes of Richard Mahony. 1930.
Australia Felix. 1917.
The Way Home. 1925.
Ultima Thule. 1929.
The Young Cosima. 1939.

Other

Myself When Young (unfinished autobiography). 1948.
Letters to Nettie Palmer, edited by Karl-Johan Rossing. 1953.

Translator, *Siren Voices,* by J. P. Jacobsen. 1896.
Translator, *The Fisher Lass,* by B. Bjørnson. 1896.

*

Bibliography: *Richardson 1870–1949: A Bibliography to Honour the Centenary of Her Birth* by Gay Howells, 1970.

Critical Studies: *Richardson: A Study* by Nettie Palmer, 1950; *Richardson and Some of Her Sources,* 1954, *A Companion to Australia Felix,* 1962, *Myself When Laura: Fact and Fiction in Richardson's School Career,* 1966, and *Richardson,* 1967, all by Leonie Kramer; *Richardson* by Vincent Buckley, 1961; *Ulysses Bound: Richardson and Her Fiction* by Dorothy Green, 1973, revised edition, as *Richardson and Her Fiction,* 1986; *Richardson* by William D. Elliott, 1975; *Richardson* by Louis Triebel, 1976; *Art and Irony: The Tragic Vision of Richardson* by J.R. Nichols, 1982; *The Portrayal of Women in the Fiction of Richardson* by Eva Jarring Corones, 1983; *Richardson: A Critical Study* by Karen McLeod, 1985; *Richardson: Fiction in the Making* (vol. 1 of biography) by Axel Clark, 1990.

*   *   *

Although Henry Handel Richardson won most of her fame as a novelist she also published two small collections of short stories which contain several fine and much anthologised pieces. Born in Melbourne, Richardson travelled to Germany to continue a prospective career as a pianist but abandoned it to begin writing and translating. She married J.G. Robertson, a student and later a professor of German literature, in 1895 and lived the rest of her life in London, returning to Australia only for one brief visit of two months in 1912, after the death of her mother.

Mostly between her masterpiece, *The Fortunes of Richard Mahony,* and her final, disappointing novel *The Young Cosima,* Richardson wrote a number of short stories which were gathered together as *Two Studies* and *The End of a Childhood and Other Stories.* Long after her death, an Australian publisher brought out *The Adventures of Cuffy Mahony and Other Stories,* which contains these stories and new, previously uncollected ones.

The Adventures of Cuff Mahony is a kind of coda to Richardson's giant novel. It opens twelve months after the close of the novel and carries on the story of Cuffy Mahony, Richard's son, who had appeared in the final volume of the trilogy, and his mother Mary, who dies in the course of the story after suffering an infected leg. In general, the two main themes of the collection are adolescence and death. Mary broods on death continually but without coming much closer to any answers than she did in the novel. Memories of the past come back to her as she lies delirious (as they do to the title character in "Mary Christina," another of Richardson's finest) and she tries without success to fathom the workings of providence.

Nine of the stories, gathered together as "Growing Pains," are sketches of female adolescents and contain some of Richardson's best writing. Though they vary in quality and ambition, collectively they form a moving and delicate study of the pains and humiliations of growing up and entering adulthood: "shame" is probably the most repeated word in the collection and is the central experience in many of the stories. Beginning with very young adolescents, the stories move steadily closer to the treatment of sexual dilemmas, often involving a young and rather older girl. Males are absent for the most part, though an exception is "The Wrong Turning," in which a young boy and girl are out on a boat ride when they accidentally come across a group of sailors bathing naked. Their shame and humiliation ruin their embryonic relationship.

The famous and much anthologised story "And Women Must Weep" depicts the situation of a girl at a ball receiving no invitations to dance, except under duress. The note of sexual protest implicit in the story ("Oh, these men, who walked round and chose just who they fancied and left who they didn't . . . how she hated them! It wasn't fair . . . it wasn't fair") emerges more openly in "Two Hanged Women," in which a young girl is boasting to her older female friend of her new boy. The story touches most closely and delicately on quasi-lesbian themes, as it slowly becomes clear that Fred is merely an excuse for the girl to escape the competing and opposed demands on her of her friend and her mother, and that in reality she has a fear and horror of male sexuality. The story ends ambiguously with the older girl holding and stroking her but with no real solution to the implied impasse.

The remaining five stories mostly deal with death. "Life and Death of Peterle Luthy" is a grim account of a baby who is unwanted and neglected to the point where he finally dies. Henrietta, whose preoccupation with dancing had led to her child's death, displays at the end a kind of peasant-like stoicism, or perhaps merely indifference: "Her arms felt, and no doubt for a day or two would feel, strangely empty. Still, it was better so. Two were enough, more than enough. And she would take care—oh! such care . . ."

"The Professor's Experiment" is one of the longest and finest stories in the collection. A stuffy bookworm of a man marries a young woman who is full of charm and spirit. They go to live with the professor's domineering sister Annemarie and the two make life highly unpleasant for the young bride. After she dies in childbirth, however, Annemarie unexpectedly comes to see the emptiness of her own life and the false god she had been serving in her brother, and the story ends of a note of ominous rebellion.

"The Coat" is interesting largely as a rare excursion into at least partial fantasy. "Succedaneum," similarly, is significant in its author's body of work as the most direct and simple treatment of the relationship between life and art, a question that preoccupied Richardson throughout her life. "Mary Christina" is a fine story that is reminiscent in many ways of Tolstoi's "The Death of Ivan Illich." Written in 1911 upon the death of her mother and originally titled "Death," it ends characteristically on a note of scepticism: "Now, she asked for rest—only rest. Not immortality: no fresh existence, to be endured and fought out in some new shadow-land, among unquiet spirits."

Critics are divided as to Richardson's status as a short story writer and the shorter work tends in any case to be concealed by the novels. But had she written only these stories she would still have had a place in Australian literature. The best of them are fine pieces, written in a spare, compressed but delicate style, but without abandoning the hard-headed realism and maturity that were always Richardson's trademarks.

—Laurie Clancy

RIVE, Richard (Moore). South African. Born in Cape Town, 1 March 1931. Educated at Hewat Training College, teacher's certificate 1951; University of Cape Town, B.A. 1962, B.Ed. 1968; Columbia University, New York, M.A. 1966; Oxford, D.Phil. 1974. Teacher of English and Latin, South Peninsula High School, Cape Town; visiting professor, Harvard University, Cambridge, Massachusetts, 1987; lecturer in English, academic administrator, and head of English department, from 1988, Hewat College of Education. Fulbright scholar, 1965–66. Recipient: Farfield Foundation fellowship, 1963; Heft scholar, 1965–66; Writer of the Year (South Africa), 1970. *Died (murdered) 4 June (?) 1989.*

PUBLICATIONS

Short Stories

African Songs.   1963.
Advance, Retreat: Selected Short Stories, illustrated by Cecil Skotnes.   1983.

Novels

Emergency.   1964.
Buckingham Palace, District Six.   1986.
Emergency Continued.   1990.

Plays

Resurrection, in *Short African Plays,* edited by C. Pieterse. 1972.
Make Like Slaves, in *African Theatre,* edited by G. Henderson.   1973.
Buckingham Palace, District Six.

Other

Selected Writings: Stories, Essays, and Plays.   1977.
Writing Black (autobiography).   1981.
The Black Writer and South African Prose (criticism). 1987.

Editor, *Quartet: New Voices from South Africa.*   1963.
Editor, *Modern African Prose.*   1964.
Editor, *Olive Schreiner Letters 1871–1899.*   1988.

*

Bibliography: "Rive: A Select Bibliography" by Jayarani Raju and Catherine Dubbeld, in *Current Writers,* October 1989.

Critical Studies: "Form and Technique in the Novels of Rive and Alex La Guma" by B. Lindfors, in *Journal of the New African Literature and the Arts* 2, 1966; interview by L. Nkosi and R. Serumaga, in *African Writers Talking,* edited by D. Duerden and C. Pieterse, 1972; "South African History, Politics and Literature: Mphahlele's *Down Second Avenue* and Rive's *Emergency*" by O O. Obuke, in *African Literature Today* 10, 1979.

* * *

Short story writer, novelist and playwright, Richard Rive has as the ethos of all his work the now demolished, so-called "coloured" ghetto of District Six in Cape Town in apartheid-ridden South Africa. This leads to his stories, as he himself saw them, having a tightly constructed framework of both time and place.

Rive's opposition to oppression is evident in all his short stories. Although he spoke out strongly against the status quo, he was not an active member of any political organization. Something of an anomaly among black South African writers, he chose not to go into exile, but continued his work at home; this led to the ire of some writers abroad who accused him of being a collaborator with the government, even though his works were banned for about 15 years.

He was one of the founders of the protest movement in South Africa, being a black writing against the government from within the country and directing his stories largely at white readers whom he felt could effect change, as he points out in his autobiography *Writing Black*. He was suspicious of white liberals who wrote about the tyranny of the times, but could never experience what it was really like to be discriminated against on the grounds of colour. His discomfort with and objection to their patronizing attitude is evident in several short stories, for instance, in the early story "Drive-In," which describes the gathering of several would-be writers, including a token black to whom an overly colour-conscious white woman keeps on trying to prove her liberalism but underlines differences throughout with sentences such as "I know how hard you people have to work, sweetie." Rive depicts this "you people" liberal syndrome in many of his works, including "Make Like Slaves" and the much later "Riva." Other whites are often seen to be ignorant, dull, and brutal, and the racists obviously are estranged from God, as found in the unusual (because of their religious message) stories "No Room at Solitaire" and "The Return" where Christ appears as a black, underlining the idea that "If Christ came back we wouldn't recognize him."

Rive insisted that in South Africa art had to be propagandistic rather than art for art's sake. In his stories we see how politics influences the lives of all people (rather than what the individual's effect on politics is). This is evident in the protagonist in "The Bench," who is stirred to sit on a whites-only bench at a railway station and triumphs when he is dragged away; however, he is no Rosa Parks and the impression is that his actions will have little, if any, effect on the community, let alone the country, as a whole. We find this is Rive's last short story, too, which features his most delightful and graphically depicted character, the eponymous heroine in "Mrs. Janet September and the Siege of Sinton," which gives a true, first-hand account by an elderly woman who insisted on being arrested with a group of protesting students.

This clash with the authorities is seen throughout Rive's writings, as is one-on-one physical violence (not always racially motivated) found in stories such as "Rain," "Dagga-Smoker's Dream," "Moon over District Six," "The Return," and "Willie-boy," all underlining the rabid nature of the society depicted by him.

Although most of the governmentally designated "coloureds" in the Cape have Afrikaans as their first language, Rive's characters generally seem to have English as their mother tongue, and when they do not, they still prefer to use it, especially those who aspire to some sort of social success: " . . . sophisticated Charmaine," he writes in "Rain" in 1960, "was almost a schoolteacher and always spoke English." This reference to Charmaine also appears in "Mrs. Janet September" published 27 years later, and adds to the impression that he is really writing about a cohesive group of people in a ghetto where everyone knows everyone else, and also that his stories and characters seem to be not the fruits of imagination but rather a portrayal of people and a recounting of incidents he experienced or which others had told him. We find this in stories as diverse as "The Man from the Board," which concerns a

black man who is investigated because he lives in a whites-only racial area (the incident based on Rive's own situation); "Incident in Thailand," which depicts his encounter with a grieving woman in the East, and then reflects on his own situation in South Africa; and, of course, "Mrs. Janet September," who tells her story to "Dr. Richard Rive." Rive's theme might largely be the oppression of "coloureds," and he did grow up in District Six, but he appears as something of an outsider in some of his stories, having left the area, becoming "grossly over educated" (as he regarded himself), and adopting rather sonorous tones in conversation, quite alien to those he left behind, as we see in the short story "Riva" with the "highly educated coloured" student.

Although he was opposed to "colouredism," considered himself as speaking for all the oppressed (as he states in his autobiography) and objected to himself being labelled a "coloured" (as apart from black) writer or academic, a stressing of racial differences comes out strongly in his stories. His characters are aware, often grossly conscious, of them because of their suffering, as with the "coloured" woman in an early story, "The Return," who expostulates, "I never trust a Kaffir or a White man"; and the bereft woman in "Resurrection" who remembers her mother as "old and ugly and black" as she also seems to be, whereas her siblings have all tried for white and rejected their original environment, heritage, and family as embarrassing. Rive's characters often reveal racial bigotry and a consciousness of their fitting into the "coloured" classification, as if found in "Street Corner," where several youths object to "Tom's brother" wanting to join their club because he is too dark and looks like "a bloody nigger": "Our constitution debars Africans and Moslems from our Club." Through the garrulous Mrs. Janet September, Rive mocks current terminology: objecting himself to the term "coloured" as denigrating, he uses her to poke fun at the fashionable nomenclature "so-called coloureds" by having her refer to the group as "so-calleds."

Whatever term is used, they remain almost the sole focus of Rive's writing, people whose lives he depicts as they struggle under an oppressive regime, in a bigoted environment and in which the prevailing emotion is one of anguish.

—Stephen M. Finn

ROBERTS, (Sir) Charles G(eorge) D(ouglas). Canadian. Born in Douglas, New Brunswick, 10 January 1860. Educated at the Collegiate School, Fredericton, New Brunswick, 1874–76; University of New Brunswick, Fredericton (Douglas medal in Latin and Greek; Alumni gold medal for Latin essay), 1876–81, B.A. (honours) in mental and moral science and political economy 1879, M.A. 1881. Served in the British Army, 1914–15; captain: transferred to the Canadian Army, 1916: major; subsequently worked with Lord Beaverbrook in the Canadian War Records Office, London. Married 1) Mary Isabel Fenety in 1880 (died 1930), three sons and one daughter; 2) Joan Montgomery in 1943. Headmaster, Chatham Grammar School, New Brunswick, 1879-81, and York Street School, Fredericton, 1881–83; editor, the *Week,* Toronto, 1883–84; professor of English and French, 1885–88, and professor of English and economics, 1888–95, King's College, Windsor, Nova Scotia; lived in New York, 1897–1907; associate editor, *Illustrated American*, New York, 1897–98; co-editor, Nineteenth Century series, 1900–05; lived Europe, 1908–10, England, 1911–25, and Toronto, 1925–43. Recipient: Lorne Pierce medal, 1926. LL.D.: University of New Brunswick, 1906. Fellow, 1890, and president of Section 2, 1933, Royal Society of Canada; fellow, Royal Society of Literature, 1892; member, American Academy, 1898. Knighted, 1935. *Died 26 November 1943.*

PUBLICATIONS

Collections

Selected Poems, edited by Desmond Pacey.   1956.
Selected Poetry and Critical Prose, edited by W.J. Keith.   1974.
Collected Poems, edited by Desmond Pacey and Graham Adams.   1985.
The Vagrants of the Barren and Other Stories, edited by Martin Ware.   1992.

Short Stories

The Raid from Beauséjour, and How the Carter Boys Lifted the Mortgage: Two Stories of Acadie.   1894; *The Raid from Beauséjour* published as *The Young Acadian,* 1907.
Earth's Enigmas: A Book of Animal and Nature Life.   1896; revised edition, 1903.
Around the Campfire.   1896.
By the Marshes of Minas.   1900.
The Kindred of the Wild: A Book of Animal Life.   1902.
The Watchers of the Trails: A Book of Animal Life.   1904.
The Haunters of the Silences: A Book of Animal Life.   1907.
In the Deep of the Snow.   1907.
The House in the Water: A Book of Animal Life.   1908.
The Red Oxen of Bonval.   1908.
The Backwoodsmen.   1909.
Kings in Exile.   1909.
Neighbours Unknown.   1910.
More Kindred of the Wild.   1911.
The Feet of the Furtive.   1912.
Babes of the Wild.   1912; as *Children of the Wild,* 1913.
Cock Crow.   1913; in *The Secret Trails,* 1916.
Hoof and Claw.   1913.
The Secret Trails.   1916.
The Ledge on Bald Face.   1918; as *Jim: The Story of a Backwoods Police Dog,* 1919.
Some Animal Stories.   1921.
More Animal Stories.   1922.
Wisdom of the Wilderness.   1922.
They Who Walk in the Wild.   1924; as *They That Walk in the Wild,* 1924.
Eyes of the Wilderness.   1933.
Further Animal Stories.   1935.
Thirteen Bears, edited by Ethel Hume Bennett.   1947.
Forest Folk, edited by Ethel Hume Bennett.   1949.
The Last Barrier and Other Stories.   1958.
King of Beasts and Other Stories, edited by Joseph Gold.   1967.
Eyes of the Wilderness and Other Stories: A New Collection.   1980.
The Lure of the Wild: The Last Three Animal Stories, edited by John C. Adams.   1980.

Novels

Reube Dare's Shad Boat: A Tale of the Tide Country.   1895; as *The Cruise of the Yacht Dido,* 1906.
The Forge in the Forest, Being the Narrative of the Acadian Ranger, Jean de Mer.   1896.
A Sister to Evangeline, Being the Story of Yvonne de Lamourie.   1898; as *Lovers in Acadie,* 1924.
The Heart of the Ancient Wood.   1900.
Barbara Ladd.   1902.
The Prisoner of Mademoiselle: A Love Story.   1904.
Red Fox: The Story of His Adventurous Career.   1905.
The Heart That Knows.   1906.
A Balkan Prince.   1913.
In the Morning of Time.   1919.

Verse

Orion and Other Poems.   1880.
Later Poems.   1881.
Later Poems.   1882.
In Divers Tones.   1886.
Autotochthon.   1889.
Ave: An Ode for the Centenary of the Birth of Percy Bysshe Shelley, 4th August, 1792.   1892.
Songs of the Common Day, and Ave: An Ode for the Shelley Centenary.   1893.
The Book of the Native.   1896.
New York Nocturnes and Other Poems.   1898.
Poems.   1901.
The Book of the Rose.   1903.
Poems.   1907.
New Poems.   1919.
The Sweet o' the Year and Other Poems.   1925.
The Vagrant of Time.   1927; revised edition, 1927.
Be Quiet Wind; Unsaid.   1929.
The Iceberg and Other Poems.   1934.
Selected Poems.   1936.
Twilight over Shaugamauk and Three Other Poems.   1937.
Canada Speaks of Britain and Other Poems of the War.   1941.

Other

The Canadian Guide-Book: The Tourist's and Sportsman's Guide to Eastern Canada and Newfoundland.   1891.
The Land of Evangeline and the Gateways Thither. . . for Sportsman and Tourist.   1894.
A History of Canada for High Schools and Academies.   1897.
Discoveries and Explorations in the Century.   1903.
Canada in Flanders, vol. 3.   1918.

Editor, *Poems of Wild Life.*   1888.
Editor, *Northland Lyrics,* by William Carmen Roberts, Theodore Roberts, and Elizabeth Roberts Macdonald.   1899.
Editor, *Shelley's Adonais and Alastor.*   1902.
Editor, with Arthur L. Tunnell, *A Standard Dictionary of Canadian Biography: The Canadian Who Was Who.*   2 vols., 1934–38.
Editor, with Arthur L. Tunnell, *The Canadian Who's Who,* vols. 2 and 3.   1936–39.
Editor, *Flying Colours: An Anthology.*   1942.

Translator, *The Canadians of Old,* by Philippe Aubert de Gaspé.   1890; as *Cameron of Lochiel,* 1905.

*

Critical Studies: *Roberts: A Biography* by Elsie M. Pomeroy, 1943; *Roberts* by W.J. Keith, 1969; *The Proceedings of the Roberts Symposium,* edited by Carrie Macmillan, 1984; *The Roberts Symposm* edited by Glenn Clever, 1984; *Sir Charles God Damn: The Life of Roberts* by John C. Adams, 1986.

* * *

Though his writings include translation and history, Charles G.D. Roberts is best known as an author of poetry and fiction. *Orion*, the first book of poetry published by a member of the Confederation generation, became a Canadian literary landmark, and such later poems as "Tantramar Revisited" are still recognized as minor classics. However, it is his invention, along with fellow Canadian Ernest Thompson Seton, of the realistic animal story that is his most significant contribution to world literature.

When he resigned his professorship at King's College in 1895 to pursue a full-time writing career, and then decided to leave his family in Fredericton and tackle the New York literary milieu in 1897, Roberts hoped that writing fiction would subsidize his poetry and his family. He put most of his effort into historical fiction, which was then in vogue, but the results were conventional costume romances, in no way memorable. He also published a few stories involving animals, but editors didn't feel comfortable with them (one editor described his first animal story, "Do Seek Their Meat From God" [1892] as "neither fish, flesh, fowl nor good red herring"), so Roberts discontinued them for a time. Then, in 1898, Seton—inspired in part by reading Roberts's animal stories—published *Wild Animals I Have Known*. It became a best seller, opening up the market, and Roberts found his niche.

What differentiates the over 200 animal stories of Roberts from previous ones—e.g., the anthropomorphism (human speech, reasoning, emotional patterns, psychological processes, and societal structures) of Sewell's *Black Beauty* and Kipling's *The Jungle Books*—is the emphasis on nature science and close observation. The conclusions to which scientific observation led were that instinct and coincidence alone could not explain animal behaviour: instead, "within their varying limitations, animals can and do reason," and there are such things as animal "personality" and "animal psychology." Accordingly, Roberts wrote in *The Kindred of the Wild*, "The animal story at its highest point of development is a psychological romance constructed on a framework of natural science." In other words, the author's task, through focussing on one or more animal characters, is to depict and highlight the powerful dramatic reality of everyday animal life and adventure: the competition for necessities (food, shelter, mates); the struggle for survival against predators, enemies, or harsh conditions; and the protection of offspring.

The potential for dramatic conflict in the stories is augmented by certain aspects of Darwinian theory. First, the struggle for survival among individuals and species pervades all nature, from a vast landscape to a single plant ("The Prisoners of the Pitcher-Plant"). Second, human beings, as, in theory, evolved animals, rank as extremely effective predators and share some bestial characteristics: hence a shipwrecked man who, naked, reaches the shore of the Sumatran jungle, proves himself "a more efficient animal than the best of them" by killing the tiger that hunts him ("King of Beasts"). Third, and almost paradoxically, there is a kinship of all creatures (hence the title, *The*

Kindred of the Wild), and this may have ethical implications and cause inner conflict for human beings: thus Jabe Smith decides to raise the infant cub of the bear he was forced to kill ("The Bear That Thought He Was a Dog"), and Pete Noel makes a financial sacrifice by refraining from killing more than one caribou of the herd that has saved him ("The Vagrants of the Barren"). Thus, too, the "Boy," a character in some stories who is based on Roberts as a child, "thrashed other boys for torturing . . . superfluous kittens" and regrets snaring rabbits ("The Moonlight Trails"); later, as a youth, he prefers to "name all the birds without a gun," to "know the wild folk living, not dead," though this does not deter him when marauding lynxes kill farm animals: "his primeval hunting instincts were now aroused, and he was no longer merely the tender-hearted and sympathetic observer" ("The Haunter of the Pine Gloom").

Roberts's stories usually follow one of three patterns. In the full-life animal biographies, such as "Queen Bomba of the Honey-Pots" (the biography of a bumblebee) or "The Last Barrier" (the life story of an Atlantic salmon), the stories begin with the protagonist's parentage and birth, and trace her or his growth and development—with all its challenges and perils—from infancy through adulthood. They then describe the creature's fulfilment of its basic purpose in life—mating and propagation of the species—and, where appropriate, deal with the raising of the young. This done, the stories conclude, as all biographies must, with the death of the protagonist after a relatively long and successful life.

A different pattern is found in the stories focussed on humans in the wild. They often start with a person, usually male, experiencing a crisis ("King of Beasts," "The Vagrants of the Barren") or perturbing situation ("The Haunter of the Pine Gloom"), and then show him or her confronting and overcoming natural and/or animal opposition. Such stories may include both action and reflection, but they usually cover a relatively short portion of a human lifetime, and they often end in some sort of outward victory and inward growth for the human protagonist.

Most common among Roberts's animal stories, however, are those which present a short but eventful period—less than a full lifetime—in the life of one or more animals (e.g., the much anthologized "When Twilight Falls on the Stump Lots"). Such stories typically open with a panoramic view of the scene, dwelling on its more beautiful, apparently peaceful, features (imagery such as "tender," "lilac," "green," and "seemed anointed to an ecstasy of peace by the chrism of that paradisial color"). The problem is that such appearances are deceiving; seeming is not reality. Instead, there is also an ominous element in the scene (sometimes conveyed by clouds or shadows or the like, but in this story by images of "stumps," "sparse patches," "rough-mossed hillocks," "harsh boulders," "swampy hollows," and "coarse grass"). Nevertheless, in this seemingly pleasant panorama the focus narrows to an animal protagonist (a young cow) and describes its initial activities (nursing its just-born calf). Into this picture comes a hungry predator (a she-bear) whose personality and motives are also described and often equally noble (she has two newborn cubs to feed). Conflict ensues (the cow is hurt, but the bear is mortally wounded by a long horn) and is described in metaphors and similes recalling human battles ("stamped a challenge," "lance points," "knives," "charge," "shield"), thus suggesting an equivalent heroism. Finally, the aftermath of the conflict is given in an unsentimental manner, as the cycle of life proceeds (the bear dies before reaching its den, the cubs are eaten by hungry foxes, the cow survives, and the calf is fattened but then, in a surprise ending, is sent to "the cool marble slabs of a city market"—recalling human's place in the predatory world).

In his animal stories, Roberts portrays the realities of the natural world and the interdependence of species in the continuum of life and death. In this he reveals his life-long love and respect for nature and his fellow creatures.

—John Robert Sorfleet

RODOREDA, Mercè (i Gurgui). Spanish (Catalan language). Born in Barcelona, 10 October 1909. Married her uncle (separated); one son. Journalist, *Mirador, La Rambla, La Publicitat,* and others; editor, *Clarisme* journal, Barcelona; secretary, Institució de les Lletres Catalanes, 1936–39; exiled in France, 1939–54; seamstress and translator, Geneva, Switzerland, from 1954. Recipient: Premi Crexells, for novel, 1937; Victor Català prize, for stories, 1957. *Died 13 April 1983.*

PUBLICATIONS

Short Stories

Aloma (novella).   1938; revised edition, 1969.
Vint-i-dos contes.   1958.
La meva Cristina i altres contes.   1967; as *My Christina and Other Stories,* 1984.
Semblava de seda i altres contes.   1978.
Viatges i flors.   1980.
Two Tales ("The Nursemaid" and "The Salamander"; bilingual edition), illustrated by Antonio Frasconi. 1983.

Novels

Sóc una dona honrada?   1932.
Del que hom no pot fugir.   1934.
Un dia en la vida d'un home.   1934.
Crim.   1936.
La plaça del Diamant.   1962; as *The Pigeon Girl,* 1967; as *The Time of Doves,* 1980.
El carrer de les Camèlies.   1966.
Jardí vora el mar.   1967.
Mirall trencat.   1974.
Obras completas, edited by Carme Arnau.   3 vols., 1976–84.
Quanta, quanta guerra.   1980.
La mort i la primavera.   1986.

Other

Cartas a l'Anna Muria.   1985.

*

Bibliography: in *Women Writers of Contemporary Spain,* edited by Joan L. Brown, 1991.

Critical Studies: "The Angle of Vision in the Novels of Rodoreda" by Mercé Clarascó, in *Bulletin of Hispanic*

Studies 57, 1980; "A Woman's Voice" by Frances Wyers, in *Kentucky Romance Quarterly* 30, 1983; "Exile, Gender, and Rodoreda" by Geraldine Cleary Nichols, in *Modern Language Notes* 101, 1986; "Rodoreda's Subtle Greatness" by Randolph D. Pope, in *Women Writers of Contemporary Spain,* edited by Joan L. Brown, 1991.

*   *   *

Mercè Rodoreda, a native of Barcelona, became known in the 1930's as a member of the Catalan vanguard. Exiled following the Spanish Civil War (1936-39) to France and then Geneva, she continued to write in Catalan although it was outlawed under Franco. She has been recognized as one of the greatest Catalan writers, and the American translator of several of her works has deemed her the most important Mediterranean woman writer since Sappho. Rodoreda concentrated almost exclusively upon fiction, and profound feminist insights imbue her stories, which range from the lyric and fantastic to realistic and grotesque.

Aloma, written in 1937, is a realistic novelette set in prewar Barcelona which recreates the traumatic "rites of passage" of the gentle, quiet protagonist, seduced and abandoned, pregnant, in an exploitative, deceptive "man's world." Disillusionment in love is an experience common to the majority of Rodoreda's heroines, and Aloma's solitude is shared by numerous Rodoreda characters of both genders. Like Rodoreda's major long novels *La Plaça del diamant (The Time of Doves*—an exceptional translation) and *El carrer de les Camèlies* (Street of Camellias), this deceptively simple recreation of daily life, viewed from the perspective of a working-class woman, subtly foregrounds men's use of women as sex objects and the plight of women who have no viable alternatives to becoming accomplices to their own exploitation.

La meva Cristina i altres contes (My Christina and Other Stories), is Rodoreda's most significant, original, and gripping collection, with large doses of fantasy and lyricism found only in rare cases in other story collections, *Vint-i-dos contes* (Twenty-Two Tales) and *Semblava de seda i altres contes* (It Seemed Like Silk and Other Stories). *My Christina* has considerable thematic variety while most stories collected in *Vint-i-dos contes* present male-female relationships, where women often have the same problematic relationship with the world and the opposite sex as Aloma. A major difference is that the world portrayed is that of postwar Spain, and social concerns are more prominent. Notwithstanding thematic unity, narrative technique is deliberately varied; tone is markedly reflective. Rodoreda is too much of an artist to write "thesis" stories, and her characters' plight, while dramatic, is never melodramatic. Stories depict a married couple, distanced by jealousy, a frustrated girl who fantasizes about killing the sickly cousin she once hoped to marry, domestic entrapment of both marriage partners because of the wife's illness, the problem of aging, a wife's planning suicide after learning of her husband's infidelity, and the decision of an impoverished young mother (whose child was born of rape) to drown the infant and then herself. The failure of marriage appears in half a dozen stories while eight treat the beginning of male-female relationships in terms foreshadowing the ultimate impossibility of happiness. Despite the predominance of female characters, Rodoreda also portrays men, usually atypical, lonely, suffering souls. In this collection and *Semblava de seda,* a few tales paint the plight of exiles, Spanish political refugees who fled on foot to France at the end of the war. Among the ten stories in the latter collection is one recreating the hallucinatory, pained, surrealistic delirium of a wounded young soldier, and another grim, sordid memoir of a concentration camp inmate who shared his bunk with a corpse for days to double his ration of soup. One tale, with the air of a personal memoir, evokes an exiled woman writer's visit to a doctor in Geneva. The title narrative (whose English version, "It Seemed Like Silk," is added to the stories translated in *My Christina*) presents the perspective of a woman who adopts a tomb in a foreign cemetery because "her" deceased is too far away to visit.

Loneliness, alienation, or estrangement are obsessive motifs in essentially all of Rodoreda's work. Nowhere are they clearer than in the 17 stories of *My Christina*. The title novelette, presented last, is an allegory of masculine exploitation of the feminine, not in a sexual or erotic context, but of woman's nurturance and care. Set outside real or historical time, this beautiful, powerfully symbolic tale presents the feminine principle (Christina) as sacrificial or expiatory, incapable of self-defense, much less retaliation. A whale swallows a shipwrecked sailor (thereby saving him) and he names the whale Christina; he becomes increasingly parasitic, tearing away at her innards like a malignant tumor until, mortally weakened, she disgorges him onshore. Covered with pearl-like secretions, totally unaccustomed to fending for himself, he cannot cope in the outside world and belatedly laments his treatment of his benefactor. Other, briefer tales in this collection capture irrational dream states or nightmarish delusions, while a few, more realistic and matter-of-fact, depict the dreary, sordid world of the shantytown child or the pedestrian, trivial concerns of the live-in nursemaid. Solitary, extremely timid characters appear in three stories, with their reticence in each case preventing their establishing relationships that might alleviate their anguished loneliness. All social levels and ages appear, and narrative perspective varies from that of the small child to adolescent servant to titled aristocrat, and from an educated, intelligent viewpoint to perceptions of the mentally or emotionally disturbed. A linguistic tour-de-force, the collection displays Rodoreda's mastery of numerous and widely varied registers of discourse, including the adolescent servant who baby-talks to her young charge ("The Nursemaid") and the mentally retarded maidservant ("Therafina") who innocently lisps her history of exploitation and abuse. "A Flock of Lambs in All Colors" symbolically recreates the generation gap, the significance of illusion in a developing life distanced by parental authoritarianism. In "The Gentleman and the Moon," whose viewpoint is fantastic, a lonely senior citizen finds a way to climb the moonbeams, transcending his solitude. Marginal mentalities abound, including the psychotic family heir in "The Dolls' Room" who relates only to his doll collection, and the amateur fisherman in "The River and the Boat," a "fish out of water" among humankind who is metamorphosed into a fish. All but two tales employ first-person narration, or a variant such as the epistle ("A Letter," "The Dolls' Room") or one-sided dialogue ("The Nursemaid," "Love," "Therafina," "Memory of Caus"). These techniques allow Rodoreda to retain maximum objectivity without excluding irony and simultaneously increase impact through their directness.

—Janet Pérez

See the essay on "The Salamander."

ROSA, João Guimarães.   See **GUIMARÃES ROSA, João.**

ROSS, Martin.   See **SOMERVILLE and ROSS.**

ROSS, (James) Sinclair. Canadian. Born in Shellbrook, Saskatchewan, 22 January 1908. Graduated from high school, 1924. Served in the Canadian Army, 1942–46. Staff member, Union Bank (now Royal Bank) of Canada, in Abbey, 1924–27, Lancer, 1928, and Arcala, 1929–32, all Saskatchewan, and in Winnipeg, 1933–42, and Montreal, 1946–68; lived in Athens, 1968–71, Barcelona, 1971–73, Málaga, Spain, 1973–80, Montreal, 1980–81, and Vancouver from 1981.

PUBLICATIONS

Short Stories

The Lamp at Noon and Other Stories.   1968.
The Race and Other Stories, edited by Lorraine McMullen. 1982.

Novels

As for Me and My House.   1941.
The Well.   1958.
Whir of Gold.   1970.
Sawbones Memorial.   1974.

*

Bibliography: by David Latham, in *The Annotated Bibliography of Canada's Major Authors 3* edited by Robert Lecker and Jack David, 1981.

Critical Studies: *Ross and Ernest Buckler* by Robert D. Chambers, 1975; *Ross* by Lorraine McMullen, 1979; *Ross: A Reader's Guide* by Ken Mitchell, 1981.

* * *

Fiction has long been considered the strongest of all genres in the writing of the three prairie provinces of Canada, though in recent years a strong current of poetry writing has also appeared in that area. Both fiction and verse tend to concentrate on the brief but dramatic evolution of what we think of as an agrarian prairie society which, with the big immigrant settlements in the 1890's and 1900's, superseded the earlier nomadic and hunting culture—the bison culture—of the Plains Indians and the Métis. With the bison extinct and the hunters humbled after the defeat of the Riel-Dumont rebellion of 1885, the drama shifted to the farmer—often a transplanted North or East European peasant—fighting to conquer the inhospitable land with plough and harrow. Many of the earlier prairie novels—those of Frederick Philip Grove (Greve) and Maria Ostenso for example—were primarily concerned with this struggle, but by the early years of the 20th century a New West had emerged, characterized by the broad fields of its wheat monoculture and by the villages and small towns clustered around the cubistic towers of its railwayside grain elevators.

This was Sinclair Ross's world, into which he was born and in which he grew up as a smalltown bank clerk. His first writing, emanating from his experience with farmers and tradespeople trying to survive in the Depression, took the form of the short story. His talent was evident from the start. His first published story, "No Other Way," won third prize in 1934 in an English competition judged by Somerset Maugham and Rebecca West. It later appeared in *Nash's Magazine*, an English popular monthly, and through the rest of the 1930's Ross published stories occasionally, sometimes in popular magazines, but most often in *Queen's Quarterly*, of Queen's University in Kingston, Ontario, whose editors early recognized his importance. Stories like "Cornet at Night," "The Lamp at Noon," and "One's a Heifer" documented with sharp insight the way of life or survival of farming families in those troubled years of the 1930's when the apparent assurance of a precariously established agricultural order gave way under the impact of the Depression. What Ross was constantly illustrating in his stories was the hardness of homesteaders' lives even without the special and crushing burdens of dustbowl drought and unstable world grain markets, controlled by merchants and financiers far away. His men usually see no alternative to the dreadful physical struggle against the land, the climate, international economic conditions. The women at least have more time to be lonely and dream of something different and better, and Ross's great theme of inner solitude is established through a tough unsentimental vision and in a taut, undecorated prose.

Ross's first novel, *As for Me and My House*, did not create a sensation when it appeared in 1941, partly because it moved outside wartime preoccupations. It was a novel written with beautiful spareness, but perhaps its lack of a broad appeal was also due to the fact that what it told was too near to the recent past of Depression experience, and the community of "Horizon" which Ross imagined was too reminiscent of the places which so many of its potential readers were hoping some time to escape. Only as the "Horizons" of reality began to pass into history did it gain a popular readership. But it quickly won its place as a classic of Canadian fiction and Ross, as Margaret Laurence among other remembered so warmly—became an example for younger novelists, though none of his later longer works equalled *As for Me and My House*.

Ross continued to write stories and occasionally publish them, though in recent years illness has reduced his energy and his production as he has retreated to a largely reclusive life, first in Spain and now in Vancouver. But, curiously, he never seemed strongly moved to publish a collection, even when publishers began once again to show interest in the short story during the 1960's. It was his fellow writer and admirer, Margaret Laurence, who persuaded Ross to put together a collection and then persuaded Jack McClelland to publish the result—*The Lamp at Noon and Other Stories*—in his New Canadian Library in 1968. When Ross's second collection of stories, and doubtless his last, appeared as *The Race and Other Stories* in 1982, it was

again through the initiative of a fellow writer, the critic Lorraine MacMullen, who edited them and arranged their publication through the press of her university, the University of Ottawa.

This kind of hesitation reflects a quietness and a modesty that seem to run through Ross's personal manner, for he is the most modest of men to meet, to his writing. His prose evades the devices of eloquence; it is simple, penetrating, the perfect vehicle for his lucid perceptions of human beings, their lacks and their struggles to overcome them, often in some way through art, where he can be marvellously at one with his characters.

—George Woodcock

See the essay on "The Lamp at Noon."

ROTH, Philip (Milton). American. Born in Newark, New Jersey, 19 March 1933. Educated at Weequahic High School, New Jersey; Newark College, Rutgers University, 1950–51; Bucknell University, Lewisburg, Pennsylvania, 1951–54; A.B. 1954 (Phi Beta Kappa); University of Chicago, 1954–55, M.A. 1955. Served in the United States Army, 1955–56. Married 1) Margaret Martinson in 1959 (separated 1962; died 1968); 2) the actress Claire Bloom in 1990. Instructor in English, University of Chicago, 1956–58; visiting writer, University of Iowa, Iowa City, 1960–62; writer-in-residence, Princeton University, New Jersey, 1962–64; visiting writer, State University of New York, Stony Brook, 1966, 1967, and University of Pennsylvania, Philadelphia, 1967–80. Since 1988 Distinguished Professor, Hunter College, New York. General editor, Writers from the Other Europe series, Penguin, publishers, London, 1975–80. Member of the Corporation of Yaddo, Saratoga Springs, New York. Recipient: Houghton Mifflin literary fellowship, 1959; Guggenheim fellowship, 1959; National Book award, 1960; Daroff award, 1960; American Academy grant, 1960; O Henry award, 1960; Ford Foundation grant, for drama, 1965; Rockefeller fellowship, 1966; National Book Critics Circle award, 1988; National Jewish Book award, 1988. Honorary degrees: Bucknell University, 1979; Bard College, Annandale-on-Hudson, New York, 1985; Rutgers University, New Brunswick, New Jersey, 1987; Columbia University, New York, 1987. Member, American Academy, 1970.

PUBLICATIONS

Short Stories

Goodbye, Columbus, and Five Short Stories.   1959.
Penguin Modern Stories 3, with others.   1969.
Novotny's Pain.   1980.

Novels

Letting Go.   1962.
When She Was Good.   1967.
Portnoy's Complaint.   1969.
Our Gang (Starring Tricky and His Friends).   1971.
The Breast.   1972; revised edition in *A Roth Reader*, 1980.

The Great American Novel.   1973.
My Life as a Man.   1974.
The Professor of Desire.   1977.
Zuckerman Bound (includes *The Prague Orgy*).   1985.
The Ghost Writer.   1979.
Zuckerman Unbound.   1981.
The Anatomy Lesson.   1983.
The Prague Orgy.   1985.
The Counterlife.   1987.
Deception.   1990.
Operation Shylock: A Confession.   1993.

Play

Television Play: *The Ghost Writer,* with Tristram Powell, from the novel by Roth, 1983.

Other

Reading Myself and Others.   1975; revised edition, 1985.
A Roth Reader.   1980.
The Facts: A Novelist's Autobiography.   1988.
Patrimony: A True Story.   1991.
Conversations with Roth, edited by George J. Searles. 1992.

*

Bibliography: *Roth: A Bibliography* by Bernard F. Rodgers, Jr., 1974; revised edition, 1984.

Critical Studies: *Bernard Malamud and Roth: A Critical Essay* by Glenn Meeter, 1968; "The Journey of Roth" by Theodore Solotaroff, in *The Red Hot Vacuum,* 1970; *The Fiction of Roth* by John N. McDaniel, 1974; *The Comedy That "Hoits": An Essay on the Fiction of Roth* by Sanford Pinsker, 1975, and *Critical Essays on Roth* edited by Pinsker, 1982; *Roth* by Bernard F. Rodgers, Jr., 1978; "Jewish Writers" by Mark Shechner, in *The Harvard Guide to Contemporary American Writing* edited by Daniel Hoffman, 1979; introduction by Martin Green to *A Roth Reader,* 1980; *Roth* by Judith Paterson Jones and Guinevera A. Nance, 1981; *Roth* by Hermione Lee, 1982; *Reading Roth* edited by A.Z. Milbauer and D.G. Watson, 1988; *Understanding Roth* by Murray Baumgarten and Barbara Gottfried, 1990.

* * *

Although Philip Roth is best known as a novelist, his early short stories earned him wide public attention and a reputation for controversy that has continued to dog his heels. If a writer like Bernard Malamud justified his aesthetic by insisting that "All men are Jews," Roth took a gleeful delight in proving the converse—namely, that all Jews were men. Indeed, he went about the business of being a satirist of the Jewish American suburbs as if he were on a mission from an angry Old Testament prophet. He enjoyed holding conventional Jewish American feet to the fire.

"Goodbye, Columbus" is, of course, the classic instance of social realism with an angry, satiric twist, but it is hardly the only case. Ozzie Freedman, the religious school rebel of "The Conversion of the Jews," seems at once a younger brother of Neil Klugman (the angry young Jewish man of "Goodbye, Columbus") and a foreshadowing of Alexander

Portnoys to come. He is pitted against Rabbi Binder, a man bedeviled by Ozzie Freedman's embarrassing questions. Their names are, of course, meant to be symbolic, especially if one reads the story as a shorthand for Ozzie's wish-fulfilling dream of becoming a "freed man," no longer bound by his rabbi's parochialism.

The literal level of the story gradually fades into the background at the traumatic moment during "free-discussion time" when Ozzie again presses his point about why God "couldn't let a woman have a baby without having intercourse." After all, Ozzie argues, can't God do anything? At this point, Rabbi Binder's loses patience and Ozzie raises the psychic stakes by screaming "You don't know anything about God!" When Rabbi Binder responds with an uncharacteristic, but very authoritarian slap, Ozzie bolts from the synagogue's classroom to its roof, where his declarations take on the character of a rebellious id pitted against constraining superegoes. Considered mythically, Ozzie emerges as an ironic Joseph, one whose dreams are filled with authority figures bowing before his will. Indeed, all the standard representatives of societal force are there—preacher, teacher, fireman, cop—and Ozzie, for the moment at least, reigns supreme: "'Everybody kneel.' There was the sound of everybody kneeling. . . . Next Ozzie made everybody say it [that God can make a baby without intercourse]. And then he made them all say that they believed in Jesus Christ—first one at a time, then all together."

The story's title comes from a line in Andrew Marvell's "To His Coy Mistress" ("And you should if you please, refuse/'Till the conversion of the Jews"). Thus, Roth's vision combines a fantasized Day of Judgment with a symbolic death wish as Ozzie plunges into the very fabric of his dream—"right into the center of the yellow net that glowed in the evening's edge like an overgrown halo." No matter that "The Conversion of the Jews" was tightly structured, or even highly poetic—many rabbis were not amused. Nor were Jewish-American veterans pleased with "Defender of the Faith" a story, set in an army training camp, that includes a cast of unpleasant (goldbricking) Jewish stereotypes. But it also includes—and this may be the more important point—a protagonist (Sergeant Marx) who comes to terms with the vulnerability of his nearly forgotten Jewishness and its potential to turn him into an exploited "victim."

Indeed, the crux of "Defender of the Faith" revolves around the central question posed in nearly all of Roth's short stories—namely, what are other Jews to me or me to them that they should expect, even demand, preferential treatment? "Eli, the Fanatic" complicates the matter further by forcing its protagonist to choose between his assimilated Jewish neighbors and members of an Ultra-Orthodox yeshivah. As one of the former puts it, "Tell this Tzuref where we stand, Eli. This is a modern community." As a lawyer familiar with zoning restrictions and the like, Peck is the logical choice to be Woodenton's "defender of the [assimilated] faith." But Tzuref, the yeshivah's principal, turns out to have arguments of his own. "The law is the law . . . and then of course the law is not the law. When is the law that is the law not the law?" The result is not only a movement from sympathy to symbolic identification but also a desperate leap into mental breakdown that might, or might not, represent clear moral vision. As Eli exchanges his Ivy League suiting with the hasid's traditional black garb, he becomes the "fanatic" of Roth's title—a ripe candidate for the tranquilizers that the assimilated, in fact, administer and the hasidic sainthood he may, or may not, merit.

The stories collected in *Goodbye, Columbus* pit the Jews of stereotype against the more human ones. Some, like "Epstein," the story of a sad, middle-aged Jewish adulterer, score their satiric points at the expense of rounded characterization and suggest that, at the age of 26, its author could be a very young, young man; others, like "You Can't Tell a Man by the Song He Sings," belabor a small point about Joseph McCarthyism as it trickles down to a high school level. But in his best stories ("Goodbye, Columbus," "The Conversion of the Jews" "Eli, the Fanatic," and "On the Air," a wildly inventive romp that prefigures the zany, postmodernist experimentation he would more fully exploit in his novels about Nathan Zuckerman's rise and fall) Roth turns the environs of Newark into the stuff of literature, no small accomplishment.

—Sanford Pinsker

See the essays on "The Conversion of the Jews" and "Goodbye, Columbus."

———

RULFO (Viscaíno), Juan. Mexican. Born in Sayula, Jalisco, 16 May 1918. Educated at an orphanage to age 15, Guadalajara; at the universities of Guadalajara and Mexico City: studied law. Held various odd jobs: university staff member, and clerical worker, Immigration Department, Mexico City; publicity worker, B.F. Goodrich, 1945; worked for rubber company, Veracruz, 1947–54; film and TV script writer; accountant, Mexico City; director of the editorial department, National Institute for Indigenous Studies, Mexico City, from 1962. Adviser, and Fellow, Centro Mexicano de Escritores. Recipient: Asturias prize. *Died 1 January 1986.*

PUBLICATIONS

Short Stories

El llano en llamas.   1953; revised edition, 1970; as *The Burning Plain and Other Stories,* 1967.

Novel

Pedro Páramo.   1955; translated as *Pedro Páramo,* 1959, and 1992.

Other

Autobiografía armada, edited by Reina Roffé.   1973.
Obra completa, edited by Jorge Ruffinelli.   1977.
El gallo de oro y otros textos para cine.   1980.
Para cuando yo me ausente.   1983.
Donde quedo nuestra historia: Hipotesis sobre historia regional.   1986.

Editor, *Antologia personal.*   1978.

*

Critical Studies: in *Into the Mainstream: Conversations with Latin American Writers* by Luis Harss and Barbara Dohmann, 1967; *Paradise and Fall in Rulfo's Pedro Páramo* by George Ronald Freeman, 1970.

*   *   *

Juan Rulfo published *El llano en llamas (The Burning Plain and Other Stories)*, his sole collection of short stories, in 1953. Successive editions have added further stories, numbering 17 in all. The title places his fiction in the harsh, dry plains of Jalisco where Rulfo was born and which condition the lives of the *mestizo* (half-caste) peasants, their poverty, and the violence surrounding them. All the stories are linked by this environment, by the inarticulacy of the ignorant people, by their isolation from mainstream, post-Revolutionary Mexican life. For a peasant, place is more meaningful than history or culture.

His primitive characters live through impulse and instinct rather than reasoning. Rulfo called these illiterate Jalisco peasants "hermetic," with "limited vocabularies," who "hardly talk." Most of Rulfo's stories end in disaster, with outbursts of violence the only form of communication. In this survival world people fend for themselves, unable to feel pity for others. Rulfo claimed that "life matters little" to these people who show no sense of society, tenderness, or love.

This view of his protagonists is reinforced by the techniques used, beginning with a dependence on solitary voices, often a first-person narrator, or a monologue. There is little description, and no attempt at psychological understanding or exploration of motivation. Rulfo tends to work with images, vivid physical details suggestive of the economy and suggestive power of a poem. He offers minimal information, forcing the reader to enter the peasants' opaque mentality. The absence of authorial intervention makes it hard to assess Rulfo's own attitudes towards his protagonists. His short stories work effectively because he links an intense dramatic urgency, a poetic concision, and sparks of black humour.

The opening story "Macario" (first published in 1945) sets the tone by throwing a reader abruptly, without explanation, into the mind of the village idiot, Macario, who tells his own tale. We sense his hunger, his inability to recall; he bangs his head, and hunts frogs to eat. He depends on Felipa, and feeds on her breast milk. His age, his relationship with Felipa, who he really is, we never know.

The second story of the collection, "They Gave Us Land," is narrated by a peasant in a group walking to claim their plot of land in the wake of the 1917 Revolutionary constitution's promised but never realized land reform. In this ironic story, the land given was just a patch of dust. Rulfo emphasises the aridity, the lack of rain, the heat. The plains are compared to dried cow hide, to a hot stone for cooking tortillas, to a crust. The story is based on negatives. The absence of rain, symbol of fertility (and hope) becomes the protagonist of the story, when a black cloud passes over and one drop falls to the ground: "making a hole in the ground and leaving a paste rather like a gob of spit." This is no meteorological description, but a damnation, the flames of hell implicit in the title of the collection. When the peasants complain to an official he tells them to write it down, not to attack the government, but the old land owners. The first-person narrator does not complain, just accepts his fate.

The title story, "The Burning Plain" (first published in 1950), situates the reader directly in the Cristero revolution where priests and enraged Catholics took up arms against the official atheist post-Revolutionary government in the late 1920's, a reactionary war that cost Rulfo's father and an uncle their lives. From the opening sentence we see this revolution as horror, in the midst of an unexplained skirmish. Pointless violence links all the episodes together as the characters themselves do not understand why they are fighting: "We all looked at Pedro Zamora asking him with our eyes what was happening to us. It was as if speech had dried out in all of us, as if our tongues had turned into balls." It gives the so-called revolutionaries a sadistic pleasure to watch the maize fields burn. At the end the narrator returns to his woman (whose father he killed) and meets his son. But unlike the symbolic meeting of father than son in Mariano Azuela's classic account of the Revolution, *The Underdogs* (1916), the narrator here confesses his guilt, ending the story with "I lowered my head."

"Tell Them Not to Kill Me!" exemplifies Rulfo's world of hermetically sealed beings. In this story a wretched old man clings on to his life at the expense of everybody and everything else. He confesses, "I didn't want anything. Just to live." Juvencio kills his *compadre* (buddy) Lupe, for when it comes to survival compadre means nothing. The story narrates the break-down of Juvencio's life; his wife leaves, he loses everything and lives in terror on the run. He claims that he had to kill don Lupe, implying some alien force, or fate, that absolved him of responsibility. But we learn that don Lupe was viciously hacked down by a machete, with an ox pike stuck into his belly. The story ends with Juvencio's son chatting with his father's corpse. Instead of the "mercy killing" promised, Juvencio's face was riddled with bullets. In this hallucinatory story, with long monologues, we see how words are used in deceitful ways that typifies Rulfo's peasants from Jalisco.

The world of these outcasts echoes William Faulkner, in technique (monologues in *As I Lay Dying*), and the marginalized geographic area (Yoknapatawpha), as well as Surrealism's dismissal of reason and logic as ways to understand behaviour. Despite these sources Rulfo has created a pessimistic fictional world on the wane, where Luvina, and later Comala (in his only novel *Pedro Páramo*), stand for the ghost towns created by the Revolution, and the drift to Mexico City. Rulfo is both nostalgic about the passing of this world and critical of its reactionary peasants.

—Jason Wilson

See the essays on "Luvina," "Talpa," and "We're Very Poor."

S

SACASTRU, Martín. See **BIOY CASARES, Adolfo.**

SAKI. Pseudonym for Hector Hugh Munro. Scottish. Born in Akyab, Burma, of British parents, 18 December 1870; grew up in Pilton, Devon. Educated at Pencarwick school, Exmouth, Devon; Bedford Grammar School, 1885–87; travelled with his father in Europe, 1887–90; tutored at home, 1891–92. Served as a corporal in the 22nd Royal Fusiliers, 1914–16: killed in action in France, 1916. Military policeman in Burma, 1893–94; returned to Devon, and moved to London, 1896; as Saki wrote political satires for the Westminster Gazette from 1900; foreign correspondent, London Morning Post, in the Balkans, 1902, Warsaw and St. Petersburg, 1904–06, and Paris, 1906–08; freelance sketch writer from 1908; parliamentary columnist, Outlook, 1914. *Died 14 November 1916.*

PUBLICATIONS

Collections

Works. 8 vols., 1926–27.
Short Stories. 1930.
The Novels and Plays. 1933.
The Bodley Head Saki, edited by J.W. Lambert. 1963.
The Complete Works. 1976.
Selected Stories. 1978.
Selected Stories 2, edited by Peter Haining. 1983.

Short Stories and Sketches

Reginald. 1904.
Reginald in Russia and Other Sketches. 1910.
The Chronicles of Clovis. 1912.
Beasts and Super-Beasts. 1914.
The Toys of Peace and Other Papers. 1919.
The Square Egg and Other Sketches, with Three Plays. 1924.

Novels

The Unbearable Bassington. 1912.
When William Came: A Story of London under the Hohenzollerns. 1914.

Plays

The East Wing, in *Lucas' Annual*, 1914.
The Watched Pot, with Cyril Maude (produced 1924). In *The Square Egg*, 1924.
The Death Trap, and *Karl-Ludwig's Window*, in *The Square Egg.* 1924.

The Miracle-Merchant, in *One-Act Plays for Stage and Study 8*, edited by Alice Gerstenberg. 1934.

Other

The Rise of the Russian Empire. 1900.
The Westminster Alice. 1902.

*

Critical Studies: *The Satire of Saki* by G.J. Spears, 1963; "The Performing Lynx" by V.S. Pritchett, in *The Working Novelist*, 1965; *Munro (Saki)* by Charles H. Gillen, 1969; *Saki: A Life of Munro, with Six Stories Never Before Collected* by A.J. Langguth, 1981.

*   *   *

H.H. Munro was born in Burma in 1870, where his father was a senior official in the Burma Police. Young Munro was sent back to England and brought up in Devonshire. He began writing political sketches for the *Westminster Gazette,* and travelled in the Balkans, Russia, and France as a foreign correspondent for the *Morning Post.* Many of his short stories first appeared in the *Westminster Gazette* under the pseudonym "Saki," which he took from the last stanza of Fitzgerald's *Rubáiyát.* In all, Saki published five collections of short stories, and also wrote three novels and several plays.

Saki's two most famous stories are "Srvedni Vashtar" — sometimes regarded as an example of almost the perfect short story — and "Tobermory," both from his collection *The Chronicles of Clovis.* "This gifted Lynx," as V.S. Pritchett called him (in *The Working Novelist*) was part of the sadistic revival in English comic and satirical writing which arose during the final decade of the 19th century and the first decade of the 20th century. He belonged to the world in which Wilde flourished; the world of Hilaire Belloc's *A Bad Child's Book of Beasts* and Harry Graham's *Ruthless Rhymes.*

The stories in the first two collections, *Reginald* and *Reginald in Russia*, positively cascade sardonic aphorisms, some of which were clearly inspired by Wilde. As Pritchett observed, the characters are "done in cyanide," though "the deed is touched by a child's sympathy for the vulnerable areas of the large mammals." Or, as Walter Allen puts it, in Saki's stories, the real world is "ever so slightly rearranged."

The unreal social world of Mrs. Jollett, the Bromly Bomefields, Bassington, the Baroness, and Clovis Sangrail was blown to pieces by the guns in Flanders. It is as impossible to imagine the writings of a postwar Saki as it is the music of an elderly Mozart. The escapades of Saki's characters belong to an age where relationships are both superficial and artificial. Only the verbal wit survives.

"Tobermory" affords the author a brilliant device for unmasking hypocrisy. A guest at Lady Blemly's house party, Mr. Cornelius Appin, has been invited because someone has said he was clever. For 17 years he had been working on thousands of animals trying to get them to speak. At last he had succeeded with the cat Tobermory, who is brought before the company to be tested. To the consternation of all, the cat's answers to patronizing questions strip away the conventional pretenses of its questioners. Major Barfield tries to return the conversation to cat matters, asking Tobermory, "How about your carryings-on with the tortoise-shell puss up at the stables, eh?"

They agree that Tobermory would have to be disposed of, and attempts are made to induce it to eat poisoned food. The cat did, indeed, die, but in a cat-like manner: "From the bites in its throat and the yellow fur which coated his claws it was evident that he had fallen in unequal combat with the big Tom from the Rectory."

Saki's prose is crisp and economical, his debunking of human snobbery and upper class fatuity merciless, his wit sharp and seemingly inexhaustible. His gifts are displayed to their best advantage in his short stories, where what today we would call his "black" humour can be employed in a more deadly precise manner than in the more extended compass of his novels. Within his limitations, the sharp-eyed chronicler of upper-class English society foibles of behaviour in late Victorian and Edwardian times, was undoubtedly a master of the short story, if an amusingly mannered master.

—Maurice Lindsay

See the essays on "The She-Wolf," "Sredni Vashtar," and "The Unrest Cure."

SALINGER, J(erome) D(avid). American. Born in New York City, 1 January 1919. Educated at McBurney School, New York, 1932–34; Valley Forge Military Academy, Pennsylvania (editor, *Crossed Sabres*), 1934–36; New York University, 1937; Ursinus College, Collegetown, Pennsylvania, 1938; Columbia University, New York, 1939. Served in the 4th Infantry Division of the United States Army, 1942–45: Staff Sergeant. Married 1) Sylvia Salinger in 1945 (divorced 1946); 2) Claire Douglas in 1955 (divorced 1967), one daughter and one son. Has lived in New Hampshire since 1953.

PUBLICATIONS

Short Stories

Nine Stories.   1953; as *For Esme-With Love and Squalor and Other Stories,* 1953.
Franny and Zooey.   1961.
Raise High the Roof Beam, Carpenters, and Seymour: An Introduction.   1963.

Novel

The Catcher in the Rye.   1951.

Bibliography: *Salinger: A Thirty Year Bibliography 1938-1968* by Kenneth Starosciak, privately printed, 1971; *Salinger: An Annotated Bibliography 1938-1981* by Jack R. Sublette, 1984.

Critical Studies: *The Fiction of Salinger* by Frederick L. Gwynn and Joseph L. Blotner, 1958; *Salinger: A Critical and Personal Portrait* edited by Henry Anatole Grunwald, 1962; *Salinger and the Critics* edited by William F. Belcher and James W. Lee, Belmont, 1962; *Salinger* by Warren French, 1963, revised edition, 1976, revised edition, as *Salinger Revisited,* 1988; *Studies in Salinger* edited by Marvin Laser and Norman Fruman, 1963; *Salinger* by James E. Miller, Jr., 1965; *Salinger: A Critical Essay* by Kenneth Hamilton, 1967; *Zen in the Art of Salinger* by Gerald Rosen, 1977; *Salinger* by James Lundquist, 1979; *Salinger's Glass Stories as a Composite Novel* by Eberhard Alsen, 1984; *In Search of Salinger* by Ian Hamilton, 1988.

* * *

Although J.D. Salinger has achieved extraordinary fame as the author of *The Catcher in the Rye,* his successes in the short story form, a form he concedes being most comfortable with, have been no less impressive. Salinger's literary apprenticeship began in earnest when he took Whit Burnett's short story writing course at Columbia University in 1939. Between 1940 and 1953, the year *Nine Stories* garnered generally enthusiastic reviews, he published 30 stories in journals as various as *Cosmopolitan, Collier's, Esquire,* and Burnett's own *Story* magazine, outlets where formulaic writing was encouraged. These early efforts, none of which deserve to survive on merit, display a distinct gift for limning psychological depths through quirky mannerisms and acute observations even as they pursue conventional plot denouements, usually focusing on conflicts inherent in marital and other family relations. Two of them—"I'm Crazy" and "Slight Rebellion Off Madison" (his first *New Yorker* story)—offer crude versions of episodes that would surface in *The Catcher in the Rye.*

Reflecting the influence of Lardner, Fitzgerald, and especially Hemingway in their penchant for ironic understatement and haunting consciousness of a universe intent upon crushing frail romantic sensibilities, Salinger's novice fictions also revealed a fierce need to impose moral dimensions, a genuine spiritual hunger for goodness in a cruel world. That pervasive cruelty, frequently incarnated as insensitive louts thoughtlessly wounding sensitive alter egos, seemed confirmed by Salinger's combat experiences, which triggered a mental breakdown. War became a prime eidilon for narrative indictments of reality's implacable, if banal, onslaughts against his estranged protagonist-victims in stories such as "Last Day of the Last Furlough," "A Boy in France," "This Sandwich Has No Mayonnaise," and "The Stranger," which also played variations on the motif of childhood's redemptive innocence, projecting intense concern over a younger sibling as possible casualty and/or savior figure.

Another major theme, which exhibited traits of a very American, almost prepubic distrust of women and sex as well, emerged in "The Inverted Forest" (1947), a long (24,000 words), archly symbolic reification of the eternal battle between art and artist and the opposing thrust of love and marriage. More important, Salinger had located his mature voice and means, a deft fusion of satire, educated conversation, and sparse naturalistic details in search of Joycean epiphanies amid an urbane upper-middle-class scene nearest to his own Manhattan nurture. A year later, he signed an exclusive contract with *The New Yorker* that both signalled his artistic arrival and helped refine his talent for exploring subtle emotional complexities.

All but two of the tales in *Nine Stories* debuted in the *New Yorker*, and this ruthlessly select harvest of recent fictions showcased Salinger at the peak of his considerable powers. Three of the stories—"A Perfect Day for Bananafish," "Uncle Wiggily in Connecticut," and "For Esmé—with Love and Squalor"—have entered the canon, and the book has a significant cumulative impact. James Lundquist and others have outlined the Zen Buddhist dynamic governing *Nine Stories*, which is prefaced by the koan of "one hand clapping," but appear insufficiently aware that the tension and consequent strength of its best stories stem precisely from unresolved struggles between desired Zen transcendence of self and obdurate neuroses.

In the Esmé story, for instance, Salinger's surest masterpiece, the brilliant manipulation of a familiar crisis—devastated soldier finds an escape from his Dostoievskean hell through the kindness of a precocious girl—climaxes in a moment of karma that sidesteps the darker issue of the protagonist's patent narcissistic fixation. Similarly, the suicide of Seymour Glass at the conclusion of "A Perfect Day for Bananafish" savagely contradicts the Zen perspective established by his interaction with the little girl on the beach, the bananafish allegory working equally well with a Freudian reading of his pathological condition and pedophillic excitement.

Salinger's aesthetic judgment deteriorated steadily after the publication of *Nine Stories* as he became obsessed with chronicling the Glass family, fiction and autobiography perilously enmeshed, in several lengthy stories. The pair in *Franny and Zooey* follow Franny Glass to her sad collapse in a restaurant ladies' room, stimulating much critical discussion about a possible pregnancy, only to have her saved from a dangerous depression by "Zooey," her brother Zachary, who phones her from their brother Seymour's room to suggest Jesus Christ can be anyone. The next two installments in the Glass saga comprise *Raise High the Roof Beams, Carpenters, and Seymour: An Introduction*, but the bathic nadir came with the 1965 publication of "Hapworth 16, 1965" in the *New Yorker*, a tedious, self-indulgent letter from Seymour, age seven, at summer camp introduced by his brother Buddy. Essential distance between creator and creation had narrowed to the point of art's near extinction—the story terminates with a list of Seymour's favorite books—and Salinger's subsequent public silence.

—Edward Butscher

See the essay on "A Perfect Day for Bananafish."

———

SANSOM, William. English. Born in London, 18 January 1912. Educated at Uppingham School, Rutland, and in Europe. Served in the National Fire Service in London during World War II. Worked in a bank, as a copywriter for J. Walter Thompson advertising agency, and as a scriptwriter; full-time writer from 1944. Recipient: Society of Authors scholarship, 1946, and bursary, 1947. Fellow, Royal Society of Literature, 1951. *Died 20 April 1976.*

PUBLICATIONS

Short Stories

Fireman Flower and Other Stories.   1944.
Three.   1946.
South: Aspects and Images from Corsica, Italy and Southern France.   1948.
The Equilibriad (story).   1948.
Something Terrible, Something Lovely.   1948.
The Passionate North: Short Stories.   1950.
A Touch of the Sun.   1952.
Lord Love Us.   1954.
A Contest of Ladies.   1956.
Among the Dahlias and Other Stories.   1957.
Selected Short Stories.   1960.
The Stories.   1963.
The Ulcerated Milkman.   1966.
The Vertical Ladder and Other Stories.   1969.
The Marmelade Bird.   1973.

Novels

The Body.   1949.
The Face of Innocence.   1951.
A Bed of Roses.   1954.
The Loving Eye.   1956.
The Cautious Heart.   1958.
The Last Hours of Sandra Lee.   1961; as *The Wild Affair*, 1964.
Goodbye.   1966.
Hans Feet in Love.   1971.
A Young Wife's Tale.   1974.

Other

Jim Braidy: The Story of Britain's Firemen, with James Gordon and Stephen Spender.   1943.
Westminster in War.   1947.
Pleasures Strange and Simple (essays).   1953.
It Was Really Charlie's Castle (for children).   1953.
The Light That Went Out (for children).   1953.
The Icicle and the Sun.   1958.
The Bay of Naples.   1960.
Blue Skies, Brown Studies.   1961.
Away to It All.   1964.
Grand Tour Today.   1968.
Christmas.   1968; as *A Book of Christmas*, 1968.
The Birth of a Story.   1972.
Proust and His World.   1973.
Skimpy (for children).   1974.
Grandville.   1975.

Editor, *Choice: Some New Stories and Prose.*   1946.
Editor, *The Tell-Tale Heart and Other Stories*, by Edgar Allan Poe.   1948.

Translator, Chendru: *The Boy and the Tiger*, by Astrid Bergman.   1960.

*

Critical Study: *Sansom: A Critical Assessment* by Paulette Michel-Michot, 1971.

* * *

Although he is the author of novels, travel books, and a critical biography of Proust, William Sansom owes his reputation to his eleven collections of stories. It was during World War II that, having joined the National Fire Service, he discovered in the monastic solitude of his post at Hampstead the inspiration and the time to write. Being an artist at heart—he was a musician but also liked to paint and to act—Sansom gives pride of place to sensory impressions: all the senses are involved in his stories, sight in particular. Effects of light and shade often determine the atmosphere ("The Ball Room") or are brought to bear on events ("Cloudburst") and on characters' moods ("The Little Fears"). The weather, the light, the time of day, and the atmosphere of a place are in such close relationship that a Sansom story like "Eventide" can be essentially the result of their interaction. Evidence of Sansom's sensory perceptiveness is his demythification of prevailing beliefs concerning climate and colours, landscapes and skies: his Mediterranean settings are not dazzling with colours but rightly white or gray. Flat countries do not give an impression of infinity; on the contrary, the sky in Holland "approaches closer than everywhere else . . . the world appears finite" ("How Claeys Died").

But if Sansom likes to describe well-known, even touristic places, he often chooses much more fanciful settings, like huge vaulted rooms or glass houses, a water junction, a lighthouse, where the light plays tricks upon characters and where normality and oddity intermingle; the precision of sensory impressions contributes to blur their limits. Places that might be considered as "ordinary," devoid of particular characteristics, like a pub or coffee house at the corner of a street, are suddenly endowed with a soul and keep the imprint of a past crowded with people and events. The countryside is credited with intentions, nature is often malevolent and threatening ("A Country Walk"). The sea, particularly, appears as an evil, devastating, and repulsive monster. Countryside and sea are liable to wreak havoc with people's hopes: in "The Little Sailor" the only survivor of a crew of 41 is adrift in his frail boat on the wide blue ocean at Christmas time. On Christmas Eve, he sees palm tufts on the horizon, but the moment he is driven near the shore, the current bears away his now dead body. In many cases, Sansom's characters have done nothing to deserve such a fate, but they suffer from a *difficulté d'être* and from so many fears that we are led to believe they anticipated their destiny. In spite of there being scarcely any religious undertones in Sansom's stories, he seems to imply that some guilt haunts us all and that a punishment lies in wait for us, whatever we do to propitiate fate ("To the Rescue"). In fact the recurrence of certain animals like spiders and octopuses in threatening circumstances, or of impending falls from a height ("The Wall"), mysterious prohibitions ("The Forbidden Lighthouse"), claustrophobic places ("The Little Room"), seems to reflect Sansom's own obsessions. Childhood is considered retrospectively as a blessed moment, free, in general, from terrors of all kinds and graced with the miracle of first impressions, the memory of which will later be tinged with beauty and wistful poetry ("The Windows"). For this reason, the past and all that can evoke it—photos, postcards, engravings—are considered with nostalgic reverence in Sansom's stories.

The flight of time is one of his leitmotif, hence the importance his characters attach to clocks, watches, time-markers of all kinds. In their haste to accomplish their destiny, many Sansom protagonists are egotistic, unlovable characters; his female characters in particular are seldom attractive, even more seldom interesting. We sometimes wonder if Sansom does not revel in ugliness ("A Contest of Ladies"). There are indeed few love stories in his collections, and they do not end well, perhaps because they are not given the time to develop. In other respects, he excels at rendering duration and at creating suspense, by playing on the elasticity of time and the racing intensity of events; for what seems an eternity, he will halt a wall in its fall, protract the death of an old man lying on the floor, delay the consequences of the face-to-face encounter, in zoological gardens, of a man and a lion that has escaped from its cage ("Among the Dahlias"). In the story of this encounter, for example, only a few seconds elapse between the moment the protagonist, Doole, catches sight of the lion in the middle of the path in front of him and the moment he starts crying, which triggers the action. But these few seconds are fraught with a tight succession of various, almost simultaneous impressions the enumeration of which fills nearly four pages.

It is precisely Sansom's clever handling of words which Eudora Welty and Elizabeth Bowen have so much admired, and which himself praised in Edgar Allan Poe: "the description of a minute's fear [inflates] that minute into dreadful hourlong insistence." Such is the compelling power of the circumstances Sansom creates that we accept, breathlessly, the taxing of our patience. This feat, together with his superb handling of words, his exploitation of their musicality, his clever juxtaposition of abstract connotations with concrete evocations—which contributes to his creation of a surrealistic universe—amply compensates for certain flaws in his manner, like his predilection for pointlessly long sentences, far-fetched comparisons, or over-explicit comments.

—Claire Larriere

See the essay on "Fireman Flower."

———

SARGESON, Frank. New Zealander. Born in Hamilton, 23 March 1903. Educated at Hamilton High School; University of New Zealand; admitted as solicitor of the Supreme Court of New Zealand, 1926. Estates clerk, New Zealand Public Trust, Wellington, 1928–29; also journalist. Recipient: Centennial Literary Competition prize, 1940; New Zealand Government literary pension, 1947–68; Hubert Church Prose award, 1951, 1968, 1972; Katherine Mansfield award, 1965; New Zealand scholarship in letters, 1974, and award for achievement, 1978. Litt.D.: University of Auckland, 1974. *Died 1 March 1982.*

PUBLICATIONS

Short Stories

Conversation with My Uncle and Other Sketches.   1936.

A Man and His Wife. 1940.
That Summer and Other Stories. 1946.
I for One . . . (novella). 1954.
Collected Stories 1935–1963, edited by Bill Pearson. 1964; revised edition, as *The Stories 1935–1973,* 1973.
Man of England Now (includes *Game of Hide and Seek* and *I for One . . .*). 1972.

Novels

When the Wind Blows. 1945.
I Saw in My Dream. 1949.
Memoirs of a Peon. 1965.
The Hangover. 1967.
Joy of the Worm. 1969.
Sunset Village. 1976.
En Route, in Tandem, with Edith Campion. 1979.

Plays

A Time for Sowing (produced 1961). In *Wrestling with the Angel,* 1964.
The Cradle and the Egg (produced 1962). In *Wrestling with the Angel,* 1964.
Wrestling with the Angel: Two Plays: A Time for Sowing and The Cradle and the Egg. 1964.

Other

Once Is Enough: A Memoir. 1972.
More Than Enough: A Memoir. 1975.
Never Enough! Places and People Mainly. 1977.
Conversation in a Train and Other Critical Writing, edited by Kevin Cunningham. 1983.

Editor, *Speaking for Ourselves: A Collection of New Zealand Stories.* 1945.

*

Bibliography: in *The Stories 1935–1973,* 1973.

Critical Studies: *The Puritan and the Wolf: A Symposium of Critical Essays on the Work of Sargeson* edited by Helen Shaw, 1955; *Sargeson* by H. Winston Rhodes, 1969; *Sargeson in His Time* by Dennis McEldowney, 1977; *Sargeson* by R.A. Copland, 1977; *Barbed Wire and Mirrors: Essays on New Zealand Prose* by Lawrence Jones, 1987.

*   *   *

Frank Sargeson shares with Katherine Mansfield the place of greatest honour in the history of the short story in 20th-century New Zealand. Though he also wrote four full-length novels, at least seven novellas and short novels, two plays, and three volumes of autobiography, it is with nearly 50 short stories and sketches, which he began publishing in the radical periodical *Tomorrow* in the mid-1930's, that he was to establish and dominate the genre of the naturalistic short story in New Zealand. The formal antecedents from which he took his models were American rather than British, but he was to identify and locate his stories indisputably in his own country, revealing the society and the landscape, both urban and rural, in an economical and subtly ironic prose of great precision.

Most of the stories that Sargeson wrote between 1935 and 1945 are set in a materially and emotionally depressed society, where economic and spiritual limitations unite to confine the characters to such an extent that joy, love, and even speech itself seem stunted. The characters often seem to be only semiarticulate, whether they narrate the stories or simply take part in the action that the authorial voice describes. The stories in which they are involved will tell of their tangible worlds and experiences, but the characters will seldom speak of the emotions that might be detected beneath the narrative surface, perhaps because the articulation of these emotions might force upon them recognitions too painful to be borne.

They are characters who are solitary and vulnerable, usually either men alone, or children observing a future that seems to promise that same isolation. They inhabit a world of potential or actual violence, as exemplified in the stories "Sale Day" and "A Great Day," they see domesticity as a fate to be avoided, as in "The Hole That Jack Dug," and, like the anti-hero of "A Man of Good Will," they will find no fruitful rewards for whatever honest endeavours they may labour at. Sargeson's vision, though compassionate and occasionally sentimental, seems finally an idiosyncratic and highly personal one in its view of social reality. Yet from his writings, and particular from his short stories, a tradition of social realism in New Zealand fiction can be traced. It says much that is disturbing about his country that Sargeson's vision was accepted by a generation of readers as a naturalistic and inherently truthful vision of the experiences of a male working class in New Zealand. Part of this acceptance involved the recognition that Sargeson had an unerring skill with dialogue. His recording of the New Zealand working class vernacular has not been surpassed and has seldom been matched by later writers. The idiomatic speech, with its flattened cadences, its laconic and sometimes wry ironies, and its cautious and limited vocabulary, became intimately associated with his distinctive sketches and stories.

Many of the works take the form of casually told yarns where the story is ostensibly being narrated to the listener-reader, but where the personality and character of the narrator becomes an important element. Sometimes, as in "An Affair of the Heart," an evidently insightful narrator recalls both a childhood experience and an adult's attempt to recapture it, in the full recognition of its beauty and terror. More often the classic Sargeson narrator, in stories such as "A Man and His Wife" and "The Making of a New Zealander," finds himself verbally if not emotionally limited, telling a story whose full significance may elude him.

In the Sargeson world, relationships between men and women and between parents and children seem almost always unsatisfactory. A strong tone of misogyny seems to permeate many of the stories, perhaps because of the narrators' half-recognized prejudices rather than from any overt authorial antipathy, but the stories are expressive of a limited and sometimes fearful view of human relationships. Often the only effective emotional reality for the characters seems to be the uneasy camaraderie of "mateship" between the men in the stories. In this world, marriages are too often blighted, as in the comic but grotesque depiction of Mr. and Mrs. Crump in "The Making of a New Zealander," or stretched to breaking point, as in "A Man and His Wife," or non-existent, as in "An Affair of the Heart" or "An Attempt at an Explanation"; in each case the absence of the husband/father is never alluded to though it is always apparent.

Arguably the finest sustained narrative that adopts the style of the semi-articulate narrator inhabiting this emotional twilight world is the extended story "That Summer," first published by John Lehmann in *Penguin New Writing* in 1943-44. It is a story that tells in the first person singular the experience of two unemployed men in a New Zealand city during the Depression. They form a platonic bond, as caring and mutually supportive as any orthodox "marriage," during one golden summer. The protagonist is innocently unaware of the moral and sexual darkness that surrounds him and his more worldly "mate," and the poignancy of his ultimate loss is the more touching for its being only half-recognized. The story is among Sargeson's most subtly underwritten, and among his finest.

In the 15 years after his 60th birthday Sargeson published three new novels and several novellas, as well as half a dozen more short stories, most of the latter published between 1964 and 1969. In these later fictions Sargeson used a more eloquent style than he formerly had, with a frequently self-mocking urbanity that suggested the influence of Smollett. He now examined the lives of characters who differed from his earlier creations in being seemingly more materially secure (or bourgeois) more articulate, and more susceptible to pain. Generally now they were no longer limited by the constrictions of language that had been imposed on the earlier narrators through limited education or social opportunity. But perhaps the fact that they could speak more confidently meant only that they could recognise and articulate more clearly a vision which is still at least metaphorically "unspeakable." The later stories, such as "City and Suburban" and "Just Trespassing, Thanks," seems still to express a vision that is bleak and melancholy, with little joy or optimism finally able to be derived from the material improvement of society. The ultimate condition of humanity in Sargeson's world seems always to be loneliness, lightened only by the compassion of the author's vision.

—William Broughton

See the essay on "The Making of a New Zealander."

———

SAROYAN, William. American. Born in Fresno, California, 31 August 1908. Educated at public schools in Fresno to age 15. Served in the U.S. Army, 1942–45. Married Carol Marcus in 1943 (divorced 1949; remarried 1951; divorced 1952); one son (the writer Aram Saroyan) and one daughter. Worked as grocery clerk, vineyard worker, post office employee; clerk, telegraph operator, then office manager, Postal Telegraph Company, San Francisco, 1926–28; co-founder, Conference Press, Los Angeles, 1936; founder and director, Saroyan Theatre, New York, 1942; writer-in-residence, Purdue University, Lafayette, Indiana, 1961. Recipient: New York Drama Critics Circle award, 1940; Pulitzer prize, 1940 (refused); Oscar (for screenplay), 1944. Member, American Academy, 1943. *Died 18 May 1981.*

PUBLICATIONS

Collections

My Name Is Saroyan, edited by James H. Tashjian. 1983.

Short Stories

The Daring Young Man on the Flying Trapeze and Other Stories. 1934.
Inhale and Exhale. 1936.
Three Times Three. 1936.
Little Children. 1937.
The Gay and Melancholy Flux: Short Stories. 1937.
Love, Here Is My Hat. 1938.
A Native American. 1938.
The Trouble with Tigers. 1938.
Peace, It's Wonderful. 1939.
3 Fragments and a Story. 1939.
My Name Is Aram. 1940.
Saroyan's Fables. 1941.
The Insurance Salesman and Other Stories. 1941.
48 Saroyan Stories. 1942.
Best Stories. 1942.
Thirty-One Selected Stories. 1943.
Some Day I'll Be a Millionaire: 34 More Great Stories. 1943.
Dear Baby. 1944.
The Saroyan Special: Selected Short Stories. 1948.
The Fiscal Hoboes. 1949.
The Assyrian and Other Stories. 1950.
The Whole Voyald and Other Stories. 1956.
Love. 1959.
After Thirty Years: The Daring Young Man on the Flying Trapeze (includes essays). 1964.
Best Stories of Saroyan. 1964.
My Kind of Crazy Wonderful People: 17 Stories and a Play. 1966.
An Act or Two of Foolish Kindness: Two Stories. 1977.
Madness in the Family, edited by Leo Hamalian. 1988.
The Man with the Heart in the Highlands and Other Early Stories. 1989.

Novels

The Human Comedy. 1943.
The Adventures of Wesley Jackson. 1946.
The Twin Adventures: The Adventures of Saroyan: A Diary; The Adventures of Wesley Jackson: A Novel. 1950.
Rock Wagram. 1951.
Tracy's Tiger. 1951.
The Laughing Matter. 1953; as *A Secret Story,* 1954.
Mama I Love You. 1956.
Papa You're Crazy. 1957.
Boys and Girls Together. 1963.
One Day in the Afternoon of the World. 1964.

Plays

The Man with the Heart in the Highlands, in *Contemporary One-Act Plays,* edited by William Kozlenko. 1938; revised version, as *My Heart's in the Highlands* (produced 1939), 1939.
The Time of Your Life (produced 1939). In *The Time of Your Life* (miscellany), 1939.
The Hungerers (produced 1945). 1939.
A Special Announcement (broadcast 1940).
Love's Old Sweet Song (produced 1940). In *Three Plays,* 1940.
Three Plays: My Heart's in the Highlands, The Time of Your Life, Love's Old Sweet Song. 1940.
Subway Circus. 1940.
Something about a Soldier (produced 1940).
Hero of the World (produced 1940).

The Great American Goof (ballet scenario; produced 1940). In *Razzle Dazzle*, 1942.
Radio Play (broadcast 1940).   In *Razzle Dazzle*, 1942.
The Ping-Pong Game (produced 1945).   1940; as *The Ping Pong Players*, in *Razzle Dazzle*, 1942.
Sweeney in the Trees (produced 1940).   In *Three Plays*, 1941.
The Beautiful People (produced 1941).   In *Three Plays*, 1941.
Across the Board on Tomorrow Morning (produced 1941). In *Three Plays*, 1941.
Three Plays: The Beautiful People, Sweeney in the Trees, Across the Board on Tomorrow Morning.   1941.
The People with Light Coming Out of Them (broadcast 1941).   In *The Free Company Presents*, 1941.
There's Something I Got To Tell You (broadcast 1941).   In *Razzle Dazzle*, 1942.
Hello, Out There, music by Jack Beeson (produced 1941). In *Razzle Dazzle*, 1942.
Jim Dandy (produced 1941).   1941; as *Jim Dandy: Fat Man in a Famine*, 1947.
Talking to You (produced 1942).   In *Razzle Dazzle*, 1942.
Razzle Dazzle; or, The Human Opera, Ballet, and Circus; or There's Something I Got to Tell You: Being Many Kinds of Short Plays As Well As the Story of the Writing of Them (includes *Hello, Out There, Coming Through the Rye, Talking to You, The Great American Goof, The Poetic Situation in America, Opera, Opera, Bad Men in the West, The Agony of Little Nations, A Special Announcement, Radio Play, The People with Light Coming Out of Them, There's Something I Got to Tell You, The Hungerers, Elmer and Lily, Subway Circus, The Ping Pong Players*).   1942; abridged edition, 1945.
Opera, Opera (produced 1955).   In *Razzle Dazzle*, 1942.
Bad Men in the West (produced 1971).   In *Razzle Dazzle*, 1942.
Get Away Old Man (produced 1943).   1944.
Sam Ego's House (produced 1947).   In *Don't Go Away Mad and Two Other Plays*, 1949.
Don't Go Away Mad (produced 1949).   In *Don't Go Away Mad and Two Other Plays*, 1949.
Don't Go Away Mad and Two Other Plays: Sam Ego's House; A Decent Birth, A Happy Funeral.   1949.
The Son (produced 1950).
The Oyster and the Pearl: A Play for Television (televised 1953).   In *Perspectives USA*, Summer 1953.
A Lost Child's Fireflies (produced 1954).
Once Around the Block (produced 1956).   1959.
The Cave Dwellers (produced 1957).   1958.
Ever Been in Love with a Midget (produced 1957).
The Slaughter of the Innocents (produced 1957).   1958.
Cat, Mouse, Man, Woman and *The Accident*, in *Contact 1*, 1958.
The Dogs; or, The Paris Comedy (as *The Paris Comedy; or The Secret of Lily*, produced 1960; as *Lily Dafon*, produced 1960).   In *The Dogs; or, The Paris Comedy and Two Other Plays*, 1969.
Settled Out of Court, with Henry Cecil, from the novel by Cecil (produced 1960).   1962.
Sam, The Highest Jumper of Them All; or, The London Comedy (produced 1960).   1961.
High Time along the Wabash (produced 1961).
Ah Man, music by Peter Fricker (produced 1962).
Four Plays: The Playwright and the Public, The Handshakers, The Doctor and the Patient, This I Believe, in *Atlantic*, April 1963.
The Time of Your Life and Other Plays.   1967.

Dentist and Patient and *Husband and Wife*, in *The Best Short Plays 1968*, edited by Stanley Richards.   1968.
The Dogs; or, The Paris Comedy and Two Other Plays: Chris Sick; or, Happy New Year Anyway, Making Money, and *Nineteen Other Very Short Plays*.   1969.
The New Play, in *The Best Short Plays 1970*, edited by Stanley Richards.   1970.
Armenians (produced 1974).
The Rebirth Celebration of the Human Race at Artie Zabala's Off-Broadway Theatre (produced 1975).
Two Short Paris Summertime Plays of 1974 (includes *Assassinations* and *Jim, Sam, and Anna*).   1979.
Play Things (produced 1980).
Warsaw Visitor [and] Tales from Vienna Streets, edited by Dickran Kouymjian.   1991.

Screenplays: *The Good Job* (documentary), 1942; *The Human Comedy*, with Howard Estabrook, 1943.

Radio Plays: *Radio Play*, 1940; *A Special Announcement*, 1940; *There's Something I Got to Tell You*, 1941; *The People with Light Coming Out of Them*, 1941.

Television Plays: *The Oyster and the Pearl*, 1953; *Ah Sweet Mystery of Mrs. Murphy*, 1959; *The Unstoppable Gray Fox*, 1962; *Making Money and Thirteen Other Very Short Plays*, 1970.

Ballet Scenario: *A Theme in the Life of the Great American Goof*, 1940.

Verse

A Christmas Psalm.   1935.
Christmas 1939.   1939.

Other

Those Who Write Them and Those Who Collect Them. 1936.
The Time of Your Life (miscellany).   1939.
Harlem as Seen by Hirschfeld.   1941.
Hilltop Russians in San Francisco.   1941.
Why Abstract?, with Henry Miller and Hilaire Hiler. 1945.
The Bicycle Rider in Beverly Hills (autobiography).   1952.
The Saroyan Reader.   1958.
Here Comes, There Goes, You Know Who (autobiography). 1962.
A Note on Hilaire Hiler.   1962.
Me (for children).   1963.
Not Dying (autobiography).   1963.
Short Drive, Sweet Chariot (autobiography).   1966.
Look at Us: Let's See: Here We Are: Look Hard: Speak Soft: I See, You See, We all See; Stop, Look, Listen; Beholder's Eye; Don't Look Now But Isn't That You? (us? U.S.?). 1967.
Horsey Gorsey and the Frog (for children).   1968.
I Used to Believe I Had Forever; Now I'm Not So Sure. 1968.
Letters from 74 rue Taitbout.   1969; as *Don't Go But If You Must Say Hello to Everybody*, 1970.
Days of Life and Death and Escape to the Moon.   1970.
Places Where I've Done Time.   1972.
The Tooth and My Father (for children).   1974.
Famous Faces and Other Friends: A Personal Memoir. 1976.
Morris Hirshfield.   1976.

Sons Come and Go, Mothers Hang In Forever (memoirs). 1976.
Chance Meetings.   1978.
Obituaries.   1979.
Births.   1983.

Editor, *Hairenik 1934–1939: An Anthology of Short Stort and Poems.*   1939.

*

Bibliography: *A Bibliography of Saroyan 1934–1964* by David Kherdian, 1965.

Critical Studies: "What Ever Happened to Saroyan?" by William J. Fisher, in *College English* 16, March 1955; *Saroyan* by Howard R. Floan, 1966; *Last Rites: The Death of Saroyan,* 1982, and *Saroyan,* 1983, both by Aram Saroyan; *Saroyan: My Real Work Is Being* by David Stephen Calonne, 1983; *Saroyan* by Edward Halsey Foster, 1984; *Saroyan: A Biography* by Lawrence Lee and Barry Gifford, 1984; *Saroyan: The Man and the Writer Remembered* edited by Leo Hamalian, 1987.

*   *   *

As Howard Floan point out, William Saroyan's career can be divided into four periods, each one distinguished by Saroyan's choice of literary genre. In the closing years of his life, for example, Saroyan wrote several autobiographical volumes, thereby concentrating on a genre that had been implicit in his work from the beginning. Prior to that phase he had focused his attention on the novel, producing in 1943 one of his best-known works, *The Human Comedy.* An interest in drama (1939-43) preceded his novelistic phase. In the earliest years of his long career (1934-39), before he started writing plays, Saroyan wrote several collections of short stories. Many critics feel that these will prove to be his most significant contribution to American literature.

The collections are impressive both for the quality of their prose and for their number. Between 1934 and 1939 Saroyan published *The Daring Young Man on the Flying Trapeze, Inhale and Exhale, Three Times Three, Little Children, Love, Here Is My Hat, The Trouble with Tigers,* and *Peace, It's Wonderful.* With each one he developed a more sophisticated attitude toward the formal components of the short story, resisting a bit more in each collection his natural tendency to interrupt his narratives with philosophical reflections spoken in his own voice. Gradually he chose to place greater faith in his abilities as a storyteller. In 1936 he wrote, "Critics are happiest with my stuff . . . when I try for almost nothing, when I sit down and very quietly tell a little story. In a way, I don't blame them, I myself enjoy writing and reading a very simple story, that is whole and with form" (*Three Times Three*).

Despite this admission, Saroyan never equated form with formulaic plots or simplicity with an absence of ideas. From "The Daring Young Man on the Flying Trapeze," he consistently dramatized what one critic (William J. Fisher) calls a "pseudo-philosophy" and another (David Stephen Calonne) more generously refers to as a "central concern . . . [with] humanity's deepest spiritual aspirations." In Saroyan's oeuvre the short story is unique only insofar as its length forced him to integrate his ideas and beliefs more

effectively into the traditional elements of tone, plot, and characterization. In doing so it provided him with fewer opportunities to interrupt the narrative with his own distinct voice.

Even an early autobiographical story like "Seventy Thousand Assyrians" demonstrates how the genre could control Saroyan's ego. Despite its first-person narrative and conversational tone, "Seventy Thousand Assyrians" is not concerned exclusively with the inner life of the speaker; rather, it treats the ways in which the narrator responds to the world around him. Saroyan allows the world—its people, places, and language—to shape the young writer who narrates his story from a barber shop on Third Avenue in San Francisco. The Iowa farm boy, the Assyrian barber, even the distinctly "American" language that both enables him to communicate and threatens to "isolate" him, all of these elements define the narrator as principally a member of the "brotherhood of things alive." "If I have any desire at all," he concludes after his encounters, "it is to show the brotherhood of man."

This dialectic between the self and the world manifests itself less directly but no less forcefully in later stories such as "The Man with the Heart in the Highlands" and "Love, Here Is My Hat." The former dramatizes a series of exchanges between "neighbors and friends" that center around the figure of an itinerant bugler named Jasper MacGregor; the second depicts two people who can only satisfy their own appetites for life through their relationship with one another. In both cases Saroyan draws strong central characters by demonstrating how they interact with those around them; he dramatizes, in other words, a much later autobiographical admission (in *Sons Come*) in which he asserts, "I not only believe that . . . it means something that I am. . . . I [also] believe that this meaning is large, and goes far, and is not ever going to be forgotten by . . . the human family."

As many critics have noted, the consequences of this dialectic between the self and the world is twofold. The subsequent quest for human unity and harmony gives Saroyan's prose, especially in the short stories, much of its force and meaning. The dialectical nature of the quest leads readers to interpret those stories about the fragmented lives of individuals as allegories about the broken center at the heart of all 20th-century reality. "Deeply aware of the fragmentation and spiritual anarchy of life in the modern world," Saroyan, writes Calonne, "exhibits a driving impulse toward joy, self-realization, and psychic integration. Read in this manner, the stories do address what Saroyan himself (in *Three Plays*) called "the imperative requirement of our time": to "restore faith to the mass and integrity to the individual."

However, as Fisher argues, in order to fulfill this requirement Saroyan often sacrifices too much. According to Fisher, Saroyan "yearn[s] for a harmony, for an eradication of conflicts and contradictions" that tends to "eliminate *all* distinction, reducing meaning to some amorphous unit—if not to a cipher." The result is a sentimental literature that ignores evil, champions an unshakable optimism, and tries desperately "to get rid of the unpleasant realities of life."

There is an element of truth to both positions, as one might expect given Saroyan's preoccupation with his fundamental belief in the intrinsic value of life or "being." "The thing about the people one meets on arrival, upon being born," writes Saroyan, in *Chance Meetings*, "is that they are the people they *are*." One could argue that this single realization has motivated his entire career. If that is the case, then surely one also can understand how the consequences of his fiction would be as complicated and contradictory as the hearts of both his characters and readers.

—John C. Waldmeir

See the essay on "The Daring Young Man on the Flying Trapeze."

———

SARTRE, Jean-Paul (-Charles-Aymard). French. Born in Paris, 21 June 1905. Educated at Lycée Montaigne and Lycée Henri-IV, Paris; École Normale Supérieure, Paris, agrégation in philosophy 1929. Served in the French Army 1929–31, and World War 11: captured, 1940; escaped, 1941. Began lifelong relationship with the writer Simone de Beauvoir, *q.v.,* in 1929; Sartre had one adopted daughter. Professor, Lycée du Havre, 1931–32 and 1934–36; Lycée de Laon, 1936–37; Lycée Pasteur, Paris, 1937–39; Lycée Condorcet, Paris, 1941–44; travelled and lectured extensively during the 1950's and 1960's: member of Bertrand Russell's International War Crimes Tribunal, 1966; editor, *La Cause du Peuple,* from 1970, *Tout,* 1970–74, *Révolution,* 1971–74, and *Libération,* 1973–74. Founding editor, with de Beauvoir, *Les Temps Modernes,* from 1945; founder, with Maurice Clavel, Liberation news service, 1971. Recipient: French Institute Research grant, 1933; Popular Novel prize, 1940; New York Drama Critics Circle award, 1947; Grand Novel prize, 1950; Omegna prize (Italy), 1960; Nobel prize for literature, 1964 (refused). Foreign Member, American Academy of Arts and Sciences. *Died 15 April 1980.*

PUBLICATIONS

Collections

Oeuvres romanesques, edited by Michel Contat and Michel Rybalka. 1981.

Short Stories

Le Mur. 1939; as *The Wall and Other Stories,* 1949; as *Intimacy and Other Stories,* 1949.

Novels

La Nausée. 1938; as *The Diary of Antoine Roquentin,* 1949; as *Nausea,* 1949.
Les Chemins de la liberté (Paths of Freedom):
    L'Âge de raison. 1945; as *The Age of Reason,* 1947.
    Le Sursis. 1945; as *The Reprieve,* 1947.
    La Mort dans l'âme. 1949; as *Iron in the Soul,* 1950; as *Troubled Sleep,* 1951.

Plays

Bariona; ou, Le Fils du tonnerre (produced 1940). 1962; as *Bariona; or, The Son of Thunder,* in *The Writings 2,* 1974.
Les Mouches (produced 1943). 1943; as *The Flies,* in *The Flies and In Camera,* 1946.
Huis clos (produced 1944). 1945; as *In Camera,* in *The Flies and In Camera,* 1946; as *No Exit,* in *No Exit and The Flies,* 1947.
The Flies and In Camera. 1946.
Morts sans sépulture (produced 1946). 1946; as *Men Without Shadows,* in *Three Plays* (U.K.), 1949; as *The Victors,* in *Three Plays* (U.S.), 1949.
La Putain respectueuse (produced 1946). 1946; as *The Respectable Prostitute,* in *Three Plays* (U.K.), 1949; as *The Respectful Prostitute,* in *Three Plays* (U.S.), 1949.
No Exit and The Flies. 1947.
Les Jeux sont faits (screenplay). 1947; as *The Chips Are Down,* 1948.
Les Mains sales (produced 1948). 1948; as *Crime Passionnel,* in *Three Plays* (U.K.), 1949; as *Dirty Hands,* in *Three Plays* (U.S.), 1949.
L'Engrenage (screenplay). 1948; as *In the Mesh,* 1954.
Three Plays (U.K.; includes *Men Without Shadows, The Respectable Prostitute, Crime Passionnel*). 1949.
Three Plays (U.S.; includes *The Victors, The Respectful Prostitute, Dirty Hands*). 1949.
Le Diable et le bon dieu (produced 1951). 1951; as *Lucifer and the Lord,* 1953; as *The Devil and the Good Lord,* in *The Devil and the Good Lord and Two Other Plays,* 1960.
Kean, from the play by Dumas père (produced 1953). 1954; translated as *Kean,* 1954; as *Kean, or Disorder and Genius,* 1990.
Nekrassov (produced 1955). 1956; translated as *Nekrassov,* 1956.
Les Séquestrés d'Altona (produced 1959). 1960; as *Loser Wins,* 1960; as *The Condemned of Altona,* 1961.
The Devil and the Good Lord and Two Other Plays (includes *Kean* and *Nekrassov*). 1960.
Les Troyennes, from a play by Euripides (produced 1965). 1965; as *The Trojan Women,* 1967.

Screenplays: *Les Jeux sont faits (The Chips Are Down),* 1947; *L'Engrenage,* 1948; *Les Sorcières de Salem (Witches of Salem),* 1957.

Other

L'Imagination. 1936; as *Imagination: A Psychological Critique,* 1962.
Esquisse d'une theorie des émotions. 1939; as *The Emotions: Outline of a Theory,* 1948; as *Sketch for a Theory of the Emotions,* 1962.
L'Imaginaire: Psychologie phénoménologique de l'imagination. 1940; as *Psychology of the Imagination,* 1949.
L'Être et le néant: Essai d'ontologie phénoménologique. 1943; as *Being and Nothingness,* 1956.
L'Existentialisme est un humanisme. 1946; as *Existentialism,* 1947; as *Existentialism and Humanism,* 1948.
Explication de "L'Etranger." 1946.
Réflexions sur la question juive. 1947; as *Anti-Semite and Jew,* 1948; as *Portrait of an Anti-Semite,* 1948.
Baudelaire. 1947; translated as *Baudelaire,* 1949.
Situations 1–10. 10 vols., 1947–76; selections as *What Is Literature?,* 1949; *Literary and Philosophical Essays,* 1955; *Situations,* 1965; *The Communists and Peace,* 1965; *The Ghost of Stalin,* 1968 (as *The Spectre of Stalin,* 1969); *Between Existentialism and Marxism,* 1974; *Life/Situations,* 1977; *Sartre in the Seventies,* 1978.
Entretiens sur la politique, with others. 1949.
Saint Genet, Comédien et martyr. 1952; as *Saint Genet, Actor and Martyr,* 1963.

L'Affaire Henri Martin, with others.   1953.
The Transcendence of the Ego: An Existentialist Theory of Consciousness.   1957.
Critique de la raison dialectique: Théorie des ensembles pratiques.   1960; as *Critique of Dialectical Reason: Theory of Practical Ensembles,* 1976.
On Cuba.   1961.
Les Mots (autobiography).   1963; as *Words,* 1964; as *The Words,* 1964.
Essays in Aesthetics, edited by Wade Baskin.   1963.
Que peut la littérature?, with others.   1965.
The Philosophy of Sartre, edited by Robert Denoon Cumming.   1966.
Of Human Freedom, edited by Wade Baskin.   1967.
Essays in Existentialism, edited by Wade Baskin.   1967.
On Genocide.   1968.
Les Communistes ont peur de la révolution.   1969.
L'Idiot de la famille: Gustave Flaubert de 1821 à 1857.   3 vols., 1971–72; as *The Family Idiot: Gustave Flaubert 1821–1857,* 1981 —.
War Crimes in Vietnam, with others.   1971.
Un théââre de situations, edited by Michel Contat and Michel Rybalka.   1973; as *On Theatre,* 1976.
Politics and Literature.   1973.
The Writings 2: Selected Prose, edited by Michel Contat and Michel Rybalka.   1974.
On a raison de se révolter, with others.   1974.
War Diaries.   1984.
Witness to My Life: The Letters of Sartre to Simone de Beauvoir 1926–1939, edited by de Beauvoir.   1993.

*

Bibliography: *The Writings 1: A Bibliographical Life* by Michel Contat and Michel Rybalka, 1974; *Sartre: A Bibliography of International Criticism* by Robert Wilcocks, 1975; *Sartre and His Critics: An International Bibliography 1938–1980* by François and Claire Lapointe, 1981.

Critical Studies: *Sartre, Romantic Rationalist* by Iris Murdoch, 1953; *Sartre: A Literary and Political Study,* 1960, and *Sartre: A Biographical Introduction,* 1971, both by Philip Thody; *Sartre: A Collection of Critical Essays* edited by Mary Warnock, 1971; *From Sartre to the New Novel* by Betty T. Rahv, 1974; *Critical Fictions: The Literary Criticism of Sartre* by Joseph Halpern, 1976; *Sartre* by Peter Caws, 1979; *Sartre and Surrealism* by Marius Perrin, 1980; *Sartre as Biographer* by Douglas Collins, 1980; *Sartre and Flaubert* by Hazel E. Barnes, 1981; *The Philosophy of Sartre* edited by Paul Arthur Schilpp, 1981; *Sartre* (biography) by Annie Cohen-Solal, 1987; *Critical Essays on Sartre* edited by Robert Wilcocks, 1988; *In the Shadow of Sartre* by Liliane Siegel, 1990; *Understanding Sartre* by Philip R. Wood, 1990; *Sartre* by Philip Thody, 1992.

*   *   *

Jean-Paul Sartre, the most eminent philosopher of the 20th century and one of the most renowned writers of modern France, is the author of five major short stories, "The Wall," "The Room," "Erostratus," "Intimacy," and "The Childhood of a Leader." Written during the 1930's and included in the collection, *Le Mur (The Wall),* these stories stand as landmarks in the development of modern prose fiction. They are especially useful to first-time readers of Sartre insofar as they provide an introduction to the principal themes of existentialism elucidated in his later works of literature and in particular the monumental philosophical treatise, *L'Être et le neánt (Being and Nothingness).*

It is Sartre's fundamental existentialist tenet that with regard to human consciousness "existence precedes essence." On the ontological level this means that consciousness possesses no *a priori* meaning and is inherently free. It is in fact the responsibility of consciousness to choose its meaning and the meaning of the world. Because such responsibility can be overwhelming, consciousness often denies its freedom and seeks refuge in a fixed definition of self. Sartre calls this flight from freedom "bad faith." In bad faith consciousness lies to itself, taking its psychological, social, or historical circumstance as an inexorable destiny. The characters of his short stories are all guilty of a certain degree of bad faith. Whereas the heroines of "Intimacy" and "The Room" struggle between an existentialist and essentialist view of self and the world, the protagonist of "The Childhood of a Leader" is an existential anti-hero, rejecting freedom not only in himself but in others. To the extent that his bad faith is placed in the context of European fascism and the Nazi holocaust, Sartre's short stories can be seen to contain a moral dimension that foreshadows his later political commitment.

Sartre maintains that while philosophy grasps human reality from a perspective of exteriority, literature is able to capture something of the lived-experience of consciousness in the world. In his short stories he nevertheless employs the rhetorical conventions of a somewhat traditional realist discourse. His fictional style is closer to that of John Dos Passos, one of the writers whom he most admired during his youth, than to that of the French surrealists or the later practitioners of the new French novel. Moreover, his short stories are often typified by perverse characters, violence, and what was considered at the time of their publication to be a deviant sexuality. This has led some critics to examine them in the light of psychoanalytical theory. Notwithstanding, though Sartre incorporates certain aspects of psychoanalysis in "The Childhood of a Leader," he also parodies it, and his fundamental rejection of the unconscious places him in clear opposition to such theorists as Freud.

The earliest extant writing of Sartre is a short story, "The Angel of Morbidity," written when he was 17 years old. Unlike much youthful literature, this piece is incisive and strikingly unsentimental. It deals with a mediocre school teacher who is morbidly attracted to a tubercular woman. When he forces himself on her, she is overcome with violent coughing and begins to expel phlegm and blood. Fearing contagion, the man flees and eventually marries a seemingly healthy woman. In this story the young Sartre reveals the hypocrisy of bourgeois humanism, the exploitation and violence of interpersonal relations, and more importantly an intuition of the brutality of existence that lies behind the facade of conventional perceptions of reality.

In "Intimacy" a young woman, Lulu, leaves her impotent husband, Henri, and at the urging of her friend Rirette, plans to join her lover, Pierre. Though Henri claims to possess Lulu, she is the dominant figure in their relationship. With Pierre, on the other hand, she finds herself reduced to the status of a thing under his objectifying gaze. In a dramatic scene both Henri and Rirette physically struggle to control Lulu. Yet only Pierre, through his sexuality, has the real power to do so. Realizing the threat that Pierre poses to her freedom, Lulu returns to Henri. In so doing, however, she fails to transcend the subject/object dichotomy of interpersonal relationships and simply reassumes her frustrated role in marriage.

The situation of Eve in "The Room" is similar to that of Lulu, only in her case it is not a lover but her father, M. Darbédat, who poses the most immediate threat to her freedom. M. Darbédat is the incarnation of a bad faith that Sartre describes as the "spirit of seriousness." He maintains a rational but conventional notion of human nature and rejects Eve's choice to stay with her husband Pierre, who is slowly sinking into dementia. Yet Eve is also guilty of bad faith to the extent that she attempts to enter into Pierre's world (the room) and take on his identity. Pierre's madness manifests itself through a series of hallucinations in which he sees himself attacked by flying statues with fishy eyes. These statues symbolize the look of the other as well as the thing that Pierre will eventually become through his illness as it is interpreted by society. In the end Eve realizes that she can never become Pierre, and while this amounts to a recognition of her existential freedom, she postpones her choice and remains dependent on the other, without a room of her own.

The structures of bad faith are even more fully developed in Lucien Fleurier, the protagonist of "The Childhood of a Leader." Like Lulu and Eve, he too is aware of the objectifying gaze of the other, and as a result of a homosexual experience with the older Bergère, fears that a negative essence will be permanently affixed to him. Rather than exert his freedom, however, he decides to ascribe a negative essence to the other, in this case the Jewish population in his midst, and thereby assume what he believes to be the positive essence of Aryanism. In a crucial scene when he and several other fascist thugs attack a man on the street, he chooses to interpret his hatred as a force over which he has no control. His bad faith thus leads to the creation of the anti-Semite. Moreover, the wall against which his victim is pinned is no longer a category of being, as in the other stories of *The Wall*, but the concrete condition of human history as a struggle of freedom in the world.

—Robert Richmond Ellis

See the essays on "Erostratus" and "The Wall."

SCHNITZLER, Arthur. Austrian. Born in Vienna, 15 May 1862. Educated at Akademisches Gymnasium, Vienna, 1871–79; studied medicine at the University of Vienna, 1879–85, M.D. 1885. Married Olga Gussmann in 1903 (separated 1921); one son and one daughter. Medical intern, 1885–88; assistant at Allgemeine Poliklinik, 1888–93, then in private practice. Recipient: Bauernfeld prize, 1899, 1903; Grillparzer prize, 1908; Raimund prize, 1910; Vienna Volkstheater prize, 1914. *Died 21 October 1931.*

PUBLICATIONS

Collections

Gesammelte Werke.   7 vols., 1912; enlarged edition, 9 vols., 1922.

Gesammelte Werke, edited by Robert O. Weiss.   5 vols., 1961-67.
Plays and Stories, edited by Egon Schwarz.   1982.

Short Stories and Novellas

Sterben.   1895; as "Dying," in *The Little Comedy and Other Stories,* 1977.
Die Frau des Weisen: Novelletten.   1898.
Leutnant Gustl.   1901; as *None But the Brave,* 1926.
Frau Bertha Garlan.   1901; translated as *Bertha Garlan,* 1913.
Die griechische Tänzerin: Novellen.   1905.
Dämmerseelen: Novellen.   1907.
Die Hirtenflöte.   1912.
Masken und Wunder: Novellen.   1912.
Frau Beate und ihr Sohn.   1913; translated as *Beatrice,* 1926.
Viennese Idylls.   1913.
Doktor Gräsler, Badearzt.   1917; translated as *Dr. Graesler,* 1923.
Casanovas Heimfahrt.   1918; as *Casanova's Homecoming,* 1921.
Der Mörder.   1922.
The Shepherd's Pipe and Other Stories.   1922.
Fräulein Else.   1924; translated as *Fräulein Else,* 1925.
Die dreifache Warning: Novellen.   1924.
Die Frau des Richters.   1925.
Traumnovelle.   1926; as *Rhapsody: A Dream Novel,* 1927.
Beatrice and Other Stories.   1926.
Spiel im Morgengrauen.   1927; as *Daybreak,* 1927.
Therese: Chronik eines Frauenlebens.   1928; as *Theresa: The Chronicle of a Woman's Life,* 1928.
Gesammelte Schriften.   6 vols., 1928.
Little Novels.   1929.
Flucht in die Finsternis.   1931; as *Flight into Darkness,* 1931.
Viennese Novelettes.   1931.
Abenteuernovelle.   1937.
Vienna 1900: Games with Love and Death.   1973.

Novel

Der Weg ins Freie.   1908; as *The Road to the Open,* 1923.

Plays

Das Abenteuer seines Lebens (produced 1891).   1888.
Das Märchen (produced 1893).   1894.
Anatol (cycle of seven one-act plays; produced as a cycle 1910).   1893; edited by Ernst L. Offermann, 1964; as *Anatol: A Sequence of Dialogues,* 1911; as *The Affairs of Anatol,* 1933; as *Anatol,* in *The Round Dance and Other Plays,* 1982.
Das Märchen (produced 1893).   1894.
Liebelei (produced 1895).   1896; as *Light-o'-Love,* 1912; as *Playing with Love,* 1914; as *Love Games,* in *The Round Dance and Other Plays,* 1982; as *Flirtations,* in *Plays and Stories,* 1982; as *Dalliance,* adapted by Tom Stoppard, with *Undiscovered Country,* 1986.
Freiwild (produced 1897).   1898; as *Free Game,* 1913.
Das Vermächtnis (produced 1898).   1899; as *The Legacy,* in *Poet Lore,* July-August 1911.
Der grüne Kakadu, Paracelsus, Die Gefährtin.   1899; as *The Green Cockatoo and Other Plays* (includes *Paracelsus, The Mate*), 1913; *Der grüne Kakadu* also translated as *The Duke and the Actress,* 1910.
Der Schleier der Beatrice (produced 1900).   1901.

Reigen (produced 1920).   1900; as *Hands Around*, 1920; as *Couples*, 1927; as *Round Dance*, in *From the Modern Repertoire*, edited by Eric Bentley, 1949; as *Merry-Go-Round*, 1953; as *La Ronde*, in *From the Modern Repertoire*, edited by Eric Bentley, 1954; as *Dance of Love*, 1965; as *The Round Dance*, in *The Round Dance and Other Plays*, 1982.

Lebendige Stunden (includes *Die Frau mit dem Dolche, Die letzten Masken, Literatur, Lebendige Stunden*).   1902; as *Living Hours* (includes *The Lady with the Dagger, Last Masks, Literature, Living Hours*), 1913.

Der einsame Weg.   1904; as *The Lonely Way*, 1904; as *The Lonely Road*, 1985.

Marionetten (includes *Der Puppenspieler, Der tapfere Cassian, Zum grossen Wurstel*).   1906; revised version of *Der tapfere Cassian*, music by Oscar Straus, 1909; translated as *Gallant Cassian*, 1914.

Zwischenspiel (produced 1905).   1906; as *Intermezzo*, in *Three Plays*, 1915.

Der Ruf des Lebens (produced 1906).   1906.

Komtesse Mizzi; oder, Der Familientag (produced 1909). 1909; as *Countess Mizzie*, 1907, in *Three Plays*, 1915; as *Countess Mitzi; or, the Family Reunion*, revised translation, in *Plays and Stories*, 1982.

Der Schleier der Pierrette, music by Ernst von Dohnanyi (produced 1910).   1910.

Der junge Medardus (produced 1910).   1910.

The Green Cockatoo and Other Plays (includes *Paracelsus* and *The Mate*).   1910.

Das weite Land (produced 1911).   1911; as *Undiscovered Country*, 1980.

Professor Bernhardi (produced 1912).   1912; translated as *Professor Bernhardi*, 1913.

Komödie der Worte (includes *Stunde des Erkennens, Grosse Szene, Das Bacchusfest;* produced simultaneously 1915). 1915; as *Comedies of Words and Other Plays* (includes *The Hour of Recognition, The Big Scene, The Festival of Bacchus*), 1917.

Fink und Fliederbusch (produced 1917).   1917.

Three Plays (includes *The Lonely Way, Intermezzo, Countess Mizzi*).   1915.

Die Schwestern; oder, Casanova in Spa (produced 1920). 1919.

Komödie der Verführung (produced 1924).   1924.

Der Gang zum Weiher (produced 1931).   1926.

Im Spiel der Sommerlüfte (produced 1929).   1930; as *Summer Breeze*, 1989.

Zug der Schatten, edited by Françoise Derre.   1970.

The Round Dance and Other Plays (includes *Anatol* and *Love Games*).   1982.

Other

Buch der Sprüche und Bedenken: Aphorismen und Fragmente.   1927.

Der Geist im Wort und der Geist in der Tat.   1927; as *The Mind in Words and Action: Preliminary Remarks Concerning Two Diagrams*, 1972.

Über Krieg und Frieden.   1939; as *Some Day Peace Will Return: Notes on Peace and War*, 1972.

Breifwechsel, with Otto Brahm, edited by Oskar Seidlin. 1953; revised edition, 1964.

Briefwechsel, with Georg Brandes, edited by Kurt Bergel. 1956.

Briefwechsel, with Hugo von Hofmannsthal, edited by Therese Nickl and Heinrich Schnitzler.   1964.

Jugend in Wien: Eine Autobiographie, edited by Therese Nickl and Heinrich Schnitzler.   1968; as *My Youth in Vienna*, 1971.

Liebe, die starb vor der Zeit: Ein Briefwechsel, with Olga Waissnix, edited by Therese Nickl and Heinrich Schnitzler.   1970.

Briefwechsel, with Max Reinhardt, edited by Renate Wagner.   1971.

Correspondence, with Raoul Auernheimer, edited by David G. Daviau and Jorun B. Johns.   1972.

Briefe 1875–1912, edited by Therese Nickl and Heinrich Schnitzler.   1981.

Tagebuch 1909–1912, edited by Peter M. Braunworth and others.   1981; further volumes: *1913–1916*, 1983, *1917–1919*, 1985; *1879–1892*, 1987.

Beziehungen und Einsamkeiten: Aphorismen, edited by Clemens Eich.   1987.

Briefe 1913–1931, edited by Peter M. Braunworth and others.   1984.

*

Bibliography: *An Annotated Schnitzler Bibliography* by Richard H. Allen, 1966; *An Annotated Schnitzler Bibliography 1965–1977* by Jeffrey B. Berlin, 1978.

Critical Studies: *Schnitzler* by Sol Liptzin, 1932; *Studies in Schnitzler* by H.W. Reichart and Herman Salinger, 1963; *The Concept of the Physician in the Writings of Hans Carossa and Schnitzler* by Marie P. Alter, 1971; *Schnitzler: A Critical Study* by Martin Swales, 1971; *Schnitzler* by R. Urbach, 1971; *Schnitzler* by Richard Urbach, translated by Donald G. Daviau, 1973; *The Late Dramatic Works of Schnitzler* by Brigitte L. Schneider-Halvorson, 1983; *Schnitzler and His Age: Intellectual and Artistic Currents* edited by Petrus W. Tax and Richard H. Lawson, 1984; *Schnitzler and the Crisis of Musical Culture* by Marc A. Weiner, 1986; *Schnitzler* by Michaela L. Perlmann, 1987; *Hauptmann, Wedekind and Schnitzler* by Peter Skrine, 1989; *Deadly Dishonor: The Duel and the Honor Code in the Works of Schnitzler* by Brenda Keiser, 1990; *Schnitzler's Vienna: Image of a Society* by Bruce Thompson, 1990; *Schnitzler, Hoffmansthal and the Austrian Theatre* by W.E. Yates, 1992.

* * *

Arthur Schnitzler was one of the most prominent authors writing in Vienna at the turn of the century, during the final years of the Austro-Hungarian Empire. Because so many of his works are set in his own contemporary city, he has come to be regarded as the recreator of a social world long since past. As the only true exponent of social realism in Vienna at the time, he provides a unique portrayal of the life pursued by particular social groups. But Schnitzler offers something more than just a chronicle of Viennese clichés, for the overall impression created in his works is of a penetratingly critical examination of society. Moreover his understanding of human nature and his skill as an interpreter of the individual consciousness lend his works the quality of universality, which has ensured their enduring success and popularity.

In many of his shorter prose works, Schnitzler's main concern is with the individual psyche, rather than with the wider social scene. Some of his psychological studies, such as "Flowers," "Dying," and "The Murderer," take the reader into the minds of characters suffering from neurotic or psychotic disorders. Through his exposition of a character's consciousness via interior monologue, Schnitzler enables the reader to experience directly a psychotic condition. Such stories read like case histories, and as works of literature they have their limitations, for they are written in a cold, analytical style, involving a clinical exposition of symptoms. Nevertheless, the meticulous accuracy with which these studies are drawn testify to Schnitzler's thorough knowledge of depth psychology, and many of them reflect Freudian theories and discoveries. For example, the story "The Son" describes an example of a psychopathological condition induced by infantile trauma. In *Flucht in die Finsternis* (*Flight into Darkness*) he presents a remarkably accurate picture of paranoid schizophrenia, so convincingly that the lay reader can follow the mental processes taking place and experience the condition at first hand.

It has been suggested that the prevalence in Schnitzler's works of illness, decay, and death reflect the decadent and sickly mood of the *fin de siecle*. In his most successful stories the study of the psyche is also blended with an indication of the social sources of psychological maladies. In *Fräulein Else* he affords the reader direct access to the mental processes of a repressed Oedipal complex, but because Else's condition is partly the result of her social situation the social values of the time are exposed and condemned. *Frau Beate und ihr Sohn* (*Beatrice*) is a frank and powerful study of a woman's discovery of her own sensual nature, but the exposure of the facade of bourgeois respectability broadens the scope of the work beyond its essential psychological elements. *Rhapsody* is primarily a study of a marital relationship which exposes the unconscious drives in the human soul; but as an excursion into the sordid establishments of the sexual underworld it also explores the dark, unsavoury world of Viennese society, from prostitution and consequent disease, to decadent orgies involving the highest aristocracy.

Several early plays contributed most to the establishment of Schnitzler's reputation abroad. Because of the nature of their theme—the relationship between the sexes—Schnitzler has inevitably come to be seen as a writer primarily concerned with sexuality. In his treatment of sexual themes Schnitzler tends to sympathise with the female victims of social forces. Prominent examples are afforded by the various "sweet girls" who are to be found in many of his earlier works. But two of his most compassionately drawn female portraits are the heroines of his two major prose works about women, *Frau Bertha Garlan* and *Therese*. In the story of the widow Bertha Garlan, Schnitzler explores the gradual reawakening of sexual feelings after a period of abstinence. At the same time he exposes a social injustice, the conventional double standard that condemns women for attempting to grasp the pleasure that is freely available to the male. Not all of his works focus on womens' problems or on specific social issues. *Casanovas Heimfahrt* (*Casanova's Homecoming*) offers a penetrating study of the personality of the ageing libertine, and in the story *Doktor Gräsler* he provides a sensitive and moving treatment of a lonely, melancholy bachelor who fights shy of marriage to an intelligent, much younger woman. Most frequently, however, Schnitzler explores relationships within the specific social context of a strict moral code. Beneath the facade of bourgeois respectability, natural urges assert themselves, but because of the dominance of an unnatural code, the result is often hypocrisy, deception, and frustration.

The social world presented in Schnitzler's works is predominantly that of the bourgeoisie, occasionally the "little world" of the lower middle classes of the suburbs, but mainly the "big world" of the upper bourgeoisie, the cultured professional families and the wealthy industrialists of the inner city. The latter is presented particularly in his major social dramas, in which Schnitzler exposes the prejudices at the heart of bourgeois conventions. In his plays Schnitzler uses stage directions to convey the attitudes of his characters, and so penetrate the facade of their public behaviour. This is paralleled in his prose works by a meticulous attention to gestures and facial expressions. The first-hand rendering of thought processes also reveals the hidden truths behind insincere role-playing in interpersonal relationships ("The Dead Are Silent"), and behind the veneer of politeness adopted during social encounters and public behaviour. The superficial charm and cowardly hypocrisy, the politeness and prim respectability adopted during social encounters, constitute the hollow facade of the army officer, the liberal poseur, the progressive bourgeois industrialist, the primly respectable widow, and the secret adulteress. One of the major institutions exposed by Schnitzler is the Imperial Army, for example in the stories *Leutnant Gustl* (*None But the Brave*) and *Spiel im Morgengrauen* (*Daybreak*). Schnitzler's hostility towards militarism is expressed in his highly critical presentation of army life and of the temperament of the typical army officer, but most effectively in his condemnation of an out-moded and inhuman code of honour which made such harsh demands of its unfortunate victims.

Schnitzler's account of his contemporary society aligns him with the Realists of the last 19th century. Yet his realism is a very limited and refined form of referential realism. Far from describing in detail its institutions or geographical features, he is content to evoke the atmosphere of his native city. Moreover, despite his preoccupation with sexual themes, there is little attempt to shock the reader, for he normally treats sexual feelings and behaviour with tact and discretion. Schnitzler focusses on social values and norms. Thus he comes across as the social commentator and social critic rather than the realist, presenting a society whose codes of conduct contribute to a social facade that is inimical to the natural and healthy development of the individual, and incompatible with openness, sincerity, and genuineness in public life.

—Bruce Thompson

See the essay on *None But the Brave*.

———

SCHULZ, Bruno. Polish. Born in Drohobycz, in 1892. Educated at schools in Drohobycz; studied architecture in Lvov, and fine arts in Vienna. Art teacher in gymnasium, Drohobycz, 1924–39; shot in Drohobycz ghetto by German SS officer, 1942. Recipient: Golden Laurel award, 1938. *Died (murdered) 19 November 1942.*

PUBLICATIONS

Collections

Proza, edited by Artur Sandauer and Jerzy Ficowski. 1964; revised edition, 1973.

The Complete Fiction, edited by Jerzy Ficowski. 1989.

Short Stories

Sklepy cynamonowe. 1934; as *The Street of Crocodiles,* 1963; as *Cinnamon Shops and Other Stories,* 1963.
Sanatorium pod klepsydra. 1937; as *Sanatorium under the Sign of the Hourglass,* 1978.

Other

Ksiega Listow [A Book of Letters], edited by Jerzy Ficowski. 1975.
Letters and Drawings, with Selected Prose, edited by Jerzy Ficowski. 1988.
The Book of Idolatry, Xiega Balwochwalcza (illustrations), edited by Jerzy Ficowski. 1989.
The Drawings of Schulz, edited by Jerzy Ficowski. 1990.

*

Critical Studies: "Schulz's *The Street of Crocodiles*: A Study in Creativity and Neurosis" by Olga Lukashevich, in *The Polish Review* 13, 1968; "Schulz" by Henryk Bereza, in *Polish Perspectives* 9, 1966; "The 'Kafkaesque' Fantastic in the Fiction of Kafka and Schulz" by Leonard Orr, in *Newsletter of the Kafka Society of America* 6, 1982; "Metamorphosis in Schulz," in *The Polish Review* 30, 1985, and "Schulz's Sanatorium Story: Myth and Confession," in *Polish Perspectives* 30, 1987, and *Myths and Relatives: Seven Essays on Schulz,* 1991, all by Russell E. Brown; "On Schulz" by Louis Iribarne, in *Cross Currents* 6, 1987; "A Few Words on Schulz" by Czesław Miłosz, in *The New Republic* 200 (1), 1989; "Schulz and the Myth of the Book" by Piotr J. Drozdowski, in *Indiana Slavic Studies* 5, 1990; "Time in Schulz" by Theodosia S. Robertson, in *Indiana Slavic Studies* 5, 1991; "Cinnamon Shops by Schulz: The Apology of Tandeta" by Andreas Schönle, in *The Polish Review* 36, 1991; "Schulz Redux" by Susan Miron, in *Partisan Review* 59, 1992.

* * *

It has become virtually impossible to talk about Bruno Schulz without making the obligatory reference to Franz Kafka. The biographical similarities (both were born into Central European Jewish middle-class families, published relatively little during their lifetime while working at jobs unrelated to their literary careers, had unhappy personal lives, died relatively young, and owe their posthumous reputations at least in part to the efforts of a dedicated literary executor) serve to underscore the literary parallels: Schulz, like Kafka, employs the techniques of the grotesque to tear away the veil of normalcy and respectability from what might appear to be a comfortable, socially acceptable existence. Characters are thrown into a world where the laws of nature are no longer sacred; a single violation of those laws, as for instance the transformation of a person into an insect or a crab, throws social conventions and individual traits into stark relief. The protagonists are generally males, who see women either as alternatively alluring and threatening in their sexuality, or as oppressive maternal figures. It comes as no surprise to learn that Schulz edited and wrote the afterward for a Polish translation of *The Trial.*

And yet it is the differences between the two that reveal more about the essence of Schulz's originality and power. Essentially, his world is more extreme than that of Kafka. Nature itself constantly threatens: an ordinary overgrown garden becomes "a paroxysm of madness, an outbreak of fury, of cynical madness and lust" ("Pan"); a storm seems to change the very people and buildings of an entire town, creating an atmosphere of fear that penetrates even the safety of the home ("The Gale"); night becomes a labyrinth, alive with scents and sounds, and possessing the texture of a fluid ("A Night in July"). Transformations of people into creatures or objects may occur at any moment, sometimes as the realization of a metaphor. In "The Gale" Aunt Perasia's "self-destructive fury" causes her literal self-destruction: she suddenly begins to shrink and scurry about, finally dissolving into ash and nothingness. Metamorphosis also goes in the opposite direction: ordinary matter and objects are said to have feelings and personality ("Tailors' Dummies"), wallpaper assumes the nervous tic of the narrator's father and flowers arrange themselves to resemble his smile ("Father's Last Escape").

Each of the two collections that Bruno Schulz published just three years apart contains precisely 13 stories, and each shows some evidence of arrangement into a cycle. The first and last stories are clearly placed with care—thus *Sanatorium pod Klepsydra (Sanatorium under the Sign of the Hour Glass)* begins with "The Book" and its theme of searching, and concludes with the appropriately titled "Father's Last Escape," certain tales are clearly juxtaposed with others, and there is a sense of progression throughout both. Significantly, Schulz appears to have decided that some of his earliest stories (such as "Eddie" and "Loneliness") were not suitable for his first book, *Sklepy cynamonowe (The Street of Crocodiles,* also as *Cinnamon Shops and Other Stories)* which is perhaps the more tightly unified of the two, and therefore published them in *Sanatorium.* The two volumes show other differences as well: the stories in *Sanatorium* are, on the average, significantly longer and as a rule stay closer to a single topic. Some of the stories in *Street of Crocodiles* are also narrowly focused ("Nimrod," which describes a young puppy's impressions of the world; or "Mr. Charles," an account of the struggle into wakefulness by an uncle of the narrator), but others take the reader through a maze of impressions and topics. For example, "Cinnamon Shops," the title story of this collection in the Polish original, goes from a description of the narrator's father to a dream-like account of the narrator's trip home to retrieve a wallet, during which the boy experiences a series of eerie adventures that culminate in a surprisingly cheerful surrender to the magic of the nighttime atmosphere.

All the stories, though, are linked by recurring figures. The narrator himself appears at various stages of his youth; typically for Schulz, time does not always move forward in the usual fashion, and one result is that the age of the narrator seems to vary freely from story to story. A motley collection of aunts and uncles populates the tales, sometimes making a single appearance, but often, like Uncle Charles, returning in a subsequent work. Within the narrator's household, the servant girl Adela plays a most prominent role from the very beginning of the first story in *Street of Crocodiles* ("August"), where her vibrancy and sexuality already stand out. Her earthy and healthy "bourgeois" presence dominates the narrator's father, whose flights of fancy are abruptly halted by her sensuous appearance or by her threats of tickling ("Tailors' Dummies"), and whose strange projects are unceremoniously halted by her ("Birds"). The narrator's mother is for the most part a shadowy figure, who divides the narrator's loyalty and is opposed to the father in trying to impose a degree of normalcy on the family's existence.

The outstanding figure of the two volumes, though, is the narrator's father. In "Visitation," the second story of *Street of Crocodiles,* he is already fading into nothingness. He starts to imitate a stuffed vulture in his room and seems to inhabit a world all of his own; eventually he comes to disappear for days at a time into various corners of the house. At other times the father seems to occupy a disintegrating stuffed condor ("Cockroaches"), or when "definitely dead" comes back as something that resembles a crab ("Father's Last Return"). In the title story of the second collection, "Sanatorium under the Sign of the Hour Glass," the narrator visits his dead father, who is staying at a hotel where they manage to "put back the clock." This bizarre, nightmarish tale in particular shows the mythic qualities that the figure of the father assumes. His various deaths and fadings are clearly meant to be symbolic of a profound struggle with which he is involved. At the sanatorium, once he is dead, he seems satisfied to open another textile store. However, in stories depicting his "real-life" existence, where he owns a much larger business and is totally immersed in the world of ledgers and dry goods, he literally tries to soar above the cares of his everyday life but is brought back down to earth ("The Night of the Great Season," "Dead Season"). Yet he is hardly a passive individual; he is bursting with unusual theories ("Tailors' Dummies," "A Second Fall") and conducts unearthly experiments, such as turning Uncle Edward into a doorbell ("The Comet").

To the extent that the father is a dominant presence, Schulz's world categorizes the battle with and the effort to escape from a mundane, middle-class existence. That the father seems a fragile figure, more often than not the loser in his struggles with Adela, underscores the difficulty faced by the dreamer, the would-be artist, and presumably by Schulz himself to assert his identity within that society.

—Barry P. Scherr

See the essays on "Sanatorium Under the Sign of the Hourglass" and "The Street of Crocodiles."

SCOTT, (Sir) Walter. Scottish. Born in Edinburgh, 15 August 1771; spent part of his childhood in the Border country. Educated at the High School, Edinburgh; University of Edinburgh; studied law: admitted to the Faculty of Advocates, 1792. Married Charlotte Charpentier in 1797 (died 1826); four children. Sheriff-depute of Selkirkshire, 1799–1832; joined James Ballantyne in 1804 as a partner in his printing company which went bankrupt in 1826, involving Scott in the discharge of its debts for the rest of his life; clerk of the Court of Session, 1806–30; helped found the *Quarterly Review,* 1809; built and lived at Abbotsford from 1812; founding president, Bannatyne Club, 1823. Created a baronet, 1820. *Died 21 September 1832.*

PUBLICATIONS

Collections

Poetical Works, edited by J.G. Lockhart.   12 vols., 1833–34; edited by J. Logie Robertson, 1904.

Miscellaneous Prose Works, edited by J.G. Lockhart.   28 vols., 1834–36; 2 additional vols., 1871.
Short Stories.   1934.
Selected Poems, edited by Thomas Crawford.   1972.

Short Stories

Tales of the Crusaders (The Betrothed, The Talisman). 1825.
Chronicles of the Canongate: First Series: The Highland Widow, The Two Drovers, The Surgeon's Daughter. 1827; *Second Series: The Fair Maid of Perth,* 1828.

Novels

Waverley; or, 'Tis Sixty Years Since.   1814; edited by Claire Lamont, 1981.
Guy Mannering; or, The Astrologer.   1815.
The Antiquary.   1816.
The Black Dwarf, Old Mortality.   1816; *Old Mortality* edited by Angus Calder, 1975.
Rob Roy.   1817.
The Heart of Mid-Lothian.   1818; edited by Claire Lamont, 1982.
The Bride of Lammermoor; A Legend of Montrose.   1819.
Ivanhoe: A Romance.   1819.
The Monastery.   1820.
The Abbot; or, The Heir of Avenel.   1820.
Kenilworth: A Romance.   1821; edited by David Daiches, 1966.
The Pirate.   1821.
The Fortunes of Nigel.   1822.
Peveril of the Peak.   1823.
Quentin Durward.   1823; edited by M.W. Thomas and G. Thomas, 1966.
St. Ronan's Well.   1823.
Redgauntlet: A Tale of the Eighteenth Century.   1824; edited by Kathryn Sutherland, 1985.
Woodstock; or, The Cavalier.   1826.
My Aunt Margaret's Mirror, The Tapestried Chamber, Death of the Laird's Jock, A Scene at Abbotsford.   1829.
Anne of Geierstein; or, The Maiden of the Mist.   1829.
Waverley Novels (Scott's final revision).   48 vols., 1829–33.
Count Robert of Paris, Castle Dangerous.   1832.

Plays

Goetz of Berlichingen, with *The Iron Hand,* by Goethe. 1799.
Guy Mannering; or, The Gipsy's Prophecy, with Daniel Terry, music by Henry Bishop and others, from the novel by Scott (produced 1816).   1816.
Halidon Hill: A Dramatic Sketch from Scottish History. 1822.
MacDuff's Cross, in *A Collection of Poems,* edited by Joanna Baillie.   1823.
The House of Aspen (produced 1829). In *Poetical Works,* 1830.
Auchindrane; or, The Ayrshire Tragedy (produced 1830). In *The Doom of Devorgoil: Auchindrane,* 1830.
The Doom of Devorgoil: A Melo-Drama; Auchindrane; or, The Ayrshire Tragedy.   1830.

Verse

The Chase, and William and Helen: Two Ballads from the German of Gottfried Augustus Bürger.   1796.

The Eve of Saint John: A Border Ballad. 1800.
The Lay of the Last Minstrel. 1805.
Ballads and Lyrical Pieces. 1806.
Marmion: A Tale of Flodden Field. 1808.
The Lady of the Lake. 1810.
The Vision of Don Roderick. 1811.
Rokeby. 1813.
The Bridal of Triermain; or, The Vale of St. John, in Three Cantos. 1813.
The Lord of the Isles. 1815.
The Field of Waterloo. 1815.
The Ettrick Garland, Being Two Excellent New Songs, with James Hogg. 1815.
Harold the Dauntless. 1817.
New Love-Poems, edited by Davidson Cook. 1932.

Other

Paul's Letters to His Kinsfolk. 1816.
The Visionary. 1819.
Provincial Antiquities of Scotland. 2 vols., 1826.
The Life of Napoleon Buonaparte: Emperor of the French, with a Preliminary View of the French Revolution. 9 vols., 1827.
Tales of a Grandfather, Being Stories Taken from Scottish History. 9 vols., 1827–29.
Miscellaneous Prose Works. 6 vols., 1827.
Religious Discourses by a Layman. 1828.
The History of Scotland. 2 vols., 1829–30.
Letters on Demonology and Witchcraft. 1830.
Tales of a Grandfather, Being Stories Taken from the History of France. 3 vols., 1830.
Letters Addressed to Rev. R. Polwhele, D. Gilbert, F. Douce. 1832.
Letters Between James Ellis and Scott. 1850.
Journal 1825–32, edited by D. Douglas. 2 vols., 1890; edited by W.E.K. Anderson, 1972.
Familiar Letters, edited by D. Douglas. 2 vols., 1894.
The Letters of Scott and Charles Kirkpatrick Sharpe to Robert Chambers, 1821–45. 1903.
The Private Letter-Books, edited by W. Partington. 1930.
Sir Walter's Postbag: More Stories and Sidelights from the Collection in the Brotherton Library, edited by W. Partington. 1932.
Some Unpublished Letters from the Collection in the Brotherton Library, edited by J.A. Symington. 1932.
The Letters, edited by Herbert Grierson. 12 vols., 1932–37; notes and index by James C. Corson, 1979.
The Correspondence of Scott and Charles Robert Maturin, edited by F.E. Ratchford and W.H. McCarthy. 1937.
Private Letters of the Seventeenth Century, edited by D. Grant. 1948.
The Prefaces to the Waverley Novels, edited by Mark A. Weinstein. 1978.
Scott on Himself: A Selection of the Autobiographical Writings, edited by David Hewitt. 1981.

Editor, An Apology for Tales of Terror. 1799.
Editor, Minstrelsy of the Scottish Border. 2 vols., 1802; edited by Alfred Noyes, 1908.
Editor, Sir Tristrem: A Metrical Romance, by Thomas of Ercildoune. 1804.
Editor, Original Memoirs Written During the Great Civil War, by Sir H. Slingsby and Captain Hodgson. 1804.
Editor, The Works of John Dryden. 18 vols., 1808 (Life of Dryden published separately, 1808, edited by Bernard Kreissman, 1963).
Editor, Memoirs of Captain George Carleton. 1808.

Editor, Queenhoo-Hall: A Romance, and Ancient Times: A Drama, by Joseph Strutt. 4 vols., 1808.
Editor, Memoirs of Robert Cary, Earl of Monmouth, and Fragmenta Regalia, by Sir Robert Naunton. 1808.
Editor, A Collection of Scarce and Valuable Tracts. 13 vols., 1809–15.
Editor, English Minstrelsy, Being a Collection of Fugitive Poetry. 2 vols., 1810.
Editor, The Poetical Works of Anna Seward. 3 vols., 1810.
Editor, Memoirs of Count Grammont, by Anthony Hamilton. 2 vols., 1811.
Editor, The Castle of Otranto, by Horace Walpole. 1811.
Editor, Secret History of the Court of King James the First. 2 vols., 1811.
Editor, The Works of Jonathan Swift. 19 vols., 1814 (Memoirs of Swift published separately, 1826).
Editor, The Letting of Humours Blood in the Head Vaine, by S. Rowlands. 1814.
Editor, Memorie of the Somervilles. 2 vols., 1815.
Editor, Trivial Poems and Triolets, by Patrick Carey. 1820.
Editor, Memorials of the Haliburtons. 1820.
Editor, Northern Memoirs Writ in the Year 1658, by Richard Franck. 1821.
Editor, Ballantyne's Novelist's Library. 10 vols., 1821–24 (Lives of the Novelists published separately, 2 vols., 1825).
Editor, Chronological Notes of Scottish Affairs from the Diary of Lord Fountainhall. 1822.
Editor, Military Memoirs of the Great Civil War, by John Gwynne. 1822.
Editor, Lays of the Lindsays. 1824.
Editor, Auld Robin Gray: A Ballad, by Lady Anne Barnard. 1825.
Editor, with D. Laing, The Bannatyne Miscellany. 1827.
Editor, Memoirs of the Marchioness de la Rochejaquelein. 1827.
Editor, Proceedings in the Court-Martial Held upon John, Master of Sinclair, 1708. 1829.
Editor, Memorials of George Bannatyne, 1545–1608. 1829.
Editor, Trial of Duncan Terig and Alexander Bane Macdonald, 1754. 1831.
Editor, Memoirs of the Insurrection in Scotland in 1715, by John, Master of Sinclair. 1858.

*

Bibliography: Bibliography of the Waverley Novels by G. Worthington, 1930; "A Bibliography of the Poetical Works of Scott 1796–1832" by W. Ruff, in Transactions of the Edinburgh Bibliographical Society 1, 1938; A Bibliography of Scott: A Classified and Annotated List of Books and Articles Relating to His Life and Works 1797–1940 by James C. Corson, 1943; Scott: A Reference Guide by Jill Rubenstein, 1978.

Critical Studies: Memoirs of the Life of Scott by J.G. Lockhart, 7 vols., 1837–38, edited by A.W. Pollard, 5 vols., 1900; Scott by John Buchan, 1932; Scott by David Cecil, 1933; Scott: A New Life by Herbert Grierson, 1938; Scott in Italy by William Gell, 1953; Scott: His Life and Personality by Hesketh Pearson, 1954; Scott by Ian Jack, 1958; The Heyday of Scott by Donald Davie, 1961; The Hero of the Waverley Novels by Alexander Welsh, 1963;

Scott by Thomas Crawford, 1965, revised edition, 1982; *Scott's Novels* by F.R. Hart, 1966; *Scott* by John Lauber, 1966, revised edition, 1989; *Scott: Modern Judgements* edited by D.D. Devlin, 1968, and *The Author of Waverley* by Devlin, 1971; *The Achievement of Scott* by A.O.J. Cockshut, 1969; *Scott's Mind and Art* edited by A. Norman Jeffares, 1969; *Under Which King? A Study of the Scottish Waverley Novels* by Robert C. Gordon, 1969; *Scott: The Great Unknown* by Edgar Johnson, 2 vols., 1970; *Scott and His World* by David Daiches, 1971; *Scott Bicentenary Essays* edited by Alan Bell, 1973; *An Index to the Waverley Novels* by Philip Bradley, 1975; *The Siege of Malta Rediscovered: An Account of Scott's Mediterranean Journey and His Last Novel,* 1977, and *The Journey of Scott to Malta,* 1986, both by Donald E. Sultana; *Scott and the Historical Imagination* by David Brown, 1979; *Scott: Landscape and Locality* by James Reed, 1980; *The Language of Scott: A Study of His Scottish and Period Language* by Graham Tulloch, 1980; *The Laird of Abbotsford: A View of Scott* by A.N. Wilson, 1980; *Scott and History* by James Anderson, 1981; *Scott and Society* by Graham McMaster, 1981; *Scott and His Influence* edited by J.H. Alexander and David Hewitt, 1983; *Scott: The Long-Forgotten Melody* edited by Alan Bold, 1983; *The Forms of Historical Fiction: Scott and His Successors* by Harry E. Shaw, 1983; *Scott: The Making of the Novelist,* 1984, and *Scott's Last Edition: A Study in Publishing History,* 1987, both by Jane Millgate; *Secret Leaves: The Novels of Scott* by Judith Wilt, 1985; *Scott, Chaucer, and Medieval Romance* by Jerome Mitchell, 1987; *Scott's Interleaved Waverley Novels, the "Magnum Opus": An Introduction and Commentary* edited by Iain Gordon Brown, 1987; *Scott the Rhymer* by Nancy Moore Goslee, 1988; *Fiction Against History: Scott as Storyteller* by James Kerr, 1989.

* * *

Sir Walter Scott's stories are a by-product of his novels. He used them as a way of presenting materials of recollection or oral history which the novels had not required. Thus in the stories he is often closer to his actual sources than he is in longer works. Especially after his final revelation as "the author of *Waverley*" in February 1827, when he no longer had need to cover his tracks, he was willing to admit his sources and name his informants. The result was *Chronicles of the Canongate,* in which most of his notable stories are found (except for "Wandering Willie's Tale" in *Redgauntlet*).

But the end of anonymity did not mean the end of invented mouthpieces. He devotes considerable space to the delineation of the imaginary editor, Chrystal Croftangry, and the narrator, Mrs. Bethune Baliol, who was based on Mrs. Murray Keith (of whom he supplies a long genealogy). J.G. Lockhart, Scott's biographer, however, believed that features of Scott's own mother were intermingled with those of Mrs. Baliol.

Here the frame (the depiction of the narrator's character) is as important as the story she tells. Her sharp meditations on class conceptions of honour reflect on the heroic and aristocratic world about which Scott wrote so much. Her Jacobitism is wavering and eclectic, part sentiment and part sober judgment, perhaps like the author himself.

The first story in *Chronicles,* "The Highland Widow," is one of Scott's finest, memorably encapsulating the clash of cultures that is also the theme of the best of the novels. A chain of memories and family connections take us back to the rebellion of 1745. Elspat MacTavish is a demented solitary with a long brooding memory of dead husband and son. The husband had lived the life of a cattle-raider; the son has to earn his living in the new Hanoverian world, and he unwillingly enlists as a soldier. The idea of being flogged for discipline is more terrible both to mother and son than the idea of execution. The latter can be endured with dignity; the former seems to reduce a man to the level of a dog. His mother taunts him with "Hanover's Yoke," betrayal of the Stuarts, and even with the terrible tradition of the massacre of Glencoe, of whose perpetrators she considers his new masters the heirs. The mother's view of honour is simple; the son's, since he is a man of two worlds, is ambiguous. He partly shares his mother's view; but he is troubled also by his promise to serve the king as a soldier.

The climax comes when a party of soldiers arrest him for desertion, and, prompted by his mother, he fires and kills the sergeant who had befriended him. It is characteristic of Scott that the reader's dominant impression is not of these moments of drama, but of the dreary aftermath, of the long years in which the widow is left to brood on the past, and to remain as a living anachronism. In "My Aunt Margaret's Mirror" a woman, tormented by fears about her absent husband, goes to a sorcerer who shows her an image of her husband in a bigamous marriage ceremony abroad. After the deserted wife's death her sister is confronted with the erring husband in disguise, begging for forgiveness, which is refused after an inner struggle. Thus a moral issue invades a story of the marvelous. A deeper, meditative note also is introduced in the conflict between religion and superstition in Aunt Margaret's mind.

"The Tapestried Chamber" is the least remarkable of these stories, since it lacks the element of suspense. A visitor is put to sleep in a long disused room in a great house, and is troubled by a vision of a ferocious hag, whose face he later recognizes in his host's picture gallery, and hears the history of the ancestress guilty of incest and murder. By making the terrified visitor a general and brave soldier, Scott enforces the idea that spiritual terrors are far less bearable than earthly ones.

Scott, perhaps deliberately, sacrificed that formal tautness of the storyteller's art, as we find in craftsmen like Kipling, for the realistic atmosphere of a story actually told; hence his great stress on the memories and personality of the storyteller and on the questions and inner sensations of the listener. And by linking stories together, employing the same narrators again and again he contrives to give an impression of a great store of oral tradition from which he is selecting specimens. The stories are meant to supplement each other, and coalesce to give a picture of manners, traditions, and superstitions in a society that was passing away. And as such, they form a valuable pendant to his major works.

—A.O.J. Cockshut

See the essays on "The Two Drovers" and "Wandering Willie's Tale."

———

SHADBOLT, Maurice (Francis Richard). New Zealander. Born in Auckland, 4 June 1932. Educated at Te Kuiti High School; Avondale College; University of Auckland. Married 1) Gillian Heming in 1953, three sons and two daughters; 2) Barbara Magner in 1971; 3) Bridget Armstrong in 1978. Journalist for various New Zealand publications, 1952–54; documentary scriptwriter and director, New Zealand National Film Unit, 1954–57; full-time writer from 1957; lived in London and Spain, 1957–60, then returned to New Zealand. Recipient: New Zealand scholarship in letters, 1959, 1970, 1982; Hubert Church Prose award, 1960; Katherine Mansfield award, 1963, 1967; University of Otago Robert Burns fellowship, 1963; National Association of Independent Schools award (U.S.), 1966; Freda Buckland award, 1969; Pacific Area Travel Association award, for nonfiction, 1971; James Wattie award, 1973, 1981; New Zealand Book award, 1981; Literary Fund travel bursary, 1988. C.B.E. (Commander, Order of the British Empire), 1989. Lives in Auckland.

PUBLICATIONS

Short Stories

The New Zealanders: A Sequence of Stories.   1959.
Summer Fires and Winter Country.   1963.
The Presence of Music: Three Novellas.   1967.
Figures in Light: Selected Stories.   1978.

Novels

Among the Cinders.   1965; revised edition, 1984.
This Summer's Dolphin.   1969.
An Ear of the Dragon.   1971.
Strangers and Journeys.   1972.
A Touch of Clay.   1974.
Danger Zone.   1975.
The Lovelock Version.   1980.
Season of the Jew.   1986.
Monday's Warriors.   1990.

Play

Once on Chunuk Bair.   1982.

Other

New Zealand: Gift of the Sea, photographs by Brian Brake. 1963; revised edition, 1973.
The Shell Guide to New Zealand.   1968; revised edition, 1973.
Isles of the South Pacific, with Olaf Ruhen.   1968.
Love and Legend: Some Twentieth Century New Zealanders.   1976.
Voices of Gallipoli.   1988.
Reader's Digest Guide to New Zealand, photographs by Brian Brake.   1988.

*

Bibliography: "A Bibliography of Shadbolt 1956–1980" by Murtay Gadd, in *Journal of New Zealand Literature* 2, 1984.

Critical Studies: Introduction by Cherry Hankin to *The New Zealanders,* 1974; "Ambition and Accomplishment in Shadbolt's Strangers and Journeys" by Lawrence Jones, in *Critical Essays on the New Zealand Novel* edited by Cherry Hankin, 1976; "Definitions of New Zealanders: The Sto-

ries of Shadbolt and Maurice Gee" by Lauris Edmond, in *Critical Essays on the New Zealand Short Story* edited by Cherry Hankin, 1982.

*   *   *

Although he first became known as a short story writer, Maurice Shadbolt has become primarily a novelist in the course of a career of over 35 years. His short stories belong to one prolific decade, 1955 to 1964, when he wrote the 23 short stories and novellas that make up his three published volumes, as well as 10 uncollected stories. Such uncollected early stories as "The Funniest Thing" (1957) and "A Beer for Old Johnny" (1958) show that he began in the substantial shadow of Frank Sargeson, but by the time of *The New Zealanders* he had clearly found his own voice. He has said that in the 1950's he came to feel that "New Zealand fiction was stuck in rather a rut: a rut running directly out of the 1930's," and that "no one was really writing about the New Zealand in which [he] was living in the 1950's." His stories are attempts to capture that contemporary social reality.

In a sense, these stories of 1955 to 1964 are sketches towards Shadbolt's major work of realist fiction, the epic novel *Strangers and Journeys,* a work which he described as "an attempt to pull into the pages of one book an account of the New Zealanders I knew best, and the New Zealand I knew, in this 20th century." That novel incorporates three of the stories in *The New Zealanders* and two other uncollected stories of the 1950's and relates thematically to several other short works; "Knock on Yesterday's Door" from *The New Zealanders* and "The Voyagers" from *The Presence of Music* were trial runs for the novel. In the title story of the latter volume the main character writes a novel which, as Shadbolt said, "sounds very like the novel which *Strangers and Journeys* was to become."

The stories are all written in the social realist mode of *Strangers and Journeys* and share its three-stage view of New Zealand history. The first stage, the pioneer past with its first generation of European settlers bringing with them their dreams of creating a "pastoral paradise" and a "just city," is only a cultural memory in these stories—a loss for the protagonist of "Ben's Land," a family history for the main characters of "The Room" and "The Wind and the Spray." The earlier, preEuropean Maori past is there most strikingly in the carefully preserved tribal memories of the dispossessed Maori of "The People Before." The second stage, the colonial period, with its rural and smalltown society characterized by a puritan work ethic and code of sexual repression, a bleak conformity, and a cultural dependence on England, is captured in such stories as "The Strangers," "After the Depression," "The People Before," "The Woman's Story," and "Love Story." The third stage, that of transition towards a nation with a "national sensibility," is Shadbolt's focus in the most characteristic of his stories. Often, as in "The Paua Gatherers," "The Voyagers," "Figures in Light," and "The Presence of Music," he concentrates on the artist who is attempting to form the stories, myths, and images that will help define that national sensibility. In others, such as "Knock on Yesterday's Door" and "River, Girl and Onion," he deals with "the mixed and mostly tragic fate of the socialist idea," the loss of the dream of the just city. In still others, such as "Ben's Land," "The Wind and the Spray," or "Neither Profit nor Salvation," he deals with the return to the land, the mostly futile attempt to recapture the lost pastoral dream. In most of these stories he shows his characters trying to find meaning in personal relations, often discovering, as does the adolescent narrator of "Summer Fires," "how dangerous people were to one another." A story such as "Winter Country," with its counterpointing of Geoff's self-destruction and Alex's quest for personal salvation, shows how difficult and how central are human relations, especially sexual relations, in Shadbolt's world. Repeatedly he shows the dangers of self-deception, the need for and the difficulties of a responsible and knowledgeable commitment, the burdens of existential freedom.

In "The Presence of Music" one of the characters complains of the narrator's novel that "his people aren't individuals, they're just variations on a theme—in words instead of in colour or music." She might have been speaking of Shadbolt's own stories, since compared to the stories of Maurice Gee, for example, these stories lack densely realized, sharply individualized characters. The characters tend to be representative types, existing for the sake of the social themes, and the collections are structured around these themes, most obviously in the "triptych" concerning the artist and society in *The Presence of Music*. Shadbolt has said of himself, "In writing stories I often feel closer to the painter than to the novelist: the painter who sets out to exhaust the possibilities of a theme, from diverse directions, before moving to another." In the less successful stories such as "There Was a Mountain," the attempt to force social significance from rather unrealized characters leads to a strained and portentous style and a forced, melodramatic symbolism. However, in his best stories, such as "The Strangers" and "The Room," the characters are adequately realized to carry the social significance. In his last story, from 1964, "Figures of Light" (the title story of his 1978 selected stories), character, place, and thematic resonance all come together. Shadbolt has said of that story, that it was "the most near to perfect story [he] was ever to write in [his] life," and that he "had written to [his] likely limit within that form, and it was time to call it quits before [he] became a performer." He has not published another short story since then, but he has left behind him a legacy of permanent value in the genre.

—Lawrence Jones

See the essay on "The Room."

———————

SHALAMOV, Varlam (Tikhonovich). Russian. Born in Vologda, 18 June 1907. Educated at Law Faculty, Moscow University, 1926–29. Married and divorced. Political prisoner, in labor camps in North Urals, 1929–31, in Kolyma, Siberia, 1937–53. Journalist and writer, 1932–37; freelance journalist, 1956–82. Member, Russian Writers Union. *Died 17 January 1982.*

PUBLICATIONS

Short Stories

Kolymskie rasskazy.   1978; as *Kolyma Tales,* 1980.
Graphite.   1981.

Voskreshenie listvennitsy [The Revival of the Larch] (includes stories and prose), edited by Michael Heller. 1985; edited by I. Sirotinskaya, 1989.
Levyi bereg [The Left Bank].   1989.
Pechatka ili KR–2 [The Glove or KT–2].   1990.

Verse

Shelest list'ev: Stikhi [The Rustling of Leaves: Poems]. 1964.
Doroga i sud'ba: Kniga stikhov [The Road and Fate: Book of Poems].   1967.
Moskovskie oblaka: Stikhi [Moscow Clouds: Poems]. 1972.
Tochka kipeniia: Stikhi [Boiling-point: Poems].   1977.

*

Critical Studies: "Art out of Hell" by John Glad, *Survey* 107, 1979; "Beyond Bitterness" by Irving Howe, in *The New York Review of Books* 27, August 1980; "Surviving the Gulag" by George Gibian, in *The New Leader* 63, 1980; "Stories from Kolyma: The Sense of History," in *Hebrew University Studies in Literature and the Arts* 17, 1989, "A Tale Untold: Shalamov's 'A Day Off,'" in *Studies in Short Fiction* 28, 1991, and "Shalamov's Kolyma," in *The New Myth of Siberia,* edited by Galya Diment and Yury Slezkine, 1993, all by Leona Toker.

* * *

Varlam Shalamov's short stories deal with the inmates of Stalin's concentration camps. The narrating voice is usually that of a released prisoner imaginatively reliving and rethinking his past. Whether directly autobiographical or slightly fictionalized, the stories are based on real issues and events. Shalamov described them as "documentary prose" that records an authentic and highly emotional engagement with things of which the author has the most profound understanding. He sought the kind of absolute truthfulness which meant not only absence of reticences or wish-fulfilling embellishments but also freedom from literary conventions and from the language of traditional morality. His work shows, indeed, that traditional schemata are inapplicable to the experience that had fallen to his lot. For instance, the story "On Tick" starts with a sentence reminiscent of the opening of Pushkin's *The Queen of Spades* (1834), yet with telltale differences that set the atmosphere of a world in which moral barriers have been displaced, emotional responses cancelled, and human relationships transformed beyond recognition.

Most of Shalamov's protagonists are incapable of any active response to the violence they have to endure. Their physical and psychic energies have been totally depleted by chronic hunger, long hours of slave-labor, frost, filth, and abuse at the hands of the camp authorities and criminal convicts. In a physical state verging on that of the walking skeletons that one sees in documentaries on the liberation of Nazi camps, these people find that their emotions have been dulled, that the limit of the humiliations they can stand has been pushed back, and that most ethical distinctions have become ambivalent or irrelevant. The most shocking thing in "On Tick" is not the bare fact of the criminal convicts' killing a political prisoner for his refusal to give up his woolen sweater but the matter-of-fact way in which the murder is presented, with the authorial persona's final response being "now I had to find a new partner." A likewise merciless record of the prisoners' responses to atrocity ends such stories as "Berries," "Condensed Milk," and "Quiet."

Shalamov does not condemn his characters for lying, faking, bribing, not sharing food, begging for a piece of bread or a whiff of tobacco smoke, rummaging in garbage heaps—he too has done most of these things. Nor does he criticize them for failing to rise to supererogatory action— his characters, he says, are martyrs who could not, did not know how to, become heroes. He tends to present them at the stage when most of the props of their identities (education, social status, affiliations, professions, clothes, relationships, most of the flesh) have been removed or worn down, leaving no option but that of tacit passive resistance. Yet even these people can preserve their moral fiber so long as they do not inform on or bully others and do not accept what is being done to them. At the basis of their self-respect are mute anger, emotional independence, and a refusal to justify cruelty and exploitation or to accept the authorities and the criminals at their own valuation.

The stories present different aspects of the culture of the camps. Though Shalamov rejected the good/evil dichotomy in character portrayal, he believed that his stories, a truthful but not despondent or cynical testimony, are— rather than are about—the victory of good, a slap in the face of evil: testifying means restoring meaning to crushed lives; replacing sentimental illusions by a clear account of camp semiology and logistics amounts to a reassertion of individual freedom. Shalamov also believed that though writers are entitled to their own opinions, they have no right to teach the audience. His separate stories therefore frequently display a contradiction between narrative commentary and plot or images, as though the author's opinions were being tested against reality. Owing to this principle of reassessment, as well as to often puzzling collocations of carefully selected narrative details, most stories raise subtle and complex philosophical issues— even if at first they strike one as plain testimony. The deliberate uncouthness of Shalamov's laconic, almost mutilated style is peculiarly appropriate to the austere setting, thematised ethical paradoxes, and the valorization of moral/intellectual freedom.

Shalamov did not participate in the ideological debates of the post-Stalinist period: for him the rhetoric of "socialism with a human face" was as vapid as the official propaganda. Both were voided of meaning by his bland unconcern and by the totally different set of values implicit in his vocabulary. This may have rendered his prose more dangerous for the regime than the writings of active dissidents. His dream of having his stories printed in Russia did not come true in his lifetime: he did not live to see their publication after *glasnost* and *perestroika* had got under way. In a shelter for the disabled, blind, deaf, and in constantly deteriorating health, he held in his hands only the collection of his stories published in London in 1978. Amidst the frosts of 1982, in a move that meant "only madmen can think this way," he was taken to a psychiatric clinic where, according to a friend's account, he died three days later of untreated pheumonia.

—Leona Toker

See the essay on "The Snake Charmer."

SHEN CONGWEN. Chinese. Born in Fenghuang, Hunan, 28 December 1902. Attended military school; studied in Peking, 1922. Married Zhang Zhaohe in 1933; two sons. Served in army, 1918-20. Writer, from 1927; professor of Chinese literature, Shanghai, University of Wuhan, 1930-31, Qingdao, 1933, Southwest Associated University, Kunming, 1937-45, and Peking University, 1945-49; literary editor, Tianjin *Da Gong Bao*, Peking, 1933-37; underwent re-education, 1949; research worker, Museums of Chinese History, Peking, and Institute of History of the Chinese Academy of Social Sciences, from 1978. *Died 10 May 1988.*

PUBLICATIONS

Short Stories

Mi gan [Mandarin Oranges].   1927.
Yu hou ji qita [After Rain, and Other Stories].   1928.
Ludian ji qita [The Inn, and Other Stories].   1930.
Shizi chuan [The Marble Carrying Boat].   1931.
Long Zhu [name].   1931.
Kangkai de wangzi [The Generous Prince].   1933.
A-hei xiaoshi [The Story of A-hei].   1933.
Yuexia xiaojing [Under Moonlight].   1933; revised edition, 1943.
Ru Rui ji [Ru Rui Collection].   1934.
Bian cheng [The Frontier City] (novella).   1934; revised edition, 1943; as "The Border Town," in *The Border Town and Other Stories,* 1981.
Ba jun tu [Portrait of Eight Steeds].   1935.
Xiaoshuoji [Fiction].   1936.
Xin yu jiu [The New and the Old].   1936.
Zhufuji [Housewife].   1939.
Hei ye [Dark Night] (novella).   1943.
Chang he [Long River] (novella).   1943(?); revised edition, 1945.
Chun dengji ["Spring" and "Lamp" collection].   1943.
The Chinese Earth: Stories.   1947; revised edition, 1982.
The Border Town and Other Stories.   1981.

Novels

Chang xia [Long Summer].   1928.
A-li-si yu Zhongguo ji [Alice's Adventures in China].   2 vols., 1928.
Guizishou [The Executioner].   1928.
Hao guan xianshi de ren [The Busybody].   1928.
Ruwuhou [After Entering the Ranks].   1928.
Laoshi ren [The Simpleton].   1928; as *Yi ge furen de riji* [A Woman's Diary], 1932.
Nanzi xuzhi [What a Man Must Know].   1929.
Shisi ye jian [Night of the Fourteenth].   1929.
Dai guan riji [Diary of a Stupid Bureaucrat].   1929.
Shenwu zhi ai [The Shaman's Love].   1929.
Chen [Sinking].   1930(?).
Jiu meng [Past Dreams].   1930.
Yi ge nu zhuyuan de shenghuo [The Life of an Actress].   1931.
Ni tu [Mud].   1932.
Hu chu [Tiger Cub].   1932.
Dushi yi furen [A Lady of the City].   1932.
Yi ge muqin [A Mother].   1933.
Shenshi de taitai [The Gentry Wife].   1933(?).
Yumuji [The Roving Eye].   1934.
Fengzi [name].   1937.
Xiaozhai [place name, meaning "Little Stockade"].   1937.

Zhu xu [The Candle Extinguished].   1941.
Hai fengji [Black Phoenix].   1943.
Yunlu jishi [Yunlu Chronicles].   1947.
Chun [Spring].   1943; revised edition, 1949.
A-Jin [name].   1943; revised edition, 1949.

Other

Yazi [Duck] (stories, essays, poems, plays).   1926.
Bu si riji [A Pre-posthumous Diary].   1928.
Yi ge tiancai de tongxin [Correspondence from a Born Talent].   1930.
Jiaji [Collected Works].   1930.
Ziji [New Works].   1931.
Ji Hu Yeping [Remembering Hu Yeping].   1932.
Momoji [Froth] (literary criticism).   1934.
Ji Ding Ling [Remembering Ding Ling].   1934.
Zizhuan (autobiography).   1934; revised edition, 1981.
Xuanji [Selected Works], edited by Xu Chensi and Ye Wangyu.   1936.
Jie xuan [Selected Masterpieces].   1936.
Xiaoshuo xuan [Selected Fiction], edited by Shao Hou.   1936.
Xiang xing sanji [Discursive Notes on Traveling through Hunan].   1936; revised edition, 1943.
Fei yu can zha [Letters Never Mailed], with Xiao Qian.   1937; revised edition as *Yunnan kan yunji*, 1943.
Kunming dong jing [Winter Scenes in Kunming].   1939.
Xiangxi [West Hunan].   1939.
Ji Ding Ling xu shi [sequel to Remembering Ding Ling].   1939.
Rurui.   1941.
Xuanji [Selected Works], edited by Zhen Lei.   1947-49.
Xuanji [Selected Works].   1957.
Zhongguo sizhou tu an [Designs of Chinese Silk].   1957.
Tang Song tong jing [Bronze Mirrors of the Tang and Song Dynasties].   1958.
Ming jin [Ming Dynasty Brocades].   1959.
Longfeng yishu [The Art of Dragons and Phoenixes].   1960.
Sanwen xuan [Selected Essays].   1981.
Zhongguo gudai fushi yanjiu [Researches into Ancient Chinese Costume].   1981.
Xiaoshuo xuan [Selected Fiction].   1981.
Xiaoshuo xuan [Selected Fiction], edited by Ling Yu.   2 vols., 1982.
Recollections of West Hunan (essays).   1982.
Wenji [Works], edited by Shao Huaqiang and Ling Yu.   12 vols., 1982-85.
Xuanji [Selected Works], edited by Ling Yu.   5 vols., 1983.
Xiangxi fengcai [West Hunan Beauty].   1984.

Editor, with Sun Lianggong, *Zhongguo xiaoshuo shi jiangyi* [Lectures on the History of Chinese Fiction].   1930(?).
Editor, *Liu Yu shi xuan*, by Liu Yu.   1932.
Editor, *Xiandai shi jiezuo xuan* [Masterpieces of Modern Poetry].   1932.
Editor, with others, *Fushiji* [Floating World Collection].   1935.
Editor, *Xiandai riji wenxuan* [Selections of Modern Diary Literature].   1936.
Editor, with Lao Yu, *Meili de Beijing*.   1956.

*

Bibliography: in *Chinese Fiction: A Bibliography of Books and Articles in Chinese and English* by Tien-yi Li, 1968; *A Bibliography of Studies and Translations of Modern Chinese Literature, 1918–1942* by Donald A. Gibbs and Yun-chen Li, 1975; in *Chinese Studies in English* by Tsung-shun Na, 1991.

Critical Studies: in *A History of Modern Chinese Fiction 1917-1957* by C.T. Hsia, 1961; *Shen Ts'ung* by Hua-ling Nieh, 1972; *The Odyssey of Shen Congwen* (includes bibliography) by Jeffrey C Kinkley, 1987; *Fictional Realism in 20th-Century China: Mao Dun, Lao She, Shen Congwen* by David Der-wei Wang, 1992.

*   *   *

During his literary career, Shen Congwen wrote more than 50 volumes of published works. They include poems, travelogues, critical essays, art history, autobiography and biography, fables, short stories, and novels. He is best known for his signal short stories and his two novellas, *Bian cheng* ("The Frontier City") and *Chang he* ("The Long River"), which are quite Nietzschean in their treatment and outlook. Throughout his fictions Shen Congwen remains faithful to the earth; human activity is treated as a part of cosmic energy; moral codes are regarded as relative to social and political power; resentment against the rich and powerful is considered as non-productive as resentment against the world; candor, courage, and capacity to be and to survive vicissitudes are admired; the life—vivacious life—is celebrated with a mixture of joy, sympathy, and compassion.

Shen Congwen's fiction is notable for its regionalism, primitivism, and democratic humanism. The characters he treats of are usually country and small-town folk, simple people who stand in sharp contrast to the country gentry in the background. The simple people are soldiers, sailors, prostitutes, peasants, small shopkeepers, ferry-boat operators, rural small-mill owners, and even the very young and domestic animals. Their region is South China, especially near the borders of Guizhou, Hunan, and Sichvan. Shen Congwen's primitivism is displayed in his stories about the aborigines, such as the Miao tribe, who live in the mountains that rise from the plains where reside the sophisticated Han people—the ethnic Chinese—who have something to learn from the primitives. But Shen Congwen's democratic humanism is shown in his focus on the individual qualities of his characters, on each one's particularity and feelings, each one's hard work and dreams, each one's courage and endurance, each one's dignity and worth, and each one's fate. Shen Congwen's fiction says, "Everyone has his or her worth, and despite death and the tricks of fickle fate, human life is worth living."

Shen Congwen's stories often examine the ideosyncrasies of some individual human character in considerable detail in the context of certain circumstances and with the person being motivated by a zest for life and some strong desire or passion. Three such character studies are outstanding. In "Deng" (1930, "The Lamp") a retired army cook in his fifties becomes the servant of a young college professor, whose distinguished family he had served many years previously. The cook's passion to serve his young master with meticulous perfection leads him to become a "mother" who interfers in the professor's female friendships. In "Bai Zu" (1936; a personal name that literally means "cypress tree") a hardy sailor arrives in port and visits his prostitute girlfriend. And in "Yi ge da wang" (1934, "A Bandit Chief"), an excerpt from *Shen Congwen zizhuan* (Autobiography), a reformed bandit chief becomes an army commander's bodyguard and messenger. Although a man of skill, daring, and enormous vigor, the commander executes him when he learns that he plans to return to his life of crime.

Three other of Shen Congwen's stories illustrate his romantic primitivism and his interest in the Miao tribesmen (his grandmother was a Miao). His tales of the Miao, as the scholar Kinkley has noted, are not simply "pastoral," for they "mystify nature." In "Lung Chu" (1929; a personal name that literally means "vermilion dragon") a handsome young Miao prince, a paragon of perfection, defeats a girl in a courtship singing contest and wins her for his bride. In "Mei Jin Bao zi yu na yang" (1929, "The White Kid"), Mei Jin (which means "seductive as gold") and Bao Zu ("the leopard") have fallen in love because of their songs. They agree to a rendezvous in a cave to consummate their marriage, a proposed act that is taboo because a Miao girl may not marry the man who deflowers her. Nevertheless, the man agrees to exchange a "perfectly white kid" for the "virgin red blood" of the girl. However, in his search for perfection in the kid he arrives at the cave several hours after the agreed upon time to find the girl dead by her own hand. In (*Yuexia Xiaojing*) (1933, "Under Moonlight") the hero No Yu ("tender protector") and his girl carry out this act disapproved of by the gods and suffer the consequences. These Miao tales are not treated realistically but in terms of myth and legend. As Kinkley observes, Shen Congwen sees his aborigines as living "in a physical and spiritual world beyond ordinary Chinese history."

Three of Shen Congwen's tales show his efforts to adapt the modernism he had learned from Western models— Dumas *fils,* Proust, Dickens, Freud, Joyce, D.H. Lawrence—with his Chinese subject matter. In "Hui Ming" (1929, "The Yellow Chickens") the hero, Hui Ming, which means "able to understand," plays the role of "Holy Fool." An army cook, Hui Ming is a tall, thin, long-nosed man with a heavy beard. He meets insults with silence and is always in control of himself. He has an innate understanding and respect for animals and raises a flock of yellow chickens from the gift of a pet hen. "San ge nanzi yi ge nu sen" (1930, "Three Men and a Girl"), a story of army life in a garrisoned town, is a detailed character study that has a sustained and unified plot. Despite its realism, it deals ironically with a strange case of sexual perversion. The three men are two solders—a bugler and a sargeant—and the young proprietor of a bean-curd shop in the town. The girl is a teenage beauty and the mistress of two white dogs. She lives across from the bean-curd shop. The two soldiers have become infatuated with her and visit the shop nearly every day to catch a sight of her beauty. One day they learn that the girl had died by her own hand and her corpse buried. The next day they learn that her corpse had been stolen from its coffin. Later, it is discovered covered with wild blue chrysanthemums in a cave half a *li* away from the grave sight. "K'an hong lu," (1940?, "The Rainbow") is one of Shen Congwen's most experimental modernistic efforts. Showing the influences of Proust, Freud, and Joyce, the tale is a dramatized encounter between a man and a beautiful woman at her domicile on New Year's Eve. It is snowing outside but warm inside from the fire in the fireplace. The action consists of a constantly shifting, complex succession of things seen or imagined together with dialogue carried on by several autobiographical personae and the woman herself. It is divided, as Kinkley observes, "into separate conscious and unconscious levels of discourse." Like the phenomenon of the rainbow, all the colorings of desire are promoted by a range of sensations, feelings, imaginations, and microactions of restrained sexuality such as the mental undressing of the woman and the caressing of her body with the eyes. Although "The Rainbow" falls short of being successful, it is a highly interesting production.

Although Shen Congwen maintained his respect and appreciation of the old Chinese literary tradition, as a modernist he continually experimented with new literary techniques and forms. To him, writing was an act of artistic craftsmanship, and his view of it was far more aesthetic than political. When the Communists came to power and Mao Zedong laid out the principles of the new "socialist realism" at the Yenan Conference, Shen Congwen knew he was incapable of writing by such formulae and lapsed into silence as far as creative writing was concerned. Although he lived to the ripe age of 86, the heyday of his artistry ran from 1928 to 1940. But he is perhaps the most important Chinese writer of short fiction after Lu Xun.

—Richard P. Benton

See the essays on "A Bandit Chief" and "The Husband."

SHÊN TS'UNG-WEN.   See SHEN CONGWEN.

SIENKIEWICZ, Henryk (Adam Aleksander Pius). Polish. Born in Wola Okrzejska, 5 May 1846. Educated at Warsaw Gymnasium, 1858–65; Polish University, Warsaw, 1866–71. Married 1) Maria Szetkiewicz (died 1885), one son and one daughter; 2) Maria Wolodkowicz (marriage annulled); 3) Maria Babska in 1904. Journalist and freelance writer; visited the United States to search for site for a California settlement, 1876–78; co-editor, *Słowo* (The Word) newspaper, 1882–87. Given an estate by the Polish government at Oblegorek, near Kielce, 1900. Recipient: Nobel prize for literature, 1905. *Died 15 November 1916.*

PUBLICATIONS

Collections

Dzieła [Works], edited by Julian Krzyzanowski.   60 vols., 1948–55.
Pisma wybrane [Selected Works].   1976—.

Short Stories

Yanko the Musician and Other Stories.   1893.
Lillian Morris and Other Stories.   1894.
Sielanka, A Forest Picture, and Other Stories.   1898.
So Runs the World: Stories.   1898.
Tales.   1899.
Life and Death and Other Legends and Stories.   1904.
Western Septet: Seven Stories of the American West, edited by Marion Moore Coleman.   1973.
Charcoal Sketches and Other Tales.   1988.

Novels

Na marne.   1872; as *In Vain,* 1899.
Stary sługa [The Old Servants].   1875.
Hania.   1876; translated as *Hania,* 1897; in part as *Let Us Follow Him,* 1897.
Za chlebem.   1880; as *After Bread,* 1897; as *For Daily Bread,* 1898; as *Peasants in Exile,* 1898; as *Her Tragic Fate,* 1899; as *In the New Promised Land,* 1900. Trilogy
Ogniem i mieczem.   1884; as *With Fire and Sword,* 1890.
Potop.   1886; as *The Deluge: An Historical Novel of Poland, Sweden, and Russia,* 1892.
Pan Wołodyjowski.   1887–88; as *Pan Michael,* 1895.
On the Sunny Shore.   1886; as *On the Bright Shore,* 1898.
Bez dogmatu.   1889–90; as *Without Dogma,* 1893.
Rodzina Połanieckich.   1894; as *Children of the Soil,* 1895; as *The Irony of Life,* 1900.
Quo vadis?   1896; translated as *Quo Vadis?,* 1896.
The Third Woman.   1897.
Na jasnym brzegu.   1897; as *In Monte Carlo,* 1899.
The Fate of a Soldier.   1898.
Where Worlds Meet.   1899.
Krzyzacy.   1900; as *The Knights of the Cross,* 1900; as *Danusia,* 1900; as *The Teutonic Knights,* 1943.
Na polu chwały.   1906; as *On the Field of Glory,* 1906.
Wiry.   1910; as *Whirlpools: A Novel of Modern Poland,* 1910.
Legiony [Legions] (unfinished).   1914.

Other

Listy z podrózy do Ameryki.   1876–78; as *Portrait of America: Letters of Sienkiewicz,* edited by Charles Morley.   1959.
Listy z Afryki [Letters from Africa].   1891–92.
W pustyni i w puszczy (for children).   1911; as *In Desert and Wilderness,* 1912; as *Through the Desert,* 1912.
Listy [Letters], edited by Julian Krzyzanowski and others, 1977— .

*

Critical Studies: *The Patriotic Novelist of Poland, Sienkiewicz* by Monica M. Gardner, 1926; *Sienkiewicz: A Retrospective Synthesis* by Waclaw Lednicki, 1960; *Wanderers Twain: Modjeska and Sienkiewicz: A View from California* by Arthur Prudden and Marion Moore Coleman, 1964; *Sienkiewicz* by M. Giergielewicz, 1968.

*   *   *

Although a prolific writer of novels, travel sketches, plays, and short stories, Henryk Sienkiewicz is perhaps best known as a writer of historical fiction. Awarded the Nobel prize for literature in 1905, Sienkiewicz was established as the most popular writer in Poland beginning in the 1880's with his well-known trilogy—*Ogniem i mieczem (With Fire and Sword), Potop (The Deluge),* and *Pan Wołodyjowski (Pan Michael)*—a sequence of novels focused on historical conflicts and invasions that occurred in 17th-century Poland. As a short story writer, Sienkiewicz produced a considerable body of work over his lifetime—over 70 stories. Yet, his most widely known work is an historical novel, *Quo vadis?,* that depicts Nero's Rome in

the throes of conflict between a decaying empire and the revolutionary rise of Christianity. Critics have almost universally regarded Sienkiewicz as a remarkably gifted storyteller and interpreter of the Polish spirit whose narrative skill engages readers with vivid, dramatic, and fast-moving plot; at the same time, they have concurred that his more psychological novels suffer from degrees of oversimplification and, at times, sentimental treatment of character, making them on the whole less successful than his historical fiction.

Taken as a whole, Sienkiewicz's short stories reflect a completely different artistic sensibility from what appears in the historical novels. His stories are marked by concentrated dramatic conflict and sharp emotional pulls that resonate with a deep sense of the human spirit that persevered during centuries of social and political turmoil in Poland. For the most part, Sienkiewicz focused his short stories on the immediate social and human problems of peasant society in 19th-century rural Poland, making an artistic statement that pulled universal significance from the particular details observed in the simple, the suffering, and the non-glorious.

Sienkiewicz's early stories convey strong social messages derived from material focused in the profound conflicts that exist between spirited individuals and a repressive society. "The Charcoal Sketches" depicts a dispossessed and newly emancipated peasantry negotiating with a corrupt, insensitive bureaucracy; "The Two Roads" shows the marital "contest" and personal conflict between a commoner and a gentleman vying for the hand of the same woman; "From the Memoirs of a Poznan Tutor" exposes the experience of a perfectly normal Polish schoolboy made into a failure by prejudiced German teachers; and "Bartek the Conqueror" reveals aspects of a Polish peasant's suffering in life under an oppressive Prussian regime.

While the backdrop of Polish social and political history is not essential to understanding Sienkiewicz's short fiction, it is certainly helpful. Following the Three Partitions of the 18th century, Poles emerged from five generations of dispossession, foreign rule, and political oppression, facts which have led historian Norman Davies to assert that Poland was, both before and during Sienkiewicz's lifetime, "little more than an idea . . . a memory from the past, [and] a hope for the future." For generations, Poland remained a property of mind and spirit rather than material reality.

Since Sienkiewicz didn't respond to these conditions with revolutionary—and hence Romantic—tendencies, critics classify him as a positivist, one who sought rational and pragmatic conciliation through economic progress rather than insurrection. The characters in his short stories, although thoroughly grounded in realism, contain a strong current of hope as the basis for restoration of the human spirit denied by political and cultural repression. While these characters struggle to endure, they seek solutions largely through the application of industry tempered by deeply felt desire. Beneath the surface of pragmatic conciliation, the continual flame of Romantic hope seems to burn in Sienkiewicz's short stories, yielding a powerful, if often tragic, effect.

"Yanko the Musician," for example, is a story about a young peasant boy whose only possession is a promising musical genius that fills him with a passionate attraction to music. Through his gift, he transforms the everyday sounds of human society and the quiet whistlings of nature into comforting, aesthetic delight. His love provokes him to fashion a simple stringed instrument from a shingle and a horse hair, which he plays contentedly. When he spies a squire's beautiful violin, however, the boy succumbs to desire and steals it; he is convicted and finally dies in a scene that Sienkiewicz presents with great compassion, showing the spirit of eros still alive in a boy whose social existence is doomed a priori. "Yanko the Musician" captures the essence of the abrupt collision between a deep pathos and cruel ideology that characterizes much of Sienkiewicz's short fiction.

Perhaps his best short story, and the one most frequently extolled by critics, is "The Lighthouse Keeper of Aspinwall," an extraordinary portrait of a Polish political refugee named Skawinski who wanders the earth seeking a peaceful, productive existence until he finally settles as a lighthouse keeper off the coast of Panama. As an emigre, Skawinski in effect symbolizes the dispossessed plight of the Polish people, a fact supported by his incredible longing and feeling of purposelessness without the anchor of his homeland. When Skawinski one day receives a parcel of books that contains the epic Polish Romantic poem *Pan Tadeusz* by Adam Mickiewicz, he lapses into deep, passionate revery that keeps him reading all night long and causes, through his neglect, a ship to crash on the rocks. Skawinski is relieved from his post as lighthouse keeper and doomed to wander eternally, albeit with his book, *Pan Tadeusz*, clasped to his breast. This conflict is deftly portrayed with precise and deeply moving details. By bringing together the sharp contrast between hope and reality, Sienkiewicz succeeds at creating a short story masterpiece, a fiction that remains open-ended in both criticism and revery, exposing the excesses of Romanticism as well as the limitations of positivism.

It is this poignant contrast of loss and love, suffering and desire, that elevate Sienkiewicz's short fiction to the realm of provocative and powerful literary art, which speaks with a universal significance that transcends the limitations of time and space.

—Paul Sladky

SILKO, Leslie Marmon. American. Born in 1948. Educated at Board of Indian Affairs schools, Laguna, New Mexico, and a Catholic school in Albuquerque; University of New Mexico, Albuquerque, B.A. (summa cum laude) in English 1969; studied law briefly. Has two sons. Taught for 2 years at Navajo Community College, Tsaile, Arizona; lived in Ketchikan, Alaska, for 2 years; taught at University of New Mexico; professor of English, University of Arizona, Tucson, since 1978. Recipient: National Endowment for the Arts award, 1974; *Chicago Review* award, 1974; Pushcart prize, 1977; MacArthur Foundation grant, 1983. Lives in Tucson.

PUBLICATIONS

Short Stories

Storyteller.   1981.

Novels

Ceremony.   1977.
Almanac of the Dead.   1991.

Play

Lullaby, with Frank Chin, adaptation of the story by Silko (produced San Francisco, 1976).

Verse

Laguna Woman.   1974.

Other

The Delicacy and Strength of Lace: Letters Between Silko and James A. Wright, edited by Anne Wright.   1986.

*

Critical Studies: *Silko* by Per Seyersted, 1980; *Four American Indian Literary Masters* by Alan R. Velie, 1982.

* * *

Born in Albuquerque in 1948 of mixed Laguna Pueblo and German-American ancestry, Leslie Marmon Silko draws on both literary and oral traditions in her only collection of short fiction *Storyteller,* which has assumed a place of central importance in American-Indian literature. Like Silko's longer fiction and poetry, *Storyteller* juxtaposes diverse approaches to storytelling to explore the meaning of tribal traditions in an alien, and frequently hostile, world. Although they acknowledge the reality of suffering and destruction in Indian communities, Silko's stories seek to help reestablish the encompassing harmony that formed the foundation of traditional tribal life.

Storyteller montages "poetic" versions of tribal myths; bits of conversations with or letters from friends such as Euro-American poet James Wright and Acoma Pueblo writer Simon Ortiz; pieces of Silko's family history, many focusing on women storytellers such as Silko's Aunt Susie and Grandma A'mooh; and nine relatively conventional short stories concerning the struggles of contemporary Native Americans (Eskimo and Yupik as well as Laguna, Navajo, and Hopi). Highlighting the centrality of kinship and landscape to American-Indian life, the volume includes 26 photographs of Silko's family and the Arizona/New Mexico landscapes where many of the stories take place.

Both Silko's reworking of tribal legends and myths and her use of sections of *Storyteller* in her influential novels *Ceremony* and *Almanac of the Dead* underline her interest in the relationship between existing stories and contemporary experience. As she wrote in a letter to Wright, Silko is fascinated by the ways different versions of stories respond to different needs: "each version is true and each version is correct and what matters is to have as many of the stories as possible and to have them together and to understand the emergence, keeping all the stories in mind at the same time."

On one level, *Storyteller*'s focus on narrative process recalls the metafictions of Samuel Beckett or Donald Barthelme. Where Euro-American postmodernism explores the alienating and disruptive impact of a type of self-reflexive, sometimes solipsistic, awareness that calls all established traditions into question, however, Silko's characters seek to reestablish cultural continuity to transform their relationship with a real and threatening external world. Although some stories focus on contemporary cultural conflict and others on legendary tribal figures (the hero twins, Yellow Woman, Spider Woman, Coyote, Arrowboy), the opening lines of "Storytelling" accurately delineate Silko's fundamental perspective: "You should understand the way it was back then, because it is the same even now."

One of a sequence of sections focusing on women or perhaps a woman who leaves her husband and children, "Yellow Woman" exemplifies Silko's treatment of the struggle to understand the connections between modern life and tribal myth. Sensing her affinity with the legendary Yellow Woman (Kochininako), who went to the mountains with a *ka'tsina* spirit, Silko's protagonist wonders whether "Yellow Woman had known who she was—if she knew that she would become part of the stories." Repeatedly the woman attempts to distance herself from her mythic predecessor: "I will be sure that I am not Yellow Woman. Because she is from out of time past and I live now and I've been to school and there are highways and pickup trucks that Yellow Woman never saw." But Silva, who assumes the *ka'tsina* role, assures her that "someday they will talk about us, and they will say, 'Those two lived long ago when things like that happened.'" Never consciously resolving these issues, the protagonist decides not to tell her family the "true" (mythic) story when she returns home, claiming she was kidnaped by a Navajo. Yet Silva suggests, that, on levels difficult to reduce to logical propositions, Silva's awareness of the traditional story provides the strength that enables him to defeat the white rancher who attempts to take him to jail. The themes of departure, romance, and survival recur in the book's next section, a poetic narrative of Yellow Woman's departure with Buffalo Man, which ultimately provides the tribe with a trustworthy source of food.

In several stories Silko presents words as the primary weapon available to tribal people resisting European-Americans ranging from the brutal policeman in "Tony's Story" to the uncomprehending Catholic priest in "The Man To Send Rain Clouds," perhaps Silko's best-known short story. As the Laguna scout comments in "A Geronimo Story": "Anybody can act violently—there is nothing to it; but not every person is able to destroy his enemy with words." Similarly, the frequently anthologized "Storyteller" develops the theme of words as weapons. Drawing her inspiration from an old man's story of a polar bear stalking a lone hunter, a Yupik woman, lures an abusive white man to his death. Rather than establishing a tight parallel between the two narratives, Silko portrays both as attempts to recover truths threatened by European-American institutions. Even when told of witnesses who described the death as accidental, the woman refuses to disclaim her responsibility: "I will not change the story, not even to escape this place and go home. I intended that he die. The story must be told as it is."

Unflinchingly honest about the problems that have disrupted the balance fundamental to traditional American-Indian life, Silko's fiction can be viewed as a modern version of the ceremonies through which tribes reestablished the complex sense of harmony underlying their psychological, social, and environmental wellbeing. Awareness of the old stories and their connection with new situations is the prerequisite for the realization of this vision in the lives of her readers. As she writes at the beginning of "The Storyteller's Escape": "With these stories of ours we can escape almost anything, with these stories we will survive."

—Craig Hansen Werner

————

SILLITOE, Alan. English. Born in Nottingham, 4 March 1928. Educated in Nottingham schools until 1942. Served as a wireless operator in the Royal Air Force, 1946–49. Married the poet Ruth Fainlight in 1959; one son and one daughter. Factory worker, 1942–45; air control assistant, Langar Aerodrome, Nottinghamshire, 1945–46; lived in France and Spain, 1952–58. Recipient: Authors Club prize, 1958; Hawthornden prize, for fiction, 1960. Fellow, Royal Geographical Society, 1975; honorary fellow, Manchester Polytechnic, 1977. Lives in Wittersham, Kent.

PUBLICATIONS

Short Stories

The Loneliness of the Long-Distance Runner.   1959.
The Ragman's Daughter.   1963.
A Sillitoe Selection.   1968.
Guzman, Go Home.   1968.
Men, Women, and Children.   1973.
Down to the Bone.   1976.
The Second Chance and Other Stories.   1981.
The Far Side of the Street.   1988.

Novels

Saturday Night and Sunday Morning.   1958.
The General.   1960; as *Counterpoint,* 1968.
Key to the Door.   1961.
The Death of William Posters.   1965.
A Tree on Fire.   1967.
A Start in Life.   1970.
Travels in Nihilon.   1971.
Raw Material.   1972; revised edition, 1974.
The Flame of Life.   1974.
The Widower's Son.   1976.
The Storyteller.   1979.
Her Victory.   1982.
The Lost Flying Boat.   1983.
Down from the Hill.   1984.
Life Goes On.   1985.
Out of the Whirlpool.   1987.
The Open Door.   1989.
Last Loves.   1990.
Leonard's War.   1991.

Verse

Without Beer or Bread.   1957.
The Rats and Other Poems.   1960.
A Falling Out of Love and Other Poems.   1964.
Love in the Environs of Voronezh and Other Poems.   1968.
Shaman and Other Poems.   1968.
Poems, with Ted Hughes and Ruth Fainlight.   1971.
Canto Two of the Rats.   1973.
Barbarians and Other Poems.   1974.
Storm: New Poems.   1974.
Words Broadsheet 19, with Ruth Fainlight.   1975.

Day-Dream Communiqué.   1977.
From Snow on the North Side of Lucifer.   1979.
Snow on the North Side of Lucifer.   1979.
More Lucifer.   1980.
Israel.   1981.
Sun Before Departure: Poems 1974 to 1982.   1984.
Tides and Stone Walls, photographs by Victor Bowley.
    1986.
Three Poems.   1988.

Plays

The Ragman's Daughter (produced 1966).
All Citizens Are Soldiers, with Ruth Fainlight, from a play
    by Lope de Vega (produced 1967).   1969.
The Slot Machine (as *This Foreign Field,* produced 1970).
    In *Three Plays,* 1978.
Pit Strike (televised 1977).   In *Three Plays,* 1978.
The Interview (produced 1978).   In *Three Plays,* 1978.
Three Plays.   1978.

Screenplays: *Saturday Night and Sunday Morning,* 1960;
The Loneliness of the Long-Distance Runner, 1961; *Coun-
terpoint,* from his own novel *The General,* 1968; *Che
Guevara,* 1968; *The Ragman's Daughter,* 1972.

Radio Play: *The General,* from his own novel, 1984.

Television Play: *Pit Strike,* 1977.

Other

Road to Volgograd (travel).   1964.
The City Adventures of Marmalade Jim (for children).
    1967; revised edition, 1977.
Mountains and Caverns: Selected Essays.   1975.
Big John and the Stars (for children).   1977.
The Incredible Fencing Fleas (for children).   1978.
Marmalade Jim at the Farm (for children).   1980.
The Saxon Shore Way: From Gravesend to Rye, photo-
    graphs by Fay Godwin.   1983.
Marmalade Jim and the Fox (for children).   1984.
Sillitoe's Nottinghamshire, photographs by David Sillitoe.
    1987.
Every Day of the Week: A Sillitoe Reader.   1987.

Editor, *Poems for Shakespeare 7.*   1979.

Translator, *Chopin's Winter in Majorca 1838–1839,* by
    Lois Ripoll.   1955.
Translator, *Chopin's Pianos: The Pleyel in Majorca,* by Lois
    Ripoll.   1958.

*

Bibliography: *Sillitoe: A Bibliography* by David E. Gerard,
1988.

Critical Studies: *Sillitoe* edited by Michael Marland, 1970;
Sillitoe by Allen Richard Penner, 1972; *Commitment as
Art: A Marxist Critique of a Selection of Sillitoe's Political
Fiction* by R.D. Vaverka, 1978; *Sillitoe: A Critical Assess-
ment* by Stanley S. Atherton, 1979; *Working-Class Fiction
in Theory and Practice: A Reading of Sillitoe* by Peter
Hitchcock, 1989.

*   *   *

Alan Sillitoe's reputation as an authentic working-class
writer began with the success of his novel *Saturday Night
and Sunday Morning* in 1958, soon made into a successful
film, and was confirmed by the volume of short stories, *The
Loneliness of the Long-Distance Runner* in the following
year. Both books, Sillitoe writes in "The Long Piece" (in
Mountains and Caverns), profit from the advice of the poet
Robert Graves, with whom Sillitoe was friendly while
living in Majorca: "I'm sure Nottingham's a town worth
writing about, if you're thinking of doing a novel." Not
only the novel but a series of vivid and convincing short
stories show Sillitoe's grudging obsession with that city and
the way of life of its workers. The world he reveals is
usually a harsh one, with poverty and deprivation a
consistent undercurrent, but his characters usually find
some ways of fighting back and asserting themselves—
though with no sense that what they do will be of any
political significance. As to the method of writing, Sillitoe
pays tribute in the essay "Mountains and Caverns," to the
story "Sand" by the Yiddish writer, Israel Joshua Singer.
Its lesson for him as a writer was that "a tale is all the
better—and richer—for being told in an unhurried, mean-
dering and human way. Not sentimental, but moving and
respectful of life."

The stories in *The Loneliness of the Long-Distance
Runner,* including the title story, are all told in this human
way, whether by an omniscient or a first-person narrator.
Their central characters are men and boys on the outskirts
of society, trying to overcome the loneliness which seems
omnipresent. The reader is led to a close feeling for these
characters, however tarnished or reprehensible. Their efforts to find happiness, like Uncle Ernest's generosity to
two small girls in a café, is always under threat from
authorities, which are seen as repressive and irrational. For
Sillitoe characteristically writes from the point of view of
the underdog, who is probably in the long run the loser.
"Mr. Rayner the School-teacher," admiring the young girls
at work in the shop across the street, is no more in charge of
his life than the two small boys visiting the circus in
"Noah's Ark," or the mentally retarded boys' gang-leader
Frankie Buller in the final story, named after him. At the
end of "The Decline and Fall of Frankie Buller," the
narrator, on a visit to England, encounters his former
gangleader, trying to read a cinema advertisement. He has
been given shock-treatment, and is now quiet and respectable. The narrator wonders, "would they succeed in
tapping and draining dry the immense subterranean reservoir of his dark inspired mind?" He clearly hopes not,
locating in Frankie—to the hospital authorities no doubt
nothing more than a dangerous case—something of the
power of the unconscious on which his own art is built, for
the narrator Alan is a writer who lives, like Sillitoe at the
time, in Majorca.

The Ragman's Daughter appeared in 1963, and takes the
reader into very much the same world. The opening story
(made into a film directed by Harold Becker) is the first-
person narrative of a young worker who spends his spare
time "nicking" whatever he can get his hands on, and who
draws into his crimes a school-girl (her father a successful
scrap-dealer), who enjoys the kicks without needing the
money. The writing vividly conveys the excitement of their
"jobs," and their inevitable eventual failure. The narrator
is caught, and goes to Borstal, and later to jail, while the girl
dies in a motorcycle accident. By the end, however, the
narrator has settled down to "going straight" and has a wife
and two kids. But he is still haunted by a vision of the dead
Doris, representative of the romantic qualities that life will
not allow to be realized. In these stories, there is more

psychological exploration, more subtlety. In "The Magic Box," for instance, the protagonist Fred becomes trapped in an obsessive world of the Morse Code (which he learnt during his National Service) as he tries to avoid confronting the accidental drowning of a young son and the subsequent failure of his relationship with his wife. After hospital treatment he returns home, to find his wife pregnant. The resolution of the story is violent but suggestive, characteristic of the "matrimonial life" of the unfortunate. The more explicitly political of these stories is "The Good Woman," in which Sillitoe celebrates the courage and resolution of Liza Atkins, making a living during the war by washing the clothes of American soldiers. Her son Harry is killed in Korea: "There was nothing on the face of the earth that would have made her say: 'It was worth it. That's a good thing to die for.'" Later Liza is involved in a strike at the factory where she goes to work: "She felt good, being on strike; it was a way of doing damage to those who bossed the world." Sillitoe conveys clearly the resentment of those at the bottom of the social system—what we would now style the underclass. The story ends with the narrator and Liza's surviving son drinking to her memory: "She was one of the best."

Thus Sillitoe has extended his range both psychologically and politically, while keeping mainly to the Nottingham world of his early experience. *Men, Women, and Children* shows his continuing mastery of the short story form, in particular in "Pit Strike" (which effectively mediates its political subject-matter through the very unexpected figure of a miner who sees the modern world in terms of the Old Testament) and in the extraordinary "Mimic," which explores the state of mind of a man who exists only in terms of his imitations of other people. It is seen as an obsessive condition and the reader has to work hard to understand how far he or she can accept the judgments of life stemming from this strange mind, and to decide whether at the end some kind of catharsis has been achieved. The volume ends with another courageous female in "Scenes from the Life of Margaret." Sillitoe continues to justify his claim to write short stories that are "not sentimental, but moving and respectful of life."

—Peter Faulkner

See the essay on "The Loneliness of the Long-Distance Runner."

SINGER, Isaac Bashevis. American. Born Icek-Hersz Zynger in Leoncin, Poland, 14 July 1904; emigrated to the U.S., 1935; became citizen, 1943. Educated at the Tachkemoni Rabbinical Seminary, Warsaw, 1921–22. Married Alma Haimann in 1940; one son from earlier marriage. Proofreader and translator, *Literarishe Bleter*, Warsaw, 1923–33; associate editor, *Globus*, Warsaw, 1933–35; journalist, *Vorwärts* (*Jewish Daily Forward*) Yiddish newspaper, New York, from 1935. Recipient: Louis Lemed prize, 1950, 1956; American Academy grant, 1959; Daroff Memorial award, 1963; Foreign Book prize (France), 1965; two National Endowment for the Arts grants, 1966; Bancarella prize (Italy), 1968; Brandeis University Creative Arts award, 1969; National Book award, for children's literature, 1970, and, for fiction, 1974; Nobel prize for literature, 1978; American Academy gold medal, 1989.

D.H.L.: Hebrew Union College, Los Angeles, 1963; D.Lit.: Colgate University, Hamilton, New York, 1972; D.Litt.: Texas Christian University, Fort Worth, 1972; Ph.D.: Hebrew University, Jerusalem, 1973; Litt.D.: Bard College, Annandale-on-Hudson, New York, 1974; Long Island University, Greenvale, New York, 1979. Member, American Academy, 1965; American Academy of Arts and Sciences, 1969; Jewish Academy of Arts and Sciences; Polish Institute of Arts and Sciences. *Died 24 July 1991.*

PUBLICATIONS

Short Stories

Gimpel the Fool and Other Stories, translated by Saul Bellow and others.   1957; as *Gimpel Tam un anderer Detailungen*, 1963.
The Spinoza of Market Street and Other Stories, translated by Elaine Gottlieb and others.   1961.
Short Friday and Other Stories, translated by Ruth Whitman and others.   1964.
Selected Short Stories, edited by Irving Howe.   1966.
The Séance and Other Stories, translated by Ruth Whitman and others.   1968.
A Friend of Kafka and Other Stories, translated by Isaac Bashevis Singer and others.   1970.
A Crown of Feathers and Other Stories, translated by Isaac Bashevis Singer and others.   1973.
Passions and Other Stories.   1975.
Old Love.   1979.
The Collected Stories.   1982.
The Image and Other Stories.   1985.
The Death of Methuselah and Other Stories.   1988.

Novels

Der sotn in Goray.   1935; as *Shoten an Goray un anderer Dertailungen* [Satan in Goray and Other Stories], 1943; as *Satan in Goray*, translated by Jacob Sloan, 1955.
Di Familie Mushkat.   1950; as *The Family Moskat*, translated by A.H. Gross.   1950.
The Magician of Lublin, translated by Elaine Gottlieb and Joseph Singer.   1960.
The Slave, translated by Isaac Bashevis Singer and Cecil Hemley.   1962.
The Manor, translated by Elaine Gottlieb and Joseph Singer.   1967.
The Estate, translated by Elaine Gottlieb, Joseph Singer, and Elizabeth Shub.   1969.
Enemies: A Love Story, translated by Alizah Shevrin and Elizabeth Shub.   1972.
Shosha, translated by Isaac Bashevis Singer and Joseph Singer.   1978.
Reaches of Heaven.   1980.
The Penitent.   1983.
The King of Fields, translated by Isaac Bashevis Singer, 1988.
Scum, translated by Rosaline Dukalsky Schwartz.   1991.
The Certificate, translated by Leonard Wolf.   1992.

Fiction (for children; translated by Isaac Bashevis Singer and Elizabeth Shub)

Zlateh the Goat and Other Stories.   1966.
Mazel and Shlimazel; or, The Milk of a Lioness.   1967.
The Fearsome Inn.   1967.

When Shlemiel Went to Warsaw and Other Stories, translated by Channah Kleinerman-Goldstein and others. 1968.
Joseph and Koza; or, The Sacrifice to the Vistula. 1970.
Alone in the Wild Forest. 1971.
The Topsy-Turvy Emperor of China. 1971.
The Fools of Chelm and Their History. 1973.
A Tale of Three Wishes. 1976.
Naftali the Storyteller and His Horse, Sus, and Other Stories, translated by Isaac Bashevis Singer and others. 1976.
The Power of Light: Eight Stories for Hanukkah. 1980.
The Golem. 1982.
Stories for Children. 1984.

Plays

The Mirror (produced 1973).
Shlemiel the First (produced 1974).
Yentl, The Yeshiva Boy, with Leah Napolin, from a story by Singer (produced 1974). 1979.
Teibele and Her Demon, with Eve Friedman (produced 1978). 1984.

Other (for children; translated by Isaac Bashevis Singer and Elizabeth Shub)

A Day of Pleasure: Stories of a Boy Growing Up in Warsaw (autobiographical), translated by Channah Kleinerman-Goldstein and others, photographs by Roman Vishniac. 1969.
Elijah the Slave: A Hebrew Legend Retold, illustrated by Antonio Frasconi. 1970.
The Wicked City. 1972.
Why Noah Chose the Dove. 1974.

Other

In My Father's Court (autobiography), translated by Channah Kleinerman-Goldstein, Elaine Gottlieb, and Joseph Singer, 1966.
A Singer Reader. 1971.
The Hasidim: Paintings, Drawings, and Etchings, with Ira Moskowitz. 1973.
Love and Exile: The Early Years: A Memoir. 1984.
A Little Boy in Search of God: Mysticism in a Personal Light, illustrated by Ira Moskowitz. 1976.
A Young Man in Search of Love, translated by Joseph Singer. 1978.
Lost in America, translated by Joseph Singer. 1981.
Nobel Lecture. 1979.
Singer on Literature and Life: An Interview, with Paul Rosenblatt and Gene Koppel. 1979.
Conversations with Singer, with Richard Burgin. 1985.
Conversations: Singer, edited by Grace Farrell. 1992.

Editor, with Elaine Gottlieb, Prism 2. 1965.

Translator (into Yiddish):
Pan, by Knut Hamsun. 1928.
Di Vogler [The Vagabonds], by Knut Hamsun. 1928.
In Opgrunt Fun Tayve [In Passion's Abyss], by Gabriele D'Annunzio. 1929.
Mete Trap [Mette Trap], by Karin Michäelis. 1929.
Roman Rolan [Romain Rolland], by Stefan Zweig. 1929.
Viktorya [Victoria], by Knut Hamsun. 1929.
Oyfn Mayrev-Front Keyn Nayes [All Quiet on the Western Front], by Erich Maria Remarque. 1930.
Der Tsoyberbarg [The Magic Mountain], by Thomas Mann. 4 vols., 1930.
Der Veg oyf Tsurik [The Road Back], by Erich Maria Remarque. 1931.
Araber: Folkstimlekhe Geshikhtn [Arabs: Stories of the People], by Moshe Smilansky. 1932.
Fun Moskve biz Yerusholayim [From Moscow to Jerusalem], by Leon S. Glaser. 1938.

*

Bibliography: by Bonnie Jean M. Christensen, in Bulletin of Bibliography 26, January-March 1969; A Bibliography of Singer 1924-1949 by David Neal Miller, 1984.

Critical Studies: Singer and the Eternal Past by Irving Buchen, 1968; The Achievement of Singer edited by Marcia Allentuck, 1969; Critical Views of Singer edited by Irving Malin, 1969, and Singer by Malin, 1972; Singer by Ben Siegel, 1969; Singer and His Art by Askel Schiotz, 1970; Singer, The Magician of West 86th Street by Paul Kresh, 1979; Singer by Edward Alexander, 1980; The Brothers Singer by Clive Sinclair, 1983; Fear of Fiction: Narrative Strategies in the Works of Singer by David Neal Miller, 1985, and Recovering the Canon: Essays on Singer, by Miller and E.J. Brill, 1986; From Exile to Redemption: The Fiction of Singer by Grace Farrell Lee, 1987; Understanding Singer by Lawrence Friedman, 1988; Singer: A Study of the Short Fiction by Edward Alexander, 1990.

* * *

Perhaps the best introduction to the fiction of Isaac Bashevis Singer is reading the autobiographical stories that appear in the collection called In My Father's Court. There one sees the effect of characters and events in prewar Poland on a young, impressionable, and highly sensitive boy whose father is an orthodox rabbi and whose mother was the descendant of rabbis. Although Singer later followed his brother J.B. Singer to the United States, his spiritual roots remained firmly planted in the land of his youth. There he experienced not only the religious traditions of his parents and particularly of his father's Bet Din, or religious court, but also the encroachments upon those traditions his brother experienced as he sought emancipation and enlightenment in a more modern world of art, literature, and politics.

Indeed, the conflicts between sacred and profane modes of existence inform a great deal of Singer's fiction. So does the intermingling of fantasy and reality that springs from the folktales and folklore of the humble Jews Singer most often writes about as they struggle with mundane existence—an existence enlivened by superstition, vivid dreams and ghosts, dybbuks, and demons, either imagined or real. Singer's straightforward, unembroidered style (as translated from Yiddish into English) conveys these extraordinary imaginings in such a way that they invariably disarm disbelief and captivate the reader's sense of actuality. For example, the horrendous events of the story "Blood" (Short Friday and Other Stories) end with the representation of an utterly dissolute and sinful woman as a werewolf. Incredible as Risha's transformation might otherwise seem, the course of her life makes this not only a just and proper outcome, but an almost inevitable one as well.

This intermingling of fantasy and reality is a hallmark of Singer's fiction, as of much Jewish, especially Cabbalist, writing. But Singer disclaims any links to the tradition of Yiddish literature, which he defines as more sentimental than his and more given to advocating social justice. While he is not opposed to social justice, he is strongly opposed to sentimentality, or "schmaltz." As often as not, tragic rather than poetic justice pervades his fiction, as in "The Gentleman from Cracow" (*Gimpel the Fool and Other Stories*). There, the poor Jews in the *shtetl,* or village, of Frampol find transitory relief from their grinding poverty when a rich Jew arrives in town and begins spreading about his largesse. Although devout Rabbi Ozer sees danger and tries to warn his flock against the desecrations and depredations the gentleman's advent foments, the villagers continue to justify their behaviour through extenuation and ultimately defy their rabbi outright. They are eventually caught up in a horrible frenzy of greed and lust that ends in a catastrophe from which the town never recovers. Here, too, fantasy and reality mingle and fuse, as the gentleman emerges as none other than Lucifer and his bride, Lilith. Together they bring terrible destruction to the foolish and unsuspecting villagers, whose fate is to remain forever paupers, despising all manner of riches.

The story that first brought Singer to the attention of the English-speaking world when Saul Bellow translated it in 1953, "Gimpel the Fool" is of a different order of imagination and justice. The pious if simple beliefs of religious Jews are here reaffirmed in ways both ironic and moving. Gimpel is slow-witted enough to be the butt of many in Frampol, where he lives and earns his living as a baker, and where he is persuaded (as a cruel joke) to marry a woman who has already given birth to one bastard and, while married to Gimpel, gives birth to more. Although Gimpel discovers his wife's infidelity, his love for her and the children is such that, notwithstanding his wife's lies, he decides not to seek a divorce but continues to support Elka until her death. "What's the good of *not* believing?" he says. "Today it's your wife you don't believe; tomorrow it's God Himself you won't take stock in." Gimpel thus continues to believe, even when he knows he's being deceived by his wife or by others, until he too dies, firm in the conviction that "belief in itself is beneficial. It is written that a good man lives by faith."

But Singer knows very well that faith may be broken, even among those who earlier have demonstrated similarly strong convictions. The spirit may be willing, but the body weak, as "The Unseen" demonstrates. And virtue sometimes must be its own reward, as in "Fire" (both in *Gimpel the Fool*). But occasionally even the most skeptical and unsocial of human beings may find goodness in others and in life through experiences either ordinary or extraordinary. This is what Bessie Popkin discovers in "The Key" (*A Friend of Kafka and Other Stories*), and what Rabbi Banish of Komarov learns in "Joy" (*Gimpel the Fool*). "The Key" also shows that Singer is not limited to stories of his native Poland alone. Having lived in the United States for over 50 years before his death, and having traveled elsewhere as well, he naturally extended his range to include the experiences of American-Jews and non-Jews, Argentines, Canadians, Israelis, and others. With no other agenda than to explore through his fiction the mysteries of human existence and so uncover some of its truths, Singer remained throughout his career a writer gifted with a strong sense of wonder, very much like the boy at the end of "The Purim Gift" (*In My Father's Court*), who stands "amazed, delighted, entranced" by the vastness of this world and "how rich [it was] in all kinds of people and strange happenings."

—Jay L. Halio

See the essays on "Gimpel the Fool" and "The Spinoza of Market Street."

———

SINIAVSKII, Andrei.   See **TERTS, Abram.**

———

SIONIL JOSE, F(rancisco). Filipino. Born in Rosales, Pangasinan, 3 December 1924. Educated at the University of Santo Tomas, Manila, 1946–48. Married Teresita G. Jovellanos in 1949; five sons and two daughters. Staff member, *Commonweal,* Manila, 1947–48; assistant editor, United States Information Agency, U.S. Embassy, Manila, 1948–49; associate editor, 1949–57, and managing editor, 1957–60, Manila *Times Sunday* magazine, and editor, Manila *Times* annual *Progress,* 1958–60; editor, *Comment* quarterly, Manila, 1956–62; managing editor, *Asia* magazine, Hong Kong, 1961–62; lecturer, Arellano University, Manila, 1962; information officer, Colombo Plan Headquarters, Ceylon, 1962–64; publisher, Solidaridad Publishing House, and general manager, Solidaridad Bookshop, from 1965, publisher and editor, *Solidarity* journal, from 1966, and manager, Solidaridad Galleries, 1967–81, all Manila; lecturer, University of the East graduate school, Manila, 1968; correspondent, *Economist,* London, 1968–69; consultant, Department of Agrarian Reform, 1968–79; lecturer, De La Salle University, Manila, 1984–86; writer-in-residence, National University of Singapore, 1987; visiting research scholar, Center for Southeast Asian Studies, Kyoto University, Japan, 1988. Founder and National Secretary, PEN Philippine Center, 1958. Chair, Solidarity Foundation, from 1987. Recipient: U.S. Department of State Smith-Mundt grant, 1955; Asia Foundation grant, 1960; National Press Club award, for journalism, 3 times; British Council grant, 1967; Palanca award for journalism, 3 times, and, for novel, 1981; ASPAC fellowship, 1971; Rockefeller Foundation Bellagio award, 1979; Cultural Center of the Philippines award, 1979; City of Manila award, 1979; Magsaysay award, 1980; East-West Center fellowship (Honolulu), 1981; International House of Japan fellowship, 1983; Outstanding Fulbrighters award, for literature, 1988. L.H.D.: University of the Philippines, 1992. Lives in Manila.

PUBLICATIONS

Short Stories

The Pretenders and 8 Short Stories.   1962.
The God Stealer and Other Stories.   1968.
Waywaya and Other Short Stories from the Philippines. 1980.
Two Filipino Women (novellas).   1981.
Platinum, Ten Filipino Stories.   1983.
Olvidon and Other Short Stories.   1988.

Three Filipino Women (novellas). 1992.

Novels

The Rosales Saga:
  The Pretenders. 1962.
  Tree. 1978.
  My Brother, My Executioner. 1979.
  Mass. 1982.
  Po-on. 1984.
Ermita. 1988.

Play

Screenplay: *Waywaya* (from his story), 1982.

Verse

Questions. 1988.

Other

(Selected Works). 1977.
A Filipino Agenda for the 21st Century. 1987.
Conversations with Sionil Jose, edited by Miguel Bernad. 1991.

Editor, *Equinox 1.* 1965.
Editor, *Asian PEN Anthology 1.* 1966.
Editor, *A Filipino Agenda for the 21st Century: Papers, Discussions, and Recommendations of the SOLIDARITY Conference.* 1987.

*

Critical Studies: *New Writing from the Philippines,* 1966, and *In Burning Ambush,* 1991, both by Leonard Casper; *Sionil Jose and His Fiction* edited by Alfredo T. Morales, 1990; *Conversations with Filipino Writers* edited by Roger J. Bresnahan, 1990.

*   *   *

For over half of his life F. Sionil Jose has been simultaneously a writer of "fiction with a cause," founder and editor of *Solidarity* magazine in Manila, and owner of the Solidaridad bookstore (which also serves as center for extraliterary conferences); inevitably his novels and short stories complete a single concern. His declared aim always has been to work for "social justice and a moral order." He is best known for his five Rosales novels which trace the migration of peasants from the barren Ilocos mountains of northern Luzon, to the fertile central plains, and finally to Metro Manila. In that process basic agrarian values, such as extended-family loyalty, humility before God in nature, and honesty with one's fellow humans, along with a readiness to work, gradually have been sacrificed to Western excessive individualism and love of material objects. The Rosales epic, unique among Philippine literature, extends from the 1880's to the present and is critical of elitist Filipino families who have always collaborated with foreign interests: Spanish *hacenderos*, American "liberators" at the turn of the century, Japanese wartime Occupation forces, and modern multinationals. Such Filipinos (Ferdinand and Imelda Marcos among them) who

put personal greed and oligarchic faction before the national needs are responsible, according to Sionil Jose, for the continuing impoverishment of the landless majority of Filipinos. Yet, as protest literature these novels depend less on their characters' helplessness than on their will to resist corruption and to restore ancestral traditions of openness and trust and mutual dependency. Some of the earthier portions of *Mass* and *Ermita* have even been praised for their Rabelaisian humor.

Thematically, Sionil Jose's short stories have always been consistent with the ideals reclaimed in his novels and supported both by the eleven years he spent as consultant to the Department of Agrarian Reform and his editorials in *Solidarity* (like his bookstore, named after the late 19th century group of Philippine intellectuals in Spain who solicited not rebellion but reform of their second-class citizenship). Like William Faulkner, who also wrote to restore a closer relationship with nature than with industrialization of the American South, Sionil Jose's commitment has resulted in many of his short stories being seedlings later transplanted into the Rosales epic. One early story, "The Cripples," introduces Istak's father, hanged for theft by one arm until it withers. That situation is repeated in *Po-on* as part of the gross injustice leading to the mountain men's migration southward. Istak himself becomes Antonio Samson's grandfather in *The Pretenders*. Ermi Rojo, prostitute to politicians in "Obsession," evolves into the central character in *Ermita*. One chapter in *Mass*, "Challenge to the Race," began as "Offertory," a story of official terrorism and torture under Marcos. The title story in *Platinum* presents a mirror reverse-image of the situation in *Mass*, whose young narrator is urban-poor but resolutely opposed to the Marcos dictatorship. In "Platinum" a wealthy girl works to solve the problems of the underclass, at the price of her life.

Sionil Jose has never easily identified with a single social class or political ideology. "The God-Stealer" makes clear his respect for native beliefs; yet "Waywaya" recognizes that feuds sometimes have occurred between tribes, as has the taking of slaves regardless of gender. Even certain traditional virtues he recognizes as potential vices, when carried to an extreme. A self-reliant Ilocano in "Pride" feels enslaved by his perpetual indebtedness to relatives: he can accept the principle of solidarity but not the nepotism. Similarly, in "Tong" a young Chinese girl submits to the will of her parents out of respect and marries an older man to whom they owe money. Often the ravages of World War II seem to be the origin for the decline in Filipino honor. In "Gangrene" a soldier begs not to be seen while he is an amputee and possible casualty; but in "Hero" a man accepts without qualms unearned battlefield medals (as Marcos notoriously did). Concealing one's true self from an occupying enemy (as people typically were forced to do previously under colonial powers) often takes its toll: people can become strangers even to themselves. The difference between outright collaboration for gain ("Dama de Noche") and reluctant compromise ("Voyage") narrows. Corruption flourishes where temptation is greatest: in corporate business ("The Interview") and in government bureaucracy ("Progress," "Cadena de Amor"). Increasingly, Sionil Jose has pictured opportunists (*tutas*) who rise in the ranks of the seemingly successful, yet are burdened with a sense of their being insincere because they are insecure ("Diplomacy," "Friendship," "Modesty Aside"). Meanwhile the underclass remains as powerless as it ever was under colonialism. The epidemic spread of corruption is epitomized in the title story of *Olvidon.* There a Filipino doctor treating the leader, whose skin beginning at the genitals is turning the color of a whited sepulchre, finds his own skin taking on that same deathly hue. Compared with such "political prostitution," the hard-working whores in "Obsession" and "Flotsam" appear to be a lesser evil. Unlike the characters in "A Matter of Honor" and "The Drowning" who suffer for others, neither political nor professional prostitutes understand what love is; but of the two the corrupt elitist is the worse because he confuses love with total possessiveness.

Sionil Jose regularly demands integrity of both rich and poor without exception. The suffocating control of the common *tao* ("man") by either an overbearing oligarch or by Communist strongmen, by security guards or by vigilantes, is not acceptable to the man who in 1980 won the Magsaysay award for fighting the cause of the disenfranchised millions. As Sionil Jose explained in "The Writer Who Stayed Behind," defying the possibility of detention and confiscation during Marcos's 20 year rule, he neither hid in the hills nor escaped overseas, but stayed in the Philippines as a voice raised to reassert the nation's honor. Anything less would have seemed to Sionil Jose surrender to the "enclave of privilege and affluence."

—Leonard Casper

SMITH, Iain Crichton (Iain Mac A'Ghobhainn). British. Born in Glasgow, Scotland, 1 January 1928. Educated at the University of Aberdeen, M.A. (honours) in English 1949. Served in the British Army Education Corps, 1950–52: Sergeant. Married in 1977. Secondary school teacher, Clydebank, 1952–55; teacher of English, Oban High School, 1955–77. Member, Edinburgh Committee, 1985–91, and member of Literature Committee since 1982, Scottish Arts Council. Recipient: Scottish Arts Council award, 1966, 1968, 1974, 1978, and prize, 1968; BBC award, for television play, 1970; Book Council award, 1970; Silver Pen award, 1971; Queen's Silver Jubilee medal, 1978, Commonwealth Poetry prize, 1986; Society of Authors Travelling scholarship, 1987. LL.D.: Dundee University, 1983; D.Litt.: University of Aberdeen, 1968; Glasgow University, 1984. Fellow, Royal Society of Literature. O.B.E. (Officer, Order of the British Empire), 1980. Lives in Argyll.

PUBLICATIONS

Short Stories

Burn is Aran [Bread and Water] (includes verse).   1960.
An Dubh is an Gorm [The Black and the Blue].   1963.
Maighstirean is Ministearan [Schoolmasters and Ministers].   1970.
Survival Without Error and Other Stories.   1970.
The Black and the Red.   1973.
An t-Adhar Ameireageanach [The American Sky].   1973.
The Village.   1976.
The Hermit and Other Stories.   1977.
Murdo and Other Stories.   1981.
Mr. Trill in Hades and Other Stories.   1984.
Selected Stories.   1990.

Novels

Consider the Lilies.   1968; as *The Alien Light,* 1969.
The Last Summer.   1969.
My Last Duchess.   1971.
Goodbye, Mr. Dixon.   1974.
An t-Aonaran [The Hermit].   1976.
An End to Autumn.   1978.
On the Island.   1979.
A Field Full of Folk.   1982.
The Search.   1983.
The Tenement.   1985.
In the Middle of the Wood.   1987.
The Dream.   1990.

Plays

An Coileach [The Cockerel] (produced 1966).   1966.
A'Chuirt [The Trial] (produced 1966).   1966.
A Kind of Play (produced 1975).
Two by the Sea (produced 1975).
The Happily Married Couple (produced 1977).

Radio Plays: *Goodman and Death Mahoney,* 1980; *Mr. Trill,* 1988; *The Visitor,* 1988.

Verse

The Long River.   1955.
New Poets 1959, with Karen Gershon and Christopher Levenson.   1959.
Deer on the High Hills: A Poem.   1960.
Thistles and Roses.   1961.
The Law and the Grace.   1965.
Biobuill is Sanasan Reice [Bibles and Advertisements].   1965.
Three Regional Voices, with Michael Longley and Barry Tebb.   1968.
At Helensburgh.   1968.
From Bourgeois Land.   1969.
Selected Poems.   1970.
Penguin Modern Poets 21, with George Mackay Brown and Norman MacCaig.   1972.
Love Poems and Elegies.   1972.
Hamlet in Autumn.   1972.
Rabhdan is rudan [Verses and Things].   1973.
Eadar Fealla-dha is Glaschu [Between Comedy and Glasgow].   1974.
Orpheus and Other Poems.   1974.
Poems for Donalda.   1974.
The Permanent Island: Gaelic Poems, translated by the author.   1975.
The Notebooks of Robinson Crusoe and Other Poems.   1975.
In the Middle—.   1977.
Selected Poems 1955–1980, edited by Robin Fulton.   1982.
Na h-Eilthirich.   1983.
The Exiles.   1984.
Selected Poems.   1985.
A Life.   1986.
An t-Eilean is an Canain.   1987.
The Village and Other Poems.   1989.
Collected Poems.   1992.

Other

The Golden Lyric: An Essay on the Poetry of Hugh MacDiarmid.   1967.

Iain Am Measg nan Reultan [Iain among the Stars] (for children).   1970.
River, River: Poems for Children.   1978.
Na h-Ainmhidhean [The Animals] (verse for children).   1979.
Towards the Human: Selected Essays.   1986.
On the Island (for children).   1988.
George Douglas Brown's The House with Green Shutters.   1988.

Editor, *Scottish Highland Tales.*   1982.
Editor, with Charles King, *Twelve More Scottish Poets.*   1986.
Editor, *Moments in the Glasshouse: Poetry and Prose by 5 New Scottish Writers.*   1987.

Translator, *Ben Dorain,* by Duncan Ban Macintyre.   1969.
Translator, *Poems to Eimhir,* by Sorley Maclean.   1971.

*

Bibliography: in *Lines Review 29,* 1969; *A Bibliography of Smith,* Grant F. Wilson, 1990.

Critical Studies: interview in *Scottish International,* 1971; *Smith,* 1979; *Literature of the North* edited by David Hewitt and M.R.G. Spiller, 1983; *New Edinburgh Review,* Summer 1984; Douglas Gifford, in *Chapman,* 34; Carol Gowin, in *Cencrastus,* 35; *Smith: New Critical Essays* edited by Colin Nicholson, 1991; *Mirror and Marble: The Poetry* by Carol Gow, 1992.

*   *   *

Iain Crichton Smith comes from the island of Lewis, in the Outer Hebrides. He is bilingual, writing in both English and Gaelic. First and foremost, he is one of the most distinguished poets of his generation. He has written plays in both his languages. Two of his novels in English, *Consider the Lilies* and *The Last Summer,* are already regarded in his own country as classics. Of his eleven collections of short stories, several are in Gaelic.

In his first English collection, *Survival Without Error,* the importance of threatened regional languages and cultures are asserted, sometimes through studies of separation and alienation. A son watches his mother die, and can do nothing about it. An exile returns home from America to the Highlands, and finds that he is being constantly interrogated: "What have you done with your life?" That is the question that people, without realising it, put to him simply because he chose to return. It is also the question that he himself wants answered.

Both his novels and his short stories are filled with flashes of imagery and poetic insight, as, for instance, when the Highlander, Kenneth, is writing home to his mother about his university experiences. He goes to church where, he reports, the minister "Mr. Wood isn't very impressive. He is a small stout man who seems to me to have nothing to say. The church itself is small and quite pretty and fresh. But it's his voice that I find peculiar, as if he could be thinking of something else when he is preaching. He is not in his voice."

One of Smith's recurring preoccupations is the tension between the old dogmatic narrowness of religion in the Highlands (which he must have experienced as a boy) and the challenge of modern thought and behaviour. In "The Hermit," the title story of one of his collections, the narrator is constantly urged by his mother to stick to his books, to be able to get away from it all through study, as Smith himself did.

There is another of his deftly-drawn pictures of grim Highland ministers in this story: "a very thin man with a cadaverous face, one of those faces that Highland ministers have, grained and deeply trenched so that they look like portraits of Dante in old age." The story deals with the mysterious presence in the community of a strange bicycling hermit, innocent and reluctantly tolerated. When the narrator seduces a local beauty who needs the price of a suite of furniture, the story is set about that the "quite harmless" hermit has attacked her.

In "The Missionary" a Christian minister goes to Africa to convert the heathen, where he seduces a native girl, Tobbuta, and invokes all manner of superstitious disasters. The minister believes that "murder and death" had been "a plague around him simply in order that Tobbuta would be saved," an attitude throwing a condemning light on the sophistry of religion against the claims of common humanity.

Though the contrasts and conflicts of narrow, localised religion versus worldly modernism (often represented by common sense) is deeply engrained in Smith's work, his range is refreshingly wider. He can rival Roald Dahl with surprising horror endings, as in "Macbeth," where a jealous actor playing the title role lusts after the young African wife of the actor playing Duncan, a liaison encouraged by the older actor to secure a more passionate stage performance from the younger man. When he discovers the delusion, the murder of Duncan on the last night of the run is real.

A concern for common humanity rings through all that Smith has written, in poetry as in prose, nowhere more so than in the hilariously funny story "The Professor and the Comics." Professor MacDuff, surprisingly, addresses his students on the psychological differences between Desperate Dan and Korky the Cat. His serious-minded students are outraged; others, including Stephen Mallow, think that the professor has at last aligned himself with contemporary literary values. Eventually, the local television station invites MacDuff to appear on a chat show, which he agrees to do only if a student of his choice, Stephen Mallow, appears with him. After allowing Mallow his say, the professor discusses basic human values. Of the "aargh"-like sounds the comic characters emit, he says, "They are like the sounds we would make when we came out of the slime . . . Shall I tell you something? It's the people who write comics who look down on the working man. They are saying, that is what the working man is like. This is what he prefers. He can't do any better than this. Give him any rubbish." It's more or less the profitable philosophy of commercial television.

Smith's short stories encompass characters and situations that give them an identity and an entity of significance far beyond the bounds of Scotland. While his first importance is undoubtedly as a poet, his short stories make a distinctive contribution to the European genre.

—Maurice Lindsay

See the essay on "Murdo."

———

SMITH, Pauline (Janet). South African. Born in Oudtshoorn, Little Karoo, 2 April 1882. Educated in Scotland and Hertfordshire. Moved with family to England, 1895; contributor under pen names Janet Tamson and Janet Urmson, Aberdeen *Evening Gazette,* and other Scottish journals, from 1902; close friend of Arnold Bennett; visited South Africa, 1905, 1913–14, 1926–27, 1934, and 1937; lived with sister in Dorset, England, from 1930's. *Died 29 January 1959.*

PUBLICATIONS

Short Stories

The Little Karoo.   1925; enlarged edition, 1930.

Novel

The Beadle.   1926.

Play

Radio play: *The Last Voyage* (produced 1929).   1965.

Other

A.B.: A Minor Marginal Note (biography of Arnold Bennett).   1933.
Platkops Children (stories for children), illustrated by Barbara Shaw.   1935.
South African Journal 1913–1914, edited by Harold Scheub.   1983.

*

Bibliography: *Smith Collection* edited by Leonie T. Jones, 1980.

Critical Studies: "'Quaintness' in Smith: Observations on Her Style and Dialogue" by Charles Eglington, in *English Studies in Africa* 3, March 1960; "Smith" by Arthur Ravenscroft, in *A Review of English Literature* 4(2), April 1963; *Smith,* 1969, and "Smith: The First Full-length Study," in *Lantern,* June 1970, both by Geoffrey Haresnape; *Smith: A Commemorative Introduction to Her Life and Work* by Jeanne Heywood, 1982; *Smith* by Dorothy Driver, 1983.

*   *   *

Pauline Smith's reputation as a writer rests on two slim volumes: a collection of short stories, *The Little Karoo,* and a novel, *The Beadle.* As her slender oeuvre perhaps reflects, Smith is renowned for the pared-down simplicity of her prose, a feature that scarcely disguises the complexity of her artistic vision. Her fictional locale is the Little Karoo, an expanse of land in the south-western Cape bordered by a mountain range and, beyond that, the sea on one side and on the other the Great Karoo, a vast, forbidding hinterland.

Each of the ten stories included in *The Little Karoo* (two were added to the original eight of the first edition) exemplifies Smith's remarkable ability to capture the stark, elemental quality of her rural Dutch characters and the ponderous Biblical cadences of their speech, the harsh oppressiveness of a life spent wresting the barest of yields from the reluctant earth, the austerity of their Protestant faith, and the tragic dimension in their human fallibilities. So compatible are the stories in terms of theme and setting that they have been profitably read as a "cycle."

In "The Pain" (often considered Smith's best story), Juriaan van Royen undertakes a journey to Platkops dorp to seek help for his terminally ill wife at the newly established hospital there. The humble, rustic lifestyle of the simple peasant couple—a life closely tied to the soil and the elements, and presided over by a benign but frugal God—comes up against a newer world of modern medicine and impersonal efficiency, a world with new rhythms and rationales. In this bewilderingly new setting, Juriaan's God deserts him and the central irony of the story unfolds: Deltje's physical pain, which persuades them to undertake the journey, is not cured in hospital but it is merely eclipsed by the greater pain of spiritual suffering. The couple secretly resolve to leave the hospital, and the closing passage sees them on their way back to their isolated homestead, where Deltje will await a lingering but certain death, and, with her passing—the reader is left to presume—will come the inescapable fact of Juriaan's own demise.

"The Schoolmaster" concerns the youthful, selfless love Engela feels for Jan Boetje, a man on the run from his own past. Jan Boetje becomes the teacher to the young children on Engela's grandparents' farm. He teaches the children and Engela about the far-off wonders of Europe, while Engela instructs him in local veld-lore. One day, in a fit of rage (which signifies something about his troubled past), Jan Boetje blinds a pair of mules when they refuse to cross a stream and subsequently banishes himself to a life of drawing a hand-cart across the veld, buying and selling goods to eke out an existence. In the depths of her anguish upon his departure, Engela draws comfort from the thought that what she taught him about the veld would help him in the physical and spiritual wilderness which he has damned himself to inhabit for life. In a tragically ironic final twist, the family discovers that Jan Boetje has drowned in a flood at the drift near the farm.

The story illustrates Smith's immense power as a writer in the tragic mode, and marks her position in this tradition in South African literature. "The Miller" is another example of this tendency in Smith's work. Andries Lombard, the miller, is described as "a stupid kindly man whom illness had turned into a morose and bitter one." His illness causes him to become estranged from his wife and children and this culminates in his refusal to attend the annual Thanksgiving ceremony at the local church. At the last moment, when the service is already fully underway, he suddenly desires to be reunited with his wife. He makes his way down to the Thanksgiving but collapses outside the church, coughing up blood, and, slipping from her arms, dies without achieving full reconciliation. (Significantly, the person who helps him when he collapses is Esther Sokolowsky—the "Jew-woman"—a refugee persecuted in Russia and now condemned to be an outsider in this rigidly Calvinistic community. This detail, like the minute description of the way the church congregation is segregated by gender and race, testifies to Smith's acute perceptiveness regarding matters of oppression.)

A similar tragic lack of fulfilment in a love relationship characterises "The Pastor's Daughter," while "Desolation" and "The Father" are masterpieces in portraying the harshness of the lives of the poor labouring classes and the societal forces that drive people apart and ultimately consign everyone to a bleak and lonely fate. "Desolation" traces the fate of "poor white" Alie van Staden, who suffers one harsh blow after another. She loses her son, is turned out of the house on the farm where he worked as a "bijwoner," and finally, friendless and financially destitute, she makes her way to the small town of Hermansdorp where she finds a place in the orphanage for her grandson. Succumbing to the fate which has dogged her so relentlessly, she dies.

Smith's skill as a story writer manifests itself chiefly in the austere economy of her stories—a quality perfectly commensurate with the frugal, self-denying lifestyles of the people of the Little Karoo. This gives the stories an archetypal, timeless quality: the ageless themes of thwarted love, familial conflict and betrayal, and the depredations of a baneful fate all surface again in these stories and are stripped of ornamentation, reduced to their bare, elemental features. It is not surprising, therefore, that the stories leave the impression of being ineluctably familiar, of having surfaced from the wells of a shared human unconscious.

Smith's achievement is to have traced in the geography of the Little Karoo some of the primary contours in the landscape of the human mind. The starkness of her settings, the harsh, unforgiving nature of the terrain, and the attitudes it has etched into the psyches of its inhabitants imbue her stories with an enduring, emblematic quality and attest to the unflinching steadiness of her artistic vision.

—Craig MacKenzie

SÖDERBERG, Hjalmar. Swedish. Born in Stockholm, 2 July 1869. Married 1) Märta Abenius in 1899 (dissolved 1917), one daughter and two sons; had one daughter from another relationship; 2) Emilie Voss in 1917. Briefly customs officer, then journalist, and literary critic, from late 1880's, Kristianstad; travelled frequently to Copenhagen, from 1906, and moved there, 1917. Recipient: De Nois prize, 1934; Fröding Scholarship, 1941. *Died 14 October 1941.*

PUBLICATIONS

Collections

Samlade verk [Collected Work], edited by Tom Söderberg and Herbert Friedländer. 10 vols., 1943.
Skrifter [Writings], edited by Olle Holmberg. 2 vols., 1969.
Skrifter [Writings], edited by Hans Levander. 9 vols., 1977–78.

Short Stories

Historietter. 1898; as *Selected Short Stories,* edited by Charles Wharton Stork, 1935.
Främlingarna [The Strangers]. 1903.
Det mörknar öfver vägen [Darkness Falls]. 1907.
Hjärats oro [The Heart's Unrest]. 1909.
Den talangfulla draken [The Talented Dragon]. 1913.
Resan till Rom [Journey to Rome]. 1929.
Selected Stories, edited by Carl Lofmark. 1987.

Novels

Förvillelser [Aberrations]. 1895.
Martin Bircks ungdom. 1901; as *Martin Birck's Youth,* 1930.
Doktor Glas. 1905; as *Doctor Glas,* 1905.
Den allvarsamma leken [The Serious Game]. 1912.

Plays

Gertrud [Gertrud]. 1906.
Aftonstjärnan [The Evening]. 1912.
Ödestimmen [Hour of Destiny]. 1922.

Other

Valda sidor (selection). 1908.
Jahves eld [Jehovah's Fire]. 1918.
Skrifter [Writings]. 10 vols., 1919–1921.
Jesus Barabbas [Jesus Barabbas] (essay). 1928.
Den förvandlade Messias [The Transformed Messiah] (essay). 1932.
Sista boken [The Last Book] (essays). 1942.
Makten, visheten och kvinnan [Essays and Aphorisms], edited by Herbert Friedländer. 1946.
Vänner emellan [Between Friends], with Carl G. Laurin, edited by Carl Laurin and T. Söderberg. 1948.
Kära Hjalle, Kära Bo. Bo Bergmans och Söderberg brevväxling 1891-1941 [Dear Hjalle, Dear Bo. Correspondence between Bo Bergman and Söderberg 1891–1941], edited by Per Wästberg. 1969.

*

Critical Studies: in *Is There Anything New under the Sun?* by Edwin Björkman, 1913; "Söderberg" by Eugénie Söderberg, in *The American-Scandinavian Review* 29, 1941; "Söderberg: *Doktor Glas*" by Tom Geddes, in *Studies in Swedish Literature* 3, 1975; "Söderberg: *Martin Bircks ungdom*" by Wolfgang Butt, in *Studies in Swedish Literature* 7, 1976; "Söderberg: *Historietter,*" in *Studies in Swedish Literature* 10, 1977, and "Söderberg (1969–1941): A Swedish Freethinker," in *Question* 11, 1978, both by Carl Lofmark; "A Coincidence According to the Gospel of St. James" by Johannes Hedberg, in *Moderna språk* 72, 1978; "Ethical Murder and "Doctor Glas" by Merrill Reed, in *Mosaic* 12 (4), Summer 1979.

* * *

Hjalmar Söderberg wrote prose, drama and poetry, as well as journalism and learned essays, but he is best known in Sweden as a novelist and short story writer. The collected edition of his works in nine volumes contains over 60 short stories, about half of them written while he was in his twenties and published originally in Stockholm newspapers and magazines.

Although he spent the latter part of his life as a journalist and writer in Copenhagen, Stockholm was the city where Söderberg was born and grew up, and it features in most of his prose writing. The settings are generally realistic (although he does occasionally venture into surrealistic realms), but often the plot is sparse, and Söderberg's characters are rarely more than caricatures, often passive vehicles for opinions or attitudes the author wishes to discuss in the guise of fiction. Indeed, many of the so-called short stories are little more than anecdotes—the collection he published in 1898 is called *Historietter,* an invented diminutive form of the normal Swedish word for "story."

Especially in the early stories, Söderberg's sceptical and melancholy pessimism is expressed in the "decadent" *fin-de-siècle* style fashionable in Scandinavia at the turn of the century. Several of his characters are *flâneurs,* who prefer to sit in cafés discussing questions of philosophical interest or the injustices of life, rather an actually attempting to do anything about them. Söderberg's stories are rescued from sheer gloom and doom, however, by his wry humour.

It has been suggested, perceptively, that if Strindberg wrote in oils, Söderberg wrote in water colours. His style, much admired in Sweden for its clarity and rhythmic balance, is restrained and ironic. Emotions are generally subdued, and on the rare occasions when an emotional outburst occurs, the narrator is nonplussed—in "The Sketch in Indian Ink," for instance, a simple shopgirl is unable to comprehend why the narrator has given her a landscape drawing to look at, and she bursts into tears when he is unable to answer her question, "What does it mean?" She has asked the wrong question, and here as in several other stories, Söderberg implies that questions like "What is the meaning of life?" are similarly misguided.

In later life, Söderberg wrote several works in which he attacked Christian beliefs, and lost few opportunities of ridiculing what he thought were the absurd, inconsistent, and illogical teachings of the church. His story "The Talented Dragon" is a hilarious send-up of religious faith, with farcical names, souls in bottles, a manufactured dragon, a troubadour impersonating a war-god, and a magician working "miracles." When the troubadour is sentenced to death, the High Priest "added a request that the man should be hanged in secret so that the people would not become agitated. He considered that it might be highly dangerous for religion if the truth were to leak out." Similar criticisms are levelled at the church in "Patriarch Papinianus" and "After Dinner," but Söderberg claimed he was not irreligious. In one of his best-known stories, "A Dog without a Master," he depicts a dog whose master dies: at first, the dog experiences a deep feeling of loss, but he soon grows used to his freedom. As he grows old, however, he begins to envy other dogs who can respond to the calls and whistles of their masters. One day, he hears a whistle that must, surely, be from his own master. He searches in vain, and eventually gives up, sits down at a cross-roads, and howls: "Have you seen, have you heard a forgotten, masterless dog when he stretches his head up at the sky and howls, howls? The other dogs slink quietly away with their tails between their legs; for they cannot comfort him and they cannot help him." Söderberg may have had no God, but he did not pretend that made life any easier for him.

Humbug and hypocrisy are frequent targets for Söderberg's wit and sarcasm. "Vox Populi" is an amusing story reflecting a lively debate taking place in Stockholm at the time of writing: a sculpture depicting a naked man and boy had been erected near the National Library, which scandalised the guardians of public morals. In the story, two ugly matrons gape at the statue and are vociferously horrified—but why should nakedness be immoral? The statue is aesthetically pleasing, and the old man is evidently thinking beautiful thoughts—more than can be said of the ladies, whose dogs join in the chorus of disapproval as the scene degenerates into farce. In "A Cup of Tea" a character complains about the hypocrisy of a society that encourages beer and spirits to be drunk in a tea-shop, but exposes him to censure because he orders a cup of tea. The irony goes

deeper than that, however, for the man himself is exposed as a hypocrite: people in glass houses should refrain from throwing stones.

Söderberg always sides with the underdog, but he is well aware that in a meaningless world, there is no justice. The opening sentence of "The Chimney-Sweep's Wife" informs us: "This is a sad, cruel story." And so it is, with the evil bully of a woman surviving to live happily ever after while all the people she abuses die or go mad. In "The History Teacher" the narrator tells the story of how the teacher was teased and mocked by his pupils, and cruelly treated when he fell upon hard times: "His world fell apart. There was nothing he could do but cry. And so he cried."

Admirers of Söderberg's stories tend to read them because they are stimulating and thought-provoking, and while they rarely present solutions, they raise questions over which one can ponder at length. Although some of them are well-crafted in the tradition of the German novelle ("The Fur Coat"), and although the niceties of his style are pleasing, his main attraction is his honest and persistent search for the truth, and his ironic vision that exposes hypocrisy but reinforces his humanism.

—Laurie Thompson

SOLDATI, Mario. Italian. Born in Turin, 17 November 1906. Educated at Jesuit schools in Turin; Istituto Superiore di Storia dell'Arte, Rome; University of Turin, degree in literature 1927; Columbia University, New York, 1929–31. Married twice; three children. Full-time writer; also film director; contributed regularly to *Il Giorno* and *Il Corriere della Sera.* Currently president, ANGEAT (National Association of Journalists in Cenology, Gastronomy and Agritourism); president, Centro Pannunzio, Turin, from 1988. Recipient: San Babila prize, 1949; Strega prize, 1954; Campiello prize, 1970; Bagutta prize, 1976; Naples prize, 1978; Giarre-Taormina prize, 1979; Hemingway prize, 1986; Viareggio prize, 1987; Amici del Latini prize. Lives in Turin. Publications

Short Stories

Salmace.   1929.
A cena col commendatore.   1950; as *The Commander Comes to Dine,* 1952; as *Dinner with the Commendatore,* 1953.
I racconti.   1957.
Il vero Silvestri (novella).   1957; as *The Real Silvestri,* 1960.
I racconti (1927–1947).   1961.
La busta arancione.   1966; as *The Orange Envelope,* 1969.
I racconti del Maresciallo.   1967.
55 novelle per l'inverno.   1971.
44 novelle per l'estate.   1979.
La carta del cielo: racconti.   1980.
Nuovi racconti del Maresciallo.   1984.

Novels

La verità sul caso Motta.   1941.
L'amico gesuita.   1943.
Le lettere da Capri.   1954; as *The Capri Letters,* 1955; as *Affair in Capri,* 1957.

La confessione.   1955; as *The Confession,* 1958.
La messa dei villeggianti.   1959.
Storie di spettri.   1962.
Le due città.   1964; as *The Malacca Cane,* 1973.
Fuori.   1968.
L'attore.   1970.
Lo smeraldo.   1974; as *The Emerald,* 1977.
La sposa americana.   1977; as *The American Bride,* 1979.
Addio diletta Amelia.   1979.
L'incendio.   1981.
La casa del perché.   1982.
L'architetto.   1985.
L'albero.   1985.
L'avventura in Valtellina.   1986.
El paseo de Gracia.   1987.

Plays

Pilato. 1925.

Screenplays: *Gli uomini, che mascalzoni!,*   1932; *Il signor Max,* 1937; *La Principessa Tarakanova,* 1938; *La signora di Montecarlo,* 1938; *Due milioni per un sorriso,* 1939; *Dora Nelson,* 1939; *Tutto per la donna,* 1940; *Piccolo mondo antico (Old-Fashioned World),* 1941; *Tragica notte,* 1941; *Malombra,* 1942; *Quartieri alti,* 1943; *Le miserie del signor Travet (His Young Wife),* 1945; *Eugenia Grandet,* 1946; *Daniele Cortis,* 1947; *Fuga in Francia (Flight into France),* 1948; *Quel bandito sono io!,* 1949; *Botta e risposta,* 1950; *Donne e briganti (Of Love and Bandits),* 1950; *Il sogno di Zorro,* 1951; *E l'amor che mi rovina,* 1951; *O.K. Nerone (O.K. Nero),* 1951; *Le avventure di Mandrin,* 1952; *I tre corsari,* 1952; *Jolanda—La figlia del corsaro nero,* 1952; *La provinciale (The Wayward Wife),* 1953; *La mano dello straniero (The Stranger's Hand),* 1953; *Questa è la vita (Of Life and Love),* 1954; *La donna del Fiume (Woman of the River),* 1955; *Era di venerdi 17 (The Virtuous Bigamist),* 1957; *Italia piccola,* 1957; *Policarpo—Ufficiale di scrittura,* 1959.

Other

America, primo amore.   1935.
Ventiquattro ore in uno studio cinematografico.   1945.
Fuga in Italia.   1947.
L'accalappiacani.   1953.
To Plan or Not to Plan? A Short Talk.   1959.
Canzonette e viaggio televisivo.   1962.
Vino al vino.   1969.
I disperati del benessere: Viaggio in Svezia.   1970.
Gloria dell'uomo, with Colomba Russo.   1973.
Da spettatore.   1973.
Un prato di papaveri: diario 1947–1964.   1973.
The Octopus and the Pirates (for children).   1974.
Lo specchio inclinato: diario 1965–1971.   1975.
Piemonte e Valle d'Aosta, illustrated by Folco Quilici. 1978.
Lo scopone, with Maurizio Corgnati.   1982.
Conversazione in una stanza chiusa con Soldati, with Davide Lajolo.   1983.
24 ore in uno studio cinematografico.   1985.
Ah! Il Mundial!.   1986.
Regione regina.   1987.
Rami secchi.   1989.
Opere, vol.1: racconti autobiografici.   1991.

* * *

In any consideration of Mario Soldati's literary work, it is useful to note several facts: first, he was born in Turin in 1906 of middle-class Catholic parents; second, from an early age he was as much interested in the fine arts as in literature; third, he spent an influential period of his early manhood in the United States; and fourth, he was for many years involved in the Italian film industry. All tend to be strongly reflected in his writing.

Although Soldati's first public piece, the comic play *Pilato* (Pilate), attracted little attention, a collection of short stories, *Salmace,* published in 1929 while he was still a post-graduate student at Columbia University in New York, established his reputation as a promising young writer of fiction. That helped him, on his return from the United States, to be taken on as a scriptwriter with the film production centre in Rome, Cines. Although Soldati is best-known today as a writer, the earliest part of his career was dominated by his activities in the Italian film industry, and these need briefly to be sketched here as they provided the background to several of his later novels.

Soldati began by scripting scenarios for several of the most distinguished Italian directors of the 1930's, like Alessandro Blasetti, with whom he worked on *La tavola dei poveri* (The Table of the Poor), and Mario Camerini, for whom he did *Gli uomini, che mascalzoni!* (Men) and *Il signor Max* (Mr. Max). He then graduated to direction, co-directing with F. Ozep *La principessa Tarkanova* (Princess Tarkanova), and although he turned increasingly to fiction writing after the success of his later 1930's fiction, like *La verità sul caso Motta* (The Motta Affair), he maintained his contacts with the film industry through to the 1960's. Perhaps appropriately for one whose prime interest lay in writing, as a film director he proved to be particularly good at handling adaptations of literary texts, especially those with a nostalgic bent. In the postwar period, influenced by the then dominant mode in Italian serious filmmaking, Neo-Realism, he attempted, if with only modest success, to apply something of the new realist manner to materials drawn from middle-class life, as in an adaptation of his own short story, *Fuga in Francia (Flight into France),* and in a version of Alberto Moravia's novel, *La provinciale (The Wayward Wife).* In the 1950's and 1960's Soldati was also very active in television.

Some recent critics have seen in Soldati's early stories an ironic and sceptical treatment of bourgeois values under Fascism, rather comparable to the stance and tone of other young writers of the 1930's, like Alberto Moravia. But this reading is rather forced, for there is little overt attempt in his early work to engage with politics; although it may contain implicit social and political criticism, his interests are essentially private, engaged much more with the interior life, and with personal relationships, than with expressly public concerns. Most of his work of the 1930's seems to underscore the truth of Cesare Pavese's view that the largely non-prescriptive nature of the Italian regime towards the arts encouraged many to cultivate an apolitical individualism, for the prime emphasis in many of Soldati's novels and short stories is on the psychology and sensibilities of individuals, preoccupations which in part perhaps explain the comparative neglect of his work in much postwar Italian literary criticism, which has tended to favour writing of firm political commitment.

Much of Soldati's writing appears to have a strong autobiographical dimension: this is seen as much in an early non-fiction work, like *America, primo amore* (America, First Love), as in a much later novel, *La sposa americana (The American Bride).* The former, rooted in the observations of his post-graduate years in the United

States, sifts myth and reality in European conceptions of the American way of life; its implicit nationalism struck a particularly strong cord in a nation where, following the wave of emigration in the early years of the century, most families had friends or relatives, and won for Soldati his first major literary success. *The American Bride,* one of his last novels, re-explores some of the issues of cultural difference he had examined from various perspectives in a number of stories, and is a sensitive account (if overly marked by a resort to the melodramatic) of irresolvable tensions and misunderstandings in a marital relationship.

Themes rooted in childhood and adolescent experience, more particularly the personal and moral implications of a sexually repressive education, inform some of his best work. Translation of such experience into fictional terms is seen in *L'amico gesuita* (The Jesuit Friend) and *La confessione (The Confession).*

Many of Soldati's works are concerned with self-deception in relationships. The tightly written novella *Il vero Silvestri (The Real Silvestri)* juxtaposes the opposed views held of a mutual friend by a middle-class lawyer and an attractive working-class woman: for the latter, Silvestri is a cheat and blackmailer, while the former remembers him only as the very model of kindness, consideration, and personal honesty. Gradually the lawyer appreciates how impossibly idealised was his memory of his friend, but comes to understand and feel for him all the more by accepting his human feelings.

Notwithstanding that his plots can exploit the bizarre and the extraordinary, Soldati chronicles the human ordinariness in the romantic deceptions and misunderstandings of friendship, marriage, and the intrigues of love relationships. There is, too, an element of the erotic in his work, the more powerful for never being overt or exploitative. The romantic dimension, reinforced by the sure sense of the storyteller, helped to win him in the 1950's and 1960's a wide readership in Italy and abroad. Although at times overly rhetorical, and not always persuasive in handling the psychology of relationships, Soldati shows an impressive stylistic mastery in his skilful intermingling of the formal and the colloquial; his work is eminently readable.

—Francesca Ross

* * *

SOLZHENITSYN, Aleksandr (Isaevich). Russian. Born in Kislovodsk, 11 December 1918. Educated at school in Rostov-on-Don; University of Rostov, 1936–41, degree in mathematics and physics 1941; correspondence course in philology, Moscow University, 1939–41. Served in the Soviet Army, 1941–45: captain; decorated twice; arrested and stripped of rank, 1945. Married 1) Natalia Alekseevna Reshetovskaia in 1940 (divorced), remarried in 1957 (divorced 1973), three sons; 2) Natalia Svetlova in 1973, one stepson. Physics teacher, secondary school, Morozovsk, 1941; sentenced to eight years imprisonment for anti-Soviet agitation, 1945: in prisons in Moscow, 1945–50, and labour camp in Kazakhstan, 1950–53; released from prison, and exiled to Kok-Terek, Siberia: mathematics teacher, 1953–56; released from exile, 1956, and settled in Ryazan, 1957, as teacher, then full-time writer; unable to publish from 1966; charged with treason and expelled from U.S.S.R., 1974; lived in Zurich, 1974–76, and in Cavendish, Vermont since 1976; reinstat-

ed to Union of Soviet Writers, 1989; Russian citizenship restored, 1990; treason charges formally removed, 1991. Recipient: Foreign book prize (France), 1969; Nobel prize for literature, 1970; Templeton prize, 1983; National Arts Club medal (U.S.), 1993. D.Litt.: Harvard University, Cambridge, Massachusetts, 1978. Member, American Academy of Arts and Sciences, 1969; Honorary Fellow, Hoover Institution on War, Revolution, and Peace, 1975.

PUBLICATIONS

Short Stories

Odin den' Ivana Denisovicha.   1962; as *One Day in the Life of Ivan Denisovich,* 1963.
Etudy i krokhotnye rasskazy.   1964; as *Stories and Prose Poems,* 1971; as *Prose Poems,* 1971; as *Matryona's House and Other Stories,* 1975.
Rasskazy [Short Stories].   1990.

Novels

Dlia pol'zy dela.   1963; as *For the Good of the Cause,* 1964.
Sluchai na stantsii Krechetovka; Matrenin dvor.   1963; as *We Never Make Mistakes,* 1963.
V kruge pervom.   1968; as *The First Circle,* 1968; restored complete edition, 1978.
Rakovyi korpus.   1968; complete edition, 1968; as *Cancer Ward,* 2 vols., 1968–69; as *The Cancer Ward,* 1969.
Six Etudes.   1971.
Avgust chetyrnadtsatogo.   1971; as *August 1914,* 1972; expanded version, as *Krasnoe koleso 1,* in *Sobranie sochinenii,* 11–12, 1983; revised edition, as part of *Krasnoe koleso,* 1983–86.
Krasnoe koleso: povestvovan'e v otmerennykh srokakh [The Red Wheel]:
    Uzel 1: Avgust chetyrnadtsatogo.   2 vols., 1983; as *The Red Wheel: A Narrative in Discrete Periods of Time,* 1989.
    Uzel 2: Oktiabr'shestnadtsatogo.   2 vols., 1984.
    Uzel 3: Mart semnadtsatogo.   2 vols., 1986.
    Uzel 4: Aprel' semnadtsatogo.   1991.

Plays

Olen' i shalashovka.   1968; as *The Love-Girl and the Innocent* (produced 1981), 1969; as *Respublika truda,* in *Sobraniye sochineniy* 8, 1981.
Svecha na vetru.   1968; as *Candle in the Wind,* 1973; as *Svet, koroty, v tebe,* in *Sobranie sochinenii* 8, 1981.
Pir podebitelei.   In *Sobranie sochinenii* 8, 1981; as *Victory Celebrations* (produced 1990), 1983.
Plenniki.   In *Sobranie sochinenii* 8, 1981; as *Prisoners,* 1983.
P'esy i kinostsenarii (plays and film scripts).   1981. *The Love-Girl and the Innocent* (includes *Prisoners; Victory Celebration*).   1986.

Verse

Prusskie nochi: poema napisannaia v lagere v 1950.   1974; as *Prussian Nights,* 1977.

Other

Sobranie sochinenii [Collected Works].   6 vols., 1969–70.

Les Droits de l'écrivain.   1969.

Nobelevskaia lektsiia po literature.   1972; as *Nobel Lecture,* edited by F.D. Reeve, 1972; as *One Word of Truth,* 1972.

Arkhipelag Gulag.   3 vols., 1973–76; as *The Gulag Archipelago,* 3 vols., 1974–78; abridged edition in 1 vol., edited by Edward Ericson, Jr., 1985.

Iz-pod glyb.   1974; as *From Under the Rubble,* 1975.

Mir i nasilie [Peace and Violence].   1974.

Pis'mo vozhdiam Sovetskogo soiuza.   1974; as *Letter to the Soviet Leaders,* 1974.

A Pictorial Autobiography.   1974.

Solzhenitsyn, the Voice of Freedom (two speeches).   1975.
    Bodalsia telenok s dubom (autobiography).   1975; as *The Oak and the Calf,* 1980.

Lenin v Tsiurikhe.   1975; as *Lenin in Zurich,* 1976.

Detente: Prospects for Democracy and Dictatorship.   1975.

America, We Beg You to Interfere (speeches).   1975.

Amerikanskie rechi [American Discourse].   1975.

Warning to the Western World (interview).   1976.

A World Split Apart (address).   1978.

Alexander Solzhenitsyn Speaks to the West (speeches).   1978.

Sobranie sochinenii [Collected Works].   1978 —.

The Mortal Danger: How Misconceptions About Russia Imperil the West.   1980.

East and West (miscellany).   1980.

Issledovaniia noveishei russkoi istorii.   1980 —.

Publitsistika: stat'i i rechi (articles and speeches).   1981.

Kak nam obustroit' Rossiiu [How Are We to Put Russia in Order?]   1990.

Rebuilding Russia: Toward Some Formulations.   1991.

Les Invisibles.   1992.

Editor, *Russkii slovar' iazykovogo rasshireniia.*   1990.

*

Bibliography: *Solzhenitsyn: An International Bibliography of Writings by and About Him* by Donald M. Fiene, 1973.

Critical Studies: *Solzhenitsyn* by Georg Lukács, 1970: *Solzhenitsyn: The Major Novels* by Abraham Rothberg, 1971; *Alexander Solzhenitsyn* by David Burg and George Feifer, 1973; *Solzhenitsyn: Critical Essays and Documentary Materials* edited by John B. Dunlop and others, 1973, revised edition, 1975; *Solzhenitsyn* by Christopher Moody, 1973, revised edition, 1976; *Solzhenitsyn: A Collection of Critical Essays* edited by Kathryn Feuer, 1976; *Solzhenitsyn: Politics and Form* by Francis Barker, 1977; *The Politics of Solzhenitsyn* by Stephen Carter, 1977; *Solzhenitsyn* by Steven Allaback, Taplinger, 1978; *Solzhenitsyn and the Secret Circle* by Olga Andreyev Carlisle, 1978; *Solzhenitsyn Studies: A Quarterly Survey* (journal) from Spring 1980; *Solzhenitsyn and Dostoevsky: A Study in the Polyphonic Novel* by Vladislav Krasnov, 1980; *Solzhenitsyn, Tvardovsky and "Novy mir"* by Vladimir Lakshin, 1980; *Solzhenitsyn: The Moral Vision* by Edward E. Ericson, 1982; *Solzhenitsyn's Traditional Imagination* by James Curtis, Athens, 1984; *Solzhenitsyn* by Georges Nivat, 1984; *Solzhenitsyn: A Biography* by Michael Scammell, 1984; *Solzhenitsyn in Exile: Critical Essays and Documentary Material* edited by John B. Dunlop, Richard S. Haugh, and Michael Nicholson, 1985; *Solzhenitsyn: Myth and Reality* by A. Flegon, 1986.

*   *   *

Although known primarily for his novels and longer works, Aleksandr Solzhenitsyn has produced several important short stories. "The Easter Procession" describes an Easter 50 years after the Revolution, at which a rowdy group of teenagers harasses the Orthodox faithful, mostly old women, deacons, and priests. These "hooligans" insult the spiritual event taking place by being drunk, swearing, and flashing knives. The narrator warns that this generation will "trample" on everyone else.

In contrast, in "For the Good of the Cause" young people voluntarily construct a building to house their technical school, but they lose it to a scientific research institute. The students' enthusiasm for their work is a rare example of socialism at its best. But despite the impassioned pleas of their principal that Communism must choose people over prestige, the students' needs are subordinated to the view of the party bureaucracy that the research institute is a higher priority.

Another short story, "The Right Hand," deals with sterile bureaucratic rules that override humanitarian responses. Like *Rakovui korpus (The Cancer Ward)*, this story is related by a camp survivor who is recovering in Tashkent from a life-threatening condition. At the age of 35, the protagonist has already endured ten years of camp life, and he reflects on the truth that "the true savour of life is not to be gained by big things but from little ones" (translated by Michael Glenny). Enjoying his taste of freedom at the clinic where he can ogle girls, he attempts to help a sickly veteran who seeks admittance to the hospital. Both men are rebuffed by a callous receptionist who has no sympathy for the veteran. The author infers that simple human kindness is lacking because of an inflexible bureaucratic routine.

Solzhenitsyn uses fiction as a vehicle to preserve memories of his eight years in prison camps. In 1962 the journal *Novy Mir* published *Odin den' Ivana Denisovicha (One Day in the Life of Ivan Denisovitch)*, which enjoyed immediate success. Solzhenitsyn had actually begun the novella before 1959 and called it "Shch-854." Khrushchev, who wanted to denigrate Stalin, approved publication of the work with its new title. *One Day in the Life of Ivan Denisovitch*, although fiction, is also a historical perspective — the political climate at the time precluded an objective history of the Stalinist period. Ivan Denisovitch (Shukov) represents the common individual incarcerated in a Soviet camp for an insignificant crime; his energies are devoted entirely to survival under brutal conditions.

The stories "Matrena's House" and "Incident at Krechotovka Station" were published in *Novy Mir* in 1963. Matrena, a prototypical peasant character, demonstrates spirituality and selflessness. The latter story concerns a railroad station during World War II, where a soldier is denounced by the station commandant. The story illustrates the workings of a police state in which trainloads of former soldiers, having been sentenced to prison terms, pass through the station. Zotov, the station commandant who feels sympathy for Tveritinov, a former actor who elicits his help, nevertheless, must turn him in to the police. Yet Zotov shows his sensitivity by manifesting doubt over his decision.

"Zakhar Kalita" ("Zakhar-the-Pouch") describes a summer bicycling holiday at Kulikovo Field, the scene of a battle in 1380 between the Russians and the Mongols. The narrator focuses upon the Keeper of the Field, an eccentric *muzhik* named Zakhar, who carries a pouch in which he keeps a Comments book and other articles. Seemingly a foolish figure at first, by the end of the story, Zakhar becomes the "Spirit of the Field," a faithful guardian of the best of Russian traditions, and the narrator judges Kulikovo Field as an important piece of Russian history that needs to be preserved.

Solzhenitsyn's work follows in the 19th-century tradition of realism epitomized by Tolstoii. His range of characters is broad, including persons from all levels of Soviet society. His language is simple, concrete, terse, and understated, although he often intrudes into the narration through his didactic comments. Certainly the personal experiences of the author have refined his efforts to recreate the effects of the prison camps, the loss of freedom, and the sense of exile and suffering inherent in his characters' struggles. His major themes deal with freedom and repression: the struggle to survive and achieve a sense of self-worth, in spite of a cruel and inhumane system of government.

—Shirley J. Paolini

See the essays on "Matrena's House" and *One Day in the Life of Ivan Denisovich*.

———

SOMERVILLE and ROSS. SOMERVILLE, Edith (Anna Oenone). Irish. Born in Corfu, 2 May 1858; grew up at the family home in Drishane, County Cork, Ireland. Educated at home, and at Alexandra College, Dublin; studied painting at the Westminster School of Art, London, in Dusseldorf, and at the studios of Colarossi and Délécluse in Paris. Began career as an illustrator, and continued to illustrate her own books and to exhibit after becoming a writer (one-woman shows of paintings in Dublin and London, and in New York City, 1929); organist at the parish church of Castlehaven, Drishane, County Cork, 1875–1949; lived with her cousin and collaborator, Martin Ross in Drishane, 1886 until Ross's death in 1915; with Ross, travelled extensively in Europe and lived at various times in Paris; after Ross's death continued to write (as Somerville and Ross) on her own. Master of the West Carbery Foxhounds, 1903–19. Recipient: Irish Academy of Letters Gregory medal, 1941. Litt.D.: Trinity College, Dublin, 1932. Founding member, Irish Academy of Letters, 1933. *Died 8 October 1949.* **ROSS, Martin.** Pseudonym for Violet Florence Martin. Irish. Born at Ross House, County Galway, 11 June 1862; moved with her family to Dublin, 1872. Educated at home, and at Alexandra College, Dublin. Writer from 1886; lived with her cousin and collaborator, Edith Somerville in Drishane, County Cork, 1886-1915; in failing health from 1898. Vice-president, Munster Women's Franchise League. *Died 21 December 1915.*

PUBLICATIONS

Short Stories

Some Experiences of an Irish R.M.   1899.
A Patrick's Day Hunt (by Ross).   1902.
All on the Irish Shore: Irish Sketches.   1903.
Further Experiences of an Irish R.M.   1908.
In Mr. Knox's Country.   1915.
The Sweet Cry of Hounds.   1936.

Novels

An Irish Cousin.   1889; revised edition, 1903.
Naboth's Vineyard.   1891.
The Real Charlotte.   1894.
The Silver Fox.   1898; revised edition, 1902.
Dan Russel the Fox: An Episode in the Life of Miss Rowan.   1911.
The Story of the Discontented Little Elephant (for children; by Somerville).   1912.
Mount Music.   1919.
An Enthusiast.   1921.
The Big House of Inver.   1925.
French Leave.   1928.
Little Red Riding Hood in Kerry.   1934.
Sarah's Youth.   1938.

Verse

Slipper's ABC of Foxhunting (by Somerville).   1903.

Other

Through Connemara in a Governess Cart.   1892.
In the Vine Country.   1893.
Beggars on Horseback: A Riding Tour of North Wales.   1895.
Some Irish Yesterdays.   1906.
Irish Memories.   1917.
Stray-Aways (essays).   1920.
Wheel-Tracks.   1923.
The States Through Irish Eyes (by Somerville).   1930.
An Incorruptible Irishman, Being an Account of Chief Justice Charles Kendal Bushe and of His Wife, Nancy Crampton, and Their Times, 1767–1843.   1932.
The Smile and the Tear (essays).   1933.
Records of the Somerville Family from 1174 to 1940 (by Somerville and Boyle Townshend Somerville).   1940.
Notions in Garrison (essays).   1941.
Happy Days! Essays of Sorts.   1946.
The Selected Letters of Somerville and Ross, edited by Gifford Lewis.   1989.

Editor (Somerville only), *The Mark Twain Birthday Book.*   1885.
Editor (Somerville only), *Notes of the Horn: Hunting Verse, Old and New.*   1934.

*

Bibliography: *A Bibliography of the First Editions of the Works of Somerville and Ross* by Elizabeth Hudson, 1942.

Critical Studies: *Somerville: A Biography* by G. Cummins, 1952; *Somerville and Ross: A Biography* by M. Collis, 1968; *Somerville and Ross: A Symposium, 1969; The Irish Cousins: The Books and Background of Somerville and Ross* by Violet Powell, 1970; *Somerville and Ross* by John Cronin, 1972; *Somerville and Ross: A Critical Appreciation* by Hilary Robinson, 1980; *Somerville and Ross: The World of the Irish R.M.* by Gifford Lewis, 1985.

* * *

Edith Somerville and Violet Martin (Martin Ross) were second cousins, both members of the Irish Ascendancy class, who in 1886 decided to collaborate in writing fiction. Although in the following 30 years they produced a novel, *The Real Charlotte,* that critics have greatly admired, their popular reputation has depended on a series of comic stories, the first of which were written for the *Badminton Magazine.* When published in book form in 1899 as *Some Experiences of an Irish R.M.,* they were such an outstanding success that the cousins eventually wrote the tales for two further collections, *Further Experiences of an Irish R.M.* and *In Mr. Knox's Country.*

The "R.M.," or resident magistrate, of the title is Major Sinclair Yeates who at the beginning of the series is appointed to this government position in the fictional town of Skebawn, west Cork. Despite the title, there is little interest in Yeates's official duties: few of the stories ever enter a court room ("The Boat's Share" is an exception). Instead, the location of most tales is the Irish outdoors with the major and others engaged in or attending various recreational activities: horseracing, sailing, game shooting, picnics, village festivals, but most of all, fox hunting. Violet Powell (*An Irish Cousin*) protested at the widely held view that the tales were only about the Irish gentry's pursuit of the fox. But many indeed do dramatise this subject, while others are related to it in some way, like buying horses or hounds.

The tales are remarkable for their vivid accounts of this activity, which to many now seems either quaint or barbaric. In "Philippa's Fox-Hunt," for instance, the major and fellow members of the hunt become engaged in a wild, even reckless, pursuit of hounds and fox across fields and woods and over fences. The reader is caught up in the breathless pace, and delights at Yeates's hilarious attempts at staying on his horse while his wife, Philippa, is eagerly giving advice on the whereabouts of the fox as she dashes around the countryside on a bicycle. "Philippa's Fox-Hunt" also illustrates Somerville and Ross's skill in structuring a story so that it concludes in an unexpected denouement. The fox and one hound become trapped in a culvert, but are finally brought out; the fox is dead, much to the chagrin of the naive Philippa who didn't know this was the object of the chase!

Such social events bring together a host of characters and incidents that allow the writers to present the major as an innocent abroad amidst excitable, inventive, but irrational and unpredictable Irish. His most frequent contacts are with the Knox family, most of whose members belong to the ascendancy class. Appearing in a number of stories are Lady Knox and Mrs. Knox, imperious ladies despite poverty; Flurry, master of the fox hounds and companion to Yeates; and Sally, who eventually marries Flurry. Another family of gentry, the Shutes, also feature in a number of stories. Servants of the various families and locals, the "mere" Irish, complete the cast. The major himself is, supposedly, Irish, but his sensibilities have been totally shaped by education at Oxford and Sandhurst and a career in the British army. In other words, for him, appointment to the southwest of Ireland is akin to appointment to the wilds of Borneo. Readers come to see him as an outsider bringing back to the upper-class English (readers of the *Badminton Magazine*) tales of his adventures amongst the "natives."

The comedy is often in evidence when the major is the victim of some ruse perpetrated by these wily, and more worldly, locals. In "Great-Uncle McCarthy," for example, he eventually discovers that the noises that have been disturbing his sleep have been due to squatters in the attic who, with the connivance of the servants, have been consuming his food and whiskey. In "Occasional Licences" he is cajoled into helping Flurry and Sally Knox outwit a horse dealer. The scheme involves the formidable Lady Knox's horse, and Yeates has the task of keeping her ladyship unaware of what has happened. In "The Holy Island" contraband rum is smuggled out of the district while the magistrate and police are tricked by a decoy.

The fact that the major is a naive but likeable fellow who takes the antics in good part might suggest that the Irish too are just amiable rascals, and that the tales always exist on a comic level. But more serious appraisals of the Irish do occasionally occur. Sometimes, Yeates will launch into sudden praise of the Irish character, as in "Poisson d'Avril," for example, where he reflects on "the magnificent superiority of the Irish mind to the trammels of officialdom." And certainly authorial indulgence towards the gentry is evident in his observations of Mrs. Knox's household where hallmarks of past civilised living are incongruously mixed with images of present neglect. But in the opening tale, Yeates registers, with English disdain, Flurry's "shabby pink coat and dingy breeches," his poor spelling and lack of appreciation for high-quality cigarettes. As far as the native Irish are concerned, the major does seem to share the authors' enjoyment of their linguistic dexterity, but he regularly draws attention to their smell, their inability to value fine food and their general lack of social graces. On the whole however, what saves them is a respectful attitude towards their betters. A hint of authorial nastiness is apparent when local bourgeois are featured. The Flynns, in "A Conspiracy of Silence," or McRorys in "Sharper than a Ferret's Tooth," are set up for mockery by Yeates and the gentry for their uncouth social pretensions and, in the case of the Flynns, being implicated in an ungentlemanly act of dishonesty.

At the period the "Irish R.M." stories were written, Ireland was in the midst of social, political, and cultural ferment, but little of this was allowed to filter through to Skebawn. References to political change occur mainly in relation to the decline of the ascendancy class ("The Finger of Mrs. Knox"), and they are incidental to the plots. Somerville and Ross's attitude to the future of Ireland is probably summed up in occasional appearances of "The Sons of Liberty" (in "The Waters of Strife" and "A Royal Command"), a local football club who don't know the rules and whose brass band can only play discordantly. All part of the comic routine, of course, but with an implication that the English need not fear Irish political aspirations.

—F.C. Molloy

See the essay on "Poisson d'Avril."

————

ŚRĪVĀTAVA, Dhanpat Ray.   See **PREMCAND**.

————

STAFFORD, Jean. American. Born in Covina, California, 1 July 1915. Educated at the University of Colorado, Boulder, B.A. 1936, M.A. 1936; University of Heidelberg, 1936–37. Married 1) Robert Lowell in 1940 (divorced

1948); 2) Oliver Jensen in 1950 (divorced 1953); 3) the writer A. J. Liebling in 1959 (died 1963). Instructor, Stephens College, Columbia, Missouri, 1937–38; secretary, *Southern Review,* Baton Rouge, Louisiana, 1940-41; lecturer, Queens College, Flushing, New York, Spring 1945; fellow, Center for Advanced Studies, Wesleyan University, Middletown, Connecticut, 1964–65; adjunct professor, Columbia University, New York, 1967–69. Recipient: American Academy grant, 1945; Guggenheim fellowship, 1945, 1948; National Press Club award, 1948; O. Henry award, 1955; Ingram-Merrill grant, 1969; Chapelbrook grant, 1969; Pulitzer prize, 1970. Member, American Academy, 1970. *Died 26 March 1979.*

PUBLICATIONS

Short Stories

Children Are Bored on Sunday.   1953.
New Short Novels, with others, edited by Mary Louise
    Aswell.   1954.
Stories, with others.   1956; as *A Book of Stories,*   1957.
Bad Characters.   1964.
Selected Stories.   1966.
The Collected Stories.   1969.

Novels

Boston Adventure.   1944.
The Mountain Lion.   1947.
The Catherine Wheel.   1952.

Other

Elephi: The Cat with the High I.Q. (for children).   1962.
*The Lion and the Carpenter and Other Tales from the
    Arabian Nights Retold* (for children).   1962.
A Mother in History (on Marguerite C. Oswald).   1966.

*

Bibliography: *Stafford: A Comprehensive Bibliography* by Wanda Avila, 1983.

Critical Studies: *Stafford* by Mary Ellen Williams Walsh, 1985; *Innocence and Estrangement in the Fiction of Stafford* by Maureen Ryan, 1987; *Stafford: A Biography* by David Roberts, 1988; *Stafford: The Savage Heart* by Charlotte Margolis Goodman, 1990; *The Interior Castle: The Art and Life of Stafford* by Ann Hulbert, 1992.

*   *   *

In some painful and laughable sense of the words Jean Stafford was the daughter of a writer. Her ne'er-do-well father squandered the family money on bad investments and then installed himself in the basement to write pulp fiction for magazines that virtually never bought from him. The next writers to leave a direct imprint on her life were of a loftier stripe. While she was a student at the University of Colorado, at summer writers' conferences there, her work was read and admired by such visitors as Ford Madox Ford, John Crowe Ransom, Martha Foley, Whit Burnett, and Robert Penn Warren. There also she met the young

poet Robert Lowell, who was to become her first husband. Her network of supporting friends and editors spun out from these introductions.

She had, to be sure, been preparing herself assiduously if erratically as a writer from childhood on. She once wrote that she had (figuratively) "left home at seven"—meaning she had distanced herself from a family she considered mundane to write all manner of prose pieces, many ironic and most of them rebellious in one fashion or another. Her college writings impressed the best of her instructors. By the time she was 23 years old she had completed the manuscripts of five novels (none of these ever published).

In spite of these fervid commitments to a career, it may well be the best preparation was (as she wrote in a late essay) "taking her childhood seriously." In the masterpiece among her three novels, *The Mountain Lion,* and in a rich cluster of her short stories there is a central figure of a preadolescent girl, fiercely sardonic, painfully lonely by choice, timid and feisty by turns, obsessively enthralled by literature and committed to fictionalizing the bumpkins she is obliged to live with. Surely this prototype must be the young Stafford as she saw herself from the vantage of her maturity. In "The Healthiest Girl in Town" we see this girl in her environment, a small town on the slopes of the Colorado mountains where her widowed mother cares for various tuberculars who have moved west for their health. A certain glamour attaches to the sick and they are popularly thought to be rich as well. Our healthy narrator becomes ensnared and enchanted by the bullying friendship of two daughters of a sick family and only frees herself finally by a reflex of vanity and fear, reclaiming the merit of health even if "being healthy means being a cow." The narrator of "Bad Characters," the resentful loner Stafford gets involved with the most comic shoplifter in our literature, a girl her own age who works through dime stores caching her loot in the enormous hat that wobbles atop her head. In an excess of greed and confidence she overloads the hat. When the booty spills out, the girls are apprehended, but our girl escapes with no more punishment than a lecture from a fusty judge. Now reformed, she joins the Campfire girls, repents the lone wolf urges in her nature. "A Reading Problem" is in the same vein and equally good. One feels it might be another episode from the life of Molly, who is the center of *The Mountain Lion.*

All three of these stories are distinguished by their comic irony, but there is none of this at all in "The Philosophy Lesson," though it also comes from a situation with which Stafford had first-hand experience. A college girl, posing nude for a class of art students, watches, first, the snow storm outside move in to blind the windows while she drifts in the grandiose melancholy peculiar to the boredom of modeling. Then the shocked rumor sweeps from the campus into this room that a wealthy and popular male student has committed suicide. No action follows from this dreadful news, but the posing girl's meditations are brought to a point. If someone who seemed to have so much to live for could kill himself, then why didn't she "who was seldom happy, do it herself?" No answer to that except that the "benison" of the snow "forgave them all."

Up through the writing of her first published novel *Boston Adventure* Stafford cultivated a mandarin style, deliberately compounded of the manners of Proust and James. So *Boston Adventure* is a baffling hybrid, mixing her lofty and generally tedious style with a story that is essentially soap opera. Perhaps it was the suds and bubbles in it that made it a substantial best-seller. At any rate after its publication Stafford was able to buy a house in Maine and move there with her husband Robert Lowell. Lowell had already shattered her face in a car accident and was working up to breaking her nose again with his fist. Their residence in Maine was anguished. Nevertheless from it came two particularly noteworthy Stafford stories: "A Country Love Story" and "An Influx of Poets." The first is a complete triumph. A young wife and an older, ailing husband move up into the country to be away from the strains of urban living to help his regain his health. The farmhouse they occupy is utterly banal, but parked in the yard is an antique sleigh that somehow projects a spirit of dash and adventure. As the winter drifts hopelessly on with increments of alienation piling up on the married couple like the slow sift of snow, the wife begins to attach more and more of her fantasies of escape to the eye-catching sleigh in the yard. At last in a beautifully restrained climax, the wife imagines an appropriate male driver for the sleigh. He is just as real and just as unreal as a figure of myth ought to be. Though he has no corporal reality, his ravishment and abduction of the wife are absolutely incredible. No need to ask where she has gone. "An Influx of Poets" on the other hand is crudely shaped. It is chiefly worth reading for the scornful picture it draws of Lowell and his poet buddies as they come scrounging and reciting their work into each other's faces while the summer lasts.

Always at her best Stafford tempered her aesthetic intents with raw delight in the human scene. Her vision of grief is no less poignant for being ballasted with positive merriment. She never became a reporter in the conventional sense. When she was not rehearsing the pangs of childhood she went on projecting its awful wisdom onto the havoc of adult life, as in the many stories she published in *The New Yorker*.

One of her deservedly famous stories, "Children Are Bored on Sunday," makes a strict (though tender) accounting of the emotional cost and compensations of city life. A lonely and neurotic woman is spending the afternoon in New York's Metropolitan Museum, equally afraid of mingling and of lonely isolation, uncertain whether she belongs anywhere: "She was a bounty-jumper in the war between Great-uncle Graham's farm and New York City." She will not admit to being either a rube or an intellectual. She has seen a male acquaintance whom she wants at first to avoid, but when she leaves the museum with him it has dawned on her that the two of them are cousins-german "in the territory of despair." Then how does one distinguish such recognition from love? She does not, and though the terminal language of the story is both mocking and spritely, somehow we know that in Manhattan this must pass for the real thing.

—R.V. Cassill

See the essays on "In the Zoo" and "The Interior Castle."

STEAD, Christina (Ellen). Australian. Born in Rockdale, Sydney, New South Wales, 17 July 1902. Educated at Sydney University Teachers' College, graduated 1922. Married William James Blake in 1952 (died 1968). Demonstrator, Sydney University Teachers' College, in Sydney schools, 1922–24; secretary in Sydney, 1925–28; moved to Europe, 1928, and worked as a clerk in offices in London, 1928–29, and in Paris, 1930–35; lived in the U.S., 1937–47; senior writer, Metro-Goldwyn-Mayer, Holly-

wood, 1943; instructor, New York University, 1943–44; travelled, 1948–52; lived in England (mainly in Surbiton, Surrey), 1953–73, and in Australia, 1974–83; fellow in creative arts, Australian National University, Canberra, 1969. Recipient: Arts Council of Great Britain grant, 1967; Patrick White award, 1974; Australian Premier's special award, 1982. *Died 31 March 1983.*

PUBLICATIONS

Short Stories

The Salzburg Tales.   1934.
The Puzzleheaded Girl: Four Novellas.   1967.
Ocean of Story: The Uncollected Stories, edited by R.G. Geering.   1985.

Novels

Seven Poor Men of Sydney.   1934.
The Beauties and Furies.   1936.
House of All Nations.   1938.
The Man Who Loved Children.   1940.
For Love Alone.   1944.
Letty Fox: Her Luck.   1946.
A Little Tea, A Little Chat.   1948.
The People with the Dogs.   1952.
Dark Places of the Heart.   1966; as *Cotters' England,* 1967.
The Little Hotel.   1973.
Miss Herbert (The Suburban Wife).   1976.
The Palace with Several Sides: A Sort of Love Story, edited by R.G. Geering.   1986.
I'm Dying Laughing: The Humourist, edited by R.G. Geering.   1986.

Other

A Stead Reader, edited by Jean B. Read.   1979.

Editor, with William J. Blake, *Modern Women in Love.* 1945.
Editor, *Great Stories of the South Sea Islands.*   1955.

Translator, *Colour of Asia,* by Fernand Gigon.   1955.
Translator, *The Candid Killer,* by Jean Giltène.   1956.
Translator, *In Balloon and Bathyscaphe,* by August Piccard. 1956.

*

Critical Studies: *Stead,* 1969, and *Stead,* 1969, revised edition, 1979, both by R.G. Geering; *Stead* by Joan Lidoff, 1982; *Stead* by Diana Brydon, 1987; *Stead* by Susan Sheridan, 1988; *Stead: A Life in Letters* by Chris Williams, 1990.

* * *

The first of Christina Stead's books to be published was a remarkable display of her virtuosity as a writer of short fiction. Although it does share certain preoccupations and techniques with the novels that were to come, few who read *The Salzburg Tales* when it appeared in 1934 could have predicted the directions her later work would take. Whereas her novels tend to achieve their power by accumulating naturalistic detail and concentrating on the gradual revelation of complex characters and relationships, *The Salzburg Tales* keeps moving in sprightly fashion from one narrator to another, one situation to another, one set of characters to another. R.G. Geering remarks that her masterpiece *The Man Who Loved Children* "stands firmly in the great tradition of psychological realism in European fiction"; *The Salzburg Tales* reaches back to a more ancient, richly variform tradition, springing from that inventive gusto and delight in prolific tale-telling which Chaucer and Boccaccio most notably exemplify.

Not only in its composite structure but also in its range of miscellaneous subjects and styles, Stead's debut volume seems frequently reminiscent of *The Decameron, The Arabian Nights,* and *The Canterbury Tales.* Other sources of intertextual transformation include the writings of romancers and raconteurs such as Hoffman and Hawthorne. Pervasive in *The Salzburg Tales* is a deep curiosity about ramifications and roots of the narrative compulsion itself.

Describing the group of Salzburg festival visitors who will narrate in turn the episodes that comprise this book, the prologue characterises each of them in terms of their distinctively individual kinds of imagination or speaking style and their preferred genres. Many later passages, within and between the ensuing segments of storytelling, comment further on the impulses that lead people to make their world go round by chasing their tales. However, Stead's fascination with the polymorphic abundance of fiction-making is more fully expressed in the sheer diversity of the tales themselves. Few books present such a showcase of types of narration.

In a piece she contributed to a 1968 *Kenyon Review* symposium on the short story, Christina Stead mentioned an Indian anthology called *The Ocean of Story,* and made this comment:

> That is the way I think of the short story and what is part of it, the sketch, anecdote, jokes cunning, philosophical, and biting, legends and fragments . . . ancient folklore and church-inspired moralities and some tales to shiver at which are quite clearly frightening local events . . .

There are specimens of each of these sub-genres in *The Salzburg Tales*: sketch, both of a person ("Poor Anna") and of a place ("On the Road"); anecdote ("The Sparrow in Love," "Guest of the Redshields"); joke ("Sappho," which burlesques classical and Christian myths); legend ("Gaspard," which shows how legendary materials can serve a serious end, in this case an illuminating insight into life under the moribund ancien régime); fragment ("The Wunder Gottes"); folktale (several are recounted by the Centenarist); morality ("The Gold Bride"); and a tale of frightening local events ("The Triskelion"—one of the few items in this book that have a recognizably Australian setting). And other kinds of short fiction appear as well: fable ("The Sensitive Goldfish"); snatch of dialogue ("The Little Old Lady"); whimsical episode ("Silk-shirt"); parable ("The Death of Svend"), lyrical apostrophe ("Fair Women"); and various parodies—of Poe's Gothic extravagance ("To the Mountain"), of Chekhov's sentimental irony ("A Russian Heart"), of courtroom dramas ("Speculation in Lost Causes").

The passage quoted above from Stead's symposium contribution yielded a phrase for the title of a large posthumous publication: *Ocean of Story,* comprising her previously uncollected stories, appeared in 1985. Whereas her first book had been a deliberately organised miscellany, *Ocean of Story* was a gathering up of leftovers. They had been written at various times over five decades. A few are fine short stories; but several are discarded drafts, shavings from her novels, or pieces of biography, autobiography, journalism, and other non-fiction. Though uneven, this collection shows the persistence of some of Stead's most distinctive qualities as a teller of tales. Among the most noteworthy are "My Friend, Lafe Tilly," which relates a womaniser's inability to accept the peripeteia that he undergoes, and the grotesque details of his physical decline; "A Harmless Affair," about a passion that goes nowhere; and "The Boy," a study in dependence and entrapment. In many of them the action occurs entirely indoors, often in a boarding house or a small apartment, and the focus is on psychological intensities exacerbated by a sense of enclosure.

Between those two volumes of short fiction, half a century apart, came eleven novels—and also one other book that deserves mention here: a collection of four novellas, *The Puzzleheaded Girl.* Each novella has a casual structure that incorporates abrupt changes of direction—a frequent feature of Stead's long and short fiction. Perhaps the most startling in this respect is "The Rightangled Creek." Subtitled "a sort of ghost story," it may seem on the face of it to have no narrative unity except that of place: it is set in an apparently haunted house, occupied by a succession of people. For half its length the story deals with one family group—who then, suddenly, disappear from view, and others move casually into and out of the rest of the narrative. Closer reading reveals that the story's course is often interrupted by descriptive passages which accumulate images of fecundity that invade the oddly doubled structures of the house. Any orderings of culture (the building itself, but also the domestic arrangements and vocational schemes of its inhabitants) seem subverted by inchoate impulses from the natural surroundings. The imagery of profusion, disturbing hand-made things, constitutes a self-referential narrative code, persuading readers to regard analogically as a unified whole the desultory formal features of this tale.

In one way or another, much of Stead's short fiction poses a challenge to conventional expectations. Some stories risk appearing inconsequential; others mix folktale motifs with psychological realism, gothic horror with whimsy, and so on. It is a strange and distinctive world.

—Ian Reid

See the essays on "The Marionettist" and "The Puzzleheaded Girl."

———

STEIN, Gertrude. American. Born in Allegheny, Pennsylvania, 3 February 1874; as a child lived in Vienna, Paris, and Oakland, California. Educated at schools in Oakland and San Francisco; Radcliffe College, Cambridge, Massachussetts, 1893–97; studied philosophy under William James, B.A. (Harvard University), 1897; studied medicine at Johns Hopkins Medical School, Baltimore, 1897–1901. Lived in Paris from 1903, with Alice B. Toklas from 1908; center of a circle of artists, including Picasso, Matisse, and

Braque, and of writers, including Hemingway, *q.v.*, and Fitzgerald, *q.v.*; lived in Mallorca, 1914–16; worked with American Fund for French Wounded, 1917–18; founder, Plain Edition, Paris, 1930–33; lectured in the U.S., 1934-35. *Died 27 July 1946.*

PUBLICATIONS

Collections

Writings and Lectures 1911–1945 (selection), edited by Patricia Meyerowitz.   1967; as *Look at Me Now and Here I Am*, 1971.
Selected Operas and Plays, edited by John Malcolm Brinnin.   1970.
The Yale Stein: Selections, edited by Richard Kostelanetz.   1980.

Short Stories

Three Lives: Stories of the Good Anna, Melanctha, and the Gentle Lena.   1909.
Mrs. Reynolds, and Five Earlier Novelettes, edited by Carl Van Vechten.   1952.

Novels

The Making of Americans, Being a History of a Family's Progress.   1925.
A Book Concluding with As a Wife Has a Cow: A Love Story.   1926.
Lucy Church Amiably.   1931.
Ida: A Novel.   1941.
Brewsie and Willie.   1946.
Blood on the Dining Room Floor.   1948.
Things as They Are: A Novel in Three Parts.   1950.
A Novel of Thank You, edited by Carl Van Vechten.   1958.
Lifting Belly, edited by Rebecca Marks.   1989.

Plays

Geography and Plays.   1922.
A Village: Are You Ready Yet Not Yet.   1928.
Operas and Plays.   1932.
Four Saints in Three Acts, music by Virgil Thomson (produced 1934).   1934.
A Wedding Bouquet: Ballet, music by Lord Berners (produced 1936).   1936.
In Savoy; or, Yes Is for a Very Young Man (produced 1946).   1946.
The Mother of Us All, music by Virgil Thomson (produced 1947).   1947.
Last Operas and Plays, edited by Carl Van Vechten.   1949.
In a Garden, music by Meyer Kupferman (produced 1951).   1951.
Lucretia Borgia.   1968.
D. Faustus Lights the Lights (produced 1984).
Operas and Plays.   1987.

Verse and Prose Poems

Tender Buttons: Objects, Food, Rooms.   1914.
Have They Attacked Mary. He Giggled.   1917.
Before the Flowers of Friendship Faded Friendship Faded.   1931.

Two (Hitherto Unpublished) Poems.   1948.
Stanzas in Meditation and Other Poems (1929–1933), edited by Carl Van Vechten.   1956.

Other

Portrait of Mabel Dodge.   1912.
Composition as Explanation.   1926.
Descriptions of Literature.   1926.
An Elucidation.   1927.
Useful Knowledge.   1928.
An Acquaintance with Description.   1929.
Dix Portraits.   1930.
How to Write.   1931.
The Autobiography of Alice B. Toklas.   1933.
Matisse, Picasso, and Gertrude Stein, with Two Shorter Stories.   1933.
Portraits and Prayers.   1934.
Chicago Inscriptions.   1934.
Lectures in America.   1935.
Narration: Four Lectures.   1935.
The Geographical History of America; or, The Relation of Human Nature to the Human Mind.   1936.
Everybody's Autobiography.   1937.
Picasso.   1938.
The World Is Round (for children).   1939.
Prothalamium.   1939.
Paris France.   1940.
What Are Masterpieces.   1940.
Petits poèmes pour un livre de lecture (for children).   1944; translated as *The First Reader, and Three Plays*, 1946.
Wars I Have Seen.   1945.
Selected Writings, edited by Carl Van Vechten.   1946.
Four in America.   1947.
Kisses Can.   1947.
Literally True.   1947.
Two: Stein and Her Brother and Other Early Portraits (1908–1912), edited by Carl Van Vechten.   1951.
Bee Time Vine and Other Pieces (1913–1927), edited by Carl Van Vechten.   1953.
As Fine as Melanctha (1914–1930), edited by Carl Van Vechten.   1954.
Painted Lace and Other Pieces (1914–1937), edited by Carl Van Vechten.   1955.
Absolutely Bob Brown; or, Bobbed Brown.   1955.
To Bobchen Haas.   1957.
Alphabets and Birthdays, edited by Carl Van Vechten.   1957.
On Our Way (letters).   1959.
Cultivated Motor Automatism, with Leon M. Solomons.   1969.
Stein on Picasso, edited by Edward Burns.   1970.
A Primer for the Gradual Understanding of Stein, edited by Robert Bartlett Haas.   1971.
Fernhurst, Q.E.D., and Other Early Writings, edited by Leon Katz.   1971.
Sherwood Anderson/Stein: Correspondence and Personal Essays, edited by Ray Lewis White.   1972.
Reflection on the Atomic Bomb, edited by Robert Bartlett Haas.   1973.
Money.   1973.
How Writing Is Written, edited by Robert Bartlett Haas.   1974.
Dear Sammy: Letters from Stein to Alice B. Toklas, edited by Samuel M. Steward.   1977.
The Letters of Stein and Carl Van Vechten 1913–1946, edited by Edward Burns.   2 vols., 1986.

*

Bibliography: *Stein: A Bibliography* by Robert A. Wilson, 1974; *Stein: An Annotated Critical Bibliography* by Maureen R. Liston, 1979; *Stein and Alice B. Toklas: A Reference Guide* by Ray Lewis White, 1984.

Critical Studies: *Stein: Form and Intelligibility* by Rosalind S. Miller, 1949; *Stein: A Biography of Her Work* by Donald Sutherland, 1951; *The Flowers of Friendship* (letters to Stein) edited by Donald Gallup, 1953; *Stein: Her Life and Work* by Elizabeth Sprigge, 1957; *The Third Rose: Stein and Her World* by John Malcolm Brinnin, 1959; *Stein* by Frederick J. Hoffman, 1961; *What Is Remembered* by Alice B. Toklas, 1963, and *Staying On Alone: Letters of Alice B. Toklas* edited by Edward Burns, 1973; *The Development of Abstractionism in the Writings of Stein*, 1965, and *Stein*, 1976, both by Michael J. Hoffman; *Stein and the Present* by Allegra Stewart, 1967; *Stein and the Literature of Modern Consciousness* by Norman Weinstein, 1970; *Stein in Pieces* by Richard Bridgman, 1970; *Stein: A Biography* by Howard Greenfield, 1973; *Charmed Circle* by James Mellow, 1974; *Stein: A Composite Portrait* edited by Linda Simon, 1974; *Everybody Who Was Anybody: A Biography of Stein* by Janet Hobhouse, 1975; *Exact Resemblance to Exact Resemblance: The Literary Portraiture of Stein* by Wendy Steiner, 1978; *Stein: Autobiography and the Problem of Narration* by Shirley C. Neuman, 1979, and *Stein and the Making of Literature* by Neuman and Ira B. Nadel, 1988; *A Different Language: Stein's Experimental Writing* by Marianne DeKoven, 1983; *The Structure of Obscurity: Stein, Language and Cubism* by Randa Dubnick, 1984; *Stein's Theatre of the Absolute* by Betsy Alayne Ryan, 1984; *The Making of a Modernist: Stein from Three Lives to Tender Buttons* by Jayne L. Walker, 1984; *Stein* edited by Harold Bloom, 1986; *The Public Is Invited to Dance: Representation, the Body and Dialogue in Stein* by Harriet Scott Shessman, 1989; *Stein Advanced: An Anthology of Criticism* edited by Richard Kostelanetz, 1990; *Gertrude and Alice* by Diana Souhami, 1992.

*   *   *

Gertrude Stein's writing defies classification by genre because of its variety as well as its experimental nature. Her short fiction, however, offers an attractive if unbalanced introduction to her work, beginning with *Q.E.D.*, a quasi-autobiographical novella written in 1903. It is remarkable for its sexual candor, particularly so as the work of a young American female at the turn of the century. Here Gertrude Stein explores human behavior through three women locked in an emotional vise, as their disparate characters attempt to manipulate each other both sexually and intellectually. Adele is gauche, cerebral, and bourgeois; Mabel is experienced, passionate, and aristocratic. Their combat for the beautiful but passive Helen leads to the book's stalemate, borne alternately of lesbian alliances and frustrations. *Q.E.D.* bears little resemblance to anything Stein wrote afterward. Her work progressed from startling discovery to startling discovery in form, although the content remained largely if not exclusively autobiographical.

Two years later she had completed *Three Lives*, a trio of naturalist novellas. The prose in "The Good Anna" is fairly conventional, although this German servant's spoken idiom infects the narrative with attenuated locutions. "The Gentle Lena" combines the stumbling speech of a second German domestic with a touching narrative of failure more successfully. "Melanctha," the best known and most often reprinted of the stories, indicates Stein's movement toward what she later called a "prolonged present," delaying the narrative until it had been transformed into a "continuous present." A similar but far more convoluted and repetitive prose identifies Stein's other early work, until about 1912.

After *Three Lives* she wrote a long, dense, largely plotless novel of paragraph-long and sometimes page-long sentences, *The Making of Americans*, between 1906 and 1911; but she began to experiment during that time with word portraits of people she knew, constructing them of accretive variations in similarly protracted sentences. These resulted occasionally in biographies thinly disguised as short fiction. "Orta or One Dancing," for example, is Isadora Duncan who, Stein wrote in *Two*, "was one dancing in being one being that one being the one dancing then." "Miss Furr and Miss Skeene" are Maud Hunt Squire and Ethel Mars, Paris acquaintances whose private life together, wrote Stein in *Geography and Plays*, consists—in perhaps the first use of the euphemism in print—of "being gay, they were gay every day, they were regular, they were gay, they were gay the same length of time every day, they were gay, they were quite regularly gay." "Ada" is Alice B. Toklas, who became at the time of these compositions Stein's secretary, companion, lover, and alter-ego in a symbiotic relationship that lasted until death; indeed, in "Ada," "someone was then the other one" (*Geography and Plays*).

That observation continued to inform Stein's writing for the next 25 years, during which she devoted herself to a series of experimental pieces in a variety of forms, notably plays (although they are not conventionally stageable), dialogues, and poems to celebrate the major joys and minor disruptions in her apparently happy marriage. She interrupted these often erotic compositions—all rich in the word-play and puns that characterized much of her writing—with two novels, the hermetic *A Novel of Thank You* and *Lucy Church Amiably*, accurately described on the title page as "A Novel of Romantic Beauty and Nature and which Looks Like an Engraving." Simultaneously, she began to formulate her theories about grammar and rhetoric, in a series of elliptical essays and meditations.

Then, in 1933, Stein's engaging memoirs were published as *The Autobiography of Alice B. Toklas*, written in the acerbic voice of the eponymous subject, forgoing Stein's garrulousness for Toklas's pith. The best-seller success of this curious but accessible work gave Stein both readers and royalties for the first time; afterward, she divided her energies about equally between what she called "identity" writing for an audience and "entity" writing for herself. Nearly all of her subsequent fiction fell in the latter category, beginning with *Blood on the Dining Room Floor*, a brief, unsolved murder mystery nearly as impenetrable as most of the erotic apostrophes to Toklas that had preceded it.

During a 1934-35 American lecture tour, Stein synthesized her ideas about narrative forms in a seminar at the University of Chicago. Published as *Narration*, her lectures contended that conventional narrative was no longer appropriate in the modern world, and she modified somewhat her earlier assertions about the emotional life of paragraphs rather than of sentences. She had found greater strength in the balance of the latter, she believed, and she used several examples, from popular road signs to the Old Testament, to prove her point. These considerations brought her to a revised definition of literature: "the telling of anything but in telling that thing where is the audience. . . .Undoubtedly that audience has to be there for the purpose of recognition as the telling is proceeding to be written and that audience must be at one with the writing."

Other short fiction that did not entirely adhere to this declaration followed. *The World Is Round,* written in 1939, is about a little girl named Rose who climbs a mountain with a chair, despite perilous adventures and artistic endeavors along the way. Enroute, for example, Rose carves Stein's quintessential observation, written many years before, around a tree trunk so that it meets itself to make a ring: "Rose is a rose is a rose is a rose." Here, then, are aspiration, execution fraught with dangers, and achievement—autobiography disguised as a children's story.

Stein's novel *Ida* followed in 1941, arguably her most successful short fiction and an excellent example of the kind of narrative she had referred to in *Narration* as "permanently good reading." Ida's amorous history begins when her twin Ida-Ida disappears at birth, at the end of the first paragraph. Ida then reinvents her and, when she disappears again, absorbs the twin's personality into her own. Here, Stein imaginatively rather than theoretically toys with the difference between "identity" and "entity." Ida's ensuing liaisons include a quartet of husbands before she ends up in Washington, D.C., as a celebrated hostess who has brief flings. All of these romances are spun with Stein's familiar rhyming and verbal games along Ida's erratic route; but no plot summary can impart the pleasures of *Ida,* for they lie as much in form as in content.

Stein's final work was another short novel, *Brewsie and Willie,* in 1946, about American servicemen in Paris after the war. She wrote it almost entirely in dialogue, slangy, colloquial, often passionate, but recreated through her own unique and insistent voice, like no other in American literature. Although Stein is not usually identified as a writer of fiction, much of what she did write in the genre offers an unusually accessible avenue into her often bewildering work.

—Bruce Kellner

See the essay on "Melanctha."

STEINBECK, John (Ernst). American. Born in Salinas, California, 27 February 1902. Educated at Salinas High School, graduated 1919; Stanford University, California, intermittently 1919–25. Married 1) Carol Henning in 1930 (divorced 1942); 2) Gwyn Conger (i.e., the actress Gwen Verdon) in 1943 (divorced 1948), two sons; 3) Elaine Scott in 1950. Worked at various jobs, including reporter for the New York *American,* apprentice hod-carrier, apprentice painter, chemist, caretaker of an estate at Lake Tahoe, surveyor, and fruit picker, 1925–35; full-time writer from 1935; settled in Monterey, California, 1930, later moved to New York City; special writer for U.S. Army Air Force during World War II; correspondent in Europe, New York *Herald Tribune,* 1943. Recipient: New York Drama Critics Circle award, 1938; Pulitzer prize, 1940; King Haakon Liberty Cross (Norway), 1946; O. Henry award, 1956; Nobel prize for literature, 1962; Presidential Medal of Freedom, 1964; U.S. Medal of Freedom, 1964. Member, American Academy, 1939. *Died 20 December 1968.*

PUBLICATIONS

Short Stories

The Pastures of Heaven. 1932.
Saint Katy the Virgin. 1936.
The Red Pony. 1937.
The Long Valley. 1938.
The Moon Is Down (novella). 1942.
Burning Bright: A Play in Story Form (novella). 1950.
The Short Novels. 1953.

Novels

Cup of Gold: A Life of Henry Morgan, Buccaneer, with Occasional Reference to History. 1929.
To a God Unknown. 1933.
Tortilla Flat. 1935.
In Dubious Battle. 1936.
Of Mice and Men. 1937.
The Grapes of Wrath. 1939; edited by Peter Lisca, 1972.
Cannery Row. 1945.
The Wayward Bus. 1947.
The Pearl. 1947.
East of Eden. 1952.
Sweet Thursday. 1954.
The Short Reign of Pippin IV: A Fabrication. 1957.
The Winter of Our Discontent. 1961.

Plays

Of Mice and Men, from his own novel (produced 1937). 1937.
The Forgotten Village (screenplay). 1941.
The Moon Is Down, from his own novel (produced 1942). 1942.
A Medal for Benny, with Jack Wagner and Frank Butler, in *Best Film Plays* 1945, edited by John Gassner and Dudley Nichols. 1946.
Burning Bright, from his own novel (produced 1950). 1951.
Viva Zapata! The Original Screenplay, edited by Robert E. Morsberger. 1975.

Screenplays: *The Forgotten Village* (documentary), 1941; *Lifeboat,* with Jo Swerling, 1944; *A Medal for Benny,* with Jack Wagner and Frank Butler, 1945; *La perla (The Pearl),* with Jack Wagner and Emilio Fernandez, 1946; *The Red Pony,* 1949; *Viva Zapata!,* 1952.

Other

Their Blood Is Strong. 1938.
Steinbeck Replies (letter). 1940.
Sea of Cortez: A Leisurely Journal of Travel and Research, with Edward F. Ricketts. 1941.
Bombs Away: The Story of a Bomber Team. 1942.
The Viking Portable Library Steinbeck, edited by Pascal Covici. 1943; abridged edition, as *The Steinbeck Pocket Book,* 1943; revised edition, as *The Portable Steinbeck,* 1946, 1958; revised edition, edited by Pascal Covici, Jr., 1971; 1946 edition published as *The Indispensable Steinbeck,* 1950, and as *The Steinbeck Omnibus,* 1951.
The First Watch (letter). 1947.

Vanderbilt Clinic. 1947.
A Russian Journal, photographs by Robert Capa. 1948.
The Log from the Sea of Cortez. 1951.
Once There Was a War. 1958.
Travels with Charley in Search of America. 1962.
Speech Accepting the Nobel Prize for Literature.... 1962(?).
America and Americans. 1966.
Journal of a Novel: The East of Eden Letters. 1969.
Steinbeck: A Life in Letters, edited by Elaine Steinbeck and Robert Wallsten. 1975.
The Acts of King Arthur and His Noble Knights, From the Winchester Manuscripts of Malory and Other Sources, edited by Chase Horton. 1976.
Letters to Elizabeth: A Selection of Letters from Steinbeck to Elizabeth Otis, edited by Florian J. Shasky and Susan F. Riggs. 1978.
Conversations with Steinbeck, edited by Thomas Fensch. 1988.
Working Days: The Journals of The Grapes of Wrath, 1938–1941, edited by Robert DeMott. 1989.

*

Bibliography: *A New Steinbeck Bibliography 1929–1971 and 1971–1981* by Tetsumaro Hayashi, 2 vols., 1973–83; *Steinbeck: A Bibliographical Catalogue of the Adrian H. Goldstone Collection* by Adrian H. Goldstone and John R. Payne, 1974; *Steinbeck Bibliographies: An Annotated Guide* by Robert B. Harmon, 1987.

Critical Studies: *The Novels of Steinbeck: A First Critical Study* by Harry T. Moore, 1939, as *Steinbeck and His Novels,* 1939; *Steinbeck and His Critics: A Record of Twenty-Five Years* edited by E.W. Tedlock, Jr., and C.V. Wicker, 1957; *The Wide World of Steinbeck,* 1958, and *Steinbeck, Nature, and Myth,* 1978, both by Peter Lisca; *Steinbeck* by Warren French, 1961, revised edition, 1975, and *A Companion to The Grapes of Wrath* edited by French, 1963; *Steinbeck* by F.W. Watt, 1962; *Steinbeck: An Introduction and Interpretation* by Joseph Fontenrose, 1964; Steinbeck Monograph series, from 1972, *A Study Guide to Steinbeck: A Handbook to His Major Works,* 2 vols., 1974–79, and *Steinbeck's Literary Dimenson,* 1991, all edited by Tetsumaro Hayashi; *Steinbeck: A Collection of Critical Essays* edited by Robert Murray Davis, 1972; *Steinbeck and Edward F. Ricketts: The Shaping of a Novelist* by Richard Astro, 1973; *The Novels of Steinbeck: A Critical Study* by Howard Levant, 1974; *Steinbeck: The Errant Knight: An Intimate Biography of His California Years* by Nelson Valjean, 1975; *The Intricate Music: A Biography of Steinbeck* by Thomas Kiernan, 1979; *Steinbeck* by Paul McCarthy, 1980; *The True Adventures of Steinbeck, Writer: A Biography* by Jackson J. Benson, 1984; *Steinbeck: The California Years* by Brian St. Pierre, 1984; *Steinbeck: Life, Work, and Criticism* by John Ditsky, 1985; *Steinbeck's New Vision of America* by Louis Owens, 1985; *Steinbeck, The Voice of the Land* by Keith Ferrell, 1986; *Steinbeck's Fiction: The Aesthetics of the Road Taken,* 1986, and *The Dramatic Landscape of Steinbeck's Short Stories,* 1990, both by John H. Timmerman; *Beyond The Red Pony: A Reader's Companion to Steinbeck's Complete Short Stories,* 1987, and *Steinbeck: A Study of the Short Fiction,* 1989, both by R.S. Hughes; *New Essays on The Grapes of Wrath* edited by David Wright, 1990; *The Short Novels of Steinbeck* edited by Jackson J. Benson, 1990.

* * *

Like many another American writer who got his start in the early 20th century, John Steinbeck devoted himself to writing short stories as well as novels early in his career. Magazine sales of stories were, after all, highly remunerative, and the market for longer fiction chancy. But after the enormous success of *The Grapes of Wrath,* with his financial security assured, Steinbeck's story output slowed to a trickle. Only a Japanese collection of the later stories exists, not easy to locate, and though some of the stories in it are worth study, they are likely to elude the nonspecialist reader. By the same token, a quartet of studies in recent years has made us aware of the existence of even more stories, many of them early efforts; but once again few will encounter them. For the most part, Steinbeck's considerable achievement in the short story form is found in two volumes from the 1930's, *The Pastures of Heaven* and *The Long Valley.*

Steinbeck's short fiction also possesses some unusual features that make criticism unconventional. Not only do some pieces (such as *The Pearl*) straddle the borderline between novel and novella (the work is in effect a film scenario), but Steinbeck also composed three "play-novellas" that exist in both formats, the most famous of these being the classic *Of Mice and Men.* Of the more conventional stories that deserve treatment here, the ones in *The Pastures of Heaven* can be said to constitute a novel in the form of an interlinked suite of separable stories, generally called by their central characters' names, and recent criticism has stressed their interdependence. Sherwood Anderson's *Winesburg, Ohio* can be claimed as a model for *Pastures,* and certainly its characters can be studied as Andersonian grotesques.

Steinbeck's evident narrational detachment, based on his interest in science, particularly the marine biology he investigated with his biologist—and fellow amateur philosopher—friend Edward F. Ricketts, whose laboratory is still passed by thousands of tourists each day, uncomprehending as they might be, in Cannery Row, Monterey, California. Practically all the worthwhile short stories of Steinbeck are set in California, where he grew up; and the local landscape seems inseparable from his treatment of character. Additionally confusing to early readers was Steinbeck's apparent link to the literary naturalists, whereas in fact he was a Romantic ahead of his time in terms of his prevision of metafiction. "Tularecito" and "Johnny Bear," from the works already cited, along with Lennie from *Mice,* are mental defectives; many of Steinbeck's characters are also hardly quiz kids, nor their sometimes irresponsible ways admirable. Yet they are presented, not sentimentally as some used to claim, but sympathetically, since their values stand in marked contrast to those of the success-oriented society as a whole, the standards and smugness of which Steinbeck abhorred.

Steinbeck's variegated reading shows up in his stories in ways that might surprise the reader, who at first might find them seemingly simple pieces. He was early taken with Arthurian themes, and he was familiar with researches into myth; Joseph Campbell was an early friend. His interest, with Ricketts, in what they called "is-thinking" led him to eschew moral stances in his stories, leading some to presuppose that he approved of all that he presented. These subtleties and traps still threaten the unwary, as in the *Long Valley* story "The Murder." Does Steinbeck or his unidentified narrator see Jim Moore's "foreign" (she is a Yugoslav, and strange to his culture as he is to hers) wife Jelka in animal terms, or does Jim do this, perhaps in error or misjudgment? Jim rejects his father-in-law's advice to give his wife the occasional beating as also foreign, and instead neglects her as little better than his livestock, leading to her eventual adultery with a cousin whom Jim murders. Throughout this story, the Gothic towers of a local natural formation loom, as if to epitomize Steinbeck's merging of natural landscape and European literary tradition.

Teachers who regularly assign Steinbeck works to their pupils and students often do so in the face of attempts at censorship from school boards and parents. Yet it is only fair to note that Steinbeck's fictions contain a great amount of violence that is neither judged nor condoned, and thus may elude the sensitivity of the reader not tipped off as to what he or she is expected to be upset by. Even some noted critics have missed the challenge to their own moral resources in Steinbeck's stories and have found little but lower-class humor in searingly bitter material. The often-reprinted classic, "Flight," which prefigures *The Pearl* in many respects, does not spend much time examining the rightness of the act of violence which sets young Pepé running away from his pursuers. Steinbeck is interested in the process by which the boy, in accepting the implications of his actions, becomes a man even as he loses his father's estate, a few possessions, and then his life. Here the stoicism of Indian characters, as elsewhere in Steinbeck stories set in Mexico or California, is counterpointed by the universal theme that the establishing of one's integrity and the losing of one's life are a tradeoff, as is clearly the case in our relentlessly violent contemporary society.

Similarly, "Junius Maltby" from *Pastures* is also frequently anthologized, perhaps as instruction to teachers tempted to back down from community criticism. Young Junius's son is raised on the very sort of reading that Steinbeck held in high regard, and yet the way he is being raised arouses community hackles, in spite of the sympathy of the teacher Miss Morgan. Since the boy is being raised as something of a "wild child" without conventional restraints, he must be put into a normally fitting strait jacket, which does at last occur. The story is rife with literary lore, as Steinbeck imputes to Junius many of his favorite readings; and it is also a nutshell encapsulation of Californian values as eventually embodied years later by hippies and "flower children."

Because his stories raise far more questions than they imply judgments, they are seemingly eternally fascinating to the reader. Steinbeck understood both hard toil and knightly quests after the ideal, and his stories set in balance the perils of both. The neglect of his writing in academic and critical circles through the 1950's and 1960's has been replaced by an enormous resurgence of critical and scholarly attention. His endings, even when seemingly tragically final, are ultimately open-ended and provocative of endless discussion. His treatment of human beings as animals with a difference, but basically different animals nevertheless, seems keyed to the new awarenesses of the 1990's and beyond. Boys who grow up relating to horses and women who grow old relating to flowers are all parts of his acknowledgment of the ambiguity of the human condition, so ably reflected in his major short stories.

—John Ditsky

See the essays on "The Chrysanthemums" and *The Red Pony.*

———

STEVENSON, Robert Louis (Robert Lewis Balfour Stevenson). Scottish. Born in Edinburgh, 13 November 1850. Educated at Mr. Henderson's school, Edinburgh, 1855–61; Edinburgh Academy; a school in Isleworth; Mr. Thompson's school, Edinburgh; University of Edinburgh, 1867–72; studied law in the office of Skene Edwards and Gordon, Edinburgh: called to the Scottish bar, 1875. Married Fanny Osbourne in 1880; two stepchildren, including the writer Lloyd Osbourne. Lived in Europe, mainly in France, 1875–80; contributor, *Cornhill Magazine,* London, 1876–82; lived in the U.S., 1879–80 and 1887–88, Scotland, 1881–82, Hyères, France, 1882–84, and Bournemouth, 1884–87; made three cruises in the Pacific, 1888–89; settled at Vailima, Samoa, 1890. *Died 3 December 1894.*

PUBLICATIONS

Collections

Works (Vailima Edition), edited by Lloyd Osbourne and Fanny Stevenson. 26 vols., 1922–23.
Selected Writings, edited by Saxe Commins. 1947.
Collected Poems, edited by Janet Adam Smith. 1950.
Essays, edited by Malcolm Elwin. 1950.
The Collected Shorter Fiction, edited by Peter Stoneley. 1991.

Short Stories

New Arabian Nights. 1882.
More New Arabian Nights: The Dynamiter, with Fanny Stevenson. 1885.
Strange Case of Dr. Jekyll and Mr. Hyde. 1886; edited by Emma Letley, with *Weir of Hermiston,* 1987.
The Merry Men and Other Tales and Fables. 1887.
Island Nights' Entertainments, Consisting of The Beach of Falesá, The Bottle Imp, The Isle of Voices. 1893.
The Ebb-Tide: A Trio and Quartette, with Lloyd Osbourne. 1894.
The Body-Snatcher. 1895.
The Amateur Emigrant from the Clyde to Sandy Hook. 1895.
The Strange Case of Dr. Jekyll and Mr. Hyde, with Other Fables. 1896.
Fables. 1896.
The Waif Woman. 1916.
When the Devil Was Well, edited by William P. Trent. 1921.
The Suicide Club and Other Stories, edited by J. Kenneth White. 1970.
An Old Song: A Newly Discovered Long Story; and a Previously Unpublished Short Story, Edifying Letters of the Rutherford Family, edited by Roger G. Swearingen. 1982.
The Scottish Stories and Essays, edited by Kenneth Gelder. 1989.

Novels

Treasure Island. 1883; edited by Emma Letley, 1985.
Prince Otto: A Romance. 1885.
Kidnapped, Being Memoirs of the Adventures of David Balfour in the Year 1751. 1886; edited by Emma Letley, with *Catriona,* 1986.

The Misadventures of John Nicholson: A Christmas Story.
1887.
The Black Arrow: A Tale of the Two Roses.   1888.
The Master of Ballantrae: A Winter's Tale.   1889; edited
by Emma Letley, 1983.
The Wrong Box, with Lloyd Osbourne.   1889; edited by
Ernest Mehew, 1989.
The Bottle Imp, with *American Notes,* by Rudyard Kipling.
1891.
The Wrecker, with Lloyd Osbourne.   1892.
Catriona: A Sequel to Kidnapped.   1893; as *David Balfour,*
1893; edited by Emma Letley, with *Kidnapped,* 1986.
Weir of Hermiston: An Unfinished Romance.   1896;
edited by Emma Letley, with *Strange Case of Dr. Jekyll
and Mr. Hyde,* 1987.
*St. Ives, Being the Adventures of a French Prisoner in
England,* completed by Arthur Quiller-Couch.   1897.

Plays

Deacon Brodie; or, The Double Life, with W.E. Henley
(produced 1882).   1880; revised edition, 1888.
Admiral Guinea, with W.E. Henley (produced 1897).
1884.
Beau Austin, with W.E. Henley (produced 1890).   1884.
Macaire, with W.E. Henley (produced 1900).   1885.
The Hanging Judge, with Fanny Stevenson.   1887.
Monmouth, edited by Charles Vale.   1928.

Verse

Penny Whistles (for children).   1883.
A Child's Garden of Verses.   1885.
Underwoods.   1887.
Ticonderoga.   1887.
Ballads.   1890.
Songs of Travel and Other Verses.   1896.
Poems Hitherto Unpublished, edited by George S. Hellman.
2 vols., 1916; as *New Poems and Variant Readings,*
1918; additional volume, edited by Hellman and Wil-
liam P. Trent, 1921.

Other

The Pentland Rising: A Page of History, 1666.   1866.
The Charity Bazaar: An Allegorical Dialogue.   n.d.
An Appeal to the Clergy.   1875.
An Inland Voyage.   1878.
Edinburgh: Picturesque Notes.   1879.
Travels with a Donkey in the Cévennes.   1879.
Virginibus Puerisque and Other Papers.   1881.
Familiar Studies of Men and Books.   1882.
*The Silverado Squatters: Sketches from a Californian
Mountain.*   1883.
Memories and Portraits.   1887.
Thomas Stevenson, Civil Engineer.   1887.
Memoir of Fleeming Jenkin.   1887.
*Father Damien: An Open Letter to the Reverend Dr. Hyde of
Honolulu.*   1890.
The South Seas: A Record of Three Cruises.   1890.
Across the Plains, with Other Memories and Essays, edited
by Sidney Colvin.   1892.
A Footnote to History: Eight Years of Trouble in Samoa.
1892.
The Works (Edinburgh Edition), edited by Sidney Colvin.
28 vols., 1894–98.

In the South Seas.   1896.
A Mountain Town in France: A Fragment.   1896.
The Morality of the Profession of Letters.   1899.
Letters to His Family and Friends, edited by Sidney Colvin.
2 vols., 1899; revised edition, 4 vols., 1911.
Essays and Criticisms.   1903.
Prayers Written at Vailima.   1905.
Essays of Travel.   1905.
Essays in the Art of Writing.   1905.
Lay Morals and Other Papers.   1911.
Records of a Family of Engineers.   1912; unfinished
chapters edited by J. Christian Bat, 1930.
Memoirs of Himself.   1912.
Some Letters, edited by Lloyd Osbourne.   1914.
On the Choice of a Profession.   1916.
Diogenes in London.   1920.
Hitherto Unpublished Prose Writings, edited by Henry H.
Harper.   1921.
Stevenson's Workshop, with Twenty-Nine MS. Facsimiles,
edited by William P. Trent.   1921.
*Confessions of a Unionist: An Unpublished Talk on Things
Current, Written in 1888,* edited by F.V. Livingston.
1921.
The Best Thing in Edinburgh, edited by Katharine D.
Osbourne.   1923.
The Castaways of Soledad, edited by George S. Hellman.
1928.
*Henry James and Stevenson: A Record of Friendship and
Criticism,* edited by Janet Adam Smith.   1948.
Silverado Journal, edited by J.E. Jordan.   1954.
RLS: Stevenson's Letters to Charles Baxter, edited by De
Lancey Ferguson and Marshall Waingrow.   1956.
From Scotland to Silverado, edited by J.D. Hart.   1966.
Travels in Hawaii, edited by A. Grove Day.   1973.
*The Amateur Emigrant, with Some First Impressions of
America,* edited by Roger G. Swearingen.   2 vols.,
1976–77.
*The Cévennes Journal: Notes on a Journey Through the
French Highlands,* edited by Gordon Golding.   1978.
*From the Clyde to California: Stevenson's Emigrant Jour-
ney,* edited by Andrew Noble.   1985.
The Lantern Bearers and Other Essays, edited by Jeremy
Treglown.   1988.

*

Bibliography: *The Stevenson Library of E.J. Beinecke* by
G.L. McKay, 6 vols., 1951–64; *Three Victorian Travel
Writers: An Annotated Bibliography of Criticism on Mrs.
Frances Milton Trollope, Samuel Butler, and Stevenson* by
F.J. Bethke, 1977.

Critical Studies: *Stevenson the Dramatist* by Arthur Wing
Pinero, 1903, edited by C. Hamilton, 1914; *Stevenson* by
G.K. Chesterton, 1927; *Stevenson* by Janet Adam Smith,
1937; *Stevenson,* 1947, and *Stevenson and His World,* 1973,
both by David Daiches; *Voyage to Windward: The Life of
Stevenson* by J.C. Furnas, 1951; *Portrait of a Rebel: The
Life and Work of Stevenson* by Richard Aldington, 1957;
Stevenson and the Fiction of Adventure by Robert Kiely,

1964; *Stevenson and the Romantic Tradition* by Edwin M. Eigner, 1966; *Stevenson* by Compton Mackenzie, 1968; *Stevenson* by James Pope-Hennessy, 1974; *Stevenson* by Paul M. Binding, 1974; *The Henley-Stevenson Quarrel* edited by Edward H. Cohen, 1974; *Journey to Upolu: Stevenson, Victorian Rebel* by Edward Rice, 1974; *Stevenson* by Irving S. Saposnik, 1974; *Stevenson in Hawaii* by Martha Mary McGaw, 1978; *RLS: A Life Story* by Jenni Calder, 1980, and *Stevenson and Victorian Scotland* edited by Calder, 1981; *The Prose Writings of Stevenson: A Guide* by Roger G. Swearingen, 1980; *Stevenson: The Critical Heritage* edited by Paul Maixner, 1981; *Stevenson in California: A Remarkable Courtship* by Roy Nickerson, 1982; *Stevenson* edited by Andrew Noble, 1983; *Stevenson and The Beach of Falesá: A Study of Victorian Publishing with the Original Text* by Barry Menikoff, 1984; *A Stevenson Companion* by J.R. Hammond, 1984; *RLS in the South Seas: An Intimate Photographic Record* edited by Alanna Knight, 1986; *Dead Man's Chest: Travels after Stevenson* by Nicholas Rankin, 7; *Dr. Jekyll and Mr. Hyde after One Hundred Years* edited by William Veeder and Gordon Hirsch, 1988.

* * *

Robert Louis Stevenson was a deliberate and painstaking stylist. In one of his essays he says that he was busy from his earliest years in learning to write by playing the "sedulous ape" to a large variety of writers. In his short life he achieved an international reputation for his essays, travel books, poetry, and novels, including one of the best-known of all children's books, *Treasure Island.* Throughout his whole career he was also a notable writer of short fiction.

It is misleading to regard Stevenson as an English writer, as does, for instance, a recent editor of some of his short fiction. He is very much part of the Scottish tradition. He once proposed to write a book, *Four Great Scotsmen,* on Knox, Hume, Burns, and Scott, to show the "strong current" of Scottish life "making itself felt underneath and throughout." The same is true of Stevenson, even if his poor health drove him to live in warmer climes. In his day, the influence of Walter Scott was at its height. He, like Stevenson, was an Edinburgh man, and he was one of the originators of short fiction as well as a powerful force in the development of the novel. Stevenson himself said that he felt a particular kinship with Robert Fergusson, a poet of the 18th century who wrote in Scots about the convivial and boisterous side of Edinburgh life.

This is another clue to Stevenson. As the son of a prosperous and distinguished Edinburgh family, who had been lighthouse builders for several generations, he was part of respectable society. But Edinburgh has long been a city of contrasts and Stevenson was drawn to the more Bohemian side of its life. This led to a break with his father, afterwards reflected in his great unfinished novel, *Weir of Hermiston.* Scottish literature is often said to be marked by a combination of opposites between the rational and the fantastic. Stevenson is no exception. Indeed, his short novel, *The Strange Case of Dr. Jekyll and Mr. Hyde* is the classic parable of the split personality, set in Edinburgh.

The imagination of Stevenson, like that of Scott and many other Scottish writers to this day, was nourished on the Border ballads. These are narrative poems, which have been passed on in oral tradition, telling of love, battle, and the supernatural. They are direct, economical in words and strongly evocative of mood and place. As a child, Stevenson had a nurse, Alison Cunningham, of Presbyterian and Covenanting convictions, who told him stories in good Scots, often involving moral dilemmas and encounters with the devil. All of these influences were to appear later in Stevenson's fiction.

Walter Allen in *The Short Story in English* (1981) dates the beginning of the modern short story to one which Stevenson first published in October 1877 and which afterwards appeared in his first collection, *New Arabian Nights,* in 1882. This was "A Lodging for the Night," an imaginary episode in the life of the French poet, François Villon. Nothing very much happens. Villon witnesses a murder; then, cold and penniless, he is taken in for the night by a man alone in a richly furnished house. Villon contemplates theft, but desists. That, in a sense, is all; but the atmosphere of the place and time and the suspense are striking.

Some of Stevenson's plots are ingenious and full of surprise, but he is a master of the story that depends for its effect more on its atmosphere and the tension of not knowing what might happen next than on the events or even character. He said in a letter from Samoa in 1891, about one of his last and finest stories, "The Beach at Falesa": "Now I have got the smell, and the look of the thing a good deal." That was evidently his chief aim and he very often succeeded.

Stevenson's short fiction varies in length. He made something of a speciality of the novella or short novel, divided into chapters and amounting to about 50 or 80 pages. In his first collection, "The Pavilion on the Links" is of this kind and so is the title piece of a later collection, *The Merry Men.* Both of these draw on his knowledge of the force of the sea and its tides and rocks, derived from his travels round the lighthouses with his father. Both also deal with mysterious events for which natural causes are eventually revealed. The same might be said of "The Beach at Falesa." It is written throughout in the first person as if by a trader of limited intelligence and unfortunate attitudes. He reveals more than he realises of the racist attitudes of the white settlers in the Pacific islands, a technique of self-revelation that Stevenson may have learned from the Scottish novelist, John Galt, who was a past master in the art.

Stevenson's particular skills, and the influences from his childhood, appear very strongly in his tales of the supernatural. Naturally enough, two of the best of them, "Thrawn Janet" and "Tod Lapraik" (inserted in the novel *Catriona*) are in Scots. "Markheim," another chilling tale of the devil, is in English and so is "The Body-Snatcher," although it deals with a notorious episode in the life of Edinburgh.

An impressive story, "Olalla," fits into none of these categories. It tells of the hopeless love of a convalescing officer for a mysterious girl in a sinister household in Spain. It is a fine example of Stevenson's ability to create the feel of a place and to write in the language and personality of the assumed narrator.

—Paul H. Scott

See the essays on "Markheim," "The Suicide Club," and "Thrawn Janet."

STIFTER, Adalbert. Austrian. Born in Oberplan, Bohemia, (Horní Planá, Czechoslovakia), 23 October 1805. Educated at village school; Benedictine monastery school, Kremsmünster, 1818–26; studied law at University of Vienna, 1828–30. Married Amalia Mohaupt in 1837. Tutor and painter; editor, *Der Wiener Bote,* 1849–50; school inspector, Vienna, 1850, and in Linz, 1851–65; art critic, *Linzer Zeitung,* 1852–57. Curator of Monuments for Upper Austria, 1853; vice-president, Linzer Kunstverein. Order of Franz Joseph, 1854; Ritterkreuz des Weissen Falkenordens, 1867. *Died (suicide) 28 January 1868.*

PUBLICATIONS

Collections

Sämtliche Werke, edited by August Sauer.   25 vols., 1904–79.
Werke, edited by Gustav Wilhelm.   5 vols., 1926.
Gesammelte Werke, edited by Max Stefl.   6 vols., 1939.
Werke, edited by Magda Gerken and Josef Thanner.   5 vols., 1949–61.
Werke, edited by Max Stefl.   9 vols., 1950–60.
Werke und Briefe, edited by Alfred Doppler and Wolfgang Frühwald.   1978 — .

Short Stories and Novellas

Studien.   6 vols., 1844–50; enlarged edition, 1855.
Rural Life in Austria and Hungary.   3 vols., 1850; *Pictures of Rural Life,* 1850.
Pictures of Life.   1852.
The Heather Village.   1868.
Der Hagelstolz.   1852; as *The Recluse,* 1968.
Bunte Steine: Ein Festgeschenk.   1853; translated in part as *Mount Gars; or, Marie's Christmas Eve,* 1857; as *Rock Crystal,* 1945; as "Limestone," in *Brigitta,* 1990.
Erzählungen, edited by Johannes Aprent.   2 vols., 1869.
Der Waldsteig (in English translation).   1942.
The Condor.   1946.
Erzählungen in der Urfassung, edited by Max Stefl.   3 vols., 1950–52.
Limestone and Other Stories.   1968.
Brigitta (includes "Abdias," "Limestone," and "The Forest Path").   1990.

Novels

Der Nachsommer.   1857; as *Indian Summer,* 1985.
Witiko.   1865–67.
Die Mappe meines Urgrossvaters (Letzte Fassung).   1946.

Other

Briefe, edited by Johannes Aprent.   3 vols., 1869.
Stifter: Sein Leben in Selbstzeugnissen, Briefen, und Berichten, edited by Karl Privat.   1946.
Jugendbriefe (1822–1839), edited by Gustav Wilhelm.   1954.
Leben und Werk in Briefen und Dokumenten, edited by K.G. Fischer.   1962.
Briefwechsel, edited by Josef Buchowiecki.   1965.

Editor, with Johannes Aprent, *Lesebuch zur Förderung humaner Bildung.*   1854.

*

Critical Studies: *Stifter: A Critical Study* by E.A. Blackall, 1948; *Natural Science in the Work of Stifter* by W.E. Umbach, 1950; *The Marble Statue as Idea: Collected Essays on Stifter's "Der Nachsommer"* by Christine O. Sjögren, 1972; *Stifter* by Margaret Gump, 1974; *Stifter Heute* edited by Johann Lachinger, Alexander Stillmark, and Martin Swales, 1984; *Stifter: A Critical Study* by Martin and Erika Swales, 1984.

*   *   *

Adalbert Stifter is one of the foremost writers of German fiction of the mid-19th century and an early exponent of the refined or poetic realism quintessential to German prose writing during this period, characterised by a preference for shorter prose works such as the novelle, a strong sense of regionalism, and a predilection for rural settings. In the stories of his *Studien* (Studies) and the collection *Bunte Steine* (bright stones), Stifter expresses his love for the natural world of his native Bohemia, in sensitive and often unashamedly lengthy descriptive passages. At the same time the serious tone of his dignified and elegant prose conveys a keen sense of moral values, as he explores the relationship between the human and natural spheres.

Stifter's principles are set out in the preface to *Bunte Steine,* in which he states that he is concerned essentially with the ordinary forces of nature which are recurrent but not startling (for example, the peacefully flowing river rather than the overflowing raging torrent which comes once but five years); unspectacular everyday weather rather than the occasional violent storm; the forces which preserve, rather than the forces which destroy. The small and unremarkable manifestations of natural laws are matched in the human sphere by the unspectacular qualities of simplicity, moderation, and patience, which Stifter values more highly than violent destructive passions. Stifter finds greatness in those moral and unselfish actions that aim at the preservation of humankind. Nature can thus be an example to humans, and Stifter establishes a universal law called "the gentle law," which is most firmly rooted in self-effacing human virtues and which reflects the higher moral laws of nature. It is Stifter's aim to represent in his stories examples of the "gentle law" in both the human and natural spheres.

Of the *Bunte Steine* collection the story that best embodies Stifter's principles is "Limestone," which presents in the figure of a humble, unassuming, and selfless priest a perfect illustration of Stifter's conception of a great life. The *Bunte Steine* were written for children, and Stifter tried to cultivate a naive, primitive style. In "Limestone" he achieves the childlike quality and the simplicity of moral greatness and kindness, matching perfectly the unpretentious and initially unattractive landscape. The latter's hidden beauty is revealed only slowly, paralleling the gradual revelation of the moral beauty of the shabby and seemingly unremarkable priest.

Such a harmonious union of the natural and the human is rarely achieved, however, in the earlier *Studien,* in which the relationship between humans and nature is seen to be far more problematic. In "The Hochwald," for example, the virgin innocence of the Bohemian forest is contrasted with the violent disorder of human beings who can never hope to combine innocence with naturalness. If they attempt to retreat into the natural peace and order of the forest, they do not "live." If they surrender to their own "natural" inclinations the result is violent passion, resulting in war, destruction, and ensuing sorrow. In "Abdias" the forces of nature seem to be in violent conflict with the world of human affairs. Here the hero falls victim to the cruelty of inscrutable and inconsistent natural laws which deal him a series of incomprehensible and seemingly unavoidable body-blows: the death of his wife in childbirth is compensated by the survival of the child Ditha, whom he loves and protects, only for him to discover that she had been born blind; a freak storm miraculously restores her sight, only for a second storm to take away her life. Abdias is stunned into madness by the whole experience. The sole ray of sunlight in a harsh and disturbing story is when Abdias literally opens the seeing eyes of Ditha to the beauties of the natural world in the Bohemian valley.

A number of the studies do illustrate the possibilities of harmony and the kinds of behaviour and qualities which Stifter admired. In "My Great-Grandfather's Notebook" a brawler and gambler repents the errors of his ways and becomes a "gentler" person and a happily married man. When he loses his wife when she falls into a ravine, he has to draw on his reserves of character to survive this cruel blow of fate, accepting it with resignation and devoting himself to useful agricultural pursuits as compensation. He serves as an example to a young doctor who is rejected in love and is devastated as a result. But instead of committing suicide he sublimates his grief in an even greater dedication to his patients. In these cases extreme despair gives way to a selfless patience, and good has resulted from apparent evil. These processes find their reflection in the natural world when an extremely cold and destructive winter is followed by a spring which seems all the more beautiful in comparison. The study which represents most perfectly both the harmony between the natural and human spheres, and the reconciliation in the latter of passion and moral values, is *Brigitta*. In this supreme anticipation of the principles set out in the preface to *Bunte Steine*, Stifter presents a married couple whose marriage is inspired initially by a violent passion, who consequently separate, but who later live as neighbours, devoting themselves to farming the land on their respective farms. In middle-age they become aware of each others' moral worth and their marriage is resumed in a moment of intense passion, but also on a higher spiritual level. Here the fruitful cultivation of the seemingly barren land of the Hungarian *puszta* leads to the discovery of the inner beauty of the physically unattractive Brigitta. Stifter's work reached its culmination in the great novel *Der Nachsommer* (*Indian Summer*), in some ways a much expanded version of *Brigitta*, in which the cultivation of nature accompanies the maturing of a peaceful and harmonious friendship of a man and woman in the autumn of their lives.

It must be stressed that references to the plots and events of Stifter's works do scant justice to the quality of his prose, the long flowing sentences and meticulous descriptive passages. For Stifter, the naked events of his stories are less important than the rich, highly poetic descriptions of the qualities of his characters and the natural surroundings of which they form a part. For Stifter, our individual griefs, transgressions, and extravagances are unimportant in comparison with nature's eternal cycle, to which humans can contribute with a life devoted to simple, fruitful, and virtuous pursuits.

—Bruce Thompson

STORM, (Hans) Theodor (Woldsen). German. Born in Husum, Schleswig-Holstein, 14 September 1817. Educated at local schools and the Gymnasium, Lübock; studied law at Kiel University, 1837–42. Married 1) Constance Esmarch in 1846 (died 1865), seven children; 2) Dorothea Jensen in 1866, one child. Set up legal practice in Husum, 1843–53; forced into exile in Potsdam in 1853 after the Danish occupation; assignment, Prussian civil service, Potsdam, 1853–56; magistrate, Heiligenstadt, 1856; chief legal and administration officer, 1864 and chief judge, 1874, Husum. *Died 4 July 1888.*

PUBLICATIONS

Collections

Gedichte, edited by Hans Heitmann.   1943.
Sämtliche Werke, edited by Peter Goldammer.   4 vols., 1956; 4th edition, 1982.
Werke, edited by Gottfried Honnefelder.   2 vols., 1975.
Sämtliche Werke, edited by Karl Ernst Laage and Dieter Lohmeier.   4 vols., 1987–88.

Short Stories and Novellas

Immensee.   1851; as *Immensee*, 1863; as *Immen Lake*, 1881.
Ein Grünes Blatt (stories).   1855.
Auf dem Staatshof.   1859.
In der Sommer-Mondnacht (stories).   1860.
Drei Novellen.   1861.
Im Schloss.   1863.
Auf der Universität.   1863; as *Lenore*, 1865.
Zwei Weihnachtsidyllen (stories).   1865.
Drei Märchen.   1866; as *Geschichten aus der Tonne*, 2nd edition, 1873.
Pole Poppenspäler and *Waldwinkel.*   1875.
Viola tricolor.   1874; translated as *Viola Tricolor*, 1956.
Psyche.   1876.
Aquis submersus.   1877; translated as *Aquis Submersus*, 1910; as *Beneath the Flood*, 1962.
Renate.   1878; translated as *Renate*, 1909.
Carsten Curator.   1878; translated as *Carsten Curator*, 1956.
Eekenhof, with *Im Brauer-Hause.*   1880; translated as *Eekenhof*, 1905.
Die Söhne des Senators, with *Der Herr Etatsrath.*   1881; *Die Söhne des Senators*, as *The Senator's Sons*, 1947.
Schweigen.   1883.
Zwei Novellen.   1883.
Hans und Heinz Kirch.   1883.
Zur Chronik von Grieshuus.   1884; as *A Chapter in the History of Greishuus*, 1905.
Ein Fest auf Haderslevhuus, with *John Riew'.*   1885; as *A Festival at Haderslevhuus*, 1909.
Bötjer Basch.   1887.
Ein Doppelgänger.   1887.
Bei kleinen Leuten (stories).   1887.
Der Schimmelreiter.   1888; as *The Rider on the White Horse*, 1915; as *The White Horseman*, 1962; as *The White Horse Rider*, 1966.
Gesammelte Schriften.   10 vols., 1877–89.

Novels

Im Sonnenschein.   1854.
Hinzelmeier.   1857.

Eine Malerarbeit.   1867.
Von Jenseit des Meeres.   1867.
In St. Jürgen.   1868.
Zerstreute Kapitel.   1873.
Ein stiller Musikant.   1875.
Zur Wald-und-Wasserfreude.   1880.
Vor Zeiten   1886.
Ein Bekenntniss.   1887.
Es waren zwei Königskinder.   1888.

Verse

Liederbuch dreier Freunde.   1843.
Gedichte.   1852; revised edition, 1856.

Other

Der Briefwechsel zwischen Storm und Gottfried Keller, edited by Albert Köster.   1904.
Briefe an Friedrich Eggers, edited by Hans Wolfgang Seidel. 1911.
Briefe, edited by Gertrud Storm.   4 vols., 1915–17.
Briefwechsel zwischen Storm und Eduard Mörike, edited by Hanns Wolfgang Rath.   1919.
Storms Briefe an seinen Freund George Lorenzen 1876 bis 1882, edited by C. Höfer.   1923.
Blätter der Freundschaft. Aus dem Briefwechsel zwischen Storm und Ludwig Pietsch, edited by V. Pauls.   1939; revised edition, 1943.
Storm als Erzieher. Seine Briefe an Ada Christen, edited by O. Katann.   1948.
Garten meiner Jugend (autobiography), edited by Frank Schnass.   1950.
Der Weg wie weit (autobiography), edited by Frank Schnass.   1951.
Bittersüsser Lebenstrank (autobiography), edited by Frank Schnass.   1952.
Der Briefwechsel zwischen Storm und Gottfried Keller, edited by Peter Goldammer.   1960.
Storms Briefwechsel mit Theodor Mommsen, edited by H.E. Teitge.   1966.
Storm und Iwan Turgenjew. Persönlichkeit und literarische Beziehungen, Einflüsse, Briefe, Bilder, edited by K.E. Laage.   1967.
Storm—Emil Kuh, Briefweschel, edited by E. Streitfeld. 1985.

Editor, *Deutscher Liebeslieder seit Johann Christian Guenther eine Codification.*   1859.
Editor, *Hausbuch aus deutschen Dichtern seit Claudius eine kritische Anthologie.*   1870.

*

Critical Studies: *Studies in Storm* by Elmer O. Wooley, 1943; *Storm's Craft of Fiction: The Torment of a Narrator* by Clifford A. Bernd, 1963; *The Theme of Loneliness in Storm's Novellen* by Lloyd W. Wedberg, 1964; *Storm's Novellen: Essays on Literary Technique* by E. Allen McCormick, 1964; *Techniques of Solipsism: A Study of Storm's Narrative Fiction* by Terence J. Rogers, 1970; *Sound and Sense in the Poetry of Storm: A Phonological-Statistical Study* by Alan B. Galt, 1973; *Storm: Studies in Ambivalence: Symbol and Myth in His Narrative Fiction* by David Artiss, 1978; *Storm* edited by Patricia M. Boswell, 1989; *Storm* by Roger Paulin, 1992.

* * *

Although Theodor Storm himself considered his lyric poetry his crowning achievement, today he is remembered primarily as a writer of short stories. His earliest stories appeared in the 1840's in a provincial periodical. Anxious to express radical views without antagonizing censors, editors, or readers, he elaborated artistic means of cloaking his message while manoeuvering his readers towards new positions. Superficially, "Marthe and Her Clock" is a typical edifying tale. In fact, the distance between heroine and fictional narrator highlights the plight of unmarried daughters in a backward society dominated by authoritarian fathers. *Immensee* ironically became a best-seller among the wealthy female clientele of an arch-conservative Berlin publisher. In the story, having lost his childhood sweetheart Elisabeth to the entrepreneur Erich, Reinhardt visits the couple's splendid estate years later. After moments of sultry temptation and nocturnal heart-searching, he leaves, never to return. While apparently upholding the sanctity of marriage, the story arraigns a system that estranges individuals from their true happiness. Society is depicted as a lions' den. During the repressive 1850's Storm created one masterpiece, *Auf dem Staatshof* (At King's Farm). Marx, a member of the educated middle class, seeks to persuade the reader to accept his version of the life and death of Anne Lene, a patrician. The text suggests contrary significances. Indeed, Marx contributes substantially to the heroine's suicide.

In the early 1860's, when hopes of a liberal democratic, unified Germany were high, Storm sought to contribute more overtly committed stories to the influential middle-class family magazines with their large circulation and high fees. *Im Schloss* (In the Castle), with its shifting perspectives and its communication of significances lost on the heroine herself, follows the career of an aristocrat, Anna, who despite responding to the democratic, atheist ideas of her middle-class tutor, Arnold, denies her true saviour and marries an aristocrat. The marriage violates her deepest feelings. After her husband's insistence—on the basis of unfounded rumour—on a separation, she retires, alone, to the bleak castle and is only rescued from a living death by the deus ex machina of her husband's death. Only then is the Feuerbachian gospel of human love proclaimed. *Auf der Universität* (translated as *Lenore*) pursues the recurrent theme of an innate human aspiration for a beautiful life which is frustrated by social factors. Again, Storm highlights his middle-class narrator's inadequacies. Bismarck's harrying of oppositional civil servants and authors restricted Storm's scope, and when after 1866 many liberals endorsed the Bismarckian settlement his reservoir of like-minded readers shrank significantly. Disillusioned with politics and obsessed by private worries, Storm underwent a severe artistic crisis.

After 1870 he embarked on a series of experiments. "Eine Halligkfahrt" (A Holm Trip) revises the allusive, cloaked critical techniques of E.T.A. Hoffmann and Heinrich Heine. "Draussen im Heidedorf" (Out in the Moorland Village) employs, for Storm, a novel milieu: a dark, superstitious peasant community, and a new objective, impassive presentation: a judicial investigation into the disappearance of a married farmer consumed by passion for a Slav outsider. Appalled by his sons' promiscuity, Storm gravitated to a much more conservative view of the family and gender roles in the humorous idyll "Beim Vetter Christian" (At Cousin Christian's), while in *Viola tricolor* he sought to exorcise the traumas of his second marriage.

The story's pathos and creaking symbolism pall on the modern reader as does the classicizing of *Psyche. Aquis submersus,* in contrast, constitutes a highpoint in his fiction. The first of his chronical novellas, it employs fictional narrators and the framework technique in order to contrast the violent, fanatical past of the inner story and the Biedermeier world of the outer frame. A painter, Johannes, sets out hopeful of achieving happiness in a still feudal society dominated by church and aristocracy. Yet, crushed, he and his aristocratic lover, Katharina, sink back into notions of guilt and sin and of the vanity of mortal life. The theme of individuals groping towards enlightened, human norms in the face of hostile institutions and ideologies is at the heart of Storm's later works. Hereditary or genetic disabilities, ageing, and illness compound the obstacles. The superstitious, petty-minded mass confronts isolated champions of enlightenment.

His sons' descent into alcoholism, dissipation, and syphilis impelled Storm—despite his own Poetic-Realist beliefs—towards disturbing, "base" themes. Editors, critics, and friends made disapproving noises. The father-son problem moved to the fore. *Carsten Curator* depicts the futility of the efforts of a father and wife to save a son from his genetic make-up, while in *Hans und Heinz Kirch* a son is denied and sacrificed on the altar of his father's social ambitions. The depraved hero of *Der Herr Etatsrath* is depicted as a beetle-cum-primeval monster who destroys his son and condones the corruption of his daughter within the home itself. Storm's later historical or chronicle novellas vary in quality: *Zur Chronik von Grieshuus (A Chapter in the History of Grieshuus)* powerfully combines dramatic and epic elements; *Eekenhof* is derivative and insubstantial; and *Ein Fest auf Haderslevhuus (A Festival at Haderslevhuus)* marks a nadir in Storm's fiction. Topics like syphilis were tabu in whatever form. Thus, in *Schweigen* (Silence) Storm substituted for syphilis a pathological fear of recurrent mental illness and insanity. As his subject matter became more sordid and realistic, he felt driven to compensate for this by idealising and poeticising the presentation: *Schweigen* is modelled on Weber's opera *Der Freischütz.*

Storm's later stories grapple with the social problems of industrialisation and urbanisation. *Bötjer Basch* (Basch the Cooper) offers an unconvincing synthesis of modern, American technology and older, German community values. *Ein Doppelgänger* (A Doppelgänger) accuses a society that never allows an ex-convict to recover his honour and human dignity. The hero meets an agonising end when he falls down a well attempting to save his daughter from starving by stealing potatoes. But this indictment is balanced by a framework in which his daughter appears as a loving wife and mother married to a well-to-do, kindly forester. Despite common themes and concerns, the gap separating Storm the Poetic-Realist from the naturalists remained.

—David Jackson

See the essay on *The Rider on the White Horse.*

SUÁREZ LYNCH, B.   See **BIOY CASARES, Adolfo,** and **BORGES, Jorge Luis.**

T

TAGORE, (Sir) Rabindranath. Indian. Born in Calcutta, 6 May 1861; son of Maharshi Tagore, grandson of Prince Tagore. Educated privately, and at University College, University of London, 1878–80. Married Mrinalinidebi in 1884; one son and one daughter. Managed family estates at Shileida from 1885; founded the Santiniketan, a school to blend Eastern and Western philosophical educational systems, Bolpur, Bengal, 1901, which later developed into an international institution called Visva-Bharti; visited England, 1912; contributed regularly to the *Visvabharati Quarterly*; Hibbert lecturer, Oxford University, 1930. Painter from 1929: exhibitions in Moscow, Berlin, Munich, Paris, and New York. Recipient: Nobel prize for literature, 1913. D.Lit.: University of Calcutta; Hindu University, Benares; University of Dacca; Osmania University, Hyderabad; D.Litt.: Oxford University. Knighted, 1915; resigned knighthood in 1919 as protest against British policies in the Punjab. Wrote in Bengali and translated his own works into English. *Died 7 August 1941.*

PUBLICATIONS (IN ENGLISH)

Collections

A Tagore Reader, edited by Amiya Chakravarty. 1961.
Collected Essays, edited by Mary Lago and Ronald Warwick. 1989.

Short Stories

Glimpses of Bengal Life. 1913.
The Hungry Stones and Other Stories, translated by C.F. Andrews and others. 1916.
Mashi and Other Stories. 1918.
Broken Ties and Other Stories. 1925.
More Stories from Tagore. 1951.
The Runaway and Other Stories, edited by Somnath Maitra. 1959.
Selected Short Stories, translated by Mary Lago and Krishna Dutta. 1990.

Novels

The Parrot's Training. 1918.
The Home and the World, translated by Surendranath Tagore. 1919.
The Wreck. 1921.
Gora. 1924.
Two Sisters, translated by Krishna Kripalani. 1943.
Farewell My Friend, with The Garden, translated by Krishna Kripalani. 1946.
Four Chapters, translated by Surendranath Tagore. 1950.
Binodini, translated by Krishna Kripalani. 1959.
Caturanga, translated by Asok Mitra. 1963.
Lipika, translated by Indu Dutt. 1969; translated by Aurobindo Bose, 1977.

The Broken Nest, translated by Mary Lago and Supriya Sen. 1971.

Plays

The Post Office, translated by Devabrata Mukerjee (produced 1913). 1914.
Citra. 1914.
The King of the Dark Chamber. 1914.
Malini, translated by Kshitish Chandra Sen (produced 1915). In *Sacrifice and Other Plays*, 1917.
The Cycle of Spring. 1917.
Sacrifice and Other Plays (includes *Malini; Sanyas, or, The Ascetic; The King and the Queen*). 1917.
Sacrifice (produced 1918). In *Sacrifice and Other Plays*, 1917.
The King and the Queen (produced 1919). In *Sacrifice and Other Plays*, 1917.
The Fugitive. 1918.
The Mother's Prayer (produced 1920). 1919.
Autumn Festival (produced 1920).
The Farewell Curse, The Deserted Mother, The Sinner, Suttee (produced 1920).
The Farewell (produced 1924).
Three Plays (includes *Muktadhara, Natir Puja, Candalika*), translated by Marjorie Sykes. 1950.

Verse

Gitanjali. 1912.
The Gardener. 1913.
The Crescent Moon: Child-Poems. 1913.
Fruit-Gathering. 1916.
Lover's Gift, and Crossing. 1918.
Poems. 1922.
The Curse at Farewell, translated by Edward Thompson. 1924.
Fireflies. 1928.
Fifteen Poems. 1928.
Sheaves: Poems and Songs, edited and translated by Nagendranath Gupta. 1929.
The Child. 1931.
The Golden Boat, translated by Chabani Bhattacharya. 1932.
Poems, edited by Krishna Kripalani. 1942.
A Flight of Swans, translated by Aurobindo Bose. 1955.
Syamali, translated by Sheila Chatterjee. 1955.
The Herald of Spring, translated by Aurobindo Bose. 1957.
Wings of Death: The Last Poems, translated by Aurobindo Bose. 1960.
Devouring Love, translated by Shakuntala Sastri. 1961.
A Bunch of Poems, translated by Monika Varma. 1966.
One Hundred and One. 1967.
Last Poems, translated by Shyamasree Devi and P. Lal. 1972.
Later Poems, translated by Aurobindo Bose. 1974.

Selected Poems, translated by William Radice.   1985.

Other

Sadhana: The Realisation of Life.   1913.
Stray Birds (aphorisms).   1916.
My Reminiscences, translated by Surendranath Tagore.   1917.
Letters.   1917.
Nationalism.   1917.
Personality: Lectures Delivered in America.   1917.
Greater India (lectures).   1921.
Thought Relics.   1921.
Creative Unity.   1922.
The Visvabharati, with C.F. Andrews.   1923.
Letters from Abroad, edited by C.F. Andrews.   1924; revised edition, as *Letters to a Friend*, 1928.
Talks in China.   1925.
Lectures and Addresses, edited by Anthony X. Soares.   1928.
City and Village.   1928.
The Religion of Man.   1932.
Collected Poems and Plays.   1936.
Man (lectures).   1937.
My Boyhood Days.   1940.
Eighty Years, and Selections.   1941.
A Tagore Testament.   1953.
Our Universe, translated by Indu Dutt.   1958.
Letters from Russia, translated by Sasadhar Sinha.   1960.
Tagore, Pioneer in Education: Essays and Exchanges Between Tagore and L. K. Elmhirst.   1961.
A Visit to Japan, translated by Shakuntala Shastri.   1961.
Towards Universal Man.   1961.
On Art and Aesthetics.   1961.
The Diary of Westward Voyage, translated by Indu Dutt.   1962.
On Rural Reconstruction.   1962.
The Cooperative Principle.   1963.
Boundless Sky (miscellany).   1964.
The Housewarming and Other Selected Writings, edited by Amiya Chakravarty, translated by Mary Lago and Tarun Gupta.   1965.
Imperfect Encounter: Letters of William Rothenstein and Tagore 1912–1941.   1972.

*

Bibliography: *Tagore: A Bibliography* by Katherine Henn, 1985.

Critical Studies: *Tagore, Poet and Thinker* by Mohinimohana Bhattarcharya, 1961; *Tagore: A Biography* by Krishna Kripalani, 1962, revised edition, 1971; *The Lute and the Plough: A Life of Tagore* by G.D. Khanolkar, 1963; *Ravindranath's Poetry* by Dattatuaya Muley, 1964; *Rabindranath* by Sati Ghosh, 1966; *The Volcano: Some Comments on the Development of Tagore's Aesthetic Theories*, 1968, and *The Humanism of Tagore*, 1979, both by Mulk Raj Anand; *Tagore: His Mind and Art* by Birenda C. Chakravorty, 1971; *The Poetry of Tagore* by S.B. Mukherji, 1977; *Tagore*, 1978, by Mary Lago, and *Tagore: Perspectives in Time*, 1989, edited by Lago and Ronald Warwick, 1989; *Tagore the Novelist* by G.V. Raj, 1983; *Tagore: His Imagery and Ideas* by Ajai Singh, 1984; *Tagore: A Critical Introduction* by K.R. Srinivasa Iyengar, 1986; *Perspectives on Tagore* edited by T.R. Sharma, 1986; *Tagore* by Sisirkumar Ghose, 1986; *In Your Blossoming Flower-Garden: Tagore and Victoria Ocampo* by K.K. Dyson, 1988; *The Art of Tagore* by Andrew Robinson, 1989.

*   *   *

When Rabindranath Tagore began to write short stories in the 1890's, Bengal had no tradition of really modern short fiction. It had a folk literature, principally in the oral tradition. Its classical literature was in Sanskrit or highly-Sanskritized literary Bengali, the only mediums approved by the pundits for serious, artistic literature.

Tagore's stories came out of his experiences, first, as overseer of his family's extensive estates in rural and riverine eastern Bengal. It was his first close contact with the Bengali *ryot*, the tenant-farmer peasant. Incidents, conversations, and personalities all became his working materials. A second group of stories came from his own background as a member of an affluent Calcutta family whose solution to the collision between Indian traditions and Western influences was to find a middle road between old and new: a new synthesis for a new Bengal. A third group of stories sprang from his activities as a leader of the protest movement that began in 1905 against the partition of the province into East and West Bengal. In all three types, Tagore questions the status quo, an exercise to which the modern short story, brief, elliptical, and open-ended, is particularly well adapted. It can ask questions about personal and social predicaments and problems without providing answers: the reader must do that. The genre was also eminently suited to the situation in Bengal in the 1890's and the early years of the 20th century, for those who openly questioned or criticized British rule risked being suspected of sedition.

"Shāsti" (1893, "Punishment") is a powerful example from the first group. Two brothers, Chhidam and Dukhiram, and their wives live together, and the brothers work together as tenant farmers. Their tragedy begins on a day when the landowner forces them to repair one of his properties when they should be harvesting their own rice crop. They come home weary, wet through, and hungry, for they have not eaten all day. When Dukhiram finds that his wife Radha has no meal prepared, he mindlessly strikes her with his billhook. She dies at once. Chhidam and the village Brahmin, who fancies himself an expert on British law, persuade Chhidam's wife Chandara to say that she struck back when Radha attacked her with a kitchen-knife. The Brahmin coaches her in what he thinks are foolproof answers to cross-questioning. The key to this plan is Chhidam's statement, "If a wife goes, I can get another, but if my brother goes I can't get another." In the courtroom Chandara repays her husband for his betrayal by insisting that she is guilty as charged. The brothers, confused, both claim the guilt, and the English magistrate, who has tried to be lenient, concludes that they are only trying to protect Chandara, who must indeed be guilty. She refuses to see Chhidam again before she dies, saying with harrowing irony, "I'd rather be dead!" British justice decrees her punishment, but she punishes her husband for reasons that the magistrate cannot comprehend. Chandara's tragedy is a consequence of the brothers' own tragedy. Illiterate, inarticulate, too trustful of the Brahmin's supposed learning, and too poor and unsophisticated to find other sources of advice and guidance, they are typical of a large and important sector of the Bengali population from whom the rising urban middle class draws ever farther apart.

When Tagore turned to that urban middle class he depicted Calcutta family life as he himself knew it. At the center of "Nashtanir" (1901, "The Broken Nest") is Bhupati, a husband who is neither illiterate nor poor; he is obsessed with the English language and with the English-language newspaper of which he is both proprietor and editor. He is a 19th-century Bengali type, outwardly confident but inwardly confused when forced to choose between tradition and innovation. He loves Charulata, his young wife, who has intelligence and curiosity but nowhere to invest them. She cannot compete with that newspaper for her husband's attention. She passes her empty days reading inferior bengali romantic essays and novels. Her talents begin to blossom when Bhupati's young cousin Amal comes to live with them while he attends Calcutta University. He aspires to a literary career and inspires Charulata to try her hand as a writer. Tagore has set up a literary triangle that replicates the trends of that time in Bengal: Bhupati, who longs to be a political editorialist in Western style; Amal, who writes in florid imitation of the Sanskrit classics; Charulata, who can only write simple colloquial memories of life in her childhood village. Both Amal and Charulata get their essays published in literary journals, and Tagore introduces his own preference when he has the critics judge Charulata's diction and style to be the wave of the future—as, in fact, Tagore's own diction and style were to become for several generations of Bengali writers. At that very time he was in the midst of controversy over his "Kshanikā" (1900, Ephemera), lyric poems written in colloquial Bengali.

A personal triangle parallels the literary. Bhupati, who so wishes to be seen as a modern man, is crushingly condescending toward Charulata's writing; serious literature is for men only. She is too sheltered, too naive to realize how dependent she has become on Amal for what she thinks is the emotional satisfaction from their writing together. But the critics' verdict destroys their collaboration and opens Amal's eyes to dangers of which she remains unaware. Bhupati finds him a wife, and Amal leaves to complete his education in England. Much too late, Bhupati's eyes too are opened: "He saw that he had always distanced his own life from Charu's, like a doctor examining a mortally ill patient. And so he had been unaware when the world had forcefully attacked Charu's defenceless heart. There had been no one to whom she could tell all. . . ." But still he takes his wife for granted, and this would-be modern man can only think of running away—to an editorial position in another city. Charu is alone in their Calcutta house, once again vanquished by a newspaper, and now she has no resources of her own. "The Broken Nest" brought the wrath of conventional Bengalis down upon Tagore, for he was all too correct about the outside forces that seemed to threaten the stability of the Bengali family. They saw his story striking home.

Stories that dealt with Bengali politics not only risked charges of sedition; they angered some Bengali nationalists who perhaps saw in them their own failures and foibles. Tagore added some slyly sarcastic stories to his personal protests against extremist terrorism, a tactic that only lost ground for nationalist hopes. In "Namanjur Galpa" (1925, "The Rejected Story") a convicted nationalist protester manages to get off with a jail sentence while his fellow agitators go either to the gallows or to prison camps in the Andaman Islands. He cooperates so fully with prison authorities that he is released early. He installs himself in his aunt's house as an invalid. When a newspaper editor asks for an account of his most harrowing experience as a patriot, he produces one in which his uneasy conscience becomes the protagonist. He allows a group of village girls, his philanthropist aunt's protegées, to wait on him, thus paying homage to his supposed sacrifices and ill health. At first he is flattered, then he begins to feel embarrassed. At last his reviving conscience shames him into sending them away. Among them is one young woman who has been conspicuously devoted to projects proclaiming the New Bengal, until she sees that her enthusiasms are both shallow and ridiculous. An equally enthusiastic young man wishes to marry her—until he discovers that she is illegitimate and therefore without caste. Our hero explains, "The sins of the forefathers fell away at her birth. . . .She is like a lotus; there is no trace of mud upon her." But the suitor so devoted to the New Bengal takes flight. The girl returns to her neglected college classes, to prepare seriously for a role in the New Bengal. The recovered hero, it is implied, returns to useful work. The editor, who wanted patriotic "derring-do" is disappointed at getting the truth instead, and he rejects the story.

In his stories Tagore brilliantly practised what he had preached to Bengal. Although English literature was the cornerstone of the Indian educational system under the British, he made the French story writers of the 19th century his teachers, in particular, Maupassant and Daudet. Thus he took a great Western literary tradition, combined it with indigenous themes representative of Bengal, and produced a new synthesis to serve the new India.

—Mary Lago

TANIZAKI Jun'ichiro. Japanese. Born in Tokyo, 24 July 1886. Attended Tokyo University, 1908–10. Married 1) Chiyoko Ishikawa in 1915 (divorced 1930); 2) Furukawa Tomiko in 1931 (divorced); 3) Nezu Matsuko in 1935. Recipient: Mainichi prize, 1947; Asahi Culture prize, 1949; Imperial Cultural medal, 1949. Member, Japan Academy of Arts, 1957; Honorary Member, American Academy, 1964. *Died 30 July 1965.*

PUBLICATIONS

Collections

Zenshu [Collected Works]. 28 vols., 1966–70.

Short Stories

Shisei [Tattoo] (includes plays). 1911.
Momoku monogatari [A Blind Man's Tale]. 1932.
Ashikari. 1933; translated as *Ashikari,* with *The Story of Shunkin,* 1936.
Shunkin Sho. 1933; as *The Story of Shunkin,* with *Ashikari,* 1936; as "A Portrait of Shunkin," in *Seven Japanese Tales,* 1963.
Bushuko hiwa. 1935; as *The Secret History of the Lord of Musashi,* with *Arrowroot,* 1982.
Ashikari, and The Story of Shunkin. 1936.
Neko to Shozo to Futari no Onna. 1937; as *A Cat, a Man, and Two Women,* 1990.
Yoshino Kuzu. 1937; as *Arrowroot,* with *The Secret History of the Lord of Musashi,* 1982.

Yume no ukihashi [Floating Bridge of Dreams]. 1960.
Seven Japanese Tales. 1963.
The Secret History of the Lord of Musashi, and Arrowroot. 1982.

Novels

Akuma [Demon]. 1913.
Osai to Minosuke [Osai and Minosuke]. 1915.
Otsuya-goroshi. 1915; as *A Spring-Time Case*, 1927.
Ningyo no Nageki [Mermaid's Grief]. 1917.
Kin to Gin [Gold and Silver]. 1918.
Chijin no ai. 1925; as *Naomi*, 1985.
Kojin [Shark-Man]. 1926.
Tade kuu mushi. 1929; as *Some Prefer Nettles*, 1955.
Manji [A Swastika]. 1931.
Setsuyo Zuihitsu. 1935.
Sasameyuki. 1948; as *The Makioka Sisters*, 1957.
Rangiku monogatari [Story of Tangled Chrysanthemums]. 1949.
Shoso Shigemoto no Haha [The Mother of Captain Shigemoto]. 1950.
Kagi. 1956; as *The Key*, 1960.
Futen Rōjin Nikki. 1962; as *Diary of a Mad Old Man*, 1965.

Plays

Hosshoji Monogatari [Story of Hosso Temple] (produced 1915).
Okuni to Gohei [Okuni and Gohei] (produced 1922).
Aisureba koso [Because of Love]. 1923.
The White Fox, in *Eminent Authors of Contemporary Japan*, edited by E.S. Bell and E. Ukai. 1930.
Shinzei [Lord Shinzei]. 1949.

Other

Zenshu [Collected Works]. 12 vols., 1930; and later editions.
In'ei raisan. 1933; as *In Praise of Shadows*, 1985.
Bunshu tokuhon [On Style]. 1936.
Yōshō-jidai [Boyhood]. 1957.
Setsugoan jawa [Reminiscences]. 1968.

Translator (into modern Japanese), *Genji monogatari*, by Murasaki Shikibu. 26 vols., 1939–41.

*

Critical Studies: *The Search for Authenticity in Modern Japanese Literature* by Hisaaki Yamanouchi, 1978; *The Moon in the Water: Understanding Tanizaki, Kawabata, and Mishima* by Gwenn Boardman Petersen, 1979.

* * *

Tanizaki Jun'ichiro's life and writings, which spanned the first three imperial reigns of Japan's modern era, both affected and were affected by the development of modern Japanese literature. Constantly at odds with the Japanese *bundan*, the literary mainstream, Tanizaki boldly set forth his ideas about fiction and forged his own style. From the start he opposed the major literary trends of his day, namely Japanese naturalism and the I-novel. Both these trends incorporated strong autobiographical tendencies, linking life and literature through a sincere, confessional style. Tanizaki believed that fiction involved using the imagination, telling lies not truths, telling a good story. He expressed these views in his famous debate with fellow writer Akutagawa Ryūnosuke in 1927. Throughout the debate Tanizaki emphasized the importance of plot and story in creating and constructing fiction. Throughout his career he explored numerous ways of implementing such ideas. In his writings he strove to create distinct and complete worlds with a reality all their own. Tanizaki played with various narrative devices, including diaries, as in *Kagi (The Key)*, retrospection ("The Bridge of Dreams"), and confession ("The Thief"), created dream-like worlds (*Ashikari*, "Longing for Mother," "Aguri") and worlds of shadows and darkness ("A Portrait of Shunkin," "A Blind Man's Tale") where fact and fiction were often indistinguishable, and developed a rich, eloquent, often lyrical style, as in *Ashikari* and *Yoshino Kuzu (Arrowroot)*. Although he initially built his reputation on short stories and novellas, his complete works also include novels, plays, essays, memoirs, and several translations into modern Japanese of the Japanese classic *The Tale of Genji*.

Tanizaki's work is often neatly divided into two phases: his infatuation with the West and things Western through the mid 1920's, and his return to Japan and things Japanese thereafter. However, the reversal was never complete as he continually interwove Japanese and foreign elements, always mindful of Japan's modernization even as he sought an irretrievable past. This modern-traditional dichotomy was often a function of geography, Japanese geography that is, with Tokyo representing the stark, chaotic, disruptive nature of modernization and the Kansai area (Osaka, Kyoto, Kobe) representing the beauty and charm of Japan's past. Most of Tanizaki's early writings do take place in Tokyo and its environs, with a transition to the Kansai area in the mid to late 1920's, shortly after Tanizaki himself moved there. It is during this middle period that Tanizaki not only sought Japan's past in the Kansai area, but experimented with the world of historical fiction as well. (*Arrowroot*, "A Blind Man's Tale," "The Secret History of the Lord of Musashi," "A Portrait of Shunkin"). He manipulated history in order to create a separate world and fabricated "documents" to lend authenticity to the form. Tanizaki's next major work to be set in Tokyo was the novel *Futen Rōjin Nikki (Diary of a Mad Old Man)*, near the end of his long career.

The major recurring themes in Tanizaki's writing revolve around a sense of longing. Tanizaki grew up in Tokyo's *shitamachi*, or downtown, where merchants and artisans lived, and where traditional Japan and modernizing Japan came together creating a diverse urban culture. A decline in the family fortune and increasing Western influence robbed Tanizaki of the comfortable world that he loved. Tanizaki's longing for the lost world of his childhood was a stimulus for his nostalgic and loving recreations of both the recent and distant past. *Sasameyuki (The Makioka Sisters)* was his most sustained and successful tribute to a vanishing way of life, that of the pre-World War II, upper-middle class. Tanizaki is probably most famous for his longing for and pursuit of the Ideal Woman. Pathologoical and/or sado-masochistic elements are indispensable to his quest for absolute beauty, thus linking beauty with evil. In many cases Tanizaki's longing for the Ideal Woman becomes a longing for Mother, or vice versa. Other favorite themes include an obsession with feet, excretory processes, food and eating, a fear of madness and self-destruction, and glimpses of perversity in human nature.

Tanizaki's writing is often compared with that of Edgar Allan Poe. Their similarities include explorations of the worlds of fantasy, terror, and shadow, fascination with the Eternal Woman and sadomasochism, and lack of didacticism. Yet, in depicting the power struggle between the sexes inherent in the quest for absolute beauty Tanizaki drew his inspiration not only from Poe and the Western Romantic tradition, but from the 17th- and 18th-century erotic and sadistic stories of Japanese picture books and kabuki. Tanizaki's femme fatale stories reveal a masochistic desire on the part of the protagonist to submit completely to a woman, and often one of lower social status, thus opposing Buddhist and Confucian teachings on two counts—elevating women and crossing class lines.

"The Tattooer" is classic Tanizaki. He creates a world where beauty is the ultimate authority. Seikichi, a tattooer renowned for the bold eroticism of his art, revels in the pain his needles cause and dreams of creating his masterpiece on a beautiful woman. He discovers the essence of woman in a young, apprentice geisha and enacts the male fantasy of forced submission (through the use of a Western drug) that leads to sexual awakening. As he tattoos her drugged body, he pours his own being into her. Drained and exhausted, he watches his masterpiece come to life and willingly submits to the power he has created. Through submission he validates his achievement. Other male protagonists participate to varying degrees in molding women to suit their fantasies, leaving the reader to wonder whether submission signifies a loss or gain in power. Okada is literally wasting away from his obsession with an overindulged young bar girl ("Aguri"). Professor Rado is a middle-aged, self-important, eccentric but respected public figure whose startling private obsessions, involving a maid and a chorus girl, are uncovered by an inquisitive reporter ("Professor Rado"). In a comic yet touching piece, two women vie for the love of a man who is totally consumed with love for his cat ("A Cat, A Man, and Two Women"). Tanizaki also treats the theme of dominance and submission by examining a non-erotic relationship between teacher and pupil ("The Little Kingdom"). All these stories entail a power reversal and the questions remain; who has control and at what cost?

Tanizaki's theme of longing for Mother is strongly connected with an idealized image of his own dead mother, as well as his fascination with *The Tale of Genji*, where the pursuit of a lost mother is central to the plot. As in *Genji*, the longing for mother carries with it strong erotic undertones. A young boy searches for and finds his dead mother in a dream sequence that is evocative, surreal, and nostalgic ("Longing for Mother"). Tsumura helps his friend gather material for a historical novel while actually pursuing a woman who resembles his dead mother (*Arrowroot*). Tadasu is raised by a stepmother who was instructed and encouraged by the father to be exactly like the dead mother ("The Bridge of Dreams," also the title of the last section of *Genji*). In all three stories the mother figure remains eternally young and beautiful, whether through dream, memory, or transference.

Tanizaki's carefully constructed fictional worlds expose the reader to exotic, erotic, and nostalgic fantasies, as they simultaneously reveal glimpses of a modernizing Japan. His insights into human psychology both delight and cause alarm. Tanizaki combines all this with a rich, imaginative style and succeeds in creating a distinctive and memorable body of literature.

—Dina Lowy

See the essay on "A Portrait of Shunkin."

TAYLOR, Peter (Hillsman). American. Born in Trenton, Tennessee, 8 January 1917. Educated at Vanderbilt University, Nashville, 1936–37; Southwestern College, Memphis, Tennessee, 1937–38; Kenyon College, Gambier, Ohio, 1938–40, A.B. 1940. Served in the United States Army, 1941–45. Married Eleanor Lilly Ross in 1943; two children. Teacher, University of North Carolina, Chapel Hill, 1946–67; visiting lecturer, Indiana University, Bloomington, 1949, University of Chicago, 1951, Kenyon College, 1952–57, Seminar in American Studies, Oxford University, 1955, Ohio State University, Columbus, 1957–63, and Harvard University, Cambridge, Massachusetts, 1964; professor of English, University of Virginia, Charlottesville, from 1967. Recipient: Guggenheim fellowship, 1950; American Academy grant, 1952, and gold medal, 1979; Fulbright fellowship, to France, 1955; O. Henry award, 1959; Ford fellowship, for drama, 1960; Ritz Paris Hemingway award, 1987; Pulitzer prize, 1987. Member, American Academy, 1969. Lives in Charlottesville.

PUBLICATIONS

Short Stories

A Long Fourth and Other Stories.   1948.
The Widows of Thornton.   1954.
Happy Families Are All Alike: A Collection of Stories. 1959.
Miss Leonora When Last Seen and 15 Other Stories. 1963.
The Collected Stories.   1969.
In the Miro District and Other Stories.   1977.
The Old Forest and Other Stories.   1985.
The Oracle at Stoneleigh (includes plays).   1993.

Novels

A Woman of Means.   1950.
A Summons to Memphis.   1986.

Plays

Tennessee Day in St. Louis (produced 1956).   1957.
A Stand in the Mountains (produced 1971).   Published in *Kenyon Review,* 1965.
Presences: Seven Dramatic Pieces.   1973.
The Early Guest: A Sort of Story, A Sort of Play, A Sort of Dream.   1982.

Other

Conversations with Taylor, edited by Hubert H. McAlexander.   1987.

Editor, with Robert Penn Warren and Robert Lowell, *Randall Jarrell 1914-1965.*   1967.

*

Bibliography: *Andrew Lytle, Walker Percy, Taylor: A Reference Guide* by Victor A. Kramer, 1983; *Taylor: A Descriptive Bibliography* by Stuart Wright, 1988.

Critical Studies: *Taylor* by Albert J. Griffith, 1970, revised edition, 1990; *Taylor: A Study of the Short Fiction* by James Curry Robinson, 1988.

*   *   *

Despite having written two well-received novels, *A Woman of Means* and *A Summons to Memphis,* which won a Pulitzer prize, and a clutch of plays, Peter Taylor's distinguished career has been built on his short stories. Born in Tennessee in 1917, he attended Kenyon College, where he was roommate of Robert Lowell and friend to Randall Jarrell, both poets having followed John Crowe Ransom from Vanderbilt University.

Taylor began teaching English and creative writing, and his academic career permitted him to pursue the short story form during a time when it was neither financially nor critically popular. He published three collections by 1969, the same year that *The Collected Stories of Peter Taylor* appeared.

Influenced by Ransom and the conservative Agrarian movement, as well as his own Southern background, his fictions tend toward the traditional, favoring first-person narratives, though obviously, sometimes heavily, aware of Freudian dynamics. What is absent or off-stage are the violence and fierce sexuality of O'Conner and Faulkner, though he shares the latter's obsession with the invidious impact of the New South on the Old, closer perhaps to Eudora Welty in his focus on subtle psychological revelations. His major characters are usually well-educated members of a faded and/or dying upper class in conflict with a present time and clime, searching the past for clues to the self.

History, local and regional, threads together many of his narratives, which can at times get buried under gossipy details and a too careful, even loquacious expository structure. At his best, however, as in "Two Pilgrims" and "A Spinster's Tale," he integrates social and character insights with a seamless craftsmanship that simulates a memoir's relaxed authenticity. In the former, the familiar figure of an aged narrator scrutinizing a misunderstood past recounts an auto trip in which he drove his cotton-broker uncle and his lawyer from Memphis to rural Georgia. En route, they encounter a fire in a shack, and the uncle risks his life trying to save a child who had already been removed by the father. The husband slaps his wife in front of the men when he discovers she had lied to them about the child's whereabouts. Most important, the event helps the protagonist span the generation gap. "A Spinster's Tale," which also replicates a diary's easy flow, if too glib in its manipulation of psychoanalytic symbolism, has a more dramatic climax — an act of cruelty against a scape-goat drunk — that leaves an old woman still uncertain of childhood's influence.

Taylor's next two collections, *In the Miro District* and *The Old Forest and Other Stories,* evinced a continuing mastery of a sophisticated regionalism intent upon preserving a way of life and a cast of characters disappearing rapidly from Tennessee's urbanized landscape. *In the Miro District*'s eight stories suggest a degree of impatience with the form itself, four of them phrased in poetic terms, albeit without much success. "The Captain's Son," on the other hand, achieves a nagging power in its dispassionate depiction of an odd marriage between emotional cripples from upper-class Nashville and Memphis that deteriorates into alcoholic madness. Only "The Throughway" is eccentric enough to escape a formula feel, although the long title story, digging beneath familiar excess, strikes occasional gold in unearthing the dramatic struggles and underlying similarities of a Civil War survivor and his randy grandson.

This notion of a hidden generational bond and need for one another's waywardness, a defiant male life force, animates both "The Gift of the Prodigal" and "Promise in the Rain" in *The Old Forest and Other Stories,* Taylor's ripest, surest-handed collection. Among its gems is "Allegiance," a minor Jamesian masterpiece that dramatizes a brief but momentous meeting between a soldier nephew and a hated aunt (her crime never identified) in wartime London, peeling away layer after layer of sensibility and covert motives without reaching a deliberately ambiguous core even as the soldier ends up viewing his idealized dead mother in an uncomfortably new light.

Similarly, in "Rain in the Heart," a sensitive young drill sergeant and his bride, both from genteel Memphis backgrounds, find their shared sense of union against a brutal world compromised by his lapse into existential chaos, "the sense that no moment in life had any relation to another," before being saved by rain's arrival and the prospect of a sensual bonding. Other stories, specifically "Porte Cochere" and "The Scoutmaster," are almost as effective, despite the former's tendency to rely again too heavily on a reductive Freudianism, but two stories with blacks as their focus are embarrassing in their provincialism — blacks in Taylor's fictional world are either deranged outsiders or shackled by a servant's vantage, however sympathetically drawn.

The Oracle at Stoneleigh Court, which contains one novella, ten stories, and three one-act plays, shows Taylor trying to expand his range, at least in confronting more directly the "jolly corner" where James's alter-ego found the ghost of his own lost self and environment. Spirits and supernatural plot devices dominate, if still hitched to an obsessive drive to tame the past's unruly psychological impact, and very few of the stories evidence any significant falling off of Taylor's rich narrative talent.

—Edward Butscher

TELLES, Lygia Fagundes. Brazilian. Born in São Paulo, 19 April 1924. Educated at various institutions: holds a teaching credential and degrees in physical education and law. Married 1) Gofredo da Silva Telles (divorced 1961); 2) Paulo Emílio Salles Gomes (died 1977). Recipient: Afonso Arinos prize, 1949; Instituto Nacional do Livro prize, 1958; Boa Leitura prize, 1961; Cannes Festival grand prize, for short fiction, 1969; Guimarâes Rosa prize, 1972; Brazilian Academy of Letters award, 1973; Pedro Nava award, 1989. Elected to Brazilian Academy of Letters. Lives in Rio de Janeiro.

PUBLICATIONS

Short Stories

Porão e sobrado.   1938.

Praia viva.   1944.
O cacto vermelho.   1949.
Histórias do desencontro.   1958.
Histórias escolhidas.   1961.
A confissão de Leontina.   1964.
O jardim selvagem.   1965.
Antes do baile verde.   1970; revised and enlarged edition, 1971.
Seleta.   1971.
Seminário dos ratos.   1977; as *Tigrela and Other Stories,* 1986.
Filhos pródigos.   1978.
A disciplina do amor: fragmentos.   1980.
Mistérios: ficções.   1981.
Os melhores contos, edited by Eduardo Portella.   1984.
10 contos escolhidos.   1984.
Venha ver o por-do-sol & outros contos.   1988.

Novels

Ciranda de pedra.   1954; as *The Marble Dance,* 1986.
Verão no aquário.   1963.
As meninas.   1973; as *The Girl in the Photograph,* 1982.
As horas nuas.   1989.

Other

Telles (selected works and criticism).   1980.

*

Critical Studies: "New Fiction: Telles" by Jon M. Tolman, in *Review* 30, 1981; "The Baroness of Tatui" by Edla Van Steen, in *Review* 36, 1986; "The Guerilla in the Bathtub: Telles's *As Meninas* and the Irruption of Politics" by Renata R. Wasserman, in *Modern Language Studies* 19(1), 1989.

* * *

Although Lygia Fagundes Telles has written four novels, she is better known for her short stories. In the 1940's she published what she later called "impulses of a literary adolescence:" the volumes of short stories *Praia viva* (Live Beach), and *O cacto vermelho* (The Red Cactus). *Tigrela and Other Stories,* Telles's only collection of short stories in English, is a compilation of stories that appeared in Brazil at different times in different books.

Telles's stories deal with the bourgeoisie, with people who have had unhappy marriages and who long for the lost joys of youth. Her characters, mostly adults, are depicted in a moment of crisis, when they have to settle accounts with their past. There are also stories, such as "Rat Seminar," and "The 'X' in the Problem," that comment on Brazilian political and social situation. One of the stories of *Tigrela and Other Stories,* "Herbarium," is unique in the sense that its main character is a young girl. However, even in "Herbarium," Telles's distinguishing characteristics are present: the girl falls in love with her older cousin, who is staying in her house to recover from a long illness. He introduces her to botany and to the joys of collecting leaves. In the end, when he is about to depart with his fiancé, the girl has to face a painful moment of truth, when she gives him a leaf that represents death.

Indeed, Telles's stories are explorations of the theme of love and life, and of the moment of death. In "The Touch on the Shoulder" the character is introduced within a dream. He is in a garden with a bench, a dry fountain, and a decaying marble statue of a young woman in the middle of the fountain. All seems lifeless, the lack of water, or even butterflies, and the scent of herbs and flowers is strange. The man feels the invisible presence of a stranger who at any moment will touch him lightly on the shoulder and tell him it's time to go. He forces himself to wake up, just to realize that his life is barren of joy or feelings. In the end, he takes his car to escape his fear, but he suddenly sees himself back in the garden, and this time he does feel the touch on his shoulder.

In "Yellow Nocturne" a middle-aged woman is with her husband on their way to a party. That their marriage, after so many years, has become a succession of ready-made questions and answers. When they stop to fix a flat tire, the woman, Laura, feels the smell of a flower, "Lady-of-the-Night." This smell leads her to a garden, in the middle of which stands her old family home. In the lit atmosphere of the living room, Laura is made to face her past sins—promises not kept, betrayals of her relatives, the guilt over a man's attempted suicide—and the pain over a love misspent. This settling of accounts, which happens in a dreamy atmosphere, takes no time in the actual world. When she comes back from the garden, the car is fixed and they leave the place.

Smell is also the trigger of memories in "The Sauna." A successful middle-aged painter goes to a sauna; the scent of eucalyptus takes him back to a time when he was still young and poor. In the foggy atmosphere, the past becomes present, and he is invaded by memories of his first love, Rose. By the time he leaves the sauna, the man has cried, reviewed his whole past, and admitted to his sins. The story, however, ends on an ironic note, when the painter says to the sauna attendant that he is a bit worn out, but clean.

Some of Telles's stories have insects and animals as characters. In "The Ants" two college students rent a room in the attic of a run-down house. The previous tenant has left a box of bones in the room, and one of the students discovers that the bones are a dwarf's skeleton. At night, a strange smell comes upon the place; a row of red ants invades the room and goes inside the box. After two days, the students find that the skeleton is being put together by the ants. The two escape the house in the middle of the night, terrified of something they can't name. In "Rat Seminar" a group of bureaucrats from Brazil and the United States have a seminar to discuss what to do with the rat population plaguing the nation. It is a narrative full of references to the political situation of Brazil, where the people are equated to rats, subversives, and "reds." In the end, the rats invade and destroy the house completely. The only survivor evades death by hiding inside the refrigerator. When he finally escapes the house, he can hear that the rats are holding their own seminar in the Conference Room. In another story, "Tigrela," a tigress is raised in an apartment owned by an unhappy woman who has been married many times. The story is weaved around a vaguely fantastic atmosphere. The tigress, we learn in the end of the story, is a young woman. We do not learn whether she has always been a woman, or if her humanity will only be revealed when she dies.

In Telles's fiction, no matter how trivial the subject—a family watching a TV show, in "The 'X of the Problem," or a young couple's fight in a Paris garden, in "Lovelorn Dove (A Story of Romance)," or a young woman getting dressed for a carnival dance, in "Green Masquerade," or a poor mother taking her son to a doctor in "Natal na barca" (Christmas on the Boat)—there is always room for a sharp commentary on human frailties, the pain of love, the changing flow of life, and the moment of confrontation with death.

—Eva Paulino Bueno

See the essay on "Rat Seminar."

———

TERTS, Abram. Pseudonym for Andrei (Donatovich) Siniavskii. Russian. Born in Moscow, 8 October 1925. Educated at Moscow University, degree 1949, candidate of philological sciences 1952. Served in the Soviet Army. Married Maria Rozanova-Kruglikova; one son. Senior research fellow, Gorky Literary Institute, Moscow, until 1966; lecturer in Russian literature, Moscow University, until 1965; arrested for alleged anti-Soviet writings, 1965, sentenced to seven years' hard labour, 1966: released from prison, 1971; emigrated to France, 1973; assistant professor, then professor of Slavic studies, the Sorbonne, Paris, from 1973; Russian citizenship restored, 1990. Founder, *Sintaksis* literary journal. Recipient: Grolier Club Bennett award, 1978. Lives in Fontenay-aux-Roses.

PUBLICATIONS

Short Stories

Sud idet (novella).   In *Kultura*, 1960; as *The Trial Begins*, 1960.
Fantasticheskie povesti.   1961; as *Fantastic Stories*, 1963; as *The Icicle, and Other Stories*, 1963.
Liubimov (novella).   In Polish as *Lubimow*, 1963; in Russian, 1964; as *The Makepeace Experiment*, 1965.

Novel

Spokoinoi nochi.   1984; as *Goodnight!*, 1989.

Other (as Andrei Siniavskii)

Kto kak zashchishchaetsia [Who Defends Oneself Thus]. 1953.
"Chto takoe sotsialisticheski realizm?" (as Abram Terts). In *L'Esprit*, February 1959; as *On Socialist Realism*, 1961.
Istoriia russkoi sovetskoi literatury [History of Soviet Russian Literature].   1961.
Lysukha (Naturalist Stories).   1961.
Poeziia pervykh let revoliutsii, 1917–20 [The Poetry of the First Years of the Revolution], with A.N. Menshutin. 1964.
Mysli vrasplokh (as Abram Terts).   1966; as *Unguarded Thoughts*, 1972.
Druzhnaia semeika [Friendly Family].   1966.
Fantasticheskii mir Abrama Tertsa [Fantastic World of Abram Terts] (as Abram Terts).   1967.
Medvezhonok Taimyr [The Bear Cub Taimyr].   1969.
Khrabryi tsyplenok [The Brave Chicken].   1971.
For Freedom of Imagination.   1971.

V nochnom zooparke [In the Night Zoo].   1973.
Golos iz khora (as Abram Terts).   1973; as *A Voice from the Chorus*, 1976.
Progulki s Pushkinym [Strolls with Pushkin] (as Abram Terts).   1975.
V teni Gogolia [In the Shadow of Gogol] (as Abram Terts). 1975.
Kroshka Tsores [Little Tsores] (as Abram Terts).   1980.
Syntaxis: réflexion sur le sort de la Russe et de la culture russe.   1981.
"Opavshie list'ia" V.V. Rozanova [V.V. Rozanov's Fallen Leaves].   1982.
Osnovy sovetskoi tsivilizatsii. As *La Civilisation Soviétique*, 1989; as *Soviet Civilization: A Cultural History*, 1992.
Sny na pravoslavnuiu Paskhu [Dreams of Orthodox Pashka].   1991.

*

Critical Studies: *On Trial: The Case of Sinyavsky—Tertz—and Daniel–Arzhak,* edited by Leopold Labedz and M. Hayward, 1966, revised edition, 1980; "Sinyavsky in Two Worlds: Two Brothers Named Chénier" by Richard Pevear, in *Hudson Review* 25, 1972; *Siniavsky and Julii Daniel', Two Soviet "Heretical" Writers* by Margaret Dalton, 1973; "Siniavskii: The Chorus and the Critic" by Walter F. Kolonsky, in *Canadian-American Slavic Studies* 9, 1975; "The Sense of Purpose and Socialist Realism in Tertz's *The Trial Begins*" by W.J. Leatherbarrow, in *Forum for Modern Language Studies* 11, 1975; *Letters to the Future: An Approach to Sinyavsky-Tertz* by Richard Lourie, 1975; "On Tertz's *A Voice from the Choir*" by Laszlo M. Tikos, in *International Fiction Review* 2, 1975; "The Literary Criticism of Tertz" by Albert Leong, in *Proceedings of the Pacific Northwest Conference on Foreign Languages,* 28(1), 1977; "The Bible and the Zoo in Sinyavsky's *The Trial Begins*" by Richard L. Chapple, in *Orbis Litterarum* 33, 1978; "Narrator, Metaphor and Theme in Sinjavskij's *Fantastic Tales*" by Andrew R. Durkin, in *Slavic and East European Journal* 24, 1980; "'The Icicle' as Allegory" by Grace Anne Morsberger, in *Odyssey,* 4(2), 1981; "Sinyavsky's 'You and I': A Modern Day Fantastic Tale" by Catharine Theimer Nepomnyashchy, in *Ulbandus Review,* 2(2), 1982; "The Writer as Alien in Sinjavskij's 'Pkhens'" by Ronald E. Peterson, in *Wiener Slawistischer Almanach* 12, 1983; "Conflicting Imperatives in the Model of the Russian Writer: The Case of Tertz/Sinyavsky" by Donald Fanger, in *Literature and History: Theoretical Problems and Russian Case Studies,* edited by Gary Saul Morson, 1986; "*Spokojnoj noci*: Andrej Sinjavskij's Rebirth as Abram Terc" by Olga Matich, in *Slavic and East European Journal* 33(1), 1989.

* * *

In Moscow from 1956 until arrest in 1965 Andrei Siniavski led a double existence as a university lecturer and literary critic, while under the pseudonym Abram Terts he was sending out to the West free-thinking essays and fantastic tales. Between 1966 and 1971, while serving his sentence in the labour camp, he continued to write, sending out his work in sections disguised as fortnightly letters to his wife. His book on Pushkin was smuggled out in this way and the material that became the camp memoir *A Voice from the Chorus*. It was there too that he conceived and started his book on Gogol. He has lived near Paris since 1973, where he has continued to lead his double life, publishing under the signatures of both Terts and Siniavski.

This continuing free coexistence of Siniavski and Terts has made plain that the pseudonym is more than just a cover. Terts functions rather as a double, an alter ego who, though not differing fundamentally from his creator, is bolder, more playful and less bound by conventions of form, language, and style. It is not a matter of a straightforward distinction between fictional (Terts) and non-fictional (Siniavski) identities, rather between works of the imagination and academic works. The literary studies of Pushkin and Gogol and the autobiographical work *Spokoinoi nochi (Goodnight!)*, for example, though non-fictional, are signed by Terts, while scholarly studies and the earlier brilliant essay on Boris Pasternak are signed Siniavski. But between the two selves there is, as his old friend Hélène Zamoiska put it, "a dialogue in which there were no contradictions."

The story of the evolution of Abram Terts should not stifle interest in the initial motivation for the splitting of identity in the 1950's, nor dull appreciation of the conscious act of moral courage behind the sending work out of Russia. Siniavski was fully aware at the outset that the Soviet authorities would see it as a gesture of political subversion, and, if proof were needed, there was the example of the hounding of Pasternak following the publication of *Doctor Zhivago* in the West in 1957. But, like Pasternak, Siniavski was no longer content to write privately "for the drawer," as had writers like Bulgakov in the days of the Stalinist terror. An insistent motif in Terts's early fiction is the narrator's compulsion not just to write, but for his voice to be heard. The voice of Terts is a voice of doubt, of dissent and protest, but, Siniavski reveals himself the true heir to the Russian literary tradition, the medium he chooses is not political polemic, but literature. Under Stalin, as he argues in his provocative essay *On Socialist Realism,* writers had been turned away from their proper function of exploring reality into propagandists for the glorious purpose, the future of world communism. What was needed after Stalin's death when the truths of his brutal regime were coming to light was not a sham cardboard representation of an ideal reality but an art that would examine the complexities and brutal disjunctions of the times. It would be a grotesque, fantasmagoric art— fantastic realism.

The world of the early stories deals with the everyday Russia of his times, but it is a world out of joint, sometimes comically or grotesquely distorted and fragmented, infiltrated by the paranormal or the extraterrestrial. In "The Icicle," for example, the narrator develops an uncanny ability to see into both the prehistoric past and the distant future. When he gazes inwards upon himself he sees a motley assortment of incarnations of former and future selves, good and bad with no perceivable advancement on the evolutionary scale. By contrast, when he looks at his interrogating officer, the KGB colonel, he sees a refinement of the force of power, from past incarnations as Tsarist police officials to that blind purpose in the form of a giant sentient icicle. Significantly, the tragic accident the narrator foresees, but is powerless to avert, is the death of his girlfriend Natasha, killed by an icicle falling from a roof. With Natasha's death, the narrator instantly loses his psychic gift. His motive for writing the account, as he puts it, is like a note thrown into the sea in a bottle, a letter addressed to a future incarnation of himself with the message of the enduring triumph of love over blind necessity.

The subversive questioning of the teleological principle of Communism and the pervasive atmosphere of paranoia, betrayal, and arrest found here and in the novellas *Sud idet (The Trial Begins)* and *Liubimov (The Makepeace Experiment)* tie Siniavski's writing to the political realities of post-Stalinist Russia. His themes of alienation, loneliness, and the dehumanising effect of modern urban life are themes common to much 20th-century Western literature, and he has many affinities with Western modernists, in particular, surrealism and magic realism. However, he sees himself "linked by an invisible chain" with the Russian modernist writing of the earlier part of the century, which had been stifled after 1930. He is reviving the tradition of the imaginative fantastic writing practised by Babel, Olesha, Zamiatin, Zoshchenko, and Bulgakov (which was a development of the fantastic realism of 19th-century writers like Leskov, Dostoevskii and Gogol.) When he said in a 1975 interview, "For me fantasy and fiction are primarily the means of discovering *this* world . . . a way to the metaphysical foundations of being," he is only echoing what Dostoevskii wrote in a letter over a century earlier: "I have my own idea or reality in art; and what most people call fantastic and exceptional is sometimes for me the very essence of reality."

Siniavski's later writings show him developing and deepening his meditations on art, history, and the nature of good and evil. The irony, self-deprecation, and doubt are still present, but they are counterpoised by a greater serenity and a positive statement of religious faith. *Goodnight!*, which he formally styles a novel, is a loosely linked series of autobiographical "short fictions" which, in their close kinship with the earlier works, illustrate vividly just how fantastic was the life experience out of which the fiction was fabricated. The last chapter gives a factual basis for the psychic foreknowledge that the narrator has in "The Icicle." Siniavski describes an attempt by the KGB to enlist him in a plan to entrap his student friend Hélène, the daughter of a French naval attaché. The third chapter reveals that the psychoscope dreamed of by the secrete service men in *The Trial Begins* and the psychic magnet that imparts hypnotic powers in *The Makepeace Experiment* are a fictional transposition of the author's father, who believed that his brain had been tampered with while in prison and that his thoughts were still being monitored by the KGB.

Goodnight! is essentially an account of the making of the writer Terts. Its key episodes all turn on an acceptance of responsibility, both for the innocent and for the guilty. It is an idea replayed in fantastic vein in the story "Kroshka Tsores" (1980, "Little Jinx"), where a fictional Siniavski confesses to being the unwitting cause of the death of all five of his brothers. The suspension of disbelief ends with the end of the confession, when the five brothers turn into the writer's five fingers resting on top of the finished manuscript. There is more than an echo here of the debate that is at the centre of Dostoevskii's world in *The Brothers Karamazov*: what should be the response to gratuitious evil and innocent suffering? Siniavski has sought to dissociate himself from the strong didactic tradition in Russian literature, yet, as his later writing makes clear, he has a very definite sense of vocation. If he does not presume to know the purpose being worked out for humans through history and nature, he can perceive a pattern, a design. He sees it as the job of the artist to be attentive to that pattern, to make and record the connections. "I am in no way a preacher or a moralist; it is something which is lacking in me." In 1986 he said, "It's true that as a writer you do fulfil a kind of moral function, but that happens not because you embark from some moral aim, but because it's impossible to write without love."

—Jane Grayson

See the essay on "Pkhentz."

———————

THOMAS, Audrey (Grace, née Callahan). American; Canadian Landed Immigrant. Born in Binghamton, New York, 17 November 1935. Educated at Smith College, Northampton, Massachusetts, B.A. 1957; University of British Columbia, Vancouver, M.A. in English 1963. Married Ian Thomas in 1958 (divorced); three daughters. Emigrated to Canada, 1959; lived in Kumasi, Ghana, 1964–66; visiting professor, Concordia University, Montreal, 1989–90; Scottish-Canadian Exchange Fellow, Edinburgh, 1985–86; writer-in-residence, University of Victoria, British Columbia, University of British Columbia, Vancouver, Simon Fraser University, Burnaby, British Columbia, and David Thompson University Centre, Nelson, British Columbia, Victoria College, University of Toronto. Recipient: *Atlantic* First award, 1965; Canada Council grant, 1969, 1971, 1972, 1974, and Senior Arts grant, 1974, 1977, 1979; British Colombia Book prize, 1985, 1990; Marion Engle award, 1987; Canada-Australia prize, 1989. Lives in British Columbia.

PUBLICATIONS

Short Stories

Ten Green Bottles.   1967.
Ladies and Escorts.   1977.
Personal Fictions, with others, edited by Michael Ondaatje. 1977.
Real Mothers.   1981.
Two in the Bush and Other Stories.   1981.
Goodbye Harold, Good Luck.   1986.
The Wild Blue Yonder.   1990.

Novels

Mrs. Blood.   1967.
Munchmeyer, and Prospero on the Island.   1972.
Songs My Mother Taught Me.   1973.
Blown Figures.   1974.
Latakia.   1979.
Intertidal Life.   1984.
Graven Images.   1993.

Plays

Radio Plays: *Once Your Submarine Cable Is Gone . . . ,* 1973; *Mrs. Blood,* from her own novel, 1975.

*

Critical Study: "Thomas Issue" of *Room of One's Own* 10 (3–4), 1986.

*   *   *

Though Audrey Thomas has published six novels, she is still best known in Canada as a writer of short fictions. Her first story appeared in *The Atlantic Monthly* in 1965, and it set the tone for much of the short fiction that followed. "If One Green Bottle" is an impressionistic, ellipsis-filled fiction, which follows the ebb and flow of a woman's memories of a painful miscarriage. The imagery of the sea surfaces repeatedly throughout the story, and the reader feels virtually sucked under the tide of pain and disorientation. These features recall Virginia Woolf's *The Waves,* and so it is not surprising that Thomas has defended her experimental method by invoking that powerful foremother of contemporary women's writing: "I'd like to demonstrate through my literature that you can do whatever you like. If you want to have seventeen points of view, have them, if you want to chop your thing in the middle, do it. Virginia Woolf was doing that sort of thing all the time, she didn't care."

This willingness to experiment, to play with the conventions of fiction, is a trademark of Thomas's work, placing her among her postmodernist contemporaries. In her 1977 collection of stories, *Ladies & Escorts,* Thomas opens one story by meditating self-consciously on the story that precedes it: "Writers are terrible liars," she begins. She then imagines a series of possible explanations for the central mystery of that preceding story, some of which directly contradict others. For Thomas, "lies" are the very stuff of fiction, and anyone who expects her short stories to hand over what Woolf called in *A Room of One's Own* the "nugget" of truth will be challenged and surprised.

It may seem, then, surprising to some readers that a writer who eagerly embraces the postmodernist concept of fabulation draws much of her fiction from her own life. That early story "If One Green Bottle" is loosely based on Thomas's own experience of a miscarriage in Ghana, and that episode is repeated in a number of fictions, most spectacularly in her novel *Mrs. Blood.* Other situations and even snippets of dialogue echo throughout the fiction; for example, in a number of her fictions, a lover/husband who seeks to break off a relationship cruelly opens the subject with the warning: "There is no nice way of saying this." Another repeated scenario is the married man in his forties finding narcissistic adulation in a relationship with a younger woman, while the 40-ish wife bitterly looks on. No matter what the precise extent of the autobiographical material may be, Thomas is, like her fellow Canadian story writer Clark Blaise, writing a fiction of self-conscious autobiographical fiction, what I would call meta-autobiography. Clearly, Woolf is not Thomas's only influence; so too are the confessional poets, particularly Sylvia Plath.

Like Plath, Thomas has searing indictments to offer about the power relationships between men and women. Though much of her energy in the 1970's was taken up with her trilogy of novels, *Mrs. Blood, Songs My Mother Taught Me,* and *Blown Figures,* in the latter part of the decade Thomas turned to short fiction once again, and produced during those years some of her most pointed critiques of gender relations. In fact, she described those stories, collected in *Ladies and Escorts,* as particularly concerned with the male-female relationship. In "A Monday Dream at Alameda Park," for example, a restive professor wishes to return to a naive memory of the 1960's, and so he dumps his wife in favour of a belated flower child. Always, it is the husband who has the option of choice, and the wife who angrily grinds her teeth, and must sit on the sidelines to watch the antics of the aging Peter Pan.

In the short fiction of the 1980's, however, Thomas—and her heroines—have moved on. Several of the stories in *Real Mothers* and *Goodbye Harold, Good Luck* show women recovering from these failed relationships and taking the initiative to form new ones, even if they, too, promise further rounds of the war between the sexes (for instance, "Real Mothers"). Some of these heroines reveal this new mobility and choice in the act of taking to their heels when a relationship proves too stifling ("Goodbye Harold, Good Luck").

Obviously, Thomas's fiction places an emphasis on heterosexual relationships; or, it might be more accurate to say that she is obsessed with them, too. This bias is closely related to her art of meta-autobiography; as Thomas once reflected, "I think everybody writes autobiography. I think everybody writes one story, has one thing that really interests them, and I suppose what really interests me is the relationship between men and women and how we lie to one another." Although her more recent fiction does not break with this obsession, there is a new direction in stories like "Crossing the Rubicon" from *Real Mothers*: an increasing concern with the mother-child bond. Indeed, the new strands of Thomas's fiction of the 1980's cross; a number of the stories deal with the implications of a woman's new relationship with a man on her growing children.

Like other women writers of the Canadian West Coast, Thomas shows a willingness to experiment formally, which brings her closer to the postmodernist poems and short fictions of Quebecois women like Nicole Brossard than to the central-Canadian writers. But what sets Thomas apart from almost any other writer in Canada is her rich melange of self-conscious fabulation, feminism, and autobiography.

—Lorraine M. York

———

THOMAS, Dylan (Marlais). Welsh. Born in Swansea, Glamorganshire, 27 October 1914. Educated at Swansea Grammar School (editor of school magazine), 1925–31. Married Caitlin Macnamara in 1937; two sons and one daughter. Copyreader, then reporter, *South Wales Evening Post*, Swansea, 1931–32; freelance writer, from 1933; lived in London, with periods in Wales and Hampshire, 1934–45; worked for Strand Films, making documentaries for the Ministry of Information, during World War II; broadcaster and scriptwriter, 1946–49; lived in Laugharne, Wales, 1949–53; made four poetry reading tours of the U.S., 1950, 1952, 1953. Recipient: *Sunday Referee* prize, 1935; Foyle poetry prize, 1952; Etna-Taormina prize, 1953; Italia prize, for radio play, 1954. *Died 9 November 1953.*

PUBLICATIONS

Collections

Collected Prose. 1969.
Selected Writings, edited by J.P. Harries. 1970.
The Poems, edited by Daniel Jones. 1971; revised edition, 1974.

Selected Poems, edited by Walford Davies. 1974.
Collected Poems 1934–1953, edited by Walford Davies and Ralph N. Maud. 1988.

Short Stories

The World I Breathe (includes verse). 1939.
A Prospect of the Sea and Other Stories and Prose Writings, edited by Daniel Jones. 1955.
Adventures in the Skin Trade and Other Stories. 1955.
Two Tales: Me and My Bike, and Rebecca's Daughters. 1968.

Novels

Portrait of the Artist as a Young Dog. 1940.
Rebecca's Daughters. 1965.
The Outing. 1971.
The Followers. 1976.
The Death of the King's Canary, with John Davenport. 1976.

Plays

Return Journey (broadcast 1947). In *New Directions: Five One-Act Plays in the Modern Idiom*, edited by Alan Durband, 1961.
The Doctor and the Devils, from the Story by Donald Taylor (film-script). 1953.
Under Milk Wood: A Play for Voices (broadcast 1954). 1954.
The Beach of Falesá (film-script). 1963.
Twenty Years A-Growing: A Film Script from the Story by Maurice O'Sullivan. 1964.
Me and My Bike: An Unfinished Film-Script. 1965.
The Doctor and the Devils and Other Scripts (includes *Twenty Years A-Growing, A Dream of Winter, The Londoner*). 1966.

Screenplays: *Balloon Site 568*, 1942; *Wales*, 1942; *New Towns for Old*, 1942; *Our Country*, 1944; *When We Build Again*, 1945; *The Three Weird Sisters*, with Louise Birt and David Evans, 1948; *No Room at the Inn*, with Ivan Foxwell, 1948.

Radio Writing: *Quite Early One Morning*, 1944; *The Londoner*, 1946; *Return Journey*, 1947; *Under Milk Wood*, 1954.

Verse

18 Poems. 1934.
Twenty-five Poems. 1936.
The Map of Love: Verse and Prose. 1939.
New Poems. 1943.
Deaths and Entrances. 1946.
Twenty-Six Poems. 1950.
In Country Sleep and Other Poems. 1952.
Collected Poems 1934–1952. 1952; as *The Collected Poems*, 1953.
Two Epigrams of Fealty. 1954.
Galsworthy and Gawsworth. 1954.
The Notebook Poems 1930–1934, edited by Ralph N. Maud. 1989.

Other

Selected Writings, edited by John L. Sweeney. 1946.

Quite Early One Morning: Broadcasts.   1954; revised edition, 1954; *A Child's Christmas in Wales* published separately, 1955.
Conversations about Christmas.   1954.
Letters to Vernon Watkins, edited by Vernon Watkins. 1957.
Miscellany: Poems, Stories, Broadcasts.   1963.
The Colour of Saying: An Anthology of Verse Spoken by Thomas, edited by Ralph N. Maud and Aneirin Talfan Davies.   1963; as *Thomas's Choice: An Anthology of Verse Spoken by Thomas,* 1964.
Miscellany Two: A Visit to Grandpa's and Other Stories and Poems.   1966.
The Notebooks, edited by Ralph N. Maud.   1967; as *Poet in the Making: The Notebooks of Thomas,* 1968.
Early Prose Writings, edited by Walford Davies.   1971.
Living and Writing, edited by Christopher Capeman. 1972.
Miscellany Three.   1978.
Collected Letters, edited by Paul Ferris.   1985.

*

Bibliography: *Thomas: A Bibliography* by J. Alexander Rolph, 1956; *Thomas in Print* by Ralph N. Maud and Albert Glover, 1970, *Appendix 1969–1971* by Walford Davies, 1972.

Critical Studies: *Thomas: Dog among the Fairies* by Henry Treece, 1949, revised edition, 1956; *The Poetry of Thomas* by Elder Olson, 1954; *Thomas: A Literary Study* by Derek Stanford, 1954, revised edition, 1964; *Thomas in America: An Intimate Journal* by John Malcolm Brinnin, 1955, and *A Casebook on Thomas* edited by Brinnin, 1960; *Leftover Life to Kill* by Caitlin Thomas, 1957; *Thomas* by G.S. Fraser, 1957, revised edition, 1964, 1972; *Thomas: The Legend and the Poet* edited by E.W. Tedlock, 1960; *A Reader's Guide to Thomas* by William York Tindall, 1962; *Entrances to Thomas' Poetry* by Ralph N. Maud, 1963; *Thomas* by T.H. Jones, 1963; *The Religious Sonnets of Thomas: A Study in Imagery and Meaning* by H.H. Kleinman, 1963; *Dylan: Druid of the Broken Body* by Aneirin Talfan Davies, 1964; *The Days of Thomas* by Bill Read, 1964; *Thomas: His Life and Work,* 1964, *Welsh Dylan,* 1979, and *A Thomas Companion,* 1991, all by John Ackerman; *The Life of Thomas* by Constantine FitzGibbon, 1965; *Thomas* by Jacob Korg, 1965; *The Craft and Art of Thomas* by William Moynihan, 1966; *Sound and Sense in Thomas's Poetry* by Louise Murdy, 1966; *Thomas: A Collection of Critical Essays* edited by C.B. Cox, 1966; *The Growth of Milk Wood* by Douglas Cleverdon, 1969; *An Outline of the Works of Thomas* by Richard Morton, 1970; *Thomas's Early Prose: A Study in Creative Mythology* by Annis Pratt, 1970; *The World of Thomas* by Clark Emery, 1971; *The Saga of Prayer: The Poetry of Thomas* by Robert K. Burdette, 1972; *Thomas: The Code of Night* by David Holbrook, 1972; *Thomas: New Critical Essays* edited by Walford Davies, 1972, and Thomas by Davies, 1976; *The Country of the Spirit* by Rushworth Kidder, 1973; *Thomas: Poet of His People* by Andrew Sinclair, 1975, as *Thomas: No Man More Magical,* 1975; *Thomas: The Poet and His Critics* by R.B. Kershner, Jr., 1976; *Thomas: A Biography* by Paul Ferris, 1977; *My Friend Thomas* by Daniel Jones, 1977; *Portrait of a Friend* by Gwen Watkins, 1983; *Thomas's Places: A Biographical and Literary Guide* by James A. Davies, 1987; *The Prose Writing of Thomas* by

Lin Peach, 1988; *Thomas: Craft or Sullen Art* edited by Alan Bold, 1990.

*   *   *

There are writers whose gift is to put down roots within the world of dreams, the logic of whose work is the logic of the dreaming and not the waking mind. Dylan Thomas's stories, no less than his more widely acclaimed poetry, inhabit such a world, the tales of "good old three-adjectives-a-penny belly-churning Thomas, the Rimbaud of Cwmdonkin Drive."

At his worst, in *The Map Of Love* and the posthumous *A Prospect Of The Sea,* he had a genuine storytelling talent submerged by willful and self-indulgent oddity, a narratorial gift imprisoned within a style which could not register the depth of seriousness his ostensible subject required. Yet at his best, in *Portrait of the Artist as a Young Dog* and his radio stories, the personal recollections heightened by a more mature style and dramatic presentation are as unforgettable as they are powerful.

The distinction between his earlier surreal prose and his later more naturalistic style is one commonly accepted by critics. Thomas himself, referring to the early stories with characteristic humour as "the death and blood group," felt that they suffered from "immature violence, rhythmic monotony, frequent muddleheadedness and a very much overweighted imagery." Despite this, they introduce many of his recurrent themes that were to persist throughout his career: a preoccupation with birth and death, a sacramental vision of the natural world, an obsession with Biblical symbols, and the myth and mysticism of Welsh folklore. Only on rare occasions, as in "The Burning Baby," "The Enemies," and "The Dress," do these elements not overwhelm the narrative with their symbolism. This is all the more unfortunate, because a close reading of these stories often reveals a serious concern to try to comprehend the origins of sexual violence and sadomasochism, as in "The True Story" and "The Vest," or a radical overturning of established religious myths and associations, as in "The Tree" and "The Holy Six."

His morbid preoccupation with images of incest, violence, and horror, apart from reflecting the adolescent mentality of his heavily-mined notebooks and a passing acquaintance with Freud, also pay homage to the influence of Caradoc Evans, a man widely castigated in Wales for his brutal and excessive satires of Welsh peasantry. It will surprise few that Thomas's favourite quote about Evans came from a fearsome Welsh journal, *The Nonconformist Objector,* which charged Evans with possessing "an imagination like a sexual pigsty."

The passing of the 1930's revolution in middle-class sensibility, and its obsession with the spontaneity of inchoate power, marked a change in Thomas's stories. Responding to Richard Church's suggestion that he concentrate on narratives inspired by his early years in Swansea, Thomas produced his finest collection of stories, *Portrait of the Artist as a Young Dog,* A Joycean sequence rooting the dreams, obsessions, and frustrations of the individual in a clearly delineated sense of place, the urban and rural locale of South West Wales.

The stories work by retaining an instinctive innocence and humour which is contrasted with the stark social realities and despair of the 1920's and 1930's. As lamented by the narrator of "An Extraordinary Little Cough," they are set in a time "some years before I knew I was happy."

The finest achievement, "One Warm Saturday," achieves its epiphanic moments by relating to the structuring image of Victorian romanticism by means of Tennyson's poem, "Come into the Garden Maud." The narrative plays on the similarities and dissimilarities between the two: the Victorian Gardens, the youth and his "dream girl" reading poetry to her, desiring to be buried, losing her in the house and his ensuing madness. There is a fruitful tension between the narrative prose story and the poetic prose dreams contained within its form, as if the protagonist and the characters are constantly reimagining the story from the inside as it unfolds:

> As he thought this, phrasing her gentleness, faithlessly running to words away from the real room and his love in the middle, he woke with a start and saw her lively body six steps from him, no calm heart dressed in a sentence, but a pretty girl, to be got and kept.

The stoic clarity of the final sentence encapsulates the unfulfilled romantic dreams of a generation whilst still managing to retain the cadence and flow of a born storyteller:

> The light of the one weak lamp in a rusty circle fell across the brick-heaps and broken wood and the dust that had been houses once, where the small and hardly known and never-to-be-forgotten people of the dirty town had lived and loved and died and, always, lost.

The finer achievement in his later prose was made possible by the fusing of the visionary power of his interior world with an economy of implication which allowed the serious and the comic, the surreal and the naturalistic, to thread simultaneously through the same story. At the outbreak of war Thomas was employed as a scriptwriter for films and as a writer and broadcaster for radio, both of which contributed to the development of his later stories. The narrative economy, the sustaining of atmosphere and character, and the evocative sense of place demanded by those mediums resulted in such autobiographical gems as "A Visit to America," "A Story," "Reminiscences of Childhood," and "Holiday Memory." The near devastation of Swansea by bombing produced the uproarious comedy and wry sadness of "Return Journey," and the finest Christmas story of them all, "A Child's Christmas In Wales."

Thomas's imaginative and comic prose gifts showed no signs of diminution, as *Under Milk Wood* and his proposed collaboration with Stravinsky on a libretto will testify. His early death in 1953 at the age of 39 robbed the world, not only of a great poet, but also of a prodigious and underrated storyteller.

—Simon Baker

See the essay on "A Child's Christmas in Wales."

————

THURBER, James (Grover). American. Born in Columbus, Ohio, 8 December 1894. Educated at Ohio State University, Columbus, 1913–14, 1915–18. Married 1) Althea Adams in 1922 (divorced 1935), one daughter; 2) Helen Wismer in 1935. Code clerk, American Embassy, Paris, 1918–20; reporter, Columbus *Dispatch,* 1920–24, Paris edition of Chicago *Tribune,* 1925–26, and New York *Evening Post,* 1926–27; editor, 1927, writer, 1927–38, then freelance contributor, *The New Yorker;* also an illustrator from 1929: several individual shows. Litt.D.: Kenyon College, Gambier, Ohio, 1950; Yale University, New Haven, Connecticut, 1953; L.H.D.: Williams College, Williamstown, Massachusetts, 1951. *Died 2 November 1961.*

PUBLICATIONS

Collections

Vintage Thurber: A Collection of the Best Writings and Drawings.   2 vols., 1963.

Short Stories and Sketches (illustrated by the author)

The Owl in the Attic and Other Perplexities.   1931.
The Seal in the Bedroom and Other Predicaments.   1932.
My Life and Hard Times.   1933.
The Middle-Aged Man on the Flying Trapeze: A Collection of Short Pieces.   1935.
Let Your Mind Alone! and Other More or Less Inspirational Pieces.   1937.
Cream of Thurber.   1939.
The Last Flower: A Parable in Pictures.   1939.
Fables for Our Time and Famous Poems Illustrated. 1940.
My World—and Welcome to It.   1942.
Men, Women, and Dogs: A Book of Drawings.   1943.
The Thurber Carnival.   1945.
The Beast in Me, and Other Animals: A New Collection of Pieces and Drawings about Human Beings and Less Alarming Creatures.   1948.
The Thurber Album: A New Collection of Pieces about People.   1952.
Thurber Country: A New Collection of Pieces about Males and Females, Mainly of Our Own Species.   1953.
Thurber's Dogs: A Collection of the Master's Dogs, Written and Drawn, Real and Imaginary, Living and Long Ago. 1955.
A Thurber Garland.   1955.
Further Fables for Our Time.   1956.
Alarms and Diversions.   1957.
Lanterns and Lances.   1961.
Credos and Curios.   1962.
Thurber and Company.   1966.

Fiction (for children)

Many Moons.   1943.
The Great Quillow.   1944.
The White Deer.   1945.
The 13 Clocks.   1950.
The Wonderful O.   1955.

Plays

The Male Animal, with Elliott Nugent (produced 1940). 1940.
A Thurber Carnival, from his own stories (produced 1960). 1962.

Wrote the books for the following college musical comedies: *Oh My! Omar,* with Hayward M. Anderson, 1921;

Psychomania, 1922; *Many Moons*, 1922; *A Twin Fix*, with Hayward M. Anderson, 1923; *The Cat and the Riddle*, 1924; *Nightingale*, 1924; *Tell Me Not*, 1924.

Other

Is Sex Necessary? or, Why You Feel the Way You Do, with E.B. White.   1929.
Thurber on Humor.   1953.
The Years with Ross.   1959.
Selected Letters, edited by Helen Thurber and Edward Weeks.   1981.
Conversations with Thurber, edited by Thomas Fensch. 1989.
Collecting Himself: Thurber on Writing and Writers, Humor, and Himself, edited by Michael J. Rosen.   1989.

*

Bibliography: *Thurber: A Bibliography* by Edwin T. Bowden, 1968; *Thurber: An Annotated Bibliography of Criticism* by Sarah Eleanora Toombs, 1987.

Critical Studies: *Thurber* by Robert E. Morsberger, 1964; *The Art of Thurber* by Richard C. Tobias, 1969; *Thurber, His Masquerades: A Critical Study* by Stephen A. Black, 1970; *The Clocks of Columbus: The Literary Career of Thurber* by Charles S. Holmes, 1972, and *Thurber: A Collection of Critical Essays* edited by Holmes, 1974; *Thurber: A Biography* by Burton Bernstein, 1975; *Thurber's Anatomy of Confusion* by Catherine McGehee Kenney, 1984; *Thurber* by Robert Emmet Long, 1988.

* * *

Not the least of the difficulties in writing about James Thurber's short fiction is to discover which among the thousands of short pieces covering a number of modes — fable, parody, autobiography, social commentary — can be reasonably defined as fiction. "A Box to Hide In" (1931), for instance, falls somewhere between comic prose commentary and fiction, while stories like "Doc Marlowe" (1935) and "The Wood Duck" (1936) read as if they are personal anecdotes. But the mass of his comic prose writings tends to conceal the fact that Thurber, one of the most famous American comic writers, is a short story writer of considerable distinction and formal adventurousness.

The one story for which he is unquestionably famous is "The Secret Life of Walter Mitty," in which he established the archetype of the hen-pecked husband who sustains himself on a life of rich inner fantasy. Many of his stories are variations on this theme. "The Catbird Seat" (1942), for instance, involves the conflict between a meek man and a domineering woman, but here they are fellow employees, not a married couple. Mrs. Barrows has won the confidence of the head of the firm and commences a radical reform of it. She goads the meek, long-serving, tee-totalling Mr. Martin to the point where he makes private plans to murder her. When he arrives at her apartment he loses the nerve to carry the scheme through but proceeds to engage in wild behaviour, drinking and smoking, and finally insulting her employer. Martin has his way, after all: the next morning when Mrs. Barrows reports his behaviour she is not believed and is assumed to be a cracking up. In

another variation, "The Lady on 142" shows a train traveller and his quarrelsome wife involved in a heavily melodramatic intrigue about a spy, that both parodies and pays homage to Alfred Hitchcock movies and Dashiell Hammett novels (both mentioned in the text). At the end, of course, we find that the husband has dreamt the whole thing. In "The Private Life of Mr. Bidwell" (1933) a man develops eccentric habits — holding his breath for as long as possible, multiplying numbers in his head — possibly to bring about (unconsciously) the event that occurs; his wife leaves him. The gesture of private insurrection becomes a compulsive one; there is a last, pathetic glimpse of him at the end of the story walking along a road — he is trying to see how many steps he can take without opening his eyes. "The Remarkable Case of Mr. Bruhl" (1933) is yet another experiment along the same lines.

If there is one theme that is worth isolating, it is the battle of the sexes, the title of the film made from "The Catbird Seat." Thurber's men, ineffectual, dithering, indecisive, are dominated by their strong-minded wives. For instance, *The Owl in the Attic* (1931) has a series of eight stories about a young couple called the Monroes. In "Tea at Mrs. Armsby's" Mrs. Monroe is drunk and launches into a monologue about her husband's mania for collecting objects such as pencils ("My husband has eight hundred and seventy-four thousand pencils"). Mr. Monroe is forced into a desperately quick-witted confirmation and even embellishment of the bizarre claim ("I became interested in pencils in the Sudan. . . .The heat is so intense there that it melts the lead in the average Venus or Faber") until he can get her into a taxi and escape from the gullible guests. It is Thurber's wit at its best — the straight-faced dealing with the most preposterous situations. More often, though, the woman is in charge of the relationship. When Mr. Monroe dares to have an affair, his wife calls on the other woman and ends it by pleasantly informing her of Mr. Monroe's gross ineptitude in all practical matters.

Sometimes this ascendancy can take a relatively benign form: "Little Mrs. Monroe, burdened with coats and bundles, rosy, lovely, at length appeared. Mr. Monroe's heart leapt up, but at the same time he set himself as if to receive a service in tennis." (Thurber is also good at the incongruous contrasts between emotional responses and physical situations.) At other times it can be painfully humiliating. "A Couple of Hamburgers" (1935) is a chillingly detached portrait — conveyed largely through dialogue — of a failed marriage in which husband and wife take turns scoring points off each other. Thurber is very good, too, in his grasp of how a trivial incident can have disastrous consequences. In "The Breaking Up of the Winships" (1936), a husband's irritation at his wife's worship of Greta Garbo leads to his responding to her challenge to name a better actor by nominating Donald Duck. The absurd argument continues to escalate to the point where both husband and wife feel their whole ego is committed to their respective beliefs, and the marriage ends in tatters. Despite its underlying comedy, the tone of the story is sombre.

Many of Thurber's best stories, especially from the 1930's centre around failing marriages and aggressively sparring couples, their antagonism often exacerbated by alcohol, but there is a range of other themes as well. "The Black Magic of Barney Haller" (1932) is a very funny story that rests around the atrocious pronunciation of the narrator's hired man, Barney Haller. Its most attractive feature is Thurber's obvious delight in language and especially invented words and the suggestions they can convey. "The Figgerin' of Aunt Wilma" (1950) is different from most of Thurber's work in its loving conjuring up of an Ohio town in 1905. "The Man Who Hated Moonbaum" (1940) is Thurber's only Hollywood story, but his versatile talents extend even to the apocalyptic satire of "The Greatest Man in the World" (1931), which ends with the president of the United States silently ordering the assassination of an aviator who proves inappropriate as a hero, and "You Could Look It Up" (1941), a grotesque story about a baseball-playing dwarf. There is also the melancholy of "One Is a Wanderer" (1935) and the posthumously published "The Other Room," fine stories in which the usual humour is largely absent. There are also several stories about writing figures, such as "Something to Say" (1932), which read like comic or parodic versions of stories by Henry James on the same themes. Thurber is a subtle, dispassionate observer of American (mostly middle-class, urban) mores. In this and in his use of a style at once comic and sadly ironic, the writer he most anticipates is John Cheever.

—Laurie Clancy

See the essay on "The Secret Life of Walter Mitty."

———

TOLSTAIA, Tatiana (Nikitinichna). Russian; great-grand-niece of Lev Tolstoi, *q.v.*; granddaughter of Aleksandr Nikolaevich Tolstoi. Born in Leningrad, 3 May 1951. Educated at Leningrad State University, 1968–74, degree in philology 1974. Married Andrei Lebedev in 1974; two sons. Junior editor, Eastern literature division, Nauka publishing house, Moscow, 1974-83; writer-in-residence, University of Richmond, Virginia, 1988, and Texas Tech University, Lubbock, 1990; senior lecturer in Russian literature, University of Texas, Austin, 1989. Lives in Moscow.

PUBLICATIONS

Short Stories

Na zolotom kryl'tse sideli.   1987; as *On the Golden Porch and Other Stories,* 1989.
Sleepwalker in a Fog.   1992.

*

Critical Study: "Tolstaia's 'Dome of Many-Colored Glass': The World Refracted Through Multiple Perspectives" by Helena Goscilo, in *Slavic Review* 47(2), 1988.

* * *

Tatiana Tolstaia's short stories first appeared in print in the late 1980's when Mikhail Gorbachov's *glasnost* was already in full swing. Tolstaia's world is the Soviet-Russian metropolis (mainly the former Leningrad) and the surrounding summer resorts. Her time is the 1970's and early 1980's, but the past informs the consciousness of many stories. The overwhelming majority of the writer's oeuvre is her shorter fiction: its strong personal stamp—both

structural and thematic—differs from all published literature of the Soviet period since the 1930's. Tolstaia's stories never treat politically sensitive issues and yet their publication under the stern reign of Soviet-style "socialist realism" would have been all but inconceivable. Her characters are ostentatiously non-heroic, average people depicted in a private world of domestic life; often they are children and old people or men and women captured in a world of dreams and fantasies. Tolstaia is uninterested in the collectivized atmosphere of the workplace, the school, and other social institutions. Her characters live their unmistakable and utterly non-idealized Soviet lives, surrounded by communal flats and drab, exhausting, and embittering daily routines. They dream about the good life, suffused with the crudest images of Western commercialism, vague memories of prerevolutionary Russia and the distant and unavailable outside world in which East Germany, Syria, and Australia unite in their "exoticism."

Tolstaia's short stories offer intimate glimpses into banal lives, but her rare ability to create aesthetic experiences out of the flotsam and jetsam of triviality reminds readers that the significance of life for most of us lies in little details rather than in much-publicised drama. It appears, from the intensity and lyricism of these accounts, that Tolstaia's childhood stories ("Loves Me, Loves Me Not," "On the Golden Porch," "Most Beloved") draw on personal experiences. However, her stories about adults, her almost grotesque portraits of lower-middle-class *poshlost* (mostly embodied in women, such as Vera Vasilevna in the "Okkervil River" and Zoya in "Hunting the Wooly Mammoth") seem to be far removed from the privileged circles of Tolstaia's own family: this world of the favoured intellectual elite does not inform her fiction.

Each of Tolstaia's quintessentially Soviet-Russian stories captures universal human experiences. Sexuality lurks as a motivating force behind the action of many stories: her main interest lies in such areas as coming to terms with unresolvable contradictions between dreams and reality, health and illness, and with rejection. In "Fire and Dust" Rimma's hopes of occupying both rooms of their two-room flat and of living a life of some interest, turn out to be more unreal than the crazy Pipka's accounts of fantastic adventures. The flat remains communal, and instead of exoticism, all she gets is an out-of-style and overpriced blouse from a profiteer who is distinguished by having been to Syria.

Loneliness and old age contrast with memories of the past: Zhenechka in "Most Beloved" and the protagonist of "Sweet Shura" appear important and interesting in their own tales, whose audience is largely restricted to themselves. Upon their death all that is left of them is heaps of their treasured rubbish and old dwellings, which nobody wants to protect in loving memory. In "Hunting the Wooly Mammoth" Zoya, one of Tolstaia's females with no redeeming features, wants to hook a husband who can deliver her the lower-middle-class dream lifestyle of chic long cigarettes, East German dressing gowns, and Yugoslav lamps. In what is, no doubt, one of Tolstaia's wittiest parodies, we see Zoya picturing to herself a proposed visit to her boyfriend's artist friend and then her own aggrandized image and the dream artist completely debunked when the meeting takes place in a tawdry studio. The artwork is completely incomprehensible to Zoya and so is the conversation.

An abandoned child and an orphaned child, respectively, are the main characters in "Peters" and "The Moon Came Out." Meaningful vignettes summarize lives in a nutshell. Raised by oppressive grandmothers, Peters and Natasha were denied the chance of befriending people of their own age group; instead of a happy childhood, they received inhibitions powerful enough to prevent them from ever feeling comfortable. As their dreams of love remain unrealized and their disastrous relationships pass, they wake up to find that the best part of their lives is over and nothing good has ever happened to them. A life of rejection is, perhaps, best suggested in the epiphany in "Most Beloved": the man whom Zhenechka loved never noticed her. She never forgot his most meaningful words to her: "Good tea, Evgeniia Ivanovna. It's hot."

Of all of Tolstaia's stories, the most universal ones seem to deal with ill people surrounded by the healthy. In "Night," a mentally retarded man lives in complete dependence on his 80-year-old mother in a communal flat. Incapable of understanding the world around him as other people see it, or his own mature sexuality, Alexei Petrovich, endowed with the mind of a four-year-old, confronts the bestiality of modern society. In "Heavenly Flame" Korobeinikov was operated on supposedly for an ulcer, but we know and he guesses that the flaming pain inside his body signifies his approaching death from cancer. He forgets about the pain when he visits Olga Mikhailovna and her husband at their dacha. They find him and his stories highly amusing and this sense of approval keeps the ill man's spirits up. But a pseudo-artiste, Dmitrii Ilych, turns up and resents that he does not receive all the attention. He lies about the past of Korobeinikov, a man whom he has never before encountered. As a result, the dying man and his stories grow unwelcome. The vulgar hostess now deems his illness to be the "heavenly flame" meted out as his punishment: her discourse and behaviour provide one of the most eloquent examples of *poshlost* in modern Russian literature.

Perhaps the most intriguing feature of Tolstaia's stories is their style. No writer in Russia since the 1920's has come close to her in creating such a richly multi-voiced text. Her sentences do not attempt to "reflect" a narrowly-defined lacklustre reality, but, allude and imply through their use of abundant metaphors ("love—a homely, barefoot orphan," from "Most Beloved"), synecdoches, and images pasted together by the logic of dreams. In fragmented sentences she leads her reader—saturated by propagandistic or ineffective Soviet literature—towards hackneyed conclusions that never materialize. Instead, she produces *ostranenie* by her carnivalesque denial of the insincere official literary consciousness, the only consciousness allowed under the dictates of socialist realism. She consistently shuns institutionalised literary kitsch with its ready-made solutions and trite closures.

Her pastiche is unmatched by any contemporary Russian writer: she juxtaposes such diverse styles as that of children, semi-educated people, and the voices of the street (completely ignored, incidentally, by Soviet official literature). Certainly, her stylistic parodies of pretentious discourse, such as the poems by Maryvanna's "Uncle" in "Loves Me, Loves Me Not," are probably some of the finest in Russian literature. Tolstaia's narrative technique pluralizes the test still further. Third-person narrators imitate the characters talking to a particular audience, as in "Heavenly Flame," where the narrator's irony merges with the banal Olga Mikhailovna's attempt to impress her lover: "She loves truth, what can you do, that's how she is." Frequently, several consciousnesses are at work in the narrator's voice: the child's impressions merge with the omniscient adult narrator's viewpoint in "On the Golden Porch." In "Night" the narrator's perspective incorporates the retarded man's childlike viewpoint with that of an adult outsider: as a result, our conventional, dulled perception of reality is challenged into recognizing the abnormality of the normal.

The author of some 30 stories, Tolstaia has earned herself the kind of recognition Russians give only to great writers. Her fiction does not imitate any of her literary predecessors, but it is clearly founded in the best traditions of Russian prose. Indeed, she has marked her territory by developing an idiom recognizably her own: in her anthropomorphic universe people are not judged, but are allowed to have their little pretences and innocent or harmful lies as they go about their lives fraught with hardships and failures. Tolstaia's creatures, even the mice ready to move into a dilapidated house, or the cat fed up with all the meat she is given, talk, explain, implore, and fend for themselves; it is a world where the ugly and the petty are made radiant in the kaleidoscope of language.

—Peter I. Barta

TOLSTOI, Lev (Count Lev Nikolaevich Tolstoi). Russian. Born at Iasnaia Poliana, near Tula, 28 August 1828. Educated at home, in Moscow, 1837–41, and in Kazan, 1841–44; Kazan University, 1844–47. Married Sofiia Andreevna Bers in 1862; 13 children; also one son from another relationship. Landowner on his inherited estate, 1847–48; in Moscow, 1848–51; visited his brother's military unit in Caucasus, and joined artillery battery as noncommissioned officer, 1851–54, then transferred to a unit near Bucharest, 1854, and, as sub-lieutenant, in Sevastopol, 1854–55: resigned as lieutenant, 1855; after some travel, a serious landowner: set up school, and edited the school journal *Iasnaia Poliana*, 1862–63 (and member of local educational committee, 1870's); social and religious views widely disseminated in last decades of his life, and religious views excluded him from church, 1901; because of censorship, many works first published abroad. *Died 7 November 1910.*

PUBLICATIONS

Collections

Polnoe sobranie sochinenii.   90 vols., 1928–58.
Centenary Edition (in English).   21 vols., 1929–37.
I Cannot Be Silent: Selections from Tolstoy's Non-Fiction, edited by W. Gareth Jones.   1989.
Tolstoy's Short Fiction, edited by Michael R. Katz.   1991.

Short Stories

Sevastopolskie rasskazy.   1855–56; as *Sebastopol,* 1887; as *The Sebastopol Sketches,* edited by David McDuff, 1986.
Kreitserova sonata.   1891; as *The Kreutzer Sonata,* 1890.
Khoziain i rabotnik (novella).   1895; as *Master and Man,* 1895.
The Death of Ivan Ilyich, edited by Michael Beresford. 1962.
The Kreutzer Sonata and Other Stories, edited by David McDuff.   1985.

Novels

Semeinoe schast'e.   1859; as *Katia*, 1887; as *Family Happiness*, 1888; as *My Husband and I*, 1888; as *The Romance of Marriage*, 1890.
Kazaki.   1863; as *The Cossacks*, 1878.
Voina i mir.   1863–69; as *War and Peace*, 1886.
Anna Karenina.   1875–77; translated as *Anna Karenina*, 1886.
Voskresenie.   1899; as *Resurrection*, 1899.

Plays

Vlast' t'my (produced 1888).   1887; as *The Dominion of Darkness*, 1888.
Plody prosveshcheniia (produced 1889).   1889; as *The Fruits of Enlightenment*, 1891.

Other

Detstvo, Otrochestvo, Iunost'.   3 vols., 1852–57; as *Childhood, Boyhood, Youth*, 1886.
Azbuka [An ABC Book].   1872; revised edition, 1875; as *The Lion and the Puppy and Other Stories* (for children), 1986..
Ispoved'.   1884; as *A Confession*, 1885; as *Confession*, 1983.
V chom moia vera?   1884; as *My Religion*, 1885; as *What I Believe*, 1885.
Tak chto zhe nam delat'?   1902; as *What to Do*, 1887; uncensored edition, 1888.
The Long Exile and Other Stories for Children.   1888.
O zhizni.   1888; uncensored edition, 1891; as *Life*, 1888; as *On Life*, 1902.
Gospel Stories.   1890.
Kritika dogmaticheskogo bogosloviia.   1891; as *God Sees the Truth But Waits*, 1986.
Soedinenie i perevod chetyrekh evangelii.   3 vols., 1892–94; as *The Four Gospels Harmonized and Translated*, 1895–96; shortened version, 1890; as *The Gospel in Brief*, 1896; as *The Gospel According to Tolstoy*, edited by David Patterson, 1992.
Tsarstvo Bozhe vnutri vas.   2 vols., 1893–94; as *The Kingdom of God Is Within You*, 2 vols., 1894.
Pis'ma o Genre Dzhorzhe [Letters on Henry George]. 1897.
Kristianskoe uchenie.   1898; as *The Christian Teaching*, 1898.
Chto takoe iskusstvo?   1898; as *What Is Art?*, 1898.
Rabstvo nashego vremeni.   1900; as *The Slavery of Our Times*, 1900.
Letters, edited by R.F. Christian.   2 vols., 1978.
Diaries, edited by R.F. Chrstian.   2 vols., 1986.
Mahatma Gandhi and Tolstoy Letters, edited by B. Srinivasa Murthy.   1987.
Writings on Civil Disobedience and Nonviolence (essays). 1987.
Tolstoi for Children: Stories, Fables, Tales, Epics, edited by Anne Zwerin.   1987.
The Lion and the Honeycomb: The Religious Writings, edited by A.N. Wilson.   1987.

*

Bibliography: "Tolstoy Studies in Great Britain: A Bibliographical Survey" by Garth M. Terry, in *New Essays on Tolstoy* by Malcolm Jones, 1978.

Critical Studies: *Tolstoy: His Life and Works* by John C. Kenworthy, 1902; *The Life of Tolstoy* by Aylmer Maude, 2 vols., 1910; *Tolstoy*, 1946, *Introduction to Tolstoy's Writings*, 1968, and *Tolstoy*, 1973, all by Ernest H. Simmons; *The Hedgehog and the Fox: An Essay on Tolstoy's View of History* by Isaiah Berlin, 1953; *Tolstoy or Dostoevsky* by George Steiner, 1959; *Tolstoy's "War and Peace,"* 1962, and *Tolstoy: A Critical Introduction*, 1969, both by R.F. Christian; *Tolstoy* by Henri Troyat, 1965, translated by Nancy Amphoux, 1967; *Tolstoy and the Novel* by John Bayley, 1966; *Tolstoy: A Collection of Critical Essays* edited by R.E. Matlaw, 1967; *Tolstoy: A Critical Anthology* edited by Henry Gifford, 1971, and *Tolstoy* by Gifford, 1982; *Tolstoy and Chekhov* by Logan Spiers, 1971; *Tolstoy: The Making of a Novelist* by Edward Crankshaw, 1974; *Tolstoy: The Comprehensive Vision* by E.B. Greenwood, 1975; *Tolstoy* by T.G.S. Cain, 1977; *Tolstoy's Major Fiction* by Edward Wasiolek, 1978; *New Essays on Tolstoy* by Malcolm Jones, 1978; *Tolstoy: Resident and Stranger* by Richard F. Gustafson, 1986; *Lev and Sonya: The Story of the Tolstoy Marriage* by Louise Smoluchowski, 1987; *Tolstoy* by A.N. Wilson, 1988.

*   *   *

Lev Tolstoi's collected works fill 90 volumes in the standard Russian edition. Considered one of Russian literature's finest stylists and a master of psychological analysis and physical description, Tolstoi also possessed great moral vision. Not content with describing the wide sweep of Russian life, he burrowed beneath the surface to find out why we act the way we do, how we should be acting, and how we should face the fact of death. He tackled the problems of religion, war, relations between the sexes, and social injustice with fierce intelligence, compassion, and biting wit. His best effects are achieved through his habit of writing in small scenes, making his points through showing rather than telling. He usually strives to present the various aspects of an issue, rather than didactically presenting only one point of view.

In his long career, Tolstoi wrote three novels, *Voina i mir* (War and Peace), *Anna Karenina*, and *Voskresenie* (Resurrection), and several long pieces that are often considered novels, such as the trilogy *Detstvo, Otrochestvo, Iunost'*, (Childhood, Boyhood, Youth), "Hadji Murad," and *Kazaki* (The Cossacks). Among his short works, "The Death of Ivan Ilyich," written in the 1880's, is the best-known. The stories of the 1850's already contain many of the themes that point the way to the great novels of the following two decades. From the very beginning, Tolstoi's stories are marked by careful style and word choice, clever construction, and descriptions using a few vivid and telling details. He is exceptionally good at creating characters of various types, and at differentiating their speech by social class and personality. Drawing on his own experience and sparing himself nothing, he bares his—and our—inmost thoughts, often disjointed, inappropriate, and contradictory. He is able to capture on paper long streams of thought, showing how the important is mixed up with the inconsequential, the noble with the trivial. Always, he seeks for meaning.

Particularly successful among the early stories are the three Sebastopol tales, "Sebastopol in December," "Sebastopol in May," and "Sebastopol in August." The first story is addressed directly to "you," and is set in Sebastopol during the Crimean War, so that we experience as closely as possible the sights, sounds, and emotions in that place during the siege. We visit the living, the wounded, and the dying, and experience the mingled pride, pleasure, and fear of those times. In the second story, an extraordinary passage sets down the thoughts of a soldier as he is wounded and dies. In this story, Tolstoi describes the horror of war and the bloodshed, and questions why Christians don't fall down repentant at what they have done. The third story describes the feeling of shame, anger, and despair at the fall of Sebastopol. Taken together, these stories are a powerful indictment of war.

In "Sebastopol in May" Tolstoi uses contrast, one of his favorite devices, to show the difference in attitude between an eager, reckless new soldier and cautious, more experienced soldier. In another early story, "Albert," Tolstoi uses contrast to explore the power of art (in this case, music) and the nature of genius. Tolstoi compares the weak-willed but talented artist with the pedestrian gentleman who wants to save him, to show that genius is not necessarily accompanied by high morals or by a strong personality. In "Two Hussars" the impetuous, passionate, loose-living father is seen to advantage compared to his cold son who wins money from his hostess at cards and pursues her daughter. In "Three Deaths" Tolstoi contrasts the death of a querulous rich woman with the death of a peasant, whose passing causes much less fuss. The death of a tree cut down for a grave marker, described in a stunningly beautiful passage, is the most natural and least disruptive death of all.

Even as Tolstoi delineates the differences in people, he also is interested in the idea of the oneness of humanity. He explores what cuts people off from others, and what draws them together. In "Snowstorm," one of Tolstoi's most beautiful and subtle stories, a character lost in a snowstorm is led on a journey to self-knowledge by his contacts with others and by his dreams. He learns that to submit to what we fear (death) brings release from that fear, and also learns that all humans are one.

No one is a stranger to Tolstoi, not the rich, nor peasant, nor soldier; not even animals. In "Polikushka," which details the effects forced army service has on peasant families, he features a peasant who hangs himself after accidentally losing money he was entrusted with. In "Family Happiness," a study of how married people can grow apart and of how the nature of love changes in a marriage, Tolstoi probes the woman's viewpoint. In "Strider" Tolstoi writes most of the story from the horse's viewpoint.

Among Tolstoi's later works are some didactic stories like "God Sees the Truth but Waits," which describes how a prisoner is moved to confess to an old crime and ask forgiveness of the man who was unjustly convicted for it. Another example is "How Much Land Does a Man Need?" We learn that he needs only six feet when he falls dead after greedily racing around a huge area to claim ownership.

In the period after *Anna Karenina,* the themes of death and sex dominate several of the best-known stories. *Khoziain i rabotnik, Master and Man* returns to the theme of death and the oneness of all humans. The master, lost in a snowstorm, lies down on his servant's body to keep him warm and alive. Though the master dies, he lives on because his servant survives. "The Devil," a study of the destructive force of passion, tells how a married man kills himself when he is unable to handle his attraction to a former mistress. In "Father Sergius," the character keeps his feelings under control by cutting off his finger. "Kreutzer Sonata," the most famous of these stories of passion, examines the whole concept of physical love and marriage, and poses the idea that both men and women would be better off without sex. In the story, the jealous husband kills his wife, and only then remorsefully can see her as a fellow human.

Tolstoi examines the fundamental problems facing us as humans: how are we to live, how are we to face death, how are we to handle war and sex. His profound understanding of our myriad emotions and quirks, his joy in the beauty of the physical world, and the gracefulness of his prose, all combine to create some of the best stories in world literature.

—Sydney Schultze

See the essay on "The Death of Ivan Ilyich."

TOOMER, Jean (Nathan Eugene Toomer). American. Born in Washington, D.C., 26 December 1894. Educated at high schools in Brooklyn, New York, and Washington, D.C.; University of Wisconsin, Madison, 1914; Massachusetts College of Agriculture; American College of Physical Training, Chicago, 1916; New York University, Summer 1917; City College, New York, 1917. Married 1) Margery Latimer in 1931 (died 1932), one daughter; 2) Marjorie Content in 1934. Taught physical education in a school near Milwaukee, 1918; clerk, Acker Merrall and Conduit grocery company, New York, 1918; shipyard worker, New York; worked at Howard Theatre, Washington, D.C., 1920; studied at Gurdjieff's Institute in Fontainebleau, France, 1924, 1926: led Gurdjieff groups in Harlem, 1925, and Chicago, 1926–33; lived in Pennsylvania after 1934. *Died 30 March 1967.*

PUBLICATIONS

Collections

The Wayward and the Seeking: A Collection of Writings by Toomer, edited by Darwin T. Turner.   1980.
Collected Poems, edited by Robert B. Jones and Margery Toomer Latimer.   1988.

Fiction

Cane (includes stories and verse).   1923; edited by Darwin T. Turner, 1988.

Play

Balo, in *Plays of Negro Life,* edited by Alain Locke and Montgomery Gregory.   1927.

Other

Essentials (aphorisms).   1931.
An Interpretation of Friends Worship.   1947.
The Flavor of Man.   1949.

*

Bibliography: "Toomer: An Annotated Checklist of Criticism" by John M. Reilly, in *Resources for American Literary Study,* Spring 1974.

Critical Studies: *In a Minor Chord* (on Toomer, Cullen, and Hurston) by Darwin T. Turner, 1971; *The Merrill Studies in Cane* edited by Frank Durham, 1971; *The Grotesque in American Negro Fiction: Toomer, Wright, and Ellison* by Fritz Gysin, 1975; *Toomer* by Brian Joseph Benson and Mabel Mayle Dillard, 1980; *Toomer, Artist: A Study of His Literary Life and Work 1894–1936* by Nellie Y. McKay, 1984; *The Lives of Toomer: A Hunger for Wholeness* by Cynthia Earl Kerman and Richard Eldridge, 1987; *Toomer's Years with Gurdjieff: Portrait of an Artist 1923–1936* by Rudolph P. Byrd, 1990.

*   *   *

After Jean Toomer wrote *Cane,* he went on to write a number of plays, essays, poems, and short stories, many of them never published. One of the leading voices to be associated with the Harlem Renaissance, Jean Toomer was born in Washington, D.C., December 26, 1894. His grandfather, P.B.S. Pinchback, a leading political figure in Louisiana during Reconstruction, was said to have African blood in his ancestry, setting up a racial ambivalence in Toomer which he attempted to resolve throughout his life. Toomer often lived in white communities, though his brilliance as a writer emerged when he became steeped in his black heritage. The pressures of a segregated America finally overwhelmed him, until he refused in later life to believe that his heritage included any African blood. He held a number of different jobs, including that of car salesman and physical education director, and he worked for a time in a business firm and settlement house.

In 1921 Toomer accepted a temporary teaching post in rural Georgia. Travelling through the South he became absorbed in the life of blacks, experiencing a personal regeneration that amounted to a spiritual awakening. As a result of his experiences in Georgia, he began writing *Cane* on his journey back up North.

Cane stands as a classic of American experimental fiction, anticipating such later writers and experimenters in form as William Faulkner, Donald Barthelme, and Joan Didion. *Cane* has been read both as an extended poem-novel, as well as a series of separate short stories, poems, and a dramatic piece. Toomer himself referred to an integral design throughout which allowed *Cane* to be read as a cohesive whole.

Cane is a prose-poetic vision of the black people's quest for integrity within a world fragmented by "corkscrew words," by hostile restrictions and cruel contradictions. The reader of *Cane* encounters a series of narratives circumscribed by fierce passion and debilitating prejudice. Personal histories circle against a natural backdrop of wilderness, canefields, and the changing light of the sun. The dusky colors of the setting sun intensify the poignancy of individual experience as they peak, then become extinguished, casting geographic space and lingering time in lineaments of mysticism and sensuality.

The first section of *Cane* deals primarily with women in the South and their response to a world divided by prejudice. These historical narratives contained by the parameters of individual female personalities at the same time blend into and become part of nature in a lyrical commingling and spirituality. There is the exotic Fern who

longs for fulfillment but is not satisfied by the men she attaches to herself by her insatiability. Fern becomes immobilized by her suffering, by words that issue forth from her in strange, broken sounds. Esther, too, finds her reality diminished. Esther begins to dream when her love for King Barlo is disrupted, and her passion becomes converted into flames that light the notion shop, the fire department rescuing a child she claims as her own. Condemned by society for being born white to a wealthy black father and white mother, she becomes like a dead person, unable to live life.

But it is the rebellious Karintha, her beauty causing men to be overwhelmed by her perfection, whose story resonates throughout *Cane.* The men who know her seek to violate Karintha before she is fully grown, to possess that perfection until she reacts by becoming a prostitute who burns her unwanted child in the sawmill pile in the woods. Smoke rises up from the sawdust pile to remind the town of its sins, of the materialism and carelessness of the masculine sensibility that has violated and destroyed Karintha.

Toomer, disturbed by the dying out of the tradition of folk songs in the South, makes Karintha's pain emblematic of the tragedy of other black souls, and yet linguistically gestures toward comfort and solace in a world that makes spiritual transcendence difficult, yet desired: "Smoke is on the hills. . . . O rise/And take my soul to Jesus." Throughout *Cane,* the human plight of the women trapped by external forces is attested to and witnessed by the negro spiritual.

The second section of *Cane* opens on "Seventh Street"—"a bastard of Prohibition and the war. A crude-boned, soft-skinned wedge of nigger life breathing its loafer air, jazz songs and love, thrusting unconscious rhythms, black reddish blood into the white and whitewashed wood of Washington." Here a black masculine sensibility is affirmed against the sterility of materialism and industrialism that empties the soul out into a blankness, a white nothingness that is a reminder of the void the individual is cast into by prejudice.

In section three of *Cane*'s "Kabnis," Lewis is a visionary who discerns promise in the character of Kabnis. Kabnis is a Christ image gone wrong, being "suspended," crucifixion-like, above the soil that would renew him. He is a confused, "completely artificial man" who, coming from the North, struggles but cannot respond to the possibility for regenerative vision held by the beauty of his heritage. Rather Lewis, as the man who has been most in touch with his black heritage, appears as the messiah to Carrie Kate: "The sun-burst from her eyes floods up and haloes him. Christ-eyes, his eyes look to her."

Yet within *Cane,* there is no possibility for redemption from the sins of slavery and segregation as the narratives spin and circle against each other throughout, clashing and resonating. There is finally no possibility for the violence of human experience to be healed by the appearance of a different savior within *Cane,* one who wields the power of a new language and artistic face. The sounds of suffering are too great, the words of the spiritual bend before the weight of human pain, and though religion offers comfort, the fragmented conditions of society can bring only hope for a future healing.

Cane ends with Carrie Kate invoking the coming of the savior as she whispers, "Jesus, come." United with her past in the personality of Father John she is viewed through the "soft circle" of a halo, becoming the last potential madonna figure of a series of thwarted black women in *Cane.* Outside, nature shares in Carrie Kate's longing as her hope is shaped by words into the linguistic creation of a "child" in the sun (son) that will regenerate the world: "The sun arises. Gold-glowing child, it steps into the sky and sends a birth-song slanting down gray dust streets and sleepy windows of the southern town."

Toomer sought throughout his life for an integrity to his personal experience, embracing at one point socialism, at another the teachings of Gurdjieff. But in his greatest fictional achievement, *Cane,* he came closest to realizing the profundity of human experience as it was cast within societal blindnesses and the obliteration of space and time.

—Olga Pelensky

———

TORGA, Miguel. Pseudonym for Adolfo Correia da Rocha. Portuguese. Born in São Martinho da Anta, 12 August 1907. Educated at schools in São Martinho da Anta, and in Brazil, 1913–16, 1924–25; University of Coimbra, graduated as doctor 1933. Practicing physician: in São Martinho da Anta, Vila Nova de Miranda do Corvo, Leiria, and since 1940, in Coimbra. Recipient: International grand prize for poetry (Belgium), 1976; Montaigne prize; Morgado de Mateus prize; Almeida Garrett prize; *Diário de Notícias* prize; Camões prize, 1989; Association of Portuguese Writers Vide Literária prize, 1992; Prémio do Correspondentes Estrangeiros, 1992. International Miguel Torga prize named for him. Lives in Coimbra.

PUBLICATIONS

Short Stories

Pão ázimo.   1931.
Bichos.   1940; revised edition, 1970; as *Farrusco the Blackbird and Other Stories,* 1950.
Montanha: contos.   1941; enlarged edition, as *Contos da montanha,* 1955, 1969, 1976, 1982.
Rua: contos.   1942; revised edition, 1967.
Novos contos da montanha.   1944; enlarged edition, 1952, 1959, 1967, 1975, 1977, 1978, 1979, 1980, 1981, 1982, 1984.
Pedras lavadas.   1951; revised edition, 1958.
Tales from the Mountain (selection).   1991.

Novels

A criação do mundo: os dois primeiros dias.   1937; revised edition, 1948, 1969, 1981.
O terceiro dia da Criação do mundo.   1938; revised edition, 1952, 1970.
O quarto dia da Criação do mundo.   1939; revised edition, 1971.
O senhor Ventura.   1943; revised edition, 1985.
Vindima.   1945; revised edition, 1965, 1971.
O quinto dia da Criação do mundo.   1974.
O sexto dia da Criação do mundo.   1981.

Plays

Teatro: Terra firme, Mar.   1941; revised edition of *Mar,* 1977, 1983.
Terra firme (produced 1947).   Included in *Teatro,* 1941; revised edition, 1977.

Sinfonia.   1947.
O Paraíso.   1949.

Verse

Ansiedade (as Adolfo Correia da Rocha).   1928.
Rampa.   1930.
Tributo.   1931.
Abismo.   1932.
O outro livro de Job.   1936.
Lamentação.   1943.
Libertação.   1944.
Odes.   1946; revised edition, 1951, 1956, 1977.
Nihil Sibi.   1948.
Cântico do homen.   1950.
Alguns poemas ibéricos.   1952.
Penas do Purgatório.   1954.
Orfeu rebelde.   1958; revised edition, 1970.
Câmara ardente.   1962.
Poemas ibéricos.   1965.
Antologia poética. 1981; revised edition, 1985.
Torga (selection).   1988.

Other

A terceira voz.   1934.
Diário 1–15.   1941–90.
Portugal.   1950; revised edition, 1967.
Traço de união.   1955; revised edition, 1969.
Fogo preso.   1976.
Lavrador de palavras e ideias.   1978.
Trás-os-Montes, illustrated by Georges Dussaud.   1984.
Camões.   1987.

*

Critical Studies: *Humanist Despair in Torga* by Eduardo Lourenço, 1955; "Torga: A New Portuguese Poet," in *Dublin Review* 229, 1955, and "The Art and Poetry of Torga," in *Sillages* 2, 1973, both by Denis Brass; "The Portuguese Revolution Seen Through the Eyes of Three Contemporary Writers" by Alice Clemente, in *Proceedings of the Fourth National Portuguese Conference,* 1979; "Madwomen, Whores and Torga: Desecrating the Canon?" by Maria Manuel Lisboa, in *Portuguese Studies* 7, 1991.

*   *   *

Miguel Torga is well known for the quality of his work in both poetry and short stories. Many of his best stories have been translated by Ivana Carlsen in *Tales from the Mountain,* which offers a representative selection of his narrative technique and choice of subject. In his stories, Torga achieves a harmonious match between form and content. Indeed, because of the brevity of these tales, the reader might almost overlook the care with which they have been crafted. Torga exploits the stylistic possibilities of the short story to great effect, making the fullest possible use of its potential for concentration, intensity, and unity of impression. In the majority of his tales, the narrator selects and freezes a particular moment in time, either revealing a way of life ("Mariana," "Fronteira"), or illustrating an outstanding quality in his characters, such as the personal courage of a man who goes hunting in the belief that he will be killed in a hunting accident ("The Hunt"), or that of

Gonçalo fighting off the wolf in "Young May." The short story permits the writer to pinpoint a key moment, such as the loss of childhood innocence and illusion ("Sesame," "The Gift") or the unmasking of a deep-seated jealousy.

An enormous range and diversity of characters is depicted in *Tales from the Mountain*. Torga chooses as his protagonists the men, women, and children of Trás-os-Montes. His stories never focus on the experiences of a character in isolation: they are always shown in their wider relationship to the community to which they belong, even when they have been ostracized or rejected ("The Leper," "Peace of Mind"). Sometimes two or three characters are given prominence (the unhappy lovers in "Destinies"), and sometimes he opts for a collective protagonist (the villagers in "The Leper"). His stories have in common the same setting, the remote, backward, inward-looking northern region of Trás-os-Montes. This does not impose any limitations on his creativity or artistry. Setting is as important an actor in these tales as any of his characters, conditioning the way the villagers and peasants live and die. The clear delineation of a geographical, physical, and social space also allows the author to explore in depth the issues and themes that arise within that space. Torga focuses on a microcosm and reaches conclusions about human behaviours and experiences, characteristics and emotions, that far transcend the local and regional, having a universal applicability.

He is particularly concerned with the social structures, customs, moral values and laws (written and unwritten) that bond and bind the families, communities, and villages of the north. However, it would be simplistic to see a merely deterministic relationship between the harsh environment, oppressive socio-political structures and the behaviour of Torga's protagonists and antagonists. Rather, he demonstrates how many qualities that might be perceived as negative are undoubtedly those qualities that have enabled his northern peasants to survive the deprivation and isolation of their far-flung communities. Among those things that he conveys with piercing clarity are his love of the land, his sense of belonging to the mountains and valleys, the joy that men experience in going hunting and feeling at one with nature ("Mariana," "The Hunt," "The Hunter'," "The Shepherd Gabriel").

Torga's writing is characterized by great integrity. Notwithstanding his great love for the inhabitants and the landscape of Trás-os-Montes, he does not flinch from showing the darker, more bestial side of his people, writing about them without illusions. Never an actor in his own narratives, his is a discreet presence. He looks into the community with the privileged insight of one who knows it extremely well, and is able to produce a third-person, omniscient narrative that selects key moments and incidents for our attention, but without uttering explicit moral judgments or criticism of his people.

Not a few of his characters are driven by violence, among them Lopo in "Lopo," both Grande and Issac in "Alma Grande," Lomba in "Peace of Mind," the Gomes woman in "Witchcraft," and the villagers in "The Leper," who are more than a little reminiscent of the villagers in Bernardo Santareno's *O Crime de Aldeia Velha*. And yet, for every negative element, there is a reverse, a positive. Although Torga shows people driven by hatred and the desire for revenge, these are balanced against other, more positive elements. If the villagers in "The Leper" are capable of violence and inhumanity, those in "Sesame" have a sense of community that sustains them throughout the harsh months of winter in the mountains. Or there is the figure of the mother, for instance, strong, nurturing, protective of

her young, like Mariana in the story of the same name. Felisberta, in "Renewal," shows strength and the determination to save her only surviving child, Pedro, after an influenza epidemic has killed her husband, daughters, and grandchildren. Teodosia weeps for her inarticulate son who cannot bring himself to declare his love for Natalia, and so loses her.

It is not difficult to understand why Torga's writing did not find favour with the censors, or, indeed, why he should have been arrested and imprisoned in the Salazar's period in Portugal. The picture he presents of Portugal is too stark, too brutal, in many ways akin to the universe of Santareno, whose plays also were subject to censorship. Here is no idealized vision of a happy people, working the land and finding contentment. His vignettes of country life have little of the idyllic. Instead, he tends to depict the lawless and the outlawed, characters who more often than not are seen to challenge or "get round" the law, like the village of smugglers in "Fronteira." No reader could forget Torga's description of the police and their brutal treatment of the innocent suspects in "The Confession." The idea of imprisonment is present in several of Torga's stories, the physical gaol to which people may be condemned unjustly, or the figurative space where people's spirits are held captive, the prison of oppression, fear, loneliness, or guilt. At the same time, the forces of law and order are often reluctant to intervene when they should protect the people ("Peace of Mind"). As Torga wrote in the preface to the second edition of *Novos contos da montanha*, September 1945, "social hardships have been added to the natural adversities, and the law walks hand in hand with the south wind to dry up the eyes and the springs."

Torga's characters refuse to conform to the conventional morality of the day, particular the prevailing sexual mores. In fact, he seems to exhibit greater warmth and sympathy for his fecund earth-mother Mariana than the virginal, puritanical Marília of "Mariana." Nor is there any criticism, explicit or implicit, of the unmarried mother Matilde in "Revelation," or the healthy young protagonist of "The Shepherd Gabriel," who trains his flock to graze in other people's fields, and who services a young girl—a "creature in heat"—in the same way that his ram would mate with a ewe. The hunter Tafona ("The Hunter") holds the village gossip at gunpoint to allow a young couple to make love, uninterrupted, in the field. Likewise, there are the wily, picaresque figures of Gimpy ("Gimpy"), Faustino ("The Theft"), and Garrrinchas ("Christmas"). Humour it must be said, is an important element of Torga's narrative; in "The Hunt" even the antagonists' dogs growl at one another. Like the other principal institutions of society, the Church, responsible for education and pastoral care, is also found wanting, frequently failing to offer succour and comfort to its flock (as witnessed by the demoralizing effect achieved by tolling the church bells in "Renewal"; or the lonely old age and even lonelier death imposed on Felisberto in "The Sacristan's Position"). It is clear that the Church has done little or nothing to eradicate superstitions and beliefs that have not altered since the Middle Ages ("Witchcraft"). Only on rare occasions does he show the potential of the Church to help and heal the people, as in "The Lord," when the priest intervenes to save Filomena and deliver her baby.

The Portuguese title of an early collection of short stories, *Bichos*, is very suggestive. *Bicho* has several possible meanings: "Any kind of animal," "worm," "grub," "vermin," "insect," "ugly person," "ugly customer." Of the 14 stories, four have as their protagonist a human being, and each of these is in some way abnormal: Ramiro the shepherd does not speak or communicate with other human beings. Magdalen is an unnatural mother, Nicholas the entomologist is a Kafka-esque figure who virtually metamorphoses into one of the insects he collects, and Jesus, it is suggested, is the son of a virgin mother. Thus, all of the protagonists of this collection are *bichos* of one kind or another, either literally or figuratively. (In the English translation of *Bichos, Farrusco the Blackbird and Other Stories*, a certain ambivalence may have been lost, but more weight has been given to clarity and accessibility. In some ways, this may be due to a conscious adherence to the Western European fable tradition, in which we find titles such as "The Fox and the Raven," and "The Ant and the Grasshopper." Onomatopoeia is lost in one or two instances, for instance "Cega-Rega" becomes the less evocative "The Cicada," and the symbolism of some of the animals' names disappears, but this is an inevitable consequence of the act of translation.)

These tales will inevitably be read in the light of the Bible, Aesop's *Fables*, the medieval bestiary tradition (see *De bestiis et aliis rebus*, a work found in 14th-century Portuguese under the title of *Livro das Aves*) which finds its continuation in sermons and popular tales, and, inevitably, La Fontaine's 17th-century *Fables choisies*, among other texts. Although he shares the didactic, moralizing intention of these works, Torga by no means adheres to traditional views and conceptions; in some instances he seems to be rewriting pothe myths and subverting the status quo. Thus, Bambo the toad is neither evil nor malign, and Vincent the Crow is not a bird of ill omen, but a symbol of all that is strong and courageous.

Although Torga is anthropomorphic in the literal sense, his animals are not the saccharine specimens that adorn the conventional Christmas card. *Bichos* contains the same mixture of grim humour and pathos that is so essential an ingredient of the *Tales from the Mountain*. Thus, Don Juan the Rooster is well aware of what fate has in store for him—a starring role in this year's harvest pie. Torga's animals are sentient creatures, subject to the same feelings and emotions as human beings. Mago the Cat and Miura the Bull experience feelings of pain and humiliation; Morgado the Mule's faces death with full consciousness of his master's ingratitude and betrayal; and more than one of his characters takes pride in his ability to procreate—Don Juan the Rooster, Mago the Cat. One message that comes through very strongly is that animals are no better, and no worse, than the human beings to whom they are supposedly inferior. Ramiro, who commits murder when one of his ewes is accidentally killed, is the exact opposite of "The Shepherd Gabriel," but may well be an adult version of the youthful protagonist of "O Sésamo." Farrusco the Blackbird does not approve of the cuckoo's behaviour and sets out to redress the balance, while Vincent protests against injustice. "Farrusco the Blackbird" is considered by many to be the best story in the collection, and it is the subject of several penetrating critical studies.

The themes, motifs, and symbols of *Bichos* are identical to those found in his *Contos da montanha* and *Novos contos da montanha*. Universal values are expressed by apparently regional preoccupations: the harshness of life in Trás-os-Montes; the natural cycle of birth, life, and death; the eternal struggle between good and evil (although the author's perception of these does not always correspond to traditional Catholic dogma). Torga demonstrates in *Bichos* the same preoccupation with balance and economy, characterization and symbolism (the recurring symbol of the mountain, for example), the search for evocative, poetic language, and the all-important ending, not always pleas-

ing, sometimes shocking, but never inappropriate in the literary universe he has constructed.

More than anything, Torga's stories are an author's testament to the enduring resistence of his people, despite what he called "four decades of oppression." If their most notable quality is, perhaps, the ability not to succumb, one of Torga's lasting literary and human achievements has certainly been to immortalize their strengths and weaknesses with honesty, compassion, humour, and affection.

—Patricia Anne Odber de Baubeta

TREVOR, William. Pseudonym for William Trevor Cox. Irish. Born in Mitchelstown, County Cork, 24 May 1928. Educated at St. Columba's College, Dublin, 1942–46; Trinity College, Dublin, B.A. 1950. Married Jane Ryan in 1952; two sons. Teacher, Armagh, Northern Ireland, 1951–53; art teacher, Rugby, England, 1953–55; sculptor in Somerset, 1955–60; advertising copywriter, Notley's, London, 1960–64. Recipient: *Transatlantic Review* prize, for fiction, 1964; Hawthornden prize, for fiction, 1965; Society of Authors travelling fellowship, 1972; Allied Irish Banks prize, for fiction, 1976; Heinemann award, for fiction, 1976; Whitbread award, 1976, 1983; Irish Community prize, 1979; Jacob award, for television play, 1983. D.Litt.: University of Exeter, 1984; Trinity College, Dublin, 1986; D.Litt.: Queen's University, Belfast, 1989; D.Litt.: National University, Cork, 1990. Member, Irish Academy of Letters. C.B.E. (Commander, Order of the British Empire), 1977. Lives in Devon.

PUBLICATIONS

Short Stories

The Day We Got Drunk on Cake and Other Stories. 1967.
The Ballroom of Romance and Other Stories. 1972.
The Last Lunch of the Season (story). 1973.
Angels at the Ritz and Other Stories. 1975.
Lovers of Their Time and Other Stories. 1978.
The Distant Past and Other Stories. 1979.
Beyond the Pale and Other Stories. 1981.
The Stories. 1983.
The News from Ireland and Other Stories. 1986.
Nights at the Alexandra (novella). 1987.
Family Sins and Other Stories. 1990.
Two Lives (includes *Reading Turgenev* and *My House in Umbria*). 1991.
The Collected Stories. 1992.

Novels

A Standard of Behaviour. 1958.
The Old Boys. 1964.
The Boarding-House. 1965.
The Love Department. 1966.
Mrs. Eckdorf in O'Neill's Hotel. 1969.
Miss Gomez and the Brethren. 1971.
Elizabeth Alone. 1973.
The Children of Dynmouth. 1976.
Other People's Worlds. 1980.
Fools of Fortune. 1983.

The Silence in the Garden.   1988.

Plays

The Elephant's Foot (produced 1965).
The Girl (televised 1967; produced 1968).   1968.
A Night with Mrs. da Tanka (televised 1968; produced
    1972).   1972.
Going Home (broadcast 1970; produced 1972).   1972.
The Old Boys, from his own novel (produced 1971).
    1971.
A Perfect Relationship (broadcast 1973; produced 1973).
    1976.
The 57th Saturday (produced 1973).
Marriages (produced 1973).   1973.
Scenes from an Album (broadcast 1975; produced 1981).
    1981.
Beyond the Pale (broadcast 1980).   In *Best Radio Plays of
    1980,* 1981.
Autumn Sunshine from his own story (televised 1981;
    broadcast 1982).   In *Best Radio Plays of 1982,* 1983.

Radio Plays: *The Penthouse Apartment,* 1968; *Going
Home,* 1970; *The Boarding House,* from his own novel,
1971; *A Perfect Relationship,* 1973; *Scenes from an Album,*
1975; *Attracta,* 1977; *Beyond the Pale,* 1980; *The Blue
Dress,* 1981; *Travellers,* 1982; *Autumn Sunshine,* 1982; *The
News from Ireland,* from his own story, 1986; *Events at
Drimaghleen,* 1988; *Running Away,* 1988.

Television Plays: *The Baby-Sitter,* 1965; *Walk's End,* 1966;
The Girl, 1967; *A Night with Mrs. da Tanka,* 1968; *The
Mark–2 Wife,* 1969; *The Italian Table,* 1970; *The Grass
Widows,* 1971; *O Fat White Woman,* 1972; *The School-
room,* 1972; *Access to the Children,* 1973; *The General's
Day,* 1973; *Miss Fanshawe's Story,* 1973; *An Imaginative
Woman,* from a story by Thomas Hardy, 1973; *Love Affair,*
1974; *Eleanor,* 1974; *Mrs. Acland's Ghosts,* 1975; *The
Statue and the Rose,* 1975; *Two Gentle People,* from a story
by Graham Greene, 1975; *The Nicest Man in the World,*
1976; *Afternoon Dancing,* 1976; *Voices from the Past,* 1976;
Newcomers, 1976; *The Love of a Good Woman,* from his
own story, 1976; *The Girl Who Saw a Tiger,* 1976; *Last
Wishes,* 1978; *Another Weekend,* 1978; *Memories,* 1978;
Matilda's England, 1979; *The Old Curiosity Shop,* from the
novel by Dickens, 1979; *Secret Orchards,* from works by
J.R. Ackerley and Diana Petre, 1980; *The Happy Autumn
Fields,* from a story by Elizabeth Bowen, 1980; *Elizabeth
Alone,* from his own novel, 1981; *Autumn Sunshine,* from
his own story, 1981; *The Ballroom of Romance,* from his
own story, 1982; *Mrs. Silly* (*All for Love* series), 1983; *One
of Ourselves,* 1983; *Aunt Suzanne,* 1984; *Broken Homes,*
from his own story, 1985; *The Children of Dynmouth,* from
his own novel, 1987; *August Saturday,* from his own story,
1990; *Events at Drimaghleen,* from his own story, 1991.

Other

Old School Ties (miscellany).   1976.
A Writer's Ireland: Landscape in Literature.   1984.
Juliet's Story (for children).   1991.

Editor, *The Oxford Book of Irish Short Stories.*   1989.

*

Critical Studies: "Trevor's System of Correspondences" by
Kristin Morrison, in *Massachusetts Review,* Autumn 1987;
Trevor: A Study of His Fiction by Gregory A. Schirmer,
1990.

*   *   *

"The Table," the opening tale of William Trevor's first
collection, is typical of the characters, situations, and
themes to be found in many of his stories. Mr. Jeffs, from
whose point of view the story is narrated, is a social
outsider—a rapacious Jewish dealer living alone amidst
the furniture he buys and sells, who unexpectedly becomes
involved in the marital problems of a customer, whom he
accuses of refusing to face the truth of her husband's
infidelity. Miss Winton, the elderly spinster wrongly accused of damaging a luxury flat in "The Penthouse
Apartment," is another solitary figure who attempts "to
speak the truth," not so much to vindicate herself as "to
promote understanding" between the occupants and their
spiteful caretaker, but "no one bothers to listen." Edward
Tripp, in another early story, is equally unsuccessful when
he tries to confess "the honest truth" about his sister, who
he believes is punishing him for the tricks he played on her
when they were children; instead of giving him the comfort
and understanding he seeks, his neighbour tells him it is no
concern of hers.

Failure of human sympathy is also the theme of the
ironically entitled "A Meeting of Middle Age," in which an
aggressive divorcee sets out to humiliate the timid bachelor
hired to act as her co-respondent. This tale is typical, too,
of Trevor's way of building a story round an encounter or
confrontation between a single man and an unhappily
married woman ("In Isfahan" and "A Complicated Nature"), in which the man's sexual and other inadequacies
are revealed. In "Raymond Bamber and Mrs. Fitch," for
example, a shy, repressed bachelor rejects the "awkward
truths" spoken by the drunken woman he meets at a
cocktail party; ignoring the evidence of his eyes and ears
about her husband's infidelity, Bamber accuses Mrs. Fitch
of "transferring the truth about herself to other people,"
ironically unaware that this is precisely what he himself is
guilty of doing.

Many of Trevor's finest stories, like John Updike's,
anatomise failed or ailing marriages together with the self-
deceptions and pretences of the parties involved. In "The
Grass Widows," for instance, a headmaster's wife, angered
by years of selfish neglect, urges the newly-wed wife of one
of her husband's proteges to leave him on their honeymoon. Mrs. Angusthorpe's decision to speak out for the
first time in her married life is motivated less by a desire to
prevent Daphne from repeating her own mistake, than by
the opportunity it gives her of registering a "small triumph" over her domineering husband. Daphne, however,
is unable or unwilling to see the truth about her marriage:
"It's different for us," she says at the end—a claim
undermined by what we are actually shown of the young
couple's relationship.

In "Angels at the Ritz" Trevor explores the sexual games
played by those who live "in the outer suburb" in order to
revive their "wilting marriages." At the same time, he
presents a bleak picture of the kind of moral compromises
that people make in their middle years. Again the story
features two couples, one of whom sets out to seduce the
other by exploiting their long friendship and shared past.
Trevor's narrative mastery is seen not only in the way he

keeps both seductions going simultaneously by deftly cutting between them, but also in his handling of the tale's dominant image, the song that gives the story its title. This sentimental reminder of their younger innocence, which both the Ryders use in their attempt to seduce the Dillards, becomes for Polly Dillard a moral index of the extent to which the two couples have "fallen" during the intervening years. Although it is clear to Polly how the others have fallen, it is not until the end of the story, when she finds herself unable to ask her husband not to return to the Ryders' party "because the request seemed fussy," that she realises the nature of her own lapse: the "middle-age calmness" with which she is prepared to accept without protest or complaint her best friend's treachery and her husband's infidelity.

One character who does speak out against her best friend's treachery, her husband's infidelity and her own blindness is Cynthia Strafe at the end of "Beyond the Pale," Trevor's most ambitious treatment of the theme of self-deception. For the truth which Cynthia's companions refuse to face—in their comfortable belief that the "troubles" in Northern Ireland are nothing to do with them, any more than the fate of the Belfast couple whose tragic story Cynthia relates—is political and historical as well as personal. "England," she claims, "has always had its pales." The story's moral theme is also cleverly dramatised by Trevor's choice of Strafe's mistress as its unreliable narrator, since she ironically exposes herself as a smug, selfish, and hypocritical self-deceiver—"the voice," according to G.A. Schirmer, "of everything that Trevor is writing against."

No one listens to Cynthia any more than to the elderly Protestant school-mistress in "Attracta" who loses her job when she tries to share with her pupils the story of how her parents' murderers sought to atone for their act of violence by befriending her, and "the gleam of hope" it contains of escape from the deadly cycle of sectarian hatred. Attracta fails, not because her listeners are insulted from terrorist bloodshed, but because this is all too familiar a part of their lives. Without the kind of imaginative sympathy shown by Cynthia and Attracta, however, the truth can destroy rather then heal, as Trevor demonstrates in "Torridge" or "Another Christmas," where Dermot's insistence that I.R.A. violence is the consequence of the oppression of generations of Ulster Catholics alienates both his kindly English landlord and his own wife. Not that Trevor discounts the importance of history—it is, he points out, inescapable in a country like Ireland; what he opposes is the way history is twisted by fanatics like Harold in "Autumn Sunshine" or Fogarty in "The News from Ireland" in order to justify the perpetuation of violence.

—Graeme Roberts

See the essay on "The Ballroom of Romance."

———

TROLLOPE, Anthony. English. Born in London, 24 April 1815; son of the writer Frances Trollope. Educated at Harrow School, Middlesex, 1822–25 and 1831–33; Winchester College, Hampshire, 1825–30. Married Rose Heseltine in 1844; two sons. Classical usher at a school in Brussels, 1834; worked for the British Post Office, 1834–67: surveyor's clerk, later deputy surveyor, in Bang- her, Clonmel, and Belfast, Northern Ireland, 1841–54; chief surveyor, Dublin, 1854–59; chief surveyor of the Eastern District, London, 1859–67; suggested the use of letter boxes; made official visits to Egypt, 1858, the West Indies, 1858–59, and the U.S., 1861–62, 1868; lived at Waltham House, Hertfordshire, 1859–71, in London, from 1872, and at Harting Grange, Sussex, until 1882; a founder, *Fortnightly Review,* 1865; editor, *Pall Mall Gazette,* 1865–66, and *St. Paul's Magazine,* 1867–70; Liberal parliamentary candidate for Beverley, 1868; travelled in Australia and New Zealand, 1871–72, Australia, 1875, and South Africa, 1877. *Died 6 December 1882.*

PUBLICATIONS

Collections

The Trollope Reader, edited by Esther Cloudman Dunn and Marion E. Dodd. 1947.
The Oxford Illustrated Trollope, edited by Michael Sadleir and Frederick Page. 15 vols., 1948–54.
Complete Short Stories, edited by Betty Jane Breyer. 5 vols., 1979–83.

Short Stories

Tales of All Countries. 2 vols., 1861–63.
Lotta Schmidt and Other Stories. 1867.
An Editor's Tales. 1870.
Why Frau Frohmann Raised Her Prices and Other Stories. 1882.

Novels

The Macdermots of Ballycloran. 1847; edited by Robert Tracy, 1989.
The Kellys and the O'Kellys; or, Landlords and Tenants: A Tale of Irish Life. 1848.
La Vendée: An Historical Romance. 1850.
Barsetshire series:
  The Warden. 1855; edited by David Skilton, 1980.
  Barchester Towers. 1857.
  Doctor Thorne. 1858.
  Framley Parsonage. 1861.
  The Small House at Allington. 1864; edited by James R. Kincaid, 1980.
  The Last Chronicle of Barset. 1867; edited by Stephen Gill, 1981.
The Three Clerks. 1858; edited by Graham Handley, 1989.
The Bertrams. 1859.
Castle Richmond. 1860; edited by Mary Hamer, 1989.
Orley Farm. 1862.
The Struggles of Brown, Jones, and Robinson, by One of the Firm. 1862.
Rachel Ray. 1863; edited by P.D. Edwards, 1988.
Palliser series:
  Can You Forgive Her? 1864; edited by Andrew Swarbrick, 1982.
  Phineas Finn, The Irish Member. 1869; edited by Jacques Berthoud, 1982.
  The Eustace Diamonds. 1872; edited by W.J. McCormack, 1983.
  Phineas Redux. 1874; edited by John C. Whale, 1983.
  The Prime Minister. 1876; edited by Jennifer Uglow, 1983.

The Duke's Children.   1880; edited by Hermione Lee, 1983.
Miss Mackenzie.   1865; edited by A.O.J. Cockshut, 1988.
The Belton Estate.   1866; edited by John Halperin, 1986.
The Claverings.   1867(?).
Nina Balatka.   1867.
Linda Tressel.   1868.
He Knew He Was Right.   1869; edited by John Sutherland, 1985.
The Vicar of Bullhampton.   1870; edited by David Skilton, 1988.
Sir Harry Hotspur of Humblethwaite.   1871.
Mary Gresley.   1871.
Ralph the Heir.   1871; edited by John Sutherland, 1990.
The Golden Lion of Granpère.   1872.
Lady Anna.   1873; edited by Stephen Orgel, 1990.
Harry Heathcote of Gangoil: A Tale of Australian Bush Life.   1874.
The Way We Live Now.   1875.
The American Senator.   1877; edited by John Halperin, 1986.
Christmas at Thompson Hall.   1877; as Thompson Hall, 1885.
Is He Popenjoy?   1878; edited by John Sutherland, 1986.
How the Mastiffs Went to Iceland.   1878.
The Lady of Launay.   1878.
An Eye for an Eye.   1879.
John Caldigate.   1879.
Cousin Henry.   1879.
Dr. Wortle's School.   1881; edited by John Halperin, 1984.
Ayala's Angel.   1881.
The Fixed Period.   1882.
Marion Fay.   1882.
Kept in the Dark.   1882.
Not If I Know It.   1883.
The Two Heroines of Plumplington.   1882.
Mr. Scarborough's Family.   1883; edited by Geoffrey Harvey, 1989.
The Landleaguers (unfinished).   1883.
An Old Man's Love.   1884.

Plays

Did He Steal It?   1869; edited by R.H. Taylor, 1952.
The Noble Jilt, edited by Michael Sadleir.   1923.

Other

The West Indies and the Spanish Main.   1859.
North America.   2 vols., 1862; edited by Robert Mason, 1968.
Hunting Sketches.   1865.
Travelling Sketches.   1866.
Clergymen of the Church of England.   1866.
The Commentaries of Caesar.   1870.
Australia and New Zealand.   2 vols., 1873; *Australia* edited by P.D. Edwards and R.B. Joyce, 1967.
Iceland.   1878.
South Africa.   2 vols., 1878; revised abridgement, 1879.
Thackeray.   1879.
The Life of Cicero.   2 vols., 1880.
Lord Palmerston.   1882.
An Autobiography, edited by H.M. Trollope.   2 vols., 1883; edited by Michael Sadleir, 1947.
London Tradesmen, edited by Michael Sadleir.   1927.
Four Lectures, edited by Morris L. Parrish.   1938.

The Tireless Traveller: Twenty Letters to the Liverpool Mercury 1875, edited by Bradford A. Booth.   1941.
The New Zealander, edited by N. John Hall.   1972.
Trollope-to-Reader: A Topical Guide to Digressions in the Novels of Trollope, edited by Mary L. Daniels.   1983.
Letters, edited by N. John Hall and Nina Burgis.   2 vols., 1983.
The Irish Famine: Six Letters to the Examiner 1849–1850, edited by Lance Tingay.   1987.

Editor, *British Sports and Pastimes.*   1868.

*

Bibliography: *Trollope: A Bibliography* by Michael Sadleir, 1928, revised edition, 1934; *The Reputation of Trollope: An Annotated Bibliography 1925-1975* by John C. Olmsted, 1978; *The Trollope Collector: A Record of Writings* by and Books about Trollope by Lance Tingay, 1985; *Trollope: An Annotated Bibliography of Periodical Works by and about Him in the United States and Great Britain to 1900* by Anne K. Lyons, 1985.

Critical Studies: *Trollope: A Commentary* by Michael Sadleir, 1927, revised edition, 1945; *The Trollopes: The Chronicle of a Writing Family* by Lucy Poate Stebbins and Richard Poate Stebbins, 1945; *Trollope* by B.C. Brown, 1950; *Trollope: A Critical Study* by A.O.J. Cockshut, 1955; *Trollope: Aspects of His Life and Work* by Bradford A. Booth, 1958; *The Changing World of Trollope* by Robert Polhemus, 1968; *Trollope: The Critical Heritage* edited by Donald Smalley, 1969; *Trollope* by James Pope-Hennessy, 1971; *Trollope: Artist and Moralist* by Ruth Roberts, 1971, as *The Moral Trollope,* 1971; *A Guide to Trollope* by Winifred Gerould and James Gerould, 1975; *Trollope: His Life and Art* by C.P. Snow, 1975; *The Language and Style of Trollope* by John Williams Clark, 1975; *Trollope and His Contemporaries: A Study in the Theory and Conventions of Mid-Victorian Fiction* by David Skilton, 1976; *The Novels of Trollope* by James R. Kincaid, 1977; *Trollope and Politics: A Study of the Pallisers and Others* by John Halperin, 1977, and *Trollope Centenary Essays* edited by Halperin, 1982; *Trollope: The Artist in Hiding, 1977, and A Trollope Chronology,* 1989, both by R.C. Terry, and Trollope: *Interviews and Recollections* edited by Terry, 1987; *Trollope: His Art and Scope* by P.D. Edwards, 1977; *Trollope's Later Novels* by Robert Tracey, 1978; *Trollope's Palliser Novels: Theme and Pattern* by Juliet McMaster, 1978; *Trollope* by Arthur Pollard, 1978; *Trollope,* 1980, and *Trollope: The Barsetshire Novels: A Casebook,* 1983, both edited by T. Bareham; *Trollope and His Illustrators* by N. John Hall, 1980, and *The Trollope Critics* edited by Hall, 1981; *The Art of Trollope* by Geoffrey Harvey, 1980; *The Novel-Machine: The Theory and Fiction of Trollope* by Walter M. Kendrick, 1980; *Trollope in the Post Office,* 1981, and *The Chronicler of Barsetshire: A Life of Trollope,* 1988, both by R.H. Super; *The Trollope Critics* edited by N. John Hall, 1981, and *Trollope: A Biography* by Hall, 1991; *The Reasonable Man: Trollope's Legal Fiction* by Coral Lansbury, 1981; *The Gentleman in Trollope: Individuality and Moral Conduct* by Shirley Robin Letwin, 1982; *The Androgynous Trollope: Attitudes to Women Amongst Early Victorian Novelists* by Rajiva Wijesinha, 1982; *Trollope: Dream and Art* by Andrew Wright, 1983; *Trollope and the Law* by R.D. McMaster, 1986; *Trollope: Barchester Towers* by Graham Handley, 1987; *Writing by Numbers: Trollope's*

Serial Fiction by Mary Hamer, 1987; *Trollope* by Susan Peck MacDonald, 1987; *Women in Trollope's Palliser Novels* by Deborah Denenholz Morse, 1987; *Trollope and Comic Pleasure* by Christopher Herbert, 1987; *The Chronicler of Barsetshire: A Life of Trollope* by R.H. Super, 1988; *Trollope and Character* by Stephen Wall, 1988, as *Trollope: Living with Character,* 1989; *A Guide to Trollope* by A. Craig Bell, 1989; *Trollope: A Victorian in His World* by Richard Mullen, 1990; *Trollope* by Victoria Glendinning, 1993.

* * *

Anthony Trollope is not regarded as a great short story writer, and since he wrote 47 substantial novels his output of shorter fiction is often ignored. He did, however, produce 42 short stories which have usefully been divided, in a recent edition into five categories.

The first category is called "Editors and Writers." Trollope was of course a writer all his life, and between 1867 and 1870 he was editor of the *St. Paul's Magazine.* This gave rise to eight stories, of which "The Spotted Dog" is the longest, best and best-known, concerning the struggles of authorship and the trials of editorship. A persuasive account is given, in the Grub Street mode, of those who turn to their pens as a last resort in a financially desperate situation and of the difficulties an editor faces in trying to get rid of such importunate people.

The second category, which also numbers eight items, is that of Christmas stories. These were a highly popular genre in mid-Victorian times and Trollope, although he professed dislike of the clichés involved, managed to turn out some respectable examples. The happy ending required evidently went somewhat against the grain (in his best fiction Trollope sees life as too complex for simple resolutions), but in these tales of hitches in young love being smoothed out by goodwill and Christmas cheer he manages to put forward his most optimistic side. Again, typically for Trollope whose forte was the extended narrative, the longest story is the best: "Two Heroines of Plumplington" is a simple tale of paternal objection to the suitors of two young women; love triumphs in the end quite predictably, so we are forced to see that the interest in the story centres around character portrayal and handling of dramatic scene rather than around the plot.

In the third category are the ten stories based on Trollope's extensive travels round the world. In these we see a grimmer world than in the English Christmas scenes but also a world of immense vigour and some comic potential. Whether in the Middle East, Jamaica, or Belgium, Trollope's English abroad are empire-builders and tourists of the middling sort whose exploits are more likely to concern marriage, meals, and getting value for money out of the natives than anything more elevated or political. As with the stories of editors and writers, we have here a strong strain of pleasant autobiography but there is also a bleaker dimension, for the mid-Victorian travellers and colonialists risked their lives to a degree almost unimaginable in the late 20th century. Students of the British imperial period would do well to read "Returning Home" or "George Walker at Suez."

The fourth category comprises eight stories about travel and foreigners, less about Empire and tourism than about the quirks and coincidences of daily life. Mostly set in Europe, they foreshadow some of E.M. Forster's preoccupations with the meaning of the English experience of the continent. Confrontations between the different cultures inevitably generate tensions which make worse the small but infuriating problems that beset Trollopian characters. "The Journey to Panama" is a superb example of realism in which the everyday, in the close confines of a ship, becomes almost intolerable for one whose major preoccupation, love, is going wrong.

The eight stories in the fifth category (called "Courtship and Marriage") are closer to Trollope's more usual territory; as in his novels he is concerned here with the whole complex social and personal comedy of human pairing. "Alice Dugdale" could be read as a miniature version of a number of his novels and "The Parson's Daughter of Oxney Colne" is as good a short story as many by Hardy or other recognised masters of the genre.

Trollope's stories are always entertaining if sometimes slightly predictable. They do not conform to our usual expectations of the genre, however, in that, Trollope being incapable of writing except at length, they are not neat or pithy or cryptic or rounded off with a piquant twist. Instead they are somewhat inconclusive slices of life wrapped up rather faster than the author would evidently have liked. But Trollope's greatest strength was his ability to bring characters together and allow us to watch them interacting. This he does in every story he wrote, immediately and vigorously.

These stories offer unusually frank insights into aspects of Victorian society; most of them were written in the 1860's and they could usefully be set alongside the paintings of the period. We find sentimentality in them ("Mary Gresley") and a certain preoccupation with Christian themes (charity in "The Widow's Mite") but for the most part they help to make the Victorians more normal to us.

—Lance St. John Butler

See the essay on "The Parson's Daughter of Oxney Colne."

TSUSHIMA Yūko. Japanese. Born Tsushima Satoko in Tokyo, 30 March 1947; daughter of the writer Dazai Osamu, *q.v.* Educated at Shirayuri Women's College, M.A. in English literature 1969. Has one daughter. Recipient: Izumi Kyōka prize, 1977; Women's Literature award, 1978; Kawabata Yasunari prize, 1983; Yomiuri prize, 1987. Lives in Tokyo.

PUBLICATIONS

Short Stories

Ōma monogatari [Twilight Stories].   1984.
The Shooting Gallery and Other Stories.   1988.

Novels

Dōji no kage [Shadow of Child].   1973.
Mugura no haha [The Mother in the House of Grass].   1975.
Yorokobi no shima [Island of Joy].   1978.
Chōji.   1978; as *Child of Fortune,* 1983.
Hikari no ryōbun [Territory of Light].   1979.

Yama o hashiru onna. 1980; as *Woman Running in the Mountains,* 1991.
Moeru kaze [Burning Wind]. 1980.
Suifu [City in the Water]. 1982.
Hi no kawa no hotori de [On the Bank of the Fire River]. 1983.
Danmariichi [The Silent Traders]. 1984.
Yoru no hikari ni owarete [Driven by the Light of Night]. 1986.
Mahiru e [Toward Noon]. 1988.
Yume no kiroku [Record of Dreams]. 1988.
Kusamura: jisen tanpenshū. 1989.
Oinaru yume yo, hikari-yo [Enormous Dream, Light!]. 1991.

*

Critical Study: in *Off Center* by Miyoshi Masao, 1991.

* * *

Tsushima Yūko has been a consistent and prodigious, interrogating female voice ever since she was recognized by the Japanese literary establishment in 1971, at the age of 24. Over the years her copious short stories, as well as several novels, have won numerous prestigious literary prizes and been translated and published abroad. Taken together, her works are a collection of installments, of glances from different angles at a particular persona coming into being within a concrete age and place, modern Tokyo. This type of Japanese fiction is written to be read as an extended acquaintance with a textual shadow of the author; and the reader's sense, from story to story, of being drawn into the inner depths of a single character's psyche is confirmation of Tsushima's skill.

Like many other writers of her postwar generation, she has taken the family as a predominant theme, treating each literary work as another exploration of this nexus of physical and social bonds, of prescribed roles and obligations. Yet Tsushima's "family" is an exploded image, an absent core that nonetheless refuses to give up its form. It is a scattering of shining, refracting fragments that draws her back again and again—that she is constantly forced to call up in order to deny. The narrator of "A Bed of Grass" returns to live with her mother after the death of her baby and desertion of her abusive husband. Although they live in the same house, the weight of the protagonist's failure as woman and mother so oppresses her relationship with her own mother that the two do not speak. Her only two friends are a slightly retarded young man (with whom she plays a playfully cruel, asexual sisterly role), and an unattractive, unclean woman, who is a single mother (with whom she has an ambiguous relationship that presses against but never quite breaks through boundaries of gender and sexual orientation).

What does it mean to be a mother, a father? What does a mother expect of her children and lovers? Or of her own mother? Where in this framework does one turn for protection, indulgence, "love"? The Japanese family, like Japanese society in general, is defined by negotiations between interdependent members in fixed positions. Within this network, coherence is maintained by and depends upon the figure of a nurturing, sacrificing, selflessly devoted mother. Therefore it is this paradigm at its very heart that is under interrogation in Tsushima's writings. In "The

Shooting Gallery" a selfish and inattentive mother imagines herself as a bright golden dragon, only to awaken into a dream of shrinking into a tiny ant and being stomped on by her two young sons. By the end of the story, as these three watch the owner of a shooting gallery, we feel the mother's relief at having the young man take control, at being released into the position of a child. Tsushima's literature is filled with children who fear abandonment, mothers who have babies to fill the place of parents, and fathers who are abusive or absent altogether.

The author herself was the youngest of three children, with a sister six years older and a mentally-handicapped brother three years her senior. Her father (the celebrated writer Dazai Osamu) committed suicide when she was just over a year old, leaving her mother to head the family alone. Tsushima is now a single parent living in Tokyo. These people and configurations of the writer's life powerfully shape her works. Japanese society's insistence on conformity necessarily exiles the different; and the characters in her works are forever possessed by the shadows of suicide, single parenthood, and mental retardation. Here, family is a web of emotional bondage that grips with the threat of dismissal more often than the promise of gratification.

Probed from the shadowy depths of dream, recollection, fantasy, and desire, Tsushima's writing opens an incisive world of personal reality. Repeatedly emerging from this textual swirl of past, present, and imagination is the figure of a woman/mother/ daughter/sister/lover—an unordered kaleidoscope of role-fragments through which the reader senses a self or selves that shift and overlap and constantly re-form. In "Missing" the protagonist is a mother waiting through the night for the return of a daughter she knows will not be restored to her; in "South Wind" she is a woman at the end of an affair, looking back over the transformations of the past six years, wondering at former selves that were mother and wife. In "A Sensitive Season" the narrative perspective makes a rare shift, to the view of a young boy abandoned by his mother, left with his aunt and grandfather. The aunt has been forced to quit her job in order to become a full-time caretaker for the two males. Through the boy's childishly needy and yet not-entirely-innocent eyes, the text insightfully explores the ways in which even those who are "used" willfully manipulate those by whom they are used. "The Chrysanthemum Beetle" reveals, through the painful relations of a jealous lovers' triangle, how ghost-tale horrors are lived out in our real lives.

For Tsushima's characters there is one escape: nature, the exotic wild of profuse vegetation, endless oceans, and untamed creatures—an other place sometimes reached by travel and other times flourishing within the walls of a park, but always a space that is not city and that escapes the unbending structures of society. The sun and the south wind lavish their warmth on all alike, unconditionally and without judgement. Lush green hillsides offer freedom and protection from the responsibilities and demands of personal and economic reality as in *Yama o hashiru onna (Woman Running in the Mountains).* But nature is also crushingly powerful, threatening utter disintegration, the dissolution of the abyss; and this deliciously terrifying aspect is exactly what makes it so desirable, what one is horrified to face and yet unwilling to turn away from. In "Clearing the Thickets" abundant and uncontainable grass, which the protagonist's mother and older sister have demanded she help clear, becomes a symbol of her wild and frightening love for her family, the child she carries, the man who has left her, and for herself. In "The Silent

Traders" the unknowable depths of a park open a silent space that makes possible tacit, imaginable relationships between absent fathers and their children.

Tsushima's narrative is built of the repetition of these motifs—wild nature, family, pregnancy, the quest for selfless love—and yet never reduced to them. Her straightforward prose never diminishes the complexity, the multiplicity of lives absorbed by the mysterious contradictions that entangle and confuse desire, present, past, and dream.

—Pamela Abee-Taulli

TURGENEV, Ivan (Sergeevich). Russian. Born in Orel, 28 October 1818. Educated at home; briefly at Armenian Institute and Weidenhammer's boarding school in Moscow; University of Moscow, 1833–34; University of St. Petersburg, 1834–37; University of Berlin, 1838–41; completed master's exam in St. Petersburg, 1842. Civil servant in Ministry of the Interior, 1843–45; then mainly interested in country pursuits, especially hunting; went to France with the singer Pauline Viardot and her husband, 1845–46, and again in 1847–50; exiled to his country estate for a "faulty" obituary of Gogol, 1852–53; in Western Europe again for long spells after 1856, often in Baden-Baden after 1863, and in Paris with the Viardots, 1871–83. Corresponding Member, Imperial Academy of Sciences, 1860. Dr. of Civil Laws: Oxford University, 1879. *Died 3 September 1883.*

PUBLICATIONS

Collections

Novels. 15 vols., 1894–99.
The Borzoi Turgenev, edited by Harry Stevens. 1950.
Polnoe sobranie sochinenii i pisem. 28 vols., 1960–68.

Short Stories

Dnevnik lishnego cheloveka (novella). 1850; as *Diary of a Superfluous Man,* 1984.
Zapiski okhotnika. 1852; as *Russian Life in the Interior,* 1855; as *Annals of a Sportsman,* 1885; as *A Sportsman's Sketches,* 1932; as *Sketches from a Hunter's Album,* 1990; as *A Huntsman's Sketches,* 1992.
Povesti i rasskazy [Tales and Stories]. 1856.
Rudin (novella). 1856; as *Dmitri Roudine,* 1873.
Asia (novella). 1858; as *Annouchka,* 1884; as *Asya,* in *Three Novellas about Love,* 1990.
Dvorianskoe gnezdo (novella). 1859; as *A Nest of Gentlefolk,* 1869; as *Lisa,* 1872; as *Home of the Gentry,* 1970.
Nakanune (novella). 1860; as *On the Eve,* 1871.
Pervaia liubov' (novella). 1860; as *First Love,* 1884; in *First Love and Other Stories,* 1982.
Dym (novella). 1867; as *Smoke,* 1868.
Neschastnaia (novella). 1869; as *An Unfortunate Woman,* 1886.
Stepnoi Korol' Lir (novella). 1870; as *A Lear of the Steppe,* with *Spring Floods,* 1874.
Veshnie vody (novella). 1872; as *Spring Floods,* with *A Lear of the Steppe,* 1874; as *Spring Torrents,* in *Three Novellas about Love,* 1990.
First Love and Other Stories. 1982.

Three Novellas about Love (includes *Asya, First Love,* and *Spring Torrents*). 1990.

Novels

Ottsy i deti. 1862; as *Fathers and Sons,* 1867; edited by Ralph E. Matlaw, 1989; as *Fathers and Children,* 1991.
Nov'. 1877; as *Virgin Soil,* 1877.
Klara Milich. 1883.

Plays

Neostorozhrost' [Carelessness]. 1843.
Bezdenezh'e [Lack of Money]. 1846.
Gde tonko, tam i rvet'sia (produced 1851). 1848; as *Where It's Thin, There It Tears,* in *Plays,* 1924.
Zavtrak s predvoditelia [Lunch with the Marshal of the Nobility] (produced 1849). 1856.
Kholostiak (produced 1849). 1849; as *The Bachelor,* in *Plays,* 1924.
Razgovor na bolshoi doroge (produced 1850). 1851; as *A Conversation on the Highway,* in *Plays,* 1924.
Provintsialka (produced 1851). 1851; as *The Provincial Lady,* in *Plays,* 1924.
Mesiats v derevne (produced 1872). 1855; as *A Month in the Country,* in *Plays,* 1924; as *A Month in the Country,* edited by Richard Freeborn, 1991.
Nakhlebnik (produced 1857). 1857; as *The Family Charge,* in *Plays,* 1924.
Vecher v Sorrente (produced 1884). 1891; as *An Evening in Sorrento,* in *Plays,* 1924.
Plays. 1924.

Verse

Parasha. 1843.
Razgovor [The Conversation]. 1845.
Andrei. 1846.
Pomeshchik [The Landowner]. 1846.
Senilia. 1878; as *Stikhotvoreniia v proze,* 1882; as *Poems in Prose,* 1883; as *Senilia: Poems in Prose,* 1890.

Other

Sobranie sochinenii. 5 vols., 1860–61, and later editions.
Literaturnye i zhiteiskie vospominaniia. 1874; revised edition, 1880; as *Literary Reminiscences and Autobiographical Fragments,* 1958.
Nouvelle correspondance inédite, edited by Alexandre Zviguilsky. 2 vols., 1971–72.
Lettres inédites à Pauline Viardot et à sa famille, edited by Alexandre Zviguilsky. 1972.
Letters (selection), edited by A.V. Knowles. 1983.
Letters (selection), edited by David Lowe. 2 vols., 1983.
Flaubert and Turgenev: A Friendship in Letters: The Complete Correspondence, edited by Barbara Beaumont. 1985.
Flaubert-Ivan Turgenev: Correspondance, edited by Alexandre Zviguilsky, 1989.

*

Bibliography: *Turgenev in English: A Checklist of Works by and about Him* by Rissa Yachnin and David H. Stam, 1962; *Turgenev: A Bibliography of Books 1843–1982 by and about Turgenev* by Nicholas G. Zekulin, 1985.

Critical Studies: *Turgenev: The Man, His Art, and His Age* by A. Yarmolinsky, 1959; *Turgenev, The Novelist's Novelist: A Study* by Richard Freeborn, 1963; *Turgenev: The Portrait Game* edited by Marion Mainwaring, 1973; *Hamlet and Don Quixote: Turgenev's Ambivalent Vision* by Eva Kagan-Kans, 1975; *The Clement Vision: Poetic Realism in Turgenev and James* by Dale E. Peterson, 1976; *The Gentle Barbarian: The Life and Work of Turgenev* by V.S. Pritchett, 1977; *Turgenev: His Life and Times* by Leonard Schapiro, 1978; *Turgenev's Russia: From "Notes of a Hunter" to "Fathers and Sons"* by Victor Ripp, 1980; *Turgenev and England*, 1980, and *Turgenev and George Sand*, 1981, both by Patrick Waddington; *Turgenev* by Henri Troyat, 1985, translated by Nancy Amphoux, 1988; *Turgenev* by A.V. Knowles, 1988; *Worlds Within Worlds: The Novels of Turgenev* by Jane T. Costlow, 1990; *Beyond Realism: Turgenev's Poetics of Secular Salvation* by Elizabeth Cheresh Allen, 1992; *Turgenev and the Context of English Literature 1850–1900* by Glyn Turton, 1992.

*　　*　　*

Ivan Turgenev started his literary career as mainly a poet, and this early discipline helped him develop a lyrical tone and a stylistic elegance that became permanent qualities of his writing. Through the early 1850's he wrote a number of plays, including at least one, *Me siats v derevne (A Month in the Country)* that remains in the standard repertory today. From the latter 1840's on, however, he concentrated more and more on prose narrative, especially after he became famous in 1852 for his widely influential collection *Zapiski okhotnika (A Sportsman's Sketches,* also *A Huntsman's Sketches)* which portrayed the life of serfs, in the days before their emancipation, so vividly and sympathetically that the volume is said to have helped bring about that emancipation, in 1861. These "sketches" are primarily just that: snapshots, as it were, of individual peasants and some of their owners. In many ways the volume amounted to a temporary experiment; Turgenev seldom thereafter wrote about the underclasses, and he soon abandoned the snapshot technique in favor of more developed narratives: novellas, novels, and short stories in the modern sense. Certain qualities in *A Sportsman's Sketches* do point toward his later, more characteristic, and fully imaginative work. Such pieces as "Bezhin Meadow," for example, are sketches but have overtones also of the short-story form, and the combination in the *Sportsman* volume of intense interest in individual lives and character with social-political commentary, along with the author's penchant for using nature as tonal atmosphere and powerfully evocative symbol, anticipates what we find in many of his major works to come.

Distinguishing Turgenev's novels from his short fiction is problematical; in a sense, all his fiction is short. Only two of the six works he himself chose to call novels—*Ottsy i deti (Fathers and Sons)* and *Nor' (Virgin Soil)*—attain the length we normally expect in novels, and the other four—*Rudin, Dvorianskoe gnezdo, (Home of the Gentry)*, *Na Kanune (On the Eve)*, and *Dym (Smoke)*—range, so far as sheer length is concerned, along the spectrum running from short novel to novella. *Veshnie Vody (Torrents of Spring)*, if we look at length in itself, could have been called a novel. Quite a few of Turgenev's works are of fairly standard novella length, including *Dnevnik lishnego cheloveka (Diary of a Superfluous Man)*, *Asia (Asya)*, *Pervaia liubov' (First Love)*, *Neschastnaia (An Unfortunate Woman)*, and *Stepnoi*

Korol' Lir (A Lear of the Steppes). Although he also wrote a considerable number of short stories proper, even they tend often to be long—"Mumu" (1852), for example, his best-known story, a study in pathos centering on a deaf-mute peasant who, having lost his beloved when she is forced into a marriage, takes a pet dog as a surrogate and finally is forced by his cruel owner to drown it.

We can probably best focus on Turgenev's achievement in short fiction by looking at the works of intermediate length, longer than the true short stories and shorter than the two full-length novels. That the classification by scale should be so difficult, that an intermediate length should be so common for him, is itself revelatory of two important things about Turgenev: that "blockbuster" spiritual or social panorama-novels in the vein of his contemporaries Dostoevskii and Tolstoii were not his vein, and that Turgenev needed, for his characteristic psychological amplitude and subtlety, a larger canvas to work on than the short story proper normally affords.

The often-drawn contrast of Turgenev with Dostoevskii and Tolstoii is in some ways misleading, though, despite obvious differences in the size of their canvases, for all three are visionary realists, mimetically rendering the texture of human experience but infusing into that texture an arresting hyper-vividness. The special area of Turgenev's visionary power is partly nature but, more especially, the subjective experience of romantic love. In such works as *First Love, Asya,* and *Smoke,* he evokes the feeling with piercing intensity, rendering the euphoria of love's dawning and the poignancy of lost love about as powerfully as that can be done. Turgenev's commentators repeatedly remind us that romantic love in his world is, invariably, sadly impermanent, which is true enough but not in itself very surprising or interesting; after all, we are talking about *romantic* love, not love in general. Romantic love in Turgenev is not so much a link between persons as a voucher for the supercharged energy that life in general can have at its most intense, for better and worse, and Turgenev seems to imply that such intensity cannot in any arena of human existence be maintained for more than brief lightning-flashes. The sadness of love's impermanence is the sadness of the perishability of all life's visionary experiences. When Gregorii Litvinov, protagonist of *Smoke,* abandons his fiancée Tatiana for a glamorous young woman named Irina who had already, in the past, thrown him over once, he moves from the value-system defined by love in general into the different kind of system—beautiful, terrible, daemonic, visionary—defined by the specifically romantic variety of love. This is what the works we call love stories are all about, and to recognize the distinction is to see how irrelevant are the objections one sometimes hears to the effect that happy endings in love stories ignore the inevitable stresses that lie beyond the wedding. *Smoke,* in fact, does have a "happy" ending: Gregorii and Tatiana do come together again some years after their broken engagement. But what we have is no longer romantic love. As for the enchantress Irina, she ends in the lonely gaiety of the social whirl she has preferred over Gregorii, which obviously is not romantic love either. To judge whether she or Gregorii ends up happier is, for the visionary purposes of the love story, of no consequence at all.

Turgenev's characters, though highly individualized in a way, include several recurrent types. He once identified what he considered two archetypal categories of people; the Hamlets (indecisive, introspective, paralyzed) and the Don Quixotes (adventuresome, impulsive, questing). In his *Diary of a Superfluous Man* he introduced a specimen of ineffectual maleness that popularized a vogue, especially in Russian literature; the title protagonist of *Rudin*, gifted with inspiring eloquence but unable to follow through and commit himself when the heroine, Natalia, offers herself to him, is such a type. Indeed, Turgenev's women are almost invariably strong, far stronger than his men, more endowed with vital energy, more capable of commitment, and, even when deeply flawed in character—like Irina in *Smoke* or Maria, the aggressive temptress in *Torrents of Spring*–more compelling.

Perhaps the prototype of Turgenev's strong women is Elena, the idealistic heroine of *On the Eve;* defying her conventional parents, she throws in her lot with Insarov, a Bulgarian exile and nationalist. She leaves with him for his country on the eve of its imminent revolution. He dies before he can go into action, but Elena goes forward on her own, into a dangerous but heroic future. (It is no wonder that the American novelist Henry James, also preoccupied with forceful young women, extravagantly admired *On the Eve,* as he admired Turgenev generally.)

The characteristic combination in Turgenev's work of love story with political-social commentary is sometimes organically effective, sometimes not. In *Smoke* the two strands seem almost independent of each other; in *Rudin* they are connected, but a little loosely; in *On the Eve,* where the heroine's boldness as lover blends with her boldness in the service of a cause, the blend is a more successful fusion.

—Brian Wilkie

See the essays on "Bezhin Meadow" and *First Love.*

TWAIN, Mark. Pseudonym for Samuel Langhorne Clemens. American. Born in Florida, Missouri, 30 November 1835; moved to Hannibal, Missouri, 1839. Married Olivia Langdon in 1870 (died 1904); one son and three daughters. Printer's apprentice and typesetter for Hannibal newspapers, 1847–50; helped brother with Hannibal *Journal,* 1850–52; typesetter and printer in St. Louis, New York, Philadelphia. for Keokuk *Saturday Post,* Iowa, 1853–56, and in Cincinnati, 1857; apprentice river pilot, on the Mississippi, 1857–58; licensed as pilot, 1859–60; went to Nevada as secretary to his brother, then on the staff of the Governor, and also worked as goldminer, 1861; staff member, Virginia City *Territorial Enterprise,* Nevada, 1862–64 (first used pseudonym Mark Twain, 1863); reporter, San Francisco *Morning Call,* 1864; correspondent, Sacramento *Union,* 1866, and San Francisco *Alta California,* 1866–69: visited Sandwich (i.e., Hawaiian) Islands, 1866, and France, Italy, and Palestine, 1867; lecturer from 1867; editor, *Express,* Buffalo, New York, 1869–71; moved to Hartford, Connecticut and became associated with Charles L. Webster Publishing Company, 1884; invested in unsuccessful Paige typesetter and went bankrupt, 1894 (last debts paid, 1898); lived mainly in Europe, 1896–1900, New York, 1900–07, and Redding, Connecticut, 1907–10. M.A.: Yale University, New Haven, Connecticut, 1888; Litt.D.: Yale University, 1901; Oxford University, 1907; LL.D.: University of Missouri, Columbia, 1902. Member, American Academy, 1904. *Died 21 April 1910.*

PUBLICATIONS

Collections

The Writings (Definitive Edition), edited by Albert Bigelow Paine. 37 vols., 1922–25.
The Portable Twain, edited by Bernard De Voto. 1946.
The Complete Short Stories, edited by Charles Neider. 1957.
Selected Shorter Writings, edited by Walter Blair. 1962.
The Complete Novels, edited by Charles Neider. 2 vols., 1964.
Twain Papers, edited by Robert H. Hirst. 1967–.
Works (Iowa-California Edition), edited by John C. Gerber and others. 1972–.
Mississippi Writings (Library of America), edited by Guy A. Cardwell. 1982.
The Innocents Abroad and Roughing It (Library of America), edited by Guy A. Cardwell. 1984.
Collected Tales, Sketches, Speeches, and Essays (Library of America), edited by Lewis J. Budd. 2 vols., 1992.
The Science Fiction of Twain, edited by David Keterer. 1984.

Short Stories and Sketches

The Celebrated Jumping Frog of Calaveras County and Other Sketches, edited by Charles Henry Webb. 1867.
A True Story and the Recent Carnival of Crime. 1877.
Date 1601: Conversation as It Was by the Social Fireside in the Time of the Tudors. 1880; as *1601,* edited by Franklin J. Meine, 1939.
The Stolen White Elephant. 1882.
Merry Tales. 1892.
The £1,000,000 Bank-Note and Other New Stories. 1893.
Tom Sawyer Abroad. 1894.
Tom Sawyer Abroad, Tom Sawyer, Detective, and Other Stories. 1896; as *Tom Sawyer, Detective, as Told by Huck Finn, and Other Tales,* 1896.
The Man That Corrupted Hadleyburg and Other Stories and Essays. 1900.
A Dog's Tale. 1904.
The $30,000 Bequest and Other Stories. 1906.
Extract from Captain Stormfield's Visit to Heaven. 1909; revised edition, as *Report from Paradise,* edited by Dixon Wecter, 1952.
The Mysterious Stranger: A Romance (novella). 1916; *Mysterious Stranger Manuscripts,* edited by William M. Gibson, 1969.
The Curious Republic of Gondour and Other Whimsical Sketches. 1919.
The Mysterious Stranger and Other Stories. 1922.
A Boy's Adventure. 1928.
The Adventures of Thomas Jefferson Snodgrass, edited by Charles Honce. 1928.
Jim Smiley and His Jumping Frog, edited by Albert Bigelow Paine. 1940.
A Murder, A Mystery, and a Marriage. 1945.
The Complete Humorous Sketches and Tales, edited by Charles Neider. 1961.
Satires and Burlesques, edited by Franklin R. Rogers. 1967.
Twain's Hannibal, Huck, and Tom, edited by Walter Blair. 1969.
Twain's Quarrel with Heaven: Captain Stormfield's Visit to Heaven and Other Sketches, edited by Roy B. Browne. 1970.

Early Tales and Sketches, edited by Edgar M. Branch and Robert H. Hirst. 2 vols., 1979–81.
Wapping Alice. 1981.
Huck Finn and Tom Sawyer among the Indians and Other Unfinished Stories, edited by Dahlia Armon and Walter Blair, 1989.

Novels

The Innocents Abroad; or, The New Pilgrims' Progress. 1869.
The Innocents at Home. 1872.
The Gilded Age: A Tale of Today, with Charles Dudley Warner. 1873; *The Adventures of Colonel Sellers, Being Twain's Share of The Gilded Age,* edited by Charles Neider, 1965; complete text, edited by Bryant Morey French, 1972.
The Adventures of Tom Sawyer. 1876.
A Tramp Abroad. 1880.
The Prince and the Pauper. 1881.
The Adventures of Huckleberry Finn (Tom Sawyer's Comrade). 1884; as *Adventures of Huckleberry Finn,* 1885; edited by Sculley Bradley and others, 1977.
A Connecticut Yankee in King Arthur's Court. 1889; as *A Yankee at the Court of King Arthur,* 1889; edited by Allison R. Ensor, 1982.
The American Claimant. 1892.
Pudd'nhead Wilson. 1894; augmented edition, as *The Tragedy of Pudd'nhead Wilson, and The Comedy of Those Extraordinary Twins,* 1894; edited by Sidney E. Berger, 1980.
Personal Recollections of Joan of Arc. 1896.
A Double Barrelled Detective Story. 1902.
Extracts from Adam's Diary. 1904.
Eve's Diary. 1906.
A Horse's Tale. 1907.
Simon Wheeler, Detective, edited by Franklin R. Rogers. 1963.
Twain at His Best, edited by Charles Neider. 1986.

Plays

Ah Sin, with Bret Harte (produced 1877). Edited by Frederick Anderson, 1961.
Colonel Sellers as a Scientist, with William Dean Howells, from the novel *The Gilded Age* by Twain and Charles Dudley Warner (produced 1887). In *Complete Plays of Howells,* edited by Walter J. Meserve, 1960.
The Quaker City Holy Land Excursion: An Unfinished Play. 1927.

Verse

On the Poetry of Twain, with Selections from His Verse, edited by Arthur L. Scott. 1966.

Other

Twain's (Burlesque) Autobiography and First Romance. 1871.
Memoranda: From the Galaxy. 1871.
Roughing It. 1872.
A Curious Dream and Other Sketches. 1872.
Screamers: A Gathering of Scraps of Humour, Delicious Bits, and Short Stories. 1872.
Sketches. 1874.
Sketches, New and Old. 1875.

Old Times on the Mississippi. 1876; as *The Mississippi Pilot,* 1877.
An Idle Excursion. 1878.
Punch, Brothers, Punch! and Other Sketches. 1878.
A Curious Experience. 1881.
Life on the Mississippi. 1883.
Facts for Twain's Memory Builder. 1891.
How to Tell a Story and Other Essays. 1897; revised edition, 1900.
Following the Equator: A Journey Around the World. 1897; as *More Tramps Abroad,* 1897.
Writings (Autograph Edition). 25 vols., 1899–1907.
The Pains of Lowly Life. 1900.
English as She Is Taught. 1900; revised edition, 1901.
To the Person Sitting in Darkness. 1901.
Edmund Burke on Croker, and Tammany. 1901.
My Début as a Literary Person, with Other Essays and Stories. 1903.
Twain on Vivisection. 1905(?).
King Leopold's Soliloquy: A Defense of His Congo Rule. 1905; revised edition, 1906.
Editorial Wild Oats. 1905.
What Is Man? 1906.
On Spelling. 1906.
Writings (Hillcrest Edition). 25 vols., 1906–07.
Christian Science, with Notes Containing Corrections to Date. 1907.
Is Shakespeare Dead? From My Autobiography. 1909.
Speeches, edited by F.A. Nast. 1910; revised edition, 1923.
Queen Victoria's Jubilee. 1910.
Letter to the California Pioneers. 1911.
What Is Man? and Other Essays. 1917.
Letters, edited by Albert Bigelow Paine. 2 vols., 1917.
Moments with Twain, edited by Albert Bigelow Paine. 1920.
Europe and Elsewhere. 1923.
Autobiography, edited by Albert Bigelow Paine. 2 vols., 1924.
Sketches of the Sixties by Bret Harte and Twain. . . from The Californian 1864–67. 1926; revised edition, 1927.
The Suppressed Chapter of "Following the Equator." 1928.
A Letter from Twain to His Publisher, Chatto and Windus. 1929.
Twain the Letter Writer, edited by Cyril Clemens. 1932.
Works. 23 vols., 1933.
The Family Twain (selections). 1935.
The Twain Omnibus, edited by Max J. Herzberg. 1935.
Representative Selections, edited by Fred L. Pattee. 1935.
Notebook, edited by Albert Bigelow Paine. 1935.
Letters from the Sandwich Islands, Written for the Sacramento Union, edited by G. Ezra Dane. 1937.
The Washoe Giant in San Francisco, Being Heretofore Uncollected Sketches, edited by Franklin Walker. 1938.
Twain's Western Years, Together with Hitherto Unreprinted Clemens Western Items, by Ivan Benson. 1938.
Letters from Honolulu Written for the Sacramento Union, edited by Thomas Nickerson. 1939.
Twain in Eruption: Hitherto Unpublished Pages about Men and Events, edited by Bernard De Voto. 1940.
Travels with Mr. Brown, Being Heretofore Uncollected Sketches Written for the San Francisco Alta California in 1866 and 1867, edited by Franklin Walker and G. Ezra Dane. 1940.
Republican Letters, edited by Cyril Clemens. 1941.

Letters to Will Bowen, edited by Theodore Hornberger. 1941.

Letters in the Muscatine Journal, edited by Edgar M. Branch.   1942.

Washington in 1868, edited by Cyril Clemens.   1943.

Twain, Business Man, edited by Samuel Charles Webster. 1946.

The Letters of Quintus Curtius Snodgrass, edited by Ernest E. Leisy.   1946.

Twain in Three Moods: Three New Items of Twainiana, edited by Dixon Wecter.   1948.

The Love Letters, edited by Dixon Wecter.   1949.

Twain to Mrs. Fairbanks, edited by Dixon Wecter.   1949.

Twain to Uncle Remus 1881–1885, edited by Thomas H. English.   1953.

Twins of Genius: Letters of Twain, Cable, and Others, edited by Guy A. Cardwell.   1953.

Twain of the Enterprise, edited by Henry Nash Smith and Frederick Anderson.   1957.

Traveling with the Innocents Abroad: Twain's Original Reports from Europe and the Holy Land, edited by Daniel Morley McKeithan.   1958.

The Autobiography, edited by Charles Neider.   1959.

The Art, Humor, and Humanity of Twain, edited by Minnie M. Brashear and Robert M. Rodney.   1959.

Twain and the Government, edited by Svend Petersen. 1960.

Twain-Howells Letters: The Correspondence of Samuel L. Clemens and William Dean Howells 1872–1910, edited by Henry Nash Smith and William M. Gibson.   2 vols., 1960; abridged edition, as *Selected Twain-Howells Letters*, 1967.

Your Personal Twain. . . .   1960.

Life as I Find It: Essays, Sketches, Tales, and Other Material, edited by Charles Neider.   1961.

The Travels of Twain, edited by Charles Neider.   1961.

Contributions to The Galaxy 1868–1871, edited by Bruce R. McElderry.   1961.

Twain on the Art of Writing, edited by Martin B. Fried. 1961.

Letters to Mary, edited by Lewis Leary.   1961.

The Pattern for Twain's "Roughing It": Letters from Nevada by Samuel and Orion Clemens 1861–1862, edited by Franklin R. Rogers.   1961.

Letters from the Earth, edited by Bernard De Voto.   1962.

Twain on the Damned Human Race, edited by Janet Smith. 1962.

The Complete Essays, edited by Charles Neider.   1963.

Twain's San Francisco, edited by Bernard Taper.   1963.

The Forgotten Writings of Twain, edited by Henry Duskus. 1963.

General Grant by Matthew Arnold, with a *Rejoinder* by Twain (lecture), edited by John Y. Simon.   1966.

Letters from Hawaii, edited by A. Grove Day.   1966.

Which Was the Dream? and Other Symbolic Writings of the Later Years, edited by John S. Tuckey.   1967.

The Complete Travel Books, edited by Charles Neider. 1967.

Letters to His Publishers 1867–1894, edited by Hamlin Hill.   1967.

Clemens of the Call: Twain in California, edited by Edgar M. Branch.   1969.

Correspondence with Henry Huttleston Rogers 1893–1909, edited by Lewis Leary.   1969.

Man Is the Only Animal That Blushes — or Needs To: The Wisdom of Twain, edited by Michael Joseph.   1970.

Fables of Man, edited by John S. Tuckey.   1972.

Everybody's Twain, edited by Caroline Thomas Harnsberger.   1972.

A Pen Warmed Up in Hell: Twain in Protest, edited by Frederick Anderson.   1972.

What Is Man? and Other Philosophical Writings, edited by Paul Baender, in *Works*.   1973.

The Choice Humorous Works of Twain.   1973.

Notebooks and Journals, edited by Frederick Anderson and others.   1975 — .

Letters from the Sandwich Islands, edited by Joan Abramson, 1975.

Twain Speaking, edited by Paul Fatout.   1976.

The Mammoth Cod, and *Address to the Stomach Club*. 1976.

The Comic Twain Reader, edited by Charles Neider. 1977.

Interviews with Clemens 1874–1910, edited by Louis J. Budd.   1977.

Twain Speaks for Himself, edited by Paul Fatout.   1978.

The Devil's Race-Track: Twain's Great Dark Writings: The Best from "Which Was the Dream" and "Fables of Man," edited by John S. Tuckey.   1980.

Selected Letters, edited by Charles Neider.   1982.

Plymouth Rock and the Pilgrims, and *Other Salutary Platform Opinions*, edited by Charles Neider.   1984.

Twain Laughing: Humorous Stories by and about Clemens, edited by P.M. Zall.   1985.

Letters (1853–1866), edited by Edgar M. Branch and others.   1987; *Letters (1867–1868)*, edited by Harriet Elinor Smith and Richard Bucci, 1990.

Translator, *Slovenly Peter* (Der Struwwelpeter).   1935.

*

Bibliography: *A Bibliography of the Works of Twain* by Merle Johnson, revised edition, 1935; in *Bibliography of American Literature* by Jacob Blanck, 1957; *Twain: A Reference Guide* by Thomas Asa Tenney, 1977; *Twain International: A Bibliography and Interpretation of His Worldwide Popularity* edited by Robert H. Rodney, 1982.

Critical Studies: *My Twain: Reminiscences and Criticisms* by William Dean Howells, 1910, edited by Marilyn Austin Baldwin, 1967; *Twain: A Biography* by Albert Bigelow Paine,   3 vols., 1912, abridged edition, as *A Short Life of Twain*, 1920; *The Ordeal of Twain* by Van Wyck Brooks, 1920, revised edition, 1933; *Twain's America*, 1932, and *Twain at Work*, 1942, both by Bernard De Voto; *Twain: The Man and His Work* by Edward Wagenknecht, 1935, revised edition, 1961, 1967; *Twain: Man and Legend* by De Lancey Ferguson, 1943; *The Literary Apprenticeship of Twain* by Edgar M. Branch, 1950; *Twain as a Literary Artist* by Gladys Bellamy, 1950; *Twain and Huck Finn* by Walter Blair, 1960; *Twain* by Lewis Leary, 1960, and *A Casebook on Twain's Wound* edited by Leary, 1962; *Twain and Southwestern Humor* by Kenneth S. Lynn, 1960; *The Innocent Eye: Childhood in Twain's Imagination* by Albert E. Stone, 1961; *Twain: Social Philosopher*, 1962, and *Our Twain: The Making of a Public Personality*, 1983, both by Louis J. Budd, and *Critical Essays on Twain 1867–1910*, 1982, *Critical Essays on Twain 1910–1980*, 1983, and *New Essays on Adventures of Huckleberry Finn*, 1985, all edited by Budd; *Twain: The Development of a Writer* by Henry Nash Smith, 1962, and *Twain: A Collection of Critical Essays* edited by Smith, 1963; *Discussions of Twain* edited by Guy A. Cardwell, 1963; *Mr. Clemens and Mark Twain: A Biography,* 1966, and *Twain and His World,* 1974, both by Justin Kaplan; *Twain: The Fate of Humor* by James M. Cox, 1966; *Twain as Critic* by Sydney J. Krause, 1967; *Twain: God's Fool* by Hamlin Hill, 1973; *Plots and Characters in the Works of Twain* by Robert L. Gale, 2 vols., 1973; *The Dramatic Unity of Huckleberry Finn* by George C. Carrington, Jr., 1976; *The Art of Twain* by William M. Gibson, 1976; *Twain: A Collection of Criticism* edited by Dean Morgan Schmitter, 1976; *Twain as a Literary Comedian* by David E.E. Sloane, 1979; *Twain's Last Years as a Writer* by William R. Macnaughton, 1979; *Critical Approaches to Twain's Short Stories* edited by Elizabeth McMahan, 1981; *Twain's Escape from Time: A Study of Patterns and Images* by Susan K. Harris, 1982; *Writing Tom Sawyer: The Adventures of a Classic* by Charles A. Norton, 1983; *Twain* by Robert Keith Miller, 1983; *The Authentic Twain: A Biography of Clemens* by Everett Emerson, 1984; *One Hundred Years of Huckleberry Finn* edited by Robert Sattelmeyer and J. Donald Crowley, 1985; *The Making of Twain* by John Lauber, 1985; *Huck Finn among the Critics: A Centennial Selection* edited by M. Thomas Inge, 1985; *On Twain: The Best from "American Literature"* edited by Louis J. Budd and Edwin H. Cady, 1987; *A Reader's Guide to the Short Stories of Twain* by James D. Wilson, 1987; *Twain* by John C. Gerber, 1988; *The Man Who Was Twain: Images and Ideologies* by Guy Cardwell, 1991; *Comedic Pathos: Black Humor in Twain's Fiction* by Patricia M. Mandia, 1991; *Mark and Livy: The Love Story of Twain and the Woman Who Almost Tamed Him* by Resa Willis, 1992.

* * *

Samuel Langhorne Clemens, or Mark Twain, will always be best known for his masterpiece, *The Adventures of Huckleberry Finn,* the book from which, Ernest Hemingway said, "all modern American literature comes." It is very unlikely, however, that Twain could have written that novel without the benefits of a decades-long apprenticeship in the writing of shorter pieces, only some of which can be properly called short stories. Included among his shorter writings are sketches, travel letters, anecdotes, burlesques, and the feature stories and reportage associated with his experiences as a newspaper journalist. Twain's genius throughout his career is most apparent in the richly rendered episode, and many of his most anthologized short pieces are excerpts from longer works such as *Roughing It, The Innocents Abroad,* and *Life on the Mississippi.* Twain himself lifted the so-called "Raft Passage" from the manuscript of *Huckleberry Finn* and inserted it into his Mississippi River memoir.

His first publication, "The Dandy Frightening the Squatter" (1852), is Twain's immature version of a much-told anecdote. But even with its defects it hints that Twain was gradually discovering the terms of the art of southwest frontier humor and the form of the tall tale that he would come to perfect and transform. Self-educated, what Twain came to know well was the tradition of American humor from its beginnings—Yankee and "Down East" as well as southwest frontier. What he seems to have possessed by nature was an ear for the cadences of vernacular speech patterns; whether by instinct or deliberate discipline and cultivation, Twain's was an aural imagination. His boyhood experiences listening to the tales of Uncle Dan'l, a slave on Twain's uncle John Quarles's farm, and his experiences as a cub-pilot and pilot on the Mississippi put him in close touch with an oral tradition of literature that would lead to Huck's opening sentence: "You don't know about me, without you have read a book by the name of 'The Adventures of Tom Sawyer,' but that ain't no matter." His relish of "talk" he captured first in "Jim Smiley and His Jumping Frog" (1865), and his career was launched.

That Twain customarily began writing with virtually no well-conceived plan in mind is attested to not only by his essay "The Art of Authorship" (1890) but also by his two revisions of the Jim Smiley story and his almost eight years of composing *Huckleberry Finn.* In "How to Tell a Story" (1895), however, he described brilliantly many of the essential components of the American humorous story. It depends upon "the *manner* of its telling," not the *matter;* that manner is "deadpan," "the teller [doing] his best to conceal the fact that he even dimly suspects that there is anything funny about [the story]"; its contents are ingeniously digressive and "string incongruities and absurdities together in a wandering and sometimes purposeless way." There is not more apt explication of what happens in the framed narrative of "Jim Blaine and His Grandfather's Old Ram" (1872). Like "Jumping Frog," the tale is a framed narrative that pits the decorous, correct language of the East against the vernacular vitality of the western mining camp. The old miner Blaine tries still once again to tell "the stirring story of his grandfather's old ram," but, since he "is comfortably and sociably drunk. . . .tranquilly, serenely, symmetrically drunk," he as usual loses sight of his subject in his third sentence and appears to meander through a maze of uncontrollable memories. Along the way he describes "Old Miss Wagner," who "was considerable on the borrow, she was." The good lady we learn, in careful steps, was lacking an eye and borrowed a glass one from old Miss Jefferson, had only one leg and borrowed Miss Higgin's wooden one "when she had company and things had to be done," was "bald as a jug" and so borrowed Miss Jacops's wig. Miss Jacops, we discover in the following sentence, "is the coffin-peddler's wife—a ratty old buzzard, he was, that used to go roosting around where people was sick." Before Blaine surrenders to sleep in mid-sentence he mentions a man named Wheeler, who "got nipped by the machinery in a carpet factory and went through in less than a quarter of a minute." All this grotesquerie and violence are embraced by an imperturbable humor and Blaine's certitude about the orderly design of the universe: "Prov'dence don't fire no blank ca'tridges, boys." Twain's persona, like Jim Smiley and the frame's narrator in "The Jumping Frog," "perceived that [he] was 'sold.'" Twain would use variations on such alternative narrators and points of view repeatedly and effectively in numerous works.

Likewise light-hearted are many of his burlesques such as the companion pieces, "Story of the Bad Little Boy" (1865) and "Story of the Good Little Boy" (1870), which satirize the pieties of Sunday School pamphlets and look forward to *Tom Sawyer.* The Snodgrass letters exploit the illiteracy of its author, the butt of a hoax, and "A True Story" (1874) shows Twain's ability to capture black dialect in the slave Aunt Rachel's tale. Others, such as "The Babies" (1879) and the notorious "Whittier Birthday Speech" (1877), exemplify Twain as raconteur, master of stand-up oral performance. "The Private History of a Campaign That Failed" (1885), a personal memoir of his very abbreviated Civil War experiences, parodies a then popular and widespread form of narrative. Its humor vanishes at the end when the band of raw recruits fire collectively at a single rider and kill him.

"The Facts Concerning the Recent Carnival of Crime in Connecticut" (1876), a dialogue between Twain's persona and a diminutive dwarf identified as his conscience, has a darkening, grimmer humor that looks forward to Twain's later despairing works on "the damned human race." Having banished conscience, the narrator "killed thirty-eight persons during the first two weeks," "swindled a widow and some orphans out of their last cow," and so on. The narrative is much closer to "The Man That Corrupted Hadleyburg," *The Mysterious Stranger,* and *Letters from the Earth,* works in which his humor has failed him.

—J. Donald Crowley

See the essays on "The Man that Corrupted Hadleyburg" and "The Notorious Jumping Frog of Calaveras County."

U

ULIBARRÍ, Sabine R(eyes). American. Born in Tierra
Amarilla, New Mexico, 21 September 1919. Educated at
University of New Mexico, Albuquerque, B.A. 1947, M.A.
1949; University of California, Los Angeles, Ph.D. 1959.
Served in U.S. Air Force, 1942–45: Gunner (received
Distinguished Flying Cross and Air Medal four times).
Married Connie Limón in 1942; one child. Teacher, Río
Arriba County, 1938–40, and El Rito Normal School, both
New Mexico, 1940–42; associate professor, 1947–68, pro-
fessor of Spanish, from 1968, chair of modern and classical
languages department, 1971–80, now professor emeritus,
University of New Mexico; director, National Defense
Education Act Language Institute, Quito, Ecuador,
1963–64; director, Andean Study Center, University of
New Mexico-Quito, 1968. Vice-president, 1968, president,
1969, American Association of Teachers of Spanish and
Portuguese. Recipient: Governor's award for literature,
1987; Hispanic Heritage award, 1989. Lives in Albuquerque.

PUBLICATIONS

Short Stories

Tierra Amarilla: Cuentos de Núevo México. 1964; as
  Tierra Amarilla: Stories of New Mexico. 1971.
*Mi abuela fumaba puros y otros cuentos de Tierra Amarilla
  / My Grandma Smoked Cigars and Other Stories of
  Tierra Amarilla* (bilingual edition), translated by Uli-
  barrí; illustrated by Dennis Martínez. 1977.
Primeros encuentros/First Encounters (bilingual edition),
  translated by Ulibarrí. 1982.
El gobernador Glu Glu and Other Stories (bilingual edition),
  translated by Ulibarrí. 1988.
El Cóndor, and Other Stories (bilingual edition), translated
  by Ulibarrí. 1989.

Verse

Al cielo se sube a pie. 1966.
Amor y Ecuador. 1966.

Other

Spanish for the First Grade. 1957.
*El mundo poético de Juan Ramón: estudio estilístico de la
  lengua poética y de los símbolos.* 1962.
Fun Learning Elementary Spanish. 2 vols., 1963–65.
El alma de la raza. 1971.

*

Bibliography: in *Chicano Perspectives in Literature: A
Critical and Annotated Bibliography* by Francisco A. Lomelí and Donald W. Urioste, 1976.

Critical Study: in *Chicano Literre: A Reference Guide*
edited by Francisco A. Lomelí and Julio A. Martinez, 1985.

* * *

Sabine R. Ulibarrí is a major contributor to the cultural
heritage and memory of New Mexico and the Southwest.
His two books of stories, *Tierra Amarilla* and *Mi abuela
fumaba puros/My Grandma Smoked Cigars,* remain classic
portrayals of Ulibarrí's childhood home, the village of
Tierra Amarilla, and the people, ethnic values, and overall
atmosphere of northern New Mexico.

Both books serve, on one level, as reminiscences of
Ulibarrí's own childhood spent growing up in that region,
his friends and family influences, and, on another level, as
a native son's modern account of the continuing historical
and cultural presence of the Spanish settlers who first
populated the region in the 16th century following the
expeditions of Juan de Oñate and other conquistadors. In
both respects, as autobiography and ethnological case
study, Ulibarrí's stories of Tierra Amarilla and New
Mexico are tributes to the lives and landscapes of the
people and places of his "tierra del alma" (soulscape).

Ulibarrí's two books of stories may be read as one
volume—or as companion volumes of the closest kinds of
thematic and structural ties. The narrators of both works
are obvious analogs of the author's own autobiographical
persona, a successful man of letters with a reverence for
words and the mysteries of language, pausing in his
maturing to cast a retrospective eye over the ghosts of his
past. His tone is respectful but humorous, in that the
people and lives he imaginatively recasts and reanimates
into words were shaped by both the sadness and the joy of
life.

Thus Ulibarrí's sense of what the Spanish heart and soul
intuit as "la tristeza de vida" (the sadness of life), is colored
and revived by a counterbalancing exuberance and zest for
life, regardless of its hardships. Each of these 17 stories
thereby provide the pleasure and catharsis of tragicomedy,
reinforced by Ulibarrí's urbanized and sophisticated self,
looking back at his rural beginnings. And this dualistic
somewhat ironic sense, is further underscored by the
bilingual texts. Ulibarrí's Spanish/English fluency is apparent within and between both versions, both "translations,"
set conveniently side by side so as to enhance mutual
Spanish/English, Hispanic/Anglo linguistic and cultural
understanding.

Tierra Amarilla contains short anecdotal accounts of
vaqueros (cowboys), priests, village merchants, local families, near and distant relatives, along with one long story,
almost a novella, "Hombre sin nombre," "Man Without a
Name," of an author's anguished attempts to escape the
psychic dominance of his father suddenly and strangely
become himself.

The initial story, "Mi caballo mago" "The Wonder
Horse" is a more innocent father/son story involving a

teenage boy's youthful quest for masculinity, dramatized here in the pursuit and capture of a white, gloriously wild mustang. This wonder horse, a magnificent stallion, symbolizes the narrator's individualism and identification with manliness. In finding and roping the stallion the boy revels in his prize and the pride it brings him in his family and in his community. It is, however, in the horse's escape that the boy finds real maturity. With the solidarity and empathy shown by his father, the boy realizes that such a horse exists forever as a transcendent spirit, escaping, symbolically, into the rising sun.

This theme of innocence lost turns darker in "Hombre sin nombre," a story in the tradition of the doppelganger. Here the narrator, retreating to his home village to write a story about his father, becomes convinced that his father has usurped his own motive and identity. He attempts to rid himself of this psychic horror by returning to his home in the city and the comforting embraces of his wife. To his ever greater horror he comes to see that his wife is his own mother. He is lost, a man without a name, in a long, tormented dark night of the soul. His book takes on that very name, and troubled though he is, he attempts to save himself in the act of writing yet another book outlining his former self's experiences since returning to the city to his disturbing "discoveries."

Mi abuela fumaba puros similarly deals with triumph and travail. The titular story is a great tribute to the strength of the narrator's grandmother. She survives the grief of her own widowhood by adopting the cigar smoking habits of her deceased husband. And when the narrator's father commits suicide she rages against him and the wages of death with such vehemence that she wards off insanity for the narrator's forlorn and grieving mother.

In a more humorous accounting of death's visitations, "El Negro Aguilar," the narrator recounts the ribald exploits of a black cowboy who shocks the village, especially the women, and also endears himself to them. His earthy stories and songs, and his uncouth antics, elicit avowed public condemnation but inner admiration. Even at his funeral he literally rises from his casket with a smile on his face and a silent song of life.

All of Ulibarrí's stories are flavored with the earthiness of folk tale and the passion of people deeply and passionately engrossed in living out their cultural and familial destinies. His retrospective analyses and dramatizations are loving even in their moments of satire. Through Ulibarrí's microcosmic rendering of one small northern New Mexico village, the reader finds a joyous, reaffirming window on the human condition.

—Robert Franklin Gish

UNAMUNO (y Jugo), Miguel de. Spanish. Born in Bilbao, 29 September 1864. Educated at Colegio de San Nicolás, and Instituto Vizacaíno, both Bilbao; University of Madrid, 1880–84, Ph.D. 1884. Married Concepción Lizárraga Ecénarro in 1891; nine children. Professor of Greek, 1891–1924, 1930–34, and Rector, 1901–14, 1934–36, University of Salamanca; exiled to Canary Islands for criticism of Primo de Rivera government, 1924, then lived in Paris, 1924, and Hendaye, 1925–30; under house arrest for criticism of Franco government, 1936. Cross of the Order of Alfonso XII, 1905. *Died 31 December 1936.*

PUBLICATIONS

Collections

Obras completas, edited by Manuel Garcia Blanco.   16 vols., 1966–71.
Selected Works, edited by Anthony Kerrigan.   7 vols., 1967–84.

Short Stories

El espejo de la muerte.   1913.
Abel Sánchez: Una historia de pasión.   1917; translated as *Abel Sanchez,* 1947.
Tres novelas ejemplares y un prólogo.   1920; as *Three Exemplary Novels,* 1930.
San Manuel Bueno, mártir y tres historias más.   1933.
Abel Sanchez and Other Stories.   1956.

Novels

Paz en la guerra.   1897; as *Peace in War,* 1983.
Amor y pedagogía.   1902.
Niebla.   1914; as *Mist,* 1928.
Tulio Montalban y Julio Macedo.   1920.
La tía Tula.   1921.

Plays

La Venda, La princesa, Doña Lambra.   1913.
Fedra.   1924.
Sombras de sueño.   1931.
El otro.   1932; as *The Others,* in *Selected Works,* 1976.
Raquel.   1933.
El hermano Juan; o, El mundo es teatro.   1934.
La esfinge.   1934.
Teatro completo, edited by Manuel García Blanco.   1959.

Verse

Poesías.   1907.
Rosario de sonetos líricos.   1911.
El Cristo de Velázquez.   1920; as *The Christ of Velazquez,* 1951.
Rimas de dentro.   1923.
Teresa.   1923.
De Fuerteventura a París.   1925.
Romancero del destierro.   1928.
Poems.   1952.
Cancionero: Diario poético.   1953.
Cincuenta poesías inéditas, edited by Manuel García Blanco.   1958.
Last Poems.   1974.

Other

De la enseñanza superior en España.   1899.
Tres ensayos.   1900.
En torno al casticismo.   1902.
Paisajes.   1902.
De mi país.   1903.
Vida de Don Quixote y Sancho.   1905; as *The Life of Don Quixote and Sancho,* 1927.
Recuerdos de niñez y de mocedad.   1908.
Mi religión y otros ensayos breves.   1910; as *Perplexities and Paradoxes,* 1945.
Por tierras de Portugal de España.   1911.
Soliloquios y conversaciones.   1911.

Contra esto y aquello.   1912.
El porvenir de España, with Angel Ganivet.   1912.
Del sentimiento trágico de la vida en los hombres y en los pueblos.   1913; as *The Tragic Sense of Life in Men and in Peoples*, 1926.
Ensayos.   8 vols., 1916–18; revised edition, 2 vols., 1942.
Andanzas y visiones españolas.   1922.
La agonía del cristianismo.   1925; as *The Agony of Christianity*, 1928.
Essays and Soliloquies.   1925.
Cómo se hace una novela.   1927; as *How to Make a Novel*, in *Selected Works*, 1976.
Dos artículos y dos discursos.   1930.
La ciudad de Henoc: Comentario 1933.   1941.
Paisajes del alma.   1944.
Algunas consideraciones sobre la literatura hispano-americana.   1947.
Madrid.   1950.
Mi Salamanca.   1950.
Epistolario, with Juan Maragall.   1951; revised edition, 1976.
Autodiálogos.   1959.
Pensamiento político, edited by Elías Diaz.   1965.
Our Lord Don Quixote and Sancho with Related Essays.   1967.
Diario íntimo, edited by P. Félix García.   1970.
Epistolario, with Alonso Quesada, edited by Lázaro Santana.   1970.
Cartas 1903–1933.   1972.
The Agony of Christianity and Essays on Faith.   1974.
Escritos socialistas.   1976.
Unamuno "agitador de espíritus" y Giner: Correspondencia inédita, edited by D. Gómez Molleda.   1976.
Articulos olvidados sobre España y la primera guerra mundial, edited by Christopher Cobb.   1976.
Gramatica y glosario del Poema del Cid, edited by Barbara D. Huntley and Pilar Liria.   1977.
The Private World: Selections from the Diario íntimo and Selected Letters, 1890–1936, edited by Allen Lacy.   1984.
Escritos de Unamuno sobre Portugal, edited by Angel Marcos de Dios.   1985.
Cartas íntimas: Espistolario entre Unamuno y los hermanos Gutierrez Abascal, edited by Javier Gonzalez de Durana.   1986.
Epistolario completo Ortega-Unamuno, edited by Laureano Robles Carcedo.   1987.
Azorín-Unamuno: Cartas y escritos complemetarios, edited by Laureano Robles Carcedo.   1990.

Translator, *Etica de las prisiones, Exceso de leglslación, De las leyes en general*, by Herbert Spencer.   3 vols., 1895.
Translator, *Historia de la economica política*, by J.K. Ingram.   1895(?).
Translator, *Historia de las literaturas castellana y portuguesa*, by Ferdinand J. Wolf.   2 vols., 1895–96.

*

Critical Studies: *The Lone Heretic: A Biography of Unamuno* by Margaret Thomas Rudd, 1963; *Death in the Literature of Unamuno* by Mario J. Valdés, 1964; *Unamuno: The Rhetoric of Existence* by Allen Lacy, 1967; *Unamuno: An Existential View of Self and Society* by Paul Ilie, 1967; *Unamuno* by Martin Nozick, 1971; *Unamuno's Webs of Fatality* by David G. Turner, 1974; *Unamuno: Abel Sánchez* by Nicholas G. Round, 1974; *Unamuno: The Contrary Self* by Frances Wyers, 1976; *Unamuno: San Manuel Bueno, Mártir* by John Butt, 1981.

*   *   *

Miguel de Unamuno came late to fiction, having published numerous volumes of essays, plays, and poetry before his first collection of short stories, *El espejo de la muerte* (Death's Mirror), appeared in 1913. Individual stories are not remarkable, although most of Unamuno's major preoccupations appear; given the unity of his work and thought, Unamuno expresses certain nuclear ideas regardless of genre. Many stories were preliminary sketches for themes later developed fully as novels, theatrical works, or essays. Important concepts treated include personality conflict or splitting, humanity's internal battles against itself or others, the contrast between public and private persona, and the problem of faith versus doubt. The difficulty of truly knowing oneself, the desire for immortality, the need for proof of God's existence, and the relationship between creator and creation are repetitive concerns. Love, death, parenthood, the conflict between reason and passion or faith, and various existential questions are also major themes: human's destiny, life's ultimate meaning, the nature of physical reality, the absurdity of existence, radical solitude, the impossibility of communication.

Unamuno's most significant contribution to fiction is his own peculiar creation, the *nivola*, born of his reaction against canonical Realism and Naturalism as well as his rejection of Modernism and his scorn for the concept of genres. Unamuno claimed to write without a preconceived plan, freeing his characters from the constraints of plot. He eliminated descriptions and background details (customs, characters' prior lives) to focus on dialogue as reflecting their internal drama, passion, and striving. Characters were termed "agonists," sufferers. His open-minded narratives allegedly had no rules but included important novelettes whose inherent theatricality resulted in frequent dramatic adaptations.

"Nada menos que todo un hombre" ("Every Inch a Man"), one of Unamuno's most characteristic and best-known novelettes, paints the enigmatic portrait of a marriage whose partners neither coincide in sentiments nor succeed in communicating—until it is too late. Julia dreams of living a great love like that of Romantic heroines, while Alejandro considers novels stupid and talk of love beneath the dignity of a real man. Driven to desperation and adultery in her efforts to provoke some show of emotion from Alejandro, Julia is confined to an asylum by her husband. Alejandro terms his wife "a thing of his," incapable of infidelity by definition; therefore, she must remain institutionalized until she renounces the crazy notion that she has been unfaithful. Her spirit finally broken, Julia "confesses" her fidelity, regains her liberty, and dies—provoking Alejandro's suicide. Readers must attempt constantly to define and redefine the pair's true feelings in the face of silence, contradiction, paradoxical acts, and outright lies. Most of Unamuno's novelettes are studies of an overwhelming passion or monomania; here two obsessions lock in mortal struggle.

In 1920, Unamuno published *Tres novelas ejemplares y un prólogo* (*Three Exemplary Novels*) containing the novelettes "Dos madres" ("Two Mothers") "El marqués de Lumbria" ("The Marquis of Lumbria"), plus "Every Inch a

Man." Although all three study failed marriages, portray husbands who have past histories as libertines (something Unamuno sternly disapproved), and end tragically, both new stories emphasize maternal instinct or drive as overpowering urges. Both pit iron-willed, domineering women against more scrupulous and decent younger women for the possession of a weak and pusillanimous man, the "right" to motherhood, and control over the future child. Wealthy and beautiful Raquel in "Two Mothers," believing herself too old for childbearing, forces her lover Juan to marry an impoverished younger woman, sire her child, and deliver it to Raquel. The women's battle for the baby drives the weak-willed Juan to escape through a fatal automobile accident. By contrast, "The Marquis of Lumbria" focuses upon the decadent aristocracy (despised by Unamuno, an erstwhile socialist). The two daughters of the old marquis (who has no sons) fight to bear the future marquis; when the younger Luisa becomes engaged to Tristan, the elder Carolina seduces him and manages to give birth to an illegitimate son before the legitimate heir is born. The sisters' struggle, Tristan's passivity, and postpartum complications end Luisa's life, and Carolina forces the weak-willed widower to marry her and legitimize her firstborn. While less hermetic than "Every Inch a Man," these two tales present "agonists" locked in mortal combat, with victors who believe they are in control yet are hostage to their own passions. Unamuno's women are typically stronger than his men, even if their roles are minor; here they occupy center stage.

In 1933, Unamuno published a volume containing "La novela de don Sandalio, jugador de ajedrez" ("The novella of Don Sandalio, Chess Player"), "Un pobre hombre rico o el sentimiento cómico de la vida" ("A poor Rich Man, or the Comic Sentiment of Life"), "San Manuel Bueno, mártir" ("Saint Emanuel the Good, Martyr," the title story), and "Una historia de amor" ("A Love Story"). Seen as the definitive formulation of Unamuno's religious quandary and philosophical position, "Saint Emanuel the Good" has very much overshadowed other contents of the volume. Nevertheless, "The Novella of Don Sandalio" is one of Unamuno's most interesting literary experiments. A series of letters written by the unnamed narrator to Felipe implies the latter's response—Felipe's replies are critiqued although his letters are not included. The one-sided correspondence chronicles the narrator's passive relationship with don Sandalio in the casino of a small coastal resort where he is spending the summer. While proclaiming his dislike for stupidity, banal conversations, and polite society, the narrator flees solitude, frequenting the casino where he needs not establish any relationships. Observing Sandalio, the local chess wizard, and noting his taciturnity, he imagines Sandalio's sentiments mirror his own. Their silence continues after becoming chess partners, but the narrator's curiosity grows; he fantasizes about Sandalio's thoughts, feelings, and life, projecting his own preferences, creating a figure to his own liking if not exactly in his own image. Startled when Sandalio disappears, he is dismayed, even revolted to hear he has been jailed, not because of moral scruples, but because his version of Sandalio must be modified. Still more upset by a visit from Sandalio's son-in-law, he learns that Sandalio not only had a family but had discussed the narrator with them. He is quite relieved when Sandalio dies. Fraught with chess imagery and ploys, the novella is part game, part serious treatise on the creation of a literary character and characters' ultimate autonomy, as well as a meditation on the role of illusion in human relationships. Like most of Unamuno's tales, this one is dense, susceptible of multiple interpretations, and rich in intellectual and philosophical nuances.

—Janet Pérez

See the essays on "Every Inch a Man" and "Saint Emmanuel the Good, Martyr."

UPDIKE, John (Hoyer). American. Born in Shillington, Pennsylvania, 18 March 1932. Educated at public schools in Shillington; Harvard University, Cambridge, Massachusetts, A.B. (summa cum laude) 1954; Ruskin School of Drawing and Fine Arts, Oxford (Knox fellow), 1954–55. Married 1) Mary Pennington in 1953 (marriage dissolved), two daughters and two sons; 2) Martha Bernhard in 1977. Staff reporter, *The New Yorker,* 1955-57. Recipient: Guggenheim fellowship, 1959; Rosenthal award, 1960; National Book award, 1964; O. Henry award, 1966; Foreign Book prize (France), 1966; New England Poetry Club Golden Rose, 1979; MacDowell medal, 1981; Pulitzer prize, 1982, 1991; American Book award, 1982; National Book Critics Circle award, for fiction, 1982, for criticism, 1984; Union League Club Abraham Lincoln award, 1982; National Arts Club Medal of Honor, 1984; National Medal of the Arts, 1989; Pulitzer prize, 1990; National Book Critics Circle award, 1990. Member, American Academy, 1976. Lives in Beverly Farms, Massachusetts.

PUBLICATIONS

Short Stories

The Same Door.   1959.
Pigeon Feathers and Other Stories.   1962.
Olinger Stories: A Selection.   1964.
The Music School.   1966.
Penguin Modern Stories 2, with others.   1969.
Bech: A Book.   1970.
The Indian.   1971.
Museums and Women and Other Stories.   1972.
Warm Wine: An Idyll.   1973.
Couples: A Short Story.   1976.
Too Far to Go: The Maples Stories.   1979; as *Your Lover Just Called: Stories of Joan and Richard Maple,* 1980.
Problems and Other Stories.   1979.
Three Illuminations in the Life of an American Author.   1979.
The Chaste Planet.   1980.
The Beloved.   1982.
Bech Is Back.   1982.
Getting Older.   1985.
Going Abroad.   1987.
Trust Me.   1987.
The Afterlife.   1987.
Brother Grasshopper.   1990.

Novels

The Poorhouse Fair.   1959.
Rabbit, Run.   1960.
The Centaur.   1963.
Of the Farm.   1965.

Couples.   1968.
Rabbit Redux.   1971.
A Month of Sundays.   1975.
Marry Me: A Romance.   1976.
The Coup.   1978.
Rabbit Is Rich.   1981.
The Witches of Eastwick.   1984.
Roger's Version.   1986.
S.   1988.
Rabbit at Rest.   1990.
Memories of the Ford Administration.   1992.

Plays

Three Texts from Early Ipswich: A Pageant.   1968.
Buchanan Dying.   1974.

Verse

The Carpentered Hen and Other Tame Creatures.   1958;
   as *Hoping for a Hoopoe,* 1959.
Telephone Poles and Other Poems.   1963.
Verse.   1965.
Dog's Death.   1965.
The Angels.   1968.
Bath after Sailing.   1968.
Midpoint and Other Poems.   1969.
Seventy Poems.   1972.
Six Poems.   1973.
Query.   1974.
*Cunts (Upon Receiving the Swingers Life Club Memberships
   Solicitation).*   1974.
Tossing and Turning.   1977.
Sixteen Sonnets.   1979.
An Oddly Lovely Day Alone.   1979.
Five Poems.   1980.
Spring Trio.   1982.
Jester's Dozen.   1984.
Facing Nature.   1985.
A Pear Like a Potato.   1986.
Two Sonnets.   1987.
Recent Poems, 1986–1990.   1990.
Collected Poems, 1953–1993.   1993.

Other

The Magic Flute (for children), with Warren Chappell.
   1962.
The Ring (for children), with Warren Chappell.   1964.
Assorted Prose (includes stories).   1965.
A Child's Calendar (for children).   1965.
On Meeting Authors.   1968.
*Bottom's Dream: Adapted from William Shakespeare's "A
   Midsummer Night's Dream"* (for children).   1969.
A Good Place.   1973.
Picked-Up Pieces (includes story).   1975.
Hub Fans Bid Kid Adieu.   1977.
Talk from the Fifties.   1979.
Ego and Art in Walt Whitman.   1980.
*People One Knows: Interviews with Insufficiently Famous
   Americans.*   1980.
Invasion of the Book Envelopes.   1981.
Hawthorne's Creed.   1981.
Hugging the Shore: Essays and Criticism (includes stories).
   1983.
Confessions of a Wild Bore (essay).   1984.
Emersonianism (lecture).   1984.

*The Art of Adding and the Art of Taking Away: Selections
   from Updike's Manuscripts,* edited by Elizabeth A.
   Falsey.   1987.
Self-Consciousness: Memoirs.   1989.
Just Looking: Essays on Art.   1989.
Odd Jobs: Essays and Criticism (includes stories).   1991.

Editor, *Pens and Needles,* by David Levine.   1970.
Editor, with Shannon Ravenel, *The Best American Short
   Stories 1984.*   1984; *The Year's Best American Short
   Stories,* 1985.

*

Bibliography: *Updike: A Bibliography* by C. Clarke Taylor,
1968; *An Annotated Bibliography of Updike Criticism
1967–1973,* and *Checklist of His Works* by Michael A.
Olivas, 1975; *Updike: A Comprehensive Bibliography with
Selected Annotations* by Elizabeth A. Gearhart, 1978.

Critical Studies: interviews in *Life* 4, November 1966,
Paris Review, Winter 1968, and *New York Times Book
Review,* 10 April 1977; *Updike* by Charles T. Samuels,
1969; *The Elements of Updike* by Alice and Kenneth
Hamilton, 1970; *Pastoral and Anti-Pastoral Elements in
Updike's Fiction* by Larry E. Taylor, 1971; *Updike: Yea
Sayings* by Rachael C. Burchard, 1971; *Updike* by Robert
Detweiler, 1972, revised edition, 1984; *Updike: A Collec-
tion of Critical Essays* edited by David Thorburn and
Howard Eiland, 1979; *Updike* by Suzanne H. Uphaus,
1980; *The Other Updike: Poems/Short Stories/Prose/Play,*
by Donald J. Greiner, 1981; *Updike's Images of America* by
Philip H. Vaughan, 1981; *Married Men and Magic Tricks:
Updike's Erotic Heroes* by Elizabeth Tallent, 1982; *Critical
Essays on Updike* edited by William R. Macnaughton,
1982; *Updike* by Judie Newman, 1988.

*   *   *

John Updike published his first story, "Friends from
Philadelphia," in *The New Yorker* in 1954, joining the staff
of the magazine a year later. In many ways, over the next
three decades and more, he would serve as the quintessential *New Yorker* fiction writer in the mold of colleagues J.D.
Salinger and John Cheever: urbane, witty, sensitive, comfortably white middle class, more interested in psychological nuances than plot.

Updike's first collection, *The Same Door,* distinguished
by a lapidary style and acute eye for significant detail, also
reveals a yearning for an essentially Christian perspective
and ethic. The latter is reflected in his quest for moments of
"grace," Joycean epiphanies, among the many polite wars,
often marital, being waged by his conflicted protagonists.
In "Tomorrow and Tomorrow and So Forth," for instance,
perhaps the collection's strongest story, there is a climactic
lurch of insight (typically ambivalent) shared by a high
school teacher and the pretty adolescent girl who had
tricked him into believing she had a crush on him. "Ace in
the Hole," foreshadowing a major theme and preliminary
sketch for *Rabbit, Run,* offers a modest case study of a
representative American male's inability to mature.

From an historic vantage, the most significant story in
The Same Door might be "Snowing in Greenwich Village,"
which introduces Joan and Richard Maple in a simple but
subtly persuasive domestic drama involving the first seri-

ous threat to their young marriage. The Maples also figure in several later collections, the evolution and dissolution of their adultery-battered marriage crudely paralleling the course of Updike's own first marriage. Their stories were eventually collected in *Too Far To Go: The Maples Stories,* which became a television movie as well. The effectiveness of the Maple tales, more direct in narrative thrust than usual for Updike, has much to do with their author's painful empathy for both sides of the marital Punch-and-Judy show, though sympathy patently alights easier on Richard's consciousness.

Updike's second collection, *Pigeon Feathers and Other Stories,* established his mastery of the form. The title story and "A&P" are among his most anthologized, and "Should Wizard Hit Mommy?" is almost as strong. If marriage is Updike's central focus, both as arena and as possible stoa for his moral scan of our culture's pressure points, then childhood, especially coming-of-age moments, runs a close second. "Pigeon Feathers," for example, set in Olinger, the eastern Pennsylvanian village modeled on Updike's hometown and scene for a number of serial stories—the bulk of them in *Olinger Stories, A Selection*—and for *The Centaur,* climaxes with its anguished, dislocated 14-year-old protagonist finding divinity in the beautifully intricate plumage designs of the pigeons he had been ordered to kill by his grandmother. For Sammy, the 19-year-old narrator of "A&P," which weaves a comic spell that deftly enhances its harsh denouement, the moment of truth is less sublime, his romantic moral gesture (quitting his job) revealing only "how hard the world was going to be to me hereafter."

The Music School abandons childhood, adolescence, and maturational passages for dives into the murky undercurrents of failing marriages. Except for two Maple stories, "Giving Blood" and "Twin Beds in Rome," the familiar stress on delicate probings of psychological sore spots deteriorates into a willful muffling of plot explosions at the expense of literary impact. Relaxed, observant, always in control, Updike seems more concerned with stylistic conceits than satisfying larger fictional expectations; many of the stories are mere sketches, autobiographically etched meditations on the high price paid for lost ideals and an absent godhead.

The narrator of the title story, a writer, envisions his friends and himself as "all pilgrims, faltering toward divorce," but juxtapositions of a senseless murder with his domestic discomfit never coheres into an affecting social portrait. In fact, the expected moment of grace—being ravished by the appearence of his daughter when he comes to pick her up at the school he has transformed into a symbolic sanctuary—betrays a stunted psychosexual growth pattern almost Victorian in its sentimental pedophilia. Mary Allen and other critics have traced the limitations of Updike's vision of women, though not always fully cognizant of the distance between artifice and artisan.

Through the next two decades, Updike continued to supply his quota of expertly tailored short fictions. But the heart of his prolific creative energy was being poured into his novels, particularly the *Rabbit* quartet, where his relentless (at times pornographic) obsession with sex as transcendent hope and replacement for lost spiritual imperatives could have freer expression, as could his worrying the religious question in a broader cultural and aesthetic framework. Very few of the stories in *Museums and Women, Problems and Other Stories,* or *Trust Me,* can match the harsh brilliance of the portrait of contemporary America rendered by *Rabbit at Rest.* "Trust Me," for example, fluent and cleverly structured upon the thrust

required for any love relationship to thrive, is far too pat in plot design to achieve much emotional weight, however psychologically acute. And the title story of "Museums and Women" actually reinforces a Manichean reduction of female realities to caricature.

Nevertheless, Updike's most durable stories, mainly from the early collections and the Maples's chronicles, provide a series of vivid literary x-rays of the once-dominant American self—male, white, Northeastern middle class—at a crisis stage of its deconstruction when Puritan inheritance and consequent social and political assumptions could no longer neutralize urgent existential anxieties. They also depict, with frequently touching poetic exactitude, the sufferings attendant upon growing up in a family environment where parental love is skewed by manipulative power conflicts, limning, in addition, the flawed marriages that must result when the offspring of such unions wed.

—Edward Butscher

See the essays on "A&P" and "Lifeguard."

URQUHART, Fred(erick Burrows). British. Born in Edinburgh, 12 July 1912. Educated at village schools in Scotland; Stranraer High School, Wigtownshire; Broughton Secondary School, Edinburgh. Worked in an Edinburgh bookshop, 1927–34; reader for a London literary agency, 1947–51, and for MGM, 1951–54; London scout for Walt Disney Productions, 1959–60; reader for Cassell and Company, publishers, London, 1951–74, and for J.M. Dent and Sons, publishers, London, 1967–71. Recipient: Tom-Gallon Trust award, 1951; Arts Council of Great Britain grant, 1966, bursary, 1978, 1985; Scottish Arts Council grant, 1975. Lives in Lothian, Scotland.

PUBLICATIONS

Short Stories

I Fell for a Sailor and Other Stories.   1940.
The Clouds Are Big with Mercy.   1946.
Selected Stories.   1946.
The Last GI Bride Wore Tartan: A Novella and Some Short Stories.   1948.
The Year of the Short Corn and Other Stories.   1949.
The Last Sister and Other Stories.   1950.
The Laundry Girl and the Pole: Selected Stories.   1955.
Collected Stories :
    The Dying Stallion and Other Stories.   1967.
    The Ploughing Match and Other Stories.   1968.
Proud Lady in a Cage: Six Historical Stories.   1980.
A Diver in China Seas.   1980.
Seven Ghosts in Search.   1983.
Full Score: Short Stories.   1989.

Novels

Time Will Knit.   1938.
The Ferret Was Abraham's Daughter.   1949.
Jezebel's Dust.   1951.
Palace of Green Days.   1979.

Other

Scotland In Colour.   1961.

Editor, with Maurice Lindsay, *No Scottish Twilight: New Scottish Stories.*   1947.
Editor, *W.S.C.: A Cartoon Biography* (on Winston Churchill).   1955.
Editor, *Great True War Adventures.*   1956.
Editor, *Scottish Short Stories.*   1957.
Editor, *Men at War: The Best War Stories of All Time.* 1957.
Editor, *Great True Escape Stories.*   1958.
Editor, *The Cassell Miscellany 1848–1958.*   1958.
Editor, *Everyman's Dictionary of Fictional Characters,* by William Freeman, revised edition.   1973.
Editor, with Giles Gordon, *Modern Scottish Short Stories.* 1978; revised edition, 1982.
Editor, *The Book of Horses: The Horse Through the Ages in Art and Literature.*   1981.

*

Critical Studies: review by Janet Adam Smith, in *New York Times Book Review,* 31 July 1938; Alexander Reid, in *Scotland's Magazine,* February 1958; Iain Crichton Smith in *The Spectator,* 24 May 1968; *History of Scottish Literature* by Maurice Lindsay, 1977; "Praise the Lord for Short Stories" by Douglas Gifford, in *Books in Scotland* 8, Autumn-Winter 1980; *A Companion to Scottish Culture* edited by David Daiches, 1981; "Urquhart: Lad for Lassies" by Graeme Roberts, in *Scottish Review,* May 1982; *Modern Scottish Literature* by Alan Bold, 1983; *The Macmillan Companion to Scottish Literature* by Trevor Royle, 1983, as *Companion to Scottish Literature,* 1983; *Guide to Modern World Literature* by Martin Seymour-Smith, 1985; "A Man Who Can Write about Women" by Isobel Murray, in *The Scotsman,* 9 September 1989.

*   *   *

Fred Urquhart published his first short story in 1936. During the next two decades he produced no fewer then seven volumes of stories, as well as three novels, earning from Alexander Reid the accolade of "Scotland's leading short story writer of the century." The publication of his *Collected Stories* in 1967 and 1968 won for his work the admiration of a new generation of readers and critics; the appearance of three more volumes of stories, many dealing with supernatural or historical themes, has consolidated Urquhart's reputation as a master of the genre.

It was Urquhart's portrayal of female characters that caught the attention of early admirers, such as Compton Mackenzie, who praised his "remarkable talent for depicting women young and old." Longing for escape from the monotonous drudgery of working-class life is a characteristic theme of many of these stories. Sometimes that longing ends in bitter disillusionment, as in "The Bike," where a girl saves for three years to buy a gleaming red racing cycle. Her joy of ownership of this symbol of freedom is shortlived, however, when the bike is damaged beyond repair by the carelessness of her drunken boyfriend: "She knew that something more than her bike had been broken. Nothing would ever be the same again."

Another story that displays what Alan Bold describes as Urquhart's emphasis "on the way dreams are defeated by hostile circumstances" is "Washed in the Blood." Its young heroine longs to be saved by an exotic black revivalist, only to have her childish faith rudely shattered when she discovers that "Jesus was a carpenter" like the local atheist drunk. The effectiveness of this story depends on the way Urquhart maintains an ironic distance between the naive childish self whose experiences are recorded and the knowing adult self who narrates them.

Perhaps Urquhart's finest story about working-class girls is "We Never Died in Winter." This moving account by a tuberculate patient of her nine months in hospital is a remarkable study of courage and resilience in the face of physical discomfort and disappointed hopes. Its tragic power is primarily due to the flat, matter-of-fact tone of the narrative, which by playing down the pathos inherent in the heroine's situation, sets off the cheerfulness and wry humour—epitomised by the story's title—with which she adjusts to her illness and faces the loss of love, hope, and ultimately life itself. Urquhart's achievement in such stories is to transfigure the commonplace by realising the tragic potential of shopgirls and factory hands.

Sympathetic insight is the hallmark of Urquhart's best stories, the product not only of observation and imagination, but also of careful attention to details of language and tone. It is this that enables him to avoid what he calls the "sentimental clutch of the Kail Yard," particularly in his Auchencairn stories, which are set in the Mearns countryside south of Aberdeen, where Urquhart spent part of the war. Nowhere is this insight better exemplified than in "The Ploughing Match," which won the Tom-Gallon award for 1952-53.

In the story Annie Dey has dreamed for 50 years of holding a ploughing match on the family farm. Now at last her girlhood ambition is about to be realised, but she is paralysed and bed-ridden, restricted to watching the contest through a "square of window" with the aid of a pair of spying glasses, and forced to relinquish to her son's "ill-gettit quaen of a wife" the glory of playing hostess and presenting the prizes. Moreover, instead of the "horses with beribboned manes and tails" that Annie remembers, this match has only tractors—"a lot of new-fangled dirt." And although she waits all day to receive visitors, arrayed in her best pink nightdress, none of her late husband's friends or the local gentry takes the trouble to pay their respects to her. Summarised thus, the irony inherent in Annie's situation seems likely to be drowned in a welter of pathos. That this does not happen is due not only to Urquhart's unsentimental conception of Annie's character, but also to his control of language and tone. Notice how the physical helplessness and frustration of Annie, deprived by a stroke of the use of her tongue and compelled to communicate her needs to an impudent servant girl by means of paper and pencil, is brought into sharp focus by a single image:

> The old woman sucked in her lower lip, clamping down her hard gum on it. She looked at her set of false teeth in the tumbler beside the bed, and she closed her eyes in pain. To be beholden to other folk to get them put into her mouth . . .

It is the blow to her pride that Annie finds hardest to bear, a feeling that Urquhart articulates with economy and precision in a couple of brisk vernacular phrases:

She that had aye a tongue on her that would clip cloots to be lying here speechless! . . . And the old woman writhed as she thought of what the grieve and the ploughman childes must say out there in the tractor-shed: "Only an act o' God would make the auld bitch hold her tongue!"

The peasant humour, vigour, and candour of these comments establishes the unsentimental narrative tone at the very start of the story, enabling Urquhart to introduce a series of potentially pathetic situations without producing a maudlin effect.

Many of Urquhart's characters are the natural underdogs beloved of the traditional short story writer from Gogol to Malamud: comic figures from the lowest rungs of society, like the wall-eyed Lizzie in "Beautiful Music," or the malicious Rosie in "Win Was Wild," or the Hogarthian landlady in "Dirty Minnie," or the chorus of Rabelaisian washerwomen in "Dirty Linen," fighting over a pair of cami-knickers in their local steamie. These stories exemplify that "gusto, passion, rumbustiousness, and vigour" that Urquhart has identified as the distinguishing characteristic of the Scottish short story.

—Graeme Roberts

See the essay on "Alicky's Watch."

V

VALENZUELA, Luisa. Argentinian. Born in Buenos Aires, 26 November 1938. Educated at Belgrano Girls' School; Colegio Nacional Vicente Lopez, Buenos Aires; University of Buenos Aires, B.A. Married Théodore Marjak in 1958 (divorced); one daughter. Lived in Paris, 1958–61; assistant editor of Sunday supplement, *La Nación*, Buenos Aires, 1964–69; freelance journalist in the United States, Europe, and Mexico, 1970–73, and Buenos Aires, 1973–79; writer-in-residence, Columbia University, New York, 1980–83; contributing writer, *The Village Voice* and *The New York Time Book Review*, 1980; visiting professor, New York University, 1984–89; fellow, New York Institute for the Humanities; lived in New York, Buenos Aires, and Tepoztlán, Mexico, 1978–89. Recipient: Fondo Nacional de las Artes award, 1966, 1973; Fulbright fellowship, 1969–70; Instituto Nacional de Cinematografía award, 1973; Guggenheim fellowship, 1983. Honorary doctorate: Knox College, Illinois, 1991. Lives in Buenos Aires.

Publications

Short Stories

Los heréticos. 1967; as "The Heretics," in *Clara: 13 Short Stories and a Novel*, 1976.
Aquí pasan cosas raras. 1975; translations in *Strange Things Happen Here: 26 Short Stories and a Novel*, 1979.
Clara: 13 Short Stories and a Novel. 1976.
Strange Things Happen Here: 26 Stories and a Novel. 1979.
Cambio de armas. 1982; as *Other Weapons*, 1985.
Donde viven las águilas. 1983; as *Up Among the Eagles*, in *Open Door*, 1988.
Open Door. 1988.
The Censors: A Bilingual Selection of Stories. 1992.

Novels

Hay que sonreír. 1966; as *Clara*, in *Clara: 13 Short Stories and a Novel*, 1976.
El gato eficaz. 1972.
Como en la guerra. 1977; as *He Who Searches*, in *Strange Things Happen Here: 26 Short Stories and A Novel*, 1979.
Libro que no muerte. 1980.
Cola de lagartija. 1983; as *The Lizard's Tail*, 1983.
Novela negra con argentinos. 1990.
Blame. 1992.

Plays

Realidad nacional desde la cama. 1990.

Screenplay: *Hay que sonreír.*

---

*

Critical Studies: "Women Writing About Prostitutes: Amalia Jamilis and Valenzuela" by Amy Kaminsky, in *The Image of the Prostitute in Modern Literature*, 1984; "Valenzuela: From *Hay que sonreír* to *Cambio de armas*," in *World Literature Today* 58, 1984, "Valenzuela's *Cambio de armas*: Subversion and Narrative Weaponry," in *Romance Quarterly*, 1986, and *Reflections/Refractions: Reading Valenzuela*, 1988, all by Sharon Magnarelli; "Valenzuela's *The Lizard's Tail*: Deconstruction of the Peronist Mythology" by Z. Nelly Martínez, in *El Cono Sur*, edited by Rose S. Minc, 1985; Valenzuela issue of *Review of Contemporary Fiction*, Fall 1986; "Fragmentation in Valenzuela's Narrative" by Patricia Rubia, in *Salmagundi* 82–82, 1989.

* * *

Luisa Valenzuela is best known for her short stories, especially those collected in *Aquí pasan cosas raras* (*Strange Things Happen Here*), and *Cambio de armas* (*Other Weapons*).

Since her earliest pieces Valenzuela has concentrated on three interrelated topics: language, politics (or religion, as in *Los heréticos*, her first collection of short stories), and male-female relationships in patriarchal societies. Her prose, often playful and humorous, and always iconoclastic, underscores the basic ambiguity of the human being and the world, and the fact that language is an untrustworthy means of expression and communication. Individuals inherit linguistic systems laden with tendentious meanings, often of a political or sexual nature, which constitute invisible but powerful and oppressive traps. They not only distort reality, but they also contaminate individual and social interactions. Most individuals are unaware of such contamination and very few escape it. This constitutes a fundamental concern of the collection *Strange Things Happen Here*.

Characters in the stories of *Donde viven las águilas* (*Up Among the Eagles*), explore the dimensions of non-discursive language as a means of transcending the pollution of contemporary western societies. Most of them take place in the Mexican highlands where vestiges of preColumbian cultures are still present. In these "upper worlds" reason and magic coexist; individuals experience closeness to nature, and the possibilities of communicating "interpreting pauses, intonations, facial expressions, and sighs," allow the characters to pierce the boundaries of reason into pre-linguistic, subconscious, and oneiric realms. Those who ascend in "Up Among the Eagles" or "The Attainment of Knowledge," strip off their masks, erase their faces, and become one with nature, a process which is only possible away from contemporary urban societies.

Language in Valenzuela's stories often becomes an instrument of distortion of reality for those in power. The meaning of specific words, for example, is substituted for its antithesis; in "United Rapes Unlimited, Argentina," the verb "to defend" means "to rape." In her stories political discourse serves to hide state-sponsored violence, torture, and murder behind linguistic masks denoting order, peace, and happiness. Consequently, people exist in absurd and chaotic worlds characterized by the inversion of values and the legitimization of deceit.

Strange Things Happen Here is Valenzuela's most overtly political work. Its stories were inspired by the dirty war unleashed against the Argentinean population by that country's military dictatorship, in the mid 1970's and early 1980's. The stories explore the psychological and social effects of sustained and systematic violence. One of its most immediate consequences is the immobilizing effect of fear, which translates in people's unwillingness to recognize that strange things are happening, that nothing is normal anymore. The character of "Who, Me a Bum?" for example, regards the moaning and groaning he overhears at night as a mere impediment to his sleep. Also, while at a metro station, he comments on the anger of commuters because a suicide victim is holding up the train. Nobody questions the motive of the incidents, and all continue unbothered about their business.

Another consequence of state-sponsored terrorism is the debasement and reification of individuals. Characters' lives are materially, psychologically, and socially impoverished to such an extent that they become lonely entities leading meaningless, nightmarish existences. One character in "Strange Things Happen Here" is addressed at one point as "the jacket," and in "The Celery Munchers" humans contaminate rats. The most dramatic example, however, is "The Best Shod," which, in Valenzuela's characteristical black humor, "celebrates" how well shod beggars invading Buenos Aires are, thanks to the availability of good shoes found on the numerous tortured and often mutilated bodies in "vacant lots, sewer conduits, and fallow fields."

The five stories in *Other Weapons*—all of them narrated by a female voice—explore the ways in which women resist the images, values, and codes of behavior imposed on them by the patriarchy. The title not only refers to the violence of the dirty war, of which women were primary victims, but also to the recourses available to women in their struggle for identity, fulfillment of their sexuality, and attainment of freedom. In stories such as "Fourth Version" and "Other Weapons," the political and the erotic are inextricably bound, and constitute the main source of conflict between men and women. It is possible for women to extricate themselves from the seductive powers of men ("Rituals of Rejection") but the punishment imposed by the patriarchy on "liberated" women is severe. In "Other Weapons" torture reduces "so-called Laura," a leftist revolutionary, to a vegetable-like state, devoid of memories and volition. She becomes the sexual object of her husband/torturer who deprives her of physical and psychological freedom. In their struggle against a tradition of passivity, submission, and acquiescence, Valenzuela's women need to charter new ground, and explore the untapped resources of their imagination and erotic impulses.

The power and significance of Valenzuela's short fiction lie not only in the intrinsic interest of the themes it develops, but also, as "Other Weapons" demonstrates, in her constant search for a feminist discourse. Although she is not the only Latin American female writer to embark in such a project, her fiction undoubtedly has broken new ground for women's writing in Latin America.

—Patricia Rubio

VALLE-INCLÁN, Ramón (Maria) del (Valle Peña). Spanish. Born in Villanueva de Arosa, Pontevedra, Galicia, 28 October 1866. Educated at University of Santiago de Compostela, studied law, 1888–1890. Married Josefina Blanco in 1907 (divorced 1932); six children. Newspaper journalist and war correspondent, *El Imperial*, France, 1916; professor of ethics, Madrid School of Fine Arts, 1916–1933; director, Spanish Academy of Fine Arts, Rome, 1933–35. *Died 5 January 1936.*

PUBLICATIONS

Collections

Obras completas. 2 vols., 1944.
Obras escogidas, edited by Gasper Gómez de la Serna. 1958; vol. 2, 1971.
Antologia, edited by Florentino M. Turner. 1963.
Valle-Inclán: Antología, edited by Rafael Conte. 1966.

Short Stories

Femininas: seis historias amorosas. 1895.
Epitalamio (novella). 1897.
Sonatas. Memorias del Marqués de Bradomín. 1941; as *The Pleasant Memoirs of the Marquis of Bradomín*, 1924.
    Sonata de ontoño. 1902.
    Sonata de estío. 1903.
    Sonata de primavera. 1904.
    Sonata de invierno. 1905.
Corte de amor. 1903.
Jardín umbrío. 1903; expanded edition as *Jardín novelesco*, 1905.
Flor de santidad. Historia milenaria (novellas). 1904.
Historias perversas. 1907; expanded edition as *Historias de amor*, 1909.
Cofre de sándalo. 1909.
Las mieles del rosal. Trozos selectos. 1910.
Flores de almendro. 1936.

Novels

La guerra Carlista (Los cruzados de la causa, El resplandor de la hoguera, Gerifaltes de antaño). 3 vols., 1908–09.
La lámpara maravillosa. Ejercicios espirituales. 1916; as *The Lamp of Marvels*, 1986.
Tirano Banderas. 1926; as *The Tyrant*, 1929.
La corte de los milagros. 1927.
Baza de espadas. 1958.
El truedo dorado, edited by G. Fabra Barreiro. 1975.

Plays

Cenizas (produced 1899). 1899; as *El yermo de las almas*, 1908.
Aguila de blasón. 1907.
El marqués de Bradomín. 1907.
Romance de lobos. 1908; as *Wolves! Wolves!*, 1957.

Cuento de Abril (produced 1909).   1910.
Voces de gesta (produced 1912).   1911.
La marquesa Rosalinda (produced 1912).   1913.
El embrujado.   1913.
La cabeza del dragón (produced 1909).   1914; as *Farsa de
    la cabeza del dragón,* 1914; as *The Dragon's Head,* in
    Poet Lore 29, 1918.
Farsa de la enamorada del rey.   1920; as *Farsa italiana de
    la enamorada del rey,* 1920.
Divinas palabras.   1920; as *Divine Words,* 1977.
Comedias bárbaras.   1922.
Farsa y licencia de la reina castiza.   1922.
Cara de plata.   1922.
Luces de Bohemia.   1924; as *Lights of Bohemia,* 1969; as
    Bohemian Lights, 1976.
Los cuernos de don Friolera.   1925.
Las galas del difunto.   1930.
Teatro selecto, edited by Anthony N. Zahareas.   1969.

Verse

Aromas de leyenda.   1907.
La pipa de kif.   1919.
El pasajero.   1920.
Valle-Inclán: Sus mejores poesías, edited by Fernando
    Gutiérrez.   1955.
Páginas selectas, edited by Joseph Michel, 1969.

Other

Opera omnia.   22 vols., 1912–28;   24 vols., 1941–43.
La media noche.   1917.
Cuentos, estética y poemas (includes story and verse).
    1919.
Ligazon; auto para silvetas.   1926.
Vísperas de la gloriosa.   1930.
Publicaciones periodísticas anteriores a 1895, edited by
    William L. Fichter.   1952.
Autobiography, Aesthetics, Aphorism, edited by Robert
    Lima.   1966.
Artículos completos y otras páginas olvidadas.   1987.

Also translated works by Paul Alexis, José María Eça de
    Queiroz, and others.

*

Bibliography: *A Bio-bibliography and Iconography* by José
Rubia Barcía, 1960; *An Annotated Bibliography* by Robert
Lima, 1972.

Critical Studies: *Valle-Inclán, An Appraisal of His Life and
Works* edited by Anthony Zahareas, 1968; *Valle-Inclán:
Tiranos Banderas* by Verity Smith, 1971; *Valle-Inclán* by
Verity Smith, 1973; *Dominant Themes in the Sonatas* by
Rosco N. Tolman, 1973; *The Primitive Themes in Valle-
Inclán* by R. Spoto, 1976; *"Ruido ibérico": A Popular View
of Revolution* by A. Sinclair, 1977; *Time and History in
Valle-Inclán's Historical Novels and Tirano Banderas* by
Peggy Lynne Tucker, 1980; *Valle-Inclán's Modernism* by
Claire J. Paolini, 1986.

* * *

The Spanish novelist, dramatist, poet, and short story
writer Ramón de Valle-Inclán was born of impoverished
rural gentry in Pontevedra (Galicia), Spain's most northwestern province—agrarian, backward, feudal and atavis-
tic. This Galician background is evident in the Celtic
influences, legends, superstitions, and mythological figures
of his early stories, and regional folklore continues flavor-
ing some mature works. Valle-Inclán, usually included with
the "Generation of 1898," established himself from 1895
onward in Madrid, leading a bohemian literary existence.

His first collection of short stories, *Femeninas,* cameo
portraits of women, contained some germs of plots later
expanded. His penchant for reworking and recycling his
materials aroused critical imputations of limited originality, yet Valle-Inclán was one of the most profoundly original
creative personalities in all Spanish letters. Parnassianism,
Symbolism, Decadentism, and Latin-American Modernists
influenced his initial period (1895–1905). His first major
achievement in the Modernist manner, *Sonata de otoño*
("Autumn Sonata") was one of four novelettes keyed to the
seasons, constituting the gallant memoirs of an aging Don
Juan, the Marquis of Bradomín. Each recreates a season of
Bradomín's life (spring-youth, summer-prime, autumn-
middle age, winter-old age) with everything harmonizing,
from the lady love of the hour to mood, setting, decor, and
rhetoric. The titles evince Modernist efforts to equate
literature with music (as with plastic arts). *Sonata de estío*
("Summer Sonata") and two collections of Modernist short
stories, *Corte de amor* (Court of Love) and *Jardín umbrío*
(Shaded Garden) appeared in 1903, and *Sonata de primavera* ("Spring Sonata") and the novelette, *Flor de santidad*
(Saintly Flower) the following year. After completing the
cycle with *Sonata de invierno* ("Winter Sonata"), Valle-
Iclán moved from Modernism toward Expressionism. He
married actress Josefina Blanco, and began writing more
for the theater while working on a novelistic cycle treating
the 19th-century Carlist wars. He is best known for his
mature theater and novels based on the *esperpento,* an
aesthetic of his own devising, defined as the heroes and
values of yore reflected in distorting mirrors—a grotesque,
caricaturesque reversal of orthodox values and parodic,
Expressionistic deformation of humanity (human is dehumanized, seen as a puppet, an animal, or a bad actor).
Because of the force, daring, and licentiousness of some of
his works, they were banned from the Spanish stage until
nearly a half-century after his death.

Story collections or anthologies published after 1905
added little new material. *Corte de amor* contained three
stories, two from *Femeninas,* plus the novelettes "Rosita"
and "Augusta," the latter published separately in 1897 as
Epitalamio (Epithalamium). Later editions included "La
Condesa de Cela" (Countess Cela) and "La Generala" (The
General's Wife), both first published in *Femeninas* and
subsequently in literary reviews. *Jardín novelesco* (Novel-
esque Garden), an expanded version of *Jardín umbrío,*
added five stories, with more in subsequent editions. *Cofre
de sándalo* (Sandalwood Box) repeated four of the six
stories from *Femeninas,* and two from *Corte de amor,* etc.
"La nina Chole" from *Femeninas* formed the basis for
Sonata de estío, while "Adega," published in a magazine in
1899, was expanded to become *Flor de santidad. Historias
perversas* includes eight stores, all from previous collections, six of them repeated in *Historias de amor* (Love
Stories), which adds only one story not found in collections
already cited. Usually each edition incorporates modifications, sometimes significant.

Need for funds obliged Valle-Inclán to keep publishing fiction, but being an exquisite craftsman and consummate stylist who continually polished and refined his work, he recycled material from earlier collections rather than dashing off new stories. This makes it impractical to treat collections as entities, but two basic divisions exist: the novelettes and all story collections except *Jardín umbrío* (later *Jardín novelesco*) are exclusively portraits of "noble and modest ladies"; as titles of subsequent collections indicate, they are also love stories, often adulterous, semiclandestine, and perverse, involving libertines, or are parodies of Romanticism, which Valle-Iclán despised. The remainder (especially those in the final expanded edition of *Jardín novelesco*, subtitled "Stories of Saints, Souls in Torment, Demons and Thieves") are fused with the millenary, medieval Galician ambient of ruins, superstition, witchcraft, satanism, lyricism, decadence, brutality, madness, and savagery. *Flores de almendro* (Almond Flowers), the most complete anthology of his short stories, includes both types of his brief fiction, the erotic and gallant, and Galician tales of mystery, fantasy, and the supernatural. Determining how many stories are in Valle-Inclán's corpus is problematic: quite a few published separately were later incorporated verbatim into the various Sonatas, *Flor de santidad*, or his novel-length theatrical works, the *Comedias bárbaras* (Barbarian Comedies), raising questions as to whether they are fragments or independent works; the existence of multiple extant variants, some widely divergent, is another problem, as is his practice of changing titles. Most counts set Valle's brief fiction somewhere between 50 and 70 titles, including stories and novelettes.

The decadent aristocracy, inauthenticity, and artificiality of social behavior, seen in the gallant tales and the *Sonatas*, contrast with Valle-Inclán's love for the idyllic, pastoral world of rural Galicia, a landscape of fable and legend, bucolic forests and rivers, but also of primitive passions, stark misery, and tragedy, appearing in a majority of the other stories. In *Flor de santidad*, an innocent, devout shepherd girl shares her tent with a mendicant pilgrim that she believes is Christ; he seduces her, and she prophesies that she will bear a divine child. Pronounced bewitched and exorcised, she ends by going to the servants' market. "Spring Sonata," set in Italy where the youthful Bradomín is serving as an envoy to the Vatican, depicts his involvement in intrigues as a background to his pursuit of a virginal adolescent destined for the convent. His diabolical snares and stalking of María Rosario indirectly cause her little sister's death and lead to madness in which María Rosario equates him with Satan. "Summer Sonata," set in tropical Mexico during Bradomín's prime, features a mature, sensual, amoral Creole, involved in an incestuous "marriage" with her father. She eventually becomes the Marquis's lover (this is the only sonata which does not end tragically). The other two sonatas are set in Spain, "Autumn Sonata" in Galicia, and "Winter Sonata" in the Pyrenees of Navarre where the silver-haired Bradomín is fighting on the side of the Carlist insurrection against government troops. Wounded, his arm amputated, he is nursed in a convent by a novitiate he recognizes as his illegitimate daughter from a long-ago affair. Nonetheless, he seduces her, provoking her suicide, which does not prevent his subsequently enjoying a night of love with her mother. Valle-Inclán deliberately emphasizes the satanic side of Bradomín and further titillates his readers by intertextual references to writings of the Marquis de Sade and other 19th-century pornographers. While the sonatas are the best known of Valle-Inclán's works, and are fully characteristic of the erotic subgrouping of his stories, they differ greatly from his theater and his mature, historical novels of political criticism and satire, on which the author's enduring reputation rests.

—Janet Pérez

See the essay on "Autumn Sonata."

———

VERGA, Giovanni. Italian. Born in Catania, Sicily, 2 September 1840. Educated at home, and privately, 1851–60; studied law at University of Catania, 1860–65. Lived in Florence, 1865–70, and Milan, 1870–85; then returned to Catania. Made a senator, 1920. *Died 27 January 1922.*

PUBLICATIONS

Collections

Tutte le novelle (stories).   2 vols., 1942.
Le Opere, edited by Lina and Vito Perroni.   2 vols., 1945.
Opere, edited by Luigi Russo.   1955.
Edizione nazionale delle opere di Verga.   1987—.

Short Stories

Nedda.   1874; translated as *Nedda,* 1888.
Primavera ed altri racconti.   1876.
Vita dei campi.   1880; as *Cavalleria Rusticana and Other Tales of Sicilian Life,* 1893; as *Under the Shadow of Etna,* 1896.
Novelle rusticane.   1882; as *Little Novels of Sicily,* 1925; as *Short Sicilian Novels,* edited by Eric Lane, 1984.
Per le vie.   1883.
Drammi intimi.   1884.
Vagabondaggio.   1887.
I ricordi del Capitano d'Arce.   1891.
Don Candeloro e C.i.   1894.
The She-Wolf and Other Stories.   1958.

Novels

I carbonari della montagna.   4 vols., 1861–62.
Una peccatrice.   1867.
Storia di una capinera.   1873.
Eva.   1874.
Tigre reale.   1875.
Eros.   1875.
I vinti:
    I Malavoglia.   1881; as *The House by the Medlar Tree,* 1890.
    Mastro-don Gesualdo.   1889; edited by Carla Riccardi, 1979; as *Master Don Gesualdo,* 1893.
Il marito di Elena.   1882.

Plays

Cavalleria rusticana, from his own story (produced 1884). 1884.
La lupa; In portineria, from his own stories.   1896.
La caccia al lupo; La caccia alla volpe.   1902.
Dal tuo al mio.   1906.
Teatro (includes *Cavalleria rusticana, La lupa, In portineria, La caccia al lupo, La caccia alla volpe*).   1912.
The Wolf Hunt, in *Plays of the Italian Theatre,* edited by Isaac Goldberg.   1921.
Rose caduche, in *Maschere 1.*   1929.

Other

Lettere a suo traduttore (correspondence with Édouard
    Rod), edited by Fredi Chiappelli.   1954.
Lettere a Dina (correspondence with Dina Castellazzi di
    Sordevolo), edited by Gino Raya.   1962.
Lettere a Luigi Capuana, edited by Gino Raya.   1975.
Lettere sparse, edited by Giovanna Finocchiaro Chimirri.
    1980.

*

Critical Studies: *Verga* by Thomas G. Bergin, 1931; *Verga's
Milanese Tales* by Olga Ragusa, 1964; *Verga: A Great
Writer and His World* by Alfred Alexander, 1972; *Language in Verga's Early Novels* by Nicholas Patruno, 1977;
*The Narrative of Realism and Myth: Verga, Lawrence,
Faulkner, Pavese* by Gregory L. Lucente, 1981.

*   *   *

Giovanni Verga's short stories were introduced to English
readers in the 1920's by D.H. Lawrence, who translated
two of his collections, *Vita del Campi (Cavalleria Rusticana
and Other Tales of Sicilian Life)* and *Novelle Rusticane
(Little Novels of Sicily)*. These two collections belong to the
period of approximately ten years, starting in 1880, in
which the Sicilian writer produced all his mature work. His
two great novels, *I Malavoglia (The House by the Medlar
Tree)* and *Mastro-Don Gesualdo)*, and the best of his short
stories also appeared during these years. Leaving behind
the romantic stylistic mode of his previous sentimental
novels and stories (all set in the bourgeois and aristocratic
milieu of Italian northern cities), Verga decided to focus his
attention on the life of poor Sicilian people and thus
discovered his most authentic poetics.

A native of Sicily and a son of a local landowner, Verga
spent his first 25 years there before moving first to Florence
(1865-1871) and then to Milan (1872-1893) where he came
in touch with literary circles and participated in the
contemporary cultural debate surrounding French naturalism and the novels of Émile Zola. The Italian version of
naturalism was called *verismo,* from the Italian word for
"true" ("vero"). Giovanni Verga and his friend Giovanni
Capuana were among the most influential promoters of this
new artistic theory. Both trends called for an impersonal
and detached narration. While French naturalism was
more interested in depicting the urban proletariat and
explaining its moral decadence in pseudo-scientific terms,
Italian *verismo* returned to regional and peasant reality,
evoking primitive modes of life bluntly and without
sentimentality. In Verga's case, experiments with *verismo*
and impersonal narration brought him to elaborate an
autonomous style—a skillful mixing of written language
and oral dialect—best fit to describe "the naked and
unadulterated fact ... without having to look for it
through the lens of the writer" ("Gramigna's Mistress";
translated by Giovanni Cecchetti). Verga achieved his
effect of "the invisible author" through stylistic devices
such as choral narration—where events are reported
through the comments of the village—or free indirect
discourse and interior monologue—where the characters'
thoughts are related as events and there is a constant shift
between direct and indirect representation.

The Sicily that becomes the permanent setting for Verga's
mature prose is described at length with topographical
precision. Its scorching sun, the roughness and aridity of its
landscape, its merciless weather conditions, are all such
imposing presences in Verga's stories that they acquire
symbolic value in spite of their naturalistic connotations.
Verga's Sicily is a country as implacable and cruel as the
destiny of suffering and poverty under which the author's
"vanquished" are condemned to live and die. At times the
landscape becomes one with the character who inhabits it
(the red-sand quarry and the red-haired protagonist of
"Rosso Malpelo"), owns it (Mazzarò and his land in
"Property"), or hides in it (the prickly pear cactuses and
the bandit Gramigna in "Gramigna's Mistress").

The lifelong challenge for the peasants' society is to
transform their miserly soil into fertile land. To this
purpose the land is constantly watched, nurtured, blessed,
or cursed as a whimsical goddess who is able to bestow
prosperity or, more often than not, misery. A wheat field
waving in the wind excites the same sexual desire as the
breasts of the beloved ("Black Bread"). In "War Between
Saints," in a mixture of Christian and pagan beliefs, people
fight over the abilities of Saint Rocco and Saint Paschal to
effect a miracle and send rain to their sun-scorched wheat
field.

Throughout all Verga's stories, a constant presence in
Sicilian landscape is malaria, the fever which strikes
everyone and kills randomly. Human medicine is powerless
against it: quinine is only as good as any other exorcism
and it often serves merely to add to the characters' debts.
Malaria even becomes the main character in one homonymous story: "Malaria gets into your bones with the bread
you eat, and when you open your mouth to speak, as you
walk on the roads that suffocate you with dust and sun, and
you feel your knees give away, or you sink down on the
saddle as your mule ambles along with its head low."
Nonetheless, where the danger of getting the disease is
highest, the land is more fertile than anywhere else. Malaria
thus becomes the ultimate symbol of Verga's Sicily, a
malevolent and cynical destiny against which human
beings are condemned to lose in one way or another.

Within such an inhospitable environment, Verga's characters are constantly engaged in a struggle for the most
elementary means of survival. Humanity at its simplest
seems to be ruled by economic interests which often cause
their tragedy. Money is mentioned obsessively and counted
not only by landowners and day workers, by husbands and
wives, by young women and their suitors, but even by
priests and small children. Property is the only good
capable of demeaning the value of money; in "Property,"
for instance, Mazzarò keeps accumulating land and farms
"because he didn't want filthy paper for his things." Yet
even when he becomes the richest man in the region, he
retains the psychological insecurity of the poor and this
leads him to insanity.

It follows that human feelings in the society of these
stories are interpreted as contracts: weddings are planned
with the same care one opens a bank account, marriage is
viewed as division of labor ("like two oxen under the same
yoke"), care for a father as insurance for one's own old age,
charity as making providence your debtor. Although a few
young characters neglect these emotive economics and
Verga does describe a few poetic moments of love (The
Redhead and Santo at the beginning of "Black Bread," Ieli
and his Mara in "Ieli") and friendship (Ieli and Don
Alfonso, Rosso Malpelo and Frog), each is later severely
punished for such naiveté.

Verga's anthropological vision is that of a pessimist, with no allowance for change or hope. In "Freedom" the masses of the poor revolt against the rich with the cry: "Down with the *Hats! Hail to freedom.*" They will have to pay dearly for the consequences of believing that a new political order would bring land and wealth to everyone.

—Anna Botta

See the essays on "Cavalleria Rusticana" and "The She-Wolf."

VIK, Bjørg (Turid). Norwegian. Born in Oslo, 11 September 1935. Educated at a journalism school. Married Hans Jørgen Vik in 1957; three children. Worked as a journalist in Porsgrunn, five years. Recipient: Riksmål prize, 1972; Aschehoug prize, 1974; Norwegian Critics' prize, 1979; Porsgrunn prize, 1981; Cappelen prize, 1982; Booksellers' prize, 1988. Lives in Porsgrunn.

PUBLICATIONS

Short Stories

Søndag ettermiddag [Sunday Afternoon].   1963.
Nødrop fra en myk sofa [Cry for Help from a Soft Sofa].   1966.
Det grådige hjerte [The Greedy Heart].   1968.
Kvinneakvariet.   1972; as *An Aquarium of Women,* 1987.
Fortellinger om frihet [Tales of Freedom].   1975.
En håndfull lengsel [A Handful of Longing].   1979; as *Out of Season and Other Stories,* 1983.
Snart er det høst [Soon It Will Be Autumn].   1982.
Når en pike sier ja.   1985.

Novels

Gråt, elskede mann [Weep, Beloved Man].   1970.
En gjenglemt petunia [A Forgotten Petunia].   1985.
Små nøkler store rom.   1988.
Poplene på St. Hanshaugen.   1991.

Plays

To akter for fem kvinner [Two Acts for Five Women].   1974; as *Wine Untouched* (produced New York).
Hurra, det ble en pike! [Hurray—It's a Girl!].   1974.
Sorgenfri: fem bilder om kærlighet [Free from Sorrow: Five Pictures of Love].   1978.
Det trassige håp [The Obstinate Hope] (radio play).   1981.
Fribillet til Soria Moria.   1984.
Vinterhagen [The Winter Garden].   1990.
Reisen til Venezia [The Journey to Venice].   1991.

Radio Plays: *Daughters,* 1979; *Myrtel* [Myrtle], 1981.

Television Play: *Fribillett til Soria Moria.*

Other

Gutten som sådde tiøringer.   1976.
Jørgen Bombasta.   1987.

*

Critical Study: "The Norwegian Short Story: Vik" by Carla Waal, in *Scandinavian Studies* 49, 1977.

*   *   *

Although Bjørg Vik has written plays, novels, and children's books, her reputation rests mainly on her eight short story collections, two of which have been translated into English. Vik is known as a feminist writer, and most of her stories deal with women at various stages in life. She describes women in transition, from childhood to adolescence, to adulthood, to old age, and depicts female sexuality honestly and forthrightly.

Reconciling the need for freedom with the need for love and connectedness with others, she examines the fates of ordinary men, women, and children searching for warmth and growth in an impersonal and oppressive society. Though sometimes criticized for portraying women as resigned victims, her work reflects solidarity with other women, and her characters achieve insight leading to hope.

Protagonists often remain nameless, and locations are always unidentified. Nevertheless, characters and settings are vividly described. Vik captures a mood in just a few words, revealing a character's psychology in brief scenes or exchanges of dialog. The heavy burden of nouns shows how things can define a person's life. Images and metaphors are always polished and precise.

Kvinneakvariet (An Aquarium of Women) is Vik's most overtly feminist work. Each section of three stories represents a different stage in women's lives. The first story ("Sunday 43") features adolescent girls learning about adult life. The girls get conflicting messages about their femininity, as one mother explains to her daughter what a "tart" is, and her aunt tells her she'll soon be "a little lady, a dangerous little lady." The nameless girl in "It's Good to Be on the Bus" realizes that she is valued for her appearance, and experiences the contrasting masculine and feminine worlds of nature outdoors and the home indoors. The bus ride is a metaphor for the girl's journey into unfamiliar territory and the comfort of returning home with the knowledge she has gained there.

The second section portrays adults. The first title, "Climbing Roses," suggests the theme of middle-class social climbing. Trapped by the materialism of a consumer society, the adults are mercilessly skewered in the diary entries of a clear-sighted but unforgiving teenage girl. Taking place over several years and telling of five families from one neighborhood, this story demonstrates Vik's unique ability to encompass a long time period and multiple stories within a few pages. In "Liv" a working class woman is exhausted and enervated by her double shift. The factory work is hard and repetitious, dulling both mind and body. When not at her job, she is working at home. Now and then she explodes in anger, but most of the time she is too tired to react, certainly too tired to participate in protest meetings. Finally she realizes that she is not solely responsible for the way her life is. The reader is left to wonder whether her new insight will lead to positive change. Though Emilie ("Emilie") is a middle-class professional, her life is not appreciably easier. Exhaustion combined with her craving for autonomy and freedom leads to a breakdown. The story ends on a note of hope, as Emilie writes to tell her husband of the quest she is about to embark on—to find her true femininity in sympathy and solidarity with other women.

The final trio of stories features "liberated" women, and addresses issues of political as well as personal freedom. In the last story, aptly titled "After All the Words," a woman travels, meets a man, and reflects on her situation and that of all women. This story is the most sexually explicit, and also the most explicitly political and feminist piece. The protagonist reflects that "no-one can liberate women except *women. . . .and we know that we are many."* (Vik's emphasis.) Women "imprisoned in the myth of femininity" will be impatient together, and will find new happiness together.

The Norwegian title of *En håndfull lengsel* (A Handful of Longing) reveals its theme of people—women mostly—longing for a little closeness and warmth, a little recognition, an opportunity to develop their talents. Unfortunately, the English title, *Out of Season*, misses this point. Vik portrays the longing of a working-class girl to fulfill her potential as an artist ("Spring"), of a middle-aged woman for a romantic relationship outside of marriage ("The Annexe"), of two widows for warmth and contact ("The Widows"), of a twice-divorced woman for love from a man who will not physically or emotionally abuse her ("Soffi"), of an old man for love and attention from a young woman ("Crumbs for an Old Man"). The final story, "Oppbruddet" ("The Break-up"), portrays a woman telling her husband she is in love with another man and is leaving him after 16 years of marriage. Though told from the woman's point of view, the man's emotions are clearly revealed. Images of light permeate this story—the weak winter sun, warning beams from lanterns and lighthouses, a flickering light bulb, the flat, chilly February light. All these images come together in the last sentence: "The winter sun fell on the sidewalk, surrounding the bowed figure with a merciless stream of light." In one of the two translations of this story the last sentence is omitted. Vik's ending is ambiguous and inconclusive; unfortunately, this is lost in the mistranslation.

One feminist reviewer criticized this collection, finding the mood too dark, the tone too resigned, and the characters too weighed down by their fate. A closer reading reveals growth in the characters' understanding of their relationships, and their realization that freedom means more than the loosening of external bonds.

Vik's fiction is calm, reflective, and deeply satisfying. The entrapment, frustration, and desperate longing in her earlier work is frequently replaced in her later stories by reconciliation and harmony. With subtle psychological insight she creates totally believable characters and situations. Diving below the surface of the mundane lives of ordinary people, she brings them to life for the reader.

—Solveig Zempel

VILLIERS DE L'ISLE-ADAM, (Jean-Marie Mathias Philippe) Auguste (Comte) de. French. Born in Saint-Brieuc, Brittany, 7 November 1838. Educated in Brittany. Served in Franco-Prussian War, 1870. Married Marie Dantine in 1889; one son. Moved with family to Paris, 1859; journalist and playwright, from 1860's. Founding editor, *Revue des Letres et des Arts*, 1867. *Died 18 August 1889.*

PUBLICATIONS

Collections

Œuvres complètes.   11 vols., 1914–31.
Œuvres, edited by Jacques-Henry Bornecque.   1957.
Contes crueles et Nouveaux contes cruels, edited by A. Lebois.   1963; edited by Pierre-Georges Castex, 1968.
L'elu des reves (stories and novellas), edited by Claude Herviou.   1979.
Œuvres complètes, edited by A.W. Raitt and Pierre-Georges Castex.   2 vols., 1986.

Short Stories

Les Contes cruels.   1883; as *Claire Lenoir* (selection), 1925; as *Queen Ysabeau* (selection), 1925; as *Sardonic Tales*, 1927; as *Cruel Tales*, 1963.
L'Amour suprême.   1886.
Akëdysséril (novella).   1886; as *Le Secret de l'échafaud*, 1888; as *Akëdysséril et autres contes*, 1978.
Tribulat Bonhomet.   1887.
Nouveaux Contes cruels.   1888.
Histoires insolites.   1888.
Nouveaux Contes cruels et Propos d'au-delà.   1893.
Histoires souveraines.   1899.
Trois Portraits de femmes Hypermnestra, Isabeau de Bavière, and *Lady Hamilton*).   1929.

Novels

Isis.   1862.
Maison Gambade père et fils succ.   1882.
L'Ève future.   1886; as *Eve of the Future Eden* (bilingual edition), 1981; as *Tomorrow's Eve* (bilingual edition), 1982.

Plays

Elën (produced 1895).   1865.
Morgane.   1866; as *Le Prétendant*, edited by Pierre-Georges Castex and A.W. Raitt, 1965.
La Révolte (produced 1870).   1870; in *The Revolt and The Escape*, 1901.
Le Nouveau-monde (produced 1883).   1880.
Axël.   1890; translated as *Axël*, 1925.
L'Evasion (produced 1887).   1891.

Verse

Deux essais de poésie.   1858.
Premières poésies, 1856–1858.   1859.

Other

Chez les passants (stories and essays).   1890.
Reliques (fragments), edited by Pierre-Georges Castex.   1954.
Correspondance générale, edited by Joseph Bollery.   2 vols., 1962.
Histoires insolites, suivies de nouveaux condes cruels, et de lettres à Charles Baudelaire, illustrated by Louis James.   1963.
Nouvelles Reliques (fragments), edited by Pierre-Georges Castex and J.-M. Bellefroid.   1968.
Contes et récits, edited by Jacques Chupeau.   1970.

Lettres: correspondance a trois (Villiers de l'Isle-Adam, Leon Bloy, J.-K. Huysmans), edited by Daniel Habrekorn. 1980.
Textes politiques inedits de Villiers de l'Isle-Adam. 1981.

*

Critical Studies: *Villiers de l'Isle-Adam* by William Thomas Conroy, 1978; *Life of Villiers* by A.W. Raitt, 1981.

*   *   *

Villiers's generic range was broad. He began as a poet. In 1858-1859 he produced *Deux essais de poésie* (Two Attempts at Poetry) and *Premières poésies* (First Poems). By the 1860's he was writing novels, plays, and short stories. His first novel was the unfinished *Isis* and his first play *Elën*. His first short stories were *"Claire Lenoir" (1867)* and *"L'Intersigne" (1867; "The Sign," 1963)*. Although his poetry displays some evidence of his genius, it is predominantly derivative. His novels are slow paced and lack sustained drive, the narrative energy being impeded by verbose observations and strained melodramatic actions. As for his plays, they are largely poeticized closet-dramas much too long for practical production on the stage. Performed but rarely, they were poorly received. However, his drama *Axël* has been highly praised by some critics and considered a literary monument because of its introduction of Symbolism. There is no doubt, however, that Villiers's full genius came out in his short stories, especially in his elegantly written satiric-ironic stories collected in *Les Contes cruels (Sardonic* Tales, and *Cruel Tales),* his real masterpiece. His other collections of stories are less consistent in quality and have not been translated into English.

A descendant of an aristocratic but poor family, Villiers disclaimed the bourgeois world for its materialism, gross sensuality, scientism, money grubbing, and *vox-populi* politics. He dreamed of escaping from this cesspool of corruption to an ideal world of the spirit. A Roman Catholic, he was also deeply interested in occult forces and powers as well as in German idealistic philosophy and the music drama of Wagner. As to literary influences, Villiers was influenced by E.T.A. Hoffman's tales and especially by those of Edgar Allan Poe as translated into French by Baudelaire. Since the fiction of these authors concerns itself with the theme of escape from mundane reality, it strongly appealed to Villiers.

Villiers's "Claire Lenoir" at first seems a commonplace case of adultery, but by its end it turns out to be the wildest kind of science-fiction melodramic horror tale that in some ways resembles Joseph Conrad's "Heart of Darkness." Told in the words of the sinister bourgeois doctor Tribulat Bonhomet, he tells of the unhappy marriage of Claire and Césaire Lenoir. Claire's taking of a lover, Sir Henry Clifton, has caused much anger on the part of her husband. When Bonhomet visits the married couple to treat Césaire for his addiction to snuff, his incompetence causes the husband's death.

When Bonhomet meets the widow Claire a year later, she has become blind and wears big, round, blue spectacles to conceal her nearly sightless eyes. The doctor also learns that Sir Henry Clifton has been killed in the South Seas by a black savage. Claire dies in the presence of Bonhomet. Her last words are uttered amidst shrieks that she has experienced a horrible vision of some kind. The doctor removes Claire's spectacles and probes the pupils of her eyes with hideous instruments. He sees on her retina the image of a black savage whose features resemble those of Césaire. The savage is brandishing the severed head of Sir Henry while chanting a war song. This episode suggests the idea of metempsychosis: Has Césaire's soul been reincarnated in the body of a black savage? Was it the revengeful spirit of Césaire inhabiting the savage's body that killed Sir Henry? When people die, is what they have seen at the moment of death preserved on their retina until decomposition sets in?

According to A.W. Raitt, "Claire Lenoir" consists of "an astonishing amalgam of themes and techniques" to serve "an intransigent philosophical idealism." This kind of presentation became typical of much of Villiers's later fiction. His method is to present some basic ideas to serve as a background for melodramatic actions. In "Claire Lenoir" these ideas came from several sources: Poe, Hegel, scientism, Hinduism, and occultism. Villiers's creation of Tribulat Bonhomet was meant to represent Philistinism; he was Villiers's Babbitt and "*l'archétype de son siécle,*" through whom he could express his contempt of the bourgeois world. Finally, his method included a carefully controlled and elegant style. Villiers designed "Claire Lenoir" to satirize the overconfidence and overoptimism the bourgeoisie expressed in "scientism."

"The Sign" is a satire that hits people's scepticism regarding the existence of a supernatural world that holds sway over the natural world and that dismisses preternatural phenomena as hallucinatory. It pits the philosophy of the real against the philosophy of the spirit: a Parisian aristocrat, Baron Xavier, against a Roman Catholic priest, the Abbé Maucombe, of the Breton village of Saint-Maur. To get away from the pressures of urban life, the baron journeys to visit his old friend, the priest. While staying at the priest's rectory, the baron experiences the play of preternatural phenomena, and he has two visions which prove premonitory. While the baron is talking to the priest, whose face depicts health, the former sees that the latter's face is suddenly transformed for a second into that of a dying man. On another occasion, the baron hears a knock at his bedroom door. When he opens the door he sees a tall, dark figure of a priest possessed of fiery eyes standing before him in the corridor holding out a black greatcoat. Terrified, the baron slams the door shut.

The baron is unexpectedly recalled to Paris to meet an emergency. Back home he receives the news that his friend, the priest, died three days after he had left for Paris. When the baron had left, an icy rain had begun to fall. Since he had left his greatcoat at an inn near the railway station, the priest had offered him his and requested him to return it when he reached the inn. The priest had acquired his coat in the Holy Land where it had "touched 'The Sepulchre.'" "The Sign" has echoes of Poe, but Villiers's treatment of his theme is original and his point is made with a perfectly straight face.

In "Véra" (faith, truth) Villiers seeks to disorient the reader sufficiently to force him to at least entertain the possibility of immortal life after death in an age of scepticism. His fascinating story is apparently based on Solomon's premise: "Love is stronger than Death." "Véra" is the story of the passionate physical love of the young Count d'Athol for his beautiful wife Véra when one evening love overcame her heart and death struck her down quickly. The count, however, is unable to accept reality, and he immediately dreams her back into life.

Set in Paris, the story begins with Véra's funeral and burial in the family vault. Having stayed with his dead wife for six hours, the count returns to his mansion on the

Faubourg Saint Germain. He goes immediately to the chamber where Véra died. There he reminisces about his and Vera's love for each other. He recalls the evening when the two of them "had plunged into the oceans of those languid and perverse pleasures in which the spirit mingles with the mysteries of the flesh," and it is at this point that he dreams Véra back into existence again. Having done so, he acts—and instructs his old servant to act—as if Véra were alive and had never died. The count entertains this fantasy for a considerable period, until one day while holding a dialogue with Véra he suddenly addresses her: "'But now I remember! What is the matter with me? You are dead!" These words strike the atmosphere like a sound frequency breaks glass. At once Véra and all the objects in the room that the count had perceived vanished into thin air. If the tale at first seems high Romanticism in the vein of Hugo, its Romanticism is smashed to pieces at the conclusion. Also, the tale shows that by the 1870's Villiers had advanced beyond Hegel's phenomenology of spirit, or the certainty of our perceptions, to a new illusionism, or the view that nothing can actually be known except one's own thoughts—everything else, including our perceptions, being illusions.

These outstanding early stories illustrate some of Villiers's styles of representation, tone of treatment, final effect, and themes except for the comic grotesque that had been used by Poe. In "Claire Lenoir" the representation is bizarre, the tone satiric, the effect one of horror, and the theme that scientism cannot be applied fruitfully in all fields of knowledge. In "The Sign" the representation is mixed naturalistic-occult, the tone straightforward but uncertain, the effect ambiguous, and the theme the idea that occult phenomena may possibly exist. In "Véra" the representation is fantastic-idealist, the tone Romantic, the effect one of beauty, and the theme the idea that an individual's imagination may prove wildly delusive.

Other outstanding stories include two whose effect is of terror and suspence: "Catalina" (in *L'Amour suprême*) and "La torture par l'esperance" ("The Torture of Hope") in *Nouveaux Contes cruels*).

"Catalina" is set in the Spanish seaport of Santander. The narrator is there to visit a naval officer friend. The friend is obliged to return to his ship, while the narrator is invited to sleep in the officer's hotel room in the presence of Catalina, a "flower girl of the wharf." During the night the narrator hears "old wood splitting" and a pendulum appears to be swinging back and forth in his room, while Catalina is shivering with terror in her bed. People are fleeing the hotel and the narrator asks them to explain their flight. They answer that he is mad "to sleep with the Devil in the room!" He ignites a rolled-up newspaper to light up the darkness in the room. To his horror he sees a huge python that had broken free of most of its ropes, a fine treasure his friend had brought from his stay in Guiana, one of the specimens he was bringing to the Madrid Museum. The narrator and Catalina flee from the scene. It was evidently the swinging of the python against the walls of the hotel room that had deceived the narrator's senses. Or was it merely a dream, a horrible nightmare, produced after a reading of Poe's "The Pit and the Pendulum"? What about Catalina—had she been possessed by the devil? Ambiguity is the watchword! What is clear is that sense experience can be distorted by the imagination, and that is the theme of this marvelous story.

"The Torture of Hope" is set in Spain in the 16th century during the time of the third Grand Inquisitor, Pedre Arbuez d'Espila. It is the story of the next-to-the-last torture of a Jew of Aragon, Rabbi Abarbanel, accused "of usury and pitiless scorn for the poor." Having been tortured daily for over a year, he is informed by the Grand Inquisitor himself that his torture will end on the morrow because then he will be included in the auto-da-fé.

Left alone in the darkness of his prison, he sees the light of lanterns through a chink between the door and the wall. This fancy makes him wonder if the prison door is closed. That thought also arouses "a morbid idea of hope in his chest." To test his theory he drags himself across the floor to the door where he slips his finger into the chink and finds the door unlocked. Pulling the door open, he slides out to find himself in a long corridor.

After advancing slowly, sometimes terrified by footsteps which pass by him in the darkness, he keeps hoping to find an escape route. Finally, he comes to a door that opens outward. He cries, "Halleluia!" But in a few minutes he finds himself grabbed by the Grand Inquisitor. Now the rabbi realizes that his "escape" is actually his next-to-last torture and that this "torture of Hope" had been cleverly designed by the Grand Inquisitor as a practical joke.

Two other stories are worthy of mention, examples of Villiers's "bitter irony." In "Les Demoiselles de Bienfilatre"(1874, "The Bienfilatre Sisters") two sisters, Olympe and Henriette, professional prostitutes, sit at a table in a Paris cafe, waiting for customers. The daughters of poor concierges, they became ladies of the evening. They conduct their business in a business-like-way. They owe nobody and they put money aside for a rainy day and retirement. All is well until Olympe disobeys her moral duty in respect to her class and profession by falling love with a customer. Her conscience troubling her, she confesses her "sin" to a priest—she had been guilty of having a lover for mere pleasure! The story, then, comically illustrates the moral relativity that is a reality in the world.

In *Le Secret de l'échafaud* ("The Secret of the Old Music") the members of the Paris Opera are assembled to learn the "new music" of a certain composer said to have invented it, but who is now forgotten. The conductor is obliged to announce that, because of the obsolescence of the instrument called the "Chinese pavilion" and the lack of a professor who knows how to play it, it is impossible to perform the new German music.

Then the cymbalist speaks up and declares that he knows the whereabouts of "an old teacher of the Chinese pavilion" who is "still alive." Forthwith, a deputation leaves the Opera to find this venerable master. They bring him to the opera house. He tries to play the work of the German composer (who hated the Chinese pavilion) but finds the score too difficult. So indignant does he become that he collapses and falls into the bass drum, where he disappears "like a vision vanishing from sight." This story obviously is a satire directed at the bourgeois public for their reluctance to accept the "new music" of Richard Wagner, Villiers's favorite composer.

Villiers also wrote stories of the grotesque in the manner of Poe's "Loss of Breath" or "The Man That Was Used Up." The grotesque present persons, things, or actions in an exaggerated fashion that is laughingly absurd. One outstanding grotesque is "L'Afflichage céleste" (1876, "Celestial Publicity"), in which the idea of projecting powerful streams of magnesium or electric light into the sky, in the form of advertising slogans, is proposed, to profit the advertiser and make the sky productive.

As a writer of short stories, Villiers cannot match Hoffmann's imaginative depth nor Poe's rhetorical power. Unlike Maupassant and Chekhov he cannot go far in creating a human being but only a caricature like Bonhomet. His tales have none of the somber, dark romanticism of Hawthorne nor the light, adventurous romanticism of Stevenson. However, Villiers is a precursor of the Argentinian fiction writer Borges. Like Borges, Villiers sought to undermine the reader's confidence in mundane reality. But unlike Kafka, he never touches on the existentialist predicament of the modern individual's alienation, which was his own position. Further, his predominant interest in ideas to the detriment of storytelling for its own interest, and his straining to achieve an unusual style are faults that prevented him from being a major short story writer. Nevertheless, he has his own virtues: he conferred an intellectual dimension on the short story, and he is a master satirist. At its most tempered, his elegant style has both power and beauty. Although Villiers is altogether a lesser writer than such masters as Poe and Chekhov, he has his own unique genius, as A.W. Raitt has said, "for imparting simultaneously emotional excitement and intellectual stimulation," and he has "a voice which is unmistakably his own." If Villiers is a minor writer, he is a "great minor writer."

—Richard P. Benton

W

WALKER, Alice (Malsenior). American. Born in Eatonton, Georgia, 9 February 1944. Educated at Spelman College, Atlanta, 1961–63; Sarah Lawrence College, Bronxville, New York, 1963–65, B.A. 1965. Married Melvyn R. Leventhal in 1967 (divorced 1976); one daughter. Voter registration and Head Start program worker, Mississippi, and with New York City Department of Welfare, mid–1960's; teacher, Jackson State College, 1968–69, and Tougaloo College, 1970–71, both Mississippi; lecturer, Wellesley College, Cambridge, Massachusetts, 1972–73, and University of Massachusetts, Boston, 1972–73; associate professor of English, Yale University, New Haven, Connecticut, after 1977; Fannie Hurst Professor, Brandeis University, Waltham, Massachusetts, Fall 1982. Distinguished Writer, University of California, Berkeley, Spring 1982. Co-founder and publisher, Wild Trees Press, Navarro, California, 1984–88. Recipient: Bread Loaf Writers Conference scholarship, 1966; *American Scholar* prize, for essay, 1967; Merrill fellowship, 1967; MacDowell fellowship, 1967, 1977; Radcliffe Institute fellowship, 1971; Lillian Smith award, for poetry, 1973; American Academy Rosenthal award, 1974; National Endowment for the Arts grant, 1977; Guggenheim grant, 1978; American Book award, 1983; Pulitzer prize, 1983; O. Henry award, 1986. Ph.D.: Russell Sage College, Troy, New York, 1972; D.H.L.: University of Massachusetts, Amherst, 1983. Lives in San Francisco.

PUBLICATIONS

Short Stories

In Love and Trouble: Stories of Black Women.   1973.
You Can't Keep a Good Woman Down.   1981.

Novels

The Third Life of Grange Copeland.   1970.
Meridian.   1976.
The Color Purple.   1982.
The Temple of My Familiar.   1989.
Possessing the Secret of Joy.   1992.

Verse

Once.   1968.
Five Poems.   1972.
Revolutionary Petunias and Other Poems.   1973.
Good Night, Willie Lee, I'll See You in the Morning. 1979.
Horses Make a Landscape Look More Beautiful.   1984.
Her Blue Body Everything We Know: Earthling Poems 1965–1990.   1991.

Other

Langston Hughes, American Poet (biography for children). 1974.

In Search of Our Mothers' Gardens: Womanist Prose. 1983.
To Hell with Dying (for children), illustrated by Catherine Deeter.   1988.
Living by the Word: Selected Writings 1973–1987.   1988.
Finding the Green Stone, with Catherine Deeter (for children).   1991.

Editor, *I Love Myself When I am Laughing . . . and Then Again When I Am Looking Mean and Impressive: A Zora Neale Hurston Reader.*   1979.

*

Bibliography: *Walker: An Annotated Bibliography 1968–1986* by Louis H. Pratt and Darnell D. Pratt, 1988; *Walker: An Annotated Bibliography 1968–1986* by Erma Davis Banks and Keith Byerman, 1989.

Critical Studies: Special Walker issue, *Callaloo,* Spring 1989; "Walker: The Achievement of the Short Fiction" by Alice Hall Petry, in *Modern Language Studies,* Winter 1989; "Tradition Walker's 'To Hell with Dying'" by Michael Hollister, in *Studies in Short Fiction* 21, Winter 1989.

* * *

Alice Walker's short stories, like her other fiction, are marked by her concern with African-American life, and in particular, with African-American women. Walker's literary influences include those of Zora Neale Hurston and Jean Toomer, but by far the greater influence on her work is her own personal and cultural background. From this she draws on a rich oral tradition for her stories, and invests her realism with mystical experience. Her folk material is often used for political and psychological purposes rather than the mere provision of local colour. This tends to create a dialectic between liberal ideology in her work, and the folk values which serve to subvert ideological claims to absolute truth.

In "Everyday Use" Dee wants nice things: "At sixteen she had a style of her own: and knew what style was." Her sister, Maggie, burnt in a house fire, knew she was not bright: "Like good looks and money, quickness passed her by." Maggie's mother, the narrator of the story, attempts to mediate between her daughters. The conflict is effectively that of the city-slick African-American perception of race, and the more homely perceptions of the unsophisticated rural dwellers. When Dee returns home for a visit, she has taken an African name, Wangero Lee-wanika Kemanjo, and a man friend with a name "twice as long and three times as hard." She sports an African-American hair-do and wants to bring her mother and sister into the "new day." She also wants the churn top as a centre-piece for her alcove table, and will "think of something artistic to do with the dasher." The other things Wangero wants are the quilts Grandma Dee had made from scraps of dresses 50 years before, and when asked what she will do with them, she replies that she will hang them: "As if that were the only thing you could do with quilts." Her mother, in an interesting reversal of the prodigal son theme, feels something hit her, "just like when I'm in church and the spirit of God touches me." As in many of Walker's characters, the mystical experience is a precursor to personal growth, and, recognizing the worth of her second daughter, she gives Maggie the quilts: "This was Maggie's portion," and it is she who will put them to "everyday use."

Many of the stories in *In Love and Trouble* take up the theme of women victimized by men. The title to the collection suggests the dual focus of women who must deal with a life full of love, but one which also includes violence, injustice, and oppression. In "The Child Who Favoured Daughter," a sister named Daughter is cast out of her family for desiring sexual freedom. The story explores the ambiguous nature of her brother's feelings toward her, and, when confronted by his own daughter's burgeoning sexuality he, horribly, cuts off her breasts. Many of the men in Walker's stories are the emasculated casualties of racism, but in turn they vent their frustration and anger on women who are punished for wanting an identity of their own. In this sense African-American folk culture provides nurture for such women, and it is the daughters who must learn to speak for their mothers. This function is implied, if not overtly stated, in Walker's essay, "In Search of Our Mother's Gardens." It is one which seems to motivate much of Walker's own work.

The distinction between fiction and ideological discourse is not always explicit in Walker's work, and the stories in *You Can't Keep a Good Woman Down* represent a departure in that several are ideological statements in fictional form. "Coming Apart" and "Porn" demonstrate the effects of pornography on relations between the sexes, while "1955" fictionalizes the exploitation of African-American blues singers. In a thinly disguised version of Big Mama Thornton and Elvis Presley, who turned Thorton's "Hound Dog" into a commercial success himself, the white male singer is shown obsessed with a mystical African-American culture, represented by the song, which he can never quite own, nor quite understand. In Walker's work it is, perhaps, the perception of God in everything that renders it possible to forgive even great evils. It creates a form of magical realism in which even the pain of being female and black is offset by an inherent capacity to endure. Her work is exemplified by companionable and strong women who, like Maggie and her mother, who have the fortitude to watch the dust settle, and afterwards say, "I asked Maggie to bring me a dip of snuff. And then the two of us sat there enjoying, until it was time to go in the house and go to bed."

—Jan Pilditch

See the essay on "To Hell with Dying."

———

WARNER, Sylvia Townsend. English. Born in Harrow, Middlesex, 6 December 1893. Educated privately. Worked in a munitions factory, 1916; member of the editorial board, *Tudor Church Music,* Oxford University Press, London, 1918–28; lived with the writer Valentine Ackland, 1930–69; joined Communist Party, 1935; Red Cross volunteer, Barcelona, 1935; contributor to *The New Yorker,* from 1936. Recipient: Katherine Mansfield-Menton prize, 1968. Fellow, Royal Society of Literature, 1967; honorary member, American Academy, 1972. *Died 1 May 1978.*

PUBLICATIONS

Collections

Collected Poems, edited by Claire Harman.   1982; *Selected Poems,* 1985.
Selected Stories, edited by Susanna Pinney and William Maxwell.   1988.

Short Stories

Some World Far from Ours; and Stay, Corydon, Thou Swain.   1929.
Elinor Barley.   1930.
A Moral Ending and Other Stories.   1931.
The Salutation.   1932.
More Joy in Heaven and Other Stories.   1935.
24 Short Stories, with Graham Greene and James Laver.   1939.
The Cat's Cradle-Book.   1940.
A Garland of Straw and Other Stories.   1943.
The Museum of Cheats: Stories.   1947.
Winter in the Air and Other Stories.   1955.
A Spirit Rises: Short Stories.   1962.
A Stranger with a Bag and Other Stories.   1966; as *Swans on an Autumn River: Stories,*   1966.
The Innocent and the Guilty: Stories.   1971.
Kingdoms of Elfin.   1976.
Scenes of Childhood.   1981.
One Thing Leading to Another and Other Stories, edited by Susanna Pinney.   1984.

Novels

Lolly Willowes, or, The Loving Huntsman.   1926.
Mr. Fortune's Maggot.   1927.
The Maze: A Story to Be Read Aloud.   1928.
The True Heart.   1929.
Summer Will Show.   1936.
After the Death of Don Juan.   1938.
The Corner That Held Them.   1948.
The Flint Anchor.   1954; as *The Barnards of Loseby,* 1974.

Verse

The Espalier.   1925.
Time Importuned.   1928.
Opus 7: A Poem.   1931.
Rainbow.   1932.
Whether a Dove or a Seagull, with Valentine Ackland.   1933.
Two Poems.   1945.
Twenty-eight Poems, with Valentine Ackland.   1957.
Boxwood: Sixteen Engravings by Reynolds Stone Illustrated in Verse.   1957; revised edition, as *Boxwood: Twenty-one Engravings,* 1960.
King Duffus and Other Poems.   1968.
Azrael and Other Poems.   1978; as *Twelve Poems,* 1980.

Other

Somerset.   1949.
Jane Austen 1775–1817.   1951; revised edition, 1957.
Sketches from Nature (reminiscences).   1963.
T.H. White: A Biography.   1967.
Letters, edited by William Maxwell.   1982.

Editor, *The Week-end Dickens.*   1932.
Editor, *The Portrait of a Tortoise: Extracted from the Journals and Letters of Gilbert White.*   1946.

Translator, *By Way of Saint-Beuve,* by Marcel Proust. 1958; as *On Art and Literature 1896–1917,* 1958.
Translator, *A Place of Shipwreck,* by Jean René Huguenin. 1963.

*

Critical Studies: *This Narrow Place: Warner and Valentine Ackland: Life, Letters, and Politics 1930–1951* by Wendy Mulford, 1988; *Warner: A Biography* by Claire Harman, 1989.

* * *

In recent years, the work of Sylvia Townsend Warner has been rediscovered by a new generation of readers through reprints of her novels, poems, and short stories, mainly from feminist presses. Warner lived long enough to see this revival of interest in her writing, a fact which, as Claire Harman's biography suggests, both pleased and surprised her: "It is the most astonishing affair to me," Warner wrote in 1978, the year of her death, "to be taken notice of in my extreme old age." During her career, Warner published eight volumes of short stories, many of which originally appeared in *The New Yorker* magazine over a period of 40 years, and two further volumes were published posthumously (*Scenes of Childhood* and *One Thing Leading to Another*). Warner's work increasingly is anthologized in short story collections, such as *The Virago Book of Love and Loss* (1992), marking the recognition of Warner as a significant writer of short stories.

Unlike her novels, which display immense diversity in terms of plot, narrative technique, and setting (from *Summer Will Show,* which takes place in the Revolutionary Paris of 1848, to *The Flint Anchor,* set in 19th century Norfolk) Warner's short stories present variations on a number of overlapping themes. A central concern is often what Warner herself described as an attempt at "understanding the human heart" in all its complexity. Within this, the stories focus on the relationship between art and life (often with a central character who is a writer, as in "Absalom, My Son"); the gulf between representation and reality (as in "Boors Carousing"), and the underside, the eccentricities and extraordinary moments in the details of everyday life.

Whilst often thematically linked, Warner's stories range from longer and fuller narratives such as "A Love Match," to sketch-like stories in which considerations of plot have been replaced by a concern for a brief, fleeting intensity and, very often, an elliptical and ambiguous atmosphere. A good example of such writing is "A Widow's Quilt" (in *One Thing Leading to Another*), which tells the story of Charlotte, a married woman who becomes obsessed with a quilt she sees in a museum, made for a widow's bed. She begins to make her own quilt, which she acknowledges as a mark of her desire for escape from her dreary, mundane existence with her husband Everard:

> This was her only, her nonpareil, her one assertion of a life of her own. . . .She was stitching away at Everard's demise.

Ironically, the fantasy of escape symbolised by the quilt is not to be realised, as Charlotte dies before completing it. Her husband never learns the true meaning of the quilt, although he unknowingly comes close to it when telling a friend the cause of death, "There was something wrong with her heart." Just before Charlotte dies, she drops a paper bag containing threads for the quilt down the stairs: "Two reels of thread escaped from it, rolled along the landing, and went tap-tapping down the stairs." The image of cotton reels "tap-tapping" away down the stairs captures something of the experience of reading these sketches, with little or no context for the narrative and many loose "threads" at the end of the text.

The fantasy of escape is fulfilled in one of Warner's longer stories, "But at the Stroke of Midnight," in which Lucy Ridpath steps out of her conventional middle-class existence, to take a new identity, that of her dead aunt, Aurelia Lefanu. The story explores the possibilities of such a change:

> Aurelia, the replacement of Lucy, was a nova—a new appearance in the firmament, the explosion of an aging star. A nova is seen where no star was and is seen as a portent, a promise of what is variously desired.

Whilst much of the narrative is taken up with Aurelia's new-found freedoms, the final section of the story emphasises just how illusory and fragile the new identity, and indeed any identity, is. Aurelia befriends a cat whom she calls Lucy, obviously representing her former identity and when the cat dies, the central character is thrown into an "agony of dislocation" from which neither of the identities seems tenable; "she could not call back the one or the other," and she drowns herself. The atmosphere of the story completely changes in the last few paragraphs: what has been an often humourous and fairly light tale, becomes a disturbing, claustrophobic narrative of schizoid identities. As the protagonist feels at her moment of dislocation, "it admitted no hope."

"A Love Match" is a text that moves towards "understanding the human heart" when it is afflicted by almost intolerable suffering, the effects of war on a brother and sister, Julian and Celia Tizard. Both have been profoundly affected by World War I: he returns injured and traumatised from service; she has lost her fiancé in battle. They begin an incestuous relationship as Celia tries to soothe Julian from a nightmare: "They rushed into the escape of love like winter-starved cattle rushing into a spring pasture." At the end of the story, they are killed by a bomb in World War II, and their bodies are discovered together. In a touching and humane final scene, those who find the bodies invent their own narrative to account for the scene: "'He must have come in to comfort her. That's my opinion.' The others concurred. . . .No word of what they had found got out." What is most noticeable about the story, and its source of power, is the lack of any authorial intrusion or moral standpoint in the text. Suffering and the response to it are laid bare for the reader without any comment, and with a sensitivity to the emotional needs of the "winter-starved" individuals in the horrors of war.

Towards the end of her career, Warner began to write stories set in Elfland, and she relished the possibilities offered by the nonrealist text, as the narrator of "The One and the Other" suggests: "Fairies can take any shape they will: so much is agreed by the best authorities." Warner's last work represented a whole new beginning for her: "I never want to write a respectable, realistic story ever again," she said.

—Elisabeth Mahoney

See the essays on "Poor Mary" and "Uncle Blair."

WARREN, Robert Penn. American. Born in Guthrie, Kentucky, 24 April 1905. Educated at Guthrie High School; Vanderbilt University, Nashville, Tennessee, 1921–25, B.A. (summa cum laude) 1925; University of California, Berkeley, M.A. 1927; Yale University, New Haven, Connecticut, 1927–28; Oxford University (Rhodes Scholar), B. Litt. 1930. Married 1) Emma Brescia in 1930 (divorced 1950); 2) the writer Eleanor Clark in 1952, one son and one daughter. Assistant professor, Southwestern College, Memphis, Tennessee, 1930–31, and Vanderbilt University, 1931–34; assistant and associate professor, Louisiana State University, Baton Rouge, 1934–42; professor of English, University of Minnesota, Minneapolis, 1942–50; professor of playwriting, 1950–56, professor of English, 1962–73, and professor emeritus, from 1973, Yale University. Member of the Fugitive group of poets: co-founder, *The Fugitive,* Nashville, 1922–25; founding editor, *Southern Review,* Baton Rouge, Louisiana, 1935–42; advisory editor, *Kenyon Review,* Gambier, Ohio, 1942–63. Consultant in poetry, Library of Congress, Washington, D.C., 1944–45; Jefferson Lecturer, National Endowment for the Humanities, 1974. Recipient: Caroline Sinkler award, 1936, 1937, 1938; Houghton Mifflin fellowship, 1939; Guggenheim fellowship, 1939, 1947; Shelley Memorial award, 1943; Pulitzer prize, for fiction, 1947, and, for poetry, 1958, 1979; Screenwriters Guild Meltzer award, 1949; Foreign Book prize (France), 1950; Sidney Hillman prize, 1957; Edna St. Vincent Millay Memorial prize, 1958; National Book award, for poetry, 1958; Bollingen prize, for poetry, 1967; National Endowment for the Arts grant, 1968, and lectureship, 1974; Bellamann award, 1970; Van Wyck Brooks award, for poetry, 1970; National medal for literature, 1970; Emerson-Thoreau medal, 1975, Copernicus award, 1976; Presidential Medal of Freedom, 1980; Common Wealth award, 1981; MacArthur fellowship, 1981; Brandeis University Creative Arts award, 1983. D.Litt.: University of Louisville, Kentucky, 1949; Kenyon College, Gambier, Ohio, 1952; Colby College, Waterville, Maine, 1956; University of Kentucky, Lexington, 1957; Swarthmore College, Pennsylvania, 1959; Yale University, 1960; Fairfield University, Connecticut, 1969; Wesleyan University. Middletown, Connecticut, 1970; Harvard University, Cambridge, Massachusetts, 1973; Southwestern College, 1974; University of the South, Sewanee, Tennessee, 1974; Monmouth College, Illinois, 1979; New York University, 1983; Oxford University, 1983; LL.D.: Bridgeport University, Connecticut, 1965; University of New Haven, Connecticut, 1974; Johns Hopkins University, Baltimore, 1977. Member, American Academy, American Academy of Arts and Sciences; Chancellor, Academy of American Poets, 1972; U.S. Poet Laureate, 1986. *Died 15 September 1989.*

•

PUBLICATIONS

Short Stories

Blackberry Winter. 1946.
The Circus in the Attic and Other Stories. 1948.

Novels

Night Rider. 1939.
At Heaven's Gate. 1943.
All the King's Men. 1946.
World Enough and Time: A Romantic Novel. 1950.
Band of Angels. 1955.
The Cave. 1959.
Wilderness: A Tale of the Civil War. 1961.
Flood: A Romance of Our Time. 1964.
Meet Me in the Green Glen. 1971.
A Place to Come To. 1977.

Plays

Proud Flesh (in verse, produced 1947; revised [prose] version, produced 1947).
All the King's Men, from his own novel (as *Willie Stark: His Rise and Fall,* produced 1958; as *All the King's Men,* produced 1959). 1960.

Verse

Thirty-Six Poems. 1936.
Eleven Poems on the Same Theme. 1942.
Selected Poems 1923–1943. 1944.
Brother to Dragons: A Tale in Verse and Voices. 1953; revised edition, 1979.
To a Little Girl, One Year Old, in a Ruined Fortress. 1956.
Promises: Poems 1954–1956. 1957.
You, Emperors, and Others: Poems 1957–1960. 1960.
Selected Poems: New and Old 1923–1966. 1966.
Incarnations: Poems 1966–1968. 1968.
Audubon: A Vision. 1969.
Or Else: Poem/Poems 1968–1974. 1974.
Selected Poems 1923–1975. 1977.
Now and Then: Poems 1976–1978. 1978.
Two Poems. 1979.
Being Here: Poetry 1977–1980. 1980.
Love. 1981.
Rumor Verified: Poems 1979–1980. 1981.
Chief Joseph of the Nez Perce. 1983.
New and Selected Poems 1923–1985. 1985.

Other

John Brown: The Making of a Martyr. 1929.
I'll Take My Stand: The South and the Agrarian Tradition, with others. 1930.
Who Owns America? A New Declaration of Independence, with others, edited by Herbert Agar and Allen Tate. 1936.

Understanding Poetry: An Anthology for College Students, with Cleanth Brooks. 1938; revised edition, 1950, 1960, and 1976.

Understanding Fiction, with Cleanth Brooks. 1943; revised edition, 1959, 1979; abridged edition, as *The Scope of Fiction,* 1960.

A Poem of Pure Imagination: An Experiment in Reading, in *The Rime of the Ancient Mariner,* by Samuel Taylor Coleridge. 1946.

Modern Rhetoric: With Readings, with Cleanth Brooks. 1949; revised edition, 1958, 1970, 1979.

Fundamentals of Good Writing: A Handbook of Modern Rhetoric, with Cleanth Brooks. 1950.

Segregation: The Inner Conflict in the South. 1956.

Selected Essays. 1958.

Remember the Alamo! (for children). 1958; as *How Texas Won Her Freedom,* 1959.

The Gods of Mount Olympus (for children). 1959.

The Legacy of the Civil War: Meditations on the Centennial. 1961.

Who Speaks for the Negro? 1965.

A Plea in Mitigation: Modern Poetry and the End of an Era (lecture). 1966.

Homage to Theodore Dreiser. 1971.

John Greenleaf Whittier's Poetry: An Appraisal and a Selection. 1971.

A Conversation with Warren, edited by Frank Gado. 1972.

Democracy and Poetry (lecture). 1975.

Warren Talking: Interviews 1950–1978, edited by Floyd C. Watkins and John T. Hiers. 1980.

Jefferson Davis Gets His Citizenship Back. 1980.

A Warren Reader. 1987.

Portrait of a Father. 1988.

New and Selected Essays. 1989.

Editor, with Cleanth Brooks and John Thibaut Purser, *An Approach to Literature: A Collection of Prose and Verse with Analyses and Discussions.* 1936; revised edition, 1952, 1975.

Editor, *A Southern Harvest: Short Stories by Southern Writers.* 1937.

Editor, with Cleanth Brooks, *An Anthology of Stories from the Southern Review.* 1953.

Editor, with Albert Erskine, *Short Story Masterpieces.* 1954.

Editor, with Albert Erskine, *Six Centuries of Great Poetry.* 1955.

Editor, with Albert Erskine, *A New Southern Harvest.* 1957.

Editor, with Allen Tate, *Selected Poems,* by Denis Devlin. 1963.

Editor, *Faulkner: A Collection of Critical Essays.* 1966.

Editor, with Robert Lowell and Peter Taylor, *Randall Jarrell 1914–1965.* 1967.

Editor, *Selected Poems of Herman Melville.* 1970.

Editor and part author, with Cleanth Brooks and R.W.B. Lewis, *American Literature: The Makers and the Making.* 2 vols., 1973.

Editor, *Katherine Anne Porter: A Collection of Critical Essays.* 1979.

Editor, *The Essential Melville.* 1987.

*

Bibliography: *Warren: A Reference Guide* by Neil Nakadate, 1977; *Warren: A Descriptive Bibliography 1922–79* by James A. Grimshaw, Jr., 1981.

Critical Studies: *Warren: The Dark and Bloody Ground* by Leonard Casper, 1960; *Warren* by Charles H. Bohner, 1964, revised edition, 1981; *Warren* by Paul West, 1964; *Warren: A Collection of Critical Essays* edited by John Lewis Longley, Jr., 1965; *A Colder Fire: The Poetry of Warren,* 1965, and *The Poetic Vision of Warren,* 1977, both by Victor Strandberg; *Web of Being: The Novels of Warren* by Barnett Guttenberg, 1975; *Twentieth-Century Interpretations of All the King's Men* edited by Robert H. Chambers, 1977; *Warren: A Vision Earned* by Marshall Walker, 1979; *Warren: A Collection of Critical Essays* edited by Richard Gray, 1980; *Critical Essays on Warren* edited by William B. Clark, 1981; *Warren: Critical Perspectives* edited by Neil Nakadate, 1981; *The Achievement of Warren* by James H. Justus, 1981; *Then and Now: The Personal Past in the Poetry of Warren* by Floyd C. Watkins, 1982; *Homage to Warren* edited by Frank Graziano, 1982; *Warren* by Katherine Snipes, 1983; *A Southern Renascence Man: Views of Warren* edited by Walter B. Edgar, 1984; *In the Heart's Last Kingdom: Warren's Major Poetry* by Calvin Bedient, 1984; *Warren and American Idealism* by John Burt, 1988; *The Braided Dream: Warren's Late Poetry* by Randolph Runyon, 1990; *Warren and the American Imagination* by Hugh M. Ruppersburg, 1990.

*   *   *

An illustrious man of letters in virtually every genre— poetry, drama, the novel, literary criticism, biography, intellectual history—Robert Penn Warren spent a relatively brief segment of his 65-year career on short fiction. Gathered into a single book named after its title novella, *The Circus in the Attic,* these stories were written in the span between 1930 and 1946, and they reflect two constraints that cut short his story-writing career. One constraint, he admitted in an interview, was the hand-to-mouth financial exigency of the Great Depression that moved him to grind out some stories mainly to make a fast dollar—a mercenary motive that was superseded by the huge financial success of his novel *All the King's Men* in 1946. The other, more unusual constraint, which he declared in interviews, was that his short stories kept turning into poems, particularly after he discovered his gifts for narrative poetry in his major opus of 1943, "The Ballad of Billie Potts."

Within these constraints, Warren's most successful shorter fiction encompassed two novellas, "The Circus in the Attic" and "Prime Leaf," and one classic short story, "Blackberry Winter." Because of their length, complexity, and wide range of characters, the two novellas come closer to the novel form than that of the short story. Apart from "Blackberry Winter," the other entries in *The Circus in the Attic and Other Stories* display a spectrum of achievement that ranges from rather thin, immature story-writing to strongly competent but not first-rate work. The critic Allen Shepherd has described these stories as "by-blows," or works that claim our interest mainly because of their correlations with Warren's more substantial work of the time in poetry and fiction.

The least successful category of Warren's stories are those given over to the cheap ironies of "The Life and Work of Professor Roy Millen" (who undermines a brilliant student's application for study abroad), "The Confession of Brother Grimes" (a tale loaded with sarcasm about its protagonist's unwarranted religious faith), and "The Patented Gate and the Mean Hamburger" (which ends with an O. Henry-like triumph of plot over characterization). The best of these tales, however, bear out the correlation that usually obtains between technical virtuosity and the intensity of imagination. "Goodwood Comes Back" is one such tale, which traces out the career of an actual friend of Warren's boyhood who became a big-league pitcher until he was done in by alcohol. This story later turned into a superb poem, "American Portrait: Old Style," in the Pulitzer-prize winning volume *Now and Then.* And "The Love of Elsie Barton: A Chronicle" joins with its sequel, "Testament of Flood," to represent a deepening of the author's imagination concerning the conflict between passion and marriage in the mores of small town America. Collectively, the stories in *Circus in the Attic* depict the ironies of small town life much in the fashion of *Winesburg, Ohio, Our Town,* and *Spoon River Anthology*—three works that exerted great influence during Warren's formative period as an artist.

One story of village life, the widely anthologized "Blackberry Winter," ranks with the finest initiation stories ever written. Its theme, the fall from childhood's Eden into an adult's knowledge of loss and loneliness, had from the beginning pervaded both Warren's poetry, gathered from a 20-year spread in *Selected Poems 1923-1943,* and his novels, including *All the King's Men*—whose title, we recall, evokes the "Great Fall" of Humpty Dumpty (a fall shared by all that book's main characters). The title "Blackberry Winter" serves the theme in referring to a cold snap that commonly affects the weather in June, otherwise the most Edenic of months, bringing with its chilly air a premonition of the boy-narrator's imminent lapse into tragic knowledge. This story too turned into a poem, or actually two poems, in *Promises:* "Summer Storm (Circa 1916), and God's Grace" and "Dark Night of."

Epitomizing his reluctance to enter the adult world-view, the boy, nine-year-old Seth, evades his mother's orders to wear shoes as he goes out into the morning's chilly landscape. But the aftermath of the night's fierce storm moves the boy toward inescapable discovery of time and loss and corruption, which Warren dramatizes in a series of child-adult encounters. The first and last encounter, in Warren's circular plot-line, is between Seth, comfortably secure in his family and community, and a tragically rootless, wandering bum—in Warren's work a recurring figure of the fall into a ruined world. The job that the bum does for Seth's mother, burying chicks that drowned in the storm, gives the boy his first intimate view of death: "There is nothing deader looking than a drowned chick. The feet curl in that feeble, empty way which . . . , even if I was a country boy who did not mind hog-killing or frog-gigging, made me feel hollow in the stomach."

The second scene of awakening occurs at the bridge where townspeople gather to measure their losses—in crops and livestock—because of the storm. Here Seth, riding on his father's fine horse, gets his first notion of desperate poverty when the drowned cow that comes tumbling downstream turns out to belong to the town's poorest family, evoking some conversation about whether "anybody ever et drowned cow." Seth's third initiatory encounter comes when he visits the meticulously neat cabin of Dellie, the family servant, only to find her yard awash in symbolic filth and trash that the storm has washed out from under her cabin. Thanks to her sufferings in menopause, her personality has also changed radically for the worse, and

her husband Jebb extends her "Womanmizry" to encompass earth-mother significance: "this-here old yearth is tahrd . . . and ain't gonna perduce."

By the time he returns home, Seth's barefoot condition can no longer fend off the new awareness of social inequity that he discerns in adult footwear when comparing his father's fine boots with the bum's "pointed-toe, broken, black shoes, on which the mud looked so sad." Though his father sends the bum packing with a coin for his labor, the boy is jolted out of his family nest as the story ends, feeling compelled to follow the tramp so as to learn more about him. The bum's last words, ("You don't stop following me and I cut yore throat, you little son-of-a-bitch,") echo down through the story's coda, which marks a 35 year passage of time during which all manner of ruination has ensued: the death of Seth's parents; the imprisonment of his black playmate, Dellie's son, for murder; and, ironically, the continuing life of Old Jebb, who has come to regret God's answer to his prayer for longevity ("A man doan know what to pray fer, and him mortal"). The bum's words, repeated in the closing lines, evoke the one positive effect of the day's insights—the making of an artist. Though warned not to follow this menacing fellow, the writer says "I did follow him, all the years." By working out how to live in "the world's stew," as he later called it, Robert Penn Warren built his career, in a sense, on this day of discovery.

—Victor Strandberg

WAUGH, Evelyn (Arthur St. John). English. Born in Hampstead, London, 28 October 1903; younger brother of the writer Alec Waugh. Educated at Lancing College, Sussex (editor of the school paper); Hertford College, Oxford (senior history scholar), 1921–24; Heatherley School of Fine Art, London, 1924; studied carpentry at Central School of Arts and Crafts, London, 1927. Served in the Royal Marines, 1939–40, and the Commandos, 1940–42; major; served in the Royal Horse Guards, 1942–45. Married 1) Evelyn Gardner in 1928 (divorced 1930; marriage annulled 1936); 2) Laura Herbert in 1937, three daughters and three sons, including the writer Auberon Waugh. Teacher, Arnold House, Denbighshire, Wales, 1925–26, and schools in Aston Clinton, Berkshire, 1926–27, and Notting Hill Gate, London, 1927; staff member, London *Daily Express,* 1927; full-time writer from 1928; joined Roman Catholic church, 1930; lived at Piers Court, Stinchcombe, Gloucestershire, 1937–56, and Combe Florey House, Somerset, 1956–66. Recipient: Hawthornden prize, for biography, 1936; James Tait Black Memorial prize, 1953. Fellow, and Companion of Literature, 1963, Royal Society of Literature. *Died 10 April 1966.*

PUBLICATIONS

Short Stories

Decline and Fall: An Illustrated Novelette.   1928.
Mr. Loveday's Little Outing and Other Sad Stories.   1936.
Scott-King's Modern Europe (novella).   1947.
Work Suspended and Other Stories Written Before the Second World War.   1949.
Love among the Ruins (novella).   1953.

Tactical Exercise.   1954.

Novels

Vile Bodies.   1930.
Black Mischief.   1932.
A Handful of Dust.   1934.
Scoop.   1938.
Put Out More Flags.   1942.
Work Suspended: Two Chapters of an Unfinished Novel.
    1942.
Brideshead Revisited.   1945.
The Loved One.   1948.
Helena.   1950.
Sword of Honour (shortened and revised version of trilogy).
    1965.
    Men at Arms.   1952.
    Officers and Gentlemen.   1955.
    Unconditional Surrender.   1961; as *The End of the
        Battle,* 1962.
The Ordeal of Gilbert Pinfold.   1957.
Basil Seal Rides Again; or, The Rake's Regress.   1963.

Verse

The World to Come.   1916.

Other

*PRB: An Essay on the Pre-Raphaelite Brotherhood
    1847–1854.*   1926.
Rossetti: His Life and Works.   1928.
Labels: A Mediterranean Journal.   1930; as *A Bachelor
    Abroad,* 1930.
Remote People.   1931; as *They Were Still Dancing,* 1932.
*Ninety-Two Days: The Account of a Tropical Journey
    Through British Guiana and Part of Brazil.*   1934.
Edmund Campion.   1935; revised edition, 1946, 1961.
Waugh in Abyssinia.   1936.
Robbery under Law: The Mexican Object-Lesson.   1939;
    as *Mexico: An Object Lesson,* 1939.
When the Going Was Good.   1946.
Wine in Peace and War.   1947.
The Holy Places (essays).   1952.
The World of Waugh, edited by C.J. Rolo.   1958.
The Life of the Right Reverend Ronald Knox.   1959; as
    Monsignor Ronald Knox, 1959.
A Tourist in Africa.   1960.
A Little Learning (autobiography).   1964.
The Diaries, edited by Michael Davie.   1976.
A Little Order: A Selection from His Journalism, edited by
    Donat Gallagher.   1977.
The Letters, edited by Mark Amory.   1980.
The Essays, Articles, and Reviews of Waugh, edited by
    Donat Gallagher.   1983.
The Letters of Waugh and Lady Diana Cooper, edited by
    Artemis Cooper.   1992.

Editor, *A Selection of the Occasional Sermons of Ronald
    Knox.*   1949.

*

Bibliography: *Waugh: A Reference Guide* by Margaret
Morriss and D.J. Dooley, 1984; *A Bibliography of Waugh*
by Robert Murray Davis and others, 1986.

Critical Studies: *Waugh* by Christopher Hollis, 1954;
Waugh: Portrait of an Artist by F.J. Stopp, 1958; *Waugh* by
Malcolm Bradbury, 1964; *The Satiric Art of Waugh* by
James F. Carens, 1966, and *Critical Essays on Waugh*
edited by Carens, 1987; *Waugh: A Critical Essay,* 1969,
and *A Reader's Companion to the Novels and Short Stories
of Waugh,* 1989, both by Paul A. Doyle; *Waugh* edited by
Robert Murray Davis, 1969, and *Waugh, Writer,* 1981, and
Brideshead Revisited: The Past Redeemed, 1990, both by
Davis; *Masks, Modes, and Morals: The Art of Waugh* by
William J. Cook, 1971; *Waugh* by David Lodge, 1971;
Waugh and His World edited by David Pryce-Jones, 1973;
Waugh: A Biography by Christopher Sykes, 1975; *Waugh's
Officers, Gentlemen, and Rogues: The Fact Behind His
Fiction* by Gene D. Phillips, 1975; *Waugh* by Calvin W.
Lane, 1981; *The Picturesque Prison: Waugh and His
Writing* by Jeffrey Heath, 1982; *The Will to Believe:
Novelists of the Nineteen-Thirties* by Richard Johnstone,
1982; *The Writings of Waugh* by Ian Littlewood, 1983;
Waugh: The Critical Heritage edited by Martin Stannard,
1984, *Waugh: The Early Years 1903–1939,* 1986, and
Waugh: The Later Years 1939–1966, both by Stannard;
Waugh on Women, 1985, and *Waugh,* 1988, both by
Jacqueline McDonnell; *Confused Roaring: Waugh and the
Modernist Tradition* by George McCartney, 1987; *Waugh*
by Katharyn Crabbe, 1988; *The Brideshead Generation:
Waugh and His Friends* by Humphrey Carpenter, 1989;
Waugh's World: A Guide to the Novels of Waugh by Iain
Gale, 1990; *From Grimes to Brideshead: The Early Novels
of Waugh* by Robert R. Garnett, 1990.

*   *   *

Evelyn Waugh's career as a writer was a relatively short
one—he died when he was only 63 years old and his later
years were largely unproductive—but he was a prolific
author who wrote 17 novels, three collections of short
stories, eight travel books, three biographies, an unfinished
autobiography, and a multitude of essays, reviews, and
short articles. In his day he made a handsome living from
his writing and, in some respects, regarded literature as
much as a profession as a calling. His first literary attempts
were prompted by a desire to break free from the shackles
of middle-class life as a schoolmaster and to rediscover the
social excitement he had sensed at Oxford. Certainly, there
is a strong element of the autobiographical in his earliest
short stories—and a hint of the direction his future writing
would take.

In "The Balance: A Yarn of the Good Old Days of Broad
Trousers and High-Necked Jumpers" (1925) he tells the
story of Adam Doure, a youth torn between action and
culture, who attempts suicide after failing to win Imogen
Quest. (At the time, Waugh, too, had been rejected in love
and had tried to take his own life.) Opting to kill himself
through a life of dissipation, Adam befriends the shadowy
Ernest Vaughan whose violent death shocks him back into
sobriety. Vaughan makes a surprise reappearance in "The
Tutor" (1927), another autobiographical short story, and
many of the darker aspects of his personality were to
resurface in Basil Seal, a recurring character in Waugh's
fiction.

As he grew older Waugh always insisted that his work was
"external to himself," but, as his voluminous diaries and
letters make clear, his own personal experiences were

central to just about everything that he wrote. This is not to say that his fiction is veiled autobiography: rather, Waugh transmogrified real life characters and encounters as a means of creating a fictional world that would help him confront life's central issues. For example, "Charles Ryder's Schooldays" (1945) was both an intended sequel to *Brideshead Revisited* and an attempt to recreate Waugh's own religious self-questioning while a schoolboy at Lancing.

While Waugh never made any great claims for his prewar short stories he was prepared to recycle many of the ideas, characters, and themes in his later fiction. "The Man Who Loved Dickens" (1933) found its way into *A Handful of Dust*, "An Englishman's Home" was used extensively for *Put Out More Flags*, and "Compassion" for *Unconditional Surrender*. For the most part, these stories are highly stylised pieces in which characters like Henty in "The Man Who Loved Dickens" are little more than stereotypes and the differences between good and evil, loneliness and boredom, are more clearly drawn. (These, too, were preoccupations of Waugh's at the time.)

After the publication of *Brideshead Revisited* in 1945 a harsher and more sombre tone enters Waugh's writing as he steadily began to withdraw from what he thought was a drab new world. Typical of this mood was the story "Tactical Exercise" in which the central character John Verney is a villain who plans to murder his wife because she is having an affair with a Jewish colleague. Unbeknownst to him she, too, is planning to kill him and does so by the very methods he was intending to employ. Verney is a deeply flawed character, consumed by a deep loathing of the world around him, a hatred Waugh was also coming to share.

More engaging is the eponymous central character of the novella *Scott-King's Modern Europe*. A somewhat dim and solitary middle-aged bachelor, Scott-King is catapulted from his work as a classics master into the postwar world of Neutralia to attend the celebrations of their national poet Bellorius. To his dismay he finds that his Europe has disappeared and classical culture, fine wine, and good food have been replaced by "the victories of barbarism." It transpires that Neutralia (a thinly disguised Yugoslavia) has ulterior purposes in celebrating Bellorius, and after giving a peroration in Latin at his memorial, Scott-King is prevented from leaving the country. After a series of preposterous adventures he ends up in a refugee camp in Palestine where he is rescued by one of his pupils, once a classics student but now a doctor. As Waugh makes clear in this sharp little fable, the new Europe has abandoned classical grace in favour of a sterile modernism.

He returned to the theme in a later novella *Love among the Ruins*, which began as a short story before going through several drafts to become a Jamesian "long" short story. Set in a monstrous rehabilitation centre in the indeterminate future, it follows Miles Plastic's vain attempts to kick against a system in which criminals are "the victims of inadequate social services." Himself a pyromaniac, Miles is incarcerated in the lavish surroundings of Mountjoy Castle where he falls in love with Clara, a ballet dancer. Inevitably she betrays him and, having glimpsed the vestiges of an older and more cultivated past, Miles turns again to a life of crime. Not a great work, *Love among the Ruins* is nonetheless a harsh attack on the leveling drabness of state interference which Waugh saw as one of the worst features of the postwar world.

A feature of Waugh's short stories is his preoccupation with many of the themes that run through all his fiction — the conflict between faith and reason, and the relationship between loneliness and estrangement and cruelty and death.

—Trevor Royle

WELLS, H(erbert) G(eorge). English. Born in Bromley, Kent, 21 September 1866. Educated at Mr. Morley's Bromley Academy until age 13: certificate in book-keeping; apprentice draper, Rodgers and Denyer, Windsor, 1880; pupil-teacher at a school in Wookey, Somerset, 1880; apprentice chemist in Midhurst, Sussex, 1880–81; apprentice draper, Hyde's Southsea Drapery Emporium, Hampshire, 1881–83; student/assistant, Midhurst Grammar School, 1883–84; studied at Normal School (now Imperial College) of *Science, London* (editor, Science School Journal), 1884–87; teacher Holt Academy, Wrexham, *Wales,* 1887–88, and at Henley House School, Kilburn, London, 1889; B. Sc. (honours) in zoology 1890, and D. Sc. 1943, University of London. Married 1) his cousin Isabel Mary Wells in 1891 (separated 1894; divorced 1895); 2) Amy Catherine Robbins in 1895 (died 1927), two sons; had one daughter by Amber Reeves, and one son by Rebecca West, the writer Anthony West. Tutor, University Tutorial College, London, 1890–93; full-time writer from 1893; theatre critic, *Pall Mall Gazette,* London, 1895; member of the Fabian Society, 1903–08; Labour candidate for Parliament, for the University of London, 1922, 1923; lived mainly in France, 1924–33. International president, PEN, 1934–46. D. Lit.: University of London, 1936. Honorary fellow, Imperial College of Science and Technology, London. *Died 13 August 1946.*

PUBLICATIONS

Short Stories

The Stolen Bacillus and Other Incidents. 1895.
Select Conversations with an Uncle (Now Extinct), and Two Other Reminiscences. 1895.
The Plattner Story and Others. 1897.
Thirty Strange Stories. 1897.
Tales of Space and Time. 1899.
A Cure for Love (story). 1899.
The Vacant Country (story). 1899.
Twelve Stories and a Dream. 1903.
The Country of the Blind and Other Stories. 1911; revised edition of *The Country of the Blind,* 1939.
The Door in the Wall and Other Stories. 1911.
Tales of the Unexpected [of Life and Adventure, of Wonder], edited by J.D. Beresford. 3 vols., 1922–23.
Short Stories. 1927.
The Shape of Things to Come: The Ultimate Resolution. 1933; revised edition, as *Things to Come* (film story), 1935.
Man Who Could Work Miracles (film story). 1936.
28 Science Fiction Stories. 1952.
Selected Short Stories. 1958.
The Valley of Spiders. 1964.
The Cone. 1965.
Best Science Fiction Stories. 1966.
The Man with the Nose and Other Uncollected Short Stories, edited by J.R. Hammond. 1984.
The Complete Short Stories. 1987.

Novels

The Time Machine: An Invention.   1895; edited by Harry
   M. Geduld, 1987.
The Wonderful Visit.   1895.
The Island of Dr. Moreau.   1896.
The Wheels of Chance.   1896.
The Invisible Man: A Grotesque Romance.   1897.
The War of the Worlds.   1898.
When the Sleeper Wakes: A Story of the Years to Come.
   1899; revised edition, as *The Sleeper Wakes*, 1910.
Love and Mr. Lewisham.   1900.
The First Men in the Moon.   1901.
The Sea Lady: A Tissue of Moonshine.   1902.
The Food of the Gods, and How It Came to Earth.   1904.
A Modern Utopia.   1905.
Kipps.   1905.
In the Days of the Comet.   1906.
*The War in the Air, and Particularly How Mr. Bert
   Smallways Fared While It Lasted.*   1908.
Tono-Bungay.   1908; edited by Bernard Bergonzi, 1966.
Ann Veronica.   1909.
The History of Mr. Polly.   1910; edited by Gordon N.
   Ray, 1960.
The New Machiavelli.   1911.
Marriage.   1912.
The Passionate Friends.   1913.
The World Set Free: A Story of Mankind.   1914.
The Wife of Sir Isaac Harman.   1914.
Boon.   1915.
Bealby.   1915.
The Research Magnificent.   1915.
Mr. Britling Sees It Through.   1916.
The Soul of a Bishop.   1917.
Joan and Peter.   1918.
The Undying Fire.   1919.
The Secret Places of the Heart.   1922.
Men Like Gods.   1923.
The Dream.   1924.
Christina Alberta's Father.   1925.
The World of William Clissold.   1926.
Meanwhile: The Picture of a Lady.   1927.
Mr. Blettsworthy on Rampole Island.   1928.
The King Who Was a King: The Book of a Film.   1929.
The Autocracy of Mr. Parham.   1930.
The Bulpington of Blup.   1932.
The Croquet Player.   1936.
Star Begotten: A Biological Fantasia.   1937.
Brynhild.   1937.
The Camford Visitation.   1937.
The Brothers.   1938.
Apropos of Dolores.   1938.
The Holy Terror.   1939.
Babes in the Darkling Wood.   1940.
All Aboard for Ararat.   1940.
You Can't Be Too Careful: A Sample of Life 1901–1951.
   1941.
The Wealth of Mr. Waddy, edited by Harris Wilson.
   1969.

Plays

Kipps, with Rudolf Besier, from the novel by Wells
   (produced 1912).
The Wonderful Visit, with St. John Ervine, from the novel
   by Wells (produced 1921).
Hoopdriver's Holiday, from his novel *The Wheels of
   Chance*, edited by Michael Timko.   1964.

*The Prophetic Soul: A Reading of Wells's Things to Come,
   Together with His Film Treatment Whither Mankind
   and the Postproduction Script*, by Leon Stover.   1987.

Screenplays: *H.G. Wells Comedies* (*Bluebottles, The Tonic,
   Daydreams*), with Frank Wells, 1928; *Things to Come*,
   1936; *The Man Who Could Work Miracles*, with Lajos
   Biro, 1936.

Other

Text-Book of Biology.   2 vols., 1893.
Honours Physiography, with R.A. Gregory.   1893.
*Certain Personal Matters: A Collection of Material, Mainly
   Autobiographical.*   1897.
*Anticipations of the Reaction of Mechanical and Scientific
   Progress upon Human Life and Thought.*   1901.
The Discovery of the Future (lecture).   1902; revised
   edition, 1925.
Mankind in the Making.   1903.
The Future in America: A Search after Realities.   1906.
Faults of the Fabian (lecture).   1906.
Socialism and the Family.   1906.
Reconstruction of the Fabian Society.   1906.
This Misery of Boots.   1907.
Will Socialism Destroy the Home?   1907.
New Worlds for Old.   1908; revised edition, 1914.
*First and Last Things: A Confession of Faith and Rule of
   Life.*   1908; revised edition, 1917.
Floor Games (for children).   1911.
The Labour Unrest.   1912.
War and Common Sense.   1913.
Liberalism and Its Party.   1913.
Little Wars (children's games).   1913.
*An Englishman Looks at the World, Being a Series of
   Unrestrained Remarks upon Contemporary Matters.*
   1914; as *Social Forces in England and America*, 1914.
The War That Will End War.   1914; reprinted in part as
   The War and Socialism, 1915.
The Peace of the World.   1915.
What Is Coming? A Forecast of Things after the War.
   1916.
The Elements of Reconstruction.   1916.
War and the Future.   1917; as *Italy, France, and Britain at
   War*, 1917.
God the Invisible King.   1917.
A Reasonable Man's Peace.   1917.
In the Fourth Year: Anticipations of a World Peace.   1918;
   abridged edition, as *Anticipations of a World Peace*,
   1918.
British Nationalism and the League of Nations.   1918.
History Is One.   1919.
*The Outline of History, Being a Plain History of Life and
   Mankind.*   2 vols., 1920 (and later revisions).
Russia in the Shadows.   1920.
The Salvaging of Civilisation.   1921.
*The New Teaching of History, with a Reply to Some Recent
   Criticisms of The Outline of History.*   1921.
Washington and Hope of Peace.   1922; as *Washington and
   the Riddle of Peace*, 1922.
The World, Its Debts, and the Rich Men.   1922.
A Short History of the World.   1922; revised edition, 1946.
Socialism and the Scientific Motive (lecture).   1923.
*The Story of a Great Schoolmaster, Being a Plain Account of
   the Life and Ideas of Sanderson of Oundle.*   1924.
The P.R. Parliament.   1924.
A Year of Prophesying.   1924.
Works (Atlantic Edition).   28 vols., 1924.

A Forecast of the World's Affairs.   1925.
Works (Essex Edition).   24 vols., 1926–27.
Mr. Belloc Objects to The Outline of History.   1926.
Democracy under Revision (lecture).   1927.
Wells' Social Anticipations, edited by H.W. Laidler. 1927.
In Memory of Amy Catherine Wells.   1927.
The Way the World Is Going: Guesses and Forecasts of the Years Ahead.   1928.
The Open Conspiracy: Blue Prints for a World Revolution. 1928; revised edition, 1930; revised edition, as What Are We to Do with Our Lives?, 1931.
The Common Sense of World Peace (lecture).   1929.
Imperialism and the Open Conspiracy.   1929.
The Adventures of Tommy (for children).   1929.
The Science of Life: A Summary of Contemporary Knowledge about Life and Its Possibilities, with Julian Huxley and G.P. Wells.   3 vols., 1930; revised edition, as Science of Life Series, 9 vols., 1934–37.
The Problem of the Troublesome Collaborator.   1930.
Settlement of the Trouble Between Mr. Thring and Mr. Wells: A Footnote to The Problem of the Troublesome Collaborator.   1930.
The Way to World Peace.   1930.
The Work, Wealth, and Happiness of Mankind.   2 vols., 1931; revised edition, 1934; as The Outline of Man's Work and Wealth, 1936.
After Democracy: Addresses and Papers on the Present World Situation.   1932.
What Should Be Done Now?   1932.
Experiment in Autobiography: Discoveries and Conclusions of a Very Ordinary Brain (since 1866).   2 vols., 1934.
Stalin-Wells Talk: The Verbatim Record, and A Discussion with others.   1934.
The New America: The New World.   1935.
The Anatomy of Frustration: A Modern Synthesis.   1936.
The Idea of a World Encyclopaedia.   1936.
World Brain.   1938.
Travels of a Republican Radical in Search of Hot Water. 1939.
The Fate of Homo Sapiens: An Unemotional Statement of the Things That Are Happening to Him Now and of the Immediate Possibilities Confronting Him.   1939; as The Fate of Man, 1939.
The New World Order, Whether It Is Obtainable, How It Can Be Obtained, and What Sort of World a World at Peace Will Have to Be.   1940.
The Rights of Man; or, What Are We Fighting For?   1940.
The Common Sense of War and Peace: World Revolution or War Unending?   1940.
The Pocket History of the World.   1941.
Guide to the New World: A Handbook of Constructive World Revolution.   1941.
The Outlook for Homo Sapiens (revised versions of The Fate of Homo Sapiens and The New World Order). 1942.
Science and the World-Mind.   1942.
Phoenix: A Summary of the Inescapable Conditions of World Reorganization.   1942.
A Thesis on the Quality of Illusion in the Continuity of Individual Life of the Higher Metazoa, with Particular Reference to the Species Homo Sapiens.   1942.
The Conquest of Time.   1942.
The New Rights of Man.   1942.
Crux Ansata: An Indictment of the Roman Catholic Church. 1943.
The Mosley Outrage.   1943.

'42 to '44: A Contemporary Memoir upon Human Behaviour During the Crisis of the World Revolution.   1944.
Marxism vs. Liberalism (interview with Stalin).   1945.
The Happy Turning: A Dream of Life.   1945.
Mind at the End of Its Tether.   1945.
Mind at the End of Its Tether, and The Happy Turning. 1945.
The Desert Daisy (for children), edited by Gordon N. Ray. 1957.
Henry James and Wells: A Record of Their Friendship, Their Debate on the Art of Fiction, and Their Quarrel, edited by Leon Edel and Gordon N. Ray.   1958.
Arnold Bennett and Wells: A Record of a Personal and Literary Friendship, edited by Harris Wilson.   1960.
George Gissing and Wells: Their Friendship and Correspondence, edited by R.A. Gettmann.   1961.
Journalism and Prophecy 1893–1946, edited by W. Warren Wagar.   1964; abridged edition, 1965.
Early Writings in Science and Science Fiction, edited by Robert M. Philmus and David Y. Hughes.   1975.
Literary Criticism, edited by Patrick Parrinder and Robert M. Philmus.   1980.
Wells in Love: A Postscript to An Experiment in Autobiography, edited by G.P. Wells.   1984.
The Discovery of the Future, with The Common-Sense of World Peace and The Human Adventure, edited by Patrick Parrinder.   1989.

Editor, with G.R.S. Taylor and Frances Evelyn Warwick, The Great State: Essays in Construction.   1912; as Socialism and the Great State, 1914.

*

Bibliography: Wells: A Comprehensive Bibliography, 1966, revised edition, 1968; Wells: An Annotated Bibliography of His Works by J.R. Hammond, 1977.

Critical Studies: The World of Wells by Van Wyck Brooks, 1915; Mr. Bennett and Mrs. Brown by Virginia Woolf, 1924; Wells by Norman Nicholson, 1950; Wells: A Biography by Vincent Brome, 1951; The Early Wells: A Study of the Scientific Romances by Bernard Bergonzi, 1961, and Wells: A Collection of Critical Essays edited by Bergonzi, 1976; Wells: An Outline by F.K. Chaplin, 1961; Wells and the World State by W. Warren Wagar, 1961; Wells and His Critics by Ingvald Raknem, 1962; The Life and Thought of Wells by Julius Kargalitsky, 1966; The Future as Nightmare: Wells and the Anti-Utopians by Mark R. Hillegas, 1967; Wells by Richard Hauer, 1967, revised edition, 1985; Wells: His Turbulent Life and Times by Lovat Dickson, 1969; essay in A Soviet Heretic by Yevgeny Zamyatin, 1970; Wells by Patrick Parrinder, 1970, and Wells: The Critical Heritage edited by Parrinder, 1972; The Time Traveller: The Life of Wells by Norman and Jeanne MacKenzie, 1973, as Wells: A Biography, 1973, revised edition, as The Life of Wells, 1987; Wells: Critic of Progress by Jack Williamson, 1973; Wells and Rebecca West by Gordon N. Ray, 1974; The Scientific Romances of Wells by Stephen Gill, 1975; Anatomies of Egotism: A Reading of the Last Novels of Wells by Robert Bloom, 1977; Wells and Modern Science Fiction edited by Darko Suvin and Robert M. Philmus, 1977; Wells: A Pictorial Biography by Frank Wells, 1977; The Wells Scrapbook edited by Peter Haining, 1978; Who's Who in Wells by Brian Ash, 1979; An H.G. Wells Companion, 1979, and Wells and the Modern Novel,

1988, both by J.R. Hammond, and *Wells: Interviews and Recollections,* edited by Hammond, 1980; *Wells, Discoverer of the Future: The Influence of Science on His Thought* by Roslynn D. Haynes, 1980; *The Science Fiction of Wells: A Concise Guide* by P.H. Niles, 1980; *The Science Fiction of Wells* by Frank McConnell, 1981; *Wells and the Culminating Ape: Biological Themes and Imaginative Obsessions* by Peter Kemp, 1982; *The Logic of Fantasy: Wells and Science Fiction* by John Huntington, 1982; *The Natural History of Wells* by John R. Reed, 1982; *Wells* by Robert Crossley, 1984; *Wells: Aspects of a Life* by Anthony West, 1984; *The Splintering Frame: The Later Fiction of Wells* by William J. Scheick, 1984; *Wells* by John Batchelor, 1985; *Wells: Desperately Mortal: A Biography* by David Smith, 1986; *Wells: Reality and Beyond* edited by Michael Mullin, 1986; *Wells* by Michael Draper, 1987; *Bennett, Wells, and Conrad: Narrative in Transition* by Linda R. Anderson, 1988; *Wells* by Christopher Martin, 1988; *Wells under Revision* by Patrick Parrinder and Christopher Rolfe, 1990; *The Invisible Man: The Life and Liberties of Wells* by Michael Coren, 1992.

* * *

One of the most prolific writers of the 20th century, H.G. Wells produced in just over 50 years a body of work which includes more than 40 novels; political, sociological, and philosophical treatises; textbooks and histories; autobiographies and biographies; journalism and letters; as well as his scientific romances and some 70 short stories. The most artistically fruitful period of his career spans the first 15 years, during which time he wrote his best short fiction such as *The Time Machine, The War of the Worlds,* and almost all of his collections of short stories. Critics generally agree that his highest literary achievement remains the scientific romances. By 1911 Wells largely abandoned telling a story merely for its own sake; the fiction became less entertaining as it gradually took on a blatantly didactic tone.

Though generously laced with humor, the short stories are usually pessimistic—a consequence of Wells's being both a true product and a reflection of his times. Growing up in the Victorian age as the son of an impecunious father whose business failed and an ambitious mother who did everything possible to keep the family solvent, including entering service, Wells knew first hand the trials and tribulations of the "little man" who tries to make it on his own in the world. This type became a fixture in Wells's fiction. Having been educated as a scientist and trained in biological disciplines under Thomas Huxley, Wells fell under the influence of the prevailing theories of the age, especially Darwinian evolution as applied both to the natural world and social structures. This led to a dismal view of human destiny, with humankind hopeless in the face of social and cosmic forces beyond its control.

The themes that occupied Wells throughout his career first appeared in the short stories. He saw nightmare visions of an apocalyptic war, after which a world state would emerge. Though Wells had hopes for such a state, he also feared its inherent dangers. He saw the possibilities of the emergence of a totalitarian state, which he vigorously condemned. Wells recognized that dangers for humanity come from within and without; though outside forces may conspire to annihilate humankind, humans have the potential to destroy themselves, especially through an innate tendency to deceive themselves by thinking they are safe.

In order for the world to survive, humans must evolve into a higher, more intelligent being. With this in mind, Wells portrays in several stories the striking contrast between human "bestial" tendencies and the civilizing process of education.

But Wells perceives even in learning hidden perils. He warns his readers to be careful of science, which when used improperly, can lead to amorality through obsessive solipsistic behavior. Wells also sees danger for humanity in humans' aspirations, especially if used as a means of escape from reality.

It is no wonder, then, that a recurring motif in Wells's fiction, as Robert P. Weeks has noted, revolves around his characters' need to escape, to disentangle themselves from the complexities and circumstances of their lives. While this motif manifests itself most obviously in the scientific romances and comic novels, it also runs through a majority of the short stories in one way or another. On a basic level, in "The Purple Pileus," Mr. Coombes, sick of life, his business, and his unpleasant wife, decides to end it all by eating poisonous mushrooms. Instead the fungi transform him into a man enraged. He eventually takes control of his life, only to fall into another trap: complacency. Other characters seek relief from the quotidian only to be destroyed or to see their situations worsen: the nameless little man of "The Beautiful Suit," the morbidly obese protagonist of "The Truth About Pyecroft," as well as the eponymous heroes of "Filmer" and "The Plattner Story."

As a consequence of an accident connected with a scientific experiment, Gottfried Plattner disappears for days into a parallel universe inhabited by spirits of the dead, only to return as a mirror image of himself, with all external features and internal organs transposed. Other stories that explore parallel worlds include "The Stolen Body," "Mr. Skelmersdale in Fairyland," "In the Abyss," "Under the Knife," "The Crystal Egg," and "The Remarkable Case of Davidson's Eyes." Rejection of this parallel world and the opportunities it offers can ultimately lead to death, as it does for Lionel Wallace in "The Door in the Wall."

As a child Wallace once opened a door to a secret garden of delights, but elected to return to this world. The door appeared to him at various times, always when he had to choose between the promise beyond the door and the task at hand. By always choosing the latter, Wallace becomes famous, yet always discontent. One night he seeks and finds the door, only to walk through it and fall to his death in a construction pit. Here Wallace's decision to escape has fatal consequences.

Wells pursued his favorite themes in various subgenres of the short story: the adventure tale ("The Flying Man"); tales of magic and the occult ("The Magic Shop," "The Red Room," "The Inexperienced Ghost"); prophecies ("A Dream of Armageddon," "The Land Ironclads," "Argonauts of the Air"); social comedies ("My First Aeroplane," "The Hammerpond Park Burglary"); romances ("The Jilting of Jane," "In the Modern Vein: An Unpopular Love Story"); anti-utopian warnings ("A Story of the Stone Age," "A Story of the Days to Come"); and tales of menace ("In the Avu Observatory," "The Empire of the Ants," "Aepornys Island," "The Sea Raiders," "The Star"). Many even see Wells's stories as parables.

The characters who people Wells's stories are usually stylized caricatures or comic creations. He normally puts commonplace, dull characters in extraordinary situations and lets the external events rather than internal motives propel the plot. Very few women appear as characters in Wells's stories. Instead his favorite heroes are men destroyed by their obsessions ("The Lord of the Dynamos," "The Moth"), often perverted scientists ("The Stolen Bacillus," "Slip Under the Microscope").

Wells's style is as uncomplicated as his characters. He preferred a straightforward style with minimal extraneous material. He includes very few country landscape descriptions, though his realistic, accurate portrayals of London and its environs in the scientific romances make the tales credible. Wells excels in his manipulation of the reader through skillful narrational techniques, especially his use of details.

In his explanations of his characters' more bizarre adventures, Wells includes just enough detail to make his premise plausible. He manages to conceal logical objections to improbable inventions and situations by reverting to a scientifically precise, detached tone. Wells's readers willingly enter into a pact with the narrator to suspend their disbelief during the telling of the tale.

Wells did not succumb to his contemporary, Henry James, and his theory of narration with its insistence on "showing" rather than "telling." Instead he preferred an obtrusive, Victorian storyteller who often called attention to himself and the very process of narration. By establishing early on his first-hand knowledge either of the characters and/or events and then quickly taking the reader into his confidence, Wells's narrator makes a potentially improbably story believable. He also makes it interesting.

Wells believed that the most important trait in a narrator should be imagination; therefore, he bestowed on his storytellers all of the wealth of his own inventive resourcefulness. The sense of urgency and immediacy in his early works builds the suspense which attracts and sustains the reader's attention. Unfortunately as his later works, especially the "idea" novels, became more didactic in spirit and tone, they lost the spontaneity and appeal of the short stories and scientific romances. Wells's early works not only established his reputation as a writer, but secured it for posterity.

—Christine A. Rydel

See the essays on "The Country of the Blind" and "The Stolen Bacillus."

WELTY, Eudora (Alice). American. Born in Jackson, Mississippi, 13 April 1909. Educated at Mississippi State College for Women, Columbus, 1925-27; University of Wisconsin, Madison, B.A. 1929; Columbia University School for Advertising, New York, 1930–31. Part-time journalist, 1931–32; publicity agent, Works Progress Administration (WPA), 1933–36; temporary staff member, *New York Times Book Review,* 1946. Honorary Consultant in American Letters, Library of Congress, Washington, D.C., 1958. Recipient: Bread Loaf Writers Conference fellowship, 1940; O. Henry award, 1942, 1943, 1968; Guggenheim fellowship, 1942, 1948; American Academy grant, 1944, Howells medal, 1955, and gold medal, 1972; Ford fellowship, for drama; Brandeis University Creative Arts award, 1965; Edward MacDowell medal, 1970; Pulitzer prize, 1973; National medal for literature, 1980; Presidential Medal of Freedom, 1980; American Book award, for paperback, 1983; Bobst award, 1984; Common Wealth award, 1984; Mystery Writers of America award, 1985; National Medal of Arts, 1987. D.Litt.: Denison University, Granville, Ohio, 1971; Smith College, Northampton, Massachusetts; University of Wisconsin, Madison; University of the South, Sewanee, Tennessee; Washington and Lee University, Lexington, Virginia. Member, American Academy, 1971; Chevalier, Order of Arts and Letters (France), 1987. Lives in Jackson.

PUBLICATIONS

Short Stories

A Curtain of Green. 1941.
The Robber Bridegroom (novella). 1942.
The Wide Net and Other Stories. 1943.
Music from Spain. 1948.
The Golden Apples. 1949.
Selected Stories. 1954.
The Bride of the Innisfallen and Other Stories. 1955.
Thirteen Stories, edited by Ruth M. Vande Kieft. 1965.
The Collected Stories. 1980.
Moon Lake and Other Stories. 1980.
Retreat. 1981.
A Worn Path. 1991.

Novels

Delta Wedding. 1946.
The Ponder Heart. 1954.
Losing Battles. 1970.
The Optimist's Daughter. 1972.

Verse

A Flock of Guinea Hens Seen from a Car. 1970.

Other

Short Stories (essay). 1949.
Place in Fiction. 1957.
Three Papers on Fiction. 1962.
The Shoe Bird (for children). 1964.
A Sweet Devouring (on children's literature). 1969.
One Time, One Place: Mississippi in the Depression: A Snapshot Album. 1971.
A Pageant of Birds. 1975.
Fairy Tale of the Natchez Trace. 1975.
The Eye of the Story: Selected Essays and Reviews. 1978.
Ida M'Toy (memoir). 1979.
Miracles of Perception: The Art of Willa Cather, with Alfred Knopf and Yehudi Menuhin. 1980.
Conversations with Welty, edited by Peggy Whitman Prenshaw. 1984.
One Writer's Beginnings. 1984.
Photographs. 1989.

Editor, with Roland A. Sharp, *The Norton Book of Friendship.* 1991.

*

Bibliography: by Noel Polk, in *Mississippi Quarterly,* Fall 1973; *Welty: A Reference Guide* by Victor H. Thompson, 1976; *Welty: A Critical Bibliography* by Bethany C. Swearingen, 1984; *The Welty Collection: A Guide to the Welty*

Manuscripts and Documents at the Mississippi Department of Archives and History by Suzanne Marrs, 1988.

Critical Studies: *Welty* by Ruth M. Vande Kieft, 1962, revised edition, 1986; *A Season of Dreams: The Fiction of Welty* by Alfred Appel, Jr., 1965; *Welty* by Joseph A. Bryant, Jr., 1968; *The Rhetoric of Welty's Short Stories* by Zelma Turner Howard, 1973; *A Still Moment: Essays on the Art of Welty* edited by John F. Desmond, 1978; *Welty: Critical Essays* edited by Peggy Whitman Prenshaw, 1979; *Welty: A Form of Thanks* edited by Ann J. Abadie and Louis D. Dollarhide, 1979; *Welty's Achievement of Order* by Michael Kreyling, 1980; *Welty* by Elizabeth Evans, 1981; *Tissue of Lies: Welty and the Southern Romance* by Jennifer L. Randisi, 1982; *Welty's Chronicle: A Story of Mississippi Life* by Albert J. Devlin, 1983, and *Welty: A Life in Literature* edited by Devlin, 1988; *With Ears Opening Like Morning Glories: Welty and the Love of Storytelling* by Carol S. Manning, 1985; *Welty* by Louise Westling, 1989; *Welty: Eye of the Storyteller* edited by Dawn Trouard, 1989; *Welty: Seeing Black and White* by Robert MacNeil, 1990; *The Heart of the Story: Welty's Short Fiction* by Peter Schmidt, 1991.

* * *

Known for her novels and short stories set in the South, Eudora Welty was often dismissed by critics as a regionalist, early in her career. Though the label remains accurate, Welty's work is now recognized for the broadness of its themes and its complexity and depth. On the surface Welty's work often reads like small town gossip, folksy, meddlesome, and comic, due to her masterful use of colloquial speech and her extraordinary gift for storytelling. However, as stated by one critic upon the publication of her collected stories, Welty "is bigger, and stranger, than we have supposed."

Throughout her career Welty has freely discussed her artistic creed, in interviews, lectures, and essays. This material enhances Welty's critical stature and clarifies the universality of her topics. In *One Writer's Beginnings* she speaks of her family life, childhood interests, and the values that influenced her work, emphasizing how she never "invades" the lives of real people, particularly someone she knows and loves. Rather, she develops composite, imaginative characters. "My imagination," she says, "takes its strength and guides its direction from what I see and hear and learn and feel and remember from the living world." Welty's fiction typically examines the complexities in the lives of seemingly uncomplicated people. Her characters live outside the dominant fabric of society and range from a feeble-minded young woman, a battered wife, an adulterer, and a deaf-mute couple, to a circus freak, field hands, and hitchhikers.

Her most imaginative character development came in *The Golden Apples*, a collection of short stories some critics have called a novel, though Welty rejects the classification. All the stories revolve around the lives of eight families, their friends, servants, neighbors, and the villagers of the fictional town of Morgana, Mississippi. Welty's creation of an imagined town has led her to be readily compared to William Faulkner and to James Joyce, though the stories in Joyce's *Dubliners* do not intersect, as do Welty's. *The Golden Apples* has also been compared to a photography show, where the artistic effect is cumulative.

This sense of place, epitomized by *The Golden Apples*, but prominent throughout Welty's work, is a cornerstone of her fiction. In "Place in Fiction" from *The Eye of the Story* Welty wrote that "it is by knowing where you stand that you grow able to judge where you are. . . . Sense of place gives equilibrium; extended, it is sense of direction too. . . . Place absorbs our earliest notice and attention, it bestows on us our original awareness; and our critical powers spring up from the study of it and the growth of experience inside it. . . . It never really stops informing us, for it is forever astir, alive, changing, reflecting, like the mind of man itself." While Welty roots her characters in a particular place, like Morgana or along the Old Natchez Trace (as with the eight selections in her second collection, *The Wide Net and Other Stories*), she nevertheless develops around them themes of remarkable breadth and catholicity. She may narrate events in small town life, but the tension in her stories derives from basic human needs and frustrations, such as the failure to be understood. In the words of Robert H. Brinkmeyer, Welty's fiction "explores the dynamics of growth, or the missed opportunities for growth, that occur in the charged relationship between a person and something other than the person."

Frequently the missed opportunity for growth is a consequence of failed communication among Welty's characters. The absence of communication and understanding leads to both real and imagined violence in more than a few of Welty's stories. For example, in "A Piece of News" an abused wife imagines that she reads in the newspaper about her own death at the hands of her husband, while in "Clytie" an old maid commits suicide in a rain barrel rather than live with her alcoholic brother, her badgering older sister, and her speechless father, a stroke victim. In "A Curtain of Green" a depressed widow briefly contemplates stabbing her gardener. All three of these women feel cornered by life, and each is unable to share or to move beyond her personal anguish. In "Powerhouse" a lonely jazz singer improvises a song about his wife's suicide. He fabricates the death to explain why he has the blues. Even though he can give voice to his depression, Powerhouse discovers that some of his listeners are more concerned about the truth of the tale than they are about its creator's troubled condition.

Robert Penn Warren viewed the thwarted communication in Welty's fiction as being symptomatic of a larger theme, which he called love and separateness. Welty's characters "are compelled to seek one another in the hope of forming permanent bonds of mutual service," he said, "not primarily from an instinct to continue the species, but from a profound hunger, mysterious in cause, for individual gift and receipt of mutual care. So intense is the hunger however that, more often than not, it achieves no more than its own frustration—the consumption and obliteration of one or both of the mates." Such is the case in "The Key," "The Whistle," "Flowers for Marjorie," "The Wide Net," "Livvie," "At the Landing," and "No Place for You, My Love."

Ruth M. Vande Kieft describes this same aspect of Welty's vision as a "doubleness," in which the seeming opposites of life are aligned to emphasize their actual closeness, love being close to hate, hope to despair, and living to dying. For example, in "First Love" Welty erases the lines between dreams, visions, and reality when a deaf-mute becomes convinced that Aaron Burr secretly uses his room while plotting a defense. Welty's deliberate vagueness and her intentional blurring of usually polarized experiences makes much of her fiction elusive, enigmatic, and charged with mystery.

Doc, in Welty's story "The Wide Net," gets to the heart of what this doubleness signifies when he says, "The excursion is the same when you go looking for your sorrow as when you go looking for your joy." As Gail L. Mortimer has pointed out, Welty cautions us not to overlook the journey that is living, as we preoccupy our lives trying to achieve the destinations we envision. For instance, in "Death of a Traveling Salesman" R.J. Bowman sells shoes on the road and assumes that he outfits his customers to meet life's adventures. Yet, Bowman's life of travels is a shallow model. Lost on some backroads, he drives off a ravine and entangles his car in grapevines. Seeking assistance, he walks to the home of an inarticulate field hand whose wife is pregnant. After the husband uprights the car, Bowman wishes he could spend the night. The couple share a private bond, which the salesman suddenly desires. Self-absorbed, he had neglected to consider life's meaning. The couple refuse his attempt to leave money, for their happiness is not purchaseable. Bowman then dies of a massive heart attack as he approaches his car.

As an avid photographer in her younger years, Welty gained an eye for detail, nuance, and shade. When discussing her snapshot album of Depression-era Mississippi, *One Time, One Place*, Welty explained how the camera taught her "a storywriter's truth: the thing to wait on . . . is the moment in which people reveal themselves." Her descriptive capabilities led Reynolds Price to characterize her work, particularly the early stories, as being "compulsively metaphoric." Welty's experiments with point of view are at their most masterful in "June Recital," when the narrative freely shifts between past and present events, and between the observations of Cassie and Loch Morrison, as each relate events in the life of Miss Eckhart, a German-speaking piano teacher. Throughout her work Welty employs an amazing range of narrative styles, including farce, satire, horror, lyric, pastoral, and mystery. Her versatility in style and genre has led to her ready comparison to Anton Chekhov, one of her own favorite authors.

—Barbara A. Looney

See the essays on "Petrified Man," "Why I Live at the P.O.," and "A Worn Path."

WENDT, Albert. Samoan. Born in Apia, Western Samoa, 27 October 1939; member of the Aiga Sa-Tuala. Educated at New Plymouth Boys High School, New Zealand, graduated 1957; Ardmore Teacher's College, diploma in teaching, 1959; Victoria University, Wellington, 1960–64, M.A. (honours) in history 1964. Married Jennifer Elizabeth Whyte in 1964; two daughters and one son. Teacher, 1964–69, and principal, 1969–73, Samoa College, Apia; senior lecturer, 1974–75, assistant director of Extension Services, 1976–77, and professor of pacific literature, 1982–87, University of the South Pacific, Suva, Fiji; professor of English, University of Auckland, since 1988. Director, University of the South Pacific Centre, Apia, Western Samoa, since 1978. Editor, *Bulletin,* now *Samoa Times,* Apia, 1966, and Mana Publications, Suva, Fiji, 1974–80. Coordinator, Unesco Program on Oceanic Cultures, 1975–79. Recipient: *Landfall* prize, 1963; Wattie award, 1980. Lives in Auckland.

PUBLICATIONS

Short Stories

Flying-Fox in a Freedom Tree.   1974.
The Birth and Death of the Miracle Man.   1986.

Novels

Sons for the Return Home.   1973.
Pouliuli.   1977.
Leaves of the Banyan Tree.   1979; as *The Banyan,* 1984.
Ola.   1990.

Plays

Comes the Revolution (produced 1972).
The Contract (produced 1972).

Verse

Inside Us the Dead: Poems 1961 to 1974.   1976.
Shaman of Visions.   1984.

Other

Editor, *Some Modern Poetry from Fiji [Western Samoa, the New Hebrides, the Solomon Islands, Vanuatu].*   5 vols., 1974–75.
Editor, *Lali: A Pacific Anthology.*   1980.

*

Critical Studies: "Towards a New Oceania" by Wendt, in *Writers in East-West Encounter: New Cultural Bearings,* edited by Guy Amirthanayagam, 1982; chapter on Wendt in *South Pacific Literature: From Myth to Fabulation by Subramani,* 1985.

* * *

In addition to being a novelist, poet, and critic, Albert Wendt is the author of two collections of short stories, *Flying-Fox in a Freedom Tree* and *The Birth and Death of the Miracle Man.* The two collections constitute a small but significant portion of the total corpus, complementing the thematic concerns of the novels while expressing a particular reality by exploiting the formal attributes of the short story form. As in the novels, an enduring concern in Wendt's fiction is self-possession, of the affirmation and discovery of an identity and reality that never found adequate expression. The dismantling of essentialist and romantic formulations and the regeneration of a true self become central concerns that unite the short stories. As Wendt himself remarks in *Writers in East-West Encounter,* "our writing is expressing a revolt against the hypocritical, exploitative aspects of our traditional, commercial, and religious hierarchies, colonialism and neocolonialism, and the degrading values being imposed from outside and by some elements in our societies."

The world of the *papalagi* is never absent for long in the short stories. The cultural and economic hegemony of Europe is evoked by references to New Zealand, mission schools in Western Samoa, or to history, as in the memorable story "Prospecting" (*Miracle Man*) where the pastor's

greed for gold leads him to an ancient site of massacre. The
discovery of gold is thus transformed into the discovery of
"white" skeletons, the latter an obvious but grim reminder
of a brutal past. The skeletons thus become a complex
symbol of both wealth and torment, and the mass Christian
burial given to them by the village serves as a moment of
regeneration and hybridization. What could have been a
tendentious tale is subverted by ironies, by the syncretism
of including an empathetic *papalagi* in the discovery of the
skeletons. Binaries are dismantled in the story as new
realities are affirmed with the consciousness that the past
can neither be forgotten nor totally restored.

If the past entailed suppression and domination, the
present involves mimicry and "cultural cringe." "The
Coming of the Whiteman" and "Declaration of Independence" in *Flying-Fox* are both concerned with mindless
aping of Western values and the consequent loss and
humiliation endured by the community. The former, a
particularly complex story, is concerned with notions of
moral and ethical choice, with guilt and betrayal, and with
the perpetuation of collective illusion in a world of
transition. Neocolonialism is also the central concern in
"Flying-Fox in a Freedom Tree," in which the Tagata, the
"dwarf" (a significant symbol of colonial subjugation)
writes: "The *papalagi* and his world has turned us, and
people like your rich but unhappy father and all the
modern Samoans, into curious cartoons of themselves,
funny crying ridiculous shadows on the picture screen."

Mautu and the Barter from an earlier story reappear in
"Daughter of the Mango Season," another story preoccupied with the past. But the focus now is less on the
dichotomy between *papalagi* and Samoan and more on the
nuclear family threatened by division and rebellion. The
assertion of self now gives way to a referential surface
where traditional roles are questioned and new rules
emerge. The paradigm of the family, which could serve an
essentialist and tendentious purpose, is now subverted to
reveal fissures and implosions as the daughter Peleipu
leaves home and returns on her own terms. As Wendt
himself remarks, "individual dissent is essential to the
healthy survival, development and sanity of any nation—
without it our cultures will drown in self-love."

The dismantling of paradigms that serve romantic ends
becomes the focus of the first story in *The Miracle Man*,
entitled "A Talent," in which the trickster figure, Salepa,
finally overreaches himself. Episodic, comic, and picaresque, the story records the adventures of Salepa who seeks
to be a *matai* (titled head of the extended family) while
shirking the responsibilities of his role. His subversion of
the system is hilarious until the end when the freedom he
demands is literally denied to him as he is sent to prison
and his family disintegrates. The formal strategy of opposing linearity with circularity, freedom with imprisonment,
community with the individual, has the effect of asserting
the beauty and strength of a culture while preventing any
easy romanticising of the experience.

While the metonymic is never absent from Wendt's
stories, it is in those that combine the metonymic with the
metaphoric that the author is at his best. The fusion
enables the story to encompass the specific and the local
while demonstrating a preoccupation with the colonial and
historical. A case in point is "I Will Be Our Saviour from
the Bad Smell" (*The Miracle Man*), an allegorical tale of a
village suddenly struck with a disease—a bad smell—
whose eradication requires the skill and perseverance of
the entire community. Its symbolic undertone is evident in
the narrator's comment that "the whole area *occupied* (that

was the appropriate description) by the Bad Smell was
oval-shaped and our church building was its centre." Not
surprisingly, the story invites a variety of modes, from the
realistic to the fabulous, and the narrator, resentful of
others who oppose his methods, comments, "in every
community there is always that hard-hearted realist who,
whenever our imaginations lift us up into dizzy poetic
speculations, drag us back down to our body odour and
juices and pain." Despite the narrator's complaints, the
narrative remains experimental and open-ended as it
creates elaborate structure to fuse the efforts of tradition,
science, and Christianity to dispel the smell that afflicts the
community. It is a story that is compelling in its fusion of
realism and fabulation, demonstrating, as Wendt himself
points out in a different context, that "one human being's
reality is another's fiction."

—Chelva Kanaganayakam

WHARTON, Edith (Newbold, née Jones). American. Born
in New York City, 24 January 1862. Traveled in Italy,
Spain, and France as a child; educated privately. Married
Edward Wharton in 1885 (divorced 1913). Lived in
Newport, Rhode Island, after her marriage, and in Europe
from 1907; close friend of Henry James, *q.v.*; helped
organize the American Hostel for Refugees, and the
Children of Flanders Rescue Committee, during World
War I. Recipient: Pulitzer prize, 1921; American Academy
gold medal, 1924. Litt.D.: Yale University, New Haven,
Connecticut, 1923. Chevalier, Legion of Honor (France),
1916, and Order of Leopold (Belgium), 1919; member,
American Academy, 1930. *Died 11 August 1937.*

PUBLICATIONS

Collections

A Wharton Reader, edited by Louis Auchincloss.   1965.
Collected Short Stories, edited by R.W.B. Lewis.   1968.
Novels (Library of America; includes *The House of Mirth,
    The Reef, The Custom of the Country,* and *The Age of
    Innocence*), edited by R.W.B. Lewis.   1986.
The Stories, edited by Anita Brookner.   2 vols., 1988–89.
The Muse's Tragedy and Other Stories (Library of Ameri-
    ca), edited by Candace Waid.   1990.
Novellas and Other Writings (Library of America), edited
    by Cynthia Griffin Wolff.   1990.

Short Stories

The Greater Inclination.   1899.
Crucial Instances.   1901.
The Descent of Man and Other Stories.   1904.
Madame de Treymes (novella).   1907.
The Hermit and the Wild Woman, and Other Stories.
    1908.
Tales of Men and Ghosts.   1910.
Ethan Frome (novella).   1911; edited by Blake Nevius,
    1968.
Xingu and Other Stories.   1916.
Summer (novella).   1917.

Old New York: False Dawn (The 'forties). The Old Maid (The 'fifties). The Spark (The 'sixties). New Year's Day (The 'seventies).   1924.
Here and Beyond.   1926.
Certain People.   1930.
Human Nature.   1933.
The World Over.   1936.
Ghosts.   1937.
Fast and Loose: A Novelette, edited by Viola Hopkins Winner.   1977.

Novels

The Touchstone.   1900; as *A Gift from the Grave,* 1900.
The Valley of Decision.   1902.
Sanctuary.   1903.
The House of Mirth.   1905; edited by Elizabeth Anomons, 1990.
The Fruit of the Tree.   1907.
The Reef.   1912.
The Custom of the Country.   1913.
The Marne.   1918.
The Age of Innocence.   1920.
The Glimpses of the Moon.   1922.
A Son at the Front.   1923.
The Mother's Recompense.   1925.
Twilight Sleep.   1927.
The Children.   1928; as *The Marriage Playground,* 1930.
Hudson River Bracketed.   1929.
The Gods Arrive.   1932.
The Buccaneers.   1938.

Plays

The Joy of Living, from a play by Hermann Sudermann (produced 1902).   1902.
The House of Mirth, with Clyde Fitch, from the novel by Wharton (produced 1906). Edited by Glenn Loney, 1981.

Verse

Verses.   1878.
Artemis to Actaeon and Other Verse.   1909.
Twelve Poems.   1926.

Other

The Decoration of Houses, with Ogden Codman, Jr. 1897.
Italian Villas and Their Gardens.   1904.
Italian Backgrounds.   1905.
A Motor-Flight Through France.   1908.
Fighting France: From Dunkerque to Belfort.   1915.
Wharton's War Charities in France.   1918.
L'Amérique en Guerre.   1918.
French Ways and Their Meaning.   1919.
In Morocco.   1920.
The Writing of Fiction.   1925.
A Backward Glance (autobiography).   1934.
Letters, edited by R.W.B. and Nancy Lewis.   1988.
Letters 1900–1915, with Henry James, edited by Lyall H. Powers.   1989.

Editor, *Le Livre des sans-foyer.*   1915; as *The Book of the Homeless: Original Articles in Verse and Prose,* 1916.
Editor, with Robert Norton, *Eternal Passion in English Poetry.*   1939.

*

Bibliography: *Wharton: A Bibliography* by Vito J. Brenni, 1966; *Wharton and Kate Chopin: A Reference Guide* by Marlene Springer, 1976; *Wharton: A Descriptive Bibliography* by Stephen Garrison, 1990; *Wharton: An Annotated Secondary Bibliography* by Kristin O. Lauer and Margaret P. Murray, 1990.

Critical Studies: *Wharton: A Study of Her Fiction* by Blake Nevius, 1953; *Wharton: Convention and Morality in the Work of a Novelist* by Marilyn Jones Lyde, 1959; *Wharton,* 1961, and *Wharton: A Woman in Her Time,* 1971, both by Louis Auchincloss; *Wharton: A Collection of Critical Essays* edited by Irving Howe, 1962; *Wharton and Henry James: The Story of Their Friendship* by Millicent Bell, 1965; *Wharton: A Critical Interpretation* by Geoffrey Walton, 1971, revised edition, 1982; *Wharton: A Biography* by R.W.B. Lewis, 1975; *Wharton and the Novel of Manners* by Gary Lindberg, 1975; *Wharton* by Margaret B. McDowell, 1976, revised edition, 1991; *Wharton* by Richard H. Lawson, 1977; *A Feast of Words: The Triumph of Wharton,* 1977, and *Wharton's Prisoners of Shame: A New Perspective on Her Neglected Fiction,* 1991, both by Cynthia Griffin Wolff; *The Frustrations of Independence: Wharton's Lesser Fiction* by Brigitta Lüthi, 1978; *Wharton's Argument with America* by Elizabeth Ammons, 1980; *The Female Intruder in the Novels of Wharton* by Carol Wershoven, 1982; *Wharton: Orphancy and Survival* by Wendy Gimbel, 1984; *Wharton: Traveller in the Land of Letters* by Janet Goodwyn, 1989; *Wharton and the Art of Fiction* by Penelope Vita-Finzi, 1990; *Verging on the Abyss: The Social Fiction of Kate Chopin and Wharton* by Mary E. Papke, 1990; *The House of Mirth: A Novel of Admonition* by Linda Wagner-Martin, 1990; *Wharton and the Unsatisfactory Man* by David Holbrook, 1991; *Wharton's Letters from the Underworld: Fictions of Women and Writing* by Candace Waid, 1991.

*   *   *

In addition to 14 novels, Edith Wharton wrote distinctive short fiction: 13 novellas and 86 short stories. Even before her 15th birthday in 1877, she wrote *Fast and Loose,* a lively satirical novella, and by 1891 completed "Bunner Sisters," a novella that reflects interest in the poor, weighs the difficulties of marriage against those of spinsterhood, and develops for the first time her recurring theme that unselfishness ironically brings suffering to a good individual. In her stories as in her novels, she focuses on the complexities in a judgmental society of sex, marriage, divorce, unmarried cohabitation, and on the status of women; and she calls attention to the uneven ramifications for men and for women if they break genteel conventions. A third of her short stories and the majority of her novellas focus on these topics.

The best of Wharton's early novellas is her polished *Madame de Treymes,* a deliberate imitation of Henry James, with whom she took a motor trip in France the year the novella appeared. In exquisite detail she presents two women: Fanny Malrive, a divorced American living in

France, who faces the loss of her son's custody to his father's wealthy family, if she marries her American fiancé, and Madame de Treymes, who disingenuously offers help her. Wharton insists on a realistic, rather than romantic, resolution of the problem, and Fanny Malrive escapes the sordid situation only by relinquishing her plans to marry.

Two other fine novellas, *Ethan Frome* and *Summer*, set in rural New York, near Wharton's home, present simple people in the most restrictive surroundings, who become emblematic of the human struggle to survive with dignity and courage. Their significance goes beyond the literal to the universal.

Four novellas, each representing a decade in New York society in the 19th century, appeared together in *Old New York*. The most praised of the quartet, "The Old Maid," balances the admirable and the destructive elements over two decades in the life of an unmarried mother, who is determined both to protect and to possess her child in ways that contrast with—but also parallel—the struggles and compromises of Charity Royall in *Summer*. This comparison between the two women suggests how gracefully Wharton shaped similar situations and themes into remarkably different works of art.

As her novellas, Wharton's short stories often possess such careful ordering of detail that they attain the psychological complexity in characterization and the moral insight that one expects to find only in novels. Her earliest stories, including "A Journey," "Souls Belated," "The Mission of Jane," "The Other Two," "The Quicksand," and "The Lady's Maid's Bell," are often epigrammatic and slowed by authorial comment. "Xingu," published years after it was written, is a highly amusing satire on the intellectual pretensions of a group of women. Far more bitter is the satire in "The Eyes," which coldly explores the aesthetic temperament of a cultured literary critic, who subtly woos the admiration of young writers and then destroys them. Wharton's masterful ghost stories increasingly have received critical interest. The symbolic power, the subtlety of autobiographical disclosure, the oblique sexual elements, and the deep moral implications in her tales of the supernatural link them with the philosophical fiction of Hawthorne. These fine stories include "The Lady's Maid's Bell," "Miss Mary Pask," "Bewitched," "After Holbein," "Pomegranate Seed," "All Souls," "Kerfol," and "Mr. Jones."

In "Kerfol" ghostly dogs return on a certain date each year to stand sad witness to a murder and to a woman's powerlessness over a man's cruelty. "Bewitched" focuses not only on the fearsomeness of the incubus that sucks away a man's vitality, but also on the bitter intensity of his wife, who keenly perceives that his mysterious malady may derive from guilt as well as fear. She suspects that he was tempted sexually by a young neighbor. In fury, she demands that a group of men hammer a stake through the breast of a girl, who was recently buried, to prevent her rising from a snow-covered grave to seek out the man and to draw him back with her to the graveyard.

In "After Holbein" no acknowledged supernatural events occur, but the confusion that imprisons the minds of old Anson Warley and Evalina Jaspar, their moldering memories of a lost aristocracy, and the skeletons on the collection of Holbein wood-carvings all suggest decay and death. The atmosphere itself is smothering and ghostly, and as Anson and Evalina perform their dance of death, they are caricatures of a dead New York society. Although Wharton's single criterion for a good ghost story was that it send a shiver down the spine, her own penetrating stories leave the reader reflecting upon deeper meanings and unseen truth.

—Margaret B. McDowell

See the essay on "The Other Two."

WHITE, Patrick (Victor Martindale). Australian. Born in London, England, 28 May 1912; taken to Australia, 1912. Educated at Tudor House, Moss Vale, and other schools in Australia, 1919–25; Cheltenham College, England, 1925–29; King's College, Cambridge, 1932–35, B.A. in modern languages 1935. Served in the Royal Air Force, in Sudan and Egypt, 1940–45: intelligence officer. Worked on sheep stations in New South Wales, 1929–32; lived in London and travelled in Europe, 1935–38; travelled in the U.S., 1939–40; after 1945 lived with Manoly Lascaris in Castle Hill, New South Wales, and later Sydney. Recipient: Australian Literature Society gold medal, 1939; Miles Franklin award, 1958, 1962; W.H. Smith award, 1959; National Conference of Christians and Jews Brotherhood award, 1962; Nobel prize for literature, 1973. A.C. (Companion, Order of Australia), 1975 (returned 1976). *Died 30 September 1990.*

PUBLICATIONS

Short Stories

The Burnt Ones.   1964.
The Cockatoos: Shorter Novels and Stories.   1974.
A Cheery Soul and Other Stories.   1983.

Novels

Happy Valley.   1939.
The Living and the Dead.   1941.
The Aunt's Story.   1948.
The Tree of Man.   1955.
Voss.   1957.
Riders in the Chariot.   1961.
The Solid Mandala.   1966.
The Vivisector.   1970.
The Eye of the Storm.   1973.
A Fringe of Leaves.   1976.
The Twyborn Affair.   1979.
Memoirs of Many in One.   1986.
Three Uneasy Pieces.   1988.

Plays

Bread and Butter Women (produced 1935).
The School for Friends (produced 1935).
Return to Abyssinia (produced 1947).
The Ham Funeral (produced 1961).   In *Four Plays,* 1965.
The Season at Sarsaparilla (produced 1962).   In *Four Plays,* 1965.
A Cheery Soul, from his own story (produced 1963).   In *Four Plays,* 1965.
Night on Bald Mountain (produced 1964).   In *Four Plays,* 1965.
Four Plays.   1965; as *Collected Plays 1,* 1985.
Big Toys (produced 1977).   1978.
The Night the Prowler (screenplay).   1977.
Signal Driver: A Morality Play for the Times (produced 1982).   1983.
Netherwood (produced 1983).   1983.
Shepherd on the Rocks (produced 1983).

Screenplay: *The Night the Prowler,* 1979.

Verse

Thirteen Poems.   1930(?).
The Ploughman and Other Poems.   1935.
Habitable Places: Poems New and Selected.   1988.

Other

Flaws in the Glass: A Self-Portrait.   1981.
White Speaks.   1989.

*

Bibliography: *A Bibliography of White* by Janette Finch, 1966.

Critical Studies: *White* by Geoffrey Dutton, 1961, revised edition, 1971; *White* by Robert F. Brissenden, 1966; *White* by Barry Argyle, 1967; *Ten Essays on White Selected from Southerly* edited by G.A. Wilkes, 1970; *The Mystery of Unity: Theme and Technique in the Novels of White* by Patricia A. Morley, 1972; *Fossil and Psyche* by Wilson Harris, 1974; *White as Playwright* by J.R. Dyce, 1974; *White* by Alan Lawson, 1974; *The Eye in the Mandala: White: A Vision of Man and God* by Peter Beatson, 1976; *White: A General Introduction* by Ingmar Bjøksten, translated by Stanley Gerson, 1976; *White's Fiction* by William Walsh, 1977; *White: A Critical Symposium* edited by Ron E. Shepherd and Kirpal Singh, 1978; *White* by Manly Johnson, 1980; *White* by Brian Kiernan, 1980; *A Tragic Vision: The Novels of White* by A.M. McCulloch, 1983; *Aspects of Time, Ageing and Old Age in the Novels of White 1939–1979* by Mari-Ann Berg, 1983; *Laden Choirs: The Fiction of White* by Peter Wolfe, 1983, and *Critical Essays on White* edited by Wolfe, 1990; *White* by John Colmer, 1984; *White* by John A. Weigel, 1984; *The World of White's The Vivisector* by Beyla Burman, 1984; *The Warped Universe: A Study of Imagery and Structure in Seven Novels of White* by Karin Hansson, 1984; *White's Fiction: The Paradox of Fortunate Failure* by Carolyn Bliss, 1986; *White: Fiction and the Unconscious* by David J. Tacey, 1988; *White* by May-Brit Akerholt, 1988; *Vision and Style in White: A Study of Five Novels* by Rodney Stenning Edgecombe, 1989; *Dissociation and Wholeness in White's Fiction* by Laurence Steven, 1989; *White: A Life* by David Marr, 1992.

*   *   *

Patrick White, Australia's most famous writer, was born in London in 1912, at the age of six months went with his family to Australia, where he was educated in New South Wales, and returned to England at the age of 13. After a few false starts in writing (his primary ambition was to be a playwright) he served in the Royal Air Force in the Middle East as an intelligence officer. Somewhat reluctantly, he returned to Australia after the war with his lifelong companion Manoly Lascaris, and, despite his frequent excorations of Australians, most notably in his famous essay "The Prodigal Son," he lived there until his death in 1990.

While White is best known for his ten full-length novels, among the mass of other material that he wrote are two collections of shorter work, *The Burnt Ones* and *The Cockatoos.* White has said that he wrote short stories only when he was travelling and had not the resources to work on a novel but even his stories are often ambitious, some of them stretching into the length of novellas. The six pieces in *The Cockatoos,* for instance, range in length between 20 and 85 pages. Though the themes are often identical with those of the novels they tend, not surprisingly, to take more simplified, expository forms, the dualities with which White is characteristically concerned spelled out in a starker, more polarised way. This is especially true of the stories to do with Sarsaparilla, the mythologised outer suburb of Sydney that White employed in his novels, stories and plays to express his disgust with contemporary urban Australian life.

The title of *The Burnt Ones* comes from the Greek "oi kaymenoi," meaning "the burnt ones" or "the poor unfortunates," but the kind of compassion this suggests for the less fortunate members of society is only intermittently present at best; very often the tone is harshly and blackly satirical or even frankly contemptuous, with only occasional moments of epiphanic understanding or discovery emerging, as at the end of "Down at the Dump." Four of the stories ("A Glass of Tea," "The Evening at Sissy Kamara's," "Being Kind to Titina," and "The Woman Who Wasn't Allowed to Keep Cats") deal with Greek protagonists or have Greek settings; the other seven have Australian backgrounds.

The opening and longest story of the collection, "Dead Roses," is also one of the best. Its protagonist, Anthea Scudamore, is that characteristic White figure, a repressed and dutiful woman. Early in the novella Barry Flegg makes sexual advances to her and she responds involuntarily to his "hard, human body, which, she had been taught, it must be her duty to resist," but immediately she controls herself, remembering the advice of "Mummy," and drifts into marriage with a dried up, elderly man, Mortlock. The whole courtship is sketched in by a few brief passionless glimpses of the couple—Mortlock taking her hand, the two of them stopping the car for a view—before Anthea abandons herself to a life of sterility.

White skilfully juxtaposes his sadly satirical account of the marriage against that of Flegg, the man she might have surrendered herself to sexually, until eventually they come into contact with one another for one last time. Flegg is totally unaware of her continued thoughts of him and merely wishes in his embarrassment to get away as quickly as possible. The tact and restraint about the treatment of Flegg and Anthea in this part of the story is not always characteristic of White. As Thea Astley observes, "Anthea Scudamore is burnt, without doubt, but her husband largely conducts the *auto da fe,* and White helps it along with stoking comments on Anthea's middle-class habits."

More typical is the satirical comedy of suburban mores in "Willy-Wagtails by Moonlight," a diabolically funny story about a dinner party at which the playing of a tape recording of bird calls inadvertently captures calls of a more urgent kind, to the humiliation of the husband in the story. "Being Kind to Titina" is something of a surprise, as the plump unattractive child of the title, who wets herself and is teased by others, is transformed into an exquisitely desirable adult.

The stories in *The Cockatoos* are marked by pointed contrasts between fulfilled and unfulfilled lives. In "A Woman's Hand," for instance, the animus is heavily evident in the contrasts drawn between the elderly retired couple Harold and Evelyn Fazackerley and the silent Clem Downson and the woman he marries, Nesta Pine. Evelyn is a predatory, sterile woman who is described with revulsion even down to her make-up ("Her mouth dripped with light and crimson"), while her husband is kinder but a weak, subservient man who plans to reread *War and Peace* in retirement but of course never gets around to doing so. His old school friend Clem is marked by "resilient stillness" while Nesta suffers the predictable fate of visionaries and writes letters from the asylum to which she has been consigned and where she kills herself.

The women in "Five-Twenty" and "Sicilian Vespers" are similar in some ways but more obviously sexually frustrated. In the latter story, the main characters are a retired couple, Charles and Ivy Simpson. In an extraordinary climax to the story Ivy makes love to an American tourist in an Italian church while a service is being conducted, and the savagery of White's writing bursts out: "Like two landed fish, they were lunging together, snout bruising snout, on the rucked-up Cosmati paving. She wrapped herself around him, her slimy thighs, the veils of her fins, as it had been planned, seemingly, from the beginning, while the enormous tear swelled to overflowing in the glass eye focused on them from the golden dome." Almost from the beginning of the story, Ivy's barren rationalism is under fire and by the end it has been totally consumed in the inferno of her desires.

Set in Greece, "A Full Belly" is mainly notable for supplying the title of White's later autobiography: of the prodigy Costa we are told that "at least he didn't flinch on recognizing his own flaws, moral as well as physical, when he caught sight of them in the glass." In "The Night, the Prowler," which was made into a film with a screenplay by the author, a young woman is allegedly raped by a nocturnal intruder and sets out to avenge herself. White speaks of Felicity's efforts to expend, by acts of violence, the passive self others had created for her; and of "her failed intention to destroy perhaps in one violent burst the nothing she was, to live, to be, to know." In some form or other, most of the stories are about the question of identity. In the most hopeful and perhaps finest of them, the title story, the cockatoos in the park come to mean different things to the various characters who are mostly defined in terms of their relationship to the birds, but above all seem emblems of salvation, rising above the disgust and anger that dominates most of these short fictions.

—Laurie Clancy

See the essays on "A Cheery Soul," "Clay," and "Down at the Dump."

WILDE, Oscar (Fingal O'Flahertie Wills). Irish. Born in Dublin, 16 October 1854. Educated at Portora Royal School, Enniskillen, County Fermanagh, 1864–71; Trinity College, Dublin, 1871–74; Magdalen College, Oxford (classical demyship; Newdigate prize, for poetry), 1874–78, B.A. (honours) in classical moderations 1878. Married Constance Lloyd in 1884 (separated 1893; died 1898); two sons. Moved to London, 1878; art reviewer, 1881; engaged by Richard D'Oyly Carte to lecture in the U.S. and Canada on the aesthetic movement, 1882; lived in Paris, 1883; gave lecture tour of Britain, 1883–84; regular reviewer, *Pall Mall Gazette*, mid–1880's; editor, *Woman's World*, London, 1887–89; sued the Marquess of Queensberry for slander, 1895, but revelations at the trial about his relations with Queensberry's son Lord Alfred Douglas (whom Wilde met in 1891) caused him to be prosecuted for offenses to minors; tried twice: first trial ended with hung jury, second trial with guilty verdict: sentenced to two years hard labour in Wandsworth prison, London, then Reading Gaol, 1895–97; after release lived in Berneval, near Dieppe, and then in Paris; joined Roman Catholic church, 1900. *Died 30 November 1900.*

PUBLICATIONS

Collections

The Portable Wilde, edited by Richard Aldington.   1946; as *Selected Works*, 1946; revised edition, edited by Stanley Weintraub, 1981.
Complete Works, edited by G.F. Maine.   1948.
Selected Essays and Poems.   1954; as *De Profundis and Other Writings*, 1973.
Poems, edited by Denys Thompson.   1972.
Complete Shorter Fiction, edited by Isobel Murray.   1979.
The Picture of Dorian Gray and Other Writings, edited by Richard Ellmann.   1982.
The Annotated Wilde, edited by H. Montgomery Hyde.   1982.
(Selections), edited by Isobel Murray.   1989.

Short Stories

The Happy Prince and Other Tales.   1888.
Lord Arthur Savile's Crime and Other Stories.   1891.
A House of Pomegranates.   1891.

Novels

The Picture of Dorian Gray.   1891; edited by Isobel Murray, 1974; edited by Donald L. Lawler, 1988.
The Portrait of Mr. W.H.   1901; edited by Vyvyan Holland, 1958.

Plays

Vera; or, The Nihilists (produced 1883).   1880.
The Duchess of Padua: A Tragedy of the XVI Century (as *Guido Ferranti*, produced 1891).   1883.
Lady Windermere's Fan: A Play about a Good Woman (produced 1892).   1893; edited by Ian Small, 1980.
A Woman of No Importance (produced 1893).   1894; edited by Ian Small, in *Two Society Comedies*, 1983.
Salomé (in French; produced 1896).   1893; as *Salome*, translated by Alfred Douglas, 1894.
An Ideal Husband (produced 1895).   1899; edited by Russell Jackson, in *Two Society Comedies*, 1983.
The Importance of Being Earnest: A Trivial Comedy for Serious People (produced 1895).   1899; edited by Russell Jackson, 1980; 4-act version edited by Ruth Berggren, 1987.
A Florentine Tragedy, one scene by T. Sturge Moore (produced 1906).   In *Works* (Ross Edition), vol. 6, 1908.
For Love of the King: A Burmese Masque.   1922.

Verse

Ravenna.   1878.
Poems.   1881.

The Sphinx. 1894.
The Ballad of Reading Gaol. 1898.

Other

Intentions. 1891.
Oscariana: Epigrams. 1895; revised edition, 1910.
The Soul of Man. 1895; as *The Soul of Man under Socialism,* 1912.
Sebastian Melmoth (miscellany). 1904.
De Profundis. Expurgated version, edited by Robert Ross, 1905; revised edition, 1909; *Suppressed Portion,* 1913; *The Complete Text,* edited by Vyvyan Holland, 1949; complete version, in *Letters,* 1962.
Decorative Art in America, Together with Letters, Reviews, and Interviews, edited by R.B. Glaenzer. 1906.
Impressions of America, edited by Stuart Mason. 1906.
A Critic in Pall Mall, Being Extracts from Reviews and Miscellanies. 1919.
To M.B.J., edited by Stuart Mason. 1920.
Essays, edited by Hesketh Pearson. 1950.
Letters, edited by Rupert Hart-Davis. 1962; *Selected Letters,* 1979; *More Letters,* 1985.
Literary Criticism, edited by Stanley Weintraub. 1968.
The Artist as Critic: Critical Writings, edited by Richard Ellmann. 1969.
Sayings, edited by Henry Russell. 1989.
Oxford Notebooks: A Portrait of Mind in the Making, edited by Philip E. Smith II and Michael S. Helfand. 1989.
The Fireworks of Wilde, edited by Owen Dudley Edwards. 1989.
The Soul of Man and Prison Writings, edited by Isobel Murray. 1990.

*

Bibliography: *A Bibliography of Wilde* by Stuart Mason, 1908, edited by Timothy d'Arch Smith, 1967; *Wilde: An Annotated Bibliography of Criticism* by E.H. Mikhail, 1978.

Critical Studies: *Wilde: His Life and Confessions* by Frank Harris, 2 vols., 1916, *New Preface,* with Alfred Douglas, 1925, edited by Frank MacShane, 1974; *A Study of Wilde* by Arthur Symons, 1930; *The Life of Wilde* by Hesketh Pearson, 1946, as *Wilde: His Life and Wit,* 1946; *Wilde* by Edouard Roditi, 1947, revised edition, 1986; *The Paradox of Wilde* by George Woodcock, 1949, as *Wilde: The Double Image,* 1989; *Wilde: A Present Time Appraisal* by St. John Ervine, 1951; *Son of Wilde,* 1954, and *Wilde: A Pictorial Biography,* 1960, as *Wilde and His World,* 1960, both by Vyvyan Holland; *The Fate of Wilde* by Vivien Mercier, 1955; *The Three Trials of Wilde* edited by H. Montgomery Hyde, 1956, and *Wilde: The Aftermath,* 1963, and *Wilde: A Biography,* 1975, both by Hyde; *The Art of Wilde* by Epifanio San Juan, Jr., 1967; *Wilde: A Collection of Critical Essays* edited by Richard Ellmann, 1969, and *Wilde* (biography) by Ellmann, 1987; *Wilde: The Critical Heritage* edited by Karl Beckson, 1970; *Wilde* by G.A. Cevasco, 1972; *The Unrecorded Life of Wilde* by Rupert Croft-Cooke, 1972; *Wilde* by Martin Fido, 1973; *Into the Demon Universe: A Literary Exploration of Wilde* by Christopher S. Nassaar, 1974; *Wilde* by Sheridan Morley, 1976; *Wilde* by Louis Kronenberger, 1976; *Wilde* by Donald Ericksen, 1977; *The Plays of Wilde* by Alan Bird, 1977; *Wilde: Art and Egotism* by Rodney Shewan, 1977; *The Moral Vision of Wilde* by Philip K. Cohen, 1978; *Wilde: Interviews and Recollections* edited by E.H. Mikhail, 2 vols., 1979; *The Importance of Being Oscar: The Wit and Wisdom of Wilde Set Against His Life and Times* by Mark Nicholls, 1980; *Wilde's Life as Reflected in His Correspondence and His Autobiography* by Anita Roitinger, 1980; *Wilde* by Robert Keith Miller, 1982; *Mrs. Oscar Wilde: A Woman of Some Importance* by Anne Clark Amor, 1983; *Wilde* by Richard Pine, 1983; *Wilde* by Katharine Worth, 1983; *Hues of Mutability: The Waning Vision in Wilde's Narrative* by Jean M. Ellis D'Allessandro, 1983; *Idylls of the Market-place: Wilde and the Victorian Public* by Regenia Gagnier, 1986; *Wilde* by Peter Raby, 1987; *The Wilde File* by Jonathan Goodman, 1988; *Wilde: The Works of a Conformist Rebel* by Norbert Kohl, 1989; *Wilde and the Theatre of the 1890's* by Kerry Powell, 1990; *File on Wilde* edited by Margery Morgan, 1990.

*   *   *

Oscar Wilde attempted most of the available literary forms of his day, beginning with poetry. But his *Poems* were widely scorned, and his next and more successful genre was the short story. Where he was accused of minimal originality in his early poems, each of his stories is stamped with its author's personality, grace, and wit.

A few were contemporary. Particularly memorable is "The Canterville Ghost," where the author/narrator contrives to satirise a number of targets simultaneously. The rich Americans who come to stay at Canterville Chase have patent cures and nostrums for everything, from three-hundred-year-old bloodstains, nightly renewed, to rusty fetters, robustly refuse to be afraid of the ghost, and worship "according to the simple rites of the Free American Reformed Episcopal Church." The presentation of the ghost in his dramatic roles and his atrocious history mock and outdo the most fearful products of a century that revelled in ghost stories and melodrama.

But Wilde's most perfect modern short story is "Lord Arthur Savile's Crime," the story of a young man who has his palm read by a fashionable "cheiromancer," and learns it prophesies murder. The success of the story is entirely dependent on tone, and on the kind of inspired through-the-looking-glass logic Wilde was not to sustain so thoroughly again until *The Importance of Being Earnest.* Lord Arthur belongs in the convention-ridden Victorian world of moral decision (the subtitle is "A Study of Duty"), but his first and lasting response is the key: he "was fully conscious of the fact that he had no right to marry until he had committed the murder." He makes two attempts to do away with harmless relatives he likes (this is no time to indulge prejudices), but one dies naturally, having left him her small fortune, while the exploding clock secretly obtained from Russian nihilist conspirators for the other seems as dangerous as a child's cap pistol. The wedding is called off, and Lord Arthur is in despair. One night he happens to meet the cheiromantist, who he pushes into the Thames, and he is happy ever after, with a great respect for cheiromancy. If Tennyson's King Arthur was doubly fated to defeat, Wilde's Lord Arthur, with his devotion to duty, is wholly justified.

In his two volumes of fairy tales, Wilde purports to use the traditional styles of Andersen and the Grimms, but this impression does not last. In not one of the nine stories is there a central conventional love affair (the swallow-loves-statue and nightingale-loves-love are a little unusual); in not one of the stories is there an unqualified conventionally happy ending. The stories in *A House of Pomegranates* are longer and more elaborate than those in *The Happy Prince*, but Wilde said both collections were "an attempt to mirror modern life in a form remote from reality—to deal with modern problems in a mode that is ideal and not imitative." The problems are generally concerned with poverty and privilege, egotism and self-absorption, beauty and cruelty. They have several levels of appeal. They have always been favourites with children, but children will inevitably miss a great deal; Wilde said, "Now in building this *House of Pomegranates* I had about as much intention of pleasing the British child as I had of pleasing the British public."

In "The Happy Prince" the eponymous hero is dead, after a life of careless happiness, but his statue develops the pity he forgot to feel for his people, and he determines to strip himself of wealthy ornament to help individuals in need. In turn he is loved by a swallow that refuses to leave him, facing certain death in the hard winter. The story is framed by comments from self-seeking town councillors, which reduces sentimentalism, and the swallow is an entertaining mini-egotist, one who has read Gautier and beguiles the prince with all the glories of Egypt. Even the prince has reservations: "the living always think that gold can make them happy." God's last-minute intervention to save the leaden heart of the statue and the body of the dead bird cannot tip the tale back into conventional Victorian sentimentality.

In many ways the most subtle and entertaining story is "The Devoted Friend," where Wilde tackles a theme very important to him. Are love and self-sacrifice the same? Should they be? In the story the humble little Hans is proud of his friendship with Hugh the Miller; the miller endlessly dilates on the theory of friendship, while poor Hans is confined to the practice, undertaking ever greater self-sacrifices to please his rich friend. A first reading may cause the reader to admire and wonder at the devotion of the brave and selfless little fellow: a second or third begins to suggest that though the miller's selfishness is abominable, Hans's self-abnegation is excessive. Wilde's other work suggests that self-realisation or self-development is preferable to self-sacrifice, and I think that is the tenor of this story too. The miller neglects Hans in winter when he might need help ("Flour is one thing and friendship is another") while his young son offers to share his food with Hans, and the miller's wife admires her husband's eloquence ("I feel quite drowsy. It is just like being in church"). The whole story is more carefully framed than "The Happy Prince," with a debate about friendship going on among pond creatures, and a selfish water-rat who is apoplectic with rage when he finds he has been told a story with a moral. Significantly the main story has been told by a Green Linnet. The ironies of Wilde's fairy tales make them uniquely provocative.

—Isobel Murray

WILDING, Michael. British. Born in Worcester, 5 January 1942. Educated at Royal Grammar School, Worcester, 1950–59; Lincoln College, Oxford (editor, *Isis,* 1962), B.A. 1963, M.A. 1968. Primary school teacher, Spetchley, Worcestershire, 1960; lecturer in English, University of Sydney, 1963–66; editor, *Balcony,* Sydney, 1965–66; assis-

tant lecturer, 1967–68, and lecturer in English, 1968, University of Birmingham, senior lecturer, 1969-72, and since 1972 reader in English, University of Sydney; Australian editor, *Stand,* Newcastle-upon-Tyne, since 1971; editor with Frank Moorhouse, *q.v., Tabloid Story,* Sydney, 1972–76; general editor, Asian and Pacific Writing series, University of Queensland Press, 1972–82; director, Wild and Woolley, publishers, Sydney, 1974–79; editor, *Post-Modern Writing,* Sydney, 1979–81; visiting professor, University of California, Santa Barbara, 1987; George Watson Visiting Fellow, University of Queensland, St. Lucia, 1989. Fellow, Australian Academy of Humanities, 1988. Recipient: Australia Council senior fellowship, 1978. Lives in New South Wales.

PUBLICATIONS

Short Stories

Aspects of the Dying Process.   1972.
The West Midland Underground.   1975.
Scenic Drive.   1976.
The Phallic Forest.   1978.
Reading the Signs.   1984.
The Man of Slow Feeling: Selected Short Stories.   1985.
Under Saturn: Four Stories.   1988.
Great Climate.   1990; as *Her Most Bizarre Sexual Experience,* 1991.

Novels

Living Together.   1974.
The Short Story Embassy.   1975.
Pacific Highway.   1982.
The Paraguayan Experiment.   1985.

Plays

Screenplay: *The Phallic Forest,*   1972.

Television Play: *Reading the Signs* (documentary), 1988.

Other

Milton's Paradise Lost.   1969.
Cultural Policy in Great Britain, with Michael Green. 1970.
Marcus Clarke.   1977.
Political Fictions.   1980.
Dragons Teeth: Literature and Politics in the English Revolution.   1987.

Editor, with Charles Higham. *Australians Abroad: An Anthology.*   1967.
Editor, *Three Tales,* by Henry James.   1967.
Editor, *Marvell: Modern Judgements.*   1969.
Editor, with others, *We Took Their Orders and Are Dead: An Anti-War Anthology.*   1971.
Editor, *The Portable Marcus Clarke.*   1976.
Editor, with Stephen Knight, *The Radical Reader.*   1977.
Editor, *The Tabloid Story Pocket Book.*   1978.
Editor, *The Workingman's Paradise,* by William Lane. 1980.
Editor, *Stories,* by Marcus Clarke.   1983.
Editor, with Rudi Krausmann, *Air Mail from Down Under.* 1990.

*

Critical Studies: "The Short Stories of Wilding and Moorhouse" by Carl Harrison-Ford, in *Southerly* 33, 1973; interviews with Rudi Krausmann, in *Aspect* 1, 1975, David Albahari, in *Australian Literary Studies* 9, 1980, Kevin Brophy and Myron Lysenko, in *Going Down Swinging* 3, 1982, Giulia Giuffre, in *Southerly* 46, 1986, and Peter Lewis, in *Stand* 32, 1991; "Recent Developments in Australian Writing, with Particular Reference to Short Fiction" by Brian Kiernan, in *Caliban* 14, 1977; "The New Novel" by Leon Cantrell, in Studies in the *Recent Australian Novel* edited by K.G. Hamilton, 1978; "Uncertainty and Subversion in the Australian Novel," in *Pacific Moana Quarterly* 4, 1979, and "Character and Environment in Some Recent Australian Fiction," in *Waves* 7, 1979, both by Ken Gelder; "Laszlo's Testament, or Structuring the Past and Sketching the Present in Contemporary Short Fiction," in *Kunapipi 1,* 1979, "A New Version of Pastoral," in *Australian Literary Studies* 11, 1983, and "Paradise, Politics, and Fiction: The Writing of Wilding," in *Meanjin* 45, 1986, all by Bruce Clunies Ross; "The New Writing, Whodunnit?" by G.M. Gillard, in *Meanjin* 40, 1981; "Wilding: Post Modernism and the Australian Literary Heritage" by Hans Hauge, in *Overland* 96, 1984; "The Social Semiotic of Narrative Exchange" by Ian Reid, in *Semiotics, Ideology, Language,* edited by T. Tweadgold, E.A. Grosz, G. Kress, and M.A.K. Halliday, 1986; "Lost and Found: Narrative and Description in Wilding's 'What It Was Like, Sometimes'" by Simone Vauthier in *Journal of the Short Story in English* 12, 1989, and "Reading the Signs of Wilding's 'Knock Knock'" by Vauthier, in *European Perspectives: Contemporary Essays on Australian Literature,* edited by G. Capore, 1991; *The New Diversity: Australian Fiction 1970–1988* by Ken Gelder and Paul Salzman, 1989.

*   *   *

The experience of migration is central to Michael Wilding's fiction. Like Elizabeth Jolley, also from the English Midlands, Wilding shows figures caught between English and Australian cultures. Whereas Jolley's "new country" is the suburbs and hill country near Western Australia's capital city Perth, the younger Wilding moved in 1963 to Australia's east coast metropolis, Sydney. There, like the native-born Frank Moorhouse, Wilding has been a leading proponent of "new writing" since the 1970's.

The first of Wilding's collections, *Aspects of the Dying Experience,* sets his scene. In a number of stories, a hesitant English persona is bemused by Sydney's extrovert, hedonistic youth culture—the beaches, parties, and booze. The volume's title suggests the "dyeing" as an immigrant changes colour in his new country, and is also a pun on sexual initiation rites. D.H. Lawrence and Henry James have left their mark on the writer's early style and subject matter. In "Odour of Eucalypts" the autobiographical narrator is temporarily drawn to an English shipboard companion who retains her aloofness from Australians. A more threatening encounter occurs in "Joe's Absence," in which a possible sexual relationship with a young woman is deferred because of her lover Joe, who is a strong personality and rival writer even in his absence. This is the first of many references in Wilding's work to fellow Sydney writer Frank Moorhouse. The story opens up speculation about the power of published fiction over human lives. (The

typescripts which Joe has left near his typewriter inexorably impose his presence on the young man and woman.) Other writers enter this volume too. The story "And Did Henry Miller Walk in Our Tropical Garden," for example, introduces this American novelist into the discourse; other American authors alluded to include Burroughs, Kerouac, and Brautigan.

Wilding's English inheritance comes to the fore in his second book of stories, *The West Midland Underground.* In "Canal Run" a first-person narrator recalls, Sillitoe-like, his claustrophobic sense of schooldays in the West Midlands (around Worcester). Sexual repression mirrors class repressions: "[sex] was wrong and furtive and C stream; which was another way of saying lower class." A sociopolitical consciousness, born of class and regional differences in England, informs much of Wilding's fictional and non-fictional writings. But social realism is not his preferred mode. In the title story "The West Midland Underground" he becomes a metaphor man: the underground holds an ambiguous set of possibilities, including entrapment and the subconscious. Personal freedom is imagined in organic surroundings beyond the men of order who hold economic and industrial control.

Wilding's literary preference in the 1970's was for postmodern experiment like that of Borges, Barth, Barthelme, Brautigan, and others. His principal thematic concern was with involvement in or withdrawal from socio-political action. A quite short piece, "The Silence of the Seer," touches both concerns. Its narrative manner is that of a fable, which offers a dispassionate recounting of the stages of withdrawal and silence of a 20th-century prophet who "on 5 January 1970 . . . died by his own hand and his own necktie." While the fable purports to offer a durable image of the temptations and perils of withdrawal from the world, Wilding's witty allusions to cults and fads of the 1970's anchor it to a particular decade.

In Wilding's novel about short story writers, *The Short Story Embassy,* a character comments that the coming of the contraceptive pill has opened up "a whole different anthropology." But in order to write this new anthropology, Wilding and others had to overcome taboos of subject matter and vocabulary. The literary rebellion by Wilding, Moorhouse, and others against "bourgeois social repression" took place in underground newspapers or the less established literary magazines. Wilding and Moorhouse (with Brian Kiernan) even started their own packaged short story magazine *Tabloid Story.*

Wilding's contributions to the literary sex revolution are most apparent in his volumes *Scenic Drive* and *The Phallic Forest.* The wit and ironic allusiveness of stories in these volumes takes them beyond pornography, reinforcing the importance of the fantasy life that links sexual and fictional expression. Ambiguity is the keynote of these stories and comedy emerges from surprising juxtapositions of literary and sexual domains. "The Girl Behind the Bar is Reading Jack Kerouac" works in this way. "Emma: Memoirs of a Woman of Pleasure" is a literary tour de force, intercutting paragraphs of John Cleland's *Fanny Hill* to Jane Austen's *Emma,* revealing that literary and sexual play can be analogous. Similarly in the story "Phallic Forest" (which has been filmed) the focus is on the medium of language itself and its capacity for "jouissance."

The signs are generally not good for sexual and narcotic hedonism in Wilding's fifth volume *Reading the Signs.* Greater emotional force is evident in the title story, recalling a childhood incident in England in which the narrator's attempts to revive his parents' memories of a flying saucer fail. His mother has repressed the incident.

His father has written to the local newspaper: "As an iron-moulder, it seemed to me like a glowing red ball of molten iron." The son wants to share this apocalyptic moment but the reality is his mother's middle-class shame at the public exposure of her husband's working-class occupation.

Personal and social emancipation is sought by many Wilding characters but is seldom achieved. The long story "Among My Books" (in *Reading the Signs*) sensitively evokes the pleasures, terrors, and anxieties of an affair during the autobiographical persona's Oxford days. Dialogue and interior monologue intertwine rhythmically to produce a story of unsentimental poignancy, in which a life of freedom among books survives the feared romantic entrapment. Another long story, "In the Penal Colony," recalls a writer's tour of Tasmania in which an older narrator is still seeking personal and sexual emancipation. The island's convict past gives a historical dimension to the wayward behaviour of contemporary writers on the freedom trail. In recalling Marcus Clarke more than Kafka, Wilding reveals again his sense of transportation to an Australia of equivocal freedoms.

The four long stories in Wilding's recent volume of new work, *Under Saturn*, traverse some familiar territory. "Writing a Life" returns to an ivory tower Oxford and "Campus Life" satirises a university conservatism, which seems hardly touched by the days of student protest marches and sit-ins. A more complex situation is evoked in the title story "Under Saturn," a story carried forward principally by dialogue, in which the protagonist's conspiracy theories and paranoia are projected onto sunny Sydney—a city, in Wilding's hands, where deception and brutality prevail. The story's dilemma is the one faced by D.H. Lawrence's protagonist Somers in *Kangaroo* of sociopolitical involvement or withdrawal. The conspiracy theories of Wilding's protagonist include the CIA, UFOs, breakins, and sexual entanglements. The principal alternatives seem to be social activism or some form of spiritual engagement. Instead, the sign of Saturn triumphs as the protagonist withdraws gloomily from the world.

—Bruce Bennett

WILLIAMS, William Carlos. American. Born in Rutherford, New Jersey, 17 September 1883. Educated at a school in Rutherford, 1889–96; Chateau de Lancy, near Geneva, Switzerland, and Lycée Condorcet, Paris, 1897–99; Horace Mann High School, New York, 1899–1902; University of Pennsylvania, Philadelphia, 1902–06, M.D. 1906; intern at hospitals in New York City, 1906–08; post-graduate work in pediatrics, University of Leipzig, 1908–09. Married Florence Herman in 1912; two sons. Practiced medicine in Rutherford, 1910 until he retired in the mid-1950's; editor, *Others*, 1919; editor, with Robert McAlmon, *Contact*, 1920–23; editor, *Contact: An American Quarterly*, 1931–33. Appointed consultant in poetry, Library of Congress, Washington, D.C., 1952, but did not serve. Recipient: Loines award, 1948; National Book award, 1950; Bollingen prize, 1952; Academy of American Poets fellowship, 1956; Brandeis University Creative Arts award, 1958; American Academy gold medal, 1963; Pulitzer prize, 1963. LL.D.: State University of New York, Buffalo, 1956; Fairleigh Dickinson University, Teaneck, New Jersey, 1959; Litt.D.: Rutgers University, New Brunswick, New

Jersey, 1948; Bard College, Annandale-on-Hudson, New York, 1948; University of Pennsylvania, 1952. Member, American Academy. *Died 4 March 1963.*

PUBLICATIONS

Collections

The Williams Reader, edited by M.L. Rosenthal.   1966.
Selected Poems, edited by Charles Tomlinson.   1976.
Collected Poems, edited by A. Walton Litz and Christopher MacGowan.   2 vols., 1987–88.

Short Stories

A Novelette and Other Prose 1921–1931.   1932.
The Knife of the Times and Other Stories.   1932.
Life along the Passaic River.   1938.
Make Light of It: Collected Stories.   1950.
The Farmers' Daughters: The Collected Stories.   1961.

Novels

A Voyage to Pagany.   1928.
Trilogy:
    White Mule.   1937.
    In the Money.   1940.
    The Build-Up.   1952.

Verse

Poems.   1909.
The Tempers.   1913.
Al Que Quiere!   1917.
Kora in Hell: Improvisations.   1920.
Sour Grapes.   1921.
Spring and All.   1923.
Go Go.   1923.
The Cod Head.   1932.
Collected Poems, 1921–1931.   1934.
An Early Martyr and Other Poems.   1935.
Adam & Eve & the City.   1936.
The Complete Collected Poems 1906–1938.   1938.
The Broken Span.   1941.
The Wedge.   1944.
Paterson, Book One.   1946; *Book Two*, 1948; *Book Three*, 1949; *Book Four*, 1951; *Book Five*, 1958; *Books I-V*, 1963.
The Clouds.   1948.
The Pink Church.   1949.
Selected Poems.   1949.
The Collected Later Poems.   1950; revised edition, 1963.
The Collected Earlier Poems.   1951.
The Desert Music and Other Poems.   1954.
Journey to Love.   1955.
Pictures from Brueghel and Other Poems.   1962.
Penguin Modern Poets 9, with Denise Levertov and Kenneth Rexroth.   1967.

Plays

Betry Putnam (produced 1910).
A Dream of Love (produced 1949).   1948.
Many Loves (produced 1958).   In *Many Loves and Other Plays*, 1961.

Many Loves and Other Plays: The Collected Plays (includes *A Dream of Love; Tituba's Children; The First President,* music by Theodore Harris; *The Cure*).   1961.

Other

The Great American Novel.   1923.
In the American Grain.   1925.
The Autobiography.   1951.
Williams' Poetry Talked About, with Eli Siegel.   1952; revised edition, edited by Martha Baird and Ellen Reiss, as *The Williams-Siegel Documentary,* 1970, 1974.
Selected Essays.   1954.
John Marin, with others.   1956.
Selected Letters, edited by John C. Thirlwall.   1957.
I Wanted to Write a Poem: The Autobiography of the Works of a Poet, edited by Edith Heal.   1958.
Yes, Mrs. Williams: A Personal Record of My Mother. 1959.
Imaginations: Collected Early Prose, edited by Webster Schott.   1970.
A Beginning on the Short Story (lecture).   1974.
The Embodiment of Knowledge, edited by Ron Loewinsohn.   1974.
Interviews with Williams: Speaking Straight Ahead, edited by Linda W. Wagner.   1976.
A Recognizable Image: Williams on Art and Artists, edited by Bram Dijkstra.   1978.
Something to Say: Williams on Younger Poets, edited by James E.B. Breslin.   1985.
Williams and James Laughlin: Selected Letters, edited by Hugh Witemeyer.   1990.

Translator, *Last Nights of Paris,* by Philippe Soupault. 1929.
Translator, with others, *Jean sans terre/Landless John,* by Yvan Goll.   1944.
Translator, with Raquel Hélène Williams, *The Dog and the Fever,* by Francisco de Quevedo.   1954.

*

Bibliography: *A Bibliography of Williams* by Emily Wallace Mitchell, 1968; *Williams: A Reference Guide* by Linda W. Wagner, 1978.

Critical Studies: *Williams* by Vivienne Koch, 1950; *Williams: A Critical Study* by John Malcolm Brinnin, 1963; *The Poems of Williams,* 1964, and *The Prose of Williams,* 1970, both by Linda W. Wagner; *The Poetic World of Williams* by Alan Ostrom, 1966; *Williams: A Collection of Critical Essays* edited by J. Hillis Miller, 1966; *An Approach to Paterson* by Walter Scott Peterson, 1967; *The Music of Survival* by Sherman Paul, 1968; *Williams' Paterson: Language and Landscape* by Joel Connarroe, 1970; *Williams: An American Artist* by James E.B. Breslin, 1970; *Williams: The American Background* by Mike Weaver, 1971; *A Companion to Williams's Paterson* by Benjamin Sankey, 1971; *Williams: The Later Poems* by Jerome Mazzaro, 1973; *The Inverted Bell: Modernism and the Counterpoetics of Williams* by Joseph N. Riddel, 1974; *Williams* by Kenneth Burke and Emily H. Wallace, 1974; *Williams: The Knack of Survival in America* by Robert Coles, 1975; *Williams: Poet from Jersey* by Reed Whittemore, 1975; *Williams: The Poet and His Critics,* 1975, and *Williams: A New World Naked,* 1981, both by Paul L.

Mariani; *The Early Poetry of Williams* by Rod Townley, 1976; *Williams and the American Scene 1920–1940* by Dickran Tashjian, 1978; *Williams's Paterson: A Critical Reappraisal* by Margaret Glynne Lloyd, 1980; *Williams: The Critical Heritage* edited by Charles Doyle, 1980, and *Williams and the American Poem* by Doyle, 1982; *Williams and the Painters 1909–1923* by William Marling, 1982; *Williams: Man and Poet* by Carroll F. Terrell, 1983; *Williams: A Poet in the American Theatre* by David A. Fedo, 1983; *Ezra Pound and Williams* edited by Daniel Hoffman, 1983; *Williams and Romantic Idealism* by Carl Rapp, 1984; *The Visual Text of Williams* by Henry M. Sayre, 1984; *American Beauty: Williams and the Modernist Whitman* by Stephen Tapscott, 1984; *The Transparent Lyric: Reading and Meaning in the Poetry of Stevens and Williams* by David Walker, 1984; *Williams and the Meanings of Measure* by Stephen Cushman, 1985; *A Poetry of Presence: The Writing of Williams* by Bernard Duffey, 1986; *Williams and the Maternal Muse* by Kerry Driscoll, 1987; *Virgin and Whore: The Image of Women in the Poetry of Williams* by Audrey T. Rodgers, 1987; *The Early Politics and Poetics of Williams* by David Frail, 1987; *The Early Prose of Williams, 1917–1925* by Geoffrey H. Movius, 1987; *Williams: The Art, and Literary Tradition* by Peter Schmidt, 1988; *Williams and Autobiography: The Woods of His Nature* by Ann W. Fisher-Wirth, 1989; *Williams: A Study of the Short Fiction* by Robert F. Gish, 1989.

*   *   *

William Carlos Williams is best known as a modern American poet. In recent years, however, his achievement as a novelist and writer of short fiction has been recognized. He was also a doctor who specialized in pediatric medicine. As a physician his education and his vocation reflected his abilities as a scientist, his outlook of life growing out of the assumptions of the scientific method. He remained dedicated to the medical profession throughout his life.

His short stories, in particular, evidence the ways in which he reconciled the concerns of medicine, its motive toward healing, its empathy for the sick; its wonderment in the presence of the mysteries of life and death. His passion to write drove him to scribble down ideas for poems and stories between appointments with patients. A clinical notation was likely to be either preceded or followed by an artistic insight, a line of poetry, a character profile— science and art blending. In more than one instance his patients became the characters of his stories, as individuals or as composites.

His compassion for humanity and its predicaments led him into the politics of class and of economics and ethnicity. Generally his sympathies came down on the side of the lower classes, the proletariat. As a physician and an artist he was himself a member of the privileged, upper middle class. He was for a time drawn quite strongly to Europe and the ostensibly higher levels of culture, and especially the Anglo-European impulses and traditions. But his devotion to things American, American cities, American art, American people, the egalitarian and democratic premises of government, the melting-pot of diverse immigrants combined to provide his subject, in his stories, his poems, and in his masterpiece of revisionist history, *In the American Grain.*

Williams's short stories bespeak all of these scientific, aesthetic, sociological, and political concerns, and his democratic, albeit bohemian, leftist leanings. His style and his facility with metaphor combine with the austerity and objectivity of scientific description to form a special kind of imagistic, objectivist, and minimalist prose.

His subjects, broadly, take on the categories of "doctor" stories and stories of the urban poor and the disadvantaged. His allegiance to American speech, to what he touted as the "American Idiom" celebrate the cadences and the vitality of the speech, of utterances such as are found emanating "out of the mouths of Polish mothers." His popularity in the 1960's as an anti-Puritan free thinker, free lover, and spontaneous writer is somewhat diminished today, among feminist readers in particular, in that his tone and personae seem paternalistic and condescending. His precise attitude toward women—as a man and as an author—remains fascinating in an era of gender analysis and "political correctness." He loved women, to be sure; just how well he loved them as narrator, physician, and person, remains rather problematic. However, many of his stories are used in courses in medical ethics in the training of physicians.

Williams's collected stories include *The Knife of the Times and Other Stories, Life along the Passaic River, Make Light of It,* and *The Farmers' Daughters.* Several of his stories, such as "The Use of Force," "Jean Beicke," and "The Girl with a Pimply Face," are frequently anthologized. All of his published stories, some 50, are rewarding at both casual and more critical levels. "The Knife of the Times""The Colored Girls of Passenack—Old and New," and "Old Doc Rivers" are especially worthy.

"Knife" deals with a long-repressed expression of lesbian love of Ethel for her friend, Maura. Maura reciprocates and the "knife" of repression and social conformity cuts through to new awareness and sensuality. "Colored Girls" represents Williams's one autobiographical recording of his enduring attraction to black women, and he writes about the five or so who gave physical form to his youthful and adult yearnings. "Doc Rivers" offers a case study of the sins and abuses (sex, drugs, violence) of a prominent physician—from the heights of acclaim to the skids of defamation. "Jean Beicke" is an account of the love and care extended by a physician and nurses to a deformed infant. Jean dies; the vivid description of the autopsy performed on her underscores the deep pathos of the neglect and abandonment which was her inheritance—of the poor like her. In this story in particular Williams's softer, more directly stated elegiac regard, his sigh for humanity comes through. In "Pimply Face" a physician, called to attend the baby of an impoverished family, is taken with the adolescent sister, her blemished face, her life. His prescription goes beyond acne to advice about returning to school.

Williams believed that the short story allowed him a medium for "nailing down a single conviction." His stories, individually and collectively, reveal just how deeply he commiserated with and celebrated humankind. He knew his patients and his characters virtually inside and out—anatomically and psychologically—and he declared them "rare presences" all.

—Robert Franklin Gish

See the essay on "The Use of Force."

————

WILSON, (Sir) Angus (Frank Johnstone). English. Born in Bexhill, Sussex, 11 August 1913. Educated at Westminster School, London, 1927–31; Merton College, Oxford, B.A. (honours) in medieval and modern history 1936. Served in the Foreign Office, 1942–46. Staff member, British Museum, London, 1937–55: deputy superintendent of the reading room, 1949–55; Ewing lecturer, University of California, Los Angeles, 1960; Bergen lecturer, Yale University, New Haven, Connecticut, 1960; Moody lecturer, University of Chicago, 1960; Northcliffe lecturer, University College, London, 1961; Leslie Stephen Lecturer, Cambridge University, 1962–63; lecturer, 1963–66, professor of English literature, 1966–78, and from 1978, professor emeritus, University of East Anglia, Norwich; Beckman Professor, University of California, Berkeley, 1967; John Hinkley Visiting Professor, Johns Hopkins University, Baltimore, 1974; visiting professor, University of Delaware, Newark, 1977, 1980, 1983, University of Iowa, Iowa City, 1978, 1986, Georgia State University, Atlanta, 1979, University of Michigan, Ann Arbor, 1979, University of Minnesota, Minneapolis, 1980, University of Pittsburgh, 1981, University of Missouri, Columbia, 1982, and University of Arizona, Tucson, 1984. Member of the Committee, Royal Literary Fund, 1966; member, Arts Council of Great Britain, 1966–69; chairman, National Book League, London, 1971–74; president, Dickens Fellowship, London, 1974–75, and Kipling Society, 1981–88. Recipient: James Tait Black Memorial prize, 1959; Foreign Book prize (France), 1960; *Yorkshire Post* award, for nonfiction, 1971; Focus award, 1985. D. Litt.: University of Leicester, 1977; University of East Anglia, 1979; University of Sussex, Brighton, 1981; Litt. D.: Liverpool University, 1979; Hon. Dr.: the Sorbonne, Paris, 1983. Honorary fellow, Cowell College, University of California, Santa Cruz, 1968. Fellow, 1958, Companion of Literature, 1972, and since 1982 president, Royal Society of Literature; commandant, Order of Arts and Letters (France), 1972; honorary member, American Academy, 1980. C.B.E. (Commander, Order of the British Empire), 1968. Knighted, 1980. Lives in Suffolk.

PUBLICATIONS

Short Stories

The Wrong Set and Other Stories.   1949.
Such Darling Dodos and Other Stories.   1950.
A Bit off the Map and Other Stories.   1957.
Death Dance: Twenty-Five Short Stories.   1969.
Collected Stories.   1987.

Novels

Hemlock and After.   1952.
Anglo-Saxon Attitudes.   1956.
The Middle Age of Mrs. Eliot.   1958.
The Old Men at the Zoo.   1961.
Late Call.   1964.
No Laughing Matter.   1967.
As If by Magic.   1973.
Setting the World on Fire.   1980.

Plays

The Mulberry Bush (produced 1956).   1956.

Television Plays: *After the Show,* 1959; *The Stranger,* 1960; *The Invasion,* 1962.

Other

Emile Zola: An Introductory Study of His Novels.   1952; revised edition, 1965.
For Whom the Cloche Tolls: A Scrapbook of the Twenties, illustrated by Philippe Jullian.   1953.
The Wild Garden; or, Speaking of Writing.   1963.
Tempo: The Impact of Television on the Arts.   1964.
The World of Charles Dickens.   1970.
Dickens Memorial Lecture 1970, with Kathleen Tillotson and Sylvère Monad.   1970.
The Naughty Nineties.   1976.
The Strange Ride of Rudyard Kipling: His Life and Works. 1977.
Diversity and Depth in Fiction: Selected Critical Writings, edited by Kerry McSweeney.   1983.
Reflections in a Writer's Eye: Travel Pieces.   1986.

Editor, *A Maugham Twelve,* by W. Somerset Maugham. 1966.
Editor, *Cakes and Ale, and Twelve Short Stories,* by W. Somerset Maugham.   1967.
Editor, *Writers of East Anglia.*   1977.
Editor, *East Anglia in Verse and Prose.*   1982.
Editor, *The Portable Dickens.*   1983.
Editor, *Essays by Divers Hands.*   1984.

*

Bibliography: *Wilson: A Bibliography 1947–1987* by J.H. Stape and Anne N. Thomas, 1988.

Critical Studies: *Wilson* by Jay L. Halio, 1964, and *Critical Essays on Wilson* edited by Halio, 1985; *Wilson* by K.W. Gransden, 1969; *Harvest of a Quiet Eye: The Novel of Compassion* by James Gindin, 1971; *Wilson: Mimic and Moralist* by Peter Faulkner, 1980; *Wilson* by Averil Gardner, 1985.

*   *   *

Angus Wilson began his career as a writer almost by accident. Recovering from a nervous breakdown after World War II, he was advised by his therapist to try writing. He decided to try short stories, which could be conceived and written during a single weekend spent in the country and away from his regular job as assistant superintendent of the reading room in the British Library. "Raspberry Jam," his first story, was soon followed by others, and before long he had enough for a collection. *The Wrong Set* was the first volume to be published and contained several stories that had already appeared in literary magazines such as Cyril Connolly's *Horizon.* Widely acclaimed, this volume was followed by another, *Such Darling Dodos,* which became a Book Society recommendation. Wilson's career as a fiction writer was launched.

Although he eventually gave up shorter fiction for novels and biographies, Wilson's reputation for many years hung on the vivid impression his stories had made. At first regarded as one of Britain's "Angry Young Men," the soubriquet was unmerited for several reasons. In the first place, Wilson was of an earlier generation than Osborne,

Kingsley Amis, and others in that group; for another, his stories, while often satiric, even bitter, were not "angry." Wilson was more interested in exposing the deceptions and self-deceptions of otherwise well-meaning people, like Lois Gorringe in "A Story of Historical Interest" (the title, like many others, is fully ironic). When Lois finally awakens, with a shock, to realize that the father whom she has cared for over many years is neither grateful nor deserving of her ministrations, she appears rather cold-hearted when the old man lies on the brink of death. But this is only a natural reaction to what she has experienced. Sentimentality might dictate a different response, but Wilson is never sentimental in his fiction. It is his clear-sighted recognition of unpalatable truths that gives his stories their strength— and their undeserved reputation for being brutally misanthropic.

A careful reading of his stories reveals that Wilson does not despise his fellow human beings. If anything, he pities the weaker ones among us, but more typically he tries to show courage in the face of adversity—psychological adversity above all. Hence in "Heart of Elm" Constance Graham exhibits great strength in the face of her children's sentimental attachment to their old nurse, Ellen, who lies dying. She refuses to allow either the children or herself to wallow in mistaken and misguided feelings of affection and insists that all three of them break free at last of the sticky bonds that have fettered them to an actually unlovely past. Similarly, in "A Visit in Bad Taste" Malcolm and Margaret Tarrant face up to the problem that Margaret's brother, Arthur, has brought them. Recently released from prison on a morals charge, Arthur clearly does not "fit in" with the Tarrants' way of life, and Margaret for one is determined to tell him. She does, and in so doing wins her husband's admiration. She also makes him vaguely uneasy, however, as he suspects she has somehow been too strong, too willing to face up to reality. The reader is even more uneasy, recognizing in Margaret's actions a singular absence of compassion for her poor old brother, whom she is quite ready to send off to "the colonies" or even to suicide so that her life with Malcolm—"individually alive, socially progressive"—may remain undisturbed by his presence.

As these stories and others show, Wilson is very much the social critic. He is at his best, perhaps, in satirizing the pretensions and hypocrisies of middle-class people in post-World War II English society, as in "A Flat Country Christmas." There, attempts at hearty camaraderie, earlier developed between Eric and Ray during their Army days, break down miserably, as together with their wives the men try to bridge gaps of social class and privilege that hitherto have separated people like themselves—and apparently still do. But if satire is mingled with compassion for suffering human beings in that story, the bitchiness and snobberies of others, like June Raven in "More Friend than Lodger," come in for largely unmitigated pillorying, as also in the title story of the collection, *A Bit off the Map,* which merges social with political satire. A socialist all his life, Wilson opposed Britain's invasion of Suez in 1956 and mocked the futility of attempts to revive her imperialist past. Those attempts are satirized indirectly in the neo-Nietzschean palaver of the "crowd" in "A Bit off the Map" and dramatized when mad old Lieutenant-Colonel Lambourn unfolds his secret maps to Kennie Martin, a deeply disturbed "Teddy boy," earnestly trying to discover the truth. Their meeting ends in disaster.

Wilson tends to see social gatherings and the interactions of human beings generally in the form of a dance, a "Totentanz" (the name of one of his stories), or "Death Dance" (as a later collection is called). But the interactions are not always deadly, and often they are very funny, as in "What do Hippos Eat?" Wilson peoples his stories with many colorful types, some of which may seem dated now, such as the "Raffish Old Sport" ("A Story of Historical Interest"), the "Intense Young Woman" or "Man" ("Fresh Air Fiend"), and "The Widow Who Copes" ("Sister Superior"). But more often than not, deftly using such devices as the interior monologue ("Et Dona Ferentes"), he penetrates beneath the type to the common core of humanity, so that even as he exposes their follies and foibles, or worse, his characters emerge as people who still deserve some measure of sympathy. Limited or twisted as they may be by class consciousness, social background, or political beliefs, they are still recognizable as human. Thus Wilson no more deserves to be called a misanthrope than does his great 18th-century forebear, Jonathan Swift. Whatever they may have thought of the human race generally, their compassion—even love—for the individual remained undiminished.

—Jay L. Halio

See the essay on "Such Darling Dodos."

———

WODEHOUSE, (Sir) P(elham) G(renville). American. Born in Guildford, Surrey, 15 October 1881; lived in Hong Kong, 1882–86; moved to the U.S., 1910; became citizen, 1955. Educated at schools in Croydon, Surrey, and Guernsey, Channel Islands; Dulwich College, London, 1894–1900. Married Ethel Rowley (née Newton) in 1914; one step-daughter. Clerk, Hong Kong and Shanghai Bank, London, 1900–02; full-time writer from 1902; columnist ("By the Way"), London *Globe*, 1903–09; drama critic, *Vanity Fair*, New York, 1915–19; scriptwriter in Hollywood for MGM, 1930, and RKO, 1936; lived in Le Touquet, France, 1934–39; interned by the Germans in Upper Silesia, 1940–41; lived on Long Island, New York, from 1947. D.Litt.: Oxford University, 1939. Knighted, 1975. *Died 14 February 1975.*

PUBLICATIONS

Collections

Vintage Wodehouse, edited by Richard Usborne.   1977.
Wodehouse Nuggets, edited by Richard Usborne.   1983.
Four Plays (includes *The Play's the Thing; Good Morning, Bill; Leave It to Psmith; Come On, Jeeves*), edited by David A. Jasen.   1983.

Short Stories

Tales of St. Austin's (includes essays).   1903.
The Man Upstairs and Other Stories.   1914.
The Man with Two Left Feet and Other Stories.   1917; expanded edition, 1933.
My Man Jeeves.   1919.
Indiscretions of Archie.   1921.
The Clicking of Cuthbert.   1922; as *Golf Without Tears*, 1924.
The Inimitable Jeeves.   1923; as *Jeeves*, 1923.
Ukridge.   1924; as *He Rather Enjoyed It*, 1926.

Carry On, Jeeves!   1925.
Meet Mr. Mulliner.   1927.
Mr. Mulliner Speaking.   1929.
Very Good, Jeeves!   1930.
Mulliner Nights.   1933.
Mulliner Omnibus.   1935; revised edition, as *The World of Mr. Mulliner*, 1972.
Blandings Castle and Elsewhere.   1935.
Young Men in Spats.   1936.
Lord Emsworth and Others.   1937; as *The Crime Wave at Blandings and Other Stories*, 1937.
Eggs, Beans, and Crumpets.   1940.
Dudley Is Back to Normal.   1940.
Nothing Serious.   1950.
Selected Stories, edited by John W. Aldridge.   1958.
A Few Quick Ones.   1959.
Plum Pie.   1966.
The World of Jeeves.   1967.
The Golf Omnibus: Thirty-One Selected Golfing Short Stories.   1973.
The World of Psmith.   1974.
The World of Ukridge.   1975.
The Swoop! and Other Stories, edited by David Jasen.   1979.

Novels

The Pothunters.   1902.
A Prefect's Uncle.   1903.
The Gold Bat.   1904.
The Head of Kay's.   1905.
Love among the Chickens.   1906; revised edition, 1921.
The White Feather.   1907.
The Swoop! How Clarence Saved England: A Tale of the Great Invasion.   1909.
Mike: A Public School Story.   1909; part 2 reprinted as *Enter Psmith*, 1935; revised edition, as *Mike at Wrykyn* and *Mike and Psmith*,   2 vols., 1953.
The Intrusion of Jimmy.   1910; as *A Gentleman of Leisure*, 1910.
Psmith in the City: A Sequel to Mike.   1910.
The Prince and Betty.   1912; revised edition, as *Psmith, Journalist*, 1915.
The Prince and Betty (different book from the previous title).   1912.
The Little Nugget.   1913.
Something New.   1915; as *Something Fresh*, 1915.
Uneasy Money.   1916.
Piccadilly Jim.   1917.
Their Mutual Child.   1919; as *The Coming of Bill*, 1920.
A Damsel in Distress.   1919.
The Little Warrior.   1920; as *Jill the Reckless*, 1921.
Three Men and a Maid.   1922; as *The Girl on the Boat*, 1922.
The Adventures of Sally.   1922; as *Mostly Sally*, 1923.
Leave It to Psmith.   1923.
Bill the Conqueror: His Invasion of England in the Springtime.   1924.
Sam the Sudden.   1925; as *Sam in the Suburbs*, 1925.
The Heart of a Goof.   1926; as *Divots*, 1927.
The Small Bachelor.   1927.
Money for Nothing.   1928.
Fish Preferred.   1929; as *Summer Lightning*, 1929; as *Fish Deferred*, 1929.
Big Money.   1931.
If I Were You.   1931.
Doctor Sally.   1932.
Hot Water.   1932.

Heavy Weather. 1933.
Thank You, Jeeves. 1934.
Right Ho, Jeeves. 1934; as *Brinkley Manor*, 1934.
The Luck of the Bodkins. 1935.
Laughing Gas. 1936.
Summer Moonshine. 1937.
The Code of the Woosters. 1938.
Uncle Fred in the Springtime. 1939.
Quick Service. 1940.
Money in the Bank. 1942.
Joy in the Morning. 1946.
Full Moon. 1947.
Spring Fever. 1948.
Uncle Dynamite. 1948.
The Mating Season. 1949.
The Old Reliable. 1951.
Barmy in Wonderland. 1952; as *Angel Cake*, 1952.
Pigs Have Wings. 1952.
Ring for Jeeves. 1953; as *The Return of Jeeves*, 1954.
Jeeves and the Feudal Spirit. 1954; as *Bertie Wooster Sees It Through*, 1955.
French Leave. 1956.
Something Fishy. 1957; as *The Butler Did It*, 1957.
Cocktail Time. 1958.
How Right You Are, Jeeves. 1960; as *Jeeves in the Offing*, 1960.
The Ice in the Bedroom. 1961; as *Ice in the Bedroom*, 1961.
Service with a Smile. 1961.
Stiff Upper Lip, Jeeves. 1963.
Biffen's Millions. 1964; as *Frozen Assests*, 1964.
The Brinkmanship of Galahad Threepwood. 1965; as *Galahad at Blandings*, 1965.
The Purloined Paperweight. 1967; as *Company for Henry*, 1967.
Do Butlers Burgle Banks? 1968.
A Pelican at Blandings. 1969; as *No Nudes Is Good Nudes*, 1970.
The Girl in Blue. 1970.
Much Obliged, Jeeves. 1971; as *Jeeves and the Tie That Binds*, 1971.
Pearls, Girls, and Monty Bodkin. 1972; as *The Plot That Thickened*, 1973.
Bachelors Anonymous. 1973.
Aunts Aren't Gentlemen. 1974; as *The Cat-Nappers*, 1974.
Quest. 1975.
Sunset at Blandings, edited by Richard Usborne. 1977.

Plays

The Bandit's Daughter (sketch), with Herbert Westbrook, music by Ella King-Hall (produced 1907).
A Gentleman of Leisure, with John Stapleton, from the novel by Wodehouse (produced 1911); as *A Thief for a Night* (produced 1913).
After the Show, with Herbert Westbrook (produced 1913).
Brother Alfred, with Herbert Westbrook (produced 1913).
Nuts and Wine, with C.H. Bovill, music by Frank Tours (produced 1914).
Pom Pom, with Anne Caldwell, music by Hugo Felix (produced 1916).
Miss Springtime (lyrics only, with Herbert Reynolds), book by Guy Bolton, music by Emmerich Kalman and Jerome Kern (produced 1916).
Have a Heart, with Guy Bolton, music by Jerome Kern (produced 1917). 1917.

Oh, Boy!, with Guy Bolton, music by Jerome Kern (produced 1917); as *Oh, Joy* (produced 1919).
Leave It to Jane, with Guy Bolton, music by Jerome Kern, from play *The College Widow* by George Ade (produced 1917).
Kitty Darlin' (lyrics only), book by Guy Bolton, music by Rudolf Firml (produced 1917).
The Riviera Girl (lyrics only), book by Guy Bolton, music by Emmerich Kalman and Jerome Kern (produced 1917).
Miss 1917, with Guy Bolton, music by Jerome Kern and Victor Herbert (produced 1917).
Oh, Lady! Lady!, with Guy Bolton, music by Jerome Kern (produced 1918).
See You Later, with Guy Bolton, music by Jean Schwartz and Joseph Szulc (produced 1918).
The Girl Behind the Gun, with Guy Bolton, music by Ivan Caryll (produced 1918); as *Kissing Time* (produced 1919).
Oh, My Dear!, with Guy Bolton, music by Louis Hirsch (produced 1918).
The Rose of China (lyrics only), book by Guy Bolton, music by Armand Vecsey (produced 1919).
The Golden Moth, with Fred Thompson, music by Ivor Novello (produced 1921).
The Cabaret Girl, with George Grossmith, Jr., music by Jerome Kern (produced 1922).
The Beauty Prize, with George Grossmith, Jr., music by Jerome Kern (produced 1923).
Sitting Pretty, with Guy Bolton, music by Jerome Kern (produced 1924).
Hearts and Diamonds, with Laurie Wylie, music by Bruno Granichstaedten, lyrics by Graham John (produced 1926). 1926.
Oh, Kay!, with Guy Bolton, music by George Gershwin, lyrics by Ira Gershwin (produced 1926).
The Play's the Thing, from a play by Molnár (produced 1926). 1927; in *Four Plays*, 1986.
Her Cardboard Lover, with Valerie Wyngate, from a play by Jacques Deval (produced 1927).
Good Morning, Bill, from a play by Ladislaus Fodor (produced 1927). 1928; in *Four Plays*, 1986.
The Nightingale, with Guy Bolton, music by Armand Vecsey (produced 1927).
Rosalie (lyrics only, with Ira Gershwin), book by Guy Bolton and Bill McGuire, music by George Gershwin and Sigmund Romberg (produced 1928).
A Damsel in Distress, with Ian Hay, from the novel by Wodehouse (produced 1928). 1930.
The Three Musketeers (lyrics only, with Clifford Grey), book by Bill McGuire, music by Rudolf Friml (produced 1928). 1937.
Baa, Baa, Black Sheep, with Ian Hay (produced 1929). 1930.
Candle-Light, from a play by Siegfried Geyer (produced 1929). 1934.
Leave It to Psmith, with Ian Hay (produced 1930). 1932; in *Four Plays*, 1986.
Who's Who, with Guy Bolton (produced 1934).
Anything Goes, with Guy Bolton, music by Cole Porter (produced 1934). 1936.
The Inside Stand (produced 1935).
Don't Listen Ladies, with Guy Bolton, from a play by Sacha Guitry (produced 1948).
Nothing Serious (produced 1950; also produced as *Springboard to Nowhere*, and *House on a Cliff*).
Come On, Jeeves, with Guy Bolton (produced 1956). 1956; in *Four Plays*, 1986.

Screenplays: *Oh, Kay!*, with Carey Wilson and Elsie Janis, 1928; *Those Three French Girls*, with others, 1930; *The Man in Possession*, 1931; *Anything Goes*, with others, 1936; *Damsel in Distress*, with Ernest Pagano and S.K. Lauren, 1937; *Her Cardboard Lover*, with others, 1942.

Television Play: *Arthur*, from a play by Molnár.

Verse

The Parrot and Other Poems.   1988.

Other

William Tell Told Again.   1904.
Not George Washington, with Herbert Westbrook.   1907; edited by David A. Jasen, 1980.
The Globe "By the Way" Book: A Literary Quick-Lunch for People Who Have Only Got Five Minutes to Spare, with Herbert Westbrook.   1908.
Louder and Funnier (essays).   1932.
Nothing But Wodehouse, edited by Ogden Nash.   1932.
Wodehouse (selection).   1934.
Bring on the Girls! The Improbable Story of Our Life in Musical Comedy, with Pictures to Prove It, with Guy Bolton.   1953.
Performing Flea: A Self-Portrait in Letters, edited by W.T. Townend.   1953; revised edition (including text of five Berlin radio broadcasts), 1961; as *Author! Author!*, 1962.
America, I Like You.   1956; revised edition, as *Over Seventy: An Autobiography with Digressions*, 1957.
The Uncollected Wodehouse, edited by David A. Jasen.   1976.
Wodehouse on Cricket.   1987.
Yours, Plum: The Letters of Wodehouse, edited by Frances Donaldson.   1990.

Editor, *A Century of Humour.*   1934.
Editor, with Scott Meredith, *The Best of Modern Humor.*   1952.
Editor, with Scott Meredith, *The Week-End Book of Humor.*   1952.
Editor, with Scott Meredith, *A Carnival of Modern Humor.*   1967.

*

Bibliography: *A Bibliography and Reader's Guide to the First Editions of Wodehouse* by David A. Jasen, 1970, revised edition, 1986; by Eileen McIlvaine, in *Wodehouse: A Centenary Celebration*, 1981.

Critical Studies: *Wodehouse at Work: A Study of the Books and Characters*, 1961 (includes bibliography), revised edition, as *Wodehouse at Work to the End*, 1977, *A Wodehouse Companion*, 1981, and *The Penguin Wodehouse Companion*, 1988, all by Richard Usborne; *Wodehouse* by Richard J. Voorhees, 1966; *Wodehouse* by R.B.D. French, 1966; *Homage to Wodehouse* edited by Thelma Cazalet-Keir, 1973; *Wodehouse: A Portrait of a Master* by David A. Jasen, 1974, revised edition, 1981; *The Comic Style of Wodehouse* by Robert A. Hall, Jr., 1974; *Wodehouse: A Critical and Historical Essay* by Owen Dudley Edwards, 1977; *Wodehouse: An Illustrated Biography* by Joseph Connolly, 1979, revised edition, 1987; *In Search of Blandings* by N.T.P. Murphy, 1981; *Wodehouse: A Centenary Celebration* edited by James H. Heineman and Donald R. Bensen, 1981; *Wodehouse: A Literary Biography* by Benny Green, 1981; *Wodehouse at War* by Iain Sproat, 1981; *Thank You, Wodehouse* by J.H.C. Morris, 1981; *Wodehouse: A Biography* by Fras Donaldson, 1982; *Who's Who in Wodehouse* by Daniel Garrison, 1989.

*   *   *

The fictional world of P.G. Wodehouse is peopled by eccentric earls, an amiable but bone-headed aristocracy, and hearty, healthy country folk. Such a world, together with its urban extension, offered Wodehouse, the greatest English humorist of the 20th century, endless material to turn irreverently on its head.

Wodehouse's father, a judge in Hong Kong, was connected to the Earls of Kimberley. Wodehouse was brought up in England and then by a succession of aunts, one of whom provided the prototype of his own fictional Aunt Agatha, "who eats broken bottles and wears barbed wire next to the skin," and left him with a humorous anti-aunt complex. Not surprisingly, he was an introspective, lonely boy, deprived of a normal home life and starved of parental affection. He began writing at the age of seven and never really wanted to do anything else. On leaving school, Wodehouse was employed by the Hong Kong and Shanghai Bank, but hated both the bank and the place. Back in England, he got a job as a columnist with *The Globe* newspaper. His first book, *The Pothunters*, appeared in 1902. *Mike* first introduced the character Psmith, whereupon, in Evelyn Waugh's words, "the light was kindled which has burned with glowing brilliance for half a century."

During his long writing career Wodehouse produced about two hundred books (including various compilations and collections), some 30 stage plays, and, during a few years working in Hollywood, more than a dozen film scripts. Since his death, much of his material has appeared on television. His fiction includes about 150 short stories. It is difficult to settle for an exact number, because some of his novels are really extended short stories or novellas, while others are so episodic—variations on a single theme—as to be really loosely linked short stories.

The early stories, like the novels written before about 1918, deal mainly with school life. These stories first appeared in publications like *The Captain*, a magazine for public schoolboys, at that time by far his most regular market, and in *Chums* and *The Public School Magazine*. They were mostly written in formula for *The Captain*, good yarns full of games, raggings, and study teas. *Mike* has been called "perhaps the best light school story in the English language." Some of the best of these early short stories are in *Tales of St. Austins*, which introduce the quirky schoolmasters Pullingford and Mellish.

The mature stories were written mostly during the 1920's and 1930's, the marketable heyday of the short story, when *The Strand Magazine*, in London, paid Wodehouse as much as five hundred guineas for a single tale. He wrote for *The Saturday Review* and *The American Magazine* in the United States, this last making him the record payment of six thousand dollars for one story. According to Richard Usborne (in *Wodehouse at Work to the End*), 12 short stories could earn Wodehouse £20,000 from magazine fees alone, with, of course, book royalties to follow.

The essence of a Wodehouse short story is an irreverent look at some particular aspect of English life: sex (though the Wodehouse lovers never get past enthusiastically wooing their girls and their mothers), golf, cricket, children, aunts and uncles, politicians, policemen, old age, royalty and even the church. Especially in the short stories he was an excellent deviser and twister of ingenious plots, the Jeeves stories usually having an extra twist in the tail. The critic Owen Dudley Edwards (in *P.G. Wodehouse: A Critical and Historical Essay*) described them as "extremely crafty, never arty—always mechanically good and often very funny in themselves."

Wodehouse's character Ukridge (his only unpleasant narrator), who believed in "giving false names as an ordinary business precaution," defined the whole race of Wodehousian butlers, including Jeeves: "Meeting him in the street and ignoring the foul bowler hat he wore on his walks abroad, you would have put him down as a Bishop in mufti, or at the least, a plenipotentiary at one of the better courts." Butlers, mostly Jeeves (who began life as "Jevons" in a story, "Creatures of Impulse," published in *The Strand* in 1914) appear in some 80 books.

Wodehouse was a master of witty yet accurate metaphor and simile: "Jeeves coughed that soft cough of his, the one that sounds like a sheep clearing its throat on a distant mountainside"; "The Duke's moustache was rising and falling like seaweed on the tide"; "He felt like a man who, chasing rainbows, has had one of them suddenly turn and bite him in the leg." Such felicities abound on almost every page Wodehouse wrote.

Appreciation of Wodehouse since the war has steadily grown. Sir Compton Mackenzie, for instance, praised "the ingenious plot, the marvellous simile, the preposterous characters which came to life and remain alive and the continuously dynamic dialogue." Best of all, perhaps, was Evelyn Waugh, who observed, "for Mr. Wodehouse there has been no fall of man; no 'aboriginal calamity.' His characters have never tasted forbidden fruit. They are still in Eden. The Gardens of Blandings Castle are that original garden from which we are all exiled. The chef Anatole prefers the ambrosia for the immortals of high Olympus. Mr. Wodehouse's idyllic world can never stale."

He is, indeed, one of the 20th century's most original English short story writers, reminding us, in Auberon Waugh's words, "that the best jokes ignore everything in which men of authority try to interest us."

—Maurice Lindsay

See the essay on "Uncle Fred Flits By."

————

WOOLF, (Adeline) Virginia. English. Born in London, 25 January 1882; daughter of the scholar and writer Leslie Stephen; younger sister of the painter Vanessa Bell. Educated privately. Married the writer Leonard Woolf in 1912. Moved to Bloomsbury, London, 1904; associated with her sister and with the economist J.M. Keynes, the art critic Roger Fry, the painter Duncan Grant, the writers E.M. Forster, *q.v.,* and David Garnett, and others, later known as the Bloomsbury Group; reviewer, *Times Literary Supplement,* from 1905, and other periodicals; teacher of adult education classes, Morley College, London, 1905; founder, with Leonard Woolf, Hogarth Press, Richmond, Surrey, later London, 1917–41. Recipient: Femina-Vie Heureuse prize, 1928. *Died (suicide) 28 March 1941.*

PUBLICATIONS

Collections

The Woolf Reader, edited by Mitchell A. Leaska.   1984.
The Complete Shorter Fiction, edited by Susan Dick. 1985.
The Essays, edited by Andrew McNeillie.   1986—.

Short Stories

Two Stories, with Leonard Woolf.   1917.
Kew Gardens (story).   1919.
Monday or Tuesday.   1921.
A Haunted House and Other Short Stories.   1944.
Mrs. Dalloway's Party: A Short Story Sequence, edited by Stella McNichol.   1973.

Novels

The Voyage Out.   1915; revised edition, 1920.
Night and Day.   1919.
Jacob's Room.   1922.
Mrs. Dalloway.   1925.
To the Lighthouse.   1927; draft version, edited by Susan Dick, 1982.
Orlando: A Biography.   1928.
The Waves.   1931; draft versions edited by J.W. Graham, 1976.
Flush: A Biography.   1933.
The Years.   1937.
Between the Acts.   1941.
The Pargiters: The Novel-Essay Portion of The Years, edited by Mitchell A. Leaska.   1977.

Play

Freshwater, edited by Lucio P. Ruotolo.   1976.

Other

Mr. Bennett and Mrs. Brown.   1924.
The Common Reader.   1925; second series, 1932; first series edited by Andrew McNeillie, 1984.
A Room of One's Own.   1929.
Street Haunting.   1930.
On Being Ill.   1930.
Beau Brummell.   1930.
A Letter to a Young Poet.   1932.
Walter Sickert: A Conversation.   1934.
Three Guineas.   1938.
Reviewing.   1939.
Roger Fry: A Biography.   1940.
The Death of the Moth and Other Essays.   1942.
The Moment and Other Essays.   1947.
The Captain's Death Bed and Other Essays.   1950.
A Writer's Diary, Being Extracts from the Diary of Woolf, edited by Leonard Woolf.   1953.
Hours in a Library.   1958.
Granite and Rainbow: Essays.   1958.
Contemporary Writers, edited by Jean Guiguet.   1965.
Nurse Lugton's Golden Thimble (for children).   1966.
Collected Essays, edited by Leonard Woolf.   4 vols., 1966–67.
Stephen versus Gladstone.   1967.
A Cockney's Farming Experiences, edited by Suzanne Henig.   1972.
The London Scene: Five Essays.   1975.

The Letters, edited by Nigel Nicolson and Joanne Traut-
mann. 6 vols., 1975-80; *Congenial Spirits: The Select-
ed Letters,* edited by Joanne Trautmann Banks, 1989.
Moments of Being: Unpublished Autobiographical Writings,
edited by Jeanne Schulkind.   1976.
The Diary, edited by Anne Olivier Bell.   5 vols., 1977–84;
A Moment's Liberty: The Shorter Diary, 1990.
*Books and Portraits: Some Further Selections from the
Literary and Biographical Writings,* edited by Mary
Lyon.   1977.
Women and Writing, edited by Michèle Barrett.   1979.
Reading Notebooks, edited by Brenda R. Silver.   1982.
The Widow and the Parrot (for children).   1988.
A Passionate Apprentice: The Early Journals 1897–1909,
edited by Mitchell A. Leaska.   1990.

Translator, with S.S. Koteliansky, *Stavrogin's Confession,*
by Dostoevskii.   1922.
Translator, with S.S. Koteliansky, *Tolstoi's Love Letters.*
1923.
Translator, with S.S. Koteliansky, *Talks with Tolstoy,* by
A.D. Goldenveizer.   1923.

*

Bibliography: *A Bibliography of Woolf* by B.J. Kirkpatrick,
1957, revised edition, 1967, 1980; *Woolf: An Annotated
Bibliography of Criticism* by Robin Majumdar, 1976.

Critical Studies: *Woolf* by Winifred Holtby, 1932; *Woolf*
by E.M. Forster, 1942; *Woolf* by David Daiches, 1942,
revised edition, 1963; *Woolf: Her Art as a Novelist* by Joan
Bennett, 1945, revised edition, 1964; *Woolf: A Commentary* by Bernard Blackstone, 1949; *Mimesis: The Representation of Reality in Western Literature* by Erich Auerbach,
1953; *Woolf's London,* 1959, and *Woolf,* 1963, both by
Dorothy Brewster; *An Autobiography* by Leonard Woolf,
5 vols., 1960–69; *Woolf's Black Arrows of Sensation: The
Waves* by R.G. Collins, 1962; *The Narrow Bridge of Art:
Woolf's Early Criticism 1905–1925* by E.A. Hungerford,
1965; *Woolf and Her Works* by Jean Guiguet, 1965; *Woolf*
by Carl Woodring, 1966; *Feminism and Art: A Study of
Woolf* by Herbert Marder, 1968; *Critics on Woolf* edited by
Jacqueline E.M. Latham, 1970; *Woolf: To the Lighthouse:
A Casebook,* 1970, and *Critical Essays on Woolf,* 1985,
both edited by Morris Beja; *Woolf: The Inward Voyage* by
Harvena Richter, 1970; *Twentieth-Century Interpretations
of To the Lighthouse* edited by Thomas A. Vogler, 1970;
Woolf: A Collection of Critical Essays edited by Claire
Sprague, 1971; *Woolf: A Biography* by Quentin Bell,   2
vols., 1972; *Recollections of Woolf by Her Contemporaries*
edited by Joan Russell Noble, 1972; *Woolf and the
Androgynous Vision* by Nancy Topping Bazin, 1973; *Woolf:
The Echoes Enslaved* by Allen McLaurin, 1973; *The World
Without a Self: Woolf and the Novel* by James Naremore,
1973; *Woolf* by Manly Johnson, 1973; *Woolf: A Personal
Debt* by Margaret Drabble, 1973; *The Novels of Woolf: Fact
and Vision* by A.V.B. Kelley, 1973; *Woolf: A Critical
Reading* by Avrom Fleishman, 1975; *Woolf: The Critical
Heritage* edited by Robin Majumdar and Allen McLaurin,
1975; *Woolf and Her World,* 1975, and *Thrown to the
Woolfs: Leonard and Virginia Woolf and the Hogarth Press,*
1978, both by John Lehmann; *Woolf: A Collection of
Criticism* edited by Thomas S.W. Lewis, 1975; *Woolf's
Mrs. Dalloway: A Study in Alienation* by Jeremy Hawthorn,
1975; *The Razor Edge of Balance: A Study of Woolf* by Jane

Novak, 1975; *The Reader's Art: Woolf as Literary Critic* by
Mark Goldman, 1976; *The Novels of Woolf* by Hermione
Lee, 1977; *Woolf: Sources of Madness and Art* by Jean O.
Love, 1977; *A Marriage of True Minds: An Intimate
Portrait of Leonard and Virginia Woolf* by George Spater
and Ian Parsons, 1977; *The Seen and the Unseen: Woolf's
To the Lighthouse* by L. Ruddick, 1977; *The Novels of
Woolf: From Beginning to End* by Mitchell A. Leaska,
1978; *Woman of Letters: A Life of Woolf* by Phyllis Rose,
1978; *Woolf* by Susan Rubinow Gorsky, 1978, revised
edition, 1989; *The Unknown Woolf* by Roger Poole, 1978;
Continuing Presences: Woolf's Use of Literary Allusion by
Beverly Ann Schlack, 1979; *Woolf: A Study of Her Novels*
by T.E. Apter, 1979; *Woolf: Revaluation and Continuity: A
Collection of Essays* edited by Ralph Freedman, 1980;
Woolf's First Voyage: A Novel in the Making, 1980, and
*Woolf: The Impact of Childhood Sexual Abuse on Her Life
and Work,* 1989, both by Louise A. DeSalvo; *Woolf's Major
Novels: The Fables of Anon* by Maria DiBattista, 1980;
Woolf's Quarrel with Grieving by Mark Spilka, 1980; *New
Feminist Essays on Woolf,* 1981, *Woolf: A Feminist Slant,*
1983, and *Woolf and Bloomsbury: A Centenary Celebra-
tion,* 1987, all edited by Jane Marcus, and *Woolf and the
Languages of Patriarchy* by Marcus, 1987; *Woolf's The
Years: The Evolution of a Novel* by Grace Radin, 1981; *The
Elusive Self: Psyche and Spirit in Woolf's Novels* by Louise
A. Poresky, 1981; *Between Language and Silence: The
Novels of Woolf* by Howard Harper, 1982; *Woolf and the
Politics of Style* by Pamela J. Transue, 1982; *All That
Summer She Was Mad: Woolf, Female Victim of Male
Medicine* by Stephen Trombley, 1982; *Woolf: Centennial
Papers* edited by Elaine K. Ginsberg and Laura Moss
Gottlieb, 1983; *Comedy and the Woman Writer: Woolf,
Spark, and Feminism* by Judy Little, 1983; *Woolf's Literary
Sources and Allusions: A Guide to the Essays,* 1983, and
Woolf's Rediscovered Essays: Sources and Allusions, 1987,
both by Elizabeth Steele; *Woolf: New Critical Essays* edited
by Patricia Clements and Isobel Grundy, 1983; *Woolf: A
Writer's Life* by Lyndall Gordon, 1984; *The Short Season
Between Two Silences: The Mystical and the Political in the
Novels of Woolf* by Madeline Moore, 1984; *Woolf: A
Centenary Perspective* edited by Eric Warner, 1984; *Woolf
and London: The Sexual Politics of the City* by S.M. Squier,
1985; *The Invisible Presence: Woolf and the Mother-Daugh-
ter Relationship* by Ellen Bayuk Roseman, 1986; *The
Singing of the Real World: The Philosophy of Woolf's
Fiction* by Mark Hussey, 1986; *The Interrupted Moment: A
View of Woolf's Novels* by Lucio P. Ruotolo, 1986; *Woolf
and the Real World* by Alex Zwerdling, 1986; *Woolf: The
Waves* by Eric Warner, 1987; *The Victorian Heritage of
Woolf: The External World in Her Novels* by Janis M. Paul,
1987; *Woolf and the Problem of the Subject: Feminine
Writing in the Major Novels* by Makiko Minow-Pinkney,
1987; *Woolf: The Frames of Art and Life* by C. Ruth Miller,
1988; *To the Lighthouse and Beyond: Transformations in
the Narratives of Woolf* by Virginia R. Hyman, 1988;
Woolf, Dramatic Novelist by Jane Wheare, 1988; *Woolf:
Feminist Destinations* by Rachel Bowlby, 1988; *Woolf: To
the Lighthouse* by Stevie Davies, 1989; *Woolf* by Susan
Dick, 1989; *A Study of the Short Fiction* by Dean R.
Baldwin, 1989; *A Woolf Chronology,* 1989, and *Woolf,*
1990, both by Edward Bishop; *Woolf and the Literature of
the English Renaissance* by Alice Fox, 1990; *Woolf and the
Poetry of Fiction* by Stella McNichol, 1990; *Woolf and the
Fictions of Psychoanalysis* by Elizabeth Abel, 1990; *Woolf
and the Madness of Language* by Daniel Ferrier, 1990; *The
Reading of Silence: Woolf in the English Tradition* by
Patricia Ondek Laurence, 1991.

* * *

Virginia Woolf established her reputation primarily as a novelist and an essayist; she published only one book of short stories during her lifetime, *Monday or Tuesday,* of which a reviewer wrote in the *Daily News,* "all this bereft world of inconsequent sensation is but a habitation for those lonely, dishevelled souls who are driven about by the great wind which blows through Limbo."

According to her husband Leonard Woolf, it was Woolf's habit to sketch out the rough idea of a story and file it away. Later, if an editor asked for a piece of short fiction or "if she felt, as she often did, while writing a novel that she required to rest her mind by working at something else for a time," she would pull out a sketch for a story. Not long before her death, she had decided to put together a collected edition of her shorter work, including most of the stories from *Monday or Tuesday,* others which had appeared over the years in magazines such as *Harper's Bazaar, Harper's Magazine, The Athenaeum,* and *The Forum,* and some which had never been published. The posthumous result was *A Haunted House and Other Short Stories.*

With the exception, perhaps, of stories like "The Legacy," "Lappin and Lapinova," and "The Duchess and the Jeweller," which involve conflicted and complicated affairs of the heart but are fairly traditional stylistically, Woolf's work is generally impressionistic, imagistic, and experimental. Lyrical and melancholy, often quite beautiful, the stories revolve not so much around character or plot as consciousness and identity. According to the critic Phyllis Rose, Woolf's work involves the "radical questioning of what it is important to notice, what character consists in, what structure, if any, life has, and what structure [fiction]."

"Of all things," Woolf writes in "Together and Apart," "nothing is so strange as human intercourse . . . because of its changes, its extraordinary irrationality." In a story like "A Haunted House," which T.S. Eliot admired, not even death can interfere with essential connections; Sasha Latham, on the other hand, believes in "A Summing Up" that the human soul "is by nature unmated, a widow bird." Somewhere between these two poles lies the elusive "truth" of relationships, language, and the mind's "astonishing perceptions."

A number of the stories involve confrontations of the individual with society, generally in the setting of the upper middle class, "idle, chattering, overdressed, without an idea in their heads." On the one hand, Woolf gives us Prickett Ellis in "The Man Who Loved His Kind," a lawyer who runs into a friend from school he hasn't seen in 20 years and reluctantly accepts his invitation to a party. "Pitted against the evil, the corruption, the heartlessness of society," Ellis feels he must justify himself, but ironically this "man of the people" finds human contact and conversation almost impossible. Mabel in "The New Dress" suffers a similar fate for different reasons; rather than putting herself above everyone else, she has had a lifelong sense "of being inferior to other people." The situation in this story, as in all of Woolf's short fiction, appears deceptively simple: Mabel shows up at a party where she is suddenly struck by the sense that her appearance is unacceptable; she has chosen the wrong dress. In the third-person interior monologue so typical of Woolf, Mabel recalls the feeling she had had at the dressmaker's when she was in the mirror, briefly, "the core of herself, the soul of herself," a beautiful woman who pleased her. But here

reflected through the eyes of others, she feels "condemned, despised," for being "a feeble vacillating creature" leading a wretched "kind of twilight existence." Over the course of the evening she comes to believe that "*this* was true, this drawing-room, this self, and the other false." Several of Woolf's stories involve, either centrally or peripherally, "the true man, upon whom the false man was built" ("Together and Apart," "A Summing Up"); perhaps the most extreme example of this interplay "between one's eyes and the truth" is found in "The Lady in the Looking-Glass," where little by little the image of Isabella Tyson is stripped away until "here was the woman herself. . . . And there was nothing."

In one way or another, all of Woolf's stories deal with perception and consciousness. Central to Woolf's vision is the idea expressed in "Solid Objects" that "any object mixes itself so profoundly with the stuff of thought that it loses its actual form and recomposes itself a little differently in an ideal shape which haunts the brain when we least expect it." Her texts are constructed of splashes and patches, shadows, reflections, color, the play of light, a constant flood and flux of images and sensations which both reflect and transform reality.

Ultimately Woolf's work is about "moments of being," the title both of a collection of Woolf's autobiographical writings published after her death and of the story "Moments of Being" (originally called "Slater's Pins Have No Points"), where Fanny Wilmot observes that there is always the danger in life that one will "not possess it, enjoy it, not entirely and altogether." Woolf's reflections are poignantly expressed in "The Searchlight," in which a party of people sit watching air force maneuvers as "rods of light" scan the sky, momentarily illuminating objects over which they pass; the text itself begins to imitate the movement—broken, fragmented, interrupted by ellipses—as if to illustrate Woolf's understanding that although one tries to embrace the "adorable world" ("An Unwritten Novel"), "the light . . . only falls here and there."

—Deborah Kelly Kloepfer

See the essays on *Kew Gardens* and "The Mark on the Wall."

———————

WRIGHT, Richard (Nathaniel). American. Born near Natchez, Mississippi, 4 September 1908; brought up in an orphanage. Educated at local schools through junior high school. Married 1) Rose Dhima Meadman in 1938; 2) Ellen Poplar; two daughters. Worked in a post office in Memphis, Tennessee, at age 15; later moved to New York; worked for Federal Writers Project, 1937, and Federal Negro Theatre Project; member, Communist Party, 1932–44; Harlem editor, *Daily Worker,* New York; lived in Paris from 1947. Recipient: Guggenheim fellowship, 1939; Spingarn medal, 1941. *Died 28 November 1960.*

PUBLICATIONS

Collections

The Wright Reader, edited by Ellen Wright and Michel Fabre.   1978.

Short Stories

Uncle Tom's Children: Four Novellas.   1938; augmented
    edition, 1940.
Eight Men.   1961.
The Man Who Lived Underground (story; bilingual edition), translated by Claude Edmonde Magny, edited by
    Michel Fabre.   1971.

Novels

Native Son.   1940.
The Outsider.   1953.
Savage Holiday.   1954.
The Long Dream.   1958.
Lawd Today.   1963.

Plays

Native Son (The Biography of a Young American), with
    Paul Green, from the novel by Wright (produced 1941).
    1941; revised version, 1980.
Daddy Goodness, from a play by Louis Sapin (produced
    1968).

Screenplay: *Native Son,* 1951.

Other

How Bigger Was Born: The Story of "Native Son."   1940.
The Negro and Parkway Community House.   1941.
*12 Million Black Voices: A Folk History of the Negro in the
    United States.*   1941.
Black Boy: A Record of Childhood and Youth.   1945.
Black Power: A Record of Reactions in a Land of Pathos.
    1954.
Bandoeng: 1.500.000.000 Hommes, translated by Hélène
    Claireau.   1955; as *The Color Curtain: A Report on the
    Bandung Conference,* 1956.
Pagan Spain.   1957.
White Man, Listen!   1957.
Letters to Joe C. Brown, edited by Thomas Knipp.   1968.
American Hunger (autobiography).   1977.

*

Bibliography: *Wright: A Primary Bibliography* by Charles
T. Davis and Michel Fabre, 1982; *A Wright Bibliography:
Fifty Years of Criticism and Commentary, 1933–1983* by
Keneth Kinnamon, 1988.

Critical Studies: *Wright: A Biography* by Constance Webb,
1968; *Wright* by Robert Bone, 1969; *The Art of Wright* by
Edward Margolies, 1969; *The Most Native of Sons: A
Biography of Wright* by John A. Williams, 1970; *Twentieth-
Century Interpretations of Native Son* edited by Houston A.
Baker, Jr., 1972; *The Emergence of Wright: A Study of
Literature and Society,* 1972, and *New Essays on Native
Son,* 1990, both by Keneth Kinnamon; *Wright* by David
Bakish, 1973; *The Unfinished Quest of Wright* by Michel
Fabre, translated by Isabel Barzun, 1973, *The World of
Wright,* 1985, and *Wright: Books and Writers,* 1990, both
by Fabre; *Wright: Impressions and Perspectives* edited by
David Ray and Robert M. Farnsworth, 1973; *Wright's
Hero: The Faces of a Rebel-Victim* by Katherine Fishburn,
1977; *Wright: The Critical Reception* edited by John M.

Reilly, 1978; *Rebels and Victims: The Fiction of Wright and
Bernard Malamud* by Evelyn Gross Avery, 1979; *Wright* by
Robert Felgar, 1980; *Wright: Ordeal of a Native Son* by
Addison Gayle, Jr., 1980; *The Daemonic Genius of Wright*
by Margaret Walker, 1982; *Critical Essays on Wright*
edited by Yoshinobu Hakutani, 1982; *Wright: A Collection
of Critical Essays* edited by Richard Macksey and Frank E.
Moorer, 1984; *Wright's Art of Tragedy* by Joyce Ann Joyce,
1986; *Wright,* 1987, and *Wright's Native Son,* 1988, both
edited by Harold Bloom; *Wright, Daemonic Genius* by
Margaret Walker, 1988; *Voice of a Native Son: The Poetics
of Wright* by Eugene E. Miller, 1990; *Native Son: The
Emergence of a New Black Hero* by Robert Butler, 1991.

*   *   *

Richard Wright's stature as a major American writer rests
primarily on his novels of social protest concerning the
violence, hostility, and oppression experienced by African-
Americans in northern urban environments. The most
famous of these novels is *Native Son,* a novel having
generated so much critical interest as to obscure the fact
that Wright began his career as a short story writer with the
publication of *Uncle Tom's Children* in 1936.

Uncle Tom's Children is a collection of four novellas
depicting the lives of African-Americans in the south. Even
though these stories were written while Wright was interested in Communist ideology, most of the characters in this
collection lash out against their oppressors from a desire for
freedom and personal dignity rather than as advocates of
any political ideology or collective philosophy. The result is
a collection of stories free from lapses into political rhetoric
one finds in the latter novels. In *Uncle Tom's Children,* and
virtually all of Wright's fiction, one encounters a world
where violence and racial hatred render life chaotic and
meaningless. As a result, his African-American characters
feel outside of and excluded from the American dream of
progress, dignity, and opportunity, and they are forced to
come to terms with life on their own. Because of the effects
of racism, including lack of education, Wright's characters
are unable to express themselves in conventional ways, and
often resort to violent acts against whites and other
African-Americans. Since Wright deals largely with uneducated and inarticulate characters, he focuses on what they
do rather than what they think or feel. Wright is concerned
with their reactions to specific situations. Violence is
frequently the central action of the story and he portrays it
as deliberate and senseless when it is perpetuated by white
characters, and a last resort, a reflex reaction, or revenge
motivated when perpetuated by black characters. The
obvious exception is Wright's novel *Savage Holiday* which
contains only white characters.

In "Long Black Song" a white salesman seduces the wife
of a black farmer named Silas. When Silas returns home he
discovers her infidelity and attempts to whip her. She flees
from him but sneaks back the next day for her infant child.
She watches as two white men return to their farm, where
one of them is whipped by Silas and the other is killed. A
lynch mob surrounds the house and burns Silas alive inside
because he refuses to be taken by them. Silas achieves a
sense of dignity and control over his destiny only after
choosing to control the manner of his own death. Silas's
acts of violence are motivated by revenge and his refusal to
surrender announces his refusal to be exploited any longer
by the values of racist, white culture in the South.

In the most famous story in this collection "Big Boy Leaves Home," Big Boy witnesses the murder of three of his friends and while he is hiding, waiting to make his escape, he fantasizes about killing white people in the same manner he had earlier killed a snake—by whipping them, and kicking their heads against the sand. Revenge or flight are not the only responses of black characters to racial oppression. In "Bright and Morning Star" the two central characters are murdered, but they die believing that the cause for which they have been sacrificed will some day be realized. In "Fire and Cloud," the progression of the central character Reverend Taylor moves from a simple, unassuming, God-fearing minister to one of active social participation. Central here is the theme of the relationship between the white power structure and black leadership, a theme Wright explores in greater detail in his novel *The Long Dream.*

Wright's second collection of short stories, *Eight Men*, published two months after his death in 1961, is a collection of fiction previously unpublished in book form. One of these stories, "The Man Who Went to Chicago," is an excerpt from an unpublished chapter of his autobiographical novel, *Black Boy*. Two stories deal with the oppression of African-Americans in the South and were written in the 1930's. "The Man Who Saw the Flood" was originally published in 1938 in *New Masses* under the title "Silt." The other piece, "The Man Who Was almost a Man" was first published in *Harpers Bazaar* in 1939 as "Almo's a Man." His stories written during the 1940's and collected in *Eight Men* deal with the African-American as an outsider, whom Wright places in an urban environment. These stories are "The Man Who Went to Chicago," "The Man Who Lived Underground," and "The Man Who Killed a Shadow." In his stories of the 1950's Wright focuses on black nationalism and portrays blacks as virile and proud in the face of whites, displaying pride in their African-American identity. These stories are "Man of all Work," "Man, God Ain't Like That," and "Big Black Good Man."

This collection reveals Wright's range of experimentation and movement away from actions with clearly identifiable motives to a world of arbitrary, meaningless, almost unavoidable violence. These portrayals have led many critics to describe this perspective as Wright's "existentialism."

In "The Man Who Killed a Shadow" a black janitor "inadvertently" kills a white librarian. A blond, blue-eyed, white woman attempts to seduce a black janitor by demanding he look at her legs. When he refuses she screams, causing him to panic. He brutally beats her in an attempt to silence her. Finally he stabs her in the throat, hides the body, and flees. The story is a bit contrived in that Wright goes to great lengths to portray the protagonist as a victim of a racist society, but he appears to be as much a victim of his own stupidity. While trying to drag the woman's body away, her wedding ring falls off her hand and he places it in his pocket. When he discovers it in his pocket while at home, he places it in his drawer. He also hides his bloody clothes and the knife he used to kill her in the corner of his closet. While at home he places his gun in his pocket, "for he was nervously depressed." Consequently, this characters fails in comparison to Bigger Thomas in *Native Son*, who is far more frightening and more believable.

Wright's short stories display a wide range of plot, setting, and characterization, as well as revealing in embryonic form characters and subject matter appearing in many of his novels. In addition to affinities with other African-American writers, he has much in common with Nelson Algren and James T. Farrell. Wright's career transformed the limitations and expectations imposed on black writers while still managing to expose the violence, hatred, and frustration experienced by African-Americans to a larger audience of white readers than any of his predecessors.

—Jeffrey D. Parker

See the essays on "Big Boy Leaves Home" and *The Man Who Lived Underground.*

Y

YEHOSHUA, A(braham) B. Israeli. Born in Jerusalem, 9 December 1936. Educated at Jerusalem Hebrew Gymnasium; Hebrew University, Jerusalem, B.A. 1961; Teachers College, graduated 1962. Served in the Israeli Army, 1954–57. Married Rivka Kirsninski in 1960; one daughter and two sons. Teacher, Hebrew University High School, Jerusalem, 1961–63; director, Israeli School, Paris, 1963–64; secretary-general, World Union of Jewish Students, Paris, 1963–67; dean of students, 1967–72, and since 1972, professor of comparative literature, Haifa University; visiting fellow, St. Cross College, Oxford, 1975–76; guest professor, Harvard University, Cambridge, Massachusetts, 1977, University of Chicago, 1988, and Stanford University, California, 1990. Member of board of art, Haifa Municipal Theatre; adviser to drama editorial board, Israeli Television Network; member of editorial board, *Keshet* literary magazine, 1967–74; editorial consultant, *Siman Kria, Tel-Aviv Review,* and *Mifgash.* Recipient: Akum prize, 1961; Municipality of Ramat-Gan prize, 1968; University of Iowa fellowship, 1969; Prime Minister's prize, 1972; Brenner prize, 1983; Alterman prize, 1986; Bialik prize, 1989; National Jewish Book award (U.S.), 1990; Israeli Booker prize, 1992. Honorary doctorate: Hebrew Union College, Cincinnati, Ohio, 1990. Lives in Haifa.

PUBLICATIONS

Short Stories

Mot hazaken [Death of the Old Man] (novella). 1962.
Mul haye'arot [Facing the Forests] (novellas). 1968; as *Three Days and a Child,* 1970.
Tishah sipurim [Nine Stories]. 1970.
Bithilat kayits 1970 (novella). 1972; as *Early in the Summer of 1970,* 1977.
The Continuing Silence of a Poet: Collected Stories. 1988.

Novels

Sheney sipurim. 1970–71.
Ad choref 1974: mivchar. 1975.
Hame'ahev. 1977; as *The Lover,* 1978.
Gerushim me'ucharim. 1982; as *A Late Divorce,* 1984.
Molcho. 1987; as *Five Seasons,* 1989.
Mar Maniy. 1990; as *Mr. Mani,* 1992.

Plays

Laylah beMai (produced 1969). As *A Night in May,* in *Two Plays,* 1974.
Tipolim acharonim (produced 1973). As *Last Treatment,* in *Two Plays,* 1974.
Two Plays: A Night in May and Last Treatment. 1974.
Chafetsim [Possessions] (produced 1986).
Tinokot laylah [Children of the Night] (produced 1992).

Screenplays: *Sheloshah yamim veyeled* [Three Days and a Child], 1967; *Hame'ahev* [The Lover], 1986; *The Continuing Silence of a Poet* (Germany), 1987.

Other

Bizechut hanormaliyut. 1980; as *Between Right and Right,* 1981.
Israel, with Frederic Brenner. 1988.
Hakir vehahar: metsi'uto hasifrutit shel hasofer beYisrael [The Wall and the Mountain: The Literary Reality of the Writer in Israel]. 1989.

*

Critical Studies: "An Appraisal of the Stories of Yehoshua" by Baruch Kurzweil, in *Literature East and West* 14(1), 1970; "Yehoshua as Playwright" by Anat Feinberg, in *Modern Hebrew Literature* 1, 1975; "A Touch of Madness in the Plays of Yehoshua" by Eli Pfefferkorn, in *World Literature Today* 51, 1977; "Distress and Constriction" by Haim Shoham, in *Ariel* 41, 1976; "Multiple Focus and Mystery" by Leon I. Yudkin, in *Modern Hebrew Literature* 3, 1977; "A Great Madness Hides Behind All This" by Gershon Shaked, in *Modern Hebrew Literature* 8(1–2), 1982–83; "Casualities of Patriachal Double Standards: Old Women in Yehoshua's Fiction," in *South Central Bulletin* 43(4), 1984, and "The Sleepy Wife: A Feminist Consideration of Yehoshua's Fiction," in *Hebrew Annual Review* 8, 1984, both by Esther Fuchs; "Possessions as a Death Wish" by Gideon Ofrat, in *Modern Hebrew Literature* 12(1–2), 1986; "Yehoshua: Dismantler" by Chaim Chertok, in his *We Are All Close: Conversations with Israeli Writers,* 1989; "Yehoshua" in *The Arab in Israeli Literature,* 1989, and "Yehoshua and the Sephardic Experience," in *World Literature Today* 65(1), 1991, both by Gila Ramras-Rauch; "Yehoshua's 'Sound and Fury': *A Late Divorce* and Its Faulknerian Model" by Nehama Aschkenasy, in *Modern Language Studies* 21(2), 1991.

* * *

A.B. Yehoshua, one of Israel's most beloved writers, also provokes controversy and even anger in his country for some of the themes he poses in his writing. One of Yehoshua's fundamental beliefs is that Israelis must break free from their past in order to live successfully and freely in the present and future, an idea that is dramatized repeatedly in his novels and stories. Yehoshua is vehemently opposed to the idea of Jews living in the Diaspora (countries other than Israel); he argues that such exile is and has always been voluntary and self-imposed. In his work, such self-exiled Jews are shown to be selfish and cowardly—takers rather than givers.

"Death of the Old Man" (1962) exemplifies a recurring theme in Yehoshua's work: conflict between the generations and their total inability to understand or communicate with each other. In this novella, an old man is eventually buried alive by the other tenants in his apartment building. The surreal elements reflect the influence of Kafka; the bizzare action reflects both the need to shed the past and the danger of doing so without vision for the future. As in other of Yehoshua's works, we also witness the eruption of violent and destructive human urges.

From 1963 to 1968 Yehoshua lived in Paris, and this temporary exile brought about changes in his artistic style. The distance gave him an ability to look at and represent Israel with more realism, and he began to modify the surreal images in his writing. In 1968 he published a collection of novellas called *Mul haye'arot* (Facing the Forests), containing "Three Days and a Child" (the title story of the collection in English). "Three Days and a Child" offers some small sense of hope for the future. The main character is a typical Yehoshua anti-hero: frustrated in love, disappointed in life and relationships. The story begins as his ex-lover calls and asks him to take care of her child for three days while she and her husband cram for university exams. For the next three days he does his best to make the child sick— exhausting him with outings and trips, and allowing a friend to let a snake loose in the house. When his parents finally retrieve him, the child is feverish and bleeding. But there is hope at the end. He realizes with shock how much the father loves the child, and he returns with some sense of resignation to his partner.

The novella "A Long Hot Day, His Despair, His Wife and His Daughter" deals with the disintegrating family. It deals with the same characters and similar situations as Yehoshua's novel *Hame'ahev (The Lover)*. The father, a character who appears repeatedly in Yehoshua's fiction, is a middle-aged man, losing control and power to his wife, who grows stronger and more dominant as she begins to take classes at the university. The father had worked in Africa, returning because of a mysterious sickness, at first thought to be cancer. He is waiting for a new position with his old company. His adolescent daughter becomes the focus of his sexuality; he takes naps on her bed and vacillates between encouraging her would-be boyfriend and hiding the young man's letters in the tool box of his car. At the end of the story, his duplicity is discovered, and he lies in the driveway waiting for his wife to come home—"this time she will crush him indeed." Another hopeless and despairing middle-aged man appears in the story "Missile Base 612": he hasn't spoken with his wife for months, and his child is lost in the silence between them.

Yehoshua also treats the themes of war and loss so resonant in Israeli life. In *Bithilat kayits 1970 (Early in the Summer of 1970)* an elderly Bible teacher is told that his son has been killed in a border skirmish with Jordan. As he travels to identify the body, all sense of linear time is lost; even though it is not his son's body after all, the trauma of the event has shaken him so deeply that he keeps retelling it to make sense of it. This story also bears an allegorical resemblance to the barely averted sacrifice of Isaac in Genesis.

In an interview with Joshua Cohen, Yehoshua made the distinction between "world writers" and "subject writers," suggesting that he is a subject writer—one who focuses on developing issues rather than creating a fictional world.

—Carla N. Spivack

See the essays on "The Continuing Silence of a Poet" and "Facing the Forests."

YU DAFU. Chinese. Born in Fuyang, Zhejiang Province, 7 December 1896. Studied at Jiaxing Secondary School and an American missionary school, Tokyo, 1913-16; studied political economics at Imperial University, Tokyo, 1916-22. Married 1) Sun Quan in 1920, two sons and one daughter; 2) Wang Yingxia (divorced 1940), three sons; 3) He Liyu in 1943, one son and one daughter. Writer, editor, and translator, Shanghai, from 1923; lecturer, Peking University, 1923-24; professor of literature, Wuchang, 1925, Sun Yat-sen University, 1926; German instructor, Shanghai Law Faculty, 1927; editor, *Torrent* and *Mass Literature,* and at Shanghai University of Fine Arts, 1928-30; co-editor with Lu Xun, q.v., *PenLiv,* 1928-29; professor, University of Anhui, 1930; lived in Hangzhou, 1933-35; editor and government worker, Fujian, 1936-38; local government council worker, Wuhan, 1938; editor and journalist, Singapore Daily newpaper, 1938-42; moved to Sumatra under assumed name Zhao Lian, forced to serve as interpreter for Japanese military police, 1942; wineshop owner, 1942-45. Founding editor, *Creation Quarterly,* 1921-24, *Creation Weekly,* 1923-24, *Creation Monthly,* 1926. Co-founder, Creation Society, 1921. Founding member, League of Left Wing Writers, from 1930. *Died 17 September 1945.*

PUBLICATIONS

Collections

Wenji [Collected Works].   12 vols., 1982-85.

Short Stories

Chenlun [Sinking].   1921; as *Chenlunji qita* [Sinking and Other Stories], 1947.
Wei bing [Stomach Trouble].   1921.
Nan qian [Moving South].   1921.
Mangmang ye [Deep Night].   1922.
Feng ling [Wind Bell].   1922.
Xue yu lei [Blood and Tears].   1922.
Li san zhi jian [Before Parting].   1923.
Qiu lin [Autumn Willows].   1923.
Cai shiji [Coloured Cliff].   1923.
Niaoluo xing [Marital Episodes].   1923.
Huanxiangji [Returning Home].   1923.
Qing yan [Bluish Smoke].   1923.
Qiu he [Autumn River].   1923.
Luo ri [Sunset].   1923.
Haishang tongxin [Correspondence Written at Sea].   1923.
Yi feng xin [A Letter].   1923.

Chunfeng chencui de wanshang [Intoxicating Spring Night]. 1924; as "Nights of Spring Fever," in *Nights of Spring Fever and Other Writings,* 1984.
Zhong tu [In the Middle of the Road].   1924.
Beiguo de weiyin [A Weak Voice from the North of the Country].   1924.
Shiyi yue chu san [November the Third].   1924.
Song Fangwu de xing [Seeing Fangwu Off].   1925.
Huaixiang bingzhe [Homesick].   1926.
Yan ying [The Shadow of Smoke].   1926.
Han xiao [Cold Night].   1926.
Shen lou [Mirage].   1926.
Lingyuzhe [A Superfluous Man].   1927.
Bo dian [A Humble Sacrifice].   1927.
Xiaochun tianqi [Gossamer Weather].   1927.
Haigu milianzhe de duyu [Monologue of a Collector of Decaying Bones].   1927.
Guoqu [The Past].   1927.
Qingleng de wuhou [Fresh Afternoon].   1927.
Weixue de zaochen [Snowy Morning].   1927.
Jijinji [Chicken Ribs] (novella).   1927.
Mi yang [The Lost Sheep] (novella).   1928.
Deng'e maicang zhi ye [The Night of the Moth's Funeral]. 1928.
Zai han feng li [In the Cold Wind] (collection).   1929.
Mafeng de duci [Wasp's Sting].   1929.
Zhibi de tiaoyao [Dance of the Banknotes].   1930.
Yangmei shaojiu [Strawberry Brandy].   1930.
Shisan ye [Thirteen Nights].   1930.
Mayinghua kai de shihou [Blossom Time of the Maying Flower].   1932.
Dong Zi Guan [name].   1932.
Chi kuihua [Late-Blooming Cassia].   1932.
Bilianghu de qiuye [Autumn Night in Bilianghu].   1933.
Chanyuji [Repentance] (collection).   1933.
Qi mu [At the Decline of Years].   1933
Chu ben [A Start].   1935.
Nights of Spring Fever and Other Writings (selection). 1984.

Novels

Chun chao [Spring Tide] (unfinished).   1923.
Gushi [Legend].   1928.
Ta shi yi ge ruo nuzi [She Is a Weak Woman].   1932; as *Raoliao Ta* [Forgive Her!], 1933.
Jihen chuchu [Footprints Here and There].   1934.

Verse

Shi ci chao [Collected Poetry], edited by Lu Tan-lin. 1962.

Other

Niaoluoji [Wisteria and Dodder] (prose).   1923.
Gei Mo Ruo de jiuxin [An Old Letter to Mo Ruo].   1924.
Xiaoshuo lun [On the Novel] (literary criticism).   1926.
Yi ge ren zai lushang [A Lonely Man on a Journey].   1926.
Nanxing zaji [Various Notes of a Journey to the South]. 1926.
Qi yuan [Source of Prayers].   1927.
Riji jiu zhong [Nine Diaries].   1927.
Gei yi wei wenxue qingnian de gongkai zhuang [An Open Letter to a Young Writer].   1927.
Quanji [Complete Works].   7 vols., 1927-33; 1st vol. as *Hanhuiji* [Cold Ashes] (stories), 1927.
Er shiren [Two Poets].   1928.

Bizhouji [Battered Brooms] (prose).   1928.
Qilingji [Fugitive Fragments] (prose).   1930.
Xian shu [Books for Idle Hours] (prose).   1936.
Xuanji [Selected Works].   1942.
Wenxue nan tan [Random Talk on Literature]. n.d.
Riji [Collection of Diaries].   1947; numerous other editions.
Suoyi duan pianji [Collected Essays].   1965.

Editor, *Xiandai mingren qingshu* [Love Letters of Contemporary Celebrities].   1936.

Translator, *Yu Dafu suoyi duan pianji* [Collected Short Stories Translated by Yu Dafu].   1935.

*

Critical Studies: in *Three Sketches of Chinese Literature* by Jaroslav Prusek, 1969; *Yü Ta-fu: Specific Traits of His Literary Creation* by Anna Doležalová, 1971; in *The Romantic Generation of Modern Chinese Writers* by Leo Ou-fan Lee, 1973; "Yu Dafu and the Transition to Modern Literature" by Michael Egan, in *Modern Chinese Literature in the May Fourth Era,* edited by Merle Goldman, 1977; "Yu Dafu's Superfluous Hero" by Mau-sang Ng, in *The Russian Hero in Modern Chinese Fiction,* 1988.

*   *   *

The earliest and most successful of Yu Dafu's short fiction is associated with the Creation Society. The society was formed under the leadership of scholar-writer Guo Moro (1892-), who engaged the interest of other young post-May 4th Movement (1919) literati, among them Yu Dafu, then studying in Japan. The society's founding publication, in 1921, featured Yu Dafu's collection of stories under the title *Chenlun* (Sinking) (including "Sinking," "Moving South," and "Silvergray Death"), which created an immediate sensation in China. In 1928, disaffected from the Creationists' increasingly leftist views, Yu Dafu quit the society. He wrote for other groups, helping establish the League of Left Wing Writers (1930), but eventually he turned from political themes to more subjective content.

Subjecting Yu Dafu's work to extraordinarily intense scrutiny, critics focus upon its apparent autobiographical nature. They invariably note Yu Dafu's own preface to "Sinking," which claims that all literature is autobiographical, but gives various degrees of credence to the statement. C.T. Hsia sees the story as "unabashedly autobiographical," noting the close identity between the author's background and that of his protagonist, and complains that Yu Dafu fails to transform his personal experience into literary medium. Jaroslav Prusek agrees that Yu Dafu writes almost exclusively about his own experience and feelings, but discerns that while Yu Dafu draws upon diaries, notes, and letters for his fiction, he does "apply *belletristic* processing of this personal experience as a basic artistic principle." Yu Dafu's writing is not, Prusek claims, after all a record of personal experiences but fiction for the "anonymous reader." Yu Dafu, he observes, writes in the third person and "actual incidents . . . are practically submerged beneath a truly fantastic whirl of emotions and imaginings." But even in the late 1980's, other authoritative critics still assert that the autobiographical element in Yu

Dafu's fiction is paramount; Mau-sang Ng explains that the author makes himself the protagonist, "attempting to go beyond himself to create visions of himself through his writings."

A more thoughtful view discounts Yu Dafu's own assessment and warns against what William Wimsatt called the "intentional fallacy," that is, "deriving the standard of criticism from the psychological *causes* of a text." From this standpoint, criticisms of Yu's work as autobiographical emerge as misinterpretation.

The view specifically refutes charges that Yu Dafu's output is what Hsia calls "maudlin sentimentality" and "emotional dissipation," or that "Sinking" is a "mawkish tale of adolescent frustration and guilt." On the contrary, as a pivotal writer in the transition to modern Chinese fiction, Yu Dafu introduces, according to Merle Goldman, "an extremely important and subtle innovation, the use of irony." Goldman observes that the "objective narrative technique [in 'Sinking'] serves instead as an ironic counterpoint that undercuts the hero's sentimental view of himself, emphasizing the basic absurdity of his self-image." The theory is convincing. In each situation, the reader is shown how the protagonist invariably misconstrues his predicament, which is invariably of his own making. Patently, Goldman concludes, such writing is not "the predominance of a literal imagination fascinated by the narrow world of his private sensations and feelings," but rather "an objective, and ironic presentation of a *character* with a mistaken and sentimental view of *himself.*"

As a Chinese student in Japan, the protagonist in "Sinking" feels that his Japanese classmates are racially prejudiced against him. However, his own sense of intellectual superiority, or artistic integrity, also pits him against his fellow Chinese. The reader sees him isolated through his own misperceptions, and not as the pitiable, lonely figure of his self-evaluation. However much Yu Dafu may have shared the protagonist's experience, he presents the material objectively for the reader's evaluation, not as a sentimental recollection.

In a long tradition of cheerful pornography, Yu Dafu's treatment of sex was sensational. His modernity lay in his honest exposure, through the protagonist, of his own sexual fantasies. As such, sex is elevated in his fiction above the merely prurient to moral and psychological abstraction. In "Sinking," for example, the hero finds himself impotent in his relations with women, and resorts instead to the guilty voyeurism and masturbation that lead to his implied suicide.

Patriotism was another motif that found ready response among the youth of Yu Dafu's day. Critical appraisal might consider the theme only superficially grafted onto Yu Dafu's more deeply felt interests, but his contemporaneous audience was convinced by the merging of the protagonist's frustration at both the national humiliation and his individual impotence. The hero's final invocation ("O China, my China, you are the cause of my death!") might ring hollow in modern Western ears after the entirely self-directed introspection of the narrative, but to his Chinese audience, the call to arms was clear.

The sources of Yu Dafu's inspiration have equally been scrutinized. The author was well-versed in traditional Chinese literature and in European, Russian, and Japanese works. It is no affectation that his hero, at the beginning of "Sinking," is "seen strolling with a pocket edition of Wordsworth's poems." Chinese writers traditionally expressed their disdain for the mundane world and corrupt officialdom; the European and Japanese so-called "decadent" writers provide extensive models for the outcast hero. In particular, the protagonist's self-pity in "Sinking" is most commonly identified with Goethe's *The Sorrows of Werther* (1774). Yu Dafu's approach in other works, like "The Superfluous Man," is also judged to have been significantly influenced by the 19th-century Russians, for example, Dostoevskii's "Underground Man" and Turgenev's "The Diary of a Superfluous Man."

Yu Dafu's early work, especially "Sinking," generally considered to be his best, continues to generate critical controversy. Its autobiographical foundations and exploration of intimate sexuality arouse outrage, exasperation, or admiration, or all, in the reader. The overlay of patriotism and national shame may seem artificial in today's view, but such concerns were overriding in Yu Dafu's time, and were appreciated by his youthful audience. His Chinese and foreign literary scholarship is also admired, and absorbing interest is exhibited in the antecedents that shaped his attitudes and styles.

—John Marney

See the essays on "Nights of Spring Fever" and "Sinking."

Z

ZAMIATIN, Evgenii (Ivanovich). Russian. Born in Lebedian', 20 January 1884. Educated at Progymnasium, Lebedian', 1892–96; gymnasium in Voronezh 1896–1902; studied naval engineering at St. Petersburg Polytechnic Institute, 1902–08; arrested and exiled for student political activity, 1906 and 1911. Naval engineer, 1908–11, and lecturer from 1911, St. Petersburg Polytechnic Institute; supervised the construction of ice-breakers in England, 1916–17; associated with the Serapion Brothers literary group, from 1921; editor, *Dom Iskusstva* (House of the Arts), 1921, *Sovremennyi zapad* (Contemporary West), 1922–24, and *Russkii Sovremennik* (Russian Contemporary), 1924; editor, with Kornei Chukovskii, English section of World Literature series; victimized from the late 1920's, and removed from the leadership of Soviet Writers Union; left Soviet Union, 1931; settled in Paris, 1932. *Died 10 March 1937.*

PUBLICATIONS

Collections

Povesti i rasskazy [Tales and Stories].   1963.
Sochineniia [Works].   2 vols., 1970–72.

Short Stories

Uezdnoe [A Provincial Tale].   1916.
Ostrovitiane.   1922; title story translated as *The Islanders,* 1978; as *The Islanders, and The Fisher of Men,* 1984.
Bolshim detiam skazki [Fairy Tales for Grown-Up Children].   1922.
Nechstivye rasskazy [Impious Tales].   1927.
The Dragon: Fifteen Stories.   1967; as *The Dragon and Other Stories,* 1975.

Novels

Na kulichkakh [At the World's End].   1923.
My.   1952; translated as *We,* 1924.
Zhitie Blokhi ot dnia chudesnogo ee rozhdeniia . . . [The Life of a Flea from the Day of Its Miraculous Birth . . .].   1929.
Navodnenie [The Flood].   1930.
Bich Bozhi [The Scourge of God] (unfinished).   1939; as *A Godforsaken Hole,* 1988.

Plays

Ogni sviatogo Doninika [The Fires of St. Dominic].   1922.
Blokha [The Flea] (produced 1925).   1926.
Obshchestvo pochotnykh zvonarei [The Society of Honorable Bellringers] (produced 1925).   1926.
Sensatsiia, from the play *The Front Page* by Ben Hecht and Charles MacArthur (produced 1930).

Atilla, and *Afrikanskii gost'* [The African Guest], in *Novy zhurnal 24* and *73, 1950, 1963.*

Screenplays: *Severnaia liubov'* [Northern Love], 1928; *Les Bas-Fonds (The Lower Depths),* 1936.

Other

Robert Mayer.   1922.
Gerbert Uells [H.G. Wells].   1922.
Sobranie sochinenii [Collected Works].   4 vols., 1929.
Litsa [Faces].   1955; as *A Soviet Heretic: Essays,* edited by Mirra Ginsburg, 1969.

*

Critical Studies: *Zamyatin: A Russian Heretic* by David J. Richards, 1962; *The Life and Works of Evgeny Zamyatin* by Alex M. Shane, 1968 (includes bibliography); *Zamyatin: An Interpretative Study* by Christopher Collins, 1973; "Literature and Revolution in *We*" by Robert Russell, in *Slavonic and East European Review,* 1973; *Brave New World,* 1984, and *We: An Essay on Anti-Utopia* by Edward J. Brown, 1976; "The Imagination and the 'I' in Zamjatin's *We*" by Gary Rosenshield, in *Slavic and East European Journal,* 1979; *Three Russian Writers and the Irrational: Zamyatin, Pil'nyak, and Bulgakov* by T.R.N. Edwards, 1982; "Adam and the Ark of Ice: Man and Revolution in Zamyatin's The Cave" by Andrew Barratt, in *Irish Slavonic Studies 4,* 1983; *Zamyatin's "We": A Collection of Critical Essays* edited by Gary Kern, 1988.

* * *

Although Evgenii Zamiatin is far better known in the West for his novel *We,* his short fiction is arguably the greater achievement. Of the approximately 50 stories and sketches, fewer than half have appeared in English, along with just a couple of the 20 "fairy tales" that are clearly aimed at an adult audience. Still, the translated works include most of his finest prose, and they give a clear idea of the qualities that have established him as a major figure in 20th-century Russian literature.

To some degree the stylistic distinctiveness of his writing comes through even in translation. The characters in "A Provincial Tale," his first work to attract wide attention, speak in a peasant dialect that conveys the rhythms and syntactic peculiarities of the living language; these people are a world removed from the gentry society described in much 19th-century Russian literature. The narrative voice is equally distinctive: at times it too employs the turns of speech and incomplete sentences that typify the characters, but it is equally notable for presenting the story in a fragmentary, elliptical fashion. The action jumps from one figure to another, the significance of individual scenes is often left unexplained, and as a result a coherent picture emerges only gradually. Zamiatin was a master of the intricate style that came to be called "ornamental prose," which in his case is especially notable for its dense imagery and grotesque descriptions.

Zamiatin deals with primitive forces that overwhelm any decency or civilizing tendencies. Many of his provincial characters seem motivated only by their animal-like instincts and by a selfish need to satisfy their own desires, at whatever cost to those around them. Thus, in "A Provincial Tale" Chebotarikha's obesity is matched only by her insatiable sexual drive. Baryba, a loutish young man whom she has used for that purpose, eventually accepts a bribe to give false testimony against a friend, who is then hanged. "A Godforsaken Hole" deals with soldiers at a remote garrison, where the military figures have yielded to the apathy and depravity of their surroundings. The small handful of worthy people within this milieu are eventually caught up in the wanton actions of the other military people and their lives are destroyed as a result. Daria ("In Old Russia") chooses which of her suitors to marry by drawing a slip of paper; when she is courted by another, a poisonous mushroom ends up in her husband's supper, and she is free to remarry.

Although Zamiatin's stories are filled with brutality and horror, most are not unrelievedly gloomy. Often, the most vicious deeds are juxtaposed with scenes of incongruous humor, particularly in some of the works that deal with the manner in which the Bolshevik revolution takes hold in provincial Russia. "The Protectress of Sinners" has as forboding a beginning as any of Zamiatin's works. Three peasants have been assigned to take funds from a convent to aid the others in their village; the "decree" that the villagers have passed contains a garbled example of revolutionary terminology. At night they violently overpower the guard, and the stage is set for further mayhem inside. But instead the good-natured Mother Superior, who has always treated the nuns as though they were her own children, cheerfully treats the men to cake and wine, solicitously asks about the injured hand of one man, and totally disarms the three, who run off and slink back without any money. In "X," a story that weaves together Zamiatin's favorite themes of revolution, religion, and love, the tone remains relatively light throughout. The main figure is a former deacon who has switched his loyalties from the church to the new civil order; he comes upon the beautiful Marfa when she has gone for a swim, and he switches; now he is no longer a Marxist but a Marfist. A much grimmer vision appears in "Comrade Churygin Has the Floor," where the comic elements (Churygin mangles ideological phraseology; one character mistakes a statue of Mars for that of Marx) are mingled with horrific images: the narrator comes to the home of a neighbor, just back from the front, and finds him propped up against a trunk like a sack of oats, both his legs having been shot off in the war. The story ends with a bloody confrontation between the villagers and an estate owner, motivated largely by a grotesque misunderstanding of the events in the outside world. In Zamiatin's tales revolutionary ideals cannot change or even penetrate through the deeply ingrained barbarity that rules these people's lives.

Several of the postrevolutionary works that have an urban setting are constructed around a single dominant image. "Mamai" is based on a darkly ironic comparison between the hero and the historical figure who shares his name, the leader of the Tatar forces at the 1380 battle of Kulikovo field, where the Russians attained their first victory against the Golden Horde. This Mamai, a meek book collector who

has managed to save up money in order to add to his library, finds that his cache has been eaten by a mouse; he rises up in fury and runs the mouse through with a sword, just as mercilessly as his namesake. "The Cave," the most widely anthologized of Zamiatin's stories in English, takes place in Petersburg after the revolution, where the cold and hunger are depicted in terms of a return to the ice age, with mammoths and glaciers seeming to reappear and the apartments compared to caves. The couple in the story are still surrounded by the accoutrements of culture from prerevolutionary times; now, however, their lives are ruled by a new god, the cast-iron stove whose appetite they can no longer satisfy. The husband steals some firewood to enable his sick, frail wife to celebrate her name-day, and at the end he allows her to use the one vial of poison they have stored away to end her misery.

Zamiatin was opposed to all forces that crushed the individual, be it the revolution (which he initially supported), the savagery of provincial life, or religion. In this fairy tale "The Church of God" he tells of a man who resolves to build a church, but who steals and kills in order to get the money. At the dedication ceremony, the church turns out to be pervaded by a smell of death that drives everyone away. As a naval engineer, Zamiatin spent part of World War I in England, and he came away with a dislike of righteous church people who attempt to impose their morality on others; two stories with an English setting, "The Islanders" and "Lovets chelovekov" (The Fisher of Men), depict the passions that eventually disrupt surface appearances of respectability, much as in his novel *My (We)*, where the demand for order confronts the powerful force of human emotions.

The fatal effects of repression come out most clearly in "The Flood," where the usual social and political themes give way to an exploration of the human psyche, which is ultimately Zamiatin's chief concern throughout his stories. Sofia's inability to have children is symbolic of an inner closedness, and she breaks out of this state through a kind of fertility rite: the murder of a young girl whom she and her husband had taken in and who had become the husband's lover. The rich layers of imagery, the startling cold-bloodedness of the murder, and the deep psychological insights combine to make this story one of Zamiatin's finest.

—Barry P. Scherr

See the essay on "A Story about the Most Important Thing."

ZHANG AILING. Chinese. Born in Shanghai, 30 September 1920 (some sources say 1921). Lived in Beijing and Tianjin as a child; returned to Shanghai in 1929. Educated at the University of Hong Kong, 1939–42: returned to Shanghai in 1942 because of war. Worked for *The Times* and *Twentieth Century,* Shanghai; moved to Hong Kong in 1952; worked for *The World Today*; moved to the United States in 1955; associated with Chinese Study Centre, University of California, Berkeley, from 1955; visiting writer, Cambridge University, 1967, and Miami University, Oxford, Ohio; associate scholar, Radcliffe Institute for Independent Study, Cambridge, Massachusetts.

PUBLICATIONS

Short Stories

Jin suoji [The Golden Cangue].   1943.
Chuanqi xiaoshuoji [Selected Romances].   1944.
Xiaoshuoji [Selected Short Stories].   1954.
Qingcheng zhi lian: duanpian xiaoshuo xuan [Love in a Fallen City: Short Stories].   1985.

Novels and Novellas

Chenxiangxie [Bits of Incense Ashes].   1943.
Moli xiangpian [Jasmine Tea].   1943.
Xinjing [Heart Sutra].   1943.
Qingcheng zhi lian [Love in a Fallen City].   1943.
Fengsuo [Sealed Off].   1943.
Liuli pian [Glazed Tiles].   1943.
Deng [Waiting].   1943.
Hongyingxi [Happiness].   1943.
Hua diao [Withered Flowers].   1943.
A Xiao bei qiu [A Xiao's Sad Autumn].   1943.
Lianhuan tao [Chain of Rings].   1944.
Nianqing de shihou [Time of Youth].   1944.
Hong meigui bai meigui.   1944; as *Red Rose and White Rose*, 1978.
Yinbao yan song hualouhui.   1944.
Liu qing [Mercy].   1945.
Chuang shiji [Genesis].   1945.
Chuanqi [Romances].   1947.
Yang ko. As *The Rice Sprout Song,*   1955.
Jidi zhi lian. As *Naked Earth,*   1954.
Wu si yi shi [Remnants from May 4th Movement].   1958.
Yuan nu [The Embittered Woman].   1966.
The Rouge of the North.   1967.
Wang ranji [Disappointment].   1968.
Liu yan [Gossip].   1969.
Zhang kan [Zhang's View].   1976.
Xiao tuanyuan [Reunion].   1976.
Se jie [Threshhold of Eroticism].   1979.
Haishanghua liezhuan [Biography of Prostitutes].   1981.
Zhang Ailing juan [Zhang Ailing].   1982.
Lian zhi bei ge.   1983.
Yin Bao Yan kan Hualouhui.   1983.
Sheng ming de yue zhang [Music of Life], with Lin Haiyin.   1983.
Chuanqi [Romance].   1986.
Si yu [Whispers].   1990.

Other

Sanwenji [Selected Prose].   1945.
Shi ba chun [Spring of 18].   1948.

Translator, *Fool in the Reeds,* by Chen Chi-ying.   1959.

*

Critical Studies: in *A History of Modern Chinese Fiction, 1917-1957,* 1961, and *Modern Chinese Stories and Novellas: 1919-1949,* 1981, both by C.T. Hsia; "Eileen Chang's Bridges to China" by Jeannine Bohlmeyer, in *Tamkang Review* 5(1), 1972; "Themes and Techniques in Eileen Chang's Stories" by Stephen Cheng, in *Tamkang Review* 8(2), 1977; "Fiction and Autobiography: Spatial Form in *The Gold Cangue* and *The Woman Warrior*" by Lucien Miller and Hui-chuan Chang, in *Tamkang Review* 15(1–4), 1984–85; "Moon, Madness and Mutilation in Eileen Chang's English Translation of *The Golden Canque*" by Shirley J. Paolini and Chen-Shen Yen, in *Tamkang Review* 19(1–4), 1988–89.

*   *   *

Zhang Ailing (Eileen Chang), an eminent fiction writer and translator, has been recognized by the critic C.T. Hsia in *Modern Chinese Stories and Novellas: 1919-1949* as the most talented Chinese writer of the 1940's. Since she is proficient in Chinese and English, Zhang Ailing has translated some of her works. Among these is the brilliant novelette, *Jinsuo ji* ("The Golden Cangue"), modelled upon the *Dream of the Red Chamber,* an 18th-century Chinese novel. "The Golden Cangue" has spawned two further versions: *Yuan nu* (The Embittered Woman) and *The Rouge of the North* (composed in English). Zhang Ailing's "Nightmare in the Red Chamber" offers insights into the classical source of "The Golden Cangue."

Departing from classical inspiration, Zhang Ailing tragic novel, *The Rice Sprout Song (Yang ko),* which she wrote in English), is set in China during the land reform in the 1950's. On a similar note, *Jidi zhi lian (Naked Earth)* chronicles Communist rule in China from the land reform period through the Korean War. Broader in scope than *The Rice Sprout Song,* the novel deals with adversity, friendship, and love.

Besides her novels, Zhang Ailing has mastered the short story form. She has been compared to Eudora Welty, Katherine Mansfield, and other contemporary women writers. Well-drawn short stories include "Little Finger Up," which deals with the issue of concubinage and the distress of the legitimate wife and her powerless position in marriage, and "Stale Mates," where divorce and remarriage cause problems. "Stale Mates" relates a tale of ill-feeling and marital pride, but in a lighter vein than the author's usual mode. "Shame, Amah" tells about a maid in Shanghai, whose employer is a foreigner and man-about-town.

Some universal themes in Zhang Ailing's fiction include survival and suffering, the elusiveness of romantic love, the importance of family, and the clarification of individual identity with respect to the group. Duty and convention rankle against self-fulfillment or self-indulgence. In her works, Zhang Ailing presents generational clashes between mothers and daughters-in-law and conflicts between spouses and brothers and sisters. She shows the hierarchical structure of Chinese families, whether they be mandarins or farmers. She depicts the world of servants, concubines, and slaves. Often her stories use Shanghai or its environs as their locale.

In *The Rice Sprout Song,* for example, Zhang Ailing creates the predicament of village folk in the countryside outside of Shanghai. In simple, direct language she relates the tale of Chinese villagers who suffer from poverty and hunger after Mao's revolution. Zhang Ailing shows the hypocrisy of the government that officially proclaims its achievements in the countryside while the people starve.

Zhang Ailing portrays an authentic picture of Chinese villagers—their familial and social interactions. She demonstrates the interrelationships between generations, mothers-in-law and new brides, spouses, and parents and children. With directness, Zhang Ailing powerfully exposes hypocrisy and lies. She uncovers the reality under Party rhetoric: her truth is the hunger and desperate condition of the people in spite of the government's efforts to gloss over its problems.

While *The Rice Sprout Song* focuses upon the poor, "The Golden Cangue" illustrates the decadence of the mandarins. Located in Shanghai, the novelette reveals the situation of Qi Qiao, who marries into a well-born family despite her lowly origins. The "golden cangue" symbolizes the destructiveness of the protagonist who, while metaphorically bearing the frame used to hold prisoners in old China, is both imprisoned and imprisoning.

Developed from the story of "The Golden Cangue," *The Rouge of the North* portrays an in-depth study of the heroine, Yindi (Qi Qiao). The third-person narration focuses upon the consciousness of Yindi, who marries into the rich Yao family and documents her struggles as a daughter-in-law vis-a-vis the Old Mistress and her constant battle for acceptance. After a brief liaison with her brother-in-law, she attempts suicide, but she survives. No such suicide occurs in the first story. Like the heroine of "The Golden Cangue," Yindi falls victim to her opium habit, and she manipulates the life of her only son after her invalid spouse dies, and she achieves independence. Contrary to the original story, there is no daughter in *The Rouge of the North*, but the sufferings inflicted by Yindi upon her son's wife are detailed in both works.

Similarities occur in both stories when the heroines fail to find fulfillment in love or marriage, and they dominate their sons and daughters-in-law. *The Rouge of the North* is more developed with details of the characters' habits and backgrounds than "The Golden Cangue," and it offers information on family social structure, styles of living, and conversation. While focusing upon the theme of love lost, *The Rouge of the North* lacks the symbolism and brevity of "The Golden Cangue," which paints a more devastating picture of its protagonist's destructiveness.

Zhang Ailing's body of work succeeds in revealing family relationships, especially the plight of her female protagonists as they attempt to work out their conflicts. Her heroines are strong, memorable characters. Whether mandarins or villagers, her characters are drawn in sharp, deft strokes, and she captures conversation with a practiced ear in a realistic and descriptive style.

—Shirley J. Paolini

See the essay on "The Golden Cangue."

ZOSHCHENKO, Mikhail (Mikhailovich). Russian. Born in Poltava, the Ukraine, 10 August 1895. Studied at the Faculty of Law, Petersburg University, 1913. Married Vera Vladimirovna Kerbits in 1921. Served in army, 1915–17: ensign to second captain (wounded and decorated). Held odd jobs: shoemaker, carpenter, office clerk, and government employee for railways, post office, telephone company, border patrol, Petrograd, 1917–20; joined Red Army, 1918-1919; translator and critic, Petrograd, from 1919; evacuated to Kazakhstan, 1941; editor, journal *The Star,* from 1946. Recipient: Banner of Red Labor medal, 1939. Member, Serapion Brothers, from 1921. Member, All-Russian Union of Writers (expelled 1946; readmitted 1953). *Died 22 July 1958.*

PUBLICATIONS

Collections

Sobranie sochinenii [Collected Works].   6 vols., 1929–31.
Sobranie sochinenii v trekh tomakh.   1930–31; edited by Daniil Aleksandrovich Granin and Iu Tomashevskii, 1986–87.
Izbrannye proizvedeniia v 2-kh t [Selected Works in 2 Vols]. 1968.
Izbrannye v dvukh tomakh.   1978.

Short Stories

Rasskazy Nazara Ilycha gospodina Sinebriukhova [Stories Told by Nazar Ilycha sir/gospodina Sinebriukhov]. 1922.
Sobachii niukh [The Dog's Scent].   1926.
Obez'ianii iazyk [Monkey Language].   1926.
Tsarskīe sapogi [The Tsar's Boots].   1927.
Uvazhaemye grazhdane [Esteemed Citizens].   1927.
Nad kem smeetes'.   1928.
Nerveze mentshn.   1929.
Semeinyi kuporos [Family Vitriol].   1929.
Pis'ma k pisateliu [Letters to a Writer].   1929.
Michel Siniagin (novella).   1930.
Izbrannye rasskazy i povesti [Selected Works].   1931; 2 vols., 1978.
Vozvraschonnaia molodost' (novella).   1933; as *Youth Restored,* 1984.
Golubaia kniga [A Skyblue Book].   1935.
Russia Laughs (selection).   1935.
Kerenskii.   1937.
Rasskazy.   1938.
Rasskazy o Lenine [Stories about Lenin] (for children). 1939.
The Woman Who Could Not Read and Other Tales. 1940.
The Wonderful Dog and Other Tales.   1942.
Povesti i rasskazy.   1952.
Rasskazy, fel'etony, povesti.   1958.
Rasskazy i povesti.   1959.
Scenes from the Bathhouse and Other Stories of Communist Russia.   1961.
Rasskazy, fel'etony, komedi.   1962.
Nervous People and Other Satires, edited by Hugh McLean. 1963.
Ispoved' [The Confession].   1965.
Liudi [People], edited by Hector Blair.   1967.
Rasskazy dvatsatykh godov: Stories of the 1920s (in Russian), edited by A.B. Murphy, 1969.
Pered voskhodom solntsa. Porest' (sketches).   1972; as *Before Sunrise,* 1974.
A Man Is Not a Flea (selections).   1989.
Twelve Stories (in Russian), edited by Lesli LaRocco and Slava Paperno.   1990.

Plays

Parusinovyi portfel' [The Canvas Briefcase].   1944.

Screenplay: *Soldatskoe schast'e* [Soldier's Luck],   1943.

Other

Rasskazy, povesti, fel'etony, teatr, kritika.   1937.
Taras Shevchenko, with others.   1939.

*

Critical Studies: "The Tragedy of a Soviet Satirist" by Rebecca A. Domar, in *Through the Glass of Soviet Literature,* edited by Ernest J. Simmons, 1953; "Zoshchenko in Retrospect" by Vera Von Wiren, in *Russian Review,* October 1962; "Zoshchenko and the Problems of *Skaz*" by Irwin R. Titunik, in *California Slavic Studies* 6, 1971; *Zoshchenko: A Literary Life* by A.B. Murphy, 1981.

* * *

Mikhail Zoshchenko's satiric short stories were so popular during the early days of Soviet rule (1920's-1930's) that the absurdities of daily life under the new regime were often characterized as "straight out of Zoshchenko." His unique talent enabled him to work within a genre disrespected at that time (the very short story, vignette, anecdote), and turn it into high art form. He accomplished this through his use of language, narrative technique, and elusive, subtly ironic tone. Zoshchenko's satiric sketches are descendants of both Anton Chekhov's humorous and poignant short stories and Nikolai Gogol's absurdist tales.

Although Zoshchenko himself was descended from the gentry, his first-person narrator is always a man of the people—uneducated, bumbling, but stridently confident of his own worth and opinions. He reveals his ignorance through his views and his language, which is full of incorrectly used words, Soviet bureaucratese, neologisms, and colloquialisms. Brilliant and idiosyncratic, his prose is almost as difficult to translate as poetry. Zoshchenko is regarded as one of Russian literature's finest practitioners of *skaz*, a literary technique that offers the illusion of oral speech and involves a form of narrative that differs markedly from the accepted literary norm. The resulting stylistic distance and dissonance between author and narrator, not to mention the reader, often serve to cast doubt on the narrator's judgment.

From the beginning, Zoshchenko published his short works in mass market, cheap editions, taking as his subject matter the challenges of day-to-day existence in the Soviet Union: securing housing, using a public bath, buying moonshine liquor, visiting the doctor, sharing a communal apartment, learning how to use new-fangled equipment, attending the theatre. The language and subject matter were such a far cry from the serious literature of 19th-century Russia that they were seen as totally in keeping with the new revolutionary spirit of the regime, and the reading public embraced the writer with gusto.

Among his most famous works, "The Bathhouse" (1925) begins with the narrator supposing that public baths in America are excellent, and he describes them in ways that make them sound just like Russian bathhouses, only cleaner, more orderly, with better service. He is quick to add that one can get washed in Russian bathhouses, too, although he asks, "Where does a naked man put a claim check?" Once admitted to the bathing area in the bathhouse, the narrator discovers that all of the buckets are taken and when he tries to pry one loose from a fellow who has gathered three for himself, the owner of the buckets threatens to him him right between the eyes with the tub. The narrator replies, "This isn't tsarist Russia . . . to go around hitting people with tubs." Later he steals a tub from a drowsy old man, but he finally gives up when he can't find a place to sit down and is surrounded by people doing their laundry in the bathing area. Of the two claim checks

he was issued (one for his clothing and one for his outerwear), one has been washed away and the attendant refuses to give him his coat in exchange for the string that remains. When he finally describes his coat (torn pockets, all buttons missing but the topmost one), the attendant grudgingly hands it over. Outside, he realizes he has forgotten his soap, but cannot be readmitted without undressing again. He gives up. All of this activity is related in language that is highly colloquial and unliterary. To prove his political correctness, the narrator says that while bashing people with tubs might have been acceptable in prerevolutionary Russia, it is impermissible now under the Soviets. He asks, What kind of public bath is this? And he answers himself, "The usual kind." Readers easily identify with the unsanitary conditions, poor management, shabby clothing, and shabbier behavior among the bath customers, all described in colorful language that captures the essence of oral speech.

In "The Crisis" (1925) the narrator begins his tale with a paean to the building campaign in progress at the time and looks forward to a time when the housing crisis will be solved and "we'll sleep in one room, receive guests in another, do something else in the third." His search for an apartment in Moscow takes so long that he loses his bundle of worldly possessions and grows a beard. Finally, a landlord agrees to set him up in an empty bathroom, telling him that he can fill himself a whole tubful of water and dive in it all day long if he wants. Noting that he's not a fish and would prefer to live on dry land, the narrator nevertheless agrees to the arrangement and moves in immediately. Soon he marries and his wife joins him, claiming that "lots of nice people live in bathrooms." When their first child is born a year later, they give him a bath every day. The only trouble is that when the other 32 tenants of the communal apartment want to use the bathroom at the end of each day, the narrator and his family are forced to move out into the hall. Eventually, his mother-in-law arrives and settles down behind the hot-water tank. The news that his wife's brother may spend his Christmas vacation with them spurs the narrator to leave town in disgust and promise to send money to his family from afar. Russia's ubiquitous housing shortage is carried to almost believable satiric extremes.

Zoshchenko also wrote longer, more literary, novella-like stories that parodied contemporary practitioners of 19th-century poetics by showing just how absurd such genres and language were for describing life under the new regime. Later, he also began to collect and combine his very short stories into book-like works. *Vozvraschonnaia molodost'* (Youth Restored), *Golubaia kniga* (A Skyblue Book), and *Pered voskhodom solntsa* (Before Sunrise) form a trilogy, each one an attempt to fashion connecting and overarching structures around existing stories in such a way as to make the end result greater than the sum of its parts. A lifelong depressive, Zoshchenko gradually moved away from humor and satire in his works, as he tried to cure his depression by creating positive works and a positive self. His literary experiments with short forms came to a bitter end after Andrei Zhdanov, Stalin's cultural commissar, targeted him for a vilification campaign in 1946, and he produced little of note from then until his death in 1958.

—Linda H. Scatton

See the essay on "The Lady Aristocrat."

WORKS

A

A&P
by John Updike, 1962

Reduced to a plot summary, John Updike's "A&P" is unpromising: a grocery store manager admonishes some girls for shopping in their bathing suits, and a young cashier quits his job because he has been attracted to one of them and wants to make an impression. Updike, however, has constructed a highly entertaining moral tale in "A&P," guaranteed to amuse but in the end to instruct with bittersweet wisdom that grows from the magic in the telling.

The girls are merely summer visitors who will leave at the end of the season, just as they leave at the end of the story, while Sammy, Updike's teenage narrator, must stay on. But this is only one of the distinctions between work and play, innocence and experience, public and private codes of morality, that enhance "A&P." Updike achieves this through Sammy's slangy speaking voice. His casual vocabulary and eye for highly selective details give the story both its humor and its truth. Moreover, Sammy's easy transitions from present tense to past tense and back again allow for an off-the-cuff monologue to keep its seeming innocence intact until the conclusion, while at the same time being faithful to his point of view. As its narrator, Sammy knows the story's end before he begins to tell it. Inevitably that must influence his narration to reflect what he knows; he never loses his cheeky voice, but subtly it has been colored throughout by what has already happened.

Written over 30 years ago and included in Updike's *Pigeon Feathers and Other Stories* (1962), "A&P" reflects a more decorous time through the social mores it details, but readers—especially those of Sammy's age—are likely to find it astonishingly contemporary. Even long after the so-called sexual revolution, Sammy is easily recognizable and, withal, sympathetic to anyone who ever fell in love at first sight and learned to see more clearly afterward. Updike's timeless fable insures that through its careful language, as any number of seemingly inconsequential details demonstrate. When Sammy first sees the girls, he is standing with his hand on a box of crackers and cannot remember whether or not he had rung them up. They might have been Ritz or Saltines or even unidentified, but they are "HiHo crackers": accidentally or by design an invitation, a greeting. Similarly, as Sammy watches the girls parade up one aisle and down the next, Updike arranges appropriate backdrops: the girls stroll by the meat counter, which provides the butcher an excuse to be "patting his mouth and looking after them sizing up their joints" before they disappear from sight momentarily "behind a pyramid of Diet Delight peaches." Updike might have placed them at some other counter or built that pyramid of some other canned goods, but the story is richer because he did not.

Sammy sees "these three girls" in the first paragraph of the story; in its last paragraph they have become "my girls." In between, as he follows them on their journey in search of a jar of herring snacks, fiction's artifice seems unerringly natural. Sammy reflects exactly what the grocery store manager will eventually pronounce: "You know, it's one thing to have a girl in a bathing suit down on the beach, where what with the glare nobody can look at each other much anyway," but in the A&P, the lights are fluorescent, and bare feet look naked on a rubber-tile floor. Sammy first registers the chubby girl with "a sweet broad soft-looking can," wearing a two-piece green suit, then the tallest one, who is "the kind of girl other girls think is very 'striking' and 'attractive' but never quite makes it, as they very well know, which is why they like her so much." But they are merely attendants to "the queen," later "Queenie," who, Sammy says, "made my stomach rub against the inside of my apron." Her suit is "a kind of dirty-pink—beige maybe" and of a nubbly material, with its shoulder straps down. Although Sammy does not consciously realize it—surely he would say so if he did—she must look quite nude from the distance. Later the effect is even more staggering for Sammy when the girl comes to his register and "lifts a folded dollar bill out the hollow at the center of her nubbled pink top," or as Sammy describes it, stashed "between the two smoothest scoops of vanilla I had ever known were there."

Although Sammy focuses almost exclusively on the girls, Updike weaves into his narrative a succession of casual observations that open the intentions of the story to embrace an entire range of social variations. When Sammy first hears Queenie's voice, "so flat and dumb yet kind of tony, too," he has a momentary fantasy about a party her family will give, the men in bow ties and the women in sandals, all drinking martinis, while his own family would serve lemonade or, "if it's a real racy affair Schlitz." His distance from the girls exacerbates his distance from the older generation in other instances as well, for in a broader sense he cares not only about the girls but about the rest of a younger generation's punishments. In a throwaway line, he complains that "about twenty-seven old freeloaders [are] tearing up Central Street because the sewer broke again," while the story verifies through seemingly impertinent details that he takes some implicit pride in his day's labor at the grocery store. Even so, he resents the "plastic toys done up in cellophane that fall apart when a kid looks at them anyway," and mothers "screaming with her children about some candy they didn't get." Adults are the enemy: Lengel, the "pretty dreary" manager who "teaches Sunday school and the rest"; "a witch of about fifty with rouge on her cheekbones and no eyebrows," who bawls out Sammy when he gets sidetracked by the girls and rings up her HiHos twice; the "sheep, pushing their carts" and the "houseslaves in pincurlers." Customers and manager alike have power over the younger generation in various ways, even though Sammy's smart mouth is no more innocent than the actions of the girls who are clearly aware of the effect they are making. "We *are* decent," the leader of the three retaliates when Lengel tells her that their bathing suits are against A&P policy. "That's policy for you," Sammy says to himself. "Policy is what kingpins want. What the others want is juvenile delinquency." Sammy's bravado in quitting is vainglorious but only partly romantically so: the girls have disappeared by the time he gets to the parking lot, and when he registers that, he adds, "of course."

On first reading or last, the words on the pages of "A&P" do not change, but Sammy changes. He comes to learn "how hard the world was going to be . . . hereafter." So, perhaps, does the reader who looks closely at Updike's canny tale.

—Bruce Kellner

ADAM'S BRIDE
by Elizabeth Jolley, 1983

When "Adam's Bride" was first published as "The Bench" in 1980, Elizabeth Jolley was beginning to attract attention amongst Australian readers and critics outside her adopted state of Western Australia. For 20 years, her stories had found outlets mainly in regional periodicals, and her two collections of stories had been published in Western Australia. But 1980 marked the publication of her first novel, *Palomino* and of this story in *Meanjin*, both in Melbourne. "Adam's Bride" was collected in *Woman in a Lampshade* in 1983.

Like that first novel, "Adam's Bride" is an unusual treatment of such themes as relationships and the fate of marginal figures in our society, and also is concerned with the acquisition of land and the role of creativity in people's lives. Its mixing of the realistic and bizarre, humorous and tragic, signalled an approach to writing that would become characteristic of Jolley's later work.

The story is set in an unspecified town, probably in the countryside east of Perth where a number of her stories are located. The focus of the town is the courthouse, a kind of alternative theatre for the locals, conventional residents who enjoy the exposure of others' crimes. Jolley clearly intends us to sample one such exposure; but, as she has explained in an interview, she does like to "suspend things a bit . . . have a little sense of drama." So, the reader is first introduced to the magistrate and Robinson, a young lawyer. As the "Bench," the magistrate represents the solidity of the law, although he appears anything but solid; he is bitter at marriage, suffering from haemorrhoids and later from guilt at abandoning his pet bantam rooster. An unlikely combination of afflictions, one might conclude, but not atypical in an Elizabeth Jolley tale. There is even a hint of homosexuality about the magistrate: "he looked at Young Robinson with tenderness," and he also relies on him for succour.

Evidently, relationships, and marriage in particular, is a theme, emphasized by recurring references to doves cooing in the courthouse roof. An epigraph from Wordsworth's "Resolution and Independence" ("Over its own sweet voice the stock doves brood") alerts the reader to the harmony in the natural world so clearly absent in the human. The magistrate can think only in cynical terms of the doves, believing that they peck each other in a cage as people do in marriage.

With the major theme in place, the narrative returns to the courtroom and a sitting interrupted by the sudden arraignment of a woman, Evie May Adams, accused of murder. Equally melodramatic is the appearance of her husband in her defence. The lack of plausibility here—no legal formalities or swearing in of Adams—is easily set aside as he launches into the story of their marriage. What emerges is for the most part unexceptional: Adams, a drifter, dreaming of owning land (a recurring theme in Jolley's stories), marries Evie, a village girl with few brains but a five acre plot as her dowry. The dreams turn sour when the land is found to be barren. He finds that summers that scorch the earth are followed by frosty winters, and only weeds will thrive. Frustration gives way to despair and despair turns to cruelty against Evie and their idiot daughter. A dreary milieu matches the marriage, with Adams referring to the house as a "cage," an echo from the magistrate's earlier comment on the doves.

Sections of narrative presenting this evidence are balanced by those recreating the drab Adams household, the whole carefully constructed to support Jolley's commitment "to write of those who fail to meet expected social achievement." Adams and Evie are the kind of marginal figures that fascinate her because they "often form a vehicle for the expression of my picture of life". That this "picture" can develop in unexpected ways is evident when she introduces the possibility of Adams's despair being relieved by creativity. He buys a pencil and writing pad, and a rumour spreads that he is writing a book. But this is another impossible dream: Adams can do no more than indulge in a fantasy of being a writer, and the tension mounts to the discovery of his impotency. Violence erupts again. Evie runs away, steals a truck and, perhaps accidentally, kills the store keeper's wife and her own child.

The magistrate, devastated by the spectacle of human misery before him, yet persuaded by the eloquence of the testimony, acquits the woman. But he seems suddenly overwhelmed by the impossibility of any human relationship, even with Robinson, and rushes outside straight into a passing car. The original title of the story reminds the reader that the magistrate was initially Jolley's main subject, and his despair points to a bleak conclusion.

But there are other possibilities. The story's opening sentence, "All small towns in the country have some sort of blessing," alludes to the possibility of religious overtones, something confirmed by the presence of the doves and the ironic Garden of Eden connotations in the names of the principal characters. Certainly, here is confirmation that human relationships have been vulnerable since the beginning of time. However, the reference to "bride" in the title is more than just irony. The reader can see Adams's wife as being like Eve, created by her husband. In the dock she never speaks; she is a character totally presented by him, if not in writing, then in oral narrative. And his creation of this character, whom he claims to love despite his cruelty, and description of their life together results in a kind of victory—for them if not for the magistrate.

This carefully constructed story is totally engaging because it illustrates Jolley's determination in her writing: "to concentrate and to refine—to reject non-essentials and all that the reader can supply for himself." Such a commitment to the writing craft has certainly contributed to a growing reputation for her novels, but her achievements in the short fiction form are also worthy of serious attention.

—F.C. Molloy

AGHWEE THE SKY MONSTER (Sora no kaibutsu Aguii)
by Ōe Kenzaburō, 1972

Ōe Kenzaburō, arguably the most important contemporary Japanese writer, is known in his home country as a prolific and exceptionally imaginative creator of novels, essays, and short stories. His fiction runs the gamut from his autobiographical 1964 novel *Kojinteki na taiken* (*A Personal Matter*), the story of a young man's panicky reaction to the birth of his brain–damaged first son, to the angry 1979 fantasy *Dojidai gemu*, in which Ōe posits what is essentially an alternative history to modern Japan, a history seen from the perspective of the margins. His short story *Sora no kaibutsu Aguii* ("Aghwee the Sky Monster") combines both the central autobiographical motif of *A Personal Matter*, that of the father and brain–damaged child, with the surreal play on perspectives exemplified in *Dojidai gemu* to produce one of his best and most unique works, a narrative that is both grotesquely funny and unsentimentally poignant.

The plot of "Aghwee" is, by Ōe's standards, relatively simple. An unnamed young student, (the narrator), is hired to look after D, an eccentric composer who believes that he is being haunted by a huge phantom baby, whom he calls Aghwee. The student soon learns that the composer himself has just lost his own child, a baby born with a brain tumour who was allowed to die in the hospital, and he deduces that it guilt towards his lost child that causes D's hallucinations. The student's job consists in following D around Tokyo, often witnessing the composer's one-sided exchanges with Aghwee when the baby apparently descends from the sky. One day, however, the composer, seemingly deep in discussion with the phantom child, steps in front of a truck and is killed. The narrator then decides that Aghwee was simply a pretence for the composer to prepare his own suicide. He confronts the dying man, shouting, "I was about to believe in Aghwee!"

Although Japanese critics tend to see "Aghwee" as a form of alternative autobiography, the fantasy correlative to the more strictly realistic *A Personal Matter*, in which the protagonist decides to fight for his baby's life, the story can actually be interpreted on many levels. As the narrator's last accusation suggests, "Aghwee" is a story revolving around problems of perception, belief, and guilt. Vision, both of the real and the unreal, is a fundamental key to the story.

Thus, the young student theorizes that the composer is trying to show his dead child the world he missed by bringing Aghwee on his explorations around Tokyo. At the same time, the composer shows the student something as well, a fantasy world where "lost" things, (people, animals, and experiences) still exist unperceived in the sky. Although the student himself has often been lost in his own fantasy world of obsessive movie viewing, (he immediately conflates Aghwee with the giant rabbit in the Jimmy Stewart film *Harvey*, for example), it takes him until the end of the story to really understand the composer's message. This is shown in "Aghwee"'s coda, when the narrator loses his eye in an accident. As he says in the story's last lines, "When I was wounded . . . and sacrificed the sight in one eye . . . I had been endowed if only for an instant with the power to perceive a creature that had descended from the heights of my sky."

This tension between different modes of perception also contains an implicit social criticism as well. Those who do not "see," are usually characterized as members of the establishment, such as D's businessman father who only worries about guarding his family from any scandal caused by his "lunatic" son, or D's former wife, a "tomato faced" newspaper magnate's daughter who sees her ex-husband's actions as simply "escapist." Ranged against these establishment characters are the marginal figures of D, who, as an eccentric and a composer, is doubly an outsider, and the student narrator who eventually comes almost to believe in Aghwee.

As for Aghwee himself, he is another "marginal," in his status of both victim and phantom. However, as Michiko Wilson points out, Aghwee is not content to remain a passive victim. In fact, he performs a trickster function, "haunting" his guilt-obsessed father and thereby shocking his straitlaced grandfather. This theme of revenge by the marginals is another important aspect of Ōe's work, coming to perhaps its most complete fruition in his long fantastic novel *Pinchiranna chōso* (*The Pinch-Runner Memorandum*), in which a father and brain-damaged son head an army of grotesque marginals, including the living dead, in a march against the Tokyo establishment.

The fantasy in "Agwhee" is more contained but no less effective. Indeed, "Agwhee" is also impressive as an almost textbook exposition of Todorov's structuralist theory of the fantastic, in which the fantastic is characterized by a hesitation between a natural explanation or a supernatural one. Ōe brilliantly maintains this tension between the two alternatives, not letting either reader or narrator know for certain if "Agwhee" is really the composer's hallucination (the natural explanation) or if at some other level the phantom might actually exist (the supernatural explanation). Ultimately, however, the narrative goes beyond the formal pleasures of the fantastic to suggest a moral dimension as well; often it is those who are slightly outside the real world, due to mental or physical abnormalities, who see another, richer, world around them. At its best, as in "Agwhee", Ōe's work allows the reader to see that world as well.

—Susan J. Napier

ALICKY'S WATCH
by Fred Urquhart, 1950

Towards the end of the 19th century there flourished in Scotland a development in fiction which its opponents were to classify as *The Kailyard*, meaning the "cabbage patch." Kail or kale in Scotland becomes curly greens in England. The implication was that the writers' vision went no further than the kitchen garden. Thomas Knowles described the school: "In its 'classic' form, the Kailyard is characterised by sentimental and nostalgic treatment of parochial Scottish themes, often centred on the church." Some writers specialised in idealised, tear-jerking death scenes and sentimental funerals. The more skillful Kailyard writers—Barrie was one—spread their interests wider, but a refusal to allow readers to face the facts was characteristic. The distortion of rural life gave rise to the fierce reaction in fiction of George Douglas Brown and Lewis Grassic Gibbon.

It might be thought that such subject matter as a funeral would not attract Fred Urquhart, yet the entire tale of "Alicky's Watch" is taken up with the preparations, the journey to and from the funeral, and the festivity thereafter. Indeed add one word to the title of his story, *Little*, and a potential reader ignorant of the author might well have placed it in the 19th century kailyard. It is, of course, the treatment of the subject that matters: the difference is between a travesty of a reality and what appears to be a transcript of reality: the conventions and rituals at a funeral of working people are faithfully recorded, and each character is individual within the context of the situation. The final imaginative touch is the perspective on grief determined by Alicky's concern for his grandfather's watch. A cursory reading will reveal the tale's perfect simplicity, and attract by its humour and pathos, but the ironies that rise out of the discrepancy between the attitudes and feelings the solemn occasion expects of the participants and their actual attitudes and feelings bring the whole affair close to the theatre of the absurd, close to but not into, for the genuineness of boyhood at the end claims the attention.

Far removed in content from the *Collected Stories*, Urquhart considered the story worthy to be one of the 25 selected. He also selected it for inclusion in *Scottish Short Stories* (1957). In his preface he shows himself keenly aware of the Kailyard School, as when he refers to Ruthven Todd's *The Big Wheel* as "a welcome antidote to the sickly, sentimental stories of the Kail Yard school." Nevertheless none of the stories in the book are as immediately sharp as "Alicky's Watch"

The first word of the first sentence displays the gap between what Alicky is to himself and to his friends and what he is presumed to be for the solemn occasion: "Alexander's watch stopped on the morning of his mother's funeral." The grandeur is sustained for the announcement of his inheritance, his grandfather's watch, given him on his seventh birthday. He was nine when his mother died, and now the death of the watch bulked much larger in his mind than it should, not that he was alone in the problem of sustaining the correct atmosphere: "And there was the genteel bickerings between his two grandmothers, each of them determined to uphold the dignity of death in the house, but each of them equally determined to have her own way in the arrangements for the funeral." A feature of the tale is the apportioning of nice distinctions of sensitiveness to propriety, "genteel bickerings," and of the guffaws of rude men on the return journey with the tragedy already far out of mind. Alicky's mind is on his broken watch. He shows no interest in the games the others play: "He put his watch to his ear and shook it violently for the fiftieth time." For him time had stopped.

At the funeral tea, as the minister prays, Alicky notices the cat nosing a large plate of ham, but is held back from action by the thought that he might be called "a wicked ungodly wee boy for not payin' attention to what the minister's sayin' about yer puir mammy." But the minister saves the situation: "He stopped in the middle of a sentence and said calmly in his non-praying voice: 'Mrs. Peebles, I see that the cat's up at the boiled ham. Hadn't we better do something about it?' After the minister has gone the party is free to give vent to its own double standards, to its rough enjoyments, its gentility, while Alicky, ignored, pries into his watch. Also on the sidelines is Alicky's father. His wish to have his wife's body cremated was overruled. The information that he is 31 years old surfaces and is ignored.

In this imagined world, there is a place for the free expression of coarse enjoyment as part of a human comedy, but the unnoticed players on the sidelines, the father and Alicky, in their integrity, are the measure of behaviour. The absence of the author's explicit judgement is the measure of his art.

—George Bruce

THE ALOE.   See PRELUDE.

ALONG RIDEOUT ROAD THAT SUMMER
by Maurice Duggan, 1963

"Along Rideout Road that Summer" was begun by Maurice Duggan towards the close of 1960, the year in which he held the Burns Fellowship at Otago University. It was published in 1963 in *Landfall*, New Zealand's premier literary journal of the period, and later collected with eight other stories in *Summer in the Gravel Pit*, which was published in London and in New Zealand in 1965. This was only Duggan's second collection of stories but was greeted in New Zealand as a major literary event. The Burns Fellowship had allowed Duggan to write free from financial pressures for the first time in his life, and was a period of unparalleled productivity and growth in an output which he himself often acknowledged as limited. "Along Rideout Road that Summer" is a bravura piece, marking the culmination of Duggan's intense work over the year 1960 and the successful break at last by the New Zealand short story from the traditions of high Modernism and social realism that had preceded it.

The basis of the story is very simple; indeed Duggan had used the same material once before in a sketch entitled "Six Place Names and a Girl." A teenager named Buster O'Leary relates the tale of his running away and finding himself in the morning at the farm of Puti Hohepa, "a mere dozen miles from the parental home." Buster's father is a rural storekeeper, of European descent, and a narrow-minded disposition, while Puti Hohepa is a farmer and a Maori (Polynesian), who takes an unhurried attitude both to life and the husbanding of his land. Buster, "a bookish lad," is fond of quoting poetry and dreamy philosophising, but he does labour work on the farm and begins an idyllic sexual relationship with Fanny, Hohepa's largely uneducated daughter. Eventually Mr. O'Leary arrives to ask his son to return home, and, after various appeals to propriety, he is made to leave in abject defeat. However, by the next day, Buster has begun to realize that his stay with the Hohepas can only be temporary. After saying goodbye to Fanny he eventually departs by hitching a ride with a passing car that drives off "through the tail-end of summer."

With its contrasts of character and lifestyle, "Along Rideout Road that Summer" is a story at the heart of traditional New Zealand literary themes, but it is Duggan's use of language that overwhelms us on first reading the story and that leaves the most lasting impression. Duggan has made skillful use of the double perspective provided by an older Buster recalling the events of his youth, and is able to incorporate successfully a number of different registers within the story at once. In the space of a paragraph, as Neil Besner has shown, Duggan is able to employ the language of traditional European romanticisation of the

Maori race, of fashion and fashionable phrase imported from abroad, highly literary rhetoric and its parody, and colloquial New Zealand idiom. That Duggan is able to make these cohere in what Buster himself calls a "verbose review" is a remarkable achievement, due partly to Duggan's success with monologue and partly to the well-known nature of the plot for readers of New Zealand fiction. Buster appears to be addressing an audience in a self-conscious manner, but the nature of his relation to that audience, and even the audience itself, changes subtly with the story's changes in register. This richness of language has provoked a number of literary critical interpretations.

It is the exuberance of Duggan's writing that carries the reader through the story's linguistic complexities. "Along Rideout Road that Summer" sparkles with jokes, ironies, and asides. In it many of the components usually associated with the early, colloquial stories of Frank Sargeson, Duggan's mentor and widely regarded as the father of New Zealand literature, are examined, inverted, and finally rejected. Buster cannot find escape from the world into Puti Hohepa's pastoral halfway-farm, and in any event the farm itself is too rundown and dilapidated to be the proper stuff of pastoral. Fanny is at once "a picture of rustic grace" and a "collapsible sheila," Puti Hohepa a "dignified dark prince" and a "chocolate old bastard." Buster describes his own emotions in qualified terms as "almost happy," his reaction to his father's departure as "an impossible pairing of devotion and despair." Buster leaves the Hohepa farm in a passing hearse and there is a sense at the story's end of a loss of Edenic innocence, but his reemphasised happiness suggests a concomitant sense of new-found freedom.

The flexibility of Duggan's style means that "Along Rideout Road that Summer" is able to touch on many areas of importance to New Zealand literature, but one of the most famous occurs in the scene when Buster meets Fanny for the first time. Duggan describes at length Buster driving a battered Ferguson tractor back and forth to plough one of Puti Hohepa's paddocks, reciting Coleridge's "Kubla Khan" while Fanny sits perched on the gate and strums her ukelele. For Buster, and for most New Zealanders, despite their Euro-centred education and expectations, someone like Fanny can be the only indigenous Abyssinian maid and a Hohepa-like farm the only Xanadu. Buster's rich elaboration "of how to cope with the shock of recognition of a certain discrepancy between the real and the written" is performed "in riddles and literary puddles," and has become a seminal moment in New Zealand fiction. His acknowledged failure to make the differing parts converge throughout the story contributes to its final, paradoxical sense of loss and release.

Some critical debate has occurred in New Zealand in recent years over race relations in the story and Buster's attitude to the Maori. W. H. Pearson has argued that the young Buster's view is a limited one, containing much of his fellow countrymen's prejudice of Maori as second-class citizens but tempered and occasionally brought into ironic relief by the views of the older narrator. Terry Sturm sees the younger Buster as inclined to sentimentalise the Maori. Buster has illusions about the sexual freedom of his relationship with Fanny and of Puti Hohepa as a superior father-figure, only to have them punctured by Hohepa's unwanted advice: "A boy shouldn't hate his father; a boy should respect his father." C. K. Stead has argued that "Along Rideout Road that Summer" contains no such moralising and that Buster's story is one of self-discovery, of recognition of his closeness to and distance from his father, and of the experience of love. That the story is able

to sustain all three interpretations is testament to its fecundity and its enduring relevance. Many critics have called it Duggan's masterpiece, and some have claimed it as the best short story ever written in New Zealand fiction.

—Ian Richards

AMERICAN DREAMS
by Peter Carey, 1974

Peter Carey is acknowledged as one of the most exciting writers to have emerged in Australia within the past 20 years. His reputation is due largely to his adoption of various styles and disregard for traditional modes of Australian fiction, which Patrick White once described as "the dreary dun-coloured offspring of journalistic realism." His stories in particular draw on science fiction, surrealism, fantasy, and magic realism, and Carey readily admits to being more influenced by American writers than by Australian. Yet he has succeeded in making his work accessible to a wide audience both at home and overseas by writing in a simple, straightforward but engaging manner.

Carey has asserted that he is "always writing about how the world is now," and the contemporary flavour of his material also accounts for its popularity. "American Dreams," however, seems to break away from current issues and take the reader back to an earlier Australia, of the 1950's. This story was written later than others published in his first collection, The Fat Man in History, and lacks that cold, occasionally surreal quality in, for example, the title story, "Crabs," and "A Windmill in the West." There is a softer tone here, even a hint of nostalgia. Carey admits that he drew on memories of the town where he grew up, Bacchus Marsh, for such details as names of characters and his childhood love of bicycles. He certainly succeeds in recreating the atmosphere of a small Australian town of 40 years ago.

From the beginning, however, it is evident that this tale is not merely a personal trip down memory lane. It opens with the narrator trying to work out what he and other townsfolk might have done to offend an unassuming little man called Mr. Gleason. The reader is immediately intrigued to find out what Mr. Gleason did to warrant such self-examination. And so a strange story is launched, of this man's retirement project of building a large, forbidding wall around a plot of land on a hill overlooking the town. The townsfolk were initially puzzled, but, given their Australian habit of reticence, were reluctant to question the man, and eventually they put the project down to oddity. For years no one knew what was behind the wall, even though there was clearly some reason to build the wall high and keep the project a secret.

Another label applied to Carey's work is "fabulist," and a reading of "American Dreams" illustrates why. Gradually what is disclosed here is a fable for our time. When Gleason dies, his wife has the wall pulled down to reveal a miniature version of the whole town with every building and person carefully constructed. The narrator had earlier mentioned in passing that people believed their town was second-rate. They had seen films of the "outside" which had filled their heads with dreams, "dreams of the big city, of wealth, of modern houses, of big motor cars: American dreams, my father has called them." The revelation of the miniature town prompts a question in the narrator's mind: was this why Gleason built his model, to encourage the locals to take pride in their town and keep it untainted by outside influences? Or did he realise that such an elaborate model could have tourist potential, that in fact it would lead to an influx of outsiders, so that the people might fulfil their American dreams without going away? Part of the story's intrigue is that no one can ever work out what Gleason's motives were.

More significantly for the outcome of this fable is that the tourists do come. Americans with their dollars arrive, and their needs are met by locals who become entrepreneurs. But while business people make money and generally "get ahead," for most there is no sense of fulfilment. The narrator and others become weary from having to act like performing animals for the eager tourists. They also change while the models remain timeless. And strangely, or perhaps not so strangely, the tourists come to prefer the models. They seem more real than the living people who are turning into specimens of humanity similar to the tourists themselves. The story concludes with the narrator sadder and wiser, feeling that some irreversible process has been started, some dilution of Australianness.

Peter Carey has commented on another of his fables, "The Chance": "Everybody [is] believing in change, chance, another go; somehow they think it will all get better. It's a drugged-out society. Everyone believes in newness." He rails against this obsession Australians have with what usually turns out to be tacky or barren or destructive values created elsewhere. For him, these values are summed up in the word "American," and he believes that Australia has been colonised, as it were, by America, socially, culturally, and economically. In this story located away from the cities, he seems to suggest that the nationalist myth of sturdy pioneers venturing into the outback and establishing communities with a distinctive ethos is no longer valid. Modern Australians don't want to be different; they just exploit their land while dreaming of being elsewhere. It is a bleak picture, although one can read into the fable's conclusion a message for Australians that they must resist colonisation and reassert their own identity.

In a discussion about the writing of "American Dreams," Carey said that it started from the idea of "this guy building this wall." His stories usually begin with ideas, not people, and the ideas always remain prominent. The townsfolk are rarely more than names. Yet he never loses sight of the need to keep readers entertained. There is a strong narrative line here that makes it all the more likely that Australians might listen to his message.

—F.C. Molloy

APOCALYPSE AT SOLENTINAME (Apocalipsis de Solentiname)
by Julio Cortázar, 1978

Like so many Latin American writers, like his countryman Jorge Luis Borges, Julio Cortázar often stages his stories in the middle ground between fact and fiction, suggesting perhaps that the real is imaginary and the imagination is real—a particularly Borgesian notion. Thus, in "Apocalipsis de Solentiname" ("Apocalypse at Solentiname"), collected in Territorios (1978), the unnamed

narrator is a writer, an expatriate who has returned for a visit to his native Latin America, the author of the short story which served as the basis for Michangelo Antonioni's film Blow Up—in short, Julio Cortázar himself. The other characters are real people, too: Carmen Narranjo, the Costa Rican novelist and poet; Samuel Rovinski, a fiction writer, also Costa Rican; Sergio Ramirez, Nicaraguan author and political activist. The story finds one of its points of focus in Father Ernesto Cardenal, the Nicaraguan poet and political leader who founded the religious community of Solentiname on the island of Mancarron in the archipelago at the southern end of Lake Nicaragua in 1966. The Solentiname community involved local people in political action against the Somoza regime and also gave rise to a significant body of painting, poetry, and commentaries on the Gospels. Somoza's National Guard attacked the community and destroyed it in 1977, killing a number of its members. Later, after the fall of Somoza and the coming to power of the Sandinista government, Father Cardenal served as Nicaragua's Minister of Culture.

"Apocalypse at Solentiname" offers virtually none of this information. Cortázar merely assumes that the reader knows the historical background of the situation. In the story, the writer has left his home in Paris to visit a number of Caribbean and Central American countries, giving press interviews and promoting his books, when he gets the opportunity to visit Solentiname. There he takes pictures of the people living their daily lives in the community and taking part in Sunday mass, and he also photographs their paintings of "ponies and sunflowers and fiestas in the symmetrical fields and palm groves."

He continues his tour and eventually returns to the safety and comfort of Paris—"once more the life of wristwatch and merci, monsieur, bonjour, madame, committees, movies, red wine and Claudine, Mozart quartets and Claudine." Eventually, he gets around to having his rolls of film developed, and he settles down alone in his home to look at the slides, but he finds that the pictures he has received are not the pictures he took.

The peaceful scenes from Solentiname have been replaced by scenes of violence—a boy being shot through the head by a soldier, a field of bodies laid out face up under a gray sky, an exploding car, a woman being tortured, a man facing a firing squad, Salvadoran poet and revolutionary Roque Dalton being assassinated. This is what the horrified writer sees projected on the screen, but when Claudine returns home from work and looks at the slides, she sees only the original snapshots. "They came out so well," she says. Somehow, the writer has caught a glimpse of the coming apocalypse at Solentiname as well as the violence that takes place daily throughout Latin America "in the heart of a city that could be Buenos Aires or Sao Paulo . . . on a Bolivian or Guatemalan hillside. . . ."

Is this a true story? It is true that, in 1976, one year before the attack on Solentiname, Julio Cortázar visited the community, entering Nicaragua secretly from Costa Rica. It is true that Solentiname was violently broken up by Somoza's soldiers, that people there were killed. It is true that violence is not at all unusual in some Latin American countries. And yet certainly "Apocalypse at Solentiname" is a work of fiction, carefully structured, carefully written. All of the elements are perfectly in place. For example, the theme of the commentary during the mass is Jesus's arrest in the garden, "a theme that the people of Solentiname treated as if they were talking about themselves." The parallel between this theme and the violence that will appear later in the story is too perfect. Certainly such correspondences happen only in works of fiction, in art, not in reality.

Even so, the characters are based on real people, the events on real events. Indeed, in this story, the distinction between the real and the fictive is unclear, and that, in fact, is the whole point. Anyone who has ever spent time in Central America knows that it is a beautiful land. The beauty is quite real, but there is another hidden and violent reality that turns that beauty into a fiction, because the violence can overwhelm the beauty at any moment. And yet the beauty is still real, just as art is real and can, in its turn, overwhelm the violence of life.

The writer's experience with the photographs reminds him of the violence in the New World that he has left behind, a violence he already knows about, as he already knows about the powers of art and imagination, as he already knows about the ongoing dialectical exchange between fact and fiction which informs not only "Apocalypse at Solentiname" but every aspect of human life. Near the end of the story, when he is about to view his slides for the first time, the writer decides to look at the paintings from Solentiname first, before screening the slides depicting real life—"Why the paintings first, why the professional deformation, art before life, and why not, the one said to the other in their eternal unresolvable fraternal and rancorous dialogue, why not look at the Solentiname paintings first since they're life too, since it's all the same."

"Apocalypse at Solentiname" is an arena in which the form of fiction and the violence of fact can come together and comment on each other. It, too, is life and art—politically involved art about the life of political involvement—"since it's all the same."

—Welch D. Everman

ARCTURUS, THE HUNTING DOG (Arktur—gonchii pes)
by Iurii Kazakov, 1958

Arktur—gonchii pes (*Arcturus, The Hunting Dog,* also translated as "Arcturus, the Hound") is the title story of Kazakov's collection of short stories published in 1958. In his diaries Kazakov describes writing this story, which he worked on for two years, from 1955 to 1957. The original version was entitled "Homer" and focused more on the heroine than the blind dog of the later version. Kazakov changed the name of the dog from the transparent "Homer," a name directly pointing to the dog's physical handicap, to "Arcturus"—"the name of a never-fading blue star." This name acquires a new symbolic meaning. It emphasizes the unique qualities of Arcturus, the ability to shine without being physically able to see.

Not only is Arcturus the protagonist of the story, but the whole structure of the story is built around him. Two other characters, the doctor and the author-narrator himself, are described in terms of their interactions with Arcturus. All events in the outside world are grouped and selected according to their connection with the blind dog.

The narration is presented by the author-narrator in the form of a reminiscence, an episode from the life of the author himself. It is clearly autobiographical in nature. But the information the author reveals about himself is so devoid of detail that he takes on a rather sketchy character.

The description of the third character, the doctor, is also lacking in detail. Arcturus's biography, on the contrary, is given in great detail. The author-narrator offers several versions of it, leaving to the reader the right to choose what to believe about the past of this amazing dog. Thus Arcturus appears in town long before the arrival of the author. His appearance is steeped in mystery. No one really knows how he turned up in this provincial town. There are several versions of the story: he was abandoned by gypsies, or he arrived "floating in on a cake of ice in flood time." The reader also learns about his birth, his mother, his siblings, and about his first sensations concerning his handicap—his blindness. Actually, Arcturus does not even realize that he is blind: "It was not given him to know. He accepted the life that was his lot."

Arcturus is a loner, like many other characters in Kazakov's stories ("The Outsider," "An Easy Life"). He is lonely not only because of his blindness, but also because he possesses an unusual gift, about which, for the time being, he has no idea. On the outside Arcturus differs little from other dogs of his breed. He is strong and powerful, but a vague feeling of uncertainty is hidden in his being, causing a certain guardedness. Arcturus is the embodiment of the best human traits: he is honest, brave, and capable of deep feelings of devotion. Out of his love for the doctor he is able to overcome his repulsion to the smell of eau de cologne, "an odor never to be found in nature." His sense of smell replaces his eyes; it is his only compass in a hostile and unseen world.

Along with smells, sounds play a crucial role in Arcturus's life. For him everything resounds, and each object has not only its own particular smell, but also its own particular sound. All the faintest sounds, unheard by human beings, serve as guideposts in his life. Kazakov, a former musician, describes with realistic exactness the combinations of sounds that the hunting dog hears, so that the reader can really believe the guiding function of sounds in Arcturus's life. Sounds and smells form Arcturus's inner world.

Arcturus's contact with the human world is essentially represented by his relationship with the doctor and the author. Other contacts (for example, with shepherds who whip him) simply serve as examples of the cruelty of the unseen outside world toward him, whereas the doctor and the author comprise the inner world, visible only to Arcturus himself. The absense of detail in their descriptions transforms them into mutually interchangeable figures, as it were. While the doctor saves the dog from hunter and beatings, the author helps him find his true calling and unwittingly becomes the source of his destruction.

While wandering through the woods one day, tagging along with the author, Arcturus suddenly discovers what the meaning of his life is. It is hunting, although blindness would seem to be an insurmountable barrier to self-fulfillment in this manner. Arcturus keeps returning to the woods, where, by hunting, he can perform the task he was destined to do, and his life becomes meaningful. For his devotion to this task he pays a terrible price—constant physical pain and, eventually, his very life—but no one can stop him. Having found himself, the dog is transformed, his uncertainty disappears. Throwing caution to the wind he fearlessly rushes forward, and in the end perishes by crashing into a branch. Such is the price for blindly following one's passions without acknowledging the limitations that life has dealt one.

In his essay on Russian short fiction Deming Brown writes that "conflict is still the heart of the Soviet short story." Kazakov's *Arcturus, The Hunting Dog* gives us an example of an inner conflict, the conflict between physical possibilities and life's destiny.

In Soviet criticism of the 1960's, Kazakov was often criticized; Igor Kuzmičev wrote "insufficient contemporary social content, for pessimism and morbidity, and for featuring passive, estranged, and otherwise negative heroes spiritually unworthy of emulation by Soviet citizens." The story of a blind dog following his calling to the fatal end takes on a completely different character if read in the political context of the late 1960's. The desire of the gifted individual to fulfill his or her destiny at all cost, to be dedicated to one's gift without compromising or wavering from one's true path—this is what can be read in Arcturus's fate.

—Marina Balina

_____

THE ASPERN PAPERS
by Henry James, 1888

Published first in 1888, and revised for James's *Novels and Tales* (New York Edition) 20 years later, "The Aspern Papers" is a novella with a suspenseful plot, characters who embody qualities inherent in James's greatest fiction, and a first-person narrative form. In his preface to the New York Edition James attributes the "germ" of his narrative to an anecdote about a biographer who attempted to persuade the half-sister of Shelley's wife to entrust him with highly personal letters which Shelley had written to her years before, only to discover that his marrying the lady's niece would be part of her "bargain." James altered his story to make the poet an American, Jeffrey Aspern, a romantic writer of Nathaniel Hawthorne's generation. The biographer and first-person narrator is an American literary critic, who idolizes Aspern, much as James did Hawthorne. Famous for his international fiction, James located the ensuing events in Venice.

Miss Juliana Bordereau, the elderly spinster, once the object of Aspern's passionate intentions and now a disagreeable recluse, conceals under a sinister green visor the only vestige of her former beauty, her clear, fierce-looking eyes. The biographer/narrator has chosen an alias in order to inveigle his way into the Bordereau household, but he never reveals his assumed name or his real one to the reader although he confesses it late in the story to the younger Miss Bordereau. Miss Tina, the niece, (called Miss Tita in the New York Edition) is the story's one innocent person. Lonely and reclusive by necessity, she is depicted as being neither intelligent, nor beautiful, nor young. Yet she has the spirit to become engaged in life and to offer her love and trust to the narrator. Like Catherine Sloper in James's *Washington Square*, she is a dull, good person, capable of ardor and loyalty, who is betrayed by a callow, self-interested male. Rejected by those whose love they are most eager to claim (Catherine by her father and Morris Townsend; Tina by her aunt and the narrator), they nevertheless survive rejection without embitterment or loss of dignity.

Juliana claims to have her niece's interests in mind when she extorts a high fee for renting her rooms to the narrator, but significantly Tina comments after the old lady's death that she was neither "just nor generous." Justice and generosity are essential virtues in a rounded Jamesian character which none of his truly admirable protagonists lack. The conflict in this international tale does not occur between Europeans and Americans but within a group of Americans who exploit the legendary past of a dead compatriot for their own gain.

James, who valued both the moral and the aesthetic sense, recognized that individuals with exquisite tact and artistic sensibilities were capable of moral insensitivity. The narrator professes a great love of Aspern's poetry and also appreciates the beauty of Venice, but he is willing to manipulate two vulnerable women, to exploit their friendship without concern for their privacy or emotional needs.

Like Hawthorne, James often used garden settings to allude to the myth of Eden. Here he unexpectedly places a garden inside the walls of a dilapidated Venetian palazzi in which the narrator, as a paid lodger, will grow flowers for the Bordereau women. Claiming that he will "work the garden" as part of his strategy for gaining their confidence, the narrator identifies himself to the reader as a Satanic tempter, and he ultimately enlists the younger lady's assistance in obtaining the papers. Miss Tina mistakes his familiarities as courtship rituals. The garden itself, unexpected in a city constantly threatened by watery erosion, is reminiscent of a Hawthorne tale, such as "Rappacini's Daughter." One senses that perversity and tragedy will result from its cultivation.

Hidden from all but a handful of people, it parallels the isolation of the narrator, the Bordereaus, and perhaps James the author, who may have paid the cost of his privacy with a limiting emotional isolation.

What secrets did James take to his grave and at what price of personal fulfillment? The lonely bachelors of his later fiction often came to an awareness of what they had missed in life. John Marcher at May Bartram's graveside in "The Beast in the Jungle" is a prime example. Critic Millicent Bell has suggested that subtle changes in "The Aspern Papers" for the New York edition indicate that the narrator might have come to recognize the opportunity for love and trust which he sqaundered. While in the original version the narrator concluded "when I look at it, my chagrin at the loss of the letters becomes almost intolerable," James alters his confession in the New York edition: "when I look at it I can scarcely bear my loss—I mean of the precious papers." The subtext of his remark is that he recognizes too late the absence of emotional commitment in his life.

Although James is often grouped with authors such as William Dean Howells as a realist, he also shares traits of writers in the romantic and naturalistic modes. Juliana Bordereau regards her love affair with the late Jeffrey Aspern as the defining moment of her life. After his death, she secluded herself, preserving Aspern's love letters as if they were sacred relics. Eschewing publicity or even the opportunity to document her importance to the poet in terms of literary posterity, she inhabits the empty stage of her own romantic drama of the imagination. When she makes contact with the real world at all, it is as an imperious manipulating spinster with a secret, thrilling past arranging a marriage for her lonely niece.

But James also appreciates the inevitability of Juliana's self-entrapment. A woman not only immortalized but also compromised by Aspern's verses, Juliana becomes less than respectable, a woman about whom the narrator says, "there hovered about her name a perfume of reckless passion, an intimation that she had not been exactly as the respectable young person in general."

The narrator, having devoted himself to the canonization of Jeffrey Aspern, imagines that the late poet appears to him as a ghost, encouraging him in his quest for the love letters which he perceives as an heroic exploit rather than a self-serving intrusion. At one point the obliging spirit of Aspern encourages the narrator to extremes of expedience, pleading "get out of it as you can, dear fellow." When Miss Tina realizes that the narrator feels marrying her may be too high a price to pay for Aspern's letters, she burns them and tells the narrator she no longer wishes to see him. She has freed him of an unwanted obligation and herself of a temptation to barter documents for the illusion of being loved—a paradigm of the Jamesian renunciation.

Even though James suggests that the protagonists of "The Aspern Papers" spin romantic fantasies at the same time they are capable of moral choice, he is sympathetic to circumstances of their lives that inhibit them as free agents. Like a character in naturalistic fiction, the narrator is psychologically incapable of participating fully in life. He is one of James's "marginal" males in that he has been consigned to a sexually ambivalent limbo, less interested in pursuing women as sexual partners than in venerating a dead poet's youthful exploits with a now elderly Juliana. The old lady's opportunities for marriage would surely have been diminished by the notoriety of her affair. Finally, her niece has been isolated by her limited circle of acquaintances, her plainness, and her financial dependency on her elderly relative. While James's plot contains adventurous episodes, the outcome of his extended anecdote seems inevitable. The story of "The Aspern Papers" reveals James's artistic mastery of many fictional modes and may also be a parable of his refusal to expose his own vulnerabilities. Its lasting appeal is verified by Dominick Argento's opera adaptation, performed in New York in 1990.

—Kimball King

AN ASTROLOGER'S DAY
by R.K. Narayan, 1947

The fiction of R.K. Narayan is marked by a persistently ironic apprehension of life, the irony varying from the simple and the situational type producing comedy to tragic irony revealing the deep-seated ambiguities and existential dilemmas of the human condition. It is also a fiction strongly imbued with the "spirit of place," as much rooted in its native soil as is the work of William Faulkner. However, unlike the American novelist, Narayan employs a style that is disarmingly simple.

Narayan's short stories are, on the whole, characterized by these three basic traits, though it is possible to argue that by and large, the irony that operates in them is usually of the light-fingered variety. "An Astrologer's Day," the title story of a 1947 collection, is a short story eminently representative of Narayan's talent.

The actual narrative element in "An Astrologer's Day" is rather slight. A town astrologer coaxes a rather reluctant client into consulting him at the end of a day, when he is about to shut up shop. The client wants to know when he would be able to locate his enemy, who had tried to kill him years before in their village, so that he could avenge himself. Little does the client know that the enemy whom he seeks is the astrologer himself, before whom he is squatting at the moment. He does not recognize the man because the latter, with his "painted forehead," dark whiskers, and saffron-coloured turban, looks every inch an astrologer. However, the astrologer recognizes the client as the victim whom he had knifed years before. No wonder, he is able therefore to recapitulate the client's past so thoroughly that absolute belief in his prediction of the future now becomes possible for the poor client. The astrologer cooly tells the client that his enemy is now dead, "crushed under a lorry." His advice to the client is to "take the next train and be gone. I see once again great danger to your life if you go from home." He particularly emphasizes the necessity of the client's avoiding another visit to the town. The story ends with the astrologer returning home and telling his wife, "Do you know a great load is gone from me today? I thought I had the blood of a man on my hands all these years. That was the reason why I ran away from home, settled here, and married you. He is alive."

At first reading, "An Astrologer's Day" appears to be a somewhat uncomplicated story, rather amusing in the O. Henry-like twist, administering a mild shock of surprise to the reader at the end. But Narayan's is an art that conceals art. The deceptive simplicity of the story really hides a multiplicity of ironies. First, as pointed out by the narrator himself, the astrologer is a charlaton, with neither the requisite expertise nor the proper training; he just gets by, on the strength of common sense, keen observation, and shrewd guesswork. It is ironic that the false prediction of a fake astrologer should radically change the lives of two men for the better. This might even raise for the perceptive reader the eternal question of "Action" and the "Fruit of Action"—an ethical question raised in the Indian religious classic: *The Gita*. In many other respects the entire situation is ironical: the astrologer is himself the subject of the client's query, and it is his own future he is asked to predict; never perhaps is prediction so easy for the astrologer, and so certain to come true; the astrologer is at first extremely reluctant to advise the client, once he recognizes him, and is actually forced by the man to do his job; had he really declined to predict, he would not have had a great weight lifted from his mind, nor would he have been able to ensure a life of peace for himself. Furthermore, in this game of one-up-manship, each has won, in his own way: the astrologer has obviously won, by getting rid permanently of an old foe, but the client too has gained a little victory—he had promised a rupee to the astrologer but has actually fobbed him off with only twelve and a half annas; nevertheless, basking in the satisfaction of having saved about a quarter rupee, the poor client is left blissfully unaware of the great opportunity he has missed.

Like most of Narayan's stories, "An Astrologer's Day" is a story neatly structured, with its action briskly moving towards the snap, surprise ending. The opening, with its rather long description of the astrologer's personal appearance, and the setting in which he operates, may at first appear to be a little too leisurely for a short story. But with its skilful use of colour and small details, it recaptures evocatively the small-town scene. Thus, the astrologer, with his forehead "resplendent with sacred ash and vermilion," his dark whiskers, and the saffron-coloured turban around his head, presents a colourful figure. Telling details like the place being lit up by "hissing gaslights," "naked flares stuck up on poles," "old cycle lamps," create the proper atmosphere for the astrologer's dark predictions.

The story is written in a direct and lucid style, almost Spartan in its unadorned simplicity. Narayan uses no similes and no metaphors. His sentences are mostly short, and his diction unpretentious, with Indian words like "jutka," "jaggery," and "pyol" providing the proper local colour to a story that is essentially Indian in every way.

—M.K. Naik

ASTRONOMER'S WIFE
by Kay Boyle, 1936

Kay Boyle published over 30 books in her career, including 14 novels, 7 story collections, and 5 volumes of poetry. Yet, her work and its influence on American letters has received relatively little scholarly attention. Early in her career, as one of the Lost Generation writing in Europe in the 1920's and 1930's, Kay Boyle crafted fiction that developed from experimental and intensely personal expression characterized by innovative language and narrative structures to a more conventional technique that communicated social concerns about a shared social world common to her readers.

"Astronomer's Wife" appeared in *The White Horses of Vienna and Other Stories* in 1936 and reflects in many ways a transitional story in this early period. It looks backward to her earliest thematic concerns—the quest for identity, the hunger and need for human love and contact—and forward to the simpler, less experimental narrative style of later years. In terms of subject, the story is also forward-looking. It deals with the loss and recovery of a woman's sense of self in an oppressive marriage, a subject that, at the time, was a dilemma widely experienced by women but not widely discussed. In this sense, "Astronomer's Wife" trumpets a brilliant herald for the feminism that lies decades ahead.

"Astronomer's Wife" expresses an archetypal mind/body conflict that expands into opposition between intellect and intuition, contemplation and action, love and denial. The story centers concretely on the relationship between Mr. and Mrs. Ames, the astronomer and his wife. Mr. Ames is a solitary dreamer who contemplates an abstract, theoretical world; Mrs. Ames is a woman of concrete, physical animation whose actions reveal a life without reflection, the busy removal of spots from her husband's vest or the thrashing of mayonnaise for his lunch. While the astronomer's deep thoughts have, to his mind at least, reached dignified status, they are so intellectually top-heavy that they remain incomprehensible to his wife. As a result, the astronomer's soaring thoughts "sounded in her in despair" and returned her "in gratitude to the long expanses of his silence" where she withdrew in bewildered self-doubt.

Much of the story's power rests in the fact that Mr. Ames remains asleep in bed throughout the story, an offstage character revealed only through the mental and emotional effect he has on Mrs. Ames. He spends his life pursuing questions that have no answers, "to which there could be no response," punctuated by his scorn for anything mundane or non-intellectual. By contrast, Mrs. Ames connects with the world through active engagement of flesh and bone. When the morning brings its "evil moment on awakening when all things seem to pause," she immediately fills up the "interval gaping" with action that seems more necessity than pleasure. For Mrs. Ames, "questions to which true answers would be given" are the thing, not questions like her husband's which pursue mere illusion,

addressing "the nameless things that cannot pass between the thumb and finger."

The story's tension centers inside Mrs. Ames, who steps gingerly around Mr. Ames's sleeping presence, treating him and what he might say or do with complete reverence. In the end, although never stated directly, this expectation proves soul-sapping beyond endurance. By presenting the antagonist through his effects on Mrs. Ames, the story obviates the need for explicit confrontation. This structure successfully creates such a strong sense of repression that the plumber's arrival to repair the broken water closet—symbolic of Mrs. Ames's life—offers tangible relief.

The plumber represents symbolic choice for Mrs. Ames. In his earthy sexuality and belief that every problem is solvable by merely asking the right question—to which true answers will be given—he presents the path to epiphany where Mrs. Ames can realize her own self-worth. The symbolism of earth (life/vitality/action) and sky (mind/thought/contemplation) provides the contextual frame for Mrs. Ames's choice.

Near the end, the archetypal character of the plumber emerges literally from the earth so full of symbolism that the moment carries much of the force and meaning of the story. With his hair "shining, like a star," he delivers Mrs. Ames, in effect, to herself. The plumber's intuitive confidence in action, so unlike the paralyzing effect of her husband's intellectual judgment, causes Mrs. Ames to liberate herself. Suddenly, she recognizes her connection to a tangible world she has always cared deeply about, a connection free from scorn and judgment. When the plumber says, "There's nothing at all that can't be done over for the caring," Mrs. Ames is validated.

The story ends on a brilliant poetic note—perhaps a bit too glaring in its brilliance. The golden-haired plumber describes the cow he once fed "flowers and things and what-not" when she lost her cud, presenting a powerful image of salvation and redemption, two crucial dimensions of life that Mrs. Ames has been missing until this point. The final image of her clutching the plumber's arm as they descend into the heart of the earth is ripe with symbolism shaded, perhaps a bit too heavy-handedly, by romance. Yet, considering this subject and its conflict, a velvet hammer might not, to some readers, seem objectionable.

The story reflects Boyle's undying concern with individual action in a social world and marks, partially, the early transition of a writer concerned with personal expression to a writer concerned with communicating social meanings to an audience situated in a problematic world. Mrs. Ames surely aims in that direction.

—Paul Sladky

AT THE BAY
by Katherine Mansfield, 1922

Katherine Mansfield's reputation rests primarily on four expansive stories set in and around Wellington, New Zealand: "Prelude." "At the Bay," "The Garden Party," and "The Doll's House." The last three of these, along with "The Voyage," were written in an inspired creative burst in Switzerland between August and October, 1921. At the time, Mansfield entertained thoughts of amalgamating them, along with other material, to form a novel, *Karori*.

But, like other earlier projects for novels, this one was never fulfilled.

"Prelude" (under an earlier title, *The Aloe*) was begun much earlier, in 1915 shortly after her younger brother, Leslie ("Boy"), visited her in London, on his way to the battlefront, where he died in October of the same year. Her conversations with him—and the shock of his death—evidently unlocked a series of childhood memories and she determined, ostensibly as a tribute to Leslie, to "make our undiscovered country leap into the eyes of the Old World. It must be mysterious, as though floating. It must take the breath. It must be 'one of those islands'." It is in "At the Bay" that this ambition is most explicitly fulfilled; the little seaside community of Crescent Bay floats up out of the mist in the first of the story's twelve sections, and disappears back into the darkness at the end.

The group of characters in the story correspond very closely to the extended family in which Mansfield, as Kathleen Beauchamp, grew up. Kezia Burnell, her older sister, Isabel, and the younger Lottie correspond respectively to Kathleen, Vera (or Charlotte), and Jeanne Beauchamp. "The boy" (as the baby in the story is called) occupies Leslie's position in the family, and bears his nickname. The Burnell parents, Stanley and Linda, closely resemble Harold and Annie Beauchamp. Linda's unmarried sister, Beryl, and their mother, Mrs. Fairfield (a bilingual pun on "Beauchamp"), live with the family, as did Annie's sister (Belle) and mother (Mrs. Dyer). Sharing the Burnells' holiday at the beach are Linda's brother-in-law, Jonathan Trout, and his two boys (Pip and Rags). Their surname puns on that of Kathleen's uncle, Valentine Waters, and his sons, Barrie and Eric. The Crescent Bay of the story corresponds to Muritai Beach (across the harbour from Wellington city), where the Beauchamps and the Waters spent their summer holidays.

At a deeper level too the story can be seen as autobiographical. Mansfield's biographer, Antony Alpers, believes that she had her first sexual experience with a man at Muritai Beach in 1908. This strange blend of English and French was written in her *Journal* that evening.

> Night. J'attends pour la premiere fois dans ma vie le crise de ma vie. As I wait a flock of sheep pass down the street in the moonlight. I hear them cracking the whip—and behind, the dark heavy cart—like a death cart il me semble—and in all this sacrificial light I look lovely. I do not fear—I only feel. . . .Ah come now soon. Each moment il me semble is a moment of supreme danger—but this man I love with all my heart. . . .It comes—I go to bed.

"At the Bay" begins with the passage of a flock of sheep along the beachfront in the early morning. It examines the topic of death at some length in section seven. And it ends with Beryl longing for love and undergoing a close encounter with the sinister Harry Kember. While Kezia corresponds to the young Kathleen Beauchamp, Beryl may be seen as a projection of the mature Mansfield who wrote the story.

As Beryle is threatened by Harry Kember, "the sea sounded deep, troubled." Once she escapes from his clutches, its sound becomes "a vague murmur, as though it had waked out of a dark dream." Here and elsewhere (e.g., when the young Lottie is frightened by "an old whiskery" wave in the fifth section, or when Stanley and Jonathan take utterly different approaches to their early morning swim in section two) the treatment of the sea underlines an important distinction in the story between childish (or, in Jonathan's case, childlike) innocence and adult experience.

The distinction is akin to Kristeva's between "the semiotic" and "the symbolic." Those who accept the sea in effect access what Kristeva calls "the archaic contact with the maternal body," which is a prerequisite for creativity. Those who resist it are locked in the phallocentric symbolic order which children enter after they have passed through "the mirror phase" and acquired linguistic competence. It is interesting that little Lottie, who retreats from the "old whiskery" wave, is just over the threshold of language. Mansfield herself defined the distinction between child and adult along more traditional Romantic lines. In a book review written late in her life, she presented this version of the Wordsworthian maxim that "the child is father of the man":

> It is implicit in the belief of the child that the dream exists side by side with the reality; there are no barriers between. It is only after he has suffered the fate of little children—after he has been stolen away by the fairies—that the changeling who usurps his heritage builds those great walls that confront him when he will return.

The imaginative games played by the children in sections four and nine of "At the Bay" demonstrate their capacity to shift back and forth between reality and dream.

In all of Mansfield's stories the degree to which adults can empathize with children is generally a measure of their human worth. The brusque, self-centered Stanley fails this test of character, as do the cynical Kembers. Similarly, the philistine tastes of Alice (the maid) and Mrs. Stubbs (the local shopkeeper) are ruthlessly pilloried in the eighth section of the story (Mansfield subsequently dismissed this episode as a "black hole in my book").

In contrast, old Mrs. Fairfield has a delightful rapport with her grandchild, Kezia. Jonathan (who describes adult life as a Wordsworthian prison-house at some length in section ten) still has intimations of childish freedom, and when he first appears in the story (in section two) he unsettles Stanley with talk of his dreams. His sister-in-law Linda is initially immune to the delights of childhood, but—in what is really the only palpable development in this long, leisurely "slice of life"—she finally learns to appreciate "the boy" at the end of the sixth (and central) section. Even the narrator adopts a childish point of view—especially in sections one and seven.

Overall, then, what Mansfield liked to call "joy" triumphs over "satire" in "At the Bay"—as it does in almost all her New Zealand stories. In her English stories, on the other hand, satire ("a cry against corruption," as she termed it in a famous letter to J.M. Murry) is generally the norm.

—Richard Corballis

———

AUGUST 2026: THERE WILL COME SOFT RAINS
by Ray Bradbury, 1951

"August 2026: There Will Come Soft Rains" addresses the central fear of its time—nuclear holocaust. This is not uncommon for a work of science fiction written in the 1950's. In 1945, for the first time in human history, the end of the world became a real possibility, and writers of Ray Bradbury's generation were witnesses to that event. What is uncommon about "August 2026," then, is not its theme of nuclear disaster but its view of the technology that had made such a disaster possible.

In general, from the time of Jules Verne and H.G. Wells to the present, science-fiction writers have been faced with two mutually exclusive views of technological progress. Technology can offer the promise of a future paradise in which mechanization will set humans free from labor, hunger, and disease. Or, technology threatens to eliminate humans completely by making them, quite simply, obsolete. For Bradbury, this either/or perception of the possibilities of technology is too simplistic. In "August 2026," he argues that utopia and dystopia are the same place.

The opening lines of the story introduce the reader to a house without inhabitants in a city without survivors in a world which may well be devoid of human life. The house seems to be the only structure still standing in Allendale, California, and all that is left of the McClellan family, who once lived there, are the silhouettes of their bodies left on the outside of the west wall by the nuclear firestorm. In this posthuman story, it is the house that is the central character.

The house is fully automated, capable of waking its inhabitants in the morning, reminding them of appointments and bills to be paid, preparing their meals, doing the dishes, cleaning, setting up tables for an afternoon bridge game, even reading them poetry in the evening. It operates without the need for human intervention or decision, and so it continues to do its various tasks, even though those it once served are gone. The house does not know this, of course, though it does seem to have a kind of electronic awareness and even to be capable of thought. Bradbury offers the house an emotional life of sorts by giving it a maternal voice ("Rain, rain, go away; rubbers, raincoats for today") and instilling it with "an old maidenly preoccupation with self-protection which bordered on a mechanical paranoia."

The story chronicles the last day in the life of the house, August 4, 2026, almost 81 years to the day after the first atomic bombs were used against a civilian population in Japan. The day seems ordinary enough, despite the fact that there is no family within the walls of the house and perhaps no world outside. But of course this is not an ordinary day. At noon, the family dog appears at the door, sick with radiation poisoning. The house recognizes its voice and lets it in, but it soon dies, and the cleaning mechanisms dispose of it coldly and efficiently.

At ten o'clock, "the house began to die." There is an accident; the wind blows a tree branch through the kitchen window, and a bottle of cleaning solvent splatters across the hot stove. The fire spreads quickly, and though the house tries to save itself with its built-in defense mechanisms, it fails. By morning, only one wall is left standing, and an electronic voice repeats the same words over and over: "Today is August 5, 2026, today is August 5, 2026, today is. . . ."

Of course, the technology that makes this utopian house possible is the same technology that makes nuclear war possible, and Bradbury does not want us to overlook this connection. In fact, he implies that the difference between the house and the bomb is only one of degree. The technology of the mechanized house has already rendered human beings superfluous. The technology of war merely brings that process to its logical end.

Is it possible that the weapons of war in 2026 are also fully automated, computerized, free of human input, and

so, like the house, capable of acting on their own? The story does not address this question directly, but, even if there was no human decision behind the nuclear war that has put an end to human life, neither nuclear technology nor the house is responsible for that cataclysmic event. The truth is that humans have simply abdicated their position as dominant species, if indeed that ever really was their position on earth. Despite technology, the end of human life in Bradbury's story is the result of a human crime, a crime of conscious omission.

The house is in the habit of reading poetry to Mrs. McClellan in the evening, and it does so even on this evening, choosing to read the Sara Teasdale poem which gives the story its title.

> Not one would mind, neither bird nor tree,
> If mankind perished utterly;
> And Spring herself, when she woke at dawn
> Would scarcely know that we were gone.

The poem states that the natural world does not need us in order to exist, that it would be as it is even if we humans were not here to know it. There is nothing particularly profound about this suggestion in itself, but Bradbury's use of the poem in this particular story makes an unusual connection between the natural world and the world of technology, which also does not seem to need us in order to exist. Though it is the natural world that all but destroys the technology of the house, technology itself—like the world of nature—is also able to go on without us.

What "August 2026" suggests then is more than a simple conflict between civilization and nature. Rather, in this story, Bradbury notes that human life is poised quite precariously between the natural world which we believe we have left behind and the technological world which has outdistanced us, and, to our misfortune, neither of these worlds needs us to be what it is.

—Welch D. Everman

AURA
by Carlos Fuentes, 1962

Aura, one of Carlos Fuentes's most characteristic novellas, evinces extensive acquaintance with mythology and number symbolism. Fuentes's use of the occult, archetypes, and witches are significant. Equally important are phases of what Robert Graves calls "the White Goddess," the triple deity of birth, love, and death, manifest in the new, full, and waning moon. Her cult subsumes that of her consort (son/husband), a sacrificial hero-god periodically slain, then reincarnated in a successor.

Aura's young male protagonist (like the hero of Fuentes's story, "In a Flemish Garden") enters a strange, unnatural, magic house or garden with its own climate and remnants of the past (signifying a different, independent temporal dimension), meets the goddess first as hag and then as maiden, and is ultimately unable to leave the place whose tomblike aspects represent death-in-life. Water or dampness, seasonal change, witchcraft, the cave, night, fertility, vegetation, the numbers three and five, all have primal significance in lunar myths where the moon provokes lunacy or obsession, connoting the evil potential of the feminine principle. All appear in *Aura,* Fuentes's recreation of the mythic White Goddess and her dying/reviving consort.

Felipe, a struggling 27-year-old history teacher, answers an advertisement for a man versed in French to edit, complete, and publish the memoirs of Consuelo's late husband. The job requires living in an old, decaying, aristocratic section of Mexico City in the moldy, crumbling mansion of the ancient widow. Convinced after meeting the beautiful "niece" Aura, he plunges into the surreal, dreamlike, diabolic [under]world of night, full of rotting plants. The cavelike house and night reveal Hecate, the hag (final phase of the triple goddess), incarnate in Consuelo, who predictably possesses powers of magic and witchcraft. Votive lights in her bedroom reflect off silver objects and a mirror, both associated with the moon. The white rabbit on the bed, Consuelo's white hair, her dress, and pallor evoke the White Goddess. The "worn-out red silk of the pillows," the only other color associated with the widow, symbolizes the second lunar phase (love goddess). Aura's green eyes and dress evoke water, the sea, and Venus (in Hispanic literature, green denotes eroticism). The room assigned to Felipe repeats red in the rug and red velvet chair, green in the leather desk top.

Despite a working lightswitch, Aura appears repeatedly holding a candelabra (identifiable with its functional equivalent, the torch, an attribute of Hecate), subtly underscoring the identity of Aura/Consuelo. The single menu—liver and onions, wine, broiled tomatoes—invariably served at every meal, obviously transcends mere nourishment. Tomatoes belong to the same family as other plants Aura cultivates in the damp, dark patio, including henbane, belladonna, and deadly nightshade, whose narcotic or poisonous effects, as Felipe recalls, include weakening the will (overcoming his will to survive) and reducing pains of childbirth (i.e., Consuelo's pangs in producing Aura). The bell Aura rings to summon Felipe to dinner symbolizes creative power and may function magically to maintain Aura in the "real" world. The repetitive motif of the keys—another attribute of Hecate—symbolizes mystery, enigma, or a task to be performed (the obvious relevance of the key to the general's papers, entrusted by Consuelo to Felipe).

Hecate's symbols include dogs, goats, mice, and torches, all appearing in Consuelo's Black Mass celebration and paraphernalia (which reinforces identification with the devil) and the dog's head door-knocker. The garden yew and brambles—not native to Mexico, and therefore contrived (like the climatological manipulations in "In a Flemish Garden")—are discussed by Graves as significant in Druidic rites. The yew, a death-tree throughout Europe, was sacred to Hecate in Italy and Greece; the bramble was sacred to the Triad and Pentad of seasonal goddesses (its leaves on a single stalk vary between three and five). Cats, traditionally associated with witchcraft, populate the general's memoirs, which mention Consuelo's torturing a cat, and Felipe has a fleeting glimpse through the skylight of several writhing, burning cats. Given the general's special fondness for cats, their death could symbolize his "spirit death," an essential prerequisite to reincarnation in Felipe. Felipe's last name, Montero ("hunter") evokes the consort of the huntress, Diana (one of many names of the White Goddess). Felipe symbolically assumes the general's identity upon agreeing to complete his memoirs/autobiography; they share mutual interests in history and French, and—after Felipe's second night in the house—the same woman. The aging photographs of Consuelo and her husband make the dualities unmistakable, as Felipe identifies the youthful

Consuelo as Aura and has only to cover the general's beard and imagine black hair to see himself. One photograph of Consuelo/Aura suggests the nymph ("Aura with her green eyes, her black hair gathered in ringlets, leaning against a Doric column").

The house—labyrinth, womb, and tomb—is Felipe's inescapable destiny. His obsessive dreams evince unconscious realization that remaining means death, although Aura's nocturnal visits submerge his survival instincts in a torrent of eroticism. Discovery of Aura beheading a kid in the kitchen follows shortly after espying the old woman in an ecstatic, orgiastic dance; both acts belong to the cult of Artemis (Diana). When the narrator first meets Aura, she appears about 20 years old. The second time Felipe makes love to her, she is a mature woman (the full moon) whose age he estimates at 40; she is Demeter, the mother (explaining her "maternal" treatment of the lover). Consuelo's appearance the following day in an ancient, yellowed bridal gown—no mere senility—follows the sacrilegious, parasacramental exchange of vows between Aura and Felipe the previous night with Aura's profanation of the Host. Maiden, nymph, and hag, Consuelo/Aura is the triple goddess of past, present, and future: in the darkened room, Felipe embraces the woman he believes to be Aura, as a moonbeam reveals the toothless gums and withered, naked body of the old woman. Sacrificing his youth, he renounces his former life, becoming the reincarnation of the dying/reviving consort of a modern Mexican Diana/Hecate.

—Janet Pérez

AUTUMN SONATA (Sonata de otoño) by Ramón del Valle-Inclán, 1902

Sonata de otoño (1902, "Autumn Sonata," in *The Pleasant Memoirs of the Marquis de Bradomín,* 1924) is the first of four interrelated novelettes composed by Ramón del Valle-Inclán. It illustrates the Modernist penchant for attempting to erase the boundaries between literature and other arts—literature and painting—here the approximation of literature to music. In his series of four "sonatas," Valle entitles each with the name of a season: *Sonata de estío* ("Summer Sonata"), *Sonata de primavera* ("Spring Sonata"), and *Sonata de invierno* ("Winter Sonata"). In each sonata, Valle-Inclán carefully keys everything to the title concept and the stage in life of the central character who links the works. "Autumn Sonata," for example, takes place in the autumn of his life (probably approaching the age of 50), and in the autumn of the year. Setting, mood, imagery, and the lady of the hour are likewise autumnal, melancholic, contemplative, and marked by approaching death. Thus, there is an emphasis on falling leaves, wilting flowers, dried herbs, darkening skies, chill in the air, and numerous omens of fatality (seen in retrospect, these constitute foreshadowing).

One of the major influences in "Autumn Sonata" is Decadentism, notable not only in the exquisite refinement of style, the emphasis on the artificial (the museum-like atmosphere of the palace and gardens) and abnormal (the narrator-protagonist is degenerate to a point approaching the pathological), but also the Decadent belief in the superior beauty of dead or dying things. Thus, the heroine—who is dying of consumption—appears to the narrator as possessed of ethereal beauty with her wan pallor, which he irreverently likens to a Mater Dolorosa. Narrative content is subordinated to creation of an artistic whole through impressionistic techniques and musical, sensuous prose, to evoke a strong response, not so much intellectual as emotional or sensual.

The most characteristic creation of Valle-Inclán's early period (1895-1905) is his narrator-protagonist, the Marquis of Bradomín, an inveterate Don Juan, a Carlist (conservative monarchist), and a Catholic, whose religion serves most frequently to heighten his perverse pleasure as he reflects that the deadly sin then being committed may result in his (or her) eternal damnation. The Galician Marquis, the quintessential Decadent hero, incorporates aspects of Baudelaire's dandy and Neitzsche's Overman, as well as being vaguely satanic. Insofar as he resembles literary models, Bradomin is metaliterary and intertextual; however, some commentators have also identified him as an alter ego of Valle-Inclán, pointing to the author's amputated left arm and Bradomín's suffering a similar mutilation in the final sonata. Nevertheless, certain passages leave little doubt as to Valle-Inclán's ironic distancing of himself from the character, his sly parodies of literary models, and burlesque attitude.

The atmosphere is thoroughly aristocratic, with aesthetic values foregrounded and objects subtly calculated to underscore nobility and wealth. The elaborate, polished, highly lyrical style uses numerous Modernist techniques and motifs, incorporating archaisms, alliteration, lyric cadence, and bits of Galician dialect. In Impressionist fashion, Valle-Inclán stresses light and dark, the play of sunlight on windows, moonlight on the floor, shadows in the garden, candlelight on a wall, reflections of light on metals, water, and mirrors, all of which contributes to an air of unreality, a dreamlike ambient. The author emphasizes jewelry, tapestry, statuary, paintings, rich fabrics, antique furniture, heavy draperies and hangings, carved goblets, portraits of titled ancestors, marble staircases, patterned gardens, gushing fountains—all the trappings of affluence and power—and everywhere he places art objects, from illuminated Medieval manuscripts to hand-carved chests and golden ornaments. In common with Spanish Modernist writing, this is a mannered work, a period piece reminiscent of museum reproductions, with deliberate exaggeration and stylization.

Valle-Inclán juxtaposes death and eroticism, piety and satanism, prurience and purity; the narrative consciousness frequently displays a sacrilegious bent. The action is largely confined to the Galician palace of Brandeso where Bradomín goes upon receipt of a letter from his cousin and former lover, Concha, informing him that she is dying of consumption; her last wish is to see him again. Her paleness and terror of dying in mortal sin paradoxically stimulate his desire. Bradomín persuades her to spend the night with him despite her wish to remain chaste in order to go to confession in the morning. His pleasure is enhanced by thoughts of her dying during their lovemaking, as indeed happens. Valle-Inclán employs auditory and visual impressions to evoke fear in his readers, an aspect of his skillful composition found in his stories of Galician ambient, mystery, superstition, witchcraft, and the supernatural.

When Bradomín goes to alert another cousin, Isabel, to Concha's death, Isabel misinterprets the motive of his visit, and rather than disillusion her, he makes love to Isabel also before taking Concha's body back to her own bedroom. Feigning ignorance the following morning, he sends Con-

cha's young daughters to discover the body, and the work ends with their terrified shrieks and sobbing.

Like many writers from Romanticism onward, Valle-Inclán professed a scorn of the bourgeoisie and shared the common artistic desire to shock or scandalize. Therefore, Bradomín's actions are reinforced by his allusions to the Marquis de Sade and other well-known pornographers of the 19th century, as the narrator-protagonist parades his own sexual prowess and knowledge of erotica. That this was not Valle-Inclán's alter ego seems clear, however, from the unmistakable sociopolitical critiques of his mature works and his own contrasting personal life. "Autumn Sonata" is the best of the four novelettes, probably because it treats the region Valle knew best, and it epitomizes the first stage of his evolution, diametrically opposed to his later development.

—Janet Pérez

AXOLOTL
by Julio Cortázar, 1964

The Jardin des Plantes is located near the Sorbonne in one of the oldest and most appealing neighborhoods of Paris, just along the Left Bank of the Seine. It is a place the Argentine author Julio Cortázar might well have spent an afternoon during his expatriate years, for it serves as the occasion for a story both sympathetic in its appreciation of the city's charms and foreboding in its essential loneliness. It is also subtly unnerving in its combination of realistic and fantastic elements, especially so as the joining of the two is virtually seamless.

Scarcely two thousand words in length, the story "Axolotl" (collected in *Final de juego*) is representative of fiction crafted by South American writers known as "magical realism," a style of work that introduces patently preposterous subjects and events in an offhand manner and then explores their natures in a closely detailed way. The title itself would be meaningful only to a marine biologist, and so the story's narrator takes time to look up the name in a library: "axolotls are the larval stage (provided with gills) of a species of salamander of the genus Ambystoma." Although he does not identify himself as Latin American, the narrator notes carefully that the creatures are Mexican in origin and Aztec in facial appearance. Where in the city, "one spring morning when Paris was spreading its peacock tail after a wintry Lent," can they be seen? In the aquarium at the Jardin des Plantes, where the narrator has begun his tale, advising that "there was a time when I thought a great deal about the axolotls," and revealing, just two lines later in the story's first paragraph, "Now I am an axolotl."

The gap between the narrator's two confessions (of interest, of identity) create the space Cortázar's story must fill. That the action begins "by chance" makes its tone all the more effective, for terror disarms best when presented as happenstance (a feature of Poe's tales of the fantastic set in a Paris of a century and a half before). Justification for the ultimate transfer of being from human to beast can be found in the stylistics of the story's first page, where the narrator customarily uses the personal pronoun to identify the zoo's animals during his frequent visits: he gets off "my bike" to look at "my panther." But the big cats (whom he describes as "friends") are either asleep or looking sad (another anthropomorphic projection), so he drifts into the aquarium building, is bored with the fish, but "unexpectedly . . . hit it off with the axolotls."

Unable to think of anything else, the narrator immerses himself in dictionary definitions and descriptions—a handy device to both educate and intellectually seduce his readers, for such seduction is what is happening to him as the axolotls command more and more of his attention. Even though his frequent visits confuse the aquarium guards, he returns to spend more and more time in front of the axolotl's tank. "There's nothing strange in this," he advises, "because after the first minute I knew we were linked." Which is strange indeed, all the more so as the language and mood behind it take on a tone of compulsion, a confession that "something infinitely lost and distant kept pulling us together." He has looked up the creatures' Spanish name and related them to Aztecs, but other features remind him of Chinese glass figurines. His rapt attention is complemented with (and even justified by) the information he provides; much as a casual browser can become caught up unsuspectingly in a random encyclopedia entry and the wealth of knowledge it contains, so too does the narrator let himself be figuratively devoured by the little aquatic beings (who are, his library research tells him, edible and productive of a fluid useable as cod-liver oil).

But how does he *become* an axolotl? For this, Cortázar guides the reader through several careful stages. First his narrator picks one axolotl for study, its tiny hands and slim fingers (with almost human nails) suggesting personal identity. With one such creature singled out and allowed to be itself, the narrative's motion becomes the animal's own, the miniscule motion of its gills described with the attention usually given only to matters of great scope and importance. And that this point the personal pronoun makes its almost subliminal reappearance: "It's that we don't enjoy moving a lot, and the tank is so cramped." Yet the axolotl's barest movement has been noted, and that

close notation has made the center of perception the axolotl's own.

Close study also breeds a philosophical fascination, a perception of the animal's "secret will to abolish space and time with indifferent immobility." Their eyes, so physically different from those of human beings, "spoke to me of the presence of a different life, of another way of seeing." The eyes know more than he does; they know that, despite all claims to the contrary, they are *not* animals, but just another order of sentience the narrator has learned to share.

A subsequent paragraph debates mythological propositions, but dismisses them. Instead, an indentification of being (and not just allusion) has taken place. Nor is there a simple, common explanation in psychology, that "my own sensibility was projecting a nonexistent consciousness upon the axolotls," for that would be the device of traditional and not magical realism, an excuse for everything fabulous that has transpired.

By the story's end, the narrator is speaking as always with his face to the glass—only now it is inside, looking out at the human being who comes each day to visit. The window and its reflective nature make this transfer mechanically possible, just as the structural situation of a human staring at the animals staring at the human creates an infinitely replicable narrative. That there can be closure to this method is grammatical: the last paragraph begins with the pronoun "He" to describe the visitor while the "I" is not just an animal, but an animal that can wonder if "perhaps he is going to write a story about us"—a plural form that includes both animals and human being—"that, believing he's making up a story, he's going to write all this about axolotls."

—Jerome Klinkowitz

B

BABYLON REVISITED
by F. Scott Fitzgerald, 1931

In a letter to his daughter, Fitzgerald wrote, "I not only announced the birth of my young illusions in *This Side of Paradise* but pretty much the death of them in some of my last *Post* stories like 'Babylon Revisited.'" While "Babylon Revisited" was not in fact among his last stories published in *The Saturday Evening Post,* he did place it at the end of *Taps at Reveille,* and it stands at the end of his career as well: he was working on a film version in Hollywood when he died. Chronologically the story fits nicely into the middle of Fitzgerald's career. He wrote it in December 1930, a decade after the publication of his first novel, and ten years before his death. Its setting of Paris during the Depression recalls the story "The Bridal Party"; its self-destructive hero suggests Bill McChesney of the earlier "Two Wrongs" and Dick Diver of the later *Tender Is the Night,* both of them, like Charlie Wales, modified self-portraits of their creator.

The meeting of the author's past and future in the story corresponds to the central concern of "Babylon Revisited," the protagonist's desire to recover something important that he has lost. In the late 1920's Charlie Wales had joined the crowds of rich Americans in Paris, the Babylon of the title, in their dissipated, extravagant behavior. He loses his money in the crash of 1929, but by then his wife has died, his child, Honoria, has been taken from him, and his drinking has impaired his health to the extent that he has gone to a sanitarium. As he tells Paul, the bartender at the Ritz, "I lost everything I wanted in the boom."

He has returned to Paris from Prague, where he has again become financially successful, to reclaim his daughter, whose name represents the honor he has lost and wants to recover, and she also stands for his hopes for the future. The girl is being cared for by Marion Peters, Charlie's sister-in-law, and her husband, Lincoln. Their names, too, are emblematic, Lincoln standing for the older American values that Charlie senses in their presence. Significantly, Lincoln did not share in the prosperity and dissipation of the 1920's. The Peters are solid, as the Latin derivation of their name, "petrus" (rock), implies. Before they will surrender custody of Honoria they want proof that the former goodtime Charlie has become what he—and only he—calls himself, the sober Charles.

Charlie willingly confronts his past, returning to the bar of the Ritz where he had spent so much of his time and money. The opening scene establishes Charlie as a survivor: all the other members of the old crowd have succumbed to death, disease, or disgrace. Charlie demonstrates his strong character by taking one drink, but only one, to show that he can confront temptation without reverting to his former self. Yet questions about his reformation linger. In the evening when he rides past his former haunts, he no longer finds them alluring, but he does buy a ticket to watch Josephine Baker's nude dancing. He also "incautiously [puts] his head inside" an "ancient rendezvous" before retreating, and he leaves his in-laws' address for Duncan Schaeffer and Lorraine Quarles, "ghosts out of the past" who will return to wreak their revenge.

Marion's doubts about Charlie's transformation may therefore not be groundless, though much of her resentment derives from jealousy. Charlie prospered without working, while the Peters worked hard and earned far less. Now again Charlie is making more money than they. Yet she reluctantly agrees to give up Honoria, until Duncan and Lorraine appear, drunk as usual, at the Peters's apartment. The ghosts of Charlie's past destroy his opportunity, at least for now. In the final scene Charlie remains faithful to his code of taking only one drink, despite the temptation to drown his grief. He asks the bartender what he owes; Charlie is willing to pay for his drinks and his mistakes, but he thinks, "They couldn't make him pay forever." But perhaps they can.

Charlie's plight mirrors that of his country and his creator, deluded for a time by an overeasy prosperity and trying to regain the values lost during that strange interlude. Charlie discovers that the past cannot be obliterated. In the 1920's one imagined that even such erasure was possible; dollars or francs could do anything. "If you didn't want it to be snow, you just paid some money." Now he recognizes, in T.S. Eliot's words, "Time present and time past/Are both perhaps present in time future." Two images reenforce this motif of time. At the end of the third section Charlie dreams of his wife, Helen, "swinging faster and faster," like a pendulum, and in the fourth section Lincoln Peters swings Honoria "back and forth" in the same way.

Fitzgerald creates sympathy for Charlie by emphasizing his history of hard work and his devotion to Honoria. The third person point of view nevertheless creates an objective distance that allows the reader to recognize Charlie's past errors and present flaws. The organization of the story also reveals Fitzgerald's careful craftsmanship. The five sections correspond to the five acts of a play, and the first, second, and fourth move from light to darkness, with the fifth set entirely at night. Only the middle section partially and temporarily reverses this progression, as Charlie is at the height of his fortune, having secured Marion's consent to take Honoria. Yet even this section concludes, like all the others, with Charlie's isolation. Structure thus intensifies the melancholy mood that pervades the story.

Like the future of America and Fitzgerald, Charlie's future remains unclear. Unlike Bill McChesney of "Two Wrongs," and Dick Diver of *Tender Is the Night,* Charlie perseveres. Yet he ends where he began, in the bar of the Ritz, alone. Not least among the charms of "Babylon Revisited" is its open-endedness. Will Charlie's Babylonian exile end in restoration, or will he be weighed in the balance and be found wanting?

—Joseph Rosenblum

632

BALL OF FAT (Boule de Suif)
by Guy de Maupassant, 1880

When the war between Prussia and France broke out in 1870, the 19-year-old law student Guy de Maupassant enlisted as a private in the French army. He served in Normandy with a regiment that was badly equipped and rather futile. The regiment retreated in disarray and Maupassant was almost taken prisoner. In less than a year, the French lost the war. But Maupassant's brief army service provided him with the background material for "Boule de Suif" ("Ball of Fat").

When peace returned to France, Maupassant settled in Paris. He went to work for the Ministry of the Navy and he began to write fiction. His writing mentor was the great novelist Gustave Flaubert, a close friend of his mother. Through Flaubert, Maupassant came to associate with some of the great writers of the day—Zola, Daudet, Edmond de Goncourt, and Turgenev. Along with other writers, Maupassant regularly visited Zola at his home in Medan. In 1880, a book of short stories, *Les Soirées de Medán* (Evenings at Medan), was a result of these gatherings. The book contains six stories by six different writers on the subject of the Franco-Prussian War. Maupassant's contribution was "Ball of Fat," his first published story, a story that Flaubert called a masterpiece.

What makes this story a masterpiece is its symmetrical structure, its descriptions, its characterizations, and the power of its irony and satire. Maupassant brings together on a winter morning in Rouen ten travelers who represent easily distinguishable types in French society. There are the count and countess, the cotton magnate Carré-Lamadon and his wife, the wine merchant Loiseau and his wife. Here we have, therefore, in the order of decreasing social status, "the strong, established society of good people with religion and principle." They of course are the chief targets of the young Maupassant's satire. On the journey to Dieppe, he shows that what these pillars of society have most in common is their hypocrisy.

From these "good people with religion and principle," we would expect to see such qualities as compassion and generosity, loyalty and patriotism, gratitude; Maupassant shows that under the surface these qualities are completely lacking. Among the ten are two nuns; for them as well, convenience takes precedence over principle. Two of the great achievements of this story are the characters of Cornudet the democrat and the woman after whom the story is titled. Relentlessly, Maupassant reveals Cornudet, the supposed defender of the common people, to be nothing more than an artful posturer. And the "Ball of Fat" who sells herself is shown to be the most genuine person among the ten.

On the first day of the journey, Maupassant begins the process of stripping away respect for the respectable people and building admiration for the prostitute. Ball of Fat is the only traveler who has had the foresight to bring along food and drink. Despite their scornful manner towards her, she offers to share her provisions with the others. She does not, however, win their gratitude. Indeed, the ladies become even more scornful and "they would have liked to kill her, or throw her and her drinking cup, her basket, and her provisions out of the coach into the snow of the road below." Nevertheless they do partake of her food and drink.

At the Commercial Hotel in Tôtes, where the travelers are to spend the night, an unexpected problem develops. The Prussian officer who lives at the hotel wants Ball of Fat to go to bed with him. Surprisingly, she refuses. Out of her love of France, she will have nothing to do with an officer of the enemy. She already has repulsed Cornudet, because she will not do what she usually does when there are Prussians in the house. Ball of Fat refuses to go to bed with the Prussian officer, and he, in turn, refuses to let the travelers proceed with their trip. What was to be an overnight stop could turn into an indefinite stay. Her fellow travelers are being inconvenienced, and they become angry. Why must she be so stubborn? What has she to lose? All the pillars of society, their wives, and one of the nuns attempt to break her resolve. On the third day, it is the count who takes her for a walk, determined to wear down her resistance—with kindness, logic, guilt, flattery, with whatever it takes. And finally he succeeds. It is the aristocrat—one of the best—who persuades Ball of Fat to abandon her principles and not be so patriotic.

When the journey is resumed, the pillars of society cannot allow themselves to be grateful to the prostitute; instead, their scorn is greater than ever. In the haste and confusion of the departure from Tôtes, Ball of Fat did not bring provisions for the rest of the trip. The others have. But they do not share with Ball of Fat, for after all she has shamed herself by going to bed with the Prussian. Cornudet, with four hard-boiled eggs, does not offer one to Ball of Fat; instead he taunts her by humming the *Marseillaise*. That, we realize, is Cornudet's purpose in life—to taunt. With this contrast to the earlier scene in which Ball of Fat gladly shared her food and drink, Maupassant achieves a most pleasing symmetry.

He also achieves a pleasing effect through the narrowing of the focus from beginning to end. For the story begins with the brilliantly described scenes of the bedraggled French army in retreat and the city of Rouen under enemy occupation. At the end of the story the scene is the narrow confines of the coach. Within that small space, the pillars of society finally are able to cast out and exile the prostitute. But by that point only she has the reader's sympathy. And of the three men who would regard themselves as pillars of Rouen society, it is the coarse and vulgar wine merchant who is the least unlikable; for he is the least hypocritical. While Maupassant is at times heavy-handed in his satire, at other times he is quite subtle, as with the characterizations of the nun, Mme. Carré-Lamadon, and Cornudet. All in all, Flaubert was right. "Ball of Fat" is a masterpiece of the short story.

—Paul Marx

THE BALLAD OF THE SAD CAFÉ
by Carson McCullers, 1951

The Ballad of the Sad Café is Carson McCullers's most nearly perfect treatment of her most common theme—the mystery of the love relationship. It is also a classic example of what has come to be known as southern gothic or southern grotesque. Forsaking any attempt at realism, the story is a lyrical parable or fairy tale that takes place in a world less physical than poetic, involving characters less real than mythical. As critics have pointed out, the genius of the work depends on the voice of the narrator who transforms what otherwise might be either foolish or repellent into the stuff of legend and dream.

The plot has the simplicity of myth and the triangular set of characters that constitute it have the mythic aura of the transcendent—from the giant man/woman Miss Amelia, to her equally giant adversary Marvin Macy, to the trickster figure of the dwarfish little hunchback Cousin Lymon. The story is so filled with narcissistic mirror reflections that it turns inward on itself like the crossed eyes of Miss Amelia, which are "turned inward so sharply that they seem to be exchanging with each other one long and secret gaze of grief." It is as though the story springs from a single projective consciousness for whom all the characters are poetic embodiments of desire.

As the central expository passage of this long story or novella suggests, the basic theme is the relationship between the lover and the beloved. The narrator argues that although love is a joint experience between two people, the lover and the beloved come from "different countries." The beloved is merely a stimulus for the stored-up love within the lover, and the lover suffers because he or she knows that love is a solitary thing. The beloved can be of any description, says the narrator, for the quality of any love is determined by the lover. Thus, everyone wants to be the lover, for the state of being beloved is intolerable to most. "The beloved fears and hates the lover, and with the best of reasons. For the lover is forever trying to strip bare his beloved."

McCullers's story is a grotesque working out of these philosophic truths. Although the central part of the plot revolves around the mysterious arrival of the hunchback and the equally mysterious transformation of the formerly forbidding Miss Amelia into the doting lover of the indifferent and exploitative Cousin Lymon, the background for the story focuses on Miss Amelia's marriage many years before to Marvin Macy, for whom she was the beloved. But Miss Amelia rejects this role and sends her despondent lover Macy away. When Macy, now a famed criminal who has served time in prison, returns and becomes the beloved to Cousin Lymon, the story moves inevitably toward a classic battle between the two giants for the little man. The story reaches its climax when just as Miss Amelia is about to triumph, Cousin Lymon leaps on her back like a small animal and helps turn the tide in Macy's favor. The hunchback's departure with his beloved leaves Miss Amelia cracked and broken.

Serving as the backdrop for this triangular relationship is the town itself, a classical chorus for whom the central god-like figures serve as a necessary unifying force. When Miss Amelia becomes the lover of the hunchback, the community becomes unified around the café, "the warm center of the town," in communal gatherings inspired by the magic liquor distilled by Miss Amelia. Cousin Lymon is a magical creature who has an "instinct to establish immediate and vital contact between himself and all things in the world." He is the archetypal mysterious stranger; no one knows who he is, how old he is, or where he came from.

When Cousin Lymon runs off with Marvin Macy, the town becomes lonesome and sad, "like a place that is far off and estranged from all other places in the world." Instead of joining them in a communal oneness, the only liquor available makes the people dream themselves into a dangerous inward world. The story, however, ends with a coda that suggests that in spite of the break-up of the communal order established by the lover between Miss Amelia and the little hunchback, there still remains a metaphor of unity, albeit a unity in despair, in the

description of "The Twelve Moral Men." The narrator describes a chain gain of seven black men and five white men who sing a song both somber and joyful that seems to come not from the men themselves but from the earth itself.

The Ballad of the Sad Café is one of the best known modern examples of what might be called short fiction's tendency toward the principle of incarnation. Even as the world of the story is that of hard physical reality, the poetic power of the storyteller transforms profane reality into the realm of the sacred, projecting human desire in its most elemental forms.

—Charles E. May

———

THE BALLOON
by Donald Barthelme, 1968

One of the targets in Barthelme's second collection of short stories, *Unspeakable Practices, Unnatural Acts*, is society's blind gropings for truth. Barthelme probes the problems, if not the impossibility, of discovering meaning both in the external world and one's own consciousness. Words, he seems to conclude, are our only connection with the inner and outer worlds, but they are seductive in making us believe we can traverse the gap between question and knowledge. The collection treats a number of specific subjects—e.g., the relationship between war and mechanized society, the search for meaning in politics, art, science, and personal relationships, the privacy of love, the failure of language. One of Barthelme's richest stories is "The Balloon." Funny, complex, and replete with verbal and visual acrobatics, it incorporates all but the first of the themes just enumerated.

The plot is simple. A balloon suddenly appears in New York, covering the area from 14th Street to Central Park. Had it a name like "Goodyear," those who saw it could have handled it and thus placed it into perspective—into a category of mind. But because the nameless balloon is merely suspended, for 22 days, it is treated as a situation. Such a state of the unknowable, the unclassifiable, the mysterious, evokes a variety of responses.

For seven or so pages, the speaker then describes the balloon's texture and numerous reactions to it. Some people find it fascinating and argue about its meaning. When these intellectual discussions prove unsatisfying, some decide to physically enjoy the balloon, and they jump, stroll, race, and bounce on it. Others—and every response is dependent upon one's basic, innate temperament—are timid or hostile; they are frustrated by the balloon. One group performs secret tests to try to make the balloon go away. All, however, "interpret" it according to their own frames of reference, and Barthelme has a heyday tracing the gamut of responses. In the end, most people cope with the balloon pragmatically, and it becomes a meeting place. As Barthelme puts it, "marginal intersections offered entrances."

The speaker, however, warns: "Each intersection was crucial, none could be ignored." In other words, to each person, his or her own intersection or "reading" was as valid as any other one. Finally, "it was suggested" that the virtue of the balloon, given all these intersections, was its "randomness." That is, it offered people any number of possibilities and hence the possibility of the "mislocation of the self," a way of getting out of a rut.

This sort of material fills seven pages. Only in the last paragraph does the speaker explain: "I met you under the balloon, on the occasion of your return from Norway; you asked if it was mine; I said it was . . . a spontaneous autobiographical disclosure, having to do with the unease I felt at your absence, and with sexual deprivation." The speaker, so it would appear, has subsequently removed and stored the balloon, "awaiting some other time of unhappiness, sometime, perhaps, when we are angry with one another."

On close reading and rereading (which most of Barthelme's fictions demand), it becomes clear that from the beginning, the balloon—like one's story, or one's words, or one's comprehension of life—has been controlled by the speaker. The balloon is meaningful to him alone (and not his lover, and not even Barthelme!). He admits at the start: "*I* stopped it." He continues: "*I* asked the engineers to see to it." The reader's pleasure in the story lies in Barthelme's playfulness toward the human need, and yet frequent failure, to understand signs and his parody of social science jargon. In describing how critical opinion toward the balloon was divided, for example, he writes:

::::::: "abnormal vigor"
"warm, soft, lazy passages"
"Has unity been sacrificed for a sprawling quality?"
"Quelle catastrophe!"
"munching"

In another funny passage that uses the word "sullied" several times, Barthelme spoofs the reading of foreign signs. On a more serious level, he says: "It is wrong to speak of 'situations,' implying sets of circumstances leading to some resolution, some escape of tension; there were no situations, simply the balloon hanging there." And with his usual satire on the experts, and word-play on "inflation," he writes: "Now we have had a flood of original ideas in all media, works of singular beauty as well as significant milestones in the history of inflation, but at that present moment, there was only this *balloon*, concrete particular, hanging there."

Barthelme does something extraordinary here, only suggested in the volume's other excellent stories "Indian Uprising" and "Me and Miss Mandible." Here, in this metafiction—another story about writing stories—he takes Stephen Dedalus's definition of the dramatic artist, in *A Portrait of the Artist as a Young Man*, and pushes it as far as he can. Joyce defines the dramatic artist as standing totally aloof from his creation and "paring his fingernails." Barthelme here focuses on the impersonality not just of the artist but of the word itself (what he calls "the concrete particular"). He writes a story, a "distraction," that really has no need for the reader as interpreter. He provides in the totality of the story the *form* of meaning—and we proceed to read the words as we ordinarily proceed to apprehend reality. But Barthelme has done this without any fixed, definable material behind his structure. What he illustrates is how form is only form, rather than meaning. In other words, the meaning of the balloon is that the balloon has no meaning. It is all air within a structure or a covering.

And yet the deeper irony is that the story ultimately does mean something. As the balloon is to the speaker, so is the story to the balloon. Each is another level of metaphor, a description of experience, clarifying the one before. That is, first the balloon is the emblem or externalized symbol of what the speaker—not Barthelme—is feeling, and this is

totally personal *to the speaker*. The narrator gives it only the most general (sexual) significance, and both the reader and Barthelme remain in the dark as to its precise significance. It is the speaker's balloon.

But the balloon—an utterly wonderful life image—as it is described, goes beyond its emotional or sexual significance to inevitably become the "concrete particular," since the speaker's (or anyone's) communication of (felt) experience must be clothed in images, or concrete particulars, in language. As such, it is both literally and figuratively removed from life; it is a balloon, both as metaphor and as concrete (or imagined) reality.

Finally, the balloon, like the story, like all words and like life, expands and connects, and in its state of infinite movement, it elicits (or means) as many things as one can attribute to it. It lacks an absolute and fixed meaning, as it simultaneously elicits a variety of responses and significations. To paraphrase Barthelme, it offers the possibility and the process of interpretation, where at "any intersection" one can react in any number of ways. The participant—the reader, like the lover-narrator—becomes the ultimate artist or creator, and depending upon his or her system, grid, or frame of reference, constructs, or manipulates, or rejects, or simply plays with, whatever responses the balloon elicits. These then inevitably color the reader's experience, which indeed, for the time one is involved with these responses, change and "mislocate" reality. We are left with the same internal contradiction about the meaningful/meaningless nature of words, roles, and experience itself.

—Lois Gordon

———

THE BALLROOM OF ROMANCE
by William Trevor, 1972

William Trevor is one of the leading short story writers in the British Isles. Trevor's overall accomplishment is so various and strong that none of his 90 or so published stories has become a chestnut. Relatively few of them have been anthologized. His own favorite seems to be "In Isfahan" from *Angels at the Ritz* (1975), which Graham Greene deemed the best collection of stories in English since *Dubliners*. That was true until the publication of Trevor's *Lovers of Their Time* (1978).

"The Ballroom or Romance," the title story of an earlier collection (1972), is one of Trevor's stories of provincial life in Ireland, life as endured in straitened circumstances by the poor and lower-middle class. That Trevor knows what goes on during the days and nights of such folk, laboring people who work unremittingly on small farms and in small shops, is but one representative instance of the vast range of the characters and experience that appear in his fiction.

Bridie, the protagonist and viewpoint character of "The Ballroom of Romance," is a "girl" of 36 years who is immured on a small farm owned by her crippled father, a widower. Her life is frozen in its accustomed patterns and will be until he dies; the same applies to most of the middle-aged bachelors of her acquaintance, men who are bound to their hard-hearted widowed mothers and to their own timid and lethargic ways. "The bachelors would never marry. . . . They were wedded already."

Trevor here permits himself a few such small instances of humor, but none at Bridie's expense. People, especially Justin Dwyer, owner of the shabby but remunerative Ballroom of Romance, ask after her father but have no intention of visiting the one-legged man. Only the priest does that. Each week Dwyer worries about the middle-aged bachelors like Bowser Egan, Tim Daley, and Eyes Horgan who come "down from the hills like mountain goats, released from their mammies and from the smell of animals and soil," and who drink on the sly. They required Dwyer's close attention, as his wife reminds him at the dance hall each Saturday night. Eyes Horgan and the rest, including Egan, are little more than randy overgrown boys whose sexual impulses outrun their actual performances by a long measure. It is the bachelors whom Trevor satirizes, not their mothers or the objects of their attention in the dance hall. He sees the sad prospect of Bridie and the other middle-aged women who are unmarried, making it painfully clear that marriage to one of the hopeless bachelors is worse than the present circumstances of these aging women.

In such a world Saturday night offers a brief surcease from toil and tedium, but Saturday night in this world is so routine to these people that to most of us it is itself tedious, dull, banal. The Saturday night during which the action of "The Ballroom of Romance" unfolds enables the author to reveal the whole story and tenor of Bridie's circumscribed existence and to reveal the weather of the society in which she lives. What Trevor accomplishes in about 8,000 words is astonishing: he gives us her life history up to this Saturday night, which will have been her last occasion of its kind in her misspent middle age. Bridie decides that she is now too old to return to the Ballroom of Romance and that she must wait for Egan, one of the "homemade bachelors," to claim her hand—after her father and his mother have died. The prospect is bleak at best, and when we see Bridie, the best part of her life, including her failed romance with Patrick Grady, now married and working in England, is long behind. Bridie is a victim of circumstance and duty.

The story is not presented as a bleak chronicle of woe, however. Bridie is inured to her condition and does not feel sorry for herself except on rare occasions, and she has accustomed herself to waiting for the next small turn in her life. Her sudden and complete failure with Patrick has resulted in her being shrewder and more guarded about her prospects. She realizes that her prospects of marriage with Dano Ryan, the drummer in the little band at the Ballroom of Romance, have run out when Dano tells her that the widow who rents him a room has gotten him an appointment with a doctor. "It was a natural outcome," she thinks, "for Mrs. Griffin had all the chances, seeing him every night and morning and not having to make do with weekly encounters in a ballroom." Bridie's revelation continues:

> She thought of Patrick Grady, seeing in her mind his pale, thin face. She might be the mother of four of his children now, or seven or eight maybe. She might be living in Wolverhampton, going out to the pictures in the evenings, instead of looking after a one-legged man. If the weight of circumstances hadn't intervened she wouldn't be standing in a wayside ballroom, mourning the marriage of a road mender [Dano] whom she didn't love. For a moment she thought she might cry. . . . In her life, on the farm or in the house, there was no place for tears. Tears were a luxury.

Poor Bridie has no luxuries, even tears, except for her daydreams; and she dreams the outlines of three marriages—to Patrick, to Dano, to Bowser—each less romantic and hopeful, each more realistic.

Bridie, who is otherwise unnamed (and her father remains nameless), is no bride of Christ; she might be called an instance of the Irish grass widow, although in the exact sense of the term "grass widow" she is neither a renounced mistress nor a wife long separated from her husband. Her foreshortened name, or nickname, is as ironic as her general circumstances; and as the action makes clear, by the time she becomes a bride, Bridie's life will be over, Bowser Egan, her "intended," as she knows, is no catch. She knows him for what he is—lazy, trifling, inclined to excessive drink.

We are interested in Bridie and the sad history of her life because she remains loyal to her father and true to herself with her dignity intact. She does not give up her virtue any more than she abandons her poor crippled father and her work on the farm, upon which they both depend. In a changing world Bridie remains unchanged despite the reversals and frustrations in her life, and so we admire her despite the pathos of her life. Such is one of Trevor's best reports of life in the Irish countryside, a story that might be called an instance of hard pastoral, of bleak life fully imagined and rendered.

—George Core

A BANDIT CHIEF (Yi ge da Wang)
by Shen Congwen, 1934

"Yi ge da Wang" is chapter 16 of *Shen Congwen zizhuan* (Shen Congwen's Autobiography). It was titled "Ta Wang" by Ching Ti and Robert Payne in their translation of Shen Congwen, *The Chinese Earth* (1947) and "A Bandit Chief" by William L. MacDonald in his translation in *Anthology of Chinese Literature* (vol. 2, 1973).

"A Bandit Chief" is a memorable story of character, presenting the dominant character in Liu Yunting, the reformed bandit chief, and two lesser characters, the confessional narrator "I"/"we," who in reality is Shen Congwen as a fictional character; and Wang Yao-mei, the attractive female bandit chief captured and held prisoner by the Sichuan Army. Character depends on time, locale, circumstance, choice, and action. Sometimes locale may be the first element in a situation, for it can be responsible for both atmosphere and action. The details of characterization in the short story, however, must be more selective and brief in extent, more exploited and intensified than in the case of the novel. Although the short story often focuses on character in terms of some single character trait, it is rare that a short story presents a more or less fully developed characterization. "A Bandit Chief" is outstanding in this respect and rivals Robert Louis Stevenson's character drawing in "A Lodging for the Night," a characterization of the criminal-poet François Villon.

The character of a person is shown especially in conjunction with a circumstance that involves complication, causes action and reaction, and demands resolution. In "A Bandit Chief" the protagonist, Liu Yunting, has had his life spared by the commander of the Kan Army, who has "come up through the ranks," and has given up banditry for an army career. He serves the commander "with the loyalty of a slave," having the rank of a sergeant with "the salary and status of a captain." Although of small stature, he is strong, courageous, and a veritable dare-devil. He has killed 200 enemies with his bare hands and has had 17 wives. He is familiar with such crimes as arson, rape, and murder. He subtly conveys how the commission of "such crimes, intolerable to society," still nurtures "such a strong and violent soul."

The Kan Army of West Hunan undertakes a pacification campaign against the numerous bandits in Sichuan in conjunction with the Sichuan Army. As the Kan Army advances, the command post has to stay in Lungtan. Meanwhile, the Sichuan Army pulls out of the garrison area, but stations a platoon at a Buddhist temple on the other side of the river. It is at this temple that the bandit chief finds himself unable to resist temptations, which leads to Liu's tragic downfall —but his choices are freely chosen. The Sichuan Army holds an unusual prisoner—an attractive girl bandit, Wang Yao-mei, a bandit chief at the age of 18. Several young Sichuan officers had gone mad over her and two junior officers "had even killed each other over her." When she had been brought to brigade head-quarters, all the officers had wanted to get at her but were prohibited. Liu Yunting, however, apparently already known to her, visits her in company with the narrator. The narrator finds the female bandit enclosed by a fence and sitting on a bright red rug. On their appearance she arises and walks towards them. She is wearing leg irons. The narrator judges her figure superior to her face. He also learns that she and the great bandit chief have woven a plot together.

Despite Wang Yao-mei's attractiveness, she had a reputa-tion for brutality. The Sichuan commanding officer would have decapitated her except that she had 70 rifles buried somewhere. (At this time rifles were scarce and sold at a premium.) Having made friends with the commanding officer, Liu Yunting gained access to the woman. He persuades her that he had 60 rifles buried on the Hunan border, and that he was trying to bring about her release so that they could recover the rifles and resume the bandit life together.

The next morning the Sichuan officers and soldiers learn that the sergeant had stayed with her during the night. What the sergeant had done was taboo in the military. A non-commissioned officer, he had taken what had been forbidden to commissioned officers. Furthermore, he was an outsider, not a member of the Sichuan Army but of the Kan (Hunan) Army. The Sichuanese persuade themselves that the sergeant was guilty of rape, considered a horrible taboo by a society trained in Confucian principles. The troops of the platoon block the gate so that the sergeant could not pass through and return to his Kan unit. He buckles on his cartridge belt and draws his two pistols, so they let him go. They drag the girl bandit from her quarters and decapitate her. While waiting the blow of the sword on her neck, she is calm and utters no word: "When her head fell to the ground, her body did not fall over." Her bravery in the face of death would give her "face" with her kin and her village. In facing decapitation, she knew how to kneel so that her headless corpse would face up and thus benefit her reincarnation, an idea fully developed by Chinese Buddhists. A pool of blood was left at the spot where she had been beheaded, as well as a pile of white ash. The white ash resulted from the burning of paper money, otherwise known as "spirit money." According to Chinese folklore religion, the living are obliged to protect the spirits of deceased family members. The passage from this world into the next involves many expenses such as for guides, passports, visas, even for bribes, since the bureaucracy of the spirit world is as corrupt as the bureaucracy of this world. Hence, when a person dies "spirit money" is burned to assure that the person's spirit will be able to meet all the expenses occurring in the spirit world.

When the sergeant learns what had happened to Wang Yao-mei, he is downcast and guilt-ridden. He says to the narrator; "Yao-mei died because of me, so I wept for seven days, but now it's all right." It is not long, however, before he covets a launderer's wife, which gets him in trouble with the commander. When Liu Yunting begs the commander for mercy, the commander replies: "Don't say anything to make you lose more face." While the narrator watches, the great chief is pushed out, and he never sees him again.

In Chinese society, if a person does something that is socially unacceptable, that person is said "to lose face" (qui mian zi). If, however, a person behaves correctly according to society's view, or if a person's status is raised, then that person is said "to save face" (bao quan mianzi), which is to gain and not lose face. In China, if a person fails to keep one's temper, that person "loses face." The loss of face is a serious matter in China, and the great chief's loss of face in a variety of ways causes his personal tragedy. Any military organization requires its members to subordinate their personal wishes to those of the whole.

The narrator sketches in his own character very well. As a soldier he is an enlisted man and a raw recruit. At the same time he is educated and cultured. He practices calligra-phy—"the law of the brush"—and carries with him several volumes of collections of famous examples of calligraphy. He also reads traditional prose and poetry. He treasures poems by Li Shang-yin (fl.836), whose work is noted for its "elegance and obscurity." Liu Yunting, also, has a cultural side to him. He could sing arias from old-style Chinese military operas such as Chua-chu san lu (Taking the Three Passes) and Po huai si men (Destroying the Four Gates).

"A Bandit Chief" ends with a kind of moral based on the theme that "those who live by the sword die by the sword." The narrator points out that following the execution of Liu Yunting by Commander Chang, Chang himself was assassi-nated in Chenchou, Hunan, by Captain Tian. Then the Hunan chairman, Ye Kai Yin, assassinated Tian. All this implies, it would seem, that the warlords of this period in the early 1920's were little better than bandits themselves, a rather cynical view. The establishment of the Chinese Republic in 1912 introduced for China a long period of instability. Droughts, floods, starvation, and lack of moder-nization played havoc with China's economy. Both the government and the army fell apart. Bandit armies ravaged the countryside until political organization lapsed into warlordism. The story of "A Bandit Chief" takes place during this unsettled and disunified period.

—Richard P. Benton

BARN BURNING
by William Faulkner, 1938

"Barn Burning" was born in the intense activity of William Faulkner's most brilliant decade. *Absalom, Absa-lom!* behind him, he gave increasing thought to the Snopes family, poor whites with stories worth telling—as he had already intimated in *As I Lay Dying* when Anse Bundren, his mules having drowned, is forced to buy a team from Flem Snopes. For writers in the 1930's, stories about the poor were seemingly mandatory, but Faulkner presented his characters from a much larger perspective than did most fiction writers of the time. He placed them in a context that demanded that they be seen in a history and a locale, not merely as victims of a flawed economic system. Like the monied and established families of his fiction, Faulkner's poor are held accountable for their moral failures. Whereas much proletarian fiction of the 1930's now seems dated, Faulkner's Snopeses continue to intrigue and to challenge readers. Rooted in the lower class, they are larger than their class and speak across it.

Among Faulkner's most brilliant efforts in the short story, "Barn Burning" is regularly anthologized. In 1980 a dramatization of it appeared on the Public Broadcasting System as part of the "American Short Story" series produced by the National Endowment for the Humanities. The series included only writers who had made a substantial contribution to the genre. "Barn Burning" was a fitting choice to represent Faulkner; the story stands with such classics as "The Man That Corrupted Hadleyburg," "The Blue Hotel," and "Soldier's Home."

Were there no Snopeses elsewhere in Faulkner's fiction, "Barn Burning" would still command attention. The story is, however, interesting as a prelude to the Snopes trilogy— *The Hamlet*, *The Town*, and *The Mansion*. Flem Snopes, the most outrageous member of their tribe, is the unifying character of the trilogy. Although "Barn Burning" portrays Flem and his parents, Flem's name (unpleasant in the extreme) never appears in the story. Nor is he its major character. Primary focus is on Abner Snopes, Flem's father, and on Sarty, Flem's younger brother. The story asks readers to ponder how two brothers in the same family could be so different. Flem accepts the vision of the world that his father expounds; Abner declares that family loyalty is the only reality. Unfortunately, he pushes that premise to an extreme: vindication of the self transcends the well-being of his family. Thus, family pride becomes a mockery, something worthy of ridicule. Ridicule is central to the comic mode of the novels, but there is little that is comic in "Barn Burning." As Faulkner's title suggests, Abner Snopes is a threat to the community; his path leads to destruction and to death. Faulkner shows that the Snopeses as well as the Compsons (*The Sound and the Fury*) and the Sutpens (*Absalom, Absalom!*) can touch the tragic notes.

By the time of the action of "Barn Burning," the course of Flem Snopes's life is set. Abner can trust him absolutely. But when brought to trial for burning a barn, Abner senses that his younger son is inclined to speak the truth. For Sarty, there may be loyalties that transcend family loyalty. Abner intends to teach his son otherwise, and that becomes his primary goal when the family takes up a new sharecropping contract in another community. As he begins that contract, he takes Sarty with him to see Major DeSpain— intending to make his son see DeSpain as the oppressor. Thus, "Barn Burning" becomes a story of education in which parent and child make a journey together and discover more than either anticipated (it may be likened to Hemingway's "Indian Camp" or Ernest Gaines's "The Sky Is Gray" in this basic pattern). In the lesson of moral outrage that Abner tries to teach his son, he is close to Mark Twain's Pap Finn when he lectures Huck. Huck's instinct tells him that his father is morally bankrupt. Increasingly, Sarty's does too.

Unquestionably, Abner's outrage is genuine (Faulkner humanizes him as Twain never humanizes Pap Finn), and his mistake is attempting too much at one time. He wants not only to teach Sarty but also to force his new landlord to take notice of Abner Snopes—just as his numerous barn burnings have made other landlords remember him. Approaching DeSpain's house, he discovers the opportunity to make a similar impression. He does not veer from the fresh horse droppings in the path leading to the DeSpain door, but plants his foot in the droppings, and then on Mrs. DeSpain's rug. Coming down that same path, Sarty gets a vision Abner did not intend. Looking at the house, Sarty feels "a surge of peace and joy," and the narrator takes us into Sarty's thoughts: "They are safe from him. People whose lives are a part of this peace and dignity are beyond his touch, he no more to them than a buzzing wasp; capable of stinging for a little moment but that's all; the spell of peace and dignity rendering even the barns and stable and cribs which belong to it impervious to the puny flames he might contrive."

Sarty makes two more trips to the DeSpain's house (Abner has made moving a way of life for his family—and motion is a principal structuring device of this story). The next trip comes because Abner wants his son to see his second insult to the DeSpains as he returns the rug that he has purposely ruined in order to make his "signature" indelible. Sarty makes the third trip because he feels morally obligated to do so—his sense of fair play demanding that DeSpain be warned that Abner is going to burn the barn in protest to the judge's ruling that Abner make modest reparation for ruining the rug.

Although Sarty does not hesitate in his decision to warn DeSpain, Faulkner brilliantly conveys the price that Sarty pays for his difficult moral choice. Sarty's dilemma is the central issue of the story: he loves his father, but his sense of rightness demands that he oppose him. Having warned DeSpain, Sarty does not break his frenzied run. When he hears gun shots, he knows that Abner is dead: "springing up and into the road again, running again, knowing it was too late yet still running even after he heard the shot and, an instant later, two shots, pausing now without knowing he had ceased to run, crying "Pap! Pap!', running again before he knew he had begun to run, stumbling, tripping over something and scrabbling up again without ceasing to run, looking backward over his shoulder at the glare as he got up, running on among the invisible trees, panting, sobbing, 'Father! Father!'" Twain's *Pap* is elevated to the more moving *Father*, catching biblical echoes of Jesus's crucifixion and reminding Faulkner's readers of another son's anguished call for acknowledgement from his father in *Absalom, Absalom!*

Although a part of Sarty still wishes to believe in a core of integrity in his father, Faulkner's narrator overrides Sarty's voice, declaring Abner a man without honor. As the story ends, Sarty, having chosen the path of honor, walks into the future with some courage: he does not look back. And he is never again heard from in Faulkner's many stories of the Snopeses.

Sarty carries with him the moral values that his longsuffering mother has tried to maintain, values that she may have asserted most forcefully for her son by naming him for Colonel Sartoris.

—Joseph M. Flora

BARTLEBY, THE SCRIVENER: A STORY OF WALL STREET
by Herman Melville, 1853

In the 1853 story "Bartleby," Herman Melville antici-pates the alienation theme so common to contemporary American writers. He poses the question, "Why would someone prefer the independence of homelessness to the meager security that society offers the homeless?" By asking and not answering this question, he offers a puzzling story, unusually open to interpretation.

Generally called simply "Bartleby," the story's full title is significant: "Bartleby, The Scrivener: A Story of Wall Street." At the beginning of the story, the title character is a scrivener, i.e., a law-copyist, the mid-19th-century equiva-lent of a human Xerox machine. But very soon, he ceases to scriven.

When Bartleby stops, is he still the scrivener? Can he be? Does he, and do we, acquire identities only through work? Or do people have inherent value whether or not they produce labor? The analogy between Bartleby and all of humankind becomes explicit in Melville's final two sen-tences: "Ah, Bartleby! Ah, humanity!" The concerned tone of this last line, and of the story, belongs to a narrator who, like his money-driven society, ironically drains Bartleby's life of energy even while mouthing pious personal concern for him (as argued in Louise K. Barrett's 1974 Marxist reading of the story, "Bartleby as Alienated Worker").

The subtitle, "A Story of Wall Street," drives home this point. Although Bartleby works for a Wall Street lawyer, not a stockbroker, his placement in the nation's financial center has obvious economic implications. Wall Street is also an important verbal symbol. Walls of many kinds recur in the story, making Bartleby like a laboratory subject trapped in a maze with no exit. Dead ends, blank walls, or dead walls reinforce this image of hopeless. As Leo Marx's 1953 essay "Melville's Parable of the Walls" points out, Bartleby works in a stultifying office: on Wall Street, its two windows look out on a white wall and "a lofty brick wall, black by age," located within "ten feet of" the office workers. In the office itself Bartleby is seated near a small window, "which originally had afforded a lateral view of certain grimy backyards and bricks but which owing to some subsequent erections commanded at present no view at all. Within three feet of the panes was a wall" to further enclose Bartleby. The lawyer-narrator whose office is divided in two by "ground-glass folding doors" has even "procured a high green folding screen which might entirely isolate Bartleby from my sight."

Having stopped work, Bartleby continues living at his desk, eating little, responding "I would prefer not to" to his employer's and fellow-workers' requests. "For long peri-ods," the narrator relates, "he would stand looking out . . . upon the dead brick wall," "behind his screen . . . in one of those dead wall reveries of his," around the clock, seven days a week. Wall Street is compared to Petra, a mid-eastern city desolated in the ninth century A.D. and covered by sand until archeologists uncovered it in 1812. ("Petra," the Greek word for "rock," draws a further analogy between Wall Street and Petra as two lifeless sealed tombs.) In his dismal abode Bartleby stays, even after the narrator fires him. The narrator later finds him in "The Tombs," the city jail, staring at "a high wall." The architecture of the Tombs was distinctly Egyp-tian-looking, with formidable walls and pillars. References to Egypt and Petra and Carthage aside, much of "Bartleby" is rooted in the ancient world, particularly the Bible.

Melville, a lifelong rebel against his strict Dutch Re-formed upbringing, juxtaposes Biblical ethics with those of contemporary Wall Street, most scathingly by quoting Jesus from John 3:34: "A new commandment give I unto you, that ye shall love one another." Though briefly inspired by the command to treat Bartleby kindly, the narrator quickly reverts to ignoring it, behaving as if the absolute command were limited to occasions when such love is convenient, or when the recipient is suitably grateful. The narrator soon blithely rationalizes his disobe-dience.

Passively, the narrator abdicates the limited responsibili-ty for Bartleby he had assumed, and lets his ex-landlord charge Bartleby with vagrancy. Even the narrator's actions are passive: he doesn't act on his emotions as much as they act on him.

This passivity mirrors Bartleby's, although the narrator stays unaware of any parallel between himself and his clerk. As he tells the story, his mood ranges from patient to angry to Christian to vengeful, and finally to compassionate, while Bartleby is resolutely phlegmatic. As the story's conflict heightens, Bartleby grows increasingly passive. The effect is comical. The narrator seriously claims to seek an active solution. His extreme moodswings, however, show his self-deception, while Bartleby's nihilistic calm speaks to his self-knowledge.

Bartleby also represents Jesus Christ, the master whose commandment the narrator ignores. Accepting his impend-ing death calmly, Bartleby responds to his persecutors' questions indirectly but with omniscient contempt. (Don-ald M. Fiene's 1970 essay "Bartleby the Christ" exhaus-tively lists and interprets the Biblical allusions in the story. See also John Gardner's 1962 essay "Bartleby: Art & Social Commitment.")

Further parallels have been suggested: between the narra-tor and Pontius Pilate (in John Seelye's 1970 *Melville: The Ironic Diagram*); between the narrator and Melville's father-in-law (Robert L. Gale, 1962); between Bartleby and Henry Thoreau (Elbert S. Oliver, 1945) and between Bartleby and numerous others, particularly Melville him-self (Richard Chase, Joel Porte, and Leo Marx).

Like Bartleby, Melville had made a comfortable living as a scrivener of sorts: his adventurous sea tales of the 1840's had great commercial success. But in the 1850's Melville refused to plagiarize his adventure stories. Instead, he insisted on writing his own way, a way that seemed to spell his artistic extinction; the dense *Pierre* and the dark *Moby-Dick* practically destroyed Melville as a commercial writer. Yet to continue copying themselves, Melville and Bartleby could not.

—Steven Goldleaf

THE BEAR
by William Faulkner, 1942

There are four published texts of all or part of Faulkner's "The Bear": "Lion," an experimental germ of the story published in *Harper's Magazine* in December 1925; "The Bear," a four-part hunting story published in *The Saturday Evening Post* on May 9, 1942; "The Bear," a chapter in the novel *Go Down, Moses* which adds a fifth section (as a new section four) published by Random House in late 1942; and

"The Bear," the *Post* story placed in a new setting, to introduce fiction of outdoor sport in *Big Woods* (1955). While the two shorter versions can stand independently and are simpler and more straightforward than the longest version, Faulkner always stoutly claimed that this last, in *Go Down, Moses*, could not be read independently of the rest of the book, even though the first (and subsequently withdrawn) printing of the novel was titled, without Faulkner's knowledge, *Go Down, Moses and Other Stories*. Both the texts called "The Bear" have been reprinted and anthologized: whatever Faulkner's claim or intention, even the longer chapter from the novel can be read independently although in doing so it loses some of its force of reference and powers of association.

This longest, fullest version actually radiates in its turn from a commissary scene on the McCaslin plantation where two second cousins, the ascetic Ike McCaslin and the plantation manager McCaslin Edmonds confront each other and their radically differing philosophies as exposed by family ledgers found in that plantation store. While Cass sees them as they were doubtless meant to be seen—as the careful accounting of property bought, earned, and dispensed—Ike, noting that black slaves of the McCaslin family (the parallel Beauchamp family) are also treated as property, so that an apparently neutral ledger is really a revealing and damning chronicle of Southern race relations and a singular family diary which suggests the present responsibility for the past. The most elusive entries, about the slave girl Eunice and her daughter, which no McCaslin has attended to since earlier brothers quarreled about their significance, is unscrambled by Ike to show that their own forebear had violated a mulatto daughter by incestuous relations with a black slave woman. Horrified, Ike sets out to repair the damage by seeing that the descendants of this bastard line receive three times the money that was first promised them. What Cass sees as a sad if telling reminder of the Southern burden of the past, Ike sees as a tormented and bitter indictment of his own blood line and kin. In time, his mission of reparation and reconcilement will end in defeat, since one descendant is dead (or unlocatable), one has already claimed his inheritance as property and lives a proud and separate life, and one refuses to accept any guilt-ridden blood money. As a further penalty, Ike withdraws from the plantation, asking no further support, instead marrying a carpenter's daughter; when that marriage fails, he takes what little he can from the plantation and lives a lonely and isolated life in the city of Jefferson.

This added fourth section to "The Bear" for *Go Down, Moses*, then, is a compact history of the South in terms of race, economy, and social life, of clan caste, and class. The guilt of the past is visited upon the sons, and the sons find the burden unbearable, the situation irresolvable. The three sections that precede this take place at an earlier time, in the young boy Isaac's youth, when, at the age of 16, he joins the older hunters on their annual ritual hunt for "Old Ben," the gigantic wounded bear. This time, unlike other times, Isaac has a prescience that it will be their last hunt. "It was like the last act on a set stage. It was the beginning of the end of something, he didn't know what." When the killer dog Lion helps the part-Indian Boon Hogganbeck kill Old Ben after Old Ben has killed their pet fyce, Ike's mentor Sam Fathers, half-black, half-Indian, the natural man of the woods, dies too, and Ike reluctantly is given permission to stay with Boon to bury the dog and the old man. Although this is a moment of deep anguish for Isaac, he learns anew from Boon as he had from Sam about the cycles of all nature, the cycles of birth and growth and death, of generation and decay, of gift and of loss. This is not what

Cass understands; returning to fetch Ike, Cass accuses Boon of killing Sam, not understanding the ways of the woods, the ways of nature, or even the ways of the human heart. In retaliation, Boon refuses to return to the plantation. It is the first quarrel between Ike and Cass and looks forward directly to the commissary scene added later in order to give the full genealogical background to the cousins who no longer communicate.

The death of Old Ben takes the heart out of the annual fall hunting expeditions in northern Yoknapatawpha County, Mississippi, Faulkner's fictional version of Lafayette County (just as the hunting camp is based on the camp of General Stone, the father of Faulkner's childhood friend and patron Phil Stone). But two years later, at the age of 18, Isaac feels the strong urge to return to the old hunting grounds in order to understand more completely the meaning of the bear, the old mentor, and the despairing Boon. He is filled with grief on the trip. The woods are being ransacked by a lumbering company, slowly but irrevocably destroying them forever. A train passes its way through the countryside, linking the commerce of the lumber camp with the economic forces of the town. A snake appears. And then, seated at the foot of the ancient, sacred gum tree, surrounding by chattering and scrambling squirrels, Boon is knocking powerfully and unsuccessfully at the barrel of his gun. "Get out of here! Dont touch them!" Boon shouts. "Dont touch a one of them! They're mine!" While it is unclear if Boon is destroying or repairing his gun, whether in fact living in a nature being gutted and annihilated around him he is sane or mad, the sharp diminishment of the game available for the hunt and the sad demise of the one hunter who remains links the degeneration of history and the decline of humanity with the growth of a sense of possession.

All versions of "The Bear" conclude at this point, although the longer version, with Ike seen at the age of 21 in the commissary, traces out the long life that follows as a much-diminishing thing. In either version, however, the forces of American commerce and materialism are placed in stark and damaging contrast with the beauty of the woods and the shared secrets of game to hunt and the canny game that made a ritual of being hunted. What the fourth section adds is the matter of genealogy and the force of racial hatred. Reemphasizing the first chapter of *Go Down, Moses*, entitled "Was," the fourth part added to "The Bear" shows how possession of nature (the woods by the lumber industry) is analogous to the possession of slaves (to foster the cotton crops); how the impersonality, exploitation, and greed of the woods was matched in the whites' treatment of blacks, even when those blacks were their own descendants. This understanding of brother conquering brother (and cousin, cousin) suggests to the older Ike that the Civil War has never really ended, that brotherhood is a myth, and that progress, let alone prosperity, is ever possible in human society. The whites who hunt to kill are, later, and at home, hunters who destroy human dignity and human life. Ike's condemnation is searing and total; and the last scene in the longer "The Bear" chronologically, in which Ike's laughing wife refuses ever to give herself to him again, although she had wanted both him and his inheritance, may suggest that she and the lonely, ineffective Ike have themselves been somewhat maddened by their experiences. Only the later chapter "Delta Autumn," in which the 70-year-old Ike hunts deer, not bear, shows that he continues to live, but his life is now void of purpose, and, when he denies a mulatto woman who turns out to be his old blood-relative once more, he also seems himself, finally, woefully inadequate to his own best

symbol of slaves

intentions and uneducable to the lessons he once thought he had learned.

Faulkner's entire career was spent, except for a few early novels and two later ones, charting through fiction the history of the South by way of its chief family lines. But only in *Go Down, Moses* are so many generations pulled together, and only in "The Bear" is the matter of race—the chief concern and sin of that history—made so powerfully and singularly clear. It is Faulkner's strongest testament, as it is his most excruciating revelation, of his past as well as his present time and place.

—Arthur F. Kinney

THE BEAST IN THE JUNGLE
by Henry James, 1903

In "The Art of Fiction" Henry James advised the aspiring writer to be one "upon whom nothing is lost." Perhaps no writer has better lived up to this credo than Henry James himself. His stories evince this determination to miss nothing that is relevant to our understanding of human nature. Frequently, the fun of a James story derives from the distance between what characters miss about themselves and what the perceptive reader so clearly sees. No better example exists than his great story, "The Beast in the Jungle."

Especially upon first reading, James's stories often appear to be more difficult than they really are. The difficulty arises from two technical factors: his sentence style and his preferred point of view. "The Beast in the Jungle" (in *The Better Sort*, 1903) is a good example. The sentence structure is involved, convoluted, labyrinthine. The narrative voice is also typical of James: third person limited to an unreliable point of view, in this case the protagonist's, John Marcher's. James's technical choices are organic: that is, they grow out of and contribute to theme and characterization. The labyrinthine sentence structure, for instance, is very near what a few years later would be called "stream of consciousness." John Marcher is an intensely introspective, self-involved, searching yet passive character; and the sentence style—dominated by the passive voice—perfectly mirrors his personality. Despite Marcher's searching introspection, however, he constantly misses the point about himself and his condition. The narrative point of view, limited to him, must be correspondingly unreliable. Hence, the reader is made an active participant in trying to figure out Marcher. If the reader finds the answer long before Marcher, that too is appropriate.

It is the terrible irony of the story—James would call it an "operative irony"—that in one sense Marcher does not miss the point at all; he is in fact correct in his essential view of himself, but it is a view that is ultimately destructive. James frequently took as his theme the "destructiveness of an idea." Marcher's idea is a common one (occurring to many children, probably, but most outgrow it): that he is reserved for something unique, a terrible thing, perhaps, but something for himself alone. The problem is that Marcher is so captivated by this childish notion that other potentialities of his life are eliminated or reduced to anemic supporting roles. Chief among the "supporting cast" is May Bartram. It is obvious to all but John, certainly obvious to May, that she should have been his leading lady, but John is too intent on waiting for "the beast." She may wait with him, at her peril, if she chooses, but with the understanding that she can never be first in his life. And so appears the operative irony. And so appears the beast. Only John Marcher does not yet realize it.

The first scene of the story is a good example of John's problem. In touring a lovely old English home, Marcher is vaguely aware that he has met another party in the tour once before—where and when, he is not certain. Appropriately, that other party, May Bartram, does remember. They had met in Naples nearly ten years before when they were both in their twenties. What could be more romantic: two young people meeting on a holiday in Naples. The scene becomes vivid to John, however, only when May reminds him that he had told her the secret of his life—the beast. Already by the time of his young manhood, then, Marcher was obsessed to the point of ignoring what to anyone else might seem reason enough to consider one's life extraordinary: the potential for love.

Indeed, "The Beast in the Jungle" can easily be read as a love story—but an unhappy one. May, one senses, would have been quite happy to have seen their relationship assume a more romantic aspect back in Naples. She would, no doubt, be happy to entertain such a notion ten years later, at the start of the story. But again, John must wait for his beast. May waits with him—for the beast, he thinks, but really for him to come to his senses—as the years pass.

By the time of the climactic fourth section of this six-section story, it is clear that Marcher's dominating idea is destructive not merely in the abstract. Both have aged; May in fact had noticeably (even to dull John) aged in the ten years since Naples. Now, May not only is older but is ill, perhaps near death. Still there is time—time for love. John, as always, is concerned with the beast. Was he wrong all along? Here, at the end of his life, has he missed the extraordinary thing that was to happen, he asks. No, May replies, gliding over to him, presenting herself to him. The extraordinary thing is still possible; she of course means love, means herself. But what is the thing, he demands. Finally realizing that he will never see, May virtually collapses. "What then has happened?" John pleads to know. May replies, "What *was* to."

What May refers to is, of course, the beast. It savages John in the April scene, but then it had been savaging him—stealing his life away, his receptivity to love—all along, from the first moment he conceived his destructive idea. John himself finally realizes it in the story's last scene, before May's grave, where he witnesses a mourner whose face is scarred by grief. He suddenly realizes that he himself has never been so moved by anything, that his unique destiny is to be the one man to whom nothing ever happens. Recoiling from the beast, which rises like a phantom before him, Marcher throws himself on May's grave—one more turn of the Jamesian screw. What will he do tomorrow if the opportunity for love presents itself? Abjure it once more, no doubt, in his dedication to his new beast: the memory of May Bartram.

"One's in the hand's of one's law," John says earlier in the story. His fate bears out the terrible truth of that remark.

—Dennis Vannatta

BEATTOCK FOR MOFFAT
by R.B. Cunninghame Graham, 1902

The most highly rated of R.B. Cunninghame Graham's short stories, "Beattock for Moffat," first collected in

Success, has appeared in several collections and anthologies and has been much admired for the author's skill in dealing with the awkward subject of death and exile. By maintaining a low key throughout and by refusing to sentimentalise his subject, Graham steers a watchful course in his tale of a dying Scotsman's return to his native land, travelling north by train from London to Beattock, where he will be taken to Moffat and his last resting place.

From the very outset Graham signals his intentions by providing Andra, the dying man, with companions who refuse resolutely to bow to any false hopes. Their immediate task is to make sure that he survives the night and gets as far as Beattock. This is a favourite literary technique of Graham's—the drawing together of different people and the evocation of past experience through their thoughts and memories.

Jayne, the wife, is a Londoner, tearful yet self-sufficient, who only dimly understands her husband's primal need to return to his homeland. The brother is a different but equally recognisable type, the brusquely sympathetic upland sheep farmer who is tied to the land and takes his strength from its harsh rhythms.

Like others of his kind, especially Scots, Jock's religious beliefs are anchored in the knowledge that his work brings him face to face with God and that fear of the Lord is the beginning of wisdom. Whereas Jayne tries to comfort her husband with thoughts of a heaven that is more music hall than Christian paradise, Jock responds with the fundamentalist belief that Andra was not the man to want an eternity in such a place, "daunderin' aboot a gairden naked, pu'in soor aipples frae the trees." However, it is a measure of Graham's sympathy for his characters that Andra intervenes with the thought that they should set their minds on getting him home before they start thinking about the nature of paradise.

Once started, the train journey takes on the aspect of a pilgrimage and from the outset it is impossible not to admire Graham's powers of observation and his ability to make even the smallest detail count. Old sandwich papers are tossed into the air in the train's wake as it leaves Euston, the London terminus; as it pushes on through England the flickering light inside the compartment contrasts eerily with passing brightly lit stations; ironworks light up the night and in the country places bright frost sparkles over the surrounding hills and meadows. If this is a lovingly described journey through the real England, it is also an account of the making of a man's soul before death.

As the train travels ever further north it is also a race against time. In the dark watches of the night Jock and Jayne fall asleep while Andra counts the miles to Scotland, wondering whether or not his strength will fail him. At Shap, the long gradient over the Cumbrian hills, he gets the first scent of the winds of home and believes that it might be possible to survive the night. Here sentimentality could easily descend into bathos—aided and abetted by the brothers' homely Scots speech—but Graham is alive to the danger and refuses to be drawn into anything so romantic or escapist.

Instead, the two brothers launch into a reasoned discussion about the funeral, Andra taking great pleasure in Jock's description of the new hearse that will carry his body to the cemetery. Jayne is scandalised by their conversation, "holding the English theory that unpleasant things should not be mentioned, and that, by this mean, they can be kept at bay." Knowing that his fellow countrymen take considerable interest in the subject and that death and funerals are a natural topic of conversation in Scotland, Graham takes obvious delight in contrasting the opposing points of view as the train crosses over the border into Scotland and home.

The only hint of emotion is reserved for the final homecoming as the train passes names familiar to both men and Jock is allowed to brush a tear from his face "as angrily as it had been a wasp." At Beattock station in the wet early morning, the sad little party leave the train with Andra barely alive. But there is to be no last-minute salvation; death comes to him on the platform with a porter's voice ringing in his ears, "Beattock, Beattock for Moffat."

As Jayne weeps silently beside her dead husband, Jock draws out a whisky bottle and salutes his brother with the thought that he had made a good fight of it. After the undertaker has been summoned, Jock walks out into the early morning rain whistling a lively Scots air and the story ends with him remarking that whatever else has happened, his brother will at least get a decent ride in the new Moffat hearse.

Satisfying though it is to end the story on such an ironic note, it would be wrong to think that Graham had severed his emotional involvement with his characters. On the contrary, his awareness of the rhythms of their speech and the strength of their quiet philosophy reveals a shrewd familiarity with the background that made them. Also, in no other story did he identify so completely with the lives and concerns of the characters he created.

—Trevor Royle

BENITO CERENO
by Herman Melville, 1855

In the story "Benito Cereno" Amaso Delano, an American sea captain commanding the *Bachelor's Delight*, is anchored off the shore of southern Chile when he spots another ship moving about mysteriously in the waters. Without apparent concern for his own safety, although pirates are in the area, Delano packs food into a small boat and leaves to bring aid, if aid is needed, to fellow seamen. At first unable to understand the nature of the strange ship because of the persistent fog, Delano gets closer and realizes the *San Dominick* is a Spanish merchant ship carrying a cargo of slaves. But the *San Dominick* is more than Delano is able to apprehend. It is actually a microcosm of gigantic proportions, and herein lies the real story that Herman Melville tells.

"Benito Cereno" is about perception and those factors that inhibit it, causing humans to persist in behavior that is violent, shameful, warlike, and inhuman. Aboard the *San Dominick* are representatives of three cultures: the new world, the old world, and the third world. Amaso Delano, the American ship captain, commands with firm hand and good order the *Bachelor's Delight*. He is a man respected by his crew, fair, honest in his dealings, pragmatic in his practices, a man who moves immediately to correct problems. Delano believes himself to be protected by his religious beliefs that deny inherent evil in humans and extol good works. Benito Cereno, the Spanish ship captain, is a scion of old world aristocracy, dressed in old world finery, with a body servant constantly at his side. He appears ill and unable to act except autocratically. To Delano, the Spanish captain appears as a perfect example of the decay of an outmoded civilization. Benito Cereno is so weak he needs to be supported to walk; he seems incompetent, both physically and mentally. The ship he commands is in great disarray, filthy, and rotting. The association of the *San Dominick* with catholicism is clear and, as we learn, evil is prevalent in Cereno's world. The third world is typified by Babo. Masquerading as Cereno's body servant, Babo is the leader of the insurectioners, for a time the real commander of the ship and all aboard it.

On board the slave ship conditions are abominable. Though Aranda, owner of the slaves, allows them certain freedoms, he does so at his peril. The ship's sternpiece makes the point clearly, if symbolically: "But the principal relic of faded grandeur was the ample oval of the shield-like sternpiece, intricately carved with the arms of Castile and Leon, medallioned about by groups of mythological or symbolical devices; uppermost and central of which was a dark satyr in a mask, holding his foot on the prostrate neck of a writhing figure, likewise masked."

This figure of the masked satyr holding his foot on the body of a writhing figure, also masked, points to the ironies of the reversals to follow and asks the essential question: "Who is master, who is slave?" Or does not the situation enslave master as well as slave? When Babo and his people can, they revolt and slave becomes master: when Delano arrives he is able to free Cereno and to capture those who had previously been in authority.

Babo and compatriots fight for freedom; their behavior during the revolt is horribly atrocious. What they do to Aranda's body is too terrible for many Westerners to conceive; but from another point of view, one based on knowledge of tribal practices, totem figures, and religious ceremonies, the behavior of the blacks seems completely credible. Nor can one say that any of the three civilizations represented are without sin or free from shameful practices. What the Spaniards do to Babo after he is captured is evidence enough and points to perhaps a final irony. At his death, Don Benito does follow his leader, but who is the leader? Aranda whose skeleton is tied to the figure head or Babo whose head is stuck on a pole in the town square?

Point of view in the story is intricate and thematically functional. When the story begins readers identify with Delano, who is the dominant point of view character for some pages into the narrative. But an omniscient narrator carefully guides reader responses as it becomes clearer that a mystery exists on board ship and that the mystery involves more than Delano is able to perceive. Delano's perceptions are guided by his stereotypical beliefs about the three cultures represented on ship. Once readers begin to recognize this fact, they must begin to disassociate from Delano and to peer over his shoulder rather than see through his eyes.

A series of events arranged in climatic order provides evidence against Delano's reliability, especially the penultimate shaving scene in which Babo uses the Spanish flag as a shaving apron draped about Cereno's neck. However, so skillful is Melville in running suspense parallel with foreshadowing that most American readers doubt Delano's conclusions even though they may reach the initial revelation simultaneously with Delano.

This revelation is, however, not the climax of the story. There is much more to come: Melville discards Delano as point of view character as readers follow the American sailors in putting down the rebellion. There follows the lengthy deposition in legal language of the time. Only now after sufficient time has passed can Delano and Cereno be brought together again and the reader join them in what is the true climax of the story, occurring several pages before the end. Delano says to Cereno: "'You are saved: what has cast such a shadow upon you?'" Don Benito's reply ("The negro") carries with it the immense ethical and political implications of slavery, the kind of people who engage in it, and the horrible atrocities both masters and slaves commit in its name.

Babo dies in punishment for his "crimes." Cereno dies, unable to achieve absolution in his own mind and soul. Delano escapes, hardly touched by the horror around him, his innocence and naivety protecting him from experiencing true terror. But Delano is not free from guilt whether he knows it or not, and he can come to know terror. He supports the idea of slavery, rejects the blacks as less than human, and will not speculate upon meaning. Surely Melville meant "Benito Cereno," published in 1855, to be, among other things, a word of warning to his own countrymen on the eve of the Civil War.

—Mary Rohrberger

THE BEWITCHED (El hechizado)
by Francisco Ayala, 1944

"The Bewitched," by Francisco Ayala, originally published separately as *El hechizado* (1944), was incorporated into the collection *Los usurpadores* (1949; *Usurpers,* 1987). The seven tales in *Usurpers* are unified by a common theme: all power exercised over others is a usurpation. Ayala's first collection after the Civil War never mentions the war in which his father and brother were executed by Fascists under Franco, but several tales treat prior civil conflicts in the peninsula. Context is crucial to interpreting Ayala, whose subtexts must be divined by analogy—here, that Franco and his regime are the latest in centuries of usurpers.

With varying fidelity or fancy, the *Usurpers* stories present characters in Spanish history from the 11th to the 17th centuries; all combine fictitious characters with historical ones, none better known to Spanish readers than the unfortunate King Carlos II (1661-1700), last of the Hapsburg kings. The nickname "the Bewitched" originated when Carlos II became convinced he was possessed of the devil or bewitched and had himself exorcised—a shameful and degrading process. To appreciate Ayala's tour de force, one must understand the background Spanish readers bring to bear: Generations of royal intermarriage intensified negative, recessive genes, and the king was malformed, sickly, mentally retarded—probably suffering from cretinism. Yet he reigned during Spain's greatest "glory" in extent of domain, the microcephalic head of a gigantic empire whose grandeur the traditionalist Franco regime exalted and hoped to emulate. Although married to a granddaughter of Louis XIV, Carlos II was impotent or sterile, and fortunately, the degeneracy was not transmitted.

Ayala achieves maximum impact with a "non-story" (nothing happens but bureaucratic delays until the final paragraphs) with a startling ending despite readers' knowing the facts in advance. He employs a framing tale (story-within-a-story structure), and a device familiar to all readers of Cervantes, the "found manuscript." The narrator of the framing tale, whose name is a disguised form of Ayala's own, claims to be the editor of another's "historical" work, fooling many critics who believed him a genuine philologist. A professional Hispanist and Cervantine scholar in addition to journalist, diplomat, sociologist, novelist and law professor, Ayala incorporated the "found manuscript" often in his fiction, and utilizes literary borrowing, intertextual allusions, or "updated" classical tales in contemporary, innovative contexts. The framing story in "The Bewitched," a pseudo-academic essay, comprises the editor's pedantic comments and speculations that the extensive folios will never be published. Questions raised by the narrator's reading completely miss the point of the manuscript (a self-referential or self-critical technique often used by Ayala to humorous effect). Another joke on readers is that they never see the manuscript in question (just as "The Message," the sole topic of discussion in the novella by that name in *The Lamb's Head,* remains invisible).

The same narrator summarizes the lengthy manuscript, whose author (the "Indian" González Lobo) recounts a pilgrimage originating in the remotest Andes, an arduous and protracted journey including a three-year delay in Seville, and ending in the imperial Spanish court following years of desultory, labyrinthine questing whose sole purpose is to pay homage to the great monarch.

Not to be forgotten is that Spain's Hapsburg dynasty (Felipe II in the 16th century) invented bureaucracy, archiving the most trivial documentation; the Franco regime carried archival and bureaucratic detail to absurd extremes. That these fill González Lobo's manuscript is therefore no coincidence. This persona never criticizes or comments; supposedly a primitive, unworldly, mountain aborigine, he views everything with impassive detachment, resignation, and seeming acceptance. His feet trace slow, intricate patterns through a maze of corridors and antechambers as he silently, sadly, threads his way through moral, economic, and administrative roadblocks, interminable waits, repeated visits to the same secretariats and new clerics, adjutants, and ministers—all clearly baffled by his not requesting favors or emoluments but merely to present his obeisance, to kiss His Majesty's feet.

Rooms filled with bookshelves, replete with folders, desks piled with dockets, misplaced dossiers, broken appointments when the worthy fifth clerk of the third secretariat appears late or not at all—extensively detailed episodes repeated three or more times so identically as to be distinguished solely by their dates—constitute González Lobo's account. Representative minutiae include the 46 steps in the stairway of the palace of the Inquisition, the exact description of a beggar to whom he gives alms before entering church, his confessor's Teutonic inflections, particulars of the liturgy each Sunday, the luxuriant opulence of the church decor.

Years of waiting with other postulants (a bustling swarm of suppliants all trafficking in influence, with applications for exemptions, purchasing positions, petitions for pardons or procurement of privileges) suddenly end by chance—an encounter so absurd, a resolution so facile, that the entire system is trivialized without a word. González Lobo meets the king's dwarf who demands a ring to introduce him into the royal presence. Traversing courtyards, gates, vestibules, guards, corridors, antechambers, galleries, stairways, enormous doorways, and halls lined with mirrors, he suddenly glimpses His Majesty: thin, limp legs richly shod, hair colorless, lace collar soaked with slobber, black velvet suit exuding a stench of urine because of lifelong incontinence. Although the monarch extends his hand to be kissed upon the dwarf's prompting, a monkey distracts him, demanding to be petted; González Lobo understands that the interview is over and withdraws in respectful silence.

"The Bewitched" begins and ends with silence and is filled with silences (a significant technique of the rhetoric of dissent under Franco), silences eloquent of Spain's centuries of censorship, tradition of orthodoxy enforced by the Inquisition, and the Franco regime's silencing of political differences by imprisonment and execution. Although the head of state is so manifestly unfit to govern that no comment is necessary or even possible, the system is so entrenched that not a single voice is raised. The usurpation of power is absolute, Ayala implies, for its hypnotic fascination affects both those who hold it and those who submit to it.

—Janet Pérez

BEZHIN MEADOW (Bezhin lug)
by Ivan Turgenev, 1852

"Bezhin lug" ("Bezhin Meadow"), one of the pieces collected in Ivan Turgenev's 1852 volume *Zapiski Okhotnika* (*A Sportsman's Sketches,* also *A Huntsman's Sketches*), is indeed more sketch than short story proper: it is held together not by a linear plot but by a set of contrasting yet interlocking motifs. It is like certain masterful drawings or paintings, motionless but full of palpable dynamic tensions of theme, line, mood.

The general structural composition of the Turgenev piece is fairly simple, framed by two specimens of the lyrical nature-writing for which he is famous. Many of the sketches in the collection begin with a statement by the narrator about how, during his shooting excursions, he happened to be in a certain locality and how he ran into the people he intends to acquaint us with. "Bezhin Meadow" departs from this pattern; not until after a full page chronicling the progress of earth and sky on a perfect July day—the keynotes are serenity, settledness, a vitality that is also peace—does he locate himself at all, and then only briefly, because he promptly gets lost. There follows an atmospherically uncanny description of his hapless wanderings, through landscapes that have suddenly become both less reassuring and more eerily haunting. We are now in a world more visionary than the beatifically normal one described at first, and utterly lonely except for the narrator, the wild creatures he encounters, and his hunting dog, a creature of tamed, almost humanized instinct. (Throughout the sketch, animal and human behavior repeatedly are juxtaposed, as if to invite comparisons between the human and nonhuman.) Night having fallen, the hunter arrives at a precipice where another step or two might have plunged him to his death. Only now is he ready to introduce us to the human actors in his sketch, whom we have been prepared to see as exotic fantasy creatures.

And yet they are utterly normal, "natural" boys after all, on a delightful but commonplace mission: night-grazing some horses. We and the protagonist have happened on this group by a scenic and psychological route resembling those in fairy stories, yet what we find is not in the least otherworldly. On the other hand, there is something wondrous about the boys, although we can see that better than they can themselves. In this double vision of the boys we come near the heart of what Turgenev is doing in "Bezhin Meadow": exploring the relationship of the wondrous to the ordinary, of what is supernatural to what is natural, of the fantastic to the human.

To the five boys, there is nothing extraordinary about the natural world—except in the still-childlike imagination of the youngest one, the seven-year-old Vanya, and even he, entranced by the stars, compares them in a homely way to swarming bees. Nor is there any sign that the boys think of themselves as anything very special. They are almost entirely unselfconscious; even the oldest, Fedya, interested in girls and aware of his somewhat superior background, is nevertheless still essentially naive. For these youngsters, the wondrous lies not in or around them, but in ghosts and ghost stories. They are touchingly unaware that the world they actually live in, the "merely" natural world, and indeed they themselves, are a good deal more interesting and wonderful than water goblins and noisy but invisible revenants. They are too young to understand or appreciate the poignant human implications, on the naturalistic level, of the story about Gavrila, the village carpenter who, having used the sign of the Cross to drive off a flirtatious water fairy as unholy, thereby reduces her grief and himself to perpetual despondency. The boys can see the riskiness in Pavel's going to fetch water from the goblin's river habitat, but they cannot appreciate the human courage he displays when he faces up to wolves and dismisses fatalistically the supernatural ill omens that he too believes. The ironies in all this are not directed against the youngsters; they are simply too inexperienced to appreciate such things. A more cutting irony implicates the kind of adults whose imaginations can respond to lurid fantasy but not to the truly human, the truly natural—in short, the vein that realist writers such as Turgenev adopted as their own.

Nature is not merely mood-enhancing in "Bezhin Meadow," nor is it merely a backdrop. It is a principal agent—posed against the supernatural agencies in the ghost tales—and, along with the boys, is the foregrounded material of the sketch. By the time we begin to hear the boys' supernatural tales, we have already seen actual nature, in two guises—the edenic July day and the eerie, haunted landscape through which the lost narrator wandered—both of which are vastly more evocative than what passes in the story for being beyond or above nature. And during the tale-telling, the focus moves, often very rapidly, between the two arenas of imagination. Pavel's practical errand to fetch water from the river modulates quickly into concern over the peril he faces from the water goblin, then into a fanciful story (based on actual unhappiness in love, however) of a woman driven mad by that goblin, then into the more realistic story of Vasily and his mother Feklista (another woman driven mad), then back into the supernatural as Pavel tells us that Vasily has called out to him from his watery grave, then into a cry that, naturalistically enough, Pavel identifies as coming from curlews.

A final irony emerges in the last sentences, following the description of a world awaking to a fresh, exhilarating new morning: after this end-frame, as we had thought it, we learn that Pavel died in a fall from a horse. (The horse is, as it were, a sub-irony.) We are not privileged to hear either a ghost story version of that death from the boys nor the narrator's version, despite his professed admiration for Pavel. We can hardly help wanting more by way of explanation of the boy's end than we get in the understated last words of the sketch. And what our curiosity demands is not a ghost story but a human account.

—Brian Wilkie

BIG BLONDE
by Dorothy Parker, 1930

Dorothy Parker first attracted attention as a flippant and bittersweet poet and irreverent and acerbic satirist whose aim at the shallow and superficial social customs and social climbers often turned on a *bon mot,* a turn of phrase or perspective or a pun that was both striking and memorable. Closer attention to her work, however, shows a talented and dedicated artist whose persistent concern with spare, economical, pure language—even when clichéd and colloquial, which she often used for effect—drew both on her classical education at Dana's School in Morristown, New Jersey, a private secondary school where she took several years of Latin, and her less formal teachers, especially Ernest Hemingway. Like him, she learned to foreshorten time and place in her short stories, so that the central characters and events were always prominently in focus. She learned to rely more on monologue or dialogue than on description. She sought the typical that was also archetypal. Thus however a "slice-of-life" her fiction might seem, the real emphasis often resembles that of James Joyce, whom she also admired. Whether acts and the people who perceive them are substantial or trivial, her stories deal with epiphanic moments of self-awareness or self-exposure (leading to the reader's new judgment and awareness). She frequently spoke of Hemingway as a model and convinced *The New Yorker* to pay her sea voyage to Paris so that she could interview him there, producing the first profile in that magazine ("The Artist's Reward," November 30, 1929). But she also praised F. Scott Fitzgerald, from whom she learned the value of particular, selected objects as symbols of broader social significance, and Ring Lardner, who taught her how to use colloquial dialogue.

The strategy for her fiction—both the early, obvious satires and the later, more sophisticated ones—is often the same: the energy and significance reside in irony, where one shallow person condemns another or is in turn exposed. Nearly all her short stories chart the same course: they affect sophistication while nevertheless displaying the manners of an ignorant "bambosie." But if some of their customs and behavior seems obvious or transparent now, such revealing stories in the 1920's and 1930's had significant power. The bohemian style following World War I, affected and derivative, fit awkwardly with the Puritan values that were still prevalent among Parker's readers, and a considerable part of her strength and importance as a writer lies in her awareness that both strains that together constituted American culture had their serious weaknesses. Her fiction thus constantly turns to the disjunction between intention and performance, pretended knowledge and real ignorance, feigned concern and real pride and greed. In her short stories, the barbed and acid criticism of her satirical verse is still central, but it is both more incisive and more subtle. Gilbert Seldes's praise of Lardner fits her equally well: "the swift, destructive, and tremendously funny turn of phrase, the hard and resistant mind, the gaiety of spirit," but compounded, in Parker's case, with great labor and care. "It takes me six months to do a story. I think it out and then write it sentence by sentence," she once told Marion Capron in an interview; "I can't write five words but that I change seven." This caution, purchased at such cost, was also necessary to keep guard over Parker's more sentimental, sympathetic side, the kind of emotion she could show in public but ruthlessly exempted from her writing.

The best example of all her qualities is seen in her most successful, most anthologized, and most enduring story, "Big Blonde" (first published in 1929, and collected in 1930 in *Laments for the Living*). It is also her most daring story, for it recounts unflinchingly her own alcoholic depressions and attempts at suicide in the years immediately preceding its composition. Like Parker, the story's protagonist, Hazel Morse, is terrified of loneliness and despair, even when she is thought by her friends to be a party girl, a barrel of laughs, always ready for a carefree time. While the stark and unrelieved tragedy of Hazel was new for Parker, a risk that seriously challenged her popular reputation as a wit, on which her career had relied so completely, the story of "Big Blonde" is masterfully rendered, told with astonishing power and technique. Parker reduces the long and despairing years of a woman's life into short panels and compresses an entire autobiography into the strictly limited range of the short story. It is both startlingly panoramic and severely concentrated. In its portrait of the birth and growth of alcoholism and suicidal despair and in its clinical analysis, painfully detailed and piercingly accurate, it is an unrelenting study of the possibility of the brutality of life—the brutality of an uncaring society and of an uncaring self, without self-esteem. The close and steady focus on Hazel Morse's decline and fall is Parker's searing attempt to record society's victimization of its more vulnerable members, and the self-victimization of those who cannot earn even self-respect.

From the start, Hazel Morse finds no advantage in living. She never knew the pleasure of family; her later popularity is artificial. But she has no distorted sense of herself; she is willing to settle for the nearly worthless Herbie Morse to gain some security and stability. Herbie leads Hazel to alcohol, which in turn produces tenderness, self-pity, "misty melancholies." Herbie finally leaves her, despising himself, despising him in her, and she becomes a party girl, seeking favors from anyone willing to give them to her, however temporarily.

Hazel Morse is mirrored in her husband, the speakeasies, her lovers, and finally, the maid, yet all these painful doublings are not nearly so pathetic as the comparison Parker makes between Hazel and a wretched horse nor as tragic as Hazel Morse looking at herself in an actual mirror when taking Veronal. Here, at the moment of suicide, the best she can manage is a bad joke: "Gee, I'm nearly dead, . . . That's a hot one!"

But that is not the end of Hazel Morse. As she survived desertion by her husband and by a string of anonymous lovers, so she survives the deadly poison: her punishment is to remain alive amid the squalor of the poor and unfortunate yearning to breathe free. Yet what survives is at best what we see when Hazel Morse, drugged, is at greatest peace with herself: "Mrs. Morse lay on her back, one flabby, white arm flung up, the wrist against her forehead. Her stiff hair hung tenderly along her face. The bed covers were pushed down, exposing a deep square of soft neck and a pink nightgown, its fabric worn uneven by many launderings; her great breasts, freed from their tight confiner, sagged beneath her arm-pits. Now and then she made knotted, snorting sounds, and from the corner of her opened mouth to the blurred turn of her jaw ran a lane of crusted spittle." The spittle doubtless descends from that of her literary prototype, the suicide Emma Bovary of Flaubert, from whose mouth at death trickles black bile. But Emma leaves a respectable husband, a doctor, and their

daughter. Hazel lives rather than dies, and she still has no one. She remains, at the close of the story, symbolically limp and weakened in bed, a bottle close to her hand—but no more pills.

From more than 2,000 entries in 1929, the unrelenting story of the "Big Blonde," the good-time girl, was awarded the eleventh annual first prize of $500 in the O. Henry Memorial Prizes for the best short story appearing in an American magazine for that year. It was instantly a classic. From as far away as Cannes, Fitzgerald himself was elated. He urged his agent to take up Parker as a client: "Just now she's at a high point as a producer and as to reputation," he wrote Max Perkins, "I wouldn't lose any time about this if it interests you." For him as for many later critics, this was masterful storytelling. However closely it scraped along the bones of Parker's own life, they were bones with the beauty of artifice stripped bare and a detail clean with truth. But like Hazel Morse, alone at the end, feeling unwanted and unsuccessful, there is no record that Parker ever knew what her model Fitzgerald thought of the story or what he said of it.

—Arthur F. Kinney

BIG BOY LEAVES HOME
by Richard Wright, 1938

Richard Wright's short story "Big Boy Leaves Home" first appeared in 1936 in the anthology *The New Caravan*, edited by Alfred Kreymborg, Lewis Mumford, and Paul Rosenfeld. It also appears as one of four novellas in *Uncle Tom's Children* published in 1938. All of the stories in this collection focus on black rural life in Mississippi.

The action of "Big Boy Leaves Home" takes place over a period of 24 hours and begins with Big Boy and three friends, all having skipped school for the day, enjoying a walk through the woods where they eventually decide to swim naked in the creek. The opening setting is intentionally idyllic, emphasizing youthful innocence and exuberance. Relying more heavily on dialogue written in African-American dialect than on description or other forms of authorial intrusion found in Wright's later works, he allows the characters to discuss topics with varying degrees of racial overtones, including hostility to blacks by Mr. Harvey, the owner of the land they are walking on. In spite of their apprehension, they swim naked in the creek and startle a white woman who is standing on the creek bank. The woman backs away from them towards the tree where the boys have hidden their clothes. A white man with a rifle arrives on the scene after hearing her screaming. In the ensuing scuffle Big Boy sees two of his friends shot and killed; he wrestles the rifle away and shoots the white man to protect himself.

The two survivors, Big Boy and his friend BoBo, run home to escape from a lynch mob. Big Boy's family and three friends arrange for his escape by hiding him in a brick kiln where he will wait for a truck driver to drive him to safety in Chicago. Although Big Boy is successful in his escape, his friend BoBo is not so lucky. BoBo was supposed to meet Big Boy at the brick kilns but is captured by the lynch mob. From his hiding place, Big Boy watches as the lynch mob tars, feathers, and burns his friend.

"Big Boy Leaves Home" shares a number of themes typically found in American literature, such as the initiation of youth and the subsequent flight to a new land. In "Big Boy Leaves Home" the concept of flight is ironic since Big Boy flees not to a new and open free territory, but to the violent urban landscape of Chicago. The theme of initiation, particularly to violence and an attempted escape from it, is a central part of Wright's novels, including *Native Son, The Outsider,* and *The Long Dream,* as well as several of his short stories.

Wright begins the story with an Edenic setting where four boys are enjoying themselves, in harmony with nature. The environment changes sharply as the story progresses. The warm sun is replaced by the chill of the cold water which prefigures what follows. Although the story focuses on racism and its effects on blacks and whites in rural Mississippi, Wright's narrative resists this convenient generalization, and he successfully prevents the reader from arriving at simplistic conclusions or suggesting ineffective remedies such as those he warns against in his prefatory essay to *Native Son,* "How Bigger Was Born." The result is a clear and effective portrayal of the precarious nature of African-American life in the South. It is the element of chance, of arbitrariness, of a meaningless and insignificant encounter fueled by racial prejudice and fear, that becomes magnified to such a level of violence. It is not just the acts of violence that should draw our concern here, it is the basis for these acts and the degree to which human beings are willing to escalate violence before it becomes shocking and repulsive.

The level of violence and its impact on the human personality is developed in transitions between the idyllic natural landscape to a human or psychological landscape characterized by fear and terror. At the beginning of the story, Big Boy appears as a bit of bully to the extent that his three friends gang up on him to overcome his dominance. Although this is a more or less playful scene, Big Boy almost strangles BoBo and tells him if people gang up against you "you put the heat on one of them n make im tell the others t let up." Although this may seem innocent enough, it prefigures the tar and feather scene later in the story, as well as the lynch mob burning Big Boy's home because his parents would not reveal his hiding place.

Later when Big Boy hides in the brick kiln he is startled by a rattlesnake. In a frenzy, Big Boy beats the rattlesnake to death with a stick while imagining the angry lynch mob chasing him. After wishing he had taken his father's shotgun with him for self-defense he lapses into a dream of killing his attackers and imagines the newspaper's headlines: "Nigger Kills Dozen Of Lynch Mob Befo Lynched" and "Trapped Nigger Slays Twenty Befo Killed." Here violence appears again in an imaginative context, but in this instance, it is clear how the external environment has affected Big Boy's consciousness. It is in part due to progressively violent and hostile imaginings of Big Boy that one can begin to address the irony inherent in Big Boy's name. He is no more than a boy, as the story indicates, but he is forced to become big, to become as threatening to others as others are to him. In Big Boy's case he threatens or overpowers no one, he merely survives by escaping.

Escape, especially to the North, is rendered symbolically with the existence of north-bound trains in the story. The North is seen as a place of escape from racial oppression, but as Wright chronicles in his later fiction, the city, Chicago in particular, was not the haven African-Americans expected it to be. It is ironic that the theme of flight from the rural South exists as a central theme in much of Wright's fiction since many critics, both black and white,

accused Wright of abandoning his own people by fleeing the South and eventually his country when he moved to Paris. More importantly, the reader of "Big Boy Leaves Home" should not breathe a comfortable sigh of relief or congratulate Big Boy on his escape as a solution to the conflict. In Wright's most famous novel, *Native Son,* published in 1940, the protagonist commits the brutal murder of two women—his name is Bigger Thomas.

—Jeffrey D. Parker

BILLY BUDD, SAILOR: AN INSIDE NARRATIVE
by Herman Melville, 1924

Left unfinished at the time of Melville's death, "Billy Budd, Sailor" was discovered and first published in 1924; its definitive version was brought out by Harrison Hayford and Merton M. Sealts in 1962. Like most of Melville's fiction, the story raises complex issues in which ethics, psychology, and metaphysics shade into one another.

The plot of "Billy Budd" is partly reminiscent of the events that took place on the USS *Somers* in 1842, but Melville sets the action on an English man-of-war and in 1797, a few months after "the Great Mutiny" at Spithead and the Nore, when British naval authorities had reason to fear the spread of rebelliousness through the fleet engaged in the war with revolutionary France.

The story stages the classical conflict of innocence and evil. The former is represented by William Budd, an outstandingly handsome and generally beloved young sailor who has been impressed (arbitrarily enlisted) into service on the outward-bound gunship *Bellipotent*—symbolically, the merchantman to which he bids farewell at the beginning of the story is called "Rights-of-Man." The bearer of the theme of evil is Claggart, the *Bellipotent*'s master-of-arms, whose duties, at the time, were those of a disciplinarian and chief of the ship's secret police. Billy is an almost extreme romantic version of the noble savage with only an occasional speech impediment to remind one of the doctrine of humanity's post-lapsarian condition. Innocent to the point of inability to suspect maliciousness in others, he fails to notice Claggart's ill will toward him. By contrast, Claggart is presented as a case of "natural depravity," a mysterious turpitude in the constitution not of people in general but of a few rare individuals. Although capable of an intellectual appreciation of Billy's character, he is determined to destroy him—out of envy that fosters irrational suspiciousness and, as is indirectly suggested, perhaps out of a warped homosexual attraction. Yet during the confrontation that follows Claggart's attempt to denounce Billy as a mutineer, it is Billy who, handicapped by his speech impediment, instinctively strikes out and causes Claggart's death.

This paradoxical development gives rise to a set of ambivalences that leave no further space for the good/evil dichotomy. Though the captain of the ship is convinced of Billy's loyalty and innocence of any intent to murder Claggart, he nevertheless convenes a drumhead court and practically forces it to sentence Billy to death.

Captain Vere's immediate view of the situation is expressed in his impulsive remark that Claggart has been struck dead "by the angel of God" yet that "the angel must hang." A sailor's violence to an officer is a capital offense;

at the time, extenuating circumstances would be overruled by the vague fear of mutiny. Yet it is not for the sake of expedience in the prevention of unrest but rather out of a single-minded adherence to the principles of military discipline that Captain Vere consciously sacrifices natural justice: "do these buttons that we wear attest that our allegiance is to Nature? No, to the King." Significantly, he has been presented as a conservative not out of his class interests but out of conviction and as an intellectual who reads books not for new ideas but for the confirmation of his old ones. Owing to an almost mystical fervor of his single-minded commitment, he strikes the ship's surgeon as "unhinged."

True to his name which is etymologically linked with the Latin for "truth," Captain Vere never stoops to distort facts, either in giving evidence to the drumhead court, or, the narrator suggests, in explaining the sentencing and his own role in it to Billy. His feelings for Billy, who is a foundling of apparently noble descent, are presented as paternal; and Billy himself seems to have been in search of a father-figure in the course of his brief life. It is to his ideology that Vere, like the Biblical Abraham, appears to sacrifice Billy—and Billy accepts the necessity of this sacrifice, calmly, and perhaps with a sense of fulfillment at the completion of a quest. His hanging is described in a language that associates him with Christ; and there is a suggestion of the supernatural in the absence of the involuntary muscular spasm that usually follows hangings. "Belli" and "Budd" happen to be the names of a Celtic god ritually sacrificed for the sake of victory: soon after the event, the *Bellipotent* vanquishes the French ship *Athée* (the *Atheist*).

This is also the thematic framework for Melville's references to Sir Horatio Nelson in "Billy Budd." Melville notes that in 1797, off the Spanish coast, Nelson was ordered to shift his pennant to a ship that had newly arrived from the mutinous English shores: he would not terrorize the crew into submission but won them over by the sheer strength of his heroic personality. Though "military utilitarians" eventually condemned Nelson's "ornate publication of his person" in the battle of Trafalgar, the effect and the meaning of such an act, tantamount to placing oneself on a sacrificial altar, were, according to Melville, beyond rational explanation. Captain Vere, who, unlike Nelson, is not a natural leader, instinctively sacrifices a person who represents another charismatic archetype, that of the Handsome Sailor.

As if to complement this layer of significance, Melville refers to the cagy older sailor to whom Billy has clung on the *Bellipotent* as "the *Agamemnon* man." The Greek king after whom old Dansker's ship was named had sacrificed his daughter for the sake of victory. Unlike Aeschyllean Agamemnon, however, Captain Vere does not dismiss the clash between the systems of value among which he has to choose, nor does he waive his feelings for Billy. His choice of asserting an abstract set of principles at the price of an innocent human's life sharply contrasts with his keen awareness of the dilemma and his profound emotional engagement.

The story ends with two outside narratives of Billy's death: a newspaper report that transforms Billy's image into that of a foreign-born traitor and a ballad, "Billy in the Darbies," that presents a third version of his character and fate. The inside narrative seems to be a true account of the inside politics and of the clash of individual and social goals. Yet the subtitle of the story also points to the inner dynamics of the work of imagination that explores the branching multi-level significances of human acts, critiques mendacious or simplifying ways of representing them, and places itself amidst the multiplicity of incomplete and perhaps incommensurable human perspectives.

—Leona Toker

THE BIRTHMARK
by Nathaniel Hawthorne, 1846

Humankind can never know whether its relation to nature is adversarial or harmonious. While nature creates and nourishes, it also blasts and destroys. As far as we can conjecture it is utterly indifferent to human ideas of perfection. The riddles with which nature confronts humankind proliferate constantly in practical and emotional terms in all types of literature, but it is characteristic of Nathaniel Hawthorne that almost all of his stories and novels should be cast in the mold of romantic allegory and that they are pushed into metaphysical realms for resolution. His great novel *The Scarlet Letter* has less to do with the New England past or with illicit love than with sin and redemption. His story "Ethan Brand" traces to its absolute extreme the course of a stylized character who in his pride repudiates the world.

"The Birthmark" (collected in *Mosses from an Old Manse*)—readily comparable to another of Hawthorne's more ambitious stories "Rapaccini's Daughter"—tells of a scientist's passion to overcome what he deems to be the imperfection of nature. In each of these stories it is a lovely woman whose physical body bears the intolerable flaw, and in each case the woman dies as a result of relentless attempts at purgation. This repeated allegorical design strongly suggests Hawthorne's conviction that woman, as incarnation of nature, may be perfect *because* of her nominal imperfections and that the whole scientific agenda for correcting nature may be wrong-headed and impious if not downright evil.

The three main characters of "The Birthmark" are designed specifically to serve symbolic functions in the allegorical action. Aylmer is the greatest scientist of his age, skilled not only in the physical sciences but in medicine and organic chemistry. His wife Georgiana is the most beautiful of women, except for the little birthmark on her cheek. (That the birthmark has the shape of a handprint suggests it has been laid on by nature to signify its hold on the woman's life.) Aminadab the laboratory assistant is ugly, hairy, primitive in appearance to signify that he belongs entirely to the material world, not to the spiritual one for which Aylmer longs. It is Aminadab who, at one point, admonishes his master, "If she were my wife, I'd never part with that birthmark."

But it is the focus of Aylmer's overreaching pride to find means for correcting what he can only see as nature's mistake, he can only love Georgiana as she might be without the birthmark. For her part, she does not in the beginning consider the mark to be a defect at all, claiming plaintively that former suitors have called it an addition to her other charms. It is less for her own sake than from noble and finally sacrificial loyalty that she submits to be the subject of her husband's experiments with her.

In the fashion of his time Hawthorne intrudes repeatedly to warn that Aylmer's aspirations are misguided and likely to cause irredeemable mischief. "The crimson hand expressed the ineludible gripe in which mortality clutches the highest and purest of earthly mould . . ." and " . . . our great creative Mother, while she amuses us with working in the broadest sunshine is yet severely careful to keep her own secrets, and, in spite of her pretended openness, show us nothing but results." When timorous Georgiana summons courage to peer into her husband's library she finds in the older works of alchemists and scientists only a compilation of quaint errors, while in her husband's own voluminous record of his experiments she finds that "his most splendid successes were invariably failures, if compared with the ideal at which he aimed."

She tries her best to warn of impending failure. In his pride and frustration he brushes aside her warnings and determines on greater efforts—until at last he bends to warn her there may be danger in continuing. Then the peripety occurs as, in the full stretch of her nobility, she drives him to press on to a conclusion of what has been begun.

That conclusion, of course, is her death. Aylmer's supreme concoction works, though not just as intended. The birthmark begins to fade as Georgiana slips into unconsciousness. By "a strange impulse" the husband kisses the fading blemish, though essentially he is exultant with the appearance of success. He crows about it to Aminadab, as if the earthly servant, too, had been conquered.

At this moment of frightful joy the dying Georgiana wakes to console him from the plane of her superior compassion. "My poor Aylmer . . . you have aimed loftily; you have done nobly. Do not repent that with so high and pure a feeling you have rejected the best the earth could offer. . . ." And now, beholding her death, Aminidab finds his turn to laugh—surely in contempt of Aylmer's lofty aims as well as their grim result. It is the laughter of the everlasting night in which humankind persists with no hope of certainty.

But the story does not end with such pessimistic simplicity. The author, indeed, admonishes us to believe that with a "profounder wisdom" Aylmer would have left well enough alone. That, however, is really no better than Aminidab's advice, laid in earlier. It leaves out of account Georgiana's compassionate and lofty instruction, "do not repent." She has chosen, with her life, to side against complacency and in favor of aspiration. May it not be that Aylmer's defiance of nature is what nature intends of humans? This stunning paradox has blazed through some of the greatest literature of our civilization from the Prometheus legend to the Faust myth.

—R.V. Cassill

THE BLACK DOG
by A.E. Coppard, 1923

Coppard's short stories belong more to the tradition of the folktale than to that of modern literary fiction. Though Coppard's work has its sophistications they are not the sophistications of the 20th century novel. Though in temperament, and *weltanschauung,* very different from Hardy, there are affinities in the way the two use the materials of folktale and ballad. Coppard's themes are the eternal verities of the folk narrative; love and death, jealousy and suicide. There is a wryness of method and outlook, a refusal to overwrite, which prevents such materials from becoming merely melodramatic. In "The Black Dog" this elemental world is mediated through the presence of a far from elemental protagonist, the Honourable Gerald Loughlin.

Loughlin is a figure both of fun and of pathos. He is "handsome and honest," with a "decent gentlemanly mind." The story begins with Loughlin about to return to London after a stay in the country. He gets as far as the station, but then breaks his journey and walks back to the village (a pattern of interrupted journeying that will be very significantly repeated later); he does so because he has fallen in love with Lady Tillington's companion, Orianda Crabbe. Loughlin's infatuation draws him into a social world of which he has no knowledge, and of which he has only the most patronising and idealised conceptions—conceptions of which experience is gradually to disabuse him.

Orianda is the daughter of an innkeeper (his inn is "The Black Dog" of the story's title) and hurdlemaker. Loughlin's upper-class values leave him almost wholly at a loss to understand the codes of behavior that govern Orianda's environment. There is absurdity in his initial approach to Orianda: "Are you related to the Crabbes of Cotterton—I fancy I know them?" But Orianda refuses to be drawn into Loughlin's world of social connections. Her insistence that she is "nobody at all, my father keeps an inn" is a declaration of truth to self, which reflects that greater strength—and greater truth to her feelings—that we shall see more of later. As Orianda narrates her family history (her mother's running away from her father; Orianda's own theft of money from her father, whom she insists she loves, and her flight to join her mother, whom she finds living with another man), Loughlin is immediately out of his depth. Loughlin has no experience of a world where social morality (and social appearance) can so readily be subordinated to the higher values of personal happiness and truth to feeling. His ponderous affirmations—"I am sure life is enhanced not by amassing conventions, but by destroying them"—never ring true, and are the product only of his infatuation. Orianda, on the other hand, finds her new environment, with Lady Tillington, unsatisfying, since, though "it is polite and soft, like silk," she finds it insufficiently "barbarous."

Loughlin escorts Orianda back to her father; there is a wonderfully effective moment in the meeting of father and daughter when "his heavy discoloured hands rested on her shoulders, her gloved ones lay against his breast." The two worlds, one open to all the powers of nature and instinct, the other covered up against them, are crystallised in these pairs of hands. Loughlin is inclined to see rural life as a "parade of Phyllis and Corydon." The truth is that Orianda's father has taken a mistress; Orianda sets about getting rid of her, and in the process drives her to suicide. Loughlin has earlier been moved to speculate, unconsciously keeping an anthropologist's distance, "Have they no code at all?"

Orianda herself has no illusions and is entirely aware that "this is a very dirty Eden." The decisive moment, at which Loughlin might reenter that Eden from which his adherence to social convention has excluded him, is clear enough. He and Orianda, returning from a picnic, have to cross the river; the bridges are inconveniently far away. The two decide to strip off and swim over, carrying their clothes; Gerald retires to a discreet distance. He returns, "humming a discreet and very audible hum" as a warning of his approach, to find Orianda "scantily clothed" and lying on the ground. The "Honourable Gerald" (Coppard is wholly alert to the absurd ties of the appellation) can only react in a "decent gentlemanly" fashion:

> "I beg your pardon," he said hastily and full of surprise and modesty walked away. The unembarrassed girl called after him,"Drying my hair."

Orianda, it seems to Gerald, displays "a contempt for good breeding," while Orianda is clear that Gerald doesn't know what love is. She tells Loughlin it is "a compound of anticipation and gratitude"; he still does not understand. The anticipation and the gratitude, Orianda has to explain, are "for the moment of passion," and she sounds almost Lawrentian in her mock solemn pronouncement: "Honour thy moments of passion and keep them holy." Gerald is quite incapable of living by such a code; as Orianda aptly observes, he is a "timid swimmer." Orianda knows she could never marry him, she would feel like "a wild bee in a canary cage." It is a typical Coppard image, both homely and poetic."

Gerald packs his bag and leaves, even though Orianda "grew more alluring than ever." The last two paragraphs startle by their abrupt transition to the present tense; Gerald has left behind Orianda's world; he considers returning but, in the final words of the story "he does not do so." It is "a dirty Eden" he is incapable of regaining.

—Glyn Pursglove

THE BLACK MADONNA
by Doris Lessing, 1966

The formal aesthetic elegance of "The Black Madonna" coupled with its political content make it one of Lessing's best African stories. It offers a biting socio-political and cultural commentary on the social structure and British colonial attitudes in Zambesia, once part of Southern Rhodesia, now the independent nation of Zimbabwe. The politics of the 1990's are very different from those in the 1940's when the story takes place and in the 1960's when it was first published. Nonetheless, this story stands up very well over time. Lessing's control of the narrative voice, her very considerable descriptive skills, and her ability to meld fact and invention to create a plot that carries the weight of her socio-political commentary all manifest her extraordinary talent. Initially, Lessing's progressive critique of apartheid contributed to the popularity of both her novel *The Grass Is Singing* (1950) and her stories of Africa collected in *The Black Madonna* (1966). Recently the critical response to her ideological views has been more mixed, in part reflecting the dramatic changes in the geopolitical world. An understanding of her subject position as an author helps to explain the mixed responses her story produces.

Lessing is a white woman, born in Persia (now Iran), who grew up in Southern Rhodesia under British Colonial rule before she moved permanently to England in 1949. When she tried to return to South Africa, she was denied entrance by the government who found her Communism and politics unacceptable. She also has been condemned by others of a more liberal and progressive persuasion for being too slow to break with the Communist party at a time when many left due to Stalin's excesses. In an essay in *In Pursuit of Doris Lessing* (1990), Anthony Chennells analyzes the views of Lessing's Zimbabwe critics, reporting

that they find her Rhodesian stories deficient. They think that her criticism of colonialism and the West does not go far enough. Although "The Black Madonna" identifies with the plight of the Africans driven into hard-work by their colonial oppressors, it does not look to the Africans to regain their tribal authority and create an independent African nation. Lessing's narrator is scathing in passages depicting the ways in which the general in the story and the white colonialists exploit the hardworking Africans. The narrator shows how the Africans are trifled with by the leisured wives of those wielding power. The story starkly displays white arrogance, describing the ways in which men like Captain Stocker use the African women sexually while denying them respect or personhood. It can be admired for its critique of colonialism but it can also be seen as a force that perpetuates the modes of representation of the oppressors. Lessing's studied attempt to give a "masculine prose style" to the narrator of the story whose gender often appears to be feminine is further evidence of Lessing's concessions to patriarchy. In these many ways it is possible to see how a postcolonial critique of Western cultural and writing practices and Lessing's constructedness illuminates her stories.

Lessing writes in the tradition of Isak Dinesen, Olive Schreiner, and Joseph Conrad, all exiled writers who criticize British Colonialism and its oppressive regime in Africa. However, her own subject position makes her an agent of oppression, reproducing the kinds of representations of patriarchy and colonialism that she condemns. Her imagery of Captain Stocker's native mistress participates in the stereotype of the black native's primitive, unselfconscious sexuality. She exoticizes the native Africans and in many of her stories she imbues the African veld with savagery and mysticism, relying heavily upon romantic and apocalyptic tropes. A less romantic immersion in the narrative of exploration and discovery and the quest for identity in the heart of Africa would fashion the veld differently, seeing it not as a vast, savage landscape, awesome in its size and silence, but as a landscape filled with ancestral voices and intimately connected to the spirit world. Her account of Captain Stocker's double-life, the one inside the African bushstations with his native wife, the other in the African cities with his white wife, would be written differently if Lessing were not entangled in Western fictions of travel and exploration and the consequent displacements they cause.

"The Black Madonna" is set in Zambesia at the end of World War II. It explores the relationship between Michele, a feckless Italian prisoner of war who paints to while away the time and gain favor during his period of imprisonment in a Zambesian internment camp, and Captain Stocker, a military figure assigned to supervise him. When the story starts, Michele is the benefactor of Italy's swift transformation from the status of enemy to honorary ally. Free in Zambesia, with little to do but paint for the leisured wives of the military, he is fetched into labor by the general, who is planning a Military Tattoo to lift the morale of the civilian population and boost the war effort. Captain Stocker is to supervise Michele while he constructs an artificial city which can be spectacularly bombed in the climax of the Military Tattoo. Captain Stocker, with his Northern temperament, prejudice against the Italian enemy, secret admiration for Hitler, and military precision, stands in stark contrast to Michele, with his indolent, sensuous, Southern temperament and his capacity to feel. Michele is ordered to use his artistic skills (actually he is a bricklayer) to construct this artificial city. While a prisoner in the camp, he had assisted in the decoration of the interior of a church, painting sensuous murals. His murals depicted the swarthy Italian peasantry gathering grapes with dancing Italian girls and dark-eyed children playing. In the midst of the happy Italian scene, he painted the Virgin Mary and the baby Jesus. The turning point of Lessing's story comes when a drunken Michele paints Captain Stocker's bush-wife, giving her the appearance of a black Madonna complete with a halo and rendering her as every bit as appropriate to Captain Stocker's black world as the Madonna is to the Italian people.

Captain Stocker and Michele are each complicit in the other's transformation and undoing in ways not unfamiliar to those who have studied the relationship between captive and oppressor. Captain Stocker initially chastizes Michele for his careless dress, his lack of respect, his drunkenness, and his easy talk. Later, Captain Stocker is found seated on the campground, careless of appearance, and drunk himself. The two men, who initially loathe each other, bond in a drunken camradery, confessing to each other their private lusts and loves. Lessing's description of Michele and the words she gives him to utter call forth images of Christ and his last words on the cross. With deep irony, Lessing's story reveals how Michele's inherent goodness and the innocence that lies behind his depiction of women as Madonnas are both misunderstood by Captain Stocker and the colonial institutions that have shaped him. In the misunderstanding lies Lessing's condemnation of a culture that has produced a Captain Stocker with his schizoid life and the civilization that fails to understand the right relationship between art and ethics, wantonly playing at imperialistic fantasies of domination and militarism, making a mockery of human values.

The final line of Lessing's story imitates James Joyce's epiphany, offering a sudden illumination of the "whatness" (quidditas) of the thing. It reveals Captain Stocker, a man in the midst of breakdown, weeping silently at the loss of his friend, Michele, the artist of sorts who has painted him a native, young, plump woman with her dress falling off her shoulder, a black Madonna with her black baby slung in a band of red cloth. Michele, sensing Stocker's harsh disapproval of the image, strips the woman of the halo, and poignantly offers the gift of the revised painting to Stocker. At the same time, he apologises for it, saying it's a black Madonna for a black country. But Captain Stocker cannot acknowledge the gesture, nor the innocence of this Christ-like Michele, and he sinks back into the role of a lost man, unable to assimilate the parts of his life, ordering Michele to leave, taking the gift away. Dumbly, Captain Stocker hears the soul-breaking words— "yes, *Sir*"—as Michele salutes and leaves, mocking the unfeeling military values that Captain Stocker cannot abandon. The unbearable burdens of the irreconcilable ironies of colonial life undo Captain Stocker. The story ends with an indictment of colonialism, militarism, and the senselessness of war.

Today, Lessing's story provokes a more penetrating analysis of colonialism, forcing us to consider the ways in which she is implicated in colonialism and patriarchy, and how various modes of representation enforce the very realities they are overtly criticizing. Nonetheless, the story is sufficiently supple in its treatment that it can withstand the critique and still remain vital. Perhaps this is one of the earmarks of great literature.

—Carol Simpson Stern

———

BLACKBERRY WINTER.   See the Writers entry on **WARREN, Robert Penn**.

———

BLOW-UP (Las babas del diablo)
by Julio Cortázar, 1959

Julio Cortázar's story "Las babas del diablo" ("Blow-Up") received exceptional popular acclaim, thanks in part to Italian film director Michelangelo Antonioni's film version in the late 1960's. Unfortunately, very little of Cortázar's story remains in the motion picture, which retains only certain specifics, so that the moviegoer experiences very little of the original text. The English translation likewise fails to convey a totally adequate impression of the original, and, particularly, its symbolism. Whether the translator missed the symbolic nature of certain passages or opted for other reasons to minimize those aspects, the fact remains that the symbolism is considerably less perceptible in the English version. An especially significant instance involves the title, which in the original is "Las babas del diablo," literally "The devil's drooling," alluding to a comparable term used in French. It refers to the early morning fog that resembles gossamer filaments also called "threads of the virgin."

In the story, first collected in *Las armas secretos* (1959), Cortázar explores the artist's relationship to his art and to the reader, examining the narrator's role in this relationship. The ostensible narrator of "Blow-Up," an authorial construct, is both a persona of Cortázar and an embodiment of the narrative consciousness and perspective. Initially, he exists outside the incident to be narrated, that is, the story qua story (his existence is prior to the events), but he will have a role in those incidents.

The protagonist-narrator is Roberto Michel, a French-Chilean translator whose consuming passion is photography, to which he devotes much of his spare time. His life is external to the occurrence narrated, but tangential thereto. In the telling of the incident, however, he is not only the narrator but also a participant. Cortázar questions the relationships of fact to fiction and literature to reality: this persona retells an incident experienced as real, and he himself is presented as real, in the world external to the event. But where is reality? Is it relative? Is his interpretation of reality false? Does objective reality correspond to his perception or interpretation, and are the characters as he has judged them? Ultimately, the reader must inquire how reliable Michel is in his role as narrator.

Michel, bored with a translating job from which he is repeatedly distracted, first recalls and then determines to narrate an event of a month earlier, which he inadvertently photographed (an enlargement displayed on the study wall, across from his worktable, providing the English title for the story). While sitting in a small park a month before, Michel was intrigued by his observation of an encounter between a mature, fortyish woman and a boy of perhaps 15 years. From attitudes and gestures (for he is unable to hear the conversation), he makes certain inferences, deciding to take a picture of the two. From the boy's nervousness, Michel postulates an attempt on the woman's part at seduction. Upon noticing the photographer, the boy runs away, "like a gossamer filament of angel-spit in the morning air." But, the reader is informed almost immediately, "filaments of angel-spittle are also called devil-spit," a reference to the original Spanish title. The relativity of literary interpretation (linked to reader-response, the narrative voice, or both) begins with language itself, as exemplified in the two almost diametrically opposed terms referring to one and the same phenomenon. The reader realizes that the latter phrase is equally relevant when Michel discovers yet another actor in the momentary street drama he had witnessed, a man watching from a parked car, resembling "a flour-powdered clown," apparently waiting for the woman to procure the boy for him. Stereotypical suggestions of homosexuality or effeminate mannerism appear in Cortázar's description of the man: "walking cautiously as if the pavement hurt his feet. . . ." The woman's anger at Michel's interference and the man's demand for the film give Michel some satisfaction at having intervened. When he develops the film, the event is recalled so forcefully that he enlarges the photograph, becoming so obsessed by the comparison between memory and what the photograph has retained that he enlarges it again.

Contrast between the two time planes becomes part of the self-consciousness of the text, developed as two interwoven narratives, the second presented in parentheses that separate it visually as well as temporally from the primary one. In the secondary narrative, Michel as author/narrator includes his impressions and perceptions of the present, experienced during the course of the narrative act (retelling the event in which he is both narrative perspective and minor character). The decision to undertake the narration (an integral portion of Cortázar's meditation upon the relationship between the artist and his art) results from a conflict between Michel's role as a translator (external to the fiction), and his role as a minor character or marginal participant in the event within the fiction. That conflict occurs as the translator is unable to do his job because the character/observer is obsessed with the incident, requiring his assumption of yet another role as author/narrator. Thus, the artist is not free but is compelled by his art. The photograph symbolizes that compulsion or fixation.

Sometimes, particularly late in the narration, when the shifting time planes are further blurred and almost fused, Michel feels that the incident is repeating itself and will have a different, negative outcome because he will be unable to intervene. Therefore, he screams to break the narrative distance and thus save the child and prevent evil's triumph.

—Genaro J. Pérez

THE BLUE JAR
by Isak Dinesen, 1942

Isak Dinesen is a Danish author best-known for her three volumes of Gothic and Romantic short stories, *Seven Gothic Tales, Winter's Tales,* and *Last Tales,* and her memoirs *Out of Africa.* She wrote these tales in English first and then translated them into Danish. Her stories fall into the oral tradition of *The Arabian Nights,* often distanced in time or set in exotic locales. Her characters experience trials that would test a Job, yet are rewarded by a moment of epiphany in which the pattern of their lives is revealed, allowing them to accept their destiny.

Dinesen's story "The Blue Jar" is actually a story within the story of "The Young Man with the Carnation" in *Winter's Tales.* It may have been influenced by Mallarmé's poem, "L'Azur." It has all the elements of the fable, the once-upon-a-time-ness we expect, the lack of physical description of the characters, the pointed moral of the story at the end. We know little about the characters' lives except for their obsessions. These rich aristocrats can afford to indulge their whims. The father is perfectly blind to the real needs of the daughter, whose name, Lady Helena, echoes "the face that launched a thousand ships."

The brevity of "The Blue Jar" and its finely honed craftsmanship, make this story-within-a-story a model for Dinesen's art. The father cares for nothing but collecting ancient blue china. Apparently he cares little for his daughter, for he abandoned her easily when his ship was sinking. Arriving on the deserted deck, she is saved by a young English sailor. The two "fugitives" have escaped both death by drowning and the ordinary lives they lived before. For nine magical days they sailed together as stars ran across the sky and seemed to fall into their boat, as the sea glowed phosphorescent from the fire of the burning ship, as the blue of the ocean and the blue of the sky held and rocked them. And as we later learn, in the midst of that blue world, their hearts "beat gently," "innocent and free."

The state of unity that Lady Helena enjoyed is a rare state that many wish for: a kind of relaxed joyfulness that children, in their innocence, have known. In such a state, at one with nature, all the elements of air, earth (the clay jar), water, fire, and god's creatures come together, balanced in harmony for a few precious moments. Such harmony is lost when the lovers are parted by the unfeeling father. At the end of her life, Lady Helena regains this sense of unity when she finds the true blue porcelain, and dies at peace with the world.

The "blue jar" that is never quite the perfect blue is symbolic of her quest in search of the bliss she once shared with the sailor, floating in a brilliant blue sea, with a beautiful blue sky above. The separation she feels, and the intensity of the quest, is symbolized by her mystical image of the earth as a blue orb with water above and below, her ship sailing on one side while below under the sea, the shadow ship of her lover accompanies her.

The values of the father contrast with the values of the daughter in their divergent views of the sailor. The father's sense of class distinctions make it impossible for him to see the sailor as a suitable partner for his daughter. Thus he pays the sailor to sail on the other side of the world, because he finds it unpleasant that a "peer's daughter" and "a young sailor, who made his bread in the merchant service," spent nine days alone together. The daughter, on the other hand, thinks, "If I stopped sailing, what would those poor sailors who made their bread in the merchant service do?" She sees the sailor with compassion and love, and foretells that when she dies, he will die with her: "In the end my ship will go down, to the center of the globe, and at the very same hour the other ship will sink as well — for people call it sinking . . . and there we two shall meet."

The daughter both follows and rejects her father's vocation of a collector of blue china. While she too sails the world searching for the blue jar, rejecting all other meaningful pursuits, she is really searching for her lover. And unlike the father, she is looking for the one true blue.

Frequently in fables, the father, a symbol of the powerful, patriarchal culture, separates the young lovers. In these tales, the young man often becomes the focus of the story as he braves the wrath and power of the father to attain his love. In a marvelous twist on this old take, Dinesen focuses the story on the daughter; the sailor disappears, and the woman takes charge of her life.

In "The Young Man with The Carnation" Dinesen addresses the dilemma of the writer who becomes isolated from nature by focusing on words. Her solution, and that of the main character who narrates "The Blue Jar," is that the artist and the sailor alike must submit their lives to a divine destiny. Each are compelled to be what they are, and by their submission to divine will, they are ennobled creatures. Dinesen includes in her pantheon of superior beings the aristocrat, based on the dichotomy she witnessed between her own repressed middle-class mother and her aristocratic, free-thinking father, whom she adored. In the pattern of her life, she experienced moments of intense joy in her union with nature in Africa, and like Lady Helena, she was forced to separate from that bliss by the demands of her powerful family. Dinesen turned to writing to recapture the joy of her formerly happy years through imaginative recreation.

In "The Blue Jar" Dinesen connects the themes of nature and art, showing how imagination is the force that unifies all opposites. Love, art, the sea, and the quest for the ideal are recurrent themes in this story. To Dinesen, the quest is the holy task, which must be fulfilled, no matter what the cost, no matter how senseless it may appear to others.

—Judith Rosenberg

BLUEBEARD (Blaubart)
by Jacob and Wilhelm Grimm, 1812

The fairy tale motif of the forbidden room has appeared in tales from many different cultures and centuries. Besides appearing in the Grimms' fairy tales "Bluebeard," "The Virgin Mary's Child," and "Fichter's Bird," the motif can be found in works such as the *Thousand and One Nights* (or *Arabian Nights*); Charles Perrault's French tale "La barbe bleue" from his collection *Contes du Temps passé* (1697); the Romanian story "The Enchanted Pig" (in Andrew Lang's *The Red Fairy Book,* 1890), and most recently in the title story of Helga Schubert's 1982 East German collection, *Das verbotene Zimmer* (The Forbidden Room), in which "the forbidden room" represents West Berlin.

"Blaubart" ("Bluebeard") is a mixture of Perrault's tale "La barbe bleue" and the oral rendition of the Hassenpflug sisters, members of a magistrate's family in Kassel with a Huguenot background, who had become close friends and relatives of the Grimms (Dorothea Grimm married Ludwig Hassenpflug). The Hassenpflug sisters were among the more than 25 women that contributed the majority of the 86 stories in the first volume of Grimms' 1812 collection. Because of the important precedence of the Perrault tale "La barbe bleue," Jacob and Wilhelm Grimm decided to omit "Bluebeard" from their collection beginning with the second edition in 1819. (For the same reason, the tale "Puss in Boots" was omitted from the Grimms' 1819 collection). In spite the fact that "Bluebeard" is among the 32 tales that were relegated to the section of "omitted tales" in Grimms' *Kinder- und Hausmärchen* (*The Complete Fairy Tales of the Brothers Grimm,* translated by Jack Zipes, 1987), the Grimms' "Bluebeard," a tale of the

horribly "beastly" bridegroom and his beautiful young bride, is included in many fairy tale collections and anthologies. Bluebeard's violent actions against his string of wives and his controlling and misogynist demeanor have frequently been viewed by feminist critics as model representatives of 19th-century patriarchal violence in the domestic realm.

Another widely applicable motif in "Bluebeard" is the disobedience of a young curious woman during her passage from girlhood to womanhood. Seen from this vantage point, "Bluebeard" contains implicit allusions to the Biblical story of the Fall (Genesis 3:1-7) and suggests a link between Eve and the unnamed female in the tale. The allusion to Eve is particularly evident when the motif of the forbidden room in "Bluebeard" is placed next to its related Grimms' tale "The Virgin Mary's Child." In the latter tale it is the Virgin Mary who holds the key to the forbidden room and who punishes transgressions. In both Grimm tales, the female figures evoke images of Eve as scapegoats for the origin of evil in Western civilization. Just as the myth of Eve has been used in Western religious history to rationalize male fear and negation of women, "Bluebeard" can be read as a warning for women not to succumb to sexual curiosity, Eros, and fantasy because it might result in male brutality and anxiety. The female protagonist's unlocking of the forbidden room in the Grimms' tales closely resembles Eve's daring act to eat from the forbidden fruit, the tree of knowledge.

That the forbidden room in "Bluebeard" clearly refers to an unlocking of sexual desires is suggested by the Grimms' tale of "Fichter's Bird," another variation of the "Bluebeard" story. Here it is not the key to the forbidden room that is dropped by the woman into the blood flowing out of the room. Instead an egg, associated with the female role in reproduction, is dropped into the blood in the forbidden room of a sorcerer. Both the egg and the key result in a magic indelible bloodstain. Significantly, the female protagonists in "Bluebeard" and in "Fitcher's Bird" are terribly frightened of marriage and of having to be dutiful, virtuous wives to husbands that they find repulsive. The young bride in "Bluebeard" asks her brothers several times to protect her from "Bluebeard." The title "Fitcher's Bird" refers to the scared bride, who outwits her groom, a sorcerer, that she would engage in wedding preparations when she actually prepares her own escape from patriarchal violence by disguising herself as a bird. In order to clarify the Grimms' adaptation of Perrault's tale to 19th-century male-dominated German society, a short overview of the story line of Grimms' "Bluebeard" follows.

As in many other Grimm tales, the setting is the enchanted world of the German forest. A beautiful young female resides in a forest surrounded by the protection of her father and three brothers (no mother is mentioned) until a king happens by and asks the father for the hand of his daughter. Because the unusual blue beard immediately repulses the daughter, she has no interest in marrying him. Only upon her father's insistent urging and her brothers' promise to come to her aid instantly whenever she would call for their help, does she finally agree to leave with the king. Even in the splendor of the castle, she continues to feel frightened each time she looks at his beard. After a while, the king decides to take a trip (no doubt to provide a testing ground for her curiosity) and forbids the queen to enter a particular room in the castle. Because she is entrusted with a golden key to the room, she cannot resist the temptation to unlock it and finds in it the bodies of the king's former wives. Upon this discovery, she recognizes that she is doomed to die just like the wives before her unless she can outsmart the cruel king. The golden key, however, endowed with magic power, becomes the outward sign of her betrayal. After the queen accidentally drops the key into stream of blood that flows toward her out of the secret room, the blood sticks to the key resisting her efforts to wipe it off. (One might interpret the clinging power of the blood as a projection of her guilt onto the key.) Upon Bluebeard's return, he immediately discovers her disobedience when the blood-stained golden key is missing. He prepares for her to join the other dead wives in the secret room, while her screams for help from her three brothers (who happen to be in a nearby forest drinking wine while guarding her safety) brings them to the palace just in time to prevent her slaughter. Thereupon, they kill the king with their sabers and hang him in the bloody room next to the murdered wives. In the end, justice has been restored and she returns home with the brothers and inherits Bluebeard's treasures.

In Perrault's version, by contrast, the woman is not totally dependent on her brothers for help—she has a sister and two brothers. Thus she is not only surrounded by males in her family but can also develop bonding with a female. She need not helplessly rely on only the males as rescuers. The brothers in Perrault's story are not idly sitting in a forest close to the king's castle eagerly awaiting their rescue missions; they had already arranged a visit as a guest to her house on that day. In Perrault's version, the sister does not live forever happily in dependency on her brothers and father but she remarries and sets out for a life of her own.

It has been widely documented that the Grimm brothers changed details from Perrault's stories and all the other written and oral sources in order to accommodate 19th-century values and perceptions of German bourgeois society. Female sexuality was suppressed and women's marginal and dependency-oriented place in society underscored. Whether one applies Freudian, Jungian, Marxist, or feminist perspectives to "Bluebeard," the Grimms' beastly Bluebeard symbolizes the power-structures of 19th-century ossified German patriarchy that still needed the forbidden room to keep women's curiosity and desire for independence in check. As Jack Zipes has shown in his study, *The Brothers Grimm: From Enchanted Forests to the Modern World,* for the brothers Grimm and the German romantics, old alluring forests harbored cultural heritage, collective history, laws, and customs, and were an arena in which dangerous elements could be overcome. Today, we need a double focus when we read the Grimms' *Märchen*: a child's eye that hungrily absorbs the charm, magic, and fantastic elements of the tale and the mature 20th-century eye, exploring traces that break the magic spell of enchanted forests and shed light on social issues and gender questions in the modern world.

—Barbara Mabee

THE BLUES I'M PLAYING
by Langston Hughes, 1934

Many critics consider Langston Hughes the father of black modernism, for he "made it new" by employing unequivocally black literary forms. As he announced in 1926 in his groundbreaking essay, "The Negro Artist and the Racial Mountain," black artists should embrace their own culture as the source of their works without apology. His collection of poems, *The Weary Blues*, set the standard. Hughes's poems helped establish the blues as the basis of black life and, concomitantly, black literature. In poems such as "The Weary Blues" and "Jazzonia," the author celebrates the black voice and its expression of joy and pain, repeats and revises key themes, and highlights the black person's ability to improvise in order to survive insurmountable obstacles. Hughes establishes black modernism by incorporating the blues, first in poetry and with equal mastery in prose.

"The Blues I'm Playing" represents an early example of the author's use of the blues in fiction. Hughes initially wrote "Blues" for *Scribner's Magazine*; it was published in the short story collection *The Ways of White Folks* in 1934. The inextricable connection between art and life is the crux of the story, for it examines the role white patrons played in the Harlem Renaissance and the black artist's search for personal fulfillment.

That "Blues" functions on so many levels is a testimony to Hughes's genius. The story of Oceola Jones, a young black pianist, and her wealthy white patron, Mrs. Dora Ellsworth, synthesizes issues specific to the Renaissance and to African-Americans. Not only does the story treat the issue of white patronage, but it also explores the distinction between blacks' and whites' perceptions of art, the psychosexual dynamics underlying the racial tensions, and the black expatriate's experience. In five episodic sections, an omniscient narrator presents the plot and characters.

Mrs. Ellsworth, reminiscent of Mrs. Charlotte Osgood Mason (patron of both Hughes and the novelist Zora Neale Hurston), insinuates herself into Oceola's life and work. Captivated by the young woman's renditions of European classical music, Mrs. Ellsworth removes Oceola from her native Harlem and relocates her in such white artistic enclaves as Greenwich Village and Paris. The older woman attempts to superimpose her esoteric vision of art onto the younger one. Also, during her tenure as Oceola's benefactress ("the period of Oceola"), Mrs. Ellsworth not only attempts to define Oceola's artistic vision but her personal life as well. Fervently, she discourages Oceola from pursuing a romantic interest in a young black medical student because she must "sublimate her soul" for the sake of art. Hughes brings both artistic and sexual conflicts to the fore when Mrs. Ellsworth shares her protege's bed: "Then she would read aloud Tennyson or Browning before turning out the light, aware all the time of the electric strength of that brown-black body beside her, and of the deep drowsy voice asking what the poems were about."

Hughes explores both the quest of the black artist and myriad issues surrounding race relations in the 1920's. References to *Nigger Heaven* add further resonance; the novel's author, Carl Van Vechten, played a crucial and controversial role in Hughes's career just as Mrs. Ellsworth does in Oceola's. The tale's many oppositions—black/white, old/young, black art/white art, latent lesbianism/brazen heterosexuality, Paris/Harlem—demonstrate Hughes's ability to integrate several themes and create a heightened sense of tension and drama. Indeed, the story provides a panoramic portrait not only of the Harlem Renaissance specifically, but of the charged racial climate in America in general.

That Hughes builds the story's tension so deftly foregrounds his dramatic abilities; in addition to prose and poetry, he wrote dramas such as *Mulatto* and *Don't You Want to Be Free?* His philosophy of art becomes most evident in the climactic fifth section of "Blue." The story's denouement marks the birth of the Hughesian artist when

Oceola vehemently rejects her patron's hackneyed, sterile conception of "art for art's sake." As she begins playing the blues on Mrs. Ellsworth's piano, Oceola declares, "This is mine. . . . Listen! . . . How sad and gay it is. Blue and happy—laughing and crying. . . . How white like you and black like me. . . . How much like a man. . . . And how like a woman. . . . Warm as Pete's [her black lover] mouth. . . . Those are the blues. . . . I'm playing" (Hughes's ellipses). One can see Oceola's thematic function in the story most markedly here, for she presents the blues as the reconciliation of disparate and antithetical elements of the African-American experience. Thus, Hughes brings to the short story the blues motifs and forms he inscribes so meticulously in his poetry. Crucially, the narrative voice gives way to Oceola's, and her confession or blues "performance" emphasizes African-American oral traditions. The author's innovative use of ellipses further illustrates how gaps, syncopation, and improvisation lie at the heart of the blues text. As the story ends, Hughes incorporates lines from blues music, again illustrating how the black *written* artifact comes into being from black *oral* expression—the telling of the black person's tale in America.

"The Blues I'm Playing" is a landmark short story. As Peter Bruck notes, "It marks one of Hughes' outstanding achievements in this genre and established him as a serious writer of satirical short fiction." Its rich autobiographical references provide insights about the "Poet Laureate of Harlem" and his cultural milieu. Equally important, "Blues" paved the way for works such as James Baldwin's story "Sonny's Blues." Indeed, "The Blues I'm Playing" shows Hughes as a consummate craftsman, a chronicler of the African-American experience, and a shaper of the black aesthetic.

—Keith Clark

THE BRIDE COMES TO YELLOW SKY
by Stephen Crane 1898

"The Bride Comes to Yellow Sky" is one of Stephen Crane's most popular stories, with critics and professors of American literature as well as with general readers. It is the strange tale of Jack Potter, an insecure marshal of a small Texas town on the Rio Grande, Yellow Sky. He has supposedly committed an extraordinary crime and failed heinously in his duty to the "innocent and unsuspecting community," by not informing the townspeople that he was going to San Antonio to court and marry "a girl he believed he loved." Returning with his plain, under-class bride, the guilt-ridden man fears a big nasty "scene of amazement, glee, reproach." There is indeed a critical showdown, with the town badman, Scratchy Wilson, the marshal's longtime trigger-happy adversary. He has been on a rampage just before the arrival of the newlyweds, and now in his drunken rage vents his fury on Potter. But Scratchy, on hearing Potter's announcement that he has gotten married and that he wasn't looking for another of their gun battles (law vs. disorder) when he brought home his bride, takes the news very badly. To this "simple child of the earlier plains" marriage is unfathomable. Since their customary feud is now effectively cancelled, the crushed and disillusioned outlaw holsters his weapons and trudges disconsolately away.

Taking the story as a whole, critics have read it as a kind of satire of, or humorous commentary on, the passing of the Old West, as that region in time is giving way to Eastern influences and the force of progress. Crane actually complained, after his 1895 trip to the West and to Mexico, about the way the West was being transformed. Clearly Crane's story, with the badman's "reversal of intention" at the end, suggests that the contemporary West is not what it used to be, but the narrative conveys much more than that. The variety of critical interpretations indicates the complexity of symbolic patterns, allusions, and perspectives it contains. Among the plethora of structural elements are the following: the appellations (Jack Potter, Scratchy Wilson, Yellow Sky, the Weary Gentleman Saloon); the story's dualisms (old and new, East and West, old and young, static and kinetic landscapes, guilt and innocence, lawlessness and order); linguistic analysis (phonological and morphological). Yet a very significant subtext in the narrative has been generally overlooked, despite the frequent references in the critical literature to Crane's having parodied the feud and showdown of local badman and town sheriff. Apparently only one critic, Tibbetts, noting here "a sort of visual comedy . . . close to slapstick" and "the comedy of the confrontation of the 'ancient antagonists' . . . involved in a burlesque of the Western feud," has even approached the story within the story.

Experiences from Crane's own life bear directly on the story. Crane's late father had been a Methodist minister, his late mother had been the daughter of a Methodist minister. A year or two before he wrote "The Bride Comes to Yellow Sky," Crane had taken up with the madam of a house of prostitution in Jacksonville, Florida. He was well aware of how impossible it would be to bring such a woman back to his home territory, where relatives, friends, and acquaintances were still living. During the period from 1891 to 1896, Crane lived mostly in New York (aside from brief trips to the West and Mexico in 1895), producing reportage and fiction for various local papers. In New York the raffish and footloose Crane took liberal advantage of what such purlieus as the Bowery had to offer. Beer, Crane's early biographer, colorfully describes this spicy, unruly district of shabby buildings, saloons, prostitutes, and what O. Henry called "waifs and strays," and then adds, "The Bowery, though, was funny. Comedians aped its dress on the stage of Koster and Bial's improper vaudeville and speakers at banquets recited Bowery jokes. There was no other slum in America so settled of speech and habit. It was supposed that the Bowery invented words." It is this latter element that actually provides a means for an understanding of the structure as well as the contents of "The Bride Comes to Yellow Sky."

The text itself bespeaks not merely a dramatic performance involving rituals, as some commentators have indicated, but an actual vaudeville show. The matter of basic stage setting—scenery and music—is made clear at certain points in the narrative. Sheriff Potter recalls, as he and his bride are riding toward Yellow Sky, that the town has a brass band of sorts, and he imagines without pleasure what kind of uproarious parade and escort the band would provide for them from the train station to his home, if the townspeople knew about their marriage and expected their arrival. Back in Yellow Sky, across from the Weary Gentleman Salon, there were "vivid green grass-plots" so striking in appearance as to arouse "a doubt in the mind" because of their exact resemblance to "the grass mats used to represent lawns on the stage."

Then there are a number of extended and closely interrelated skits, as well as a certain amount of stage business, to provide the general outlines of a lively vaudeville production. The opening skit is set in a lavishly decorated, dazzlingly appointed parlor car. The bride is neither pretty, nor young, nor very bright, nor even of her husband's modest social background; both are ill at ease amid their fancy surroundings in the parlor car and in the dining car. Added to their essential nervousness and trepidation about Yellow Sky's reaction to their arrival, is their inexperience as a domestic duo, which is so obvious that they attract the derisive attention of fellow passengers, the porter, and the waiter. Crane's creation of this mirthful scene, awkward newlyweds unintentionally playing clown roles, is in the best vaudeville tradition of the innocent as comic victim. The author's intention here, though misinterpreted by a number of commentators in the last several decades, is highlighted in the text: "Historically there was supposed to be something infinitely humorous in their situation."

The next vaudeville routine is set in the Weary Gentleman Saloon, across from the grass plots resembling stage-prop lawns. It involves a stand-up comic of sorts, actually a drummer (travelling salesman), telling funny stories about farcical situations to his taciturn audience of bar patrons (three Texans and two Mexican sheepherders). The drummer's tale about an old man and an old woman carrying heavy burdens and taking a tumble on the stairs is interrupted by the herald of a new comic sequence. A young man rushes in to announce that Scratchy Wilson is on the loose again, in fact is on a drunken rampage. This is the prelude to another skit, consisting of some hustle and bustle, and a bit of comic wisecracking, all as a result of this supposedly life-threatening situation. The two Mexicans quickly exit through the back door, while the frightened and confused drummer acts like the butt of an in-group joke concocted at his expense. Hardly satisfied by the answers to his questions, the unnerved drummer is forced by the bartender to get down on the floor behind the bar. Again he is made the "fall guy" in an impromptu Western-style drama.

Another skit follows: a solo performance by the drink-crazed Scratchy Wilson (recalling the drunken hall-porter scene in *Macbeth*). Bellowing, threatening, spoiling for a fight while brandishing his two long revolvers—with his little fingers now and then playing "in a musician's way," the madman occupies center stage. He torments the barkeeper's dog by shooting near it, tries in vain to get through the barred door of the saloon, and fires at it. Then he remembers "his ancient antagonist" and decides to go to his house and get him to fight. Making his way there he chants "Apache scalp-music." But Potter is not at home to meet his howling challenges, and the infuriated Scratchy churns himself "into deepest rage" and reloads the revolvers.

At last comes the fitting climax to the extended burlesque of the Wild and Woolly West, which has not only been enlivened with jolly good vaudeville numbers, but has also been made into a burlesque of the nuptial process. The closing act, a sham showdown, with its strange pair of newlywed *naifs,* its spurious air of impending doom (which some commentators have taken seriously, and its exaggerated histrionics such as the bride's being "a slave to hideous rites, gazing at the apparitional snake"), is the fitting final touch to Crane's Western Follies show. The Armageddon won't take place after all. In fact the sheriff has a new partner with whom to entertain the town from now on, and so the old act with Scratchy Wilson, one of the problems on his mind during the train ride home, is finished.

The result of all this for Crane's audience is a vaudeville marriage, the newly-wedded state, that is, as imagined by a young writer-adventurer who himself has entered into a problematical, irregular union with a lady. He uses the story to fearfully anticipate dire consequences, which he finally dispels by burlesque logic.

—Samuel I. Bellman

C

CAFÉ NIAGARA (Niagara Nagykávéház)
by István Örkény, 1963

Niagara Nagykávéház ("Café Niagara") is a short story by the Hungarian writer and playwright István Örkény. It was written in the late 1950's but it evokes the atmosphere of the Stalinist period, which in Hungary can be dated from 1948 to 1953. On a wider scale, it is about the conditions created by a totalitarian state with complete control over the life of its individuals.

The heroes of "Café Niagara" are a married couple from the provinces, Mr. and Mrs. Nikolitch. They come to Budapest on holidays and go to the opera to see an operetta and a Soviet play. (The notion that to see a Soviet play is somehow expected of people firmly dates the story in the Stalinist period. They also visit the "recently remodeled" Niagara Café, which is said to be a fashionable coffee-house (or night club). It is, however, not easy to find the café, for it is not listed in the telephone directory and the desk clerk in the Nikolitchs' hotel has never heard of it. Thanks to a well-informed taxi driver, however, they manage to find the café.

Once inside, the Nikolitchs are disappointed. There is no music or dancing, not even a waiter in sight. The place is full and the patrons are waiting for something. Across the room there is a bar, at the end of which is a door "concealed by curtains." After a long and boring wait, the curtains part and a "stocky, red-necked man" appears "in a fishnet shirt." The patrons are called behind the curtains one by one; they reappear after a while flushed but "wearing a satisfied smile." This makes Mr. Nikolitch very curious and he keeps fidgeting to catch the stocky man's attention.

First Mrs. Nikolitch and, after her return, Nikolitch himself is called behind the curtains. He walks into an empty kitchen where three people are waiting for him; he is asked whether he would like to undress. Nikolitch decides to keep his clothes on. He is beaten up by the three individuals; afterwards "he had a headache and his knees were shaky, but otherwise he felt fine. Surprisingly, he felt light and free, as though he had just been given a massage, or had returned from a tiring but satisfying climb in the mountains. The secret anxiety which had tortured him was gone" (translated by Carl R. Erickson).

Örkény suggests that in a totalitarian system most people have a sense of guilt about unknown crimes or about past shortcomings for which they may be called to account. There is an atmosphere of ubiquitous fear, an intangible anxiety pervading society: one never knows when the system will find it necessary to pounce. In such circumstances a totally unwarranted, in fact "ritual," beating by unknown people is a relief; once one is "chastized" there is no need to worry about further punishment.

The interpretation of "Café Niagara" given above seemed a plausible one to the Communist authorities as well. Although the story was published in a Budapest monthly in 1963, it created a furore. Örkény, otherwise an author favoured by the Kádár regime, was asked not to include it in his collections of short stories. "Café Niagara" was translated into English and published in Albert Tezla's anthology *Ocean at the Window, Hungarian Prose and Poetry Since 1945* (1980) and is now regarded as a representative piece of Örkény's short prose.

—George Gömöri

CARMILLA
by Sheridan Le Fanu, 1872

"Carmilla" is the last of the five stories constituting Sheridan Le Fanu's most important collection, *In a Glass Darkly* (1872). This Gothic tale of vampirism is narrated by the heroine, whose survival from her ordeal can thus be taken for granted from the outset; her narrative is, however, distanced in two ways. Like the other stories in the collection, "Carmilla" is framed by being supposedly offered a case-history of medical and psychological interest by a learned German physician, Dr. Martin Hesselius, whose papers have been edited by an unnamed fellow-physician who has been his friend and assistant. Furthermore, the prologue to the tale notes that the narrator, who had communicated her story to Dr. Hesselius many years earlier, had died in the interval.

This distancing of the narrative voice and use of a period setting, clearly intended to counteract in some measure—or perhaps by contrast to heighten—the dark and lurid elements of the tale of horror, are matched by geographical remoteness. Almost inevitably for a story so firmly in the Gothic tradition, it is set in Central Europe and in, as the opening description makes clear, a very lonely place: a Gothic castle, surrounded by moat and drawbridge, and set deep in a forest miles from the nearest habitation. In view of the sexual elements in the story that follows, it seems legitimate to detect sexual symbolism in this setting.

Here the heroine lives with her father and governesses; like many another heroine of a Gothic tale she is motherless. An early reference to an abandoned village nearby is not expanded upon and creates, or adds to, a mood of mystery that will not be resolved until a much later stage. Into this small and archetypally isolated setting another character is introduced, the eponymous young woman who will first appear to fill the role of much-needed friend and substitute-sister, then will emerge as an intense and frightening lover, and finally will be seen as a would-be murderess. Carmilla is introduced, appropriately, through a violent carriage accident that is graphically described and that guarantees her admission as a long-term guest in the castle.

At this point the reader familiar with Coleridge's "Christabel" will be reminded of a similar incident. In that famous Romantic poem (never completed but published in 1816), the witch-woman Geraldine takes the form of a damsel in distress and, befriended by the heroine, is taken to her father's castle, being carried in her weak state over the threshold. Le Fanu's story uses a similar incident, and this and other resemblances make it seem likely that he had Coleridge's poem in mind.

Carmilla's true nature as a vampire is not revealed until later in the story, and at first she is presented as a young lady surrounded by mystery (she refuses to answer any questions about her home, her family, or her past) but acceptable without recourse to the supernatural. There are, however, hints, carefully and unobtrusively planted, that, in the light of subsequent knowledge, can be interpreted as pointing to the truth. An old picture in the castle, newly cleaned, shows a face identical with Carmilla's as belonging to a woman long dead whose name is an anagram of Carmilla's own (though the clue is not picked up by the other characters at the time). Carmilla does not appear during the earlier part of the day, though it seems that, at times when she is believed to be in her room with doors and windows locked, she is sometimes seen roaming outdoors. Her moods alternate between periods of feverish excitement and phases of extreme weariness ("languid" is a recurring epithet applied to her). And the heroine has a number of dreams or visions in which she is attacked by a nocturnal visitor. Le Fanu skilfully assembles these and other hints before disclosing the vampire's real identity.

In its early manifestations, Carmilla's yearning to make the heroine her victim takes the form of an intense romantic attachment, and for modern readers this is of interest as suggesting an attempt to depict lesbian passion. There is, for example, a remarkable passage in the fourth chapter which effectively contrasts the vampire's possessive determination and the heroine's innocent unawareness: "It was like the ardour of a lover; it embarrassed me; it was hateful and yet overpowering; and with gloating eyes she drew me to her, and her hot lips travelled along my cheek in kisses and she would whisper, almost in sobs, 'You are mine, you *shall* be mine, you and I are one for ever'." This cleverly exploits the ambiguity of a situation capable of interpretation without recourse to the idea of vampirism but, in the event, entirely consistent with that outcome. The use of the first-person narrative contributes to this effect in that the heroine, ignorant alike of lesbianism and vampirism, is baffled as well as frightened by Carmilla's behaviour and desperately seeks commonplace explanations such as a fit of insanity.

The climax of the narrative involves the discovery of the vampire's grave, where she lies in a living state, and her destruction by the traditional devices of impaling, decapitation, and burning. It becomes clear that the passion felt by Carmilla for her victim has blended the erotic with the homicidal, or perhaps used the erotic as a mask for the homicidal, and some of her fervent but puzzling declarations come to be seen in their true light—for example, in the passage already cited, "In the rapture of my enormous humiliation I live in your warm life, and you shall die—die, sweetly die—into mine."

As this summary suggests, "Carmilla" embodies many of the traditional elements of the vampire tale and ought probably to be seen as an important influence on a better-known work published later in the century by another Irish writer, Bram Stoker's *Dracula* (1897), which has many ingredients in common with Le Fanu's tale. In the 20th century "Carmilla" was the inspiration for a remarkable and very early sound film, *Vampyr* (1932), by the Danish director Carl Dreyer. Historically speaking, "Carmilla" is thus an important link between the Gothic fiction of the Romantic period and later examples of the Gothic horror story and specifically the vampire story.

—Norman Page

THE CASK OF AMONTILLADO
by Edgar Allan Poe, 1846

One of Edgar Allan Poe's finest stories, "The Cask of Amontillado" is especially notable for two reasons: its subtle, ironic treatment of a passionate but coldly-calculated plot to bury a man alive to satisfy an aristocrat's honor; and its superb dialogue between its protagonist, the insulted nobleman, Montresor, and his antagonist, the gross bourgeois Italian who has a purchased title, Fortunato. This dialogue amounts to a duel with words, and it is unusual because Poe rarely depended on much dialogue in constructing his stories.

If "The Cask" seems simply a story of a clever and successful revenge, it is also the story of a failed quest that goes much beyond the simple quest for the cask of Amontillado, a dark-colored Spanish sherry, various images in the text suggesting archetypal acts such as the quest for the original substance or the universal solvent, the quest for the Holy Grail, and the quest for Solomon's Secret Vault and the Stone of Foundation connected with the Tetragammaton (a Jewish and later a Masonic concern). As a whole "The Cask" consists of two narratives, each of which has its appropriate dialectic and rhetoric. Montresor tells of the motive and the execution of the perfect crime he committed in the fictional past (50 years previously) to a silent, unidentified listener in the fictional present.

The story as a whole takes place in 18th-century France. "Montresor" was not a family name but is of French origin. It was the name of a countship, i.e., of a fief designated by that name. Montresor is the Count of Montresor. A real Count of Montresor, Claude Bourdeille (1606-1663), conspired to assassinate Cardinal Richelieu. Poe knew him from Hamilton's *Count of Gramont* (1811) and possibly other sources. On the other hand, "Fortunato" is the Italian form of the Latin "*fortuna*" or "*fortunatus*" and means "fortunate" and "rich." When Fortunato refers to his wife, he calls her "Lady Fortunato," hence he himself is a nobleman and a "Lord," Poe preferring to use English rather than French titles. But his indifference to Montresor's coat of arms and his lack of manners peg him as a bourgeois Italian and newly endowed with a purchased title, an *anoblis*, whereas Montresor is a *noblesse d'épée*, but a man of the country instead of the court.

The murder of Fortunato takes place in the dungeons of Montresor's Italian Renaissance styled *château*, although in his pride of place he calls it his "palazzo." It is evidently located on a river somewhere in the Loire river valley. The telling of the murder takes place in Paris, and the catacombs mentioned are the so-called "catacombs of Paris" since they were originally the limestone quarries from which limestone was taken for building the city. The trouble was that Paris had only one burial-ground, *La Cimetière des Innocents*. But in 1785 the Council of State "decreed that the cemetery should be cleared of its dead," and it was decided that the bones taken from the Cemetery of the Innocents should be deposited into the abandoned limestone quarries underneath the *Plaine de Mont-Souris.* This action was performed and in 1786 the catacombs were consecrated by the Church authority. Hence the action of Poe's "The Cask" can be almost precisely dated. The story cannot have taken place after the French Revolution that began in 1789 because Montresor would not have possessed the privilege of wearing a sword after the Revolution occurred as he sports a rapier in Poe's tale. Further, the telling cannot have taken place before 1786, since before this date there were no catacombs in Paris. Therefore, the telling must have taken place in 1787 or 1788. Since the murder took place 50 years previous to the telling, it would have occurred in 1737 or 1738. Of course, Montresor's "long sword," or rapier, had become somewhat out of date by the beginning of the 18th century, having been replaced by the "short sword," or *colichemarde,* which then became the aristocratic weapon of choice for this century. On the other hand, his wearing of the heavy, knee-length coat called the *roquelaire* is up to date since it was at the height of fashion in the 1730's and 1740's.

The keys to the revenge plot and its motivation in "The Cask" are class conflict and the aristocratic social codes called the "*point d'honneur*" and the "*duella a la mazza.*" In the stratified society of the *Ancient Régime* in France, honor coincided with social status as did justice and the mode of punishment. The code of behavior called "the point of honor" was exclusively a possession of the aristocratic class, whose men held the honorific privilege of wearing a sword with everyday dress. An offense against one's honor called for justice and punishment in the "duel to the death." However, the honor of an aristocrat could not be satisfied in the performance of a duel unless the impugner was a social equal. If a commoner was the offender, the aristocrat either ignored the matter or hired some thugs to beat the fellow up. Because Fortunato is of bourgeois origin, Montresor cannot challenge him to a duel with swords. But Montresor is full of aristocratic pride reflected in his thoughts of titles of nobility, genealogy, escutcheons, coats of arms, quarterings, the bones of ancestors, fiefs, and inheritable property. The motto on his coat of arms is "*Nemo me impune lacessit*" ("No one insults me with impunity"). He cannot challenge the ignorant Fortunato; besides, with his purchased title he holds some official post in the government, is perhaps an *intendant,* and is thus a personification of the evils that had been foisted on the provincial aristocracy by the crown. Since Fortunato has power, Montresor resorts to murder.

What Poe does in "The Cask" is parody the social codes of "the point of honor" and "the duel to the death" by arranging the dialectic exchange between Montresor and Fortunato in a manner suggestive of a *duel with swords.* The dialogue is so arranged as to suggest the basic maneuvers of swordplay: the attacker lunges and thrusts; the defender parries and counterparries. But it is not a real duel he provides but simply a *duel with words.* An important aspect of duelling in the first half of the 18th century was the "chance meeting" of French duellists who were prohibited by royal law from duelling at all. By prearrangement they would agree to meet somewhere "as if by chance." When they met, they would proceed to walk into fields or woods where they would duel. In "The Cask" Poe has Montresor meet Fortunato "as if by chance" when it is clear that Montresor had foreknowledge of Fortunato's attendance during the *Mardi gras* celebration at a banquet, it appears, at the local Freemason's lodge. When Montresor leads the intoxicated Fortunato into the blind wall in the subterranean passages of the *château* and takes him prisoner, he already has mortar and trowel prepared for walling up his victim. Since Fortunato had given Montresor a Masonic sign and inquired if he were a Mason, an inquiry that elicited the response that he was nothing more than a real stone mason and he laughingly displayed the real trowel he had brought with him, it is plain that Poe is also parodying French Freemasonry, whose motto was "*liberté, égalité, fraternité.*"

Poe's parody of Masonry extends the quest for the Amontillado to the Masonic legend of the Secret Vault and the search for the Lost Word. This legend links the Temple of Solomon with the Temple of Zerubabel. At the conclusion of his tale Montresor states his political attitude by telling his silent listener: "Against the new masonry [i.e., against the new Freemasonry] I re-erected the old rampart of bones" [i.e., the bones of his ancestors]. To him Fortunato's insults had not merely injured him but also his ancestors. His last words, a quotation from the Requiem Mass, are directed not at Fortunato but at the bones of his ancestors. He says, "*In pace requiescat!*" or "May it [the bone pile] rest in peace!" It is to be noted that the Latin quotation is not in its normal linear order, the actual text is "*Requiescat in pace!*"

The theme of "The Cask" is perhaps a mixture of such sayings as "Revenge is sweet" (Southerne) and "What passes will be sweet" (Pushkin). Montresor's narrating voice displays an inner satisfaction and a pride in reliving in the present the performance of a masterful trick in the past. He is so pleased with himself that he proudly exhibits every detail—every act, word, and gesture—of his treatment of Fortunato. A positive attitude about the past is to be observed of persons when they are old, and in the fictional present Montresor is about 75 years old if he committed his perfect crime at about age 25. Despite his age he appears healthy and vigorous and in no imminent danger of dying. There is no sign that he considers what he did to Fortunato as wrong. He is definitely not, as some readers have thought, penitently confessing his sin to a priest.

Montresor tells his story to the silent listener, whom he addresses simply as "you." He says, "You, who so well know the nature of my soul . . . " It is clear that the listener knows him well because of a long-standing intimacy that began well after his youthful manhood. It is also clear that he desires to enhance himself in the narratee's eyes. The narratee says nothing but remains all attention. The narratee seems a woman, for clever women are good listeners in men's words. Is she Montresor's mistress?

What is the final effect of "The Cask" on the reader? The reader is most likely completely shocked. The reader is surprised to hear a gentleman recount so coldly and yet with such exuberance the circumstances of a murder he committed that could have led him to the gallows. Even if the narratee is shocked by his tale, Montresor surely expects the narratee to sympathize with his moral aim. Readers must make their own judgments. At any rate, "The Cask of Amontillado" is one of the finest examples of Poe's concentrated, closely woven, and rigorously controlled tales featuring superb dialogue. Such a construction and such a style is proof of Poe's full consciousness that he was "writing" and not simply "telling" his tale. It is not simply a Poe masterpiece but one of the great short stories of world literature.

—Richard P. Benton

CATHEDRAL
by Raymond Carver, 1983

Many of the cathedrals of Europe took hundreds of years to build. Historians of architecture and culture have marveled at these wonders, noting that they are best understood as monuments to people who find value and meaning in doing. At first blush, it would seem that the world of the makers of Europe's great cathedrals could not be further removed from the world of working class people in Raymond Carver's fiction. But a more leisurely reflection upon the cathedral builders and the characters in the title story of Carver's collection *Cathedral* opens the possibility that some of the late stories of Carver offer a promise of resurrection which he usually so brutally denies.

At one level, the postmodern world in Carver's fiction is understood as one in which the mechanical age of reproduction strips objects and images and art of its aura, its meaning and value as something original, leaving in its place only the simulacrum, the hyperreal. This interpretation of postmodernity accounts for much of the experience charted by Carver. His stories are about people who work mindlessly, drink, have broken marriages, and take in life, not directly, but through an immersion in mediated images, be they received visually through the T.V. screen, or aurally through listening to mediated messages reported on T.V., or transmitted through popular culture, most frequently in the lyrics of songwriters. The American playwright Eugene O'Neill created language to capture the lyrical stammering of the fog people in his famous play, "A Long Day's Journey into Night." Carver's alcoholics lack even the eloquence of O'Neill's fog people. They are often crude and utterly lacking in the powers of introspection. They cannot express what they mean but they want to tell stories. Very often they quite literally have nothing to do: they are out of work or about to be fired. They know they once had hopes and ideas about the kind of people they should be and how they should live their lives (having a job, wife, and maybe children), but they do not know how to connect the everyday reality in which they live with the dim, second-hand ideas they have about who they should be and why. Their lives are measured out in bouts of drinking or long stints in front of the television, interrupted most frequently by visits to the refrigerator and some trysts in bed. They are full of prejudices. One narrator does not like fat people, another dislikes blind people, still another dislikes anyone who seems different. His narrators, male or female, want to be taken seriously but when they think about it, they are not sure why they should be. They are afraid and hide behind bravado and alcohol to avoid confronting themselves. "Cathedral" needs to be understood against this background.

Carver's writings typically take the working class man or woman as their subject. With an economy of style that has caused many to describe Carver as a "minimalist" of short fiction, these stories usually depict the emotionally impoverished lives of people who cannot speak their thoughts in words and who cannot accept responsibility. His people are, indeed, workers—"doers" we might say—but they, unlike the builders of Europe's cathedrals, take little pleasure in their work and accord it even less meaning or value. They do not understand their lives, nor why they execute the ritual of work.

The story "Cathedral" reflects a breakthrough in Carver's style. It begins disarmingly enough with one of his familiar unnamed narrators, a working-class, married man musing over an impending visit from an old friend of his wife's, a blind man whose impairment bothers the narrator. But the story moves towards a moment of illumination and transformation, taking the limited narrator to a rare epiphanal moment typical of the kind found in James Joyce's short stories. This moment is achieved through a simple kind of doing. The blind man, Robert, and the narrator drink and smoke dope into the wee hours of the morning. Irritated that his wife has not stayed awake and handled the burden of the unwanted guest, the narrator flicks the channels on T.V., searching for something to watch. He finds a program on the church and Middle Ages. To his annoyance, he cannot find anything else and turns apologetically back to the first program. Robert wants to know what the cathedrals of Europe look like. In an amazing moment of trust, the narrator, after struggling to define the word "cathedral" and admitting that cathedrals do not mean anything special to him, agrees to try to show the blind man the meaning of the word by drawing a cathedral. The narrator has confessed that he only knows about cathedrals through watching late-night T.V., but Robert does not accept his explanation. He insists that he and the narrator draw cathedrals together in order to teach him what they are. Urged on, the narrator fetches paper and a pen and begins by drawing a box that looks like a house and adding windows, and arches, and flying buttresses. The blind man runs his fingers over the image and then rides his fingers on the narrator's fingers as his hand passes over the drawing paper and the narrator completes the image of a cathedral with his eyes closed. Prompted by Robert, he puts people in the cathedral and closes his eyes as the two of them continue to draw. The narrator does not want to open his eyes. With his eyes closed he knows he is in his own home, but for once he does not feel that he is inside anything. He feels liberated. The closing line of the story is his simple utterance describing what he feels. "It's really something," he says, leaving the reader in that puzzling realm so familiar in Carver's stories. The words are inadequate for the occasion. What, after all do they mean? Are they just the clichéd observation of a man who does not know his own meaning? Or, is he asserting that the image that he cannot see with his eyes but that he does see with his mind's eye is really something remarkable? Or, is his statement ironic, and are we to understand that he actually has never escaped the four walls of his home, and by extension, of his provincial, limited life in which few experiences are authentic, with their own aura, and most are mediated replicas of the experiences of others?

Throughout most of the stories collected in *Will You Please Be Quiet, Please*? and many of those collected in the volume of short stories entitled *Cathedral*, Carver's narrators belabor their narratives. "Fat" opens with typical lines: "I am sitting over coffee and cigarettes at my friend Rita's and I am telling her about it. Here is what I tell her." The narration is oddly sparse, with the speaker seeming not to know the point of his or her own narration. The stories often conclude abruptly with the narrators feeling depressed and wondering what actually they are waiting for. They feel helpless to affect the direction of their lives. They sense their life is going to change but nothing in the story has indicated that they play any important part in bringing about the changes. Several of the stories in *Cathedral* such as "Feathers" and the title story depart from this mold, revealing a more forgiving author. In addition, "A Small, Good Thing," a rewrite of an earlier, much bleaker story on the same subject, gave many critics as well as Carver reason to believe that he had evolved into a writer of greater substance, capable of capturing transcendent values and a modicum of hope.

Carver's stunning achievement in a story like "Cathedral" lies in his ability to capture the textures of the narrator's life and yet permit him a moment of recognition when he glimpses something much bigger than the world he knows. Carver's craft with words has always earned him high praise but many thought that the relentless bleakness of his vision would finally limit him as a writer. Carver thought otherwise and often pointed to his story "Cathedral" as evidence of a new turn in his evolution as an artist. Part of the brilliance of the story lies in his ability to breathe new life into an old literary theme—the theme of the partially blind man who sees, a theme as old as Oedipus and as recent as T.S. Eliot's creation of one-eyed Reilly in "The Cocktail Party," the seer in the play. In "Cathedral" it is the blind friend who holds a precious kind of knowledge. The narrator is right to be jealous and worried about his wife's friend: he does know the narrator's wife well; he has lived fully and known a whole love for his wife before her death from cancer. But more important is Carver's understanding of the bodily knowing that can connect a blind man to a sighted one. Dylan Thomas wrote one of his most memorable poems about the subject of the hunchback in the park. In a moment of exquisite pathos he pictured forth in words the image of the contorted body of the hunchback in his hovel in the dark, drawing the lovely image of a whole and perfectly shaped woman. Victor Hugo treats a similar theme in *The Hunchback of Notre Dame.* Carver fully enters, imaginatively, the domain of the blind man, reporting that not only does he have one T.V., but that he has two and that he enjoys listening to both and that from sound he discovers sight. The narrator, too, learns this precious lesson. He moves from a posture where he cruelly mocked the condition of blindness, confiding that he knows nothing about blindness except from seeing a blind man on T.V., to a position where he will close his eyes and draw, letting the blind man speak the drawing, and allowing their two blind hands to travel over the page together seeing images that neither man has actually ever seen. Part of the thrill of the last line is that it achieves such dazzling feats, spanning great spaces, like the cathedrals, and yet built by a man who at one level only knows the very smallest part of the edifice he builds. And, yes, it is the doing of the drawing, just as it was the doing of the cathedral building, that gives the action moment. Once as a child I watched my father sitting late at night sketching the massive head of his blind friend, talking to the man with great ease as his charcoal traced the lines of the head on the white paper. I have never forgotten the image. The blind friend was an eminent scholar from Oxford, blinded in his childhood from glaucoma. My father at the time was an historian in the United States who had not seen his college friend for over a decade. Neither thought it odd that the form of my father's tribute to and affection for his friend found its expression in a visual drawing that one of them could not see but could know. Carver captures this same enigmatical truth with all its possibilities of transcendence in his story. It is a great loss that Carver did not live longer and leave further proof of his growth as a writer. "Cathedral" and several other stories show him to be a writer deeply knowledgeable about a certain kind of blue collar worker but also charitable and forgiving, capable of depicting worlds where humans can connect and an aura, almost metaphysical, is in reach.

—Carol Simpson Stern

CAVALLERIA RUSTICANA
by Giovanni Verga, 1880

The publication of "Cavalleria Rusticana," collected in *Vita dei Campi* in 1880, signalled a new departure in Verga's fiction, the application of narrative techniques which, even more than the choice of subject, form the basis of what is known as *verismo.* Though he later dramatised the story as a vehicle for the actress Eleanora Duse and a libretto was adapted for Mascagni's opera, the original has a particular power which owes everything to its author's penetrating imagination and consummate craftsmanship.

Verga had begun by writing historical romances whose conventions derive from Scott and Dumas, and from the mid-1870's short stories and *contes,* which show the influence of Flaubert, Maupassant, and Zola. The first of these, *Nedda* (1874), has for its principal character a poverty-stricken peasant girl and for its setting rural Sicily. Though the theme constitutes a move towards social realism, the handling of the tale, especially in the well worn opening, remains within conventions which predate Verga's remodelled approach to narrative as he embarked on the series of regional novels beginning with *I Malavoglia* (*The House by the Medlar Tree*). In "Cavalleria Rusticana," "La Lupa" ("The She-Wolf") and the other stories published in *Vita dei Campi* and subsequent collections, Verga applied innovative theories about realism, objectivity, and fictional truth in ways that profoundly affect the narrative stratagems open to the author.

Like many of his stories about *i vinti,* the defeated and dispossessed Sicilian peasantry, "Cavalleria Rusticana" was founded on a true incident. Destined at first for incorporation in *The House by the Medlar Tree,* it was removed in the course of rewriting and developed into a free-standing story which was first published in the literary weekly *Fanfulla.* It is a tragic tale of dishonour revenged.

Turiddu, a poor widow's son, returns from military service to his native village, expecting to resume his courtship of Lola, a farm manager's daughter. She meanwhile has become engaged to Alfio, a well-to-do carrier, and rejects Turiddu. Finding employment as a farm hand, Turiddu starts to court Santa, the only daughter of a prosperous wine seller. Lola, now married, overhears their flirtations and encourages Turiddu to visit her during Alfio's absence, to Santa's chagrin. On Alfio's return Santa tells him of Lola's infidelity. Alfio challenges Turiddu; the two fight it out with knives, and Turiddu is killed.

Verga's handling of the plot shows both originality in the authorial approach and a masterly control of balancing internal cross references, whose cumulative effect is woven into a complex unified design.

The authorial approach is dictated by Verga's own thoughts about realism in fiction. The author should not intrude as commentator. The unfolding of the story should be managed by the objective reporting of successive acts or by advancing the narrative through dialogue. The actions and motivations of individuals should be presented as the participants would themselves perceive them, and be expressed in language appropriate to their perceptions. In this way the author would achieve the realisation of artistic truth to the events and emotions he sought to portray. It is worth noting that Verga preferred to talk of *verità,* truth, rather than *verismo,* realism; he expressed some distrust of critical theorising and of labelling -isms on individual writers and their work.

A close reading of "Cavalleria Rusticana" shows that the development of the plot is carried forward almost entirely in passages of objectively reported narration. The passages of dialogue, on the other hand, are dramatised illustrations of the impact on the characters of events that have already been revealed. The conversations between Turiddu and Lola, Turiddu and Santa, Santa and Alfio, and finally Alfio and Turiddu, carry the main weight of the psychological insights into the minds and emotions of these individuals, and within these conversations Verga introduces the network of cross references that help to knit the story together.

The notions of personal honour implicit in Sicilian society, and of the appropriate sanctions when the code of honour has been transgressed, are probably well enough understood by most readers; but there are certain details whose import may require explanations and which pose problems for translators that cannot be solved by a footnote gloss. This is unfortunate when the details are part of the referential complexity mentioned above—for instance, the contrast between Turiddu's military cap with its swaggering tassel and Alfio's cap worn over the eyes, a habit of the *mafioso*. Similarly the formalities of Alfio's challenge to Turiddu in the tavern may at first cause surprise with its initial embrace, which is a ritual preliminary to the exchange of *il bacio della sfida,* the kiss of challenge, sealed by Turiddu's formal biting of the challenger's ear in acceptance.

Other balancing details in the patterning of the story are more easily picked up. In his first encounter with Lola, Turiddu speaks of Alfio's four mules: "but my mother, poor thing, had to sell off our bay mule and our patch of vineyard on the highway while I was away on service." Again, Alfio is a native of the neighbouring village of Licodia; and when Turiddu determines to get his own back by flirting with Santa under Lola's very eyes, he says to Santa, "Your mother's from Licodia, we know! Hot blood you've got! I could just eat you up with my eyes!" This thread is picked up again in the final dialogue between Turiddu and Alfio; Turiddu, confessing that he is in the wrong and therefore should let Alfio kill him, is nevertheless determined to kill Alfio (a further transgression of the code) in order to spare his old mother's tears—"she seems never out of my eyes." "Open them up then, those eyes!," yelled Alfio at him. The handful of dust that blinds Turiddu permits Alfio's last fatal knife thrusts.

The inevitability of this retribution, the increasingly doom-laden tension, and the swift tragic climax of the tale have been managed with extraordinary skill. They fully vindicate Verga's self-imposed constraints in his search for artistic truth.

—Stewart F. Sanderson

THE CHEAPEST NIGHTS (Arkhas layālī)
by Yusuf Idris, 1954

"Arkhas layālī" ("The Cheapest Nights") the title piece from Yusuf Idris's first collection of short stories, published in 1954, is one of the author's best-known works. It demonstrates many characteristics of his short fiction: a small town or village setting, characters drawn from Egypt's hardworking lower classes, uncomfortable descriptions of poverty and ignorance, and a style that mixed both literary and colloquial forms of language.

Set in a small town, probably not unlike the many Nile delta towns in which Idris spent a number of years as a youth, the story opens with an ironic juxtaposition of evening prayers at the mosque and "a torrent of abuse gushing" from the mouth of the protagonist, Abdel Kerim, "sweeping Tantawi and all his ancestors in its wake." One does not know why Abdel Kerim is angry, nor known who Tantawi is. However, the curses are many, and the anger fervent. It would seem that Tantawi has done something unforgivable to Abdel Kerim. Thus, a certain dramatic tension is built up immediately.

As he passes the children "scattered like breadcrumbs" in the lane, Abdel Kerim "lash[es] out at them vituperating furiously against their fathers and their forefathers, the rotten seed that gave them life, and the midwife who brought them to existence." He bears a grudge against all children because he is the father of six, whom he cannot feed, in spite of his hard work. He is comforted that half the children in the lane will starve to death while the remainder will die of cholera.

Gradually the reason for his spleen becomes clear: earlier in the evening he had accepted a glass of very strong black tea from Tantawi the watchman. As a result, Abdel Kerim had to rush through evening prayers, presumably because of the need to empty his full bladder. The tea was so strong that his head continues to spin. As he gains his composure, he finds himself fully awake and agitated. He realizes that he is alone on a cold winter night in the middle of the deserted square. Except the wild children in the lane, almost everyone else is home in bed. He has nothing to do, nowhere to go, and does not know what to do with himself. He cannot afford to go to the local cafe for coffee and smoke a water-pipe, or listen to the blaring radio and watch better-off men joke and play cards. He thinks of his friend Sama'an, who is out of town at his father-in-law's, making up with his estranged wife.

Thinking of Sama'an and his wife makes Abdel Kerim think about going home to his wife, who would be "lying like a bag of maize with her brood of six scattered round her like a litter of puppies." He hopes that she might have saved him some food or even a little tea. But then he realizes that his six hungry children have probably eaten everything. Thinking for a long time about what he should do, he finally decides to return home. He makes his way in the darkness past his children, and he settles down next to his wife, whose knuckles he starts to crack and whose mud-caked feet he starts to tickle. Eventually she awakens as he fumbles with his clothes "preparing for what was about to be," his cheapest form of entertainment.

Months later, his seventh child arrives. And even more months and years later, additional children are born whom he cannot afford to feed. As if oblivious of cause and effect, Abdel Kerim "still wondered what pit in heaven or earth kept throwing them up."

This story can be read as a blistering critique of Egypt's inability to deal with its overwhelming population problem and the ineffectiveness of its birth-control programs. Idris seems to be saying that men from this particular class of Egyptian society—indeed, society at large—are caught in a double bind. On the one hand, they do not have enough money for a glass of tea, much less birth-control devices; yet they must have some sort of pleasure in their lives. What seems like a cheap form of entertainment is, in fact, over the life of a resulting child, a very expensive proposition that will cost the parents, and by extension the country, dearly.

Here sex, as in many of Idris's early stories, is depicted entirely from the male point of view. It is all urgency and need, lacking in intimacy or finesse. Even in the later stories Idris's protagonists seem to view woman as objects, to be pursued and possessed. This is especially well depicted in "Dregs of the City," the title story from his 1959 collection, where the protagonist, Judge Abdollah, is caught up in a hapless round of sexual conquests.

In Abdel Kerim's curses and angry remarks, one can also see features of one of Idris's major stylistic contributions to the modern Arabic short story: the juxtaposition of classical Arabic in the narrative, but highly colloquial Arabic in the speech of lower-class characters. A rough approximation to this situation in English is found in the contrast between the narrative prose and the speech of Huck and Jim in Twain's *Huckleberry Finn.*

One of Idris's most popular stories, "The Cheapest Night" has been widely translated into European, Asian, and African languages, and is regularly anthologized in collections of Middle-Eastern literature.

—Carlo Coppola

A CHEERY SOUL
by Patrick White, 1962

"A Cheery Soul" is one of only two short stories by Patrick White upon which he based a work in another genre. This tale, an anatomy of what one character calls "the sin of goodness," began as a short story which appeared in the *London Magazine* in September 1962. But White's biographer David Marr reports that even as he wrote the story, White was visualizing it as a play and hearing the voice of actress Nita Pannell in the lead role of Miss Docker. With some misgivings, Pannell accepted the enormous challenge of playing a woman who, because she wields love as a weapon, is herself what Pannell termed "completely *unloved.*" Plans went forward, and the three-act play *A Cheery Soul* premiered in Melbourne in November 1963.

This was the third of White's plays to be staged in his native Australia, and the one he thought his best to date. Thus he was confident of a warm reception. Instead, audience and critics were surprisingly hostile. White offered this summary of the response; "Almost all the Melbourne critics condemned it (one of them in one line) saying that I am without wit, humour, love, or even liking for human beings. . . . [On its opening night] there were people stamping up and down in the intervals saying the theatre should be locked to keep such stuff out of it."

The offence taken by the play's audience can probably be traced to the difficulties they encountered in recognizing Miss Docker's peculiar brand of villainy. This is because Miss Docker is a conventionally "good" person: she is charitable even when she can't afford to be, responsive to the sufferings of others, and always ready to offer her services. According to White, the character was based on an actual person, a woman called "Scottie" who came to help out with the gardening when White lived in Castle Hill, a suburb of Sydney. Although many spoke of her with apparent affection, Scottie was a non-stop talker and colossal bore who considered herself an authority on everything and would buttonhole people with anecdotes and photos of her youth. Still more annoying was her habit of confronting even casual acquaintances with home "truths" she felt they needed to hear. She once said to White, "I am praying that someday you will write some-thing good." This to the man who would soon become Australia's first (and so far only) Nobel Laureate in literature.

All of what White knew of Scottie he transferred to the character of Miss Docker. Like Scottie, she converts to Christianity after reading the Bible cover to cover and then starts to manage and subsequently empty the neighborhood Anglican church. Again like her prototype, Miss Docker has a box of photographs to which she subjects anyone within range, and she radiates destructive candor in all directions. White masterfully captures the essence of her character in the first speech he gives her in the story. She has just arrived at the home of the Custances, a middle-aged and childless couple who have reluctantly decided that their Christian duty compels them to take her in. Mrs. Custance is meeting the taxi or "hire car" in which Miss Docker has arrived:

"Well, now," Miss Docker was saying, "isn't it lovely to be amongst friends? What would we do without them? I, for one, would be homeless in the world. Neat place they've got"—she was addressing the hire-car man—"only, as a matter of personal taste, I would have painted it cream and green."

We can see Miss Docker's entire *modus operandi* here. In a few short sentences she reminds her benefactors of the extremity of her need. Yet she refuses the role of grateful petitioner. Instead, she adopts the posture not merely of Mrs. Custance's equal, but of one in a position to be critical, demanding, and judgmental of Mrs. Custance and her way of life.

Such a person would be apt to inspire guilt and resentment in those around her, as in fact, Miss Docker has already done in the Custances. But White makes Miss Docker more than merely a nuisance or a source of guilty discomfort, and it is this added dimension which must account for the fact that the play's audience so recoiled from her and from acknowledgment that such people exist. For Miss Docker is *dangerous*, all the more so because she doesn't know it. In her, the laudable impulse to serve has assumed monstrous proportions, mutating into a means to manipulate, control, and destroy. As one of her victims observes, "her goodness is a disease. She is sick with it." That disease worsens as the story progresses. But unlike the cancer White employs as its metaphorical equivalent, Miss Docker's disease consumes others rather than herself.

White structures his story in three sections, each built around the experience of a loving couple threatened by Miss Docker's version of love. In part 1, the effect of Miss Docker's advent upon the hidebound, but rewarding marital relationship of the Custances is imaged in the effect produced by the tallboy which Miss Docker insists on moving into her room. It dominates the space, blocks the light from the windows, and smashes a little bookshelf which Mr. Custance had put up for Miss Docker's things. The Custances' eventual decision to send Miss Docker to an old folks' home is clearly an act of last-ditch self-defense against the similar mayhem she inflicts upon their emotional lives.

The Custances are saved by ridding themselves of Miss Docker, but the Lillies were not so fortunate. In part 2 of the story, Miss Docker arrives at the Sundown Home to find Millicent, Tom Lillie's widow, already in residence there. Through Millie's memories, we learn that Miss Docker had attached herself to the Lillies after Tom's first stroke, ostensibly to help with the nursing chores. But as Tom weakened, the vampire-like Miss Docker grew in strength, more and more preempting control of her patient and separating him from his wife. Millie could not forgive her for coming between them at the moment of his death and managed to leave her behind when his funeral procession paused to check directions. But even this blatant act of rejection fails to deflect the "avalanche of kindness" with which Miss Docker bears down on people.

In part 3, it engulfs Mr. Wakeman, the young Anglican rector, whose lawn she cares for while lecturing him on his inadequacies as a preacher. Reverend Wakeman does manage one memorable sermon—on Miss Docker's "sin of goodness"—but collapses and dies in the midst of it. His bewildered wife accuses Miss Docker of having killed her "saint" and perhaps her God as well.

Ironically, White puts into Miss Docker's mouth the lesson the rector should have preached, one she should have learned: "failure is not failure if it is sent to humble. The only failure is not to know." Wakeman understands the spiritual lesson inherent in his failure, while Miss Docker does not. White suggests that because she fails to grasp the meaning of her failures, she will never achieve the "illumination" in which Reverend Wakeman dies.

"A Cheery Soul" appeared in the 1964 collection of White's short fiction called *The Burnt Ones*. He has explained this title as a literal translation of the Greek lament *oi kaymenoi*, which is an "expression of formal pity" for "the poor unfortunates," people for whom "nothing can be done." Appropriately, the stories in this volume are filled with characters who seem irremediably maimed, people in whom some vital capacity for living and loving has atrophied or been amputated by events. Miss Docker is memorable, even among these emotional cripples. All three of the couples she menaces have aligned themselves with life. They express, cherish, and nurture their love for each other, even if circumspectly. But Miss Docker is an agent of sterility, death, and dissolution. White once said that in his view, the greatest sin was to destroy in another the ability to love. This remark seems to describe Miss Docker's whole agenda, all the more insidious because it masks itself as selfless love and cheerful service.

—Carolyn Bliss

THE CHILD OF QUEEN VICTORIA
by William Plomer, 1933

One of the finest South African stories ever written, "The Child of Queen Victoria" (the title story of the 1933 collection) complements William Plomer's pioneering novel, *Turbott Wolfe* (1926), in developing the theme of love across the colour bar: an English trader in "Lembuland," Frant, falls unsuccessfully in love with a beautiful Lembu girl. As in the novel, the girl in the story, Seraphina, has an uncommonly light complexion. Though it may well have been that Plomer was drawing from a living person with complete accuracy, that both his black heroines should need to undergo this bleaching process would not on its own be a notable testimony to his colour-blindness, so it is a relief to find him assuaging this slightly embarrassing aspect by the unapologetic qualifications in the following portrayal of Seraphina:

though unmistakably negroid, her features were in no sense exaggerated. Her nose, for example, though the nostrils were broad, was very slightly aquiline . . . and though one side of her face was marked with a long scar, this only drew closer attention to its beauty.

The three qualifications beginning with "though" are unapologetic because, while an unambiguously exultant nigritude would undeniably be more acceptable to present-day orthodoxy, they show Plomer, concerned as he is to present his black character in the best possible light, is nevertheless able to rise above the narrowly racial aspects of difference and, far from suppressing them, to make them a justification: the scar that may make Seraphina's face additionally attractive to another African is also able to draw the white man's "closer attention to its beauty." More ordinary black characters would be less tricky subjects, no doubt, in avoiding any hint of the "honorary white" condescension related to the kind of patronizing Plomer deplored in "an Englishman's praise of a foreigner for not behaving like a foreigner." But his African characters refuse to be shackled by any ethnic generalizations, and even that physically typical Lembu, Umlilwana, who is (it transpires in the end) engaged to be married to Seraphina, is not left ethnically "naked except for a fur codpiece and some bead ornaments," but carries "a large black cotton Brummagem umbrella, to shelter himself from the sun." More problematic, ultimately, is not Plomer's treatment of blacks, who are neither patronized nor idealized, but his thumb in the scale against white characters like the archetypally awful trader MacGavin: "You've always given me the impression of being a bit too fond of the niggers," says MacGavin in one typical yet convincing utterance. But then, with a disquieting inevitability, the angry young author tips the balance a little too far to add, "treating them a bit too much as if they were really human beings."

Seraphina herself is fully human, and full of character. She appreciates irony, her speech contains much good-natured humour, and, by making him a gift of the skin of a python she has killed, she takes some of the initiative in her relationship with Frant. The tender yet awkward nature of this relationship is conveyed primarily by direct presentation rather than commentary, which is reserved for when Frant is alone, with the exception of his encounter with Umlilwana, whom he takes to be Seraphina's brother. Umlilwana tells him, with no threat or condemnation, that it is not good for him to like a black girl, for "we are all people, but we are different." The implications of this conversation reverberate throughout the story, dominating much of Frant's thinking. The lonely youth's strongest feelings are aroused by "the immediate physical presence of the Lembus," and he is "sensual by nature and sexually repressed," the greatest repression being the wall of racial segregation.

The title of the story comes from the half-affectionate, half-ironical salutation, *S'a ubona, umtwana ka Kwini Victoli!* ("Greeting, child of Queen Victoria!"), given to both Plomer himself in real life and the fictional Frant by a vagabond old Zulu/Lembu. But this amusing old man, though drawn from life in the person of one Nkiyankiya, is not a superfluous appendage to the fictional story. He appears again with almost supernatural effect at the end, all the comic trappings—like his teasing of MacGavin's sour wife with his assortment of *cache-sexes*—forgotten in the drama of the storm.

In the build-up to the immense climax, the weather mirrors the emotional climate of the story. As Frant's turbulent feelings mount without release, torturing him with unfulfilled desires, so the heat mounts every day and it seems the anticipated rain will never come. After the tension has increased almost unbearably, catharsis is finally achieved in a virtuoso resolution, the long-awaited storm exceeding expectations and in one terrifying night flooding the river and submerging the Lembu village. On the tableland above the valley, from where Frant sees the devastation of Seraphina's home, he meets the transformed old man, whose revelations about Seraphina, drowned in the flood, combine with the terror and destruction of the apocalyptic storm to make him feel "all was finished, all was destroyed . . . like the end of the world," though he knows he must return to his world, his life. In its "great symphony," this is the greatest of several storms in Plomer's work, bringing to a desperate but satisfying close this unhappy, deeply impressive story.

—Michael Herbert

THE CHILDHOOD OF ZHENIA LUVERS.   See **ZHENIA LUVERS' CHILDHOOD.**

A CHILD'S CHRISTMAS IN WALES
by Dylan Thomas, 1955

Between his finest collection of prose, *Portrait of the Artist as a Young Dog* and his last work, *Under Milk Wood*, Dylan Thomas's stories tended towards more autobiographical pieces, mainly prepared for radio broadcast during the 1940's. The surrealistic imagery, naturalistic detail and narrative patterns held in a constant tension in his earlier work are subordinated to a more overt concern with the creative potential of memory. In his later poetry and prose Thomas became fascinated with the perennial Welsh theme of "remembrancing." As defined by the novelist Emyr Humphreys, this entails the actual process of trying to recall, with all of its delight and amusement, and all of its pain and despair. It has been a central feature of Welsh storytelling for centuries, the mythopoetic quality of an oral tradition focused on the rhythms of the speaking voice, and its desire to constantly recreate and reimagine the past.

"A Child's Christmas in Wales" (collected in *Adventures in the Skin Trade*, 1955) is perhaps the best example of this remembrancing technique, being a fusion of two earlier stories, "Memories of Christmas" and "Conversation about Christmas." The solitariness of the lone perspective used in earlier stories such as "Peaches" and "One Warm Saturday" is replaced by a strong sense of family ties and communal bonds. Linden Peach has pointed out that the narrative combines three sets of myths, those associated with childhood (the myth of lost innocence), Christmas (the myths of family and community kinship), and Wales (the cultural myths of singing, the harp, and women dressed in shawls and red petticoats). The story follows a rough chronology, an accumulation of humorous anecdotes and acute observations charting the weather, presents, games, food, tales, singing, and finally bed. Thomas the adult writer hovers above Thomas the innocent child, tempering the gleeful memories with constant wry acknowledgements that such details are as much fantasy as fact: "Our snow was not only shaken from whitewash buckets down the sky, it came shawling out of the ground and swam and drifted out of the arms and hands and bodies of the trees." The vast white landscape, "eternal, ever since Wednesday," in turn becomes the "inscape" of the middle-aged writer, a metaphor for his dive into memory: "I plunge my hands in the snow and bring out whatever I can find. In goes my hand into that wool-white bell-tongued ball of holidays resting at the rim of the carol-singing sea, and out comes Mrs. Protheroe and the firemen."

The way in which Thomas holds the adult and childlike versions of reality in a perfect tension is the most obvious strength of the narrative technique. The comparisons and contrasts, the ambivalence and the blending of realistic details with surreal exaggeration, aspires to the condition of that contemporary South American phenomenon, mythic realism. The boys, hands wrapped in socks for warmth and greater accuracy, snowball the "horrible-whiskered, spitting and snarling" cats, before dividing their presents into "Useful" and "Useless" piles. Yet Thomas is rarely interested in grasping people or events precisely, only in exaggerating them precisely. Many of the memories become progressively more ludicrous as fantastic images occur to the author's imagination: "when there were wolves in Wales, . . . when we sang and wallowed all night and day in caves . . . before the motor-car, before the wheel." The "mis en abyme" technique favoured by Thomas in many of his stories, the creation of a frame within a frame, is particularly evident in "A Child's Christmas in Wales." The narrator creates a young boy to whom he regales his memories, a boy similar to the young Thomas who in turn listens to "the tall tales" of his uncles before bedtime. One of his remembered presents turns out to be a metaphor for his later profession: "and a painting book in which I could make the grass, the trees, the sea and the animals any colour I pleased, and still the dazzling sky-blue sheep are grazing in the red field under the rainbow-billed and pea-green birds."

The past and the present, the child and the adult, appear to be one and the same at such moments. The ambivalence between the excesses of an imagined past and their prominence and importance to the adult in the present recurred throughout Thomas's later stories. Two phrases from "Reminiscences of Childhood" will serve as an example. In the final section the narrator sadly admits of the Swansea he has recreated, "never was there such a town." Yet the story still ends on the wistful certainty that "the memories of childhood have no order, and no end." It is similar to Proust's concept of "the involuntary memory," the significance of minor details which linger on for no apparent reason, time investing them with an often incomprehensible significance, even when we know they are imagined. "A Child's Christmas in Wales" represents the creating of a medium of expression that used the full potential of language to evoke, visually and aurally, a sense of place and time. Its ending prepares us for the sense of community rarely found in Thomas's poetry, but realised in *Under Milk Wood*:

I could see the lights in the windows of all the other houses on our hill and hear the music rising from them up the long, steadily falling night. I turned the gas down, I got into bed. I said some words to the close and holy darkness, and then I slept. The story celebrates the fact that the actual value of memory lies in the insight that nothing is past. It recalls the sentiments of T.S. Eliot's poem "Little Gidding":

We shall not cease from exploration And the end of all our exploring Will be to arrive where we started And know the place for the first time.

—Simon Baker

A CHRISTMAS CAROL
by Charles Dickens, 1843

The first and much the best of Dickens's long series of Christmas books (1843-48) and stories (1850-67), *A Christmas Carol* had suddenly occurred to him in early October 1843, when he was visiting Manchester to speak at a fundraising occasion. Though busy producing his monthly serial installments of *Martin Chuzzlewit* (1843-44), he went furiously to work on it and completed it in time for the Christmas market. It was immediately recognized as a classic celebration of Christmas, most eloquently by his future rival Thackeray, who called it "a national benefit, and to every man or woman who reads it a personal kindness" (*Fraser's Magazine,* February 1844). Already Thackeray could assume that it was as superfluous to recapitulate the story of Scrooge as to remind the reader of the plot of *Robinson Crusoe,* another definitively mythic story.

Before becoming a novelist, Dickens had proclaimed in "Christmas Festivities" and "The New Year" (published in the 1835-36 Yuletide period and collected in his *Sketches by Boz*) his strong and sincere devotion to the sentiment and celebrations of this season, and his first novel, *Pickwick Papers,* had included a "good-humoured Christmas Chapter" followed by a story, closely anticipating the *Carol,* about a misanthropic old bachelor who, after some supernatural events and visions on Christmas Eve, becomes "an altered man," repentant, reformed, and wiser. When Dickens died in 1870, a Cockney costermonger's girl was heard to say "Dickens dead? Then will Father Christmas die too?" With his many returns to the subject, he had identified himself with the Christmas spirit, even for the illiterate (who could be familiar with his works through the numerous stage versions. The *Carol* has always been, and still remains, notably popular in stage, radio, film, and television adaptations, and his own solo rendering of it (from 1853 onwards) was the central item in his public readings repertoire.

As often in his fiction, Dickens suggests his positives through a negative—Scrooge (finely named for his function), whose automatic response to Christmas jollity and benevolence is "Bah! Humbug!" In the opening "Stave" he is seen rejecting the seasonal claims of family and of charitable giving, and being penny-pinchingly mean to his clerk Bob Cratchit; in the final "Stave" these denials are all rectified by the overnight-reformed Scrooge, who thenceforward "became as good as friend, as good a master, and as good a man, as the good old city knew." His conversion is mythical and magical, not a psychological process (Dickens called his method here "a whimsical kind of masque which the good humour of the season justified"). By supernatural means, Scrooge revisits his past and sees what he has lost by sacrificing love to money-lust, and he glimpses the bleak future that he and those dependent on

him risk unless he mends his ways. In the "Christmas Present" episodes, Dickens celebrates Christmas positively, with the animated descriptions of the streets and shops on Christmas Eve, the superbly inclusive presentation of the Cratchit family's Christmas dinner (it has every appropriate anticipation, worry, triumph, congratulation, and sentiment, with due attention to the children for whom Christmas is so special an event), and the fun and jollity in Scrooge's nephew's household. There is a sharp final reminder, too, of those excluded from the feast, symbolized by the two allegorical children, Ignorance and Want, "wretched, abject, frightful, hideous, miserable." A typically Dickensian note of pathos is introduced by the crippled Tiny Tim, and the story appropriately ends with Scrooge's becoming "a second father" to him, "who did NOT die" (as he had done in Scrooge's vision of the future: Dickens thus eats his cake—the pathos of the Cratchits' grief over their bereavement—but has it complete when Tim survives.)

"He went to church," we hear of the reformed Scrooge on Christmas Day, but that is almost the only reference to religion. It is a secular winter-solstice festival that Dickens celebrates: the weather is appropriately "cold, bleak, biting . . . foggy withal" on Christmas Eve, with no fog on Scrooge's joyful Christmas morning, but "clear, bright, jovial, stirring cold; cold, piping for the blood to dance to," cold to offset by contrast the physical and emotional warmth of the festive hearth and home. The stress is on benevolence, generous sentiment, family togetherness, and simple enjoyment to young and old and rich and poor—"a kind, forgiving, charitable, pleasant time," as Scrooge's nephew says on Dicken's behalf, "the only time . . . when men and women seem by common consent to open their shut-up hearts freely, and to think of people below them as if they really were fellow travellers to the grave, and not another race of creatures bound on other journeys." Scrooge's early unseasonable misanthropy does not threaten the ambient benevolence and high spirits. He is a thoroughly enjoyable miserly mugwump: as G.K. Chesterton remarked, "there is a heartiness in his inhospitable sentiments that is akin to humour and therefore to humanity; he is only a crusty old bachelor, and had (I strongly suspect) given away turkeys secretly all his life."

Dicken's annual Christmas items continued, almost uninterrupted, for 20 years, becoming a national institution, and he returned to the subject in his novels too, but he never again achieved such a perfect and (save in its religious dimension) comprehensive evocation of the Christmas spirit. Nor has any British writer before or since rivalled him in creating so potent a myth of this annual festival, experienced by many but surprisingly under-represented in our literature. Henceforth, wrote a reviewer on 23 December 1843, anyone who wants to "understand what the real enjoyment of Christmas is . . . will have to read" this story—a pardonable exaggeration and an extraordinary prophetic accolade for a book then four days old.

—Philip Collins

CHRONOPOLIS
by J.G. Ballard, 1971

By the late 1960's, J.G. Ballard was one of the most innovative writers in the English language, but he began his career as a writer of more or less conventional science fiction. "Chronopolis" is a good example of his early work, not only because it does what good science fiction ought to do but also because it illustrates how and why even Ballard's earliest stories are only "more or less" conventional. The story was first published in 1961, and was the title story of a 1971 collection.

The science-fiction story is almost always a projection into the future. Generally speaking, the writer says, "If life continues in this way, here is what things will be like later on." Also, in general, the science-fiction story addresses the issue of technology—what it is and what it might be in some future time. Science fiction *is* science fiction precisely because of these two components: the future (fiction) and technology (science).

"Chronopolis" is a blend of futuristic fantasy and technology, and yet, as is characteristic of Ballard's work, this future is not particularly distant and the technology is not exotic. Apart from a few differences, "Chronopolis" could be set in our own time. And the technology does not involve spaceships or time machines or super-computers; it involves ordinary timepieces—wristwatches and clocks.

Conrad Newman is in jail, waiting to stand trial for murder, in a world where timepieces have been abolished. People use timing devices—more or less elaborate egg timers—to wake them in the morning or to measure the length of the work day, but no one ever knows precisely what time it is.

Newman, however, is obsessed with time. He has built a sundial in his holding cell, and he is able to amaze the other prisoners by predicting daily events (inspection, roll call, breakfast) which are measured out according to timers and which, therefore, take place at regular intervals. He understands the purpose that timepieces once served: to regulate, to standardize, to make life predictable. It is precisely this sense of order that the world of "Chronopolis" has lost.

The story moves back to Conrad's childhood when he first notices clock towers in the older, rundown sections of his town. In every case, the hands and inner mechanisms of the clocks have been removed, and when he asks adults about these unfamiliar devices, they either cannot or will not answer him.

As an adolescent, Conrad builds his own water clock which allows him to regulate his life. As a result, he excels at school, because he can make better use of his time than his fellow students: "The water clock had demonstrated that a calibrated timepiece added another dimension to life, organized its energies, gave the countless activities of everyday existence a yardstick of significance."

He still does not understand why timepieces are illegal, and eventually he asks his English teacher, Mr. Stacey:

"It's against the law to have a gun because you might shoot someone. But how can you hurt anybody with a clock?"

"Isn't it obvious? You can time him, know exactly how long it takes him to do something."

"Well?"

"Then you can make him do it faster."

Stacey takes Conrad to "Chronopolis, the Time City." Clearly, the city is London, now abandoned, and Conrad learns that he has spent his life in one of the suburbs of this "vast dead center forty or fifty miles in diameter." The city is full of clocks, all stopped at 12:01.

Conrad, not convinced of the evils of time, escapes when Stacey, a secret member of the Time Police, tries to kill

him. He meets old Marshall, who is dedicated to starting the clocks again, and in time they get the master clock working. The people of the suburbs hear the chimes and fondly remember "the ordered world of the past." The police arrest Newman, and Stacey is killed by Marshall, but Conrad takes the blame to allow his friend to continue with their work.

Is Conrad Newman a hero or a villain? Typically, Ballard refuses to offer any simplistic judgments. A world without clocks is disorderly and uncomfortable, even meaningless; a world with clocks is slavery. For Ballard, technology is what makes modern life possible, but it is also what makes modern life impossible, and he never suggests a resolution to this dilemma.

In the end, Newman is sentenced to 20 years, and he is thrilled to find a working clock in his new cell. Newman finds this ironic and amusing at first. "He was still chuckling over the absurdity of it all two weeks later when for the first time he noticed the clock's insanely irritating tick. . . ." It seems that, for Newman and perhaps for all of us, clocks are both a salvation and a punishment.

—Welch D. Everman

THE CHRYSANTHEMUMS
by John Steinbeck, 1938

On 25 February, 1934, John Steinbeck wrote George Albee that he had completed a new story, "The Chrysanthemums," and commented that "it is entirely different and is designed to strike without the reader's knowledge. I mean he reads it casually and after it is finished feels that something profound has happened to him although he does not know what nor how." Ever since its publication in *Harper's* (October 1937) and *The Long Valley* (1938), this story has been "striking" readers more forcefully than any of Steinbeck's other stories, leading André Gide to call it "remarkable for its adroitness" and Mordecai Marcus to praise it as "one of the world's great short stories." Steinbeck foresaw correctly when he jotted "This is to be a good story" on the first page of the draft.

Set in the foothills of California's Salinas River valley during the Depression years of the early 1930's, "The Chrysanthemums" chronicles a crucial Saturday afternoon in December in the life of Elisa Allen, perhaps Steinbeck's most memorable depiction of a repressed woman. Henry, her husband, has managed to sell 30 three-year-old steers to the Western Meat Company and offers to take Elisa to dinner and perhaps a "picture show" in Salinas that evening. He then rides off with a ranch-hand to herd in the steers. Thus Elisa's adventure begins.

With astounding deftness and economy, Steinbeck quickly establishes the complexities and depths of the 35-year-old Elisa in this study of the repression of her feminine, sexual, and creative impulses. Elisa, whom Joseph Warren Beach has called "one of the most delicious characters ever transferred from life to the pages of a book," enters the story looking "blocked and heavy," wearing a man's hat, heavy gloves, and a print dress "almost completely covered by a big corduroy apron." From a distance, she could easily be mistaken for a man. She channels her frustrated energies into caring for her "hard-swept looking" house, her red geraniums, and her "forest of new green chrysanthemum sprouts." Henry longs for Elisa to exercise her creative, nurturing "planter's hands" in practical ways on the ranch's apple orchard, but she reserves her "gift" for the flowers. Paul McCarthy has noted the ironic contrasts developing early in the story between "the rich land and the sterile marriage, the fertile plants and Elisa's inner emptiness" to enrich the story.

This day, though, things change, because the antagonist, an itinerant tinker traveling turns into the ranch road as Elisa reroots her chrysanthemums. Exotic, sexually attractive in an unkempt way, and extremely skillful at exploiting potential customers, the tinker immediately discerns Elisa's vulnerabilities, joking with her about his dog's reaction to the ranch's dogs, complimenting her chrysanthemums, and capturing her sympathies by describing her flowers as looking "like a quick puff of colored smoke." Elisa responds, doffing her gloves, tearing off her hat, and shaking out her "dark pretty hair," in ways not unlike Hester Prynne in *The Scarlet Letter*. As he encourages her to talk more about her flowers, Elisa's voice grows "husky," her "breast swell[s] passionately," and she "crouche[s] low like a fawning dog" before him. When Steinbeck revised the story for *The Long Valley*, he cut several explanatory passages and made Elisa's sexuality much more explicit. Expressing her wish that women could be as free to lead the life he does, she claims an equality, even a superiority to, the tinker. As she pays him 50 cents for repairing two saucepans, she brags, "I could show you what a woman might do."

Awakened sexually and creatively, perhaps for the first time in many years, Elisa goes into the house and subjects her body to a cleansing, almost a ritually purifying bath, appraises her body's reflection in a mirror, then dresses slowly in her "newest underclothing" and her dress, "the symbol of her prettiness." When Henry returns from rounding up the steers, he is startled by her transformation, telling her that she looks "nice . . . different, strong, and happy." Her appearance so discomposes him that he breaks into metaphor, telling her "you look strong enough to break a calf over your knee, happy enough to eat it like a watermelon," an image to which numerous Steinbeck critics have objected as being inappropriate, but one which surely alludes to the Dionysian energies with which she has been infused.

This new self collapses, however, during their drive to Salinas, because she sees the chrysanthemums she had so carefully prepared for the tinker dumped on the road. She feels crushed and discarded. He had kept the "bright new flower pot" but threw away the shoots Elisa had packed. She surprises Henry asking about the bloodiness of prize fights, and the story ends with her "crying weakly—like an old woman." When one weighs the symbolic weight of the chrysanthemums, the crucial question remains whether or not Elisa has been destroyed. She had told the tinker that chrysanthemums needed to be pinched back, but not so far as to be killed. Has Elisa been "pinched back" just enough to ensure later blooms, or has she been "pinched back" so far as to destroy her? This point remains tantalizingly ambiguous, and critical opinion remains much divided over the extent to which "The Chrysanthemums" is or is not a feminist story, especially since the reader is never allowed access to Elisa's own thoughts.

—David Leon Higdon

THE CINDERELLA WALTZ
by Ann Beattie, 1982

Ann Beattie's short story "The Cinderella Waltz" first appeared in *The New Yorker* in 1979. Later it was included in *Prize Stories, 1980: The O. Henry Awards* and her collection *The Burning House*. It was Beattie's sixth book to be published. Two novels and three collections of short stories preceded its publication, but the stories in *The Burning House* were heralded as the best she had written. Carolyn Porter writes, in *Contemporary American Women Writers* (1985), that the stories in *The Burning House* are "marked by understatement, caustic dialogue, and an unsentimental view of social relations." Porter adds that Beattie's technique of representing "surfaces of a world perceived as surface . . . have now begun to serve as a ground on which to build a more complex narrative."

An aspect of this complexity is her use of objects. Beattie strews objects on the path or plot of the narrative, not unlike Hansel and Gretel who threw pebbles on the forest path, so that the reader will follow the object-strewn path, mapping a way to meaning. Raymond Carver, who, like Beattie, is often linked with the minimalist school, writes in his essay "On Writing," (in *Fires*), that "it's possible, in a poem or a short story to write about commonplace things and objects using commonplace language and to endow those things—a chair, a window-curtain, a fork a stone, a woman's earring—with immense, even startling power. It is possible to write a line of seemingly innocuous dialogue and have it send a chill along the reader's spine—the source of artistic delight, as Nabokov would have it."

In "The Cinderella Waltz" the objects serve, in some cases, as icons of meaning, but because meaning is elusive and mutable, Beattie refrains from tagging or naming, and the objects, like the ivy, the tulip-shaped glasses, the glass slippers, and the glass elevator reflect mobility and, consequently, mutability—Americans moving, always moving, in spaces, and among or between objects, looking for meaning, looking for roots.

This is apparent in "The Cinderella Waltz." Objects lie on the surfaces in a seemingly casual or haphazard manner, but as the story unfolds the objects take on a kind of patina, as it were, of interest and meaning. Among these objects in the story are a blue, moth-eaten scarf, a coleus, a blue bowl, Beckett's *Happy Days*, an octascope, and various and sundry glasses, including references to glass slippers and a glass elevator which become significant, reinforcing an aura of vulnerability, in particular, the vulnerability of the child Louise. Thus, these objects are invested with meaning beyond the understated, seemingly casual placement in the landscape of the story. The glass elevator that figures in the end of the story is an example of such an object—an objective correlative. Louise's father, who is leaving New York for the west coast, promises her that when she visits him, he will take her up in a glass elevator, but at this point in the narrative, the reader knows that the glass "box" functions as an encapsulation of the daughter to the whims and desires of her father, "the prince."

Porter notes that Beattie's "characters are attached to people and often to plants or dogs; their mobility is a characteristic of their lives. It is also a trail of that 'something lost,' a rootlessness of the American character which Beattie portrays in her short fiction." This mobility and rootlessness pervades the lives of her characters. In "The Cinderella Waltz" it manifests itself on physical and psychological levels. The four characters are in constant motion: the husband and father, Milo, leaves the house in Connecticut to live in New York City; the nine-year old daughter Louise travels, most weekends, to visit her father in New York City. But just when the pattern or routine is established for the daughter, her father decides to move out to the west coast. Although the other two characters seem to move about less than Milo and Louise, psychologically they have adjusted to quantum leaps—Milo's ex-wife to his leaving her for a man, Bradley, and Bradley to Milo's lackadaisical commitment in their relationship. It is significant that the child Louise is trying to root a plant for Bradley; she carries the ivy with her as she goes from her mother's home to her father's. She typifies the Beattie character stranded in spaces too vast to navigate. The characters in "The Cinderella Waltz" are adrift in space, but it is a peculiar American space, as the characters are American characters. One finds them portrayed throughout American fiction, not only by Beattie, but also by such writers as Raymond Carver, Joan Didion, Joyce Carol Oates, Saul Bellow, and John Irving.

In "The Cinderella Waltz" the focus of the relationships centers on the child, Louise. Children and their relations to adults often figure in Beattie's fiction. In an interview with Beattie, conducted by Steven R. Centola, in *Contemporary Literature* (1990), she says that "the nuclear family has broken down, so there's a different set of realities. I think adults often make the mistake of thinking they understand children. I think children are always watching and understanding but may not be quite as comprehensible to the parents as they think." In "The Cinderella Waltz" the child is watching and understanding, but nevertheless unable to control the direction of the events that overtake her, and it is her dilemma that adds poignancy to a story told with restraint and without sentimentality.

In "The Cinderella Waltz" Beattie articulates this complexity through her use of objects and through her sense of what it means to live in American spaces, and to live in a state of constant mobility, balancing the precarious relationships we so devoutly seek and need.

—Alice Swensen

THE CIRCULAR RUINS (Las ruinas circulares)
by Jorge Luis Borges, 1944

In the story "Las ruinas circulares" ("The Circular Ruins") Jorge Luis Borges offers a fascinating perspective on the ontological question of *causa sui*. Can someone or something be its own cause? Some critics have seen the story, collected in *Ficciones* (1944), as a metaphor for the creative process, and others as a parable concerning the fallibility of a less than omnipotent God. The tale's simplicity conflicts with the profound statement(s) and paradox(es) it proposes. The epigraph ("And if he left off dreaming about you. . . .") from Carroll's *Through the Looking-Glass* sets the tone for the arrival of the "gray man" from an imprecise South where "lepers are rare." Such an onset catapults the reader into strange and exotic surroundings where the baroque style and the erudite vocabulary submerge him in an alien world, while suggesting a timeless, Eastern setting. Reality is suspended and the reader is ready for the uncanny. The gray man establishes

camp near ancient circular ruins and begins his toil, which is to dream a man. This task, resembling a mystic quest, requires that he dream for long periods of time, searching for the perfect pupil. Among many "dream students he selects one who seems promising and begins an arduous pedagogical undertaking. Unfortunately, the gray man suffers prolonged, acute insomnia, rendering him unable to continue dreaming. He decides to follow another method as the shaping of dreams is among the hardest things that anyone can attempt. Before resuming his labors, he awaits the full moon, cleanses himself in the waters of the river, worships the gods, ultimately falling asleep. These mystic, ritual actions draw upon various religions, ancient and modern, Oriental and Occidental. He dreams about a beating heart. From this heart the rest of the body slowly develops in successive dreams until finally the heart becomes a whole man, sleeping within the dreamer's dream. Eventually, the dreamed young man awoke and thereafter the magician spent two years instructing him into the mysteries of the universe and the worship of fire. When this apprenticeship was complete and the time had come for the spiritual son to be born, the creator-magician kissed him and ordered the young man to proceed to a distant temple. So he might never know he was just a dream, the sorcerer erased all memory of the apprenticeship years. Curiously, during the extended pedagogical process, the gray man had been haunted by the impression that all this had already happened. After several "half-decades" he heard of a magic man in a northern temple who walked on fire without being burned. Believing him his offspring, he worried that his son would discover his origins and be humiliated at the realization he was merely someone's dream. The cessation of his trepidations arrived one day in the form of encircling sheets of flame that devoured everything around him. As a result of the conflagration, he discovered to his humiliation that the fire did not affect his flesh and drew the logical conclusion that he too was the product of someone's dream.

Some critical studies have suggested the parallel between the magician and the magical process of creating or dreaming a son with the situation of the writer and process of creating a text. As the author struggles to "procreate" or "give birth" to the characters, some are discarded and others developed, and eventually the finished product appears. The result, in some instances, is a reflection of the author who in turn has a similar parallel relationship with his God (who, Borges implies, might in turn have his own God, and so on ad infinitum). The notion of a sleeping deity dreaming creation is drawn from the idealist philosophy of Berkeley and was echoed for Spanish readers by Miguel Unamuno with his prayer, "Dream us, Oh God." Although Borges was certainly familiar with Unamuno's works and Berkeley's speculations, his approach lacks the anguished personal involvement of the former and is more accessible than the intellectual abstractness of the latter. Indeed, it approaches the ludicrous.

Borges declared once that he took up the same idea in a pair of sonnets about chess. The chessmen do not know they are guided by the players; the players do not know they are guided by God; and God, in turn, is not aware of being directed by other gods, and so on. Just as the closed circle is infinite because it has no end, the implied regression (dream within a dream or game within a game within yet another more encompassing one) is susceptible of infinite repetition. Similarly, if one imagines ever-decreasing concentric circles, the number which will fit inside a given circular configuration extends to the infinitely small. The central conceit of the masterful Borges tale alludes by analogy to the concept of infinite concentric circles.

Furthermore, the title of the story with its reference to the circle evokes ramifications of the geometric figure considered the most perfect by philosophers and also held sacred by many religions. The circle as a mystical figure carries within it a myriad of connotations and denotations. Significantly, as a sphere, the circle suggests the Pythagorean and Eastern concepts of time, and thus by implication, extends the analogy beyond the spatial to the temporal plane.

Calderón, the 17th-century Spanish playwright whose play entitled *Life Is a Dream* fascinated Unamuno and was incorporated into the latter's concept of dreaming life, is also an inescapable intertext for Borges. Unlike Borges, however, Calderón does not suggest any control over dreams. In "The Circular Ruins" Borges attempts to validate his theme of controlled dreaming and regulated hallucinations. Such oxymorons imbue the magician's attempts to create a being as he must not only "manage" his dreams and also rationally control the irrational and produce a result—a product—that can transcend the dreamworld and the dream, carry over into the wakening world, and, by implication, outlive the dreamer.

—Genaro J. Pérez

CIVIL PEACE
by Chinua Achebe, 1972

In the preface to his collection *Girls at War* (1972), Chinua Achebe has argued that his short stories have provided only "a pretty lean harvest" and that he cannot lay any great claim to the literary form—but this is only the protest of a naturally modest writer. Running through all his short fiction is the same economy of language and sharpness of observation that informs his early novels.

Above all, though, his best short stories have a distinct focus: the disastrous and tragic civil war which raged in Nigeria between 1967 and 1970 and which cost over one million lives. Much ink has been spilt over this conflict which followed the secession of Biafra from the newly independent republic, and it inspired a number of west African writers to come to terms with it, not just from the standpoint that it was a human tragedy but also because it was a war in which sides had to be taken.

One response is Achebe's short story "Civil Peace," which is set in the first days of the uneasy peace settlement of 1970. Its title is deeply ironic. At first reading it signifies a state of normality but "civil" is normally applied to war: as the main protagonists discover, for all the hopeful signs, the conflict is not over for them. On that level it is a classic rendering of the old saying that a bad peace is worse than war itself.

The mood is set in the opening paragraph when Jonathan Iwegbu, the central character, gladly associates himself with the greeting that has gained a sudden currency in the first days of peace: "Happy survival!" In fact, Jonathan has good reason to be pleased. His wife and three out of their four children have managed to weather the fighting and have come through the experience unscathed. So too has his beloved bicycle, which at one point had almost been commandeered by a bogus army officer.

A bigger miracle awaits them when they return to their home base in the mining town of Enugu to find their small house still standing. Soon the family is back in its stride and flourishing. The children are sent to pick mangoes and sell them to soldiers' wives, his wife cooks meals for the villagers, and Jonathan opens a small bar selling palmwine. Their good fortune is in stark contrast to the fate of his fellow coalminers who have been made destitute by the war and who face a troubled future. To cap it all, he is able to change his Biafran money back into 20 pounds of Treasury currency—a considerable sum which he is careful to hide in the safety of his house.

Throughout these short opening scenes Achebe invokes the Iwegbu family's good fortune and their ensuing domesticity in language that is redolent of the scriptures (the house is a "blessing"; his "overjoyed" family carry five heads on their shoulders). This is reinforced by Jonathan's constant exclamations that "nothing puzzles God," and by the comparisons between their happy lot and the misfortunes which have engulfed the rest of the country. At this point, with Jonathan closing his fist over the notes—nicknamed "egg rashers" because no one can pronounce their official name—Achebe makes it clear that for the Iwegbu family at least, the war is over.

Significantly, the change of mood is presaged by the onset of night when the friendly neighbourhood noises die down one after another to leave the world in darkness. The stillness is interrupted by a thunderous knocking on Jonathan's door: thieves have come to rob the Iwegbu family who are powerless to save themselves. Passionate pleas to their neighbours go unanswered—Achebe does not make clear the reasons for their refusal but they do not intervene—and the "tief-men" demand that Jonathan hands over his money. This order they back up with a short burst of automatic fire.

Frightful though the scene undoubtedly is, the real horror lies in the thieves' apparently reasonable statements that they mean no harm because the war is over and that they are acting under the constraints of "civil peace." Having survived the war, Jonathan stands in great danger of losing everything once more. The tension is increased further by Achebe's device of keeping the thieves unseen: only their menacing voices are heard by the hapless Iwegbu.

Inevitably, Jonathan is forced to hand over the money to the raiders and he is left with nothing, a poor reward for having survived the war. In the light of day his neighbours arrive to commiserate with the family but Jonathan puts a brave face on his misfortune. What are the "egg rashers," he asks, compared to the fact that he and his family are safe and well? Like everything else he has experienced, the loss of the money seems to be part of a larger plan.

Although Achebe's message is bleak, that the war has transformed Nigeria utterly and that nothing can be the same again, there is a strong sense of hope in the creation of Jonathan Iwegbu. Like other great survivors of warfare—Hasek's Schweik comes to mind—Jonathan gets by because he refuses to take life too seriously.

All around him his country is in ruins and he himself has been robbed but these disasters count for nothing provided that life goes on as before. With optimism like Jonathan's, Achebe seems to be saying, nothing is so terrible that humans cannot overcome it.

—Trevor Royle

CLAY
by Patrick White, 1964

According to its author Patrick White, the story "Clay" is "very peculiar and surrealist." Written in 1962 and dedicated to the Australian comic Barry Humphries (better known as Dame Edna Everidge), and the actress Zoe Caldwell, it was included in White's first collection of short stories, published in 1964, *The Burnt Ones*.

The general title, *The Burnt Ones*, is a literal translation of a Greek term, the *oi kaymenoi*, used to mean the poor unfortunates. From *The Aunt's Story* (1948) onwards, White often used a fire metaphor to suggest a numinous, transcendental illumination. Clay, the eponymous hero of this short story, is one of White's usual poor unfortunates, or *illuminati*. Like White, he is a writer and artist. Again like White, he suffers from being different; he is even called a freak by his mother, as White was by his mother. The word "freak" returns in *The Vivisector* (1970), White's long novel devoted to describing the life of the painter Hurtle Duffield, called "a freak, an artist." The reason for Clay and Hurtle Duffield's sense of exclusion is that, as artists, they have been "burnt" by a knowledge of inner life (Clay is described as "born with inward-looking eyes"), which pushes them to transmit an artistic vision at the price of pursuing a normal occupation and lifestyle.

In the story White focuses on various time periods in the life of Clay Skerritt. We see the five-year-old boy, the adolescent, and the married man. In a way the short story is a miniature version of *The Vivisector*, which also begins with the theme of difference. White exposes two ideas at the beginning of the story: the sense of alienation, exclusion, and loneliness felt by Clay (he has a strange name, he looks different—his hair is too short), as well as the close emotional relationship between Clay and his mother, Mrs. Skerritt. Typical of White's literary representation of the family, the mother is the dominant authoritative figure. White's fathers tend to be sick, absent, or dead. The dead Mr. Skerritt is remembered as a curious mixture of virility ("those thick thighs, rather tight about the serge crutch") and debilitation. Clay remembers the smell of yellow skin and the sick sheets of his cancerous father, a forerunner of another weak, sick, and departed father figure, Alfred Hunter in *The Eye of the Storm* (1973).

The essential elements of the action are simple: young Clay is beaten up by his peers because he is different; as an adult he has a mundane job at Customs and Excise, he marries a girl called Marj, his mother dies, he begins to write a poem or novel, and he is haunted and pursued by an imaginary feminine figure, Lova. In the final denouement, Marj interrupts Clay holding a white shoe, and screams. The real interest of "Clay" lies behind these events, and is not immediately obvious. White's use of surrealism (the profusion of interconnecting images), the ambiguous and deliberately open-ended conclusion, and the often sibylline dialogue, force the reader to consider more closely the use of metaphor and the chains of repeated images in order to find meaning.

Two symbolic worlds are operating in "Clay." The most important character other than Clay is Mrs. Skerritt. Marj and Lova are both associated with her by means of the repetition of key images (fretted lace, maidenhair, ferns). Marj is a substitute mother figure, and Lova is a phantasmatic revenant of Mrs. Skerritt, a product of Clay's disturbed psyche. Given the predominance of these three maternal figures, it is not surprising to see that one of the symbolic worlds operating in "Clay" is that of feminine womb-like containers: the house where the Skerritts live, the garden, the bay, the white bridal shoe in the wedding photograph of Clay's parents, which is compared to a great boat. Opposed to this symbolic register, is the masculine "world of pointed objects": the heel of the shoe, the barber's clippers, the axe in Clay's writing, the pointed teeth of Lova.

These two symbolic worlds are made to coalesce by means of a series of repeated images, to assume new and different symbolic patterns throughout the story. Recurrent images include feminine hair (fretwork, fretted lace, maidenhair, asparagus ferns, sea-lettuce), connected with feminine, soft, tactile details (satin, breasts, wet mouths, kumquats). Clay is very much attracted by this feminine world of protection and sensual pleasure, which symbolises the creative sphere of the imagination. This seems to be in conflict with the masculine world symbolised by threatening pointed objects (scissors and broken bottles, a pointed shoe the boys chasing Clay carry). Clay has difficulty coping with a highly developed imagination which demands expression (his dreams, fantasy, and inventiveness), whereas mundane existence, his work and marriage, try to make him other than what he is.

Clay is gradually possessed by the feminine side of his personality. White's constant use of water imagery in connection with Clay and Lova, the repetition of the colour green and the threatening femme fatale quality of Lova, give a mythological dimension to the story. Lova reminds us of one of the lorelei, a water nymph, siren and seductress of men. The seduction scene suggests that finally Clay opts for the world of the imagination and fantasy, even at the price of being different.

—David Coad

A CLEAN, WELL-LIGHTED PLACE
by Ernest Hemingway, 1932

Since its publication, the quiet tensions of "A Clean, Well-Lighted Place," have haunted readers. More than any other in the collection, the story captures the spiritual angst of *Winner Take Nothing* (1933), Ernest Hemingway's third story collection. For many readers, it exemplifies the existential plight of modern humanity.

For 60 years, scholars have judged the story pivotal in the Hemingway canon, though they have argued about the degrees of despair and hope that it offers. Shortly before Hemingway's death, the grounds for discussion shifted. Some critics began claiming that the printed version of the story did not make complete sense and that in the extended dialogue between the two waiters, Hemingway had apparently lost track of who was speaking which lines. Following the lead of F. P. Kroeger and William Colburn, John Hagopian argued in 1964 that an "obvious typographical error" occurred and that it should be corrected to provide "order" to Hemingway's masterpiece. In 1965, acting upon Carlos Baker's advice and with Mary Hemingway's concurrence, the publishing company Charles Scribner's Sons made the suggested alteration. By moving one sentence ("You said she cut him down") up one line to make it part of the preceding speech, Scribner's gave readers a text where the dialogue between the two waiters alternated neatly—although the alteration required that some readers rethink the identity of the speaker of the opening lines.

For the past 20 years, most readers coming to the story for the first time read the altered version. Those readers find no footnote identifying the alteration and the possibility for a variant reading. No matter that in 1956 after Judson Jerome brought the issue of the "confused" dialogue to his attention, Hemingway reread the story and said that the published story continued to make sense to him. No matter that no galley exists to prove a printer's error. Because manuscript evidence does not prove the case for the "corrected" version, some scholars have requested that the version Hemingway knew and approved be restored. At the very least, readers should be alerted that they are reading a variant. The publishing history of the story provides a fascinating instance of textual "authority." Not only do words slip, slide, perish (as T. S. Eliot has it), so do texts.

Like many of Hemingway's stories, "A Clean, Well-Lighted Place" is brief. Its characters are few, and its external action minimal. In accordance with the early morning hour of the "action," the dialogue is muted, much of it scarcely above a whisper. As its title suggests, the story is concerned with the search for refuge and for transcendent meaning. That should surprise no one. Hemingway's protagonists typically battle the demons of chaos. Images of light and dark pervade his work, and they are certainly in abundance in the stories of *Winner Take Nothing*. The famous "Our nada" prayer of "A Clean Well-Lighted Place" recalls other prayers and other praying in Hemingway's work.

The story is essentially dramatic in method, similar to such Hemingway works as "ToDay Is Friday" and "Hills Like White Elephants." Authorial presence in the story is minimal, establishing setting and providing a few crucial "stage directions." Two waiters watch an old man who sits outside a cafe in the shadows that the leaves make against the electric light. He's a very old man—an image for pondering the ultimate significance of life in the face of impending death. Although he is deaf, the old man can feel the quietness of the late hour. Hemingway's story is about such nuances, and deciphering nuance quickly becomes the primary challenge to its readers.

The opening line of dialogue and its tag define the challenge: "'Last week he [the old man] tried to commit suicide,' one waiter said." The reader will have to hear more dialogue before deciding which waiter has broken the silence. The story asks that readers listen carefully; in only a few instances will the narrator provide unequivocal identifications for the speaker of lines.

The opening line not only sets up this task for the reader, it foregrounds the religious dimension of the story. Suicide, against the backdrop of Catholic Spain, is not the incidental topic that it seems to be to the speaker of the line. For the orthodox, suicide is the gravest of sins because it results from despair—the condition that denies God's mercy and places the suicide beyond God's mercy.

In the course of dialogue that moves toward monologue and becomes interior monologue, the traditional judgment of suicide seems inadequate. With the older waiter, we not only sense the isolation of the old man, we also cherish his dignity. Sitting up late, looking into the darkness, the old man appreciates a clean, well-lighted place. He longs for order in a universe that seems to provide mainly darkness and chaos. Order lacking or minimal, he behaves as if he knows a sustaining code. When he leaves the cafe, he attempts the difficult feat, "walking unsteadily but with dignity."

Although the old man has not wished to inconvenience anyone, his presence has annoyed the younger waiter, who is eager to close the cafe and to get home to his bed and wife. Much of the story contrasts his impatience, his glibness, his insensitivity with the empathy of the older waiter—the telling contrast evident long before the narrator, usually effaced, charges the young waiter with stupidity. The older waiter pays careful attention not only to what the old man does, but attends carefully to what his companion says. Thus, in the text Hemingway published, it is the young waiter who breaks the silence in the opening dialogue, reporting on the old man's attempted suicide. Attempted suicide is a topic that has more than passing interest for the older waiter—for he knows much about loss and isolation. For him, the explanation "nothing" has a philosophical meaning that his companion cannot grasp. He takes very long views, and he is looking to his own future as he looks at the old man—and as he observes, "He must be eighty years old." Hemingway does not identify the speaker of the line nor the speaker of the line that follows it. But the "sound" of the next line ("Anyway I would say he was eighty") resonates in that same gentle voice—a quiet line, one in marked contrast to the unmistakably impatient line of the young waiter that follows. As sometimes happens in plays and often in life, a character follows his own line. Here the older waiter speaks to himself as much as to the other character. This dramatic device, indeed, opened the memorable exchange: "'He's drunk now,' he said. 'He's drunk every night.'" Both of those sentences, in their original publication, are spoken by the impatient, increasingly disgusted younger waiter. They contrast with the meditative "double" speeches on the old man's age. In a story teeming with religious overtones, Hemingway admonishes those with ears to hear.

In the story's concluding episode the older waiter becomes a customer in an all-night bar, though the narrator continues to identify him as "waiter," one of Hemingway's most successful puns. Readers should catch what the barman who serves the waiter misses. In the face of the barman's impatience and incomprehension of his words, the waiter emulates the old man. Politely, with dignity, he walks into the darkness. More than any other characters in *Winner Take Nothing*, he and the old man exemplify the epigraph Hemingway invented for the book: "Unlike all other forms of lutte or combat the conditions are that the winner shall take nothing; neither his ease, nor his pleasure, nor any notions of glory; nor, if he win far enough, shall there by any reward within himself."

—Joseph M. Flora

THE CLOCKMAKER.   See **SAM SLICK, THE CLOCKMAKER.**

THE CONSTANT TIN SOLDIER.   See **THE STEADFAST TIN SOLDIER.**

THE CONTINUING SILENCE OF A POET (Shtikah holechet v'nimshechet shel meshorer) by A.B. Yehoshua, 1968

In A.B. Yehoshua's seminal story, "Shtikah v'nimshechet shel meshorer" ("The Continuing Silence of a Poet"), collected in *Mul haye'arot* (1968), an old man is bewildered—in fact tormented—by a young son born to him in his old age. The boy's existence is a complete and excruciating mystery to the father. These two characters embody one of Yehoshua's central themes: the estrangement and lack of understanding between generations.

The birth of this son coincided with the beginning of the father's silence. An established poet, he discovers that he cannot write anymore, that he has "lost the melody." The poetry of new, younger poets is incomprehensible to him; his own works have lost their audience. Through this character, Yehoshua expresses his concern that the older generation has lost its ability to communicate, to articulate its thoughts and dreams.

There is a sinister element to the estrangement between parent and child. After the death of the mother, her pictures disappear from the house—the son has buried the slashed pictures in a hole in the garden. The idea that the younger generation is involved in a struggle to the death with its parents is an oft-repeated one in Yehoshua.

The boy's family tries to ignore or even hide him from visitors and acquaintances, and in school he is isolated from the other children and considered hopeless by the teachers. However, eventually he does find a way to fit in by turning himself into a kind of servant. It begins at home, where he emerges from his room when guests arrive and silently hands around trays of biscuits and lights cigarettes, and he helps wash up in the kitchen. Later, in school, he gets chosen to be class monitor, responsible for cleaning blackboards. He draws his father's baths for him and prepares meals. The one person he strikes a friendship with at school is the janitor. Yehoshua's disturbing suggestion is that the older generation regards its children as acceptable if they agree to devote their lives to the roles of caretaker and servant.

The son discovers that his father is, or has been, a famous poet when one of his poems is taught in class. The son rushes home to assault his father with "violent emotion," demanding that he read his works and show him all his old notebooks. From this point, the boy becomes obsessed with writing poetry. He steals his father's old scraps of paper, hides them in his room, memorizes them, and tries to put words together on his own. He neither understands what he reads, nor produces anything comprehensible. Without understanding he throws back at the father fragments of his own verse on torn pieces of paper, leaving them around the house. In a way, this peculiar exchange between the poet who no longer writes and the son who tries desperately, without success, to understand and recreate his father's words summarizes what Yehoshua sees as the problems of communication between the generations.

In spite of the fact that the child is incapable of understanding, the father eventually turns the task of writing over to his son, refusing to help him. The father, for his part, is planning to leave the country and live out the rest of his life somewhere else—"an attic in a decaying city," perhaps the Greek islands. The desertion of Israelis is also one of Yehoshua's recurring themes; he stresses repeatedly that the Diaspora has always been voluntary, and that choosing to live in a country other than Israel is a kind of betrayal.

Before his departure, the old man wanders through the house, reconciled to his silence, to the fact that, as he puts it, "there is nothing to write about any more." He enters his son's room and looks at the sleeping boy. He notices sheets from newspaper on the floor; in their margin he finds a poem—a poem of sorts, for the lines are mixed up, the words senseless. He sees his own name across the top.

Yehoshua's disturbing vision of the translation from one generation to the next is completed with this final act. The old man leaves without being able to communicate his vision or dreams to the young son; the son, lacking this vision, struggles to reproduce images he does not understand.

—Carla N. Spivack

A CONVERSATION WITH MY FATHER by Grace Paley, 1974

Grace Paley is best known as a short story writer whose work undertakes the socially realistic business of questioning patriarchal structures and celebrating the positive powers of womanhood while employing techniques more commonly associated with experimental, nonrepresentational fiction. Called by some critics an "experimental realist," she draws on the sociology of metafiction to present pictures of women intent upon writing themselves into a validly accepted existence.

"A Conversation with My Father" is overtly metafictional in that it not only shows the writer at work creating her story but, in its collected form, features the author describing her intentions and naming this story's antagonist. For its 1972 appearance in *The New American Review,* a journal featuring much overtly experimental work by such innovators as Donald Barthelme and Robert Coover, "A Conversation with My Father" is already sufficiently self-apparent, for the narrator is cast as a writer not only historically much like Paley but who is writing stories in Paley's manner as the narrative proceeds. But when Paley includes it in her second collection, *Enormous Changes at the Last Minute* (1974), its theme is thrown into higher relief by the volume's disclaimer: "Everyone in this book is imagined into life except the father. No matter what story he has to live in, he's my father, I. Goodside, M.D., artist, and storyteller.–G.P." Placed as one of the book's concluding stories, it interrogates Paley's own manner of writing while explaining the necessary pathos of such activity.

Although the story's situation is not exceptional—a middle-aged daughter visiting her 86-year-old father in the rest home, where they discuss her career—Paley takes care to show how its real action is the creative and insightful use of language. As for any person that age, the old man's health is an issue, but Paley's narrator engages the question with a startlingly physical image: "His heart, that bloody motor, is equally old and will not do certain jobs anymore." Yet it "still floods his head with brainy light," another striking image, and it is within these two contrasting views that the story's action takes place. Physically old yet intellectually quite sharp, he presents a historical challenge to his daughter's flights of fictive fancy, arguing for factual necessity and moral judgment even as she tries to create characters less burdened by such fates.

A child of the 19th century and an immigrant from Czarist Russia, the narrator's father has had success; in his daughter's words from a companion story, "Enormous Changes at the Last Minute," he saw the U.S. flag for the first time on Ellis Island: "Under its protection and working like a horse, he'd read Dickens, gone to medical school, and shot like a surface-to-air missile right into the middle class." In "A Conversation with My Father," however, he is present to argue with such metaphysically extravagant imagery and call for work not just more like that of Dickens but of Maupassant and Chekhov, for stories about "recognizable people" where she can "write down what happens to them next."

This the Paley narrator resists. The notion of beginning with "There was a woman . . . " and following it with a logically deduceable plot is something she and the real Grace Paley have sought to counter: "the absolute line between two points which I've always despised. Not for literary reasons, but because it takes all hope away. Everyone, real or invented, deserves the open destiny of life." Yet to please her father she drafts a story that has been evolving in her neighborhood, about a mother who in order to bond with and help her heroin-addicted son becomes an addict herself, and who is then rejected in disgust by the son when he cures himself and goes straight. Though not a Paley story per se, this piece—which is summarized in just one hundred words—is cut from the same cloth as the volume's other narratives. None of Paley's stories, published or (in the manner of Jorge Luis Borges) described as if they were written and published (and thus eminently quotable), fit the style of Turgenev or Chekhov, as the narrator's father points out: too much is omitted, such as the character's looks, her hair, what her parents were like, and the situation in which her child was conceived (out of wedlock, he is told, and he complains, "For Godsakes, doesn't anyone in your stories get married? Doesn't anyone have the time to run down to City Hall before they jump into bed?").

A second version, several pages long and fleshed out in somewhat more traditional style, follows. Yet the father isn't pleased, because it still remains an essentially Paley-esque tale: quirky in its imagery, explosive in its insights, and open-ended in its implications for one's fate. The narrator tries to give her father the last word, a stern admonition that the character must be punished, but allegiance to the woman she has created wins out: "I'm not going to leave her there in that house, crying. (Actually neither would Life, which unlike me has no pity.)"

As an argument against male authority, the ironclad rule of history that determines a culture's voice and authenticates only certain styles of discourse, "A Conversation with My Father" sounds a stirring feminist call. Yet Paley locates her theme even more personally, for as author she does allow the father (her father, as the book's disclaimer states) the final word. "How long will it be?" the old man asks. "Tragedy! You too. When will you look it in the face?" The answer does need to be spoken, any more than the narrator need further defend her denying the inevitable, for the death of an aged and infirm parent is an ultimately universal tragedy for any daughter or son.

—Jerome Klinkowitz

THE CONVERSION OF THE JEWS
by Philip Roth, 1959

"The Conversion of the Jews" is a young man's fantasy. Philip Roth wrote it by the age of 23, and it concerns Roth's youngest protagonist, Ozzie Freedman, age 12. The simple conflict in "The Conversion of the Jews" is developed in Roth's later, complex, fully-adult fiction, as his protagonists challenge the values of their oppressive communities.

Ozzie succeeds in this challenge as Alex Portnoy, David Kepesh, and Roth's other adult protagonists can only imagine succeeding. In the course of the fantasy, Ozzie literally compels a crowd of Jews to kneel "in the Gentile posture of prayer" and to "say they believed in Jesus Christ."

Ozzie's aim isn't to humiliate his rabbi, his mother, or other members of his synagogue, although he surely does that. Rather, his goal is perversely to proclaim the power of their God. As he puts it, if God can do anything, how can his rabbi so smugly deny Christ's divine birth?

Roth's story was received by the Jewish community much as Ozzie's questions were received by his: with fierce hostility. Why would Roth expose the Jewish people, critics asked, as small-minded bigots who suppress Ozzie's inquiries? The reason is the same for both Roth's affront and for Ozzie's: because, by restricting free discussion, the community harms itself while claiming to defend itself. (In the story's Hebrew school, "when free discussion time rolled around, none of the students felt too free," a paradox that also applies to the nominal freedom Jewish writers of the 1950's felt in criticizing contemporary Jewish values.)

Characters' names in "The Conversion of the Jews" highlight the issue of individual freedom. (In broad farces such as Our Gang and The Great American Novel, Roth's characters took emblematic names such as Senator Innuendo and Word Smith and Gil Gamesh and Base Baal.) Ozzie's last name is Freedman, and his repressive rabbi is named Binder.

The struggle between individual freedom and binding authority, in Roth's view, is eternal. Outsiders will always want in, so their struggles will always have a comic tinge, too. Whether these outsiders are Jews, adolescents, sexual libertines, idealists, or any other marginalized figures Roth might use, they resist and seek to purify the values of the mainstream into which they wish to assimilate. "The Conversion" offends its audience by addressing a serious theme in terms of low-comic characters.

Always particularly sensitive to lampooning, the Jewish community took offense at Roth's work because, like Ozzie's, his voice has resounded with earnest articulation. The opening scene of "The Conversion" mixes serious literature with travesty: the dignified Jamesian device of the *ficelle* (a *confidant* functioning as the protagonist's sounding board) here takes the ludicrous form of Ozzie's friend Itzie, a coarse Hebrew-school truant whom Ozzie fills in on the events leading up to the story's conflict. The comic pair, Ozzie and Itzie, discuss the rabbi's denial of Mary's virgin motherhood. "'That stuff's all bull. To have a baby you gotta get laid,' Itzie theologized. 'Mary had to get laid.'" Over Itzie's vulgar inanities, Ozzie outlines his serious intellectual problem: what can restrain an omnipotent God from performing any miracle he chooses?

Itzie's prurient interruptions isolate Ozzie from his friends just as surely as Binder's attempts to mute Ozzie's inquiries isolate him from his enemies. Ozzie, Roth's youngest "good Jewish boy," yearns to cleanse his community of muddied ideas, but he wants more to be his own man. The need for autonomy estranges Ozzie from his culture, and he needs to be alone.

After Rabbi Binder tries bullying him into agreeing that New Testament miracles are more absurd than Old Testament miracles, Ozzie flees to the synagogue's roof, where he is misconstrued as threatening suicide. This misunderstanding gives Ozzie the power to make the crowd of Jews below swear to Jesus Christ's divinity. "The Conversion of the Jews," a title drawn from Andrew Marvell's poem "To His Coy Mistress," where it signifies the end of recorded time, ironically signifies here a very short-lived conversion. No reader expects Ozzie's converts to embrace Christianity once he is safely off the roof. But the story ends with Ozzie still triumphant, having imposed his individual beliefs on his community.

Roth celebrates the individual's primacy in much the same boisterous spirit as Ralph Waldo Emerson did a century before Roth was born. Both Roth and Emerson earned the scorn of their religious communities by stressing individual intellectual freedom. Both writers, curiously, made an issue of the divinity of Christ, the Christian-rebel Emerson by denying its necessity, the Jewish-rebel Roth by affirming its possibility. In his Divinity School Address, Emerson castigated the Unitarian ministry for turning religion into "a hollow, dry creaking formality," charging that wherever "the pulpit is usurped by a formalist then is the worshipper defrauded"; soon afterwards, he resigned his ministry. Jewish formalism is Roth's target in "The Conversion" where Ozzie suspects one elderly Jew muttering prayers of having "memorized the prayers and forgotten all about God."

Like Emerson, Ozzie is a purifier of a religion he sees as corrupt and defiled. He yearns to have his eyes opened, but his religion insists he follow its forms blindly: Rabbi Binder "asked him petulantly why he didn't read more rapidly. He was showing no progress. Ozzie said he could read faster but that if he did he was sure not to understand what he was reading. Nevertheless, at the rabbi's repeated suggestion Ozzie tried. . . ." Ozzie's heartfelt wonderings about God are subordinated to the primacy of mere appearance: the rabbi wants Ozzie to seem to understand the text he reads, far more than he wants Ozzie genuinely to understand it.

The imagery in "The Conversion of the Jews" is visual: Rabbi Binder repeatedly averts his eyes from the sight of Ozzie on the edge of the roof, as if not seeing Ozzie would make him disappear. Ozzie finally threatens to jump off the roof only because he "wanted to see Rabbi Binder cover his eyes one more time."

Roth expresses the conflict from the community's point-of-view: "the boy had to come down immediately before anybody saw." Before any passing Christian, that is, saw the scandalous sight. Even the rescuing fireman's "net started up at Ozzie like a sightless eye." (Eyes and vision, unsurprisingly, are Emerson's favorite metaphors: "I become a transparent eyeball, I am nothing, I see all," he exults in "Nature," whose ultimate image is of a man achieving oneness with God, specifically "a blind man . . . restored to perfect sight." Roth, a graduate student in American studies around the time he wrote "The Conversion of the Jews," was certainly reading and noting his Emerson.) Ozzie restores the sight of his blinded community and, however briefly, returns them to oneness with God.

—Steven Goldleaf

THE COUNTRY HUSBAND
by John Cheever, 1958

While reminding us of Cheever's fame as a *New Yorker* writer who chronicles suburban life, the title of Cheever's justly famous "The Country Husband" suggests as well the complexity of his work. A portrait of a middle-aged husband who embodies the values of 20th-century suburbia, the story plays against William Wycherley's risqué comedy of manners *The Country Wife* (1675). Like Wycherley's Restoration play, it exposes the superficiality and emptiness of the very society that it celebrates. The allusion also emphasizes the current of sexual conflict that underlies human life. Wycherley's title is but the starting point for the dense allusive style of Cheever's story; it effectively highlights the comedic approach that is Cheever's forte.

"I'm in love, Dr. Herzog," Francis Weed confesses to a psychiatrist at a climactic moment of the story. The affliction, whatever one calls it, has made the middle-aged country husband behave absurdly and destructively. His awareness of his mortality (he had just escaped serious injury and death when his airplane was forced to make an emergency landing) may have been a factor in his pursuit of the attractive girl who sits with his children when illness has kept Mrs. Henlein, the usual sitter, away. Francis risks separation from his capable (if somewhat neurotic) wife Julia and the emotional security of his four children—two girls and two boys, the ideal combination for the ideal family. His futile pursuit of Anne Murchison also threatens Shady Hill, the paradise that Francis and his peers have endeavored to create.

Through the good work of Dr. Herzog, Francis regains his perspective. The comedy ends, as comedy should, with restoration and unity. The Weeds will not separate. Shady Hill (ambiguously named as it is) survives. Cheever's last look in the story is humorously, even mythically, focused on the community. As night falls, Cheever emphasizes the restlessness underneath the order of the suburban kingdom. Mrs. Masterson warns the wandering child Gertrude to return to her home. A nude Mr. Babcock chases his nude wife from their house to the hedge-screened terrace. Once again Mr. Nixon shouts his formulas at the squirrels in his bird-feeding station. Julia Weed tries to rescue the cat, "sunk in spiritual and physical discomfort" because it wears a doll's hat and a dress (Cheever's neuter pronoun tells us that the cat has endured more decisive violence); "'Here, pussy, pussy, pussy!' Julia calls. 'Here, pussy, here poor pussy!'" The dog Jupiter, ever disruptive of the order of paradise, prances through the tomato vines, carrying "in his generous mouth the remains of an evening slipper." Understandably, Cheever adored the final sentence of the story: "Then it is dark; it is a night where kings in golden suits ride elephants over mountains."

Comedies of manners never put much emphasis on plot, and audiences seldom remember those plots. They recall, usually, a situation and a few characters. A Cheever story is likely to be remembered in much the same way. Because events are numerous and varied and involve many characters, however, "The Country Husband" would not readily be translated to the stage. (It is the opposite of most of Hemingway's stories, in which characters are few and dialogue central.) It could effectively be translated to film, but such a translation would likely require feature-length treatment.

Although characters in comedies of manners usually exist to bandy witty dialogue, only a few scenes of Cheever's story rely on dialogue. The first such is between Anne Murchison and Francis as he drives her home; she explains the reason for her tears—her alcoholic father. Cheever relies on dialogue to portray the dramatic change that has come upon Francis. The next morning, waiting for his commuter train, he insults grande dame Mrs. Wrightson. The evening of that day Clayton Thomas, a college student, comes to pay for theatre tickets; he discusses his future with Julia and Francis, then voices condemnation about Shady Hill people. Francis is shocked when Clayton reports his plan to marry Anne Murchison. Clayton's visit produces the most extended dialogue of the story, provoking the crisis between the husband and wife.

For the most part, the memorable lines of "The Country Husband" belong to the narrator. His elegance threads the story, uniting the many scenes. (Thread is one of the story's important metaphors.) His voice provides the allusive texture, creating the comic distance, even as it insists on the ultimate seriousness of the issues. Finally, the country of the husband is the country we all inhabit, precarious at best, fallen certainly, but always holding seeds for a more happy flowering.

Consider the opening sentences: "To begin at the beginning, the airplane from Minneapolis in which Francis Weed was traveling East ran into heavy weather. The sky had been a hazy blue, with the clouds below the plane lying so close together that nothing could be seen of the earth. Then mist began to form outside the windows, and they flew into a white cloud of such density that it reflected the exhaust fires." The passage evokes Genesis as well as John's gospel. With the four elements clearly in evidence, the possibility for creation seems as great as the possibility for destruction. The name "weed" plays against the story of Eden, that earlier paradise. As he charts the domestic battle of the Weeds, Cheever frequently plays domestic strife against global strife, reminding readers often of the ongoing cosmic struggle between chaos and creation. Through a range of allusions (biblical, classical, contemporary), Cheever deftly balances the ordinary and the extraordinary in such a way that the extraordinary is always becoming ordinary, the ordinary extraordinary.

"The Country Husband" gives abundant evidence of Cheever's skill as a social realist. We usually hear it in the extended scenes of dialogue—especially in the scene depicting the visit of Clayton Thomas and the crisis between Julia and Francis it produces. The crisis is, in fact, the most mundane part of the story—precisely because Cheever renders it so mimetically with the narrator fairly effaced.

That domestic crisis comes fairly late in the story, however. If we compare it with Francis's homecoming after his near brush with the Angel of Death (to use Cheever's image from his opening paragraph), we find Cheever working in a very different mode. The narrator shuns the strictly mimetic; turning to present tense, he utilizes an exaggerated comedic style to portray the non-welcoming. The younger children are in tears in the midst of fierce combat, daughter Helen lies on her bed reading *True Romance,* and Julia attempts to keep peace and to get the family through the evening meal. The narrator uses some lines of direct discourse, but they are immersed in long paragraphs, working with effective indirect discourse that adds to the sense of speed and chaos. The scene ends with Julia in tears as she carries the youngest child upstairs to bed. Cheever concludes an episode that is representative as well as unique: "The other children drift away from the battlefield, and Francis goes into the back garden for a

cigarette and some air." The narrator's metaphors, his blend of direct and indirect discourse, and his pace, have made the common event seem a good deal more.

Even as it insists on the ordinariness of the Weeds, Cheever's story recounts numerous events that are out of the ordinary, the airplane crisis initiating them. Their clustering in a short time span adds to the sense of the extraordinary. The day after the airplane crash, the Weeds have dinner at the Farquarsons. The maid who serves dinner, Francis recalls, is the French girl he had seen disgraced in her French town for having lived with a German soldier during the occupation. That same night Francis first meets Anne Murchison. The next morning as he waits for his train, he sees "an extraordinary thing": in one of the passing sleeping-car compartments, he views a naked woman sitting and combing her golden hair—Venus incarnated. (That very night he steals a kiss from Anne.) In the context of this cluster, his insulting of Mrs. Wrightson takes place, a signal of how far from the path of reason he has wandered. Chaos seems destined to triumph. The string of extraordinary events reaches a high moment when Francis makes his initial visit to Dr. Herzog, to be greeted by a policeman who orders him to freeze, then frisks him for weapons.

Thematically considered, the most instructive of these events is the least dramatic—Francis's memory of the French maid. In the face of Shady Hill's strenuous efforts to keep the ugliness of the world at bay, his vivid recollection of the scene in the French village asserts the importance of memory and history. Try as it might, Shady Hill cannot create a world in which the present and future inevitably dominate. (The narrator's cultural memory enhances the values implicit in Francis's particular memory; the allusions keep reminding readers of stories of love, war, disaster, and death.)

Memory, in fact, leads Francis to his resolution. Reflecting on the aborted plane crash, the Farquarsons' new maid, and Anne Murchison, he is reminded of the one time in his life that he had been lost in the north woods: "He had now the same bleak realization that no amount of cheerfulness or hopefulness or valor or perseverance could help him find, in the gathering dark, the path that he'd lost. The feeling of bleakness was intolerable, and he saw clearly that he had reached the point where he would have to make a choice." As Francis confronts these personal memories, Cheever's readers confront Dante's famous image in the opening lines of *The Divine Comedy:* "Midway life's journey I was made aware/ That I strayed into the dark forest,/ And the right path appeared not anywhere." In a very different kind of comedy, Cheever awakens cultural memories to bring his readers to contemplation of Dante's theological realities.

—Joseph M. Flora

THE COUNTRY OF THE BLIND
by H.G. Wells, 1911

Like other fantasies by H.G. Wells, such as *The Island of Dr. Moreau,* "The Country of the Blind" is a parable. It is not realism, although the story has a pseudo-historical introductory section and some convincing details, nor is it modernist in any way in spite of the date of its publication (1911). It is a meditation on the nature of power, culture, self-knowledge, and the purpose of life (Wells did not make a virtue of modest ambitions).

The preamble is supposed to lend a veneer of verisimilitude to the lesson that will follow. It tries to present a plausible case for the existence of a lost kingdom in the Andes and it even includes a spurious reference to an authority on Andean exploration ("Pointer"). From such sources we are offered a reconstruction of the story of Nuñez who, climbing in the Andes, has an immense fall down snow-covered slopes into the lost valley where everyone has been blind for 15 generations. In this Happy Valley or Eldorado (the story is intertextually connected with Johnson's *Rasselas* and with a general mythology of South American remoteness), a modestly successful society has become established by the unseeing inhabitants. It lacks many of the things that a sighted society has, but it is rational, peaceful, and clean; its religion, of course, is limited to what it knows. For its inhabitants the valley is the world and their culture has its own simple creation myth which includes "angels" fluttering and singing above the heads of the blind people and a roof of smooth rock over all.

Nuñez imagines that he will easily dominate the simple people of this country; he repeats to himself the adage that "In the country of the blind the one-eyed man is king." But the blind have developed their other senses to the point that they can control him, and, above all, as they cannot understand what he means when he tries to explain to them the advantages sight gives him, he is regarded as a species of idiot. Eventually he submits and begins to accept life as the blind live it, but when he falls in love with a blind girl it is declared that he can only become a suitable husband for her if his strangeness is cured by an operation to remove his eyes. He agrees but then goes out and looks at the world anew and realises that he cannot go through with the operation. He leaves the valley and begins to climb the rocky mountains that surround it.

Nuñez, we infer, falls to his death at the end of the story and the questions it poses are by then clear. Is it better to live confined but happy, like the blind in their country, or is it better to be open to the wider world with its sights and far horizons? Nuñez is called, by the blind people, "Bogotá" because he uses that place-name when he first arrives to try to explain where he has come from and what the great outside world is like. They cannot understand him but the reader is left in no doubt as to the value of those three syllables: Bogotá is a great and wonderful city whose impressiveness is rather overstated by Wells for purposes of comparison.

The story also questions whether a connection with other people, rendered most clearly in the matter of love, is more important than what might be called an individual's own self. Wells has it both ways here: love is set not against romantic individualist isolation but against more general and liberating connections with the greater world—he calls it "the great free world" to emphasise its value to the individual but it consists of multitudes of other people.

Another question is posed, whether we can escape from our own cultures. The blind people are self-sufficient and quite able to deal with intruders but they are incapable of seeing what they cannot see; similarly, Nuñez is incapable of becoming so estranged from his culture that he will abandon its values. He comes very close to agreeing to lose his sight but he cannot do it; he chooses what, as a mountaineer, he must know is almost certain death instead.

The morals drawn from these questions are evidently posed by the story. Twice in the story Nuñez lies in the snow above the Country of the Blind. The first time he is almost miraculously lucky to be alive after his fall and is taken by the inhabitants as a creature new-born from heaven; the second time he lies, at the end of the story, dead but peacefully dead, on the Andean mountainside. Birth, childhood, basic existence, ordinary work, love and harmony, are miracles in their way, but there is another side to being human: there are mountains to climb, immense vistas to see, ships discernible on the horizon, a whole world to live in. There is a parallel here with Nietzsche's distinction between the will to security, represented by the Country of the Blind, and the will to power, represented by the thoroughly Nietzschean symbol of the mountains that are to be conquered and the wonderful views from their summits.

—Lance St. John Butler

THE CRICKET ON THE HEARTH
by Charles Dickens, 1845

In contrast to the labyrinthine darknesses of his greatest novels, Dickens's *Christmas Books* resolve themselves in happy catharsis. Each ends with a celebration of the domestic situation, with families and individuals restored to a harmonious ensemble, after the threat of discord has been encountered and removed. They are essentially festive comedies, and the imminent disruptions faced by the characters are real enough, but they are snatched away from disastrous realization at the climactic moment. Festive equilibrium is affirmed. The pleasures of holiday are earned.

Dickens wrote *The Cricket on the Hearth* after returning to England from a year abroad. He was planning to produce a weekly periodical which would publish cheerful tales, anatomizing humbug and putting everybody in good temper. Instead, his ambitions in journalism were focused on the establishment of a national paper, the *Daily News,* which embraced Liberal causes and exercised his fervent social and political passions. *The Cricket on the Hearth* is a counterpoint to this overt and direct writing. It is ornate, intricately designed, and full of homely pathos. All of these qualities are splendidly depicted in the original illustrations by Leech, Doyle, and Maclise. It was popular from its first publication (though the critics disliked it), and it was revised as a drama for professional actors as soon as it appeared. It also was turned into a popular opera with spoken dialogue and a splendid overture by the inexcusably neglected Victorian composer Sir Alexander Campbell Mackenzie. Dickens himself gave a number of public readings to audiences of hundreds of avid listeners.

Indeed the theatricality of the tale is woven into its verbal fabric. It reads well aloud, and suggests a firm pact between the narrator of the tale and his audience. Much of the action of the story is called up by the spoken voice of the narrator, rather than objectively depicted in a dispassionate way. The title suggests this dramatic fictionality. After the voice of the narrator himself, the cricket and the kettle are the first voices we hear; they maintain a running commentary on the action from the viewpoint of the domestic hearth.

The story lends itself to a dramatic rendering; but it is also rich in suggestive themes germane to its Victorian milieu. As the narrator introduces us to Mr. and Mrs. Peerybingle, or John and Dot, and their "Baby" ("a live Baby . . . a very doll of a Baby") and then to Tackleton the Toy-merchant, Caleb Plummer and his Blind Daughter, and the rest of the small cast, Dickens's theatrical imagination is highly engaged. For example, Caleb has kept from his daughter the knowledge of the state of disrepair of their dwelling-place; he has turned her blindness into a blessing by describing a splendid world of his own imagination which, lacking the ability to see for herself, is the world his daughter inhabits. Describing this situation, Dickens lists the things the blind girl has *not* seen, thus giving us a vivid picture of her actual situation, contrasting it with "the picture in her mind."

This example reflects thematically upon the principle matter of the story itself, the supposed infidelity of a young wife, Dot Peerybingle, as imagined by her husband John, who is considerably older. In one case, the imagination is the source of tortured agonising and self-doubt, in the other it is a solace, balm and sustenance. Typically, Dickens keeps this theme alive with fresh variations of incident, increasing suspense as the disclosure of the husband's anxious doubt seems more and more likely, and a number of minor characters who vary the pace and tone of each of the story's three "Chirps."

The ambiguous quality of the life of the imagination, the liability as well as the blessing of such brim-topping plenitude of mind, is Dickens's subject here, but the tone of the story is playful and diverting, rather than morally earnest or didactic. The story opens with an exclamation and ends in a dance. As if to bring the theme directly to bear upon his own practice as a writer, however, Dickens adds a short final paragraph wistfully describing his characters vanishing into air, and leaving him alone beside the props of the tale with which he began.

The enigmatic sexuality in the story is a revealing instance of Dickens's analysis of Victorian morality. In the elaborate fretwork of a cosy and domestic Christmas fireside story, he offers us a constantly surprising reading of the nature of sexual jealousy, and the tense relationship between possessiveness, propriety, and greed. The sexual subjugation of women and the tyranny of the hearth lie underneath the blissful domesticity of home. But neither the banality of sentimental homeliness nor the vulgarity of strident protest are allowed to hold full and final sway. Dickens is masterly in suggesting the really fearful threat of a shattered domestic world, and he leaves us with a sense of compassionate understanding about the interweave of social convention and the security of love in marriage. Law and grace are reconciled.

—Alan Riach

D

THE DAFFODIL SKY
by H.E. Bates, 1955

The story collection *The Daffodil Sky* has been called the crowning achievement of H.E. Bates's later years; the title story both exhibits the hallmarks of his earlier writing and is colored by an increasing maturity, a sensibility altered by World War II, and a recognition of the inescapability of time's passage.

Like many of Bates's stories, "The Daffodil Sky" is highly charged visually, marked by "the direct pictorial contact between eye and object, between object and reader," which Bates admired in Hemingway and discussed in *The Modern Short Story: A Critical Survey*. In the first few paragraphs alone, Bates evokes a spectrum of colors (dusky yellow, prussian blue, "a strange sharp green," "stencillings of silver," "a stormy copper glow") not to mention the impact of a farmer's cart full of plums, peas, broccoli, apples, and daffodils. The text is suffused not only with visual images but an intensely sensory contact with the environment: skin "cold and wet with splashes of hail," the smell of "steam-coal smoke and stale beer and cheap strong cheese," the sound of pike "plopping in the pools of the backwater."

Much of Bates's work is characterized by stark, stripped down plots which turn on situations rather than on a series of developed events; this is one reason, perhaps, that his short fiction was often more successful than his many novels. "The Daffodil Sky" takes place within the space of a few hours, the time frame ruptured by a flashback. The color of the sky is the controlling image, the shuttle that moves back and forth weaving past and present. Bates is known for his striking nature imagery, and here it is the coursing clouds, the discoloured sky, and its sudden clearing "fresh and brilliant, shot through with pale green fire" like daffodils, which trigger for the nameless narrator the memories through which his story is revealed.

While waiting out a storm in a pub he once haunted, he asks after Cora Whitehead, a woman he once knew; Bates (whose short fiction, according to the critic Dennis Vannatta, often "works by inference rather than exposition") gives the reader no initial clue to the complexity of the narrator's relationship with Cora. He remembers his instant physical attraction to her in a similar rainstorm many years ago — the "racing flame" of her "running hot through his blood and choking his thinking." One of Bates's recurring preoccupations, for which he has been compared to D.H. Lawrence, is the conflict between passion and repression, the ways in which culture and psychological inhibitions strangle natural impulses or, conversely, the ways in which passion short-circuits propriety or reason.

Indeed, the central event revealed in the flashback is a murder. The narrator, a young farmer, recalls the days when his life seemed full of promise. The man from whom he rented his land proposed to sell him the property; having insufficient funds, he accepted Cora's offer to go in with him on the deal, an offer contingent on the help of a friend of hers, Frankie Corbett. Overcome with the vision of his future, the narrator rather impetuously asked Cora to marry him and then became "blinded with the stupor of a slow-eating jealousy," which intensified with Cora's pregnancy. Unable to tolerate the thought that the child might be Corbett's, the narrator confronted him one night on the street; the ensuing violence between them led to Corbett's death and the narrator, apparently, was sentenced to jail.

The story ends with the narrator returning to Wellington Street to "have the last word," to tell Cora what he thinks of her having testified against him. He is a man of 40 years now, Bates tells us, his dreams long ago "eaten by the canker." A young woman opens the door. The narrator is struck by how little Cora has changed; he feels "the flame of her stab through him again exactly as it had done on ... the day of the daffodils." Slowly, however, he realizes that this is not Cora but her daughter. It is pouring rain, and the girl, whose mother is not at home, offers to get an umbrella and walk the stranger at her door back to the bridge where he can get a bus. He accepts, and this non-event, so typical in Bates, is the situation upon which the entire story hinges.

The text becomes filled with sexual imagery — the "rising steam of rain in the air," the heat and thickness, his blood beating in "heavy suction strokes in his throat," the girl's arms "full and naked and fleshy" like her mother's. She is coy and seductive; he is desperately attracted to her even as he considers telling her who he really is. Looking at the "haunting yellow sky," overcome, sickened by "an awful loneliness," he is, apparently, just about to proposition her when a rather phallic train comes "crashing and flaring" under the bridge where they have stopped; the girl waits for it to pass and asks the stranger, whose body is shaking, whether he had intended to ask her out. Instead, the train passed, the storm clearing, he settles for a drink with the girl who is perhaps his daughter, steering clear of the bridge blocked with a notice stating, symbolically, "Bridge Unsafe. Keep off. Trespassers will be prosecuted."

Clearly there is the suggestion here of incest, only one of the many boundary issues in the story. There are many violations: Cora violates, perhaps, fidelity; the narrator violates the law; reality violates dreams; the present violates the past. Although Bates has been compared to Maupassant, his endings are often more ambiguous than ironic, an ambiguity echoed in the title. The reader is left unsure which sky controls the landscape — the "pure and clear" sky and the "fierce, flashing daffodil sun" of the narrator's youth or the dusky yellow sky "with spent thunder" that the narrator finds upon his return to town. The importance lies perhaps in a recognition of complexity: appearances are deceptive; things both are and are not what they seem; past and present intersect, become confused, coexist. Both inner and outer landscapes are wracked by storms of violence, passion, and loss, but nature also offers the "light of after-storm, ... a great space of calm, rain-washed daffodil sky."

—Deborah Kelly Kloepfer

———

DAISY MILLER: A STUDY
by Henry James, 1878

Henry James's first contribution to a British magazine, "Daisy Miller" appeared in the illustrious *Cornhill* (June and July, 1878). It had been rejected by an American magazine, perhaps because, a friend suggested, it seemed "an outrage on American girlhood," maybe (as James suspected) because its length, over 20,000 words, put editors off, though he adored "the dear, the blessed *nouvelle*" form. Immediately, as James reported, "a really quite extraordinary hit," this story remained "the ultimately most prosperous child of my invention," as he wrote in his preface to the New York edition reprint (1909). He also wryly recorded "the sweet tribute" of its being pirated in America, where British publications were unprotected by copyright—a "tribute" he "hadn't yet received and was never to know again." Daisy Miller hats appeared in shops, and her name caught on to signify a recognizable type of American girl. In a designedly companion-piece story, "Pandora" (1884), James even has a young German diplomat reading *Daisy Miller* in preparation for visiting the New World, and wondering how much Pandora Day, another "remarkable specimen" of this remarkable American species, the "self-made girl," resembles Daisy.

The story established James internationally as a notable author, and for long afterwards he was "the author of *Daisy Miller*," to his embarrassment when he had turned to other topics and modes. It appeared in book form with two kindred stories in 1879. For the New York edition the text was significantly revised, and that 1909 text is cited here. He also made it into a play (*Daisy Miller: a Comedy*, 1883, never performed), adding new characters, altering others, and greatly changing the plot.

Years later, when contemplating another episode in his "international" series, he remarked that it "really, without forcing the matter or riding the horse to death, strikes me as an inexhaustible mine." *Daisy Miller* was not the first nor by any means the last of his "international" stories, but it was the most immediately striking, and he was seen to have invented this genre and made it peculiarly his own. He was eminently equipped to do so, as a New Yorker and New Englander who had spent years of his boyhood and young manhood in Europe before settling permanently there in 1875, at the age of 32, by which time he had a decade of writing (reviews, stories, novels) behind him. Like the story's hero, Frederick Winterbourne, his education had included periods in Geneva, and he was familiar with the Swiss and Italian locations of the narrative. He had also perforce had much opportunity and incentive to note and reflect upon differences between American and European behaviour, manners, and assumptions, particularly among the more affluent classes, and the possibilities of misunderstanding and misjudgment when one culture meets another.

The story is seen through the consciousness of the 27-year-old expatriate American bachelor Winterbourne, though there is an un-named impersonal narrator who occasionally raises questions about him ("I hardly know whether it was the [Swiss/American] analogies or differences that were uppermost in [his] mind," "Poor Winterbourne . . . ," "Winterbourne—to do him justice, as it were . . . "). At a hotel by Lake Geneva he encounters an obstreperous undisciplined American boy, Randolph Miller, unwillingly being dragged through Europe by his foolishly insouciant mother and his charming and exceed-ingly pretty sister Daisy. Mr. Miller remains prosperously at work in Schenectady (an industrial town in New York state). Daisy finds Europe "perfectly sweet . . . she had had ever so many dresses and things from Paris"—she is not a sophisticated or cultured girl—but cannot discover what she recognises as "any society" in which to mix. Winterbourne finds her charming but impossible to assess: her readiness to go on expeditions with him, unchaperoned, delights but disconcerts him, though he realizes that, living so long abroad, "he had become dishabituated to the American tone." His strait-laced aunt Mrs. Costello has no doubt that the Millers are "very common" and that Daisy (whom she refuses to meet) is "dreadful." She warns Frederick that, if he continues to meet her, he "is sure to make some great mistake."

He reencounters Daisy in Rome, where she is outraging the American colony by her nonchalantly unconventional behaviour, notably her unchaperoned association with a handsome but unacceptable Italian fortune-hunter, Giovanelli. Her indiscretions culminate in a nocturnal stroll with him in the Colosseum, an adventure notoriously unhealthy besides being socially imprudent (but, as Giovanelli says, "when was the Signorina ever prudent?"). She dies of a fever contracted there. Giovanelli, who recalls her as the most innocent as well as the most beautiful and amiable young lady he ever knew, assures Winterbourne that she would never have married him. Winterbourne comes to realize that he was indeed "booked to make a mistake," though not the way his aunt had predicted, and feels guilty over doing Daisy an "injustice." If through her ignorance (and lack of parental guidance) her behaviour seemed outrageous, it was fundamentally innocent. Winterbourne (the "winter" in whose surname is significant) has never been quite sure how far he is attracted to her, nor how to comprehend her: perhaps he has lived abroad too long to take the measure of this "new type" of American womanhood. Daisy is the most lively character of the story to which she gives her name, but it is "A Study" and the often baffled student Winterbourne is a major subject of it, not just a puzzled witness.

—Philip Collins

DANTE AND THE LOBSTER
by Samuel Beckett, 1934

One of the first things to be published by the great novelist and playwright, "Dante and the Lobster" is regarded as one of Beckett's best short stories from the 1934 collection *More Pricks Than Kicks*. Beckett would go on to write short fiction that would test the limits of the genre and was still experimenting in this form at the very end of his life. Even in the *More Pricks* collection he would write wilder and weirder stories than "Dante and the Lobster," but here, at the start of his publishing career, he writes a fairly straightforward story in the mould of Joyce's *Dubliners*.

Beckett, part of the Joyce circle in Paris at the time this story was written, had Irishness, iconoclasm, erudition, and other qualities in common with the older writer. "Dante and the Lobster" is set in Dublin where its hero, Belacqua

Shua, is a student, apparently of Italian, with great erudition and a misanthropic view of the world. Like the hero of Beckett's first published novel (*Murphy*), Belacqua is evidently torn between body and mind. The story moves confidently between the physical and mental, or even spiritual levels. Its language reflects this play most accurately.

Initially we appear to be reading about Belacqua's deep studies, but then noon strikes and "at once he switched his mind off its task." The body begins to take over as his mind "subsides," and we witness the making of a bizarre lunch. Belacqua burns toast and spreads it with mustard and Gorgonzola specially purchased for the purpose, the result ("it was like eating glass") is an eye-watering sandwich for which, however, his hunger is "more of mind, I need scarcely say, than of body." While drinking beer after this gastronomic exploit, Belacqua hears of the imminent execution of the murderer McCabe. A petition for mercy has been rejected. Belacqua takes delivery of a lobster for his aunt. Then he goes for his Italian lesson. Here he brings up, as a linguistic topic, the translation of a line in Dante that puns on the two meanings of *pietà*: pity and piety. His teacher refuses to translate it, and in due course he takes the lobster on to his aunt's where he discovers that it is still alive and that his aunt is about to boil it in that condition. The story ends: "Well, thought Belacqua, it's a quick death, God help us all. It is not."

The narrator here is very close to the actions and thoughts of his protagonist. The focus of the story moves in and out of Belacqua's head, sometimes as his thoughts expressed directly, sometimes a free indirect speech that echoes his thoughts, and sometimes the narrator's external thoughts. Thoughts expressed directly can be relatively simple: "he ventured to consider what he had to do next." Free indirect speech is very effectively handled; it is hard to say exactly where Beckett is quoting Belacqua's thoughts and where the omniscient narrator is talking to us in a passage such as the following:

> It was now that real skill began to be required, it was at this point that the average person began to make a hash of the entire proceedings. He laid his cheek against the soft of the bread, it was spongy and warm, alive. But he would very soon take that plush feel off it, by God but he would very quickly take that fat white look off its face.

Most of the story is like this, an amalgam of narration from a third person perspective and the thoughts of Belacqua expressed in his idiosyncratic language; thus "the average person" is a colloquial expression, "by God but" is likewise unusual in written prose, even in Ireland, while the conditional "he would" when first used sounds like the narrator until we realise, when it is repeated, that it is a pedantic version of a colloquial "I'll take that look off your face" and comes from Belacqua's own thoughts.

Among the technical brilliance of this surface the clues to Belacqua-Beckett's concerns are readily identifiable: the bread is "alive" and "warm" but must be "vanquished"; the lobster, already cold, will become dead by being heated to the maximum; McCabe, in spite of the mercy petition, will "swing at dawn" in the appallingly named Mountjoy prison, and he will "relish one more meal." The dilemma is that of Hardy's Arabella Don and Jude Fawley when they kill their pig: Jude cannot bear the cruelty but Arabella points out that "poor folks must live." On the one hand, there are physical necessities (lunch, lobsters) and ethical requirements (piety, justice); on the other there is mercy,

pity, and the life, warm or cold, of those as yet unsacrificed to either of these things.

Beckett is unusually direct in this story and it is perhaps his least experimental short fiction. He states his theme quite openly; the dilemma is clearly expressed in the Italian pun on *pietà* and then made even more explicit in the narrator's comments (they are Belacqua's thoughts too): "Why not piety and pity both, even down below?" But things are as they are: "'Where are we?' said Belacqua. . . . 'Where are we ever? Where we were, as we were.'" cries his Italian teacher.

—Lance St. John Butler

THE DARING YOUNG MAN ON THE FLYING TRAPEZE
by William Saroyan, 1934

There are several contexts in which one can read "The Daring Young Man on the Flying Trapeze." Published and set in 1934, William Saroyan's story about the Depression dramatizes the plight of a sensitive young man who starves to death because he cannot find work. As Saroyan's first successful story, "The Daring Young Man" holds a prominent place within the author's literary corpus: it announces the basic affirmation of life or "being" that recurs throughout his writings. In this story as in others, the specter of death serves to stimulate the protagonist's awareness of life; its proximity leaves this young man "thoroughly awake," "lithe and alert," and hypersensitive to details as mundane as the smell of "a cut melon" or the feel of a smooth, polished penny.

A third context in which to read "The Daring Young Man" is the one Saroyan provided when he positioned it in a collection of stories by the same title. Like "Seventy Thousand Assyrians," "Aspirin is a Member of the NRA," "Common Prayer," and others, "The Daring Young Man" has for its main character a writer and as a central aspect of its plot the problem of how to write when neither the inner self nor the external environment will cooperate. The letter-writing protagonist of another story from the collection, "A Cold Day," summarizes the predicament in a most straight-forward manner when he writes: "That's the fix I'm in: waiting to write and not being able to."

Why can't so many of Saroyan's writers in this collection write? Ostensibly, the main character of "A Cold Day" cannot write "because of the cold." However, as that story and its 1930's context implies, the real reason he is unable to write is that he earns too little to heat his small room. A similar but much graver situation confronts the daring young man of the title story, who will starve because he writes "prose" for a world that values only "good penmanship" and the ability to "use a typewriter." In the social worlds represented by the stories in this collection there is no place for the writer or the perspective on social reality that he articulates.

This situation is both unfortunate and ironic, because Saroyan's writers are not necessarily social critics. "Let this be your purpose," the protagonist of "A Cold Day" advises himself and his reader; "to suggest this great country." In "The Daring Young Man" a similar conviction, which Saroyan represents most clearly through the protagonist's fascination with a penny he finds in the street, deepens the irony to the point of tragic loss. As Saroyan's young writer polishes the penny he ruminates over the collection of sacred phrases that decorate its surface: "E Pluribus Unum One Cent United States of America . . . In God We Trust Liberty." During this delirious reading we realize the full dimensions of his problem: he is a writer who will starve to death in a society that defines its primary values in writing.

According to this third context, therefore, Saroyan's story dramatizes the dilemma of the writer who does not produce the right kinds of texts for his social order, who cannot earn the words on the coin with the words that fill his imagination. Saroyan highlights this dilemma at the end of the story as the young man dares to leave incomplete his *Application for Permission to Live*. Without this document, he dies. But as Saroyan points out, such a death amounts to nothing less than a new life that is "dreamless, unalive, perfect." In the final scene the world that requires documentation of this sort, the world of employment agencies and "department store" jobs, "circles away." "With the grace of the young man on the trapeze" the protagonist soars away to become "all things at once." His destination, Saroyan tells us, is the source of all life, that ground of "being" that at some level motivates all of Saroyan's fiction. Significantly, this vast unknown territory appears to him as "an ocean of print undulat[ing] endlessly and darkly," perhaps the ultimate metaphor for the writer's experience of heaven.

—John C. Waldmeir

THE DAUGHTERS OF THE LATE COLONEL
by Katherine Mansfield, 1922

It was the New Zealand of her childhood and girlhood that inspired Katherine Mansfield's best work, yet as the critic Ian Gordan has recognized, it was not New Zealand itself that matters to her but her exile from her family. This accounts for the quality of her meditation on the family theme in "The Daughters of the Late Colonel," set in London.

An innovator in the art of the short story, Mansfield characteristically almost dispenses with plot and breaks with chronology and sequence. She artfully engages in shifts of time and place and, though the time compass of the story is only one week, she telescopes the whole life history of her two main characters, Josephine and Constantia. The reader's interest is held by her sensitive perception of human behaviour and the delicacy of her prose which verges on the poetic. The underlying theme, depersonalization, unifies the story and is its steady focus.

The title is itself significant: Josephine and Constantia have no personalities as such; they are merely the daughters of the late colonel. The story opens at a moment of crisis. At the death of their father, the sisters are experiencing a complete upheaval and trying to adjust to it.

In these circumstances, Constantia's urge to giggle seems odd at first, but, becomes suggestive of the sisters' true characters—a long preserved girlhood, with no chance to mature and grow. Constantia's nickname for Josephine, Jug, also is childish. As they anxiously debate the externals of mourning, it looks as though their sensitivity to the constraints of society, its conventions and piety, is not prompted by love (for their father). Even when Josephine

weeps 23 times over the sentence "We miss our dear father so much," repeated in her replies to sympathy letters, this seems conventional mourning and also an unconscious mourning for themselves, all they have lost by way of opportunities and experiences.

Their want of affection becomes understandable when the character of their father is revealed in a flashback. He is, in fact, unlovable and has been a stern Edwardian paterfamilias. The final parting was grotesque. The dying man opens one eye only and glares. The daughters feel that "the eye wasn't at all a peaceful eye," suggesting memories of unpleasant scenes and scoldings. Their father had such a terrible and strong impact on them that, even after his death, they could not possibly believe that he was never coming back. At the cemetery, Josephine had experienced a moment of "absolute terror" when she realized that they were burying their father without his permission!

The father, in effect, had crushed their personalities. Their mother had died in Ceylon when they were young. Their brother, Benny, with masculine advantage, had escaped to Ceylon and marriage with Hilda, leaving the sisters to carry out their duties as females—and miss all their rights as females. They had become meek and mild.

Two other characters assume dominant roles in the sisters' lives. Nurse Andrews, who looked after their father, is a contrary and constricting force in the house—still there one week after his death, by their invitation prompted by a conventional recognition of her services. Kate, their maid, adopts a haughty attitude towards them. Her youth forms a striking and painful contrast to their arid age. She is called "the enchanted princess," recalling their main imaginative nourishment, fairy tales.

The object on which Josephine and Constantia lavish their starved affections, maternal and otherwise, the one thing they can love, is their nephew Cyril: "Cyril to tea was one of their rare treats." They sacrifice their necessities, Josephine's "winter gloves" or "the soling and heeling of Constantia's only respectable shoes," to produce a treat for Cyril. When Cyril confirms their view that his father was "most frightfully keen on meringues," although he had no memory of this, they are overjoyed. Their sources of pleasure are minute and pathetic.

Josephine and Constantia have a great deal in common, but they are differentiated too. Josephine, as the elder, is more decisive, seemingly stronger. Constantia is the more imaginative, dreamy, impulsive, and bolder. When they first enter their father's room after his death, they are frightened by the change circumstances visually present— the blinds down, a cloth over the mirror. It is Constantia who locks the wardrobe and urges postponing dealing with things.

Procrastination, irresoluteness, indecision are their notable tendencies. It reflects the seriousness of the damage inflicted on their personalities by their father's tyranny. Their will has been broken. When the window blind of their dead father's room flies open there is a suggestion that they are free at last, a sense of swift liberation: "The little tassel tapped as if trying to get free. That was too much for Constantia." Even after their father's death, they are too timid to face the implications of freedom. They cannot break through the prison-life structured by his demands and commands.

The story reaches its climax and the prose becomes most poetic during the final episode. A barrel-organ strikes up in the street below. Josephine and Constantia unconsciously smile as they realise the music and go on unchecked by their father. The abundance and sweetness of life are suggested: "a perfect fountain of bubbling notes shook from the barrel-organ, round, bright notes, carelessly scattered." The sun, a symbol of life, comes out and Josephine responds to it. Constantia remembers her rituals and songs, impelled instinctively by the moon and the sea. Both awaken simultaneously, but only vaguely and momentarily. It is too late and futile. "A big cloud" soon appears "where the sun had been." The story is a tragi-comedy from first to last.

—D.C.R.A. Goonetilleke

THE DAUNTLESS TIN SOLDIER.   See **THE STEADFAST TIN SOLDIER.**

THE DEAD
by James Joyce, 1914

"The Dead" is the capstone story of James Joyce's *Dubliners,* first published in 1914, and it centers around the consciousness of Gabriel Conroy, a teacher and literary man in turn of the century Dublin. Gabriel and his wife Gretta are attending a holiday party given each year by his aunts Kate and Julia Morkan and their niece Mary Jane, and Gabriel is relied upon annually to keep things in order and to provide the traditional afterdinner speech. It is in Gabriel's interactions with several of the guests and in his talk with Gretta in their hotel room after the gathering, that Joyce presents a portrait of a representative, ineffectual 20th-century consciousness. The story is a triumph of literary modernism.

Despite the fact that Gabriel would seem to be confident and in charge, things do not go well for him right from the start. As Lily the caretaker's daughter helps him off with his overcoat, he jokes that she will probably be married someday soon, but he is confused and taken aback by her bitter reply. ("The men that is now is only all palaver and what they can get out of you"). He can only thrust a coin at her to resolve an awkward situation, and even this gesture is more insulting than considerate. Later, Gabriel is chided by Molly Ivors, an Irish nationalist, about writing reviews for an English newspaper and taking his vacation on the Continent, rather than in the west of Ireland, and once again he is uncomfortable and unable to reply: "Gabriel glanced right and left nervously and tried to keep his good humour under the ordeal which was making a blush invade his forehead." He is even unsure of his upcoming afterdinner remarks, pompously assuming that they will be too intellectual for his lowbrow audience.

Irritated and out of sorts, Gabriel will reveal, without perhaps knowing it, the extent of his paralysis and alienation as he attempts to deal with Gretta after the party. Driven by the rush of sexual desire for his wife, Gabriel does not realize that she is in a different mood altogether. As the festivities are breaking up, the tenor Bartell D'Arcy sings an old Irish ballad that reminds Gretta of Michael Furey, a young suitor of hers who died when he was only 17 years old. Nostalgia for the past has made Gretta sad, though she loves her husband and Furey died many years ago, but Gabriel is totally unable to empathize with her

feelings. At first angry that she would think of anyone else but him, his mood quickly changes from coldness to awkwardness to humiliation. He is unable to reach outside of his own consciousness, since he is immersed in his own solipsistic world and can respond to others only as they have some relation to his personal feelings. His utter egoism is the culmination of the series of dissociated pictures that Joyce has drawn throughout the *Dubliners* collection.

Ultimately, Gabriel can only revel in self-pity, as he celebrates what he considers to be his own worthlessness. In something of a masochistic way, he negates the reality of his relationship with his wife and family, choosing yet again to see himself as the suffering victim and not realizing how ridiculous he looks. His many years of marriage mean nothing, if he has not been the one and only center of his wife's existence: "It hardly pained him now to think how poor a part he, her husband, had played in her life. He watched her while she slept as though he and she had never lived together as man and wife." His childish reaction to the events of the evening turns his thoughts away from the exuberance of life to the oncoming gloom of death. Just as he sees that Gretta is growing older, Gabriel notes that Aunt Julia and Aunt Kate will soon be dead, and that he too will eventually join them. Rather than striving to celebrate his own life for what it is, with its significant milestones that have accrued over the years, he gives up passively to the sleep that absolves him from the responsibility of objective self-examination: "His soul had approached that region where dwell the vast hosts of the dead. He was conscious of, but could not apprehend, their wayward and flickering existence."

The narrational point of view of "The Dead" has been firmly lodged in the mind of Gabriel Conroy, but in the final paragraph Joyce moves the reader back and away from the immediate action, like a movie camera recedes from a close-up to an objective overview. The focus is upon the snow, falling "general all over Ireland," and it is "falling faintly through the universe and faintly falling, like the descent of their last end, upon all the living and the dead." The ultimate irony in this concluding description is that Joyce has upended the meanings of both "living" and "dead." Though Michael Furey may indeed be dead in body, he lives on in the memories of both Gretta and Gabriel, and his validity cannot be erased. Conversely, alive in the flesh, Gabriel has proven to be dead in spirit, and it seems that nothing can be done to resurrect his essence. An overwhelming self-involvement has dulled Gabriel's possibility of any productive interaction with the other human beings around him, and he has joined the ranks of the contemporary walking dead, inhabitants of what T. S. Eliot called a modern wasteland. "The Dead" sums up the dilemma that Joyce will confront head on, later in his artistic career, in *A Portrait of the Artist* and *Ulysses.*

—Michael H. Begnal

THE DEAD MAN (El hombre muerto)
by Horacio Quiroga, 1926

"El hombre muerto" ("The Dead Man") first appeared in *La Nación* on 27 June 1920, then in a collection *Los desterrados* in 1926. Dating from Quiroga's pioneering period in Misiones, Argentina, "The Dead Man" reflects his perennial preoccupation with death, nature, and the darker side of the frontier experience, and it offers a perfect illustration of his narrative technique. The plot may be summed up in three words: a man dies. While clearing weeds from his banana plantation, a farmer falls on his machete, and takes approximately half an hour to die. The title of the story precludes any attempt to build suspense, or supply a twist in the ending. Rather, it suggests that the outcome has been decided long in advance.

The short story is a particularly appropriate vehicle for Quiroga's choice of subject matter. Concentrated and intense, it singles out and focuses on a moment of crisis. Quiroga uses this medium to depict human beings in extreme situations. The struggle between humans and nature is a constant theme of the (American) short story and Quiroga's characters are engaged in a perpetual struggle with their environment. Occasionally they are successful ("The Incense Tree Roof," 1922), more often they are defeated ("The Son," 1935). Nature never appears as mere background in Quiroga's stories: the river Paraná, the jungle, the natural hazards of heat or flood— these are all part of human existence, obstacles to be overcome, dangers to be conquered. There is no reward for the fight, the quality of an individual's life is in the struggle, and this alone is the meaning of existence.

Nature is mutely present throughout the story, the river Paraná "sleeping like a lake," but capable of great damage should it awake, the midday sun so hot that the farmer's horse is covered in sweat, the virgin bush lying in wait beyond the fenced-off land. The wire fence, mentioned eight times in the text, is simultaneously a symbol of his unceasing attempts to keep nature at bay, and of the futility of his efforts. We might compare this with "The Son," where a young boy trips over a wire fence and blows his head off with a shotgun: it is almost as if nature were showing the pointlessness of a person's attempts to fence it in. The dead man is never named. Quiroga always shows his protagonists in action, either carrying out a task or going on a difficult journey, and this man is defined by his work. He is first described as satisfied with the work he has completed so far, then as he lies dying, he contemplates the results of "ten years in the woods": the fence he has put up, the grass he planted, the paddock it took him five consecutive months to clear, "the work of his own hands," the flood ditch, the banana grove—"work of his hands alone." From the outset he is linked to the tool that kills him: "the man and his machete had just finished clearing the fifth row of the banana grove," "they still had two rows to clear." The machete is an extension of the farmer and an actor in the drama, while the man, who believes himself in control, becomes an object, or victim.

Short stories frequently depict a moment of revelation or an epiphany, and "The Dead Man" is no exception, presenting the protagonist's growing awareness that he is no longer in control, his life is ended. From the initial mood of complacency, there is the realization that he is fatally wounded. This is immediately followed by a refusal to accept his predicament. As he lies on the ground, surrounded by his possessions, within earshot of his family, he is conscious of the normality of external events in contrast to the abnormality of his situation. His perspective changes, and he now perceives himself as a small figure lying on the grass, the insignificance of his life and labours marked by the repetition of the adjective "trivial." There are no superfluous elements in a Quiroga short story. All the parts of the narrative work together to produce the single effect that he, like Edgar Allan Poe, sought to achieve. His style is economical and terse. None of the paragraphs is particularly long, and some are extremely short in order to make a specific point or create a contrast. The first paragraph sketches in as much background as the reader requires, with no lengthy preliminaries, merely setting the scene, while other details are inserted at later stages. The narrative fulfils two functions: it tells us about the last ten years of the dying man's life, and it shows us his growing awareness of the futility of those years. The story is narrated from an omniscient, third-person point of view, interspersed with paragraphs containing either narrator's philosophizing, marked by first-person plural verb forms, pronouns, and possessive adjectives, or the dying man's last conscious thoughts. Through the "camera-eye" of the narrator, there is the slow-motion sequence of the fatal accident, a series of panning shots from where the man lies dying, and finally, an overhead shot that shows the small, crumpled body of the dead farmer on the grass below.

The chronological time of the narrative is fairly short, half an hour at most, in contrast with the psychological time, much greater because of the digressions that represent the fluctuations of his consciousness and his growing awareness of precisely what has happened to him. The imperfect tense provides a backdrop, the preterite advances the action, and the present, present perfect, and future tenses denote his growing awareness. Deictics locate the action in time and space, reinforce the time scheme and point of view, and underline the helplessness of the man as he lies dying—he is surrounded by his possessions, but they cannot prevent his death. Adjectives are normally determinative in the more clinical third-person narrative stretches, and qualificative in the subjective stream-of-consciousness paragraphs. Quiroga relies quite heavily on adverbs, not just for deixis, but also to intensify, reinforce, and affirm emotional attitude. Accumulation is an important device in his writing, either by repetition of certain key words, such as "wire fence," or the triple structure, three adverbs, three adjectives, or nouns placed together: "coldly, fatally and unavoidably." Irony is also a key factor in Quiroga's narrative. The man plans to enjoy a well-earned rest, but "rest" in the story becomes a euphemism for death. He takes great pride in his work and possessions, but in the end they kill him. Quiroga does not glorify his pioneer; for this man, as for so many others, the frontier becomes the final resting place. Human life and effort are presented as puny and ephemeral, only the land achieves permanence and grandeur.

—Patricia Anne Odber de Baubeta

DEATH IN THE WOODS
by Sherwood Anderson, 1933

It was as a short story writer that Anderson won his first and lasting fame when he published the collection *Winesburg, Ohio*. It consists of loosely linked depictions of individuals in a single Midwestern town. In this highly successful book readers encountered an author who was going to reform the texture and aims of American fiction. By his chosen subjects and his sympathies with the endemic loneliness of small town life he revised the common perception of what America had come to be in the early 20th century.

His career began in a time of literary ferment in America and abroad, but Anderson was hardly suited to be an intellectual theorist of the revolution in which he played a part. He liked to call himself a "story teller," suggesting a modest distinction between him and disciplined literary practitioners. But this is misleading. In fact, he invented new forms to sustain his informalities. Without schematic programs or impressive philosophic baggage, he felt his way into narrative methods that are as technically admirable as they are well-suited to the emotional content of his work. Many writers of the next generations are indebted to him. His innovative fictional strategies for shaping a story are not yet exhaustively exploited.

An example is his use of the first person narrator of "Death in the Woods." The narrator is an eye witness to some part of what he has to tell us about, but as the story moves toward its deep core of revelation, we are told he has *seen* concrete specifics that never passed before his eyes. Thus the concept of witnessing and of perception are disassembled and rearranged to permit the articulation of a truth only to be apprehended by the imagination.

The narrator was not exactly a witness to the death of an old farm woman, struggling in the snow on her way home after a pathetic trip to town to get provisions. The boy (as he was at the time of the event) gets only one poignant glimpse of the woman as her body is turned over by a member of the search party, and he is literally quite wrong about what he sees. He sees a beautiful woman, a frozen princess, a character of high romance. He admits (in the voice of an adult recollecting this at a later time) that "it may have been the snow clinging to the frozen flesh, that made it so white and lovely, so like marble." Nevertheless, if what he saw was illusionary, it retains a force equal to the inferences, hearsay, and parallel sense perceptions of which the story is compounded.

The narrator definitely does not proclaim "I was there" as witnessing narrators usually do in fiction. By insisting he was not present to behold much of what happened on the fatal night, he highlights the question of what it means to see. The thing witnessed becomes "like music heard from far off." It is difficult to locate the real truth of memorable events.

In a sense, Anderson has fused two stories—the story of the old woman's death, and the story of the narrator's coming to maturity as an artist. There is no possible distinction between this narrator and the author, nor is there intended to be. A storyteller understands by making associations, assembling from far and near whatever may fit together, and tuning the disparate chords of experience until they resonate the "music heard from far off" as a literal record could not.

The old woman rendered by the composite vision is not sharply individualized. Among other things she is representative of the lower fringe of farm women of her time and place, brought into life with no advantages, bandied from man to man as a sexual provider, but mostly as a slavey whose main obligation is to "feed animal life." She accepts a low concept of duty in lieu of any personal aspirations. She is scrupulous in seeing that the mean chores get done. When she takes her meager produce to town, she appeals to the butcher for scraps of meat to piece out the diet back on the farm.

The storyteller does not pretend he knows this woman, except that he knows her through learning about the nature of the lives of farm women in general. He does not know about her transaction with the butcher except as he has glimpsed the practices of small-town butchers and invented for this one a minimal charity. As for the dogs that circle in ritual observance as the old woman lies dying the snow—well, the storyteller has seen sometime in his life a similar, haunting performance by another dog pack. With a hiking friend he has seen the ugly ferocity of the dogs on the place where the woman once lived.

It is finally with himself that the narrator must come to terms about the riddle of the woman, and here inferences from general observation will not help. He must somehow reconcile the appearance to his eyes of a beautiful woman dead in the snow with the drabness of what he can know of her existence. Prompted by the music he can not quite grasp or define, he gropes to a primal level where she was an enduring source in the cosmic scheme of things. Sufferings and shortcomings quite aside, she prevailed like a divinity on whom all else depended. The dogs that ran around her without attacking expressed a mystic dependence on humans, dependence on whatever distinguished dogs from wolves.

It may have been some occult glimpse of divinity that met the boy's eyes when he stood among the men who found her dead and saw her glorified by the fatal snow, freed from the rags and squalor of her individual existence.

—R.V. Cassill

DEATH IN VENICE (Der Tod in Venedig) by Thomas Mann, 1912

Der Tod in Venedig ("Death in Venice"), which was made into a highly successful film starring Dirk Bogart by Luchino Visconti in 1976 and was brilliantly adapted by Myfanwy Piper to provide Benjamin Briten with the libretto for his last opera in 1973, is probably the best known of all the works of the Nobel-prize winning Thomas Mann. Though there is, of course, much to be said for *Buddenbrooks, Der Zauberberg* (*The Magic Mountain*), and other novels by Mann, the fact remains that much of what the author stood for is fairly represented in this finely crafted, thoughtful, and deeply evocative tragic tale which, as well as acquiring the status of a modern classic, is also a splendidly accurate presentation of the spirit of the educated and cultured well-to-do European bourgeoisie in the years before World War I.

Gustav Aschenbach—or rather von Aschenbach, as it is pointed out in the very first sentence, for he had been ennobled on his 50th birthday—is a worthy representative of high German culture in the early years of the 20th century. He had won fame with the general public and esteem with the more discerning critics with his works, which included a prose epic on Frederick the Great, novels that make sense of the complexities of existence, and criticism that stands comparison with the greatest works of German Classicism. High standards are expected of him, and despite a constitution that is far from robust he conceives it his duty to live up to them at all times, in his writing, his behaviour, and even his dress and appearance. Perhaps that is a reflection of his origins in the strict milieu of North Germany, where his forebears had all devoted their lives to the service of the state, but now he resides further south, in the elegant city of Munich. As a child he had been brought up without much contact with other children, and now he lives alone, for his wife died young, leaving a daughter who had married and gone away.

For a man so thoughtful, Aschenbach's decision to take a vacation in Venice was rather impulsive, though the journey there from Munich is, of course, not a particularly long or arduous one. But even at the start of the story we sense something ominous: it is strange that Aschenbach's eyes should linger upon the inscriptions on the monuments in a graveyard, and there is a mysterious stranger whose unexpected presence seems to have some hidden significance. The journey, too, though essentially realistic in its detail, has its odd touches, and the sense grows that Aschenbach is somehow being caught up in a destiny he cannot fully control. Finally he arrives, taking a room in a grand, cosmopolitan hotel. There, among the guests from America and all over Europe, he sees, under the charge of a governess, a party of young Poles, three teenage girls and a long-haired boy of about 14 years, and with astonishment he notes "the boy's perfect beauty," a beauty still not spoiled by any contact with the world.

Aschenbach is hesitant and coy as his love develops; he envies those who come into close contact with Tadzio, as he is called, yet cannot bring himself to do more than worship from a distance, following him as he is taken to see the sights of Venice. Now, however, another sinister element enters the story. Throughout the 19th century Europe had feared the onset of cholera, which, it was thought, came in from the East through the Italian ports, and Mann deftly builds up the sense of horror as Aschenbach begins to suspect that the dread disease is threatening Venice, that the hotel is like a fortress besieged by the pestilence, and, worst of all, that Tadzio might fall victim to it. In fact the boy remains healthy, and it is Aschenbach who dies, still bewildered by beauty and, as is emphasised in an episode when a barber dyes his hair and makes up his face with cosmetics, with the very essence of his being under threat.

Set in a city whose fine buildings are reflected in the rise and ebb of the surrounding tidal waters and whose location is traditionally seen as standing half way between the sage European world and the greater mysteries of the East, "Death in Venice" is no less rich in its symbolism than it is vivid in its topographical and human situations. Nothing is quite what it seems, yet the importance of appearance is stressed time and again. Another layer of significance is added to this straight-forwardly plotted third-person narrative by Mann's inclusion of a good deal of discussion of aesthetics, with particular stress on the opinions of Plato on the relationship between beauty and morality. Moreover, through the unfulfilled tender relationship between Aschenbach and Tadzio, Mann has created a powerful image of the nature of the artist which, with its origins in Romanticism, has remained valid throughout the 20th century.

—Christopher Smith

———

THE DEATH OF IVAN ILYICH (Smert' Ivana Il'icha)
by Lev Tolstoi, 1886

Lev Tolstoi's career falls into two fairly distinct phases: the master of realism as demonstrated in his two great novels *Voing i mir* (*War and Peace*) and *Anna Karenina*, and the religious mystic whose fiction sometimes resembled polemical tracts more than traditional stories. Many readers find that the second phase suffers, in purely literary terms, compared to the first. In at least one work, though, "Smert' Ivana Il'icha" ("The Death of Ivan Ilyich"), the two phases meet in one of the most memorable short stories ever written.

Until the very end of the story, Tolstoi's later concerns—religion and mysticism—seem hardly in evidence. Throughout most of Ivan's life, his interest lay in everything but the spiritual; since the story is an account of his life, it is only proper that little, quantitatively, concern the spiritual. But that is exactly the point.

The title of the story is both highly appropriate and appropriately misleading—"appropriately" because the reader, like Ivan himself, is fooled into thinking that death has been the important issue when the climax of the story clearly shows that death is irrelevant.

This is not to say that death is given slight shrift in the story. Indeed, one could argue that no more vivid, harrowing, and moving account of dying has ever been written. The reader is spared none of the physical and emotional trama of a wasting illness: a floating kidney, according to the doctors, but the story warns against putting too much faith in the medical profession. Here is Tolstoi the realist with his matchless eye for physical and psychological detail: the wife's bad breath, the bowel movements, the numerous but futile tricks with which Ivan tries to convince himself that he is getting better, but most of all the pain, incessant and remorseless. Ivan screams for three days before his death.

A large portion of the story is taken up with this graphic account of Ivan's dying—but not all of it. The accident that eventually leads to his death is not introduced, in fact, until one-third of the way into the story. Furthermore, if this is merely the story of a man's dying, why does the entire lengthy first section transpire after Ivan's death? Indeed, Ivan and perhaps even the reader does not realize his experience's true relevance until it occurs to him that his dying is so terrible because, "Maybe I did not live as I ought to have done" (translated by Louise and Aylmer Maude). At that point, it is obvious that Ivan's life, not his death, has been Tolstoi's chief concern.

What kind of life was it? The perceptive reader will not be as easily fooled as Ivan into believing that before the accident his life passed, as the story's refrain would have it, "pleasantly and properly." To be sure, Ivan seemed to be successful in all the outward, material ways, but that is just the issue for Tolstoi, the religious mystic who believed that one should live simply and spiritually, governed only by the most fundamental Christian precepts: love God, love one another.

The first section of the story, then, is indeed of little consequence if the story's theme is how Ivan died; but if we concern ourselves rather with how he lived, the first section is illuminating. The evidence shows, sadly, that Ivan left little mark on the people—colleagues, friends, and relatives—to whom he was closest. The story opens with the announcement of Ivan's death. His colleagues are momentarily taken aback, but their principal concern is soon evident: how they might benefit from his judge's position being vacated. In a very few moments they are joking once more, making plans for a game of cards, trying to decide if there is any recourse from the irksome task of attending his funeral. At the funeral the reader encounters Ivan's grieving wife, but clearly her emotion is aroused more by her own suffering ("For three days he screamed incessantly. . . .I cannot understand how I bore it") than for her late husband's. In accepting condolences from Ivan's best friend (who could not think of a reasonable excuse for avoiding the funeral), she is more interested in his opinion of her chances of receiving a large pension than in his fond remembrances of Ivan. Only Ivan's son, glimpsed fleetingly, shows what appears to be genuine grief.

Why did Ivan elicit so little regard from friends and family? Essentially, they gave back what they got from him: little worth having. He married his wife, for instance, not because of any profound love but because she fit into his picture of what comprised a pleasant life. When she begins to upset his pleasant routine by making "unreasonable" demands on his time and patience—when she becomes pregnant—his solution is not to become more understanding, patient, and loving, but to leave the house, devote himself to his friends and career. The fact that his children are barely mentioned in the subsequent account of his life is not evidence that Tolstoi ignored them, but that Ivan ignored them.

When he is injured, then, tortured by pain and fear, he elicits the same degree of devotion and compassion that he offered his family: precious little. Indeed, it is the lack of love and understanding that plagues him even more than his floating kidney. Significantly, his only solace comes through the person of Gerasim, a simple peasant who tends him with honest goodness and caring. Ivan's pain stops only when Gerasim holds his legs up—testament to Ivan's craving for human contact.

It is another human touch that leads Ivan to his final epiphany. Thrashing about in his death agony, Ivan touches his son's head. The grieving son catches his father's hand and kisses it. For perhaps the first time in his life Ivan puts someone else's feelings before his own; he realizes he is making others wretched. At the same time, he realizes that death is natural, inevitable, and, compared to the simple virtues of living, inconsequential. Instead of fearful darkness before him, he sees a joyous light. His last thought is "Death is finished. It is no more."

The most somber and forbidding of stories, "The Death of Ivan Ilyich" is also the most optimistic. It shows that a man can live his entire life in darkness but in the final moment be resurrected into the light.

—Dennis Vannatta

THE DECAPITATED CHICKEN (La gallina degollada)
by Horacio Quiroga, 1917

"La gallina degollada" ("The Decapitated Chicken") was first published on 10 July 1909, in *Caras y Caretas,* then in the collection *Cuentos de amor, de locura y de muerte* in 1917. It offers one of the clearest examples of Quiroga's fascination with madness and the macabre (see Peter Beardsell's commentary), and his debt to Edgar Allan Poe and the other masters he lists in his "Decálogo del perfecto cuentista" (Ten Commandments for the Perfect Short-Story Writer), Chekhov and Maupassant. The story contains the three elements of the title of the collection: love, madness, and death. A couple, deeply in love, marry and have children. Their four sons all sicken and are reduced to a state of idiocy because of congenital disease. They then

have a daughter who is healthy and normal, but this child is butchered by her four brothers.

The narrator focuses on a particular moment in time, the day before the tragedy occurs. He sets the scene briefly but with precise detail (the ages, physical and mental condition of the children, and the state of their parents' marriage), and then steps back in time to fill out additional background, all of which is intended to prepare the reader for the eventual outcome of the tale. There is then a shift to the present time of the narrative, with a relentless progression towards the ghastly climax.

The story is not just about madness and violent death; it chronicles the breakdown of a relationship, with loss of respect, affection and hope. Clinical description ("Their tongues protruded from between their lips; their eyes were dull; their mouths hung open as they turned their heads") alternates with more subjective matter marked by qualificative adjectives ("profound despair"), rhetorical questions and exclamations intended to convey the parents' fears and anguish ("So it was their blood, their love, that was cursed! Especially their love!"). With the birth of their first son all their hopes seem to have been fulfilled. However, at the age of 20 months the child is overtaken by illness and is damaged to the point of imbecility. The doctor attributes the illness and its effects to hereditary disease, which the reader may deduce to be syphilis. At the same time, the child's mother is showing the first signs of consumption. The couple feel guilty and bereft, but place their hopes in a second child. At 18 months, this son also suffers convulsions and is left an idiot. When the couple try again, Berta gives birth to twins, with exactly the same result. The young parents love their subnormal offspring, and care for them as best they can. However, after three years they begin to long for another child, to make up for the four "beasts" they have already produced. Because Berta does not conceive straight away, they become bitter and resentful, no longer supporting one another, but making veiled accusations about who is to blame for the children's illness. The couple become reconciled, and have another child, this time a daughter. By now they have shifted from "great compassion for their four sons" to overt hostility, demonstrated by the increasingly strong language used to describe the boys—"monsters," "four poor beasts"—and the fact that they are kept in the yard. On her fourth birthday Bertita falls ill, having eaten a surfeit of sweets; in contrast with her brothers, she is spoiled and over-indulged. The couple have a violent argument, in which the accusations are no longer veiled. Berta openly blames Mazzini's father for the children's idiocy, and he blames her consumption. The little girl recovers from her indigestion, but on the next day Berta coughs up blood. One horror has receded, but now another threatens their happiness. The couple decide to go out for the day with Bertita. During the morning the four sons see the maid killing a chicken and are fascinated by the sight of blood draining from the bird's neck. In the afternoon, Bertita escapes from her parents and wanders into the yard. Her brothers seize her, carry her off into the kitchen, "parting her curls as if they were feathers." The parents hear her screaming for help, but arrive to find the kitchen floor covered in blood.

Quiroga makes use of foreshadowing and irony. The relevance of the title is not immediately apparent, but it does presage a violent death, as do the descriptions of the boys' animal behaviour, particularly when they see the chicken slaughtered. Nor does the fact that Berta coughs up blood portend a happy ending. The irony lies in the fact that the couple's only healthy child dies at the hands of her brothers on the very day when they have cause for celebration: Bertita has come through her illness unscathed. There is also a kind of reverse symbolism. Light and sunshine normally represent positive qualities, virtues, but here the sun becomes a symbol of the boys' bestiality, and the day of the tragedy is splendid and sunny.

It is possible that some of the inspiration for "The Decapitated Chicken" came from Joseph Conrad's short story "The Idiots," first published in 1898. In the Conrad tale a couple have four idiot children (twin boys, another boy then a girl), the wife kills her husband because he tries to force her to have another child, then commits suicide by leaping from a cliff. Both tales depict growing hopelessness and the breakdown of a once happy marriage. Like Conrad's idiots, Quiroga's "monsters" are never given names or any individualizing characteristic: they function as a collective, almost a herd: in Quiroga there are eight references to animal qualities: they live in the "deepest animality," make mooing noises and all their feelings and responses are "bestial"; in Conrad, the children are described as "worse than animals who know the hand that feeds them." Both sets of parents grow to detest their children, keeping them out of sight as far as possible. Religious themes run through both stories: in Conrad, the anti-clerical protagonists Jean-Pierre seeks a solution to his problems in religion. When neither solution nor solace are forthcoming, he turns against the Church with renewed anger. In "The Decapitated Chicken" Mazzini and Berta try to "redeem once and for all the sanctity of their tenderness," and are desperate for the "redemption of the four animals born to them." In both stories there are hints of the Biblical idea that the sins of the father are visited on the children, and their children's children. In Quiroga there are comments such as "paying for the excesses of their grandfathers," "the terrifying line of descent," "rotten progeny." In "The Idiots" Susan's father was "'deranged in his head' for a few years before he died," and Susan's mother "now began to suspect her daughter was going mad." "The Decapitated Chicken" illustrates how Quiroga's essential themes and narrative technique work together to produce the greatest possible effect, in this case, one of horror and repulsion. Disaster is inevitable, all that remains to be revealed is the unfolding of the tragedy.

—Patricia Anne Odber de Baubeta

THE DEMON LOVER
by Elizabeth Bowen, 1945

Elizabeth Bowen's "The Demon Lover" is a striking example of what critic Tzvetan Todorov has called the "fantastic." Todorov says that if a fictional event occurs in a world that seems to mirror our own, but that cannot be explained by the laws of our world, there are two possible explanations: Either we or the characters are the victims of an illusion, in which case the laws of our world remain; or else the event has actually taken place, in which case we are in a world controlled by laws unknown to us. The first constitutes the genre of the "uncanny"; the second comprises the realm of the "marvelous"; the "fantastic," says Todorov, occupies the period when we are uncertain.

Such uncertainty has characterized critical comment on "The Demon Lover." While Allan Austin in his book on Bowen calls the work a ghost tale, Douglas Hughes in a shorter study argues that it is a story of psychological delusion. The problem centers on the mysterious letter the protagonist Mrs. Drover finds in her boarded-up London home when she visits it from the country where the family has retreated to escape World War II bombing. The letter, which bears no stamp but has the current day's date, is from a man that Mrs. Drover knew 25 years before but who was reported missing in battle during World War I. It reminds her of a promise she made to the young man and tells her to expect him on this day they had arranged.

As the title suggests, the story makes use of the legend of the demon lover. Although there are many different versions of the story, the basic plot focuses on a young woman's promise to love her young man forever and to await his return from battle. However, when he is reported dead or missing, she meets and plans to marry another man. Usually on the wedding day, the lost lover returns, in its most melodramatic versions as a rotting corpse, and carries the young bride away to join him in death. The legend is part of the medieval romance tradition that asserts the ideal of love eternal, implying that the promise of love cannot be broken, even by death, and affirming that the only way lovers can be truly united is in death. Mrs. Drover recalls the young man's feeling for her was "not love, not meaning a person well," but rather absolute desire, irrational passion.

Mrs. Drover is an example of a common short fiction protagonist whose "prosaic" nature and "utter dependability" must be challenged, whose notion of love and life is so safe and comfortable that her habit of her life must be invaded by some basic irrational force. The brief flashback to her parting with the young man in the past suggests that the visitation is in retribution for her previous lack of commitment. Although her own feelings for the soldier were not passionate and she seemed relieved when he left, she did indeed make the promise to him—an "unnatural promise" that cuts her apart from the rest of human kind: "No other way of having given herself could have made her feel so apart, lost and foresworn. She could not have plighted a more sinister troth." Realizing that what made her make the promise was that she was not herself (for she felt a "complete suspension of her existence" during that period), when she finds the letter she goes to a mirror, polishes a clear patch in it, and looks in to confirm her identity.

Bowen's treatment of the demon lover myth largely depends on the residue of the past in the boarded-up house. "Dead air" meets her as she opens the door, and she is "perplexed" as she looks around at the traces of her former habit of life—a yellow smoke stain on the fireplace, a ring left by a vase on a table, the bruise in the wallpaper where the doorknob hit it, clawmarks left by the piano on the parquet floor. These "traces" of the past establish a metaphoric motivation for the appearance of the letter which makes a past promise a present reality. Bowen makes this connection clear: "The desuetude of her former bedroom, her married London home's whole air of being a cracked cup from which memory, with its reassuring power, had either evaporated or leaked away, made a crisis—and at just this crisis the letter-writer had, knowledgeably, struck."

The story reaches its climax when Mrs. Drover leaves the house and hails a taxi, intending to bring the driver back to the house for her parcels. When the taxi driver makes a turn to go back to her house, even before she tells him where it is, she scratches on the dividing panel, making his stop abruptly and throwing her face up close to the glass. When the driver looks around, she screams and continues to scream as the taxi, "accelerating without mercy, made off with her into the hinterlands of deserted streets." Bowen does not resolve our uncertainty about the nature of Mrs. Drover's visitation, for what matters is the story's theme of the past's claim on the present and its basic structural use of the demon lover legend—both of which are delicately developed in this fantastic fable.

—Charles E. May

_____

DÉSIRÉE'S BABY
by Kate Chopin, 1892

The first paragraphs of Kate Chopin's "Désirée's Baby" read like a fairy tale. The wealthy Monsieur Valmondé discovers a foundling sleeping in his gateway and presents her to his wife, who loves her like the child she has never had. Eighteen years later, this beautiful foundling, Désirée, is discovered standing in the same gateway by Armand Aubigny, yet another wealthy man, who falls in love with her, makes her his wife, and takes her home with him to L'Abri (the shelter). At this point, Chopin works a turn on the fairy tale, moving from romance to gothic horror. Désirée gives birth to a son, and although Aubigny initially shares his wife's delight, as weeks pass, his delight turns to the darkest displeasure. Désirée cannot fathom the change in her husband, until one afternoon she finds herself studying the similarities between a half-naked quadroon boy and her son. Confused, frightened, Désirée says to Aubigny, "Look at our child. What does it mean?" And Aubigny answers, "It means that you are not white." This pronouncement, and Aubigny's obvious abhorrence of his wife, prompt her suicide; with her son in her arms, she walks into the bayou.

Some weeks after Désirée's death, while burning her effects, Aubigny comes upon the remnant of a letter from his mother to his father in which his mother thanks God that Aubigny "will never know that his mother, who adores him, belongs to the race that is cursed with the brand of slavery."

Early readers of "Désirée's Baby" commented upon its tightness of plot, praise its poignancy, and compared it favorably to the stories of Maupassant, stories admired by Chopin. Most placed it within the tradition of local color. Not till in the 1970's did "Désirée's Baby" begin to receive the critical attention it deserves. Cynthia Griffin Wolff, in "Kate Chopin and the Fiction of Limits: 'Désirée's Baby,'" (*The Southern Literary Journal* Spring 1978), reads Chopin's story as representative of Chopin's work as it concerns the instability of boundaries with which we hope to contain and control our lives. Wolff shows how obvious color line violations in "Désirée's Baby" find echoes in violations between goodness and evil, life and death, civilization and the bayou. As Woolf observes, Chopin writes a "fiction of limits," focusing upon "the persistent shadow-line that threads its way through all of the significant transactions of our lives."

Anna Shannon Elfenbein, in *Women on the Color Line*, (1989), also attends to lines of demarcation in Chopin's story, highlighting the ways in which Aubigny imposes rigid categories on experience and Désirée acquiesces to these categories. The product of a patriarchal and racist culture, this husband insists upon a wide gap between positions of power and powerlessness; he assumes determinative power over his wife and children, deciding who bears his name, who belongs to his family. Désirée, meanwhile, accedes to Aubigny's determinations; she defines herself on the basis of how he positions her.

Informed by Wolff and Elfenbein, one might further highlight issues of gender and interpretive authority articulated within "Désirée's Baby." Like Georgiana in Hawthorne's "The Birthmark" (1843) and the unnamed narrator in Gilman's "The Yellow Wallpaper" (1892), the heroine of Chopin's story is figured as a blank page, as a text to be written upon and read by men.

Numerous features of "Désirée's Baby" contribute to this figuration. First is Désirée's unknown parentage; discovered by M. Valmondé, she is a cipher. It falls upon M. Valmondé to determine what kind of life she shall have, and he does so by taking her to his wife and by bestowing a name upon her ("desire": the sign of lack; and "Valmondé," the sign of this particular family). Interestingly, when found by M. Valmondé, Désirée does speak, but her speech is limited to "Dada," as if to suggest her complete subjection to the rule of the father. Second, the story imagines Aubigny "discovering" Désirée under the same gateway that Valmondé found her 18 years earlier. The parallelism suggests that once again Désirée is lacking—and of course she is; she has no husband, and despite her years at Valmondé, "she [is] nameless." So Aubigny inscribes her with his name, and she shows her gratitude by being the wife he wants her to be and producing the son he desires. But this son proves flawed. Surrendering authority to her husband, Désirée begs him to tell her what it means, to interpret it for her. When he does so, she utters her one cry of protest: "It is a lie. . . .Look at my hand; whiter than yours, Armand." For the first time, Désirée offers an interpretation of her own, and evidence in its support, but Aubigny scornfully challenges her evidence: "As white as La Blanche's." His reply is definitive: a slave at L'Abri, La Blanche looks white and her name signifies whiteness but she has given birth to quadroon boys (possibly fathered by Aubigny, who spends time at her cabin).

Désirée writes to Madame Valmondé, asking for a refutation, but Madame refuses to challenge the interpretation of a husband, offering instead a mother's love and encouraging Désirée to return home. Silent, white, "like a stone image," Désirée lays Madame's offer in front of Aubigny, and asks if she should go. In doing so, she again presents herself as a text to be written by her husband.

The final lines of "Désirée's Baby" take on a peculiarly horrific irony given the story's insistent positioning of men as interpretive authorities over women. The words written by Aubigny's mother suggest that she has not remained a blank page; she has co-authored a life with a man who loves her, a life which allows her to produce both the letter read by Aubigny, and Aubigny himself. The return of this letter to Aubigny, like the return of the repressed, speaks of the terrible costs to both men and women when the former claim complete interpretive power, and the latter acquiesce.

—Madonne M. Miner

_____

THE DEVIL AND DANIEL WEBSTER
by Stephen Vincent Benét, 1937

Primarily a poet, Stephen Vincent Benét won the Pulitzer prize with his narrative poem of the Civil War, *John*

Brown's Body. His interest in American themes is also represented in the short story, "The Devil and Daniel Webster," which received unanimously the first prize in an O. Henry Memorial award. As one of the judges remarked, "This has as fine a chance to approach immortality as any short story can attain. It is typically American, and typically New England. It is also a folk legend."

The story is a legend, combining a traditional myth with a specifically American tale. The myth is that of Faust, the man who sold his soul to the devil in return for a period of worldly fulfillment. Early versions of the myth concerned a scholar who was willing to sell his soul in exchange for knowledge. Probably the most famous versions are those of Christopher Marlowe, who created a Renaissance tragedy about the aspiring hero who ultimately is damned, according to the demonic pact, and of Johann Wolfgang von Goethe, whose 18th-century epic poem introduces a significant change, in that the doomed hero, Faust, actually achieves salvation at the end. Many variants have been composed, among them the Benét story, which adds an interesting patriotic twist.

The Faust figure in this story is Jabez Stone, a farmer in New Hampshire, who is down on his luck. His wife and children are ailing, his field is not producing crops, and his horses suddenly become ill. He is so depressed with his lot that, although he is a religious man, he vows he would sell his soul to the devil to improve his wretched fortunes. Naturally the devil shows up the very next day, in the guise of a well-dressed and soft-spoken lawyer. The pact is made. Jabez experiences seven years of prosperity, after which he persuades the devil to grant him an extension of three more years. At the end of the decade, Jabez, in desperation, asks Daniel Webster, a fellow New Hampshire man, to take on his legal case and defend him.

The story is told in the third person from the viewpoint of an omniscient observer. The story begins with the casual remark, "It's a story they tell in the border country, where Massachusetts joins Vermont and New Hampshire," and concludes with another reference to the three states. The voice is that of a rural speaker, in colloquial language, somewhat resembling that of farmer Stone. The reader has a sense of immediacy throughout.

The major characters are the unhappy farmer, Jabez, his lawyer, Daniel Webster, and the devil who prefers to be called Scratch. Jabez Stone, whose very name sounds like the hardy, struggling New England farmer, is a decent though desperate man. When he realizes that his request may endanger the soul of the great orator, Daniel Webster, he pleads with his would-be savior to leave before the devil gets him. Webster, however, in many ways a man of similar nature, an educated and rhetorical version of the down-to-earth farmer, asserts that he has never left either a case or a jug unfinished. He stays on the case, remaining calm even when the devil shows the little black box with air holes in the lid, in which he carries the souls of people he has bought.

Webster begins the case by insisting on an all-American jury. "Let it be the quick or the dead!" The members of the jury selected by the devil are a gallery of traitors and criminals, all actual figures from American history, including such notables as the pirate Teach and the cruel governor Dale, who broke men on the wheel. The judge, fittingly, is Hawthorne, who presided at the witch trials in Salem and never repented of the convictions.

Webster's appeal to the jury is brilliantly handled by Benét. At first, the doughty lawyer simply "got madder and madder," determined to "bust out with lightenings and denunciations." But as he stares at the wild glitter in the eyes of these damned souls, he realizes that would be a mistake. Instead he decides to address them as men, the men that they were rather than the damned that they have become.

At this point Benét wisely decides to resume indirect narration. He does not attempt to repeat Webster's speech word for word, but rather tells us what he talked about. He does not condemn or revile but instead talks about what makes a man a man. He speaks of the simple things, of the meaning of America and the part that even traitors have played in its development. He speaks so movingly that the diabolic glitter disappears from the eyes of the jurors who seem to return to being simply men once more. Walter Butler, the loyalist terrorist of the Revolution, delivers the verdict, astonishing the devil by finding for the defendant.

After the evocative account of Webster's appeal, the author returns to the word-for-word exchange of devil and lawyer. At this point Benét introduces a new angle, which has nothing to do with the Faust myth but much to do with his characters. The devil offers to tell Webster's fortune. The device is effective, for it brings the theme of American history full circle. Webster learns what we know, that he would never become president but that his beloved union would survive. At that final prediction, Webster characteristically bursts into comic, good-natured invective. "Why, then, you long-barreled, slab-sided, lantern-jawed, fortune-telling note shaver, . . . I'd go to the Pit itself to save the Union!" The story ends with homespun humor and with a new legend in the making. The devil, being worsted by Dan'l, has never dared to return to New Hampshire.

With its blend of down-to-earth realism and mythic imagination, the story captures the reader on many levels. It was also made into a successful one-act folk opera, with music by Douglas Moore, as well as a Hollywood film entitled *All That Money Can Buy*.

—Charlotte Spivack

THE DIAMOND AS BIG AS THE RITZ
by F. Scott Fitzgerald, 1922

Fitzgerald's "The Diamond as Big as the Ritz," written in 1921 and published the following year in *Tales of the Jazz Age*, has elicited a great deal of critical interest for many reasons; Matthew J. Bruccoli has called it a masterpiece. Fitzgerald had married in 1920; his daughter (and only child) was born in 1921. Setting aside the psychological adjustments involved in his being a newlywed and, soon after, a new father, at least one other matter apparently was working on his mind to shape his fictive fantasies. His scholastic record at Princeton from 1913 to 1917 was a drawn-out misadventure. The numerous course failures, coupled with his realization that he was unable to meet Princeton's rigid standards, shattered his hopes and dreams about proving himself academically, as a prelude to achieving even greater success in the outside world. The disillusionment resulting from his self-confessed unwillingness to do what Princeton required for its bachelor degree, coupled with the sorry results of that compelling refusal, had an effect on his outlook, which had a lasting effect on his personality. When he received rejections from editors or sustained other comparable setbacks, his emotional vulnerability was intensified.

"The Diamond as Big as the Ritz" is about the immature disillusionment of the schoolboy protagonist and his girl, at the end of the action-packed story, as they separately announce that their youth was a dream. It reveals Fitzgerald's dislike of the very rich (an animosity noted by at least one critic), as also expressed in his 1926 story, "The Rich Boy," with its explanation of just how the very rich "are different from you and me."

This ominous and grandiose story concerns young John T. Unger, from "a small town on the Mississippi," sent to an elite school near Boston, St. Midas. In his second year he is invited by a schoolmate from Montana, Percy Washington, to come home with him for the summer. As a result of this he finds himself in a death trap, at the same time that he is being allured by Percy's two beautiful sisters, Jasmine and Kismine. Percy's father—the richest man in the world—Braddock Washington, possess an extraordinary diamond mountain bigger than the Ritz-Carlton Hotel. Fearful of outside threats to his treasure trove, he keeps his family isolated and secured, though he allows Percy to attend the far-distant St. Midas School. Occasionally a fellow-student, such as John, may be invited to this precious-stone fastness of the Washington family, but that unlucky individual will not be permitted to return alive. Yet someone, a teacher of Italian, has recently escaped to tell the tale. Just before John himself is in immediate danger from his scheming host, there is an aerial attack on the paradisaical hideaway.

Desperate to save his domain, Mr. Washington makes a serious effort to bribe God, with a large chunk from his diamond-mountain, and the promise of cutting, setting, and ornamenting the diamond, in an unprecedentedly splendiferous manner. There is no reply. Seeing no other course to follow, he blows up his entire glittering alp. John and Percy's two sisters somehow manage to gain their freedom. At the end of the story John and his chosen one, Kismine (Jasmine is reduced to being a hanger-on), in a sort of wacky love duet among the ruins, utter platitudes about the end of the dream they have supposedly just experienced, and thus the end of their youth. Seeming to accept the temporary nature of their relationship, they will try to keep warm against the night chill, and go to sleep.

According to Kenneth Eble's study of Fitzgerald's literary career, "The Diamond as Big as the Ritz" may be traced to his having been invited to spend part of the summer of 1915 at the ranch of an old friend, "Sap" Donahoe. The two were kindred spirits and schoolmates, first at Newman, a wealthy Catholic boarding school in New Jersey, and later at Princeton. Andrew Turnbull, in his biography of Fitzgerald, remarks, of the two months Fitzgerald spent at Donahoe's Wyoming ranch, that while outdoor life did not appeal to him, he made himself accompany the rustlers in their occupational activities and joined in their recreations—drinking and poker playing, but incurred the hatred of the ranch manager for finding out about his secret liaison. The complexity, multiplicity of thematic elements, and density of symbols and allusions in the resulting story have several sources apart from Fitzgerald's time at the ranch.

There is first of all the title and primary symbol. The untold benefits a Ritz-size (or larger) diamond mountain might offer suggest an old folksong that Fitzgerald might have heard: "The Big Rock Candy Mountains," which describes a hobo's utopia that offers all manner of delights to have-nots with a sizable want list. Then there are traces of Dante's *Divine Comedy*, as well as a number of allusions to the Bible and Christianity, transposed out of traditional contexts to suggest that Fitzgerald meant to rewrite or reinvent certain elements of the culture in which he was raised. The more obvious of these references have been noted by Joan M. Allen in her book on Fitzgerald's Catholic sensibility. For example, the "Dantesque motto" over the gates of Hades, John's hometown: presumably "All hope abandon, ye who enter here," yet the actual words do not appear in the story. Then the little settlement of Fish, suggesting the Greek word-symbol of Jesus; and the 12 Godless apostle-like men of Fish waiting daily for the Transcontinental Express, all within an ambience devoid of Christianity.

John's early life in Hades seems to represent the *Inferno* stage of human experience. Fitzgerald includes a number of gags about the heat in Hades, worthy of college humor magazines of the early 1900's, but which appear vapid to a reader in the 1990's. John's stay at St. Midas School would then represent the *Purgatorio* stage, to the extent that John was being prepared spiritually or psychologically for the *Paradiso*. John's guide here to that next stage is Percy Washington. But Percy, a direct descendant of George Washington (who in reality had no direct descendants), takes him to another kind of *Inferno*, where outsiders should be forewarned by the familiar sign, "All hope abandon, ye who enter here." Escaping from that other *Inferno*, The Diamond As Big As The Ritz, John at the end of the story is bedded down near his girl, Kismine, on a high cliff, under the stars, and they contemplate their future life together, in a kind of travesty of paradise.

If this possible linkage (however twisted) with Dante seems far-fetched, another citation involving a kind of religion may be more understandable, on closer analysis. The scene in which Percy's father attempts to bribe God—with what Fitzgerald aptly calls "a quality of monstrous condescension"—is given relatively brief notice by the critics. But the implications of the man's attempt at bribery should be considered more closely, in light of Fitzgerald's remarks on the scene he has described. Fitzgerald reminds the reader, using a reference from Greek mythology to help make his point: "Prometheus Enriched" was demonstrating sacrifices, rituals, and prayers that had become obsolete before Jesus was born.

A broad range of satire informs the entire story: suggestive wordplay (a Rolls-Pierce motorcar, symbolizing both Rolls-Royce and Pierce-Arrow, Kismine using her name to invite John to kiss her); ridicule or insult (certain references to the living habits of Braddock Washington's black slaves, one of whom is named Gygsum ["Some Jig"?]); romantic comedy (the first meeting of John and Kismine); and, among other things, socio-religious criticism (the effect of the absence of religion in Fish, and the workings of the money religion at St. Midas School and within Braddock Washington). Considering the fact that Fitzgerald was hardly the one to correct society's foibles in the area of purse-pride, the much-commented-on social satire running throughout "Diamond" ought not to obscure other important aspects of the story not yet touched on here.

The influence of Mark Twain merits some consideration. Matthew Bruccoli cites evidence of Fitzgerald's exposure to a number of works by and about Mark Twain, and credits Twain with being an early influence on Fitzgerald. He makes two significant comments: first, Twain had "minimal direct influence" on what Fitzgerald wrote; and second, the coal mountain in Twain's (and co-author Charles Dudley Warner's) *The Gilded Age* may have suggested the diamond mountain in the present story. While the second statement seems farfetched, the "minimal direct influence" idea should be considered in the light of the following points: John Unger's family came from a small town on the Mississippi River; Mark Twain grew up in the town of Hannibal, Missouri, situated on the Mississippi River, and he immortalized that town in his best-known stories; Fitzgerald himself was born in a town on the Mississippi River, St. Paul, Minnesota. Though the coal mountain in *The Gilded Age* seems to have very little in common with Fitzgerald's diamond mountain, the money-madness that informs the present story may be found in some form throughout Twain's writings, including the bitterly nihilistic novelette, *The Mysterious Stranger*. Fitzgerald had already read *The Mysterious Stranger* by the time he wrote "The Diamond as Big as the Ritz," as noted in a letter to his editor at Scribners, Maxwell Perkins, dated December 12, 1921.

"The Diamond as Big as the Ritz" has much in common with the boys' adventure stories of the late 19th and early 20th centuries. An individual boy or a small group of boys ventures into totally unfamiliar territory—possibly involving a cave, an underground domain, a hitherto inaccessible region—encountering deadly danger but finding no way to get out. Eventually at least one escapes, somewhat transformed by the experience, which (in some versions) may serve as an initiation into manhood. Often a taboo violation is involved, which puts the adventurer(s) in dire peril. Charlotte Perkins Gilman, for example, adapted this format for her boy-men in her 1915 feminist adventure novel, *Herland*. There the three jolly chums intrude into a two-thousand-year-old realm "For Women Only," with surprising results. Fitzgerald's schoolboy appears at the end, as he and his girl speculate about the future, to foreshadow the way his creator would appear from time to time in the coming years: fatuous, frivolous, and juvenile.

—Samuel I. Bellman

THE DIARY OF A MADMAN (Kuangren riji)
by Lu Xun, 1923

"Kuangren riji" ("The Diary of a Madman," also "A Madman's Diary") is Lu Xun's first successful story. It was written twelve years after he abandoned his medical studies at Sendai, Japan, believing, as he put it, that medical science was less important than "changing the spirit" of "the people of a weak and backward country." The story was first published in *La Jeunesse* (New Youth), a radical magazine advocating democratic revolution. When it first appeared, in April 1918, at the dawn of the New Literature Movement in China, the story took readers by storm. Liberal critics all over China hailed the story as epoch-making. It was included in Lu Xun's first collection of short stories, *Na Han* (*Call to Arms*), in 1923, and regularly anthologized from the 1920's to the present. Today, it is recognized world-wide as marking the beginning of contemporary literature in China, and its author is regarded as the father of modern Chinese literature.

The story is relatively plotless, beginning with a brief introduction by an unnamed narrator informing us that his former schoolmate had kept a diary during a period of mental illness. It then plunges directly into the apparently chaotic, turbulent self-revelations of the madman's diary, presented in 13 sections of varying lengths. However, elements in the story are highly symbolic. Its central, gruesome image of cannibalism should be viewed at two levels. On the surface, it presents a shocking, paranoid narrative of cannibalism as a driving force throughout Chinese history to the present: "Last year they executed a criminal in the city, and a consumptive soaked a piece of bread in his blood and sucked it." At a deeper level, it also serves as a symbol of old Confucian Chinese culture. "The whole book" of Chinese history, according to the madman, is "filled with the two words—'Eat people'." Of the other symbolic scenes in the story, one at the end of section ten deserves particular attention for its obvious social relevance. Here the madman imagines himself confined in a "pitch dark" room, trapped under a mounting pile of beams and rafters. This reinforces the tragic image of the madman as a conscious fighter suppressed and imprisoned in "an iron house having not a single window and virtually indestructible." However, the deliberate arrangement of the 13 sections of the protagonist's diary may suggest a way out of the narrative of entrapment. At the end of a "perfect cycle" (for which the number is twelve in Chinese horoscopes), there appears an "extra" 13th section. Although consisting of only two brief sentences, it signifies the possibility of both a formal and prophetic break from established frameworks: "Perhaps there are still children who haven't eaten men?"

Most critics of Lu Xun's work agree that the story's historical significance lies in the revolutionary appeal of its new theme. Through a madman's voice, obsessed with cannibalism, the author lodged a powerful protest against orthodox social conventions. It was a forceful "call to arms" to the Chinese people, most of whom were then still deep in slumber in the dark "iron house."

Critics also noted the story's importance in promoting the use of vernacular Chinese at the time, for serious creative purposes, as well as its unusual employment of the diary format to generate an unprecedented intensity of focus on the subjective, interior life of the madman. Lu Xun himself commented on "The Diary of a Madman" that, "I must have relied entirely on the hundred or more foreign stories I had read and a smattering of medical knowledge." It is obvious that the intense psychological probings of the madman and the stirring voice of the narrator of the story were the result of borrowings from foreign literature. (Critics and Lu Xun himself have all referred to Gogol, whose similarly titled story appeared in 1834.) However, his assimilation of both foreign literary influences and the vernacular elements gave his work a wholly original flavour.

Recent critics, especially from the West, have been more interested in the technical aspects of the story. The juxtaposition of what are in effect two texts—an utterly conventional preface written in classical Chinese declaring that the madman had "recovered some time ago" and gone somewhere "to take up an official post," alongside an extraordinarily unconventional diary written in vernacular Chinese demonstrating the chaotically tortured mind of the protagonist—produces an effect similar to that of surrealistic art and literature. Drawing on his knowledge of medicine, and his personal experience with a relative suffering from a persecution complex, Lu Xun succeeds in portraying vividly the incoherent, nightmarish world of a psychopath. This authentic portrait is enclosed in a pretentious narrative framework, which undermines the illusion that the protagonist is simply mentally deranged. It also generates powerful narrative ironies. The madman, who is in reality awakened to the evil of his society, is "treated and cared for" by "healthy people" whose souls and bodies are in fact poisoned by the traditional norms; the seemingly random thoughts that tell the truth are prefaced by apparently fluent, elegant words that disclose nothing but stale clichés.

Another strikingly new feature of the story is the absence of any naturalistic delineation of physical background, time scale, or character—resulting in expressionist or symbolic effects, which some Western critics claimed were evidence of foreign influence. Chinese scholars have nevertheless argued that he learned such apparently modern expressionist techniques from local Chinese operas. Lu Xun himself wrote: "The old Chinese theatre has no scenery, and the New Year pictures sold to children show a few main figures only." While consciously borrowing from abroad, and incorporating innovative vernacular elements in his writing, Lu Xun certainly also inherited a great deal from the rich tradition of Chinese art and literature. In this combination lies the strength and charm of "The Diary of a Madman."

—Shifen Gong

DID YOU EVER SLIP ON RED BLOOD?
by Joyce Carol Oates, 1972

No one story can typify Joyce Carol Oates's enormously varied short fiction, but "Did You Ever Slip on Red Blood?" (from *Marriages and Infidelities*, a volume thematically concerned with variations on betrayal), is typical in the sense that it could hardly have been written by anyone else. Its collocation of sex and violence, its evoking of the fevered Vietnam War era and of the trappings of U.S. pop culture, its picture of psychosis as something recognizable, almost familiar, and above all, the nonjudgmental distance the narrator maintains—all attest that we are in Oates's America. It is a place both banal and lurid, where intimacy and impersonality somehow coexist, creating an explosive mixture that frequently does in fact explode.

The typical Oatesian combination of intimacy with her characters and nonjudgmental detachment from them is especially functional in this story, which is essentially about ways of knowing. It is a love story, a powerful one, but even the lovers hardly like one another. Oberon, the FBI sharpshooter, is convinced that "no one knew Marian Vernon except him," but Marian's half-hysterical question *"did you ever slip on red blood yourself?"* epitomizes a fundamental separation even from him. Emotional contact between people is an impossibility; even physical contact is fenced around by pain and danger. To Severin the very breath, the touch of his accomplice Jacob Appleman are abrasive; the first meeting even of the lovers Marian and Oberon takes place across a locked and chained door, one of several closed or slightly cracked apertures in the story. The extent of failed communication is revealed, in a half-comical but startling way, by the curious incident in which Marian asks Oberon how much his wife "knows." He thinks she is concerned that the wife may "sense" the adulterous love affair, but Marian refers to the impossibility of the wife's—or anyone else's—understanding what the killing of Severin felt like, literally or figuratively.

The two sensory modes of knowing in the world of the story are tactile and optical. The first of these is Marian's mode. For her, one knows about red blood by touching it, *slipping* on it. She never reads; even when her picture and Oberon's appear in the newspaper she traces their outlines with her fingertips. In the story's first paragraph she shuts her eyes to invite her lover's stare. The blinds of their dim-lighted love nest are closed, like the shutter of a camera; "here he had to see her with his hands." From her end of the long trajectory leading back from Severin's body, pressed against her own, to Oberon's eye, rifle, and sniperscope, she insists that *"I felt the kick myself. I felt it. I felt you."* This is a story in which normally abstract metaphors become startlingly palpable: red-bloodedness, guts (Severin's bowel problems), getting a kick out of something.

Oberon's way of knowing (and Severin's too, though in a more ambiguous way) is through the eyes, and typically through artificial, technology-aided images and close-ups. Oberon is proud of his "perfect" vision. Unlike Marian, he is a reader, and although he never actually writes his plaintive letter to the celebrity folk singer Jacob Appleman, Oberon obviously thinks in such telespatial terms. Both he and Severin are associated repeatedly with optical and visual instruments: a magnifying telescopic rifle sight (which turns physical distance into simulated closeness), a television set, a movie screen. Severin imagines his image on such a screen as "blown up, enlarged, exaggerated." (His $1.98 aviator's glasses are a ludicrous but revealing parody of such optical sophistication.) Oberon defines his identity through his presence in an imagined group photograph. When he is not in Marian's physical presence, she slips "out of focus." The distance between Marian's tactile mode and the male visual mode in the story is epitomized in a small, telling detail from one of the love scenes: "a strand of her hair stung his eye."

The most urgent problem in the story is the relation between love and violence. Marian and Oberon are drawn to each other exactly because of their joint involvement, from opposite ends, in the gory incident. Sexual parallels emerge in the phrasing and images: Oberon's sharpshooter eyes are "like muscles, tensing, erect, . . . getting to know [the stranger's face] closely, intimately"; Severin dies orgasmically: "She caught the fullness of his weight . . . , his body gone heavy, the blood gushing from him and onto her." In the work of most other writers, it seems fair to say, the connection of the killing with lovemaking would amount to an ironically moralizing, probably cynical, commentary on love or society, and although there is nothing to keep us from reading the Oates story too that way, it is by no means clear that we should do so. In "Did You Ever Slip on Red Blood?" sex and violence are not so much analogous as, almost, synonymous; Oberon's wrestling in sexual play with Marian blends with a demonstration of how easily he could have overcome the less potent Severin, who also had once pressed up against Marian in an intimacy that was "an embrace and yet not an embrace." This powerful story probes deeper than social commentary on the Vietnam era, deeper even than commentary on American society in general. Without registering overt disturbance, it says something disturbing about the ultimate, and mysterious, recesses of human motivation.

—Brian Wilkie

THE DOLL
by Edna O'Brien, 1982

Commentators on Edna O'Brien's work often point out that coming to terms with the trauma of personal loss is a recurring concern. In addition, there is widespread agreement that when this theme is given an Irish location, the author's control of her material is more assured. Both personal loss and Irish setting are most in evidence in a collection of stories with a significant title, *Returning*, published in 1982. All nine stories are located in the environment of her first novel, *The Country Girls*: the rural west of Ireland in the 1940's—even some of the village characters from that novel reappear here. In each, the adult narrator is dwelling on memories of her childhood as a young girl, a farmer's daughter, very much part of the community, the "parish."

"The Doll," originally published in *Redbook*, a New York magazine for young women, in December 1979, is the shortest story in the collection. In it the major themes are most clearly foregrounded. Unlike her longer tales, which enjoy a freedom to explore village characters and interesting episodes, the focus here remains on the emotions of the narrator. The opening sentence ("Every Christmas there came a present of a doll from a lady I scarcely knew") immediately introduces the subject and establishes that perspective of looking back. It also leaves an impression of wistfulness, supported later in the opening paragraph by memories of childhood Christmases as times of family "bustle and excitement," times that implied that "untoward happiness was about to befall us."

The narrator's thoughts are soon concentrated on one doll in particular. It was special—"the living representation of a princess"—and childish wonder at its lifelikeness is fondly recalled. There is an intimation that it evoked a world beyond the confines of the village, some romantic, glamorous place where life might be very different. There is an added suggestion, then unrecognised by the child, that it symbolised some fulfillment in life she might aim for later.

The scene quickly shifts to the local school and a teacher's daily cruelty towards the girl. This was inexplicable at the time but is perceived by the adult narrator as motivated by jealousy of a bright, intelligent child. One Christmas the adoption of her favourite doll as the Blessed Virgin in a school play was welcomed by the bewildered girl as a way of ameliorating her teacher's attitude. The doll proved to be one of the few successful features of the play, but rather than being grateful, the teacher kept it, without any explanation. The reason seems to be that she not only begrudged the girl her potential for a better life elsewhere, but wanted to make a gesture at aspiring towards something more fulfilling for herself.

The story may be short, but the timespan is long. The narrative moves suddenly to the narrator's adult life in some cosmopolitan centre, her description introduced by reflections on how impressions of people from childhood are infused in everyone we later meet: "Those we knew, though absent, are yet merged inextricably into new folk, so that each person is to us a sum of many others . . ." The "new folk" turn out to be drifting, rootless people, only sketchily presented here, but with enough detail to confirm the narrator's disillusionment that a better life has not been achieved simply by going away.

The change of scene is matched by a change of style. To readers this proves unsettling, and some commentators have seen the wrench out of the childhood story as a weakness. It is possible instead to see it as a device to prevent the reader from just "returning" to familiar O'Brien territory and not attending to the narrator's attempt at making sense of her experiences.

A short final section centres on her inevitable return home as an adult. This visit only increases feelings of alienation. The doll is long faded, the teacher dead, and her

son full of unease at how to treat this urban stranger. The story moves to a close as the narrator walks down the village street, "where I walk in memory, morning noon and night," filled with thoughts of "wretchedness" rather than of achievement. However, the gloom does lift momentarily. She experiences anew relief at having escaped, and steps out with renewed determination to continue striving for some personal fulfillment. A futile goal, we conclude, but still worthy of the attempt.

The prevailing mood in "The Doll" is reflective and sombre. While there are glimpses of happiness, in the family preparations for Christmas, for instance, the concentration on the narrator's emotional trauma and her increasing awareness of pain confirms there will be little light. In addition, as in the first story in the collection, "The Connor Girls," the distance between childhood immersion in village life and adult alienation is emphasised by that entry of the narrator into the story.

In an interview with Philip Roth in *The New York Times Book Review*, O'Brien commented on her obsession with her childhood: "One is dogged by the past—pain, sensations, rejections, all of it. I do believe that this clinging to the past is a zealous, albeit hopeless desire to reinvent it so that one could change it." Nowhere is such intense emotional involvement with her past better illustrated than in this brief tale.

—F. C. Molloy

THE DOLL QUEEN (La muñeca reina)
by Carlos Fuentes, 1964

"The Doll Queen" originally appeared as "La muñeca reina" in *Cantar de ciegos* in 1964. It is one of several tales by Carlos Fuentes that involve variations on the theme of the triple lunar goddess (maiden, matron, and witch or hag), deity of birth, love, and death, visible as the new, full, and old or waning moon. Worshipped under many names, the goddess is associated with numerous sacred animals, emblems, and other attributes, as well as with madness, obsession, fertility, spiritual love, and lust, death-in-life and life-in-death. Fuentes, well-acquainted with myths from many cultures, is interested also in the occult and in exotic religions, likewise relevant to understanding "The Doll Queen."

Narrated by a male protagonist, the tale recounts his impulsive search for a long-lost friend, Amilamia who 15 years before used to play near the place where he studied in a garden or park. Memories of Amilamia reconstruct her as an idealized version of the child or maiden, associated with symbols of the White Goddess: she appears in a "lake of clover," water and three-leaved plants being emblems of the moon goddess. She wears a white skirt (visible sign of virginity) and invariably carries a pocketful of "white blossoms" (associated with the casting of spells). Amilamia is remembered in the wind, "her mouth open and eyes half closed against the streaming air" (the White Goddess traditionally controls the winds). The second stage of the Goddess, nymph or goddess of love, is suggested as a dream of the narrator, "the women in my books, the quintessential female . . . who assumed the disguise of Queen . . . the imagined beings of mythology," and as a potential of

Amilamia/Aphrodite, insinuated when their last romp acquired unexpected erotic undertones.

Amilamia is not a normal or usual name, but one invented by Fuentes, probably referring to the *lamia,* another legendary being, commonly represented in classical mythology with the head and breast of a woman and the body of a serpent. Lamias were female demons, reputedly vampires, believed to lure youths to where they could suck their blood. In Mexican mythology (especially relevant for a Mexican writer), they are associated with the loss or death of children, specifically with women whose children have died. Amilamia's death proves to be figurative, but such connotations allow Fuentes to suggest the monstrous and to hint at danger while keeping the details of his narrative within the bounds of reality.

After Amilamia disappears from the garden—a microcosm of earth—and the hero goes to seek her, there are analogies with Demeter's search for Persephone (and Amilamia is Kore or Persephone) and Orpheus's seeking Euridice. The hero must figuratively enter the underworld, "descend the hill . . . cut through that narrow grove" and cross a busy avenue, a figurative Styx, to reach a "gray suburb," "dead-end streets," a tomblike house whose Greek adornments subtly indicate the presence of myth beneath the narrative surface. "Harsh, irregular breathing" heard through the door betrays a sort of Cerberus (watchdog of Hades) whose function is to prevent intercourse between the two worlds, and indeed, the initial attempt at entry fails. Later description of this guardian terms him an "asthmatic old bear" who wears a "turtle's mask," a composite mythological beast like the lamia and the three-headed hound of Hades with snakes protruding from its neck and shoulders.

Returning under the pretext of conducting an assessment, the narrator discovers a woman of fifty, "dressed in black . . . with no makeup and her salt-and-pepper hair pulled into a knot," with eyes "so indifferent they seem almost cruel." The witchlike appearance and chaplet she carries—a figurative key—identify the woman with Hecate, the Terrible Mother, associated with cruelty and the lower world (death). A clue indicating Amilamia's presence in the tomblike abode is the symbolic fruit "where little teeth have left their mark in the velvety skin and ocher flesh," clearly evoking Persephone and the pomegranate.

When forced to confess the true motive for his visit, the narrator is conducted to the funereal chamber holding the dolls and forgotten toys of Amilamia, with its sickly floral scent and small coffin displaying the "doll queen who presides over the pomp of this royal chamber of death." The doll-cadaver maintained in the bedroom is death-in-life, one aspect of the White Goddess. The spectacle convinces the nauseated narrator that Amilamia had died long years before, and he leaves the underworld overcome with sympathy for the bereaved parents. Only chance determines that the story does not end with the supposed revelation of death.

Accidentally discovering the child's card months afterward, he returns in the belief it may assuage the parent's grief. As he approaches the door, several motifs evoke the goddess of fertility or vegetation (another aspect of the lunar goddess): "Rain is beginning to fall . . . bringing out of the earth . . . the odor of dewy benediction that stirs the humus and quickens all that lives." The dwarfish, deformed body of the "misshapen girl" found in the wheelchair with a "hump on her chest" incarnates a degraded variant of the myth; the comic book suggests she may also be mentally retarded. The guardian's reaction is that of Cerberus preventing contact with the outsider: "Get back!

Devil's spawn! Do I have to beat you again?" Persephone imprisoned, Amilamia appears here as the goddess of death-in-life, unable to leave the tomb or participate in the world beyond.

As a self-conscious writer, admirable critic and literary theoretician well aware of the mythological sources of his inspiration, Fuentes (who is well read and fluent in English) may have been familiar with *The White Goddess* or *The Golden Bough,* or may have used original myths. The usefulness of mythic analysis of Fuentes's works using Aztec deities as the archetypes has been repeatedly demonstrated; classical mythology is a comparably significant instrument.

—Janet Pérez

DOWN AT THE DUMP
by Patrick White, 1964

The story "Down at the Dump" (in *The Burnt Ones,* 1964) revisits and successfully reworks a theme the Australian writer Patrick White explored repeatedly during his half-century career as creator of novels, plays, short fiction, poems, and finally political polemic. This theme provided the focus and title for his second novel, *The Living and the Dead* (1941), but can be seen to operate throughout his *oeuvre*. It is that of a choice of allegiances. White often categorizes his characters in terms of their brave affirmation of life and its cyclic processes, or their retreat toward death and its allies: sterility, rigidity, moral prudery, fear of growth and change, the worship of convention, and the abhorrence of nature. Ironically, of course, death triumphs over those who enlist under its banner. Only by aligning oneself with life can death be understood and encompassed within a wider scheme.

In this story, the battle lines between opposing camps are drawn early. Residing in houses that face each other across a road in White's fictional Sydney suburb of Sarsaparilla are two families, the Whalleys and the Hogbens. Middle-aged, sagging, and down at the heels, the Whalleys resell junk and live in chaos. But their profession is made emblematic of their central function in the story: to proclaim and assist the process of resurrection, by means of which life invades and conquers death. Just as their junk dealership gives a new life of usefulness to discarded objects, The Whalleys' abiding love and recurring lust for each other continually renew their relationship. Early in the story, White says of them: "Their faces were lit by the certainty of life."

The Hogbens, however, are certain only of death. The immediate occasion for this knowledge is the death of Mrs. Myrtle Hogben's sister Daise, whose burial is to take place that day. But White associates the Hogbens with death in many other ways as well, especially with Myrtle. Mrs. Hogben is thin, dry, withered, and terrified of her own mortality. She is also ferociously attached to the perishable, that is, to status and possessions, a quality White gives to only his most despicable characters. Most telling as a sign of her alliance with death is her small-minded resentment of her sister's large, gracious, and generous life.

Two young emissaries from these warring factions—the teenagers Meg Hogben and "Lum" (William) Whalley—are brought together over the body of Daise Morrow, a woman related by blood to the Hogbens, but by temperament to the Whalleys. Daise recycles people as the Whalleys do trash. She has reignited the fires of life and love in Jack Cunningham, the long-suffering husband of an invalid wife, and in an old derelict named Ossie Coogan, whom she finds lying amidst horse manure and brings home in the wheelbarrow she had intended to use for the fertilizer. The linkage of feces and the catarrhal old man is typical of White in its suggestion that even repugnant manifestations of life are valuable and can be redeemed. Daise acts the role of redeemer here: manuring her garden into luxuriant growth and offering Ossie a rejuvenating love which is at once maternal, spiritual, and sexual. Ossie is restored by Daise's simple belief in the necessity of loving "what we are given to love."

At Daise's funeral, Meg and Lum discover that they have been given each other to love. They meet and enjoy their first, tentative kisses after Meg has wandered away from her aunt's interment and Lum from his parents' pursuit of the salvageable in the dump which abuts the cemetery. White's point in establishing this unlikely juxtaposition seems to be that both dump and graveyard are sites of potential resurrection. As the story progresses, Daise Morrow and the two young people will all undergo resurrections of sorts.

Meg Hogben is clearly identified as Daise's spiritual heir, and is thus possessed of her aunt's transformative imagination. She and Daise can both reshape life as poetry, seeing carnations as "frozen fireworks" melting into dizzying motion in the early morning sun. Meg also projects Lum Whalley into his own future, one in which the unpretentious profession of truck driving becomes his contribution to poetry. In this passage, Meg imagines herself as Lum's wife, riding with him on a night run in his truck:

> She saw it. She saw the people standing at their doors, frozen in the blocks of yellow light. The rushing of the night made the figures for ever still. All around she could feel the furry darkness, as the semi-trailer roared and bucked, its skeleton of coloured lights. While in the cabin, in which they sat, all was stability and order. If she glanced sideways she could see how his taffy hair shone when raked by the bursts of electric light. They had brought cases with toothbrushes, combs, one or two things—the pad on which she would write the poem somewhere when they stopped in the smell of sunlight dust ants. But his hands had acquired such mastery over the wheel, it appeared this might ever happen. Nor did she care.

The heroic stature which Meg accords Lum here remakes him as a worthy partner, just as Daise's tenderness transfigured Ossie.

The engine driving all these metamorphoses is love, which is the force a resurrected Daise celebrates in the speech White imagines she might have given to those gathered around her grave. The text of her sermon is life everlasting:

> Truly, we needn't experience tortures, unless we build chambers in our minds to house instruments of hatred in. Don't you know, my darling creatures, that death isn't death, unless it's the death of love? Love should be the greatest explosion it is reasonable to expect. Which sends us whirling, spinning, creating millions of other worlds. Never destroying.

White's version of immortality locates it securely within this life, where it can be as fertile and procreative as other forms of love. That Meg and Lum will achieve these several kinds of love is suggested by the story's closing paragraph, in which Meg senses a "warm core of certainty," which recalls the Whalleys' faces "lit by the certainty of life," and which White associates with nature's persistent resurrections.

This paean to life's victories over death is placed last in a 1964 collection of White's short fiction called *The Burnt Ones*. The story strikes one of the few affirmative notes in a volume peopled, for the most part, by those who are morally and/or spiritually damaged, those whose capacity for engagement with life has been scorched by events. Meg and Lum are clearly of a different ilk. They are among the privileged few in White's work who search for and even sometimes find what he has called "the extraordinary behind the ordinary, the mystery and the poetry which alone could make [life] bearable. . . ." In "Down at the Dump" Meg and Lum begin to explore one of life's deepest mysteries. While the parson reminds the mourners that "in the midst of life we are in death," the boy and girl learn that the reverse is equally true. Life penetrates death as well. Garbage nurtures seeds, and abandoned junk is swathed in living vines. This knowledge of the interdependence of life and death comes only to the *illuminati* in White's fiction. The fact that he ends his volume with a story of initiation into such awareness indicates that the fires that singe so many of "the burnt ones" can also light up the darkness.

—Carolyn Bliss

E

END OF THE GAME (Final del juego)
by Julio Cortázar, 1956

Along with Gabriel García Márquez, Mario Vargas Llosa, Carlos Fuentes, José Donoso, and others, the Argentine Julio Cortázar made possible the "boom" in Latin American fiction. Famous for both his novels and short stories, Cortázar contributed significantly to the modern short story by stretching it in a number of different directions. He excelled in stories of the fantastic and metempsychosis with works such as "La noche boca arriba" ("The Night Face Up") and "Axolotl." He wrote excellent psychological stories that are often open-ended, such as "Carta a una señorita en Paris" ("Letter to a Young Lady in Paris"), and, at the same time, he wrote fine examples of what is usually called realism. As a translator and theorist of the short story, he made significant contributions. In "Algunos aspectos del cuento" ("Some Aspects of the Short Story"), he observed that the novel was like a movie and the short story like a photograph.

Cortázar is often credited with being a master at depicting the psychology of children and adolescents. A number of his stories, among them "Siesta," "Los venenos" ("Poisons"), and "La señorita Cora" ("Nurse Cora"), present very serious themes filtered through the perspectives of young people. "Final del juego" ("End of the Game"), the title story of a 1956 collection, is such a story. Like "Siesta," it is an example of cross-gender writing, in this case of a male author describing the emotions of a female protagonist.

"End of the Game" involves three girls: Leticia, Holanda, and the narrator. These cousins in their early teens create their imaginary "kingdom," a place of escape where they play a game called "statues and attitudes." Located near their home in Palermo, a neighborhood of Buenos Aires, the "kingdom" is a grove of willows near a railroad track. There they have a daily audience on the 2:08 commuter train for whom they pose as either attitudes (envy, shame, fear, jealousy) or statues (Venus, for example). The game, which has been going on for more than a year, allows the girls to escape the ordinary world of the kitchen chores and the authority of their mother and aunt.

The game turns serious when a series of notes are thrown from the train by a young man named Ariel B. In one of the notes, Ariel declares that the prettiest is also the laziest, and the girls know that he is referring to Leticia. Ariel's final note says that he will visit the girls the next day. Leticia suffers from an unspecific disease, but one that is clearly paralytic and crippling, and she chooses not to meet Ariel; instead she writes a letter to him that Holanda delivers.

The climax of the game and story occurs the following day, when Leticia secretly takes both her mother's and aunt's jewelry, adorns herself for her final and most impressive statue, and Ariel leans out the window to look at her. The narrator and Holanda run to catch her and see the tears streaming down her face. The next day Leticia is ill, and Holanda and the narrator return to watch the train pass. As they imagine that Ariel is seated on the other side of the train looking at the river, they realize that the game has ended.

This poignant story reveals the confusion and despair that the girls feel when they must face reality in their make-believe kingdom. Although the reader sympathizes with and hurts for Leticia, the main focus finally falls on the narrator, who undergoes a process of growth or initiation. Because of Cortázar's imagination and talent, the reader sees the world from the viewpoint of the young girl, whose innocence and limitations give the story its flavor. At first, the narrator is jealous of Leticia because of the favors that are granted to her by the watchful mother and aunt. But, as she witnesses Leticia's reaction to Ariel's overtures, she slowly begins to realize the enormous burden that Leticia must bear permanently.

Cortázar enriches the story by choosing the name Ariel. Although not uncommon in Argentina, the name clearly is an allusion to José Enrique Rodó's *Ariel,* a work exhorting the young people of Latin America to eschew materialism in favor of idealism. *Ariel* is an ironic intertext for the story, for all of its optimism and hope for the future seems contrary to the unspoken loss of dreams that the girls suffer when they realize what the future holds for Leticia.

Hemingway's famous "iceberg principle" from *Death in the Afternoon* is particularly suitable for this story. Because the reader must rely on the young narrator for all of the information in the story, there are obvious details that are missing. For example, the reader is not told what Leticia said in the letter nor what disease she has. Still, Cortázar does a splendid job of cross-gender writing through his revelation of the mind and emotions of the young narrator. The story has been recognized as a fine study of juvenile psychology.

—Wendell M. Aycock

EROSTRATUS
by Jean-Paul Sartre, 1939

When he wrote "Erostratus" in 1936, Jean-Paul Sartre was seven years out of college. He had begun a very close relationship with Simone de Beauvoir which would, however, permit physical infidelities on both sides, he had completed his military service, he had gone through a considerable inheritance left to him by his grandmother, and he had spent a year working at the French Institute in Berlin in order to study with the German philosopher Husserl, who had developed a particular brand of "phenomenology" from Hegel.

Sartre was teaching philosophy at a Le Havre school, and Beauvoir was at Rouen, about 75 kilometres away. Sartre was having a liaison with Olga Kosakiewicz, one of

Beauvoir's pupils. He had rewritten a rejected first novel, *The Diary of Antoine Roquentin,* to be published in French as *La Nausée* in 1938, but in 1936 he had published nothing, although a publisher, Alcan, had accepted the reworked and less original first part of his thesis, to be published that year as *L'Imagination* (*Imagination: A Psychological Critique*). He did not vote in the 1932 or 1936 elections, although he was drifting steadily towards the left, and had supported the Front Populaire in a rejected newspaper article in 1936. He had read Kafka, had begun to regard Dos Passos as "the greatest writer of our time," and, in pursuit of his study of image-formation in the brain, had injected himself in hospital with mescalin. It took him six months to get over the hallucinations.

When "Erostratus" was published in 1939, it accompanied four other pieces of short fiction in *Le Mur* (*The Wall and Other Stories,* also *Intimacy and Other Stories*). When he wrote it, Sartre had the *Roquentin* novel, which still needed pruning. Like the novel, it was the product of Sartre's need to explore fictionally the sort of mental experience he was also philosophically analysing in the course of his academic career. He had been hurt by Gallimard's initial rejection of his novel, and was looking for a philosophy to explain his own experience.

The commercial viability of synchronized sound in the cinema dates from 1930, from which year date the earliest popular "talkies." Chaplin had established his idiosyncratic personal style in the days of silent films, relying on his peculiar gait, jerky movements, ineptitude with mechanical contraptions, and perky ability to come out on top against the odds, and after 1930 remained determinedly out-of-date. At Easter in 1936 Sartre and Beauvoir saw the recently released and ironically named silent Chaplin movie *Modern Times* twice in a Paris cinema. They found irresistible the incongruity on which Chaplin's humour is based, and Sartre called his great postwar cultural review *Les Temps modernes* after the Chaplin film, a private joke he shared with Beauvoir. There is a grim humour in "Erostratus" which has its origins in Chaplin.

"Erostratus" concerns the way in which individual experience relates one to the world in which one lives. So stated, that is the theme of virtually all Sartre's fiction and drama, but all five of the short stories published in the 1939 collection focus on the isolation of individuals in the world, and thereby emphasize the centre of Sartre's imaginative concern in a way a single novel could not. "Erostratus" has a first-person narrator, and one of the other characters, Massé, tells him that he is like Erostratus, remembered for having gratuitously burned down the temple at Ephesus, one of the seven wonders of the world, simply in order to be famous. We realise from the opening that the narrator, too, is groping for some way to affirm his individual identity.

The story starts with what is presented as a reflection in the mind of the narrator, conscious of something that separates him from others. The statement is neutral, "Men, you must see them from above. I put out the light and went to the window." From on top people look bizarre. How does a bowler hat look from a sixth-floor balcony? The people in the street do not know how to fight the great enemy of "the Human," which is its de-humanizing vertical perspective. The narrator laughs.

That first paragraph is skilful. It establishes an ambiguity that will only increase. Is the narrator mad, sad, isolated, alienated, lucky, or unlucky to feel no association with the people in the street? What sort of irony is implied by referring to the collectivity of human beings as "the Human," with a capital letter? Why, we might ask, are they

as incongruous to the narrator as Chaplin's antics are to us? Any glance back at the history of western European literature since before Proust reveals an increasing need to explore the boundaries between the sane and the insane, the rationally ordered conscious and the riotously uncontrolled images that obtrude into it with apparent spontaneity from outside. It was that boundary that interested Sartre philosophically, and which he here explores imaginatively.

The narrator wonders whether his physical elevation above the passers-by is a sign of moral superiority. He reflects how unpleasant it is to be among the others in the street, physically, but also morally part of the collectivity. If you are on their level, you cannot think of them as ants. Morally as well as physically? The narrator makes up his mind that humanity is hostile. People love one another, would have shaken his hand. But they would have beaten him up if they had known who he really was. He buys a gun, caresses its butt in his pocket, practises shooting at a fair, takes a prostitute to a room, makes her undress, thinks of shooting her in the hole between her legs, decides not to, makes her beat him, gives her a lot of money, and goes home. Three nights running he dreams of making six bullet-holes round her navel. The style is casual and conversational, clipped as in American gangster fiction. The reader is made to feel sympathy for the bewildered prostitute, understandably frightened by the revolver, although unharmed by the encounter.

The narrator feels despised, he misses work, he is dismissed, he throws away what money he has left, and he writes 102 copies of a letter to popular authors to explain that he is going to shoot five people. He reveals that his name is Paul Hilbert. He cannot bring himself to go out because it would have meant mixing with people. He stays in, closes the shutters, finds his eyes changing in intensity, and thinks of himself in the third person, capitalizing the "He." What is the point, he thinks, of killing people who are already *dead* (his italics)? In the end he does randomly shoot someone, using three of his six bullets. He escapes, fires two more, goes into a café, through into the lavatory, and cannot bring himself to kill himself with his last bullet. He surrenders. The parable of inadequacy is over.

—A.H.T. Levi

EVELINE
by James Joyce, 1914

"Eveline," the fourth story in *Dubliners,* illustrates both James Joyce's thematic concerns and his meticulous treatment of language and structure. Like most of the characters in the book, Eveline is oppressed by her circumstances, and like many others she considers the possibility of escape, but when she is offered a positive opportunity to leave, she refuses.

Most of the story is mediated through Eveline's consciousness as she explores three well-defined stretches of time: her past, her present, and her doubtful future. She evokes images of all three only to find that they need painful revision. She has memories of a happier, freer past which is a parody of Eden: Eveline is a little postlapsarian Eve, remembering a time before she had to earn her bread in the sweat of her brow. As a child she had lived in circumstances that, in contrast with her adult life, seemed (a verb Joyce uses with ironic force) a muted version of paradise. She played in fields which have now disappeared: " . . . they seemed to have been rather happy then. . . .That was a long time ago." Now, in a dusty fallen world, she hopes for salvation and thinks at first that the Messiah may indeed have arrived: Frank, her sailor suitor, "would take her in his arms, fold her in his arms. He would save her." In the end, she refuses his bell-like litany: "Come! . . . Come!" Along with this clear, but not schematic pattern, Joyce emphasizes ambiguities. Eveline's twilight musing on home and the adventurous alternative to which she "had consented," poses the explicit question, for reader and character, "Was it wise?"

Even in this very early work Joyce demonstrates his mastery of form. He divides the story into three distinct parts that, though related to the three periods of time on which Eveline focuses, are more than a simple chronological sequence. "Eveline" is cast in a formal pattern found often in *Dubliners:* a long initial expository passage, exploring problems but containing little action that might lead to a climax, is followed by a short conclusion in which possibilities of further development come to nothing. The first two parts of this story, in which Eveline sits at the window, make up the exposition, while the third contains the brief flurry of action and inaction at the wharf. Especially characteristic of Joyce's stylistic skill is the way the first two parts are related. Part one begins with the description of Eveline at the window:

She sat at the window watching the evening invade the avenue. Her head was leaned against the window curtains and in her nostrils was the odour of dusty cretonne. She was tired.

After her first long evocation of past, present, and future, Joyce returns to that opening to begin the short second part:

Her time was running out but she continued to sit by the window, leaning her head against the window curtain, inhaling the odour of dusty cretonne.

Now the dust of the curtains is not simply "in her nostrils"; she actively inhales it. The addition of the verb is indicative of Eveline's growing change of heart, as Joyce prepares us for her final rejection of salvation.

Repetition with variation is central to Joyce's quasimusical methods of composition both in this story and throughout his career. In this very brief short story, the important words "home" and "house" occur with varying resonance 18 times. After the opening of the second part, the first important motif to be reconsidered is the relationship of music to promises. In part one, Eveline remembers the "yellowing photograph" of the priest which "hung on the wall above the broken harmonium beside the promises made to Blessed Margaret Mary Alacoque." Unlike the principal characters in *Dubliners,* the priest has managed to escape (to Australia). In part two, music and promises are again juxtaposed as Eveline hears a street organ and thinks it strange "that it should come that very night to remind her of the promise to her mother, her promise to keep the home together as long as she could." She also remembers an occasion on which her father ordered an Italian organ player to go away: "Damned Italians! Coming over here!" Both passages are closely related to the promises made by Frank to Eveline. Music has played an important part in their courtship. He "was awfully fond of music," he sang her "The Lass that Loves a Sailor," and he took her to see

The Bohemian Girl. Now he promises her a better life. Her father, however, who dismissed the Italian organ grinder, now effectively orders Frank away too: "her father . . . had forbidden her to have anything to say to him."

Early in the story Joyce indicates through Eveline's use of language why she will not, in fact, be able to escape. Dublin has so reduced her that she is unworthy to do so. She thinks in clichés: "the invariable squabble for money on Saturday nights had begun to weary her unspeakably"; "as she mused the pitiful vision of her mother's life laid its spell on the very quick of her being . . . "; Frank, whose apparently genuine affection she does not reciprocate, is her "lover." In the same vein she thinks, in part one, "Everything changes. Now she was going to go away like the others, to leave her home." These last two sentences are characteristic of Joyce's method. While there have been superficial changes in Dublin and in Eveline's personal circumstances, they have made no significant difference to the patterns of people's lives. Similarly, although the early parts of the stories often give the impression of containing much busy activity, it is rare for anything important to happen.

While Eveline's verbal imagination dominates the first two parts of the story, juxtapositions and the narrative content induce the reader to see beyond it. When she thinks, in the second paragraph, that "few people passed," the reader is prepared for the "passage," twice mentioned, which Frank has booked for her and which she will reject. In the third part the narrator begins to take more positive control. Eveline's style slowly gives way to a voice, familiar elsewhere in much of Joyce's work before *Finnegans Wake,* which speaks in quiet, rhythmic cadences and uses formal diction unavailable to Eveline: the boat has "illumined portholes"; Eveline "kept moving her lips in silent fervent prayer"; and, "her eyes gave no sign of love or farewell or recognition." While Eveline herself is unable to escape, Joyce quietly extracts the reader from the pitiful but deadening effects of her imaginative world.

—Clive Hart

EVERY INCH A MAN (Nada menos que todo un hombre)
by Miguel de Unamuno, 1916

"Nada menos que todo un hombre" ("Every Inch a Man") is one of Unamuno's more peculiar pieces of fiction and a fitting conclusion to the volume entitled *Tres novelas ejemplares y un prólogo (Three Exemplary Novels).* The story is significant both in terms of the thematics of the volume as a whole and because of the way it adumbrates the notion of exemplarity. The prologue—which is usually not included in English translations of the stories—emphasizes that exemplarity is to be understood in the same sense that Cervantes used the word in the title of his own *Exemplary Novels.* As Unamuno points out, this means that "llamo ejemplares a estas novelas porque las doy como ejemplo—así, como suena—ejemplo de vida y de realidad" ("I call these novels exemplary because I offer them as an example—that's right, just as it sounds—as an example of life and of reality"). And Unamuno goes on to offer the interpretive key to the three stories, including "Every Inch a Man": "Sus agonistas, es decir, luchadores—o si queréis los llamaremos personajes—son reales, realísimos, y con la realidad más íntima, con la que se dan ellos mismos, en puro querer ser o en puro querer no ser, y no con la que le den los lectores" ("The agonists, that is, combatants—or if you wish we'll call them characters—are real, very real, and with that most intimate reality that they confer upon themselves, in the pure wanting to be or in the pure wanting not to be, and not the reality that might be conferred upon them by readers").

The "real" characters of "Every Inch a Man" are Julia Yañez and Alejandro Gómez. She is the local beauty of the town of Renada, who must save her family's economic fortunes through marriage; he is quite literally a self-made man who, having married into and made his fortune in Mexico, returns to Spain to make his home in Renada. Once Alejandro sets eyes on Julia, he must have her for his very own. So he settles the Yañez family's debts and marries the beautiful young woman. If Julia had anticipated feeling nothing for the man to whom she would eventually be virtually sold, she realizes that, to her surprise, she is deeply in love with Alejandro. After their initial correspondence, she muses over their mutual salvation, "Here is a real man. Will he save me? Will I save him?" But when she later attempts to find out if he in turn loves her, he answers, "Only fools talk about such things." The crux of the story comes down to the question of love. There is the question of the depth of Julia's love for Alejandro, and of whether or not Alejandro truly loves Julia, or can be inspired to love her through jealousy. There also is the question whether or not love is dependent merely upon individual will and desire, or if it of necessity implies the existence of another and of another's desire.

Frustrated by her husband's lack of affection, Julia begins to see more of Alejandro's friend the Count of Bordaviella, an unhappily married and somewhat inept Don Juan. She finally reveals to her husband that the count is her lover. But, rather than responding as a jealous spouse, Alejandro has Julia declared insane for her delusions of infidelity. As he explains it to the count, "So then you thoroughly understand, Count, either my wife is declared insane or I will blow out your brains and hers, too." Only once she is able to admit that she was indeed mad is Julia allowed to leave the sanatorium. And at that point she asks Alejandro once again if he loves her. With tears in his cold eyes, Alejandro admits, "Do I love you, my dear child, do I love you! I love you with all my soul, with all my blood, and with all my being, more than my own self!" With this admission, Alejandro lets Julia see into the "depths of the terrible and reticent soul which this wealthy, self-made man had kept jealously concealed." He then takes her home, whereupon she takes deathly ill. Although he tries desperately to save her, even offering his blood and life in exchange for that of his wife, Julia escapes him. As he holds her during the final moments of her life, Julia whispers to him, "Won't you tell me now who you are, Alejandro?" In a play on the title of the story, Alejandro answers, "I? Oh, just a man—the man you have made of me."

Julia's death sends Alejandro in search of himself and his past, of that "life of his which he had concealed from everybody—even from himself." After kissing his son goodbye, Alejandro closets himself with the body of his dead wife and swears, "Death has taken you away and now I am going to come and get you." The story ends with these words: "When later on, they had to break down the door of the death chamber, they found him with his arms around his wife. He was pale and deathly cold and bathed in the blood that had been drained completely from him."

The play in the story between the related notions of economy and honor, redemption and salvation, desire and fulfillment, reality and appearance, comes down to Alejandro's reluctant admission of his love for, and dependence on, a woman. The man who asserts that "I live by realities and not appearances," and that "I am only a man, but I am a real man," (literally: but every inch a man) finally realizes that, in fact, he only becomes what he defines as a man when he admits that his desire—in Unamuno's terms, his wanting to be—is contingent upon his wife's love for and recognition of him and on his awareness that he is "the man you have made of me."

Of course, Julia is likewise what Alejandro makes of her, since, for Unamuno, one "is" to the extent that one is part of another. But the couple can never really enjoy their newly-discovered oneness or unity. As the possibility of a spiritual communion in their mutual love becomes more real, death approaches. And it is in the darkly ironic and ultimately empty final image of the story that the true exemplarity of these "real" agonists is to be found. Such oneness is itself a fiction, and Alejandro's desire for transubstantiation—the one true redemption—can never occur and the man is condemned to aspire to the status of fiction, of completion and wholeness, while living the reality of insufficiency.

—James Mandrell

EVERYTHING THAT RISES MUST CONVERGE
by Flannery O'Connor, 1965

The short story, Flannery O'Connor once wrote, has an extra dimension, one which comes about "when the writer puts us in the middle of some human action and shows it as it is illuminated and outlined by mystery." O'Connor's own capacity to charge her prose with mystery is demonstrated by the enigmatic title, "Everything That Rises Must Converge" (winner of the O. Henry award, 1963). The title is usually taken to refer to the philosophies of Pierre Teilhard de Chardin, in whose work O'Connor found, if not answers, at least a different set of questions. It is a title charged with mystery, but in the story that follows the incidents related are so mundane (a weight reducing class and a ride on the bus), and the points of convergence so funny (unlikely mothers and the wearing of the same hat), that an opposite and entirely comic view continuously threatens to overwhelm the tragic and mysterious. Such are the tensions of O'Connor's work.

As in many of O'Connor's stories, "Everything That Rises Must Converge" has as its fulcrum a mother. Julian's mother has sacrificed to send her good looking and intelligent son to college. She has managed to maintain appearances in the midst of squalor and Southern decline and thinks it is fun to struggle and to look back on the hard times now that she has won. Julian is not grateful. He realises that he is too intelligent to be a success and is already as disenchanted as a man of 50 years: "he could not forgive her that she had enjoyed the struggle and that she thought she had won." The action, seen through the eyes of Julian, shows him as a pre-eminently rational and reasonable man embarrassed by his mother's refusal to adjust to the modern world. Within this conflict O'Connor seeds the possibility of revelation.

Typically O'Connor's characters move toward a personal epiphany in which the rational and reasoning world of everyday occurrence is stripped away, leading to the recognition of a universe of spirit, in which sin and moral choices are still an issue. Julian is a rational man, but reason says O'Connor "should always go where the imagination goes." Julian's rationalism and imagination are at odds, so that, although he does not like to consider all that his mother has done for him, he nevertheless does take her to her weight-reducing class. As his mother prevaricates over the new hat, in which, she has been assured by the shop assistant, she won't meet herself "coming and going" Julian appears pinned to the door frame, waiting, "like Saint Sebastion for the arrows to begin piercing him." Julian's mother not only affronts his sense of reality with her "imaginary dignity," but also challenges his self-righteous liberalism by openly advocating difference in the newly integrated South: "They should rise, yes, but on their own side of the fence." The narrative voice of O'Connor's work, however, is rarely impartial.

O'Connor is, in essence, a satirist, and her narrative voice often that of a fundamentalist preacher who, like the satirist, inhabits a world of clear-cut good and evil with a sort of monumental certainty about which is which. Julian's hypocrisy is relentlessly uncovered. He childishly fusses about wearing the tie his mother insists upon, he ostentatiously seats himself next to an African-American and wishes to engage his neighbour in conversations about art, or politics, or any subject that would be "above the comprehension of those around him," and he succumbs to an "evil urge" to break his mother's spirit. "True culture" Julian insists, "is in the mind," but his actions are so far dislocated from his professed ideas that his mother acquires dignity in direct relation to Julian's loss. At least she knows who she is, and to know oneself is also, as O'Connor has remarked, "to know the world." It is the way to overcome regionalism, and, paradoxically, it is a form of exile from the world: "to know oneself is above all to know what one lacks . . ." In these terms O'Connor herself transcends the regional and material settings of her stories to consider the nature of human spirituality.

Julian, blissfully unaware of what he lacks, moves from ignorance to knowledge. When an enormous African-American seats herself beside him while he seats beside his mother, Julian maliciously allows his amusement to show. They have symbolically swapped sons, and although his mother could not comprehend the symbolism, "she would feel it." There is a look of dull recognition in her eyes, but what his mother has recognized is both more mundane and more womanly. The large African-American woman is wearing the same hat. This vision breaks upon Julian with the "radiance of a brilliant sunrise."

O'Connor views the symbol as an integral part of her art, and allows a given symbol to accrue meaning until "it is turning or working the story." The language of her fiction invites imaginative response which is rewarded with meaning. The son's rise at this point in the story is short-lived, for his mother is able to withstand even this blow to her dignity: "With a sinking heart, he saw incipient signs of recovery on her face and realised that this was going to strike her suddenly as funny and was going to be no lesson at all."

The point of convergence is entirely comic, and the reader, like Julian, can be beguiled into what Melville would have called "horrible allegory." It is, however, part of O'Connor's craft that her shift from Southern comedy to Southern grotesque is as swift as it is terrible. As the party alights from the bus, the large African-American woman, whose anger is stoked by centuries of indignities, finds the offer of a penny to her son unbearable. She hits Julian's mother and sends her reeling for home. The reader, surprised by the sudden shift in emphasis, is forced to experience, with Julian, the loss of complacency. The pleasure of puzzle solving in order to arrive at meaning gives way to textual uncertainty and ambiguity just as Julian's pleasure, at seeing his mother finally receive a lesson, gives way first to indignation, then fear, and at last to blind panic as he realises that she is, in fact, about to die. He feels the tide of darkness sweeping him back to her, "postponing from moment to moment his entry into the world of guilt and sorrow."

Symbolic meaning is complex, and in O'Connor's work, rational meaning must be brought into correlation with possible meaning. It is not that one does not understand Julian's frustration with his mother, but that one is rhetorically engaged with a persona insisting upon a transcendent signifier. In a letter of 16 December 1955, O'Connor explains that she has no foolproof aesthetic theory, and that the moral basis of her work was to be found in the Jamesian sense of a "felt life." The writer, she thought, should have a moral sense which coincided with the dramatic sense. Her own moral sense, that of the confirmed Christian writing for an audience who, she said, thought God was dead, informs all of her work. In her own words her writing tends to be "more terrible than it is funny . . . or only terrible because it is funny."

—Jan Pilditch

F

FACING THE FORESTS (Mul Haye'arot)
by A.B. Yehoshua, 1968

The early short stories of the leftist Israeli writer A.B. Yehoshua, those written during the 1960's, have been often described as the Kafkaesque nightmares of alienation and isolation experienced by the "generation of the state," persons who came of age after 1948, the year in which the State of Israel was proclaimed. In these stories, Israel is not the land of hope and fulfillment usually depicted in the works of other Israeli writers and reflected in the hopes of the Zionist ideologues who created that country. Instead, Yehoshua's Israel is a place of pessimism and despair inhabited by dislocated people concerned with the moral dilemmas that arise from, among other things, the Palestinian presence in Israel and the danger of holding on too assiduously to the Zionist vision of the previous generation without taking into account the reality of these Palestinians and their demands.

Yehoshua powerfully depicts these dilemmas in "Mul Haye'arot" ("Facing the Forests"), the title novella of his 1968 collection, (in English as *Three Days and a Child*). A highly controversial work that provoked extensive, sometimes acrimonious, debate both inside and outside of Israel (some thought it subversive), the story concerns a shiftless, lonely, unnamed graduate student of modest intellectual means who, for want of something better, takes "a marginal job" as a forest ranger. He is interviewed for the position by the head of the Afforestation Office, "a worthy character edging his way to old age." In the silence and isolation offered by the job (he is to watch for fires), he hopes to complete extensive readings in Latin for a thesis of some sort dealing with the Crusades. The forest grows over land where an Arab village used to stand until it was razed by the Israelis. The ranger's Arab servant lives in the firewatch tower with his daughter; he used to live in that village, where his wives were somehow murdered. Occasional visitors include hikers, foreign dignitaries and tourists who come when donor name plates are placed on rocks and dedicated to the memory of loved ones, and the ranger's middle-aged mistress.

Though initially weary of the ranger, the Arab and his daughter warm to the young man, who is vaguely sexually attracted to the girl. He learns that the authorities believe the Arab is saving kerosene to burn the forest. One night the ranger lights a bonfire from pine needles, as if to give the Arab "a lesson" on how to burn down the forests. On the night before the ranger is to leave, the Arab sets fires to the forests; because the telephone lines have been cut, the ranger cannot call for help. Taking the girl with him, he escapes the holocaust; and though fire engines eventually come, nothing can save the forests.

The next day the police and the old Afforestation officer arrive; the latter, enraged at the loss of the forest, holds the ranger responsible. Both the ranger and the Arab are relentlessly interrogated; eventually, the Arab is accused. As he is led away, his daughter clings to him. The ranger demands that, somehow, she be taken care of. At this suggestion the Afforestation officer attacks the ranger, who is then roughed up and driven to town by the police. Looking like "a savage," he eats and tries to sleep. He can only drowse as visions of green forests spring up before him. His friends abandon him, treating him like a "wet dog begging for fire and light," a pariah.

In this story, the Arab-Israeli conflict is depicted as a three-sided affair; the old director of Afforestation, an articulate and organized person, representing the older generation that established Israel, wields power on behalf of and takes pride in the forests, a symbol for Israel; the rootless, uncertain student, whose competence the older man seems to question and who, at first, does not even believe that the forests exist; and the Arab, whose tongue has been cut out, by either other Arabs or by the Israelis, a symbol of the silent, unheard Arabs living in Israel, performing menial jobs and capable of violence.

During the job interview, the older man, wishing to think the best of the young man, asks whether he is writing his dissertation; the younger replies evasively that he is not quite that far along. The implication here is that the older man's expectations of the younger are not met, or are perhaps inflated, unrealistic. When the older man comes to the forest with visiting dignitaries, the younger man notices that he is "darting troubled looks about him, raising his eyes at the trees as though searching for something." The older man introduces the younger to visitors by the hyperbolic title of "scholar." Later the officer holds the ranger responsible for the fire and attacks him when the ranger seems to show more concern for the young Arab girl than for the forests.

The Crusades, the ranger's thesis topic, holds powerful metaphorical meaning in the story. These were events in which zealous yet rapacious Europeans invaded the Middle East based on ostensibly justifiable religious reasons, and established short-lived, so-called "Latin" (European) kingdoms there. The analogy between the Crusaders and their ephemeral kingdoms, and latter-day European Jewish occupiers of Israel is stark. That Israel, like the kingdom of the Crusaders, might disappear, due in part to the lack of commitment of younger Israelis, is blasphemous for many, especially Zionists convinced of the God-given right of Jews to this land.

Highly symbolic and, in light of the *intifada* (uprising) among the Palestinians in the occupied territories of Israel, even prophetic, "Facing the Forests" is one of Yehoshua's most politically disturbing stories. Though his later works are, by comparison, more muted, this story may be viewed as Yehoshua's appeal that, though Israel may wish to gloss over the presence of Palestinians by planting forests, both actually and symbolically, it cannot do so. Israel must face the possibility that what is buried beneath these "forests" will come forth not merely as trees but as Arab grievances and, perhaps, even conflagration as well.

—Carlo Coppola

FAITH IN A TREE
by Grace Paley, 1974

Although Grace Paley has not yet received much scholarly attention (only one book-length study by Jacqueline Taylor published in 1990), her 45 short stories have been widely anthologized and admired by writers and critics as well as a general reading public. "Faith in a Tree" appeared in the second of three story collections, *Enormous Changes at the Last Minute,* and illustrates many features that have lead critics to regard her as "a writer's writer": careful craft, inventive narrative technique, original voice, and a language that is freshly unique.

While Paley's stories deal with non-heroic characters engaged in everyday life, usually set in Greenwich Village, New York, her fiction is colored by a penetrating vision of contemporary social-political reality. As in most of her work, Paley articulates a female-centered consciousness in "Faith in a Tree" that cuts deeper than the usual surface problems facing women in a male-dominated society. At the end of the story, the narrator, Faith, acts with initiative and quietly bold resistance to the dominant tradition, a form common among Paley's protagonists. Instead of ending in resignation or despair, the story resolves with a hope that celebrates strength in "doing" and faith in change which, as one critic points out, circumvents the standard "resolutions for a female protagonist: marriage or death."

In similar fashion, when Alexandra, the protagonist in the story "Enormous Changes at the Last Minute" becomes pregnant, she doesn't ask the child's father to come live with her, but instead invites three pregnant teen-age girls to share her house so she can "make good use of the events of her life." It is this spirited theme of action that blossoms at the end of "Faith in a Tree."

The story opens with Faith sitting literally in the arm of a sycamore tree watching her women friends and their children—including her own, Richard and Tonto—interact with the world below. From this suspended perspective, Faith reports on a world that seems odd and quirky in its logic, or, rather, "logics," which represent the multiplicity of principles that govern human action.

In the third paragraph, Faith describes the park in language that exposes three of the "logics" frequently used to explain and justify the ways of the world: "*democratic time,*" "God," and "springtime *luck.*" In one sentence, this juxtaposition establishes a universe of logically incompatible congruence that subtly fuses reason, faith, and chance. When we read of "the deer-eyed eland and kudu ... grazing the open pits of the Bronx Zoo," we hardly notice the logical contradictions: can a "pit" really be "open"? Can a "zoo" really be a place for "grazing"? Who, in a state of numbed familiarity, ever bothers to ask?

Paley defamiliarizes scene after scene by revealing the simultaneity of contradictory logics. She does this so frequently that illogic itself becomes the subject of the story. Faith is in a tree, animals graze in a zoo, and park policemen refuse to allow kids to strum their guitars in the grass because the sound "could be the decibel to break a citizen's eardrum," a form of "civic" logic here defamiliarized to absurdity.

Male characters enter the story bearing the "male" logic of transience and detachment. Ignorant of the children he has fathered ("I think I have a boy who's nine"), Philip is nevertheless ready to adopt Tonto, Faith's youngest, on the basis of mere acquaintance after hearing Tonto expose the logic of fatherhood: "Mostly nobody has fathers," Tonto

says, substantiating his claim by reporting that Kitty's daughters have none, he himself has one who disappeared in an Equatorial jungle, and his friend Judy has two, one being Dr. Kraat who will, quite appropriately, "take care of you if you're crazy." Philip responds by saying, "Maybe I'll be your father," and with this ironic sword, draws figurative blood from his own foot.

Much of the illogic Faith reports is humorous—the P.T.A. president fired when authorities discover he has no children; Philip deciding to become a comedian even though he isn't funny—but also ironic, especially in its implicit revelation of male attitudes. As in much of Paley's fiction, there are moments when the world's illogic and contradiction seem of no more consequence than Philip's turning out to be a bad comedian who cannot make people laugh. However, when Faith describes the Vietnam War protesters who enter the park pushing their children in strollers, carrying placards that depict napalmed babies beneath the query WOULD YOU BURN A CHILD? and the response ONLY WHEN NECESSARY, illogical logic is revealed as anything but inconsequential.

The story gains force through the use of collaborative narration where characters are allowed to correct the narrator's version of events, a technique that appropriately undermines the dominant logic of traditional narrative in a story whose subject is the challenge of dominant logic. The narrator herself comes to realize that, from another point of view, her own logic is equally imperfect. When her son Richard says, "We're really a problem to you, Faith, we keep you not free," she can only find an exasperated response: "How can you answer that boy?"

It is Richard's action that reveals to Faith the "suppressed woman" logic which has kept her powerless. When the cop asserts civic dominance to expel the protesters from the park, Richard reacts with livid anger and berates the adults who sit passively in the face of dangerously flawed logic. In responding, Faith discovers inside herself the most valid logic of all: protest. Richard mocks adults and Faith changes, enormously, at this last minute. No longer suspended indecisively in the arm of a sycamore tree, Faith commits to "changing," she says, "my hairdo, my job uptown, my style of living and telling." When the protesters move outside the park beyond the cop's jurisdiction, they reveal an effective logic for functioning in an illogical world. When Faith descends from the tree and follows her inner sense, she discovers a related logic that indeed makes good use of the events of her life.

—Paul Sladky

THE FAITHLESS WIFE
by Sean O'Faolain, 1976

The great figures of Irish literature who flourished in the early years of the century, notably James Joyce and W.B. Yeats, have inevitably tended to overshadow writers of the succeeding generation. Yet these writers, whose material derived from the world made by the ideals and ideologies of their elders, offer with quiet artistry innumerable trenchant and cogent views of a people attempting to establish the social meaning of the political independence they had won. The most important member of this generation, which began to consolidate its claim to cultural relevance from the 1930's onwards, is Sean O'Faolain. His preoccupation with the mores and vagaries of Ireland and the Irish sustained him throughout a long literary career, the best-known accomplishment of which is his short fiction.

An instance of this preoccupation may be found in "The Faithless Wife," published in O'Faolain's last collection of new stories, *Foreign Affairs and Other Stories,* published in 1976. The story represents both O'Faolain's fascination with his material and the distance he feels from it. The author's detached involvement with his subject matter is seen in the narration, from the foreign point of view of Ferdy, the undiplomatic embassy official. The use of Ferdy's perspective provides both an adroit focus on Celia's elusive reality and an occasion for the story's most revealing component, O'Faolain's tone of worldly amusement. Without this tone, which is relentlessly deployed throughout, there is a danger that the story might become a tiresome allegory dealing with attempts to tame and codify that femme fatale of the author's career, Mother Ireland. This danger is averted by the deliberate excess of O'Faolain's approach. The story's sheer linguistic and cultural variety, its wilful writing-off of the canon of Irish fiction, the galloping prolixity of some of its sentences, its motif of the chase and the influence this exerts over the work's tempo and timing, combine to make "The Faithless Wife" a most engaging account of the madness of romance. O'Faolain manages to be satirical without being bitter, farcical without being cruel, knowing without being didactic. Conceived of in terms of its highly polished surface, "The Faithless Wife" is both a sophisticated romp and the work of a master of the form. The possibility of alternative responses to the story seems obtuse and heavy-handed, so accomplished and assured is the author's controlling presence in the work.

However, in view of O'Faolain's commitments and preoccupations as the leading Irish man of letters of his generation, it seems inadequate to regard this late story as merely an instance of O'Faolain perfecting his master of the short story, even if "The Faithless Wife" represents his last word on the critique of romance (to which much of his later work was devoted). The exuberance and extravagance of Ferdy's point of view address what Ferdy perceives as the phenomenon of Celia. Part of the story's sophistication, however, resides in the fact that Ferdy's perceptions cannot be quite aligned with Celia's reality. Inexplicably, as Ferdy sees it, ignoring such evidence of her independence as her boutique and the affair itself, Celia exists not for him but for herself. And this fact of life, while clearly contributing to the comedy of cultural dissonance, extends that comedy beyond the bedroom.

The story's cultural conflicts arise not only from the obvious fact of different nationalities, but from misguided conceptions, on Ferdy's part, of what those nationalities should embody. His attempts to locate a dependable definition of Irish women is as laughable as his unreflecting portrayal of the Gallic lover, complete with champagne and roses. Just as this portrayal proves irrelevant to the reality of love-making, so Celia's failure to embody what Ferdy understands Irish women to be may be taken as the signature of her reality. In doing nothing other than being herself, Celia expresses a combination of amoral freedom and convenient responsibility which leaves the ostensibly more experienced Ferdy at a loss, as his closing words reveal.

The nature of Celia's freedom does not derive from her affair with Ferdy. Rather it is a quality she brings to the affair, and is conceived of, in typical O'Faolain fashion, in terms of the cultural and social actualities of post-independence Ireland. Celia's clever reading of the cultural geography of Dublin meetingplaces, early in the affair, amusing in its own right, is a clear indication of her desirable status. This status is not indebted either to her husband's scissors-making or the Catholic Church, yet Celia remains loyally associated with both emblems of convention, the better to cloak her own disloyal and unconventional activities. By thinking these attachments illogical and hypocritical, Ferdy misses the point about Celia, the apparent irrationality of whose behavior is an expression of an autonomy and unself-consciousness hitherto unrecorded in the annals of Irish independence and its complicated, liberated consequences.

—George O'Brien

THE FALL OF THE HOUSE OF USHER
by Edgar Allan Poe, 1839

To his artistic successors, Edgar Allan Poe seemed a man ahead of his time. This was one reason why Baudelaire and Mallarme translated him into French, why D.H. Lawrence gave him a laudatory chapter in his *Studies in Classic American Literature,* and why Allen Tate wrote his essay "Our Cousin, Mr. Poe." To judge from Poe's most celebrated short story, "The Fall of the House of Usher," the main question is how far ahead of his time he was. Translated to film (as it has been several times: Jean Epstein's French version in 1929, and Roger Corman's American film in 1960) this gothic tale of "struggle with the grim phantasm, FEAR" evokes a Poe who was at least the Alfred Hitchcock of his time, a master of mood superbly weaving his spell for the sake of entertainment. To Allen Tate, Poe was more likely the Schopenhauer or Kafka of his time, a proto-Modern nihilist going against the Transcendentalist grain of his time by creating in Roderick Usher "a mind from which darkness . . . poured forth upon all objects of the moral and physical universe in one unceasing radiation of gloom." D.H. Lawrence, seeing "spiritual vampirism" in Roderick Usher's total domination of his sister Madeline, was most interested in the theme of psychological perversity—Poe as a Freudian precursor. In this view, Usher's wicked work in the underground crypt, not only sealing Madeline up alive but screwing shut her coffin lid for good measure, made Poe an explorer in the "horrible underground passages of the human soul." Even T.S. Eliot claimed Poe as an ancestor in his essay "From Poe to Valery," probably because a portrayal like Usher's suits well the ambience of Eliot's Hollow Men living in a spiritual/moral Waste Land.

In addition to all these highly credible responses, scholars have also noted various resemblances between Usher and his creator. Physically, Usher's appearance could pass as a portrait of the author, featuring "a cadaverousness of complexion; an eye large, liquid, and luminous . . . ; lips somewhat thin and very pallid; . . . [and] an inordinate expansion above the regions of the temple." Usher's characterization too recalls some depictions of Poe, depending on which biographer one consults. (Poe's executor,

Rufus Griswold, willfully defamed his subject, probably as Poe had wanted). Thus we have Usher's manic-depressive temperament, "alternately vivacious and sullen," suggestive of "the lost drunkard, or the irreclaimable eater of opium." Like Poe, Usher is also an artist, a poet whose morbid sensibility brings forth "The Haunted Palace." This poem, in turn, illuminates a theme that Poe often dramatized in his verse and fiction, the precarious struggle against oncoming madness. And the essential motive for Usher's madness, the imminent death of his neurasthenic sister, evokes the two traumas that Poe suffered at the opposite ends of his life—his mother's untimely death in his early childhood (after his father had abandoned the family), and the invalid weakness that portended the early death of his child-bride, Virginia Clemm. Little wonder that in Usher's library his "chief delight . . . was found in the perusal of . . . the *Vigiliae Mortuorum*"—"Services for the Dead"—in an ancient church manual. One could easily see this story, like many others, as effecting the psychotherapy of art for this grief-haunted, anxiety-ridden writer.

Apart from these levels of meaning, Poe's technical virtuosity has made this work a classic short story. Despite Poe's contempt for allegory, expressed most potently in his review of Hawthorne's *Twice-Told Tales,* he unmistakably depicts the gloomy mansion as representing the house of the psyche. With its "vacant eye-like windows" and "a barely perceptible fissure" crossing its wall, the edifice resembles Usher's precarious psychic condition, which is further allegorized in the master metaphor of "The Haunted Palace." Here "the monarch Thought's dominion" is initially "a fair and stately palace" with yellow banners on its roof (Usher's hair), a door "with pearl and ruby glowing" (his teeth and lips), a "troop of Echoes" singing (his voice), and "two luminous windows" revealing "Spirits moving musically/To a lute's well-tuned law." This happy, healthy image gives way, however, to the assault of "evil things, in robes of sorrow," bringing on the displacements of madness—"red-litten windows" for eyes, "discordant melody" for a voice, and "a hideous throng" supplanting the troop of Echoes. All that remains is for Usher to enact his madness by premature burial of his cataleptic sibling. In D.H. Lawrence's reading, that misogynistic action brings on the revenge of the female, as Madeline returns from the crypt just long enough to bring her errant brother and the house itself to their rightful end.

Because of this multiplicity of meanings, ranging from high entertainment value to powerful psychological insight, "The Fall of the House of Usher" can satisfy an unusually wide spectrum of reader responses. This fact, together with Poe's technical mastery of the short story medium, helps explain why "The Fall of the House of Usher" has attained classic status, more so than any other instance of Poe's fiction.

—Victor Strandberg

FATHER AND I (Far och jag)
by Pär Lagerkvist, 1924

Pär Lagerkvist came of traditional peasant stock. His parents were deeply religious, accepting God without question and seeing his hand in the world around them. Although Lagerkvist loved and respected them, at an early age he rejected their religion and their traditions. As station foreman Lagerkvist's father lived in the station house and for Lagerkvist the powerful locomotives in the station yard symbolised new technology and the fast-moving uncertain life which swept away his parents' calm, ordered existence.

Following periods of intense, anguished searching for a doctrine to replace his childhood faith, Lagerkvist produced the autobiographical play *Gäst hos verkligheten* (*Guest of Reality*), which depicts the child and adolescent torn between his loving, secure but stifling home and the harsh frightening but fascinating world outside. The previous year, 1924, Lagerkvist had published a collection of short stories entitled *Onda sagor* (Evil Tales). The dominant strain is misanthropic and satirical: the hero is a fool, the saviour is an idiot, the angels are evil and the romantic lovers die. One of the stories, however, "Far och jag" ("Father and I"), which had first appeared in *Svenska Dagbladet* in 1923, points toward *Guest of Reality* and puts in the author's struggle between two worlds into both an autobiographical and universal context.

"Father and I" is written in the first person, the narrator being a ten-year-old boy. The narrative line is thin. Father, a railway man, and son go out walking one Sunday, and they both enjoy the sunshine and beautiful, natural surroundings. When dusk falls the boy's fears grow and reach a crescendo when an unscheduled train hurtles towards them out of the darkness. The style is simple and in places naive, as Lagerkvist projects the thoughts and fears of a ten-year-old.

The story is a study in contrasts, creating a tension between two different worlds, the smiling daylight walk representing a rural idyll with ancient beliefs, and the dark, terrifying homeward journey adumbrating a dangerous unknown outside world soon to be experienced by the boy. In the first part all the sounds, scents, and movements are pleasurable: "There was a twittering of finches and willow warblers, thrushes and sparrows in the bushes, the hum that goes on all around you as soon as you enter a wood. The ground was white with wood anemones, the birches had just come out into leaf, and the spruces had fresh shoots; there were scents on all sides, and underfoot the mossy earth lay steaming in the sun." Above all there is a feeling of familiarity and of security in the setting. When a train comes along, "Father hailed the engine driver with two fingers to his Sunday hat and the driver saluted and extended his hand." They passed a field of oats "where a crofter we knew had a clearing" and went down to a stream which "flowed past where Father had lived as a child." Here the familiarity is allied to continuity.

The change occurs with sunset. The child grows anxious—"the trees were so funny. They stood listening to every step we took, as if they didn't know who we were." By the time they come to the bridge across the stream it is quite dark. The stream, which previously had "murmured in the hot sun, broad and friendly," now "roared down there in the depths, horribly, as though it wanted to swallow us up; the abyss yawned below us." On the outward journey the telegraph poles "sang as you passed them" but now they "rose, ghostly to the sky. Inside them was a hollow rumble, as though someone were talking deep down in the earth and the white porcelain caps sat huddled fearfully together listening to it."

The familiarity gives way to alienation. The child whispers "Why is it so horrible when it's dark?" Father replies, "No, my child, you mustn't think that. Not when we know there is a God." The child feels separated by his fear, and the chasm widens when a black train unexpectedly hurtles past. In direct contrast to the friendly driver in the first part, this driver "stood there in the light of the fire, pale, motionless, his features as though turned to stone." This time the father doesn't recognise him. The alienation is complete as the boy, filled with dread, stands "gazing after the furious vision. . . .I sensed what it meant: it was the anguish that was to come, the unknown, all that Father knew nothing about, that he wouldn't be able to protect me against. That was how this world, this life, would be for me; not like Father's, where everything was secure and certain. It wasn't a real world, a real life. It just hurtled, blazing, into the darkness that had no end."

It is typical of Lagerkvist that he can introduce natural objects and then in simple, deliberately naive language turn them into symbols for disturbing emotional and philosophical problems. The realistic childhood setting suddenly opens into a yawing gap between two generations and an angst-ridden view of a world void of religious belief. "Father and I" becomes important not just as a key to Lagerkvist's personal dilemma, which was the spring-board for much of his writing, but also as an example of a symbolic use of ordinary phenomena to imply existential problems.

—Irene Scobbie

FATIMAS AND KISSES
by John O'Hara, 1966

Novelist and short story writer John O'Hara still remains best-known for his realistic style and his ear for conversational dialogue to reveal his characters' natures. A chronicler of life in 20th-century America, O'Hara said in 1960, "I want to record the way people talked and thought and felt, and to do it with complete honesty and variety." O'Hara began his writing career as a journalist, and his observational, nonjudgmental training remained with him in his writing of fiction. A character who appears throughout O'Hara's short story collections, as well as in his novel *Butterfield 8,* is autobiographical James Malloy, who, like O'Hara, is the son of a doctor who becomes a journalist. "Fatimas and Kisses," collected in *Waiting for Winter* (1966), deals with the character of James Malloy from childhood to young adult. As the reader follows the central character's growth, Malloy observes and reports on the events of the Lintz family, who create an atmosphere of middle-class America gone bad.

The story opens with Malloy, the reader's guide, describing the Lintz's family business. Donald Lintz and his wife Lonnie own and operate a neighborhood store. Malloy describes Lintz as having once been in the Marine Corps stationed in New Jersey. This hardly seems a glamorous assignment, yet Lintz dwells on his tour of duty as if it were. Considering what Malloy reveals about Lintz's wife, the reader tends to agree. One day, the young Malloy, not yet sent off to boarding school, stops in the store for cigarettes for himself and his young girlfriend. No one is attending the counter, so Malloy opens and shuts the door again. Lonnie comes running downstairs. Malloy asks her where her husband is, and when she answers and questions his curiosity, Malloy looks out toward the sidewalk and sees a driverless delivery truck. Lonnie believes he knows of her adultery and bribes him with free cigarettes. Malloy muses, "They never knew—older people—at just what age

you started to notice things like a driverless truck and a husband's absence and a delayed appearance." He keeps his discovery to himself and joins his girlfriend outside: "She was a girl, and in ten years or maybe less she was going to be my wife. Then I might tell her some of those things, but now Fatimas [a brand of cigarettes] and kisses were as much as she was ready for." His chivalric attitude, though sexist, is touching in one so young.

When Malloy returns from school as a cub reporter in his hometown, Lintz begins inviting him for drinks at a neighborhood saloon. Malloy reflects that Lintz has no men friends and is in the habit of coming to the saloon daily for drinks before the afternoon rush at the store. Malloy feels that Lintz needs someone to talk to, and he allows the store keeper to recount his exploits in the Marines as long as he continues to supply the drinks. From his experiences in whorehouses, Lintz unthinkingly proceeds to some revelations about his wife Lonnie; she adds items to the housewives' monthly bills and so steals well over a thousand dollars a year. Lintz doesn't seem worried that she might have affairs: "Some girls didn't care what they looked like after they got married, and Lonnie was one of them. Well, which was worse: the ones who didn't care, or the ones who cared about nothing else and flirted with every son of a bitch with pants on?" Apparently, Lintz is unaware of how his wife entertains the delivery men. Malloy feels some ethical difficulty, since Lintz uses the store's money, stolen from the housewives, to pay for their drinks together. He tries to justify his acceptance in two ways: the housewives don't realize that they're being cheated, and Lonnie owes him for his silence regarding her activities. Earlier in his life, Malloy wanted to protect his girlfriend from the unseemly side of life by not telling her of his discovery concerning Lonnie. Now, Malloy reveals his struggle of growing into adulthood: "My ethics and morals and my conscience were taking a continual beating in other areas as well. I was giving myself trouble over girls and women and love and theology and national politics and my uncontrollable temper. Not the easiest of my problems was my willingness to spend as much time with a man whom I regarded as a moron."

With these dilemmas still on his mind, Malloy visits a commercial hotel and overhears one salesman telling another of a customer's willingness to entertain (so to speak) her salesmen. Horrified, Malloy realizes that it is Lonnie who is being discussed. He knows that there is going to be trouble since Lonnie is behaving so blatantly, so he stops his drinking with Lintz. Malloy then theorizes, with foreshadowing, that Lintz's suspicions of his wife begin now that he no longer has anyone to talk to: "He was left entirely with his thoughts, and his world was very small. He had a wife, two kids who gave him no pleasure, and the clientele of his store for whom he had no respect." Lintz sits in the saloon staring at the only decoration in the place, a brewery advertisement depicting a goat in Bavarian costume raising a beer stein.

A full year passes when Malloy receives a tip at the newspaper office that Lintz has shot his wife and the latest salesman dead in the couple's bedroom. More chilling, he has also murdered his two children.

Malloy interviews Lintz, who reveals a persecution complex—Lonnie and their son were conspiring to kill him and a foreigner with whiskers and funny clothes had been visiting Lonnie. Ironically, Lintz wants to give Malloy a picture of himself dressed as a private in the Marines to put in the paper with the story of the murder, almost as if he were a war hero, but he doesn't want pictures of Lonnie and the children. Malloy ends the intriguing story with a reference to how individuals judge and compare each other, something Malloy as narrator and O'Hara as writer are unwilling to perform.

—Judith M. Schmitt

———

FIREMAN FLOWER
by William Sansom, 1944

William Sansom's first collection of stories, *Fireman Flower,* was partly inspired by his experience as a fireman during the Blitz. The stories in this volume present common features and in many ways foreshadow characteristics of Sansom's themes and manner in his subsequent works. The stories in *Fireman Flower* are not all about fires and firemen, but all of them have allegorical undertones. In most of them, owing to the author's metaphysical preoccupations, the human condition is represented metaphorically. "Fireman Flower," besides being openly an allegory of humanity's progress towards self-awareness and the understanding of their condition, is the story of a fireman in search of the "kernel of a fire" in a huge city warehouse. As in his other "fireman stories," Sansom finds here an opportunity to explore the gamut of sensory impressions; he also exploits the high emotional potential represented by a building on fire. More strikingly still, his desire to extend the experience of his protagonist to that of all humanity transforms the setting and the events of his story: coloured by his imagination, these undergo a subtle metamorphosis, become unreal and at times surreal. The adventure of fireman Flower can be seen, in Sansom's words, as a "surreal romance." It is also a realistic fantasy, in which we recognize Kafka's influence, acknowledged by Sansom. The abundance of realistic details referring to the warehouse on fire stresses its strangeness: "great embattled cogwheels, lifeless pistons, curved shapes of rough-cast metal, stanchions, rods, the immense cylinders of two riveted boilers." From one huge room to another, each place is endowed with characteristics that make it both easy to visualize and strange to conceive.

All the Sansom imagery, including his bestiary, appears in the story; pipes become coiling snakes, a mobile steel ladder "extends swiftly like the neck of a lusting reptile." Some characters whom Flower meets in the course of his search evince typically Sansomian peculiarities, like the unreliable and falsely reassuring fireman who shows, as he smiles, "two regular rows of false and pelleted teeth," whose "ordered achievement he fondly caresses." The variations of light, from "dull luminosity" and the "sluggish light of a pearl" to a "furnace glare," as well as the wide range of smells, sounds, tactile perceptions, ceaselessly surprise Flower and sharpen his alertness. They also sharpen our own expectation of ever new stages in Flower's progress towards wisdom.

The first stage, which corresponds to his encounter with the man with false teeth, teaches Flower that freedom from doubt is dangerous, for it is "the greatest deception of all." The second one results from Flower's fall into a lake of delight, filled with the scents from hundreds of bottles of perfume that have exploded in the fire. His colleagues, who have reached a state of drunken bliss, appear as unreliable as the man with false teeth, and Flower learns not to yield to the pleasures of the senses. As he continues his search for the centre of the fire, he is confronted with another temptation: the appeal of the past. But the past assumes successively two different forms; first that of a moth-eaten fur coat hanging in a wardrobe at the farther end of a deserted moonlit room; the coat appears like a headless human shape. This garment, which may be seen as a metaphor of a sterile past, is furiously hacked to pieces by Flower. But behind the wardrobe, the back of which he has cut through, he discovers another room and in it an old friend of his, who no doubt represents a past enriched by the memory. Flower is lulled by his nostalgic evocations: the past becomes more real than the present, it is seen as the only real experience, after which "what we imagine to be a recurrence of sensation is really a memory of [this] first experience; or, of the first time that the taste, smell, sound, sight, was fully experienced." But Flower has to tear himself away from these typically Sansomian considerations in order to resume his search—providentially, his helmet has fallen over his face in the course of his conversation with his friend, and this helps him sever himself from over-sweet evocations. At this juncture Flower is saved by the memory of his girlfriend Joan, who obviously embodies the necessity of ever struggling forward, "with the will to create." The disappearance of a big mirror where Flower had seen his own image some time before leads to another temptation, that of rejecting reality in favour of nightmare, because the latter is more vivid, more enticing. Having escaped this temptation, Flower resumes his advance towards various fires which reveal themselves as secondary ones, though their beauty magnetizes him. His journey is punctuated by philosophical considerations on his part, and symbolic elements introduced by the author to emphasize his point. Both philosophical considerations and symbolic elements somewhat tend to weigh the story down, but the reader is sometimes struck by the fine wording and the true ring of a statement, as when Flower discovers a room burnt with white and bright yellow light and filled with flour which lies silted in beautiful deep drifts: "His previous exhilaration faded beneath a sensation of profound and calm joy, so intense a joy that in its roots he perceived sadness." In "Fireman Flower" Sansom's visual power is given free rein and finds its expression in striking comparisons—among which that of a green curtain, torn and discoloured, lying on the floor, with "a drowned old woman." And we seldom meet in Sansom's stories such straightforward and loving characters as Flower, who finds in friendship a driving force and in his love for his sweetheart the poetic expression of his love for his fellow creatures. Having found numberless fires, none of which is the central one, Flower, who at the end of his search has arrived at the top of the huge building, gazes at the roofs around him and understands that his quest mattered more than its goal, that the apparent confusion and oppositions which he has perceived have become explainable: he is filled with a love which encompasses everyone, good and bad, beautiful and ugly, and all manifestations of life "so that he loved a single rusted nail as he loved the Giaconda smile, the factory's time clock as he loved the mold of autumn leaves, a mausoleum as he loved the crèche, a cat's head in the gutter as he loved the breasts of Joan." In spite of some overlong passages, the story stands as an exceptionally successful combination of philosophy, poetry, and imagination.

—Claire Larriere

———

FIRST CONFESSION
by Frank O'Connor, 1951

Frank O'Connor was the best-known Irish short story writer of his generation. Widely published, he has been credited generally with providing a version of post-independence Ireland that sustains a sense of his fellow countrymen's charming if foible-ridden behavior. While O'Connor certainly concentrated on the various complexities of human behavior, and while his work has almost invariably an Irish setting, the standard view of his work can be misleading. In particular, the significance of a somewhat maverick element in his stories, and this element's relationship to the stories' broad cultural background, is frequently overlooked. Even in such a typical O'Connor story as "First Confession," first published in 1944 and collected in *Traveller's Samples* (1951), the disarming mannishness of Jackie tends to be regarded by critics as sufficient to the artistic occasion.

"First Confession" is a typical O'Connor story for a number of reasons. It belongs to the cycle of stories of childhood upon which his international reputation as a writer of short fiction is based. This cycle, components of which are to be found throughout O'Connor's career, include such familiar works as "My Oedipus Complex," "The Drunkard," and "Christmas Morning." These stories draw on the author's impoverished background, and their invariably youthful narrators are all fully sensitive to the various deficiencies of their family situation, even if they are not always able to understand its origins or confront its implications. The references to money in "First Confession," and the likelihood that Gran's presence in the household is necessary for economic reasons, though these are beyond the narrator's grasp, is an instance of these stories' method and orientation. "First Confession" is also typical in its use of the tone of a child's perception for gently ironic and satirical purposes. And the story's style and structure combine the open and the tentative to reproduce with winning fidelity the child's moral world.

The existence and delineation of this world is the subject of "First Confession," confession being a medium through which the existence of right and wrong is acknowledged. It is important for O'Connor's standpoint in the story that the occasion in question is Jackie's first confession, and that the confession itself be an informal, guilt-free, exercise in innocence and its inevitable limits. Jackie is clearly in need of such an exercise, given the crudeness with which he specifies his own moral nature, expressed in his response to Gran and Nora. These responses are grounded in such primitive emotions as fear, greed, violence, and a general, incomprehending hostility to whatever disturbs him. It is impossible for Jackie to identify Gran as a person from a different environment than his own, with different codes and practices. O'Connor is careful not to sentimentalize Gran's peasant practices, a gesture of some cultural relevance to Irish readers at the time the story first appeared. But he is also careful to allow her behavior to be asserted in its own right. The harmlessness and lack of malevolence in her activities is the basis on which it remains immune from judgement, and why, in the confession itself, the priest endorses this immunity.

Gran is the pretext for Jackie's realisation that the world changes. The possibility of moral individuation exists through forming an adequate judgment of, and relationship to, a changing world. This possibility is made available in institutional form through the Church. However, the quality of the Church's contribution is critical, as O'Connor makes clear by providing such a clear contrast between Mrs. Ryan and the young confessor. Mrs. Ryan's view of sin is purely eschatalogical, a view which in its crude rhetoric and vulgar financial underpinnings resembles Jackie's primitive and self-interested morality. Yet, Mrs. Ryan's orthodoxy cannot be dismissed as an old woman's apocalyptic rambling. Despite differences in articulation, the crime-and-punishment view of sinner and sinning also informs Nora's outlook.

This connection, in addition to hinting at the structural pattern of "First Confession," with its reliance on kinship, affiliation, and allegiance, also has the effect of making Jackie appear singular. And his singularity is underlined by his attempt to hide behind a toothache and thereby avoid confessing, as well as by the perhaps unnecessary knockabout comedy of his activities in the confessional. Yet it is to Jackie's singularity that the priest responds. Jackie's confession does not consist of a formulaic recitation of childish peccadilloes but in "a rush" of confiding his human troubles. The magnitude of these troubles is ironically perceived through the means by which Jackie proposes to eliminate them. It is the priest's role to restore some sense of proportion, some degree of active evaluation and judgement, between objective conditions and subjective reactions to them, between self and world. The priest is required to be an agent in the human world, rather than an executive of eternity, such as Mrs. Ryan.

The implications of that requirement smuggle into "First Confession" a resonance that reaches far beyond young Jackie. His experiences, precisely because they are authorised by his own nascent moral intelligence in which his individuality is encoded, are paradoxically not merely valuable for him. Jackie is not yet in a position to appreciate or utilise the value of his experiences. His story, however, has an exemplary value, which can be characterised in two ways. The first is that Jackie's insistence on his entitlement to his own story, underlined by the first-person narration of "First Confession," as well as by the confessional aspect of first-person narration, is a manifestation of his individuality. The second is that the story represents the Church as a potential ratifier of that individuality. In the morally restrictive, clergy-dominated Ireland in which O'Connor wrote "First Confession," such findings have a far greater importance than any underwritten by the story's superficial, if undeniable, charm.

—George O'Brien

FIRST LOVE (Pervaia liubov')
by Ivan Turgenev, 1860

The seemingly ingenuous title of Turgenev's novella *Pervaia liubov* (*First Love*) is actually ironic. It implies that the principal narrator, Volodia, has gone on to experience other loves, but apparently he has not, and his elegiac tone at both the beginning and the end of the story further implies that his early love was unique. Conversely, *First Love* implies that adolescent love is somehow special, but by the end of the story we see that love affects people of all ages in much the same way. Among those reduced to helplessness by love (or, more exactly, by romantic love, "being in" love) are Zinaida's assortment of suitors, from the green Volodia to the middle-aged Dr. Lushin, Volodia's father, Zinaida herself, even the 40-year-old Mark Antony (romantically assumed by the ignorant in the story to have been a youth when he loved Cleopatra). This story is not so much about "first" love as about romantic love. Ultimately, in fact, it is about something even broader. It is about vitality, what it means and feels like to be fully alive. Romantic love is important to the story primarily because people in love feel the life within and around them more intensely than others do.

This view of the story brings a number of its elements into sharper focus. For one thing, we see that the lyrical descriptions of nature—for which Turgenev is famous—are more than atmospheric mood music; nature also functions as an objective correlative to the young Volodia's emerging sense that life can have aliveness, and experience can have intensity. Even before he meets Zinaida, he senses these new, "feminine" presences: "But through the tears and through the sorrow inspired by some melodious poem, or by the beauty of the evening, a joyous feeling of youthful and effervescent life sprang up like grass in spring" (translated by Harry Stevens, *The Borzoi Turgenev*). Later, correlating with the boy's tense awareness of rivalry in his love and of dangerous glamour in Zinaida's situation, the nightscape becomes portentous and uncanny: "suddenly everything grew profoundly still all around me. . . .Even the crickets ceased to chirrup among the trees. . . .I felt a strange agitation, as though I had been to keep an assignation and had been left waiting alone and had passed by another's happiness."

Among the more perishable essences in literature are the nuances of sexual desirability and, especially, of sexual charm. *First Love* depends heavily on our feeling Zinaida's attractiveness, which consists in a combination of seductiveness and imperiousness not necessarily in keeping with the tastes (male or female) of a later age. Probably the fascination in the mock-punishments and mock-beatings (with flowers, for example) that Zinaida metes out to her male worshipers is conditioned by a paradox of female imperiousness that, today, seems less sheerly paradoxical. Fortunately, however, in light of the main thrusts of the story, these beatings (the first time we see Zinaida she is delivering one of them) are part of a thematic counterpoint that loses none of its force with changing times; pain and violence continue to be as intelligible today as ever. Zinaida, the female focus of all the love vectors in the story, repeatedly gives and takes punishment, taking it most climactically in the brutal blow Volodia's father deals her on the arm when he visits her in Moscow. Her kissing of the wound in this scene both confounds the watching Volodia and confirms for him the meaning, depth, and power of what he now recognizes as authentic love.

It is important that we not respond to this incident as mere brutality, any more than we should respond that way to the playful beatings Zinaida doles out earlier, or even the genuine pain she inflicts on Dr. Lushin when she forces him to laugh despite the shame and pain he feels when she pushes a pin hard into his skin. Nor is this a way of saying that love is sadomasochistic. The upshot, rather, is to define love as intensity of feeling—whether pleasurable or the opposite—and to contrast it as such with the various ways of being half-responsive and half-alive. The opening frame of the story—the clichéd situation of after-dinner storytelling, along with the utter banality of the first two men's reminiscences—is one way of conveying this half-aliveness, as is the physical and moral shabbiness of Zinaida's mother and home surroundings. The idle warnings given Volodia by the middle-aged—Dr. Lushin and Volodia's father himself—about the dangers of romantic love ("that happiness, that poison") amount to warning

him away from life itself, which is exactly such an oxymoronic mixture of intensely vital feelings. Neither of the two older men is the worse person for being unable to take his own advice.

It is often remarked that Turgenev, characteristically, portrays romantic love as doomed to impermanence. The comment is exasperating, not only because such impermanence is an obvious fact of general human experience but, more importantly, because the comment misses the point and Turgenev's tone. *First Love*, for example, is a sad story, even tragic, but its final effect is to affirm vitality, however painful. The dwelling on death in the last pages, including the painful story of the old woman who so tenaciously and illogically clings to a life that has been sheer misery, complements the dwelling on half-aliveness at the beginning: both front and end frames are chiaroscuro that lends brilliance and color to the explosiveness and wonder of life, which is most vividly realized through romantic love. After the blissful but painful experience of Zinaida's farewell kiss, Volodia tells us, "I would never wish it to be repeated, but I would regard myself as unfortunate if I had never known it." Looking back from middle age, he adds later, "what is left to me more fresh, more precious than the memory of that swiftly passed, vernal thunder of my morn?" The key fact is not that such vernal thunder has passed away but rather that it has existed.

—Brian Wilkie

FISHMONGER'S FIDDLE
by A. E. Coppard, 1925

"Fishmonger's Fiddle," the title story of Coppard's 1925 collection, at first promises to be a fairly stereotypical seduction story in which an abandoned wife will further compromise her middle-class status with a reckless, ill-advised romance with a musician. Although it may be tighter in construction than some of Coppard's stories and lacking the detailed countryside and the detailed vernacular, it still provides a surprising twist to the expected conclusion.

Maxie Morrisarde, married but six months to a "one-time amiable tobacconist" who has absconded to America, "her little fortune" in hand, has come to live with her uncle and aunt, Ethelbert and Ida Vole, and their dog Toots, in their sea-side villa, Crag Dhu. The Voles and their dog are caricatured, generally remaining on the margins of the action. One day Maxie attempts to lighten tea-time by talking about a man she has seen carrying a cello entering a fishmonger's shop. Mr. Vole appreciates the incongruity, but Mrs. Vole seems unable to fathom the incident further than to tell her niece she "shouldn't go that way again." To Aunt Vole, fiddlers and all such musicians "are all for self." Inevitably, Maxie meets the cellist a few days later. He is sitting on a bench and is covered with pigeons eating peas from his outstretched hands. The dog Toots snaps up one of the birds.

One afternoon, Maxie again visits the pier, this time without Toots. She feels it "exhilarating, and yet almost terrifying" to recognize the young man of the cello and the pigeons. He walks her to the pier gate and asks to see her again. She meets Arnold Blackburne, as the musician is called, several times, and even tells him about her absent husband. Feeling "like an insect caught in a web that the spider had forsaken," Maxie thinks of divorce, much to the scandal of the Voles, and she thinks even more of Arnold's sexual overtones. He encourages her to come away with him one day for a holiday, and the reader surely fears the inevitable. Maxie slips off her wedding ring and tosses it into the river before they walk further upstream to an inn for lunch. Arnold's questions about divorce disturb her, and he reminds her that after seven years Maxie will be free of her husband if she has not heard from him. Even this, though, does not cajole her into accepting his very frank advances and proposals.

Later Aunt Vole melodramatically makes her swear on the Bible never to see Arnold again. Maxie's eyes light on a verse in Psalm 38: "My heart panteth, my strength faileth me; as for the light of mine eyes, it also is gone from me." The verse certainly captures Maxie's mood; however, this act of divination known as *sortes biblicae* does not disturb her. She does not join her aunt in prayer but rather contemplates "a wonderful shining with eternity, and far-off ineffable joys." After all, she has achieved that state of postponed beauty through her denial of Arnold.

"Fishmonger's Fiddle" has been much admired for its pointed satire of Aunt Vole's merciless noncomformist views, its telling delineation of the fates waiting an innocent schoolmistress, and its unexpected turn at the end where Arnold's "fiddle" or his nonsensical triflings and liberties with Maxie suddenly are reversed against him. Maxie has actually been "fiddling" with Arnold. As H.E. Bates concluded, Coppard was indeed "a man with ripe powers of description, an uncanny knack of weaving a tale . . . a sense of both humour and tragedy."

—David Leon Higdon

FLOWERING JUDAS
by Katherine Anne Porter, 1930

In an important essay on Katherine Anne Porter ("The Eye of the Story"), Eudora Welty, one of Porter's contemporaries and her equal in the delicate art of short fiction, says that by using only enough of the physical world to meet her needs, Porter makes us see the "subjective worlds of hallucination, obsession, fever, guilt." The great critic/artist Robert Penn Warren, in another well-known essay ("Irony with A Center"), however, notes that Porter's stories are characterized by "rich surface detail scattered with apparently casual profuseness and the close structure which makes such detail meaningful."

Although these two famous comments may initially sound contradictory, they actually complement each other and perceptively pinpoint the central quality of Porter's art—her ability to make mere physical reality resonate with moral significance. By means of a tactic that has dominated modern short fiction since Anton Chekhov, Porter makes such stories as her most famous one, "Flowering Judas," appear to be realistic situations about people caught in specific moral dilemmas while at the same time they are spiritual allegories in which characters and objects are emblems of universal moral issues.

Although the conflict in "Flowering Judas" takes place, as Welty says about most of Porter's stories, in the interior of the protagonist's life, the story is less a psychological study of one individual's act of renunciation than it is a symbolic parable of the basic nature of renunciation. Laura, named perhaps for the unattainable and thus idealistic object of Petrarch's love in his famous sonnets, is caught between her desire to embody her own ideals as a Marxist revolutionary in Mexico and her realization that it is the very nature of idealism that it cannot be embodied.

The story appropriately opens with Laura face to face with the revolutionary leader Braggioni, who is so much an incarnation of flesh that his every action compels both Laura and the reader to confront his bodily being. He sits "heaped" over his guitar, "heaves" himself into song, scratching the instrument as it were a pet animal, taking the high notes in a "painful squeal." He "bulges" marvelously in his clothes, "swelling" with "ominous ripeness" over his ammunition belt. Porter says Braggioni has become the symbol of Laura's "many disillusions, for a revolutionist should be lean, animated by heroic faith, a vessel of abstract virtue."

Laura is caught in the disillusionment of all idealists—feeling "betrayed irreparably by the disunion between her way of living and her feeling of what life should be." Externally, she projects the image of one who has rejected the flesh, preferring instead to wear the "uniform of an idea"—sound blue serge and a nunlike round white collar—and thus nobody touches her, even though they praise her "soft round underlip which promises gaiety yet is always grave.'" Braggioni tells her she only thinks she is cold and puzzles on the "notorious virginity" of the simple girl who "covers her great round breasts with thick dark clothe and who hides long invaluably beautiful legs under a heavy skirt."

The many dichotomies in the story—Laura's Catholicism and her socialism, her sensuality and her ascetic renunciation, her dedication to the people and her renunciation of genuine involvement—coalesce in the symbolic dichotomy of Braggioni, who affirms life even though it means throwing himself into the physical and becoming a "professional lover of humanity," and Eugenio, the imprisoned revolutionary who maintains his idealism but who negates life and wants to die because he is bored. The key mythic figures who embody this antithesis in the story are Judas, who gives it its title, and Christ, the one he betrayed.

Given the powerful universal significance of these dichotomies, it is little wonder that they cannot be solved in actuality, but must be resolved aesthetically in a dream—typical of medieval dream visions that the story in some ways resembles. In Laura's dream she refuses to follow Eugenio to death because he will not take her hand. In a dream-distorted reversal of the Christian Communion, Eugenio gives her bleeding flowers from the Judas tree, (the tree from which Judas hanged himself), which she greedily eats. However, rather than affirming the inextricable union of body and spirit as does the Christian Communion, Laura's act is a negative one of betrayal for helping Eugenio to escape life. The story ends with the "holy talismanic word" Laura always uses that keeps her from being led into evil but which also keeps her from being involved in life—"No."

—Charles E. May

FRAIL VESSEL
by Mary Lavin, 1956

Apart from two novels, Mary Lavin's literary reputation rests exclusively on her short fiction, of which she has published ten volumes, together with numerous other selected and collected editions. "Frail Vessel," from *The Patriot Son and Other Stories* (1956), is typical of the stories of her middle period, being less generalized than her earlier work and less discursive than her later fiction.

"Frail Vessel" is set in the small-town provincial Ireland in which Lavin grew up and with whose middle class she was intimately familiar. Reared in the fledgling years of the Irish Free State, as the newly independent country was then called, Lavin was exposed to the full force of cultural austerity and moral timorousness that characterised Irish social life in this period. The marks of this formative environment, and in particular its effects on the lives of women, are to be found throughout her accomplished output. Her stories are an exemplary chronicle of a submerged population group within a generally submerged population. The full significance of her work, from both a cultural and artistic point of view, has yet to be given its due recognition.

As in many of her stories, setting is rendered so sketchily as to seem makeshift. Yet despite the place's anonymity—a relative rarity in Irish writing—Lavin deftly depicts its mean streets, indifferent housing, and lack of opportunity. These are represented as the devitalised facades behind which an inner reality, consisting of a narrow economy and an exploitative morality, thrives. In addition, depriving the setting of a name draws attention to the story's expertly controlled orchestration of motifs of face-making, face-saving, shamefacedness, and related concerns, all of which have a bearing on the kind of name Bedelia believes her sister is making for herself in her hapless marriage to Alphonsus O'Brien.

As though to emphasise the relevance of names, the story's twin protagonists' are named so as to suggestively evoke their characters: beadle-like Bedelia and somewhat giddy Liddy. It is at the point at which such facile evocations no longer suffice, however, that the characters' reality transpires. Liddy is not merely a picture of youthful flightiness. And Bedelia fails in her attempt to police her young sister's destiny. Just as Lavin reveals the forces that sustain the moribund town, a place to which the reader is introduced by way of a funeral, so she unmasks the human consequences of either adopting or resisting the spirit of such a place.

The revelation is accomplished by means of a carefully structured system of dualities. This embraces not only the two sisters but also their husbands, the feckless and opportunistic Alphonsus and the careful, clerkly Daniel. The contrast between the two men is highlighted by their financial scrupulousness, though the limited, economically-determined role each man plays underlines the unrewarding social context in which he is expected to function. Under the circumstances, Alphonsus's inability to comply with such expectations slyly speaks in his favor. This view is necessary since there must be some objective basis for Liddy's attachment to him. If such a basis is missing, there is a risk of reading Liddy's marriage, and her view of it, as an act of self-deception, thereby rendering spurious her resistance to Bedelia's baleful influence.

It is that resistance, however, that substantiates Liddy's triumph. Impoverished, pregnant, possibly abandoned, obliged to "creep back" to her domineering sister, Liddy yet possesses what Bedelia cannot comprehend. What this possession consists of is also kept at a somewhat intriguing distance from the reader, as is Liddy's marriage itself. In this way, Lavin creates a sense of the ineffable fulfillment Liddy experiences in her relationship with Alphonsus. This fulfillment does not derive from the marriage as such, or at least not from the marriage institutionally considered, which is Bedelia's perspective on it.

On the contrary, as the closing words of the story make clear, Liddy's bliss derives from a sense of intimacy whose components the reader may infer without being shown. By means of such sympathetic inference, Bedelia's inhibiting presence in the story may be circumvented, so that the reader experiences something of Liddy's ultimate autonomy and authenticity. The realignment of forces that "Frail Vessel" proposes reduces the power of that somewhat empty vessel, Bedelia, whose view of life is determined by a strongly-developed attachment to social pomp and circumstance. In place of that attachment is Liddy's somewhat wayward, unpredictable, ostensibly inappropriate, and socially unsuccessful marriage to Alphonsus. The very unlikelihood of that relationship gives it a distinctiveness, daring, and intrigue which makes it far more substantial for Liddy than all Bedelia's oppressive orthodoxies, though whether this inner substance can protect Liddy remains a painfully open question, rendering her frailty both a spiritual strength and a social weakness.

Lavin's implicit endorsement of Liddy's spirit is conveyed in the story's spontaneous, intimate style. Here again, the story functions in terms of a telling duality. Bedelia is characterised by means of stream of consciousness. Yet that consciousness belies its flow and emerges, rather, as a scheming, self-regarding instrument. In contrast, no direct access is provided to Liddy's thought processes. But her speech, over which she is not always able to exercise appropriate control, reveals her openness, lack of guile, integrity, and self-respect. This artful verbal complement, which underwrites the story's more prominent structuring of duality, emphasises Lavin's literary economy and imaginative resourcefulness, and shows how she, like Liddy, finds much in what appears to be so little.

—George O'Brien

FRANCIS SILVER
by Hal Porter, 1962

It is difficult to avoid questions of autobiography in Hal Porter's short fiction. Many of his stories are told in the first-person voice and can be traced to incidents in his life experience, whether they are set in his native state of Victoria, Australia, or in places he has lived in or visited, including Rome, London, Athens, Tokyo, or Venice. In a typically mischievous comment, Porter remarked in 1969 on his "lack of imagination," comparing his "reportage" to the activities of a "shoplifter" from his past. Nevertheless, he admitted to the techniques of an "illusionist," especially regarding written conversation in fiction: "The reader has to be tricked with a selection of words which *look* like what is supposed to be heard."

Porter's story "Francis Silver" was published in 1962 in the second of his seven volumes of short stories, *A Bachelor's Children*. Autobiographical accuracy is indicated by many reported details of Porter's early life. A meticulous collector of the bric-a-brac of furniture, songs, architecture, photographs, and idioms in his fiction, Porter felt that "an anachronism mars all." Important though such details are in Porter's short fiction, however, they are not the heart of it.

"Francis Silver" is the story of a middle-aged man (the first-person narrator) whose mother has died at the age of 41 when he was only 18 years old. The oldest of seven children, he, the firstborn, is the one destined to carry the memory of his mother, his mother's memories. Indeed, the story turns on the nature of memory, its fragility and its notorious unreliability. The emotional impact conveyed to the reader is of a young man who identifies deeply with his mother and for whom his father is a shadowy insubstantial figure. The loss of the mother is a crisis for the young man, though it provokes no emotional death-bed scenes in the story. Rather, the story's focus is on a son's capacity to recall his mother's memories and to place them in his own life experience.

Who then is Francis Silver? He is the principal myth figure of the narrator's mother's memories. Throughout childhood, he is the invisible "other" in his mother's domestic life—the lover whom she left to marry the boy's placid father:

> In marrying the country wooer, my father, and darning [his] socks, mother left the suburb for a country town set smack-flat on the wind-combed plans of Gippsland. She also left behind Francis Silver, whom she never saw again, at least not physically. He lived on, remarkably visible, in a special display-case of her memories.

In a separate album, among all the postcards of the prewar period of his mother's young womanhood, those of Francis Silver have "a sacred quality." To the eldest son, Silver comes to represent all that his father is not. A picture-framer with his own business, he is presented to the son as "artistic and sensitive":

> He smoked Turkish cigarettes, did not drink, was popular with other sensitive young men, wore a gold ring with a ruby in it, was very proud of his small feet, and loved the theatre.

Francis Silver thus becomes a talisman of the boy's links with his mother. Silver's image emerges from the boy's hallowed world of domesticity which the mother has animated with her vivacious presence, making even the rituals of ironing the sheets a sacred event. Before she dies, the mother entrusts her son with the task of returning the album of postcards to their sender and of personally burning a lock of her hair in an envelope with Francis Silver's name on it.

Faithful to his mother's wishes, the son has carried out these tasks. What gives a special force to the concluding part of this tightly constructed story, with its artfully contrived flashbacks, is the scope its author leaves for both ironic reflection and feeling. The irony is evoked by the boy's first-hand observations of the myth figure from his childhood, when he visits him at his shop. The "real" Francis Silver is short and fat and lisps. Moreover, he has totally forgotten the boy's mother. How can this person be his alternative father? The boy/man's confusion is patent: "Scraps of the past were blowing about my brain like the litter at the end of a perfect picnic." Disillusion is inevitable but is not dwelt upon: the middle-aged narrator is better able to give an ironic perspective to the boy's confrontation between myth and physical reality. Moreover, the rites of initiation have a further twist. The boy prepares to tell a saving lie to his father, for whom Francis Silver has been a necessary imaginative counterpart throughout his married life—the invisible, imagined rival.

In the recognition that inventive lying is necessary, the narrator reconfirms that he is his mother's son.

In this perfectly proportioned rites of passage story, the conclusion returns us to the young man's moment of pain. Porter once remarked that he thought of his conclusions first and wrote towards them. The concluding sentence in this story captures the narrator's momentary perception of the burning of his mother's envelope to Francis Silver with a lock of her hair in it: "It writhed and writhed in an agony I could not bear to watch." He has fulfilled her dying wish. Is he now his own man or forever hers?

—Bruce Bennett

FREE JOE AND THE REST OF THE WORLD
by Joel Chandler Harris, 1884

Though written in the post-Reconstruction era, "Free Joe and the Rest of the World" presents Joel Chandler Harris's anatomy of the antebellum society of middle Georgia. At the top of this social order are the slaveowners, Judge Alfred Wellington and "Spite" Calderwood, who respectively exemplify the conventional good and bad masters. Under the guardianship of the former, Free Joe and his enslaved wife, Lucinda, enjoy a pastoral existence: Lucinda is "well provided for," and Joe has no trouble meeting his needs. When Calderwood inherits the plantation, their lives change. The new owner bars Joe from his property even though the freedman has a legal pass, and when Calderwood learns that Lucinda and her husband continue to meet secretly, he takes the woman to Macon, 60 miles away, and sells her.

While Harris thus acknowledges the tyrannical power and cruelty of Calderwood, the story does not indict the system that allows him to flout the law and divide families. Harris's slaves are happy: they "laughed loudly day by day, . . . sang at their work and danced at their frolics." None of them envies Joe's lot, and Free Joe recognizes that because he has no master he has no friend; because he has no single owner he is subservient to everyone.

As Harris depicts pre-Civil War Hillsborough, the lower class whites are socially inferior to the slaves. Had Joe not been free he would have scorned the company of the Staleys, who are, in Harris's words, "poor white trash." They nonetheless provide the freedman with the little sympathy and help he receives. That sympathy is indeed limited; Harris does not gloss over their racist attitudes. When Free Joe tells the Staleys that he has not seen his wife in nearly a month, Becky replies, "It hain't a-gwine to hurt you," and her brother, Micajah, offers a stereotypical view of black fickleness: "Maybe she's up an' took up wi' some un else. . . .You know what the sayin' is: 'New master, new nigger.'" Only after his sister's conjuring indicates that Lucinda has undertaken a journey does Micajah recall that he had seen Calderwood taking her away. The matter was not important enough to remember, Free Joe too insignificant to be told. At the same time, only the Staleys condemn Calderwood's actions and glimpse Joe's humanity beneath his black skin. In a passage that may be the source for Gavin Steven's comments in chapter 19 of Faulkner's *Light in August,* in which the lawyer attributes some of Joe Christmas's actions to his black blood and others to his white heritage, Becky distinguishes between Free Joe's grinning, which is "nigger," and his barely restrained tears when he hears Lucinda's name.

At the bottom of the social order is the freed slave. Plantation owners fear his influence; yeoman whites are at best ambivalent and often hostile; slaves despise him, lose "no opportunity to treat him with contumely," and inform Calderwood of his clandestine meetings with Lucinda. His only companion is his dog, Dan, whose moods reflect Free Joe's, and whose death foreshadows his master's. In the world of antebellum Hillsborough, Dan and Free Joe are social equals.

Harris sympathizes with Free Joe, whose soul at the end of the story is "summoned as a witness before the Lord God of Hosts." This story was Harris's favorite, not least because the title character's isolation mirrors his own. Less consciously, the story reflects Harris's ambivalence towards blacks. Free Joe is a good person, but Harris presents him, in stereotypical racist terms, as lazy, childishly naive, and unperceptive. Similarly, when Dan summons Lucinda to meet Free Joe, she "gives the incident a twist in the direction of superstition."

This ambivalence extends to Harris's attitude toward the Old and New South. Unlike some other local color writers of the period who presented unblemished portraits of plantation life, Harris, himself an outsider to that world, recognized its flaws. Yet he disliked the mercantile mentality that characterized the South after the Civil War. The serpent in the garden of Hillsborough is Major Frampton, a slave trader. He comes to prey on the town, and though it proves wiser than he, Free Joe is his legacy.

As a character sketch and as a local color story "Free Joe" offers pleasurable reading. As a measure of its author's mind it exposes his sense of isolation and his divided loyalties. Different as this story is from the "Uncle Remus" tales, it embodies the same values and contradictions. Like them, too, it reveals Harris's ear for dialect, which mirrors social class. Calderwood's is closest to standard English, but it contains colloquial and ungrammatical elements that emphasize the man's ignorance and question his fitness for the position he holds. The blacks and poor whites sound very much alike, as they would in reality, but the former say "de" for "the," "kyards" for "cards." Harris also allows Becky Staley to lapse occasionally into standard English to lend authority to her statements.

"Free Joe" demonstrates how far the South had progressed in its racial attitudes since the Civil War. It also shows how far it still had to go.

—Joseph Rosenblum

G

THE GARDEN OF FORKING PATHS (El jardín de senderos que se bifurcan)
by Jorge Luis Borges, 1941

"El jardín de senderos que se bifurcan" ("The Garden of Forking Paths") was published for the first time in a small collection of the same name, in 1941, and again in a larger collection of Borge's stories, *Ficciones (Fictions)* in 1944. It was translated by Donald A. Yates in *Labyrinths: Selected Stories & Other Writings* (1964). It is a story in which every phrase functions on several levels of meaning, and in which the central metaphor, that of an infinite book never completely written, serves as a paradigm of Borges's own conception of the ideal literary work. The story opens with an introductory paragraph by an "editor" making a reference to a specific page in a history of World War I, and goes on to refer to a manuscript, lacking its first two pages, which supposedly elucidates the events described in that history. The rest of the story consists of a "transcription" of that manuscript. At the very opening, the authorship or point-of-view of this story is multi-layered and the events occurring in it are seen from more than one perspective simultaneously.

Although the central metaphor of the story turns out to be a book, which, among other things, is a tautological metaphor for the story itself, it is first presented as a garden. The manuscript's narrator is a Chinese man living in England during World War I and working as a German spy. He, Yu Tsun, has been found out by Captain Richard Madden, who is pursuing him. Before he is caught, Yu Tsun must send a message to Germany about the location, in the city of Albert, of a British artillery park, so the Germans can bomb it. He chooses to send that message by murdering a man named Stephen Albert, a name he finds in the telephone book, but who, seemingly by coincidence, turns out to be a sinologist with an interest in the work of Yu Tsun's distant ancestor. The narrator would be caught, and the murder reported in the newspapers, thus alerting the Germans as to the whereabouts of the artillery park. He succeeds, is caught by Madden, and the city of Albert is bombed. This spy story, however, appears to merely float on the surface of the narration, and seems quite incidental to its real content. The story is very much like the observation Albert makes to the narrator, in the course of their conversation, about the book by Yu Tsun's ancestor in which the one word that never appears is its central theme: time. This story, which slyly purports to be less ambitious than that novel, is referred to here, I believe, and "time," and humankind's consciousness of it, is its own central theme.

That theme is presented first, however, not as time, but as an idea of a labyrinthine garden, which was purportedly designed or conceived of by the narrator's ancestor in China. It is clear from a number of references in the story that this garden is presented as a kind of metaphor for the world, and perhaps for the world's origin: the Garden of Eden certainly comes to mind. The narrator, entering Stephen Albert's Chinese-style garden, with its labyrinthine paths, says it is "like those of my childhood." The instructions he receives about how to get to the garden, to keep turning left, are instructions often used to guide one through a labyrinth, but they also describe a square: for if one keeps turning to the left, one arrives at one's place of origin. It is also significant that early in the story, the moon is described not as "full" but as "circular," which in this context is a clue to the circular nature of the world here presented. In using the location of a reproduction of an ancient Chinese garden as a means of communicating to the German military, the narrator has superimposed his own distant, ancestral past upon the present, as if time were circular, or in some way complete, total.

The garden presents another image, however, which is not circular, but labyrinthine, and it is this image that is predominant in the story. The "garden of forking paths" of the narrator's ancestor turns out to have been not a garden, but a labyrinthine and infinite book that he had started to write but never completed, and which had been lost. Stephen Albert had the manuscript of the book, which to most readers seemed a confused mess of disconnected fragments, contradictory plots, and rough sketches. What the ancestor had tried to do, however, was present an image of the world in which all possible outcomes of all possible events co-existed simultaneously, as if reality were not a single chain of events, but a swarm of all possible events, all occurring in the present, and of which a human being was only fragmentarily aware. This image of time and reality is referred to frequently by the narrator: at the very start of the story, for example, he speaks of thinking that "everything happens to one precisely, precisely now." Further on, as he plans the murder of Albert, he says that the person planning a horrible act must imagine that he has already done it, that the "future is as irrevocable as the past." He also speaks of feeling "vulnerable, infinitely so," and of feeling an "intangible swarming," and that the "afternoon was intimate, infinite."

The "plot" of this story, then, that of the characters acting in history, is quite deliberately treated as an incidental part of a much larger picture. That picture, as represented by the book and the garden, is one of a universe in which any particular "story" is merely one string of events in an innumerable forking of events, of possible different outcomes, all of which may exist, and exist at the same time. No particular sequence is of any greater importance. The story as a whole reflects, and is immersed in, this model of the universe. The pathos is, that it is perceived from the viewpoint of the human dilemma, or perhaps tragedy: that the individual can only be aware of a tiny fragment of it all, and at best only sense that "intangible swarming" of the larger reality. As Yu Tsun's ancestor put it, "I leave to the various futures (not to all) my garden of forking paths."

The primary response to this model of the universe (in which all time and space are conflated into the present, and all possible outcomes of all possible events occur, in an infinite web or net) seems to be one of fatigue and hopelessness: the narrator's last line states, "no one can know . . . my innumerable contrition and weariness." This would seem to be the response, as in many of Borges's stories, to the loss of belief in the idea of an individual's having any kind of true free will or uniqueness. And yet the characters in these stories all have a kind of persistence and autonomy about them in spite of the world they think they have discovered: they are all in pursuit of something, intent on understanding or on following through to the end a particular process of thought or investigation. Yu Tsun, the narrator in "The Garden of Forking Paths," intent on completing his mission as a German spy, comes to understand his place in the universe; Stephen Albert is in pursuit of an understanding of an ancient labyrinthine book; and Richard Madden is in pursuit of a German spy. All of them complete their goals, in a sense. The paradox is that their goals are none of them quite what they had imagined them to be, and there is a resultant sense of tragedy or disillusionment: Albert dies, Madden does not understand the meaning of Albert's death, and Yu Tsun experiences a great "contrition and weariness." The greater understanding that really occurs in this story is the reader's, perhaps; a kind of global or non-individuated understanding, as if knowledge, and humankind, did not exist in individuals, but as a kind of supra-knowledge, the consciousness of the swarm or whole, which is perhaps what Yu Tsun sensed when he felt that "intangible swarming" in the "intimate, infinite" afternoon.

—John M. Bennett

THE GARDEN PARTY
by Katherine Mansfield, 1922

Katherine Mansfield published *The Garden Party and Other Stories* in 1922, the same year that T.S. Eliot published *The Waste Land*, and James Joyce published *Ulysses*. Mansfield's collection similarly represents the mature progress of her artistry. It contains some of her finest work, and illustrates the artistic usefulness of her New Zealand background. The title story, "The Garden Party," tells of a lavish occasion. The marquee has been erected, the flowers arranged, the women of the household dressed, and the guests are about to arrive when the news is brought: a young man, a carter, who lived in the poor cottages in the road below the house, has been killed in an accident. The sensitive Laura wishes to abandon the party, but practicality prevails. The grieving household is ignored until the party is over, when Laura, still in party attire, is sent with a basket of sandwiches and cream cakes to comfort the grieving family. Anthony Apiers, the eminent Mansfield biographer, once asked Mansfield's sister Vera about the veracity of the tale. Had there been a garden party, and was there an accident? She is said to have replied, "Indeed there was. . . .And I was the one who went down with the things." Such is the tenuous relation between fact and fiction.

The fictional version, however, demonstrates the immediacy with which Mansfield absorbs the reader into her stories. The story begins, "And after all the weather was ideal. They could not have had a more perfect day for a garden party if they had ordered it. Windless, warm." The narrator piles on detail, acutely observed: gardeners are mowing and sweeping, there are dark flat rosettes where the daisy plants had been, and the green bushes are bowed with roses. Laura's voice is heard rather than described, and character is swiftly depicted in a brief interchange with her mother and sister. Laura is young, but old enough to feel gauche. The workmen look impressive and she "wished now that she was not holding that piece of bread and butter. . . .She blushed and tried to look severe and even a little bit short sighted as she came up to them." Laura, the artistic one, was to supervise the placement of the marquee.

Mansfield, no less than James Joyce, demonstrates a preoccupation with the growth of an artistic sensibility. Laura must negotiate the difficult terrain between the values inculcated by her upper-middle class upbringing and those of a working class which lie, largely, outside of her experience. She must do so in a sparsely populated New Zealand where utility and practicality are, of necessity, revered. Thus, it is the workmen who dictate the placement of the marquee: "Against the karakas. . . .And they were so lovely, with their broad, gleaming leaves, and their clusters of yellow fruit . . . Must they be hidden by a marquee? They must." Nevertheless, Laura experiments with the working-class role. Class distinctions were absurd, and she preferred the broad-shouldered workmen who care for the smell of lavender to the silly boys who came to Sunday night supper. To show how much she despised stupid conversation Laura took a big bite of bread and butter: "She felt just like a working girl."

The adolescent oscillation of Laura's emotions allows the development of a tightly controlled tension in "The Garden Party." Beneath Laura's sadness and genuine emotion lies the grotesquely humorous incongruity that must attend the death of a man who has had the bad taste to get himself killed on the day of a garden party. Godber's man tells his tale with relish, and Laura's extravagant wish to stop the party is beyond comprehension. After all, warns sister Jose, "If you're going to stop a band playing every time some one has an accident, you'll lead a very strenuous life." Laura is equally astonished by her mother's behaviour. On being told that a man has been killed, her mother says, "Not in the garden?" Mansfield's humour at such times is Wildean; her characters demonstrate a similar incapacity to distinguish between the relative importance of deaths and cups of tea. Only Laura wonders if the grieving widow will like a basket of sandwiches and cream puffs.

It is, then, to Laura that the glimpse of transcendence is given. Urged to view the dead body of the young man, Laura discovers him remote and peaceful, given up to his dream: "What did garden parties and baskets and lace frocks matter to him? He was far from all those things. He was wonderful, beautiful. . . .All is well, said that sleeping face. This is just as it should be. I am content." The unique moment passes, and Laura returns to character. On such occasions one is expected to cry, or to say something: "Forgive my hat," she says.

Later, only Laura's brother understands. Mansfield's own brother, of course, died on 7 October 1915 as the result of a hand grenade accident in World War I. In January 1916 she wrote in her journal: "Now—now I want to write recollections of my own country. Yes I want to write about my own country until I simply exhaust my store. . . .My brother & I were born there . . . in my thoughts I range with him over all the remembered places."

—Jan Pilditch

GEORGY PORGY
by Roald Dahl, 1960

The title of Dahl's story "Georgy Porgy" (in *Kiss, Kiss,* 1960) comes from the old English nursery rhyme:

Georgie Porgie, pudding and pie,
Kissed the girls and made them cry;
When the boys came out to play,
Georgie Porgie ran away.

According to Peter and Iona Opie, in *The Oxford Dictionary of Nursery Rhymes,* "numerous guesses have been hazarded that an historical character is portrayed . . . no evidence is vouchsafed." The rhyme is surely about sexual furtiveness and timidity, the theme of this story. The tale belongs to the genre dating from the 19th century in which the narrator is a madman whose craziness is gradually revealed, with a startling climax at the end. Towards the end of the 19th century, the Gothic tradition drew on the divided self, giving stories of the unconscious. Freudianism, with its emphasis on the concealed, was a gift to the genre, and Dahl seized on it, writing a horror story beneath a smooth social surface, intermittently disrupted. Dahl is the heir of Poe in the ability to give the reader a *frisson.*

The rationale is clear to us, though not entirely so to the protagonist. It is immediately apparent that there is a gap between the narrator's perceptions and our own: George tells us he is "moderately matured and rounded" and makes the odd claim that he "speaks Greek and Latin." While many educated gentlemen can claim literacy in those languages, to write of speaking them immediately alerts us to possible eccentricity. Mention of speaking in "the pulpit" at the end of the first paragraph informs us that the narrator is a clergyman. He confesses to a horror of women, manifested in a phobia about touching them. His interpretation of this anxiety is eccentric: in the schoolboy, says the narrator, "it is simply Dame Nature's way of putting on the brakes and holding the lad back until he is old enough to behave himself like a gentleman. I approve of that." A strange view of nature is established here. George's manifestly ugly physique is described with equally imperceptive smugness. Clearly the narrator is out of touch with his own feelings and the reader's unease is aroused, unease tinged with amusement. George admits to longing for the "full-blown violent embrace" — on the dance floor. As a country vicar he is of course surrounded by women and is therefore "as jumpy as a squirrel."

George remembers his "wonderful" mother, who to us is a flashy eccentric: she smoked incessantly and had "progressive" notions about children tasting alcohol and being informed about the facts of life — there should be no secrets from children. She embarrasses her husband by starting to tell the son the facts of life and forbids either of them to feel embarrassed.

Soon afterwards, George is woken in the middle of a cold night and dragged outside to watch the pet rabbit giving birth, accompanied by running commentary on nature's wisdom from his mother, who identifies the rabbit mother with herself. She gushes that the rabbit mother is "fondling and kissing it all over" but George sees that the mother rabbit, unable to avoid the humans' intrusive curiosity, is actually eating the baby. Identifying the mothers one with the other, George sees her mouth as a "big round gaping hole with a black centre" (implicitly a hell mouth with traditional sexual overtones). She touches him and he runs away across a main road and she is killed. George concludes "she gave me a nasty fright with those rabbits, but it wasn't her fault and anyway queer things like that were always happening between her and me. I had come to regard them as a kind of toughening process."

The spinsters of the parish decide that the shy vicar needs "loosening up": when one presumes to squeeze his hand, he feels "as though a cobra was coiling itself around my wrist." Similar advances reduce him to a "nervous wreck." We read that George was "mad about women" — as a guilt-ridden voyeur.

Having acquired some pet rats, he sets up a social experiment, segregating males and females, identifying the females with his intrusive parishioners. It is the females who electrocute themselves by trying to cross the barrier, while the males remain passive. George's interpretation is characteristic: "In one stroke I had laid open the incredibly lascivious . . . nature of the female. My own sex was vindicated; my own conscience was cleared." He toys with the idea of electrifying his own garden fence.

On a social occasion, the ladies slyly give George an alcoholic fruit drink. He is captivated by a large "uncommonly fine" woman who is, we learn with a shock, no "more than forty-eight or nine." Innocently, he gets drunk, and she attempts to seduce him, or at least get him to kiss her. Suddenly he panics at the sight of her open mouth and starts hallucinating: he is convinced that she has swallowed him alive, "just like that baby rabbit."

He passes out and overhears women's voices commiserating and talking about "a sex maniac" and a damaged mouth. The narrative blandly continues: George is convinced that he is living in "the duodenal loop, just before it begins to run vertically downward in front of the right kidney." He is, of course, in a padded cell.

It is left to the reader to recognize that George hated and feared his mother, that he has transferred this complex of emotions to women in general, that he is perversely attracted by large mature women who pleasurably threaten him, and that he is indeed a "sex maniac" but of the guilt-ridden and passive kind, in no way active until dangerously and irresponsibly provoked. And like all victims of delusory systems, he regards his own reactions as normal. The effectiveness of the story comes from the tension between what is described and the way we, the readers, feel about it. Fear and repulsion towards female sexuality can characterise male adolescence and may survive in the adult: thus the story, although occasionally almost too explicit, earns response.

—Valerie Grosvenor Myer

THE GIFT OF THE MAGI
by O. Henry, 1906

A prolific writer, O. Henry turned out over 250 short stories between 1899 and 1910. These stories have been widely read and enjoyed throughout the world, and even though in the eyes of some they may not be considered first-rate literature, they have become a significant part of the short story genre. "The Gift of the Magi," collected in *The Four Million* (1906), stands as a clear example of O. Henry's mastery of the sentimental story with the surprise ending.

More a short short story, "The Gift of the Magi" covers only a few pages, but it has a variety of appeals to popular and traditional sentiment. The two main characters, Della and Jim, are a happily married couple living near the edge of poverty in an eight dollar a week flat, each with the same problem of trying to figure out how to buy a Christmas present for the other. How they solve their mutual problem is the essence of the story.

"One dollar and eighty-seven cents. That was all. And sixty cents of it was in pennies." Thus does O. Henry pique the interest of his reader at the opening of the story—and thus does Della Dillingham Young ponder on Christmas Eve how to get a present worthy of her husband Jim. Catching a reflection of herself in a strip of pier glass between the windows of the flat, Della finds her inspiration. O. Henry quickly points out here that Della and Jim each have a prized possession: she has beautiful long hair that ripples and shines "like a cascade of brown waters" and he has a gold watch that was his father's and his grandfather's before that. Della's inspiration is to sell her hair to a hairgoods store and to use the money to buy Jim a fob chain for his watch. With the 20 dollars she receives for her hair, she ransacks the stores and finds a chain that she know Jim will be proud of.

Della's excitement about her gift for Jim fades a bit when she wonders how her husband will like her new hair style— "tiny, close-lying curls that made her look wonderfully like a truant schoolboy." When he arrives home, she runs to his arms explaining what she has done and assuring him that her hair will grow back quickly. Momentarily stunned, Jim takes a small package from his coat pocket and throws it upon the table, telling Della that nothing could change his feelings for her. Della opens the package and to her astonishment finds the set of combs for her hair that she has been worshipping for so long in a Broadway store window—"pure tortoise shell, with jewelled rims—just the shade to wear in the beautiful vanished hair." Again reminding Jim that her hair grows fast, Della gives Jim his present. When he opens it, she asks for his watch so that they can see how it will look with the new fob. Jim's response is to tumble down on the couch with his hands behind his head, saying that they should put their presents away and "keep 'em for a while. They're too nice to use just as presents. I sold the watch to get the money to buy your combs."

And so the story ends with O. Henry making a moral point that though Della and Jim may have unwisely sacrificed for each other their greatest treasures, yet "in a last word to the wise of these days let it be said that of all who give gifts these two were the wisest."

If short stories can be divided between those considered quality stories and those considered craft or commercial stories, "The Gift of the Magi" would fall into the latter category. And surely the reader of this story sees clearly the craftmanship of O. Henry. Utilizing a plot of very little action and two characters about whom little is told, he presents a story of foreshadowing, suspense, and surprise that holds the reader to the end. Focusing on the precarious financial situation of Della and Jim and on their love for each other, he tells the reader only what is necessary to elicit sympathy for the couple. Della's predicament at the opening of the story is mundane enough as is her crying about it; as O. Henry points out, "life is made up of sobs, sniffles, and smiles, with sniffles predominating." And it is Della's story until near the end when Jim comes home. We are shown explicitly the love and loyalty that she feels for her husband, but we can only wonder whether these feelings are returned. As Della waits in both anticipation and some trepidation for Jim's arrival, so too does the reader. With the ending of that suspense, of course, comes

the surprise that each character has given up the one thing that the other hoped to embellish.

"The Gift of the Magi" is, to be sure, a sentimental, surprise-ending story, the type that is passé now. Certainly, as an example of that kind of story, it stands on its own merit. But more than that, "The Gift of the Magi," in its stark simplicity, touches a common cord of understanding of, and yearning for, the basic relationship of mutual love and sacrifice exhibited by Della and Jim. Indeed, in the story's final words, "They are the Magi."

—Wilton Eckley

GILLETTE, OR THE UNKNOWN MASTERPIECE.
See **THE UNKNOWN MASTERPIECE.**

GIMPEL THE FOOL
by Isaac Bashevis Singer, 1957

Singer's best work is found in his short fiction, and "Gimpel the Fool" is one of his masterpieces. It features a kind of character associated with Singer—"the wise or sainted fool," in Irving Howe's phrase.

Singer subtly subverts the customary associations of "fool" from the very beginning of his story. Gimpel, the main character, realizes that he has been deceived when he initially believes the villagers' statement that "the rabbi's wife has been brought to childbed," but he continues to accept their stories even when they become truly fantastic. He accepts them because in the long run it is conducive to peace and quiet—otherwise they shout at him and disturb the tenor of his life—and as long as he resists, the episode (and its unpleasantness) last longer. But the situation is ironical too: since he does not really believe what the villagers say and is not taken in, it is he who is fooling them—not the other way round as they think. In fact, Gimpel serves to expose the inanity of the villagers: the folly of spending so much time in cooking up, elaborating, and collaborating on such silly stories, all to trick one man they consider an idiot, is evident.

Singer thus suggests that Gimpel is not the fool he seems to be. His wisdom lies in his forethought and his realistic acceptance of the world as it is. When the community proceeds to force him to marry an unchaste woman, Elka, it may, he realises characteristically (though the matter is far more serious), make for harmony and an easier life for him if he accepts. Yet the fact is that he himself happens to fancy her. Shrewdness is not lacking either. He and Elka do not do badly, financially, from their marriage. He sees that the village can afford to pay for its fun. They demand and receive a dowry of 50 guilders and a collection. Gimpel possesses practical (if well-concealed) wisdom.

There are, however, more aspects to his wisdom. It is based on goodness. It is emphasized that Gimpel is good-natured, not vicious. He remains so although he is aware of being fooled, aware of people's bad motives, and also aware of his own physical strength. His goodness appears a quality inborn and deeply implanted.

His character goes even deeper. He philosophizes thus on his impending marriage to Elka: "you can't pass through life unscathed, nor expect to." After she has given birth to a child, obviously not his own, four months after their marriage, he thinks, "shoulders are from God, and burdens too." This perhaps shows Gimpel's acceptance of God's will. (Singer's is, after all, a Yiddish story, set in an East European Jewish village.)

Elka does not stop her infidelities after her marriage to Gimpel, but he persists in believing in her primarily because he continues to love her. His desire to indulge her, his outpouring of affection of which he obviously has an immense store and which he can afford to expand unreturned, makes him reluctant to deprive himself of the happiness of her presence and that of the child. His realistic acceptance of the world also helps him to accept errors and imperfections—even Elka's rank faults.

The values Gimpel embodies, kindness, love, and the love of living quietly at peace, are life-affirming because they are based on a lack of awareness. His patient suffering of Elka's temper and his cuckolding—he realizes that others would not put up with it and is fully aware of the extent of his own tolerance—is contrasted with the aimless malice of the villagers.

Gimpel's character undergoes significant changes. Elka's confession of her infidelity on her deathbed provokes and tempts him to revenge himself on society. An orphan, a village baker's poor employee, now a baker himself, he pours a bucket of urine into the dough. He then sees Elka in a dream (reflecting his conscience and belief) and, black-faced, she says: "Because I was false, is everything false too?"—an affirmation of standards that exist apart from the individuals who violate them. Gimpel repents and rejects evil: he buries the bread made with that dough.

He then decides to leave the village—to liberate himself from his history and to free himself from the pattern of life tied to earning a living at the bakery. When he is old and wiser, "having heard a great deal, many lies and falsehoods," he nevertheless discovers paradoxically that "there were really no lies," and also that "the world is entirely an imaginary world, but it is only once removed from the true world." These insights confirm and sanction his earlier behaviour: an objective or subjective truth, the phenomenal world and the interior world, govern his life only as much as he permits; Gimpel's acceptance of the situations and deceptions imposed on him have given him just as much control over his own life as he would have had if he insisted on questioning or rejecting them. Finally, he looks forward to death—because it promises him the happiness of an ultimate, unquestionable reality; but since he is assured of it only in wish-fulfilling dreams, the validity of his belief is left an open question.

Singer himself in this story seems to prefer faith to skepticism. In the final analysis, he suggests that faith offers consolation, and leads to a positive approach and release from self-tormenting anger and doubt.

Simplicity is the fundamental principle of Singer's narration. It shows itself in this story in two ways—in the form and in his characterization. In the first place, Singer appears a master storyteller. In fact he believed that it is the primary task of a writer of fiction to relate a story. He said: "I still believe in the old-fashioned storytelling. The writer should tell a story and the essays should be written by critics." Moreover, he seldom or never attempts to explain the story or character. In this story, the choice of the first-person point of view is particularly effective because it leaves matters open: since all is seen from Gimpel's viewpoint, no judgement is given—except by the reader.

The art of this story is wholly without artifice. It is like the art of Chaucer in the great stories of *The Canterbury Tales*—simple, apparently artless, yet profound.

—D.C.R.A. Goonetilleke

A GLORIOUS MORNING, COMRADE
by Maurice Gee, 1975

The last four stories in Maurice Gee's collection *A Glorious Morning, Comrade* (1975) concern old men. All of them are Gee's attempts to portray his own grandfather, a charismatic figure finally captured in the novel *Plumb*, the first of the Plumb trilogy. When asked once why so many of his stories deal with older people, Gee replied, "Perhaps it comes from an interest in the architecture of the old life. There's the fullness, on the one hand, of experience, and the narrowing down of time on the other. So as one increases and fills out the other is decreasing. You've got a huge imbalance.... Also there's the possibility that it's easy to write about old people, in the sense that so many of them have strongly marked traits and quirks. There's a good deal to latch on to, in a physical way—and in a mental way too. Things so often come out of their minds in a marvellously graspable shape...."

Gee's world is based on power relationships and on a deep mistrust between the sexes—a mistrust that some might argue to be typical of New Zealand society, at least in its earlier, colonial period, in which sexual relationships are constrained by personal limitations or public disapproval, men are territorial and underdeveloped emotionally, and women are managing and possessive. "A Glorious Morning, Comrade" is the last in the eponymous collection. In *Critical Essays on the New Zealand Short Story* (1982), Lauris Edmond notes that the story seems to celebrate "that spark of absurd but indestructible energy" in Pitt-Rimmer that helps him rise above a petty provincial society. Yet a closer reading shows him to some extent as a symptom of the very society he scorns.

Pitt-Rimmer is a bored old man, probably in his late eighties. He has had a distinguished career as a judge, but unlike many retired men, he seems not to need the reflection of these past glories for his sense of self-worth. He gets that by despising his two daughters, but unlike King Lear he conceals his scorn, "pitying their innocence." Because the story is told completely from Pitt-Rimmer's point of view, the reader tends to sympathise with him and his sarcastic judgments of his daughters, their conventional friends, and life in general. His views have that "marvellously graspable shape" that Gee talked about in older people. There is a refreshing iconoclasm, for example, in Pitt-Rimmer's summation of Gallipoli, the great Anzac expedition, as "a very great piece of nonsense." Having been a judge in a small town, Pitt-Rimmer has the lowdown on many of the people (particularly women) he meets, and enjoys excoriating them for their middle class pretensions and hypocrisy, for example when he reminds himself how the mother of the three Bailey girls "broke their hearts by choosing to live in an old people's home."

He will not give his own daughters the satisfaction of getting out of their lives. On the contrary, he will make life as difficult as possible for them by playing his game of escaping. He manoeuvres himself through the town like a chess-piece. Indeed he is proud of the fact that he prefers chess to the far less intellectual game of bridge, at which his daughters excel, and he considers himself the equal of Capablanca. It's only when we see him in scenes of dialogue that we see another light cast on him. In these scenes Gee opens up his character to other judgments, especially the idea that he's a cantankerous, bullying, opinionated old man who uses his age and infirmity to get his own way. When he slyly informs Maisie that her mother had had an affair with his own son-in-law, we see in action someone using his insider knowledge to wield power—always over women—for the sheer pleasure of it. He reveals his misogyny when he confesses to a little boy, "The conspiracy starts at the cradle." His malice reaches its nadir when he tries a final, physical assault on Christine Hunt, and when that doesn't work, draws on his memory of her court case to give a malicious schoolboy snigger about her "frillies."

At this point Gee brilliantly moves the reader back to sympathy for Pitt-Rimmer. He has become hopelessly dependent on his daughters. His curling "into a ball to defeat the cold" is a pitiful image evoking the fetus curled up in the womb, totally dependent. At his moment of greatest triumph he is at his most vulnerable, becoming weary, cold, and dizzy. He asks desperately for his daughters. Pitt-Rimmer's "little victory" by running away and beating his old record is a "life line" to save him from a deep sense of depression and loss. He hints at this existential despair when he says, "I walk on the pipe, Mercy. If I'd fallen off you would never have been born." When he is eventually found and taken home, we begin to sense that he is held captive by these over-protective sisters, who insist on mothering their very able father. The very first line sounds this sadistic note, with the ironically mis-named Mercy (mis-named, Pitt-Rimmer later points out, by his wife and not by him) tying her father's scarf "in a mean granny knot." She and her sister are mean; they exacerbate the familial difference between them and their father by talking to him patronisingly like a baby ("dad-dums") and by describing their card-playing friends as the "girls." As in *King Lear,* there's also a power struggle between the two women. Mercy, the one who stole her sister's husband, is destined to lord it over Barbie; as Pitt-Rimmer observes, "Barbie will be the invalid when I'm dead."

His annotations in a library book continue to win our sympathy for Pitt-Rimmer. They show a man intellectually starved ("he corrected one split infinitive") by small-minded people in a small town, and physically starved—he underlines the mention of breasts and writes at the end of the book, *"Help! I have not had a piece of meat for twenty years."* This is the final of his italicised missives, and the only one to be actually written down. To follow this italicised series within the story is to chart Pitt-Rimmer's slippage from confidence to lonely desperation; eventually, he has no audience except the next borrower of his public library book.

Gee captures brilliantly and obliquely the various facets of old age: the demeaning incontinence, the frustration of a lively mind in an enfeebled body, the frank desire for physical pleasure in a society that presumes age is good only for vegetables and naps, and the inevitable pettymindedness that comes from being looked after. The unstinting realism of Gee's portrayal of Pitt-Rimmer makes the reader accept even more readily his eventual superiority, and admire the way he manages to "walk the pipe," to balance the "huge imbalance" of old age, to stand on the "rim" of the "pit" of mediocrity when everything—society, family,

body—conspire to force him to slide meekly into second childhood and mere oblivion.

—David Dowling

THE GOLDEN CANGUE (Jin sou ji)
by Zhang Ailing, 1943

Zhang Ailing (Eileen Chang), an important novelist and short story writer, has achieved fame in China's postrevolutionary period. A talented Chinese-English translator, Zhang has translated her own novellette, *Jin sou ji* ("The Golden Cangue"), inspired by the *Dream of the Red Chamber*, an 18th-century Chinese novel. "The Golden Cangue" story continues in new, lengthier versions: *Yuan nu (The Embittered Woman)* and *The Rouge of the North* (which she wrote in English). Zhang Ailing's "Nightmare in the Red Chamber" discusses the classical source of "The Golden Cangue."

"The Golden Cangue" illustrates the decadence of the idle rich. Set in Shanghai, the novellette unfolds the degeneration of the heroine, Qi Qiao, and her family. The "golden cangue" symbolizes the destructiveness of the protagonist who metaphorically bears the frame used to hold prisoners in old China; she is both imprisoned and imprisoning. She uses the golden cangue as a way of mutilating others psychologically while this instrument ironically stands for her own exploitation. The motifs of moon, madness, and mutilation, and the themes of exploitation, moral degeneration, and destruction, merge with images and symbols of moon, gold, and green, and the cangue.

The repetition of the motifs evolve through the narrative perspective. At the beginning of the story the moon functions not just as an image, but as a symbol, seen from the viewpoint of the authorial "we." The perspective is of a futurist present, looking backward to the Shanghai of 30 years ago. The Shanghai moon frames both the beginning and the ending of the tale. The point of view shifts from the "we" at the start to an omniscient third person who centers upon the protagonist.

Tragically, the heroine of humble origins, who marries a cripple, suffers an unhappy and unfulfilled life. The third-person narration focuses upon the consciousness of Qi Qiao, who marries into a rich family, and documents her struggles as a daughter-in-law of the Old Mistress and her constant battle for acceptance. As the spouse of the disabled second son, Qi Qiao, the daughter of a sesame oil shopkeeper, was saved from being a concubine by her brother who arranged her marriage through a matchmaker. The heroine discovers she has escaped concubinage only to fill the lowliest role in the family. She learns that women fight for power in the household's hierarchy, illustrating the point that women of lower status suffer in Chinese society.

The novella's plot consists of two parts: the period from the protagonist's marriage to the death of her mother-in-law and her husband, and the period after their demise. In the first part Qi Qiao lacks freedom; in the second part she achieves control over others. After a brief flirtation with her brother-in-law, Qizi, she becomes disillusioned with love because Qizi tries to exploit her financially. Qizi professes his love for the heroine in an effort to gain her trust, but his real intention is to take away her money in a property transaction. Torn by the possibility of love and her disdain for his motives, Qi Qiao, realizes he only wants to use her and continue the pattern of exploitation in her life. When she angrily throws her fan, and sour plumb juice spills on his clothes, the juice becomes the objective correlative of her emotions. Love, like Qizi's robe, is spoiled and soiled. The woman's refusal to negotiate costs her the one chance for love and happiness, however flawed.

When the heroine fails to find fulfillment in love or marriage, she dominates her children and daughter-in-law and falls victim to her opium habit. She manipulates the life of her son after her invalid spouse dies, and she gains independence. The sufferings inflicted by Qi Qiao upon her son's wife and her daughter, Chang An, are detailed. In particular, Chang An, a less-handsome version of her mother, suffers her erratic orders. For the daughter, her mother's madness passes for normalcy. Chang An leaves school because of embarrassment over her mother's scenes. She breaks her engagement with Shi Feng because she realizes her mother's interference will ruin any chance for happiness. Even her opium habit has been instigated by her mother.

Not content with manipulating her daughter's love affair, Qi Qiao causes the death of her daughter-in-law, whom she ridicules by using metaphors of mutilation to expose her planned destruction. Jealous of her son's bride, the mother-in-law keeps her son at her side at night while smoking opium and while making him reveal his sexual intimacies with his wife. She even gives her son a concubine and makes him smoke opium to drive him further from his wife. Finally, the ill-fated bride dies under the garish light of a huge white moon.

At the conclusion of the story, Qi Qiao lies in an opium stupor, reflecting upon her ruined life and the hatred of those around her:

> For forty years now she had worn a golden cangue.
> She had used its heavy edges to chop down several
> people. She knew that her son and daughter hated her
> to death, that the relatives on her husband's side
> hated her and that her own kinfolk also hated her.

The protagonist destroys or mutilates every close relationship, but at the end she is conscious of the bitterness of her life and the hatred she had engendered. She realizes that the golden cangue that imprisoned her has cut her off from those who loved her.

The story offers information on family social structure, styles of living, and conversation. While focusing upon the theme of love lost, "The Golden Cangue," through brevity and symbolism, paints a devastating picture of its protagonist's destructiveness.

Zhang Ailing's brief fiction recreates the traditional world of Chinese families and culture and the hierarchical order of households. In "The Golden Cangue" she also shows her Modernist side in her use of time and symbols. The issue of the exploitation of women strikes a resonant note with Western readers, as do the power struggles among women family members and servants. However, the juxtaposition of love and hate, and jealousy and revenge, creates universal themes and symbols. Zhang Ailing's acute perception of female consciousness and her often ironic observations point to her movement from the traditional to the modern.

—Shirley J. Paolini

———

GOOD COUNTRY PEOPLE
by Flannery O'Connor, 1955

Perhaps there was a time when Flannery O'Connor was regarded chiefly as a cult author adored by Catholic readers on the basis of her unusual southern Catholic background, but those days are gone forever. Her fiction and her nonfiction are distinguished by a religious ardor, to be sure, but the former is never tendentious or preachy. Rather, O'Connor is artist enough to let her characters hang their own moral selves, generally on the basis of that pride that goeth before a fall, or that fails to anticipate its own shortcomings in the face of other forms of pride, and other follies and vices as well.

An often-anthologized story in this mode is "Good Country People." Though its title drips with O'Connor's usual caustic irony as regards folk sententiousness, it expands as the story proceeds to hoist as well those who think themselves superior to such simplistic usage. In her more public utterances, O'Connor noted that we are inclined to accept the southern grotesque as the local norm when we might well refuse its applicability to our own lives. In O'Connor's work, we are all, northern and southern, capable of grotesquerie, in just the way Sherwood Anderson employed the term. In O'Connor's unremitting world view, we are all monsters in some sense or other.

Ironical too are the names of the two women whose conversations parenthesize O'Connor's story. Mrs. Hopewell is heard talking to her employee Mrs. Freeman, whom she has hired because she and her husband were reputed to be "good country people," at the beginning and the ending of the story. Mrs. Hopewell and Mrs. Freeman are quick to slip into the dialogue of maxims that apparently marks "good country people":

> "I've always been quick. It's some that are quicker
> than others."
> "Everybody is different," Mrs. Hopewell said.
> "Yes, most people is," Mrs. Freeman said.
> "It takes all kinds to make the world."
> "I always said it myself."

These banal routines of oneupmanship morning banter are overheard by Mrs. Hopewell's daughter, "large hulking Joy," as early as the latter's morning bathroom visits, and O'Connor begins to shift the story's focus to this ungainly woman of 32 years who has lost a leg, acquired a Ph.D. in philosophy—which in her mother's mind becomes redundantly useless—and changed her legal name to "Hulga," a switch from a "beautiful name" to "the ugliest name in the language," apparently the former Joy's claim to having addressed her identity candidly.

It would hardly be surprising if the intellectual O'Connor might not have intended to parody herself in the person of Joy/Hulga. O'Connor was killed early on by the disease lupus, while Hulga, maimed in a hunting accident, has a "weak heart" and "might see forty-five" at best. Hulga contents herself with a philosophy that abhors the contemplation of nothingness and an attitude that holds her above the "nice young men" of the region. That is, at least until the Bible salesman comes calling.

Manley Pointer, with his hilariously phallic name, ingratiates himself with Mrs. Hopewell, even though she has no desire to buy one of his Bibles, because he is also "good country people"; Hulga, operating at a supposedly more sophisticated level of insight, might have found him attractive because she feels his superiority as an unbeliever, or because they share the same "heart condition." He admires her wooden leg and her glasses; she meets him by prior arrangement, having imagined seducing him and thus getting "an idea across even to an inferior mind," her "true genius" being able to deal with his expected remorse.

Only through the logic of threes does the reader note O'Connor's suggestion that Hulga's defects include not only defective vision and a missing leg, but also her status as a conscious nonbeliever. Finding that she can endure his kisses with detachment, Hulga goes further in her pride and reveals her nonbelief, which the young boy accepts with "admiration" as though she were a "fantastic animal at the zoo." She even leads him to the barn loft where he removes her glasses, after which, with unwitting irony, she pities him: "I don't have illusions. I'm one of those people who see *through* to nothing"; she claims to have achieved "a kind of salvation by having taken her blindfold off. Insisting on honesty between them, she tells him that she is "thirty years old"—shaving off a couple of years—and that "I have a number of degrees." "I don't care a thing about all what all you done," he replies, as though she had confessed to a sordid past; and he demands to be told that she loves him, which she does after a series of ardent kisses, congratulating herself on having "had seduced him." The reader notes the sexual role-reversal here, the boy asking for assurances of love, the woman seducing, or thinking she is.

As if to play up that aspect of the story, O'Connor has the young man request that she remove her artificial leg for him, something she "took care of . . . as someone else would take his soul." It is what makes her different, he says, tallying with the notion of soul. Faced with his innocence, she complies, and she finds in her quasi-sexual yielding that "It was like losing her own life and finding it again miraculously, in his." This parody of Christian paradox makes the boy her false savior, and almost immediately, the boy takes from his case of Bible samples one that actually contains a flask of whiskey, a box of condoms, and a pack of pornographic playing cards. He startles her by saying that though he is "good country people," he is no "perfect Christian" but someone who has been believing in "nothing" since birth. In a grotesque ending worthy of Faulkner, the young man scrambles out of the barn loft with Hulga's artificial leg, her glasses, and, one hopes, her self-deception. But the narrational camera pans back to Mrs. Hopewell and Mrs. Freeman, who reflect in their ignorance on how "simple" the good country boy is. In this masterful moral tale, Flannery O'Connor shows us a character who, with her useless Ph.D. in Philosophy, might instead have better studied the one about the farmer's daughter and the traveling salesman.

—John Ditsky

A GOOD MAN IS HARD TO FIND
by Flannery O'Connor, 1955

Flannery O'Connor claimed always to center her fiction on the extraordinary moments of God's grace, when it touches even the most maimed, deformed, or unregenerate of people—especially those; proper Christian literature,

she remarked, is always "an invitation to deeper and stranger visions." Yet however willingly the most devoted reader might listen to such remarks, precisely those extraordinary moments when God's grace is meant to enter the lives of her characters have been the most troubling, even for such an admirer as Thomas Merton, a Trappist monk for whom she sustained the highest respect. Speaking once of another of her stories, "The Lame Shall Enter First," he notes that her good characters are bad and her bad people finally not so bad as they first seem, while her crazy people turn out to have a kind of sanity.

There are reasons for this difficulty. Throughout O'Connor's short stories and novels, God seems to spend his grace on the unlikeliest of people. Usually they do not appear to deserve his blessing; almost as often they appear to learn nothing from it. Nor is grace dramatized as a dazzling joy, a sweep of awareness. Rather, it can come in an act of random violence, a forceful accident, a blinding pain. It can be unexpected, intrusive, unwanted, ignored, baffling, misidentified, forgotten. It can bring suffering, wretchedness, even annihilation. Walter Sullivan has counted its cost. In the 19 stories published in her lifetime, he notes, nine end in one or more violent deaths, three others end in physical assaults and bodily injury and, in the remaining seven, one ends in arson, another two theft. This problem has left her apologist Frederick Asals to note that her fiction is meant to catch the reader unawares by being anthropotropic rather than theoropic, concentrating more on people than on God despite her concern with grace.

Yet throughout her life O'Connor was an ardent Catholic. She grew up in Savannah, Georgia, living in the shadow of the great spire of the cathedral and attending its convent school. When she later moved to Milledgeville, in central Georgia, her family contributed to the building of a Catholic parish church which she regularly attended until her death. Her own library, now at Georgia College, has a large collection of books on theology, Catholic history and dogma, and Christian apologetics. Her letters, collected as *The Habit of Being*, display everywhere a concern with her faith in terms even more passionate than her concern with her fiction. In a letter of 4 May 1963, she writes that the gospels give testimony that "it was the devils who first recognized Christ and the evangelists didn't censor this information. They apparently thought it was pretty good witness. It scandalizes us when we see the same thing in modern dress only because we have this defensive attitude toward the faith." She felt compelled to write about an oddness that she claimed was odd to her readers, from their perspective, but not odd to God's, from his. Nor should a reader think her lacking in sympathy for those invalided by handicap or disease: from the age of 25 until her death at age 39, she was herself increasingly debilitated by the rare and progressive lupus erythematosus, a disease that caused her bones to decay, forced her onto crutches, and finally ate its pain into her hands so that she found it agony to continuing writing, although she continued working on fiction until the end of her life. Looking for grace was her aim, her vocation, and her necessity. The same was true, for her, of understanding evil. "To insure our sense of mystery," O'Connor once said at Hollins College, since grace is also mysterious, "we need a sense of evil which sees the devil as a real spirit who must be made to name himself, and not simply to name himself as vague evil, but to name himself with his specific personality for every occasion." Thus the function of O'Connor's fiction is to recognize sin for what it is and to get the reader to recognize and condemn it. But the subject of her fiction, as she persistently said, was the action of grace and the manifestation of that was conversion, however fleeting.

"A Good Man Is Hard to Find," which became the title story of her first collection of short fiction, remains one of her most difficult, if her most popular, short story. It centers on Bailey's mother and a criminal called The Misfit (which she based on a real person and incident). At the start Bailey's mother, the grandmother of the story, is exactly described as sneaky (she deliberately deceives Bailey about the family cat which she smuggles on their vacation and which will cause the deaths of the entire family) and she is proud (everything she does is centered about her own satisfaction, such as protecting the cat, or her own future pleasure, such as recording mileage so as to center later conversation on her special knowledge). Following a brief nap, she awakes to recall a plantation house she once visited, a house which her own son has, pointedly, never provided her and his family. She forces this loss by seducing the children to insist on visiting the ruins: she tells them it has a secret panel and some lost silver. Their curiosity and the family's greed thus provoke the fatal error of going there: her own selfish desire corrupts them.

Next to these repeated acts of pride and wrongdoing, a stockpile of venial sins without care or caution by the grandmother, The Misfit appears suddenly as a former gospel singer and one who, hounded by thoughts of Christ, is theologically alert and religiously wise. A mentally disturbed child, he has been imprisoned for killing his father without premeditation or awareness—or so it is claimed by "a head-doctor at the penitentiary." Although the reader is never certain that The Misfit was originally innocent or guilty of crime as sin, The Misfit does sense that "something" is wrong and that he is trapped in a life that he sees as a narrow room with walls right and left; his own feelings are both abstract and urgently real. He also sees the grandmother's manners as selfish, superficial, and condescending, and he condemns her greed by noting his lack of it. But the grandmother, free and with no criminal past by legal standards, fails to see this and in their lack of communication, O'Connor inscribes her sense of religion.

"Jesus, Jesus," the grandmother says, "meaning Jesus will help you, but the way she was saying it, it sounded as if she might be cursing." For The Misfit, Jesus as loving saviour "thrown everything off balance" because he responded to injustice (his Crucifixion) with mercy. This torments The Misfit because it shows him his own cupidity and culpability: he will seek revenge on Christ's mercy by killing God's children as they deserve to be killed for his sake. "No pleasure but meanness" he tells the grandmother. Her reply is even more shocking: "Maybe He didn't raise the dead." Given the opportunity to confess her sins before he kills her, she denies the divinity of Christ himself. By contrast, The Misfit, a sinner, is not unregenerate; he is agonizing about the state of his (and human's) condition and he asks for some kind of revelation. And when the grandmother reaches out to him, dressed in her son's shirt, in a vision of him as her son, The Misfit gets the love he wants and denies. He is doubly shocked. He cannot accept an act of grace because he is too aware of his own sins; and he cannot accept the stupid and shallow grandmother as God's agent of revelation and grace, of love and faith.

Yet that is just what this is. In reaching out with honest if dazed compassion, the grandmother who denied Christ nevertheless learns actively his atonement: "You're one of my own children." Thus she not only brings The Misfit face to face with the occasion of grace he wants desperately to avoid but she makes him into the agent of her own occasion of grace. She saves them both in spite of them both. So does

he. By instinct, she throws off manner and convention and finds love. At this moment of sobering responsibility, he recoils from her help and shoots her. "I don't want no hep," he says, the responsibility of redemption being too much for him to bear. He has characterized life as meanness, as no real pleasure. But the selfish grandmother overcame meanness in a blind, overpowering moment, as with Paul on the road to Damascus. She dies, but at the moment of love and so grace; and The Misfit is left confronted with his own shortcomings—the kind of anguishing challenge that can lead him, too, to a sense of insignificance which is the first stage of redemption. For the Catholic O'Connor, who found such challenges more dramatic for Protestants, who lacked the help of church ritual, than for Catholics, this is her most powerful, a quintessential, story.

—Arthur F. Kinney

———

GOODBYE, COLUMBUS
by Philip Roth, 1959

"Goodbye, Columbus" first appeared in the autumn-winter 1958-59 issue of the *Paris Review* and shortly thereafter in *Goodbye, Columbus, and Five Short Stories* (1959). This collection brought Philip Roth recognition as one of America's most important fiction writers.

"Goodbye, Columbus" treats many of the themes for which Roth is best known: acculturation and assimilation of second and third generation Jews into American life; their attempts to fulfill the American dream; their relationship to their heritage, both American and European; and the tension between wealth and intellect. The story's central character and narrator, Neil Klugman, embodies all of these themes. Living with his Aunt Gladys in the Jewish section of Newark, he meets and falls in love with Brenda Patimkin, daughter of Ben Patimkin, who made a fortune in kitchen and bathroom sinks. The Patimkins live in Short Hills, New Jersey, an affluent suburb. As Neil drives there, he feels that he is approaching heaven. When he arrives, he is struck not only by the Patimkins' affluence but also by their athletic prowess and their eating ability as they all sit at one table and gorge themselves. Neil contrasts this meal to the meals in his aunt's home, where Gladys feeds each person separately, one after the other.

The title of the story derives from a record Ron Patimkin, Brenda's brother, owns. It recounts the events of his senior year at Ohio State University in Columbus, Ohio, and it ends with the words, "goodbye, Columbus . . . goodbye, Columbus . . . goodbye . . ." Yet the story's title also refers to Christopher Columbus. Neil too is a discoverer of a new world, the world of the Patimkins, one that promises fulfillment for all Neil's worldly dreams. But it demands a sacrifice in return: to become a part of that world, he must, he feels, become a Patimkin. When Ron decides to marry, Ron abandons his dream of being a physical education teacher to meet his "responsibilities" by entering the Patimkin business. At Ron's wedding, Ben says to Neil and Brenda, "There's no business so big it can't use another head," implying that if Neil marries Brenda, he too will enter the business. But Neil ultimately rejects the Patimkin world.

Neil connects his trips to Short Hills with a little black boy's coming to the library to look at a book of Gauguin's paintings of Tahiti. In a key dream, Neil pictures himself and the child on a ship moving inexorably away from an island in the Pacific. The female natives on the island throw leis at them and say the concluding words of Ron's record. Neither the child nor Neil wants to leave, but neither can do anything about it. In the dream, Neil is Columbus, and the land he must leave is the world of Brenda. He ultimately decides that he is unwilling to become a Patimkin, and he realizes the truth of what he thinks earlier: "No sense carrying dreams of Tahiti in your head, if you can't afford the fare."

When Neil spends his two-week vacation just before Labor Day at the Patimkin household, he realizes that he has fallen in love with Brenda, but he also gets a taste of what life as a Patimkin would be. Shortly after moving in, he sees the hostility between Brenda and her mother as they argue concerning Neil's visit, which occurs just after Ron has announced that he is getting married in two weeks. As Brenda runs from her mother, Neil finds himself sitting on his one Brooks Brothers shirt and pronouncing his own name aloud. Neil's last name, Klugman, is a Yiddish word for clever or smart one, but it also means cursed one. In fact, the story's title inevitably connects Neil's name with a saying ubiquitous in Jewish immigrant neighborhoods in east coast cities around the turn of the 20th century: *a klug tzu Columbus,* a curse on Columbus, the discoverer of the land in which the immigrants found themselves suffering so much. Ben's brother Leo assumes Neil will marry Brenda. At Ron's wedding, Leo tells Neil that Neil is "a smart boy" who will "play it safe" and not "louse things up." But after Neil apparently decides to ask Brenda to marry him, he discovers that he cannot.

Towards the end of his stay at the Patimkin house, Neil asks Brenda to buy a diaphragm. She initially refuses, indicating, Neil feels, her lack of commitment to their relationship. Then, she relents, but when she goes back to Radcliffe at the beginning of the school year, she leaves her diaphragm in a drawer at home, where her mother finds it. Neil visits her in Cambridge, where she tells him what happened. Neil feels, with what seems justification, that Brenda left the diaphragm on purpose to hurt her mother. He apparently feels that Brenda has been using him all along. He tells her, "I loved you, Brenda, so I cared." She responds, "I loved *you.*" Then, both realize what tense they have used, and Neil leaves.

Before he calls a cab to take him to the train station, he looks through a window into the Harvard University library, where he knows Patimkin sinks have been installed. He sees his own reflection in the window and beyond sees the stacks with their "imperfectly shelved" books. He returns to Newark in time to go to work the next morning.

Ultimately, Neil is unable to stay in the New World that Brenda represents. He is unwilling or unable to pay the fare. Instead, he returns to the imperfect world of Newark and his job at the Newark Public Library, with its own "imperfectly shelved" books.

In 1969 "Goodbye, Columbus" was made into a popular film directed by Larry Peerce, starring Richard Benjamin, Ali MacGraw, and Jack Klugman.

—Richard Tuerk

———

THE GOOPHERED GRAPEVINE
by Charles Waddell Chesnutt, 1899

Chesnutt's story "The Goophered Grapevine" is a complex response to the difficult situation of African-American writers at the beginning of the 20th century. It adapts the folk practice of "masking" to counteract the racial stereotypes held by its predominantly white audience. Originally published in *The Atlantic Monthly* (1887), "The Goophered Grapevine" was reprinted as the first story in Chesnutt's *The Conjure Woman,* a collection which both resembles and questions the "Plantation Tradition" tales popularized by Joel Chandler Harris.

Like Harris, Chesnutt structures his story around a tale told to white listeners by an old black man. Seemingly child-like and devoted to his white employers, Chesnutt's Uncle Julius McAdoo shares numerous characteristics with Harris's Uncle Remus. Visually, he fulfills the stereotype of the "happy darky"; he first appears "smacking his lips with great gusto" over a pile of grapes and later smacks his lips and rolls his eyes. Meanwhile, his supernaturally-tinged dialect stories delight an audience conditioned by racial images popularized in minstrel shows. Echoing the stereotypical association of blacks with nature (rather than culture), Chesnutt images the haunted ("goophered") slave Henry as an extension of the grapevine. Chesnutt remains highly conscious of the preconceptions of his white audience, represented in the story of John and Annie, white northerners who eventually decide to purchase the old plantation where Julius lives.

Chesnutt's contemporary readers seem to have accepted his story at face value, reading it as support for the "Plantation Tradition" belief that, despite occasional abuses, Southern paternalism (and the institution of slavery) were beneficial to both whites and blacks. Chesnutt's decision to abandon the Uncle Julius stories in favor of more direct political commentary during the 1890's, and to stop writing fiction at all between 1905 and his death in 1932, suggests a tormented awareness that, like Julius, he was being perceived almost entirely in stereotypical terms.

Nonetheless, a careful reading of "The Goophered Grapevine" reveals numerous ambiguities and complexities in Uncle Julius and his creator. Both structurally and rhetorically, the story subverts many of the conventions and beliefs it was originally understood to support. Writing during the period when segregation was beginning to dominate racial relations in the United States, Chesnutt challenges the system in several ways. Assuming the authority of the white voice, Chesnutt presents the frame story from the perspective of the hard-headed white businessman John, who views all art as inferior to commerce. In addition, Chesnutt explicitly alerts readers to the story's ironic dimensions. The setting is "a quaint old town, which I shall call Patesville, because, for one reason, that is not its name." Although John accepts the racist belief attributing intelligence solely to "white blood," his description of Julius warns that the story is not as simple as it appears: "There was a shrewdness in his eyes, too, which was not altogether African."

Julius's shrewdness operates on several levels. William Andrews's excellent book *The Literary Career of Charles Chesnutt* alerted readers to the complexity of Julius's economic motivation. Early readers seem to have believed that Julius tells the story of the haunted vineyard to "scare off" John and Annie, thereby maintaining control of the grape harvest for himself. It seems more realistic, however, to credit Julius, a black man living in the post-Reconstruction era, with an awareness that his economic control cannot continue indefinitely. Rather than the simplistic greed John sees as its motive, the tale advertises the desirability of the vineyard, which is presented as a source of high profits, and of black workers including Julius. The images of the white master whose profits accrue almost entirely from the black man Henry and the Yankee owner (whose ignorance of local conditions nearly destroys the plantation's profitability), in fact appeal to John to buy the plantation, thereby keeping it out of the hands of southern whites, who are associated in the story with violence against blacks.

On another level, Julius educates Annie, the relatively sympathetic white woman, about the evils of slavery. Repeatedly invoking the phrase "befo' de wah"—a standard element of Plantation Tradition defenses of slavery— Julius embeds a subversive image of slavery in the midst of his tale. Although Julius avoids direct political commentary, he counteracts the stereotype of benevolent white masters and lavish feasts with matter of fact observations concerning the reality of black suffering: "befo' de wah, in slab'ry times, a nigger did n' mine goin' fi' er ten mile in a night, w'en dey wuz sump'n good ter eat at de yuther enn'." Subsequently, he provides an understated warning concerning the possibility of black violence. Although he claims ignorance—"I dunner how it happen"—his description of the shooting of slavemaster Douglas McAdoo contradicts the stereotypical image of happy, passive slaves.

On its most complex level, "The Goophered Grapevine" can be read as Chesnutt's meditation on the role of the African-American artist. Both Chesnutt and Julius attract audiences by playing off stereotypes they know to be destructive. Both understand that the same story can transmit different messages to different listeners. Purely entertainment for John, Julius's story educates Annie in order to enlist her as an ally. Like the northern white women who formed a core audience for abolitionist literature, Annie understands Julius's basic points concerning the human destructiveness of slavery. In alter stories in *The Conjure Woman,* she uses her influence to temper John's purely economic responses. Yet Julius's success, like Chesnutt's, is limited. He finds work; he corrects some fundamental, and relatively obvious, misconceptions in some of his white listeners. But Annie neither alters the oppressive system nor accepts blacks as equals. Nonetheless, "The Goophered Grapevine" plays a major role in African-American literary history by providing a model in the dilemma of the black artist writing in a world that consistently underestimated black writers and the richness of the African-American cultural tradition.

—Craig Hansen Werner

GOOSEBERRIES (Kryzhovnik)
by Anton Chekhov, 1898

Like all great writers Anton Chekhov not only reflected on timeless, universal themes, but also exemplified the spirit of his own time and place. The disintegration of feudal Russia in the 1890's resulted in increased poverty for the lower classes; apathy, boredom, and frustration for the middle classes; and a kind of cocooning paralysis throughout Russian society as a whole. The uncertainty, loneliness, and failure of what O'Connor called "the

submerged population" is all too apparent in Chekhov's mature stories. This societal paralysis transmutes itself into physical and mental inertia, and poetic vision and strength of expression take precedence over outward movement.

Chekhov's concern with social breakdown produced narratives not concerned with resolving dilemmas, but intent on revealing a state of affairs. It is rather similar to Beckett's play *Endgame,* which the author claimed did not signify "the end of the game," but an arrested "state of play," caught for a brief but timeless moment (the implication being before complete dissolution). "Gooseberries" and its fellow stories, "Man in a Case" and "Concerning Love," form a trilogy linked by common characters, designed to exhibit precisely this paralysis. The direct or indirect focus in each story falls on Nikolai Ivanich, Belikov, and Alekhin consecutively, three men whose automaton-like nature exemplifies the moral degeneracy and egotism inculcated by a complacent society.

The basic narrative detail of "Gooseberries" is, not surprisingly, uninspiring. Ivan Ivanich and Burkin take shelter from the rain in the farmhouse of an acquaintance, Alekhin. After bathing Ivan Ivanich recounts the story of his brother Nikolai, a minor government official, whose sole aim in life is to acquire a country estate with gooseberry bushes. To achieve his desire, he lives in virtual penury, saving all his money, even to the point of starving to death the wealthy wife he calculatingly has married. Visiting him on this estate, his brother Ivan is overcome by the pettiness, bigotry, and self-deceit of Nikolai, and implores his two listeners not to fall into the same habits. Burkin and Alekhin are unimpressed, and all three retire to bed as the storm rages outside.

The power of the story lies in its ability to convey emotion which surpasses the words used to describe such a feeling. Joyce was concerned with the same thing when he said "its absence was as its presence." Chekhov achieves it not by the psychology of extended description and analysis, but by investing significance in a concrete symbol more readily assimilated by the imagination. The gooseberries of the title perform this function in the story. They symbolise the rapacious, miserly, and pathetically self-deluding aspirations of Nikolai:

Speechless with emotion, he popped a single gooseberry into his mouth, darted at me the triumphant glance of a child who has at last gained possession of a longed-for toy, and said—"Delicious!" And he ate them greedily, repeating over and over again: "Simply delicious! You try them." They were hard and sour.

(translated by Ivy Litvinov)

The incident convinces the narrator that all human happiness is "a kind of universal hypnosis," concealing the injustice of "intolerable poverty, cramped dwellings, degeneracy, drunkenness, hypocrisy, lying." Happiness is a delusion, concealing a hard and sour reality. The gooseberries are what Chekhov called "a living image," giving visual immediacy in the same way the blood-soaked potatoes on the floor in the superb story "The Murder" add poignancy to Yakov's realisation that he has killed his brother. Yet Ivan's plea, "Do good!," falls on deaf ears; indeed the reader is likely to be suspicious of his diatribe against happiness because of his earlier delight in the natural landscape and sensuous pleasure when swimming in the rain. The final scene resolves nothing beyond suggesting the inevitable movement towards death in a world seemingly incapable of change:

> They were allotted a big room for the night, in which were two ancient bedsteads of carved wood, and an ivory crucifix in one corner. Ivan Ivanich undressed in silence and lay down. "Lord have mercy on us sinners," he said, and covered his head with the sheet. . . . . The rain tapped on the window panes all night.

The subtleties of this fine story are barely explicable in so short a space: the "story within a story" technique giving Chekhov a control that is barely visible; the patterning of the characters adding to the many grim ironies, particularly the obvious similarities between Nikolai, Ivanich, and Alekhin; the Gogolian echoes of the bestial images, especially associated with pigs; and the sense of a whole society, a brooding mass of insignificant, frustrated individuals standing behind each character. The lack of any overt didactic purpose, other than the fallible and ignored assertations of Ivan Ivanich, makes "Gooseberries" all the more remarkable for its effect on the reader. The petty domestic bliss and trivial amusements seem all the more obvious for being understated. If a great story is not what it says, but what it whispers, "Gooseberries" stands alongside the finest of Chekhov's achievements.

—Simon Baker

GORILLA, MY LOVE
by Toni Cade Bambara, 1972

In the forefront of the new African-American consciousness, Toni Cade Bambara has had experience in theatre, review panels for arts councils, affirmative action projects, workshops, museums—wherever a talented and energetic voice may be heard. Writing almost consistently from a female viewpoint and creating mainly black characters who come from widely varied segments of contemporary life, she presents without rancor the distinctly black experience. Her characters, artists, singers, civil rights workers, midwives, doctors, healers, and rapists, speak rich and varied dialects, confront aspects of black life that sometimes surprise themselves, even while they live by the codes and traditions of their people, and seldom remotely fit any of the stereotypes. With typical exactness in the black idiom, "Gorilla, My Love" appeared as the title story in a 1972 collection of 15 stories, reprinted from a variety of publications in 1960—her first book, which established her reputation.

It is the story of a small black child, Hazel, who is tough, brilliant, and streetwise. She is self-confident and secure in the matters of handling herself and others, with a strong family backing, and much hard irreverence for the general system of sentiment. Underneath, however, are the fears and uncertainties of a small child.

Hazel remembers the year when Hunca Bubba, her uncle, changed his name; henceforth, because he is in love and plans to be married, he is to be called by his real name Jefferson Winston Vale. This announcement of the name change conveys a vague knowledge that the affectionate relationship between Hazel and her uncle has ended. The authentic name sounds "very geographical weatherlike" to her, and the forecast bodes no good. The crisis occurs on the return from a trip south for pecans. Hazel's tone of hard calculation and her vulnerability are conveyed in her refusal to sit in back with the pecans that are sometimes dusty and slip as if "maybe a rat in the buckets." Yet the favored uncle and Baby Jason sit there with no problem.

Hazel's other reason for sitting in the front "navigator seat" is her pride in following the map and directing her grandfather's driving; but she learned to read maps while keeping the light on at night for fear of the dark.

Emerging from her reminiscent self-confession are three themes: the sacrament of a name, a distrust of grownups, and a child's failure to realize the unavoidable contradictions in normal human affairs. To her, a promise is forever.

The distrust of grownups is focused in her excursion to the movies with her two brothers, Big Brood and Baby Jason. Three theaters are "too far, less we had grownups with us which we didn't," and the two nearer are eliminated for other reasons, leaving only the Washington playing *Gorilla, My Love*.

The child thinks she's tough, and brags about the adulation of Baby Jason and the necessity to fight for Big Brood, but the pranks she plays in order to manage her world are a child's pranks. She thrills with the independence of buying potato chips and delights in giving "some lip" to the matron and creating enough disturbance to "turn out" the theater. She becomes the leader and the spokesperson for juvenile injustice. Big Brood mutters protests, but she has to take action, as in hiding the money when older boys demand it, or jumping on the back of an older boy who takes a basketball.

Therefore, it follows that Hazel will erupt into action in response to the theater's cheating by showing a picture about Jesus instead of *Gorilla, My Love*. Hazel complains, "Grownups figure they can treat you just anyhow." Against the yelling and stomping, the technician turns up the sound; eventually a matron fondly called Thunderbuns subdues the crowd, and there follows a very humorous version of the Christ story as it would be played in the Vale household.

When Hazel demands her money back, the manager thrusts her bodily out the door. She has stolen matches and the ensuing fire closes the theater for a week. Instead of beating her, her father accepts her explanation: "Cause if you say Gorilla, My Love, you suppose to mean it." Even gangsters in the movies say, "My word is my bond."

Hazel provides additional examples of the necessity that one's word be kept, but the slight variation creeps in. Granddaddy has little memory and "sometime you can just plain lie to him." However, she was raised to speak her mind and take the consequences.

She speaks her mind when demanding the truth about Hunca Bubba's intentions. Overlooked in her indignation about the name change is the fact that Hazel is not addressed by her own name but given baby names: "Scout," "Miss Muffin," "Peaches," and "Precious." The climactic revelation and the secret in her turmoil is the uncle's former promise to marry her when she grows up; and now, with her faith in the spoken word demolished, she's "hurtin." The grandfather and the guilty party agree that the name change means a different person made the promise. To call him another name ("You a lyin dawg") is her only defense.

This tough girl weeps like a baby, and Baby Jason joins in. Together they make two babies crying against the world of grownups, in which adults treacherously play change-up and turnaround every day. Instead of enjoying the security of her uncle's love, she beats futilely against the cage of childhood. Childish vulnerability is represented poignantly in a picture show fraudulently named on the marquee and that reveals shamelessly the victimization of children: "No gorilla my nuthin."

—Grace Eckley

GREEN TEA
by Sheridan Le Fanu, 1872

Sheridan Le Fanu, a 19th-century Irish writer and grand-nephew of playwright Richard Sheridan, was a prolific author, with 14 novels and many short stories to his credit. He is most remembered for his great mystery novel *Uncle Silas,* which has been translated into several continental languages and adapted to film, in England as *The Inheritor* and in the United States as *Dark Angel.* Most of his other novels, however, are inferior to the shorter pieces. Altogether Le Fanu wrote some 30 supernatural tales, most of which appeared initially in periodicals. Although many Victorian authors wrote ghost stories, Le Fanu was distinguished by his intense interest in psychology and his emphasis on the implications of supernaturalism for the personality of the believer. He had read widely in the psychological theorists of the time, as well as in the mystical theories of Emmanuel Swedenborg. As a result, his stories are a sophisticated blend of natural and supernatural, of conscious and unconscious, and of the symbolic linkages between the outside world and the human mind.

"Green Tea" was published in the collection *In a Glass Darkly,* a group of tales connected as narratives reported by a German physician, Dr. Hesselius, who is interested in exploring the relationship between the unconscious and the supernatural. As in much Gothic fiction, the narrative is even more indirect, for it is introduced by Dr. Hesselius's secretary who is ostensibly reproducing (after translating) the doctor's letters.

After a brief explanatory prologue, the rest of the tale is related in eleven brief chapters. Minor characters remain peripheral, for the focus is on two figures, the analytical Dr. Hesselius, through whose reactions we witness the events, and the disturbed Rev. Jennings, who has turned to the doctor for help in his desperation. The Rev. Jennings is a well-to-do bachelor who functions only intermittently at his vicarage because of some mysterious illness which frequently afflicts him during services. As he confides to the doctor, the illness is seemingly not physical at all, however, but involves his perturbation over a "spectral illusion" of a monkey, which has been haunting him. Since Dr. Hesselius is professionally interested in such apparent supernatural manifestations and their connection with the human mind, he is eager to record the whole sequence of events, then transmitted to the reader in this letters to a friend. We learn of the monkey's first appearance in an omnibus in which the reverend was the sole rider, then of its increasingly ominous appearances, when it attempts to interrupt his prayers and even to urge him to suicide.

The title of the story refers only obliquely to these apparitions. The Rev. Jennings has developed a passion for green tea, which he sips while staying up late at night writing. As Dr. Hesselius reveals to us, a sensitive fluid in the nervous system may be adversely affected by overindul-gence in green tea, thereby disturbing what he calls the "interior vision" of the nerves.

Le Fanu handles the first-person narrations brilliantly. The voice of Dr. Hesselius is that of the objective, scientific observer, humane but dispassionate. He also is a subject in his own right, however, for he shares with the reader his personal philosophy, explaining that he believes the natural world to be an expression of the spiritual world. The essential human is a spirit, hence "the material body is, in the most literal sense, a vesture, and death . . . simply his extrication from the natural body." Although his professional concern is to apply this belief to medicine, clearly this mental outlook is especially receptive to such phenomena as "spectral illusions."

The Rev. Jennings also narrates his experiences with the monkey on a first-person basis, directed to the doctor. His voice is one of fear, anxiety, and profound perturbation. The three chapters called "The Journey: First Stage, Second Stage, and Third Stage" are all related in the first person. His growing sense of terror over knowing the monkey to be always there, even though unseen by others, is effectively captured in vivid language. In the last stage of the journey, the monkey tries to persuade him to commit suicide by jumping into an empty mine shaft. Only the presence of his niece prevents him from doing so. This episode in particular suggests the close connection between the apparition and the viewer's perturbed state of mind. When he does ultimately take his own life, it seems inevitable, although the reader suspects the monkey's malign presence caused him to act.

At once a symbol and a haunting presence, the monkey is an important factor in the story. In "Green Tea" Le Fanu is anticipating Jungian psychological theory. The monkey represents the archetypal shadow in the collective unconscious of the Rev. Jennings. Much Gothic fiction of the 19th century is concerned with projections of the shadow, or dark side of an individual, onto a double, one of the most famous being *Dr. Jekyll and Mr. Hyde.* Le Fanu's shadow works more like the shadow figure in Ursula Le Guin's *A Wizard of Earthsea,* where the protagonist sees an actual shadow, which then pursues him until he learns to recognize it as part of himself. The unfortunate Rev. Jennings never reaches this recognition. The monkey represents the dark side of the personality in that it is a primate, not a human creature. The shy, courteous, and generous Rev. Jennings would never think of himself in such primitive terms, so that the shadow has been repressed all his life. This lonely bachelor has never learned to know himself.

—Charlotte Spivack

THE GUEST (L'Hôte)
by Albert Camus, 1957

"L'Hôte" ("The Guest") is one of the six short stories comprising the collection *L'Exil et le royaume (Exile and the Kingdom),* the last major work the Nobel prize-winning novelist, dramatist, and essayist Albert Camus completed before his death. Written in the laconic style of a classic short story, with a conclusion that comes with brutal suddenness to make a lasting impression on the reader,

"The Guest" brings into focus many of the themes that obsessed Camus throughout his life.

The story is set in Algeria, the country in which Camus was born, and the time is the era of the postwar, anticolonial protests which demanded so much of the attention not only of the large numbers of French settlers in North Africa but also of the general public in France. More generally, "The Guest" explores the theme of the loneliness of individuals forced to make their own moral choices without reference to transcendental principles or convictions; the consequence is an anguished conscience, and the sense of isolation is increased when it turns out that decisions and actions are misunderstood.

In the story it is midwinter and very cold up in the inhospitable mountains inland from the North African coast where Duru, who was born in these parts, lives in the spartan schoolhouse. He is a teacher, and French readers might respond especially to that detail, for the idea that lay education had an important moral role to play in the colonies by introducing French ideas is one that is very familiar to them. Because of the time of year, classes have been suspended, and Duru has little to do but ensure that certain supplies of grain are doled out to the local population when starvation threatens. Apart from that, he has nothing to do but sit and wait alone with his thoughts. But one day he sees coming towards him up the steep and stoney slope two figures. One of them, riding on a horse, is Balducci, an old gendarme from Corsica; behind him, with his hands tied, his prisoner comes stumbling along. He is an Arab, and, as Balducci explains, in trouble for the crime of killing a cousin in a quarrel.

Duru and Balducci have known one another for a long time, but their relationship is not cordial. The old gendarme, as might be expected, takes a conservative view of things, expecting nothing good to come from anticolonial protests, and he has little sympathy for his captive. He does not take long telling Duru that he is now entrusting him with the duty of seeing that the Arab is taken to the next settlement and handed over to the authorities. Duru, who has not agreed with much in Balducci's words or attitudes, does not relish assuming this responsibility either, but he has no choice in matter.

Duru is left with the Arab, and the fact that his name is not given symbolises neatly the difficulty of making any human contact with him. Duru, however, shares his own meagre rations with him and tries to make him as comfortable as possible when he beds down in the schoolroom, but the atmosphere remains tense, as the schoolmaster worries about his own safety and wonders whether the Arab will try to escape. In a way Duru would have welcomed that, for it would take the responsibility off his shoulders if the Arab ran away. But he does not, and Duru seems to have no alternative but to obey instructions and walk over the hills to the settlement with the Arab and deliver his captive to the authorities.

At a point where the road forks Duru stops, however, and makes clear to the Arab that by turning in one direction he will be able to walk away from a future of punishment and captivity and live in freedom with people of his own race. Duru gives him the choice, but, to his chagrin, he sees that the Arab prefers, for what reason is not made clear, the path to prison. Anxious and disappointed, but unwilling to interfere further, Duru returns to the school, only to discover that on the blackboard an unknown hand has scrawled the words "You handed over our brother. You will pay for that!" The imperatives of current politics cut crudely across the doubts and worries of the sensitive Duru, leaving him feeling more alone in his actual and metaphorical solitude than ever. Rich in observed detail, full of human compassion, scarred by the horrors of the end of the colonial period in North Africa, "The Guest" is a fine brief summary of Camus's vision of the bleakness of the human condition.

—Christopher Smith

GUESTS OF THE NATION
by Frank O'Connor, 1931

Frank O'Connor's "Guests of the Nation," with its wonderfully ironic title, is one of the most memorable short stories ever written about Ireland's struggle for political independence from England. Set during the Troubles or the revolutionary period between the Easter Rising in 1916 and the signing of the Home Rule treaty at the end of 1921, O'Connor's narrative of rebels and hostages reveals the conflicts, not just between the Irish and their unwelcomed "guests," but among the revolutionaries themselves.

Like so many of O'Connor's stories, "Guests of the Nation" (the title story of a 1931 collection) is told from the first-person point of view to give the narrative the quality of oral storytelling. Unlike the typical O'Connor storyteller, who narrates an event that has happened or been told to someone else, the narrator in "Guests of the Nation" is someone who has taken part in an action so emotionally and morally disturbing that it has altered his life. Speaking with the voice of his own Cork region, while imitating the accents and expressions of the English hostages, O'Connor's narrator, called Bonaparte by his fellow rebels, recounts his reluctant role in the execution of two English soldiers in retaliation for the deaths of four Irish rebels. The success of O'Connor's narrative, however, lies not so much in the description of the event itself, common enough during the Troubles, but in O'Connor's intimate study of the humanity of the rebels and their prisoners and the personal ordeal experienced by O'Connor's narrator.

"Guests of the Nation," one of several early O'Connor stories about the Irish gunman, reflects his own experiences while fighting on the losing Republican side during the Irish Civil War. During the final days of the war, O'Connor, while suffering acutely from the constant danger of life on the run, was puzzled by the cold resourcefulness of some of his companions, who actually appeared to enjoy the danger and the violence. Afterwards, Daniel Corkery, O'Connor's old teacher and fellow short story writer, suggested that O'Connor had witnessed the critical moment in a revolution when control shifts from the dreamers, those caught up in the Republican ideal, to the professionals, those caught up in the political expediency and emotion of the violence and killing.

In "Guests of the Nation" O'Connor develops this conflict between revolutionary attitudes in the strained relationship between the narrator and Jeremiah Donovan, the experienced rebel, who has the responsibility for carrying out the battalion order to shoot the English prisoners. Their differences are played out as the narrator and his youthful compatriot, Noble, become familiar with the Englishmen, while they stand guard over them. When the narrator eventually finds out that the prisoners are actually hostages, he bitterly complains to Donovan, only to be told that the English have also held their Irish prisoners over a long period of time. This moral and emotional blindness or indifference to the closeness that has developed between Noble, the narrator, and their prisoners is what most clearly defines Jeremiah Donovan and what most troubles O'Connor's narrator when he is finally told to carry out the executions. While he recognizes the necessity of an act of reprisal—one of the executed rebels was sixteen years old—the narrator is deeply disturbed by the order to shoot two men whom he has come to regard more as companions than as the enemy.

The most compelling scene in "Guests of the Nation" occurs when the English prisoners are taken to the end of the bog where a hole has already been dug for their bodies. O'Connor's early narrative strategy of developing the personalities of the two Englishmen now takes on dramatic force as Hawkins, the more garrulous of the prisoners, pleads for his life, even by offering to join the rebels, before he is shot in the back of the neck by Donovan. After Hawkins is executed, finished off with a shot fired by Bonaparte, the narrative shifts its attention to the usually taciturn Belcher, whose words, just before his death, take on a dignity and humanity in sharp contrast to the bumbling and grotesque behavior of his executioners.

Once the executions and burial are over, Bonaparte and Noble return to the house used to hide the Englishmen, thereby shifting the narrative back to the emotional and moral impact of the deaths on those closest to the prisoners. While Noble and the old woman of the house fall to their knees in prayer, O'Connor's narrator goes outside to watch the stars and listen to the now dying shrieks of the birds. At story's end, the narrator turns briefly to his own emotional state immediately after the killings and to the effect of the deaths on his life ever since. He remembers vividly that the executions and the praying figures seemed at a great physical distance from him and that he felt as lonely as a lost child. He also confesses that he has never felt the same about anything since that night. Apparently compelled to tell this story, O'Connor's rebel appears to recognize at the close of his narrative that this single, terrible act of revolutionary violence destroyed his youth and left him permanently disillusioned and emotionally isolated from the human condition no matter what the cause.

—Richard F. Peterson

GUY DE MAUPASSANT (Giui de Mopassan)
by Isaak Babel, 1932

After the mid-1920's Isaak Babel published relatively little, but several of these later pieces, including "Giui de Mopassan" ("Guy de Maupassant") are regarded as among his finest. Although he dated the manuscript of this story "1920-1922," it first appeared in 1932, and critics have discussed it more often than his other late works. If for no other reason, the story would be notable for a pair of pithy remarks about style, which seem to summarize Babel's view on the subject. But it is also one of the stories in which Babel is concerned most pointedly with the role of the artist; the encounter between art and reality is presented with a vibrancy, humor, and ultimately pathos that make the work memorable.

Babel takes on the role of first-person narrator and protagonist; as in the story, he was in fact in St. Petersburg in 1916, a would-be writer with virtually no income. He describes being taken in by Alexei Kazantsev, a teacher of literature who supplements his meager income by translating the Spanish novels of Blasco Ibáñez. Through Kazantsev he gets a job: the lawyer Benderskii owns a publishing house, and his wife, Raisa, has been attempting to translate the works of Maupassant for a projected Russian edition. Her efforts have not been successful, so the young Babel is hired to help out. He works closely with Raisa and apparently seduces her one evening, when the two get drunk while working on a translation. Babel returns home and reads a biography of Maupassant, in which he learns of the French writer's struggle to write while coping with the ravages of congenital syphilis. After noting Maupassant's descent into madness and his death at the age of 42, the narrator concludes by describing how the presentiment of some truth touched him.

As always, Babel has a wonderful eye for detail, and in particular for the sensual. He sees in Raisa one of those women who have transformed their husband's money "into a pink layer of fat on the belly, the back of the neck, and the well-rounded shoulders." The colors pink and red surround her; she lives in a house with pink columns and a red carpet, and she has pink eyes and reddish eyelashes. The narrator seems constantly aware of her flesh, which he describes in terms of barely adequate restraints; thus he refers to her efforts to control the swaying of her hips, to her legs swathed in stockings, her constrained breast, her half-opened lips. There is, though, no small measure of self-irony in the way that Babel's narrator, who is clearly revealing his own sexual longings, describes women. Raisa's maid, with her gray eyes and haughty manner, would seem to be a quite different type, but the narrator sees lewdness in her eyes and imagines what she must be like as a lover. Later, after he receives an advance from the Benderskiis, he throws a party for those in his apartment. He gets drunk and dreams that he is passionately kissing Katia, a 40-year-old laundress who lives below. The next morning he goes down to get a good look at this person whom he has barely seen, and he finds a worn-out, grey-haired woman.

The narrator's fascination with Raisa is not purely sexual. She and her husband represent the wealthy, assimilated Jews who have succeeded among the Russians; it is a world as alien to Babel's own Jewishness as that of the impoverished Polish Jews whom he describes in his *Konarmiig (Red Cavalry)* stories. The Benderskiis have all the trappings of wealth and art serves as just another decoration—it is no coincidence that the husband is dabbling in publishing, that icons and paintings decorate their home, and that Raisa says Maupassant is the one passion of her life.

But pretense is not culture. Their spiritual poverty is symbolized by the flatness of Raisa's translations. And it is in this regard that Babel' makes his pronouncements about style. He says that a sentence at its birth is simultaneously good and bad; the secret is in a scarcely perceptible twist, and the lever that performs this trick must be turned once, not twice. Later, when Raisa asks him how he managed to transform the stories, he uses a military metaphor, talking of armies of words and of the various weapons at their disposal. No iron, he says, can so pierce the heart as a period placed at the right moment. Art, in other words, involves intuition and talent, two qualities lacking in the Benderskii's bourgeois household.

The narrator's wildly comic seduction of Raisa comprises the brief story's major scene. He comes to see her with a translation of Maupassant's "L'Aveu" just as she is having a boisterous dinner party with her sisters and their husbands. Everyone else leaves for the theater, but Raisa, somewhat the worse for drink, wants to get to work on Maupassant. She opens a bottle of 1883 Muscatel, and the unthinking narrator quickly downs three glasses of the precious liquid. They go over the story, which tells how the coachman Polyte constantly propositions Céleste, who twice a week takes his carriage to town. (In this outline Babel shifts the focus of Maupassant's story and adds a few details, such as the "pink lips" of Polyte's horse, to make the imagery parallel his own.) Céleste routinely rebuffs the driver, but one day, after two years, she gives in. At this point in the retelling, the narrator turns to Raisa, using the same words as Polyte. She at first fends him off, and then, half-drunk, he leaps out of his chair, knocking all 29 volumes of the Maupassant collection off the shelf. Art and reality merge.

Or do they? The story implies that such a merger is always more apparent than real. Through his love of Spain,

Kazantsev knows every physical feature of that country, even though he had never been there. Yet his wretched surroundings serve as a reminder of his ordinary life. The narrator's passionate dreams of Katia are deflated by reality, and his brief fling with Raisa is dispelled by his reading of Maupassant's biography. The actual point of the story appears here. At the beginning of the story Babel' talks of turning down a good office job that would have exempted him from military service; instead, he chooses to dedicate himself to his writing. True art, he seems to be saying, requires the kind of risk that he himself has taken as well as the courage that Maupassant showed in battling his illness. Art may indeed influence others—it inspires Kazantsev and for that matter Raisa—but talent is a calling and a challenge; it remains apart from and in defiance of ordinary life.

—Barry P. Scherr

H

HAIRCUT
by Ring Lardner, 1929

"Haircut" was collected in *Roundup*, probably Ring Lardner's best book. In any case this is the finest story that Lardner wrote during his short, intense career. It shows his trademarks—exact dialect, surface clarity of character and event colored by irony, the accurately detailed small-town scene, and, most of all, masterly use of the dramatic monologue.

This story could unfold at nearly anytime during this century save for the fact that men now seldom go to a barbershop for a shave. Otherwise it has an almost timeless quality, although the careless reader might think it too saturated in midwestern local color. In fact the action might occur in nearly any small town outside the metropolitan areas of the United States.

The person getting a haircut is a silent stranger who is, of course, you the reader. The stranger says nothing because he doesn't know the town or the story. The speaker is the typical garrulous barber who has bored countless victims with interminable stories, especially gossip and other small talk, and who has moved some exasperated customers who, when asked how they want their hair cut, to reply, "In silence." That response would do little to check our narrator, who is as talkative as he is obtuse.

Our barber, who is as nameless as his listener, tells what he thinks of the story of a "plain accidental shootin'" that resulted owing to the addled nature of Paul Dickson, whom he believes shot Jim Kendall by accident. In fact we know better. Paul shot Jim for having played the worst—the most callous and coarsest—of his many practical jokes.

Kendall is at once the protagonist and antagonist of the story: everyone else, including Paul, Julie Gregg, and Dr. Stair, has a relatively minor role. The barber, without knowing it, presents not only the anatomy of a murder but the case history of a bully, not a mere joker or card, as the narrator would have it. Our barber keeps saying such things as "He certainly was a card!" and "He *was* kind of rough, but a good fella at heart." But it takes no expert in abnormal psychology to perceive that Jim was a wretch with nothing to recommend him. A lazy and self-indulgent alcoholic, he bestirred himself to action only in playing vicious jokes on people, especially when someone had crossed him. His victims included not only his long-suffering wife but his children, strangers, acquaintances, and friends such as our barber. Jim Kendall was responsible to no one, loyal only to himself, and effective only as a practical joker and bully.

It might be objected that Lardner stacks the deck too easily against Kendall, whose fall is drastic and final; but, with such a scenario, the ending of the story could not have been otherwise. Paul, the mentally disabled boy who has been mistreated by Kendall and helped by Julie (the object of Kendall's thwarted lust and then his malicious revenge) and the man she loves, Ralph Stair, the new doctor in town, has been shaped by events to strike out against Kendall.

And Kendall, in the manner of all practical jokers, has overreached himself, going beyond petty cruelty into outright malevolence. His punishment is swift and just, and his killer could not be found legally guilty, even if he were tried. The story is worthy of a first-rate writer of police procedurals or detective fiction.

As has been pointed out more than once, our barber is a perfect instance of the innocent narrator who reports exactly what he has seen and heard but doesn't know the full significance of what he reports. He is an innocent eye and I, as it is said—an almost perfect instance. One is reminded of Huckleberry Finn, among other such figures in American literature. Behind Lardner looms the shadow of Mark Twain.

"Haircut" has many other virtues. Its verisimilitude is partly secured by the time it takes to read the story aloud—15 minutes, the time it ordinarily takes to get a haircut. The barbershop, like the saloon in the past, is the hub of this town's life, especially among its males. In no other setting could the story be so effective, the listener so silent. The story is a triumph of the dramatic monologue, as good in its way as anything that Robert Browning wrote—and, to repeat, the best instance of Lardner's art, which is often repetitive and tedious—but not here.

Until the 1960's this story was often anthologized and with good reason. Many authors, especially the minimalists of the present time, could profit by a close study of its art. Part of Lardner's success here lies in his having concealed the considerable art and artfulness of this great story. The ordinary reader is as likely to overlook Ring Lardner's mastery in "Haircut" as his barber and narrator was in overlooking Jim Kendall's murder.

—George Core

HANDS
by Sherwood Anderson, 1919

Sherwood Anderson's *Winesburg, Ohio* is an important literary document in the history of the American short story, for the collection marked a definite shift from the ironically patterned and linearly plotted stories of Edgar Allan Poe and O. Henry to a form that focuses on lyrical moments of realization structured around feelings and impressions. Although Henry James and Stephen Crane made use of these impressionistic techniques long before Anderson, it is in *Winesburg, Ohio* that they become the primary characteristics of the modern short story. A series of thematically and symbolically related images rather than temporal plot holds Anderson's stories together and gives them their sense of reality. In his *Memoirs* Anderson said, "There are no plot stories in life."

"Hands" is one of the most clearly impressionistic stories in the collection and thus a central example of Anderson's development of what critics have called the modern lyrical story. Instead of being dependent on a straightforward plot line, the story revolves around the central image of hands in such a way that the main character is revealed by various reactions to them. The story focuses on Wing Biddlebaum, a "fat little old man" who lives alone in Winesburg and is befriended only by George Willard, a young reporter for the local newspaper who serves as the major linking device in the stories. Biddlebaum is a former schoolteacher who was driven out of another town 20 years previously because he, quite innocently, "touched" the young boys in his class. However, as Anderson says, the real story of Wing Biddlebaum is "a story of hands."

Anderson laments throughout the story that revealing the secret of Biddlebaum's hands is a job for a poet. Thus, as a prose writer he struggles with the problem of trying to communicate something subtle and delicate with words that are coarse and clumsy, for all he has to work with are the tools of story—event and explanation. What he needs is a way to use language, the way the poet does, to transcend language. This inadequacy of language is why the central metaphor of this story is Biddlebaum's "talking with hands." However, what Biddlebaum aspires to is not hands but, as the name given to him by some obscure poet of the town suggests, "wings," which enable one, like the poet, to fly. The use of hands as a central image also suggests many other implications in the story, such as the magic of "laying on of hands," the injunction to "keep your hands off," and the need to maintain "clean hands."

Biddlebaum wants to transcend the merely physical and genuinely communicate with the other, but the only way he can "touch" someone is with his hands, which, by their very nature, are physical. The problem Anderson faces in the story is trying to express the kind of love Biddlebaum has for the boys without it sounding crude or being misunderstood; it is not flesh that is at stake here but spirit, and spirit is difficult to communicate. Motifs throughout the story suggest this counterpoint between the spiritual and the physical: dreams becoming facts for the half-witted boy who accuses Biddlebaum of "unspeakable" things which happen only in his dreams, doubts becoming beliefs for the men of the town who beat Biddlebaum up and chase him out of town, and the hard knuckles of the men versus Biddlebaum's fluttery winglike hands. The most emphatic example is the image at the end of "Hands," in which Biddlebaum's mundane task of picking up crumbs from the table is transformed into a gesture that could be "mistaken for the fingers of the devotee going swiftly through decade after decade of his rosary."

Biddlebaum's dilemma in the story—trying to convince George Willard of the need to dream and struggling to paint a picture of young men in a kind of pastoral golden age who come to gather about the feet of an old man—is the same as the dilemma Sherwood Anderson as a writer complains of in this story—the difficulty of communicating the Platonic ideal when one has only physical reality and ordinary language with which to do so.

Central to the success of "Hands," and typical of the technique Anderson inherited from Anton Chekhov, is the sense Anderson creates of maintaining an objective distance and a sympathetic identification both at the same time by projecting himself within the central character. Such a technique makes it possible for his stories, like Chekhov's, to focus on objective reality and to maintain a subjective power simultaneously. Poet Hart Crane once said of Anderson: "He has a humanity and simplicity that is quite baffling in depth and suggestiveness."

—Charles E. May

HAPPINESS
by Mary Lavin, 1969

As her career developed, Mary Lavin's short fiction went through some subtle but important changes. These developments have the overall effect of making more explicit and deliberate tendencies which recur throughout her large output. Apart from such obvious features as a continuing preoccupation with the lives of women and the moral climate and cultural atmosphere of provincial Ireland, Lavin's short stories are also marked by distinctive formal features. Among these are a certain inclination towards the anecdotal and also towards a certain looseness of structure, with a resultant lack of emphasis on plot. As with many other Irish writers, the emphasis is first and foremost on character. In addition, Lavin's work also has tended away from the vignette, preferring greater temporal and spatial scope, so that her stories are generally longer, and to a certain extent more old-fashioned, than many contemporary works in the genre.

The more pronounced presence of many of these features dates from the appearance of the 1969 volume of Lavin's short fiction, of which "Happiness" is the title story. One of the effects of the greater emphasis on the distinctive character of Lavin's imagination is fiction with a stronger autobiographical component. In "Happiness" a mother's early widowhood, a family of three daughters, and rural domicile is identical to the situation in which the author found herself. The presence of Father Hugh also has an autobiographical dimension. More important than, or perhaps the ultimate expression of, this autobiographical emphasis is the greater imaginative freedom of much of Lavin's later stories.

This freedom may be discerned in the broad time-span of "Happiness." Rather than a story, it is more in the nature of a life-story. The narrator's role and the final scene indicate as much. Another expression of the increasing breadth of Lavin's work is the persistence with which Mother is depicted as a character who typically occupies a space larger than that prescribed by merely domestic circumstances. "Happiness" is notable in the first instance, therefore, for the ways in which it reconfigures the author's deployment of time-space relationships. And it is these reconfigurations that give the story its open and unplotted air.

There is more to the story, however, than its technical accomplishments, however relevant an appreciation of these are for an adequate judgement of an author who has perhaps not always received her artistic due. The openness, rapid movement, and interweave of anecdotes that characterise the technique of "Happiness" also relate directly to the story's somewhat mysterious theme. The theme's strangeness derives from the fact that the central experiences of Mother's life—widowhood, debt, an unsatisfactory relationship with her mother—can hardly be considered a recipe for happiness. The story's point is much less simple than its title, and much less simple than the claims the mother wishes to make for the presence of happiness in not just her own life, but life in general. So unapparent is the meaning of happiness that the reader may well consider that perhaps the momentum, spontaneity, and naturalness of the narrative is as convincing an explication of what is meant as anything that the characters affirm.

This view is suggested by the use of the word "rhetoric" to describe Mother's perception and evaluation of her life and experiences. But, as in the case of "happiness," the finality of the word does not necessarily express the spirit of phenomenon. From the perspective of her daughters, whose lives have understandably taken a different trajectory from Mother's, insistence on happiness may seem purely rhetorical, a knowing sublimation of the effort to look on the bright side, to keep going despite the vicissitudes of death and taxes, and an implicit declaration of a need to find value in that effort. Such a perspective, however, merely addresses Mother's continual use of the word "happiness," and does not address the more dramatic manifestations of the spirit which she intends "happiness" to describe.

In particular, the striking incident of attempting to bring the heaps of daffodils to her dying husband's bedside surpasses both the scope of rhetoric and the seemingly cogent rationality of Father Hugh. But Father Hugh's observations are based on a life barren of the kind of bloom that inheres in Mother's extravagant, life-enhancing gestures. Because of such gestures, Mother cannot be regarded as merely all talk, nor can her talk merely be dismissed as a tissue of self-serving, self-deceiving fabrications. The detailing of action, with its implications of an objective, problematic world beyond the self, gives Mother a vitality which is not merely the signature of an appealing personality but which also argues for the existential viability of her outlook. The culmination of Mother's actions in gardening, with its connotations of nature and nurture, of energy and effortlessness, acts as a gloss on the other versions of the life process which have similarly engrossed her.

Moreover, as additional proof of the unsentimental challenge of objective reality, Lavin concludes "Happiness" with the daring intimacy of a death-bed scene. Clearly, death is antithetical to the spirit of survival and overcoming that is characteristic of Mother's viability. Yet, despite the obvious difficulties, harshly dramatised by Bea's contribution, Mother ultimately seems to embrace the fact of death as comprehensively as she identified with the nature of life. This unsettling ending makes the greatest demands on the reader's credibility, and is Lavin's most incisive reminder that "Happiness" is less a story in the conventional sense of the term, despite its superficially conventional form, than a meditation, that its method is not so much a narrative of idiosyncratic events as an exploration of the means whereby those events may be rendered tolerable, and that its subject is not merely the facts of a certain life as the necessary freedom to perceive the spirit of those facts.

—George O'Brien

HAUTOT AND HIS SON (Hautot Père et Fils)
by Guy de Maupassant, 1889

Guy de Maupassant was born and educated in Normandy, and though he excelled in the depiction of Parisian life in the last two decades of the 19th century and in his evocations of the great horrors of the German invasion of France in 1870, his portrayal of his home region has a strength and insight that is not surpassed. The provincial Normandy that he presents offers a contrast to the cosmopolitan Paris of so many of his other tales; it is more old-fashioned, slower moving, yet full of character, and the extravagance, in more than one sense, of the capital is set off against the careful conservatism of country ways. In "Hautot Père et Fils" ("Hautot and His Son"), which first appeared in the newspaper *Écho de Paris* on 5 January 1889, and was collected in *La main gauche* in the same year, Maupassant creates, albeit in just a few pages, some sense of the slowness of life in his native province in a tale which, like so many, leaves us with a conclusion that is not only unexpected and ironic but also puzzling. We might wonder whether the author is not saying something a bit more profound, even something sympathetic about humanity in its loneliness. Tight-lipped as ever no less in explanations than in his laconic realism, Maupassant declines to give us any hint about his attitudes, leaving us to respond to the story for ourselves—his tales, like life itself, do not give answers; they confront us with human situations that we must puzzle out for ourselves.

In the story Hautot is a contented man who enjoys the good things of life. He is a successful farmer with a fine old house, and, almost adopting the style of a lord of the manor, he is celebrating the start of the hunting season by inviting a couple of old friends for some shooting with himself and his son César. Fate strikes almost at once. Hautot brings down a partridge, dashes into some undergrowth to pick up the bird, trips, and is wounded when the other barrel of his gun goes off. His wound is dreadful, and he knows perfectly well that he is dying. Characteristically he does not let the doctor fool him with talk of recovery, and he has little patience with the clergyman either, but he does want a word in private with his son.

He tells the 24-year-old Césare to stop snivelling and explains what is worrying him. Left a widower seven years ago while still in his late thirties, he had not married again because he had promised his late wife not to do so. But he had found he could not get by without some female company, so he had been in the habit of spending some of his time in the provincial capital, Rouen, with a young woman called Caroline Donet, whose address he keeps on repeating. Now, Hautot explains, he had not made a will because he knows that that sort of thing only leads to trouble and disputes, so he wants his son to swear he will see that Mademoiselle Donet will be well provided for. Césare, puzzled by this confession and naturally devastated by his father's dreadful accident, promises he will do just as he has been asked, and old Hautot dies soon after, not saying another word to anyone.

A few days later Césare dutifully sets forth to Rouen, thinking over the financial arrangements he ought to make. He has some difficulty in finding Mademoiselle Donet's flat and, in a nicely ironic touch, asks a clergyman the way because he is a bit ashamed about what other people might think if he enquired of them. What greets him when he arrives at the flat is a perfect scene of quiet domesticity. In the neat flat the table has already been laid, the red wine is uncorked, warmed and waiting to be poured, and the crust has been removed from the bread by one of the plates because old Hautot had trouble with his teeth. Mademoiselle Donet is a calm, pleasant young woman, and she is genuinely upset by the totally unexpected news that old Hautot has been killed in an accident. The next surprise in store for Césare is the discovery of the existence of a charming little boy who is, of course, the son of Mademoiselle Donet and of his father; in other words this is his stepbrother.

The situation that develops does not becoming distressing, largely because of Mademoiselle Donet's simple good sense. Showing an instinctive concern for Césare's wellbeing, she insists that he should have something to eat, looks after him well, lets him enjoy the chance of getting to know her little boy. Césare departs, only to return a week later, finding a good meal waiting for him, but on this occasion he discovers that the crust has been left on the bread. When he realises a little later that he has left his pipe at home, Mademoiselle Donet quickly finds him one that his father used to smoke. As he leaves, he readily agrees that he will be back next Thursday. We can easily see what is going to happen, but in this beautifully crafted story it is left to us to decide exactly how to interpret it all.

—Christopher Smith

_____

HEART OF DARKNESS
by Joseph Conrad, 1902

Conrad's intention in "Heart of Darkness" is not to provide an accurate description of Africa, and the Africa in the tale is the continent as seen through European eyes. Certainly, "Heart of Darkness" possesses elements of realism. Marlow relates the story as if it were firsthand experience. The most powerful influence on Conrad's choice of narrative convention would have been the mode of the *sahib* recounting his colonial experiences. Conrad uses it ironically to subvert the *sahib* views of imperialism.

On one level, "Heart of Darkness" is a serious commentary on imperialism, what Conrad called "the vilest scramble for loot that ever disfigured the history of human conscience and geographical exploration." Marlow's portrayal is, from one aspect, a part of this theme and his suitability as a narrative vehicle is crucial to its presentation. In four instances, Marlow is compelled to compromise with truth, but for a worthy purpose; we feel that he is as honest as possible in an imperfect world.

That Marlow is a certain type of Englishman is also important. His honesty and exceptional humanity qualify him to be a suitable narrator. But is his usefulness limited by his British imperial-mindedness? Conrad is able to treat this side of Marlow critically just as he does the other aspects. Marlow provides one way by which he can bring Britain into his concerns. He can plausibly employ Marlow to convey his themes as fully as he understands them partly because Marlow's national sentiment would not be on the defensive, as a hindrance to clear-sightedness and frankness, in confronting the imperial entanglements of a foreign country, Belgium.

Conrad's presentation of the imperial theme begins when Marlow is on board a yawl in the Thames at dusk with four cronies. Suggestions of darkness in Great Britain's (Roman) past and present history converge. Marlow's cronies comprise a director of companies, a lawyer, and an accountant, each pillars of capitalism, and thereby implicated in his tale.

The action gathers momentum as the scene shifts to Brussels, the headquarters of the Belgian Empire. The whole city seems to Marlow "a whited sepulchre." Its deathlike attributes link with the inhumanity in the empire and Conrad suggests how the attributes of the metropolitan country are founded on imperialism. When Marlow leaves Brussels for the Congo, the realities en route are an integral part of the portrayal of imperialism: "the merry dance of death and trade goes on."

When the action moves on to the Congo, Conrad presents the imperial entanglements of Western civilization and primitive culture in the colony itself. The structure of the tale is provided by Marlow's journey to and from the heart of Africa, a linear structure, with a unifying centre, a pivotal concern, in Marlow himself and his growth.

In "Heart of Darkness," Marlow is extraordinary in his powers of observation, not in his attempts at analysis. What distinguishes him is his openness to impressions. However, Marlow is a narrator who only partially understands his experiences. The most fundamental irony of the tale is that Marlow narrates experiences but is unaware of their full import, which emerges through prose rich in implication, through the fine selection and juxtaposition of scenes.

It is commonly argued that Marlow is the hero of the tale, but his role as a character in his own right is of secondary importance. He is mainly a vehicle through which Conrad conveys the entanglements of Western civilization and primitive culture.

At the story's climax, when Kurtz tells his story of the heart of Africa, the imperial theme expands to include an account of moral isolation. At the same time, the symbolic level of the journey into the Congo becomes more pronounced, a journey into the depths of the unconscious. Indeed, "Heart of Darkness" is more symbolic than realistic.

Kurtz has lofty ideals, but the tragedy is that he deteriorates to the lowest possible levels. Marlow thinks that Kurtz's problems are solitude and silence, but his chief problem is one of freedom. Deprived of the protective power of society, of civilized restraints, he is faced with the terrible challenge of his own self, the knowledge that he is free, with all the dangers that attend this awareness. The strong drives in human nature then emerge in all their force. Kurtz is unable to control his lust for women, his lust for power, and the lure of the alien.

Kurtz's role in the story suggests meanings on political, economic, social, religious, moral, and psychological levels. It also intimates archetypal and philosophic levels. Behind Kurtz stands the Christian legend of Lucifer. Kurtz is guilty of pride, and the pride of self. Kurtz rebels against the limitations and imperfections of the human condition. He sets himself up as a demigod and comes to grief partly as a consequence. His final cry, "The horror! The horror!" is rich in meaning. It is interpreted by Marlow as "complete knowledge" and "a moral victory"; on one level, as rejection of "going native." It also can be understood as a recoil from the whole mess of European rapacity and brutality into which he is being returned. Perhaps Kurtz also sees a vision of hell and the damnation awaiting him.

Kurtz becomes than a representative of imperialism and European civilization; he acquires significance both as a human being and ultimately as a symbol of evil. The heart of darkness is the centre of Africa, the unknown, the hidden self, and, above all, the evil in humankind.

"Heart of Darkness" was first published in *Blackwood's Magazine* in 1899 and revised for publication in *Youth* (1902).

—D.C.R.A. Goonetilleke

_____

HELL HATH NO LIMITS (El lugar sin límites)
by José Donoso, 1966

El lugar sin límites (1966, *Hell Hath No Limits,* 1972), José Donoso's third novel, is more properly termed a novella or novelette, like the two before it, and like them, it represents the deterioration of the Chilean upper class. A major difference—one which relates it to the author's fourth novel, *El obsceno pájaro de la noche* (1970; *The Obscene Bird of Night,* 1973)—is the rural setting; earlier works portrayed decadent families in the capital, Santiago. The rural aristocracy in the latter two works is symbolized by the figure of the *hacendado,* owner of vast *haciendas* (ranches or other lands), typifying the system known as *latifundismo,* whereby the majority of the rural population work as sharecroppers or daylaborers for the landlord. Although some Chilean critics originally saw *Hell Hath No Limits* as part of the turn-of-the-century movement known as *criollismo* (a variant of regional realism emphasizing rural customs, traditions and legends, type characters, and confrontations between the individual and nature), this is only Donoso's point of departure. Clearly aware of literary tradition (and tradition weighs heavily in the novel), Donoso stylizes and distorts for aesthetic effect. Parodic inversion adds another, subversive dimension of interpretation. There is no hero—the dominant character is instead an anti-hero—and unlike the traditional regional novel that portrayed rural landowners as benevolent, paternalistic figures, the *hacendado* in *Hell Hath No Limits* is egotistical, short-sighted, and capricious, with no interests beyond his own material well-being.

Chronologically, the limits are tight, less than 24 hours: from around ten o'clock on a Sunday morning until about five A.M. the following day. Narration is basically linear and chronological, with the exception of a flashback in chapters 6 and 7, to a moment 20 years before, explaining the origins of certain key relationships; given the frequent focus upon characters' memories, however, all but the last two chapters contain considerable retrospective material. Setting is narrowly circumscribed; everything takes place in a sordid, miserable village near the city of Talca, in Chile's wine-producing region, largely in a brothel managed by one of the main characters, more briefly in the church and at the hacienda (the emblematic nature of these locales is self-evident). Narrative viewpoint is fairly complex, beginning with a free indirect style used by a seemingly traditional third-person narrator who is soon replaced by the first-person narrative consciousness of "la Manuela," half owner of the brothel and principal narrator. Other narrative perspectives belong to Manuela's 18-year-old daughter, Japonesita, and the truckdriver Pancho (something of a rebel who has rejected working for the local landowner and political boss don Alejo). The remaining significant players are don Alejo, Octavio (Pancho's brother-in-law), and don Céspedes, don Alejo's foreman.

One noteworthy peculiarity of the narrative perspective concerns Manuela, the dominant narrative consciousness. While the third-person narrator avoids pronouns, the adjectives describing self employed by Manuela are feminine, and Manuela remembers with delight several past performances as a Spanish flamenco dancer with high heels and sequined dress—a prized possession—plus supposed artistic triumphs and drunken celebrations. Because details appear elucidating Manuela's present decrepit, toothless condition and residence in the run-down brothel, the reader suspects a capacity for self-delusion in references to fragile girlhood, but does not realize until later that "she" is actually a male homosexual and transvestite. Manuela's perspective is used not only for unfolding "her" thoughts but also for presenting and considering the attitudes and desires of other characters, often misinterpreted or incompletely understood, which results in a deformed perception and distorted world-view. Donoso thereby portrays decadence in rural Chile, and more generally, life's existential precariousness.

Basically, three natural subdivisions can be distinguished, with the five initial chapters devoted to anticipation and dread, the interlude consisting of the flashback to two decades before, and a third section of encounters in which events anticipated or dreaded initially are played out. Manuela's original malaise results from news of Pancho's return: the stereotyped bully and *macho,* he has beaten and threatened Manuela on previous occasions—usually after drinking bouts in the brothel (the only place in town). Despite Manuela's self-deception, the reader realizes that her fear is ambivalent and mixed with desire, as Pancho's strength, virility, enormous stature, and brutish attractiveness are repeatedly noted. Pancho has designs on Manuela's daughter, Japonesita, still a virgin despite growing up in a brothel (Pancho's only interest is deflowering her; she is thin, plain, and still prepubescent). Japonesita has talent for business and bookkeeping; too realistic to dream of escaping her background, she reflects that "If I'm going to be a whore, I might as well begin with Pancho."

Two decades before, don Alejo planned a drunken orgy in the brothel to celebrate an election victory, and Manuela was imported as a special entertainer. Don Alejo bet the madame, Japonesa Grande (so nicknamed because of Oriental features) that she could not seduce the homosexual; to make it worth her while, she insisted upon betting the brothel (which stood on his land) and won by exploiting Manuela's notion of being female, playing out a fantasy lesbian relationship; becoming pregnant with Japonesita was not part of the plan. Manuela was paid with half-interest in the business, and Japonesita inherited the other half upon her mother's death. Ironically, Pancho's much-anticipated evening visit to the brothel does not lead to Japonesita's sexual initiation, for Manuela's flirtatious "final dance" sparks his latent homosexuality; Octavio's reprimand when Manuela attempts to kiss Pancho (placing his *machismo* in jeopardy) leads to brutal beating, sado-masochistic rape, and Manuela's death.

Financial focus revolves around possible electrification of the area, which might infuse life into the moribund village. Don Alejo favors this only so long as it may bring a highway, increasing the value of his land; when his plans go awry, he thinks instead of doing away with the village entirely and expanding his vineyards. Economically, there is no hope for the villagers, condemned to continue in their degraded, infernal world (both Pancho and don Alejo have satanic attributes). This is the significance of the epigram from Marlowe's *Dr. Faust,* when Mephistopheles replies, to Faust's query concerning hell's location, that it has no limits, but is where we are, and where it is, we must stay. Donoso's vision of the human condition and what he suggests of metaphysical reality are equally horrendous.

—Janet Pérez

THE HILL OF EVIL COUNSEL (Har haetsah haraah)
by Amos Oz, 1974

The novella "Har haetsah haraah" ("The Hill of Evil Counsel") by Amos Oz, chronicles in microcosm the physical and psychological rites of passage that European Jewish emigres to Palestine endured during 1946 and 1948, the twilight of the British Mandate. Actual events, such as World War II and political incidents in Palestine during this period, anchor the story in a specific historical context wherein the ineffectual inhabitants of Tel Arza, a forlorn village just outside of Jerusalem, live out their tense lives. These include: Dr. Hans Kipnis, a gentle, rumpled veterinarian from Silesia, the nephew of the famous geographer Hans Walter Landauer; his elegant wife, Ruth, who, as a child of a secular, wealthy family in Warsaw, was adept at watercolors and reciting Polish nationalistic poetry; and their son, about six or seven years old, the precocious, pudgy, asthmatic Hillel, who, like Oz, was born in Jerusalem.

Because he came to the medical assistance of the high commissioner's sister-in-law, Lady Bromley, at a public celebration, Kipnis receives an invitation to the May Ball at the high commissioner's palace, located atop the Hill of Evil Counsel. As Kipnis and Ruth prepare to attend, their backgrounds and those of their neighbors emerge through flashbacks, showing how they have come to Palestine. Some, like Kipnis, had emigrated for ideological or religious reasons; others, like Ruth, had come for a visit but were forced to remain because of the outbreak of World War II.

Powerful secondary characters add further texture and depth to the story. The best-drawn is the fanatical leftist Mitya. Compulsively neat and usually meek, he is sometimes prone to verbal outbursts that are oracular in diction and filled with images of violence and destruction. The musicians Madame Yabrov and her niece, Lyubov, babysit young Hillel while his parents attend the May Ball. After plying the boy with a large meal, they put him to bed. Here, in that uncertain state between awakening and sleep, Hillel feels someone touching his penis. It is unclear whether it is one of the women or Hillel himself. The engineer Brzezinski rigs up a gigantic radio antenna to receive news and builds a telescope because "he would be the first to see them when they arrived." Who "they" are remains unspoken, but "they" are probably Arabs who someday will attack the village.

Educated, urban, and dislocated, the adults are overwhelmed by the gaping differences between their former circumstances and their new ones. Chamber music and Beethoven's "Eroica" offer a counterpoint to the muezzin's call to prayer and the howl of jackals. Though a master of modern Occidental technology, Brzezinski gets drunk on arak, a "frightful Oriental drink." Hillel is fed Quaker Oats, while Arab men drink strong, black coffee in tiny cups. As if to retain their identity and resist integration with the new land, these inhabitants, and by extension, most, if not all, Jews in Palestine, cling to their "us against them" siege mentality. According to Oz, they seem to be thinking only in terms of "self" and "other."

But there seems to be no agreement among the various "selves" either. Mitya rants against latter-day "Hellenizers," a term referring to Jews who in earlier periods of history adopted Greek (that is, European) ideas and abandoned their essential Judaism. However, the photograph of Kipnis' famous uncle is ever-present. A proud, successful, assimilated (that is, "Hellenized") Jew who, as a geographer, possessed a vast world view, he looks down from the wall with patronizing disdain on the events in the Kipnis household, in the neighborhood, and, more globally, in all of Palestine. Kipnis and Ruth seem to be caught somewhere in between, but there seems to be an unspoken hope of some kind for the Jerusalem-born Hillel.

At the ball Ruth meets a dashing British naval hero, who dances with her all evening. They run off together. Learning of this, Hillel climbs a high tree, creating turmoil among the adults, who try to coax him down, and he leaps "up to the last leaf, to the shore of the sky." One is left to conjecture what actually happens to the boy.

In the coda of the story, the State of Israel is established, and the fate of the various inhabitants of Tel Arza is revealed. The village itself eventually becomes a part of Jerusalem and braces itself for attack from its enemies.

The destructiveness of anti-Semitism, a major theme in Oz's works, is harrowingly depicted here. First, in the ironic story title itself. During the waning days of the Mandate, the British offered everything but good council to either the Zionists or the Arabs. Lady Bromley is viciously amused as she devastates Kipnis, to whom she refers disdainfully as "a Jew," with the news that Ruth has run off.

Semi-autobiographical, "The Hill of Evil Counsel" is the title piece of a collection of three loosely connected novellas, each of which has a young boy as a central character. The stories also share a common time period, locale, and several minor characters.

—Carlo Coppola

HILLS LIKE WHITE ELEPHANTS
by Ernest Hemingway, 1927

Since its publication in 1927, "Hills Like White Elephants" has become regarded as the quintessential Hemingway story for its restraint and subtlety. In only a few pages, Hemingway develops a tense conflict between a man and a woman who are deeply divided about a decision that will affect the rest of their lives. In accord with Hemingway's "iceberg theory" that an essential element of a story could be implied but never stated, the woman's pregnancy and the man's insistence on an abortion are never directly articulated, even though the issue becomes increasingly evident as the conversation progresses. Even the titular reference to "white elephants," metaphorically an item of considerable value that is too troublesome and expensive to keep, would seem to underscore the heart of the drama.

Hemingway was no stranger to Spain, having become intrigued with bullfighting and Spanish culture, and the earliest drafts of the story have a biographical basis. When Hemingway's first wife, Hadley, became pregnant in 1923, he complained that he was not ready for the responsibilities of parenthood and the imposition of his time that a child would represent. In an early sketch, Hemingway explored the central situation, writing in first person and calling the woman "Hadley." The tone of this draft was positive, however, expressing the relief the two of them felt to be travelling away from the arguments that had ruined the Pamplona fiesta of 1925.

When he returned to this subject in May 1927, he had divorced Hadley and was about to marry Pauline Pfeiffer, and he transformed the plot into a third-person narrative with a tense unstated conflict at the heart of the action. He retained the setting and the elephant simile of the earlier draft, but he changed the central figures into an anonymous American man and a woman called "Jig."

The central plot of the published story is deceptively simple. A man and a woman are at a station in the valley of the Ebro waiting 40 minutes for the train to Madrid. They have conversation over drinks; he carries their luggage to the other side of the station, has a drink alone at the bar, and returns to his companion. What gives this simple action interest is the tension of their dialogue, the implications of their comments, and the subtle suggestions of their personalities and the irreconcilable conflict between them.

The story opens with them seated at a table ordering beer on a hot day. Jig looks at the Spanish hills and comments that they look like white elephants, the first occurrence of the phrase in the story. When the man remarks that he has never seen one, she counters, "No, you wouldn't have," in a tone of bitterness and resentment. It is clear in the ensuing conversation that they have travelled together, staying in hotels, and that he wants her to submit to an abortion. She is reluctant, fearing the consequences for their relationship: "Then what will we do afterward?" His suggestion that they will be just the way they were before does not reassure her, and she is skeptical that other couples who have gone through the procedure were happy afterward. He professes love for her, and she seems to acquiesce: "Then I'll do it. Because I don't care about me." The conversation that follows makes it clear that the tension has not been relieved, that he is aware of her resentment and continues to argue his case.

When the waitress informs them that the train is coming in five minutes, he takes the bags to the other side of the station and stops in the bar for a drink on his way back to her. He seems to enjoy this moment apart from her, noting how reasonable the people in the bar all seem. Then he returns to her, and she says, "There's nothing wrong with me. I feel fine." Less than an hour has elapsed, the conflict remains unresolved, and the story ends.

Part of the genius of Hemingway's fiction is his ability to do so much with so little, to create a tense scene without direct physical or verbal conflict. Her repeated comments about white elephants suggests a deep awareness of their situation that he does not recognize, and scholars have seen this allusiveness as an indication of her superior imagination and knowledge. She seems more mature, to want commitment, a child, a life together. His comments reflect a desire for a carefree existence, adventure, a relationship free of obligations. Structurally, his comforting drink alone at the bar portends eventual separation for the couple, the fulfillment of her apprehensions.

The subtlety of the story has generated a good deal of critical attention. Gary Elliott has suggested that the bamboo bead curtain at the entrance to the bar is a reference to rosary beads, indicating that Jig must be a Catholic, thus understandably resistant to an abortion. Joseph DeFalco reads the story as focusing on the man's refusal to accept the "natural processes of life" and the woman's capitulation in an attempt to save the relationship, a tragic ending in that she is clearly the more sensitive and insightful of the pair. Sheldon Grebstein argues that the conflict is dynamically unresolved at the end, still a smoldering issue that threatens to tear them apart. However the conclusion is read, it is evident that Hemingway has presented a dramatic conflict built on subtle implication and inference, making this brief narrative a masterpiece of short fiction.

—James Nagel

THE HITCHHIKING GAME (Falešný autostop)
by Milan Kundera, 1965

Milan Kundera's international reputation as one of the most renowned writers of the 20th century rests almost entirely on the novels he began publishing in 1967 and hardly at all on the ten short stories he wrote during the half-decade leading up to the shortlived Prague Spring, which ended with the Soviet invasion and occupation of Czechoslovakia in 1968. This was just three days after the completion of the last of his three-volume collection: Směšné lásky (Laughable Loves), Druhý sešit směšných lásek (A Second Book of Laughable Loves), Třetí sešit směšných lásek (A Third Book of Laughable Loves). (Kundera revised the collection as Směšné lásky, and it was translated into English as Laughable Loves.) Far from being mere apprentice work or just a sidelight to his dramas and novels, the stories are in style, structure, and substance clearly the work of an already mature writer who conceives of writing as a series of explorations in form and theme.

"Falešný autostop" ("The Hitchhiking Game"), from the second book, is a case in point. Here in miniature one finds Kundera's characteristic philosophical playfulness, classically precise anti-Romantic style, and the theme and variation approach that Kundera inherited from his father, a musician and musicologist. The story is less a conventional short fiction than it is an aesthetic and existential inquiry, a search for a new literary form through which to understand the human situation in the modern, posthumanist (and perhaps even posthuman) world. Its overall theme and variation approach incorporates a number of diverse elements, most notably the Sartrean gaze, film (which Kundera taught), and theater, while retaining fiction's capacity for entering the minds of its characters. As a result, "The Hitchhiking Game" reads less like a story and more like a sketch for a script involving a very limited number of characters ("the young man," and "the girl,") and settings (a sportscar, a petrol station, a restaurant and room, both in the same hotel). The story's basic situation is no less deceptively simple. The couple, lovers for some time, are on their way to the mountains (the Tatras) for a well deserved vacation: she from her tiresome job and sick mother, he from an office that "infiltrates" and scrutinizes his every move (a reflection of the totalitarian state): "Its omnipotent brain . . . did not cease knowing about him even for an instant."

Their relationship, like their vacation, provides a respite from their otherwise confining, more or less official lives. However, even though he values her modesty (which she experiences as shame of a body she believes he will eventually abandon for one more attractive and accessible), the young man nonetheless plays with, or on, that modesty in a way that gives him pleasure but that causes her pain. (It is of course a relationship that looks ahead to that of Tomas and Tereza in L'Insoutenable Légéreté de l'être (The Unbearable Lightness of Being) and back to Chaucer ("The Clerk's Tale"), Boccaccio, and Petrarch.) The game he plays is this: he drives until the car runs out of gas and then, hidden, watches as she hitches a ride from another man to the nearest petrol station, during which time he fantasizes about what she and the driver may be doing. Alternatively, he drives until she, despite her shame, must ask him to stop so that she can urinate.

Soon after he announces that the car is running out of gas, they unexpectedly come to a station (much to her delight and his disappointment) where he fills up while she relieves herself. Then, instead of returning to the car, she walks ahead and, as he pulls up, she puts out her thumb for a ride. He is suddenly no longer the young man, instead, first a stranger and later a gallant seducer; she is no longer the girl, instead, first a damsel in distress and then an "artful seductress." The permutating possibilities do not stop there as the role playing leads each to believe that the part of the other more accurately represents who that other actually is and has always been. The mind-body dualism that troubles the girl suggests that the story is a variation on the familiar Descartean theme of "cogito ergo sum," revised here to "I play, therefore I am." In her role as hitchhiker, the girl can "do anything: everything was permitted her" because she has become "the woman without a destiny," or more narrowly and ironically, without a destination.

If the road they take from the city to the mountains suggests their desire to escape their official selves not only by vacationing but by vacating their usual roles as worker and as daughter, then their turning from the plot of their usual game offers them a new but also disconcerting and even dangerous freedom not only from scrutiny and shame (two sides of the same coin) but from themselves as well. Similarly, when he unexpectedly turns off the road to the mountains and towards Nowy Zamky, their game, shifting like his sports car into a higher gear, begins to develop a logic of its own. Borders are crossed, boundaries blur, as the self begins to take on the unsettling look of a double exposure: "The game merged with life. The game of humiliating the hitchhiker became only a pretext for humiliating his girl" (whose "amorphous," no longer "pure" soul now disgusts him). Like the jokes in another of Kundera's *Laughable Loves*, "Nobody Will Laugh," and in his first novel, *Zert* (*The Joke*), the game has turned serious.

Although "The Hitchhiking Game" begins as a broadly drawn existential cartoon, its conclusion is decidedly horrific. The horror, which is existential rather than Gothic, begins with the young man's debasement of the girl and includes her finding pleasure in her own debasement as well as his awareness "of the emptiness" of "her pitiful tautology" ("I am me, I am me, I am me"). The horror does not end, as the story does, with the ironic statement, "There were still thirteen days' vacation before them." It ends with the realization that in pursuing freedom the young man and the girl have come to embody the very tyranny they sought to escape, becoming as it were the mirror of the larger political situation. In their sexual and emotional being, they have fallen victim to the totalitarian tyranny and absolute skepticism that Kundera has elsewhere said the modern world has become.

—Robert A. Morace

THE HOLLOW MEN (Kida lee mansen)
by Gaṅgādhar Gādgil, 1948

A leading and prolific modern Marathi short story writer, Gādgīl has written stories in different veins, including the starkly realistic, the surrealistic, the psychological, the semi-mystical the comic, and the farcical. But he is probably at his most characteristic when he probes with rare precision and penetration the mind of the urban middle class, to which he himself belongs.

"Kida lee mansen," ("The Hollow Men"), is collected in *Kaḍū aṇī god*, is easily one of the most memorable depictions of urban middle-class life and values in Marathi short fiction. The story describes an eventful day in the normally humdrum life of the inhabitants of a crowded *chawl* (a large tenement house) in a typical middle-class suburb in Bombay. On that day, there is an outbreak of communal violence in the city, attended by gang warfare, murder, and arson. A band of ruffians has just broken into a Muslim shop opposite the tenement, and the story narrates how the Hindu tenants react to this event, revealing the characteristic weaknesses—big and small—of middle-class psyche.

The opening description of the tenement and its residents sets the tone of the story, by striking a strong ironic note. The tenement is a "castle of the puissant nation of office-clerks"; the four traditional stages of the Hindu's life are reduced here to landing a clerical job, marrying, educating the children, and earning a small pension. The boss's favour and a rise are the focal points of the life of a man here, and one's husband's salary and the extent of one's own good looks the acid-test of a woman's worth. The burning questions of this culture are how to obtain supplies of sugar and kerosene (then scarce commodities owing to the war).

The reactions of these people to the violence and the looting taking place at their very doorstep are varied, but they are all typical of the middle-class mind. First, then is the thrill of something exciting happening, right in front of their eyes, breaking the monotony of their insipid diurnal routine. Young Damu, who always has a "nose for news," and who is therefore naturally the first to disclose the wonderful tidings, represents this aspect of middle-class psychology. But the middle-class people know that they can never be actors in the drama of life: at best they are only passive spectators; hence, they can only enjoy adventure vicariously. Ainapure, the armchair politician in the *chawl* illustrates this. A rabid Hindu, he bravely talks about teaching the Muslims a lesson, and rejoices that the shop being looted belongs to a Muslim, though he has no courage to join in the fray. Gharuanna's rejoinder to Ainapure reveals how narrow are the horizons of the middle class: "What's the use of discussing politics? Tell me about a political strategy that will improve my salary." The author adds, "And he looked around in the belief that he had said something very clever; everybody agreed with him, and precisely for this reason, no one like what he said."

But it is not merely innate pusillanimity nor inborn narrowness that renders the middle class incapable of action; taboos and inhibitions drilled into them for generations are equally instrumental. Thus, it is a North Indian milk vendor who is the first to grab a pair of new shoes from the burglarized shop. The tenement people's reaction to this is "a happy collective laugh. . . .for that simple fellow had translated into action what everybody had in his heart of hearts longed to do." Soon, others on the street join in the fray (but not the tenement-people, of course). The author underscores the point by adding: "Ainapure, almost unaware of what he was doing . . . turned hastily towards the stairs. 'Are you too joining in the looting?' asked Gharuanna in mocking tones. Ainapure suddenly realized the enormity of what he was about to do."

Middle class greed can sometimes prove stronger than all its ethical imperatives. Young Damu, wise beyond his years, boldly joins the looters and returns with his trophy—a nice pair of new shoes for his father. Gharuanna's reaction is typical of middle-class hypocrisy: "You fool, . . . you mustn't. . . .but well, now that you have them. . . ." Once a dreaded taboo is broken, the floodgates are opened. So, Damu's mother now actually gives him a cloth-bag to collect more loot, and he gleefully sets out for another foray. His shining example inspires the neighbour's wife Radhabai to admonish her son Madhu, "Go, go down, you good-for-nothing fellow; see what a clever boy is Damu." But Damu's second expedition is an unmitigated disaster. As he is returning with the loot, a burly hooligan slaps him and snatches away his satchel. Upon his inglorious return, Damu is sternly reprimanded for losing his bag as well—an unpardonable offence against middle-class thrift.

The story ends with the arrival of the police and the dispersal of the mob. The last sentence carries not only ironic but almost symbolic overtones: "In the vanguard [of those who ran] was a clerk, escorting a couple of women and a large band of urchins shouting in terror, without looking back: 'Run, run, have you all gone lame?'" There could not be a better symbol of middle-class cowardice, helplessness, and escapism.

"The Hollow Men" is a brief but acute study of a representative segment of modern Indian society caught in a moment of crisis. Imbued with a strong social and psychological awareness, it drives home its point with ruthless honesty and sharp irony.

—M.K. Naik

A HORSE AND TWO GOATS
by R.K. Narayan, 1970

"A Horse and Two Goats," by R.K. Narayan appeared, in a somewhat different form, in *The New Yorker* in 1965. It was first published in its present form in the collection *A Horse and Two Goats* (1970), and was later included in *Under the Banyan Tree*, a selection of Narayan's stories to 1984.

Narayan is admired as a writer whose novels and stories are remarkably consistent in quality. Yet one or two works do stand out—like the novel *The Guide* (1958) and the short story "A Horse and Two Goats." To many, Narayan is best known as the creator of Malgudi, one of literature's most enduring and endearing fictional worlds, so it is somewhat ironic that "A Horse and Two Goats" is one of only a handful of Narayan's stories not to be set in the brilliantly-realised world of Malgudi. Nevertheless, it is a tale that perfectly displays his mastery of the short story form.

Muni, the central character of the story, is a typical Narayan hero who has achieved little, and who feels he has been dealt with unsympathetically by the world around him, and by fate. Unlike most of Narayan's heroes, though, he is a lower-class village peasant, rather than the usual middle-class Malgudi-dweller, and he is very poor, as the appalling conditions of his life, always present behind the humour of the story, attest. Indeed, on one level this tale provides the non-Indian reader with a glimpse of the type of poverty and hardship that must be endured by the millions of Indians who, like Muni, have barely enough food to keep them alive:

> His wife lit the domestic fire at dawn, boiled water in a mud pot, threw into it a handful of millet flour, added salt, and gave him his first nourishment of the day. When he started out, she would put in his hand a packed lunch, once again the same millet cooked into a little ball, which he could swallow with a raw onion at midday.

Narayan has, on occasions, been criticized for focussing on middle-class urban India in his stories, thereby excluding the poor of rural India who continue to make up the vast majority of the Indian population. But Narayan's purpose as a storyteller has never been to educate the non-Indian reader about India. So although we can learn specific things about village life in India from this story, it isn't about Indian problems or about Indian sensibilities as such. While what happens in "A Horse and Two Goats" is accurate to the particular of the Indian experience, it deliberately deals with themes that are quintessentially human, also. William Walsh has suggested it is a story about misunderstanding, a story about the gap between supposed and real understanding, a story about the element of incomprehension in human relationships.

"A Horse and Two Goats" is typical of Narayan's pre-Modernist, village storyteller style of writing. In a deceptively simple, linear narrative Narayan unfolds the story of Muni, an old goatherd. In keeping with his usual narrative formula, Narayan carefully follows Muni as he goes about his daily, frequently humiliating existence—eating his meagre breakfast, visiting the local shopkeeper in a typically unsuccessful attempt to get a few items of food on credit, and then taking his two scraggy goats to graze near the foot of the horse statute at the edge of the village. He spends the rest of his day crouching in the shade offered by the clay horse, or watching the traffic pass on the highway.

Once the nature of Muni's world has been established, both the plot and the comedy of the story hinge on the disruption of that routine (as they do with the arrival of Vasu in *The Man-Eater of Malgudi*, or Tim in *The World of Nagaraj*). This is a formula Narayan uses frequently, and always with consummate skill. In "A Horse and Two Goats" the seemingly timeless routine is interrupted when a car stops and a "red-faced foreigner," an American whose vehicle has run out of petrol, asks for directions to the nearest gas station.

This is where the comedy of misunderstanding takes over. After initially thinking he is being questioned about a crime by the khaki-clad foreigner, whom he assumes must be either a policeman or a soldier, Muni concludes that the man wants to buy his goats. Meanwhile the red-faced American, assuming the Tamil peasant owns the clay horse statute, which to the villagers, as Muni explains, "is our guardian, it means death to our adversaries," sets about trying to buy it, so he can take it back to the United States to decorate his living room: "I'm going to keep him right in the middle of the room . . . we'll stand around him and have our drinks."

The humour and the irony of this tale lies in the total benign incomprehension that exists between the two, not only in the way neither understands the other's language, but also in the absolute contrast of their cultural and economic backgrounds, emphasised by the way each values the clay horse. Much of this is conveyed through the wonderful double discourse that makes up a significant part of the story, with each of the characters happily developing his own hermetically-sealed interpretation of the other's words and gestures. The story's charm lies in the way Narayan refrains from passing judgement.

—Ralph J. Crane

THE HORSE DEALER'S DAUGHTER
by D.H. Lawrence, 1922

"The Horse Dealer's Daughter" is a story from the middle period of D.H. Lawrence's writings, and was collected in 1922 in *England My England and Other Stories*. In the story, after the death of the horse dealer, life seems to be over for the rest of the family as well. The eldest son plans to get a job by marrying the daughter of a steward of a neighboring estate: "He would marry and go into harness. His life was over, and he would be a subject animal now." The daughter, 27-year-old Mabel, refuses this kind of death-in-life, preferring to follow her beloved mother into death. She attempts suicide, but the young doctor, Jack Fergusson, rescues her from drowning and restores her to life literally. When she kisses him, "this introduction of the personal element" is to him a distasteful "violation of his professional honour." Her eyes, her drawing him to her, his touching of her shoulder, which seems to burn his hand— all cause him to yield to her, and then he finds he wants to remain holding her "for ever, with his heart hurting him in a pain that was also life to him." She suddenly feels she must seem horrible to him: it is a reaction he did in fact have earlier, but now he wants to marry her, soon.

This kind of summary does little justice to the subtleties of Lawrence's story, its psychological shifts, its range of effects. For one thing, the story does not have the finished quality such an outline suggests: it begins and ends *in medias res*, opening casually in the midst of a desultory conversation, turning back in time in the middle to give the previous history of the Pervins, and ending not with the actual wedding, or anything about their future married life, but with Fergusson's repeated declaration that he wants Mabel, uttered "with that terrible intonation which frightened her almost more than her horror lest he should *not* want her." The story is open at both ends, with a sense of life going on both before and after, and this gives it a distinctively modern and indeed modernist feel.

What is distinctively Lawrence, however, is a matter not so much of structure as of subject and style. This is a story about the psychological dynamics of relationships in a family and between a man and a woman, a story about love and the links between love and a series of other things: family ties and tensions, power, sex (in its repelling as well as attractive, physical as well as emotional aspects), death, and rebirth. Few writers could handle such large concerns in a short fiction without any hint of strain or cliché or oversimplification, and with a compelling sense of truthfulness to the complexities of the central human experiences presented, as when Fergusson at last admits to Mabel that he loves her:

"Yes." The word cost him a painful effort. Not because it wasn't true. But because it was too newly true, the *saying* seemed to tear open again his newly-torn heart. And he hardly wanted it to be true, even now.

The nuances here persuade the reader of a genuine insight, a fidelity of response to varieties of delicate feelings.

The intensity of the writing matches the intensity of the psychological and emotional themes. The presentation of the drowning scene, for example, uses recurrent references to death in the grey wintry afternoon, blackened by industrial smoke and the grey clay beneath the black water of the pond: the afternoon is referred to as "deadened" and "deadening" as well as "dead," the word repeatedly used of the cold water. Death is also prominent in the story as a whole: particularly striking is Mabel's identification with her dead mother, for "the life she followed here in the world was far less real than the world of death she inherited from her mother." She looks forward to being transformed in death as "her fulfilment, her own glorification, approaching her dead mother, who was glorified." The religious language draws attention to the religious aspects of the story, especially when Mabel's later "transfiguration" is not into death, but a resurrection, a rebirth she shares with the doctor. As frequently happens in Lawrence, this is brought about through physical touch, as well as through the power of eyes, so often referred to throughout the story, both magnificently combining with the death theme and threat in the sentence "He could not bear the touch of her eyes' question upon him, and the look of death behind the question." Touching and looking at one another brings the triumph of affirmation to make this not a story of death but of new life, through new love.

Lawrence's original title was overtly religious: "The Miracle." In combining so many aspects with such easy mastery, from religious reverence for life down through acute psychological penetration to the little details of characterization such as the animal imagery in Mabel's brutish horsey brothers and her own "bull-dog" fixity and determination, this story is indeed a miracle.

—Michael Herbert

THE HOUSE ON THE HILL
by Hal Porter, 1970

"The House on the Hill" is set in Japan and is a product of Hal Porter's second visit to that country. The author's first visit to Japan was for a period of two years after World War II as a schoolteacher of children of the Australian Occupation Forces. He also used the time to acquaint himself with Japanese people and the land and cityscapes of this temporarily defeated country. A talented artist, Porter sketched scenes as well as wrote about the Japanese. His novel *A Handful of Pennies* (1958; revised 1980) was an outcome of this first visit. Porter's return visit in 1967 led to a travel book, *The Actors: An Image of the New Japan* (1968)—illustrated with his own drawings—and a collection of short stories, *Mr. Butterfry and Other Tales of New Japan* (1970), which contains "The House on the Hill."

Porter's two visits to Japan provide an important context for understanding his fiction that is set there. In the novel *A Handful of Pennies*, as Mary Lord has observed in her 1980 book on Porter, "the Westerners in occupation not only corrupt the vanquished Japanese, each corrupts the other and himself." Even in defeat, Lord observes, these Japanese have the advantage of "an ancient culture and transcending philosophy." The literary products of Porter's second visit to Japan, 18 years after the first, show a continuing fascination with the country but a sharper satiric eye for the Japanese people, who have largely lost their traditional ways in imitation of urbanized Western automatism. Porter's Australian country-bred conservative values can only see the disappearance of the old Japan, still vestigially present in the early postwar years, as a tragic loss. This sense of loss lies behind Porter's satiric treatment of the "new Japan."

"The House on the Hill" introduces its third-person protagonist Perrot (who reemerges from the earlier story "Say to me Ronald!") as an artist who has returned to Japan for a six-months' sketching tour. Having braced himself for "near-skyscrapers instead of *après-guerre* ruins, for near-arrogance rather than *après-guerre* mock-humility," he finds things even worse than expected. Nor is he braced for the astronomical costs of accommodation. It is this latter complication that leads to the story's principal focus—a house which he is lent by an Australian family returning to their home country for four months.

Porter's houses of childhood and youth in country Gippsland develop in his writings a Dickensian vivacity in which objects become strangely animated and develop a life of their own. These houses are the forebears of the incongruous house Perrot inhabits temporarily on the outskirts of Tokyo in the late 1960's. The house is "a quasi-folly, Western, *circa* 1912, brick, in an ex-fashionable but still far from unfashionable suburb of Tokyo, a hilltop suburb." But the hilltop location cannot totally escape the rampaging city:

> This relatively bucolic area was ringed about by a mesa-and-butte horizon of office blocks, department stores, glassy factories, and scenes of Meccano-like towers. At each day's end chemically gorgeous sunsets ..owed up beyond them to be replaced each night, by the topless coal-blue cliffs of night and the hideous splendour of twitching and feverish neon advertisements.

In this location the house stands and becomes the story's central character. But like human figures in stories it raises questions. What are its origins? Who owns it (or is owned by it)? What spirit inhabits it? The danger of giving a house such a central role is that description will take over from action or dialogue. Although this story is weighted towards description, it is description of a peculiarly vivacious baroque kind, in which a strange history of Eastern and Western rivalries is revived:

> Those Japanese, wealthy and upstart, who had, thirty and forty and fifty years before, sat disloyally on imitation Queen Anne chairs to nibble Huntley and Palmer biscuits and sip Twining's tea from cups with handles, had left the miasmata of their queerness and nullness to thicken slightly the contours of the inglenook lead-lights, to blur the crab-shaped designs on the brocaded wall-paper above the panellings, to tarnish the pelmets over the embrasures of bow windows through the sea-green diamond panes of which European shrubs, local hybrid roses, and smudges of Korean grass had once attempted to reproduce a St. John's Wood garden and lawn.

Behind such meticulous attention to detail is a fascination with the bizarre twists and turns of history: the rules of one generation are ruled in the next. Japan is a crossroads.

Although Westerners (Australians) are presented as the current occupiers of this house, the presiding spirits are Japanese. These come in the form of three Japanese *au pair* girls hired by the Australian family, who stay on in the house while Perrot lodges there. Porter contrives a paranoiac belief in his protagonist that these three women, like ugly witches, are watching him. He senses their relief when he leaves for sketching-trips in different parts of Japan. The story's crisis is precipitated when Perrot returns early from one of these trips and discovers the house "lit up as a casino" and a party going on. Perrot realises he has made a social blunder when he enters the house, talks to the party-goers, and proceeds to bed. His discovery of the *au pair* girls' "unsanctioned social spree" can only be humiliating to them; and, he cogitates, "nothing less than suicide or revenge could restore [their] lost face."

In another story from the *Mr. Butterfry* volume, "They're Funny People," the loss of face of a Japanese tourist guide leads to his suicide. In "The House on the Hill" the incident sparks revenge. First, Perrot is "sent to Coventry" by the girls whose party he has witnessed. But then comes the *coup de grace*. When the family returns, Yukiko, the leader of the trio of house-sprites tells the Australian mistress of the house that Perrot has assaulted her. He is rapidly expelled. The revenge for his invasion of the house has succeeded.

The story builds towards its conclusion around a tapestry of ancient wrongs and cross-cultural misunderstandings. Trivial in itself, perhaps, the incident recalls this wider history. The Australian artist, a social outsider, cannot be humiliated by the incident, because he cannot lose face. The mistress of the house and her Japanese *au pairs,* on the other hand, have customs to observe, appearances to uphold.

The tone of the story is comic-grotesque, recounting a small but illustrative chapter in the history of a haunted house:

> an imitation Hazeldene or Craigholme perched on its hill, from the time of the assassination- and earthquake-riddled reign of the insane Emperor Taisho, like an exotic granary of phantoms, malformed charms, alien affectations, and the uneasy ardours of expatriates.

Here, as elsewhere, Porter is a fatalist, concerned to record a consciousness of history rather than to change it.

—Bruce Bennett

HOW I CONTEMPLATED THE WORLD FROM THE DETROIT HOUSE OF CORRECTION AND BEGAN MY LIFE OVER AGAIN
by Joyce Carol Oates, 1970

"How I Contemplated the World from the Detroit House of Correction and Began My Life Over Again" is typical of Joyce Carol Oates's fiction in its devastating portrait of the sterility of suburban life and the horrifying brutality of urban America. It is atypical in the unusual narrative technique she uses to convey these ideas.

The story is told by the principal character, whose name we never learn (she calls herself "the girl"). It consists of notes she is recording for an essay to be written for an English course at the private school she attends. The notes focus on her experiences during the past year when she was 15 years old. The narrator, therefore, is an adolescent reflecting upon the "debris" of her recent life to fulfill a school writing assignment. As the details of her experiences are revealed in blunt and laconic fashion, the reader becomes increasingly aware of the pathos of the story she will write and the tragedy of the life she has lived.

As a writer, the girl is obviously an amateur. Her title (the story's title) is too long, awkward, and confusing. Her notes are packaged in simplistic categories, incongruously arranged. She makes numerous false starts. She places trivia next to significant detail. As the real author, Oates is flawless, placing herself in the mind of a deeply disturbed juvenile unwittingly revealing the sources of conflict in her life. The reader's challenge is to sift through the welter of incoherent details in order to see connections, causes, and motivational factors the girl herself unconsciously denies or fails to understand.

We learn that this "innocently experienced" girl comes from a wealthy family living in a fashionable suburb of Detroit. She has everything money can buy. What she does not have is love. Her father is a physician "of the slightly sick," but prefers to spend his time playing squash and golf, dining at his country club, and cavorting with medical cronies at conventions. Her socialite mother fills her time with cultural events and club activities. They make time for their passions by shuffling their children off to private schools and summer camps.

The girl's response is to become a kleptomaniac. As early as age eight, she has been stealing things she neither needs nor wants—a copy of *Pageant Magazine*, a package of Tums. She steals to be noticed, and to be caught. When apprehended, she hopes for attention from her parents. Instead, they use their influence to have the charge of shoplifting dropped and try to buy her compliance to behavior less embarrassing to them ("If you wanted gloves, why didn't you say so? Why didn't you ask for them?" her mother chastises her).

Equally disturbing is the girl's total absorption in herself, also the result of parental neglect. She has learned one lesson well from them, self-centeredness. This is evident in her consciousness of her physical appearance, but is especially revealed in her ignorance of the larger world around her. The year is 1968—the year of the turning point of the war in Vietnam with the launching of the Tet Offensive, of President Lyndon Johnson's decision not to run for reelection, of the assassination of Martin Luther King, of the assassination of presidential candidate Robert Kennedy, of serious antiwar and civil rights demonstrations at the Democrats' convention in Chicago, of an acerbic presidential campaign—one of the most turbulent years in U.S. history. In the category the girl creates to take notes on world events for her essay, she writes one word: "Nothing."

The girl is twice victimized—first by her parents, and then, Oates implies, by the American society of the 1960's. This child of an increasingly permissive age with mottoes like, "tune in, turn on, and drop out" and "make love, not war," runs away from home. She ends up in Detroit where she is brutally exploited by Simon and Clarita, who force her into prostitution to support their drug habit. Apprehended on a number of charges, she mistakingly believes

she has achieved a refuge in jail from the streets, and the security and discipline her parents never gave her. "I won't go home I want to stay here," she says. But she changes her mind after being mercilessly beaten in the lavatory by two other inmates.

Released from a hospital, she returns to her parents' home, where she exhibits the trauma of her recent experience in the bizarre attachments she has formed. She has developed an obsessive preoccupation with Raymond Forrest, the man who decided not to prosecute her for shoplifting. In the confused state of her feelings, he has assumed the role of surrogate father—generous, benevolent, caring, and even omnipotent ("this man who is my salvation"). He is one of two characters she lists in her notes that she will be "forever entwined with." The other is the grotesque and repulsive addict, Simon. The extent of her emotional deprivation is underscored by her affection for the man who raped her, shared her with his male friends, and introduced her to streetwalking. She calls him her "dear friend," and, when she poses the question, "Would I go back to Simon again? Would I lie down with him in all that filth and craziness?" she replies, "Over and over again."

In her fixation on Simon, the girl has reshaped reality to filter out the pain and humiliation of the experience. In the last of her new attachments—to the objects in her parents' house (chandeliers, carpets, the toaster, faucets, etc.)—she makes one final adjustment of reality as she frantically seeks "a happy ending" for her story. Unable to rely upon the affection of her parents, she follows their example and fixes her emotions on things. "I love everything here. I am in love with everything here," she desperately asserts. A line from one of Simon's poems, "There is no reality only dreams," crosses her mind as she prepares to transform her notes into a finished essay with a happy ending. The observant reader will infer from these same notes a more realistic future of woe and anguish for the girl.

—Joseph Flibbert

HOW I GOT MY NICKNAME
by W.P. Kinsella, 1984

As a university-trained fiction writer adept at producing eminently marketable material, W.P. Kinsella has cleverly appropriated two highly saleable topics: Iowa-grown baseball and American Indian life in the Pacific Northwest. Though neither an Iowan nor an Indian, Kinsella nevertheless presents a reliable account of each activity, sometimes ridiculously comic but always with the assurance of an ultimate insider—which, of course, he isn't, making the occasion of "How I Got My Nickname" (in *The Thrill of the Grass*) an especially effective tall tale.

Like many of Kinsella's baseball storytellers (notably Ray Kinsella of the novel *Shoeless Joe*, filmed as *Field of Dreams*), narrator William Patrick "Tripper" Kinsella is an Iowan, in this case a rather bookish high school student whose reward for showing a prize calf at the All-Iowa Cattle Show and Summer Exposition is a trip to New York to see the 1951 New York Giants for part of that year's pennant race. Because his father is a professor and eminent classicist, "Tripper" is a guest in the country home of translator

Robert Fitzgerald, in the company of another holiday visitor, the just-emerging writer Flannery O'Connor.

From these two elements, classic baseball and serious literature, Kinsella performs the writers' workshop tricks of generating as much action as he can without having to introduce other concerns and making his combinations of sports and literature as daring as possible without losing his narrative's smoothly progressive force.

The story's brilliance can be traced to great potency within his two initial choices. The year 1951 was a vintage one for major league baseball; even those only tangentially familiar with the game will have heard about the colorfulness of manager Leo Durocher, the hard and sometimes mean play of Eddie Stanky, the roster of future Hall of Famers who played for the Giants that year, and the thrill of the Giants's amazing come-from-behind success that necessitated an unprecedented play-off game with their blood rivals, the Brooklyn Dodgers—an equally famous and colorful team that was defeated with a heroic, game-ending home run by Bobby Thompson, a rising line-drive to the left field stands celebrated ever after as "the shot heard round the world." These events are among the most famous lore of baseball, many of them enshrined as hallowed memories and thus becoming subjects in themselves. In similar manner the writing field was being treated to an equally brilliant crop of rookies: not only Flannery O'Connor but Bernard Malamud (whose first novel, *The Natural*, would mythologize baseball), J.D. Salinger, and others working in or visiting New York about this time. Just as Salinger himself became such a talked-about subject that he can function as a useable fictive character in *Shoeless Joe*, so did the ballplayers in that fabled summer of 1951—and so Kinsella's combination of the two areas of legend is an appropriate move.

What is accomplished with the combination, however, stretches the reader's imagination to a point just artfully short of breaking completely. Not only does "Tripper" become the nonchalant confidant of Miss O'Connor, but at the Polo Grounds his naive request to take a few swings in batting practice (a sign of pure Iowa hickishness—a common feature in Kinsella's work, similar to his comic demeaning of American Indians) leads to an invitation to join the team. This action invokes another tradition, that of the old-fashioned sports story of fantasy film in which a little kid joins a major league team and propels them to their greatest success. Assuming correctly that his readers are familiar with this by now campy narrative twist, Kinsella makes a metafictional move: having his storyteller not simply rewrite history but actually skewer events in increasingly improbable ways so that the history we all know as recorded fact can be allowed to happen as remembered.

For this to happen, Kinsella must establish a premise that by itself would be unacceptable, but which in combination with another otherwise unacceptable premise forms a proposition that can be worked out with simple, almost ironclad logic. The key to this combination is a seemingly endless line of dualisms: Iowa hickishness and New York sophistication, being a spectator and becoming a participant, reading narratives as opposed to serving as a shaping factor in them, and, as the basis for all these contrasts, the sometimes unmanageable distance between youth and maturity, innocence and experience, and fantasy and reality.

"Tripper" Kinsella is the narrator who can bridge these gaps. Fresh from an unexceptional few words with Flannery O'Connor, he blunders into a New York Giants's dugout where the otherwise vulgar, tobacco-spitting players are reading the great works of world literature and discussing their authors' experiments with theme and technique. If this is a modification of expectable behavior, it is no more exceptional than "Tripper" chiding Eddie Stanky for tagging him too hard and receiving a polite, heartfelt apology in return—and certainly no more exceptional than the narrator's hitting exploits. All these actions proceed in a manner of utter nonchalance, the baseball action and literary discussion each proceeding according to stereotype, with the only real surprise being that they happen side by side.

The major challenge to the reader's expectations is not that the Giants come from behind with the kid's help (for their pennant drive is commonly accepted as a miracle finish), but that in the decisive play-off game Leo Durocher is seen planning to lift Bobby Thompson for a pinch hitter. If such an action were to happen, reality would indeed be changed; and so at the last minute, "Tripper" Kinsella reaches out and trips the unsuspecting substitute as he heads for the field. Injured, he cannot play; Bobby Thompson keeps his rightful place in the order, stepping up to hit against Ralph Branca; and the rest, as they say, is history— which answers the title's question of how the narrator got his nickname.

—Jerome Klinkowitz

HOW I MET MY HUSBAND
by Alice Munro, 1974

"How I Met My Husband" (collected in *Something I've Been Meaning To Tell You*) is one of Alice Munro's most humorous stories, with a surprise ending that is neither gimmicky nor really surprising. It embodies many of Munro's favourite themes, and portrays small-town life with the irony and sensitivity for which she is best known.

The story portrays the infatuation of a 15-year-old girl for an itinerant pilot who arrives offering rides in the nearby fairgrounds. Edie is working for Dr. and Mrs. Peebles, a snobbish but cheap couple with little understanding of, or interest in, the town's social rules; for instance, Edie is shocked when they invite Loretta Bird for dessert, "not knowing any better," because the Birds are country people who do not farm and are therefore, in Edie's opinion, lower in class than farmers like herself. Mrs. Peebles refers dismissively to farmers without realizing Edie is included in the term. When Dr. Peebles learns why the pilot has come, he says, revealingly, "I'd like to see this neighborhood from the air." Clearly, his curiosity and social pretensions mesh nicely. On the other hand, neither Edie nor, it seems, the Peebles realize how unusual it is for a "hired girl" to eat with her employers. Both Edie and her employers therefore have strong senses of social superiority, but are not always certain precisely what the rules are.

Much of the story's charm derives from the voice of Edie, the narrator. She is a simple girl from a poor background who nonetheless possesses a strength of spirit and independence that leads her to express strong opinions of her own; for example, she ridicules the Peebles's belief that they are working her hard, since they have appliances like a washer and dryer that her own family could only dream of. She is shy, but not entirely self-conscious; like Del Jordan of Munro's *Lives of Girls and Women* she admires her own body. For all her disdain, born of reverse snobbery, Edie aspires to be like Mrs. Peebles, as evidenced by her donning of her employer's finery while the Peebles family is away. The pilot, Chris Watters, comes by looking for water while she is dressed and made-up in Mrs. Peebles's things, and his compliments on her appearance enchant her. Yet because she is young she does not see all the implications of his flirtation, nor fully understand her own responses. All she can think of is the fear that he will tell Mrs. Peebles about her unauthorized "borrowing" of the clothes, and visits him late one night to ask him to keep her secret.

Alice Kelling, Chris's fiancee, arrives in town, and Chris greets her appearance with little enthusiasm. We learn that his barnstorming is his way of keeping his distance from her. Alice is put up at the Peebles, much to Edie's jealous chagrin (which is made evident through very subtle hints, such as her inability to sleep while Chris and Alice are out on a date). She yearns to take Alice's place: "I go back in bed and imagined about me coming home with him. . . ." The next day Edie is asked to deliver a message to Chris, and visits him armed with a freshly baked cake. They begin kissing, but Chris wisely stops things from going too far when he remembers her age. He promises to write her a letter. When Edie returns home a brief misunderstanding about their "intimacies" ensues, one that reveals both Edie's naivete and the true state of Alice's and Chris's engagement.

Chris's letter becomes a source of hope for Edie for many weeks, until one day she realizes that it will not come. She ends up marrying the postman who sees her at the mailbox every day, and there is no hint in the story that her second choice is a disappointing one, or one she regrets. Edie has romanticized her relationship with Chris, but not to the point of being crushed by reality. She recognizes that people often live with illusions, but is too wise to cling to them for long: "He always tells the children the story of how I went after him by sitting by the mailbox every day, and naturally I laugh and let him, because I like for people to think what pleases them and makes them happy." To the end Edie remains independent, keeping her cherished secrets to herself.

The story reflects an aspect of Munro's work that is seldom noticed: her very strong consciousness of class. The town in which Edie lives and works is highly stratified, and operates on definite social rules. The Birds are at the bottom of the social totem-pole; Edie is scandalized by Loretta's use of "youse." Edie does not see herself as lower than the Peebles, however; her own pride is too strong. Yet she does notice the marked difference in lifestyle between her family and the Peebles, especially in their labor-saving devices, and feels somewhat uncomfortable making use of their facilities, such as their bath—something that is, to her, very elegant. We must remember, however, that what we see of the town comes through Edie's eyes, and she has social pretensions of her own that lead her to treat Loretta Bird with hilarious contempt. Still, the stratification portrayed is a valid portrait of small-town society.

"How I Met My Husband" is one of Munro's funniest stories. Throughout the story we are led to expect that Chris is one of the title characters, but if we are attentive to the story and not ourselves subject to romantic delusions, the ending should not come as much of a surprise. Edie's wait for the letter gives her temporary respite from the mundane world of the Peebles, but she is too smart and independent to see that respite as anything *but* temporary: "If there were women all through life waiting, and women busy and not waiting, I knew which I had to be. Even though there might be things the second kind of woman have to pass up and never know about, it still is better." Edie triumphs by growing up, and finding happiness where it really exists, not where it exists only as a fantasy or a vain hope.

—Allan Weiss

HOW SLEEP THE BRAVE
by H.E. Bates, 1943

"How Sleep the Brave" was the title story of a collection by H.E. Bates, first published in 1943 by Jonathan Cape on behalf of the British Publishers Guild, a co-operative venture launched in the early 1940's to publish "important books of universal appeal," and to ensure that scarce supplies of rationed paper were put to good use. Bates's story of a night-bomber shot down over the North Sea after a raid on Germany, the crew's three nights in an open dinghy, and the co-operation and common purpose that ensured their survival had obvious appeal and importance as both a celebration of air force heroism and an allegory of effective response to the war for both civilians and combatants.

The crew comprises a cross section of class, age, temperament, and nationality whose mutual reliance on and support of one another implies that the petty discriminations of peacetime have no place in a united front against a common threat. The narrator contrasts the petty selfishness of his prewar marriage with the harmonious relations he and the crew enjoy, and considers his status and experiences as an airman responsible for his improvement as a citizen. Flying, as such, functions as a metaphor for the dangers, duties, and rewards of wartime citizenship: "flying had beaten some of the selfishness out of me. My self was no longer assertive. It had lost part of its identity, and I hoped the worst part of its identity, through being part of the crew." The civilian, cast into uncertainty by the war, is part of a larger crew whose survival, like that of the airmen, depends upon each fulfilling his duty and subordinating the individual to the common good.

The narrator's self-effacement (we never learn his name and have only a few details about his life before the war) is a powerful, formal endorsement of the self-denial that characterises the crew, sustains the war effort, and promises ultimate success. The crew's status as both symbols and very real objects of sacrifice is implied in a striking series of parallels between the narrator's experiences and the suffering and death of Christ. From the outset of the mission the narrator complains of numbness in his feet and a taste "congealed between my chest and throat . . . something horribly sour like vinegar." After the raid, when the plane is hit and parts of the fuselage are ablaze, the narrator badly burns his hands fighting the flames. Wounded hands, "dead" feet, and the sour taste of vinegar, all features of Christ's suffering on the cross, prepare us for the narrator's ultimate sacrifice when, in a final effort to save his own life and the lives of his colleagues, he casts himself upon the flames, arms outstretched, and lies momentarily crucified on the burning fuselage: "at last because I could not throw my hands against the flames I threw my whole body. I let it fall with outstretched arms against the fuselage." A little crude perhaps, but the implication is clear—they suffer that others might live in hope, hence their self-sacrifice is a lesson to us all.

For a story about a World War II bombing raid, there are remarkably few references to Germany or the Germans. In fact, the narrator implies an equivalent threat from the weather, whose assaults on the plane and its crew are indistinguishable from enemy anti-aircraft fire. This equivalence indicates that the Germans are only one, and by no means the most deadly, of the perils faced by the bomber crews, a point driven home by the death of the wireless operator Allison from a combined assault by the hostile elements and the *Luftwaffe*. We know more about Allison than any other crewman, in particular the cause of the "cancerous emptiness" which eats him away until there is so little of him left that he is barely distinguishable from his surroundings. When Allison crawls into the ruins of his house to recover the body of his daughter killed in an air raid, his clothes were "plastered white as a limeworker's from the dust of debris washed by rain." When the cold weather closes in aboard the dinghy, this deathly pallor penetrates deep beneath Allison's clothes: subdued by and submerged in the surrounding elements he reifies and reflects the lifelessness of the sea and the snow as he is conquered by despair: "the face of Allison, thin and quite bloodless, had something of the grey whiteness of broken edges of foam that split into parallel bars the whole face of the sea . . . . His eyes, reflecting the snow, were not dark. They were cold and colourless."

Yet like the crucifixion, over which the crewmen's experiences are inscribed, this is not a story about death and loss but a proclamation of individual and collective salvation through self-sacrifice. That the story is set close to Christmas promises hope, confirmed when the dinghy makes lanfall after three days at sea. Just as the crew triumphed by rationing and sharing their scarce resources, caring for the weak and wounded, and by each cheerfully filling his allotted task, so, implies Bates, can the community as a whole. The crew have risked self-immolation, suffered trial by ordeal, and endured the worst that the elements and the enemy could throw at them, and are ready to do it all again: "We had been out a long way, and through a great deal together. We have been through fire and water, death and frost, and had come home. And soon we should go out again." The community must be prepared to make similar sacrifices. Allison's death implies that the price may be high: but the alternative is unthinkable.

In 1943, with the war still hanging in the balance, it is little wonder that the British Publishers Guild expended a little of their scarce paper supplies on such an exemplary parable of self-denial, sacrifice, and collective triumph.

—Kevin Foster

HOW THE DEVIL CAME DOWN DIVISION STREET
by Nelson Algren, 1945

"How the Devil Came Down Division Street" is arguably one of Nelson Algren's two or three best short stories. It is certainly his most popular one—so popular in fact that by the mid-1970's he was withholding reprint permissions on it, in any language, fearing over-publication; much as Hemingway feared over-publication of "The Killers."

The story's popularity rests partly at least on its familiarity, its recognizability, and at the same time, partly on its incredibility, its grimly surprising twist. The ironic tension within this paradox results finally in an almost believable and strangely satisfying balance, a naturalistic choice between undesireable but inevitable alternative explanations for a pre-determined situation. And all the while, it's a comic story, imbued with Algren's dark folksy humor.

The story takes place in Chicago, in his favorite ethnic neighborhood. It begins and ends in the Polonia Bar where four drunks, Symanski, Oljiec, Koncel, and Czechowski, are trying to decide who is the biggest drunk on Division Street. The argument is stalemated until Poor Roman Orlov enters. Poor Roman clearly is the winner, for he has been drunk so long that no one can remember him as sober. Poor Roman spends his time going from bar to bar cadging double shots ("The devil lives in a double-shot") in order to drown the worm that he says grows at his insides: "Every day I drown him and every day he gnaws."

Given a double shot he tells his story, which explains why he had become the biggest drunk on Division Street before he was 30 years old.

When he was 13 years old, Roman, his mother and father, his sister Teresa, and his twin brothers moved into a three room flat with two double beds. Mama O. cooked in a Division Street restaurant all day, and Papa O. played the accordian for pennies in Division Street taverns all night. The sleeping arrangements were the problem in the family. Roman slept between the twins in one bed, Mama O. and Teresa slept in the other. Papa O. stayed out all night, got drunk, and slept under Roman's bed when he got home — unless the dog, Udo, was there before him, in which case, he crawled under Mama's bed.

This unsatisfactory situation continued until the flat began to be haunted. Papa O. heard knocking at the door while the rest of the family was at Sunday Mass; but there was no one there. Roman heard knocking in the night at the closet door, but there was no one in it. Then Mama had a terrible dream, "all night, of a stranger waiting in the hall: a young man, drunken, . . . with blood down the front of his shirt and drying on his hands." And the next morning, Papa came home without his accordian; no one, including Papa, ever knew whether he had sold it or lost it or loaned it.

Knowing they were haunted, Mama consulted another tenant. Yes, Mama Zolewitz said, the young man was a ghost. She had said nothing to warn the Orlovs at the landlord's behest. The young man had come home drunk and had murdered the young woman with whom he was living out of wedlock, and then had hanged himself in the closet. They were buried without a priest in unsanctified ground. The young man, Mama Z. says, only seeks peace, and she urges Mama O. to pray for him.

That night, and every night thereafter, the Orlovs prayed for the young man—as a family, for now, without his accordian, Papa O. stayed at home, and resumed sleeping with Mama O. That caused some shuffling about. Teresa now slept between the twins, and Roman had to compete for space with Udo.

But the knocking stopped, and the priest said that their prayers had redeemed the ghost and that God had rewarded them by giving Papa O. back to Mama O. instead of to his accordian. Papa became the best janitor on Noble Street, the landlord brought gifts and forgave back rent, and Teresa, who had been abused by her classmates, became the most popular girl in her class. And the twins, who used to fight so badly that someone had to sleep between them, became the best of friends and allies.

And Poor Roman became the biggest drunk on Division Street. At the age of 17, he took to roaming the taverns all night because he could not sleep beneath the squeaking beds. He slept, when at all, during the day. He took his father's place, except without an accordian, killing the nights until dawn, which he called "the bitterest hour of the day."

The story ends back at the Polonia Bar with the narrator suggesting alternative interpretations: "Does the devil live in a double-shot? Is he the one who gnaws all night, within?" Do we drown the worm which is the devil who lives in the double-shot we drown him with? Is that why Poor Roman cannot drown the worm no matter how many double-shots he takes? "Or is he the one who knocks," the narrator asks, "on winter nights, with blood drying on his knuckles?" Mama O. believes that "the young man who knocked was in truth the devil. For did she not give him, without knowing what she did, a good son in return for a worthless husband?"

The irony in this grim paradox creates the balance that makes the incredibility of the story not only credible but inevitable, not only grim but comic, in the same way and for the same reasons that the idea of a catch-22 is comic. And that's the reason for its popularity as well. It's recognizable even in its surprises, for Algren eschews the falsity of an O'Henry-like sentimentalism.

—Joseph J. Waldmeir

A HUNGER ARTIST (Ein HungerKünstler)
by Franz Kafka, 1924

The haunted and suffering look in the standard photograph of Franz Kafka expresses his sensitivity to religious and political hatreds in his native city of Prague, ruled by the Austro-Hungarian monarchy in his youth, and later, after World War I, subject to bureaucratic government typified in his novel *Der Prozess* (*The Trial*). His friend Max Brod preserved the manuscript of *Ein HungerKünstler* ("A Hunger Artist") among Kafka's works that he had directed to be burned, and Brod published it posthumously. The story reflects the aspirations of a middle-class Jewish artist, his preoccupation with suicide, and the wasting away of tuberculosis that eventually killed Kafka.

The details of the plot perhaps developed from a 40-day fast accomplished by Dr. Tanner in New York City in July and August of 1880. Widely reported abroad, the fast drew hoards of onlookers (many of them elegant ladies), as well as accusations that Tanner secretly took food, misconceptions of Tanner's motives, and comparisons with animals.

The stereotype of the starving and misunderstood artist developed in the 19th century. Kafka's artist lives in a cage instead of a garret, and makes his hunger a lifework and a performing art, with the added complication that in seeking perfection he wills his death. The public for a time callously entertains itself with his artful suffering, demonstrates a macabre and ghoulish pleasure in the moribund state, and even selects the butchers who comprise a continual guard; hence the public would appear to bear the blame for his progressive mistreatment, neglect, and eventual death. But the dedicated artist defies and refuses assistance to maintain life while exhausting himself with his lifework.

With a martyr complex, he exploits his animal nature: living in a cage, dressing in black tights with his ribs prominently displayed, and sitting in straw. The animal, it would seem demands to be fed. But the artist conversely refuses both food and exercise. The animal, in contrast with the man, is said not to have a soul; but as evidence that he has a soul, the hunger artist keeps foremost the human passions for integrity and perfection. He is willing to die for these.

Contrary and unreasoning, and proud of his professional achievement, the artist for a time sustains himself with the egotism of the esoteric-versus-exoteric conflict; at the height of his glory he consoles himself with the thought that a few initiates understand and appreciate the honor of his profession and recognize his professional supremacy. The initiates, however, are not permitted to share his innermost secret—how easy it is to fast. Gradually the esoteric assurances are dissipated for him amid doubts that both the initiates and the public share about his artistic integrity; unobserved, they suspect, he might take a surreptitious morsel. Eventually he becomes the only spectator and, ironically, the only skeleton at his own fast.

The Christ analogies, in part exploited by the impresario, are more than obvious. The watchers, similar to the soldiers at Christ's death who threw dice, play at cards; and death on the cross was reported to be a matter of dehydration and starvation. The impresario fixes the term of fasting to 40 days, and typically, at the moment of extreme faintness lifts his arms "as if inviting Heaven to look down upon its creature here in the straw, this suffering martyr." Like paintings of Christ being taken from the cross, the artist's head lolls on his breast, his body is hollowed out; his legs, close to each other at the knees, scrape the ground; and, like the women tending Christ, fainting ladies assist him.

With his performance routine established and the viewers' behavior anticipated, the hunger artist lives for many years with the aura of a Christ—"in visible glory"—with only himself dissatisfied and "troubled in spirit." The impresario who, among all the others, should understand, fails to appreciate that the artist's work is still not perfected, that his work, which always exhausts him, should not be limited and prematurely ended at 40 days and himself cheated of his fame. Others do not grasp the ethic-esthetic connection; even his protests are misunderstood and masterfully exploited by the impresario, so that the artist grows discouraged with the task of fighting against a whole world of misunderstanding.

After the struggle to establish his fame and the incomparable excellence of his performance through many European settings, the artist finds that the public's enthusiasm gradually diminishes; when the older generation recalls him for the younger, his art seems to have been only a fad, and revulsion sets in. He parts from the impresario and hires himself to a circus.

Unfortunately, this transfer only speeds the process of decline, disinterest, and revulsion. The public hastens past his cage and, instead of honoring his achievement, seems to shrink from him. His chief competition is the exact opposite of himself, the lively circus animals, and gradually he comes to accept the fact that his presence is only an impediment for those visiting the menagerie. As the signs announcing his art fade and he becomes forgotten, a rare passerby dredges up the old charges of swindling. The artist, however, with deepening depression, continues to work hard at fasting.

He becomes a nuisance mostly forgotten; when too late he is discovered among the straw, his last words also recall those of Christ on the cross: "Forgive me, everybody." The overseer, like the public, still fails to understand. The artist's confession, when he faces the truth of his existence, climaxes the story; the overseer should not admire him because he could not do otherwise, because he could not find the food he liked.

The denouement reveals the artist replaced by a healthy black panther, as if the former garment of black tights had foreshadowed the artist's fate. The public's former fascination for the hunger artist is now transferred to his opposite; and the crowds admire the panther as if it were an artist.

The artist, then, lives an existence trapped in his own nature, and between two worlds of pleasing others and pleasing himself. If he were not an artist, no system could make him one; because he is an artist, no system can prevent his being so.

—Grace Eckley

———

THE HUSBAND (Chang-fu)
by Shen Congwen, 1930

Shen Congwen is not classified as a local colorist in modern Chinese fiction, but many of his characters that have enduring interest and universal appeal are drawn against a landscape rich in folklore and scenic beauty—the landscape of his native West Hunan, along the River Yuan. The story, "Chang-fu" ("The Husband"), collected in *The Chinese Earth*, is set in this area.

Although this story is not pastoral like Shen Congwen's famous novella "The Border Town," it is invested with the same nostalgic overtone: "Idlers drinking tea in Four Seas Teahouse, if they leaned out of a window over the river, had a fine view of 'misty rain and red blossom' by the pagoda on the other shore. . . . This convenient proximity enabled people . . . to hail their acquaintances." Sentimental touches are no less discernible, especially if we compare it with a similar story that was published in the same year, "A Hired Wife," by Rou Shi. While "A Hired Wife" is unrelenting in its naturalistic delineation of a young woman whose husband hires her to a landlord in order to support their family, "The Husband" is marred by a sentimental outlook on the demimonde. The harsh, squalid reality in this story is softened by the hospitable madam, the sympathetic river warden and the idealized wife-prostitute, who is able to retain her innocence and freedom.

Most of the characters, including the protagonist, are unnamed; they seem to be presented as types rather than individuals, though enough vivid details are provided to make them round and three-dimensional. The author's main interest is obviously theme, not characterization. A self-styled "countryman," Shen Congwen never fails to stress the superiority of simplicity to artificiality, or rustic life to "citified" existence; a dominant theme in his fiction is how girls manage to beat the odds and retain their trustfulness and innocence.

"The Husband" has a very old romantic theme: the return to nature, as illustrated by the story's incredible plot of how a country bumpkin goes to visit his wife, who has been sent on a boat near a small town to be a prostitute, and how, despite tremendous temptations, he and his wife are able to give up all that a "citified" life has to offer and return to the country. Bizarre as the plot may sound, it is set up as a typical situation: "There were many, many husbands like this. . . . The place bred healthy girls and honest fellows. But the soil was really poor, . . . It was hard to make ends meet. . . . They were only twenty *li* to the wharf where the women went to make a living. The man could see all the advantages of this."

Poverty forces these country husbands to fall victim to the temptation of prostituting their wives, yet some of them can resist it or give up its "benefits." In this story, for instance, the husband himself is by no means mistreated (he has been invited by the madam to see an opera and to go to the teahouse, and by the river warden to enjoy a "feast"), but he cannot stand the way his wife is treated by her "visitors" and rude soldiers. He decides that to share a simple, poor life with his wife and to have children is far better than being the husband of a prostitute and receiving money from her. The wife seems able to endure and even enjoy her life on the boat and does not plan to go back to the country. The fact that eventually she does return to her husband proves her to be essentially a pure-hearted woman who chooses to follow her husband.

But this choice is certainly not an easy one for a poor woman, especially in the 1920's, one of the most terrible decades in modern Chinese history. The author has provided us with ample evidence that the 1920's were a dark age with widespread prostitution, illustrated by the "business" of many poor wives; drug-abuse, depicted by the numerous opium-eaters; superstition, exhibited by the popularity of incense-burning; and lawlessness, exemplified by the presence of robbers and drunken soldiers everywhere. Short as the story is, it contains several episodes that reveal the corruption of the government and the hardship of the poor, who have to endure tyrannical warlords, rude soldiers, "midnight" search parties, unwarranted police investigations, and other types of abuse.

Shen Congwen is noted for his plain narrative and unadorned style. He has been called "a rough diamond" rather than a polished gem; however, "The Husband" is undeniably subtle and symbolic enough to be ranked with his best works. Rich in detail and narrated with exuberance and a throbbing vitality, this story gains additional strength through its skillful use of imagery, which emphasizes the contrast between the urbane and the rustic. Indeed, much of the thrust of the theme is reinforced by the contrasts of images. For instance, the husband brings chestnuts (a symbol of the children he has never had) to his wife; she, having become "citified," offers him cigarettes that taste "strange" to him. The husband remembers piglets at home as "his sole friends, his family"; the river warden wears a pair of pigskin boots. Boots are a recurring image, succinctly representing the tyranny and evil of the rich in the city. The husband's dependence on the small sickle, an indispensable tool, and his delight in the fiddle, a free gift, are contrasted with the townspeople's dependence on and pride in wealth. For example, the wife's client is described as looking "like a boat-owner or shopkeeper, in cowhide jackboots. From one corner of his pocket protruded a thick, bright silver chain." The river warden sports "an enormous gold ring" and possesses a "deerskin pouch" so "proudly bulging" with money. He is depicted with more verve than is any other character, and his portrait is more subtle. For all his sympathy and generosity, he is by no means an exemplary character; his crooked personality is suggested by the fact that he has only one eye, is well-off, and plays the role of the "godfather" to most prostitutes. All of these characteristics smack of the stereotyped ruffian from a syndicate of organized crime. This point is illustrated by another powerful image of him: to the husband, his square-jawed face seems to be made up of "distillers' grain and blood."

With the image of his wife's protector and patron changed in his mind from "fatherly" to "bloody," the poor husband has no choice but decide to go home tomorrow with his wife—"back to the land," as the author puts it. Thus the couple completes their round trip—a journey away from nature to the dissolute city, and a journey back to nature after awakening.

—Sherwin S.S. Fu

I

I WANT TO KNOW WHY
by Sherwood Anderson, 1921

"I Want to Know Why," published in the collection *The Triumph of the Egg: A Book of Impressions of American Life in Tales and Poems* (1921)—Sherwood Anderson's fifth book—reflects the many menial jobs in his youth that familiarized him with the people and procedures of livery stables and race-horse stables. He enjoyed companionship with jockeys, grooms, and trainers. In concert with the roving freedom of the young men of this story, his dominant interests and his many jobs prevented his completing high school—articulated here and in other works in a groping search for meaning among fragmented experiences.

A variation of a journey of initiation, "I Want to Know Why" presents a boy of 15 years teetering on the verge of sexual discovery, suffering a shock to his innocence, and a year later—though he speaks of maturity—being still mystified. The theme, however, is a betrayal of standards rather than a sexual awakening.

The call to adventure is the horse race at Saratoga in upstate New York. With all the markings of a boy's adventure, the narrator steals away without telling his parents, leaving Kentucky with three friends, hopping freight cars and following—in his mind—not adventure but something much more important, his love of horses. The black man Bildad, doing odd chores at livery barns in the winter and working as cook at racetracks in the summer, serves in the role of guide and protector. Saratoga is the "Eastern track," the land of beginnings where initiations occur on the important "first day in the East."

The narrator's sense of values soon emerges from his self-confession. His faith resides in two standards about which his opinions are stated as absolutes: "niggers" and horses. He wishes he were a black with the freedom to hang around livery barns, and his kinship with a quality horse enables him to interpret the horse's thoughts. Regarding blacks, he feels, "You can trust them." Regarding horses, he says, "There isn't anything so lovely and clean and full of spunk and honest and everything as some race horses." Ultimately, however, the quality of a person, in his judgment, depends on that person's appreciation of horses.

At the difficult age between childhood and maturity, the narrator no longer expects his lawyer father to buy him things. Maturing, he earns his own money, wants to be a man and to think straight. Yet he knows he cannot be a stableboy because his father won't let him, and he risks being caught and sent home for viewing the horses in the paddocks before races.

The boy expresses self-confidence, but uncertainties intrude and foreshadow the climactic befuddlement. A horse the narrator picks will win unless "they've got him in a pocket behind another or he was pulled or got off bad at the post or something." By the same ratio, a trainer will be admired unless the boy observes the trainer violating what he thinks are their common standards.

The sexual element remains suppressed throughout. The narrator recognizes two winners: Middlestride, a gelding; and Sunstreak, a stallion who is "like a girl you think about sometimes but never see," and who is "hard all over and lovely too. When you look at his head you want to kiss him." Good breeding means that a thoroughbred "sired right and out of a good mare" and trained right can run; the narrator makes no assessment of stud purposes but knows a horse to serve only one of two purposes, running in races or pulling a plow.

Between the absolutes of the narrator's talent for picking reliable blacks and winning horses resides the trainer, and the trainer Jerry Tillford causes the bewilderment stated in the title. Knowledge occupies the realm of the metaphysical, far beyond the physical qualities of speed and appearance; and a touch of mysticism that enables the narrator to see inside a horse provides the emotional connection with Jerry Tillford, in whose eyes he finds a shared knowledge about Sunstreak's success, and at a glance "I loved the man as much as I did the horse because he knew what I knew." The narrator knows the trainer's pride is like that of a mother for her child, and he likes the trainer even more than he likes his own father.

After the race, desiring to be near the trainer and without knowing why, the boy walks in the direction he had seen an automobile travel and arrives at a ramshackle farmhouse in which Jerry Tillford and other white men from home flirt with prostitutes. While he spies on them, the shameful talk and behavior and the barnyard odor fill him with disgust and challenge his standards: "A nigger wouldn't go into such a place." The boy has decided he would not be a gambler, but the professional gambler Rieback ("a nice man and generous") is the only white man from home who refuses to enter the brothel.

At crisis is the narrator's democratic social consciousness; he judges people and horses on their own merits. Other boys' fathers discourage association with a gambler like Henry Rieback's father, but the narrator doesn't see "what it's got to do with Henry or with horses either." At a younger age, he wanted to be a jockey or a stableboy. At this time, he wants to be an owner or a trainer. Blacks can make you laugh, whereas whites cannot; blacks "won't squeal on you" and are "squarer with kids." He dislikes Henry Hellinfinger, who is "too lazy to work."

In general, he favors blacks and trainers because, like them, picking a winner is in his blood. At the crucial scene in the farmhouse, he overhears the trainer Jerry brag as Sunstreak never would; nor would a proud mother claim credit due her child. Jerry claims that he rather than Sunstreak won the race. But most disappointing of all, Jerry looks at the prostitute with his eyes shining just as they had shone when he looked at Sunstreak, and then kisses her. The narrator's love for Jerry turns to hatred.

With the same touch of mysticism that provides knowledge without words, and a sense that more is to be revealed, the narrator keeps secret this observation and this disappointment. A year later, a new colt frolics with Sunstreak

748

and Middlestride, but the former pleasures are spoiled; beauty has been betrayed. The narrator has not found a means to change his standards; women and horses, still, belong in a special category, and Jerry Tillford should have been selective of both. Democracy tempered by nearness to horses has not encouraged a removal of trainers from the special category they occupied earlier, and the boy remains puzzled.

The story seems to scrape the surface of a profound meaning that resides in the narrator's fine sense of tuning regarding women and horses. When the sexual awakening occurs, he will not bestow his attentions on any female as Jerry Tillford did but only on a thoroughbred.

—Grace Eckley

THE ICE WAGON GOING DOWN THE STREET
by Mavis Gallant, 1964

In many of Mavis Gallant's short stories, characters suffer from an unwillingness to grow; they become trapped in self-images engendered by their pasts, and refuse to recognize the passage of time. As such, they become, in the words of David O'Rourke, "exiles in time": they continue to think and behave in habitual ways, remaining wilfully blind to whom they have become.

Two such characters are Peter and Sheilah Frazier in "The Ice Wagon Going Down the Street" (collected in *My Heart Is Broken*). Peter sees himself as a man of leisure, a member of a patrician family experiencing only temporary financial difficulties. He belongs, he feels, to a higher class than most and therefore deserves suitable employment for someone of his standing. Until he is able to find such a position, he will accept nothing that is more in keeping with his true status. Sheilah shares and reinforces his pretensions.

"Now that they are out of world affairs and back where they started," the story begins, revealing immediately the high opinion both Peter and Sheilah have of themselves. We learn that they and their daughters have descended on Peter's sister and become her houseguests for 17 weeks, considering the free room and board to be their right. Indeed, Peter believes the world owes him a living, and not just any kind, either: his daughters wonder, "What job will Peter consent to accept?" Peter and Sheilah retain a distinct class-consciousness while their daughters, representing a younger generation, are "more cautious than their parents; more Canadian." Social conditions have changed, but not the way Peter and Sheilah think.

Of course, the Fraziers consider their current economic state to be none of their own fault. They believe they are simply insufficiently ruthless, "crooked," or vulgar to succeed today. The story then portrays their memories of past glories: plans in Paris, Germany, and Geneva by which they would be set for life. But Peter will not do the demeaning things necessary to earn some actual money, until he finds a job working in a minor office of an international agency. But even then he succeeds in doing very little; he is one of Gallant's most ineffectual exiles and holdovers from a long-dead past.

Peter's efforts to secure a job reveal much about him and his relationship with Sheilah. At a wedding reception, when he drunkenly makes fun of the groom, Sheilah cautions him, "every single person who can do something for you is

in this room. If you love me, you'll get up." Love appears to be a small element in their relationship. They need each other, because they are partners in parasitism. Peter's sister Lucille manages to get him the filing job, but Peter is convinced that someone "higher up" must have been watching out for him, despite all evidence to the contrary.

As noted, Peter handles the job with his usual incompetence, and Sheilah copes by pretending "they were in Paris and life was still the same." In other words both continue to live in the past, shutting their eyes to present circumstances or necessity. Peter continues to believe something much better will come along, and sees himself as in a state of temporary exile. Then their pasts begin to haunt them. Peter learns from his friend Mike Burleigh that Sheilah had been a poor child, and her upper-class English accent is revealed as a very recent acquisition. We then learn about Peter's own poverty-stricken childhood, after the family fortune had been squandered by earlier generations. But he will not give in to the truth: "Even in Geneva . . . he had a manner of strolling to work as if his office were a pastime, and his real life a secret so splendid he could share it with no one except himself."

The past almost literally comes alive in the form of Agnes Brusen, a fellow Canadian coworker. Peter comforts himself in his delusions of importance by ridiculing her as a mole, dismissing her as a child of recent immigrants, someone without class. To his horror, "the others couldn't tell Peter and Agnes apart. There was a world of difference between them, yet it was she who had been brought in to sit at the larger of the two desks." As we learn, her success is the result of her hard work and competence. In his mind Peter is superior to her, the reverse of reality. Peter is a parasite and a fraud; Agnes is a self-made woman. She must be there to spy on him, Peter supposes. Agnes represents everything Peter might have become, had he tried to succeed instead of expecting to simply by virtue of his name. As so often happens in Gallant's fiction, a character with a fossilized self-image comes face to face with a double or mirror-image. Peter realizes that Agnes "was the true heir of the men from Scotland; she was at the start." She is Peter at an earlier stage, but the choices they have made could not be more different.

To the Fraziers' horror, Agnes has even achieved social superiority over them; she has been invited to the parties held by the Burleighs, a couple whom the Fraziers had considered their friends (in other words, suitable candidates for their leeching). At a costume party, Agnes gets drunk and Peter helps her home, and during the experience Peter sees—briefly—the connection between them. They come close to having an affair, but then the connection snaps, and Peter draws away from the one true communion he might ever possess, returning to his old self-deluding ways.

Two symbols represent the contrast between past ideals and present reality in the story. One is the Balenciaga gown Sheilah holds onto through all their travels; it symbolizes their elegant past to which she clings. The other is the ice wagon that Agnes watched as a child during solitary summer mornings. It represents an ideal, particularly a world of innocence, that is now irretrievably lost. All three characters are exiled from their pasts, finding comfort only in those brief trips home they can take though their memories.

—Allan Weiss

THE IMITATION OF THE ROSE (A imitação da rosa)
by Clarice Lispector, 1960

Clarice Lispector's story "A imitação da rosa" ("The Imitation of the Rose") can be read as a gentle sequel to Charlotte Perkins Gilman's story "The Yellow Wallpaper." It tells the story of Laura, an urban housewife, upon her return from hospital treatment for a mental breakdown. Like "The Yellow Wallpaper," Lispector's story is widely seen as a critique of traditional gender and family roles, as well as a glimpse at the madness lurking just below the surface of an unnaturally constrained creative (female) mind. It is one of the most extensive explorations of these themes in Lispector's stories. The story was first collected in *Laços de família* (1960, *Family Ties*) and was the title story in a 1973 collection.

The Gilman story achieves its intensity by placing the reader squarely in the mind of the protagonist during her descent into madness. In this manner the reader can feel the claustrophia of confinement in the room, in the marriage, and in the mind gone out of control. The success and the uniqueness of Lispector's story also derive from its method of narration. Rendered in a mix of limited omniscience, third-person narration, and free indirect discourse, the story hovers at the boundaries between Laura's mind and that of the narrative consciousness. This narrative technique, with its intentional blurring effects, highlights the process by which Laura struggles to define her subjectivity, or sense of self.

The reader, with this same perceptual margin, follows Laura as she careens from one defining horizon to the next. In the context of her marriage, Laura projects with pleasure the return to an "insignificant role," one which now frees her husband Armando to ignore her at dinner and converse freely with another man. Her friend Carlota imposes an "authoritarian and practical goodness" upon her, a bold and somewhat reckless sense of self which mocks the cautious piety and fastidiousness which Laura applies evenly to her religious faith and her household routines. Contradictory orders from the doctor force Laura into a perceptual contortion which will let her drink the prescribed milk and release herself from compulsive rituals. She solves the dilemma by sitting calmly in her living room while drinking the milk. Through these silent pressures Laura's family and associates conspire to forget Laura's illness and to ease her back to a sense of moderation and wellness.

Each of these horizons—represented by individuals and enhanced by details of Laura's past—evokes a critical basis for reading the story. Among the most common is the issue of gender roles, a unifying concern in the *Family Ties* collection. Under such readings, Laura's plunge into madness represents her only means of escape from the tyranny of a confining marriage. With irony the narrator casts marital intimacy as the freedom to ignore one's spouse.

Other horizons include those of religion, mysticism, and madness. Laura read Thomas A. Kempis's *The Imitation of Christ* superficially as a child and reacted with increased devotion to her faith. The state of alertness, mental clarity, and independence that characterize her madness also set her apart in a manner often associated with mystics. All of these paradigms intersect in the motif of ritual, as Laura's penchant for detail spins into compulsion. Thoughts and actions that would be acceptable as religious devotion seems absurd when channeled to the rituals of domesticity.

The central object of the story, a bouquet of roses Laura has bought at the market, offers a legacy of figurative and thematic horizons as well. In the same way that madness and mysticism overlap, however, the roses inspire a number of competing impulses in Laura, each of which struggles to define her sense of self. Laura is not clear herself if she wanted the flowers or if the vendor has intimidated her into buying them. Nor can she decide if she wants to keep them or send them to Carlota. As she arranges and admires the roses, she awakens into the heightened state from which she is trying to recover. The flowers themselves reverberate with multiple values: perfection, isolation, selfishness, and selflessness.

Plato's concept of art and imitation—expressed in "The Myth of the Cave"—might serve as the ultimate horizon of the story. As Laura seeks to imitate the roses, with their multiple and conflicting figurative values, the break between the object (or subject) and its ideal becomes apparent, if not to Laura, then to the reader. Perfection is revealed as its own shadow, and it becomes apparent that Laura's obsession with being the model housewife has made her boring and petty. As Laura withdraws "like a train that had already departed," the reader is left abandoned with Armando. But unlike Armando, the reader has the option to review the process through which Laura struggled to define herself.

The danger in assessing Laura's search for self, however, lies in relying too heavily upon any one thematic or structural horizon. Laura's emerging self clearly passes through all of the interpretive frameworks given here. Yet the method of narration prevents the reader from attributing any given thought to Laura herself. In one instance, Laura contemplates the results of giving away the roses with a direct thought: "They would not last long; why give them away then?" This attributed thought is followed by an external observation: "The fact that they would not last long seemed to free her from the guilt of keeping them, in the obscure logic of the woman who sins." The next moment these thoughts fuse into free indirect discourse: "All right, but she had already spoken to Maria and there would be no way of turning back. Would it be too late then?" Although these comments build the image of a character wresting with important moral questions, the extent of Laura's conscious participation in this struggle remains unclear.

In her conscious thoughts Laura also comes to embrace inconsistency. Because the doctor has told her she is well, she rationalizes her mixed feelings for the roses: "So she was not obliged, therefore, to be consistent, she didn't have to prove anything to anyone, and she would keep the roses" (in spite of her announcement to the maid that she would give them to Carlota).

In combination, the inconsistencies and the narrative blurring of consciousness serve as a warning against too simple an interpretation of Laura and of the story itself. To seize upon one theme or horizon would be to join the silent conspiracy of friends who would limit Laura's subjectivity or halt those excursions into boundless worlds upon which her well-being seems to thrive.

—Rebecca Stephens

THE IMMORALIST (L'Immoraliste)
by André Gide, 1902

André Gide was an exceedingly self-conscious writer—he published his own diary and he was always aware of himself as the author of the work he was writing, even when he used a narratorial voice, and of the multiplicity of meanings that could be conveyed in a single sentence, or even word. He set out in 1919 to write a great novel, which he called *Les Faux-monnayeurs* (*The Counterfeiters*), and he published it in 1926; in the same year he published an account of how he wrote it. In 1947 he won the Nobel prize largely on account of it. A bright schoolboy, he had as a young man considered a career as a concert pianist, and he had written intensely lyrical, then allegorical work before, for a variety of largely personal reasons, including the discovery of his homosexuality, he turned to the literature of moral and spiritual values.

His first major work, called by Gide a "récit" (narrative), but in fact more complex than that title suggests, *L'Immoraliste* (*The Immoralist*), published twice in 1902. It was expected and intended to shock, published very carefully in a blue-covered edition on luxury paper limited to 300 copies; later the same year, it was published in a yellow-covered edition on ordinary paper, with an important preface covering the work's façade with a whitewash of moral neutrality. Everything about the book, its title, its later description as a "récit," its launch, its two editions, and its preface, was carefully and, as far we can tell, accurately calculated.

Gide wrote nothing else of significance for five years. In the wake particularly of the revelations about Oscar Wilde, whom Gide had met in Paris in 1891, and who must have prompted Gide to reflect about some of the values advocated in the récit by Ménalque, the subject of homosexuality between adult and adolescent males was delicate. On the surface, the three-part récit *The Immoralist* is about a rich, adult, male, atheist scholar who marries, is sexually disturbed by adolescent Arab boys, falls ill on a journey to North Africa, is cured ambiguously either by his wife's nursing or by her prayers, takes up invigorating pursuits like swimming in icy water, physically fights a belligerent coachman, consummates his marriage the same night, and eventually falls into a moral degeneracy. He is not present when his wife has a miscarriage, and fails to save her from death when she falls ill.

Nothing in Gide is ever quite as simple as that. To start with, Gide's preface begins with such an absurdly affected sentence that we know that what follows is going to be a pseudo-naivety. The preliminary Psalm quotation is ironic, and the dedication to a Catholic a tease, well understood in the exclusive literary circle in which Gide was known. Michel's story of his marriage and his sexual inclinations is presented by an unidentified member of a trio of friends who had listened to the narrative. He sends his account of Michel's narrative in a letter to an influential acquaintance to try to get Michel a job. The letter is the text of the book, so that the reader does not know whether Michel's implied moral judgement on himself is too harsh, too indulgent, correctly reported, or reasonably glossed by the letter's writer.

Since we have the work's manuscript, we can say, although not from the text as printed, that Gide toned down Michel's self-condemnation, making his moral position more ambiguous, and the whole work therefore more provocative. What is left of Michel's self-condemnation is still strong enough. When his wife, Marceline, reproaches him, Michel's reaction suggests an acknowledgement of guilt.

There are other ways in which Gide has finely tuned his ambiguities, like the blatant abuse of probability. Michel's connivance at the theft of a pair of sewing scissors from Marceline by an Arab boy is clearly depicted as an emotional betrayal of his wife for the boy; the way the scissors turn up in Ménalque's possession in Paris lifts the whole narrative near the level of fable, parable, or allegory. Then Gide deliberately blurs any dividing line the reader may bring to the distinction between moral and aesthetic values. Michel's recovery of health sharpens his aesthetic sense as well as increases his awareness of physical sensation and the intensity of his sexual drive, so that we scarcely know how much we are being told when Michel reports his decision to shave off his beard. We do know that Michel's recovery was due to his wife's moral strength, although Michel, the atheist, leaves open the possibility that it was due to her prayers.

Michel's narrative includes a long account of an interview with Ménalque, who represents a way of life discreet enough to be socially acceptable, but which is totally free of moral, or even more than trivial social constraints. Ménalque's personal philosophy is not Michel's, and not necessarily Gide's. It is impracticable, but is is presented as attractive. Ménalque suggests that pleasure is the only morally legitimizing aim in life, which only ever consists in the present. He has money, indulges cultivated tastes, and travels, but he will not own property, write memoirs, or be circumscribed by family obligations. That is the form of happiness he has chosen, but no reference is made to its obvious limitations other than to imply its disregard for the weak. The reader is left to reflect on its inadequacies. The life of a philosopher, Ménalque says, is a form of poetry, and the life of a poet is itself a philosophy.

It is easy to link strands in Ménalque's thought with Schopenhauer, Nietzsche, or Wilde. It is not difficult to dissect the literary techniques and list the parallels, antitheses, and trivial changes in behaviour that denote the clash of important and opposing moral visions in the text. Michel keeps his appointment with Ménalque on the night Marceline is symbolically delivered of their still-born child; Michel's relationships with his farm tenants and employees, with whom he poaches his own game, mirrors his interior moral development.

Michel's story ends with the funeral of Marceline. The letter-writer takes up again. Had Michel's behaviour been made more acceptable by being recounted? If so, the reader, like the trio of listeners to Michel's narrative, has also connived, even by reading. The text is not a simple récit at all. It is a delicate invitation to look at the legitimacy and viability of a set or moral attitudes opposed to many of those normally accepted by various sections of the educated French public in 1902. The title *The Immoralist* carries an implied question mark. Gide provoked exactly the range of public reactions he counted on. He did not regard Ménalque's philosophy as sustainable, nor Michel's behaviour as admissible, but he was mischievous, and thought the reaction would be agreeable to watch. *The Immoralist* is much cleverer than its deceptively naive tone suggests. As a tentative exploration of the possible base for some of society's moral assumptions, it is a classic.

—A.H.T. Levi

IN A GROVE (Yabo no naka)
by Akutagawa Ryūnosuke, 1921

The adoption of Western ideas during Japan's Meiji Period (1868-1912) had a profound effect on its literature and gave Akutagawa Ryūnosuke the opportunity to read from various translations of European, American, and Russian literature. Exalting truth over art, the Japanese literary establishment came to believe that only "true" stories from the author's life made suitable subject matter for fiction, ironically relegating all "fictional" elements of literature to the popular novel. With the publication in 1906 of Tayama Katai's confessional novel *Futon* (*The Quilt*), Japanese naturalists began the transformation of European Naturalism into the *shishōsetsu* or "I-novel," consisting of intimate disclosures about the authors' personal lives. Convinced that the undermining of imagination and creativity was a dead end, Akutagawa and other young writers, all associated with the magazine *Shinshicho* and such established writers as Mori Ogai and Natsume Soseki, searched out a new direction for Japanese literature. By 1921, when Akutagawa published his short story *Yabu no naka* ("In a Grove"), he was a literary figure whose work drew mixed reviews from the critics, the more negative of which indicted him for narrative detachment and aestheticism.

Although based on an episode in the *Konjaku*, a vast collection of ancient folk tales, "In a Grove" has a peculiarly modern appeal. Simply stated, a samurai, Takehiko, and his wife, Masago, encounter the bandit Tajomaru along their travels on the Yamashina highway outside Kyoto. Appealing to the husband's greed, the bandit lures Takehiko into the woods, where Tajomaru beats and gags him, ties him to a tree, and then rapes his wife while the husband looks on silently. Afterwards, the husband dies, but the true cause of his death remains a mystery. On the surface, a fairly simple story, but the plot is much more complex.

Divided into seven parts, the tale opens with four sections, subtitled "testimonies," reported by a woodcutter, a priest, a policeman, and an old woman. The woodcutter says he found the samurai's body in a bamboo grove, but he found no weapons, only a piece of rope. The priest's testimony consists mostly of a physical description of the woman. The policeman explains how he captured Tajomaru, and the old woman, Masago's mother, confirms the body is that of her son-in-law. Interestingly, the police commissioner who questions them is never introduced, nor are his queries ever revealed, leaving the reader to fill in the gaps.

Tajomaru's speech, subtitled a "confession," makes up the fifth part of "In a Grove." He immediately claims responsibility for Takehiko's death, but the wife's "confession," which makes up the sixth part of the story, contradicts his claim, as she also confesses to killing Takehiko. Adding even more to the confusion, in the final part—the only one subtitled a "story"—the dead husband reveals, through a medium, that he killed himself. Since the glut of inconsistencies makes it impossible for readers to solve the mystery, they are left instead trying to account for the cause of so many discrepancies.

Rather than attempt to solve the mystery, readers must try to understand the cause of all the contradictions. As some critics have suggested, egoism is partially responsible: the bandit's machismo is the most obvious example. His final words suggest his motivation in taking the blame for a murder he perhaps did not commit: "I know that my head will be hung in chains anyway, so put me down for the maximum penalty" (translated by Takashi Kojima).

Language, of course, is also partially responsible for contrary statements, and in some instances, the lack of language forces too heavy a reliance on sight. Each character interprets expressions in the eyes of the others and then accepts those interpretations as "truth." After the bandit has violated Masago, she says, "Just at that moment I saw an indescribable light in my husband's eyes. Something beyond expression . . . his eyes make me shudder even now. That instantaneous look of my husband, who couldn't speak a word, told me all his heart." Yet the husband says, "I winked at her many times, as much as to say 'Don't believe the robber.' I wanted to convey some such meaning to her. . . .To all appearance, she was listening to his words. I was agonized by jealousy." But she interprets his expression differently. She says, "Beneath the cold contempt in his eyes, there was hatred."

As many critics have suggested, "In a Grove" comments on the reliability of the *shishōsetsu*. Having written some autobiographical works during his life, Akutagawa experienced misgivings about that genre's capability for truth since he knew he had presented only a partial picture of himself. Believing there are as many true accounts of an event as there are perspectives, Akutagawa once expressed the belief that everything exists merely because we believe it exists. Rather than being a search for "truth," "In a Grove" explores the obstacles which make that pursuit impossible to fulfill.

Akira Kurosawa's 1951 film, *Rashomon*, which borrows its title and frame from Akutagawa's short story of the same name, relies heavily on "In a Grove" for its story. A brilliant film, it won the 1951 Venice Festival grand prize and the 1952 Academy award for Best Foreign Film.

—Gretchen Thies

IN THE PENAL COLONY (In der Strafkolonie)
by Franz Kafka, 1919

In October 1914, Franz Kafka interrupted his work on the novel *Der Prozess* (*The Trial*) to write a novella titled *In der Strafkolonie* ("In the Penal Colony"). It was published by Kurt Wolff in 1919. Thematically the novella is closely related to *The Trial* which depicts Josef K. in search of the cause for his arrest. Josef K. gets lost in the impenetrable maze of a court system that he can neither comprehend nor locate in his bourgeois world, because the court in *The Trial* is not of this world. But the novella is also the novel's thematic counterpart in that it focuses exclusively on the process of judgment and punishment which are not described in the novel. Like Josef K., the condemned man in the novella does not know that he was condemned, he does not know the verdict, and he had no opportunity to defend himself. Although the settings of novel and novella are different—*The Trial* takes place in a large city like Prague, whereas the novella is set in French penal colony—it is obvious that both fictions are allegories about the way in which human's relation to the metaphysical realm has been perceived and ordered within the Judeo-Christian tradition. Although the goal of the court and of the commandant in the penal colony is to administer justice, the man's fate is never in doubt. An officer explains to the explorer who has come to witness an execution in the penal colony: "Guilt is never to be doubted"; and the verdict is always that the man must die. Against the process of life (the trial) there is no defense and no appeal.

The story opens *in medias res.* An explorer visiting a penal colony is confronted with an execution apparatus. It was invented and constructed by the old commandant of the colony and has fallen into disfavor with the new, more lenient commandant. It is now operated by the former president of the court, one of the last followers of the old commandant. The officer explains the tripartite structure of the machine to the explorer: the naked prisoner is laid out on the vibrating bed covered with cotton; a Harrow descends on him to tattoo a law into his body according to a blueprint stored in the Designer above the Harrow. The verdict is always the same: "whatever commandment the prisoner has disobeyed is written upon his body by the Harrow." Hence it is unnecessary to inform the condemned of the verdict, because "he'll learn it on his body." This sentence is based on a German colloquialism; it is a metaphor, which Kafka takes literally in the deadpan fashion already employed in "The Metamorphosis."

In the case witnessed by the explorer the crime of the condemned, who is now chained to a soldier and waiting patiently, was that of Adam, disobedience. The law to be inscribed on him is the basis of any religion: "Honor thy superior." The more the officer explains, the more the explorer is offended by the old commandant's notion of justice. But the officer misreads the explorer's silence and tries to persuade him to take his side. The officer spells out an elaborate plan describing how the explorer should speak up in defense of the old system during an assembly held the next day. When the explorer refuses, the officer replies enigmatically, "Then the time has come." He frees the condemned, sheds his uniform and prepares his own execution. He inserts the verdict "Be just!" into the Designer and is fastened to the bed by the condemned. The machine starts working smoothly, but soon it disintegrates. Instead of inscribing the verdict into the officer's body, the Harrow "was only jabbing." During the sixth hour of torture, the officer had claimed, the condemned begin to decipher the script on their bodies; with understanding come recognition, acceptance, redemption, and death. But this is not what happens now. The explorer realizes too late that the machine simply murders the officer. In the dead man's face "no sign was visible of the promised redemption; what others had found in the machine the officer had not found." After a search for the hidden grave of the old commandant, the explorer leaves the island.

Although some critics tried to see in the tyrannical old commandant a representation of Kafka's dominating father, it is obvious that Kafka was not simply "drawing on the story of his own personal life," as Malcolm Pasley pointed out; "he was at the same time envisaging more widely the problem of emancipation from old codes and laws." More specifically, the novella can be read as an allegory of the transition from the stern, purifying notion of justice in Judaism to the softer, seemingly more charitable and humanitarian attitude in Christianity. The old commandant, who had always been remote and has now been superseded, was, like Yahweh, "soldier, judge, mechanic, chemist and draughtsman," whereas the new commandant is surrounded by women like Christ. The officer, who carries around what Pasley calls the "calligraphic commandments," which, like the Torah scroll, can only be deciphered by those trained in its language, resembles Moses carrying the tablets of the Law inscribed by God. Many details, like the officer's handwashing, his ceremoni-

al clothing, his reverence for the old commandant's handwriting, and the centrality of justice, are reminiscent of Jewish rituals and modes of thought, which Kafka knew well.

In *The Trial* and later in *Das Schloss* (*The Castle*), Kafka undertook to review the history of metaphysics in order to prove by way of literature the possibility of a purely spiritual existence. The narrative form he chose wavers between parody and allegory. We know that we have not yet fully deciphered Kafka's esoteric system of allusions. Taking time off from *The Trial,* Kafka explored a very limited problem in his novella, namely the possibility to capture the Judeo-Christian view of human's relation to the world of transcendence. Kafka's choice of the judicial metaphor was in keeping with a tradition that considered human's guilt predetermined (original sin) and punishment inevitable. Kafka moves on from here, but encodes his view, in a set of rebuses, such as the execution machine, that call for interpretation. Theodor W. Adorno said, "The reader who succeeds in solving such rebuses will understand more of Kafka than all those who find in him ontology illustrated."

—Susanne Klingenstein

IN THE ZOO
by Jean Stafford, 1964

Jean Stafford began her career by writing three novels, before shifting in the next 25 years to the production of mostly short stories. During the final years of her life, she turned away from all fictional work and concentrated on essays and book reviews. Stafford had no children herself, but she often wrote about the helpless and powerless status of young people. Maureen Ryan has noted how the youthful characters of Stafford's fiction are most often female. They are handicapped by their inefficacy and by their limited knowledge and understanding. One of Stafford's most successful stories, "In the Zoo," explores the consequences of powerlessness. First published in *The New Yorker* in 1953 and collected in *Bad Characters* in 1964, the story moves beyond childhood trauma and examines the lingering and damaging effects of girlhood events on two middle-aged sisters. As in many other of her stories, Stafford demonstrates a remarkable insight into a child's mind.

Daisy, the older sister, lives west of Denver, and the younger sister, the story's unnamed narrator, lives on the east coast. While waiting for the narrator's train to depart, following her visit to Colorado, the sisters visit the Denver zoo. An aging polar bear reminds Daisy of Mr. Murphy, a childhood friend, and the association triggers the sisters' recollection of their unhappy and guilt-ridden youth.

Like so many other children in Stafford's stories, the girls are orphans. At ages eight and ten they moved from New England to Adams, Colorado, to live with Mrs. Placer, a childless boardinghouse operator and acquaintance of their grandmother. Though a life insurance policy paid some of the sisters' expenses, Mrs. Placer never allowed them to forget her "sacrifice." The boardinghouse was filled with "cruel, uncushioned furniture," "dour and dire pictures," and an assortment of lodgers, who shared Mrs. Placer's cynical manner and spent their evenings on the front porch "tasting their delicious grievances."

Stafford's piece is structured around two zoos: the Denver zoo, which frames the story, and the zoo-like boarding-house, recalled by the sisters' painful memories. Mrs. Placer treated the occupants of her home like captured animals: she fed and quartered them, she subjugated them with her criticism, and she ensnared their self-esteem with her negativity.

To escape "Gran," the girls often visited Mr. Murphy, an alcoholic ne'er-do-well who lived alone with a menagerie of animals, and who amused himself with gin and solitaire. He became the girls' only friend and gave them a puppy, which Gran surprisingly allowed them to keep as a watchdog. Laddy slept with the girls and escorted them to school. In a display of independence and sociability, he disappeared on a hunting trip with the firehouse dog, and returned three days later, dirty and covered in cockleburs and ticks. Gran set out to remake Laddy. First she changed his name to Caesar. Then she instructed him with "stamina-building cuffs," chained him to prevent his walking to school, and kept him at her bedside. Before long, the dog was transformed from "a sanguine, affectionate, easygoing Gael . . . into an overbearing, military, efficient, loud-voiced Teuton."

Learning of Laddy's plight, Murphy upbraided the sisters for surrendering their dog. With a monkey atop his shoulder and colorfully dressed more like a clown than a defender of moral righteousness, Murphy marched to the boardinghouse to challenge Gran. The old woman met him at her door with Caesar. Unrestrained he bounded through the screen and killed the monkey. Gran admonished Caesar with only a light slap, saying, "You scamp! You've hurt Mr. Murphy's monkey! Aren't you ashamed?" Murphy cried bitterly and got his revenge the following day by feeding Caesar poisoned meat. The girls never again visited Murphy, but they did often pass by his house and observed him graying, withering, and maneuvering more slowly over his cards, in a manner the polar bear would prompt them years later to recall.

Gran's domination of Laddy graphically illustrated her capacity to bring out the worst in life. The girls viewed her lodgers as both "victims" and "disciples," yet they were unable to inoculate themselves against her penetrating bitterness. Nurtured on lies, accusations, and insults, the sisters "grew up like worms." While at the Denver zoo, they puzzle over why they did not escape the boarding-house, and they conclude that they were trapped by guilt. "We were vitiated, and we had no choice but to wait, flaccidly, for her to die," writes the narrator.

Though Gran's death physically released the sisters, her legacy of pessimism lives on in them. On the train platform, Daisy suggests that her sister obtain a roomette. "If there are any V.I.P.s on board, I won't have a chance," charges the narrator. Mounting the train steps she tells Daisy, "It will be a miracle if I ever see my bags again. Do you suppose that black-guardly porter knows about the twenty-dollar gold piece in my little suitcase?" Then as the train pulls away, Daisy cautions, "Watch out for pickpockets." Settled in her train car, the narrator writes to Daisy and shares her suspicions about the only other occupant of her car, a Roman Catholic priest. "That is to say, he is *dressed* like one," she writes to Daisy. Then, as she looks out the window, it occurs to her that the fields below are most likely "chockablock with marijuana." Suddenly the narrator erupts in an "unholy giggle," as she recognizes her odious connection to Gran. She has assumed the old woman's view that life is essentially a matter of being "done in, let down, and swindled." The story culminates in this tightly focused moment when the narrator realizes that she cannot escape the influence of her past. She may have loathed Gran's manner, but she cannot purge herself of the old woman's imprint.

Ryan has noted how Stafford commonly organized her stories to produce self-revelatory experiences like the one captured by "In the Zoo." The connection between youthful experience and mature reflection intrigued Stafford and appears elsewhere in her work. Maybe because her own childhood was unhappy and unsettled, and her first two marriages were troubled, Stafford was capable of writing so piercingly about family life and relationships in much of her fiction.

—Barbara A. Looney

INDIA: A FABLE
by Raja Rao, 1978

Raja Rao's acknowledged reputation as a major Indian English novelist perhaps has obscured the importance of his work in short fiction, though he has written some of the finest short stories that have come from modern India. Remarkable as his early stories are for their strong social and political awareness, it is in the later stories that we find his characteristic world view expressed more substantially. "India: A Fable" is a typical example of this.

"India: A Fable" is a meaningful parable treating the cognate themes of the discrimination between illusion and reality and the radical contrast between India and the West. The narrative element in the story is slight, but every single telling detail reverberates with symbolic significance. The Indian narrator visits the Luxembourg Park on a spring day, dressed in a long coat with gold buttons, and sits under the statue of Queen Anne of Austria. Here he meets Pierrot, a small French boy, accompanied by his young nanny, who is escorted by her lover. Pierrot has lost his mother, and his father is an army officer in Morocco. He plays with his wooden toy camel, around which he has constructed a whole world of romantic fantasy: the animal is a wedding present from Rudolfe, "Prince of the Oasis" to Princess Katherine. Taking the Indian to be a prince, Pierrot asks him about India and the narrator's tale contrasts the French boy's world of fantasy and the essential India: the desert of the former with the teeming forests of India, the oases with the Ganges, and the camel with the Indian elephant. In place of Princess Katherine, the Indian prince has two goddesses, on his left and right respectively, riding elephants, and they are to be married, one by the light of the sun, and the other in moonlight. Enthused by this description, Pierrot discards his own world of fantasy, throws his toy camel into the garden pool, and imagines himself riding an elephant at the wedding of the Indian "prince." When the boy and the narrator meet again several days later, Pierrot has a new, middle-aged nanny, and he too seems to have grown. He wears a new suit with gold buttons and declares, "I know now, I am a Maharaja. I ride the elephant. The wedding is over."

The epigraph to this strange narrative suggests its central theme (it is from Sankarāchārya, the ancient Hindu philosopher): "Non-duality alone is auspicious"—that is, the realization that this world is an illusion, that the individual soul is identical with the divine soul, alone leads to the fulfillment of the spiritual quest for salvation. The title, "India: A Fable," indicates how this quest has actually been achieved in India.

The setting itself is symbolic: the garden, with its traditional divine associations, is the right place for the spiritual education of the protagonist. The season is spring, the archetypal time for rebirth. The difference in the ages of the French boy and the middle-aged Indian indicates the spiritual maturity of India, against Western immaturity. Pierrot himself is contrasted with his other countrymen in the park, none of whom has his imagination: the old men read newspapers, the old women gossip; the youths sleep, and even the serious-minded Sorbonard girls read D'Alembet, the scientist, and Henri Becque, the social satirist.

The narrow vision of the Sorbonard girls is only one aspect of the limitations of Western womanhood (and it is the woman who is the true custodian of a country's culture); another is seen in Queen Anne of Austria, a symbol of an unhappy wife. Since wedding (the union between the individual soul and the oversoul) is a key symbol here, the fact that Pierrot's father lost his wife early is significant. This gentleman, a colonel in Morocco, is the image of the Westerner as conqueror and colonizer, around whose romantic notions of the Orient, Pierrot's world of fantasy is built. The arid desert of this world is pitted against the spiritually fertile Ganges-region of India, the camel of the desert being replaced by the elephant, which has divine associations in Hinduism and Buddhism.

The suggestion behind Prince Rudolfe in the world of fantasy being replaced by the Indian narrator, who is obviously a plebian (though his gold buttons are more real than Rudolfe's "horse of gold") is plain: the symbolic "wedding" can be achieved in India even by a plebian. The two goddesses who replace Princess Katherine are reminiscent of the two consorts of God Ganesha or the two wives of the *Purusha* (the divine as the male principle). Pierrot's throwing of the camel into the pool, and his own fall into it, suggest his discarding of his world of romantic illusion, after his enlightenment by the Indian, and his own baptism into a new life of spiritual awareness. When the two meet again, Pierrot has therefore grown; an external symbol of his maturity is his new middle-aged nanny. (The wedding motif is again suggested in that the previous young nanny perhaps has married and left). Pierrot's final comment reveals how his education from illusion to reality is now complete. Earlier, he was only a witness to a fantasy wedding in a nonreal desert. Now, he himself is a Maharaja, he rides the elephant—"The wedding is over." Its effective symbolic statement of Hindu philosophical thought makes "India: A Fable" one of the finest short stories to come from India.

—M.K. Naik

THE INDIAN UPRISING
by Donald Barthelme, 1968

"The Indian Uprising" is one of the earlier Donald Barthelme stories that mark this innovative writer's surprising emergence in that most aesthetically cautious magazine, *The New Yorker*. Beginning his fictionist's career in 1961 with a startlingly new stylistic approach in such little magazines as *Contact* and *First Person*, Barthelme by 1963 had broken into the pages of America's most highly regarded venue for the short story; "The Indian Uprising" (collected in *Unspeakable Practices, Unnatural Acts*) was the 11th of over one hundred *New Yorker* contributions he would make until his death in 1989, an activity that educated an entirely new readership to the intricacies of fiction that explores the reality of its own making.

Such self-regarding, writerly work is often known as "metafiction." "The Indian Uprising" employs metafictional techniques, but the story remains accessible because of its satiric perspective. Consider the story's opening line: "We defended the city as best we could." A typical invocation to the familiar seige narrative, it prompts readerly expectations for a story of any of several guises. But then the second sentence contradicts these expectations with the equally familiar but contextually dissonant reference to an entirely different style of warfare, the frontier conflict of cowboys and Indians: "The arrows of the Commanches came in clouds." The clichéd nature of this statement makes the disjunction all the more emphatic, for two stereotypical situations are presented in tandem, as a result producing a third entity so far from being stereotypical that it becomes fascinatingly new.

Barthelme's method in such juxtapositions is that of collage. There are such happenings in the real world as cities beseiged by armies, just as a staple of American historical lore is the frontier Indian attack. By placing them together, in the manner of pasting a cartoon sketch of Snoopy the Dog on a dollar bill where George Washington should be, Barthelme creates a new entity in which both compositional elements retain their identity; indeed, it is the commentary these elements make about each other that forms the created work of art. The story's metafictional dimension results from the reader being able to see such obvious traces of the creator at work, especially because both types of narrative are already known.

Throughout "The Indian Uprising," Barthelme continues collaging in elements in a predictable but satisfying way. His city is an American one, with streets named after military heroes in a European manner: the Boulevard Mark Clark, Rue Chester Nimitz, George C. Marshall Alée, and Skinny Wainwright Square. The reader is expected to play along with the increasingly dissonant nature of these terms, until the last general is memorialized by his nickname. When barricades need to be erected in these streets (as they always are, in any urban warfare narrative), they are made not of the usual paving stones and commandered vehicles but "of window dummies, silk, thoughtfully planned job descriptions (including scales for the orderly progress of other colors), wine in demijohns, and robes." Again, these are collage elements: real things in themselves, but improbable in combination. Their nature fits the story's theme, for as the Indian attack proceeds the narrator and his companion maintain a rather studied, mannered lifestyle developed from just such items. As war clubs clatter on the pavements and earthworks are thrown up along the boulevards, people "try to understand." This phrase, itself a psychobabble cliché, prompts the sentences that follow: "I spoke to Sylvia. 'Do you think this is a good life?' The table held apples, books, long-playing records. She looked up. 'No.'"

The life Sylvia and the narrator live is a contrived one. Their dangling conversations about philosophy and the arts often touch upon absurdities, such as the habit of playing Fauré's "Dolly" at different speeds to fit the desired mood. Friends travelling abroad send messages back via "International Distress Coupon," a seemingly ridiculous device that for all the author knows may have been actually invented by the time his story saw print. (What reports do such coupons bear? Things like being beaten up by a dwarf in a bar on Tenerife.) Barthelme's satiric approach is evident as his characters support a ghetto army by sending it heroin and hyacinths and caring more for how people dress than what they do. When, as in the typical seige narrative, romantic liaisons are formed among the combatants, their behavior is played out as if they are sharing cocktails at a garden party. Even the warfare is contrived, as during a particularly fierce struggle between "the forces of green and blue" across Skinny Wainwright Square. "The referees ran out on the field trailing chains," which is a reminder that much of what transpires in this story is as much a spectator sport as Sunday afternoon football viewed in the stadium or on television. "I might point out," a character insists, "that there is enough aesthetic excitement here to satisfy anyone but a damned fool," to which the narrator replies with "solemn silence."

The narrator, for certain, is bored—but not the reader. Instead, "The Indian Uprising" offers a collagist's view of fashionable urban American life around 1965, an era in which the dullness of the Eisenhower years had given way to the excitement of Kennedy style and almost feverish economic growth, only to be threatened by the specter of looming racial discontent and political volatility. Because it is presented as a collage, the story invites the reader to take part in the act of assembling, to ask why one item is being juxtaposed with another and to guess what comes next— not just in terms of narrative action but in anticipating which objects can be drawn from the storehouse of contemporary artifacts and combined in an amusingly new way. In a literary age that had begun to question whether all available themes and techniques had been exhausted, Donald Barthelme here shows how fictive creation can always come up with something entertainingly and instructively new.

—Jerome Klinkowitz

THE INTERIOR CASTLE
by Jean Stafford, 1953

Although Jean Stafford published five collections of short fiction, three novels and over sixty articles and reviews during her career, she is perhaps best remembered for her *Collected Stories,* which won the Pulitzer prize in 1970. Described by one biographer as "the earliest absolute first rate story to come from her pen," "The Interior Castle" was first published in *Partisan Review* in 1946, later anthologized in five collections, including *The Best American Short Stories of 1947,* and collected in *Children Are Bored on Sunday* in 1953.

In her work, Stafford created a fictional landscape that ranged from the Colorado desert to coastal Maine and the neighborhoods of old Boston, always presenting characters with the adroit perception of a literary psychologist subtly revealing the dramatic terms of human perception. A frequent pattern in Stafford's stories is the depiction of a private and highly idiosyncratic subjective interior encroached upon by some dimension of the publicly-shared, socio-cultural universe.

Often, her protagonists suffer the disenchantment of failed expectation in a world quite inhospitable, if not openly hostile, to individual desire. In "A Country Love Story," for instance, a wife trapped inside a bickering marriage finds solace only within the subjective fantasy of an imaginary lover. In "Polite Conversation" a young woman is buried in her own mind under the unbearable weight of "neighborly" expectation. In "The Hope Chest" a loveless but longing monologue spins in the head of a lonely spinster confronting isolation at the end of her life. Interestingly, these stories are grouped with "The Interior Castle" in a subsection of *The Collected Stories* called "The Bostonians, And Other Manifestations of the American Scene," an ironic title considering the manners, expectations, longing, and repression the stories portray of middle-class American life.

In "The Interior Castle" Stafford writes from a source she claimed to rarely tap for fictional incident: her own life. Based on a car accident she experienced in 1939, the story details the pain and fear that protagonist Pansy Vanneman endures during hospitalization and surgery to remove bone fragments from her shattered nose, an operation Stafford herself underwent following her automobile accident.

Situated in a "bland and commonplace" hospital surrounded by a freezing landscape as "pale and inert [as] a punctured sac," Pansy chooses to remain so stubbornly immobile in her hospital bed that the sterile room and inert landscape seem to become extensions of herself. Without so much as rumpling the sheets, she takes great pleasure in baffling the nurses with her staunch passivity, boldly circumscribing an external bodily shell and retreating literally and metaphorically into her "interior castle."

The crass and boorish hospital staff follow misdirected perceptions that lead them to know only the surface of Pansy's being and not her soul, a fact which causes Pansy to withdraw deeper into the glimmering "jewel" of her consciousness.

A central thematic question concerns the extent that human subjectivity can be bridged, and the degree that one human being can truly know the interior of another. The hospital staff, including her primary antagonist, Dr. Nicholas, reveals the limitations of the single mechanism available to humans for bridging the inter-subjective gap. Through observing her passivity, the staff can only infer that Pansy is a "frightful snob" living in a "final coma" for which "she might as well be dead," a series of inferences derived from surface observation and all completely erroneous considering the interior vitality of Pansy's monologue. The truth is, Pansy Vanneman is far from comatose, and the mechanism of inference is quite inadequate for knowing that fact.

Angered, Pansy retreats inward to pure consciousness, that "innermost chamber of knowledge . . . perhaps . . . the same as the saint's achievement of pure love." Within herself, her spirit seems complete, unfettered, and pure, a state so desired that Pansy self-induces deliberate pain to achieve it, not because she values pain inherently, but because the pain transports her to a consciousness akin to the saintly ecstasy of love.

As with most of Stafford's work, it is difficult not to view this story as an articulation of feminine consciousness. By seeking fulfillment in subjectivity, struggling against a reduced object status, Pansy is emblematic if not prototypic of women repressed in a male-dominated society. Her retreat into the castle of consciousness establishes a universe grounded solely in the present, a state free from interpreted memory where Pansy is not intruded upon to "love anything as ecstatically" as she loves the spirit "enclosed within her head."

A tragic ending unfolds when this protective castle crumbles under the violent intrusion of Dr. Nicholas's scalpel, a rape-like action that puts the surgeon "at her brain" and disrupts subjective integrity in a way that jars Pansy into distastefully pragmatic submission. The time will come, she unhappily realizes, "when she can no longer live in seclusion . . . [but] must go into the world again and . . . be equipped to live in it." The nose itself is symbolic of this movement: Pansy "banally acknowledges that she must be able to breathe."

"The Interior Castle" is a challenging and difficult story. Stafford's technique remains close to the surface and refrains at every turn from offering easy generalizations to help the reader interpret events. Thus, form brilliantly reinforces meaning by making the story itself "unknowable" by easy inference. As a subjectivity, its heart can only be known by those willing to struggle with uncovering the spirit beneath its observable surface. The story does not beckon readers who resemble Dr. Nicholas, "young and brilliant" by appearance but "nose-bigots" beneath the surface, ensconced in a mechanistic psychology that keeps them blandly unaware of the human spirit within.

Of course, that Pansy Vanneman herself falls victim to the limitations that haunt her antagonists—emotional inferences about the "heartless" and "evil" Dr. Nicholas—reveals Stafford's artistic genius as well as the truly enormous difficulty, perhaps impossibility, of moving to the place her art suggests: from observable surface to spiritual depth. In this, even her protagonist must fail.

—Paul Sladky

J

JACOB AND THE OTHER (Jacob y el otro)
by Juan Carlos Onetti, 1965

Juan Carlos Onetti's story "Jacob y el otro" ("Jacob and the Other"), first published in 1961 and later the title story of a 1965 collection, received an honorable mention in an international competition organized by *Life* in 1960. The story treats the themes of disillusionment, desire, and deceit, with an air of decadence and corruption permeating the narration of the events. The setting for the story, Onetti's legendary town, Santa María, serves as a backdrop for the wrestler Jacob van Oppen and his manager, Prince Orsini, who have come to challenge any man to fight for a purse of 500 pesos. His challenger, a gigantic young Turk, does so at the insistence of his fiancée who is pregnant and wants money for the wedding. The story's three parts are entitled "The Doctor's Story," "The Narrator's Story," and "The Prince's Story"; the narration is presented from these three perceptions. The three narrators use different time sequences for the events in question, resulting in a sort of three-piece puzzle that the reader must put together in order to have a clear understanding of the actual chronological sequence of incidents and possible cause-effect relationships.

The story begins with the narration by a doctor who is called to the hospital to treat a large man who has been injured. The tone and manner employed to describe his surroundings (the theater, the club) and the hours spent playing poker suggest that the doctor's existence is not only rather boring but that he has little to be happy about: he sleeps very little and apparently drinks far too much. As the story progresses, the patient's already serious condition deteriorates and the doctor must perform an operation. He manages to save the dying man, to the admiration of many, and he recalls how Orsini and the wrestler van Oppen had arrived in town with the fanfare of free publicity received from the local newspaper. Interestingly enough, however, readers remain in the dark as to whether the injured man is van Oppen. The only clue to identity of the victim—and one that will be overlooked by most until the end—is the description of an angry woman who kept spitting at the moribund man.

The "Narrator's Story" introduces more details, providing considerable insight into the different characters—an omniscient narrator tells this portion of the tale. The reader consequently discovers that the aging Champ drinks a bit too much, and that he usually manages to fall asleep only after the prince sings "Lilli Marlene" (a nostalgic World War II song sung by German soldiers), while crying from melancholy and drunken stupor. Evidently, the pair make their livelihood travelling through small South American towns challenging all comers without anyone responding to the challenge.

"The Prince's Story" presents Orsini's perspective on the morning of the fight. When the manager informs Jacob that another reason for not wrestling is their lack of 500 pesos to match the challenge, Jacob surprises him by producing an amount of money he had secretly been saving. The wrestling encounter ends with van Oppen lifting and throwing the Turk out of the ring.

Several commentators have stressed the story's title in their critical analyses, suggesting a biblical allusion to Jacob's dream of a ladder to heaven and his wrestling with an angel. No one, however, has suggested that Jacob is actually wrestling with another part of himself: the aging, decadent side he wants to conquer and to some extent does overcome. The other characters, Orsini and the Turk's fiancée, particularly, are portrayed as liars, cheats, and materialistic dregs of society whose lives are pathetic. Like many of Onetti's existentially inauthentic characters, they are condemned to live in their purgatory of Santa María. Jacob, however, managed to wrestle with his destiny, successfully overcame decadence, and momentarily relived his greatness as a wrestler. His willingness to believe in himself and to risk his reputation and savings purchased the measure of existential authenticity the story's other characters lack. For this reason, Jacob achieves a dynamism rare in Onetti's fictional world.

—Genaro J. Pérez

JAMILA (Jamilá)
by Chingiz Aitmatov, 1959

Called "the most beautiful love story in the world" by the French writer Louis Aragon, the short story "Jamilá" was the first celebrated foray into the Russian literary world by the Kirghiz author Chingiz Aitmatov. The story appeared in August 1958 in the literary journal *Novyi Mir* (New World) when it was still under the stewardship of Aleksandr Tvardovsky, famous for having published Solzhenitsyn's *One Day in the Life of Ivan Denisovich*. This was not Aitmatov's first published work; earlier stories had appeared in local Kirghiz periodicals, but "Jamila," translated from the Kirghiz by A. Dmitrieva, was the first sensation in what would prove to be a succession of works from Aitmatov, works that skirted the limits of the permissible in the regulated world of Soviet literature. "Jamila" launched the hitherto unknown Central Asian author from literary obscurity onto not only the Soviet but the world literary scene.

The story begins with the musings of an artist over his favorite picture, that of a couple trekking across the Kirghiz steppe: "If the travelers were to take another step they would seemingly walk off the canvas" (translated by James Riordan in *Mother Earth and Other Stories,* 1989). "Jamila" is the story of an eponymous protagonist and her lover, the wounded soldier Daniyar, the travelers in the picture. The story takes place during World War II, and is set, as are almost all of Aitmatov's works, in the author's native Kirghizstan. The story is related through the eyes of a 15-year-old narrator, Seit, stepbrother-in-law to Jamila.

Jamila's husband is at the front, and she is an object of desire of the few men who remain in the village, and those that return from the front. The heroine, however, is a proud young woman, and she roughly snubs all advances. Daniyar's arrival and assignment to work with Seit and Jamila change little at first. The slightly built and lame recluse does not cut the figure of one to sweep anyone off their feet, let alone the beautiful Jamila, but he doesn't try. A starry ride home one evening spurs Jamila to song, and her demand that Daniyar also sing uncovers his exceptional voice and spirit. Daniyar's songs prove the spark that fuels Jamila's love and finally leads to her flight with him from the society that will not accept what she will not deny, her love for a man other than her husband. The power of music is so strong in the story that the title was originally to have been "Obon," Kirghiz for "melody," before Tvardovsky changed it.

The songs also have their effect on the young narrator, stirring feelings that subtly parallel the mature emotions of the central characters: "His singing made me want to fall to the ground and kiss it, as a son to a mother, grateful that someone could love it so keenly. For the first time in my life something new awoke within me, something irresistible . . . a need to express myself." In an attempt to satisfy this need Seit returns to a hobby abandoned in early childhood—painting—and puts in a picture of Daniyar and Jamila what he cannot express in words. Though reproached by his family, the boy refuses to forsake the couple, as they had refused to forsake their love, and like them he pursues his passion; he becomes an artist.

Compositionally, the conclusion brings the story around full circle; "Jamila" begins and ends with a picture of the couple. Like the boy and his picture, Aitmatov has carefully framed his story. This sort of attention to literary form, especially the symmetry of the framed tale, attests to the strong influence of classical Russian literature on Aitmatov, particularly that of Aleksandr Pushkin. The character Jamila herself can be seen as the product of a long heritage of strong women in Russian literature and Aitmatov's upbringing in a fatherless family. His father fell victim to Stalin's purges in 1937 before the boy was ten, and he grew up surrounded by women forced to make the best of horrible circumstances. The liberation of women, an important theme in many of Aitmatov's stories, originates in Jamila, but she has a long list of Russian literary predecessors including Pushkin's Zemfira (in "Aleko"), and Lermontov's Bela (*A Hero of Our Time*). The perspective of a boy recalls Turgenev's "First Love," and the description of the power of music evokes scenes from that author's *A Sportsman's Sketches*. Aitmatov's story is steeped in the classic Russian literary tradition combined with authentic Khirghiz settings, characters, and conflicts.

The broad vistas of the story's Kirghiz setting provides a background that underscores the isolation of the lovers. The setting also highlights the universality of their plight by revealing that the dilemmas of love are the same be they in the center of an elite Moscow or on the expanses of a traditional Central Asia. The child narrator (found in a number of Aitmatov's stories) allows Aitmatov to present Jamila's decision to abandon her husband nonjudgmentally, even positively, despite society's proscriptions. Though the narrator's insights sometimes seem too sophisticated for a boy of 15 years, the perspective offers a fresh view on the timeless dilemma, personal love versus demands of society, and the reader cannot help but sympathize with the heroine.

This short work spawned a 1969 film version of the same name (screenplay by Aitmatov), and an operatic rendition (score by Raukhverger, libretto by Aitmatov and Bogomazov, 1970). By virtue of its artistic merit and the strength of its message, "Jamila" is a work of lasting worth not only in Kirghiz and Russian letters, but in world literature as well.

—Nathan Longan

THE JEWBIRD
by Bernard Malamud, 1958

Although many of his stories and novels are written in a strictly realistic mode, some of Bernard Malamud's most compelling fiction combines realism and fantasy in ways that recall the tradition of Yiddish writers and artists such as Sholem Aleichem and Marc Chagall. On occasion his blending of these elements is extremely subtle, so that readers of his first novel, *The Natural*, may miss its mythic aspects and regard it purely as a baseball book, just as readers of Mark Twain's *The Adventures of Huckleberry Finn* may find that novel to be simply a boy's adventure story and nothing more. But there can be no mistaking the combination of fantasy and reality in such important stories as "Angel Levine," "Take Pity," "Idiots First," and above all, "The Jewbird."

Malamud's basic technique in these stories is to combine fantasy and reality so that the fantasy appears almost as mundane, as natural, as the realism that surrounds and includes it. In "Take Pity," for example, it is not until the end that we become more fully aware that the entire interview between Davidov, the census-taker, and Rosen, the ex-coffee salesman, takes place in a kind of otherworldly limbo, or purgatory. In "Idiots First" at the start we scarcely recognize Ginzburg as an angel of death since he speaks in the same cadences and accents as Mendel, who is trying to scrape together enough money to send his retarded son to a relative in California before the hour of his death approaches—as it does at the very end of the story. The black angel in "Angel Levine" tests both our credulity and Manischevitz's, until we finally concede with the poor tailor that such things—a black man who seems to come straight out of Harlem (where Manischevitz later finds him)—may indeed be a Jewish angel trying to earn his wings.

So in "The Jewbird," the credible incredible (an expression Philip Roth has used about some of his own fiction) occurs: one summer's evening a skinny crow calling himself Schwartz flies through the open window of the Cohens' apartment on First Avenue near the lower East River in New York City. "That's how it goes. It's open, you're in. Closed, you're out and that's your fate," the anonymous narrator comments, doubtless voicing the opinion of the world-wise bird who speaks English bountifully sprinkled with Yiddish words and phrases. For the elder Cohen, whom some critics see as an assimilationist, anti-Semitic Jew (though he has not changed his quintessentially Jewish name), Schwartz is a *schnorrer*, a beggar who does not merit any consideration from either him, his wife, or his young son, Maurie. But Cohen's family is more tender-hearted and compassionate. They see nothing wrong in yielding to Schwartz's request for "a piece of herring and a crust of bread" (typical Jewish fare). By contrast, the elder Cohen's reply is, "This ain't a restaurant." Furthermore he wants to know what brings Schwartz to his address.

"I'm running. I'm flying but I'm also running," Schwartz says. "From whom," Cohen's wife, Edie, asks. "Anti-Semeets," comes the reply. The entire family reacts with amazement. How can a bird, a crow, be the victim of anti-Semitism? Schwartz explains that he is a "Jewbird," fleeing from all kinds of anti-Semites, "also including eagles, vultures, and hawks." He adds: "And once in a while some crows will take your eyes out." Thus Malamud introduces the idea of Jewish anti-Semitism, one of the story's central themes. For at the end, despite all of Schwartz's help to little Maurie—a nice kid, but not very bright—Cohen does him in. He just can't stand Schwartz and all he represents.

On that first evening, after identifying himself as a Jewbird, Schwartz begins dovening (praying). "He prayed without Book or tallith [prayer shawl], but with passion." Respectful of his attitude, Edie bows her head, and even Maurie rocks back and forth in imitation of Schwartz, but not Cohen. After the prayers, Cohen continues the conversation, inquiring about Schwartz's background. Though his skepticism mounts, the reader's does not. Malamud has so skillfully developed the dialogue that we suspend disbelief more than willingly to hear all of what Schwartz has to say and its effect on the Cohens. The more Jewish Schwartz appears, the greater the antagonism grows between him and Cohen, who nevertheless yields to Edie and Maurie's pleading to let the bird stay for awhile.

Schwartz stays longer, into the start of the school year in September. Although he prefers a "human roof" over his head, he settles into the birdhouse on the balcony that Edie buys him, but is allowed indoors a couple of hours a night to help Maurie with his schoolwork and violin. (Remarkably, Maurie improves in both.) Schwartz balks, however, when Cohen brings home a bird feeder filled with dried corn. "Impossible," Schwartz complains. His digestion can't take it. So Edie feeds him herring, surreptitiously slipping an occasional piece of potato pancake or a bit of soupmeat.

As these events concerning Schwartz's diet indicate, "The Jewbird" contains a good measure of ironic Jewish humor. But neither Schwartz's wit nor Maurie's evident improvement in his studies assuages Cohen's hostile feelings, and he orders Schwartz to head south when winter comes. When Schwartz refuses, Cohen embarks on a campaign of secretly harassing the bird, even bringing home a cat— ostensibly a pet for Maurie, but in reality a ferocious enemy to Schwartz. The campaign has its comic moments, but both the humor and the comedy have their darker side.

In the end, his limited patience exhausted the day after his mother dies and Maurie gets a zero on an arithmetic test, Cohen directly attacks Schwartz, who vainly tries to fight back. They are alone, and when Edie and Maurie return, Schwartz is gone and Cohen greets them with a badly wounded nose. In the spring Maurie finds a dead black bird in a small lot near the river—his wings broken, his neck twisted, and both bird-eyes plucked out. Maurie weeps and asks his mother who killed Schwartz. "Anti-Semeets," Edie explains, as the reader recalls that Schwartz earlier said crows sometimes pluck out other crows' eyes.

—Jay L. Halio

———

JOURNEY BACK TO THE SOURCE (Viaje a la semilla)
By Alejo Carpentier, 1944

The Cuban novelist who invented the phrase "lo real maravilloso americano," Alejo Carpentier considered "Viaje a la semilla" ("Journey Back to the Source") to be the story from which his maturity as a writer began. First published in 1944, the same year as Jose Luis Borges's *Ficciones,* and collected in *War of Time* (1970), "Journey Back to the Source" starts from an idea so simple and so universal that a six-year-old has uttered it: "what if we could live our lives backwards?" The story answers that, living forward or living backward, we end in the same place: clay returns to clay. What signifies, then, is not the source, but the journey, the stories people spin out in idleness as they wait for death, a destination reached by the "hours growing on the right-hand side of the clock."

Unlike Carpentier's later work, where the "marvelous" accrues from the juxtaposition of different realities, this story depends on a magician and an explicitly literary trick. A mumbling old man roves the ruins of a dilapidated colonial mansion being demolished by workmen. With the workmen gone for the day, the old black man twirls his stick over "a graveyard of paving stones"; the house magically puts itself back together, and the old black enters the house where the Marqués de Capellanías lies dead. Once he has reset time's direction and lit the lamps, the Afro-Cuban sorcerer and his magical reality vanish into the text. Although the story includes other Afro-Cubans, he is none of them. Nor does the story propose (as Carpentier's later work will) that his magic is real in his world though not in ours: unelaborated, the sorcerer's world is not contrasted to our rationalist one. The character derives from Carpentier's interest in Afro-Cuban culture, music, and magic—evident in his first novel, *¡Ecue-yambo-Ó!* (1933) and his next, *El reino de este mundo* (*The Kingdom of This World*). But here the sorcerer's trick constitutes the reality of the text and so resembles the *trompes l'oeil* that begin *Los pasos perdidos* (*The Lost Steps*) and *El recurso del método* (*Reasons of State*).

Outside the house, before the old man acts, a rich, baroque, typically encrusted description establishes the simultaneity of decay and renewal. Walls have sloughed their paper like snakes shed their old skins; capitals lie fallen, against their natural propensities, yet the vines recognize their affinity with the acanthus of fallen columns and twine round them. A door frame lets in the darkness. Once the house is reassembled, in the room where the marqués lies, the tall candles grow longer and longer until the nun puts them out with a light. When the doctor shakes his head to indicate there is no hope, the dying man feels better at once. Thus, gradually, delightedly, the reader realizes that he is moving not forward, but backward in time.

Going back, everything passes much more quickly. The ruined marqués trades bankruptcy for mourning, mourning for romance, romance for spiritual crisis, spiritual crises for toy grenadiers, the groom, and the only true perspective on a house—the one from the floor. Finally he renounces the light, and all grows dark, warm, moist again. As he "slips towards life," everything else in the house rushes still faster and further back: wool gloves unravel to return to their sheep, palm trees close their fronds and slip into the earth, metal dissolves, all things return to their original state, and a desert appears where the house once was. The next day the workmen return, but the house they were to demolish is gone, the statue of Ceres carted off and sold. So they sit out the day. One tells the story of the drowning of the Marquesa de Capellanías, but no one marks it "because the sun was travelling from east to west, and the hours growing on the right-hand side of the clock must be spun out by idleness—for they are the ones that inevitably lead to death."

Like Laurence Sterne in *Tristram Shandy,* whose hero tells his story from the moment of his conception, or Machado de Assis in *Epitaph for a Small Winner,* whose hero begins his story just after his death, Carpentier starts from a conceit, a smart, clever, ingenious idea. Nor does he spoil it in the telling: while accounts of the story emphasize its portentous allegory, the tale itself, the reader's journey, is ironic, witty, and fun. Carpentier is not the first author to put time in reverse: Manuel Durán supplies examples from Quevedo to H.G. Wells and observes that film runs its action backwards or forwards with equal ease (in "El Cómo y el porqué de una pequeña obra maestra," *Recopilación de textos sobre Alejo Carpentier* [1976]). Carpentier makes explicit the fictive and/or magical nature of this backward movement, by setting the marqué's reversed time within ordinary, realistic, forward-moving time and by paralleling the storyteller at the end with the magician at the beginning. The storyteller makes comprehensible (and forces the reader *back* through the text) the otherwise indecipherable death of the marquesa by water. He thus supplements the other story we have just been told and returns us to our own forward time.

With its search for (illusory) origins, its loving descriptions of colonial luxury, its contrast between past and present, its typical rather than individual protagonist, and its account of the material decline of an effete aristocracy, the story adumbrates much of Carpentier's later writing. Critics dispute whether the conclusion represents a glorious return to nature or a dismal annihilation of the human race. The antithesis is too simple, since the fiction enacts an exuberant, uniquely human contemplation of the dismal reality, always and forever impending, of the annihilation of our last trace. In Spanish, the title of the story, "Viaje a la semilla," means literally "journey" or "voyage" to the "seed," feminine. Since "seed" in English denotes semen, masculine, spurting out to join the egg, it cannot be used to describe the trip back up the vaginal canal to our source. Yet the ironic balance is maintained: of two deaths in the story, one takes us to water, the other to clay. Though the new growth may be unrecognizable, seeds in clay and water do come up again.

—Regina Janes

THE JUDGMENT (Das Urteil)
by Franz Kafka, 1916

Franz Kafka's story *Das Urteil* ("The Judgment") is famous for at least two reasons. First, it was almost the only one of his works with which Kafka himself seemed pleased; he wrote it in the space of a single night in September 1912, read it personally in public at least four times and had it published early in 1913. Second, it is even more absolutely enigmatic than most of his other pieces. What makes it so difficult is that it has a purely realistic opening and never deviates very far from a naturalistic surface; yet its inexplicability forces the reader to speculate about symbolic and other meanings.

"The Judgment" was originally to have been collected, in a volume to be entitled *Sons,* along with "The Metamorphosis" and "The Stoker"; its title reminds us of *Der Prozess* (*The Trial*). It has been said that it contains in miniature the essence of Kafka's themes and techniques as developed in his later work. The author of this comment, Angel Flores, went so far as to publish an edition of the story with eleven essays appended that consider its various meanings and the history of its critical reception. Few short fictions can have had so much close attention devoted to them.

The judgment in question is the judgment of a father upon his son. The constant Oedipal struggle evident in Kafka is brought brutally to the surface here. What is so peculiarly Freudian is the fact that the struggle is presented in a welter of oblique symbols which bear to the central theme the same relation that Freud's dream-symbols bear to the matter signified. Thus the plot of the story, such as it is, appears to turn on whether or not Georg, the hero, should send a letter to a friend who lives in St. Petersburg. The letter takes on a role that it would hardly have in the work of most other writers; so does the absent friend. Adorno commented that every sentence of Kafka's says, "Interpret me," and nowhere in his work is this truer than in the case of "The Judgment"; elements in the story seem almost free of immediate significance and are thus virtually constituted by the interpretations placed on them.

In the first half of the story we learn of the correspondence between Georg and his friend; Georg gives an excessive amount of consideration to the question of what to tell his friend and it becomes apparent that the friend is in fact some sort of alter ego of Georg's; thus the friend is resigned to bachelorhood while Georg has become engaged and now questions the wisdom of telling his friend this; the friend's business is failing while Georg's is thriving, and so on. In a characteristic moment, Kafka said in a letter to Milena that writing letters was "an intercourse with ghosts . . . with the ghost of the recipient . . . with one's own ghost." The friend is utterly alienated from Georg's world, apparently; he has not been home for three years and is completely stuck in his Russian loneliness. Georg needs isolation and bachelorhood to pursue his writing (symbolised by his writing the letter, where all is well until he starts to involve another—his father) and his friend has achieved these things although he appears to have paid a price in terms of his health and prosperity. Against this harsh requirement to suffer and write is set the figure of Georg's fiancée who, even while "breathing faster under his kisses" protests at Georg's reluctance to tell his friend of their engagement. "If you've got friends like that, Georg, you should never have got engaged," she tells him, and, indeed, if the friend is in fact a part of Georg, she is right to object.

In the second half of the story, Georg crosses the hall to his father's room and their conversation forms the main action. Here the strangeness thickens; everything in his father's room seems at once to be inside and outside Georg, a figment of his anxious imagination and an objective statement of fact. A hallucinatory quality is produced by such unexplained touches as his father's size—at first he is "still a giant of a man" but later Georg is easily able to lift him up and carry him across to his own room. Evidently Georg's perceptions form a greater part of the narrative than is at once apparent; the father is clearly an internalised figure operating in Georg's psyche, even the letter turns out to have only a dubious sort of existence.

In the final three paragraphs of the story the father sentences Georg to death, Georg runs out of the house, bumps into the charwoman ("Jesus," she cries and "covers her face with her apron"), jumps over the railings by the river and drops into it, saying, "Dear parents, I did always love you." The thematisation of parenthood is unmistakable but an erotic element in the final, single-sentence paragraph is easier to miss: "At that moment the traffic was passing over the bridge in a positively unending stream." Perhaps, as Lacan said, the father is the symbolic originator of the dynamics of desire and signification. In "the Name of the Father" we write and we love; paternal permission is needed to send the letter to Russia (Georg's father doesn't even believe in the existence of the friend, it turns out) and, of course, to marry. The strange episode in the father's room symbolises, perhaps, this Oedipal permission-seeking, the denial of permission and the resultant life-in-death as the son's psyche returns to the dark flow of the river and accepts that other releases are forbidden him.

—Lance St. John Butler

JULIA CAHILL'S CURSE
by George Moore, 1903

"Julia Cahill's Curse" is a frequently anthologized story from George Moore's seminal 1903 collection, *The Untilled Field* (it was first published in Gaelic in 1902). In addition to being a finely crafted story in its own right, it is the single story that is most strongly and compactly representative of the collection's central interrelated concerns: spiritual paralysis, clerical abuse of power, individual exile, and the general depopulation of the Irish landscape. The phrase, "untilled fields," which suggests that Ireland's potential is going to waste, actually appears in this story.

The story is told by a first-person narrator who is an "agent of the Irish Industrial Society," a group working to revitalize rural Irish industries such as weaving, in an attempt to stem the tide of emigration due to the lack of employment. One of the story's goals is to show that the curse of so much emigration has come about not so much because there are no jobs but because the clergy are creating a joyless, intolerable atmosphere that is driving Ireland's brightest and most spirited people away. The interaction between the narrator and the young car driver, who is shuttling the narrator about the countryside, suggests the beginnings of the oral storytelling method Moore was later to perfect at great length in *A Story-Teller's Holiday* (1918). Part of Moore's method here also is to develop what he called the "melodic line," a flowing effect that he sought to cultivate in his prose, especially toward the later stages of his career, which relies heavily on the repeated use of the coordinating conjunction "and."

After some coaxing from the narrator, the initially reticent car driver tells the story of Julia Cahill, the parish's most independent-spirited and sexually attractive young woman and the one who seems to feel the greatest joy of life. She is described as "nearly always laughing" and as moving "with a little swing in her walk," traits that draw the attention of all the young men. Because she enjoys the courting of many young men more than the limitations of marrying any one of them, she is considered immoral by the new priest, Father Madden, who denounces her from the altar. The fear inspired by Madden quickly spreads and soon Julia's own family puts her out and no one in the parish will speak to her. Taken in by a blind woman— significantly the only communicant at Father Madden's mass—she is sheltered until some money arrives from America, after which, as a testament to her active indomitable spirit, she walks barefoot the ten miles to the station on her way into exile in America. The last thing she is observed to do prior to leaving is to curse the village, a curse in whose effectiveness the villagers fully believe because they have superstitiously assumed that she has gained sinister powers from the fairies in the mountains. Julia's "curse" is that eventually all the villagers will leave the parish until it is entirely depopulated, despite its exceptionally rich farmland.

Moore makes sure, however, that we see the actual curse as being the pernicious influence of priests who abuse their clerical power in an attempt to exert virtually complete control over their parishioners. The narrator says of Madden that "the religion he preached was one of fear," his sermons "filled with flames and gridirons, and ovens and devils with pitchforks." Soon after his arrival in the parish, Madden outlaws courting, dancing, the telling of fairy tales, and even bowling. Instead of marriages for love, which develop through courting, Madden promotes marriages arranged by parents for financial gain—especially since he is then assured of receiving a hefty fee for performing the sacrament. Moore purposefully shifts the story's scene temporarily to Madden's "well-furnished" cottage so that we may see the relative luxury in which this little potentate lives while his parish remains almost entirely destitute. Toward the industrial or economic changes being promoted by the narrator and toward "new ideas" or any change in general, Madden is cynical. He acknowledges the undeniable depopulation, but, taking a *laissez faire* approach, he feels that that circumstance is inevitable and beyond temporal amelioration.

In sharp contrast, Moore gives us a few glimpses of Father O'Hara's bordering parish, a progressive, flourishing place that is already embracing the modernization offered by the narrator. O'Hara is described as being "a wise and tactful man" who deals with even harsh landlords "on terms of friendship" and who is also "energetic and foreseeing." Loved by his people, O'Hara is obviously intended as the antithesis of Madden and is offered by Moore to afford a sense of balance: not all priests are like Father Madden, although enough are that Ireland's brightest individuals continue to flock to America. This attempt at balance is typical of most stories in *The Untilled Field*.

It should be emphasized that the narrator is, clearly, speaking for Moore most of the time, as when he announces that "the only idealism that comes into the lives of peasants is between the ages of eighteen and twenty [because] afterwards hard work in the fields kills aspiration"—and, in other words, begins a lifetime of spiritual paralysis. Madden ultimately kills the joy of life in his parishioners, and this joy of life is what Moore always valued most highly, instead of acquiescence to clerical demands in the hope of gaining eternal salvation once the potential "next life" begins. In his novel, *The Lake* (1905), Moore completes his clerical indictment by having his protagonist, a priest, renounce his vows and go into exile to seek exactly this quality: life. In "Julia Cahill's Curse," Moore tells us through the narrator that, in Ireland, "religion is hunting life to the death." It was perhaps Moore's most heartfelt ideological concern.

—Alexander G. Gonzalez

K

KAA'S HUNTING
by Rudyard Kipling, 1894

"Kaa's Hunting," the second story in *The Jungle Book* (1894), tells of an early adventure in the life of Mowgli, the boy brought up by wolves, and their associates, Bagheera the panther and Baloo the bear, who teaches him the law of the jungle. Mowgli is abducted by the Bandar-log, or monkeys, and taken to a ruined Indian city, known as the Cold Lairs, from which he is rescued by Baloo and Bagheera acting in concert with Kaa, a huge python and the terror of the monkeys.

"Kaa's Hunting" belongs primarily to two genres that have always been popular in children's fiction, the beast fable and the adventure story, both of which are exploited to the full. The adventure story elements are most obvious in the battle with the monkeys, cunningly led up to and excitingly paced, full of action and injury. The combining of animal and human has been described by Angus Wilson as the chief glory of Kipling's art in the Mowgli stories. Wilson also saw an English boys' school flavour in these stories, with Mowgli as a kind of head prefect and Baloo his housemaster; this is an element some readers reject as didactic moralizing about the law, especially the socio-political thrust against those who do not obey it, as seen in the despised leaderless anarchic chattering monkey-people, whose slaughter is perhaps a matter of too much cruel relish on Kipling's part. However, this is also where Kipling shows his great power: the scene on the moonlit palace terrace of "the Dance of the Hunger of Kaa," with the endlessly uncoiling python mesmerizing his monkey prey into swaying helplessly towards him in lines, is not only one of the most macabre and horrific but also one of the most gripping and evocative passages in all Kipling's work.

The descriptive passages are perhaps the most notable achievement in the story. Not all readers respond well to such explicit drawing of a moral, or to the archaic speech of the characters, whose other humanoid features may strike an unsettling anthropomorphic note. There are many humorous as well as human touches, as when Baloo sets up a hullabaloo that seems more Lear than bear, even one with a sore head, after his man-cub is kidnapped: "Put dead bats on my head! Give me black bones to eat! Roll me into the hives of the wild bees that I may be stung to death." But many readers will be as mesmerized as Kaa's monkeys by Kipling's descriptive powers. Mowgli's abduction is brilliantly done, from the acute depiction of him being swung through the trees, when "the terrible check and jerk at the end of the swing over nothing but empty air brought his heart between his teeth," to the use of sea imagery as he looks for miles over the jungle canopy like a man on a mast or is lashed by leaves as the "waves of the branches" close over him. This kind of precision in description makes it hard to believe Kipling is not writing from first hand experience of the jungle, though critics generally believe he learnt about it mostly from photographs. He did, however, visit abandoned cities in Rajasthan, and one such as Chitor

lies behind the Cold Lairs, magnificently evoked with its roofless houses "looking like empty honeycombs filled with blackness," the shattered temple domes sprouting wild figs, the split and stained marble of the palace overgrown by vegetation. The Cold Lairs is one of Kipling's most stunning creations or recreations of place, and the spirit of place.

One typical feature of Kipling's writing, an obsession with humans and their machines, is absent, apart from an incidental and very effective brief description of the fighting power in Kaa's blunt head and long body: "a lance, or a battering ram, or a hammer weighing nearly half a ton driven by a cool, quiet mind living in the handle of it." With such economical touches, even conveying some light characterization, combined with such lavish effects of scene and action, this is a story to appeal to children of all ages.

—Michael Herbert

THE KERCHIEF (HaMitpahat)
by S.Y. Agnon, 1935

S.Y. Agnon won the Nobel price for literature in 1966, nearly 60 years after the publication of his first story, "Agunot" (1908). The deceptive simplicity of his two hundred folktales, with their luminous evocations of the *stetl*, gave him a relatively limited audience until the 1940's, when the darker shadows and alienation of his characters were recognized. While Agnon uses the form of the Hebrew or Yiddish folktale, his ethos is existential. As critic Miriam Roshwald explains in *International Fiction Review* (1977), "What Kafka did in German, Joyce and Beckett in English, and the existentialists and avant garde writers in French, Agnon did in Modern Hebrew." By contrasting a time when the world was harmonious with a modern awareness of the disintegration of meaning and wholeness, Roshwald says that Agnon captures "the haunting fear, the sense of sin and guilt which pursue modern man's consciousness, and the . . . gradual dissolution of the whole web of familiar culture. . . ."

In "HaMitpahat" ("The Kerchief"), collected in *BeShuvah uveNachat*, Agnon sends the reader headlong into the world of the *stetl*, a tiny Jewish hamlet in eastern Europe, where numerous customs and holy days are not merely observed, but treasured as gifts from a benevolent God. Of the 613 commandments an Orthodox Jew must follow, Agnon focuses in this story on *siddukkah*, or charity to the poor. This commandment is a *mitzvah*, which carries the triple meanings of good deed, blessing, and obligation. One gives to the poor not only because God commands it, but because to do so is a good deed, and doing good brings a blessing upon the giver and the receiver. It would be easy for the reader to focus on the moral tone of this folktale, for Agnon sketches a tale of piety and charity. He draws the character of the mother from biblical models: she epitomizes "a woman of valour who can find? . . . her price is far above rubies. . . .Her children rise up and call her blessed. . . ."

The narrator, a young Jewish boy from Agnon's native Galicia, lives in a world where Sabbath angels routinely accompany worshippers home from Friday night services, where the Messiah's arrival is daily awaited, and where the Master of Dreams whispers a child's wishes. But the boy is an unreliable narrator, whose view of both the parents and the times are heavily steeped in nostalgia, and whose native beliefs and sense of awe are only infrequently interrupted by the voice of the adult Agnon. The boy's idealized remembrances are so lyrical that one might miss the nightmarish visions skillfully woven into the text.

To the boy, home and family form a sanctuary free from the evils of the outside world. The reader realizes that sanctuary is easily imperiled. The family mourns the father's absence on an annual business trip to a small town marketplace and likens it to the destruction of the Temple in Jerusalem, because thieves attacked and nearly killed the father the first time he went to the fair in Lashkowitz. In an extrasensory trance, the mother "saw" her husband strangled hundreds of miles away, sent him aid, and by a miracle, he was saved. Thus, Agnon introduces evil into the story as an attack upon the family.

While the father is away, the boy is rescued from a terrifying dream of thorns and monsters by the miraculous return of the father. But the return is not real, only part of the dream. When the father does return from the fair with a chest of gifts, the boy fearfully recalls a story about evil thieves at the inn who stole treasures from a chest and replaced them with dust. Miracles restored the gifts in both stories. Evil here looms as a disturbing reminder of the imminent loss of harmony. As the adult Agnon recalls his late parents, our sense of his loss is heightened by the numerous references to his father "of blessed memory" and his mother, "peace be with her." And no miracle will restore them.

The father resembles the all-knowing, all-seeing, all-loving, and all-powerful God in whom the boy believes implicitly. He is a bearer of gifts, a deliverer of happiness. He gives his wife a silk brocade kerchief that miraculously never becomes soiled. Because the kerchief is a material thing, one must not value it, for only spiritual things have currency in this rarified world of religious ecstasy. It represents the purity, unity, and love of the family, the goodness that counters evil in this world. The boy loses it, not by carelessness, but by *siddukkah.* Thus, the boy gains spiritual redemption, as his gift of the kerchief to the beggar becomes a *mitzvah,* an unselfish act on the day he becomes a man. Symbolically, the loss of purity, harmony, and unity can never be regained, as the kerchief will never return, soiled now by the beggar, who may well have been the Messiah.

In this story, the balance of good and evil teeters precariously. The parents are viewed by the boy as saintly, while the community in which they function contains both good and evil. The boy yearns for the coming of the Messiah, yet the reader is aware that he waits in vain. If the Messiah would come, the world would end, the dead would live again, and the kerchief, which was lost forever, would be restored, unstained. The lack of charity in the world, exemplified by the townspeople's rebuff of the beggar, would be transformed into goodness, as the gift of the kerchief transformed the material into the spiritual.

Agnon begins with the extrasensory and moves to the miraculous. Amidst so many miracles, the end of the story is not unexpected, but is easily overshadowed by the glow of pride in the eyes of the narrator's mother. The contrast between the ideal harmonious vision of Agnon's childhood and the reality of the modern world with its enormous potential for evil surfaces. Some critics claim that Agnon's stories are colored by or anticipate the events of the Holocaust, and that the poignancy of the lost world of the *stetl* is heightened by the remembrance of the millions who were rounded up from those tiny hamlets to die in the gas chambers. Yet even without that resonance, "The Kerchief" reminds us of a simpler, more pious time when everyone knew what the rules were, and it highlights the subsequent sense of alienation and absence of meaning that grips our world.

—Judith Rosenberg

KEW GARDENS
by Virginia Woolf, 1919

Kew Gardens was first published as a small book by Leonard and Virginia Woolf's Hogarth Press (1919) and later included in the volume *Monday or Tuesday* (1921). Woolf herself judged it "slight and short" and wrote in her diary, "the worst of writing is that one depends so much upon praise. I feel rather sure that I shall get none for this story; & I shall mind a little." Later, however, she was consoled by numerous orders for copies, "a surfeit of praise" from influential friends, and a favorable review in the *Times Literary Supplement.*

More recent critics find *Kew Gardens* an important transitional piece in which Woolf "worked out the lyrical, olbique approach in which her best later works would be written." The story, which on one level is simply about "the men and women who talk in Kew Gardens in July," is highly descriptive and visually charged with a sensuous, almost microscopic vision: describing the "heart-shaped or tongue-shaped leaves" on "perhaps a hundred stalks" rising from a flower-bed, Woolf writes, "The petals were voluminous enough to be stirred by the summer breeze, and when they moved, their red, blue and yellow lights passed one over the other, staining an inch of the brown earth beneath with a spot of the most intricate colour." Four couples pass across the field of vision: a middle-aged married couple with their two children; a confused old man, accompanied by a young male companion, who hears voices; two "elderly women of the lower middle class . . . frankly fascinated by any signs of eccentricity betokening a disordered brain, especially in the well-to-do"; and a young man and woman "in the prime of youth, or even in that season which precedes the prime of youth"—awkward, inexperienced, excited.

One of the curious features of the story is that it is narrated in the third person from the point of view of a snail in the garden, "a unique but ultimately disappointing vantage point," according to one critic, "from which to observe the flow of life. Woolf has not yet found a fictional body to inhabit."

While not entirely successful, *Kew Gardens* does lay the groundwork for many of the strategies and concerns developed in Woolf's later work. The older couple evokes

Woolf's preoccupation with the passage of time and the ghosts of the past. The old man embodies the thin line between eccentricity and genuine madness, an issue of particular interest to Woolf, who was prone to episodes of debilitating depression throughout her life, finally committing suicide in 1941. The young couple are caught in another space compelling to Woolf where the function and efficacy of language itself are called into question, a space punctuated with "words with short wings for their heavy body of meaning, inadequate to carry them far." In the section involving the two old women "piecing together their very complicated dialogue," Woolf examines the "pattern of falling words" and begins to experiment textually: "Nell, Bert, Lot, Cess, Phil, Pa, he says, I says, she says, I says, I says—" This scene later troubled Woolf, and she worried that it "discredited" the story a little.

She is nonetheless at the beginning here of her lifelong literary project to explore language, substance, human intercourse, consciousness, and, ultimately, reality. "Stylistically, formally," the critic Phyllis Rose finds the story "exciting" but "ultimately unsatisfying," in part because although *Kew Gardens* represents "daring innovations in technique," the author "had not yet found a subject which would allow her to express her humane experience of life." And yet finally Woolf is not simply experimenting with form but writing about "depth of contentment," "passion of desire," and "freshness of surprise" as she attempts to catch, according to Rose, "the fragmentary, transient nature of what *is* real, people passing, wisps of conversation, nature in motion, the wafting of life."

The story ends with a long paragraph of dissolving "substance and color" as all life in the garden—"yellow and black, pink and snow white, shapes of all these colours, men, women, and children"—appears and then seems to evanesce. But if one truly listens, Woolf maintains, "there was no silence; . . . like a vast nest of Chinese boxes all of wrought steel turning ceaselessly one within another the city murmured; on the top of which the voices cried aloud and the petals of myriads of flowers flashed their colours into the air."

—Deborah Kelly Kloepfer

KIND KITTY
by Eric Linklater, 1935

Kynd Kittok, to give her name in its original form, was a mythical character who appeared in a short Scottish ballad of the 15th century. It told, in a genial and tolerant spirit, of a poor old woman, who dies of thirst when the drink ran out. To the amusement of God, she managed to get into heaven. There she spent seven years as the hen wife of Mary, but she found the company of the place uncongenial and the beer sour. She managed to escape to an ale-house outside the gates of heaven where she felt more at home. There she remains, always ready to have a drink with the thirsty traveller.

The author of this poem is unknown, but it has been attributed without evidence or support from its style to one of the great Scottish poets of the period, William Dunbar. It was so attributed by Hugh MacDiarmid in his anthology, *The Golden Treasury of Scottish Poetry* (1940). Eric Linklater also attributes the poem to Dunbar in the few lines he

quotes at the beginning of his story "Kind Kitty." Dunbar was important to Linklater because he regarded him as a key figure in the Scottish literary tradition, of which he was himself a part. He translated some of Dunbar's poems into modern English and there is much affinity of feeling between the two men in their robust, Rabelaisian humour and their delight in exuberant language.

Linklater's treatment of the theme in "Kind Kitty" (collected in *God Likes Them Plain*, 1935) is one of the best-known and most highly regarded of his short stories. He transfers the action of the poem to the Edinburgh of the time he wrote it, the 1930's, when the lot of the poor had little support from a welfare state. The ballad had given only the essentials of the story. Linklater expands it with circumstantial detail which gives life and blood to the characters and a substantial feel of place. His Kitty lives in the Canongate, a part of town which was then an insalubrious slum. She keeps a few hens and lives on a pittance, most of which she spends on drink. To return the hospitality of a friend, she borrows against her pension to give a Hogmanay (that is, a New Year) party that "would put the Old Year to bed with joy and splendour." So it does, but a day or two later, with no money and no drink left, she, like her 15th-century namesake, succumbs to thirst. She abandons heaven for the more welcoming atmosphere of the inn outside the gates.

This theme gave Linklater an opportunity to do two things. First, he gives a memorable and sympathetic portrait of the old reprobate, so palpable that you can virtually smell her. Then he celebrates her conviviality, resilience, and generosity of spirit. It is a challenge to the qualities and standards of respectable society. The implication is that heaven, and therefore respectable society on earth, is full of people who are rather dull company and less kindly and warm-hearted than the reprobates who are kept out. It is a theme that seems to strike a particular cord in Edinburgh. A few years after Linklater's story, Sydney Goodsir Smith, an Edinburgh poet, based a long poem about the city, *Kynd Kittock's Land*, on the same legend. In this story and elsewhere Linklater made it clear that in his scale of values those of Kind Kitty had a high place.

—Paul H. Scott

KING OF THE BINGO GAME
by Ralph Ellison, 1944

Ralph Ellison's career in American letters depends almost exclusively on two major texts: one, *Invisible Man*, has been heralded as a masterpiece of the modern novel and a benchmark of African-American literature, and the other, *Shadow and Act*, has been celebrated as a perceptive collection of personal essays and criticism informing both Ellison's own writing and that of his peers. (Another collection of nonfiction, *Going to the Territory*, was published in 1986.) In addition, he has written numerous short stories, many of which, like "King of the Bingo Game," (in *Tomorrow*, November 1944), have been widely anthologized, although they have yet to be published in one collection. Nevertheless, Ellison's relatively meager output has been questioned, and even criticized, by those who expected much more from him, given his obvious talent and the excellence of what he did produce. This is not to say that Ellison somehow fell short in his full potential as a writer, however, because he imbued virtually everything he wrote with the rich complexity of his own vision of the modern African-American experience, a fully complete vision, even in the ambiguity and ambivalence of its fictional expression. "King of the Bingo Game," for example, represents in microcosm the whole of Ellison's work, especially in its stylistic and thematic anticipation of the key motifs he would develop later in *Invisible Man*: the counterpoints of north/south, black/white, dream/reality, isolation/integration, agency/bondage, identity/invisibility, and life/death.

Like *Invisible Man*, "King of the Bingo Game" features a displaced Southerner seeking his fortune in the North, ostensibly the land of freedom and opportunity, but the protagonist finds himself estranged from even his fellow African-Americans: "Folks down South stuck together that way; they didn't have to know you. But up here it was different." The Bingo King's hunger, literal and figurative, cannot be appeased in this urban setting because of its alien notion of community and hospitality which, instead of welcoming him, sets him apart as a stranger, a country hick from "Rock' Mont, North Car'lina."

Although the Bingo Game pretends to be color blind ("Anybody can win the jackpot as long as they get the lucky number, right?") it actually functions as one of the white culture's racial controls. Much like state lotteries, it sells the lower-class African-Americans on the hope of dreams, even against the odds of achieving them, subtlety diverting them from significant social change by enticing them as paying customers to their theaters with the possibility of winning a measly $36.90. A white man runs the game and collects the entrance fees, backed up by the police, who finally give the Bingo King "what all the winners received"—a kick in the head.

Two dreams run parallel to each other in the story, each emblematic of the other, counterpoints to the reality that finally intrudes on them. The first is represented by the film's depiction of a bound and beaten woman held captive by some unnamed agent but awaiting rescue at the hands of the film's hero. The second involves the Bingo King's plan to rescue Laura by winning enough money to pay a doctor to cure her. A third dream, the runaway train, foreshadows the inevitability of the protagonist's fate and underlines his own need of rescue.

The tension between the Bingo King's yearning for membership in the African-American community and his feelings of isolation among them at the theater creates a bipolar conflict of pride/shame for him: "All the Negroes down there were just ashamed because he was black like them. . . . Most of the time he was ashamed of what Negroes did himself." His winning a chance at the bingo wheel isolates him further from the rest of the audience and sets him apart, ironically "one of the chosen people." His stall tactics make him even more the focus of their anger and frustration as they displace their real complaints against the larger cultural racism.

As long as the bingo wheel of fate keeps spinning, the Bingo King can exist in a powerful free space between possibility and finality, set against the question of self-determinism and the ongoing pressure of time: "He felt vaguely that his whole life was determined by the bingo wheel. . . . Didn't they know that although he controlled the wheel, it also controlled him?" He cannot release his hold on the button that controls the wheel because it represents life, both his own and Laura's, and also because he wants to defer fate's final spin on his existence.

Ironically, at the height of the Bingo King's power, he experiences both an assertion and a loss of selfhood. He achieves "a sense of himself that he had never known before," but immediately realizes that he has forgotten his own name, "given him by the white man who had owned his grandfather." He screams the question "Who am I?" at the crowd, but they cannot respond because of their own loss of identity. They are invisible in white culture even when they take center stage.

With his renaming of himself as the Bingo King, the protagonist experiences a rebirth of sorts, although the new name reflects as much bondage as the old one did. With the bingo wheel finally coming to rest on the double zero jackpot number, he has a fleeting glimpse of the possibility of Laura's rebirth. In reality, however, the double zero signifies death for both of them as the curtain is rung down on the bingo game and their lives.

Perhaps Ellison quit writing fiction because he had said everything he had to say and simply refused to waste his time going back over ground already well covered in his work. He may, in fact, be waiting for the time when he can resume his career by writing something new about the African-American experience—for the time when the Invisible Man can feel free to move out from his underground isolation, or for the time when the Bingo King can find succor outside the Bingo Game, where the racist wheel of fate turns everyone into a loser regardless of what number comes up.

—Phillip A. Snyder

KNEEL TO THE RISING SUN
by Erskine Caldwell, 1935

Erskine Caldwell was a prolific writer of novels, documentaries, and short stories, the most successful of which were about his native Georgia. His modernistic techniques enabled him to create intense, economical, and aesthetically near-perfect short fiction that rivals the finest ever written. Thematically, his concern for social injustice conformed well to the Depression era, the period in which his works first began to be published.

Between 1931 and 1940, Caldwell published 14 books, including the strongest he would write. Although he denied any affiliation with communism, his works about Southern poverty provided vivid support for many of that decade's revolutionary assertions about economic and social injustice. Commenting on his first book of stories published in 1931, a reviewer wrote in the *New Masses,* "We need writers like Caldwell. He should go left."

"Kneel to the Rising Sun," first published in *Scribner's* four years later, then collected in Caldwell's third book of stories under the same title, serves almost as a response to that reviewer's urging. It is a story about a black and a white sharecropper, Clem and Lonnie, whose poverty and struggle against exploitation at the hands of a brutal landlord, Arch Gunnard, provide them with a basis for solidarity. Ultimately, however, the landlord's appeal to Southern racial prejudice foils the workers' union, makes of Lonnie a cowardly Judas, and ensures Clem's lynching.

The Left was never entirely happy with Caldwell, for all of his promise. His characters lacked class consciousness, and their proletarian virtue was more often than not shrouded by proletarian vice. Whatever Caldwell's political ideals, he rarely created a character without foibles. In the case of Lonnie, weakness, cowardice, and disloyalty are salient. Although the sight of his friend's lynching stirs him to try "to say things he had never thought to say before," the end of the story finds him "slumped down" with "his chin falling on his chest."

Recognizing that African-Americans were often the scapegoats of Southern society, Caldwell never allowed his black characters to sink to the degraded level of his poor whites. Whereas poor-white Lonnie cowers in fear, Clem stands up for himself and Lonnie, helps Lonnie find his starving father, and objects to Arch Gunnard's sadistic behavior. In return, Lonnie tenders only weakness and betrayal. In this and Caldwell's other stories of lynchings, such as "Saturday Afternoon" (1930) and *Trouble in July*, racial violence is shown to occur because of white character flaws and in spite of the complete innocence of the black victims. Clem's crime is actually the virtue of retaining his dignity in vicious surroundings.

Caldwell first published in little magazines, small circulation periodicals that featured experimental works by what would turn out to be some of the finest writers of the 20th century. From these publications, he was exposed to modernistic techniques such as imagism, which he uses with effectiveness in his finest short stories.

In "Kneel to the Rising Sun," several concrete, vivid images serve to convey the story's message economically. For example, Lonnie's "sharp chin" effectively emblematizes his malnutrition. When it is jabbing into his chest, it also illustrates the dejected, defeated posture with which he responds to his exploitation. The "fattening hogs" in Arch Gunnard's pigpen symbolize the landlord's greedy feeding off his sharecroppers. And the rising sun at the story's end is replete with possible meaning. James Devlin regards it as a Christian motif, representing the ascension (the sun/son rising into heaven) following Clem's betrayal and crucifiction. The emphasis on the sun's redness and Lonnie's struggle with a new consciousness may also imply the birth of the communist revolution, a political force arising from the experience of social and economic injustice. Finally, the image of Lonnie kneeling before the mysteriously rising orb suggests nature worship in a savage world in which people are hunted and killed like animals.

This use of concrete images to suggest abstract ideas can be found throughout the story. With Lonnie's dog Nancy, Caldwell uses what T.S. Eliot termed an objective correlative. When Arch Gunnard beckons to Nancy, she crawls to him on her belly wagging her tail, then turns over on her back with paws in the air in complete surrender. This image of Arch's complete mastery over the dog correlates with the absolute power he wields over his sharecroppers and the community at large. That he is willing to use physical force to maintain his power is demonstrated when he kicks the dog in the stomach. Ultimately, Caldwell carries the brutal landlord's violence into the realm of sadism in the scene in which he cuts off the dog's tail with his knife. The cropping of the dog's tail parallels Lonnie's relinquishing of his manhood to Arch and demonstrates that he cannot stand up for himself or his family, let alone his dog. In a final bizarre touch, Caldwell establishes that Arch keeps a collection of cropped dogs' tails in a trunk at home. Thus an almost surrealistic dimension is added to the malevolence of this landlord/collector arch-fiend who owns his tenants body and soul.

Another aspect of Caldwell's technique is the use of repetition. As Scott MacDonald has pointed out, certain repeated phrases or motifs serve as indices to character or to build suspense, increasing their implications with each occurrence. In section I of "Kneel to the Rising Sun," Arch repeats several times that Nancy does not need such a long tail; each repetition increases the reader's sickening realization of what will inevitably happen. In section II, the phrase "the fattening hogs" occurs periodically as Lonnie and Clem search for Lonnie's father until the horrible meaning of the phrase becomes apparent: the hogs are literally fattening on Mark Newsome.

With the help of these technical innovations, Caldwell creates a world in which civilized values seem too fragile to withstand the brutal forces that drive both human and beast.

—William L. Howard

L

THE LADY ARISTOCRAT (Aristokratka)
by Mikhail Zoshchenko, 1923

From the early years of the Soviet regime to the present, the enduring fame of Mikhail Zoshchenko rests chiefly on his satiric sketches. He became a household word in Russia because the situations he described were drawn directly from the daily lives of Soviet citizens at home, at work, in bars, shops, restaurants, and theatres. Writing in an environment in which art was judged according to its level of service to the State, Zoshchenko worked in satire and created a series of first-person narrators whose language and judgments were seen as the writer's "mask." By the 1930's, critics were questioning the future of the genre itself, noting that satire was surely nearing extinction because, in the ideal State soon to be realized, it would be irrelevant and unnecessary.

One of Zoshchenko's most famous creations is "Aristokratka" ("The Lady Aristocrat"), in which the narrator recounts his attempts at romancing a woman who lives in the apartment building where he works as a superintendent. In typical Zoshchenko fashion, the narrator starts his tale with a blanket statement, a generalization that, in the end, tells the reader more about the character of the narrator than about its ostensible subject: "You guys—I don't like ladies in hats. If a lady has a hat on, if she's wearing silk stockings, or carrying a puppy dog around in her arms, or she has a gold tooth, then as far as I'm concerned, an aristocrat like her is no lady at all: she's total nothing to me." He admits, however, that he did fancy such ladies in the past and recounts how his relationship with such an "aristocrat" faltered at the point where she "revealed her ideology in full force."

At first, the narrator courts his aristocrat by regularly knocking at her apartment door to ask about the plumbing in his most official tone: "How's everything as regards malfunctioning of the toilet and plumbing? Is it all working?" After she warms to his repeated solicitations and he takes her for walks in town, she suggests that he take her to the theatre. As luck would have it, the local party committee is giving out free opera tickets the next day, and he gets one on his own behalf and an extra one from a pipefitter friend who doesn't want to go. The tickets are not together, however, and the narrator and his ladyfriend can barely see each other once they are seated. At intermission, they meet in the lobby, where he offers to treat her to a meat pastry. Then he watches in horror as she quickly downs one, then another, and then a third. Furtively, he counts the available cash in his pocket and worries that he won't have enough. He tries to distract her from her eating by suggesting that perhaps intermission is over, or that it's not good to eat so much on an empty stomach. Unable to stand it when she reaches for the fourth pastry, he snaps at her, "Put that back!" When the man behind the counter attempts to charge him for four pastries, he insists that his ladyfriend ate only three and refuses to pay for the fourth. A crowd gathers to debate whether the fourth pastry shows

toothmarks or is slightly squished, while the narrator turns his pockets inside out to come up with the money. Finally he finds enough small change to cover the pastry and tells her to go ahead and eat it. The aristocrat, however, is too embarrassed to continue eating, and an old man quickly steps forward to eat the disputed pastry. At the end of the opera, she tells the narrator that he shouldn't ask ladies out if he doesn't have money. He counters, "Money can't buy happiness, if you'll excuse the expression." After they part, he concludes, "I don't like aristocratic types."

This tale of aristocratic (read "bourgeois") pretensions and working-class discomfort and ineptitude for the refinements of romance and culture is told in language that veers constantly from one sociolinguistic extreme to the other. Interlarded with the narrator's highly colloquial, slangy, and unlearned speech are Soviet slogans, Marxist buzzwords, incorrectly used foreign words, and antiquated terms of address from the tsarist era. Although the narrator is uneducated, he has absorbed the Soviet rhetoric that praises him as a worker and scorns those who belong to the bourgeoisie. His descriptions of his courtship and the fateful evening with the lady aristocrat reveal just how out of place he is, and how inaccurate is his assessment of what went wrong. The reader finds the narrator's statements and opinions to be unacceptable, and his authority is undermined.

In his hundreds of short stories and feuilletons, Zoshchenko's narrator is almost always unreliable, and it is this tension between the storyteller's assessment of the situation and the reader's normative understanding that makes his stories unique exercises in short-form narration.

—Linda H. Scatton

THE LADY WITH THE LITTLE DOG (Dama s Sobachkoi)
by Anton Chekhov, 1899

"Dama s Sobachkoi" ("The Lady with the Little Dog") is one of the most anthologized of Chekhov's short stories. It is typical of his work in that it combines realism—accentuated by the avoidance of obvious literary devises and of moral or philosophical comment—with an understated symbolic quality, a combination which gives his work its unique atmosphere. The content of the story is on the surface very conventional, but it is Chekhov's treatment of this content, particularly the kind of concrete detail he supplies, which creates recognition and identification on the part of the reader yet is also defamiliarizing, that gives the work its power.

Gurov, a bank official from Moscow whose marriage offers him no fulfilment and who has had numerous affairs, is attracted by a new arrival in Yalta, where he is on holiday alone, a young woman with a Pomeranian dog. When they meet it is significant that she is the first one to speak. She blushes and lowers her eyes, indicating an attraction towards him, and it is clear that the philandering Gurov will have little difficulty in persuading her to have an affair with him. Her name is Anna and clearly her life is as unfulfilled as his. A week later they begin an affair. Afterwards they are sitting looking at the sea and there is a striking passage in which the roar of the waves suggests the eternal sleep of death and nature's indifference to humanity. Yet paradoxically, Gurov feels part of a never-ceasing movement of life and he reflects that everything in the world is beautiful. When Anna has to return home Gurov does not seem particularly unhappy, regarding it at this point as just one more affair.

Back in Moscow he expects to forget Anna within a month but he finds that he cannot. All of the activities of his life, at home, at work, and at leisure, seem pointless. He therefore decides to travel to the town where Anna lives and eventually meets her. She discloses that she has also been unable to forget about him, but his arrival fills her with dread. Shocked by his kisses, she promises to see him in Moscow.

Chekhov conveys the change that takes place in Gurov by the artful use of detail. Gurov tries to tell a friend about what happened in Yalta but all he says is that the fish they had for dinner was off. This provokes in Gurov disgust with the waste and triviality of his and other people's ordinary lives. Chekhov describes Gurov's hotel room as having a grey carpet, a grey blanket, and an inkstand covered in grey dust on the table, with a headless horseman surmounting it. With the use of such detail Chekhov builds an atmosphere with symbolic overtones. Indeed the colour grey pervades the story: Anna has grey eyes, her dress is grey, the fence surrounding her house is grey and studded with upturned nails, and at the end of the story Gurov notices that his hair is turning grey. This greyness is contrasted with the whiteness of the dog and the whiteness of the clouds as they look over the sea in the second section. No definite meaning is attached to such colours and many readers will see them merely as part of the story's realism, but they suggest other levels of meaning.

Both Anna and Gurov are reconciled to leading double lives. Gurov finds it difficult to understand why she loves him. Although they look forward to a time when they can escape their lives of deception and live freely, they accept by the end of the story, that the most difficult part of their lives is only beginning.

The story does not make clear why these two people love each other so intensely. In numerous other works Chekhov shows love to be based on illusion and egotism. That is not denied in this story, but it is less important than Gurov and Anna's desire to find something in life that gives their lives meaning and significance. Their love has to be understood in the context of the barrenness and banality of their ordinary lives. Social pressures and conventions have driven them into marriages and domestic situations which do not offer satisfaction to their deeper sense of self. The price of confining life to the social level is repression. The love of Gurov and Anna is a rebellion against such repression.

Chekhov is often seen as a writer who sees the human predicament in tragic terms. But his work can also be read as an indictment against society and its repressions. The world that confines Anna and Gurov in dead marriages and offers no outlet to their desires for some kind of transcendence is not unchangeable. This story, like many other Chekhov works, contains a Utopian vision in Gurov's

realization that the world is beautiful and that human beings have a higher purpose. Often those who have such visions, such as Trofimov in *Vishnevyi sad* (*The Cherry Orchard*), are treated ironically, but that irony does not mean that vision or yearning is invalid. They at least offer the hope of a better life and a better world.

It is probably no accident that the heroine of this story is called Anna, suggesting an allusion to Tolstoii's *Anna Karenina* (1875-77). Tolstoii's Anna is destroyed by rejecting her social life and social self in favour of a new self that does not inhibit passion and impulse. Though Tolstoii dramatizes Anna Karenina's desires with great power, he is convinced that they are fundamentally wrong and will inevitably prove destructive. In contrast, Chekhov presents the desire to escape repression and liberate impulse in a positive light, though he is well aware that the chances of success are slight. Both negative social forces and the self's vulnerability to boredom and egotism have almost overwhelming power. Yet there remains some hope in the story, which ends with the lovers expecting a new and beautiful life, aware of the many difficulties and complications that lie ahead.

—K.M. Newton

THE LAMP AT NOON
by Sinclair Ross, 1968

Sinclair Ross is one of Canada's best-known prairie realists. His novels and short stories present nature as a force beyond human control, one that reduces us to our most elemental selves as we struggle to survive. Lines of communication, most notably between husband and wife, break down as men and women are left isolated before the nature's onslaught. Civilization is a thin facade, built upon social niceties that are easily swept away. Also, Ross's works are often set during the Depression, so that the economic environment is as harsh and unforgiving as the natural one.

"The Lamp at Noon" portrays such a breakdown in communication. Paul is a farmer who refuses to give up despite years of drought. Ellen, his wife, feels trapped in their house, and vulnerable to nature's fury represented and symbolized by the dust storm raging outside. She can no longer cope with the failure and isolation, but her attempts to tell Paul what she is feeling fail. He will not surrender, remaining oblivious to the cost of his decision to go on despite her desperation.

At the beginning of the story Ellen is lighting a lamp against the daytime darkness. The lamp is a symbol of both hope and hopelessness: it is a challenge to the dust storm, but the very fact she has to light it proves how desolate their life is. She sees the dust storm as invading her home and, we realize, it is invading her mind as well. In an oft-quoted passage, she sees the wind as predatory:

There were two winds: the wind in flight, and the wind that pursued. The one sought refuge in the eaves, whimpering, in fear; the other assailed it there, and shook the eaves apart to make it flee again. Once as she listened this first wind sprang into the room, distraught like a bird that has felt the graze of talons on its wing; while furious the other wind shook the walls, and thudded tumbleweeds against the window till its quarry glanced away again in fright.

Her home is her garrison, but one unable to provide her with any real protection. The dust invades everywhere: "The table had been set less than ten minutes, and already a film was gathering on the dishes." Similarly, her sanity is a thin shield against the madness besieging her.

Paul, like many male characters in Ross's fiction, is stoic and impatient with displays of emotion. Ellen yearns to rush out to the stable to find him, but there "was too much grim endurance in his nature ever to let him understand the fear and weakness of a woman." They had quarreled earlier, contributing to the silence between them; what he cannot see is that her combativeness is the product of "the dust and wind that had driven her."

As a naturalist writer, Ross portrays a world of inevitable hardships; all we can do as individuals is learn to cope. His characters are stripped of anything grafted on by civilization, and are forced to grow up quickly: for instance, although Paul is only 30 years old, Ellen notices "the strength, the grimness, the young Paul growing old and hard, buckled against a desert even grimmer than his will." Paul has placed his faith in nature but it has betrayed him; nevertheless, he retains his hope. But rather than being strengthened by hardship Ellen is progressively destroyed: "the same debts and poverty had brought a plaintive indignation, a nervous dread of what was still to come. . . . It was the face of a woman that had aged without maturing, that had loved the little vanities of life, and lost them wistfully." Unlike Paul, she does not have the hope necessary to shield her from the harsh reality of their existence: "It's the hopelessness—going on—watching the land blow away," she tells him.

Ellen tries to tell him that the farm is doomed, but he is blinded by hope, and pride as well as he refuses to accept the alternative—working for her father. Their lives and particularly their youths are being wasted here, as Ellen sees clearly and Paul will not.

When he storms out to return to the stable she pleads with him not to go. She is tortured as much by the loneliness as the hopelessness, and needs his comfort and affection. But he cannot show tenderness. In the stable, as he looks out over the fields, Paul's eyes open:

Suddenly he emerged from the numbness; suddenly the fields before him struck his eyes to comprehension. They lay black, naked. . . .before the utter waste confronting him, he sickened and stood cold. Suddenly like the fields he was naked. Everything that had sheathed him a little from the realities of existence: vision and purpose, faith in the land, in the future, in himself—it was all rent now, all stripped away.

He now sees the truth as clearly as Ellen, but it is too late. He returns home to discover she is missing. He finds her out in the storm clutching their dead baby—another symbol of their hopes now blasted. She has gone mad and, ironically, in her madness expresses the hope that he in his own stubborn refusal to face the truth had always expressed. Their roles are thus now reversed; it seems that the truth is so painful only illusions—even to the point of madness—make it bearable.

—Allan Weiss

THE LEGEND OF SLEEPY HOLLOW
by Washington Irving, 1820

Like a number of writers of his time, Washington Irving faced the question of what to write about. A new nation, the United States had no sense of the past and was, moreover, preoccupied with the pragmatic and the materialistic. Indeed, if there was anything that might be considered old, it had to be sloughed off in favor of the new. Irving, an exponent of the genteel tradition, was not comfortable in such a setting. If Whitman and Emerson were to find their creative inspirations in an active existence in the present, Irving was to find his in his romantic affection for the legends and relics of the past. "The Legend of Sleepy Hollow" (in *The Sketch Book*) is a clear example of the tension that Irving felt between the imaginative endeavor and the American cultural tendency.

Anyone who has ever journeyed to the Catskill Mountains and the Hudson River that meanders among those high hills should have little difficulty in feeling the drowsy, dreamy influence that hangs over the land and pervades the very atmosphere surrounding Sleepy Hollow, the setting that Irving describes in his story. The people, he says, "are given to all kinds of marvelous beliefs; are subject to trances and visions; and frequently see strange sights, and hear music and voices in the air." So does Irving set the stage for the wondrous tale of the schoolmaster Ichabod Crane and the Headless Horseman of Sleepy Hollow. As he does in "Rip Van Winkle," Irving goes to some lengths to create a sense of the past in "The Legend of Sleepy Hollow" that the United States did not have. In this by-place of nature, he says, "there abode, in a remote period of American history, that is to say, some thirty years since, a worthy wight of the name of Ichabod Crane." Ichabod is indeed a comic figure—"tall, but exceedingly lank, with narrow shoulders, long arms and legs, hands that dangled a mile out of his sleeves, feet that might have served for shovels" and "with huge ears, large green glassy eyes, and a long snipe nose, so that it looked like a weathercock perched upon his spindle neck." He is also a person with a strong imaginative faculty, who enjoys spending winter evenings with old Dutch wives exchanging frightening tales of ghosts and goblins, but then fearing on his walk home all the strange shapes and shadows that "beset his path amidst the dim and ghastly glare of a snowy night." He is particularly concerned that he might one night meet the legendary Headless Horseman, that Hessian soldier who lost his head to a cannonball.

Ichabod, too, has an eye for the women, especially the plump and rosy-cheeked Katrina Van Tassel, a lass of 18 years whose father is a farmer of some wealth. Not only does Katrina fire the schoolmaster's imagination, so too do the treasures of her father's farm: the geese, ducks, pigs, along with the fields of wheat, rye, and Indian corn. But another also is interested in Katrina, one Brom Van Brunt, a strong, arrogant, fun-loving, double-jointed man always ready for either a fight or a frolic. Often called Brom Bones because of his strength and power of limb, he is also a skilled horseman. Though he would have welcomed the opportunity for a physical contest with Ichabod, the latter is too wise to provide such, and, frustrated, Brom Bones is left to playing practical jokes on the schoolmaster, often in front of Katrina.

Both Ichabod and Brom Bones are invited to a quilting frolic at Mynheer Van Tassel's. Ichabod arrives on a broken-down plough horse with his knees nearly up to the pommel of the saddle, while Brom Bones gallops in on his handsome and spirited steed Daredevil. During the ensuing dancing, however, it is Ichabod who, with his feet clattering and limbs flying, is the talk of the other dancers, including his partner Katrina, leaving Brom Bones to sulk in a corner. Following the dancing, Ichabod speaks with Katrina, convinced that he now has won her affections. Irving declines to divulge this conversation except to say that the schoolmaster leaves "with the air of one who had been sacking a hen-roost rather than a fair lady's heart." Poor Ichabod mounts his decrepit horse and disconsolately begins his travel homewards.

As he approaches a bridge that has played a role in some of the legends of the area, Ichabod hears a sound and sees a ghastly shape looming off to the side. It is the Headless Horseman, with his head held on the pommel of his saddle. As the schoolmaster frantically attempts to flee, the apparition hurls his head at Ichabod, tumbling him from his horse. Following this meeting with the Headless Horseman, Ichabod is not to be seen again in Sleepy Hollow. All that searchers find is the poor fellow's horse and saddle and a crushed pumpkin lying nearby. The old Dutch wives, of course, believe that he has been spirited away. A more likely story is probably that of a traveler who maintains that he has seen the schoolmaster in New York and that he is now a lawyer and judge. Either way, it is Brom Bones who takes Katrina to the altar and who often laughs at the mention of the crushed pumpkin.

Like Rip Van Winkle, Ichabod Crane lives too much in the world of his imagination and does not fit into the mold of the success ethic of American development. Caught up in his own fears of the supernatural, he is not able to realize the maturity necessary for finding a place in the society of his time, at least in Sleepy Hollow. If he has found a new life in New York, then, also like Rip Van Winkle, he has made a success of his own failure—in his case by synthesizing reason and imagination as a lawyer and judge.

"The Legend of Sleepy Hollow" stands as one of Irving's best efforts in the short story and as a salient contribution to that genre. A master of style, he blends humor and sensibility in this story to give it both a charm and picturesqueness. Perhaps he did, as Herman Melville said, deal only smooth topics and did not attempt anything beyond his abilities. Still, he remains a significant voice in American letters.

—Wilton Eckley

———

LENZ.   See the Writers entry on **BÜCHNER, Georg.**

———

LEOPOLDINA'S DREAM (Los sueños de Leopoldina) by Silvina Ocampo, 1959

In "Los sueños de Leopoldina" ("Leopoldina's Dream"), collected in *La furia* in 1959, as in so many of Silvina Ocampo's short fictions, the possible and the impossible are brought together so effortlessly that we as readers are forced to question what we think we know about possibility and impossibility. The narrator of the story is Changuito, and he tells the story about a family in which all the women's names begin with the letter "L," from the youngest, Ludovica and Leonor, to Leopoldina who, by her own estimate, is about 120 years old. There is a significant generation gap between oldest and youngest. Leopoldina lives in a world in which miracles are commonplace. Ludovica and Leonor believe in miracles, too, but their faith is more worldly, more practical. Early on, they imagine their fame if they were to have a vision of the Virgin Mary.

For Leopoldina, however, miracles are simply a way of being in the world, not a way of getting ahead in it. Like so many of Ocampo's characters, she has the gift of prophecy. For 30 years, she has not left the house, and yet she knows everything that is going on outside, even before it happens—when the rains are coming, when the crops are ready for harvest.

Leopoldina's special gift is her ability to dream and often to bring objects out of her dreams and into the real world. Her dreams are modest, and so are the things she brings forth, stones, branches, feathers. No one has ever considered her ability to be of any particular value, but Ludovica and Leonor see the potential in it. They want her to dream of "precious stones, of rings, of necklaces, of bracelets. Of something that's good for something. Of automobiles."

At first, the girls are content to watch over Leopoldina as she naps in her wicker chair, hoping something valuable will turn up. When this doesn't happen, they encourage her to spend more of her time asleep by giving her heavy meals and strong wine and eventually by threatening to give her injections of narcotics to force her to sleep. Her dreams change, but she still doesn't manage to bring forth anything of interest to the girls.

Ludovica and Leonor threaten her again, and Leopoldina dreams a final dream, though she comes out of it apparently with nothing. The girls want to know what she dreamed about, but she and the narrator simply leave the house in silence. In that instant, without warning, a devastating storm sweeps across the land, destroying livestock and crops and carrying Leopoldina and Changuito away, out of the material world, like saints ascending into heaven.

Did Leopoldina foresee the storm or did she bring it out of her dream? Is the future already there, waiting for us, or is it something we create, willingly or unwillingly? Ocampo raises this question often in her writing, but it is a question she never answers. It seems clear, however, that miracles, if there are such things, are not solely for our benefit and exploitation. Leopoldina knows how to live with miracles and feels no need or desire to question them. For her, the gift is exactly that, a gift given freely, for no purpose, and received as such. When she is no longer permitted to accept the gift for what it is, she escapes, perhaps by her own choice, perhaps because of a higher power, or perhaps by chance.

There is another dimension to "Leopoldina's Dream." At the close of the story, Changuito informs us that he is Leopoldina's lap dog, the author of the story in his mistress's dream, and so it seems that the pages she brought out of that dream are the very pages we have been reading. Is this another miracle, a dog that can write? But who is the author here? Not Changuito, certainly, because he "wrote" the story only in a dream. Leopoldina? Again, this is not a simple question to answer. She dreamed the story, her own story, the story that creates her as a character in a fiction, but was the dream her own creation or another gift?

Ocampo is raising an interesting question about the very process by which literature comes into being. Perhaps the writer is not responsible for his or her stories, as Leopoldina is not responsible for her dreams. Perhaps the stories that create the writer as surely as the writer seems to create them are written by another, by a character in a dream, as Changuito writes the story of his mistress. Perhaps the writer's job is not necessarily to be creative but to be receptive, to receive the dream and bring the pages out into the waking world.

There is something viciously circular in all this. It is the writer who, in some sense, makes the dream, the dream that makes the story, and the story that makes the writer who makes the dream. As readers, perhaps our task is to read the stories, as we have read Leopoldina's story, and so learn to dream for ourselves, discover our own stories written there, and bring those stories out into the world where they will create us. As Ocampo has said, "What matters is what we write: that is what we are, not some puppet made up by those who talk and enclose us in a prison so different from our dream."

—Welch D. Everman

THE LETTER
by Somerset Maugham, 1926

So tightly plotted and richly characterised are Somerset Maugham's 90-odd short stories that quite a few have transferred very successfully to stage and screen. "Rain," which eventually was to earn its author a million dollars one way and another, has been dramatised, filmed three times, turned into a musical, and even formed the basis of a ballet. "The Letter" has done almost as well, both as a long-running play featuring Gladys Cooper and as a classic Hollywood film starring Bette Davis.

"Fact is a poor story teller," Maugham once observed. It rambles, is haphazard, and tails off untidily. The writer, he claimed, needs to impose the discipline of a beginning, a middle, and an end. In the case of "The Letter," however, he used material taken direct from real life, and, except for one element, remained faithful to the facts. On his travels around Malaya he had been told by a lawyer in Singapore about a notorious murder trial of 1911. A headmaster's wife in Kuala Lumpur had shot the manager of a local tin mine when he called on her one evening in her husband's absence. He attempted to kiss her, she said, and after he turned out the light she groped for the switch, somehow touched a revolver, and fired, not once but six times. The prosecutor established that she had previously been on intimate terms with the man and that, since then, he had acquired a Chinese mistress. Public opinion sympathised with her and saw her as a heroine defending her honour. She was found guilty but received a pardon after a petition on her behalf. The one element Maugham added to this ready-made plot was a letter in which she had begged the man to come and see her that evening while her husband was away. According to Maugham's version, this letter is in the hands of the jealous Chinese mistress who only agrees to release the incriminating document in return for a large sum of money raised by the husband.

Maugham himself, a successful and experienced playwright, dramatised "The Letter": it opened with the stage in darkness and the sound of six shots fired rapidly one after another. By that time, fortunately for the author, the woman who had inspired his story was dead. While another of his works set in Malaya, *The Painted Veil,* evoked the threat of a libel action which he was obliged to settle out of court, "The Letter" escaped any hint of legal problems. Even so, his habit of putting people and places into his Malayan stories with only a slight change of name caused much indignation in the colony among those who had shown him hospitality and spoken freely to him. It was as well that he never went back there after the 1920's.

"The Letter" was published in 1926 in a collection entitled *The Casuarina Tree* along with other Malayan stories. The characters are firmly drawn with Maugham's usual economy: the husband Robert Crosbie, a big fellow, gentle but stupid; the wife Leslie Crosbie, outwardly graceful and fragile, inwardly made of steel; the lover Geoff Hammond, a handsome and dashing ex-soldier; and the Crosbies' lawyer, the discreet and worldly-wise Mr. Joyce, through whose eyes the action is described. Another character, one of the few Chinese depicted in any detail by Maugham, is the clerk Ong Chi Seng, a Cantonese. After studying at Gray's Inn, Ong is working in Mr. Joyce's office to gain further experience. He is the go-between who alerts Joyce to the letter, arranges the negotiations (with a satisfactory commission for himself), and ensures that the letter and its revelation about Mrs. Crosbie's affair with Hammond is suppressed. Interestingly enough, the device of the crucial letter was a standby in the Edwardian theatre (Lonsdale was to use it also in his play *The Last of Mrs. Cheyney*) when Maugham wrote his first plays. The invention of the telephone put paid to that.

Why did Mrs. Crosbie shoot her attempted seducer six times? This is the only point that worries the cool, analytical lawyer Mr. Joyce. It is also the factor that sustains interest in what would otherwise be a straightforward case. Each time Mrs. Crosbie gives her account of the incident she remains composed and does not vary it in the smallest detail. The man tried to rape her, she repeats, and as for the six shots, well, her memory must have failed her at this juncture. Joyce reflects to himself, in typical Maugham style, "The fact is, I suppose, that you can never tell what hidden possibilities of savagery there are in the most respectable of women." Then, when the existence of the letter is revealed through the agency of Ong, he realizes that Hammond, as she later confesses to him, had been her lover for years. Her anger at his desertion of her for the Chinese mistress became uncontrollable, and that was why she fired at his corpse until there were no more bullets left in her revolver.

Since Mr. Joyce and his wife are close friends of the Crosbies, the lawyer is ready to commit an unprofessional act. The letter is duly bought at a price which nearly bankrupts Crosbie, the damning evidence is destroyed, and Mrs. Crosbie is acquitted amid public acclamation on grounds of justifiable self-defence. The story does not have such a happy ending as all that, for the dull-witted husband at last sees that his marriage is ruined and his wife continues to be tortured by her lover's rejection of her. A frequent theme with Maugham is the unexpected depths that a human being can reveal under stress: here it is Mrs. Crosbie who proves his point. Wracked by pain and rage, her normally placid face turns into "a gibbering, hideous mask," and one "would never have thought that this quiet, refined woman was capable of such fiendish passion." To a certain extent the lawyer Mr. Joyce, who plays the part of *raisonneur*, is Maugham himself, urbane, unshockable, studying human emotion with the clinical remoteness of the doctor he once was. Although the content of "The Letter" is melodramatic—as a play it was highly sensational—its luridness is contained by Maugham's deliberately matter-of-fact style. He often used a professional man as the medium for telling a story, thus adding to the authority and credibility of the narrative. After all, you do not lightly challenge the opinions of your lawyer or your medical adviser.

—James Harding

A LETTER ABOUT EMILIA (Carta sobre Emilia)
by Adolfo Bioy Casares, 1962

The complexity of love is a predominant theme in much of Adolfo Bioy Casares's work. Such titles as *Guirnalda con amores* (1959, Garland with Love) and *Historias de amor* (1972, Love Stories) indicate the prevalence of the love theme. The story "A Letter about Emilia" ("Carta sobra Emilia") originally from the collection *El lado de la sombra* (1962, The Shady Side), opens with the epigraph "crazy love." The love relationship between Emilia and the narrator reveals itself to be complex role play in which each character assumes the identity of another in a reversal of male and female roles. Thus Bioy Casares plays with double realities.

The first-person narration from the artist seems reliable and is the only source of descriptions of his love for Emilia. The artist details this love relationship in a letter to Mr. Grinberg, the artists' father figure. Grinberg warns him against losing his identity by working with many different women instead of concentrating on finding the one universal image of woman.

When the artist sees Emilia being photographed by Mr. Braulio he remembers Grinberg's advice and becomes inspired. He requests Braulio to ask the girl to model for him. Emilia reluctantly appears at the artist's stately home and says that she will work for him although she has limited experience. At the moment she enters the house, the narrator believes that he falls in love with her.

The artist begins a very rigid daily routine. After completing his chores, he draws from memory until early evening when Emilia arrives to sit for him. After the sitting, she leaves and goes to a club. She first asks the artist to accompany her, but to prove his superiority, he refuses. The ambiguous relationship between Emilia and the narrator has sexual overtones. They have discussed marriage, an idea to which, supposedly, both partners show disdain. They are both set in their own ways, and, as later discovered, Emilia has another lover.

Emilia relates all of her experiences from the club to the narrator, including advances made by other men. The narrator, concerned about her promiscuous behavior at the club, asks her to be careful. She remonstrates him for worrying about advances that she considers inconsequential. Emilia claims that she will reform her behavior since she is now a "different" woman with stronger and renewed feeling for the narrator. After listing the names of other men with whom Emilia has had romantic encounters, the narrator states that she has finally reformed. He uses as proof the fact that she stops relating stories of new adventures to him.

Emilia proposes a change in their daily schedule. Throwing caution to the wind, she spends the night with the artist. The following morning they walk back to her house as the sun is coming up. The narrator experiences a momentary feeling of invincibility. After this emotional high he begins to suspect that their love affair is not a normal one. His fears are confirmed the night of their anniversary celebration, when Emilia, contrary to her normal behavior, orders him to close the window he left open for her. The role reversal deepens when the narrator notices that Emilia is imitating his walk and acting more masculine. Believing that her change in mannerisms indicates her growing impatience to leave, the artist suggests that they go out. The woman opposes leaving and addresses the narrator as Emilia, arrogantly demanding that he be quiet. The misidentification of the male protagonist—Emilia assigning her role to the narrator—at first is interpreted by the narrator as an affirmation of their love for one another. He believes Emilia is the perfect lover since she is losing her individual identity. Upon further thought, however, he decides that his lover's behavior is the result of another man's influence. The artist reasons that Emilia is in love with another man and that she fantasizes about being with the other man when she is with him. She assumes the persona of the other male and therefore places the artist in the role of Emilia.

The narrator accepts this situation, stating that all love is absurd, and that, since communication is illusory, no one can really know what others are thinking and feeling. He resolves to remain in his relationship even if it is determined by another man's actions. As long as Emilia and the other lover do not interact differently, the relationship of the narrator and Emilia also remains constant. If the actions of the other man change dramatically, then the narrator would see the effects in Emilia's actions towards him.

The existence of double roles emphasizes the importance of the search for reality and identity within the text. The change of identities confuses the narrator's perceived reality. Love impairs the judgement of the narrator to the extent that living a double identity is preferable to his own identity. The artist's conviction, stated early in the story, that nothing is so bitter as to lead a double life, is forgotten. He accepts his role play and allows himself to be manipulated by Emilia, therefore appearing as many of Bioy Casares's characters in a game of multiple identities and realities.

—Joan E. Clifford

THE LIBRARY OF BABEL (La biblioteca de Babel)
by Jorge Luis Borges, 1944

Jorge Luis Borges's standing as one of the greatest and most influential writers in the history of the short story seems assured. At least a half a dozen of his stories are widely and frequently anthologized and appear destined to survive the test of time. Perhaps the most famous of these is "La biblioteca de Babel" ("The Library of Babel"), collected in *Ficciones* (1944).

"The Library of Babel" is characteristic of Borges's short fiction in any number of ways. It is stylistically adventuresome, provocatively witty, and profoundly philosophical. It is also deceptively personal— "deceptively" because it is not always easy to find Borges the man behind the coolly ironic facades employed by his narrators.

Perhaps the facet of Borges's short fiction that the reader will be drawn to first is his style. In the early part of the 20th century, writers began rejecting the label "tales" in favor of "short stories," implying a movement away from the romantic, supernatural, and melodramatic and toward the sort of realism that we now associate with James Joyce, Katherine Mansfield, Sherwood Anderson, and others. Borges signaled another sea-change in the short story a half-century later by adopting the label "fiction" in place of "story." "The Library of Babel" shows why the fiction label is more appropriate. "Story" implies certain givens: a few richly drawn characters with whom we are concerned, a conflict, action rising toward a climax, and some sort of resolution of conflict. But where is the action in "The Library of Babel," rising or otherwise? What, exactly, is the conflict? One could not spend more than a short paragraph discussing any or all of the "characters" in the fiction. Rather than reading "The Library of Babel" as a story, the reader will more profitably view it as a fictional essay, with an introduction of subject matter (thesis), an exposition of ideas, and a conclusion—and it comes complete with footnotes!

Not all of Borges's fictions follow an essay format, but "The Library of Babel" and similar works show his willingness to forego any of the traditional assumptions about what makes a story a story in favor of whatever suits his purposes. It is this breaking the stranglehold of the realistic short story that makes Borges such an important and influential figure.

The revolution was not just stylistic, of course. The vast majority of writers before Borges (and his mentor, Kafka) had striven to capture in their fictions a mundane, quotidian reality. Borges showed that one could write about anything, real or imagined. Again, "The Library of Babel" is a marvelously entertaining example. The setting is no less than the universe, which here is made up of an infinite number of hexagonal galleries containing shelves of books and populated, of course, by librarians. The galleries are connected by narrow hallways, down which the librarians roam in their quixotic and almost always failed quests to find certain bits of information or, more generally, the ultimate truths of the library-universe. The term that best describes Borges in this and other fictions is "witty," but witty in the 18th century sense of intellectually fanciful, ingenuous.

Borges is rarely merely witty, however, certainly not in "The Library of Babel." He, his narrator, and the librarians who haunt their carrels are concerned with the most fundamental questions: Where are we? Why are we here? What is *here*? How do we know what we know? As is always the case with Borges, by the end we are no more—indeed, far less—certain than we were at the beginning. The reason for the uncertainty is the nature of the library (universe). The vast majority of the books contain what appears to be gibberish, or at least languages unknown to the librarians. The occasional recognizable phrases—"*Oh time thy pyramids*" (translated by James E. Irby)—are generally as inegmatic as life. The only thing certain about the exceedingly rare books (frequently fragments) written in a recognizable tongue is that somewhere in the universal library is another that contains the first's refutation. Where, then, is truth, certainty? Nowhere in the Library of Babel.

Borges's stories are so fanciful and his narrators so coolly and distantly analytical that it is sometimes difficult to sense Borges the man. But he is there, a profoundly affecting presence for those who read sensitively. Perhaps the fact that he worked as a minor functionary in a library while writing the story (and later was director of the Argentine national library) helps the reader to locate him. It is also interesting that Borges once observed that the most important event of his youth was his father's library. One might expect that an occurrence, a happening, would be that most important event—not a static *thing*. But the paradox is an important and painful irony for Borges. Throughout his writing is opposed the man of action and the man of contemplation—rarely to the latter's advantage and, hence, rarely to Borges's. Throughout "The Library of Babel" one senses more than anything else the total futility of the librarians' pursuits. Their world is the world of the intellect, of language, of literature; and it is ultimately a loveless, meaningless chaos.

Near the end the narrator notes that suicide among the librarians has grown more frequent over the years. The reader finds little solace in the narrator's prediction that although "the human species—the unique species—is about to be extinguished . . . the library will endure." And probably Borges didn't either.

—Dennis Vannatta

———————

THE LIBRARY WINDOW
by Margaret Oliphant, 1879

Of the 36 or so short stories, some almost novellas, written by Margaret Oliphant, twelve deal with the supernatural. All but two of them—"A Christmas Tale" (1857) and "The Secret Chamber" (1876)—date from the last 17 years of her long working life. It was a life of ceaseless literary industry, a wider range of travel experience than fell to the lot of most Victorian women writers, a less than happy marriage, and the burden in widowhood of having to support a tribe of hard-up and generally unsuccessful relations; hers was a life of human loss and disappointment, since most of those on whose behalf she had laboured were invalids or failures who predeceased her.

Her attitude to the supernatural was, of course, related to her views on religion. Brought up in the Free Church of Scotland, which she rejected because of its narrow views, she viewed the High and Low harsh rivalries of Victorian England, in which she spent her mature years, with a greater degree of detachment than Trollope. Unlike previous writers on the supernatural, from Defoe to Poe and Radcliffe, Oliphant was not so much concerned with creating horrorful suspense as using the device, in Margaret K. Gray's words, to "create in the reader feelings of sympathy and understanding for the beings who came back into the world of the living." In other words, to make us reexamine our own sense of human values.

"The Library Window," published in *Blackwood's Edinburgh Magazine* in January 1896, and collected in *A Beleaguered City* (1879), became the most popular and frequently reprinted of all Oliphant's stories. It differs from her other supernatural stories in that its central spirit is earthbound, and that a kind of secular consolation supplants any religious overtones.

The narrator, a young girl, dreaming and much given to poetry, has gone to stay with her aunt, Mistress Mary Balcarres, in a house in "the broad High Street of St.

Rules." A window recess looks out onto a library window on the other side of the street. It is not difficult to establish that the fictional St. Rules is, in fact, St. Andrews, a place Oliphant visited as a girl, and where there is a row of windows such as are described in the story, along the library buildings in South Street.

The story takes place around St. John's Eve (Midsummer Eve), when, in the north of Scotland, there is scarcely any night, and in the curious sub-daylight people often "see things." Aunt Mary is holding a party for her "old ladies," described with wonderful vividness. They include the sinister old Lady Cornbee wearing a diamond in a claw-like setting that to the niece seems sinister—to bite and sting, a symbol of sexual passion, perhaps. Present, too, is dapper little old Mr. Pitmilly. The talk turns to the library window opposite the house. Is it a real window, or merely a painted imitation, such as the dummy windows blocked out to evade Pitt's window tax (not abolished until 1851)?

Aunt Mary's unsureness, attributed to the misting sight of her declining years, arouses the girl's curiosity. For hours she secrets herself in the recess and stares across at the window, until she sees deeper and deeper into a dark room where, before a large picture, a man wearing ruffs sits writing at a desk. Eventually, he looks round and waves at her, but without recognition. Then she can no longer see anything. The illusion vanishes. A Baker's boy throws a stone at the window, and the stone falls back to the street. Against her will, she is taken to a *conversatzione* in the library. An open window where the painted bars should have been lets in air and light.

The image of the writing man at the window recalls Lockhart's memorable account (in his *Memorials of the Life of Sir Walter Scott*) of just such an image of Scott (Oliphant's literary hero) seen writing in the study of his house in Castle Street, Edinburgh, and may have suggested the initial theme of this story.

But the denouement is disturbingly original. The narrator, on losing her vision, becomes pale, ill, and distressed. No one else can see anything but a false window. In the end, Aunt Mary, who clearly knows more than she at first pretends, realizes that the girl is what she calls "one of us" ("of that kind," different from the rest). "It is a longing all your life after," Aunt Mary explains. "It is a looking—for what never comes. The eye is deceived as well as the heart." The ghost is that of a scholar who preferred his books to his lady, "one of us," though "a light woman." In vain did that lady sit in the recess, wearing the claw-set diamond ring as a token sign to her lover who never came. Eventually, her brother found out about her abandonment and avenged her by killing the scholar, the ghostly writer wearing ruffs.

Oliphant creates a remarkable sense of unease, not only in the story's setting, but in the ambivalence of the relationship of the various characters. Sir Walter Scott, through his Edinburgh window, was seen throwing down each completed sheet to the floor. The scholar never seemed to get to the end of a sheet. What was he writing? Why did he desert his lady for the pursuit of some strange unspecified sort of knowledge? What made her, seemingly constant, "a light woman"? Was there not some moral, an over-extreme justification, in the brother's anger? What are Aunt Mary and her niece? The memorable quality of the story is created precisely because none of these mysteries are ever really answered. The figures flit before our imagination as if in a tragedy really seen behind silent glass. When a very old Lady Cornbee dies and leaves the ring to the narrator, she locks it in a box and leaves it in a house she never thereafter visits.

In later life, widowed young (like Oliphant), the narrator fancies she sees the scholar's face looking at her from a crowd. Momentarily, such glimpses were consoling; once, returning from India, with no one to welcome her, she suddenly saw his face on the quay, but when she had got ashore "he had disappeared as he did from the window, with that one wave of his hand."

There is no horror, just a sad image of lost possibility without even moral justification, the rights and wrongs of it all, called into question.

"In the end, one cannot *explain* "The Library Window," says that champion of the recent Oliphant revival, Merryn Williams. "It was part of her creed that a great many things could never be explained by limited human beings, which is why so many of her stories have an open ending." Yet the image of that scholar at the window lingers in the mind's eye long after many a mere corporeal fictional image has dissolved from the reader's memory.

—Maurice Lindsay

LIEUTENANT GUSTL.   See NONE BUT THE BRAVE.

LIFEGUARD
by John Updike, 1962

The story "Lifeguard" by John Updike was first published in *The New Yorker* and then included in the collection *Pigeon Feathers* (1962). One wonders, at first, whether the story should be considered a piece of fiction at all; the piece is entirely a meditation by the speaker, punctuated by only the most perfunctory kind of "action," in the form of the predictable pastimes of the crowd on the beach. In the end, though, one sees that the absence of events in the story is itself a reflection of its religious theme: the relationship of a teeming world and human race to a rather lonely, if superior, person (divine or human) who is, or thinks of himself as being, above that world, involved in but also detached from it, both its creator and its helpless observer. The substance of the story, then, becomes fiction in a somewhat altered sense, a rendering of various modes of imagining, making, creating.

It is easy enough to read "Lifeguard" as an allegory in which the speaker stands for God, as for a kind of portrait. As God, the lifeguard sits high on his "elevated . . . throne," surmounted by a (red) cross, "attentively perched on the edge of an immensity" and privileged with a panoramic view of space and time (which he can play backwards, like a film). He feels amusedly superior to the fumbling or superficial efforts by theologians and other religious writers, serious and popular, to understand him. He finds it hard to envisage his own ceasing to exist. He utters edicts: "Be Joyful is my commandment." The early reference to the skin as a disguise invokes the Christian doctrine of the Incarnation. His great "exercise" (a pun, for the lifeguard/God is the only inert figure on the scene) is "to lift the whole mass into immortality," a heavy task in light of the commonplace unworthiness of human beings en masse. Above all, his role is to save, though so far no one has called on him to do any such saving.

One can also read "Lifeguard" more literally, as a self-portrait of a young man who, presumably conditioned by his career as divinity student, has acquired the habit of taking cosmic views, of the world, of people, and of himself. ("Divinity student" is another pun; the protagonist is both divinity and human student, a word that, incidentally, comes from the Latin for "being eager," or "desiring.") He, too, exists to save people, though up to now there has been no real call for his help, despite the adulation paid him; as with God, his protective surveillance of his flock amounts to mere admonitions from above, alarmed tweetings of a whistle.

Perhaps the most significant thing about "Lifeguard," whether we read it allegorically or literally, is the view it takes of humanity. When the speaker says that he grounds his sermon in the complementary relationship between the "texts of the flesh" and "those of the mind," he means by "flesh" not merely the near-"naked" beachgoers but also whatever is incarnate, that is, human. As divinity or divinity student, the lifeguard is disturbingly ambivalent toward the myriad creatures under his care. He regards all this teeming, often banal, fleshliness—the "vast tangle of humanity"—with paternalistic solicitude mixed with repulsion, but he also regards it with ineffectual desire. As human lifeguard, the speaker is powerful and superior, but he confesses wistfully that he "would love" and hopes, just as wistfully, that "someday my alertness will bear fruit; from near the horizon there will arise, delicious, translucent, ... the call for help, the call, a call, it saddens me to confess, that I have yet to hear." An act of deliverance, the lifeguard has already told us, is how he envisages love: in loving intercourse, we descend into a world of "grotesque and delicate shadows," in effect, a submarine world, so that we can bring the loved one "into this harbor," this "security." An all-powerful chivalric rescuer, he is impotent until and unless someone acknowledges a need to be rescued. The speaker has, as yet, found no one who wants to share this amatory immersion with him, no equivalent of the "vivacious redhead" flirting with her boy friend and "begging to be ducked."

As deity, the lifeguard represents a god who, being God, likewise enjoys plenary power but is also dependent on a reciprocal recognition by human beings that they need to be saved. The humans on the beach are, at most, only vaguely aware of such a need. Like the literal lifeguard's admiring public, the teenage satellites who pay him impersonal homage (he is "edible" but not one of them), this God is remote, isolated, lonely, unfulfilled. Science has begun to discredit his reality as a person and nature's ruler: the ocean "no longer comfortably serves as a divine metaphor; the immortality to which he wishes to lift "the whole mass," the "clot" of humanity, has become a matter of the survival of cells, the biological cells of the body or the communal cells that constitute the beehive. Confused by sheer human multitudinousness, he is not confident that he can adequately manage the Last Judgment, or "final Adjustments Counter." The "sea of others exasperates and fatigues" him most on Sunday mornings, when church attendance has depressingly declined. Like the actual lifeguard, this God is the only being in the entire vulgar, seething scene who sits idle, isolated from activity, honored but essentially ignored. His commandment "Be Joyful" seems less a gesture of magnanimity toward human beings than an acknowledgement of his own removal from human joy.

The speaker is entirely accurate, then, in telling us that the "sermon" we are hearing has to do with the relationship of flesh to mind, that is, of humanity to the transcendental. This holds true on both literal and allegorical levels, the levels of both poignant human longing for love and uneasy divine hegemony. Either way, to quote William Blake, "Eternity is in love with the productions of time."

—Brian Wilkie

THE LIFTED VEIL
by George Eliot, 1859

George Eliot was well-known as a rationalist and agnostic. Her story "The Lifted Veil," initially rejected by her publisher, John Blackwood, appears at first sight uncharacteristic: it combines a Gothic story of second sight with science fiction (a transfusion of blood into the veins of a corpse immediately after death). The title comes from Shelley's "Sonnet": "Lift not the painted veil which those who live/Call Life." The poet warns that "behind, lurk Fear/and Hope ... I knew one who had lifted it ... he sought,/For his lost heart was tender, things to love,/But found them not, alas."

This is the plight of Latimer, the story's narrator. He is unloved by his elderly father, scorned by his athletic brute of an elder brother. Latimer is sickly but with the ambiguous gift of telepathy: he carries the burden of the thoughts, often vulgar and trivial, of those around him but for self-protection conceals this talent. We learn at the beginning that Latimer also has second sight: he foresees his own approaching death when "no one will answer by bell." Latimer is educated, not at Eton and Oxford like his brother, but at Geneva, where young George Eliot, similarly deprived of formal education, reinvented herself by first starting to write her journal. There he makes a friend, Meunier (a name taken from a celebrated preacher Eliot heard there). This story, apart from *Impressions of Theophrastus Such*, is her only first person narrative.

The story is about the pain and danger of the power to "see" more than other people. Latimer is a poet *manqué*: he has "the poet's sensibility without the voice," a fear Eliot was possibly overcoming, painfully, for herself at the time of writing, when she had already published *Scenes of Clerical Life* and *Adam Bede*. The loss of visionary power was an anxiety that remained with her, as shown by the poem "Armgart" and the fate of Alcharisi in *Daniel Deronda* (1876): both singers, Armgart and Alcharisi end up singing out of tune. Latimer's brother Alfred is engaged to the enchanting, but cold and scheming, Bertha, whom Latimer is also fascinated by.

The name Bertha resonates as that of the destructive dark madwoman in Charlotte Brontë's novel, *Jane Eyre* (1847). The destructive blonde beauty looks forward to Rosamond Vincy in *Middlemarch* (1872) and Gwendolen Harleth in *Daniel Deronda*. Latimer has a prevision of Bertha as his wife, hating him and secretly wishing he would kill himself. "I saw the great emerald brooch on her bosom, a studded serpent with diamond eyes. I shuddered—I despised this woman with the barren soul and mean thoughts, but I felt helpless before her."

Before going to Prague, Latimer has had a grim vision of the city as like something out of Dante: "the blackened statues, as I passed under their blank gaze, along the unending bridge, with their ancient garments and their saintly crowns, seemed to me the real inhabitants and owners of the place, while the busy, trivial men and women, hurrying to and fro, were a swarm of ephemeral visitants infesting it for a day." He imagines these stone bodies as "worshipping in the stifling air of the churches." When he reaches Prague, it is as he has imagined it.

F.C. Pinion believes that this is "the heart of the story": in it "lies the more generalised fear of an era when the old, other-worldly religion is dead, and people, without a new religion, pursue their activities mechanically, with no high purpose." He also suggests that "her feelings of rejection by kindred and friends are implicit in the hero's bitterness; and her own religion, as opposed to . . . other-worldly religion . . . is heard in the brief overtone of 'I thirsted for the unknown: the thirst is gone. O God, let me stay with the known.' . . . It is noticeable that, the more spiritually deadened Latimer becomes through being cut off from his fellow-men, the more subject he is to visions like that of Prague."

Latimer visits a synagogue. Using almost the same words from her own journal, Eliot has Latimer say, "I felt a shuddering impression that this strange building, with its shrunken lights, was of a piece with my vision. Those darkened dusty Christian saints, with their loftier arches and their larger candles, needed the consolatory scorn with which they might point to a more shrivelled death-in-life than their own."

The elder brother is killed in a riding accident, and Latimer inherits. He marries Bertha, who persuades him she loves him. Her thoughts, alone among those of his acquaintance, remain impenetrable to him. She is cold and distant. When a servant dies, Meunier carries out an experiment in blood transfusion, which briefly revivifies the corpse. The dead woman reveals she has bought poison, at Bertha's instigation: "You mean to poison your husband." After this, Bertha and Latimer separate, and Latimer, knowing he is about to die that day, September 20, 1850, struggles to write his story. He associates Bertha with water-nixies, malignant water-spirits in Germanic legend, and with Lucrezia Borgia, seen in a picture attributed to Giorgione.

Sandra M. Gilbert and Susan Gubar, in *The Madwoman in the Attic*, give a 20-page analysis. They identify Bertha with Milton's Eve in association with Satan, point to her "great rich coils" of hair and the serpent brooch "like a familiar demon on her breast." They also associate Latimer, in his vulnerability and isolation, with the monster created by Mary Shelley's Frankenstein.

Bertha also carries reminiscences of John Keats's poem, "Lamia," about a sorceress-serpent who is implicitly compared to Nereids, water spirits, and who glitters in "sapphires, greens and amethyst/And rubious argent." Falling in love with a young man, she manages to change her outward form to that of a beautiful woman, and marries him, but after marriage reverts to her true form as a deadly snake.

—Valerie Grosvenor Myer

LINEMAN THIEL (Bahnwärter Thiel)
by Gerhart Hauptmann, 1888

Of the ten short stories Gerhart Hauptmann wrote during his long career *Bahnwärter Thiel* ("Lineman Thiel") is the

best known and the finest. One of his earliest works, it was first published in 1888 in the Munich-based naturalist periodical *Die Gesellschaft*. Set in the countryside southeast of Berlin where Hauptmann, then a sympathiser of social democracy, was living, the story grew out of his frequent contacts with local working people, including railwaymen. In many respects it can be seen as a representative work of naturalism. Sexuality and crime, two typical naturalist themes, both figure prominently; the central character Thiel is firmly situated in a working-class milieu; and Hauptmann adopts a quasi-scientific approach in exploring the factors determining his behaviour.

The story traces Thiel's development from the death of his first wife Minna in childbirth, leaving him a small son Tobias, to his second, rapidly concluded marriage with the dairy-maid Lene, who bears him another child. Because of his sexual dependence on her, Thiel for a period tolerates Lene's maltreatment of her step-son, but when Tobias is fatally injured by an express train on his stretch of track, the lineman's subsequent derangement culminates in the violent murder of Lene and her baby, after which he is admitted to a mental asylum in Berlin. The events, though shocking in the manner traditional to the novella as genre, are not sensationalised. Hauptmann grants the railway accident just a few lines, viewed from the limited perspective of Thiel, whilst the murders are not described at all. His concern is rather to explore character and milieu, hence the subtitle "A Novella-like Study."

As the title proper suggests, Thiel's character dominates the tale. Whilst the wives remain one-dimensional, Minna characterised by her spiritual hold on the lineman, Lene by her physical one, Thiel himself is the subject of a complex, finely drawn portrait. Significantly, we never learn his first name. He remains *lineman* Thiel because the job in large measure makes the man. A cog in the efficient machine of the Prussian railway system, Thiel himself leads a routine life, organized on systematic lines and with a fixed schedule. His behaviour is often mechanical, like the trains in whose service he is employed. This service resembles that in the army, Thiel taking great pride in his uniform and manning his post with all the discipline and punctuality associated with the Prussian military ethos. His workplace deep in the pine forest also isolates him from human company for long hours, thus intensifying his propensity to brood on things, and, importantly, encouraging his mystical tendencies.

A regular church-goer, steeped in Protestant tradition, Thiel makes his workplace a sacred shrine to his late wife Minna, of whom he has ecstatic visions during night-long sessions of Bible-reading and hymn-singing. This "spiritual intercourse" is intended to quell the pangs of conscience he feels about his abject sexual dependence on Lene, his puritanical upbringing having led him to associate desire with depravity. However, his guilt and self-disgust are compounded when he realizes how much he is neglecting Tobias's welfare to satisfy his own physical needs. By dwelling on Thiel's Herculean physique, Hauptmann also indicates a potential for violence, although this is held in check by a fundamentally phlegmatic temperament. He is a giant, but a gentle one, his metabolism rendering him so sluggish and passive that only a severe shock to his system will prompt a violent reaction.

All these factors—social, cultural, psychological, and physiological—interact to determine and make plausible Thiel's breakdown and the ensuing murders. Yet they are not sufficient causes. He is not simply a victim of circumstances or a creature of physical impulses. Hauptmann often portrays him deep in thought, implying that he has genuine options, however limited, and because we witness him wrestling with awkward alternatives, we sympathise with, rather than merely pity, him.

A wide variety of techniques encourage this sympathetic response. For long stretches, an impersonal narrative voice provides an objective, analytical account, investigating cause and effect in a detached, non-judgemental manner consistent with the scientific approach of naturalism. But this omniscient stance is not maintained throughout. Less reliable passages of reported opinion and deceptive appearances intervene to complicate the picture, whilst at points the narration is subtly reticent, hinting at Thiel's complex inner life, but leaving the content of his broodings to the reader's imagination. Switches in perspective are also exploited. Sometimes we view Thiel through Lene's eyes, on one occasion through Tobias's, but in the build-up to the accident and the murders Hauptmann increasingly adopts Thiel's own perspective, forcing us to share his reactions, either by using interior monologue or, more frequently, free indirect discourse. The immediacy thus achieved is further enhanced by a switch to the present tense for fully two pages after Tobias's accident, ensuring that we remain "on the spot" throughout the lineman's most traumatic experience.

Another device used to chart Thiel's progressive disorientation is description, mainly of natural landscape, but also of the railway track and the passing trains. Five lengthy descriptive passages interrupt the otherwise economical narrative, all symbolically evoking Thiel's state of mind or mirroring his situation. Thus the imagery of a monstrous iron mesh for the railway track and the web of a giant spider for the telegraph wires alludes to his ensnarement by Lene, whilst a violent storm reflects his inner turmoil and threatened loss of control. The fact that Thiel is acutely impressionable, hypersensitive to sounds, colours, and light partly justifies the view of many critics that Hauptmann's descriptive technique is Impressionist. But in instances where Thiel is unconscious of his surroundings, grotesque imagery and garish colours seem rather to anticipate the techniques of German Expressionist writing. These devices can appear somewhat forced, especially when compared to the understated symbolic effects Hauptmann derives from the concrete particulars of Thiel's everyday life, but they do extend the story's stylistic range beyond the confines of programmatic naturalism, thus contributing to its lasting appeal.

—David Horrocks

LITTLE RED RIDING HOOD (Rotkäppchen) by Jacob and Wilhelm Grimm, 1812

"Rotkäppchen" ("Little Red Riding Hood"), a fairy tale whose canonical version comes down to us from the brothers Grimm, is considered, by the critic Linda Degh, to be one of the most popular stories of all time. While the original version was a traditional folktale, and the brothers Grimm claimed to reproduce exactly the traditional version, the way that they combined features of different regional versions to make a tidy fictional narrative converted it into a short story.

According to their notes, they put together several plots from several regions to make the fairy tale more attractive.

They wanted to present many versions as one, and in this, according to folklorist Alan Dundes, "they committed a cardinal sin in folk lore." But if it was inaccurate as folklore, it was highly successful as an aesthetically satisfying and entertaining fictional narrative.

The Grimms got their version of the tale from a French Huguenot storyteller, Marie Hassenpflug, which leads many researchers to suspect that she led them to Charles Perreault's version. Thus, according to Jack Zipes, we have the Grimms' "literary reworking of a literary reworking of the original oral tale." The main change that the Grimms made was in giving the story a happy ending, which probably accounts for its great popularity.

As most readers will remember, "Little Red Riding Hood" tells the story of a charming little girl whose mother sends her to take some bread and wine to her sick grandmother. Since the way to the grandmother's house passes through a forest, she is warned by her mother not to go off the path, or to speak to anybody. On her way through the forest she runs into the wolf, and despite all the warnings of her mother, she stops to chat with him. By cleverly questioning her the wolf discovers where the grandmother lives, and, distracting Little Red Riding Hood into picking a pretty bouquet, he beats her to the house. He devours the grandmother, and, disguising himself in her cap and gown, lies down in her bed to wait for his next victim, Little Red Riding Hood. When the girl arrives, she is surprised to find the door open, but, despite her anxious feelings, she walks into the house. She notices that her grandmother looks very different and that her cap is pulled down to partially conceal her face. In a famous dialogue, Little Red Riding Hood notices that her grandmother's ears, eyes, and hands are strangely larger than before. When she says, "Grandmother, what a terrible big mouth you have!," the wolf leaps out of bed and gobbles her up. In Perrault's version, this is the end of the story, but the Grimms provide a convenient huntsman, who, finding the satiated wolf snoring in the grandmother's bed, cuts open the wolf's stomach and liberates Little Red Riding Hood and her grandmother. After this close call, Little Red Riding Hood piously decides that she will always stay on the path and never disobey her mother again.

The Grimms also extend the plot of the fairy tale with a second encounter with a wolf who tries to entice Little Red Riding Hood off the path on her way to her grandmother's. But this time, she goes straight on her way and tells her grandmother about it. By the time the wolf arrives and pretends to be Little Red Riding Hood, they have prepared a terrible punishment for him. When they won't let him in, he hides up on the house roof to wait for Little Red Riding Hood to come out so that he can sneak up and devour her under cover of darkness. But the grandmother tells Little Red Riding Hood to fill the big stone trough in front of the house with the water she has used for making sausage; the wolf smells the sausage, stretches his neck further and further toward it, and finally slides off the roof and drowns in the water.

The Grimms' version of this fairy tale became not only the subject of folklorists' criticisms, but also evoked a wide range of interpretations from literary critics of different schools. The myth/ritual interpretation falls into two kinds: seasonal ritual where Little Red Riding Hood represents spring, escaping from the winter wolf; or puberty rites, where Little Red Riding Hood's journey symbolizes the various stages of the girl leaving home, experiences the onset of menses, and fulfilling set tasks in preparation for marriage and maturity. Psychoanalytic critics since Freud have paid an incredible amount of attention to this fairy tale. A characteristic reading is that of Erich Fromm, who finds in every detail a symbol of the dangers of sex. Fromm sees the "little cap of red velvet" as a symbol of menstruation and the mother's warning "not to run off the path" as a clear warning against the sexual danger. For him, the tale "speaks of the male-female conflict; it is a story of triumph by man-hating women, ending with their victory." Jack Zipes, on the other hand, argues that the story is "a male creation and projection . . . and viewed in this light, it reflects man's fear of women's sexuality—and of their own as well."

But however complicated and varied these theoretical interpretations become, they have had little effect on the tale's continuing popularity with readers. Though the Grimms did not intend to address an audience primarily of children, it is as a children's story that the tale of Little Red Riding Hood achieved lasting appeal.

—Marina Balina

THE LONELINESS OF THE LONG-DISTANCE RUNNER
by Alan Sillitoe, 1959

"The Loneliness of the Long-Distance Runner" by Alan Sillitoe, is a first-person monologue, spoken by a 17-year-old inmate of an English Borstal, or reform school. Smith, the only name this character receives, has been imprisoned for the break-in of a local bakery and received a two-year sentence, but he has discovered a way to improve the conditions of his stay in jail. The warden of the reformatory has his heart set on the winning of the Borstal Blue Ribbon Prize Cup for Long-Distance Cross-Country Running (All England), and Smith, the fastest runner in the institution, needs to do nothing but train for the race. He can trade his daily chores for the mitigated freedom of early morning runs in the countryside around the reformatory.

Yet things are not quite as simple as they seem, and the nature of the monologue, crude and colloquial in language and tone, underlines the tremendous class distinction between what the narrator Smith terms the "in-laws" and the "out-laws." In-laws, like the warden and his cronies, speak Oxford English and support and perpetuate the system, while the residents of the Borstal are denizens of the working class who have nothing to lose. It might seem that Smith would have little choice or desire not to play along with the powers that be, but during his stay in prison he has developed his own personal and idiosyncratic sense of morality. For him, to win the race would be tacitly to accept the premises of a self-serving establishment, and his own sense of defiance and self-worth can only be maintained by his individual conception of honesty. As he says, "It's a good life, I'm saying to myself, if you don't give in to coppers and Borstal-bosses and the rest of them bastard faced in-laws."

While it might appear that Sillitoe is simply delineating a social and economic struggle between the classes in postwar England, in a short story that was first published in 1959, the situation is much more complicated. In Smith's world, there is no such thing as solidarity and brotherhood among the underclass. In a series of flashbacks that illuminate his early life and the robbery that got him into his immediate trouble, we find that he has always been alone. Smith and his pal Mike are clever enough to hide their loot so that the police will not catch on to two teenagers who have suddenly become relatively wealthy, but the boys are even more wary of their own neighbors who will turn them in out of spite and jealousy. Loyalty is something that simply does not exist in this circumstance, and trust is a silly idea for fools. In the end, one can only be true to one's self, a self that can make mistakes but will never let you down. Loneliness becomes a natural condition; as Smith says, "I knew what the loneliness of the long-distance runner running across country felt like, realizing that as far as I was concerned this feeling was the only honesty and realness there was in the world."

Smith's own experience bears out his conclusions, especially in his family life, where his father died horribly of stomach cancer after a lifetime of slaving away in a factory and his mother was constantly unfaithful to her husband while he lived. The death benefit of five hundred pounds is quickly spent on clothes, cream cakes, a television set, and a new mattress for his mother and her "fancyman," and things are immediately back where they began. Thievery is all that the boy knows, and even the army can provide no outlet. As far as Smith is concerned, patriotism is another false idea concocted by the government to protect its own advantage, and life in the army is little different from life in prison. At least, in declaring himself a robber and an outlaw, Smith is overtly acknowledging the state of warfare that exists between people like him and the people in power, landowners and politicians who look like fish gasping for breath when the sound is suddenly turned down in the middle of their speeches on the television set.

Powerless as he may be in an England that views him as only another cog in the economic machine that grinds out more comfort for the rich, Smith seizes on the moment to shake his fist in the faces of the in-laws as he turns toward home in the Borstal race. Though he is far ahead of his nearest competitor, he slows down and then stops before the finish line, allowing his rival enough time to catch up and to win the race. Smith's gesture is meaningless to everyone but himself. "The governor at Borstal proved me right; he didn't respect my honesty at all; not that I expected him to, or tried to explain it to him, but if he's supposed to be educated then he should have more or less twigged it." But, if nothing else, the long-distance runner has remained true to himself, has not been duped into believing the false promises that would only enslave him even further. There is virtually no hope of social change in the bleak universe that Sillitoe has created, but there remains a kind of comfort in the affirmation of the individual human spirit that will not be broken down. If truth and honesty can exist anywhere, Sillitoe asserts, they survive in one's ability to look squarely at one's self in the face of all the odds. Paradoxically, honesty may reside in recognizing and accepting the dishonesty of contemporary existence.

—Michael H. Begnal

LOOKING FOR MR. GREEN
by Saul Bellow, 1968

One of Bellow's most famous fictional creations, Herzog, wonders "what it means to be a man. In a city. In a century.

In transition. In a mass." Bellow has said that Herzog appeals "to those who yet hope to live awhile." The hero of "Looking for Mr. Green" (published in 1968 in *Mosby's Memoirs and Other Stories*), George Grebe, is one of those who yet hope to live awhile. Grebe is Bellow's typical 20th-century character, having "an immense desire for certain durable human goods—truth, for instance, or freedom, or wisdom" (from his acceptance speech for the Nobel prize for literature in 1976). As the epigraph from Ecclesiastes makes clear, Grebe also believes in doing a job well, and by the end of the story he is himself a modern "Koheleth" (Hebrew for the Greek "Ecclesiastes" or "preacher")—although not as confident and conclusive a one as some critics argue.

Bellow's philosophical meditation on the human condition is played out in this story, as in his other fiction, against the landscape of Chicago, that "cultureless city pervaded nonetheless by Mind." For Bellow, the city challenges its inhabitants to combine the physical and spiritual, just as America does. The narrator of Bellow's *The Bellarosa Connection* laments his lack of a European Jewish tradition: "You pay a price for being a child of the New World." That price is, quite literally, dollars. Indeed, according to one interpretation, the whole story is an allegory of this condition of consumer capitalism. If a lawyer's client does not pay him, the lawyer asks for the case to be delayed by saying, "Mr. Green is not here"—meaning he hasn't been paid yet.

The story is mostly written in free indirect discourse, from Grebe's point of view. From the outset, we are given contradictory images of Grebe's work. On the one hand he "feels like a hunter" in pursuit of his quarry; on the other, the relief checks in his pocket remind him of "player-piano paper," as if humans are ciphers who will emit the appropriate noise when called upon. Grebe is similarly contradictory, both a thinker and someone avoiding "definiteness of conclusion." The sentence "Nothing was deliberately hidden" catches Grebe's ambiguousness perfectly, since something *may* still be hidden, by chance, and the sentence refers equally well to the city he tries to penetrate.

His boss Raynor (his name suggesting "rain or snow") encourages Grebe and the reader to think symbolically. "The closer you come to your man the less people will tell you," he says, echoing what Marlow discovers in his similar search for Kurtz in "Heart of Darkness." Raynor adds an overt metaphysical dimension to Grebe's quest: he suggests that he and Grebe might swap positions, save for his law degree (later we learn that the two of them work in what used to be a factory, reinforcing the anonymity of a dystopian bureaucracy); he and Grebe are similarly cultured, quoting Latin to each other, trying to reconcile their learning with expediency, the city with the mind. Raynor admits that "there ain't any comparison between twenty-five and thirty-seven dollars a week, regardless of the last reality"; he gets a bonus for seeing life (in a parody of Matthew Arnold's terms) "straight and whole." Aware that he lives in what he calls "the fallen world of appearances," Raynor nevertheless yearns for "the last things that everything else stands for." His talk of Tanganyika reminds us that even civilization is a culture-specific veneer, and that our notion of meaning may not fit there, or even in Chicago, where black people cower in the honeycomb of rundown tenements.

The allegorical dimension of Grebe's quest thus established is reinforced by his first descent into the underworld, the furnace room of his first building. Indeed, as he questions person after person the reader senses a pilgrim-age, perhaps through Dante's rings of hell. Grebe hopes that each one may be a possible guide through this inferno, this "terrific, blight-bitten portion of the city" where everyone seems an immigrant or refugee, and destitute. Staika is perhaps the most obviously allegorical character in that she lives by literally giving her blood to the system. Grebe sees her as representing "the war of flesh and blood" which will wear down governments and nations, but which has nothing to do with the desires of the spirit. The unemployed who are Grebe's clients and about whom Staika rails may be more deeply alienated than she suspects, may be rejecting the whole "fallen world of appearances" out of a profound spiritual revulsion.

The quest takes on a mood of increasing absurdity and black humour: from the Italian shopkeeper with his horror of alien immigrants, to the old man who refuses to accept a check until his identity is truly established. Both voice truths: that each culture has its own sign system, and that western society's system is based on the cash nexus (in Field's pun, "Money, that's d' sun of human kind").

The reading process parallels Grebe's ("he needed experience in interpreting looks and signs") as we are confronted with realistic details which sometimes do, and sometimes do not, seem to slot into an allegorical pattern. What are we to make of his card which reads "TULLIVER GREEN—APT 3D"? Is his quarry like the quester, since his name begins with the same three letters? Is he a pastoral ideal (see Hardy) at odds with this squalid inner city ghetto? Is he relevant or "apt" to Grebe's own condition? Should he be found and realized in "three dimensions"?

Grebe's splendid meditation reminds one of Thomas Pynchon on entropy, Henry Adams's imaging of the United States as a dynamo. Grebe sees his city as "a faltering of organization that set free a huge energy"; he finds this energy revitalising rather than entropic. If he can only sort out those who need relief checks from those who do not (like Pynchon's "Maxwell's demon"), he will be doing his part to maintain the system in its differentiation. He becomes heartened by the constant rebuilding of Chicago. The city reminds him of the covenant or agreement of its citizens to transform, by sheer imagination, appearance into reality. He almost succeeds in finding intellectual satisfaction in the cash nexus, until he contemplates on the one hand, the millionaire Yerkes's interest in astronomy, and on the other the continuing poverty of the inner city. The system fails materially (why are people starving?) as well as spiritually (why else would Yerkes "offer money to be burned in the fire of suns"?).

His final confrontation, not with Mr. Green but with a naked woman in a surreal "high box" of a house, is deliberately fantastical. It does not connect with anything, although Grebe makes it connect by an act of will, his decision that "the woman stood for Mr. Green." This is not enough to assuage his spiritual anxiety, for he realizes that he comes as "emissary from hostile appearances"—that is, from the world of money and signs which pit people against each other and do not satisfy the soul. The verb form of Grebe's conclusion ("he could be found") is carefully chosen to slip between enacted past and conditional future, since Grebe is unwilling to rest with a semantic agreement and "yet hopes" for a centre where the minotaur will stand revealed.

One detail typifies Bellow's genius for threading onto one spool the contingent and the allegorical: as the woman signs the check, Grebe "came near believing that someone was standing on a mountain of used tires in the auto-junking shop next door." Who is this person? Someone who is observing his deceit to report to Raynor? Someone (God?)

who approves of his decision and blesses it? Or the devil atop his entropic garbage heap, laughing?

—David Dowling

THE LOONS
by Margaret Laurence, 1970

Throughout her life and work, Margaret Laurence maintained an abiding interest the Métis, that crossbreeding of French, Scots, and Indians which began during the days of the fur traders in the area of the Red River, in what is now Manitoba, Canada. As she said, in *A Place to Stand On* (edited by George Woodcock, 1983), "There are many ways in which those of us who are not Indian or Métis have not yet earned the right to call Gabriel Dumont [Louis Riel's lieutenant] ancestor. But I do so, all the same. His life, his legend, and his times are a part of our past which we desperately need to understand and pay heed to." Theirs is a story of repression which recapitulates the theme of female oppression of much of Laurence's writing: just as the Métis tried to maintain their independence from a paternalistic Canadian government in Ottawa, so Vanessa MacLeod struggles to escape the Brick House and her Grandfather Connor's influence, and Morag Gunn tries to reassert her inheritance.

"The Loons" is the fifth of eight stories collected into the story sequence/novel *A Bird in the House* (1970). The main force of the book comes from Vanessa as she recalls (and sometimes recalls recalling) scenes from childhood, with varying degrees of insight. Here we see her trying to comprehend Piquette first as "other," then as outsider, and finally perhaps as "sister." "The Loons," tells us that the Tonnerres "did not belong" anywhere, but in *The Diviners* we learn from Piquette's brother that their father "was pretty tough on my mother. She was Métis, too, from up Galloping Mountain way. She thought Manawaka was gonna be the big city." On the first page of *A Bird in the House* we are told that Vanessa's grandfather brought tree seedlings from Galloping Mountain for his property, because "they were the trees for him" (he also wears a coat made from a bear from that same mountain). If Piquette is a descendent from that wild north, so is Vanessa. In 1885, Métis leader Louis Riel led the North West Rebellion, was defeated, and executed; in the story Vanessa says, "the voices of the Métis entered their long silence." After a long silence she, too, is learning to use her voice by writing her story; that is why, according to Peter Easingwood, Piquette's story "still remains to be realised as a vital part of Vanessa's own background and cultural heritage."

Everything in Laurence's economical writing is both realistic and symbolic: the wild strawberries beautiful in their setting but adulterated when a Tonnerre youngster sells them "bruised" door to door; the squirrels at the cottage which will be tame by summer's end; the reason Piquette is there—it's a convenient way of getting rid of Ewen's mother with her wearying aristocratic pretensions. Even names are important: "Piquette Tonnerre" means literally "the thunder which pricks or stings"; Diamond Lake is renamed Lake Wapakata even as the tourists move in and the Indians move out. If Piquette is true to her father's name, Lazarus, she is in need of a miracle, to raise her not from the dead but from her tubercular lameness. If she is true to her own name, she will rouse Vanessa in some way—but perhaps not, since the only thunder in the story comes from the café jukebox.

Taking her cue from Métis poetess Pauline Johnson (1861-1913), Vanessa is convinced of Piquette's indigenous nobility, but soon discovers that "as an Indian, Piquette was a dead loss." It's with her father rather than with Piquette that Vanessa listens to the call of the loons. The scene is made richer by a knowledge of the whole book; Vanessa felt her father's life had been wasted by female oppression, a fact confirmed by her discovery after his death of secret love letters from a French girl he had met during the war; also, the dominant motif is the trapped bird, and the loon contributes to this idea that only the freed bird can truly sing. Vanessa's feeling that she had "somehow failed" her father links these two ideas together: had she uncovered Piquette's native nobility and helped her "sing," she would also have affirmed her father's secret spiritual freedom.

Four years later, Vanessa's disappointment with Piquette has changed to "pique" and even revulsion. She looks at Piquette (earlier her expression was "as though she no longer dwelt within her own skull") "unmasked" (another motif from the book) in its desire for happiness, and glimpses the predicament of the "marginalised indigene."

Three years later (at the age of 18) Vanessa returns to the lake and equates the "half mocking and half plaintive" loon with Piquette's "unconscious" knowledge of her own impending destruction. Just as Ewen's dock has been replaced by the "government pier" and the lake shore by tourist cottages, so the indigenous Indian has become extinct, unable to find a place to be. As Vanessa's mother says, "Piquette didn't get out."

But there's still something of the younger Vanessa in this easy explanation—the would-be writer who liked the idea of doom and destruction, especially for someone like Piquette who tries to cross boundaries and exchange the loon for the Flamingo dancehall. The careful use of tenses ("It seemed to me now") makes it clear that we are getting the 18 year old's judgments, not those of the 40 year old writer, who can therefore play an ironic light on these conclusions. The story is full of images of not knowing or not wanting to know ("I did not want to see her"), which should warn the reader against taking Vanessa's insights as exhaustive or indeed valid. Contrast this dangerous sentimentality with Morag Gunn (in *The Diviners*) who ponders Piquette, arrested "for outrageously shrieking her pain aloud in public places. . . . What went wrong? Or did it go wrong so long ago that there is now no single cause or root to be found?" At the end of that novel there are several songs written by Jules, including "Piquette's Song," with the final stanza, "My sister's eyes/Fire and snow—/What they were telling/You'll never know." Both these appraisals point to the complexity of human motivation and psychology rather than to Vanessa's notions of racial otherness and doomed extinction. After Morag gives Jules her eye-witness account of the burning of Piquette, he tells her, "By Jesus, I hate you . . . I hate all of you." That is a far more raw reaction, more difficult to deal with. Perhaps it's that hatred that Vanessa wants to avoid. Piquette's tragedy, therefore, is not that of the vanished Indian, nor that of the marginalised "other," but of the oppressed "other," usually the female. After all, Piquette's life with her own people is as cruel as her life with white people, not because she is Métis but because she is a woman.

When Laurence wrote to her editor about this story that "it isn't the strongest story in the collection," she was sensing the complexity of the subject and its unfinished treatment here. But when we place the story into its larger contexts, *A Bird in the House* and Laurence's other work, we can see "The Loons" as embodying her best qualities: an apparent economic simplicity masking and exposing some of the most complex problems of contemporary living.

—David Dowling

LOST IN THE FUNHOUSE
by John Barth, 1968

John Barth is no doubt best known as a novelist, but his one collection of short stories, *Lost in the Funhouse: Fiction for Print, Tape, Live Voice*, is so startling in its virtuosity that Barth's place in the history of short fiction is also assured.

"Lost in the Funhouse" is the pivotal story in a collection of related fictions that trace the conception, youth, maturity, decline, and renewal of not only a writer (Ambrose) but also life and fiction in general. In "Lost in the Funhouse" Ambrose travels to an amusement park on the Maryland shore with his parents, brother Peter, and Peter's girlfriend Magda. As the title suggests, Ambrose gets lost in the funhouse. More important, by the end he realizes the direction he will henceforth take in reference to art (being a writer) and life (specifically in terms of sex and love). The tragic implications are felt through the realization that the choice between art and life of necessity excludes thereafter the one not chosen. Ambrose, a good deal reluctantly, chooses art.

The story is an example of metafiction—as are most others in the collection—because it is not only about Ambrose's trip to the park but also about writing a story about Ambrose's trip to the park. The narrator—Barth? an older Ambrose?—frequently steps in and comments on the writing strategy he is at that moment using. For example, after the introductory section the narrator observes, "The function of the *beginning* of a story is to introduce the principal characters, establish their initial relationships, set the scene for the main action," etc. The narrator seems to be trying not so much to instruct his reader but to keep straight in his own mind what he should be doing. Indeed, the narrator is having as much trouble with his story as Ambrose is with puberty. At the end of the same paragraph in which the narrator summarizes the purposes of the beginning, he suddenly realizes that he is five pages into his story without having gotten past the beginning: "And a long time has gone by already without anything happening; it makes a person wonder. We haven't even reached ocean city yet: we will never get out of the funhouse."

Already we can see the funhouse taking on at least two connotations. It is the physical structure in which Ambrose gets lost; it is also the story that we are reading and with which the narrator is struggling, constantly getting bogged down or lost, introducing events out of sequence, jumping ahead to the funhouse before the family even reaches the park, offering more than one ending, and so on.

The funhouse is also sex and love, as the opening lines suggest: "For whom is the funhouse fun? Perhaps for lovers. For Ambrose it is *a place of fear and confusion*" (emphasis Barth's). Why cannot Ambrose simply relax and have fun? For one thing, Ambrose is just entering adoles-

cence, and the funhouse has clear sexual connotations for him and the narrator (a confused adolescent of a writer): "If you knew your way around in the funhouse like your own bedroom, you could wait until a girl came along and then slip away without ever getting caught, even if her boyfriend was right with her. She'd think *he* did it! It would be better to be the boyfriend, and act outraged, and tear the funhouse apart. . . . Not act; *be*." The direction the thought takes in this passage is from furtiveness (the phantom molester) and dissimilation (*act* outraged) to actual passion (*be* outraged). It is a path Ambrose would like to take, but cannot.

His problem is not simply that he is an adolescent, typically confused about sex and wary of the future, but that he is a budding writer, a calling that will set him apart from life-beyond-art. His recollection of an earlier sex game with Magda indicates his problem. He recalls during the sex act, "standing beside himself with awed impersonality"; and recalling the same scene later in the story, "But though he'd breathed heavily, groaned as if ecstatic, what he'd really felt throughout was an odd detachment, as though someone else were Master. Strive as he might to be transported, he heard his mind take notes upon the scene: *This is what they call* passion. *I am experiencing it.*" What Ambrose is already doing, obviously, is distancing himself from experience, taking notes, preparing to write. Later, fantasizing about finding his great love, he imagines her as someone who will appreciate him as a writer.

The end of the story finds Ambrose lost in the funhouse of fiction, committed to it, but committed with a sense of resignation and loss: "He wishes he had never entered the funhouse. But he has. Then he wishes he were dead. But he's not. Therefore he will construct funhouses for others and be their secret operator—though he'd rather be among the lovers for whom funhouses are designed."

One of the most provocative short stories of the post-World War II period, "Lost in the Funhouse" shows Barth at the top of his form: as a great innovator whose fictions would be worth the reader's time for their technical virtuosity alone but also as a writer with a profound grasp of the human spirit in conflict with itself, its world, and its art.

—Dennis Vannatta

THE LOTTERY
by Shirley Jackson, 1949

First published in *The New Yorker*, as many of Jackson's stories were, "The Lottery" was an early narrative of a kind of existentialist, world-weary angst that shocked readers. Mail at the magazine was heavy with readers' reactions to the calmly objective recounting of the ritualized murder of the unlucky housewife and mother, Tessie Hutchinson. In the 1940's and the 1950's, when the story quickly became a classroom staple, few people felt it was significant that the victim of the orderly fertility process was a woman. Today, that recognition underlies much of the effect of the story.

Married to literary critic Stanley Edgar Hyman, Shirley Jackson bore four children and tried to face their unconventional life with humor, most of the time avoiding the depression that troubled her intermittently. Much of her fiction is either purposefully unrealistic or it is focused on the darker side of family life (*Hangsaman*, about a schizophrenic adolescent; *We Have Always Lived in the Castle*, about a demonic child). Its tone resembles that of "The Lottery" in its gradual accumulation of relentless—yet seemingly harmless—details. Part of the horrific effect of Jackson's writing stems from the author's technique of unfolding plot as if it were conventional, even though it is not.

In "The Lottery," for example, the reader is first lulled into an appreciation of the beautiful June 27th morning, when the 300 people of the village are gathering stones, positioning themselves to await the drawing, and beginning the interaction that Jackson describes so carefully, and so naturally. Her use of archetypal names for the leaders of the benevolent patriarchy—Mr. Summers, Mr. Graves—seems mundane, until the reader comes to realize that one of the members of the close-knit community is about to be stoned to death by the other residents. Then the idyllic quality of the "summer" quickly metamorphoses into the solemn tone of "graves."

The interaction between men and women of the community is also telling. The men, particularly Old Man Warner who is drawing for the 77th time, accept the meaningless ritual, and will not hear of questioning its reason or its propriety. When Mr. Adams, whose name suggests some power to originate, tells old Warner that a nearby village is thinking of giving up the lottery, Warner's reply is "Pack of crazy fools." Like other primitive fertility rituals, this one supposedly enhances the crop, brings the community prosperity, and is life-affirming. But others in the crowd lament how quickly the years go by, and that it seems as if last year's lottery has just been held. Clearly, opinion within the community is divided as to the usefulness and the efficacy—not to mention the humanity—of this lottery.

Yet when Tessie Hutchinson complains after her husband Bill has drawn the marked slip of paper, it is Bill who tells her to shut up. The polarization of the crowd as they hope it is not any of the children who are chosen shows again the persuasiveness of the patriarchal order: sons have priority as do children in general; mothers, however, are expendable. To Tessie's low-voiced comment that "It isn't fair," none of the villages responds with sympathy; even her best women friends throw rocks at her, under the justification that the old custom, the old order, is the right premise for living life. And with unexpected rapidity, after the first stones are thrown and Old Man Warner urges everyone to continue the stoning, and Tessie protests more loudly, Jackson's narrative ends abruptly: "'It isn't fair, it isn't right,' Mrs. Hutchinson screamed, and then they were upon her."

Jackson's brilliance is to convince the reader that the residents of the community are normal, ordinary people; and that the rule that they accept so unquestioningly is no more extreme than other orders that comprise patriarchal law. Once the reader has accepted this premise (a convention that the quiet conversation among the villagers makes possible—just as no one is upset about this, so the reader can maintain tranquility), Tessie's lateness, her complaining, and her protests at her incipient death seem almost annoying. The reader quickly fits into the community, and accepts the arguments of Old Man Warner as if he or she also had some vested interest in the traditions of the ritual. Society is like that: it makes people behave, and forces established customs on them in lieu of the new.

Worse, the reader in irritation with Tessie almost echoes Bill Hutchinson's voice when he tells his wife to shut up, inhumane and indefensible as such a reply is. At that point in the story, Tessie is worried for her husband and her children as much as for herself; and her protests are what one might expect from any person who cared about her family. The disjuncture between the community's quiet and Tessie's voicing her concern about her husband's drawing the marked slip of paper—behavior which is itself very normal—is part of Jackson's powerful irony.

Bringing in the small children as she does, from early in the story (they are gathering stones, piling them up where they will be handy, and participating in the ritual as if it were a kind of play), creates a poignance not only for the death of Tessie the mother, but for the sympathy the crowd gives to the youngest Hutchinson, little Dave. Having the child draw his own slip of paper from the box reinforces the normality of the occasion, and thereby adds to Jackson's irony. It is family members, women and children, and fellow residents who are being killed through this orderly, ritualized process. As Jackson herself once wrote, "I hoped, by setting a particularly brutal ancient rite in the present and in my own village, to shock the story's readers with a graphic dramatization of the pointless violence and general inhumanity in their own lives." "The Lottery" has made many a reader do just that, as well as to question their unthinking acceptance of tradition.

—Linda Wagner-Martin

LOVERS OF THE LAKE
by Sean O'Faolain, 1957

Although he has produced books in almost every genre of writing, Sean O'Faolain's literary significance must be judged by his own admission and by the opinion of the critics on his carefully wrought short stories. O'Faolain has acknowledged the influence of Chekhov and Turgenev. He lauded their effectiveness in conveying atmosphere and mood and their ability to combine realism and lyricism. Chekhov, in particular, was significant, O'Faolain said, because he probed "the inscrutable mystery of human suffering," and because he was an author who seemed "to compass all life and balance all life, and yet leave us questioners of life at the end." Such a writer has "detachment without loss of emotion; passion without loss of justice; judgment without loss of sympathy."

O'Faolain's story "Lovers of the Lake" (collected in *The Finest Stories of Sean O'Faolain,* 1957) fulfills the Chekhovian canon in observing a middle-aged couple, Dr. Robert Flannery and his mistress Jenny. They have been romantically involved for six years, but in the story they reveal unknown qualities to each other and surprise themselves with hidden depths of conflict and ambiguity. Jenny's sudden decision to go on a religious pilgrimage to Saint Patrick's Island confounds not only her lover, but even astonishes her. The pilgrimage is not a mere visit. It is a penitential ordeal where one must endure a sparse liquid fast for two days, walk barefoot on stones for hours, and pray endlessly, staying awake all night in the island's basilica. Although hundreds of visitors participate in this ritual, Jenny often finds herself isolated among the crowds, stripped spiritually and emotionally bare as she ponders the mystery of her own personality and the contradictions and ambivalence of her love affair.

Even more surprisingly, the apostate Flannery belatedly visits the island and half-heartedly submits himself to some of the spiritual activities. He too is caught in a love-hate process. He cannot know himself, but he wants to participate in his mistress's deepest reflections and aspirations. Flannery rejects St. Augustine and his cry, "O God, make me chaste, but not yet," but he realizes Augustine's conflict is stirring in the turmoil of Jenny's heart and mind, even though she fights to deny this call. O'Faolain demonstrates the never-ending lure of religion on the Irish Catholic, which as James Joyce, for example, attested can never be totally removed from the Irish mind even when it is outwardly rejected.

O'Faolain subtly analyzes the struggle between the pull of the spirit and the weakness of the flesh, the appeal of mysticism and imaginative longings which haunt the Irish psyche. Jenny feels her adulterous affair is sinful but she cannot bring herself to break away from the physical desires that overwhelm her. Yet she performs her yearly Easter duty in which she promises to give up her lover. The struggle is not clear-cut. There are tugs in both directions, both felt and unfelt. At times the disparate elements seem to unify; on other occasions the ambivalence is intense.

Flannery is filled with disbelief, but, recalling his childhood religious training, he too feels the lure of the spiritual despite his medical profession and his rigid scientific training. Late in the story, his skepticism appears to waver somewhat, but his physical passion for Jenny seems to be too powerful to be more than temporally allayed by the island experience. He decided to visit Lough Derg to observe Jenny's spiritual exercises, but he is stunned to find mystical stirrings within himself.

The ambivalence of the lovers toward the island's mystical effects is subtly underscored by atmospheric contrasts. Away from the island the lovers live in a world of physical and sensuous delight. They eat and drink lavishly in the most expensive restaurants, romance and dance magically, watch fashionable tennis matches, and mingle in the best society. This carefree existence is contrasted with the somber, penitential life on the isolated lake island surrounded by nearby mountains of grim beauty. The ambivalence is not in humanity alone; nature interlinks with its grandeur and majesty, although soon turns into a fury by a deluging rainstorm that churns the island's surrounding water in a frightening manner.

Both Jenny and her lover are amazed by the spiritual depths they have experienced, but the lovers acknowledge that the lure of the flesh is just as strong as ever. Richard Bonacorso speaks of the couple's "inability to exactly and finally know who they are and what they believe." By enduring this state of mind, the protagonists underscore O'Faolain's emphasis on the spiritual-physical conflict that in some form or fashion engulfs all human hearts. Even if no apparent change has occurred in the lovers' relationship, they have come to realize uncertainties in the midst of certainty. O'Faolain is non-judgmental. He emphasizes that there are no simple solutions to life's complexities and ambiguities and that underneath the apparent happiness of various experiences an eternal note of sadness can never be separated from humanity's existence.

—Paul A. Doyle

THE LUCK OF ROARING CAMP
by Bret Harte, 1870

Bret Harte's "The Luck of Roaring Camp," originally published in the San Francisco *Overland Monthly* in August 1868, as the title story of an 1870 collection, and reprinted widely throughout the United States, established its author's reputation. It also set the form for the local color story, where setting is all-important: the events could occur in no other place, and character is shaped primarily by location. Harte was the first to describe the life of California Gold Rush mining camps for Easterners eager to hear what they were like. Even though his knowledge of them was not profound—he was a skilled urban journalist, not a miner—he conveyed a vivid picture that at the time appeared new and daring; in fact, he shocked prudish readers by making the baby's mother a prostitute and by letting his character repeat "d—d."

Harte prided himself on creating realistically mixed characters, meaning that his rascals are always capable of performing "a virtuous or generous action" (preface to 1870 collection of stories). "The Luck of Roaring Camp" aims to show that there is goodness and refinement of feeling in the most crude and degraded of human beings. When the only woman in Roaring Camp dies in childbirth, the men resolve to raise the baby and to provide him with a proper setting to grow up in. The significance of the child's arrival is indicated by parallels with the Christian story: Tommy Luck is the son of an unmarried mother and an unknown father; right after his birth, the miners file past to look at him and give him gifts; he elicits improvement from everyone who comes in contact with him. This theme lends itself to sentimental treatment, and indeed the story has been witheringly condemned as mawkish and false (see early editions of *Approaches to Literatures,* edited by Cleanth Brooks). "The Luck" is not vitiated by sentimentality: the events are sufficiently probable to make Harte's point, and, for the most part, he does not attempt to draw more pathos from the situation than is warranted. Surely it is true that the most unpromising men and women may have some potential for good, some aspirations toward achieving self-respect by maintaining decent standards of behavior. Harte never suggests that any of them are totally reformed. The first effect Tommy Luck produces is natural: the first man who files in to gawk at the baby takes off his hat without thinking; the others follow his example of showing respect, because good and bad actions are indeed catching among people who are neither all good nor all bad. From then on, the men develop altruism and propriety in about equal measure. Stumpy is chosen to take charge because he is the only man with paternal experience (obtained, comically, from fathering two families he has walked out on). He selflessly devotes himself to rearing the child as best he can. Personal washing, abstention from swearing, and whitewashing the houses mark improvements in social refinement. The events in Roaring Camp symbolically represent the actual history of the West, as the roughest frontier settlements became respectable towns.

It is plausible that an exceptional event could stir a community of normal men, debased principally by their social setting, into an altruism they had never shown before and a longing for the civilized standards they had left behind them. The advent of a baby could be sufficiently startling and new to regenerate their outlook and values, at least temporarily (Tommy is around for less than a year). It would indeed be a sentimental exaggeration if the miners developed a Wordsworthian love of nature from contact with the baby, but it is quite possible that, in looking for pretty things for him to play with, they would see a beauty in bits of quartz that they had missed when their only concern was finding gold. Kentuck reacts with fatuous sentimentality when he interprets Tommy's reflexive clutch of his finger as an expression of particular affection, but the fatuity is not Harte's. Many people who know babies better than Kentuck does are irrationally touched by this gesture from an utterly helpless creature that seems to be claiming our protection, a totally innocent one that seems to be expressing spontaneous affection for us. Although born of a degraded mother, Tommy is the one human untouched by the sordid influences of Roaring Camp. Indeed, a new-born infant is the only totally unspoiled member of any society, and thus it represents the natural potential for good in humankind and the never-failing possibility of a fresh start.

There are some undeniably sentimental bits in "The Luck of Roaring Camp." When the baby cried his first cry, "the pines stopped moaning, the river ceased to rush, and the fire to crackle. It seemed as if Nature had stopped to listen." Possibly the wind stopped bending the trees, although hardly because of Luck's birth; but obviously the river must have continued to rush and the fire to crackle. The ending, in which Kentuck is happy to die because "the frail babe" is "taking me with him" to heaven, is a blatant attempt to extract tears. Other unfortunate characteristics of popular 19th-century American prose might be noted, such as pompous diction (Cherokee Sal's "rude sepulture") and coy humor (Kentuck's neglect of washing as the result of "the carelessness of a large nature").

Nevertheless, "The Luck" shows high technical skill, for example, in the deft way Harte sets up the essential characteristics of Roaring Camp in his first paragraph. His portrayal of life in the mining camps has been attacked as superficial, but Mark Twain, who knew them well, greatly admired this story. And, beyond the vivid setting, the humor, and the pathos, there is a Romantic theme of some validity and lasting appeal—that there is potential goodness in all humans, despite what society has done to us.

—Katharine M. Rogers

LUVINA
by Juan Rulfo, 1953

Juan Rulfo became well known in Latin America in 1953 with the publication of his book *El llano en llamas (The Burning Plain)*, a collection of 15 stories. "Luvina" is one of the six published for the first time. The book, which introduces the reader to a world where fantastic and realistic motifs intermingle, was an immediate success in all Spanish-speaking countries. After 1955, when Rulfo published his novel *Pedro Páramo*, in which that same world is magnified, "Luvina" attracted added attention from critics, who found in the story certain elements that appear in the novel. However, "Luvina" stands by itself; in its few pages Rulfo was able to create an unforgettable tale based upon the description of a ghostly town, which becomes the real protagonist of the story, with its howling black wind, its white dust, its old people, its lonesome women—a dying place where dogs do not bark at silence, for they have all died.

Unlike many other authors, Rulfo wrote "Luvina" and his best fiction before he ever traveled outside his own country. All his fiction has as a setting his native state of Jalisco, in central Mexico, and his characters and anecdotes are drawn from that region. Central to his fiction is his technique of letting his characters tell the story in their regional language, but artistically elaborated. Thus, not only in "Luvina," but in all his stories, the reader finds a deep sense of place. As Octavio Paz has stated, Rulfo is the only Mexican writer "to have given us an image—rather than a mere description—of our physical surroundings."

An important aspect of those surroundings is to be found in "Luvina," and, two years later, on a larger scale, in the novel *Pedro Páramo*. Comala, where the action of the novel takes place, and Luvina, are both dilapidated towns where the few surviving inhabitants are presented as living ghosts. The origin of Rulfo's sense of place can be found in his first seven stories published between 1945 and 1951, although in none of them is the description of a desolated town the central theme of the story. One story ("The Hill of the *Comadres*") ends when the people begin to abandon the town, but the haunted nature of the community is not the theme of the story, as in "Luvina."

What Rulfo has said about the origins of his novel can be applied to "Luvina." As he stated during an interview, "*Pedro Páramo* represents the desire to give life to a dead town; that town lives again in the imagination of my characters." And that is precisely how the story of Luvina is presented. The school teacher, after having lived in Luvina for 15 years, relates his experiences to a person who is on his way there. Unlike the protagonist in *Pedro Páramo*, who dies soon after arriving in Comala, the narrator in "Luvina" was lucky enough to get out and tell about his horrible experiences.

The reader is taken to Luvina only through the imagination and words of the unnamed teacher, who meets the other person at a country store and there, while drinking warm beer and mezcal, unfolds his vivid recollections. His story becomes starker by the silence of his listener, whom the reader assumes is there, eagerly taking in every word of the speaker. Neither does the storekeeper, Camilo, interrupt the narrator's monologue. The only other voices heard are those of children playing outside in the dusk. There are, however, a few interruptions by an omniscient narrator, as when he mentions the children's shouts, and at the end when he tells the reader that the teacher has fallen asleep, and the only sounds now are those of a near-by river and the faraway shouting of the children.

The teacher cannot forget the lost years spent in Luvina; but he especially remembers the first night, when he arrived with his wife Agripina and his three children. The first night was the most horrible in his life, without food, and without a place to sleep, for the town had no eating place or inn. They finally slept in the church, an empty old shed with a leaky roof, without doors, and not even saints to pray to. And there was always the wind. He soon discovers that the few inhabitants of Luvina are old men and women abandoned by their husbands, who come to see them once a year, like the rain storms.

When the teacher first heard the name Luvina, he says, it sounded like a name made in heaven; but it turned out to be a purgatory, a place where death was the only hope. The creation of this magical atmosphere is accomplished by associating strong emotions with popular realistic images, a common stylistic device in Rulfo's prose: Luvina "is the place where sadness rests . . . like a large plaster weighing on the living flesh of the heart"; you can feel the constant wind of Luvina "boiling inside you, as if it were removing the hinges of your bones"; if it stops, the sun gets too close to Luvina and it sucks out your blood and the little water you have left in your skin, according to the old men who live there.

As the story unfolds the reader passes from the real to the unreal, or vice versa, as when the bats in the church turn out to be women dressed in black; or like the old men who cannot leave town because they are taking care of their dead, who "live" there and cannot be left alone. These and other phantasmagoric images, with which the narrator reconstructs his years in Luvina, are contrasted to the realistic images of the place where the story is being told. It is a place where there is life, food, drinks, happy children, a river. This weaving of fantastic and realistic images gives the story a magic realism tonality, a characteristic found not only in "Luvina" but in all of Rulfo's fiction, which has made his work so popular and influential in the Hispanic world.

—Luis Leal

M

A MADMAN'S DIARY.   See THE DIARY OF A MADMAN, by Lu Xun.

THE MAGIC BARREL
by Bernard Malamud, 1958

Critics have long regarded "The Magic Barrel" as quintessential Malamud—in form, content, and perhaps most of all, in moral vision. In the story, Leo Finkle, an unmarried rabbinical student more familiar with books than with life, had been advised that he would find it easier to land a pulpit if he were married. Since Finkle has had virtually no experience in matters of the heart, he reluctantly agrees to engage the services of a professional matchmaker. Thus the wheels of Finkle's amorous quest and its ironic initiation are set into motion. Pinye Salzman is not only a matchmaker as colorful as Finkle is drab, but he is also the catalyst who forces Finkle to see how sterile, how spiritually improverished, his life has been.

Initially, the shy rabbinical student is radically different from the mercurial matchmaker (Finkle represents the force of law while Salzman stands for the power of flesh), but it soon becomes clear that Salzman, for all his vulgarisms, betrays a "depth of sadness" that Finkle uses as a convenient mirror for his own.

The progress of the typical Malamud protagonist nearly always involves identification with suffering and some strategy for taking on the burdens of others. In Malamud's most earnestly serious novels, similar movements are chronicled both with a straighter face and a tongue more prone to lashing out at social injustice than lodging ironically in its cheek. Nonetheless, comic misfortunes dog his protagonists' collective heels. In Finkle's case, sympathy is as much his leitmotif as Salzman's is fish. Each of the much-handled cards from Salzman's "magic barrel" represent a person whose aloneness is a counterpart of his own.

That Salzman plays the con man to such a willing dupe is hardly surprising, for Finkle has the words "live one" written all over his face. At a used-car lot he would no doubt kick tires and play the role of a discriminating consumer; at the matchmaker's he eyes each new prospect with similar suspicions. No matter, because so far as Salzman's sales pitches are concerned, the two commodities are virtually the same: "Sophie P. Twenty-four years. Widow one year. No children. Educated high school and two years college. Father promises eight thousand dollars. Has wonderful wholesale business. Also real estate. On the mother's side comes teacher, also one actor. Well known on Second Avenue." In this way, the juxtaposition of Finkle's growing hesitation about "buying" and Salzman's increasingly aggressive brand of "selling" create what might have been a purely comic situation. However, Finkle gradually comes to see Salzman's portfolio of marital candidates as a microcosm of the world's suffering and his shoulders as the proper place on which it might rest.

Finkle, in short, no longer imagines a world in which hundreds of cards—each one longing for marriage—are churned about and finally brought together. Rather, the "much-handled cards" of Salzman's portfolio make it clear that others also suffer the loneliness and indignation of being damaged, passed-over goods, and Finkle's traumatic meeting with Lily Hirschorn forces him to realize, for the first time, "the true nature of his relationship to God, and from that it had come to him, with shocking force, that apart from his parents, he had never loved anyone." "The Magic Barrel" is, then, a love story, one that operates simultaneously on the levels of eros and agape. That Finkle's learning leads him to admit his essentially loveless condition, his particular death of the heart, is a necessary precondition for the comic victimhood that will follow.

And yet, Lily Hirschorn, important though she might be as a wake-up call to Finkle's slumbering soul, is simply another frantic figure yoo-hooing after a life that had already passed her by. There are dozens of similar stories in Salzman's magic barrel. Moreover, if Finkle had been conned by Salzman, so had Lily. After all, she expected to meet a biblical prophet, a man "enamored with God," and instead she found herself walking with a man incapable of passion either in the physical or the spiritual senses of the term. In the Finkle-Salzman-Hirschorn triangle, the end result is initiation; Finkle finds out how and what he is, and in the context of the story this information provides the tension, the essential ground condition, that moral bunglers are made of.

By contrast, Stella, Salzman's wayward daughter, provides the occasion for Finkle to finally act. Unlike the typical Salzman profile, Stella's dime store photo suggests that she "had *lived*, or wanted to—more than just wanted, perhaps regretted how she had lived—had somehow deeply suffered." In a world where suffering is the standard for one-upmanship, she is the hands-down winner. A Lily Hirschorn may have wanted to live, Finkle himself has the urge to try, but it is Stella who has actually been there. And it is through the figure of Stella (her name suggesting the ironic star that guides Finkle's destiny) that the prospective rabbi hopes to "convert her to goodness, himself to God."

Indeed, it is Finkle's highly stylized movement toward Stella that turns him into a saintly fool, at least in the sense that his goal of spiritual regeneration is incommensurate with his activity. The story's concluding tableau crystallizes the matter of Finkle's salvation and/or destruction without providing the luxury of a clear reading direction. Finkle runs toward Stella, seeking "in her, his own redemption" in ways that make this now passionate rabbi akin to the biblical Hosea. However, Salzman remains just "around the corner . . . chanting prayers for the dead." Is this *kaddish* for Finkle? For Stella? Or, perhaps, for Salzman himself? In much of Malamud's early fiction, ironic affirmations become an essential part of his aesthetic, as if movements toward moral change were not enough, but total regeneration is not possible. And in Malamud's greatest stories, like "The Angel Levine," "Take Pity!," "The Jew Bird," moral allegories slip easily from the gritty surfaces of realistic detail to surrealistic fancy, and back again. At their most achieved, Malamud's short fictions have the feel of Marc Chagall paintings.

—Sanford Pinsker

MAHOGANY (Krasnoe derevo)
by Boris Pil'niak, 1929

Boris Pil'niak's *Krasnoe derevo* ("Mahogany") defies attempts to place it within the confines of a well-defined literary form. It certainly comes across as a relatively long story in the category of short fiction. Neither the Western European term *novelle* nor the Russian *povest'* can accommodate its decidedly modern form: it has no central characters and no coherent plot; the narrator mixes stylistic levels as well as ideological assumptions cleverly enough to efface himself. Constructed as an elaborate collage, the story's events and characters loosely relate to each other through a few leitmotifs. One overriding concern prevails, however: material and spiritual dispossession.

The title refers to 18th- and 19th-century mahogany furniture which outlives its builders and its owners and represents some permanence amid confusion and transitoriness. The chairs, tables, and wardrobes which two Moscow art dealers buy up from the residents of a town in the country had witnessed Russian history in the making. Originally, Russian peasants were sent to Europe in the 18th century to learn the craft of carpentry. Upon their return to the primitive conditions of their homeland, they adapted their skill to meet local needs and created an indigenous Russian mahogany style. The knowledge was handed down from generation to generation and the furniture ended up in the homes of the nobility and the merchant class.

As the narrator accounts for the fate of pieces of furniture as they pass into the possession of the antique dealers, Russian history becomes a prominent theme in the story. The liberation of the serfs in 1861 signalled the rise of the furniture factory and the end of privately built pieces. By the beginning of the 1920's, mahogany chairs and tables become treasured antiques which their owners must sell greatly under value; they must part with their cherished objects and artworks in the face of starvation.

The story takes place in a town the narrator keeps referring to as the "medieval Russian Bruges, imperial Russia's Kamakura." Allusions to a Japanese and a Belgian city point to the division of Russia geographically and spiritually between East and West. Furthermore, Bruges, immortalized in literature by Georges Rodenbach, also symbolizes the "dead city." The narrator never directly refers to the city by its real name, Uglich. Lying by the river in the heart of the Russian countryside, the town looks back on its dark history: the last member of the Rurik dynasty, Tsarevich Dmitri, was murdered here. Boris Godunov, the murderer, "sentenced" the church bells to death. His work is completed in the 1920's: during the course of events in the story, the bells are destroyed and the carillon is heard no more. People outside the new power hierarchy of the Communist Party face severe discrimination. The narrator paints a devastating picture of the corrupt ruling elite who live in seclusion to hide their luxuries from the eyes of the public whose wealth they embezzle and waste. In equally lucid terms, the narrator uncovers the sufferings and destruction of the peasantry even before the full brunt of collectivization.

An ominous, dark, and mud-filled world surrounds the town. As Communism—an original European import—takes hold and develops its indigenous Russian variety (much like mahogany furniture did two centuries earlier), daily customs reflecting the pre-Petrine spirit of Russia's austere *Domostroi* retain their tight grip over the older generation. The young unlearn the old values but nothing replaces these.

The only people who have faith are the "okhlomons." They are a group of mentally unbalanced men who supported the Revolution during the Civil War but became profoundly disillusioned with the Soviet state. They live in a commune and own nothing. Like his predecessors, the holy fools who were much veneered by superstitious Russian folk, the chief "okhlomon" seems to be endowed with prophetic powers: he predicts a "time of troubles" to come.

"Mahogany" resembles a painting: its fragments create a lasting impression as they mutually illuminate each other. They radiate a sense of melancholy before the approaching storm of the worst excesses of Stalinism in the 1930's. The "okhlomon's" dark forebodings become real: Pil'niak was one of the first writers to be arrested and killed in the 1930's.

—Peter I. Barta

THE MAKING OF A NEW ZEALANDER
by Frank Sargeson, 1940

"The Making of a New Zealander" was first published in the Christchurch periodical *Tomorrow* early in 1939, then Sargeson entered it in the Centennial Literary Competition (where it was judged first equal) and collected it in his 1940 volume, *A Man and His Wife*. The generalizing title points towards the kind of cultural reference that is left implicit in the story itself and that underlies much of Sargeson's work.

The story is typical of Sargeson's classic period (1935-45) in its method, world, and attitude. The method turns on point of view. It is first-person narration told by an involved observer who is looking back on the experience but still uncertain of its significance (if any): "What I want to tell is about how I sat on a hillside one evening and talked with a man. That's all, just a summer evening and a talk with a man on a hillside. Maybe there's nothing in it and maybe there is." The title points to a significance beyond the narrator's ability to articulate. From this point of view follows the language, appropriate to the narrator—laconic, understated, vernacular, literal. Also from the point of view comes the structure, that of the anecdotal yarn appropriate to such a speaker, open-ended, seemingly casual, yet implicitly epiphanic.

The world of the story is that of most of Sargeson's early work. The place is rural North Island New Zealand, perhaps North Auckland, during the Depression of the 1930's. The society in the background is dour, joyless, puritan, and conservative. Its primary representative in the story is Mrs. Crump, the hard-working wife of a farmer. She is dominating and judgemental, approving of her neighbour Nick only because he works hard and is loyal to his mate. Also representative of New Zealand society is the narrator, a casual laborer with a real feel for work on the land, a man of some sensitivity and intelligence, but rootless and repressed. At the center of the story is Nick, a Dalmatian immigrant trying to succeed as an apple-grower on marginal land. He works hard (and puts too much manure on his apple trees) in order to succeed in the New Zealand way, but he finds real meaning only in mateship, and he is sure that somehow "it's all wrong" in a society where the concern is "money, money, money, all the time," where even marriage is sacrificed to economic necessity. Thus, as he proclaims to the narrator, he is a communist. He knows that Mrs. Crump would not approve, but then he sees her as a woman who would be happier in a less commercially individualistic and more communal society such as the Dalmatian, although he also knows that she is not aware of that.

The plot of the story, such as it is, is the conversation between Nick and the narrator, and its aftermath. Nick states his sense that something is wrong, the narrator thinks Nick may be right but disapproved of his politics. When Nick says that he is a New Zealander, the narrator knows that he is not really one, but that he is not a Dalmatian any longer either. They agree to talk again, but the narrator is sacked the next day for telling Mrs. Crump that her heart is in the wrong place (he meant that she should be in Dalmatia), and he goes to town to drink and to get Nick off his mind.

To be a New Zealander, the story implies, is to be relentlessly practical, materialistic, lacking any close relationship with the land and valuing only the money to be made from it. Thus despite his efforts to adapt, Nick cannot be a real New Zealander because he is too emotional and wants more from life than material success. The story thus implies that New Zealand society, as it has formed over its first 100 years, is in some ways unnatural, running counter to some basic human needs and values, not "God's own country" (as it would like to believe), but a place where it is "all wrong." The narrative method, asking the reader to read between the lines and see what the narrator cannot articulate or even allow himself to feel, makes this meaning all the more powerful because of the necessity of readerly participation to make sense of the story. As in much of Sargeson's work, less is more.

—Lawrence Jones

THE MAN THAT CORRUPTED HADLEYBURG
by Mark Twain, 1900

"The Man That Corrupted Hadleyburg" was published in *Harper's Magazine* in 1899, and collected in *The Man That Corrupted Hadleyburg and Other Stories and Essays* in 1900. It is considered one of Twain's most tightly written, and best, short stories. The story covers several of the major themes that characterize most of Twain's work: the corruptible influence of money, the weakness of people's spirit in the face of temptation, and the basic lack of goodwill in those most professing to be Christian. Written toward the end of his lifetime, the story's tone extends from

the despair and misanthropy that imbued Twain's final works. Twain was always subject to periods of depression which his writings reflected, but his last ten years of writing particularly emphasized his dark view of humanity.

In "The Man That Corrupted Hadleyburg" the plot centers around a town that embodies what Twain saw as the fundamental and flawed teachings of the Christian church. Hadleyburg has earned a national reputation for raising citizens who are above corruption. Raised with the principles of honest dealing, "the mere fact that a young man hailed from Hadleyburg was all the recommendation he needed when he went forth from his natal town to seek for responsible employment." Raised without temptation to commit an act of dishonesty, the townspeople believe themselves above corruption. Twain stresses the lack of temptation, to emphasize his belief that a will untested is unlikely to endure.

The townspeople offend, in an unspecified manner, a man passing through town. The stranger makes it his goal to wound the people of Hadleyburg in a way that would affect everyone. He offers a large sack of gold to be given to the man who, through various machinations, can prove that he donated $20 to a beggar who has lost all his money in gambling. This supposed donor was to have given advice to the beggar that changed his life, and the knowledge of this advice is the key to receiving the reward.

The stranger then instructs each of the townspeople by way of a letter the method of claiming the money. The stranger includes in each letter some hesitation to the right of the recipient to that claim, but assures him that "I know that I can trust to your honor and honesty, for in a citizen of Hadleyburg these virtues are an unfailing inheritance, and so I am going to reveal to you the remark, well satisfied that if you are not the right man you will seek and find the right one . . . " Each of the letters includes the exact same information.

Barclay Goodson, dead before the advent of the tale, is the one townsperson who neither takes pride in the town's reputation nor believes it to be well founded. He is also the one that everyone privately believes to be the only possible donor of a large sum of money to an impoverished gambler. The other residents would have all summarily dismissed such a beggar without thought to his state in life. Goodson, while alive, was reviled by the community. He labels the townspeople "honest, narrow, self-righteous, and stingy," a view Twain held of many professed Christians.

When the day comes to claim the money, all the letters are revealed to have the same incorrect phrase. The town is nationally shamed by this attempted forgery of claim to the money. Richards, the one man left out of the embarrassing letter reading, has been protected by Burgess, the reader of the letters, to return a favor done by Richards.

In the story, two charitable services are mentioned. The first is one done by Richards for Burgess. Burgess has been accused of an undescribed crime, which is never pursued in court, but for which he is ostracized by the community permanently. Burgess is able to escape the attack of the townspeople because of advance warning from Richards. Richards did this because his conscience bothered him in not revealing Burgess's innocence in the crime. Richards alone could have proved Burgess's innocence but chooses not to, to avoid his own possible ostracism by the residents of Hadleyburg. Although this event occurred years before the incident in the story, Twain uses it to portray the moral cowardice of the villagers. In much of Twain's writing, the sin of inaction and omission play heavily in characters. They are not unredeemable characters, but they let their belief in their own moral correctness give them the right to passiveness in correcting the injustices of the world.

The second charitable act is that of Burgess protecting Richards from ridicule at the public reading of the letters. Richards, unable to view any act as motivated by kindness, sees this as an attempt by Burgess to hold Richards up to blackmail later. Richards believes that Burgess wants to punish him for his earlier cowardice, although Burgess is never aware of those inactions. Eventually this guilt drives Richards and his wife mad. The last man with a decent reputation confesses on his deathbed his sins of inaction and deceit. The stranger's revenge is accomplished by besmirching the reputation of every single resident of Hadleyburg through their own behavior.

The first test of virtue is the offer of the money. Twain viewed money not as the root of evil but as evidence of humanity's evil by their manner of keeping and taking money. At the point in Twain's life when this story is composed, Twain had just ended years of paying off debts incurred from a failed business. He did everything he could to earn money and saw it as the source of much misery. Twain witnessed and experienced the greed and stinginess of those who could easily assist the less fortunate.

In the second test of virtue set up by the stranger, the townspeople must search their souls for a gift to Goodson of "a very great service once, possibly without knowing the full value of it." In this test, Twain has the main character, Richards, struggle through the test, trying to come up with one small favor done to Goodson in the many years he lived in Hadleyburg. He can, of course, come up with nothing. Richards decides nonetheless to claim the money. Twain writes that the other residents are in the same predicament. Reflecting Twain's views of the effects of the teachings of the Christian church, the townspeople have never extended a considerate gesture or act to another, particularly someone they did not personally care for. Yet they all determine that they must have, somehow, done a service to Goodson for which they should be rewarded.

In the story, the only character with openly spiteful and wicked intent is the stranger who precipitates the plot. The townspeople, equally guilty in Twain's eye of wickedness, are only brought to recognize their own flaws through the extreme actions of the story. It was Twain's belief, enhanced by the end of his lifetime, that people are basically moral cowards, blind to their own flaws, perpetuating the misery on earth.

—Carol Summerfield

THE MAN WHO INVENTED SIN
by Sean O'Faolain, 1947

"The Man Who Invented Sin" is the title story of Sean O'Faolain's 1948 collection (first published as *Teresa and Other Stories* in 1947). In his own view, it represents his first proper adjustment to the realities of Irish life, after the comparative romanticism of the earlier collections. In the preface to the 1959 edition, he outlines the dimensions of the problem: by the time I had more or less adjusted myself to the life about me, it suddenly broke in on me that Ireland had not adjusted herself to the life about her in the least little bit." Irishmen, he said, were still thinking about themselves in romantic terms, while at the same time

making good hard cash and carefully compiling another contradictory image composed of terms like "pious, holy prudent, sterling, gorsoons . . . ancestors, deeprooted, olden, venerable . . . " This "double-thinking or squint-thinking" mode is used as a means of dodging "more awkward social, moral and political problems than any country might . . . hope to solve in a century of ruthless thinking." O'Faolain's task, as he perceived it, was thenceforth to chart this ambivalence, though he was aware that to succeed he had to devise a totally new fictional approach. But he wanted to avoid both satire and anger. For all his wonder that he could bear to return to a country that he describes, in the "O'Faolain Issue" of *Irish University Review* (Spring 1976), as "run by a cowardly, priest-bullied, ignorant, bigoted mob of bourgeois, gombeen-men," he was aware that he did not begin to write until he had suffered "enough mortal shocks to shatter those three refracting lenses, Family, Fatherland and Faith, that up to that moment of time prevented me from seeing with my own eyes at least some little bit of the nature of life as it is really lived"; he admitted he loved Ireland and its people too much for satire: "all any artist should ask of his country is his freedom, and all he should promise it in return is his disloyalty. If he achieves both, he will serve his country well."

O'Faolain can be seen, no matter what genre he works in, to be the most balanced and intelligent of analysts of the malaise of post-1922 Ireland. He has been described as working "all his life to bring a parochial, nationalistic and clerical Ireland into the mainstream of modern culture." Since this was his aim, he rarely adopts the narrative stance of the innocent and naive child, but chooses rather the mature, detached, knowledgeable, retrospective view. "The Man Who Invented Sin" is a story of innocence corrupted, of spontaneity perverted in the interests of clerical dominance and social conformity. The impact depends crucially on the tone of the narrator, on his ability both to recreate the lost Eden of innocence and to realize the significance of what has taken place. The note of nostalgic reminiscence is struck immediately: "in our youth" the young people of Ireland were in a mood of energetic idealism. A newly created state was re-establishing its own sense of identity and thousands of people flocked to the Irish-speaking areas, to learn to speak their own language and to debate pressing questions of national identity. The natural setting is beautiful, the predominant mood is one of merriment with a pagan undertone. The story centres on two sets of monks and nuns, forced by overcrowding to lodge somewhat apart from the other summer visitors, and drawn by proximity and shared interests and background into openness and communication with each other. They are presented throughout mainly as children, transforming their ludicrously inappropriate clerical names to childish nicknames (Chrysostom to Chrissie, Majellan to Jelly), and often, as lonely, homesick children. Their spontaneity, naturalness, and gentleness is emphasized; "Brother Virgilius was a countryman with a powerful frame and a powerful voice, round red cheeks, and no nerves"; Brother Majellan, "a gentle, apple-cheeked man with big glasses, a complexion like a girl's, teeth as white as a hound's, and soft, beaming eyes." In sharp contrast is the local curate, who, by misinterpreting their behaviour, invents sin, and by creating a sense of guilt irremediably corrupts everyone. He is, in keeping with the central irony of the story, presented throughout as satanic. He is physically violent, fat, pompous and cocksure, with a "black barrel of a body," nicknamed Lispeen (a frog). At the end as he walks away surrounded by respectful salutes, the narrator sees "his elongated shadow (waving) behind him like a tail." Although the curate laughs off the effect of his actions, the narrator is aware that he has not only destroyed the natural, wholesome, and consolatory interaction between the four young people, creating in them a puritan suspicion and concern for rigid social observance at the expense of personal growth, he has also corrupted the natural world, changing it from benign to threatening, and, ultimately, negated the possibility of creating an Edenic world that can nurture idealism and creativity. As the story ends the mountains are empty, Majellan is stooped and grey, existing in a "smelly slum" and denying the truth of his own memories, while the curate, elevated in the church, self-satisfied and unchanged in appearance, is the inheritor of the earth.

—Anne Clune

THE MAN WHO LIVED UNDERGROUND
by Richard Wright, 1961

With the publication of his novel *Native Son* (1940), Richard Wright became a cultural celebrity, who was not only identified as a spokesperson for African-Americans but a best-selling author. When his autobiographical *Black Boy* (1945) was submitted for publication, his editors at Harper Brothers lopped off the conclusion as too critical of the Communist Party that was favorably portrayed in *Native Son*. (The excised material appeared, well after Wright's death, as *American Hunger,* 1977). In the previous year he published in venues apart from Harper two lengthy pieces—one an autobiographical narrative, "I Tried To Be a Communist," which was very famous in its time (in part because it was reprinted in Richard Crossman's anthology *The God that Failed,* 1949); the other is Wright's best single piece of imaginative writing, *The Man Who Lived Underground*.

When read together, these signal a turning point in the development of his interpretation of experience. The first piece deals critically with the initial affirmation of Wright's intellectual career—his experience within the orbit of the American Communist Party. The theme of this memoir is that the party was always more interested in expanding and solidifying its power than in helping Wright, or any other African-American, advance. What makes this memoir a transitional work in Wright's intellectual development is the enormous change in his concept of how good and evil function in social reality. In his early fiction, such as *Native Son,* some characters clearly shined as friends of African-Americans, and others were patently his enemies; and Wright's attitude toward these figures was decisive. In this and his later work, distinctions in Wright's world become less clearly defined.

The Man Who Lived Underground represents Wright's first wholly imaginative attempt at creating a more fluid and ambiguous moral universe. Where crimes were once determined by social conditions and, therefore, as in *Native Son,* sometimes rationalized, now they are acts of accidental impulse. Where the earlier book saw "reality" in the most ordinary activities, here Wright describes events that are often preposterous, whose causes are usually mysterious.

A young African-American, escaping from the police, jumps into a manhole to find himself imprisoned in the underground darkness. The police, it seems, have accused him of murdering a Mrs. Peabody; whether he actually committed the crime we never finally know. Sloshing through the slime, the young man encounters various alternatives; and unlike the desperate Bigger Thomas, who is forced to take whatever aid will come to him, Wright's generally nameless protagonist scans all choices with the cold eye of a gambler. Death, the eternal escape, is the first alternative that fate offers to him. Seeing the tiny nude body of a baby snagged in sewer debris, he contemplates its significance for himself only to kick it loose from its mooring, propelling it down the stream.

Through a crack in the wall of an abandoned sewer case, he peeks into the basement of a black church and surveys African-American religion, which he finds ludicrously unable to cope with the problems of life:

> His first impulse was to laugh, but he checked himself. They oughtn't to do that, he thought. But he could think of no reason *why* they should not do it. Just singing with the air of the sewer blowing in on them.

Seized by the desire to shout that their singing is all in vain, he squelches that impulse.

Fundamentally, *The Man Who Lived Underground* is, like Dostoevskii's *Crime and Punishment,* about the perils of the social-political choice of complete isolation—a kind of emigration from America which Ralph Ellison in his prophetic 1945 article on Wright christened "going-underground." Like Dostoevskii before him, Wright meticulously illustrates how separation from the world slowly debilitates the outcast's moral character and, eventually, his human essence. First, the protagonist progressively loses any recognition of how his actions relate to others, as well as any sense of moral value and any pragmatic awareness of actual effect. He burrows into a radio shop and steals some merchandise that he cannot use. As he later observes the owner of the shop accusing an employee of theft, he wonders why he is unable to feel guilty, conjecturing that the major reason for the absence of feeling is his inability to relate goods to people. That is, he cannot recognize that he is taking something from somebody. In a later scene, after he robs a safe, he watches the police physically beat its watchman into making a confession; and to his surprise, he feels little remorse. In discovering that anything is possible, he makes the collateral discovery that nothing is morally unjustifiable. "Maybe anything is right he mumbled. Yes, if the world as men have made it was right, then anything else was right, any act a man took to satisfy himself, murder, theft, torture."

Upon emerging from the hole into the midst of traffic, the young man finds that cars swerve "to shun him and the gaping hole," and a voice screams, "You blind, you bastard?" (which is to say blind to worldly realities). Soon after, he enters a black church, hoping for solace. An anonymous voice complains that "he's filthy," and an usher escorts him back into the street. Later, the young man inexplicably goes directly to the police station and confesses to his crime. The policemen reveal that someone else has already confessed to the Peabody murder, and they attempt to dismiss him as a crank. However, the man who lived underground no longer comprehends the worldly reality of social "freedom"; instead, he insists that the police arrest him and, to clinch their case, accompany him to his cave. Embarrassed, the officers follow the man to his sewer; and once he descends the ladder, they shoot him.

Wright's explanation for this metamorphosis in character resembles Dostoevskii's: Once the man becomes the sole inhabitant of his own universe, he becomes his own God. "Sprawling before him in his mind," Wright says of his protagonist, "was his wife, Mrs. Wooton for whom he worked, the three policemen who had picked him up. . . . He possessed them now more completely than he ever possessed them when he had lived aboveground." Once the man becomes the sole ultimate judge of his actions, he also becomes his own God; anyone so emancipated from extrinsic authority is capable of both crime without guilt and honesty without prudence. The man who lived underground loses his human identity. When he first steals a typewriter, he picks the name "freddaniels" [sic], which may or may not be his own; but once he returns to his cave, he attempts the same task, only to discover that he had forgotten his name. Earlier, coming upon a lunch basket, he gobbles up the sandwiches and fruit with the greed of an uninhibited animal: "Then, like a dog, he grounds the meat bones with his teeth." Wright's final point is that escape into total isolation, while it may seem at first attractive, if not inevitable, condemns the escapee to qualities not fully human.

Perhaps the surest measure of the imaginative impact of this Wright fiction is that Ralph Ellison's *Invisible Man* (1953), begun soon after the publication of *The Man Who Lived Underground,* opens with a likewise nameless man underground, now speaking in the first person, rather than Wright's third person. Remembering Ellison's interest in jazz, one can speak of Ellison's blowing riffs on Wright's tune. In my book *Politics in the African-American Novel* (1991), I read *Invisible Man* as an implicit commentary on Wright.

The Man Who Lived Underground was initially published as a "novelette" in *Cross-Section: A Collection of New American Writing* in 1945 (which incidentally also contains Ralph Ellison's "Flying Home") and was collected in Wright's *Eight Men* in 1961. It was published in a bilingual edition in 1971.

—Richard Kostelanetz

THE MAN WHO WOULD BE KING
by Rudyard Kipling, 1888

Rudyard Kipling achieved an artistic coherence in his short stories that he never attained in his episodic longer fiction. "The Man Who Would Be King," collected in *Under the Deodars* in 1888, is one of his best early stories, illustrating the skill with which he transformed apparently simple tales into multi-leveled fictions. Early readers like Henry James and Edmund Gosse admired his portraits of ordinary soldiers, whom he portrayed with keen psychological insight. These early stories offer strikingly ironic pictures of British India and of the cultural divisions between the colonial rulers and their subjects.

"The Man Who Would be King" works on different levels, combining a tale of adventure with a realistic frame story. The sophisticated and skeptical narrator provides a frame of reference for the reader, knitting together the exotic and the familiar. By presenting divergent accounts of the exotic east, that of the jaded newspaper reporter and that of the romanticists, Dravot and Carnehan, Kipling disturbs conventional attitudes to colonial India. His blend of realism and fable is powerfully illustrated in the story's finale, when the crucified Peachy displays Dravot's head, its withered, blind-eyed grimace symbolizing the blindness that destroyed the would-be king. Kipling's account of the red-bearded man's last public appearance is realistic, whether we accept Peachy's story or challenge it as a product of his hallucinated state.

Early in the story Kipling gives a vivid account of the newspaper office were the narrator works, detailing the frantic rush to meet deadlines and the hours of ennervating boredom, the demands by strange ladies to have visiting cards printed and the repeated appeals for work from "every dissolute ruffian" who passes by. The precision with which this dreary place is described establishes the narrator's claim to be an accurate reporter, not only of items in his paper, but of the character and appearance of Dravot and Carnehan. These two men represent a breed who have come to India looking for plunder and found to their disappointment that it is no longer possible to make a fortune in the tame lands under British rule.

"We are going away to be kings," says Peachy to the reporter during his first visit, meaning they are escaping from colonial mediocrity. The narrator concedes that they are too big for the cramped room where he performs his editorial duties. He can't resist a sneaking admiration for these tricksters, who are both naive and endlessly resourceful, like the more genteel marauders who created the Empire in times gone by. Drawing a parallel between past and present adventurers (Dravot dreams of ceding conquered territories to Queen Victoria and being knighted for his services), Kipling suggests that the Empire is still mainly concerned with loot. Dravot and Carnehan represent the Empire's underlying rapacity, as it was before it was domesticated and turned into a government. They have made a contract, expressing their English love of legal formalities, regardless of how lawless the actual business involved may be. In this they parody the colonialist system of plundering subject states under the guise of normal commerce. Theirs is a cautionary tale about the dangers that await empire builders, and Kipling's blend of biblical language and racy speech provides an effective medium for that warning.

Carnehan's narrative is tinged throughout by our awareness of the storyteller's crippled state. The fable of a man who allows himself to be worshipped as a god suggests Conrad's "Heart of Darkness," written ten years later, which also describes a colonialist who is lured to his death by dreams of unlimited power. Like Conrad's novella, Kipling's "The Man Who Would Be King" reveals the underlying psychology of imperialism, especially the fall into megalomania, in ways which the author himself may not have intended. Critics of the stories, like Jeffrey Meyers, have pointed out "the difference between their intended and actual effect. [Kipling's] art is sometimes in conflict with his thought." The narrator partly undermines the theme of "The Man Who Would be King" by romanticizing the two adventurers; he fails to distance himself from the racist attitudes that underlie their enterprise. Nevertheless, the tale itself exposes the madness of claims to racial mastery. Dravot's belief in English superiority leads him to play god, and sustains him till his subjects discover, as they must, that he is only human. Even Dravot's absurd attempt to narrow the racial gap by claiming the indigenous people as England's lost tribes rests on racialism and further undermines his hold on reality. He is seduced by a vision of unlimited possibilities. "I won't make a nation," he says, "I'll make an Empire."

Dravot is corrupted by power, lust, and money. This petty adventurer who falls to his death from a precarious rope bridge illustrates the weaknesses of the colonial system, though the cynical narrator, distrusting large claims, keeps the focus on Dravot and Carnehan's personal tragedy. Still, Kipling's ironic vision admits the more universal reading. His art, as Henry James said, is "so mixed and various and cynical and, in certain lights, so contradictory of itself." Dravot's story, moreover, evokes Kipling's patriotic poem, "Recessional." While celebrating the British Empire, "Recessional" warns that human empires melt away, destroyed by the power-madness of their rulers. "The Man Who Would be King" implicitly challenges English pride of conquest. At the end of the story, with the disappearance of Dravot's withered head, not a shred of evidence remains that his "kingdom" ever existed.

Kipling's naturalistic frame and romantic adventure blend into a successful hybrid form, half way between the popular tale and the modern short story. The use of an ironic narrator and the Christian and Masonic echoes add their special resonances. "The Man Who Would Be King" forms a complex whole that is greater than the sum of its parts.

—Herbert Marder

THE MARINE EXCURSION OF THE KNIGHTS OF PYTHIAS
by Stephen Leacock, 1912

"The Marine Excursion of the Knights of Pythias" is the third story in Stephen Leacock's *Sunshine Sketches of a Little Town*. The story cycle portrays various sides of life such as the economic, religious, and political, in the town of Mariposa. In this story Leacock shows us something of the Mariposans' social life during the course of a holiday excursion on the *Mariposa Belle*, which ultimately becomes more than a steamboat; it comes to represent the town itself. The story contributes to our understanding of the town's main entrepreneur, Josh Smith (arguably the entire book's main character), and the way the townspeople think. Indeed, in no other story does the narrator of *Sunshine Sketches* identify so often and so closely with the mentality of the town.

The narrator's voice throughout *Sunshine Sketches* is quite variable, occasionally speaking as an outsider but mostly speaking in the voice of a townsperson. The opening of the story reveals the narrator's ironic acceptance of Mariposan values:

Half-past six on a July morning! The *Mariposa Belle* is at the wharf, decked in flags, with steam up ready to start. Excursion day!

The narrator's expressed excitement is that of the town, and throughout the story he speaks of the excursion in the overblown terms with which the townspeople would describe the event. The town's pretensions to greatness are portrayed in the narrator's dismissal of European natural splendors: "Lake Wissanotti in the morning sunlight! Don't talk to me of the Italian lakes, or the Tyrol or the Swiss Alps." Nothing in foreign lands could compare to Mariposa's gala. As the extremely strict time of departure keeps being moved back, as the number of members of the "Knights of Pythias" grows, as the grandeur of the scene is undercut by the sound of bottles clinking in passengers' pockets, we learn the reality behind the mock-heroic account of the ship's departure.

Like the town itself, the *Belle* "seems to vary so" in size, depending on how long one has been in the town and influenced by its scale of values. After "a month or two" the ship appears to be as large as the *Lusitania,* and the accident it suffers deserves the great build-up given to it by the narrator and the tension experienced by the reader. Leacock parodies other ship disasters by focusing on the absurdly strange circumstances that allowed many of the townspeople to escape being aboard the ship when it sinks. The parody at once prepares us for a real disaster and undercuts that expectation as we see the nature of the supposed coincidences. Also, the parody makes the narrator as much a figure of fun as the townspeople.

The townspeople's excitement at this outing proves to be very short-lived. Complaints arise about seating conditions, and the women retire to the lower deck where, "by getting round the table with needlework, and with all the windows shut, they soon had it, as they said themselves, just like being at home." In other words, the ship might as well be the town, for all the difference in the townspeople's behavior.

While on the way home the ship begins to sink. Our anticipation of a real emergency is undercut by the calm way in which the passengers receive the news; they appear unconcerned, and we remain puzzled until the narrator explains:

What? Hadn't I explained about the depth of Lake Wissanotti? I had taken it for granted that you knew; and in any case parts of it are deep enough, though I don't suppose in this stretch of it from the big reed beds up to within a mile of the town wharf, you could find six feet of water in it if you tried.

He then berates us for having the intimations of catastrophe that he himself has provoked. The joke is on us, then, if we insist on taking the narrator at his word; we are now in Mariposa, and must relinquish our city-based, sophisticated values in favour of the town's. The sinking is an inconvenience, not a threat, in keeping with the collection's overall tone of gentle, or Horatian, satire. The townspeople are fools, not villains, and thus the objects of sympathetic rather than damning ridicule.

Once we are told that the "sinking" is a minor affair, the rhetoric shifts again and the narrator implies that in its way this sinking is as frightening as one on the open seas, if not more so. Mariposan pretensions, then, never falter, or escape attack. The rescue that follows similarly contrasts what are superficial similarities to a maritime emergency to the real thing; women and children leave first, but only in order to test the lake-worthiness of the boat, and the brave rescuers are the ones in most need of rescue—by those they tried to save. At last, the *Mariposa Belle* itself floats into view, thanks to the efforts of Josh Smith, who once more demonstrates his shrewdness and basic practical intelligence. As an outsider to the town he is not quite subject to their ideals and illusions, and therefore capable of acts too fundamentally sensible for most of the townspeople to conceive of.

The story is a delightful parody of sea calamities. It holds the Mariposans up to ridicule, but of a gentle sort. As elsewhere in the book, the Mariposans here are satirized, but in a way that makes them seem more charming than despicable. These are foolish human beings—possessed of a grand self-image, but no more so than any of us. As such, Leacock suggests, they deserve smiles of recognition, not sneers of disdain.

—Allan Weiss

MARIO AND THE MAGICIAN (Mario und der Zauberer)
by Thomas Mann, 1930

Mario und der Zauberer ("Mario and the Magician") presents Thomas Mann's European backgrounds in the form of a visitor from his native northern Germany vacationing in southern Italy, who experiences the initial onslaught of totalitarianism in the hands of the artist-magician Mario, who commands his subjects to dance at his will before an audience that lacks self-discipline. Dated 1929 and first published in 1930, "Mario and the Magician" was collected in English in *Stories of Three Decades* (1936), translated by H.T. Lowe-Porter.

In the story, an unnamed narrator, with his wife and two children, visits the Italian seaside resort Torre di Venere, the Tower of Venus, in August 1929. Immediately upon arrival and sequentially thereafter, the visitors find themselves subject to humiliations originating in patriotic fervor. The town itself becomes a microcosm for the state under Mussolini, with diminished hospitality for its international clientele, and a common consciousness of the lost grandeur of Rome.

In the throes of a fascist state, the conflict focuses on freedom of will, of submission and domination of the personal and patriotic will. The visitors should enjoy hospitality and some immunity from politics, but inexplicably and against their desire they submit to the prevailing conditions, wherein their companions are common people, and the magician—a crippled Mussolini—arrives to crack his whip in aristocratic exploitation of their will and their weaknesses.

Why the narrator permits himself to be drawn into submission and extends his visit continually perplexes himself, but his persistence is an natural as the fact that everybody has to live somewhere.

They cannot sit at a chosen table in the Grand Hotel because it is "reserved for clients" (of which they are one party); then they must change their room because the Principessa X objects to the child's cough. Outraged by this "Byznatinism" but submitting without protest, they remove to the Pensione Eleonora, presided over by Signora Angiolieri and her husband, whose special reverence in the community derives from her having been wardrobe mistress to Eleonora Duse (1859-1924). The narrator's attitudes begin to formulate an allegory in which his personal experiences equal those of an upper-class citizen of the state, squeezed out of aristocratic company and forced among proprietors and servants, just as Mussolini's "corporate state" represented employers and workers. The narrator experiences many "collisions with ordinary humanity, the naive misuse of power, the injustice, the sycophantic corruption."

The middle-class mob on the beach pierces the family's recreation with shouts Homeric only in volume, and the narrator's sociable children suffer numerous insults from patriotic playmates. When the eight-year-old daughter rinses her swimsuit in the waters, her momentary nudity offends the national dignity; the father must apologize and pay a fine to officials of the Italian government.

After 18 days of discomfort, when other visitors have departed, the family remains and the magician arrives. Walking through streets leading "from the feudal, past the bourgeois into the proletarian," the family enters a performance hall with stalls but no boxes and the "manhood" of "the awakened Fatherland" standing in the back—among them the children's favorite waiter Mario.

The magician has taken for himself the aristocratic title of "Cavaliere" and his name "Cipolla" means onion, to signify, perhaps, that he peels the layers of dignity off his willing subjects, whom he selects carefully among the employers and workers. He advocates "division of labor" while repeatedly insulting the local speech, which he calls "the national cement, the mother tongue," and ridiculing the "lady-killers" of Torre di Venere. His own sexual prowess has been, obviously, diminished by an undefinable physical defect that appears to be a hips or buttocks hump, only approximately deemed a hunchback. He boasts that he conquers life with his mental and spiritual powers and that the brother of *Il Duce* once attended one of his performances. He speaks well, and speech, he says, serves as a measure of personal rank.

Through a series of arithmetical contests and various commands, the magician demonstrates hypnotism and complete mastery of the workers in the audience; even the more select members of the audience, as objective witnesses, tolerate the disgraces and the insults of their compatriots as inexplicably as the narrator extended his visit under increasing discomfort. Not a mere prestidigitator or stage magician, Cipolla demonstrates clairvoyance and other talents of the higher degrees of occultism, so that an uncomfortable suspicion arises that he has implanted by mental telepathy the numbers his victims call forth. He explains that "freedom of the will does not exist, for a will that aims at its own freedom aims at the unknown."

If this assertion is fact, then the astounding action of Mario in his climactic shooting and killing of the magician is not an act of resentment or free will but the result of post-hypnotic suggestion. Later the narrator remembers Mario's "absent and pensive smile" during the intermission. Throughout his performance, the magician begs for the sympathy of the audience; he appears ill and exhausted and must fortify himself repeatedly with cognac and cigarettes. All his life he has been deprived of the pleasures of "the fair sex." In other words, on this evening Cipolla commits suicide.

The magician maintains that commanding and obeying form a unity, as "people and leader were comprehended in one another," or murderer and victim would be comprehended in one another. Demonstrating this unity in one scene, Cipolla reverses the procedure and makes himself subject to the common will; he finds and carries a bit of costume jewelry and kneels to present it to Signora Angiolieri while speaking the required words with difficulty in French.

Cipolla praises Signora Angiolieri for having served a great artist, the Fatherland's immortal songstress. An artist himself, and now the audience's "lord and master," Cipolla announces intermission at this suspenseful moment, during which—with the children falling asleep and the parents concerned with the lateness of the hour—the narrator consents to remain rather than take them out of harm's way, as if his own will is paralyzed, with logic and parental solicitude both suspended. In retrospect he analyzes the personal-communal layers as an excuse for submission: "as things had been in Torre in general queer, uncomfortable, troublesome, tense, oppressive, so precisely they were here in this hall tonight." He consoles himself that the children are too young to understand the disreputable side of the entertainment.

The magician's series of "attacks upon the willpower, the loss or compulsion of volition" resume and continue past midnight, with his liquor glass and claw-handled riding whip the secrets of his "demoniac fires." Sitting on a rigid, entranced subject lying stretched between two chairs, Cipolla announces himself the person suffering, the person to be pitied. After additional demonstrations of his power to overcome the will of others, Cipolla lights upon the unresisting Signora Angiolieri and bids her follow him, enslaved, while her husband implores her to return. As proof of his power, the audience learns that her name, ironically, is Sofronia, meaning "of sound mind."

A young Roman gentleman challenges Cipolla to make him dance against his will, and yields. The narrator speculates that between willing and not willing there may lie too small a space for the idea of freedom to squeeze into, which also would explain a people's inertia under a dictator. The dancers in his care, Cipolla insists, cannot tire because it is not they who dance but himself.

Just as Signora Angiolieri's great pride and accomplishment had been a position of servitude, so Cipolla's last victim, Mario the waiter, personifies obedience. Nothing in his background, with his father a petty clerk and his mother a washerwoman, would suggest resistance to Cipolla, at this late hour "throned and crowned" in the estimation of the audience. Cipolla has had Mario in his eye "this long while" and proceeds with his denigration of Mario by invoking his attraction to women. On the basis of cupbearer to Zeus, Cipolla calls Mario a Ganymede, but Zeus's love for Ganymede was the god's only homosexual liaison. The most atrocious of Cipolla's commands, therefore, is that Mario kiss him.

Not entirely free of self-knowledge, when the crack of the whip brings Mario out of the trance he beats his temples in shame. Offstage he turns and fires a small gun twice, and the children and all watch Cipolla die. The demoralization of a people has been accomplished in this evening's entertainment, in which Cipolla has demonstrated that hypnotism—against the popular appraisal of it—can persuade people to commit indecencies against their will. He has not demonstrated—if Mario's supreme action is self-initiated—that the victims will not eventually seek recompense. Or—and here lies the narrator's interpretation of the final scene—the death has been a liberation. This implies that self-pitying Cipolla has willed his own death.

—Grace Eckley

THE MARIONETTIST
by Christina Stead, 1934

The story "The Marionettist" is placed near the beginning of Christina Stead's collection *The Salzburg Tales*, a highly significant position. Being the first story of the first day's round of narration, it serves to prepare readers for some of the most distinctive qualities of the 40 stories (along with scene-setting preliminaries, linking sections and an epilogue) that comprise the volume as a whole.

The image of the marionettist, made salient by the story's title, has a particular aptness as a figure for the kind of literary artist who produces stories such as those Stead has written for this collection. The overt manipulation of character and plot, the free adaptation of traditional narrative motifs and the scant regard for psychological realism—these puppeteerings are all recurrent features of Stead's extraordinary tales.

The narrator who unfolds this first story to the group of festival visitors is the Salzburg town councillor. He produces it when one of them asks whether "Salzburg always lost its sons to Vienna and the great cities," and his response begins in a way that seems to situate modern Salzburg in a timeless perspective, as a folktale might. "When winter came round, James's mother would look out at cloaked figures making tracks in the snow along the Nonnthalgasse beneath black Hohensalzburg, and say: 'I dreamed last night that Peter and Cornelius knocked at the door on a day like this . . .'" The iterative implication ("came round . . . would look out") may suggest that seasonal and narrative cycles are moving in step, and it is almost as if the tale itself belongs to the mother's dream trance.

Further affinities with folktale conventions soon appear. We seem close to the familiar three-sons formula when we learn that Peter and Cornelius, the two eldest, have run away from home years before and that the parents fret about the likelihood that James, the remaining one, will soon be lost to them now that he wants to train as a sculptor in Vienna. But the ensuing events give an odd twist to any expectations that derive from those seemingly formulaic premises. Although James promises them that he will return as soon as his studies end, he falls in love with a fellow-student, marries her, stays in Vienna, and is faced before long with parental responsibilities. He makes wooden dolls for his young children, using each new puppet "to tell them a new chapter in an endless story that he made up as he went along, one which sprang naturally out of events of their daily life, with incidents he read in the newspapers, and memories of his childhood pieced in." This sounds like a partial account of Stead's own method of composition—and, again like James, who would recount "ancient themes" from European myth and fantasy, the author of *The Salzburg Tales* is also fond of the often-told, the legendary, the archetypal.

James eventually decides to establish himself commercially as the operator of a marionette show. The whole family willingly shares the business tasks associated with this. As scripts for his marionette shows James invents stories that rework aspects of his family history in extravagant analogies. One of these, "The Pot of Gold" (shades of Hoffmann), tells how "two brothers went out after adventure and were variously reported as lost by accident, or as beggars, while a third brother stayed at home and became an honest butcher."

Then, with the kind of abruptness that so often enters Stead's short fiction, the narrator reports simply: "James left home when he was in his thirty-eighth year." There is no warning, no explanation, and no attempt to provide the kind of narratorial meditation that takes up much of Nathaniel Hawthorne's story "Wakefield," which tells of a man who leaves home and stays away for years without any evident motive. The family in Stead's story continues to run the marionette theatre. One of James's brothers, long-lost Peter, appears briefly on the scene and disappears again. After 15 years of absence, James casually turns up one day and is surprised that his family is not overjoyed at this reappearance.

The story proceeds with a couple more twitches of the narrator's own marionette strings. This is the first one: "They had no room for James in the house so they rented a small room for him not far away, and he stayed there and did some fancy articles in wood ordered by a shop selling cheap objets d'art. When winter came on he went away from Vienna one morning and his family never heard from him again." And the second twitch of the marionettist's strings follows at once, partly repeating the story's opening sentence ("But James's mother looked out at the cloaked figures making tracks in the snow . . . ") and its oneiric motif (she dreams of James's return) as a prelude to the wanderer's arrival in his parental home, whereupon he becomes a character in his mother's tale: repeatedly she "told the women about her son the sculptor who had travelled all over the world." He, in contrast, continues to withhold any mention of his wife and children "or his marionette theatre, for James knew that she would think a marionette show a come-down for a sculptor."

In this concluding irony of mild misrepresentation one might see again an implicitly self-referential narratorial comment. In a sense, this story wanders just as James does; and although some readers may want to see it as "sculpture"—as immobolised high art—its generic alignment is with the more popular cultural form of the marionettist's show.

—Ian Reid

THE MARK ON THE WALL
by Virginia Woolf, 1921

"The Mark on the Wall," which Virginia Woolf wrote in one sitting in 1917 while recuperating from a long illness, was her breakthrough into a new experimental form of fiction. Concentrating on the narrator's thoughts and mental states, Woolf tested the limits of the short story form by placing her emphasis on the inner life rather than on external action. Variations of stream-of-consciousness or interior monologue techniques like those in "The Mark on the Wall" were also being explored at the time by James Joyce and D.H. Lawrence, but Woolf combined modernist techniques with a new feminist consciousness.

The narrator's play on immobility and the supple movements of her thought anticipate Samuel Beckett's immobile, speculative characters. Woolf's emphasis on philosophical reflections, as critics like James Hafley and Avrom Fleishman observe, makes the story resemble an imaginative essay, but the subtle characterization of the speaker places it in the realm of fiction.

The story is an epistemological satire about the narrator's attempts to identify a mark on the wall across the room without getting up from her chair. Speculating about the mark, she recognizes the forces that prevent her from seeing the world as it is. She is limited on the one hand by rigid social and intellectual conventions and on the other hand by purely subjective fantasies. The fantasies seem liberating, but they bring their own distortion, blurring her

vision at times so that she cannot distinguish men and women from trees. She keeps reminding herself that she must refer to an external reference point, like the mark on the wall, but without moving to discover what it is. The unreliability of her efforts to know the world is mitigated by the solidity of natural phenomena, though the narrator is for the moment too involved in her speculations to check their relation to the truth.

Her thoughts circle round and round the mark on the wall, repeatedly going off on tangents, but gradually getting closer. At first she sees the mark as a depression or hole in the wall, then as a blemish, like a leaf on the surface, and finally she judges correctly that it is a round protuberance, like the head of a nail. This is as close as she can come by means of speculation. In order to reach the truth it is necessary to move close enough to examine the thing itself.

Since the story imitates spontaneous thought, its underlying logic is at first less obvious than the above summaries suggest. Its effect depends on the humor with which Woolf presents the narrator's wayward reflections, while at the same time shrewdly staying on course toward the final disclosures.

Early in the story the narrator ponders the flow of time, considering whether life is entirely accidental or whether on the contrary, it follows an intelligible pattern. Is there any rhyme or reason in things, she asks, any way to explain how she could lose such bulky objects as a coal scuttle and a hand organ, which just seemed to disappear off the face of the earth? The practical people who run the world do not recognize such mysteries. Theirs is a domain of "generalizations," barren formulas that regiment and limit the mind. She remembers the Victorian world of her childhood when society was governed by rigid rules for everything from parliamentary procedure to the way to sew table cloths. This dominant "masculine point of view which governs our lives" leaves hardly any room for imagination. But she believes there is another sphere "after life," a more spiritual state in which, perhaps, some sign of a larger purpose can be found. She imagines withdrawing into a purely subjective dream state where she can be free, as if floating weightless under water, but of course she knows that the old social and political rules still dominate the surface world. Can she connect those two worlds? For a moment she thinks of Shakespeare, who managed to be both a practical man of the theater and a poetic genius, but no—his example cannot help her because she knows so little about him. Shakespeare is merely a "historical fiction" and she needs something tangible to guide her.

The mark on the wall, still unidentified, represents the external facts of life against which it is folly to rebel, facts from which one cannot stray very far without risking great confusion. The mark recalls her to awareness of the actual room where she is sitting. Concentrating on that, she brushes aside rigid social and intellectual categories and ponders the objectivity of nature. Her position illustrates what S.P. Rosenbaum has described as Woolf's philosophical realism. The mark on the wall, the narrator says, represents "the impersonal world which is proof of some existence other than ours." Whatever it is, the mark offers a mediating term between the abstract generalizations of the masculine order and the escapism of a purely subjective vision. As Rosenbaum has observed, Woolf believes that "sanity and sense involve the interrelation of thought *and* external reality, of consciousness *and* the objects of consciousness."

The story is amplified by the disclosures at the very end. The final angry remark about World War I broadens the frame of reference; Alex Zwerdling has properly described

"The Mark on the Wall" as a war story. The war is symptomatic of an imbalance between outer and inner realms, a clash between social order and the private self which, as the narrator says, blurs our vision, ultimately also creating the need to fight. The snail, on which the story focuses at the end, suggests the moderating influence of nature. With its mollusc shell round a soft inner body, the snail symbolizes a harmonious union of outer and inner spheres.

In its mediating vision "The Mark on the Wall" (collected in *Monday or Tuesday*, 1921) anticipates Woolf's major novels such as *Mrs. Dalloway* (1925) and *To the Lighthouse* (1927). Although the story implicitly suggests an epistemological theme, its appeal to most readers, as Woolf's biographer, Lyndall Gordon, points out, is based on a humorous evocation of simple objects and ordinary domestic life.

—Herbert Marder

MARKHEIM
by Robert Louis Stevenson, 1887

First published in 1885 in an annual aimed at the Christmas market, "Markheim" was an unlikely candidate for such a volume. True, the story is set on Christmas day, it opens with an ostensible quest for a last minute present, and there is an encounter with the supernatural. But this is no pleasantly spine-tingling ghost story; rather it is a complex study of the problem of good and evil.

Stevenson had already tried his hand at the supernatural in stories exploiting the folktales of witchcraft, bogles, and warlocks he had heard as a child. "Markheim" (collected in *The Merry Men* in 1887) reflects a different sector of his Scottish upbringing. The Calvinist preoccupation with the polarities of good and evil, freewill and predestination, the elect and the damned, were art and part (in the Scots legal phrase) of the Scottish consciousness. Henley unerringly listed amongst his friend Louis's attributes "something of the Shorter Catechist." The individual's struggle with conflicts of vice and virtue forms the very stuff of "Markheim" and *The Strange Case of Dr. Jekyll and Mr. Hyde*. The latter is the more powerful foray into the territory of *The Confessions of a Justified Sinner*, but "Markheim" combines an equally original approach with a narrative treatment of remarkably close texture.

The opening paragraphs set both scene and theme economically:

> "Yes," said the dealer, "our windfalls are of various kinds. Some customers are ignorant, and then I touch a dividend on my superior knowledge. Some are dishonest," and here he held up the candle, so that the light fell strongly on his visitor, "and in that case," he continued, "I profit by my virtue."

> Markheim had but just entered from the daylight streets, and his eyes had not yet grown familiar with the mingled shine and darkness in the shop. At these pointed words, and before the near presence of the flame, he blinked painfully and looked aside.

We learn from the dealer's continuing speech that it is Christmas day when he is known to be alone and balancing his books, that he has previously bought articles from Markheim, and that he suspects they were come by dishonestly.

From this point the story is developed swiftly in dramatised dialogue. Clues are distributed as deftly as in the opening paragraphs—Markheim's instability, twinges of guilt, barely controlled violent impulses; the dealer's shady equivocations, now the *faux bonhomme*, now the bargainer with the upper hand; increasing tension as the dealer tries to conclude their business and get rid of his visitor. There is a rapid climax as Markheim leaps on his victim and stabs him to death.

The pace of the narrative is then suddenly relaxed. The viewpoint alters; Markheim's perceptions and reflections follow. A brooding atmosphere is built up—silence broken by the sound of innumerable clocks; the mirrored faces of portraits and china figures apparently moving in the trembling candlelight while the dealer's body lies motionless on the floor; the contrast between the shadowy shop and the steady light from the door open to the rooms above. These also are polarities, though it is open to question whether Stevenson deliberately contrived their parallel symbolisms; perhaps they are the unconscious product of his creative imagination.

As Markheim fills his pockets with loot and considers his crime he is totally impenitent. The boy who had shuddered at pictures of murderers has grown into a man unmoved by the murder he has committed. He fears neither God nor the day of judgment, only that by planning his crime imperfectly he may be caught and brought to trial. Action is resumed when he goes upstairs to look for the dealer's money, confidence returning as he discovers that the house is deserted, as he had guessed earlier on seeing the servant girl leave. But as he searches he hears footsteps, followed by the opening of the door:

> What to expect he knew not, whether the dead man walking, or the official ministers of human justice, or some chance witness blindly stumbling in to consign him to the gallows.

But the visitant (as Stevenson calls him) glances round, nods, smiles, withdraws. Markheim desperately calls him back, and there follows a conversation on the nature of evil which the visitant conducts with worldly courtesy.

Commentators usually refer to this character as the devil, but this is too simple a reading. Stevenson presents him ambiguously:

> The outlines of the new-comer seemed to change and waver like those of the idols in the wavering candle-light of the shop; and at times Markheim thought he knew him; and at times he thought he bore a likeness to himself; and always . . . there lay in his bosom the conviction that this thing was not of the earth and not of God. "What are you?" cried Markheim, "the devil?" "What I may be," returned the other, "cannot affect the service I propose to render you."

That service is knowledge of where to find the hidden money and thus escape before the servant returns. Though Markheim's interlocutor professes an interest in both sins and virtues, he declares that he lives for evil, manifested not in individual acts but inherently in evil character. Markheim protests that both evil and good run strong in him, but his visitant predicts an irreversible progress in evil which will be halted only by death. "You will never change; and the words of your part on this stage are irrevocably written down."

This is truly the doctrine of predestination. But Stevenson tips the balance towards freewill. Urged to murder the maidservant when she rings the doorbell, Markheim retorts that his love of good may be damned but his hatred of evil remains. By applying his interlocutor's own logic he can break with further evil by giving himself up to justice and thus to sentence of death; "the features of the visitor began to undergo a wonderful and lovely change: they brightened and softened with a tender triumph, and, even as they brightened, faded and dislimned," a transformation at odds with Calvinistic notions of the devil seeking whom he may devour. Stevenson's innovative treatment of the theme is both complex and subtle, his stance redemptive.

—Stewart F. Sanderson

THE MARQUISE OF O (Die Marquise von O)
by Heinrich von Kleist, 1810

"Die Marquise von O" ("The Marquise of O") caused an outrage in polite German society when Kleist first published the story in 1808 (collected in *Erzählungen* in 1810). Today the work lays claim to being one of the greatest pieces in the entire canon of German short fiction, a masterpiece that within its modest length touches on issues that lie at the very heart of human existence as it is played out in its social context: male and female sexuality, filial bonds, family status and honour, the fragility of social order in times of war or catastrophe, the nature of forgiveness, and that key question to Kleist and Western philosophy—how does one prove to others what one feels to be true?

Kleist's subject matter was by no means original: a woman finds herself pregnant and does not know how. The theme can be found in Montaigne and Cervantes, but Kleist's treatment takes the story well beyond the bounds of mere curiosity, although it is by means of the curious that Kleist typically seizes his reader's attention at the very beginning of the story. In an opening sentence, that is both a cascade of information and an intricate linguistic web characteristic of the story as a whole, the incredulous reader is told that a certain titled lady, a widow and mother of impeccable character, has announced through the newspapers that she finds herself inexplicably with child and would be prepared to marry the father if he would declare himself. Having caught the reader's imagination, Kleist immediately meets the desire for further information by giving a detailed, business-like account of the lady's background and the events that have led to this bizarre public announcement. Only a second or third reading will betray to the careful reader the subtle shifts in narrative perspective and the presence of a distancing irony. By the end of the story, which a superficial reading would reduce to a mere gothic precursor of the detective story, the reader is in possession of all the external facts: the Marquise was raped whilst in a swoon by a Russian officer, the Count F, who had led the storming of the citadel commanded by the Marquise's father. This young Russian had only moments before saved the lady from the hands of his own soldiers, and her impression of him before she lost consciousness

was that of her saving angel. Once order has been restored to life in the citadel, Count F displays an ardent concern for the Marquise's well-being, culminating in a seemingly impetuous request for her hand in marriage. Her family are both touched and disconcerted by this ardour and press their daughter's rescuer to be patient. Military duties compel the Russian to travel away, and it is during his absence that the Marquise's changing physical condition plunges her into confusion and despair and Kleist brings us to the heart of the matter. The Marquise's awareness of her own unblemished conduct stands in total contradiction to what her senses tell her: "Oh God! said the Marquise, beginning to convulse, how can I set my mind at rest? Do not my own inner and all too familiar feelings tell against me?" (my translation). Her avowal of innocence to her mother and her plea for confirmation of her condition provoke the most exquisite oxymoron in the German language as the Marquise's mother retorts, "A clear conscience and a midwife!" Yet the Marquise is both blameless and pregnant. Her inner senses are indeed a finer guide than her conscious perception of her social behaviour, which, as with all human beings, is far from being complete and infallible.

Rejected by her family, who now perceive their once cherished daughter as little more than a mendacious whore, the Marquise retreats to her country estate with her children to prepare for her labour and enters a moment of private idyll, a familiar device in Kleist and one that shows his delicate control of narrative pace. It is here she decides upon the unprecedented action of announcing her condition in the newspaper. (This unprecedented event is entirely in keeping with the tradition of the German novelle.) With tremendous technical verve, Kleist prepares the appearance at the appointed hour of the respondent to the Marquise's announcement with impeccable dramatic timing, and even permits an element of comedy. The respondent is the Russian Count, and this diabolical revealing of an unbearable truth causes the Marquise once more to faint.

Unlike many of Kleist's stories, harmony is restored at the end of this work: between the man and the woman, between the parents and the child. And the participants even gain a high degree of insight into the nature of existence. The Marquise understands why she swooned a second time on the day all was revealed, for as she confides to the Count, "he would not have appeared to her a devil if at his first appearance to her he had not seemed an angel." But not the Marquise is aware that both categories were false perceptions, a third way of seeing him was necessary. And the Russian's sense of being reconciled is also based on an inner feeling, a belief that he has been forgiven because all now accept his crime reflected the "fragile order of the world."

It was not the rape itself that concerned Kleist. The text reduces that incident to the smallest typographical possibility available to him: a mere dash. Yet it is instructive to recall Erich Rohmer's acclaimed film version of the story to see how easy it is to distort the complex, hypotactic structure of Kleist's language. Rohmer's camera has to motive the rape by lingering over the Marquise's prostrate body, whilst the timing of the act completely misunderstands Kleist's intentions. In the film the Count commits his crime after he has taken control of the citadel, thus when order prevails, yet in the text the rape takes place exactly at that point in the siege when neither party is in charge, namely at that very moment when the all too fragile order of Kleist's world had collapsed.

—Anthony Bushell

MATEO FALCONE
by Prosper Mérimée, 1833

Prosper Mérimée was just 26 years old, and a literary hopeful of still quite modest achievements, when he published his very first short story, in the prestigious *Revue de Paris,* on 3 May 1829. It turned out to be a major literary event. Critics hailed its exceptional concision, and the concentrated power of its spare plot; and, because it was a story about Corsica, they congratulated the author on the accuracy and truth of his portrayal of the island's local color. What the critics did not know was that Mérimée had never set foot on the island of Corsica, but had invented his details about Corsican topography and customs purely on the basis of his reading. That reading had clearly been effective, since everyone seemed to find "Mateo Falcone" convincingly authentic. Indeed, Mérimée himself reported, when he finally did visit Corsica a decade later, that he was amazed to see how accurate he had been.

What the critics and other readers had recognized in "Mateo Falcone," we now know, was the sudden appearance of something new on the literary scene, a short story unlike anything they had seen previously, a composition so conscientiously researched and so painstakingly constructed that no superfluous detail had been allowed to intrude upon the reader's attention, or deflect the reader from following the relentless course of the action toward the cruelly inevitable dénouement. In other words, "Mateo Falcone" seemed driven, from the first word, by carefully controlled artistic principles willed by the author. In 1829 it was seen as a new kind of French short story, and almost instantly became the standard by which subsequent French short stories would be judged. Eventually, 20th-century scholars comparing the development of the short story in many different cultures, would come to the conclusion that Poe and Hawthorne in the United States, and Pushkin and Gogol in Russia, had arrived independently and at about the same time at the same concept of an artistically controlled and thematically unified short story as Mérimée had invented, but that a confrontation of dates seemed to show that, with the publication of "Mateo Falcone" on 3 May 1829, Mérimée simply had the honor of getting into print first with a published specimen. Critical consensus today thus considers the publication of "Mateo Falcone" as a major *international* literary event, marking the start of the modern short story as a new literary genre.

It is useful to review, briefly, the elements of "Mateo Falcone" that persuaded readers in 1829 that this was indeed something new, meriting, for the first time in the long history of the short story, the implied claim that it was a genuine work of art. Structurally, Mérimée seems to have followed the principles of French Classic tragedy: there is but one action towards which everything in the story tends, and it all happens in one day, and in one place: the house of Mateo Falcone in the hills above Porto-Vecchio. A five-part division can be perceived in the plot, akin to the five acts of a classical tragedy: exposition of the character, family, and environment of Mateo Falcone; the fateful decision of the parents, one day, to leave their son in charge of their house, and the arrival of the wounded bandit seeking shelter; the arrival soon after of the government soldiers, and their confrontation with Mateo's son; the climactic return of Mateo and wife just as the bandit, betrayed by the son, Fortunato, is taken prisoner; the precipitation of the family tragedy once everyone else has departed. Equally classical is the terse, stripped down prose of the narration, with few modifiers or subordinate clauses to qualify or complicate the account of the action. One notices, indeed, that as the action grows more tense, the sentences tend to get shorter, and by the end there is scarcely any narration, only the staccato exchange of speech fragments reminiscent of the stychomythia of Greek, and French, classical tragedy. Particularly noticeable, after the first few pages of exposition, is the almost complete disappearance of authorial intervention, in the form of psychological analysis or comment. The author seems deliberately to avoid informing the reader of the emotions felt by the characters, almost effacing himself by the spare style, and leaving the reader alone and helpless, forced by the momentum of events to follow the horrifying action unaided by the comfort of a narratorial voice.

While the ending is a shock, because of the utter absence of even a flicker of emotion in the prose, it is certainly not unexpected by the reader. Rather it is felt, in classical terms, as inevitable and hence a relief to the reader, now purged of the emotions of pity and fear. It is the dry, hard, disciplined prose of the concluding pages on which Mérimée particularly relies to impart to his reader the sense that his brief tale is not sordid but tragic.

Mérimée must have sensed that, in "Mateo Falcone," he had somehow created a masterpiece with his first try at this literary form. Perhaps it was out of a kind of gratitude that he became almost exclusively a short story writer thereafter, in his creative work, forsaking all the other forms in which he had dabbled till then. "Mateo Falcone" made its appearance in book form, four years later, as the proud "lead piece" in Mérimée's first collection of short stories, entitled *Mosaïque (Mosaic).* That volume, published in 1833 and frequently reprinted since, truly launched Mérimée's career as a writer.

—Murray Sachs

MATRENA'S HOUSE (Matrenin dvor)
by Aleksandr Solzhenitsyn, 1964

One of Aleksandr Solzhenitsyn's most memorable pieces of short fiction is "Matrenin dvor" ("Matrena's House"). The time and setting of the story is the summer of 1953 in rural Russia. The first-person narrator is a man returning from prison and exile to teach mathematics. Much like the author, the narrator has experienced life in the prison camps and exile in the desert. Wishing to start life anew, he heads for a teaching post in Torfoprodukt, a settlement among the peat bogs. Over the hill is a village called Talnovo, which holds the "promise of backwoods Russia."

Framing the tale with his personal views and perspective as an outsider, the schoolteacher's moving eye focuses on Matrena, an elderly, unattractive woman who reluctantly accepts him as a lodger in her house. She is ill—"yellow and weak." Besides her decaying house, she owns only a lame cat and a goat. Matrena functions as the prototypical Russian peasant, following in the tradition of Dostoevskii, Chekhov, and Tolstoi (especially his portrayal of the serfs). She illustrates a spirituality that eschews greed and self-interest.

In contrast to the acquisitiveness of her fellow villagers, Matrena is singularly selfless. She finds it impossible to say "no" and consequently finds herself being asked to work by the *kolkhoz,* even though she no longer is officially attached; she joins work parties to plant gardens. She helps feed the herdsmen with delicacies she denies herself. Although she is exceedingly poor, she never asks for pay.

Her only possession of value is her home, yet she loses it through her generosity. Before World War I, Matrena became engaged to Faddy Mironovich, who went to war and returned several years later to find his betrothed married to his brother Effim. Faddy curses Matrena and marries another woman of the same name. After Matrena loses the six children she bears to Effim, both she and her neighbors believe her to be cursed. When Effim is called up in World War II and never returns, Matrena is left alone in her house. In the present time of the narrative, Matrena is asked to give her top room to her foster daughter, Kira (Faddy's daughter), whom she has raised as her only child.

The episode of the devastation to Matrena's home, symbolized by the removal of the top room, points to her exploitation by her family. Even before she is dead, her family covets her house. In her zeal to help out, she accompanies the moving party and is killed along with her nephew by a train. The ill-fated top room serves as the culmination of Faddy's threat of 40 years earlier when he said, "If it wasn't my own brother, I'd chop the two of you to bits." Matrena at the end is mutilated and literally chopped to bits by the train. Although the heroine has placed little stock in earthly goods, her sisters and brother-in-law wage a bitter fight over the remains of the house. They descend to the level of dogs fighting over a bone. Solzhenitsyn shows their greediness and pettiness with his relentless description of the funeral wake.

At the end of the story, the narrator realizes the true worth of Matrena, and he recites an epitaph:

> She was misunderstood and abandoned even by her husband. She had lost six children, but not her sociable ways. She was a a stranger to her sisters and sisters-in-law, a ridiculous creature who stupidly worked for others without pay. She didn't accumulate property against the day she died.

Further, he judges her to be the "righteous one" whom no village or country should be without.

Only the schoolteacher, having lived through the horror of the camps, is able to discern Matrena's spiritual depth and beauty in the face of a materialistic society. Logically, the moral is that, if there were more Matrenas, Russia would be redeemed. Moreover, the narrator implies that people do not appreciate the righteous among them until they are dead. The villagers took Matrena's goodness for granted. Since the narrator acts as the observing consciousness, he sees what the villagers do not see—the intrinsic worth of the heroine.

The narrative style is realistic, simple, and direct. At times, the descriptions are stark and serve to indict the thoughtless and self-serving villagers. In contrast, the schoolteacher and Matrena are kindred souls. Like Kostoglotov, the released prisoner in *The Cancer Ward,* who meets a kind functionary at the novel's conclusion, the narrator finds in Matrena's character and deeds a cause for optimism. Like Matrena, the narrator is happy to have food, shelter, and company. He appreciates the smile on her round face. Like her, he has risen above the petty occupations of a property-fixated society. His relationship to Matrena is that of a surrogate son. She cooks and cares for him like the son she never raised to manhood. Their life exists in an equilibrium until her untimely death. Thus, the author juxtaposes the themes of materialism and spiritualism, selfishness and selflessness, and greed and love. Harkening back to Dostoevskii's *The Brothers Karamazov,* (1880), Solzhenitsyn might agree that Alesha's all-encompassing love is the only corrective to the evil wrought by humankind.

—Shirley J. Paolini

MELANCTHA
by Gertrude Stein, 1909

Gertrude Stein had already written *Q.E.D.* and *Fernhurst,* novellas about love triangles both lesbian and heterosexual, and an early version of *The Making of Americans,* before she began writing the stories of the three lower-class women, collectively published as *Three Lives* in 1909, that would make her a pioneer of 20th-century realism. In the first written stories, "The Good Anna" and "The Gentle Lena," Stein described German immigrant working women's lives. Heavy with the irony that, for all their "goodness" and "gentleness," both women died miserable, their only happiness coming from friendships with other women, Stein's fiction was marked by a continuous and ever modulating repetition and the use of very common language.

When she began "Melanctha," the last of the three lives, in the winter of 1905–06, she was living in Paris and sitting for the portrait that Pablo Picasso was painting of her. During the more than 80 sittings for the painting, Stein's use of repetition intensified, and her presentation of the mulatto protagonist of this novella was both more complicated, and more sympathetic, than her characterizations of Anna and Lena had been.

Stein's description of Melanctha Herbert was both innovative and risky. The style of incremental repetition attracted readers' attention, but sometimes drove them away from the text; once into it, however, the fact that Melanctha was bisexual might also drive readers away. In the fragmented narrative that Stein chose, it is clear that Melanctha explored heterosexual relationships during her adolescence; she spent much time "wandering" at the docks. Later she became intimate with the alcoholic Jane Harden who, at age 23, was sexually adept. Stein says clearly, "It was not from the men that Melanctha learned her wisdom. It was always Jane Harden herself who was making Melanctha begin to understand." The two years of the women's relationship pass quietly, Melanctha spending "long hours with Jane in her room," a description that echoes love-making scenes from *Q.E.D.* Melanctha's later liaison with Rose, which is the story that opens the novella, adds to the lesbian strand of the story and suggests Melanctha's double injury when Rose betrays her—first by marrying Sam and then by ending their affair.

After 35 pages of Melanctha's varied bisexual history, Gertrude introduces Jeff Campbell, the black doctor who grows to love Melanctha while he tends her dying mother. The story then becomes an extended dialogue between the arbitrarily rational Campbell and the purposefully inarticulate Melanctha, a tour de force of voiced dialogue unlike anything in published literature of the time. During the lengthy Jeff-Melanctha interchanges, Stein draws Jeff as the rational speaker who wants permanence, exclusivity, security. His polemical insistence is shown to be absurd, however, when contrasted with Melanctha's meaningful silences. She loves through acts; she gives Jeff what she has to give and does not talk about it. While he accepts her love, he verbalizes all parts of their relationship and forces her into language that becomes destructive. Whatever Melanctha says, Campbell argues with. By the end of the 50-page dialogue, the reader sees that Stein has constructed a classic discourse between reason and emotion. Because the language sounds so much like real people's speech— circular, repetitive, boring—its classic pattern has been entirely overlooked.

Stein's fiction continued what was becoming her life process, melding the knowledge she had acquired from her studies of philosophy and psychology at Radcliffe College and her studies of brain anatomy and medicine at Johns Hopkins Medical School, with those of literature and painting. Her main interest was presenting the person; her fascination with the "portrait" was a culmination of years of formal study as well as the result of the contemporary artistic excitement over Cezanne, Picasso, and Matisse as they worked to change the nature of painting, particularly through their portraits. In "Melanctha," Stein created a double portrait—or, rather, the fictional portrait of herself as a deeply divided person. Although the long dialogue between Jeff and Melanctha has been described as typical of conversations Stein and her female lover often had, with Stein represented by Jeff Campbell, Stein portrayed herself too in the character of Melanctha. Born of very different, and irreconcilable, parents and later isolated from her family, the maturing Melanctha—like Stein—tried to escape her feelings of difference and looked to sexual love for self-knowledge. Jeff and Melanctha's impasse mirrors Stein's own conflicted sense of her emotional loyalties to different aspects of her self.

One of the on-going points of interest about "Melanctha" is that it is a very early fiction about a black character— written by a white woman who seemingly knew very little about black life. Despite the story of Richard Wright's later reading the work aloud to black workers, with good response, today's readers must be sensitive to what appears to be racial stereotyping. But in some ways, Stein's identification with Melanctha wipes out what seems to be racism in the text. In her notebooks, Stein repeated that her own nature was "dirty": "the Rabelaisian, nigger abandonment . . . daddy side, bitter taste fond of it." Locating herself in the camp of the sensual, Stein used the stereotype of the sexual black woman as a kind of self-portrait. Her aligning Melanctha with "her black brute" of a father instead of with her better-born mother is a means of justifying Stein's own family alliance, and her own sexuality—though we still deplore her choice of language.

Critics have cited as important influences on *Three Lives* the painting of Madame Cezanne hanging above Stein as she wrote, as well as her reading Flaubert's lyric story of the servant Felicite, "Un Coeur Simple." While these influences should be mentioned, the real radicalism in Stein's "Melanctha" was her choice of a lower class, bisexual, mulatto character as a protagonist, and the comparatively unsympathetic style she used to present her. This was fiction without the expected apparatus: how did the reader know what the author felt, and therefore, how did the reader know how he or she was supposed to feel about the characters? Without the use of conventional narrative clues, however, Stein made clear the unhappiness of both Melanctha and the other two women in *Three Lives*; and her work, privately published in 1909, served as an admonition for women who would accept cultural mandates about what kind of life would make them "happy."

—Linda Wagner-Martin

THE METAMORPHOSIS (Die Verwandlung) by Franz Kafka, 1915

One night in September 1912, in a single eight-hour sitting, Franz Kafka wrote the novella *Das Urteil* ("The Judgment"). It was his first successfully completed longer work. "*This* is the *only way* to write," Kafka noted in his diary, "with such cohesion, with such total opening of body and soul." He now felt encouraged to approach the novel form again. On September 25, Kafka began the second version of his *Amerika* novel. Between November 17 and December 6, he interrupted his work on the novel to write *Die Verwandlung* ("The Metamorphosis"), which was published in October 1915. Because of its proximity to "The Judgment" and "The Stoker" (the first chapter of the incomplete *Amerika* novel), stories in which the father-son conflict is prominent, "The Metamorphosis" has often been read as yet another psychological *conte à clef,* in which Kafka works out his complicated relationship to his father. The story depicts a son who takes over the role of the father as caretaker of the family, finds himself transformed into an enormous insect, and is left to die in his room by his visibly revived family. In much of the critical literature Gregor Samsa's transformation into a giant bug is either taken to signify his sense of guilt and desire for punishment for having usurped the role of the father; or, to symbolize both a libidinous rebellion and the condemnation of such a rebellion; or, to represent a rebellious assertion of unconscious desires and energies that are identical with the primitive and infantile demands of the id. Yet despite their profusion and persistence, psychological readings of "The Metamorphosis" remain unsatisfactory because they leave too much unexplained.

Theodor W. Adorno, by contrast, recommended "the principle of literalness," an approach to Kafka that seems to go to the heart of "The Metamorphosis." "The first rule," wrote Adorno, "is take everything literally; cover up nothing with concepts invoked from above. . . . Only fidelity to the letter . . . can help." Thus we are inescapably confronted with the story's famous first sentence: "As Gregor Samsa awoke one morning from uneasy dreams he found himself transformed in his bed into a gigantic insect." Despite the strange nonchalance with which Gregor accepts his transformation, the course of the story makes clear that "it was no dream."

The story's first part is desperate slapstick. It shows Gregor struggling with comic and terrifying questions: What do you do when you are a bug? How do you get out of bed? How do you present yourself to your family and your boss? When Gregor finally manages to open the door of his room and reveals himself to his assembled family and his boss, their horrified reaction confirms that he is indeed a giant cockroach.

In part two the family settles into living with a bug. The narrative focus, however, is still inside Gregor's room. We follow his movements and share his gratitude when his mother and sister gradually transform the outfit of his cell from a human bedroom into the habitat of an animal. Part two ends, like part one, with Gregor breaking forth from his room and his father driving him back. But instead of shooing Gregor back as before with the help of a stick and a newspaper, the father now pelts him with apples. One of them gets stuck in Gregor's back and becomes a festering wound.

With part three the narrative focus shifts to the living quarters of the family. They no longer relate to Gregor individually (as sister, mother, and father), but react to him only as a group. They no longer see in Gregor a transformed family member, but primarily an animal. The separation of the animal from the human beings is complete. This development is emphasized as much by the contrast between the family's newly developed commercial energies and Gregor's idleness, as by the introduction of new characters. The family is renting a room to three bearded boarders and employs a strong-willed charwoman, who shows a certain disgusted fondness for the roach. She greets Gregor every morning with a colloquial abuse German speakers apply to human beings: "Du alter Mist-käfer" (You old dung beetle). Kafka, who was impressed by the unsubtle energies of the working class, took servants seriously. It is no surprise then to find the basis for the story's conceit comes from the mouth of an immensely vulgar woman. Kafka's story takes the servant's abusive metaphor literally. Each sentence in the story is literal and each signifies; "nowhere in Kafka," said Adorno, "does there glimmer the aura of the infinite idea."

And yet Kafka modifies his literalness when he allows Gregor to react to music. The sister, who had brought Gregor all his food, now plays the violin for the boarders: "Was he an animal," Gregor reflects, "that music had such an effect on him? He felt as if the way were opening before him to the unknown nourishment he craved." Here Kafka points to the realm of infinite idea, which is not accessible to those confined to earthliness. Confusingly, it is precisely the sister who condemns Gregor to death when he upsets the boarders with his third and final emergence from his room. "We must try to get rid of it," she says. As if to indulge and oblige his family one more time, Gregor dies during the following night and it thrown out into the garbage by the charwoman the next morning. The remaining family members celebrate their liberation by taking a day off from their jobs and embarking on a trainride into the countryside.

"The Metamorphosis" abounds in enigmatic details, such as the father's edenic missiles or the bearded trinity, that refuse to fit squarely into a psychological interpretation. Yet they call for interpretation while the story itself insists on their literalness. Those who succumb to the temptation to read the story symbolically, perhaps as a metaphysical allegory, soon find themselves in a maze of contradictions. What remains real about Kafka's story, however, is the moment of pain when Gregor understands that he is no longer himself, a person, but a thing. At that point, concentrating into a single moment Kafka's acute insight into the human condition, which for the Jews of Prague would soon become an inescapable fate, the story stops being a joke, metaphysical, psychoanalytical, or otherwise.

—Susanne Klingenstein

MICHAEL KOHLHAAS
by Heinrich von Kleist, 1810

Though Heinrich von Kleist is remembered above all for the dramas that he wrote in the course of his short and tragic life, his stories too have power, passion, and the ability to confront his readers with uncompromising and unsettling depictions of humanity under pressure. "Michael Kohlhaas" was begun in 1804 and about a quarter of the text was printed in 1808 in the sixth issue of the short-lived literary magazine *Phöbus*. The complete story, which takes up the text from *Phöbus* virtually unchanged, was first published along with other tales by Kleist in his *Erzählungen* (Tales) in 1810.

The basis of "Michael Kohlhaas" is an episode from Germany's troubled history in the early 16th century. A certain Hans Kohlhase (Kleist altered the name slightly in his story), smarting from a sense of injustice, raised a small band of followers and terrorised Saxony over a period of some 18 years, from 1522 to 1540; he was finally executed, along with his companion Georg Nagelschmidt, in Berlin. From this material Kleist constructs a story whose major interests are not so much military or political as psychological and moral. The central issue throughout is the nature of justice.

Michael Kohlhaas is, we learn in the suspiciously calm opening of this quite long tale, a successful man, and his success is largely due to his readiness to explore matters carefully before taking a decision. But once he has made up his mind, nothing can make him swerve from the course once he has decided. We first meet him when, in his 30th year, he is riding out from Brandenburg into Saxony with a string of young horses which he is intending to sell. He soon falls victim to petty tyranny: the new lord, Junker Wenzel von Tronka, is introducing a new tax on horses passing through and even insists on a permit. All this is news to Kohlhaas, unwelcome news at that, and he is distressed to have to leave behind a pair of fine black horses with a groom to look after them as pledges while he goes on to investigate the legitimacy of the new practices. What follows is almost Kafkaesque in its account of how a well-meaning man is defeated by the system. No one in an official position wants to listen to Kohlhaas, for von Tronka has friends and relations in high places, and meantime both the pair of horses and the groom are villainously ill-treated. Kohlhaas, a kindly family man who is devoted to his wife and children, is slow to take offence: he is careful to evaluate all the evidence about von Tronka, questioning the groom most carefully, and he repeatedly seeks redress through legal channels.

Finally his patience snaps, and then his vengeance is swift and terrible. Not content with razing von Tronka's castle to the ground, he pursues his fleeing persecutor from town to town. Kleist evokes all the horrors of the 16th-century Peasant Wars with the intensity of a man living through the Napoleonic campaigns that had wreaked such havoc in German-speaking lands. Gradually we become aware, however, of the warping of Kohlhaas's mind. His sense of outrageous injustice is strengthened when his dear wife dies after being struck by a guard when she goes to court to present a petition on her husband's behalf. After that there is no controlling him. In a grand apocalyptic vision he sees himself as an emissary of Saint Michael the Archangel charged with punishing with fire and the sword all who sided with his persecutor von Tronk. The population quails before him, and his ferocious determination enables him and quite small numbers of followers to defeat the considerable forces marshalled against him by the authorities, who are shown as effete and corrupt.

A meeting with Martin Luther provides a turning point, for Kohlhaas respects him as an authority on moral questions. The second half of the story reveals what happens to Kohlhaas when he gives himself up, trusting that the justice of his cause will be his salvation. Once again, it is all too obvious that Kohlhaas's opinion that society is founded on genuine moral principles is shown to be naive in the extreme. He rejects opportunities to back out of the situation: for instance, when a gypsy woman gives him a capsule containing information which the Elector of Saxony wishes to know about, he rejects the opportunity of ingratiating himself by handing it over. It is significant that when he is executed, Kohlhaas is not broken on the wheel like his historical counterpart. Instead, he receives a more honorable death, by beheading, and the Elector orders that his sons should be well-treated. Thus ends Kleist's account of the life and death of a character from Germany in the 16th century, which we can see is also a portrait of a Romantic hero who feels he has no choice but to follow the dictates of his own inner convictions. That this should lead only to tragic despair and to doubt about all values is characteristic of Kleist's vision of the human predicament.

—Christopher Smith

MIDNIGHT MASS (A missa do galo)
by Joaquim Maria Machado de Assis, 1899

"A missa do galo" ("Midnight Mass") is a classic Brazilian short story. Not only is it obligatory reading for any educated person in Brazil, it is also one of the most anthologized stories since it was first collected in 1899 in *Páginas recolhidas,* and a supreme example of Machado de Assis's craftsmanship. The very simple plot has intrigued generations, who sometimes debate whether there was adultery, or whether the narrator knew what the woman's intentions toward him were.

One proof of the text's ambiguity is the fact that six celebrated Brazilian writers—Antonio Callado, Autran Dourado, Julieta de Godoy Ladeira, Lygia Fagundes Telles, Nélida Piñon, and Osman Lins—published *Missa do galo; variacões sobre o mesmo tema* (Midnight Mass: Variations About the Same Theme) in 1977. In this book, each writer takes up a different point of view and tells the story all over again. Still, Machado's original version remains with all its force.

"Midnight Mass" is narrated by an adult, Mr. Nogueira, who remembers a Christmas eve spent in Rio around 1861 or 1862. On this occasion, as is customary, the Catholic Church has a special mass at midnight. The young Mr. Nogueira, a student from the province then boarding at the notary Menezes's house, stays up late to go to the mass. While he's waiting for a friend to come pick him up, the notary's wife, Conceição, keeps him company. Their dialogue never leaves the confines of what is appropriate: they talk about novels, the characteristics of masses in the provinces and in the big city, and the two engravings she has on the wall.

However, as any reader of Machado's fiction knows, even as simple an occasion as a seemingly banal conversation between a younger man and an older woman gives rise to all sorts of play between what is said and what is implied. One important thing to consider in this story is its original title, "A missa do galo" (The Rooster's Mass), as the Christmas Eve mass is referred to in Portuguese—a rooster is said to have crowed at midnight, the time Jesus is supposed to have been born. The symbol of the rooster—a sexually mature bird—as the usher of a new day for Christendom, can of course be understood, in this context, as the sign for the birth of the man Nogueira out of the conversation he has with the lonely Conceição, whose husband, it is made clear, has a lover whom he visits constantly.

Because the narrator of the story is a mature Nogueira looking back on that crucial moment of his life, when he was just 17 years old, he can muse about perceptions and understandings which were probably not available to him when the conversation took place. At the time the young Nogueira, however, can only feel the ambiguous vibrations of Conceļão's words and his feelings. The older Nogueira can only remark how he never quite understood the conversation: too much time has passed, too many things have changed, and he might misrepresent what happened.

Indeed, representation, misrepresentation, and insinuation are at the center of the story. When Conceição first speaks to Nogueira, he is holding a copy of *The Three Musketeers,* a favorite with young boys. As the subject wanders to novels, a classic of young women's sentimental fiction, Macedo's *The Little Sweetheart,* is mentioned. It seems clear that Conceição is inviting Nogueira to grow from the adventure stories to love stories, with all that might imply. As Nogueira pretends to resume his reading, Conceição's "chaste disarray" allows him to see parts of her forearms, and when she paces between a window and the door of her husband's study, he notices the rhythm of her body.

The subject then falls on the appropriateness of the engravings on the wall. For Conceição, those two pictures, one representing Cleopatra and the other some feminine figures, would be better in a barber's shop. Of course, she has never been to a barber's shop. But she believes that such pictures belong in these places, as well as in bachelors' quarters. What she would have instead, she says, is saints' pictures. She refers to a statue of Our Lady of the Immaculate Conception that she has in her little oratory.

The contrast between what her house displays—two inappropriate pictures of secular women—and the religious icon she has hidden in her room signals the ambiguous nature of Conceição's representation. In the eyes of the young Nogueira, there can only be the Conceição in the flesh, unavoidably associated with the engravings he can see on the wall. However, even as she calls his attention to these pictures, Conceição assures him of the existence of another, hidden, immaculate Conception.

The two do not even touch. Nogueira's friend knocks at the window at the appointed hour and they go to the midnight mass—the rooster's mass. And Nogueira's life goes on eventlessly after he returns to his parents' house. The news that the notary Menezes dies and Conceição marries her husband's apprenticed clerk is given in the last lines of the story. Nogueira does not comment on this new fact of her life. He also abstains from analyzing the nature of the feelings the news arises in him. Desire, both in the form of the young Nogueira's nascent sexuality and the mature Nogueira's longing for a magical moment in his youth, cannot be represented as such. What the reader is left with is the representation of its impossibility, personified in a night shortly before the rooster crowed.

—Eva Paulino Bueno

THE MONKEY (Aben)
by Isak Dinesen, 1934

Considered by many readers and scholars to be Isak Dinesen's most compelling tale, "The Monkey" ("Aben") is included in her widely acclaimed collection, *Seven Gothic Tales,* published in 1934 soon after she returned to Denmark from nearly two decades abroad in Africa. (She wrote the stories in English first, and then translated them into Danish herself.) "The Monkey" borrows from the tradition of transformation used by such disparate writers as Ovid, Mary Shelley, and Nikolai Gogol; it is most indebted to Kafka's "The Metamorphosis," which helped usher in modernism.

"The Monkey" at first appears to be made for readers of adult fairy tales and romance. A soldier visits his aunt, the prioress of Closter Seven, who is, we are told, part of an institution whose "proud and kindly spirit of past feudal times seems to dwell in the stately buildings and to guide the existence of their communities." The prioress is delighted to offer advice on finding a suitable marriage mate for her nephew Boris. Boris's professed interest in marriage, we learn, is to relieve him of the scandal associated with his sexual dalliances among the soldiers in his regiment. Marriage he now views with pleasant detachment, and he shows no resistance when his aunt suggests a woman who is large, much larger than he is, and, as it turns out, capable of turning aside his forced sexual advances to the point of knocking out his front teeth. A toothless Prince Charming does not daunt the narrator, nor, it seems, us as readers.

Boris sets out to woo his aunt's choice, Athena, who is more than a maiden, a very *valkyrie,* the warrior her name implies. Athena does not share Boris's newly discovered enthusiasm for marriage, and she refuses his proposal. Furious, the prioress decides to match wits with Athena, planning a seduction supper with Boris as her instrument. During an evening of intoxicating wine, Boris precociously and erotically undresses his intended imaginatively, surrealistically proceeding in his thinking to her bones, her very skeleton which appeals to him even more—disconcertingly delivering us into the Gothic realm.

After a rather muddled sexual encounter, Boris is bested and turned aside by Athena's greater strength. But the prioress is counting on the naiveté of Athena when she informs her the next morning that a child will result from the kiss Boris managed to press on her lips and teeth. Athena reacts incredulously: from *that* will she have a child?

The aunt is not unreasonable to count on Athena's naiveté, for after all Athena has never seen herself in a mirror. To have never seen oneself in a mirror suggests intriguing possibilities. We can assume that Athena's existence cannot be entirely defined by the boundaries of flesh and bone a mirror would reflect back—certainly not in her own mind, even if Boris is thus tempted; her sense of self is much larger in scope, reaches more easily to the ether of the gods, to the goddess whose name she carries. She escapes the self-consciousness of being human, the vanity and folly of human beings; she cannot marvel at the beauty of her human features in an act of narcissism, but instead she can participate in an instinctive grasp of herself within the human flux— for the feeling of being human, without the glass in the mirror, must stay on the level of the senses, the knowledge of self remain partially formed.

We come to the transformation, which is the problematic issue in "The Monkey." It appears at the moment when Athena seems lost to Boris. What is it exactly that happens from the beginning of the tale to the end? The tale begins with a poised, almost demure, confident prioress who commands respect among her peers, and it ends as a wild, unrestrained animal claws and clatters up the Closter Seven wall after breaking through the glass of the window, sending the prioress into a frenzy before she is forced into transformation.

Dinesen delighted in paradox, in creating endings to her tales that were equipoised between opposite intention, without the linguistic details suggesting where the balance was meant to be heaviest. Here the temptation becomes to decide who indeed *is* the real prioress: it seems we can trust the narrative which insists that the "true Prioress" emerges at the end, if only because the previous one seems to have behaved fairly badly, not in keeping with the proprieties expected from a prioress—now she can be given another chance. From this newly evolved prioress we do not expect an arranger of seductions.

From Dinesen's private papers we learn that in early drafts of "The Monkey" the prioress was referred to as a witch, one whose power as a chaste older woman came from being associated with the supernatural, an idea Dinesen on occasion encouraged in thinking about herself, her claim to have psychic powers in a Denmark that tended to have a no-nonsense attitude toward people.

"The Monkey" reflects Dinesen's own life-long struggle with maintaining a stable sense of being; the tale is modern in its shattering of identity and concomitant retrieval of that identity. But unlike Kafka, for whom Gregor's insect in "The Metamorphosis" exemplifies a modern world in which forms of bourgeois existence bring ruin, here Dinesen playfully chucks the reader back to a more graceful century and whimsically speeds up Darwinian evolution, leaving us acutely aware of the glass fragments lying on the floor as our reading of "The Monkey" closes. The shattering of glass has broken our hold on fixed meaning, has reminded us that to imagine any human existence in the past is subject to the modern circumscription of self and perception as less than intact, predictable, or consolingly firm as the text and gender are deflated, our romantic expectations overturned. We are left with a tale whose linguistic turns have deflated us, leaving instead a suspect uniting of the reconciled couple, Boris and Athena, who have witnessed the transformation as an extremity of experience. Momentarily they face the world as a unity, which they were incapable of doing before and may well be incapable of doing in the future.

Dinesen would on occasion advise people facing troubles to let the monkey out as the solution to their dilemmas. Within the tale, significantly, the monkey lands on a bust of Kant, the purveyor of reason, in a reminder that as humans, we falter if we embrace reason only and forget that fate as meted out by the gods can cause eccentric quirks in our existence, can thwart us unexpectedly with humorous results that discomfit us. Only those with a fluid sense of reality (those who realize that good and evil flow into the same space at points, are not always distinguished, and *should* not, for Dinesen, be easily distinguished) are able to retrieve themselves, "a little out of breath from the effort," in a modern world that has lost the emotional organization of feudal times, the spirit of which is here nostalgically and aristocratically remembered. To "learn justice, and not to scorn the gods," as the Latin inscription at the close of "The Monkey" cautions us, is to aim at balanced reason. But one must realize there is a place reason does not reach—that hidden void where we find ourselves unwitting subjects of destiny.

—Olga Pelensky

THE MONKEY'S PAW
by W. W. Jacobs, 1902

Although W.W. Jacobs is best known for his humorous short stories and was, indeed, hailed as a master by P. G. Wodehouse, he did, on occasion venture into other forms. He left, for example, five novels which are still agreeable to read, although one senses that he was not entirely at ease with the genre. They lack the organic development of plot that the form demands and give the impression of episodes deftly knitted together. He was at his happiest within the discipline of the short story, rewriting and revising the taut narrative at a laborious rate of a hundred words a day. He did not always restrict himself to comedy. Sometimes he verged on what a later age would describe as "black" humour, and this led him to experiment with the macabre. A chilling example is "The Interruption" (*Sea Whisper*), about a man who murders his wife for her money and is afterwards blackmailed by his housekeeper. When he plans to poison her as well, the scheme goes awry and he meets his own death. Another exercise in the macabre is "Jerry Bundler" (*Light Freights*), a ghost story which is highly believable since in Jacobs's skillful narrative no ghost actually makes its appearance. His most macabre story is "The Monkey's Paw" (*The Lady of the Barge*), written around 1900 when he was at the height of his powers. Since then it has been the subject of a play and a film. ("The Lady of the Barge" was also successful as a play, and ("The Boatswain's Mate" as an opera by Dame Ethel Smyth.)

The plot of "The Monkey's Paw" is unfolded with rigorous logic. It opens with a typical piece of economical scene-setting. What, in contrast with the eerie events to follow, could be more commonplace than the suburban home known as "Laburnum Villa"? Outside, the rain is falling viciously and the road is a streaming torrent:

Without, the night was cold and wet, but in the small parlour of Laburnum Villa the blinds were drawn and the fire burned brightly. Father and son were at chess; the former, who possessed ideas about the game involving radical changes, putting his king into such sharp and unnecessary perils that it even provoked comment from the white-haired old lady knitting placidly by the fire.

They are awaiting the arrival of their old friend Sergeant-Major Morris, now back in England after long service in India. He at last finds his way through the storm, and, in the course of conversation, shows them a monkey's paw,

dried to a mummy. A fakir, he explains, has put a spell on it in order to show that people who interfere with fate do so to their own sorrow. The fakir decreed that three separate men should each have three separate wishes from it. Mr. White's son Herbert jocularly asks the sergeant if he has had his three wishes. The sergeant, white faced, hand trembling, replies that he has. "The first man had his three wishes," he adds. "I don't know what the first two were, but the third was for death. That's how I got the paw." It has caused enough mischief, he says, and he throws it on the fire. Mr. White hastily snatches it back despite the sergeant's warning. The paw is forgotten as the rest of the evening passes in tales of adventure in the mysterious East.

When the sergeant has gone, late at night, the family discuss the sinister talisman he has given them so unwillingly. Herbert suggests his father wish for £200 to pay off the mortgage. Mr. White, a little shamefaced, holds the monkey's paw and speaks his wish. The thing twitches, like a snake. Uneasily, they go to bed. Next day a representative of Herbert's employers calls. He tells the old couple that their son has died in an accident with machinery. He offers compensation in the form of £200.

The days pass in mourning. Mrs. White urges her husband to make a second wish that their boy return alive. Very reluctantly he does so. Nothing happens. Then, in the darkness of the night, a fusillade of knocks is heard at the door. Mrs. White hurries downstairs while her husband, petrified with fear, begs her not to open. She struggles with the bolt as he gropes for the talisman. He finds it, and, frantically, makes his third and last wish. As he does so the knocking ceases, the door opens, and the street lamp flickers on an empty road.

As in "Jerry Bundler," Jacobs creates an atmosphere of horror by avoiding direct description and concentrating on subtle detail: the heavy rain, the darkness, the imagined appearance of a ghastly simian mask in the dying embers of the fire, the squeaky stair, the rustle of a scurrying mouse, the cold wind rushing up the staircase after the wife has opened the door. There is no need for him to depict "the mutilated son" whom Mr. White fears he will see if his third wish is granted. The style is spare and precise: not a word could be added, not a word taken away without damaging the effect. Incidents which in themselves are harmless become hauntingly significant in the context: "The candle-end, which had burned below the rim of the china candlestick, was throwing pulsating shadows on the ceiling and walls, until, with a flicker larger than the rest, it expired." When the sergeant is asked whether he has had his three wishes granted, he says no more than "I did," but "his glass tapped against his teeth." The participants in the drama are drawn with swift, indelible strokes: the veteran sergeant who knows more than he cares to tell, the youthfully facetious son, the doting mother, the incredulous father. "The Monkey's Paw" is not to be dismissed as an ordinary ghost story. It is a little masterpiece of horror by an unusually gifted writer.

—James Harding

MOTHERS
by Endō Shūsaku, 1979

Although much of Endō's shorter fiction can be seen as a precursor to a full-length work devoted to the same, or related, themes, there are a few stories that clearly occupy an integral position in his oeuvre. Of these stories, possibly the most impressive is "Mothers." Developing the theme that recurs throughout Endō's work to that date—the issue of whether the Christian God first introduced into Japan by the Western missionaries in the 16th century could be moulded into a figure with whom the Japanese could feel an affinity—the story adds significantly to the image of the divine as representing not merely the strong paternalistic figure of the Old Testament, but also the more maternal figure, the "compassionate weakling" that Endō claimed to see encapsulated by Christ in the New Testament. As evidenced, for example, in *Silence*, Endō had long sought a literary depiction of Christ, whose very strength lay paradoxically in his weakness, but it is in "Mothers" that the author succeeds as never before in incorporating within this image the various elements he had been seeking to reconcile in previous works.

The text itself is carefully crafted to incorporate both the present and the past. Narrated entirely in the first person by a young novelist engaged in research on Japan's "Christian century" (1550-1650), the story intersperses depictions of his current field trip to Kyushu island with a variety of flashbacks—recollections of his childhood and, in particular, of certain incidents involving his mother. The link between the two levels is, however, far from tenuous: the focus of the narrator's study is the *Kakure* (Hidden) Christians, the descendants of those who had succumbed to *shogunate* pressure to perform an outward act of apostasy towards the end of the "Christian century," and who had subsequently been forced underground. Discovering the existence of a small number of determined locals who had refused to revert to traditional Christianity even following the readmission of the foreign missionaries towards the end of the 19th century, the narrator is initially attracted to the psychology of those who have been forced to come to terms with their own weakness (for agreeing to apostatise). Increasingly, however, as the story develops, the narrator comes to discern in the experience of the *Kakure* parallels, not merely with so many contemporary Japanese Christians struggling to reconcile the perceived clash between their faith and their native culture, but also with his own experience of having been unable to live up to the expectations of religious piety that his mother had struggled so hard to impose on him.

On one level, the story contains frequent references to the similarities the narrator perceives between his own situation and that of the *Kakure*. On arrival in Kyushu, for example, the narrator is met by a series of Catholic parishioners who will serve as his local guides. Immediately, he is reminded of the intensity of his mother's faith, but confrontation with such powerful spirituality only serves to heighten his feelings of empathy for the "weak" *Kakure*, leading him to conclude, "If I had been born in such a time, I [too] would not have had the strength to endure punishment" (translated by Van Gessel). The more he contemplates their situation, the more he comes to realise that, just as the *Kakure* had been forced to endure the critical gaze of "stronger" people around them, so he too has been subjected to the censorious gaze of others as a result of his callous, occasionally deceitful, treatment of his mother. As he admits, "I am interested in the *Kakure* for only one reason—because they are the offspring of apostates. Like their ancestors, they cannot utterly abandon their faith . . . sometimes I catch a glimpse of myself in these *Kakure*, people who have had to lead lives of duplicity, lying to the world and never revealing their true feelings to anyone."

It may be the awareness of this mutual burden of guilt that initially attracts the narrator to the *Kakure*, but the more he comes to contemplate their situation, the more he comes to accept that, just as the *Kakure* had learned of the impossibility of merely abandoning God with no subsequent pangs of guilt, so too, he is unable to simply forget his own mother. The result is a juxtaposition of scenes devoted to the *Kakure* with those involving recollections of the narrator's mother and the explicit acknowledgement that, "to the *Kakure*, God was a stern paternal figure, and as a child asks its mother to intercede with its father, the *Kakure* prayed for the Virgin Mary to intervene on their behalf."

This process of fusion of images is gradual, and is accompanied in the narrator's mind by a mellowing of the initial recollections of his mother. As the story develops, the image of the pious woman with the "hard, stone-like face" that so troubles him at the beginning is tempered, developing gradually into a more tender, maternal figure who stands "with her hands joined in front of her, watching [him] from behind with a look of gentle sorrow in her eyes."

The depiction echoes a recurring image of Endō's literature of the time and represents his most concerted attempt to date to fuse the image of the mother with this vision of Christ as human companion, symbol of love and compassion. Seen in this light, the "mother" in the story is an idealised figure, and again the text provides ample evidence of this intent. In the first flashback scene, for example, the narrator is portrayed as dreaming of his mother standing at his hospital bedside, although, as he subsequently acknowledges, "My wife . . . was the one who watched over me through every night after each of my three operations." Already, reality and imagination have become blurred, and, as the author himself was ultimately to concede, the creation of this absolute mother figure owes much to the concept of the "great mother" archetype as outlined by Carl Jung. The more the narrator seeks to abandon this image, the more he is forced to recognise the mother as the personification of selfless love—and to acknowledge that, in the creation of this image, he had "superimposed on the face [of his mother] that of a statue of 'Mater dolorosa', the Holy Mother of Sorrows, which [his] mother used to own."

The result is a single image—a fusion of the mother, the Virgin Mary, and of Christ—that is the key to an understanding of this and so much of Endō's work. This is overtly acknowledged by the narrator towards the end when he says, "When the missionaries had been expelled and the churches demolished, the Japanese *Kakure*, over the space of many years, stripped away all those parts of the religion that they could not embrace, and the teachings of God the Father were gradually replaced by a yearning after a Mother—a yearning which lies at the very heart of Japanese religion." Significantly, however, the story does not end with this moment of insight. As this realisation revives memories of his mother, the narrator's thoughts wander to the painting he has just seen—a picture of a Japanese farmwoman suckling her baby—and he comes to view this as representative of the maternal element inherent in the Japanese religious sensitivity.

The conclusion is indicative of the progress made during the course of the story in the attempt to establish the framework for the process of indigenisation of Christianity. At the same time, however, this further juxtaposition of images provides testimony to the degree to which, in the composition of this story, the author has been obliged to confront his own conscience. As a work of fiction, the extent to which Endō may have drawn upon autobiographical information may be irrelevant. As an examination of a series of emotions shared by the author and his narrator, however, "Mothers" can be seen as establishing new parameters for the modern Japanese short story.

—Mark Williams

MOZAIL
by Sādat Hasan Mānṭo, 1950(?)

The 1947 partition of the British colony of India into the two independent states, India and Pakistan, is an important event treated in numerous novels and short stories of many Indian literatures, especially Urdu, Hindi, Bengali, and Punjabi, languages spoken in the areas most profoundly affected by this cataclysmic event. In the wake of partition, about three million people lost their lives in rioting and insurrection growing out of the flight of 15 million people from one side of the border to the other.

Considered one of Sādat Hasan Mānṭo's best short stories and set against these political events, "Mozail" was written in the early 1950's after the author had immigrated from India to Pakistan. The story, first translated into English in *Another Lonely Voice* in 1979, highlights two of Mānṭo's favorite themes: sex and violence.

"Mozail" is told from the point of view of Tarlochan Singh, an orthodox Sikh who lives in Bombay. Like any orthodox Sikh, he has never cut his hair and does not smoke. Because of these traits, he is, like all Sikhs, readily recognizable and often made the butt of jokes. He meets and falls in love with a highly unconventional Jewish woman, Mozail, a salesperson who, among other things, wears distinctive wooden sandals. She says she will marry him only if he cuts his hair. He does, and she agrees, but she unexpectedly meets a former lover with whom she leaves town.

Though shattered, Tarlochan recovers, meets, and then proposes to a simple Sikh girl, Karpal, the complete antithesis of Mozail. She and her family live in a Muslim neighborhood, and because communal riots have broken out as a result of partition, Tarlochan worries about her safety. The strictly enforced curfew has prevented him from contacting her.

Mozail returns and grows irate when she learns that Karpal and her family are holed up in their apartment in a Muslim neighborhood. She demands that Tarlochan do something to get them out. He is reluctant to go into that neighborhood without his turban for fear of offending the young girl's religious sensibilities; yet if he goes there with a turban, he will be taken for a Sikh and attacked by Muslims. Mozail says she will help him rescue the girl and her family.

Through bluffing, bribes, and winks, Mozail gets them through the riot-stricken neighborhood and to Karpal's apartment. Because looters are systematically making their way through the building and will be knocking on the apartment door in a few moments, Mozail quickly takes off her kaftan, under which she is naked, and makes Karpal put it on, saying the Muslims will now take her for a Jew and spare her. Mozail says that when the looters arrive, she will run up the stairs naked; stunned, the looters will go after her, at which time Karpal is to escape. When the looters do come to the door, she throws it open, and as she predicted, they chase after her as she rushes upstairs. However, she slips on her wooden sandals, falls head first on the stairs, mortally gashing her head. As she lies dying, she further bluffs, saying that the turbaned man is her Muslim lover who is so "crazy that I always call him a Sikh." As Tarlochan takes off his turban to cover her nakedness, she refuses the turban saying, "Take away this rag of your religion. I don't need it," and she dies.

This story derives its power from two sources: the portrayal of Mozail, one of Mānṭo's most bewitching characters, and the Maupassant-style ending. Everything about Mozail is unorthodox, big, and loud: her hair is cut short in a westernized style, and she wears lipstick so thick that her lips look like "beefsteaks." Her large, loose kaftan, under which she wears no undergarments, is cut so low that her large, bouncing breasts are exposed. It also covers "her generous thighs," which she readily scratches or exposes. Her wooden sandals are large, and their clatter loud. Going out of her way to be a good friend, she sometimes leaves Tarlochan sitting alone in a restaurant or movie while she goes and talks to old friends she might meet. Her willingness to accompany Tarlochan into the Muslim neighborhood and even to die protecting him is the ultimate expression of friendship. More overtly sexual than Tarlochan, which hints that she might be a prostitute on the side, Mozail is unpredictable, uninhibited, and unrefined.

By contrast, Tarlochan, a Sikh, whom one would expect to be tough, aggressive, even mean, is a laid-back counterpart to Mozail. He is embarrassed that she does not wear undergarments; he is frightened, while she is not, as they pass through the Muslim neighborhood. She is a free spirit; he is circumscribed by religious orthodoxy; she is a playful tease; he a stolid idealist.

The ending of the story is a powerful indictment of the partition. Whereas unspeakable acts are being committed matter-of-factly all around her, Mozail is willing to place herself in jeopardy, and even die, for her friend Tarlochan. Her refusal to take his turban to cover her nakedness at the end of the story is masterfully ambiguous: does she refuse it out of genuine disdain for his religious orthodoxy (she teases him defiantly about his beard and often puffs cigarette smoke into his face), or is it one last selfless act whereby he can take back his turban so he can appear before his fiancée appropriately attired? This vagueness adds complex dimensions and rich texture to the story.

Some critics, such as Leslie A. Flemming, (in *Another Lonely Voice*) have referred to "Mozail" as "unrealistic, idealized and romanticized" in its portrayal of the partition experience. While this may be so, the story remains one of Mānṭo's most popular, and Mozail one of modern Indian literature's most independent and self-empowered women.

—Carlo Coppola

MRS. BATHURST
by Rudyard Kipling, 1904

Though Rudyard Kipling wrote *Kim,* arguably the greatest novel of India by a non-Indian writer, it is as a writer of short fiction that he is best remembered. Of all Kipling's stories, perhaps the most famous, and most argued about, is the haunting, enigmatic story, "Mrs. Bathurst." Set in

South Africa, it was first collected (uneasily alongside some of his most abominably jingoistic fiction) in *Traffics and Discoveries* (1904).

Though he is rightly most frequently associated with India, Kipling's travels took him to a great many other countries, including South Africa and New Zealand. In his autobiographical work, *Something of Myself,* he recalls the origin of "Mrs. Bathurst" in his visit to Auckland:

> All I carried away from the magic town of Auckland was the face and voice of a woman who sold me beer at a little hotel there. They stayed at the back of my head till ten years later when, in a local train of the Cape Town suburbs, I heard a petty officer from Simonstown telling a companion about a woman in New Zealand who "never scrupled to help a lame duck or put her foot on a scorpion." Then—precisely as the removal of the key-log in a timber-jam starts the whole pile—those words gave me the key to the face and voice at Auckland, and a tale called "Mrs. Bathurst" slid into my mind, smoothly and orderly as floating timber on a bank-high river.

This passage highlights the fact that "Mrs. Bathurst" owes its genesis to the memory of specific images, and this emphasis on seemingly random images is maintained in the story.

The story opens with an accident, a series of coincidences that bring together the narrator (who is never named), Hooper, Pycroft, and Pritchard in an empty railway carriage at a place called False Bay (a name that warns us to be wary of false impressions, false starts, false surfaces). The emphasis at the outset of the story is clearly on chance, on accident, on the random nature of life.

Having met, the four men drink beer and tell each other a series of stories which at first glance appear to have little in common. Yet the story of the maidservant who gave Sergeant Pritchard a bottle of beer because she mistook him for someone called MacClean, and the story of Boy Niven, who lured a group of eight seamen and marines, including Pycroft and Pritchard, into the woods on an uninhabited island off the coast of British Columbia with a story of a generous uncle and the promise of free land, effectively act as frame narratives, which precisely anticipate the themes of mistaken identity and desertion that pervade the central story of Vickery and Mrs. Bathurst.

Some critics, notably C.S. Lewis, have suggested that Kipling cut too much out of this story and that as a result it is impenetrable. But Elliot Gilbert has convincingly suggested that the peculiar structure of "Mrs. Bathurst" is constructed along the lines of a cinematograph newsreel (indeed many critics have commented on the excellent use Kipling makes of what was then a new phenomenon, an untested metaphor), which presents a series of stories that at first appear to have little connection with one another, but which actually serve to emphasize once more the randomness of life, already seen in the chance meetings that bring the four storytellers together.

The narrative is also linked throughout by what is effectively an unseen leitmotif—Vickery's false teeth. Early in the story Hooper is about to take something out of his waistcoat pocket when he is interrupted by the arrival of Pyecroft and Pritchard. His hand returns to his waistcoat pocket in the middle of the tale, at the outset of the central narrative, when Vickery's nickname, Click, is explained and his false teeth mentioned. Then, as the story draws to its conclusion, his hand travels to his waistcoat pocket once more, only to be brought out empty for a third time. It is

only as the story of Vickery and Mrs. Bathurst is told that the mystery of the "curiosity" or "souvenir" in Hooper's waistcoat pocket is explained. Yet because we never actually see the teeth, we never know for certain that they are there. In this way the teeth also highlight the essential mystery of "Mrs. Bathurst," and the unanswered questions the reader is left to consider at the close: What happens to Mrs. Bathurst after she walks out of the cinematograph? Who is the second burnt-out corpse? And, of course, does Hooper really have Vickery's false teeth in his waistcoat pocket? Thus Kipling neatly juxtaposes the inexplicable—the false teeth, the corpses, and, of course, Mrs. Bathurst.

In this story Kipling shuns the traditional Victorian ideology of description and rational explanation in favour of "random" memories and "newsreel" techniques. The magical, yet disturbing image of Mrs. Bathurst walking out of a newsreel of images, together with the equally disturbing, conclusive-yet-inconclusive image of the two charred corpses in the teak forest, one of them undoubtedly Vickery, the other unknown (though there is just a hint, albeit one which should quickly be dismissed, that it may in fact be Mrs. Bathurst herself), are at the heart of Kipling's story. Far from being impenetrable, "Mrs. Bathurst," with its emphasis on the enigmatic nature of life over rational explanation, is a triumph of storytelling that anticipates the advent of modernism.

—Ralph J. Crane

A MUNICIPAL REPORT
by O. Henry, 1910

One of O. Henry's less familiar stories today, "A Municipal Report," (collected in *Strictly Business* in 1910), was widely appreciated in earlier times, perhaps because of its clever stylistic devices and the odd psychology of its storyline. Stephen Leacock in 1916 spoke of "the master genius that penned 'The Furnished Room' and 'A Municipal Report.'" In 1917 Carl Van Doren called it "one of his truest stories." Twenty-two years later he and his brother Mark Van Doren referred to it as "probably his best short story." In 1936 Arthur Hobson Quinn attributed the excellence of the story to the way in which a key figure in the proceedings is deliberately held to a subordinate if not a marginal position in the storyline. To V.S. Pritchett "A Municipal Report" was O. Henry's masterpiece. Yet in 1965 Eugene Current-Garcia asserted that the story "is perhaps justly famed as one of O. Henry's finest efforts, but it hardly deserves any longer the extraordinary praise given it forty or fifty years ago." And in 1970 Richard O'Connor referred to a 1914 *New York Times* symposium wherein readers voted it the greatest American short story, to which he responds, "Needless to add, its literary rating has since depreciated considerably."

In light of O. Henry's own diversified geographical settings for his fictions, the epigraph of "A Municipal Report" at first glance seems inconsequential. It begins with a quotation from Rudyard Kipling to the effect that "The cities are full of pride, Challenging each to each," followed by a quote from Frank Norris stating that only three big American cities are *story cities: not,* for example, Chicago, Buffalo, or Nashville, but New York, New Orleans, and San Francisco. Then the first-person narrator, in answer to this perceived challenge to his honor as a storyteller, proceeds to show how romance (i.e, a story worth the telling) can come out of Nashville. Seemingly to enhance Nashville's reader appeal, he occasionally inserts descriptive passages, apparently taken from a guidebook, about the location, history, commerce, and general significance of the city. A number of references within the story proper deal with the issue of whether there is really "anything doing" in Nashville.

O'Connor cites two contemporaneous explanations for the origin of "A Municipal Report," the first—understandably enough–being the disparaging remark by Norris and O. Henry's consequent annoyance. The second explanation, which O'Connor traces to O. Henry's memoirist Robert Davis, has O. Henry telling a guest that a competent writer with a functioning imagination could produce a story from the paltriest object of consideration; upon the guest's daring him, by proffering a pocket guide to Nashville, O. Henry wrote "A Municipal Report." Praiseworthy or overpraised, the tale has an odd, disturbing quality. The contrived storyline with its caricatured dramatis personae gives the impression of having emerged from the murky mental depths of a professional storyteller.

The narrator, a business traveler, has landed in Nashville, and finds to his dismay that it is a dull, rainy, torpid city. He is there not by choice but on commission from a literary periodical in the North. His task is to sign up a woman writer, Azalea Adair, whose unsolicited contributions (essays and poems) have greatly impressed that magazine's editors. The latter want her future work to be contractually pledged to their publication, at the rate of two cents per word, before another publisher tempts her away with a promise of five to ten times that amount. Two men of very different backgrounds enter his life before he is in a position to meet the lady, and he takes an intense dislike to each, for seemingly unrelated reasons. One, who intrudes upon him in the hotel lobby, is a so-called major, Wentworth Caswell. He represents the type of Southerner that the narrator, a Southerner himself who wants to keep a low profile just because of that, loathes and considers a rat. Caswell is a loud, vulgar, self-important braggart whose unexpected sudden attachment is difficult to endure and hard to break off. The second is Uncle Caesar, an elderly black carriage driver, with the features of an African king, wearing a tattered but once-splendid coat, possibly that of a Confederate Army officer. The narrator treats him, and describes him, with marked contempt. (Near the beginning of the story another black carriage driver is also depicted in a dismissively degrading manner.)

Uncle Caesar reluctantly conveys the narrator to where Azalea Adair lives, and he finds her to be a poor but proud lady evincing more than decayed Southern gentility and cultivated literary taste: genuine imaginative power and a compelling poetic eloquence. On his return visit to the lady, when again Uncle Caesar is the cab driver, the sympathetic narrator, having received editorial approval in the interim, offers her eight cents per word for future contributions, and on his own initiative gives her a 50-dollar advance. But now the actions of the two men referred to earlier take on major significance. It appears that Major Caswell is Azalea Adair's husband, and he has been wringing from her whatever amount of cash she is able to scrape up, so that he can spend it convivially on liquor. As for Uncle Caesar, whatever the narrator might think of his lowly status, it turns out that he is really descended from an African king. Moreover, he has been supporting the lady, daughter of his former master in slave

days, from his cab fares; he has even charged the narrator four times the normal amount, for this private purpose.

When Uncle Caesar discovers that Caswell has taken the desperately-needed 50 dollars (advance money) away from his long-suffering wife, he kills the scoundrel, under circumstances that will conceal the murderer's identity from all but the narrator. The latter finds (and reveals to no one in the story) that the victim, at the time of his death, which resulted from a fierce struggle with his assailant, was clutching a button torn from Uncle Caesar's tattered coat.

There are a number of meaningful patterns here which offer a range of perspectives on this strange revenge tale. Three of these patterns (the second and third being closely intertwined) are: municipal memorabilia, the Southern tradition, and fictionalized autobiography as an escape from self. The events in the story could have been invented, with only minor topographical changes, against the background of a number of other Southern towns besides Nashville, in the early 1900's. O. Henry's "municipal report," notwithstanding the guidebook quotations and other comments on the Tennessee capital, does not by any means make it a story city distinctive enough to be on the literary map with New York, New Orleans, and San Francisco. The story's concluding line, "I wonder what's doing in Buffalo!" hints at nothing more than another staging area for a contrived plot with oddball characters and a mix of virtues and vices. But O. Henry's authorial opinion on this whole matter appears to have been vindicated to this limited extent, at least; if he could not make a story city out of just any municipality, at least he could make a story from one.

It appears that O. Henry is settling a number of old scores and releasing a variety of long-harbored mixed emotions within the story. A number of biographers, Current-Garcia prominently included, have dealt with the author's literary use of his Southern heritage. Growing up in Greensboro, North Carolina, during the period of the Civil War and Reconstruction, the closely observant, imaginative William Sidney Porter (whose shame, resulting from his prison sentence for embezzlement, elicited the famous pseudonym) became familiar with a variety of recognizable Southern character types, which he would transmute into story characters. His fictional Nashville, then, is inhabited by certain characters who might well have come out of Greensboro, and it is pervaded by the spirit of Porter who had had unhappy dealings with the law, to say nothing of his financial troubles as a professional writer.

Major Caswell was a representative of the kind of Southern gentleman that was anathema to Porter, whose formerly well-to-do family fell apart in the course of the Civil War. His father, a physician, lost much of his medical practice, his mother and infant brother died, and the rest of the family went to live with his Aunt Evelina and her mother. Dr. Porter, no longer able to cope, let his practice dwindle away. Considering the author's reduced circumstances, he might well have loathed and fled from a man such as the Major, that is, a tobacco-chewing professional Southerner, with typical attire, and extravagant claims to family lineage and property (as well as war losses).

The narrator's shabby treatment of Uncle Caesar, who is presented first as a figure of fun, and then as a murderer, is to be seen in light of the author's having grown up in the South during the 1860's and 1870's, and having absorbed the common prejudices of the time and place. Uncle Caesar is depicted not only as an old raggedy ex-slave, but as one who would still do anything for his mistress, even kill for her. (One of the boyhood games Porter played with his fellows was "KKK.") Uncle Caesar's murder of Major

Caswell reads like a psychological shifting of blame by the narrator, with the saving grace that the killer goes scot-free. However, as at least one commentator has noted, there is at one point in the story a moment of tacit mutual understanding about doing whatever one can for Azalea Adair, based on a Southern code of behavior, between the narrator and Uncle Caesar. The character of the refined, sensitive, poetic Azalea Adair has been traced to Porter's teacher, Aunt Evelina, who was largely responsible for his wide reading interests and probably also his highly developed verbal skills. Azalea Adair's rescue from unscrupulous editors, by the narrator, who could not bear to see her so badly underpaid as they intended, seems to be one of Porter's clearest insertions in the story of his own concerns. The genteel lady author is to receive the satisfactory payment she so richly deserves. Dark as the "municipal report" is, it contains enough plot twists and colorful characters to provide lively reading entertainment in the traditional O. Henry manner.

—Samuel I. Bellman

THE MURDERS IN THE RUE MORGUE
by Edgar Allan Poe, 1841

"The Murders in the Rue Morgue" is the first detective story written in the Western world to be intended as such. ("Detective stories" of a kind were produced in China in the early 17th century—Ming dynasty—which featured magistrates as investigative officers of the law courts.) Poe wrote his tale in Philadelphia in March 1841. It was first printed in April 1841 in *Graham's Magazine*, of which he was the editor. It was translated in France by three different translators from 1846-47. It attracted the famous Goncourt brothers. They hailed it in their journal for 16 July 1856, recognizing it as a new kind of literature that looked forward to the 20th century when the "heart" would give way to the "head," "love" being replaced by "deductions." The poet Baudelaire was also deeply affected, feeling a "strange commotion" and recognizing Poe as his "spiritual brother."

Despite the artistry of "Murders," no writer picked up on this new sub-genre until the 1860's when the Frenchman Émile Gaboriau produced the novels *The Lerouge Affair* (1866) and *File 113* (1867). He was followed in Ireland by Sheridan Le Fanu, with his novels *Wylder's Hand* (1864) and *Checkmate* (1871). By the late 1880's Fergus Hume's *The Mystery of a Hansom Cab* (1886) and Sir Arthur Conan Doyle's first Sherlock Holmes novel, *A Study in Scarlet* (1888), made the detective story an established popular form.

Poe was apparently inspired to invent the detective story from learning of the life and the police career of the ex-criminal turned detective, François-Eugène Vidocq (1775-1857). Having decided to reform, Vidocq offered his services to the prefect of the Brigade de Sûreté. Hired as a police informer, Vidocq organized the plain-clothes division in 1811, and soon he became its head. After a spectacular career as a detective, he retired in 1827. He produced his *Mémoires* (1828-29). In 1838-39 two articles were published in the American *Burton's Gentlemen's Magazine* titled "Unpublished Passages in the Life of Vidocq," by one J.M.P., Poe having become the editor of this magazine in 1839. However, in "Murders" Poe did not model his detective-hero, C. Auguste Dupin, on Vidocq, who was much more physical than intellectual. His model was the distinguished engineer and mathematician François-Pierre-Charles, Baron Dupin (1784-1873), who made significant contributions to differential geometry; and he also put himself and his predilections for the problematic and mysterious into his characterization.

Since Poe decided to write a detective story in 1841, his choice of Paris, France, as the locale for his story was a necessity. Paris was the only city in the Western world to have a coherently organized, professional police force with a brigade of plain-clothes detectives. Having chosen the Baron Dupin as the model for C. Auguste, Poe chose the Baron's contemporary, Henri-Joseph Gisquet, to be the model for the Chevalier's competitor, the fictive "G—." Gisquet was the real prefect of the Paris police from 1831 to 1836. In other words, Poe's "Murders" takes place during the time of the early July monarchy when Louis-Philippe was the "citizen king" and title aristocrats were "in," and one might be living with an American friend. In fact, at this time the Brigade de Sûreté, located in the Petite rue St. Anne, was again, temporarily, being headed by Vidocq, who had been brought out of retirement to cope with the riots of 1832.

As to detectives in London and New York of a professional type, there were none. Although in London there was a detective force called the Bow Street Runners, they were in effect private detectives who demanded private payment before taking a case. The detective division of Scotland Yard (the Metropolitan Police of London), called the Criminal Investigation Department (C.I.D.), was not formed until 1842. In New York, and elsewhere in the United States, there were no professional detectives until 1850 when Allan Pinkerton founded the Pinkerton National Detective Agency, and these were private detectives.

As for Poe's "The Murders in the Rue Morgue" as a literary narrative and a work of art, it was a new sub-genre of the romance, if by "romance" we mean an adventure story featuring a hero/heroine who is larger than life in the ordinary sense. Set in Paris, France, in the early 1830's, its primary characters are three: a detective-hero, a young but impecunious aristocrat, the Chevalier C. Auguste Dupin, living in an old mansion in the Faubourg St. Germain, practically a synonym for aristocratic Paris. This area on the Left Bank was now shabbier than in the days of its splendor of the 18th century. Dupin lives with an American friend, unnamed, a visiting lawyer, who acts as both discussant and narrator of the tale. Dupin's rival and foil in the effort to solve the mystery of the horrible double murder, in a locked room, of one Madame L'Espanaye and her unmarried daughter, is the prefect of the Paris police, Monsieur G—. Having read in the newspaper of the murders committed on the Right Bank, in the St. Roch quarter, at the house in the Rue Morgue (a purely fictional street) said to be between the Rue St. Roch[e] and the Rue [de] Richelieu, Dupin's curiosity is piqued. Being well acquainted with the Prefect G—, he asks his permission to visit the murder house and to inspect the premises, a permission which G— readily grants. The plot of the story, then, concerns Dupin's examination of the premises, his consideration of the testimony of witnesses and the medical examiners, his collection of evidence, and the reasoning by which he arrives at his solution that identifies the murderer and frees the accused but innocent man, Le Bon.

The story begins, however, not with narrative but with dialectic, with a discourse by the narrator—most of it perhaps learned from Dupin—on the nature of the analytical faculty of the mind and its power together with its relation to mathematics. According to the narrator, analysis is "that moral activity which *disentangles*" and the exercise of this faculty gives the analyst much pleasure. Consequently, he is fond of enigmas, conundrums, hieroglyphics, and such like obscurities that challenge his analytical talent and acumen. His solutions and results are brought about "by the very soul and essence of method" and appear intuitive. The narrator then speaks of the faculty of "re-solution" and its relation to mathematics. "Re-solution" has to do with the capability of solution and proof—especially proof by assuming the result and then deducing a valid answer by reversible steps. The narrator suggests that mathematical study might possibly invigorate the faculty of resolution, but he points out that calculation is not in itself analysis.

The narrator now enters into analyses of the social games of chess, draughts (British for "checkers"), and whist. In these analyses he looks forward 80 to a hundred years into the future, because they anticipate the modern branch of applied mathematics called "the theory of games." This theory considers any kind of situation subject to analysis that involves two or more persons in a contest of interest and control that will produce a "payoff" in either profit or loss. Developed out of the theory of probability, the theory of games was first proposed by Émile Borel in 1921. However, it was not until 1944 that the first full treatment of the theory of games was produced by John von Neumann and Oskar Morgenstern in their treatise *Theory of Games and Economic Behavior*. Using symbols of quantitative operations and the solution of quantitative problems, the narrator intimates, ought not be confounded with the "faculty of analysis," which is strongly psychological and imaginative. It is reserved for those "important undertakings where mind struggles with mind." The truly imaginative person is "never otherwise than analytic." Hence analysis has a poetics.

The narrator is awestruck by Dupin's "peculiar analytic ability" and the "vivid freshness of his imagination." He then furnishes a prime example of its workings: One night they were strolling down a street near the Palais Royal, the residence of King Louis-Philippe and his queen. Neither man had spoken for 15 minutes when Dupin addressed the narrator, saying, "he is a very little fellow, that's true, and would do better for the *Theatre des Variétés*." This announcement was the result of Dupin's reading his thoughts by interpretating the narrator's facial expressions and bodily movements as well as by tracing a chain of word associations to their origin. Such thought-reading, or "*lecture de la pénsee*," is often referred to as "mind-reading." However, it has nothing to do with the modern conception of "telepathy," or "extra-sensory perception," since Dupin's thought-reading is empirical and depends on his close observation and his "superior acumen." Public performers of thought-reading in modern times, such as Dunniger and Kresge, called themselves "mentalists." An Italian mentalist, the Chevalier Joseph Pinetti, assisted by his wife, offered a performance of a "mind-reading" act in Paris in 1784. When Dupin exercises his analytical talent, according to the narrator, he becomes a changed person. His manner becomes "frigid and abstract," and his "eyes and voice" lose their normal qualities. The narrator amuses himself "with the fancy of a double Dupin—the creative [i.e., the synthetic] and the resolvent [i.e., the analytic]." This idea of Dupin's split-personality suggests the old concept of *der Doppelgänger*, or the ghostly counterpart and companion of a person.

The narrator summarizes the newspaper account of the murders in the Rue Morgue. On the night of the crime the neighbors of the murdered women were awakened by their screams. A party gathered in front of the women's house. After gaining forceful entry to it, they rushed up the first flight of stairs where they heard two voices in contention coming from above. One voice was gruff, the other shrill. When the group got to the top of the second flight of stairs, all was quiet. When the party got into the fourth-floor apartment, everything was in the "wildest disorder." On a chair was a razor, "besmeared with blood." On the fireplace hearth were some chunks of gray human hair. Mademoiselle L'Espanaye's body was found wedged up the chimney. Examination showed she had been strangled. Her mother's body had been thrown out the window into the paved yard at the rear of the house. She had been practically decapitated. Although the apartment was wrecked, nothing seemed to have been stolen. It also appeared that the apartment had been locked, doors and windows, from the inside.

Dupin learns that the bank clerk, Le Bon, has been imprisoned for the murders, and he decides to investigate them. He and his companion visit the scene, where Dupin not only examines the front and rear of the house but the whole neighborhood. They ascend the stairs to the bedroom where the body of Mademoiselle's L'Espanaye had been found. After scrutinizing everything, Dupin asserts that the crime evidences certain peculiarities that make it unique: the murders were an atrocity; they had to be committed by a third party; the voices of this third party were those heard in contention; witnesses agreed that the gruff voice spoke French; none could identify the nationality of the shrill voice, which lacked syllabification; the idea that the bedroom was wholly locked on the inside must be false, for there must have been ingress and egress; and the most likely opening was one of the windows.

When Dupin examines the windows, he finds they are fastened with hidden springs and also with single nails. But the "window which looked upon the bed" had its nail severed; it was the one through which the murderer entered and left, closing it in leaving. Dupin collects a tuft of tawny unhuman hair clutched in the hand of Madame L'Espanaye. He makes a "*fac-simile* drawing" of the fingernail indentations on the throat of Mademoiselle L'Espanaye and compares them with the size of the human hand; they are not human. Also, the shrill voice without syllabification cannot be human. Dupin consults the French naturalist's famous *Regne Animal* (1817) and comes up with a description of an "Ourang-Outang" that matches the hair and fingernail marks he had collected. He concludes that such a beast had done the horrible deed, using as its means of ingress and egress a lightning rod and the nearest shutter at the window. The gruff voice was the owner of the animal which had evidently escaped while imitating its master in the act of shaving. Having picked up a ribbon tied in a certain knot, Dupin infers that the owner of the beast is a Maltese sailor, who by the words he uttered at the crime scene was an innocent man. Putting an advertisement in the newspaper, Dupin and his companion trap the man, who explains the circumstances of the murders to the police. Le Bon is freed. The "Ourang-Outang" was captured in the *Bois de Boulogne*. It is returned to its owner. He sells it to the *Jardin des Plantes*. The prefect of Police, Monsieur G—, is mortified by Dupin's success.

—Richard P. Benton

MURDO
by Iain Crichton Smith, 1981

Iain Crichton Smith is one of Scotland's foremost poets and writers. He has published numerous volumes of poetry in both Gaelic (his native language) and English, as well as novels and short stories. The poet frequently elbows the prose writer in his lyrical descriptions of character and landscape.

Murdo Macrae, the eponymous hero of "Murdo," the title story of Smith's collection published in 1981, was a bank clerk until, to the consternation of his wife, Janet, and her stolid family, he resigns from his post to become a writer. Janet's father, "the quintessence of normality," and to whom Murdo leaves a stone in his will, cannot understand such a man. Murdo's claim to a position of conventionality and conformity is a flair for figures, and the stereotypical appearance of a bank clerk—thin and pale faced. As a boy, he was capable of remarkable calculations, to the astonishment of the headmaster.

The story is a study in alienation and of increasingly exuberant behaviour which borders on a total mental breakdown. Physical and mental exhuberance of any kind, however, are quite beyond the comprehension of Janet and her family, who have little understanding of Murdo, as he is perplexed by his wife's zeal for tidiness and the precise positioning of the furniture and ornaments in their home.

The white, snow-covered mountain, at which Murdo is forever gazing, dominates his thoughts and aspirations, and seems to represent an unattainable ideal. He longs to leave the imprint of his footsteps in its virgin snow, an ambition he does not achieve any more than his ambition to be a writer. The sheet of paper before him remains as unsullied as the mountain's snow. He is always "trying" to write, but never actually writes anything.

There are indications in Murdo's earlier behaviour that he would always be an original, if not a buffoon. For instance, he wears a cabbage leaf in his button-hole on his wedding day. Told to write an essay entitled "My Home" he describes it as "a place where there are large green forests, men with wings, aeroplanes made of diamonds, and rainbow-coloured stairs." The exercise earned him "two strokes of the belt."

Janet considers him to be a philosopher, but feels she has an unnatural person living with her—an understatement if ever there was one, in view of his subsequent behaviour.

His increasingly bizarre antics embrace much that is basic childish humour. He wears a red rubber nose when collecting newspapers and renders deeply nervous a female bystander whom he accosts and subjects to a stream of inane repetitive remarks about the weather. On his way home, he spreads out the newspaper on a large piece of ice, lays an old boot (found in a nearby ditch) on top of it so that passers-by could read the headline ("I still love him though he killed for me"). Smith's ironic sense of humour shows in Murdo's description of the *Daily Record*: "those sublime pages that tell us about the murders that have been committed in caravans in the south."

Murdo's obsessions deepen—the colours yellow and green dominate his mind. Drunk, in the moonlight, he shouts to the stars: "Lewis" (Smith's native island); "Skye" (another Scottish island); "Betelgeuse," which he accuses of putting skin on his bones, and a worm in his head. He suffers from headaches, implicit indications, surely, of severe mental disturbance.

The joker in Murdo performs absurd acts; he writes to Dante inquiring how and when the poet first began writing, and encloses a stamp for his reply. He thinks everyone needs a friend, he tells Dante, an indication perhaps of his awareness that no one understands him and that he has no true kindred spirit. He advertises for a man between a hundred and a hundred and two, with a knowledge of Kant, who would work on the roads for three weeks in the year. He asks for nonexistent books in the library, and thinks how much easier the librarian's life would be were the shelves lined with "nonexistent, unwritten books." He makes up words like "blowdy" to describe "the kind of marbly clouds that you sometimes see in the sky on a windy day."

The happy, carefree, childlike vision of much of Smith's earlier prose now gives way to the horrendous qualities of a child's nightmare. To Murdo, the sun appears like blood across the white mountain, and in his own nightmares, the witch carries a cup of blood, like a cup of tea. Hideousness and normality are now co-mingled in his mind.

Perhaps the most significant explanation of Murdo's psyche lies in his unpublished letter to his local newspaper, *Is Calvin Still Alive?* The religion of the Free Kirk (the epithet could be considered a misnomer) and its strict adherence to the observance of the Scottish Sabbath is still practised in the Western Isles of Scotland, though less ardently than in previous days. Smith was brought up on the Island of Lewis where, in certain quarters, the adherents of that faith can still envisage physical hell-fire, a kind of literalness that can in normal circumstances, stimulate a rigid observance of daily duties, but could easily lure an imaginative child into apocryphal forebodings and fancies, such as Murdo experiences.

The jerky, episodic nature of the story resolves ultimately into a quietly melancholic ending as Murdo watches his father dying. He demands bitterly, "What did he get out of life? What did he get?" He cannot answer, but he knows what he has to do—"write a story about his father . . . and if he couldn't defeat the mountain, he knew also what he would do." Smith has posed the age-old questions in this strangely haunting story.

—Joyce Lindsay

MURKE'S COLLECTED SILENCES (Doktor Murkes gesammelten Schweigen)
by Heinrich Böll, 1958

Because so many of Heinrich Böll's early stories deal with the events of World War II and its aftermath, it is impossible to separate that period from the central thrust of his writing. The war and the Nazis helped to shape modern Germany, and while most Germans would prefer to forget the past, or, at least, put it to one side, Böll refuses to let go. His message is clear and simple: we are what we have made ourselves to be; and we cannot alter that simple fact.

Not that Böll wants to glorify the war in any way: for him it is a banal and meaningless activity which destroys not only life but also the imagination. That tension between the historical feeling for real events—Böll is careful to place his stories in real time and space—and artistic form provides Böll with the starting point for a coherent literary response to the problem of postwar Germany.

While *Doktor Murkes gesammelten Schweigen* ("Murke's Collected Silences") is not a war story, there are many echoes from the conflict and Böll makes it clear that its cast and setting, producers in a radio station, have all been influenced by earlier events. Above all, he insists that although the story is realistic, the characters and their activities are basically absurd. For example, one producer admits that he was cured of Nazism by listening three times to one of Hitler's four-hour speeches in order to cut three minutes from it.

The mood is set in the opening paragraphs which describes the arrival at Broadcasting House of Murke, a producer in the Cultural Department. Instead of going directly to his office, Murke insists on continuing upwards in the lift until he reaches the upper floors. This "existential exercise" is repeated on a daily basis because Murke fears that the lift might fail: the subsequent anxiety, or "panic-breakfast," provides him with the necessary tension to begin work on the station's cultural output. It is also a metaphor for the meaninglessness and pretentiousness of much of Murke's own efforts.

Having set the scene Böll introduces the central dilemma. Murke has been entrusted with an unusual and special task—the removal of the word "God" from two talks on "The Nature of Art," given by Dr. Bur-Malottke, a noted academic. Due to a crisis of conscience the great man had insisted that the word be replaced with the formula "that Higher Being Whom we revere," and it falls to Murke to ensure that this is done.

Absurdity is heaped upon absurdity when Bur-Malottke refuses to re-record the talks and insists that the tapes must simply be recut. To do this, he has to return to the studios to record the phrase "that Higher Being Whom we revere" a total of 27 times, not just in the nominative case but also in the vocative and genitive.

As might be expected, this is a richly comic scene and Böll makes the most of it, investing Murke with an insouciance which is in stark contrast to the discomfort felt by Bur-Malottke. Indeed, as becomes increasingly plain during this scene, Bur-Malottke emerges as a focus for Böll's satirical view of a common postwar German type—the aesthete who is also an opportunist. As Böll makes clear, there is something pathetically ridiculous about the man's conversation at a politically propitious moment in 1945.

Set against Bur-Malottke's views on the nature of art is a telling scene in the canteen where Murke observes three writers arguing about "art." Each time he hears the word Murke feels that he is being whipped, and to assuage his feelings he takes refuge in the knowledge that earlier he pinned a tawdry religious print outside the drama production office. This small action is his protest against the sterile modernity of the studios in which design has been subordinated to art.

The real nature of his discontent, though, is revealed towards the end of the story. From the edited tapes Murke collects silences—the places where a speaker pauses for a moment—and keeps them on tape. It is his pleasure to play the tapes in his spare time both as a respite from the demands of his work and as a means of keeping sane. Like the scene with Bur-Malottke, the description of Murke sitting at home with his collected silences is both comic and deeply ironic. In view of the thousands of words he has to produce each day, Murke believes that the only justifiable attitude to take to language is silence.

There is another aspect to the introduction of silence. As in Böll's earlier short fiction, silence is taken to be a motif for meaninglessness. In "That Time in Odessa" the soldiers have nothing left to say to one another and lapse into silence, and in the novella *Wo warst du, Adam?* (*And Where Were You, Adam?*) the soldier Feinhals relapses into silence as a means of avoiding the unbearable horror of war.

Unlike the earlier war stories "Murke's Collected Silences" is not a first-person narrative but unfolds through the points of view of the individual characters. This allows Murke's actions to be seen against the functional pragmatism of the radio station, a world Böll clearly believes is too closely involved with bureaucracy, and in Böll's eyes bureaucracy, the enemy of art, is clearly identified with fascism.

—Trevor Royle

MY FIRST GOOSE (Moi pervyi gus')
by Isaak Babel, 1926

Although he tried his hand at a number of literary genres, Isaak Babel is pre-eminently a master of the short story. His reputation rests largely on the collection *Konarmiig* (*Red Calvary*), some 35 impressionistic tales that reflect the writer's experience as a correspondent attached to the Soviet Calvary during the 1920 Polish campaign. Laconic and polished in style, dealing with violence in an atmosphere of extreme moral ambiguity, the stories are both brilliantly made and deeply disturbing. Crafted for intensity of effect, they reveal character and theme not through lengthy narration or probing psychological analyses, but through vivid imagery and the dramatic rendering of speech and action. The language of the stories exhibits a great variety of tonalities: documentary objectivity alternates with first-person lyric melancholy and both of these with patches of vulgar dialogue. The abrupt transitions and sharply contrasting stylistic levels assault the reader with a variety of conflicting impressions, and often the stories' ambiguities and ironies are left unresolved.

Babel is an intensely personal, even autobiographical writer, and questions of private identity play a central role in his art. Many of the *Red Cavalry* stories deal with his response to the conflicting claims of culture and nature, a clash of values dramatized in the tensions between the stories' narrator, a Jewish intellectual much like Babel himself, and the half-literate, often brutal, yet virile Cossacks with whom he serves. The narrator, for all his apparent cultural advantages, refuses to adopt an attitude of moral superiority; something in the Cossack ethos, however antithetical to traditional Jewish values, appeals to him—not the violence certainly, but something akin to it, the physical vitality or the primacy given the sensual self.

At the opening of "Moi pervyi gus'" ("My First Goose") the narrator, newly appointed to the staff of a combat division, observes his Divisional Commander with an almost naive envy and admiration:

I wondered at the beauty of his giant's body. He rose, the purple of his riding breeches and the crimson of his tilted cap and the decorations stuck on his chest cleaving the hut as a standard cleaves the sky. A smell of scent and the sickly sweet freshness of soap emanated from him. His long legs were like girls sheathed to the neck in shining riding boots.

(translated by Walter Morison, from *Isaac Babel: The Collected Stories*)

The commander, learning that his bespectacled new recruit is a law school graduate, reacts with disdain. The narrator, denied by his superior the "satisfaction" of serving at the front, sets off to find a billet, and a home, with the Cossack troop. The newcomer is greeted with a barrage of taunts and insults. One of the soldiers overturns his trunk, scattering his manuscripts and belongings about the yard. Humiliated, hungry, and lonely, the narrator settles down by himself and tries to read a speech of Lenin's in *Pravda,* but the Cossacks continue to torment him. Resolving on a face-saving action, he puts aside his newspaper and accosts the peasant landlady with a demand for food. When she responds with a mildly muttered complaint he picks up a sword lying nearby:

> A severe-looking goose was waddling about the yard, inoffensively preening its feathers. I overtook it and pressed it to the ground. Its head cracked beneath my boot, cracked and emptied itself. The white neck lay stretched out in the dung, the wings twitched.
>
> "Christ!" I said, digging into the goose with my sword. "Go and cook it for me, landlady."

The sacrifice produces the desired effect. The Cossacks, "immobile and stiff as heathen priests," invite him to join them, to share their food, and to read to them from the text of Lenin's speech. The price of community has been paid, but a brief and telling image reveals the inner revulsion that now infects the narrator's perception of the world: "the moon hung above the yard like a cheap earring."

The narrator's action, successful with the Cossacks, strikes us as tawdry and perverse, and the story itself resembles a travesty of a tale of initiation. The "hero" has faced no formidable challenge, only an old woman and her goose; even the title sounds like a mocking variant of grimmer alternatives such as "My First Kill" or "My First Rape." Furthermore, the killing is linked to a repressed and perverse sexuality. The quartermaster's suggestion that the newcomer gain acceptance by "messing up a pure lady" hints at a kind of symbolic matricide, the destruction of the maternal sway in order to gain the affection of the Cossack brotherhood. But the killing of a bird turns out to be less an appropriate rite of passage than a mutilation of the narrator's own deepest self. In two other Babel tales, "The Story of My Dovecote" and "First Love," which deal with the writer's childhood, we find a kind of dialectic with the present story. In one there is a scene in which a crippled cigarette vendor, frustrated by his inability to join in the looting during a pogrom, seizes the narrator's newly-bought pet pigeon and crushes it against his face. In the other story the boy is comforted by the Russian woman in whose house he and his violated family have found shelter, a women for whom he feels the first stirrings of sensual desire. Here again then, the slaying of a bird, this time the narrator's own, is linked to the discovery of harsh truths and to sexuality. Our sense of Babel's irony and of his narrator's conflicted spirit is further heightened when we recall that in another story from *Red Cavalry* the narrator is likened to Francis of Assisi, the saint with the failing eyes, who especially loved birds and sought to protect them from wanton destruction.

Near the end of "My First Goose" even the narrator's attainment of community is cast into doubt. Reading aloud from Lenin's speech, he exults in the intellectual's pleasure of "spying out the secret curve of Lenin's straight line"; but the Cossacks admire Lenin's directness, the way he "strikes at truth straight off, like a hen at grain." The narrator thus has not become one with his comrades after all; their "straight" way is not his, neither in brute action nor in its justification. With the coming of night he is overwhelmed with an ambivalent longing for the rejected mother and with a poignant sense of the loss of innocence: "Evening wrapped about me the quickening moisture of its twilight sheets, evening laid a mother's hand upon my burning forehead." When he lies down with the others to sleep, for all their physical closeness, he is still alone, estranged from himself as well as from the Cossacks, troubled by harsh and discordant dreams:

> We slept, all six of us, beneath a wooden roof that let in the stars, warming one another, our legs intermingled. I dreamed; and in my dreams saw women. But my heart, stained with bloodshed, grated and brimmed over.

—James E. Falen

MY HEART IS BROKEN
by Mavis Gallant, 1961

Although she has written many essays and reviews, two novels and a play, Mavis Gallant's reputation in Canadian literature rests on her short stories. Of these, "My Heart Is Broken" is one of the best crafted and most frequently anthologized.

The occasion for the story is Jeannie's rape; the focus is the response of the victim and her best friend, Mrs. Thompson. At first, the two women appear to be foils: Jeannie is young, attractive, silly; Mrs. Thompson is mature, plain, sober. Their reactions to the attack are also contrasted: Jeannie seems unnaturally detached as she calmly polishes her fingernails; Mrs. Thompson seems maternal and concerned. As the story progresses, however, their positions shift. It gradually becomes clear that Jeannie is in shock; far from being abnormal, her behaviour is typical of a rape victim.

But the more Mrs. Thompson talks, the stranger she seems. What at first sounded like moral and emotional support for Jeannie increasingly resembles attack as she flip-flops from one disjointed statement to another, seeking an almost prurient clarification of the details of the rape, advising Jeannie of her legal rights, accusing Jeannie of not being willing to adjust to mining-camp life, criticizing Jeannie for her deficiencies as a housekeeper, and blaming her for having provoked the attack by her overly generous use of the perfume "Evening in Paris." Her remarks are a jumble of stock responses that range from viewing Jeannie as a victim to judging her the culprit.

Despite their superficial differences, at the end of the story Jeannie's remarks and Mrs. Thompson's thoughts converge. In the final paragraphs, Jeannie, who has made only meagre responses through most of the story, presents her fullest version of the rape. She tells Mrs. Thompson that if the attacker had been friendly, she would not have made a fuss. According to Jeannie, the really shocking aspect of her rape was that, for the first time in her life, she encountered someone who did not like her. "My heart is broken, Mrs. Thompson, My heart is just broken." Even taking into account Jeannie's emotional state, this is a bizarre response. Jeannie suggests that she might have accepted the rape if the rapist had been nice to her. And Mrs. Thompson, who, until now, has had no shortage of punchy comments, responds to Jeannie's words indirectly by tapping her foot and "trying to remember if her heart had ever been broken, too."

Abandoning her buckshot anger, Mrs. Thompson identifies with Jeannie as the heroine of a romance with an unhappy ending, a romance that Mrs. Thompson enviously craves as a justification and fulfilment of her own empty life. Using Jeannie's terminology of "the broken heart," she tries to recall a more romantic moment in her life when a man might have found her desirable. Flying in the face of Jeannie's violent experience, both Jeannie and Mrs. Thompson connect rape with sexual attraction, and they both fantasize that rape can be nonviolent. Through the tired appeal to the broken heart, the women come to terms with sexual violation and bestow on it a romantic glow.

The story suggests that this perverse attitude is fostered and sustained by movies. The first paragraph establishes a relationship between Jeannie and Jean Harlow in Mrs. Thompson's mind as she announces that the death of the actress Jean Harlow was the most terrible shock she has ever experienced, more shocking, apparently, than Jeannie's rape. From the very start, Mrs. Thompson firmly links Jeannie and the rape to Hollywood fantasies of torrid sexual desire in which Jean Harlow is the star.

Mrs. Thompson has clearly never overcome her adolescent fixations. She not only gives Jean Harlow abnormal attention, she enjoys listening to dwarfs singing silly songs on antique records, she hangs pictures of herself and her husband as children over beds that are filled with teddy bears and dolls, and she takes her dolls out for walks in a pram. The vast emptiness of northern Quebec, the geographical setting of the story, is an accurate setting for a mining camp, but it is also an objectification of her intellectual and emotional state. Nature, however, abhors vacuums. So Mrs. Thompson fills the empty emotional and intellectual spaces with attitudes and language unconsciously borrowed from a ready-to-hand, commercial Hollywood culture that trades in romantic dreams.

If Mrs. Thompson is a grotesque example of arrested development, Jeannie, the child bride with Harlow-like peroxided hair and a name reminiscent of the actress's, is a more attractive version of the same condition. Jeannie's attitudes, like Mrs. Thompson's, are derivative. She is a vulnerable, unconscious tease who models herself after the Hollywood image of the dumb blonde in whom assertive sexuality and the appearance of pervasive stupidity are equally represented. And, like the Hollywood dumb blonde, she invariably finds herself in sexually ambiguous circumstances. But whereas the innocence of the Hollywood dumb blonde is a calculated effect based on sophisticated sexual experience, Jeannie's innocence is a blend of cultural deprivation, excessive provincialism, and authentic inexperience. Although married, Jeannie does not appear to have progressed much beyond the notion of sex as an impenetrable mystery, an idea she extrapolated from a Lana Turner movie.

What the Harlow-type movies have neglected to tell her, just as they have neglected to tell Mrs. Thompson, is that rape has less to do with sexual desire than with male anger, frustration, and the need to assert power. So strong is the hold of the Hollywood deceptions concerning sexuality that even after the rape, neither Jeannie nor Mrs. Thompson can recognize or acknowledge its true significance. Both Jeannie and Mrs. Thompson are disabled by the false assumptions of cinema romance that consistently sugarcoat violent sexual behaviours, and they thus do not experience the therapeutic personal and social effects of a righteous anger. Jeannie's rape is simultaneously a criminal act and a persuasive metaphor for the psychological and emotional assault that movies (and, by extension, other manifestations of the popular culture) commit on the minds and hearts of Gallant's characters.

—Bernice Schrank

MY OEDIPUS COMPLEX
by Frank O'Connor, 1963

Following the publication of his first collection of stories in 1931, Frank O'Connor became established in Ireland as a major writer of fiction. Like his contemporary and fellow Corkman, Sean O'Faolain, he did write novels but felt uneasy about the form, and even argued that Ireland was better suited to stories. His best work is considered to be that which focuses on the mores of the Catholic middle classes in the decades following independence, a time he believed of increasing social repression. His achievements were praised by W.B. Yeats, who once commented that "O'Connor was doing for Ireland what Chekhov did for Russia," an acknowledgement of his mastery of the short story form as well as for a commitment to broadly social themes.

"My Oedipus Complex" has an unusual reputation in the O'Connor canon: it is frequently included in collections and has achieved widespread recognition outside Ireland, but is subject to some disparagement at home. Certainly the story, broadcast on BBC radio in November 1950 and published a month later in *Today's Woman*, has been reprinted many times and translated into many European languages. It has, in short, been made available to more readers than any other O'Connor work. However, when Irish commentators in particular review O'Connor's fiction, they rarely do more than glance at this story, preferring instead to concentrate their critical gaze elsewhere.

The reasons for the story's popular appeal are not hard to find. There is a universal quality about this tale of a child whose cosy relationship with his mother is rudely disturbed by the return of his father, a soldier in World War I. The child, Larry, had developed a partiality for daily routines with his mother: early morning chats in her big bed, pleasant walks into town for Mass and shopping, and later perhaps into the countryside, and evenings which concluded with prayers for a father who seemed as mysterious as Santa Claus. When this father does return, there is no longer room for Larry in the big bed, nor of course is he the centre of mother's attention at other times of the day. Father has taken his place: so in Larry's eyes he's no less than a "monster" and "very wicked." They become "enemies, open and avowed," a situation leading to all kinds of petty conflicts. A truce is declared only when both feel ignored by the mother who is now giving all her attention to a new-born child. The story concludes with the boy reflecting in a happier frame of mind on the nice model railway his father bought him for Christmas, an ironic echo of the earlier reference to Santa Claus.

These family scenes are presented through the child's eyes but from an adult perspective: a technique that ensures a warm response from many readers, and one that is skillfully handled. What is also attractive is Larry's personality: his rich imagination, evident for example in the little dialogues between his two feet, Mrs. Right and Mrs. Left, and in his articulateness and self-assurance. His lack of understanding of such adult matters as marriage, war, and where babies come from, together with puzzlement at his mother's inexplicable concern about his father's well-being, adds to the humorous quality of the narrative. The author, drawing on his own memories of childhood, clearly delights at such childish misconceptions. And many readers can share his delight.

However, for some critics, there is a shallowness about "My Oedipus Complex." The author is perceived to be indulging himself in personal reminiscences and neglecting larger social issues. This story, it is pointed out, is just one of a number from the 1950's featuring Larry Delaney where O'Connor seemed to prefer dwelling on the personal. These stories are compared unfavourably with "Uprooted," "The Luceys," "In the Train," "The Mad Lomasneys," and others, which are praised for their portrayal of provincial Irish life. In contrast, there is nothing that can be identified as social or political about "My Oedipus Complex," and little indeed to identify the milieu as specifically Irish. There is a lack of toughness here, it is concluded, a retreat into sentimentality, or even into exploiting his childhood for material with commercial possibilities.

There is however more to this story than such criticism would allow. As one critic, Eavan Boland, did indicate, the theme of "My Oedipus Complex" is loss of innocence and the acquisition of cunning. Larry's childhood idyll, typified by a purity of early mornings "feeling myself rather like the sun, ready to illumine and rejoice," is replaced by a gradual adult sense of the need for allegiances and strategies to fight a hostile world. One can even see in the boy foreshadowings of the lonely characters O'Connor explored in other stories. Moreover, that growth in self-awareness is presented in a narrative that does not slip into nostalgia but maintains a distance between the teller and the tale.

O'Connor said in a *Paris Review* interview that for him having "a story to tell" was essential; he had to work with experiences that had an extraordinary aspect to them that would captivate listeners everywhere—and "listeners" rather than "readers" was his preferred term. He added elsewhere that "the tone of a man's voice speaking" was also an essential ingredient in a good tale. Nowhere are these attributes better illustrated than in "My Oedipus Complex." Although the resulting intimacy between writer and reader/listener is another reason for adverse criticism—a contemporary, Francis Stuart, referred to his writing as "soft-centred"—it has undoubtedly helped to make this story one of the best-known in the modern period.

—F.C. Molloy

N

THE NECKLACE (La Parure)
by Guy de Maupassant, 1885

First published in the daily newspaper *Le Gaulois* on 17 February 1884 and then included in 1885 in *Contes du jour et de la nuit* (Stories of Day and Night), "La Parure" ("The Necklace") is rightly one of the most famous of all Maupassant's short stories. In just a few pages it vividly evokes a situation with which every reader—especially female Parisian readers at the time of the Third Republic towards the end of the 19th century—could easily identify. This is a story of aspirations and fears, and then there is a conclusion rich in ambiguities that has the force and heart-breaking irony of tragedy. All this Maupassant recounts vividly, without wasting a word and not commenting on what has been taking place, but leaving us to find what response we may to the situation.

Monsieur Loisel is a minor clerk in the Ministry of Instruction (just as Maupassant himself had been a couple of years before writing this story), and things are beginning to go reasonably well for him in their modest way. He has a little money put aside and is promising himself a few hunting trips with his friends next summer. That does not mean, however, that he is anything but very happy to be at home, in his little flat in Paris where his very pretty young wife, Mathilde, always waits for him after his day's routine work with an economical but tasty meal. One evening he arrives home in particularly good spirits because he is sure he has achieved something that will delight his wife: he has managed to get an invitation for them both to attend an official reception at the Ministry.

What he does not know is that Mathilde has been eating her heart out at home. Like any pretty young woman—but perhaps the thought came more easily to Mathilde when she reflected what the possibilities might well be in Paris for someone like her at this particular period in French history—she thought there was no limit to what she might have achieved, if only she had not been so poor. In an age when the expression "articles de Paris" was synonymous with luxury and high style, she felt frustrated by poverty, and waiting at home preparing supper for her husband seemed a poor substitute for a brilliant social life of restaurants and evening parties. But, to her husband's surprise, if not to the reader's, Mathilde is far from pleased when she hears her husband proudly tell her about the invitation to the Ministry reception. Of course, she could not possibly go, she argues, for she has nothing suitable to wear. She does not even have to wheedle, however, for her husband very quickly decides to sacrifice his savings and offers her a suitable sum of money for a new gown.

As the great day comes closer, however, Mathilde begins to fret again: she really must have some jewelry to set off the new gown. The idea of wearing some flowers is just silly, in her view; she cannot think of anything more humiliating than looking poor in the company of rich women. This time her husband cannot come up with cash, but he has an idea, and he does not have too much difficulty in persuading Mathilde to borrow some jewelry from a friend. Madame Forestier, who seems well provided for, is only to pleased to oblige by lending a fine diamond necklace, and at the Ministry reception Mathilde really does feel that she is the belle of the ball.

On the way home, disaster strikes. Somehow, somewhere, the clasp of the diamond necklace must have come undone. Mathilde and her husband search everywhere desperately and make enquiries in all the right places, but all in vain. Rather than face the disgrace of going and telling Madame Forestier of the loss, they buy a replacement. The price is enormous. All Monsieur Loisel's savings, including a small inheritance, have to be paid over, and he contracts debts with a number of his friends. Now begins a desperate race against time to pay off everything.

The couple move into a smaller flat, dismiss their maid; Monsieur Loisel takes on miserably paid over-time jobs, and Mathilde loses her youthful freshness and prettiness as she becomes a hard-natured housewife, doing all the household cleaning herself and fighting with shopkeepers over every centime as she struggles to make do on the least possible amount of money each month.

Heroically the couple wins its battle and manages to pay off the debt. Mathilde can take some pride in that, and when she meets Madame Forestier she cannot resist telling her the whole story of the loss of the necklace and the gigantic effort that she and her husband have made to pay for its replacement. Madame Forestier is moved, but, in a last line that leaves us to answer a thousand questions about values, appearances, and bourgeois respectability that must flood through Mathilde's mind, reveals that the diamonds in the necklace were not real ones, just paste and not worth very much at all.

—Christopher Smith

NEIGHBOUR ROSICKY
by Willa Cather, 1932

"Neighbour Rosicky," first published in 1928, was later collected in *Obscure Destinies*. The story is that rare masterpiece in modern American literature, a celebration of good life and the good person. The key line is the story's last, a reflection of Ed Burleigh: "Rosicky's life seemed to him complete and beautiful."

Burleigh is the bachelor doctor of a farming Nebraska community, where Anton Rosicky, a Czech immigrant, has preferred to make small profits rather than sacrifice familial and neighborly cohesion. Burleigh's judgment comes after Rosicky's death, as if to affirm the ancient Greek principle: Call no man happy while he is alive. Depiction of virtue has always been more difficult than the depiction of the mean, the tawdry, the vicious. Using the young doctor as a framing device for her story gave Cather several advantages for creating virtue. Burleigh provides a perspective of someone whose daily affairs keep him in contact with the community. Part of him looks at suffering and death scientifically; dedicated to his profession, he emerges as a trustworthy guide. His perspective helps Cather avoid the sentimental. In "Neighbour Rosicky" goodness seems good without being cloying.

Burleigh's bachelor status is a significant element in the story—not only to accent his role as disinterested surveyor of the community, but also to heighten the story's concern for the perpetuation of Rosicky's values. There is no suggestion that Burleigh will be able to find a helpmeet who could enable him to duplicate the achievement of Anton Rosicky. He seems destined to be an observer, an evaluator—like an author of fiction.

Burleigh's vision alone would not be sufficient to create a convincing representation of the uncommon success of Rosicky's life. Cather also used an omniscient narrator to reveal Rosicky at moments when Burleigh is not present, a narrator to take the reader close to the private Rosicky. That narrator enables the reader to witness Rosicky in interaction with his wife and family, no outsiders present; and that narrator permits the reader to share moments when Rosicky is alone. A significant part of "Neighbour Rosicky" portrays Rosicky remembering. The reader has ample opportunity to test Burleigh's judgment on Rosicky.

While creating the picture of an individual (her title reflects this goal), Cather is careful to make that picture comment on the greater American experience, contrasting Rosicky's life in Nebraska with his European roots (he has lived in London as well as in Czechoslovakia) and with his years in New York City. Written and published during the era of Coolidge prosperity, "Neighbour Rosicky" challenges the assumptions of a galloping materialism and asks what place, if any, the Jeffersonian ideal of the small farmer living in close contact with the land might yet have. Many of Rosicky's neighbors are opting for dreams of great fortunes, moving as rapidly as possible to big machinery—forgetting to ask the most fundamental question: What is the good life? To emphasize the larger implications of her story of Rosicky, Cather recounts a defining day, the Fourth of July, in Rosicky's past. Although uncommon heat destroyed the summer's crop, Rosicky and his wife had a family picnic, in celebration that they still had their land, their faith, their health, and each other.

Rosicky had taken to Nebraska the best of the old world. He is a man unafraid of feeling, a trait that Cather emphasizes by calling attention to Rosicky's creative hands—gypsy hands, we are told. A tailor in London and New York, farmer Rosicky still occupies himself usefully with needle and thread; like his wife Mary, he is not victimized by rigid gender roles. His greatest gift is loving people, enjoying their fellowship.

In cities, Rosicky had found pleasure in great music. But industrial tensions gradually made the assets of the cities not worth their price. He increasingly met urban foulness, misery, brutality—the very things that Jefferson found in the industrial cities of Europe and had hoped would not be exported to an America he envisioned as essentially rural. Searching for a better life, Rosicky moved west.

In Nebraska, he realized the Jeffersonian ideal. He obtained land (his family had never owned land in the old world), and he took a wife, also Czech. Mary enjoys farm life and is comfortable with herself; the Rosickys are more comfortable with their bodies and their emotions than are their Protestant neighbors. (Cather is careful to keep Rosicky removed from doctrinal religion; she aims instead

at suggesting Rosicky's spiritual essence.) Mary is also a good cook, and Cather's story teems with food images, images that enforce the Rosicky code: Good food is symbolic of quality living.

The ultimate test of good living is, inevitably, one's dying. How Rosicky responds to the news that his time is limited provides the structure of Cather's story. Having lived 65 years, Rosicky is not alarmed by Dr. Burleigh's declaration that he has a "bad heart." Without being foolish, he continues to enjoy the things that he has always enjoyed. But he does have some unfinished business, business that allows Cather to expand her consideration of the American dimensions of her story. In the American melting pot, Rosicky's oldest son, Rudolph, has married someone who is not Czech, not even Catholic. Having a difficult time at farming, Rudolph is considering moving to Omaha for his wife Polly's sake. Rosicky does not instruct the young couple, but he does understand the tensions they feel. Through the power of his example and sympathy, during his last days and weeks he conveys his vision to Polly. Before he dies he is gratified to hear her call him father and to know the secret that she is pregnant. Rosicky's values will outlast him.

At story's end as Dr. Burleigh surveys the graveyard where Rosicky is buried, Cather reminds her readers of the cities Rosicky has fled. Burleigh thinks of "city cemeteries; acres of shrubbery and heavy stone, so arranged and lonely and unlike anything in the living world. Cities of the dead, indeed; cities of the forgotten, of the 'put away.' But this was open and free, this little square of long grass which the wind for ever stirred." In his prairie grave, Rosicky is not "put away." For Burleigh, for others, he is still neighbor. In Cather's quiet story, not only has the American dream had uncommonly satisfying fulfillment, but death has lost its sting.

—Joseph M. Flora

A NEW ENGLAND NUN
by Mary E. Wilkins Freeman, 1891

Though Mary E. Wilkins Freeman wrote many novels, she is best known for her short stories. Her subject matter in much of her fiction was life and character as she had observed them in the villages and countryside of her native New England. She is skilled in describing settings and in evoking atmosphere, but her main focus in her best stories is on character. She is especially interested in the New England will and conscience in their extreme, sometimes neurotic, manifestations. Life in Freeman's New England was frequently stormy.

Yet in "A New England Nun" a pastoral calm lies over the village in which the action takes place. Published in *Harper's Bazar* (sic) in 1887 and as the title piece in *A New England Nun and Other Stories* in 1891, the story opens by describing, in terms that recall, apparently intentionally, the opening stanzas of Gray's "Elegy Written in a Country Churchyard," the onset of dusk in a New England village street—the lowing of cows, a farm wagon and laborers returning home, insects flying about in the warm air. The scene then shifts to the livingroom of Louisa Ellis, a single woman approaching middle age, who has been placidly sewing all afternoon and is about to prepare her evening tea. The room is spotlessly clean and painstakingly neat. Every object rests precisely in its prearranged place. A canary dozes in its cage near a window. Louisa serves her tea "with as much grace as if she had been a veritable guest to her own self." Her way of life is regulated by a compulsive daintiness and formality that she obviously considers expressive of her femininity. There is only one discordancy in her dainty menage. In her garden, chained to his little house, is the ironically named dog Caesar, who 14 years earlier had bitten a neighbor and had been chained ever since, because Louisa and the other villagers consider the animal to be savagely vicious, much too dangerous to go free. Louisa keeps him because he had belonged to a beloved brother long since dead.

Fifteen years earlier Louisa had become engaged to a local man, Joe Daggett. A year after the engagement Joe had gone to Australia to make his fortune preparatory to marriage. After 14 years, having accomplished his purpose, he returned to New England. During his absence he and Louisa had exchanged a few letters and had remained steadfastly faithful to one another. Such lengthy engagements were, in fact, not uncommon in New England at the time; they are found quite frequently in Freeman's stories. Also during Joe's absence, Louisa's mother and brother died; left alone in the family house, Louisa underwent a subtle change. "Her feet had turned into a path, smooth maybe under a calm serene sky, but so straight and unswerving that it could only meet a check at her grave, and so narrow that there was no room for any one at her side."

But once Joe returned, plans for the marriage went ahead. Freeman describes one of Joe's twice-weekly visits to his fiancée during this time. With heavy tread he almost bursts into the immaculate room, tracking in dust, waking the canary, disturbing the careful arrangement of some books that Louisa immediately replaces in their ordained positions. After an hour of discussion of the weather and other trivialities, Joe leaves, tripping over a carpet and knocking Louisa's sewing basket to the floor. When he has gone Louisa sweeps up the dust he has tracked in. This man with his, to her, rough, hearty ways fills her with consternation. Especially upsetting is his avowal that after their marriage he is going to unchain the luckless Caesar, who thus becomes a symbol of masculine aggressiveness and sexuality so frightening to Louisa.

Both Joe and Louisa begin to have secret misgivings concerning their marriage, but are determined to abide by their vows. Then, one evening while on an evening stroll, Louisa overhears a conversation between Joe and Lily Dyer, his mother's hired girl. Lily is healthy, pretty, and lively, and the conversation between her and Joe reveals that they are in love but are resolved to forgo their own happiness rather than have Joe break his engagement. When Louisa returns home that evening she realizes that Lily, not she, should be Joe's wife. The next day she and Joe come to an understanding, reached mainly on her initiative, and the engagement is terminated. Louisa "that night, wept a little . . . ; but the next morning, on waking, she felt like a queen who, after fearing lest her domain be wrested from her, sees it firmly insured in her possession. . . . If Louisa had sold her birthright she did not know it, the taste of the pottage was so delicious. . . . Serenity and placid narrowness had become to her as the birthright itself." The dog Caesar would remain chained, the canary could doze peacefully in its cage, and Louisa would be spared the disruption that marriage would bring to her way of life.

Freeman has left to the reader a decision as to the merits of Louisa's choice. Her own attitude seems to have been ambivalent. From the time of its publication the story caused Freeman's friends to wonder whether Louisa was not, in part at least, a self-portrait of the author. Freeman herself did not marry until she was 50 years old. She was extremely feminine, even doll-like in appearance, dainty in her ways, concerned with clothing, and interested in interior decoration and housekeeping in general. Of Louisa, Freeman writes that she "had almost the enthusiasm of an artist over the mere order and cleanliness of her solitary home." Recent critics have pointed out that Louisa's chosen way of life is a valid alternative marriage. Another of Louisa's activities also suggests a relationship with Freeman. Louisa, we are told, has a little apparatus with which she extracts the "aromatic essences" of various herbs and flowers—an equivalent, perhaps, of Freeman's extracting and preserving in her stories some of the qualities of life in her New England environment. But aside from any possible autobiographical element, "A New England Nun" with its deft symbolism, its evocation of atmosphere, and its delicate but vivid characterization is one of Freeman's finest stories and an outstanding contribution to American short fiction.

—Perry D. Westbrook

NIGHTS OF SPRING FEVER (Chenfeng Chencui de Wanshang)
by Yu Dafu, 1924

Chenfeng Chencui de Wanshang ("Nights of Spring Fever") was first published in 1924, one year after Yu Dafu had completed his studies in Japan and returned to China; later the story was included in the first volume of his complete works, *Hanhui Ji* (1927, Cold Ashes). (It is the title story of a 1984 collection of Yu Dafu's stories in English.) During his first several years back in China, Yu Dafu was actively involved in editing and publishing the *Creation Quarterly,* and he had opportunities to meet some of China's most eminent writers. As a result, his fiction from this period showed significant changes. In a preface of his complete works, he recalled that "these three stories, including 'Nights of Spring Fever,' 'A Humble Sacrifice,' and 'Snowy Morning,' have more or less a socialist tinge." This may be a contemporary ideological remark, but it also implies that the author is more concerned about people around him. And, from a literary point of view, "Nights of Spring Fever" demonstrates a more integrated narrative structure and some relatively matured literary techniques.

The protagonist in "Nights of Spring Fever" is a desolate young intellectual drifting from place to place in a city. In dire straits, he is compelled to move into a very small attic room in a house located in a slum area in Shanghai. Here he meets his neighbor, Chen Er'mei, a 17-year-old girl, who works in a cigarette factory. After a period of suspicion and observation, the young woman begins to talk to him, and they become friends. Later, the young man's habit of taking night walks in the streets makes her feel suspicious again. She thinks he must be involved in illegal affairs. In the end, his sincerity and explanations resolve her suspicion. The two people brought together by fate become more understanding and sympathetic to each other.

The autobiographical approach in "Nights of Spring Fever" is evident, as in other stories like "Sinking." Some physical features and the experiences of the protagonist are identical to Yu Dafu's life. But in the former story the protagonist is portrayed as a more mature and steady young man. Although he is still over-sensitive, he is not as sentimental and hysteric as the protagonist in "Sinking."

In "Nights of Spring Fever" Yu Dafu shows a masterful control over his unique lyric-like prose; the language is fresh, smooth, and graceful. He also adopts more subtle and indirect devices in creating atmosphere and settings and thus makes the character stand out vividly. His language and technique bring alive the image of a superfluous man in the story. As the protagonist first appears in the scene, he is a nobody, nameless, homeless, and jobless, having just moved into his attic room. The room is so pitch dark and small that if he stretches out his arms, they will pierce through the roof. His destitution is so dreadful that he has no belongings, only two piles of books and a painting frame which is used as his desk during the day and bed at night. The landlord is a confused old man, hunchbacked with a wrinkled and filthy face covered by coal dusts. He makes a living by collecting scraps from garbage dumps along the streets. Because there is no communication between the protagonist and the old man, the protagonist feels deeply depressed and isolated. He is like a prisoner in a small jail cell, doing nothing but smoking and facing the emptiness and darkness. The depiction of the gloomy and brutal life is animate and nerve wrenching, but it is done economically, with only a few words and phrases.

Chen Er'mei an orphan, is portrayed as pale-faced, slim and fragile. She has to tolerate her manager's sexual harassment and to work overtime for her meager wages, barely enough for her rental and food. The helpless protagonist can only express his sympathy and feel sorry for her. The two contrast each other. He is eager, but has failed to find job; she has a job, yet she hates it. He is educated and sophisticated; she is uneducated and naive. He has too much time and feels useless, she has too much work and feels exploited. These contrasts create a situational irony: in one way or the other, they simply cannot escape from being caught by poverty and hopelessness. As the story unfolds, the theme gradually emerges in another form of continuous contrast. They are trapped in a life of misery and poverty, and they barely survive starvation; however, they find love in their friendship and refuse to submit themselves to their fate. One particularly touching scene is the one in which they share a meal. All they have are a few pieces of bread and two bananas, but they want to share with each other. Their feelings for each other, so pure and unconditional, ease their sorrow and make them believe life is worth living. It is this kind of goodness that transcends their misery and gives meaning to their existence.

The story has a well designed structure. It is divided into four parts, each focusing on one episode and linked to each other. The first episode introduces the settings and the young man's psychological stress. In their first encounter the man and the girl exchange only a few words, but their curiosity is stirred. Curiosity leads to the girl's inquiry and to the second episode in which they talk more often and feel close. Their personalities and good intentions are revealed slowly through their conversations. The third episode creates a small suspension in which his night walks and a registered letter from the publisher make her believe that his illegal business has been busted and he is receiving an arrest warrant. In the last episode, he buys some delicacies with the money from his publisher and explains

everything to her. At the moment she expresses to him her concern and care, he is so touched that he feels an impulse to embrace her, but restrains himself and goes out for a walk. The first-person narration and the numerous monologues in this episode are skillfully manipulated. The ending is sentimental and open-ended. While walking in the street on a chilly night, he is saddened by a melancholy song sung by a Russian émigré girl. Gazing into the sky, he sees the dark grey clouds, "piling up heavily like decaying corpses," as if burying the endless grief and sorrow.

—Pin P. Wan

NO ONE WRITES TO THE COLONEL (El coronel no tiene quien le escriba) by Gabriel García Márquez, 1961

The Nobel prize winning Colombian Gabriel García Márquez began to publish his work in the early 1960's. His monumental best-seller *Cien años de Soledad (One Hundred Years of Solitude,* 1967) established a distinguished literary career that continues to the present.

Published four years after it was written in Paris, and considered by the critics as one of García Márquez's most finished works (he has said that he rewrote the story more than eleven times), *El coronel no tiene quien le escriba* ("No One Writes to the Colonel") demonstrates the qualities that were to earmark García Márquez's style. Parting from the single image of a solitary old man who waits in vain—a technique the author himself has identified as the basis for most of his works—the story communicates repression and violence in a subdued and pathos-ridden village.

The action covers a few months in the life of a colonel whose pension, delayed 15 years by an overwhelming bureaucracy in a marginalized world, becomes an obsession. Reduced to penury and near starvation despite his veteran status, the protagonist and his asthmatic wife live in anticipation of his pay. But every Friday the mail launch, the only apparent contact with the outside world, comes and goes with the same declaration from the postmaster, "Nothing for the colonel. No one writes to the colonel."

An understated tone and quotidian descriptions typify García Márquez's prose. Along with the townspeople's attitudes of resignation, these stylistic qualities offset an implied reality of violence and repression, to create a heightened sense of irony. Martial law reigns in the town. Everything, including the movies, is censored. Yet, the repressive observances are such a part of daily life that they have become ingrained in a familiar pattern. On his way to a funeral the colonel observes, cynically, that the dead man is the first to die of natural causes in many years. During the procession he is reminded that a burial must not pass before the police barracks. There are constant references to clandestine activity that seems to lead nowhere and be taken seriously by no one. When the colonel mentions the possibility of elections, the town doctor says, "Don't be naive. We're too old to be waiting for the Messiah."

Despite the repression, the inhabitants appear not to be in immediate danger. Habituation, rather than fear, drives them forward in their daily activities. The potential for tragedy remains implicit with Agustín, the colonel's son who was murdered nine months earlier for distributing clandestine leaflets at a cockfight. We expect a similar outcome near the story's end. During a heart-stopping moment Agustín's killer, cocked gun in hand, blocks the colonel's path. In his characteristically ironic way, however, García Márquez deflates the scene. Demonstrating the courage and strength that he must have displayed as a young soldier, the immutable old colonel passes without incident, noting that his enemy, "small and Indian looking," emits a "baby scent."

As in all of García Márquez's work, the story contains an implicit social protest toward Latin American politics and society. Don Sabas, the colonel's *compadre,* is "the only leader of his party who had escaped political persecution." True to type, however, as the doctor characterizes him to the colonel, Sabas is the double-crossing land baron who has accumulated great wealth at the expense of the weak and the poor. The politicians, also through the enlightened doctor, are portrayed as anonymous forces with no immediate impact. Yet their repressive practices remain tacit in the consciousness of the apathetic people. Not even the colonel escapes criticism as his wife admits with shame that she "even went to the Turk's" to sell the clock.

Perhaps the most important aspect of the story resides in García Márquez's ability to create resonance with a single, concrete object. Agustín's rooster, a legacy to his parents and a representation of his rebellion and demise, constitutes the greatest element of redemption for the colonel and the town. Secondary to the promise of the money it will earn in January as the cockfighting season begins, the rooster augurs hope for change. During the entire story, the hunger motif makes itself felt as the colonel and his wife sacrifice their food to the bird. They peddle it to Agustín's friends and don Sabas with the expectation of getting as much as 900 pesos. But in the end, as he rescues the rooster from a trial fight, the colonel has a revelation, feeling "that he had never had such an alive thing in his hands before." Reminiscing about better days when his son was alive, the colonel decides that the rooster is not for sale. As his wife asks what they will eat if they keep the rooster, the old man ends the story with his powerful, one-word reply: "Shit!" In the rooster's palpitating heart, Agustín has returned to the town, fulfilling his father's lifelong hope of assertiveness and action.

As García Márquez successfully accomplishes later in *Crónica de una muerte anunciada (Chronicle of a Death Foretold),* he creates characters whose earnestness and persistence allow the reader to hope against the inevitable in "No One Writes to the Colonel." Along with the protagonist, we lift our expectations to prevent sorrow and hopelessness from settling into our consciousness. The novella's deadpan style, which recalls oral storytelling at its best and which often reaches very humorous levels, provides a vivid experience that shows us how grace and courage can overcome repression and fear.

—Stella T. Clark

NONE BUT THE BRAVE (Leutnant Gustl)
by Arthur Schnitzler, 1901

Arthur Schnitzler wrote his most famous novella, *Leutnant Gustl* ("None But the Brave") within the span of six days in July 1900. The story appeared in the Viennese newspaper *Neue Freie Presse* on 25 December, 1900, and caused a scandal. The officers' corps of the Austrian-Hungarian army felt insulted by the novella about a 24-year-old lieutenant stationed in Vienna. The conservative military paper *Reichswehr* printed a fierce attack on Schnitzler, and it was generally expected that as a reserve officer Schnitzler would defend his honour by challenging his attacker to a duel. When it became clear at last that Schnitzler had no intention to do so—one point of his story having been precisely the mindlessness of duels—a military court adjudicating matters of honor convened and relieved Dr. Schnitzler of his officer's title. It was an extraordinary step; but the judges felt that Schnitzler's disrespectful fiction as well as his subsequent cowardice called for such a severe punishment. The honor of the Hapsburg army was at stake, challenged by a Jewish intellectual.

Schnitzler's story, which consists entirely of Lieutenant Gustl's interior monologue, was indeed designed to expose an unglamorous core concealed beneath a glittery uniform. Schnitzler's narrative form, the monologue novella, which he thus introduced into German literature, fits its function perfectly. The reader is allowed immediate access to the protagonist's thoughts, even those Gustl might wish to hide. Rather than criticize army officers through an omniscient narrator, Schnitzler creates an effect of self-revelation, which magnifies Gustl's shortcomings. Schnitzler's interior monologue differs from James Joyce's stream of consciousness through greater narrative coherence. The sentences are better ordered; but they still resemble spoken language in their simple, paratactic structure, and by being sometimes left incomplete. Unlike Joyce, Schnitzler keeps his readers informed about his character's actions through sentences such as this one: "Let's see what time it is . . . perhaps I shouldn't look at my watch at a serious concert like this."

Gustl's monologue begins in a concert hall. Bored by the music, he fumbles for his watch. The opening sentence, "How much longer is this thing going to last?", is one of the story's leitmotifs. Gustl recently challenged a doctor to a duel, who had remarked that not everyone who joined the army did so to serve the fatherland. The duel is to take place in the afternoon of the next day; and Gustl is now killing time. The novella is focused on Gustl's waiting, on his wavering between impatience and boredom. On one level Schnitzler thus comments on the uselessness of the army; on another level the story's structure parodies the Catholic view of life, which is a waiting for redemption from death. This is indeed what Gustl is waiting for. As soon as the concert is over, he hurries to retrieve his coat and gets into an argument with a bulky man waiting in line. Gustl tells him to shut up and recognizes too late the man as the baker who frequents the same coffeehouse as Gustl. The man, furious at Gustl's insult, takes a firm hold of Gustl's sword, the symbol of his prestige, power, and masculinity, and threatens to break it if Gustl does not "hold his peace." Horrified at the baker's insult, but unwilling to risk a scandal, Gustl backs down. The baker leaves, and Gustl looks around to see whether their quarrel had been overheard. Gustl's anxious concern about the opinions of other people is the story's second leitmotif, which appears as early as the third sentence. Recurring phrases like "but no one will see me," or, "Heavens, I hope nobody heard it," structure the text and alert the reader to an incongruence between Gustl's outer and inner world. He does not want to be found out. The idea of honor, however, implies a congruence between appearance and reality, between inside and outside. In the defense of honor an incongruence is rectified. In the course of the story, which can also be read as Gustl's pursuit of honor, the reader learns that Gustl's notion of honor is simply a concern for appearances. He is all shell and no core. He thinks in clichés and stereotypes that show him to be a true product of his time and his place; he lacks all individuality.

Left behind in the concert hall, Gustl is dumbfounded. He cannot challenge the baker to a duel, because being neither an aristocrat, nor an officer, nor an academic, the baker cannot offer "satisfaction." The only way to restore his honor is to kill himself. Gustl wanders aimlessly around the city reasoning with himself that suicide is his only option, because even if nobody witnessed his humiliation, he, Gustl, would know: "And even if [the baker] had a stroke tonight, I'd know it. . . .I'd know it. And I am not the man to continue wearing a uniform and carrying a sword if such a disgrace is on me! . . . So, I've got to do it, and finished— There's really nothing to it." During his peregrinations through Vienna, Gustl's mood changes from aggression to sentimentality. He reviews his life and thus reveals not only his prosaic reasons for joining the army, but also his sexual promiscuity and love of gambling, vices then half-condoned in officers by Austrian society. Politically, Gustl embraces militarism, antisemitism, and antisocialism; he worships Richard Wagner and hates intellectuals. Gustl's aggressive views, however, turn out to be a defense mechanism; he has always felt second class. The pose of aggression protects him, just as a career in the army compensated his inferiority complex.

When morning comes Gustl walks into his old coffeehouse. He learns by chance that the baker has died of a stroke during the night. Overjoyed to be so unexpectedly redeemed, Gustl vows "to make mince meat" of the doctor in the afternoon.

Like his character Gustl, Schnitzler's story is clearly a product of its time and place. Its unique narrative form, Gustl's free-associating interior monologue, was chosen by a Viennese writer who was equally aware of the first stirrings of Freudian psychoanalysis, as of Ernst Mach's then celebrated philosophy of impressionism. Schnitzler's monologue novella, that grants the reader no access to Gustl's outer world, illustrates dramatically Mach's view that the outer world has no reality independent from that registered in an individual's sense impressions. In short, Gustl is imprisoned in a world defined by the limitations of his body which he cannot transcend.

—Susanne Klingenstein

NOON WINE
by Katherine Anne Porter, 1937

Though written and first published in 1937, and reprinted with the title story and "Old Mortality" in *Pale Horse, Pale Rider: Three Short Novels* (1949), *Noon Wine* is dated "1896-1905" by subtitle and located in a "Small South Texas Town," which parallels the time and place of Katherine Anne Porter's own childhood. Such specifics are important in a Romantic sense, a confessional grounding of scene and character for what seems almost mythic in its bleak determinism, but they also help explain the story's realistic conviction, memoir-like persuasiveness.

The main character, Royal Earle Thompson, a genial farmer resigned to failure, wed to a delicate, sickly former Sunday School teacher, father of two healthy sons, is not large enough for tragedy but decent enough to center the heightened pathos required for domestic melodrama. His fatal flaw is a "feeling for the appearance of things, his own appearance in the sight of God and man," a deep concern for "his dignity and reputation." The arrival of Olaf Eric Helton, a mysterious Swede from North Dakota who becomes the Thompson family's financial savior by dint of his herculean, albeit taciturn, labors over the next nine years, is one of those trusty plot turns that a writer fine-schooled in the literature of James, Cather, and Joyce inevitably uses to plumb dark modernist undercurrents, anticipating, in this very Southern case, the bitter Catholic thrashings of Flannery O'Conner's doomed Gothics.

George Hendrick has noted that *Noon Wine* grapples "with one of the central problems in Porter's fiction: the efforts of man to cope with evil." When the sin-greased wheels of the sad denouement commence to spin into madness with the intrusion of yet another stranger, the odious, money-hungry Homer T. Hatch, intent upon returning Helton to the mental institution from which he had escaped, ethical waters are muddied beyond resolution. The dream-like explosion of violence that ensues as Thompson hits Hatch with an ax after seeing him apparently stab Helton, who then runs off only to be tracked to his death by a brutal posse, rolls implacably into ironic complications. Freed by a jury of a murder charge, like the peasant protagonist in Mauppasant's "A Piece of String," Thompson cannot cease seeking to justify his actions to sceptical neighbors, mangling himself into an obsessed, guilt-ridden pariah in the process.

In the end, in true Porter fashion, irony assumes the guise of a pessimistic Angel of Death, and Thompson finds himself condemned by his own family. His ultimate, inescapable self-destruction and desperate suicide note of explanation leaves crucial moral issues unclarified. Porter herself subsequently dismissed her suffering characters with a contemptuous shrug: "There is nothing in any of these beings tough enough to work the miracle of redemption in them." Happily, the art of the story is much deeper than its author's harshly narrow religious vision would intimate. More relevant might be the acute view of Ellen, Thompson's wife, anent her husband's savage act and the typical male violence unleashed by the men restraining the frenzied Swede, whose senseless murder of his brother (Cain-Abel reprised) over a mere harmonica injects its own moral enigma: "Yes, thought Mrs. Thompson again with the same bitterness, of course, they had to be rough. They always have to be rough."

The durable power of *Noon Wine,* its title derived from the single tune Helton ever played on his beloved harmonica, a Scandinavian folk song about the regrets of a worker after having greedily drank up all his wine before the noon break, resides in the ethical ambiguities engendered by a frontier context. It echoes Porter's steady focus on the clash, usually bloody, between primitive and more cultivated outsider forces in her early Mexican stories, especially "Maria Concepcíon." Self-delusion and unconscious impulse are key motivating factors that provide a partial catharsis for the reader, without releasing him or her from the claws of unavoidable destiny, intimations of original sin, Adam's crime of having been born human, although the equally powerful "The Jilting of Granny Weatherall" would seem to confound any attempts to impose a traditional Catholic interpretation.

The obsession at the heart of *Noon Wine,* and at the pith of most Porter artifices—to sketch in action the terrible price paid for our inherited existential dilemma—demands sufficient courage to gaze without blinking at the cruelties of a human world and an inhuman universe, the kind of courage she claimed her fictional people lacked and she obviously possessed in sardonic abundance.

—Edward Butscher

_____

THE NOSE (Nos)
by Nikolai Gogol, 1836

"Nos" ("The Nose") is the second of Gogol's St. Petersburg stories—the others are "The Nevsky Prospect," "The Portrait," "The Overcoat," "The Carriage," and "Diary of a Madman"—a cycle in which he took as his model the French newspaper feuilletons that described the streets and thoroughfares of the great city and showed how the urban environment influenced the people who lived in it. Gogol's concern in these tales is, however, much less sociological than ethical. "The Nose" is primarily a study in vanity and ambition, and concerns Platon Kuzmich Kovalyov, a run-of-the-mill civil servant newly risen to the rank of collegiate assessor, who wakes up one morning to find that his nose has disappeared. The story is about his attempts to find and retrieve his nose, which has acquired an independent and quasi-human life of its own.

The story gains its uniquely dreamlike quality from the unusual way in which the action is presented. We do not encounter Kovalyov straight away; instead, the opening scene presents, in the style of a newspaper column ("On 25 March there occurred in St. Petersburg an unusually strange event"), the shock received by Kovalyov's barber, Ivan Yakovlevich (his surname has been "lost") on discovering a nose in the roll that has been freshly baked for him by his wife. Seized by fear that the police may arrest him for having cut off the nose of one of his customers while drunk, Ivan Yakovlevich goes out into the streets in order to find some suitable place where he can get rid of the nose. But whenever he tries to drop it or throw it away he is spotted by someone he knows, who invariably tells him that he has dropped something. In the end, he decides to go to Isakievsky Bridge and throw the nose, wrapped in a rag, into the Neva. After he has done this, he is accosted by a surly policeman who refuses to believe his protestations of innocence. At this point the narrative becomes shrouded in mystery: "Of what happened after that, decidedly nothing is known."

The scene now shifts to the quarters of Major Kovalyov. Kovalyov's rank of "collegiate assessor" has been gained not in Russia but in the Caucasus, where such distinctions are more easily acquired, and throughout the story we are made aware of his feelings of unease and inferiority which stem from this fact. The loss of his nose, which he discovers upon taking a mirror to examine a pimple he has had, devastates him, for it attacks him where he is most vulnerable—in his personal vanity. Instead of a nose he has nothing, "a completely smooth place." Gogol places great emphasis on the "nothingness" experienced by Kovalyov. Covering his face with a handkerchief, he sets off immediately to report the loss to the chief of police. On his way he goes into a pastry-cook's shop to examine the

"smooth place" again, and coming out of the shop he sees his nose getting out of a carriage. The nose is dressed in the uniform of a very senior civil servant, a councillor of state, and Kovalyov does not at first even dare to approach the august personage. When, in the interior of the Kazan Cathedral, during a religious service, he does accost the nose, it treats him with cold disdain, drawing attention to the great discrepancy in their ranks. After this, it disappears again, and Kovalyov continues on his way to see the chief of police. But the chief is not in his office, and so he goes to the offices of a newspaper in order to place an advertisement requesting the return of his nose.

The story describes Major Kovalyov's fruitless attempts to make the newspaper's editor accept such a suspicious advertisement for publication, his visit to the local police station to report the loss, his crisis of despair, and the mysterious return of his nose to him by the police, who have arrested it as it was about to leave the city. Gogol' leads the reader constantly between reality and fantasy, material and spirit, until by the last short chapter a sense of total absurdity has been created. "Complete nonsense happens in the world," Gogol writes, to underline the apparently meaningless and trivial nature of his plot: after all the panic occasioned in the major by his nose's disappearance, the nose suddenly turns up in its proper place again, on the major's face. Kovalyov can hardly believe it; he has to have several people confirm that the nose is there before he will concede that he is not dreaming. And then, his spirits thoroughly restored, he goes to the Gostiny Dvor and buys a medal ribbon, even though he has never been awarded any medal. In conclusion, Gogol reflects on the absurd tale, declaring that "what is most incomprehensible of all is how authors can choose such plots. I confess that this is completely unfathomable, this is almost . . . No, no, I do not understand at all. In the first place, it brings decidedly no advantage to the Fatherland; in the second . . . but in the second there is also no advantage. I simply do not know what it is." And yet, he reflects, "if you think about it, in all this, truly, there is something. Whatever you may say, similar events take place in the world—rarely, but they do take place."

Like the other St. Petersburg stories, "The Nose" is a semi-comic, semi-tragic meditation on the nature of reality and its inseparable relation to morality. It is Kovalyov's vanity that deprives him, temporarily, of his nose—to him orders, decorations, ranks, and medals are of more account than his own humanity. His moral blindness acquires a life of its own and torments him by fusing with the inhuman, dreamlike environment of the city itself. At one level, Gogol appears to be saying, this is a world in which reality is determined by what is in humans, or missing from them.

—David McDuff

_____

NOTES FROM UNDERGROUND (Zapiski iz podpol'ia)
by Fyedor Dostoevskii, 1864

Zapiski iz podpol'ia ("Notes from Underground") is the first major work of the second phase of Dostoevskii's fiction in which psychological, existential, and philosophical concerns take over from his earlier social realism. It is in two parts, the first an attack by the narrator, who is never named, on science and determinism, and the second recounting a number of episodes from the narrator's life. The most powerful element in the story is the narrator himself: a tortured, intense, guilt-ridden, outsider. The story is an attack on scientific rationalism and positivist thinking, but it does not merely condemn these on abstract grounds; rather the narrator exposes the dire effects they have had on his own personality and behaviour, which we see in the second part of the story.

The "Underground Man" is essentially a Romantic in terms of his sensibility, comparing himself, for example, with Byron's Manfred. But unlike Romantic heroes he suffers from a disabling self-consciousness that perverts his Romantic nature, making it impossible for him really to believe in or take seriously Romantic attitudes. He is so conscious of himself, of what others might think of him, that his emotional energy can find no authentic outlet. He cannot break free from his own subjectivity, with the result that his feelings lack spontaneity and it is virtually impossible for him to act decisively. The dark cellar he lives in is a kind of metaphor for the condition of being trapped inside one's own ego.

The first part of the story is crucial since it helps us to understand what has made him as he is. He addresses directly his contemporaries who quite unthinkingly believe in scientific and material progress. Underlying such belief is an acceptance of deterministic thinking, that there are laws governing the world, society, and human nature. The Underground Man does not claim that determination is false. He does not have any alternative theory. What he is concerned with is the consequences of deterministic thinking. If human beings come to believe that everything they think and do can be understood in terms of psychological and sociological laws, analogous to the way that the world can be understood in terms of scientific law, then any concept of freedom of action disappears.

Though the Underground Man accepts determinism, he has a deep emotional need to believe that he is free. He knows that everything he does or thinks can be explained in terms of psychological, sociological, or behavioural laws, and therefore that freedom is a fiction, but the implications of this, he claims, have not been understood. In the past people believed that they were free and therefore could act with spontaneity and without self-consciousness. People identified themselves with their actions. But since determinism shows that people are merely the product of various sets of laws, the self has no independent status. This creates people who are characterless, who are content to be mere cogs in the system, while those who still believe they are free are merely too stupid to understand the consequences of determinism.

The second part of the story illustrates the effects of this on the Underground Man's life. He is committed to making his life significant in the face of the nullifying effect of deterministic thinking. Though a minor civil servant involved in trivial work that is of no value in itself, he refuses to become one of the crowd and conform. But the price he pays is that he is regarded as an eccentric, a figure of ridicule. He tries to feel superior but his sense of self is so fragile that he finds it difficult to oppose the judgements of others. The incidents he recounts all concern his effort to resist nullification by asserting his dignity and significance.

In the first episode he describes his tortuous efforts to be noticed by an army officer who insults him. All these efforts fail until he meets the officer by chance in the street, and, before he can become self-conscious, he bangs shoulders with him. Although the officer does not even look round, he feels that his existence has been acknowledged.

The next episode recounts the difficulty he has in asserting a sense of his own significance in the face of the contempt in which he is held by some of his former school acquaintances. Though he feels contempt for them, their contempt for him has the greater force; in order to overcome this threat to his ego, he must find a way of making them accept him as significant. After an embarrassing scene that only seems to increase their contempt for him, he finds a device to restore some sense of his dignity by writing a letter to one of his former school companions apologizing and blaming his behaviour on having too much to drink. The letter allows him to create a dignified image of himself without having to encounter again his former school acquaintance.

Probably the most crucial episode of the story is his meeting with a prostitute. For the first time he meets someone who treats him with sympathy and who offers him a human relationship. On the surface this might seem to provide him with the basis for believing that his life has significance and importance. But when she calls to see him he insults her and drives her away—he has just been outfaced by his servant and needs to compensate for that humiliation by exerting his power over someone else. He cannot allow himself to be sincere and open with another person since that would leave his ego too exposed and vulnerable if he were laughed at. Relationships for him, therefore, can exist only in a context of power, and for him that power can be fuelled only by spite. Spite is central to his sense of identity because, psychologically at least, spite seems to resist determinism since it is difficult to account for it in causal terms. It remains hidden within, in contrast to other emotions, such as anger, which have an outward manifestation. The Underground Man can keep it bottled up inside him, cultivate it, and use it to generate the power necessary to sustain a sense of self in the face of his intellectual belief that that his life has no significance. But the price he pays for forging an identity through spite is that he has to reject any genuine contact with other people, even with someone like the prostitute who offers him a relationship.

The Underground Man is a representative figure; he is a product of the modern, industrialized, godless civilization which Dostoevskii saw emerging in Europe and which he detested. The Underground Man is desperately fighting to preserve a human identity. The motto for the modern self, Dostoevskii implies, is: I am spiteful and rancorous, therefore I am.

—K.M. Newton

THE NOTORIOUS JUMPING FROG OF CALAVERAS COUNTY
by Mark Twain, 1867

According to Twain, "The 'Jumping Frog' was the first piece of mine that spread itself through the newspapers and brought me into public notice." The San Francisco Alta California testified to the tale's immediate popularity, claiming that it had been "voted the best thing of the day." At first embarrassed to be judged by this example of Southwestern humor, Twain soon recognized his achievement, describing "The Notorious Jumping Frog of Calaveras County" as "the best humorous sketch in America."

Although several published versions of a frog race predate Twain's account, Twain claims to have first heard the story from Ben Coon, who recounted the adventure in a straightforward, deadpan manner. Sam Wheeler presents his account of Jim Smiley in the same way, but Wheeler, unlike his prototype, knows exactly what he is about. Wheeler is following the advice Twain would offer later in "How To Tell a Story": "The humorous story is told gravely; the teller does his best to conceal the fact that he even dimly suspects that there is anything funny about it." That is the manner of the humorist Artemus Ward (Charles Farrar Browne), to whom Twain addressed the story in its original 1865 epistolary form.

"The Notorious Jumping Frog" is, therefore, self-reflexive, a narrative about narrative. Wheeler, understanding how to recount a humorous tale, which Twain distinguishes from a witty one, "never smiled . . . never frowned . . . never betrayed the slightest suspicion of enthusiasm — but all through the interminable narrative there ran a vein of impressive earnestness and sincerity."

Wheeler also knows how to build to a climax. He begins with several brief examples of Jim Smiley's addiction to betting. Many of these instances are comical, but none extends beyond a sentence. Wheeler then devotes a short paragraph to an unlikely-looking horse that Smiley owned. Despite its appearance, it always outraced its opponent. Wheeler gives slightly more attention to Smiley's dog, which, unlike the horse, has a name — Andrew Jackson. In this section Smiley is at last outwitted through an absurd but effective ruse. Finally comes the episode that gives the story its title, and again Smiley, after numerous successes, loses a bet to a stranger, whose frog outjumps Smiley's Daniel Webster because in Smiley's absence the stranger has filled Smiley's frog with lead shot.

The theme of the frog race (and of the dog fight as well), that of the biter bit, the deceiver deceived, is echoed in the frame of the fiction. The Mark Twain of the story (whom the reader must not confuse with the author of the story) wants to learn about the Reverend Leonidas W. Smiley, a minister, but instead must listen to an account of a gambler with a similar name. The narrator suspects, no doubt correctly, that Artemus Ward (in the 1865 version), or, in later renditions, an unnamed friend from the East, knowing how Wheeler will respond to the inquiry, has tricked him (Twain) into this predicament.

Like Smiley, though, Mark Twain is not a wholly innocent gull. Smiley poses as the naif. His mare appears to be so rheumatic and slow that opponents give her a few hundred yards' head start, and she allows them to pass her before she charges ahead to win. Similarly, his dog looks worthless and lets his opponent "bite him, and throw him over his shoulder two or three times." Then, once the audience has bet heavily on the other side, Andrew Jackson grabs the other dog's leg and holds on until the opposition yields. Appropriately, Smiley finally is defeated by another seeming innocent. When Smiley boasts to him that his own frog can outjump any other in the county, the stranger claims to see nothing special about that animal. He adds that he'd gladly wager on a frog race — if only he had a frog. Preying on Smiley's love of betting, he tricks the gambler into going off to find one, thus permitting the stranger to weigh down Daniel Webster to the extent that the frog cannot even move.

While Mark Twain complains of being the naif taken in by Sam Wheeler, (and by whomever sent him to the storyteller), the narrator sees himself as superior to the westerner. He does not appreciate Wheeler, whom he regards as "simple," Wheeler's story (an "infernal reminiscence . . . long and tedious," he calls it), or Wheeler's storytelling technique, which he considers "exquisitely absurd." Whereas Wheeler uses colorful images and speaks a salty vernacular, Twain's language is stilted and overwrought. Twain refers to the old mining camp as "this village of Boomerang," and he calls Leonidas W. Smiley "a young minister of the gospel."

Southwestern humor often uses a frame that serves to celebrate the triumph of the native intelligence of the westerner over the urban sophistication of his eastern interlocutor. "The Notorious Jumping Frog" at once preserves and reverses that element. Just as in the naming of Smiley's animals Andrew Jackson and Daniel Webster the author mocks both Democrats and Whigs (S.J. Krause's "The Art and Satire of Twain's 'Jumping Frog' Story" in *American Quarterly* 16, 1964, points out the numerous similarities between the political figures and their namesakes), so he allows both East and West their victories. An Easterner gulls Twain into asking about Leonidas W. Smiley, and Twain later called the man who wins the frog race a Yankee. At the same time, a seemingly innocent westerner (Wheeler) outwits a stranger (Mark Twain) who regards himself as superior. In technique, too, Twain fuses Southwestern humor with eastern satire. Writing in the shadow of the Civil War, Twain rejects sectionalism to create a truly American story. Similarly, he subverts narrative conventions to find his own voice.

—Joseph Rosenblum

NOW THAT APRIL'S HERE
by Morley Callaghan, 1934

"Now that April's Here" is a marvellously, closely observed tale that is a telling monument to the crucial role that a sojourn in Paris played in the cultural life of North American writers in the decade after World War I. Morley Callaghan spent his early years in his home town, Toronto, and it was there that in 1923 he met Ernest Hemingway, who was making a brief return visit from Europe and encouraged the younger man to carry on writing. Subsequently, some of Callaghan's first stories were published in Paris, and finally, in the spring of 1929, immediately after getting married, he crossed the Atlantic with his bride and spent some months in Paris, getting to know all the other American writers and publishers gathered there. Edward Titus bet Callaghan and Robert McAlmon that they could not write stories presenting their views of a couple of young Americans who were familiar figures around Montparnasse. McAlmon lost out, but Callaghan, in his usual tight-lipped, economical manner, wrote "Now that April's Here," using as his title what was then the very familiar first line of Robert Browning's poem "Home Thoughts from Abroad." The story first appeared in the October-December issue of the Paris-based magazine *This Quarter*. Callaghan must have set some store by his story, first published in 1929; when he included it in a 1936 collection of 35 stories he used it as the title story.

In the story Charles Milford is four years older than Johnny Hill. They are bored with life in their native town in the Middle West; they are convinced that America has nothing to offer talented people such as themselves and have been influenced above all else by George Moore's

Confessions of a Young Man (1888). So they have come to Paris together in late autumn. Fortunately Johnny has $100 a month to spend, and he is happy to give some financial support to Charles who is, he is sure, going to become a famous writer.

We have an early glimpse of the pair as they peer into the windows of an art gallery, making patronizing remarks about Foujita's draftsmanship. Soon they settle down to a life of sitting for hours in boulevard cafés, talking to friendly girls, looking at the luminaries of the literary scene, and hoping against hope that they are themselves being looked at, too. They certainly pick up something of the style of milieu they frequent in such a self-conscious manner, but they don't get far with their writing. For a fortnight Charles does devote himself to his latest book, and Johnny, who is typing it out, assures his friend that no modern author since Henry James had anything like his perceptiveness or delicacy. An authorial aside first assures us that Charles "did write creditably enough," but then devastatingly undermines that praise by adding, that "everything he did had three or four good paragraphs in it." The strain of creativity (or perhaps a realization that persisting was unlikely to pay dividends) leads to the desire for a break, so Charles and Johnny decide to go south. They stay in Nice, spending more than they can afford on drink and hotel bills and finally making a surreptitious get-away without paying. In April they return to Paris, expecting the city to live up to its reputation as the ideal spot in spring time, but they are disappointed by the raw weather.

It is at this juncture that Johnny decides he must go over to London where his father is spending a few months, and the parting of the two friends, though only for a short while, is the turning point in the seemingly loosely structured story. Charles finds that for some reason people do not care much for him when Johnny is away, and there is talk of the danger that the younger man might take up with some woman in London. In fact, Johnny has a violent row with his father, who suggests it is about time he made some effort to earn his living. Once he is back in Paris, however, the pair soon begin to fall out over a girl called Constance Foy whom they had met in Nice. They try to patch things up, but it is no good: the spell is broken, and Johnny decides to return to the United States, taking Constance with him. We last see Charles alone in a café one cool evening; on his head he has the black hat that he had bought specially to create the right sort of impression before crossing over to Europe but had somehow never got around to wearing. This makes a fine, open-ended conclusion to the tale that Callaghan makes both vivid and laconic, richly comic in its portrayal of two conceited young men and genuinely touching in its account of the deep relationship between them. It may be significant that after writing "Now that April's Here" and turning down Edward Titus's offer of the editorship of *This Quarter,* Callaghan returned to Canada to pursue his distinguished career there.

—Christopher Smith

O

AN OCCURRENCE AT OWL CREEK BRIDGE
by Ambrose Bierce, 1891

In spite of the fact that "An Occurrence at Owl Creek Bridge" seems merely a trick to shock the reader, Ambrose Bierce's tale of the man who imagines he has escaped hanging in the moment before he comes to the end of his rope is one of the most famous and frequently anthologized stories in American literature. The story is primarily a tour de force of technique, in which the content is merely a pretext for a game Bierce plays with the conventions of narrative time and fictional endings. Collected in *Tales of Soldiers and Civilians,* the story's theme—the human need to escape death—is established by Bierce in the only way it can be, by means of the imagination, a truth that Bierce develops through an elaborate bit of fiction-making that the reader initially takes to be actuality.

"An Occurrence at Owl Creek Bridge" is made up of three sections corresponding to the basic fictional elements of static scene, exposition, and action—all of which are presented in such an ironic way they are undermined. Although part I of the story is the only one in which something is "actually happening," it seems as static and dead as a still picture. Part II, which seems to exist to provide the realistic motivation for the protagonist's dilemma, is more important for providing the aesthetic motivation for the story's manipulation of narrative time. Although part III is an exciting chase sequence that seems to be happening in the physical world, it is actually a psychic event taking place only in the mind of the protagonist.

Bierce cues the reader to the fictional nature of his story at the crucial moment just as Farquhar falls beneath the railway crossties. Standing there on the brink of death, he thinks hypothetically, "If I could free my hands . . . I might throw off my noose and spring into the stream." Bierce notes, "As these thoughts, which have here to be set down in words, were flashed into the doomed man's brain rather than evolved from it, the captain nodded to the sergeant. The sergeant stepped aside."

This is the central passage in Bierce's tale, for it is actually a self-reflexive reference to the story itself, calling attention to the most notorious characteristic of fiction—the impossibility of escaping time. It is a reminder to the reader that in spite of the author's desire to communicate that which is instantaneous or timeless, the reader is trapped by the time-bound nature of words that can only be processed one after another. It is thus only because of the time-bound nature of discourse that Farquhar's imaginative invention of his escape makes the reader believe that it is taking place in reality.

Although at the end of the story the reader may feel tricked, Bierce actually plays quite fairly, providing a number of clues throughout the last section to indicate that what the reader thinks is happening is not really happening at all. For example, the words used to describe Farquhar's feelings as he falls into the water suggest an illusory experience, as agonies "seemed" to shoot through him and pains "appeared" to flash along well defined lines. On coming to the surface, his senses seem so "preternaturally keen and alert" that he can see the veins of leaves and the dewdrops on blades of grass on the shore. Against all odds, after escaping from the hangman's noose, he escapes from drowning and from the fire of Federal rifles and cannon. Finally, on the way home he passes through an unfamiliar and uninhabited region that surprises him with its wildness, and he looks up at stars grouped in strange constellations that seem to have a secret and malign significance. It is only the reader's sympathetic involvement with the reality of Farquhar's escape that allows him or her to ignore such obvious unrealities.

At the conclusion of the story when Farquhar reaches home, he sees his wife and springs forward to greet her with extended arms. At this point, the verb tense of the account abruptly shifts from present to the ultimate past tense as he feels a stunning blow on the back of his neck and all is darkness and silence: "Peyton Farquhar was dead; his body with a broken neck, swung gently from side to side beneath the timbers of the Owl Creek Bridge."

Although in the past Ambrose Bierce has been scorned as a mere sensationalist, he is now belatedly gaining the attention he deserves as a serious writer with a profound understanding of the psychological nature of reality and a shrewd awareness of the complexities of narrative. "An Occurrence at Owl Creek Bridge" is not a cheap trick; it is a sophisticated model of Bierce's mastery of short fiction.

—Charles E. May

ODOUR OF CHRYSANTHEMUMS
by D.H. Lawrence, 1914

The final version of "Odour of Chrysanthemums" was written during the period of *The Rainbow* (1915), Lawrence's peak period as a writer and collected in *The Prussian Officer.* The story is of the essence of Lawrence and it is in the central line of his artistic development.

One of Lawrence's major interests as a writer was in the conditions of life of modern humans as brought about by industrialism. The story begins with a description of a mining village brings out the ugliness of industrialism, how it ensnares and victimizes people. It radiates beyond description to become representative of the plight of humans in industrial society. Lawrence's own interest is less in the milieu and more in individual human destinies, on the consequences of the industrial system on individual human lives and on personal relationships. The miner's home is a "dirty hole," cramped, untidy, infested with rats. The miners have to live frugally: the child John's trousers and waistcoat "were evidently cut down from a man's clothes"; at night, Mrs. Bates wants to light a candle only when indispensable. Soon after she hears that her husband has had an accident, she thinks of its financial implications, not because she is callous, but because she is in the grip of poverty. Lawrence thus shows how industrial capitalism works for the benefit of a few, not for the majority.

The duration of the action of the story is only a single evening, yet it is a highly significant moment and Lawrence telescopes the entire marital history of the Bateses and a phase of British social history. The central theme of the story is failure in human relationships, shown through the relationship of the Bateses.

Mrs. Bates, the main character, is conventional. Her conventionality is not merely a matter of her prim appearance and outward conduct, but goes deeper and has affected her inner being. This is confirmed in the early scene when she meets her father. She censures him for remarrying (in her view) too soon, yet the reader tends to sympathize with the bluff parent who had wanted to save himself from loneliness. Criticism of Mrs. Bates's values is also implied by the actions of her son and daughter. Their behavior (John goes outside on his own, playing by himself; Annie comes late from school) suggests a kind of independence which Mrs. Bates does not permit and, in their own way, a more natural way of life.

The neighbors, the Rigleys, form a striking contrast. Mrs. Bates's house is neat, Mrs. Rigley's an untidy mess. Mr. Bates is a toper; Mr. Rigley goes to the pub but is not an addict. Mrs. Rigley is kind, sympathetic, and helpful. The Rigleys represent natural, instinctive life, different from Mrs. Bates's rigid conventionality.

Mr. Bates, alive, is not a character in the story. He appears only at the end, as a corpse. He is portrayed through the conversation, thoughts, and attitudes of the others. Mrs. Bates and her father see him as an alcoholic brute, and Mrs. Bates holds him responsible for all the family problems. Yet Lawrence's implied criticism of Mrs. Bates suggests that her view of her husband is righteous rather than accurate. His addiction to alcohol is established as a fact, but Mrs. Bates regards it as an inherent flaw of character. The truth is suggested unmistakably only at the end, yet the reader doubts her view early on. Mr. Bates appears a comradely kind of person, natural and instinctive in his responses down in the pits and in the pub.

Thus, Mr. and Mrs. Bates represent two different ways of living and the failure of their marriage is the result of the conflict between these two. His alcoholism is shown to be not the cause of the failure but a consequence of Mrs. Bates's attempt to impose her way of life on him. Incapable of self-criticism, she is bitter against the life she and her family are forced to lead and also bitter against her husband: this is all she is capable of, intellectually, in the circumstances.

Lawrence introduces chrysanthemums ("dishevelled," "ragged wisps") in the opening scene as a part of the background. They suggest the disfiguring of nature by industrialism and the sombre atmosphere of the story, and prepare the reader for a sad human situation. Mrs. Bates associates the flowers with crucial stages in her life: "It was chrysanthemums when I married him, and chrysanthemums when you (Annie) were born, and the first time they ever brought him home drunk, he'd got brown chrysanthemums in his buttonhole." Towards the close of the story, one of the miners carrying Mr. Bates's body knocks off a vase of chrysanthemums. This symbolizes the end of the marriage of the Bateses as Mrs. Bates used to think of it as well as the shattering of her views. Whether the symbolism of the chrysanthemums is integral to the story or external, is debatable.

The main emphasis of the story, however, is on the change that comes over Mrs. Bates at the climax. Mrs. Bates's conventionality and her view of her marriage are ingrained, disrupted only by her husband's death. She realizes that they had not understood each other and that she is responsible for the failure of their marriage. She concedes that he had been "living as she never lived, feeling as she never felt." It is he, not she, who has lived the instinctive life which Lawrence values. She is the only one who could have adjusted their relationship, yet comprehension comes too late.

The story is tragic, but not despairing. Lawrence's outlook is, in the final analysis, positive. The industrial system is destructive, but human beings can survive it provided they can adjust themselves to their environment.

—D.C.R.A. Goonetilleke

OLD MORTALITY
by Katherine Anne Porter, 1939

Katherine Anne Porter chose to call "Old Mortality," *Noon Wine*, and *Pale Horse, Pale Rider* short novels. Though "Old Mortality" is complete in itself as a carefully structured work that develops the single theme of frustrated search for truth, a familiarity with Porter's seven "Miranda" stories (most of which appeared in "The Old Order" section of *The Leaning Tower and Other Stories*) enhances appreciation of "Old Mortality." These brief stories explore significant moments in the childhood and adolescent development of the autobiographical figure, Miranda, particularly as she appears in "The Circus," "The Grave," and "The Fig Tree." The grandmother who raised the motherless Porter children provided the prototype for the domineering grandmother in Porter's short fiction. Though she is the most significant influence in Miranda's life, she never quite gains her trust. Miranda regards her relatives—especially her father, Harrison, and her grandmother—as conspirators who keep her from discovering truth as she seeks to separate it from Southern romance and evasive idealism.

Throughout "Old Mortality" Miranda remains unsure about what to reject and what to salvage from legends, myths, and little lies that preserve the respectability and romantic penchant of the family. In "Old Mortality," as in the other stories, her thoughts and anxieties revolve around beauty, death, love, and unhappiness, but she protects herself with an armor of cynicism. Themes related to slavery in the stories are absent from the novel. An ironic humor underlies Porter's mostly sympathetic presentation of Miranda in "Old Mortality." By subtle authorial remarks, Porter encourages readers to smile knowingly at Miranda's intensely serious—and somewhat arrogant—search for truth. She pursues wisdom in an idealistic and over-simplified way, denying the inevitable complexity of life and of contradictory truths or individual perceptions of reality. While criticizing her family's preference for fantasy over fact, Miranda fails to acknowledge her own appetite for the romantic and sensational and finds education that stresses factual knowledge unspeakable boring. Contrasting with its psychological complexity, the story's simple structure consists of three chronological sections: (1885-1902, 1904, and 1912). The symbolic figure of the beautiful, mysterious Cousin Amy, who died in 1885, provides a thread connecting all three. In part one, as Miranda (age twelve) and her sister, Maria (age eight), study a picture of Amy (now a singing angel according to her tombstone), they are unimpressed by her fabled beauty. The truth they want is more revealing gossip about family secrets related to Amy's engagement to Gabriel, a dashing heir-apparent and owner of race horses. They speculate about what really happened the night Amy's old beau appeared at a ball and danced with her before Harrison shot at him and then fled across the border to Mexico after his "defense of a woman's honor." The girls wonder also about Amy's mysterious death in New Orleans while on her honeymoon.

Two years later in part two the sisters, bored by the routine of their convent school in New Orleans, wish their nuns were like the evil ones they read about in a forbidden paper-back book, nuns in dungeons who helped other nuns hide strangled newborns under rocks. Ecstatic when their father arrives to take them to a race track where they will finally meet the dashing Gabriel, they soon are disillusioned by the fact that he is a heavy-drinking fat man with a big red nose. Their celebration at winning a hundred dollar bet on his mare is cut short when their father collects the money to deposit in the bank. Miranda gives up her dream of becoming a jockey after she sees the mare suffering nosebleed from over-exertion. The afternoon worsens as they visit Gabriel's home, a shabby apartment in Elysian Fields, and Gabriel's second wife, Miss Honey, a rude woman who resents the years of talk about Amy and resents more Gabriel's continued glorification of his brief marriage to the "angel." It is significant that Miranda and Maria, though disappointed in their anticipated afternoon of fun, are not shocked at the discrepancy between the family story and the new knowledge of Gabriel. They have long been cynical about family versions of history. Back at school, they wash their hands for supper and shrug their shoulders when asked about the adventures of the day.

In part three the Amy/Gabriel legend again becomes central. Miranda, who eloped from the convent at age 16 and is at age 18 awaiting an annulment, is on a train speeding back to the family from whom she had escaped by running away to marry, just as she is now running away from marriage. After a year's estrangement from her family, she is returning to attend the funeral of Gabriel, who has died from alcoholism, and has been returned to Texas to rest beside Amy's grave, rather than Miss Honey's. On the train Miranda is confronted accidentally by the homely, bitter spinster, Cousin Eva Parrington, whose conversation demystifies the romantic Amy/Gabriel legend and substitutes for it a harsh reality. In spite of Miranda's long quest for truth, she resents Cousin Eva's talk of Amy's wildness and flirtations, Gabriel's drinking, Harrison's careless use of a gun, Amy's lung hemorrhages, and her suicide by overdosing on her medication. Miranda turns away from Eva, cherishing the old legend of love and a beautiful death. Miranda realizes that she eloped because of her "early training" (Grandmother's tales about ideal romance and Cousin Amy's rebellious spirit). As the train carries her back and as she meets her father at the station, Porter rushes the reader through dizzying shifts in Miranda's moods and "silent declarations." She has longed for an affectionate welcome from her father and sister and for the security of sleeping one more night in the bed she slept in as a child. Her father, however, remains distant after being estranged since the elopement. At the station, he and Cousin Eva immediately close her out of their "family" talk. Miranda declares to herself that she is through with love and being loved. She then—like Amy—desperately

questions the value of life itself, but she is saved from a "beautiful death" by suicide as she recalls her grandmother's belief that life must be shaped by each individual. After Miranda's silent victorious declaration of courage—that she can at least "know the truth of what happens to me, making a promise to herself"—the author's voice interrupts with the ironic phrase: "in her hopefulness, her ignorance." The story thus ends on a note of cynicism after its dramatically effective third section.

"Old Mortality" was first published in *The Southern Review* in 1938 and collected in *Pale Horse, Pale Rider* (1939).

—Margaret B. McDowell

THE OLD NURSE'S STORY
by Elizabeth Gaskell, 1852

Charles Dickens much admired Elizabeth Gaskell, whose story "Lizzie Leigh" opened the first number of his weekly *Household Words* (30 March 1850). She became a regular contributor (*Cranford* and *North and South*, among other items), though her craftsmanship often vexed him and she could be patronizing about the "Dickensy periodical . . . I did so hope to escape it," and could regard as "good enough for Dickens" stories unworthy of classier magazines. "The Old Nurse's Story," her first ghost story, was contributed, by invitation, to the 1852 Extra Christmas Number, *A Round of Stories by the Christmas Fire*; several others appeared in later ones. (The story was later collected in 1865 in *Cousin Phillis and Other Tales*.) She loved telling ghost stories, and on one occasion she claimed to have seen a ghost.

Dickens called "The Old Nurse's Story" "a very fine ghost-story indeed. Nobly told, and wonderfully managed." In his six letters about it he suggested, and even sent a draft of, an alternative ending; he claimed that her conclusion weakened the terror. She did alter the ending, but not in his fashion.

In the story the old nurse Hesther tells how, when 17 years old, she took her beloved five-year-old charge Miss Rosamond, recently orphaned, to Furnivall Manor house, an impressive though rundown mansion near the Cumberland Fells. It was owned by the girl's relative, Lord Furnivall, though now is inhabited only by his aged and "hard sad" great-aunt Miss Grace Furnivall, her "cole and grey, and stony" companion Mrs. Stark, and a few servants. Strange and sinister events accumulate. An organ plays weird music, though Hesther finds that its mechanism is broken ("my flesh began to creep a little"), but she gets used to it (it "did one no harm"). Then little Rosamond is lured, one wintry evening, up the Fells by a pretty little girl who beckons her from the garden. She is discovered, frozen and asleep, when revived, she tells how a weeping lady had welcomed her there and lulled her to sleep. But only one set of footprints lead up through the snow! The girl continues to haunt Rosamond, beating at the window to be let in. Hesther's fellow-servants are reluctant to disclose the family history underlying these mysteries, but eventually she discovers that the special organist is an earlier Lord Furnivall, a vicious tyrant who nevertheless was an ardent music lover. His two beautiful daughters, Grace and Maude, both fell in love with a foreign musician who annually visited the Manor to perform; he flirted with both, but clandestinely married Maude, who bore him a daughter. Furnivall, enraged by this disgrace to a noble family, turned mother and child out into the snow, where the girl soon died and her mother went crazy. The climax comes with a re-enactment of this event, on a suitably tempestuous January night, witnessed by all the household. The aged Miss Furnivall tries to stop her father striking the child, but her younger self is seen mercilessly looking on. The old lady drops "death-stricken" and dies realizing that "what is done in youth can never be undergone in age!" Rosamond survives and prospers, through Hesther's heroic efforts to prevent her being lured to her death by the phantoms.

As Miriam Allot points out (in *Notes and Queries*, 1961), the storm is a link between Emily Brontë's *Wuthering Heights* (spectral girl clamouring at the window to be let in, an old house in northern England, tempestuous weather) and Henry James's *The Turn of the Screw*, another story told "round the fire" at Yuletide (and another mansion, with Gothic weather and a young governess gradually becoming aware of a supernatural threat to her charge(s) and striving—vainly in James's story—to save them). Like Brontë's Nelly Dean and James's Mrs. Grose, Hesther is a sensible, wholesome down-to-earth domestic, whose very ordinariness helps to credibilize the strange, disturbing, and violent narrative she tells.

Dickens's notion for "a very terrific end" was that in the climactic episode everyone should hear the noises and see the ghost-child, but only Rosamond should see the other spectral figures, "crying out what it is she sees, and describing the phantom child as shewing it to her as it were." This would certainly have made a stronger ending, remark the editors of Dickens's *Letters*: other commentators argue otherwise. Unfortunately neither Gaskell's original ending, nor Dickens's draft revision, nor her replies to his letters have survived.

—Philip Collins

OLD RED
by Caroline Gordon, 1963

The story "Old Red," by Caroline Gordon, describes a quiet crisis in the life of Aleck Maury, who at a family reunion reviews his 60 years of life and finds them wanting. Maury is viewed as the family idler and wastrel, a failed classics teacher, now a widower, whose only passion in life has been hunting and fishing, rambling the woods with black fieldhands and poor white trash tenants.

Maury contemplates his daughter Sarah and her young husband Stephen, whose innocent love for writing and literature disgusts the world-weary Maury. He rejects the life of the mind and of art that Stephen and Sarah represent, and he meditates on fleeting time, as if a narrator of a *carpe diem* poem:

> *Time,* he though, *time!* They were always mentioning the word, and what did they know about it? Nothing in God's world! ... Where, for instance, had this year gone? He could swear he had not wasted a minute of it, for no man living, he thought, knew better how to make each day a pleasure for him.

Escape is much on his mind; Aleck has consciously evaded family responsibilities and powers for a half century, in exchange for a life in nature, a life among the poor, unpretentious rural people who live close to nature, who can "smell out fish." While young Stephen, with his whole life ahead of him, spends his days indoors meditating on the sonnet "in the form in which it first came to England" and on such esoterica as the poetry of John Skelton, Maury admires Jim Yost of Maysville, "a man of imagination" who makes the Devil Bug lure, although Maury regretfully boasts, "I myself had the idea thirty years ago and let it slip by me the way I do with so many of my ideas."

Aleck Maury reviews his past, thinking of himself and his dead wife Mary "when they were the young couple in the house." His marriage seems a failure, a domestic war of attrition. His life has been a series of constraints and defeats, Maury feels, and now his old age and impending death represent the ultimate skirmish.

Maury takes his son-in-law fishing, to induct him into a world of freedom and intuitive knowledge, the hard-won empiricism of humans against nature. It is experiential learning, the use of time, that he seeks to teach, in contradistinction to the precious book-learning he has rejected: "His daughter had told him once that he ought to set all his knowledge down in a book. 'Why?' he had asked. "So everybody else can know as much as I do?'" When Stephen asks if he prefers fishing to hunting, Maury says "A man has got to come to himself early in life if he's going to amount to anything." By the measure of his family and genteel middle class society, Aleck Maury—once an esteemed professor—has failed to amount to anything, but by his own lights he has seized the day and wrung out its value. He crafts gentle irony in summarizing the fishing expedition to Stephen: "Ain't it wonderful ... ain't it wonderful now that a man of my gifts can content himself a whole morning on this here little old pond?"

In the course of his reminiscence, Maury recalls a fabled quarry, "one fox, they grew to know him in time, to call him affectionately by name. Old Red it was who showed himself always like that there on the crest of the hill." Old Red becomes a totem for Maury, an emblem of escape, freedom, imagination, self-sufficiency, everything he values in life. Through his imagination, he becomes a foxhunter, then a companion of the fox, and finally by empathetic alchemy the fox itself.

Maury then conceives a foxy plan to escape the constraints of his family, the present, and go fishing. Like the old fox, the animal he has studied all his life, the old professor will have stolen away, lost to the baying hounds of respectability and responsibility, the traps and barbs and snares of life. Aleck's life is back in order, he is himself again.

—William J. Schafer

ON THE WESTERN CIRCUIT
by Thomas Hardy, 1894

"On the Western Circuit" is dated Autumn 1891; it was collected in Thomas Hardy's 1894 volume of short stories, *Life's Little Ironies.* In Hardy's writing career it thus comes between the novels, *The Woodlanders* (completed and published, February 1887) and *Tess of the d'Urbervilles* (completed October 1890, published 1891), and just before *Jude the Obscure* (conceived, according to Hardy himself, from 1887 to 1890, written from 1893 to 1894, and published in 1895). With each of these works it shares the same theme of marriage and the alliance, or misalliance, of temperaments and education. There are also some particular points of resemblance: Fitzpiers in *The Woodlanders*, like Raye in "On the Western Circuit," is a professional man with metropolitan interests caught between a country girl (though Grace is better educated than Anna) and a more sophisticated woman; Angel Clare in *Tess* is also allied to a comparatively simple country girl, and, like Raye, finds on his wedding day that an important fact about their relationship has been kept from him; and Jude, in the novel named after him, is torn between two women, Sue and Arabella, of very different temperaments and background, and trapped into marriage with Arabella by deceit. Associated issues of class, sex, and respectability are likewise important in each work, and pregnancy outside wedlock is a significant feature in all except *The Woodlanders*.

These connections indicate certain underlying preoccupations in Hardy's work of the late 1880's and early 1890's, which spring out of tensions in his own life, and perhaps relate to difficulties experienced in his own marriage to his first wife, Emma. More emphatically, however, they reveal him as a writer increasingly critical of the contradictions and hypocrisy rife in 19th-century England, dissatisfied with the smug ethic of its conventional Christianity, and becoming more acutely aware of the woman's point of view in a male-oriented society. Inhibited by the conventions of Victorian publishing which forbid outspokenness, especially in sexual matters, he is nonetheless becoming more impatient with its restraints. As he asserts in his essay, "Candour in English Fiction" (January 1890), "Life being a physiological fact, its honest portrayal must be largely concerned with, for one thing, the relation of the sexes, and the substitution for such catastrophes as favour the false colouring best expressed by the regulation finish that 'they married and were happy ever after,' of catastrophes based upon sexual relations as it is."

It is appropriate to set "On the Western Circuit" in this context. But it must also be recognised as a story meant to entertain—as arising out of these preoccupations, but less earnest, less mordant in its expression of them than the contemporary novels. Anna's fate is not tragic as Tess d'Urberville's is; and though it is evidence, like Grace Melbury's, of Hardy's determination to have done with the regulation" they were married and were happy ever after" ending, it is a fate to be contemplated ruefully, not despairingly. Even for the cheated husband his situation is one to be accepted, at the worst, "with dreary resignation" (the last words of the tale). And it is suitably ironic, one of "life's little ironies," that the foot-loose seducer, a clever lawyer, should get his come-uppance from a simple country girl.

Of course, that is not quite how the story is told; nor is it quite how it looks from either Raye's or Edith's point of view. As the situation is triangular, so the possibilities of interpretation are threefold—fourfold, if the narrator's tacit complicity with the reader is also taken into account. The story is simple enough: Anna, an illiterate girl fresh from the country working as maid to a sympathetic mistress in the cathedral town of Melchester, is picked up by the smart Londoner, Charles Bradford Raye, on one of his visits on the legal "western circuit." She is drawn into a correspondence with him that is actually written on her behalf by the lady she works for, Edith Harnham. Through this vicarious contact Edith becomes sentimentally involved, while Anna, meeting her lover from time to time, becomes pregnant. Raye is so impressed by the elegance of her letters that he decides to marry her, only to discover too late that the style is the mistress's not the maid's.

Thus far it is a contrast between physical and spiritual courtship—a contrast imaginatively introduced by the vividly impressionistic opening of the story, which plays off the darkly glimpsed Melchester cathedral, "the most homogeneous pile of mediaeval architecture in England" (recognisably based on Salisbury) against the Dickensian vulgarity, but also vitality, of a nearby fair. It is there that the attraction of Anna's fresh country beauty, enhanced in its sexual appeal by her "crimson skirt, dark jacket, brown hat and brown gloves," is first felt by Raye, drawing him into flirting with her as any middle-class Victorian young man might do, without any thought of her as a social equal and potential marriage partner. Her very spontaneity ("She was absolutely unconscious of everything save the act of riding") is a powerful polar opposite to his "vague latter-day glooms and popular melancholies"; a physical "circuit" is set up between them, which proves more potent for both as the story develops. But Anna is also instinctively aware that her social inferiority is a serious barrier, and that the one possibility of overcoming it is denied her by her lack of education. It is here that her mistress's help is essential, leading to the irony of the deception that persuades Raye that the sexual satisfaction he has had (which has made the girl pregnant) may be matched by the social accomplishments society expects in a professional man's wife, and so to his proposal of marriage.

However, the situation Hardy has created is more complex than this. A significant detail in the original fairground meeting is that the mistress, having gone out in search of the maid, finds her in Raye's company, is secretly attracted by him, and by accident has her hand caressed by him when he thinks he is seducing Anna. This physical contact (one inevitably thinks of the significance of touch in the later tale by D.H. Lawrence, "You Touched Me") remains as an undercurrent to her vicariously spiritual affair with him conducted through their correspondence; and it has a slightly sinister reinforcement from the circumstances of her own marriage to an older man—a loveless, and childless, marriage of convenience that has clearly left her physically unfulfilled. These circumstances also provide the artistic justification for what might otherwise be a somewhat melodramatic climax to their indirect relationship: when Raye discovers that Edith is the author of the letters, he demands a kiss—on the cheek only if all was "pure invention," but otherwise on the lips; and lips it is.

For Edith the outcome is tragic. She feels that she has "ruined" Raye, because she "would not deal treacherously" towards Anna; and there is the unspoken implication that she has ruined herself by lacking the courage to break out of a loveless marriage. Raye's ruin, however, is more operatic than real, expressed in the overblown simile, "She [Anna] did not know that before his eyes he beheld as it were a galley, in which he, the fastidious urban, was chained to work for the remainder of his life, with her, the unlettered peasant, chained to his side." Nevertheless, he is not angry. He can speak to her "gently"; and he can even acknowledge that "It serves me right." And for Anna things are not as bad as they might be; at the end of the story she is not a ruined maid, but a married woman.

Readers can savour the irony of physical and spiritual mismatchings, of illusions shattered, and of the contrast between an ending of prose and a beginning of vividly contrasted poetry. But it may also be felt that of the two marriages of convenience, that between London sophisticate and Wessex innocent is less stale than that between middle-class old man and middle-class young woman; and that the astringency of the ending is not incompatible with a degree of comic laughter.

—R.P. Draper

ONE DAY IN THE LIFE OF IVAN DENISOVICH
(Odin den' Ivana Denisovicha)
by Aleksandr Solzhenitsyn, 1962

During Khrushchev's partial de-Stalinization campaign of the early 1960's, Aleksandr Solzhenitsyn lived in the town of Ryazan', worked as a schoolteacher, and secretly wrote about his experience in Stalin's concentration camps. Recollecting Tolstoii's suggestion that a whole novel could be devoted to one day in the life of a simple peasant, he once attempted to describe a schoolteacher's day, but then, under the pressure of his major concerns, he switched over to a detailed account of a day in the life of a concentration-camp inmate. The times seemed propitious for getting the story into print; therefore, Solzhenitsyn "lightened" his story, that is, removed the most shocking and politically subversive material. After great difficulties and the intervention of Khrushchev himself *Odin den' Ivana Denisovicha* (*One Day in the Life of Ivan Denisovich*) came out in *Novyi Mir,* the country's most influential literary journal. Khrushchev had been partly won over by the peasant origins of the story's protagonist, yet Solzhenitsyn's choice of the peasant hero was mainly a hint at the fate of the millions of peasant victims, eclipsed by the much smaller number of intellectuals and party leaders "liquidated" under Stalin and rehabilitated, with fanfare, during the so-called "thaw."

The publication of the story was a major event in Soviet literature: it seemed to signal that writers henceforth would be allowed to present sincere and truthful views of their country's past and present. For many readers the story was the first reliable aid to imagining what it was really like in the camps. It is now common knowledge that in the majority of Soviet labor camps the conditions were much harder than those of Ivan Denisovich; and in the story itself, it is mentioned that the protagonist almost died in his previous camp. Yet the relatively livable setting of the story, which got it past the censorship, is a matter not of misrepresentation but of the choice of the place and time: the camp, modeled on the author's own Ekibastuz, is located among the relatively warm Kazakhstan steppes; its inmates are employed on construction sites; the time is around 1950, when the political offenders were separated from the criminal convicts, yet the regime in their camps was not as murderous as a couple of years before. The day described is a particularly lucky one: all of the protagonist's little projects and self-protective infringements of the rules have succeeded (it is suggested that this may have turned out otherwise). Nevertheless, the story powerfully evokes a sense of life reduced to the marrow amid chronic hunger, deprivation, terror, absurdities, and humiliations; it also builds up a complex picture of the veteran prisoners' adjustment and their struggle for physical and moral self-preservation.

The story presents a great deal of information without turning the protagonist's experience into a mere pretext for describing the camp. Clever and alert, Ivan Denisovich Shukhov, the third-person, center-of-consciousness protagonist, always considers the spectrum of the possible outcomes of every situation, as well as the alternative conduct options. Moreover, the information about camp food, medical service, the frisking, parcels from home, and so on is distributed so that it never interrupts the account of the action, but rather fills in such stretches of the story time as the protagonist's waiting in a queue or marching back from work.

Through the letters that Shukhov receives from home and the conversations that he hears, Solzhenitsyn expands the ideological repertoire of the story, thus embracing broader social and aesthetic issues. It cautiously is suggested that the camp is but a condensed expression of the tendencies at work in the country as a whole, tendencies that cripple individual lives, deform personal relationships, and vitiate both official and folk art. Oblique touches of self-reflexivity also hint that similar tendencies still threaten the integrity of the narrative itself.

By not idealizing his protagonist, not endowing him with eccentricities beyond endearing folk beliefs, and by avoiding accounts of excess atrocities, Solzhenitsyn creates the impression that *Ivan Denisovich* depicts a characteristic slice of camp life. The account of what seems to be a more or less typical day is comprehensive, from reveille to lights out, with a logical interconnection of the elements of the setting, yet without a strict thematic control of such narrative details as inset stories of other prisoners. These features of the narrative further contribute to its "reality" effect; and though the testimony that the story bears has been "lightened," at the time of its publication it proved to be sufficiently consciousness raising. By shaping Shukhov's camp experience, not as a marginal, but as a representative phenomenon, Solzhenitsyn practically institutionalized the Gulag subject as ample and vitally important material for literary exploration. The regime's rather prompt suppression of the camp memoirs that started flowing into editorial offices after the publication of *Ivan Denisovich* came to be perceived as violence that left the Soviet literature of the next two decades largely handicapped and drained.

Occasionally criticised as a piece of covert journalism, *Ivan Denisovich* actually proved to be a major literary event. It legitimized a new literary genre—Gulag documentary prose, fictionalized or directly autobiographical—in the eyes of the reading public throughout the world.

—Leona Toker

THE OPEN BOAT
by Stephen Crane, 1898

"The Open Boat" is one of the most celebrated, and most frequently anthologized, stories in English. For nearly a century, this tale of four men struggling for survival at sea in a ten-foot dinghy has touched something central to the appeal of a narrative, and it has been analyzed and discussed from a rich diversity of perspectives.

The biographical background and composition history of the story are nearly as compelling as the published work itself. In the late autumn of 1896, Crane was hired by the Bacheller newspaper syndicate to cover the Cuban revolution. Crane went immediately to Florida and, on December 31, 1897, sailed on the *Commodore* for the short journey. There was a heavy fog that evening, however, and the ship struck a sand bar leaving the harbor. Once the vessel was free, the captain ordered the voyage to continue, and it was not until they were well at sea that the crew discovered the extensive damage to the hull and the order to abandon ship was given. Crane worked calmly and steadily with the lifeboats until he and the injured captain, the cook, and an oiler named Billy Higgins were left with only a small dinghy to row to safety. Meanwhile, one of the lifeboats had capsized in the heavy waves, and the seven men aboard returned to the ship. They were looking to the dinghy for assistance as the ship sank and they were drowned. Crane and his companions rowed toward land, spending a night just off the breakers in rough water, until they capsized and swam to shore, the oiler dying in the attempt. A few days later, Crane published a newspaper account of the incident in the New York *Press* (7 January 1897) as "Stephen Crane's Own Story."

Later in the year, Crane used these events as the basis for "The Open Boat," adding to the basic facts of the adventure the thematic values of psychological transformation, of life as a struggle for existence, of human isolation in a hostile world. He told the story with a shifting point of view, stressing how the incident would be interpreted from a multiplicity of points of view, from the perspective of each of the participants and from the vantage point of an objective observer. But he gave primary emphasis to the consciousness of the "correspondent," who is best able to formulate and interpret the meaning of the events. Collectively, the men protest against an abstract fate, who seems intent on drowning them: "If this old ninny-woman, Fate, cannot do better than this, she should be deprived of the management of men's fortunes." As the events progress, however, they come to see nature and the sea as less hostile than indifferent, and they realize that they are not important in the grand scheme of things. They contemplate the meaning of a "high cold star," its distance and indifference, and it reveals to them the true pathos of their situation. On the personal level, this realization changes the attitude of the correspondent toward a character in Caroline S. Norton's poem "A Soldier of the Legion," and he comes to feel compassion for the man dying in Algiers without sympathy. This humane view enriches the experience for the correspondent and places in perspective the death of the oiler as the men struggle through the breakers to shore: "When it came night, the white waves paced to and fro in the moonlight, and the wind brought the sound of the great sea's voice to the men on shore, and they felt that they could then be interpreters."

These dramatic events have given rise to scores of critical readings from different assumptions. Leedice Kissane analyses the language of the story, arguing that the metaphoric style has the effect of emphasizing the futility of a struggle against nature. Charles R. Metzger gives a realistic interpretation, stressing the irony of the death of the oiler, the strongest member of the crew. Richard P. Adams, on the other hand, explores the interplay between omnipotent naturalistic forces and the desires of individual human beings. James Nagel places the emphasis on the perspectives of the men, on their progressive ability to perceive and interpret the world around them. More recently, David Halliburton has discussed how the sinking of the ship transforms the roles of the men, making them play reduced roles in their precarious circumstances. Collectively, these varied points of view testify to the thematic richness and artistic skill of Crane's most important story.

—James Nagel

THE OTHER BOAT
by E.M. Forster, 1972

E.M. Forster is best known as author of *A Passage to India* but he also wrote five other novels and a number of short stories, two volumes of which, *The Celestial Omnibus* (1911) and *The Eternal Moment* (1928), and *The Collected Tales* (1947), were published in his own lifetime. *The Life to Come* appeared posthumously in 1972 and comprises all that the editor, Oliver Stallybrass, was able to salvage of the manuscript stories extant at Forster's death in 1970. "The Other Boat" was published in this edition.

The versions of the unpublished stories that Forster left behind him were, as Oliver Stallybrass explains in his introduction to the volume, untidy and confused. "The Other Boat" and parts of it exist, variously, in typescript, manuscript additions, and alterations, and a published version of the first part, which appeared in *The Listener* on 23 December 1948 as "Entrance to an Unwritten Novel." The first part of the story dates from about 1913; the remainder from 1958. The story as it appears in *The Life to Come* is Stallybrass's attempt to make sense of the various manuscript, typescript, and printed sources and to offer a version as close as possible to what he believed were Forster's "latest intentions."

It is quite clear why Forster did not himself attempt to publish "The Other Boat" in its complete form, for its explicit homosexual love-making scenes would not have been acceptable in the prevailing sexual climate which governed during most of his own lifetime. By the time of his death social mores had changed and first *Maurice* in 1970 and then *The Life to Come* were published without too much sensationalism.

The setting of "The Other Boat" belongs to the earlier part of this century, during the days of the British Empire. The two principal characters are Cocoanut and Lionel March, two boys from different races, of different nationalities, and from widely different social classes. The whole story takes place on two boats and it is divided into five parts; the first part records the events of less than an hour on a journey back from India during Cocoanut and Lionel's childhood; the incidents in the remaining four parts occur on a single night some years later on a journey to India when the two boys are young men, Lionel a captain in the army on a colonial posting and Cocoanut with a job in shipping.

In part 1 Forster sets a social scene familiar to the reader of *A Passage to India*; the passengers on the boat are divided into two classes—Mrs. March and her family belong to the ruling classes, Cocoanut to the inferior and subjugated races. The children, however, have few inhibitions and they play happily together, not noticing that Cocoanut is different from the rest because he has a "touch of the tarbrush." Forster's portrayal of Mrs. March confirms his hostility to the womenfolk of colonial administrators, which he spells out explicitly in *A Passage to India*. Mrs. March is snobbish, prejudiced, and ill-educated; unwilling to look after her children herself whilst she can be escorted around the ship by Captain Armstrong, she nevertheless accuses them of selfishness when they demand her attention. It is clear that she is attempting to pass on her prejudices to her children and the frustration that she feels at their constant association with Cocoanut finds voice in her final words to the little boy, "You're a silly idle useless unmanly little boy."

Cocoanut, however, is the centre of attention for the children, and Lionel shows a special preference for his company, ominously (in view of the outcome of the story) seeing him as "the only one who falls down when he's killed." At this stage, too, though the March children do not realise it, it is Cocoanut who takes the lead in their games and who dominates their entertainments; at the same time he is flattered by their attentions and shows himself adept at leading them to follow the pursuits he has chosen.

Part 2 begins with the marvellously linguistically revealing letter from Lionel to his mother: "Hullo the Mater!" places the March family accurately and exactly on a point in the social scale which most contemporary readers will see as archaic. The letter serves to remind of the previous voyage, the words "touch of the tar-brush" are recalled in reference to Cocoanut and the scene is set for the conclusion of the tale.

Once again, it is Cocoanut who takes the lead; memories of his childhood pleasure in Lionel's attentions have blossomed into love and he fails to understand the ephemerality of a shipboard affair; when he seduces Lionel he hopes for a lasting partnership but Lionel's behaviour is deeply influenced by his class and race consciousness, so that the affair between him and Cocoanut is a matter of shame that must be hidden from his peers. Moreover, it is his fear of what his fellow officers and other British people will think that makes him decide, despite his love, that he must repress his natural instincts and leave Cocoanut. The final tragedy, in which Lionel murders Cocoanut during the act of love and then commits suicide by jumping into the sea, is perhaps the only possible end for such a story.

The story contains many of the hallmarks of Forster's fiction: the fatherless family, the dominant and class-conscious mother, the British repression of natural instincts, the intrusion into the story of a lively and life-loving foreigner. Though by no means autobiographical, it also reflects aspects of Forster's own life, suggesting his disillusion with colonial rule and his concern at racial discrimination; in particular, however, it recalls his own first real love for el Adl, the poor Egyptian tram-conductor from a subject race. The "ecstasy" and the "agony" of the union between Lionel and Cocoanut no doubt owes much to Forster's memory of the union between himself and el Adl.

—Hilda D. Spear

THE OTHER TWO
by Edith Wharton, 1904

Although most literary scholars tend to think of Edith Wharton as a novelist, she was in fact one of the most accomplished story writers among American authors of the past century. She began her career as a writer of tales in *Scribner's* in 1891 and continued to practice this genre throughout her career. In all, she wrote 86 stories and 11 novellas, most of them first published in magazines and then collected in 11 volumes. For Wharton the story was not a means of apprenticeship before writing novels but an end in itself. She used stories to work out ideas and explore themes that later found treatment in her novels.

Wharton was no innovator for form in the story, but she developed and blended plot, character, setting, and theme with extraordinary skill. She greatly admired the Russian story writers, of whom she said in *The Writing of Fiction* (1925): "Instead of a loose web spread over the surface of life, they have made it [the story], at its best, a shaft driven straight into the heart of human experience." So did Wharton at her best, and at the same time she leavened her tales with irony and subtle humor.

In her memoirs written late in life (*A Backward Glance*, 1934), Wharton could not remember the time when she did not want to make up stories. Before she could even read or write, she would pick up a book and walk about turning pages and inventing tales. She had to overcome formidable odds, however, to become a writer, as she was born in a socially prominent New York City family that expected a daughter to grow up to be a society matron, mother, and hostess, not an intellectual or writer. She also was married early to a Boston dilettante with no literary interests and endured 28 years of unhappy married life before divorcing her husband.

These facts about her life figure prominently in her short fiction. As in "The Other Two," Wharton wrote extensively about the dynamics of marriage, and her settings are often the high society in which she grew up. Characters in her stories live in mansions staffed by butlers, up-and-down-stairs maids, footmen, governesses, coachmen, and later chauffeurs. They have boxes at the opera, second homes at fashionable places like Newport, and they travel to Europe frequently in the days when only the rich could afford to do so. But the problems they face in their human relationships are universal.

"The Other Two," which tells the story of Alice Haskett-Varick-Waythorn from the point of view of her third husband Waythorn, shows Wharton's preoccupation with the problem of woman's role in a world dominated by men. The story, written early in her career and published in *The Descent of Man* (1904), takes place at a time when even woman suffrage was a long way off. The story opens with Alice newly married to number three, a rich New York broker, who views her romantically as the perfect wife. The humor and irony of the story come in Waythorn's gradual realization that Alice's perfection as a wife has come from experience with her previous husbands.

Waythorn's awakening begins when he first meets husband number one, a man Alice has led him to believe was a brute. It turns out that Haskett was a small businessman in upstate New York, dull and colorless, but gentle and intensely devoted to the daughter who now lives with Alice and Waythorn. He has sold his business and moved to the city to be near his daughter. The meeting between Waythorn and Haskett comes over visiting rights when the daughter is sick and can't visit her father. Waythorn finds it distasteful to have to meet the first husband, but he gets used to it.

With her second husband Alice is able to move to the big city. This is Gus Varick, a socially prominent New Yorker—but shallow, improvident, and unfaithful—and Alice has discarded him for the solid, middle-aged bachelor Waythorn. Soon after his marriage, however, Waythorn meets Varick a couple of times by chance, then to his dismay is forced because of his partner's illness to handle some business transactions for him. Thus through circumstances beyond his control he is thrown together with both of Alice's former spouses. It is all rather distasteful, but Alice handles matters adroitly.

The wonderful denouement takes place when Haskett comes to discuss with Alice the child's education after Waythorn comes home from his office and before Alice, who has been out for the afternoon, has returned. Waythorn takes Haskett into his library, gives him a cigar, and just then the servants usher in another visitor, none other than Varick, who has to see Waythorn on business. So Waythorn gives Varick a cigar, and all three men stand there uncomfortably. Then in walks Alice just as the maid brings in the tea things. The tale ends with Alice handing around cups of tea to all three of her husbands.

This story is a masterpiece of social comedy by a master storyteller. Wharton's biographer, R.W.B. Lewis, calls it "the most nearly perfect short story that Edith Wharton ever wrote." It's a cautionary tale about what a woman had to do in the late 19th century to get what she wanted out of life, but Alice ends up the winner. Her third husband admits to himself that he's like a member of a syndicate who holds so many shares in his wife's personality and "his predecessors were the partners in the business." In the final analysis, however, he concludes that perhaps it were better "to own a third of a wife who knew how to make a man happy than a whole one who had lacked opportunity to acquire the art."

—James Woodress

OTHER VOICES, OTHER ROOMS
by Truman Capote, 1948

Other Voices, Other Rooms, Truman Capote's first book, remained on the *New York Times* best-seller list for nine weeks, a remarkable achievement for such an unconventional work. In its probing psychological insights into previously tabooed areas, the short novel was, in Capote's words, "an attempt to exorcise demons." Graced with lush descriptive language, it confirmed the young author's place at the forefront of post-World War II literature.

Other Voices, Other Rooms is an initiation story. Joel Knox, a troubled 13-year-old whose mother has recently died, is invited to live with his father on an old plantation called Skully's Landing. Struggling to form his adult identity, Joel still seeks "the far-away room," a world of his imagination, even though as he grows older he finds it more and more inaccessible. One of the characters in that room is the father he has never known, whom he imagines is courageous and strong. But the handsome imaginary man who buys his son a .22 rifle and hunts possum with him is not the pitiful invalid Joel finds at Skully's Landing. Joel's initiation into adulthood is further complicated by adult deceptions. The invitation that brings him to the Landing is a ruse perpetrated by his father's second wife and her cousin Randolph. Joel tries to hang onto previously instilled values, but ultimately his initial instinct to reject the decadence of Skully's Landing is replaced by an acceptance of it.

Another complicating factor in Joel's passage to adulthood is his struggle with his sexual identity. Early in the story, Radclif, the truck driver who brings Joel to Noon City, thinks the boy lacks masculinity and questions the

flowery, dainty handwriting on the letter supposedly from Joel's father: "What the hell kind of man would write like that?" Later, Joel futilely attempts to assert his manhood over a neighborhood tomboy, but it is she who takes his sword from him and vanquishes a water moccasin as she holds Joel safely behind her. Ultimately, Joel cannot fill a conventional male role, and it is suggested that, at the end, he only discovers his true identity when he accepts his homosexuality, for then "he knew who he was."

Although Capote denies being a regionalist, *Other Voices, Other Rooms* nevertheless bears a strong resemblance to writings of the Southern gothic tradition. He uses the American South's deteriorating plantation houses and ghost-haunted sense of a former life to evoke that brooding and terrifying atmosphere common to the gothic novel. Each year the plantation house sinks several inches into the marsh and, to Joel, the house emits "settling sighs of stone and board, as though the old rooms inhaled-exhaled constant wind." The sense of ruin and decay is illustrated by the garden, "a jumbled wreckage," and a burned wing of the house, only the pillars of which remain. Joel observes "luminous green logs that shine under the dark marsh water like drowned corpses." The very atmosphere seems to exude decadence and to threaten to engulf the boy: "a sea of deepening green spread the sky like some queer wine."

A little over a decade before *Other Voices, Other Rooms* was published, Ellen Glasgow complained of writers such as Erskine Caldwell and William Faulkner whom, she felt, overemphasized degeneracy and "fantastic abominations." According to William Van O'Connor, by preferring "weirdly distorted images," these writers challenged the "bland surfaces of bourgeois customs and habits" and created a new genre that blurred the division between the tragic and comic. Like Caldwell and Faulkner, Capote creates several grotesque characters as part of the Southern ambience of his short novel: the owner of R.V. Lacey's Princely Place with her single, antenna-like hair growing from a facial mole; the gnome-like Jesus Fever who, asleep at the reins, drives Joel to Skully's Landing; the congregation of town loafers who look "like a gang of desperadoes in a Western picture-show"; and Miss Wisteria, the love-thwarted carnival dwarf who weeps "to think little boys must grow tall."

With Cousin Randolph, however, Capote takes the grotesque character further than his predecessors. Although Randolph's affectations immediately qualify him as another of the grotesques filling Joel's view of the Southern landscape, his importance in the boy's development transforms him from simply part of the bizarre scenery into a figure whom Joel eventually embraces for the love he has failed to find elsewhere.

Randolph's decadence complements the decadent setting. His world-weary languid manner, manicured toenails, "silver-tongued" flattery, and caustic sarcasm are reminiscent of Oscar Wilde. His bedroom, which he terms "a rather gaudy grave," is closed off from natural light. Eventually, we learn that he is the mysterious person dressed like an 18th-century French countess standing in the plantation window, whose identity puzzles Joel. Whereas Faulkner and Caldwell might have created a bizarre character and even might have described the person with compassion, they maintained a distance from him, just as Capote's protagonist does early in the story. But Capote's novel differs from earlier ones in that Joel eventually accepts and chooses to participate in the grotesque world, the world of "other voices, other rooms." His coming of age is sealed by his acceptance of the transvestite

Randolph. Moreover, his decision is described in affirmative terms.

The relationship of Randolph and Joel clarifies one of the major themes of the novel, and of other Capote works: that "love, having no geography, knows no boundaries. . . .Any love is natural and beautiful that lies within a person's nature." Although there are numerous ways in which Joel is betrayed by the adult world, in particular by Randolph, at the end of the story, the boy forgives the older man and accepts him in his most fantastic metamorphosis. Capote suggests what William Van O'Connor says is the propensity of the writer of the grotesque to find the sublime in "weirdly distorted images." Perhaps Joel accepts Randolph because of the older man's soul-baring story of his doomed love for the Mexican boxer, Pepe Alvarez, and his subsequent loneliness, with which Joel can certainly identify. Perhaps he accepts him because Randolph sits faithfully by the boy's bedside during a long illness. At any rate, Randolph becomes the answer to Joel's prayer, "God, let me be loved."

Beneath Capote's substantial public reputation lies a novel powered by an intense private vision, a work that, according to one reviewer, is "artistically exciting." In identifying influences on his first novel, Capote himself stressed that "the real progenitor was my difficult, subterranean self." The young author's life as an unwanted child who eventually affirmed his homosexuality clearly informs *Other Voices, Other Rooms*. As he said of it, "The book set me free."

—William L. Howard

THE OTHER WOMAN (La Femme cachée)
by Colette, 1924

"La Femme cachée" ("The Other Woman") is the title story in Colette's 1924 collection. It was only the second time that Colette had published under her own name; her famous *Claudine* novels were signed in her first husband's name, "Willy," and work after 1904 under the pen name of Colette Willy. The title of "The Other Woman" plays on the double meaning of the word *femme*, which in French means both "woman" and "wife."

In the story a couple, in all likelihood on their honeymoon, stop for lunch whilst touring. Instead of allowing themselves to be led to a vacant table by the window overlooking the bay, Marc insists that he and Alice should sit in the middle of the room. The restaurant is busy, the waiter over-worked and perspiring. After ordering lunch for them both, Marc explains that the move was in order to prevent Alice sitting next to his first wife, who is also unexpectedly there.

In the three brief pages of the tale Colette unobtrusively underlines the contrast between the two women, coincidentally in the same place as their husband in common. Alice's blonde, wavy hair is enclosed within the veil of her fashionable hat; bronzed from the holiday sun and generously proportioned, she exudes the immoderate happiness of a newly-married young woman. The blinding midday light tellingly changes the colour of her eyes from blue to green. The first wife, who is never named, also has blue eyes, something Alice had not previously known. She is dressed in white, a serene parallel to the opalescent sky and

the bleached sea of high summer. Her smooth brown hair is uncovered, glossily reflecting the sun and the sea, and amidst the throng of other diners in large sun hats, and children in red, she sits calmly smoking, self-contained and indifferent both to her surroundings and to the couple. The composure and sophistication of the first wife reflects on Alice, making her appear both naive and youthfully dependent on her husband's praise.

Marc is possessively proud of his young wife, teasing her about putting on too much weight, complimenting her on her looks; rather smugly he compliments himself about her feelings and attitude towards him: "The way you indulge me is so charming, darling. . . .You're an angel. . . .You love me. . . .I'm so proud when I see those eyes of yours." He is clearly affluent, with a chauffeur who is eating his lunch elsewhere. He has well manicured hands, but there is no suggestion that he is handsome; his features are ruddy and regular, his hair is turning grey.

The presence of his ex-wife, however, imposes subconscious alterations in the couple, and Colette shows how this changes their behaviour. Marc sits up straighter during the protracted meal, controlling his posture, while Alice sometimes laughs too loudly, as if they are ill at ease with the situation. This is reflected in their conversation, for though each thinks the other has forgotten the first wife, they inevitably return to her. Early during lunch Marc had explained their incompatibility, their amicable, quick, divorce. Towards the end of the meal, however, Marc makes the mistake of trying to explain further the breakdown of their relationship: he says to Alice that, "To tell you honestly, she wasn't happy with me. . . .I just didn't know how to make her happy, that's all. I didn't know how." Alice angrily and triumphantly denounces the woman as difficult, the reaction of someone unconsciously trying to bolster her creeping self-doubt, and the word is taken by Marc to underline his own lack of responsibility for the failure in his first marriage.

But as they are making ready to leave, while Marc is paying the bill and calling for the chauffeur, Alice cannot help wondering, out of curiosity and envy, what this other wife knew that she does not, what she had discovered to be lacking in her husband, what makes her appear, in short, to be her superior.

Colette is at her unsentimental best in vignettes such as this one—analytical, observant, and exact. "The Other Woman" has no hero or heroine; it merely points out in a subtle, unemphatic way that a relationship is coloured not only by the memories and aspirations of the two involved, but also by the psychological adjustments that have to be made following a small and seemingly insignificant revelation.

—Honor Levi

THE OUTCASTS OF POKER FLAT
by Bret Harte, 1870

Local color writing was an important part of the American literary chronicle during the latter 19th century, and many writers tried their hand at it. One who made a significant contribution to the genre was Bret Harte, an Easterner turned Westerner, who found in the mining camps of California his own gold mine of material for his literary efforts.

Harte had a deep feeling for those pioneer gold seekers, gamblers, and prostitutes who lived their lives in a devil-may-care, reckless fashion, but who at the same time had the capacity for love and compassion in a setting that was not the most conducive for such. In "The Outcasts of Poker Flat" (first published in 1869, then collected in *The Luck of Roaring Camp*) Harte focuses on the theme of the regenerative power of human love in a world where nothing can be assumed. He also presents an ironic contrast between self-righteousness and self-sacrifice.

Poker Flat, like most California mining camps of the time, is not a model of social decorum, but, as occasionally happens in communities, some of the leading citizens feel that the place needs to spruce up its image. Several thefts and a murder give rise to a kind of pseudo moralistic stance that demands a scapegoat or two to redeem Poker Flat's honor. Indeed, as John Oakhurst, the gambler who appears in a number of Harte's stories, ventures out on the street one morning, he senses a "Sabbath lull in the air, which in a settlement unused to Sabbath influences, looked ominous." Oakhurst, in fact, has been targeted as one of several undesirables to be run out of town in a cleansing ritual by some of the more upstanding citizens. His companions include two prostitutes, the Duchess and Mother Shipton, and Uncle Billy, a town drunk—an apt set of characters for a Harte story.

Left by their escort at the edge of Poker Flat, the four outcasts set off toward Sandy Bar, another mining camp, where they hope to resume their normal lives. The Duchess, however, tires before they get out of the mountains and refuses to go any further. Despite Oakhurst's admonitions against stopping, "Uncle Billy passed rapidly from a bellicose state into a stupor, the Duchess became maudlin, and Mother Shipton snored." Looking at his companions, Oakhurst thinks of his own past life and where it has led him. Upon this scene come Tom Simson (the Innocent) and Piney Woods, his fiancée, who are eloping. Against Oakhurst's advice the two lovers decide to join the outcasts—thus setting the stage for the tragedy to follow.

The three women take refuge in a ruined cabin, and the men sleep on the open ground. The next morning Oakhurst awakens to a heavy snow falling and the discovery that Uncle Billy has run off with the horse and mules. Stranded, the pathetic group tries gamely to survive their situation on the little food they have and by keeping their spirits up with singing and storytelling. It is at this point that Harte shows the regenerative power of human love. Ironically, the Duchess takes care of Piney, and Mother Shipton starves herself to death by secretly saving her own food rations for the young girl.

After convincing the Innocent to go back to Poker Flat for help, Oakhurst piles up enough firewood to last a few days more, then he also leaves the cabin. The Duchess and Piney are left alone. When Piney admits to the Duchess that she does not know how to pray, the latter seems relieved and rests her head on the young girl's shoulder: "And so reclining, the younger and purer pillowing the head of her soiled sister upon her virgin breast, they fell asleep." And the next morning, when help arrives, they are found that way—dead. Oakhurst, too, is found not far from the cabin, gun in hand and a bullet through the heart—"who was at once the strongest and yet the weakest of the outcasts of Poker Flat."

"The Outcasts of Poker Flat" shows clearly Harte's penchant for basing sentimental plots on a formula that contrasts appearance and reality and for populating those plots with stock characters. And certainly he made it work. This story, along with the others that he wrote focusing on the early mining camps of California, brings to life the boiling potpourri of characters and incidents that made that time such a rich part of American development. In "The Outcasts of Poker Flat," as in so many of his other stories, Harte was able to move above the level of sheer sentimentality through a deft blending of humor, parody, irony, and deep feeling.

—Wilton Eckley

THE OUTSTATION
by Somerset Maugham, 1926

Although the much-travelled Somerset Maugham is famous for his short stories with a Malay setting, he did not spend all that much time in the country. He first visited what was then the British Colony of the Federated Malay States in 1921. His stay lasted for six months, three of them passed in a sanatorium in Java due to illness. His second and last visit came in 1925 when he was there for four months. This was enough, however, to collect the material he sought. During his travels through remote jungle places he would put up for the night at the homes of colonial officials who had not seen a compatriot for months on end and who accordingly were bursting with chat and tales to tell. In the capital, Kuala Lumpur, he talked with people in clubs and carefully stored up the gossip, stories, anecdotes, and reminiscences they were only too glad to pass on. Unlike certain other Malayan stories, "The Outstation" cannot be traced directly to a real person or place, although it probably had its germ in something told to Maugham over a hospitable gin *pahit*. It vividly illustrates his primary interest, which was to study the reactions of his compatriots when placed in an exotic context. "The Outstation" first appeared in the collection entitled *The Casuarina Tree* (1926).

In the story Mr. Warburton, the resident of a distant outstation in Borneo, always dresses for dinner at a set time every night, chooses his courses from a menu in French, and is waited on by Malay servants immaculately turned out. He peruses *The Times*, especially the social news of lords and ladies, even though it arrives six weeks late, having disciplined himself to read each issue in strict sequence, however much he is longing to know the course of certain events. When on duty his attire is invariably perfect, for he believes that if a man succumbs to the influences around him and loses his self-respect he will also lose the respect of the natives. Warburton is the complete snob. Yet over the years he has evolved into a skilful administrator and has acquired a profound knowledge of, and affection for, the Malays, their customs and their language, although he remains an English gentleman who will never "go native."

An assistant is sent out to help him with the extra work that has grown up. The assistant, a shabby, blunt-spoken man named Cooper, is everything that Warburton is not, and he is at first amused by the stately dinner routine and chuckles at the resident's pomposity. Cooper has been neither to public school nor to university, and during the war he served in the ranks. "I wonder why on earth they've sent me a fellow like that?" Warburton thinks to himself, especially when he learns that his assistant, a colonial with an inferiority complex, bullies the Malays and treats them harshly. In return Cooper earns their dislike. Small irritations become large ones between the two men. The impious Cooper tears open Warburton's sacrosanct copies of *The Times* and dares to read them first, untidily. Then Warburton is obliged, for perfectly valid reasons, to countermand one of Cooper's orders to his men. Their mutual antagonism erupts into a violent confrontation when Cooper accuses him openly of being a snob and humiliates him by reporting that he is a standing joke for that reason among his colleagues up and down the country. But Warburton has the last laugh. Cooper sacks his Malay servant, having held back his wages, treated him with injustice, and insulted him. Warburton, from his deep acquaintance with the passionate and vengeful mind of the Malays, warns him that he is running a grave risk. Cooper disdains him. A few days later he is found in his bed, a dagger through his heart. Warburton settles down again happily to his ceremonious dinners for one, in full evening dress, and to his thrilled absorption in the social columns of *The Times*.

It is one of Maugham's great strengths that he does not take sides and lays out the facts with apparent objectiveness in order to round out his characters. Yes, Warburton is a quite outrageous snob, but he is also a just administrator who is respected by the Malays, whom he instinctively understands and among whom he wishes to be buried when he dies. And yes, Cooper is a racist cad, tactless and uncouth, but within his limits he is conscientious and hard-working, grimly determined to get the most out of those whom he is employed to supervise. Local colour is deftly touched in to highlight the encounter between two types of men who, because of their different social classes, would never have met in England, whereas in Malaya their close juxtaposition emphasises the unbridgeable gulf that separates them. Maugham's eye for dramatic effect lends the narrative a power that propels the story on to its inevitable end. Speaking of the stories in *The Casuarina Tree* Maugham observed, "I have the impression that they are rather tight and I believe that I could attempt with advantage a greater looseness of construction. Have you not noticed that the tightrope walker skips now and then in order to rest his audience from a feat too exactly done?" However that may be, "The Outstation," which the contemporary critic Edwin Muir declared to be "one of the best stories written in our time," remains a prime example of Maugham's gift for taut structure. Here, as in the other stories in the volume, he builds up an intricate mosaic through the accumulation of significant detail which only a master craftsman knows how to distinguish and apply.

—James Harding

THE OVERCOAT (Shinel')
by Nikolai Gogol, 1841

"Shinel'" ("The Overcoat") the story of a lowly clerk in a government office, marks an important stage in the development of 19th-century realism. Gogol wrote it in 1840 in Vienna, while undergoing a religious crisis. His account of Akaky's suffering translates his own spiritual unrest into the simplest and most universal terms. Using a fussily pedantic narrator whose outlook is not far removed from Akaky's, Gogol expresses moral urgency and at the same time distances himself from his character, avoiding self-pity and special pleading. This satirical mode has influenced both Russian and world literature.

Gogol's style is digressive and sometimes arbitrary, as at the beginning of Akaky's search for a new overcoat, when the narrator offers a sketch of the tailor, because, as he says, it is fashionable to describe every character in a story. He mimics the historian or reporter: "We'd better say a word about [the tailor's] wife, but unfortunately very little is known about her." This mock objectivity contrasts with the story's charged, almost surreal atmosphere. The Russian formalist critic, Boris Eichenbaum, calls this mode the literary grotesque. The grotesque style, he says, requires that the action "should be enclosed in a fantastically small world" that is removed from ordinary reality. This estrangement allows the author to play with and rearrange experience in accordance with his artistic aims. In this artificial reality "any trifle can grow to colossal proportions"—as in this case Akaky's overcoat does.

The underlying fantastic element surfaces explicitly in the story's final scenes with the appearance of Akaky's ghost. Since this is Gogol's only reference to the supernatural, some readers regard these scenes as an awkward coda that impairs the story's unity. For others, however, they grow logically out of the grotesque mode and confirm the story's spiritual implications.

Some critics see Akaky's love of the overcoat as a religious parable, though they draw varying conclusions about its meaning. Anthony Hippisley, for example, argues that the overcoat stands for Akaky's spiritual regeneration, the putting on of a new man. On the other hand, Dmitri Chizhevsky infers that Akaky is guilty of loving the things of this world too much, which results in his final fall from grace. The story is resonant enough to carry the reader beyond such competing views, offering the overcoat as an inclusive symbol of human passions and needs. The story's universality is founded on Gogol's skillful evocation of a specific historical time and place. For all its mysterious atmosphere, "The Overcoat" is filled with concrete, familiar details, which keep the reader grounded in day-to-day life and which account for the story's role in the development of literary realism. It is the most powerful of the many Russian works—over two hundred, according to one count—on the theme of the downtrodden civil servant or poor clerk. Tolstoii's often-quoted remark about the writers of his generation—"We all come out of 'The Overcoat'"—refers to Gogol's pioneering realism.

Akaky is one of the humblest and most insignificant of protagonists—only Kafka's Gregor Samsa, who turns into an insect, can challenge him as the quintessential human without qualities. Akaky is too vacant to turn into an insect. This absence of personal traits enables Gogol to focus on Akaky's humanness plain and simple. He is hardly more, Sean O'Faolain remarks, than an old overcoat. While maintaining his emphasis on the grotesque, the narrator describes in detail just how much Akaky, like all poor folk, suffers from the Russian winter. He paints this picture with compelling realism. When the hard freeze sets in, the wind whips through Akaky's threadbare clothes and his short walk to the office is a daily torment that leaves him shaken. In the arctic Russian climate Akaky's overcoat can make the difference between life and death. The narrator is appropriately exact about how much it costs to buy this necessity: one-fifth of a clerk's annual salary—the equivalent of thousands of our dollars. Additional details realistically define the meaning of poverty—the other necessities

Akaky has to forgo: the candle in his room, the evening cup of tea he gives up in order to pay for the new overcoat.

The story reminds us that the deadly cold can kill—and it does kill Akaky in the end. Having been abused by a callous bureaucrat, an "important personage," he gives up and dies, but his health has already been undermined by cold and deprivation.

Akaky's overcoat, as Eichenbaum suggested, takes on colossal proportions, symbolizing the human need to cover one's nakedness, as Adam and Eve covered theirs after the fall. Not only clothes, but houses, families, and civilization itself—all things emerge from and merge into the overcoat. Akaky's biblical complaint, only half of which he speaks aloud—"Let me be. Why do you do this to me? . . . I am your brother"—echoes Cain's speech in Genesis: "Am I my brother's keeper?" and Jesus's last words about his tormentors, "Father, forgive them, for they know not what they do."

The discipline and self-sacrifice Akaky displays in order to buy the overcoat reveal a certain dignity, though of a very humble and qualified kind. For Akaky even the breezy congratulations of the other clerks, who use the overcoat as an excuse to throw a party, represent a break with his ordinary faceless anonymity. Like some worldly success, the party dazzles and befuddles him. He allows himself to be lured into drinking champagne; he strolls the unfamiliar streets, lusts after a fascinating woman, and so wanders on to his downfall. Having lost his overcoat to thieves, he turns to the bureaucratic official for help—a quest that destroys him.

Akaky's illness and death seem pre-ordained; like his life, they are marked by obscurity and insignificance. But the ghost at the end, wresting his overcoat from the smug official, reverses the balance of terror between oppressor and oppressed. In the light of later Russian history, it seems a prophetic act. Through it Gogol amplifies the universal message implied by Akaky's unspoken words, "I am your brother." No sufferer's claim may be ignored, no human being may be dismissed as insignificant. The humanist vision, as exemplified by "The Overcoat," provided the moral foundation of 19th-century realism and inspired later writers to portray humble and neglected lives.

—Herbert Marder

P

A PAIR OF SILK STOCKINGS
by Kate Chopin, 1897

Born in 1851 in St. Louis but a resident of Louisiana after her marriage, Kate Chopin began writing after her husband's death in 1882. Drawing on what she had learned from wide reading, particularly of Mary E. Wilkins Freeman and Sarah Orne Jewett, and from translating stories by Guy de Maupassant, she was able to support herself and her six children by publishing stories in leading magazines, at least so long as those stories were the expected exotic "local color" accounts of life in the Creole culture of the South.

In 1894, after Chopin published the popular *Bayou Folk*, her first collection of short fiction, her themes began to change subtly. "A Pair of Silk Stockings" illustrates her ability to draw women characters so that they are recognizable, but also so that they are more than stereotypes. Here, the protagonist is clearly conflicted in what appears to be her dutiful performance of daily responsibilities. A young woman with four children, "little" Mrs. Sommers has a windfall of 15 dollars and plans a day of shopping for her children's clothes. But unexpectedly, and the structure of Chopin's story shows how unexpected her change of direction is, Mrs. Sommers begins buying things for herself.

Chopin's narrative emphasizes the woman's lack of plan by stressing how long it has been since she has had anything for herself, how difficult her life providing for the children has been. Wearied from the interminable struggle, Mrs. Sommers (who is never given any name except this identification by her role in society) sits down at a counter and finds that her hand has fallen on a pile of soft silk stockings. Chopin makes the reader feel the sensation, and the joy it brings the deprived woman:

> By degrees she grew aware that her hand had encountered something very soothing, very pleasant to touch. She looked down to see that her hand lay upon a pile of silk stockings. . . . a young girl who stood behind the counter asked her if she wished to examine their line of silk hosiery. She smiled, just as if she had been asked to inspect a tiara of diamonds with the ultimate view of purchasing it. But she went on feeling the soft, sheeny luxurious things—with both hands now, holding them up to see them glisten, and to feel them glide serpent-like through her fingers.

Chopin's marvelous description, the sensuality of the feeling of the fabric pushing beyond known language ("sheeny"), is echoed a few paragraphs later as Mrs. Sommers chooses her pair from among lush colors, and then goes to the ladies' room to put the stockings on in place of her cotton ones. Through Chopin's details, the reader is completely won to the protagonist's side. This woman needs this luxury. And the matter-of-fact way Chopin continues the story—with Mrs. Sommers next buying herself boots, gloves, high-priced magazines, an expensive lunch, and a ticket to a matinee—is a masterful nod to the psychological accuracy of the woman in need. The author says plainly, "She was not thinking at all. She seemed for the time to be taking a rest from that laborious and fatiguing function [of mothering] and have abandoned herself to some mechanical impulse that directed her actions and freed her of responsibility. How good was the touch of the raw silk to her flesh."

Chopin's departure from a plot-oriented narrative, to the emphasis on the inner motivation of her character, was as important as her abandonment of the details of local color writing. There is so little specific description of place in "A Pair of Silk Stockings" that Mrs. Sommers's story becomes Everywoman's, and her urgency and lack of guilt become feelings any reader understands. With the succinct brilliance of this characterization, Chopin finds a way to intrigue readers, suggesting even as they read the ostensibly simply story that women's lives—domestic and predictable as they may seem—are as filled with drama as the most adventurous of men's. It is truly a revisionist narrative.

The story also works differently from most turn-of-the-century short fiction. Rather than relying on plot to keep the reader attentive, Chopin abandons any pretense of the formulaic "rising action-climax-denouement" structure. She in fact begins the story with the climax, when Mrs. Sommers chooses to buy the silk stockings for herself. And she saves it from a predictable close with another stroke of brilliant writing: having Mrs. Sommers, still defined with the word "little," still modest in her assumptions and in her role, attract the attention of a male observer on the cable car, a man whose "keen eyes" are bemused by an expression in the woman's face he cannot decipher. Rather than Mrs. Sommers being suffused with satisfaction, with the satiety that a day of self-pleasuring might bring, Chopin creates an ambiguity in her character that opens the story at its end, rather than closing it. She writes that the authoritative male observer has noticed the woman's "poignant wish, a powerful longing that the cable car would never stop anywhere, but go on and on with her forever."

In this relinquishment of the importance of mothering, in Mrs. Sommers's willingness to give up her role and leave her place in life, Chopin suggests questions about the prescription of women's roles that had to be bothersome for her readers. Much as she did in "The Story of an Hour," her 1894 narrative of a woman dying when she learns that her husband has lived through a train accident, Chopin here reverses the reader's expectations—that Mrs. Sommers would find her pleasure tinged with guilt when her children realized she had spent the money on herself.

When Chopin followed her inclination to tell the truth about women's lives, and published her controversial *The Awakening* in 1899, she brought a burst of clarity to the lives and the work of many women writers. When they saw how much Chopin could achieve through the ambivalent narrative of Edna Pontellier—the woman who demanded to be a sentient, sexual person as well as a wife and mother—women's writing took a new turn, one expressly away from the narrative conventions of mainstream, male fiction.

—Linda Wagner-Martin

THE PARSON'S DAUGHTER OF OXNEY COLNE
by Anthony Trollope, 1861

Originally published in *The London Review* in 1861, this story was collected in Trollope's *Tales of All Countries* (1863). One of its interests is that the story contains material developed in a different way in Trollope's novels. For example, it has strong connections with his novel, *The Belton Estate* (1866). In that novel the heroine, Clara Amedroz, who has no fortune, receives proposals of marriage from two men, one of whom, Captain Aylmer, is a gentleman, the other, Will Belton, a rich farmer. Clara accepts Aylmer's proposal by declaring her love for him, at which point, his love declines and he has doubts about the marriage. When Clara finally breaks off their engagement, Aylmer's love for her sparks into life but by that time it is too late, and she eventually marries Belton.

"The Parson's Daughter of Oxney Colne" is an earlier work of similar material. Patience Woolsworthy is courted by Captain John Broughton, a gentleman who is well connected and who is likely to inherit riches. Though in love with him she has not succumbed as it would not be regarded as a good match from his point of view. He returns to London and the main events of the story take place on his return to Oxney Colne. Captain Broughton proposes again to her and this time she accepts him.

Whereas in *The Belton Estate* the heroine had to decide between a man of gentlemanly status and a man who was not a gentleman by conventional standards, in the short story this conflict is undeveloped. We are told that Patience had a suitor who was a farmer and had rejected him but this is merely mentioned. The story focuses on the one relationship. But as with Clara Amedroz, when Patience responds to Captain Broughton's proposal by warmly declaring her love for him, the effect is to reduce the intensity of feeling of the proposer. He begins to view the marriage in a more detached and prudent frame of mind, doubting the wisdom of uniting himself with someone who has no fortune and who is much beneath him in social status. When he tells her that she ought to bear in mind that this marriage will raise her considerably in social rank, she, a person of great pride, tells him he dishonours her. She breaks the engagement. At the end of the story she remains unmarried while he eventually marries someone else.

In most fiction in which love is a central theme, when two lovers who have been divided finally declare their love for each other, the story is usually nearing its resolution. Often in Trollope this is when problems start. One of his major interests is the psychological aspect of love. Trollope suggests that if love and desire are to maintain intensity there has to be an element of insecurity in the relationship. By straightforwardly declaring her love Patience removes that insecurity from Captain Broughton. This psychological insight is similar to Schopenhauer's pessimistic philosophical view that the will perpetually seeks gratification but when the gratification is achieved it never satisfies.

Another typical Trollopian theme in the story is that of pride. Patience feels her dignity and self-esteem are undermined when Captain Broughton tries to make her accept her social inferiority. Though marrying him would be greatly in her self-interest she would rather reject marriage and live as an old maid than perform an act she feels is irreconcilable with her sense of her own dignity and integrity. This act is treated ambiguously in the story, and the effects of her rejection are very severe. She throws away a life of great promise with a man who loves her, in favour of a narrow existence in a small parish that clearly cannot offer her any fulfillment.

Once a man has proposed to a woman, the conventional view is that he has made a commitment that should not be broken, and any man who does break the engagement will risk being held in contempt by society, as Trollope shows in several of his novels. However, women are regarded as having the right to break engagements. Thus Captain Broughton could not easily have broken his engagement to Patience despite the change in his feelings but there was nothing to stop her from ending it. The story concludes with him, after marrying someone of more appropriate status, "a gratified smile" on his face when he thinks of Patience.

—K.M. Newton

A PASSION IN THE DESERT (Une Passion dans le désert)
by Honoré de Balzac, 1837

"Une Passion dans le désert" ("A Passion in the Desert") was first published in the 26 December 1830 issue of the *Revue de Paris,* a literary magazine whose policy was to encourage young writers, which had started appearing only a year before. Honoré de Balzac was a writer whose fertile imagination was matched by a fondness for grandiose plans for ever more ambitious schemes, embracing not only the works he had already completed but also many others, which were, in many cases, no more than an embryonic idea that never developed to maturity. He dreamed up a number of ideas of larger structures in which to insert "A Passion in the Desert." First he thought of putting it, with various other texts, in a collection to be called *Fantaisies.* Next he decided to incorporate it in his *Scenes of Military Life,* but then changed his mind and published it in 1837 with his *Études philosophiques* (Philosophical Studies), only to print it next, in 1844, with "Modeste Mignon." Finally, two years later the story was restored to the series *Scenes of Military Life,* the 15th volume of *La Comédie humaine (The Human Comedy).*

"A Passion in the Desert" reflects a number of interests Balzac shared with the French public in the days of Romanticism. The tale is set in a desert of North Africa. This was a region that had loomed large in the French imagination since the time of the Crusades; attention which had been fired by reports of Napoleon's campaigns in Egypt in 1797 became even more intense with French military involvement in Algerian affairs during the Restoration period. Painters, poets, and novelists all strove to satisfy the public's interest about the area, and Balzac, characteristically, did not let the fact he had never been there stop him from placing his story in a North African setting and imaginatively evoking the loneliness of the desert with great feeling. In taking a soldier as his hero, Balzac also was responding to the spirit of the age, as French readers reflected on the past Napoleonic glories and wondered whether something similar might be in the offing now that Louis-Philippe was on the throne. The theme of the possibilities of a relationship between human and beast, though age-old, was also one that fascinated the French at the time. There was, of course, the basic problem of human's dual nature, of the beast within the individual, which is fundamental to Romanticism, but to this must be added a fascination with the loyalty and intelligence of animals.

According to Balzac's sister Laure Surville, it was a visit to Martin's menagerie in Paris that gave him the idea for the story, but it has been suggested that he had in fact gone there at the suggestion of Victor Ratier, the editor of the review *Silhouette,* specifically to gather material for a story. However that may be, "A Passion in the Desert" begins at the menagerie when a lady expresses her horror at the sight of Martin handling a hyena. Conversation soon focuses on the question of whether animals have feelings, and the narrator tells the exciting story of an old Provençal soldier. While serving in Egypt he had been captured by nomads, but he managed to escape and fled across the desert. After suffering from hunger and thirst, and being taken in by mirages, he came at last to some palm trees where he was able to rest in a cave. To his surprise and horror he discovered when he woke up that the exit was blocked by a huge she-panther.

The soldier's first response was to reach for his musket, but there was no room to raise it, and he was doubtful that he could kill the fierce animal with his knife either. So he had to wait as patiently as he could, and gradually a relationship grew up between the man and the beast. It is made all the more probable because Balzac brings out behavioural similarities between the panther and its zoological relative, the domestic cat, with which all his readers were familiar. There are some particularly fine passages in which Balzac describes how the soldier grew bolder and ran his hands over the panther's fur and felt its muscles rippling over the powerful skeleton underneath. The panther is referred to as "a strange Friday" in a rather odd anthropomorphic literary allusion to *Robinson Crusoe,* Defoe's novel which had become popular with French readers at the time. The soldier calls the animal "Mignonne," the name (meaning "darling") he had given to his first mistress, a beautiful girl possessed of a most uncertain temperament. The name expresses the ambiguities of his relationship with the panther. Finally the inevitable break-up came, and the soldier was fortunate to escape almost unscathed, but he had had an experience he would never forget.

—Christopher Smith

PATRIOTISM (Yukoku)
by Mishima Yukio, 1966

Mishima Yukio committed ritual suicide, or seppuku, on 25 November 1970, in an attempt to restore Japan to what he saw as its history and tradition. As late as 1960, Mishima had described himself as a nihilist, but the beginnings of his nationalism and emperor worship may be traced back to stories like *Yukoku* ("Patriotism"), written in the same year, and inspired by the Army Rebellion of 1936.

On the morning of 26 February 1936, 21 young officers in the Japanese Imperial Army attempted to overthrow a government that they considered traitorous. The rebels meant to restore the emperor to supreme command of the armed forces, and they executed three of his ministers in their homes. Refusing the advice of his counselors, Emperor Hirohito himself declared the officers "mutineers," and refused to issue an imperial command demanding that they die in his name. They were executed by their fellow officers on 28 February. "Patriotism" concerns itself with this same day. In the story Lieutenant Shinji Takeyama discovers that his colleagues were among the insurgents, and he realizes that he will be unable to join the attack against them. He has been kept from the conspiracy because he is newly married. He decides to disembowel himself in the traditional samurai manner, and his wife Reiko decides to die with him—she stabs herself in the neck with a dagger.

The "patriotic" impulse that the story describes is more than a love for one's country. For Mishima, it becomes a religious devotion to the ideals of the Japanese spirit that transcend particular national circumstances. The story reinforces this insulation from society and never moves beyond the walls of the young couple's house: "this house rose like a solitary island in the ocean of a society going as restlessly about its business as ever." The lieutenant recognizes that what is at stake is his individual integrity, and it is his dedication to his personal moral ideals rather than a political interest that makes his decision necessary: "His was a battlefield without glory, a battlefield where none could display deeds of valor: it was the frontline of the spirit." Reiko's devotion to her husband involves her in his commitment, and the couple finds themselves "encased in the impenetrable armor of Beauty and Truth."

A detailed description of the couple's last night together blurs the boundaries between erotic desire and death. Their suicide pact stirs sexual desire in both husband and wife. The lieutenant experiences a "healthy physical craving" and Reiko's senses are "reawakened" in every corner of her body. As the lieutenant waits for Reiko in the bedroom, he asks himself, "Was it death he was now waiting for? Or a wild ecstasy of the senses?" While they make love they are constantly aware of death's presence, and the descriptions of their actions foreshadow their end. Reiko's throat "reddened" beneath the lieutenant's kisses, and the lieutenant's face "rubbed painfully" against Reiko's breast, "digging into her flesh." Death offers the couple a superior consummation, and their awareness of the "The Last Time" serves to heighten their physical sensitivity: "Not that joy of this intensity—and the same thought had occurred to them both—was ever likely to be re-experienced, even if they should live on to old age." Separation seems impossible during sex, but it is only through death that Reiko can truly enter "a realm her husband had made his own." The anticipation of death fuels erotic desire, until they become what the lieutenant describes as "two parts of the same thing."

By the final section of story only Reiko remains. She serves as her husband's witness, and feels separated from him by his pain. Throughout the story she is described as "following" her husband, and her obedience is repeatedly emphasized: "Ever since her marriage her husband's existence had been her own existence, and every breath of his had been a breath drawn by herself." The lieutenant is repeatedly described as the sun, "about which her whole world revolved." She is troubled by the disposition of her small china collection, but the small animals looking "lost and forlorn" are overshadowed by "the great sunlike principle that her husband embodied." But it is in Reiko that the lieutenant finds his strength and determination, and her "heroic resolve" is repeatedly emphasized. By the end of the story, through her dedication to her husband, Reiko is able to become his spiritual equal. She releases the bolt on the door, which initially prevents her reunion with her husband and moves beyond her obedience to a transcendent ideal:

> Reiko sensed that at last she too would be able to taste the true bitterness and sweetness of that great moral principle in which her husband believed. What had until now been tasted only faintly through her husband's example she was about to savor directly with her own tongue.

In the story, the physical reality of seppuku serves as a direct contrast to the purity of the couple's mental determination. A trail of blood "scattered everywhere" and a "raw smell" prompts the narrator to remark, "It would be difficult to imagine a more heroic sight." The detailed graphic description of the lieutenant's disembowelment causes the reader as well as the lieutenant to ask, "Was this seppuku?" This gulf between spiritual devotion and body that Mishima explored throughout his work and life, emphasized in "Patriotism."

—Mary U. Yankalunas

PAUL'S CASE
by Willa Cather, 1905

As its subtitle suggests, "Paul's Case" is also "A Study in Temperament," confirming the reader's suspicion that the story is intended to be a case history of a particular pathology, in this case a hypersensitivity that makes Paul uneasy company for his high school peers and his teachers. Collected in *The Troll Garden,* this early piece of Cather's, roughly contemporary with Gertrude Stein's pioneering usage of her own clinical training to write fiction, spends its first pages offering the reader data on which to venture a judgment of Paul's "case." His theatrical use of eyes of a "certain hysterical brilliancy" and size is, for example, compared to the effects of belladonna addiction, though as the narrator knowledgeably notes, "there was a glassy glitter about them which that drug does not produce." Clearly, Cather intends to introduce Paul as a scientifically observed character who nonetheless remains something of a mystery until his own demise.

Nor is Paul a typical member of his peer group. He works as an usher at Pittsburgh's Carnegie Hall, and we observe him rushing off to work whistling the Soldiers' Chorus from Gounod's *Faust,* unusual musical fare for a young man then or now. Cather's character is a belated descendant of 19th-century European Romanticism, German and French varieties especially; and his stifling American surroundings have not given him the release he senses in the Parisian and Venetian scenes that hang in the orchestra hall's picture gallery and that "exhilarated him." Cather, no more a sentimentalist about the American landscape

than Hamlin Garland or her mentor Sarah Orne Jewett, nevertheless judged character against the standard of interiorized harmony with nature. But even in the presence of such interior harmony, the world of art could prove a disruptive force, a catalyst that could cut a person adrift from his or her moorings. Or as a popular song of the era would put things, how could you hope to keep a person down on the farm after he or she had glimpsed "Paree." Paul knows no farm, but he thinks he has seen Paris.

As Paul works as usher, he grows "more and more vivacious and animated, and the colour came to his cheeks and lips." The soprano soloist has for him a "world-shine" that makes her seem to him "a veritable queen of Romance." Paul follows the singer to her hotel and sees it as "the fairy world of a Christmas pantomime," whereas the house he must return to on Cordelia Street is Christian, conservative, and tawdry. Not a reader, Paul wants most of all "to see, to be in the atmosphere" of the world of art, to which the local theatre was "the actual portal of Romance." Paul is punished by being taken out of school, deprived of his usher's job, and cut off from his theatrical contacts. Ripe for radical change in his life, Paul is almost immediately seen en route by train to New York.

Paul's capacity to lie convincingly and his theft of money from his employer have taken him to a room in the Waldorf, where, for the first time, he feels freed of the dread that has haunted him all through his life. New York is filled with "the rumble and roar, the hurry and toss of thousands of human beings as hot for pleasure as himself," and Paul burns "like a faggot in a tempest." Paul feels at home with people who are like himself but whom he has no desire to know, and he wonders how there could be any honest people in the world, given the opportunity to steal—and to have what he has had. Hearing that his farther is in pursuit of him, "he had the old feeling that the orchestra had suddenly stopped, the sinking sensation that the play was over." Back in Pittsburgh, they have decided that "Paul's was a bad case." But he has no regrets; he plays his role like an actor, and rejects the theatrical ending of death by revolver-shot. He makes his feverish way back to New Jersey, watches his characteristic red carnations droop, and jumps in front of a Pennsylvania Railroad locomotive.

Paul's death is indeed theatrical, and at the moment he jumps to it he seems to feel "as though he were being watched." The narrator's voice becomes extraordinarily omniscient, as in Paul's last split seconds of life he could not only regret the "folly of his haste," but also "the vastness of what he had left undone." Again, "there flashed through his brain, clearer than ever before, the blue of Adriatic water, the yellow of Algerian sands." In a sense, Paul's death recapitulates Crane's soldiers, dying in Algiers, even as it foreshadows Camus's Meursault and the futility of his existence.

The story "Paul's Case" straddles two centuries of action and idea, and like many a more recent fiction, it ends openly, equivocally. "Paul's Case" is in the end also a police report, and a testament to our inability to come up with a wholly convincing answer as to why we do what we do. Her hasty character dies with the blues and yellows of an Impressionist landscape in his brain. Yet these also fade at once to black, "the immense design of things." What design; whose design? The story teases by means of what it does not say; our towns are filled with Pauls whom we will never understand.

Paul had lived on Cordelia Street, which he found depressing. He also lacked a mother, and we know little about what the protofeminist Willa Cather might have said about that lack, nor whether in this early story we are meant to read "Paula" for "Paul." Death by locomotive was, after all, already a convention of late romantic/early realist fiction by the time of Tolstoi. The missing Ms. Lear may or may not be part of why we cannot yet say with any certainty that Paul's case is closed.

—John Ditsky

A PERFECT DAY FOR BANANAFISH
by J.D. Salinger, 1953

When "A Perfect Day for Bananafish" appeared in *The New Yorker* in 1948, readers were stunned. The American version of French existentialism drew on the tradition of understated narrative and idiomatic language that began with Twain's *Huckleberry Finn* and appeared again in Hemingway's fiction. Salinger's story of the damaged World War II veteran Seymour Glass gave readers everything they needed to understand its characters, but in near-comic scenes that bore little relationship to the tragic suicide that closed the story.

The story begins with description of of Seymour Glass's young wife, Muriel, waiting to place a call to her worried mother in New York. Reading women's magazines and doing her nails, Muriel epitomizes the beautiful but dumb woman, hungry for attention and pleasure. The phone conversation makes clear that Seymour, recently returned from war, is terribly disturbed—clearly paranoid—but in the vacuous women's eyes, not much changed from his prewar self. The real object of satire in the scene is not Seymour but rather the women, and their elite culture, that fails to recognize a troubled psyche. Salinger's juxtaposition of the mother's questions about fashionable hem lengths and her instructions that Muriel fly home to escape the madness of her husband creates such an absurd text the reader is bewildered. If people are worried about Seymour, why is Muriel alone, on vacation, with him? Toward the end of the conversation (which is the longest section of the story), Muriel reproves her mother ("you talk about him as though he were a raving *maniac*—"), but then describes him lying on the beach, covered by his robe so that no one will see his tatoos (which are non-existant). Salinger has prepared his reader well for the obviously comic closing line from Muriel's mother, "Call me the *instant* he does, or *says*, anything at all funny—you know what I mean."

By now alerted to the fact that the war veteran is seriously disturbed, the reader is next introduced to another dialogue scene, this one between the six-year-old Sybil Carpenter (known as Pussy) and her fashionable mother. Sybil-Pussy, whose name introduces what is going to become a sexualized text as she is taught what beach beauties do and are, is chanting the name of her new friend, "See more glass." As she runs to the beach to find her bath-robed buddy, her primary motivation is jealousy: Seymour has allowed a 3-year-old girl to sit beside him on the piano bench.

As Sybil flirts through the child-adult dialogue with Seymour, Salinger's pattern of non-sequiturs increases the sexual intensity, and Glass—calling Sybil "Baby"—creates the metaphor of the title. Because it is, he says, "a perfect day for bananafish," he is going into the ocean. The bananafish are ogres, stuffing themselves on so much of the underwater fruit (found only in banana holes) that they later swell and can never escape the hole. Although the child misses the sexual allusions in the nonsense, Seymour's courtly treatment of her in the water, placing her carefully on his inflated float and forcing her over a wave until "her scream was full of pleasure," continues the analogy. The bananafish metaphor suggests that Glass's sexual hunger for Muriel led him into the hole of this mindless, irrelevant life; and his bitingly ironic answer to Sybil's question of where "the lady" (Muriel) is confirms his angst. Seymour explains, using the same comic tone of the rest of their dialogue:

> "The lady?" The young man brushed some sand out of his thin hair. "That's hard to say, Sybil. She may be in any one of a thousand places. At the hairdresser's. Having her hair dyed mink. Or making dolls for poor children, in her room." Lying prone now, he made two fists, set one on top of the other, and rested his chin on the top one. "Ask me something else, Sybil," he said. "That's a fine bathing suit you have on. If there's one thing I like, it's a blue bathing suit."

> Sybil stared at him, then looked down at her protruding stomach. "This is a *yellow*," she said. "This is a *yellow*."

> "It is? Come a little closer."
> Sybil took a step forward.
> "You're absolutely right. What a fool I am."

Seymour's "What a fool I am" is his only comment on his life, the only information the reader gets before he returns to his and Muriel's room, looks at her asleep on the bed, takes out his automatic, "and fired a bullet through his right temple."

Salinger created texts that purposefully engaged readers to think past their endings. Rather than follow the traditional paradigm of beginning action, rising action leading to climax, and denouement, he chose to arrange events to reflect a kind of systematic chaos. As the reader felt more and more bewildered, he or she began to construct an alternative narrative—a kind of "what if?" construction. In this fiction, the reader could wonder what would have happened if Seymour had gotten the kind of helpful attention he needed; or, more darkly, what would have happened if he had shot Muriel too, or instead of himself; or if he had taken his anger out on Sybil so far from the hotel beach that no one would have seen him. The immediacy of Salinger's narratives, the way they pulled the reader into the act of reading and deciphering, paralleled his interest in zen and the involvement of the human psyche in thought. Salinger's writing anticipated the experimentation, the questioning, and the freedoms, of the 1960's to come.

"A Perfect Day for Bananafish," collected in *Nine Stories* in 1953, is in some respects a typical Salinger story. For the next decade, his *New Yorker* stories of the Glass family and his immensely popular novel, the Holden Caulfield story, *The Catcher in the Rye* in 1951, gripped American readers. But as Salinger became reclusive, and forbade his fiction to appear in anthologies and collections, his enigmatic fiction became less popular.

—Linda Wagner-Martin

PETRIFIED MAN
by Eudora Welty, 1941

Central in Eudora Welty's "Petrified Man" (collected in *A Curtain of Green*, 1941) are two conversations, a week apart, between Leota, owner of a shabby beauty shop, and her regular customer, Mrs. Fletcher. In the first dialogue, Mrs. Fletcher, already angry at learning she is pregnant, becomes more so when Mrs. Pike, a newcomer in town, guesses her secret, since she may have an abortion to keep from becoming ugly. In this conversation Leota is light-hearted, enthusiastic about her new friend, Mrs. Pike from New Orleans, and fascinated by a fortune teller's information—that an old high school boy friend may soon be "available" again. In their dialogue during Mrs. Fletcher's shampoo-set appointment a week later, gossip has spread about Mrs. Fletcher's pregnancy. Leota's mood is melancholy and angry. Concerned only about money, she now declares Mrs. Pike a traitor.

In this story of selfish, angry, jealous, and often cruel women, some of whom thirst for the sensational or perverse, the women with their "wild hair" become Medusa figures, who turn their men to stone. The husbands seem to be a sorry lot, lazy, unemployed, paralyzed or petrified in body, mind, and spirit—and are seen only through the women's descriptions.

The description of the beauty parlor significantly reinforces the satire of women's pursuit of beauty, because that pursuit occurs in a very dirty, run-down setting, where wet towels are piled in heaps, Leota flicks her cigarette ashes on the dirty towels, and three-year-old Billy Boy Pike, for whom she is caring, plays with wave clips on the floor under the sink and eats stale peanuts taken from the depths of Leota's purse (which also contains loose cigarettes that taste like face powder.) In ironic contrast, pastel colors supposedly suggest gentleness and feminine beauty—shelves, swinging doors of the booths, and combs are all lavender. A violent element is suggested by Leota's blood-red fingernails as she digs them into Mrs. Fletcher's scalp. The violence seems related to pregnancy, to women giving orders to submissive men, or to the women's fascination for rapists and failure to have compassion for their victims. The lavender comb brings up a cloud of reddish henna dust from Mrs. Fletcher's head as Leota announces Fletcher is losing her hair because of pregnancy; and in this "den of curling fluid" women are "cooked" by being attached to the permanent wave machine, while Leota links their screams to the shrieks of a woman in labor.

Though this story is largely a bitter satire, one might argue that it is also Welty's strongest accomplishment in the juxtaposition of comedy and harsh reality. Viewed in this way, the story almost certainly exceeds Welty's successes in "Why I Live at the P.O." and "Ponder Heart." Perhaps the greater achievement in this story can be explained by her presenting most of the action here in two relatively short dialogues, rather than in a single monologue. If Mrs. Fletcher in "Petrified Man" is not an especially vivid character, she is a lively and critical prompter or interrupter of what would otherwise be a less varied monologue delivered by Leota. An even more probable reason for the story's success lies in the robust vulgarity, liveliness, and basic common sense of Leota, who is more perceptive, outgoing, and able to express herself and to interact with others than are Edna Earle in "Ponder Heart" and Sister in "Why I Live at the P.O." While Leota's language and the topics of her conversation are those of a small town Southerner in the 1930's, she has an awareness and interest in things beyond the parochial. Leota welcomes Mrs. Pike

so quickly and unconditionally because Pike is somewhat older, has lived elsewhere, and imagines exciting ways to live and find romance. She tells Leota stories of New Orleans, introduces her to New Orleans Jax beer, recommends a superb fortune teller, and takes Leota to the freak show, where they marvel at pygmies, a petrified man turning to stone, and two full-term babies in a jar, who are joined at the waist. Now that Leota has been married for eight months, Pike reassures her that she is normal, for passion that Leota shared in a rumble seat (the day she met her husband Fred and found herself halfway to the alter) does not last. When Pike urges Leota to pay another fee to have her other palm read at the freak show, in case her two sides don't agree, thrifty Leota doubts the fame of Lady Evangeline, because she has "the worst manicure I ever saw on a living person." Leota admires Pike's acute eye that sees through others, because she herself is something of a psychologist and judge of her clients.

The story speeds to a miserable close after Mrs. Pike identifies Mr. Petrie, who is wanted for five rapes of California women, and gets $500 for information leading to his arrest. He is her former New Orleans neighbor, the petrified man in the freak show, and also the man pictured in Leota's *Startling G-Man* magazine. Leota contends her ownership of the magazine qualifies her for part of the reward. Finally, she takes out her frustration on Billy Boy Pike instead of his mother. Mrs. Fletcher gleefully grabs him and holds him as Leota spanks the child and he kicks both women hard. All the customers with towels covering their "wild hair" come forth from their booths to applaud the scene. Even in so miserable an ending, Welty manages to insert a moment of humor as Billy Boy, sassy as ever, stomps out of the door yelling the words that will most annoy Leota: "If you're so smart, why ain't you rich?"

—Margaret B. McDowell

A PIECE OF STEAK
by Jack London, 1911

Jack London is generally regarded as a master of naturalistic fiction. As such, his stories deal with the larger assumptions of naturalism that are based on both Darwinism and Marxism. In London's fiction humanity is ultimately reduced to representing the larger forces of class struggle and the survival of the fittest.

Humanity, reduced to presumptions about its brutish, animalistic faculties and motives, is involved in a struggle with external forces, both societal and cosmic, which, whether by design or neglect, will inevitably squelch optimism, hope, and significant achievement. Or, such hopes of success and attainment, if reached, will only be experienced for a short time due to powerful forces of attrition and defeat at work in the naturalistic scheme of things.

Certainly such assumptions, even about the natural, inherent qualities of animals, are even more problematic when applied to human nature. London's story, "A Piece of Steak," (collected in *When God Laughs and Other Stories*), dramatizes the strength and weakness of such naturalistic assumptions in an obvious but quite effective way. "Steak," because of its technique and its theme, is a classic work of naturalism and a classic story about boxing and all of the attendant imagistic and metaphorical implications of prize fighting.

The focus of the story is the final fight, the last attempt, of an Australian boxer named Tom King, to win a fight with an up-and-coming youthful New Zealand challenger named Sandel. The prize in question is 30 quid. But winning would give Tom more than money to buy groceries and provide for his wife, Lizzie (and their two children); it would enhance his drastically waning career as a prizefighter. Sandel, as Tom's human antagonist, hardly needs the money. His motive is to climb the career ladder as a challenger, a position Tom in past years enjoyed. In terms of larger forces, the story dramatizes a fight between youth and age, between stamina and conditioning. Tom knows as he contemplates the fight—before, during, and afterwards—that "Youth was the nemesis . . . and would be served." Thus the outcome of the fight and the story is no surprise: Tom almost wins but loses in the final moments. Why? Ultimately because he had no money, before the fight, to have the needed piece of steak which would serve him when he needed the power of a decisive, knock-out punch. And he would never again have the needed money for "a piece of steak." Steak is only for winners, for the wealthy.

London masterfully allows us to follow Tom King's expectation, anguish, and resignation, both from an external, omniscient perspective and from Tom's own point of view as he is defeated mentally and physically. Never really a champion, King's name is offered ironically by London throughout. Tom remembers that early in his fighting career he once defeated a veteran boxer named Stowsher Bill and reduced him to tears. The "stake" for that fight had also, ultimately, been for more than a piece of "steak." It meant the end of Bill's boxing career.

London drives home the parallelism of that event. At the end of the story, Tom, in the dressing room, covers his face and he too cries, for the loss to Sandel, for his previous defeat of Bill, for Lizzie's now dashed expectation, for the fight and the plight of humanity. Short of meliorism, London counts out the story with utter pessimism. Even Sandel has his youthful challenger, Pronto, waiting on the side line and this character's name is not lost on the reader. Any person's time comes fast, comes "pronto."

London's plotting of the story reinforces other ironies and progressions of theme and style, characterization and setting. The animal attributes of Tom are clear in his looks, especially his eyes, as well as in his actions. The story opens as he wipes his plate with a final morsel of bread and chews slowly in meditation. And, as mentioned, in the end he cries, albeit more from the pain of a broken spirit than from the pain in his hands and knuckles. Tom controls that pain, at least partially transcends it, because of his experience, his wiles as a boxer, the strategies he has for preserving his strength and energy, and his attempts to wear down the youthful enthusiasms of his opponent.

London takes Tom and the reader through a blow-by-blow, round-by-round account and count of Tom's demise. At the age of 40, Tom's life is essentially over. He will have to find navvy work now, assuming his battered hands can hold a shovel. At the end Tom is hungry for food and for a future. The assumptions and forces of naturalism in defeating Tom have won yet again. As pure story, "A Piece of Steak" is a triumph.

—Robert Franklin Gish

THE PIECE OF STRING (Le Ficelle)
by Guy de Maupassant, 1884

Chekhov and Maupassant, widely acclaimed as the two most important influences on the modern short story, brought to the genre two very different talents. If Chekhov is the master of mood and atmosphere, then Maupassant is the model for the succinct and terse narrative. Flaubert's advice to the young Maupassant that "talent is a long patience" was well heeded, for all of his three hundred stories written between 1880 and 1890 display an acute concern with detailed exactitude, the single precise observation that will continue the narrative—and nothing more. The vast majority of his tales deal with a limited number of themes: the Franco-Prussian war, adultery, prostitution, and the avaricious cunning of the Norman peasant. The influence of Schopenhauer affected his outlook on life sufficiently so that he saw cruelty, lechery, and duplicity everywhere, although often viewed with a wry sense of humour. This led Henry James to call him "the lion in the path" because of his apparent unconcern with questions of morality, which James found troubling in so fine an artist.

"Le Ficelle" ("The Piece of String"), collected in *Les Soeurs Rondoli* (1884), is a classic example of Maupassant's technique, style, and theme. The bare outline of the plot is commonplace enough. When a peasant, Maître Hauchecorne, picks up a piece of string on the road, his enemy, Maître Malandain, accuses him of finding a lost purse. After the purse is found and returned, people still doubt his innocence. Finally, he dies of worry and indignation, with his last breath proclaiming his innocence. The story's strength derives from the sense of a whole community behind Hauchecorne. His cunning thrift is reflected throughout the entire Norman peasantry, which is why his innocence is not believed.

At least half of Maupassant's stories begin with a preliminary discussion or scene, which serves to introduce the main action. In 19th-century French literature this device is known as a "cadre," and "The Piece of String" begins with an unusually long and informative example of such a frame. The scenes on the road and in the market square of Goderville, both thronging with local peasants intent on buying and selling their wares, are reminiscent of the panoramic, crowded paintings of Pieter Breugel, "The Procession to Calvary" and "The Battle Between Carnival and Lent" being the most obvious examples. The details of the "plodding" peasants, "legs deformed by hard work," dressed in bright blue smocks "like balloons ready to fly away," are similar to the acute, socially satirical pictures favoured by Breugel, the peasants' weary mundanity in sharp contrast to the image of balloons, associated with delight and airy freedom. There is little distinction made between men, women, and animals, the "confused mass" pictured as "the horns of the bullocks, the tall beaver hats of the well-to-do peasants, and the coifs of the peasant women." The "wild, continuous din" of voices merges with the "long lowing" of the animals, as if people and beasts lived on one and the same level.

The peasants are obsessed with thrift and deceit, "always afraid of being taken in," openly admiring the innkeeper as "a cunning rascal who had made his pile." The battle of wits which constantly engages them leads to Hauchecorne's downfall, for he is at first too shamefaced to admit his miserliness over the string in front of Malandain, who in turn uses the incident to vex and humiliate his enemy. The characters are pared down to their essentials in a rigorously economical style, so that all we learn of Hauchecorne is that he is "a thrifty man like all true Normans." Even the mention of his rheumatism serves only to underline his avarice, "bent double" in pain for the sake of a piece of string.

Hauchecorne's obsession with proving that he has been unjustly accused over the theft of the purse is a perennial theme in Maupassant's stories, the self-prepossession and moral myopia of the inadequate individual. Monsieur Sacrement's life-long desire to be publically honoured in "The Decoration" is of the same order, even at the price of self-deceit and cuckoldry. The oblique illumination of Hauchecorne when he realises his dilemma is all the more painful for his realisation, and that of the reader, that there is nothing he can do to resolve his situation:

> He returned home ashamed and indignant, choking with anger and embarassment, all the more upset in that he was quite capable . . . of doing what he was accused of having done, and even of boasting about it. . . . He dimly realized that . . . it was impossible to prove his innocence, and the injustice of the suspicion cut him to the quick.

> (translated by Roger Colet)

Maupassant has no need to add to Hauchecorne's own realisation of his folly, which haunts him into an early grave. As Percy Lubbock has said, he is rarely an intrusive narrator; "the scene he evokes for us is contemporaneous. . . .But the effect is that he is not there at all, because he is doing nothing that ostensibly requires any judgement, nothing that reminds us of his presence . . . the story occupies us, the moving scene, and nothing else."

Reading of Hauchecorne's ludicrous demise reminds one that Maupassant was a soulmate of W.H. Auden's "Epitaph on a Tyrant" in at least one respect: "He knew human folly like the back of his hand." Like so many of his stories, "A Piece of String" presents human behaviour at its worst. Although I mentioned Bruegel earlier, perhaps the closer resemblance is to Hieronymous Bosch, the story being akin to "The Garden of Earthly Delights" brought to life; vanity transformed into absurdity, wordly ambition reduced to facile farce.

—Simon Baker

PIERRE MENARD, AUTHOR OF THE *QUIXOTE*
(Pierre Menard, autor del *Quixote*)
by Jorge Luis Borges, 1944

Among the short fictions that brought renown to Jorge Luis Borges, his story "Pierre Menard, autor del *Quixote*" ("Pierre Menard, Author of the *Quixote*") is something of a legend. Conceived and started in a hospital bed, where Borges lay convalescing from a home accident that had brought him near-death, it was his first major narrative piece, published in *Sur,* May 1939. The story, gathered thereafter in the volume *Ficciones,* went on to enjoy an astounding influence among literary people, its clever thoughts giving rise to aesthetic theories that went well beyond anything Borges had probably intended.

"Pierre Menard" is a prime example of the "essay-fiction" genre fashioned by Borges. It presents itself as a posthumous literary appreciation of the recently deceased Menard, as told by an unnamed and typically snobbish French rightist. The list he gives of Menard's published works shows the dearly departed to have been a narrow, claustrophobic sort whose interests lay chiefly in self-enclosed fields such as chess, metrics, symbolic logic, and the retranslating of translated books back to their originals. One of the titles tells all: *Les problèmes d'un problème* (The Problems of a Problem).

Menard's unpublished masterwork, however, was the fulfillment of his fond ambition, namely, to write—independently, and verbatim (and not copy)—*Don Quixote.* The project, we are informed, went through thousands of drafts, but Menard finally came up with some two chapters. How he got there is a complex matter. At first he had contemplated reliving Cervantes's life, but soon realized that his aim was to write *Don Quixote* not as a 17th-century Spaniard, but as Menard the 20th-century Frenchman. In the meantime he devoured all of Cervantes's works —save for the *Quixote.* The latter he had already read at the age of twelve, and thus existed in his mind much as an unwritten work of art does, furnishing him the initial germ for his "creation."

The main substance and wit of the story are in the prissy narrator's subsequent "commentary." To him, Menard's *Quixote* is actually more impressive than Cervantes's, inasmuch as the Frenchman was writing in a language not his own and moreover was encumbered with all the quaint stereotypes (conquistadors, gypsies, *Carmen*) of later European vintage. Moreover, one of the passages that Menard "wrote" is the mad knight's spirited defense of arms over letters—easy enough for Cervantes, who had been a soldier, but not so for a bookish, reclusive Menard. The narrator deftly attributes this choice to influence from Nietzsche and also to Menard's ironizing habit of saying things the opposite of what he really felt.

The most famous moment in the piece comes when the narrator compares two brief passages dealing with the subject of "truth," one from Cervantes and the other from Menard. Though the two extracts seem identical, Menard's, he argues, is actually the better one, because Cervantes's is mere commonplace rhetoric of the time, whereas Menard echoes the ideas of his contemporary pragmatist William James. To cap the story, the eulogist sums up Menard's real achievement, a revolutionary new technique of reading in disregard of chronological sequence or authorial fact —for example, thinking of the *Aeneid* as coming before the *Odyssey,* or the *Imitation of Christ* as written by Céline or Joyce. On this wild speculation the piece ends.

"Pierre Menard" is several things at once. On the most basic level it is a broad satire of the debates, polemics, and tempests-in-teapots of literary criticism. The narrator fittingly deploys such typical literary criticism "weapons" as erudite allusion, high sophistry, and thick irony, and along the way provides vivid instances of critical subtypes: ideological aesthetics, literary memoir, philological enumeration, genetic explanation (how Menard's *Quixote* originated), influence study (the role of Nietzsche), historical scholarship, and evaluative criticism. The choice of the *Quixote* is not accidental. Cervantes's masterwork itself starts out as a satire of genre, and his mock-romance has since been subjected to every conceivable interpretation, from didactic to Christian or existentialist. Menard's eulogist's is only the latest installment in a long series.

At the same time Borges's spoof raises weighty points concerning the place of literature in an age of decline. Coming as he does at the end of French Symbolism, poor Menard can only write what has been written before, though with irony and on a Quixotic scale. Such a pessimistic prospect has in fact been part of the 20th-century climate, and parodying past works is among the outstanding devices in modern art: Joyce's *Ulysses* and the *Odyssey,* Duchamp and the *Mona Lisa,* Stravinsky's *Pulcinella* and Pergolesi, to cite but a few examples. "Pierre Menard" in this respect also inaugurates what we now see as the post-Modern sensibility, where in all art tends to ironic quotation, and history is flattened out into a timeless present.

In its original intent, of course, Borges's piece was largely humorous. He was devising a complex mental joke, not propounding a new aesthetic. Nonetheless the "ideas" in this story were eventually to be picked up on and further elaborated by influential men of letters. The French critic Gérard Genette in his essay "L'utopie littéraire" (1966) bases an entire theory of ahistorical literary space on "Pierre Menard." Alain Robbe-Grillet in *Pour un nouveau roman* (1963, *For a New Novel*) expressly defends Borges's (actually Menard's friend's) notion that two identical texts can mean different things. And the American novelist John Barth in his well-known essay "The Literature of Exhaustion" (1967) takes "Pierre Menard" as a starting point for what he, Barth, sees as the necessity of parody in our time. (Some of Barth's own novels, in turn, are parodies of 19th-century narrative.)

None of this, of course, could have been foreseen by Borges as he imagined "Pierre Menard" within his hospital room. Still, the comments and quasi-manifestoes elicited by this little piece speak for its intellectual richness, its power to quicken the mind and suggest possibilities. "Pierre Menard, Author of the *Quixote*" is a funny story that inspires serious thoughts—much as is the case with the first *Quixote* of Cervantes.

—Gene H. Bell-Villada

PKHENTZ
by Abram Terts, 1966

"Pkhentz" was the last of Andrei Siniavski's writings to be sent out to the West under the pseudonym Abram Terts before his arrest in 1965. Although it was referred to at the trial, it did not figure in his indictment. The story was published in English and Polish translation in 1966 and in the original Russian in 1967. It was included in the anthology *Soviet Short Stories* in 1968 and is one of his best-known works. Perhaps not his most accomplished work, its simple story line and well judged blend of pathos and grotesque humour make it accessible and immediately appealing.

Because of its subject—the visitation of a creature from outer space—"Pkhentz" belongs to the category of science fiction. However, it is characteristic of much of Terts's writing in that it evades conventional classification. Terts is a self-consciously literary writer who makes frequent play with intertextual reference, pastiche, and parody. In "Kroshka Tsores" ("Little Jinx"), for example, he inverts the plot of a Hoffmann story, "Little Zaches." In "Pkhentz" he reverses the plot line of H.G. Well's *The War of the Worlds* (1898). The point of view is changed to that of a harmless alien, the sole survivor of a galactic accident who for years has been living incognito in a Moscow communal flat. He is more akin to a plant than a human or animal, needing only warmth and water as nourishment, but his many-limbed and many-eyed form is maimed and blinded because he was bound up for so long in the disguise of a hunchback. What we are reading is the irregular diary of this character, Andrei Kazimirovich Sushinskii, in which he records his failing health and his final decision to use his savings to return to the Siberian forests, where he originally landed, and perish there.

Obviously, the novelty of Terts's approach is somewhat lost on a generation of cinema-goers familiar with the movie *E.T.* The similarities between the story and the film may or may not be purely coincidental: E.T.'s disorientation and fear at being stranded on a strange planet, his anxiety about returning "Home," the danger that he will become a victim of scientific curiosity, the final departure from the forest clearing. But Terts's interest could not be further removed from Spielberg's sentimental reminder of the value of retaining a child's imaginative understanding and communication skills in a depersonalised, high-tech adult world. Still less is he interested here in exploring the utopian, dystopian possibilities of the science-fiction genre. In "Pkhentz" the focus is firmly on the present. It is a story of alienation and lack of communication in which the science-fiction convention functions as a device of defamiliarisation. As such, it is closer to the literary tradition of the foreign visitor or traveller from an antique land—like Le Sage's *Le Diable Boiteux,* Montesquieu's *Les Lettres Persanes,* and Swift's *Gulliver's Travels*—than to classic science fiction.

"Pkhentz" is an example of fantastic realism, which Terts advocated at the end of his essay "What is Socialist Realism?"; he called it the art best suited to conveying the grotesque anomalies of Soviet life. The last page of the essay, like "Pkhentz," was sent out separately to the West. At his trial Siniavski acknowledged that it was his own literary credo. In his final plea he quoted a sentence from "Pkhentz," which he said could apply to himself: "Just because I'm different must you immediately curse me?" Siniavski slips small but unmistakable autobiographical touches into the assumed identity of his outsider. The assumed name echoes his own and hints at his Polish ancestry. Self-deprecation and a tendency to conceal his feelings behind a protective casing of irony is very much a part of Siniavski's writing manner. It is a trait he recognises, as he has written in his observations on Russian culture and as he commented at his trial, as being typical of the Russian character. But what he is also challenging here, with his sympathetic portrayal of a monstrosity, are conventional notions of beauty in art. In a poignant central scene the alien (it is tempting to call him Pkhentz, but this is in fact a cherished remembered word from his lost language, denoting some indescribable beautiful warm radiance) uncovers himself and bathes his strange argus-eyed form in view of a mirror. He says "It's no good measuring my beauty against your own ugliness. I am more beautiful than you and more normal." This is the voice of Terts the embattled romantic, stoically echoing Victor Hugo's declaration of the inseparability of the sublime and the grotesque in art. Yet in the context of this story, the romantic view is challenged both from without, by the unrelenting harshness of everyday reality, and from within, by the author's own difficulty in reconciling the animal and the spiritual sides of human nature, the body and the soul. From the alien's estranged viewpoint, practically everything he encounters is threatening and repulsive. He visits a fellow hunchback whom he erroneously suspects of being a fellow alien (in fact, the hunchback, in a subtle yet pointed allusion to Soviet anti-Semitism, is an "alien," of sorts—

he is a "closet" Jew). He undergoes a succession of violent assaults on his senses: a yapping dog, a yelling child brandishing a sabre, a landlady reeking of cheap perfume, audible whispers of nosy neighbours commenting on his repulsiveness. But the greatest threat comes from a woman, Veronica, a lonely neighbour attracted to him as a fellow lonely creature. It is an acquaintance that provides the opportunity for a neat parody of the pillory scene in *Notre Dame de Paris,* where Esmeralda offers water to the thirsty Quasimodo. In "Pkhentz" the thirsty hunchback also cries out for water and Veronica ministers to the tormented sufferer. She misunderstands; he does not need the water to drink, but to pour over his parched body. However, when Veronica offers herself to this fastidious ascetic, she is transformed in his eyes from a sister of mercy into a monster from hell. With imagery borrowed from mediaeval representations of the sinfulness of sex—the woman's sexual organs depicted as a little old man baring his teeth— Terts seeks to convey the disgust of raw human sexuality. The tensions and contradictions that Terts touches upon here show that his concerns extend beyond the observation of social and political anomalies and divisions, and go deeper than any trendy liberation from Soviet sexual and linguistic taboos. "Pkhentz," despite its comic elements, remains one of the author's bleakest comments on the human condition and specifically on sex.

—Jane Grayson

———

A POET'S CONTINUING SILENCE. See **THE CONTINUING SILENCE OF A POET.**

———

POISSON D'AVRIL
by Somerville and Ross, 1908

Although the novels of Somerville and Ross, detailing the economic and cultural threats to Anglo-Irish landowners at the turn of the century, constitute their most important work, these authors' reputation rests to a considerable extent on the three volumes of sketches and stories known by the collective title, *Experiences of an Irish R.M.* Of these, "Poisson d'Avril," from *Further Experiences of an Irish R.M.,* though not quite a typical example of the works' locale and subject matter, is representative of their tone, style, and quirky artistry.

The reason that "Poisson d'Avril" is an exception to the general rule of the narrator's experiences is that it is set outside his normal sphere of operations, which is based on the area around the market town of Skibbereen in West Cork, where Edith Somerville lived. And his experiences usually involve fox-hunts and horseflesh, from the uncertainties of which a loyal retinue of colorful locals preserve him. The narrator in question, identified in "Poisson d'Avril" merely as "Sinclair," is the R.M., Major Sinclair Yeates. As the R.M., or Resident Magistrate, it is his duty to uphold British law and order in rural Ireland, a place which in the official mind is synonymous with backwardness and chaos. The historical context of the *Experiences of an Irish R.M.,* should be borne in mind. The stories were written in the wake of the Land War of the 1880's, when violence against landlords, police, and magistrates was commonplace, initiating the beginning of the end of the system of land tenure then dominant in Ireland.

As members of the land-owning class, Somerville and Ross were fully aware of the shift in social relations brought about by the Land War and government responses to it. Their perspective, however, overlooks the institutional and juridical questions of the day in favor of an intimate portrait of ruler and ruled, the main features of which are geniality and harmlessness. The idea of order may be a slippery one, as "Poisson d'Avril" slyly suggests, and the career of the official who believes in the idea is prey to certain unavoidable contradictions and misprisions. The most serious outcome of Irish irregularity and elusiveness, however, is loss of face rather than any more revolutionary loss. The ties between the law and its subjects seem as relaxed as the embrace of family members. Such unanimity, *Experiences of an Irish R.M.* argues, articulates the value of the union between Britain and Ireland more cogently than anything that politics might assert. One of the station-masters in "Poisson d'Avril" acts as if silence on politics is the better part of courtesy. And courtesy, or the "personal element," is the story's preferred version of the social contract.

If on the superficial levels of setting and personnel "Poisson d'Avril" differs from the typical R.M. story, at a more fundamental level it consolidates the general orientation of those stories. The cross-country dash by unreliable train may be a substitute for the more familiar fox-hunt, and the waywardness of rural life finds a replica in the inefficiency of the railroad. Nevertheless, "life and its troubles" prove essentially negotiable. Major Yeates's many adventures all have the ultimate effect of securing his safe passage through what is, judging by the weather and the landscape and the glimpses of town life, an inhospitable country. The only mistake that makes a significant difference is the one which the major makes himself, snatching in his haste the accoutrements of Jimmy Durkan. When the mistake is discovered, Major Yeates is bereft of the support system that rectified his other errors. Perhaps the personal element will also come to his rescue in Gloucestershire, though the final words of "Poisson d'Avril" suggest that it is not necessarily as freely available among the major's own people as it is in Ireland.

Among the gentry of a Gloucestershire country house party, the R.M. is merely "Sinclair," who leaves at least one of his intimate acquaintances and social equals "cold." In Ireland, his presence is distinguished and made viable by the aggreeableness of all who come his way. The Irish characters in "Poisson d'Avril" are the major's social inferiors. Yet, despite the various demands, delays, and discomforts of his journey, there is a sense in which he assents to, or at least tolerates, the style of public behavior responsible for his travail. His is not the head that sticks out the carriage window, asking various relevant yet somehow inappropriate questions in "a wrathful English voice." His encounter with the peasant women and their conversation regarding the salmon may not be intended to contrast with the story's closing scene. However, the contrast in social styles and social expectations is revealing not only from an amateurishly anthropological point of view but from an appreciation of "the comfortable mental sleekness" the major feels as a result of the encounter.

This complacent feeling is amusingly ironic, in view of the fact that Major Yeates has just discovered that he is, in effect, an accomplice to the crime of poaching, one of the most common offenses against property heard in his courtroom. The piquancy of these and other quirks of circumstance are expertly rendered by the author's animated style, whose combination of vivid demotic speech and punctilious, animated prose not only depicts some Irish realities of the day, but illustrates the dual character of the Anglo-Irish experience. Major Yeates's journey between the two poles of this experience hints, in its darkness, uncertainty, inclemency, and unforeseen outcome, at some of the insecurities of the times, against which the wryly stoical comedy of Somerville and Ross may be seen as an eloquent defense.

—George O'Brien

THE POOR MAN
by A.E. Coppard, 1923

In the foreword to his *Collected Tales,* A. E. Coppard argues that the short story, far from being sprung from the same fictional principles as the novel, is "an ancient art originating in the folk tale," far more ancient than printing, and "minister[s] to an apparently inborn and universal desire to hear tales." Indeed the loose, wandering narrative of the tale can be seen in many of his stories. "The Poor Man" collected in (*The Black Dog*), is typical, not only in its structure, but also in Coppard's creation of setting, use of rural village folk, and loving attention to dialect. It is these very qualities that led Frank O'Connor to praise Coppard for his "uncanny perception of a human's secretiveness and mystery."

Although at first "The Poor Man" seems only a collection of random incidents covering four years in the life of Dan Pavey, it is actually one of Coppard's most ironically Hardyesque tales, treating the insignificant human in the grasp of patterned destiny, brought on in part by the hubris of Dan, who strives "to be no better than he should be." Dan, a 35-year-old man who lives with his mother Meg in Icknield vale, earns his living, to all appearances, by turning chairs in beech wood and delivering papers in six villages. (Coppard evokes England's rural past extraordinarily deftly with names: Thasper, Cobbs Mill, Kezzal Predy Peter, Buzzzlebury, Trinkel, and Nuncton.) He delights the villagers on his rounds by singing in a fine tenor voice: hymns and anthems early in the week, "modestly secular tunes" by mid-week, and "entirely ribald and often a little improper" tunes by the end of the week. His bowler hat and ugly nose distinguish him less, though, than do his poaching game, getting drunk, and collecting bets on horse races from the villagers, activities he is specifically warned against by the Reverend Faudel Scroppe and Mrs. Scroope. Dan denies involvement, telling his mother, "I do as other folks do, not because I want to, but because I a'nt the pluck to be different. . . .You never taught me courage, and I wasn't born with any."

One Bonfire Day (Guy Fawkes Day, November 5), almost as if to challenge Scroope, Dan brings his five-year-old illegitimate son home with him, and Scroope expels him from the church choir. "Your course of life . . . reveals not only a social misdemeanor but a religious one—it is a mockery of God," he tells Dan. When Dan replies that "we can only measure other people by our own scales," the rector responds with a providential tale of an atheist who was deafened, then blinded, for his mockery.

Within days, Dan is singing a "savage libel" in the White Hart about Scroope. He becomes a chorister in a distant village, not heeding the gap between his actions and the words of the songs he so delights in singing.

At this point in the tale, Coppard shows his full mastery of narrative art by inserting a brief, highly symbolic, but also highly realistic scene, involving Martin, Dan's son. While playing at Old John's cottage, Martin calls attention to the crooked chimney. John responds, "My chimney's crooked, a'nt it, ah, and I'm crooked too." John's perceived analogy between the line of the chimney and the ethics of a man relate to Dan Pavey's life and his refusal to take responsibility for what he has become. During the next three years, Martin and Dan grow very close, and Dan repeatedly warns his son, "never take pattern by me."

At the end of these three years, just when Martin seems to have brought good luck into the Pavey household, Dan is jailed at hard labor for poaching and for attempting to murder a gamekeeper. He is innocent of the latter charge but unable to convince the jury. In one day, Dan has lost his dog, poisoned by bait the gamekeeper had put out, and his freedom. Six months later, Martin drowns in a boating accident. When he hears this news, Dan collapses, dazed, as though he has suffered a stroke, unable to speak anything other than three lines of a "jig." In his mind, these "punishments" have come to him as surely and as inevitably as did deafness and blindness to Scroope's parishioner. One can easily see that Coppard learned much from Thomas Hardy's *Life's Little Ironies.* Coppard's keen perceptions into the tragedy of life caused him to value "The Poor Man" highly, and he accorded it third position in his *Collected Tales.* His contemporary, H.E. Bates, was surely correct when he said that stories such as "The Poor Man" are as "sturdy and sound in grain as oak, as delicate and oddly scented as hawthorn."

—David Leon Higdon

POOR MARY
by Sylvia Townsend Warner, 1947

"Poor Mary" was first published in *The Museum of Cheats* in 1947, a collection that concentrates on the effects of war on British life. The stories work almost as a series of vignettes, with a markedly different tone from much of Warner's other writing, which may stem from her interest here in representing contemporary social conditions. Claire Harman suggests in her biography of Warner that the irony and satire of her early stories has been replaced here by a "texture . . . which had to form a suitable vessel for the sad, shabby, petty, and pitiable characters Sylvia was observing."

Although the texture may be different, the central themes in the story are familiar enough to readers of Warner's stories. The story is a brief glimpse into the lives of a couple separated by war: Nicholas, a conscientious objector, and his wife Mary, a volunteer in the A.T.S. The narrative focuses on a visit home by Mary, after four years away, gradually revealing a relationship which has been deadened and then brutalized by the war around it. The space and differences between them forms the concern of the story. Not only have they taken opposite stances with regard to the war, but their separation during it has irrevocably altered their relationship:

> She smells of metal, he thought, as I smell of dung. . . . Just as there was a difference between their smells and a difference in their gait, there was a difference in their manner of speech.

The distance between them is marked symbolically both by everyday detail (Nicholas is unable to remember whether Mary takes sugar, for example) and finally by their lovemaking at the end of the text, only bearable, it seems, because they no longer have to maintain the pretence of communication:

> Their smells of dung and metal would mingle, her shoulder would feel like greengages and her hair would get in his mouth, and she would be silent. It was one of her graces that she was silent in bed.

It is the texture of the writing, as Harman suggests, that pushes the loneliness at the centre of this story into the realm of abjection and brings the horror of this narrative to the surface. This is achieved both through the mode of narration and the intrusion of disturbing, surreal images throughout the story.

Although called "Poor Mary," Mary's voice and experience is almost effaced in the story (except through dialogue) and the point of view presented in the narration is always that of Nicholas, however bizarre, fragmented, and disturbing. Despite a third-person narration, we get access to his internal thoughts and the narratives he constructs about Mary:

> She was going to have a baby, no doubt of it. It accounted for everything, for her nerves, for her legs, for her appetite, for her arrival. Poor Mary! . . . And the next instant he was thinking: My poor Mary, I hope it wasn't a rape. Meanwhile his indifferent body was complying with the schedule of his daily life, and he felt himself to be growing more and more sleepy.

It is indeed the indifference that is so striking throughout the story and the sense of irritation at the disruption of "his daily life," more than any concern for Mary's welfare. When she tells him that she has fallen in love during the four years they have been apart, he is only aware of the kettle for tea he is holding ("Would nothing rid him of these turbulent kettles?").

The figurative language and surreal detail give the story its disturbing power and mark this from the beginning as something other than a conventional romance narrative, which we otherwise might expect from the opening scene (Nicholas picking flowers for his wife's homecoming). As in her story "A Love Match," a story dealing with the taboo of incest, Warner alerts us here to a different discourse by the image of the hedge, in the second paragraph, as "like a black wave breaking into lips of foam." The natural landscape, like the emotional one in the story, is sterile ("the leafless hedge"); everything within it is tainted and deadened. This atmosphere is carried into the interior of Nicholas's home, a space as small and enclosed as the narrative. When Mary comments on the candles in the kitchen, he explains:

> I bought them at a sale. They're called corpse candlesticks. The idea is that you leave them by the body all night, you see, and the rats can't knock them over.

Thus gradually a narrative perspective is established that is almost wholly contaminated by the horror of war, the same horror that Warner highlights in her story "A Love Match." Here though, the partial nature of the narrative, its sketch-like quality, is crucial to the atmosphere of the text. "Poor Mary" ends with another disturbing image: after they have made love, we are told that Nicholas will sleep, "letting the day's fatigue run out of his limbs as the fleas run out of the body of a shot rabbit," emphasising once again the horrific filter through which the lives of Mary and Nicholas are seen and lived.

—Elisabeth Mahoney

THE POPE'S MULE (La mule de Pape)
by Alphonse Daudet, 1869

The stories contained in Daudet's *Lettres de mon moulin (Letters From My Windmill)* are more various then is often realised; their emotional range is also quite considerable. The note of tragedy is at least approached in "The Beaucaire Stagecoach" and "The Two Inns," for example; still, the predominant note is that narrative charm for which the volume is most famous, and this quality is perhaps nowhere more fully displayed than in the tale "La mule de Pape" ("The Pope's Mule"). "The Pope's Mule" was invented to supply a meaning for an otherwise enigmatic Provençal proverb. Daudet's interest in the folk-idioms of the region was profoundly stimulated by his connections with Frédéric Mistral and the other members of the Félibrige—a society for the study of Provençal lore and literature. So far as "The Pope's Mule" is concerned, one particular member of the Félibrige was perhaps of especial importance. This was Joseph Roumanille who had a scholarly (and nostalgic) interest in the folklore of his native region, especially its traditional linguistic idioms, proverbs, and superstitions. It is with words that Roumanille might have written (and which Daudet had perhaps heard him speak) that "The Pope's Mule" begins:

> Of all the striking sayings, proverbs and adages with which our peasants of Provence flavour their talk, I know none more picturesque than this one. For fifteen leagues around my mill, when they speak of a spiteful, vindictive person, they say; "Beware of that man! He's like the Pope's mule who saved up her kick for seven years."

(translated by Frederick Davies)

Diligent, but unavailing, enquiry as to the source of the saying has been undertaken, the narrator tells us. Even his friend Francet Mamaï, the fife-player learned in the folklore of Provence, can offer no explanation. His suggestion is that the answer to the mystery will only be found "in the cicadas' library."

It is a characteristic piece of whimsy that Daudet should describe himself undertaking a week's research in the "cicadas' library" ("on my back," as he explains). Whimsical it may be, but the whimsicality does not entirely conceal a serious point; it is Daudet's declaration that the story is offered not as the purely subjective creation of a modern individual, but as a kind of articulation of truths contained in the countryside itself.

The resulting tale is a delightful fantasy. It has its full share of Daudet's brilliantly evocative writing. The early description of Papal Avignon is masterly. In long, accumulative sentences, Daudet creates an extraordinary picture— very specifically a *moving* picture—of abundant activity. People process and dance, the wind blows flags and banners, the shuttles of lacemakers dart back and forth; soldiers sing (in Latin), lutes sound, bells ring and drums are beaten.

There is delightful human warmth in the portrait of the fictional Pope Boniface, affable and friendly, devoted to vineyard (and mule) more than to higher matters. Though we are told that Boniface has a certain shrewdness of mind, the tale is concerned more with his gullibility and how easily—and repeatedly—he is deceived by Tistet Védène. There is wit and liveliness of mind in Tistet's initial deception of Boniface—extravagantly praising his mule in the shrewd knowledge that nothing could more delight the Pope. The deception seems a harmless one—even an engaging one. Our attitude changes as we find that Tistet is not satisfied by the considerable dividends he reaps from the deception; he mistreats the mule and encourages his toadies to do likewise. He leads the mule to the very top of the highest bell-turret in the Papal palace, exposing it there to public ridicule and to the humiliation of being lowered back down by pulleys and ropes; this has a splendid and perverse inventiveness about it, but seems to go beyond the boundaries of tolerant amiability in the tale's world. Our sympathies now are entirely with the mule as it anticipates the chance of revenge.

The unfortunate animal is denied the opportunity of immediate revenge by Védène's departure to the Court of Naples. There is delightful irony in what follows. Seven years later the rogue returns to seek the newly vacant post of First Mustard Cup Bearer—a title that has become a proverbial phrase to describe someone with an excessively conceited idea of their own abilities and importance. Védène resorts to his tried and tested tactic of lauding the mule—in doing so he prompts the Pope's promise that he shall be taken to see the creature. When this happens on the following day Védène is at his most flamboyantly self-satisfied. Before long he stands in precisely the right place for the mule to let fly with its long delayed revenge:

And the kick she let fly was so terrible, so terrible, that in far-off Pampérigouste they saw the smoke of it, vast clouds of yellow smoke in which there fluttered an ibis feather [from Védène's cap]; all that was left of the unfortunate Tistet Védène!

Much of the charm of "The Pope's Mule" comes from the apparent artlessness of Daudet's narrative method; it is, of course, an impression created by considerable art of an unorthodox nature. Daudet described his style as "littérature debout" (literature standing-up); by this he meant to indicate how his writing sought to find a literary approximation to the methods of oral narrative. Daudet was himself an accomplished storyteller amongst his friends and acquaintances; it is the essential achievement of "The Pope's Mule" that the reader, too, is made to feel that he or she is sitting in the charmed circle of the storyteller.

—Glyn Pursglove

A PORTRAIT OF SHUNKIN (Shunkin sho)
by Tanizaki Jun'ichiro, 1933

When Tanizaki Jun'ichiro published his short story, *Shunkin sho* ("A Portrait of Shunkin") in 1933, he was still engaged in a bitter public debate with fellow author, Akutagawa Ryūnosuke, as to the appropriate role for the author's imagination in the formulation of fiction. In response to the latter's public advocacy of the "plotless novel," Tanizaki argued passionately in favour of "complicated stories that are embellished with maximum intricacy"—and nowhere is this determined advocacy of the author's duty to "construct" his fictional world by giving free rein to his powers of creativity more evident than in "A Portrait of Shunkin."

Immediately acclaimed by the majority of his critics as the embodiment of much that Tanizaki had long been propounding for his fiction, at first sight the work conforms to the author's express desire to "reconstruct the psychology of a woman of Japan's feudal past." The consequent portrayal of the blind Shunkin suggests a woman who, though "blessed with aristocratic grace and beauty" (translated by Howard Hibbett), has become so accustomed to having her own way (especially from her dutiful servant Sasuke) that any hint of questioning of her absolute authority is met with a stubborn, even ruthless assertion of her dominance.

To interpret the story in such terms, however, is to reckon without Tanizaki's extraordinary "power to construct"— and to overlook the story's complex narrative strategy which the author was subsequently to attribute to his reading of Stendhal and Hardy. Reviewed thus, far from the uncomplicated, objective portrayal of the spoilt mistress and her obedient servant, the story comes to be seen as an increasingly complex framework of carefully constructed, though often seemingly conflicting, messages, and it is only in penetrating the various levels of narration that the reader gains access to the issue at the core of the work—a questioning of the very nature of truth itself.

To achieve his ends, Tanizaki frames the entire story through the introduction of the narrator-researcher who seeks to piece together an "accurate" portrait of Shunkin from the limited sources at his disposal. Thereafter, by casting increasing doubt on the objective reliability of each of these sources, the author succeeds in disarming his reader to such an extent that, by the end, the veracity of the narrator himself is called into question.

The sources of information concerning Shunkin available to the narrator are varied but, as the story develops, each of these is provided with plausible grounds for presenting a somewhat "economical" truth. At the outset of the work, as the researcher visits the graves of Shunkin and Sasuke, he is introduced to the old lady, Teru, who had served both so faithfully and who now tends both their graves. However, in emphasising her blind devotion to the couple—and hinting at a possible relationship between Sasuke and Teru following Shunkin's death—a question mark is deliberately introduced over the disinterested nature of the information with which she supplies the narrator. A similar element of uncertainty surrounds the other source on which the narrator relies heavily, a biography entitled *The Life of Mozuya Shunkin*. As the narrative is quick to point out, the work was apparently compiled at Sasuke's behest and Sasuke "undoubtedly supplied all the material and may well be regarded as the real author." Given the confused nature of the relationship between Sasuke and Shunkin, described by one critic as "at once brutal and sublime" (Ito, *Visions of Desire*, 1991), the reader hardly needs to be reminded that Sasuke's "remarks cannot be taken at face value since he was accustomed to humbling himself while praising her to the skies."

The subsequent text is presented through a combination of conjecture, description, and several lengthy quotations from these "primary sources," with the narrator seemingly intent on maintaining a clear delineation between his own hypothesis and the various "facts" at his disposal. The text, however, gradually erodes this distinction, and, as fact and flights of imagination become ever more interwoven, so increasing doubt is cast on the authenticity of the fundamental "portrait" itself—to the extent that, confronted with the incident in which Shunkin is deliberately disfigured by someone pouring boiling water over her face, the suggestion that, rather than any of the potential culprits considered by the narrator, the crime is of Sasuke's doing, though not raised explicitly, is not far beneath the surface. Even Sasuke's subsequent and inexplicable blinding fails to clarify the issue. As the narrator confesses, considerable discrepancy exists between the depiction of this event in *The Life of Mozuya Shunkin* (which describes the "strange turn of fate [whereby] within a few weeks Sasuke began to suffer from cataracts"), or Sasuke's own account offered some ten years later, of his sacrificial act of self-immolation to ensure that he would never been in a position to witness Shunkin's disfigurement. Whatever the "truth," the incident itself is pivotal; it calls into question the very nature of the relationship between Shunkin and Sasuke, raising the possibility (discussed at length by Ito) that, for all his apparently unquestioning acquiescence to his mistress' every whim, it is actually Sasuke who exercises the dominant role, ensuring to the end that Shunkin remains totally dependent on her "servant."

In suggesting that, through his blindness, Sasuke acquires a new vision—an "inner vision in place of the vision he had lost"—the narrator appears to be hinting that a resolution of the various questions raised by the story will be achieved. But, in enveloping even this comment in the countless layers of narrative that intervene between reader and the "real" Shunkin, the author succeeds in maintaining the ambiguity to the end, thereby retaining the focus on the questions of truth and objectivity that, from the outset, Tanizaki had sought to construct.

—Mark Williams

THE POST OFFICE
by Liam O'Flaherty, 1956

After serving in the Irish Guards in France, Liam O'Flaherty travelled around the world, between the years 1918 and 1921, earning his way in the odd jobs available to a vagabond. These experiences are recorded in "The Post Office," in which he poses the Irish native provincials with the cosmopolitan visitors. An uncharacteristic story for O'Flaherty, "The Post Office" was collected in *The Stories of Liam O'Flaherty* (1956).

In the story O'Flaherty creates a comical portrait of a clash between wealthy and sophisticated American-Irish and natives of a small Irish town west of Galway in Connemara. It is pension day in the early 1950's and the villagers, mostly old, come to the post office not only to collect their money but also to entertain themselves at the expense of the postmaster Martin Conlon. The bane of his existence and the symbol of the new technology is the telegram, which entails use of an anachronistic telephone with crank handle. Three tourists, a man and two women, arrive in a sky-blue Cadillac convertible "of the latest model," asking to send a telegram. This sends the assembled natives into contortions of laughter at the discomfort of Conlon. Somewhat dimwitted without knowing it and naturally incapable, Conlon fears for his position and he thinks that the handsome young man driving the car is a spy. All three visitors are dressed in the latest expensive fashion, daring and outlandish next to the local women in shawls and aprons.

The American speaks the local dialect of the Gaelic language with no apparent roots in the area. The natives' knowledge of local families extends a hundred years back to the Great Famine, but they don't ask his name or who he is. A "mocker by nature" and a "smiling rogue" who feeds on the humor of the situation, he seems more an American than a "rich Dubliner" or a "Government official"; but he knows the local history and temperament.

The visitors are models of sophistication in the languages they speak, their clothing, car, and worldly experience. The villagers, their hosts, reveal provincial behavior, Irish colloquialism, insults and threats of violence, and ignorance of the world, which is balanced with native wit and humor.

To avoid the devilment of sending a telegram, Conlon tries to persuade the young man of the futility of such a transaction but finds himself defeated by the "facts" presented, which are in part inspired by his pronouncing the Cadillac "the king of all motor cars." The young Spanish woman is the daughter of a duke, invited to dine in Dublin with the president of the Republic. She desires to send a telegram from the town, Paiseach, because her friend in Los Angeles had a great-great-grandmother who came from Paiseach. The natives quickly seize upon the name O'Graudain and provide the family history.

Meanwhile, an old hag wants to know what disease the women have, with their painted toenails; when told they were infected when imprisoned in the Brazilian forest, she departs swiftly in terror. Father Tom the priest arrives searching for his dog and, on learning about the telegram, commiserates the postman with the traditional words of bereavement ("I'm sorry for your trouble") and departs with gales of laughter. Conlon fears that the telegram written in Spanish—a quotation from Federico García Lorca—may be obscene, whereupon the young visitor requests the Spanish girl to recite "avec force." Intelligence for the message means nothing; the listeners are carried away with her dramatics and call out "God be with you, noble lady!. . . . "Brightness of all brightnesses!" Ironically, what she has said in Spanish is exactly the opposite.

The popular applause persuades Conlon that he must attempt to send the telegram. In speaking on the antiquated telephone, he encounters a roar of thunderous voices, a prankster selling fish, then a person grieving the death of a native after an operation at a nearby hospital. On reporting this to the assembly he elaborates, "They didn't leave a drop of blood in him that they didn't draw." A soldier, a sensible old veteran of the Boer War, contradicts the consensus about the corpse: "It was no good for him to be alive and the way he was."

Conlon, on the telephone again, encounters a school teacher with a wrong number, then someone trying to reach Carna by telephone, who laughs on finding he has reached Paiseach, for the town is aptly named; in Gaelic it means "confusion, disorder, and shapelessness." He expresses Conlon's philosophy: "We were much better off when we had only donkeys and carts and row-boats."

The triumph of American technology, as represented in the visiting American, climaxes at this point, where Conlon collapses in defeat. The American girl steps forward, seizes the telephone, connects immediately, and proceeds to convey the telegram in Spanish with phonetics: "Muerto. M for Mary, U for Una. . . ." The soldier, much impressed, appraises the American girl's physical assets and advises the young man to marry her. The mystery of the young man's identity is only partly solved in his response: "I'm just a poor Dublin lad studying sculpture in Paris."

Conlon, with his telegraph responsibilities discharged vicariously, turns character completely and brusquely orders the audience into position to receive their pensions amid their good-humored cheers.

The mixture of nationalities represented by the visitors clashes with the provinciality of the Irish, and the unspoken message is that life and love lie elsewhere. The great opportunity, as the soldier insists, is in the Irish mating with American technology.

—Grace Eckley

PRELUDE
by Katherine Mansfield, 1920 (as *The Aloe,* 1918)

Katherine Mansfield's "Prelude" was published by Leonard and Virginia Woolf's Hogarth Press under the title *The Aloe.* The story was revised and retitled by Mansfield (and collected in *Bliss and Other Stories*), apparently to bring it more in line with her growing appreciation of the form of the short fiction she was writing but had a difficult time defining. ("What form is it?" she asked of a friend in a letter, published in *Letters.* "As far as I know, it's more or less my own invention.") With an *in medias res* beginning and lack of a sustained overt plot line, the story proceeds by images clustering into symbolic patterns that stand in harmonic relationships to each other and direct meaning. In speaking about "Prelude," in another letter, Mansfield says "[the story] just unfolds and opens" (also in *Letters*).

Her original writing of "Prelude" followed a visit from her brother with whom she shared memories of childhood and also coincided with an awakening from a kind of artistic fatigue. Her revision of the story prior to publication followed her brother's death in the war and her interest in creating a story in his honor. Based in both their childhood memories, "Prelude" was apparently to end with an announcement of a pregnancy that would herald the birth of a boy child, her brother just deceased. But the story stops before the pregnancy is announced, although images suggest that the mother, Linda, is pregnant.

The appearance of a boy child is delayed for a dozen years when he is introduced in another New Zealand story, "At the Bay," which follows so closely to themes and motifs found in "Prelude" that a reader might desire to consider the two stories a diptych, for what is started in "Prelude" is found in "At the Bay." Both stories have at various times and by various readers been declared Mansfield's best. But regardless, all Mansfield readers agree that these two stories taken together with some 12 or 15 others declare Mansfield the great writer she hoped to be.

"Prelude" tells about three days in the life of the Stanley Burnell family at the time of their move to a larger house befitting Stanley's achievements in business. The Burnell family consists of husband Stanley; wife Linda; daughters Isabel, Lottie, and Kezia; Linda's sister Beryl; and their mother Mrs. Fairchild. In most short stories characters are flat rather than round, a circumstance attributed to the story's symbolic underpinnings as well as its short length.

This is not to say *ipso facto* that round characters are better than flat characters. Rather, characterization is suited to need in any given short story. What is notable here is the manner in which Mansfield achieves characterization with the limited time and space of the writer of the short story by juxtaposing her characters so that they double over and comment on each other. One knows Linda by getting to know Mrs. Fairchild, Beryl, and Kezia. One understands Kezia by recognizing some of Beryl's traits and some of Linda's in the child. The female characters are spread along a spectrum from child to mature woman; from Kezia just learning to differentiate her female ego from that of others, to Isabel clearly patterning herself after what she understands Beryl to be, to Beryl dreaming of a lover and fighting her "false self," to Linda whose serene aspect belies her anger and frustration at the role she finds herself playing, to Mrs. Fairchild, beloved of Linda who returns that love and special attention while she carefully and deliberately puts the new house in order, postponing her fears of the future.

Surrounding the new house is a garden and while the women put the house in order, moving from one room to another, Kezia explores the garden, moving through the neatly arranged flowers and well laid-out orchards. Surrounding the garden, though, is the bush in all its frightening aspects. From her safe position Kezia is aware of the tangle of trees, the strange scents, the cream flowers that buzz with flies, and she knows, as do the other members of her family, that the reality of nightmares is embodied in the dark bush and that life, after all, is a prelude to death.

Stanley Burnell is the only male in the immediate family. He is the cock in the henhouse and the bull in the china shop. He is loved but also tolerated; his needs are carefully tended to and he is the center around which the household dances until he leaves for work and the woman sigh and relax their ways through the day. Other male characters in the story seem peripheral but are really central as they comment on the masculine role in the society. Pat, the handyman, wears an earring, which astonishes Kezia. He is kind and gentle with the children but capable of beheading the duck in a way that frightens Kezia into hysteria. Rags and Pip Trout are cousins, sons of another of Mrs. Fairchild's daughters. Rags resists the masculine role. He is still young enough to play with dolls and he does, though he knows that what he does is "shameful." Pip, somewhat older, adopts the stance of a stereotypical male ordering his cousins about and "training" his dog Snooker.

The theme of sexual frustrations and anxieties is one of several important to overall meaning in the story. Linda loves Stanley; but he frightens her. His desire for a son is apparent in his every move; and Linda fears for her life. She has already had three children and she has been diagnosed as having a heart condition that could kill her. The aloe with its tall, stout, swelling stem has special significance for Linda. It represents male power, the means to escape. For Mrs. Fairchild the aloe is the century plant, blooming once every 100 years, marking a family's movement in time and through generations. Beryl's desire for a lover expresses itself in various ways, in her annoyance with Stanley for moving the family to the country, in her flirting with Stanley, which seems both an act of revenge as she watches him respond to her moves and a practice exercise in anticipation of future lovers.

If sexual activity is fraught with difficulty and pain, still it is the basis of generational movements timed with the movements of the planets, as Mansfield parallels historical time with a family delineated in all its tenses—past, present, and future. The century plant is coming into bloom and it will bloom again in another century as it has in the past.

—Mary Rohrberger

THE PRUSSIAN OFFICER
by D.H. Lawrence, 1914

Whether "The Prussian Officer" is, as some critics claim, one of the world's masterpieces of short fiction," most agree that it is one of D.H. Lawrence's best stories, representative of his favorite theme of so-called "blood consciousness" and his customary narrative technique of combining the realistic with the mythic. The plot of the story is so simple and its two characters are so stark as to be archetypal. An aristocratic Prussian captain becomes obsessed with his uncomplicated young orderly but deals with the obsession by repressing it, humiliating and physically mistreating the young man. The story reaches its climax when the orderly kills the officer, an act that destroys the world of everyday reality for the young man, launching him into an alienated psychic state that eventually leads to his own death. Just as the officer seems driven by forces outside of his control and understanding, the orderly responds in a primitive unthinking manner. In fact, as is usual in Lawrence's stories, it is not rational thought but rather primitive instinct that motivates the action of "The Prussian Officer."

Although the Prussian officer's sadistic treatment of the young man is a result of his repressed sexual desire for him, as in other Lawrence works of fiction in which homosexuality seems to play a role, sex is a metaphor for something deeper. As Aldous Huxley once wrote about Lawrence, his special gift was for "unknown modes of being." The significance of sexuality for Lawrence, suggested Huxley, was that in it "the immediate, non-mental knowledge of divine otherness is brought, so to speak, to a focus—a focus of darkness." Indeed, the most basic myth substratum of "The Prussian Officer" is the story of *Paradise Lost*, in which Satan, tormented by thought, yearns for the innocent and instinctive Adam; however, frustrated by the impossibility of regaining that lost innocence, he can only scorn it and try to destroy it.

As opposed to the officer, who is bound to the rules of the aristocracy and the military, the orderly is one who seems "never to have thought, only to have received life direct through his senses, and acted straight from instinct." It is this "blind instinctive sureness of movement of an unhampered young animal" that so irritates the officer. Realizing this, the orderly feels like "a wild thing caught" and his hatred in response to the officer's passion grows; as the

officer seems to be going irritably insane, the youth becomes deeply frightened.

Whereas the first half of the story focuses on the consciousness of the officer who tries not to admit the passion that has seized him, gradually the focus shifts to the orderly as the captain begins to grow vague and unreal. However, the officer's passion makes the orderly feel similarly unreal. He has a sense of being "disemboweled, made empty, like an empty shell. He felt himself as nothing, a shadow creeping under the sunshine." More and more he feels in a "blackish dream" and all those around him seem to be "dream people."

This movement toward unreality in which the two characters become transformed by their very passion is a typical Lawrentian structural device by which conventional characters are transfigured into depersonalized representatives of states of mind. The orderly's murder of the captain is presented in unmistakable sexual terms. He leaps on the older man, pressing his knee against his chest and forcing the officer's head over a tree stump, "pressing, with all his heart behind in a passion of relief, the tension of his wrists exquisite with relief." Exulting in his "thrust," he shoves the officer's head back until there is a little "cluck" and a crunching sensation, and heavy convulsions shake his body, horrifying the young soldier, yet pleasing him too.

The murder completes the young man's alienation from the ordinary world. "He had gone out from everyday life into the unknown, and he could not, he even did not want to go back." As he wanders alone through the forest, the world becomes a ghostly shadow to him. His actual death seems an inevitable and even anticlimactic consequence of his complete distancing from the world.

As more than one critic has suggested, "The Prussian Officer" is about the "divided self," for the two central characters represent the split between fallen intellect and prefall innocence, or between repressed consciousness and the instinctive unconscious. This basic tension between life as stiff and repressed and life as vital and dynamic can be seen in the final image of the story; the two men lie side by side in the mortuary—the officer frozen and rigid and the orderly looking as if any moment he might rouse into life again.

—Charles E. May

THE PSYCHIATRIST (O Alienista)
by Joaquim Maria Machado de Assis, 1882

Like his novels, Machado's stories can be divided into early and late periods. *Papéis avulsos* (Odd Papers), the first of the mature collections, appeared in 1882, one year after *Bráz Cubas (Epitaph of a Small Winner)*. The stories and the novel both reveal sharp changes in theme, form, and technique. From the late 1870's the author was increasingly a biting satirist of the social structure and leisure middle class of Brazil's Second Empire and early republic (1840-90). The reader is particularly aware that the well-being of the characters who are the butt of Machado's satire depends on those lower than they in the hierarchy.

Among the best-known narrative of *Papéis avulsos* is "O Alienista" ("The Psychiatrist"), in which the author satirizes Positivism, the philosophy of Auguste Comte prevalent in 19th-century Western Europe, and therefore in urban centers in Brazil, that science held the solution to every human problem. Possibly suggested by the theme of Jonathan Swift's "A Serious and Useful Scheme to Make a Hospital for Incurables," Machado's satire, like many ironic modern treatments of ontology and epistemology, goes much farther than Swift's, or other precursors', to obliterate the boundary between reason and madness. The theme was a favorite of Poe's, as well as of broadly defined realists such as Maupassant, and naturalists such as Chekov, to mention only a few writers and thinkers of the 19th century who influenced Machado. Those preoccupied by the impressionistic interpretation of ethical matters are numerous; as Anatole France pointed out so appropriately in a speech at the Sorbonne in 1909, Machado deserved to be classified among them as precursor and contemporary.

Like his other stories, "The Psychiatrist" means different things to different readers. Its satire may be aimed at the scientific rationalism and complete authority of the psychiatrist for whose typically Brazilian ways of thinking Machado had little love. *Bacamarte,* the name of the psychiatrist, means "good-for-nothing" in Portuguese, after all. Or, the writer who created the characters of Braz Cubas and Dom Casmurro may have believed in Bacamarte's definition of insanity, so comprehensive that almost every normal individual may be considered insane. Can one really know the meaning of "insane" and therefore of being insane?

As in *Dom Casmurro,* the structure of the story rests on an ironic inversion of roles. The learned psychiatrist, who at the outset dedicates himself to committing people to the "Green House," ends up judging them all sane—cured by him?—and committing himself. Again, what is the relationship between meaning and knowledge? Like the arbitary, imprecise tool of language that it must use for definitions, as the structuralists point out in their basic precepts, science fails to offer perfect understanding of the human condition.

Typically cold and rigid, the doctor bases his choice of a wife on her health rather than her beauty. Biologically, she should give him good children, but she proves barren. She loves and admires him, so long as his knowledge remains purely theoretical for her. In practical terms, the diet he prescribes is not for her, and she becomes jealous when his studies preempt her in his concerns. The setting of a small city especially reveals the petty, egotistical side of human behavior which is the object of the pychiatrist's practice. A gentle madman, the rationalist Bacamarte does not inspire sympathy as does the daydreamer Don Quijote. Nor does his Sancho Panza, the opportunistic pharmacist, or any of the other secondary figures with which Machado surrounds the master in this work reminiscent of aspects of *Madame Bovary.* All are deemed mad by the psychiatrist in this story that is neither a tragedy nor a comedy. Before his arrival, the dangerous ones were locked up in their rooms for life, the docile ones left free to go about their business. But Bacamarte finds even the most normal persons to be mad, and after a while he comes to question his own mental balance. He advances a new, entirely opposed and absurd theory of insanity, according to which the well are now sick, but also rational. Although undisturbed by his reversal of positions, he does wonder if all the asylum's inmates whom he now releases were in fact insane, if he really cured them all, or if mental balance is so natural and inherent that it eventually asserts itself. After another 20 minutes of "rational" inquiry, Bacamarte discovers in himself the one he sought, the individual with all the virtues of a well-balanced yet insane person. Embodying both the theory and practice of his new scientific doctrine, Bacamarte sets out to cure himself, as the omniscient narrator remarks that

some of the Green House's former inmates have suggested that the doctor was the only madman ever committed to the asylum.

Reacting to his contemporaries' superficial treatment of Brazilian reality, Machado probes his characters to reveal highly complex behavior. His world view is a subjective, ambiguous one, for truth and reality are always relative. As Machado explores the consciousness of his characters, in which time is expanded and contracted at will, his reader attempts to make sense of the experience. Machado's sense of time is relative, too, however, and therefore what he experiences, albeit perhaps the most tangible part of his work, remains fluid. Machado's extensive use of suggestion for communication permits him to convey a great deal in a compact space. Whether in his novels or stories, he has the principal action reside in the character and develops it with the greatest possible economy of means and stylistic precision.

—Richard A. Mazzara

THE PUZZLEHEADED GIRL
by Christina Stead, 1967

Best-known for *The Man Who Loved Children* (1940), Christina Stead was productive for over five decades. In addition to novels, her output included novellas and short stories. A distinguished example of her achievement in short fiction, *The Puzzleheaded Girl* (1967), comprising four tales, has contributed to her reputation as one of the important writers of our time.

First published in *Kenyon Review* in 1965, the opening narrative and title-piece, "The Puzzleheaded Girl," depends for its chief setting on the writer's observations of New York. It also draws on her experience of London and the continent. After leaving her birthplace, Australia, in 1928, Stead spent stretches of her life in Europe and America, taking imaginative possession of the trans-national domain of modern Western culture. The period of composition of the stories which comprise *The Puzzleheaded Girl* has been identified by R.G. Geering as spanning the 1950's and early 1960's, following the completion (in substance) of *Dark Places of the Heart* (1966), entitled *Cotters' England* in England. At this time, Stead and her American husband, novelist William Blake, were living in London.

Her habit of mind, learned from a father who was a naturalist, is strongly empirical, to the extent that she maintains a scrupulous openness to evidence—including evidence which might actually cast doubt on scientific disinterestedness. "The Puzzleheaded Girl" (told in the third person) reports in a factual way on the observations and reflections of a left-wing intellectual who, against his inclination, is compelled towards a vision of truth as passion, i.e., as experienced by involved subjects. This movement away from truth as objectivity occurs as Augustus Debrett, a New York businessman with a social conscience, attempts to come to terms with the periodic appearance in his life of a young woman who is the embodiment of mystery. Debrett is a haunted man. But what is it that haunts him?

At the outset, Debrett and his business colleagues are simply presented with a spectacle of poverty in the form of a new addition to their staff, the young typist Honor Lawrence, who turns out to be the daughter of an Italian fruit-seller. Debrett employs the girl on a whim, won over by her ingenuousness and quaint air of intellectual seriousness. However, as she begins to affect his life, to the point of influencing his family's move to France, he begins to see that the power she has over him is disproportionate to the straightforward demands she makes on his charity. In her portrait of Homer, Stead reworks the character of Teresa Hawkins, the protagonist of *For Love Alone* (1944). The bond, which exists from the moment Debrett recognizes something unusual in the girl's frank and detached manner, recalls the earlier novel's account of the meeting of Teresa and her future partner, James Quick, although in this case the relationship never reaches the point of sexual encounter. Honor appears not to desire it. Or does she? This is one of the mysteries surrounding this woman *manquée* who is puzzling to herself as well as to others. Interestingly, both fictional meetings imitate the real-life situation—of boss and young employee—in which Stead met her own husband.

Honor Lawrence works out her destiny in relation to other important characters in the story in a series of episodes which show her poised enigmatically on the cusp of dependence and independence, obsession and detachment, innocence and experience. Unconscious of conventional restraints, she importunes her bosses and their wives, seeking advice, money, an invitation to dinner or to stay. Debrett's wife, Beatrice, is especially put out by the girl's behaviour. She senses the danger of an affair, at the same time as she shrugs off the idea as ridiculous. It is clear to all that Honor, who narrowly escapes the designs of two lesbian patrons, is sexually naive. Baffling to the people who are driven to help her through compassion, the girl both pursues and does not pursue her benefactors. To Debrett it seems that she is simply there as a fact of life.

In this character, Stead combines the traits of her earlier passionate searcher, Teresa Hawkins, and Teresa's terrible super-ego, Jonathan Crow. Honor aspires to be an artist like her brother, Walter Lawrence. It is said of her, by a friend from her adolescent years who is infatuated with her and to whom she proposes marriage, that she is a person with "great gifts," who has created herself as a work of art. At times she seems to possess preternatural knowledge of Debrett, tracking him down after the break-up of his marriage to Beatrice. Debrett shares with his second wife, Mari, the puzzle of this creature who seems to be set on integrity, yet so often acts out of desperation, shocking others with her unwitting opportunism. He learns from Honour's "husband," Jay Hewitt, that a story she previously told him, about a South African marriage and a lost child, exists in another version in which Debrett is himself cast as the lover, accused of cold-bloodedly handing her on to a South American. Debrett is stunned by this challenge to his idea of Honor as a truth-teller.

At the end of the story we encounter an Honor who, approaching death, repudiates any notion of love: "Love, I spit, I spit it out. . . . It kills you." It is left to Mari to throw some light on the power of this vagrant who, even after she is gone, upsets Debrett's evenness of mind: "She's the ragged, wayward heart of woman that doesn't want to be caught and hasn't been caught. . . . She never loved anyone." Mari's husband, however, does not choose to believe her. A 1968 reviewer of *The Puzzleheaded Girl* collection described Stead's portraiture as "cubist," evoking the Picasso double profile. This is an illuminating way of drawing attention to the complex perspectives of the title-piece, a tale of pursuit that sets out to confront both the objective and the subjective faces of truth.

—Patricia Dobrez

Q

THE QUEEN OF SPADES (Pikovaia dama)
by Aleksandr Pushkin, 1834

Aleksandr Pushkin, a poet, first turned to prose fiction in 1830 with his *Tales of Belkin*. Russian prose writing was still in its infancy and, indeed, *Pikovaia dama* (*The Queen of Spades*) is the first major Russian prose work. To write it, Pushkin had to invent a new literary language. Hitherto the language of popular prose writers such as Bestuzhen-Marlinskii had been elaborately flowery, with a surfeit of adjectives, similes, and metaphors. Pushkin opted for a pared, clipped style, akin almost to telegraphese, with a minimum of subordinate clauses and an almost total absence of all but the most basic adjectives and figures of speech.

The basic plot of the story would have been familiar to readers of the pulp fiction of the day. P. Mashkov's *Three Crosses* (1833) was just one of a long line of card-playing stories, usually involving a foolproof winning formula of supernatural origin, a love intrigue, and a twist at the end of the story. Pushkin's radical reworking of this tired formula involves Hermann, a half-German officer in the Engineer corps, and the 87-year-old countess, reputedly the guardian of a secret winning formula, and her ward Liza. Through pretending to pay court to Liza, Hermann gains access to the countess's room with the intention of eliciting the formula from her. The shock is too great for the old woman, who dies before revealing her secret. She subsequently appears to Hermann, apparently as a ghost, and reveals her secret—ace, three, seven. Armed with this formula, Hermann, an extremely cautious man who has never gambled in his life, takes on the formidable gambler Chekalinskii at faro. The three and the seven win for him and he stakes all his winnings on the ace. Thinking he has won again, he turns the card over only to discover it is the queen of spades, which bears an uncanny likeness to the old countess. Hermann goes mad and is confined to a lunatic asylum.

Although *The Queen of Spades* is ostensibly a tale of the supernatural, Pushkin tantalises the reader by suggesting rational explanations for all the events in the story. The ghost, for example, may be explained by the effect of alcohol on Hermann's brain, while the apparently magical substitution of the queen of spades for the ace may simply be a case of "misdrawing" a card from the pack, an event common enough in the game of faro to merit its own technical term. Pushkin, who was known to the secret police more as an obsessive card player than as a political subversive, was well aware of such mishaps and, indeed, litters his story with the jargon of the professional card player.

The apparent simplicity of the story, however, is highly deceptive. As the poet and Pushkin scholar Anna Akhmatova remarked, "How complex it is: layer upon layer." Among the layers is the character of Hermann himself, the self-made man of will with "the profile of Napoleon and the soul of Mephistopheles," who is a precursor both of Lermontov's Pechorin and of a whole range of Dostoevskii's heroes, from the Underground Man to Ivan Karamazov. Others have seen the story as an essay in numerology, a subject that fascinated Pushkin. Certainly the numbers one, three, and seven recur repeatedly throughout the story to the point where, at the very end, Hermann is incarcerated in room 17. Still others have detected a consistent pattern of masonic symbolism and point to Pushkin's active involvement in the movement. There are autobiographical elements and a highly complex narrative technique with the *fabula* (what actually happens) and *sujet* (how the reader learns about it) widely separated. The complexity of the narrative technique stems not only from Pushkin's desire to elaborate an existing genre but also from his desire to underline the theme of time, youth and age. This is one of the dominant themes in Pushkin's work as a whole and is seen nowhere more clearly than in the portrait of the countess, la Vénus Moscovite of a bygone age.

Above all, this is a work of parody. The traditional dashing hero of Romantic fiction is replaced by the calculating Hermann whose means do not permit him to "risk the necessary in the hope of acquiring the superfluous." Liza, cast in the role traditionally reserved for the heroine-victim in the mould of Karamzin's "Poor Liza" (1792), is conventional, dull, and ultimately happy while the countess, far from being a traditional villain, displays, even in extreme old age, both style and spirit. There are many elements of parody, from the spoof epigraphs, all of them Pushkin's own invention, to the celebrated scene in which the concealed Hermann witnesses the undressing of the old countess by her maids after the ball.

The story has been made into a play (by Aleksandr Shakhovskii), several films and, most notably, an opera by Petr Chaikovskii.

—Michael Pursglove

R

THE RAILWAY POLICE
by Hortense Calisher, 1966

Better-known for her often protracted and intricate novels and for many memorable short stories, Hortense Calisher has written half a dozen pieces of fiction in a novella form, not uniquely her own but marked by her unmistakable voice. Arguably, they are illustrated best by "The Railway Police." It is in distinguished company with Henry James's "The Beast in the Jungle" or Katherine Anne Porter's *Noon Wine,* or, more recently, Jim Harrison's "The Woman Lit By Fireflies" or Jane Smiley's "Good Will," in which neither extraneous plot lines nor judgmental authorial asides intrude to deflect the reader from a concentrated stare at human behavior in the process of coming to terms with the limitations of the self. In such works, either the extraordinary is made to seem ordinary or the ordinary is made to seem extraordinary—in "The Railway Police," the true and the false, what lies beneath the human masquerade—and by their conclusions the reader may be hard-pressed to defend which is which. This is a familiar theme in Calisher's work: the masks that human beings wear for survival.

In the introduction to a volume of her *Collected Stories,* Calisher observed that a story was "an apocalypse, served in a very small cup." In "The Railway Police" the cup is only slightly larger—a 70-page monologue—but the apocalypse deserves capitalizing. A bald woman decides to face the world without her disguising wigs, insisting in that act that neither art imitates life nor that life imitates art. Instead, they are equidistant from a self only discovered when it refuses to let life and art masquerade as each other.

In the novella, an unnamed narrator relates the events of the 24 hours preceding 22 March, the first day of spring, the beginning of a new cycle, a rebirth. On a train bound for Boston, she witnesses the railway police take a man into custody. He has been hiding in the washroom, just sufficiently badly dressed to give himself away as a vagrant rather than a passenger. The epiphany that the narrator experiences at that moment will alter her life, for she determines to become a vagrant too, an "honor-bright refuser of houses, clothing, income and other disguises," an action that has "boiled up out of meditation" for 20 years.

Systematically, she disposes of her portfolio and her girdle in the washroom; she flies back to New York as soon as she reaches Boston, tossing her jewelry into the plane's washroom ventilator once she is airborne; she empties her safety deposit box of money and calls on her lawyer to alter her will, leaving her estate to the Seamen's Institute; and she returns to her apartment for a final confrontation with herself. In her transformation there will be no "drama," no "travesty," no public display. Divesting herself of her clothing in favor of stout shoes and slacks, she bundles her many wigs—"the very psalm of my life, as sung by somebody else," she says—and locks the door behind her with the keys deliberately inside, to face the future as a hobo. Whether she will "beg, steal, or wash dishes" she does not

know, since "circumstances must be [her] moral instruction." After dispersing her money among her clients as anonymous gifts, she settles under a viaduct, curls up next to another vagrant, shares her coat with him for warmth, and is "born."

Pervading the whole of "The Railway Police" is the ongoing identification of "the sterner exquisite I am to become" with her wigs and what they represent, through a series of references to earlier events. She has visited Bangkok to see the hairless monks, the shaven widows in mourning, and others bald merely to be sanitary. In a swimming pool, a man once tried to flirt by pulling off her bathing cap, only to fear he has accosted a nun. In her wig closet, 20 stylish coiffures in subtly varying hues are her secret coven, until 20 oval headshapes greet her in a multiple mirror-image when she has whipped away their stylish curls, "lyric abstracts of the human head, . . . one sad step away from art."

Calisher's assessment of art, or artifice, and its adversary as well as its alter-ego, life, or actuality, give "The Railway Police" its staggering power. No plot summary can convey the rich texture of her prose nor the way in which this novella is constructed, in execution as well as in effect. As the narrator proceeds to relate the chronological events from impetus to action, she interweaves her history, in the process offering deadly accurate illustrations of at least three social masquerades. First, the inequity of the sexes: the narrator's twin brother—their congenital baldness had begun at puberty—is a Hollywood sex symbol whose glamorous appeal lies entirely in his hairlessness, while hers must be disguised. Second, class distinctions: a kindly client she has called on warns her about bedbugs in the couch, saying, "Dun sit, dolling. Om afraid fom de boggles, dun sit dere." Yet on a last visit, when the narrator is on her way to her viaduct, the client willingly joins her, now a bald hobo, on the couch and confesses that she has known all along about the wigs. "It's no trick at all to come down in the world," the narrator ruefully observes. And third, aesthetics: her lover is ardent and intelligent, and he worships baldness in art, but a moment after she offers her bald skull to his lips, he shudders. Afterward he sends her a note: "Forgive me, . . . and forget me. I am a dilettante." "The Railway Police" draws its authority not only from such details but also from the narrator's voice. Calisher's locutions are often indirect and occasionally arch; a mandarin's calm pervades many of her novels and stories. Scenes potentially revulsive or hilarious are, instead, deeply moving. When first the narrator of "The Railway Police" offers herself to her lover without her wig, a moment toward which she has privately progressed with lethal humor to allay her apprehension, she observes that "Men know earlier and better than we what the razor can do and what it can't." "Art and life is it?" she asks after he has rejected her, "I had taught him the difference."

The novella concludes not with an end but with a beginning: "Come, you narks, cops, feds, dicks, railway police, members of the force everywhere! Run with us! If the world is round, who's running after who?" The narrator has rejected a kind of art in favor of a kind of life, but as she cannot know the future, she may well be anticipating an observation Calisher makes in *Herself,* a subsequent, autobiographical work: The "inner life" of her ego seems to her "a pilgrim still in progress, shedding fears like skins, which with age . . . may well form again. . . ." There is no authorial aside of this nature in "The Railway Police," but it is clearly felt throughout Calisher's remarkable fable.

—Bruce Kellner

———

THE RAINY MOON (La Lune de pluie)
by Colette, 1940

"La Lune de pluie" ("The Rainy Moon") was printed in 1940, along with "Chambre du hôtel" ("Hotel Room"), the title story of the collection. By then Colette was in her late sixties, but the story has many of the psychological and literary qualities that have made her famous. "The Rainy Moon" is a first-person narration, told with a passionate involvement that makes no secret of inviting the reader to identify the author and the narrator. In both the detailed and affectionate depiction of the Parisian scene and the deeply empathetic portrayal of woman's lot, there is much that is vintage Colette, especially in the way past and present are linked as a single continuous whole. The tale is, in fact, really little more than a situation, but there is a verbal brilliance in the presentation of three female characters, the creation of atmosphere, and the setting up of a most unusual situation, which is resolved in the laconic manner of classic short stories.

Set, like many of Colette's richest tales, in Paris in the earlier part of the 20th century, "The Rainy Moon" begins with the first encounter between the narrator, a woman of some experience who has been a relatively successful fiction writer, and Mademoiselle Rosita Barberet. She is younger and makes a meagre living by typing literary manuscripts. Oddly, Rosita currently occupies the same apartment where the narrator had spent her adolescence. The evocation of this strange, even slightly unsettling circumstance is masterly. We are told how the narrator responds to everything around her, whether in the street outside or inside the apartment; her hand, without thinking about it, will close around a doorknob, and her feet somehow seem to know their way down the stairs. Everything seems so familiar, yet she knows that much has changed. She feels locked out of part of what used to be hers and scarcely knows how to react. The narrator herself remarks that for her, as for many other writers such as Marcel Proust, "the past is a far more violent temptation than the craving to know the future." This leads her to look forward to future opportunities of calling on Rosita, and sometimes she does not hesitate to invent occasions for doing so. The desire grows within her to explore further her former home. In particular she wants to go into what used be to her bedroom, but Rosita seems most uneasy about permitting her to do so.

At last the narrator manages to have her way. What she discovers is that her old bedroom is currently being used by Rosita's sister, a pretty girl named Adèle who prefers, however, to be called by the more romantic name of Délia. She is ill, upset, and something of a recluse, and it is only little by little that the cause of her distress is explained. She is, in fact, married, but her husband has left her. Though the story moves slowly at this point, tension grows as we realise that just as the narrator had responded emotionally to the fact that the apartment was her old home, so too she becomes aware of the similarities between Délia's emotional predicament and the heart-breaking stresses and strains of her own experiences of love. In this tale of three lonely women, the non-appearance of men is a significant factor. The narrator tries in vain to cut herself off from the Barberet sisters; however, there is something that impels her to keep up the uneasy relationship.

The final phase of "The Rainy Moon" takes an unexpected direction. Rosita goes to see the narrator in her apartment. She is persuaded to have a drink and she talks of notions of witchcraft, of occult practices by which a rejected wife tries to wreak her revenge on an errant husband. The narrator, who is not unfamiliar with the séances that attracted some interest in the France of the Third Republic, is surprised, if not shocked. The crisp conclusion of the tale, however, is arresting.

Fascinating in its psychological insight, "The Rainy Moon," which takes its title from a strange effect caused by the play of light that produces a strange pattern on the wall when it streams in through the coarse glass in one of the window panes, is no less notable for the richness of Colette's verbal texture, which is, of course, here given a certain plausibility since the narrator is presented as being herself a writer. The basis of the story is the close observation of remembered reality, but to this is added a poetic delight in the evocative power of words which invests everything that is described with extraordinary life and vitality.

—Christopher Smith

———

RAPPACCINI'S DAUGHTER
by Nathaniel Hawthorne, 1844

"Rappaccini's Daughter" was first published in the *United States Magazine and Democratic Review* in 1844, entitled "Writings of Aubépine," with the interior title, "Rappaccini's Daughter." It first appeared in book form in *Mosses from an Old Manse* in 1846 under the title "Rappaccini's Daughter." It is prefaced with a humorous note in which Hawthorne explains that it is taken from the lengthy and tedious writings of M. de l'Aubépin (the French word for hawthorn). Aubépin's writings, given as comprising many volumes, have titles that are French translations of Hawthorne's own short stories.

This humorous introduction precedes a tale that is anything but humorous. It tells of Giovanni Guasconti, who comes from the south of Italy to study at the University of Padua. He finds lodgings overlooking a magnificent garden owned by Dr. Giacomo Rappaccini. As Giovanni looks into the garden, he sees the doctor, wearing his scholar's garb and thick gloves, tending his plants. Giovanni wonders whether he is looking into "the Eden of the present world." In the center of the garden stands a beautiful but poisonous purple shrub. Its poison is too great for Rappaccini to tend it himself, but his beautiful daughter, Beatrice, tends it without any form of protective covering and calls it her sister.

Eventually, Giovanni enters the garden, where he meets Beatrice. He is too shallow to fall in love with her, but he finds her very attractive. Still, he is wary of her, since he thinks he has seen her killing an insect with her breath and causing a bunch of flowers to wither at her touch.

Professor Pietro Baglioni is one of Giovanni's father's friends and a professional rival of Rappaccini. He fears that Rappaccini intends to replace him at the university with Rappaccini's own daughter. Baglioni detects a perfume in Giovanni's breath that he eventually associates with the poisons in Rappaccini's garden. He decides that both Giovanni and Beatrice have been made poisonous by Rappaccini, and he gives Giovanni an antidote.

On his way home from his interview with Baglioni, Giovanni buys flowers that he intends to give to Beatrice to see whether they really wither in her grasp. Instead, they wither in his grasp. When he discovers that his breath can kill a spider, he realizes that Baglioni was right: he also has become poisonous. He enters the garden, feeling and showing hatred for Beatrice, who feels and shows only love for him. When he tells her about the antidote, she takes it, asking him to wait to see its effects on her before taking any himself. Her father than approaches and says that he has blessed both Giovanni and Beatrice by giving them a marvelous gift which no human power or strength can withstand. Beatrice responds that she would rather have been loved than feared. She says to Giovanni, "Oh, was there not, from the first, more poison in thy nature than in mine," and dies. Rappaccini is "thunderstricken." Baglioni, who watches the whole scene from a window, calls out "in a tone of triumph mixed with horror": "Rappaccini! Rappaccini! and is *this* the upshot of your experiment!"

Critics compare Rappaccini to Aylmer in "The Birthmark" and Chillingworth in *The Scarlet Letter;* Rappaccini is Hawthorne's typical man of science, willing to sacrifice even his daughter for the sake of knowledge. He plays the role of creator in his garden. When toward the end of the story he approaches Giovanni and Beatrice, he grows "erect with conscious power" and spreads his hands over the two young people "in the attitude of a father imploring a blessing upon his children."

Baglioni also is a corrupt man of science who allows his jealousy of a rival to make him launch his own scientific experiment resulting in Beatrice's death. Hawthorne supplies no explanation of why, at the story's end, Baglioni would be at a window overlooking the garden or how long he has been there. That he should not be there, however, is obvious. His horrible, inappropriate words of triumph at the end of the story indicate that he also lacks concern for human life and feeling.

More important than Rappaccini and Baglioni are Beatrice and Giovanni. Early in the story, Hawthorne alludes to Dante. In *The Divine Comedy,* Beatrice leads Dante to heaven. Hawthorne's Beatrice could similarly lead Giovanni to a kind of heaven. She offers him true, unconditional love. But he is too shallow and self-centered to make the trip. Although he agrees to believe of Beatrice only what he hears from her own lips, he assumes that she has been involved in making him poisonous and that she is a vile, evil creature. His lack of commitment appears most forcefully as he stands back and allows Beatrice to try the antidote rather than taking it first himself.

"Rappaccini's Daughter" has been made into a one-hour movie as part of the American short story series produced for the Public Broadcasting System. The movie, filmed in Puerto Rico, has a beautiful setting but lacks the force and the multiple levels of meaning of the short story.

—Richard Tuerk

RASHOMON (Rashōmon)
by Akutagawa Ryūnosuke, 1917

During the summer of 1915, Akutagawa Ryūnosuke spent his time reading Gothic novels, including Matthew Lewis's *The Monk* and Mary Shelley's *Frankenstein*; the effects of his reading appear in his short story, "Rashomon," published in the November 1915 issue of *Teikoko Bungaku*, where he used the pseudonym Yanagawa Ryūnosuke for the last time. A year and a half later, Akutagawa also titled his first collection of short stories *Rashōmon*, published in May 1917.

About half of the more than one hundred stories Akutagawa wrote during his short life are indebted to earlier literary sources. "Rashomon" is based on an episode found in the *Konjaku*, an ancient collection of over one thousand folk tales and parables produced during the Heian Period (794-1184) and compiled in the Kamakura Period (1185-1333). Despite critics who label some of Akutagawa's stories "historical fiction," he does not attempt to document history faithfully. Although Akutagawa painted settings from a colorful spectrum of locations and time periods, while certainly an indication of how well read he was, they serve only as backdrops for close-up examinations of his themes, often focused on human frailties.

The dilapidated Rashomon, the two-storied south gate of Kyoto, presages many of the themes of Akutagawa's early story, "Rashomon." Set in Kyoto toward the end of the 12th century, Akutagawa chooses a period fraught with civil war. As feudalism developed, the Imperial court in Kyoto fell into obscurity. Also, religious thinkers of the time believed they were witnessing the final phase of Buddhism. Because Kyoto, once the capital city of Japan, had suffered so many natural disasters, "broken pieces of Buddhist images . . . were heaped up on roadsides to be sold as firewood" (from "Rashomon," translated by Takashi Kojima), as much an earth-to-earth image as the rain-induced erosion of the thick gate. Its former glory deemed unimportant, the neglected gate in the story signifies physical decay just as firewood made of Buddhas signifies spiritual decay. That the Rashomon serves as a hiding place for thieves and robbers as well as a dumping place for unclaimed corpses further emphasizes the story's theme of decay.

Akutagawa's tale opens on a chilly evening outside the crumbling gate on Sujaku Avenue. Surprised to find himself alone on a normally busy street, a recently unemployed servant tosses between thievery and starvation, an archetypal battle between body and spirit. As the weather becomes more violent, the thinly-dressed man enters the gate in search of shelter, the one provision the Rashomon still has to offer. Moving inside, where erosion's pace slows a little, the ex-servant finds "a broad lacquered stairway leading to the tower over the gate." Halfway up, he detects movement above, and fear of the unknown, so prevalent in the original version of this story, sets in. "He had expected only dead people inside the tower." He had not expected to be forced into a decision so soon.

Finally summoning enough courage to creep to the top of the stairs, he is met with a fragmented view of decomposing bodies, only some of them clothed. After stopping his nose from the stench, as straight a shot of *memento mori* as he can stomach, he catches sight of an old woman pulling hair out of the skull of a corpse. Still fearful but suddenly noble and angered by what he considers "an unpardonable crime," he questions the frightened woman, who explains that she uses the hair to make wigs. Disappointed by so earthly an explanation, the ex-servant's fear transforms into hatred. Sensing his contempt, the old woman claims as her defense that the previous owner of the hair, herself a dishonest vendor, would empathize with the old woman. The ex-servant mocks, "Are you sure?" She assents, and he, having made his choice at last, responds, "Then it's right if I rob you. I'd starve if I didn't." He then strips the old woman of her clothes, kicks her down onto the corpses, and flies off into the night.

Critics have called "Rashomon" a simple case of egoism, but the characters' sins are of varying degrees. While the old woman admittedly shows disrespect for the dead, she at least causes no harm to the living. Even the former owner of the hair can only be accused of selling dried snake as fish, a trade apparently not lucrative enough to keep her from dying while her hair was still black. But the servant's crime is worse: he targets the old woman like a crow targets road kill, and as a result, he looks small and cowardly.

After the ex-servant has "rushed down the steep stairs into the abyss of night," the naked woman drags herself to the top of the staircase and peers through her gray hair down to the bottom step: "beyond this was only darkness . . . unknowing and unknown." This final scene parallels the earlier one in which the young man had been frightened of the unknown as he entered the gate, yet the only thing he needs to fear is himself. The old woman, however, in spite of remaining relatively stationary throughout the story, fell in the path of danger and now looks with fright at the mysterious world outside the old gate.

Although "Rashomon" received no critical attention at the time of its publication, more recent critics have praised its precise style and see in it a foreshadowing of Akutagawa's later works. It is perhaps best known in the West as Akira Kurosawa's 1951 film *Rashomon*, which owes an even heavier debt to Akutagawa's 1921 short story, "In a Grove."

—Gretchen Thies

RAT SEMINAR (Seminário dos ratos)
by Lygia Fagundes Telles, 1977

Lygia Fagundes Telles has published four novels, and 14 books of short stories in four decades. In all these works, Telles discusses love, hatred, and life in the immediacy of death. The stories are usually set in several regions of Brazil. *Tigrela and Other Stories,* her only collection of short stories in English, has a sample of some of Telles's main themes.

"Seminário dos ratos" ("Rat Seminar"), the title story of a 1977 collection, is set in the politically repressive Brazil of the mid-1970's. The working metaphor here is "rats," functioning both as a source of danger and as a reminder that the silent, repressed masses can at any moment explode into revenge and political activity. In another short story, "The 'X' of the Problem," Telles also comments on a specific historical phenomenon, the enslavement of the people to a (malfunctioning) TV set. Here, however, the people are alienated, narcotized by the media, and will not take measures to change their situation.

In "Rat Seminar" the theme is corruption, involvement of foreigners—Americans—in internal affairs, and the fear the powerful feel of the repressed. In the beginning of the story, the narrator informs that there have been problems with the rodent population in the country: they are multiplying by the millions, despite all efforts to destroy them. A special office, RATESP, has been formed to coordinate the war against the rodents. Now in its seventh seminar, the RATESP members are gathered in an isolated country house especially restored for this purpose. Among the authorities gathered for the seminar is an American from Massachusetts, guest of the director of the Armed and Unarmed Forces. In the conversation that opens the story, the chief of Public Relations informs the secretary of Public and Private Welfare that the American is a specialist in rats and in electronic journalism. The secretary protests, "The rats are ours, the solutions have to be ours. Why demonstrate our flaws to everybody else?" The American, he says, will "go tooting his horn all over."

Foreign interference in internal affairs is but one of the problems: even the secretary is afraid his telephone has been bugged. Of course the American is the first suspect: "Wherever these people are, there's always a cursed tape recorder." They drop the subject, exactly because they are afraid somebody is listening to them.

At one point of the conversation, the secretary asks the chief if he has heard something, a sound that gets "louder and softer . . . in waves, like the sea." The chief says that he hasn't heard anything. The secretary then remarks that he hears too well, and then relates an episode during the Revolution of '32, when he was the first one in his group to sense the approach of enemies.

The noise disappears, and the conversation continues with the chief commiserating to the secretary about his gout. The chief says, "It could be a drop of water! It could be a drop of water!" Here Telles is playing with two levels of signification. On one level, there is the play between the Portuguese word "gota," which means both "drop" and "gout." But it also refers to Chico Buarque de Holanda's protest song, "Gota d'água," very popular in Brazil in the mid-1970's. When the chief excuses himself by saying that this is merely a song people sing, the secretary retorts that "the people are nothing but an abstraction."

The contrast between the living conditions of the starving population and that of those in power is immediate. For the authorities gathered for the seminar, the dinner will be lobster and Chilean wine. Obviously, only a wine from a country under an even more repressive regime is above suspicion. Pinochet's name is mentioned affectionately.

Things begin to happen quickly: the rats, which by now have chewed the wires of telephones and cars wires, invade the whole house. The chief only escapes death because he barricades himself inside the refrigerator. When he finally leaves it, the house is completely destroyed, the food eaten, the furniture broken. Not an abstraction or background noise anymore, the rats themselves are now holding their own seminar in the Conference Room. There are no other humans to be seen.

In this story, Telles uses an element of the uncanny to represent other tensions. Death is a common theme in her stories, in this case, it is the death of a political regime: the corrupt old order is replaced by another, now composed by those who were previously threatened with extermination.

—Eval Paulino Bueno

A RECLUSE
by Walter de la Mare, 1930

The reader of de la Mare's short stories is never likely to forget that they are the work of a considerable poet. His stories are as exactly shaped as his poems; they deal, very often, with the same tricks of atmosphere and mood that characterise the poems. Like the poems, the best stories are simultaneously precise and nebulous, both exactly solid and teasingly ethereal. "A Recluse" (collected in *On the Edge,* 1930), one of de la Mare's finest stories, is all of these things. It fuses the humdrum and the extraordinary in a remarkable tale of terror—terror made all the more menacing by the insistent obliquity of the narrative, and by the number of questions left unanswered.

In outline the story is simple. The narrator, Mr. Dash, reads in *The Times* an advertisement for the sale of a house (Montrésor) and is reminded of an experience he had there. He recounts his adventure: he stopped his car to look at what he thought was an empty house, was tricked into spending the night there by its solitary occupant, Mr. Bloom, and discovered his host to be a spiritualist whose experiments took him beyond the "edge" (an important word in the story). Mr. Bloom produced phenomena that induced the narrator to make an early morning flight from the house, driving his car away at speed, absurdly dressed in "a purple dressing-gown and red morocco slippers," which he has borrowed from another occupant of Montrésor, lately dead. The materials are those of many a lesser ghost story. This, however, is no ordinary ghost story, and its special character resides as much as anything in the exactness and evocativeness of de la Mare's language.

The story might be said to begin with the narrator's reaction not just to the advertisement in *The Times,* but to the linguistic idiom of that advertisement. Montrésor is described as "imposing," and as a "singularly charming freehold Residential Property." It is the idiom of the stable, middle-class commercial world; it expresses a world view that was perhaps that of the narrator prior to his adventure at this very house. Prior to his encounter with Mr. Bloom, we meet the narrator climbing into his "cosy two seater." There is smugness in the false poeticism with which he presents himself and his car: "a lime-tree bower her garage was." Later, however, he is no longer able to feel so confident of the kind of certainties that the language of the estate agent so complacently articulates. As he proceeds to tell his remarkable story, moving into more questionable areas of experience, the narrator's language more and more effectively creates the sense of the unexplained (and perhaps inexplicable) and the uneasy. A dense texture of allusion and reiterated images draws us into a world more mysterious and nearly ineffable than the journalistic idiom can encompass.

Relatively early in his dealings with Mr. Bloom, the narrator confidently, and contemptuously, dismisses the whole world of spiritualism as a silly and dangerous waste of time. By the end of his experiences at Montrésor he feels that his earlier objections "seemed now to have been grotesquely inadequate." His realisation now is that "this house was not haunted, it was infested." But infested with quite what? That remains essentially unknowable. The narrator knows not what kind of company it was that shared Mr. Bloom's "charming house" (that such a phrase should thus recur in the closing sentences of the story is piece of malevolent irony). He can only comment that "here edges in the obscure problem of what the creatures of our thoughts, let alone our dreams, are 'made on.'" The Shakespearean allusion (to Prospero's speech in act IV of *The Tempest*) recognizes the essential insubstantiality of human life itself and implicitly raises questions about the nature of any after life: "We are such stuff/ As dreams are made on; and our little life/ Is rounded with a sleep." Earlier, the narrator has reminded us of one of Hamlet's most famous soliloquies in talking of that "'other side's' borderline from which, according to the poet, no traveller returns" (*Hamlet,* III.i). For Hamlet the "other side" may be an "undiscovered country"; for Mr. Bloom it is a country from which he is unable wholly to escape. Mr. Bloom asserts that "there are deeps, and vasty deeps": the echo this time is of Glendower's claim in *Henry IV* part I (III.i): "I can call spirits from the vasty deep." It will be remembered that the claim prompts a rejoinder from Hotspur: "Why, so can I, or so can any man, / But will they come when you do call for them?" The spirits have certainly come when Mr. Bloom has called them; now, however, they come uninvited, and their entry cannot be refused. It is as a defence, in his solitude, against the inhabitants of that "other" country that Mr. Bloom so much desires to detain the narrator.

In presenting Mr. Bloom and his house (and the two are frequently identified metaphorically, in the best traditions of the supernatural tale), de la Mare is concerned that we should see both of them as being simultaneously of the utmost physical solidity and yet characterised by an ominous vacancy. Their physicality—especially in the case of Mr. Bloom—is not enough, of itself, to make them altogether real. Earlier, when faced with the "ordinary" presence of Mr. Bloom, the narrator is moved to question the very nature of things: "What made him so extortionately substantial, and yet in effect, so elusive and unreal? What indeed constitutes the *reality* of any fellow creature." "The Recluse" is perhaps best seen not merely as a tale of the supernatural but as yet another of those meditations on metaphysical problems that are to be found everywhere, irrespective of genre, in de la Mare's work.

—Glyn Pursglove

THE RED PONY
by John Steinbeck, 1937

John Steinbeck's *The Red Pony* is a series of four vignettes dealing with the young boy Jody during his formative years on his father's California ranch. Each story focuses on a specific aspect of Jody's passage from childhood to the threshold of adulthood.

In the opening story, "The Gift," Jody at one point gazes at the ranch from a nearby hill and feels "an uncertainty in the air, a feeling of change and of loss and the gain of new and unfamiliar things." And as this story and the succeeding three unfold, change is the central theme. The gift is a red pony colt that Carl Tiflin, Jody's father, gives him. Naming him Gabilan, Jody devotes every spare moment he has to the colt and his welfare. On a cold day in the fall the pony is left in the corral and gets soaked by rain. Although Billy Buck, the ranch hand who is an expert with horses, assures Jody that rain can't really hurt a horse, the pony does take cold. Billy Buck and Jody desperately work to save the pony, but one morning they find that the pony has escaped from the barn. Searching frantically, Jody finds the dying pony surrounded by buzzards. Plunging into their circle, he grabs one by the neck, holds it to the ground, and smashes it with a piece of quartz.

In this story Jody learns that Billy Buck, a man in whom he had the greatest confidence, like all human beings is not infallible. He also learns that in nature's scheme of things, one cannot always wreak vengeance on a principal cause. Carl Tiflin explains to him that the buzzards did not kill the pony. "I know it," Jody responds wearily.

The second story, "The Great Mountains," is about an old man named Gitano, who was born on the land now comprising the Tiflin ranch. He has returned to his roots to die. Carl Tiflin's reaction, however, is barely hospitable as he offers the man a meal and a night's sleep in the bunkhouse, telling him that he should not come to die with strangers. Curious youngster that he is, Jody engages Gitano in conversation. He is particularly intrigued when he learns that as a child the old man had gone into the mountains with his father—an area that Jody has always wanted to see. The boy also learns that Gitano's prize possession is a "lean and lovely rapier with a golden basket hilt . . . pierced and intricately carved." To Jody's questions about the origin of the rapier, Gitano says that he doesn't know, that he just keeps it. Jody realizes at this point that he must never tell anyone about the rapier. "It would," he realizes, "be a dreadful thing to tell anyone about it, for it would destroy some fragile structure of truth." Although he may not be able to verbalize such a truth, Jody has reached another level in his growth from child to adult. And when Gitano takes an old horse from the ranch and rides off into the mountains, Jody lies down in the grass near the brush line, covers his eyes with his arms, and is "full of a nameless sorrow."

In "The Promise" Jody gets the chance to have a colt of his own. After the mare Nellie is bred, the youngster waits impatiently for the birth of his colt. When that time finally arrives, however, Billy Buck recognizes that something is terribly wrong. The colt is turned wrong, and Billy has no choice but to kill Nellie with a hammer blow to the head and cut a gaping hole in her stomach to bring the colt out. With his face and arms dripping blood, Billy lays the colt at Jody's feet, whispering, "There's your colt. I promised. There it is. I had to do it—had to." As Jody goes for hot water and a sponge, "the tired eyes of Billy Buck hung in the air ahead of him." Jody recognizes here that adults too can feel a sense of loss, just as he himself did at the earlier loss of his pony.

The last story, "The Leader of the People," focuses on the visit of Jody's maternal grandfather, whose biggest experience in life was leading a group of emigrants west in days long past. In response to her husband's complaint that all the old man does is talk of this experience, Mrs. Tiflin says, "That was the big thing in father's life. He led a wagon train clear across the plains to the coast and when it was finished, his life was done. It was a big thing to do, but it didn't last long enough." Jody, of course, is eager to hear his grandfather's stories, and it is to the boy that the old man can express his true feelings. It is not the stories themselves that are his main concern, but the way he wants

people to feel about them—the whole idea of "westering." "We carried life out there," he says, "and set it down like those ants carry eggs. And I was the leader." To Jody's comment that perhaps some day he too could lead the people, his grandfather replies, "There's no place to go. There's the ocean to to stop you." He goes on to say that westering has died out of the people, that there is no hunger for it anymore. And again Jody feels the pain of sadness and loss.

Taken in chronology, these stories cover approximately three years in the life of Jody Tiflin—each representing a new stage in his maturation. His parents play only a secondary role in this process. Of primary importance are Billy Buck, Gitano, and his grandfather. Through his relationships with these men Jody moves from a naive and somewhat selfish child to a person who has a glimmer of understanding of the sense of accomplishment and of loss that is so much a part of human existence. He learns that one cannot really count on anything in the natural course of events, that death is as much a part of life as is the living of that life, and that love may be defined in various ways.

—Wilton Eckley

THE RED-BACKED SPIDERS
by Peter Cowan, 1958

Peter Cowan was born in Western Australia in 1914 and has lived and worked there all his life. A regional writer, he carefully mines the same territory in his stories in ever more reticent ways. His primary interest is in the outback to the north of Perth where, as he says, "there are stretches of quite pitiless but utterly attractive landscape." His stories are dominated by barren landscapes that dwarf the few isolated human figures who dwell among them. Although he has written two novels and several biographical and historical works, his sparse, almost minimalist prose, influenced by Hemingway especially in his early collections, is best suited to the demands of the short story. The development of his work over many years is towards silence, truncation, the almost entire elimination of words themselves.

"The Red-Backed Spiders," from his second collection *The Unploughed Land*, is one of the most representative stories from his early period. The setting is typical, a small, isolated, infertile farm, a place of "indifferent soil and slow yields, [of] quiet and total involvement that was imprisonment," on which live a farmer, his wife, and two children. The action is observed by a sharp-eyed itinerant worker, who is reluctant to become involved in the tensions among the family. However, violence is never far from the surface in Cowan's world, and the narrator becomes reluctantly involved. "The Red-Backed Spiders" opens with the farmer striking his daughter while the wife anxiously urges the narrator not to intervene.

With a kind of generous but helpless understanding, the narrator recognises the tension that is apparent in every one of the farmer's gestures, the blows, the impatient jerking of the reins of his horse, his quick, jerky walk, the "constant irritability that was part of his make-up." He recognises, too, that although the two women have turned away from the man, the boy is still in need of some kind of understanding and communication: "He was trying to look into an adult world that simply did not hold meaning for him."

The boy himself is a common figure in Cowan's fiction, a kind of artist in the way that his imagination reveals itself in the superb castle he makes out of old jam tins and meat cans. Because red-backed spiders (one of Australia's few venomous species) could be found among the jam tins, the man had forbidden his son to play with them. In one of the story's few climactic moments, the man strides towards the boy, kicks the castle down, and then hits him across the head and kicks him. The violence and frustration are very simply categorised by the narrator: "If an animal went like that you would shoot it." That evening the man himself is bitten by a spider and taken to hospital.

Cowan's stories work, like most short stories, by understatement and oblique suggestion. The implication at the end seems to be that the boy caused his father to be bitten (the narrator had seen him carrying tins towards the house) and that the father, finally recognising his son's hatred and the futility of his own life, allowed himself to die. There is a strong element of fatalism in Cowan's work: "I realized how it must have come to the man, how he must have seen it all then with a sudden clearness, how this had happened, and beyond this, to the way it had all become set so there was no changing of anything, and he had had no strength and knew it was no use to go on." When the narrator sees the man being comforted by his wife as he drives them towards the hospital, he realises that there must have been a period earlier in their lives when things were different.

By the standards of Cowan's later work, "The Red-Backed Spiders" is overwritten and too heavily explanatory but it movingly conveys the desolation of the lives of the four people, the intimidating effect the landscape has on them, and the barrenness of a world in which a dump, used tins, and venomous spiders can become a child's favourite toys. The women, as often in Cowan's fiction, are hardly glimpsed, but in the child's desperate act of revenge he suggests the same tensions that led to the creation of the magnificently improvised castle. "The Red-Backed Spiders" is a story that suggests the influence of Raymond Carver, but in a uniquely Australian setting.

—Laurie Clancy

REDEMPTION
by John Gardner, 1981

Of the 19 stories in John Gardner's two published collections, *The King's Indian* (1974) and *The Art of Living* (1981), "Redemption" remains the most potent and memorable. Perhaps not accidentally, it is also the most personal and direct, least given to the sort of metafiction fireworks often on display in its companion pieces, as well as in the bulk of Gardner's virtuoso novels.

"Redemption," which originally appeared in *The Atlantic Monthly* (May 1977), processes a traumatic event from the author's rural childhood handled less successfully by "Stillness" (1975), also in *The Art of Living*. Age eleven at the time, Gardner was driving a tractor home, younger sister in his lap, younger brother astride a bar yoking the tractor to a two-ton cultipacker, when the tractor suddenly shuddered to a stop from lack of gas. His brother fell off the bar and under the cultipacker, dying almost instantly.

There seems to have been little that Gardner could have done to save his brother, but natural guilt intensified over the years, sharpening the author's always keen ethical focus. In "Redemption" as first tracked by John M. Howell, the actual incident is altered to deepen young Gardner's responsibility (and hence his moral dilemma). Named Jake Hawthorne, probably as a spur to recall the original-sin context of Nathaniel Hawthorne's Puritan allegories, the protagonist recollects the event with near masochistic clarity: "Even at the last moment he could have prevented his brother's death by slamming on the tractor's brakes . . . but he was unable to think, or, rather, thought unclearly."

The story's initial concentration is on the father, limned as a genial, sensitive, intelligent man with a talent for writing and reciting poetry, "a celebrity, in fact, as much Romantic poet-hero as his time and western New York State could afford," who takes to suicidal broodings, aimless motorcycle trips, and a string of casual adulteries in the wake of his son's death. His ironic "redemption," coming home to kneel and receive tearful forgiveness from a willing family, contrasts acutely to Jake's lonely self-savagings, but Jake's whispered "I hate you" is unheard by his father and the rest of the family.

The complexity of Jake's response, accusing himself of a monstrous evil, then projecting himself in his fantasies as a noble sufferer, which causes further self-castigation, drills to the hard heart of the tale's obsession with the artist figure—a modernist leit motif woven through most of Gardner's playfully postmodernist fictions. It also abets a familiar Shakespearean doubling device as Jake seeks solace through learning the French horn (a mother's gift) and comes under the sway of the sort of father surrogate 20th-century scepticism loves to supply as a priest's replacement: arrogant Arcady Yegudkin, principal horn player in the Czar's own orchestra before the Russian Revolution sent him across the ocean.

Yegudkin is the kind of artist character Gardner tended to push into mythic, shaman extremes—as done with Taggert Hodge in *The Sunlight Dialogues* (1972), for example—but realistic restraint governs here to good effect. Although suitably outlandish in his affectations, which included arriving every Saturday morning to give lessons "like some sharp-eyed old Slavonic king" and being "one of the last men in Rochester, New York, to wear spats," the 70-year-old refugee stays within the realistic boundaries of the story. At the climactic moment, testing a new horn, he gives a brilliant performance that causes the stunned hero to blurt out, "You think I'll ever play like that?"

Yegudkin's incredulous, equally thoughtless response ("Play like *me*?") thuds home like Abraham's knife, leaving the shaken Jake at the edge of extinction, the extinction haunting him since his brother's death. Recognizing the terrible truth of Yegudkin's assessment of his aesthetic limitations, he is dazed and weeping as he heads home through a crowd of "Saturday-morning shoppers herding along irritably, meekly, through painfully bright light."

The power of the ending resides in Gardner's uncharacteristic refusal to let sentiment soften the cruel ambiguity of his alter-ego's situation. If "home" is a key word, faintly intimating possible salvation, it is undercut by the mocking image of a "herd" of "meek" Christian souls dominating an indifferent earth and the apparent dearth of any firm positive alternative to the loss of art's redemptive potential. Lack of genius in a universe where talent, not virtue, reigns supreme seems to leave scant room for imagination's magic. There is, in other words, no redemption, except for the author of the story in being able to write with such bleak precision about a private agony.

In contrast to *The Art of Living*'s title story, similarly convincing in regional texture but overburdened by conscious design, a forced sense of arty poignancy, the resonance achieved by "redemption" stems from the harsh absence of an overt ethical grid. Jake's return to the street, to brute life and "home," offers a possible reprise of Gilgamesh's return to kingly duties after banishing the ghost of Enkidu (best friend and self's animal half) in the Sumerian epic Gardner translated (with John Maier). Furthermore, home offers the healing female forces of mother and sister, the child who brought him lunch when he was working in the field and incarnated life's simpler gifts.

Like literature and its creators, "Redemption" thus spirals inward to replicate the process of enduring an existence stained foul by mortality and a lost godhead, which guarantees its own survival.

—Edward Butscher

REGRET FOR THE PAST (Shang shi)
by Lu Xun, 1925

"Shang shi" ("Regret for the Past"), collected in *Pang Huang (Wandering)* in 1925, is one of Lu Xun's best stories, with a lyric élan rare among modern Chinese writings. When compared with the author's other stories, which are often satirical rather than sentimental, this one seems to have a peculiar appeal in its indulgence for human foibles, but its treatment of the pathetic elements of life and the tragic aspects of love remains uncompromising from start to finish. The tone is chastening and dark with premonitions of doom.

Told in the first-person-central point of view, the story is a confession of the protagonist, Juansheng, containing little dialogue but much reminiscence and soul-searching. Some critics, notably Lyell and Lee, tend to downplay or ignore the significance of this confession, yet there is no denying that the intensity of Juansheng's remorse somewhat redeems his guilt: "If only there really were a hell! . . . In the whirlwind and flames I would put my arms round Zijun and ask her pardon or let her take her revenge!" Therefore, the author's attitude is not unsympathetic. Instead of ironically exposing the protagonist as mean and silly in a cool and aloof style, Lu Xun seems not so detached, as can be seen in the narrative prose which takes on an earnest, passionate glitter. Another engaging element about this story lies in the haunting picture it invariably presents to the reader: two lonely lovers moving against a desolate background, fighting not only tradition and other people, but each other, while despair closes in on them.

The story successfully evokes the ambience of Beijing during the 1920's, one of the darkest periods in the long history of China. This period was a time when ordinary people lived under numerous restrictions, as suggested by the repeated image of a bird in a narrow cage forgetting how to flap its wings. As we are told in the story, "man's place in nature" is only somewhere "between the dog and the chicks." The chicks, which cannot survive the destitution of the family, are symbolic of Zijun; and the dog, deserted like Zijun, symbolizes the homeless Juansheng.

The 1920's was also a time when honest people could barely eke out a precarious living by hard work, and a time when a discharge slip was almost tantamount to a death sentence. Superior knowledge or better education did not help one land a decent job, because what really mattered was *who* one knew and not *what* one knew. Both Juansheng and Zijun are members of the younger, better-educated generation, a new breed in the wake of the May Fourth Movement of 1919, yet their knowledge of Western literature and foreign languages is more of a liability than an asset, turning them into liberals spurned by their contemporaries.

Zijun's case seems even more desperate. When she says, "We can make a fresh start," she knows deep in her heart that this is just a false hope. Because she is a woman, the burdens of tradition and old customs are especially heavy on her. For all her courage in cutting her hair short and cohabitating with the man she loves, she cannot free herself entirely from "the trammels of old ideas." For instance, she feels embarrassed to look at a picture of the English poet Shelley because he is male, although he died more than a century ago, and she never tries to find a job because a decent girl is not supposed to work. Thus, after being "disowned" by her uncle and jilted by her lover in Beijing, she has no other choice but to be "taken away" by her father who comes, presumably, from a much more conservative city or village. It is understandable that Zijun, susceptible as she is, cannot survive such a rigid, uncongenial milieu, because her father and other people would certainly regard her as a shameless "hussy" deserted by a reckless villain, a much worse position than that of a jilted wife: "What a fearful thing it is . . . , walking . . . one's path in life amid cold looks and blazing fury! This path ends, moreover, in nothing but a grave without so much as a tombstone." Though the cause of her sudden death is not mentioned, it must be suicide.

Unlike Zijun, Juansheng manages to avoid the impending doom by virtue of what may be called his survivalism. In his opinion, "the first thing in life is to make a living." He would jettison everything else in order to survive: the chicks are served for food at his "insistence," the dog abandoned, and even a "clean break" with Zijun is sought because "all she could do was cling to someone else's clothing, making it hard for even a fighter to struggle, and bringing ruin on both." Survive he does, only to learn too late what a selfish coward he is. This kind of self-knowledge is often hard to come by. In Juansheng's case its price is terribly high: he loses Zijun and her love. He can obtain self-knowledge only through an agonizing, futile journey in which he moves out of the hostel with Zijun in search of happiness and moves back to it alone, in great distress. He eventually realizes that it is selfishness and timidity rather than honesty that prompted him to tell Zijun he did not love her any more. He learns too late that he mistook Zijun's intrepidity for an ability to take care of herself after their separation, and it never occurs to him, while he is taking refuge in the public library, how lonely and cold Zijun must feel, being left home alone in a loveless, heatless room. He does not understand what is love or how to love. Compared with him, Zijun appears noble and brave, capable of sacrificing herself for love at any cost, completely fearless and impervious to people's "sarcastic smiles or lewd and contemptuous glances." If Juansheng feels that the way he proposed to her is laughable and even "contemptible," to her it is no joke—love is too serious a matter to be joked about. While Juansheng insists that a man must make a living before there can be any place for love, Zijun could argue that without love, life is not worth living. When her father comes to take her away, she "solemnly" leaves all their worldly goods ("salt, dried chili, flour, half a cabbage, and a few dozen coppers") for Juansheng to eke out his existence "a little longer." It is apparent that, heartbroken as she is, still she loves him.

With Zijun gone, nothing remains but emptiness for Juansheng. The only way for him to make a fresh start is through confession, and the first step is to record his remorse and grief for Zijun's sake as well as for his own. This record turns out to be a superb story of tragic love. Indeed, nowhere else does Lu Xun brood more darkly over the themes of love versus existence and sacrifice versus selfishness, and nowhere else in modern Chinese literature do we find a young couple so desperate in their struggle to survive and so alienated from society.

—Sherwin S.S. Fu

THE RESERVOIR
by Janet Frame, 1963

First published in *The New Yorker* in 1963, "The Reservoir" became the title story of one volume of a two-volume set of short fiction that Janet Frame published the same year. The subtitle of the volume, *Stories and Sketches*, set it off from the other volume in the set, *Snowman, Snowman*, which was subtitled *Fables and Fantasies*, and indicated that these works were not in Frame's more allegorical or fabular mode. Thus the story can be read, at least on an initial level, as an example of Frame's relatively literal mode, both in its world and in its method.

The story's world of "Ohau" in Otago, South Island, New Zealand, is recognisably based on Oamaru, Frame's "Kingdom by the Sea" as later described in the first volume of her autobiography. *To the Is-Land*. The story is about an outing by the children in a family during the long hot summer of an infantile paralysis epidemic. The outing is ostensibly an exploration of "their" creek, but it turns into an expedition to the forbidden reservoir, the source of the creek. The expedition is successful; the children see the reservoir and then flee home in fright. They do not tell their parents where they have been, finding them in their repeated prohibitions "out of date" and "actually afraid."

This simple, literal story is told by an appropriate method to capture the impressions of the children. The narration is from a first person point of view, retrospective in its use of the past tense, but put back into a child's way of seeing. The "I" often becomes "we," for the narrator is speaking for all of the children in the family. Her style incorporates elements of the language of the children, with something of their idiom and their images (the wild sweet peas by the creek are "boiled-lolly pink," the moths come in the windows "with their bulging lamplit eyes moving through the dark and their grandfather bodies knocking, knocking upon the walls"). The children's experience is caught very well in this way—their sense of endless time, of mysterious space; their fears, excitement, and sense of promise and menace; their games, dares, rhymes, and mispronunciations.

Thus the story is a very successful evocation of a literal childhood experience. However, it is more than that. While it is not a parable or an allegory, it does resonate with meaning beyond itself. The reservoir and the journey to it are associated with geographical distance ("the end of the world"), with mysterious technology (the water is "treated" with chemicals "to dissolve the dead bodies and prevent the decay of teeth"), with sex (the courting couples lying down in the long grass by the creek), and with loneliness (the sighing pine trees and the owls). The narrator's mental image for it is "a bundle of darkness and great wheels which peeled and sliced you like an apple and drew you toward them with demonic force." It is associated with disease (a boy who defied the ban on going there contracted infantile paralysis) and with death by drowning, while at the same time it is the mysterious source that controls the flow of the creek. It comes to represent to the children all the mysterious and partially known aspects of adult life that they will have to face, but not yet: "We would some day visit the Reservoir, but the time seemed almost as far away as leaving school, getting a job, marrying." When they do see the reservoir, it seems to represent in its "wonderful calm and menace" fears that are already there in their unconscious: "In the Reservoir there was an appearance of neatness which concealed a disarray too frightening to be acknowledged except, without any defence, in moments of deep sleep and dreaming."

Thus the reservoir and the journey to it assume an archetypal suggestiveness, and the simple story of a childhood adventure becomes suggestive of a journey of initiation into the mysteries and terrors of adult existence. The children's feeling of superiority to their frightened parents at the end becomes both understandable and ironic, for the reader knows as the children do not that this is just a preliminary foray out of the "cowslip's bell" of childhood and into the truly frightening adult world where "owls do cry," the world that they are doomed to inhabit. Not a parable or allegory, yet the story is more than a piece of literal impressionism, and it resonates with the primary themes of Janet Frame's fiction—death, time, and the plight of conscious human beings in an unconscious universe; social conditioning, and the plight of the sensitive individual in a conformist society.

—Lawrence Jones

THE RETURN OF A PRIVATE
by Hamlin Garland, 1891

Hamlin Garland, who believed that the American artist's responsibility was to find a form and content original to American experience, realized his literary ideals in the collection *Main-Travelled Roads*. Determined to avoid hackneyed traditional themes, he rejected the myth of idyllic agrarianism and portrayed farm life as harsh, unjust, and spirit-killing. At the same time, he could not adopt a strictly naturalistic vision of humans degraded and made powerless by their environment. His characters, although worn by their struggle, nevertheless persevere and even have brief moments of grandeur in which their humanity rises above their condition.

"The Return of a Private," collected in *Main-Travelled Roads*, is typical of Garland's artistic vision. In many respects a grim story, it shows a common Civil War soldier, significantly named Private Smith, who has survived the ravages of war only to return to a life of physical hardship and economic injustice on his Wisconsin farm. Mixed with the harshness of the portrait, however, is the tenderness of his fellow veterans toward him and his joy in being reunited with his wife and three young children.

A populist and reformer, Garland first published "The Return of a Private" in *Arena*, a journal of radical political thought. He objected to the injustices of economic policies toward mid-Western farmers. In fact, Joseph B. McCullough argues that *Main-Travelled Roads* accurately describes the frustrations over farm conditions that led to the populist revolt in the 1890's. "The Return of a Private" strikes a populist theme in contrasting the generosity of the private with the stinting behavior of the rich: "While the millionaire sent his money to England for safe-keeping, this man, with his girl-wife and three babies, left them on a mortgaged farm, and went away to fight for an idea."

William Dean Howells noted the political stance of the story in his introduction to *Main-Travelled Roads*, calling it "a satire of the keenest edge." Indeed, the beginning of the story bitterly contrasts the soldiers' return with their departure for the war three years before. Now there are no crowds or bands playing, only the indifferent looks of the town loafers. This indifference is juxtaposed with a careful description of the price Private Smith and his fellow soldiers have paid for their country. They are variously pale from long bouts with illness, scarred, or limping. All are emaciated. Besides the physical costs exacted, Smith is emotionally scarred by the memory of a young friend's gruesome death in battle. Another of the veterans is returning to an empty house. His wife died from pneumonia contracted as she worked in the fields in the rain.

Garland's aroused sense of justice is also evident as he describes the financial doom awaiting the private: "the inevitable mortgage [stood] ready with open jaw to swallow half his earnings." While Smith sacrificed at the war, no one looked out for his wife, his young children, or his farm. In fact, an unscrupulous renter absconded with some farm machinery and a neighbor put the Smiths' crops at risk as he tended to his own welfare first.

Whereas a naturalist might have shown the Smiths devolving into degraded conduct as a result of their plight, Garland belonged to what Jane Johnson has called "the gentler school of realism." Even among the bitterest scenes of suffering, he might include redeeming moments of human triumph. Reminiscent of Walt Whitman's democratic vision of the common soldier in the "Drum Taps" section of *Leaves of Grass*, the generic Private Smith and men like him emerge as the true heroes of the war. To his son, Smith's return is "epic," and his honorable conduct a valued family heritage. This is apparently what Garland means when he insists that the American artist find among the common lives of Americans inspiration for his art. At the end of the story, Private Smith is transformed into an archetypal common hero; "his figure looms vast . . . he rises into a magnificent type."

Garland termed his artistic technique "veritism." While it relies on realistic accuracy in creating the external world, it also insists on the writer's adding to that superficial creation his sense of moral truth. The description of the gaunt private might be enough for the realist, but the veritist is compelled to add the private's transformation into an archetypal hero according to the artist's inner conviction of the basic goodness of the common person. Influenced by Whitman, Garland coupled with realism a form of romantic individualism that raised his common characters above their environment, even if only temporarily.

In *Main-Travelled Roads*, the metaphor of the road is used as what one critic calls the "structural center" of the book. According to Garland's headnote, the road is "long and wearyful" and "it is traversed by many classes of people, but the poor and the weary predominate." In "The Return of a Private," the weary soldier literally returns on a road, and his wife looks anxiously down it for him. But the road also functions as a metaphor for the difficult lives led by the Smiths. When the emaciated private reaches the top of a ridge overlooking the valley of his home, the narrator suggests, "He is looking down upon his own grave." The road, then, evokes in a single, concrete image the pain and struggle and the harshness and sublimity of the common person's destiny. Moreover, the road seems a particularly apt metaphor to represent Garland's philosophy and its differences with naturalism. It suggests a quietly paced inevitability that leads characters to their destinies naturally. Although the paths can be bitterly difficult and wear one down, characters choose those paths, rather than being driven down them by inexorable forces. Garland insists on his characters' free choice and on their grace under duress. Their individualism ennobles them even in the midst of harsh conditions.

—William L. Howard

REVELATION
by Flannery O'Connor, 1965

In "Revelation," Flannery O'Connor juxtaposes humor and tragedy, inverts traditional assumptions about the judging of individuals to be good or bad, exaggerates certain characteristics of the people she creates, indirectly expresses her belief that only those humble enough to ask forgiveness can receive spiritual grace and goodness, and focuses on a single character in need of a revelation about self, others, and God—a divine alert that may come in time or may not and that may be accepted by the targeted individual or may not.

She develops the story in four scenes. The first in a doctor's office and the last in a pig parlor are the most dramatic, while the other two offer brief transitional glimpses of Mrs. Turpin to detect a very gradual change in her during her day-long struggle with humiliation, physical pain, anger, and fear. O'Connor's succinct descriptions of even minor characters make them unforgettable.

Avoiding an introduction or opening frame, O'Connor thrusts the reader at once into a volatile situation where fires are already smoldering. The reader will understand from watching and responding as an eye witness while the action unfolds and cannot distance himself or herself emotionally from it. From the first sentence, Mrs. Turpin, the prideful owner (with her husband, Claud) of a modernized hog farm and unsuspecting that she is in danger of losing her soul because of her arrogance, commands attention as she enters the doctor's tiny waiting room and "looms" over the magazine table in the center of the crowded space. Large and self-assured, she scrutinizes the lesser people and waits impatiently for one to rise politely and offer a seat to this imposing newcomer.

The story seems at first to be only a comical satire on human foibles. We laugh easily at Turpin's amusing games—for example, as she methodically establishes in a moment the status of the folk in the waiting room by observing the shoes each wears: the stylish red and grey pumps of the "pleasant lady"; the Girl Scout shoes and ankle socks of the "ugly girl," a college student afflicted with severe acne; Mrs. Turpin's own high-quality black pumps; the white-trashy woman's tennis shoes; and the bedroom slippers worn by the grandmother of the little boy with a runny nose. But the tone of the satire shifts radically as the appearance of a black delivery boy moves the conversation in the room to the issue of all blacks being sent to Africa and Turpin's notion that it would be easier to send them north to New York to "improve" their color through intermarriage. Turpin's insomniac's game that places each person in order—with blacks at the bottom and white rich owners of land at the top—brings O'Connor's strongest indictment as she links it with Hitler's cramming less desirable people into box cars. Class discrimination and racial hatred pervade the conversation of the women in the room, as does each one's attempt to establish her own status or respectability. While Mrs. Turpin boasts of her fine pig parlor, the "white-trashy woman" insists that she is above such things as raising pigs, because they stink. Only the "ugly girl" refuses to enter the conversation and glares in hostile silence. (Ironically, she is the daughter of the woman Turpin has named the "stylish lady" or the "pleasant lady"; ironically, her name is Mary Grace, a name with connotations of sainthood and the giving of blessings; and ironically the book she reads is *Human Development*.)

In the three parts of this long scene in the doctor's waiting room, O'Connor skillfully shifts the tone: the lightly humorous beginning; the dreadful insensitivity and scramble for pride in the women's conversation; and finally the sudden shift to the religion theme of humility and spiritual revelation by a violent convergence, which remains shocking and, to a degree, mysterious or unfathomable. Mary Grace, her face almost purple, hurls her book, leaps across the table with a howl, and with hands like clamps, begins to strangle the prostrate Ruby Turpin (the only time Mrs. Turpin is referred to as Ruby in the story and the first time she hears her new name: Wart-Hog from Hell!) Moments later, Mary Grace lies like an innocent baby, with her head buried in her mother's lap and sucking one finger. Later that day, after great anger and pain, Turpin experiences a second violent revelation that follows her curious discourse with God, a defensive prayer uttered as she cleanses her fine pig parlor. The discourse closes abruptly when, in response to her angry cry, she hears the voice of God calling "Who do you think you are?" Seeing a cloud of dust in the distance, she fears that her blaspheming has caused Claud to wreck his pick-up truck. Humbled by the voice of God and by her fear of losing the one person she unconditionally loves, she gazes beyond the sunset, has a vision of a rag-tag crew dancing along in raucous fashion as they enter heaven and she takes her place near the back of the line. A lesser artist could have made this story into a simplistic morality play or a pedantic parable, but O'Connor manages to manipulate the ending into a somewhat comical and even hopeful close. A crack has appeared in Turpin's implacable pride and through fear of God and love of Claud she has experienced a touch of humility—the quality that allows one to ask forgiveness and receive grace. Looking into the sunset, she has turned her head in the direction of light. In O'Connor's world, the need to have sins washed away is less crucial than the need to have one's virtues burned away. While O'Connor recognizes a world of mystery and wisdom beyond the earthly, her sense of humor and commitment to realism control her blending of the mystic and the down-to-earth reality, and she refuses to compromise the literary demands of either. Her boisterous humor

thrives on the stubborn resistance and determination of Mrs. Turpin, who may still be willing to wrestle an angel to keep her soul, who has shown she can dearly love one person, and who is alert enough to know that when she marches toward heaven, she and people like her may still wonder whether their song is "alone on key."

"Revelation," first published in *Sewanee Review* in 1964, won the O. Henry award that year. It is collected in *Everything That Rises Must Converge* (1965).

—Margaret B. McDowell

THE REVOLVER (El revólver)
by Emilia Pardo Bazán, 1895

Pardo Bazán's "El revólver" ("The Revolver") addresses, however obliquely, issues related to the status of women in 19th-century Spain. Similar to other of her works in which these questions are broached—in novels like *Un viaje de novios (A Wedding Trip)* and *La Tribuna* and elsewhere in the stories—Pardo Bazán uses the narrative of "The Revolver" to explore the oppressive environment in which women of necessity live in relationship to men at the same time that they are subject to masculine desires. Yet what results in the few pages of this story is neither as simple as an exposure of patriarchy's destructive force nor as reductive as mere summary would serve to indicate.

"The Revolver" opens with an unidentified narrator's observation of a sickly 35- or 36-year-old woman. This woman, who is linked to nature by means of her name Flora, displays all of the characteristic symptoms of the 19th-century "female" illness of hysteria: "the woman suffering from heart trouble told me about her illness, with all the details of chokings, violent palpitations, dizziness, fainting spells, and collapses, in which one sees the final hour approach." The narrator shrewdly notes that physical illness rarely induces the intense suffering experienced by the woman and begins to probe for other possible causes by initiating a discussion on the inevitability of death. Flora responds with the curious suggestion that "Nothing is anything. . . .Nothing is anything . . . unless we ourselves convert this nothing into something."

This line of thought proves crucial to understanding "The Revolver," as it bears directly on Flora's illness, both on the origin of her malady in her relationship with her husband Reinaldo and on his crippling jealousy. As Flora tells the narrator, she married a much older man who at first took great pleasure in his wife's vivacity. Gradually, however, his personality changed and he became irrationally jealous of his wife. Reinaldo's desire for Flora is so powerful and confining that the two begin to spend their time at home alone. Flora neither goes out with her friends as before nor entertains at home, and she withdraws from Reinaldo, too: "I often wept, and did not respond to Reinaldo's transports of passion with the sweet abandonment of earlier times."

Reinaldo's solution to this dilemma is cunningly simple. Showing Flora a revolver that lies in a drawer in their bedroom, he tells her that she is free to do as she likes: "But the day I see something that wounds me to the quick . . . that day, I swear by my mother! Without complaints or scenes, or the slightest sign that I am displeased, oh no, not that! I will get up quietly at night, take the weapon, put it to your temple and you will wake up in eternity." This draconian threat has its intended effect. Flora immediately faints from mortal fright. And when she returns to her senses she begins to live a haunted existence. Reinaldo never threatens her, never reproaches her, never expresses any disapproval. But this apparent passivity in and of itself terrifies Flora, who is paralyzed with fear despite her love for her husband.

For four years she lives in fear for her life, experiencing symptoms of hysteria. Her torture comes to an end when Reinaldo is thrown from a horse and dies instantly. At this point, Flora, who sends the servant to remove the revolver, learns that the gun was never loaded. Reinaldo's was quite literally an empty threat. Flora realizes that "an unloaded revolver shot me, not in the head, but in the center of my heart, and believe me when I tell you that, in spite of digitalis and all the remedies, the bullet is unsparing."

It is tempting to see in "The Revolver" yet another instance of woman's suffering at the hands of a man and a male-dominated society. Flora, the creature of nature, experiences the world around her with an enviable delight only gradually to find herself imprisoned by her husband's corrosive jealousy. Acting from what he himself admits is a feverishly overweening love, Reinaldo threatens his wife and turns her into an emotional invalid with all too real physical symptoms. Only with Reinaldo's death is Flora free of the immediate threat of death; yet she continues to live as an invalid, unable to shake off the ills of the past.

However, it is important to note how first Reinaldo and then Flora create "something" from "nothing," how, in essence, Reinaldo's unfounded suspicions fed on his wife's innocent pastimes and how Flora's fear turned an unloaded gun into a potential instrument of revenge and death. If "The Revolver" is about the status and role of women in 19th-century Spain—and, indeed, it is—then it is also about the questionable powers of observation, of the ways in which we often can see only what we most fear or desire. Pardo Bazán, a quintessential Realist author, asserts in these brief pages a possible critique of Realist texts as mirrors held up to the world even as she suggests the dangers of unrestrained imagination and unchecked fabulation.

—James Mandrell

THE RIDER ON THE WHITE HORSE (Der Schimmelreiter)
by Theodor Storm, 1888

Der Schimmelreiter (The Rider on the White Horse, 1915, also translated as *The White Horseman,* 1962, and *The White Horse Rider,* 1966) was the last work published by the poet and storyteller Theodor Storm, who died in 1888 at the age of 70 a few months after its first publication. It is, in many ways, a summation of all his work. The setting is the storm-battered coastland of Nord Friesland in the province of Schleswig—the subject of the disputes between Prussia and Denmark in the 19th century which ended, to Storm's personal satisfaction, with Prussian claims prevailing. Storm was born in these parts and he had an intimate knowledge of the local people and their ways, of the abundant and still unspoilt wild life of the region and of the folktales that were repeated by firesides on winter nights.

Storm presents *The Rider on the White Horse* through a number of narrative frames, gradually taking us further and further back from the present into the past in a manner that is typical of the German novella of the 19th century. A first-person narrator, whom we might well be tempted to identify with Storm himself, tells us how he read a tale in some old magazine on which, of course, he cannot lay his hands any more. The author of the magazine article relates how one stormy day he had set out to ride along the Nord Friesland shore in dirty weather when suddenly he saw what seemed to be a ghostly figure galloping on a white horse along the dike; the apparition was all the more eery because he heard no sound of the hooves beating the ground. In some alarm, the traveller went into the next inn he came to. When he related what he thought he had seen there was a stir of interest, and after a little persuasion the village schoolmaster prepared to tell the old tale. The frame has served to transport us back from the present to a more remote past, and the scepticism of the schoolmaster in particular makes the reader more curious about the superstitious side of a story packed full of homely detail about the everyday life of this rural community in a coastal region, where there is a constant duel between land and sea.

The basic concern of this community is the reclaiming of rich farming land from the shallow sea and protecting it from the waves and tides by maintaining dikes. The official in charge of this highly responsible task has the title of "dike master," an important personage in local affairs. But Tede Volkerts is old, idle, and stupid, and when the young, intelligent, and enterprising Hauke Haien enters his employ, what happens is predictable enough. Tede soon comes to rely on him, and, though Hauke has to overcome the resentments of the older workers, he wins some respect by displaying physical prowess in the village winter games on the ice. He ends up, as good apprentices so often do in 19th-century fiction, by both marrying his master's daughter and taking over his office of dike master. He then sets out to implement a policy of further land reclamation, designing dikes on a new, more efficient model. Hauke's proposals meet with opposition from the local people who do not wish to change their ways; they resent the intellectual superiority of a young man at whose social ascension they look askance.

All of this looks as though it belongs to the familiar traditions of 19th-century bourgeois optimism, with a certain novelty given by the rural setting, which can in turn be delightful and threatening. But there are darker forces at work too. When Hauke purchases from a mysterious stranger a white horse, there is some whispering about the skeleton of a horse which used to lie on a sandbank bleaching in the sun at low tide and has now disappeared. There is also the blow of the birth to Hauke and his wife of a baby who is feeble-minded, and Hauke is himself taken ill. While still weak, he consents to proposals made by an old rival for inadequate upkeep to the old dike, and in a storm the next winter the inevitable occurs. Hauke rides to the scene on his white horse, surveys the damage, and sees that his wife and daughter, instead of staying at home in a house on higher land, are in danger of being swept away by the swirling waters as they drive down to look for him. In despair, as if to expiate his guilt for not insisting on proper repairs and also, it seems, to satisfy the local superstition that some living sacrifice must be made if the breach is to be sealed, Hauke spurs his white horse and dashes into the water. He is drowned, and so is his family. The next morning the storm subsides and, uncannily, the bones of a horse, it is said, are seen again on the sandbank off shore.

The Rider on the White Horse is a gripping tale. Homely realism in the depiction of the existence of ordinary folk living close to the land and the sea provides a fine setting for a well-observed account of social pressures in a small community. Hauke is something of a Romantic loner, though his marriage provides him with some measure of integration, and the conflict of a thoughtful man with the natural forces of the sea is another Romantic theme. The exploration of superstitions adds another dimension, and Storm's clever narrative technique, which includes some effective use of symbols, enhances a tragic story that has been acclaimed as one of the finest examples of the German novella.

—Christopher Smith

RIP VAN WINKLE
by Washington Irving, 1820

"Rip Van Winkle" may be the most important short story ever written. Though the text is routinely misread (books seldom reprint the story as Irving wrote it) and though the story's comic tone tends to deflect serious criticism, it remains one of the world's great short stories—a peer of Gogol's "The Overcoat" and Kafka's "The Metamorphosis."

Historically, "Rip Van Winkle" sparked the success of *The Sketch Book of Geoffrey Crayon, Gent*, which assured the reputation of Washington Irving and for the first time in history made American literature worthy of international esteem. Never has a single short story been more responsible for establishing a rising culture's literary respectability. Since 1820 virtually no American has been able to write in ignorance of "Rip Van Winkle." Irving's story sowed literary seed reaped in future decades—the pattern of Rip's tall tale swallowed whole by the overeducated outsider Knickerbocker helped ground frontier humor, a literary mode that began to flourish in the 1830's and eventually climaxed in Rip's illegitimate offspring, *Huckleberry Finn*. The local color movement that dominated American literature after the Civil War followed the example "Rip Van Winkle" set in highlighting peculiarities of local mores, fashions, geography, and folklore.

Since Joseph Jefferson first staged the story as an immensely popular play late in the 19th century "Rip Van Winkle" has metamorphosed into films, television programs, cartoons, children's books, and songs, appearing in virtually every conceivable medium. Within a century, the story's central motif—Rip's startled waking to a changed world after 20 years—has entered world folklore; only a tiny number of stories can claim a similar grip on the global imagination.

More important from a literary perspective, before "Rip Van Winkle" the short story as a genre did not really exist in Western literature. Tales abounded, as did countless other versions of brief narrative, but before 1820 short stories in the modern sense appeared as rarely and with as little impact as European visitors to America before Christopher Columbus. Irving created the modern short story by marking Western literature's first cross fertilization of the tale tradition and the essay-sketch tradition.

From the tale tradition Irving borrowed dramatic incident as formal skeleton—the long sleep and astonished waking. In the story's ultimate note, the muddleminded Knickerbocker denies, thus encouraging us to believe, that "Rip Van Winkle" actually originated in Teutonic folklore (H.A. Pochman names an old German tale, "Peter Klaus the Goatherd"). Historically, similar strong incident patterns dominated the tale tradition and most short fictions before "Rip Van Winkle."

From the essay-sketch tradition, specifically the scenic sketch, Irving borrowed the subtly detailed descriptions of place which dominate the first two paragraphs following the opening headnote. In fact, the story at first almost masquerades as a travel sketch ("Whoever has made a voyage up the Hudson must remember"). A second category of sketch, the character sketch, dominates the next few paragraphs. Tale tellers habitually rushed from incident to incident; Irving seems to value characterization for its own sake, his phrasing graceful, sophisticated, and unhurried. Such detailed observation of places and people had virtually no place in the tale tradition before "Rip Van Winkle."

Perhaps the element from the essay-sketch tradition Irving adapted most fruitfully involved the narrative persona. In the Romantic period the familiar or personal essay peaked in popularity, the central feature being an intimate sense of voice, the experience of a psychologically rich personality revealing deeply personal thoughts and feelings to the reader. The close analysis of self which familiar essayists exploited, Irving diverted toward his central character, Rip. That technical shift more than any other transformed the tale into the modern short story.

We see the technique most clearly from the point at which Rip wakes. Earlier the story largely focuses on the world Rip experiences; afterward the story highlights Rip's experience of that world. Rip's first perceptions of difference—closely described—tend to be external, relatively unimportant, and easily explained: a rusty old gun in place of a new, the disappearance of his dog, stiffness in his joints, and a stream flowing in a previously dry gully. Rip grows increasingly disturbed to discover social differences—a crowd of new faces in the village, unaccustomed fashions of clothing—and astonished to discover a beard on his own chin. Next he observes more momentous changes: the village's buildings have altered, as have the names on the houses—even his own home has utterly decayed. Despite never deserting his comic tone, Irving subtly guides the story toward profound darkness when Rip discovers his family has disappeared. The ultimate shock occurs when Rip tries to reclaim his name and identity; sceptical villagers point to an apparent double of Rip himself as when he disappeared 20 years ago. Rip, his confused despair climaxing in a moment of profound psychic horror, fears himself lost in madness: "I'm not myself . . . I can't tell what's my name, or who I am!" Lear could sympathize.

The story's beneficent comic tone refuses to desert Rip, however, and the pattern of graduated losses reverses, altering to one of dramatic gains. Rip's now grown daughter appears, the apparent double turns out to be Rip's son, and in a crowning bit of luck Rip learns that his shrewish wife recently died when she "broke a blood-vessel in a fit of passion at a New England peddler." Rip ultimately claims a post of honor at the inn, surrounded by a few old cronies, making a career of weaving his yarn.

The description above outlines the core story most readers recognize, but Irving's frame—headnote, endnote, and postscript—identify the story's putative author, Diedrich Knickerbocker, as a naive dunderhead who has swallowed hook, line, and sinker a fantastic tale which locals themselves are sensible enough to discredit. The core story's last line asserts that the neighborhood's henpecked husbands often yearn for a drink of the flagon that released Rip from his nagging wife. Read in the version Irving published, the story leaves us little room to doubt that Rip simply ran away from home, returned on his shrewish wife's death 20 years later, and invented a preposterous story to explain his absence.

Reading Rip without the headnote, endnote, and postscript we seem to have an omniscient narrator's endorsement of the six paragraphs which deal with the supernatural crew and magic draught of wine; reading the full story we understand that the only narrative authority for the supernatural events is the knuckleheaded Knickerbocker. The skillful metafictional play helps make "Rip Van Winkle" more than Western civilization's first significant short story, more than one of the best ever written—after eight generations of readers the story still seems one of the most modern.

—Walter Evans

THE ROAD FROM COLONUS
by E.M. Forster, 1942

In his introduction to his *Collected Tales* (1947), E.M. Forster was careful to identify these as "fantasies." The title makes it clear that he thought of them as exercises in marking the defining moment: the sense of something beyond the real that promised an epiphany, a new life. Forster saw nature as an agent of that newness, but, he wrote, "there is no hope of writing down Nature: we can write down man. We employ similes for Nature, which the imagination revivifies. But to describe their source is hopeless. The imagination won't wake" (from his unpublished diary, courtesy of King's College, Cambridge). The aspirant must settle for a symbol, a metaphor, some transcendental state of mind. Forster even tried to fall into a trance by repeating a name, but without success. The pull of reality was too strong.

At rare intervals, however, the creative imagination comes wide awake and gets close enough to nature to inscribe something magical upon the senses. "The Road from Colonus" is the product of such a moment in his visit to Greece in 1903, and it is about such a moment in the life of an elderly man. It proves to be his last chance at such an epiphany. "The whole of *The Road form Colonus* hung ready for me in a hollow tree near Olympia," Forster wrote. He combined his acute observations of the English as tourists abroad, with motifs from his classical studies; he placed the bored and elderly Mr. Lucas and his boring daughter Ethel at Colonus, the village near Athens that was Oedipus's birthplace and also his chosen place of death. Unlike Oedipus on his return from Thebes, Mr. Lucas is not physically blind, but age and social conventions have smothered him at home, and in Greece it is the tourist conventionalities of his companions (in addition to Ethel, Mrs. Forman, and a younger Mr. Graham). They are merely "doing" Greece, but Mr. Lucas has realized a lifelong dream. "Forty years ago he had caught the fever of Hellenism, and all his life he had felt that could he but visit that land, he would not have lived in vain." He is a version of G. M. Trevelyan's composite character, "poor Muggleton," who drudged his way through the classics at school and university, hating the manner of teaching but loving the subject matter, and finally achieving intellectual and emotional apotheosis when at last he visits Greece. Mr. Lucas is a version also of Oedipus, complete with daughter and a wish not to be rushed away from Colonus. Oedipus gets his wish, but Mr. Lucas does not. He has reckoned without Ethel, who equals Antigone in determination but is uninterested in martyrdom. Mr. Lucas tries to "settle down to the role of Oedipus, which seemed the only one that public opinion allowed him."

Modern Greece has fallen short of his romantic expectations: "Yet Greece had done something for him, though he did not know it. It had made him discontented. . . . Something great was wrong, and he was pitted against no mediocre or accidental enemy." Old age is the enemy, and Greece makes him want to put up a fight, to "die fighting." His companions aid and abet that enemy, and Forster develops them with stinging touches to which his victims would have been oblivious. Mr. Lucas eludes them long enough to discover something magical: a hollow tree beside a tiny khan, or inn, inside which are votive offerings, and a living spring gushing from its base. He adds his own offering, a little figure of a man. When the others catch up with him Mrs. Forman calls it "all very Greek"; Colonus is useful for validating her coy conceit of calling Ethel Antigone. Mrs. Forman babbles about "a place in a thousand!" She could "live and die there"—if she were not expected back in Athens. She does not mean a word of it. But Mr. Lucas is serious about wanting to stay overnight at that inn. The others do not take him seriously and "had to turn away to hide their smiles."

Ethel has never taken him seriously, which is perhaps her unconscious retort to the family's assumption that her father is her responsibility in his old age. When she finds him inside the hollow tree that seems to him so magical, she treats him like a child: "Why, here's papa, playing at being Merlin." She degrades him further by fussing over his wet feet and burbles insincerely about staying overnight: "You mean a week papa! It would be sacrilege to put in less." He takes her at her word, and "his heart was leaping with joy." At once she professes incredulity that he could have believed her. To pacify him she pretends to inspect the inn's bedrooms while the muleteer, astonished but delighted, starts to lead Mr. Lucas's mule toward the stable.

Then young Mr. Graham, who is "always polite to his elders," shows his true colors. "'Drop it, you brigand!' shouted Graham, who always declared that foreigners could understand English if they chose. He was right, for the man obeyed." Ethel pronounces the bedroom unacceptable, but her father clings to his vision of a defining moment. They "became every minute more meaningless and absurd. Soon they would be tired and go chattering away into the sun, leaving him to the cool grove and the moonlight and the destiny he foresaw"—some "supreme event . . . which would transfigure the face of the world." Even Ethel is no match for this vision until she calls up Mr. Graham as reinforcement. Literally and metaphorically the polite young man pulls the rug from under Mr. Lucas, picks him up, and plants him firmly on the mule that has been sneaked up behind him. The Greek children say farewell by shying stones at them. "That's the modern Greek all over," says Graham. They wanted only Mr. Lucas's money. Had he been brutal? "No indeed. I admire strength," says Ethel.

There is an epilogue. Mr. Lucas is at home in foggy London, querulous and complaining, obsessed with neighborhood annoyances, particularly water running in the pipes. He has forgotten the enchanted spring in the hollow tree. Ethel is about to be married—one assumes, to Mr. Graham—and her father is being bundled over to the care of an unattached aunt. The morning post brings a parcel of asphodel bulbs from Greece wrapped in a Greek newspaper. It imparts the news that a great tree had blown over on the inn and killed its inhabitants, on the very night that Mr. Lucas had wished to stay there. Ethel thinks of providence. Mr. Lucas thinks only of his letter of complaints to the landlord. His defining moment at Colonus might as well never have happened. Dying at the inn could have been the "supreme event" that transfigured, but if he lived on for years and years such a moment would never come again. To miss the defining moment, says Forster, even if it is one's last, is the great tragedy of life.

—Mary Lago

_____

THE ROCKING-HORSE WINNER
by D.H. Lawrence, 1933

The final stories of D.H. Lawrence, written in the middle and late 1920's, represent a period of formal experimentation, in which he moved away from traditional narrative realism and the settings of rural and urban England to the realm of the mythical, supernatural fairy story. As Frank O'Connor said, the withdrawal of the sense of actuality pushes the stories, closer to the tales of Puskin and Poe rather than the studious realism of Chekhov and Maupassant. Yet that sense of the miraculous always present in Lawrence's narrative saves them from becoming mere exercises in the occult and uncanny.

"The Rocking-Horse Winner" (collected in *The Lovely Lady,* 1933), Lawrence's second attempt to write a contribution for a collection of ghost stories compiled by Lady Cynthia Asquith in 1926, is a fusion of various narrative modes. Perhaps closer to the German Märchen (in its bleakness) than the fairy story, it is a conscious artistic adaptation of the oral storytelling technique. It combines elements of the supernatural and the fable with a variety of Lawrence's favourite traits, such as the unhappy marital relationship, the capitalist obsession with money and work, and the pervasive sexual and religious symbolism. The characters only live in so far as they progress the narrative, making the story similar to Doyle Springer's definition of an "apologue," an overt and stylized parable where the characters are never our prime concern, since some idea shapes the whole.

The basic plot concerns a middle-class couple who live beyond their means, and the effect this has on their young son. Upset by his mother's unhappiness, and mindful of her belief that the family are "unlucky," he sets out to discover "luck," and thereby obtain wealth. He secures both by riding his rocking-horse to the point of frenzy, and magically coming up with the names of winners in classic races, aided by his uncle and the gardener. However, the fortune he amasses doesn't bring his mother the happiness he had expected, and in an effort to pursue still greater wealth he collapses and dies at the very moment of his greatest victory.

The suspension of incredulity required by the reader is barely apparent because of the subtlety with which Lawrence narrates the events:

There was a woman who was beautiful, who started with all the advantages, yet she had no luck. She

married for love, and the love turned to dust. She had bonny children, yet she felt they had been thrust upon her, and she could not love them.

The fairy tale simplicity of the opening sentence is echoed in his next story, "The Man Who Loved Islands," a more overt moral fable. The short sentences, divided into two or three syntactical clauses each time, impart the sense of a fixed, eternal unfolding of events with their nursery rhyme simplicity, especially the repetition of "she," "yet," and "and" at the beginning of each clause. This linguistic repetition is themed throughout the narrative, with the stresses falling on the phrases "there must be more money," "luck," and "when I'm sure." The spectral quality is reinforced by the first of those phrases being given to inanimate objects, the satire on the consumerism and rapacity of polite society emphasized by the house furnishings:

And yet the voices in the house, behind the sprays of mimosa and almond-blossom, and from under the piles of iridescent cushions, simply trilled and screamed in a sort of ecstasy: "There must be more money!"

The avaricious nature of the capitalist ethos is wryly parodied by the number of proverbs and clichés that are either directly stated or associated with the tale. The phrase "lucky in money, unlucky in love" assumes the mantle of a double entendre as the events unfold; "the wooden horse that takes its rider nowhere" symbolises the capitalist urge for advancement merely to maintain the status quo.

A tribute to Lawrence's narrative control are the astonishing number of symbolic patterns in the text, which defy any single, coherent reading. The two most obvious are images associated with sex and religion. Paul has an Oedipal urge to replace his failed father in a family where money is taken as the nexus of affection. The symbolism of sexual activity centres on Paul's "mount," which is "forced" onwards in a "furious ride" towards "frenzy." Readers familiar with "St. Mawr," or the famous description of Gerald Crich and the stallion in *Woman in Love,* will need no introduction to Lawrence's suggestiveness in such descriptions. Likewise, it is impossible to ignore the allusions toward masturbation in Paul's "secret of secrets" (especially in his death scene) if one recalls Lawrence's sentiments in his essay "Pornography and Obscenity": "Masturbation is the one thoroughly secret act of the human being. . . .The body remains, in a sense, a corpse, after the act of self-abuse."

The religious symbolism is more apparent but less easy to understand. Bassett perceives Master Paul as a seer, telling Oscar in a "secret, religious voice" that "it's as if he had it from Heaven," an irony considering Paul's claim that "God told" him of his luck. Yet the Märchen framework is that of a hero who bargains with evil powers for forbidden knowledge and wealth, and his mother's fear in the final scene ("What in God's name was it?") turns into a nightmare when her "poor devil" of a son collapses and dies during his last vision. The diversity of narrative modes and the complexity of the symbolism make "The Rocking-Horse Winner" much more than a neat parable about an acquisitive society's implicit deathwish. As Brian Finney has noted, the reversal of expectation, the breaking of literary conventions, and the movement towards verbal play and self-conscious artifice makes this story a forerunner of Borges and Beckett, and one of the finest achievements of postmodernist prose.

—Simon Baker

―――――

THE ROOM
by Maurice Shadbolt, 1962

First published in the periodical *Landfall* in 1962 and then collected in 1963 in Shadbolt's second book of stories, *Summer Fires and Winter Country*, "The Room" typifies Shadbolt's particular kind of social realism. As in much of his fiction, the focus is on personal relations, but the characters are seen more as social representatives than as unique individuals, and their relationship to New Zealand social history is emphasized.

The story is set in Auckland in the 1950's, but that urban environment is juxtaposed with the rural North Island farm inhabited by the Hamilton family since the pioneering days four generations before. The first Hamilton brought with him to New Zealand a "dream of happiness" that he hoped to bring to fruition by his pioneer venture, but his vision was defeated by the truth of the struggle with the land, "the stripped, sunburned acres which had drained all wonder, hope and memory." This pioneer vision is symbolized by the library room on the family farm, a room central to the hopes of its builder but viewed only as a curiosity by the "less introspective" succeeding generations. It becomes central again only to the protagonist, Sonny, and Margaret, his older sister, who gain from it a new version of the dream of happiness, one that leads them to the university and the city, the world of learning, art, and freer human relationship. They move from the library to the room in the boarding house in the city, first Margaret and then Sonny, becoming representatives of a generation, Shadbolt's own, that was moving out from a provincial, post-pioneering society in search for something more challenging and exciting, more metropolitan. The story focuses on Sonny's first evening in the room, which he has taken over from Margaret, who had died suddenly and shockingly from an illegal abortion two months before. The movement of the story is psychological, towards an epiphany as Sonny seeks to "unriddle whatever secret remained . . . behind that quickly-shut door" of the room that his sister had inhabited. He searches both for the meaning of her death and for the possible meaning of his own future in the city.

The crucial instruments in Sonny's search are a tiki (a Maori fertility symbol), and a poem and an unfinished letter by his sister. The poem uses Margaret's and Sonny's earlier discovery of a Maori burial cave as an image for her exploration of the forbidden area of sexual love, an area also evoked by the tiki, which gave "a vision, tantalizing and terrible, of an older, darker, god-begun world." The poem and tiki force Sonny to "see the colour of his loneliness," to face the "vast void uncovered" within himself when he realizes that he loves his sister, that he has lost her forever, and that he is angry (and even jealous) that she had moved into a sexual world beyond his experience. The letter, to her ex-lover who had returned to England, telling him of her unexpected pregnancy, reveals that she had planned to have an abortion to be free to help Sonny through his first year in Auckland. Thus he sees that "he might, after all, have been important to Margaret."

The rooming house itself also contributes to Sonny's epiphany, for he receives a telephone call for his sister from someone who does not know that she has died, and he is forced to acknowledge publicly that painful fact of her death. The rooming house also contributes the sound of a girl crying in the next room, "trapped as securely in her privacy as he was in his own," an indication of "the condition on which life here was lived." Poem, tiki, letter, phone call, and girl all come together for him in a moment when he senses the "strange and terrible" in life, an experience "like contemplating the dark spaces beyond the stars from the porch steps on the farm at night." When he had earlier visited his sister in the city, it had seemed to him that she and her male companion were "talking in an elaborate code" of a metropolitan world of which he knew nothing, and that their eyes were "signalling in an even more mysterious code." In the narrative present he has not yet cracked the codes of metropolitan culture or of sexual love, but he realizes that he is beginning the learning process. His sister had wanted to help him to enter this process, and, the story implies, she has actually done this through her almost sacrificial death.

The story is thus one of initiation into adulthood, an initiation perhaps more cultural and historical than individual and psychological. For Sonny is not a sharply individualized and fully developed character, but is rather a representative of a generation moving rather uncertainly towards a cultural adulthood. The analogy between individual growth and the development of a national culture is assumed, not explored or questioned in the story.

The story's representative quality is both its strength and its weakness, as is the case in much of Shadbolt's fiction. On the one hand, the story reverberates with cultural significance, and every detail seems relevant to its themes; on the other hand, the rather heavy-handed prose reveals the strain of reaching for that significance, as does the too obvious artifice of the detail. An impressive thematic pattern has been defined, but at some cost to particular life.

—Lawrence Jones

―――――

THE ROOSTER AND THE DANCING GIRL
(Niwatori to Odoriko)
by Kawabata Yasunari, 1926

The short story's appeal has depended on its brevity and intensity. In this way it can produce emotion and meaning whether in shaping a plot, creating a character, or producing a mood. In terms of length, however, its range is relatively wide. At its briefest it can range from 500 to 2,000 words (whereupon it is called a "short-short story"). At its longest it can amount to 7,000 or 8,000 words (whereupon it is called a "novella," or short novel). Prominent practitioners of the short-short story in English include Edgar Allan Poe ("Shadow—A Parable" and "Silence—A Fable") and O. Henry ("The Gift of the Magi" and "The Furnished Room").

The Japanese Nobel prize winning author Kawabata Yasunari devised a unique kind of short-short story. His stories (as in some of Poe's) are so poetic in style, so delicate in sensibility, and yet so coolly detached in their objectivity that if they are not prose poems they resemble them. In Japanese the short-short story is ordinarily called "*chopen shōsetsu*" or "*kyo shōsetsu*." But Kawabata called his stories "*tenohira no shōsetsu*" ("palm-of-the-hand stories"). Seventy-four of this kind of story by Kawabata have been translated into English by Lane Dunlap and J. Martin Holman and appear in one volume titled *Palm-of-the-Hand Stories*.

The question of what Kawabata meant to convey by his "palm-in-the-hand story" has some interesting implications. Certainly he considered the palm, a part of the hand, as a unit of measure, suggesting that one of his stories was condensed enough to be written on the palm of his hand. (The concept of "hands," of course, has been used as a measure in determining the height of horses.) Secondly, Kawabata's idea suggests "prestidigitation," or the use of "sleight of hand" that is quick, clever, and deceptive—as in the card or coin tricks of a stage musician. And thirdly, the idea of palm suggests divination by "palmistry" (*shusōjutsu*), or the reading of the lines and marks of the human hand and the form of the fingers to determine intelligence, character, and future fortune. Many of Kawabata's stories end on a note of prophecy—as is the case with "Niwatori to Odoriko" ("The Rooster and the Dancing Girl").

In "The Rooster and the Dancing Girl" a teenage girl living in Tokyo has completed her dance training and is rehearsing at a theater in the district of Asakusa, Taitō Ward, preparatory to making her debut before a public audience. The girl lives with her mother somewhere near Hongō Avenue in Bunkyō Ward, which is west of Taitō Ward, and when walking to Asakusa goes from Hongō Avenue eastwardly into Kototoi Avenue and her destination.

At home the girl's mother raises chickens and naturally employs roosters or cocks as well as hens to produce eggs and chicks. The mother visits her daughter in her dressing room at the theater to inform her that one of the roosters crowed at night. Such an action by a rooster is regarded by the Japanese as an ill omen. Therefore, to avoid a calamity the mother requests the dancing girl to carry the rooster to the Kannon Temple in Asakusa and donate it as a sacred bird in honor of Kannon, a popular bodhisattva, and at the same time utter a prayer of supplication to this figure. Before carrying out her mother's request, the girl informs her that a strange man has been observing the windows of the room where the dancing girls shower, although the glass of the windows is frosted and the man can see nothing but drops of water. The next evening the girl carries the rooster to the Kannon Temple, sets it free, feels pity for the rooster, and prays. She is surprised to see four chickens roosting in a tall ginko tree.

On her way to the theater the next day she wonders what the rooster is doing and stops to see it at the Kannon Temple. The rooster approaches her. She runs and the rooster chases her. She blushes and people stare at them.

In several days the rooster regresses to a more primitive form and becomes wild, able to fly and swagger about the temple grounds. But the girl never passes in front of Kannon again, and "even if she had, the rooster had forgotten her," presumably because it had become its primitive ancestor, the red jungle fowl, *Gallus bankiva*, the indigenous fowl of India that had been the ancestor of the Japanese chicken.

Now 20 chicks have hatched at the dancing girl's house, but again a rooster has crowed at night. Hence her mother insists that she dispose of it at the Kannon Temple at Asakusa in the same manner that she had the very first prophetic rooster. The dancing girl smiles, because she had thought her mother had discovered her secret. The girl

thinks of the 20 chicks that have hatched and wonders if she might be allowed to have 20 men during her lifetime.

The prophecy of the rooster has nothing to do with her desire for 20 men, but with the intrusion of the strange man, who represents evil. He approaches her when she is carrying the second rooster to Kannon Temple, and proposes that she help him in a scheme to blackmail the male admirers of the dancing girls who write them love letters. The girl tries to run away, but he grabs her. She shoves the rooster in his face; its flapping wings terrify him and he flees.

The next morning the girl walks in front of Kannon, whereupon the rooster of the previous night comes running after her. This time she stifles a laugh and does not run away. When she returns to the dressing room at the theater, she instructs the other girls not to throw their love letters into the trash and thus protect public morality. Now it is suggested that she may turn out to be a great dancer.

Although the above summary is more or less straightforward, causal, and chronological, and may be practically useful, it is a complete distortion of Kawabata's own narrative structure. His narration frees instead of enclosing space, allowing it to be open-ended. It often ignores temporal sequence and the logic of cause-and-effect, presenting effect before cause and allowing events to occur by chance. Kawabata's narrative depends mainly on evocative images that are often symbolic and that are invested with mental and emotional energy, pictorial images often appearing on the screen of our consciousness like rapid snapshots in a TV commercial. The critic Masao Miyoshi has noted that Kawabata's narratives tend "to remain flexible and open-ended like individual verse-stanzas in a *renga* (linked poem)." Images require background and background is important in Kawabata's writings.

Further, what "The Rooster and the Dancing Girl" is really about and what its significance is is not revealed in the above summary. This story is essentially about sexuality. It is about male and female, fertility, reproduction, propagation, polygamy, and voyeurism. Finally, it is about sexual maturity together with artistic maturity and creativity.

This sexuality begins with poultry raising. The mother raises chickens and she requires her dancing daughter to associate with roosters or cocks. In Japanese folk belief a rooster is a symbol of male vigor and courage. It can even ward off evil and prophetize. In poultry raising its importance is acknowledged in that it is said to constitute "one-half of the flock" because it is ordinarily mated with from ten to twenty hens. It is polygamous and promiscuous.

The heroine of the story is a dancing girl. Her dancing consists of rhythmic and patterned bodily movements, usually performed to music. Although dancing can be a healthy form of entertainment, it can easily deviate, even in a ballroom environment, into "dirty dancing" and otherwise turn into eroticism that produces sexual arousal. Animals, birds, insects, and human beings have been known to engage in courtship or mating dances. The heroine is sexually aware and knows the role of the rooster; when chicks are born of her mother's flock the girl thinks of the men she might have.

When the heroine carries the first rooster to the Kannon Temple and releases it on the grounds, she pities it and looks up into the ginko tree where she sees four chickens roosting. The ginko tree, a deciduous tree prevalent in Southeast Asia, is sexually peculiar because its male flowers grow on quite separate trees from its female flowers, with pollen producing motile sperm cells in autumn.

The dancing girl is a worshiper of the Buddhist bodhisatt-va Kannon, whose name means "the one who hears the cries of suffering beings." A bodhisattva is one who, having perfected himself to become a Buddha and to enter the state of *nirvana*, compassionately refrains in order to save others. In Japan Kannon is worshipped as a deity and hence is commonly referred to as the God/Goddess of Mercy, because Kannon can assume any incarnate form, male or female, according to the status of the worshipper. In representation, Kannon was originally male, but latterly began to take on a feminine appearance, so that in China from the 8th century (known as Kuan-yin) and in Japan from the 10th century, the image of this deity became predominantly female. (The Kannon Temple at Asakusa is now called Senroji.) No image of Kannon is to be seen in the temple because it is supposedly buried underneath the building. At any rate, one can speak of the bisexuality of Kannon. In prewar Japan Asakusa was the seat of popular entertainment in Tokyo.

In sum, Kawabata's story is a *fabula* showing the development of sexual and artistic maturity in a young dancing girl.

—Richard P. Benton

A ROSE FOR EMILY
by William Faulkner, 1931

In his Nobel prize address of November 1950, William Faulkner declared his allegiance to the heroic view of life, much as though we were still living in the age of Homer: "The poet's, the writer's, duty is . . . to help man endure by lifting his heart, by reminding him of the courage and honor and hope and pride and compassion and pity and sacrifice which have been the glory of his past." The story "A Rose for Emily" (collected in *These Thirteen*) poses an important challenge to Faulkner's Nobel purpose: Does this story about a pathological necrophiliac murderess lift its reader's heart?

At first reading, the gothic horror of the tale will likely rule out a heart-lifting experience. But in the end, this story can be seen as the quintessence of Faulkner's art, and failure to grasp the heroic nature of Emily Grierson will probably portend an inability to understand Faulkner's oeuvre at large. What connects Faulkner's Nobel senti-ments with his necrophiliac murderess is the existentialist concept that every life contains some possibility of genuine free choice, despite the psychological determinism that severely limits the area of free will in many cases. It is only within that area of freedom, however small, that the dignity and meaning of anyone's life can be predicated.

With his customary economy of style, Faulkner indicates Emily's huge burden of psychological determinism in a visual image—"a tableau; Miss Emily a slender figure in white in the background, her father a spraddled silhouette in the foreground, his back to her and clutching a horse-whip." By driving away her suitors so as to keep her housekeeping services for himself, Emily's father has ruined her chances for a normal life and thereby grossly deformed her personality. But crazed as she is, after her father dies Emily attains a tiny area of genuine free choice—her chance to find and hold Homer Barron as lover and husband—and it is solely within this area that Emily can be judged. Faulkner's overall design leads our judgment to work greatly in Emily's favor, highlighting the virtues of courage, honor, and endurance in her life story.

The narrative design of "A Rose for Emily" is typical of much Faulknerian fiction: we begin in time present, as it were, with the death of Emily; then we move far back into the past to examine several character-revealing episodes; and finally we return to time present, having gained deeper insight into the opening scene. The story's five sections are unified by the heroic theme announced at the outset of part II: "So she vanquished them, horse and foot." That last phrase, referring to a medieval army, indicates the dimen-sions of Emily's string of victories over the townspeople, having nothing more than bare will power with which to repel their crude invasions. In part I, she expels the tax board from her house despite the legal powers they embody regarding tax delinquents; in part II, the townspeople are reduced to skulking about her place after midnight spread-ing saltpeter against the mysterious bad smell (a nice clue for the detective format); in part III she flouts the law concerning rat poison (another clue); in part IV, the Baptist minister, epitomizing this society's moral authority, de-parts from her home a broken man; and in part V we discover her private victory over time, death, and spinster-hood.

This crucial last scene is nicely adumbrated in the way Emily had earlier handled the death of her father: "She met [the ladies] at the door, dressed as usual and with no trace of grief on her face. She told them her father was not dead. She told them that for three days." After finally giving in to the townspeople's version of reality—"and they buried her father quickly"—she infallibly learned never to do so again, and so withdrew totally from their sphere of influence, not even allowing installation of a mail box. The next time they would have no chance to pronounce her love object dead, and so Homer could take the place she had reserved for him among the rose-colored objects and silver bridegroom's articles in the attic. It is very important to Faulkner's heroic view of character that, crazy as she is, Emily does not rely on mere fantasy to fulfill her need for the status of wife and lover. Instead she obtains a palpable human body to esconce within an actual bridal chamber. That difference between wishing and willing—between fantasy and reality—is precisely the measure of heroic aptitude.

There is no denying that the image of Homer Barron's mummified body, with Emily's tell-tale hair next to its head on the pillow, violates conventional standards of morality, just as her courtship with a Yankee of low class ("a Northerner, a day laborer") violates the conventional code of a Southern lady. But suspension of conventional mores is an indispensible feature of Faulkner's heroic vision. It is only by occupying the inner consciousness of his madmen, scapegoats, and outlaws that we can have any hope of understanding the Faulkner protagonist, whose circumscribing contingencies will typically make conven-tional standards inapplicable. Emily is thus the prototype of many Faulknerian heroes: the idiots Benjy and Ike Snopes in *The Sound and the Fury* and *The Hamlet*; the abortionist doctor in *The Wild Palms*; the murderer-protag-onist in *Light in August*; the "nigger dopefiend whore" in *Requiem for a Nun*. Ultimately, Emily's unbreakable will power, the basis of her total victory over the combined force of the townspeople, links together the necrophiliac's secret chamber and the great hall in Stockholm where a voice speaks nobly about the old verities of the heart.

—Victor Strandberg

ROTHSCHILD'S VIOLIN (Skripka Rotshil'da)
by Anton Chekhov, 1894

Anton Chekhov probably had the first idea for "Skripka Rotshil'da" ("Rothschild's Violin") in 1892, but it was not published until 6 February 1894 in the newspaper *Russiye Vedomosti* (Russian Bulletins). It first appeared in a collective volume of Chekhov's tales and stories in Moscow from 1899 to 1906. In its tone and moral gravity "Rothschild's Violin" is considered to have been influenced by the moral stories of Tolstoii, which had made a deep impression on Chekhov a few years earlier. But in this instance the didactic element is kept strictly in check, which means that the reader is more likely to respond positively to the tale and the characters, especially since the author reveals his usual insight into the quirkiness of humanity.

In the story Jacob is an old man, 70 years old, and he lives in a wretched small town, hardly bigger than a village. He reflects with grim irony that its elderly inhabitants are so slow to die that his trade as a coffin-maker languishes and he is forced to live in poverty. He has some pride in his trade, it is true, taking particular care to do a good job of work when a coffin is required for one of the gentry. Things are made all the more difficult for him, however, because it is not permissible for him to work on Sundays or saints' days, or on Mondays either, because that would bring bad luck, and from time to time he falls to calculating just how much money he has lost because of this enforced idleness and even how much interest he might have received annually if only he had been able to work all the time and bank the proceeds.

Jacob also plays the violin with a Jewish band that generally performed at weddings in the town, which is another minor source of income. But the miserly Jacob can never forget that the tinker who conducts generally pockets half the fee, and, though he does not think much of the Jewish musicians, he has a particularly low opinion of Rothschild, named after the famous financier only in heavy-handed mockery of his utter destitution. As a musician he was known as a flute player who generally made even the merriest tunes sound miserable, and he and Jacob often nearly came to blows. Despite his annoyance with the band, Jacob does get some consolation in his wretched existence when he plays his violin.

Things take a turn for the worse for Jacob when his wife Martha dies. She is old and decrepit, and the staff at the hospital make little effort to save the life of an impoverished woman. As she lies dying, waiting for the last rites, Martha tries to make her husband remember happier days, 50 years before, when the couple had a baby and sat under the willow trees by the riverside. Jacob finds, to his horror, that he has no recollection whatsoever of all that. The only satisfaction he has is that of seeing his wife buried, decently and at a very moderate expense, in a coffin he had made for her shortly before her death.

As he returns from the burial Jacob begins to feel ill, and he is in anything but a good mood when Rothschild comes to tell him that he is needed to play at a wedding. Jacob's temper flares. There is a good deal of the anti-Semitism that plagued Russia in the 19th century in Jacob's abuse of Rothschild, and he is rather pleased when he hears that the Jew has been bitten by the dogs that chase him off. But then, as Jacob comes to the river, he begins to be reminded of the past. He starts asking himself what has happened to him over the decades to alienate him so thoroughly from the rest of humanity. "Life," he reflects, "has flowed past without profit, without enjoyment—gone aimlessly, leaving nothing to show for it." And now he knows that the future holds nothing for him either. What good had it done, he wonders, to spend his time cursing and threatening people with violence.

The next day Jacob goes to the hospital, though he is perfectly aware that there is no treatment that can cure him. He finds some comfort in the wry reflection that at least he won't be spending much on himself anymore. As he lies on his deathbed, Rothschild comes again to call him to play at a wedding, and this time there is some regret when he has to say that he cannot come. A little later, after he has made his confession to the priest and is invited by him to think over the sins of his life, he has the idea of asking for his violin to be handed over to Rothschild.

—Christopher Smith

———

ROYAL BEATINGS
by Alice Munro, 1978

"Royal Beatings" is the first section of Munro's volume of interconnected stories, *Who Do You Think You Are?* (published in the United States as *The Beggar Maid*). It originally appeared, like many of Munro's stories, in *The New Yorker* (March 1977).

"Royal Beatings" introduces us to Rose, the character who will provide the interconnecting thread for the stories of the volume. She is an imaginative girl from small-town Ontario who moves from an early life of poverty to middle-class existence on the Canadian West Coast, though the transition is never an easy or complete one. In fact, this opening story shows Rose's past invading her present; Rose can never escape the various "beatings" which she has experienced physically (at the hands of her father) or fictionally (at the hands of that inveterate storyteller, her stepmother Flo). Years later, living in Toronto, supposedly sanitized of all contact with Hanratty violence, Rose hears a radio interview with one of the men who severely beat Becky Tyde's abusive father. But the media of radio and time have sanitized him, too: "Horsewhipper into centenarian. Photographed on his birthday, fussed over by nurses, kissed no doubt by a girl reporter. . . .Living link with our past." It is Rose's part, in the stories that follow in *Who Do You Think You Are?*, to de-sanitize the past, to acknowledge under the affable centenarian-like surfaces of her present life the horsewhipping nightmares of her past. Indeed, such a project is Munro's, in all of her short fiction.

Another Munrovian feature that looms large in this story is the figure of the verbally imaginative young girl, living in surroundings of poverty, ignorance, and violence, and yet deriving creative energy from those unlikely sources. The story opens, in fact, with the young Rose's puzzling out of Flo's phrase "Royal Beating." "How is a beating royal?" Rose wonders, and she proceeds to construct an elaborate scene, full of ceremonial savagery. This opening passage, too, is emblematic of much of Munro's fiction, for the pairing of ceremony ("royal") with grimy detail ("beatings") is one that many so-called magic realist writers would recognize. Time after time, in "Royal Beatings,"

Rose tries to bring ceremony and detail together; looking at some prettily patterned (but worn) egg cups which once belonged to her own mother, Rose weaves a myth of a "far gentler and more ceremonious time." Rose's father, too, participates in this pastime, though he endeavours to hide and disown that part of himself; from his worked drift snatches of words—words that also meld detail and ceremony or art: "Macaroni, pepperoni, Botticelli, beans—"; "The cloud-capped towers, the gorgeous palaces" (a line from *The Tempest*).

But, for Rose, this habit of mind—that of the artist—produces more tempests than palaces. Oddly enough, her father is the one who attempts to beat this propensity out of her. One of the royal beatings of the story is the horrifying one that Rose's father gives her, and it is brought on by imaginative, verbal crime: "Two Vancouvers fried in snot! Two pickled arseholes tied in a knot!," sings Rose to her younger half-brother Brian, thus incurring the wrath of Flo, and the intervention of Rose's father. When he beats her, Rose recognizes that he looks at her not merely with anger but with hatred—hatred, presumably, for that part of himself that produces those cloud-capped words in his grimily everyday workshed. This generational dynamic is a common one in the stories of Alice Munro; parents and children often express hatred for or shame at each other, not for being so different from what they are, but for representing a part of themselves that they are not yet ready to acknowledge—usually, the imaginative, creative, questioning part.

This story also introduces a familiar Munrovian figure, that of the grotesque. Becky Tyde, deformed by polio as a child, physically abused by her father (some Hanrattyians even say, impregnated by him), is described as "a big-headed loud-voiced dwarf, with a mascot's sexless swagger." And yet, like other Munro "grotesques," such as Bobby Sherriff from *Lives of Girls and Women*, she reminds the artist-character that the bizarre often appears in the sheep's clothing of the everyday; sitting in Flo's store, munching cookies, she seems a calm survivor of an extravagantly violent past. As such, she plays an important role in the volume of stories as a whole, for she prefigures that wonderful eccentric of the final, title story, Milton Homer, an artist figure by virtue of his twin names, if nothing else.

In this story, however, another early proof that art may be lurking under the cover of domesticity appears in the character of Flo, Rose's grumbling, choleric stepmother. After Rose's royal beatings, Flo becomes a ceremonial bearer, of sorts, carrying a tray full of fancy sandwiches and cookies and chocolate milk to the bruised Rose. And, on a similar occasion, once family harmony has been established, Flo does an amazing trick: placing her head and feet on chairs, she rotates her body. "There was a feeling of permission, relaxation, even a current of happiness, in the room," an older Rose remembers. Occasionally, in the domestic world of Hanratty, art and ceremony are "permitted"; as she matures, Rose will struggle to find the exact conditions for their coexistence.

—Lorraine M. York

S

THE SAD FORTUNE OF THE REV. AMOS BARTON
by George Eliot, 1857

"The Sad Fortune of the Rev. Amos Barton" is George Eliot's first published work of fiction. It originally appeared in *Blackwood's Magazine* in 1857 and was included with two other stories in her *Scenes of Clerical Life* (1858). Being her first attempt at fiction it embodies more than any of her other works her philosophy of fiction as stated in essays and letters. Fundamental to that philosophy is a commitment to realism and a rejection of idealization. In one of her best-known essays, "The Natural History of German Life" (1856), she states:

> Our social novels profess to represent the people as they are, and the unreality of their representations is a grave evil. The greatest benefit we owe to the artist, whether painter, poet, or novelist, is the extension of our sympathies. . . . Art is the nearest thing to life; it is a mode of amplifying experience and extending our contact with our fellow-men beyond the bounds of our personal lot. All the more sacred is the task of the artist when he undertakes to paint the life of the People. Falsification here is far more pernicious than in the more artificial aspects of life.

She attacks Dickens's representation of children and the poor since this encourages "the miserable fallacy that high morality and refined sentiment can grow out of harsh social relations, ignorance and want," and claims that "we want to be taught to feel, not for the heroic artisan or the sentimental peasant, but for the peasant in all his coarse apathy, and the artisan is all his suspicious selfishness."

These views underlie her approach in "Amos Barton." The title of the story indicates that its eponymous hero will not have a happy life, but it is not made easy for the reader to sympathize with him by representing him as a man of admirable character or attractive qualities. The narrator states explicitly that he is "in no respect an ideal or exceptional character." Nor does he have the kind of interest that readers of fiction might expect: he "had no undetected crime within his breast . . . had not the slightest mystery hanging about him, but was palpably and unmistakably commonplace." Eliot's dual aim in this story is to make such a character interesting in fictional terms and also to make the reader feel sympathy with him without resorting to idealization.

It is clear that the influence of Wordworth's poems in the *Lyrical Ballads* was strong at this stage of Eliot's career. In *Lyrical Ballads* Wordsworth endeavoured to interest an audience brought up to believe that poetry was remote from life and written in an artificial form of language in poems that dealt with basic human situations and were written in what appeared to be "unpoetic" language. In order to do this the poems embody various devices designed to undermine the audience's expectations and encourage it to read and respond in a new way. Similarly, in "Amos Barton" Eliot's narrator encourages the reader to reject idealization in fiction and overcome the kind of prejudices that would prevent the reader taking a character like Amos seriously. Thus there are numerous direct addresses to the reader. These have often been criticized, but at this early stage of her career Eliot felt the need to create an audience for the kind of fiction she wished to write. This story, therefore, is as much about the relation between the reader and the fiction as about the characters and situations.

The culminating point of the story comes when Amos's wife Milly dies. The reader, like the people of Shepparton, who had held him in extremely low regard, cannot ignore his suffering and thus are able to feel human solidarity with someone for whom they had previously felt only contempt. Details, such as the children's inability to feel grief for the death of their mother because they cannot understand what death means, enhance the effect since this realistic representation of children's responses in such a situation is more moving than to have idealized them in the manner of conventional fiction. Amos himself, in recognizing that "he could never show her love any more, never make up for omissions in the past by filling future days with tenderness," increases in human stature, indicating that even people who have no special qualities are fully human and must be recognized as such. Eliot's implicit humanism is also present; though the story is about a clergyman there is no suggestion of the possibility of a metaphysical consolation beyond the human, though her rejection of religion is never directly stated.

It could be argued that Eliot does not herself avoid idealization in that Milly Barton appears to be a faultless wife, an angel in the house. There is, however, something ironic about such a woman being the wife of a mediocrity like Amos Barton. Milly represents a conventional ideal of womanhood but doubt is cast on this ideal by Amos's unworthiness of it. The story is perhaps questioning the appropriateness of such an ideal of womanhood. Amos is directly responsible also for the death of his wife, both by his insensitivity to the intolerable strain that she is under and by the fact that he gives her more children than she can cope with. The narrator informs us of one of Amos's few good qualities: "Amos was an affectionate husband and, in his way, valued his wife as his best treasure," but ironically the consequences of that "affection," which Amos seems oblivious to, finally kill Milly.

—K.M. Newton

THE SAINT
by V.S. Pritchett, 1966

With comic seriousness, "The Saint," the title story of V.S. Pritchett's 1966 collection, recounts an adolescent boy's progress from an illusory disregard for catastrophe to a realization of humanity's mortal fate. But in this spiritual journey, the hero discovers the rightness of his own orientation to the world. The boy himself, at the age of 33, tells of his brief membership in, and final apostasy from, the Church of the Last Purification, of Toronto, Canada. The satiric telling is never bitter and—as finale—the narrator displays a generous understanding of his momentary guru, the pseudo-saint, Mr. Hubert Timberlake.

The story is more about gain than loss, its initial comic utterance notwithstanding: "When I was seventeen years old I lost my religious faith." The faith in question entails two familiar absurdities. First, evil is unreal because an omnipotent God cannot intend the suffering of his creatures (especially economically). Second, it is "Error" to assert that anyone suffers, an idea as conceivable to the devout as a square circle to a logician. The boy inherits these beliefs in the usual, familial, not unkindly, but mandatory fashion.

That the Church's home is Toronto amuses us as readers. Not because we are Pritchett's English neighbors, but because we find amusing the provincial enshrinement of a metaphysical worldview. That a religion so wedded to money is so grandly titled and has originated in Toronto tickles us like the idea that the Second Coming is destined for Kansas City. We want the boy to see through this blather and are not disappointed. Yet we know that he is delicately poised on the brink of adulthood and will pay for his insight. Pritchett has created in him, as the narrator's tone reveals, a character capable of growth, one inclining inevitably to a healthy but perplexing view of human experience.

This inevitable growth is woven carefully into the story. The uncle is struggling through a depression. When the Church greases his palm with a tad of cash, it falls to him to start a congregation, appropriately at the Corn Exchange, a not exactly other-worldly parish. The boy is included, no options. Yet he experiences evil and begins to break away. Then the fabulous Timberlake, the sage of purification, arrives and compels his allegiance again. Not, of course, because the boy believes this man has raised the dead. It is because Timberlake gives the uncle a barb, about being funny, commensurate with the one his uncle had given the boy, about thinking. He can abandon the trapped authority who mocks him for one who defends him. Momentarily, Timberlake shines; no matter that his witticism is part of a plot, including the uncle, to rein in a wayward sheep. But an *ad hominem* ascent is never wise. In fact, Pritchett is all but gratified by the struggle of the young against authorities, who often enforce beliefs at odds with experience and desire. Surely, the cynical teacher's hilarious response to the boy's justification of his Pollyanna theology is a judgment we share. Yet the schoolmates also look at the boy "with admiration," because his dissent, while ludicrous, represents idealistic resolve and independence.

It is these qualities, in conjunction with the boy's experience of the world in its beautiful and calamitous reality, that make his rejection of this religion a happy certainty. The boy loves the river, has "water on the brain," as his uncle likes to jest. Pritchett's joke transcends the uncle's, because the boy is not just happily stupid but instinctively and socially drawn to the most irreducible element of nature, to the instrument of purification, of baptism. Fortunately, he does have water "on the brain." When he casually offers his detailed image of the river, and of all that is on, under, and beside it, he conveys a spontaneous, unerring attachment to life. He is alive on the river because he knows the water and the willows are lovely

and dangerous at once, and that their capacity to make one suffer is as real as their friendly allure. On the other hand, Timberlake's uncomprehending and detached confrontation with both the river and the field of buttercups reveals the death at the marrow of his spuriously religious nature. What properly animates the boy is reduced by Timberlake to the commercial grin and the innocuous word "fine," the latter a bit of verbal disease the boy catches, but only in passing.

At the heart of the story are water and passion. Half in and half out of the faith, the boy first sees Timberlake as a reformed merchant captain who, though once contaminated by the sea, has left it for money. This suggests the boy's unconscious wish that his religious leader share some authentic relation to water. Yet the "merchant" element implies that even unconsciously the boy knows this prophet has long been deeply shallow. He has never been properly "at sea." Timberlake's name is thus amusing; he could be neither a seaman nor a Hubert Rivers. After all, spiritually serious Christianity tries to confront the problem of evil, of a fallen nature, through baptism, originally by immersion in the river Jordan. Poor Timberlake, denies his immersion in the river. He doesn't sufficiently have "water on the brain." He doesn't know how to go properly crazy. So, he could by "no word . . . acknowledge the disasters or the beauties of the world." Besuited, soaked, and dipped in buttercups, he re-entered the "husk" of his life only as sanctified as the gilded statue of a saint.

Nothing in this story is hostile to any religion that acknowledges suffering and is not founded on the love of money. But its deepest values are strictly human. It sees that each of us carries, within, the "ape" of evil. Timberlake's denial of the "ape" only proves that he saw the truth and found it unendurable. Yet to deny evil is to deny its contrary, those "beauties" that come with those "disasters." Acknowledging the "ape" makes possible a complete and passional life and genuine feeling, especially sympathy, not that "glaze" on the faces of the faithful.

—David M. Heaton

SAINT EMMANUEL THE GOOD, MARTYR (San Manuel Bueno, Mártir)
by Miguel de Unamuno, 1933

"San Manuel Bueno, Mártir" ("Saint Emmanuel the Good, Martyr") is one of the most profound and enigmatic fictional texts of Miguel de Unamuno. Written in 1930, published in magazine form in 1931, and as the title story of a 1933 collection, it is the story of a Catholic priest unable to believe in the afterlife and perhaps even in the existence of God, but who nevertheless practices his vocation in an effort to spare his parishioners the anguished knowledge of their mortality and nothingness beyond the grave. Through this character Unamuno makes a final though by no means conclusive statement on the basic philosophical, religious, and aesthetic themes introduced in his earlier essays and works of literature.

The simple and straightforward plot of "Saint Emmanuel the Good, Martyr" is complicated by the narrative structure. Most of the text is the memoir of the fictional Angela Carballino, a follower and friend of Emmanuel who sees him as a holy man plagued by doubts but fundamentally a believer. She also recounts the perceptions of her atheist brother, Lázaro, who regards Emmanuel as a non-believer, and the villagers, who revere him as a man of God and a saint. Rather than clarify her portrait of Emmanuel, these various perspectives, as Unamuno intends, undermine the narrative and leave the reader in a state of uncertainty regarding the truth of the protagonist.

The action of the story takes place in a small village, Valverde de Lucerna, located at the edge of a lake and at the foot of a high mountain. On the bottom of the lake lie the remains of a former village and on the mountainside the ruins of a Medieval monastery. Though a similar setting was discovered by Unamuno during a visit to the lake of Sanabria in Spain, which in fact contains the remnants of an ancient village, its function within "Saint Emmanuel the Good, Martyr" is symbolic. The solidity and permanence of the mountain is suggestive of eternal life, whereas the religion of the past, as revealed by the monastery, is no longer a viable means of achieving immortality. The water of the lake is indicative of the nothingness of human reality, reflecting the illusion of being through the image of the mountain while concealing its own deep secret of death and annihilation.

Certain left-wing readers have criticized Unamuno for the political stance of Emmanuel. When Lázaro approaches him with a plan for making a parish church the headquarters of an agrarian syndicate, Emmanuel responds that the purpose of religion is not to resolve political and economic conflicts but rather to provide humanity with the illusion of immortality. In an astonishing passage he accepts the Marxian premise that religion is the opiate of the masses, and through an ironic twist insists that it is precisely for this reason that religion should be maintained and fostered. From the political perspective his position is clearly reactionary. Yet, although he minimizes the importance of pressing social problems, he simultaneously implies that the faith of the Church is a lie. Through the creation of Emmanuel, therefore, Unamuno does not, as a superficial reading might suggest, reject the importance of political activism or the need for social progress; instead, he forces his readers to question and perhaps even doubt whatever religious beliefs they might hold.

It must be noted, however, that for Unamuno Christianity is enriched through doubt to the extent that doubt involves suffering. Emmanuel is unable to believe with the simple faith of his parishioners, but as a result of his doubt he experiences an overwhelming agony that not only inspires in him a profound compassion for the suffering of others but reveals an even Christlike nature. Indeed, the name "Emmanuel" (in Hebrew "God with us") is synonymous with "Messiah" or "Savior." Moreover, his suffering and doubt are linked specifically to the passion of Christ through the lament, "My God, my God, why hast thou forsaken me," which echoes throughout the text.

Emmanuel never explicitly denies a belief in God but only in human immortality. Yet for some critics this is enough to make of him an atheist, and through the identification of Emmanuel with Christ they argue that Unamuno intended to suggest that Christ himself was a non-believer whose sole aim was to save the world from anguish. Although such an interpretation can be justified through textual analysis, it does not deny the possibility that for Unamuno non-belief (as a form of salvific suffering) might in reality be a dimension of belief. In this context Angela concludes that both Emmanuel and Lázaro died believing they did not believe, but believing nevertheless through their very desolation.

At the end of "Saint Emmanuel the Good, Martyr," Unamuno intervenes in the narrative to comment on the characters and their motivations. With regard to the fictional Angela he claims she is actually real and that he believes in her reality more than in his own. This is reminiscent of such earlier texts as *Niebla* (1914, *Mist*) in which he establishes a relationship between himself and his fictional narrator and characters, as well as *Vida de Don Quixote y Sancho* (1905, *The Life of Don Quixote and Sancho),* where he argues that literary characters are more real than their authors to the extent that they are continually recreated through the imagination of readers. Unamuno also invokes a passage from the epistle of Saint Jude, in which the archangel Michael contends with the devil for the soul of Moses, who, like Emmanuel, led others to a promised land that he himself was unable to enter. Unamuno identifies with his namesake, Michael, and in so doing seems to reject the rational interpretation that a figure like Emmanuel is an atheist unworthy of salvation and to ascribe to him, as did Angela, the passion of a tormented believer.

Notwithstanding, the mystery regarding the faith of Emmanuel, like that of Unamuno himself, is never fully resolved. Although it has been argued that for Unamuno belief is ultimately a quixotic affirmation of an ideal that the human heart desires but that reason denies, the dialectic of belief and non-belief remains operative throughout his entire literary and philosophical corpus and is in fact the source of his creative genius.

—Robert Richmond Ellis

THE SALAMANDER (La salamandra)
by Mercè Rodoreda, 1967

"La salamandra" ("The Salamander"), one of Mercè Rodoreda's most powerful stories, appears in *La meva Cristina: altres contes* (1967; *My Christina and Other Stories,* 1984)—in David Rosenthal's translation is outstanding. The first-person narrative recounts the experiences of the nameless protagonist—a village girl living at an indefinite time in centuries past—when she is accosted in the forest at nightfall and assaulted by a married man (it is a rape, but her resistance erodes when the episode is repeated). Her attacker is known to her, and she asks about his wife; in reply, he swears he has no wife. Surprised *in flagrante delicto* by the jealous wife, the narrator is accused of witchcraft by the wife, who drags the husband home without a word of reproach. The narrator suffers several attacks as a suspected witch before being burned at the stake by superstitious neighbors (they apparently had burned the girl's mother when she was small). She spots her lover in attendance at the burning, with his arm around his wife. In extremes of torment in the flames, she is metamorphosed into a salamander, eludes pursuit, and takes refuge beneath her lover's bed. Discovered and routed by the wife, attacked by villagers again, badly beaten, she finally slips into a pond where her wounded paw is chewed off by eels before she escapes into mud and mire at the bottom.

Rodoreda combines the most prosaic realism with the fantastic; realistic details abound in initial descriptions of the setting—pond, willow-tree and watercress, frogs and lengthening shadows—and the fantastic metamorphosis, unexplained and unelaborated, is connected to earlier reality by the unchanged narrative voice, unchanged setting, and characters. Even though the reader encounters an event (the narrator's transformation into a salamander) that contravenes the laws of science, compounded by the realization that the metamorphosis has not changed her human consciousness, feelings, and reactions, continuity in other elements prevents the sense of a break with reality. And Rodoreda wants to maintain contact with quotidian, domestic reality, because (like many other stories in *My Christina*) this is a commentary on the feminine condition, albeit one which contains a degree of violence and a sense of terror not typically found in her work.

The timeless, mythic chronology and non-specific, rural locale convey a universality transcending the more specifically 20th-century Spanish contexts evoked by most of Rodoreda's fiction. While the stubbornly scientific reader may view the metamorphosis as a symptom of psychosis or pain-induced hallucination, it is clear that Rodoreda would prefer another reading. Her allusions to witches and witchburning have a double function: appeal to superstitious credulity and a tradition whereby salamanders were alleged to appear in similar circumstances may induce suspension of disbelief, while witches and the persecution thereof exemplify the epitome of man's inhumanity to woman.

Lyricism combines with the grotesque in this account of the simple village girl—alone in the world, without defenders, with the stigma of her mother's having been burned as a witch—with her sensitivity to nature and total, unquestioning acceptance of the world around her and the actions of others. It is no mere coincidence, of course, that she (like the wife) abstains completely from criticizing the man's deeds, and in no way protests the unfairness with which she is treated (she lacks the feminist consciousness that would perceive the injustice of her situation, but the reader almost inevitably will notice—herein lies much of the irony).

Significantly, metamorphosis is not the end of the salamander's suffering, but the beginning of prolonged torment which has not terminated when the story concludes. The metamorphosis (occurring at what realistically might be the point of death) is not the end, simply because the exploitation and abuse of women which Rodoreda foregrounds has not ended. The fact that the story is continued by a consciousness still partly human, situated beyond the loss of her human condition (or life), gives a sense of immediacy and intensity of suffering, perhaps because of its unexpectedness; continuing persecution indicates that no escape is possible for women in patriarchal society. And society is more at fault than the man: even though he sneaks up behind her in the woods, chases her when she runs away, and pins her to a tree until she can struggle no more, then rapes her—these are the least of the outrages she suffers. Insulted and vilified by the wife (society's traditional reaction to the "other woman"), ostracized, stoned, persecuted in various ways, even exorcised—her situation recalls the moral environment of *The Scarlet Letter,* except that in "The Salamander" the adulterous man is known and goes free, hypocritically leaving her alone to face public disgrace and official punishment. Certainly Rodoreda indicts much of society, for all take part in persecuting the salamander, from elders and priest to the young men who come to break down her door and drag her from the house, the boys who help pile on the wood, and the old woman who brings dry heather when the fire fails to start. Loss of self-esteem from ostracism and disgrace is externalized by physical change to a lower

animal, one which must crawl on its belly and live in the mire. Yet the salamander's societal conditioning and values remain with her, as evinced by her crawling out from beneath the bed to pray at a spot where moonlight and windowpane projected a luminous cross upon the floor.

Dragging herself to the pond which she desperately envisions as a haven, she is set upon by three eels who eat off her broken hand. The transparently phallic nature of the eels and their taking advantage of her helplessness suggests an allegory of societal relegation of the "fallen woman" to prostitution, especially because the eels play with their victim until they tire of the game, leaving her in the slime. These events with a less skillful writer might degenerate into melodrama or bathos, but the salamander's understated, impersonal tone and near absence of reference to her sentiments or physical pain let the horror of events achieve full impact. Rodoreda has chosen an extreme example, but by no means uncommon historically and combined it with women's widespread silence about rape and abuse to produce an implicit condemnation of the double standard and its contribution to the victimization of women in patriarchal society.

—Janet Pérez

THE SALT GARDEN
by Margaret Atwood, 1983

In Margaret Atwood's story "The Salt Garden" (collected in *Bluebeard's Egg*), the protagonist, Alma, is involved in a bizarre web of relationships that leaves her bewildered. She is separated from her husband Mort, but is still seeing him. His lover does not know of Alma's existence, so Alma finds she is the one who has to be discreet with her own husband: "He sneaks out on Fran to see Alma and calls Alma from telephone booths." She is meanwhile having an affair of her own. Nothing is certain, nothing is secure; she finds herself being carried away by circumstances, fearing resolution.

The story's themes and symbols revolve around her contradictory feelings about time: she wants to know what is going to happen, but is afraid of what she might lose, and so wants to stop time from moving. For example, she thinks back to her childhood, although she dismisses her nostalgia with the thought that it shows "she's getting old." Instead of choosing, she would rather let life take her where it will. She is also disturbed by her daughter Carol's wish to grow up, wondering why children are so desperate for time to pass quickly: "It upsets Alma to see them trying on her high heels and putting lipstick on their little mouths. . . . They wiggle their hips, imitating something they've seen on television." Alma would prefer time to slow down.

But her fears about the future cannot be denied, and she suffers periodic blackouts accompanied by hallucinations about the outbreak of nuclear war. These apocalyptic visions represent her terror that the careful balance of emotions she has established in her relationships with her husband and lover, and the other women in their lives, will be upset and everything will come crashing down. In her calmer moments she treats her visions sardonically, wondering how she could survive a real nuclear attack, and makes vague plans about buying a farm far from Toronto, one fully equipped with a root cellar and, magically, enough food and water to sustain the survivors. The plans, of course, do not stand up to very close scrutiny; Alma is too down-to-earth to let her imagination run away with her. But suppressing her fears only cause them to break out in violent ways. Her intimations of disaster even invade her more lucid thoughts about nuclear war: in her daydream the "hill of the root cellar, honeycombed with tunnels, too thoroughly mined, fell in upon itself, and all perished."

Her first blackout occurs just after Mort has attempted to discuss with her "how things could be arranged better." She does not want to face the implications of her situation, especially the fact that it cannot go on forever. Mort has his own way of trying to prevent apocalypse: he marches and signs petitions. Her lover Theo "deals with the question by not dealing with it at all. . . . Theo has said he doesn't see any percentage in negative thinking." We sense that he represents for Alma a successful denial of the future, one to which she aspires.

The story also contains references to magic and the occult, familiar themes in Atwood's work. Atwood often parodies and structures her works, notably in *Lady Oracle*, on gothic romances, which are so much a part of women's cultural mythology. At one point Alma compares her hallucinations to religious visions:

> She suspects that other people are having similar or perhaps identical experiences, just as, during the Middle Ages, many people saw (for instance) the Virgin Mary, or witnessed miracles: flows of blood that stopped at the touch of a bone, pictures that spoke, statues that bled.

Nowadays, Alma suggests, our need to find something outside our mundane existence expresses itself in accounts of alien abductions and health-food stores containing "magical foods that will preserve you from death." Perhaps we can prevent the end of the world with talismans: "you could . . . carry around oranges stuck with cloves."

The story's central symbol, the "salt garden" one can make with thread and a supersaturated solution, combines these two main themes. It is a form of magic, as we see in her childhood chemistry set's instruction book: *"Astonish your friends. Turn water to milk. Turn water to blood. . . . How to make a magical salt garden."* Through chemistry she can gain apparent control over her environment. It also represents a timeless, perfect little world of her own: she remembers "the enclosed, protected world in the glass, the crystals forming on the thread." Making the garden is her expression of her desire for stasis in an "'alternative' wordless language of symbol and aphoristic gesture," to use Frank Davey's words.

At the end of the story two events conspire to drop Alma back into the real world. One is an accident in which the doors of the streetcar she is on close on the arm of a woman. Despite cries from passengers to stop, the streetcar driver continues to drag the woman. Like Alma, the woman suffers pain in virtual isolation: "The most frightening thing must have been not the pain but the sense that no one could see or hear her." Alma visits Theo, hoping to postpone choice: "She wants it to go on the way it is forever." But after she and Theo make love he says, "'I hope . . . that when this is all over we won't be enemies' . . . he didn't say 'if,' he said 'when.'" The finality of his words, the implication that there will be a future, provokes another fainting spell, another vision of nuclear apocalypse. Her final image is of the comforting timelessness of the salt garden: "It is so beautiful. Nothing can kill it. After

everything is over, she thinks, there will still be salt." If only our uncertain lives could be so easily crystallized.

—Allan Weiss

SAM SLICK, THE CLOCKMAKER
by Thomas Chandler Haliburton, 1835

Haliburton's fame rests on his invention of Sam Slick, a Yankee clock peddler who draws on his insight into "natur and human natur" to make his sales, and who endlessly, and amusingly draws attention to the failings of Nova Scotians (Bluenoses), the enlightened progressiveness of Americans, and the intolerable pride and disdain of the British. Like all great humorists, Haliburton is ambivalent. Sam's boasting is warranted; the achievements of Americans are to be admired if their manners are not. Sam is one of the memorable humorous figures of the mid-19th century, and Haliburton published a number of Sam Slick books. *The Clockmaker; or, The Sayings and Doings of Samuel Slick of Slickville* has gone through more than 70 editions. It is not so much the figure as the force of his language, shot through with colourful turns of phrase and marked by acute and pithy perceptions of human behaviour, that makes Sam Slick memorable; and Haliburton is credited with such familiar phrases as "upper crust," "stick-in-the-mud," "as quick as a wink."

"The Clockmaker" was the second in a series of sketches, "Recollections of Nova Scotia," begun in the Halifax *Nova Scotian* in 1835. The practice of commenting ironically on local matters in a series of linked letters or sketches was already well-established in Nova Scotia as in New England. Seba Smith's *Life and Writings of Major Jack Downing, of Downingsville, Away Down East, In the State of Maine* (1833) was one widely admired precedent, and locally Thomas McCulloch's *Letters of Mephiboseth Stepsure* (1821–22) was another. The Sam Slick sketches were so well received that after about 20 of them had been printed the series was stopped, and those (with minor but interesting changes) were collected together with the rest of the sketches Haliburton had submitted, and published as a volume in 1836. An unauthorised volume published by Bentley in London in 1837 was an instant success. London was ripe for an "inside" view of the Americans, following the severe account of Trollope's *Domestic Manners in America* (1832) and other such works. Dickens would later reinforce the image of Americans as culturally grotesque.

Haliburton's satire was initially directed at regional political concerns, but with Sam's insistent intrusion of the American model, larger questions of political principle and the kind of interest the individual should take in political affairs displace anecdotes of political chicanery. Ultimately the rights and wrongs of a war of independence also are taken up. Haliburton's conservatism revealed itself more openly as the series progressed; eventually Sam resembles something more like a Jeffersonian republican than a Jacksonian democrat. Neither Sam nor Haliburton had much regard for the unthinking populace.

Haliburton had served a term in colonial politics, making several radical speeches. Then he became a circuit judge (as Sam's travelling companion, the squire, is) and with the Sam Slick sketches he began an enormously successful career. Sam Slick was as well known as Dickens's Sam

Weller; Artemus Ward is reputed to have acknowledged Haliburton as "the father of American humour."

It is humour of a colonial kind, energetic rather than polished, bold to the point of indecency, prepared to be offensive for a bit of fun, and "altogether nateral." For all Haliburton's delight in puns, his humour has none of the starched fussiness of early *Punch,* and rests not on wittiness but on a thing well and vigorously said.

"The Clockmaker" depicts Sam's strategy in selling his wares. He relies on flattery and vanity to gain his initial point, and inertia to clinch it. Once the Flints have become accustomed to an article they don't really need, they will find it difficult to give up.

Yet such homespun matter is the least of the sketch. It is sustained by all sorts of resonance and allusion. Sam begins his pitch by admiring the deacon's farm: "If I was to tell them in Connecticut there was such a farm as this away down East here in Nova Scotia. . . ." Nova Scotia is even further "down East" than Connecticut, or Maine. Sam appears to be flattering, but he is making a joke against the place too. Then there is a rather gratuitous crude playfulness about the deacon's fine deep bottom and running a ramrod into it, and this prurience leads on to a Sternean whisper about the deacon's continuing vitality, which in turn prepares the way for the risque business from *Tristram Shandy,* about Mrs. Flint promising to remind her husband to wind up the clock every Saturday night—a better regulated clock than Walter Shandy's. The disappointment is that Haliburton signals his effects: Sam hands the key to the deacon "with a sort of serio-comic injunction," and the deacon had seemed to wish the experiment with the ramrod to be tried in the right place. The humour, and the criticism, is all the more effective when not flagged in that way. Sam notices that the idle folks of Nova Scotia "do nothing in these parts but eat, drink, smoke, sleep, ride about, lounge at taverns, make speeches at temperance meetings, and talk about 'House of Assembly'." The contradictory inclusiveness of these activities is in the manner that Stephen Leacock would take up. It is in what becomes the characteristically Canadian manner of resisting categories.

The sketch is carefully organized to demonstrate a standard moral proposition about how to put time to good effect. Precept and example reinforce each other. Yet here too the point is ambiguous, for Sam puts time to his own advantage, and keeps his eye upon the time, whereas the Flints and the Bluenoses appear not to know its proper value. Sam's 600% mark-up on his clocks is a harsh and unsentimental way of making the point. Sam's unyielding readiness to make a speculation is an aspect of his authenticity as a figure, and his slightly intimidating authority as a commentator on colonial affairs.

—Adrian Mitchell

SANATORIUM UNDER THE SIGN OF THE HOURGLASS (Sanatorium Pod Klepsydra) by Bruno Schulz, 1937

"Sanatorium Pod Klepsydra" ("Sanatorium under the Sign of the Hourglass") is the title story of Bruno Schulz's second (and last) collection of short fiction, first published in Poland in 1937. The story's length makes it something of an anomaly in the author's small but important body of work. Only "Spring," in the same volume, is longer. However, Schulz's collections are virtually novels in their own right, even, like Thomas Mann's *Joseph and His Brothers* (1933-43), an important influence, parts of a single multivolume work. Length aside, "Sanatorium under the Sign of the Hourglass" is wholly characteristic of Schulz's extraordinary prose. It offers, to borrow Schulz's description of his first collection, *Sklepy Cynamonowe (Cinnamon Shops),* "a certain recipe for reality, posits a certain special kind of substance, the substance of that reality exists in a state of constant fermentation, germination, hidden life. It contains no dead, hard, limited objects. Everything diffuses beyond its borders, remains in its given shape only momentarily, leaving his shape behind at the first opportunity."

In "Sanatorium under the Sign of the Hourglass" not even the narrator's dead father remains dead. Modelled on the author's father, Jakub Schulz, a successful textile merchant who died in 1915, several months after fire destroyed his business, the father plays as important a part in this story, and indeed in much of Schulz's fiction, as Kafka's father Hermann did in his son's writings. However, where Kafka's father-figure is a petty but nonetheless powerful tyrant engaged in an Oedipal struggle that inevitably ends with the son's defeat, the father in Schulz's fiction is a far more sympathetic if ultimately ineffectual figure whom the son admires rather than fears.

In Schulz's fiction the factual and autobiographical are never more than points of departure for the author's prodigious imagination, which runs towards fantasy and fable. The son's journey by rail to the nameless sanatorium run by the enigmatic and elusive Dr. Gotard (modelled on the one in Thomas Mann's *The Magic Mountain,* as well as the health resort at Truskawiec where Schulz frequently vacationed) is rendered in terms of myth and dream. Once he has arrived, these elements become still more pronounced as time loses its linearity and becomes at once multiple and synchronous. Dead in one time, the father lives in another, and not just lives but lives as it were a double existence. He is the patient confined to his bed who reproaches his son for neglecting him, and he is the merchant who has opened a new shop, small but thriving (a success that makes the son's visit seem unnecessary).

The son finds himself in a world that appears at once strange yet strangely familiar. Arriving at the father's shop by a curiously direct route, he learns that a letter has arrived for him, but what his father calls a letter turns out to be a parcel, which does not contain the pornographic work he ordered (and which he now learns is out of stock) but a "certain object" that the sender believes will interest his client. This "certain object" defies the son's ability to know or even name it except by a relay of expressive yet ultimately inadequate similes. (These similes, like Schulz's larger style, reveal meaning as if through a veil and revel in their own imaginative excess.) Compared at first to a folded up accordion, the "certain object" is subsequently likened to a telescope, an enormous phallic bellows, a labyrinth of black chambers, a long complex of camera obscuras, an automobile, a theatrical prop, a paper butterfly, a large caterpillar, a paper dragon.

Nearly everything and everyone in the story undergoes similar, often ceaseless metamorphosis, including the father, of course, and a dog, which the son greatly fears and which turns out to be a harmless old man whom the narrator-son soon abandons. The structure of the story follows a similarly Ovidian course, with the abrupt transitions between its five sections rendered as if the parts do make up a single, seamless, continuous whole (which in a very different sense they do). "The quick decomposition of time" that so disconcerts the narrator upon his arrival at the sanatorium soon begins to afflict the reader as well through the agency of a narrative that blurs all distinctions between dream and reality, fact and fiction, cause and effect. The chief exception to the uncertain reality of the sanatorium and its environs, with its sweet air, black vegetation, bands of roving dogs, and occupation by invading army, is the group of girls the son sees walking as if in possession of an inner rule, "the idee fixe of their own excellence." This is an "excellence" that, even though nothing more than a flattering delusion, is often sufficient to defeat the men in many of Schulz's stories and in most of his drawings.

As the story progresses, either conditions worsen or Joseph chooses to believe they do. Either his father is quite well bustling about his shop or he is dying in his bed. Either the son was right to place his father in the sanatorium and thus save the father's life, or he and his family have been "misled by skillful advertising. . . .Time put back—it sounded good, but what does it come to in reality?" For the son, time proves cyclical rather than progressive. Deciding on no factual basis whatsoever that his father is dead, he exits the maze ("Where am I? What is happening here? What maze have I become entangled in?") by boarding the same train that brought him to the sanatorium earlier. This, however, is a train he is doomed never to leave, the train on which he will himself grow old, eventually forced to sing for his supper, to repeat his story over and over, dressed in the same shabby railway uniform as the old man he met at the very beginning of his story. For Schulz, who found life interesting solely as the "raw material" for his writing and who claimed that his "ideal goal [was] to 'mature' into childhood," and who, believing in the mythologizing of reality, contended that the tracing of the individual spirit must necessarily end in "mythological delirium," the son's fate may constitute, in its own strange way, less a defeat than a celebration of the powerful imagination of an author able to conjure densest fantasy out of thinnest reality.

—Robert A. Morace

THE SAND-MAN (Der Sandmann)
by E.T.A. Hoffman, 1816

Although *Der Sandmann* ("The Sand-Man") is carefully crafted short fiction, it also combines in an articulate narrative a pattern of childish fantasies including foreboding, terror, longing, frustration, and self-destruction. Typical of a general fascination with the grotesque by no means confined to German authors at this period, "The Sand-Man" is of particular importance on three accounts; it is technically an exceedingly accomplished and complex piece of writing; thematically it makes clear that what are linked together into a narrative with the perfunctory logic of mental association are in fact the apparently desperate conceptualizations of deep psychic sensations to which Hoffmann seems to have had unusually immediate access; and psychologically the story itself narrates the panic-stricken and in the end unsuccessful efforts of the central character, Nathanael, to preserve his sanity partly by

affectively exteriorizing into a coherent conceptual and narrative pattern his deepest and most interior feelings of horror.

"The Sand-Man" was written in 1815, shortly after E.T.A. Hoffman had finished his only completed novel, *Die Elixiere des Teufels (The Devil's Elixir)*, but after only the first dozen of his 50 or so short stories. It was published as the first of four stories in the first volume of *Nachtstücke* in 1816. All eight stories in the two volumes are linked by a theme, possibly inspired by Novalis's 1799 *Hymns to Night,* which joins a consideration of the deeper and darker recesses of the personality to a background of nighttime when most of the incidents occur, and darkness of colour, occasionally illuminated by brilliant shafts of light, as in the paintings of Rembrandt which Hoffman, caricaturist and painter as well as professional musician, much admired. Hoffman first became known in English-speaking countries through the 1824 Edinburgh publication of *The Devil's Elixir,* of which extracts were also published by Blackwood's *The Edinburgh Magazine.* This provoked Sir Walter Scott's 1827 "On the Supernatural in Fictitious Composition; And Particularly on the Works of E.T.A. Hoffmann," whose treatment of "The Sand-Man" as psychotic raving was particularly harsh, and was at the origin of the story's neglect for well over a century. In contrast, interest in Hoffmann has concentrated on it since 1970.

In the story, the communication of the efforts of Nathanael's imagination to exorcize his childhood terrors by exteriorizing and conceptualizing them into narrative was sufficiently powerful to give new life to the Pygmalion myth, in which a human artefact is endowed with real life, in its inverted form, in which a real person, the Olimpia of the story, turns out to be lifeless doll. Freud used the story as the subject for psychological interpretation in one of his more important essays, the 1919 "Das Unheimliche" (The Uncanny), seeing the theme of threatening eyes, even more emphatic in earlier drafts of the story, in terms of fear of castration. Freud has more recently been controverted by Jochen Schmidt and others, and eleven essays more or less specifically devoted to controverting Freud's interpretation of the story, together with a score of other interpretations published between 1970 and 1988, have been listed in Gerhard Kaiser's 1988 *E.T.A. Hoffman* (in German).

"The Sand-Man" starts with three letters; a lengthy letter in a highly artificial style, with passages of conversation and a deliberate self-consciousness, containing an elaborately written-up account of incidents from the student Nathanael's past to his friend Lothar, which reaches Lothar's sister, Clara, to whom Nathanael is engaged; a shorter letter from Clara to Nathanael; and a short letter from Nathanael to Lothar. From the first letter we learn that a few days earlier, at midday on 30 October, a peddlar of barometers, Coppola (whose name is connected by resonance to the Italian for eye-socket, "coppa") had called on Nathanael trying to sell his wares and, on being threatened with forcible ejection, had gone quietly away. Something in Nathanael's memory was stirred by this trivial event, whose time Nathanael so precisely records, and he explains to Lothar that as a child he had been sent to bed with the threat that the sandman was on his way. His mother had explained that that was just a way of saying that the children were tired and could no longer see out of their eyes, "as if sand had been scattered over them."

His sister's governess had a different story. The sandman was a threatening monster who threw sand into the eyes of children who would not go to bed, so that their eyes bled and sprang out of their sockets. The letter recounts how

Nathanael became obsessed with fear of the sandman. One night, when he was ten years old, he hid in his father's study and waited for the sandman to come. The person who came, and had therefore to be the sandman, was the fearsome but familiar lawyer, Coppelius, who used to come to lunch. Nathanael saw them doing frightening things, in fact performing alchemy experiments, but Coppelius, when Nathanael was discovered, had threatened to put out his eyes with burning coals. Nathanael had had fever for several weeks afterwards. On the last night of the experiments, undertaken much against Nathanael's mother's wishes, there was an explosion that killed his father. The letter ends by saying that the barometer peddlar was none other than Coppelius, now known as Giuseppe Coppola.

Clara's letter contains a perfectly normal explanation of Nathanael's childhood fears, confusing the frightening old man with the fair-tale monster and, although she does not use the terminology, suggests that Nathanael was projecting inner insecurity on to externalized objects. Lothar and she do not believe in the powers of darkness. In the third letter Nathanael reproaches Lothar that Clara had seen his previous one. Coppola has turned out not to be Coppelius. The new professor of physics, Spalanzani, has long known Coppola, and vouches for the fact that he is Italian, whereas Coppelius had been German. Spalanzani is a good-looking man, with protruding eyes and a beautiful daughter, Olimpia, whom Nathanael has seen.

These letters cover over a third of the way through the text. After the unintroduced letters, Hoffmann switches to a first-person narrator, a friend of Nathanael's, who directly addresses the reader, is himself in turmoil about how to understand, and whether to recount, what happened. The narrator tells the reader that, not having known how to start, he simply reproduced the three letters, without introduction or comment. Hoffmann, of course, had ensured that the first letter contained enough information for the reader to know roughly who was writing to whom, and who Clara was. The narrator now tells us that he is going to get on with the story, and fills us in. Lothar and Clara were orphans, distant relatives, and had been brought up by Nathanael's mother. The engagement of Clara and Nathanael was not only reasonable, but desirable. Before he goes on, however, the narrator tells us, he wants to tell us about Clara, who is the opposite of Nathanael, innocent, fun-loving, unafraid, sensitive and kindly, statuesque, but not pretty.

There is a first gap in the paragraph layout after the letters, and another two-thirds of the way through the story. In the second part Nathanael pushes Clara from him, saying, "You lifeless, damned automaton," and Clara stops Nathanael and Lothar from fighting a duel over the incident. Nathanael goes back to his university and finds his room burnt out. A fire had broken out at the chemist downstairs.

Some of the paragraphs of the final section are immensely long. Nathanael, we are told, bought a small pocket telescope from Coppola, thought he heard a "death sigh," looked at Olimpia through the telescope, and fell in love with Olimpia, much encouraged by her father, Spalanzani. Olimpia had played the piano at a concert before a ball, but had behaved strangely and unresponsively as Nathanael made his declaration. She could only sigh. Others, too, had found her lifeless. She behaved more and more oddly. One day Nathanael, totally obsessed, found her father Spalanzani and Coppola packing her up, disputing the relative importance of their roles in her creation. She was a lifeless doll, animated by alchemy. When Nathanael discovered that, he returned to Clara. They were admiring the view from a mountain when Nathanael went mad, and tried to throw Clara over the parapet. Lothar heard screams, and saved her. Nathanael heard Coppelius beckoning him from below to jump, and leapt to his death. The narrator tells us that Clara got over it all and married, and that she would not anyway have been happy with Nathanael.

—A.H.T. Levi

SATURDAY AFTERNOON
by Erskine Caldwell, 1931

Although Erskine Caldwell gained fame writing novels, his short stories may be his finest artistic achievements. In the decade of the 1930's, over 30 of his stories appeared on the honor rolls of Edward J. O'Brien's *Yearbook of the American Short Story*. Six were listed among the best stories of the year, and *Kneel to the Rising Sun* was ranked the best short story collection of 1936. "Saturday Afternoon," which first appeared in 1930 in the "little magazine" *Nativity* and then was included in *American Earth* (1931), is one of his best short stories.

Caldwell consistently maintained that he was a mere storyteller without artistic pretensions, but the works of his early career are as disciplined in their craftsmanship as Ernest Hemingway's. Like Hemingway, Caldwell was a minimalist who used a striking image rather than explanation to convey his message. Indeed, Caldwell preferred the short story genre because it avoided the "excessive verbiage" and "contrivances" of the novel. The consequences of the young author's careful study of methodology are stories distinguished for their simplicity and economy.

"Saturday Afternoon" is a representative example of this aesthetic. It is simply plotted. Opening on a humdrum Saturday afternoon in Tom Denny's smalltown butchershop, the plot thickens when Tom's assistant interrupts his nap to announce a lynching. The excitement created by the lynching is more what one might associate with a sporting event than a murder. The lynching itself is hardly described at all; instead, Caldwell focuses on the holiday atmosphere and stresses the callousness of the participants. After the lynching, the butchershop routine is described again, almost identically to the description in the exposition. Although the plot is simple in outline, its function is complex. It reinforces Caldwell's portrait of a community inured to its ritualistic racial violence. The lynching fits comfortably into an afternoon of buying meat for Sunday dinner.

Caldwell uses an equally simple method of characterization. He delineates his characters with a few select images so that the reader gains an impression of them and the society in which they live, but no attempt is made to provide a fuller portrait. For example, the salient features of Will Maxie, the lynching victim, are that he takes the grass out of his cotton before he harvests it and that he has none of the vices whites expect blacks to exhibit. This impression of Will is all the reader really needs to understand the motives of his lynchers—they envy and feel threatened by the black man—which are Caldwell's focus in the story. The characterization of Tom Denny is only slightly more developed. His folksy, colloquial voice as he waits on his customers establishes that he is well accepted in the community, even though his shop is unsanitary and he fills everyone's order—whether for pork, veal, or ham—using the same side of beef. News of the lynching stimulates him out of his beastlike stupor, but there is no sense in which his intellectual or moral faculties comprehend the event. The overall effect created by the two characterizations is a clear contrast between Will's competence and decency and Tom's sloppiness and near bestiality.

An important aspect of Caldwell's technique is the rigidly non-committal perspective of his narrator. One reviewer called his work, in which brutal events are depicted without comment, "the poetry of unfeeling." This hard-boiled technique was common during the 1920's and 1930's. In an age of growing political and commercial propaganda, the artist chose not to compromise the integrity of his vision with commentary or persuasive appeal, but rather let it speak for itself.

That Caldwell used a sophisticated set of techniques that omitted his personal voice does not mean that he was insensitive to social injustice. Critics often grouped him with a growing tide of committed, left-leaning writers of the 1930's. In a *New Masses* review of *American Earth,* Norman Macleod commented that "Saturday Afternoon" proved Caldwell "capable of good proletarian work," and then suggested that he "go left." Powerful images such as the town doctor's sending his son to a lynching to sell Coca Cola and a burning black man's being shot "so full of lead that his body sagged from his neck where the trace chain held him up" provided graphic testimony in an era anxious to rectify social inequities.

Some 50 years after the publication of "Saturday Afternoon" in a foreword to a collection of his stories, Caldwell referred to Southern race relations as "a savage heritage." Through his ability to exert rigorous control over his materials, he was able to evoke with power that shocking heritage for his readers.

—William L. Howard

A SCANDALOUS WOMAN
by Edna O'Brien, 1974

The publication of *A Scandalous Woman and Other Stories* (1974) followed closely on the success of Edna O'Brien's early novels. Those novels won almost instant admiration for making an art of naiveté, for their intimate and sensitive portrayals of young women growing up, dealing with their burgeoning sexuality in an unusually repressive society and, inevitably, being disappointed in love.

A constant theme throughout O'Brien's work is the entrapment of women by societal pressures, by the expectations of family and religion, and by their own desire for "romance." Her women, generally sensitive and self-sacrificing, value themselves only when they are needed by men who selfishly use and then discard them, leaving them, at worst, completely destroyed, or, at best, going through the external motions of an empty life. In "A Scandalous Woman" Eily Hogan, vivacious and gifted, with the face of a Madonna, conceives a desperate infatuation for a worthless man, and after a brief, self-deluding moment of happiness is forced, because she has become scandalously pregnant, into a loveless marriage with him. It is a marriage that leaves her, initially, mad and haggard, with her "lovely hair" falling "out in clumps," and eventually, with all "the feelings drugged out of her."

"A Scandalous Woman" clearly demonstrates O'Brien's most notable quality as a writer, her ability to evoke vividly the world of rural Ireland in the 1940's. The method is to focus on a single idiomatic phrase, or an apparently trivial detail, in order to create a picture of an impoverished rural economy, where unremitting drudgery is commonplace and excitement scarce. It is a society of rigid social distinctions, and even more rigid social and moral expectations and controls, monitored by the Catholic Church and cruelly reinforced by the family. Most specifically these controls apply to sexuality, or rather, to the suppression and repression of sexuality, and its constant association with a sense of guilt and expectation of punishment. It is, clearly, a society in which women are dominated by their husbands and fathers. The narrator's father goes "to bed in a huff, because she had given him a boiled egg instead of a fry for his tea," Eily Hogan's father is "a very gruff man who never spoke to the family except to order his meals," and Eily, as a child "always lived under the table to escape her father's thrashings." Mrs. Hogan is a terrified, demoralised woman; the wreck of her expectations is pathetically evoked in the description of her attempt to give birds some of the pleasure of which she is deprived: "She liked the birds and in secret in her own yard made little perches for them, and if you please hung bits of coloured rags, and the shaving mirror for them, to amuse themselves by." In this isolated world, backward looking, superstitious and tribal, glamour and excitement can be found only in the hell-fire exhortations of a visiting missionary or in those whispers of the modern world that creep in through bad films, tacky furnishings, and cheap perfume with suggestive names. These, for a brief moment, delude young women into believing that there are some, even if vaguely imagined, possibilities for self-fulfilment.

O'Brien has a fondness for the apparently guileless, child-like, first-person, confessional narrator. This story deals with the brief and spontaneous flowering of Eily and its destruction by the perverted rigidity of the adult world. It is narrated by a younger child who shares many of the attitudes of the community but who is distinguished by a very accurate ear (the crassness of male attitudes to women evoked by the description of Peter the Master spitting into the "palm of his hand" and saying "didn't she strip a fine woman"), by an immediate, sensuous relationship to experience (the pink jelly which is the only thing her mother can eat at Eily's wedding is "like a beautiful pink tongue, dotted with spittle, and it tasted slippery"), and by an ability to isolate a single image that encapsulates the full significance of the events she has witnessed:

> It was a wonderful year for lilac and the window sills used to be full of it, first the big moist bunches, with the lovely cool green leaves, and then a wilting display, and following that, the seeds in pools all over the sill and the purple itself much sadder and more dolorous than when first plucked off the trees.

The innocence and freshness of the child's response can reveal the hypocrisy and comic incongruity of much adult behaviour, as when the men sing a song or two after they have threatened, bullied, and beaten Jack into marrying Eily. For the most part, then, (apart from the somewhat irritating "you" form of narrative), the style is effective and appropriate. It is especially effective when O'Brien speaks through her naive narrator and, by exploiting the superstition and folklore that are a part of the child's everyday reality, expands the range of references and thus elevates Eily into a symbol of Ireland herself, moving in a recognised metaphorical pattern from Madonna to scandalous woman, or from Cathleen or Houlihan to the hag/crone figure suggested by the witch, whom Eily comes to resemble.

It is arguable, however, that the ending, given from the perspective of an adult, experienced, rationalising narrator, negates, with its tendentiousness, the immediacy of the naive narrative and its movement to a deeper mythological level: "It was beginning to spot with rain, and what with that and the holy water and the red rowan tree bright and instinct with life, I thought that ours was indeed a land of shame, a land of murder and a land of strange sacrificial women." The last sentence appears to be unnecessary and indicates a lack of confidence on the part of the writer in her readership, a lack of trust in the accumulated impact of the story.

—Anne Clune

SEATON'S AUNT
by Walter de la Mare, 1923

The short story "Seaton's Aunt," collected in *The Riddle and Other Stories,* provides a good example of Walter de la Mare's sense of the macabre. Though the aunt of the title eventually dominates the story, the author is careful to begin with a narrative and characters conventional enough to set off her strangeness. Seaton, the unpopular schoolboy, desperately clinging to a half-unwilling friend, and Withers, too embarrassed to refuse a treat he does not want, are at first little different from stock characters in innumerable school stories. The adolescent fear of sentiment, of unfamiliar experience that escapes the crude and simple categories of schoolboy tradition, is conveyed in ordinary schoolboy language.

The setting, too with a coach house, rambling orchard, pond-like stream, and meadow, is redolent of late Victorian ease and confidence. But instead of the expected crowd of sisters and servants, we find our attention focused on a single strange being. Though we see and hear enough to form a judgment of our own, we also have an artful contrast of points of view. Seaton's view is different from Wither's, and the boyish perception of each is different from his later adult understanding. The atmosphere is built up by the contrast between Seaton's mixture of real apprehension with an exhibitionist desire to impress his friend, and the friend's sturdy attempts at scepticism. As Withers is also the narrator, there is a contrast between the strange things he describes, and his contemptuous rejection of Seaton's interpretations. Some of Seatons's suspicions may be mere fantasy. How can we know whether the aunt "as good as killed" his mother? But the scoffing Withers is gradually affected by the atmosphere, so that the two boys, normally so lacking in mutual sympathy, are driven by fear to hide together in the cupboard in the aunt's bedroom, and must cling to each other for support.

The aunt's sinister quality is maintained in two opposite ways. She is mostly absent. Her face is "fixedly vacant and strange"; she seems to be living a more intense life in an unseen world. But when she speaks, she is able to turn commonplaces about a "fleeting world" or "dust to dust" into messages or personal malevolence towards her nephew. She is a master of particularizing the general. This becomes more apparent in the later adult scene, when Seaton's fiancée Alice has been added to the party. Her dark hair becomes a text for a sermon on mortality, that is also a personal threat: "Consider, Mr. Withers; dark hair, dark eyes, dark cloud, dark night, dark vision, dark death, dark grave, dark DARK!"

But the threat also goes beyond death, when she quotes Withers: "As for death and the grave, I don't suppose we shall much notice that." This foreshadows the story's climax when on Withers's last visit to the house, after Seaton's death, she calls to him by Seaton's name. Her expression at finding herself in the presence of the living suggests that her real enjoyment is in tormenting the dead. Similarly, previous hints about ghostly companions are given definite expression, when she rebuts the suggestion of loneliness:

I was never lonely in my life. I don't look to flesh and blood for my company. When you've got to be my age, Mr. Smithers (which God forbid), you'll find life a very different affair from what you seem to think it is now. You won't seek company then, I'll be bound. It's thrust on you.

In a story full of ambiguities, that "God forbid" is the most poignant. Does it spring out of malevolence, or pity? If the second, then we may find something almost unselfish in her pessimism. Perhaps she means that life only becomes sadder as it goes on longer.

After this, Withers escapes, like so many de la Mare characters in other stories, to the railway station. He feels guilty because he does not go to look for Seaton's grave in the churchyard; he does not clearly know why this is. The story's last sentence, which might easily be dismissed as a mere formality, is worth special attention:

My rather horrible thought was that, so far as I was concerned—one of his extremely few friends—he had never been much better than "buried" in my mind.

There is a general point here, which will help us to define the differences between de la Mare and writers of ordinary ghost stories. The ghostliness is subordinate to general human values, which do not differ from those embodied in literary forms usually considered more weighty then the ghost story. In the end what matters most is not just the eeriness of paranormal experience, but human relations. We suddenly see Seaton and his ill-requited dependence on his friend in a new light. We experience vicariously opportunity irrevocably lost; Seaton is beyond Wither's help, even if he may not be beyond his aunt's interference.

A similar general point could be made about de la Mare's lifelong obsession, in his prose and verse writings, with death. Spooky, eerie, artful it often is. But it is more than that. It has also the dignity of radical questioning about life; since until we form a view about the meaning of death we cannot have a coherent view of life. We might miss the hint here, if the point had not been more explicit elsewhere, for instance in de la Mare's "Peacock Pie" or in the eloquent passage about "Mors" in "Ding Dong Bell": "It means, well, sleep, or nightmare, or dawn, or nothing, or—it might mean everything." On the whole, there are more questions than answers on the meaning of death. But the questions never became mere literary devices. In age, as in youth, the curiosity about the overwhelming question retains its freshness.

—A.O.J. Cockshut

THE SECRET LIFE OF WALTER MITTY
by James Thurber, 1942

As a comic short story writer, James Thurber had few rivals in the mid-20th century. "The Secret Life of Walter Mitty" (collected in *My World—and Welcome to It,* 1942) is arguably the best of his stories and is still cited as an exemplar of its form during that period.

Thurber's story has its roots in American cultural tradition. His chief character, Walter Mitty, has forerunners in native folklore and fiction. Carl M. Lindner points out that "Mitty is a descendant of Rip Van Winkle and Tom Sawyer" in serving to orchestrate the theme of conflict between the individual and society, and "he dream-wishes qualities customarily exhibited by the legendary frontier hero." At the same time, the main theme of the story, the craving for power, is presented in a distinctively modern context.

Mitty's occupation is not specified, but the suggestion generated by his lifestyle is that he is some type of clerk. The story is about craving for power by the powerless. Whereas Shakespeare's Macbeth, in his quest for power, crosses the border between thought and action, and seeks power in reality, Thurber's Mitty is placed in circumstances that permit him to enjoy power only in fantasy and offer him no avenue of achieving it in real life.

The story begins with an episode of fantasy. Mitty imagines that he is a Navy commander piloting a hydroplane through the worst storm in 20 years of flying. Modern American life is bedevilled by mechanical devices, technology, the demand for super-efficiency, and Mitty dreams that he is a master of it all. His description of himself in this episode suggests a man of steel. But the fantasy is suddenly juxtaposed with fact, the basic technique of the story. The eight-engined hydroplane is played off against a car and the hero against a mild, ordinary human being whose domineering wife snaps, "Not so fast!" Mitty typifies the male whom critics have called "the Thurber man," while his wife represents the female characterized as "the Thurber woman." Thurber's view of the battle of the sexes in 20th-century America is that the women have won it.

It is ironical that when Mitty's imagination is working, his wife feels that he needs medical treatment, psychiatric treatment in particular, in which Americans place trust, markedly so in Thurber's period. Mrs. Mitty gets out of the car at the hairdresser's with a parting order to her husband to wear his gloves. He rebels against her momentarily and takes them off, significantly, after she has departed. But when a cop snaps at him at the traffic lights, Mitty confuses his voice with that of his wife and hastily pulls on his gloves.

Characteristically in this story, surroundings trigger the fantasies. These gloves of Mitty are transformed into surgical gloves in his mind and he imagines that he is a surgeon. His patient, the millionaire banker Wellington McMillan, has Mitty's initials and Mitty's psychiatrist reappears as a surgeon inferior to him. As Mitty, in his dream, confidently gets ready to perform the impossible operation on McMillan and save him from certain death, it becomes clearer that what he craves is absolute power, the power over life and death. Thus, he is Thurber's most ambitious hero.

During the operation, Mitty (once again) handles a complicated machine, a defective "anesthetizer" with competence and nonchalance, with practical resource too, using a fountain pen to replace a faulty piston. The fantasy is then juxtaposed with reality. Mitty, in fact, is unable to handle his own car. He is in the wrong lane, and, in contrast to him, a parking-lot attendant backs Mitty's car up "with insolent skill."

A newsboy's shout about the Waterbury trial releases him from worry about a forgotten item in his shopping list, and he begins to imagine himself the cool accused in a court room scene. He shows super-efficiency even as a murderer. His concluding reference to "cur" in his imagined scene reminds him of the missing item on his shopping list—"puppy biscuit." He cannot remember its brand name, but the effect of American advertising agencies is evident—he remember the advertising slogan, "Puppies Bark for it."

Mitty then goes to the hotel to wait for his wife. He picks up an old copy of *Liberty* and the title triggers a dream about the threat of domination posed by Germany during World War II. Mitty imagines himself the pilot of a giant bomber, setting off amidst firing cannons, machine guns, and flame-throwers, to knock out an ammunition dump. Mrs. Mitty interrupts his fantasy.

In depicting Mitty's fantasies, Thurber uses deceptive terms that are really non-existent (the "streptothricosis" or "ductal tract" during the operation) or inaccurate ("coreopsis" is not a medical term as used in the story but a genus of plants; in war slang the Germans were not "Archies" but "Jerries"). These subtly underline Mitty's ignorance of heroic experience while remaining oblivious of his mistakes as he persists in his fantasies regardless. The result is both amusing and pathetic.

Mrs. Mitty remembers that she has something to purchase and goes to the drugstore on the corner. Mitty then imagines his last fantasy, the story closing in the same vein it began. He is facing a firing squad, scorning to be blindfolded—a victim with a touch of the heroic. It is true that Mitty is unable to cope with the petty demands of life, but the possibility is not negated that he could handle more important tasks if given a chance. Thurber did insist that the perceptive reader would detect in his work "a basic and indestructible thread of hope." Mitty is a projection, not of the author, but of aspects of the American national psyche.

—D.C.R.A. Goonetilleke

THE SECRET SHARER
by Joseph Conrad, 1912

Joseph Conrad's "The Secret Sharer," written in late 1909, explores his favorite theme of how individuals come to know and define themselves. More intense and intellectualized than his earlier fiction, the story possesses a design, characters, setting, and style that turn in upon themselves to imply how the process of self-realization unfolds. The result is a modernist masterpiece of implication and suggestion. As a consequence, the story has drawn a good deal of critical attention, is frequently anthologized, and—along with "Heart of Darkness," which it in some ways resembles—is usually regarded as being among Conrad's best and most evocative works.

Because of the story's construction, the sparseness of characters and paucity of action complicate rather than resolve meaning. The captain-narrator appears to relate in a reasonably straight-forward fashion the events that occurred soon after he took charge of his first ship's command in the Gulf of Siam, but questions soon arise. The narrator remains unnamed and his character is never objectively delineated; his story is revealed to have occurred at a "distance of years" from the time of its telling; and the precise nature of his relationship with his "secret sharer," a seaman named Leggatt, is especially puzzling and never defined. Although Leggatt represents some powerful force for the narrator-captain, the nature of that force remains open to a range of different interpretations. The story is built around only a few major actions, but these events, too, are complicated by the narrative framing, interpolated stories, and the first person point of view. Even Leggatt's story (while serving as chief mate of the *Sephora* he accidently killed a sailor and has escaped by swimming away) requires explication. What is clear is that to the narrator suffering in the solitude of his first command, all details become loaded with an excruciatingly acute significance, and the strong bond he feels with Leggatt invests every circumstance with metaphorical import. The Eastern setting and the relative isolation of his ship at sea compound feelings of alienation. His identification with Leggatt, a criminal, conflicts with his untried sense of authority and duty to legalities. His investigation of this relationship is his way of exploring "how far I should turn out faithful to that ideal conception of one's own personality every man sets up for himself secretly," a concern he has raised early in his narrative.

The peculiar thematic intensity of the story derives primarily from its descriptive style, from the way that events are perceived rather than from what actually happens. Although surface details are rendered with typical Conradian precision, they take on an enigmatic or cryptic quality as they emerge through the brooding consciousness of the introspective narrator. The first sentence describing the lines of fishing stakes observable from the narrator's ship immediately establishes this quality: the stakes resemble "a mysterious system of half-submerged" fences, "incomprehensible" in its design and "crazy of aspect." Later the riding light—which attracts Leggatt—is described as having a "clear, untroubled, as if symbolic flame . . . in the mysterious shades of the night." Much of the secret partnership with Leggatt—the hushed whisperings, the concealment in the captain's cabin, the necessary duplicity towards the crew—is described in similar terms. In such a context it is not surprising that interpreters discover deep archetypal significance in facts such as Leggatt's initial appearance from the sea at night, naked, and seeming to be a headless corpse. The "L" shape of the captain's quarters; the similar size, appearance, and background of the two major characters; the hidden significance in the few proper names that are revealed; the preponderance of doubled images; and the series of references like "my double" or "my second self" all compound possibilities of meaning. Many readers feel Leggatt represents an instinctive capacity for action or imaginative strength and symbolizes one side of the captain's conflict between public and private values; Archbold, the captain of the *Sephora,* may embody the other side, and the narrator is caught between the two.

Much critical energy has been spent exploring the significance of particular details and actions. The captain's risking his crew and ship to come as close to the island of Koh-ring as possible, for example, is usually perceived in terms of a crucial rite of passage, or the Captain's hat, which remains floating on the water in the final scene, is scrutinized as being a particularly important symbol. The large number of classical and Biblical allusions in Conrad's writing promotes such interpretive concerns, especially for scenes like the final one where the ship is described as being like "a bark of the dead floating in slowly under the very gate of Erebus." His style helps transform otherwise ordinary events into a ritual night sea passage, a descent into the underworld, or a Cain and Abel story.

The story's involved moral questions capture many of the modernist concerns with the quest for identity, the nature of evil, the pervasiveness of guilt, the value of codes of conduct, the friability of institutions. Although the denouement seems positive—the captain feels "the perfect communion of a seaman with his first command," and his secret sharer is "a free man, a proud swimmer striking out for a new destiny"—it still is never clear whether Leggatt is an evil that has been exorcised, or whether his brief relationship with the captain has simply provided a timely opportunity for greater understanding. Most interpreters feel, however, that in spite of the final sense of affirmation, the story suggests that the process of self-definition is both exceedingly complex and that it is rooted in tragedy. The enduring popularity of "The Secret Sharer" seems to confirm this vision.

—Thomas Loe

SEIZE THE DAY
by Saul Bellow, 1956

Published between two of his most expansive novels, *The Adventures of Augie March* and *Henderson the Rain King*—two "loose, baggy monsters," to borrow Henry James's term for such works—is Saul Bellow's tautest composition, *Seize the Day.* All of the action in the novella takes place within the compass of a few blocks on New York's West Side during several hours of what the protagonist, Tommy Wilhelm, senses from the outset will be his day of reckoning. Far from sharing the ebullience of Augie March or Henderson, Tommy is among the most abject and passive of Bellow's heroes, and yet he resembles the protagonists of the big novels in being "a visionary sort of animal. Who has to believe that he can know why he exists." Unlike the two of them, Tommy has never seriously attempted to plumb that question. What he has not actively sought is, nonetheless, seeking him. Bellow recounts the story almost entirely from Wilhelm's point of view, albeit with a psychological penetration and a power of expression of which the protagonist himself is scarcely capable. As Daniel Fuchs's study of the successive drafts of *Seize the Day* reveals, Bellow is as scrupulous a pursuer of the *mot juste* as Flaubert or James, however much his racy, nervous idiom departs from theirs. The novella is Bellow's most patterned narrative; every word is made to count.

Seize the Day is the story, played out with a nearly Greek inexorability, of a failed actor, failed salesman, failed husband, ineffectual father, and fading lover, who on the day in question sees his last seven hundred dollars go up in smoke on the commodities market and experiences his own father's definitive repudiation of him. For most of these disasters—his career as a Hollywood extra, his marriage to the exacting Margaret, his financial dealings with the confidence man Tamkin—Tommy has set himself up: "After much thought and hesitation and debate he invariably took the course he had rejected innumerable times." At the root of this compulsion to err lies Wilhelm's relationship to his parents, to the mother whose brooding, tender-hearted nature he has inherited and whose memory he adores, as well as to the chilly, egocentric physician father whose professional success and impeccable demeanor constitute a standing reproach to the slovenly 44-year-old who still feels as though he were the doctor's "small son" and whose blessing he continues to crave. In all his ties Tommy endlessly re-enacts his mother's humiliation at his father's hands.

Nowhere is this disposition more evident than in his affinity for "Dr." Tamkin, into whose investment schemes he allows himself, in spite of better knowledge, to be drawn. His doing so is in part a desperate wager, a hope that the survival artist Tamkin "would get through this crisis too and bring him, Wilhelm, to safety also," but beyond this, and more fundamentally, he is seeking in Tamkin the solicitude his father has denied him. Unfortunately the chief resemblance between Dr. Tamkin, whose pointed shoulder, bald head, and claw-like nails suggest a buzzard, and Dr. Adler (German for "eagle") is their preying on others' emotions. Much of the time Tamkin mouths half-digested formulas out of Wilhelm Reich. "Biologically," he intones in his wonderfully fatuous fashion, "the pretender soul takes away the energy of the true soul and makes it feeble, like a parasite. It happens unconsciously, unawaringly, in the depths of the organism." And yet Tommy's sense that Tamkin does, finally, speak "a kind of truth" is not altogether wide of the mark. The doctrine of the two souls in particular touches a nerve.

Seize the Day concerns itself, above all, with the protagonist's yearning to be restored—or raised up for the first time—to his essential being. "Tommy Wilhelm," the identity he has assumed during his Hollywood days, he acknowledges a pretender. Even Wilky, the name his parents have given him, seems a merely social self. "Might the name of his true soul," he speculates, "be the one by which his old grandfather had called him—Velvel?" Ultimately, he realizes, his essence cannot receive a personal name; it lies beyond individuality. The true soul consists in a "larger body" in which all of us are joined, an oversoul. This intimation stems from his experience in a dark tunnel under Times Square, a surreal moment in which the commonplace is revealed to be the extraordinary: "in the haste, heat, and darkness which disfigure and make freaks and fragments of nose and eyes and teeth, all of a sudden, unsought, a general love for all these imperfect and lurid-looking people burst out in Wilhelm's breast. . . . And as he walked he began to say, 'Oh my brothers—my brothers and my sisters,' blessing them all as well as himself." How seriously is one to take this? Tommy himself is unsure. Perhaps it is just a figment that has surfaced out of some obscure corner of the psyche, with no more significance than—the analogy is his—a casual erection. The vision will not, however, admit of such vulgar dismissal. In this his hardest hour it offers, he decides, "the right clue. . . . Something very big. Truth, like." Neither the terms in which this affirmation is cast nor anything leading up to it will incline the reader to repose much trust in Tommy as a spiritual authority. All the same, the subway epiphany is

pivotal. From this point on it becomes more difficult to view Wilhelm's suffering as mere pathology; one begins to look for a redemptive meaning in it.

The concluding scene of *Seize the Day* is one of the supreme moments in short fiction, akin to Gabriel Conroy's rapprochement with Michael Furey in Joyce's "The Dead" or the protagonist's acceptance of his mortality in "The Death of Ivan Ilyich." In Tommy Wilhelm's case an unnamed corpse laid out in a Broadway funeral parlor becomes his secret sharer. "A man—another human creature," he reflects compassionately, but his lamentation quickly shifts to his own concerns; it is Tommy he grieves for. This may be a distinction without much of a difference. "The man's brother, maybe?" asks one of the mourners, awed and baffled by the intensity of Tommy's feeling. And so he is, in the sense he has recognized in that tunnel beneath Times Square. The last lines of the story depict him as having sunk "deeper than sorrow," to a depth it may be where he understands that he is "only on loan to [him]self." The phrase is Tamkin's, but that does not render it invalid. "One hundred falsehoods," remarks Tommy, "but at last one truth."

—Richard K. Cross

THE SHAWL
by Cynthia Ozick, 1988

First published in 1981 in *The New Yorker* magazine, "The Shawl" was combined in 1988 with another piece of short fiction, "Rosa," to comprise a novella also titled *The Shawl*. Although the two segments are correlated, the 1981 story certainly has a power and integrity sufficient to stand on its own merits for its rendering of the Holocaust in searingly vivid sensory impressions of the cold, filth, starvation, and paralytic fear that afflicted its death camp victims. At the same time that these horrors arouse our sympathy, however, Ozick's strongly held Judaic ethos puts her victim-hero's maternal passion in conflict with the central basis of Jewish identity. "The single most serviceable . . . description of a Jew," she has written, is "someone who shuns idols." An idol, in turn, is anything that is treasured "instead of" God. And there is no doubting that Rosa Lublin, in *The Shawl*, reveres her martyred infant instead of God, going so far as to worship the shawl it had slept in as a sacred totem.

Even the child's name, Magda—a cognate of "magic"—evokes the realm of occult power that classic Judaism repudiates. In fact, Ozick's general choice of names reinforces her theme of cultural conflict. Although Rosa's last name, Lublin, is a powerful reminder of the Holocaust atrocities associated with Poland's second largest city (after Warsaw), where 200,000 Jews were liquidated, her first name, along with that of Stella and Magda, suggest a peculiarly Christianized sensibility. Traditionally, the rose, as in a cathedral's rose window, symbolizes the Incarnation of Christ, while the other two names, Stella and Magda, evoke Latinate analogies with the Advent of the Christ child, the former with the star of Bethlehem and the latter with the Magi who came bearing gifts. (To Orthodox Judaism, an icon such as a crucifix is a graven image and the Trinity represents polytheism, making Christianity a pagan religion). Deepening this dilemma of Jewish identity under siege is the apparent paternity of the child, whose blond eyes and blue hair lead Stella to call her "Aryan"— "You could think she was one of *their* babies." (In "Rosa," the evidence favors Magda's father being an SS guard.)

A consummate stylist in her other writings, Ozick here works to the outer reach of her talent, combining a mastery of metaphor with brutally precise diction for her most unforgettable effects. The filth in the barracks, for example, comes across in the "thick turd-braids, and the slow stinking waterfall that slunk down from the upper bunks, the stink mixed with a bitter fatty floating smoke that greased Rosa's skin." Outside, in "the ash-stippled wind," Rosa's teen-age niece, Stella, looks skeletal—"Her knees were tumors on sticks, her elbows chicken bones. . . . Rosa and Stella were slowly turning into air." Surrounding the camp meanwhile, in heartless mockery, is the burgeoning glory of nature: "The sunheat murmured of another life, of butterflies in summer . . . . green meadows speckled with dandelions and deep-colored violets . . . innocent tiger lilies, tall, lifting their orange bonnets." The two contrasting realms, of nature's beauty and human brutality, seem to join for one paralyzing moment when the infant, Magda, is flung by a guard into the fence, making her appear to Rosa, from a distance, "like a butterfly touching a silver wire." But the electrified fence, when the child hits it, becomes animate with Moloch-like hunger: "the steel voices went mad in their growling."

At this moment, Rosa too goes mad with the maternal frenzy which would sustain her idolatrous daughter-worship undiminished through a lifetime. In the novella at large, though not in "The Shawl," we discover the reason for Rosa's cultural inadequacy. Before the war, she had been raised in a wealthy family so totally assimilated into the Polish aristocracy as to make her utterly de-Judaized. As a result, her major grievance against the Warsaw ghetto is her family's forced proximity to its class inferiors: "we were furious because we had to be billeted with such a class, with these old peasant Jews worn out from their rituals and superstitions, phylacteries on their foreheads sticking up so stupidly, like unicorn horns." The conflicting claims of maternal idolatry, class bias, and the Judaic ethos in *The Shawl* form a rich texture of ideas and feelings to which "The Shawl" is prologue. And in its own right, despite her reluctance to make art of the Holocaust (which delayed publication for several years), "The Shawl" figures to rank as a classic work on the subject, with an interior grasp of Holocaust horror that is graphic enough to be unsurpassed in the realm of imaginative literature.

—Victor Strandberg

THE SHE-WOLF
by Saki, 1914

Throughout 1912, "Saki" published a series of stories in the *Morning Post* and the glossy weekly *Bystander* at the rate of one or two per month. In 1914, when 36 tales had been written, John Lane published the collection known as *Beasts and Super-Beasts* (an ironic hint at George Bernard Shaw's *Man and Superman*, which appeared in 1905). "The She-Wolf" is the first story in the collection.

An upper class of witty, deprecating, and ironic people, whose habitat is the country house before the onset of World War I—these are the characters and context of "The She-Wolf." Its humour is perfectly measured, poised upon the brink of awful revelation, dissolving into reassurance as the joke is played out to its audience. It is a world both fragile in its constructions of imagination and resourceful in its devious scorn for platitude.

Though Munro is often thought of as an English writer, he was born in Burma of Scottish parents, and, like many of his best stories, "The She-Wolf" displays themes and attitudes typical of Scottish fiction. Saki's short fiction is related to that of James Hogg, Walter Scott, and R.L. Stevenson, in its balance upon the edge of some terrible supernatural manifestation, in its double focus on materialist society and the imminent metaphysical world, which is conspicuous by its absence but always on the point of breaking through, in its use of comic convention to abet a serious argument, and in its attitude towards the characters, simultaneously ironic and sympathetic.

"The She-Wolf" concerns the come-uppance of Leonard Bilsiter, a "drawing-room visionary" whose brief acquaintance with East European folklore turns him into a houseparty bore on the subject of the "esoteric forces" of "Siberian magic." Baited by his hostess and challenged to turn her into a she-wolf ("it would be too confusing to change one's sex as well as one's species at a moment's notice"), Bilsiter is thrown into horrified distress along with the rest of the company, when the hostess disappears behind a setting of fern and azaleas, and a large, evil-looking timber wolf appears in her place.

The reader has been in on the game. A third party, Clovis Sangrail, overhearing the initial conversation, has acquired a tame wolf from the menagerie of Lord Pabham. In connivance with the hostess, he has brought the she-wolf to take her place in an impish practical jape which has the desired effect of producing shocked consternation in Bilsiter. Lord Pabham decoys the animal out of the room and when Mrs. Hampton reappears, she claims to have woken from mesmerized sleep, finding herself in the game larder, being fed with sugar by Lord Pabham. After protesting his innocence, Bilsiter has now lost the opportunity to claim responsibility for the magical changes the company has witnessed. Clovis comes forward and takes his bow, explaining, not the facts of the subterfuge, but that he himself had lived for years in northeastern Russia, becoming quite conversant with the strange powers of "Siberian magic," and doesn't like to hear "a lot of nonsense being talked about them." This leaves Bilsiter feeling that if he could have transformed Clovis at that moment, "into a cockroach and then have stepped on him he would gladly have performed both operations."

At one level, "The She-Wolf" is an adult version of the nursery tale "The Boy Who Cried Wolf"; but it is also full of delightfully self-conscious language, whose precision the reader may savour. On Bilsiter's visit to Eastern Europe, the railway strike leaves him "in a state of suspended locomotion." The euphonious quality of Bilsiter's own name is itself wickedly suggestive of a conversationalist of spurious value. Moreover, vulnerable creatures are a veiled presence beneath the elegant humour and moral imperatives of the tale. Bilsiter's Aunt Cecilia ("who loved sensation perhaps rather better than she loved the truth") has already paved the way for his indulgences in vanity, averring that she had already seen him turn a vegetable marrow into a wood-pigeon. And a nice touch is the moment when Mrs. Hampton feeds the macaws in the conservatory, just before she appears to turn into the wolf that looks as though it might eat the same birds. Such a sense of creatural vulnerability, human susceptibility and vanity, counterpoints the network of planning, co-operation, and trust by which characters rise above their weaker fellows. This is the significance of the ironic title of the book in which "The She-Wolf" first appeared.

The conspiracy of Clovis, Mary Hampton, and Lord Pabham is ultimately benign, for it is a justified game to trounce the hapless Bilsiter, and it is played with the reader as one of the silent conspirators, whose engagement confirms the justice of the judgement, and whose sense of the credibility of the action enhances the pleasure in the comic effects of its performance.

—Alan Riach

———

THE SHE-WOLF (La Lupa)
by Giovanni Verga, 1880

Between March and July 1880 Giovanni Verga published a number of short stories dealing with peasant life in Sicily. They included "Cavalleria Rusticana" and "La Lupa"("The She-Wolf"). Republished in book form at the end of the year under the title *Vita dei Campi,* the collection was moderately well received: reviewers recognised a new voice speaking in an original way about a world strikingly different from the urban society whose mores preoccupied French realist authors.

The novelty and unity of Verga's material partly obscured the diversity of his experiments in narrative technique in the various stories. In "Cavalleria Rusticana," for instance, he illuminates the progress of events by presenting different facets of the interrelationships of the characters, set by set, in a complex close-knit design. The structure of "The She-Wolf" is altogether simpler and starker. Here attention is concentrated on one overwhelming tragic passion and the treatment is narrowly compressed.

The short opening paragraph is powerful in its concision: "She was tall, thin; she had the firm and vigorous breasts of the olive-skinned—and yet she was no longer young; she was pale, as if always plagued by malaria, and in that pallor, two enormous eyes, and fresh red lips which devoured you." It is an arresting portrait. The selection of details is both economical and charged with reverberations. We do not know who she is nor what will happen, nor to whom; we see and more forcibly feel the presence of a woman of sexual power, sensuality, and consuming mystery.

The next paragraph fleshes out some of these traits. She is known as "the She-Wolf, because she never had enough—of anything"; she prowls about on her own like a wild bitch, devouring sons and husbands and even the parish priest, "a true servant of God [who] had lost his soul on account of her"; she "never went to church, not at Easter, not at Christmas, not to hear Mass, not for confession"; when she appears the women of the village make the sign of the cross. She is both She-Wolf and She-Devil.

The next brief paragraph introduces her daughter Maricchia, a good girl whom no one will marry despite her sizeable dowry. Then in the fourth paragraph the dramatic action starts. It too is handled with the same concision as the introductory setting.

The She-Wolf falls in love with a young man with whom she works in the fields, he reaping corn, she gathering and binding the sheaves. The thirst induced by the torrid June sun is mirrored in the fire the She-Wolf feels in her flesh. Following close at the indifferent Nanni's heels, she never stops to drink from her flask; her sexual desire remains equally unslaked. The images reinforce each other powerfully and economically. One is reminded of Hemingway's dictum that a writer may omit things "and the reader, if the writer is writing truly enough, will have a feeling of those things as strongly as if the writer had stated them" One evening the She-Wolf answers Nanni's repeated question: "What is it you want, Pina?" "It's you I want. You who are beautiful as the sun and sweet as honey. I want you!" "And I want your daughter, instead, who's a maid," answered Nanni laughing.

The She-Wolf walks away. But in October she reappears when Nanni is working near her house. She offers him her daughter in marriage and her house as an extra dowry, reserving a corner in the kitchen for her own sleeping quarters. The daughter objects to Nanni but the She-Wolf threatens to kill her if she refuses him.

In the next episode the passage of time is unobtrusively compressed. The She-Wolf no longer haunts people's doorways; the lapse of years is handled in the phrase, "Maricchia stayed at home nursing the babies, and her mother went into the fields to work with the men," even in the heat of August, "in those hours between nones and vespers when no good woman goes roving around." The proverbial phrase is neatly deployed with its folkloric overtone, the belief that malignant spirits are abroad at that time. The scene in which the She-Wolf rouses Nanni from his afternoon slumber and seduces him is a superb example of description suppressed, as are the subsequent intense brief glimpses of Nanni's mingled desire and revulsion. Maricchia, now in love with her husband and protecting her babes like a young she-wolf herself, denounces the incestuous pair to the police sergeant, who threatens Nanni with the gallows but ignores his desperate plea to be jailed to keep him from temptation. The power of the state does nothing for him; the power of the church when he is at the point of death is just as impotent, and operates to save him only through the She-Wolf's own decision to leave the house and let the priest hear Nanni's last confession. But Nanni recovers and threatens to kill the She-Wolf when she returns to tempt him again. "Kill me," she answers, "I can't stand it without you."

The final scene when Nanni, wild eyed, advances on the She-Wolf axe in hand, is once more starkly drawn, with its swift ambiguous climax as the She-Wolf walks towards him, her hands laden with red poppies, her black eyes devouring him, while Nanni stammers, "Ah! damn your soul!"

Verga had spent periods of his boyhood and youth at his family's country properties, when the conditions, attitudes, and values of the impoverished Sicilian peasants had come as a revelation to him. Doomed to lives of toil and hardship, defenceless before the authority of landlords, church and state, they were people whose frustrations were apt to erupt in uncontrollable passion and violence. Verga found the matter of his tales in real events; he turned them into art by exploring their psychological wellsprings in new narrative modes. For him, fictional realism demanded that the author "should disappear"; he aimed at some kind of impersonal objectivity of presentation which would be true to life.

Acclaimed today as the master of Italian *verismo,* he fought shy of such labels. To his French translator he wrote in 1899, "I think that in an original writer his own method is of supreme importance and that his so-called school matters very little. . . .I would say that I tried to put myself under the skin of my characters, tried to see things with their eyes, and express things with their words—that's all."

In point of fact the author does not and cannot "disappear," as Benedetto Croce pointed out in the first major critical study of Verga's work. However seemingly objective his narrative technique, the writer is always there, selecting, shaping, presenting—in Verga's case with supreme artistry in conveying a tragic view of life.

—Stewart F. Sanderson

THE SHORT HAPPY LIFE OF FRANCIS MACOMBER
by Ernest Hemingway, 1936

No story by Ernest Hemingway is more famous than "The Short Happy Life of Francis Macomber." Popular with general readers, it has also attracted an enormous amount of scholarly attention—and debate. Long aware of the basis of the story in Hemingway's first African safari, scholars have over the years identified numerous literary parallels and influences, ranging form Stephen Crane and Leo Tolstoi to Captain Marryat. The debate began in the 1960's when the traditional reading of Margot Macomber as the archetypal bitch of American fiction became suspect. Had she really intended to end the life of Francis Macomber after he discovered his manhood?

The story is in many ways atypical for Hemingway. Few of his short stories foreground physical action to the extent that we find it in the Macomber story. Usually Hemingway portrays his protagonists confronting themselves very privately, though the context may be physical action such as war (numerous Nick stories) or crime ("The Killers"). "The Snows of Kilimanjaro," Hemingway's other African story, is closer to the norm of private or inner conflicts. Also a story with important analogs to Tolstoi's "The Death of Ivan Ilych," "Snows" may be profitably seen as a companion story to "The Short Happy Life." Indeed, Hemingway wrote it immediately after finishing "The Short Happy Life." These two stories answer the bad reviews he had received for *Green Hills of Africa*, his nonfictional account of his African safari. Although Hemingway continued to write short stories almost until the end of his life, he completed his major contribution to the genre with the African stories.

"The Short Happy Life of Francis Macomber" is unique among Hemingway short stories in highlighting the name of its protagonist. Not only does the full name rest boldly in the title, Hemingway also uses "Francis" or "Macomber" frequently throughout the story, the first name a telling part of the uncomfortable given of Macomber's indecisive manhood. He is white-livered, his wife charges by calling him, "Francis, my pearl."

F. Scott Fitzgerald, with the hidden first name, Francis, was on Hemingway's mind when he worked on both African stories. (In the magazine version of "Snows" he had angered Fitzgerald by referring directly to "Scott" and the very rich.) In both African stories, written during the middle of the Great Depression, Hemingway took the very rich—Fitzgerald's terrain—as his subject. He was also haunted by Fitzgerald's article in *Esquire* about Fitzgerald's "crack-up." Fitzgerald's manhood was always a worry to Hemingway, but in the African stories he also seemed intent on warding off any "crack-up" for Ernest Hemingway.

There is little mystery about Francis Macomber's character. Born to money and good looks, he is an idle dabbler. He has not had to forge an identity; the inherited Macomber name and wealth have been sufficient. Now in mid-life, he is married to a beautiful woman, Margot. Together they seek adventure on an African safari, Macomber subconsciously eager to realize his manhood or to satisfy his wife's doubts about it. Certainly, he seeks the symbols of such manhood. Although he bolts when the lion he has wounded charges, in the next day's hunt he discovers that fear of death need not control him. He proves the point by not bolting when the wounded buffalo charges. And whatever Margot's motivation when she shoots Macomber, he is transformed, or, with safari leader Robert Wilson's concurrence, thinks that he is, which may be the same thing. Macomber's death means, of course, that there will be no long-term testing of his manhood. That makes his death "fortunate"; if his bravery is only illusion, he keeps it intact.

As he worked on "The Short Happy Life," Hemingway considered an exceptionally large number of titles, twenty-six. The majority of these titles refer to marriage, portraying it as an enormous power struggle—the most deadly. In the last 25-years, criticism has given more attention to that dimension, often inviting readers to see Margot Macomber more sympathetically, to see her as victim as much as Francis—not an easy step for some readers given their sense of Hemingway's bias against women. For them, Margot is proof that the female is the most deadly of the species. Margot indeed has many good lines that challenge the assumptions and authority of the males—and some of her own actions as well. She, after all, was eager for the safari, seems to have instigated it. But from the start she questions its meaning. She tells Wilson that he was "lovely" as he killed the lion; "That is if blowing things' heads off is lovely." (Her qualification is a grim foreshadowing of the story's ending.) She questions a good deal more before the story's end—the ethics of the chase and certainly the meaning of Francis's transformation. That is something that she first desires, then fears. Although Wilson turns harshly against Margot after she shoots Francis, his earlier thinking has demonstrated a good deal of sympathy for her. He senses *her* complexity. "What's in her heart, God knows," he thinks—a line that should caution readers that Wilson does not.

As readers have been more willing to consider Margot with sympathy—seeing her as victim of her class, her culture, and ineffectual males—they have tended to turn against Wilson. He has been charged with sexism, racism, opportunism—reversing early readings that made him the admired tutor to Francis the tyro. His anger with Margot at the story's end may tell us more about Wilson and his inadequacies than it does about Margot and hers. Wilson's greatest moment of exaltation in the story corresponds with Macomber's. He marks it by quoting the lines of another Francis (Shakespeare's (Feeble): "By my troth, I care not; a man can die but once; we owe God a death and let it go which way it will he that dies this year is quit for the next." But the sentiment provides Wilson with no consolation after Macomber lies dead before him.

In fact, none of the characters of "The Short Happy Life" is without flaw. None shows much understanding of self—though Macomber moves in that direction; Margot's "accidental" killing of Francis may reflect the complexity of her transformation. Arguably, Wilson's anger is displaced anger against himself, a reflection of his own miscalculations. In narrating the Macomber safari, Hemingway uses multiple centers of consciousness (though significantly not Margot's), emphasizing the inadequacies of any single viewpoint and the flaws of each member of his triangle. By taking readers briefly into the consciousness of the wounded lion, he underscores the importance of the multiple perspectives to his tale. Thus, readers who sense Margot's better side trust the omniscient narrator on a crucial issue when he reports that she "shot at the buffalo" as it "seemed about to gore Macomber." Her weapon is a "Mannlicher," an ironic touch that still persuades some readers of an intention different from the stated one in the narrative. Hemingway's tale teems with ironies and paradoxes, however. A story that once seemed among his simplest now ranks among his most complex.

—Joseph M. Flora

THE SHROUD (Kafan)
by Premcand, 1936

Published in 1936, just months before Premcand's death, "Kafan" ("The Shroud") is generally thought to be the author's best, blackest, and most powerful short story. Set in an Indian village, the milieu of Premcand's best works, on a dark, chilly winter night, it is the story of the father, Ghisu, and his son, Madhav, who sit at the door of their hut roasting potatoes, potatoes stolen from a neighbor's field. Budhiya, Madhav's young wife of one year, is inside groaning in childbirth. Neither man responds to her moans. In fact, Madhav is annoyed. His father urges him to look in on the girl, and he asks, "If she's going to die why doesn't she get it over with? What can I do by looking?"

Lazy, dishonest, and superstitious, Ghisu and Madhav are members of the untouchable leather-worker caste, the poorest and lowest members of India's highly structured social hierarchy. Both father and son refuse to do farm work that is readily available in the community. Instead, they prefer to take handouts or cheat others to maintain themselves at a subsistence level. Though Budhiya has been a good wife and had established some order in the men's chaotic lives, neither wishes to spend money to get her help. Believing her to be "possessed by some ghost," they will not enter the hut. Moreover, they believe that "God will provide," as he always seems to have done in the past. Speaking editorially, the author notes that Ghisu is smarter than most Indian peasants, for he has managed to earn himself the lowest reputation in the village, yet survive without engaging in honest working.

As if to negate the horror of the woman dying in childbirth, Ghisu recalls a sumptuous wedding feast he attended 20 years before. Yearning for the olden days, he complains, "Nobody feeds us like that now." Instead, people are taken with "economizing and hoarding." Finishing their potatoes, they curl up and fall asleep, "just like two enormous coiled pythons."

The next morning Madhav goes into the hut and finds his wife dead, the baby having died inside the womb. Both men go about the village beating their chests wailing "according to the old tradition." They receive consolation from the other villagers, and, to get money for the shroud and firewood needed to cremate the dead woman, they go the the village's major landowner and beg. Though the landowner knows them to be cheats, he reluctantly throws them a few rupees. They then make the rounds, collecting money for the cremation from other people. They end up with five rupees, in addition to other gifts of grain and wood.

The men decide they have enough wood, then start to have second thoughts about purchasing a shroud, since the corpse will be taken from the hut at night and no one will see it. Moreover, why spend money on something that is going to be burned anyway? Wandering through the market, the two find themselves, "by some divine inspiration or other," in front of the village liquor store. They order a bottle and some food. As they drink and eat "in the lordly manner of tigers enjoying their kill in the jungle," the second allusion to their animal-like behavior, they gradually sink into drunkenness. Initially they have qualms about not purchasing a shroud, but rationalize their decision with praises for the dead woman: "even dying she got us fine things to eat and drink." When they are about to leave the tavern, Ghisu magnanimously offers a famished beggar their leftovers, asking him to bless the dead woman through whose bounty he will eat.

Their mood changes again, this time to grief and despair. Sounding like priests at a cremation, they console one another by saying they should "be glad she's slipped out of this maze of illusion and left the whole mess behind her," and that she "was very lucky to escape the bonds of the world's illusions so quickly." They start to chant a religious song that decries the "deceitful world" of illusion, and, "intoxicated right to their hearts," they start to dance frantically until "finally they collapsed dead drunk."

Aside from a few editorial comments about the Indian caste system, "The Shroud" shows Premcand's prose at its most succinct and leanest, but the author at his most disillusioned and vulnerable. The narration is fast-paced; the dialogue bristles with anger and irony, as it does in many of the stories Premcand wrote toward the end of his life. The solution the two men find for their sadness is only a temporary one. The next morning both will have to face the problem of cremating without a shroud a woman whose goodness they seem to acknowledge only at her death. Little will have changed in their lives, except that now Madhav, too, will have a fond memory of a feast, not as grand as the one his father narrates earlier in the story, but a feast all the same.

This story is Premcand's final salvo against what he considered India's most intractable problems: poverty and ignorance. The two leather-workers are despicable not from any inherent evil in them, but rather because Hindu society has made them that way. The social system, buttressed by religion, sharply circumscribes their lives and dictates the roles they must play. They have rejected the basic societal norms that demand that they live out their lives in poverty and oppression. Instead, they seem to take every opportunity to "beat the system." In so doing, they have become heartless and annealed to the suffering of others. Unable to bond with anyone but one another, they can only think of themselves and behave selfishly. They rationalize their behavior with corrupt religious rhetoric, which, in fact, runs counter to the true message of Hinduism. In short, Hindu society is responsible for the perversion of the real norms of this great religion, a theme that is found in many of Premcand's stories and novels.

Thought by many critics to contain an intended pro-Marxist subtext, "The Shroud" has been adapted for radio and theater performances by several prominent Marxist writers in India's various languages. It is translated into English as the title story of a 1972 collection.

—Carlo Coppola

THE SIGNALMAN
by Charles Dickens, 1866

Some 20 years before publication of "Mugby Junction" and the story known as "The Signalman" (Dickens's own title for the story, "No. 1 Branch-Line," was dropped), Dickens had become the first writer to capture the railway age for the creative imagination. In *Dombey and Son,* the railways had been exciting, their rapid movement a symptom of an exuberant, forward-looking age. Afterwards, in most of his major works, Dickens reverted to the coaching age, as if *Dombey and Son* had contained everything he wished to say about railways. When eventually in "The Signalman" he returned to the topic, the contrast with his earlier treatment was marked. Sinister silence replaces the bustle and clatter, solitude broods where gregariousness reigned; in place of the bright light of the sun, we have the faint light of the stars, and the feeble red lamp that marks the entrance to the tunnel. Like so many ghost stories, this one is set at night. By the 1860's, of course, railways had acquired that tedious familiarity we associate with old novelties, like sputniks and space travel today.

There is a pervasive downward movement; the narrator has a long and difficult climb down to reach the signalman, who is himself a man of education who has come down in the world. He contrasts strongly here, in general character and spirits, with the cheerful uneducated "Lamps" in the other parts of "Mugby Junction." Although we are told he goes off duty and returns, the impression given is almost as if the signalbox is his prison, and both the narrator and the trains running up and down the line are like visitors to a cell.

Dickens, more than other novelists, stresses and analyzes work; it is characteristic that the signalman does not rest in his horror of the spectral visitant, but wants to know what it means. He is anxious about its effect on his duties; he is able to control his fear in the interests of his responsibility. His pain of mind is most pitiable to see. It is the mental torture of a conscientious man, oppressed beyond endurance by an unintelligible responsibility involving life.

His perplexity about what sort of alarm he shall give, what sort of danger to report, is convincing; and it functions excellently as the link between the uncanny and the normal, which represents the main technical problem in all ghost stories with a realistic rather than fantastic setting. If he reports danger, but can give no facts, no details, he will not only be disbelieved, but may arouse suspicions about his reliability, or even his sanity. Dickens's unequalled power of description of urban settings, which makes his London streets and Coketown in "Hard Times" so memorable, is used here to intensify the impression of dull, depressed, yet dutiful life: "On either side, a dripping-wet wall of jagged stone, excluding all view but a strip of sky; the perspective one way only a crooked prolongation of this great dungeon; the shorter perspective in the other direction terminating in a gloomy red light, and the gloomier entrance to a black tunnel, in whose massive architecture there was a barbarous, depressing, and forbidding air."

The story's structure depends on the simple phrase "Below there" which so neatly combines colloquial familiarity with a shadowy suggestiveness. The three occasions on which it is used mark the beginning, middle, and end of the story. The narrator uses it by accident, and then finds that the same words are reported by the signalman as those of the spectral visitor. Finally, the words are used by the engine driver in warning the signalman to save himself by getting off the line. The ghostly gesture of putting the arm before the eyes is repeated by the driver who cannot bear to look at the death his train will cause. Here lies the story's main ingenuity. There are many ghost stories in which a ghost repeats words that have before been uttered by the living. Here a living man is mistaken by the signalman for a ghost because he repeats ghostly words that he has heard before. Thus, at the end we have in very small compass a stark opposition of points of view; the driver's humane horror at being the innocent cause of death; the signalman's inability to react to obvious danger because earlier experience has made him unable to grasp that the oncoming train and driver are solidly real.

The idea of combining the inventions of the new industrial society with a ghost story is peculiarly Dickensian. Whereas the Gothic novelists had generally associated the preternatural with far countries and distant ages, so that the strangeness of an esoteric setting should seem to vouch for strangeness of event, Dickens takes the opposite course. His ghost is enmeshed in the new, the prosaic, the familiar. So while we are reading, we suspend our disbelief in the transformation of our ordinary world into a place of hidden terrors.

This helps to maintain the continuity in Dickens's work between the specialized world of the ghost story and the plentiful inventions of his work in general, just as the descriptive passages about the railway line would be acceptable in a perfectly realistic narrative. Indeed, we may well feel a great truth to life, more in this preternatural story than in some examples of the other aspects of his Christmas spirit, the sentimental. If so, the reason is clear; in the latter, human motives and characters may be simplified or distorted. In this story, once granted the original donee, the feelings are real. We can imagine people we know acting as the signalman and the narrator do.

"Mugby Junction" was no doubt intended to be read as a whole; Dickens's annual Christmas story had long been an institution. The reader who absorbed at the same time the honest cheerfulness of Lamps and his daughter, the sombreness of "The Signalman," and the comic indignation of the attack on English catering methods in the refreshment room would be able to admire once again the versatility of the great entertainer who was also the master craftsman.

—A.O.J. Cockshut

SIGNS AND SYMBOLS
by Vladimir Nabokov, 1958

"Signs and Symbols" was first published in *The New Yorker* in 1948, and later collected in *Nabokov's Dozen.* The story describes a Friday afternoon and night of an elderly Jewish immigrant couple in an American city. This is their son's 20th birthday; the boy is incurably deranged, and it is with great care that they have chosen an inoffensive gift for him, a basket of fruit jellies. Yet, on reaching his sanitarium, they are told that he tried to commit suicide that morning and should not be disturbed. They take the gift back home, so that it does not get mislaid in the office. Unable to sleep at night, the father declares that they must remove the boy from the sanitarium: the doctor can come to see him at home, and they will take turns watching him at night. The monologue is twice interrupted by mistaken telephone calls from an anxious girl looking for someone called Charlie; the second time, the mother explains to the girl that she had been dialling the letter O instead of zero.

Having made the decision to bring the boy home the following morning, the couple sit down to "unexpected festive midnight tea." Yet while the father is spelling out, with difficulty and pleasure, the labels on the jelly jars, the telephone rings again. The reader is left wondering whether this third call is another unlikely case of the wrong number or whether it carries the message that the couple have reason to fear.

In a few spare strokes the author sketches the history of the couple's leaving Russia after the revolution, their relatively affluent life in Germany, and their difficult move to the United States on the eve of World War II. In their new country they are financially dependent on the husband's younger brother, an American of 40 years' standing. The "signs" to which the title refers are the tell-tale code that evokes their way of life amidst an alien culture, in straightened circumstances but not real poverty: the father's Russian-language newspaper, his new yet ill-fitting dental plates, his toothless, wordless helplessness with strange phone calls, the old overcoat that he prefers to his bathrobe; the mother's cheap black dresses, plain hairdo, absence of make-up, her worn pack of cards, and the picture album with snapshots of her child who is now largely beyond her reach and a relative who has perished in the Holocaust. These narrative details are signs rather than symbols: black clothes are versatile and convenient; the third landing on which the couple's two-room apartment is located makes one of the minor discomforts that make up their daily life. The story, however, tempts its readers to see the black dresses as symbols of mourning, and the third landing as the third country in which the exiles must make their home.

Even stronger is the readers' temptation to interpret the recurrent motifs of death (the subway train loses its "life current" for a while between two stations, a half-dead unfledged bird is twitching in a puddle) as symbolic of the boy's suicide at the end of the day. Such a reading, however, is dangerously in tune with the boy's own "referential mania." His disease consists in a logically intricate conviction that everything in the outer world "is a veiled reference to his own personality and existence": clouds transmit information about him, at nightfall "darkly gesticulating trees" discuss his innermost thoughts, pebbles and stains are coded messages about him, storms misinterpret his acts, and "the very air he exhales is indexed and filed away."

The boy's radical paranoia is an extreme literalization of the Jewish experience in Europe under the Nazi rule, when the whole universe seemed to be alertly hostile. Yet it is supplemented by his belief in a mysterious transcendent reality which can be found in the metaphysical background of most of Nabokov's works. The boy wishes "to tear a hole his world and escape." Gifts of gadgets or other hand-made objects distress him by evoking the gross malevolent utilitarianism of the artificial second-order reality in which he feels trapped.

Nabokov believed that people live in individual worlds that are at least partly of their own making. The world of the boy's mother contains "immense waves of pain," yet it also contains tacit understanding and family feelings, as well as an "incalculable amount of tenderness," which evidently keeps resurging on being "crushed, or wasted, or transformed into madness." The symbols of the story are the images, whether seen by the characters (the half-dead young bird), or vaguely remembered ("neglected children humming to themselves in unswept corners"), or imagined ("beautiful weeds that cannot hide from the farmer and helplessly have to watch the shadow of his simian stool leave mangled flowers in its wake"), that, unlike the polysemous yet decipherable "signs," pertain not so much to the plot or the problematic open ending as to the ineffable coloring of genuine emotion, the only treasure that the unhappy old refugees have still retained.

—Leona Toker

SILENT SNOW, SECRET SNOW
by Conrad Aiken, 1934

"Silent Snow, Secret Snow," collected in *Among the Lost People*, is one of Conrad Aiken's best stories. Hearing the title, its hissing, alliterative sibilants, and pondering the connotations of "*silent*" and "*secret*," we begin to feel our way toward its terrifying heart. Conspiracy and treachery are implicit. That these are the attributes of a coldly suffocating entity seems right, but that a boy of 12 years is ardently fond of such a thing is chilling. We have here, of course, an intriguingly intimate account of that boy's unalterable decline into psychosis, probably schizophrenia. It is a progress tracked from a relatively late moment in the onset of his hallucinatory state right up to its immanent usurpation of his sanity, an oncoming moment when the pernicious hissing of that snow in his psyche will become a "roar."

Paul Hasleman loves this snow, even thinks it "warm," because it distances him from his father, mother and, pre-eminently, the postman. It enables him to envision just ahead a "heavenly seclusion." But such a state really bespeaks the snow's ever increasing capacity to muffle "the world, hiding the ugly, and deadening . . . above all . . . the steps of the postman." By silencing the postman's steps, the snow "said peace . . . remoteness. . . ." The heavenly seclusion is consequently a veritable death, a termination of the world and its incessant messages of the real. This explains Aiken's fascination with the geography class and its social ambience. For Paul, Deirdre's freckles have no charm except in forming a constellation "like the Big Dipper" (so cold, so remote). And Miss Buell's friendly humor, warm eyes, and talk of the equator and the great wheat-producing areas of North America and Siberia, which supply the staff of life, cannot penetrate his moribund fascination with the vast ice fields of the arctic and antarctic.

In the course of the narrative, Paul journeys from his geography class to his bedroom, all the while adrift in the euphoric onrush of madness, a state he will achieve deliberately, "at whatever cost to himself, whatever pain to others." We understand, certainly, that he cannot choose insanity. But his acquiescence in his delusion is his uttermost wish; it is preferable to a world full of "items of mere externality" and to a mother and father who are but "hostile presences." Why? It is fair to call the origin of this divorce oedipal, given Paul's feeling for "Father's voice" during the "interrogation" in the living room: "The voice was the well known 'punishment' voice, resonant and cruel." No surprise, then, that the culminating and imperative gesture he makes in severing his bond to the family is to shout his hatred of his mother. Whether the father is less cruel and the mother less the father's ally than Paul finally makes them out to be is not to the point. It is his sense of them that counts.

Everything pertinent to that sense can be found in a few figures of speech and images provided in the narrator's depiction of Paul's trek homeward from school. By this point we feel the utter identity of the narrator with Paul's unconscious life. He is not only sympathetically attuned to every fluctuation in the boy's conspiracy with the snow; he grants Paul the perfect point of balance between choosing the snow and being chosen by it. The language in question entails a conjunction of "lost twigs" fallen from "parent trees" with a "fragment of eggshell." Surely Paul feels his fate in the twigs shed by their parents and in the fractured shell of embryonic life. Horribly, this waste of infant existence is visible not simply on the "lip of a sewer," but, from Paul's perspective, "in a delta of filth." And when he arrives home, the "eggshaped stones" at the gateway to his house appear to be "cunningly balanced . . . as if by Columbus." Thus the child, who feels his very life to be broken, has only a precarious hold on his family identity, one maintained by a trick, a deception. As a consequence, the *H* on the wall beyond the gateway has become unintelligible to Paul, suggesting his alienation from his parents and the inappropriateness of their house as his proper habitation. He enters it to challenge his parents, whose antagonistic allegiance, for Paul, is manifest in the phalanx of their slippers and in the doctor they have elected to bring against him.

Because Paul is sensitively, if selectively, observant, because he is too fragile for the actual explorations of Hudson, Peary, Scott, Shackleton, and Columbus (all of whom pass abruptly through his musings), because he refuses the postman's news, he might seem to typify the youthful artist. The poet, after all, is able to replace what is banal or unlovely or intolerable with a consolatory fabrication. Such a reading renders Paul's personified snow world an early fruit of artistic imagination. But it is not so. His snow is not sufficiently of his own inventing. It comes only with a "half-effort." And it insulates both the actual world and his consciousness rather than enabling their vital reciprocation. It is chosen, if volition pertains, out of despair and hatred. For Baudelaire, who brought flowers from the mire, the ugly and quotidien were fecund in the light of imagination and thus essential to art. For Paul Hasleman, they sadly compel retreat and mere delusion.

—David M. Heaton

A SIMPLE HEART (Un coeur simple)
by Gustave Flaubert, 1877

"Un coeur simple" ("A Simple Heart") is by far the best-known, and most often reprinted, of the trio of stories Flaubert published in 1877, in a small volume simply titled *Trois contes* (*Three Tales*). Although it was the second of the three stories to be completed, Flaubert chose to place it first in the published volume, perhaps because it was, in subject matter, the closest of the three to Flaubert's private life and feelings. The story is set in his native Normandy, during the middle decades of the 19th century, and the protagonist, a humble servant named Félicité, was modeled on a woman who had been a servant, of fond memory, in Flaubert's own family.

The reason for its greater popularity than that of the other two stories, one of which is a medieval legend, the other a tale of Biblical times, may also be its greater immediacy for the modern reader, and perhaps too its thematic resemblance to Flaubert's most popular novels, *Madame Bovary* and *L'Education Sentimentale* (*Sentimental Education*), both of which also depict, in realistic detail, the personal world in which Flaubert grew up, but are very long. "A Simple Heart" is therefore often recommended as the best brief introduction to Flaubert's literary world and to his writing manner.

It is true that "A Simple Heart" does depict, in scrupulously accurate detail, the drab and loveless life of a poor, uneducated servant. Getting the details right was part of Flaubert's method, in all he wrote. But Flaubert's artistic energy is chiefly invested here, not in depicting a surface reality, but in the far more important goal of deeply probing the inner truth of Félicité's spirit, and of the spirit of the bourgeois society she serves, in order to understand and reveal the reasons for their mutual failure ever to develop any meaningful human contact with one another. "A Simple Heart" is a painful study in human limitations and the spiritual isolation they can impose. In that respect, it does indeed resemble both *Madame Bovary* and *Sentimental Education* which study similar human limitations and their consequences, but it has always been a crude oversimplification, as Flaubert himself protested, to identify any of these works as mere exercises in literary realism. Flaubert is much more profound.

The opening chapter of "A Simple Heart" identifies Félicité as the longtime envy of Pont-L'Evêque's womenfolk, not as a person, but as an invaluable possession of Mme. Aubain's. Everyone sees in Félicité, as the chapter's last sentence states, a mechanical female, made of wood. No one imagines that she has any human feelings. The following three chapters flash back to recite the raw materials that make up her life, namely, a long series of unrequited attachments, to a farmhand named Théodore, to Mme. Aubain, to Mme. Aubain's daughter Virginie, to her belatedly discovered nephew Victor, to Polish soldiers, to a sick old outcast of a man, le père Colmiche, thought to have committed atrocities during the Reign of Terror in 1793, and finally to a parrot. None of these attachments satisfies any of Félicité's needs but one: her boundless need to give unstintingly of herself to others. All of these attachments soon vanish or die, including the parrot. However, she has the parrot stuffed, and in old age takes to worshipping it, mistaking it, in her senile confusion, for the Holy Ghost.

The stuffed parrot becomes the last attachment of her life, revealing the unbroken lifelong pattern of her existence, and the meaning of the story's title. For Félicité is nothing but heart, whose simple and only function is to love—to give of herself. She is also simple in the sense of uneducated, and uncomplicated. She is not given to anything so sophisticated as introspection, self-doubt, or doubts about others. She loves, simply and without second thoughts. The pattern of her life is therefore tragic, for she can neither stop herself from loving, nor ever be loved in return, since others see her as made of wood and functioning automatically.

About the character of Félicité, and the meaning of Flaubert's title, there is a strong critical consensus, but the interpretation of the concluding paragraph has sharply divided critics. As Félicité smilingly draws her last breath, is she being rewarded for her simple faith and selfless existence by being vouchsafed a vision of the Holy Ghost escorting her to heaven? Or does that vision of the Holy Ghost, in the fantastic guise of a gigantic parrot, signify rather that with her last breath she is experiencing one last illusory love, making of the visionary parrot the mocking symbol of her bitter destiny on earth, which was to be ever the victim of love unrequited? With the achingly beautiful prose of that final paragraph, is Flaubert inviting the reader to understand that Félicité's is a blissful death, because she believes she has reached that beatific state promised by her given name? Or is he, instead, solemnly reminding the reader of the pattern of Félicité's whole life of bitter disappointment, and inviting the reader to ponder sympathetically the bleak tragedy symbolized by the vision on which her life ended?

Flaubert has clearly left ample room, in the text of "A Simple Heart," to allow for different, and even diametrically opposed, interpretations of the story. Whatever interpretation readers might favor, however, agreement is universal among all readers that "A Simple Heart" is a deeply moving and supremely beautiful work of art.

—Murray Sachs

_____

SINKING (Chenlun)
By Yu Dafu, 1921

Yu Dafu was one of the most versatile and prolific writers of the May Fourth Period. He wrote traditional poems (*gushi*), essays, fiction, editorials, political criticism, and literary criticism. Although his traditional poems were highly praised by Lu Xun and other critics as the finest among his contemporaries, it was his fiction that established his nationwide reputation and gained him recognition as one of the prestigious founding members of the influential Creation Society. "Chenlun" ("Sinking") is the title piece of Yu Dafu's first publication, which is also the first short story collection of China's "New Literature."

The protagonist in the story is a young Chinese student sent by his family to pursue a college education in Japan, an alien country where he constantly feels humiliation and hostility brought about by his inferior nationality. Living in tormenting loneliness and impelled by his thriving sexual desire, he has involuntarily segregated himself from his Chinese friends and indulged in sexual fantasy and masturbation. Although his earlier education upholds a strong sense of ethics and moral purity, he is too weak to resist sexual temptation and is caught in a perpetual, yet always losing, battle against haunting erotic desire and sinful voyeurism. One morning, while walking along a small path in the countryside, he accidentally overhears the bewitching talk between a Japanese man and woman who are making love behind bushes. Aroused by fantasizing the scene, that afternoon he wanders onto trolley and then transfers to a ferry, without knowing the destination. Going ashore, he

suddenly finds himself pacing in front of a brothel; in a trance he walks into the brothel and spends an evening there. That night, sobered from wine and driven by unbearable shame and sinfulness, he walks into the sea and drowns himself.

The story, as well as many of Yu Dafu's later stories, adopts an autobiographical confession approach; that is, in the story the basic tone is one of persistent self-condemnation and the protagonist's experiences often reveal conspicuous similarity to the author's real personal life. Yu Dafu's use of this approach stems from his belief in the concept of "literature reflecting life" and from the influence, in China of the European decadents and Romantics. He once stated in an article that "all literary works are the autobiographies of the writers." In "Sinking" this approach is particularly evident, and it cannot be ignored in interpreting the story.

The plot of "Sinking" shows neither a pattern of rising climax/descending action, nor a formula of conflict/resolution, as normally found in fiction. The story is told by a third-person narrator who is omnipresent and omniscient, always ready to disclose every single thought or feeling of the protagonist. The exposure starts immediately from the first line, telling of the protagonist's biting solitude. Every action contributes to the portrayal of the protagonist's character—over-sensitive, highly sentimental, unstable and unpredictable. At one moment he is so touched by the beauty of nature—a gentle breeze, a pitiable quivering blade of grass, or a fragrant and delicate flower—that he sheds tears and soothes himself in fantasy, seeing Cupid-like angles dancing and soaring around him. When he is desperately seized by melancholy, he grumbles to himself and bears grudge against his Japanese classmates, simply overwhelmed by his bitter hypochondria and megalomania dubbed with patriotism.

The use of third-person point of view in the story is successful in two accounts: it is possible to reveal the protagonist's inner feelings by using a number of monologues, and it allows the story to shift back and forth freely between the present scene and past reminiscences. The protagonist's psychological conflicts. A psychological tension is created by combining the third-person point of view with the forthright and unveiled self-exposure of the protagonist. The tension is created precisely at the point where his sexual impulse and his moral vision of self clash against each other; to use Yu Dafu's own words, "it is a clash between soul and desire." This clash takes not a linear form, but an alternate form of development. For example, a momentary peace is broken by his aroused desire of peeking at the landlord's daughter while she is taking a shower. This leads to the condemnation from his other "self" constructed by his moral vision. As a result, his guilt causes him to escape to a recluse life in a mountain house, where he regains his tranquility. Before long, however, he accidentally overhears amorous love making which again stirs his lust. The struggle between his carnal self and moral self carries on and accumulates enormous frustration and pressure inside him, making him a victim torn by guilt and shame. The tension ultimately causes the total breakdown of his spiritual loftiness when he visits the brothel. At the end, he drowns himself in the sea. The title "Sinking" implies a dual meaning of falling into the water and the falling of his soul.

The self-exposure, particularly the depiction of his lustful desire and erotic fantasy, is blunt and straight. It is tinged by the influence of the then prevailing Japanese "Self-novel" (*watakushi shōsetsu*), a style highly charged with subjective and personal inner feelings and inclined to be direct. One interesting aspect of the "Self-novel" in "Sinking" is the intimate relationship between the protagonist and nature; he is constantly searching for consolation and tranquility in nature. The story is structured in such a way that his triumph and defeat in the battle of resisting sexual temptation parallel the presence and absence of nature. In this sense, nature becomes a symbolic sanctuary. Yet, sometimes this kind of detailed exposure of his inner feelings seems too trivial and superficial. More often than not, it diminishes the artistic effect. This is largely caused by the selection of materials from Yu Dafu's autobiographical accounts and the excessive readiness of using these accounts. It contributes particularly to the superficiality of character portrayal and the unwieldiness in narrative.

However, these flaws tend to be insignificant and bring no real blemish to the story. Yu Dafu succeeded in portraying a desperate young man's psychological conflicts and sexual frustration through his admirable lyric style and faithful attitude to realism. "Sinking" presents a theme of human suffering, not merely a breakthrough of the forbidden sexual theme. It is a genuine avant-garde work in China's new literature.

—Pin P. Wan

THE SNAKE CHARMER (Zaklinatel' Zmei)
by Varlam Shalamov, 1954

Most of Varlam Shalamov's stories deal with specific aspects of camp life. The phenomenon examined in "Zaklinatel' Zmei" ("The Snake Charmer") is the criminal convicts' love of listening to narratives of adventure and romance. Numerous memoirs by Gulag survivors interpret this as a form of cultural life. Shalamov, who, in a series of essays, would criticize the literary convention of romanticizing professional criminals, harshly demystifies even this feature of their camp life.

"The Snake Charmer" begins with a prologue-type conversation between two prisoners seated on a fallen larch-tree, probably during a short recess—most episodes of camp literature are, for obvious reasons, set during such "moments of reprieve," as Primo Levi has called them. One of the two is the narrator, the authorial persona; the other is his friend, the script-writer Andrei Fedorovich Platonov. Platonov mentions a year that he spent in Jankhar, one of the most deadly camps of Kolyma. He survived that year by doing what Shalamov himself would never stoop to—telling stories to criminals in return for extra food, clothing, and protection. He adds that if he lives to see his release, he will write a story about his experience as a "novelist" in Jankhar and call it "The Snake Charmer." Three weeks later Platonov dies, evidently of a heart attack, falling down like the tree that has provided the setting for the prologue. The narrator, who has likewise been tossed from camp to camp, is familiar with the ways of the criminals, and he survives Kolyma. He decides to write "The Snake Charmer" for Platonov. Thus, the story about storytelling is presented as a self-conscious fictional construct erected on a factual basis.

The narrator composes the Jankhar episode out of sparse "typical" touches, such as the long nail on the criminal chieftain's little finger: in the camps an "honest thief" would not work; he would get by through abusing political prisoners, brazenly appropriating the lion's share of all the available clothes and food, and corrupting the guards (the camp authorities were, in any case, lenient to the criminal convicts as "socially closer" to the working class than the "enemies of the people"). On the day described, the camp's seven hardened criminals have been playing cards on the barrack bunks instead of working outside with the rest of the prisoners. At night, when all the regular prisoners are overcome with fatigue, the criminals are bored and restless. Fedia, their chieftain, whiles away some of the time by abusing the newcomer Platonov, who is referred to as "Ivan Ivanich," a jargon term for naive city-dwellers. Then he orders a pretty boy called "Mashka" (a female nickname given to young thiefs used by the veterans for homosexual diversion) to scratch his heels—another favorite form of entertainment. Then a flunky suggests that they try the newcomer in the capacity of a storyteller. As Platonov agrees to tell Fedia "novels," he immediately becomes the criminals' protegé, is given some bread, and obliquely promised impunity for sleeping his fill at the worksite.

His new status becomes apparent next morning: a country boy who had slept on the bunks throughout the night's "novel" pushes him but then, on learning that he is a "novelist," is embarrassed and asks him not to complain to Fedia—this is also typical both of the brutality that young peasants adopted as a way of life in the camps and of their uncritical acceptance of the criminals' rulings. Platonov is safe, but for how long? His reassuring answer, "I won't tell," the punchline of the story, reminds us that he will not live to tell his version of the events.

Shalamov emphasizes the fictionalized nature of the Jankhar episode by making it contradict a detail of the prologue. Platonov has told the narrator that the first two or three months of his stay in Jankhar were difficult, but the narrator turns Platonov into a "novelist," a "snake charmer," on his very first day in that camp. By thus disowning the authority conventionally granted to omniscient narrators, Shalamov invites us to be critical of the generalizations made in the story. Indeed, three different views are presented in the account of Platonov's thoughts on being offered the job of the "novelist." Platonov first wonders whether he should "become a jester in the court of the duke of Milan, a clown who was fed for a good joke and beaten for a bad one"—Fedia's entourage is, indeed, a sordid replica of a nobleman's court. Then he decides to think that he would acquaint criminals with real literature, "become an enlightener," and so do his real work, his duty. Recoiling from this sentimental illusion, the narrator comments that Platonov does not wish to recognize that he would simply earn an extra bowl of soup by what was "more like scratching a thief's dirty heels than enlightenment." Yet this third view is also a private opinion rather than absolute truth: each prisoner draws his or her own line between what should and what should not be done for a bowl of soup, and there are many shades of grey between honor and humiliation.

The problem of the limits of compromise is associated with an issue frequently raised in Shalamov's stories, the ambivalence of people's use of their intellectual and spiritual life for the sake of physical survival. Platonov is shown musing on the peculiar clinging to life which allows people to endure Kolyma better than horses—"a physical tenacity to which [one's] entire consciousness is subordinated." He survives Jankhar by, Shalamov believes, debasing his gifts at the service of those who make an obscene mockery of the so-called spiritual needs. Averse to preaching, Shalamov does not say that some part of one's consciousness should be kept away from the exigencies of the struggle for survival. "The Snake Charmer" bears witness and pays a tribute to a fallen friend; it does not judge him or extract a moral from his experience.

—Leona Toker

THE SNOWS OF KILIMANJARO
by Ernest Hemingway, 1936

Often considered one of Hemingway's major short stories, "The Snows of Kilimanjaro" shows the mature author working at the top of his talent to combine spare idiomatic style with richly layered narrative. The story comes more than a decade after Hemingway began writing superb short fiction as if prose were poetry, under the tutelage of Ezra Pound and following the example of James Joyce. Unlike such stories from his 1920's collections as "Indian Camp," "The Undefeated," "Hills Like White Elephants," and "Big Two-Hearted River," "The Snows of Kilimanjaro" allowed him to draw on a complicated tapestry of personal memory and formal narrative.

Hemingway wrote the long story he originally called "The Happy Ending" between February and April of 1936. Exuberant after finishing another African story, "The Short Happy Life of Francis MaComber," he worked on this narrative through many versions, at least one of them typed by his wife Pauline. Manuscript evidence suggests that he incorporated some previously written materials as he composed (manuscript versions of the story are housed at the University of Delaware and the University of Texas, Austin; and the John F. Kennedy Library, Boston). Published in the August 1936 issue of *Esquire*, the story then had no epigraph. It also attributed the praise of the rich to "poor Scott Fitzgerald." When Fitzgerald objected to the use of his name, Hemingway changed it to "Julian," a reference to the autobiographical hero of Fitzgerald's story "The New Leaf." But besides references to living people, the story reflects more personal involvement than Hemingway's fiction usually evinced. Near the end of his second marriage, unsettled by European conflict and comparatively hostile reactions to his recent writing, Hemingway was experiencing the bleakness that the character Harry bitterly expresses.

Autobiography aside, "The Snows of Kilimanjaro" became a central Hemingway story because in it the author dealt explicitly with themes of broad significance—a person's need to make a good death, the fickleness of fate, the moral guidance a primitive, natural world such as Africa gave cynical Americans. The story also questioned the hold wealth and privilege had upon the American imagination, because even during the Great Depression, value continued to be measured by materialistic standards.

Accompanied by the epigraph about the frozen leopard found near the western summit of Kilimanjaro, a park called "The House of God," the story forces the reader to make universal what appears to be a personal memory narrative as Harry faces his death from gangrene. Infected after a minor scratch on his leg, Harry—the frustrated and unfulfilled writer on safari—never shares his wife Helen's belief that the rescue plane they are awaiting will, in fact, save him. Harry will die from this macabre wound, although he has formerly survived much more serious injuries. Hemingway's implication is that the rot that will cause Harry's physical death is a corollary for the spiritual and moral rot that living with the wealthy—and neglecting his talent—has occasioned.

Hemingway's story is about Harry's spiritual death as much as his bodily one. In the devastating dialogue between the writer and his rich, supportive wife, that spiritual death dominates. After he announces his approaching death ("The marvellous thing is that it's painless"), he brutally suggests that Helen either cut off his leg, though he doubts that amputation would save him, or shoot him. Irrationally blaming her for his failure as a writer, Harry uses his tirade to denounce her and her money, ending with his denial that he has ever loved her.

Within the story, Hemingway softens Harry's objectionable character by including a quantity of flashbacks, set in italics, which pose as fragments of autobiography—the first man Harry sees killed in World War I, begging for death in order to escape the pain of his ruptured body; Harry's happiness while writing in Paris when the spirit of the new was everywhere; the beauty of skiing in Austria; the warmth of eating well after hunger. In these flashbacks Hemingway shows a man who has not yet been defeated, who is not yet "bored," as he cruelly answers Helen's question about their life together. Taken with the driving narrative (we read to know whether or not Harry will survive), these reflective moments-out-of-time form a montage that reflects life in its complexity.

Hemingway saves Harry for the reader through his use of animal metaphors. The story is filled with vultures hovering as they wait for Harry's death, and later, with mysterious but stinking hyenas lurking nearby for the same reason. Described with deft imagery, the hyena may exist only in Harry's reverie, but the mention of animals forces the reader back to the epigraph with its noble, but dead, leopard. Searching for some unknown, traveling too high up the mountain, the frozen leopard had died in pursuit. Through juxtaposition, Hemingway equates Harry and his writing life with the leopard, and almost makes the equation work.

He creates a positive effect, finally, by writing two different endings, playing on the narrative expectation that what appears at the end of any story *is* its ending. His working title, "The Happy Ending," suggested an ironic oversimplification of the storytelling process, for just as Harry was an ambivalent character rather than any kind of "hero," so his story would be more complex than a conventional "happy" or "sad" conclusion could convey. The first ending, presented without the reader's awareness that there will be a second, describes the plane arriving and rescuing Harry, then flying toward the mountain peak. The euphoria of his delivery is beautifully phrased: "there, ahead, all he could see, as wide as all the world, great, high, and unbelievably white in the sun, was the square top of Kilimanjaro. And then he knew that there was where he was going."

In the second ending, Helen awakes at the sound of a crying hyena (which had crouched over the sleeping Harry and extinguished his breath, killing him in a scene the reader assumes is fantasy). She finds her husband dead. Her resulting grief has no connection with the triumph of Harry's assent in the previous ending, and the layering of the two scenes forces the reader to question, what is valuable? What is moral? How does culture judge any person's life, or death? The narrative then circles back to Julian's wistful comment about the lives of the rich, making the reader face the fact that wealth had brought Harry only unhappiness—if his view of his life was credible.

"The Snows of Kilimanjaro" has been one of the most often anthologized of Hemingway's stories during its 50-year-history. Not only a complex tapestry of writing style, it also provides the opportunity for discussion of gender roles and social issues, particularly because of the way Hemingway creates ambivalence in the character of Harry. The story has also been filmed. It receives new critical treatment in Mark Spilka's *Hemingway's Quarrel with Androgyny.*

—Linda Wagner-Martin

SOMETHING OUT THERE
by Nadine Gordimer, 1984

Nadine Gordimer's 1984 novella "Something Out There," from the anthology of the same name, shares with her novels a complexity of idea and structure, and with her stories an economy and neatness of form. In this exemplary text, Gordimer disaggregates South African life into numerous constituent parts and examines each in turn, from affluent golf-playing doctors to gangs of black youths on city streets. Her tone is typically wry and acerbic for large parts of the text, becoming sombre and prophetic at its end. Her satire has seldom been crisper, especially at the points when she writes about that which she knows best: the consciousness, foibles, and lifestyles of prosperous white South Africans.

The phrase "something out there" provides the key to Gordimer's conceptual mechanisms in the novella. Through it she responds to the apartheid government's ideological onslaught against South Africa's (then exiled) liberation movements in the 1970's and 1980's. In the popular media and in parliament, the Afrikaner Nationalists propagated an image of a dangerous, subhuman, foreign force lurking on and within the country's borders. Far from acknowledging the desperate social conditions from which the liberation groups were born, the Nationalists insisted on the mysterious, hostile, and bestial nature of black fighters. Numerous age-old racist stereotypes (such as the idea of blacks being kin with monkeys) were employed in this official version of liberation groups.

Gordimer overturns and questions these stereotypes by creating her own countertypes, and by knowingly playing upon the idea of blacks as apes or objects. Half the novella is devoted to describing the activities of a small underground cell of revolutionaries (both black and white) who are encamped outside Johannesburg and who are planning to blow up an electrical power plant. Gordimer places herself outside the position from which governmental pictures of rebels emanates, and offers a set of different perceptions on the nature of "something out there." What she gives us is a homely, domesticated portrait of the guerillas: their loves, their hates, their needs. The descriptions of Vusi producing "muffled, sweet" sounds on a home-made flute, or of Charles back from his run "panting like a happy dog, shaggy with warm odours," set up the revolutionaries as knowable, fallible, and laudable, as human.

The novella consists of two interwoven narratives: that describing the guerrillas, and a second, describing the path of an errant monkey who is causing panic in Johannesburg's white suburbs. Gordimer employs the figure of the monkey as an astute and often humorous means of exploring white paranoia. Feeling ever more threatened by the prospect of thoroughgoing political change, and believing official "bad press" about the liberation movements, many white South Africans from the 1970's on have expended massive financial and psychic resources on their own security. Only at the end of the novella is the monkey found to be a monkey. Up until that point it is a shadowy and amoeboid shape that steals in and out of white lives, defying burglar bars and alarm systems and stringing the suburban figures together in a consensus of fear.

The supreme irony of the story is that the "something out there" so dreaded by the suburban dwellers, and incarnated in the monkey, indeed exists in the form of the guerilla cell. Between the reality of the guerillas and the willingness or ability of whites to recognise the former's existence, stands the baboon. The divergent parts of South African life have the peculiar quality of being invisible to each other. Gordimer attempts to convey a sense of social totality by making both parts visible to her reader, using the gorilla as a mischievously improbable metaphoric bridge.

The novella functions powerfully through contradiction between interiors and exteriors. The many houses in the text are all sites of containment, fortresses against fear and change. By contrast, the guerillas and the monkey are on the loose, marginal and yet ubiquitous in the panic they engender. The monkey's forays into various kitchens signals that that which is "out there" is in fact very close by, or even inside the heart of white privilege and consciousness. A similar point is made in the episode in which one of the revolutionaries, Eddie, makes a forbidden journey into the city after years of homesickness and exile, and mingles with others "like him." Again the suggestion is that "something out there" is in fact "in there." The allegorical parallelism between gorilla and guerillas continues until near the novella's end, at which point the baboon is found dead and, of the revolutionary cell, one is killed and three escape. Gordimer suggests that, unlike the baboon, the other "something out there" is not wholly destroyed and will return again, as the repressed is always likely to return.

Not only does Gordimer attempt to dilute and question racist stereotypes in this novella, she also juxtaposes various stereotypes of femininity present in South African society. The white revolutionary, Joy, must be seen alongside the whole gamut of South African women which flashes by in the novella: the slavish young wife of the security policeman whose venison is stolen by the baboon, the "girl" or black domestic servant who arbitrarily loses her job; the pleasure-bent lover interrupted at her tryst; and Mrs. Naas Klopper, queenly but gullible wife of the Afrikaans estate agent from whom the revolutionaries rent a property. Joy represents the subversion of all these situations: she is their "something out there" or alternative. This is not to say that Gordimer's portrait of Joy is entirely sympathetic. The author's attitude to feminist women is a highly complex and ambiguous one. However, what Gordimer demonstrates is her knowledge of the multiple ways of being available to women and men in her society. She leaves the reader to weigh up the options.

—Karen Ruth Lazar

SONNY'S BLUES
by James Baldwin, 1965

"Sonny's Blues," first published in 1957, was collected in James Baldwin's *Going to Meet the Man* in 1965. It is one of Baldwin's most skillfully crafted works of short fiction, and one of his most revealing. It reflects his preoccupation with problems of identity—particularly racial identity—but examines those problems both in the context of the experience of the African-American in the United States of the mid-20th century and in the more universal framework of human experience, regardless of time or place.

That larger context is suggested toward the end of the story as the two principal characters—Sonny, a blues musician, and his brother, a high school mathematics teacher seven years older than Sonny—watch a street revival meeting on Seventh Avenue in New York. Sonny associates the power of the street singer's hymn with the suffering she has experienced. His brother (never identified by name) replies, "But there's no way not to suffer—is there, Sonny?" Sonny agrees, one of the few things the two brothers, separated by more than age, can agree upon.

The view that suffering and sorrow are inevitable is, of course, the tragic view of life. About the time he was writing this story, Baldwin—recently returned to the United States from a decade of expatriotism in Europe—commented in *Nobody Knows My Name* on what he calls the Old World vision: "a sense of the mysterious and inexorable limits of life, in a word, of tragedy." But he also asserts that the American artist has the task of fusing the vision of the Old World with that of the New World, "a sense of life's possibilities." That is precisely what is happening in this story, not a story of defeat, but one in which the principal character, Sonny, finds hope and meaning in tragedy, and inspires others to that view.

With a Hawthornean eye, Baldwin uses images of darkness throughout the story to suggest a certain feeling experienced by his characters. Young children are "filled with darkness" as they listen to their parents talk on Sunday afternoons of "the darkness outside." Teenagers, aware of "the low ceiling of their actual possibilities," begin to discover "the darkness of their lives," even as they seek escape from it in the darkness of movie theatres. The darkness of the road Sonny's uncle was killed on (struck by a car filled with white men) stays with Sonny's father for the rest of his life. The streets in which Sonny grew up seem to darken as he passes through them, and convey their mood to him.

The feeling experienced by these characters—all African-American—is deep and heavy, akin to melancholy and depression, impossible to explain, just there. It's called the blues, a mental and emotional state arising from recognition of limitation imposed—in the case of African-Americans—by racial barriers to opportunity.

One can try to escape the blues. The teenagers attempt to stifle the inner darkness in the fantasy world of the movies; the adults in the housing projects turn away from the windows that disclose the ominous shadows of the streets, and watch TV. Those who try to escape on the streets find themselves "encircled by disaster." In his adolescence, Sonny succumbs to the streets, and ends up hooked on dope and in prison. For Sonny's father and uncle, it was liquor. Both Sonny and his brother try to escape through military service. Sonny's brother believes his college education and respectable job as a teacher will eliminate the blues.

But Sonny and his brother need to learn that "there's no way not to suffer." The difference between them is that Sonny's brother decides submissively to "take it," and Sonny decides to "do something to give it meaning." That's when Sonny begins to play the piano, initially with enthusiasm, eventually with consuming passion. He takes no lessons. He plays from the soul. The improvisational rhythms he creates reflect the darkness in him. Through the power and beauty of Sonny's music, Baldwin reveals the intimate relationship between the blues as a state of mind and as a musical tradition in African-American culture. Sonny has found a way, not to escape the blues, but to give it meaning. Moreover, as an artist, he has found a way to transcend tragedy; he not only uses the blues as an outlet for feeling and as an expression of his states of mind, but he also shares and communicates those feelings and, in the process, makes his music into an affirmation of life.

While the story focuses mostly on Sonny's development as a blues musician and, through Sonny's music, on his brother's gradual acceptance of his African-American identity, it also displays the many forms that expression of the blues takes in the lives of ordinary African-Americans: a boy on the street whistling a tune that is "cool and moving" and "pouring out of him" is whistling the blues; a barmaid dances the blues to the music of a jukebox; the old folks talk the blues after Sunday dinner; Sonny's mother hums the blues as she murmurs an old church song; she verbalizes the blues in a moving account of the death of his uncle; the uncle played the blues on his guitar; Sonny's cool walk is an expression of the blues; even Sonny's brother whistles the blues to keep from crying after an altercation with Sonny.

At this point, Sonny's brother is a brother in name only. He is not a "brother," in the African-American sense; he doesn't even know who Charlie Parker is. To become a brother in that sense, he must accept his heritage of suffering rather than attempt to escape from it. This he does in the concluding scene in a dimly lit night club, on a dark street, as he listens for the first time to Sonny playing the blues. In the music he hears, he sees his mother's face, and that of his little girl who died of polio. The powerful incantations of Sonny's art reach his soul, and for the first time, he listens to the dark voice within. "For, while the tale of how we suffer, and how we are delighted, and how we may triumph is never new, it always must be heard. There isn't any other tale to tell, it's the only light we've got in all this darkness."

—Joseph Flibbert

SORROW-ACRE (Sorg-Agre)
by Isak Dinesen, 1940

Born into an old family of Danish nobility and writing both in Danish and in English under her maiden name at times, at times under the best-known of her pseudonyms, Isak Dinesen became world famous for her reminiscences about her 17 years' experience in British East Africa, *Out of Africa* (1937), a book that decades later served as the basis for a widely popular Hollywood movie version. Both her first two collections of short stories (which she wrote in English and then translated into Danish), *Seven Gothic Tales* (1934) and *Winter's Tales* (1942), enjoyed large sales as Book-of-the-Month Club selections. Originally published in her second collection and later appearing in *Ladies' Home Journal* (May 1943), as did numerous other fine stories such as "Babette's Feast," "Sorrow-Acre" ("Sorg-Agre") is commonly considered Dinesen's masterpiece.

Dinesen's imagination like that of Nathaniel Hawthorne, was typically stirred by events of a distant past, and she found her inspiration for "Sorrow-Acre" in a spare little folktale from a South Jutland village of Ballum dating from 1634. In roughly 250 words the folktale tells of a mother whose son has been condemned to death for having killed a robber trying to steal the family's property. She gains a promise of clemency from a ruling count on the condition that she mow, between sunrise and sunset, a field of barley said to be so large as to require the labor of four men. Accomplishing this Herculean task and winning her son's freedom, she falls dead from a broken back. Buried in the church-yard, the woman is etched on her gravestone holding a sickle and a sheaf. The legendary converges with accurate historical fact in the conclusion, where we learn that the field of the nameless woman's labors is "known [still] as 'Sorrow-Acre.'" Dinesen's concluding paragraph only begins to suggest the elaborate changes she makes in what turns out to be a story of about 14,000 words: "In the place where the woman had died the old lord later on had a stone set up, with a sickle engraved in it. The peasants on the land then named the rye field 'Sorrow-Acre.' By this name it was known a long time after the story of the woman and her son had itself been forgotten." In Dinesen's revision of her ancient source the memory of individual identity and, indeed, historical factuality give way to a haunting sense of legendary, parabolic enchantment.

The folktale is but a skeletal fragment of the story that becomes Dinesen's, and one she takes great liberties with for the purposes of telling a richer, denser saga. The largest changes are at once novelistic and romantic. She fleshes out as major characters the unnamed lord, his new 17-year-old bride whom he has married after the death of her intended, his one remaining son; the lord's bailiff and the crowd of a hundred peasants, as well as the old woman's son, come to play roles as an active audience. Dinesen adds still another major character, the lord's nephew and potential heir, the young Adam, who, having grown up in "the big house at the top of the avenue, the garden and the fields [that] had been his childhood paradise," now returns after a nine years' absence on the very day of the peasant woman's ordeal. He has spent his time travelling in Rome and Paris and is currently a member of the Danish Legation in London, where he "had come in touch with the great new ideas of the age: of nature, of the right and freedom of man, of justice and beauty." Adam's return is "to make his peace" with these scenes of his childhood before emigrating "to America, to the new world."

Dinesen thus sets the stage for a dramatized conflict between radically disparate world views, and to do so she shifts the folktale's action from 1634 to the late 18th century between the American (1776) and French (1789) revolutions and thus just prior to Denmark's own liberation of its peasant-serfs in 1787. Not only are Old World and New World political, social, and cultural conflicts— feudal hierarchical orders as against the age of enlightenment and the ideal of the perfectability of the common individual—conflated here. So too is a Christian/sacral history. The peasant-mother Dinesen names Anne-Marie, the lavishly described landscape is edenic, the lord's rule is awesomely absolute, his new bride bears names regal and Biblical (Sophie-Magdelena). In the single scene devoted to her she takes an Eve-like gaze into her own mirrored nakedness. And the tormented son's embrace of his dying mother symbolizes an inverted Pietà. Thus is Anne-Marie's sacrifice recast as a performance acted out in front of the

two opposing views of the lord and Adam, the manorial and the modern respectively.

Dinesen knew not only the original folktale but a 1931 retelling by another Danish writer, Paul la Cour, whose story presented the action from the point of view and anguished feelings of the mother herself. Dinesen recenters the drama by framing the widow's labors with a dialogue between the lord and Adam, and in the process it is Adam who undergoes a profound transformation and resolves to stay in his old hereditary home. As the lord tells him Anne-Marie's story, Adam comes to learn that the charges against her son might be false, that Anne-Marie was herself not well thought of by the villagers, rumor having it that "as a girl she had a child and did away with it." Dinesen's lord comes to assume a tragic burden similar to that of Melville's Captain Vere in *Billy Budd*. For Adam, "more dominantly even than the figure of the woman struggling with her sickle for her son's life, the old man's figure . . . kept him company through the day." Initially fearing his uncle as despotic and self-indulgent "in senile willfulness," Adam gradually realizes that the man is possessed of an ennobling vision of existence that, however paradoxically, involves him integrally in the widow's rite of sacrifice and celebrates the heroic nature of her destiny. Adam bears witness finally to the fact that peasant and lord share the same suffering and that he himself was able to "comprehend in full the oneness of the world . . . the unity of the universe." The landscape itself had mystically "spoken" to him. Born into a new, heightened consciousness, Adam knows that "this hour was consecrated to greater emotions, to a surrender to fate and to the will of . life."

—J. Donald Crowley

THE SPECKLED BAND
by Arthur Conan Doyle, 1892

The Sherlock Holmes stories are perennially popular, and "The Speckled Band" is among the best. It was its author's personal choice, coming atop of a list of twelve as "the grim snake story," "an echo of which," Doyle said could be found "in all parts of the world." As if to confirm this, one of the characters in Paul Scott's *Raj Quartet* (1975) remembers that it was her favourite as a child: "I used to read it by torchlight under the bedclothes at the school Sarah and I went to at home. 'The Speckled Band' reminded me of India. Because of the snake . . . "

This power of imminent suggestion attaches to the Holmes stories. They are incipient "ripping yarns," Victorian-Edwardian melodrama, but Holmes himself maintains the authority of the calculus and the elemental table, the abstract mathematical exactness of algebra and logarithms. The slightly overinflated and unsteady magniloquence of Doyle's prose counterpoints the restraint and precision of Holmes himself. However, Holmes's famous ingenuity of observation is secondary to the postures struck in the various set scenes in each story. In "The Speckled Band" the scenes are instantly familiar to anyone who knows the Holmes canon, but they are also superbly evocative to anyone coming to the stories fresh.

They were written for *Strand Magazine,* carefully structured, appealing to an increasingly enthusiastic public and developing a predictable formula upon which individual adventures worked variations. "The Speckled Band" comes from the earliest volume of collected short stories, *The Adventures of Sherlock Holmes,* published in 1892. Scholars consider that the events of "The Speckled Band" took place on 4 April 1883. That they take place during the course of a single day and night gives some impression of the gathering tension the story generates and for which it is memorable.

The title alludes to the dying exclamation of Miss Julia Stoner to her sister: "It was the band! The speckled band!" Recounting the events surrounding her sister's mysterious death to Holmes and his friend and chronicler Dr. Watson in their rooms in Baker Street, Helen Stoner inclines to the view that a band of gypsies camped in their father's estate might have been responsible, and the observation of their spotted-handkerchief headgear provides a visual suggestion of their unrealized threat. There are also a cheetah and baboon at large in the grounds, strange whistling sounds in the night and unusual noises, like the clang of metal falling. The circumstances that surrounded her sister's death are recurring, and Miss Stoner is in fear for her own life as the story begins.

Musing upon her tale, Holmes and Watson are suddenly interrupted by her father, whose very name bespeaks the oppressive authority typical of the era of late Victorian patriarchy: Dr. Grimesby Roylott. In furious temper, he warns Holmes off by twisting the fireplace poker into a curve. After he leaves, Holmes coolly performs the impossible feat of straightening it out again. Such melodrama enhances the appeal of the ostensibly rational deductive processes Holmes engages upon. We know that there are anomalies in the story: snakes are deaf and don't like milk, and cheetahs don't inhabit India. Nevertheless, our disbelief is willingly suspended by virtue of the great detective's supreme competence and professional pride. We know that Holmes will solve the mystery when he and Watson travel to the manor to Stoke Moran, and in getting to the solution, pace is more important than the pedantries of credible procedure.

It is tempting to subject the story's symbolism to close analysis. Roylott, for example, enters wearing a black top-hat, frock-coat, high gaiters and hunting-crop, with his large face seared with a thousand wrinkles, burned yellow by the sun of India and marked with every evil passion. His deep-set, bile-shot eyes and the high, thin, fleshless nose make him resemble a bird of prey. His pet baboon resembles a hideous and distorted child, and along with the cheetah, is a nocturnal dweller in the garden. Such images suggest the dominance of adult authority and its oppressive attitude towards the impressionable, curious, xenophobic, childish imagination. The speckled band is a night-time threat, a phallic symbol, and Holmes, who lashes the snake with his own cane, turning it back upon its master to wreak its revenge, represents the more acceptable and attractive version of adult authority. Though equally disciplinarian, he is protective, physically dependable, and wise. To do this, however, is to over-read a story whose attractions arise not from explicit but from latent tendencies. It is also to indulge in pastiche in a degree that the actual stories never quite permit themselves.

Doyle turned the story into a play in 1910 when he quickly needed to fill a theatre in which he had invested. Written in three weeks, the play is much weaker than the story, but it proved popular. The use of a dummy snake was preferred after Doyle found that it gave a more convincing performance. The story also gave its name to the American Holmes enthusiasts' "Speckled Band Club" and it has been the subject of at least one "sequel" by Edward D. Hoch, "The Return of the Speckled Band" (1987). Doyle himself used the sinister-sounding name "Moran" again for the villain who takes over from Professor Moriarty after the latter's death, in "The Empty House" (1905).

But perhaps the most significant legacy of the story is the impression it gives of Holmes as an arbiter of moral justice. Before the final confrontation, he comments to Watson, "When a doctor does go wrong he is the first of criminals. He has nerve and he has knowledge. Palmer and Pritchard were among the heads of their profession. This man strikes even deeper, but I think, Watson, that we shall be able to strike deeper still."

—Alan Riach

THE SPINOZA OF MARKET STREET
by Isaac Bashevis Singer, 1944

When Singer first published "The Spinoza of Market Street" in Yiddish in 1944 under the title "Der Spinozist: Dertseylung," he signed it Yitskhok Bashevis, combining his masculine first name with his mother's. The androgynous signature perfectly suits this tale of the union of opposites, represented by Dr. Nahum Fischelson, the Spinozist, and Black Dobbe.

Dr. Fischelson lives on the fifth floor of a Warsaw apartment house. Singer thus places him in a middle state between earth and heaven, flesh and spirit. Fischelson, however, rejects this status. For 30 years he has studied and annotated Spinoza's *Ethics,* until he has become almost a double of the Jewish philosopher. In an enlightening article, "Spinoza in Singer's Shorter Fiction," (in *Critical Views of Isaac Bashevis Singer*), Samuel I. Mintz examines the numerous similarities between Dr. Fischelson and his mentor. Fischelson cannot enjoy even a cool breeze without citing the authority of the *Ethics.* Despite the summer's heat Fischelson, ignoring the physical discomfort, wears a long black coat, stiff collar, and bowtie. When he looks out his attic window at the stars, he feels himself one with them and experiences that "Amor dei Intellectualis," that love of the divine intelligence, that Spinoza deemed "the highest perfection of the mind."

For the mundane, on the other hand, he has only contempt. He scolds the moths flying too close to the candle flame; he regards them as no wiser than people, who seek only "the pleasure of the moment." Whereas his vision of the sky is serene and happy, he regards Market Street as an image of hell, filled with noise, smoke, fire, strife, and crime. On the street emotion reigns, and Fischelson shares Spinoza's contempt for passion. When a tomcat howls in front of Fischelson's window, the Spinozist chases him away as another representative of the irrational and the passionate. Similarly, he rejects Immanuel Kant's *Critique of Pure Reason* and the writings of Kant's disciples, since pure reason is Fischelson's ideal.

Yet the sensate world insists on intruding. Fischelson feels the heat in his apartment, however much he may try to deny its existence. His stomach hurts, his knees shake, his vision blurs. He knows that Spinoza condemned anger, but he becomes furious when he reads what he regards as distortions of Spinoza's views. His dreams do not yield to his efforts to devise rational explanations.

Next door to him lives Black Dobbe, his antithesis. Whereas he is a creature of the heavens, she belongs to the earth. He visits the marketplace once a week to buy necessities; she sells cracked eggs there daily. He speaks and writes Hebrew, Russian, German, French, and Yiddish, and he reads Spinoza in Latin; she is illiterate. His father was a rabbi; her parents worked in a slaughterhouse. He enjoys the content of books; she admires their gold tooling. He talks to her about philosophy; she shows him her trousseau.

Fischelson's opposite, Black Dobbe is also his salvation. Set during World War I, his quarterly pension from Berlin is stopped and stores close so that he cannot buy food. War, that epitome of chaos, thus intrudes to disturb his cosmos. Faint from heat, hunger, and contact with the jostling, irrational crowd, Fischelson returns to his apartment to die. Seeking someone to read a letter that she has received from her brother in America, Black Dobbe enters Fischelson's room and finds him in bed, unconscious. She nurses him back to physical health and, to the surprise of all who know them, they marry.

This union with Dobbe rejuvenates the philosopher. He had thought himself impotent but discovers that he is "again a man as in his youth." Instead of talking to Dobbe about the metaphysics of Spinoza as he had previously, he quotes Romantic poetry to her—Klopstock, Lessing, Goethe. His perception of Market Street also changes. Looking out his window at dawn he still sees the beauty of the heavens, but below the gas lamps flicker like stars; the black shutters of the shops match the black arc of the sky.

Fischelson apologizes to Spinoza for becoming a fool by marrying—Spinoza remained a lifelong bachelor—and thus abandoning pure reason. However, Singer demonstrates that real foolishness lies in disregarding passion. The very fact that initially Fischelson looked into the night sky and then, after his wedding, peers into the dawn suggests that here is a long night's journey into day, a movement from darkness into light. Singer would agree with Hamlet that there are more things in heaven and earth than are dreamt of in philosophy. As his stories about *dybbuks* and demons demonstrate, Singer believes in the existence and power of the inexplicable. Black Dobbe does not represent the ideal any more than Fischelson. She has been unhappy and as isolated as the philosopher. When he asks about her past she is surprised because no one else had ever inquired. She, too, therefore gains from the marriage. Those who are partial to one party or the other believe that the marriage is a mistake, but what Singer shows of their life together belies that view. Their marriage saves them because each complements the other. Alone each is a half truth and therefore only half a person. "The Spinoza of Market Street" can be read as a retelling of Aristophanes's myth in the *Symposium*. There the playwright imagines that people once had four legs and four arms, but their attempt to assault the gods angered Zeus, who divided them. Each person therefore seeks his or her other half, love being the quest for wholeness. The author's duality—masculine and feminine, reason and mysticism—and the Jewish traditions of Haskalah (rational enlightenment) and Chassidism (passionate religion) find their expression and reconciliation in this, one of Singer's finest stories.

—Joseph Rosenblum

SPOTTED HORSES
by William Faulkner, 1931

Through much of his career after his first Yoknapatawpha novel, *Flags in the Dust* (first published as *Sartoris* in 1929), Faulkner wrote of his fictional county in free-standing episodes that he would later combine into novels. "Spotted Horses," first published in *Scribner's Magazine* in June 1931, was later incorporated into *The Hamlet* (1940), the first volume in the trilogy of the Snopes family. Although this long story, or novella, continued to appear with the divorced half of another novel, *The Wild Palms* (1939), "Old Man," there is reason to believe that Faulkner finally saw both of these shorter works as primarily important if possibly discrete portions of the later novels.

In either version, "Spotted Horses" is the best example of Faulkner's tall tales, exercises in Southern or Southwestern humor which he first appreciated in the work of Thomas Banks Thorpe ("The Big Bear of Arkansas") or Mark Twain ("You Can't Pray a Lie" from *Huckleberry Finn*, for instance). At the same time, the wild auction at the center of "Spotted Horses" reveals Flem Snopes's greed as menacing, since it victimizes both the dreams and the life savings of his fellow country people of northern Mississippi. But as it betrays them, the auction also allows them to betray themselves: the people of Frenchman's Bend are without hesitation or encouragement anxious to buy what they neither want nor can afford, and what is of no use to them as well. In their instinctive reactions to ownership and status, most of the characters of "Spotted Horses" serve as embodiments of American capitalism at its most representative.

The entrepreneur is Flem Snopes, himself the poverty-stricken backwoods son of a manipulative con artist who gains employment through intimidating landowners by threatening to burn their barns. Buying his way into a country store and then taking ownership of it, the dissatisfied, ambitious Flem decides to climb to the highest social status in Yoknapatawpha, and to the greatest fortune. To aid his career, the impotent Flem elopes with an unmarried pregnant woman and, returning from his Texas honeymoon, takes that opportunity to bring with him some wild Texas ponies which he can sell to credulous country people like Henry Armstid. The wild horses become symbols of the country folk, clattering over wooden bridges and running through houses and down moonlit roads, unrestrained (and untrainable) properties which, when they have escaped, can not be tied in any legal way to Flem.

Flem is accompanied in his scam by a Texan who disappears with the horses after the auction, and whom Flem holds accountable as the sharp trickster who robbed his customers and neighbors of their money and their pride. The situation of the Armstids is meant as metonymic. When Mrs. Armstid, gaunt in a shapeless garment and stained tennis shoes, comes to Flem for the five dollars that her husband gave for the horse he has lost, Flem unblinkingly tells her that the Texan has disappeared with all the money. When she stands there, forlorn and unmoved, he adds that perhaps the Texan forgot to return the money. When she leaves, he offers her a small striped paper bag of candy for her children as an inappropriate and inadequate recompense. She retrieves her dignity by minding her manners, by thanking Flem for his thoughtfulness without a trace of irony, but Faulkner underscores Flem's crassness by having a store clerk, watching the scene, slap his thigh and see it as the clever joke of a clever salesman.

At once more assured and foolishly confident, Vernon Tull's wife sues Flem Snopes for damages. One of the spotted ponies belonging to Eck Snopes had upset Tull's team and her husband was injured when his team ran away. The justice trying the case asks Eck if the horse is truly his, and Eck, one of the more honest of the Snopes clan, confesses it is. When he begins to ask the judge how much he owes Mrs. Tull, Eck is interrupted by her—she is so relieved to triumph at last against those who would cheat her, that she pronounces that "at least forty men heard that Texas murderer give that horse to Eck Snopes. Not sell it to him, mind; give it to him." Such a remark causes the judge to question whether or not Eck is the owner and decides that Eck had no horse he could claim as his, since at best he had received it by word of mouth, and so he is innocent of any damages. Moreover, if ownership can be transferred by simple pronouncement, the judge continues, then Eck himself could have transferred possession of the wild pony to Vernon Tull when he lay unconscious under the bridge. Still, the legal statutes provide the responsibility for any claim. Since the owner of the horse—if it is the Texan—will not or cannot assume liability and since Eck never owned the horse at all, the Tulls must themselves bear the costs of any damages which the wild horse has incurred or will incur. When Mrs. Tull, now thoroughly outraged, turns all her anger on the justice, he dismisses the hearing.

Flem is unmoved by these complaints. In the first action against him, he is exonerated by the perjury of one of his own kin; while obvious, the perjury cannot be proven. In the second case, the law itself comes to his rescue. The situation, then, is at once a tall tale, and a story of victimization. In some ways, it is the culture that is to blame; in other ways, it is the ambition of Flem; but, yet again, it is the ambition of a Henry Armstid or a Vernon Tull. "The comedy of the situation," Cleanth Brooks writes, "and the gusto with which the whole episode is recounted provide the proper undercutting of any argument put too seriously or symbolism set forth too nakedly."

Of Faulkner's broad, exaggerated, and indulgent humor there can be no doubt. "A little while before sundown the men lounging about the gallery of the store saw, coming up the road from the south, a covered wagon drawn by mules and followed by a considerable string of obviously alive objects which in the levelling sun resembled vari-sized and -colored tatters torn at random from large billboards—circus posters, say—attached to the rear of the wagon and inherent with its own separate and collective motion, like the tail of a kite. 'What in the hell is that?' one said." The suddenness, energy, and wildness of the untamed horses—which the Texan and Flem promise will be easy to train—captures the tall tale-telling just as Faulkner's language embodies the oral tradition from which such preposterous tales are derived. These "transmogrified hallucinations of Job and Jezebel," as the stranger, the anonymous Texan, calls the spirited horses, emphasizes their ghostly qualities and the improbability of the horses and what is to happen with them. At the same time, these hilarious references to the Bible speak of suffering and treachery. Their "phantom" quality, like the rail fence that cannot contain them, argues the underlying unruliness of mercenary dreams, and their breaking loose, confronting Ratliff as he is dressing and Mrs. Littlejohn as she is bringing laundry back into her house, suggests their essential wildness. "The horse," goes Faulkner's account, "whirled around without breaking or pausing. It galloped to the end of the veranda and took the railing and soared outward, hobgoblin and floating, in the moon. It landed in the lot still running and crossed the lot and galloped through the wrecked gate and among the overturned wagons and the still intact one in which Henry's wife still sat, and on down the lane and into the road."

"Spotted Horses" is one of Faulkner's most successful narratives in its ability tonally to combine the fantastic, the wildly comic, and the seriously consequential. While other stories sometimes combine these ingredients, such as the Indian stories, "Lo!" and "A Courtship," or the later story of Lucas Beauchamp and hunting for buried treasure, "The Fire and the Hearth," none of them reaches quite the exuberance or fantasy of "Spotted Horses." And with Flem always standing, brooding, over the tale, none has the same unsettling quality either.

—Arthur F. Kinney

SPRING SILKWORMS (Chun can)
by Mao Dun, 1933

Mao Dun, a voluminous writer, concentrated his creative energies on fiction, producing ten novels, several short story collections, and a large body of essays. *Chun can* ("Spring Silkworms"), Mao Dun's best short story, is perhaps the outstanding achievement in Chinese left-wing literature.

An outstanding realist writer, Mao Dun emerged in the 1920's after China's May Fourth Movement against imperialism and feudalism. He helped establish the Literary Research Society, one of the earliest organizations to advocate a new outlook in Chinese literature and art, served as editor of *Xiaoshuo Yuebao* (Short Story Monthly), and engaged in political action during the Revolutionary Civil War. Mao Dun established a unique fictional style and touched on practically every phase and corner of contemporary Chinese life; he describes the gradual spiritual corrosion of the young intellectuals, the unscrupulous manipulations of the bankers and industrialists, and the forlorn apathy of the peasants.

In "Spring Silkworms," the first of a three-story trilogy, Mao Dun turns his attention to China's luckless rural community. The plot revolves around the collapse of China's rural economy under the combined depredations of imperialism and feudalism. During a typical silkworm-raising season, the old peasant Old Dung Bao and his family strain to care for the worms and to provide them with enough mulberry leaves. The family reap an abundant crop of cocoons; but before they can rejoice, they learn to their dismay that most silk factories have shut down as a consequence of armed conflict between Chinese and Japanese in the Shanghai area (the 28 January Incident of 1932) and there is no demand for cocoons. Old Dung Bao's family sell the crop at a great loss and are much the worse for their season's worry and work.

"Spring Silkworms" gives a masterful characterization of several members of a peasant family. Old Dung Bao is the protagonist and the father of two sons. Like many other peasants in his village, Old Dung Bao and his family are hard-working, honest, and frugal. In Dung Bao's memory, during his father's era, his family was successful in cocoon raising and had lives typical of rich peasants. His family possessed "three acres of rice paddy, two acres of mulberry grove," and was "the envy of the people of East Village." The family fortunes quickly declined as the whole nation deteriorated economically. Finally Old Dung Bao himself has no land of his own, and is "over three hundred silver dollars in debt." As one of the old fashioned and submissive peasants under feudal rule, Old Dung Bao believes in "fate"; he also instinctively feels that all his countrymen are approximately the same as they were before the war, but that China has changed since "the foreign devils have swindled our money away." He is also convinced that "the world's going from bad to worse." Old Dung Bao neatly epitomizes thousands of Chinese peasants, his destiny a microcosm of the peasantry's bankruptcy under the dual pressure of traditional usury and foreign aggression.

A Duo, a rebellious young son of Old Dung Bao, neither shares his father's worries nor believes that "one good crop, whether of silkworms or of rice, would enable them to wipe off their debt and own their own land again." He knows they will never "get out from under" merely by toil and thrift even if they break their backs in hard work, but he enjoys labor and works with a will. He likes to help others, freely assisting when any of the village women need help carrying heavy burdens or fishing something out of the stream. Unlike his father, A Duo rejects taboos and superstitions. The village taboo against Lotus, whom the community consider an unlucky woman, convinces him something is wrong in the scheme of human relations, although he cannot figure out exactly what it is.

The action of "Spring Silkworms" follows one season of cocoon-raising. Nurturing silkworms in the traditional Chinese manner is a primitive but exacting endeavor, almost a form of religious ritual, one that peasants believe calls for love, patience, and the favor of the deity. Mao Dun captures this reverence and invests the family, especially Old Dung Bao, with the kind of unquestioned piety habitual to Chinese peasants, whose lives reflect their unsparing diligence and unfaltering trust in a beneficent heaven. Although Mao Dun intends to discredit such a feudal mentality, his celebration of the dignity of labor communicates his affection for good peasants at their traditional tasks.

The story takes place in a small southern community, one of the so-called "land of abundance" villages. The shiny green canal water is described, with several small boats occasionally passing by and breaking the mirror-smooth surface, rippling the reflection of the earthen bank and long line of mulberry trees into a dancing gray blur. Later in the story Mao Dun reveals unhealthy women and malnourished children, wearing old and torn clothes; an old, hard working man deeply in debt; a young woman, originally a household slave, married to a prematurely aged man. Through the season's grueling work, people become thinner each month, eyes sunk more deeply in their sockets, throats increasingly rasping and hoarse. Their ultimate reward is to sink more deeply in debt.

Mao Dun seeks to communicate the real life of ordinary Chinese people. He considers literature a weapon of social reform, one that stimulates the human mind, helps waken the common people, and gives them strength. Because of his literary creation, Mao Dun and his "Spring Silkworms" have earned the Chinese people's profound respect.

—Liping Guo

SREDNI VASHTAR
by Saki, 1912

As a professional journalist and star foreign correspondent, Saki (pseudonym for H.H. Munro) had all the resource of the ready writer who, strictly on time, never fails to supply the precise number of words to fill the precise amount of space, no more and no less. These limitations helped him to achieve the balance and economy so characteristic of his best stories, among which "Sredni Vashtar" (in *The Chronicles of Clovis*, 1912) is certainly one. Although he wrote two full-length novels, he was most at home with the medium of the short story. His stories, often no more than anecdotes, are exquisitely constructed and beautifully proportioned. In the course of his short life he produced over a hundred and twenty of them, all written at speed to meet a deadline. Not a word is superfluous, not a phrase too long. The prose glitters with Wildean epigrams ("To have reached the age of thirty is to have failed in life") and others that are pure Saki, for example the most famous one: "She was a good cook as cooks go, and as cooks go she went." He is on the side of children against adults, of life-enhancers against bores, of frankness against pomposity. Beneath the sparkling surface is a moralist who satirises greed, cupidity, hypocrisy, and snobbery. He can be very cruel, sometimes playfully, as when he writes: "Waldo is one of those people who would be enormously improved by death." Most of us have a Waldo in our life and have, on various occasions, felt that way about him. At other times the cruelty can be implacable and chilling. "Sredni Vashtar" is very typical of him, both in his fellow-feeling for children and in his detestation of interfering adults.

When Saki was a boy his much loved pet had been a Houdan cockerel. It fell ill, and although a veterinary surgeon could have saved it, the aunt under whose domination the boy Saki lived ruled that it should be put down. His misery was intense. Thirty years later he used the incident, still agonising in his memory, as the basis of "Sredni Vashtar." The protagonist, 10-year-old Conradin, belongs reluctantly to the household of an elder female cousin who is his legal guardian. She delights in thwarting his every pleasure and loves to forbid him from doing the things he enjoys. It is all, she explains prissily, "for his good." (One is reminded of another Saki story, "The Jesting of Arlington Stringham," where a woman is annoyed by a page-boy who delivers an unwelcome message: "Eleanor hated boys, and would have liked to have whipped this one long and often. It was perhaps the yearning of a woman who had no children of her own.") Conradin hates "The Woman," as he calls her, and takes refuge in his imagination. He often wanders about the dull and cheerless garden in flight from the woman's peremptory demands and joyless embargoes. One of the few delights Conradin has left him is a dilapidated shed in an overgrown corner of the garden. Here lives a ragged Houdan hen on which he lavishes his affection, as did the young Saki. Here, also, is a hutch containing a large polecat ferret which a friendly butcher's boy has smuggled in for a handful of silver. Conradin baptises the animal Sredni Vashtar and invents pagan rituals in his honour. Sredni Vashtar grows into a god and a religion much more potent to Conradin than the Sunday outings on which the woman drags him to the local church. The shed is a haven, a place where for the time being he can forget his tyrannical guardian and can summon up phantoms and beings remembered from history and from his own musings. The ferret is a lithe beast with sharp fangs which Conradin secretly fears but dearly treasures. Every Thursday he performs a mystic ceremonial at the shrine of the great Sredni Vashtar. In summer he lays flowers at the shrine, and in winter scarlet berries. The woman suspects something is going on in the shed. "It is not good for him to be pottering down there in all weathers," she decides. The Houdan hen is promptly taken away and sold overnight. She peers expectantly at Conradin, white-faced but silent. Determined not to give her satisfaction he stares back impassively. The secret worship of Sredni continues. There is a special thanksgiving one day when the woman suffers from an agonising toothache and the boy convinces himself that Sredni Vashtar is responsible.

The woman remains suspicious about his persistent visits to the shed. She ransacks his bedroom and finds the secret hiding place where he keeps the key. "What are you keeping in that locked hutch?" she demands. "I believe it's guinea-pigs. I'll have them all cleared away." That night Conradin prays earnestly: "Do one thing for me, Sredni Vashtar." Sredni Vashtar, being a god, must surely know what it is that the suppliant asks of him. He watches the woman stalk down to the shed. He imagines her going in, peering short-sightedly at the animal, perhaps poking clumsily at the thick straw. In his mind he sees her coming out with the pursed smile on her lips which he knows and loathes so heartily, and his ferret being carried away by the gardener. And he foresees a future dominated more and more by her insufferable dictatorship. In the misery of defeat he chants a defiant hymn:

Sredni Vashtar went forth, His thoughts were red thoughts and his teeth were white. His enemies called for peace, but he brought them death. Sredni Vashtar the Beautiful.

Soon he is rewarded. Out through the doorway ambles "a long, low, yellow-and-brown beast, with eyes a-blink at the waning daylight, and dark wet stains around the fur of jaws and throat. Conradin dropped on his knees. The great polecat-ferret made its way down to a small brook at the foot of the garden, drank for a moment, then crossed a little plank bridge and was lost to sight in the bushes. Such was the passing of Sredni Vashtar."

The maid starts to look for the woman. "She went down to the shed some time ago," says Conradin. He hears the search being made for her, the scream when she is discovered, the sobbings, the sound of something heavy being borne into the house. "Whoever will break it to the poor child? I couldn't for the life of me!" exclaims a voice. Conradin spreads a lavish allowance of butter on his toast and eats it with enjoyment. Toast with his tea was among those things which the woman had usually denied him because she knew he liked it.

—James Harding

THE STATIONMASTER (Stantsionnyi smotritel) by Alexander Pushkin, 1830

Generally recognized as the best of *Povesti pokoinogo I.P. Belkina* (*The Tales of Belkin*), "Stantsionnyi smotritel" ("The Stationmaster"), typifies Aleksandr Pushkin's prose style at its finest. Though it seems merely a straightforward account of seduction and betrayal, its apparent simplicity actually masks a complexity of narration, composition, and theme. The story begins with a prologue about the plight of stationmasters in early 19th-century Russia. After generalizing about these civil servants, the narrator turns to particulars and relates events surrounding the decline and death of one stationmaster, Samson Vyrin.

On his first visit to Vyrin's, the narrator meets a hearty fellow who lives at the travel station with his 14-year-old daughter, Dunia. The narrator soon focuses his attention on the girl, for she keeps order in the station and calms unruly travelers when they must wait for fresh horses. So charming is the girl that the narrator is reluctant to leave. But when he does, Dunia accompanies him and grants his request for a goodbye kiss.

When the narrator returns about four years latter, he finds the travel station and Samson Vyrin in sad repair. A few glasses of rum punch loosen the stationmaster's tongue; he tells the tale of how a young hussar carried Dunia away to Petersburg, and how he went to the city to bring his daughter back. Failing to rescue his "lost lamb," he returned to live a solitary life. Upon his third visit the narrator discovers that Vyrin has died, most likely from trying to console himself in drink. He visits the stationmaster's grave with a "one-eyed little boy in tatters," who relates how a wonderful lady in a magnificent carriage, along with her three children, nanny, and dog, came to visit Vyrin, only to discover that he had died. On hearing this sad news, the fine lady went to the cemetery where she threw herself upon the old man's grave, prostrate with grief. After hearing this account from the boy, the narrator says that he regrets neither the journey nor the seven rubles he spent on it.

Identified in the introduction to the tales only as Titular Councillor A.G.N., the narrator proves to be both highly manipulative and obviously unreliable. By muddling the dates of his story, he makes it impossible for the events to have taken place when he said they did. And if he had travelled as long as he claims, Belkin would have written down his version of A.G.N.'s account after his own death. Pushkin may have included such incongruities only to remind the reader that he indeed is reading a work of fiction by invented narrators, a form of Romantic irony.

Such narrative play sets the tone of the entire collection, where a publisher, A.P., edits the final text of the five stories and presumably adds the epigraphs to each tale, which Belkin has written down after having heard them from various people, among whom is A.G.N., who relates the events told to him by Samson Vyrin, the stationmaster himself. (Of all the Belkin tales, only "The Shot" surpasses "The Stationmaster" in narrative complexity.) Belkin first allows Vyrin to tell his story in his own language, but then switches over the A.G.N.'s own idiom—presumably because Pushkin himself disliked writing in dialect. However, we have no way of knowing whether A.G.N. grew impatient with dialect and began to relate the events his own way or whether Belkin decided to abandon the difficult task of writing in Vyrin's style. And because Samson Vyrin has taken to drink out of self-pity, his account is also implicitly unreliable and biased. In addition A.G.N. remains sympathetic to Samson Vyrin and ready to take his side. In fact, he tries to manipulate the reader into doing the same by describing the stationmaster in most pathetic terms. Presumably the more prosaic Belkin undercuts the sentimental tone by drawing our attention to the fact that Vyrin has a fondness for rum punch, the most likely source of his copious tears.

On one level "The Stationmaster" parodies N.M. Karamzin's sentimental tales, especially "Poor Liza" (1792), a peasant girl who commits suicide after having been abandoned by Erast, a gentleman of much higher station. Like that story, "The Stationmaster" begins with a prologue. A.G.N. almost mimics Karamzin's narrator in his use of sentimental vocabulary and tone; he even calls Vyrin's daughter "poor Dunia." The contemporary reader would immediately recognize in this usage an allusion to the earlier work and would expect Dunia to end as badly as did Liza and all the poor damsels of sentimental tales who fell in love with men above their station. As Paul Debreczeny has noted, such a false assumption becomes the basis for the entire work.

Begun as a simple parody, Pushkin's story evolves into a more complex phenomenon: a parody with a twist. Unlike Liza, Dunia does not perish; instead she lives splendidly in Petersburg with her three children. The second story does not completely reverse the first because Pushkin does retain some of the original elements.

The engravings on the wall which A.G.N. notices the two times he enters the stationhouse provide the source for yet another "incomplete reversal," the parody of the New Testament parable, "The Prodigal Son." In spite of the fact that Pushkin rarely clutters his prose with many details, no one even noticed the engravings until 1919 when M. Gershenson discussed their significance. Once again the reader falsely expects Dunia to turn into a "Prodigal Daughter" and come back to beg her father's mercy after having lived her life in poverty and degradation. But in this case the father, not the child, becomes the prodigal. Here Pushkin flouts sentimental and romantic convention which demanded that Dunia perish. Instead, the father, the apparent "victim," dies of drink. However, Pushkin does not really make the parable itself the subject of his parody, but the sentimental German verses which interpret the original text. This parody within a parody of an interpretation of the parable goes farther and farther from the original source, not unlike the series of unreliable narrators who deviate from the truth a little more with each retelling.

One more reversal reinforces the reader's false expectations. In the New Testament the parable of the Lost Sheep directly precedes that of the Prodigal Son. And when Samson Vyrin tells A.G.N. of his trip to Petersburg to bring Dunia home, he says that he went after his "lost lamb." The biblical shepherd returns and rejoices over the one lost sheep, but Vyrin returns home alone.

The narrator sets up false expectations in his method of narration as well as in the parodies. For example A.G.N. begins by asking a rhetorical question about who has not cursed stationmasters. He then supplies a list of reasons why one would want to send them to the devil. And just when the reader expects a condemnation of stationmasters, A.G.N. begins an apologia for them in anticipation of his sympathetic introduction of Vyrin. The negative epigraph about the "despots of the posting station" confuses the reader even more.

The complexity of "The Stationmaster" raises it above the other stories in the collection; its inherent ambiguity sets it apart from other works of the period. Although Dunia appears to be married, no concrete evidence in the story points to such a conclusion. When A.G.N. asks whether she is married, Vyrin does not respond. By ending his story with an unanswered question, Pushkin creates a modern story in spite of its sentimental roots.

—Christine A. Rydel

THE STAUNCH TIN SOLDIER. See **THE STEADFAST TIN SOLDIER.**

THE STEADFAST TIN SOLDIER (Standhaftige tinsoldat)
by Hans Christian Andersen, 1838

"Standhaftige tinsoldat" ("The Steadfast Tin Soldier," also "The Constant Tin Soldier") was published in Hans Christian Andersen's *Eventyr* (Fairy Tales), which appeared from 1835 to 1842. In the 19th century, the strong impetus for imaginative literature for children, encouraged by the works in folklore of the brothers Grimm, gained power with the efforts of Andersen. Andersen did not collect folklore, but used its effects creatively with a special sympathetic touch for the lonely child who endows inanimate objects with life.

Although deemed a fairy tale, "The Steadfast Tin Soldier" is an adventure story. In a setting of childhood play, it presents the ideals of the life history of a tin soldier who remains constant in duty. Although a pawn to "higher powers" in the form of a little boy, the toy soldier is willing to die in uniform as a soldier should. Conscious of his place and his training, he does not move his eyes, nor does he shout or change his position when distracted or threatened; he never winces with pain.

He is, however, odd man out, the rare exception. Cloned with 24 others from the same old tin spoon, his origin as number 25 in a box that should end, one would suppose, with two dozen, leaves him minus a leg; there was not enough tin to make him like the others. Unlike "The Ugly Duckling," he cannot grow out of his deformity.

Never despairing of his shortcoming, he proceeds with a singular life denied to the common lot. He alone among them finds a ladylove, a paper dancer standing on one leg in the doorway of a paper castle. She, too, is disproportioned in that the spangle that adorns her scarf is larger than her face. The soldier—possibly because he does not fit—is left to lie beside a snuffbox where he can gaze at her indefinitely.

Resistance to confinement characterizes all the tin soldiers, who are animated when the lid is taken off the box and they find themselves placed on a table with other toys, chief of which is the paper castle with realistic setting and the dancer in the doorway. The soldier assumes she must be one-legged like himself and desires her for his wife.

A blending of rigidity befitting a toy and consciousness resembling living beings characterizes the telling. The tin soldier's concern for propriety enters the scene; she lives in a palace and he only in a box, but he must try to make her acquaintance. The toy soldier does not remove his gaze from the lady, and behind the snuffbox he watches her continue to stand without losing her balance.

At evening when the 24 soldiers are returned to the box, the other toys play their own games—except for the dancer and the one-legged soldier, who do not move. At the stroke of midnight the lid of the snuffbox flies open to disclose the soldier's enemy, a jack-in-the-box type of goblin who requests that the soldier remove his gaze; as soldiers on parade must do, he "feigned not to hear." From this point on he suffers the vicissitudes of nature and the goblin's curse. "You just wait till tomorrow," the goblin threatens.

The children next day place the one-legged soldier on the window sill, from which a puff of wind blows him from the third story to the ground where the owner, searching, cannot find him. The soldier does not think it proper to shout when in uniform. Other children find him and make a paper boat to sail him in the gutter. Amid much danger as he floats, he holds his position as a soldier should and looks straight before him.

Entering the darkness of a sewer, his soldier life continues when a rat demands a pass and payment of a toll, but he only holds tighter to his gun and floats faster than the rat can swim to the end of the "tunnel" where he is emptied into the canal. Floating swiftly and dangerously he holds himself stiff and does not wince. As the paper gives way and the boat sinks, he remembers the refrain "Onward! Onward! Soldier!/ For death thou canst not shun." Knowing a soldier's supreme duty is to die, as the paper gives way, he is swallowed by a fish.

With magical coincidence, after the awareness of intense darkness comes a piercing flash of light. The fish had been caught, sold, purchased, and carried to a cook, who lifts out the toy soldier. He is not famous; everyone wants to see him. Miraculously, he finds himself placed among the toys on the same table as before, where he can resume watching the dancer, who also is steadfast. The soldier cannot yield to tears, which are not proper to his calling; and they gaze at each other.

The goblin's curse returns; a boy flings the soldier into the fire, and as he melts he keeps himself erect. A gust of wind catches up the little dancer and floats her also into the fire. The next morning among the ashes the soldier is a lump in the shape of a small tin heart and nothing is left of the dancer but her blackened spangle.

The soldier's destiny is completely realized: adventures that no one else can equal; a series of opportunities that enable him to prove himself able and loyal; the traditional journey of the hero delineated by Joseph Campbell, complete with departure, the "belly of the whale" initiation, and return, the "meeting with the goddess," and the dramatic transformation in fire. With the dross of the mortal body burned away, the immortal part, the heart that has made him steadfast, remains with the spangle—both symbols of immortality.

—Grace Eckley

THE STOLEN BACILLUS
by H.G. Wells, 1895

H.G. Wells wrote "The Stolen Bacillus" in the same period he wrote *The Island of Dr. Moreau, The Time Machine, The Invisible Man,* and *The War of the Worlds.* This curious tale, therefore, is significantly placed among some of Wells's most celebrated scientific romances. Indeed, "The Stolen Bacillus" is itself a tale about a scientist, beginning in sombre tone with a quickly developed plot suggesting the possibility of a terrifying threat to humankind. However, the bizarre twist with which the tale ends, makes it less interesting as a work of thriller fiction than as an almost perfect example of the use of bathos in literature.

"The Stolen Bacillus" concerns a bacteriologist who entertains a mysterious stranger, referred to at first as "the pale man." As the bacteriologist exhibits various deadly cultures in his laboratory, the visitor demonstrates a morbid fascination with them. Looking at a test tube containing what the bacteriologist describes as "the celebrated Bacillus of cholera," the pale man remarks, "It's a deadly thing to have in your possession."

It soon becomes clear that there is something hazardous about the pale man. His eyes shining, he observes, "These Anarchist-rascals . . . are fools, blind fools—to use bombs when this kind of thing is attainable." After his visitor has left, the bacteriologist discovers that the vial, of what he had flippantly referred to as "Bottled cholera," is now missing from the laboratory. It is obvious that the pale man is, himself, an anarchist and has stolen a deadly virus with which he intends to bring some terrible fate on society.

The anarchist escapes in a hansom cab, intending to release the bacillus into the drinking-water system of London. The bacteriologist gives pursuit (followed, in turn by his wife, alarmed at seeing her husband fleeing through the streets without hat and coat). There follows a hair-raising chase during which the anarchist inadvertently breaks the test tube. He swallows what is left of the virus and, when the bacteriologist finally catches up with him, laughs defiantly and cries out, "*Vive l'Anarchie!* You are too late, my friend. I have drunk it! The cholera is abroad!"

Only as the anarchist strides off towards Waterloo Bridge, "jostling his infected body against as many people as possible," does Wells deliver the bathotic denouement to the story. The bacteriologist explains to his wife that, in the hope of astonishing his visitor (who he had not known to be an anarchist) he had shown him "a cultivation of that new species of Bacterium . . . that infest, and I think cause the blue patches upon various monkeys; and like a fool, I said it was Asiatic cholera."

The sense of anticlimax is tremendous, but Wells quickly dispels the reader's sense of disappointment or, possibly, annoyance: "Of course I cannot say what will happen," the bacteriologist confides to his wife, "but you know it turned that kitten blue, and the three puppies—in patches, and the sparrow—bright blue. But the bother is, I shall have all the trouble of preparing some more."

This amusing conclusion, coupled with the remembrance of earlier narrative details which suddenly make sense, such as the bacteriologist's exclamation of "Blue ruin!" as he rushes out of the house after the anarchist, might lead the reader to dismiss the story as a piece of spoof sensationalism—an entertaining joke on those mad scientists and crazy revolutionaries so popular in late-Victorian fiction (they are found in the Sherlock Holmes stories of Arthur Conan Doyle as well as in the novels of G.K. Chesterton). Yet the seriousness with which the bacteriologist speaks of the dangers inherent in the viruses he handles ("mysterious, untraceable death, death swift and terrible, death full of pain and indignity"); and the zeal with which the Anarchist shapes his schemes demand that the reader seek a deeper purpose to the story.

In his 1951 biography of Wells, Vincent Brome has said of Wells's scientific romances that "it was ideas that mattered more than characters"; that is certainly true of "The Stolen Bacillus," where the characters are nothing more than caricatured archetypes.

Although Wells gives several physical descriptions of the anarchist—his "limp white hand . . . lank black hair and deep grey eyes, the haggard expression and nervous manner"—this is done merely to unsettle the reader, and signal the character as sinister and potentially dangerous; and there is no description whatsoever of the bacteriologist. Also, whilst Wells gives names to the bacteriologist's wife and even to the drivers of the hansom cabs; his central protagonists are named only by their profession or calling—bacteriologist and anarchist. In doing this, Wells clearly makes them representational characters and draws a distinction between the common man and woman, who have names like us, and the nameless forces who shape and influence the world—in this case a man of science and a political activist.

Additionally, both men are primarily motivated by a desire for self-glorification: the bacteriologist regards his work as an end in itself, rather than as a means to an end (the eradication of disease); the anarchist plots revolution not because he has ideals of social equality, but because he wants to be avenged on individuals whom he believes despise him. Both act wilfully and irresponsibly, and are utterly complacent about the effects of their actions on others. Perhaps, Wells seems to be saying, there is little to chose between an extremist determining to overthrow a society and a respected member of society who, nevertheless, risks placing it in peril.

—Brian Sibley

A STORY ABOUT THE MOST IMPORTANT THING (Rakaz o samom glavnom) by Evgenii Zamiatin, 1923

One of Zamiatin's most interesting and unusual fictions, "Rakaz o samom glavnom" ("A Story about the Most Important Thing") demonstrates a cosmic breadth of theme, an action running on several planes, and a combination of lyrical and epic features that is typical more of a full-fledged novel than of a short story. Symptomatic of this thematic richness—and also characteristic of Zamiatin and other contemporary Russian "ornamental" writers— is the shifting, relativistic narrative voice that alternates between authorial omniscience and embodiment in the form of various protagonists, animal, human, and extraterrestrial. All this reinforces Zamiatin's theory of literature in a revolutionary age, developing a narrative style and technique apposite to the post-Einsteinian era, in which timescales are confused and relative, and where even "the most important thing" seems contingent and totally contextual. Nevertheless, all is ultimately unified and contained within a single philsophic vision, one sign of which is the employment throughout the story of a pervading and cohesive set of leitmotifs, or recurring phraseological formulae: the curling ash on the cigarette, the lilac, the broken watch.

The story opens with the revelation of three different worlds. One is that of the lilac bush, "eternal, immense and boundless," in which a pink and yellow worm of the *Rhopalocera* genus lives out its final mute and agonising hours before "dying" and becoming a cocoon. The single, most important thing for this larva is to "die," turn into a chrysalis, then re-emerge as a butterfly, and thus enact part of the eternal process of life. The second world is that of the Russian revolution: a river spanned by a bridge that connects the pro-Soviet peasants of Orlovka in their clay-colored shirts and the anti-bolshevik peasants in the village of Kelbuy. The third world is that of a faraway star whose last few inhabitants are about to perish from lack of air.

Although the action in these worlds proceeds independently, the three planes of existence are shown as intersecting and interacting: the *Rhopalocera* larva plummets down from a branch and lands in the lap of Talia as she talks with Kukoverov, leader of the Kelbuy peasantry. The larva's imminent death is echoed in the fate of Kukoverov, for whom time is also running out. He is captured by the bolsheviks. Dorda, their leader, and Kukoverov in an earlier life shared a cell as political prisoners. For Dorda,

now a servant of the revolution, the most important thing is defeat of the opponents, and Kukoverov thus faces execution by his former friend. As a humane gesture, however, Dorda allows him to spend his last night with Talia, and thus their love (for this couple, the "most important thing") is consummated before his final extinction. Thoughtlessly Kukoverov has overwound his watch. The spring snaps, and the hands whirl round madly, a hundred times faster than before. Yet in his final moments with Talia, he is lifted out of himself and experiences a mystic, illuminating sense of timelessness: "Hugely, easily, like the Earth, Kukoverov suddenly understands all. And he understands: yes, this is so, this is necessary. And he understands: there is no death."

Events on the earth are mirrored by those on the dying star. The last four inhabitants are unnamed and identifies only as a mother, man, woman, and a blind boy. Echoing acts of revolutionary murder on earth, the man kills his blind brother so as to enjoy a few more breaths of life. Like *Rhopalocera*, the mother is prepared to die, yet is full of sympathy for her elder son who murdered in order to survive; he meanwhile embraces the other woman. Like Kukoverov and Talia, "the two are one. And the other one, the older one, the Mother, stands over them. Her profile is etched against the red glow of the sky." Meanwhile as their lives end, the distant star itself hurtles on towards a final collision with the earth. The fates of earth-and star-dwellers are thus made to coincide.

Despite its seeming conclusion in science fiction, the story is ultimately a reflection by Zamiatin on earthly— and, more narrowly, Russian— history. Despite the acceleration of time in a revolutionary age, the "most important thing" in human relations is the timeless love of man and woman, and it is only this that offers an escape from time. In the final immolation scene, Zamiatin's narrator steps back once again from the action and perceives a greater good that might one day emerge. But his message is one that belittles and ultimately negates any bolshevik masterplan for human history, even though it too offers a utopian vision. As star and earth are about to collide, "the Earth opens her womb wider—still wider—all of herself—in order to conceive, in order that new fiery creatures may come forth in the scarlet light, and then, in white warm mist—still newer, flowerlike forms bound to the new Earth only the slenderest stem. And when these human flowers ripen . . . "

—Christopher Barnes

THE STORY OF SHUNKIN.   See **A PORTRAIT OF SHUNKIN.**

STRAIT IS THE GATE (La Porte étroite) by André Gide, 1909

In *L'Immoraliste* (*The Immoralist*) André Gide had tentatively explored the moral consequences of a particular type of self-centred and, by innuendo, atheistic hedonism. By implication Gide's text had rejected it. *La Porte étroite*

(*Strait Is the Gate*) explores and rejects the opposite possibility that the summit of human achievement lies in the renunciation of all earthly joys. It is the story of Jerome, told 13 years later, and of his love as a young adolescent for his cousin Alissa, who turns him down, wastes away, and finally dies.

The ambiguities are carefully built up; Gide uses a narrator, speaking directly in the first person. His feelings are too involved in the narration for his judgements to be accepted without reflection, even now he is no longer young. Alissa's point of view is presented, in letters and in the substantial section of her diary copied verbatim by Jerome, and inserted into his narrative after he had given his own version of what had happened. There is an abundance of allusions contemporary readers might miss; the writing is too self-consciously artistic to be taken entirely at face value.

There is ample evidence in the text to show that, as Gide later said, there is something "forced and excessive" in Alissa's view, but the element of falsification is quite subtly insinuated, for instance in Alissa's implied but consciously literary self-identification with Pascal in her diary entries, although, as if aware that he may have been over-allusive, Gide makes the distortion of authentic spiritual values more straightforwardly obvious in the "depoetization" Alissa undergoes in pursuit of her ascetic endeavours. She gets rid of her literary books, and her piano.

Against a background of delicately portrayed adolescent love, as seen by one of the participants ten years after the death of the other, Gide uses an extraordinary miasma of half-tones. The reader is expected to pick up tiny adolescent pomposities, slight excesses in literary allusiveness, covert allusions to Claudel's texts, and to Goethe's concept of "elective affinities" or spiritual relationships, trivial behavioural spontaneities betraying in painful surface emotions the vulnerably raw reactions of adolescence.

Alissa is incapable of enduring any physical contact with Jerome, and yet when, three years after their last meeting, Jerome is by chance again at Le Havre, and has indulged his nostalgia sufficiently to go to the country house where Alissa lives and where he had so often stayed, he finds that she knew he was coming; for three days she had been coming down to the garden gate to meet him. This was the gate which together they had previously used; the gate was also the symbolic barrier between them, the multivalent gate of the title. The reader is expected to pick up the almost exquisitely subtle inadequacy of the reasons of exaggerated shame and self-deceiving selflessness which make Alissa unwilling to marry Jerome, and drive her to neglect her mind, aesthetic pleasure, her taste, her music, her appearance, and finally her health, to protect some analogue with her of emotional anorexia.

Gide leaves Alissa's incapacity for shared intimacy ambiguous almost to the end, when Jerome reproduces the diary extracts. Indeed Alissa's spiritual power remains such that the ambiguity extends beyond her death. One of the reasons she had alleged for not marrying Jerome was that her sister, Juliette, loved him. Juliette's daughter is called Alissa, and looks like Juliette's sister. A family resemblance with her mother's sister, no doubt, but Gide delights in leaving the reader to wonder. The infant also looks like the woman loved by the man her mother really loved, not her husband, the father.

Gide's characters are sufficiently sheltered from economic problems for the fiction to concentrate on their spiritual anguishes. *Strait Is the Gate* is set against a background of a large French family in which uncles and aunts take turns holding family reunions on great family estates during the holidays. Gide rightly thought in 1910 that it was the best piece he had yet written, although he was taken aback at the way his Catholic friends wrongly welcomed the book as a sign of imminent conversion.

The narrative opens just after Jerome, aged twelve, has lost his father. His mother had moved to Paris from Le Havre, and the background to most of the story is the estate at Fongueusemare where Jerome's creole aunt, his father's sister, lives with her children, Alissa, Juliette, and Robert. Jerome devotes several pages to his aunt, and three successive paragraphs begin with her name. She wore bright colours and low-cut dresses, rose at midday, spent her time in an apparent dream, and had a way of lingering on the chords when she played Chopin's mazurkas. Jerome feels strange one day when she undoes one of the buttons of his sailor's shirt.

At this point in the story, he breaks off, addressing the reader, "It's time I told you about my cousin," and Gide makes his syntax falter to betray his emotion. The first major incident occurred when Jerome was 14 years old, and, unexpectedly free for the afternoon, he called on Alissa. He passed his aunt's room, where his aunt was lounging, making jokes at his uncle's expense, and sharing a cigarette with a lieutenant in the presence of Juliette and Robert. He finds Alissa in her room, on her knees, crying. Alissa is clearly concerned that her father should not know what went on, and the reader realises only slowly that Alissa comes to use the shame she feels at her mother's behaviour as an excuse for her own frigidity. The whole of the story's interest lies the ambiguity of Alissa's behaviour, and the delicate depiction of her growing self-deceit.

There are subtle ironies, as when Alissa dreams that Jerome has died and she has to make a huge effort to find him. In fact she does make the effort, but she is the one who dies. An amethyst cross becomes a symbol of their union. There is a brilliant set piece as the older children and young adults perform the rite of decorating the Christmas tree and Juliette tells Jerome that Alissa wants her to marry before Alissa herself does. Alissa has no more reason not to marry Jerome on Juliette's account than she has on account of exaggerated shame at her mother's behaviour. The *récit* is the story of her unfolding self-deception as she forces herself self-destructively through the narrow gate of an immature asceticism. The story, apparently guileless, is a highly sophisticated literary artefact, scintillating with resonances, a strong candidate for the most brilliantly written short fiction to have appeared in France in the 20th century.

—A.H.T. Levi

THE STREET OF CROCODILES (Ulica Krokodyli) by Bruno Schulz, 1934

"Ulica Krokodyli" ("The Street of Crocodiles") is the title piece of the American edition of the first of Bruno Schulz's two collections of short fiction, *Sklepy Cynamonowe* (1934; also translated as *Cinnamon Shops*, 1963). Like all of Schulz's stories, "The Street of Crocodiles" is narrated in the first person (by a character elsewhere identified as Joseph) and is based on the author's life, particularly his childhood, in Drohobycz in what was then southeastern Poland and is now part of Russia. Schulz's father, an assimilated Jew, owned a thriving textile shop in the Market Square section of a city that the discovery of oil had transformed into a modern if still provincial metropolis. It is also a city transformed by the genius of a writer often and favorably compared to Franz Kafka. Although Schulz's stories are just as "polysemantic, unfathomable, not exhausted by interpretation" as Kafka's existential parables (as Schulz himself described them in the afterword to his Polish translation of *The Trial*), they are far more elliptical and wildly disassociative, less logical in their absurdity and more fabulous. They are not so much (like Kafka's "The Metamorphosis") about transformation as they are themselves in transformation in the audacity and brilliance of Schulz's disjunctive plots and riotously excessive language. Capable of transforming a market square into a labyrinthine street of wholly metaphorical crocodiles, his painterly prose combines the eerie geometry of Giorgio de Chirico and the differently dream-like work of Marc Chagall. (The pictorial quality of Schulz's fiction derives from his own work as painter, illustrator, engraver, and art teacher.) In this way, Schulz ultimately seems less "the Polish Kafka" than the precursor of magic realists such as Gabriel García Márquez.

Appearing (or, to be more precise, not appearing) on his father's wall-size city map as a terra incognita, the Street of Crocodiles stands in vivid contrast to the "baroque panoramas" of the nameless city's other parts, including the one described in the companion story, "Cinnamon Shops," named for the stores' rich wood panelling and array of exotic goods. The Street of Crocodiles is by contrast sober and colorless in appearance, commercial and utilitarian in character. Everything there, from the construction materials to the goods displayed, seems ephemeral and false, every store merely a front for some still less savory enterprise. Behind the tailor shop that specializes in cheap elegance, that stocks a library of false labels, and that is staffed by transvestites and women of flawed beauty, is an antique shop devoted to licentious books and pictures. The street itself proves no less strange with its indistinct passersby, driverless cabriolets, papier-mâché trams, and trains that arrive and depart according to no known schedule, and from makeshift stations that suddenly appear and then just as suddenly disappear. In "that area of sham and empty gestures," the narrator discovers "a fermentation of desires prematurely aroused and therefore impotent and empty." The reality may be thin, but the air is thick with the futility of desires aroused but forever left unfulfilled. However, there is an irony here. The metonymic street arouses not only false hopes but also false suspicions, for it is "we" who invest the "ordinary banality" of the street with its air of decadence and depravity that on closer examination turns out to be "thin" and theatrical.

To some extent the story is, as Ewa Kuryluk has noted, an attack on the modern culture of mass production. However, it is also considerably more than that. It is, for example, certainly, albeit ambivalently, sympathetic to the cheap goods that Kuryluk too readily dismisses. "The Street of Crocodiles" and "Cinnamon Shops" do not, therefore, so much oppose as complement one another, offering two versions of the same story of desire that informs nearly all of Schulz's stories, including "The Book" (young Joseph's transformation of the advertisements for cheap goods and quack cures into "pure poetry") and "Treatise on Tailors' Dummies" (the father's call for a second genesis that will improve on the first by devoting itself to the making of ephemeral "trash"). As Schulz explained in his 1936 essay, "The Republic of Dreams," "Embedded in the dream is a hunger for its own reification,

but this reification, or realization, must remain at best incomplete and at worst a disappointment, even a delusion," like the fantastic birds that the father conjures in several stories, which are cruelly destroyed by the townspeople as the birds fly overhead. Only then the father realizes they were "nothing but enormous bunches of feathers, stuffed carelessly with old carrion" ("The Night of the Great Season"). Against that inevitable realization Schulz steadfastly but with characteristically self-conscious irony holds out the counter possibility that he found best expressed in Rilke's poetry, that "the tangled, mute masses of things unformulated within us may yet emerge to the surface miraculously distilled."

—Robert A. Morace

A STRING.   See THE PIECE OF STRING.

SUCH DARLING DODOS
by Angus Wilson, 1950

Angus Wilson began his writing career with the short stories of *The Wrong Set* in 1949, followed the year after with *Such Darling Dodos*. Once he started on his novel-writing career, however, the flow of short stories rapidly fell off, the only further volume being *A Bit off the Map* in 1957. Nevertheless, the short story is a form that suited his exuberant and disturbing talent particularly well, and is brilliantly exemplified in "Such Darling Dodos" with its comic observation and satiric bite.

The story does not depend on its action, which is minimal. An ageing Roman Catholic, Tony, has come to visit his cousin Priscilla in Oxford, having received her letter telling him that her husband Robin is mortally ill. What is important is the contrast in values between the two characters, which Wilson conveys through his vivid mimicking of their respective voices and his careful descriptions of their appearance and possessions. Tony employs an imitation Jane Austen speech to address his academic relatives, which gives him a pleasing sense of social superiority. Priscilla and Robin, left-wing intellectuals whose heyday was the 1930's, speak in a less affected manner. Tony at the age of 55 keeps up his looks by means of hair dye and cold cream; Priscilla looks "like a giant schoolgirl," and has the capacity to make whatever dress she wears "seem like hand-woven djibbahs." Details like these give a clear sense of the opposing ways of life represented by the characters. No doubt Tony is the more obviously satirised, but the slightly self-righteous high-mindedness of Priscilla and Robin does not escape.

Moreover Tony's visit to Oxford, which is actually an embarrassment to his secularly-minded hosts, is an act of genuine concern on his part in response to Priscilla's panicky letter. He wants to offer the possible comforts of his Catholic faith to the dying man and the wife who will survive him, and he is allowed to put forward his ideas at some length, even describing the house in which he is staying as "a very dark corner of pagan England." But Priscilla certainly feels that he has taken advantage of her distress to introduce religious ideas in an entirely inappropriate way, and she stands up vigorously for her own view of life. While they are arguing, Robin himself arrives dramatically, and attempts to conciliate them both. When Tony refuses to respond, Robin asserts his socialist ideas forcefully: "I'm afraid though, Tony, I remain satisfied not with the amount of what I have done, God forbid, but with the kind." And he refuses to rise to Tony's characterisation of his concerns as "drains and baths and refrigerators."

However, Wilson's stories usually have a sting in the tail. For a young couple, postwar undergraduates, are coming to lunch, and they bring the contrasting values to a striking focus. Tony is surprised to hear Priscilla describing the young people as "awful," but at lunch he comes to see why she feels this. For Michael and Harriet Eccleston, recently demobilized respectively from the Army and the Wrens, prove to be very different in political outlook from their hosts. Michael does not find chapel a bore, and Harriet wonders whether "freedom was quite the issue when one looked at India, after all responsibility was important." And neither of them is in favour of the abolition of the death penalty. The political gap becomes ever wider, and it takes a good deal of social effort "to end the occasion on an easier note." Tony walks with the young couple as far as St. Giles, and assures them that not all of his generation thought like Priscilla and Robin. Tony agrees with Harriet that they are living in the past and, feeling himself very "modern," makes the final judgment that gives the story its title: "'They're dodos, really, but,' he added more kindly, 'such darling dodos.'"

This is extremely neat and amusing, and certainly characteristic of Wilson's short stories. But it also makes serious social observations and raises important issues. Do human beings need religion? Can we live by "drains and baths and refrigerators" alone? Were the left-wing thinkers of the 1930's too austere or humanly unaware? Another question might concern the accuracy of Wilson's social observation. After all, it is generally argued that the ex-soldiers of 1945 put into power the Labour Government that tried to change British society towards real democracy. How representative are the Ecclestons of the new generation at Oxford? Literature is better suited to raising questions than to finally answering them, and the success of the story is that is makes us see vividly two contrasting ways of life, and encourages us to judge them both. But it does this in a way that is consistently entertaining. Wilson's brilliant accuracy of social observation expresses itself in relevant details. Michael Eccleston addresses Tony as "Sir," and the narrator comments, "he loved old-world manners." Wilson's method is to make us look carefully into what manners of all kinds reveal.

—Peter Faulkner

THE SUICIDE CLUB
by Robert Lewis Stevenson, 1882

Stevenson was, from childhood, a reader and admirer of *The Arabian Nights*. In "A Gossip on Romance" (1882) Stevenson said of the collection that its reader would "look in vain for moral or for intellectual interest. . . . Adventure, on the most naked terms, furnishes forth the entertainment and is found enough." In the same year Stevenson's *New*

Arabian Nights, which includes "The Suicide Club," first appeared in book form.

"The Suicide Club" is by no means a simple imitation of *The Arabian Nights*. Its settings are not in medieval Baghdad but in 19th-century Paris and London; yet these modern cities are the locations for adventures as gloriously improbable as anything narrated by Scheherazade. There are many echoes of the original. So, for example, the first part of "The Suicide Club" is entitled "The Story of the Young Man with the Cream Tarts." The allusion is to the story of Hasan Bedr-ed-Deen and Nour-ed-Deen Ali, in which the skill of Bedr-ed-Deen's mother as a cook of cream-tarts is a crucial element in the narrative. At the end of this first part of "The Suicide Club" there appears a linking passage very reminiscent of the *Arabian Nights*:

> Here (*says my Arabian author*) ends THE STORY OF THE YOUNG MAN WITH THE CREAM TARTS, who is now a comfortable householder in Wigmore Street, Cavendish Square. The number, for obvious reasons, I suppress. Those who care to pursue the adventures of Prince Florizel and the President of the Suicide Club, may read the HISTORY OF THE PHYSICIAN AND THE SARATOGA TRUNK.

There, in microcosm, is the special world of this tale—its attractive juxtaposition of the exoticism of medieval romance and the "comfortable" realities of Stevenson's own world. The tale this link promises again contains echoes of *The Arabian Nights*, since Silas Q. Scuddamore's discovery of a dead body, which he resorts to packing away in his trunk has direct precedents in *The Arabian Nights*. When, in the final part of "The Suicide Club," Lieutenant Brackenbury Rich is spirited to Colonel Geraldine's mysterious party in a lavishly appointed London villa, and then witnesses all its luxuries begin removed, revealing it as "the mushroom of a single night which should disappear before morning," we have a slightly more prosaic version of Aladdin's magic palace.

The chief protagonists of the adventure of "The Suicide Club" are Prince Florizel of Bohemia and his Master of the Horse, Colonel Geraldine. The two are in the habit of disguising themselves and seeking out adventures on an "evening ramble." The parallel is surely clear; these are Stevenson's versions of Harun al-Raschid and his Vizir Jaafar who, in *The Arabian Nights*, frequently wander the nighttime streets in disguise. Of course, the motif of the disguised rules is an archetypal one, rich in significance. At the end of "The Suicide Club" Stevenson drily records:

> To collect, *continues my author*, all the strange events in which this Prince has played the part of Providence were to fill the habitable world with books.

Yet there is a real sense in which Prince Florizel's adventures have offered us playful exempla of providence at work. Stevenson's *New Arabian Nights* are not, perhaps, so entirely free of "moral or intellectual interest" as he asserted the original *Arabian Nights* to be.

One of the would-be suicides wishes to be dead because he was "induced to believe in Mr. Darwin," and cannot bear to be descended from an ape. Some of the most remarkable and vivid writing in the story comes in the presentation of one of the "victims" who needs the repeated threat of impending death to give any meaning to his life, Mr. Malthus. The name is surely no accident. Another of the would-be suicides tells us, "I wish no more than a bandage for my eyes and cotton for my ears. Only they have no cotton thick enough in this world." There is real anguish in the cry, and more than once this note of profound disturbance and unease penetrates the comic-romantic surface of the story, which for all its wit and vivacity is by no means wholly frivolous in its apprehensions of human futility and evil. One of Stevenson's letters to W.E. Henley (written in May 1884) proclaims that his "view of life is essentially the comic; and the romantically comic." Stevenson's sense of what these terms mean is not, however, a simple one. "Tragedy," Stevenson continues, "does not seem to me to come off" for it too often ignores laughter—"laughter, which attends on all our steps in life, and sits by the deathbed, and certainly redacts the epitaph." Stevenson's concern is for "the comedy which keeps the beauty and touches the terrors of our life . . . telling its story, not with the one eye of pity, but with the two of pity and mirth." That precarious compound finds one especially vivid form in "The Suicide Club," with its sense both of the mere mortality of human flesh and the possible vivacity of the human spirit. Stevenson's humour plays on the complications of life lived "chained to a dead Englishman doubled up inside a Saratoga trunk" with an energy and sense of absurdity worthy of Ionesco; it reflects on the powerlessness of human power; it explores "the stimulating . . . atmosphere" of a London in which the individual is "surrounded by the mystery of four million private lives." Everywhere is Stevenson's sense of what the prince calls "this precarious stage of life," on which our triumphs and disasters alike are played out. "The Suicide Club" is brief, and seemingly lightweight; but its brevity is dense with invention and meaning, and its lightness of tone, while real enough, must not be allowed to distract us from the recognition of how fully it articulates its author's sense of the pity and the mirth of human existence.

—Glyn Pursglove

———

SUMMER NIGHTS
by Elizabeth Bowen, 1941

The wartime London of 1940 forms the background of several of Elizabeth Bowen's best stories. The story "Summer Night" (collected in *Look at All Those Roses* in 1941) has an Irish setting, and the war is a distant presence. The main structure of this story of unusual complexity is created by the use of two houses, Emma's home and the scene of her adulterous surrender, which is never described. They are linked by her awareness of leaving one and approaching the other, and by the telephone ringing in each as she calls. A series of unobtrusive indications show her uncertainty and regret. When she telephones her prospective lover (we gather that the arrangement of the meeting has been casual and impulsive), she is repelled by his calm, self-satisfied acceptance of her approach. When she says, sardonically, "You're a fine impatient man," she is implicitly pleading for a keener recognition of the enormity of her sin and the greatness of her sacrifice. When he asks after her husband, as if all three could remain friends in the face of the contemplated betrayal, he shows himself unaware of her feelings.

When Emma telephones home, unable to reveal the cause of her unease, her husband, who has seen her off a few hours before, is puzzled. But the reader understands her feeling of guilt, her wish to assure herself that the scene of her normal life is still there, her absurd, contradictory wish to atone by words of affection.

These calls prepare us to visualize the scene within each house. In one house, Robinson, the lover who is separated from his wife, talks with his unwanted visitors the deaf Queenie and her brother Justin. Robinson fears an embarrassing encounter with the approaching Emma. At Emma's house, her husband is the only person unaffected by the hidden influence of her guilty unease. The children are affected; one wanders round the house, and displays herself, anointed with coloured chalks before the mirror in her mother's bedroom, feeling "anarchy all through the house." "This is a threatened night," reflects Aunt Fran, unconsciously making the link between aerial conflict on the other side of the Irish sea and Emma's night of passion.

Emma feels "the shudder of night, the contracting bodies of things," and this too is proleptic. Looking at photographs of Robinson's children, she projects her sense of betrayal of her own children on to his: "I wish in a way you hadn't got any children." Her request to go into the garden is like a useless gesture of defence against the bedroom to which she will soon be taken. They are near a wilderness belonging to a castle burnt down years before. Emma's vague awareness of this forms a link with the consciousness of the deaf Queenie, alone in her bedroom, who is thinking of another summer night 20 years before, when she had wandered in the garden with a man she had never seen again and whose face she had forgotten.

The sexual encounter at the heart of the story is omitted from the narrative; even the couple's anticipation of it is only present by implication. By showing with such delicacy the shock waves it sends, the author suggests that it is far more important in its consequences than in itself. Adultery is seen as a social, or anti-social, act despite its triviality as experience. The virtual nullity of Robinson's character, his inability to understand feeling (Justin's or Emma's), or to respond to it, is right too. He is the gap of incomprehension, yet the cause of complex feelings, subtly expressed in the story's other characters.

—A.O.J. Cockshut

———

SWANS
by Janet Frame, 1951

"Swans" is a story from Janet Frame's earliest collection *The Lagoon*, published in 1951. It offers the response of two children, and occasionally their mother, to the events, sights, and sounds of a particular day. The children's spontaneous and uncluttered perceptions disclose truths that often elude rationalising adult minds.

The story is a credible account of a mother and two small girls who set out by train to attend a picnic. They disembark at the wrong place and find their way to a beach, which they call, with an irony that amuses the reader, "the wrong sea." The secure and familiar beach with its merry-go-rounds, swings, and slides is replaced by a "different and sad" sea. The anticipated scene is exchanged for its opposite. Instead of the clamour, chatter, and laughter of families, there is the desolate sound of the sea, or a strange silence.

The margin between sea and land is a familiar image in Frame's work. It is significant in *Owls Do Cry*, *The Edge of the Alphabet*, *The Rainbirds*, and *Daughter Buffalo*, as a metaphor for the way life and death are inseparably aspects of each other. Frame's work shows death to be ever-present within life. Generally, however, the noise and bustle of life tends to masque the presence of death. But in times of unexpected quietude or darkness, its existence can be imagined. The visit to "the wrong sea" leads the family to a nearby lagoon which emits the requisite darkness and quiet.

While seeming to be a story about children, "Swans" reflects attitudes with which everyone is familiar. It expresses a longing for security and permanence. The word "always" forms an ironic refrain. "Mother knew always" and "there were Mother and Father always, for ever." Having confidence in "for ever" and "always" is mocked in this story, just as it is mocked in "Snowman, Snowman," where the protagonist, a snowman, believes himself to be immortal. Mother does not know "always"; in fact, she is frequently wrong. Furthermore, the children's discovery of the reality of death anticipates a time when mother and father, too, must die.

The story is beautifully crafted, opening with the alarm at the sickness of Gypsy, the children's cat, and concluding with the discovery at the day's end that the cat is dead. The interim explores and illustrates the truth that death exists within life. A series of contrasts provide analogies for this premise: light and darkness are inter-dependent, as are movement and stillness, noise and silence.

Images of death and darkness are contrasted with others evoking colour and movement: "the seagulls crying and skimming and the bits of white flying and look at all the coloured shells, look a pink one like a fan, and a cat's eye." But this reminds the children of Gypsy and their anxiety for her. An impression of security is given by the nearness, warmth, and caring of the mother, and by images like the "ball of wool hanging safe and clean from a neat brown bag with hollyhocks and poppies on it." But the brightness and orderliness of the knitting bag is undetermined by an alarming possibility. The bag displays "a big red initial, to show that you were you and not the somebody else you feared you might be, but Fay and Totty didn't worry they were going to the Beach." Thought of the mystery of one's identity is put aside all too rapidly, affirming an underlying alarm at the inadequacy of our knowledge.

The familiar complacent belief in the superiority of human knowledge is mocked. Father is one for "showing this and that and telling why." The children do not doubt the wisdom of their parents: "Mother always said things would be all right, cats and birds and people even as if she knew and she did know too." As the story unfolds and the mother's insecurity and lack of knowledge become increasingly apparent, a simple truth is expressed by the child-narrator. "Did anyone in the world ever know why? Or did they just pretend to know because they didn't like anyone else to know that they didn't know? Why?" The story is a testimony to the limitations of human knowledge. Unlike those who are dogmatic and sure about everything, the mother observes, "Oh things are never like you think they're different and sad."

Frame depicts the precariousness of life. In addition, she makes almost visible a vast unknown realm. Towards the conclusion of the story, the mother and children pass by a lagoon which has "dark black water, secret." The black shapes of swans hover at the far edge of vision against a backdrop of darkness. The barely visible swans were quite invisible moments earlier. The image is analogous to a concept of death as something constantly present but unseen. The lagoon with its silent water seems like "another world that had been kept secret from everyone and now they had found it." The children have new knowledge of the continuous presence of another dimension. This anticipates the reality of the death of Gypsy.

"Swans" is not a simple story about children, but a complex one that contrasts the human tendency to avoid the truth of death with an acceptance that death is an integral part of life. The concept has been offered with great clarity. The ease with which the children enlarge their understanding proffers an example to the reader who may follow suit. At the same time, "Swans" raises questions to which no answers are given: Do we ever know who we are? And do we ever know why? These questions can be explored by those who have retained an imaginative capacity that is so often lost upon entering adulthood.

—Judith Dell Panny

SWEAT
by Zora Neale Hurston, 1926

Written during Hurston's years of active participation in the Harlem Renaissance, "Sweat" typifies her writing at its best. Clear focus on well-defined characters combined with poignant and accurate dialogue and some touches of macabre humor makes a Hurston story both readable and informative. Trained as she was in anthropology at Barnard College, under Franz Boas, Hurston used accurate cultural information in all her fiction. Her incorporation of local color and detail was exceptional because she understood that the detail of life provided its substance.

Focused on black characters, Hurston's fiction is unusual because it stays within the black community for its action. A decade later, fiction written by Richard Wright, Ralph Ellison, and other black male writers often set up a white-black antagonism, so that the actions of black characters might be seen as reflecting racial struggle. Hurston seldom wrote fiction dependent upon that plotline. Rather, her stories deal with the positive and negative poles of characters in an enclosed black culture, complex and self-sustaining in its own right. Similarly, in Hurston's best-known novel, *Their Eyes Were Watching God*, the black community provides ample setting for Janie Starks's bildungsroman.

What Hurston achieves in this simple but dramatic story of Delia Jones, a Florida washwoman, is remarkable. Her economic emphasis on the value of work for this black woman is never maudlin or sentimental, but the narrative makes clear that Delia's only value to her husband Sykes is financial. She works hard to make money; with her money she has bought the house that Sykes wants to give to his current lover. (He does not work regularly, and is known for his laziness.) With her money, Delia has bought her independence—independence to go to church and take comfort in its community (particularly since her husband has long since abandoned any pretence of loving her), and independence to make and spend her money as she wishes. The value of Delia's work is emphasized both through the movement of the story, and the focus of key scenes on the piles of dirty clothes and the activity of washing them; and through the forceful title. Delia plans her week so that her Monday washings receive priority; here, at 11 p.m., she is sorting the mounds of clothes that will be washed, by separated color, the next day—and the next and the next.

Connected through archetypal images, the parts of Hurston's fiction cohere to reinforce thematic integrity. The opening scene is that of Delia sorting the clothes, only to be frighted by a "long, round, limp and black" object—Sykes's bullwhip. Trying to frighten her into thinking the whip is a snake, of which Delia is deadly afraid, Sykes plots to run his wife out of her house. Because Delia stands up to her abusive husband for one of the first times in their marriage, he realizes that she will fight for her house—and that stronger measures than fear might be called for. Later Sykes brings a snake to the house, still trying to frighten her away from the valuable property; but the resolution of the narrative lies in the way the snake works justice upon Delia's husband.

Hurston involves the community regularly so that the reader understands that Delia's point of view can be trusted. A separate section of the story is devoted to a long description of Joe Clarke's porch where the village men are gossiping. When Delia approaches, the men lament the loss of her looks—which they attribute to Sykes's mistreatment. They also chastise him for that behavior: "'Taint no law on earth dat kin make a man be decent if it aint in 'im. There's plenty men dat takes a wife lak dey do a joint uh sugar cane. . . .dey squeeze an' grind, squeeze an' grind an' wring tell dey wring every drop uh pleasure dat's in 'em out." Then, says Joe Clarke, such men just throw the chew away—as Sykes has Delia. Nodding agreement, Old Man Anderson advises the group that they should kill Sykes. The men who have spoken are those with power: the storekeeper and the sage.

For 1926, Hurston's undisguised criticism of macho behavior on the part of black men was unusual. Sykes's behavior would not necessarily have met with the kind of disapproval Hurston metes out for him, telling the story as she does from Delia's perspective—and buttressing her views with male community voices. This scene clearly anticipates, and erases, the guilt Delia may feel at the end of the narrative.

Another section describes Sykes's relationship with the ample Bertha, and makes even clearer his intention to run Delia out of the coveted house. His first vengeful act is to bring a six-foot rattlesnake in a soap box and locate it beside the steps to the house. His second is to place the snake in Delia's clothes hamper so that as she sorts her wash, she will be bitten by the now-hungry reptile. When Delia finds the snake, however, and sees it "pouring his awful beauty from the basket upon the bed," she runs away, and the snake remains free in the dark room.

Returning to the house during the night, Sykes hopes to find his problems resolved. But instead of a dead wife, he finds only the snake in the dark room. The tragic climax of the story is that Delia, who has slept in the haymow, upon hearing Sykes's calls after he has been bitten by the rattler, must decide whether or not to save her betraying husband. Hurston finesses any moral dilemma by having Delia approach the house and look through the door, and when she sees Sykes's "horribly swollen neck and his one open eye shining with hope," she is tempted to help him. But only briefly. Common sense comes to her rescue, and she knows what his appearance means: death. Help is too far away. Her husband is too far gone. Reality solves her moral dilemma. And so Sykes dies.

By allowing the story to end with Delia's waiting outside until the process ends, Hurston avoided all post-mortems, all need to justify any act (or its lack), and any chance to dwell on abstract meanings. By implication, Hurston tells

the reader that Delia will resume her sweating washwoman's life, living in her house and going to her church, a dried out cane-like woman who had found happiness through her work. Hurston's picture in "Sweat" is close to idyllic. It is a realistic, yet positive, picture of the stubbornness of a character who should have been beaten by her poor life, yet instead found strength and energy in it.

—Linda Wagner-Martin

THE SWIMMER
by John Cheever, 1964

Masterful as so many of John Cheever's stories are, none quite matches the compressed power and inexorable logic of "The Swimmer." The story's greatness derives in large measure from its being distilled from 150 pages of notes for and manuscript of the novel Cheever had originally planned to write. The origins of "The Swimmer" also can be traced to a story entitled "The Music Teacher," published five years earlier: "The night was dark, and with his sense of reality thus shaken, he stood on his own doorstep thinking that the world changed more swiftly than one could perceive—died and renewed itself—and that he moved through the events of his life with no more comprehension than a naked swimmer."

The story that developed from that image begins in a deceptively beguiling comic-realistic manner: a number of well-off suburban couples are seen sitting around a backyard pool on a sunny Sunday afternoon, accounting for their present malaise in terms of having drunk too much the night before. The tone here is gently satiric, as typically Cheeveresque as the suburban setting modelled on the author's own Westchester. The titular hero, Neddy Merrill, seems equally familiar: youthful (though not young), athletic, well-to-do, yet also somewhat aloof, yearning for something more. In Neddy's case this longing takes the curious and clearly comical form of deciding to swim home, eight miles and fifteen pools to the south. Humorous as his prank seems, it is also imbued with a mythic resonance. One is reminded of the similar though more ambitious method that James Joyce employed in Ulysses: as T.S. Eliot explained, the author's "manipulating a continuous parallel between contemporaneity and antiquity" as "a way of controlling, of ordering, of giving a shape and significance to the immense panorama of futility and anarchy which is contemporary history."

The unity of "The Swimmer" depends less on Cheever's version of the modernists' mythic method however, than on the incremental repetition that typifies folk ballads and many of Cheever's stories and novels. Thus the structure of "The Swimmer" proves surprisingly and deceptively simple. Playing the role of legendary explorer, Neddy sets out for home; an odyssey back to innocence, purity, and youth. The story's plot follows Neddy from pool to pool, and is paced in a way that allows the reader not just to read about but actually to experience Neddy's initial exhilaration and subsequent exhaustion. After two pages of exposition, the story gets off to a fast start: five pools in the next half page. Obstacles such as sharp gravel underfoot and a thorny hedge seem at this point more like realistic details than ill omens.

As the pace begins to slow over the next few pages, the signs of Neddy's growing separation from familiar natural and social worlds begin to increase, and when halfway through he tries to cross a divided highway his odyssey comes to a momentary halt. The tone here, like the day, turns darker, even colder; from this more detached point of view, Neddy seems no longer boyishly enthusiastic and sympathetic but pitifully unprepared and exposed, unable to turn back and unsure when and where his little game began to turn so deadly serious. Once across a highway drawn in part from Greek myth (the rivers Styx and Lethe), Neddy enters the hell of a public pool. Here he is assaulted by loud noises and harsh smells and is jostled by the kind of people he has spent his well-to-do suburban life successfully avoiding. Yet even here Neddy finds himself excluded; lacking the proper identification tag, he is ordered to leave. With each new "breach in the succession"—finding that his former mistress has a new lover, being snubbed by a couple he had formerly dismissed as social upstarts—Neddy's alienation from all that is familiar and therefore reassuring increases until, dispossessed in various ways, he arrives at his home, now dark, empty, and locked.

The mythic parallels deepen and dignify a story that might otherwise have been little more than one more social parable about the dark side of the American dream. Indeed, "The Swimmer," for all its density of social fact and examination of the suburban experience, proves as dreamlike as the stories of Poe, Hawthorne, and Kafka. Cheever transforms a comedy of manners into dream fantasy and ultimately nightmare. Just as it is impossible to tell exactly where and how the real turns into the fantastic or how a single summer afternoon lengthens to become months, even years, it is impossible to say whether at story's end Neddy Merrill finally confronts his past and present—waking to reality as it were—or only confronts a future possibility in the form of a dark dream. What is clear is that in "The Swimmer" Cheever manages to transform realistic details, myths (especially those of Odysseus and Rip Van Winkle), and his very personal fears of financial and emotional ruin into a masterwork of 20th-century literature.

—Robert A. Morace

THE SWITCHMAN (El guardagujas)
by Juan José Arreola, 1951

Juan José Arreola owes his reputation to his short stories, even though he has also published a novel, two plays, and many essays. His best-known and most anthologized tale, "The Switchman" exemplifies his taste for humor, satire, fantasy, and philosophical themes. The story, first published as "El guardagujas" in *Cinco Cuentos* in 1951, is translated in *Confabulario and Other Inventions* (1964).

Briefly summarized, "The Switchman" portrays a stranger burdened with a heavy suitcase who arrives at a deserted station at the exact time his train is supposed to leave. As he gazes at the tracks that seem to melt away in the distance, an old man (the switchman) carrying a tiny red lantern appears from out of nowhere and proceeds to inform the stranger of the hazards of train travel in this country. It seems that although an elaborate network of railroads has been planned and partially completed, the

service is highly unreliable. Therefore the horrified stranger, who keeps insisting that he must arrive at his destination "T" the next day, is advised to rent a room in a nearby inn, an ash-colored building resembling a jail where would-be travelers are lodged. The switchman then relates a series of preposterous anecdotes, alluded to below, illustrating the problems that one might encounter during any given journey. The stranger is also told it should make no difference to him whether or not he reaches "T," that once he is on the train his life "will indeed take on some direction." In the final lines of the story a whistle is heard in the distance, indicating the train's arrival. But upon inquiring again where the stranger wants to go, the switchman receives the answer "X" instead of "T." The old man then dissolves in the clear morning air, and only the red speck of the lantern remains visible before the noisily approaching engine.

As demonstrated by its numerous interpretations, "The Switchman" is fraught with ambiguity. It has been seen as a satire on Mexico's railroad service and the Mexican character, as a lesson taught by the instincts to a human soul about to be born, as a modern allegory of Christianity, as a complex political satire, as a surrealistic fantasy on the illusive nature of reality, and as an existentialist view of life with very Mexican modifications. The latter comes closest to the most convincing interpretation, namely, that Arreola has based his tale on Albert Camus's philosophy of the absurd as set forth in *The Myth of Sisyphus,* a collection of essays Camus published in 1942. (Three years later Arreola received a scholarship to study in Paris, where he may well have read these highly acclaimed essays.)

Camus writes that neither humans alone nor the world by itself is absurd. Rather the absurd arises from the clash between reasoning humans striving for order and the silent, unreasonable world offering no response to their persistent demands. The absurd human is one who recognizes a lack of clear purpose in life and therefore resolves to commit himself or herself to the struggle for order against the unpredictable, fortuitous reality he or she encounters. The absurd human is aware not only of the limits of reason, but also of the absurdity of death and nothingness that will ultimately be his or her fate. Awareness of the absurd human condition can come at any moment, but it is most likely to happen when, suddenly confronted by the meaninglessness of hectic daily routine, he or she asks the question, "Why?" The answer to this question, according to Camus, should be to accept the challenge of the absurd, to live life to the fullest and, through action, to become an absurd hero.

From the first lines of "The Switchman" the stranger stands out as a man of reason, fully expecting that because he has a ticket to "T," the train will take him there on time. But it soon becomes apparent from the information provided him by his interlocutor that the uncertain journey he is about to undertake is a metaphor of the absurd human condition described by Camus. Thus the stranger's heavy suitcase symbolizes the burden of reason he carries about, and the inn resembling a jail, the place where others like him are lodged before setting out on life's absurd journey. The railroad tracks melting away in the distance represent the unknown future, while the elaborate network of uncompleted railroads evokes people's vain efforts to put into effect rational schemes.

The switchman's anecdote about the founding of the village "F," when a train accident stranded a group of passengers—now happy settlers—in a remote region, illustrates the element of chance in human existence. Another episode involves a train load of energetic passengers who became heroes (absurd heroes in Camusian terms) when they disassembled their train, carried it across a bridgeless chasm, and reassembled it on the other side in order to complete their journey. And the conductors' pride in depositing, without fail, their deceased passengers on the station platforms prescribed by their tickets suggests that humans' only certain destination is death, a fundamental absurdist concept.

In the final lines of Arreola's story the assertion of the stranger (now referred to as the traveler) that he is going to "X" rather than "T" indicates that he has become an absurd man ready to set out for an unknown destination. The image immediately thereafter of the tiny red lantern swinging back and forth before the onrushing train conveys the story's principal theme: the limits of reason, that is, the small light of reason, in a world governed by chance. Why, then, does the switchman vanish at this moment? Because he has fulfilled his role as the stranger's subconscious by not only asking the Camusian question "Why?" but also by switching the stranger from the track of reason onto the track of the absurd, which explains the title of the story.

Arreola's ingenious tale exudes a very Mexican flavor, but above all else it is a universal statement on existential human's precarious place in the world.

—George R. McMurray

SYLVIE
by Gérard de Nerval, 1854

Gérard de Nerval was in his mid-forties, near the tragic end of his troubled life, when "Sylvie" was first published on 15 August 1853 in the *Revue des Deux Mondes*, the prestigious fortnightly French literary magazine. In 1854 he included it in *Les Filles du feu* (*The Daughters of the Fire*), a strange volume which, superficially at least, seems to be something of a miscellany for it is made up of stories, essays, a one-act play, and the marvellously evocative collection of twelve sonnets called *Les Chimères* (*The Chimeras*). "Sylvie" has been hailed not only as a work that is the very quintessence of Romantic sensibility but also as the forerunner of a trend seen later in France in Rimbaud, Proust, and the Surrealists, which places a particularly high value on subjectivity and finds in dreams and memories the most satisfactory means of exploring reality.

"Sylvie" takes the form of a first-person narrative, and though there is always a risk in identifying a narrator with the author of a work of fiction, there is no doubt that there is much of Nerval in his story, both in a host of allusions and references which are never more than rather transparently disguised, precisely as if to invite us to penetrate them, and in the tone, spirit, and intellectual orientations of the tale. Owing much to observation and experience, "Sylvie" also hovers on the brink of a dream-world made up of personal reminiscence and artistic predilections, so that we are introduced to a curiously unstructured but none the less intoxicatingly seductive amalgam of the present and the past, the real and the imagined. Everything is interpreted in terms of the cultural revolution taking place in France since the time of Jean-Jacques Rousseau. Here we do indeed find much that is individual to Nerval himself, but "Sylvie" is likewise testimony to the extent to which his own attitudes and outlooks were themselves shaped by his reading.

The structure of "Sylvie" serves to transport us back further and further into the past. The first of the story's 14 short chapters takes us back from the present (the 1850's) to an earlier period in the narrator's life when he frequented the Parisian theatres, not so much to enjoy the plays as to pay silent homage from afar to the leading actress. It is fairly clear that this is a transposition into fiction of aspects of Nerval's tempestuous love affair with one of the young actresses at the Opéra-Comique, Jenny (or, more properly, Marguerite) Colon, who had died in 1842. More interesting than these autobiographical links is the narrator's highly significant remark that he has preferred not to become too well-informed about the actress "for fear of spoiling the magic mirror that reflected her image towards me."

The preference for the imaginary over the real, which might ruin it, is a theme that is continued for the rest of the story. After talking briefly with some friends the narrator returns home where, falling asleep, he dreams of his past. What he recalls is an idyllic period where old-world customs were still maintained in the countryside of the region formerly known as the Valois, which corresponds roughly with the present Aisne and Oise "departments," north of Paris. The constituents of the narrator's dream fall into patterns that psychoanalysis has made familiar. Along with the memories that come crowding in, there is first the theme of the journey, which is interrupted and never really completed, and the time structure is loose. The tale shows an uneasy juxtaposition of relationships with women which threaten to become entangled and which, likewise, do not reach their fulfilment. Sylvie is there, of course, delightful and fresh, yet her nature changes somewhat, not because of experience but because she is unsettled by reading Rousseau's epoch-making novel *The New Heloïse* (1761). The narrator's relationship with her is complicated by the role of Adrienne, though it is not clear whether she is real or a figment of the narrator's imagination. The most facinating episode comes in the fourth chapter entitled, in a reminiscence of Jean-Antoine Watteau's famous painting of 1717, "A Voyage to Cythera," with a marvellously poetic evocation of beautiful countryside by night while the young people enjoy the delights of this "fête galante." The 13th chapter brings the narrator back to Paris where he makes contact with the actress, but though she agrees to take the leading role in a play he writes during an absence of some months in Germany, she cannot believe that he loves her. "Sylvie" concludes quite strangely; one day the narrator asks Sylvie whether the actress is not very like Adrienne. The reply is that the latter had died many years ago in a convent, and we are left with a slightly uneasy sense that in life there is no ending, but rather a pattern of never-ceasing cyclical return.

—Christopher Smith

T

THE TAGUS (El Tajo)
by Francisco Ayala, 1949

The title of "El tajo" ("The Tagus") one of four novellas by Francisco Ayala included in the original edition of *La cabeza del cordero* (1949; *The Lamb's Head,* 1971), involves a complex play on multiple meanings of the word "tajo." First, it is the name of the Tagus River, which winds around three sides of Toledo, where a decisive incident occurs. It also means a violent cut or slice, both literally and figuratively relevant: a cut in the earth (the Tagus gorge, but also the valley separating the entrenched armies) and cutting off a life (cf. the Furies cutting threads of mortal existence). Finally, the Spanish Civil War constituted a *tajo* in the nation's life, terminating the Republic.

Narratives of *The Lamb's Head,* written during Ayala's exile in Argentina, treat aspects of the Spanish Civil War and its aftermath; only "El tajo" presents the war directly. As a disciple of Ortega y Gasset, an intellectual architect of the Republic, Ayala served in diplomatic capacities, and would have been executed if caught by Fascist rebels (who shot his father and brother). His treatment of the war—impartial, objective, and dispassionate—disconcerts readers aware of Ayala's background. He does not even name the war or opposing factions, and even denied in interviews and his prologue that the conflict portrayed relates to the Spanish Civil War, probably hoping eventually to have his work published in Spain (a vain hope, as the work was prohibited until 1972). Many Ayala prologues are apocryphal or ironic, and this one is no exception.

The Spanish Civil War generated more fiction than any event in history (one bibliography lists more than 8,000 novels), and *The Lamb's Head,* cannot be read adequately while assuming that the conflict described is abstract or imaginary, despite Ayala's allegorico-symbolic presentation. Some critics were fooled, if the censors were not, believing that nothing in the story suggests authorial preference for either side. The war is paradigmatically reduced to a single encounter between two combatants representing the opposing sides, a cultured bourgeois officer and an unschooled working-class militiaman (a sufficiently skewed choice of "generic" antagonists to contradict assertions of impartiality).

During 1938, the opposing armies dug into positions in respective mountain ranges, facing each other across a no-man's land along the Ebro front in Aragón, waiting for months without firing a shot in an ultimately decisive battle. Republican resistance was crumbling, and desertions mounting; only months later, no obstacles to Franco's advance remained. This is the setting of the symbolic encounter emblematic of the war, a strategically insignificant occurrence one sweltering August afternoon. During the lethargy of the siesta, Lieutenant Pedro Santolalla alleviates his boredom by strolling to the valley vineyards, where he is startled to observe an enemy soldier picking grapes. The man's back is turned, his rifle on the ground, but Santolalla kills him, taking his victim's wallet and rifle

as evidence of his "heroism." Santolalla becomes the butt of jokes by comrades who realize taking the victim prisoner would have meant no risk. As the body of Anastasio López Rubielos rots, the stench blows into Santolalla's camp, and his companions wax sarcastic.

Ayala traces the ethical evolution of Santolalla's conscience from initial self-satisfaction to uneasy realization that the killing was unnecessary to a progressively more guilty conscience and unacknowledged remorse. López Rubielos's identity card becomes a symbol of Santolalla's guilt; attempts to rid himself of it by giving it away fail, most resoundingly so when, after the war, he seeks out the victim's impoverished family in Toledo, pretending to be a wartime buddy wanting to return the documents to the family.

Although Ayala uses none of the terms normally denoting the contending factions (Loyalists, International Brigades or Republicans, on the one side; Falangists, rebels, Nationalists or Fascists for the Francoists), subtle clues leave no doubt as to which side each antagonist represents: no militia supported the Franco side (López Rubielos is a militiaman), and Santolalla—the narrative consciousness—calls the enemy "Reds," the Franco regime's generic term for Communists, fellow travelers, and all who supported the Republic. The victim's documents identify him as a member of the Workers' Socialist Party and unobtrusively supply the information that he is barely 18 years old. Conversely, Santolalla's being on the winning (Falangist) side is evident, given his position and advantages after the war.

Ayala's message, while subtle, is far from unintelligible or unbiased. The implicit ethical question concerns just how Santolalla's act differs from war crimes. Killing an enemy in battle may be heroic, but the same act in peacetime is criminal. The differentiating element legally is circumstantial—a state of war existed—but morally the difference is blurred. Ayala portrays a peaceful interlude, a quiet front—almost an unofficial cease-fire—and a confrontation without danger. Had the war already ended, Santolalla's act would have been a gratuitous homicide.

When the "generic" antagonists become Falangists and Republican Loyalists, the implications are unmistakable. Franco and the Falangists revolted against Spain's legal government; had they lost, they would have been charged with insurrection and crimes against the Republic. Allied with the German and Italian Fascists, they received the latest military technology and help from Hitler and Mussolini, while poorly-armed Republican militia fought with their forefathers' antiquated hunting rifles, pitchforks, or whatever was at hand. That Santolalla kills an unarmed enemy is thus not fortuitous. Ayala's narrative economy is exemplary: there are no superfluous words or details. Irony abounds, however, and his works are seldom simply what they seem. Extratextual data illuminate his stories which (like many written under censorship) are often allusive or elliptical, requiring readers to figure out a picture which closer examination shows to be a puzzle.

—Janet Pérez

—————

TALPA
by Juan Rulfo, 1953

A segment of a distinguished but small literary production, the story "Talpa" contains many elements that characterize the Mexican Juan Rulfo's fiction. Like his landmark novel *Pedro Páramo* (1955), the 1953 story collection *El llano en llamas (The Burning Plain and Other Stories)* depicts characters doomed to roam an arid landscape, bearing the weight of their sins. "Talpa," a tale of adultery, death and remorse, is an integral part of Rulfo's Dantesque scheme.

The stories of *The Burning Plain* fall in the category of "regionalism," a prominent subgenre in 20th-century Latin American literature. Behind the realistic, clearly Mexican topographic, social, and cultural elements, however, a strong mythical reality imbues Rulfo's unique world, recalling William Faulkner's phantasmagoric landscape. Rulfo, like many other Latin American writers of his time, greatly admired his American predecessor; but he went a step farther, to create the atemporal perspective of "wandering souls" whose raw emotions he conveys in strong visual images. Successfully, he incorporates the afterlife with his characters' existence amidst an ethereal, yet strongly delineated, reality.

By means of an interior monologue, the protagonist of "Talpa" traces the progressive intensification of his guilt at his brother's death. In a quiet, understated manner that belies his inner torment, the narrator describes Tanilo's severe disease, his own physical relationship with his sister-in-law, Natalia, and the trio's journey to Talpa in search of a cure.

The five-part story opens with the protagonist's shocking self-accusation as his brother's killer, a technique that reveals the outcome from the beginning. Since the reader soon finds out that Tanilo succumbed to his leprosy-like illness, the author removes the expected element of suspense that we usually find in a crime story. Instead, he shifts the tension toward the causes of the guilt. As the action unfolds in a series of flashbacks, the focus turns toward the adulterers' feelings of remorse and suffering. The narrator discloses the events that have led to the "present," including the pilgrimage, the love triangle, Tanilo's horrible death, the quick burial, and the two surviving characters' hell on earth.

Tragic irony pervades the narrative, revealing an insight into the characters' psyche in a manner intensified by the unexpected and by the force of the rural environment. The arid and hostile landscape, vividly and tersely portrayed, communicates the characters' inner world with immediacy. The understated and sparse, yet highly suggestive, imagery hides tense and dramatic conflicts. The tension between stark reality and complex passion, moreover, creates a powerful sense of movement and dynamism.

The six-week pilgrimage to Talpa, a place of redemption and salvation, takes priority in the narrative space. The arduous trip, including the 20-day lag that takes the unfortunate trio only as far as the road, seems to last an eternity. Rulfo stretches time by shifting our attention to the characters' perception of the landscape away from their feelings. His rural characters have no perspective on their own situation. They see everything in literal terms, visible and concrete. As the couple drags Tanilo unwillingly toward his death, a fine dust clings persistently onto a caravan of pilgrims that they have joined. The sky above them hovers "like a heavy gray spot crushing . . . from above." Passion and desire come from "the heat of the earth" rather than from their psyches. As the adulterers give in to their guilt, they feel "bent double" as if "something was holding [them] and placing a heavy load on top of [them]."

The narrative contains an oscillation between Talpa and Zenzontla, invented places that sound real. Talpa becomes a shrine and a mecca, home to the Virgin of the same name, where the sick and the dying seek a miracle. Sustaining his ironic mode, Rulfo presents the journey to that town as the cause of Tanilo's death. A pathetic figure ravaged by wounds and "giving off a sour smell like a dead animal when he passed by," he dies shortly after the group reaches Talpa. It is at that moment, toward the story's end, that the narrator reiterates what he stated earlier as he admitted his crime: "But we took him there so he'd die, and that's what I can't forget."

Zenzontla, like Talpa, is "home," where Natalia seeks solace and a chance to cry in her mother's arms. The narrator speculates, nevertheless, that this town is only a place where they are "in passing, just to rest." Their guilt and the memory of Tanilo has turned Zenzontla into an alien place, the living hell from which none of Rulfo's characters seems to escape.

Time in the story manifests itself in only two dimensions—the present and the immediate past. This technique serves to stress the characters' flat and simple perceptions of their actions and consequences. The past incorporates the affair, the journey to Talpa, the quick burial of Tanilo and the return. The "now" (a word which is repeated to underscore the protagonist's living hell) is more of a consciousness than a time frame. The "then" and "now" interweave with Talpa and Zenzontla, to blur the boundaries between paradise and hell, salvation and damnation. Only the guilt, which has taken a life of its own, survives, giving Tanilo the best revenge possible.

In "Talpa" Rulfo portrays a world that is clearly identified with Jalisco, his native state—the arid landscape, the stoic people, the belief in miracles, the moral customs. With that strong identification with his homeland he proceeded, in all of his work, to combine his vision of Mexican rural life with a view of humanity's great capacity to confront death, alienation, and guilt with dignity and courage.

—Stella T. Clark

—————

TELL ME A RIDDLE
by Tillie Olsen, 1961

In 1980, Lee Grant directed a feature film version of Tillie Olsen's story, "Tell Me a Riddle." Although it received generally favorable reviews, the film failed financially. Its failure is easily explained (in December 1980, a *Variety* reviewer observed: "Tell Me a Riddle" is "a very morose story about very old people and thus a challenge to today's commercial market"); less explicable is Grant's initial decision to film Olsen's story, a story essentially without plot, action, or typically heroic characters. And yet, one sympathizes with Grant's desire to bring Olsen's "Tell Me a Riddle," the title story of her 1961 collection, to a movie-going audience, because this is a story that makes its readers feel the pain, anguish, and joy of everyday, common life.

Married for 47 years, David and Eva find themselves riven apart by a quarrel. Ostensibly, this quarrel focuses on their immediate future. He would like to sell their house and retire to his lodge's "Haven," where he might dispense with "the troubling of responsibility, the fretting with money," and engage in "happy communal life." She, having spent her years intensely engaged in the communal life of seven children and a husband, looks forward to the peacefulness of her nearly empty home, to the solitude of moving to her own rhythms. The disagreement between husband and wife goes beyond the question of where to spend their next years, however; this dispute is over how they are to live these years—"how," not materially, but philosophically: what are David and Eva to live for?

As the story proceeds, we learn that before marriage and children, David and Eva were politically active in a Russia undergoing change and revolution (1905). "Hunger; secret meetings; human rights; spies; betrayals; prison; escape"— such are the components of their lives in Olshana. The 16-year-old Eva rebelled against her father's objections and learns to read. Her teacher, a Tolstoian, impressed Eva with the holiness of life and of knowledge; teacher and student spent a year imprisoned in Siberia. After this year, Eva, along with David, escaped west, to America, land of "opportunity." Their middle years are spent trying to realize this opportunity: how to put bread on the table? how to make a soup of meat bones begged from the butcher? Most often, there's no time left for anything beyond the daily demands of the body: no time for reading, for developing the mind and the soul, for touching the sacred in individual human life.

But now deaf, half-blind, Eva insists on taking advantage of a new opportunity. She has retained scraps of melodies from her idealistic youth, memorized phrases from revolutionary readings, and, most importantly, her belief in a progressive humankind. She wants now to live differently, to return to those early songs. David, however, seems to have lost touch with the songs; instead, he is caught up in the babble of America.

The two argue over the course they are going to chart, and in the process of doing so, Eva loses her health. An initial diagnosis of kidney disorder leads to further tests, surgery ("the cancer was everywhere"), and the realization that Eva has, at best, a year to live. The children agree that Eva must not be told, that David must act as though she is recuperating. This act propels David and Eva on yet another westward journey, to visit the children and grandchildren: Connecticut to Ohio, to California. This journey, in direction parallel to that from Olshana to America, raises questions again about the meaning of human life: for what does one live? What might one teach to and learn from others? In order to ask and answer these questions, Eva must protect herself against maternal springs of emotion, holding her newest grandchild away from her, and escaping from her daughter Vivi's memories by crouching in the children's closet. In California, Eva comes close to answers; she approaches life's "transport," its "older power," as she skips in the ocean, picks up sand, and looks "toward the shore that nurtured life as it first crawled toward con-

sciousness the millions of years ago." But California, like America and like Russia, is a contradiction, providing both revivifying sea air and then the horrors of smog ("she walked with hands pushing the heavy air as if to open it, whispered: who has done this?"). Eva's sense of that contradiction (life offers both beauties and horrors) grows as she grows sicker. Her fear that humankind will destroy itself increases, as does her sense of hope and her iteration of idealistic lines from Victor Hugo.

Eva dies, but before doing so, she carries her message of despair and hope to her granddaughter Jeannie and, more importantly, to David. As he listens to her babbling, a sense of bereavement and betrayal overwhelms him; he mourns not just for what he is losing, but for what he has lost. For a moment, he counters this loss with the thought of his American grandchildren, "whose childhoods were childish, who had never hungered," who would be "nobility" to those in Olshana. But then he asks himself, in the voice of Eva, "And are there no other children in the world?"

Such is the plot of "Tell Me a Riddle." As in a play by Chekhov (one of Eva's favorite authors), little happens. Time passes, and a character dies. No one performs any particularly large or heroic action. Instead, we get wisps of conversations, threads of thought, a hodge-podge of hope and regret. But also as in a Chekhov play, we attain a sense of these characters as human beings like ourselves, growing older, often losing touch with "that joyous certainty, that sense of mattering, of moving and being moved." Eva, wife of 47 years, mother of seven children, conveys not only to David, but also to us, her belief in that certainty.

—Madonne M. Miner

THE TELL-TALE HEART
by Edgar Allan Poe, 1843

One of the most powerful contributions that Edgar Allan Poe made to the short story genre was his insistence that every element of the work contribute to the story's overall effect. Poe frequently gave this aesthetic demand realistic motivation by making his central character or narrator so psychologically obsessed with a mysterious phenomenon that everything in the story irresistibly revolves around it, held in place by the psychological equivalent of centrifugal force. Some metaphoric examples of this central force are the tarn in "The Fall of the House of Usher," the pit in "The Pit and the Pendulum," and the whirlpool in "The Descent into the Maelstrom"; purely psychological equivalents are embodied in the sense of the perverse in such stories as "The Imp of the Perverse," "The Black Cat," and "The Tell-Tale Heart."

Although there are ostensibly two characters in "The Tell-Tale Heart"—an old man and the younger man who lives with him—the story is really about only one character psychically split in half. To understand the ingenious way Poe develops this story about a split in the self, one must examine the nature of the narrator's obsession. He insists that he loves the old man, has no personal animosity toward him, does not want his money, has not been injured by him. Instead, he says he wishes to kill the old man because of his eye. Although there is no way to understand this kind of motivation except to declare the narrator mad, the reader must try to determine the method and meaning of the madness. For Poe, there is no such thing as meaningless madness in fiction.

However, the only way to understand what the "eye" means to the narrator is to take Poe's own advice and look for the relevance of other themes and ideas throughout the story. In addition to the theme of the "eye," there are two primary motifs: the identification of the narrator with the old man and the concept of time. The narrator says at various points in the story that he knows what the old man is feeling as he lies alone in bed, for he himself has felt the same things. He says the moan the old man makes does not come from pain or grief, but from mortal terror that arises from the bottom of the soul overcharged with awe: "Many a night, just at midnight, when all the world slept, it has welled up from my own bosom, deepening with its dreadful echo, the terror that distracted me."

Throughout the story the narrator is obsessed with time. The central image of the beating of the heart he associates with the ticking of a clock; he says the old man listens, just as he has done, to the death watches (a kind of beetle that makes a ticking sound) in the wall; he emphasizes how time slows down and almost stops as he sticks his head into the old man's room. The meaning of time for the narrator is suggested by the title, for the tale that every heart tells is the tale of time—time inevitably passing, with every beat of the heart bringing one closer to death.

If we relate the motif of the narrator's identification with the old man to his obsession with the eye, we can see that Poe makes use of a kind of dream logic distortion; what the narrator really wishes to destroy is not the "eye," but that which sounds like "eye"—that is, the "I." There is a kind of method to the narrator's madness. The only way he can defeat the inevitability of time is to destroy that which time would destroy, that is, the self. However, to save the self by destroying the self is a paradox that the narrator can only deal with by displacing his need to destroy the "I" on to a need to destroy the "eye." Ultimately, by destroying the old man's eye, the narrator indirectly does succeed in destroying himself, for he confesses his crime in the end.

Reading "The Tell-Tale Heart" is like trying to solve the mystery of motivation in a detective story. However, for Poe the key to motivation is the aesthetic concept that there is some central core to the story, some basic idea or effect that holds it together. As a result, everything coheres around this effect and radiates out from it. If we think of the core of the story as being like an obsession, then it follows that the obsession can be identified by the principle of repetition, for a character who is obsessed repeats himself, always coming back to his obsession. It is this transformation of a psychological obsession into an aesthetic principal that has earned Poe his reputation as a principal innovator of 19th-century short fiction and the form's first important theorist and critic.

—Charles E. May

A TERRIBLY STRANGE BED
by Wilkie Collins, 1856

"A Terribly Strange Bed" was the first of numerous contributions by Wilkie Collins to Charles Dickens's magazine *Household Words*, where it appeared on 24 April 1852. Collins subsequently included it in his collection *After Dark*. Like many of Collins's stories it sets the main narrative within a "frame"—an appropriate metaphor, since the initial narrator is an artist. Confronted with the task of painting the portrait of a sitter who seems unable to relax, he is relieved when the sitter begins to tell the story of an adventure that befell him in France many years earlier: engrossed in his storytelling, the sitter loses his self-consciousness and the artist is able to produce a good likeness. The story thus draws attention both to the narrative act and to the power of narrative art.

Leading a dissipated life in Paris, the narrator-protagonist goes one evening to a gambling-house and succeeds in "breaking the bank," winning a fortune at the card game *rouge et noir*. An old soldier who befriends him (and who later turns out to be the proprietor of the gambling house) first plies him with champagne and then gives him black coffee containing a narcotic. He is then taken to a bedroom in the house, finding himself in no condition to make his way home. The coffee has, however, been too effectively drugged, and the effect is to make him intensely wakeful.

In this state he passes the time in examining the room and its contents, especially a four-poster bed with a heavy canopy and valances. To his horror he discovers that the top of the bed is gradually descending and, had he been asleep, would certainly have suffocated him. Escaping through the window, he goes to the police station, the house is raided, and the criminals—who have played the same trick more successfully on other lucky gamblers—are arrested.

The story depends for its effectiveness almost entirely on the rapid and economical narrative, and there is virtually no development of character or analysis of motive and relatively little description. The narrator's horrified realization that the bed is designed to kill him is graphically depicted, and the narrative as a whole gains from the use of the first person method. As in much of Collins's fiction, the tradition of Gothic horror tales has been modified and domesticated so that an important element is the existence of appalling wickedness and ingenious crimes in commonplace, even banal settings. At one point in the story this become explicit: as he discovers the true nature of the bed, the narrator reflects that it is "in the 19th century, and in the civilised capital of France" that he has stumbled upon "such a machine for secret murder by suffocation, as might have existed in the worst days of the Inquisition, in the lonely Inns among the Hartz Mountains, in the mysterious tribunals of Westphalia!" And as in much Gothic fiction, what at first appears to be inexplicable and uncanny turns out to have a rational explanation: the "terribly strange bed" is in fact a piece of ingenious machinery designed for a specific purpose.

Collins himself said that the idea for the story was given him by an artist-friend, W. S. Herrick. The French setting may owe something to Edgar Allan Poe, who uses a similar setting in such stories as "The Murders in the Rue Morgue," as well as to the French writer Eugène Sue, whose novels describe the Parisian underworld. Joseph Conrad's story "The Inn of the Two Witches" (1913), which has some strikingly similar features, in turn may have been influenced by "A Terribly Strange Bed," and the resemblance was in fact noted by a reviewer; Conrad however, denied any knowledge of Collins's story, and as Catherine Peters has suggested, the two stories may have been derived from a common source.

When Collins decided to follow Dicken's lucrative example and give readings from his own work in the United States, he prepared a version of "A Terribly Strange Bed" and gave a trial reading at the Olympic Theatre in London on 28 June 1873. This was extensively reviewed, not always sympathetically—some reviewers pointing out, not unfairly, that Collins did not possess Dicken's histrionic powers and should adopt a less dramatic style of reading. Later one member of the audience recalled that Collins "seemed to think that the word '*bed*stead' was full of tragic meaning, and we heard again this '*bedstead*' repeated till it became almost comic." In the event Collins substituted another story for his American readings.

Robert Ashley has described "A Terribly Strange Bed" as "the most exciting short story Collins ever wrote and a first-rate story by any standard, Victorian or modern." There is perhaps some exaggeration here, for by the standard of psychological realism that we might apply to, say, a short story by D. H. Lawrence of Katherine Mansfield, Collins's tale can hardly be taken seriously. As an example of pure narrative, however, it does have considerable pace and power, and the cool, almost scientific detachment of Collins's always lucid prose contributes to the effect. Part of Collins's distinctive achievement in his fiction is to combine disturbing and even violent incidents with a manner and style that are notable for their control of structure and syntax and their precision of detail. He could excel in the very long and complex narrative, as his great novels of the 1860's testify, but "A Terribly Strange Bed," a very early example of his work, proves that he was also a master of the shorter form.

—Norman Page

THEY
by Rudyard Kipling, 1904

Rudyard Kipling's short story "They" (collected in *Traffics and Discoveries,* 1904) has acquired an adventitious interest as one source of the first section of Eliot's "Burnt Norton" ("for the leaves were full of children, / Hidden excitedly, containing laughter"). The story occupies a central place among Kipling's more than three hundred stories. It is one of only a handful with a clear autobiographical impulse, much of its imaginative energy deriving from Kipling's attempt to find in his new life in rural Sussex some comfort for the death of his daughter, Josephine, in 1899. It brings together two themes, healing and the supernatural, that were to dominate much of his later writing. It is the most developed example of those first-person stories, such as the early "The Story of Muhammad Din," which disclose more than the narrator is himself able to bring to order. And, like many of Kipling's later stories, it is accompanied by a poem, "The Return of the Children," which offers an alternative reading of the same experience, and suggests the provisional nature of the text in front of us.

The narrator of the story, whom we gradually realise is a bereaved father, makes three visits between the beginning and the end of a single summer to a mysterious but beautiful house, inhabited by a blind woman and filled with the laughter of children seen only momentarily, as a "glint" of blue shirt, or a girl's form behind a window. The first visit suggests the entry into a fairy tale, its highly-wrought beauty owing something to Kipling's pre-Raphaelite background. This contrasts sharply with the second visit in which a dishevelled woman, "loose-haired, purple,

almost lowing with agony," beseeches the blind woman's help for her sick grandchild, leading the narrator into a frantic search for doctor and nurse. On the third visit, the narrator for the first time enters the house, but despite all his strategems is still unable to do more than glimpse the children. Only as he suspends his efforts, while watching the blind woman deal with a devious tenant, does he feel a child's kiss pressed into the palm of his hand: "a gift on which the fingers were, once, expected to close . . . a fragment of a mute code devised long ago." At once he realises what has already become clear to the reader, that they are spirits, living in the house as children, even able to walk in the woods with their parents. Yet this discovery is for the narrator the sign that he can never return: "For me it would be wrong. For me only." No explanation is offered as to why, but the suggestion seems to be that for the narrator the pain of his bereavement has become an absolute, a part of his being that he cannot give up. Perhaps only the bereaved will recognise the truth of this.

From the beginning there have been clues that the story will be shaped by the emotional and psychological needs of the narrator. He is led to the house as if by the road itself ("one view called to another, one hill-top to its fellow"), through a landscape that already hints at the miraculous (the word is used in the first paragraph). He explains that he comes from "the other side of the country"; the blind woman acknowledges that the house is "so out of the world"; later he is unable to find it on any of his maps. And from the first there are signs that he will in the end be held back from what he seeks, as when, for example, he pulls his car up before the yew trees clipped into armed horsemen barring his way ("a green spear laid at my breast"). His conversation with the blind woman is shot through with a similar ambivalence. She is unable to tell him how many children there are in the house. Her literal blindness foreshadows his inability to see the children, while her hesitancy, and his lack of understanding, are both played off against the familiar clutter of children's toys—a rocking horse, a wooden cannon—and furniture, and still more against the calm acceptance of Jenny, who tells the narrator, "You'll find yours indoors, I reckon." The effect is to poise the story on a boundary that seems always about to be crossed.

This sense of a boundary powerful yet somehow permeable is repeated on the second visit, which begins with the narrator's car seeming to take the road to the house "of her own volition," and ends with a desperate effort to get help for the dying child. This visit also helps to suggest what it is in the narrator that debars him from seeing his own lost child. He takes advantage of a mechanical fault to his car to set out his tools as if playing shop: "it was a trap to catch all childhood." Later he speaks of "child's law," meaning the rules of play children are bound to observe; earlier he has prefaced a remark to the blind woman with "if I know children." Evidently the narrator "knows" children, and loves them, but he expresses that knowledge in terms of rules, traps, and strategems. Is it this cast of mind, this need for some mental control of his deepest feelings of love, that binds him to his grief, and eventually exiles him from the house and its woods? Kipling was most reticent. Perhaps for that reason, the three stories we can associate most closely with his own life—"Baa, Baa, Black Sheep," dealing with his childhood; "They," following the death of his daughter; and "The Gardener," after the death of his son at Loos in 1915—are laceratingly personal.

The distinction between conscious knowing, and other, more intuitive forms of understanding, is raised elsewhere in "They," when the blind woman responds with pain to an angry mood in the narrator, which she perceives as a "bad colour," black zig-zagging across red. Urged on by his questions, she also outlines the contours of the egg, an arcane symbol of the universe enclosed in a single shell. Her knowledge of the colours and of the egg is innate; the source of the narrator's knowledge is not explained. In fact, Kipling was fascinated with non-physical modes of perception. He believed that his own artistic inspiration was given, that his responsibility as a writer was to follow the instructions of his "daemon." "We are only telephone wires," he told Rider Haggard in 1919. In this story, the child whose absence is so deeply felt, yet at the same time so firmly held to by the narrator, becomes Kipling's daemon. "They" both depends on and seeks to close the gap opened up by her loss. In the pain of this paradox lies the intensity of the story, and the narrator's recognition that he can never return.

—Phillip Mallett

———

THE THIRD BANK OF THE RIVER (A Terceira Margem do rio)
by João Guimarães Rosa, 1962

João Guimarães Rosa is generally agreed to be the most important writer in the development of modern Brazilian fiction, for he signals a transition from the realistic regionalist tradition of the early part of the 20th century to the modern magical realism that has characterized the work of such better-known Latin American writers as Jorge Luis Borges and Gabriel García Márquez. Guimarães Rosa has been called a "universal regionalist," a "transrealist," and a "surregionalist"—terms suggesting that although his content focuses on the people and places of the Brazilian backlands, his style effects a transcendental transformation of these "as-if-real" settings and characters into universal spiritual emblems. "A Terceira Margem do rio" ("The Third Bank of the River") is one of Guimarães Rosa's best-known tales, having appeared in several short story anthologies. Although the story is grounded in a real place and features "as-if-real" characters, the central event in the story makes it more fabulistic than realistic. The tale centers on a son's efforts to understand a father who one day, without any explanation, goes out into the river near his home in a small boat and lives his life there by eddying about in one place. Typical of the fable conventions of magical realism, the father is not so much a specific person as he is an embodiment of the role he plays. Because all we know of him is that he is a father, his journey out on the river (combined with the fact that the central focus of the story is the son's reaction to this event) can only be explained by his paternal status. The question the story poses is: What does the father communicate to the son by wandering aimlessly on the river?

The only other significant action in the story—as the other members of the family get married, have children, and move away—is that the narrator son remains, maintaining his affection and respect for his father. Whenever someone praises him for doing something good, he says, "My father taught me to act that way." The puzzle the son cannot reconcile himself to is why, if the father does not care about his family, he does not go up or down the river, but stays so close to home. The central conflict that he faces is the sense of guilt he feels, for his father is always away and his "absence" is always with him. At the end of the story, when the son himself has grown old, he calls the father to come in and let him take his place. However, the old man seems to come from another world and the son runs away in fear. The son's final hope is that when he dies they will put his body in a small boat in the "perpetual water between the long shores" and that he will be "lost" in the river.

There is no realistic motivation for the father's behavior, nor can it be explained away as a parable of one's abandonment of his social responsibility to the family. Instead, it must be approached as an embodiment of a universal spiritual act. The critic Allan Englekirk describes the father in "The Third Bank of the River" as a "liminal" character whose apparently irrational action to define truth and reality other than the way it is usually defined sets him apart as an heroic figure, and the critic James V. Romano says that the most basic antithesis in the story is between transcendence/spiritual life represented by the father versus non-transcendence/spiritual death suggested by the son.

Because the river is a traditional metaphor for time that continually moves yet simultaneously remains timeless and for change that is also permanence, the father's action symbolizes the human need to transcend time by remaining in one place as the river constantly flows by. Human beings at their most heroic, or, some would say, at their most insane, are never willing to accept that life is contained, as within two banks of a flowing river; they insist on transcending these limitations and seeking the timeless third bank of the river instead of allowing the river to sweep them on until they die. Although this is the basic responsibility that every father passes on to every son, such an effort means casting oneself off alone; thus only a few are willing to attempt it.

In a fable such as this one, characters do not act because of realistic or psychological motivation but because the underlying theme and structure of the fable demands that they do so. Unless readers recognize the fabulistic nature of the story and the spiritual nature of its theme, they may be tempted to dismiss the father's act as madness. However, as the son says, in our house the word "crazy" is never spoken, "for nobody is crazy. Or maybe everybody."

—Charles E. May

———

THIRST (Žed)
by Ivo Andrić, 1934

Ivo Andrić has been translated into more than 30 languages, but the translations leave the mistaken impression that this famous Yugoslav writer was first and foremost a novelist. In fact Andrić saw himself as a teller of tales and was known in his country as a writer of dozens upon dozens of short stories. The quintessentially Andrićan story "Žed" ("Thirst") is among the few of the author's short works readily available in English (quotations here are from Joseph Hitrec's translation in *The Pasha's Concubine and Other Tales*, 1968).

"Thirst" is very compact (fewer than five thousand words), but it is superbly constructed, and Andrić considered it significant enough to lend its title to the sixth volume of his collected works. In its barest form the plot of

"Thirst" concerns a young Austrian army officer who has been stationed in Bosnia with his wife. While the wife pines in the Bosnian "wilderness," the officer spends days on end combing the countryside for bandits. The most powerful bandit is a certain Lazar Zelenović, whom the young officer can only dream of capturing. By a fluke of fortune, however, the Austrian does manage to seize Lazar. The wounded bandit is brought back to headquarters, where he is locked up and deprived of water for not betraying his comrades. While her husband slumbers, the officer's wife sits awake at night, riveted by the horror of Lazar's torture. Only with the rising sun do Lazar's moans fade and finally cease. The officer awakes and begins to make love to his wife. With the voice of the dying man only barely gone, the wife is aghast at the thought of her husband's desires, but she is speechless and powerless to resist. Finally she surrenders completely to the "twilit sea of familiar and ever-new pleasure. . . .Her nighttime thoughts and resolutions . . . dissolving into air one after another like watery bubbles over a drowning person."

Many of Andrić's stories derive from Bosnian legends and tales, but "Thirst," though set in late 19th-century Bosnia, is a retelling of Jesus's parable "The Rich Man and Lazarus" (Luke 16:19-31), retold with an existential twist. Jesus's beggar Lazarus, covered with sores, is an unmistakable model for Andrić's bandit Lazar, with his festering chest wound, and like Jesus's rich man, Andrić's Austrian officer is never named but is described as living luxuriously. Both "rich men" have the power to alleviate the suffering; both refuse to do so.

From here the direction of Andrić's tale diverges from its prototype. In the Bible, both men die, and in hell the rich man begs Lazarus's heavenly protector Abraham to "send Lazarus to dip the tip of his finger in water to refresh my tongue, for I am tortured in these flames." (Luke 16:24). In Andrić's version, it is Lazar who is in a hell on earth (beneath the commander's well appointed quarters) and who begs for water from his guard. Andrić's Lazar and the guard Živan come from the same town, and their families worship the same patron saint, St. John. This is significant since, besides the story in Luke, the only other Lazarus in the Bible is in "The Raising of Lazarus" in John (11:1-43). The New Testament story and "Thirst" also share a theme of isolation, but if the Biblical story holds out a chance of salvation for the lowly through grace, Andrić's existential approach seems to offer scant relief. It is unclear whether the reference to St. John is to inspire hope, or is simply ironic. Since ambiguity is a hallmark of Andrić's style, the uncertainty may indeed be intentional.

The narrative style of "Thirst" is very much in keeping with Andrić's best laconic and aphoristic tendencies. People and places beyond Bosnia are described in vague terms: "The commanding officer brought with him, from somewhere abroad, a lovely fair-haired wife. . . ." Dialogue is sparse. Though the officer "talked a great deal with his wife," there are only two lines of dialogue recorded between the two, and only Lazar's pleading for water, like the rich man's appeal to Abraham in Luke, is recorded directly at any length. Instead of psychological investigation into personalities, Andrić employs generalizations that give universal import to particular situations: "Between a person who is wide awake and his sleeping mate there is always a great and chilly chasm that grows wider with each new minute and becomes filled with mystery and a strange sense of desolation and tomblike loneliness" (this echoes Abraham: "Between you and us there is fixed a great abyss, so that those who might wish to cross from here to you cannot do so, nor can anyone cross from your side to us"

Luke 16:26). "Thirst" is full of Andrić's favorite images and artistic associations: night is not a time for sleep, but of nightmarish insomnia (a state Andrić knew well from his own terrible insomnia), "a desert of gloom." Nature is indifferent and infinite: "the mountain, which had just turned green . . . seemed as endless as the sea," and the physical need for water parallels spiritual thirst, so often unquenched.

In "Thirst" Andrić has accomplished precisely what, in the monologue "Goya," the author lay down as his own artistic/philosophical credo: "We must listen to legends. . . .One must seek [meaning] in those layers which the centuries have deposited around some of the most important of man's legends" (translated by John Loud). By recasting in his own vision an age-old story, Andrić produced in "Thirst" a work of simple beauty, profound and complex intent, and lasting significance—a new layer in which to seek meaning.

—Nathan Longan

THIS MORNING, THIS EVENING, SO SOON
by James Baldwin, 1965

The most famous story in James Baldwin's 1965 volume of short stories, *Going to Meet the Man*, is "Sonny's Blues." It is a story of brothers and of brotherhood, and the need for connecting and "communicating" (ostensibly through music but also in words), which both epitomizes and transcends the life and outlook, the failures and frustrations, as well as the triumphs of the African-American and the jazz-musician experience in the urban United States.

Another famous story in *Man*, "This Morning, This Evening, So Soon," adds a more distanced but equally universal and transcendent perspective on the African-American urban experience by juxtaposing the United States with France, New York with Paris. Both stories reflect Baldwin's own struggle to find his voice and himself, and to be heard. Hearing himself at the most authentic level and honestly expressing that to others—connecting the delight and the angst of black experiences to blacks and to non-blacks—became the controlling purpose of his art.

Baldwin's many works hit hard at one's sense of justice forsaken, and cut deep, down to the quick of the complicated issues of prejudice, racism, and overall cultural tolerance of diversity. His early years as a preacher (and his eventual disillusionment) shine through his fictions, each of them making and calling for more reader decisions, not so much for Christ in the abstract as for simple human decency, civility, and the basic Christian moral tenets of love and forgiveness.

"This Morning" dramatizes the profound effect Baldwin's expatriate stay in France had on him—and the jolts which his reentries into America caused him. Clearly Baldwin's closest analog is the movie star, celebrity singer who serves as the story's narrator, and beyond him the persona of "Chico" (a man consumed by hatred of his Martinique mother and his French father, and by anger against all black women and white men), a character whom the narrator/actor assumes in one of his most successful films.

Baldwin, seen in varying degrees in all his story's characters, is closest to the narrator's friend, Vidal, whose editorializing on film and the essences that, as a director, he must draw out of the narrator's past, reveal Baldwin's own zeal for the efficacy of art—whether on celluloid images or ink on the page.

"Morning" takes place on the eve of the narrator's return to America after 12 years in France and the attainment of celebrity status as a singer and film star. He is much in love with his Swedish wife, Harriet, and their young son, Paul. In his marriage and family, as well as in his art and friendships with persons like Vidal, who impose no stereotypes of slavery or negritude or inferiority on him, he has come to love Paris. His sister's visit reminds him of the racism of their Alabama beginnings, as do associated flashbacks of his brief visit a few years back to New York. Remembering the strategies needed to cope with ingrained prejudice of Americans angers him and makes him wish his son, Paul, could remain oblivious to such things.

The night of conviviality with Vidal and some college-age tourists before the New York departure is a poignant reminder that he must take Paul with him to America. Paul, like his father, must know the truth of his American ancestry, his birthright, blemished by prejudice though it may be. It is inevitable.

In the story's final scene, the narrator arrives at Mme. Dumont's (where Paul has been cared for during the night) and swoops him up from his sleep at early morning to prepare for the journey to New York, *"Fusqu'au nouveau monde!"* Together they ride the apartment house elevator "up," the symbolic start of the voyage all the way to the new world. And the suggestion lingers that perhaps it will be a new world, a new dawning for Paul, contrary to the narrator's own knowing in his life time, and in his father's before him.

Baldwin believed that to be black and to be an American was to live in rage. And yet, as this story proves, that rage is not without assuagement. In this sense if in no other, Baldwin, like most writers, knows the power of a "timely utterance," knows that words, communicated through art, may matter most, if not in the result, at least in the telling.

—Robert Franklin Gish

THRAWN JANET
by Robert Louis Stevenson, 1887

Of "Thrawn Janet" Henry James wrote, "a masterpiece in thirteen pages." It was the first work by Stevenson to which the epithet could be satisfactorily applied. In the same essay (*Century Magazine*, April 1888) James writes, "Before all things he is a writer with a style," and he develops the themes of Stevenson as the self-conscious craftsman. In Stevenson's early essays and travel descriptions, there were hints of the dark, wild world in "Thrawn Janet," (collected in *The Merry Men*, 1887). "Even in the names of places," Stevenson wrote in *Winter and New Year*, "there is often a desolate, inhospitable sound; and I remember two from the near neighbourhoods of Edinburg, Cauldhame and Blaweary." The latter name became Balweary in "Thrawn Janet." As a child, Stevenson heard frightening tales from his nurse, about an evil personified by the devil. Yet "Thrawn Janet" could not have been predicted from his previous writings. A considerable shift of focus was re-

quired for Stevenson to justify the name given him by the Samoans, Tusitala—the teller of tales.

The plot of "Thrawn Janet," a young, liberal minister comes to believe that the devil had entered the body of one of his parishioners, might appear to be of only anthropological interest. Stevenson himself wrote in *Note* of what he regarded as a defect, "it is only historically true, true for a hill parish in Scotland in the old days." Yet he admitted that "the story carries me away every time I read it." Elsewhere he remarked on "the Scots dialect" being "singularly rich" in wintry terms, and quotes four adjectives, "snell, blae, nirly and scowthering," but he is equally effective in creating it by the suffocating atmosphere in which the tragic and distorting events in "Thrawn Janet" happen:

> About the end o' July there cam' a spell o' weather, the like o't never was in that countryside; it was lown an' het an' heartless; the herds couldna win up the Black Hill, the bairns were ower weariet to play; an' yet it was gousty too, wi' claps o' het wund that rumm'led in the glens, and bits o' shouers that slockened naething.

This has the authority of the teller of folk tales. The storyteller is cast as "one of the older folk" who "would warm into courage over his third tumbler." Earlier in the story, Stevenson introduces the reader to the minister as he is 50 years after these strange events: "a severe, bleak-faced old man dreadful to his hearers." As a young minister he required a housekeeper at the Manse. Janet M'Clour was recommended by the laird. The folk told him Janet was "sib [bound] to the de'il," which the minister rejected as superstition. Matters came to a head when the minister intervened in an attempt to drown Janet to discover if she was a witch. On the following day the minister escorted Janet to the manse: "there was Janet comin doun the clachan—her or her likeness, nane could tell—wi' her neck thrawn, an' her heid on ae side, like a body that had been hangit, an' a girn on her face like an unstreakit corpse."

In Scotland we thraw the neck of a chicken to kill it. This is common parlance, but thrawn many also mean the face twisted, generally twisted with pain. The minister, however, "preached about naething but the folk's cruelty that had gi'en her a stroke of the palsy." Events culminated in a night that "fell as mirk as the pit; no a star, no' a breath o' wund." Hearing noise from Janet's room, he ventured to seek her there:

> An' then a' at aince, the minister's heart played dunt an' stood stock-still; an' a cauld wund blew amang the hairs o' his heid. Whatten a weary sicht was that for the puir man's e'en! For there was Janet Hanging' frae a nail beside the auld aik cabinet: her heid aye lay on her shouther, her e'en were steekit, the tongue projected frae her mouth, an' her heels were twa feet clear abune the floor. "God forgive us all!" thocht Mr Soulis, "poor Janet's dead."

The grotesque theatre in the vernacular is ended by the minister's use of King's English; his speech throughout is informed by the King James translation of the Bible. By such writing Stevenson puts himself in the Scottish tradition of the expression of evil through the figure of the devil or "deil." He may be presented as a figure of fun in the dance of the witches in Robert Burn's *Tam o' Shanter*, with horror, as he possesses the soul of Robert Wringhim, in

James Hogg's *Confessions of a Justified Sinner,* or with the zest of the storyteller set to create belief where none may seem possible in Walter Scott's "Wandering Willie's Tale." This element is in Stevenson's "Thrawn Janet," but it has the wider implication that the non-rational may destroy the reasoning mind—and this was the apprehension of Stevenson.

—George Bruce

THREE MILLION YEN (Hyakumanen senbei)
by Mishima Yukio, 1960

First published in October 1960, some ten years before Mishima's early death, "Hyakumanen senbei" ("Three Million Yen") is one of his last stories. He tended to concentrate on novels and speculative or political essays in his last years. "Three Million Yen" therefore represents Mishima's mature ironic style, a combination of self-consciously distanced narrative, strong symbolic effects and sharply-observed dialogue. One feature of this style is that it is hard to tell whether the irony serves to rein in a real sense of anger, or merely to sharpen good-humored social observation. It is probably this tension between mockery and passion, present in all of Mishima's best work, that makes the story so memorable.

In the story a young married couple, Kiyoko and Kenzo, has an appointment with an unnamed old woman later that evening. They are walking towards a modern department store housed in the New World Building. On the roof of the building is a five-story pagoda, gaudily illuminated with flashing neon lights. We are told that this pagoda has replaced a pond, now filled in, as the prime landmark of this district of the city. With the image of this rooftop pagoda, the tone and direction of the story start to emerge: this is to be an ironic exposure of the values of modern Japan and the concerns of "average" postwar Japanese people. The pagoda, evocative of quiet temple grounds and the grace of old Japan has become something lit up in neon, flickering on the roof of the building named "New World." The massive western-style department store, both symbol and propagator of consumerism, rises like a tombstone over the grave of a pleasure-garden pond, again evocative of the more refined amusements of Japan's past.

The young couple are in Western clothes in the summer heat—the man in a singlet, the woman in a sleeveless dress, clutching a pink plastic handbag. On entering the department store the atmosphere of abundant consumerism is stressed again among the mountainous piles of cheap, brightly coloured goods.

A remark about the man's fondness for toys sets the couple talking about their wish to have children, and the authorial voice tells us that they are indeed a couple united in their careful consumerism. They open special saving accounts for each item—refrigerator, washing machine, television—that they wish to acquire, and then search carefully for the best deal they can get on their chosen model. They also have a budget plan for a child, though that is still a few years off, and feel only contempt for those poor families who have children without proper economic planning. We are told that Kenzo is filled with rage when modern young Japanese say there is no hope, believing that those who respect nature and work hard will be able to make a life.

This talk about hope for the future then shades into a description of a toy flying saucer station which has attracted Kenzo's attention. On a tin base, its background cunningly painted with twinkling stars, the toy launches plastic spaceships into the humid summer air. The flying saucer that Kenzo launches lands on the packet of three "million-yen rice crackers," which provide the title of the story. (Although the English translation is "Three Million Yen," the Japanese title is literally "Million Yen Rice Crackers.") Here again we are treated to an ironic contrast of the old values and the modern consumerism. The figure on the imitation bank notes on the wrapper is that of the bald-headed owner of the department store, replacing Shōtoku Taishi, the legendary scholar-prince who is said to have introduced Buddhism to Japan and who used to be on most Japanese banknotes.

Kenzo sees the landing as a good omen and buys a packet of the crackers despite his wife's protests that they are too expensive. Much of his wife's share of the dialogue throughout the story is to say that things are too expensive. They nibble the crackers while looking round the indoor "funfair" on another floor of the building. Kenzo insists that they try out a ride called "Twenty Thousand Leagues Under the Sea," even though his wife again mutters that for the price of the ticket one could get a good bit of real fish rather than looking at a lot of cardboard ones.

In the description of the ride that follows the focus of the attention is mostly on the wife as she feels her husband's bare arms on her naked back and shoulders, and she senses that he takes a sensual enjoyment in her fear. She feels paradoxically more embarrassed by this sense of sexuality in the darkness of the ride than she would be in the daylight; she tells herself that with her husband's arms around her she could bear any kind of shame or fear.

The second attraction they try is called "Magic Land," and the dwarves suggest again the children they want to have. As they walk up the path with its row of artificial flowers lit by flashing bulbs, Kenzo remarks that they should have something like this themselves someday. In the leaning room and other wonders of distorted architecture contained in "Magic Land," the couple continue to see genuine images of future domestic happiness.

Finally it is time for them to keep the appointment mentioned at the beginning of the story, and we learn that the money they put so scrupulously aside for various projected purchases is earned by giving sex performances in the homes of the bored and wealthy.

The end of story comes as a kind of epilogue, in which the couple are shown walking along tired and spiritless, late at night, talking about how hateful the crowd they had performed for had been. Kenzo says he would like to rip up the banknotes that the bourgeois bellesdames had given them; his wife nervously offers him the remaining million-yen rice cracker as a substitute. It has become so damp and sticky that it will not tear.

Pressed together in the dark, sexually aroused and ashamed before the cold, bright eyes of artificial sea monsters, the pair reenact a version of the kind of performance by which they earn their living. Then they move from this to a "magic land," which, with its wobbly staircases and shaking passageways provides a distorted and insecure vision of the domestic bliss they hope to build out of their nightly humiliations.

This story reflects Mishima's contempt for what he considered the decadence of postwar, Americanized consumer culture in Japan, and also for bourgeois money values. He came to feel more and more that they were destroying everything of worth in traditional Japan. However, although the irony is strong and the whole structure of the story possibly a little too schematic, it is still humor rather than rage that dominates. Although we are clearly meant to see the young couple as largely unwitting victims of modern acquisitiveness, Mishima's treatment of them still contains enough indulgent warmth to allow us to be touched by their naive trust in each other and in what their relationship can do. They have sold what was best in themselves to buy into a more prosperous future, and clearly Mishima believed the same could be said of postwar Japan.

—James Raeside

TILL SEPTEMBER PETRONELLA
by Jean Rhys, 1968

Jean Rhys considered "Till September Petronella" the story which "just about saved [her] life." Originally begun as a 50,000 novel which she "cut and cut," it was written during the 1930's and initially rejected when she submitted it for publication in the 1940's as part of a collection called *The Sound of the River*. Rhys, almost always apologetic about her work, feared the stories might be "dated" or "a bit lifeless." However, she wrote in a letter in 1959, "I think there might be an idea or two knocking about. . . .Especially in the last which is called 'In September, Petronella.' Dated. But purposely." Through the offices of Francis Wyndham, Rhys managed to place the story, for which Wyndham himself wrote an introduction, in the *London Magazine*. "Petronella's" appearance in the January 1960 issue brought Rhys not only some much needed cash but a small flurry of acclaim from publishers and other writers, which pleased her greatly. Wyndham was even approached by the critic and poet Goefirey Grigson to write an entry on Rhys for *World Literature 1900 to 1960*. In 1966, after favorable reviews of her long awaited novel, *Wide Sargasso Sea*, Rhys hoped that "Petronella" might appear in *The New Yorker*, but it was not reprinted until the collection *Tigers Are Better-Looking* appeared in 1968.

The story takes up many of the concerns and themes familiar in Rhys: poverty, misogyny, exploitation, addiction, depression, and isolation. Although Rhys claimed in a letter to her daughter in 1960 that "Petronella" was "*not autobiography*," one cannot help but see the parallels between the life of Petronella Gray, the narrator, and Rhys, whose stage name during the time she toured England as a chorus girl was Ella Gray.

As Thomas Staley has observed, this important story is one of the few in Rhys's canon which is internally dated; sitting in a pub, Petronella notices a calendar marked 28 July 1914. As Staley suggests, the time frame sets the characters on the verge of war which "will only confirm the underlying human barbarism" of the relationships in the story "on a grander and more violent scale."

The plot involves a young model who leaves her dreary Bloomsbury existence for a fortnight in the country with a young painter, Marston, who, despite her lack of feelings for him, offers her "a bit of a change." Staying at his country cottage are a cynical music critic, Julian, to whom Petronella is attracted, and Frankie Morell, Julian's current lover. It is clear immediately that class is an issue in the story, as in much of Rhys's work: Frankie speaks to Petronella in a "patronizing voice" of opera, Marston taunts her for having "no money, no background," and Julian, in a drunken outburst, condemns her as "fifth rate," a "ghastly cross between a barmaid and a chorus-girl."

Even more marked, however, is the pervasive misogyny, seen in both men's barely disguised disgust with women and women's animosity towards each other. There is no escape in Rhys's world as Petronella passes from one encounter to another, from the women in street markets staring at her "with hatred" to Julian who condemns her as a "female spider" to Marston who sees her as a "poor devil of a female, female, female, in a country where females are only tolerated at best!"

Finally unable to bear the cruelty and vindictiveness of this odd menage à quatre, Petronella leaves the house, intending to return to London. As she walks along the main road, formulating her plan, a car stops and she accepts a ride with a man who identifies himself as a farmer on his way to market. As in much of Rhys, the story is constructed around a series of non-events: she waits in a pub for the farmer while he attends to business; he drives her back to Marston's to pick up her belongings; he drops her at the depot and she takes the train back home. Issues cover the text like standing water; no one swims or dives or even drowns although early on Petronella confesses, "the thought came to me suddenly, like a revelation, that I could kill myself any time I liked and so end it. After that I put a better face on things."

Back in London, Petronella shares a cab with a stranger named Melville, then dines with him, sleeps with him, and lets him take her home. "I daresay he would be nice if one got to know him," she thinks as they exchange banter and she tells him of her failed theatrical career, due to her inability to say lines on cue. The irony here is not to be missed, for in much of Rhys, it is just this problem which haunts women: the inability to perform, to say or do what other people, usually men, want. Petronella still seems resilient enough to absorb the emptiness of her encounters; she doesn't seem to realize, as do Rhys's older women, that no one ever "gets to know" anyone and has not yet, as Staley notes, "progressed very far along that inevitable downward spiral of life" so familiar to Rhys's older heroines. The story is still somewhat open-ended—the phrase "till September" echoes twice, as both Marston and Melville part and promise to see Petronella in the fall. But as Judith Kegan Gardiner has observed, the title also presages the guns of August, connecting "world war with the battle between the sexes."

For Rhys, however, the sustaining metaphor is not battle but a kind of cruel passivity, seen in the striking last scene of the story when Petronella stands looking out the window in her sitting room, remembering the night on stage when she forgot her lines. She is fixated by the face of a man in the front row whom she sees "quite clearly" and whom she wills to help her, to tell her what she has forgotten. "But though he had looked, as it seemed, straight into my eyes, and though I was sure he knew exactly what I was thinking, he had not helped me. He had only smiled. He had left me in that moment that seemed like years."

"Till September Petronella" is significant in that artistically it articulates this key Rhysian "moment" and yet historically, in a sense, ruptures it, for it was through this story that Rhys looked out again after many years of despair into the face of her audience and saw, if only briefly, what it was she had forgotten.

—Deborah Kelly Kloepfer

A TIME TO KEEP
by George Mackay Brown, 1969

In the short opening sentences of "A Time to Keep" Brown serves notice of his immediate thematic intentions: he is concerned with the eternal verities of marriage, procreation, and death. Bill, the narrator, has just married Ingi and they are walking across the white virginal snow towards their new home in the farming valley of Rackwick on the Orkney island of Hoy. It is the middle of winter, death's season, but the couple are bringing hope of renewal to the dwindling community. Seeing the smoke rise above the farmhouse, Bill observes that the first true fire has been lit.

For all the familiar imagery, though, this is not a simple fable of life returning to a moribund society through the infusion of new blood. Bill is free-thinker and atheist who shuns the company of his fellow crofters and scorns the church. Although the dubious company of the alehouse still claims him, he is an isolated figure who turns away the hand of companionship. With his respectable father-in-law, a merchant and pillar of the community, he has no relationship at all.

Despite his unwillingness to accept Christian doctrine, Bill is not without religious feeling. He is aware of nature's subtle rhythms and of the continuity between seasons. In his wife, home, plough, and boat, he can sense a new beginning, the birth of a life different from the decay of older generations. At its most intense the emotion comes alive in his relationship with his natural surroundings. To him the valley is a green hand, open and giving; but the sea is a blue hand which takes more than it gives. Because he is a good fisherman who realises that the sea can never belong to any human—unlike the land—in his mind it will always takes precedence over the valley.

But Ingi is out of place in her new home. Brought up outside farming life she cannot cook or brew ale, and has difficulty keeping house, however much she wants to please her husband. Worse still, she has never lacked for money or belongings and has difficulty understanding Bill's constant admonitions to be careful as "we're poor people." The crisis comes when her father arrives at the croft to take her home but she refuses to leave because she is pregnant.

Her condition is mirrored by the surroundings. In the fine summer weather the cornfields ripen beneath the soft wind which "blessed it continually, sending long murmurs of fulfilment." But in that happy hour, as the crofters await their turn to help one another bring in the harvest, there is a double tragedy.

First, rain falls on the day of Bill's harvest and his cornfield is left "squashed and tangled." The ruination forces him to accept a loan from his father-in-law, thereby restricting his independence. Then, following hard upon this disaster there is a second calamity when Ingi dies in childbirth. That the unhappy events are related is made clear by Brown, who compares Ingi's "damp hair sprawled over the pillow" to the ruined corn in the fields outside the croft.

With his customary stoicism Bill is able to endure the heavy loss and after his wife's burial he insists that he will remain an emancipated man. However, he is not prepared for the kindness and good sense of the people of the valley who take him and the newborn child into their care and protection. His neighbours, the Two-Waters family, agree to run his croft while he does the fishing for both homes. It is also tacitly agreed that Anna, their plain daughter, will move in with him at the end of the year to help bring up the child. And there the story ends, with snow again on the ground and Anna marvelling anew at the miracle of the nativity.

Although this is a bleak tale with little human comfort, the desolation is softened by the lyrical beauty of Brown's physical descriptions. On a fine day the green hand of the valley and the blue hand of the sea are linked in the summer dawn as if in prayer. Physical pleasure is found in the naked power of hard work and in the benison of food and drink at the day's end. The harsh landscape yields beneath the sweat of the men and women who work it while the sea is celebrated in a chance meeting between Bill and fishermen from the Scottish mainland.

Constructed in short sharp sentences, Brown's prose has a timeless quality: pails of water ring like bells, dead lambs resemble red rags, the cliffs towering over Bill's fishing boat are as grey as ghosts, the baby is blessed by a fleck of spindrift as it lies in Bill's arms. All these are accepted images in Brown's prose and help to soften the uncompromising brutality of the central plot.

Within that symbolic framework Brown has fashioned other strands, the most notable being the promise of renewal contained in the twinning of the pre-Christian winter solstice with the New Testament account of the nativity. This is made manifest in the birth of a child through the sacrifice of its mother and the consciousness of impending salvation in the depths of winter when night is at its darkest.

In the penultimate passage, as Anna returns from the Christmas church service, Bill notices the beasts kneeling in the byre, just as they had done before the Christ-child in his mean and squalid stable. In that sense, Brown seems to be saying, every birth is a miracle in its own right, being in some small measure a reenactment of the nativity of Jesus.

—Trevor Royle

TO BUILD A FIRE
by Jack London, 1910

During his relatively short life, London produced numerous novels and stories as well as political journalism and travel writing. Though most of his work is both eloquent and compelling, some obviously was written so that London could survive in a world he increasingly came to see as "red in tooth and claw." Perhaps because of these hack productions, but more likely because of the exotic settings and characters of even his best work, few critics have given him a place of high acclaim in American literature. He writes of the Klondike and South Seas islands, of pirates, boxers, hobos, and Socialists, not the home town fare of such contemporaries as Sinclair Lewis or Sherwood Anderson. London was a man of the Pacific before America knew how important that ocean was to become.

The Pacific and the down-and-out were what London knew best. "To Build a Fire" was drawn from the year he spent in Canada's Yukon Territory, aged 21 and suffering from scurvy, during the height of the gold rush there in 1898. One of his finest short stories, it reflects the heavily Naturalistic flavor he has come to be known for, and it pits one man, alone, against the overwhelming forces of nature, a setting many critics have claimed to be his best. Yet "To Build a Fire" is more than a naturalistic story of "one against nature," more than a vivid local color narrative; it is part of the great American pioneer experience, and can be read as allegory, in the tradition of *Moby-Dick*, for the solitary and doomed journey of human existence.

Among the most interesting features of "To Build a Fire" is that it comes in two versions: the first published in May 1902 in *Youth's Companion*, the second published in *Century Magazine* in August 1908 and later collected in *Lost Face* in 1910. Unless otherwise specified, the latter story is the one critics refer to. The two versions provide a rare insight into the evolution of a writer, as the first comes from the beginnings of London's writing career and the second was written in the glow of his first financial success and literary acclaim.

The 1902 version reads as a simple adventure story. Only a third of the length of the later version, its hero has a name, Tom Vincent, and he survives his ordeal of breaking through the ice in temperatures approaching -75 degrees Fahrenheit, albeit not without some bodily damage. This version lacks suggestive imagery, its action lacks development (as its length indicates), and its narrative is devoid of the more cosmic and philosophic elements of the later version: its tone more resembles the tale-telling of a journalist than that of a fiction writer. Vincent, lacking the dog of the later version, is foolishly over-confident in the face of the cold: "At such times animals crawled away in their holes and remained in hiding. But he did not hide. He was out in it, facing it, fighting it. He was a man, a master of things." As its publication in a magazine for adolescents might bode, it ends in a facile moral nutshell.

Though noticeably not of the quality of the 1908 version, the 1902 text still shows the promise of London's later writing. The suspense is gripping: Will he get the fire built in time? Will he live? London writes the 1902 story with descriptive realism about the snowy tundra, the numbness of frozen feet, the agony of burning flesh. If the 1902 story lacks irony and subtlety, we realize it primarily because we have the 1908 version to compare it to.

The man with no name of the 1908 version has become an Everyman, trekking through a naturalistic universe. The absolute zero of outer space has dropped the "spirit thermometer" to 107 degrees below freezing. He tramps alone, but for his suspicious dog, in sunless twilight through endless tracts of white snow. His humanity hovers precariously just above the level of a dumb beast: he lacks the instinct of his dog, yet, despite his vigilance and keen observation, he lacks imagination and thoughts about the significance of things, and he trudges in the silence of his "ice-muzzle" formed by the frozen tobacco juice in his beard, seemingly oblivious to the minor pain of frost-nipped cheeks. Indeed, the man and the dog become more similar as the story progresses. The man is muzzled; the dog breaks through a hidden ice patch when the man sends it to test a suspicious spot, and together they break the ice from between its toes; the man seems as much a "toil-slave" as his dog.

The naturalist focus of the 1908 test, in contrast to the 1902 version, closes on the inevitable extinction of the man. His death comes through no lapse of observation, no lack of diligence, no real folly, but through the nature of himself and his environment. Like his fire, his life is simply extinguished by the overwhelming forces that surround him, his belief that "All a man had to do was keep his head, and he was all right" proving hopelessly naive.

Arising from London's first-hand observations of the Yukon, "To Build a Fire" creates vivid depictions of arctic conditions and eerily realistic descriptions of what it feels like to freeze. But it also creates London's vision of naturalistic determinism without diminishing the story's tight, life-and-death suspense, its engrossing narrative action. London claimed, in the Twain tradition, that he wrote as he spoke; he is a powerful and persuasive story-teller.

—Karen Rhodes

TO HELL WITH DYING
by Alice Walker, 1973

More than anything, Alice Walker's "To Hell with Dying" is about her roots as a writer. It represents, for example, one of her first real successes in African-American literary circles and her first published story, in 1968. (It was also later published in the collection *In Love and Trouble: Stories of Black Women,* 1973.) Langston Hughes included the story in his collection *The Best Short Stories by Negro Writers: An Anthology from 1899 to the Present* (1967) to illustrate what "the new young writers of the sixties" were producing; he comments in the introduction that "Neither you nor I have ever read a story like [it] before." Yet, despite such praise, it seems impossible that even Hughes could have anticipated the career that lay ahead for Walker. Neither could Hughes have envisioned the story's latest incarnation as a children's book, lavishly and brightly illustrated by Catherine Deeter (1988), return, in spirit at least, to the story's other roots in Walker's own life, as evidenced by the illustrations clearly depicting Walker as the story's narrator and by the edition's dedication: "To the old ones of my childhood who taught me the most important lesson of all: That I did not need to be perfect to be loved." The story thus uncannily anticipates Walker's continuing preoccupation throughout her writing—perhaps most notably in *The Color Purple*—with the construction or restoration of communities, with the recovery of those community's outcasts, and with the power art has to mediate difference and transcend time. (Certain other details in the story, such as a reference to the narrator's finishing a doctorate in Massachusetts, however, do not match Walker's biography, so we may be better served by calling "To Hell with Dying" an example of "autofictography.")

"To Hell with Dying" works beautifully as a children's story. A first-person narrative, it embodies the charm and magic of that narrator's youth, tempered by the perspective of experience and adulthood but still told with an innocence that is knowing rather than naive. Mr. Sweet's essential goodness may be the center of the story, but it exists alongside more negative aspects of his existence, of which the narrator certainly has been aware from her earliest childhood, such as his alcoholism, his lost ambition, his occasional fits of depression, his largely unhappy marriage to Miss Mary, his shiftless son who may not even be his son, and his long lost love "now living in Chi-ca-go, or De-stroy, Michigan." In this sense, "To Hell with Dying" is a truly bitter-sweet story. That Mr. Sweet finds acceptance and support in his community bears ample witness of its tolerance and of Walker's own value system, especially as they allow him a relationship with their children: "He had great respect for my mother for she never held his drunkenness against him and would let us play with him even when he was about to fall in the fireplace from drink. . . . His ability to be drunk and sober at the same time made him an ideal playmate, for he was as weak as we were and we could usually best him in wrestling, all the while keeping a fairly coherent conversation going."

Indeed, Mr. Sweet's relationship with these children makes his ritual, death-bed revivals possible, as if their proximity to birth and the freshness of their lives can somehow pull him backwards toward them and away from death's door. "To hell with dying, man," the narrator's father would proclaim at Mr. Sweet's bedside—after the physician had done what he could and warned them all away from the "death room"—"these children want Mr. Sweet." The children then swarm all over Mr. Sweet's bed to tickle him back to life. In their childish innocence they do not question the ultimate efficacy of their "revivaling" and suppose that their power over death was universal and not restricted to Mr. Sweet: "It did occur to us that if our own father had been dying we could not have stopped it, that Mr. Sweet was the only person over whom we had power." Whether this power was indeed divine, or merely given by Mr. Sweet, is not clear in the narrative; what is clear, however, is that this power has a limited efficacy because it finally fails to save him on his 90th birthday even though the now 24-year-old narrator immediately rushes to his bedside as she has so many times before. Perhaps she herself has grown too old to cheat death and nature yet again. In any case, Mr. Sweet must have sensed the inevitable, for he had arranged some months before to have her father give her his guitar: "He had known that even if I came next time he would not be able to respond in the old way. He did not want me to feel that my trip had been for nothing." This inheritance from Mr. Sweet, the guitar on which he played the blues for so long, symbol of his one great talent, tempers this final loss and represents some kind of passing on of the artistic, creative impulse from Mr. Sweet to the narrator. As she plucks the strings and hums "Sweet Georgia Brown," she understands that "the magic of Mr. Sweet lingered still in the smooth wooden box." It lingers too in the short story "To Hell with Dying." Perhaps that is the real "revivaling" power in operation here—the power of art.

—Phillip A. Snyder

TO ROOM NINETEEN
by Doris Lessing, 1963

"To Room Nineteen," first published in the collection *A Man and Two Women* in 1963, pursues Doris Lessing's intense interest in the consciousness of women under the stresses of modern life. It reflects the concerns of the period in which it was written and foreshadows the sort of feminist explorations that were to become much more common after 1970. Its ancestry is traceable to D.H. Lawrence, Katherine Mansfield, and other writers of the earlier part of the century. And it looks forward to the work of Fay Weldon and others.

The Rawlings appear to have everything that a couple could want; having married late "amid general rejoicing" (Lessing deliberately offers us this cliche to put us on our guard), they have four healthy children and create what seems to be a stable and comfortable home. Matthew Rawlings is briefly unfaithful, which seems acceptable but which puts a small piece of grit into the perfect machine of their marriage. Nothing else goes wrong but the result is that Susan Rawlings goes slowly mad inside the meaninglessness of her life. She finally commits suicide. There is not much more to the plot than that, but this forces readers into a strongly hermeneutic position—they are obliged to explore the text in detail to try to see exactly what it is that drives Susan to such desperate lengths when there is so much that is right with her life and so little that is wrong.

The story is delicately balanced between possible explanations: Susan may be a victim of her class and place in the world (bored middle-class housewife stereotype), or of her gender (things go wrong because, once she has given up "being herself" in order to be a wife and mother, she cannot recapture what she once was), or of the human condition (her suicide seems to transcend local or gender questions to some degree—life is just too much for the sensitive perhaps). All three levels are hinted at in the opening paragraph, where the narrator obtrudes into the fiction to make the apparently reliable observation that "This is a story" about "a failure in intelligence." At first this seems to mean that Susan fails to live up to the ideals of being sensible and rational that are stressed in her marriage to Matthew. When she becomes irrational and even mad she can no longer function as wife, mother, or anything else. But then we begin to wonder if intelligence is not rather lacking in Matthew's sensible world, for he is unable to help or to understand Susan when things start to go wrong. There may even be a suggestion that "intelligence" should bear its military meaning: what is lacking is the right sort of information about the nature of human life and relationships.

What seems to be missing in the apparently ideal world of the Rawlings is pain. They are forever sensible (the word is repeated half a dozen times) and balanced; they always choose the right ways, so they have managed an "abstinence" (curious word) from "painful experience," they are excluded from a "painful and explosive world." For this reason, perhaps, they have no reason for living. Lessing explicitly canvases the options: children or Matthew's work cannot in themselves provide a reason for living; their love for one another seems a good candidate, but if even that becomes hollow, not so much because of Matthew's infidelity as because everything always was too perfect and too sensible, there is nothing to live for. Where "intelligence forbids tears" and nothing can happen that is unforeseen, a void opens in Susan's heart. One of the merits of the story is that we can feel the madness that this brings on Susan; the void is first "something waiting for her at home," then "the enemy," then "a demon," then "a devil," then a sinister man with gingery whiskers whom she thinks she sees in her garden. Like the reader, Susan is quite aware that these are symptoms of madness.

Susan has lived a lie. She needs to learn that emotions, however absurd they may be, are still *felt*, but it is too late;

once Matthew has "diagnosed" her as unreasonable she does indeed lose her reason. Smaller doses of unreason and irrationality, taken earlier, might have saved her. Once her life-illusion of perfection has collapsed she cannot bear to be anything at all—she retreats to a hotel room and simply sits there, away from the demands of a now meaningless world. Her only freedom now is stasis and this soon becomes a logical desire for the final stasis of death.

The final paragraphs of the story try to demonstrate the sanity of Susan's madness. Normal life is represented by planning to deceive her husband into believing that the lover whom she has invented really exists (Matthew needs the *rational* explanation of a lover to understand his wife's distress and she invents one for his sake). As Susan comments, in free indirect speech, "How absurd!" So much for the normal. The mad world of suicide, however, is represented in a series of largely positive images: Susan slips into a dream which is "fructifying" and which caresses her "inwardly" like her own blood. The impression given is that her madness signals the absence of an essential dimension, the dimension emphasised by D.H. Lawrence following Nietzsche, the dimension of true selfhood, creativity, and a true knowledge of the body. The story ends with a covert reference to Lawrence as Susan "drifts off into the dark river" of her death.

—Lance St. John Butler

THE TOMORROW-TAMER
by Margaret Laurence, 1963

"The Tomorrow-Tamer," the title story for Margaret Laurence's West African collection (1963), was written in Vancouver, British Columbia, published in *Prism International* in the fall of 1961, and awarded the President's Medal of Excellence (University of Western Ontario) for the year's best Canadian short story. However, the germ for the story came from Laurence's encounter, approximately five years earlier, with an African bridgeworker on the Volta River in Gold Coast (now Ghana) who, a few days later, died in a fall from the top of the bridge he was building. It was not an easy story to write—she thought about the accident for many years and rewrote the story ten times—but it became for her a symbol for the clash between two quite different cultures, the misunderstandings and human costs occasioned by the clash, and the insights gained and adjustments made.

The Tomorrow-Tamer stories, as well as her novel *This Side Jordan,* are set in a time of transition from colonial rule to independent nationhood, a time when the racial, religious, cultural, political, economic, technological, and related tensions between the colonizers and the colonized were highlighted. As an outsider both from the African and European communities, Laurence could see the vested interests, the strengths, and the limitations of both sides, and she had her perspectives clarified and contextualized by her reading in 1960 of Octave Mannoni's *Prospero and Caliban: A Study of the Psychology of Colonization.*

In brief, "The Tomorrow-Tamer" deals with the effects on a traditional African village of the building of a bridge where previously there had been only a ferry crossing one-half-mile downriver. Laurence's cultural and artistic sensitivity in communicating details gives the story its power.

Central to the story is Owura, the god or spirit of the river and its sacred grove, from whom the village Owurasu and its people take not just their name but their overall identity and on whom they "model their behaviour." Theirs is an animistic world, one where river and forest are spiritually alive and where the building of a bridge is seen as the coming of a "new being," disturbing the old divinities, a world where "everywhere spirit acted on spirit, not axe upon wood . . . nor man upon steel." The question is how the new being, the bridge, is to be fitted into the hierarchy of the traditional gods and the world-view of the villagers; their answer at the story's end is that, through the sacrifice of Kofi, whom they regard as the bridge's priest, the bridge is acknowledging the river god's primacy. The irony is that their conclusions (like the very different ones of the English construction superintendent) are based on their limited understanding of Kofi and his motivations. Further, in contrasting the remaking of Kofi's life into legends with the wonder at such depictions on the part of his mother and young wife, Laurence subtly undermines any simple answers.

Kofi, as the foregoing suggests, is the main character through whom the cultural adjustment process is portrayed. Initially "no one in particular," this teenager, over the course of the story's year-plus length, gains the status of a village man: he is the first villager to work on the bridge, he marries, and he becomes recognized by the villagers as the spokesman for his generation. But, at the same time, his perspective on the village and the bridge changes. He develops new loyalties: to the bridge, to the bridgemen. In both instances, though he has moved away from some village values and perspectives (a move further than even his family realizes), his evolving assumptions are still culture-bound. Dismayed to learn that the bridgemen, with whom he identifies himself, are individually itinerant, seeming to lack the rootedness in community that is so intrinsic to his village culture, Kofi does at one point resolve to tend the bridge after the others leave, to be its priest, but he later learns that it doesn't need a priest; and he asks in vain of his bridgeman friend (ironically named Emmanuel), "What will I do now?" Kofi's answer comes in the story's penultimate scene. On the top beam of the completed bridge, he glimpses "other villages" and "the new road" connecting them that would soon reach through the forest to his own village, a road that, he realizes in a flash of insight, "would string both village and bridge as a single bead on its giant thread." Exultant at this vision of connectedness, and at the accompanying realization that bridgemen too could separate but be linked together with their "brothers" in other villages and on other bridges, he understands his vision of community is too narrow, that other people can have different but meaningful beliefs and perspectives.

In this sense, the bridge serves as a symbolic means of crossing a cultural gap, of relating to another perspective, and the new road represents both a coherent outside world and the oncoming future, while the river, rather than simply symbolizing cultural division, becomes something that can be crossed. Similarly, Kofi is the cultural bridgeman who, though he dies because he does not yet fully understand the way to survive in the intercultural world (he looks directly up at the sun, which no regular bridgeman would do), does bring different cultures together, his death serving as a means for the villagers to reconcile old and new worlds. In this regard he truly serves as the tomorrow-tamer for his people, the one who converts the future from something threatening into something less dangerous, more understandable.

The rest of the story can also be seen in symbolic terms. When, in the second paragraph, the young Kofi runs "past" (repeated six times) the sacred grove, the shrine, the graves, the old huts, the old men, and even the good huts, the suggestion is made that Africa cannot stand still, that the traditional past will be put behind and replaced by a changing future. When this is followed by paragraphs describing the "Hail Mary Chop-Bar & General Merchant" shop and the delivery truck "God Helps Those," the intermingling of old and new religions is conveyed. When the bulldozers destroy the sacred grove, they reenact the destruction of African tradition and religion engineered by the Western European nations, an onslaught with technological and economic as well as religious, racial, cultural, and political dimensions. And, when village families are disrupted by the culturally different blacks from coast, city and desert, the difficulties of impending independence in a tribally divided nation are portrayed. In such ways is Laurence's story both sensitive and prescient.

—John Robert Sorfleet

TONIO KRÖGER
by Thomas Mann, 1903

Written in 1903 when he was 28 years old, "Tonio Kröger" is a self-portrait of Thomas Mann as an emerging artist. It is a miniature Bildungsroman that traces some elements in the making of the artist from when he is 14 years old to when he is just past the age of 30. A classic study of the Romantic conception of the artistic temperament as it had developed throughout the 19th century (Goethe's Young Werther and Byron come to mind in places), the story is perhaps the last gasp of these ideas before the fracture of modernism and world war.

Tonio Kröger, like Mann, himself, is of bourgeois family, son of a respected grain merchant; but as he is also the son of a Latin mother who is unconcerned about bourgeois values, he is at once split and somewhat alienated from his north-German contemporaries. Thus we first meet him at the age of 14, already an oddity at school, an outsider whose poetry is laughed at by boys and masters alike but who nonetheless feels a deep love for the blonde athletic Hans Hansen, unintellectual but full of an uncomplicated vivacity. The dark Kröger, all soul and mind, loves, but is infinitely estranged from, the northern blue-eyed simplicity of normal life.

At the age of 16 Kröger falls in love with Inge, the girl from the house opposite his parents' house, who is another incarnation of the blonde, blue-eyed energy of the northern races. He is gradually cured of this obsession not by another personal love but by his developing artistic life. His father dies, his mother marries an artist from the south and drifts away into an unknown blue distance, the house is sold, the grain business wound up. Kröger is alone, living primarily an inward existence—others look out of windows, Kröger stands looking at a blind without realising what he is doing, for his vision is "within."

He travels south, to lands where art is traditionally more highly valued; he tries debauchery but it palls. The central part of the story is taken up with a long explanation Kröger gives of himself to an artist friend in Munich. He realises that he wants an audience of mindless "blue-eyed ones" so

he travels north again, though this is 13 years later and he 30 years old. He revisits his old home, now a public library, and travels on to a Danish holiday resort by the Baltic. Here he recognises Hans and Inge, presumably married, in a party of day-tourists who come to a dance at the hotel where he is staying. He does not reveal himself and the action of the story closes with him lying on his bed listening to "life's lulling, trivial waltz rhythm" coming faintly from below. In a coda, a letter to his friend in Munich, Kröger proclaims his double allegiance, both to the life of art and to his own bourgeois roots.

This novella, besides having a directly explanatory role as far as Mann's own life is concerned, summarises a number of themes in his major novels. The struggle between art and other forms of life is the stuff of which his monumental Doctor Faustus is made, for instance, and time and again he would return to the figure of the suffering, sensitive soul, often an artist, and his attempts to strike a balance with the world. The themes are boldly handled. The soul of the artist, like the souls of all people, is divided between blonde and dark, that is, between the cold light of the north and the passionate darkness of the south. At first this is an unbearable division; as a young man he feels "flung about" between "icy intellect and scorching sense," or, to put it more simply, the mind and the body. At first, too, it seems that the artist must belong irrevocably to the south and to the darkness for the artist is obliged to *dance* while the Hanses and Inges *sleep*; the artist must suffer while the others exist in comfort.

However, this simple opposition has to be broken down. Kröger, even 13 years later, is jealous of Hans and Inge, he expresses a longing for "the average, unendowed, respectable human being" which is a force that has to be set against his earlier "surrender" to the "power of the word." He is a great artist but he despises the trappings of artistic bohemia. The circle is squared in the final letter to Lisabeta: he realises that although he is an artist he is a *bourgeois* artist and that his soul does not wish to reject the everyday but to use it (as Mann himself would do with such success in his own realist fiction). Above all, there is a virtue in the bourgeois world that is unknown to the cruel world of the artist (Kröger calls literature a "curse") and that virtue is love. The poet is made of his surrender to the word but he is also made of love—Mann actually quotes St. Paul's famous definition of charity in this context. The feelings of love with which the story opened, although adolescent infatuations, now take on, as Kröger watches Hans and Inge and their uncomplicated joy, a deeper meaning. He is the lonely Romantic artist and he suffers and feels alienated; his parents and house are gone; he is neither of the north or the south; but he is the artist who has loved, and out of the endless connectivity of love he will forge his art.

This story is Mann's Portrait of the Artist or even his Sons and Lovers or A la recherche. It balances "man's innate craving for the comfortable," which it does not condemn, with the torture and ecstasy of poetic creation, which it sees as a fate more than gift.

—Lance St. John Butler

A TRAGEDY OF TWO AMBITIONS
by Thomas Hardy, 1888

Thomas Hardy published four volumes of short stories in addition to his fourteen novels. These stories do not rise to the epic intensity of his greatest fiction but they are well-crafted; their tendencies are summarised in the titles of the first two collections Hardy published: *Wessex Tales* (1888) with its promise of regionality and a folk tradition, and *Life's Little Ironies* (1894) with its promise of bizarre but homely coincidence. Often these stories sketch out ideas and plots that, without being blueprints for the novels, at least deal with the same material.

"A Tragedy of Two Ambitions," in *Wessex Tales*, works some of the same ground that would be covered in *Jude the Obscure* a few years later and, like that novel, it also works over some of the material from Hardy's own life. Cornelius and Joshua are sons of a millwright, a small tradesman in much the same social position as Hardy's own father, a small builder; we first meet them studying the Greek New Testament, the book from which the call of the flesh will distract Jude. These two are training for ordination into the Anglican priesthood, as Hardy himself considered doing in spite of his humble origins. What threatens constantly to undermine their efforts is their drunken father; he wastes the small legacy that would have sent them to Oxford or Cambridge and several times seems likely to upset their careful attempts to achieve ordination by the second-best route via a theological college. In spite of adversity and the absence of a real vocation, the brothers do eventually become Anglican priests, but by then a virtual parricide has blighted their chances of happiness and success.

Joshua and Cornelius have a beloved younger sister, Rosa, whom they have managed, in spite of poverty, to educate as a lady, sending her to finishing school in Brussels. They send their increasingly unpresentable father off to Canada with his new gipsy wife. The father returns and threatens to make himself known to Rosa's about-to-be fiancé, the young squire Albert Fellmer—whose connection will set the seal on the brothers' social ambitions. Hardy manages the story's climax by having the brothers follow their drunk father across the fields towards the house where the young squire is about to propose to Rosa; they try to dissuade him from blighting their hopes by intruding on the occasion but he is adamant; as he walks ahead of them they hear him fall into a weir where he drowns; they do not attempt to rescue him until it is too late. Rosa marries the squire and the brothers rise in the church but their efforts, though outwardly successful, seem to bring them little satisfaction. At the end the elder and more ambitious of them, Joshua, even wishes he had stuck to his father's trade.

The story opens and closes with a reference to St. Paul's Epistle to the Hebrews; a passage from its is quoted, in Greek, at the end of the story and translated by Hardy: "To have *endured* the cross, *despising* the shame—there lay greatness!" Cornelius, the less worldly of the brothers, cites this passage to demonstrate the complete opposition between the brothers' idea of greatness and the spirit of a true Christianity. Instead of enduring and despising the shame, the brothers have had purely worldly ambitions, only wanting to be ordained for the social status and financial reward of being clergymen. Here is a moral tale, typical of one late-19th century view of Christianity; Hardy was able to accept many of the ethical doctrines of the church (charity, humility) but was not able to believe the metaphysical doctrines it preached and was made anxious by the worldly advantages that accrued to Anglican vicars. As the narrator comments at the beginning, however, the Epistle to the Hebrews is "difficult."

At the end of the story the brothers revisit the site of their father's death and they discover that his stick, which he had cut from a silver poplar and which they had stuck into the mud beside the water, has sprouted and is now in full leaf. This obvious reference to Aaron's rod in the Book of Numbers is puzzling. Aaron is shown to be just and true when God singles out his rod to flower and it seems hard to see how this can apply to the drunken and aggressive old millwright. Two interpretations offer themselves; one is simply Hardy's interest in murder stories and in the tradition that the murdered man will somehow make a sign that will incriminate the murderers. The other is that Joshua and Cornelius's father in fact represents something more worthwhile than we might suppose; he is, for instance, at least honest and vigorous, able to attract women, even gipsy women, and thus full of life. His sprouting rod might thus take on phallic overtones, as it does in D.H. Lawrence, and the brothers would stand condemned as having wasted their lives working away at dead languages in order to qualify themselves to be ministers of a dead religion in which, in the end, they do not even believe. The title of the story seems to hint at something like this; the tragedy is that of wasted lives and it is almost classical in its pattern: *hubris* besets the brothers, they attempt to rise too high and an action of their own condemns them not to enjoy the fruits of their efforts.

Readers of *Tess of the D'Urbervilles* will recognize some aspects of Angel Clare's brothers in Joshua and Cornelius; elsewhere in Hardy can be found a motif of floating corpses; more significantly, throughout Hardy the matter of social class is of immense importance. In this story it is put into the place that Hardy often seems to want to assign it to: pursued too ruthlessly, class ambition is deadly; even as an atheist Hardy evidently thought that a Christian life was preferable to a socially successful one.

—Lance St. John Butler

THE TRAIN FROM RHODESIA
by Nadine Gordimer, 1952

"The Train from Rhodesia" is an early story by Nadine Gordimer, one of many that reflect her concern with the relations between blacks and whites in South Africa. The story (collected in *The Soft Voice of the Serpent*) deals with the economic discrepancies between the races and the shame aroused by the resultant exploitation of poor black by rich white. Written by a less talented writer, the story could have been more like a tract than a story; but Gordimer has followed her own distinction between the propagandist, who tells others what they must do or believe, and the artist. The message is implicit in the story: instead of exhortation, it is conveyed by suggestion, above all through the experience and perception of the young woman on the train. She is nameless, like all the other characters, who are given thereby a representative quality, an archetypal reality (the stationmaster, the "piccanins" who beg, the artists trying to sell their carved animals to tourists). Even her new husband is "the young man," who bargains with "the old man" for the wooden lion she admires.

The details of the story, sharply observed but subtly woven into its delicate texture, are among its most impressive features, in the lightly drawn details of the remote rural setting and the impoverished (in many senses) characters. The time of day is given only in the "red horizon" of the "flushed and perspiring west"; the place and people rendered in an easy, unforced accumulation of little touches. Repetition achieves much, as in the suggestive references to dust and to emptiness, but its use is never obtrusive. The repetition of "one-and-six" suggests the noise of the train. Even the much-mentioned "sand" is most effective in its less obvious metaphorical applications: "the sand became the sea, and closed over the children's black feet softly and without imprint"; the woman's hot shame "sounded in her ears like the sound of sand pouring. Pouring, pouring." The psychological detailing is perhaps most notable of all, as in the gradual accumulation of hints about the woman's attitude to her recent marriage. She has an odd sense of her husband being part of the unreality of the holiday rather than somehow permanent, and her inner turmoil over the carved lion reveals a void of feeling that she had thought was something to do with her single life before her marriage, "with being alone and belonging too much to oneself."

Passages about the train itself are prominent in the story, notably in the two isolated introductory and concluding paragraphs. One aspect of its personification is extraordinary: it calls out, and gets no answer from the sky, neither when it approaches the station nor when it leaves:

> The train had cast the station like a skin. It called out to the sky, I'm coming, I'm coming; and again, there was no answer.

This is how the story ends. There is no "answer," no glib response to the questions raised by the story, but it has the suggestive resonance that has been sounded throughout. Gordimer would agree with Chekhov that, unlike the propagandist, the artist does not need to provide answers, only to pose the questions properly. She does so with immediacy, concreteness, descriptive and analytical power, and great tact in her moments of vision, hearing, and understanding.

—Michael Herbert

THE TRAVELLING GRAVE
by L.P. Hartley, 1948

If it is one of the aims of the horror tale to question our certainties and to hint at the mysterious world below the surface of everyday reality, then L.P. Hartley showed himself to be a master of the genre. In no other story did he tackle the conundrum with such wit and gusto than in "The Travelling Grave," a later piece that rests on an understanding that the visible world is surrounded by unknown forces of malignancy and evil.

That awareness is immediately apparent in the uneasy atmosphere of the opening paragraphs. Hugh Curtis, a foppish yet diffident young man, has received an invitation to spend the weekend with Dick Munt, an acquaintance of one of his friends, the vain and voluble Valentine Ostrop. Although he is intrigued by the invitation he senses a sinister undertone in the invitation which he cannot explain to himself. As the time of departure approaches, his anxiety increases and he starts thinking up absurd excuses to justify a change of plan. However, his natural diffidence prevents him from doing anything other than proceeding

with his preparations, even though a second sense warns him that all might not be well.

Hartley handles Hugh Curtis's indecision with masterly understatement: although we recognise his alarm, there is also a strong hint that his trepidation might be caused by nothing other than nerves, to which Curtis seems to be prone. Hartley has already set the seal on the man's personality by describing him as "a vague man with an unretentive mind." In other words, he takes the world for granted and it is this lack of curiosity that almost leads to his undoing.

In contrast, his friend Ostrop is all sensation and bombast. Having arrived early at Munt's country seat (remote country houses are favoured settings in Hartley's Gothic short fiction), Ostrop meets the sinister Tony Bettisher, who allows him to make a fool of himself by prattling over-eagerly about Dick Munt and his curious interests.

This is a richly comic scene in which Hartley counter-points Bettisher's taciturnity with Ostrop's foolish questions about their host. During the course of their conversation, in answer to a question about Munt's hobbies, Bettisher allows Ostrop to believe that their mutual friend collects perambulators. Tellingly, both men agree that all collecting is a form of vice.

At this point Munt makes a silent entrance and demands to know what they have been discussing. Ostrop blusters about the hobbies and starts discussing the matter of perambulators. They are good for carrying bodies, he says. They perform a useful function but he tries to avoid them because he does not "care to contemplate lumps of human flesh lacking the spirit that makes flesh tolerable." Above all, they need to be occupied yet need someone to push them.

Little does he know that Munt is a collector of coffins and that he has brought back from foreign parts one that can pursue its victims and bury them without any external assistance. Although the conversational contrast between perambulators and coffins has been carried along with great wit and humour, Hartley allows a darker mood to intrude. While the men talk dusk falls on the house and they are given a demonstration of the sinister coffin's abilities to chase after its victims.

What follows next is Hartley at his best. Munt encourages his two guests to play hide-and-seek before Hugh Curtis arrives, the better to surprise him. The symbolism is clear: the children's game becomes a motif for the coffin's purpose, a dark hint of the mysterious evil which Munt has brought into his house and means to use. (He has already ascertained that Curtis is a bachelor without close family; in other words, the ideal victim.)

However, Ostrop overhears Munt plotting to let the coffin loose on his unsuspecting guest and is thoroughly terrified by what he hears. Hartley underscores the horror of the scene by making Munt's voice seem "unfamiliar," "greedy," and "peevish," almost as if he has split into two incompatible halves. The sense of otherness and forboding is increased by the fact that all the lights in the house have been switched off at the mains and the entire action is spent in darkness. Everything in the house might seem familiar but there is evil at the hart of normality.

Just before Curtis arrives, Ostrop carries the dreaded coffin into a neighbouring room, locks the door, and goes downstairs to warn his astonished friend. On one level the conclusion is anti-climactic: the men dress for dinner but cannot find Munt. But the real horror is still to come. In Curtis's room a pair of shoes is found, soles uppermost but set fast in the floor. Try as they will Curtis and Ostrop fail to move them until they decide to unlace one of them:

inside is a sock with a human foot attached. Munt has been snapped up by the very coffin he was attempting to set on his unsuspecting guest. A further touch of irony is provided by the fact that Ostrop placed the coffin in the room meant for Curtis, not knowing that Munt was already hiding there.

Although the plot of "The Travelling Grave" is far-fetched, there is a satisfying metaphysical conceit in the symbolism of the man-eating coffin which eventually kills its devious owner. What began as a game ends in death. This is no isolated slaying but a reminder that evil has its own laws and that in disobeying them, Munt has met a deserved end.

—Trevor Royle

THE TREE (El árbol)
by María Luisa Bombal, 1941

Along with her novella *La última niebla (The House of Mist)*, "El árbol" ("The Tree") is the most recognized work by the Chilean María Luisa Bombal. The story is characteristic of Bombal's work in that it presents a poetically-rendered reality and the theme of a woman's isolated and marginalized existence in search of love, communication, and understanding.

The protagonist's tale is a recollection, during a concert, of her past life. As Brígida listens to a pianist, she evokes her solitary and misunderstood life with a family who find her simple, and a husband who ignores her. In the gum tree of the title, which not only serves as her sole companion but also shields her from the ugliness of the outside world, Brígida seeks comfort and fulfillment. Her inner sanctum is invaded, however, when the tree is cut down. The harsh, raw light and din from the city streets penetrate her solitude, bringing her tragic life into focus for both Brígida and the reader.

Although the themes of the misunderstood woman and the clash between reality and illusion border on cliche, Andrew P. Debicki asserts that the story's complex structure keeps Bombal away from this danger. By means of a delicate interweaving of the present and the past, as well as the protagonist's outer and inner realities, Bombal communicates in a concise and vivid manner a woman's existentialist plight.

The most notable element of the story is the contrast between a vigorous narrative movement and the protagonist's static life. The structure oscillates between two types of realities, the temporal and the spatial. The first establishes a three-part framework in which Brígida listens to the piano music, recreating key moments of her past. The other movement emphasizes space, with the evocation of Brígida's shady and protective bedroom and its transformation by the outside world. The denouement brings both the action and the recollection to a crashing halt as the pianist finishes his performance. The audience's applause emulates the felling of the tree, an act that invades Brígida's consciousness and solitude, merging her solitary past with the present. Reality and illusion clash vividly in this tragic outcome.

The stylistic and structural elements of the story revolve around three concrete elements—music, water, and the gum tree. As the pianist begins the concert with Mozart (or perhaps Scarlatti, Brígida speculates), the music leads the protagonist "by the hand," to evoke her youth in lyrical

terms. The scene of a young girl on a bridge, by a quiet brook, is offset by recollections of a motherless upbringing, and scorn and indifference on the part of her family. The white dress of her memory contrasts vividly with her black concert attire, which reminds the reader of Brígida's present mechanical existence. The delicate music and the brook blend powerfully to embody the strength of Brígida's illusion, which has allowed her to survive her misunderstood childhood and solitary adult life.

In the middle of the story's tripartite structure, the music shifts to Beethoven. The water image becomes that of the sea, broadening and strengthening the reader's consciousness of Brígida's tragedy. Since she demonstrates awareness of the composer in this segment of the program, we divine her maturity and understanding of her own life. Beethoven's powerful chords also suggest summer scenes, of Brígida's marriage to an older man, as well as the tree's growing prominence in her life. Luis, a condescending man who treats Brígida as a child, displays the solid qualities of the gum tree. However, unlike the tree, he offers his wife practical solutions but no sense of comfort nor protection. As the marriage deteriorates, the tree becomes a substitute for the compassionate man for whom Brígida longs. At this point in the story, Bombal presents the tree in an archetypal light, as a "world submerged in an aquarium," and a refuge for all the neighborhood birds. Recalling the Yggdrasil of Norse mythology, this joyful embodiment of nature contrasts vividly with Brígida's stuffy and glum house which, in turn, is a metaphor for her marriage.

Chopin's "Etudes," in the third part of the concert, spotlight the story's resolution. Rain, through the gum tree, enters the segment of Brígida's life that marks the end of her relationship with Luis. Ironically, at this point the personified tree becomes the stabilizing force that keeps Brígida in her place; its "knuckles" rapping on the windowpane, it urges Brígida to remain with her husband and to accept his practical and unimaginative perspective. An autumnal landscape blends with an acceptance of the tree as a mature and natural companion. Falling leaves accentuate Brígida's melancholy realization that her longing will be unfulfilled, that alienation will be her permanent condition. As she philosophizes on the impossibility of attaining happiness, the narrative pauses and Brígida reacts.

At what appears to be an intermission, time and space become blurred as we are abruptly transported to Brígida's bed chamber. The music's end recalls the axe's sound and the tree's fall; the auditorium lights evoke for the reader the "terrifying" glare that overtakes the room. Recalling Luis's justification for progress and community relations, Brígida confronts the new reality without the tree. In a powerful image, her room shrinks before our eyes, as she becomes aware of an enormous skyscraper which has replaced the tree. As she looks out the window, a narrow alley offers the picture of a bright red service station and boys playing soccer, reminders of the progressive and practical modern world to which the natural, illusory life is sacrificed. Brígida leaves Luis, resigned to a childless, lonely existence in the midst of a vulgar world.

In this story, Bombal effectively develops a conflict through her protagonist's sensitive outlook. The intricate structure and effective use of concrete imagery contribute to a vivid portrayal of the protagonist's agonies, providing the reader with a universal experience of isolation and alienation in a changing world.

—Stella T. Clark

A TREE, A ROCK, A CLOUD
by Carson McCullers, 1951

Carson McCullers's career in fiction, which she launched with her astoundingly precocious masterpiece in 1940, *The Heart Is a Lonely Hunter*, weakened in later years partly because of serious physical afflictions, including the effects of rheumatic fever in childhood, two severely damaging strokes during her twenties, repeated bouts of pneumonia, and breast cancer. The best work of her later years therefore tended to occur in the less demanding shorter forms like novellas and short stories, in which she clarified the themes she had originally dramatized in that first, major novel. The theme of loneliness, for example, is masterfully rendered in the novella *The Ballad of the Sad Café*, and the human propensity to favor illusion over reality dominates the short story, "Madame Zilensky and the King of Finland." (She will not acknowledge that Finland is a republic and has no king.)

The central achievement of "A Tree, A Rock, A Cloud" (first published in 1942, and collected in *The Ballad of the Sad Café*) is to illuminate the most important philosophical underpinning of her first novel, the pantheism of the philosopher Spinoza. This 17th-century Dutch Jew was the first Western thinker to resolve the conflict between religion and its apparent deadly adversary of that time, the newly developing natural sciences. Spinoza's contribution was to identify God and Nature as one and the same, thereby laying the foundation for the pantheism of the Romantic and Transcendentalist movements a century and a half later. "The highest good," Spinoza maintained, "is the mind's union with the whole of nature." We should note carefully the intellectual character of this construct, which emphasizes the mind's union with nature. A secondary Spinozan precept, which greatly enthralled the German Romantic poet Goethe, is the notion that those who love this God cannot expect to be loved in return: God/Nature is not a personal deity who recognizes our individual identities.

Because "A Tree, A Rock, A Cloud" develops these Spinozan precepts in cogent detail, the story is best understood in light of the Spinozan presence in *The Heart Is a Lonely Hunter*. Here four of the main characters are associated with the philosopher. Dr. Copeland religiously studies Spinoza, and he thinks John Singer, the deaf mute, "resembled somewhat a picture of Spinoza. A Jewish face." The actual Jewish character, Harry Minowitz (originally designated the book's main character), "was a Pantheist. Harry believed that after you were dead and buried you changed to plants and fire and dirt and clouds and water. It took thousands of years and then finally you were a part of all the world." And Biff Brannon, the novel's spiritual hero, is the truest Spinozan of all. Descended from "a Jew from Amsterdam" (Spinoza's city), he runs his cafe as a sort of True Church where the book's lonely people can commune together. As a reward, he is vouschafed the book's concluding vision of "the endless fluid passage of humanity through endless time." Importantly, he achieves that Spinozan overview only by relinquishing his focus on a single love-object, Mick Kelly.

In "A Tree, A Rock, A Cloud," the equivalent of Biff Brannon is the stranger who says "I love you" to a paperboy in an all-night cafe (again a site for community). This is not a homosexual overture on the man's part; it is rather his way of introducing "the science of love"—a phrase that reminds us of "the mind's union with the whole

of nature" in Spinoza. Like Biff Brannon, the man arrived at his science of love only after giving up his focus on a single love object—his wife, who has run off with another man. "All I had ever felt was gathered together around this woman," he tells the boy; "for the better part of two years I chased around the country trying to lay hold of her." Not until the fifth year of her absence did the Spinozan vision bring its healing. Its first phase required displacing the false love object (the following quotations are abbreviated from McCullers's story):

> I meditated on love and reasoned it out. I realized what is wrong with us. Men fall in love for the first time. And what do they fall in love with? . . . A woman. . . .They start at the wrong end of love. They begin at the climax. . . .Son, do you know how love should be begun? . . . A tree, a rock, a cloud.

This last phrase clearly denotes the Spinozan principle that those who love God truly cannot expect to be loved in return. "I started very cautious," he goes on to say; "I bought a goldfish and I concentrated on the goldfish and I loved it. I graduated from one thing to another. Day by day I was getting this technique." By staying with it for six years, the man has now achieved the full measure of pantheistic consciousness, the mind's union with the whole of reality without need for reciprocal love:

> And now I am a master, Son. I can love anything. . . .I see a street full of people and a beautiful light comes in me. I watch a bird in the sky. Or I meet a traveler on the road. Everything, Son. And anybody. All stranger and all loved!

As usual in McCullers's work, this state of enlightenment is not widely shared. The newsboy takes the stranger's last words— "Remember, I love you"—as a sign of derangement: "Was he drunk? . . . a dope fiend?" (Biff Brannon, too, was greatly misunderstood by the beneficiaries of his psychic generosity.) But what matters most in McCullers's fiction is the effect of the Spinozan insight on its practitioner—an ability to escape the psychological vicious cycle that moves from loneliness to love of the wrong object and back to worsened loneliness. By not requiring reciprocal love from a tree, a rock, or a cloud, the pantheistic visionary is freed from the cruel fluctuations of interpersonal emotional dependence. It is, however, a prudent concession to psychological realism on McCullers's part to portray this capacity for cosmic love as the property of only a few spiritually superior characters.

—Victor Strandberg

THE TRUE STORY OF AH Q (Ah Q zhengzhuan)
by Lu Xun, 1923

By far the most famous, if not the greatest, of modern Chinese stories, "Ah Q zhengzhuan" ("The True Story of Ah Q") was published more than 70 years ago in 1921 and collected in 1923 in *Na Han* (*Call to Arms*), and the name of its protagonist has become a household word. Lu Xun has added a vivid and striking type to the rich gallery of characters in world literature with Ah Q, who represents typical traits not only of the Chinese but of people everywhere. As one critic puts it, Ah Q is "an international everyman."

However, the extraordinary exaggerations of Ah Q's clownish propensities on occasion (for example, his disappointment in not finding enough lice in his jacket) lend an unrealistic and inhuman quality to the story, making questionable the view that this story is Lu Xun's most successful work. Even the author himself admitted that some descriptions might sound "too exaggerated," yet he defended them on the ground that life in China had become so shocking and abnormal that any realistic presentation would seem "grotesque" to foreigners or future generations. This explanation does not eliminate our impression that he is treating a character and a setting not entirely familiar to him, although his taut sentences and limpid delineations help bring into focus the lifestyle of an epoch now only dimly perceived by contemporary readers, many of whom, for instance, would not understand the protagonist's name—why the author chose the letter "Q" instead of a Chinese ideograph—if Zhou Zuoren, the author's younger brother (a famous essayist), had not revealed that Lu Xun was fascinated by the resemblance between the letter "Q" and a head with a pigtail hanging down.

The most significant part of the story is its introduction (chapter I). The style of this opening section is not that of a storyteller, but of a *zawen* (miscellaneous essay) writer— sarcastic, contentious, sophisticated, and tinged with wit and humor. The targets of ridicule happen to be researchers ("disciples of Dr. Hu Shi") and biographers, two of the many catagories of Chinese characters normally satirized by the author. This is vintage Lu Xun, who is essentially a lashing modern prose satirist rather than a narrator of fictional tales. The best portion of the story is the two accounts of Ah Q's "victories" (chapters II and III), which reveal most tellingly two sides of the protagonist: Ah Q the victim and Ah Q the clown.

Critics have dwelt extensively and repeatedly on Ah Q the victim; very little can be added to their observations. As they point out, Ah Q's "victories" are actually his defeats, and his forgetfulness is a kind of self-deception; both are necessary to alleviate the pain and misery in his life. The author suggests that in traditional society, people like Ah Q are always losers because at the critical moment progressive elements, represented by the Qian family, and conservative elements, represented by the Zhao family, always join forces to protect their own interests and to suppress and exploit weak and poor people like Ah Q. This is seen in the incident of the successful county candidate and the Bogus Foreign Devil going together to the convent to carry out their "revolutionary" activities. It is not surprising that Ah Q is manipulated to become a scapegoat. On the other hand, slave mentality also makes Ah Q, when armed with real or imaginary power, a victimizer, enslaving and persecuting his own kind, as can be seen in his mistreatments of the little nun and Young D. As an avenger, he proves just as tyrannical as, if not more cruel than, his persecutors.

Lu Xun's outlook on life is often too austere, too cynical to permit any comic vision. But this story was originally published in a column titled "Cheerful Chat" of the *Morning Post*, and, as the author explains, in order to be "cheerful," he had to add "unnecessary humor" that "did not suit" the story as a whole. This explanation accounts for the use of burlesque, which is so obvious in the portrait

of Ah Q the clown as "always exultant"—a proof of "the moral supremacy of China over the rest of the world!" Such barbed witticism in a humorous context indicates that Lu Xun, after all, is a satirist rather than a humorist. To quote his own words: "I do not like 'humor' and believe that the only gentlemen who can enjoy it are those who like to sit around and shoot the breeze. In China it is even difficult to find a translation for this word."

Chinese readers more easily comprehend the significance of "The True Story of Ah Q" than foreigners do because it bitterly reminds them of the most unforgetful part of modern Chinese history—the frustrations and humiliations inflicted upon China by Japan and Western countries. Weichuang, the setting of "The True Story of Ah Q," has been regarded as a symbol of "microcosmic China," the unnamed town as "foreign power," and Ah Q as "the incarnation of the Chinese masses." He is therefore not an individual in contemporary society, but a composite character, and "a summation of all the roles a man may play in Chinese society." It is with this exact image in mind that Lu Xun dramatizes in significant human terms Ah Q's problems of how to obtain a wife and how to make a living (in chapters IV to VI). The sting of his satire is aimed not so much at the protagonist as at his world.

Chapters VII and VIII deal with the 1911 Revolution and contain some fantastic details that make "revolution" sound somewhat like a joke. However, the author is serious here. These two chapters can lend themselves to a variety of interpretations, most of which focus on the meaning of revolution—what it means and does to the masses. Lu Xun seems to imply that the revolution, which made China a republic, only effected a change of names, not a fundamental change of heart. The new regime is as corrupt as the old. This point becomes even more obvious in the last chapter, when Ah Q is executed for a crime he did not commit. Its title alone, "The Grand Happy Ending," is ironic enough to deal a fatal blow to the claim that the 1911 Revolution was a success; in fact, it means hopes betrayed and ideals caricatured. Ah Q's unuttered cry for help in the finale is also a remarkable piece of irony, bringing home the chilling fact that his life ends at the exact moment when he begins to understand himself and his world.

—Sherwin S.S. Fu

TUESDAY SIESTA (La siesta del Martes)
by Gabriel García Márquez, 1962

Some of Gabriel García Márquez's best short stories are found in the collection first published in 1962 in Mexico, *Los funerales de la mamá grande, (Big Mama's Funeral)*. Several have been judged the most perfect examples of the genre ever written in Latin America. Most of them were written during the difficult late 1950's when García Márquez lived frugally in Europe and Venezuela. He submitted one of these stories, "La siesta del Martes" ("Tuesday Siesta,") to a short story context sponsored by the Caracas newspaper *El Nacional*, but it failed to receive even an honorable mention. Several years later his close friend Alvaro Mutis sent him a note from a Mexican prison where he was serving time, asking for something to read. García Márquez sent him the manuscript of eight short stories, and Mutis in turn lent them to the budding young

Mexican writer, Elena Poniatowska, who misplaced them. When they subsequently were found, Mutis was able to have them published by the University of Veracruz Press under the general title of the longest story, "Big Mama's Funeral." García Márquez received an advance of a thousand pesos, about a hundred dollars at the time, but the volume attracted little attention until after the publication of *Cien años de soledad (One Hundred Years of Solitude)* in 1967.

García Márquez considers "Tuesday Siesta" his best short story. It was inspired by the childhood memory of a woman and her daughter, both dressed in black with a black umbrella and a bouquet of flowers in their hands. They were walking down a dusty street in his native Aracataca in the hot afternoon sun. Someone told the young García Márquez that the woman was the mother of "that thief." This memory served as a model for "Tuesday Siesta," the tale of a proud woman and her daughter who visit a small, dusty town during the intense heat of a Tuesday afternoon. They have come for the express purpose of visiting the town's cemetery, where a week earlier the woman's son had been buried after being shot during a robbery attempt.

The heart of the story is an interview between the mother and the village priest, who controls the keys to the cemetery. The woman's daughter and the priest's sister, who serves as his housekeeper, are also present. The choice of Tuesday as the day of the action is no doubt based on the well-known Spanish proverb "martes, ni te cases ni te embarques, ni de tu familia te apartes" ("Tuesday, don't get married or take a trip, or leave your family"). The central idea, the dignity and pride of a poor woman in the face of ecclesiastical authority, is evident in the sparse dialogue between the mother and the housekeeper:

'I need the priest,' she said.
'He's sleeping now.'
'It's an emergency,' the woman insisted.

(translated by J.S. Bernstein)

When the priest finally appears, he suggests they wait until sundown. But the mother is firm and determined; the return train leaves at 3:30. The woman's son is nothing more than a petty thief in the eyes of the priest. The mother, however, sees the matter differently; he had promised her that he would never steal anything that someone else might need to survive, and he had kept his word. There is a clear delineation of the struggle between stealing in order to survive and dying of hunger. "He was a very good man," the mother concludes. "God's will is inscrutable," says the priest.

The conclusion is effectively stated in dramatic fashion. The priest and his sister, aware that groups of curious people have filled the streets, realize that the woman and her daughter will have to face a hostile crowd on their way to the cemetery. "Wait until the sun goes down," says the priest; "wait and I'll lend you a parasol," adds his sister. "Thank you . . . we're all right this way," the woman replies in a confident voice. Sure of herself and of the propriety of her actions, the mother and her daughter boldly face the ominous challenge of a hot Tuesday afternoon in the streets of an unfriendly town.

In his long interview with Plinio Apuleyo Mendoza, García Márquez recognizes his debt to Ernest Hemingway for certain "technical" aspects of this story. The most obvious technical aspect is García Márquez's use of Hemingway's "iceberg technique." Hemingway asserted that there is always seven-eighths of an iceberg under water for every part that shows; likewise, the short story should expose one-eighth of its totality, thereby leaving a large portion of the action unstated or understated. "Tuesday Siesta" is a prime example of this theory. No proper names are given to the four protagonists; the town's name is not given although there is abundant evidence that it is his legendary Macondo. García Márquez uses concise delineation of character and plot. Details of the son's past activities slowly emerge; before becoming a thief he was a boxer who tried to eke out a living for his family despite frequent severe injuries. In the process all his teeth had to be extracted. As the story develops, it affirms the social and economic disparity between the mother and daughter, and the priest and his sister.

The heaviness of the oppressive afternoon heat stands in contrast to the inner courage the mother demonstrates in the face of both the church and the unfriendly town. Her deep-seated strength and conviction make her a prototype of the strong female characters that García Márquez will evoke in future writings. It is essentially these strong female characters who hold Macondo together until its ultimate destruction at the end of *One Hundred Years of Solitude.* It should be noted that this destruction occurs only after the death of the principal matriarchal characters in the novel.

There is an important link between "Tuesday Siesta" and García Márquez's first novella, *La hojarasca* (1955; "Leafstorm," 1955). The novel's epigraph, taken from Sophocles's *Antigone,* speaks to the point of Antigone's struggle to give her brother a decent burial despite the edict of Creon, the tyrannical king, that anyone who attempts this "will die by public stoning." The defiance of a character who seeks to bury a person who has been harshly repudiated by the community is the gist of "Leafstorm." The dauntless mother in "Tuesday Siesta" is a modern Antigone who fearlessly faces the hostility of all of Macondo in order to pay her respects to her late son. *Antigone,* "Leafstorm," and "Tuesday Siesta" all end at the moment when the protagonists go out to confront a belligerent crowd. Their valor conveys a feeling of quiet dignity and moral authority.

This story outlines the theme of confrontation in a stagnant setting where change is slow if at all. Its protracted tension makes it a classic example of the best in Latin American fiction. At the same time it is important for its introduction of themes and ideas García Márquez will develop more fully in his later fiction.

—Harley D. Oberhelman

THE TURN OF THE SCREW
by Henry James, 1898

The Turn of the Screw is one of Henry James's longest stories (about 50,000 words), almost a short novel, and perhaps his most celebrated. It was instantly popular on publication (in 1898) and has remained so to the present. It is also one of the most discussed of James's works, not least because of its famous/notorious ambiguity. The story as such is crystal clear—there are no modernist obscurities; but its problems of interpretation are legion, making it a fascinating puzzle-piece. James himself seems to have preferred to keep it that way; in his series of prefaces written for the New York edition of his works, his remarks on *The Turn of the Screw* maintain an attitude of teasing inscrutability. He calls it "a piece of ingenuity pure and simple, of cold artistic calculation, an *amusette* to catch those not easily caught . . . , the jaded, the disillusioned, the fastidious"; and even in the more serious sentence which follows he speaks of it as being a study "of a conceived 'tone,' the tone of suspected and felt trouble, of an inordinate and incalculable sort—the tone of tragic, yet of exquisite, mystification."

The narrative method, as always with James, but especially his late period of the mid-1890's to the end of his career, is crucial. It is both heavily distanced—the story purports to be read by a man called Douglas to his fellow guests at a Christmas house-party from a manuscript given to him 40 years before, recording events still earlier than that—and markedly point-of-view oriented. The heroine, a governess employed by a handsome young man to look after his niece and nephew in an isolated country house called Bly, writes entirely in the first-person, a mode which James professed to dislike for its confessional fluidity, but which is here scrupulously controlled. Nothing has the authority of an omniscient narrator; everything is filtered through the governess's consciousness. To adapt what he later writes of Lambert Strether, hero of his novel, *The Ambassadors,* it is her sense of the things that happen, and hers only, which avail him for showing them. Consequently, an all-important question as to the reliability of the narrative arises; and among the many interpretative variations that result, two broad, and mutually incompatible, streams can be identified, which offer the governess as either protector of the threatened innocence of the two children, or neurotic victim of hallucinations which ultimately make her the baneful influence on her charges.

What the governess finds, or imagines, is that the children, Miles and Flora, are being haunted by the ghosts of their former governess, Miss Jessel, and their uncle's valet, Peter Quint, who reveal themselves in strange circumstances with the intention, it seems, of renewing, and deepening, the evil influence which they exercised on the children when alive. The relationship between the governess and the children proceeds, as the opening sentence of her narration indicates, "as a succession of flights and drops, a little seesaw of the right throbs and the wrong." She is astonished and delighted by the children's exceptional beauty and seemingly impeccable behaviour, but disturbed by a growing conviction that they hold an intercourse with Miss Jessel and Quint which they refuse to acknowledge, and which is all the more spiritually dangerous to them because of this refusal. It becomes the governess's mission to save them from perdition by bringing them to the point where they will of their own free will confess the true state of their relationship with Miss Jessel and Quint (who, significantly, had become the equivalent of tutor to Miles, as Miss Jessel was former governess to Flora). She sees herself as battling with vicious forces for the souls of her charges, as their guardian angel in an ultimate conflict between good and evil.

The story is powerful enough to carry this meaning, though its highly melodramatic ending casts doubt on how successful the governess has been in her struggle for the children's salvation. Her final tussle with Miles, in particular, must depend on the conviction that the loss of life (the boy dies at the moment of the governess's supposed triumph) is outweighed by comparison with the salvation of the soul. The Christian idea of the "fortunate fall" is perhaps what is alluded to when he utters "the cry of a creature hurled over an abyss," and the governess ecstatic-ally comments, "and the grasp with which I recovered him might have been that of catching him in his fall." This, perhaps, is the final seesaw of a drop followed by a flight. But even she only claims that it "might have been." The last sentence reads, "We were alone with the quiet day, and his little heart, dispossessed, had stopped." Here "dispossessed" can again be read positively, as the final casting out of the evil spirit; but the ultimate "stopped" more prosaically insists that what she truly held was a dead body. At the least an awful price has been paid for a spiritual victory. On this reading *The Turn of the Screw* is not a morality play, but a Christian tragedy.

However, another reading inevitably obtrudes itself. When the governess insists that Miles at last name the evil spirit, and he does so with "Peter Quint—you devil!" the "you" is ambiguous. It could be as much a denunciation of the governess as of Quint, whom he has never admitted to seeing, and even now still does not see. Throughout the story the only one to see the apparitions directly is the governess, which may be a tribute to her greater spiritual sensitivity, but also prompts questions about their objective existence, which, coupled with the subjectivity of the narrative itself, must raise doubts not only about her reliability, but also her sanity. On several occasions, most notably just before the climax, the governess entertains such doubts herself, and several of her own reactions she expresses in terms which suggest her awareness that they are capable of being construed as hysterical. (Her conviction that she is not "seeing things" depends a good deal on her having been able to describe to the housekeeper, Mrs. Grose, exactly what the apparition, then identified as Peter Quint, looks like, before she has any knowledge of the valet; but this is a local, rhetorical victory rather than a piece of indisputably objective evidence. *The Turn of the Screw* excites critical ingenuity, and explanations, convincing or otherwise, are not lacking.) Moreover, much of the circumstance of her story provides plausible material for regarding her as the victim of a frustrated passion for her employer (she is dreaming of him when she first "sees" Quint), and the underlying structure of reversed mirror images (gentlemanly employer versus caddish valet who wears his clothes and assumes his role at Bly; upward, if hopelessly, aspiring governess versus downward descending Miss Jessel; innocent girl and innocent boy versus their supposedly hidden, corrupt selves) points towards a fantasy-drama composed of the governess's own cult of respectability at war with unconscious and untamed desires. All of which makes for a tragedy of a different sort, part social, part psychological, of which the self-deceived governess is both the terrible and pitiable protagonist.

It may also be regarded as evidence of the narrator's unreliability that so little is revealed about the enormities supposedly committed by Quint and Miss Jessel, or the things said by Miles which led to his expulsion from school. Sex and drink, those very Victorian horrors, are vaguely hinted at; and in the background of the governess there is a veiled hint of hereditary madness. It is possible that more is not said because 19th-century society would not allow it. But the imprecision is also highly Jamesian, and done with malicious aforethought. In preface to the New York edition he insists that the work of particularisation is the reader's: "Make him *think* the evil, make him think it for himself, and you are released from weak specifications." More broadly, this is the essentially Jamesian technique of the whole story. It falls pat into the lap of modern reader-response theory. The story itself, as James puts it, is a "perfectly independent and irresponsible little fiction": the reader must construe it as intelligently as he may and shape his own meaning. It will yield different, and perhaps equally valid, interpretations. It is profoundly ambiguous, but not disablingly so, for it is a perpetual stimulus to the reader's imagination.

–R.P. Draper

TWENTY-SIX MEN AND A GIRL (Dvadtsat' shest' i odna)
by Maksim Gor'kii, 1899

Initially, the reader of "Dvadtsat' shest' i odna" ("Twenty-Six Men and a Girl") is most likely to be struck by the descriptive power of Gor'kii's writing. The story's opening has almost Dantesque quality about it. The 26 men of its title labour in an underground bakery (said to be based on Semyonov's bakery in Kazan, where Gor'kii worked for some time). The narrator is one of the 26 "animated machines." The basement in which they work is cut off from all natural light; its windows are barred, its walls filthy and mouldy, its ceiling wholly covered by cobwebs and soot. Fed on "putrid offal," the men's repetitive work is the very archetype of alienated labour. A cauldron bubbles in their cellar, which is dominated by the oven-furnace and its flames:

> From morning till night logs burned in one section of the oven, and the red reflections of the flame quivered on one of the walls of the bakers as if in mute mockery of us. The huge oven resembled the deformed head of a fabled monster. It seemed to project from under the floor, its gaping jaws bristling with bright fire, to breathe scorching heat upon us, watching our endless labors through a pair of black, hollow vents above the mouth of the oven. These two deep hollows were like the eyes—the pitiless and dispassionate eyes—of a monster: they always stared at us with the same dark gaze, as if tired of watching slaves at work and expecting nothing human from them; and they hated the slaves with all the frigid contempt of wisdom.

> (translated by George Reavey)

In some respects, the machine has more about it that is "human" than the men do; categories, categories essential to the retentions of human dignity, are blurred. If the 26 men are not yet in hell, they work daily before a veritable Hell-Mouth.

They find, and hold on to, a single speck of light—"a substitute for the sun"—in their darkness. This is Tanya, a sixteen-year-old housemaid who comes each morning for pretzels. She stands at the door of the basement, and the "dirty, ignorant deformed men" look up at her, since the door is at the head of the steps into the basement. Symbolically placed on her pedestal, Tanya serves as a kind of Petrarchan idealisation, a reassurance, or at any rate a token of the possibility, that there might be goodness and meaning in the world—however unattainable. The men "love" Tanya since, as the narrator observed, they had nobody else to love. But their love is founded so completely upon an idealisation that it can find no room for the actuality of Tanya's individuality. She becomes an idol rather than a person. They perform services for her—chopping wood and so on—but when one man asks her to repair his only shirt the request is deemed absurd.

There arrives, to work at the superior bakery next door, an ex-soldier, a devil-may-care seducer. In response to his bravado and his tales, the pretzel-makers offer their idol, Tanya, as a challenge: "We were terribly eager to test the fortitude of our idol: with great intensity we demonstrated to each other that our idol was a strong idol, that it would emerge victorious from this conflict." Tanya, of course, is ignorant of all this. Two weeks is agreed for the term of the test. For the men it is a time of heightened intensity—they are more alive, more intelligent than they have ever been.

On the last day of the "challenge" the men watch the soldier take Tanya to the cellar—that the snow on the roofs, as they watch and wait, should be "covered with a dirty brown deposit" is enough to tell them (and us) what has happened. As the two emerge from the cellar, the soldier appears unchanged, but Tanya has a new joy on her lips and in her eyes. "This we could not quietly accept," says the narrator. Their "love" for Tanya is not one that can bear to see her gain her happiness through the expression of her own natural sexuality. The 26 men surround and insult her; their idol has fallen, their lady has shown herself to be a human girl. Tanya walks away "upright, beautiful, and proud." The 26 men must return to their basement, this time deprived of the illusory comfort from their idealisation of Tanya.

The story may be read as wholly nihilistic. Or we may see in the conclusion the possibility, at least, that the 26 men, robbed of their escape into idealism, may now come to a fuller understanding of the nature of their own existence. Certainly the excitement of the challenge and the intensity of their reaction give them a momentary experience of a kind of vitality otherwise denied to them. Or we may feel that the tale's positives reside in the vitality of the ex-soldier and in Tanya's fulfilment of her own womanhood, her achievement of a confident selfhood beyond anything possible for her at the beginning of the tale. There is much that is ambiguous in Gor'kii's tale, a tale that is resonant with possibilities and power, a tale which is simultaneously a fable and a naturalistic narrative. In that simultaneity resides one of the many justifications for Gor'kii's subtitling his tale "Poem." There are reiterated images—of animals, religious ceremonial, light and heavenly bodies, for example—which give the narrative a densely worked poetic texture, and which carry much of its meaning and emotional power. Though "Twenty-Six Men and a Girl" is deeply embedded in the social conditions of the period in which it was composed (it was first published in the magazine *Zhizn* in 1899), it is in no sense limited by those circumstances; it raises issues of a much wider nature.

—Glyn Pursglove

THE TWO DROVERS
by Sir Walter Scott, 1827

Sir Walter Scott is known more than read nowadays. His achievement in bringing fiction and history (especially that of Scotland) into a mutually enriching relationship was celebrated by Georg Lukacs in *The Historical Novel,* but there is still a tendency to see his novels as picturesque and romantic, the bases for children's television series, rather than, in F.R. Leavis's favoured term, mature. Certainly the novels—favourite family reading for the Victorians—may now seem over-long. But the short stories brought together in *Chronicles of the Canongate* in 1827 show Scott as a careful observer of society as well as a benign moralist.

Scott's narrative mode is certainly a leisurely one. The reader of "The Two Drovers" is given a full account of the habits of the Highland drovers, who took the cattle the several hundred miles from the Scottish markets to the farms of their purchasers in England, before the introduction of the two central characters. The narrator gives plenty of information about the Highlanders, often using Gaelic terms like *skene-dhu*, but explaining them ("dirk, or black-knife") as he goes along. The reader is clearly being invited to look at the manners and behaviour of a social group not likely to be familiar to him or her.

The story itself, as is characteristic of Scott, suggests the folktale in its simplicity. We see the lively and attractive young Scot, Robin Oig, about to set out, and accosted at the last minute by his aged aunt, Janet of Tomohourich, who performs a ceremony of farewell that is suddenly interrupted with her exclamation, "Grandson of my father, there is blood on your hand." This she then describes as "English blood," calling on Robin not to go to England, or at least not to wear his dirk. Robin humours her by giving the dirk to a Lowlander, who is travelling the same route, to carry for him.

All this is before the reader has been introduced to Robin's friend and fellow-drover, the Yorkshireman Harry Wakefield, a strong man and an expert wrestler. The prolepsis is obvious. The reader will certainly expect something disastrous to occur between the two young men, and this is exactly what the narrative reveals. They drive the cattle happily together through the Waste of Cumberland, but find themselves at odds in making arrangements for pasturage. While Harry Wakefield makes an arrangement with the bailiff of a Cumbrian farmer, Robin Oig meets the farmer himself and arranges to have the use of the same field at the price of six "stots" (bullocks). Thus Wakefield's cattle have to be driven further on, and his pride is hurt. Moreover, the pasturage he eventually finds, let to him by the landlord of the alehouse, is poor. By the time Oig comes to the alehouse, the English assembled there have taken Wakefield's side against the Scot. They encourage a fight between the two friends, which inevitably leads to Wakefield's defeating the much smaller Oig. Oig is understandably indignant, and makes off into the moonlight. He then realises that he does not have his dirk with him, and recalls the old woman's prophecy. But rather than being warned by it, he sets off to find the Lowlander who has the dirk, and gets it back. He then returns to the inn where, although Wakefield seeks reconciliation, Oig insists on using the dirk and killing his friend: "I show you now how the Highland Dunniewassel fights." Wakefield dies instantly, and Oig surrenders himself to a peace-officer who is in the inn. He is taken to Carlisle to be tried at the next Assizes.

Scott concludes the story with a detailed account of the trial ("I was myself present," the narrator says.) The judge's charge to the jury is given at length, and shows a very rational and humane approach. The men are said to have acted "in ignorance of each other's national prejudices," so that their story calls forth compassion as well as judgment. But the conclusion of the charge in that the crime of murder has been committed, and that the prisoner must be found guilty, as he is. The last words are those of Oig: "I give a life for the life I took," he said, "and what can I do more?"

The story attracts the reader's attention by its tragic simplicity, and is appropriately narrated in a straightforward manner. It shows Scott's deep interest in both humanity and the particular manners and customs of individual communities, and the dialogue in particular is successful in imparting the flavour of both the Scots and the English. The story is a readerly one, to use Barthes's term—everything is made as plain as the narrator can make it. And the judge's view is clearly one which the reader is expected to accept: he points out that the idea of revenge was until recently prevalent in Scotland, as it still is among "the Cherokees or Mohawks" of North America, but that "the first object of civilization is to place the general protection of the law, equally administered, in the room of that wild justice, which every man cut and carried for himself, according to the length of his sword and the strength of his arm." Scott conveys the appeal of the romantic and primitive, but his own commitment is to Enlightenment values.

—Peter Faulkner

TWO FISHERMEN
by Morley Callaghan, 1936

Morley Callaghan's fame emanates perhaps more from the fact that he was a member of the Lost Generation of the 1920's, living the expatriate life in Paris with Ernest Hemingway and F. Scott Fitzgerald, and that he became the first renowned Canadian author outside the boundaries of his native land, than from his literary output. What is more important, however, is that in a long and productive career he published more than 20 works of fiction, including several novels and numerous short stories well worth the attention of readers and critics in Canada and elsewhere.

"Two Fishermen," collected in *Now That April's Here* (1936), one of his most famous stories, is quite typical of Callaghan's style and approach. His language here as elsewhere tends toward understatement, a simple, direct style that is reminiscent, though not necessarily derivative, of the work of his one-time newspaper colleague and comrade Hemingway. His diction is simple, elemental, like that of Sherwood Anderson in his best short stories. Although his Roman Catholicism is always an influence on Callaghan's work, the environment in which his characters live their often painful, confused, and even desperate lives is naturalistic. His characters themselves are usually simple, common people, weak, capable of blunders, but admirable for their struggling against whatever limitations fate may have assigned them.

"Two Fishermen" belongs to a number of subgenres of the short story: it is, for example, a rites-of-passage story of a young man, in many ways like George Willard, the protagonist of Anderson's *Winesburg, Ohio*, yearning to escape his small hometown for the big city; it also belongs to that time-honored category of "newspaper fiction," with the young reporter, in this instance Michael Foster, witnessing his first execution and experiencing mature emotions he has never before felt.

The motifs and themes with which Callaghan works in "Two Fishermen" include not only the initiation of the young to the bloody and painful realities of life, but also the spontaneous nature of true friendship, the pleasures and moral obligations one friend owes to another, and the pervasive presence of shame and guilt in human nature. When Michael Foster sets out to meet the hangman who has come to the small town to execute Thomas Delaney, a young man convicted of murdering a man who molested his wife, he gets much more than he bargains for: a new friend and new insights into the drama of human life. The hangman, Smitty, is a small, gray-haired, married man with five young children, simple, ordinary, affable, in short, Michael decides, "a nice little guy." An immediate amiability develops between the two as they fish and discuss the exigencies of the hangman's trade.

In this important scene, Callaghan cleverly shifts the point of view from Michael to Smitty, who thinks that the reporter believes that he, Smitty, should be ashamed, but he is not. He tells Michael, "Somebody's got to do my job. There's got to be a hangman." Irony of situation and of language is skillfully woven throughout the narrative, as when the two drink Scotch from Smitty's flask and toast each other ("Happy days") and when the hangman observes, "we're having a grand time, aren't we?"

The second part of "Two Fishermen" opens with an abrupt and stark contrast to the camaraderie and the pastoral tone of the first part: "At seven o'clock next morning Thomas Delaney was hanged in the town jail yard." Michael, though he feels it "his duty as a newspaperman" to observe the execution, is unable to do so. Afterwards, he encounters Smitty, who, seemingly unmoved by the chore he has just completed, gives his new friend two trout he had caught early in the morning, before the hanging. In the melee that ensues, angry townsmen attack the hangman outside the jail, tossing sticks, stones, and other objects as he attempts to flee and then falls. As Smitty looks desperately around for someone to come to his aid, Michael, his moral strength failing an important test, moves back into the crowd, "betraying Smitty, who last night had had such a good neighbourly time with him." Although he tries to convince himself that "it's different now," the young man is overcome with the strong sense of shame that he had attributed to the hangman the day before.

When a member of the mob, significantly identified as a "big fisherman," demands to know why Michael does not participate in the assault, the reporter, betraying his new friend as Peter denied Christ, insists, "He just doesn't mean anything to me at all." After the furious man grabs Smitty's gift from Michael's hands and throws the two fish at "the little man," the hangman, endeavoring to rise from the ground, stares at the fish "with his mouth hanging open." Michael, "hot with shame," tries to flee from the scene. Parallels to the Biblical betrayal and denial of Christ by Judas and Peter and the symbolism of the fish are subtly handled to underscore the flaw in Michael's character. Callaghan, however, as in most of his fiction, makes no judgment but merely portrays his characters with their ironic and even paradoxical strengths and weaknesses.

The force and power of this brief story are achieved through Callaghan's skillful use of several major tools of the fiction writer's craft. His juxtaposition of contrasting events and the understated language with which he describes not only everyday occurrences—two men in a boat fishing, for example—and the idyllic small-town and rural settings, but also the events before and after the execution, intensify the irony of the situation. Skillful use of Biblical parallels and the careful manipulation of symbols that are not merely tacked on to the story but emanate naturally from the events serve to make the emotional impact on Michael and Smitty, his new betrayed friend, all the stronger. One finishes reading "Two Fishermen" with a troubled, unsettled feeling that these are real people and real events and that somehow a total resolution to the dilemmas proposed here must occur, if at all, within the reader's own consciousness and conscience.

—W. Kenneth Holditch

TWO LOVELY BEASTS
by Liam O'Flaherty, 1948

Liam O'Flaherty has been described as "a poet in prose, who chose the short story as a medium" and as someone who "probably has more faults than any of the other outstanding Irish writers of short stories." The faults are clear: an inclination to slide into melodrama and sentimentality, a proclivity to humanise his animal subjects and bestialise or idealise his humans, and some stylistic uneasiness. It is equally clear why he should have been described as a poet. Most of his stories present an impassioned picture of humans and animals struggling for survival, imbued with violent, elemental passions, set against a backdrop of the harshness of the natural world.

"Two Lovely Beasts" is more characteristic of the strengths than the weaknesses of O'Flaherty. There is at times a somewhat jarring movement from dialectal speech ("God between us and harm . . . what happened to you?") to the latinate syntax of the narrative voice ("It was some time before Kate desisted from her lamentation."). Equally, O'Flaherty's use of animal imagery in characterisation is evident: Colm Derrane "was a big awkward fellow with pigeon toes and arms that were exceptionally long, like those of an ape." There are moments when the placing of the heroically enduring peasant against the hostility of the natural world seems familiar, if not clichéd:

His shoes were in tatters. His frieze trousers were covered with patches of varying colours. His grey shirt was visible through the numerous holes in his blue woollen sweater. . . . Yet he looked splendid and even awe-inspiring, in spite of his physical ugliness and his uncouth dress, as he stood poised that way on the brink of the tall cliff above the thundering sea.

The story presents a complex and impressive picture of an impoverished community, eking out a subsistence living, at the mercy of fate, bad luck, and the weather. The traditional nature of the society is evoked in the separate meeting places for men and women where communal decisions are made and collective norms asserted. Life is a matter of back-breaking, unremitting toil, in an attempt to scrape a living from land that is more rock than soil, desperately short of the arable land on which the survival of the family depends. Andy Gorum enunciates the social realities:

That's how we live here in our village by helping one another. Our land is poor and the sea is wild. It's hard to live. We only manage to live by sticking together. Otherwise we'd all die. It's too wild and barren here for any one man to stand alone. Whoever tries to stand alone and work only for his own profit becomes an enemy of all.

Colm Derrane, however, does attempt to stand alone and work for his own profit so that he can leave his people behind, "still land-slaves and at the mercy of everyone else." "Two Lovely Beasts" is the story of a man escaping from the peasantry by hard work and imagination, but also having to deny the needs of traditional society. Derrane has to face social ostracism, and, in the process of transforming himself into O'Flaherty's (and Ireland's) most hated figure, the "gombeen man," loses his humanity and warmth, terrorises his wife, starves his children, and turns his back on the natural compensations and joys which his life has also offered. For example, in taking on the feeding of a second calf Colm deprives the town of milk, flouts traditional wisdom and breaks "the law of God and of the people."

This story of a peasant community is a microcosm of the whole world of capitalism. Colm Derrane leaves the socialist mode and becomes a capitalist by putting his individual ambition before the communal needs of the people. He sacrifices everything to feed the calves, yet even when he has enough and more than anyone else, he still wants more and completes his removal from the people by becoming a town-based shopkeeper. There is nothing remarkable about Colm except his willingness to work and his unwillingness to "turn aside from an opportunity to earn an extra shilling." The reader experiences horror and revulsion at the choice he makes and its human consequences but is equally (and this is what makes the story satisfying) filled with admiration for his courage, imagination, energy, and persistence, and with sympathy for his desire to escape the slavery of his existence.

Kate represents temptation, like the serpent cunningly whispering in his ear—offering him the earth as Satan tempted Christ in the desert: "You'll be the richest man in the village. You'll be talked about and envied from one end of the parish to the other." His conflict is presented as a conflict between two mortal sins; it would be a sin to let the neighbours go without milk and a sin to have the calf slaughtered. The resolution is presented, however, in terms of something more elemental. There is a mythological element in the Homeric description of the "young bull-calf that had a wine-dark skin." Colm becomes "intoxicated" with the idea of possessing both calves and the text makes it clear that this is the kind of divine intoxication that leads to the sin of hubris. Colm is tempting the gods, but the ironic basis of the story resides in the fact that the gods of trade bless him with success, and this casts doubt on the traditional wisdom:

It what he is doing is bad, why does he prosper? Isn't it more likely that God is blessing his effort to rise in the world. Maybe it's us that are wicked on account of our laziness.

There is, of course, damnation and a price to be paid for Colm's ambitions, though this is unperceived. As Colm achieves his dreams, he becomes "cold and resolute and ruthless," and, in O'Flaherty's terms, suffers the ultimate punishment of living death, inhumanity and separation from all that is vibrant and energising in life.

—Anne Clune

TYPHOON
by Joseph Conrad, 1902

The preface to *Typhoon*, one of Joseph Conrad's most revealing, shows that his casual hearing of an anecdote about a money-quarrel below decks provided him with the first hint of the story, and that he invented Captain MacWhirr as the catalyst who could unify a "bit of a sea-yarn," with a well-shaped novella. Conrad wrote, "MacWhirr is not an acquaintance of a few hours, or a few weeks, or a few months. He is the product of twenty years of life. My own life. Conscious invention had little to do with him."

He must have been conscious of paradox here. Could anything be less like a great novelist than the story's hero? MacWhirr's unimaginativeness is even overstressed. It goes well beyond what we expect in the practical man, devoted to a craft, so as to be at times comical.

Jukes is more imaginative than MacWhirr, but he is really more like the author, because to him MacWhirr's unimaginativeness is simply a lack, about which he writes home with contemptuous amusement. For Conrad, it is not only at the heart of the story, but near the heart of the spirit of the England he loved, and of the merchant navy, of which he was proud to be a member.

The contrast between the two is well illustrated by their argument about the flag. For MacWhirr, Jukes's complaint about the flag only needs to be checked against the Signal Codebook. When he finds it correct, MacWhirr says, "Length twice the breadth and the elephant exactly in the middle. I thought the people ashore would know how to make the local flag. Stands to reason." For Jukes, with his wider, but more superficial, view, the question is, What are Englishmen doing sailing under a Siamese flag?

This flag becomes important again near the end of the story, when the ugly situation below decks makes them wonder if they will need outside help, and Jukes is afraid (and MacWhirr still uncomprehending) that they will be unable to make themselves known as British. It is characteristic of MacWhirr that he can only contemplate the mystery of death by means of something visible, a matchbox, which he may perhaps be clutching for the last time. One or two other characters (apart from the anonymous squabbling Chinese) become momentarily vivid, for example, Rout, who understands that the dullest ass makes a better captain than a rogue, and the lonely, bitter second mate. He never writes any letters, but the letters of the other three have an importance which is sometimes overlooked. The brief but vivid account of their correspondents, and of the way their letters are received, not only place each one in his home context, but emphasises that, though for certain purposes a Conrad ship may be a microcosm, we are not to forget that it is not so for the protagonists. A sailor is always thinking of returning to land; there is no alternative except drowning. There is poignancy in Mrs. MacWhirr's boredom with her dutiful husband's letters, and her "abject terror" of the time when he would come home for good. Rout's wife and mother enjoy his letters, and startle the curate with little jokes depending on his having the same name as the Hebrew king Solomon. Jukes writes to an old ship-mate. Thus Conrad arranges to give his characters a home context, and to afford the reader some relief from the claustrophobic world of the threatened ship. In describing the typhoon itself, Conrad was on his guard against the danger of mere descriptive writing, as in a superior travel brochure. He avoids it by always maintaining a contrast between the exuberant effects of nature's violence and the exhaustion of lonely endurance, when even a man's companions in the ship are almost inaccessible to communication.

Jukes's memories are important here; his fears, which he strives to conceal from himself, cause him to dwell on the deaths of his parents, and on playing cards with sailors since lost at sea. Conrad's seamen (with occasional exceptions) are brave, but more outwardly then inwardly. They feel fear while they do brave things. This explains their tendency when conditions are adverse to personalize the elements, and to feel as if they are engaged in a contest against a conscious opponent of irresistible power and resource. The threat of anarchy among the Chinese below decks serves two purposes. It is a kind of miniature allegory of life without tradition, discipline and obedience, giving almost a Hobbesian view. And it illustrates the practical superiority of MacWhirr over the more imaginative Jukes. While Jukes is willing to allow the Chinese "to fight it out among themselves, while we get a rest," MacWhirr's pedantic sense of order becomes a source of true humanity and civilization. He insists, even in the face of the unimaginable violence of nature, in being "fair to all parties." When, in the last sentence, Jukes gives MacWhirr a half contemptuous accolade ("I think he got out of it very well for such a stupid man"), we are to feel that he still has not grasped the idea of MacWhirr's real superiority. Not being English himself, Conrad had a special appreciation of English understatement. He imitates it with seasoned appreciation, when he comments on MacWhirr's dislike of losing the ship: "He was spared that annoyance."

—A.O.J. Cockshut

U

ULA MASONDO
by William Plomer, 1927

"Ula Masondo," a long short story by William Plomer, is also, as Edith Sitwell told its author, "a *great* short story"; great in itself, and great in its influence. For Ula Masondo, the man of the people, is the prototype of the innocent tribal African who leaves his family hut in the rural reserves and goes to seek money in the white man's city, invariably Johannesburg (or "Goldenville," as Plomer calls it in earlier printings), and its effect is as invariably malign and corrupting. Ula Masondo is more than a mere "type": he is a living character, an individual whose development the reader can follow from the day he buys a blanket and dances down the mountain path with it in childlike ecstasy, through his journey to and experiences in the frightening, exciting city of gold, where he is soon initiated into the ways of the sophisticated detribalized Africans, until his return to "Lembuland" as a prodigal dandy, adorned with rings and high-heeled shoes and a cane. The simple and dutiful son who set out from his tribal village at the beginning of the story has become a superior "Westernized" and "Christianized" African who repudiates his aged mother as a "bloody heathen" and goes to live with a prostitute he met in the city; his mother hangs herself.

The characterization of Ula Masondo is done with the sure touch of a master storyteller, near-miraculously entering into the very being of his creation to convey how Ula thinks and feels and even (in a risk-taking poetic phantasmagoria after a mining accident) dreams. In achieving these things, Plomer displays technical knowledge of goldmining as well as an extraordinary sense of intuitive sympathy with his hero, and the mining terms—of which Ula would probably be ignorant, even if he knew the things to which they referred—give way touchingly to convincing poetic comparisons of the kind Ula could make himself:

When one came off shift at midday the sky was dusty grey like the pelt of a donkey, and the air was full of the perennial roar of the stamps rising and falling . . . on revolving cams in the battery . . . shaking the ground, as the ground trembles to a war-dance of warriors, or summer thunder in the mountains of Lembuland.

Nor is Ula never allowed his own words, without authorial transmutation or explanation. His attractively naïve earlier character, for instance, is allowed to show itself in his speech, as when he, a novice in this new world of Western clothing, money, drink, drugs, gambling, and syphilis, an innocent who does not understand that sleeping with a friend for warmth and company risks a flogging for sodomy, is taken under the wing of the fast-living, fast-talking Vilakazi. Plomer's close observation of the speech patterns of the customers of his father's trading store in Zululand is evident in his careful dialogue between the greenhorn and the veteran:

"*Wé*, Vilakazi," said the younger man, "I have a letter."
"Where is it from, that letter?"
"From my home."
"What does it say?"
"This letter? It says I am the chief of my father's people."
"What!"
"It says I am the king of the white people."
"What!"
"It says you must give me money. It says only ten shillings."
"You are cheating me, my friend."
"It is true. Read my letter."

The letter is itself a small masterpiece, of which follows not only the melodramatic but moving and authentic ending:

I cannot sleep always always I am coughing and your father has fever he is sick and all the people send greetings but they are dead as to their stomachs send if it is a pound only o my child my beloved greeting from your mother.

The unprincipled Vilakazi pretends to his illiterate protégé that the letter contains only greetings, and pockets it himself:

"If you have it you will lose it, and it is safe with me. Some day we shall answer it; I will tell you when."

Ula Masondo made no answer. It was Sunday afternoon, and he wanted an excitement of the blood, he wanted to drink and shout, to drink and forget.

The foregoing quotations may help to demonstrate the closeness of Plomer's identification with and empathetic understanding of Ula, and to counter any suggestion that nothing is seen through Ula's eyes, for his characterization is an impressive mixture of external detail and inner revelation. The white characters are the merest sketches, appropriately maintaining the illusion of their being seen primarily from Ula's point of view, as in the brilliant presentation of the anonymous overlords of the mine only through Ula's awareness of their gleaming limousine, "its fat tyres treading richly on the gravel"; the commentary given to two white couples is a disfigurement, forming an unnecessarily explicit framework to Ula's story. But the other black characters are also distinct personalities: the moody giant, Vilakazi; the eloquent gangster, Stefan, whose analysis of the white race makes Ula feel the first stirrings of resentment; the voluptuous and abandonedly exuberant Emma; and Isimayili, called Smile by the white people, who think him a cheerful houseboy and know nothing of the violent sadist his drunken off-duty self reveals. Smile's brand of Christian dandyism becomes a model for the young, impressionable Ula, who is much taken with Smile's Sunday manner, as, with a Bible in his pocket and a cane in his hand, he dispenses scorn ("*Hau!* He's just a heathen!") or praise ("Truly, this tobacco is Christian!") according to his idiosyncratic criteria. The white storekeeper who sells the blanket to the "decent" Ula at the beginning of the story, bewails this influence above all the others at the end of it, when Ula returns to Lembuland.

"Ula Masondo," collected in the volume *I Speak for Africa* (1927), remains one of the few undeniably great stories to have come out of South Africa, and, though not flawless, is perhaps the greatest of all, a story to which one can return again and again with profit, which on each reading reveals new depths to its brilliance and, in Roy Campbell's words, "makes one's blood dance."

—Michael Herbert

THE ULTIMATE SAFARI
by Nadine Gordimer, 1991

One of the frequent complaints about Nadine Gordimer by her South African critics is that her work lacks humor. It is true that Gordimer has no pretensions to being funny, but she nevertheless uses a powerful kind of irony loaded with historical contingency. Such historically-engaged irony is apparent in "The Ultimate Safari" (in the collection *Jump*), in which the author invokes the notion of "safari" to describe the desperate *trek* of a starving group of Mozambiquan refugees across the Kruger Park game reserve to the ironically-conceived "sanctuary" of South Africa.

It is one of Gordimer's strengths as a writer to invoke an implicit series of ironic reversals in the mere choice of plot and character in her southern African stories. In this case, complex conjugations of colonialism and neo-colonialism, and the long history of unequal distribution of human value in southern Africa, are brought into the story's implicit framework. The journey of the Mozambiquan refugees is a reverse version, and an indirect result of, the European holiday safari "into Africa"; the refugee *trek* literally proceeds in the opposite direction, out of the wild, and on empty stomachs, in stark contrast to the well-fed European holiday journey into the romantically-conceived Kruger Park "bush." Indeed, the refugees pass near the cosy holiday-cottages, smell the tourist barbecues, and consider raiding their dustbins for rich leftovers. But they dare not, for fear of being caught and sent back to Mozambique, where death and starvation await them.

Gordimer cites in an epigraph to the story a recent travel advert from the *London Observer* promising that "The African Adventure Lives On. . . .You can do it! The ultimate safari or expedition with leaders who *know* Africa." By doing this, the author juxtaposes two images of Africa, and suggests their interdependence. The Western-er's safari Africa is a sub-textual suggestion in the shadow of the main text, which deals with the African's real Africa: the starving children of war, their raped and murdered mothers, and their dead or dying fathers. But it is not as simple as a mere contrast of images. The modern safari Africa is the heir to a destructive colonialism which convulsed an earlier, preindustrial Africa and slowly turned it into a state of colonial dependence. A further conjugation is that whereas the colonial adventurers of Africa severely damaged the fabric of social and cultural life-systems in their artificially constituted "states," the neo-colonial African governments, in reaction, and working within the gutted remains of colonial infrastructure, imposed destructive nationalisms on impoverished people and bred new conflicts, new corruptions, and new wars. The characters in this story are the victims of this double colonisation, and in their effort to escape they have to traverse, in a literal, historical, and metaphorical return journey, to the source of their condition, a prime terrain of land appropriation, the game park. They return as a colonial/apartheid nemesis (as refugees) to the centre of stolen power and wealth—white South Africa.

Also implicit in the story is the idea that two Africas have bred two classes of people in South Africa: the predominantly (but not exclusively) white middle class, whose idea of Africa is at least partly framed in the romantic terms of its game parks and its environmental delights (these are the heirs of imperialists and settlers who made Africa conform to such a scheme of things, partly by forcing people off land to be designated as "game parks"); and the underclass, who, in the most severe cases such as portrayed in this story, do not entertain secondary notions of "game" and "parks" because they are hungry and homeless (the descendants of colonialism's victims). For them, land is either shelter or it must be traversed in search of shelter; animals are either food or a mortal threat. In today's camouflaged language, which seeks to efface moral responsibility, these two classes of people are incorporated in the terms "first" and "third" worlds. But implicit in Gordimer's story is the idea that the passage of years since the end of formal colonialism has not dissolved the moral and historical interconnections between the two versions of Africa and the two kinds of people in it. For every tourist safari, there are many more "ultimate safaris" of starving refugees. For every slab of barbecue-rump on a safari fire, a couple of kids die of starvation beyond the charmed spaces of affluence and privilege. Gordimer reminds her readers just how interdependent the moral economy of southern Africa is with the economy of resources and the history of appropriation and dispossession.

Increasingly in her career as a writer, Gordimer has tried to escape the confines of her own white middle class background by attempting the impossible in a world of apartheid: to write from within the subjective experiences of apartheid's others. In addition, Gordimer often concretises complex historical issues in the figure of one protagonist and in the first person narration of this protagonist's life. In this story, Gordimer makes a difficult imaginative leap into the mind of a little African girl of about ten years who describes the arduous journey, by foot, of at least 100 kilometres across the Kruger Park. Gordimer's choice of a child narrator makes the leap a lot easier. She can discount cultural difference and narrate in a more general child's language of fear, hope, and longing. In doing this, she also suggests that there is in fact a level of experience not obscured by the immensely complex intercultural dynamics of southern Africa. That level of experience is constituted by the suffering children of Africa.

The girl, who is nameless, narrates how her mother simply disappears one day when what remains of her family are still living in the shell of a semi-destroyed dwelling in Mozambique. Presumably, the mother has been abducted and/or murdered by Renamo bandits. War has taken the father some time ago. The girl, her younger brother, their grandmother, and grandfather, join a group of refugees who set off for the ironic freedom of South Africa. The group walks around the electrified border-fence marking South African territory, and into the Kruger Park. For weeks the starving refugees trudge on, leaving behind those too weak to continue. They have to negotiate a passage inhabited by elephants, lions, and other animals to whom they may become prey. When they eventually emerge at a refugee tent-camp in South Africa beyond the Kruger Park, they have lost the grandfather on the way, and the younger brother seems to have suffered brain-damage as a result of malnutrition. They have no home and no prospects. When a white journalist asks the narrator's grandmother whether she wants to "go home," the grandmother replies, "There is nothing. No home."

But the narrator herself asks, "Why does our grandmother say that? Why? I'll go back. I'll go back through that Kruger Park. After the war . . . our mother may be waiting for us." This is a tenuous thread of hope that suggests an ineradicable human optimism even in the face of the worst cruelties and the most severe privations. Significantly, it is the women of the story who survive. The bright young girl who narrates the story is getting some kind of education in South Africa while living in the refugee tent. Against all the odds, Gordimer seems to suggest, women in southern Africa will continue to live, to hope and to nurture. The men have clearly failed.

In "The Ultimate Safari" Gordimer privileges (by her fictional focus) the least-privileged and doubly-oppressed anti-heroes of southern Africa's various colonialisms, the surviving women. In the story's conclusion, there is a clear, if faint, suggestion that the time is at hand for the women of southern Africa to take control of their lives, and that of their property, against the grain of a history of failure.

—Leon de Kock

UNCLE BLAIR
by Sylvia Townsend Warner, 1955

Sylvia Townsend Warner's prolific writing career encompassed many roles: novelist, poet, biographer, translator, editor, and short story writer. She is probably best known to American audiences for the 144 short stories published in *The New Yorker,* which are gathered, along with others, in ten collections. She wrote in a variety of styles, examining the foibles of human nature with a witty and shrewd humor. "Uncle Blair" appears in *Winter in the Air and Other Stories* published in 1955 and is portrayed in a pseudo-realistic manner. In this story, set in a small village in England, Warner lays bare the foolish and petty natures of the inhabitants and visitors whose mixed priorities make them laughable; at the same time, Warner lambastes the established medical community.

"Uncle Blair" opens with a description of the town of Tittingham and how it has prospered from the business generated by Miss Iris Foale's seminary for young ladies. The townspeople and Miss Foale had an understanding that something commemorative would be done upon her death. Warner characterizes Miss Foale distinctly. During her lifetime, "she could wish for no better memorial than the characters she had formed and the ideals she had inculcated." Later after her death, the townspeople discover that "in a delicate way, Miss Foale had bequeathed her own suggestion . . . a Tittingham Folk Museum." In the first two pages, we see what a hypocrite Miss Foale is, espousing ideals as more important than materialism when

in fact she advocated the reverse. Then Warner turns her attention to the townspeople. In order to find a proper location for the museum, they need to tear down Opie Cottage owned by a Miss Bishop. Warner illustrates the character of the townspeople as calculating and self-centered when she details how they go about securing the rights to the property: "Though she [Miss Bishop] was senile, it was felt that she was not too senile to sign an agreement to sell the property." The townspeople achieve their desires through trickery.

The stage is now set for what the rest of the story reveals: the machinations of one Aubrey Cutbush, who strongly, fiercely, almost maniacally, opposes the memorial since it caused the destruction of Opie Cottage where he had been born, though he only lived there until the age of six months. Warner caustically describes his actions as following those of any English gentleman; he goes to see his solicitor; however, his solicitor is on the Memorial Committee. Aubrey next gets a list of those giving funds to the memorial and informs all the local tradesmen who have contributed that he will no longer do business with them. Warner sarcastically portrays Aubrey as "a man of pure passions, [he] was immune from the gentility of having to appear to behave magnanimously." Even though he purports to be a gentleman, he starts a vendetta against those whose opinions oppose his own. In an anonymous letter to the newspaper, he condemns the idea of the memorial yet doesn't have the courage to print his own name. His letter does bring results, but ones he couldn't have anticipated. Dulcibella Tregurtha writes a letter to the newspaper supporting his views. It seems that Dulcibella was a former student of Miss Foale, who, the teacher had remarked, would never learn how to spell. Warner alerts the reader that "all Miss Tregurtha's zealotries stemmed from a schoolgirl's resentment." So Dulcibella is illustrated as a small-minded, childish character, much like Aubrey. Both react with immaturity and rashness.

The two arrange to meet, since Aubrey believes they have so much in common, being of like minds. However, their second meeting is arranged by Dulcibella, who surprises Aubrey at his home with a friend of hers named Jeanie, who "has got the Evil Eye" and, incidentally, a lisp Warner portrays very accurately. Here is where the elusive Uncle Blair is finally brought into the picture. Aubrey questions Jeanie on her evil eye and discovers that she got it from her Uncle Blair. Dulcibella has brought Jeanie along because of her inherited trait as a sort of secret weapon to use against their common enemy, the citizens in favor of the memorial, in case reason fails to convince them.

Poor Aubrey is overwhelmed by these two women, and Warner does an excellent job of enlisting reader sympathy for a character who earlier appeared so full of revenge for such an unfounded reason. His servants, who seem to be the only sane, stable characters portrayed in this story, are greatly amused by the plight of their employer.

When Dulcibella goes into a tirade berating Aubrey, informing him that she knows he wrote the anonymous letter to the paper, Aubrey begins to feel a "hellish draught, cold as though it were blowing on him from the wastes of Lapland." He sees Jeanie slumped on a chair looking exhausted, but he doesn't realize what's so obvious to the reader—Jeanie has been using her talented evil eye on him for his supposed betrayal of their fine intentions.

Left to himself, with no thought of the Memorial anymore, Aubrey sinks into illness, desperately trying to dismiss the superstition of the evil eye. His servants, attempt superstitious remedies to save their employer, though Warner notes that "these attentions were the more depressing since . . . everyone concerned knew that there is only one way to turn back the curse laid by an Evil Eye, and that is, to draw the blood of the bestower." As Warner carries the reader deeper into the mysterious realms of superstition, Aubrey continues to fade.

At the end, Warner presents Aubrey's eulogy, ironically, with a tribute from Dulcibella to Opie Cottage that hangs in the Tittingham Folk Museum. Is this perhaps an acknowledgment on Dulcibella's part that she contributed to Aubrey's death? More likely, Aubrey, at age 60, succumbed to old age, a cold, and his wild imagination. Warner has a gift of portraying ordinary people in ways that make them seem extraordinarily silly, foolish, superstitious, and immature. Her graceful, objective style seems effortless yet commandingly illustrates her talent.

—Judith M. Schmitt

UNCLE FRED FLITS BY
by P.G. Wodehouse, 1936

Uncle Fred, Lord Ickenham, is not as pervasive in Wodehouse's fiction as the more celebrated Jeeves, Emsworth, and Mulliner; but he is the central figure of one of the best of the longer books, *Uncle Fred in the Springtime,* where he appears as an impostor at Blandings Castle. Wodehouse occasionally allows his separate worlds to merge: in "Uncle Fred Flits By" collected in *Young Men in Spats,* 1936, both the owner of a stately home, and his nephew, a denizen of London clubland, find themselves in the respectable suburbia which was occasionally touched in the Psmith and Mike stories. The relation of uncle and nephew is based on the same serviceable comic reversal used in the Jeeves stories. Just as, in the latter, the servant has the wisdom and experience, and the master has most of the comedy, so here it is the young nephew who is anxious, conventional, and timid, while the uncle's youthful high spirits lead him into fantastic adventures, daring impersonations, and brilliant inventions about the lives of people he has never met. Lord Ickenham does not get nabbed by the police in this story, but we are constantly reminded of the day at the dog races where he had been arrested in the first ten minutes. Pongo is in constant apprehension of a similar disaster here, and the brooding presence of the sombre young man among the high-spirited members of the Drones is a keynote for what is to follow. This is presented with a characteristic Wodehouse ruthlessness:

> "He's all broken up about his Uncle Fred."
> "Dead?"
> "No such luck. Coming up to London again tomorrow."

This ruthlessness reminds us of many fairy stories, and it helps the happy ending and the extraordinary neatness of one of the author's best plots from making the effect over-sweet.

An important presence in the background is the dominant Lady Ickenham, who only occasionally allows her husband to get up to London, doles him out pocket-money, and would never have allowed him to be in possession of a hundred pounds on this occasion, if he had not been instructed to spend it at her orders. Ickenham's last triumph over his doubting nephew, after misappropriating the money in an act of reckless generosity, comes when he tells him he will explain to his wife that he spent it to save him (Pongo) from the clutches of an adventuress. The picture of a man, endlessly resourceful in London, as a domestic slave, is another characteristic reversal, as is the contrast between the solid suburban background and a tale of fantastic adventure.

Lord Ickenham's sentimental view of his boyhood is suitably sharpened with a touch of crudity: "stopping at intervals like a pointing dog and saying that it must have been just about here that he plugged the gardner in the trousers with his bow and arrow, and that over there he had been sick after his first cigar."

The process by which Ickenham learns just enough of the affairs of a stream of visitors he has never met before to impose on them a totally fictitious story about their own relations is highly ingenious, and could be quoted as a leading example of the author's technical mastery. And the linguistic surprises show the author at his best. As usual there is an adroit use of cliché ("Pongo, whose system was by this time definitely down among the wines and spirits"), combined with a contrasted freshness of language which, so to speak, places the cliché in inverted commas:

> The thing began to look to Pongo like a touch, and he is convinced that the parrot thought so, too, for it winked and cleared its throat. But they were both wrong.

The point of view is not as simple as it looks. Ostensibly, the main part of the story is told from Pongo's point of view, and we do get a strong impression of his distress. But the reader's feelings will be with the resourceful uncle, even when he is damned as "Hampshire's leading curse." Awareness of the comic shaping will make everyone sense from the first a happy ending, and make everyone admire its architect.

Ickenham himself is the master of several Wodehousian styles. He can talk like an old Times leader ("though we applaud his judgement of form, we must surely look askance at his financial methods"). But in the same sentence we have already had the casual style of the upper class at ease: "Harry, I grant you, won five thousand of the best and never looked back afterwards."

And later, Ickenham speaks the style of the expansive man-of-the-world: "If a man can smuggle cocaine and get away with it, good luck to him, say I." Different again is the style of cheerful coaxing, elder brother (rather than uncle) which he uses to spur his faint-hearted nephew. The variety fits exactly the requirements of the story, that Ickenham should be a moral Houdini, a suburban Proteus, whom no one can keep caged.

The moment when he gives away his wife's hundred pounds, in a gesture which might be a parody of Pickwick or the Cheeryble brothers, is again saved from over-sweetness, not only by the farcical accompaniments, but by the renewed emphasis of Pongo's sour point of view:

> The agony of realizing that the old bounder had had all that stuff on him all this time and that he hadn't touched him for so much as a tithe of it was so keen, Pongo says, that before he knew what he was doing he had let out a sharp, whinnying cry.

Similarly the delighted embraces of the young lovers Ickenham has rescued are deflated by Pongo's awareness that everyone seemed to be kissing the girl except him. Part of the charm and skill of the story lies here, that its tone and its plot are designed not to fit; it is a day-dream of wish fulfillment encapsulated in a narrative that combines pure farce with sharp satirical comment. The blending could scarcely be more successful.

—A.O.J. Cockshut

THE UNION BURIES ITS DEAD
by Henry Lawson, 1893

Henry Lawson's status both as part and as part-creator of Australia's national mythology is attested by his prominent appearance on the ten-dollar banknote. Traditional accounts of Australian literary achievement promote Lawson as the writer who did most to stabilise and to celebrate the characteristic virtues of his compatriots: a tough resilience in the face of the unrelenting bush, a "natural" (and therefore nondogmatic) socialism which finds expression both in union organisation and in the private camaraderie of "mateship," a hardheaded distrust of abstractions, cities, and social pretension.

Most of these values seem to be embodied in the scenario of "The Union Buries Its Dead," which was written early in 1893, first published in the Sydney magazine *Truth* on 16 April 1893, and collected in *While the Billy Boils* in 1896. A young labourer is drowned trying to swim some horses across the Darling River in outback New South Wales. Because the dead man has been a member of the General Labourers' Union (G.L.U.), his funeral is well attended by the inhabitants of the small bush township through which he passed on the previous day. Even though he was "almost a stranger in town" and a Roman Catholic when "the majority . . . were otherwise," his G.L.U. ticket ensures a public display of respect from his fellow-workers.

But this seeming validation of mateship also appears to be subtly undermined in a number of ways. Most obviously, Lawson—or, rather, the narrator—takes a whole paragraph to distance himself from the sentimental clichés with which the ethnic of the bush is conventionally celebrated:

I have left out the wattle—because it wasn't there. I have also neglected to mention the heart-broker old mate, with his grizzled head bowed and great drops streaming down his rugged cheeks. He was absent—he was probably "outback."

It is not, however, only the separate topoi of this idealising iconography that are missing in Lawson's narrative, but the aesthetic and moral coherence they might confer on the tableau of bereavement. "The Union Buries Its Dead," indeed, precisely foregrounds the fragmentation into which the fiction of solidarity quickly collapses, a fragmentation signalled as early as the first sentence of the second paragraph—"Next day a funeral gathered at a corner pub and asked each other in to have a drink while waiting for the hearse"—where the collectivity implicit in "funeral" immediately dissolves into the separate identities of which the cortege is composed. The deceased young man has been "almost a stranger in town," the mourners in the trap were "strangers to us who were on foot, and we to them," the horseman who briefly joins the procession

before dodging off to join a friend in a hotel bar is "a stranger to the entire show."

In such a milieu of nonrecognition, where social cohesion has given place to general estrangement, the decorous ritual gestures of mourning become perfunctory and are emptied of meaning. A pair of drunken shearers "covered their right ears with their hats, out of respect for the departed," and even the officiating priest "took off his hat, dropped it carelessly on the ground, and proceeded to business." Despite early claims that "unionism is stronger than creed," schismatic intolerance resurfaces as the burial rites proceed: "one or two heathens winced slightly when the holy water was sprinkled on the coffin," and an anonymous "someone" identifies the priest as "the Devil." Finally the squalid ceremony degenerates altogether into farce when a "big, bull-necked publican" officiously picks up the priest's conical straw hat and dangles it two inches above his head to protect him from the burning sun—implicitly a grotesque parody of a saint's halo or a martyr's crown. After all this, the narrator's laconic remark as "the hard dry Darling clods" (metonymically representative of the hard dry land that has occasioned this hard dry story) knock and rebound on the coffin's lid seems a wholly appropriate summation of what has gone before: "It didn't matter much—nothing does."

That line, or one very like its, had already occurred in another of Lawson's best stories, "The Bush Undertaker" (1892), and its aptness to the present text seems confirmed by the final paragraphs, in which the drowned man's identity is first revealed ("So his name's James Tyson"), then withdrawn ("J.T. wasn't his real name—only 'the name he went by'"), then revealed again ("We did hear, later on, what his real name was"), and finally cancelled once more ("we have already forgotten the name"). Naming, ultimate guarantee of the subject's uniqueness, has become a source of duplicity and confusion, its individuating function rendered problematic and at last illusory. The narrator, however, expresses no regret for his lapse of memory, and indeed, throughout the story, his tone has been disengaged, easily distracted by minutiae (he notices, for example, the way in which the drops of holy water leave "little round black spots" on the cloth with which the coffin is draped), digressing into anecdote ("I saw a coffin get stuck, once, at Rookwood"), unconcerned with welding his disparate perceptions into a neat structure.

And yet there is, perhaps, a hint of defensiveness in the narrator's resolute effort to distance himself from the events in which he has participated, a guarded disinclination to explore the full range of potential responses which his experience might generate. The dogged literalism with which he recounts the drowned man's last rites and the facile cynicism with which he concludes that nothing matters seem at least partly adopted to keep at arm's length the alternative of despair. A nightmare of universal estrangement and (as the dead man's anonymity implies) nonentity thus gets deflected into a wry comedy of bush manners. The speaker's determined antisentimentalism is calculated not only to establish the realistic superiority of his own narrative to falsifying stereotypes, but also to preempt any search for significance in an incident that is constructed merely as a campfire yarn (and which, in 1896, was appropriately incorporated in a collection entitled *While the Billy Boils*). And that casually discursive mode of presentation, presupposing as it does a known community of like-minded auditors, itself serves to palliate the horror that has been glimpsed. The "union" that the funeral of the dead worker has been unable to catalyse is implicitly achieved in the relationship between the narrator and his assumed readers. Alienated content coexists, and is contained by, companionable form, and this is crucial to the tale's meaning. For Lawson's story, despite its appearance of radical scepticism, can thus finally commit itself to the Australian legend of masculine solidarity—not as a comfortingly absolute value but rather as a strategy for survival on the brink of the abyss.

—Robert Dingley

THE UNKNOWN MASTERPIECE (Gillette)
by Honoré de Balzac, 1847

Given the sprawling abundance of *La Comédie humaine*, one does not immediately think of Balzac as a master of concentration. In "The Unknown Masterpiece," however, we are challenged (and delighted) not by a work of immense scale, but by a novella both stringent in design and resonant of meaning. It is a masterpiece of compression which invites critical expansion, as it were, in a great many different idioms and directions.

"The Unknown Masterpiece" was first published in the periodical *L'Artiste* in 1831. Its two sections were headed "Maître Frenhofer" and "Catherine Lescault." Expanded and amended, it appeared, in the same year, in volume three of Balzac's *Romans et contes philosophiques*. The first chapter was now headed "Gillette." For an edition of his *Études philosophiques*, published in 1837, Balzac made extensive additions (mainly involving Frenhofer's ideas on art). Other editions followed. In the edition published in 1847, *Le Provincial à Paris*, there are more differences, and, significantly, a change of title; the story is now called "Gillette." It is as "Gillette, or the Unknown Masterpiece" that Anthony Rudolf's excellent modern translation (from which quotations are here taken) was published.

This textual history gives rise to many problems which need not concern us here; of immediate significance are the changes in title. Initially we are invited to see the two points of focus as Frenhofer and Catherine Lescault— painter and subject (perhaps painter and mistress?). The first change counterpoints Gillette, the model and mistress of another painter, against Catherine Lescault. In the 1847 publication the whole work is entitled "Gillette." In narrative terms Gillette's role in the story is a relatively slight one; she can, though, be seen as a focus for many of the story's themes.

Gillette is the beautiful mistress and model (one theme is the ultimate irreconcilability of the two roles) of the young Nicholas Poussin, an impoverished artist newly arrived in Paris. He visits, uninvited, the studio of the well-established François Pourbus; he crosses the threshold "after toing and fro-ing . . . with the lack of resolve of a lover not daring to enter the presence of his first mistress." Poussin's entrance is effectively a kind of sexual initiation; throughout the tale artistic creativity is intimately bound up with questions of sexuality in general, and of sexual dominance in particular. He is a "poor neophyte"; initiation into another kind of mystery is also involved. At the studio of Pourbus, Poussin encounters a mysterious old man, Frenhofer, who fiercely criticises Pourbus's work and, in the process, makes extravagantly high demands of the "finished" work of art. With "a supernatural sparkle" in his eyes, and giving the impression that "there was a demon in

[his] body," he adds a small number of brushstrokes to Pourbus's painting of St. Mary of Egypt (formerly a prostitute). Frenhofer is rich, and is himself a painter; he has been working for ten years on a picture of Catherine Lescault (identified in the early versions of the story as a courtesan), reworking and revising the painting constantly. He is said to have, effectively bought from his master Mabuse the secret of giving to his figures an extraordinarily lifelike quality. He allows no one to see his work. When Poussin returns to his lodgings, it is to Gillette that he returns. He wishes her to sit for Frenhofer—which she feels to be tantamount to prostitution. Poussin begins to realise, for the first time, some of the agonizing conflicts set up by the conflicting demands of life and art. Chapter two opens with a scene of negotiation, central to the patterns of exchange that pervade the whole story. Poussin and Pourbus offer to "lend" Gillette to Frenhofer if he, in exchange, will allow them to see his canvas. It is to the language of sexual possession that Frenhofer instinctively turns in his reply. It would be to show them his "bride," it would be prostitution of the woman who has, for so long, "smiled" at him "with every stroke of the brush." Eventually he accepts the exchange; allowed to view his canvas Poussin and Pourbus are shocked and bewildered to find only "confused masses of colours contained by a multitude of strange lines, forming a high wall of paint." They can find no recognizable image of a woman, save a single foot which "had somehow managed to escape from an unbelievable, slow and progressive destruction." Frenhofer insists, through his tears, that he can see Catherine and that she is "marvellously beautiful." Gillette weeps, forgotten, in a corner of the studio, and declares her mingled hatred and love of Poussin. The next day it is learned that Frenhofer has burned both himself and his pictures.

One might fruitfully read the story as a fable of what men do to women in the name of art; or simply of what men do to women. Or as a prophetic fable of modern art, or as a variation on the Faustian myth of the absolute pursued to the point of self-destruction. It can be seen as an interrogation of the whole idea of artistic mimesis, insofar as it confronts the aesthetic and philosophical problems inherent in the idea that art might present realistic images of life (there are relevant implications here for Balzac's own art as a novelist). It is a vivid parable of the constant gap between the artist's conception and the realisation of that conception, of the seductions of incompleteness and revision, of infinite deferral. The relations between money and art, between creation and destruction, and between love and art are examined in complex patterns of antithesis and synthesis. We may think of Frenhofer in Faustian terms; but there are also important analogies with (and allusions to) other mythological structures and narratives—such as to the tale of Pygmalion and Galatea, to Icarus, Orpheus, and Prometheus. Such, indeed, is its richness that no reader is ever likely to feel that he or she fully knows "The Unknown Masterpiece."

—Glyn Pursglove

THE UNREST-CURE
by Saki, 1912

"The Unrest-Cure", a comic and cruel story by Saki comes from *The Chronicles of Clovis* (1912). Clovis, a witty but rather wild and wayward young man, here indulges one of his favourite forms of fun, an elaborate practical joke. The joke is at the expense of—and, to Clovis's way of thinking, to benefit—a quiet-living couple, brother and sister, who need, not the usual "rest-cure," for people whose lives are full of stress, but an "unrest-cure." For Mr. Huddle and his sister are "suffering from overmuch repose and placidity," as suggested by an anonymous friend on the train and overheard by Clovis, who copies, on "his sinister shirt-cuff" (meaning his left-hand cuff, but the other connotations of "sinister" are not inappropriate preparation of what is to come), the address-label on Mr. Huddle's bag.

The label itself appears in the very first sentence of the story: "J.P. Huddle, The Warren, Tilfield, near Slowborough." The second sentence describes the ultra-sedate Huddle as "the human embodiment of the label," but already Saki has provided the reader with suggestive proper names: as in all his stories, he chooses names for their comic or other resonances. Here, the exaggeratedly rural indicators (rabbit warren, tilled field, slow locality) have their predominantly peaceful connotations subtly undermined by hints of crowding and confusion in both "warren" and "huddle," which can mean not only to be secretive and hidden but also to be unceremoniously pushed and crowded together in hurried disorder—as happens when chaos is unleashed by Clovis, with his inventive telegrams and masquerading rigmarole, on the quiet routine of the Huddles. The initials "J.P.," repeated several times during the course of the narrative, seem hardly accidental either: the letters used after the name of a Justice of the Peace add layers of meaning when Mr. Huddle is unable to keep the peace in his own home, when he has to confront injustice and try to protect his innocent neighbours from being victims of a dreadful crime.

One critic has humorously supposed that Clovis is so named because he is "so appallingly frank"; but in this story, although it is obvious to the reader what is going on, he is far from being open to the other characters about what he is doing, as he needs to fool them by an ingenious deception, so a more appropriate connection to the Merovingian kingly name may be a shared Christian fanaticism in his inventive impersonation of "Prince Stanislaus," secretary to the imaginary bishop who plans a massacre of 26 local Jews on the Huddles' staircase. "This thing will be a blot on the Twentieth Century!" exclaims Huddle. Characteristically, the horror is combined with grim humour and word-play, as in Clovis's immediate retort to Huddle: "And your house will be the blotting-pad."

Humour is Saki's mode, and it is not always black, though it is often savage. His satirical portrayal of the Huddles is typical. Their routines have hitherto been disturbed by little more than irritation because a thrush's routine has changed. Miss Huddle is even more of a victim than her brother of Saki's comic malice, which is often misogynistic: with her appointed times for reading *Country Life,* for having curry or even for having a headache, she is not allowed any of her brother's moments of escape from caricature to character. Her response to Clovis's "Stanislaus" kissing her hand is treated in a way that smacks of both Wilde and Wodehouse: "Miss Huddle was unable to decide in her mind whether the action savoured of Louis Quatorzian courtliness or the reprehensible Roman attitude towards the Sabine women." This is farce as well as satire, and there are plenty of both in this story, as in many others by perhaps the finest of the Edwardian comic writers of short fiction.

But what makes this story is the admixture of unsettling elements: the sadism of an imagination that can add—to its pleasant send-ups of provincial English gentilities and imbecilities—the unpleasant, the uncomfortable, the cruel, the horrifying. Of course, the frightful happenings do not happen: there are not really armed men in the shrubbery; the postman, engaged to the housemaid, is not really killed by the assisting Boy Scouts; Sir Leon Birberry and Paul Isaacs are not really to be murdered "with cold steel" in cold blood. It is all, after all, a joke, an "unrest-cure" for those who have too much rest. In the end, as Clovis takes the train again, he supposes they will not be "in the least grateful for the Unrest-cure," and an unrestfulness is part of the effect this uncomfortable comic writer has on his readers.

—Michael Herbert

THE USE OF FORCE
by William Carlos Williams, 1938

When Williams wrote "The Use of Force" in 1933, as one of the contracted stories he had promised the editors of the proletarian magazine *Blast,* he was at the height of his social consciousness and his pain over the fact that many of his patients were living in poverty. America was devastated by the Great Depression, an economic disaster that lasted through the 1930's until World War II stimulated enough growth that the unemployed found jobs in war industries. Williams, a family doctor in the industrial city of Rutherford, New Jersey, knew what poverty meant—and after years of being a poet and an experimental prose writer, he began to write more clearly, more directly, about people's lives. "I lived among these people," he explained, "I was involved."

His aim in such 1930's stories as "The Use of Force," "Jean Beicke," "The Girl with a Pimply Face," "Four Bottles of Beer," and many others was to express the beauty as well as the pain of the common American. As he wrote in his *Autobiography,* "They had no knowledge and no skill at all. They flunked out, got jailed, got 'Mamie' with child, and fell away, if they survived, from their perfections. . . . They were perfect, they seem to have been born perfect, to need nothing else. They were there, living before me." "The Use of Force" appeared in Williams's second collection of short stories, *Life along the Passaic River,* a book titled to emphasize the connection between art and the people living in the hard-hit area around New Jersey's Passaic River.

Publishing his first collection of poetry more than 25 years before, Williams was a friend of Ezra Pound, H.D., and Marianne Moore during his medical school days in Philadelphia; since that time, he was considered a leading avant garde writer. He had not, however, been known as a political writer. Turning to fiction in the mid-1920's, he explored characters and themes new to modernist writing. James Joyce was mining his Irish boyhood, just as Ernest Hemingway was writing about his adolescence in Michigan and during World War I: Williams, rather then use his own earlier years as subject matter, turned to his working class patients. For him, the key question during these crucial years was "What shall the story be *about*?"

"The Use of Force" is a startling piece of fiction because it seems to have so little structure. Narrated as a physical struggle between the examining physician and the stubborn young patient, the story is a single episode, focused entirely on the battle of wills. It is written from the perspective of the male doctor, whose charge is to open the mouth of the young girl, Mathilda Olson, in order to see into her throat, to determine whether or not she has diphtheria. Held by her maudlin parents, whose dialogue with their daughter drives the brusque doctor into silence, the girl fights the physician with all the force she has. She scratches him and bites into pieces the tongue depressor he finally forces into her mouth; through the struggle, her jaws remain tightly shut and her secret guarded. The climax of the story comes when the doctor finally wrenches open her mouth and sees that she is, indeed, infected with the killing disease. The title of the story refers to both characters' "use of force."

Some readers have read the narrative as an exploration of the doctor's psyche, engaged as he is in forcing the young girl to submit to his examination. It has even been read as a rape story, privileging the erotic over the ostensible plotline in a manner that limits Williams's real genius with short fiction. What Williams has done with the figure of the physician contributes to this complex fiction: he shows the doctor as a man of passion, determined to win over the young patient, even though he admires her equally passionate will to resist his examination. But he also draws him as a man with an ironic sense of language, if not humor. The doctor talks tough: "I had to smile to myself. After all, I had already fallen in love with the savage brat."

Williams makes the reader question, here, in 1933, is this the kind of doctor I'd want for my child? Why is he calling her "a savage brat"? Why all this emphasis on the conquering role of the physician? But what the writer does is intensify the drama of a simple, daily occurrence by giving vitality to the characters' actions. The erotic undercurrents add a dimension to the struggle that is inherent in all male-female interaction, even if polite society—which the Olsens represent—denies its presence. Williams charges the story with a duel between the language of the Olsens and that of the physician: "He won't hurt you," says Mrs. Olsen. Yet the reader is caught up in the dramatic irony of knowing that the physician would indeed hurt her if he had to, because his only aim is to diagnose her illness. What he has to do to accomplish that matters little. Her parents begin labeling; they advise their struggling child to let the "nice" doctor have his way, while they call her "bad." Williams's physician sides with the child, and wonders how he could appear "nice" to her when he is struggling to overpower her so that he can jam things into her mouth.

Williams's style is both explicit and swift. No word is superfluous; everything that appears on the page is useful for the reader. But the spareness is not a skeletal journalistic treatment that oversimplifies. Rather, Williams's fiction remains intentionally suggestive and, often, refreshingly ambivalent about moral attitudes. While he is best known as a poet, having won the Pulitzer prize for poetry shortly after his death in 1963, Williams may eventually be seen as an equally important innovator in prose. "The Use of Force" remains a great American short story, precise in its delineation of character and carefully direct in its execution of narrative.

—Linda Wagner-Martin

V

THE VALIANT WOMAN
by J. F. Powers, 1947

One of the least prolific of major writers of contemporary American fiction, J. F. Powers has published only three collections of short stories and two novels in a career that now spans half a century. Nonetheless, his keen craftsmanship has established him as one of the most masterful storytellers of his time. His *Morte d'Urban,* a novel tracing the worldly rises, spiritual falls, and their reversals, of a Chicago priest, Father Urban, won the 1963 National Book award over Katherine Ann Porter's *Ship of Fools,* the work of a writer whom he considers a model of literary excellence. But Powers is equally admired for his short fiction. Most of the best of his stories dramatize with comic subtlety and shrewd psychological insight the seemingly desultory complications of midwestern Roman Catholic parish life. If his subject matter is in this sense "parochial," his skillful treatment of it is no more biased or propagandistic than, say, Joyce Carol Oates's focus on the banal terrors of teen-age shopping-mall culture. A Catholic himself, Powers has described his Church in terms, among others, of its crudeness and vulgarity; he typically writes about priests, he says, because their roles officially commit them to both the mundane/secular and the theological/sacral worlds.

The most anthologized of his stories is "The Valiant Woman," a brief early piece that appeared in *Accent* (Spring, 1947) and was collected in *Prince of Darkness and Other Stories* (1947). A brilliant example of Power's typical economy of means and method, it captures the essential terms of the entire adult life of its protagonist, Father John Firman, in just three slim scenes that take up but two or three hours on his 59th birthday. "They had come to the dessert in a dinner that was in shambles," it begins, and by the end of the first page the reader knows without the aid of any exposition that Father Firman has led a relentlessly ineffectual life, clerical and domestic alike. Joining him in this anti-celebration is another parish priest, Father Frank Nulty, who seems a vestigial companion of "bygone" better days of seminary life, commiserates silently with his host, and leaves as quickly as possible after a nervous sip of water, a quick bite of birthday cake, and a single cup of coffee. Dominating this scene and the two that follow is Mrs. Stoner, the housekeeper, whose tenure has virtually coincided with Firman's pastoral life. She had come to him years and years ago, widowed after only a year of marriage and, though "not really a girl perhaps, . . . not too old to marry again." She has long since been accustomed to saying "she had given him the best years of her life." Long since, too, has she had absolute rule of the roost, rolling up the ball of her personality out of traits descended from Irving's Dame Van Winkle, Twain's Widow Douglas, and Thurber's Mrs. Walter Mitty. Poor Father Firman is utterly feckless: there exists for him no 20 years' sleep, no raft nor river; he is denied as well the saving grace of Walter Mitty's capacities of fantasizing.

The story's central metaphor is, on its surface, an hilarious parody of married life. Powers takes his title from Proverbs (31:10-31), King Lamuel's account of his mother's description of an ideal wife, only a rare few bits of which seem to apply accurately to Mrs. Stoner, who casts her stones in every direction. The second scene, a ritual game of "honeymoon" bridge, begins with her accusing Father Firman of either having a nail in his shoe or not trimming his toenails often enough, and it ends with her "slash[ing] down the last card, a miserable deuce trump, and [doing] in the hapless king of hearts." "Skunked you!" she announces in ferocious triumph, and "the final murderous hour in which all they wanted to say . . . came out in the cards." All the while the bully-ragged priest has been too distracted taking the measure of Mrs. Stoner's character to attend to the game's intricacies. No one, he's convinced, could say that Mrs. Stoner was "a bad person": her cleanliness covered a multitude of faults, such as her inability to cook or play the organ, her snooping, her censoring of the pamphlet rack, her disapproving "of bad marriages in the presence of the victims," her hiding his books and keeping him from smoking, her picking his friends, her total lack of humor—"except at cards." The list is a veritable litany of items great and trivial. But that she is clean prevails over all: "Sometimes her underwear hung down beneath her dress like a paratrooper's pants, but it and everything she touched was clean." No wonder, then, that Father Nulty left off joshing his friend by humming "Wedding Bells Are Breaking Up That Old Gang of Mine." And no wonder that the one trick Father Firman remembers having been played in seminary days involved his getting up a New Year's morning and sitting on a freshly painted toilet seat. "Happy Circumcision! Hah," roars Father Nulty. Buffoonery aside, the remembered incident marks the moment of Father Firman's comic/symbolic castration. Father Firman needs no further spur to an indomitably celibate life, but in Mrs. Stoner he has a gilt-edged guarantee of it.

In the third scene Mrs. Stoner and Father Firman retire to their separate bedrooms, she to the much more commodious guest room, he to the "back" one whose screen door, unrepaired for decades, invites mosquitoes. One of these "wily" creatures, possessed of "preternatural cunning," lands first on the priest's back, then on a statue of St. Joseph, and then, knowing the priest's thoughts, "flew high away." Swinging in wild frustration, Father Firman whacks "St. Joseph [that most saintly of husbands] across the neck," and "the statute fell to the floor and broke." The scene is a retake of the opening pages where Father Nulty has, with aplomb, "sent [a dead mosquito] spinning with a plunk of his forefinger." All Father Firman can do in his rage is curse ("Mosquitoes—damn it!") and curse again, in his new-found knowledge—"And only the female bites!" When Mrs. Stoner rebukes him ("Shame on you, Father. She needs the blood for her eggs") and Father Firman "lunged again," the reader knows that the story has been not only an elaborate joke but a gradual revelation of the priest's character. He had been more insightful than he knew or, perhaps, will ever know, when he had "found her ferocity pardonable, more a defect of the flesh, venial, while his own trouble was in the will, mortal." In presenting his own case, then, against Mrs. Stoner, Father Firman has revealed unknowingly his own dark underside.

—J. Donald Crowley

A VERY OLD MAN WITH ENORMOUS WINGS
(Un señor muy viejo con alas enormes)
by Gabriel García Márquez, 1968

Written between his first major novels, Cien años de soledad (One Hundred Years of Solitude) and El otoño del patriarca (The Autumn of the Patriarch), "Un señor muy viejo con alas enormes" ("A Very Old Man with Enormous Wings") is one of two stories the Colombian Gabriel García Márquez designated "A Tale for Children." (The other is "The Handsomest Drowned Man in the World.") The author has never explained the heading, but both stories have at their center a fantastic person who enters, briefly, a more realistic world and transforms it in unexpected ways. Stylistically, the stories belong to the magic realism of the first part of One Hundred Years of Solitude—a world of wonders, where marvelous happenings are both impossible and innocent. Collected with La increíble y triste historia de la Cándida Eréndira (Innocent Eréndira), the two "tales for children" bring to an end the epic style of One Hundred Years of Solitude as García Márquez freed himself to develop the narrative voices of The Autumn of the Patriarch.

While "The Handsomest Drowned Man in the World" is obviously a study of the power for good of illusion (or delusion), the point or moral of "A Very Old Man" is considerably less clear, wherein resides its moral. Like its protagonist, the story provokes and resists moralizing interpretation. The very simple narrative line is complicated by details either comically insignificant or resonant with social and political implications: the reader must decide which, when, and what signifies. Closure is provided by autobiographical elements familiar from García Márquez's other work, and at the story's heart is the invention of a wackily reimagined angel, an invention that reinvents others' visions.

"A Very Old Man with Enormous Wings" starts in the sad, muddy, poor, yet still iridescent world of the Caribbean littoral, as a couple cope with crabs, rain, and the threatening sickness of their new born child. On the third day, in the mud of the courtyard, Pelayo the husband finds an old man, groaning face down in the mud, unable to rise because he is impeded by his enormous wings. After the wings, the reader's second surprise is the de-romanticization or de-sentimentalization of the angel. This "drenched great-grandfather" with wings is no angel as art has represented angels to us. His buzzard wings have parasites; he has few hairs and fewer teeth, and he stinks. To the townsfolk, as to the reader, he immediately presents a problem of interpretation: what is he? how should he be treated?

Thereafter, the angel's story follows a simple trajectory through the townsfolks' response to him. An initially brutal response to a stranger—club him to death, lock him in the chicken coop, put him on a raft with three-days' provisions—is replaced by celebrity, as others crowd to see him. Is he a supernatural creature or a circus animal? (Here an allegory of the successful artist or the imagination steps in.) Should he be mayor of the world, a five-star general, or an occasion for eugenics? (Here politics and social engineering insert themselves). The priest has doubts and suspicions, but no powerful alternative interpretation: he consults authority, without success. (Religion, its good intentions, and its futility make a bow.) From nowhere, unexplained, unsummoned, troops with fixed bayonets disperse the mob gathered at Elisenda's house. (The brutal force, usually invisible, that keeps the social order intact and possesses actual, not theoretical power, makes a fleeting appearance.) Sick, he raves like an old Norwegian. (García Márquez reminds us again that the Norse first discovered America from the west, the initial discovery having come from the east.) As the parentheses indicate, the townsfolks' multiple interpretations and the narrative's odd details spin off in different directions. The story of the angel is intrinsically coherent, but meaningless: he comes and he goes, yet just as the oddity of the angel impels the townsfolk to interpret, so the oddity of the story impels the reader to repeat their activity, interpreting them as well as the angel.

The desire for coherent interpretation, for narratives that "make sense," is worked through in the passing of the angel's celebrity. Eventually, the town's attention shifts from an indifferent, perverse angel who does not speak to them, to a more satisfying and interpretable story, the moral tale of the girl who was changed into a spider—a tarantula the size of a ram—for disobeying her parents. (Like Eréndira, in Innocent Eréndira and Her Heartless Grandmother, the metamorphosed girl had earlier appeared in One Hundred Years of Solitude.) Her story has a clear and useful meaning readily applied in daily life: honor your father and mother, or at least obey them, and do not go out dancing all night. The angel, however, does not work like that. He is irreducible and irascible and useless. He may be allegorized, but the allegorization is not he.

The story ends many years later when the angel's wings grow back and he flies away. The child he saves (or fails to take away) marks the passage of time, and the angel himself is a battered old man, a figure traceable to the author's grandfather. Such a figure, familiar from La horarasca ("Leafstorm"), El coronel no tiene quien le escriba (No One Writes to the Colonel), and One Hundred Years of Solitude, would appear transformed yet again in The Autumn of the Patriarch and, later still, as Bolívar in El general en su labertino (The General in His Labyrinth). The angel's last years as nuisance evoke the senile grandmother (Ursula in One Hundred Years of Solitude, "she" in "Bitterness for Three Sleepwalkers").

Save that his departure has something to do with the wind from the sea (inspiration? exile? freedom?) and his arrival coincided with the recovery of the sick baby, we do not know where the angel came from or where he is going. He may reflect—or incarnate—the irritation of a successful author (or his inarticulate, unprotected novel, speaking only its own language) poked at and branded, scolded and suspected, accused of not having a clear and proper moral (a frequent complaint made in Latin America against One Hundred Years of Solitude when it appeared in 1967). He may be a scrap that did not make it into that novel (where his opposite number the Wandering Jew appears and Remedios the Beauty rises into the heavens with sheets for wings): what would happen if an angel came to town, and what would an angel really look like? An image around which interpretation laps and breaks, the old angel argues the superiority of the image (and the imagination) to interpretive apparatus, while he illustrates the irresistible need to interpret.

—Regina Janes

A VILLAGE ROMEO AND JULIET (Romeo und Julia auf dem Dorf)
by Gottfried Keller, 1856

The title of Keller's story "Romeo und Julia auf dem Dorf" ("A Village Romeo and Juliet") prepares the reader for warring families, frustrated love, and tragic death, but his addition of "Village" signals a particular reworking of the Shakespearean tale. This is, in fact, a paupers' love tragedy, which was initially inspired not by Shakespeare but by a newspaper report; it consequently places less emphasis on passion and familial enmity than on the social and psychological pressures that prevent a destitute couple from marrying. The story has justifiably become the most famous of Keller's most popular collection of short stories, *Die Leute von Seldwyla* (*The People of Seldwyla*). It first appeared in 1856.

The third-person narrative has four broad sections. The first depicts a day in the life of two hard-working farmers and the carefree play of their children; it also introduces the plot of land which separates their fields, the covetous attitude both have towards it, and the fact that its rightful owner cannot prove his claim. The second section, which condenses twelve years, sketches the way in which the farmers fall out over this land, and portrays the ensuing humiliations and impoverishment to which futile litigation reduces them. During the physical fight to which they finally succumb, their children discover their love for one another. A third section covers a day and a night, and reveals the increasingly hopeless love of these young people, whose prospects are diminished even further when the boy throws a stone at the girl's father, an act that leads to the latter's dementia and eventual institutionalisation. A fourth section describes the final day and night the couple spend together before they commit suicide by drowning. This section is by far the longest, encompassing almost half of the novella.

Keller expressed satisfaction with the "simplicity and clarity" he felt he had achieved, and there are indeed few characters, a simple strand to the plot, and no complexities of time scale. The sentences are sometimes long, but they are never complex, and the language employed is also undemanding. There is a surprising amount of dialogue, and, more typically for Keller, an abundance of adjectives. Throughout the tale the author focusses in key scenes which are described in considerable detail. Such detail is heavy at times, and sometimes gratuitous; but in this novella, in contrast to many of his others, Keller does succeed in using description and apparent digression to bring out aspects of psychology and to adumbrate developments.

Keller takes pains to emphasise the sociological dimension to his plot: the barriers preventing a successful union of his lovers are not, as in Shakespeare, simply the opposition of parents. The families concerned are humble, but when the tale commences they are financially stable and proud. Their descent to poverty is demoralising and is experienced keenly by the two children, who are very much a product of their environment, are highly sensitive to changes in social standing and to moral codes, and ashamed of the behaviour of their fathers.

In contrast to their Shakespearean forebears, Keller's young couple are offered a way out of their dilemma. Although they have no hope of marrying and settling down in the bourgeois security they both long for, they are presented with an alternative way of life: the "Black Fiddler," the rightful owner of the land that has sparked the catastrophe, encourages them to escape with him and his band for a life in the woods where they can live a free, bohemian style of existence. Although initially seduced by this slightly demonic figure of temptation and the bacchic revelry in which they become involved, the lovers recognise they will be unable to forget their former way of life. Keller shows they are too keenly aware of their ingrained sense of respectability and morality. They also are disturbed by the thought that such a life might lead to infidelity, which neither wishes to contemplate. Although they maintain their sense of moral values, the pair are so roused by the Fiddler's music, wine, and the mock marriage ceremony he has acted out for them, that they cannot resist a night of sexual union; but it is immediately followed by suicide.

Much of the suggestive power of this novella is contained in the symbols, such as the fateful plot of land, the Black Fiddler, certain colours (notably red and black), and aspects of the natural world such as flowers and stones. These are interrelated, and they are also connected with the moral implications of the story, in particular the tragic consequences of greed and selfishness among the petit bourgeois.

The story is sometimes considered a prime example of German poetic realism, a loose term which refers to a period in the mid-19th century when writers, particularly of short prose, were tending towards a "filtering" of their world, a selective, imaginative approach to reality which avoided the vulgar and the political and preferred nature as a background. Keller certainly idealises parts of the world he presents. The goodness, beauty, and purity of his young lovers is beyond normal experience, and there are various idyllic touches. But the author does not overlook the misfits, failures, and socially underprivileged in the society he depicts, and the shifting tone adopted by the narrator suggests an unease with the world he is portraying. This is clearest in the final sentences of the story, which contain the severely moralising—and totally inappropriate—response of the local press to the tragedy.

—Peter Hutchinson

WAKEFIELD
by Nathaniel Hawthorne, 1835

In the development of the modern short story, Nathaniel Hawthorne has few peers. In fact, no short story writer produced work of the same calibre, complexity, and form earlier than Hawthorne. Some of his best stories were published as early as 1830, and among them are stories prototypical of the form. Typically Hawthorne's stories deal with appearance and reality and make use of symbols of guilt, isolation, secrecy, excessive ego involvement (*Hubris*), and various manifestations of what has been called the conflict between head and heart or emotion and intellect.

"Wakefield," collected in *Twice-Told Tales,* is not one of Hawthorne's best stories; but it is a fascinating one, falling into a category that seems to have been a favorite of Hawthorne's—the "What if" kind. In "Wakefield," the query is what if a man went away for a few days leaving his wife of ten years behind, stayed away for 20 years, and then returned to his wife who thought him long since dead?

In "Wakefield," Hawthorne poses the question as the initial challenge. What kind of a man could engage in so freakish a mode of marital delinquency? Not only does Wakefield leave, but he does not go anywhere, just one block from his own house. The action, Hawthorne states, is a folly of purist originality and is, therefore, worth thinking about. Readers, Hawthorne suggests, may think on their own, or, if they prefer, may "ramble" with Hawthorne seeking clues, speculating about motives, and perhaps coming upon meaning.

The story begins, "What sort of a man was Wakefield? We are free to shape out our own idea and call it by name." Here, at the very beginning of the story is where Hawthorne merges fact and fiction. It matters not whether anything that we say corresponds in any way to any facts we can discover; the truth is in the telling. "Wakefield" is a creation operating in a make-believe world; but no matter; the truth we seek is not so much related to facts of the experiential world but rather to point of view and what Hawthorne refers to as the proper use of light and shadow for distancing effects. In "Wakefield" the narrator never allows readers to forget that the man we are speculating upon is our own creation and we call him Wakefield.

In this story, the narrator invites us to agree with him that Wakefield is a man of no particularly singular attributes. He is intelligent enough but has no intellectual curiosity. He is fond enough of his wife but not so devoted to her that he cannot play the trickster. He is not exactly eccentric, but there is something strange about him, as his wife has noticed. He keeps petty secrets hardly worth revealing. She, knowing his love of secrecy, does not question him as to where he is going, nor does she protest when he says he may be gone three or four days. He, however, thinks he will perplex her by staying away a week. As Wakefield leaves his wife gets a momentary glance of his face with a slight smile upon it. Years afterwards she recalls this visage and imagines the same face and expression in a coffin or in heaven. But mostly she doubts that he is dead though all evidence points to that fact. In his musings, however, the narrator has jumped ahead of himself and must hurry to catch Wakefield. It develops that there was no hurry for Wakefield is but gone a street away and there he stays. He is sure he will be noticed, but he is not. No one looks for him.

Occasionally stopping his narrative, the narrator provides advice for Wakefield, warning him of his own insignificance, telling him to go home, for once he opens a gap in his wife's affections it will always be there. But Wakefield finds himself caught in a morass similar to the one he was in before he left home. He has moved from one "system" to another, taking up similar habits. Several times curiosity has carried him to his old house but he flees before he is noticed. And finally he is so habituated into the new system that he is powerless to act. Meanwhile, the narrator points out that Wakefield's affection for his wife remains the same. He is faithful to her, but her affection for him has probably disappeared over the years she has thought him dead.

To this point summary narrative has provided the whole story of Wakefield's drama. "Now for a narrative scene," the narrator announces, again emphasizing his own role as showman, puppeteer. For there is, the narrator admits, a certain inevitability in what has occurred. It is as though once started the train of events cannot be stopped. The red wig that Wakefield assumes becomes a substitute for his wife and he refuses to return though often his feet carry him in the direction of his former home. Some 20 years pass and on his customary walk (in the cold and rain) past his old house, Wakefield chances to see his wife sitting inside by a warm and friendly fire.

The comfort factor is too much. "Shall he remain outside?" The narrator answers for Wakefield. "Wakefield is no fool." He enters his old abode expecting his wife to be as she was and he enters with the same crafty smile that he left with. But Wakefield really is a fool if he expects to take up where he left off. His wife has had her separate life too nicely tuned without him.

"Wakefield" is a strange story about a character who exists in no real story, about a change that is no real change, concerning a new system no different from the old, and a situation more silly than tragic. Can alienation ever be its own excuse? Can one ever escape a social bond, even the most prideful?

—Mary Rohrberger

THE WALKER-THROUGH-WALLS (Le Passe-Muraille)
by Marcel Aymé, 1943

Author of an impressive body of work, including some 80 short stories, 17 novels, 12 plays, and 4 essays, Marcel Aymé did not achieve notoriety until late in his life. One reason, according to Graham Lord, may have been that "critics were particularly nonplussed by the ease with which [he] moved between reality and fantasy." Also, he had a reputation as a right-wing writer, resulting from his friendship with Brasillach and Céline, for example, in a society where the intelligentsia was vastly left-wing. Today, however, studies of Aymé have been published in France and in the United States, and some of his works, essays and articles, have been assembled by Michel Lecureur, author of several studies on Aymé, in a recently published volume entitled *Vagabondages*.

Among his 43 fantastic or supernatural short stories, "Le Passe-Muraille" ("The Walker-Through-Walls"), first published as the title story of a 1943 collection, is probably Aymé's most successful one (see J.L. Dumont in *Marcel Aymé et le merveilleux*). In contradiction to the implications of its title, "The Walker-Through-Walls" starts with two elements that are indicative of a traditional story: the name and address of the main character. This is immediately counteracted, however, by the information that Dutilleul, the main character, a "third-grade clerk at the Ministry of Registration," finds out one day that he can walk through walls. This quick shift to the supernatural done in a very matter-of-fact manner, combined with Dutilleul's lack of reaction to his "special aptitude," gives a dimension of reality to the story.

Not only can Dutilleul walk through walls, but he does it "without experiencing discomfort"; the implication is that others may have already walked through walls and did experience discomfort from doing so. Possibly Dutilleul is better skilled than others or his gift is more "complete." The doctor Dutilleul needs to be convinced of what Dutilleul is actually experiencing—not so much because of the impossibility of the occurrence, but in order to justify his prescribing the adequate medication, "tetravalent reintegration powder." The fact that such a medication exists confirms that others may have caught this "illness." The contents of the medication (rice flour and centaur's hormones) contribute to the fantastic setting as the mythological animal is found in the reality of the story.

The discovery of Dutilleul's ability to walk through walls is treated by both doctor and patient as if it were a mere headache, as if two pills could take care of it. It does not affect Dutilleul, who has "little love for adventure" and is "non-receptive to the lures of the imagination." He goes on leading his life as usual, "without ever being tempted to put his gift to the test," until one day M. Mouron, his superior at the Ministry of Registration, is replaced by M. Lecuyer. This rather ordinary event is referred to as "extraordinary" and it is going to "revolutionise" Dutilleul's life. The discovery of his "special ability" hasn't provoked the slightest stir in his imagination, but M. Lecuyer's "far-reaching reforms" ("calculated to trouble the peace of mind of his subordinate") will. To Dutilleul's horror, he is required to change the formula that he used for years to start letters, to one that is shorter and more "trans-Atlantic." "With a machine-like obstinacy," Dutilleul keeps using the former, increasing his superior's animosity, which creates an "almost oppressive atmosphere" in the Ministry. The crisis is such that Dutilleul ends up brooding over it for "as much as a quarter of an hour" before going to sleep.

The caricature is now complete. Dutilleul, the civil servant, is shown as thoughtless, lacking any intellectual substance, robot-like, and unimaginative. Through Dutilleul's "adventures" Aymé pursues one of his favorite themes as satirises the excessive and absurd uniformity of any kind of routine. He uses as an example what is viewed in French society as the epitome of repetitiveness: government work, and its effect on the human mind.

Although imagination (the "queen of the faculties," according to the French poet Baudelaire) did not disturb Dutilleul's life, pride over a very trivial item does. It causes him to be inspired when, in itself, the discovery of his ability to walk through walls has failed to do so. Now, surprisingly and ironically, "sanguinary thoughts" pop into Dutilleul's mind, and in a facetious manner Dutilleul sticks his head through the wall of the little room where he has been relegated as a punishment for his "rebellion," and he appears in M. Lecuyer's office like an insulting "trophy of the chase." Later, "having acquired a certain skill at the game," Dutilleul feels the urge to go further and terrorizes his superior with his tricks, described as demoniac by the narrator. After two weeks of this treatment Lecuyer, extremely disturbed, both physically and mentally, is finally taken into a mental home.

A new life starts for Dutilleul. He now feels a "yearning," "a new, imperious impulse"—"the need to walk through walls" to which the narrator also refers as "the call of the other side of the wall," using an animalistic terminology. In an almost philosophical tone that enhances the irony, the narrator acknowledges that walking through walls does not constitute an end in itself; as a beginning, it calls for a reward. In search of more inspiration, Dutilleul turns to the "crime column" of the newspaper. Then, without any kind of transition, the narrator very casually announces the "Dutilleul's first burglary took place in a large credit establishment on the right bank of the Seine."

This amazingly rapid transformation of Dutilleul into a burglar adds a new dimension to the world of the narration and to the satire. The dull, unimaginative, robot-like civil servant has become "the werewolf" (another animalistic term), a gentleman *cambrioleur*, an Arsène Lupin, as Michel Lecureur suggests (in *La Comédie humaine de Marcel Aymé*). Like his brilliant predecessor, Dutilleul/werewolf has a strong impact on French society. Not only is the whole Parisian population now in awe of his exploits, but any woman "with romance in her heart" lusts for him. And two ministers have to resign as a result of their failure to arrest "the werewolf."

After having finally "allowed himself to be arrested" in order to prove to his colleagues that he is the "genius," Dutilleul has the opportunity to fulfill his career, that is, to experience prison walls. As the narrator declared; "no man who walks through walls can consider his career even moderately fulfilled if he has not had at least one taste of prison." After escaping several times Dutilleul, his pride wounded, decides that he has had enough of prison life and goes into hiding. He undergoes a complete metamorphosis. But ironically, the drastic transformation simply consists of changing the four elements the narrator used early on in the story to identify the character: Dutilleul has shaved his black tuft of beard, substituted hornrimmed spectacles for his 'pince-nez', started to wear a "sports cap and a suit of plusfour in loud check," and changed his apartment.

Now comes the moralistic aspect of this tale. Dutilleul, whose disguise has now been discovered by Gen Paul, painter and friend of Aymé, is on the verge of leaving Paris for Egypt because the pyramids constitute the highest challenge for a walker-through-walls. However, he meets his fate in the person of a ravishing blonde who is immediately seduced by him because "nothing stirs the imagination of the young women of the present day more than plus-fours and horn-rimmed spectacles." His passion for this young woman (who is locked up by a jealous, but dissolute, husband who leaves her alone every night) bring about the end of his adventure. As a result of their transports Dutilleul suffers from a severe headache that will, ironically, cause the cessation of his ability to walk through walls. Instead of taking aspirin, Dutilleul takes two pills of the "tetravalent" that he had negligently thrown into a drawer. After sensing some "friction" and "a feeling of resistance" on the third night of his going through the walls to meet with his lover, Dutilleul finds himself "petrified in the interior of the wall."

However shocking and horrifying, the ending is treated in the same matter-of-fact manner already encountered at the beginning. Here again, this extraordinary occurrence appears realistic. "To this day," the narrator adds, Dutilleul is "incorporated in the stone." And not only can the birds of Paris hear Dutilleul mourn "for his glorious career and his too-brief love," but Gen Paul plays the guitar regularly "to console the unhappy prisoner." It is not Dutilleul who goes through the walls now but only the notes of the music which "pierce through the heart of the stone like drops of moonlight." The irony here is undoubtedly enhanced by the use of terms like "mourning" and "tomb," which give a macabre dimension to the story in contrast with the almost fairy-like image evoked by the last line.

Like in "Dermuche" and "The Seven-League Boots," two other Aymé stories, the fantastic in "The Walker-Through-Walls" does not find a resolution in the end. Dermuche, the criminal who has metamorphosed as a baby, is executed for a crime that he has not committed because, as his transformation went on, the crime came undone. Antoine, the poor little boy, not his richer companions, of "The Seven-League Boots" was finally given the magic pair and he finds himself "at the end of the earth"—"in ten minutes." Dutilleul, the walker-through-walls, becomes the beating heart of an object that never had a heart before, namely the wall.

—Nicole Buffard-O'Shea

THE WALL (Le Mur)
by Jean-Paul Sartre, 1939

A philosopher by training and vocation, Jean-Paul Sartre was about 30 years old when he began to experiment with the possibility that his philosophy could reach a wider public, if his ideas could be represented in literary terms. His first experiment, a novel, was completed in 1936, and published in 1938 under the title *La Nausée* (*Nausea*). In 1937, he tested public reaction to his philosophical fiction by publishing a short story about the Spanish Civil War, called "Le Mur," ("The Wall"), in one of the leading literary journals of the day. The favorable reaction led to the publication of a book of five short stories in 1939, with "Le Mur" leading off the volume, and supplying the volume's title.

The stories of *The Wall* were, like the novel *Nausea*, rather abstract in their underlying ideas, but were plainly intended to offer concrete examples of how the abstract ideas might come to the surface and find expression in the behavior of people. As a story about the Spanish Civil War, for example, "The Wall" took as its subject the reactions of a small group of three Republicans, taken prisoner by the Fascists during the civil war, who, after a brief interrogation, are told that they will be executed the next morning. Their reactions are, of course, primarily psychological and emotional, but Sartre surprises his readers by his determinedly physical approach to the psychological manifestations of his characters.

Sartre chooses one of the prisoners, Pablo Ibbieta, as the first-person narrator, and the opening sentence announces that everything will be described, in the first instance, as a physical response, which can then be interpreted by the narrator: "They pushed us into a big white room and I began to blink because the light hurt my eyes." In the same opening paragraph, Pablo observes two prisoners ahead of him in line to be interrogated, and remarks: "the smaller one kept hitching up his pants; nerves." The tone is thus established from the outset that the narrator and his companions are in a situation that produces anxiety and fear, and that the narrator gauges what is happening by observing the bodily reactions of himself and of others. Consigned to an unheated room in the cellar of the hospital that was being used for dealing with prisoners, the three Republicans soon begin to shiver from the cold, until an official comes in to announce that they have all been condemned to be executed by a firing squad the next morning. Pablo soon notices that he has stopped shivering, and that his companions have turned a peculiar shade of pale grey. He wonders if he looks the same, recognizes the greyness as the color of fear, and goes through mental reflections about being "hard" enough not to fear, and to prepare for the "clean" and dignified death he desires to achieve. When he sees his companions urinating involuntarily and without being aware of it, Pablo recognizes with disgust that his own efforts, and those of his companions, to prepare themselves for death and come to terms with the idea of dying, are doomed to failure. The observable evidence tells him that they, and he too, are unable even to control their own bodily functions. How, then, can they expect to control their thoughts, and their emotions?

About half way through the narrative, readers usually stop to reflect that the very existence of the narrative implies that Pablo, at least, is not going to be executed. If it were otherwise, the narrative they are reading could not exist. The remainder of the story is given over, less and less to the various manifestations of terror and desperation on the part of Pablo's fellow prisoners, and more and more to the separate question of how Pablo will escape execution. The account of what happens to Pablo becomes the last, necessary twist in the pattern of the story's events to underline irrefutably the philosophical point Sartre has designed his story to make: namely, that human beings cannot succeed in grasping what death signifies, nor even in controlling what one's own death will signify. One may wish a "clean" death, as Pablo does, but one has no way of making it happen by one's own will. When human beings are faced with the immediate inevitability of death by firing squad, when they are up against the wall, as the story puts it, they cannot control events or their own conduct.

Pablo is offered the last-minute chance to live if he will tell his captors where his revolutionary colleague, Ramon Gris, is hiding. Having already accepted his own death as a certainty, anyway, because he will not betray his colleague, Pablo decides to trick his captors by naming a false hiding place, just to send the Fascists on a wild goose chase, and make fools of them, before he dies. When it turns out, by pure chance, that the false hiding place was the right one, because Ramon Gris has moved, and Pablo learns that his colleague has been killed, he laughs uncontrollably at the absurd and unpredictable outcome of his "joke." Neither life nor death have meaning, Pablo seems to suggest by his reaction. The world is irredeemably absurd and senseless.

The great power of this tale lies less in the philosophical conclusion about the meaninglessness of existence—an idea that was a staple of Sartre's thought at that time—than in the vividly detailed and graphically physical account the story gives of the fear of death, and of the cold cruelty with which that kind of terror can be—and usually is—exploited by sadistic captors. Sartre's story is a new kind of literary realism: not just an accurate description of the real world, but an intense verbal evocation of the physical sensations of the way the world feels, to human beings in extreme situations when life and death are at stake, when they are "up against the wall." That is what makes "The Wall" a painfully unforgettable reading experience.

—Murray Sachs

WANDERING WILLIE'S TALE
by Sir Walter Scott, 1824

Sir Walter Scott's "The Two Drovers," published in 1827, has been described as the first short story in English, but another of his works follows a much older tradition. "Wandering Willie's Tale," which appeared as part of the novel, *Redgauntlet,* published in 1824, is a deliberate imitation of the art of the oral storyteller. This is an ancient form of popular entertainment found all over the world. It has such a strong tradition in Scotland that it still survives there and is now in the middle of a revival in defiance of the competition from modern technology.

The traditional storyteller in Scotland used, and to some extent still uses, one of the two languages native to Scotland, Scottish Gaelic and Lowland Scots. The former, which has close affinities to Irish Gaelic, is a Celtic language utterly distinct from English. Lowland Scots (or Lallans), on the other hand, shares a common origin with English. It therefore has a basic similarity to English and much common vocabulary. In the three centuries of almost continuous war between Scotland and England, from the end of the 13th to the beginning of the 17th century, Scots developed independently with influence from Gaelic and from the countries with which Scotland had a close association, France, the Netherlands, Germany and Scandinavia. In this period Scots was used by all classes and for all purposes and, especially in the 15th century, was the language of some of the finest poetry that was being written anywhere in Europe.

When Scott wrote his great novels set in Scotland it was therefore quite natural for him to use English for the narrative and Scots for the conversations of the Scottish characters. Scott was a master in his native tongue, although his English to modern ears is often somewhat ponderous. The speech in Scots in these novels (particularly *Waverley, Guy Mannering, The Antiquary, Old Mortality, Rob Roy, The Heart of Midlothian,* and *Redgauntlet*) are their most striking, moving, and entertaining passages. As

the English novelist and critic Virginia Woolf remarked, "the lifeless English turns to living Scots."

"Wandering Willie's Tale" is the longest continuous passage in Scots in all of Scott's novels. It is a tale told by one of the Scots speaking characters, a wandering blind fiddler, the sort of travelling entertainer who might easily combine storytelling with his music. The tale is about an experience of his grandfather, Steenie Steenson, a piper and tenant farmer. He lived in the "killing times" in the late 17th century when royalist troops were persecuting the Covenanters, people who refused to accept the religious settlement imposed by the king. Steenie, a tenant of a violent persecutor, Sir Robert Redgauntlet, goes to pay his overdue rent, which he had scraped together with difficulty; but before he can be given his receipt, Sir Robert suddenly dies. In the absence of this written proof, Redgauntlet's heir demands payment again. In this dilemma, Steenie, in despair, rides through a dark wood, after fortifying himself with brandy. He meets a stranger who promises to bring him to the old Redgauntlet for the receipt. So Steenie encounters him, carousing with his dead friends, in hell presumably, and gets his receipt. It is a tale of the supernatural, although with hints of a rational explanation.

The brilliance of the story, one of the best in our literature, is in the telling. There is no superfluous word and no word that could be improved. The language has the naturalness of speech, but also an unstrained felicity and lyrical flow. The historical setting, the characters, the atmosphere are all conveyed with a directness and brevity, and a combination of the eerie and the comic, that recalls the best of the Border ballads. It is in prose what Robert Burn's "Tam O Shanter" is in verse, a supreme use of what R.L. Stevenson called "this illustrious and malleable tongue." Out of the whole of Scott's vast output, impressive and widely influential as it is, this short tale is his single most perfect achievement.

The Scots language need not be an obstacle to anyone who reads English. The edition by Graham Tulloch, *The Two Drovers and Other Stories* in the World's Classics series (1987), includes glossary and notes.

—Paul H. Scott

WAR (Quando si comprende)
by Luigi Pirandello, 1919

Although Luigi Pirandello is best known as a dramatist, he himself felt that his short stories, of which he wrote over two hundred, would be his primary claim to artistic fame. Reflecting his mastery of drama, many of his stories, what the Italians, in the tradition of Boccaccio, call *novelle,* focus on character who reveal themselves primarily by dialogue. "Quando si comprende" ("War"), published in a 1919 collection and anthologized a number of times in college short story texts, is one of the best examples of this dramatic technique, for it focuses on a single situation limited in space and time in which a small number of characters reveal a hidden drama through speech. In their discussion of the story in the famous anthology *Understanding Fiction,* Cleanth Brooks and Robert Penn Warren point out the lack of physical action in the story and emphasize its debate-centered structure.

The basic thematic tension in the story centers on the difference between a mother's inarticulate and irrational grief over the loss of her son and a father's elaborate argument justifying the death of his own son. What chiefly characterizes the woman is her physical bulk; she is a "shapeless bundle" who seems to have no control and must be hoisted into the train car by her husband. Almost dehumanized under her big coat, she twists and wriggles, at times "growling like a wild animal."

The story begins with the husband's excuse for the woman's state, for he feels it is his duty to explain to the five people in the second-class carriage. When he says she is to be pitied for her son has been called to the front, the others begin to plead their own cases. One has a son who has already come back wounded twice, another has two sons at the front. The argument begins when the husband says his case is worse than the man with two sons, for he would have no one left if his only son is killed. Not to be outdone, the man replies that all love is given to each child without discrimination; thus he is not suffering half for each son but double for each.

The debate becomes further complicated when a fat man calls all this "nonsense." In response to one traveler's assertion that children do not belong to parents but to the country, the man launches into an elaborate argument about how it is "natural" that children love their country, acknowledging that children never belong to their parents, even though parents belong to them. He insists that if their sons die when they are 20 years old, they die young and happy, without having experienced the "ugly sides of life, the boredom of it, the pettiness, the bitterness of disillusionment." He urges that everyone should stop crying, thank God, and laugh as he does, because his son sent him a message saying he was dying satisfied at having ending his life in the best way he could have wished.

Then, as if protesting too much, the fat man fingers his fawn coat and boasts that he does not even wear mourning, ending his highly rational and idealistic speech with a shrill laugh "which might well have been a sob." At this point, the narrative focus shifts to the bulky and hitherto silent woman who has been listening with amazement at the fat man's speech which "amazed and almost stunned her." Intellectually, she realizes that she has been wrong and the others are right, for they are able to resign themselves stoically to the departure and even death of their sons. The contrast between her own reasonless grief and the highly reasoned and idealized rhetoric of the fat man makes her feel that she has "stumbled into a world she had never dreamt of, a world so far unknown to her."

However, in the very midst of this rational acceptance, the woman abruptly returns to her unreasoning state, and suddenly, as if she had heard nothing of the man's speech, "almost as if waking from a dream," she turns to the man and asks, "Then . . . is your son really dead?" The word emphasized here is "really," for her "silly, incongruous question" undercuts the idealism of the fat man's speech with the unspeakable sorrow of the reality. The man looks at her as if he suddenly realizes that his son is dead, and, to the amazement of everyone, he breaks down in heart-rending, uncontrollable sobs.

Although in its dependence on character and dialogue, "War" seems like a one-act play, the climax of the story, the woman's simple question, is a typical example of a central short story convention pioneered by Anton Chekhov. The question seems completely unprepared for, coming so soon after the woman's conscious acceptance of the fat man's rational and rhetorical speech. Her query about the reality of the situation undercuts everything that has been said before. As Chekhov made so subtly clear in his famous story "Misery" and Katherine Mansfield explored so memorably in her equally famous "The Fly," the ultimate mystery of loss can only be confronted in unspeakable and unreasonable grief.

—Charles E. May

WATER THEM GERANIUMS
by Henry Lawson, 1901

Australia's best-known short story writer, Henry Lawson, included "Water Them Geraniums" in his fifth collection, *Joe Wilson and His Mates* (1901). The collection consisted of four "Joe Wilson" stories—"Water Them Geraniums" is one—and 14 other tales. In the years between 1899 and 1901, Lawson had produced close to a dozen stories loosely focussed on the character of Joe Wilson. It represented an attempt, on the part of an author habituated to the journalistic sketch, to approximate at least some of the formal elements of the novel.

In fact the *Joe Wilson* sequence scarcely adds up to a novel. Rather, individual tales present discontinuous elements of a longer whole, the married life of Joe and Mary, poor smallholders or "selectors" scratching a living from the hard country of western New South Wales, the land Lawson knew so well from his boyhood in Mudgee and Gulgong. (Today the latter town, classified by the National Trust, features Lawson's image on Australia's ten-dollar note.)

Joe purports to be based on an acquaintance of the author's ("I know Joe Wilson very well . . . I met him in Sydney the other day"). He began, says Lawson, as a "strong character," but developed a "natural sentimental selfishness, good-nature, 'softness,' or weakness." He came, in short, to resemble Lawson himself, while Mary quickly became, as the author acknowledged, a portrait of Bertha, Lawson's wife. This meant that the chain of stories could be seen as a way of grappling, through the medium of fiction, with the difficulties of an actual marriage.

The sequence tells of Joe and Mary's courtship, of the sickness of a child, the momentous family decision to invest in a double buggy, a trip to Sydney involving a possible infidelity on the husband's part, the family's settlement at Lahey's Creek—all with the touch of pathos appropriate to an impending marriage breakdown, the "drifting apart" of a once-close couple. In "Water Them Geraniums" we see Joe and Mary travelling to Lahey's Creek, attempting to set up a home in the wilderness, and, above all, meeting their neighbour, Mrs. Spicer.

This last is at the heart of "Water Them Geraniums," which is not to say that the story is about her. Rather its underlying concern is with the theme of drifting apart. Mrs. Spicer's role is to show how a woman may be destroyed by a life of frontier hardship. This in turn prompts the question of domestic guilt (to what extent is the male to be held responsible?) so prevalent in Lawson's fiction—and in his own married life. In "Water Them Geraniums" this takes the form of whether or not young Mary in due course will come to resemble Mrs. Spicer.

Not that Mrs. Spicer is an unattractive character. Far from it. She embodies all those frontier or "bush" virtues so regularly extolled by Lawson and other authors of the

Australian 1890's. In fact she represents a return to that frontier female icon, in the earlier story "The Drover's Wife." Like this prototype, Mrs. Spicer lives without her husband, who is mostly away shearing sheep or working on distant stations, if not "duffing," or rustling. She has a great many ragged but lovable brats, a back-breaking workload, utmost poverty, and a great deal of tragic humanity. The pathos of her situation is her pride, her desire to do the best by her children in impossible circumstances. She is also generous, a type of frontier stoic endurance that, however, destroys something within her, reducing her to a silent despair, "past carin'."

The geraniums which must be watered at all costs (it is Mrs. Spicer's dying request to her daughter) grow beside a crude hut, a sad and impotent marker of civilization or at any rate of better things. Joe sees Mrs. Spicer labouring in summer heat, keeping starving stock alive in drought, or covered in mud under a downpour. Somehow she maintains a sense of humour. When a heifer down with the "plorer" (pleuro-pneumonia) rises inexplicably to chase her into the house, she says "I had to pick up me skirts an' run! Wasn't it redic'lus?" But bush suffering brings on "the dismals" as well, and Mrs. Spicer's repertoire of stories includes a fair share of tales of horror and suicide. Mary Wilson's reaction is to ask Joe to take her away from the bush.

There is no escape from poverty and a disintegrating marriage, however. Mrs. Spicer dies; Joe and Mary are left to ponder her fate and their own future. We are brought back to the beginning of "Water Them Geraniums," with its account of the couple's arrival at the desolation that is Lahey's Creek, their bleak first evening at the new home (a miserable wooden hut), their quarrel which prompts Joe to walk out into the bush, where he hears Mrs. Spicer's nagging cry in the darkness ("Didn't I tell yer to water them geraniums!").

It is a powerful story. The *Joe Wilson* sequence is generally regarded, with the earlier *While the Billy Boils* collection, as his best work. The sequence was put together while the author was in London, seeking to achieve the success he felt had been denied him in Australia.

—Livio A.C. Dobrez

THE WEDDING
by V.S. Pritchett, 1945

In the preface to his *Collected Stories* (1982) Pritchett talks of the short story as a form that reduces "possible novels to essentials." The writer of short stories is, he suggests, "something of a ballad-maker." "The Wedding," (collected in *It May Never Happen*, 1945) has the superficially simple lineaments of a ballad, but in a fashion that is richly suggestive of the extended psychological and social analysis we expect from a novel.

The story's opening is wonderfully evocative, and almost elegiac, in its juxtaposition of linguistic registers and of modern amenities with traditional patterns of rural life:

The market was over. Steaming in the warm rain of the June day, the last of the cattle and sheep were being loaded into lorries or driven off in scattered troupes through the side streets of the town which smelt of animals, beer, small shops, and ladies. The departing farmers left, the exhaust of their cars hanging in the air.

The paragraph establishes the cattle, and the economic reality they represent, as the ground for all that later happens. The wedding of Tom Fletcher's daughter Flo prompts much talk of love, but Pritchett never allows us to forget the money and the cattle that underly all this talk. Mrs. Jackson's romantic pieties are undermined by Fletcher's economic determinism.

Fletcher himself is described, by Messel the art teacher, as "the town bull." Pritchett describes him accompanying his daughter up the aisle like a bull about to charge, as the organ "bellowed" like Fletcher's herd. Fletcher the "bull" goes about things in his "meaty way," but, in truth, such strength as he has is deeply rooted in weakness and dependence. For all his shows of masculine dominance, he is a frightened man. His wife is dead; one daughter is now married and the other, Mary, may be carried away from him by her education—encouraged by Mrs. Jackson. He is vulnerable and lonely. So too is Mrs. Jackson, in many different ways. Each gives off an air of confidence that is largely illusory.

With Mary's aspirations there is talk of Oxford and Cambridge; Mrs. Jackson adds talk of Paris, from her past, and portraits painted by French artists. "A girl," we are told by Mrs. Jackson, "is a new thing: they have to invent themselves." Her own attempt at self-invention took her away from her origins, from her identity as the daughter of "old Charlie Tilly," seedsman and alcoholic pub-owner. But now she has returned, and is everywhere haunted by the ghost of her own childhood. When Fletcher addresses her as "Little Chris Tilly" it is a reminder of her maiden name that is both disturbing and liberating. Already her attendance at Flo's wedding has made her feel "for the first time since her divorce, unmarried." Her aspirations to refinement have taken her away from the world of cattle; "inventing" herself, however, has finally failed. She is still Charlie Tilly's daughter.

At the wedding reception any talk of love is further undermined as the men play their openly sexual game of "lassoing" the women—obviously enough a displacement of the use of their rope to control their cattle, just as Fletcher gives a slap on the bottom to a woman he wants to move. As Mrs. Jackson (she is still trying to be Mrs. Jackson rather than Chris Tilly) seeks to leave, Fletcher lassoes her. Unlike the other women she is not ready to play the game according to his rules; she struggles, she forces the rope from his hands. She leaves angrily. By next morning, however, it seems to her "a triumph" that the rope has marked her waist and "she would have liked to show it to him."

When, unsurprisingly, Fletcher comes to her cottage, ostensibly to collect his rope, their differences are beautifully captured in a characteristic piece of dialogue (especially comic after we have learned that a younger Mrs. Jackson was the author of a book entitled *Rambouillet: The Art of Conversation*):

"Well," said Mrs. Jackson. "I am not cattle. I suppose it was what one would have to call a country junket."

"I can't bear the stuff," said Fletcher innocently. "We used to give it to the girls, with prunes, when they wanted loosening."

In a tale so acute in its perception of the economic necessities at the root of most human dealings, it is unsurprising that Fletcher should be here to talk in terms of a "deal": "I want you down at the farm, and we'll do what you like about Mary." Her doubts and complaints are smothered in kisses—and her "horror was growing into a pleasure in itself."

She buys Mary's freedom to "invent herself" in agreeing to the deal. Yet is it entirely a matter of sacrifice? Does it not also offer her a means of re-integrating herself into a society at whose edges she had been uncomfortably living? Or is it the final failure of her own attempt to "invent herself"—her invented self hangs on the walls in the portrait of her by Vandenesse, which her rich husband paid for, and which Fletcher, naturally enough, sees mainly in terms of money. The story closes with Messel's wry comment that "Vandenesse was a third-rate painter with a knack of catching girls inventing themselves but no good when they had turned thirty." Are we to take it that it is only now that Mrs. Jackson has reached womanhood? Or might we not take an altogether bleaker view of things? Is this the final collapse of all her claims to individuality? It is entirely characteristic of Pritchett that we should be left to wonder—that the story's weight resides as much in what is not said as in what is made explicit.

—Glyn Pursglove

WE'RE VERY POOR (Es que somos muy pobres)
by Juan Rulfo, 1953

"Es que somos muy pobres" ("We're Very Poor") was first published in 1953 in Juan Rulfo's first book, the collection of short stories called *El llano en llamas (The Burning Plain)*. This brief story, narrated in the first person by someone who is identified only as a sibling of the central character, Tacha, tells of the tragic consequences of a family's loss of a cow in a flood. The only hope Tacha had of avoiding a life of prostitution in the city, a fate which befell her sisters, was in the wealth represented by the cow, which would have attracted a man to marry her. The story is written in what seems to be the plain speech of a peasant, but it is a language in which every word is charged with ironic meaning. This gives the impression that the narrator and his family, who seem largely unaware of these meanings, are being overwhelmed by events beyond their control or understanding. The detail and precision with which Rulfo focuses on the minutiae of a particular situation, combined with a remarkable economy of style, make this story resonate within a broad historical-social context and present strong implications about the very nature of human reality.

The historical period in which the story takes place, as with all the stories in *The Burning Plain,* is that of the late 1920's, during the last stages of the Cristero Rebellion (a period of armed rebellion by rural priests and their constituents against the anti-clerical politics of the Revolutionary Mexican government) in the Los Altos region of the state of Jalisco (west-central Mexico). Rulfo lived and worked in that area, and the landscape, culture, and colloquial language of the region are portrayed vividly and authentically.

One of the reader's first impressions of this story may be that the world it takes place in is static and "timeless," and that in spite of the characters' efforts, nothing in their lives or social condition will change. This impression is reinforced by the characters' apparent lack of full self-consciousness—which may be a lack of historical awareness (for example, the mother "can't remember . . . where she went wrong," which turns out to be quite ironic)—and the sparse natural (and stylistic) landscape they inhabit. And yet when examined more closely, it becomes apparent that that world is really in a state of change; it is a world in which the present is discontinuous with the past. As the mother says, "there have never been bad people" in her family but now her daughters end up going off to the city to become prostitutes. In other words, this is the period, following the Revolution, when the great rural-urban migrations of contemporary Mexico were just beginning, and small town, village, and peasant life, especially in the region where these stories take place, was increasingly impoverished and abandoned. (To a large extent, this abandonment was the result of failed and corrupt government policies, a criticism that underlies much of Rulfo's work.) Tacha and her family, thus, have not "gone wrong"; they have been faced with a new impoverishment and a new culture. The cause of their downfall is not the flood, but the social circumstances in which the flood occurs.

This contrast, between the static-seeming surface, and an underlying state of change, reveals one of the fundamental structural modalities of this story, and indeed, of much of Rulfo's work, that of a juxtaposition of opposites. The first example of this occurs in the very premise of the story, which is about a flood in what is normally rather arid country. The water is referred to in terms of its opposite, fire: "You could smell it, like you smell a fire." Also at the story's beginning, there is a strong juxtaposition of sleeping and waking, the water rising in the narrator's sleep as if it were a dream. The water itself is full of contradictory meanings: normally associated with fertility (especially in a dry climate), it is here a source of death and destruction. The rising water also is associated with Tacha's budding sexuality, and, because it drowns her cow, it will also destroy her hopes for a decent life:

> A noise comes out of her mouth like the river makes near its banks, which makes her tremble and shake all over, and the whole time the river keeps on rising. The drops of stinking water from the river splash on Tacha's wet face, and her two little breasts bounce up and down without stopping, as if suddenly they were beginning to swell, to start now on the road to ruin.

And although this flood of sexuality will cause Tacha's downfall in a moral or social sense, it will also prove to be her only means of survival, through prostitution.

Another form of oppositional juxtaposition in this story is the doubling of self found so frequently in Rulfo's fiction. It is here present as the narrator speaking to an absent listener, which may be the narrator speaking to him- or herself. There is even a suggestion that the narrator may be Tacha herself —speaking in the third person to distance herself from her certain doom—a suggestion supported by the intimate knowledge of and concern with her body, her situation, and her cow. The narrator might also be a younger sister of Tacha's, seeing her own future in her sister's fate, and not identifying herself in the narration as, again, a means of distancing herself from that fate.

"We're Very Poor" (a more literal translation of the title would be "It's Because We're So Poor," which perhaps more accurately reflects the lack of historical consciousness of the narrator) manages in a half dozen pages to vividly convey the circumstances of a particular life in a particular time and place while at the same time placing those particularities within a broad historical context and within a view of how human consciousness works. That consciousness is presented as a kind of bipolar structure of experience of immediate life and of experience of the self as another and/or as a being in history, in which the two levels of experience are largely unaware of each other. Although the story acquires its maximum resonance when read in the context of the others in *The Burning Plain,* it functions brilliantly as a perfectly crafted and unforgettable story on its own.

—John M. Bennett

WHAT WE TALK ABOUT WHEN WE TALK ABOUT LOVE
by Raymond Carver, 1981

Intending to have a few drinks before going out to dinner, two married couples get caught up in conversation, and still haven't made it out the door by story's end. Such is the full extent of Raymond Carver's most celebrated story, "What We Talk about When We Talk about Love," first published in hardcover in 1981, running 17 pages. It was quickly termed "minimalist" by several critics, yet Carver himself rejected the label since it emphasizes the story's form to the neglect of its human focus.

Compared to the blue-collar inhabitants of Carver's fiction, the four characters—Mel McGinnis, his wife Terri, Nick, and his wife Laura—are relatively well-educated, but they share a sense of bafflement over matters of the heart. (Ironically, Mel, the most obtuse of the four, is even a cardiologist.) The more these characters talk about love, the less they feel they know, so that rather than moving towards understanding, they are eased by the growing darkness and the guzzled alcohol into nearly stupefied befuddlement. Yet witnessing the process leads the reader, remarkably, to genuine insight.

Two anecdotes serve the party as case studies. The first is summed up in a sentence that is key to Carver's style as well as to the story's themes: "Terri said the man she lived with before she lived with Mel loved her so much he tried to kill her." Both in its staccato rhythm of monosyllables, and in its insistent pattern of repetitiveness, the sentence (like the story's title) captures the barely-furnished nature of Carver's distinctive style. The paradoxical twinning of declarations of extreme love with a violent effort to kill the beloved is what gives Mel, in particular, an insoluble riddle that nonetheless prompts much of his increasingly boozy, angry, and hurt talk.

The second anecdote, related by Mel, concerns an elderly couple very badly injured in a car crash, whom Mel has attended in the hospital. Their greatest wish, as they lay all bandaged, was to be able to see each other, and this, too—like the report of a miracle—is something that Mel cannot understand, yet cannot dismiss.

Both couples eventually reveal themselves to the reader as pairs of refugees from previous failed marriages. True love has seemed, at one time, unattainable to them, and insulating themselves from vulnerability and pain has since become second nature. Yet they feel the tug of devotion as an amputee might miss a limb, and hence they are driven to talking, talking about and around love.

The story's title implies that, on this subject at least, either we don't mean what we say, or we don't say what we mean. Imprecision and inarticulateness are the joint curses of Carver's characters, and they are delineated precisely and articulately. In a 1981 essay entitled "On Writing," Carver embraced a saying of Ezra Pound's: "Fundamental accuracy of statement is the *one* sole morality of writing." He also expounded there his own formula for achieving the discipline of economy that is exemplified in "What We Talk About . . . ": "Get in, get out. Don't linger. Go on." Yet the very redundancy of the title also shows how we bury its central concern beneath our own inarticulate words.

One of the four characters, Nick, narrates the story, but his observations and asides are kept to a minimum, leaving a fiction that, like many an early Hemingway story, is nearly all dialogue, much of it in brief spurts. The narrator, too, knows that something significant is being expressed, but he doesn't dare to express it directly. Nonetheless the stylistic exclusions and the truncated phrases succeed in pointing at the characters' frustrated attempts at numbness, and at their particular truncation of their own feelings. Defining by omission, the story makes palpable the presence of an absence. Eventually, what Carver's characters compulsively discuss yet neurotically avoid, his readers are led subtly yet memorably to feel.

Carver sculpted his prose to make it sound the way we talk. One consequence of that effort is that it looks like no one else's work on the page. Soon after the publication of the collection to which this story gave its name, *Esquire* magazine announced that Carver had "reinvented the short story." His writing has the familiar ring of originality—he writes with the true originality of the strikingly familiar. Readers of this story will continue to find in it a common fate jostled into sudden focus by his spare, lean, knowing prose.

—Brian Stonehill

WHERE ARE YOU GOING, WHERE HAVE YOU BEEN?
by Joyce Carol Oates, 1970

Known as a fascinating and prolific short story writer, Joyce Carol Oates quickly became one of the most productive of America's contemporary fiction writers. With more than 50 books published since her first novel in 1963, Oates has won the National Book award—for *Them,* her novel of inner-city Detroit, in 1969—and many other prizes, including countless O. Henry citations. A Guggenheim fellow, she is a member of the National Institute of Arts and Letters, and other prestigious groups. It is for her hundreds of moving and technically innovative short stories, however, that her audience is widest.

Nominated frequently for the Nobel prize in literature, Oates continues the work of Sinclair Lewis, who mapped life in America throughout the 1920's and 1930's. Unusually prescient about her national culture, Oates writes a socio-economic history of her times. She also cares about gender differences, but because her portrayals of women are often bleak, her fiction has seldom been championed by feminists. Little promise exists for Oates's lower and middle-class women characters, trapped as they are by lack of money and education, or by sexual misuse.

"Where Are You Going, Where Have You Been?" is representative of Oates's realistic and mythic approach to narrative. Underlying her realistic portrayal of the 15-year-old Connie who yearns to be beautiful and sexual is the paradigm of traditional, heterosexual romance. Cinderella-like, Connie separates herself from her family, waiting for a prince—any prince—to rescue her from mundane small town life. She has prepared for this role by learning to use makeup, by going to the mall and hanging out where older boys congregate, and by playing the game of flirtation that suggests she is more sexually aware than she is.

Connie, whose name places her in the 1960's as much as Oates's dedication of the story—"For Bob Dylan"—has accepted the entire package of young women's roles. Unlike her plain and dull sister, she is the pretty one, the one most like her mother. She has the promise—of catching a good man. Instead, in Oates's parable of the sex-conscious times, Connie finds herself facing the frightening consequences of her behavior.

Oates's brilliance in writing this long story is to have the reader see events through Connie's eyes. The man who comes for her, calling himself "Arnold Friend" and pretending to be her age—though even she can see he is years older, and weird—has the enigmatic, shadowy quality of a young girl's love object. She overlooks his misshapen feet (his cloven hooves?) crammed awkwardly into his boots; she paints him as she wants him to be, even denying that the slogans on his car are out-of-date. She tries to believe his representation of himself. Connie, in short, wants this romance.

If it were not for Connie's perspective being so convincing, the reader would be angry with her for her obtuse, and dangerous, behavior. All she has to do is lock the door and phone the police. Instead, she cringes toward the maniac waiting for her outside the house—and drives away with him and his macabre friend to a fate Oates does more than suggest. Yet Oates traps the reader within this tapestry of Connie's fear, sexualized because the men in the story are responding to the behavior she has so consciously learned and practiced.

Oates's dramatic irony leaves the reader in complete sympathy with Connie—who is the victim not so much of Arnold Friend as of her culture and its expectations for young women. The inevitable climax of the tale is that Connie will, voluntarily, open the door to Arnold, and one reads the whole story as a metaphor for the fact that Connie will also, just as voluntarily, open her body to him. In the culture that privileges male sexual power over honesty and love, and a woman's virginity over most of her other qualities, Connie will have lost whatever value she was developing—but she will finally know what sexuality is.

"Where Are You Going, Where Have You Been," a line from a Dylan song, juxtaposes two legends: that of the modern rock hero, as the dedication suggests, and the tale of the ancient demon lover. Tantalized by his difference, Connie is unable to resist the wrong Arnold Friend represents: her whole struggle for autonomy has been against the middle-class values of her family. The sexual is only one part of her defiance. What Oates manages to show is not that innocence is a danger, for if Connie had been completely innocent, Arnold Friend would have held no attraction at all for her. Connie's Achilles' heel, her weakness in social interaction, is her naivete. She believes everything her culture has taught her about herself as a

young woman, herself as a sexual object, and herself as a person questing for adventure. She defines "adventure" only in sexual terms. Therefore, her acquiescence before the predator rapist is predictable. Oates reverses the traditional happy ending formula for a Cinderella plot of each story is similar: girl charms older boy, who comes to "rescue" her from her conservative and protective family.

The violence that both Arnold Friend and Connie anticipate—and that Friend threatens her with (violence to both herself and her family, as well as a neighbor)—again represents Oates's clear prescience about her culture. What act is repeated again and again in the media world of today except violence? If violent behavior is not a valid currency for social interaction, why does culture credit it with value? Part of Connie's poignant naivete is that she accepts all the assumptions Arnold Friend uses, and when he threatens her with violence to her family, she feels that she must, in fact, go with him. She never questions how he expects to harm her father or other family members; she is gullible about this as about everything else he tells her. The travesty of power the story builds makes it more than a sexual parable.

Oates's story was first published in 1967 and collected in *The Wheel of Love* in 1970. It has been reprinted many times, and also has been filmed (as *Smooth Talk* in 1986).

—Linda Wagner-Martin

WHERE YOU WERE AT NIGHT (Onde estivestes de noite)
by Clarice Lispector, 1974

Clarice Lispector's later fiction defies most efforts to thematize, classify, or interpret it by any traditional standards. Beyond the consensus on her difficult style, few readers speculate upon what Alexis Levitin calls Lispector's "artistic-spiritual stance." The intensity of the voice in the stories translated by Levitin in *Soulstrom* (1989) suggests that such a stance drives these multi-generic experimental pieces, not all of which could properly be called fiction. Each clue which would lead to a general tone or mood or theme, however, undoes itself in the motion of the prose.

"Onde estivestes de noite" ("Where You Were at Night"), the title story of Lispector's 1974 collection, creates a night world that resembles a photographic negative of day and of life itself. An androgynous being, alternately the "She-he" and the "He-she," summons a group of unnamed humans to its mountain dwelling. There, in a world beyond time and life, this being fills the travelers' minds with new powers and thoughts. Moving in and out of human emotions and bodily sensations, the people resist and then succumb to the spell of this "He-She-without-name." Milk is black, pain is ecstasy, the scent of roses is stifling. Fear and terror attract the travelers to this omnipotent being, who can fill them with orgasmic waves or freeze them in a fixed position as punishment for touching her-him. Those who do not respond to the call of the night suffer "without anesthesia, the terror of being alive."

The travelers, including a Jew, a hunchbacked dwarf, a boy, a journalist, a priest, a millionaire, a perfect student, a masturbator, and an old disheveled woman, receive the thoughts of the He-she without being connected among themselves. The being suggests to them such thoughts as

"You will eat your brother," and it is "vitriolic about their not disturbing one another in their slow metamorphosis." These gestures produce a sense that the people live isolated yet parallel lives, an echo of more clearly articulated themes from Lispector's earlier fiction. The story then pushes the boundaries of communication failure to the level of horror. When the millionaire finds a voice with which to shout, the old disheveled woman responds with hostility. Others speak silently or only to themselves.

Operating outside of human time, the journey follows no narrative pattern. Chaotic and anecodotal, the account flows from an ever-moving point of perception—at one moment looking down upon the She-he and the people, then moving to "what the cat saw," and thereafter panning in and out of various individual minds. For the most part, the ebb and flow of oppositions propel the story along. In one such shift, dawn obliterates the night, and the night-time travelers appear in their beds. The earlier scenes are thus revealed as dreams, each with a different relation to the conscious mind of its host.

The butcher, we are told, is alone in carrying the night into the day. He is shown in his shop, "drunk with pleasure at the smell of flesh, raw meat, raw and bloody." Yet a number of other nighttime images resound in the minds of the now-awakened people. The journalist, for instance, wakes up inspired with an idea for a book on black magic, an echo of an unconscious association with *The Exorcist* given to him at night. Jubileu de Almeida, one of the few characters named during the night portion, wakes up longing to hear a Strauss waltz suggested by the He-she. Ironically, the waltz is "The Freethinker." A white woman gives birth to a black baby, and the narrative voice suggests, "Son of the demon of the night?" And another woman grows angry at the milk on the stove that will not boil. She suspects that, like death, the milk will reach up and grab her without notice.

Although the story seems to mock and mimic religious beliefs through the sexually-oriented rituals of the She-he, the narrative eventually funnels into the discourse of religion. As the story concludes Father Jacinto is blessing the communion wine. An irreverent exclamation of "Wow, good wine" notwithstanding, this scene confirms the existence of God through the fragrance of a flower. The He-she, we are told, has disappeared some time ago. Capitalized words ("AMEN" "AMEN" "GOD" "THE END") appear in a list, as if the story itself has been a prayer. The speaker of the epilogue confirms her religious beliefs, alluding to a "universal mind" that has guided her, suppressing thoughts of the night world "for the love of God."

This ending seems to offer two opposing interpretive choices. The story can be read as a fall into temptation, followed by salvation of the Christian faith. In a slight variation, sleep and the unconscious mind can symbolize the temptation that lurks beneath the surface of the disciplined mind. Read with attention to Lispector's more existential, religiously doubtful fiction, however, the possibility of an apocalyptic reading also exists. The nightly wrestle with darkness, portrayed through vivid sensory images, suggests itself as the permanent state of the human soul.

—Rebecca Stephens

A WHITE HERON
by Sarah Orne Jewett, 1886

Sarah Orne Jewett's celebrated story "A White Heron" was first rejected by William Dean Howells at the *Atlantic Monthly* on the grounds that it was too sentimental and romantic. Jewett kept her faith in it, however, and included it in her collection *A White Heron and Other Stories* (1886). This tale about the test of a young girl's love of nature has become one of Jewett's most popular stories.

The story concerns Sylvia, a shy little girl who, rescued by her grandmother from life in "a crowded manufacturing town," now feels at home in the Maine woods. As the story opens Sylvia is leading a cow home to be milked when the quiet of the woods is jarred by a noisy, aggressive whistle. A young man, an ornithologist from the city, is tracking a rare white heron to add to his collection. Mrs. Tilley and her granddaughter give the young man shelter for the night. When he learns how knowledgeable Sylvia is, he offers her ten dollars to help him find the heron. She accompanies the man as he walks through the woods in search of birds, which he kills. Though Sylvia "would have liked him vastly better without his gun," she watches him with "loving admiration."

In the second part of the story, Sylvia, who is still distracted by the hunter and his desires to secure the rare white bird, leaves the house before dawn to seek out the heron's nest. This journey to the heron's nesting place is described in heroic terms. Sylvia climbs an old landmark pine tree, sees the sun rise, catches a glimpse of the great world beyond the woods, and finds the heron and its mate. In her climb up the pine Sylvia is imagistically identified with the bird. Returning to the house she faces the hunter, who has vowed to himself that "now she must really be made to tell." But Sylvia remembers her beautiful moment in the pine watching the heron fly. Because of her experience in the tree, Sylvia has rekindled her kinship with the bird and has discovered she cannot betray it.

Sylvia, like many other heroines in Jewett's work, has a close relationship with nature, a relationship that is threatened by the intruder into this pastoral world. By remaining silent when the man presses her for information about the heron's nest, she chooses to preserve the heron rather than betray her woodland friend. Her choice requires that she sacrifice both the money (a sizeable sum to the girl and her grandmother) and the friendship the man has offered. The story ends with the narrator's apostrophe to nature: "Whatever treasures were lost to her, woodlands and summertime, remember! Bring your gifts and graces and tell your secrets to this lonely country child!" Sylvia, in choosing the heron over the young man, thus reinforces her relationship to the natural world.

Responding to a complimentary letter from Jewett, Mary E. Wilkins Freeman, another New England regionalist and a contemporary of Jewett's, wrote, "You are lovely to write me so about my stories, but I never wrote any story equal to your 'White Heron'." Interest in and praise for this story continues. Indeed, critics have found much to discuss in this ostensibly simple story.

Early commentators pointed out how the tale fits into the canon of the local color school. Others have moved beyond the elements of the New England landscape to explore a range of issues. Richard Cary sees Sylvia as undergoing a rite of initiation, a theme that Catherine B. Stevenson also articulates when she sees the tale as "a rite of passage from the safe world of childhood to the precarious, lonely, self-determined world of adulthood." Sarah Way Sherman sees the tale as "a *Bildungsroman* in miniature" and explores how it partakes of the paradigm of the Demeter-Persephone myth. Annis Pratt sees the story as a version of the traditional fairy tale; Theodore Hovet discusses the fairy-tale structure of Jewett's tale and also gives it a psychoanalytic reading. James Ellis and Richard Brenzo are among others who find a complex pattern of sexual symbolism in the story.

In a biographical reading of the story, Eugene H. Pool sees a parallel between Sylvia's repudiation of mature love and Jewett's own choice never to marry. Many feminist critics have seen the story as a confrontation between a patriarchal value system (the young man with his gun and money) and a matriarchal world (the female-centered natural sanctuary). Elizabeth Ammons finds embedded in this story with its traditional narrative structure, a rejection of "patriarchal prescriptions." Josephine Donovan sees this tale as consistent with Jewett's suitor pattern, and calls it a repudiation of the Cinderella text. Donovan argues that the story "culminates the antiromance tradition" that is a hallmark of women's literary realism. While some critics like Richard Cary have questioned Jewett's handling of point of view, both Michael Atkinson and Gayle L. Smith find the narrative voice, especially in the exhortations to Sylvia and to nature, enhances the theme of the story. Finally, in a short, book-length study, Louis A. Renza uses the story as a starting point for his exploration of the issues of canonical status of minor literature. The persistent interest in and variety of interpretations of this ostensibly simple tale are evidence of the richness of Jewett's classic story.

—Gwen L. Nagel

THE WHITE HORSE RIDER.   See THE RIDER ON THE WHITE HORSE.

THE WHITE HORSEMAN.   See THE RIDER ON THE WHITE HORSE.

THE WHITE HORSES OF VIENNA
by Kay Boyle, 1936

As an expatriate in Europe between the two World Wars and after the fall of France, Kay Boyle wrote novels and short stories tinged with autobiography, colored by reportorial depictions of European milieux and some of their striking personalities. In "Art Colony" she seems to be writing about her melancholy encounter with Raymond Duncan's colony in Paris. In "Rest Cure" she is drawing from the terminal illness of D.H. Lawrence in Venice. In most of her writing of that period and later her sympathies are clearly liberal, her politics inclined to the left. Therefore it is something of a shock to find in "The White Horses of Vienna" an admiration for Nazis and, by extension, Naziism.

This, to be sure, is a period piece from an era when political colorations and patterns shifted with kaleidoscopic swiftness. Specifically it is set in the time before the Nazis consolidated their control of Austria by the *Anschluss* and contains the pivotal event of the assassination of Chancellor Dollfuss. The subject is the hope and anguish of those who, like the doctor, have made a choice for "The Leader" and have found their idealism affirmed by the austere vision of those bearing the swastika. Even the Jewish character Heine is moved by the symbolism of those who set the brand of fire on the heights.

The physical setting, in the high mountain of northern Austria, near the eternal glaciers on the peaks, is played upon to represent the ideals of self-reliance and removal from a decadent urban civilization. Up here one can breathe the air of liberty and aspiration.

The unnamed doctor and his wife, who is also his assisting nurse, appear as devoted to humanitarian service as to their political cause. It is the doctor's preference, after his years as a prisoner of war, to withdraw from the festering life of cities. Presumably his responsiveness to Nazi ideology has something to do with his choice to live among the peaks. But after all he has not cut his ties with humanity. He has served the people of the mountain community until his injury severely restricts his practice. He means to continue meeting his patients' needs, though an assistant will now be required.

It is not clear that he received his injury while he was on Nazi business (setting the fires that signal resistance to the incumbent government). But a remark by the *Heimwehr* leader makes it clear enough that the doctor is well known as a Nazi activist. Therefore it comes as a complicating shock when the young doctor who arrives to assist him turns out to be a Jew.

The doctor's wife is anti-Semitic by ideology and no doubt from prejudices imbided from the people around her. She speaks of how "everyone feels" up here in their community. Gently the doctor tempers her hostility, saying that everything depends on how the young man does his work.

Heine does his work amiably, capably, and with good grace. In spite of her initial shock and her qualms about having to take her meals with a Jew, the doctor's wife slips into a smooth working relationship with him, an almost motherly rapport, though fundamental disagreements between them remain. When, as a Viennese he speaks in behalf of art and science, she replies, "What about people being hungry? What about the generation of young men who have never had work?"

This contention—in fact a microcosm of the great contentions tearing the modern world apart—is not so much resolved by the author as recapitulated by two stories within the story. The first is told by Dr. Heine, making a sort of fable of the white Viennese horses, the Lippizaner stallions who may indeed symbolize the elegance and achievement of centuries of European culture. These horses have long been the pride and the possessions of Austrian royalty. After the fall of imperial splendor and prerogative, the horses remain "still royal . . . without any royalty left to bow their heads to." As the young man speaks passionately of them they are transformed into much more than spectacle and the ostentation of the upper classes. "They were actresses, with the deep snowy breasts of prima donnas," he declares. They are beauty made flesh and flesh made beauty; they are dancers in the sublime sense celebrated by W.B. Yeats. They are an incarnation of a great city, beyond the cavil of those who might call the city (or all cities) wicked. The attempt by a maharajah to buy one of the horses away resulted in a pitiable and senseless catastrophe.

The doctor's wife says bitterly, "Even the money couldn't save him, could it?" And of course that is unarguably true. The doctor responds with a fable of his own design, acted out by some elegantly constructed marionettes put together by his cunning hands. There are just two characters in his show, a bumbling, stumbling nincompoop clown, representing the present political system and a superlatively handsome, omniscient and omnipotent grasshopper called simply "The Leader." (Who can the leader be except the German *fuhrer,* Adolf Hitler, architect and exponent of the "Leader Principle"?) The clown stumbles around carrying artificial flowers in case he comes on a grave that needs them, including perhaps his own.

In a challenge resonant with inspiration the grasshopper demands of the clown, "Why do you carry artificial flowers? Don't you see the world is full of real ones?" The clown can only collapse before this virile onslaught, going down in fading confidence that heaven may save him.

After the fables of the dancing stallions and of the leader grasshopper have been set in antithetic confrontation, there is little for the remaining action of the story to accomplish. The authorities arrive to arrest the doctor because Chancellor Dollfuss has been assassinated that afternoon and all Nazi activists are being rounded up. There is nothing anyone can do to prevent the arrest, though Dr. Heine argues emotionally against it. He feels himself buoyed up by the grand passions stirred by both the royal horses who dance in his memory and the apparently natural authority of the great grasshopper.

Yet, though there is nothing to be done, nothing that can conceivably be done to halt the foul and ruinous storm of politics and war about to strike the world, yet there are tokens of brotherhood and precious sympathy between the older and younger doctor. Dr. Heine may bring peaches to throw through the prison window when the older man is locked up. Here is a small true note in the blare of ideologies and vast rattling of armaments.

—R.V. Cassill

WHITE NIGHTS (Belye nochi)
by Fedor Dostoevskii, 1848

Pre-eminent among the world's novelists, Fedor Dostoevskii was also the author of short fiction, especially during the years before his exile in Siberia. The better known among the early stories are "The Double" (1846), "The Landlady" (1847), "An Honest Thief" (1848), and "White Nights," all of which appeared in *Otechestvennye Zapiski* (Notes from the Fatherland), an influential St. Petersburg journal. As one would expect, these stories are primarily character studies revealing Dostoevskii's usual psychological insights and his compassion for obscure and lonely misfits incapable of coping with the circumstances of their lives.

Frequently these forlorn persons retreat from reality into a world of dreams, and this is the case in "Belye nochi" ("White Nights"). The narrator-protagonist, who divulges neither his name nor the nature of his employment, is a young man of 26 years who has been in St. Petersburg for eight years (he does not say where he came from). He has

been living in a room with "grimy green walls," its "ceiling covered with cobwebs," which the slatternly landlady neglects to sweep away. After eight years in the city he has "hardly an acquaintance," and he asks, "What did I want with acquaintances? I was acquainted with all Petersburg as it was." The city, in fact, has become a substitute for human relationships. Constantly walking its streets, he has developed an attachment to it as to a person, even to the extent of feeling deep distress when he discovers that one of his favorite houses, pink in color, has been painted yellow. However, on his rambles he does notice people, sometimes "almost bowing" to an old man whom he habitually meets at a certain hour and certain spot. This is the limit of his social life.

The time of the story is late spring when nights in the latitude of Petersburg do not fully darken but remain "white." Many families have been leaving the city for their country villas, and the city "threatens to become a wilderness." Consequently the narrator on his outings goes outside the city and into the loveliness of the springtime countryside, which seems to have a liberating influence on his deeply suppressed capacity for relating with other human beings. Returning from the country late one evening, he sees a young woman leaning on the railing above a canal, sobbing softly and staring down at the water. The narrator is about to accost her, but seeing him she walks away. A drunkard across the street sees and pursues her. The narrator intervenes and thus begins his first real involvement with another person. That night, he and the girl, whose name is Nastenka, talk at length. The youth reveals himself as having lived entirely in dreams, especially in dreams of meeting and being in love with an idealized woman. He has thought at times of approaching some respectable woman in the street, telling her of his isolation and his difficulty in becoming acquainted with any woman, and begging her to say two or three sisterly words to him; but of course he has never done this. Nastenka laughs at him and tells him that he is his own enemy. She offers her friendship provided he promises not to fall in love with her. With this, the first of the "white nights" ends, but with an agreement to meet in the same place the following night.

That night Nastenka demands to know the narrator's "history." He protests that he has none, but goes on to reveal the core of his existence, and this turns out to be the core, the theme, of the story. "There are strange nooks in Petersburg," he begins, "It seems that the same sun as shines for all Petersburg people does not peek into those spots." These nooks, "painted green, grimy, dismal," resemble the room in which he lives. Those who inhabit them are friendless, but they are endowed with limitless powers of fantasy with which they create dream lives infinitely more desirable to them than anything offered by real life. Yet in that life of fantasy is "something . . . dingily prosaic and ordinary, not to say incredibly vulgar." The narrator has lived just such a life, considering any other life to be drab and pitiful. He does not foresee that sometime for him "the mournful hour may strike, when for one day of that pitiful life he would give all his years of fantasy, and would give them not only for joy and for happiness, but without caring to make distinctions in that hour of sadness, remorse, and unchecked grief." For the narrator that hour is about to strike.

When the narrator has finished his "history," Nastenka tells him hers. Brought up by a blind grandmother, her life had been narrowly restricted until a young man boarding in the house befriends both the girl and the old woman, bringing them books to read and escorting them to the opera and theater. He and Nastenka fall in love, but he has to be away in Moscow for at least a year. On his return he will marry her, though he will not bind her by a promise. When he returns he will meet her at the spot where the narrator and she have been meeting. She has learned that he has at last returned, but he has not appeared. The narrator offers to try to establish contact with the lover, for whom he has been thinking up excuses. But despite his efforts, the lover does not appear the next night, the third. Nastenka, thinking herself jilted, now realizes that the narrator is in love with her, and she does not seem displeased.

The fourth and last night the lover still does not appear. Nastenka states that she no longer loves him and declares her love for the narrator. At once they begin to make somewhat frenzied plans for their married life.

But as they talk, Nastenka's first lover arrives. She rushes into his arms, turns back to give the narrator a kiss, and then walks away with the other man. The next morning the narrator receives a letter from Nastenka describing her ecstasy at being reunited with her lover and her remorse for hurting the narrator, whose memory she vows to treasure. The narrator has had his moment of reality. Sitting once more in his room with the cobwebs, he exclaims to himself: "My God, a whole moment of happiness! Is that too little for the whole of a man's life?"

—Perry D. Westbrook

A WHOLE LOAF (Pat Shelema)
by S.Y. Agnon, 1951

An overriding theme in S.Y. Agnon's fiction is the seemingly unresolvable conflict his characters feel between traditional, ancestral past, and modern, present circumstances. The tensions inherent in this dilemma and various attempts to resolve it are treated in many of Agnon's best short stories, such as "Pat Shelema" ("A Whole Loaf") from the tenth volume of his collected fiction, *Samuel VeNireh* (1951; also called *The Book of Deeds*).

As with many of Agnon's short stories, the plot, such as it is, is deceptively simple. It is set in Jerusalem on the weekend before the feast of Purim. Because his wife and children are abroad, an unnamed, Jewish first-person narrator has failed to plan for his Sabbath meal, with the result that "the bother of attending to my food fell upon myself." After bathing, he decides that he will first attend Sabbath services, then go to a hotel for his meal. On the way he is hailed by Dr. Yekutiel Ne'eman, a prominent scholar, who asks him to mail several registered letters, which the narrator agrees to do. After services, he is not sure where he should go first: the post office or the hotel? After several changes of mind, he opts for the post office.

Just before entering, he meets Mr. Gressler, a prosperous merchant-turned-arsonist he had known abroad, who takes the narrator for a ride in his carriage. To avoid Mr. Hophni, a talkative, overbearing inventor of a special mousetrap who is coming the other way, the narrator grabs the reins and tries to steer the horses in a different direction, causing it to turn over. Both men fall out and roll about in the muck. The narrator makes his way to the hotel, where he washes off the grime and is seated the crowded dining room.

An hour later, a waiter arrives, and narrator tells him to bring anything; "But I want a whole loaf," the narrator adds gravely. After seeing other people served before him and several ensuing mix-ups, the narrator wonders about the letters, which he decides to go and mail. Jumping up, he bumps into the waiter, who drops the tray holding the narrator's meal. The hotel keeper orders him another meal, but it never arrives, not even as the restaurant closes. Waiting for his meal on into the night, he sees a mouse gnawing at leftovers on plates, and later a cat, which pays no attention to the mouse. Fearing the mouse will start nibbling him, he falls to the floor and sleeps until he is awakened by the cleaning staff. He is recognized as 'the one who was asking for the whole loaf." Because it is Sunday, he cannot go to the post office. After washing off the dirt, he leaves to get himself some food, for his wife and children "were out of the country, and all the bother of food fell on me alone."

On the surface, the story, narrated in a direct, seemingly artless style, is simple enough. The amusing, bungling, first-person narrator is typical of many of Agnon's stories, and is especially prominent in the stories of *The Book of Deeds,* a highly ironic title, since all of these anxious, slightly neurotic narrators not only fail to complete their respective deeds, but most are unable to fulfil their ritual observances.

An examination of the story's metaphorical and allegorical aspects shows its great complexity. First, the names given, or not given, to Agnon's characters is often significant. Thus, the nameless narrator could be anyone, an Every-person. "Yekutiel" was one of Joshua's associates in exploring the Promised Land; "ne'eman" in Hebrew is "faithful," an epithet of Moses, who, according to tradition, is said to have died on 7 Adar, the date on which this story takes place. Gressler's name is derived from the German *grässlich,* which means "terrible" or "shocking," referring to his arson to collect insurance. The narrator is attracted to the former, who has a Hebrew name, but both drawn to, yet repelled by, the latter, who has a German name. The scholarly doctor and the successful arsonist pose a moral dilemma for the narrator. Because of the biblical associations with the doctor's name, he represents orthodoxy and righteousness. This is underscored by the fact that the doctor's letters are "registered," in Hebrew *ahrayut,* which can also mean "obligation." Allegorically, the narrator has been charged with keeping the commandments. He fails to do so. Gressler, with his ill-gotten wealth, represents worldliness and materialism, which deter the would-be righteous person from his or her quest. Even Hophni's name is allegorical, from *hophen,* "a handful," in the sense of one who is difficult to handle.

The whole loaf, which the narrator asks for, represents not only the traditional braided challah loaf eaten at a Sabbath meal, but also the narrator's desire for spiritual completeness in and religious connectedness to the Almighty, the rewards for following the commandments. To keep his religious observances, the narrator bathes himself twice; he also falls twice, in the street and on the restaurant floor. The tale ends as it began, with a quest for food—metaphorically, spiritual sustenance—which, on another try, he might well find.

To give an allegorical sense of place, Agnon describes the night in the hotel dining room in Kafkaesque terms, a device used especially effectively in many of his earlier stories set in Eastern Europe. The hotel, in Agnon's works, is usually a place of worldly pleasure and excitement, where correct ritual observance and security are not possible, a place of danger. Such locations are often described in grotesque, threatening terms, as in the dreamlike sequence where the mouse eats scraps and the narrator fears it might start nibbling on him. The hotel cat, which he refers to as "my salvation," offers no such thing; instead of pouncing on the mouse, as the proper cat he had at home would have done, this cat ignores the mouse and helps itself to food. Even the animals in this place cannot carry out their assigned "deeds."

"A Whole Loaf" is thus a story of deeds undertaken in the pursuit of spiritual wholeness and belonging. Even though the narrator fails, Agnon leaves the reader with an underlying hope that, eventually, he—and by extension, all people—will succeed.

—Carlo Coppola

WHY I LIVE AT THE P.O.
by Eudora Welty, 1941

Eudora Welty's "Why I Live at the P.O.," first published in 1941, and collected in *A Curtain of Green* in 1941, has become one of her most popular stories and is certainly her most famous comic work. The farcical quality of the alienation of Sister, the narrator, from her family is sustained primarily through Welty's brilliant management of patterns of discourse among the characters and of references contemporary to the story's Southern setting. The story is set in China Grove, Mississippi, and explores the growing frustration of Sister with her Mama, her grandfather, Papa-Daddy, and her Uncle Rondo, as their allegiances shift from Sister to Stella-Rondo, her younger sister. Sister is the local postmistress, a job she has obtained through the influence of her grandfather, and, although she is quick to point out that her post office is "next to smallest" in Mississippi, it is clear that she has been a major force in her family and a contact with the outside world. Stella-Rondo's unexpected reappearance after separating from her husband, Mr. Whitaker, disrupts the position Sister has established, reduces her privileged status, and ultimately results in Sister's leaving home to live at the P.O. The story's strength is the manner in which Welty depicts Sister's attempts to win sympathy that instead reveal her growing neuroses.

Part of the animosity Sister bears towards her sibling results from the fact that she dated Mr. Whitaker first and believes that Stella-Rondo stole him from her. The story's opening revelation of Stella-Rondo's "deliberate, calculated falsehood," that sister "was one-sided. Bigger on one side than the other," immediately establishes both the dominating narrative voice and the highly personal terms which will help escalate its conflict. More misrepresentations from Stella-Rondo follow, and the narrator herself soon begins to distort the effect and importance of what is happening, raising questions about her own reliability. Only a few dramatic actions occur—Uncle Rondo, for instance, throws a string of firecrackers in Sister's bedroom at 6:30 in the morning in revenge for a supposed slight. How events are revealed is far more important than what happens because the hothouse atmosphere of the extended family consists largely of verbal relationships. This small group of people amuse—and define—themselves primarily by talking and by creating scenes. The stylistic texture of the narrator's speech patterns is the story's real essence,

and it provides the fabric from which Sister's world is fashioned.

Stella-Rondo's success in displacing Sister depends largely on her ability to spin mysterious and exotic connotations from her experiences. For example, her relationship with Mr. Whitaker, a Yankee from Illinois, is a source of mystery to the unconventional Rondo family. Stella-Rondo's curious flesh-colored kimono, which Uncle Rondo ends up wearing around the yard, strikes Sister as a "contraption" she "wouldn't be found dead in." To Stella-Rondo, though, it is part of her trousseau which Mr. Whitaker has taken "several dozen photographs" of her wearing. Most mysterious is the two-year-old adopted daughter with whom she returns. Sister not only suspects that Stella-Rondo was pregnant with Shirley T. when she was married, but that Shirley T., who "hasn't spoken one single, solitary word to a human being" since her arrival, may have mental problems. Shirley T., it turns out, is not only able to belt out "OE'm Pop-OE the Sailor-r-r-r Ma-a-an!" in the "loudest Yankee voice" Sister has ever heard, but is also able to tap-dance. Mama, who was also initially suspicious, responds by embracing the "little precious darling thing," and by turning against Sister. After even Uncle Rondo is alienated from Sister and he launches his firecracker attack, Sister decides to move out. The long list of belongings she decides to take with her include the electric fan, the davenport pillow she had done in needlepoint, her radio, Mama's sewing-machine motor that Sister helped pay to have repaired, the Hawaiian ukulele, and the watermelon-rind preserves. The word choice used here to describe the items defines precisely the private domesticity of this family in their rural Mississippi locale. It is through an identification with these sorts of homespun details that Sister has established her identity. Their removal helps dramatize her sense of displacement.

Welty's choice of details also unify the story. Recurring war-related images and the fact that most of the action occurs on the Fourth of July provide a military or patriotic motif that emphasizes the family's own conflict. Abundant references to commercial brand name products like a Milky Way candy bar, an Add-a-Pearl necklace and Casino and Old Maid card games, to historical personages like Nelson Eddy, or to actual locations like Mammoth Cave and Cairo, heighten the absurdity of the family's idiosyncratic, cartoon-like rivalries. Sister's predilection for extraneous description—Mama, she says, for example, "weighs two hundred pounds and has real tiny feet"—maintains a consistent humorous tone throughout the story. Perhaps most important are the recurring references to the mail and the radio, both of which provide a means of verbal communication with the outside world. These become the systems of communication that Sister attempts to control in her P.O. at the story's conclusion.

Underlying its exposure of the often hilarious flaws and self-centered complications of a Southern family, "Why I Live at the P.O." probes the mysteries and paradoxes of manipulated language. Sister's attempt to cling to and then to break out of the communal fabric of her family's words and beliefs is, in fact, an attempt at self-definition. Appreciating the distortions revealed in this masterful comic monologue should generate a good-natured skepticism about the limits of language used to define any relationships or moral attitudes.

—Thomas Loe

THE WIFE OF HIS YOUTH
by Charles Waddell Chesnutt, 1898

By the time "The Wife of His Youth" appeared in the *Atlantic Monthly* (July 1898), Charles Waddell Chesnutt had already accumulated more than 30 publications, including three previous short stories in the *Atlantic Monthly*. His early successes—especially "The Goophered Grapevine," "Po' Sandy," and "Dave's Neckliss"—had earned him a reputation, but one that he found confining: he was known as a dialect writer. As an African-American whose grandfather was white, Chesnutt may have had more cause than most when he objected to the stereotyping of his work.

In an effort to expand his reputation, Chesnutt purposely set out to write non-dialect stories. "The Wife of His Youth," after its publication in the *Atlantic Monthly,* became the title piece of his collection of these non-dialect works published in 1899, *The Wife of His Youth and Other Stories of the Color Line.* As the title suggests, each of the stories in the collection purports to examine racial issues of the time. This focus resurfaces throughout Chesnutt's canon. All of his novels—*The Marrow of Tradition, The House Behind the Cedars,* and *The Colonel's Dream*—treat the interrelationships of the races, and his one biography is of Frederick Douglass. In addition, he often explored the topic in his non-fiction as well. Essays such as "The Disfranchisement of the Negro," "Obliterating the Color Line," and "The Future American: A Stream of Dark Blood in the Veins of the Southern Whites" are representative of his interest in this theme.

Despite being a conscious departure from his dialect frame stories, "The Wife of his Youth" addresses the same topic, although it is one of Chesnutt's gentlest treatments of the race question. As he did in *The House Behind the Cedars,* Chesnutt focuses less on white oppression than on the prejudice and discrimination within the African-American community. The protagonist of this story, Mr. Ryder, is dean of a society of African-Americans that has come to be known as the "Blue Veins." The purpose of this organization "was to establish and maintain correct social standards among a people whose social condition presented almost unlimited room for improvement." That the Blue Veins's membership is composed of "individuals who were, generally speaking, more white than black," is attributed by the narrator to accident. Despite the potential for divisive commentary, the narration remains gently satiric about the pretensions of these Blue Veins.

Encased in this mildly critical treatment of those who are constantly redrawing racial boundaries is a remarkably sentimental love story. While Mr. Ryder prepares a proposal of marriage to a younger woman—a proposal he plans to deliver publicly at a Blue Vein function that evening—his meditations are interrupted by an elderly African-American woman, an ex-slave named 'Liza Jane. She has come to him seeking help in locating her long lost husband, separated from her by the random cruelty of slavery. She has been looking, she tells Mr. Ryder, for Sam for the past 25 years, but without success. Even the epitome of snobbery, Mr. Ryder, cannot help but be struck by the loyalty and determination of this woman.

At the Blue Vein dinner that evening, Mr. Ryder repeats to his guests the woman's story, onto which he grafts an apparently hypothetical conclusion. Suppose the man she seeks had since raised himself to a respected position within the community, he wonders aloud. He further asks them to suppose that the man has learned that his wife, whom he thought dead, had been seeking him for all those years. And, finally, Mr. Ryder asks, "suppose that perhaps he had set his heart upon another. . . . What would he do, or rather what ought he to do, in such a crisis of a lifetime?" After his guests tearfully respond that this hypothetical man ought to acknowledge her, Mr. Ryder introduces to them the wife of his youth.

The reunification of this long-separated couple is accomplished despite overwhelming odds. Chesnutt carefully arranges to make 'Liza Jane the epitome of what Mr. Ryder has spent most of his adult life trying to avoid. She violates the two primary unwritten principles that the Blue Veins have established, that members be light-colored and of free birth. As an ex-slave, she obviously fails the latter criterion, and as to the former, the narrator offers a definitive description: she is "very black,—so black that her toothless gums, revealed when she opened her mouth to speak, were not red, but blue." Similarly, Chesnutt has her appear on the scene as Mr. Ryder is reading poetry, and this juxtaposition emphasizes what the elite Blue Veiner would consider the deficiencies of her speech: she tells him, "I's lookin' for my husban'. I heerd you wuz a big man an had libbed heah a long time."

'Liza Jane delivers her speech to a man who, the narrator tells us, lamented the "growing liberality" in social matters that had forced him "to meet in a social way persons whose complexions and callings in life were hardly up to the standard which he considered proper for the society to maintain." In addition to Mr. Ryder's conservatism, the text points out how starkly his appearance differs from that of his wife: "His features were of a refined type, his hair was almost straight; he was always neatly dressed." Despite the apparently irreconcilable differences in social station, speech, and comportment, Chesnutt has the couple reunite.

The optimism that informs the conclusion of "The Wife of His Youth" separates this story from many of Chesnutt's other examinations of the race question. While *The Marrow of Tradition* and "The Sheriff's Children," for example, dramatize the tragic consequences of racial conflict, "The Wife of His Youth" takes a more ameliorative path: where other Chesnutt works are defined, as William Dean Howells noted, by their bitterness, this story suggests that to acknowledge, perhaps even to embrace, one's heritage can be both heroic and, ultimately, fortunate. "The Wife of His Youth" may not be the most representative of Chesnutt's canon, but it is the first, and most optimistic, work of his non-dialect career.

—Charles Duncan

WILDERNESS TIPS
by Margaret Atwood, 1991

Since the prolific Canadian writer Margaret Atwood has published, to date, seven novels and twelve poetry collections, critical evaluations of her work have tended to ignore or downplay her short fiction. "Wilderness Tips," which originally appeared in the magazine *Saturday Night*, is the title story of her seventh collection. Critical reception of this recent volume of stories was rather cool; a long-standing critic of her work, Sherrill Grace, reviewing it in the *Canadian Forum,* expressed some frustration with its replaying of by-now-familiar Atwoodian touches of irony and wit, even while she praised the stories for their sheer verbal pleasure.

"Wilderness Tips" counters Grace's charge in that it shows Atwood refining rather than mimicking her previous fictions. In particular, it shows Atwood refining a subtle form of allegory by merging psychological study and political analysis. George, a Hungarian immigrant to Canada, married to one of a trio of Canadian sisters, but dallying, intermittently with the other two, is a modern-day Paris, set among three goddesses. The apple: his sexual attentions. The three sisters—the euphonic-sounding Portia, Prue, and Pamela—embody the various strategies which women have traditionally adopted in order to placate men: Portia the long-suffering angel-in-the-house wife; Prue the risk-taking, blasphemous, sexual adventuress; and Pamela the intellectual virgin—or so it seems at first. With the denouement (the sexual encounter of George and Pamela) this neat triad dissolves, however, and the reader is forced to reconsider such neat categories. "George realizes that a good deal of what she says is directed not to him or to any other listener but simply to herself. Is that because she thinks no one can hear her? . . . He wonders if she's ever had a lover. . . ." By the end of the story, readers, too, "wonder" rather than categorize.

But "Wilderness Tips" is rich because, along with this Atwoodian concern with female scripts and revisionist mythology, Atwood has constructed a troubling political allegory. The setting of this *menage a quatre*, Wacousta Lodge, echoes the title of a 19th-century Canadian text: Major John Richardson's *Wacousta*, in which a European man disguises himself as an Indian confidant of Pontiac and plays out an old sexual vendetta against a British comrade who has ousted him in the affections of a young woman. Richardson's text has frequently been read as an exploration of the uneasy Canadian negotiation of the wilderness-civilization opposition. So, too, in Atwood's story, sexual jealousy that reaches out from these four characters' pasts raises the whole question of whether there are any "tips" for taming the "wilderness" within.

There are two approaches to this question in the story: George, as an immigrant, believes in the myth of the sacrosanct New World civilization; as Atwood's narrator points out, "He didn't want to desecrate Wacousta Lodge: he wanted to marry it." But the new generation of the lodge feels differently: a younger Prue wanted to "break some family taboo," to revel in wilderness, by introducing George to the WASPish lodge and flaunting his exoticism—and eroticism—in front of the other inhabitants. Pamela finds odd nostalgic comfort in recalling the lodge of the war years. Portia is also trapped in the past, though her entrapment consists of replaying the family dramas: "I married a man like you," she informs the dour portrait of her great-grandfather which hangs in the bathroom, "a robber king." What we have, then, is a love quadrangle which also functions as an allegorical reading of Canada at the crossroads, neither willing to embrace change and new ethnic voices nor able to feel entirely easy at the thought of being stuck in the past. As the sisters' brother Roland reflects, he has never been able to conceive of Wacousta Lodge as anything but "the repository of the family wars."

Still, George does desecrate Wacousta Lodge at the end of the story; in spite of his injunctions to himself to keep all dalliances with Prue confined to his city life, he ends up muddying the waters of the wilderness lodge—with Pamela. Just as the British officers of Richardson's *Wacousta* allow their loves and hatreds to spill over into the pristine New World, so too George's belief that he can be a peaceable intruder on Wacousta Lodge are revealed as the rationalizations of a rather greedy man. Throughout "Wilderness Tips" his sexual appetite is consistently paired with financial greed; the paper that he casts aside before sleeping with his wife's sister is *The Financial Post*. And, years before, when he engages in one of his sexual skirmishes with Prue at his office, he spills papers from his desk which concern, he recalls, "a take-over plan." For Atwood, those who wallow in nostalgia are all too likely to fall prey to a take-over plan of menacing proportions.

But Atwood inserts another variation on this Canadian nostalgia-trip: the brother Roland's old desire to be an Indian. Like Richardson's Wacousta, he "goes Indian," but in Atwood's fiction the attempt is sadly comic; the young boy runs about Wacousta Lodge with "a tea towel tucked into the front of his bathing suit for a loincloth," and his face darkened with "charcoal from the fireplace" and "red paint swiped from Prue's paintbox." Even when the nonnative dons the feather, the accessories must derive from the kitchen, the guarded domestic hearth, and the paint-by-numbers box of European civilization. Still, for all of its comedy, Roland's attempt wins Atwood's sympathy; of Roland's Indian myth, her narrator asks, "How can you lose something that was never yours in the first place?" Margaret Atwood, setting her "Wilderness Tips" in the summer of 1990, the summer when the Canadian army was sent to "subdue" Mohawk men and women at Oka, asks this question for all non-native Canadians, who lost something that summer too.

—Lorraine M. York

WINTER DREAMS
by F. Scott Fitzgerald, 1922

"Winter Dreams" rehearses the themes of F. Scott Fitzgerald's best-known novel, *The Great Gatsby*, reveals his obsessive preoccupation with the power of material wealth, and anticipates the tragedy of his own truncated career and life.

The work covers a period in the life of its principal character, Dexter Green, from 14 to 32 years of age. At the age of 14, Dexter is resourceful, energetic, and optimistic. At the age of 32, he is disillusioned, depressed, and overwhelmed by a profound sense of loss. Life has lost its glow and, despite his relative youthfulness, it will never regain its earlier sense of promise. The events that influence this radical change in outlook are the subject of the story.

Fitzgerald skillfully arranges the story's action in six sections, alternating between summary and incident to cover a period of 18 years. The first section focuses on a particular incident. Four years pass between the first and second section, which summarizes a five-year period of Dexter's life. The third section concentrates on one incident. Sections four and five summarize, respectively, the next two years and one year of Dexter's life. Seven years pass between section five and the final one, which focuses on a single incident. The six sections are connected by emphasis on Dexter's relationship with Judy Jones. The incidents in sections one, three, and six represent the stages of Dexter's attraction, involvement with, and disengagement from Judy.

The opening scene introduces us to an enterprising, middle-class midwestern boy who earns spending money during the summers by caddying for the rich at the local country club. This is the practical side of Dexter, valued by the club members because he never loses golf balls. But there is another side of Dexter—the side whose "winter dreams" focus on the power, the status, and the privileges of the rich. Those dreams inspire adolescent fantasies of defeating club members at golf, driving up to the clubhouse in a luxury automobile, and displaying his diving talents on the club raft. These are both vitalized and threatened in the first scene by Judy Jones. Even at the age of 11, she has a magnetic energy, beauty, and passion. Dexter is mesmerized. From the moment he sees her, she becomes the embodiment of all the qualities he aspires to. Ordered to caddy for her, he instinctively realizes that to do so would be the end of his dreams. Instead, he quits his job as a caddy. Dexter wants to possess Judy, not cater to her.

His first opportunity comes nine years later, after college and a year of establishing himself in business. At the age of 23, Dexter is a polished young man who went to a prestigious eastern university to learn how to act, talk, and dress like the rich. His successful laundry business uses that knowledge to cater to the clothing tastes of the elite. At the same club where he used to caddy, Dexter meets Judy again. Now "arrestingly beautiful," she encourages his advances and they become romantically involved. Dexter's dreams seem on the verge of fulfillment.

But those dreams are more complex and more elusive than they initially appear to be. Dexter seeks more than material wealth. He is not a fortune hunter. He wants to experience to the fullest extent possible "the richness of life"—an elevated, even transcendent, sense of what is fine and rare and valuable. To Dexter, Judy personifies those more ethereal goals. She is the epitome "of flux, of intense life, of passionate vitality." But in the ups and downs of their relationship over the next three years, Fitzgerald chronicles the grand failure in understanding that Dexter's perception of Judy represents. The rich young woman he idealizes is restless, bored, spoiled, fickle, and extremely unhappy. Wealth has not given her the best that life has to offer. It has merely awakened in her at an earlier age a keen sense of life's limitations, compromises, and failures, as she moves desperately from one lover to the next, seeking the same impalpable quality of richness Dexter is searching for.

Although their relationship eventually ends, Dexter is not willing to give up his dream. In the seven years that pass between their breakup and the final scene of the story, he moves East, and, after military service during World War I, becomes a wealthy New York businessman. But in a casual conversation in his office, a midwestern business associate informs him that Judy is married to a drunken philanderer who mistreats her. He also states that she is "nice" and likable, but plain and passive.

Dexter is stunned by these observations. As long as he could maintain a vision of Judy as the embodiment of genteel youth and beauty, he could continue to believe in an attainable ideal of power, freedom, and beauty. Now he sees himself as he is, a 32-year-old bachelor with no intimate relationships, locked into a pattern of mechanically accumulating money. The green and open spaces of the golf-course days in Minnesota are gone, replaced by the constricting, cold, grey cement and steel of a skyscraper. As he contemplates "the country of illusion, of youth, of the richness of life" he has left behind, he experiences a shattering sense of loneliness and emptiness.

Like Jay Gatsby, Dexter aims high. But as his materialistic pursuits converge with his idealism, they become crosscurrents in conflict with one another. Dexter makes a lot of money but never achieves his "winter dreams." In this respect, he is the prototypical American success story—one who seeks but fails to find spiritual fulfillment in material wealth. The narrator of *The Great Gatsby*, Nick Carraway, reflects upon this American dream at the end of the novel, looking over the shore of Long Island, now dotted by gawdy mansions. For the early explorers, this "fresh, green breast of the new world" represented "the last and greatest of all human dreams" as they came ashore, "face to face for the last time in human history with something commensurate to the human capacity for wonder." The wonder of America, of life itself, has passed for Dexter, like a dream.

—Joseph Flibbert

THE WOMAN DESTROYED (La Femme rompue)
by Simone de Beauvoir, 1968

Though Simone de Beauvoir has no doubt made her most lasting contribution to modern thought with *Le Deuxième Sexe (The Second Sex)*, her very influential study of the female condition, and her sequence of brilliant autobiographical writings, she also has to her credit a number of novels and short stories. These are all, to some extent, reflections of both her own experience and her philosophical attitudes. "The Woman Destroyed," "The Age of Discretion," and "The Monologue" were first published in *La Femme rompue* in 1968.

It is clear, from the differences in narrative style between the three stories, that Beauvoir is, to some degree, experimenting with different fictional modes in an attempt to persuade us to see her three heroines' predicaments from different angles. "The Age of Discretion" takes the form of a first-person narrative by the heroine; "The Monologue" is presented as a transcript of the thoughts rushing through Murielle's head; "The Woman Destroyed" is in diary form. "The Woman Destroyed," the title story, seems at first to be a straight-forward and reliable account of Monique's experiences, but we soon realise this is not the case. As the heroine herself puts it, "what an odd thing a diary is: the things you omit are more important that those you put in." Monique's life has largely been one of self-deceit, and the diary narrative is a fine expression of her essential egocentricity. This explains too why the other characters in the story are seen only from her viewpoint, and remain somewhat one-dimensional. There are critics who complain about the sketchiness of the portrayal of some of the minor figures in the story, but they overlook the fact that this is a valid expression of Monique's relationships with them.

Ostensibly all has been going well. More than 20 years before Monique had, as a young medical student, made a good marriage to Maurice, who had gone on to become a research consultant of some eminence. Now their two daughters are grown. At the start of the story, Maurice has just flown off to a scientific congress, and Monique is rather self-consciously preparing for a spell on her own. Almost at once we see a certain temperamental weakness in her as she sets about constructing relationships to spare her the agony of confrontation with herself alone; she is worried when her daughter Colette falls ill, but she subconsciously welcomes the opportunity this offers for forging anew some family links. She also takes up the cause of a female juvenile delinquent with an eagerness that is slightly alarming. Plainly she is already in a vulnerable position when Maurice tells her that he has fallen in love with another woman, Noëllie Guérard, a successful lawyer and a divorcee with a 14-year-old daughter.

The account Monique gives of the relationship between Maurice and Noëllie and her efforts to disrupt it and thus salvage a certain amount of self-respect offers us marvellous insights into the life-style of the intelligentsia in postwar Paris. If the perspective is a bit warped by her distaste for the manners and style of her rival, it only adds piquancy. At first Monique tries to give direction to her existence by struggling to regain Maurice's affections, but in this, despite the advice of her worldly-wise acquaintances, she fails. The fall in her self-respect is painful to behold, with physical decline mirroring her mental collapse. Gradually Monique comes to understand that she must stop looking for solutions to her personal problems with other people, whether they are her friends and her children, or whether she sees them as her enemies. She reflects on her position and begins to see that she must take some responsibility for the past, the present, and the future. The conclusion is anything but a conventional happy one. At the end of the story, in a state of loneliness that frightens her, Monique has at last come to an awareness of what Beauvoir understands to be the true nature of human life with each individual answerable for his or her own destiny. In this way the story is transformed from being simply a cleverly related and closely observed account of the marital misfortunes of a woman belonging to the Parisian bourgeoisie, which Beauvoir knew so well, and becomes an expression of existentialism.

—Christopher Smith

A WOMAN ON A ROOF
by Doris Lessing, 1963

In her more than 30 books and 50 short stories, Doris Lessing ranges in her fictional subjects from her early realist work to her more recent space fantasies. "A Woman on a Roof" is from *A Man and Two Women*, Lessing's collection of British stories about modern European life and culture. Mona Knapp has noted the dialectic structure of nearly all of the British stories, where each protagonist comes into conflict with a self-defining force. According to Knapp, the collective forces in Lessing's British stories fall into five categories: sexuality, role crisis, politics, history, and social ills. In "A Woman on a Roof," both sexuality and role crisis are central motifs.

While repairing a roof during a scorching heat wave, three workmen spot an attractive woman sunbathing on a neighboring roof: Tom is 17 years old, shy, and impressionable; Stanley has recently married and is both shocked and attracted by the woman's nakedness; Harry, who is married and has a son about Tom's age, is 45 years old, tolerant and practical-minded. Lessing weaves her story around each man's different response to the woman's presence and to the heat. While the woman relaxes on the stifling roof, smoking, reading, sleeping, and getting a tan, the men sweat and struggle to work under a crudely rigged blanket

for shade. Their task becomes more irritating because the sunbather ignores them.

Tom's reactions are mostly interior and secretive. Upon first noticing the sunbather, he grins excitedly, but says nothing. He joins Stanley in whistling at the woman, but when she responds with annoyance, Tom smiles apologetically, as if signaling his detachment from Stanley. Privately he watches her roll her bikini pants over her hips, and then he reports to his co-workers that she has not moved. Stanley wants the sunbather's attention, even as her boldness affronts his sense of propriety. He avows that someone will report her, though Tom defends the woman, suggesting that "she thinks no one can see." Tom views himself as an outsider, peering into the woman's intimate space, while Stanley looks at the woman as if she is on public display. He affronts her with wolf whistles, gestures, and yelling. Harry chides from his neutral position: "Small things amuse small minds."

The sunbather's presence gives Harry no reason to interrupt his work day. He borrows a blanket from a tenant and attempts to create some shade, and he leaves the work site to obtain more material. While Harry stays focused on work, Tom and Stanley periodically stop to check on the woman. Stanley gestures lewdly when she changes positions and rests on her back. His persistent whistling prompts Harry to inquire scoldingly, "What about your missus?" The older man's monitoring angers Stanley, for whom marriage should curb his wife's behavior but not his own. Frustrated by the sunbather's indifference, Stanley threatens on the second day to call the police himself. If he cannot have her attention, then he is determined no one will.

During the six days the men work, they see the sunbather every day, save one when the extreme heat drives them to the basement. By the second day Tom has fantasized imaginatively about the woman treating him tenderly at night. A crane on a neighboring building sets him to thinking that he operates the machine and can swing the woman closer to him. He feels smitten, so Stanley's anger perplexes him. The sunbather defies Stanley's need for control. He calls the woman, "Bitch," when his furious whistling on the second day prompts only a squinted glance. Tom snickers that the woman should ask the men over. Harry tries to cool this rising tension by interjecting that if the woman is married, "her old man would not like that." Stanley then challenges the potential husband by confidently telling his companions that if his wife lay about, for everyone to see, he would put a stop to it, to which Harry suggests that maybe Stanley's wife sunbathes while he works. Secure in his feelings of superiority, Stanley boasts, "Not a chance, not on our roof."

For all his criticism and supposed disgust, Stanley will not leave the sunbather alone. He postures and struts to no avail and epitomizes the man who can relate to women in only one way. When he fails, he has no other ideas. So, he reasserts his failed method with greater force. On the fourth day when the woman briefly hides her presence, Stanley assumes her husband has finally "put his foot down." It satisfies him to suppose that a man has regulated the woman's behavior, since his own efforts failed. By week's end he speaks insultingly of the sunbather. He surmises that her skin must be like a rhino's, and he sarcastically likens her aloofness to Lady Godiva's. As if to compensate for his nonsuccess with the sunbather, Stanley flirts and teases shamelessly with Mrs. Pritchett, the woman who loaned Harry the blanket. Harry watches disapprovingly and Tom with admiration at Stanley's ease in conversation. Stanley insults the sunbather again by complaining to Mrs.

Pritchett how the roof work was miserable in the oppressive heat, although some do "lie about the roof as if it was a beach."

Increasingly Tom adopts his fantasies as facts. At night he dreams of alluring encounters with the woman. She is friendly and she cares for him. He sleeps at her apartment, and he loves her. Tom is confident that the woman looks upon him as different from the other men. He envisions himself protecting her from Stanley. When she moves to a hidden spot to avoid the men's glances, Tom feels she is his because the other men cannot see her. Eventually Tom suggests that Stanley's whistling is dissuasive, and Stanley angrily retorts, "You didn't whistle, then?" Tom feels he did not. Meanwhile Harry remains detached from his coworkers' involvement. One time he whistles with the other men, but in parody of them. He reminds Stanley that the sunbather is not his wife and that she is doing no harm, and he urges Stanley to at least pretend to work, as a means of channeling his frustration.

The sixth day is the hottest yet, and Stanley finally explodes. He throws the gutters, quits work, and madly whistles with his fingers in his mouth, stamping and screaming for the woman's attention. Frightened by Stanley's ferocity, Harry takes command and packs up the tools. He tells the boss that the men are suffering from sunstroke.

The heat in Lessing's story refers both to the actual temperature and to the men's rising passions. Stanley's total irrationality and near madness make Harry fearful, while Tom loses all sense of reality. When the men finally abandon the roof, Tom stays behind on the street and finds the sunbather's apartment building. He climbs the ladder to her roof and tries to talk with her. She snubs him, suggesting that he go to the beach if he likes seeing women in bikinis. Tom assumed she would react as in his dreams, so her rebuff stymies him. He leaves resentfully and gets drunk, hating her. When it rains the following day, he thinks of the sunbather and says, "Well, that's fixed you, hasn't it now?"

By selecting three men with varying life roles, a youngster, a newlywed, and a family man, Lessing illustrates both a range of attitudes toward women and sex and how the progressive stages in life shape the men's views. Reality shatters Tom's naivete, while the erosion of his assumed dominance shocks Stanley. For Harry the incident on the roof is a catalyzing experience. He shifts from offering his companions reasonable observations to taking a paternal-like charge over them. Decisively and forcefully he prevents their encounter with the woman from escalating into a crisis.

—Barbara A. Looney

THE WONDERFUL TAR-BABY STORY
by Joel Chandler Harris, 1881

A major force in shaping racial imagery in American literature, Joel Chandler Harris's tar baby story presents a unique combination of African-American folklore and Euro-American stereotypes. Told by the stereotypical Uncle Remus, the story of Brer Rabbit's entrapment and escape articulates the anger and separatist philosophy of many African-Americans during slavery and Reconstruction.

Originally published in 1879 in Harris's popular *Atlanta Constitution* column, "The Wonderful Tar-Baby Story" circulated widely in 1881 in *Uncle Remus: His Songs and His Sayings,* the first of Harris's ten "Uncle Remus" collections. Reflecting Harris's concern with maintaining audience interest, the story was presented in two episodes, divided by a cliff-hanger ending. "The Wonderful Tar-Baby Story" focuses on Brer Rabbit's entrapment by the malicious Brer Fox. In "How Mr. Rabbit Was too Sharp for Mr. Fox" Brer Rabbit uses his wits to escape to his home in the "brier-patch."

Derived from West African folklore, the tar baby story had become a fundamental part of the African-American oral tradition by the time Harris heard it while growing up on a Georgia plantation. In numerous forms, it would exert a lasting effect on American culture generally. As a trickster who outwits more powerful adversaries, Brer Rabbit influenced familiar cartoon characters such as Bugs Bunny. The Walt Disney movie *Song of the South* adapts Harris's characters to support an image of the Old South as a benevolent patriarchy. Conversely, revisionist treatments such as Toni Morrison's novel *Tar Baby* (1981) and Ralph Bakshi's movie *Streetfight* emphasize Brer Rabbit rather than Uncle Remus while critiquing racist psychology.

Harris's original audiences in both the North and South understood the tar baby story as a charming fable reflecting the fundamentally child-like character of blacks. Contradicting the abolitionist emphasis on the brutality of slavery, the image of the loving Uncle Remus with the white boy comforted those seeking reconciliation of sections following the Civil War. In the introduction to *Uncle Remus: His Songs and Sayings,* Harris describes Uncle Remus as a "type" of the black race: "[Uncle Remus is] an old negro who appears to be venerable enough to have lived during the period which he describes—who has nothing but pleasant memories of the discipline of slavery." Although Harris presents his book as a correction of "the intolerable misrepresentations of the minstrel stage," Uncle Remus remains a reassuringly asexual version of the "happy darky" or "kindly Uncle."

Harris sensed, however, that the animal tales articulated a substantially different vision of racial relations. Some passages in his introduction anticipate revisionist understandings of the tales as racial allegories pitting symbolic blacks (Brer Rabbit) against larger, more powerful, but less intelligent symbolic whites (Brer Fox, Brer Bear). Harris wrote, "It needs no scientific investigation to show why [the negro storyteller] selects as his hero the weakest and most harmless of animals, and brings him out victorious in contests with the bear, the wolf, and the fox." The unapologetic images of violent death in "The Awful Fate of Mr. Wolf" and "The End of Mr. Bear" in fact suggest that the animal tales symbolically enact the desire for vengeance against whites.

The primary concern of the tar baby story, however, is with survival rather than revenge. The tale transmits two fundamental pieces of wisdom for blacks who, like Brer Rabbit, find themselves in a position of relative weakness in a world dominated by irrationally malicious forces. The first part of the story endorses a separatist stance as a way of avoiding conflict with whites; the second part emphasizes the importance of indirection, intelligence, and verbal agility in responding to problems once they have arisen.

The separatist reading of the tar baby story hinges on an understanding of the tar baby as a white representation of blacks. Built by Brer Fox specifically to entrap Brer Rabbit, the tar baby recalls basic stereotypes of blacks; it is dark black, foul-smelling, motionless, brainless. Brer Rabbit's first mistake is interacting with the tar baby at all. Although it can do him no harm if he chooses to ignore it, Brer Rabbit demands that the tar baby treat him with proper respect. When it fails to respond to his civil greeting, he resorts to physical violence. At each stage of his entrapment, the best strategy available to Brer Rabbit is calm withdrawal. The angrier he becomes with the tar baby, the more deeply entangled he finds himself. By the time Brer Fox leaves his rocking chair, Brer Rabbit is nearly indistinguishable from the tar baby. His desire to correct the white stereotype, to gain recognition for himself as a real human being, delivers him into the hands of the oppressor. The implications are clearly separatist. The best strategy available for blacks is simply to ignore the white folks and their inaccurate ideas.

Once Brer Rabbit has been entrapped, the story shifts focus to the use of trickster strategies for survival and escape. The most important resource for Brer Rabbit as trickster is his knowledge of the symbolic whites' cruelty toward and ignorance of blacks. Aware that "Brer Fox wanter hurt Brer Rabbit bad ez he kin," the trickster pleads to be lynched, drowned, or skinned rather than thrown into the brier-patch, an image of the true black home. Ignorant of the realities of black life and accepting the stereotype that blacks lack the intelligence needed to outthink and manipulate whites, Brer Fox falls for the trick and releases Brer Rabbit to his home.

Reflecting the fundamental realism of the folk tradition, Harris's half-conscious presentation of an African-American wisdom that belies his reassuring frame tale concludes with the situation back where it started. Brer Rabbit, the symbolic black, is no longer in the clutches of his tormentors. But those tormentors, the symbolic whites, have not gone away or changed. The continuing power of what Harris called "the legends themselves in their original simplicity" derives in large part from the continuing relevance of this vision to racial relations in the United States.

—Craig Hansen Werner

A WORN PATH
by Eudora Welty, 1941

The "unrivaled favorite" question of Eudora Welty's readers provides the title for her essay on "A Worn Path": "Is Phoenix Jackson's Grandson Really Dead?" Denying any intent to tease her audience, Welty says she "must assume that the boy is alive"; if he were not, the "truth of the story" would nevertheless "persist in the 'wornness' of the path" as the ancient grandmother makes her way to Natchez for medicine to relieve the child's suffering. The subject, Welty explains, is "the deep-grained habit of love."

One of Welty's earliest publications in a major magazine, "A Worn Path" was written in 1940 and appeared in the *Atlantic Monthly* in February 1941. Winner of the second prize for that year's O. Henry awards, it holds the important final position in *A Curtain of Green and Other Stories* (1941), Welty's first collection. Welty says the story originated in the "indelible" image of an elderly black woman whom she saw slowly crossing a wintry field. Another time, on the same road, Welty spoke with an old woman who said she was "too old at the Surrender." Welty

did not know whether this was the woman whose distant figure had so impressed her, but she felt the words belonged in the tale: "It was a case of joining two things that I had thought of, and making them into one." Although she told an interviewer that she did not begin the story with an intent to "write about the black race," Welty doubts "A Worn Path" would have been the same with a white protagonist because "it wouldn't have the same urgency about it."

As a Mississippi native, Welty found a more general source for "A Worn Path" in her familiarity with the history and the legends of the Natchez Trace, a wilderness area that forms the setting for the comic novella *The Robber Bridegroom* (1942) and for all but one piece in *The Wide Net and Other Stories* (1943). Suzanne Marrs relates "A Worn Path" to the many Natchez Trace photographs Welty took during the 1930's and suggests that Phoenix's "heroic quest for medicine" is as "enduring as the daily and seasonal cycles" of the landscape.

Welty's fascination with myths and fairy tales is evident from the opening paragraphs, as the "very old" woman begins her journey on an early morning in December. Welty has remarked that the name Phoenix is a "legitimate" symbol since it is also "an appropriate Mississippi name": "If it comes in naturally, then it can call up some overtones and I don't mean to do any more than that."

The image of the mythic Arabian bird rising every 500 years from its own funeral pyre generates overtones of self-sacrificial death and resurrection that describe the periodic trips Phoenix takes to sustain life in her only remaining relative. The "yellow burning" under her dark cheeks, her red head-rag, and her hair's "odor like copper" recall the blazing colors of the phoenix, which, in its cyclic return, is associated with the sun. Phoenix walks her treacherous path summer and winter as she, like the mythic Persephone, makes her way between worlds on errands of love. The precious medicine that awaits her in the doctor's office, at the top of a "tower of steps," has the almost magical power to restore breath to the small boy, whose throat—burned by lye a few years ago—closes up "every little while."

Louise Westling suggests that Phoenix exhibits a "distinctively feminine kind of heroism" deriving from women's roles as "guardians and nurturers of children"; men's quests, on the other hand, often involve battles for dominance and are typically concerned with "self-definition." Thus, Welty contrasts the tiny old woman with the white young hunter who helps her out of a ditch but who proves the most vicious impediment in her path. Not only does he jokingly point his gun at Phoenix, but guiltily thinks he saw her pick up a nickel that had fallen from his pocket, but he lies that he would give her a dime if he had any money. Urging her to return home, he laughs: "I know you old colored people! Wouldn't miss going to town to see Santa Claus!"

Ironically, the hunter calls Phoenix "Granny," unaware that her grandson's distress has impelled her to climb hills, tangle with a thorn bush, creep through a barbed-wire fence, and face "the trial" of crossing a creek on a log with her eyes shut and her slender cane levelled "fiercely before her." Katherine Anne Porter has identified a "mysterious threshold between dream and waking" in several of Welty's stories, and Phoenix's obstacles include a confrontation with a ghost that turns out to be a scarecrow, a hallucinatory visitation from a boy who offers her a slice of marble-cake, and a sensation that she is walking in the sleep of "old women under a spell." Welty's descriptions are characteristically figurative. "Big dead trees" are "like black men with one arm," and the "emptiness" of the scarecrow's coat is "cold as ice."

Phoenix's struggles do not end when she emerges from the shadowy woods and arrives in the "shining" and "paved city." Alert to urban decorum, she must ask a lady to tie the shoes which have been unlaced the whole journey. In the doctor's office, a "ceremonial stiffness" grips her body, and she cannot respond to the receptionist's greeting: "A charity case, I suppose." Although the nurse immediately recognizes her, Phoenix's silence leads her to ask abruptly whether the grandson is dead. Finally aroused, Phoenix confesses a lapse of memory and assures her impatient listeners that not only is the boy alive, but he is "going to

last"; moreover, she will never forget him again: "no, the whole enduring time."

The nurse marks "Charity" in her account book, and the attendant gives Phoenix a nickel, which she will pair with the hunter's unwitting contribution to buy her grandchild a paper windmill. But the most heart-felt act of giving in the story is the selfless journey which Phoenix continues, in true Christmas spirit, as her slow steps head back down the stairway, moving toward the path worn smooth by her love.

—Joan Wylie Hall

Y

THE YELLOW WALLPAPER
by Charlotte Perkins Gilman, 1892

Refused by the editor of *Atlantic Monthly* because the story made him so miserable, Gilman's now classic story of a woman suffering post-partum depression, improperly treated with isolation and inactivity, was originally considered a Poe-like Gothic tale. Narratives of supernatural horror were a staple of magazines at the turn-of-the-century, and Gilman's story—published in 1892 in *The New England Magazine,* in 1899 as a chapbook, and later reprinted by William Dean Howells in a 1920 story collection—was read without attention to the gender of the unnamed protagonist. "The Yellow Wallpaper"—revived by the Feminist Press after being out of print for 70 years—is now one of the most often read and written about stories of feminist consciousness.

Charlotte Perkins Gilman, influential economist, lecturer, and publisher, experienced depression from the time of her first marriage to Charles Walter Stetson, and that depression intensified after their daughter was born. Like Winifred Howells, Edith Wharton, and Jane Addams, Gilman too was sent to Dr. S. Weir Mitchell, whose "cures" for women were world famous. But Mitchell's treatment—of a rest cure which depended upon seclusion, massage, immobility, and overfeeding (some women gained 50 pounds during the six weeks of hospitalization)—had at its root complete mental inactivity. It is this stricture that bothers Gilman the most, this and the pervasive medical attitude that women's problems all stemmed from hysteria, and were womb-based.

"The Yellow Wallpaper" shows how well cared for the unnamed protagonist is, by both her authoritarian husband, John, who is conveniently a physician, and her physician brother, as well as by her stereotypical loving sister-in-law, who enjoys caring for the new baby as well as for the sick protagonist. But the woman's own views of what she would like (to see friends, to write, to read) are completely discounted, and her husband's treatment—like his language throughout the tale—is truly patriarchal. His wife is his child, and she doesn't know even the simplest things about what ails her. His use of diminutive names for her ("blessed little goose," "little girl") parallels his unresponsive replies: listening to her is the last thing on his agenda. Gilman provides several interchanges so that the self-serving qualities of his role are clear. After the woman tells him that she is no better, contrary to his reassurances, he replies, "Bless her little heart! she shall be as sick as she pleases! But now let's improve the shining hours by going to sleep, and talk about it in the morning!"

Shut off from all normal interaction and locked into what John calls a nursery but which smacks of a space used previously for incarceration, the woman fantasizes in a particularly meaningful way: she sees imprisoned women, trying to escape from the morass of crumbling yellowed wallpaper that covers all the surfaces of her prison. The diseased and stifling yellow, the meaningless patterns (of which the bored woman tries to make sense, and thereby creates the narrative of the trapped imaginary women), the omnipresence of the gloomy wall covering—and its moldy smell—would predictably augment a depressed person's malaise. The paper comes to symbolize her utter lack of power in the social construct: her husband John has the knowledge, earns the money, and makes the decisions. She has no role except to be his wife and the mother of his child; and when she rejects those roles, through the excuse of illness, he is more angry than he is concerned.

Gilman's brilliant use of the unnamed protagonist's voice, during a period when very few texts were written in any kind of first person, involves the reader in the woman's process of figuring out what is happening to her. At first, she writes with humility, sneaking out her forbidden journal carefully. She says all the expected things—her husband is understanding and knowledgeable and she is at fault for not responding to his care. But then a tone of complaint—a minor tone—enters her writing. Though she does not attack John directly, she knows at heart that her own treatment would have better results than his is having, and her impatience and frustration at his not listening to her colors her narrative.

But then her focus shifts, away from herself and her impasse with John and all the medical forces he represents, and she begins to explore her fascination with the woman (trapped, as she is herself) behind the wallpaper pattern. For the second half of the narrative, the purposely unnamed woman's attention is on seeing whether the woman behind the wallpaper can escape, and on whether she can help the woman to escape. Then, the woman becomes women and there are many trapped women trying to escape. In this transactive identification, the protagonist begins voicing her real anger at her husband and her society. She cannot express anger in her own persona because she has been convinced that what John does is best for her; so she creates a fantasy woman who is also caught in a similar imprisonment of male authority.

By the time of her taking action, crawling around the room and tearing off pieces of the hated, and imprisoning, wallpaper, the reader is firmly in the protagonist's camp. Her triumphal crawling over her shocked husband's body, when he faints at the destruction she has created in the room, and at what her behavior implies for her "recovery," seems to be a genuine triumph—until rational meaning returns to the reader. Gilman has created so much sympathy for the protagonist that the reader has accepted her mindset. Just as she sees her destruction, and her leaving the room, as triumph, so too does the reader.

The carefully modulated voice of the protagonist, writing secretly in the forbidden journal, is an amazingly effective means of telling the complicated story. This is a narrative with no simple right and wrong, no clear protagonist and antagonist (for John "loves" his wife and assumes that taking her to the country is a sure way of restoring her strength). In its writing, Gilman created a fable that explains, inductively, that women have rights, women have knowledge, and women have talents that need to be respected and employed. One of the primary themes of her book *Women and Economics* (1898), was that women need work that has value in the marketplace, and that their domestic work also needs to be given value. Otherwise, they face the plight of this fictional protagonist — nameless, faceless, characterless, a cypher in the work, and the life, of the real world.

—Linda Wagner-Martin

YOUNG GOODMAN BROWN
by Nathaniel Hawthorne, 1835

"Young Goodman Brown," Nathaniel Hawthorne's well-known tale of a young man's initiation into the nature of evil, is usually seen as a classic example of his allegorical method. However, even as Hawthorne suggests in the story that there is some uncertainty about whether Goodman Brown actually experienced his confrontation with the devil or only dreamed it, there is a more basic ambiguity underlying the relationship between realism and allegory in the story.

It seems as though Goodman Brown's journey into the forest is ritually predestined, that he is an allegorical figure who has no free will to act in any way other than what the allegorical nature of the story determines for him. However, his questioning of the journey and his struggles against it suggest a realistic open-endedness and that Brown is an as-if-real character with a mind of his own. This inconclusiveness is not the result of Hawthorne's faulty control of his story, but rather an indication of an important transition point in the development of short fiction in the 19th century when allegorical conventions began to be displaced by realistic ones.

The theme of Hawthorne's tale is not so straightforward as it may appear at first glance. Although we know that the story has something to do with the discovery of the concept of evil and the related concepts of guilt and sin, the work never makes it quite clear what sin or evil is. It is not so simple as to suggest that because all the people in the village are at the witches' sabbath they are therefore cruel and wicked people as individuals. Instead, sin in this story has a more basic and generalized meaning that refers to all of humanity by virtue of being human. The fact that Goodman Brown only has to make this journey once and that he has not made it before suggests, on the story's allegorical level, that it is a ritualistic journey that all humans have to make at a certain point in their lives.

This suggestion of allegorical initiation into evil thus demands an understanding of evil on its most basic level and, given the Calvinist framework of much of Hawthorne's fiction, invites comparison with the basically allegorical nature of that archetypal story of the discovery of evil in the book of Genesis in the Bible. Erich Fromm, in his study *The Art of Loving,* argues that the original couple's shame after eating the forbidden fruit should not be understood merely as the birth of sexual prudery, but as the realization of the division of their original oneness into two separate entities who must henceforth be condemned to loneliness and isolation.

According to the Christian religion the only way to heal this separation is to follow the words of Jesus to love the neighbor as the self; that is, to love the neighbor until no distinction can be made between the neighbor and the self. It is, of course, this complete loss of the self as a separate entity by sympathetic identification with the brotherhood of the race that Brown is unable to accomplish at the end of the story.

Before his journey into the forest, the young and uninitiated Goodman Brown simply assumed the sense of union. This night of all nights in the year metaphorically marks his discovery that separation is the nature of humanity. Once humans have made this discovery, Hawthorne suggests, they have only two choices: either they accept the truth of separation and try to love the other as a means to heal it, or else they fall into complete despair and hopelessness.

It is this open-ended choice that makes Hawthorne's story seem psychologically realistic. Goodman Brown's wife Faith is not merely a two-dimensional allegorical figure embodying the quality of her name; she is also a realistic example of the necessity of faith. Whereas she is able to make a leap of love and faith and welcome her husband back with open arms, Goodman Brown only looks sadly and sternly into her face and passes her without greeting. Whereas Faith can accept the inevitable fallen nature of humanity and live with that realization, Brown is an absolutist who, having been displaced from his childish illusion, cannot accept the necessary relativism of adulthood.

"Young Goodman Brown" is the best known example of Hawthorne's primary literary contribution — the psychologizing of spiritual truths once embodied in allegory and the consequent transformation of the simple one-to-one relationships suggested in that ancient form into the complex and ambiguous symbolism that formed the basis for the 19th-century short story.

—Charles E. May

The following index includes the titles of all books listed in the Short Story section of the Publications lists, and the titles of individual stories discussed in the Writer essays. Both original language and English language translations are listed. A few titles from the Collections section also are listed.

Titles appearing in **bold** are subjects of individual essays in the Works section; titles in quotes are individual stories.

The writer's name and the page number following the title directs the reader to the appropriate entry.

NOTES
ON
CONTRIBUTORS

ABEE-TAULLI, Pamela. Completing doctoral work in modern Japanese literature at Princeton University, East Asian Studies Department. **Essay:** Tsushima Yūko.

AYCOCK, Wendell M. Professor of English, Texas Tech University. Editor of *The Teller and the Tale: Aspects of the Short Story,* 1982. Editor or co-editor of seventeen volumes in the Comparative Literature Symposium Series. **Essay:** "End of the Game."

BAKER, Simon. Lecturer and Director of the M.A. course on Anglo-Welsh Literature, English Department, Swansea University. Author of numerous articles and reviews, mainly on the literature of Wales and modern short fiction. **Essays:** Frank O'Connor; Dylan Thomas; "A Child's Christmas in Wales"; "Gooseberries"; "The Piece of String"; "The Rocking-Horse Winner."

BALINA, Marina. Assistant Professor of German and Russian, Illinois Wesleyan University, Bloomington. Author of *Autobiographies of Glasnost',* vol. 7, 1992, *The Main Character in the Modern German Novel,* 1988, *Parallelism as One of the Main Structure Elements of the German Ballad,* 1988, and *Tolstoy and Canetti,* 1987. **Essays:** *Arcturus the Hunting Dog;* "Little Red Riding Hood."

BANERJEE, Soma. Freelance writer living in India. **Essay:** Ruskin Bond.

BARJASTEH, Jolene J. Assistant Professor of French, St. Olaf College, Northfield, Minnesota. Numerous papers presented at professional conferences, including "The Self as Other in Nerval's *Le Roi de Bicêtre,*" "Tragic Vision/Division in Nerval's *L'Histoire du Calife Hakem,*" "*Octavie* de Nerval: La Multiplicité de l'image féminine," and others on Maupassant, Stendhal, and Emile Nelligan. Author of *Aspects of the Double in the Works of Gérard de Nerval,* forthcoming. **Essay:** Gérald de Nerval.

BARNES, Christopher. Professor and Chair of the Department of Slavic Languages and Literatures, University of Toronto. Editor of *Research Bulletin* (Munich), 1974-75. Member of editorial board, *Forum for Modern Language Studies,* 1970-89. Author of *Boris Pasternak: A Literary Biography, Volume I,* 1989, and numerous articles and broadcasts on Russian literary and musical topics. Editor of *Studies in 20th-Century Russian Literature,* 1976. Translator and editor of *Collected Short Prose of Boris Pasternak,* 1977, *The Voice of Prose,* vol. I, by Boris Pasternak, 1986, and *People and Propositions,* vol. II, by Boris Pasternak, 1990. **Essays:** Boris Pasternak; "A Story about the Most Important Thing"; "Zhenia Luvers' Childhood."

BARTA, Peter. Professor of Russian and Comparative Literature, Director, Russian Language and Area Studies, Texas Tech University, Lubbock. **Essays:** Tatiana Tolstaia; "Mahogany."

BEGNAL, Michael H. Professor of English and Comparative Literature, Pennsylvania State University, University Park. Author of *Joseph Sheridan Le Fanu,* 1971, *A Conceptual Guide to Finnegans Wake* (with Fritz Senn), 1974, *Narrator and Character in Finnegans Wage* (with Grace Eckley), 1975, and *Dreamscheme: Narrative and Voice in Finnegans Wake,* 1988. Editor of *On Miracle Ground: Essays on the Ficton of Lawrence Durrell,* 1990. **Essays:** "The Dead"; "The Loneliness of the Long-Distance Runner."

BELLMAN, Samuel I. Professor of English, California State Polytechnic University, Pomona. Author of *The College Experience,* 1962, and *Survey and Forecast,* 1966, *Marjorie Kinnan Rawlings,* 1974, and *Constance Mayfield Rourke,* 1981, and of numerous essays, poems, and critical reviews. **Essays:** "The Bride Comes to Yellow Sky"; "The Diamond as Big as the Ritz"; "A Municipal Report."

BELL-VILLADA, Gene H. Professor of Romance Languages, Williams College, Williamstown, Massachusetts. Author of *Borges and His Fiction: A Guide to His Mind and Art,* 1981, *García Márquez: The Man and His Work,* 1990, and *The Carlos Chadwick Mystery: A Novel of College Life and Political Terror,* 1990. **Essays:** Jorge Luis Borges; "Pierre Menard, Author of the *Quixote.*"

BENNETT, Bruce. Associate Professor of English, University of Western Australia, Nedlands. Editor of the journal *Westerly: A Quarterly Review,* and the books, *New Country: A Selection of Western Australian Short Stories,* 1976, *The Literature of Western Australia,* 1979, *Cross Currents: Magazines and Newspapers in Australian Literature,* 1981, *European Relations: Essays for Helen Watson-Williams* (with John Hay), 1985, *Place, Region and Community,* 1985, *A Sense of Exile: Essays in the Literature of the Asia-Pacific Region,* 1988, and anthologies of short stories. **Essays:** Peter Cowan; Frank Moorhouse; Michael Wilding; "The House on the Hill"; "Francis Silver."

BENNETT, John M. Latin American Editor, Ohio State University Libraries, and Head of Luna Bisonte Productions. Author of numerous articles and reviews on Latin American literature and poetry, several bibliographies on Latin American literature and social sciences, and numerous books of poetry, including *Found Objects and Works,* 1973, *White Screen,* 1976, *Nips Poems,* 1980, *Antpath,* 1984, *No Boy,* 1985, *Span,* 1990, *Fenestration,* 1991, and *Was Ah,* 1992. Editor, *Lost and Found Times.* **Essays:** "The Garden of Forking Paths"; "We're Very Poor."

BENSON, Renate. Professor of German Studies, University of Guelph, Ontario. Author of *Erich Kästner, Studien zu seinem Werk,* 1973, *German Expressionist Drama: Ernst Toller and Georg Kaiser,* 1984, and *Deutsches expressionistisches Theater: Ernst Toller und Georg Kaiser,* 1987. Translator of *Die Strasse nach Altamont* by Gabrielle Roy (original title: *La Route d'Altamont*), 1970, *Beethoven, The Man and His Time* by Franz

Grassberger (original title: *Beethoven, der Mann und seine Zeit*), 1970, and of works by Louis-H. Frechette, M. Lescarbot, E. Paquin, Anne Hébert. **Essays:** Isle Aichinger; Siegfried Lenz.

BENTON, Richard P. Associate Professor Emeritus of English and Comparative Literature, Trinity College, Hartford, Connecticut. Member of the editorial boards of *Poe Studies* and the University of Mississippi *Studies in English*. Editor of *New Approaches to Poe, Poe as Literary Cosmologer, Journey into the Center--Studies in Poe's Pym*, and other symposia. Author of articles on American, English, French, Japanese, and Chinese literature. Translator in English of Chinese poetry and prose. **Essays:** Akutagawa Ryūnosuke; Shen Congwen; Auguste Villiers de l'Isle-Adam; "A Bandit Chief"; "The Cask of Amontillado"; "The Rooster and the Dancing Girl"; "The Murders in Rue Morgue."

BLISS, Carolyn. Guest Professor of the Department of English, University of Utah, Salt Lake City. Editor, American Association of Australian Literary Studies *Newsletter*. Author of *Patrick White's Fiction: The Paradox of Fortunate Failure*, 1986, and the chapter on White in *International Literature in English*, edited by Robert L. Ross, 1991. Guest editor of special Patrick White issue of *Antipodes*, Spring 1992. **Essays:** Peter Carey; "A Cheery Soul"; "Down at the Dump."

BOTTA, Anna. Assistant Professor, Italian Department, Smith College, Northampton, Massachusetts. Author of "Calvino's *Città Invisibili*: Opening an Atlas of Similitude," in *Italian Culture*, X, 1992. **Essay:** Giovanni Verga.

BRADBURY, Malcolm. Writer. Former series editor, Stratford-upon-Avon Studies, Arnold Publishers, London, and Contemporary Writers series, Arnold Publishers, London. Author of many novels (including *Rates of Exchange*, 1983, and *Cuts: A Very Short Novel*, 1987), the story collection *Who Do You Think You Are?*, 1976 (augmented edition 1984), plays, poetry, and non-fiction (including *What Is a Novel?*, 1969, *The Modern American Novel*, 1983 [revised edition 1991], *The Modern World: Ten Great Writers*, 1989, and *From Puritanism to Postmodernism: The Story of American Literature*, with Richard Ruland, 1991). Editor of numerous books and anthologies (including *The Novel Today: Contemporary Writers on Modern Fiction*, 1977 [revised edition 1990], *The Penguin Book of Modern British Short Stories*, 1987, and *Unthank: An Anthology of Short Stories from the M.A. in Creative Writing at the University of East Anglia*, with others, 1989).

BROUGHTON, William. Senior Lecturer in English, Massey University, New Zealand. Former editor, *The Journal of New Zealand Literature*. Member of the Advisory Committee of the New Zealand Literary Fund (later the Literature Programme of the Queen Elizabeth II Arts Council), 1985-90. **Essays:** Frank Sargeson; Owen Marshall.

BROWN, Russell E. Professor of German, State University of New York, Stoney Brook. Author of books and articles on German and other European literatures. **Essay:** Danilo Kiš.

BRUCE, George. Writer and lecturer. Author of *Sea Talk* (poetry), 1944, *Landscapes and Figures* (poetry), 1967, *Collected Poems*, 1970, *Perspectives*, 1987, *Festival in the North* (a history of the Edinburgh Festival), 1975. **Essays:** "Alicky's Watch"; "Thrawn Janet."

BUENO, Eva Paulino. Independent scholar. Editor of *Collages & Bricolages*, Clarion University of Pennsylvania, and *Osamayor* literary magazine, University of Pittsburgh. Author of numerous essays and reviews on Brazilian literature. **Essays:** Lygia Fagundes Telles; "Midnight Mass"; "Rat Seminar."

BUFFARD-O'SHEA, Nicole. Assistant Professor, Oakland University, Rochester, Michigan. Author of *Le Monde de Boris Vian et le grotesque littéraire*, 1993. **Essay:** "The Walker through Walls."

BUSHELL, Anthony. Head of German, Saint David's University College, University of Wales, Lampeter. Author of *The Emergence of West German Poetry from the Second World War into the Early Post-War Period*, 1989, and numerous articles on aspects of modern German and Austrian literature and culture. **Essays:** Heinrich von Kleist; "The Marquise of O."

BUTLER, Lance St. John. Senior Lecturer in English, University of Stirling, Scotland. Author of *Thomas Hardy*, 1978, *Beckett and the Meaning of Being: A Study in Ontological Parable*, 1984, *Victorian Doubt: Literary and Cultural Discourses*, 1990, *Modern Approaches to Literary Criticism: The Freedom of the Text*, 1990. Editor of *Alternative Hardy*, 1989, and *Rethinking Beckett* (with Robin J. Davies), 1990. **Essays:** Samuel Beckett; James Joyce; Anthony Trollope; "The Country of the Blind"; "Dante and the Lobster"; "The Judgment"; "Tonio Kröger"; "To Room 19"; "A Tragedy of Two Ambitions."

BUTSCHER, Edward. Author of *Aiken: Poet of White Horse Vale*, 1988. **Essays:** Conrad Aiken; J.D. Salinger; Peter Taylor; John Updike; Noon Wine; "Redemption."

CANNON, Kelly. Adjunct Assistant Professor of English, North Carolina Central University, Durham. Author of *Masculinity and Henry James: The Man at the Margins,* forthcoming. **Essay:** Ann Beattie.

CASPER, Leonard. Emeritus Professor of English, Boston College, Chestnut Hill, Massachusetts. Humanities Editor, *Pilipinas*. Former member, editorial boards of *Literature East and West*, and *Solidarity*. Author of *Six Filipino Poets*, 1955, *The Wayward Horizon: Essays on Modern Philippine Literature*, 1961, *Modern Philippine Short Stories*, 1962, *The Wounded Diamond: Studies in Modern Philippine Literature*, 1964, *New Writing from the Philippines*, 1966, *Firewalkers: Concelebrations 1964-1984*, 1987, and *In Burning Ambush: Essays 1985-1990*, 1991. **Essay:** F. Sionil Jose.

CASSILL, R.V. Writer and editor. Author of many novels, including *Clem Anderson*, 1960, and *Labors of Love*, 1980, and the collection *Collected Stories*, 1989. Editor of *Norton Anthology of Short Fiction* (4th edition), 1990. **Essays:** Erskine Caldwell; Jean Stafford; "The Birthmark"; "Death in the Woods"; "The White Horses of Vienna."

CHARTERS, Ann. Professor of English, University of Connecticut, Storrs. Author of *A Bibliography of Jack Kerouac*, 1967 (revised 1975), *Scenes Along the Road: Photographs of the Desolation Angels*, 1970 (2nd edition 1985), *Nobody: The Story of Bert Williams*, 1970, *Kerouac: A Biography*, 1973, *I Love: The Story of Vladimir Mayakovsky and Lili Brik*, with Samuel Charters, 1979, and *Beats and Company*, 1986. Editor of *The*

Beats: Literary Bohemians in Postwar America, 2 vols., 1983; *The Story and Its Writer*, 1983 (second edition 1991), and *Major Writers of Short Fiction*, 1993. **Essay:** Sarah Orne Jewett.

CLANCY, Laurie. Senior Lecturer in English, La Trobe University, Bundoora, Victoria. Author of two novels, (*A Collapsible Man*, 1975, and *Perfect Love*, 1983), two collections of short stories (*The Wife Specialist*, 1978, and *City to City*, 1988), and critical works on Christina Stead, Xavier Herbert, and Nabokov. **Essays:** Dashiell Hammett; Henry Lawson; Joaquim Machado de Assis; Katharine Mansfield; John Morrison; Hal Porter; Henry Handel Richardson; James Thurber; Patrick White; "The Red-Backed Spiders."

CLARK, Barbara. Assistant Professor of Spanish, Averett College, Danville, Virginia. **Essay:** Rosario Castellanos.

CLARK, Keith. Teaches at the University of North Carolina, Chapel Hill. Author of various critical essays. **Essay:** "The Blues I'm Playing."

CLARK, Stella T. Professor of Foreign Languages, California State University, San Marcos. Author of articles on Latin American literature. Former associate editor of *Hispania*. Manuscript reviewer for *Chasqui* and *Choice*. **Essays:** "No One Writes to the Colonel"; "Talpa"; "The Tree."

CLIFFORD, Joan E. Doctoral candidate, University of North Carolina, Chapel Hill. **Essays:** Adolfo Bioy Casares; "A Letter about Emilia."

CLUNE, Anne. Senior Lecturer in English, Trinity College, Dublin. Author of *Flann O'Brien: A Critical Introduction to His Writings* (as Anne Clissman), 1975. **Essays:** "The Man Who Invented Sin"; "A Scandalous Woman"; "Two Lovely Beasts."

COAD, David G. Lecturer in Commonwealth Studies, University of Valenciennes and Hainaut Cambrésis, France. **Essay:** "Clay."

COCHRAN, Robert B. Professor of English and Director, Center for Arkansas and Regional Studies, University of Arkansas, Fayetteville. **Essays:** W.P. Kinsella; Grace Paley.

COCKSHUT, A.O.J. G.M. Young Lecturer in Nineteenth Century Literature, Oxford University, and Fellow of Hertford College. Author of *Anthony Trollope: A Critical Study*, 1955, *Anglican Attitudes: A Study of Victorian Religious Controversies*, 1959, *The Imagination of Charles Dickens*, 1961, *The Unbelievers: English Agnostic Thought 1840-1890*, 1964, *The Achievement of Walter Scott*, 1969, *Truth to Life: The Art of Biography in the Nineteenth Century*, 1974, *Man and Woman: Love in the Novel*, 1977, and *The Art of Autobiography in 19th and 20th Century England*, 1984. Editor of *Religous Controversies of the Nineteenth Century: Selected Documents*, 1966, and *Miss Mackenzie* by Trollope, 1988. **Essays:** G.K. Chesterton; Walter Scott; "Seaton's Aunt"; "The Signalman"; "Summer Night"; *Typhoon*; "Uncle Fred Flits By."

COWAN, Peter. See his own entry.

COLLINS, Mark L. English Teacher, Scotch College, Melbourne, Australia. **Essay:** Marcus Clarke.

COLLINS, Philip. Emeritus Professor of English, University of Leicester. Author of *James Boswell*, 1956, *Dickens and Crime*, 1962 (revised 1963), *Dickens and Education*, 1963 (revised 1964), *The Impress of the Moving Age*, 1965, and *Reading Aloud: A Victorian Métier*, 1972. Editor of *Dickens: The Critical Heritage*, 1971, *Dickens: Interviews and Recollections*, 2 vols., 1981, *Thackeray: Interview and Recollections*, 1983, and *The Annotated Dickens* (with Edward Giuliano), 1986. **Essays:** Charles Dickens; George Eliot; *A Christmas Carol*; *Daisy Miller*; "The Old Nurse's Story."

COLVERT, James B. Professor Emeritus, University of Georgia. Author of *Stephen Crane*, 1984, many articles on Crane, and essays on Hemingway, Glasgow, and Southern fiction. **Essay:** Stephen Crane.

COPPOLA, Carlo. Professor of Modern Languages and Linguistics, and Director of the Center for International Programs, Oakland University, Rochester, Michigan. Editor, *Journal of South Asian Literature*. Author of *Marxist Influences and South Asian Literature*, 1988, and *Not to Darkness: The Life and Writings of Ahmed Ali; The Proletarian Episode: Urdu Poetry, 1935-1970*, forthcoming. **Essays:** S.Y. Agnon; Sādeq Hedāyat; Yusuf Idris; Nagīb Mafūz; Sādat Hasan Manṭo; Amos Oz; Premcand; "The Cheapest Nights"; "Facing the Forest"; "The Hills of Evil Counsel"; "Mozail"; "The Shroud"; "A Whole Loaf."

CORBALLIS, Richard. Senior Lecturer in English, Massey University, Palmerston North, New Zealand. Author of *Stoppard: The Mystery and the Clockwork*, 1984, and *Introducing Witi Ihimaera* (with Simon Garrett), 1984. Editor of *George Chapman's Minor Translations: A Critical Edition of His Renderings of Musaeus, Hesiod and Juvenal*, 1984. **Essays:** Patricia Grace; Witi Ihimaera; "At the Bay."

CORE, George. Editor of *The Sewanee Review*. **Essays:** "The Ballroom of Romance"; "Haircut."

CRANE, Ralph J. Lecturer in English, University of Waikato, New Zealand. Author of *Inventing India: A History of English-Language Fiction*, 1991, *Ruth Prawer Jhabvala*, 1992, and numerous articles on post-colonial literature. Editor of *Passages to Ruth Prawer Jhabvala*, 1991. **Essays:** "A Horse and Two Goats"; "Mrs. Bathurst."

CROSS, Richard K. Professor of English, University of Maryland, College Park. Author of *Flaubert and Joyce: The Rite of Fiction*, 1971, *Malcolm Lowry: A Preface to His Fiction*, 1980, and articles on Shakespeare, Lowry, Richard Eberhart, and Randall Jarrell. **Essay:** *Seize the Day*.

CROWLEY, J. Donald. Professor of English, University of Missouri, Columbia. Editor of *The American Short Story 1850-1900*. **Essays:** Nathaniel Hawthorne; Flannery O'Connor; Mark Twain; "Sorrow-Acre"; "The Valient Woman."

CURRENT-GARCIA, Eugene. Hargis Professor Emeritus of American Literature, Auburn University, Alabama. Founder and co-editor of *Southern Humanities Review*, 1967-79. Author of *O. Henry (W.S. Porter): A Critical Study*, 1965, and *The American Short Story Before 1850*, 1985. Co-editor of *American Short Stories* (with Walton R. Patrick), 1952-86 (5th edition, with Bert Hitchcock, 1990), *What Is the Short Story?* (with Walton R.

Patrick), 1961, *Realism and Romanticism in Fiction*, 1962, *Short Stories of the Western World*, 1969, and *Shem, Ham, and Japteth: The Papers of W.O. Tuggle*, 1973. **Essay:** O. Henry.

CURRY, Renee R. Assistant Professor of English, California State University, San Marcos. **Essay:** Zora Neale Hurston.

de KOCK, Leon. Lecturer in English, University of South Africa, Pretoria. Author of articles on South African and African literature. Language editor, *South African Historical Journal*. **Essay:** "The Ultimate Safari."

DINGLEY, Robert. Lecturer in English, University of New England, Armidale, New South Wales, Australia. Has contributed to *Australian Literary Studies*, *Southerly*, *Durham University Journal*, *Notes and Queries*, *Explicator*, *Parergon*, and other journals. **Essay:** "The Union Buries its Dead."

DITSKY, John. Professor of English, University of Windsor, Ontario. Author of numerous books of poetry (including *The Katherine Poems*, 1975, *Scar Tissue*, 1978, and *Friend and Lover*, 1981), and criticism (including *Essays on East of Eden*, 1977, *Onstage Christ: Studies in the Persistence of a Theme*, 1980, *John Steinbeck: Life, Works, and Criticism*, 1985, and *Critical Essays on Steinbeck's Grapes of Wrath*, 1989). **Essays:** John Steinbeck; "Good Country People"; "Paul's Case."

DOBREZ, Livio. Reader in English, Australian National University. Author of *The Existential and Its Exits, Literary and Philosophical Perspectives on the Work of Beckett, Ionesco, Genet and Pinter*, 1986, and *Parnassus Mad Ward, Michael Dransfield and the New Australian Poetry*, 1990. Currently writing a history of Australian literature. **Essays:** "The Drover's Wife"; "Water Them Geraniums."

DOBREZ, Patricia. Independent scholar in Canberra. Author of *The Art of the Boyds*. Currently writing a biography of the Australian poet Michael Dransfield. **Essay:** "The Puzzleheaded Girl."

DOWLING, David. Senior Lecturer, English Department, Massey University, Palmerston North, New Zealand. Author of *Playwriting and Playing It Right* (with David Carnegie), 1980, *Introducing Bruce Mason*, 1982, *Bloomsbury Aesthetics and the Novels of Forster and Woolf*, 1985, *Fictions of Nuclear Disaster*, 1986, *William Faulkner*, 1989, and *Mrs. Dalloway: The Price of Civility*, forthcoming. Editor of *Novelists on Novelists*, 1983, *On Stage 1, On Stage 2* (New Zealand plays for high schools), 1983, *Every Kind of Weather: The Writings of Bruce Mason*, 1986 and *Katherine Mansfield: Dramatic Sketches*, 1988. **Essays:** "A Glorious Morning, Comrade"; "Looking for Mr. Green"; "The Loons."

DOWLING, Finuala. Lecturer, Department of English, University of South Africa. Reviews current South African writing for a number of journals. **Essays:** Bessie Head; Es'kia Mphahlele.

DOYLE, Paul A. Professor of English, Nassau Community College, State University of New York, Garden City. Editor, *Evelyn Waugh Newsletter and Studies* and *Nassau Review*. Author of *Sean O'Faolain*, 1968, *Introduction to Paul Vincent Carroll*, 1971, *Liam O'Flaherty*, 1971, *Guide to Basic Information Sources in English Literature*, 1976, *Pearl S. Buck*, 1980, *A Reader's Companion to the Novels and Short Stories of Evelyn Waugh*, 1989, and of bibliographies of O'Flaherty and Waugh, and *A Concordance to the Collected Poems of James Joyce*, 1966. Editor of *Alexander Pope's Iliad: An Examination*, 1960. **Essays:** Liam O'Flaherty; "Lovers of the Lake."

DRAPER, R.P. Regius Chalmers Professor of English, University of Aberdeen, Scotland. Author of *D.H. Lawrence*, 1964, and *An Annotated Critical Bibliography of Thomas Hardy* (with Martin Ray), 1989. Editor of *Lawrence: The Critical Heritage*, 1970, *Hardy: The Tragic Novels: A Casebook*, 1975, *The Literature of Region and Nation*, 1989, and *The Epic: Developments in Criticism*, 1990. **Essays:** D.H. Lawrence; "On the Western Circuit"; *The Turn of the Screw*.

DUNCAN, Charles. Teaches at Florida State University, Tallahassee. Author of essays in *American Literary Realism* and *Frank Norris Studies*. Currently writing book about Charles W. Chesnutt's short fiction, and preparing bibliography of Chesnutt's writings (with Joseph R. McElrath, Jr.). **Essay:** "The Wife of His Youth."

ECKLEY, Grace. Adjunct faculty, Red Rocks Community College, Colorado. Author of *Benedict Kiely*, 1972, *Edna O'Brien*, 1974, *Narrator and Character in Finnegans Wake* (with Michael H. Begnal), 1975, *Finley Peter Dunne*, 1981, and *Children's Lore in Finnegans Wake*, 1985. **Essays:** Edna O'Brien; "Gorilla, My Love"; "A Hunger Artist"; "I Want To Know Why"; "Mario and the Magician"; "The Post Office"; "The Steadfast Tin Soldier."

ECKLEY, Wilton. Director of Liberal Arts and International Studies, Colorado School of Mines, Golden. Author of *E.E. Cummings*, 1968, *Harriette Arnow*, 1974, *T.S. Stribling*, 1975, *Herbert Hoover*, 1980, and *The American Circus*, 1984. **Essays:** "The Gift of the Magi"; "The Legend of Sleepy Hollow"; "The Outcasts of Poker Flat"; "The Red Pony."

ELKINS, Marilyn. Assistant Professor of English, California State University, Los Angeles. Author of *Metamorphosizing the Novel: Kay Boyle's Narrative Innovations*, 1993. Editor of *The Heart of a Man*, 1991. **Essay:** Kay Boyle.

ELLIS, Robert Richmond. Associate Professor of Spanish, Occidental College, Los Angeles, California. Author of *The Tragic Pursuit of Being: Unamuno and Sartre*, 1988, and *San Juan de la Cruz: Mysticism and Sartrean Existentialism*, 1992. **Essays:** Jean-Paul Sartre; "Saint Emmanuel the Good, Martyr."

EVANS, Walter E. Professor of English, Augusta College, Georgia. Author of essays and articles on short fiction and contemporary American writers. Editor of *The Best of Sand Hills*, 1993. **Essay:** "Rip Van Winkle."

EVERMAN, Welch D. Associate Professor of English, University of Maine, Orono. Author of *Who Says This? The Authority of the Author, the Discourse, and the Reader, Jerzy Kosinski: The Literature of Violation*, and *The Harry and Sylvia Stories*, as well as numerous short stories and essays on the arts. **Essays:** J.G. Ballard; Silvina Ocampo; "Apocalypse at Solentiname"; "August 2026: There Will Come Soft Rains"; "Chronopolis"; "Leopoldina's Dream."

FALEN, James E. Professor of Russian, University of Tennessee, Knoxville. Author of *Isaac Babel: Russian Master of the Short Story*, 1974. Translator of *Eugene Onegin: A Novel in Verse by Alexander Pushkin*, 1990. **Essay:** "My First Goose."

FAULKNER, Peter. Reader in English, University of Exeter, Devon. Author of *William Morris and W.B. Yeats*, 1962, *Yeats and the Irish Eighteenth Century*, 1965, *Humanism and the English Novel*, 1976, *Modernism*, 1977, *Robert Bage*, 1979, *Angus Wilson: Mimic and Moralist*, 1980, *Against the Age: An Introduction to William Morris*, 1980, and *Yeats*, 1987. Editor of *William Morris: The Critical Heritage*, 1973, works by Morris, *The Picture of Dorian Gray* by Wilde, 1976, *Hermsprong* by Bage, 1985, *Jane Morris to Wilfrid Scawen Blunt*, 1986, *A Modernist Reader*, 1986, and *A Victorian Reader*, 1989. Editor of *The Journal of the William Morris Society*. **Essays:** Angela Carter; Doris Lessing; Alan Sillitoe; "Such Darling Dodos"; "The Two Drovers."

FERRIER, Carole. Reader in English, University of Queensland, Brisbane. Editor of *Hecate: A Women's Interdisciplinary Journal.* Editor of *Gender, Politics, and Fiction: Twentieth-Century Australian Women's Novels*, 1985. **Essay:** Katharine Susannah Prichard.

FIEDLER, Leslie A. Samuel Clemens Professor, State Univeristy of New York, Buffalo. Former Advisory Editor, *Ramparts* magazine, and Literary Adviser, St. Martin's Press. Author of novels (*The Second Stone*, 1963, *Back to China*, 1965, and *The Messenger Will Come No More*, 1974), story collections (*Pull Down Vanity and Other Stories*, 1962, *The Last Jew in America*, 1966, and *Nude Croquet and Other Stories*, 1969), and of numerous books of non-fiction (including *The Jew in the American Novel*, 1959, *What Was Literature? Class Culture and Mass Society*, 1982, and *Fiedler on the Roof: Epistle to the Gentiles*, 1991). Editor of *The Art of the Essay*, 1958 (revised edition 1969), *Selections from The Leaves of Grass*, 1959, *The Continuing Debate* (with Jacob Vinocur), 1965, *O Brave New World* (with Arthur Zeiger), 1968, and *English Literature: Opening Up the Canon* (with Houston A. Baker, Jr.), 1981.

FINN, Stephen M. Professor of English, Pretoria University, South Africa. **Essay:** Richard Rive.

FIRTH, Felicity. Teaches in the Department of Italian, University of Bristol. **Essay:** Luigi Pirandello.

FLIBBERT, Joseph. Professor of English, Salem State College, Massachusetts. Author of *Melville and the Art of the Burlesque*, 1974, and of numerous articles on English and American literature. **Essays:** "How I Contemplated the World from the Detroit House of Correction and Began My Life Over Again"; "Sonny's Blues"; "Winter Dreams."

FLORA, Joseph M. Professor of English, University of North Carolina. Member of the editorial boards of *Studies in Short Fiction* and *The Southern Literary Journal.* Author of *Vardis Fisher*, 1965, *William Ernest Henley*, 1970, *Frederick Manfred*, 1974, *Hemingway's Nick Adams*, 1982, and *Ernest Hemingway: A Study of the Short Fiction*, 1989. Editor of *The English Short Story 1880-1945*, 1985. Co-editor of *Southern Writers: A Biographical Dictionary*, 1979, *Fifty Southern Writers Before 1900*, 1987, and *Fifty Southern Writers After 1900*, 1987. **Essays:** "Barn Burning"; "A Clean, Well-Lighted Place"; "The

Country Husband"; "Neighbour Rosicky"; "The Short Happy Life of Francis Macomber."

FOSTER, Kevin. Lecturer of English and Communications, The University of New England, Armidale, Australia. **Essay:** "How Sleep the Brave."

FU, Sherwin S.S. Professor of English, University of Wisconsin, Oshkosh. Author of books, essays, stories, and poems in Chinese, and of articles and book reviews in English. Translator of Chinese poetry and essays for anthologies and journals. **Essays:** "The Husband"; "Regret for the Past"; "The True Story of Ah Q."

GABRIELE, Tommasina. Assistant Professor of Italian Studies, Wheaton College, Norton, Massachusetts. Author of *Italo Calvino: Eros and Language*, forthcoming. **Essay:** Cesare Pavese.

GERLACH, John. Professor, Department of English, Cleveland State University, Ohio. Author of *Toward the End: Closure and Structure in the American Short Story*, 1985. **Essay:** R.K. Narayan.

GISH, Robert Franklin. Director of Ethnic Studies, California Polytechnic State University, San Luis Obispo. Author of five books, including *Songs of My Hunter Heart: A Western Kinship*, and *Frontier's End: The Life and Literature of Harvey Ferguson*, and of several articles about the West. **Essays:** Hamlin Garland; Jack London; Sabine R. Ulibarrí; William Carlos Williams; "A Piece of Steak"; "This Morning, This Evening, So Soon."

GLASS, Derek. Lecturer in German, King's College, London. Co-editor of *Berlin: Literary Images of a City* (with D. Rösler and J.J. White), 1989. Compiled annual critical bibliographies of research in "German Literature 1830-1880" for *The Year's Work in Modern Language Studies*, 1981-85. **Essays:** Georg Büchner; Annette von Drose-Hülshoff.

GOLDLEAF, Steven. Assistant Professor of English, Pace University, New York City. Author of numerous short stories, poems, and essays in journals and anthologies, including *Signet's Contemporary American Short Stories*, 1985. **Essays:** F. Scott Fitzgerald; John O'Hara; "Bartleby, The Srivener"; "The Conversion of the Jews."

GÖMÖRI, George. Lecturer in Slavonic studies, Cambridge University. Author of *Polish and Hungarian Poetry 1945 to 1956*, 1966, and *Cyprian Norwid*, 1974. Editor, with others, of *Love of the Scorching Wind* by László Nagy, 1973, *Forced March* by Miklós Radnóti, 1979, *Night Song of the Personal Shadow* by György Petri, 1991. **Essays:** Tadeusz Borowski; József Lengyel; István Örkény; "Café Niagara."

GONG, Shifen. Assistant Lecturer in Chinese language and literature, and Ph.D. candidate in comparative literature, University of Aukland, New Zealand. Author of various critical articles. Translator. **Essay:** "The Diary of a Madman."

GONZALEZ, Alexander G. Associate Professor of English, State University of New York, Cortland. Member of the editorial board of *Mid-Hudson Language Studies* and the advisory panel of *Notes on Modern Irish Literature*. Author of *Darrel Figgis: A*

Study of His Novels, 1992, and of articles on George Moore, Seumas O'Kelly, James Joyce, Liam O'Flaherty, and other Irish writers. Editor of *Short Stories from the Irish Renaissance: An Anthology*, 1992. **Essays:** George Moore; "Julia Cahill's Curse."

GOONETILLEKE, D.C.R.A. Professor of English, University of Kelaniya, Sri Lanka. Author of *Developing Countries in British Fiction*, 1977, *Between Culture: Essays on Literature, Language and Education*, 1987, *Images of the Raj: South Asia in the Literature of the Empire*, 1988, and *Joseph Conrad: Beyond Culture and Background*, 1990. Editor of anthologies of Sri Lankan poetry, fiction, and drama, including *The Penguin New Writing in Sri Lanka*, 1992. **Essays:** "The Daughters of the Late Colonel"; "Gimpel the Fool"; "Heart of Darkness"; "Odour of Chrysanthemums"; "The Secret Life of Walter Mitty."

GORDON, Ian A. Emeritus Professor of English, Victoria University, Wellington, New Zealand. Author of numerous books, including *John Skelton, Poet Laureate*, 1943, *Katherine Mansfield*, 1954 (revised 1971), *The Movement of English Prose*, 1966, and *John Galt*, 1972. Editor of dictionaries and a thesaurus, and of works by Galt, Mansfield, and William Shenstone.

GORDON, Lois. Professor of English and Comparative Literature, Fairleigh Dickinson University, Teaneck, New Jersey. Author of *Stratagems to Uncover Nakedness: The Dramas of Harold Pinter*, 1969, *Donald Barthelme*, 1981, *Robert Coover: The Universal Fictionmaking Process*, 1983, *American Chronicle: Six Decades in American Life, 1920-1979*, 1987, *Harold Pinter: A Casebook*, 1990, *American Chronicle: Seven Decades in American Life, 1920-1989*, 1990, and articles on William Faulkner, T.S. Eliot, Samuel Beckett, Philip Roth, Raymond Carver, and other writers. **Essay:** "The Balloon."

GRAVES, Peter J. Head of German Department, Leicester University. Author of *Three Contemporary German Poets: Wolf Biermann, Sarah Kirsch, Reiner Kunze*, 1985, and numerous other articles on contemporary German literature; regular reviewer for *The Times Literary Supplement* on German literature and politics. **Essay:** E.T.A. Hoffmann.

GRAYSON, Jane. Lecturer in Russian Language and Literature, School of Slavonic and East European Studies, University of London. Author of *Nabokov Translated: A Comparison of Nabokov's Russian and English Prose*, 1977. Joint editor of *Nikolay Gogol: Text and Context* (with Faith Wigzeil), 1989, and *Ideology in Russian Literature* (with Richard Freeborn), 1990. **Essays:** Abram Terts; "Pkhentz."

GUO, Liping. Nursing student, Augusta College, Georgia. **Essays:** Lu Xun; "Spring Silkworms."

HALIO, Jay L. Professor of English, University of Delaware, Newark. Chair of the editorial board, University of Delaware Press. Author of *Angus Wilson*, 1964, and *Understanding Shakespeare's Plays in Performance*, 1988. Editor of *British Novelists since 1960*, 1983, *Critical Essays on Angus Wilson*, 1985, and *As You Like It: An Annotated Bibliography 1940-1980* (with Barbara C. Millard). **Essays:** Bernard Malamud; Issac Bashevis Singer; Angus Wilson; "The Jewbird."

HALL, Joan Wylie. Instructor in English, University of Mississippi, Jackson. Author of *Shirley Jackson: A Study of the*

Short Fiction, 1993, and articles on Francis Bacon, William Faulkner, and Willa Cather. **Essays:** Shirley Jackson; "A Worn Path."

HARDING, James. Senior Lecturer in French, University of Greenwich, London. Author of many books on French music and opera, and the English theatre, including *Saint-Saëns and His Circle*, 1965, *Sacha Guitry, the Last Boulevardier*, 1968, *The Duke of Wellington*, 1968, *Massenet*, 1970, *Rossini*, 1971, *The Astonishing Adventure of General Boulanger*, 1971, *The Ox on the Roof*, 1972, *Gounod*, 1973, *Lost Illusions: Paul Léautaud and His World*, 1974, *Eric Satie*, 1975, *Folies de Paris: The Rise and Fall of French Operetta*, 1979, *Offenbach*, 1980, *Maurice Chevalier: His Life*, 1982, *Jacques Tati: Frame by Frame*, 1984, *Agate*, 1986, *Ivor Novello*, 1987, *The Rocky Horror Show Book*, 1987. **Essays:** André Gide; W.W. Jacobs; W. Somerset Maugham; "The Letter"; "The Monkey's Paw"; "The Outstation"; "Sredni Vashtar."

HARMON, Maurice. Emeritus Professor of Anglo-Irish Literature and Drama, University College, Dublin. Editor, *Irish University Review*. Author of *Sean O'Faolain: A Critical Introduction*, 1966 (revised 1985), *Modern Irish Literature*, 1967, *The Poetry of Thomas Kinsella*, 1974, *Select Bibliography for the Study of Anglo-Irish Literature and Its Background*, 1976, *A Short History of Anglo-Irish Literature from the Origins to the Present* (with Roger McHugh), 1982, and *Austin Clarke: A Critical Introduction*, 1989. Editor of works by or about Shakespeare, Synge, Richard Murphy, and Anglo-Irish poetry and fiction. **Essay:** Sean O'Faolain.

HART, Clive. Professor of Literature, University of Essex, Colchester. Author of *Structure and Motif in Finnegans Wake*, 1962, *A Concordance to Finnegans Wake*, 1963, *Joyce's Ulysses*, 1968, *A Topographical Guide to Joyce's Ulysses* (with Leo Knuth), 1975, and *Ulysses: A Review of Three Texts* (with Philip Gaskell), 1989. Editor of *Joyce's Dubliners: Critical Essays*, 1969, *Joyce's Ulysses* (with David Hayman), 1974, and *Assessing the 1984 Ulysses* (with C. George Sandulescu), 1986. **Essay:** "Eveline."

HEATON, David M. Associate Professor and Graduate Chair of English, and Chair of comparative literature, Ohio University, Athens. Author of poetry, poetry translations, and articles on Ted Hughes, Alan Sillitoe, Stanley Plumly, Alan Stephens, Ben Belitt, Marvin Bell, Jon Anderson, Toni Morrison, Joan Didion, and George P. Elliott. **Essays:** Truman Capote; J.F. Powers; "The Saint"; "Silent Snow, Secret Snow."

HENDRICK, George. Professor of English, University of Illinois, Urbana-Champaign. Author of *Katherine Anne Porter* (revised edition with Willene Hendrick), 1988, and *To Reach Eternity: The Letters of James Jones*, 1989. **Essay:** Katherine Anne Porter.

HERBERT, Michael. Lecturer of English, University of St. Andrews, Fife, Scotland. Editor of *Reflections on the Death of a Porcupine and Other Essays* by D.H. Lawrence, 1988. **Essays:** Dan Jacobson; William Plomer; "The Child of Queen Victoria"; "The Horse Dealer's Daughter"; "Kaa's Hunting"; "The Train from Rhodesia"; "Ula Masondo"; "The Unrest Cure."

HIGDON, David Leon. Paul Whitefield Horn Professor of English, Texas Tech University, Lubbock. Editor, *Conradiana*.

Author of *Time and English Fiction*, *Shadows of the Past in Contemporary British Fiction*, 1985, and various critical essays. **Essays:** "The Chrysanthemums"; "Fishmonger's Fiddle"; "The Poor Man."

HOLDITCH, W. Kenneth. Research Professor in English, University of New Orleans, Louisiana. Founding Editor and Publisher of the *Tennessee Williams Journal*, since 1988. Author of *In Old New Orleans*, 1983, and of numerous articles in journals. **Essays:** Sherwood Anderson; Stephen Vincent Benét; Isak Dinesen; "Two Fishermen."

HORROCKS, David. Lecturer in German, Keele University, Staffordshire. Author of various critical essays. Editor, with D.G. Rock, of *Gerhart Hauptmann: Bahnwärter Theil*, 1992. **Essays:** Gerhart Hauptmann; "Lineman Thiel."

HOWARD, William L. Associate Professor of English, Chicago State University. Author of various critical essays and reviews. **Essays:** Charles Waddell Chesnutt; Joel Chandler Harris; "Kneel to the Rising Sun"; *Other Voices, Other Rooms*; "The Return of a Private"; "Saturday Afternoon."

HUTCHINSON, Peter. Fellow of Trinity Hall, Cambridge. Author of *Literary Presentations of Divided Germany*, 1977, *Games Authors Play*, 1983, and *Stefan Heym: The Perpetual Dissident*, 1992. **Essays:** Gottfried Keller; "A Village Romeo and Juliet."

JACKSON, David. Lecturer in German, School of European Studies, Cardiff, Wales. Author of *Conrad Ferdinand Meyer*, 1975 and 1991, and *Theodor Storm: The Life and Works of a Democratic Humanitarian*, 1992. **Essay:** Theodor Storm.

JANES, Regina. Professor of English, Skidmore College, Saratoga Springs, New York. Author of *Gabriel García Márquez: Revolutions in Wonderland*, 1981, *"One Hundred Years of Solitude": Modes of Reading*, 1991, and articles on 18th-century British and modern Latin American literature in journals such as *Salmagundi*, *Hispanófila*, *World Literature Today*, *Journal of the History of Ideas*, and *Representations*. **Essays:** "Journey Back to the Source"; "A Very Old Man with Enormous Wings."

JEFFARES, A. Norman. Professor Emeritus of English Studies, University of Stirling, Scotland. General Editor of the Writers and Critics series and the New Oxford English series; past editor of *A Review of English Studies* and *Ariel*. Author of *Yeats: Man and Poet*, 1949 (revised 1962), *Seven Centuries of Poetry*, 1956, *Oliver Goldsmith*, 1959, *Gogarty*, 1961, *George Moore*, 1965, *A Critical Commentary on She Stoops to Conquer*, 1966, *A Commentary on the Collected Poems* (1968) and *Collected Plays* (1975, with A.S. Knowland) *of Yeats*, *Anglo-Irish Literature*, 1982, *A New Commentary on the Poems of W.B. Yeats*, 1984, and *W.B. Yeats: A New Biography*, 1988. Editor of *Scott's Mind and Art*, 1969, *Restoration Comedy*, 1974, *Yeats: The Critical Heritage*, 1977, *Poems of W.B. Yeats: A New Selection*, 1984, *Yeats's Poems*, 1989, and *Yeats's Vision*, 1990. Formerly Chair of the Literature Section of the Scottish Arts Council; life president, International Association for the Study of Anglo-Irish Literature.

JONES, Lawrence. Associate Professor of English, University of Otago, Dunedin, New Zealand. Editor, *Journal of New Zealand Literature*. Author of *Barbed Wire and Mirrors: Essays on New Zealand Prose*, 1987, and "The Novel," in *The Oxford History of New Zealand Literature* (edited by T.L. Sturm), 1991. **Essays:** Dan Davin; Maurice Gee; O.E. Middleton; Maurice Shadbolt; "The Making of a New Zealander"; "The Reservoir"; "The Room."

KANAGANAYAKAM, Chelva. Teaches in the Department of English, Trinity College, Toronto. **Essay:** Albert Wendt.

KELLNER, Bruce. Professor Emeritus of English, Millersville University, Pennsylvania. Author of *Carl Van Vechten and the Irreverent Decades*, 1968, *A Bibliography of the Work of Carl Van Vechten*, 1980, *A Gertrude Stein Companion Content with The Example*, 1988, *The Last Dandy: Ralph Barton*, 1991, and *Donald Winham: A Bio-Bibliography*, 1991. Editor of *Keep A-Inchin' Along: Selected Writings about Black Art and Letters*, 1979, and *The Harlem Renaissance: A Historical Dictionary*, 1984 (revised 1987). **Essays:** Gertrude Stein; "A&P"; *The Railway Police*.

KILLAM, G.D. Professor of English, University of Guelph, Ontario. Author of *African in English Fiction*, *The Writings of Chinua Achebe*, and *The Writings of Ngugi*. Editor of *African Writers on African Writing*, *East and Central African Writing in English*, and for ten years editor of *World Literature Written in English*. Has published numerous articles and chapters in books on African literature, and currently is editing volumes in *The Dictionary of Literary Biography* series on South Africa, Australia, India, Pakistan, and Sri Lanka. **Essay:** Chinua Achebe.

KING, Bruce. Albert S. Johnston Professor of English, University of North Alabama, Florence. Co-editor of Macmillan Modern Dramatists series. Author of *Dryden's Major Plays*, 1966, *Marvell's Allegorical Poetry*, 1977, *New English Literatures: Cultural Nationalism in a Changing World*, 1980, *A History of Seventeenth-Century English Literature*, 1982, *Modern Indian Poetry in English*, 1987, and *Three Indian Poets: Ezekiel, Ramanujan and Moraes*, 1990. Editor of *Introduction to Nigerian Literature*, 1971, *Literatures of the World in English*, 1974, *A Celebration of Black and African Writing*, 1976, and *West Indian Literature*, 1979. **Essay:** V.S. Naipaul.

KING, Kimball. Professor of English, University of North Carolina, Chapel Hill. **Essay:** "The Aspern Papers."

KINNAMON, Keneth. Ethel Pumphrey Stephens Professor of English and Head of the Department, University of Arkansas, Fayetteville. Author of *The Emergence of Richard Wright: A Study in Literature and Society*, 1972, and *A Richard Wright Bibliography: 50 Years of Criticism and Commentary 1933-82*, 1988. Editor of *Black Writers of America: A Comprehensive Anthology* (with Richard K. Barksdale), 1972, *James Baldwin: A Collection of Critical Essays*, 1974, and *New Essays on Native Son*, 1990.

KINNEY, Arthur F. Thomas W. Copeland Professor of Literary History, University of Massachusetts, Amherst. Founding Editor, *English Literary Renaissance*; series Editor for Twayne publishers. Author of numerous books, including *On Seven Shakespearean Tragedies*, and *Comedies*, 2 vols., 1968-69, *Rogues, Vagabonds, and Sturdy Beggars*, 1974, *Elizabethan Backgrounds*, 1974, *Faulkner's Narrative Poetics*, 1978, *Dorothy*

Parker, 1978, *Rhetoric and Poetic in Thomas More's Utopia*, 1979, *Flannery O'Connor's Library*, 1985, *Humanist Poetics: Thought, Rhetoric, and Fiction in Sixteenth-Century England*, 1986, *John Skelton: Priest as Poet*, 1987, *Renaissance Historicism* (with Dan Collins), 1988, and *Continental Humanist Poetics*, 1989. Editor of *Sir Philip Sidney: 1586 and the Creation of a Legend* (with others), 1986, *Sidney in Retrospect*, 1988, *Sidney's Achievements* (with others), 1990, and other collections on English and American writers. **Essays:** "The Bear"; "Big Blonde"; "A Good Man Is Hard To Find"; "Spotted Horses."

KIRBY, David. McKenzie Professor of English, Florida State University, Tallahassee. Author of *Individual and Community* (with Kenneth Baldwin), 1975, *American Fiction to 1900*, 1975, *The Opera Lover* (poetry), 1977, *Grace King*, 1980, *America's Hive of Honey*, 1980, *The Sun Rises in the Evening*, 1982, *Sarah Bernhardt's Leg* (poetry), 1983, *The Plural World*, 1984, *Dictionary of Contemporary Thought*, 1984, *Diving for Poems*, 1985, *Saving the Young Men of Vienna* (poetry), 1987, *Writing Poetry*, 1989, *Mark Strand: The Poet as No One*, 1990, *The Portrait of a Lady and The Turn of the Screw: Henry James and Melodrama*, 1990, and *Herman Melville*. **Essays:** Henry James; Herman Melville.

KLINGENSTEIN, Susanne. Research Associate, Brandeis University, Waltham, Massachusetts. Author of *Jews in the American Academy, 1900-1940: The Dynamics of Intellectual Assimilation*, 1991. **Essays:** Cynthia Ozick; "In the Penal Colony"; "The Metamorphosis"; *None But the Brave*.

KLINKOWITZ, Jerome. Professor of English, University of Northern Iowa, Cedar Falls. Author of *Literary Disruptions*, 1975 (revised 1980), *The Life of Fiction*, 1977, *The Practice of Fiction in America*, 1980, *The American 1960's*, 1980, *Kurt Vonnegut*, 1982, *Peter Handke and the Postmodern Transformation* (with James Knowlton), 1983, *The Self-Apparent Word*, 1984, *Literary Subversions*, 1985, *The New American Novel of Manners*, 1986, *A Short Season and Other Stories* (as Jerry Klinkowitz), 1988, *Rosenberg, Barthes, Hassan: The Postmodern Habit of Thought*, 1988, *Their Finest Hours: Narratives of the RAF and Luftwaffe in World War II*, 1989, *Slaughterhouse-Five: Reforming the Novel and the World*, 1990, *Listen: Gerry Mulligan/An Arual Narrative in Jazz*, 1991, *Donald Barthelme: An Exhibition*, 1991, and *Structuring the Void*, 1992. Editor of *Innovative Fiction*, 1972, *The Vonnegut Statement*, 1973, *Kurt Vonnegut Jr.: A Descriptive Bibliography* (with Asa B. Pieratt, Jr.), 1974, *Donald Barthelme: A Comprehensive Bibliography* (with others), 1977, *Vonnegut in America*, 1977, *Writing under Fire: Stories of the Vietnam War*, 1978, *The Diaries of Willard Motley*, 1979, *Nathaniel Hawthorne*, 1984, *Kurt Vonnegut: A Comprehensive Bibliography* (with Judie Huffman-Klinkowitz), 1987, and *Writing Baseball*, 1991. **Essays:** Robert Coover; "Axolotl"; "A Conversation with My Father"; "How I Got My Nickname"; "The Indian Uprising."

KLOEPFER, Deborah Kelly. Editorial Consultant to Greenwood Press, UMI Research Press, University of Texas Press, Southern Illinois University Press, and University of California Press. Author of *The Unspeakable Mother: Forbidden Discourse in Jean Rhys and H.D.*, 1989. **Essays:** Kate Chopin; Daphne du Maurier; Jean Rhys; Virginia Woolf; "The Daffodil Sky"; "Kew Gardens"; "Till September Petronella."

KOSTELANETZ, Richard. Author of many books of fiction, poetry, experimental prose, and criticism, including *The End of Intelligent Writing: Literary Politics in America*, 1974, 1977, *The Old Fictions and the New*, 1987, and *Politics in the African-American Novel*, 1991. Editor of *Gertrude Stein Advanced: An Anthology of Criticism*, 1990. **Essay:** *The Man Who Lived Underground*.

LAGO, Mary. Catherine Paine Middlebush Professor of English, University of Missouri, Columbia. Author of *Rabindranath Tagore*, 1978. Editor of *Imperfect Encounter: Letters of William Rothenstein and Rabindranath Tagore*, 1972, *Max and Will: Max Beerbohm and William Rothenstein, Their Correspondence and Friendship* (with K. Beckson), 1975, *Men and Memories: Recollections of William Rothenstein*, 1978, *Burne-Jones Talking: His Conversations Recorded by His Assistant Thomas Rooke*, 1981, *Selected Letters of E.M. Forster* (with P.N. Furbank), 2 vols., 1983-85, *Collected Essays* (with Ronald Warwick), 1989, and *Tagore: Perspectives in Time* (with Ronald Warwick), 1989. Translator of Tagore's stories, including *The Housewarming and Other Selected Writings*, with Tarun Gupta, 1965, *The Broken Nest*, 1971, and *Selected Stories of Rabindranath Tagore*, 1991. **Essays:** Rabindranath Tagore; "The Road from Colonus."

LARRIERE, Claire. Maître de conférences honoraire, Sorbonne Nouvelle, Paris, France. Past Editor-in-chief, *Paris Transcontinental*, and *Visions Critiques* (a yearly collection of essays on the short story); initiator and organizer of the first International Conference on the Short Story, Sorbonne, Paris, 1988. Author of *Victorian Short Stories* (bilingual, annotated), 1990, and of short stories published in *Short Story International*, *La Nouvelle Revue Française*, and *Europe*. Also has written numerous articles on the short story in academic reviews (*The Journal of the Short Story*, Angers, *Visions Critiques*, Paris, and *Raquam*, Strasbourg). **Essays:** William Sansom; "Fireman Flower."

LAZAR, Karen Ruth. Lecturer in English, University of the Witwatersrand, Johannesburg. Author of critical essays and reviews of Nadine Gordimer's fiction. **Essay:** "Something Out There."

LEAL, Luis. Professor Emeritus, University of Illinois, Champaign-Urbana, and Visiting Professor, Department of Spanish, Stanford University, California. Author of *Juan Rulfo*, 1983. **Essay:** "Luvina."

LEVI, A.H.T. Freelance writer and independent scholar; Buchanan Professor of French Language and Literature, University of St. Andrews, Fife, Scotland, 1971-87; also Lecturer at Christ Church, Oxford, and Professor of French, University of Warwick, Coventry. Author of *French Moralists: The Theory of the Passions 1585-1649*, 1964, *Religion in Practice*, 1966, and *Guide to French Literature 1789 to the Present*, 1992. Editor of *Erasmus: Satires*, 1986. **Essays:** Honoré de Balzac; Albert Camus; J.-M.G. Le Clézio; Robert Musil; "Erostratus"; *The Immoralist*; "The Sand-Man"; *Strait Is the Gate*.

LEVI, Claudia M.Z. Freelance journalist. **Essays:** Heinrich Böll; Roald Dahl.

LEVI, Honor. Freelance writer and independent scholar. **Essays:** Colette; "The Other Woman."

LINDSAY, Joyce. Retired English teacher. Editor, with Maurice Lindsay, of various books, including *The Scottish Dog*, 1989, and *The Scottish Quotation Book*, 1992. **Essays:** Hans Christian Andersen; Walter de la Mare; R.B. Cunninghame Graham; ''Murdo.''

LINDSAY, Maurice. Consultant, Scottish Civic Trust, Glasgow. Co-editor, *Scottish Review*. Author of more than 20 books of poetry, including *Collected Poems*, 2 vols., 1990-93; plays, travel and historical works; and critical studies, including *Robert Burns: The Man, His Work, The Legend*, 1954 (revised 1968, 1978), *The Burns Encyclopaedia*, 1959 (revised 1970, 1980), *History of Scottish Literature*, 1977, (revised 1992), and *Francis George Scott and the Scottish Renaissance*, 1980; and an autobiography, *Thank You for Having Me*, 1983. Editor, with Joyce Lindsay, of various books, including *The Scottish Dog*, 1989, and *The Scottish Quotation Book*, 1992. **Essays:** James Baldwin; H.E. Bates; Elizabeth Bowen; Margaret Oliphant; Saki; Iain Crichton Smith; P.G. Wodehouse; ''The Library Window.''

LOE, Thomas. Professor of English, State University of New York, Oswego. Author of articles on Katherine Anne Porter, Conrad, le Carré, Bellow, Dickens, Charlotte Brontë, Joyce, and Waugh in *Notes on Contemporary Literature, Conradiana, James Joyce Quarterly*, and other journals. **Essays:** ''The Secret Sharer''; ''Why I Live at the P.O.''

LONGAN, Nathan. Assisant Professor, Modern Langauges and Literature Department, Oakland Univeristy, Michigan. **Essays:** Ivo Andrić; ''Jamila''; ''Thirst.''

LOONEY, Barbara A. Teacher in the American Studies Department, University of South Florida, Tampa. **Essays:** Eudora Welty; ''In the Zoo''; ''A Woman on a Roof.''

LOWY, Dina. Instructor, Japanese Language, St. Olaf College, Northfield, Minnesota. **Essay:** Tanizaki Jun'ichiro.

MA, Sheng-mei. Teaches in the Department of English, James Madison University, Harrisburg, Virgina. **Essay:** Toshio Mori.

MABEE, Barbara. Assistant Professor of German, Oakland University, Michigan. Author of *Die Poetik von Sarah Kirsch: Erinnerungsarbeit und Geschichtsbewusstsein*, 1989, and various critical articles on German literature. **Essays:** Grimm brothers; ''Bluebeard.''

MacKENZIE, Craig. Lecturer, Department of English, Rand Afrikaans University, Johannesburg, South Africa. Author of *Bessie Head: An Introduction*, 1989. Co-editor of *Between the Lines: Interviews with Bessie Head, Sheila Roberts, Ellen Kuzwayo, Miriam Tlali* (with Cherry Clayton), 1989. Editor of *Bessie Head: A Woman Alone: Autobiographical Writings*, 1990. Co-compiler, *Bessie Head: A Bibliography*, 1992. **Essays:** Herman Charles Bosman; Pauline Smith.

MADDEN, David. Writer-in-Residence, Lousiana State University, Baton Rouge. Author of many novels (including *Pleasure-Dome*, 1979, and *On the Big Wind*, 1980), numerous short stories (including the collections *The Shadow Knows*, 1970, and *The New Orleans of Possibilities*, 1982), plays, and books of non-fiction (including *The Poetic Image in Six Genres*, 1969, *A Primer of the Novel, For Readers and Writers*, 1980, and

Revising Fiction: A Handbook for Writers, 1988). Editor of many books and anthologies (including *Studies in the Short Story*, with Virgil Scott, 1975, sixth edition 1984, and *The World of Fiction*, 1990).

MAHONEY, Elisabeth. Teaches in the Department of English Literature, University of Aberdeen. **Essays:** Sylvia Townsend Warner; ''Poor Mary.''

MALLETT, Phillip. Lecturer in English, University of St. Andrews, Fife, Scotland. Author of *John Donne*, 1983, and *Kipling Considered*, 1989. **Essays:** Rudyard Kipling; ''They.''

MANDRELL, James. Assistant Professor of Spanish and Comparative Literature, Brandeis University, Waltham, Massachusetts. Author of *Don Juan and the Point of Honor: Seduction, Patriarchal Society, and Literary Tradition*, 1992, and numerous articles on Spanish and Comparative Literature. **Essays:** ''Every Inch a Man''; ''The Revolver.''

MARDER, Herbert. Associate Professor of English, University of Illinois, Champaign-Urbana. Author of *Feminism and Art: A Study of Virginia Woolf*, 1968 and 1972, and many critical essays. **Essays:** ''The Man Who Would Be King''; ''The Mark on the Wall''; ''The Overcoat.''

MARNEY, John. Professor of Chinese, Oakland University, Rochester, Michigan. Author of *Lian Chien-wen Ti, 503-551*, 1976, *Chiang Yen, 444-505*, 1981, and *Chinese Anagrams and Anagram Verse*, forthcoming. Translator of *Beyond the Mulberries. An Anthology of Palace-Style Poetry by Emperor Chien-wen of the Liang Dynasty (503-551)*, 1982. **Essays:** Mao Dun; Yu Dafu.

MARX, Paul. Professor of English, University of New Haven, Connecticut. Editor of *12 Short Story Writers*, 1970. **Essay:** ''Ball of Fat.''

MAY, Charles E. Professor of English, California State University, Long Beach. Author of *Short Story Theories*, 1977 (2nd edition 1994), *Twentieth Century European Short Story*, 1989, *Edgar Allan Poe: A Study of the Short Fiction*, 1991, *Fiction's Many Worlds*, 1992, *The Short Story: A Study of the Genre*, 1994, and more than a hundred articles on short fiction in numerous books and journals. **Essays:** Raymond Carver; Anton Chekhov; Bret Harte; *The Ballad of the Sad Café*; ''The Demon Lover''; ''Flowering Judas''; ''Hands''; ''An Occurrence at Owl Creek Bridge''; ''The Prussian Officer''; ''The Tell-Tale Heart''; ''The Third Bank from the River''; ''War''; ''Young Goodman Brown.''

MAZZARA, Richard. Professor Emeritus, Oakland Univeristy, Rochester, Michigan. Author of many books, translations, and articles, mainly on French and Brazilian literature. **Essay:** ''The Psychiatrist.''

McDOWELL, Margaret B. Professor of Rhetoric and Women's Studies, University of Iowa, Iowa City. Author of *Edith Wharton*, 1975 (revised 1990), and *Carson McCullers*, 1980. **Essays:** Carson McCullers; Edith Wharton; ''Old Mortality''; ''Petrified Man''; ''Revelation.''

McDUFF, David. Writer and translator. Past Co-editor of *Stand* magazine. Translator of *The House of the Dead*, 1985, *Crime and Punishment*, 1991, and *The Brothers Karamazov*, 1993, all by Fedor Dostoevskii. **Essays:** Isaak Babel; Fedor Dostoevskii; Nikolai Gogol; Tove Jansson; "The Nose."

McMURRAY, George R. Professor of Spanish, Colorado State University, Fort Collins. Author of *Gabriel García Márquez*, 1977, *Jose Donoso*, 1978, *Jorge Luis Borges*, 1980, *Spanish-American Writing Since 1941*, 1987, and many articles on Spanish and Latin American literature. Editor of *Critical Essays on Gabriel García Márquez*, 1987. **Essays:** Juan José Arreola; Alejo Carpentier; "The Switchman."

MINER, Madonne M. Associate Professor of English, University of Wyoming, Laramie. Author of *Insatiable Appetites: Twentieth-Century American Women's Bestsellers*, 1984. **Essays:** "Désirée's Baby"; "Tell Me a Riddle."

MITCHELL, Adrian. Associate Professor of English, University of Sydney, Australia. **Essay:** "Sam Slick the Clockmaker."

MOLLOY, F. C. Senior Lecturer in English, Charles Sturt University, New South Wales, Australia. Author of articles on Irish and Australian literature in *Biography: An Interdisciplinary Quarterly*, *Yeats Annual*, *Irish-Australian Studies*, *Irish University Review*, and *Critique*. **Essays:** Somerville and Ross; "Adam's Wife"; "American Dreams"; "The Doll"; "My Oedipus Complex."

MORACE, Robert A. Associate Professor of English, Daemen College, Amherst, New York; lecturer on American Literature, University of Warsaw, 1985-86. Author of *John Gardner: An Annotated Secondary Bibliography*, 1984, *The Dialogical Novels of Malcolm Bradbury and David Lodge*, 1989, and essays on contemporary fiction and literary realism in anthologies and journals. Editor, with Kathryn VanSpanckeren, of *John Gardner: Critical Perspectives*, 1982. **Essays:** Donald Barthelme; John Cheever; John Gardner; "The Hitchhiking Game"; "Senatorium under the Sign of the Hourglass"; "The Street of the Crocodiles"; "The Swimmer."

MURRAY, Isobel. Senior Lecturer in English, University of Aberdeen, Scotland. Author of *Ten Modern Scottish Novels* (with Bob Tait), 1974. Editor of *The Picture of Dorian Gray*, 1974, *Complete Shorter Fiction*, 1979, *Writings*, 1989, and *The Soul of Man and Prison Writings*, 1990, all by Oscar Wilde, and *Beyond This Limit: Selected Shorter Fiction*, 1986, and *A Girl Must Live: Stories and Poems*, 1990, both by Naomi Mitchison. **Essays:** Naomi Mitchison; Oscar Wilde.

MYER, Valerie Grosvenor. Freelance writer and lecturer, Beijing Languages Institute. Author of *Margaret Drabble: Puritanism and Permissiveness*, 1974, *Jane Austen*, 1980, *Charlotte Brontë: Truculent Spirit*, 1988, *Culture Shock* (novel), 1988, *A Victorian Lady in Africa: The Story of Mary Kingsley*, 1989, *Ten Great English Novelists*, 1990, and *Margaret Drabble: A Reader's Guide*, 1991. Editor of *Laurence Stern: Riddles and Mysteries*, 1984, and *Samuel Richardson: Passion and Prudence*, 1986. **Essays:** "Georgy Porgy"; "The Lifted Veil."

NAGEL, Gwen L. Fiction writer living in Athens, Georgia. **Essay:** "A White Heron."

NAGEL, James. First Eidson Distinguished Professor of English, University of Georgia, Athens. Founder and Editor of the journal *Studies in American Fiction* and the G.K. Hall series *Critical Essays on American Literature*; Executive Coordinator of the American Literature Association; Past President, Hemingway Society. Author of twelve books, including *Hemingway in Love and War* (with Henry Villard), and more than fifty articles on American literature. **Essays:** "Hills Like White Elephants"; "The Open Boat."

NAIK, M.K. Emeritus Professor, University of Bombay, India. Author of *Mighty Voices: Studies in T.S. Eliot*, 1980, *A History of Indian English Literature*, 1982, *Raja Rao*, 1972, *The Ironic Vision: R.K. Narayan*, 1983, and *Mirror on the Wall: Anglo-Indian Fiction*, 1991. Editor of *The Indian English Short Story: A Representative Anthology*, 1984, and *Selected Short Stories* by Gangādhar Gadgil, 1994. **Essays:** Mulk Raj Anand; Gangādhar Gādgīl; Rajo Rao; "An Astrologer's Day"; "The Hollow Man"; "India: A Fable."

NAPIER, Susan J. Assistant Professor of Japanese, University of Texas, Austin. **Essays:** Ōe Kenzaburo; "Aghwee the Sky Monster."

NARAYAN, Shyamala A. Lecturer in English, Ranchi Women's College, India. Author of *Sudhin N. Ghose*, 1973, *Raja Rao: The Man and His Work*, 1988, and studies of Nissim Ezekiel, Amitav Ghosh, Salman Rushdie, Shashi Tharoor, and other Indian writers, and reviews in *Indian Literature*, *The Hindu*, *Journal of Indian Writing in English*, and other periodicals. Compiler of the Indian section of "The Bibliography of Commonwealth Literature" published annually in *Journal of Commonwealth Literature*.

NEGINSKY, Rosina. Assistant Professor of Russian, Grinnell College, Iowa. Author of numerous critical papers and articles on Russian writers. **Essays:** Chingiz Aimatov; Boris Pil'niak.

NEW, W.H. Professor of English, University of British Columbia, Vancouver. Editor of *Canadian Literature*. Author of *Malcolm Lowry*, 1971, *Articulating West*, 1972, *Among Worlds*, 1975, *Malcolm Lowry: A Reference Guide*, 1978, *Dreams of Speech and Violence: The Art of the Short Story in Canada and New Zealand*, 1987, and other books and articles. Editor of *A 20th Century Anthology* (with W.E. Messenger), 1984, *Canadian Writers in 1984: The 25th Anniversary of Canadian Life*, 1984, *Canadian Short Fiction*, 1986, *A History of Canadian Literature*, 1989, and general editor of *Literary History of Canada*, vol. 4, 1990.

NEWTON, K.M. Professor of English, University of Dundee, Scotland. Author of *George Eliot: Romantic Humanist*, 1981, *In Defence of Literary Interpretation: Theory and Practice*, 1986, and *Interpreting the Text: A Critical Introduction to the Theory and Practice of Literary Interpretation*, 1990. Editor of *Twentieth-Century Literary Theory: A Reader*, 1988, *George Eliot: A Critical Reader*, 1990, and *Theory into Practice*, 1992. **Essays:** "The Lady with the Little Dog"; *Notes from Underground*; "The Parson's Daughter of Oxney Colne"; "The Sad Fortunes of the Rev. Amos Barton."

NOVÁKOVÁ, Soňa. Assistant Professor, Department of English and American Studies, Charles University, Prague, Czechoslovakia. Author of a series of articles for Czech journals

NOVÁKOVÁ, Soňa. Assistant Professor, Department of English and American Studies, Charles University, Prague, Czechoslovakia. Author of a series of articles for Czech journals and magazines on eighteenth-century women novelists. **Essays:** Jaroslav Hašek; Bohumil Hrabal; Milan Kundera.

OBERHELMAN, Harley D. Paul Whitfield Horn Professor of Romance Languages, Texas Tech University, Lubbock. Author of *Ernesto Sábato*, 1970, *The Presence of Faulkner in the Writings of García Márquez*, 1980, and *Gabriel García Márquez: A Study of the Short Fiction*, 1991. **Essays:** Gabriel García Márquez; "Tuesday Siesta."

O'BRIEN, George. Associate Professor of English, Georgetown University, Washington, D.C. Author of *The Village of Longing*, 1987, *Dancehall Days*, 1989, and *Brian Friel*, 1990. **Essays:** Nadine Gordimer; "The Faithless Wife"; "First Confession"; "Frail Vessel"; "Happiness"; "Poisson d'Avril."

O'CONNELL, David. Professor of French and Chair, Department of Modern and Classical Languages, Georgia State University, Atlanta. Field Editor of Twayne's World Authors Series of monographs in French and German literature since 1979, also former Review Editor, and Managing Editor, of the *French Review*. Author of *The Teachings of Saint Louis: A Critical Text*, 1972, *Les Propos de Saint Louis*, 1974, *Louis-Ferinand Céline*, 1976, *The Instructions of Saint Louis: A Critical Text*, 1979, and *Michel de Saint Pierre: A Catholic Novelist at the Crossroads*, 1990. Also has written many articles and reviews for *Revue des Deux Mondes*, *Revue des Lettres Modernes*, *Revue d'Histoire Littéraire de la France*, *French Review*, *New Republic*, *Commonwealth*, and *America*. Editor of more than fifty books, including *Catholic Writers in France Since 1945*, 1983. **Essay:** Michel Aymé.

ODBER de BAUBETA, Patricia Anne. Lecturer in Hispanic studies, and Director of Portuguese studies, University of Birmingham. Author of *Anticlerical Satire in Medieval Portuguese Literature*, 1992, and several articles on Portuguese literature. Founder and commissioning editor of the *Portuguese Plays in Translation* series. **Essays:** María Luisa Bombal; Miguel Torga; "The Deadman"; "The Decapitated Chicken."

PAGE, Norman. Professor of Modern English Literature, University of Nottingham. Editor, *Thomas Hardy Journal*, and *Thomas Hardy Annual*. General Editor, Macmillan Modern Novelists and Macmillan Author Chronologies series. Author of *The Language of Jane Austen*, 1972, *Speech in the English Novel*, 1973 (revised 1988), *Thomas Hardy*, 1977, *E.M. Forster's Posthumous Fiction*, 1977, *A.E. Housman: A Critical Biography*, 1983, *A Dickens Companion*, 1984, *A Kipling Companion*, 1984, *A Conrad Companion*, 1986, *E.M. Forster*, 1987, *A Dickens Chronology*, 1988, *A Byron Chronology*, 1988, *Bleak House: A Novel of Connections*, 1990, *A Dr. Johnson Chronology*, 1990, *Muriel Spark*, 1990, and *Tennyson: An Illustrated Life*, 1992. Editor of *Wilkie Collins: The Critical Heritage*, 1974, *Thomas Hardy: The Writer and His Background*, 1980, *D.H. Lawrence: Interviews and Recollections*, 2 vols., 1981. **Essays:** Wilkie Collins; E.M. Forster; Thomas Hardy; M.R. James; Sheridan Le Fanu; "A Terribly Strange Bed."

PANNY, Judith Dell. Teaches in the Department of English, Massey University, Palmerston North, New Zealand. **Essays:** Janet Frame; "Swans."

PAOLINI, Shirley J. Professor of literature and Dean of School of Human Sciences and Humanities, University of Houston, Clear Lake, Texas. Author of *Creativity, Culture and Values: Comparative Essays in Literary Aesthetics*, 1990, and "Western Modernist Influences in Eileen Chang's *The Golden Cangue* and Li Ang's *The Butcher's Wife*, 1991. General editor of *New Connections: Studies in Interdisciplinarity*. **Essays:** Elizabeth Jolley; Aleksandr Solzhenitsyn; Zhang Ailing; "The Golden Cangue"; "Matrena's House."

PARKER, Jeffrey D. Assistant Professor of English, North Carolina A&T State University, Greensboro. Author of articles on Frank Yerby, Richard Wright, Henry Miller, and William Blake. **Essays:** James Alan McPherson; Thomas Love Peacock; Richard Wright; "Big Boy Leaves Home."

PEHOWSKI, Marian. Freelance writer and critic. Has taught comparative literature or journalism at five universities. **Essay:** Hortense Calisher.

PELENSKY, Olga. Lecturer, English Department, University of Rhode Island, Kingston. Author of *Isak Dinesen: The Life and Imagination of a Seducer*, 1991, *Isak Dinesen: Critical Views*, 1993, and articles in the *Washington Post*, *Boston Globe*, *Christian Science Monitor*, *Miami Herald*, and *Philadelphia Inquirer*. **Essays:** Jean Toomer; "The Monkey."

PÉREZ, Genaro J. Professor of Spanish and Chair, Department of Foreign Languages, University of Texas of the Permian Basin, Odessa. Editor and Publisher of *Monographic Review*. Author of *Formalist Elements in the Novels of Juan Goytisolo*, 1979, *La novelística de J. Leyva*, 1985, *La novela como burla/juego: siete experimentos novelescos de Gonzalo Torrente Ballester*, 1989, *La narrativa de Concha Alós: texto, pretexto y contexto*, 1993, and numerous articles in refereed professional journals. **Essays:** Carlos Fuentes; Juan Carlos Onetti; "Blow-Up"; "The Circular Ruins"; "Jacob and the Other."

PÉREZ, Janet. Paul Whitfield Horn Professor of Spanish, Texas Tech University, Lubbock. Author of *The Major Themes of Existentialism in the Works of José Ortega y Gasset*, 1970, *Ana María Matute*, 1971, *Miguel Delibes*, 1972, *Gonzalo Torrente Ballester*, 1984, *Women Writers of Contemporary Spain*, 1988, and numerous articles on contemporary Spanish literature. Editor of *Novelistas femeninas de la postguerra española*, 1983, *Critical Studies on Gonzalo Torrente Ballester*, 1988, *The Spanish Civil War in Literature*, 1990, and *Dictionary of the Literature of the Iberian Peninsula*, 1992. **Essays:** Francisco Ayala; José Donoso; Ana María Matute; Emilia Pardo Bazán; Mercé Rodoreda; Miguel de Unamuno; Ramón del Valle-Inclán; *Aura*; "Autumn Sonata"; "The Bewitched"; "The Doll Queen"; *Hell Hath No Limits*; "The Salamander"; "The Tagus."

PETERSON, Richard F. Professor and Chair, Department of English, Southern Illinois University, Carbondale. Author of *Mary Lavin*, 1978, *William Butler Yeats*, 1982, and *James Joyce Revisited*, 1992. **Essays:** Mary Lavin; "Guests of the Nation."

PILDITCH, Jan. Lecturer in English, University of Waikato, Hamilton, New Zealand. **Essays:** Barbara Baynton; Simon de Beauvoir; Alice Walker; "Everything that Rises Must Converge"; "The Garden Party."

PINSKER, Sanford. Shadek Professor of Humanities, Franklin and Marshall College, Lancaster, Pennsylvania. Member of the editorial board of *Studies in American Jewish Literature, Georgia Review, Conradiana,* and *Journal of Modern Literature.* Author of *The Schlemiel as Metaphor: Studies in the Yiddish and American-Jewish Novel,* 1971 (revised 1991), *The Comedy That "Hoits": An Essay on the Fiction of Philip Roth,* 1975, *Still Life and Other Poems,* 1975, *The Languages of Joseph Conrad,* 1978, *Between Two Worlds: The American Novel in the 1960's,* 1978, *Memory Breaks Off and Other Poems,* 1984, *Conversations with Contemporary American Writers,* 1985, *The Uncompromising Fictions of Cynthia Ozick,* 1987, *Bearing the Bad News: Contemporary American Literature and Culture,* 1990, *Understanding Joseph Heller,* 1991, *Jewish-American Fiction, 1917-1987,* 1992, *The Catcher in the Rye: Innocence under Pressure,* forthcoming, and many articles on contemporary fiction. Editor of *Critical Essays on Philip Roth,* 1982, *America and the Holocaust* (with Jack Fischel), 1984, and *Jewish-American Literature and Culture: An Encyclopedia* (with Jack Fischel), 1992. **Essays:** Saul Bellow; Philip Roth; "The Magic Barrel."

PURSGLOVE, Glyn. Lecturer in English, University College, Swansea. Editor of *The Swansea Review.* Author of *Francis Warner and Tradition: An Introduction to the Plays,* 1981, and *Francis Warner's Poetry,* 1988. Editor of *Distinguishing Poetry: Writings on Poetry by William Oxley,* 1989, and *Tasso's "Aminta" and Other Poems* by Henry Reynolds, 1991. **Essays:** "The Black Dog"; "The Pope's Mule"; "A Recluse"; "The Suicide Club";"Twenty-Six Men and a Girl"; "The Unknown Masterpiece"; "The Wedding."

PURSGLOVE, Michael. Lecturer in Russian, University of Exeter. Author of *D.V. Grigorovich: The Man Who Discovered Chekhov,* 1987. Translator of *Anton; The Peasant: Two Stories of Surfdom,* 1991. **Essays:** Iurii Kazakov; *The Queen of Spades.*

RAESIDE, James. Lecturer, Keio University. Author of numerous articles and reviews on Japanese literature and other topics. Former literary editor of *Asahi Evening News.* **Essays:** Dazai Osamu; Mishima Yukio; Kawabata Yasunari; "Three Million Yen."

RAWSON, Judy. Senior Lecturer and Chair of the Department of Italian, University of Warwick, Coventry. Editor of *Fontamara* by Ignazio Silone, 1977. **Essay:** Italo Calvino.

REID, Ian. Deputy Vice-Chancellor, Curtin University, Western Australia. Member of the editorial board of *Southern Review* (Australia), *Short Story* (U.S.), and *Journal of the Short Story in English* (France). Author of *The Short Story,* 1977, *Fiction and the Great Depression in Australia and New Zealand,* 1979, and *Narrative Exchanges,* 1992. **Essays:** Christina Stead; "The Marionettist."

RHODES, Karen. Lecturer, Department of English, Massey University, New Zealand. **Essay:** "To Build a Fire."

RIACH, Alan. Lecturer in English, University of Waikato, Hamilton, New Zealand. Author of *The Folding Map: Poems 1978-1988,* 1990, *Hugh MacDiarmid's Epic Poetry,* 1991, *An Open Return* (poetry), 1991, and essays and poetry in journals in Scotland and New Zealand. Editor of *The Radical Imagination: Lectures and Talks* by Wilson Harris (with Mark Williams),

1992, and *The Collected Works of Hugh MacDiarmid,* 2 vols., 1992. **Essays:** *The Cricket on the Hearth*; "The She-Wolf" (Saki); "The Speckled Band."

RICHARDS, Ian. Executive Officer, New Zealand Centre for Japanese Studies. Author of *Everyday Life in Paradise* (short stories), 1991. **Essays:** Maurice Duggan; "Along Rideout Road that Summer."

RIEDINGER, Edward A. Bibliographer for Latin America, Spanish and Portuguese, and Assistant Professor, University Libraries, and Adjunct Assistant Professor, History Department, Ohio State University, Columbus. Book Review Editor, *Phi Beta Delta International Review.* Author of *Como Se Faz Um Presidente, A Campanha de J.K.,* 1988, and *Renaissance in the Tropics, the Flowering of Brazilian Culture in the Twentieth Century,* forthcoming. **Essay:** João Guimarães Rosa.

ROBERTS, Graeme. Senior Lecturer in English, University of Aberdeen, Scotland. Editor of *Full Score: Short Stories by Fred Urquhart,* 1989. **Essays:** William Trevor; Fred Urquhart.

ROGERS, Katharine M. Research Professor of Literature, American University, Washington, D.C. Author of *The Troublesome Helpmate: A History of Misogyny in Literature,* 1966, *William Wycherley,* 1972, *Feminism in Eighteenth-Century England,* 1982, and *Frances Burney: The World of "Female Difficulties",* 1990. Editor of *Before Their Time: Six Women Writers of the Eighteenth Century,* 1979, *Selected Poems* by Anne Finch, Countess of Winchilsea, 1979, and co-editor of *Literary Women from Aphra Belu to Maria Edgeworth* (with William McCarthy), 1987, and *The Meridian Anthology of Early Women Writers,* 2 vols., 1987-91. **Essay:** "The Luck of Roaring Camp."

ROHRBERGER, Mary. Professor of English and Head, Department of English Language and Literature, University of Northern Iowa, Cedar Falls. Consultant for publications of the Modern Language Association, *American Quarterly,* University of Ohio Press, Random House, Houghton Mifflin, *Modern Fiction Studies,* Salem Press, L.S.U. Press, Garland Press, University of Texas Press, and University of Alabama; regional judge, Book-of-the-Month Club Writing Fellowship Program; Fiction Editor, *Cimarron Review,* 1970-88; Editor and Founder, *Short Story.* Author of *Hawthorne and the Modern Short Story: A Study in Genre,* 1966, *An Introduction to Literature* (with Samuel H. Woods, Jr., and Bernard Dukore), 1970, *Reading and Writing About Literature* (with Samuel H. Woods, Jr.), 1970, *The Art of Katherine Mansfield,* 1977, and *Story to Anti-Story,* 1979. Consulting Editor, *American Literature,* 2 vols., 1981, and *The American Novel,* 2 vols., 1981. **Essays:** Edgar Allan Poe; "Benito Cereno"; "Prelude"; "Wakefield."

ROSENBERG, Judith. Professor of English, College of Lake County, Grayslake, Illinois. **Essays:** "The Blue Jar"; "The Kerchief."

ROSENBLUM, Joseph. Lecturer in the Department of English, University of North Carolina, Greensboro. Author of articles in *Dickens Quarterly, Shakespeare Quarterly,* and *Studies in Short Fiction.* Editor of *The Plays of Thomas Holcroft,* 1980. **Essays:** "Babylon Revisited"; "Free Joe and the Rest of the World"; "The Notorious Jumping Frog of Calaveras County"; "The Spinoza of Market Street."

ROSS, Francesca. Freelance writer living in Germany. **Essay:** Mario Soldati.

ROYLE, Trevor. Freelance writer and broadcaster; Associate Editor of *Scotland on Sunday*. Author of *We'll Support You Ever More: The Impertinent Saga of Scottish Fitba'* (with Ian Archer), 1976, *Jock Tamson's Bairns: Essays on a Scots Childhood*, 1977, *Precipitous City: The Story of Literary Edinburgh*, 1980, *Death Before Dishonour: The True Story of Fighting Mac*, 1982, *The Macmillan Companion to Scottish Literature*, 1983, *James and Jim: The Biography of James Kennaway*, 1983, *The Kitchener Enigma*, 1985, *The Best Years of Their Lives: The National Service Experience 1945-63*, 1986, *War Report: The War Correspondent's View of Battle from the Crimea to the Falklands*, 1987, *The Last Days of the Raj*, 1989, *Anatomy of a Regiment*, 1990, and *In Flanders Fields: Scottish Poetry and Prose of the First World War*, 1991, and many articles in journals. Editor of *A Dictionary of Military Quotations*, 1990. **Essays:** George Mackay Brown; A.E. Coppard; Arthur Conan Doyle; L.P. Hartley; Glyn Jones; V.S. Pritchett; Evelyn Waugh; "Beattock for Moffat"; "Civil Peace"; "Murke's Collected Silences"; "A Time To Keep"; "The Travelling Grave."

RUBIO, Patricia. Associate Professor of Spanish, Skidmore College, Saratoga Springs, New York. Author of *Carpentier ante la critica*, 1985, and of various critical articles. **Essay:** Luisa Valenzuela.

RYDEL, Christine A. Professor of Russian, Grand Valley State University, Allendale, Michigan. Author of *A Nabokov's Who's Who*, 1993. Editor of *The Ardis Anthology of Russian Romanticism*, 1983. **Essays:** Mikhail Bulgakov; Vladimir Nabokov; Vladímir Odóevskii; Aleksandr Pushkin; H.G. Wells; "The Stationmaster."

SACHS, Murray. Professor of French and Comparative Literature, Brandeis University, Waltham, Massachusetts. Member, Advisory Board, *Nineteenth-Century French Studies*, and of the editorial board, *Romance Quarterly*. Author of *The Career of Alphonse Daudet: A Critical Study*, 1965, *The French Short Story in the 19th Century*, 1969, *Anatole France: The Short Stories*, 1974, and "The Legacy of Flaubert," in *L'Henaurme Siecle*, 1984. **Essays:** Alphonse Daudet; Gustave Flaubert; Guy de Maupassant; Prosper Mérimée; "Mateo Falcone"; "A Simple Heart"; "The Wall."

SAMBROOK, Hana. Freelance editor and writer. Author of study guides to *The Tenant of Wildfell Hall*, *Lark Rise to Candleford*, *Victory*, *My Family and Other Animals*, *Sylvia Plath: Selected Works*, and *I Am the King of the Castle*. **Essays:** Karel Čapek; Elizabeth Gaskell.

SANDERSON, Stewart F. Chair, Avron Foundation Writers Centre, Scotland. Author of *Ernest Hemingway*, 1961 (revised 1970), *Ernest Hemingway: For Whom the Bell Tolls*, 1980, and of many articles on British and comparative folklore and ethnology, and on modern literature. Editor of *The Secret Common-Wealth* by Robert Kirk, 1970, *The Linguistic Atlas of England* (with others), 1978, *Studies in Linguistic Geography*, 1985, and *World Maps*, 1987. **Essays:** Ernest Hemingway; "Cavalleria Rusticana"; "Markheim"; "The She-Wolf" (Verga).

SCATTON, Linda H. Assistant Provost for Graduate Studies and Research, State University of New York, Central

Administration (System office). Author of *Mikhail Zoshchenko: Evolution of a Writer*, 1993. Also has written reviews for the *Slavic and East European Journal*, and more than twenty reviews and notices for *Library Journal* on new publications in Russian literature (1976-81). **Essays:** Mikhail Zoshchenko; "The Lady Aristocrat."

SCHAFER, William J. Professor and Chair of English, Berea College, Kentucky. Author of *The Art of Ragtime* (with Johannes Reidel), 1973, *Rock Music*, 1973, and *Brass Bands and New Orleans Jazz*, 1987. Editor of *The Truman Nelson Reader*, 1987. **Essays:** Toni Cade Bambara; Ralph Ellison; Caroline Gordon; Ring Lardner; Dorothy Parker; "Old Red."

SCHARNHORST, Gary. Professor of English, University of New Mexico, Albuquerque. Author of *The Lost Life of Horatio Alger, Jr.*, 1985, and *Charlotte Perkins Gilman: A Bibliography*, 1985. Co-editor of *American Literary Realism*. **Essay:** Charlotte Perkins Gilman.

SCHERR, Barry P. Professor of Russian, Dartmouth College, Hanover, New Hampshire. Author of *Russian Poetry: Meter, Rhythm, and Rhyme*, 1986, *Maxim Gorky*, 1988, and of various crical articles. Co-editor of *Russian Verse Theory: Proceedings of the 1987 Conference at UCLA*, 1989. **Essays:** Maksim Gor'kii; Bruno Schulz; Evgenii Zamiatin; "Guy de Maupassant."

SCHMITT, Judith M. Instructor, Pikes Peak Community College, Colorado Springs, Colorado, and Blair Junior College. Member of the fiction staff, *Sun Dog: The Southeast Review*, 1991-92. **Essays:** Alistair MacLeod; "Fatimas and Kisses"; "Uncle Blair."

SCHRANK, Bernice. Professor of English, Memorial University of Newfoundland, St. John's. Member of the editorial board of *Canadian Journal of Irish Studies*. Author of articles on Sean O'Casey in *Twentieth Century Literature*, *Irish University Review*, and *Literature in Wissenschaft und Unterricht*. **Essay:** "My Heart Is Broken."

SCHULTZE, Sydney. Professor and Chair, Classical and Modern Languages, University of Louisville, Kentucky. Associate editor, *Russian Literature Triquarterly*, 1970-90. Author of *The Structure of "Anna Karenina"*, 1982, and several articles on Tolstoi's fiction and on other topics in Russian literature. Editor of *Meyerhold the Director* by Konstantin Rudnitsky, 1982. **Essay:** Lev Tolstoi.

SCOBBIE, Irene. Reader Emeritus in Scandinavian studies, University of Edinburgh. Author of *Pär Lagerkvist: An Introduction*, 1963, *Sweden: Nation of the Modern World*, 1972, *Pär Lagerkvist's Gäst hos verkligheten*, 1974, and articles on Lagerkvist, Strindberg, P.O. Sundman, Stig Claesson, and other writers. Editor of *Essays on Swedish Literature*, 1979, *Aspects of Modern Swedish Literature*, 1988. Also editor of *Northern Studies*, 1989-93. **Essays:** Pärs Lagerkvist; "Father and I."

SCOTT, Paul H. President, Scottish Centre P.E.N. International; Convener, Advisory Council for the Arts in Scotland; Vice-Chair, Saltire Society; Chair, Awards Panel for Scottish Book of the Year. Author of *1707: The Union of Scotland and England*, 1979, *Walter Scott and Scotland*, 1981, *John Galt*, 1985, *In Bed with an Elephant*, 1985, *The Thinking*

Nation, 1989, *Cultural Independence*, 1989, *Towards Independence: Essays on Scotland*, 1991, and *Andrew Fletcher and the Treaty of Union*, 1992. Editor of *The Age of MacDiarmid* (with A.C. Davis), 1980, *Sir Walter Scott's The Letters of Malachi Malagrowther*, 1981, *Andrew Fletcher's United and Separate Parliaments*, 1982, *A Scottish Postbag* (with George Bruce), 1986, and *Policy for the Arts: A Selection of AdCAS Papers* (with A.C. Davis), 1991. **Essays:** John Galt; Eric Linklater; Robert Louis Stevenson; "Kind Kitty"; "Wandering Willie's Tale."

SIBLEY, Brian. Writer and broadcaster. Author of *C.S. Lewis: Through the Shadowlands*, *The Land of Narnia*, and *The Disney Studio Story*. Has written and presented numerous literary features and documentaries, as well as the BBC's radio dramatizations of "The Lord of the Rings," "Tales of Narnia," and works by Ray Bradbury and others. **Essays:** Ray Bradbury; "The Stolen Bacillus."

SLADKY, Paul. Assistant Professor of Languages and Literature, Augusta College, Georgia. **Essays:** Henryk Sienkiewicz; "Astronomer's Wife"; "Faith in a Tree"; "The Interior Castle."

SMITH, Christopher. Reader in French, School of Modern Languages and European History, University of East Anglia, Norwich. Editor of *Seventeenth-Century French Studies*. Author of *Alabaster, Bikinis and Calvados: An ABC of Toponymous Words*, 1985, *Jean Anouilh: Life, Work, Criticism*, 1985, and many articles and reviews of the performing arts. Editor of works by Antoine de Montchrestien, Jean de la Taille, and Pierre Matthieu. **Essays:** "Death in Venice"; "The Guest"; "Hautot and His Son"; "Michael Kohlhass"; "The Necklace"; "Now that April's Here"; "A Passion in the Desert"; "The Rainy Moon"; *The Rider on the White Horse*; "Rothchild's Violin"; "Sylvie"; "The Woman Destroyed."

SNYDER, Phillip A. Assistant Professor of English, Brigham Young University, Salt Lake City, Utah; Alcuin Fellow. Former Associate Editor, *Encyclia*. **Essays:** Langston Hughes; "King of the Bingo Game"; "To Hell with Dying."

SOLOMON, Eric. Professor of English, San Francisco State University. Author of *Stephen Crane in England*, 1963, *Stephen Crane: From Parody to Realism*, 1966, and many articles on 19th- and 20th-century British and American fiction. Editor of *The Faded Banners*, 1960, and *The Critic Agonistes*, 1985. **Essay:** Ambrose Bierce.

SORFLEET, John Robert. Associate Professor of English and Canadian Studies, Concordia University, Montreal. Former Editor, *Journal of Canadian Fiction*. Editor of *Raymond Knister: Poems, Stories, and Essays* (with David Arnason and John G. Moss), 1975, *The Poems of Bliss Carman*, 1976, *L.M. Montgomery: An Assessment*, 1976, *Canadian Children's Drama and Theatre*, 1978, *The Work of Margaret Laurence*, 1980, *The Manor House of De Villerai* by Rosanna Leprohon, 1985, and *Politics and Literature*, 1986. **Essays:** Charles G.D. Roberts; "The Tomorrow-Tamer."

SPEAR, Hilda D. Senior Lecturer in English, University of Dundee, Scotland. Author of *Remembering, We Forget* (on the poetry of World War I), 1978, books on works by Emily Brontë, Conrad, Forster, Fowles, Folding, Hardy, and Lawrence, and

the biographical and bibliographical sections of *The Pelican Guide to English Literature 5*, 1957. Editor of *The English Poems of Calverley*, 1974, *Poems and Selected Letters* by Charles Hamilton Sorley, 1978, and *Sword and Pen: Poems of 1915 from Dundee and Tayside* (with Bruce Pandrich), 1989. **Essays:** Joseph Conrad; "The Other Boat."

SPIVACK, Carla N. **Essays:** Aharon Appelfeld; A.B. Yehoshua; "The Continuing Silence of a Poet."

SPIVACK, Charlotte. Professor of English, University of Massachusetts, Amherst. Author of *Early English Drama*, 1966, *George Chapman*, 1967, *The Comedy of Evil on Shakespeare's Stage*, 1978, *Ursula K. Le Guin*, 1984, and *Merlin's Daughters: Contemporary Women Fantasy Writers*, 1987. **Essays:** "The Devil and Daniel Webster"; "Green Tea."

STEPHENS, Rebecca. Assistant Professor of English, Carlow College, Pittsburgh, Pennsylvania. Author of "A Rogerian Invention Heuristic," in *Rogerian Perspectives* (edited by Nathaniel Teicu), 1992. **Essays:** Clarice Lispector; "The Imitation of the Rose"; "Where You Were at Night."

STERN, Carol Simpson. Professor and Chair of the Department of Performance Studies, and Dean of the Graduate School, Northwestern University, Evanston, Illinois. Member of the editorial board, *Communication Monographs*, and research consultant, *English Literature in Transition*. Author of *Performance: Texts and Contexts* (with Bruce Henderson), 1993, and of articles and theater and book reviews in *Victorian Studies* and *Chicago Sun-Times*. **Essays:** Anais Nin; "The Black Madonna"; "Cathedral."

STONEHILL, Brian. Associate Professor of English, Pomona College, Claremont, California. Former Fiction Editor, the Chicago *Review*. Author of *The Self-Conscious Novel: Artifice in Fiction from Joyce to Pynchon*, 1988, and articles and reviews for the *Los Angeles Times* and the *Washington Post*. **Essays:** John Barth; "What We Talk about When We Talk about Love."

STRANDBERG, Victor. Professor of English, Duke University, Durham, North Carolina. Author of many books, including *A Colder Fire: The Poetry of Robert Penn Warren*, 1965, *The Poetic Vision of Robert Penn Warren*, 1977, *A Faulkner Overview: Six Perspectives*, 1981, *Religious Psychology in American Literature: A Study in the Relevance of William James*, 1981, and *Greek Mind/Jewish Soul: The Conflicted Art of Cynthia Ozick*, forthcoming. **Essays:** William Faulkner; Robert Penn Warren; "The Fall of the House of Usher"; "A Rose for Emily"; "The Shawl"; "A Tree, A Rock, A Cloud."

STRUTHERS, J.R. (Tim). Assistant Professor, Department of English, University of Guelph, Ontario. Editor of *Before the Flood*, 1979, *The Montreal Story Tellers*, 1985, *New Directions from Old*, 1991, *The Possibilities of Story*, 2 vols., 1992, *Canadian Classics* (co-edited with John Metcalf), 1993, and *How Stories Mean* (co-edited with John Metcalf), 1993. **Essay:** Hugh Hood.

SUMMERFIELD, Carol. Editorial Director, Ferguson Publishing, Chicago, Illinois. **Essay:** "The Man that Corrupted Hadleyburg."

SWENSEN, Alice. Teaches literature at University of Northern Iowa, Cedar Falls. **Essay:** "The Cinderella Waltz."

THIES, Gretchen. Doctoral candidate and Teaching Associate, English Department, and Teaching Associate, Film Department, Florida State University, Tallahassee. Fiction Editor, *Sun Dog: The Southeast Review* and editorial assistant, *Journal of Beckett Studies*. **Essays:** "In a Grove"; "Rashomon."

THOMPSON, Bruce. Senior Lecturer in German, University of Stirling. Author of *Schnitzler's Vienna: Image of a Society*, 1990. **Essays:** Arthur Schnitzler; Adalbert Stifter.

THOMPSON, Laurie. Head of the School of Modern Languages, Saint David's University College, Lampeter. Author of *Stig Dagerman*, 1983. Translator of many books, including *Johnny, My Friend* by Peter Pohl, 1991, and *Island of the Doomed* by Stig Dagerman, 1992. Editor of *Swedish Book Review*. **Essay:** Hjalmar Söderberg.

TOKER, Leona. Senior Lecturer, Department of English, The Hebrew University of Jerusalem. Author of *Nabokov: The Mystery of Literary Structures*, 1989, *Eloquent Reticence: Withholding Information in Fictional Narrative*, 1992, and articles on English, American, and Russian writers. **Essays:** Varlam Shalamov; "Billy Budd"; *One Day in the Life of Ivan Denisovich*; "Signs and Symbols"; "The Snake Charmer."

TUERK, Richard. Professor of Literature and Languages, East Texas State University, Commerce. Author of *Central Still: Circle and Sphere in Thoreau's Prose*, 1975, and essays on Jewish-American literature, Emerson, Jacob Riis, and Twain. **Essays:** "Goodbye, Columbus"; "Rappaccini's Daughter."

VANNATTA, Dennis. Professor of English, University of Arkansas, Little Rock. Criticism Editor of the literary journal *Crazyhorse*. Author of *Nathanael West: An Annotated Bibliography*, 1976, *H.E. Bates*, 1983, *Tennessee Williams: A Study of the Short Fiction*, 1988, and *This Time, This Place* (stories), 1991. Editor of *The English Short Story, 1945-1980, A Critical History*, 1985. **Essays:** Franz Kafka; "The Beast in the Jungle"; "The Death of Ivan Ilyich"; "The Library of Babel"; "Lost in the Funhouse."

WAGNER-MARTIN, Linda. Haines Professor of English, University of North Carolina, Chapel Hill. Author of numerous books, including *The Poems of William Carlos Williams*, 1964, *Denise Levertov*, 1967, *The Prose of William Carlos Williams*, 1970, *Hemingway and Faulkner: Inventors/Masters*, 1975, *Introducing Poems*, 1976, *Hemingway: A Reference Guide*, 1977, *William Carlos Williams: A Reference Guide*, 1978, *John Dos Passos: Artist as American*, 1979, *Ellen Glasgow: Beyond Convention*, 1982, *Sylvia Plath: A Literary Biography*, 1987, *Anne Sexton: Critical Essays*, 1989, and *The Modern American Novel*, 1989. Editor of *Heath Anthology of American Literaure*, and co-editor of *The Oxford Companion to Women's Writing in the United States*. Also editor of works by or about William Faulkner, T.S. Eliot, Ernest Hemingway, William Carlos Williams, Robert Frost, Denise Levertov, and Sylvia Plath. **Essays:** "The Lottery"; "Melanctha"; "A Pair of Silk Stockings"; "A Perfect Day for Bananafish"; "The Snows of Kilimanjaro"; "Sweat"; "The Use of Force"; "Where Are You Going, Where Have You Been?"; "The Yellow Wallpaper."

WALDMEIR, John C. Chair, Theology/Philosophy Division, St. Mary's College, Orchard Lake, Michigan. Author of *Critical Essays on Truman Capote*, forthcoming. Also has published in the *Journal of Religion* and *Journal of American Culture*. **Essays:** William Saroyan; "The Daring Young Man on the Flying Trapeze."

WALDMEIR, Joseph J. President, Michigan Hemingway Society. Author of *Recent American Fiction: Some Critical Views*, 1963, *American Novels of the Second World War*, 1968, *Critical Essay on John Barth*, 1980, and *Hemingway from Michigan to the World*, forthcoming. **Essays:** Nelson Algren; "How the Devil Came Down Division Street."

WAN, Pin P. Assistant Professor of Chinese, St. Olaf College, Northfield, Minnesota. Co-translator of *Deathsong of the River: A Reader's Guide to the Chinese TV Series He Shang* (with Richard Bodman), 1991. **Essays:** "Nights of Fever"; "Sinking."

WEISS, Allan. Freelance writer and editor; currently teaching at York University and the University of Toronto. Author of short stories that have been published in numerous journals and anthologies, including *Green's Magazine, Fiddlehead, Year's Best Horror Stories III*, and *Tesseracts 4*. Compiler, *A Comprehensive Bibliography of English-Canadian Short Stories, 1950-1983*, 1988, and *Canadian Literature Index 1988*. **Essays:** Clark Blaise; Austin Clarke; Mavis Gallant; Stephen Leacock; "How I Met My Husband"; "The Ice Wagon Going Down the Street"; "Lamp at Noon"; "The Marine Excursion of the Knights of Pythias"; "The Salt Garden."

WERLOCK, Abby H.P. Associate Professor of American Literature, St. Olaf College, Northfield, Minnesota. Author of *Tillie Olsen* (with Mickey Pearlman), and of numerous articles on American authors, including Cooper, Faulkner, Wharton and Mourning Dove. Editor of *British Women Writing Fiction*, forthcoming. **Essay:** Tillie Olsen.

WERNER, Craig Hansen. Professor of Afro-American Studies, University of Wisconsin, Madison. Author of *Paradoxical Resolutions: American Fiction since James Joyce, James Joyce's "Dubliners": A Pluralistic World*, and *Black Women Novelists*. **Essays:** Leslie Marmon Silko; "The Goophered Grapevine"; "The Wonderful Tar-Baby Story."

WESTBROOK, Perry D. Emeritus Professor of English, State University of New York, Albany. Author of *Acres of Flint: Writers of Rural New England*, 1951, *Biography of an Island*, 1958, *The Greatness of Man: An Essay on Dostoevsky and Whitman*, 1961, *Mary Ellen Chase*, 1966, *Mary Wilkins Freeman*, 1967, *John Burroughs*, 1974, *William Bradford*, 1978, *Free Will and Determinism in American Literature*, 1979, *The New England Town in Fact and Fiction*, 1982, and *A Literary History of New England*, 1988. **Essays:** Mary E. Wilkin Freeman; "A New England Nun"; "White Nights."

WHITE, John J. Professor of German and Comparative Literature, King's College, University of London. Author of *Mythology in the Modern Novel, Literary Futurism: Aspects of the Avant-Garde*, and *Brecht's "Leben des Galilei"*, 1993. Co-author of volumes on Musil, Stramm, Grass, Kafka, Berlin, and the New German Cinema. **Essay:** Thomas Mann.

WILKIE, Brian. Professor of English, University of Arkansas, Little Rock. Author of *Romantic Poets and Epic Tradition*, 1965, *Blake's "Four Zoas": The Design of a Dream* (with Mary Lynn Johnson), 1978, *Blake's Thel and Oothoon*, 1990, and articles on major Romantic writers, including Blake, Wordsworth, Coleridge, Byron, Keats, and Austen, and on literary theory. Co-editor of *Literature of the Western World* (with James Hurt), 2 vols., 1984 (3rd edition 1992). **Essays:** Joyce Carol Oates; Ivan Turgenev; "Bezhin Meadow"; "Did You Ever Slip on Red Blood?"; *First Love*; "Lifeguard."

WILKSHIRE, Claire. Doctoral student, University of British Columbia, Vancouver. **Essay:** John Metcalf.

WILLIAMS, Mark. Lecturer in Japanese studies, University of Leeds. Author of "Life After Death? The Literature of an Undeployed Kamikaze Squadron Leader," in *Japan Forum*, 1992. Translator of *Ryugaku* by Endō Shūsaku, 1989. **Essays:** Endō Shūsaku; "Mothers"; "A Portrait of Shunkin."

WILSON, Jason. Lecturer in Hispanic poetry, University College, London. Author of *Octavio Paz: A Study of His Poetics*, 1979, *Octavio Paz*, 1986, *An A to Z of Modern Latin American Literature in English Translation*, 1989, and *Traveller's Literary Companion to Latin America*, 1993. **Essays:** Julio Cortázar; Horacio Quiroga; Juan Rulfo.

WOOD, Sharon. Teaches in the Department of Modern Languages, University of Strathclyde, Glasgow. **Essay:** Alberto Moravia.

WOODCOCK, George. Freelance writer, lecturer, and editor. Author of poetry (*Collected Poems*, 1983), plays, travel books, biographies, and autobiography (*Letter to the Past*, 1983), and works on history and politics; critical works include *William Godwin*, 1946, *The Incomparable Aphra*, 1948, *The Paradox of Oscar Wilde*, 1949, *The Crystal Spirit* (on Orwell), 1966, *Hugh MacLennan*, 1969, *Odysseus Ever Returning: Canadian Writers and Writing*, 1970, *Mordecai Richler*, 1970, *Dawn and the Darkest Hour* (on Aldous Huxley), 1972, *Herbert Read*, 1972, *Thomas Merton*, 1978, *The World of Canadian Writing*, 1980, *Orwell's Message*, 1984, and *Northern Spring*, 1987. Editor of anthologies and of works by Charles Lamb, Malcolm Lowry, Wyndham Lewis, Margaret Laurence, Hardy, Meredith, and others. **Essays:** Margaret Atwood; Morley Callaghan; Thomas Chandler Haliburton; Margaret Laurence; Alice Munro; Sinclair Ross.

WOODRESS, James. Professor Emeritus of English, University of California, Davis. Founder and Editor of *American Literary Scholarship*, 1965-87. Author of *Howells and Italy*, 1952, *Booth Tarkington: Gentleman from Indiana*, 1955, *A Yankee's Odyssey: The Life of Joel Barlow*, 1958, *Willa Cather: Her Life and Art*, 1970, and *Willa Cather: A Literary Life*, 1987. Editor or co-editor of *Voices from America's Past*, 1961, *Eight American Authors*, 1971, *The Troll Garden* by Willa Cather, 1983, and *Critical Essays on Whitman*, 1983. **Essays:** Willa Cather; Washington Irving; "The Other Two."

YANKALUNAS, Mary U. Teaches at Pennsylvania State University, University Park. **Essay:** "Patriotism."

YORK, Lorraine M. Associate Professor of English, McMaster University, Hamilton, Ontario. Managing Editor, *Essays on Canadian Writing*. Author of *The Other Side of Dailiness: Photography in the Works of Alice Munro, Timothy Findley, Michael Ondaatje, and Margaret Laurence*, 1988, *Front Lines: The Fiction of Timothy Findley*, 1990, and articles on Canadian writers, photography, and postmodernism. **Essays:** Audrey Thomas; "Royal Beatings"; "Wilderness Tips."

YUDKIN, Leon I. Lecturer in Hebrew, University of Manchester. Author of *Isaac Lamdam: A Study in Twentieth-Century Hebrew Poetry*, 1971, *Escape into Siege*, 1974, *Jewish Writing and Identity in the 20th Century*, 1982, *1948 and After: Aspects of Israeli Fiction*, 1984, *On the Poetry of U.Z. Greenberg*, 1987, *Else Lasker-Schueler: A Study in German Jewish Literature*, 1991, and *Beyond Sequence: Current Israeli Fiction and Its Context*, 1992. Editor of *Jews in Modern Culture* monograph series.

ZEMPEL, Solveig. Associate Professor, Norwegian Department, St. Olaf College, Northfield, Minnesota. Author of *In Their Own Words: Letters from Norwegian Immigrants*, 1991. Translator of O.E. Rolvaag's *When the Wind Is in the South and Other Stories*, 1984, and O.E. Rolvaag's *The Third Life of Per Smevik* (with E.V. Tweet), 1971. **Essay:** Bjørg Vik.

ISBN 1-55862-334-5